ZONDERVAN
DICTIONARY
OF BIBLE THEMES
THE ACCESSIBLE AND COMPREHENSIVE TOOL FOR TOPICAL STUDIES

**MARTIN H. MANSER, ALISTER E. McGRATH,
J. I. PACKER, DONALD J. WISEMAN**

ZondervanPublishingHouse
Grand Rapids, Michigan

A Division of HarperCollins*Publishers*

Zondervan Dictionary of Bible Themes
Copyright © 1999 by
The Zondervan Corporation. All rights reserved.

Bible Themes © 1996 by Hodder & Stoughton

Scripture Index © 1996 by Martin H. Manser

First published in the United Kingdom as
The Hodder Dictionary of Bible Themes
Copyright © 1996 by Hodder & Stoughton

Requests for information should be addressed to:

ZondervanPublishingHouse
Grand Rapids, Michigan 49530

Library of Congress Cataloging-in-Publication Data

Zondervan dictionary of Bible themes : the accessible and comprehensive tool for topical studies /
[edited by] Martin H. Manser ... [et al.].
    p. cm.
Includes index.
ISBN 0-310-20668-5 (hardcover : alk. paper)
1. Bible—Dictionaries. I. Title: Dictionary of Bible themes. II. Manser, Martin H.

BS440.Z58 1999
220.3—dc21   99-047974
                                              CIP

This edition printed on acid-free paper.

Printed in the United States of America

99 00 01 02 03 04 05 /❖ DC/ 10 9 8 7 6 5 4 3 2 1

Contents

About the Editors

Introduction

"The unfolding of your words gives light; it gives understanding to the simple."
Ps 119:130

The study of Scripture lies at the heart of the Christian faith. It is therefore important that readers of Scripture are given every means of help so that they may get as much benefit and enjoyment as possible out of reading the Bible. The Dictionary of Bible Themes is designed to allow its users to appreciate to the full the unfolding of the unity and richness of Scripture by studying its central themes.

What is Scripture all about? The Dictionary of Bible Themes was planned to allow its users to identify and explore the leading themes of Scripture–themes such as God, Jesus Christ, the Holy Spirit, the human race, sin and salvation, the Christian life, the church and the hope of glory.

This Dictionary identifies these, and many other key themes, and traces them throughout the course of Scripture. The Bible is here allowed to speak for itself, with a minimum of comment and explanation. The approach adopted in this volume allows its users to come into contact directly with Scripture, rather than having to approach it through the views of commentators. The main themes of Scripture are identified, key biblical references are provided and the mutual relationship of themes is set out clearly. Over 2,000 themes detailed in this work cover doctrinal, ethical, historical and cultural subjects. In addition to dealing with the great themes of the Christian message of salvation, the themes thus also deal with practical issues of Christian living. This approach allows a unifying of Christian wisdom, both theological and practical, for the edification of God's people.

The thematic approach The approach adopted in this work differs significantly from a more lexical approach found in some older reference works. A thematic approach is based on related ideas; a lexical approach is based on individual words. The difference between them can easily be appreciated by considering the theme of "assurance". A word-based approach would be limited to identifying biblical passages in which words such as "assure" or "assurance" appear. A thematic approach, however, goes far beyond this and explores all the basic elements of the theme. It identifies its basic ideas, its presuppositions and its consequences, in order that the theme in all its fulness can be unfolded to the reader. Thus the material that deals with assurance covers the grounds of assurance (e.g., the knowledge of God, the certainty of his word, the work of the Holy Spirit), the nature of assurance (of a relationship with God, of salvation, of eternal life and a future hope) and the relationship between assurance and the life of faith. An extensive system of indexing and cross-referencing allows the dynamic relationship of the many biblical themes to be understood and further explored.

A further advantage of the thematic approach of the Dictionary of Bible Themes is that it can be used with any Bible translation. Although the verse references provided are intended to be illustrative rather than exhaustive, the reader will nevertheless find a wealth of biblical material arranged thematically.

The thematic approach will be particularly welcomed by those who are preparing studies or talks on biblical themes and wish to ensure that they have included or referred to the central passages within Scripture. It will enable them to gain an understanding of the overall place of this theme within Scripture and to explore the way in which it relates to other themes. It will also be valued by readers of Scripture who become interested in a biblical passage or theme and wish to follow it through. The Scripture Index which allows readers to see immediately which themes are associated with the passage under study, will allow its users to turn to the Bible Themes section and discover other passages of relevance, as well as other biblical themes that cast light on the particular importance of the passage or theme being studied.

The thematic study of Scripture is also important in another respect. Tracing the great biblical themes throughout Scripture allows us to appreciate the essential unity of Scripture. As we trace the unfolding of God's purposes of redemption throughout the pages of the Bible, we come to appreciate more fully how Scripture bears witness to the same God and his same purposes throughout its entirety. The essential unity of Scripture is best appreciated by understanding the great themes that bind it together.

Application of God's word
The editors and consultant editors, compilers and publishers hope that this new work will bring a fresh quality and depth to readers' understanding and grasp of the riches of Scripture. It is a work that has been designed to meet the many needs of God's people in today's world, whether they are individual believers, or a Christian family studying Scripture in the quietness of the home, or preachers preparing to thrill and challenge a congregation with a fresh appreciation of the wonder of God's word.

As the psalmist declared, it is the unfolding of God's word that brings light and understanding to his people (Ps 119:130). It is the hope and prayer of all those involved in producing the Dictionary of Bible Themes that this new guide to the word of God will help to sustain and nourish the people of God, as they praise, proclaim and adore him for all that he is and all that he has done – and all that he has promised to do.

How to use this book

The heart of the Dictionary of Bible Themes is the section on Bible Themes: over 2,000 themes covering the key themes of Scripture. Two ways of helping readers find their way into this section are provided:

* the Alphabetical List of Themes (pages 1–15). This provides a complete listing in one single alphabetical order of all the theme titles. Selective cross-references are also provided for ease of use, e.g., at "anxiety" the reader is directed to "worry" and at "Cephas" to "Peter".

* the Scripture Index of Themes (pages 612–1232). Verses of the Bible are listed and appearing alongside each verse are the themes associated with that particular passage.

In each case, theme name and theme number should be noted and readers should use the theme number to locate the theme in the Thematic Section.

Using the Scripture Index of Themes

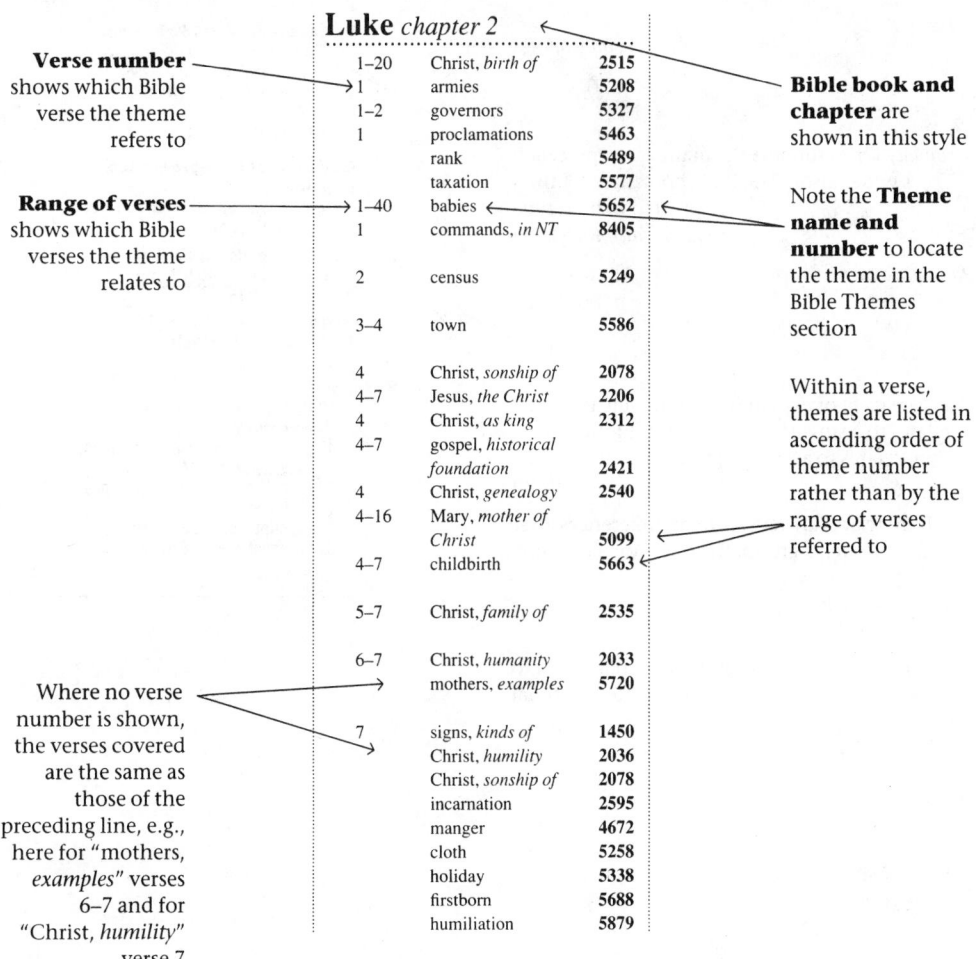

Verse number shows which Bible verse the theme refers to

Range of verses shows which Bible verses the theme relates to

Where no verse number is shown, the verses covered are the same as those of the preceding line, e.g., here for "mothers, *examples*" verses 6–7 and for "Christ, *humility*" verse 7

Luke *chapter 2*

1–20	Christ, *birth of*	2515
1	armies	5208
1–2	governors	5327
1	proclamations	5463
	rank	5489
	taxation	5577
1–40	babies	5652
1	commands, *in NT*	8405
2	census	5249
3–4	town	5586
4	Christ, *sonship of*	2078
4–7	Jesus, *the Christ*	2206
4	Christ, *as king*	2312
4–7	gospel, *historical foundation*	2421
4	Christ, *genealogy*	2540
4–16	Mary, *mother of Christ*	5099
4–7	childbirth	5663
5–7	Christ, *family of*	2535
6–7	Christ, *humanity*	2033
	mothers, *examples*	5720
7	signs, *kinds of*	1450
	Christ, *humility*	2036
	Christ, *sonship of*	2078
	incarnation	2595
	manger	4672
	cloth	5258
	holiday	5338
	firstborn	5688
	humiliation	5879

Bible book and chapter are shown in this style

Note the **Theme name and number** to locate the theme in the Bible Themes section

Within a verse, themes are listed in ascending order of theme number rather than by the range of verses referred to

This section contains over 2,000 themes, covering the key themes of Scripture. Themes cross-refer you to the various parts of Scripture at which each theme occurs and are organised under descriptive headings. You can use the resources of the Bible Themes Section in a variety of ways to support your Bible study.

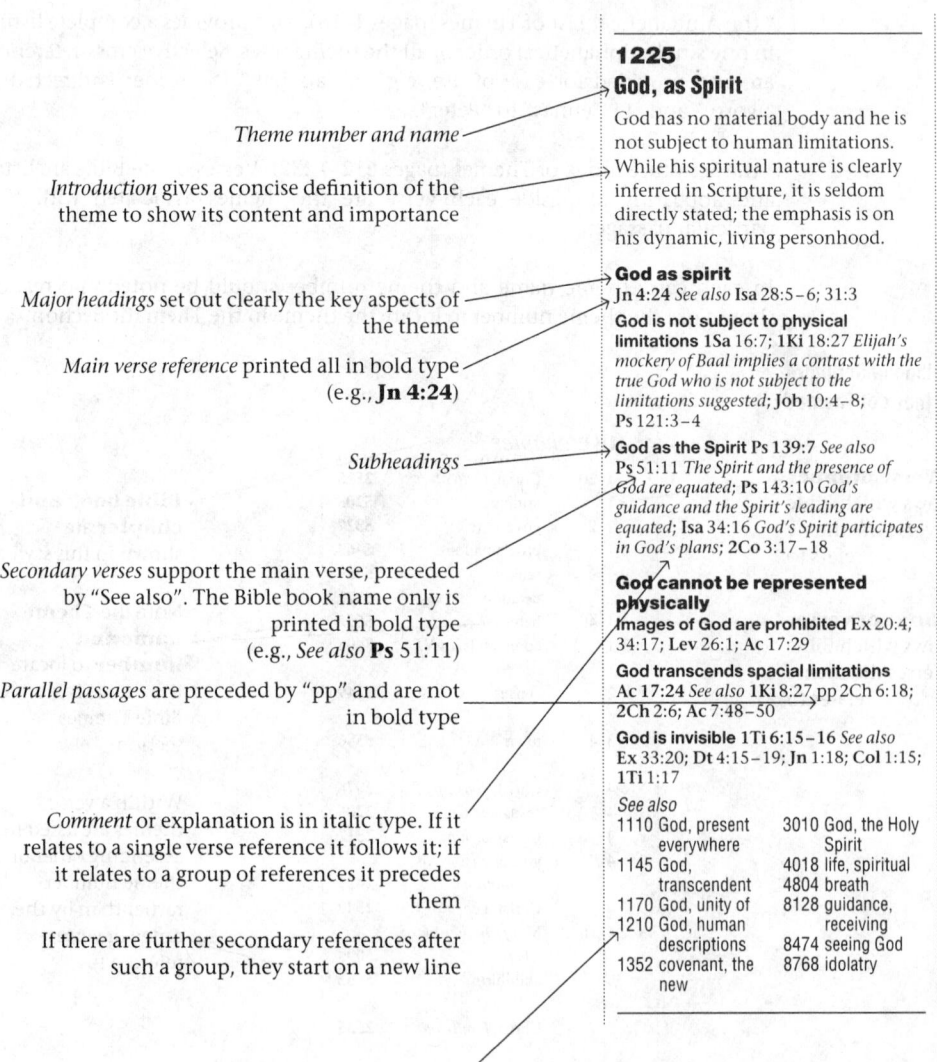

Theme number and name

Introduction gives a concise definition of the theme to show its content and importance

Major headings set out clearly the key aspects of the theme

Main verse reference printed all in bold type (e.g., **Jn 4:24**)

Subheadings

Secondary verses support the main verse, preceded by "See also". The Bible book name only is printed in bold type (e.g., *See also* **Ps** 51:11)

Parallel passages are preceded by "pp" and are not in bold type

Comment or explanation is in italic type. If it relates to a single verse reference it follows it; if it relates to a group of references it precedes them

If there are further secondary references after such a group, they start on a new line

Cross-references to other themes enable you to look up related material

---

1225
God, as Spirit

God has no material body and he is not subject to human limitations. While his spiritual nature is clearly inferred in Scripture, it is seldom directly stated; the emphasis is on his dynamic, living personhood.

God as spirit
Jn 4:24 *See also* Isa 28:5–6; 31:3

God is not subject to physical limitations 1Sa 16:7; 1Ki 18:27 *Elijah's mockery of Baal implies a contrast with the true God who is not subject to the limitations suggested;* Job 10:4–8; Ps 121:3–4

God as the Spirit Ps 139:7 *See also* Ps 51:11 *The Spirit and the presence of God are equated;* Ps 143:10 *God's guidance and the Spirit's leading are equated;* Isa 34:16 *God's Spirit participates in God's plans;* 2Co 3:17–18

God cannot be represented physically
Images of God are prohibited Ex 20:4; 34:17; Lev 26:1; Ac 17:29

God transcends spacial limitations Ac 17:24 *See also* 1Ki 8:27 pp 2Ch 6:18; 2Ch 2:6; Ac 7:48–50

God is invisible 1Ti 6:15–16 *See also* Ex 33:20; Dt 4:15–19; Jn 1:18; Col 1:15; 1Ti 1:17

See also

1110 God, present everywhere	3010 God, the Holy Spirit
1145 God, transcendent	4018 life, spiritual
1170 God, unity of	4804 breath
1210 God, human descriptions	8128 guidance, receiving
1352 covenant, the new	8474 seeing God
	8768 idolatry

---

viii

Classification of themes

The editors have given considerable thought to the arrangement and categorisation of themes. Each theme has been assigned a four-digit number, given with the aim of reflecting the theme's core subject matter and allowing both ease of reference and an understanding of the overall place of the theme in Scripture. For example, one major group of themes focuses on "God", another on "Jesus Christ" and another on "sin and salvation".

The categorisation is not intended to force a straitjacket upon the biblical material by placing any kind of arbitrary restrictions on it. Indeed, in a number of instances, a theme could have been categorised differently. The classification is simply intended to make the identification and exploration of themes as simple as possible for the benefit of readers.

Each theme number consists of four digits. The first digit stands for one of nine main groups of themes:

1000	God
2000	Jesus Christ
3000	Holy Spirit
4000	Creation
5000	Humanity
6000	Sin and salvation
7000	God's people
8000	The life of the believer
9000	Last things

Within each of the major groups of themes, themes have been arranged in subcategories. For example, under *Jesus Christ* 2000 come:

2003	Jesus Christ, qualities of
2200	Jesus Christ, titles and descriptions of
2300	Jesus Christ, ministry and work of
2400	Jesus Christ, gospel of
2500	Jesus Christ, history of

Within each subcategory, general themes are in many instances given first, followed by themes in alphabetical order.

For example, under the subcategory

2200	Jesus Christ, titles and descriptions of

comes first the general theme

2203	Jesus Christ, titles and names of

followed in alphabetical order by specific names and titles, e.g.,

2206	Jesus, the Christ
2218	Jesus Christ, Son of God
2221	Jesus Christ, Son of Man

In many cases, themes are of such importance and complexity that they have been divided in logical order into more manageable sections. For example, the theme of "the church" has been divided as follows:

7020	church, the
7021	church, OT anticipations of
7022	church, and Jesus Christ
7023	church, and Holy Spirit
7024	church, nature and foundations of
7025	church, unity and fellowship of
7026	church, leadership of
7027	church, purpose and mission of
7028	church, life of

All the themes are listed in alphabetical order in the alphabetical index at the back of the Bible. Below is a list of the major groups of themes and subcategories:

1000 God

1010	God, nature and qualities of
1200	God, titles and descriptions of
1300	God, work of
1400	God, knowledge of
1500	God, the Trinity
1600	Scripture as the word of God

2000 Jesus Christ

2003	Jesus Christ, qualities of
2200	Jesus Christ, titles and descriptions of
2300	Jesus Christ, ministry and work of
2400	Jesus Christ, gospel of
2500	Jesus Christ, history of

3000 Holy Spirit

3005	Holy Spirit, qualities of
3100	Holy Spirit, titles and descriptions of
3200	Holy Spirit, ministry and work of

4000 Creation

4100	Supernatural beings
4200	Places
4300	Metals and minerals
4400	Vegetation and food
4600	Living beings
4800	Natural and supernatural phenomena
4900	Time

5000 Humanity

5070	Individuals in OT and NT
5125	Parts of the body and clothing
5200	Human civilisation
5650	Human relationships
5760	Human attitudes and behaviour

6000 Sin and salvation

6010	Sin
6100	Aspects of sin
6500	Salvation
6600	Aspects of salvation

7000 God's people

7010	The church as the people of God
7100	Titles of the people of God
7200	History of God's people in OT
7300	Institutions and culture of OT
7500	Jews and Gentiles
7600	History of God's people in NT
7700	Leadership and the people of God
7900	The life of the church

8000 The life of the believer

8010	Faith
8100	The life of faith
8200	The character of the believer
8400	The tasks of the believer
8600	Prayer and worship of the believer
8700	Threats to the life of faith

9000 Last things

9010	Death
9100	Aspects of the last things
9200	Judgment
9300	Resurrection
9400	Heaven
9500	Hell
9600	Hope

Abbreviations

The Old Testament

The New Testament

Alphabetical List
of Themes

Alphabetical List of Themes

Hell 9500
hell 9510
　as a place of punishment 9511
　as an experience 9512
　as incentive to action 9513
helpfulness 5876
herald 5335
herbs and spices 4466
heresies 8766
hesitation 5877
high places 7374
high priest 7376
　in NT 7378
　in OT 7377
　Jesus Christ as *See* Jesus Christ, as high
　　priest 2306
highway 5336
hills 4245
hiring 5337
history 4945
History of God's people in NT 7600
History of God's people in OT 7200
holiday 5338
holiness 8266
　as separation from the worldly 8269
　as set apart for God 8270
　believers' growth in 8272
　ethical aspects of 8273
　of God *See* God, holiness of 1065
　of Jesus Christ *See* Jesus Christ,
　　holiness of 2030
　purpose of 8271
Holy of Holies *See* Most Holy Place 7396
Holy Spirit 3000
　and assurance 3203
　and grace *See* grace, and Holy Spirit
　　6670
　and love 3209
　and mission 3212
　and peace 3215
　and praise 3218
　and prayer 3221
　and preaching 3224
　and prophecy *See* prophecy 1427
　and regeneration 3230
　and sanctification 3233
　and Scripture 3236
　and worship *See* Holy Spirit, and praise
　　3218; Holy Spirit, and prayer
　　3221
　anointing of 3239
　as Counsellor 3130
　as teacher 3140
　baptism with 3242
　blasphemy against 3245
　conviction of 3248
　descriptions of 3120
　divinity of 3015
　filling with 3251
　fruit of 3254
　fulness of *See* Holy Spirit, filling with
　　3251
　gift of 3257
　gifts of *See* spiritual gifts 7966
　guidance of 3263
　in creation 3266
　in life of Jesus Christ 3269
　in OT 3272
　in the church 3275
　indwelling of 3278
　inspiration of 3281
　joy of 3020
　leading of *See* Holy Spirit, guidance of
　　3263
　life in the Spirit *See* life, spiritual 4018
　ministry and work of 3200
　mission of *See* Holy Spirit, gift of 3257
　names of *See* Holy Spirit, titles and
　　names of 3110
　personality of 3025

　power of 3030
　presence of 3035
　promise of 3040
　qualities of 3005
　resisting 3284
　sealing of 3287
　sovereignty of 3045
　the life-giver 3290
　titles and descriptions of 3100
　titles and names of 3110
　wisdom of 3050
　witness of 3293
　work in the world 3296
　work of *See* Holy Spirit, ministry and
　　work of 3200
home 5339
homosexuality 6238
honesty 8275
honour 5878
honouring God 8444
Hope 9600
hope 9610
　as confidence 9613
　in God 9612
　nature of 9611
　priority of *See* priority, of faith, hope
　　and love 8463
　results of 9615
　results of its absence 9614
hopelessness *See* hope, results of its
　　absence 9614
horn 4654
horse 4657
horticulture 4468
hospitality 8445
　a duty of God's people 8446
　examples of 8447
host of heaven 4170
hostility *See* enemies 8727
hour 4948
house 5340
house of God 7382
household gods 7384
Human attitudes and behaviour 5760
human behaviour *See* Human attitudes
　　and behaviour 5760
Human civilisation 5200
human nature 5019; 5020
human race, and creation 5002
　and God 5003
　and redemption 5005
　and sin 5004
　destiny of 5006
　the 5001
Human relationships 5650
human sacrifice *See* child sacrifice 7332
Humanity 5000
humanity, of Jesus Christ *See* Jesus
　　Christ, humanity of 2033
humankind *See* human race, the 5001
humiliation 5879
humility 8276
　of Jesus Christ *See* Jesus Christ,
　　humility of 2036
humour 5880
hunger 5341
hunting 5342
husband 5702
hymn 7927
hypocrisy 8767
hyssop 4470

idle talk *See* talk, idle 5575
idleness 5343
idolatry 8768
　in NT 8770
　in OT 8769
　objections to 8771

　idols *See* idolatry 8768
ignorance 6181
　and human situation 6182
　of God 6183
illness *See* disabilities 5296; disease 5297
image of God 5023
images *See* idolatry 8768
imagination 6184
　evil scheming 6186
　inward desires 6185
imitating 8449
Immanuel 2227
immaturity 5881
immorality 6187
　examples of sexual 6189
　nature of sexual 6188
immortality 9135
　in NT 9137
　in OT 9136
impartiality 5882
impatience 5883
impenitence 6193
　results of 6195
　warnings against 6194
imperfection 6199
　and God's purposes 6201
　influence of 6200
impetuosity *See* rashness 5925
importunity 8652
　towards God 8653
　towards people 8654
imprisonment 5344
impurity *See* clean and unclean 7340
imputation 6674
in Christ *See* union with Christ 6754
　abiding *See* abiding in Christ 8102
incarnation 2595
incense 7386
incest *See* sexual sin 6236
indecision 5884
indifference 5885
individualism 5886
Individuals in OT and NT 5070
indulgence *See* extravagance 5856; self-
　　indulgence 8821
indwelling, of Holy Spirit *See* Holy Spirit,
　　indwelling of 3278
inexperience 5887
inferiority 5888
infidelity *See* unfaithfulness 8839
influence 5345
Ingathering, Feast of *See* Feast of
　　Tabernacles 7358
ingratitude 5889
inheritance 5703
　material 5704
　spiritual 5705
iniquity *See* sin 6020
injury 5346
injustice 5347
　examples of 5349
　hated by God 5350
　nature and source of 5348
inner being 5024
innocence 8277
　examples of 8279
　teaching on 8278
innocent, suffering of *See* suffering, of
　　the innocent 5562
inscriptions 5352
insects 4660
insecurity 5890
insight 8281
insincerity *See* dishonesty 8714
insomnia *See* sleeplessness 5537
inspiration, of Scripture *See* Scripture,
　　inspiration and authority of 1611
instability 5891
instinct 5892
Institutions and culture of OT 7300

Bible Themes

The major groups of themes and subcategories:

1000 God
1010	God, nature and qualities of
1200	God, titles and descriptions of
1300	God, work of
1400	God, knowledge of
1500	God, the Trinity
1600	Scripture as the word of God

2000 Jesus Christ
2003	Jesus Christ, qualities of
2200	Jesus Christ, titles and descriptions of
2300	Jesus Christ, ministry and work of
2400	Jesus Christ, gospel of
2500	Jesus Christ, history of

3000 Holy Spirit
3005	Holy Spirit, qualities of
3100	Holy Spirit, titles and descriptions of
3200	Holy Spirit, ministry and work of

4000 Creation
4100	Supernatural beings
4200	Places
4300	Metals and minerals
4400	Vegetation and food
4600	Living beings
4800	Natural and supernatural phenomena
4900	Time

5000 Humanity
5070	Individuals in OT and NT
5125	Parts of the body and clothing
5200	Human civilisation
5650	Human relationships
5760	Human attitudes and behaviour

6000 Sin and salvation
6010	Sin
6100	Aspects of sin
6500	Salvation
6600	Aspects of salvation

7000 God's people
7010	The church as the people of God
7100	Titles of the people of God
7200	History of God's people in OT
7300	Institutions and culture of OT
7500	Jews and Gentiles
7600	History of God's people in NT
7700	Leadership and the people of God
7900	The life of the church

8000 The life of the believer
8010	Faith
8100	The life of faith
8200	The character of the believer
8400	The tasks of the believer
8600	Prayer and worship of the believer
8700	Threats to the life of faith

9000 Last things
9010	Death
9100	Aspects of the last things
9200	Judgment
9300	Resurrection
9400	Heaven
9500	Hell
9600	Hope

For an explanation of the numbering system see **Classification of Themes**, pp. ix – x.

1000
God

1010
God, nature and qualities of

1015
God

The Creator and Redeemer of the world, who reveals himself in Scripture and in Jesus Christ, and who is loved, worshipped and adored by believers. Scripture stresses the personal nature of God, and also his total reliability and trustworthiness. God is the Father of Jesus Christ and of all believers. This set of themes consists of the following:

1020 God, all-knowing
1025 God, anger of
1030 God, compassion of
1035 God, faithfulness of
1040 God, fatherhood of
1045 God, glory of
1050 God, goodness of
1055 God, grace and mercy of
1060 God, greatness of
1065 God, holiness of
1070 God, joy of
1075 God, justice of
1080 God, living and self-sustaining
1085 God, love of
1090 God, majesty of
1095 God, patience of
1100 God, perfection of
1105 God, power of
1110 God, present everywhere
1115 God, purpose of
1120 God, repentance of
1125 God, righteousness of
1130 God, sovereignty of
1135 God, suffering of
1140 God, the eternal
1145 God, transcendence of
1150 God, truth of
1155 God, truthfulness of
1160 God, unchangeableness of
1165 God, uniqueness of
1170 God, unity of
1175 God, will of
1180 God, wisdom of
1185 God, zeal of
1190 glory

1020
God, all-knowing

The omniscience of God is that attribute by which he knows all things past, present and future. What is hidden from human sight is still known by God. Scripture stresses the wisdom of God in all his actions, and often grounds this in his all-embracing knowledge.

God's unique self-knowledge within the Trinity
Mt 11:27 *See also* Jn 10:15; 1Co 2:10–11

The nature of God's knowledge
God's knowledge originates within himself Isa 40:13–14 *See also* Job 21:22; Ro 11:33–34; 1Co 2:16

God's knowledge is complete Mt 10:30 pp Lk 12:7 *See also* Ps 147:4; Isa 40:26

God knows things that are hidden from human understanding Dt 29:29 *See also* Job 37:15–16; Da 2:22; Mt 24:36 pp Mk 13:32; Ac 1:7; 2Co 12:2–4

God's comprehensive knowledge of people
God's knowledge of people's actions Job 34:21 *See also* Job 24:23; 31:4; Ps 33:13–15; 139:2–3; Jer 23:24

God's knowledge of people's needs Mt 6:8 *See also* Mt 6:31–32 pp Lk 12:29–30

God's knowledge of people's hearts and minds 1Ch 28:9 *Scripture views the heart not primarily as the seat of emotion but more particularly as the seat of the will. See also* Ps 44:20–21; 139:1–2; Jer 17:10; Eze 11:5; Heb 4:12–13

God's knowledge of individuals Ge 20:1–7 *God's knowledge of Abimelech's motives and behaviour towards Abraham's wife Sarah;* 1Sa 16:1–12 *the* LORD *to Samuel regarding David's anointing as king;* Ac 5:1–11 *God's knowledge of the deception of Ananias and Sapphira*

God's knowledge of people's sin Jer 16:17 *See also* Job 10:14; Ps 69:5; Jer 2:22; Hos 7:2; Am 5:12

God's foreknowledge
Isa 46:10 *See also* Isa 42:9; 44:7; Da 2:28

God's foreknowledge of Jesus Christ's passion Ac 2:23 *See also* Ac 3:18; 4:27–28

God's foreknowledge of those who would become disciples Ro 8:29 *See also* Jer 1:5; Ro 11:2; 1Pe 1:2

God's foreknowledge of people's free actions Ps 139:4 *See also* Ex 3:19; Dt 31:21; 1Sa 23:10–13

Implications of God's knowledge
God's knowledge ensures that all will be judged fairly Heb 4:13 *See also* 1Sa 2:3; Job 34:22–23; Ecc 12:14; Ro 2:16; 1Co 4:5

God's knowledge ensures that he knows those who are his 2Ti 2:19 *See also* Nu 16:5; Ex 33:12; Job 23:10 Jn 10:14 *See also* 1Co 8:3; Gal 4:9; 1Jn 3:19–20; Rev 3:8

See also

1025
God, anger of

The punitive and vindicatory reaction, legitimate and controlled, yet awesomely emphatic, of God the righteous judge to unrighteousness in his human creatures. Up to the present, the expression of God's anger and wrath has had the purpose of drawing sinners to repentance and conversion, but this will not be the case at the final judgment.

The nature of God's anger
It is fearsome Na 1:6 *See also* Jos 7:26; Eze 38:18

It is reluctant and short-lived Ex 34:6 *See also* Isa 54:7–8; Ne 9:16–18

It is consistent with his righteous and merciful character Ps 7:11 *See also* Hab 3:2

It fulfils God's purposes Jer 23:20 *See also* Jer 30:24

The causes of God's anger
Idolatry and unbelief Nu 25:3 *See also* Ex 32:8–10; Dt 8:19; Jdg 2:10–14; 1Ki 14:9; 16:32–33; 22:53; 2Ki 23:19 *Josiah removes idolatrous shrines;* 2Ch 28:25; 34:25; Jer 8:19; 32:29; 44:3; Jn 3:36 *the unbelief of rejecting the Son of God;* Ro 1:18–23; 2:8

Disobedience and disloyalty Jos 7:1 *See also* Dt 9:7; 2Ki 22:13; 1Ch 13:10; Ps 106:29; Jer 32:32; Zec 7:13; Eph 5:6

Ungodly living *God's judgment against the ungodly is a sign of his anger against actions that contradict his righteous character and purposes:* 2Ti 3:1–9; Jude 14–16

Pride, arrogance and hypocrisy Mt 23:27–28 *See also* 2Ch 32:25; Pr 3:34; 8:13; Isa 13:11; Hos 12:14; Mal 4:1

Complaints against, and opposition to, God's purposes Nu 11:1 *See also* Nu 14:27; 21:5

Injustice Zec 7:9–12 *See also* 2Ch 19:7; Jer 22:13; Eze 9:9; Mal 3:5; Mt 23:23

The rejection of God's servants Heb 10:29–31 *See also* Dt 32:35–36; Ps 135:14; Ne 9:26; Zec 7:12; Mt 21:33–41; Ac 7:35–37

God reveals his anger
In present times Ro 1:18 *See also* Jer 10:10

On a future "day of wrath" which is anticipated Ro 2:5 *See also* Isa 13:9,13; Eze 7:19; Zep 1:15,18; 2:2

The consequences of God's anger
God allows those who reject righteousness to remain in their sin Ro 1:18–32 *See also* 1Ki 14:16; 2Ch 12:5; Ne 9:28; Isa 54:7–8; Jer 7:27–29; 12:7–8

Punishment will be experienced by rebellious people Dt 8:19 *See also* Isa 59:18; Jer 21:14; Mt 18:34–35; 25:28–30

Punishment of death: Ex 12:12; Nu 32:13; Jos 7:25–26; Isa 13:9–13; Da 5:30; Ac 5:5,10
Punishment of exile: 1Ki 14:15; Jer 15:13–14; 25:7–11
Destruction of the whole nation of Israel: La 2:1–9; Eze 38:19–21

God will be feared as his holiness and greatness are revealed Isa 59:18–19 *See also* Eze 38:22–23

Ultimately God will purify and restore his people for service Mal 3:2–4 *See also* Jer 15:19–21

See also

1055 God, grace & mercy	2009 Christ, anger of
1075 God, justice of	5482 punishment
1125 God, righteousness	5790 anger, divine
1310 God as judge	6712 propitiation
	9240 last judgment
	9510 hell

1030
God, compassion of

An aspect of God's nature which is reflected in his sympathetic understanding of human weakness and his restoration of those in trouble.

God is compassionate by nature
2Co 1:3 *See also* Ex 33:19; 34:6; Ps 86:15; 103:8; 116:5; 119:156; Hos 1:7; Joel 2:13

God shows compassion as a parent
Ps 103:13–14 *See also* Isa 49:15–16; 63:15–16; Jer 31:20

God shows compassion to all
Ps 145:8–9

God shows compassion to those in deep trouble Isa 49:13 *See also* Ex 22:27; 2Ki 13:22–23; Ps 40:1–2,11–12; 69:16–17; Isa 30:18; La 3:22,32; Zec 10:6; Jas 5:11

God shows compassion towards sinners Ne 9:17 *See also* Dt 13:17; Ne 9:28; Ps 51:1–2; 103:3–4; Isa 54:7–8; 60:10; Da 9:9; Mic 7:19

The return from exile shows God's compassion to sinners Eze 39:25 *See also* Dt 30:2–3; Jer 12:15; 30:18; 33:26

God's deeds show his compassion
Ps 111:3–4 *See also* Ps 102:14; Isa 14:1; 63:7

God's compassion is essential to believers' well-being
Ps 119:77 *See also* Ps 77:8–9; Isa 63:15

God's compassion is reflected in acts of human compassion
Col 3:12 *See also* 2Ch 30:9; Jer 42:12; Zec 7:9; Lk 6:36; Eph 4:32

Jesus Christ reflects God's compassion
Heb 4:15 *See also* Lk 1:72; 15:20

See also

1055 God, grace & mercy	5806 compassion
1085 God, love of	5966 tenderness
2015 Christ, compassion	6652 forgiveness
2027 Christ, grace & mercy	6688 mercy, demonstration of God's
5762 attitudes, God to people	8291 kindness

1035
God, faithfulness of

God's perfect loyalty and consistency in being true to his name, his character and his word.

God's faithfulness is an integral part of his nature
Nu 23:19 *God's limitless power and steadfast love imply complete faithfulness which contrasts with human nature;* La 3:22–23 *See also* Ex 34:6; Dt 7:8–9; 32:4; Ro 4:21; 2Ti 2:13

God is faithful to his name and character
2Ti 2:13 *See also* Ne 9:8; Ps 106:8; 1Th 5:24; Heb 6:13–18

God's faithfulness is known through fulfilled promises
Jos 23:14 *See also* Jos 21:45; 1Ki 8:56; 1Ch 16:15; Ps 145:13; 2Pe 3:9

Examples of God's faithfulness in fulfilled promises
Abraham's fatherhood Ge 12:2–3; 15:4; 21:1–2; Ro 9:9; Gal 4:28; Heb 6:13–15; 11:11

The building of the temple 2Sa 7:12–13 pp 1Ch 17:11–12; 1Ki 8:17–21 pp 2Ch 6:7–11

The exile in Babylon Jer 25:8–11 *God's faithfulness will not always mean human prosperity. See also* 2Ki 25:8–12 pp 2Ch 36:17–21 pp Jer 52:12–16; Ezr 1:1–3; Jer 52:27; 29:10; Da 9:2–3,15–19

God's faithfulness is revealed to the faithful
2Sa 22:26 *See also* Gal 3:14; Heb 10:23

God's faithfulness is constant
Ro 3:3–4 *God's faithfulness is not negated by human unfaithfulness. See also* Eze 12:25; Hab 2:3; 2Ti 2:13

Jesus Christ is the ultimate evidence of God's faithfulness
Ac 13:32–33 *See also* Jn 14:9–11; Ro 15:8–9; 2Co 1:20–22; Heb 3:2–6; Rev 1:5; 19:11

See also

1150 God, truth of	6687 mercy, God's
1240 God, the Rock	7135 Israel, people of God
1345 covenant	8248 faithfulness
2021 Christ, faithfulness	8304 loyalty
5467 promises, divine	8742 faithlessness
5499 reward, divine	8839 unfaithfulness

1040
God, fatherhood of

Primarily signifying God's paternal relationship to Jesus Christ, the term also refers to God's fatherly relationship to his creation, especially to believers as the "children of God".

Aspects of the fatherhood of God
He is the Creator and provider 1Co 8:6 *See also* Dt 32:6,18; Isa 64:8; Ac 17:24–28

He shows love and compassion
Hos 11:1 *See also* Ps 103:13; Jer 3:19; 2Co 1:3

He exercises his providence and care
Ps 68:5 *See also* Mt 6:26,31–33 pp Lk 12:29–31; Mt 7:11 pp Lk 11:13

He disciplines and corrects Dt 8:5 *See also* Pr 3:11–12; Heb 12:5–6

God as the Father of Jesus Christ
Mt 3:17 pp Mk 1:11 pp Lk 3:22 *See also* Mt 11:27; Lk 2:49; Jn 5:17–18; 17:11; 20:17; Ro 15:6; Eph 1:3 1Pe 1:3 *See also* 1Jn 1:3

God is the father of Israel
He cares for his covenant people Jer 31:9 *See also* Ex 4:22; Dt 14:1; 32:6,18; Isa 63:16; Mal 2:10

He is the father of the kings of Israel 2Sa 7:13–14 pp 1Ch 17:12–13 *This description of God's fatherhood involves the maintenance of a special relationship between God and David's descendants, which ultimately includes Jesus Christ. See also* Ps 2:7; 89:26–27

God is the father of Christian believers
He has an intimate relationship with believers Mt 6:9 pp Lk 11:2 *See also* Jn 20:17; 2Co 6:18; Gal 3:26; 1Jn 2:13

He adopts believers into his family Jn 1:12–13 *See also* Ro 8:14–17; Gal 4:5–7; 1Jn 3:1

The fatherhood of God has implications for the church
Character: children are to reproduce the Father's likeness Mt 5:48

Unity: one Father means one family Eph 4:3–6 *See also* Mal 2:10; Mt 23:9; Eph 3:14–15

Status: believers are related to Jesus Christ Mt 12:50 pp Mk 3:35 pp Lk 8:21 *See also* Ro 8:29; Heb 2:11

Inheritance: believers are heirs of the Father's kingdom Ro 8:17 *See also* Lk 12:32; Gal 3:29; Col 1:12; Tit 3:7

Submission: believers are to revere the Father 1Pe 1:17 *See also* Mt 6:9 pp Lk 11:2; Eph 3:14

See also

1030 God, compassion	2375 kingdom of God
1085 God, love of	5703 inheritance
1245 God of the fathers	5895 intimacy
1250 Abba	6608 adoption
1510 Trinity, the	7115 children of God
2218 Christ, Son of God	8230 discipline

1045
God, glory of

The revelation of God's power and characteristics, sometimes accompanied by visible phenomena.

Glory as an attribute of God
Ps 24:7–8 *See also* Ps 29:3; Jn 11:40; Ac 7:2; Rev 19:1

Visible phenomena accompanying God's glory
The appearance of God's glory Hab 3:4 *See also* Dt 5:24; 2Sa 22:8–16 pp Ps 18:7–15; Ps 104:1; Eze 1:26–28

God's glory as a cloud Ex 24:15–16 *See also* Ex 33:9–10; Isa 4:5; Mt 17:5 pp Mk 9:7 pp Lk 9:34; Lk 21:27 pp Mt 24:30 pp Mk 13:26

God's glory in the tabernacle and the temple 2Ch 5:13–14 pp 1Ki 8:10–11 *The Jewish term for the outward sign of God's presence in the temple is "Shekinah". See also* Ex 40:34–35; 2Ch 7:1–3; Eze 8:4; 9:3; 10:19; 43:1–5; Rev 15:8

God's glory revealed
In Jesus Christ Heb 1:3 *See also* Isa 49:3; Jn 1:14; 13:31–32; 17:5; 2Co 4:6; 2Pe 1:17

In his people Col 1:27 *See also* Isa 60:19–21; 62:3; 2Co 3:18; Eph 3:21

In the whole world Isa 6:3 *See also* Nu 14:21; Ps 57:5,11 pp Ps 108:5; Hab 2:14; 3:3

In heaven Rev 21:23 *See also* Ro 8:17; Heb 2:9; 1Pe 5:10

In his name Ne 9:5 *See also* Dt 28:58; 1Ch 29:13; Ps 8:1; 79:9

In his works Ps 111:3 *See also* Ps 19:1; Isa 12:5; 35:2; Jn 11:40–44; 17:4

In his kingdom Ps 145:11–12 *See also* 1Ch 29:11; Mt 6:13 fn; 1Th 2:12

God's glory cannot be fully seen
1Ti 6:15–16 *To see God face to face means certain death:* Ex 33:18–20; Jdg 6:22–23; 13:20–22; Isa 6:5; Jn 1:18

God's glory experienced
Ac 7:55 *See also* Ex 3:2 *Moses;* Isa 6:1–4 *Isaiah;* Lk 2:9 *the shepherds*

The effects of God's glory
God's glory is acknowledged Ps 72:19 *See also* Ps 29:2; Ro 11:36; Rev 4:11; 5:13; 19:1

God's glory brings guilt and fear Ro 3:23 *See also* Isa 2:10,19,21; Rev 11:13; 15:8

See also
1060	God, greatness	2024	Christ, glory of
	of	2218	Christ, Son of
1090	God, majesty of		God
1190	glory	4805	clouds
1403	God, revelation	7467	temple,
1454	theophany		Solomon's

1050
God, goodness of

All God's perfect qualities are made freely available to all for the benefit of the whole world.

God alone is good
Mk 10:18 pp Mt 19:17 pp Lk 18:19

God demonstrates his goodness
In his actions Ps 119:68 *See also* 2Ch 30:18; Ne 9:20; Ps 73:1; 143:10; Ac 10:38; Ro 2:4

In his work of creation 1Ti 4:4 *See also* Ge 1:4,31; Ps 145:9

In his love Ps 86:5 *See also* 1Ch 16:34 pp Ps 106:1; Ps 25:7–8; 69:16; 100:5

In his gifts Jas 1:17 *See also* Nu 13:27; Dt 8:7; 26:11; Heb 9:11

In his promises Jos 23:14–15 *See also* 2Sa 7:28 pp 1Ch 17:26; 1Ki 8:56; Jer 29:10

In his commands Ps 119:39 *See also* Ps 19:7; Ro 7:12,16; 12:2

God's goodness is to be experienced
God is good to those who trust him Ps 34:8; Na 1:7 *See also* Ex 33:19; 2Ch 7:10; Job 42:11; Ps 31:19–20; 84:11; 86:17; La 3:25; Am 5:14–15; 1Pe 2:3

God's people can rely on his goodness Jer 32:40 *See also* Ps 23:6; 27:13; Mt 7:11 pp Lk 11:13; Php 1:6

God works positively for good in unfavourable circumstances
Ge 50:20 *See also* Ac 2:23–24; Ro 8:28; 2Co 4:17; Heb 12:10

God's goodness is to be praised
Ps 135:3 *See also* Dt 8:10; 2Ch 5:13; 7:3; Ps 86:5; 136:1; 145:7

See also
1030	God,	4464	harvest
	compassion	5187	taste
1055	God, grace &	5854	experience of
	mercy		God
1085	God, love of	7435	sacrifice, in OT
1330	God, the	8352	thankfulness
	provider	8609	prayer as
1335	blessing		praise &
4005	creation		thanksgiving

1055
God, grace and mercy of

The qualities of God's character by which he shows himself compassionate, accepting, and generous to sinful human beings, shielding them from his wrath, forgiving them, and bestowing on them his righteousness so that they can live and grow in faith and obedience. Grace and mercy are particularly expressed through God's covenant with his chosen people and through Jesus Christ's atoning death on the cross.

God's grace and mercy are made known in Jesus Christ
Jn 1:16–17

The abundance of God's grace and mercy
Eph 2:4–8 *See also* 2Sa 24:14 pp 1Ch 21:13; Ps 69:13; 84:11; 102:13; Ro 2:4; 5:17; 9:23; 1Ti 1:14

God's grace and mercy are always unearned and unmerited
Dt 7:7–8 *See also* Dt 9:5–6; Eze 36:22; Da 9:18; Ro 9:16; Eph 1:6; 2:8–9; 3:8; Tit 3:5

God's grace and mercy are a source of blessing
Ge 21:1–2 *See also* Ge 33:11; 1Sa 2:21

God's grace and mercy are expressed in the covenant relationship
Jer 31:3 *Hebrew "hesed" (translated as "love", "loving-kindness", "unfailing love") expresses specifically the grace and mercy that underlie the covenant relationship. See also* Ex 34:6; Dt 7:9,12; Ne 9:17; Ps 6:4; Isa 55:3; La 3:22,32

Salvation comes by grace
Tit 2:11 *See also* Mk 10:25–27 *Jesus Christ's words to his disciples;* Ro 5:15; Eph 1:5–6; 2:8; 2Ti 1:9–10

This is ultimately shown in the cross of Jesus Christ Ro 3:24–25 *See also* Ro 5:8; Eph 1:7; Heb 2:9; 2Pe 1:10–11

God's grace and mercy are offered to sinners
Punishment is withheld Ezr 9:13 *See also* 2Ki 13:22–23; Eze 20:15–17; Hos 11:8; Joel 2:13

Sin is forgiven Mic 7:18 ; 1Jn 1:9 *See also* Ps 32:5; Pr 28:13; Isa 55:7; Jer 3:12; 33:8; Da 9:9

Sinners' prayers are heard Ps 51:1; Lk 18:13–14 *See also* Ps 6:2–3; 123:3; Hab 3:2

The favour of God
Examples of those who found favour with God Ge 4:4 *Abel;* Ge 6:8 *Noah;* Ex 33:12 *Moses;* Jdg 6:17–18 *Gideon;* 1Sa 2:26 *Samuel;* Ezr 7:27–28 *Ezra;* Lk 1:30 *Mary;* Lk 2:52 *Jesus Christ;* Ac 7:46 *David*

Examples of those who seek the favour of God Ex 32:11 *Moses;* 2Ki 13:4 *Jehoahaz;* 2Ch 33:12 *Manasseh Nehemiah:* Ne 5:19; 13:31 Da 9:17 *Daniel*

Promises relating to the favour of God Lev 26:9 *It is given to the obedient (see Lev 26:3);* Ps 5:12 *It is given to the righteous;* Ps 30:5 *It lasts for a lifetime.*

The OT predicts a future age of God's favour Isa 49:8 *See also* Isa 60:10; 61:2; Eze 36:9

Implications for believers of the grace and mercy of God
God's grace and mercy are to influence the character and conduct of believers Ro 6:1–2 *See also* Ac 11:23; Ro 6:14; 12:1; Tit 2:11–12

Believers must humbly rely on God's grace and mercy Gal 2:21 *See also* Pr 3:34; Jas 4:6; Jnh 2:8; Ro 2:4; 2Co 6:1–2

God's grace strengthens believers for service Eph 3:7–8 *See also* 1Co 3:10; 2Co 12:7–9; Gal 1:15–16; Eph 4:7,11

Illustrations of God's grace and mercy

God shows grace to Noah, saving him from the flood and afterwards establishing a covenant with him: Ge 6:8,22; 9:9–11 *God shows mercy in saving first Jonah and then (following their repentance) the people of Nineveh;* Jnh 1:1–3,17; 2:1–3; 3:1–10; Lk 15:11–32 *The forgiving love of the prodigal's father illustrates the divine mercy of God.*

See also

1030 God, compassion	6027 sin, remedy for
1085 God, love of	6510 salvation
2027 Christ, grace & mercy	6652 forgiveness
2410 cross, the	6666 grace
2420 gospel	6688 mercy, demonstration of God's
5860 favour, divine	8602 prayer

1060
God, greatness of

God's nature, deeds and attributes are incomparable, for which he deserves all praise.

God is great
Jer 10:6 *See also* 1Ch 16:25 pp Ps 96:4; 1Ch 29:11; Ne 1:5; Isa 12:6

God's name is great
Eze 36:23 *See also* Jos 7:9; 1Sa 12:22; 1Ki 8:42 pp 2Ch 6:32

God is a great king
Ps 47:2 *See also* Ps 47:7; 48:2; Mal 1:14; Mt 5:35; 1Ti 6:15

God's deeds are great
He does great things Ps 136:4 *See also* Jdg 2:7; Isa 55:9; Jer 32:19; Lk 1:49; Eph 3:20

His acts are powerful Dt 9:29 *God's powerful acts are often associated with the exodus. See also* Ex 15:7; Dt 9:26 *His great victories in the promised land:* 1Sa 19:5; 2Sa 23:10 *His powerful act of creation:* Isa 40:26; Jer 32:17 Na 1:3; Eph 1:19–20 *His great power at work in the resurrection*

God's attributes are great
His great love Ps 108:4 *See also* Nu 14:19; 2Ch 1:8; La 3:22; Eph 2:4; 1Jn 3:1

His great mercy 1Ch 21:13 *See also* Ne 9:31; Ro 5:17; 1Pe 1:3

His great anger 2Ki 22:13 *See also* Ps 90:11; 102:10; Jer 21:5; 32:37

God's gifts are great
He bestows great gifts Da 5:18 *See also* Ge 12:2; 1Sa 26:25; 1Ch 29:25

He gives great joy Ne 12:43 *See also* Ezr 6:22; Ps 4:7; 126:3

The effects of God's greatness
God's power is known in the nations Ps 126:2 *See also* 2Ch 9:6; 20:6; Ps 99:2; Da 4:3

People are astonished Lk 9:43 *See also* Hab 1:5; Lk 5:26

God must be praised for his greatness Ps 48:1 *See also* Dt 32:3; Ps 89:1; 96:4; 145:3

God's greatness makes him unique
There is no-one like him Ps 150:2 *See also* 2Sa 7:22; Ps 71:19; 86:10; 145:3

He is greater than other gods Ex 18:11 *See also* Dt 4:7; 10:17; 2Ch 2:5; Ps 135:5; 1Co 8:4–6

God is greater than human power and pride Job 33:12 *See also* 2Ch 32:7–8; Isa 40:6–7; 1Jn 3:20

See also

1020 God, all-knowing	1165 God, unique
1025 God, anger of	1320 God as Saviour
1085 God, love of	1416 miracles
1090 God, majesty of	2069 Christ, pre-eminence
1105 God, power of	8624 worship, reasons
1130 God, sovereignty	

1065
God, holiness of

The moral excellence of God that unifies his attributes and is expressed through his actions, setting him apart from all others. Believers are called to be holy as God is holy.

God's nature is holy
He is perfect Dt 32:4 ; Isa 6:3 ; Rev 4:8 *See also* 2Sa 22:31; Job 6:10; Ps 18:30; 22:3; 71:22; 78:41; Isa 41:14; 43:15; Hab 1:13; Jn 17:11; Rev 6:10

He is uniquely holy 1Sa 2:2 *See also* Ex 15:11; Ps 77:13; Isa 40:25; Rev 15:4

God's name is holy
Eze 36:21–23 *See also* Lev 22:32; 1Ch 16:35; 29:16; Ps 33:21; 97:12; Isa 57:15; Eze 39:25; Lk 1:49

God's dwelling-place is holy
Isa 57:15 *David's palace was regarded as holy because of the presence of the ark See also* 2Ch 8:11; 30:27; Ps 2:6; 3:4; 5:7; 11:4; 15:1; 20:6; 47:8; 48:1; 65:4; Isa 63:15; Joel 3:17; Ob 16–17; Jnh 2:4; Mic 1:2; Hab 2:20; Zec 2:13; Ac 21:28 *The Jews accused Paul of defiling the temple area by bringing in Gentiles;* Eph 2:21–22 *the church as the dwelling in which God lives by his Spirit;* Heb 10:19–22; Rev 22:19

God's holiness is revealed in his righteous activity
Isa 5:16 *See also* Jdg 5:11; 1Sa 12:7; Ps 77:13; 145:17; Da 9:14,16; Zep 3:5

God's holiness affects worship
It is celebrated in worship Ps 99:5 *See also* 1Ch 16:29; Ps 29:2; 99:5; 103:1; 105:3; 145:21; Isa 6:3

Coming before a holy God requires preparation Ex 3:5 *See also* Ex 29:37; Ps 24:3–4; 1Co 11:28; Heb 10:1–2,22

Special requirements and tasks are given to worship leaders Lev 21:7–8 *the priests;* Lev 21:10–15 *the high priest*

Aaron and his family: Ex 28:1–43; Lev 21:16–23 2Ch 29:5 *the Levites*

God's holiness is to be seen in his people
God's people are to be holy because he is holy Lev 19:2; 2Ti 1:9 *See also* Ex 19:6; 22:31; Lev 11:44; Mt 5:48; Ro 12:1; 1Co 1:2; 2Co 11:2 *the church is to be pure as the bride of Jesus Christ;* Eph 1:4; 5:3; Php 4:8; Col 1:22; 3:12; 1Th 3:13; 4:3–7; Tit 1:8 *a qualification for an elder;* Heb 2:11; 3:1; 12:10; 1Pe 1:15–16

Becoming holy involves striving after God 2Pe 3:14 *See also* 2Co 7:1; 13:11; Eph 4:22–24; 1Ti 5:22; Heb 12:14; Jas 1:20–21; 2Pe 3:11–12

The holiness of believers originates from God Ex 31:13 *See also* Lev 22:9; Dt 28:9; Ps 4:3; 1Jn 3:1–3

Jesus Christ purifies Christian believers 1Jn 1:7 *See also* Heb 7:26–28; 9:26–28; 10:10,14; 1Jn 3:4–6

God's holiness makes sin objectionable to him
Hab 1:13 *See also* Jos 24:19–20; Jer 50:29

God's holiness necessitates dependence upon him for forgiveness
Ps 51:1–17 *See also* Da 9:4–19; 1Jn 1:9

See also

1100 God, perfection	6744 sanctification
1125 God, righteousness	7922 fellowship with God
1185 God, zeal of	8206 Christlikeness
2030 Christ, holiness	8266 holiness
6624 confession of sin	8333 reverence
6652 forgiveness	8622 worship

1070
God, joy of

God rejoices in the well-being and faithfulness of his covenant people, and in the repentance and conversion of sinners. He brings joy to his people, who rejoice in his presence and faithfulness.

God is the source of joy
Ps 37:4 *See also* 1Sa 2:1; Ne 1:11; 12:43; Isa 61:10; Jn 15:11; Php 4:4

God rejoices in the restoration of his people
Jer 32:41 *See also* Isa 62:4–5 *He rejoices as does a bridegroom;* Isa 65:19; Jer 31:20 *He rejoices as does a father;* Zep 3:17

Joy can be found in the heavenly presence of God
1Ch 16:27
At creation: Job 38:4–7; Pr 8:30–31 Lk 15:7 *over sinners who repent*

Causes of God's joy
His own works Jer 9:24

His chosen servant Mt 12:18; Isa 42:1; Heb 1:9; Ps 45:7

Jesus Christ Mt 3:17 pp Mk 1:11 pp Lk 3:22; Mt 17:5

The restored temple Hag 1:8

His people and their worship
Ps 149:4–9 *See also* Ps 69:30–31

Repentance Dt 30:9

Obedience, honesty and integrity
1Sa 15:22; Pr 12:22 *See also* 1Ch 29:17;
Ps 147:10–11; Pr 11:1,20

God's face shining on his people
Nu 6:25 *When God's face shines on his
people his divine pleasure and joy is
implied.*
Ps 67:1 *See also;* 80:19; 119:135
*By contrast God's face is against evil,
showing his displeasure:* Ps 34:16;
1Pe 3:12

See also

1125 God, righteousness	2039 Christ, joy of
1255 face of God	3020 Holy Spirit, joy of
1315 God as redeemer	6650 finding
1320 God as Saviour	8283 joy
	8460 pleasing God

1075
God, justice of

The moral righteousness of God is
revealed in his laws and expressed in
his judicial acts. God's commands
and judgments meet perfect
standards of justice, and his
apportioning of punishments and
rewards is also perfectly just. God's
justice is impartial. Special praise is
his for vindicating the penitent and
the needy who have no human
champions. Ultimately, all God's
ways will be seen as just and
equitable.

God's justice displays his righteousness
It conforms to his moral law Job 34:12
See also Dt 32:4; Ps 9:16; 11:7; Zep 3:5;
Ro 2:2; 2Ti 2:13; Rev 15:3

It is seen in his perfect will Ps 99:4 *See
also* Ps 40:8; Isa 53:10; Mt 6:10; 26:39
pp Mk 14:36 pp Lk 22:42; Heb 10:9–10

God acts with justice
Ps 33:5–15 *See also* Ne 9:33

**God's justice is exercised fairly and
equitably** Ps 9:7–8 *See also* Ps 96:13;
98:9; 99:4

**He judges people according to their
deeds** Rev 20:12–13 *See also*
Ex 34:6–7; Ps 62:12; Jer 17:10;
Eze 18:20; Mt 16:27; Rev 22:12

He punishes wickedness Eze 18:20 *See
also* Ex 34:7; Dt 32:35; Isa 59:18; 66:24;
Mt 25:41–46; Col 3:25; 2Th 1:8–9

He rewards righteousness Ps 58:11 *See
also* Isa 62:11; Mt 5:12 pp Lk 6:23;
Mt 25:34–40,46; Ro 2:7; 8:1–2; 2Ti 4:8

God establishes justice
He upholds the cause of the oppressed
Ps 103:6 *See also* Dt 10:18; Ps 140:12;
146:7–9; Isa 61:8; Lk 1:52–53

**He vindicates those who have been
wronged** 1Sa 25:39 *See also* 1Sa 24:15;
Ps 135:14; Ro 12:19; Dt 32:35; 1Pe 2:23

He is completely impartial
Job 34:18–19 *See also* Dt 10:17;
2Ch 19:7; Ac 10:34–35; Eph 6:9

God's ways in exercising justice
**God's justice is not always
immediately apparent** Jer 12:1 *See also*
Job 21:7; Ps 73:3–14; Ecc 7:15;
Hab 1:2–4; Mal 2:17; 3:14–15;
Mt 20:10–12

God warns before punishing
2Ch 36:15 *See also* 2Ki 17:23;
Ne 9:29–30; Jer 7:13; Jnh 3:4;
Heb 12:25

**God gives opportunity for people to
change their ways** Jer 18:8–10 *See also*
Jer 7:5–7; Eze 18:25–32; Mt 21:28–32;
1Jn 1:9

God's justice is truly equitable
Gal 6:7–8 *See also* Ge 18:25; Nu 32:23;
Ps 73:17; Lk 16:25; 18:7–8; Col 3:24–25

God's justice is satisfied by the work of Jesus Christ
Ro 3:25–26 *See also* Isa 53:10–11;
Heb 9:22; 1Jn 1:9; 2:1–2

God's justice will be established in the reign of Jesus Christ
Mt 25:31–33 *See also* Isa 9:6–7;
Ac 17:31; Rev 19:11–16

**Heaven and earth will rejoice when
God's justice is established**
Ps 96:10–13 pp 1Ch 16:30–33;
Ps 98:4–9; Rev 15:3–4; 16:5–7; 19:1–2

God requires people to reflect his justice
Pr 21:3 *See also* Lev 19:15; Dt 16:20;
24:17; 1Ki 10:9 pp 2Ch 9:8; Ps 82:3–4;
Isa 56:1; Mic 6:8; Zec 7:9–10; Col 4:1;
1Ti 5:21

See also

1095 God, patience of	5482 punishment
1310 God as judge	5498 reward
2072 Christ, righteousness	6676 justification
2309 Christ as judge	8792 oppression, God's attitude
5360 justice, God	9210 judgment, God's
5375 law	
5448 poverty, attitudes to	

1080
God, living and self-sustaining

God is alive and active. In contrast to
idols, he is uncreated and the source
of all continuing life.

God is alive
Jer 10:10 *See also* Ge 1:1; Dt 5:26;
Jos 3:10; Jer 23:36; Mt 26:63; 1Ti 3:15;
Heb 3:12; 12:22

God lives for ever
Isa 57:15 *See also* Da 4:34; 12:7;
Rev 4:9–10; 10:6; 15:7

God is self-existent
Jn 5:26 *See also* Ex 3:14; Jn 8:58;
Ac 17:25

The living God is Father, Son and Holy Spirit
Jn 6:57; 2Co 3:3 *See also* Mt 16:16;
1Co 8:6; Heb 7:24

The living God is to be worshipped
Da 6:26 *See also* Da 6:20; Ro 9:26;
Hos 1:10; 2Co 6:16; 1Ti 4:10; Heb 9:14

Turning away from the living God is sin
Heb 3:12 *See also* 1Sa 17:26,36; 2Ki 19:4
pp Isa 37:4; 2Ki 19:16 pp Isa 37:17;
Heb 10:31

The living God contrasts with dead idols
Ac 14:15 *See also* 1Ki 18:26–29;
Ps 115:2–7; Isa 46:1–4; Jer 10:3–6;
1Th 1:9

God is the source of life
Dt 30:20 *See also* Jn 1:4

God gives life to created beings Ge 2:7
See also Job 27:3; Ps 104:30; Isa 40:28;
Ac 17:25,28

God sustains the life of all people
Ps 54:4 *See also* 1Ch 29:14; Ps 3:5; 18:35;
146:9; 147:6; Isa 46:4; Heb 1:3

God gives spiritual life Jn 10:28 *See also*
Jn 5:21; 11:25; 14:6; 1Pe 1:23

God is the source of new life Ps 42:2 *See
also* Ps 63:1; 84:2; Jn 3:1–8

See also

1140 God, the eternal	4005 creation
1325 God, the Creator	4018 life, spiritual
3290 Holy Spirit, life-giver	6139 deadness, spiritual
	6645 eternal life

1085
God, love of

The deepest possible expression of
God's character. Though God loves
all people, he is especially
committed to sacrificial, loyal
relationships with his people.

God's nature is love
1Jn 4:8 *See also* 1Jn 4:16

**His love is perfectly expressed within
the Trinity** Mk 1:10–11 pp Mt 3:16–17
pp Lk 3:21–22 *See also* Jn 5:20; 10:17;
14:23; Eph 1:6; Col 1:13

Characteristics of God's love
It is eternal Jer 31:3 *See also* Ps 103:17;
136:1–26; Isa 49:15–16; 54:8,10

It is a covenant love Dt 7:9 *See also*
Ex 20:6 pp Dt 5:10; Dt 7:12; 1Ki 8:23
pp 2Ch 6:14; Ps 106:45; Da 9:4

It is lavish Ex 34:6–7 *See also* Ne 9:17;
Ps 103:8; Joel 2:13; Jnh 4:2; 1Jn 3:1

It is holy and just Ps 33:5 *See also*
Ps 37:28; 99:4; Isa 61:8

Images of God's love
God as a father: Dt 1:31; Hos 11:1–4;
Lk 15:11–32; Heb 12:6; Pr 3:12
God as a husband: Jer 31:32;
Hos 2:14–20; Rev 21:2

God's loving actions
**The gift of God's Son is a unique act of
love** 1Jn 4:9–10 *See also* Jn 3:16; 15:13;
Ro 5:7–8

God sets his love on the unlovely
Dt 7:7–8 *See also* Eze 16:1–14; Ro 5:8; Eph 2:4–5

God always acts in love towards believers
Ro 8:38–39 *See also* 2Co 13:14; 2Jn 3

God's love for his people
Israel Isa 43:4 *See also* Dt 10:15; 2Ch 9:8; Mt 15:24; Ro 9:15–16; Ex 33:19; Ro 11:28

The church Rev 1:5 *See also* Jn 16:27; 17:23

God's love for the world
Dt 10:18; Jn 3:16–17 *See also* Ps 145:9,17; Mt 5:45; Ac 14:17; 17:25

God's love for individuals
2Sa 12:24–25 *"Jedidiah" means "loved by the LORD".* See also Dt 33:12 *Benjamin* David: 2Sa 7:15 pp 1Ch 17:13; Isa 55:3 Ezr 7:28 *Ezra;* Ne 13:26 *Solomon*

God's love transforms human love
Human love must respond to God's love 1Jn 4:19 *See also* Dt 6:5; 30:6; Eph 5:1; Col 3:12–14

Human love must be modelled on God's love Mt 5:44–45 *See also* Hos 3:1; 1Jn 2:15; 4:7–8,11–12

See also

1030 God, compassion	5712 marriage, God & his people
1040 God, fatherhood	5762 attitudes, God to people
1055 God, grace & mercy	6638 election
1346 covenants	8207 commitment
2048 Christ, love of	8292 love
3209 Holy Spirit & love	8304 loyalty

1090
God, majesty of

The greatness and splendour of God, revealed in his creation and mighty works of deliverance. On account of his majesty, God is worthy of praise and adoration from all people.

God is majestic
Heb 8:1 *See also* 1Sa 15:29; Ps 24:10 *The word translated "glory" also means "majesty";* Heb 1:3–4

Majesty belongs to God
1Ch 29:11 *See also* Ps 145:12; Jude 25

God's majesty is awesome
Job 37:22 *See also* Isa 2:10,19,21

God's character is majestic
Ps 93:1 *A figurative expression indicating that God is fully majestic.* See also Ex 15:11; Ps 104:1; 145:5; Isa 24:14; 26:10

God's activity is majestic
Ex 15:6–7 *"hand" is a symbol of God's power which accomplishes his purposes.* See also Dt 9:26; 11:2–3; 2Ch 20:6; Ps 111:3; Lk 9:43

God's name is majestic
Ps 8:1 *See also* Ps 8:9

God's voice is majestic
Ps 29:4 *See also* Job 37:4; Isa 30:30

God's presence is majestic
1Ch 16:27 *See also* Ps 96:6; 2Th 1:9; 2Pe 1:17

The risen Christ shares in God's majesty
2Pe 1:16–17 *See also* Heb 1:3–4; 8:1

God's delegated majesty
To the Messiah Mic 5:4 *See also* Zec 9:9

To kings Ps 21:5 *See also* Ps 45:3–4; 110:2–3

God's majesty provides help for his people
Ps 68:34–35 *See also* Ex 15:6; Dt 33:26–27

Experiences of God's majesty
Isa 6:1–4 *Isaiah's vision;* Eze 1:4–28 *Ezekiel's vision;* Hab 3:3–6 *Habakkuk's description of God's person and work;* Rev 4:1–11 *John's vision*

Human responses to the majesty of God
An awareness of sin Isa 6:5

An awareness of insignificance *See also* Isa 40:15

Worship and adoration of God 1Ch 16:29; Ps 92:1–8; 93:1; 95:3–6; Lk 1:46

See also

1045 God, glory of	1145 God, transcendent
1060 God, greatness of	1193 glory, revelation of
1065 God, holiness of	1205 God, titles of
1105 God, power of	2051 Christ, majesty of
1110 God, present everywhere	8622 worship
1130 God, sovereignty	

1095
God, patience of

God shows forbearance in his character, decisions and actions. Above all, he waits patiently for people to turn to him for salvation.

God's patient character
God is slow to anger Nu 14:18 *"slow to anger" is the main OT expression for God's patient character.* See also Ex 34:6; Ne 9:16–17; Ps 86:15; 103:8; 145:8; Joel 2:13; Jnh 4:2; Na 1:3

God imparts patience Ro 15:5 *The Greek can be translated "God of endurance/patience". The phrase suggests that God is patient and imparts patience.* See also Jer 15:15; 2Th 3:5; 1Pe 3:20

God's patience with sinful people
God's patience lasts a long time Ac 13:18 *See also* Dt 8:2; Ne 9:30; Ps 78:38

God is patient in delaying punishment Isa 42:14 *See also* Ne 9:30–31; Ps 50:20–21; 78:38; Isa 48:9; Hab 2:3

Sinful people try God's patience Mal 2:17 *See also* Ge 18:16–33; Nu 14:27; Ps 78:41,56; Isa 1:14; 7:13; 43:24

Examples of God's patience
Ge 8:22 *with creation;* Ge 18:32 *with the city of Sodom;* 1Sa 3:10 *with Samuel* With his people: Eze 20:17; Mic 7:19 Jnh 3:1 *with Jonah*

The purpose of God's patience
Repentance Ro 2:4 *See also* 2Pe 3:9

Salvation 2Pe 3:15 *See also* Ro 9:22–24

See also

1030 God, compassion	5883 impatience
1055 God, grace & mercy	5977 waiting
	6020 sin
1085 God, love of	6510 salvation
2060 Christ, patience of	6686 mercy
	6732 repentance
5482 punishment	8318 patience

1100
God, perfection of

God is complete, faultless and totally sufficient in every aspect of his being and ways. That perfection is made known in Jesus Christ, and is the ultimate goal of the Christian life.

God's moral perfection
Ps 25:8 *See also* Ex 33:19; Ps 18:25–26; 92:15; Isa 26:7; Mk 10:18 pp Lk 18:19

Humanity should emulate God's moral perfection
Mt 5:48 *See also* Lev 19:2; 11:44–45; 1Pe 1:16; 2Co 7:1; 13:11

God's work is perfect
Dt 32:4 *See also* 2Sa 22:31 pp Ps 18:30; Ps 19:1; 40:5; 96:3; 139:14; 145:4–6; Jer 32:19–20

God's will is perfect
Ro 12:2 *See also* Ps 19:7–11

God's words are perfect
Ps 12:6 *See also* Ps 18:30; Pr 30:5

Humanity cannot always grasp the perfection of God's ways
Job 42:3 *See also* Ecc 3:11; Eze 18:25,29; 33:17–20

Examples of the perfection of God's attributes
Perfect knowledge Job 37:16; Ps 139:1–6; 147:5

Perfect faithfulness Isa 25:1

Perfect love 1Jn 3:1; 4:8–12,16–19

God's perfection is seen in Jesus Christ
Heb 7:26 *See also* Col 1:19; 2:9; Heb 2:10; 5:8–9; 7:28

See also

1020 God, all-knowing	1160 God, unchangeable
1050 God, goodness of	1165 God, unique
	1175 God, will of
1065 God, holiness of	2063 Christ, perfection
1085 God, love of	8321 perfection, divine
1105 God, power of	
1115 God, purpose of	8449 imitating

1105
God, power of

God is all-powerful (that is omnipotent), and is able to do whatever he wills. His power is limited only by his character.

God is all-powerful
Mk 10:27 pp Mt 19:26 See also Ge 18:14; Ps 93:1; Mk 14:36; Lk 1:37; 2Co 4:7

God cannot be thwarted
Job 42:2 See also Job 9:12; Isa 14:27

God's names denote his power
The uniqueness of God's power Jer 10:6

He is the Almighty
"the Almighty" is Hebrew "El Shaddai": Ge 28:3; 35:11; 43:14; Ex 6:3; Job 11:7; 31:2

He is the LORD Almighty and God Almighty
"Almighty" in these verses is usually Hebrew "Sabaoth": Ps 24:10; 89:8; Jer 10:16; 2Co 6:18; Rev 11:17; 19:6

He is the Mighty One Ge 49:24;
Jos 22:22; Ps 50:1; Isa 1:24; 10:21; 60:16; Mk 14:62; Lk 1:49

God's power is seen above all in his acts of redemption
God is powerful to save Zep 3:17

God shows his power in the exodus Dt 9:29 See also Ex 13:9; 14:31; Dt 7:8; 9:26; Ne 1:10; Jer 32:21

God shows his power through the work of Jesus Christ Ac 2:24 See also Ro 1:4; Eph 1:19–21; Col 2:13–15; Rev 12:10

God shows his power through the proclamation of the good news about Jesus Christ Ro 1:16 See also 1Co 1:18,24–25; 2Co 10:4; Col 2:12

God's power is shown in Jesus Christ's life
God's power in Jesus Christ's earthly ministry Lk 5:17 See also Lk 6:19; 8:46; Ac 10:38; 2Pe 1:16

God's power in Jesus Christ's heavenly ministry Heb 7:16 *In contrast to all other priests, Jesus Christ exercises his ministry now in heaven because death could not hold him. See also* Ac 4:10; 2Co 13:4

God's power seen in Jesus Christ's second coming Mk 13:26 pp Mt 24:30 pp Lk 21:27 See also 2Th 1:9–10

The Holy Spirit demonstrates God's power
Mic 3:8 See also Ac 1:8; 10:38; Ro 15:19; 1Co 2:4–5; 1Th 1:5

God's power in the world
God rules the created order Ro 1:20 See also Ps 19:1; 65:6; 68:34; Isa 40:26; Mt 8:26 pp Mk 4:39; Mt 21:19; Heb 1:3

God's works are powerful Dt 3:24 See also Ps 71:18; 77:12; 145:4; Jer 32:17–19; Lk 1:51

The ark symbolises God's powerful presence Ps 132:8 pp 2Ch 6:41 See also 1Sa 5:1–12; 2Sa 6:6–8,11–12; Ps 78:61

God keeps his promises Ro 4:21 See also 2Co 9:8

God gives life to the dead 1Co 6:14 See also Mt 22:29 pp Mk 12:24; Php 3:21

God's power in the lives of believers
God gives his own power to his people 1Ch 29:11–12 See also 1Sa 2:10; Da 2:27–28; 2Co 13:3–4; Php 4:13; 2Ti 1:7; 1Pe 4:11

God's power achieves his purposes in his people's lives 2Th 1:11 See also Mic 5:4; Ac 4:28; 1Co 5:4; Eph 1:20–21

God's power completes his work of salvation in believers' lives 1Pe 1:5 See also 2Ti 1:12; Heb 7:25; Jude 24

God's power gives believers inner strength Eph 3:16–17 See also Eph 1:18–19; 6:10; Php 3:10; Col 1:11

God's power is made plain through human weakness 2Co 12:9–10 See also Isa 53:1–3; 2Co 4:7; 13:4

God's power gives help to believers in suffering 2Ti 4:16–17 See also 2Ch 25:8; Ps 46:1; Da 3:17; 2Co 6:7; 2Ti 1:8

God's power is limited only by his character
God cannot deny himself 2Ti 2:13 See also Jas 1:17

God cannot tolerate evil Hab 1:13

God cannot be tempted Jas 1:13

God cannot lie Nu 23:19 See also 1Sa 15:29; Heb 6:18

God's power is to be praised
Ps 68:35 See also Ps 21:13; 118:14; 1Ti 6:16; Jude 25; Rev 5:12

See also

1115 God, purpose of	2066 Christ, power of
1205 God, titles of	2560 Christ, resurrection
1230 God, the Lord	
1265 hand of God	3030 Holy Spirit, power
1320 God as Saviour	
1325 God, the Creator	5452 power
1415 miracles	5955 strength, divine

1110
God, present everywhere

God is omnipresent in that he transcends all limitations of space and is present in the fulness of his being in every place but in varying ways.

God transcends all spatial limitations
1Ki 8:27 pp 2Ch 6:18 See also 2Ch 2:6; Ps 113:4–6

God is present throughout heaven and earth
Ps 139:7–12; Jer 23:23–24 See also Nu 14:21; Dt 4:39; Isa 6:3; 66:1; Am 9:2–3

God sees and knows everything
Pr 15:3 See also 2Ch 16:9; Zec 4:10

God is near to all human beings
Ac 17:27–28

God is present with special groups of people
God is especially close to the poor and needy Ps 34:18 See also Isa 57:15

God is especially close to those who call on him Ps 145:18 See also Ps 16:8; Isa 50:8

God's presence with his people
God is always present with his people Ex 33:15–16 See also Ps 14:5; Isa 43:2; Zep 3:17; 1Co 14:25

God's promise to be present Jos 1:9 See also Ge 28:15; 31:3; Ex 29:45; Lev 26:12; Dt 20:1; 31:8; Mt 28:20

God is present in believers through the Holy Spirit 1Co 3:16 See also Jn 14:18; Eph 2:22; 1Jn 3:24

God will be acknowledged everywhere
Ps 113:3 See also Ps 72:19; 96:7–9,11–13; Mal 1:11; Rev 5:13

See also

1020 God, all-knowing	3035 Holy Spirit, presence of
1145 God, transcendent	3278 Holy Spirit, indwelling
1305 God, activity of	8134 knowing God

1115
God, purpose of

God has a plan for his creation which he will certainly accomplish. It is carried out through the control of circumstances and his choice and use of people, and above all in the life, death, resurrection and second coming of Jesus Christ.

God's purpose will be accomplished
Isa 46:10–11 See also Ps 135:6; Pr 16:4; Ecc 3:14; Isa 14:24,26–27; 25:1; 55:11; Eph 1:11

God's purpose prevails
It stands for ever Ps 33:11 See also Job 42:2; Jer 23:20

It cannot be thwarted by human beings Pr 19:21 See also Job 9:12; 23:13; Isa 8:10; Da 4:35

It cannot be thwarted by evil powers Rev 17:17 See also 1Sa 16:14 *The implication is that evil is subject to God's control and operates within the determined limits of his sovereign purpose;* Job 1:12; 2:6; 2Co 12:7

It prevails in people's lives and circumstances Pr 16:9 See also Pr 20:24; 21:1

It is fulfilled through his choice of individuals Eph 1:11 *God's choice of individuals does not invalidate their free will to do or not to do anything, nor remove their answerability to God for their actions. See also* Ge 18:19; Ro 11:5; 1Co 1:1; Eph 1:4–5; 2Th 2:13

Examples of the actions of evil people serving God's purpose Ac 2:23 See also Ge 50:20; Isa 10:5–7

God's purpose is founded on divine wisdom

Eph 3:10–11 *See also* Ps 104:24; Ro 11:33

God's purpose is determined from eternity

2Ti 1:9 *See also* 2Ki 19:25; Isa 25:1; 46:10; Mt 25:34; Eph 1:4; Tit 1:2; 1Pe 1:20

God's purpose is for his own glory

Ex 9:16 *See also* Ro 9:17; Eze 36:22–23; Eph 1:5–6,11–12

God's purpose for his people

God reveals his purpose to his people Am 3:7 *See also* Ge 18:17; 2Sa 7:20–21; 1Co 2:9–10; Eph 1:9

Its fulness is beyond human understanding Ro 11:33 *See also* Dt 29:29; 1Co 2:9–10; Eph 1:9; 3:4–5

It is good and loving Ro 8:28 *See also* Jer 29:11; Ro 12:2; Eph 1:4–5; 2Ti 1:9

God's purpose is revealed through Jesus Christ

In the church Eph 3:10–11

It centres on the cross Isa 53:10 *See also* Ac 4:27–28; 1Pe 1:19–20; 1Jn 4:10

It is God's purpose to redeem the world through the cross Mt 26:18,45 *Jesus Christ often speaks of his appointed "hour". In John's Gospel in particular his "hour" refers to the cross. Jesus Christ refuses to allow anything except the cross to be the climax of his ministry (Jn 12:27).* pp Mk 14:41; Jn 7:6–8; 12:23; 13:1; 17:1

It is God's purpose to exalt and establish Jesus Christ as Lord Eph 1:9–10 *See also* Ac 2:36; Php 2:8–11; Col 1:18; Heb 1:2–4

Jesus Christ submits to God's purpose Jn 6:38 *See also* Mt 26:39–42 pp Mk 14:35–36 pp Lk 22:42; Jn 4:34; 5:30; Heb 5:7–8; 10:7

God's ultimate purpose is to save

The salvation of people through Jesus Christ Jn 6:40 *See also* Jn 3:16–17; Gal 1:3–4; 1Ti 2:3–4; 1Pe 1:2; 2Pe 3:9

Specific aspects of God's purpose in salvation 2Co 5:5 *knowing heavenly life;* Ro 8:29 *being conformed to Jesus Christ;* Eph 1:4 *being holy and blameless;* Eph 2:15 *becoming unified;* Eph 3:10–11 *that the wisdom of God be revealed*

God wills that people submit to his purposes

Jas 4:15 *See also* Ps 40:8; 143:10; Mt 6:10

God's people should pray for the fulfilment of his purposes

Mt 6:9–10 pp Lk 11:2

People can reject God's purposes in their lives

Lk 7:30; 19:41–42; Ac 13:46

Examples of God's purposes being worked out

Ge 45:5–9 *in the life of Joseph* Through Cyrus: Isa 41:2,25; 45:1,13; 46:11; 48:14 *In the life of Paul:* Ac 18:21; 21:14; Ro 1:10; 15:32; 1Co 4:19

See also
1020 God, all-knowing
1045 God, glory of
1105 God, power of
1130 God, sovereignty
1175 God, will of
1180 God, wisdom of
1439 revelation
2057 Christ, obedience
2354 Christ, mission
5376 law, purpose of
6638 election
7031 unity, God's goal

1120

God, repentance of

A change in God's plan or intention, often in response to human repentance, but without implying any fault or moral imperfection on God's part.

God's repentance may show his pain and sorrow

Ge 6:6–7 *God's change of purpose here involves his intention to punish. See also* 1Sa 15:11,35

God's repentance may show his compassion

Jnh 4:2 *God's change of purpose here involves his compassion for sinners: "relent" in this and other passages may also be translated "repent". See also* Dt 32:36; 2Sa 24:15–16 pp 1Ch 21:14–15; Ps 106:45; Isa 38:1–5; Hos 11:8; Am 7:1–6

God may repent in response to human repentance Jer 18:8 *See also* Ex 32:14; 2Ch 12:1–8; Jer 26:13,19; Joel 2:13; Jnh 3:6–10

God never repents of his oath or changes his character

Nu 23:19; Ps 110:4; Heb 6:17–18

See also
1030 God, compassion
1135 God, suffering of
1160 God, unchangeable
5013 heart, divine
5036 mind of God
5938 sadness
6178 hardness of heart
6227 regret
6653 forgiveness, divine
6687 mercy, God's
6733 repentance

1125

God, righteousness of

An aspect of God's nature which expresses his unique moral perfection and his readiness to save sinners. It is made known especially through the gospel of Jesus Christ.

God's nature is righteous

Ps 119:137 *See also* Dt 32:4; Ps 48:10; 97:2; 119:142; 145:17; Isa 45:21; Jer 12:1; Jn 17:25

God's righteousness shows his sovereignty Ps 71:19 *See also* Job 37:23; Ps 36:6; 97:6; Isa 5:16

God's righteousness is eternal Ps 111:3 *See also* Ps 112:3,9; 119:142,160; Isa 51:8

God's actions are righteous

Da 9:14 *See also* Jdg 5:11; 1Sa 12:7; Jer 9:24; Rev 15:3

God's rule is righteous Ps 9:8 *See also* 2Sa 23:3–4; Ps 96:13; 99:4; Jer 9:23–24

God's righteous acts are saving acts Ps 65:5 *See also* Ps 40:10; 116:4–6; 129:4; Isa 41:10; 46:13; Da 9:16; Mic 6:5

God's righteousness vindicates his people Ps 35:24 *See also* Ps 4:2–3; 7:9; 9:4; 103:6; Isa 50:8; Mic 7:9; Ro 8:33

God's righteousness shows his faithfulness Ne 9:8 *See also* Ps 4:1; Zep 3:5; Zec 8:8

God's righteousness shows his justice Jer 11:20 *See also* Ge 18:25; Job 8:3; Ps 11:7; 50:6; 51:4; Pr 21:12; Ecc 3:17; 2Ti 4:8

God's righteousness is seen in his judgments Ps 7:11 *See also* 2Ch 12:5–6; Ezr 9:15; Isa 10:22; 28:17; La 1:18; Mal 3:5; Ro 2:2,5

God's laws show his righteousness

Ps 19:8–9 *See also* Dt 4:8; Ps 33:4; 119:71,44; Ro 1:32; 7:12; 8:4

God's righteousness contrasts with human unrighteousness

Ro 3:5 *See also* Ex 9:27; Ne 9:33; Job 4:17; 9:2; Da 9:7; Ro 10:3

God's righteousness is revealed primarily in Jesus Christ

Ro 3:21–22 *See also* Isa 11:2–5; Jer 23:6; Zec 9:9; Ac 3:14; Ro 10:4; 1Co 1:30; 2Pe 1:1; 1Jn 2:1

God's righteousness is revealed in the gospel Ro 1:17 *See also* Php 3:9

God gives his righteousness to believers Ro 4:22–24 *See also* Ge 15:6; Job 33:26; Hos 10:12; Ro 3:22; 4:3–8; 5:17; 10:4; 2Co 5:21

The Holy Spirit reveals God's righteousness

Gal 5:5 *See also* Jn 16:8,10; Ro 14:17

God's righteousness is to be sought after

Mt 6:33 *See also* Isa 51:1; Zep 2:3

God's righteousness is a pattern for human living

1Jn 3:7 *See also* Ge 18:19; Hos 14:9; Eph 4:24; 1Jn 2:29; 3:12

God's righteousness is worthy of praise

Isa 24:15–16 *See also* Ps 7:17; 22:31; 35:28; 51:14; 71:15,24; 145:7

See also
1065 God, holiness of
1075 God, justice of
1320 God as Saviour
2072 Christ, righteousness
5360 justice, God
5375 law
6025 sin & God's character
6674 imputation
6676 justification
6712 propitiation
8154 righteousness

1130

God, sovereignty of

The fact that God is free and able to do all that he wills; that he reigns over all creation and that his will is the final cause of all things. This is often expressed in the language of kingship.

God is free to do all he wills
Ps 135:6 *See also* Ps 115:3; Isa 46:10; Da 4:35; Ro 9:19–21

God is able to do whatever he wills
Lk 1:37 *Gabriel speaking to Mary. See also* Job 42:2; Mt 19:26; Eph 3:20

God cannot be successfully opposed
Job 42:2 *From Job's prayer of submission and repentance. See also* 1Sa 2:10; 2Ch 20:6; Job 9:12; Ecc 7:13; Isa 43:13; 45:9–10; Ac 5:39

God rules and reigns
He is King Ps 29:10 *See also* 1Ch 16:31; Ps 47:2; Isa 6:5; 43:15; Jer 10:7,10; Zec 14:9; 1Ti 1:17; 6:15; Rev 15:3; 19:6

He is Lord of heaven and earth Dt 4:39 *See also* Ge 24:3; Dt 10:14; Jos 2:11; 1Ch 29:11; Ne 9:6; Ps 121:2; 134:3; Lk 10:21; Ac 17:24

His throne is a symbol of his sovereignty Ex 17:16; Ps 45:6; 93:2; 123:1–2; Isa 6:1 *Isaiah's commission;* Isa 66:1; Jer 49:38; La 5:19; Eze 1:26; Da 7:9 *Daniel's dream;* Mt 5:34; 19:28 *Jesus Christ teaches his disciples about things to come;* Ac 7:49; Heb 1:8; 8:1; 12:2; Rev 4:2; 20:11

God's sovereignty extends over all things
He is sovereign over creation Rev 4:11 *See also* Ps 93:1; Isa 40:22; 41:18–19

He is sovereign over human life 1Ch 29:12 *Part of David's prayer on the occasion of gifts being brought to the temple. See also* 2Ch 25:8; Lk 1:51–53; Ac 18:21; Jas 4:15

He is sovereign over the minutest details of life Mt 10:29–30 pp Lk 12:6–7

He is sovereign in electing his people Eph 1:11 *See also* Ro 8:29; 9:11,18

He is sovereign in the life and salvation of his people 1Co 1:30 *See also* Jer 18:6; 1Co 12:11; Php 2:13; Jas 1:18

He is sovereign over the sufferings of believers Php 1:29; 1Pe 3:17

He is sovereign over world history Pr 21:1 *See also* Ex 9:16; Ps 22:28; Jer 18:7–10; Da 4:35

God is sovereign over all other gods and over demonic forces
God is supreme over all gods Ps 95:3 *"gods" are part of the created order and subject to God's sovereignty. See also* Ex 18:11; Dt 10:17; 1Ch 16:26; Ps 96:5; Da 2:47; Col 1:16

Satan is defeated through God's sovereign purposes at work in Jesus Christ Col 2:15 *See also* Jn 12:31; Ro 16:20; 2Th 2:8; Heb 2:14; 2Pe 2:4; 1Jn 3:8; Jude 6; Rev 12:7–10

See also

1105 God, power of	4120 Satan
1115 God, purpose of	4135 demons, Christ's authority over
1175 God, will of	4945 history
1310 God as judge	5003 human race & God
2372 Christ, victory	6663 freedom of will
2376 kingdom of God, coming	
3045 Holy Spirit, sovereignty	

1135
God, suffering of

God suffers on account of the failures and pain of his people, and especially through his Son, Jesus Christ. Scripture often likens God to a parent who suffers pain and grief on account of children.

God feels real suffering
He suffers pain because people sin Ge 6:6 *See also* 1Sa 15:10–11,35

He is angered because people sin Ps 78:58 *See also* Dt 32:15–16; Jdg 2:12–13; 1Ki 21:22; Eze 8:17; Hos 12:14

God identifies with suffering
He suffers with his chosen people Isa 63:9 *See also* Ex 3:7; Jdg 10:16; 2Ch 36:15

He suffers with all humanity Isa 16:11 pp Jer 48:31 *See also* 2Sa 24:15–17 pp 1Ch 21:14–17 *God suffers even with those who endure punishment from his own hand;* Isa 16:9; Jer 48:32–36; Hos 11:8–9

He suffers as a parent Jer 31:20 *An indication that God suffers in both disciplining and loving. See also* Isa 42:14; 49:15; Hos 11:1–4

God's plan of salvation causes him suffering
He suffered in giving his Son Ro 8:32 *See also* Isa 7:13–14; Jn 3:16; Ro 3:25–26; 8:3; Gal 4:4; Heb 1:2; 1Jn 4:14

He suffers because he endures the rejection his Son suffers Lk 10:16 *See also* 1Pe 2:4

God's creation reflects his suffering
Ro 8:22 *See also* Ro 8:19–21

God's people share his suffering
Ro 8:17 *There is a sense in which the sufferings of Father and Son are indistinguishable. See also* Mt 16:24 pp Mk 8:34 pp Lk 9:23; Mt 20:22–23 pp Mk 10:38–39; Php 1:29; 1Pe 2:21

See also

1025 God, anger of	2078 Christ, sonship of
1030 God, compassion	
1040 God, fatherhood	2570 Christ, suffering
1065 God, holiness of	4025 world, the
1125 God, righteousness	5560 suffering
	6154 fall, the
	6214 participation in Christ

1140
God, the eternal

God transcends all limitations of time and endures for ever.

God endures for ever
Ne 9:5 *See also* Dt 32:40; 33:27; Job 36:26; Ps 48:14; 102:12; Isa 40:28; Hab 1:12

God transcends all concepts of time
Rev 1:8 *See also* Ps 90:4; Isa 41:4; 1Co 2:7; Heb 13:8; 2Pe 3:8; Rev 11:17; 22:13

He existed before time Ps 90:2 *See also* Pr 8:23; Jn 17:5,24; Eph 1:4; 1Pe 1:20

He will exist after time Heb 1:11–12 *See also* Ps 102:26–27

The eternity of God's qualities
His love 1Ch 16:34 pp Ps 106:1 *See also* 2Ch 5:13; Ps 103:17; Jer 31:3; Hos 2:19

His faithfulness Ps 100:5 *See also* Ps 117:2; 146:6

His power Ps 66:7 *See also* Ro 1:20; 1Pe 5:11

His righteousness Ps 111:3 *See also* Ps 112:3; 119:142; Da 9:24

God's word is eternal
Ps 119:89 *See also* Mk 13:31; 1Pe 1:24–25; Isa 40:8

God's covenant is eternal
Ge 17:7 *See also* Nu 18:19; Ps 105:10; Isa 24:5; 54:10; 55:3; Jer 32:40

God's kingdom is eternal
Ps 145:13 *See also* Ex 15:18; Ps 9:7; 45:6; La 5:19; Da 4:3; 7:14,27; 2Pe 1:11

God's gifts are eternal
Ro 11:29

He gives eternal life Jn 10:28 *See also* Jn 5:24; 6:47; Ro 2:7; 6:23

He gives eternal salvation Isa 45:17 *See also* Heb 5:9; 9:12

He gives eternal joy Isa 35:10 *See also* Ps 16:11; Isa 51:11; 61:7

He gives eternal possessions Ge 48:4 *See also* Ge 17:8

See also

1035 God, faithfulness	1235 God, the LORD
1080 God, living	1345 covenant
1085 God, love of	1690 word of God
1105 God, power of	2375 kingdom of God
1125 God, righteousness	6644 eternal life
1145 God, transcendent	9122 eternity & God

1145
God, transcendence of

God is far above, beyond and outside the created order.

God is outside and above all creation
Ps 113:4; Isa 40:22 *Solomon confesses that God transcends containment by the temple:* 1Ki 8:27; 2Ch 2:6

Job 37:23 *Elihu declares the LORD to be beyond reach*; Ps 8:1; 57:5,11; 97:9; 108:5; 148:13; Isa 33:5; Ac 7:49; 17:24; Eph 1:20–21 *Jesus Christ is above all, in the place of highest honour and authority*; Eph 4:6; Heb 7:26

God is able also to draw near to his creatures
Isa 57:15

The invisibility of God
God is invisible to people and hidden from their sight Ex 33:20 ; Isa 45:15 *See also* Ex 3:6
Job is unable to find God in his suffering: Job 9:11; 23:8–9
Ps 10:1; 13:1; 89:46; Jn 1:18 *Jesus Christ has made God known*; Jn 5:37; Col 1:15 *Jesus Christ is the image of God*; 1Ti 1:17; 6:16; 1Jn 4:12

OT saints who saw God Ex 33:11 *These exceptions indicate that God's invisibility is not inherent, but the result of sinful people's inability to look upon a holy God. See also* Ge 32:30; Ex 24:10; Jdg 13:22; Isa 6:5

God is made visible in Jesus Christ Jn 1:18; 14:9; 2Co 4:4,6; Col 1:15

Redeemed people will be able to look at God's face
Mt 5:8; 1Co 13:12; 1Jn 3:2; Rev 22:4

God's ways are beyond human understanding
Isa 55:8–9 *See also* Dt 29:29; Job 5:9; 11:7; 36:22–23; Ps 139:1–6; Pr 25:2; Ecc 3:11; Isa 40:28; Ro 11:33–34; 1Co 2:11,16

See also

1065 God, holiness of	1325 God, the Creator
1110 God, present everywhere	1439 revelation
1130 God, sovereignty	1454 theophany
1140 God, the eternal	1469 visions
1210 God, human descriptions	2078 Christ, sonship of
	6694 mystery
	6720 redemption

1150
God, truth of

God's unique integrity is displayed in his perfection of character and attributes. It is further emphasised by the consistent truth of his words and works, supremely shown in Jesus Christ.

God is the one and only true God
He alone is God Jer 10:10 *See also* Dt 4:39; 2Ch 15:3; Isa 43:10–11; 45:5–6,14,21; Zec 14:9; Jn 1:18; 17:3; Rev 6:10

The contrast with other "gods" Ro 1:25 *See also* Ex 15:11; Dt 4:35; 32:39; Ps 86:8; Isa 43:3; 1Th 1:9

The contrast with earthly rulers Jer 10:6–8

God is characterised by truth
Ps 31:5 *See also* Ps 40:10; 43:3; Isa 65:16; Jn 3:33; 7:28; 8:26; 1Jn 5:20; Rev 15:3

God's truth is demonstrated in the revelation of himself in Jesus Christ
Jesus Christ is "the truth" Jn 14:6 *In the light of this statement it may be concluded that truth is actually defined by the person and work of Jesus Christ. See also* 1Jn 5:20

Jesus Christ and the Spirit bring truth Jn 1:14; 14:16–17; Ro 15:8

God's words are truthful
His words are consistently true and reliable Nu 23:19 *See also* 1Sa 15:29; Ps 12:6; 33:4; 119:151,160; Ro 3:4; Tit 1:2; Heb 6:18; Jas 1:17

His words of promise are totally true and trustworthy Ps 132:11 *See also* 2Ti 2:13 *The guarantee of God's faithfulness is the truthfulness of his promises which depend in turn upon the truth that characterises God himself*; Heb 7:21; Ps 110:4

God's people live in the light of his truth
Ps 86:11 *See also* Ps 26:3; 119:141–142; Da 9:13; Jn 17:17

See also

1035 God, faithfulness	1461 truth, nature of
1065 God, holiness of	3140 Holy Spirit, teacher
1100 God, perfection	6146 deceit & God
1155 God, truthfulness	8227 discernment
1165 God, unique	8314 orthodoxy
	8722 doubt
	8768 idolatry

1155
God, truthfulness of

To call the LORD "the true God" means that he alone has in his being the fulness of deity and is worthy to be worshipped as God. He and his word are a trustworthy foundation for life because he speaks the truth and is utterly reliable and consistent in his character, his revelation of himself, his promises and his pronouncements.

Titles reflecting God's truthfulness
The true God 2Ch 15:3; Jer 10:10; 1Th 1:9

The God of truth Ps 31:5; Isa 65:16

Jesus Christ is "the truth" Jn 14:6 *See also* Jn 1:14,17; 6:32 *Jesus Christ calls himself "the true bread" meaning that he is real, substantial, reliable and life-giving*; 1Jn 5:20; Rev 3:7,14

The Spirit of truth Jn 14:17; 15:26; 16:13; 1Jn 4:6; 5:6

God is true to his character and his word
He speaks the truth Isa 45:19 *See also* 2Sa 7:28; Ps 33:4; 119:160; Jn 17:17; Rev 21:5; 22:6

He does not lie Nu 23:19 *See also* Ro 3:4; 2Ti 2:13; Tit 1:2; Heb 6:18

He is true to himself and his promises Dt 32:4; Ps 25:10; 33:4; 145:13; 146:6; La 3:23; 2Ti 2:13

The truthfulness of God undergirds the law
Ps 119:142 *See also* Ps 19:7; 119:151,160; Mal 2:6–7

The truthfulness of God undergirds the covenant
Ps 25:10 *The Hebrew word translated "faithful" can also be translated "true". The word is particularly associated with God steadfastly upholding his covenant promises. See also* Ps 145:13; Hos 2:19–20; 2Ti 2:13

The truthfulness of God undergirds the prophetic word
Eze 12:25 *See also* Isa 55:11; Jer 1:12; 28:9; Eze 33:33; Da 2:45

The truthfulness of God undergirds his promises
Jos 23:14–15 *See also* Nu 23:19; 1Ki 8:20; Ps 105:42; Ro 4:20–21

The truthfulness of God undergirds his judgment
Ps 96:13 *See also* Ps 98:9; Isa 11:3–5; Ro 2:2

The truthfulness of God undergirds the teaching of Jesus Christ
Jn 1:17 *See also* Mt 5:18; 22:16 pp Mk 12:14 pp Lk 20:21; Mk 3:28; Lk 4:24; Jn 1:51; 8:31–32; 18:37

See also

1035 God, faithfulness	3296 Holy Spirit in the world
1075 God, justice of	6146 deceit & God
1115 God, purpose of	8275 honesty
1150 God, truth of	8354 trustworthiness
1461 truth, nature of	
1690 word of God	
2363 Christ, preaching & teaching	

1160
God, unchangeableness of

God's nature, plans and actions do not change even though he is active and his relationships do not remain static. His moral consistency guarantees his commitment to unchanging principles.

God's being is unchangeable
Ps 102:27 *See also* Heb 1:12; Mal 3:6; Heb 13:8; Jas 1:17

God's characteristics do not change
God's love is constant Ps 89:2 *See also* Ps 136:1–26; 2Ti 2:13

God's purposes and plans do not change
Heb 6:17 *See also* Nu 23:19; 1Sa 15:29; Pr 19:21; Jer 44:29; Heb 7:21; Ps 110:4

God does not revoke his promises
Ps 132:11 *See also* Ps 145:13; Heb 4:1

God's word does not change
Isa 40:8 *See also* Ps 119:89; Mt 5:18; 1Pe 1:23–25

God's failure to inflict promised judgment is a sign of his unchanging grace
Hos 11:8 *See also* Ex 32:10–14; Jnh 3:10; 4:2

See also

1035 God, faithfulness	1120 God, repentance of
1050 God, goodness of	1140 God, the eternal
1055 God, grace & mercy	1170 God, unity of
1085 God, love of	1340 consistency
1115 God, purpose of	5467 promises, divine
	8331 reliability

1165
God, uniqueness of

No-one and nothing is comparable to the triune God in his nature or comparable to him in his character and activity.

There is no God except the LORD
Isa 45:5–6 *God alone stands outside nature as its Creator. All other beings are created by him. See also* Dt 4:35; 6:4; 32:3; 1Ki 8:60; Ps 83:18; 86:10; Isa 43:10–11; 44:6–8; 45:18; 1Co 8:4–6; Eph 4:6; 1Ti 2:5

There is no-one like God
Ps 89:6–8 *See also* Ex 8:10; Isa 40:18

In his creative power Isa 40:25–26 *See also* Jn 1:3; Ne 9:6; Ac 14:15; Col 1:16; Rev 4:11

In his mighty acts Ps 86:10 *See also* Ps 135:5–6

In his character and glory Ex 15:11 *See also* 2Sa 7:22; 1Ch 29:11

In his ability to save Dt 33:26 *See also* Isa 45:20–22; Jer 10:5–6

In his covenant love 1Ki 8:23 *See also* 2Sa 7:22–23 pp 1Ch 17:20–21

In his sovereignty Zec 14:9 *See also* Dt 4:39; 1Ti 1:17

Implications of God's uniqueness
God alone is to be worshipped
Ex 20:2–3 pp Dt 5:6–7 *See also* Ex 23:13,24; Lev 19:4; Dt 6:13–14; 2Ki 17:35

Idolatry is empty and worthless Jnh 2:8 *See also* Dt 4:28; Isa 44:18–20; 45:20; Hab 2:18

See also

1045 God, glory of	1240 God, the Rock
1060 God, greatness of	1320 God as Saviour
1090 God, majesty of	1325 God, the Creator
1130 God, sovereignty	1651 numbers, 1–2
1145 God, transcendent	5971 uniqueness
	8768 idolatry
	8799 polytheism

1170
God, unity of

God acts as a unity in all his deeds. The three persons of the Trinity are united in one Godhead. They are interrelated with one another, share the same attributes and co-operate in

the same work. God's characteristics are consistent, expressing his integral divine nature.

God is one
Dt 6:4 *See also* Mk 12:29,32; 1Co 8:4; Gal 3:20; Eph 4:5–6; 1Ti 2:5; Jas 2:19

The three persons of the Trinity are united in one Godhead
All three are interrelated Ro 8:9–11 *The interchange between the persons of the Trinity reflects their unity in terms of activity. See also* Jn 14:23; 2Co 13:14; Eph 2:18; 1Pe 1:2

The Son is one with the Father Jn 10:30 *See also* Mt 10:40; Mk 9:37 pp Lk 9:48; Lk 10:16; Jn 8:16; 14:9

The Spirit is one with God 2Sa 23:2–3 *See also* Ps 51:11; 1Co 3:16

The three persons are one in character
All three are eternal Ro 16:26 *the Father;* Isa 9:6 *the Son;* Heb 9:14 *the Spirit*

All three are all-knowing Isa 40:13–14 *the Father*
The Son: Jn 2:24–25; 21:17
1Co 2:10–11 *the Spirit*

All three are holy Jn 17:11 *the Father*
The Son: Mk 1:24; Ac 3:14
The Spirit: Jn 14:26; Ro 1:4

All three are called Lord and God
The Father: Mt 11:25; Ac 3:22; 1Co 8:6
The Son: Jn 1:1; 20:28; Ac 10:36; 2Pe 1:1
The Spirit: Ac 5:3–4; 2Co 3:17–18

All three are glorious
The Father: Ac 7:2; Eph 1:17
The Son: Jn 1:14; 12:41
The Spirit: 2Co 3:8,18; 1Pe 4:14

The three persons share in the same work
In creation Ge 1:1–3 *See also* Ps 33:6; 104:30; Jn 1:3–4; Col 1:16

In Jesus Christ's ministry Jn 3:34 *See also* Ac 10:38

In salvation 1Pe 1:2 *See also* 2Co 1:21–22; Tit 3:4–6

In indwelling the church Eph 2:22
The Spirit indwells believers: 1Co 3:16; 6:19
The Son indwells believers: Gal 2:20; Eph 3:17

In directing the church's mission Ac 16:6–10
The Father directs mission: Ac 14:27; Gal 1:1
The Son directs mission: Mt 28:18–20; Ac 1:7–8
The Spirit directs mission: Ac 13:2,4

God's characteristics are consistent
His love and justice are in unity
Ex 34:6–7 *See also* 2Sa 7:14–15; Ps 103:6–8; Ro 3:25–26

His wrath and mercy are in unity
Joel 2:11–13 *See also* Jn 3:16–18 *It is particularly in the cross of Jesus Christ that the perfect balance between God's wrath and justice and his love and mercy are seen;* Ro 2:4,7–8

See also

1100 God, perfection	3015 Holy Spirit, divinity
1160 God, unchangeable	7031 unity, God's goal
1165 God, unique	8138 monotheism
1510 Trinity, the	
2218 Christ, Son of God	

1175
God, will of

The intent and purpose of God, as revealed in Scripture. God's will for his creation and his people is set out in the Law and the Prophets, which find their fulfilment in Jesus Christ. A central aspect of the will of God is that his people be faithful and obedient.

The revelation of God's will
In his word 2Ti 3:16 *See also* 2Sa 7:21 pp 1Ch 17:19; Ps 103:20–21; Col 1:25–26; 1Jn 2:4–5

Through the law Ex 18:15–16; 24:12; Dt 30:16; Ps 119:43; Ro 7:12; 1Ti 1:8

Through the prophets 1Ki 22:6–7 pp 2Ch 18:5–6; 2Ki 3:11; Jer 42:3–4; Eze 12:25; Am 3:7

In the apostolic gospel Ac 20:27; Gal 1:11–12

The fulfilment of God's will
God's will is fulfilled in Jesus Christ
Eph 1:9–10 *See also* Eph 3:4–11; Col 1:27

Jesus Christ obeyed his Father's will
Jn 6:38 *See also* Mt 26:39 pp Mk 14:36 pp Lk 22:42; Jn 4:34; 5:30; Heb 10:7; Ps 40:8

Jesus Christ's death fulfilled God's will
Gal 1:3–4 *See also* Isa 53:10; Ac 2:23

God's will for the world
God desires justice and righteousness
Am 5:24 *See also* Ps 33:5; Isa 5:7; Jer 9:24; Mic 6:8

God desires honesty and truth Pr 12:22 *See also* Ex 20:16 pp Dt 5:20; Lev 19:35–36; Pr 11:1; Zec 8:16–17

God desires harmony and peace
1Ti 2:2–3 *See also* Isa 2:3–4 pp Mic 4:2–3; Isa 11:6–9

God desires the world to be saved
1Ti 2:4 *See also* Eze 18:23; 33:11; Mt 18:14; Jn 3:16–17; 2Pe 3:9

God's will for his redeemed people
God desires loving obedience
Mt 22:35–38 pp Mk 12:28–29 pp Lk 10:27 *See also* Dt 6:5
Scripture regularly makes obedience to God a higher priority than performing religious acts: Ps 51:16–17; Isa 1:11; Jer 7:22–23; 1Jn 2:5

God desires worship 1Pe 2:9 *See also* Ps 100:4; Isa 45:23; 1Th 5:18; Rev 1:6

God desires holiness 1Th 4:3 *See also* Lev 19:1–2; 1Co 1:2; Col 1:22; 1Th 4:7; Heb 10:10; 1Pe 1:15–16

God desires love for one another
Jn 13:34–35 *See also* Lev 19:18;

Mt 22:39 pp Mk 12:31 pp Lk 10:27;
Jn 15:12–13; Gal 5:14; 1Jn 3:11

God desires high moral standards
1Pe 2:15 *See also* Mt 5:16,48; 1Pe 3:4

God's will may involve suffering
1Pe 3:17 *See also* Ac 14:22; 21:13–14;
Heb 12:5–7; 1Pe 4:19

Proper responses to God's will
Discovering God's will Eph 5:17 *See
also* Ro 2:18; Col 1:9

Obeying God's will Mt 7:21 *See also*
Ezr 10:11; Mt 12:50 pp Mk 3:35;
Eph 6:6; Heb 13:21; Jas 4:15

Praying for God's will Mt 6:10 *See also*
Ps 143:10; Mt 26:42; Jn 14:13–14;
1Jn 5:14

Making radical changes to do God's
will Ro 12:2 *See also* Ro 8:5;
Gal 5:16–17; Jas 1:20; 1Pe 1:14; 4:2;
1Jn 2:15–17

Rejecting God's will
Lk 7:30 *See also* Ps 107:11; Isa 30:1;
Eze 3:7; Mt 23:37 pp Lk 13:34; Jn 8:44

**Examples of people who obeyed
God's will**
Dt 33:21 *Gad*
David: 1Sa 13:14; Ac 13:22,36
Isa 44:28–45:1 *Cyrus*
Paul: Ac 18:21; 21:14; Ro 1:10; 15:32;
1Co 4:19

Ways of discovering God's will
Ex 18:20 *teaching*; Ex 28:30 *Urim and
Thummim*; Ps 86:11 *prayer*; Ps 119:105
God's word; Da 2:22–23 *revelation*;
Jn 14:26 *the Holy Spirit*; Ac 1:26 *drawing
lots*

God's will and the human will
God's will overrules human wills
Pr 19:21 *See also* Ps 33:10–11; Pr 16:9

God's will overrides the desires of the
wicked Ge 50:20; Isa 10:5–11;
Hab 1:5–11; Ac 2:23

God's will can harmonise with human
wills 1Ch 13:2; Ps 37:4; 145:19;
Ac 15:28

God's will is sovereign
Over all things Eph 1:11

Over creation *See also* Mt 10:29;
Ro 8:20; Rev 4:11

Over evil Ge 45:8; 1Sa 2:25; Pr 16:4;
Isa 65:12; Ro 9:18

Over the gospel Mic 7:18; Mt 11:25–26
pp Lk 10:21; Jn 5:21; Ac 13:48; Ro 9:18;
1Co 1:21

In the church 1Co 1:1; 12:11,28;
Php 2:13; 2Ti 1:1; Heb 2:4

See also
1115 God, purpose of	3263 Holy Spirit, guidance
1130 God, sovereignty	5375 law
1427 prophecy	6663 freedom of will
1439 revelation	8124 guidance
1610 Scripture	8453 obedience
2525 Christ, cross of	8605 prayer & God's will

1180
God, wisdom of

Scripture declares that God alone is

wise and discerning, and that
human wisdom is often unable or
unwilling to understand his ways.
God's wisdom is expressed in both
creation and redemption.

God's wisdom described
Isa 28:29 *See also* 1Sa 2:3; Ro 16:27

God's wisdom is beyond measure
Ps 147:5 *See also* Isa 44:7; Jer 10:7;
Ro 11:33

God's wisdom is profound Isa 40:28 *See
also* Job 9:4; 28:12–24; Ps 92:5; Ecc 8:17

**God's wisdom is superior to human
wisdom** Isa 55:9 *See also* Job 21:22

God's wisdom exhibited
God's wisdom in creation Jer 10:12 *See
also* Job 28:25–27; 37:14–16; Ps 104:24;
136:5; Pr 3:19–20; Isa 40:12–14

God's wisdom as an agent in creation
Pr 8:22–31 *Wisdom here is given
personality, and may refer to the pre-
incarnate Jesus Christ.*

God's wisdom in historical events
Isa 31:2 *See also* Job 12:13–25;
Da 2:20–22

God's wisdom in knowing the human
mind 1Ch 28:9 *See also* Ps 139:2,4,6

Jesus Christ the wisdom of God
1Co 1:30 *See also* Isa 9:6; 11:2; 1Co 1:24;
Col 2:2–3

God's wisdom in the gospel
1Co 1:25 *See also* 1Co 1:18–21;
Eph 3:10

**God gives his wisdom to human
beings**
Eph 1:17 *See also* 2Ch 1:11–12;
Ezr 7:25; Pr 2:6; Ecc 12:11; Da 2:23;
1Co 2:6–16; Jas 1:5

Examples of God's wisdom
1Sa 16:7; 1Ki 3:28; Isa 28:24–29;
Lk 11:49

See also
1020 God, all-knowing	3050 Holy Spirit, wisdom
1325 God, the Creator	5026 knowledge
2081 Christ, wisdom	8355 understanding
	8361 wisdom

1185
God, zeal of

The intense and protective
commitment of God to his people
and to his purposes which seeks a
passionate and obedient response.
The zeal of God is often linked with
the idea of the "jealousy of God", in
which God refuses to contemplate
his people giving their allegiance or
affection to another.

**God in his zeal demands
exclusive loyalty from his people**
Ex 20:5 *The jealousy of God implies that
he seeks for and insists on exclusive loyalty
which is due to him and which will benefit
those who give it. See also* Ex 34:14;
Dt 4:24; 5:9; Jos 24:19; Na 1:2

**God's zeal for the honour of his
name**
Isa 42:8 *See also* Ex 20:7; Dt 32:51;
Isa 48:9–11; Eze 20:9,14,22; 36:20–23;
39:7,25

God's zeal on behalf of his people
Zec 1:14 *See also* 2Ki 19:31 pp Isa 37:32;
Joel 2:18; Zec 8:2

**God's zeal to establish the
Messiah's reign**
Isa 9:7

**God's zeal is aroused by his
people's idolatry**
Dt 32:16 *See also* Dt 29:20; 32:21;
1Ki 14:22; Ps 78:58; Eze 8:3,5; 16:38;
23:25; 1Co 10:21–22

God's zeal in judgment
He judges the nations Eze 36:5–6;
38:18–19; Zep 1:18; 3:8

He restrains his zeal in judgment
Eze 16:42 *See also* Nu 25:11

God's people appeal for his zeal to be
shown Isa 63:15 *See also* Ps 74:10–11;
Isa 26:11

God's people reflect his zeal
Nu 25:11–13 *See also* 1Ki 19:10,14;
Pr 23:17; Ro 12:11

See also
1025 God, anger of	5467 promises, divine
1045 God, glory of	8370 zeal
1065 God, holiness of	8768 idolatry
1075 God, justice of	8773 jealousy
1345 covenant	9210 judgment, God's
2230 Messiah, coming of	

glory

The distinctive feature of the
presence of God, often compared to
power, weight or brightness.
Scripture affirms that God's glory is
made known through his work of
creation, his acts of intervention in
history and supremely in the life and
resurrection of Jesus Christ.

1191
glory, of God
See 1045 God, glory of

1192
glory, of Jesus Christ
See 2024 Jesus Christ, glory of

1193
glory, revelation of

God's majestic brilliance shown to
the world through Israel and the
church, and supremely in and
through Jesus Christ.

God's glory revealed in nature
Ps 19:1 *See also* Ge 1:31; Ps 29:3–9;
104:1–4; Ro 1:20

God's glory revealed through Israel

In the exodus Ex 15:11 *See also* Ex 16:7,10; 24:9–11

At his sanctuary Ex 40:34–35 *See also* Ex 29:43; Lev 9:6,23; Nu 20:6; 1Ki 8:10–11 pp 2Ch 5:13–14; 2Ch 7:1–3; Isa 6:1; Eze 44:4; Hag 2:7

In the nation as a whole Isa 44:23 *See also* Ps 85:9; Isa 43:6–7; 46:13; 49:3; 55:5; Zec 2:4–5

To individuals in Israel
Moses: Ex 24:15–17; 33:18–23
Ezekiel: Eze 1:28; 3:23; 8:4; 9:3; 10:4,18–19; 11:22–23; 43:2–5

God's glory revealed through the church

2Co 3:18 *See also* Eph 1:12; 3:21; 1Pe 4:14

God's glory revealed to the whole earth

To all peoples Ps 57:5   pp Ps 108:5
Hab 3:3 *See also* Ps 57:11; 72:19; 97:6; Isa 6:3; 40:5

God's glory revealed in his judgments

Rev 19:1–2 *See also* Nu 14:10,21–23; 16:19–20; Isa 2:10,19,21; Eze 39:21; Rev 15:8

God's glory revealed in the future

Isa 60:19–20 *See also* Isa 4:5; 24:23; 35:2; 58:8; 60:1–2

God's glory revealed through Jesus Christ

Jesus Christ reveals God's glory
Heb 1:3 *See also* Lk 2:9; Jn 11:40; 14:8–9; Ac 7:55

Jesus Christ reveals his own glory
Jn 1:14 *See also* Lk 9:32; Jn 2:11; 12:41; 17:24; Heb 2:9; 2Pe 1:16–17

Glory revealed in Jesus Christ's death
Jn 12:23 *See also* Jn 12:27–33; 13:31–32

Glory revealed at Jesus Christ's second coming Mt 16:27 pp Mk 8:38 pp Lk 9:26; Mt 24:30 pp Mk 13:26 pp Lk 21:27; Mt 25:31; 2Th 1:10

God's glory revealed in the new Jerusalem

Rev 21:10–11 *See also* Rev 21:23

See also
1045 God, glory of
1105 God, power of
1403 God, revelation
1454 theophany
2024 Christ, glory of
2218 Christ, Son of God
2565 Christ, second coming
3030 Holy Spirit, power
4060 nature
4805 clouds
7459 tabernacle, in OT
7467 temple, Solomon's

1194
glory, divine and human

Through the death and resurrection of Jesus Christ, believers will finally be glorified. All human glory derives from God.

Human glory in the creation
Human glory as God's intention
Heb 2:6–7 *See also* Ps 8:4–5

People are created in God's image
Ge 5:1 *See also* Ge 1:26–27; 9:6; 1Co 11:7; Jas 3:9

Human beings have precedence over the rest of creation Mt 6:26 pp Lk 12:24 *See also* Mt 10:29–31 pp Lk 12:6–7; Mt 12:12

Human responsibility for creation
Ge 2:19–20 *See also* Ge 1:28; Ps 8:6–8; Heb 2:8; Jas 3:7

Human glory diminished after the fall

Ro 3:23 *See also* Ge 5:3; Ecc 7:29; Ro 5:12

The imperfect nature of human glory

1Pe 1:24–25 *See also* Isa 40:6–8; Ps 49:10–11,16–17; 103:15; 2Co 3:7–8,10,13

Human glory is given and taken by God

Ps 82:6–7 *See also* Ex 9:16; 1Ki 3:13 pp 2Ch 1:12; Jer 27:6–7; Da 2:37–39; 4:29–31,36; Jn 19:11; Ro 13:1

The temporary nature of the glory of the wicked

Php 3:19 *See also* Isa 5:15; Lk 16:25; Rev 18:14–17

The temptation associated with human glory

Mt 4:8–9   pp Lk 4:5–7 *See also* 2Ti 4:10; 1Jn 2:15

The uniqueness of God's glory
Job 40:9–10 *God shows Job the impossibility of human beings attaining the perfection of God's glory. See also* Ex 15:11; 1Ch 16:24–28 pp Ps 96:3–7; Isa 42:8; 48:11

God's glory revealed to human beings

Ex 24:17 *See also* Ex 16:10; Ps 26:8; Eze 1:25–28; Lk 2:9; Ac 7:55

Glory is not to be sought from other human beings but from God

Mt 6:2 *See also* Jer 9:23–24; Hos 4:7; Jn 5:41–44; Php 3:3; 1Th 2:4–6; Jas 4:16

It is a human duty to glorify God

Ps 34:3 *See also* Ps 63:3; 86:12; Da 4:37; Ro 15:6; Gal 1:3–5

Glory is restored to redeemed humanity by the death of Jesus Christ

Ro 8:30 *See also* Ro 9:23; 1Co 15:47–49; Col 3:10

Spiritual glory is divinely given

Jn 17:22 *See also* Ps 84:11; 2Co 3:18

Glorification when Jesus Christ returns

Col 3:4 *See also* Ro 8:18; Php 3:21; 1Th 2:20; 1Jn 3:2

See also
1165 God, unique
2580 Christ, transfiguration
4005 creation
4836 light & people of God
5023 image of God
5080 Adam
5101 Moses
5878 honour
6020 sin
6248 temptation
8664 praise
9410 heaven

God, titles and descriptions of

This set of themes consists of the following:
1205 God, titles and names of
1210 God, human descriptions of
1215 God, feminine descriptions of
1220 God, as shepherd
1225 God, as Spirit
1230 God, the Lord
1235 God, the LORD
1240 God, the Rock
1245 God of the fathers
1250 Abba
1255 face of God
1260 finger of God
1265 hand of God
1270 right hand of God

1205
God, titles and names of

These reflect the great and varied aspects of God's being and character. They are particularly used by the psalmists to speak of God as a source of strength, security, blessing and hope.

Titles which denote God's greatness
God Almighty Ge 17:1 *This was the special name by which God revealed himself to the patriarchs. The Hebrew is "El-Shaddai" possibly meaning "God the mountain", emphasising God's might. See also* Ge 28:3; 48:3; Ex 6:3; Ru 1:20–21; Job 5:17
"Almighty" is the favourite divine title in the book of Job: Job 6:4; 37:23 Ps 91:1; Rev 16:14; 19:15

God Most High Ge 14:18–20 *The Hebrew "El-Elyon" denotes the supremacy and sovereignty of God. See also* Ge 14:22; Dt 32:8; 2Sa 22:14 pp Ps 18:13; Ps 9:2; 21:7; 46:4; 47:2; 78:35; 97:9; Isa 14:14; Da 3:26
Jesus Christ as the Son of the Most High: Mk 5:7 pp Lk 8:28; Lk 1:32,35 Lk 6:35; Ac 16:17

The Eternal God Ge 21:33 *The Hebrew "El-Olam" only occurs in this verse. See also* Dt 33:27; Ro 16:26

The Ancient of Days Da 7:9,13,22

The Mighty One Lk 1:49 *See also* Jos 22:22; Ps 50:1; 132:2,5; Isa 1:24; 49:26; 60:16; Mk 14:62

The living God Ps 84:2 ; Da 6:26–27 *See also* Dt 5:26; Jos 3:10; 1Sa 17:26,36; 2Ki 19:16 pp Isa 37:17; Ps 42:2; Jer 10:10; Mt 16:16; Ac 14:15; Heb 10:31

The Holy One of Israel Isa 12:6 *"the Holy One of Israel" is a favourite divine title in the book of Isaiah. See also* 2Ki 19:22 pp Isa 37:23; Ps 71:22; 78:41; 89:18; Isa 30:12,15; 41:14; 45:11; 55:5; 60:9

The LORD Ge 4:26; Ex 6:2 *See also* Ex 3:15; 34:5–7

Titles which refer to God as Lord
Dt 10:17; 28:10; 1Ki 2:3; Ps 146:10;
Jer 14:9; Da 9:14

The Lord God Rev 1:8; 22:5

The Lord God Almighty Ps 89:8 *See also*
Ps 80:4; Jer 5:14; 15:16; Hos 12:5;
Am 4:13

The Lord Most High Ps 7:17 *See also*
Ps 47:2; 97:9

The Sovereign Lord 2Sa 7:28 *See also*
Dt 9:26; Jos 7:7; Isa 25:8; Jer 32:17;
Am 7:2

Titles referring to God as the source of light
2Sa 22:29; Ps 27:1; 84:11 *the sun*;
Isa 10:17 *the Light of Israel*; Mic 7:8;
Jas 1:17 *the Father of the heavenly lights*

Titles referring to God as the source of strength
Ps 59:9 *See also* Ex 15:2; Ps 18:1; 22:19;
28:7; 46:1; 59:17; 81:1; Isa 12:2

Titles referring to God as the source of security
A shield Ge 15:1 *See also* Dt 33:29;
2Sa 22:3 pp Ps 18:2; 2Sa 22:31
pp Ps 18:30; Ps 28:7; 84:11; 115:9;
Pr 2:7; 30:5

A refuge Ps 46:1 *See also* Ps 9:9; 61:3;
91:2,9; 119:114; 142:5; Jer 16:19;
Joel 3:16; Na 1:7

A hiding-place Ps 32:7

A fortress 2Sa 22:2 pp Ps 18:2; Ps 31:3;
62:2,6; 91:2; 144:2; Isa 17:10; Jer 16:19

A stronghold 2Sa 22:3 pp Ps 18:2;
Ps 9:9; 27:1; 37:39; 43:2; 144:2;
Joel 3:16

A defender Dt 10:18; Ps 68:5; Pr 23:11

A Rock Ge 49:24; Dt 32:4; Ps 19:14;
Isa 26:4

Titles referring to God as the source of provision
Ge 22:14; La 3:24 *See also* Ge 22:8;
Ps 73:26; 119:57; 142:5; Jer 10:16; 51:19

Titles referring to God as the source of hope
Jer 14:8 *See also* Jer 17:13; 50:7

Titles referring to God as the source of peace
Ro 15:33 *See also* Jdg 6:24; Ro 16:20;
2Co 13:11; Php 4:9; 1Th 5:23; 2Th 3:16;
Heb 13:20

Titles referring to God as the source of comfort
Jer 8:18; 2Co 1:3

Titles referring to God as the source of grace
Ex 34:6; Ne 9:31; Ps 86:15; Jnh 4:2;
1Pe 5:10

Titles referring to God as the source of love
Ps 59:10,17; 144:2; 2Co 13:11;
1Jn 4:7–16

God as shepherd
Ps 23:1 *See also* Ge 48:15; 49:24; Ps 80:1

The true God
2Ch 15:3; Jer 10:10; Jn 17:3; 1Jn 5:20

See also

1055 God, grace & mercy	1330 God, the provider
1080 God, living	2203 Christ, titles of
1105 God, power of	3110 Holy Spirit, titles of
1140 God, the eternal	
1230 God, the Lord	4354 rock
1245 God of the fathers	5042 name of God, significance
1320 God as Saviour	

1210
God, human descriptions of

Figures of speech which describe
God in human terms, sometimes
referred to as anthropomorphisms.
Since God is Spirit, these expressions
help the human mind to understand
God, and enable God to reveal
himself to human beings.

Bodily form ascribed to God
Ex 33:23 *See also* Ge 18:2–14;
Jos 5:13–15; Eze 1:26–28

His face Nu 6:25–26 *See also* Ps 27:8;
51:9; Mt 18:10; Rev 22:4

His heart 2Ch 7:16 *See also* Ge 6:6; 8:21;
1Sa 13:14; Ac 13:22

His hands Isa 14:27 *See also* 1Ch 28:19;
29:14,16; Ps 45:4; Ac 2:33–34; 1Pe 3:22;
5:6

His eyes 2Ch 16:9 *See also* Dt 11:12;
Pr 15:3; Am 9:8; Zec 4:10; 1Pe 3:12;
Ps 34:15

His feet Eze 43:7 *See also* Dt 33:3;
2Sa 22:10 pp Ps 18:9; Ps 45:5; Isa 60:13

His arm Isa 59:1; Jer 32:21 *God's arm is
particularly used as a symbol of his power
at the exodus. See also* Ex 6:6; Dt 5:15;
Job 40:9; Isa 51:9; 52:10; 63:5; Lk 1:51;
Jn 12:38; Isa 53:1

His mind Ro 11:34 *See also* Isa 40:13;
1Sa 15:29; Jer 7:31; Heb 7:21; Ps 110:4

Human actions ascribed to God
He walks Ge 3:8 *See also* Lev 26:12;
2Co 6:16

He speaks Dt 4:12 *See also* Job 40:6;
Ps 29:3–9; 33:6,9; Eze 1:24; Mt 3:17
pp Mk 1:11 pp Lk 3:22; Ac 7:6

He rests Ge 2:2 *See also* Ex 20:11;
Heb 4:4

He rides Ps 68:4 *See also* Dt 33:26;
2Sa 22:11 pp Ps 18:10; Ps 68:33; Hab 3:8

He laughs Ps 59:8 *See also* Ps 2:4; 37:13

Other actions Isa 5:26 *God whistles*;
Rev 3:20 *God knocks*

Human senses ascribed to God
He hears Ps 4:3 *God's hearing usually
refers to his answering of prayer. See also*
Ge 16:11; 2Ch 7:14; Ps 94:9; Lk 1:13;
Jn 11:42; Heb 5:7

He sees Ge 16:13 *See also* Ge 1:4;
2Ch 12:7; Ne 9:9; Pr 24:18;
Eze 8:12–13; Jnh 3:10

He smells Ge 8:21 *God's smelling refers
to his acceptance of sacrifices. See also*
Lev 1:9

God experiences emotion
He shows delight Zep 3:17 *See also*
Dt 30:9; Ps 149:4; Isa 5:7; 62:4

He is compassionate Jas 5:11 *See also*
Ps 145:9; Isa 54:10; Hos 2:19; 11:8;
2Co 1:3

He is angry Ps 95:10–11 *See also*
2Ki 17:11; Ps 78:58; 106:29; Isa 5:25;
54:8

He experiences pain Ge 6:6 *See also*
1Sa 15:11,35; 2Sa 24:16 pp 1Ch 21:15;
Eze 6:9

Human occupations ascribed to God
Isa 29:16 *God as a potter. See also* Ex 15:3
God as a warrior; Ps 23:1 *God as a
shepherd*; Heb 11:10 *God as a builder*

Human relationships ascribed to God
God as a loving husband Isa 54:5–8 *See
also* Jer 3:14; 31:32; Hos 2:16

God as a loving father Ps 103:13 *See
also* Isa 1:2–3; Jer 31:9; Hos 11:1–4;
Mt 11:27; Jn 16:27

God is not to be brought down to human levels
Hos 11:9 *See also* Nu 23:19; Job 9:32;
Ps 50:21; Isa 55:8–9

See also

1025 God, anger of	1220 God as shepherd
1030 God, compassion	1255 face of God
1040 God, fatherhood	1260 finger of God
1135 God, suffering of	1265 hand of God
1215 God, feminine descriptions	1690 word of God
	5036 mind of God

1215
God, feminine descriptions of

Some expressions attribute feminine
qualities to God, especially relating
to motherhood.

Descriptions of God relating to childbirth
God gives birth to his people Isa 44:2
*God giving birth to Israel at the exodus. See
also* Nu 11:12; Dt 32:18; Isa 44:24

God gives birth to individuals Ps 139:13
See also Ge 29:31; 30:22; Ecc 11:5;
Isa 49:5; Jer 1:5

God as a midwife Ps 22:9 *See also*
Job 10:18; Ps 71:6; Isa 66:9

Descriptions of God relating to motherhood
God nurses his people Isa 49:15

God comforts his people Isa 66:13 *See
also* Isa 40:11

**God as a mother bird protecting her
young** Dt 32:10–11; Mt 23:37
pp Lk 13:34 *See also* Ru 2:12; Ps 17:8;
91:4

See also

1030 God, compassion	5140 breasts
1210 God, human descriptions	5721 mothers, a symbol

1220
God, as shepherd

The image of God as a shepherd

points to his continual direction, guidance and care for his people.

Shepherd as a title for God
Ps 80:1 *See also* Ge 49:24; Ecc 12:11

God's people are his flock
Israel is God's flock Ps 95:7 *See also* Ps 79:13; 100:3; Jer 50:7; Eze 34:31

The church is God's flock 1Pe 5:2 *See also* Lk 12:32; Ac 20:28–29

The tasks undertaken by God the shepherd
The shepherd leads and guides Ps 23:2–3 *See also* Isa 40:11

The shepherd provides Ps 23:1 *See also* Ge 48:15; Ps 23:5–6; Hos 4:16; Mic 7:14

The shepherd protects Ps 28:9 *See also* Ge 49:23–24

The shepherd saves those who are lost or scattered Jer 31:10 *See also* Ps 119:176; Isa 53:6; Eze 34:11–16; Mt 18:12–14 pp Lk 15:3–7

The shepherd judges Eze 34:17–22 *See also* Jer 23:1; Zec 10:2–3; 11:16; Mt 25:32–46

God gives shepherds to be leaders over his people
He gives David's line Eze 34:23 *See also* 2Sa 5:2 pp 1Ch 11:2; Ps 78:70–72; Eze 34:23–24; 37:24; Mic 5:4; Mt 2:6

He gives individual leaders Isa 44:28; 63:11

He gives faithful leaders Jer 3:15 *See also* Jer 23:4; 1Pe 5:2–4

See also

1030 God, compassion	5802 care
1330 God, the provider	7130 flock, God's
	7140 people of God
1345 covenant	7733 leaders
2330 Christ as shepherd	7784 shepherd
3263 Holy Spirit, guidance	8124 guidance

1225
God, as Spirit

God has no material body and he is not subject to human limitations. While his spiritual nature is clearly inferred in Scripture, it is seldom directly stated; the emphasis is on his dynamic, living personhood.

God as spirit
Jn 4:24 *See also* Isa 28:5–6; 31:3

God is not subject to physical limitations 1Sa 16:7; 1Ki 18:27 *Elijah's mockery of Baal implies a contrast with the true God who is not subject to the limitations suggested;* Job 10:4–8; Ps 121:3–4

God as the Spirit Ps 139:7 *See also* Ps 51:11 *The Spirit and the presence of God are equated;* Ps 143:10 *God's guidance and the Spirit's leading are equated;* Isa 34:16 *God's Spirit participates in God's plans;* 2Co 3:17–18

God cannot be represented physically
Images of God are prohibited Ex 20:4; 34:17; Lev 26:1; Ac 17:29

God transcends spacial limitations Ac 17:24 *See also* 1Ki 8:27 pp 2Ch 6:18; 2Ch 2:6; Ac 7:48–50

God is invisible 1Ti 6:15–16 *See also* Ex 33:20; Dt 4:15–19; Jn 1:18; Col 1:15; 1Ti 1:17

See also

1110 God, present everywhere	3010 God, the Holy Spirit
1145 God, transcendent	4018 life, spiritual
	4804 breath
1170 God, unity of	8128 guidance, receiving
1210 God, human descriptions	8474 seeing God
1352 covenant, the new	8768 idolatry

1230
God, the Lord

God is the almighty ruler to whom everything and everyone is subject. His lordship is seen in his power and his victory over his enemies and also in his deliverance of his people and his loving care for them. He is the recipient of their obedience and their prayers. ("Lord" is the translation of the Hebrew word "Adonai" meaning "Ruler" or "Master" and is distinct from "LORD" which is the translation of the divine name "Yahweh".)

God is the almighty ruler
He is Lord of lords 1Ti 6:15 *God exercises his lordship over all creation, but especially over all humanity. See also* Dt 10:17; Ps 136:3; Da 2:47

He is Lord of all the earth Ps 97:5 *See also* Jos 3:11,13; Mic 4:13; Zec 4:14; Ac 17:24

Characteristics of God as Lord
He is great and powerful Ps 147:5 *See also* Ne 4:14; Ps 86:8; 114:7–8; 135:5; Isa 28:2; Da 9:4; Ac 4:24

He is majestic and exalted Isa 6:1 *See also* Ps 8:1,9; 2Th 1:9

He is righteous Da 9:16 *See also* Ps 97:5–6; Da 9:7

He is loving and caring Ps 86:15 *See also* Ps 62:12; 86:5

He is merciful and forgiving Da 9:9 *See also* Ps 86:3–5; 130:2–4

God, the Lord, is triumphant over his enemies
Ps 78:65–66 *See also* Ps 2:4–5; 37:13; 110:5–6

God, the Lord, delivers his people and cares for them
Ps 68:19 *See also* Ps 38:15,22; 40:17; 54:4; 59:11; 77:2; 90:1,17

God is addressed as Lord
As a mark of respect or obedience Jos 5:14 *See also* Ex 4:10,13; 5:22; Jdg 6:15; Lk 2:29

In prayer Ne 1:11 *See also* Ge 18:27,30–32; Ex 34:9; Jos 7:8; Jdg 13:8; Ps 30:8; Da 9:4,15,19

Jesus Christ is God, the Lord
Jn 20:28 *See also* Mt 22:41–45 pp Mk 12:35–37 pp Lk 20:41–44; Ac 2:34–36; Heb 1:13; Ps 110:1

See also

1060 God, greatness of	1320 God as Saviour
1090 God, majesty of	2224 Christ, the Lord
1105 God, power of	4140 angel of the Lord
1130 God, sovereignty	5394 lordship
1205 God, titles of	6720 redemption
1235 God, the LORD	7930 Lord's Day, the

1235
God, the LORD

The translation of the Hebrew name "Yahweh" which is the personal name of God whose meaning was revealed to Moses. It emphasises that God is the one who is eternal, unique, unchangeable and always actively present with his people. It expresses God's role as Israel's Redeemer and covenant Lord.

The name of God, the LORD
The LORD is the personal name of God Isa 42:8 *"The LORD" is the NIV rendering of the Hebrew "Yahweh".*

The name's meaning Ex 3:14–15 *This forms part of God's explanation of who he is. "I AM" (in Hebrew closely resembling "Yahweh") expresses the ever-present, unchanging, totally dependable character of God.*

The name is revealed to Moses Ex 6:2–3 *The name had been used previously (e.g., Ge 4:26) but its meaning was not fully understood until God revealed it to Moses in the context of the exodus from Egypt.*

The name is glorious and awesome Dt 28:58–59 *See also* Jos 7:9; 1Sa 12:22

The name is not to be misused Ex 20:7 pp Dt 5:11 *The misuse referred to here is swearing falsely by God's name. See also* Lev 19:12; 24:11,15–16 *The Jews came to believe that just uttering the name "Yahweh" was an offence and as a result its exact pronunciation has been lost. What merited the death penalty here was using God's name as a curse.*

God's character is revealed by his name the LORD
He is unique Ex 8:10; Dt 4:35,39; 1Ki 8:60; Isa 45:5,18; Joel 2:27

He is eternal Ge 21:33; Ps 9:7; 29:10; 102:12; 135:13; Isa 26:4

He is holy Lev 11:44; 1Sa 2:2; Ps 30:4; Isa 43:15

He is powerful Ex 15:6; Jos 22:22; Ps 93:4; Jer 10:6

He is majestic Ps 83:18; 93:1; 97:9; Isa 2:10,19,21; Mic 5:4

He is compassionate and gracious Ex 34:6–7; Ps 103:8; 145:8–9

He is faithful and true Ps 145:13

He is unchangeable Ps 33:11; 110:4; Mal 3:6

He is actively present with his people Dt 31:6; Jos 1:9; 1Ki 8:57; Hag 1:13

God reveals the relevance of his name the Lᴏʀᴅ by his actions
In creation Jer 33:2 *See also* Isa 42:5; 43:15 *"The Lᴏʀᴅ" is Creator of the universe but also the Creator of the people Israel;* Isa 45:18 *Human beings are the purpose of God's creation; they know God as "the Lᴏʀᴅ".*

In the deliverance of his people from **Egypt** Ex 6:6 *Deliverance is a central concept in the revelation of the divine name. See also* Ex 12:51; 14:30; 16:6; 20:2; Lev 26:13; Ps 81:10

In establishing a covenant with his **people** Ex 6:7 *See also* Ex 29:46; 2Sa 7:24 pp 1Ch 17:22; Jer 14:9

In the judgment of his enemies Ex 12:12 *See also* Ex 7:5; 8:22–23; 1Sa 17:45–47; 2Ch 14:11–13

In the restoration of his people Eze 36:36 *See also* Ps 102:15–22; Isa 60:15–22; Eze 37:6,13–14 *The theme "then you, my people, will know that I am the Lᴏʀᴅ" (with slight variations) runs throughout the book of Ezekiel and is connected to divine acts of judgment and restoration.*

God, the Lᴏʀᴅ denotes God's lordship
He is the Sovereign Lᴏʀᴅ Eze 2:4 *"Sovereign Lᴏʀᴅ" is the NIV rendering of "Adonai Yahweh", the favourite divine title in Ezekiel. See also* Ge 15:2,8; Dt 3:24; Jos 7:7; Jdg 6:22; 2Sa 7:18–29; Ps 73:28; Isa 61:1; Jer 1:6; Am 1:8

He is the Lᴏʀᴅ Almighty 1Sa 1:3 *"The Lᴏʀᴅ Almighty" is the NIV rendering of "Yahweh Sabaoth" ("the Lᴏʀᴅ of hosts") which emphasises the sovereignty of "the Lᴏʀᴅ". See also* 1Ch 11:9; Ps 24:10; 46:7,11; Isa 2:12; Jer 39:16; Hag 2:6–9; Zec 1:3–4,6; Mal 1:14

He is the Lord, the Lᴏʀᴅ Almighty Isa 1:24 *"The Lord, the Lᴏʀᴅ Almighty" is the NIV rendering of "Adonai Yahweh Sabaoth" which is often associated with the Lᴏʀᴅ's authority to rule and to judge. See also* Ps 69:6; Isa 3:15; 19:4; Jer 2:19; 46:10; 49:5; Am 9:5

As the Lᴏʀᴅ, God interacts with his people
He enforces the moral code Lev 18:1–5 *The phrase "I am the Lᴏʀᴅ" occurs over 40 times in Leviticus chapters 18–26 and is the authority behind the moral law given to God's people. See also* Lev 11:44–45; 19:2

He makes his people holy Lev 22:32 *See also* Ex 31:13; Lev 20:8; 21:8; Eze 20:12; 37:28

He is the object of his people's **worship** Ex 4:22–23 *The purpose of Israel's redemption from Egypt was that they would be free to worship the Lᴏʀᴅ. See also* Ex 12:31; 23:25; 1Ch 16:29 pp Ps 96:9; Ps 29:2; 99:5; 100:2; Jnh 1:9

Jesus Christ takes God's name to himself
Jn 8:58–59 *The form of expression used by Jesus Christ meant that he was clearly identifying himself with the divine name "I ᴀᴍ". The response of the crowd confirms this.*

See also

1035 God, faithfulness	1345 covenant
1130 God, sovereignty	2018 Christ, divinity
1165 God, unique	5394 lordship
1205 God, titles of	7160 servants of the Lord
1230 God, the Lord	9220 day of the Lᴏʀᴅ
1325 God, the Creator	

1240
God, the Rock

An OT title for God and a Messianic title signifying that God's people can rely on him for absolute protection and salvation.

Rock as a title for Israel's God
Ps 78:35 *See also* Ge 49:24; Dt 32:15,18,30; 2Sa 23:3; Ps 42:9; Isa 30:29; Hab 1:12

God the Rock is unique
2Sa 22:32 pp Ps 18:31 *See also* 1Sa 2:2; Isa 44:8

The Rock is superior to other gods
Dt 32:31 *See also* Dt 32:37

The Rock is worthy to be praised
Ps 144:1 *See also* Dt 32:4; Ps 92:15

God the Rock and his people
God the Rock is a refuge for his people Ps 62:7 *See also* Ps 28:1; 31:1–3; 61:2; 71:3; Isa 26:4

God the Rock is his people's fortress Ps 94:22 *See also* Ps 28:8; 46:7,11; 48:3; 59:9,16–17; 91:2; 144:2; Jer 16:19

God the Rock is his people's security 2Sa 22:3 pp Ps 18:2 *See also* Ps 9:9; 27:1; 37:39; 43:2; 52:7; Joel 3:16

God the Rock saves and delivers his people Ps 95:1 *See also* 2Sa 22:47 pp Ps 18:46; Ps 19:14; 62:2; 89:26; Isa 17:10

Rock as a Messianic title
The Messiah is the rock/stone on which God's living temple stands Isa 8:14; 28:16 *See also* Ps 118:22; Mt 21:42 pp Mk 12:10 pp Lk 20:17; Ac 4:11; 1Pe 2:6–7

The Messiah's kingdom is eternal and immovable like a rock Da 2:34–35 *See also* Da 2:44–45

Consequences of rejecting the rock/ **stone** Mt 21:44 pp Lk 20:18; Ro 9:32–33; 1Pe 2:4–8

See also

1205 God, titles of	5454 power, God's saving
2203 Christ, titles of	
4354 rock	5480 protection
5269 cornerstone	6510 salvation
5316 fortress	8030 trust

1245
God of the fathers

God's particular association with Abraham, Isaac and Jacob, the fathers of the nations of Israel, highlights his faithfulness in fulfilling the promises made to them. He is the God who establishes a covenant with his people for their everlasting blessing.

God's relationship with the fathers
The God of Abraham, Isaac and Jacob Ac 7:32 *See also* Ex 3:6,15; 4:5

The God of Jacob Ps 20:1 *"Jacob" is used here as a synonym for the nation of Israel. This usage is common in the Psalms as a reminder to God's people of his faithfulness to Jacob and the emergent nation of Israel. See also* Ge 32:27–28; Ps 14:7; 46:7,11; 75:9; 76:6; 114:7

Such a relationship served as an encouragement to others *Abraham's servant was encouraged to trust God in his mission by the example of Abraham's faith:* Ge 24:12,27,42,48 *God's people were frequently encouraged by the relationship they saw between God and other individuals (e.g., Jos 1:5; 2Ki 2:14):* Ge 26:24; 31:42,53 Ge 46:1–3 *Jacob learned to fear and trust God through his father Isaac.*

God's covenant with the fathers
God's promises that they will be the fathers of a great nation Ge 28:13–15 *See also* Ge 26:2–4; Ex 3:16–17

God remembers and fulfils his promises Ex 2:24 *See also* Ex 6:3–5; 32:13; Lev 26:42; Dt 1:8; Ac 7:17

God makes a covenant with his people to be their God Dt 29:12–13 *See also* Ge 17:7; Ex 6:7–8; Ps 105:8–11

Characteristics of the God of the fathers
He blesses his people Dt 1:11 *See also* Dt 30:20

He is powerful 1Ki 18:36–39

He is gracious and compassionate 2Ki 13:23

He keeps his people faithful 1Ch 29:18

He gives wisdom Da 2:23

He is the God of the living Mt 22:32 pp Mk 12:26–27 pp Lk 20:37–38

People sometimes fail to respond to the God of their fathers
Jos 18:3 *See also* Nu 32:11; Dt 6:10–12; 9:27; 2Ch 30:7

See also

1035 God, faithfulness	7140 people of God
	7145 remnant
1335 blessing	7248 patriarchs
1345 covenant	7257 promised land
5467 promises, divine	7510 Gentiles
	8124 guidance
7135 Israel, people of God	

1250
Abba

The Aramaic word "Abba" is thought to be a very intimate term for "Father" suggesting that those who use it to refer to God enjoy a close relationship with him. Jesus Christ uses the term as a consequence of his natural sonship of God; believers may use it as a consequence of their adopted sonship of God through faith.

"Abba" used in addressing God
By Jesus Christ Mk 14:36

By believers Ro 8:15; Gal 4:6

See also
1040 God, fatherhood	3221 Holy Spirit & prayer
1205 God, titles of	5895 intimacy
1510 Trinity, the	7922 fellowship with God
2078 Christ, sonship of	8104 assurance
2218 Christ, Son of God	8134 knowing God

1255
face of God

A term used to refer to the character of God, especially his favour towards his people. For God to turn his face to his people is to offer them his grace and help; for God to turn his face against his people is to withhold his favour and blessing. To seek the face of God is to seek his favour.

The face of God as a sign of blessing
Nu 6:25–26 *See also* 2Sa 21:1; 1Ch 16:11; Ps 4:6; 31:16; 67:1; 80:19; 105:4; 119:135; Eze 39:29

Parts of God's face
His ears 2Sa 22:7; 2Ki 19:28; Ps 34:15; 102:2; Isa 59:1

His eyes Ps 34:15 *See also* Dt 11:12; 2Ch 16:9; Ps 139:16; Pr 15:3

His hair Da 7:9

His lips Ps 89:34; Isa 11:4; 30:27

His mouth 2Sa 22:9; Job 15:30; Isa 45:23

His nostrils 2Sa 22:9,16

The visibility of God's face
His face cannot be seen Ex 33:20–23 *"The face of God" may mean here God's real and true self, the inference being that no-one can look on God as he is in his total purity and majesty.*

Apparent exceptions where God is seen face to face Ge 32:30 *After Jacob's wrestling with a figure whose exact identity is not explicit in the preceding verses, Jacob did experience a real encounter with God but God was in a real and approachable form, not in his transcendent and visible glory. See also* Ex 33:11; Nu 12:8; Dt 5:4; 34:10; Eze 20:35

The angels in heaven look upon the face of God Mt 18:10

God must reveal himself if people are to see his face Job 34:29 *The Greek word for "revelation" literally means "removing a veil from one's face"*

The righteous will see God's face in the life to come 1Co 13:12; Rev 22:4

When God hides his face blessing is withheld
Complaints at God hiding his face Ps 44:24 *See also* Ps 13:1; 88:14

Cries for help Ps 27:9 *See also* Ps 69:17; 102:2; 143:7

Statements concerning God's anger and judgment Isa 54:8 *See also* Dt 31:17–18; Ps 22:24; 30:7; 51:9; 104:29; Isa 8:17; 64:7; Jer 33:5; Eze 39:23–24; Mic 3:4; Rev 6:16

Other phrases synonymous with God hiding his face 2Ch 30:9; Jer 18:17; Eze 7:22

God sets his face against sinners Lev 17:10; 20:3; 26:17; Ps 34:16; Eze 14:8; 1Pe 3:12; Eze 15:7

God's face as a symbol of his favour
Seeking the face of God in prayer 2Ch 7:14 *See also* 2Sa 21:1; 1Ch 16:11; Ps 24:6; 105:4; 119:58; Hos 5:15

Seeking the favour of God Ex 32:11 *See also* 1Sa 13:12; 2Ki 13:4; 2Ch 33:12; Jer 26:19; Da 9:13; Zec 7:2; 8:21; Mal 1:9

Appearing before God in worship Ex 23:15 *The phrase seems to recall the fact that in ancient religions worshippers came before carved faces of their idols. In Israel such physical representations of God were forbidden but the phrase was still used underlining the belief that Israel's God was present in his sanctuary. See also* Ex 23:17; 34:20; Dt 16:16; 31:11; Ps 42:2; Isa 1:12

The shining of God's face upon his people indicates his blessing Nu 6:25–26 *See also* Ps 4:6; 31:16; 44:3; 67:1; 80:3,19; 119:135

God's face accompanies Israel as a symbol of his presence
Ex 33:14 *Literally "my face will go ..." Here this phrase may allude not only to God's presence but also to the manifestations of his presence (e.g., the cloud in verse 9). See also* Dt 4:37; Isa 63:9

See also
1025 God, anger of	1403 God, revelation
1110 God, present everywhere	1439 revelation
	1454 theophany
1145 God, transcendent	1670 symbols
	5150 face
1210 God, human descriptions	8474 seeing God
1310 God as judge	8602 prayer

1260
finger of God

A figure of speech which gives expression to God's creative power and authority over his creation.

God creates with his finger Ps 8:3 *See also* Isa 48:13; 64:8

God writes with his finger
He writes the law Ex 31:18 *See also* Ex 24:12; 32:16; 34:1

He writes judgment Da 5:5 *See also* Da 5:24–28

God works miracles with his finger
He sends plagues Ex 8:19

He exorcises evil spirits Lk 11:20

See also
1105 God, power of	4135 demons, Christ's authority over
1210 God, human descriptions	
1265 hand of God	5152 fingers
1416 miracles	5352 inscriptions
1439 revelation	5452 power
2351 Christ, miracles	5638 writing
2375 kingdom of God	

1265
hand of God

A figure of speech which points to God's sovereign power in creation and in his actions on his people's behalf, especially in redemption. Also used as a symbol of authority and in taking oaths.

God creates by his hand
Ac 7:50 *See also* Isa 66:2; Job 10:3,8; Ps 8:3; 19:1; 95:5; 138:8; Isa 48:13; 64:8

God holds the world in his hand
Ps 95:4 *See also* Job 12:10; 26:13; 36:32; Ps 31:15; Isa 40:12; 41:19–20; Da 5:23

God's creatures are fed from his hand
Ps 145:16 *See also* Ps 104:28; Isa 34:17

God's hand symbolises his power
God's hand is mighty Hab 3:4 *See also* 1Ch 29:12; Ps 118:15–16; Jer 18:6; Da 4:35; Am 9:2

God executes judgment by the power of his hand Am 1:6–8 *Judgment on the Philistine cities. See also* Dt 32:41; 1Sa 5:6–9; Isa 40:2; Jer 15:6; La 2:3; Eze 6:14; Zep 1:4; Ac 13:11

God's hand holds a cup of judgment Jer 25:15–17 *See also* Ps 75:8; Isa 51:17; Hab 2:16

God's hand brings trouble Job 19:21 *See also* Ru 1:13; 1Sa 6:3; Job 1:11; Ps 38:2; 39:10

God's hand causes fear Isa 19:16 *See also* Isa 23:11

Pleas for God to use his powerful hand
Ps 74:11 *See also* Ps 10:12; 60:5 pp Ps 108:6; Ps 77:10; 144:7–8

God's powerful hand used on his people's behalf
God redeems by his powerful hand Ps 138:7 *See also* 1Ki 8:41–42 pp 2Ch 6:32; Ps 98:1; Isa 11:11; Eze 20:21–22,33–34; Mic 4:10

God redeemed Israel from Egypt by his powerful hand Ex 13:3 *See also* Ex 3:19–20; 13:9,14; Dt 5:15; 7:8; Ne 1:10; Jer 32:21; Da 9:15

God's hand ensures success for his people Isa 41:10 *"righteous" has the sense of "victorious". See also* Ps 16:8; 18:35; 89:21; Isa 42:6; 49:4

God's powerful hand is invincible Jn 10:29 *See also* Ps 139:10; Isa 43:13

God's hand protects his people Ezr 8:31 *See also* Ex 33:22–23; 1Ch 4:10; Ps 121:5; Isa 41:13; 49:2,16; 62:3

God's hand inspires the prophets Jer 1:9 *See also* Isa 8:11; Jer 15:17; Eze 1:3; 3:14,22; 33:22; 37:1; 40:1

God's hand fulfils his purposes Ezr 7:6 *See also* 2Ch 30:12; Ezr 7:9,28; 8:18; Ne 2:8,18; Pr 21:1; Ecc 2:24; Isa 45:1; Lk 1:66; Ac 11:21

God's uplifted hand
Signifies his taking an oath Ne 9:15 *See also* Ex 6:8; Nu 14:30; Dt 32:40; Eze 47:14

Signifies his power Isa 9:12,17,21; 26:11

God's right hand symbolises his authority
Ac 7:55–56 *See also* Ps 110:1; Ac 5:31; Ro 8:34; Col 3:1; Heb 1:3; 1Pe 3:22

God's hand must be recognised
God requires submission under his hand 1Pe 5:6 *See also* Ro 10:21; Isa 65:2

The works of God's hand must be acknowledged Ps 28:5; 92:4; 143:5

See also

1075 God, justice of	1325 God, the
1105 God, power of	Creator
1115 God, purpose	1330 God, the
of	provider
1130 God,	1670 symbols
sovereignty	2336 Christ,
1210 God, human	exaltation
descriptions	9210 judgment,
1260 finger of God	God's
1270 right hand of	
God	

1270
right hand of God

A figure of speech that represents God's ultimate power and authority, and where the exalted Jesus Christ now sits.

The right hand of God as a symbol
A symbol of power Ps 89:13

A symbol of protection Ps 16:8 *See also* Ps 63:8; 139:10; Isa 41:13; La 2:3

A symbol of God's presence Ps 16:11 *See also* Ps 48:10; 73:23; Isa 62:8

A symbol of God's saving power Ps 60:5 pp Ps 108:6 *See also* Ps 17:7; 20:6; 80:15; 98:1; 138:7

A symbol of victory Ps 18:35; 44:3; 78:54; Isa 41:10

A symbol of the defeat of God's enemies Ex 15:6 *See also* Ex 15:12; Ps 21:8; 74:11

A symbol of God's mighty works Ps 45:4 *See also* Ps 77:10; 118:15–16; Isa 48:13

A symbol of judgment La 2:4; Hab 2:16

Jesus Christ at God's right hand
Jesus Christ is exalted to God's right hand Heb 1:13 *Comparison between Jesus Christ and the angels confirms Christ's absolute supremacy. See also* Ps 110:1; Mt 22:44 pp Mk 12:36 pp Lk 20:42; Lk 22:69; Ac 2:34; 7:55–56; Col 3:1; Heb 1:3; 12:2

Jesus Christ rules every authority at God's right hand 1Pe 3:22 *See also* Eph 1:20–21

Jesus Christ continues his work at God's right hand Ro 8:34 *See also* Ac 2:33; 5:31; Heb 4:14–16; 8:1

Jesus Christ will return at God's right hand Mt 26:64 pp Mk 14:62

Jesus Christ takes a scroll from God's right hand Rev 5:1–7 *The scroll probably refers to God's decrees for the destiny of the world.*

The right hand of Jesus Christ
The place of the righteous on judgment day Mt 25:32–34

A privileged place granted by the Father Mt 20:20–23 pp Mk 10:35–40

A place of protection for Christians Rev 1:20 *The angels of the churches are probably the church leaders. See also* Rev 1:16; 2:1

See also

1105 God, power of	2306 Christ, high
1115 God, purpose	priest
of	2336 Christ,
1210 God, human	exaltation
descriptions	5156 hand
1265 hand of God	5396 lordship of
1320 God as Saviour	Christ
2069 Christ, pre-	
eminence	

1300

God, work of

This set of themes consists of the following:
1305 God, activity of
1310 God, as judge
1315 God, as redeemer
1320 God, as Saviour
1325 God, the Creator
1330 God, the provider
1335 blessing
1340 consistency
1345 covenant
1355 providence

1305
God, activity of

God is not passive or remote from his creation but dynamically involved in all that he has made. In the past, this activity was seen in the history of Israel and in the ministry of Jesus Christ. In the present, God's activity can be seen in the life of believers and of the church.

God is active by nature
He actively works out his purposes Jn 5:17 *See also* Nu 23:19; Ps 115:3; Pr 16:4; Isa 43:13

His names reflect his activity and involvement in his people's lives Ge 22:14 *"The LORD Will Provide"*; Ex 15:26 *"The LORD, who heals you"*; Ex 17:15 *"The LORD is my Banner": this title emphasises that God is like a warrior who champions his people's cause;* Ps 95:6 *"The LORD our Maker": the Hebrew word used does not refer to original creation but to the way in which God is fashioning a people for himself.*

His word is active Isa 55:10–11 *The Hebrew for "word" can also be translated "deed" or "action". God's word is not merely a communication of abstract truth but a powerful force active in the world. See also* Ge 1:3; Eze 37:4,7

God is active in the creation
In making the universe Ne 9:6 *See also* Ge 1:1,31; 2:2; 5:1–2; Ps 102:25; Am 4:13; Ac 17:24; Rev 4:11

In sustaining the created order Ps 103:19 *See also* Ps 104:10–17; 107:33–35; Mt 6:28–30; Ac 14:17; Eph 1:11; Col 1:16–17

In bringing about changes in the weather Job 37:10; 38:22–30,34–35; Ps 107:25; 147:8; Mt 5:45; Ac 14:17

In the stars and other heavenly bodies Job 38:31–33; Ps 104:19; 147:4; Isa 40:26; Jas 1:17

In the animal creation Job 39:1–30; 40:15–24; 41:1–11; Ps 104:20–27; 147:9; Mt 10:29 pp Lk 12:6

God is active in Israel's history
In the calling and creation of Israel as a people Ex 6:6–8 *See also* Ge 1:2–3; Ex 19:3–6; Dt 4:32–34; Isa 51:2; Eze 16:6–7; Hos 11:1–4; Mal 2:10

In saving and delivering his people Ps 106:2 *This verse introduces a psalm which recounts the history of God's dealings with his people. See also* Ex 33:16–17; 2Sa 7:7–11; 1Ki 18:36–38; Ps 28:8–9; 107:2–3

In judgment Nu 25:3–4; 1Sa 2:25; 12:16–18; 2Sa 21:1

In bringing victory in battle Ex 14:27–28; 17:8–16; Nu 21:1–3; Jos 6:2; 10:30; Jdg 7:9,22; 1Sa 17:47; 2Ch 20:22–23

In raising up and sending leaders to the people 2Sa 7:8–9; 2Ch 24:19; Est 4:14; Jer 7:25; Zec 7:7

God is active in the nations of the world
His rule over the nations Ps 22:28 *See also* Ge 11:8; Dt 32:8; Jdg 2:20–23; Job 12:23; Ps 46:8–10; 66:7; Isa 41:2; Ac 17:26

Examples of nations through which God acts
Assyria: 2Ki 17:18–23; Isa 28:11
Babylon: 2Ki 24:10–14; 2Ch 36:15–18
2Ch 36:22–23 pp Ezr 1:1–4 *Persia*

God is active in human life
He determines the course of human lives Ac 17:28 *See also* 1Ch 29:12; Ps 8:3–4; 75:6–7; 139:16; Lk 1:52; Jn 1:4

Examples of God's intervention in human lives Nu 22:21–23 *Balaam;* 1Sa 1:19–20 *Hannah;* 2Ki 5:14–15 *Naaman;* Jnh 1:17 *Jonah Paul:* Ac 9:3–6; 13:1–3; 16:6,10

God is active in Jesus Christ's ministry
Ac 10:38 *See also* Lk 5:17; 11:20; Jn 3:2; 5:17–19; 9:3–4; 14:10; 2Co 5:19

God is active through the Holy Spirit
Ge 1:2; 2Ki 2:16; Eze 8:3; 11:1; 43:5

God is active in the church
1Co 12:6 *This verse comes in the context of teaching about the body of Christ and the gifts which the Spirit gives to the church. See also* 1Co 14:24–25; Gal 2:8; 3:5; Eph 3:10,20–21; Php 1:6; 2:13

See also

1080 God, living	1325 God, the
1110 God, present	Creator
everywhere	2354 Christ, mission
1115 God, purpose	3275 Holy Spirit in
of	the church
1130 God,	4945 history
sovereignty	7020 church, the
1310 God as judge	7140 people of God
1320 God as Saviour	

1310
God, as judge

As a part of his sovereignty and authority, God is executor of his righteousness within the created order. Jesus Christ shares in this ongoing work.

God has authority to judge
God's status as judge Ps 75:7 *See also* Ps 50:6; 76:8–9; Ecc 11:9; Isa 33:22; 66:16; 2Ti 4:8; Heb 12:23; Jas 4:12

He decides disputes Jdg 11:27 *See also* Ge 16:5; 31:53; 1Sa 24:15; Isa 2:4 pp Mic 4:3; Jas 5:9

He presides in the heavenly court Isa 3:13 *See also* Ps 50:4; 82:1; Da 7:9–10; Joel 3:12; Rev 20:11–15

God is judge over the whole of creation
He judges the earth Ge 18:25 *See also* Ps 9:8; 58:11; 82:8; 94:2; 96:13; 98:9

He judges every individual Eze 33:20 *See also* Ecc 3:17; Heb 9:27; 1Pe 4:5; Jude 15; Rev 20:12

He judges the nations Joel 3:12 *See also* Ps 9:19–20; 110:6; Ob 15; Zep 3:8

He judges rulers of nations Isa 40:23; Jer 25:17–27; Rev 6:15–17

He judges his own people Heb 10:30 *See also* Dt 32:36; Ps 78:62; Jer 1:16; 1Pe 4:17

He judges angels 2Pe 2:4; Jude 6

He judges Satan Ge 3:14–15; Mt 25:41; 1Ti 3:6; Rev 20:10

God's judgment is inescapable
No-one can hide from God Ob 4 *See also* Ge 3:8–9; Job 11:20; Jer 11:11; Am 9:1–4

God searches human hearts Jer 17:10 *See also* 1Ch 28:9; Ps 7:9; Pr 5:21; Jer 11:20

God reveals secrets Ro 2:16 *See also* Ecc 12:14; Jer 16:17; 1Co 4:5; Heb 4:13

Examples of God acting as judge
His judgment of the earth in sending the flood Ge 6:7,13,17; 7:21–23

His judgment of individuals Ge 4:9–12 *Cain;* Ac 5:3–10 *Ananias and Sapphira;* Ac 13:8–11 *Elymas the sorcerer*

His judgment of families Jos 7:24–25 *of Achan;* 1Sa 3:12–13 *of Eli*

His judgment of cities Ge 19:24–25 *Sodom and Gomorrah;* Jos 6:24 *Jericho*

His judgment of nations Dt 7:1–5 *the Canaanite nations*

His judgment of the rulers of nations 2Ch 26:16–21 *Uzziah;* Da 4:31–33 *Nebuchadnezzar;* Da 5:22–30 *Belshazzar;* Ac 12:22–23 *Herod*

His judgment of his own people Jdg 2:11–15; 2Ch 36:15–20; Isa 33:22

God's character is revealed through his righteous judgments
His sovereignty Ps 9:7; 96:10; 99:4; Eze 6:14

His power Ex 6:6; 14:31; Eze 20:33–36; Rev 18:8

His holiness Lev 10:1–3; 1Sa 6:19–20; Eze 28:22; Rev 16:5

His anger Na 1:2–3; Ro 2:5

His truth Ps 96:13; Ro 2:2; Rev 16:7

His impartiality 2Ch 19:7; Ro 2:9–11; Col 3:25; 1Pe 1:17

His compassion La 3:31–33; Hos 11:8–9; Jnh 3:10; 4:2

His patience Nu 14:18; Ne 9:30; 2Pe 3:9

His mercy Ne 9:31; Job 9:15; Ps 78:38; Mic 7:18

Jesus Christ continues God's work as judge
Jn 5:22 *See also* Jn 5:27; Ac 10:42

God will act as judge on the last day
Rev 20:12 *See also* Isa 2:17; Zep 1:14–18; Jn 12:48; Ac 17:31; Ro 2:16; 14:10; 1Co 4:5; 2Ti 4:1; 1Pe 4:5; 2Pe 2:9; 3:7

See also

1025 God, anger of	2309 Christ as judge
1055 God, grace &	5360 justice, God
mercy	5484 punishment by
1065 God, holiness	God
of	9210 judgment,
1075 God, justice of	God's
1095 God, patience	9240 last judgment
of	9510 hell
1125 God,	
righteousness	

1315
God, as redeemer

God alone has the ability to save his people from slavery and captivity. God's redemptive will and power is demonstrated in his deliverance of Israel from bondage in Egypt, and supremely through the death and resurrection of Jesus Christ.

God as the sole redeemer of Israel
Isa 47:4 *See also* Dt 13:5; Ps 19:14

He redeems because of his love Dt 7:8; Ps 44:26

He is able to redeem because of his power Dt 9:26; 2Sa 7:23 pp 1Ch 17:21; Ne 1:10

God acts as Israel's redeemer
Ps 78:35; 111:9; Isa 43:1; 48:17; 54:5; 63:16

He promises to redeem Israel from Egypt Ex 3:8–10 *See also* Ex 3:21; 14:4

He redeems Israel in the exodus from Egypt Dt 5:15 *See also* Dt 15:15; 21:8; 24:18; Ne 9:9–11; Ps 77:14–20; 105:23–38; Hos 13:4; Mic 6:4; Ac 7:30–36

He redeems Israel from Babylonian exile Isa 41:14 *"Redeemer" is a characteristic title for God in the second part of Isaiah. In the context of the exile Isaiah reminds Israel that God would act as redeemer. See also* Isa 43:4; 44:6,24; 49:26; 54:5; 60:16; 62:12; Jer 50:33–35; 51:12; Mic 4:10; Zec 10:8

God redeems his people from difficult personal circumstances
Ps 34:22 *See also* Isa 29:22 *Abraham was redeemed from the land of idolatry to become God's servant;* Job 19:25 *Job, in the midst of his despair, declares God to be his redeemer;* Ps 31:4–5 *part of the psalmist's prayer for deliverance when confronted by an evil conspiracy;* La 3:58 *the lamentor recognises personal redemption within the context of national despair*

He brings deliverance from enemies Ps 69:18; 106:10; 107:2; Jer 15:21; 31:11

God redeems his people from the bondage and guilt of sin
Ps 130:7–8 *See also* Ps 34:22; Isa 59:20

Those who remain sinful do not find redemption Hos 7:13 *See also* Ps 26:11 *The request for redemption is made on the basis of uprightness;* Isa 1:27–28

God redeems his people from death
Ps 49:15 *See also* Job 19:25–27; Ps 103:4

Jesus Christ is central to God's redemptive purposes
Col 1:13–14 *See also* Lk 1:68; Ro 3:23–24; 1Co 1:30; 7:23; Gal 3:13–14; 4:4–5; Eph 1:7; Heb 9:11–12; 1Pe 1:18–21

God will finally redeem all creation at Jesus Christ's second coming Ro 8:19–23 *See also* Lk 21:28; Eph 1:13–14; 4:30; Tit 2:13–14

God's redemptive work brings him praise and worship
Eph 1:3–7 *See also* Ex 15:1–21; Ps 71:23; 119:134; 136:1–26; Isa 35:4–10; 44:22–23; 48:20; 51:11; 52:9

See also

1085 God, love of	6720 redemption
1105 God, power of	6732 repentance
1320 God as Saviour	6738 rescue
2321 Christ as	7948 mission
redeemer	8624 worship,
6510 salvation	reasons
6634 deliverance	
6659 freedom, acts	
in OT	

1320
God, as Saviour

God is the only Saviour and deliverer of his people. His work of salvation is inaugurated in the OT, and reaches its climax in the work of Jesus Christ.

God is the only Saviour
Isa 45:21–22 *See also* Jdg 10:13–14; Isa 43:11; Jer 2:28; 3:23; 11:12

God's deliverance can be worked through a human agent
Jdg 2:16 *See also* Ge 45:5–7; Ex 3:10; Jos 10:6–10; Jdg 2:18; 6:14–16; 2Ki 13:5; Isa 45:1,13

Examples of God's saving deeds
God delivers his people from Egypt:
Ex 6:6–7; 14:13–14,21–23,27–28; Ps 77:19–20; Hos 13:4
God delivers David from various dangers:
1Sa 17:37; 2Sa 22:1–3 pp Ps 18:2; 2Sa 22:18 pp Ps 18:17; Ps 3:8
Da 6:16–22 *God delivers Daniel from the lions' den.*
God delivers the apostles from prison:
Ac 5:18–19; 12:6–11; 16:25–26

God's acts of deliverance reveal his nature and character
Isa 52:10 *See also* Ps 98:2; Isa 49:6; Lk 3:4–6; Isa 40:3–5; Ro 1:16

His strength is seen Ps 18:2 *"rock" and "horn" symbolise God's strength; they are frequently used to emphasise his ability to save. See also* Ex 15:2 pp Ps 118:14; 1Sa 2:1; 2Sa 22:2–3,47 pp Ps 18:46; Ps 28:8

His glory is seen Ex 14:4 *See also* Ex 14:17–18; Nu 14:22; Ps 85:9; Isa 66:19; Eze 39:21

God's deliverance is anticipated
Ps 31:2 *See also* Ge 49:18; Ps 35:4; 69:13–15; Isa 33:22; 35:4

God's deliverance is promised
Ex 6:6 *See also* Ps 50:15; 91:14; Isa 38:6; 46:4; Eze 34:12

Implications of God's deliverance for believers
God is able to deliver believers from trials and testing 2Ti 4:18 *See also* Da 12:1; Mt 6:13; 1Co 10:13; 2Pe 2:9; Rev 3:10

God is able to deliver believers from sin and death Ro 7:24–25 *God delivers both from death owing to adversity and from death that comes about as a result of sin. See also* 2Sa 12:13; Ps 33:19; Eze 37:23; 1Co 15:56–57; 2Co 1:9–10

Testimony to God as Saviour and deliverer
Ge 50:20 *See also* Ps 13:5; 18:46–48; Isa 61:10; Da 6:27; Hab 3:18; Lk 1:47; 1Ti 4:10

See also
1315 God as redeemer	6510 salvation
2324 Christ as Saviour	6634 deliverance
	6659 freedom, acts in OT
5454 power, God's saving	6720 redemption
6028 sin, deliverance from	7222 exodus, events of
6248 temptation	8289 joy of church
	9020 death

1325
God, the Creator

God's power is revealed in the initial creation and the continuing sustenance of the universe. Humanity represents the climax of the Creator's purposes.

God is the Creator
Ne 9:6 *See also* Ge 1:1; Isa 45:7; 66:2; Eph 3:9; Rev 4:11

God's creative activity demonstrates his uniqueness Ps 96:5 *See also* Isa 37:16; Jer 10:11

God's creative activity implies that he is good 1Ti 4:4 *See also* Ge 1:4,31

God creates all things
He creates the physical world Isa 45:18 *See also* Ge 1:1–25

He creates the spiritual world Ps 148:2–5 *See also* Ro 8:38–39; Col 1:16

The human race is the apex of God's creation Ps 8:3–8 *See also* Ge 1:26–28; 5:1; 9:6; Ps 100:3; 139:13; Isa 42:5; Ac 17:26–28

The Creator's agents
He creates through Jesus Christ 1Co 8:6 *See also* Jn 1:3; Col 1:16; Heb 1:2

He creates by the Spirit Job 33:4 *See also* Ge 1:2; Ps 104:30

He creates by his word Ps 33:6 *See also* Job 38:8–11; Ps 33:9

He creates by wisdom Pr 3:19 *Wisdom is personified and is active with the Creator. See also* Pr 8:30; Jer 10:12–13

He creates from nothing
Heb 11:3 *God creates out of non-existent material, which emphasises the absolute dependence of all creation upon him. See also* Job 26:7; Ro 4:17

The Creator sustains the created order
Isa 44:24 *The Hebrew indicates continuous activity. See also* Dt 30:20; Job 9:8–9; Ps 104:2–4; Isa 42:5

Examples of God sustaining creation Mt 5:45 *See also* Job 5:10; 38:31–33; Mt 6:28–30

The Creator watches over his creation
Ps 33:14 *See also* Ps 121:2–8

The creation is a vehicle for God's self-revelation
Ro 1:20 *See also* Ps 19:1; Isa 40:26; Am 4:13

God renews his creation through redemption
Jn 3:17 ; 2Co 5:17 *See also* Jn 1:12–13; Ro 4:17; 6:4; 8:19–23 *The redemption of the physical world must wait until the sons*

---

of God are revealed at the end of time;
Gal 6:15

God renews his new creation of believing people
2Co 4:16 *See also* Col 3:10

God will reveal a new universe
Rev 21:1 *See also* Rev 21:5; Isa 65:17

See also
1330 God, the provider	4110 angels
	5002 human race & creation
1440 revelation, creation	5056 rest
2303 Christ as creator	5273 creativity
	6723 redemption, NT
3266 Holy Spirit in creation	6728 regeneration
4007 creation and God	8145 renewal, people of God

1330
God, the provider

God supplies the needs of all creation, but gives special care to his own people.

God is called "The LORD who provides"
Ge 22:13–14 *The name "Yahweh Yireh" (or "Jehovah Jireh") is from the verb "to see", and means "The LORD foresees" or "The LORD will see to it". See also* Ge 22:8

God provides for the needs of all creation
He provides for the earth Ps 65:9–13 *See also* Dt 11:12,14–15; Ps 68:9; 104:10–18; 135:7; 147:8; Eze 34:26–29

He provides for the animals Ps 145:16 *See also* Job 38:41; Ps 104:27–28; 147:9; Mt 6:26 pp Lk 12:24

He provides for all people Ac 14:17 *See also* 1Ch 29:12; Ps 68:5; 107:9; Mt 5:45; Ac 17:28

He provides for the poor and needy Ps 140:12 *See also* 1Sa 2:8; Ps 35:10; 145:13–14; 146:7–9; Isa 25:4

Special instances of God's practical provision
Food and water in the wilderness:
Ex 16:13–18; 17:3–6; Nu 11:4–9,31–32
God's provision for Elijah: 1Ki 17:6,16; 19:5–8
2Ki 4:42–44 *Elisha feeds 100 men from 20 barley loaves;* Mt 14:15–21 pp Mk 6:35–44 pp Lk 9:12–17 pp Jn 6:5–13 *Jesus Christ feeds 5,000;* Mt 15:32–38 pp Mk 8:1–9 *Jesus Christ feeds 4,000*

God's special provision for his own people
He provides for their practical needs Php 4:19 *See also* Dt 2:7; Ps 68:10; 111:5; Mt 6:25–33 pp Lk 12:22–31

He provides for their protection Ps 5:12 *See also* Ge 28:15; Dt 33:27; 1Sa 2:9; Ps 91:9–13; 121:3–8; Isa 46:4; Php 4:7; 1Pe 1:5; Jude 24; Rev 3:10

He provides for their every need 2Pe 1:3 *See also* 1Co 3:21–23; Col 2:10

Examples of God's provision for his people 2Sa 7:10 pp 1Ch 17:9 *security in the promised land;* Isa 61:3 *consolation in grief;* Jer 33:6–9 *restoration from captivity;* 1Co 10:13 *a way of escape from temptation*

Implications of God's providential care
Freedom from worry Mt 6:31–33 pp Lk 12:29–31

Generosity Lk 6:38 See also 1Ch 29:14; 2Co 9:6–11; Php 4:18

Faithfulness Ro 2:4 See also Isa 5:1–7; Hos 10:1–2; 11:1–4

See also

1030 God, compassion	1355 providence
1040 God, fatherhood	1416 miracles
	4065 orderliness
	4438 eating
1130 God, sovereignty	5480 protection
1205 God, titles of	8261 generosity, God's
1320 God as Saviour	8434 giving

1335
blessing

Spiritual and material benefits given by God to be enjoyed. Blessing the name of God is also the appropriate response of believers to all that God has done for them.

God is the source of all blessing
1Ch 29:11–12 See also Ps 89:11

At creation he blessed humans with fertility and authority over the earth
Ge 1:28–30

The disobedience of Adam and Eve caused God to remove his blessing
Ge 3:16–19 See also Ge 6:5–7

After the flood God renewed his promise of blessing to Noah Ge 9:1–3
See also Ge 8:22; Job 5:10; Ps 65:9–13

The blessings promised to Abraham
The blessings included descendants and nationhood Ge 12:2–3 See also Ge 17:1–8; 18:18; 26:4; 35:11; Ex 1:6–7; Dt 1:10–11; 7:13; 1Ki 3:8; Ne 9:23; Isa 51:2

The blessings included land Ge 17:8 See also Ge 12:7; 26:3; Dt 1:8; 4:40; 11:8–12

The promises of blessing to Abraham were fulfilled in Jesus Christ
Gal 3:16 See also Ac 3:25–26; Gal 3:29

Blessings promised to Israel
Blessings of fruitfulness and prosperity Dt 7:13–14 See also Ge 49:25; Lev 26:10; Dt 15:4; 28:8,12

Blessings of good health and long life Ex 23:25–26 See also Ex 15:26; Dt 7:15

Blessings of peace and victory over enemies Dt 28:7 See also Ex 23:22; Lev 26:6–8; Dt 7:24; Ps 29:11

The promise of being blessed by future restoration Jer 31:23 See also Isa 61:9; 65:17–25; Eze 34:25–31

The conditions of God's blessings
Fear of the Lord brings blessing Jer 32:40 See also Dt 6:1–3; 10:12–20; Ecc 12:13; Isa 50:10

Obedience to the Lord brings blessing
Dt 11:26–28 See also Dt 28:1–14; 30:15–20

To bless God is to worship and adore him
Ne 9:5 See also Ge 9:26; 14:20

People may bless one another in the name of the Lord
Nu 6:24–26 There is a close link between blessing and prayer. See also Ge 27:27–29; 49:1–28; Ru 1:8–9; 1Sa 2:20; 1Ch 4:10; Mt 23:39

See also

1050 God, goodness of	8453 obedience
1620 beatitudes, the	8608 prayer & worship
5827 curse	8611 prayer for others
8117 discipleship, benefits	8622 worship
8335 reverence & blessing	8638 benedictions
	8676 thanksgiving

1340
consistency

God's nature, plans and purpose do not change. The same consistent plan of salvation can be seen throughout the OT and NT, culminating in Jesus Christ who is "the same yesterday and today and for ever". Believers are also called to show the same consistency in their faith and witness.

God's nature is consistent and unchanging
Mal 3:6 See also Ps 102:27; Jas 1:17

God's plans and purpose are consistent and unchanging
Ps 33:11 See also Nu 23:19; 1Sa 15:29; Job 36:5; Ps 89:34; Tit 1:2; Heb 7:21; Ps 110:4

God's plan of salvation is consistent
Ge 12:2–3; Heb 6:17–18; 13:8 See also Ge 18:18; 22:17–18; 26:4; 28:14; Dt 18:15,18; Ps 72:17; Jer 4:1–2; Zec 8:13; Ac 3:23–26; Gal 3:8

Believers are to live lives consistent with their profession of faith
Eph 4:1; Php 1:27 See also Mt 5:37; 1Th 4:12; 1Ti 3:7; Heb 13:7; Jas 5:12; 2Pe 3:11

See also

1035 God, faithfulness	2324 Christ as Saviour
1115 God, purpose of	5467 promises, divine
1160 God, unchangeable	5769 behaviour
	6510 salvation
1170 God, unity of	8266 holiness
1320 God as Saviour	8331 reliability

1345
covenant

God's commitment to, and requirement of, his people expressed in promise, law, judgment, faithfulness and mercy. Also used of

commitment within human relationships based upon agreements.
This set of themes consists of the following:

1346
covenants, nature of

A solemn agreement or promise, sometimes confirmed by sacrifice or by sharing in a meal, by which two or more parties commit themselves to the rights and responsibilities demanded by their relationship and their agreed course of action, and accept the serious consequences of breaking faith.

Kinds of covenant relationship
The relationship between king and people 2Sa 5:3 pp 1Ch 11:3 See also 2Sa 3:21; 2Ki 11:17; 2Ch 23:3

Terms for peace granted to a weaker party Jos 9:15 See also 1Sa 11:1; 1Ki 15:19–20; 20:34; Eze 17:13–14

A mutual commitment to peaceful relations 1Ki 5:12 See also Ge 21:27; 26:28–29; 31:44; Am 1:9

An agreement on a common course of action Jer 34:8 See also 2Ki 11:4 pp 2Ch 23:1; Ezr 10:3; Ne 9:38; Ps 83:5

The relationship between husband and wife Pr 2:17; Mal 2:14
God's covenant with Israel is likened to a marriage: Jer 2:2; Eze 16:8

An expression of friendship 1Sa 18:3 See also 1Sa 20:16–17

Sealing a covenant
By sharing a meal Ge 26:30; 31:53–54
The meal Jesus Christ shared with his disciples is an important part of the institution of the new covenant: Mt 26:26–29 pp Mk 14:22–25 pp Lk 22:17–20; 1Co 11:23–25

By offering a sacrifice Jer 34:18–19 The Hebrew expression for making a covenant means, literally, "to cut a covenant". This may refer to the solemn practice, described here, of cutting an animal in half and walking between its pieces; Ge 15:9–18; Ex 24:4–8; Ps 50:5; Heb 12:24 Sacrifice is an important part in sealing covenants made by God.

By making an oath Ge 21:31; 26:31; Jos 9:15; 2Ki 11:4; Ne 10:28–29

The obligations of a covenant
Covenant responsibilities must be honoured Nu 30:2; 1Sa 20:8 See also Jos 9:18; Mt 5:33–37; Gal 3:15

Covenant obligations are watched over by God 1Sa 20:42 See also Ge 31:48–54; Jos 9:19; Jer 34:15–16; Mal 2:14–16

The consequences of breaking covenant faith Jos 9:20 *See also* Jer 34:18–22; Eze 17:16–18; Am 1:9

Covenants with other nations are forbidden
Ex 34:12 *See also* Dt 23:6; Jos 9:7

Covenants with other nations lead to a commitment to foreign gods
Ex 23:32–33; 34:15–16; Dt 7:2–4

Covenants with other nations lead to a denial of faith in God Isa 28:15,18; 30:1–2; 31:1; Hos 12:1

See also
5205 alliance	8207 commitment
5429 oaths	8251 faithfulness to
5592 treaty	God
5708 marriage	8324 purity
5783 agreement	8711 covenant
6636 drawing near to	breakers
God	8768 idolatry
7140 people of God	

1347
covenant, God's with Noah

God's confirmation of, and commitment to maintain, his relationship with the natural order—implicit in the act of creation—whereby he promised never again to destroy the earth with a flood. This divine pledge, given unconditionally to Noah and to every living creature on earth, was accompanied by the sign of the rainbow.

The occasion of the covenant
The flood as divine judgment Ge 6:17 *See also* Ge 6:5–7,11–13; 2Pe 2:5

God's promise of salvation to Noah and his family Ge 6:18 *See also* Ge 7:23; 8:1,15–17; Heb 11:7; 1Pe 3:20

God's promise never again to destroy the earth with a flood Ge 9:11 *See also* Ge 8:21; Isa 54:9

The sign of the covenant
Ge 9:13 *See also* Ge 9:14–17

A universal covenant
God's relationship with every living creature Ge 9:8–10 *See also* Ge 7:1–3; Eze 34:25; Hos 2:18; Zec 11:10

God's relationship with the natural order Ge 8:22; Jer 33:25–26 *God's relationship with the created order is here expressed as a covenant. It is probable that this is a reference to the Noahic covenant through which the implicit relationship between Creator and creation was confirmed. See also* Ge 1:14,31–2:1; Ps 74:16–17; Jer 5:24; 33:20–21

An everlasting covenant
Ge 9:16 *See also* Ge 9:12
Isa 24:5 *The reference here is to the Noahic covenant. Though this covenant was unconditional, the prohibition of bloodshed—often described as bringing pollution to the land—was associated with it. There may be, also, a wider reference to the effects of mankind's disregard for the norms laid down at creation. See also* Ge 9:6; Nu 35:33; Isa 26:21

See also
4005 creation	7203 ark, Noah's
4845 rainbow	7227 flood, the
5106 Noah	
5467 promises,	
divine	

1348
covenant, God's with Abraham

God's gracious promise made to Abraham, and repeated to his descendants, to bless both them and, through them, the whole world. In response God calls for faithful obedience, expressed particularly in the outward sign of circumcision.

Features of the Abrahamic covenant
The covenant is based upon God's gracious promise Gal 3:18 *See also* Ge 15:4–7; 17:4–8; 18:10,14; Heb 6:13–15

The covenant was confirmed by sacrifice Ge 15:9–18

The covenant was given in perpetuity Ge 17:7 *See also* Ge 17:13,19; 1Ch 16:15–17 pp Ps 105:8–10; Jer 33:23–25

God's promises to Abraham
Ge 12:2–3

God promised the land of Canaan Ge 17:8 *See also* Ge 12:7; 15:18–21; Ex 6:4; Jos 1:3; Ne 9:8; Ac 7:5

God promised that Abraham would be the father of a nation Ge 15:5 *See also* Ge 12:2; 17:4–6 *The change of name from Abram to Abraham is a sign of God's covenant with him;* Ge 17:16; 22:17; Heb 11:11–12

God promised a relationship with himself Ge 17:7 *See also* Ge 26:24; Dt 29:13; Mt 22:32 pp Mk 12:26; Ex 3:6; Ac 7:32

The requirements of the covenant
Obedience Ge 17:9–14 *Circumcision is the sign of Abraham's commitment to God's covenant with him;* Ge 22:18 *See also* Ge 26:5; Nu 32:11 *by contrast, the consequences of disobedience;* Heb 11:8,17–19

Faith Ge 15:6; Ne 9:8 *See also* Ro 4:3,11–12,18; Gal 3:6–7; Heb 11:8–12; Jas 2:23

God's faithfulness to the covenant
God remembers his promise Ps 105:42 *See also* Ge 21:2; 50:24; Ex 33:1; Ac 7:17; Heb 6:15

God shows compassion for his people 2Ki 13:23 *See also* Ex 2:24–25; 32:13–14; Dt 9:27; Lk 1:72–73

The scope of the covenant
The covenant continued through Isaac, not Ishmael Ge 17:19–21 *See also* Ge 21:12; Ro 9:7–8; Gal 4:28

The covenant confirmed through Abraham, Isaac and Jacob Lev 26:42 *See also* Ge 26:24 *Isaac; Jacob:* Ge 28:13–14; 32:12 Ex 3:6; Dt 1:8; Ac 7:8

The people of Israel are heirs to the covenant Dt 29:12–13 *See also* Ac 3:25

All nations will be blessed through Abraham Ge 18:18 *See also* Ge 26:4; Ac 3:25; Gal 3:8–9,14,29

See also
1245 God of the	7258 promised land,
fathers	early history
5075 Abraham	7334 circumcision
5094 Jacob	8023 faith, necessity
6638 election	8453 obedience

1349
covenant, God's at Sinai

God's faithful commitment, made in pursuance of his promises to Abraham, to acknowledge the newly-redeemed Israel as his own special people. Israel's required response to the grace of God in election was to be holiness and obedience to the law.

The occasion of the covenant
The covenant fulfilled God's promises to Abraham Dt 29:12–13 *See also* Ex 2:24; 6:4–8; Dt 7:8

The covenant followed Israel's redemption from slavery Jer 34:13 *God's covenant at Sinai was made in the context of his historical acts of deliverance. Covenants ("treaties") between a supreme (suzerain) overlord and a subordinate ruler (vassal) are well known in ancient Near Eastern writings. They were not "agreements" but "requirements". See also* Ex 20:2 pp Dt 5:6; Lev 26:45

The covenant was mediated through Moses Ex 34:27; Lev 26:46; Dt 29:1; Jn 1:17

The covenant was accompanied by signs of God's presence Ex 19:18–19; 20:18–19; 24:16; Ps 68:8

Sealing the covenant
Sharing a meal Ex 24:11

Offering a sacrifice Ex 24:5–8; Ps 50:5

God's oath Dt 28:9; 29:14; Eze 16:8

Israel's promise Ex 19:8; 24:3,7

The covenant relationship
Israel as God's people Dt 7:6 *See also* Ex 19:5–6; Lev 26:12; Dt 14:2; Jer 13:11

Israel adopted into God's family Hos 11:1 *See also* Dt 1:30–31; 8:5; Isa 63:16; Mal 2:10

Israel as God's bride Jer 2:2 *See also* Isa 54:5–8; Jer 31:32; Eze 16:8; Hos 2:14–16

The blessings of the covenant
Inheriting God's promises Dt 6:3; 26:18–19; 28:9; Jos 23:5

Provision and protection Lev 26:3–13; Dt 28:1–14 *This pattern of blessings and curses is also a feature of Near Eastern political treaties.*

The requirements of the covenant
Obedience to the law Ex 24:7; 34:27–28 *See also* Dt 4:13; Jos 8:31; Ne 8:1

Holiness Dt 14:2 *Israel has been made holy through her election as the covenant people of God. The ensuing call for holiness is a call to work out the implications of that relationship and to live in accordance with its demands;* **Lev 11:45** *See also* **Lev 20:26**

Wholehearted devotion Ex 34:14; Dt 10:12 *See also* Ex 23:32; Dt 4:23; 6:5; 10:20; Jos 24:14–15

Breaking the covenant
The consequences of breaking the covenant
Disease: Lev 26:15–16; Dt 28:21–22
Drought and crop failure: Lev 26:19–20; Dt 28:23–24
Defeat by enemies: Lev 26:17,25; Dt 28:25
Exile from the land: Lev 26:32–33; Dt 28:36–37; Jos 23:16; Eze 17:19–20

Israel's unfaithfulness to the covenant Ps 78:37 *See also* 2Ki 18:12; 1Ch 5:25; Jer 3:8; 11:10; Eze 16:32; Hos 6:7

God's commitment to the covenant
God's covenant of love Dt 7:9 *"love" translates the Hebrew word "hesed", which here expresses God's loyalty and faithful commitment to his covenant people. See also* Ne 1:5; Da 9:4

The everlasting covenant Eze 16:60 *God's faithfulness to the covenant at Sinai will result in a new covenant that will never come to an end. See also* Isa 61:8; Jer 32:40

Renewing the covenant
Lev 26:40–45; Dt 29:1; Jos 24:22–25; 2Ki 23:3 pp 2Ch 34:31

See also
1035 God, faithfulness	5377 law, Ten Commandments
4269 Sinai, Mount	6020 sin
5101 Moses	

1350
covenant, God's with Israel's priests

God's promise to the Levites, and to the family of Phinehas in particular, to maintain those who serve him faithfully in a lasting priesthood.

God's covenant with Phinehas
Nu 25:12–13 *Phinehas was the grandson of Aaron. God's pledge of "a lasting priesthood", granted to him as a result of his zeal, probably means that the high priesthood would remain in his family. See also* Nu 25:10–11; Ezr 7:1–5; Ps 106:30–31

God's covenant with the Levites
An everlasting covenant Nu 18:19 *This covenant confirms the privileges and responsibilities of Aaron and his fellow Levites who have been called to Israel's priesthood. The reference to "salt" may underline the permanent nature of the covenant. God's covenant with David is also described as a "covenant of salt". See also* 2Ch 13:5; Jer 33:18–22

Requirements of the covenant
Mal 2:5–6

The Levites' portion is the LORD Dt 10:8–9 *See also* Nu 3:12

The covenant violated Mal 2:8 *By their unfaithfulness, Judah's priests have forfeited the blessings of God's promise to Levi. See also* Ne 13:29

See also
5073 Aaron, priest	7390 Levites
7364 fellowship offering	7412 priesthood
7376 high priest	7766 priests

1351
covenant, God's with David

God's promise to establish David and his descendants on Israel's throne for ever. It provided Israel with a basis for the hope of deliverance and restoration, and became a focus for the Messianic expectation which was fulfilled, ultimately, in Jesus Christ.

God's promise to establish David's line
God's election of David Ps 78:70 *See also* 2Sa 6:21; 1Ki 8:16 pp 2Ch 6:6

God's covenant is everlasting Ps 89:3–4 *See also* 2Sa 7:11–16; 23:5; 1Ki 2:45; 2Ch 13:5; Ps 18:50; 89:28–29,35–37; Jer 33:17

God's covenant is inherited through obedience Ps 132:11–12 *Though God's promise to maintain David's throne is unbreakable, individual descendants must continue to be faithful if they are to inherit the blessings promised to David. See also* 1Ki 8:25–26 pp 2Ch 6:16–17; 1Ki 9:4–5 pp 2Ch 7:17–18

God's covenant blessings are forfeited through disobedience Jer 22:4–5 *Failure to remain faithful to God brings judgment on the royal house and the people. See also* 1Ki 9:6–9 pp 2Ch 7:19–22; 1Ki 11:11–13,31–33; Jer 7:24–26; 22:6–9; 36:30–31

God's promise is fulfilled by grace 2Ch 21:7 pp 2Ki 8:19 *Though particular kings may suffer God's anger because of their sin, God's faithfulness to the house of David as a whole, and thus to the nation of Israel, will continue. See also* 1Ki 11:34–36,39; 15:4; Ps 89:30–34

The Davidic covenant as a basis for hope
God's election of Jerusalem 2Ki 21:7 pp 2Ch 33:7 *God's Name signifies his presence. God's choice of David was closely related to his choice of Jerusalem, the city established by David, as the place where the divine presence symbolised in the temple and the ark of the covenant was to be found. See also* 1Ki 8:20–21 pp 2Ch 6:10–11; 1Ki 11:32,36; 1Ch 23:25; 2Ch 6:41–42 pp Ps 132:8–10

God's promise to defend Jerusalem Isa 37:35 pp 2Ki 19:34 *See also* 2Ki 19:20; Zec 12:7–9

God's promise to restore David's house Am 9:11 *See also* Ac 15:16; Jer 33:25–26

Hopes expressed in the Davidic covenant are focused in the Messiah
The Messiah fulfils the Davidic hope Jer 23:5–6 *See also* Ps 110:1–2; Isa 9:7; 11:1–2; 16:5; 55:3; Eze 34:23–25; Zec 3:8; Jn 7:42

God's promise to David fulfilled in Jesus Christ Lk 1:32–33; Rev 22:16 *See also* Mt 1:1; 22:41–46 pp Mk 12:35–37 pp Lk 20:41–44
Many Jews in Jesus Christ's day were expecting a literal fulfilment of God's promise to restore the Davidic empire. The true hope expressed in the Davidic covenant and fulfilled in Christ is the coming of the kingdom of God: Mk 11:10 pp Mt 21:9; Lk 24:21; Ac 1:6 Ac 2:29–31; 13:34; Ro 1:3; 2Ti 2:8

See also
2206 Jesus, the Christ	2312 Christ as king
2215 Christ, Son of David	2376 kingdom of God, coming
2230 Messiah, coming of	5085 David
	7239 Jerusalem

1352
covenant, the new

The fulfilment of God's purposes of salvation expressed in the covenants of the OT, mediated by Jesus Christ and sealed in his blood. It is a covenant of grace, the benefits of which include forgiveness, a renewed relationship with God and, through the Holy Spirit, an inward transformation that enables obedience to its demands and so ensures that it will not again be broken.
Jer 31:31 *The "new" covenant is contrasted with the covenant made at Sinai which is sometimes referred to as the "old" or "first" covenant. See also* Heb 8:8

The new covenant fulfils the OT covenants
God's covenant with Noah Isa 54:9–10; Hos 2:18

God's covenant with Abraham Lk 1:72–73; Ac 3:25–26; Gal 3:14–16

God's covenant at Sinai Eze 16:60,62; 20:37

God's covenant with David Isa 55:3; Eze 34:24–26; 37:25–26; Lk 1:69

Jesus Christ, the mediator of the new covenant
The new covenant fulfilled in the Messiah Mal 3:1 *See also* Isa 42:6; 49:8

The new covenant effected through Jesus Christ's death Heb 9:15 *See also* Heb 9:16–17

The new covenant sealed in Jesus Christ's blood Lk 22:20 pp Mt 26:28 pp Mk 14:24 *See also* Ex 24:8 *Blood was an important element in sealing the Sinaitic covenant;* Jn 6:54; 1Co 10:16; 11:25; Heb 10:29

The ministry of the Holy Spirit
2Co 3:6,18 See also Isa 59:21;
Eze 36:26–27; Ro 8:2–4; 2Co 3:8

The superior blessings of the new covenant
God's grace and mercy Heb 12:24 The blood of Abel cried out to God for justice and retribution; the blood of Jesus Christ, shed to seal the new covenant, cries out for mercy and forgiveness.

A complete forgiveness Heb 8:12 See also Jer 31:34; Ro 11:27; Heb 10:17

Release from the law's condemnation 2Co 3:9; Gal 3:13–14

An inward enabling to obey God's laws Jer 31:32–33 The old covenant was broken because its demands were not met. Under the new covenant the requirements of obedience are not abolished, but in writing his laws on human hearts, God gives the ability to meet the covenant demands. See also Jer 32:38–40; Eze 11:19–20; 2Co 3:3; Heb 8:9–10; 9:14; 10:16

A new knowledge of God Heb 8:11 See also Jer 31:34; 2Co 3:15–16

A renewed relationship with God Eze 37:26–27 "peace" refers to spiritual and material well-being; real peace is possible only for those in a right relationship with God. The formula "I will be their God, and they will be my people" is associated also with the Abrahamic and especially the Sinaitic covenants. See also Jer 24:7; 31:1; Eze 34:30–31; Hos 2:19–23

A superior priesthood Heb 8:6 See also Heb 7:22; 9:24–25

A superior sacrifice Heb 9:14 See also Heb 9:20–23,26–28; 10:4,8–14

A lasting covenant Isa 61:8; 2Co 3:11 See also Jer 50:5; Heb 8:7,13; 13:20

See also
2306 Christ, high priest	5380 law and gospel
2315 Christ as Lamb	6652 forgiveness
2530 Christ, death of	6666 grace
3230 Holy Spirit & regeneration	6744 sanctification
3233 Holy Spirit & sanctification	7317 blood of Christ
	7436 sacrifice, NT fulfilment
	7933 Lord's Supper

1355
providence

The continuing and often unseen activity of God in sustaining his universe, providing for the needs of every creature, and preparing for the completion of his eternal purposes.

God's general providence
God sustains the created order Ge 8:22 A promise given by God to all peoples. See also Ne 9:6; Isa 40:26; Col 1:17; Heb 1:3

All life is dependent on God 1Ti 6:13 See also 1Sa 1:27; Job 1:21; Ps 127:3; Ecc 3:2; 9:9; Eze 24:16; Da 5:26; Mt 4:4; 10:29

God controls the elements Ps 147:8 See also Job 37:1–13; Ps 29:3–9; 135:6–7; Mt 5:45; Ac 17:25–28

God provides for the created world Ps 145:15–16 See also Job 38:39–41; Ps 104:27–28; 136:25; 147:9; Lk 12:6–7; Ac 14:17; 1Ti 6:17

God's providence through miraculous means
Job 5:9–10 God's regular activity in providing for human beings is regarded as being miraculous in just the same way as special demonstrations of his power. See also Ex 16:11–14; Nu 16:28–35; Jdg 15:18–19; 1Ki 17:5–6; 2Ki 4:42–44

God's providence in human history
God's control of human intentions Hab 1:12 See also 1Ki 22:19–20; 2Ki 19:27–28 pp Isa 37:28–29; Isa 10:15; Hab 1:6

God's providential actions on behalf of individuals Ro 8:28 See also Job 1:12; 2:6; Ps 107:12–14,24–29,33–38; Isa 38:17

God's saving purposes fulfilled through providence Ge 50:20 See also Ge 22:13; 45:5–8; 2Ch 36:22–23 pp Ezr 1:1–3; Ezr 6:14; Isa 44:28–45:1; Ac 2:23; 4:27–28; Gal 4:4–5

God's providence prepares for the completion of his ultimate purpose
God is forming a people for himself Rev 21:3 See also Ex 6:7; Jer 31:33; 2Co 6:16; Eph 2:14–16; 1Pe 1:3–5; Rev 7:9

God will bring all things under Jesus Christ's authority Eph 1:9–10 See also Isa 45:22–23; 66:23; 1Co 15:24–26; Php 2:10–11; Col 1:20; Rev 11:15

God will complete his purpose for creation Ro 8:20–21 See also Isa 65:17; 66:22; 2Pe 3:13; Rev 21:1

God directs all things for his glory Ro 11:36 See also Ps 46:10; Ro 9:23; 11:36; Eph 1:4–6,11–12

See also
1130 God, sovereignty		4854 weather, God's sovereignty	
1330 God, the provider		4969 seasons	
1416 miracles		8261 generosity, God's	
4007 creation and God		8409 decision-making & providence	
4015 life			
4065 orderliness			

1400
God, knowledge of

This set of themes consists of the following:

1403 God, revelation of
1406 burning bush
1409 dream
1412 foreknowledge
1415 miracles
1421 oracles
1424 predictions
1427 prophecy
1436 reality
1439 revelation
1448 signs
1454 theophany
1457 trance
1460 truth
1466 vision
1469 visions

1403
God, revelation of

God graciously makes himself known to humanity since people cannot discover him on their own. He achieves this in many ways, but supremely through his Son Jesus Christ.

The necessity of revelation
God is hidden from human view because of sin Isa 59:2 See also Dt 31:18; Isa 1:15; 45:15; 64:7; Eze 39:23; Mic 3:4

People are ignorant of God Ac 17:23 See also Ex 5:2; Jdg 2:10; Jer 4:22; Jn 4:22; 15:21; Gal 4:8; Eph 4:18; 1Th 4:5

People cannot know God unaided Mt 11:25–27 pp Lk 10:21–22 See also Job 34:29; 1Co 1:21

The means by which God reveals himself
In the Scriptures Ps 119:105 See also Ps 19:7–10; 119:130; 147:19; Pr 6:23; 2Ti 3:16; 2Pe 1:19–21

By the Holy Spirit Eph 1:17 See also Ne 9:20; Lk 2:26; 12:12; Jn 14:26; 1Co 2:10,12; 1Jn 2:27

Supremely in Jesus Christ Heb 1:1–2 See also Jn 1:18; 8:26; 12:49; 14:10; 17:6

In the creation Ps 19:1 See also Ps 97:6; Ac 14:17; 17:26–27

Through the prophets Am 3:7 See also Nu 12:6; 2Sa 7:17 pp 1Ch 17:15; 2Sa 7:27 pp 1Ch 17:25; Isa 22:14; 1Pe 1:12

In visions and dreams Da 1:17 See also Ge 15:1; Isa 1:1; Eze 11:24; Da 8:1; Na 1:1; Mt 1:20; 2:12,22; Ac 9:10; 16:9; 22:17–18

Face to face Nu 12:8 See also Ge 32:30; Ex 24:9–10; Jdg 13:22; Job 42:5; Isa 6:5

In the exodus Ex 7:5 See also Ex 14:4; 1Sa 2:27; Eze 20:5,9

In special signs Jdg 6:36–40 Gideon's fleece; 1Ki 13:3–5 an altar split apart; 2Ki 20:9–11 pp Isa 38:7–8 a shadow moving backwards

The nature of God's self-revelation in Jesus Christ
God reveals Jesus Christ's true identity Mt 16:17 See also Mt 3:17 pp Mk 1:11 pp Lk 3:22; Mt 17:5 pp Mk 9:7 pp Lk 9:35; Jn 1:31; Gal 1:15–16; 2Pe 1:17–18

Jesus Christ is the visible image of God Col 1:15 See also 2Co 4:4; Php 2:6; Heb 1:3

Jesus Christ's glory is still to be fully revealed Lk 17:30; 1Co 1:7; 2Th 1:7; 1Pe 1:7,13; 4:13

Things that God reveals
Hidden mysteries Da 2:22 See also Ge 41:16; Job 12:22; Da 2:28–30,47

Future events Ge 41:25 *See also* 1Sa 9:15–16; 2Ki 8:10; Jer 11:18; 38:21; Mt 2:13; Ac 18:9–10; 27:22–24

His righteousness Ro 1:17 *See also* Isa 56:1; Ro 3:21; Rev 15:4

His wrath Ro 1:18 *See also* Nu 11:1; 2Sa 6:7 pp 1Ch 13:10; Ps 7:11; Ro 2:5

His salvation Ps 98:2 *See also* Isa 52:10; Lk 2:30–32; 3:6; Tit 2:11

His glory Isa 40:5
The pillar of cloud and fire in the wilderness: Ex 16:10; 33:9; Nu 12:5; Dt 1:33; Ne 9:12; Ps 78:14; 105:39
Ex 33:18–23 *the LORD shows his glory to Moses*
The cloud of glory in the tabernacle and the temple: Ex 40:34; Lev 16:2; Dt 31:15; Eze 9:3; 10:4
Dt 5:24; Ps 97:6; 102:16; Isa 35:2; 44:23; 60:2; Ac 7:55

The mystery of the gospel Eph 3:2–3
"mystery" in the NT means "something previously hidden, undiscoverable by human means but now revealed by God".
See also Mt 13:11 pp Mk 4:11 pp Lk 8:10; Ro 16:25–26; Gal 3:23; Eph 3:5–6; Col 1:26–27; 2Ti 1:10

The revelation of God's will
Physical means by which God reveals his will
By the Urim and Thummim: Ex 28:30; Nu 27:21
By casting lots: Jos 18:6–10; Jnh 1:7; Ac 1:26
God's self-revelation makes his will plain Ro 1:20 *See also* Zec 7:11–12; Jn 9:41; 16:8; Ro 7:7

God's self-revelation is according to his own sovereign purpose
Isa 65:1 *See also* Da 2:30; Ro 10:20; Gal 1:11–12

See also
1045 God, glory of
1175 God, will of
1439 revelation
1449 signs, purposes
1610 Scripture
1690 word of God
2218 Christ, Son of God
2595 incarnation
4005 creation
6694 mystery
8135 knowing God

1406
burning bush

God spoke to Moses through a bush which burned but was not consumed
Ac 7:30–34 *See also* Ex 3:1–5; Dt 33:13–16; Mk 12:26 pp Lk 20:37; Ac 7:35
See also
4269 Sinai, Mount   5101 Moses

1409
dream

A series of images or thoughts experienced in one's mind while asleep. A means by which a divine message may be conveyed while the recipient sleeps. God may

communicate directly in the dream, or interpretation may be necessary.

Direct communication through dreams
Ge 31:24 *See also* Ge 20:3,6; 1Sa 28:6,15; 1Ki 3:5,15; Job 33:14–15; Mt 1:20; 2:12–13,19–20,22

Dreams involving unusual images
Ge 28:12–15; 31:10–13; 37:5–7,9; 40:9–11,16–17; 41:1–7; Jdg 7:13; Da 2:31–35; 4:10–17

God is the source of interpretation of such dreams
Da 2:26–28 *See also* Ge 40:8; 41:15–16,25,28; Da 4:24

Interpretation of unusual images
Ge 40:12–13,18–19; 41:26–31; Jdg 7:14–15; Jer 23:28; 31:23–26; Da 2:36–45; 4:19–26

Revelation to prophets through dreams
Nu 12:6; Joel 2:28 *See also* Da 1:17; 2:19–23; Ac 2:17

Dreams and false prophets
Dt 13:1–3 *See also* Dt 13:5; Jer 23:25–27,32; 27:9; 29:8–9; Zec 10:2

Ordinary dreams
Isa 29:7–8 *Not every dream is a vehicle for divine communication. Most are part of the natural process of sleep. See also*
Job 7:13–15; Ps 73:20; Ecc 5:3,7; Isa 56:10

See also
1020 God, all-knowing
1439 revelation
1469 visions
4428 corn
4534 vine
5263 communication
5533 sleep, physical
6694 mystery
7730 explanation
7772 prophets
8124 guidance
8281 insight

1412
foreknowledge

Foreknowledge is an aspect of God's knowledge of everything, and thus nothing can surprise him. Jesus Christ had foreknowledge of his own death, resurrection and coming in glory.

God's foreknowledge
Everything is within God's knowledge
Isa 42:9 *See also* 1Ki 22:14; Da 2:28; Mt 24:36 pp Mk 13:32
What God knows he ordains Isa 46:10–11 *See also* Ac 2:23; Ro 8:28–30; 1Pe 1:1–2
God's foreknowledge of the Messiah Ac 3:18 *See also* Isa 11:1–3; 53:7–9; Mic 5:2; Ac 2:22–23; 4:27–28; 1Pe 1:20

God's foreknowledge and his election of his people
God's sovereign choice Ro 8:29 *See also* Pr 16:4; Ro 9:11–12; 11:2; Eph 1:4; 1Pe 1:1–2,20
Human responsibility Heb 2:3 *See also* Jn 3:18,36; 1Co 15:2; 2Co 6:1–2;

Eph 5:5–6; Heb 3:12; 6:4–6; 2Pe 2:1; Heb 3:15; Ps 95:7–8

Jesus Christ's foreknowledge
Of events within his general ministry
Jn 6:64 *See also* Mt 17:27; 26:31–34 pp Mk 14:27–30; Lk 22:34; Jn 13:38
Of his suffering and departure Jn 13:1 *See also* Mt 26:18; Mk 8:31 pp Lk 9:22; Lk 12:50; 22:37; Jn 3:14; 7:33; 13:11,33; 14:28; 17:5; 18:4; 19:28
Of his coming in glory and judgment
Mt 16:27 *See also* Mt 24:30–31 pp Mk 13:26–27; Mt 25:31; Mk 8:38 pp Lk 9:26; Lk 24:26

Jesus Christ's lack of knowledge of the timing of his coming in glory
Mk 13:32 pp Mt 24:36

See also
1020 God, all-knowing
1355 providence
1427 prophecy
2024 Christ, glory of
2045 Christ, knowledge of
2230 Messiah, coming of
2309 Christ as judge
2565 Christ, second coming
5051 responsibility
5932 response
6638 election
6708 predestination

1415

miracles

Events that are totally out of the ordinary and that cannot be adequately explained on the basis of natural occurrences, such as those associated with the ministry of Jesus Christ. They are seen as evidence of the presence and power of God in the world or as demonstrating authority on the part of one of his servants.

1416
miracles, nature of

Miracles may be performed directly by God or through a human agent. Those recorded in Scripture include healing, raising the dead, miracles of nature and the casting out of demons.

Miracles demonstrate God's greatness and power
Ps 77:14 *See also* Ex 14:30–31; 34:10; Dt 3:24; 1Ki 18:37–39; Job 5:9; Ps 78:4; Lk 9:42–43

Miracles bringing God's judgment
Lev 10:1–2 *See also* Ge 19:24–26; Nu 12:10; 16:31–35; 1Ki 13:4–5; 2Ki 1:9–12; 2Ch 26:19–20; Ac 5:5,10; 13:11

Miracles which meet human need
The provision of food and water
Ex 17:6 *See also* Ex 15:25; Nu 11:31–32; 20:10–11; Jdg 15:18–19; 1Ki 17:5–6,8–16; 2Ki 2:19–22; 4:42–44; Mt 14:15–21; Mk 8:1–10
Healing Ac 5:16 *See also* Nu 21:6–9; 2Ki 5:1–14; Lk 9:6; Ac 3:1–10; 9:33–34; 28:7–9

Exorcism Ac 16:18 *See also* Mk 6:13; 9:38 pp Lk 9:49; Lk 10:17; Ac 8:7

The raising of the dead Jn 11:38–44 *See also* 1Ki 17:17–24; 2Ki 4:32–37; 13:21; Ac 9:36–41; 20:9–12

Miraculous births Ge 18:10–14 *See also* Jdg 13:2–3; 1Sa 1:20; 2Ki 4:14–17; Lk 1:34–37

Miracles involving military victory 2Ch 32:21 pp 2Ki 19:35–36 pp Isa 37:36–37 *See also* Ex 12:29–36; 14:26–28; Jos 10:12–14; 1Sa 7:10–12; 2Ki 6:18–23; 2Ch 20:22–26

Miraculous help in trouble Da 6:27 *See also* Ps 91:11–12; Da 3:19–27; 6:19–23; Mt 8:23–27 pp Mk 4:36–41 pp Lk 8:22–25; Ac 12:6–11; 16:25–26

Gifts of supernatural strength Jdg 14:5–6 *See also* Jdg 14:19; 15:1–16; 16:26–30; 1Ki 18:46

Nature miracles 2Ki 2:7–8 *See also* Ex 10:13–23; 14:15–22; Jos 3:14–17; 2Ki 2:13–14; Mt 21:18–22 pp Mk 11:12–14 pp Mk 11:20–24; Jn 2:1–11

Miracles are part of God's plan of redemption
2Sa 7:23 pp 1Ch 17:21 *See also* Mk 16:17–18; Ac 2:22–24; 14:3; Heb 2:3–4

Miracles occur at times of special significance
At the time of the exodus Ex 3:2–3; 7:3–4; 16:11–15; 17:6–7; Nu 17:8; Dt 4:34

At times of national religious crisis 1Ki 18:30–39; 2Ki 3:16–25; 4:3–7,40–41; 6:5–7

In the time of Jesus Christ Mt 14:15–21 pp Mk 6:35–44 pp Lk 9:12–17 pp Jn 6:5–13; Mt 20:29–34 pp Mk 10:46–52 pp Lk 18:35–43; Jn 11:38–44

In the time of the first Christians Lk 10:17; Ac 8:6,13; 14:8–10,19–20; 19:11–12

Miracles are God's gift
They authenticate the message of his servants Jn 10:38 *See also* Ex 4:30–31; Mt 11:2–5 pp Lk 7:20–22; Mk 9:39; 16:20; Jn 14:11; 2Co 12:12

They are given by God's sovereign will 1Co 12:8–11 *See also* Mt 10:1 pp Lk 9:1; 1Co 12:28–30; Gal 3:5

Miracles are not in themselves proof of God's work
They are no guarantee of genuine faith Mt 7:22–23 *See also* Lk 16:27–31; Jn 2:23–24; 1Co 13:1–2

They can be counterfeited Mt 24:24 *See also* Ex 7:11–12,22; 8:7; Ac 8:9–11; 2Th 2:9; Rev 13:13; 16:14; 19:20

See also
1060 God, greatness of	5333 healing
1105 God, power of	5454 power, God's saving
1265 hand of God	7966 spiritual gifts
1355 providence	9210 judgment, God's
1448 signs	9310 resurrection
2351 Christ, miracles	
4165 exorcism	

1417
miracles, of Jesus Christ

See 2351 Jesus Christ, miracles of

1418
miracles, responses to

Miracles often depend upon faith on the part of those who will benefit from them. Human responses to miracles take various forms. Some respond in faith and obedience, whilst others are confirmed in their unbelief and rebellion.

Faith and obedience required in the working of miracles
1Ki 17:13–15 *The widow gave Elijah her last meal before she could be miraculously provided for. See also* Ex 14:16,21; Nu 21:8–9; Jos 3:13–17; 1Ki 17:5; 2Ki 4:41; 5:10–14; Mt 9:6–7 pp Mk 2:10–12 pp Lk 5:24–25; Mt 9:22 pp Mk 5:34 pp Lk 8:48; Lk 1:38; Heb 11:29–30

Miracles limited by lack of faith Mt 13:58 pp Mk 6:5–6 *See also* 2Ki 4:3–6 *The number of jars limited the miraculous supply of oil;* Mt 14:28–31; 17:14–20

Positive responses to miracles
Faith Ex 14:31 *See also* Ex 4:30–31; Jn 7:31; Ac 9:33–35,40–42; 13:12

Amazement Mt 15:31 pp Mk 7:37 *See also* Da 3:24; Ac 3:10; 8:13; 12:16

Praise and worship Ac 3:8 *See also* Ex 15:11,21; Ps 9:1; Da 3:28; 4:2–3; 6:26–27; Mt 15:31; Lk 19:37; Ac 4:21–22

A closer attention paid to the word of God Ac 8:6 *See also* 1Ki 17:24

Temporary faith as a response to miracles
Jn 2:23–24 *See also* Ex 15:20–24; 16:1–3; 17:3; Nu 20:3–5; Lk 17:17–18; Jn 6:49

Negative responses to miracles
Fear Mk 5:15–17 pp Lk 8:36–37; Ac 5:5,11; 19:17

Disbelief Ac 12:14–15 *See also* Ge 17:17–18; 18:12–13; Lk 1:18,20

Hardness of heart Ex 8:19 *See also* Ex 7:3–4; 11:10; Ps 78:32; Mt 11:20–22 pp Lk 10:13–14; Jn 9:18,28–29; 10:25–26; 12:37; 15:24

Opposition Jn 11:47–48; Ac 6:8–9; 16:19–21

Disobedience Ps 106:7 *See also* Nu 14:11,22–23; Ps 78:11–22,42–43

Jealousy Ac 8:13,18–19

See also
2369 Christ, responses to	8020 faith
5624 witnesses to Christ	8453 obedience
	8622 worship
5784 amazement	8664 praise
6221 rebellion	8754 fear
6626 conversion	8834 unbelief
7757 preaching, effects	

1421
oracles

Divine utterances or messages spoken through human lips. Especially noteworthy are the oracles of Balaam. Several other prophecies are also referred to as oracles.

The oracles of Balaam
Divine inspiration is irresistible Nu 22:38 *See also* Nu 22:18–19; 23:11–12,25–26; 24:12–13

Balaam's experience Nu 24:2–4 *See also* Nu 23:3–5; 24:15–16

Balaam's oracles Nu 23:6–10 *See also* Nu 23:18–24; 24:2–9,15–19,20–24

Oracles of the prophets
Mal 1:1 *See also* Isa 13:1; 14:28; 21:1–17; 30:6–11; Eze 12:7–11 *This oracle involved actions as well as words;* Na 1:1

False oracles condemned
La 2:14 *See also* Jer 23:33–40

Wise judgment likened to oracles
Pr 16:10

Oracles of David
Ps 36:1 *See also* 2Sa 23:1–4

See also
1409 dream	5263 communication
1428 prophecy, OT inspiration	5548 speech, divine
1443 revelation, OT	5779 advice
1469 visions	5978 warning
1690 word of God	7772 prophets
3281 Holy Spirit, inspiration	7781 seer

1424
predictions

Speaking authoritatively of the future. Since God knows the future he is able to reveal it to people beforehand. Predictions, which are often but not necessarily contained in prophecies, should not be confused with promises or expressions of intention.

God's knowledge of the future
Ge 41:15–16,28 *See also* Ge 18:17; Nu 24:2–4; Isa 44:24–26

Impossible to predict the future apart from God
Ecc 8:7 *See also* Ecc 7:14; Isa 41:22–24

Jesus Christ predicted the future
Concerning his death and resurrection Mt 16:21 pp Mk 8:31 pp Lk 9:22 *See also* Mt 17:22–23 pp Mk 9:31 pp Lk 9:44; Mt 20:18–19 pp Mk 10:33–34 pp Lk 18:31–33; Jn 2:19–21; 12:32–33

Concerning the donkey on which he would enter Jerusalem Mt 21:1–3 pp Mk 11:1–3 pp Lk 19:29–31

The fall of Jerusalem Mt 24:1–2 pp Mk 13:1–2 pp Lk 21:5–6;

Mt 24:15–25 pp Mk 13:14–23
pp Lk 21:20–24

That Judas would betray him
Mt 26:21–25 pp Mk 14:18–20;
Lk 22:21; Jn 13:21,26

That Peter would deny him Mt 26:34
pp Mk 14:30 pp Lk 22:34 See also
Jn 13:38

Concerning the nature of Peter's death
Jn 21:18–19

The ability to interpret dreams and so predict the future
Ge 40:9–13,16–19; 41:28–32; Da 2:45;
8:26; 10:14

Predictions were made through OT prophets
1Sa 15:28; 28:16–17; 1Ki 11:29–32;
Heb 3:5

Predictions made through some of the first Christians
Ac 11:27–28 See also Ac 21:10–11;
Jude 17–18

False predictions
Jer 28:8–17 See also Isa 47:13–15;
Ac 16:16

The Messiah predicted
1Pe 1:10–11 Most OT references to the coming of the kingdom of God and his Messiah are not, strictly speaking, predictions but promises made by God in which he expresses his intention to save his people through the Messiah. See also
Ac 7:52

See also
1020 God, all-knowing	2411 cross, predictions
1421 oracles	2422 gospel, confirmation
1427 prophecy	
2045 Christ, knowledge of	3281 Holy Spirit, inspiration
2230 Messiah, coming of	7772 prophets
2366 Christ, prophecies concerning	7781 seer
	9130 future, the

1427

prophecy

The disclosing of the will and purposes of God through inspired or Spirit-filled human beings. The OT emphasises the importance of prophecy as a means of knowing God. Many OT prophecies find their fulfilment in Jesus Christ. The NT sets out the place of prophecy in the life of the church and gives guidance concerning the use of this gift.

1428
prophecy, inspiration of OT

The prophecies of biblical messengers are acknowledged as being of divine origin, inspired through the activity of the Holy Spirit.

God speaks through his prophets
2Pe 1:20–21 See also Ne 9:30; Zec 7:12;
Heb 1:1

God is the source of prophecy
Eze 24:20–21 The phrase "the word of the LORD came to …" is frequently used of (and by) the prophets to indicate that the message they proclaimed came directly from God. See also 1Sa 15:10; 2Sa 7:4;
1Ki 13:20; 16:1; 17:2; 2Ki 20:4; Jer 1:2;
Eze 6:1; Jnh 1:1; Hag 2:10; Zec 1:1

Prophets inspired by God speak the truth
Dt 18:22 See also Jer 28:9

See also
1150 God, truth of	3281 Holy Spirit, inspiration
1443 revelation, OT	
1610 Scripture	4155 divination
1690 word of God	7772 prophets
3272 Holy Spirit in OT	7781 seer

1429
prophecy, fulfilment of OT

All divinely inspired prophecy achieves its purpose. Scripture records the fulfilment of many prophecies.

The principle that all prophecy achieves its purpose
Isa 55:10–11 See also Dt 18:22

Fulfilment of prophecy concerning individuals in the OT
1Ki 20:35–36 See also 1Ki 8:15–21
pp 2Ch 6:4–11; 1Ki 8:23–24
pp 2Ch 6:14–15; 1Ki 13:21–22,24–26;
14:12–13,17–18; 2Ki 1:6,17;
7:1–2,16–18; 22:15–20; 23:30

Fulfilment of prophecy concerning the nation of Israel
1Ki 12:15 See also 1Ki 11:29–39

Fulfilment of prophecy concerning the royal house
1Ki 15:29 See also 1Ki 14:7–11;
16:1–7,12; 21:20–29;
2Ki 9:30–10:11,30; 15:12

Fulfilment of prophecy concerning battles
1Ki 20:13–21 See also 1Ki 22:17,35–38;
2Ki 19:20–37

Fulfilment of prophecy concerning the Babylonian exile
The rise of the Babylonians
Hab 1:6–11 See also 2Ch 36:17

The fall of Jerusalem and exile of the population 2Ki 20:17–18 See also
2Ki 21:10–15; 24:2,10–16

The fate of King Zedekiah Jer 21:3–7
See also Jer 32:3–5; Eze 12:12–14;
2Ki 25:1–7; Jer 39:1–7

The length of captivity Jer 29:10 See also
2Ch 36:21; Da 9:2

Fulfilment of prophecy concerning Jesus Christ
Lk 24:44 See also Lk 18:31; Ac 3:18

Fulfilment of other prophecy
Ac 2:14–21 See also Joel 2:28–32;
Jos 6:26; 1Ki 16:34; 13:1–3;

2Ki 23:16–18; 1Ki 17:14,16;
Mt 2:17–18; Jer 31:15; Mt 3:1–3
pp Mk 1:2–4 pp Lk 3:1–6; Isa 40:3

Prophecies modified before fulfilment
1Ki 21:20–26,27–29; Isa 38:1
pp 2Ki 20:1 Isa 38:4–5 pp 2Ki 20:4–6

See also
1055 God, grace & mercy	7217 exile in Babylon
1105 God, power of	8612 prayer & faith
1175 God, will of	8614 prayer, answers
2230 Messiah, coming of	
2366 Christ, prophecies concerning	

1430
prophecy, concerning Jesus Christ
See 2366 Jesus Christ, prophecies concerning

1431
prophecy, methods of OT

Prophets relayed their messages from God in a variety of ways, choosing methods that would make the meaning clear, attract attention or convince the people of the truth of their words.

God speaks through the prophets
Heb 1:1

Prophecy directly proclaimed
Jnh 3:1–4 See also 1Ki 13:1–3; 14:6–16;
20:22; Isa 7:13–17; Jer 26:18;
Ac 11:27–28; 1Co 14:29

Messages presented as coming from God 2Ki 7:1 Prophets often used the phrases "hear the word of the LORD" and "says the LORD" to ensure that their audience understood the divine origin of their proclamation. See also
2Ki 20:16–18; Jer 7:2; 30:3; 44:26;
Eze 34:7–10; Hos 4:1; Am 1:5; 7:16–17;
Zep 3:20; Hag 2:9; Zec 1:3; Mal 1:6

Prophecy enacted
1Ki 11:29–39 See also 1Ki 22:11;
Jer 19:1–13; 27:1–7; 28:10–11;
43:8–13; Eze 4:1–17; 5:1–3; 12:3–11;
Zec 6:9–15; Ac 21:10–11

Prophecy expressed as an allegory or parable
2Sa 12:1–12 See also Eze 15:1–8;
17:1–4; 19:2–14; 23:1–4; 24:3–5;
Mt 24:32–35 pp Mk 13:28–31
pp Lk 21:29–33

Prophecy given by vision or dream
Eze 11:24–25 See also 1Ki 22:17;
Jer 1:11–16; Eze 40:1–4; Am 8:1–2;
Zec 4:1–14

Prophecy recorded in writing
Jer 36:1–4 See also Isa 30:8; Jer 25:13;
30:2; 36:32; 45:1; 51:60; Eze 43:10–11;
Da 12:4; Hab 2:2; Rev 1:3; 22:19;
2Ch 21:12–15; Jer 29:1

Prophecy associated with music
1Ch 25:1–3 See also 1Sa 10:5; 18:10;
2Ki 3:15–19

See also

1409 dream	5611 watchman
1421 oracles	5978 warning
1448 signs	7734 leaders,
1469 visions	spiritual
5420 music	7778 school of
5438 parables	prophets

1432
prophecy, in NT

The NT describes the prophetic aspect of the ministry of Jesus Christ, and also recognises that prophetic gifts are given to believers through the Holy Spirit. It provides guidance on how such prophetic gifts are to be used.

Jesus Christ recognised as a prophet
Mt 21:11; Mk 6:4; 8:27–28; Lk 7:16; 24:17–19; Jn 4:19

Prophecy in the church
Prophecy is one among many spiritual gifts 1Co 12:28–29 *See also* Ro 12:6; 1Co 12:10; Eph 4:11

Not all are called to be prophets 1Co 12:29; Eph 4:11

Prophecy is valueless without love 1Co 13:1–2

Prophecy is for the building up of the church 1Co 14:26 *See also* Ro 12:3–6; 1Co 14:3–5; 1Pe 4:10

Prophecy superior to speaking in tongues 1Co 14:5

Prophecy in the early church
Ac 2:17; 11:27–28; 15:32; 21:9

See also

1444 revelation, NT	3275 Holy Spirit in
2318 Christ as	the church
prophet	7020 church, the
2363 Christ,	7754 preaching
preaching &	7966 spiritual gifts
teaching	

1436
reality

Scripture provides an accurate and reliable guide to the realities of the spiritual and material worlds. It affirms the reality of human sin, of the power and purpose of God to deal with sin through Jesus Christ and of the guidance of the Holy Spirit.

The reality of God
The reality of the existence of God
Job 42:4–5 *See also* 2Sa 7:22–23; 1Ki 8:23; Jer 10:10

The reality of the love of God 1Jn 4:7–9
See also Jn 3:16; Ro 5:8; Gal 2:20–21

The reality of God's salvation Ps 68:20
See also Ps 65:5; 79:9; Mic 7:7; Lk 1:47; Tit 2:11

The reality of the revelation of God
Ps 19:1–4; Jn 1:1–9; Ac 14:15–17; Ro 1:18–20

The reality of knowing God Jn 17:3; Ro 1:19; Gal 4:8–9; 1Jn 5:20

The reality of the word of God
Ps 119:160 *See also* Ps 18:30; 2Ti 3:16; Heb 4:12; 1Pe 1:23

The reality of sin
1Jn 1:8–10 *See also* Ps 58:3; Isa 59:1–2; Jer 17:9; Ro 5:12

The reality of Jesus Christ
The reality of his existence 1Jn 1:1–3

His reality foreshadowed in the past
Col 2:17; Heb 8:5; 10:1–5

The reality of his divinity Jn 1:1–2; Ro 1:3–4; Col 1:15; 2:9

The reality of his humanity Mt 4:2; Mk 6:3; Jn 8:40; 19:28; Ac 2:22

The reality of his resurrection
Mt 28:1–10 pp Mk 16:1–8
pp Lk 24:1–18; Ac 1:1–3; 10:39–43; 1Co 15:3–8

The reality of the guidance of the Holy Spirit
Jn 14:16–17,26; 15:26; 16:7–11

See also

1085 God, love of	2560 Christ,
1115 God, purpose	resurrection
of	4846 shadow
1155 God,	5173 outward
truthfulness	appearance
1460 truth	6510 salvation
2018 Christ, divinity	8135 knowing God
2033 Christ,	8779 materialism
humanity	

1439

revelation

The making known of God's person, nature and deeds, in Scripture, history and supremely the person of Jesus Christ. God is also made known, to a limited yet important extent, through his creation.
This set of themes consists of the following:
1440 revelation, through creation
1441 revelation, necessity of
1442 revelation, of God
1443 revelation, in OT
1444 revelation, in NT
1445 revelation, responses to

1440
revelation, through creation

The creation bears witness to the wisdom and power of its creator. This natural knowledge of God is limited in its extent, but is sufficient to convince human beings of the existence of God and the need to respond to him.

The creation bears witness to its creator
Ps 19:1–6 *See also* Job 36:22–37:18; Am 4:13; Ac 14:15–17

All human beings have a natural awareness of God
Ro 2:14–15 *See also* Ac 17:22–31

The limitations of a natural knowledge of God
Ro 1:18–21 *See also* Ro 1:32; 1Co 1:20–21

See also

1045 God, glory of	5548 speech, divine
1325 God, the	6183 ignorance, of
Creator	God
1403 God, revelation	8135 knowing God
5008 conscience	

1441
revelation, necessity of

Finiteness and sin make it impossible to gain adequate knowledge of God through human effort alone. God in mercy makes himself known through the incarnation of the Son and the illumination of human minds to understand him.

The impossibility of fully knowing God without revelation
God is beyond unaided human knowing Jn 1:18 *See also* Ex 33:20; Isa 55:8–9; Jn 6:46; 1Jn 4:12

The human mind is limited Job 11:7 *See also* Job 9:4,10; 23:3–9; 26:14; 36:26; 37:5,23; Ps 139:6; 145:3; Ecc 3:11; Isa 40:13–14,28; Ro 11:33

The human mind cannot discern God of its own accord 2Co 4:4 *See also* Jn 1:5; Ro 1:18–32; 1Co 1:21; 2:14; 2Co 3:14; Eph 4:17–18

God is known fully only through Jesus Christ
Heb 1:1–2; 1Jn 5:20 *See also* Jn 1:14–18; 17:3; Col 1:15–20

See also

1055 God, grace &	5135 blindness,
mercy	spiritual
1150 God, truth of	5395 lordship,
1175 God, will of	human &
2218 Christ, Son of	divine
God	8321 perfection,
3296 Holy Spirit in	divine
the world	8355 understanding
5038 mind, the	8366 wisdom,
human	source of

1442
revelation, of God

See 1403 God, revelation of

1443
revelation, in OT

The OT bears witness to God's revelation in the history of Israel and in the inspired testimony of the prophets and other writers of the period. This knowledge of God prepares the way for the full disclosure of God in Jesus Christ in the NT.

Revelation in Eden and before the flood
Ge 1:3; 2:16–18 See also Ge 1:29–30; 3:9–19; 4:6–7,9–15; 6:13–22

The covenant framework of OT revelation after the flood
God's covenant with Noah Ge 9:8–11 *This covenant covers all living creatures. See also* Ge 6:18; 9:12–17

God's covenant with Abraham Ge 17:7 *See also* Ge 15:9–21; 17:2,4,10–14; 22:16–18; Ex 6:2–6; 1Ch 16:14–18; Ps 105:8–9

God's covenant with Moses at Sinai Ex 34:27 *See also* Ex 24:3–8; 34:10–14; Dt 5:2–4 *Mount Sinai was also known as Mount Horeb;* Jer 11:2–5

God's covenant with David Ps 89:3–4 *See also* 2Sa 7:8–16; Ps 132:11–12

The promise of a new covenant Jer 31:31–34 *See also* Isa 42:6; Mt 26:27–28 pp Mk 14:24 pp Lk 22:20 pp 1Co 11:25; Heb 8:8–12; 9:15; 10:15–18

The recipients of OT revelation
The people of Israel Am 3:2 *See also* Ex 19:3–6; Dt 7:6; Isa 65:1; Eze 20:5

On occasions God spoke to people outside the covenant community Da 2:27–28 *See also* Ge 41:25,28–32; Da 4:1–37; 5:17–28

Methods of OT revelation
Direct communication Dt 18:18 *See also* Ex 4:12; Nu 12:8; 23:5; Isa 50:4; 51:16; Jer 1:9

Visions and dreams Nu 12:6 *See also* Ge 15:1; 28:12; 37:5–7,9; 46:2; Nu 24:4; Dt 13:1; Jdg 7:13–14; Job 33:14–15; Eze 1:1,26–28

Visible manifestations (theophanies) Ge 18:1 *See also* Ge 32:24–30; Ex 3:1–6; 34:4–7; Nu 11:25; 12:5; 14:10–12; Jos 5:13–15

Scripture Dt 31:9 *See also* Ex 17:14; Nu 33:2; Isa 30:8; Jer 36:2; 51:60

The content of OT revelation
Revelation of God's will and purposes Ge 17:1–2 *See also* Ge 12:1–3; 15:1–5; Ex 19:5–6; 20:1–17 pp Dt 5:6–21; Ex 22:31; Lev 11:44–45; 19:1–2; 20:7–8

Revelation of God's plan Ge 3:15 *See also* Isa 9:6–7; 11:1–10; 42:1; Mic 5:1–5; Zec 9:9–13

Revelation of God's character and being Ex 3:11–15
God's glory: Ex 40:34; 1Ki 8:11; Eze 1:28
God is just and merciful: Nu 14:17–19; Ps 143:1
God's love: Dt 7:7–8; La 3:22
God is righteous: Ps 72:2; 103:6; Isa 59:17
God is the sovereign creator: Ps 115:3; 135:5–6

The incompleteness of OT revelation
Heb 11:39–40 *The fulness of God's redemption could only become apparent with the fulness of his revelation in Jesus Christ. See also* Heb 1:1–2; 1Pe 1:10–12

See also
1115 God, purpose of
1205 God, titles of
1345 covenant
1409 dream
1431 prophecy, OT methods
1454 theophany
1469 visions
1615 Scripture, sufficiency
1690 word of God
3272 Holy Spirit in OT
4140 angel of the Lord

1444
revelation, in NT
The NT fulfils and completes the revelation of God which began in the OT. Jesus Christ is the central focus of this self-revelation of God.

The unity and progress of revelation
The unity of OT and NT Mt 5:17–18 *See also* Ro 3:21–22; 2Ti 3:14–15; 2Pe 3:15–16 *The writings of Paul are presented as having equal status with the OT Scriptures;* Rev 22:18–19 *These sanctions have the same force as those of Dt 4:2; 12:32.*

The progress of NT revelation Heb 1:1–2 *See also* Heb 2:1–4; 12:22–27

The NT fulfils and completes God's revelation of himself
Jesus Christ is the supreme revelation of God Col 1:25–27 *See also* Jn 1:9–18; 14:6; Ac 4:12; Gal 4:4; Php 2:6–8; Heb 2:14

Jesus Christ is the image of God 2Co 4:4 ; Col 1:15

Jesus Christ has the nature of God Php 2:6

Jesus Christ is the exact representation of God Heb 1:3

Jesus Christ is the incarnate Word of God Jn 1:14

The role of the Holy Spirit in revelation
He is the divine agent of revelation Jn 16:12–15 *See also* Jn 14:16–17; 15:26; 1Jn 4:6; 5:6; Rev 2:7,11,17,29; 3:6,13,22

He is the source of revelatory manifestations 1Co 12:7–11 *See also* Ac 2:1–12; Ro 12:6; 1Co 12:28–30; 13:8–12; 14:1–33; Eph 4:11

God's purposes in revelation
To reveal himself in Jesus Christ Col 1:15–20 *See also* Jn 1:14; 12:44–45; 14:9; 2Co 4:4; Heb 1:3

To reveal his plan through Jesus Christ Eph 1:9–10 *See also* Ro 16:25–27; 1Co 2:7–10; Eph 3:3–11; Col 1:19–20

See also
1315 God as redeemer
1432 prophecy in NT
2218 Christ, Son of God
2321 Christ as redeemer
2333 Christ, attitude to OT
2580 Christ, transfiguration
3140 Holy Spirit, teacher
3281 Holy Spirit, inspiration
4954 morning
6510 salvation
6717 reconciliation, world to God
7966 spiritual gifts

1445
revelation, responses to
God requires and imparts a frame of mind that receives and responds to what he has made known.

God commands that his word be heeded
Mk 4:3 *See also* Isa 1:10; Mk 4:9; Rev 2:7

People do not naturally understand what God has revealed
They fail to recognise God's revelation in Jesus Christ Mt 11:25–27 pp Lk 10:21–22 *See also* Jn 5:37–40; 6:44–45; 10:24–26; 12:37–41; 14:9; Ro 9:31–10:4; 1Co 1:18–25; 2:8; 2Co 4:4

They fail to understand God's revelation in general 1Co 2:14 *See also* Mk 4:11–12 pp Mt 13:13–15 pp Lk 8:10; Isa 6:9–10; Jn 8:43–47; 2Co 3:14–16; 2Th 2:11–13

God has given his Spirit to illuminate the human mind
He reveals and teaches truth 1Co 2:12–13 *See also* Jer 31:31–34; Mt 16:17; Jn 3:3–10; 14:16–17,25–26; 16:12–15; Php 3:15

He reveals through prayer for understanding Ps 119:18 *See also* Ps 119:12,27; Eph 1:17–18

Understanding God's revelation carries special responsibility
Lk 12:47–48 *See also* Mt 13:11–12; 25:14–30 pp Lk 19:12–27

God's revelation of himself will only be fully understood at the second coming of Jesus Christ
1Co 13:12 *See also* 1Pe 1:13; 1Jn 3:2

The consequences of responding to revelation
Repentance Ac 2:38 *See also* Mt 4:17; Ac 3:19; 26:20; 2Co 7:10

Faith Ro 10:17 *See also* Ro 10:8–10,14–15; 1Co 2:4–5

Obedience Ro 1:5 *See also* Jdg 2:17; Phm 21; 1Pe 1:2

See also
2426 gospel, responses
2565 Christ, second coming
4018 life, spiritual
5029 knowledge of God
5784 amazement
6732 repentance
8023 faith, necessity
8453 obedience
8470 respect for God
8662 meditation
8835 unbelief

1448

signs
Miraculous or supernatural confirmations of the existence and power of God or the miraculous demonstration of spiritual authority on the part of an individual.

1449
signs, purposes of
Signs are given to confirm God's

word. They may warn the rebellious
or encourage the faithful. People
may seek signs as a result of a
genuine desire to serve God.

Signs are given to demonstrate God's power
Dt 34:10–12 *See also* Dt 4:34; 6:21–22;
7:19; 26:8; 1Ch 16:11–12
pp Ps 105:4–5; Jer 32:21

Signs demonstrate the authority of God's servants
Moses and Aaron Ex 4:1–9 *See also*
Ex 4:30–31; 7:8–12; Nu 17:1–9;
Ac 7:36

Elijah 1Ki 18:36–38

Elisha 2Ki 2:13–14

Jesus Christ Ac 2:22 *See also* Jn 2:23;
3:2; 7:21; 20:30

The apostles 2Co 12:12 *See also*
Ac 2:43; 5:12; 15:12

**Signs may accompany the preaching
of the gospel** Heb 2:3–4 *See also*
Mk 16:20; Ac 8:6; 14:3

Signs may warn the ungodly of impending judgment
Ex 8:22–23
*The prophets often acted out their messages
for greater effect:* Isa 20:1–4; Eze 4:1–3;
12:3–6,11; 24:15–24
Jer 44:29–30; Lk 2:34; Php 1:28

Signs may warn God's people against rebellion
Nu 17:10 *See also* Nu 16:38; 26:10;
Dt 28:45–46; 1Sa 2:34; 12:16–18

Signs may encourage faith
By giving guidance 1Sa 14:8–10 *See
also* Ge 24:10–14; Ex 13:21–22;
2Sa 5:23–24 pp 1Ch 14:14–15;
Mt 2:9–10

By giving assurance of God's presence
Jdg 6:17–22 *See also* Ge 28:10–17;
Ex 3:1–5

**By encouraging the fearful and
doubting** Isa 38:7–8 pp 2Ki 20:8–11
pp 2Ch 32:24 *See also* Dt 7:17–19;
Jdg 6:36–40; 2Ki 6:15–17

Signs need hold no terror for the godly
Jer 10:2 *See also* Mt 24:6 pp Mk 13:7
pp Lk 21:9

Seeking signs
**When seeking signs is acceptable to
God** Isa 7:11 *See also* Jdg 6:17; Isa 38:22

**When seeking signs is condemnned by
God** Mt 16:1–4 pp Mk 8:11–12 *See also*
Mt 12:38–39 pp Lk 11:29; Lk 11:16;
12:54–56; 23:8; Jn 2:18; 4:48; 6:30;
1Co 1:22

See also

1105 God, power of	7709 apostles,
1265 hand of God	authority
1415 miracles	8128 guidance,
1454 theophany	receiving
1690 word of God	8414 encourage-
2012 Christ,	ment
authority	8425 evangelism
5978 warning	9210 judgment,
	God's

1450
signs, kinds of

Signs are miraculous events,
supernatural phenomena or
everyday things that are given a
special significance. The term is used
in John's Gospel to describe the
miracles of Jesus Christ.

Miraculous signs
2Co 12:12 *See also* Ex 10:1; Ps 78:43;
105:27; Mt 24:24 pp Mk 13:22;
Mk 16:17; Ac 2:43; Ro 15:19

The signs of Jesus Christ in John's Gospel
Jn 2:11 *John refers to the miracles of Jesus
Christ as "signs" in order to bring out the
significance of these deeds. See also* Jn 6:26
Jesus Christ, the bread of life; Jn 9:16 *Jesus
Christ, the light of the world;* Jn 11:47
Jesus Christ, the resurrection and the life

Jesus Christ refers to Jonah as a sign
Mt 12:39–41 pp Lk 11:29–32

Prophetic signs
Ex 3:12 *See also* 1Sa 10:7–9; 1Ki 13:1–5;
2Ki 19:29 pp Isa 37:30; Isa 7:14–17;
8:18; 19:19–20; Lk 2:12

Signs of protection
Ex 12:13,23; Jos 2:12–13,17–21

Signs given to guarantee promises
The rainbow Ge 9:12 *See also*
Ge 9:13–17

Circumcision Ge 17:10–11 *See also*
Ge 17:12–14; Ro 4:11

Signs serve as reminders of past blessings
Monuments Jos 4:4–7

Religious observances
Passover: Ex 13:9,16
Sabbath: Ex 31:12–17; Eze 20:12,20

Signs associated with the birth of Jesus Christ
The virgin birth Isa 7:14 *See also*
Mt 1:22–23; Lk 1:34–36

The birthplace Lk 2:12 *See also*
Lk 2:7,16

The star Mt 2:1–2 *See also* Mt 2:9–10

Signs associated with the death of Jesus Christ
Darkness at midday Mt 27:45
pp Mk 15:33 pp Lk 23:44–45 *See also*
Am 8:9

The curtain of the temple torn in two
Mt 27:51 pp Mk 15:38 pp Lk 23:45

The dead came back to life
Mt 27:51–53

Signs associated with the coming of the Holy Spirit
The sound like a violent wind Ac 2:2

Tongues of fire Ac 2:3

Speaking in other languages Ac 2:4 *See
also* Ac 2:5–11

Signs associated with the second coming of Jesus Christ
General signs Mt 24:3–8
pp Mk 13:4–8 pp Lk 21:7–11

Signs preceding the second coming
Mt 24:9–24 pp Mk 13:9–22
pp Lk 21:12–24

**Signs simultaneous with the second
coming** Mt 24:27–31 pp Mk 13:24–27
pp Lk 21:25–27; Lk 17:24; Ac 2:19–20;
Joel 2:30–31; 2Pe 3:12–13

False signs
Dt 13:1–3 *See also* Isa 44:25; Mt 24:24
pp Mk 13:22; 2Th 2:9; Rev 13:11–14;
16:14; 19:20

See also

1416 miracles	3257 Holy Spirit, gift
1427 prophecy	of
2351 Christ, miracles	4845 rainbow
2363 Christ,	9115 antichrist, the
preaching &	9170 signs of times
teaching	9312 resurrection,
2515 Christ, birth of	significance of
2530 Christ, death of	Christ's
2565 Christ, second	
coming	

1454
theophany

A temporary visible manifestation of
the presence and glory of God. This
may be in natural phenomena such
as cloud or fire, in human form or in
prophetic visionary experience.

God is manifested in nature
**God's presence in storms, thunder and
lightning** Ps 18:7–15; Ex 19:16 *See also*
Ex 20:18; Job 37:5; Ps 29:3–9; 77:18;
97:4; Isa 30:27–33; Am 1:2; Hab 3:11;
Zec 9:14; Rev 11:19

**God's presence in volcanic
phenomena** Ex 19:18 *See also* Isa 30:33

God's presence in earthquakes
Isa 29:5–6 *See also* Jdg 5:4–5; Ps 77:18;
Hab 3:6

Specific phenomena associated with the presence of God
Fire signifies God's presence Ex 3:2
*Fire in particular represents the purity,
holiness and unapproachability of God. See
also* Ex 13:21; 19:18; 24:17; Lev 9:24;
Nu 14:14; Dt 4:11–12; 5:4,22–26;
Jdg 13:20–22; Ps 97:3; Joel 2:30

Smoke signifies God's presence
Ex 19:18 *See also* Ex 20:18; Ps 144:5;
Isa 6:4; 30:27; Joel 2:30; Rev 15:8

Cloud signifies God's presence
Ex 16:10 *Cloud and smoke convey the
mystery and transcendence of God. See also*
Ex 13:21
God speaks to Moses from the cloud:
Ex 19:9; 24:15–16; 33:9; 34:5; Dt 31:15
Lev 16:2; Nu 9:15–22; 14:14;
1Ki 8:10–11; Eze 1:4; 10:3–4
The transfiguration of Jesus Christ:
Mt 17:5 pp Mk 9:7 pp Lk 9:34–35
Rev 14:14–16

God is manifested in human or angelic form
Ge 16:7–13 *See also* Ge 18:1–22;
32:24–30; Jos 5:13–15

God appears in prophetic visions

God appears on a throne Isa 6:1 *John interprets this verse to refer to Jesus Christ (Jn 12:41). See also* Eze 1:26; 10:1; Da 7:9; Rev 4:2; 20:11

God appears attended by angels and other heavenly beings Isa 6:2; Eze 1:5–18; 10:9–13; Rev 4:6–11

God appears like, or with, precious stones Ex 24:10; Eze 1:26; Rev 4:3

Functions and effects of theophanies

Theophanies reveal God's glory Eze 10:4 *See also* Ex 16:10; 24:16; 40:34–35; Lev 9:23–24; Nu 14:10; 1Ki 8:11; 2Ch 7:1–3; Ps 29:3,9; 97:2–6; Eze 11:22–23

Theophanies bring judgment Isa 30:27 *See also* Nu 12:9–10; Ps 18:13–15

Theophanies arouse the fear of God Ex 19:16; 20:18–20; Isa 6:5

Theophanies commission God's servants Isa 6:8; Eze 1:28–2:1

Theophanies authenticate God's servants Nu 12:5–8

See also

1045 God, glory of	4060 nature
1065 God, holiness of	4140 angel of the Lord
1310 God as judge	4180 seraphim
1403 God, revelation	4805 clouds
1469 visions	4826 fire
2595 incarnation	4851 storm

1457
trance

An ecstatic state in which people may be aware of God communicating with them; it may cause them to lose control of their actions or to have abnormal strength.

God communicating with people through a trance

Ezekiel Eze 8:1–3

Peter Ac 10:9–23; 11:4–18

Paul Ac 22:17–21

John Rev 1:10–13; 4:2; 17:3; 21:10

Examples of the Holy Spirit's domination of individuals in a trance-like manner

Balaam Nu 24:2–3,12–13

King Saul and his men pursuing David 1Sa 19:19–24

Under the influence of the Holy Spirit people may act with abnormal strength

Samson Jdg 14:6,19; 15:14

Elijah 1Ki 18:46

See also

1265 hand of God	3239 Holy Spirit, anointing
1403 God, revelation	
1409 dream	3272 Holy Spirit in OT
1469 visions	
3030 Holy Spirit, power	5841 ecstasy

1460
truth

Truth in Scripture is more than mere veracity. In the OT it is a moral concept, grounded in the being of God himself, which embodies the ideas of faithfulness and reliability, while in the NT the concept widens to embrace the ideas of reality and completeness.

1461
truth, nature of

God is the essence of truth and this quality should be reflected in the character of his children. Falsehood is condemned in Scripture, particularly in legal contexts, but truth is praised and advocated. God takes pleasure in truth and honesty, which are marks of an upright person.

Truth originates with God

Ps 43:3 *See also* Ps 25:5; 26:3; 86:11; Isa 65:16; Da 9:13

Truth is an aspect of God's character

It is demonstrated in his faithfulness and reliability Nu 23:19; Ps 33:4 *See also* 1Sa 15:29; Ps 31:5; 40:10–11; 119:160; Isa 45:19; Jer 10:10; 42:5; Da 10:21; Mic 7:20

It is demonstrated in his justice and mercy Ps 96:13 *The Hebraic concept of truth embraces the ideas of faithfulness, reliability and justice. See also* Ps 119:30,43–44,142,151

Truth should be reflected in the character of God's people

Zec 8:16 *See also* 1Ki 17:22–24; Ps 15:1–5; 51:6; 145:18; Pr 23:23; Jer 4:2; 5:1; Zec 7:9; 8:3,19; Mal 2:6

Absence of truth in the human character displeases God

Isa 59:14–15 *See also* Isa 48:1; Jer 5:3; 7:28; 9:3

Truth as an abstract quality

Ps 45:4 *See also* Pr 23:23; Da 8:12

Truth is the opposite of falsehood

Pr 16:13 *See also* 1Ki 17:24; 22:16 pp 2Ch 18:15; Ne 6:6; Pr 8:7; 12:17; Isa 45:19; Zec 8:16

Truth is subject to proof

Ge 42:14–16 *See also* Dt 13:12–15; 17:2–5; 19:16–19; 22:20–21; 1Ki 10:6–7 pp 2Ch 9:5–6; Job 5:27

Truth is commended in Scripture

Pr 12:22 *See also* Ex 20:16 pp Dt 5:20; Ex 23:1,7; Pr 12:19; 13:5; 14:25; 19:5,9; Eph 4:25; Rev 22:14–15

Lack of truth is a characteristic of apostasy

Jer 7:28 *See also* Ps 52:1–4; Isa 59:12–15; Jer 9:5–6; Am 5:10

Truth as an expression of affirmation

Da 11:2 *See also* Jos 7:20; Ru 3:12; 2Ki 19:17; Jer 26:15; Mt 5:18; 8:10; 21:21; Mk 8:12; 14:30; Lk 4:24; 21:32; Jn 3:3; 8:51; 21:18

Amen as a liturgical affirmation of truth

Of oaths and curses Nu 5:22 *The word "amen" is closely related to the word for "truth" in Hebrew. It constitutes an affirmation of the truth of what has been said and an acceptance of its consequences. See also* Dt 27:15–26; Ne 5:13; Jer 11:5

Of benedictions and doxologies 1Ch 16:36 *See also* Ne 8:6; Ps 41:13; 72:19; 89:52; 106:48

In general use Jer 28:6 *See also* 1Ki 1:32–37

In the NT Ro 1:25 *By NT times, the word "Amen" had become a common liturgical phrase of affirmation, used after prayers, benedictions and doxologies. See also* Mt 6:13; Ro 9:5; 11:36; 1Co 14:16; 2Co 1:20; Gal 6:18; Php 4:20; 1Ti 1:17; Heb 13:20–21; 2Pe 3:18; Jude 25; Rev 1:6–7; 7:12; 22:20

See also

1150 God, truth of	7774 prophets, false
1155 God, truthfulness	8281 insight
1436 reality	8314 orthodoxy
5202 accusation, false	8331 reliability
5466 promises	8748 false religion
	8750 false teachings
	8751 false witness

1462
truth, in NT

The NT encompasses the Greek idea of truth as reality, as well as the Hebraic concepts of faithfulness and reliability. Jesus Christ is shown as "the Truth" and the apostles present the gospel as "truth".

Truth as opposed to falsehood and lies

Eph 4:25 *See also* Jn 3:33; 4:37; 18:23; 19:35; Ac 7:1; 21:24; 24:8; 26:25; Ro 1:18; 9:1; 1Co 15:54; 2Co 7:14; Gal 4:16; Tit 1:13; 2Pe 2:22; 1Jn 2:4; 2Jn 1–2

Truth as reality

Heb 9:24 *See also* Jn 1:9; 4:23; 17:3; Eph 4:24; 1Th 1:9; 1Ti 1:2; 6:19; Tit 1:2; 3:2; Heb 8:2; 12:8; 1Pe 5:12; 1Jn 2:5,8; 5:20; Rev 19:9

Truth as trustworthy affirmations

Jn 6:47 *See also* Mt 6:2; 10:23; 16:28; 19:23; 23:36; 26:13; Mk 9:41; 11:23; Lk 12:44; 21:3; Jn 1:51; 5:24–25; 8:34; 10:7; 16:7; Php 1:15; 1Ti 3:9

Truth as faithfulness and reliability

The quality of truth Php 4:8 *See also* Jn 1:17; 3:21; 4:24; 17:17; Ro 2:20; 1Co 5:8; 13:6; 2Co 13:8; Eph 5:9; 6:14; 3Jn 12

Truth as an aspect of the character of God Ro 3:3–4 *See also* Ps 51:4; Ro 3:7; 15:8; 1Jn 5:20; Rev 3:7,14; 6:10; 15:3; 16:7; 19:2,11

Truth as a human quality Ac 11:23;
1Jn 1:8 *See also* Jn 3:21; 7:18; Ac 14:22;
Eph 4:15; Php 1:18; Rev 2:13

Jesus Christ as truth
Jn 14:6 *See also* Jn 1:14; 15:1; 18:37–38;
1Jn 5:20

The Spirit of God as truth
Jn 16:13 *See also* Jn 14:16–17; 15:26;
1Jn 4:6; 5:6

**The gospel and the Christian
faith as truth**
Eph 1:13 *See also* Jn 8:31–32; Ac 20:30;
2Co 4:2; Gal 2:5; Col 1:5; 1Ti 2:3–4;
4:6; 2Ti 2:18; 4:4; Tit 1:1; Jas 5:19;
2Pe 2:2; 1Jn 3:19

See also

2420 gospel	7915 confirmation
3296 Holy Spirit in the world	8235 doctrine
4846 shadow	8248 faithfulness
5423 myths	8275 honesty
5438 parables	8354 trustworthiness
7712 convincing	8776 lies

1463
truth, of God

See 1150 God, truth of

1466
vision

Scripture uses the term to refer to
both the physical act of seeing, and
also the gift of spiritual insight. All
things, physical and spiritual, are
seen by God.

God's vision
God views all life on earth 2Ch 16:9;
Ps 11:4 *See also* Ge 6:11; Ex 3:9;
Ps 31:22; 34:15; 139:16; Zec 4:10

**God sees the hearts and thoughts of
people** Ge 6:5 *See also* 1Sa 2:3;
Ps 139:1–4,23–24; Pr 15:11; Jer 20:12;
Mt 6:8,18; Lk 16:15; Heb 4:13; 1Jn 3:20

**The physical vision of human
beings**
It is given and can be taken by God
Ex 4:11; Ps 146:8 *See also* Lev 26:16;
Pr 29:13; Ac 9:8–9 pp Ac 22:11

**Jesus Christ restores the sight of the
blind** Lk 4:18 *See also* Mt 9:30; Jn 9:7;
Ac 9:17–18 pp Ac 22:13

Physical sight diminishes with age
Ge 27:1; 48:10; 1Sa 3:2; 4:15; 1Ki 14:4;
Ecc 12:3 *Ecc 12:2–5 is an allegory on
ageing. It gives a graphic description of a
person's progressive deterioration.*

Physical vision has its dangers
It can create fear Job 41:9; Joel 2:6;
Mt 28:3–4 pp Mk 16:5 pp Lk 24:4–5;
Rev 1:17

It gives rise to temptation 1Jn 2:16 *See
also* Ge 3:6; Jos 7:21; 2Sa 11:2–4;
Job 31:1; Ps 119:37; Mt 5:28–29

**Christians are to live by faith
rather than by sight**
Heb 11:1 *See also* Ro 8:24; 2Co 4:18; 5:7;
Heb 11:27

Visions of God
Examples of those who saw God
Ge 32:30; Ex 33:18–23; Job 42:5;
Isa 6:1,5; Rev 1:12–18

God's people will see him Mt 5:8;
1Jn 3:2 *See also* Ps 17:15; Jn 17:24;
1Co 13:12; Rev 22:4

Spiritual vision
Seeing used metaphorically for
spiritual insight 2Ki 6:17 *See also*
Pr 29:18; Isa 22:1 *Jerusalem was called
"the Valley of Vision", possibly ironically,
for although God spoke through his
prophets and dwelt there, its inhabitants
lacked insight;* Isa 29:10; Mk 8:17–21;
Lk 24:31; Jn 9:39; Ac 26:17–18

**Spiritual insight given in dreams or
visions** Ac 2:17 *See also* Joel 2:28;
Ge 15:1; Nu 12:6; Da 1:17; 2:19; 4:5; 7:1
Daniel's dream of four beasts; Da 8:1;
10:7–8 *Daniel's vision of a man;* Ac 9:12;
10:9–17 pp Ac 11:4–10 *Peter's vision;*
Ac 16:9–10 *Paul's vision of the man of
Macedonia;* Ac 26:19; 2Co 12:1

The OT prophets had visions from God
1Sa 3:15; Isa 1:1; Jer 24:1; Eze 1:1;
8:3–4; 11:24; 40:2–3; Hos 12:10; Ob 1;
Na 1:1

**False prophets in the OT lacked true
vision** Jer 14:14; 23:16; La 2:14;
Eze 7:26; 13:1–12

See also

1020 God, all-knowing	1469 visions
1409 dream	5133 blindness
1431 prophecy, OT methods	5149 eyes
	7774 prophets, false
1439 revelation	8020 faith
1454 theophany	8281 insight
	8474 seeing God

1469
visions

Mental pictures used by God to
convey messages or reveal future
events. They are normally received
in private by individuals who are
often prophets.

**God speaks to individuals in
visions**
Ge 46:2–4 *See also* Ge 15:1;
1Sa 3:10–15; Ac 9:10–12; 10:3–6;
11:5–12; 16:9–10; 18:9–10; 26:12–19

Visions may reveal future events
Da 8:17–19 *See also* Da 7:15–18,23–27;
Am 7:7–9; Lk 1:11–22; Rev 22:6

**Visions may contain unusual or
startling images**
Zec 1:8 *See also* Eze 1:4–28;
Da 4:10–17; 7:2–15; 8:2–14;
Rev 1:12–16; 4:1–11; 9:17

Visions received by prophets
Nu 12:6 *See also* Isa 6:1–4; Jer 1:11–16;
Eze 1:1; Hos 12:10; Am 7:1–9

Visions recorded by prophets
2Ch 32:32 *See also* 2Ch 9:29; Isa 1:1;
Da 7:1; 8:1; Ob 1; Mic 1:1; Na 1:1

**False visions associated with
lying prophets**
Eze 13:6–9 *See also* 1Ki 22:10–28

---

pp 2Ch 18:9–27; Jer 14:14; 23:16;
La 2:14; Eze 22:28; Zec 10:2

God may withhold visions
1Sa 3:1 *See also* La 2:9; Eze 7:26; Mic 3:6

**Visions associated with the
outpouring of the Holy Spirit**
Ac 2:17 *See also* Joel 2:28

See also

1403 God, revelation	3257 Holy Spirit, gift of
1409 dream	
1429 prophecy, OT fulfilment	4627 creatures
	6694 mystery
1431 prophecy, OT methods	7730 explanation
	7772 prophets
1439 revelation	9130 future, the
1466 vision	

1500

God, the Trinity

1510

Trinity, the

The characteristically Christian
doctrine about God. It declares that
there is only one true God; that this
God is three persons, the Father, the
Son and the Holy Spirit, each of
whom is distinct from, yet
interrelated with, the others; and
that all three persons are fully,
equally and eternally divine.

1511
Trinity, relationships between
the persons

The actual term "the Trinity" is not
found in Scripture, but the truths
implied in a trinitarian
understanding of God are clearly set
out. The OT hints at a plurality of
persons in the Godhead. The NT
affirms that the Son and the Holy
Spirit are divine.

There is only one God
Dt 6:4 *See also* Isa 43:10–11; 44:8;
1Ti 1:17; 2:5; Jas 2:19

**OT indications of plurality in the
Godhead**
God refers to himself in the plural
Ge 1:26 *See also* Ge 3:22; 11:7; Isa 6:8

The angel of the LORD Ge 16:11–13 *The
"angel of the LORD" is identified with, yet
distinct from, God. See also* Ge 18:1–33;
Ex 3:2–6; Jdg 13:3–22

The word of God
*The "word of the LORD" or "wisdom of
God" is personified and identified with, yet
distinct from, God:* Ps 33:4; Pr 8:22–31

The Spirit of God
The Spirit of God is God's personal agent:
Ge 1:2; Ne 9:20; Job 33:4; Isa 40:13 fn

The Messiah
The Messiah's divine nature is emphasised:
Ps 110:1; Isa 9:6; Jer 23:5–6

Interchangeable expressions
Word, Spirit (or breath) and LORD are used

interchangeably for God: Ps 33:6; Isa 48:16; 61:1

NT trinitarian references
Mt 28:19 *The unity of the three persons is reflected in the singular name. See also* 2Co 13:14; Eph 4:4–6; Rev 1:4–5

The unity of the three persons
The Son is fully united with the Father Jn 10:30 *See also* Mk 9:37 pp Lk 9:48; Lk 10:16; Jn 10:38; 12:44–45; 13:20; 14:7,9–11; 15:23

The Spirit is identified with God 2Sa 23:2–3 *See also* Ps 51:11; Mt 28:19; 1Co 3:16

The three persons are distinct from one another
Jesus Christ addresses the Father directly Mt 11:25–26 pp Lk 10:21; Mt 26:39 pp Mk 14:36 pp Lk 22:42; Mt 26:42; 27:46 pp Mk 15:34; Lk 23:46; Jn 11:41–42; 17:1

The Father speaks to the Son from heaven Mt 3:17 pp Mk 1:11 pp Lk 3:22; Mt 17:5 pp Mk 9:7 pp Lk 9:35; Jn 12:27–28

The Spirit speaks to the Father on behalf of believers Ro 8:26–27

Other examples of the difference between the persons Mt 12:32; 24:36; Jn 7:39; 16:7; 1Ti 2:5; 1Jn 2:1

The relationship between the Father and the Son
Jesus Christ is God's unique Son Jn 1:14 *The Greek word for "One and Only", traditionally rendered "only begotten", is actually used to signify "the only one of its kind"; "unique". See also* Jn 1:18; 3:16,18; Ac 13:33; Heb 1:5; Ps 2:7; 1Jn 4:9

The relationship of Father and Son is unique Mt 11:27 pp Lk 10:22 *See also* Jn 6:46; 7:28–29; 8:55; 10:15; 17:25

The Father loves the Son Jn 3:35 *See also* Jn 5:20; 10:17; 15:9; 17:24

The Father shares his divine life with the Son Col 2:9 *See also* Jn 5:26; 6:57; Col 1:19

The Father delegates his authority to the Son Jn 5:27 *See also* Mt 28:18; Jn 3:35; 5:21–22; 16:15; Rev 2:26–27

Father and Son indwell each other Jn 14:10–11 *See also* Jn 10:38; 14:20; 17:21–23

The relationship between the Holy Spirit and the other two persons
The Spirit is "the Spirit of God" and "the Spirit of Christ" Ro 8:9
"the Spirit of God": Ps 106:33; 1Co 2:14; Php 3:3; 1Jn 4:2
"the Spirit of Christ": Ac 16:7; Gal 4:6; Php 1:19; 1Pe 1:11

The Spirit's unique relationship with God Mt 10:20 *See also* 1Co 2:10–11

The Spirit's unique relationship with the Son Jn 1:33 *See also* Isa 61:1; Jn 14:16–17,26; Ac 10:38

1512
Trinity, equality of the persons

The Son and the Holy Spirit are equal to God the Father in eternity, nature and status. Within the Trinity the Father is head, first among equals; the Son and the Holy Spirit do the Father's will, glorifying him and making him known; and the Holy Spirit glorifies and makes known the Son.

The Son is equal with the Father
Jn 5:18 *See also* Jn 5:23; 8:16; 14:9; 17:10; Php 2:6; Col 2:9
Ro 1:7 *The equality of the Son and the Father is often implied in the opening greetings of the NT letters. See also* 1Co 1:3; Gal 1:3; Eph 1:2; 1Th 1:1; 1Ti 1:2; Phm 3; 2Pe 1:2
Rev 5:13 *Doxologies are addressed to the Father and the Son equally or just to the Son. See also* Ro 9:5; Heb 13:21; 2Pe 3:18; Rev 7:10

The Holy Spirit is equal with the Father and the Son
2Co 13:14 *See also* Mt 28:19; 1Pe 1:2; Rev 1:4–5

The obedience of the Son to the Father
The Son submits to the Father in his incarnation Php 2:6–7 *See also* Mt 24:36; Jn 4:34; 6:38; 14:28,31; Ro 5:19; Heb 5:8; 10:5–7; Ps 40:6–8

The Father is Jesus Christ's "head" 1Co 11:3 *See also* 1Co 3:23; 8:6; 15:27–28

Equality and mutuality as the three persons glorify one another
The Son glorifies the Father Ro 16:27 *See also* Jn 14:13; Eph 1:5–6; 3:21; Php 2:11; Col 3:17; 1Pe 4:11; Jude 25

The Father and the Son glorify one another Jn 17:1 *In John's Gospel, the "glory" of Jesus Christ is seen above all in the cross. See also* Jn 8:54; 13:31–32; 17:4–5,24; Ac 3:13

The Spirit glorifies the Father and the Son Jn 16:13–15 *See also* Jn 14:26; 15:26; Eph 1:13–14

1513
Trinity, mission of the persons

All three persons of the Trinity co-operate in God's work of salvation.

For this purpose, the Father sends the Son and the Holy Spirit to redeem his people on earth and to live in and among them.

The Son and the Holy Spirit do God's work on earth
In the OT, the LORD alone is Saviour Isa 43:11 *See also* Ps 19:14; 78:35; Isa 43:3; 49:26; 60:16; Jer 14:8; Hos 13:4

In the NT, the Son is the Saviour Mt 1:21 *See also* Lk 2:11; Jn 4:42; Gal 3:13; 4:5; Tit 2:13; 3:6

In the OT, the LORD lives among his people Ex 29:45 *See also* Ps 135:21; Isa 57:15; Eze 43:7; Joel 3:17; Zec 2:10–11

In the NT, the Spirit lives in the church 1Co 3:16 *See also* Jn 14:17; Ro 8:9,11; 2Ti 1:14

Father and Son in the mission of Jesus Christ
The Father sends the Son Gal 4:4 *See also* Mt 10:40; Mk 12:6; Jn 3:16–17; 7:28; 8:42; 1Jn 4:9

The Son reveals the Father Jn 8:38 *See also* Jn 1:18; 15:15; 17:6,26; Col 1:15; Heb 1:3

The Son does the Father's work Jn 5:19 *See also* Jn 4:34; 5:17; 9:3–4; 10:37; 14:10

The Son speaks the Father's words Jn 12:49–50 *See also* Jn 3:34; 8:28; 14:24; 17:8

The Father testifies to the Son Jn 5:37 *This refers to God's testimony to his Son in the OT Scriptures. See also* Jn 5:32; 8:18; 1Jn 5:9

The sending of the Holy Spirit
The Father gives the Spirit Lk 11:13 *See also* Lk 5:32; 2Co 5:5; Gal 3:5; Eph 1:17; 1Jn 4:13

The Son gives the Spirit Jn 16:7 *See also* Mt 3:11 pp Mk 1:8 pp Lk 3:16; Jn 1:33; 20:22

The Father sends the Spirit through Jesus Christ Jn 14:16–17 *The varied terminology about who sends the Spirit reflects the close co-operation between and the shared activity of the three persons. See also* Jn 14:26; 15:26; Ac 2:33

The three persons share the work of salvation
The incarnation Lk 1:35

Jesus Christ's baptism Mt 3:16–17 pp Mk 1:10–11 pp Lk 3:21–22

Jesus Christ's ministry Ac 10:38 *See also* Lk 10:21; Jn 3:34

The work of redemption 1Pe 1:2 *See also* 2Co 1:21–22; Gal 4:4–6; Eph 1:3–14; 2:18; 2Th 2:13–14; Tit 3:4–6

Commissioning the disciples Jn 20:21–22 *See also* Ac 1:7–8

Jesus Christ's exaltation Ac 7:55 *See also* Ac 5:31–32

Proclaiming the gospel Ac 2:38–39

Building the church Eph 2:22 *See also* 1Co 12:4–6

See also
2318 Christ as prophet
2351 Christ, miracles
2354 Christ, mission
2363 Christ, preaching & teaching
3130 Holy Spirit, Counsellor
3242 Holy Spirit, baptism with
3257 Holy Spirit, gift of
3296 Holy Spirit in the world
6510 salvation
6720 redemption

1600

Scripture as the word of God

This set of themes consists of the following:
1610 Scripture
1620 beatitudes, the
1630 Book of the Covenant
1640 Book of the Law
1650 numbers, significance of
1660 Sermon on the Mount
1670 symbols
1680 types
1690 word of God

1610

Scripture

The biblical writings, inspired by the Holy Spirit, have been entrusted to the church to remind it of the central teachings of the gospel, to guard it from error and to enable it to grow into holiness. The church is required to be obedient to Scripture and revere it as the Word of God.

1611

Scripture, inspiration and authority of

Those writings that are acknowledged to be the word of God to be revered as issuing from him and as having his authority.

Recognition of a body of sacred writings

In the OT Ne 8:1 *See also* Ex 24:7; Jos 8:34; 2Ki 22:8 pp 2Ch 34:14; 2Ki 23:2 pp 2Ch 34:30; 2Ch 35:12; Ezr 6:18; Ne 8:8; 9:3; 13:1

By Jesus Christ Mt 22:29 *See also* Lk 4:21; 24:27,45
Mt 21:13 *Jesus Christ frequently appealed to the OT as a recognised sacred corpus, with the expression "it is written".*
pp Lk 19:46 *See also* Isa 56:7; Jer 7:11; Mt 4:4 pp Lk 4:4; Dt 8:3; Mt 4:7 pp Lk 4:12; Dt 6:16; Mt 4:10 pp Lk 4:8; Dt 6:13; Mt 21:42 pp Mk 12:10; Ps 118:22–23; Mt 26:31 pp Mk 14:27; Zec 13:7; Mk 7:6–7; Isa 29:13; Lk 7:27; Mal 3:1; Jn 7:38

By the apostles 2Ti 3:14–15 *See also* Ac 1:15–17; Ro 1:1–2; 15:4; 1Co 15:3–4; 2Ti 3:16–17

By the early church Ac 17:11

The inspiration of Scripture
2Ti 3:16 *See also* 2Ki 17:13–14; Ne 9:30; Mt 22:43–44 pp Mk 12:36; 1Co 2:13; Heb 1:1–2; 1Pe 1:10–11; 2Pe 1:20–21

The authority of Scripture recognised in the OT
Ps 119:89; Jos 23:6 *See also* Jos 1:8; 2Ki 22:11; Ezr 10:1–4,9–12; Ne 13:1–3; Isa 40:8

The authority of Scripture recognised in the NT
Jn 10:34–36 *See also* Mt 5:17–19; Lk 21:21–23; 16:17; 1Th 2:13

Jesus Christ claims scriptural authority for his own words
Mt 24:34–35 pp Mk 13:30–31 *See also* Jn 12:47–50; 14:10,23–24

See also
1428 prophecy, OT inspiration
1439 revelation
1690 word of God
2333 Christ, attitude to OT
3236 Holy Spirit & Scripture
3281 Holy Spirit, inspiration
5215 authority
5379 law, Christ's attitude

1612

Scripture, and Holy Spirit

See 3236 Holy Spirit, and Scripture

1613

Scripture, purpose of

Scripture has been given by God to lead people to faith and salvation. Through Scripture believers are nurtured in faith and led to spiritual maturity.

Scripture is intended to lead people to salvation
2Ti 3:14–15 *See also* Ps 19:7–11; Jn 20:30–31; Ro 10:8

Scripture is intended to lead believers to maturity in faith
By its teaching 2Ti 3:16 *See also* Dt 6:6–9; Ps 19:7–8; 119:9,130; Col 3:16

By its rebuke and correction 2Ti 3:16 *See also* Ps 19:11–13; 1Co 10:11–12; Heb 4:12–13

By training in righteousness 2Ti 3:16 *See also* Dt 29:29

By its illumination Ps 119:105,130 *See also* 2Pe 1:19; 1Jn 2:8

By its encouragement and reassurance Ro 15:4; 1Jn 5:13 *See also* Ps 19:8–9; 119:50–51,76; Heb 12:5–6

By its record of God's promises 1Ki 8:56; Ps 119:140 *See also* Eze 12:25; Lk 24:44; 2Co 1:19–22

By its trustworthiness 1Ki 17:24; Ps 19:7–11; 33:4 *See also* Ps 119:151,160; Jn 21:24; Rev 21:5

Scripture is essential for spiritual growth and maturity
Ps 1:1–3 *See also* Mt 4:4; Jn 15:5–8; 17:17; Eph 6:10–17; 2Ti 3:14–17

See also
1175 God, will of
5175 reading
5902 maturity
5926 rebuke
6510 salvation
7797 teaching
8020 faith
8128 guidance, receiving
8154 righteousness
8414 encouragement
8422 equipping, spiritual
8443 growth

1614

Scripture, understanding

God intends his word to be understood and has provided the directions and means for understanding it.

Scripture is intended to be clearly understood
It is accessible to ordinary people Ps 119:130 *See also* Ps 19:7

Some sections are difficult to understand 2Pe 3:15–16 *See also* Heb 5:11

God has prescribed the way to understand Scripture
Through public reading 1Ti 4:13 *See also* Ne 8:2–8; 13:1–3

Through diligent study 2Ti 2:15 *See also* Dt 17:18–20; Ac 17:11

Through thoughtful meditation Ps 1:1–3 *See also* Jos 1:8; Job 23:12; Ps 119:15,27,48,97,148

Assistance in understanding through the Holy Spirit
1Co 2:9–12 *See also* Isa 64:4; Lk 24:45; Jn 14:26; 16:13; 1Jn 2:27

Assistance in understanding through ministers of the word
Ne 8:2–8 *See also* Eph 4:11–14; 1Ti 4:11–16; 2Ti 4:1–5

See also
3140 Holy Spirit, teacher
5026 knowledge
7464 teachers of the law
7754 preaching
7939 ministry
8234 doctrine
8355 understanding
8419 enlightenment
8602 prayer
8662 meditation
8674 study

1615

Scripture, sufficiency of

Scripture is presented as being of itself sufficient for faith and for life.

God's written revelation is sufficient
Dt 4:1–2 *See also* Dt 12:32; Jos 1:7–8; Pr 30:5–6; Jer 26:2

The NT records the completion and fulfilment of the OT
Heb 1:1–2 *See also* Jn 12:47–50; Eph 2:20

Warnings against turning from, or adding to, the apostolic gospel, as set forth in Scripture
Rev 22:18–19 *See also* Gal 1:6–9; Col 1:25–2:8,18,20–23; 2Th 2:1–2

Descriptions of Scripture point to its sufficiency

Scripture is good Ro 7:12 *See also* 1Ti 1:8

Scripture is perfect Ps 19:7 *See also* Ps 119:142; Jas 1:25

Scripture is eternal Ps 119:89 *See also* Mt 5:18; 24:35; 1Pe 1:24–25; Isa 40:6–8

See also
1460 truth	8766 heresies
2420 gospel	9612 hope, in God
8749 false teachers	

1620
beatitudes, the

The blessings pronounced by Jesus Christ in the Sermon on the Mount on those whose lives exhibit particular characteristics or qualities. These contrast sharply with popular values and outlooks.

The poor in spirit
Mt 5:3 pp Lk 6:20 *See also* Ps 69:32–33; Isa 61:1; Mt 23:12; Lk 18:9–14

Those who mourn
Mt 5:4 pp Lk 6:21 *See also* Ps 51:17; Isa 57:18–21; 61:1–3; Jer 31:13; Rev 7:17; 21:4

The meek
Mt 5:5 *See also* Ps 37:11; Zep 3:11–12; Mt 11:29

Those who hunger after righteousness
Mt 5:6 pp Lk 6:21 *See also* Isa 55:1–2; Mt 6:33; 2Ti 2:22; 1Pe 3:12

The merciful
Mt 5:7 *See also* Ex 34:6–7; Da 9:9; Mt 6:12 pp Lk 11:4; Mt 6:14–15; 18:21–35; Lk 6:36; Jas 2:13

The pure in heart
Mt 5:8 *See also* Ps 24:3–5; 51:10; 73:1; 1Jn 3:2–3

The peacemakers
Mt 5:9 *See also* Ps 34:14; Mt 5:44–45; Ro 12:18; 14:19; 2Ti 2:22; Jas 3:17–18

The righteous who suffer persecution
Mt 5:10–12 pp Lk 6:22 *See also* Jn 15:18–21; 2Ti 3:10–12; Jas 1:12; 1Pe 3:14,17; 4:12–16

See also
1335 blessing	8154 righteousness
1660 Sermon on the Mount	8276 humility
	8305 meekness
5419 mourning	8324 purity
5450 poverty, spiritual	8458 peacemakers
	8638 benedictions
6686 mercy	8794 persecution

1630
Book of the Covenant

The customary designation given to the code of law in Ex 20:22–23:33, but it may also have included the Ten Commandments (Ex 20:2–17).

Moses reads the Book of the Covenant to the Israelites
Ex 24:7 *See also* Ex 20:22–23:33 *The Book of the Covenant is the oldest, extant codification of Israelite law, where human values are constantly elevated over material ones. It can be argued that each section of the code is a further exposition of one of the Ten Commandments, giving specific case laws.*

Josiah reads the rediscovered Book of the Covenant to the people of Judah
2Ki 23:2–3 pp 2Ch 34:30–31 *See also* 2Ki 23:21 *This reference to the Book of the Covenant applies either to all or part of the book of Deuteronomy, or to the entire Mosaic Law.*

See also
1345 covenant	5377 law, Ten Commandments
1640 Book of the Law	
	8466 reformation
5375 law	

1640
Book of the Law

A documentary form of the Law placed beside the ark of the covenant as a reminder to Israel of her covenant obligation. It was rediscovered and applied during the reign of King Josiah of Judah and read publicly by Ezra after the rebuilding of the walls of Jerusalem.

The Book of the Law was written by Moses
Dt 31:24–26 *The book in question could be the material now included as chapters 1–30, although some scholars suggest it might refer to the material now included in chapters 12–26. See also* Dt 28:58–61; 29:18–21; 30:10

The Book of the Law was passed from Moses to Joshua
Jos 1:7–8 *See also* Jos 8:30–31,34–35; 23:6; 24:26

The Book of the Law during the monarchy
2Ki 14:6 pp 2Ch 25:4; 2Ch 17:9

The Book of the Law was rediscovered and applied in Josiah's reign
2Ki 22:8–16 pp 2Ch 34:15–24 *A reference to part or all of Deuteronomy or possibly the entire Pentateuch (Genesis to Deuteronomy).*

The Book of the Law was read publicly by Ezra
Ne 8:1–18 *See also* Ne 9:3

Paul refers to the Book of the Law
Gal 3:10 *Paul is teaching that justification is by faith. See also* Dt 27:26

See also
1345 covenant	5378 law, OT
1630 Book of the Covenant	8466 reformation
	8768 idolatry
5175 reading	
5377 law, Ten Commandments	

numbers, significance of

Numbers appear frequently in Scripture and in a variety of contexts. Occasionally they have a special theological significance. This set of themes consists of the following:
1651 numbers, 1–2
1652 numbers, 3–5
1653 numbers, 6–10
1654 numbers, 11–99
1655 numbers, hundreds and thousands
1656 numbers, combinations
1657 numbers, fractions

1651
numbers, 1–2

The number one is often associated with the uniqueness of God and also with the unity between God and his people. The number two is used in a variety of contexts.

One
One God Mk 12:32 *See also* Dt 6:4; Isa 44:8; 45:21; Jn 1:18; Ro 3:30; 1Co 8:4–6

One Father Mal 2:10; Mt 23:9; Eph 4:6

One Son Jesus Christ Jn 1:14; 3:16,18; 1Co 8:6; 2Co 11:2; Eph 4:5; Heb 11:17; 1Jn 4:9

One Holy Spirit 1Co 12:9,11,13; Eph 2:18; 4:4

One Saviour Isa 43:10–11; Ac 4:12; 1Ti 2:5

One Shepherd Ecc 12:11; Eze 34:23; 37:22,24; Jn 10:16

One faith Jude 3 *See also* Gal 1:8–9; Eph 4:5

One sacrifice for sin Heb 7:27 *See also* Ro 6:10; Heb 9:12,28; 10:10; 1Pe 3:18

One who acts on behalf of others Jn 11:50 *See also* 1Sa 17:8–10; Jn 18:14; Ro 5:15–19; 1Ti 2:5

One people of God Eze 37:22; Ro 12:4–5; 1Co 10:17; 12:12–13; Eph 2:16; 3:6; 4:4; Col 3:15

Christians are to be one in Jesus Christ Jn 17:21 *See also* Gal 3:28

Christians are to be one in spirit Php 2:2 *See also* Ro 15:6; 2Co 13:11; Php 1:27

Married couples become one flesh Ge 2:24 *See also* Mt 19:5 pp Mk 10:8; 1Co 6:16; Eph 5:31

One priority for all people Mk 12:28–30 pp Mt 22:36–37 *See also* Dt 6:4–5; Mt 6:33; Lk 10:42

Two
Two of every kind in the ark Ge 6:19–20; 7:2

Two brothers
Isaac and Ishmael: Ge 17:17–19; 21:10; 25:9
Jacob and Esau: Ge 25:23; Ro 9:10–13
Ge 48:1–20 *Ephraim and Manasseh*

Andrew and Simon, James and John:
Mt 4:18–22 pp Mk 1:16–20; Lk 5:10;
Jn 1:40–42
Lk 15:11 *the prodigal son and his brother*

Two wives Ge 16:3; Dt 21:15; 1Sa 1:2–7
David's wives: 1Sa 27:3; 30:5,18; 2Sa 2:2
2Ch 24:3

Teams of two: Jesus Christ's disciples
Lk 10:1 *See also* Mt 21:1 pp Mk 11:1
pp Lk 19:29; Mk 14:13

Teams of two: Paul and his colleagues
Ac 13:42–50; 14:1–3; 15:12,22;
16:19–40; 17:10; 1Co 1:1; 2Co 1:1;
Php 1:1; Col 1:1

**Two tablets of the Ten
Commandments** Ex 31:18; 34:29;
Dt 9:15,17; 10:3; 2Ch 5:10

Two cherubim Ex 25:18,22; 37:7;
Nu 7:89; 1Ki 6:25

See also

1165 God, unique	7924 fellowship in
1170 God, unity of	service
5708 marriage	7925 fellowship
5739 twins	among
5971 uniqueness	believers
6752 substitution	8461 priorities
7025 church, unity	8799 polytheism
7030 unity	

1652
numbers, 3–5

The number three, primarily
associated with the doctrine of the
Trinity, is also associated with
periods of specially significant divine
activity (e.g., "on the third day").
Four and five have a variety of
associations.

Three
The Trinity Mt 28:19 *See also* Jn 14:26;
15:26; 1Co 12:4–6; 1Pe 1:2

The triad of faith, hope and love
1Co 13:13 *See also* 1Th 1:3

Three days Ge 30:36 *Three days is a
common period, often indicating the length
of a journey or a period leading to a critical
point. See also* Ge 40:12–22; Ex 3:18;
10:22; Nu 10:33; Jdg 14:14; 1Ki 12:5
pp 2Ch 10:5

**Jesus Christ was raised after three
days** Lk 24:46 *See also* Mt 16:21
pp Mk 8:31 pp Lk 9:22; Mt 17:23
pp Mk 9:31; Mt 20:19 pp Mk 10:34
pp Lk 18:33; Mt 27:63–64; Lk 24:7,21;
Ac 10:40; 1Co 15:3–4
*Comparison between Jonah's three days in
the fish and Jesus Christ's three days in the
tomb:* Jnh 1:17; Mt 12:39–40
pp Lk 11:29–30; Mt 16:4

Three brothers
Shem, Ham and Japheth: Ge 6:10; 7:13;
9:19
1Sa 2:21; 31:6 pp 1Ch 10:6; 2Sa 2:18

Groups of three men
Job's friends: Job 2:11; 32:3,5
Jesus Christ's disciples: Mt 17:1 pp Mk 9:2
pp Lk 9:28; Mt 26:37 pp Mk 14:33
Ge 18:2; Eze 14:14–18; Da 3:23–24;
Zec 11:8; 2Sa 23:8–12 *the Three in
David's army;* 2Sa 23:13–23
pp 1Ch 11:15–25 *the three mighty men
among David's chiefs*

Three annual festivals Ex 23:14,17;
34:23–24; Dt 16:16; 1Ki 9:25; 2Ch 8:13

Three and a half
Da 7:25 *NIV footnote. See also* Da 12:7;
Rev 11:2; 12:6; 13:5

Four
**Four representing the complete
created order** Rev 7:1 *This symbol is
probably based on the four points of the
compass. See also* Jer 49:36; Eze 37:9;
Da 7:2; Mt 24:31 pp Mk 13:27

Four living creatures
*The four living creatures in Ezekiel and
Revelation represent the whole animate
creation glorifying God:* Eze 1:5–10;
Rev 4:6–7; 5:6,8; 14:3

Four kingdoms
*Human history before the coming of God's
kingdom is spanned by four great human
kingdoms, often understood to refer to the
empires of Babylon, Persia, Greece and
Rome:* Da 2:39–40; 7:17

Five
Fives in Jesus Christ's teaching
Mt 25:2,15–20; Lk 12:6,52; 14:19;
16:28; 19:18–19; Jn 4:18

Five loaves 1Sa 21:3; Mt 14:17–19
pp Mk 6:38–41 pp Lk 9:13–16
pp Jn 6:8–13; Mt 16:9 pp Mk 8:19

See also

1510 Trinity, the	2560 Christ,
2351 Christ, miracles	resurrection

1653
numbers, 6–10

The number seven is especially
associated with completeness and
perfection. The number ten is
occasionally used as a symbol of
completeness. Other numbers have a
variety of associations.

Six
The world was created in six days
Ex 20:11 *See also* Ge 1:1–31; Ex 31:17

**Human work is to be limited to six days
a week** Ex 16:26; 20:9 pp Dt 5:13;
Ex 23:12; 31:15; 34:21; 35:2; Lev 23:3;
Lk 13:14

Other important six-day periods
Dt 16:8; Jos 6:3–14; Mt 17:1 pp Mk 9:2;
Jn 12:1

**Human work restricted to six-year
periods** Ex 21:2; 23:10; Lev 25:3;
Dt 15:12,18; Jer 34:14

Seven
The seventh day is a day of rest
Ge 2:2–3 *See also* Ex 20:10 pp Dt 5:14;
Ex 31:15–17; 35:2–3; Heb 4:4

**The seventh year symbolises rest and
freedom** Lev 25:4 *See also* Ex 23:10–11;
Lev 25:2–6; Dt 15:1,12; Ne 10:31

Major festivals lasted seven days
Unleavened Bread: Ex 12:15; 23:15;
Lev 23:6; Nu 28:17; Dt 16:8; 2Ch 30:21;
35:17; Eze 45:21
Tabernacles: Lev 23:34; Nu 29:12;
Dt 16:13
Ordination of priests: Ex 29:30,35;
Lev 8:33

**The Feast of Weeks, or Pentecost,
comes seven weeks after the firstfruits
of the harvest** Lev 23:15–16; Dt 16:9

Festivals in the seventh month
Lev 16:29; 23:24,39; Nu 29:7,12

**Important rituals associated with
sevens** Lev 4:6–17; 14:7,51; 16:14;
Nu 28:11; 1Ch 15:26; Job 42:8

Ritual uncleanness for seven days
Lev 12:2; 13:4,21,26; 15:24

**Seven times indicates a completed
action** Lev 26:18; Jos 6:4; 1Ki 18:43;
2Ki 5:10; Ps 119:164

**Seven times indicates total
intensification** Ge 4:15; Lev 26:21;
Ps 12:6; 79:12; Isa 30:26; Da 3:19

The seven spirits of God Rev 5:6 *See
also* Zec 4:10; Rev 1:4; 3:1; 4:5

Seven associated with final judgment
Rev 21:9 *See also* Rev 8:2,6; 10:3–4;
12:3; 15:1,7; 17:3

Eight
Eighth day as the day of circumcision
Lk 2:21 *See also* Ge 17:12; 21:4;
Lev 12:3; Lk 1:59; Ac 7:8; Php 3:5

Eighth day as the end of major festivals
Lev 23:36,39; Nu 29:35; 2Ch 7:9;
Ne 8:18

Rituals of the eighth day Lev 14:10,23;
15:14

Nine
Jesus Christ died at the ninth hour
Mt 27:45–46 pp Mk 15:33–34
pp Lk 23:44

Ten
Ten as a symbol of completeness
Ru 4:2; 2Ch 4:6–8; Da 1:12–15; 7:24;
Rev 2:10; 12:3

Ten as an approximate number
Ge 31:7; Ru 1:4; 1Sa 1:8; Job 19:3;
Zec 8:23

Ten days as an approximate period
Ge 24:55; 1Sa 25:38; Ac 25:6

Ten plagues on Egypt Ex 7:20;
8:6,16,24; 9:6,10,22; 10:12,21; 11:5

The Ten Commandments Ex 34:28 *See
also* Dt 4:13; 10:4

Tens in Jesus Christ's parables
Mt 25:1,28; Lk 15:8; 19:13,17

See also

2357 Christ, parables	7334 circumcision
3035 Holy Spirit,	7340 clean and
presence of	unclean
4843 plague	7355 feasts &
4975 week	festivals
5056 rest	7428 Sabbath
5377 law, Ten Com-	
mandments	
5636 work & rest	

1654
numbers, 11–99

Significant numbers include twelve,
often associated with the full
number of God's people, and
multiples of ten, especially forty and
seventy.

Eleven
Eleven sons of Jacob Ge 32:22; 37:9

Jesus Christ's eleven disciples
Mt 28:16; Mk 16:14; Lk 24:9,33;
Ac 1:26; 2:14

Twelve
Twelve tribes of Israel Ge 49:28 *See also*
Ge 35:22–26; Ex 24:4; 28:21; 39:14;
Jdg 19:29; Ezr 8:35; Ac 26:7

Representatives of the twelve tribes
Dt 1:23; Jos 3:12; 4:2–3

**The church symbolised as twelve
tribes** Jas 1:1; Rev 7:4–8; 21:12

Twelve apostles Mk 3:14 *See also*
Mt 10:1–4; 19:28; Lk 9:1; 22:30;
Jn 6:70–71; Ac 6:2; 1Co 15:5 *The term
"the Twelve" is used here even though only
eleven disciples remained at the time
referred to.*

Fourteen
**Passover on the fourteenth day of the
first month** Nu 28:16 *See also* Ex 12:6;
Lev 23:5; Nu 9:2–5; Jos 5:10; 2Ch 35:1;
Ezr 6:19; Eze 45:21

**Passover on the fourteenth day of the
second month** Nu 9:10–11;
2Ch 30:2–3,15

Periods of fourteen years Ge 31:41;
2Co 12:2; Gal 2:1

**Genealogy of Jesus Christ in spans of
fourteen generations** Mt 1:17

Fifteen
Festivals on the fifteenth day
Lev 23:6,34,39; Nu 28:17; 29:12;
1Ki 12:32–33; Eze 45:25

Twenty
**Twenty as the minimum age in a
census** Ex 30:14; 38:26; Nu 1:3,18;
14:29; 26:2; 1Ch 27:23

**Twenty as the minimum age for
Levitical service** 1Ch 23:24,27;
2Ch 31:17; Ezr 3:8

Thirty
**Thirty as the age for beginning a life's
work** Lk 3:23 *See also* Ge 41:46;
1Sa 13:1; 2Sa 5:4; Eze 1:1 *The "thirtieth
year" may refer to Ezekiel's age.*

**Thirty as the minimum age for Levitical
service** Nu 4:3,23,30,47; 1Ch 23:3

The Thirty in David's army 2Sa 23:23
pp 1Ch 11:25; 2Sa 23:24;
1Ch 11:15–42; 12:4,18; 27:6

Thirty pieces of silver Mt 26:15 *See also*
Zec 11:12–13; Mt 27:3,9

Forty
Forty days Jnh 3:4 *Forty days is a
standard period, sometimes viewed as a
time of preparation or testing before a
major event.*
Forty-day periods at the flood:
Ge 7:4,12,17; 8:6
Moses fasted for forty days on Mount Sinai:
Ex 24:18; 34:28; Dt 9:9,18
Mt 4:1–2 pp Mk 1:13 pp Lk 4:1–2 *Jesus
Christ fasted for forty days in the
wilderness.*
Nu 13:25; 1Sa 17:16; 1Ki 19:8; Ac 1:3

**Forty years as a general term for a
generation**
*God's anger against Israel in the
wilderness:* Nu 14:34; 32:13; Jos 5:6;
Ps 95:10; Heb 3:9,17
God's provision for Israel in the wilderness:

Ex 16:35; Dt 2:7; 8:2–4; 29:5; Ne 9:21;
Am 2:10; Ac 7:36; 13:18

Other significant forty-year periods
Forty-year periods in Moses' life: Ex 7:7;
Dt 34:7; Ac 7:23,30,36
Forty-year periods of peace: Jdg 3:11; 5:31;
8:28
Forty-year periods of leadership: 1Sa 4:18;
2Sa 5:4; 1Ki 2:11 pp 1Ch 29:27;
1Ki 11:42 pp 2Ch 9:30; 2Ki 12:1
pp 2Ch 24:1; Ac 13:21

Fifty
The fiftieth year as the Year of Jubilee
Lev 25:10–11 *The word "jubilee" refers
to the liberation of slaves, rather than to a
fixed period of time. The number 50
represents the year following seven periods
of seven years, i.e., 49 years + 1.*

Seventy
Seventy people went down to Egypt
Ge 46:27; Ex 1:5

Seventy years of God's judgment
Jer 25:11–12 *See also* 2Ch 36:21;
Isa 23:15–17; Jer 29:10; Da 9:2;
Zec 1:12

Seventy years as the human lifespan
Ps 90:10

Groups of seventy Ex 24:1;
Nu 11:16,24–25; Jdg 9:2;
Lk 10:1 fn,17 fn

Seventy as a large number Mt 18:22
See also Da 9:24

See also

4299 wilderness	7266 tribes of Israel
5249 census	7390 Levites
7135 Israel, people of	7406 Passover
God	7482 Year of Jubilee
7217 exile in Babylon	7630 Twelve, the
7227 flood, the	8432 fasting,
7230 genealogies	practice

1655
numbers, hundreds and thousands

The words "hundreds" and,
especially, "thousands", often refer
to large quantities in general; they
are also used simply in a superlative
sense.

Hundreds
A hundred in Jesus Christ's teaching
Mt 13:23 pp Mk 4:20 *See also* Mt 13:8
pp Mk 4:8 pp Lk 8:8; Mt 18:12
pp Lk 15:4; Mt 18:28; Mk 10:30

Abraham becomes a father at 100
Ge 17:17; 21:5; Ro 4:19

People who lived to over 100
Ge 5:3–32; 9:29; 11:10–32; 25:7,17;
50:22; Dt 34:7; Jdg 2:8; 2Ch 24:15;
Job 42:16; Isa 65:20

Hundreds and thousands
**Hundreds and thousands as military
units** Ex 18:21; Nu 31:14; 1Sa 22:7;
2Sa 18:1; 1Ch 13:1; 27:1; 28:1; 2Ch 25:5

Hundreds and thousands in blessings
Dt 1:11 *See also* Ge 24:60; 2Sa 24:3
pp 1Ch 21:3; Ps 144:13

Thousands
Jesus Christ feeds thousands Mt 14:21
pp Mk 6:44 pp Lk 9:14 pp Jn 6:10;

Mt 15:38 pp Mk 8:9; Mt 16:9–10
pp Mk 8:19–20

Believers numbered in thousands
Ac 21:20 *See also* Ac 2:41; 4:4; Ro 11:4;
1Ki 19:18

God shows his love to thousands
Ex 34:6–7 *See also* Ex 20:6 pp Dt 5:10;
Dt 7:9

God has thousands of attendants
Rev 5:11 *See also* Ps 68:17; Da 7:10;
Heb 12:22; Jude 14

**God protects one believer amidst
thousands of people** Ps 91:7

**God helps one believer against a
thousand** Jos 23:10; Jdg 15:15–16

God allows thousands to be defeated
Dt 32:30; Isa 30:17

A thousand years
As a day to the Lord: Ps 90:4; 2Pe 3:8
Rev 20:2–7 *the reign of Jesus Christ with
believers for 1,000 years while Satan is
restrained*

Special numbers
Rev 13:18 *666 is a symbol of total
incompleteness;* Rev 7:4 *144,000
symbolises the perfect number of God's
people.*

God's people are without number
Ge 16:10 *See also* Nu 10:36; Rev 7:9

**God's people are compared to stars
and sand** Ge 22:17 *See also* Ge 15:5;
Ex 32:13; Dt 10:22; 1Ch 27:23; Ne 9:23;
Jer 33:22; Heb 11:12

See also

1085 God, love of	5208 armies
1335 blessing	5467 promises,
2351 Christ, miracles	divine
2363 Christ,	7105 believers
preaching &	7140 people of God
teaching	9155 millennium
4110 angels	

1656
numbers, combinations

Numbers may be combined for
making a comparison. When they
are combined in such a pattern as
"two or three" the emphasis usually
falls on the second figure.

Two and three
Two or three witnesses Dt 19:15 *See
also* Nu 35:30; Dt 17:6; Mt 18:16;
2Co 13:1; 1Ti 5:19; Heb 10:28

**Two or three as a small approximate
number** Mt 18:20 *See also* 2Ki 9:32;
Isa 17:6; Hos 6:2; 1Co 14:27,29

Two and three in a climactic pattern
Ecc 4:12 *See also* Pr 30:15

Three and four
**Three or four as a small approximate
number** Jer 36:23

Three and four in a climactic pattern
Pr 30:18–19 *See also*
Pr 30:15–16,21–23,29–31;
Am 1:3,6,9,11,13; 2:1,4,6

Other examples of the climactic pattern
Job 5:19; Pr 6:16–19; Ge 4:24; Ecc 11:2; Mic 5:5

Comparative use of multiples of ten
Am 5:3 *See also* Lev 26:8; Dt 33:17; Jdg 20:10; Mic 6:7; Lk 16:7

Numerical contrast between Saul and David
1Sa 18:7–8 *See also* 1Sa 21:11; 29:5

See also
1025 God, anger of   5359 justice

1657
numbers, fractions

Mainly associated with divisions of the people and of property, and also with sacrificial offerings.

One half
Half the people Jos 8:33 *See also* Dt 27:12–13; 1Ki 16:21; Ne 4:16; 12:31–32,38; 13:24

The half-tribe of Manasseh Dt 3:13 *See also* Nu 32:33; 34:13–14; Dt 29:8; Jos 13:29–31; 22:10; 1Ch 5:23

Halves in offering sacrifices Ge 15:10 *See also* Ex 24:6; 30:13; Lev 6:20

Significant examples of halves
2Sa 10:4 pp 1Ch 19:4 *David's men and the Ammonites;* 1Ki 3:25 *Solomon;* 1Ki 10:7 pp 2Ch 9:6 *the Queen of Sheba Half a kingdom:* Est 5:3; 7:2; Mk 6:23 Isa 44:16–20 *Idolatry*

One third
Thirds of a group 2Sa 18:2; 2Ki 11:5–6 pp 2Ch 23:4–5

Thirds in the processes of judgment
Rev 9:18 *See also* Eze 5:2,12; Rev 8:7–12; 9:15; 12:4

One fifth
A fifth of the harvest Ge 41:34; 47:24,26

A fifth in cases of restitution
Lev 5:14–16 *See also* Lev 6:5; 22:14; Nu 5:7

Redeeming what is promised to God
Lev 27:13 *See also* Lev 27:15,19,27,31

One tenth
Instructions about God's tithe
Lev 27:30–32 *The term "tithe" is the Old English word for "one tenth". See also* Nu 18:21,26; Dt 12:6,11; 14:22; Ne 10:38; Am 4:4; Mal 3:8–10

The royal tithe 1Sa 8:15,17

Examples of the tithe
Abraham: Ge 14:20; Heb 7:1–10 Ge 28:22 *Jacob The Israelites:* 2Ch 31:5–6,12; Ne 10:37 Mt 23:23 *teachers of the law and Pharisees*

See also
5741 vows   9210 judgment,
7370 guilt offering   God's
8488 tithing

1660
Sermon on the Mount

A collection of Jesus Christ's teaching on the theme of discipleship. It deals with the righteousness required of disciples, the way they are to perform their religious duties, and the blessing and persecution they will know as followers of Christ. It can be seen as a manifesto setting out the nature of life in the kingdom of God.

The setting of the Sermon on the Mount
Mt 5:1; Lk 6:17 *Either Jesus Christ taught similar material in two different locations, as is common in preaching, or else Luke more specifically identifies that he taught on a level place or plateau on the mountainside.*

The teaching of the Sermon on the Mount
The blessings of being in the kingdom Mt 5:3–12 pp Lk 6:20–23

Jesus Christ's disciples are to have a positive influence on the world
Mt 5:13–16

The relationship between Jesus Christ's message and the law
Mt 5:17–21

Jesus Christ's disciples are to exhibit a new depth of righteousness Mt 5:20 *See also* Mt 5:48

The righteousness required of Jesus Christ's disciples
Not only murder but also anger and broken relationships are wrong: Mt 5:21–24; Ex 20:13; Mt 5:25–26 pp Lk 12:58–59 *Not only adultery but also lust is wrong:* Mt 5:27–30; Ex 20:14 Mt 5:31–32 *faithfulness in marriage is called for;* Mt 5:33–37 *faithfulness in speech is called for;* Mt 5:38–48 *Retaliation must be abandoned, and enemies as well as neighbours must be loved.*

Jesus Christ's disciples are to seek only God's approval in their religious duties Mt 6:1

How religious duties are to be performed Mt 6:2–4 *Giving to the poor is to be done secretly;* Mt 6:5–8 *Prayer is not to become a public display;* Mt 6:16–18 *Fasting is to be done without show.*

The kingdom is to be valued above material possessions Mt 6:19–21 *See also* Mt 6:24–34 pp Lk 12:22–31

Jesus Christ's disciples are to avoid being judgmental Mt 7:1–2 *See also* Mt 7:3–5 pp Lk 6:41–42

Jesus Christ's disciples should pray, confident of an answer Mt 7:7–8 pp Lk 11:9–10 *See also* Mt 7:9–12 pp Lk 11:11–13

A pattern for prayer Mt 6:9–15 pp Lk 11:2–4

True disciples will obey Jesus Christ's teaching Mt 7:21 *See also* Mt 7:15–20,24–27 pp Lk 6:47–49

Characteristics of Jesus Christ's teaching in the Sermon on the Mount
Mt 7:28–29

See also
1620 beatitudes, the   8297 love for God
2375 kingdom of   8429 fasting
     God   8434 giving
5675 divorce   8452 neighbours,
5789 anger   duty to
8114 discipleship   8658 Lord's Prayer
8154 righteousness
8242 ethics, personal

1670
symbols

Objects, actions or creatures that have a deeper significance and are so understood by those who see them or use them.

Symbolic objects
The rainbow: a symbol of God's covenant Ge 9:13; Eze 1:28; Rev 4:3

A stairway: a symbol of the way to God Ge 28:11–13; Jn 1:51

Thunder, lightning, cloud and smoke: symbols of God's majesty
Ex 19:16–18; 24:17; Ps 97:2,4; Rev 4:5; 8:5; 11:19

Thunder: a symbol of God's voice Ps 29:3; 68:33

Trumpets: a symbol of God speaking Ex 19:19; Rev 8:6

The pillar of cloud and fire: a symbol of guidance Ex 13:21

A throne: a symbol of God's glory Isa 6:1; Eze 1:26; Rev 4:2; 22:3

Dry bones: a symbol of spiritual death Eze 37:1–2,11

White hair: a symbol of wisdom Da 7:9; Rev 1:14

The wind: a symbol of the Holy Spirit Jn 3:8; Ac 2:2

Fire: a symbol of the Holy Spirit Ac 2:3

Stars and lampstands: symbols of God's ministers Rev 1:20

A signet ring: a symbol of authority Est 8:10; Hag 2:23

Arrows: symbols of God's judgments Ps 38:2; 120:4

A sceptre: a symbol of God's rule Ps 2:9; Rev 2:27; 19:15

The capstone: a symbol of pre-eminence Mt 21:42 pp Mk 12:10–11 pp Lk 20:17; Ps 118:22

A rock: a symbol of stability Ps 18:2; 40:2

The human body: a symbol of interdependence 1Co 12:27

Grass: a symbol of human frailty Ps 90:5–6; 1Pe 1:24

Symbolic creatures
The serpent: a symbol of Satan's subtlety Ge 3:1; Rev 12:9; 20:1–3

Locusts: a symbol of God's judgment Ex 10:12; Joel 1:4; Rev 9:3

Beasts: symbols of earthly kingdoms Da 7:2–7,17; 8:20–22

A dove: a symbol of the Holy Spirit Mt 3:16 pp Mk 1:10 pp Lk 3:22

A lamb: a symbol of Jesus Christ's sacrifice Rev 5:6

Symbolic actions

Breaking a jar: a symbol of the destruction of Jerusalem Jer 19:10–11

The cursing of a fig-tree: a symbol of judgment Mt 21:18–19 pp Mk 11:12–14

Washing hands: a symbol of innocence Mt 27:24

Being thirsty: a symbol of spiritual need Ps 63:1; Jn 7:37

Baptism: a symbol of salvation in Jesus Christ Ac 22:16; Ro 6:3–4; 1Pe 3:21

The Lord's Supper: a symbol of union with Christ Mt 26:26–29 pp Mk 14:22–24 pp Lk 22:19–20 pp 1Co 11:23–26

Anointing: a symbol of empowering by God's Spirit 1Sa 16:13; Lk 4:18; Isa 61:1

Harvesting: a symbol of judgment day Joel 3:12–13; Mt 13:29–30; Rev 14:15

Tearing garments: a symbol of anger and sorrow Ge 37:29,34; Jos 7:6

Spitting: a symbol of contempt Isa 50:6; Mt 26:67 pp Mk 14:65

Shaking off dust: a symbol of rejection Mt 10:14 pp Lk 9:5; Ac 13:51

Sitting in sackcloth and ashes: a symbol of repentance Ps 69:11; Isa 22:12; Jnh 3:5–6; Mt 11:21

Lifting of hands: a symbol of prayer Ps 63:4; 1Ti 2:8

Covering the head: a symbol of submission 1Co 11:3–10

Symbols expressing God's nature and character

God's face: a symbol of his presence Nu 6:25–26; Ps 34:16

God's arm or hand: a symbol of his power Ps 21:8; 89:13

God's eyes: a symbol of his awareness Pr 15:3; 1Pe 3:12

God's ear: a symbol of God listening Ps 31:2; Isa 59:1

See also

1210 God, human descriptions	6732 repentance
1448 signs	7271 Zion, as symbol
1650 numbers, significance	7903 baptism
3120 Holy Spirit, descriptions	7933 Lord's Supper
5865 gestures	9210 judgment, God's

1680

types

An OT institution, person, place or event regarded as anticipating the person of Jesus Christ or some aspect of the Christian faith or life.

OT foreshadowings of Jesus Christ
Lk 24:25–27 *See also* Lk 24:44; 1Pe 1:10–12

OT institutions as types
The Sabbath: Jesus Christ's finished work Heb 4:3–6 *See also* Ge 2:2–3; Heb 4:9–10

Marriage: Jesus Christ's union with his people Eph 5:30–32 *See also* Ge 2:22–24 *Adam may be viewed as a figure of Jesus Christ, and Eve, of the church, formed in Christ, loved and united with him;* Ps 45:10–11; Mt 9:15; 25:1; Jn 3:29; Eph 5:25–27; Rev 19:7; 21:2

Circumcision: believers' union with Christ Col 2:11 *See also* Ge 17:9–14; Ro 2:29; Php 3:3

The tabernacle: Jesus Christ's coming among his people Jn 1:14 *The context shows that "The Word" is Jesus Christ; "made his dwelling" involves the idea of pitching a tent and reflects the tabernacle which was pitched among the Israelites and filled with God's glory; so Christ has pitched his tent among his people and revealed his glory. See also* Ex 25:8; 40:34–35

The tabernacle: the way to God Heb 9:11–12 *See also* Ex 25:22; 30:6,36; Nu 17:4; Heb 9:8; 10:19–22

The high priesthood: Jesus Christ as intercessor Heb 7:23–28 *See also* Ex 29:1–7; Lev 16:11–17; Heb 4:14–16; 5:1–5 *Jesus Christ, the great high priest, is both human and divine;* Heb 9:11–12; 10:11–12 *Note the contrast between the many OT sacrifices and Jesus Christ's once-for-all offering of himself.*

The priesthood: Christian worship and service Heb 13:15–16 *See also* Ex 19:6; 29:8–9; 1Pe 2:5; Rev 1:6

Sacrifices: Jesus Christ as substitute Ro 3:25 *See also* Lev 4:13–15,25–35 *Hands laid on the head of the sacrifice symbolised the transfer of guilt and its consequences to another. A perfect animal was required;* Isa 53:4–12; Mk 15:25–37; 2Co 5:15; Gal 2:20; 1Pe 3:18

Sacrifice: believers' consecration Ro 12:1 *See also* Lev 1:1–9; Nu 15:1–12; Php 2:17; 2Ti 4:6

The day of atonement: Jesus Christ as sin-bearer Heb 9:28 *See also* Lev 16:1–34; Heb 9:7

Passover: deliverance from judgment 1Co 5:7 *See also* Ex 12:1–16; Mt 26:17 pp Mk 14:12 pp Lk 22:7; Mt 26:26–29 pp Mk 14:22–25 pp Lk 22:14–20; Jn 1:29; 1Pe 1:18–19

Redemption: release from sin Mt 20:28 pp Mk 10:45 *"Redemption" and "ransom" both involve buying back that which has been lost. See also* Ex 13:11–13; 21:28–32; Job 19:25; Ps 78:35; Isa 41:14; Ro 3:24; 1Co 6:20 *Redemption from the "curse of the law":* Gal 3:13; 4:5 Eph 1:7 *Blood is the ransom price for the forgiveness of sin;* 1Ti 2:6; Tit 2:14; Heb 9:15

The temple: the church 2Co 6:16 *See also* 1Ki 6:1; 8:10–13; 1Co 3:16; Eph 2:21–22; 1Pe 2:5

OT places as types
The promised land: rest in Christ Heb 4:8–11 *See also* Jos 1:13; 11:23; 14:15

Jerusalem: the glorified church Rev 21:1–3 *See also* 2Sa 5:4–5; Ps 122:1–9; Isa 62:6–7; Zec 2:3–5;

Heb 12:22–23; Rev 3:12; 21:9–10

Babylon: enmity to Jesus Christ Rev 17:5 *Some take Babylon to represent the world, some the apostate church, some a city. See also* Isa 13:19–22; Rev 18:2–3

OT people as types
Israel: the church 1Pe 2:9 *See also* Ge 12:1–3; Ex 19:6; Ro 9:6–8; Gal 6:16; Eph 2:19

Adam: Jesus Christ as the head of his people 1Co 15:21–22 *See also* Ge 3:17–19; Ro 5:12–20 *Just as Adam was the representative of all humanity in the fall, so Jesus Christ is the representative of all who inherit salvation.*

Abraham: justifying faith in Jesus Christ Ro 4:18–25 *See also* Ge 15:6; Gal 3:6–9

Melchizedek: Jesus Christ as priest-king Heb 7:1–3 *See also* Ge 14:17–20; Ps 110:4; Heb 7:11–17

Sarah and Hagar: grace and law Gal 4:22–26 *See also* Ge 16:1–6; 21:10; Gal 4:27–31

David: Jesus Christ as king, shepherd and sufferer Lk 1:31–33 *See also* 2Sa 7:11–16; Ps 78:70–72; 89:19–37; Jn 13:18; Ps 41:9; Rev 22:16

Solomon: Jesus Christ as wise ruler Mt 12:42 *See also* 1Ki 3:5–12

OT events as types
Noah's ark: salvation 1Pe 3:20–21 *See also* Ge 7:7

Abraham offering Isaac: God giving his Son Ro 8:32 *See also* Ge 22:9–14

Crossing the Red Sea: Christian commitment 1Co 10:1–2 *See also* Ex 14:15–22

Water from a rock: Jesus Christ's provision 1Co 10:4 *See also* Ex 17:5–6

The bronze snake: Jesus Christ, the object of faith Jn 3:14–15 *See also* Nu 21:4–9

See also

1670 symbols	5089 David, significance
2306 Christ, high priest	5100 Melchizedek
2312 Christ as king	6720 redemption
2315 Christ as Lamb	6750 sin-bearer
5078 Abraham, significance	7140 people of God
5083 Adam, and Christ	7470 temple, significance

1690

word of God

The utterances of God, especially as revealed in Scripture. This may take the form of commands or promises. The term can also refer to Jesus Christ as the incarnate Word of God.

The word of God revealed as law
God has made his commands and requirements known Ps 147:19 *See also* Ex 20:1–17; 24:3; 34:27–28; Dt 5:5; Isa 2:3 pp Mic 4:2; Mt 15:6 pp Mk 7:13

2000

God's law is to be obeyed Dt 30:14 *See also* Jos 23:6; Ps 119:4; Lk 8:21; 11:28; Jas 1:22–23

Examples of disobedience and its consequences Nu 15:31; 1Sa 15:23–26; 2Sa 12:9; 1Ch 10:13; 2Ch 34:21; Isa 5:24; Jer 8:9

The word of God as prophecy

The prophets spoke the words of God Jer 1:9; 1Sa 3:1; Jer 25:3 *God's prophetic word came to Israel with varying frequency. See also* 1Ki 17:24; 2Ki 24:2; 2Ch 36:12,15; Isa 16:13; 24:3; Jer 7:1; 14:1; Am 8:11–12; Mal 1:1

Prophetic introductory formulae
"The word of the LORD came to ...":
Ge 15:1; 1Sa 15:10; 2Sa 24:11; 1Ki 6:11; 2Ki 20:4 pp Isa 38:4; Jer 16:1; Eze 6:1; Jnh 1:1; Zec 1:1
"Hear the word of the LORD": 1Ki 22:19; 2Ki 20:16 pp Isa 39:5; Isa 1:10; Jer 2:4; Hos 4:1
"This is what the LORD says": 2Sa 7:5 pp 1Ch 17:4; 2Ki 1:6; Isa 37:6; Jer 2:5; Eze 2:4; Am 1:3; Hag 2:11

Prophetic predictions fulfilled
1Ki 12:15 *See also* 1Ki 15:29; 16:12,34; 22:38; 2Ki 1:17; 9:36; 10:17; 14:25; 15:12; 23:16; 2Ch 36:21–22

The word "against" a people, indicating judgment Isa 9:8; 37:22; Jer 25:30; Am 3:1; Zep 2:5; Zec 9:1

True prophecy is inspired by God 2Pe 1:20–21 *See also* Ne 9:30; Jer 23:16,25–26,30; Eze 13:1–3; Mic 3:8

A true prophet hears from God 2Ki 3:12; Jer 5:13; 23:18; 27:18

The prophetic word is to be heeded Ex 9:20–21; Jer 6:10; 25:3; Zec 7:12

The word of God as Scripture

Scripture is the written word of God Da 9:2 *See also* Ro 3:2; 15:4

NT writings are classified as Scripture 1Ti 5:18; 2Pe 3:16

Scripture is inspired and true Jn 10:35; 2Ti 3:15

The foundational importance of Scripture
It must not be distorted or changed: Dt 4:2; 12:32; Pr 30:6; 2Co 2:17; 4:2; 2Ti 2:15; Rev 22:19
It is to be read publicly: Ne 8:1–8; 1Ti 4:13
It is to be meditated upon: Ps 1:2; 119:15,97
It is the test of orthodoxy: Isa 8:20; Ac 17:11
Mt 22:29 pp Mk 12:24
It is the basis for preaching: Ac 17:2; 18:28
1Co 4:6 *It sets the limit of authoritative doctrine.*

Jesus Christ as the incarnate Word of God

Jesus Christ is God in the flesh Jn 1:1 *See also* Jn 1:14; 12:45; Col 1:15; Heb 1:2; 1Jn 1:1; Rev 19:13

Jesus Christ speaks the Father's words Jn 8:40 *See also* Mt 22:16 pp Mk 12:14 pp Lk 20:21; Jn 7:18

Jesus Christ's words have sovereign power Mt 8:8 pp Lk 7:7; Mt 8:16; Heb 1:3

The gospel as the word of God

It was preached by Jesus Christ Mk 2:2 *See also* Mt 13:19–23 pp Mk 4:14–20 pp Lk 8:11–15; Mk 4:33; Lk 4:43 pp Mk 1:38; Lk 5:1

It was preached by the first Christians 1Th 2:13 *See also* Mk 16:20; Ac 6:2; 8:4; 11:1 *to the Gentiles;* Ac 13:5 *to the Jews;* Ac 15:35–36; 17:13; 1Co 14:36; 2Co 2:17; 4:2; Php 1:14; Col 1:25; 2Ti 4:2

It leads to numerical and spiritual growth within the church Ac 6:7; 12:24; 13:49; 19:20; Col 1:5–6; 1Th 2:13 *Paul stresses that the preached word is not merely a verbal message but a dynamic power which achieves things.*

It must be preached Ro 10:14; 2Ti 4:2

Descriptions of God's word

It is true: Ps 33:4; Jn 17:17
It is flawless: 2Sa 22:31 pp Ps 18:30; Pr 30:5
It is infallible: 1Ki 8:56; 2Ki 10:10
Ps 103:20 *It is obeyed by angels.*
It is eternal: Ps 119:89,152; Isa 40:8; 1Pe 1:25
Ps 119:103 *It is sweet and delightful;*
Ps 138:2 *It is exalted above all things;*
Isa 45:23 *It is irrevocable;* Eph 6:17 *It is the sword of the Spirit;* 2Ti 2:9 *It is not chained;* Heb 4:12 *It is living and active;* 1Pe 1:23 *It is living and enduring.*

Comparisons of the word of God with everyday things

Food: Dt 8:3; Job 23:12; Ps 119:103; Jer 15:16; Eze 2:8; 3:1; 1Pe 2:2
Ps 119:105 *light*
Fire: Jer 5:14; 20:9; 23:29
Jer 23:29 *a hammer;* Heb 4:12 *a two-edged sword*

The word of God has power

It is active Isa 55:11 *The Hebrew for "word" can also mean "action" or "deed". This indicates that God's word is active.*

It brings about creation Ps 33:6 *See also* 2Pe 3:5

It governs and maintains the created order Heb 1:3 *See also* Ps 147:18

It gives life Dt 8:3 *See also* Isa 55:2–3; Mt 4:4 pp Lk 4:4

It consecrates secular things 1Ti 4:5 *"the word of God and prayer" probably means "scriptural prayer"; i.e., on the basis of scriptural teaching the believer offers thanksgiving and prayer.*

It restrains from evil Ps 17:4; 119:11

It heals and rescues Ps 107:20

It has power to save Jas 1:21 *See also* 2Ti 3:15; 1Pe 1:23

It brings about the growth of the kingdom of God Mt 13:23 pp Mk 4:20 pp Lk 8:15

It builds up the saints Ac 20:32

See also
1403 God, revelation
1427 prophecy
1439 revelation
1611 Scripture, inspiration & authority
2420 gospel
3224 Holy Spirit & preaching
3281 Holy Spirit, inspiration
5375 law
5627 word
7754 preaching
8662 meditation
8674 study

2000

Jesus Christ

2003

Jesus Christ, qualities of

2006

God, the Son

The co-equal and co-eternal Son of the Father, who became incarnate in Jesus Christ for the redemption of the world. Scripture stresses both the divinity and the humanity of the incarnate Son of God, and the necessity and total sufficiency of his atoning death for human redemption. Through his resurrection and ascension, he intercedes for believers at the right hand of God.

This set of themes consists of the following:

2009 Jesus Christ, anger of
2012 Jesus Christ, authority of
2015 Jesus Christ, compassion of
2018 Jesus Christ, divinity of
2021 Jesus Christ, faithfulness of
2024 Jesus Christ, glory of
2027 Jesus Christ, grace and mercy of
2030 Jesus Christ, holiness of
2033 Jesus Christ, humanity of
2036 Jesus Christ, humility of
2039 Jesus Christ, joy of
2042 Jesus Christ, justice of
2045 Jesus Christ, knowledge of
2048 Jesus Christ, love of
2051 Jesus Christ, majesty of
2054 Jesus Christ, mind of
2057 Jesus Christ, obedience of
2060 Jesus Christ, patience of
2063 Jesus Christ, perfection of
2066 Jesus Christ, power of
2069 Jesus Christ, pre-eminence of
2072 Jesus Christ, righteousness of
2075 Jesus Christ, sinlessness of
2078 Jesus Christ, sonship of
2081 Jesus Christ, wisdom of

2009

Jesus Christ, anger of

Jesus Christ's controlled emotion arising from his unswerving opposition to evil and his determination to eradicate it.

Causes of Jesus Christ's anger

Petty legalism in religious observance Mt 15:3; 23:1–4; Mk 3:4–5

Attempts to prevent access to him Mk 10:14

People leading others into sin Mt 18:6–7 pp Mk 9:42 pp Lk 17:1–2

Demonstrations of Jesus Christ's anger

Purging the temple Mt 21:12–13
pp Mk 11:15–17 pp Lk 19:45–46;
Jn 2:14–16

Cursing the fig-tree Mk 11:14
pp Mt 21:19

Jesus Christ's words in anger

Against demons Mt 17:18 pp Mk 9:25
pp Lk 9:42 *See also* Mk 1:25–26
pp Lk 4:35

Against disciples Lk 9:55–56 *See also*
Mt 16:23 pp Mk 8:33

Against Pharisees Mt 23:13 *See also*
Mt 12:34; 15:7–9 pp Mk 7:6–8;
Mt 23:15–16,23–33; Lk 11:42–44;
13:15; Jn 8:44

Against unbelief Mt 17:17 pp Mk 9:19
pp Lk 9:41 *See also* Mt 12:39–45
pp Lk 11:29–32; Mk 8:38; Lk 11:50–51

Against false prophets Mt 7:15

Against the rich Lk 6:24–26

Against unrepentant cities Mt 11:20
See also Mt 11:21–24 pp Lk 10:13–15

Jesus Christ reflects the anger of God

Jn 3:36 *See also* Mt 5:21–22,29; 22:7,13;
25:30,46; Lk 21:23

The anger of the glorified Christ

Against the unbelieving world Rev 6:16

Against the wayward church Rev 2:16
See also Rev 2:5,22–23; 3:3,16

See also

1025 God, anger of	5790 anger, divine
2042 Christ, justice of	6178 hardness of heart
2072 Christ, righteousness	7552 Pharisees, attitudes to Christ
4135 demons, Christ's authority over	8749 false teachers
	8835 unbelief
5503 rich, the	9240 last judgment

2012
Jesus Christ, authority of

The right of Jesus Christ to speak and
act on his Father's behalf in forgiving
sin, pronouncing judgment and
promising eternal life to those who
believe in him.

Jesus Christ's authority underlines his divine status

Jn 8:28 *See also* Jn 8:58; 14:6; 1Co 1:24;
Col 2:10

The origin of Jesus Christ's authority

It is given by God the Father Jn 3:35 *See
also* Mt 28:18; Lk 10:22; Jn 5:26–27;
7:16; 10:18; 12:49–50; 17:2

It is limited by the Father Mk 10:40 *See
also* Mt 24:36 pp Mk 13:32; Php 2:6–8

It is questioned by others Mt 12:24–28
pp Mk 3:22–26 pp Lk 11:15–20 *See also*
Mt 21:23–27 pp Mk 11:27–33
pp Lk 20:1–8; Jn 2:18

The authority of Jesus Christ is seen in his works

He has authority over nature
Mt 8:23–27 pp Mk 4:36–41

pp Lk 8:22–25; Mt 14:22–33
pp Mk 6:45–51 pp Jn 6:15–21;
Mt 21:18–22 pp Mk 11:12–14; 20–24

He has authority over sin Mt 9:1–8
pp Mk 2:3–12 pp Lk 5:18–26;
Lk 7:37–38,44–50

He has authority over sickness
Mt 8:14–15 pp Mk 1:30–31
pp Lk 4:38–39; Mt 20:29–34
pp Mk 10:46–52 pp Lk 18:35–43;
Ac 3:16; 4:30

He has authority over evil Mk 1:23–27
pp Lk 4:33–36; Lk 10:17

He has authority over death
Mt 9:18–25 pp Mk 5:22–42
pp Lk 8:40–55; Mt 28:1–7
pp Mk 16:1–6 pp Lk 24:1–8
pp Jn 20:1–17; Lk 7:11–16;
Jn 11:38–44

The authority of Jesus Christ is seen in his teaching

**Jesus Christ claims authority for his
own words** Lk 4:18 *See also*
Mt 5:21–22,27–28; 12:41–42; 17:5
pp Mk 9:7 pp Lk 9:35; Mk 2:5,10; 8:38;
10:15 *The use of the phrase "I tell you the
truth" emphasises Jesus Christ's authority*;
Mk 13:26,31; Jn 4:24–26; 6:63;
7:15–18; 12:48–50; 13:13; 14:6 *The "I
am" sayings in John's Gospel emphasise
the divine nature of Jesus Christ's
authority*; Jn 15:3

His authority is recognised by others
Mt 7:28–29 *See also* Mt 22:33,46;
Mk 1:22,27 pp Lk 4:32

**His authority is questioned and
opposed by others** Mt 26:65–68;
Lk 4:28–30

Jesus Christ delegates his authority to others

His followers preach in his name
Mt 10:7; 28:18–20

His followers continue his works
Mt 10:1 pp Mk 6:7 pp Lk 9:1–2; Mt 10:8;
Mk 3:15; 6:13; 16:17–18; Lk 10:1–12;
Jn 14:12; Ac 3:6,16

**His followers pronounce his
forgiveness and judgment** Mt 18:18;
Mk 6:11; Lk 22:28–30; Jn 20:22–23;
1Co 6:2–3

The results of Jesus Christ's authority

He receives honour and glory
Jn 5:22–23 *See also* Jn 11:4; 17:5

He arouses amazement Mt 9:33; 12:23

He is opposed Mt 12:14 pp Mk 3:6
pp Lk 6:11

He is feared Lk 8:37 pp Mt 8:34

His disciples are opposed Ac 16:16–24

The authority of the exalted Christ

He is Lord Eph 1:20; Php 2:9–11;
Col 3:1; 1Pe 3:22; Rev 3:21

He is Lord of creation Col 1:16–17

He is Lord of the church Eph 1:22; 5:23;
Col 1:18

He is judge Ac 10:42; 17:31

He is Saviour Jn 3:15; 14:3;
Col 1:19–20; Tit 2:13; Heb 7:24–25;
9:28

He is interceder Ro 8:34; Heb 7:25;
9:24; 1Jn 2:1

See also

2018 Christ, divinity	2336 Christ, exaltation
2066 Christ, power of	
2212 Christ, head of church	2369 Christ, responses to
2224 Christ, the Lord	4165 exorcism
2309 Christ as judge	5215 authority
2312 Christ as king	6654 forgiveness, Christ's ministry
2324 Christ as Saviour	

2015
Jesus Christ, compassion of

Jesus Christ's pity and loving
concern for the lowly and the needy.
His words and deeds show God's
merciful and gracious nature in
action.

Jesus Christ shows the compassion of God

2Co 1:3 *See also* 2Ch 36:15; Ps 86:15;
Hos 11:4,8–9; Lk 1:72,78; 15:20

The compassion of Jesus Christ is the basis of Christian confidence

Heb 4:14–16 *The Greek word here
translated "sympathise" has the sense of
"be compassionate towards".*

The demonstration of Jesus Christ's compassion

In supporting the weak Mt 12:20 *See
also* Isa 42:3; Mt 19:14 pp Mk 10:14
pp Lk 18:16

In healing the sick Mt 14:14 pp Lk 9:11
See also Mt 20:34 pp Mk 10:52
pp Lk 18:42–43; Mk 1:41 pp Mt 8:3
pp Lk 5:13; Lk 13:12

In comforting the bereaved Lk 7:13 *See
also* Lk 8:50 pp Mk 5:36; Jn 11:33–35;
19:25–27; 20:14–16

In feeding the hungry Mt 15:32
pp Mk 8:2–3 *See also* Mt 14:16
pp Mk 6:37 pp Lk 9:13 pp Jn 6:5–6

In finding and forgiving lost sinners
Mt 9:36 pp Mk 6:34 *See also* Isa 40:11;
Mt 18:14; 23:37–38 pp Lk 13:34–35;
Lk 7:47–48; Jn 8:10–11

**In giving rest to those who are
burdened or abandoned** Mt 11:28–29
See also Mk 1:40–41 pp Mt 8:1–3
pp Lk 5:12–13; Lk 11:46; 15:1–2;
17:12–14

Jesus Christ's compassion is a model for Christians to follow

Lk 10:36–37 *See also* Jn 13:34; 17:18;
Php 2:1

See also

1030 God, compassion	5279 crowds
1055 God, grace & mercy	5448 poverty, attitudes to
2027 Christ, grace & mercy	5805 comfort
	5806 compassion
2048 Christ, love of	6652 forgiveness
2066 Christ, power of	6689 mercy of Christ
2351 Christ, miracles	

2018

Jesus Christ, divinity of

The equality and identity of Jesus Christ as God is clearly stated in the NT, and is also implied by the words and deeds of Jesus Christ. The OT prophecies also point to the divinity of the coming Messiah.

The NT writers affirm Jesus Christ's divinity

Heb 1:8 *See also* Ps 45:6; Jn 1:1–2,18; Ro 9:5 *NIV footnote has alternative translations: "Christ who is over all. God be for ever praised!" Or: "Christ. God who is over all be for ever praised!"*; Php 2:6; Tit 2:13; 2Pe 1:1

Statements which imply Jesus Christ's divinity

Mt 1:23 *See also* Isa 7:14; Lk 1:35; Col 1:15; 2:2,9; 1Ti 1:17; 1Jn 5:20

Jesus Christ's unity with the Father and the Holy Spirit in the Godhead

Mt 28:19 *See also* Jn 14:16; 2Co 13:14; Eph 1:13–14; 2:18,22; 3:14–17; 4:4–6

Jesus Christ's eternal nature indicates his divinity

Jesus Christ precedes creation Col 1:17 *See also* Mic 5:2; Jn 17:5,24; 2Ti 1:9; 1Pe 1:20; 1Jn 1:1; 2:13

Jesus Christ is everlasting Jn 8:58 *See also* Heb 1:12; Ps 102:27; Heb 7:3,24; 13:8; Rev 1:8; 5:13; 22:13

Jesus Christ's pre-existence indicates his divinity

Jn 6:62 *See also* Jn 3:13,31; 6:41–42; 13:3; 16:28

Jesus Christ's manifestation of God's glory indicates his divinity

Heb 1:3 *See also* Mt 17:2 pp Mk 9:2–3 pp Lk 9:29; Jn 1:14; 1Co 2:8; 2Co 4:4; Jas 2:1

Jesus Christ's divinity in the OT

The divinity of the coming Messiah Isa 9:6; 40:3; Jer 23:6; Mal 3:1

NT passages which apply OT passages about God to Jesus Christ Ro 10:13 *See also* Joel 2:32; Jn 12:40–41; Isa 6:10; Ro 9:33; Isa 8:14; Eph 4:8; Ps 68:18

Jesus Christ's claims to divinity

He claimed to be one with the Father Jn 5:17–18 *See also* Jn 10:30–33,36–38; 12:45; 14:7,9–11; 17:11,21

He demonstrated his authority to forgive sin Lk 5:20–24 pp Mt 9:2–6 pp Mk 2:5–10 *See also* Lk 7:47–48

Jesus Christ's actions imply his divinity

Mt 8:26–27 pp Mk 4:39–41 pp Lk 8:24–25 *See also* Mt 12:8 pp Mk 2:28 pp Lk 6:5; Lk 8:39 pp Mk 5:19–20

Jesus Christ's resurrection confirms his divinity

Ac 2:36 *See also* Ro 1:4; Php 2:9–11

Jesus Christ's names and titles point to his divinity

Jesus Christ as judge Jn 5:27 *In the OT, final responsibility for judgment is assigned to God. See also* Mt 25:31–33; Mk 8:38 pp Mt 16:27 pp Lk 9:26; Ac 17:31; Ro 2:16; 2Co 5:10

Jesus Christ as "I am" Jn 11:25 *"I am" is the meaning of God's name in the OT (see Ex 3:14). See also* Jn 6:35; 8:12; 10:7,11; 14:6; 15:1; 18:5–6

Jesus Christ as Saviour Ac 5:31 *According to the OT, God alone can save. See also* Ac 4:12; Eph 5:23; Heb 7:25

Jesus Christ as Lord Ro 10:9 *"Lord" was equivalent to God's name in the OT. See also* Lk 1:43; 2:11; Jn 13:13; 1Co 12:3; 2Co 4:5; Rev 19:16

Jesus Christ as creator Col 1:16 *See also* Jn 1:3,10; Ac 3:15; Ro 11:36; 1Co 8:6; Heb 1:2,10; Ps 102:25

Jesus Christ as shepherd Heb 13:20 *"Shepherd" was a well-known OT name for God. See also* Jn 10:11–16; 1Pe 2:25; 5:4

Those who recognised Jesus Christ's divinity

The disciples Jn 20:28 *See also* Mt 16:16 pp Mk 8:29 pp Lk 9:20

The demons Mk 3:11; Lk 4:41 pp Mk 1:34

The consequences of recognising Jesus Christ's divinity

Jesus Christ is worshipped as God Lk 24:52 *The fact that no-one but God may be worshipped is fundamental to Judaism. See also* Mt 2:11; 28:9,17; Jn 9:38; 2Ti 4:18; 2Pe 3:18; Rev 1:5–6; 5:12–13; 7:10

Prayer is addressed to Jesus Christ Ac 7:59–60; 9:13; 1Co 16:22; Rev 22:20

2021

Jesus Christ, faithfulness of

The total reliability and constancy of Jesus Christ is shown in his personal character, and made known by his words and works.

Jesus Christ's faithfulness is seen in his character

He is faithful by nature Rev 19:11 *A description of the exalted Christ. See also* Rev 1:5; 3:14

The promised Messiah is faithful Isa 11:5 *See also* Isa 42:3

Jesus Christ is faithful because he never changes Heb 13:8 *See also* Heb 1:11–12; Ps 102:26–27

Jesus Christ is faithful because he is the truth Jn 1:14 *"grace" and "truth" are often associated in Hebrew with love and faithfulness. See also* Jn 1:17; 14:6

Jesus Christ's faithfulness demonstrated in his obedience

He is faithful to his Father Jn 3:6 *See also* Lk 2:49; Jn 5:30; 6:38; 8:29; 14:31; Heb 3:2

He kept faithfully to his work Lk 4:43 pp Mk 1:38 *See also* Jn 4:34; 9:4; 12:27; 17:4; 19:30; Heb 2:17–18

Jesus Christ's faithfulness is seen in his words

In his predictions about events Mt 16:28 pp Mk 9:1 pp Lk 9:27 *This prediction could refer to either Jesus Christ's transfiguration or his ascension;* Mt 24:2 pp Mk 13:2 pp Lk 21:6 *This prediction was fulfilled in A.D. 70 when the Romans destroyed Jerusalem and the temple. See also* Mt 21:2 pp Mk 11:2 pp Lk 19:30 *finding a donkey and her colt;* Mt 26:21 pp Mk 14:18 pp Lk 22:21 pp Jn 13:21 *Jesus Christ's betrayer;* Mt 26:34 pp Mk 14:30 pp Lk 22:34 pp Jn 13:38 *Peter's denial;* Jn 16:20; 21:18–19

In his promises about eternal life Jn 5:24 *See also* Mt 19:28–29 pp Mk 10:29–30 pp Lk 18:29–30; Lk 23:43; Jn 6:47,53–54; 8:51

In his promise of authority for believers Mt 17:20 *See also* Mt 16:19; 18:18; 21:21 pp Mk 11:23; Mt 28:18–19; Lk 10:19

In his promise about the Holy Spirit Jn 14:26 *See also* Lk 24:49; Jn 14:16; 15:26; 16:7; Ac 1:4,8; 2:38–39; 10:44–46; Ro 5:5; 1Co 12:7

Jesus Christ's promises about the future are faithful

Jn 14:2–3 *See also* Mt 16:27; 26:64; Jn 14:28

Jesus Christ is faithful to believers in all circumstances

2Ti 2:13 *See also* Mt 18:20; 28:20; Jn 17:9; Ac 18:9–10; 2Th 3:3; Heb 10:23

2024

Jesus Christ, glory of

Jesus Christ's radiance and splendour reflects the glory of the Father, and is both revealed to and reflected in the lives of believers.

Jesus Christ's glory existed before the incarnation

Jn 17:5 *See also* Jn 1:14; 17:24

Jesus Christ's glory is God's glory

God's glory is reflected in Jesus Christ Heb 1:3 *See also* Jn 12:41 *John makes no distinction between God's glory revealed in*

Isa 6:3 and the glory of Jesus Christ;
Jn 13:32; 2Co 4:4,6

Jesus Christ brings glory to his Father
Jn 14:13 *See also* Jn 13:31; 17:1,4;
Ro 16:27; Eph 1:12; Jude 25

The Holy Spirit glorifies Jesus Christ
Jn 16:14

Jesus Christ's glory is revealed on earth

Through his miracles Jn 2:11 *See also*
Jn 11:4,40

To his disciples Lk 9:28–32
pp Mt 17:1–2 pp Mk 9:2–3 *See also*
Jn 1:14; Ac 9:3; 22:6; 26:13; 2Pe 1:17

In his death and resurrection Jn 12:23
*One of the major themes of John's Gospel is
that Jesus Christ is glorified through his
death and resurrection. See also* Jn 7:39;
12:16; Ac 3:13–15; 1Pe 1:21; Heb 2:9

The glory of the exalted Christ

His appearance Rev 1:13–16 *See also*
Ac 7:55–56; Rev 2:18; 19:11–16

He receives glory from all creation
Rev 5:13 *See also* Heb 13:21; 2Pe 3:18;
Rev 1:6; 5:11–12; 7:9–12

Jesus Christ's glory will be revealed at the second coming

Mt 16:27 pp Mk 8:38 pp Lk 9:26 *See also*
Mt 24:27,30 pp Mk 13:26 pp Lk 21:27;
Mt 25:31; 2Th 1:7; 2:8; Tit 2:13;
1Pe 4:13

Jesus Christ's glory is shared by believers

As they become like him 2Co 3:18 *See
also* Jn 17:22; Col 1:27

At the end of time 1Co 15:49 *See also*
Ro 8:17–18; Php 3:21; Col 3:4

See also
1045 God, glory of
1190 glory
2018 Christ, divinity
2051 Christ, majesty of
2063 Christ, perfection
2336 Christ, exaltation
2351 Christ, miracles
2530 Christ, death of
2560 Christ, resurrection
2565 Christ, second coming
2580 Christ, transfiguration
8440 glorifying God

2027
Jesus Christ, grace and mercy of

The qualities of Jesus Christ by
which he is compassionate,
accepting and generous. In his
ministry, Christ demonstrates these
qualities towards those whom he
encounters. Believers should model
themselves upon Jesus Christ in this
respect.

The grace and mercy of God made known in Jesus Christ

Jn 1:14,16–17 *See also* Lk 2:40,52;
2Co 8:9; Tit 2:11 *Jesus Christ shows the
grace of God in his life.*

Grace and mercy in the ministry of Jesus Christ

**Jesus Christ responds to pleas for
mercy** Mt 9:27–30 *See also* Mt 15:22;
20:29–34 pp Mk 10:46–52
pp Lk 18:35–42

**His teaching reflects his grace and
mercy** Lk 6:35–36 *See also* Hos 6:6;
Mt 6:12–15 pp Lk 11:4; Mt 9:10–13
pp Mk 2:15–17 pp Lk 5:29–32;
Mt 18:21–35 *the parable of the
unmerciful servant;* Lk 10:30–37 *the
parable of the good Samaritan;* Eph 4:32

Grace and mercy in relation to salvation

The grace of Jesus Christ Ac 15:11 *See
also* Ro 3:24; 5:15; Eph 2:4–5,8; 2Ti 1:9

The mercy of Jesus Christ Lk 23:34 *See
also* Mt 9:2 pp Mk 2:3–5 pp Lk 5:18–20;
Lk 7:37–38,48; Ro 5:6,15; 1Ti 1:13–14
*Paul speaks about his persecution of the
Christians prior to his conversion
experience.*

Eternal life is a gift of grace and mercy
Ro 5:21 *See also* Ro 6:23; Tit 3:7

The grace and mercy of Jesus Christ and the Christian life

**The need to rely upon the grace of
Jesus Christ** 2Co 12:9; 2Ti 2:1 *See also*
Eph 4:7; 2Pe 3:18; Heb 4:16

Prayers for the grace of Jesus Christ
Ro 1:7 *See also* Ro 16:20; 1Co 16:23;
Gal 1:3; 6:18; Eph 6:24; Php 4:23; 2Jn 3;
Rev 22:21

See also
1055 God, grace & mercy
1352 covenant, the new
2015 Christ, compassion
2048 Christ, love of
2324 Christ as Saviour
2351 Christ, miracles
6510 salvation
6614 atonement
6644 eternal life
6652 forgiveness
6668 grace & Christ
6689 mercy of Christ

2030
Jesus Christ, holiness of

The holiness of Jesus Christ is seen in
his divine nature and work, as he
stands apart from and above the
created world with divine power,
authority and purity. Recognition of
the holiness of Jesus Christ leads
both to a realisation of sin and
unworthiness and to worship and
adoration.

The holy character of Jesus Christ

Its divine origin Lk 1:35 *See also*
Jn 1:1–2; 3:31; 8:23; 13:3; 17:14,16

Its divine nature Col 2:9 *See also*
Jn 1:14; 10:30,38; 14:10; Php 2:6;
Heb 1:3

Its divine purity Heb 7:26 *See also*
2Co 5:21; Heb 4:15; 1Pe 1:19; 2:22;
1Jn 3:3,5

Its divine power Ac 4:30 *See also*
Ac 10:38

The holy work of Jesus Christ

He is set apart as God's servant
Ac 4:27 *See also* Mk 10:45 pp Mt 20:28;
Jn 14:31; Ac 3:26; Php 2:7–8; Heb 10:7

**His life is consecrated to the will and
purpose of God** Mt 26:39
pp Mk 14:35–36 pp Lk 22:42 *See also*
Mt 26:42; Jn 12:49–50; 14:31

He is appointed as the judge of sinners
Jn 5:22,26–27; Ac 17:31; 2Co 5:10

He makes God's people holy
Heb 13:12 *See also* Jn 17:19;
Eph 5:25–27; Heb 2:11; 10:10,14;
1Pe 2:4–5,9–10

Declarations of the holiness of Jesus Christ

By David: Ps 16:10; Ac 2:27; 13:35
Mk 1:24 pp Lk 4:34 *by demons;* Lk 1:35
by the angel Gabriel
By Peter: Jn 6:69; Ac 3:14
Rev 3:7 *by Jesus Christ himself*

Results of recognising the holiness of Jesus Christ

Awareness of sin and unworthiness
Lk 5:8 *See also* Mt 8:8 pp Lk 7:6–7

Fear Mt 8:28–34 pp Mk 5:9–17
pp Lk 8:26–37; Rev 1:17

Adoration and worship Rev 5:8–14

See also
1065 God, holiness of
2018 Christ, divinity
2057 Christ, obedience
2063 Christ, perfection
2072 Christ, righteousness
2075 Christ, sinless
2309 Christ as judge
2327 Christ as servant
2351 Christ, miracles
2369 Christ, responses to
6606 access to God
8266 holiness

2033
Jesus Christ, humanity of

Scripture stresses the total humanity
of Jesus Christ. Although sinless,
Christ shared in the general
condition of humanity, including
suffering and death.

Jesus Christ was a man

By his own claims Jn 8:40 *See also*
Mt 8:20 pp Lk 9:58

In statements made by others Jn 19:5
See also Mt 8:27; Mk 15:39 pp Lk 23:47
the centurion; Lk 15:2 *the Pharisees and
teachers of the law;* Lk 23:18; Jn 1:33;
4:42; 7:12,15 *some Jews;* Jn 7:27; 9:33;
11:47; Ac 2:22–23

Jesus Christ shared in the general condition of humanity

He assumed human nature Jn 1:14
*"flesh" here speaks not only of a material
body but also of human nature. See also*
Php 2:7–8; Heb 2:14; 1Jn 4:2

He had a human descent Ro 1:3 *See also*
Mt 1:1; 13:54–56 pp Mk 6:2–3; Ro 9:5

**He had a normal body which could be
handled and touched** 1Jn 1:1 *See also*
Mt 14:36 pp Mk 6:56; Lk 2:28; 1Ti 3:16

He had a soul Mt 26:38 pp Mk 14:34
See also Isa 53:11

Jesus Christ partook of human experience

He was born Gal 4:4 *See also* Lk 2:6–7

He grew and developed Lk 2:40,52

He was hungry Mt 21:18 pp Mk 11:12
See also Mt 4:2 pp Lk 4:2

He was thirsty Jn 19:28 *See also* Jn 4:7

He was tired Jn 4:6

He slept Mt 8:24 pp Mk 4:38 pp Lk 8:23

He was tempted Heb 2:18 *See also* Mt 4:1 pp Mk 1:13 pp Lk 4:2; Heb 4:15

He suffered 1Pe 4:1 *See also* Col 1:22; Heb 5:7–8; 10:10; 1Pe 2:24

He died Mt 27:50 pp Mk 15:37 pp Lk 23:46 pp Jn 19:30 *Jesus Christ most closely identified with the rest of humanity through his death. However Jesus Christ is distinct from human beings in that his death was an act of free will and not the inevitable consequence of sin (see Jn 10:17–18). See also* Heb 2:9,14

The risen Christ has human characteristics
Lk 24:37–43 *See also* Jn 20:27

The returning Christ retains his human identity
Ac 1:11

Jesus Christ was a sinless human being
Heb 4:15 *Sinlessness does not make Jesus Christ less human. It is sin that degrades humanity. See also* Lk 23:41,47; Heb 7:26

The necessity of Jesus Christ's humanity
As a man Jesus Christ made atonement for sin Ro 5:18–19 *See also* Ro 5:12–17; 1Ti 2:5; Heb 2:17

As a man Jesus Christ gives the gift of resurrection 1Co 15:21 *See also* 1Co 15:45; Php 3:20–21

As a man Jesus Christ is able to help others in their need Heb 2:18 *See also* Heb 4:15–5:2

As a man Jesus Christ is the perfect example Php 2:5–8

See also

2063 Christ, perfection	2575 Christ, temptation
2221 Christ, Son of Man	2595 incarnation
2515 Christ, birth of	5020 human nature
2530 Christ, death of	6203 mortality
2540 Christ, genealogy	6252 temptation & Christ
2570 Christ, suffering	6684 mediator

2036
Jesus Christ, humility of

The obedient submission of Jesus Christ to his Father, seen in his willingness to become a human being for humanity's sake, his freedom from self-interest and his willingness to serve others.

Jesus Christ's willingness to become a human being
Php 2:6–7 *"human likeness" is not mere similarity to but identity with humanity. See also* Ro 8:3; 2Co 8:9

Jesus Christ's humility predicted in the OT
Mt 12:19–20; Isa 42:2–3; 50:4–6 *The suffering servant:* Mt 8:17;

Ac 8:32–33; Isa 53:2–7; 1Pe 2:22; Isa 53:9; 1Pe 2:24 *The coming king:* Mt 21:5 pp Jn 12:15; Zec 9:9 Zec 12:10 *The shepherd struck:* Mt 26:31 pp Mk 14:27; Zec 13:7

The poverty of Jesus Christ's birth and upbringing
Lk 2:7,12,16,22–24 *Only the poorest families offered doves or pigeons.*

Jesus Christ's obedience to his human parents
Lk 2:51

Jesus Christ's obedience to his heavenly Father
Jn 5:30 *See also* Jn 8:29; 15:10; Ro 5:19; 15:3; Php 2:8; Heb 5:8

Jesus Christ's dependence on his heavenly Father
Jn 5:19 *See also* Jn 5:30; 17:7

Jesus Christ's submission to baptism
Mt 3:13–15 pp Mk 1:9 pp Lk 3:21

Jesus Christ's humble acceptance of ill treatment
1Pe 2:23 *See also* Mt 26:63 pp Mk 14:61; Mt 26:66–67 pp Mk 14:64–65; Mt 27:14 pp Mk 15:5; Mt 27:28–30 pp Mk 15:17–19 pp Jn 19:2

Jesus Christ's acceptance of the cross
Php 2:8 *See also* Mt 26:39 pp Mk 14:36 pp Lk 22:42; Mt 26:53; Lk 23:34; Heb 5:7

Jesus Christ's humility with other people
Children: Mt 19:13–15 pp Mk 10:13–16 pp Lk 18:15–17 *Beggars:* Mt 20:29–34 pp Mk 10:46–52 pp Lk 18:35–43 Mk 1:40–42 *Leprosy sufferers;* Jn 4:5–9 *a Samaritan woman*

Jesus Christ's servant attitude
Mk 10:45 pp Mt 20:28 *See also* Mt 12:19–20; Jn 13:4–5,12; 2Co 10:1

Jesus Christ's teaching about humility
Mk 9:33–37 pp Mt 18:1–5 pp Lk 9:46–48 *See also* Mt 23:8–12; Mk 10:42–45 pp Mt 20:26–28; Lk 14:7–11; 18:9–14

Jesus Christ's humility as a model for others
Jn 13:12–17 *See also* Mt 11:29–30; Eph 5:25; Php 2:5; 1Pe 2:21

See also

2057 Christ, obedience	5564 suffering of Christ
2315 Christ as Lamb	5959 submission
2327 Christ as servant	8276 humility
2570 Christ, suffering	

2039
Jesus Christ, joy of

Jesus Christ brings joy to his people, who are able to rejoice at the coming

---

of their Saviour and Lord, and all the benefits which he brings to them.

Jesus Christ's joy originates in God
From his intimate relationship with his Father and the Spirit Lk 10:21 pp Mt 11:25–26 *See also* Isa 11:2–3; Mt 3:16–17 pp Mk 1:10–11 pp Lk 3:22; Mt 12:18; Isa 42:1; Ac 2:28; Ps 16:11

From his awareness of God's purposes Heb 12:2 *See also* Jn 8:29

Jesus Christ's coming brings great joy
His birth Lk 2:10–11 *See also* Mt 2:10; Lk 1:44; 2:20,28–32

His resurrection and ascension Jn 16:20–22 *See also* Mt 28:8–9; Lk 24:40–41,50–53; Jn 20:20

Jesus Christ gives joy to his people
He brings joy to his disciples Jn 17:13 *See also* Isa 61:1–3; Jn 15:11; Ro 12:12; Php 1:26

Being in his presence is likened to the joy of a wedding Mt 22:1–10 *See also* Mt 9:14–15 pp Mk 2:18–19 pp Lk 5:33–34; Mt 25:1–10; Jn 3:29; Rev 19:7,9

To know Jesus Christ brings great joy to others Lk 15:7 *See also* Mt 8:11; Lk 15:10,22–24,31–32; Jn 8:56

See also

1070 God, joy of	2555 Christ, resurrection appearances
1115 God, purpose of	
2505 Christ, ascension	3020 Holy Spirit, joy of
2515 Christ, birth of	8283 joy

2042
Jesus Christ, justice of

The teaching and lifestyle of Jesus Christ show him to be just and impartial in his judgments and dealings with people. At the end of the age, God has appointed Jesus Christ to judge and rule with justice.

Justice was a quality displayed in Jesus Christ's life
Mt 12:18–21 *See also* Isa 42:1–4

Jesus Christ was just and impartial in his dealings with people
Jn 4:9 *with Samaritans;* Jn 4:27 *with women;* Mt 9:10–12 pp Mk 2:15–17 pp Lk 5:29–31 *with tax collectors and those classed as "sinners";* Mt 15:21–28 pp Mk 7:24–29 *with the Gentiles*

Justice in the teaching of Jesus Christ
Mt 23:23 pp Lk 11:42 *See also* Mt 5:17–48; 7:1–5 pp Lk 6:37–42; Lk 12:58–59; 14:13–14; Jn 7:24; 8:7

Parables which teach justice
Lk 18:1–8 *See also* Mt 20:1–16; 25:14–30 pp Lk 19:12–27; Lk 16:19–31

Jesus Christ will judge the nations with justice
Ac 17:31 *See also* Ps 72:1–2 *a Messianic*

psalm; Isa 11:4; Jn 5:30; 8:15–16; Rev 19:11

Jesus Christ will rule the nations with justice

Isa 9:6–7 *See also* Isa 2:2–4 *This prophecy refers to the Messianic age when Jesus Christ will rule the world as king;* Isa 32:1 *"Branch" is a Messianic title:* Jer 23:5–6; 33:15–16 Mic 4:1–3; Rev 19:11–16

See also

1310 God as judge	2372 Christ, victory
2027 Christ, grace & mercy	5360 justice, God
	5882 impartiality
2072 Christ, righteousness	6689 mercy of Christ
	9145 Messianic age
2309 Christ as judge	9240 last judgment
2312 Christ as king	
2363 Christ, preaching & teaching	

2045
Jesus Christ, knowledge of

Jesus Christ has perfect insight into God's purposes and into human nature by reason of his intimate relationship with the Father, but he has accepted limited knowledge as a consequence of his humanity.

Jesus Christ's knowledge of his Father

Mt 11:27 pp Lk 10:22 *See also* Jn 7:29; 8:26,55; 10:15; 11:41–42; 15:15; 17:25

Jesus Christ's complete knowledge

Jn 16:30 *See also* Jn 21:17

Jesus Christ's foreknowledge of events

Jesus Christ's knowledge of his mission Jn 8:14 *See also* Jn 13:1,3; 16:28; 18:4; 19:28

Jesus Christ's knowledge of his death and resurrection Mt 16:21 pp Mk 8:31 pp Lk 9:22 *See also* Mt 20:18–19 pp Mk 10:33–34 pp Lk 18:31–33

Jesus Christ's knowledge of his betrayer Jn 6:64 *See also* Mt 26:20–25 pp Mk 14:17–20; Jn 13:11,18,21–26

Jesus Christ's knowledge of the disciples' desertion and Peter's denial Mt 26:31–34 pp Mk 14:27–30 pp Lk 22:31–34

Jesus Christ's knowledge of human beings

Jesus Christ knows every human heart Jn 2:24–25 *See also* Ac 1:24; Rev 2:23

Jesus Christ discerns evil thoughts and motives Mt 22:18 pp Mk 12:15 pp Lk 20:23 *See also* Mt 9:3–4 pp Mk 2:6–8 pp Lk 5:21–22; Mt 12:14–15,24–25 pp Lk 11:15–17; Lk 6:7–8; Jn 5:42; 6:15

Jesus Christ knows those whose faith is not genuine Mt 7:21–23

Jesus Christ knows people's situations and needs Jn 1:47–49 *See also* Mk 6:34; Lk 19:5; Jn 4:16–19,28–29; 5:6

Jesus Christ's knowledge of believers

Jesus Christ knows those who are his Jn 10:14 *See also* Jn 10:27; 20:15–16; 2Ti 2:19

Jesus Christ knows those who call on him in faith Mk 5:24–34 pp Mt 9:18–22 pp Lk 8:43–48 *See also* Mt 9:2 pp Mk 2:5 pp Lk 5:20

Jesus Christ knows believers' deeds Rev 2:2 *See also* Mt 10:42 pp Mk 9:41; Mt 16:27; 25:37–40; Rev 2:3,19,23

Jesus Christ knows believers' needs Mk 6:48; Rev 2:9–10,13; 3:8

Jesus Christ knows his disciples' misunderstandings and disputes Mt 16:5–8 pp Mk 8:14–17; Mk 9:33–35 pp Lk 9:46–48; Jn 6:60–61; 16:17–19

Jesus Christ knows those who are half-hearted Rev 2:2–5; 3:1–2,15–18

Jesus Christ's knowledge of the Scriptures

Lk 24:27 *See also* Mt 4:4 pp Lk 4:4; Mt 5:21; 12:3–7; 22:29–32 pp Mk 12:24–27 pp Lk 20:34–38; Mt 24:37–39 pp Lk 17:26–29

Limitations of Jesus Christ's knowledge

Jesus Christ acquired knowledge by usual human means Mt 4:12; 14:13; Mk 6:38; 9:21; Lk 2:46,52; Jn 9:35

Things that Jesus Christ did not know on account of his humanity Mt 24:36 pp Mk 13:32 *See also* Ac 1:7

See also

1020 God, all-knowing	2081 Christ, wisdom
1412 foreknowledge	2366 Christ, prophecies concerning
1614 Scripture, understanding	3281 Holy Spirit, inspiration
2018 Christ, divinity	5026 knowledge
2033 Christ, humanity	8134 knowing God
2054 Christ, mind of	8281 insight

2048
Jesus Christ, love of

Jesus Christ's total giving of himself, shown supremely in his obedient suffering and death on the cross, reveals God's amazing love for sinners. It continues to motivate and inspire Christians today.

The supreme quality of Jesus Christ's love

Eph 3:17–19 *See also* Ro 8:35,38–39

It caused him to leave his eternal glory 2Co 8:9 *See also* Php 2:6–8

It moved him to give his life for others 1Jn 3:16 *See also* Jn 10:11,14–15; 15:13; Eph 5:2; Rev 1:5

He loves sinners Lk 23:34 *See also* Lk 13:34 pp Mt 23:37; Lk 23:43

He loves each believer 2Th 2:13 *See also* Jn 10:3–5

Examples of Jesus Christ's love

His compassion for the needy Mt 9:36 pp Mk 6:34; Mt 14:14; 15:32 pp Mk 8:1–2; Lk 7:13

His love for children Mt 19:13–15 pp Mk 10:13–16 pp Lk 18:15–17

His love for his mother Jn 19:26–27

His love for his followers Jn 13:1 *See also Lazarus:* Jn 11:1–7,17–22,32–44 *The "disciple whom Jesus loved" is widely thought to have been John, the author of the Gospel:* Jn 13:23; 20:2; 21:7,20

Jesus Christ's love stems from the Father

He receives the Father's love Jn 3:35 *See also* Mt 17:5 pp Mk 9:7 pp Lk 9:35; Mk 1:11 pp Mt 3:17 pp Lk 3:22; Jn 5:20; 14:31

His love reveals the Father's love Ro 5:8 *See also* Jn 3:16; Eph 2:4–5; 1Jn 4:9–10

Jesus Christ's love motivates the church

His love indwells believers Jn 17:26 *See also* Jn 15:9–10; Gal 2:20; 1Ti 1:14; 1Jn 4:12

His love disciplines believers Rev 3:19 *See also* Heb 12:5–6; Pr 3:11–12; Rev 3:9

His love inspires authentic Christian attitudes Jn 13:34–35 *See also* Lev 19:18; Dt 6:5; Mt 5:43–44; 22:35–39 pp Mk 12:28–31 pp Lk 10:25–27; Lk 6:27; Jn 15:12; 1Jn 3:10

His love inspires Christian marriage Eph 5:25 *See also* Eph 5:28–30

His love inspires a desire for spiritual gifts 1Co 14:1

His love motivates Christians to live for God 2Co 5:14–15 *See also* Ro 8:37; 1Co 16:14; Col 2:2; 1Th 1:3; Heb 10:24

See also

1085 God, love of	3209 Holy Spirit & love
2015 Christ, compassion	5564 suffering of Christ
2027 Christ, grace & mercy	5659 bride
2410 cross, the	5708 marriage
2525 Christ, cross of	7020 church, the
2530 Christ, death of	8292 love

2051
Jesus Christ, majesty of

The glorious splendour of Jesus Christ's royal authority belongs to him by right and is reaffirmed through his exaltation to the Father's right hand.

Jesus Christ shared in God's majesty before time began

Jn 17:5 *See also* Jn 17:24; Col 1:15; Heb 1:3; Rev 22:13

Jesus Christ renounced his majesty to become a human being

Php 2:6–8 *See also* Isa 53:2–3; Mt 20:28 pp Mk 10:45; Jn 13:3–5; 2Co 8:9

Jesus Christ's majesty seen in his earthly ministry

At the transfiguration 2Pe 1:16 *See also* Mt 17:2 pp Mk 9:2–3 pp Lk 9:29

At the entry into Jerusalem Mt 21:9–10 pp Mk 11:9–10

pp Lk 19:37–38 pp Jn 12:13 *See also*
Mt 21:5 pp Jn 12:15; Zec 9:9

Jesus Christ's majesty is reaffirmed through his exaltation
Jesus Christ is exalted to the throne of God's majesty Heb 1:3 *See also* Ac 5:31; Heb 8:1; 1Pe 3:22

A vision of the glorified Christ in his majesty Rev 1:13–16 *See also* Rev 5:6–8; 14:14

Jesus Christ is majestic in his absolute pre-eminence Col 1:18 *See also* Da 7:13–14; Ac 2:36; 1Co 15:25; Php 2:10–11; Rev 19:16

Jesus Christ's majesty is shown by his authority as judge of all Mt 25:31 *See also* Ac 17:31; 2Ti 4:1

All humanity will see Jesus Christ's majesty
Mt 26:64 pp Mk 14:62 *See also* Mt 24:30 pp Mk 13:26 pp Lk 21:27; 2Th 1:7–10; Rev 1:7; 5:13; 6:15–17; 7:9–10

See also

1090 God, majesty of	2312 Christ as king
2012 Christ, authority	2336 Christ, exaltation
2018 Christ, divinity	2565 Christ, second coming
2024 Christ, glory of	2580 Christ, transfiguration
2033 Christ, humanity	2590 Christ, triumphal entry
2069 Christ, pre-eminence	
2224 Christ, the Lord	

2054
Jesus Christ, mind of

The centre of Jesus Christ's thought, understanding and motivation, characterised by a total dedication to God. Christians are called upon to have the same mind as Christ.

The intellectual capacity of Jesus Christ's mind
In childhood Lk 2:47 *See also* Lk 2:40,52

In adulthood Jn 7:15 *See also* Mt 7:28; 13:54 pp Mk 6:2; Mk 1:22 pp Lk 4:32; Mk 11:18

Jesus Christ's mind was pure
Heb 7:26 *The purity of Jesus Christ's mind is declared by his words and actions and by his oneness with God. See also* Lk 1:35; Jn 10:30; Heb 4:15

Examples of Jesus Christ's use of his mind
In overcoming temptation Mt 4:4 pp Lk 4:4; Dt 8:3; Mt 27:42 pp Mk 15:32 pp Lk 23:37

Against opposition Mt 22:18–22 pp Mk 12:15–17 pp Lk 20:22–26

Jesus Christ's mind is more than intellect
His thinking is supported by prayer Lk 6:12–13 *See also* Lk 5:16; 22:41–43 pp Mt 26:39 pp Mk 14:35–36

His thinking is tempered by understanding Isa 11:2 *See also* Mt 9:35–36; Lk 4:22; Jn 2:24–25

His mind experiences anguish Jn 12:27 *See also* Mt 26:38 pp Mk 14:34; Mt 27:46

pp Mk 15:34; Ps 22:1; Lk 12:49–50; 22:44; Jn 13:21

Jesus Christ's mind is extraordinary
He has unusual insight Mk 2:8 pp Mt 9:4 pp Lk 5:22 *See also* Mt 12:25 pp Lk 11:17; Lk 6:8; 9:47; Jn 1:47–48; 4:17–18; 11:4

He understands the future Mk 8:31 pp Mt 16:21 pp Lk 9:22 *See also* Mt 26:21 pp Mk 14:18; Lk 22:34,37; Isa 53:12; Jn 3:14; 4:49–50; 13:33; 18:4

Jesus Christ's mind did not know all things
Mt 8:10 pp Lk 7:9; Mk 9:21; 13:32

Jesus Christ's strength of mind made him resolute
Lk 9:51 *See also* Mt 27:14 pp Mk 15:5; Jn 6:6; 12:27

Jesus Christ's mind was not always understood
Mk 9:32 pp Lk 9:45 *See also* Mk 3:21–22; Lk 2:50; 18:34; Jn 3:10; 8:27; 12:16

Christians should have the same mind as Christ
In his attitude 1Pe 4:1 *See also* 1Co 2:16; Isa 40:13; Php 2:5; 3:8; Col 2:2–3

In his knowledge of Scripture Mt 7:28–29; 22:29; Lk 2:47; 24:27; Jn 5:39

In his awareness of God Jn 8:16,28,55; 14:10–11; 17:1,6

In the love in which Jesus Christ's mind is exercised Lk 11:42; Jn 14:23; 1Co 13:2

See also

2012 Christ, authority	2366 Christ, prophecies concerning
2045 Christ, knowledge of	5037 mind of Christ
2048 Christ, love of	8206 Christlikeness
2081 Christ, wisdom	

2057
Jesus Christ, obedience of

The selfless obedience of Jesus Christ to the will of God his Father, through which the redemption of humanity is accomplished. Christ also shows himself willing to submit to earthly authorities and sets an example which believers are called to imitate.

Jesus Christ was totally obedient to his Father's will
Obedience was central to Jesus Christ's life and thought Jn 4:34; Heb 10:9 *See also* Mt 3:15; 8:9–10 pp Lk 7:8–9; Jn 5:30; 6:38; 14:31; Heb 10:7; Ps 40:7–8

Jesus Christ's obedience meant ultimate personal cost Mt 26:39 pp Mk 14:36 pp Lk 22:42; Php 2:8 *See also* Isa 50:5–6; 53:10–12; Mt 16:21 pp Mk 8:31 pp Lk 9:22; Jn 10:18; 13:1; Heb 5:8

Jesus Christ's obedience was necessary for God's salvation plan Ro 5:18–19 *See also* Mt 27:40–42

pp Mk 15:30–31 pp Lk 23:35–37; Lk 24:26; Jn 17:2–4,26; 19:30

Jesus Christ's obedience was shown in his human relationships
He was obedient to his parents Lk 2:51

He was obedient to secular authorities Mt 17:24–27; 22:17–21 pp Mk 12:15–17 pp Lk 20:22–25

He was obedient to the Jewish law Mt 5:17–18; 22:37–40 pp Mk 12:29–31 pp Lk 10:26–28; Mk 2:23–28; Jn 7:19; 10:37–38 *Jesus Christ's obedience and commitment were to the spirit of God's law; his attitudes to Jewish legalism were often seen as disobedience. Disputes over the Sabbath are one example.*

Believers should follow Jesus Christ's example of obedience
Obedience to God's will is paramount Mt 19:17 *See also* Mt 7:21; 12:50 pp Mk 3:35 pp Lk 8:21; Jn 15:10; Eph 6:6

Christlike obedience expresses love for God 2Jn 6 *See also* Jn 14:15,20–21; 15:12

Obedience should characterise believers' lives Ro 1:5 *"obedience" refers to a whole lifestyle arising from a relationship with God through Jesus Christ. See also* Ac 5:29; 2Co 2:9

See also

1175 God, will of	2510 Christ, baptism of
2036 Christ, humility	
2218 Christ, Son of God	2525 Christ, cross of
2324 Christ as Saviour	2570 Christ, suffering
2327 Christ as servant	5379 law, Christ's attitude
2339 Christ, example of	8453 obedience

2060
Jesus Christ, patience of

Jesus Christ supremely displays God's patient character in his work of salvation. The patience of Jesus Christ is seen in his relationships with people and in his perseverance through trial and suffering to death. Followers of Christ are called to demonstrate patience in all their relationships and circumstances.

The patience of Jesus Christ in his earthly ministry
His patience with people Lk 22:32–34 *See also* Mt 20:20–28 pp Mk 10:35–45; Mt 26:69–75 pp Mk 14:66–72 pp Lk 22:55–62 pp Jn 18:16–27; Mk 4:13–20; Lk 23:33–34; Jn 21:15–19

His patience with God's timing of events Jn 12:27 *Jesus Christ's life was lived under the shadow of the cross. He was concerned that people should understand his ministry and therefore he exercised great patience, being directed by the Father in the priorities and timing of his ministry. See also* Mk 1:34 pp Lk 4:41; Mk 7:36; 8:30; 9:9; Jn 2:4; 7:6,30; 12:23; 13:1; 16:32; 17:1

His patience in suffering Mt 26:39–42 pp Mk 14:35–36 pp Lk 22:42 *See also*

Mt 26:59–68; 27:28–50; 2Th 3:5;
Heb 5:7–9; 12:2–3; 1Pe 2:21–25

Jesus Christ reflects God's own patient character
Ex 34:6–7; Nu 14:18–20; Mt 18:26–27;
Ro 10:21; 1Pe 3:20; 2Pe 3:8

Jesus Christ's patience brings about God's salvation
1Ti 1:16 *See also* Ro 2:4; 2Pe 3:15

Jesus Christ's patience must be appropriated by his followers
In relation to people Eph 4:2 *See also*
Mt 18:26–35; 1Co 13:4; Gal 5:22;
Col 1:11; 3:12; 1Th 5:14; 2Ti 4:2;
Jas 5:7–8

In enduring life's circumstances and sufferings 1Pe 2:20–23 *See also* Lk 8:15;
21:19; Ro 5:3–4; 8:25; 12:12; Col 1:11;
1Th 1:3; Tit 2:2; Heb 12:1–3; Jas 1:2–4;
5:8; 1Pe 5:8–10; Rev 1:9; 13:10; 14:12

In communicating the gospel 2Ti 4:2
See also Tit 2:2

In living and waiting for the Lord's coming Jas 5:7–8 *See also* Ro 8:25;
1Th 1:3

Examples of Jesus Christ's patience found in his followers
2Co 1:5–6; 6:4–6; 2Ti 3:10–11;
Rev 1:9; 3:10

See also

1095 God, patience of	2570 Christ, suffering
2057 Christ, obedience	6652 forgiveness
	8318 patience
2324 Christ as Saviour	8418 endurance
	8459 perseverance
2339 Christ, example of	8490 watchfulness
2565 Christ, second coming	

2063
Jesus Christ, perfection of

Jesus Christ perfectly radiates the glory of God, exactly representing his Father's likeness. Christ's work is complete and he is free from all impurity.

Jesus Christ represents perfection and absoluteness
His perfection was established through obedient suffering Heb 5:8–9
See also Heb 2:10; 7:28

All things find fulfilment in Christ
Eph 1:22–23 *See also* Eph 1:9–10;
4:13,15–16; Col 1:17–18

Jesus Christ radiates God's glory
Heb 1:3 *See also* Mt 17:2 pp Mk 9:3
pp Lk 9:29 *At the transfiguration Jesus Christ's face mirrors God's glory and purity;* Jn 1:14; 2Co 4:4,6; 2Pe 1:17;
Rev 1:14–16

Jesus Christ exactly represents the Father's likeness
Heb 1:3 *See also* Jn 1:18; 12:44–45;
14:7,9–10; Php 2:6; Col 1:15

The fulness of God dwells in Jesus Christ Col 1:19 *See also* Col 2:9

Jesus Christ's work is totally complete
Heb 12:2 *See also* Heb 7:25

Christians will finally participate in Christ's perfection 2Co 3:18 *See also*
1Co 13:9–12

Jesus Christ is without impurity
1Jn 3:5 *See also* Jn 8:46; 2Co 5:21;
Heb 4:15; 7:26; 1Pe 1:19; 2:22; Isa 53:9;
1Jn 3:3,7

See also

1100 God, perfection	2306 Christ, high priest
2018 Christ, divinity	
2024 Christ, glory of	2570 Christ, suffering
2030 Christ, holiness	
2051 Christ, majesty of	2580 Christ, transfiguration
2057 Christ, obedience	8321 perfection, divine
2075 Christ, sinless	
2218 Christ, Son of God	

2066
Jesus Christ, power of

The historical and ongoing effective authority of Jesus Christ over natural elements, over human life and ultimately over sin, forces of evil, Satan and death.

Jesus Christ's power is from God
Ac 10:38

God's creative power is exercised through Jesus Christ Jn 1:3 *See also*
1Co 8:6; Col 1:16; Heb 1:2

God's infinite power is given to Jesus Christ Mt 28:18 *See also* Mt 9:6
pp Mk 2:10 pp Lk 5:24; Mt 19:26
pp Lk 1:37; Lk 1:35; Jn 3:34–35;
5:19–20; 13:3; Php 2:9

Jesus Christ's power is revealed on earth
Jesus Christ's power over nature
Mt 8:26–27 pp Mk 4:39–41
pp Lk 8:24–25 *See also* Mt 14:25
pp Mk 6:48 pp Jn 6:19; Mt 21:19
pp Mk 11:14; Mk 11:21

Jesus Christ's power over sickness
Mt 4:23 *See also* Mt 8:2–3
pp Mk 1:40–42 pp Lk 5:12–13;
Mk 5:27–30 pp Mt 9:21–22
pp Lk 8:44–46; Lk 5:17; Ac 10:38

Jesus Christ's power over human life
Mt 11:5 pp Lk 7:22 *See also* Mt 9:18–25
pp Mk 5:22–42 pp Lk 8:41–55;
Jn 11:43–44

Jesus Christ's power over his own life
Jn 10:18 *See also* Heb 7:16

Jesus Christ's power over human behaviour Mt 4:20 pp Lk 5:11 *See also*
Mt 9:9 pp Mk 2:14 pp Lk 5:27–28;
Mk 15:5; Jn 11:29; 19:10–11

Jesus Christ's power over forces of evil Mt 8:16 pp Mk 1:32–34
pp Lk 4:40–41 *See also* Mt 4:10–11
pp Mk 1:13 pp Lk 4:12–13; Mt 9:32–33;
12:22; 17:18 pp Mk 9:25 pp Lk 9:42;
Jn 14:30

Jesus Christ has power over sin and death
Jesus Christ's crucifixion defeats the power of sin Ro 6:6 *See also*

Isa 53:10–12; Mt 9:6; Jn 15:13;
1Co 15:3; Tit 2:14; Heb 9:28; 1Pe 2:24;
Rev 5:9

Jesus Christ's resurrection defeats the power of death Ro 6:9 *See also* Ps 16:10;
Jn 2:19; 5:21; 17:2; Ac 2:24,32; Ro 1:4;
Eph 1:19–20; Php 3:10

Jesus Christ's power over sin and death remains effective Heb 7:25 *See also* Jn 6:40; Ro 8:2–3; 1Co 15:22;
Heb 7:26–28; 1Pe 3:18

Jesus Christ's power remains available in human experience
Jesus Christ's forgiving power is effective today Ac 13:38–39 *See also*
Jn 20:23; Ac 5:31; Eph 1:7

Jesus Christ's enabling power is effective today Mt 28:18–20; Lk 9:1;
24:49; Jn 16:14; Ac 1:8; 1Co 12:4–6

See also

1105 God, power of	3296 Holy Spirit in the world
2012 Christ, authority	5452 power
2303 Christ as creator	6020 sin
2351 Christ, miracles	6614 atonement
2530 Christ, death of	6652 forgiveness
2560 Christ, resurrection	6676 justification

2069
Jesus Christ, pre-eminence of

Jesus Christ excels over all of creation and reigns supreme over everything in the created order.

The scope of Jesus Christ's pre-eminence
Over all people Jn 17:2 *See also*
Mt 25:31–32; Ro 10:12

Over his enemies 1Co 15:25–26 *See also* Ac 2:32–35; Ps 110:1; Eph 4:8 *Paul probably interpreted "captives" to refer to the spiritual enemies of Christ defeated at the cross.*

Over every power and authority
Col 2:15 *See also* Eph 1:21

Over all traditions and institutions
Mt 12:8 pp Mk 2:28 pp Lk 6:5

Over all things 1Co 15:28 *See also*
Mt 11:27 pp Lk 10:22; Mt 28:18; Jn 3:35;
13:3; 16:33; Ac 10:36; Php 3:21; Heb 2:8

The pre-eminence of Jesus Christ in relation to others
To other prophets Mt 3:11; 12:41
pp Lk 11:32; Jn 1:26–27,30; 3:30;
Heb 1:1–2

To the patriarchs Jn 1:17; 8:52–58;
Heb 3:3–6

To Aaron and other high priests
Heb 8:1–6 *See also* Heb 4:14; 6:20;
7:23,26–28; 9:11–14,24–26

To angels 1Pe 3:22 *See also* Heb 1:4–14

To other lords and kings Rev 17:14 *See also* 1Ti 6:15; Rev 19:16

Descriptions of Jesus Christ's pre-eminence
He is the head Col 2:10 *See also*
Eph 1:9–10,22; 4:15; 5:23–24; Col 1:18

He is the capstone Mt 21:42
pp Mk 12:10–11 pp Lk 20:17 *By so*

saying Jesus Christ applied this verse to himself. The capstone/cornerstone was the most significant stone of a building's structure. See also Ps 118:22; Ac 4:11; Eph 2:20; 1Pe 2:7

He is the Chief Shepherd Jn 10:11; Heb 13:20; 1Pe 5:4

The reasons for Jesus Christ's pre-eminence

His divine origin Jn 3:31 *See also* Jn 1:1–2; 17:24

His equality with the Father Jn 10:30 *See also* Col 1:19; 2:9

His authority derives from the Father Jn 5:22–27

He possesses the rights of the firstborn Col 1:15–17 *As the firstborn son has the rights and privileges of an heir, so Jesus Christ is heir of all things by virtue of his pre-existence and sonship. See also* Ro 8:29; Heb 1:6

He has a superior name Php 2:9 *See also* Ac 4:12; Heb 1:4

He is the First and the Last Rev 1:17 *This title implies that all things are summed up in Christ and find their purpose in him. See also* Rev 2:8; 22:13

Examples of events whereby Jesus Christ's pre-eminence is recognised

His entry into Jerusalem Mt 21:4–9 pp Mk 11:7–10 pp Lk 19:35–38 pp Jn 12:12–15; Zec 9:9

His resurrection Ro 1:4; 1Co 15:21–23; Rev 1:5

His exaltation to the Father's right hand Ac 5:31 *See also* Ac 2:33; 7:55; Eph 1:20–21; 4:8–10; Php 2:9–11; Col 3:1; Heb 8:1; 10:12; 1Pe 3:22; Rev 3:21

See also
1060 God, greatness of	2224 Christ, the Lord
2012 Christ, authority	2306 Christ, high priest
2018 Christ, divinity	2312 Christ as king
2051 Christ, majesty of	2318 Christ as prophet
2212 Christ, head of church	2336 Christ, exaltation
2218 Christ, Son of God	2372 Christ, victory

2072
Jesus Christ, righteousness of

Jesus Christ pleased his Father perfectly in his life on earth and in his death. He now gives believers a new status before God and a new power for living.

The promised Messiah will be righteous
Zec 9:9 *See also* Ps 45:7; Isa 53:11; Jer 23:5–6; 33:15

The promised Messiah will establish righteousness Ps 72:1–4; Isa 9:7; 11:3–5

Jesus Christ's own righteousness
Righteousness is characteristic of Jesus Christ Ac 22:14 *See also* Ac 3:14; 7:52; 2Ti 4:8; Heb 1:8–9; 1Jn 2:1,29; 3:7

Jesus Christ's obedience shows his righteousness Jn 8:28–29 *See also* Jn 4:34; 6:38; 12:49–50; 14:31; Php 2:8; Heb 5:8–9; 10:9

Jesus Christ judges righteously Jn 5:30 *See also* Rev 19:11

Jesus Christ is declared not guilty Lk 23:14–15 *See also* Lk 23:4; Jn 19:6; Ac 3:13

Jesus Christ's righteousness recognised by others Lk 23:47 *See also* Mk 10:17–18 pp Lk 18:18–19; Lk 23:41; Ac 10:38

Consequences of Jesus Christ's righteousness
God justifies believers on account of the righteousness of Jesus Christ Ro 5:18–19 *See also* Ro 3:23–26; 1Pe 3:18; 2Pe 1:1

All who believe share in the righteousness of Jesus Christ 1Co 1:30 *See also* Ro 3:21–22; 4:6,24; 9:30; 10:3–4; 2Co 5:21

Believers live by and for Jesus Christ's righteousness Php 1:11 *One of Paul's prayers for Christians. See also* Ro 6:18; 8:10; 1Pe 2:24

See also
1125 God, righteousness	6674 imputation
2030 Christ, holiness	6676 justification
2057 Christ, obedience	6744 sanctification
2075 Christ, sinless	8025 faith, origins of
2230 Messiah, coming of	8158 righteousness of believers
	8272 holiness, growth in

2075
Jesus Christ, sinlessness of

The complete absence of sin, only in Jesus Christ. Christ demonstrated complete obedience to God in spite of his human frailty, enabling him to be a perfect atoning sacrifice and to give his righteousness to sinners.

Jesus Christ fully experienced human weakness
Php 2:7; Heb 2:14,17

Jesus Christ was tempted to sin
Mt 4:2–3 pp Lk 4:2–3; Mk 1:12–13; 8:32 pp Mt 16:22; Mk 14:36 pp Mt 26:39 pp Lk 22:42; Mk 15:29–30 pp Mt 27:40; Lk 23:37

Jesus Christ resisted the temptation to sin
Heb 4:15 *See also* Mt 4:4 pp Lk 4:4; Mt 16:23 pp Mk 8:33

Jesus Christ committed no sin
He only spoke the truth 1Pe 2:22 *See also* Isa 53:9,7; Jn 8:46,46; Heb 7:26

He fulfilled the law Mt 5:17 *See also* Mt 3:15; Lk 24:27,44; Ro 10:4

He was fully obedient to his human parents Lk 2:51; Jn 19:26

He was fully obedient to his heavenly Father Jn 17:4 *See also* Jn 5:19,36; 8:28,49; 12:49–50; 14:31; Heb 5:7–8

He was innocent according to Roman law Lk 23:14–15 *See also* Mt 22:21 pp Mk 12:17 pp Lk 20:25; Mt 27:19,24; Lk 23:4,22; Ac 13:28

Jesus Christ's sinlessness was recognised by others
Lk 23:47 *See also* Lk 23:41

Jesus Christ was perfect
Heb 7:28 *See also* Jn 1:14; Col 1:19; 2:9; Heb 1:3; 2:10; 5:9

Jesus Christ's sinlessness qualified him to be the perfect sacrifice
2Co 5:21 *NIV footnote. See also* Isa 53:10; Ro 8:3; 1Pe 1:19; 3:18; 1Jn 3:5

Jesus Christ's sinlessness is the grounds of believers' sanctification
Heb 10:14 *See also* Isa 53:11; Ro 5:19; 8:4; Heb 10:10

See also
2030 Christ, holiness	2078 Christ, sonship of
2033 Christ, humanity	2575 Christ, temptation
2057 Christ, obedience	5375 law
2063 Christ, perfection	6674 imputation
2072 Christ, righteousness	

2078
Jesus Christ, sonship of

Jesus Christ is described as Son of David, Son of Man and Son of God. His sonship speaks of his divinity and humanity and is closely associated with his role as promised Messiah, suffering Saviour, risen Lord and coming judge and king. It also speaks of his intimate, obedient and unique relationship with his Father and of his mission to enable people to become children of God through faith in him.

Jesus Christ as the Son of David
He is physically descended from David Mt 1:1 *See also* Mt 1:2–20; Lk 1:27,32; 2:4,11; 3:23–38; Ro 1:3; 2Ti 2:8; Rev 22:16

He is the promised royal Messiah of David's line Isa 16:5 *See also* 2Sa 7:12–16 pp 1Ch 17:11–14; Ps 89:1–4; 132:11,17; Isa 9:7; 11:1; Jer 23:5–6; 33:15–16; Eze 34:23–24; 37:24–25; Zec 3:8; 6:12

He is both the Son and Lord of David Mt 22:41–45 pp Mk 12:35–37 pp Lk 20:41–44 *See also* Ps 110:1

Jesus Christ as the Son of Man
Mk 2:10 pp Mt 9:6 pp Lk 5:24; Jn 3:13 *See also* Da 7:13–14; Mk 2:28 pp Mt 12:8 pp Lk 6:5; Jn 1:51; 6:27; 8:28

Jesus Christ as the Son of God
His divine origin and divinity Lk 1:32–35 *See also* Jn 1:13,18; 5:18; 17:5,24

His intimate relationship with the Father Mk 14:36 *"Abba" was a term of intimacy and familiarity that children used with their own fathers. See also* Mt 3:17

pp Mk 1:11 pp Lk 3:22; Lk 2:49; Jn 1:18,32–34; 3:35; 5:20; 8:38; 14:31; 17:23

His knowledge of the Father's will
Mt 11:25–27 pp Lk 10:21–22 *See also* Jn 6:45–46; 8:55; 14:13–16; 15:15

His obedience to the Father's mission
Mt 26:42 pp Mk 14:36 pp Lk 22:42 *See also* Mt 3:13–17 pp Mk 1:9–11 pp Lk 3:21–22 *His baptism*; Mt 4:1–11 pp Lk 4:1–13 *His temptation*; Mt 12:50; Jn 3:17; 8:55; 10:17,36; 14:31; 17:8

His sharing in the Father's work
Jn 3:34; 4:34; 5:17,21–26; 6:40; 8:16; 9:4; 12:49–50; 14:11

His role as promised Messiah Mt 16:16
pp Lk 9:20 *See also* 2Sa 7:12–14 pp 1Ch 17:11–13; Ps 89:26–27; Isa 9:6–7; Mt 1:23; Isa 7:14; Mt 2:15; Hos 11:1; Mt 26:63–64 pp Mk 14:61–62 pp Lk 22:70; Lk 4:41; 22:29–30; Jn 1:49; 11:27; 20:31; Ac 13:33; Heb 1:5; 5:5; Ps 2:7

His sharing the Father's character and being Heb 1:3 *See also* Jn 1:14; 5:26; 6:57; 10:30; 17:5

The uniqueness of his sonship Jn 3:16
See also Jn 1:18; 3:18; Heb 1:3

Jesus Christ's disciples become children of God through him
Gal 4:4–7 *See also* Mt 12:50; Jn 3:16–18; 5:23–24; 6:40; 11:26–27; 14:1–2; 20:31; Ro 8:13–17; Eph 1:5–6

Jesus Christ as the son of natural parents
Mt 1:16,25; 13:55 pp Mk 6:3; Lk 2:7,48; 3:23; 4:22; Jn 1:45; 6:42; Ac 1:14

See also
1250 Abba	2230 Messiah,
1510 Trinity, the	coming of
2012 Christ,	2366 Christ,
authority	prophecies
2018 Christ, divinity	concerning
2215 Christ, Son of	2535 Christ, family
David	of
2218 Christ, Son of	2540 Christ,
God	genealogy
2221 Christ, Son of	6608 adoption
Man	

2081
Jesus Christ, wisdom of

Jesus Christ's deep understanding of God, people and situations derived from his relationship with God his Father and from knowledge of his word. Christ's wisdom is seen in his words, actions and dealings with people.

The wisdom of Messiah was foretold and recognised in Jesus Christ
Isa 11:2 *See also* Pr 8:22–23; Isa 52:13; Jn 1:1; 4:29; 1Co 1:24,30; Col 2:2–3

Wisdom was characteristic of Jesus Christ's childhood
Lk 2:40 *See also* Lk 2:46–47,52

Wisdom was characteristic of Jesus Christ's ministry
Jesus Christ's wisdom was exceptional Mt 13:54 pp Mk 6:2 *See also* Mt 12:42 pp Lk 11:31; Mk 11:18; Jn 7:15

Jesus Christ's wisdom in teaching Mt 7:29 *See also* Mt 11:4–5 pp Lk 7:22; Mt 13:34; 16:12; 17:13; Mk 1:22 pp Lk 4:32; Lk 24:8; Jn 2:17

Jesus Christ's wisdom in dealing with people Jn 4:29 *See also* Mt 18:2–3 pp Mk 9:36–37 pp Lk 9:47–48; Mt 20:25–26 pp Mk 10:42–43; Jn 8:10–11

Jesus Christ's wisdom in dealing with opposition Lk 14:5–6 pp Mt 12:11–12 *See also* Mt 22:18–22 pp Mk 12:15–17 pp Lk 20:23–26; Mt 27:14 pp Mk 15:5

Jesus Christ's wisdom arose from his relationship with God
It was based on prayer Mt 26:36 pp Mk 14:32 pp Lk 22:41; Lk 5:16 *See also* Mt 14:23 pp Mk 6:46; Mk 1:35; Lk 6:12

It was based on Scripture Mt 4:4 pp Lk 4:4 *See also* Dt 8:3; Mt 5:17; 22:29; Lk 24:27

Jesus Christ's life embodies the wisdom of God's will and purposes
Jn 8:29 *See also* Jn 5:30; 8:16,28; 14:10

See also
1180 God, wisdom of	2363 Christ,
2015 Christ,	preaching &
compassion	teaching
2045 Christ,	2520 Christ,
knowledge of	childhood
2054 Christ, mind of	2545 Christ,
2218 Christ, Son of	opposition to
God	8361 wisdom
2360 Christ, prayers	
of	

2200

Jesus Christ, titles and descriptions of

This set of themes consists of the following:
2203 Jesus Christ, titles and names of
2206 Jesus, the Christ
2209 Jesus Christ, as the truth
2212 Jesus Christ, head of the church
2215 Jesus Christ, Son of David
2218 Jesus Christ, Son of God
2221 Jesus Christ, Son of Man
2224 Jesus Christ, the Lord
2227 Immanuel
2230 Messiah, coming of
2233 Son of Man

2203
Jesus Christ, titles and names of

These, in their rich variety, throw light on either the person of Jesus Christ or on some aspect of his ministry.

Titles relating to Jesus Christ's identity
The exact image of God Heb 1:3 *See also* Jn 14:9; 2Co 4:4; Col 1:15

The first and last, the Alpha and Omega Rev 22:13 *"Alpha" and "Omega" are the first and last letters of the Greek alphabet. See also* Rev 1:17; 2:8; 21:6

○ **The Word of God** Jn 1:1 *See also* Mal 3:1; Jn 1:14; 1Jn 1:1; Rev 19:13

The last Adam 1Co 15:45 *See also* Ro 5:14

The bright Morning Star Rev 22:16 *See also* 2Pe 1:19

The rising sun Mal 4:2; Lk 1:78

The Living One Rev 1:18 *See also* Jn 5:26; 11:25

The Amen Rev 3:14 *See also* 2Co 1:20

The true light Jn 1:3–9 *See also* Isa 9:2; Lk 2:32; Jn 3:19–21; 8:12; 12:46

The Righteous One Ac 3:14 *See also* Jer 23:6; 33:15–16; Ac 7:52; 22:14

The Lion of Judah Rev 5:5

The king of the Jews Mt 2:1–2; 27:37

The "I am" sayings of John's Gospel
Jn 8:58 *See also* Jn 6:35 *the bread of life The light of the world:* Jn 8:12; 9:5 Jn 10:7–10 *the gate;* Jn 10:11–14 *the good shepherd;* Jn 11:25 *the resurrection and the life;* Jn 14:6 *the way, the truth and the life;* Jn 15:1–5 *the true vine*

Titles relating to Jesus Christ's ministry
The seed of Abraham Gal 3:16 *See also* Ge 12:7; 13:15; 24:7

The Root and Offspring of David Rev 22:16

The faithful witness Rev 1:5 *See also* Isa 55:4; Jn 18:37; Rev 3:14

Immanuel Mt 1:23 *See also* Isa 7:14; 8:8

The capstone Mt 21:42 pp Mk 12:10 pp Lk 20:17 *See also* Ps 118:22; Ac 4:11; Eph 2:20–21; 1Pe 2:6–7

The rock 1Co 10:4 *See also* Isa 8:14; 28:16; Ro 9:32–33; 1Pe 2:8

The bridegroom Jn 3:29 *John the Baptist describing himself as the bridegroom's friend, and Jesus Christ as the bridegroom. See also* Mt 9:15 pp Mk 2:19–20 pp Lk 5:34–35; Mt 25:1–10; Rev 19:7; 21:2

The firstborn among many brothers Ro 8:29

The firstfruits 1Co 15:23

The firstborn from the dead Rev 1:5

The heir of all things Heb 1:2

Titles relating to Jesus Christ's authority
Lord Ac 2:25 *See also* Mt 7:21; Lk 6:46; Jn 6:68; Ro 10:13; 1Co 3:5; Col 3:23; 1Th 4:16–17; 2Pe 1:11

The head of the church Eph 1:22–23; 4:15; 5:23; Col 2:19

The Chief Shepherd 1Pe 5:4 *See also* Mt 2:6; Mic 5:2; Jn 10:11; 1Pe 2:25; Heb 13:20

Prince Ac 5:31

Rabbi Jn 1:38,49; 20:16

Titles emphasising Jesus Christ's saving work
Jesus: the LORD saves Mt 1:21

Man of sorrows Isa 53:3

The Passover lamb 1Co 5:7

A horn of salvation Lk 1:69

The consolation of Israel Lk 1:68; 2:25,38

The deliverer and Redeemer Ro 11:26; Isa 59:20

The author and perfecter of salvation Heb 2:10 *See also* Heb 5:9; 12:2

Titles stressing Jesus Christ's mediatory status
The Mediator 1Ti 2:5

The high priest Heb 3:1 *See also* Heb 2:17; 6:20

The Son of Man Lk 19:10 *See also* Mt 11:19; Lk 5:24; Jn 3:13; 6:53; Ac 7:56; Rev 1:13

See also

2206 Jesus, the Christ	2306 Christ, high priest
2215 Christ, Son of David	2315 Christ as Lamb
2218 Christ, Son of God	2324 Christ as Saviour
2221 Christ, Son of Man	2330 Christ as shepherd
2224 Christ, the Lord	7160 servants of the Lord
2227 Immanuel	
2230 Messiah, coming of	

2206
Jesus, the Christ

"Christ" means "Messiah" or "anointed one". As the Christ, Jesus is the one who fulfils all OT expectations. Paul's phrase "in Christ" indicates the intimate relationship between Jesus Christ and his people.

The Christ as the anointed one
The act of anointing in the OT
1Sa 16:13 *Anointing symbolises God's calling and being equipped by his Spirit. See also* Ex 40:15; Lev 8:12; 1Sa 10:1; 1Ki 1:39

Anointed OT leaders
Priests: Ex 29:7; Lev 4:3,5; 6:20; 16:32
Kings: 1Sa 24:6,10; 26:9,11,16,23; Ps 18:50; 20:6; 132:10

The OT promise of a future anointed leader Isa 11:1–2 *See also* Isa 42:1; Jer 23:5–6

Jesus' own claims to be the Christ
Jn 4:25–26 *See also* Mt 23:10; 26:63–64 pp Mk 14:61–62; Jn 10:24–25

Jesus recognised as the Christ
Mt 16:16 pp Mk 8:29 pp Lk 9:20 *See also* Lk 2:26–32; 4:41; Jn 1:41–42; 11:27

Jesus' demand that his identity as the Christ should not be publicised
Mt 16:20 pp Mk 8:30 pp Lk 9:21 *Jesus' reluctance to be known as the Christ is*

probably due to Jewish misunderstandings of the Messiah's true role. See also Mt 12:16; Lk 4:41

Grounds for affirming Jesus as the Christ
Jesus Christ's birth in Bethlehem Mt 2:4–6 *See also* Mic 5:2; Lk 2:4–7

Jesus Christ's spiritual anointing from God Ac 10:38 *See also* Mt 3:16 pp Mk 1:10 pp Lk 3:22; Jn 3:34; Ac 4:27

Jesus Christ's proclamation of Jubilee Lk 4:17–21 *See also* Isa 61:1–2 *Isaiah's words are borrowed from the language of the Year of Jubilee (Leviticus chapter 25), which was to be a time when true freedom was restored.*

Jesus Christ's healing ministry Mt 8:16–17 *See also* Isa 53:4; Mt 11:2–5 pp Lk 7:18–23; Jn 7:31

Jesus Christ's prophetic ministry Jn 4:29 *See also* Mt 21:45–46; 26:67–68; Jn 4:19; 7:26

Jesus Christ's suffering, death and resurrection Lk 24:26 *See also* Lk 24:46; Ac 3:18; 17:3; 26:23; 1Pe 1:11

Jesus Christ's fulfilment of prophecy 2Co 1:20 *See also* Mt 1:22–23; Isa 7:14; Mt 26:21–24 pp Mk 14:18–21; Ps 41:9; Mt 21:4–7 pp Jn 12:14–15; Zec 9:9; Mt 21:8–9 pp Mk 11:9–10 pp Lk 19:37–38 pp Jn 12:12–13; Ps 118:26; Ac 2:22–36

God's establishment of Jesus Christ as king Lk 1:32–33 *See also* Ps 2:6–7; Isa 9:6; Lk 22:29

Messianic titles used of Jesus
Son of David Mt 1:1; 15:22; 21:9; 20:30–31 pp Mk 10:47–48 pp Lk 18:38–39; 2Ti 2:8

Son of God Mt 14:33; 27:54 pp Mk 15:39; Jn 1:34

The Prophet Mt 21:11; Jn 6:14; 7:40

King of the Jews Mt 2:2; 27:37 pp Mk 15:26 pp Lk 23:38 pp Jn 19:19; Mk 15:32; Jn 12:13

High priest Heb 2:17; 4:14–15; 5:5; 6:20; 7:26; 8:1

Israel's rejection of Jesus as the Christ
Jesus' messiahship was largely rejected by the Jews Mt 27:22 *See also* Jn 1:11; 8:13; 11:37; Ac 7:52–53; 17:3–5

Jesus was accused of blasphemy because of his claims to be the Christ Mk 14:61–64 pp Mt 26:63–66

That Jesus is the Christ is a central Christian belief
Jn 20:31 *See also* Jn 11:27; 1Jn 5:1

The apostles' message was that Jesus is the Christ
Ac 5:42 *See also* Ac 2:36; 9:22; 10:38; 18:5,28

Jesus Christ is the representative head of the church
Baptism is into Christ Gal 3:27 *See also* Ac 2:38; 10:48; Ro 6:3

Jesus Christ lives within believers Gal 2:20 *See also* Ro 6:8; 8:1; 16:7; 1Co 1:30; Eph 1:13; Col 3:1

See also

2212 Christ, head of church	2351 Christ, miracles
2215 Christ, Son of David	2366 Christ, prophecies concerning
2218 Christ, Son of God	2560 Christ, resurrection
2230 Messiah, coming of	7304 anointing
2306 Christ, high priest	8102 abiding in Christ
2312 Christ as king	
2318 Christ as prophet	

2209
Jesus Christ, as the truth
See 1150 God, truth of

2212
Jesus Christ, head of the church

Jesus Christ rules and governs his people and directs them towards the fulfilment of God's purposes. All power and authority within the church derive from Jesus Christ as the head.

Jesus Christ rules the universe in the interest of the church
Eph 1:22–23 *See also* Eph 1:10; Col 1:18

All power and authority within the church derive from Jesus Christ as the head
Jesus Christ is recognised as head of the church Eph 4:15 *See also* Eph 5:23; Col 2:19

Within the church Jesus Christ alone rules with authority Mt 23:8–10 *See also* Jn 13:13; 2Co 4:5

The church owes obedience to its head Jn 14:15 *See also* Jn 14:21,23; Eph 5:24; 1Jn 3:24

All human authority in the church derives from its head Eph 4:11 *See also* Gal 1:1

Jesus Christ is the cornerstone and builder of the church
Eph 2:20–22 *See also* Mt 16:18; Ac 4:11; Ps 118:22; 1Pe 2:4–6

Jesus Christ's role as head of the church
He loves the church Eph 5:25 *See also* Jn 10:11; Eph 5:2,23; 1Jn 3:16

He cares for the church Rev 7:17 *See also* Jn 10:14–15,27–28; 17:12; Eph 5:29–30

He provides for the growth of the church Col 2:19 *See also* Eph 4:15–16

He prays for the church Jn 17:20–26; Ro 8:34; Heb 7:25

He judges the church Rev 2:23 *See also* Ro 14:10–12; 2Co 5:10; Eph 6:8

He will present the church blameless before God Eph 5:27 *See also* 2Co 4:14; Col 1:22; Jude 24

See also

2012 Christ, authority	2069 Christ, pre-eminence
2048 Christ, love of	2224 Christ, the Lord
2066 Christ, power of	

See also

2309 Christ as judge	5700 headship
2330 Christ as shepherd	6754 union with Christ
5217 authority in church	7020 church, the
	7110 body of Christ

2215
Jesus Christ, Son of David

A Messianic title. Jesus Christ comes as a descendant of David to fulfil God's promises in the OT of a future king who would establish the kingdom of God on earth.

OT promises of a future king from David's line
2Sa 7:12–14 pp 1Ch 17:11–13 *These promises are known as "the Davidic covenant";* Isa 16:5 *See also* Ps 132:11–12,17; Isa 9:7; 11:1; Jer 23:5; 33:15; Eze 34:23–24; 37:24–25; Jn 7:42

NT statements verifying that Jesus Christ is descended from David
Mt 1:1 *See also* Lk 3:23,31; Ro 1:3; 2Ti 2:8; Rev 22:16

Jesus Christ inherits the throne of David
Lk 1:32–33 *See also* Lk 1:69; Jn 1:49; 18:37; Mt 27:37 pp Mk 15:26 pp Lk 23:38 pp Jn 19:19

Jesus Christ is called "Son of David"
By those seeking healing Mt 20:30–31 pp Mk 10:47–48 pp Lk 18:38–39 *See also* Mt 9:27; 15:22

At his triumphal entry into Jerusalem Mt 21:9 pp Mk 11:10 *See also* Mt 21:15

Grounds for identifying Jesus Christ as the Son of David
His human descent Ro 1:3 *See also* Mt 1:1

His birth in Bethlehem Mic 5:2; Jn 7:42

His healing ministry Mt 12:22–23 *One of the signs of the Messianic age was the healing of the sick (see Isa 35:5–6; 42:7). See also* Jn 7:31

His ultimate victory Rev 5:5

Jesus Christ is more than a merely human king descended from David
Mk 12:35–37 *Jesus Christ's claim is that he is not simply a human or political king, he is the Lord, the Son of God. See also* Ps 110:1; Jn 18:36

See also

1351 covenant with David	2351 Christ, miracles
2224 Christ, the Lord	2372 Christ, victory
2230 Messiah, coming of	2540 Christ, genealogy
2312 Christ as king	2590 Christ, triumphal entry
2345 Christ, kingdom of	5100 Melchizedek

2218
Jesus Christ, Son of God

A title emphasising Jesus Christ's

deity, his office as Messiah and his pre-eminence as the object of the church's faith and worship and as the content of its gospel.

"Son of God" in the OT
Israel as God's son Ex 4:22–23 *See also* Jer 31:9,20; Hos 11:1

The future Messiah/king as God's Son Ps 2:7 *See also* Ps 89:27; Ac 13:33; Heb 1:5; 5:5 *Jesus Christ perfectly fulfils all the OT promises concerning God's son, whether referring originally to Israel or to the Messiah.*

Jesus Christ is the Son of God
Jesus Christ affirms he is God's Son Jn 10:36 *See also* Lk 22:70 pp Mt 26:63–64 pp Mk 14:61–62; Jn 19:7; Rev 2:18

The Father affirms Jesus Christ is his Son Mt 3:17 pp Mk 1:11 pp Lk 3:22 *See also* Mt 17:5 pp Mk 9:7 pp Lk 9:35; 2Pe 1:17

Others affirm Jesus Christ is God's Son Mt 14:33 *See also* Mk 15:39 pp Mt 27:54; Jn 1:34; Ro 1:4; Heb 4:14; 2Jn 3

Demons affirm Jesus Christ is God's Son Mk 5:7 pp Mt 8:29 pp Lk 8:28 *See also* Mk 3:11; Lk 4:41

"Son of God" as a taunt
By the devil in the wilderness: Mt 4:3 pp Lk 4:3; Mt 4:6 pp Lk 4:9
By the crowd at the cross: Mt 27:40,43

"Son of God" stresses Jesus Christ's deity
Jesus Christ is the Son of God the Father Jn 3:35 *In John's Gospel in particular, the terms Son/Father are used many times to speak of Jesus Christ's unique relationship with God. See also* Mt 11:27 pp Lk 10:22; Mt 24:36 pp Mk 13:32; Jn 5:20–22; Heb 1:1–2; 1Jn 1:3; 2:22–23; 2Jn 9

"Son of God" implies Jesus Christ's equality with God Jn 5:18 *See also* Jn 5:23; 10:30,33; 14:9–10

"Son of God" implies Jesus Christ's obedience to the Father
Jn 5:19 *See also* Mt 26:39 pp Mk 14:36 pp Lk 22:42; Mt 26:42; Jn 8:28; 12:49; 14:31; 15:10; Ro 5:19; Heb 5:8; 10:9

Jesus Christ as "Son of God" is the Messiah
"Son of God" as a Messianic title for Jesus Christ Mt 26:63–64 pp Mk 14:61–62 pp Lk 22:70–23:2 *See also* Mt 16:16; Mk 1:1; Lk 1:32; 4:41; Jn 1:49; 11:27

"Son of God" as one sent by God Gal 4:4 *See also* Mt 21:37 pp Mk 12:6 pp Lk 20:13; Jn 3:16–17; Ro 8:3,32; 1Jn 4:9

Grounds for regarding Jesus Christ as the Son of God
The virgin birth Lk 1:35

Jesus Christ's resurrection Ro 1:3–4

Jesus Christ's works Jn 10:36–38 *See also* Jn 5:17,19,36; 14:11

Jesus Christ's oneness with the Father Jn 10:30 *See also* Jn 12:45; 14:10; 17:21

Jesus Christ as Son of God is the object of the church's faith
Jn 6:40 *See also* Jn 3:36; 20:31; Ac 8:37 fn; Gal 2:20; 1Jn 3:23; 4:15; 5:5,13

Jesus Christ as Son of God is the content of the church's gospel
Ro 1:9 *See also* Ac 9:20; 2Co 1:19; 1Jn 5:9–12

See also

1510 Trinity, the	2230 Messiah, coming of
2018 Christ, divinity	2354 Christ, mission
2057 Christ, obedience	2420 gospel
2078 Christ, sonship of	7754 preaching
2206 Jesus, the Christ	8020 faith

2221
Jesus Christ, Son of Man

Jesus Christ's preferred title for himself. The term points to the humanity and servanthood of Christ, but also reflects Daniel's vision of the son of man as a coming figure of judgment and authority.

Jesus Christ as the Son of Man in his human nature
OT use of "son of man" to mean "human being" Nu 23:19 *See also* Job 25:6; 35:8; Ps 8:4; 80:17; 144:3

Jesus Christ describes himself as Son of Man to stress his humanity Mt 8:20 pp Lk 9:58 *See also* Mt 11:19 pp Lk 7:34; Mt 16:13,15; Lk 6:22; Jn 9:35

Blasphemy against the Son of Man is forgivable Mt 12:32 *See also* Lk 12:10

Jesus Christ as the Son of Man in his prophetic ministry
The OT use of "son of man" as a title for Ezekiel Eze 2:1

Jesus Christ preaches God's word Mt 13:37–43

Jesus Christ offers the words of eternal life Jn 6:27 *See also* Jn 6:53,63,68

Jesus Christ as the Son of Man in his suffering and death
Jesus Christ as a servant Mt 20:28 pp Mk 10:45

Jesus Christ came to suffer, die and be raised Lk 24:6–7 *See also* Mt 12:40 pp Lk 11:30 *the sign of Jonah;* Mt 17:9 pp Mk 9:9 *the transfiguration Predictions of Jesus Christ's death:* Mt 17:22–23 pp Mk 9:31 pp Lk 9:44; Mt 20:18 pp Mk 10:33 pp Lk 18:31; Mt 26:24 pp Mk 14:21 pp Lk 22:22; Mk 8:31 pp Lk 9:22; Jn 3:14; 12:23; 13:31

Jesus Christ as the Son of Man in his authority and dominion
The vision of the son of man Da 7:13–14 *This passage provides the main OT background to Jesus Christ's understanding of himself as the "Son of Man". His main uses of the title emphasise his dominion and authority, and also paradoxically that this glory will be*

attained through the humiliation of the cross.

Son of man meaning "son of Adam"
Ge 1:26 *Jesus Christ as Son of Man (in the Hebrew "son of Adam") inherits the promise originally given to Adam of dominion over creation, which Adam forfeited because of his fall into sin. See also* Ro 5:14; 1Co 15:45; Heb 2:6–9; Ps 8:4–6

Jesus Christ had authority on earth
Mt 9:6 pp Mk 2:10 pp Lk 5:24 *Authority to forgive sins. See also* Mt 12:8 pp Mk 2:28 pp Lk 6:5 *authority over the Sabbath*

Jesus Christ is now ascended into glory Ac 7:55–56 *See also* Rev 1:13; 14:14

Jesus Christ will come to judge and reign over all Mt 16:27–28 pp Mk 8:38 pp Lk 9:26 *See also* Mt 10:23; 24:30 pp Mk 13:26 pp Lk 21:27 *the second coming;* Mt 24:44 pp Lk 12:40 *the day and hour unknown;* Mt 26:64 pp Mk 14:62 pp Lk 22:69 *Jesus Christ before the Sanhedrin;* Lk 18:8; 21:36; Jn 5:27

See also

2012 Christ, authority	2327 Christ as servant
2033 Christ, humanity	2336 Christ, exaltation
2206 Jesus, the Christ	2530 Christ, death of
2233 Son of Man	2570 Christ, suffering
2309 Christ as judge	5083 Adam, and Christ
2312 Christ as king	
2318 Christ as prophet	

2224
Jesus Christ, the Lord

A title that signifies Jesus Christ's absolute authority and the basis on which people may know him. It is especially associated with his resurrection and return.

Lord as a title of respect for the earthly Jesus Christ
Mt 8:25 *See also* Mt 15:25,27 pp Mk 7:28; Mt 21:3 pp Mk 11:3 pp Lk 19:31

Lord as a mark of Jesus Christ's authority as a teacher
1Th 4:15 *See also* Ac 11:16; 20:35; 1Co 7:10

Lord as a sign of Jesus Christ's divinity
Jesus Christ's divinity Jn 20:28 *"Lord" is a common divine title in the Greek OT and is instinctively transferred to Jesus Christ in the NT. See also* 1Co 8:6; 2Co 3:17–18; Eph 4:5; 2Th 2:16; 2Pe 1:2

The day of Christ Jesus Php 1:6 *The "day of Christ Jesus" is equivalent to the OT "day of the LORD". See also* 1Co 1:8; 2Co 1:14; Php 1:10; 2:16; Rev 1:10

Jesus Christ is ruler over all Rev 17:14 *See also* Dt 10:17; Rev 19:16

Jesus Christ is the Saviour Ro 10:13 *See also* Joel 2:32; Ac 2:21

Jesus Christ is Lord of the Sabbath
Mt 12:8 pp Mk 2:28 pp Lk 6:5

Jesus the Messiah is Lord
Ac 2:36 *"Christ" is the Greek equivalent of the Hebrew word "Messiah". See also* 2Co 4:5; Col 3:24

"Jesus is Lord" is the basic Christian statement of faith Ro 10:9 *See also* Ac 11:20; 16:31; 20:21; 1Co 12:3; 2Co 4:5; Php 2:10–11

Jesus is Lord because of the resurrection Ro 1:4 *See also* Ac 4:33; Ro 4:24; 14:9; Heb 13:20

Lord is a natural title for the risen Christ Lk 24:34 *See also* Lk 22:61; Ac 1:21; 7:59; 1Co 9:1,5; 1Th 4:17

Jesus Christ's lordship is the basis for his relationship with Christians
It is a personal relationship Php 3:8 *See also* Ac 16:15; Ro 5:11; 14:8; 1Co 6:17; 2Pe 2:20

"The name of the Lord" expresses this relationship 1Co 6:11 *See also* Ac 8:16; 15:26; 19:5; 21:13; Eph 5:20; Col 3:17

"Jesus our Lord" expresses this relationship Eph 6:24 *See also* 1Co 15:57; 2Co 8:9; Gal 6:14; Eph 5:20; 1Th 5:28; 2Ti 1:8

"In the Lord" as an expression of this relationship Phm 16 *See also* Ro 16:12; Eph 6:10; Php 1:14; 2:29; 3:1; Phm 20

The "grace of the Lord" as God's provision for this relationship 1Ti 1:14 *See also* 2Co 13:14; 2Th 3:18; Phm 25; 2Pe 3:18; Jude 21

Jesus Christ's lordship is the basis for Christian obedience
Col 2:6 *See also* Ro 12:11; Col 3:23; 2Th 1:8; 2Ti 2:19; 1Pe 3:15

Jesus Christ's lordship will be fully revealed
1Th 4:16 *See also* 1Co 1:7; Php 3:20; 1Th 5:23; 2Th 1:7; 1Ti 6:14

Jesus Christ's lordship signifies his absolute authority
Jesus Christ as judge of all 1Co 4:4 *See also* 1Co 11:32; 2Co 10:18; 1Th 4:6; 2Th 1:8–9

Jesus Christ as Lord of all Ro 10:12 *See also* Ac 10:36; 1Co 8:6; Php 2:10–11; Col 1:16–17

See also

2012 Christ, authority	2336 Christ, exaltation
2018 Christ, divinity	2560 Christ, resurrection
2051 Christ, majesty of	2565 Christ, second coming
2069 Christ, pre-eminence	5396 lordship of Christ
2206 Jesus, the Christ	

2227
Immanuel

An OT name given to Jesus Christ, meaning "God with us".

Actual uses of the name Immanuel
Isa 7:14 *The name was given originally to*

a child of Isaiah's day who would signify God's salvation and judgment for Judah; Isa 8:7–10 *The original fulfilment of the Immanuel prophecy would bring judgment on Judah;* Mt 1:22–23 *Isaiah's prophecy is fulfilled through the virginal conception of Jesus Christ.*

The significance of Immanuel
God is with his people Ge 28:15 *See also* Ex 33:14; Nu 14:9; Dt 4:7; 2Ch 13:12; Ps 46:7,11; Hag 2:4; Ro 8:31; Heb 13:5

God dwells with his people Rev 21:3 *See also* Lev 26:11–12; Eze 37:27; 2Co 6:16

Jesus Christ is always with believers Mt 28:20 *See also* Jn 14:18,23; 15:4–5,7; Ac 18:10; Gal 2:20

The Holy Spirit is always with believers Jn 14:17 *See also* Ro 8:9–11; 1Co 3:16; 2Co 1:22; Eph 2:22; 2Ti 1:14; 1Jn 4:13

See also

1035 God, faithfulness	2218 Christ, Son of God
1429 prophecy, OT fulfilment	2515 Christ, birth of
2018 Christ, divinity	2550 Jesus Christ, pre-existence of
2021 Christ, faithfulness	2595 incarnation
2033 Christ, humanity	7135 Israel, people of God
2203 Christ, titles of	
2206 Jesus, the Christ	

2230
Messiah, coming of

The coming of a figure chosen and anointed by God to deliver and redeem his people. Anointing was seen as a sign of being chosen by God for a special task of leadership or responsibility. The OT looked ahead to the final coming of such a figure to usher in a new era in the history of the people of God; the NT sees this expectation fulfilled in the person and work of Jesus Christ.

Anointing as a sign of being chosen by God
Anointing with oil Lev 8:12 *See also* 1Sa 16:12–13; 2Sa 2:4; 5:3 pp 1Ch 11:3; 1Ki 1:39; 2Ki 9:6; Ps 89:20

Anointing with the Holy Spirit Isa 61:1 *See also* Lk 4:18; Jdg 14:19; 1Sa 11:6; 16:13; Isa 11:2; Mt 12:18; Isa 42:1

Anointing as a sign of national and spiritual leadership
Anointed to be king 1Ch 29:22 *See also* Jdg 9:7–15; 1Sa 9:16; 15:17; 2Sa 19:10; 1Ki 1:34; 2Ki 9:3; 11:12 pp 2Ch 23:11; 2Ch 22:7

Anointed to be priest Ex 40:13–15 *See also* Ex 28:41; 29:7; Lev 7:35–36; 16:32; Nu 3:3

Anointed to be judge
The coming of the Spirit on some of the judges is a spiritual anointing: Jdg 3:10; 6:34; 11:29; 15:14

Anointed to be prophet 1Ki 19:16; Isa 48:16; Eze 11:5; 37:1; Mic 3:8

The expectation of a future Messiah

The future anointed king Ge 49:10; Isa 16:5 *See also* Nu 24:17; 2Sa 7:12–14 pp 1Ch 17:11–13; Ps 2:7–9; 45:6–7; 110:1–2; 132:11–12; Isa 9:6–7; Eze 37:24; Mic 5:2; Zec 9:9

The future anointed priest Ps 110:4 *See also* Zec 6:13

The future anointed prophet Isa 61:1–2 *See also* Dt 18:18

The future anointed judge Isa 2:4; 11:3–4; Mic 4:3

The future anointed servant of God Isa 42:1–4 *See also* Isa 49:1–6; 50:4–9; 52:13–53:12

See also

1427 prophecy	5358 judges
2206 Jesus, the Christ	5368 kingship
	7304 anointing
2306 Christ, high priest	7412 priesthood
	9145 Messianic age
2312 Christ as king	9150 Messianic banquet
2327 Christ as servant	
2366 Christ, prophecies concerning	

2233
Son of Man

A Hebrew and Aramaic term, often used to mean a human being in general. In the Gospels Jesus Christ uses it to refer to himself in his earthly ministry and his future death, exaltation and coming as judge and Saviour.

Sons of men as a term for humanity in general

Human beings are inferior to God Ps 115:16 *The Hebrew term here translated "man" literally means "sons of men". Many of the OT references cited in this theme follow this pattern. See also* Ps 11:4; 33:13–14; 45:2

Human beings are dependent on God's care Ps 8:4 *See also* Ps 36:7; 80:17; 107:8,15,21,31

Human beings are mortal Ecc 9:3 *See also* Ecc 3:18–19; Eze 31:14

Human beings are sinful and untrustworthy Ps 146:3 *See also* Ps 14:2–3 pp Ps 53:2–3; Mic 5:7

Son of Man as a term for individual men

The sons of Adam Ge 4:1–2 *"a man" is literally "son of Adam" in Hebrew;* Ge 5:3–4

Ezekiel Eze 2:1 *Ezekiel is called "son of man" 93 times, though this form of address is unique to him in the OT. It may emphasise his remoteness or his humanity. See also* Eze 2:3,6,8; 3:1

Other people Job 25:6; Da 8:17

A son of man as a ruler of God's future kingdom

Da 7:13 *The Aramaic "one like a son of man" stresses this person's humanity and mysterious identity;* Da 7:13–14 *He enters God's presence and is given final authority*

over God's kingdom; Da 7:27 *He shares the kingdom with God's people. See also* Da 7:18 *"saints of the Most High" have sometimes been interpreted as angels*

Son of Man as a title for Jesus Christ

Used by Jesus Christ to emphasise his humanity and authority Mk 2:10–11 pp Mt 9:6 pp Lk 5:24; Mk 8:31 pp Lk 9:22

The Son of Man receives God's kingdom Ac 7:56 *See also* Da 7:13; Mk 14:62 pp Mt 26:64 pp Lk 22:69; Heb 2:6–9; Ps 8:4–6

See also

2012 Christ, authority	2565 Christ, second coming
2078 Christ, sonship of	5001 human race, the
2221 Christ, Son of Man	5080 Adam
2375 kingdom of God	

2300

Jesus Christ, ministry and work of

This set of themes consists of the following:

2303
Jesus Christ, as creator

Scripture identifies the pre-existent Jesus Christ as involved in the work of creation, and relates this to his work in redemption, by which a new creation is brought out of the ruins of the old.

Jesus Christ's creation of the present world

Jesus Christ created all things Jn 1:3 *See also* Jn 1:10; Ac 3:15; 1Co 8:6; Col 1:15–16; Heb 1:2

Jesus Christ sustains the created universe Heb 1:3 *See also* 1Co 8:6; Col 1:17; Rev 3:14 *The word translated "ruler" can mean either "beginning" or "first in rank".*

Jesus Christ will bring the entire work of creation to perfection Eph 1:9–10 *See also* Ro 8:19–22; Col 1:20

Jesus Christ makes a new creation possible

Jesus Christ recreates people through a new birth 2Co 5:17 *See also* Jn 1:12–13; 3:5–6; Gal 6:15; Jas 1:18

Jesus Christ's work of new creation should be evident in believers' lives Eph 4:24 *See also* Eph 3:15; Col 3:10

Through Jesus Christ a new heaven and earth will be created 2Pe 3:13 *The promise was given in Isa 65:17; 66:22. See also* Rev 21:1,4–5

See also

1325 God, the Creator	3266 Holy Spirit in creation
2018 Christ, divinity	4005 creation
2069 Christ, pre-eminence	6723 redemption, NT
3230 Holy Spirit & regeneration	6728 regeneration

2306
Jesus Christ, as high priest

Jesus Christ, being a truly human high priest, perfectly represents humanity before God. He made atonement for sins by his own sacrificial death. Being a truly divine high priest, this act of Christ's was perfect, once for all and of eternal value.

The ministry of Jesus Christ as high priest

He made atonement for sin Heb 2:17 *See also* Heb 8:3; 9:7,11–12; 13:11–13

He represents human beings before God Heb 5:1 *See also* Ro 8:34; 1Jn 2:1–2

He entered the Most Holy Place Heb 9:24 *On the Day of Atonement the high priest entered the Most Holy Place (the sanctuary) which represented the presence of God. Jesus Christ fulfilled this ritual by entering heaven. See also* Heb 4:14; 6:19–20; 9:7,12

He makes believers perfect Heb 10:14 *See also* Heb 10:10; 13:12

He brings believers close to God Heb 10:19–22

He helps those being tempted Heb 2:18 *See also* Heb 4:15; 5:2

He intercedes continually Heb 7:24–25 *See also* Jn 17:20; Ro 8:34

Jesus Christ, the human high priest

As a man he is able to represent human beings Heb 2:17 *See also* Heb 5:1

He is divinely appointed Heb 5:5–6 *See also* Heb 3:1–2

Jesus Christ, the divine high priest

He is sinless Heb 7:26–27 *Jesus Christ is strongly contrasted with other high priests because he did not have to offer sacrifices for his own sins.*

He is eternal Heb 6:20 *See also* Heb 5:6; 7:17,21,28

His atoning work was completed once for all Heb 7:27 *Other high priests had to repeat their sacrifices. See also* Heb 9:12,25–26,28; 10:10

He is exalted Heb 8:1 *See also* Zec 6:13; Heb 7:26

Jesus Christ's high priesthood was of the order of Melchizedek
Heb 6:20 *The priesthood of Melchizedek resembles that of Jesus Christ because he too was king and had neither beginning nor end. See also* Ps 110:4; Heb 5:6,10; 7:1–4,14–17

Responses to Jesus Christ's high priesthood
Heb 4:14–15 *a call to keep to the faith;* Heb 4:16 *an invitation to seek God's help in times of need;* Heb 10:19–22 *an invitation to draw near to God;* Heb 12:1–3 *a call to run the race of faith;* Heb 12:28–29 *a call to offer thanksgiving and worship*

See also
2075 Christ, sinless	7378 high priest, NT
2410 cross, the	7396 Most Holy
6606 access to God	Place
6614 atonement	7414 priesthood, NT
6684 mediator	7436 sacrifice, NT
6689 mercy of Christ	fulfilment
6712 propitiation	
7308 Atonement, Day	
of	

2309
Jesus Christ, as judge

Jesus Christ executed judgment against the forces of evil through his death on the cross. Individuals will be judged according to their response to his saving grace.

Jesus Christ is appointed judge by God the Father
Jn 5:22 *See also* Jn 5:27; Ac 10:42; 17:31

Jesus Christ is a just judge
Jn 5:30 *See also* Isa 11:3–4; Mic 4:3; Jn 8:15–16; Ac 17:31; Rev 19:11

Jesus Christ's death brought judgment on Satan and evil world powers
Jn 12:31–33 *See also* Jn 16:11

Jesus Christ will act as judge at the end of time
2Ti 4:1 *See also* Mt 25:31–32; Ro 2:16; 2Th 1:7–10; 2Ti 4:8; Rev 19:11–16; 22:12

People will be judged according to their response to Jesus Christ
Jn 3:18 *See also* Mt 10:32–33 pp Lk 12:8–9; Mk 8:38 pp Lk 9:26; Jn 9:39; 12:48

Jesus Christ's teaching on judgment
Jesus Christ will separate the righteous from the unrighteous Mt 25:31–32 *See also* Mt 3:12; 13:24–30,36–42 *the parable of the*

weeds; Mt 13:47–50 *the parable of the net;* Mt 25:33–46 *the parable of the sheep and the goats*

Those who reject Jesus Christ will be punished Da 2:34–35; Mt 21:33–44 pp Mk 12:1–11 pp Lk 20:9–18 *the parable of the tenants*

Christians will stand before Jesus Christ as judge and be rewarded for what they have done Mt 16:27 *See also* Mt 25:14–30 *the parable of the talents;* Lk 19:12–27 *the parable of the ten minas;* 2Co 5:10

The day of Jesus Christ's return as judge is unknown Mk 13:32–36 *See also* Mt 24:36–44 pp Lk 17:26–37; Mt 25:1–13 *the parable of the ten virgins*

See also
1310 God as judge	2565 Christ, second
2042 Christ, justice	coming
of	4127 Satan, defeat
2324 Christ as	of
Saviour	5358 judges
2363 Christ,	5498 reward
preaching &	5897 judging others
teaching	9230 judgment seat
2372 Christ, victory	9240 last judgment

2312
Jesus Christ, as king

Jesus Christ is declared king at his birth: he descends from the royal line of David. People rejected his kingly claims at his crucifixion but God exalted him to his rightful place of power and majesty. At the end of time Jesus Christ will rule the nations for ever.

Jesus Christ descends from the royal line of David
He was the Son of David Mt 1:1 *The Messiah was expected to come from David's line. The genealogy given by Matthew follows the royal line of the kings descended from David. See also* Mt 9:27; 12:23; 15:22; Lk 1:32–33; 2:4; 3:31

He was born in Bethlehem, the town of David Jn 7:42 *See also* Mt 2:3–6; Mic 5:2; Lk 2:15–16

Jesus Christ is regarded as king
Jn 1:49 *By Nathanael. See also* Mt 2:1–2 *by the Magi;* Jn 6:15 *by the crowds;* Ac 17:7 *by Jason of Thessalonica*

Jesus Christ refused worldly kingdoms
Jn 18:36 *See also* Mt 4:8–10 pp Lk 4:5–8; Jn 6:15

Jesus Christ entered Jerusalem as a king
Mt 21:1–9 pp Jn 12:12–15 *See also* Zec 9:9

Jesus Christ's kingship is an issue at his trial
Pilate questions Jesus Christ Lk 23:2–3 pp Mt 27:11 pp Mk 15:2 pp Jn 18:33 *Pilate's first words to Jesus Christ are the same in all the Gospels.*

Jesus Christ claims to be a spiritual king Jn 18:36–37 *See also* Mt 27:11 pp Mk 15:2 pp Lk 23:3

Pilate appeals to the crowd to accept Jesus Christ as their king Mk 15:9

The crowd reject Jesus Christ as king Mk 15:12–13 *See also* Jn 19:12–15

Jesus Christ is mocked as king Mt 27:27–30 pp Mk 15:16–20 pp Jn 19:2–3

Jesus Christ is declared king at his crucifixion
Jn 19:19–22 pp Mt 27:37 pp Mk 15:26 pp Lk 23:38 *Jesus Christ's claim to be king was the "crime" for which he was executed.*

God has exalted Jesus Christ to his rightful place as king
Heb 1:3 *See also* Heb 8:1; 12:2; Rev 5:6; 7:17; 22:1–3

As king, Jesus Christ welcomes believers into his kingdom
Lk 23:42–43 *See also* 2Ti 4:18; Rev 3:20–21

Jesus Christ is king of all kings
He will rule over the nations Rev 1:5 *See also* Ps 2:7–9; Da 7:13–14; Mt 19:28; 25:31–32; Ro 15:12; 1Co 15:25; Php 2:9–10; Rev 12:5; 17:14; 19:11–16

He is king for ever Rev 11:15 *See also* Isa 9:7; Lk 1:33; Heb 1:8; Ps 45:6

See also
2215 Christ, Son of	2372 Christ, victory
David	2375 kingdom of
2230 Messiah,	God
coming of	2525 Christ, cross of
2336 Christ,	2565 Christ, second
exaltation	coming
2345 Christ, kingdom	2585 Christ, trial
of	2590 Christ,
2366 Christ,	triumphal entry
prophecies	5368 kingship
concerning	

2315
Jesus Christ, as Lamb

Jesus Christ is referred to as the "Lamb of God". This symbol points to Christ being a perfect sacrifice for sin. It also conveys his meekness and his willingness to submit to suffering and death.

The imagery of the lamb
An image of innocence and attraction Isa 11:6 *See also* Lev 23:12; 2Sa 12:3

An image of submissiveness and vulnerability Jer 11:19 *See also* Isa 40:11; Lk 10:3; Jn 21:15

An image of quiet suffering Isa 53:7

An image of sacrifice Ex 29:38 *"each day" here refers to the seven-day period of the consecration of priests. See also* Ex 12:27; Lev 3:7; 4:32; 14:13; Eze 46:13; Mk 14:12 pp Lk 22:7

Jesus Christ is likened to a lamb
Jn 1:36 *See also* Jn 1:29; 1Co 5:7; 1Pe 1:19; Rev 5:6

The symbolism of the lamb applies to Jesus Christ
Jesus Christ is innocent and draws people to himself Lk 23:41 *See also* Jn 12:32; Heb 4:15; 7:26; 1Pe 2:22; Isa 53:9

Jesus Christ was submissive and vulnerable Mt 26:38–39
pp Mk 14:35–36 pp Lk 22:41–42 *See also* Jn 3:27; 1Co 1:27; Php 2:7–8; Heb 4:15

Jesus Christ suffered quietly
Mt 27:28–31 pp Mk 15:17–20 *See also* Mt 26:62–63 pp Mk 14:60–61; Mt 27:12–14 pp Mk 15:3–5; Lk 23:8–11; Jn 19:2–3; Ac 8:32–35; Isa 53:7–8; 1Pe 2:23

Jesus Christ is seen as a sacrifice
1Pe 1:18–19 *See also* Ge 22:8; Ex 13:13; Isa 53:4–6,10–11; Jn 1:29; 1Co 5:7; Rev 12:11; 13:8

Jesus Christ as the glorious Lamb in the book of Revelation
The Lamb is worthy Rev 5:8–12 *See also* Rev 7:9–10; 15:3

The Lamb is upon the throne Rev 17:14 *See also* Rev 5:6; 7:17; 22:1–3

The Lamb will execute judgment
Rev 6:16 *See also* Rev 6:1–3; 14:10

The Lamb is the bridegroom of the church Rev 19:7–9 *See also* Rev 21:9

See also

2009 Christ, anger of	6027 sin, remedy for
2024 Christ, glory of	6614 atonement
2063 Christ, perfection	7317 blood of Christ
2075 Christ, sinless	7436 sacrifice, NT fulfilment
2570 Christ, suffering	8305 meekness
4663 lamb	8622 worship

2318
Jesus Christ, as prophet

Jesus Christ was acclaimed as a prophet by those who witnessed his miracles and heard his teaching. They recognised him as a bearer of the word of God, who spoke with authority concerning the nature and purposes of God.

Examples of those who recognised Jesus Christ as a prophet
People anticipating the coming prophet Jn 6:14 *The reference is to the promised prophet, who, like Moses, would see God face to face (see Dt 18:15,18). See also* Jn 1:21; 7:40,52

A Samaritan woman Jn 4:17–19

Witnesses of Jesus Christ's miracles
Mt 14:1–5 pp Mk 6:14–15; Mt 16:13–14 pp Mk 8:27–28 pp Lk 9:18–19

The crowd as Jesus Christ approached Jerusalem Mt 21:10–11,46

Two of Jesus Christ's disciples after his death Lk 24:19

The apostles Peter and Stephen
Ac 3:20–23; 7:37; Dt 18:15–18

Indications of Jesus Christ being a prophet
He announced coming blessing from God Jn 7:37–40 *See also* Mt 5:3–12

pp Lk 6:20–23; Mt 13:16–17
pp Lk 10:23–24; Jn 20:19–21,29

He announced coming judgment and woe Ac 3:23 *See also* Mt 11:20–24 pp Lk 10:13–15; Mt 23:13–39; Lk 6:24–26

He possessed supernatural knowledge and insight Jn 2:24–25 *See also* Mt 9:4 pp Mk 2:8 pp Lk 5:22; Lk 7:39–43; 9:47; Jn 4:16–19

He performed mighty works and miracles Lk 7:12–17; Jn 9:17

Jesus Christ's own understanding of himself as a prophet
As a rejected prophet Lk 13:31–35 *See also* Mt 13:57 pp Mk 6:4; Lk 4:24–27; Jn 5:46

As a prophet anointed by God's Spirit
Jn 3:34 *See also* Lk 4:16–21; Isa 61:1–2

As a prophet who speaks with authority Mk 1:22; 3:28; Jn 7:16; 14:10

The place of Jesus Christ in relation to other prophets
Jesus Christ is greater than other prophets Mt 12:41 pp Lk 11:32 *See also* Jn 1:15 *John the Baptist was accepted as a prophet (e.g., Mt 11:9).*

Jesus Christ is the Messiah and Son of God Mt 16:13–17 *See also* Heb 1:1–2

The exalted Christ is the source and essence of all prophecy Rev 19:10

See also

1412 foreknowledge	2366 Christ, prophecies concerning
1427 prophecy	
2206 Jesus, the Christ	3269 Holy Spirit in Christ
2218 Christ, Son of God	5098 John the Baptist
2221 Christ, Son of Man	7304 anointing
2351 Christ, miracles	7773 prophets, role
2363 Christ, preaching & teaching	

2321
Jesus Christ, as redeemer

Jesus Christ redeems believers from all forms of sinful bondage and oppression through his death and resurrection. The price of that redemption, his own death, represents a ransom paid to secure the freedom of those held in bondage to sin.

The incarnate God as redeemer
God as redeemer Isa 63:16 *See also* Job 19:25; Isa 49:26; 59:20; Lk 1:68–75

Jesus Christ as redeemer 1Co 1:30

Forms of bondage from which Jesus Christ redeems believers
Jesus Christ redeems from slavery to sin Rev 1:5 *See also* Ps 130:8; Ro 3:23–24; 6:18,22; Tit 2:14; 3:3–5; 1Pe 3:18

Jesus Christ redeems from the curse of the law Gal 3:13 *See also* Gal 4:4–5

Jesus Christ redeems from empty religion 1Pe 1:18 *See also* Gal 4:3; Col 2:20; Heb 9:14 fn

Jesus Christ redeems from the power of Satan Col 1:13 *See also* Ac 26:18; Gal 1:4

Jesus Christ redeems from the coming judgment 1Th 1:10 *See also* Ro 5:9; 8:1–2; 1Th 5:9

Jesus Christ redeems from death
Heb 2:14–15 *See also* Hos 13:14; 1Co 15:54–57

The means by which Jesus Christ has redeemed believers
Redemption comes through the incarnation of Jesus Christ Gal 4:4–5 *See also* Ro 8:3; Heb 2:14

Jesus Christ redeems by his sacrificial death Heb 9:12 *See also* 2Co 5:21; Eph 1:7; 1Pe 1:18–19; Rev 1:5

Jesus Christ redeems by paying a ransom Mt 20:28 pp Mk 10:45 *See also* Ac 20:28; Heb 9:15; Rev 5:9

The purposes for which Jesus Christ redeems believers
Jesus Christ redeems believers so that their sins may be forgiven Eph 1:7 *See also* Ac 26:18; Col 1:14; Heb 9:15; 1Jn 1:7

Jesus Christ redeems believers to make them pure Tit 2:14 *See also* 1Co 6:19–20; 7:23

Jesus Christ redeems believers so that they may receive God's promised blessings Gal 3:14 *See also* Gal 4:5; 5:1; Heb 9:15

Jesus Christ redeems believers so that they may receive final redemption
Ro 8:23 *See also* Lk 21:28; Eph 1:14; 4:30

See also

1315 God as redeemer	6027 sin, remedy for
	6652 forgiveness
2372 Christ, victory	6714 ransom
2414 cross, centrality	6720 redemption
2530 Christ, death of	6744 sanctification
4127 Satan, defeat of	7950 mission of Christ
5564 suffering of Christ	

2324
Jesus Christ, as Saviour

God's work of salvation is accomplished supremely through the cross and resurrection of Jesus Christ. Through faith, the believer is able to share in all the saving benefits won by Jesus Christ through his obedience to God.

Jesus Christ is the Saviour
Jesus Christ is called Saviour Tit 1:4 *See also* Lk 2:11; Tit 3:6; 2Pe 1:1; 3:2,18

Jesus Christ is the promised Saviour
Ac 13:23 *See also* Lk 1:69–75; 2:28–30

Jesus Christ's purpose is to save
Lk 19:10 *See also* Mt 1:21; 1Ti 1:15

Jesus Christ's qualities as Saviour
Jesus Christ is the unique Saviour
Ac 4:12 *See also* Jn 6:68–69; 10:9; 14:6; Ac 10:42–43

Jesus Christ is the complete Saviour
Heb 7:25 See also Jn 19:30; Php 3:21; Col 1:19–20; Heb 5:9; 9:26–28; 1Jn 1:9; Jude 24

Jesus Christ is the Saviour of the world
Jn 4:42 See also Lk 2:30–32; 1Ti 2:5–6; 4:10; 1Jn 4:14

Jesus Christ saves through his grace
Ac 15:11 See also Ro 3:24; Eph 5:23–27; Tit 3:4–5

Jesus Christ saves by his mighty acts
Jesus Christ saves by his death 1Pe 1:18–19 See also Mt 20:28 pp Mk 10:45; Lk 24:45–47; Jn 1:29,36; 10:15,17–18; 1Co 1:18; Rev 7:10

Jesus Christ saves by his resurrection life 1Pe 3:21 See also Ro 5:10; 2Ti 1:10

Jesus Christ saves by his coming again Php 3:20 See also Tit 2:13; Heb 9:28; 1Pe 1:5

Jesus Christ saves by defeating Satan 1Jn 3:8 See also Jn 13:31; 16:11; Heb 2:14; Rev 2:10–11

Jesus Christ saves from all forms of evil
Jesus Christ saves from physical danger Mt 8:25–26 pp Mk 4:38–39 pp Lk 8:24–25; Ac 26:17; 2Co 1:10; 2Ti 4:18

Jesus Christ saves from the power of sin 1Jn 1:7 See also Ac 5:31; Ro 3:25–26; 5:18–19; 6:6–7; Gal 1:4; Rev 1:5–6

Jesus Christ saves from the condemnation of law Gal 3:13 See also Ac 13:38–39; Ro 8:1–4; Gal 4:4–5; Eph 2:15

Jesus Christ saves from God's wrath 1Th 1:10 See also Ro 5:9; 1Th 5:9; Rev 11:17–18

Jesus Christ saves from the power of death 2Ti 1:10 See also 1Co 15:55–57; Heb 2:15; Rev 20:6; 21:4

Jesus Christ saves from Satan's power Ac 26:18 See also Lk 10:18–19; 13:16; Col 1:13; 1Jn 3:8

Jesus Christ saves to bring people to God
Jesus Christ saves for eternal life Jn 6:40 See also Jn 3:14–16,36; 5:24–25; Ro 6:23

Jesus Christ saves so that people may live for God 1Jn 4:9 See also Ro 6:8–11; 7:21–25; Gal 2:20; 2Ti 1:9; Heb 9:14–15; 1Pe 2:24; 1Jn 3:5–6; 5:18

Jesus Christ's salvation is received through faith
Ac 16:30–31 See also Ac 2:21; Ro 10:13; Joel 2:32; Ro 1:16; 10:9; 2Th 2:13; 2Ti 3:15

See also
1320 God as Saviour	2560 Christ,
2027 Christ, grace &	resurrection
mercy	6020 sin
2230 Messiah,	6510 salvation
coming of	6644 eternal life
2315 Christ as Lamb	6652 forgiveness
2321 Christ as	6717 reconciliation,
redeemer	world to God
2410 cross, the	

2327
Jesus Christ, as servant

Jesus Christ laid aside his majesty in order to serve humanity. His death is the supreme example of his servanthood: the fulfilling of the will of God his Father.

The prophets speak of the Messiah as a servant
Mt 12:17–21 See also Isa 42:1–4; 49:1–7; 50:4–9; 52:13–53:12; Eze 34:23–24; 37:24–25; Zec 3:8

Jesus Christ describes himself as a servant
Lk 22:27 See also Mt 20:28 pp Mk 10:45

Jesus Christ acts as a servant
By coming to dwell among humanity as a man Php 2:6–7 See also 2Co 8:9

By obeying God's will Jn 4:34 See also Jn 5:30; 6:38; 14:31; Heb 10:5–7; Ps 40:6–8

By ministering to his disciples Jn 13:1–17

By dying on the cross Mt 20:28 pp Mk 10:45 See also Mt 26:39 pp Mk 14:36 pp Lk 22:42; Php 2:8

The exaltation of Jesus Christ the servant
He will complete his task Jn 17:4; 19:30

He will be exalted by God Ac 3:13 See also Isa 52:13; Ac 3:26; Php 2:9–11

Jesus Christ's obedience and servanthood an example to believers
Jn 13:14–15 See also Php 2:5; 1Pe 2:21

See also
1429 prophecy, OT	5522 servants, work
fulfilment	conditions
2036 Christ, humility	5959 submission
2048 Christ, love of	7160 servants of the
2057 Christ,	Lord
obedience	8344 servanthood in
2339 Christ, example	believers
of	8454 obedience to
2530 Christ, death of	God
2570 Christ,	
suffering	

2330
Jesus Christ, as shepherd

A title for Jesus Christ indicating believers' dependence on him as he protects, tends and guides those whom he knows intimately.

Prophecies about the shepherd Messiah
Eze 34:23 See also Eze 37:24; Mic 5:2; Mt 2:6; Mic 5:4; Zec 13:7; Mt 26:31 pp Mk 14:27

Jesus Christ's role as the good shepherd
He has compassion for the helpless Mt 9:36 See also Mk 6:34; Jn 11:52

He seeks lost sheep Mt 18:12–14 pp Lk 15:3–7 See also Mt 10:6; 15:24; Lk 19:10; Jn 10:16

He knows his own sheep Jn 10:14–15 See also Mt 25:32; Jn 10:27

His sheep know his voice Jn 10:4 See also Jn 10:3,5,16,27

He provides for and protects his sheep Jn 10:9 See also Jn 10:28

He lays down his life for his sheep Jn 10:11 See also Mt 26:31 pp Mk 14:27; Jn 10:14–15,17–18

He judges the sheep Mt 25:32–46

Jesus Christ shepherds his flock
Christians are Jesus Christ's flock Lk 12:32 See also Mt 10:16; Jn 10:16; Ac 20:29; Ro 8:36

Under-shepherds are appointed over Jesus Christ's flock Jn 21:15–17 See also Ac 20:28; 1Pe 5:2–4

Jesus Christ the risen Lord is Shepherd
Rev 7:17 See also Heb 13:20; 1Pe 2:25; 5:4

See also
1205 God, titles of	7130 flock, God's
1220 God as	7789 shepherd,
shepherd	church leader
2015 Christ,	8124 guidance
compassion	8224 dependence
2230 Messiah,	
coming of	

2333
Jesus Christ, attitude to OT

Jesus Christ's teaching was based largely on the OT, which he treated as God's inspired and authoritative word, but which he had the authority to interpret.

Jesus Christ recognises the OT as Scripture
Jesus Christ calls the OT "Scripture" Jn 10:35 See also Mk 12:10,24 pp Mt 22:29; Lk 4:21; Jn 5:39; 7:38; 13:18

Jesus Christ underlines the authority of the OT
Jn 5:46–47

The OT is authoritative over Jesus Christ's opponents Mt 23:23 See also Mt 5:19–20; 23:2–3; Mk 2:24–27 pp Mt 12:2–6 pp Lk 6:2–4

The OT is authoritative over Satan Mt 4:4 pp Lk 4:4 See also Dt 8:3; Mt 4:7 pp Lk 4:12; Dt 6:16; Mt 4:10 pp Lk 4:8; Dt 6:13

Jesus Christ regards the OT as being fulfilled in himself
Jesus Christ regards his ministry as fulfilling the OT Mt 5:17–18 See also Mt 11:4–6 pp Lk 7:22–23; Mt 26:56 pp Mk 14:49; Lk 4:17–21; Isa 61:1–2; Jn 15:25; Ps 35:19; 69:4

Jesus Christ regards his death as fulfilling OT prophecy Lk 18:31–32 See also Mt 12:39–40; 26:28 pp Lk 22:20; Mt 26:31 pp Mk 14:27; Zec 13:7

Other aspects of the OT fulfilled or affirmed by Jesus Christ Mt 7:12; 11:10 pp Lk 7:27; Mal 3:1; Mt 13:14–15 pp Mk 4:12 pp Lk 8:10; Isa 6:9–10; Mt 17:11–12 pp Mk 9:12–13; Mal 4:5;

Mt 24:15 pp Mk 13:14 pp Lk 21:20;
Da 9:27; 11:31; 12:11

Jesus Christ confirms the OT teaching about judgment
Mt 12:41–42 pp Lk 11:30–32 *See also* Mt 11:23 pp Lk 10:12–15

Jesus Christ interprets OT teaching
Jesus Christ interprets OT teaching about the Sabbath Mk 2:25–28 pp Mt 12:3–8 pp Lk 6:3–5

Jesus Christ interprets OT teaching about religious practices Mt 9:13; Hos 6:6; Mt 15:7–8 pp Mk 7:6–7; Isa 29:13

Jesus Christ interprets OT teaching about purity Mk 7:18–19 pp Mt 15:17

Jesus Christ interprets OT teaching about family life Mt 5:31–32; 15:4–6 pp Mk 7:10–13; Ex 20:12; Dt 5:16; Ex 21:17; Lev 20:9; Mt 19:1–9 pp Mk 10:2–9

Jesus Christ interprets OT teaching about retaliation Mt 5:38–42

Jesus Christ refers to the OT in his teaching
Mt 19:18 pp Mk 10:19 pp Lk 18:20; Ex 20:12–16; Dt 5:16–20; Mt 22:31–32 pp Mk 12:26–27 pp Lk 20:37–38; Ex 3:6; Mt 24:37–39 pp Lk 17:26–27

Jesus Christ uses the language of the OT
Mt 27:46 pp Mk 15:34; Ps 22:1; Mk 4:29; Joel 3:13; Mk 8:18; Isa 6:10; Mk 9:48; Isa 66:24

Jesus Christ appeals to the OT in its entirety
Lk 11:50–51 *The murders of Abel and Zechariah occur in the first (Ge 4:8) and last (2Ch 24:21) books of the Hebrew OT (Chronicles comes at the close of the OT according to the Hebrew arrangement). See also Lk 24:27,44 The Law, the Prophets and the Psalms are the three divisions of the Hebrew OT.*

Jesus Christ treats the OT as a true historical record
The patriarchs: Mt 8:11; Jn 8:56,58
Moses: Mt 8:4 pp Mk 1:44 pp Lk 5:14; Mt 19:8 pp Mk 10:5
Mt 6:29 pp Lk 12:27 *Solomon*
The prophets: Mt 5:12 pp Lk 6:23; Lk 4:25–27; Jn 6:45

See also

1611 Scripture, inspiration & authority	4126 Satan, resistance to
2354 Christ, mission	5496 revenge, examples
2363 Christ, preaching & teaching	5675 divorce
	5731 parents
2366 Christ, prophecies concerning	7552 Pharisees, attitudes to Christ
2530 Christ, death of	9210 judgment, God's
2575 Christ, temptation	

2336
Jesus Christ, exaltation of

Having completed his work on earth,

Jesus Christ is raised to God's right hand where he receives honour, power and glory.

Jesus Christ is exalted to God's right hand
1Pe 3:21–22 *God's right hand is the position of authority second only to the Father. See also* Mt 26:64 pp Mk 14:62 pp Lk 22:69; Ac 2:33; 3:20–21; 7:55–56; Heb 1:3; 12:2

Jesus Christ is exalted because he first humbled himself
Lk 24:26 *See also* Php 2:6–11; 1Ti 3:16; Rev 5:6–14; 7:17; 22:3

Jesus Christ's exaltation follows his resurrection and ascension
1Pe 1:21 *See also* Mk 16:19; Ac 13:37; Eph 1:20

Jesus Christ's exaltation is predicted in the OT
As God's servant Isa 52:13 *This "servant" is a specific prediction of Jesus Christ.*

Jesus Christ is exalted by God the Father
Php 2:9–11 *See also* Ac 2:36; 5:31

The work of the exalted Christ
As Saviour Ac 5:31 *See also* Heb 7:25

As high priest and advocate Ro 8:34 *See also* Heb 4:14; 7:24–26; 8:1–2; 9:24; 1Jn 2:1

In giving the Holy Spirit and spiritual gifts to his people Ac 2:33 *See also* Eph 4:8–13

In making every authority subject to him Eph 1:20–22 *See also* 1Co 15:24–26; Php 2:9–11; Heb 2:7–9; 10:12–13; 1Pe 3:22; Rev 17:14; 19:16

Believers should lead lives that are mindful of Jesus Christ's exaltation
Believers are exalted with Jesus Christ Eph 2:6 *See also* Rev 3:21

Believers should be concerned with heavenly values Col 3:1–4 *See also* Php 3:20; Heb 12:2–3

See also

1270 right hand of God	2312 Christ as king
2012 Christ, authority	2324 Christ as Saviour
2024 Christ, glory of	2327 Christ as servant
2051 Christ, majesty of	2505 Christ, ascension
2212 Christ, head of church	2560 Christ, resurrection
2224 Christ, the Lord	5849 exaltation

2339
Jesus Christ, example of

Jesus Christ sets his disciples an example, especially in servanthood, self-denial and endurance of suffering, so that they may become like him.

Jesus Christ calls believers to follow his example
Jn 13:14–16 *See also* Heb 3:1; 12:2–3; 1Pe 2:21; 1Jn 2:6

The qualities of Jesus Christ which set an example for believers
Self-denial Php 2:4–5 *See also* Mt 10:38; 16:24 pp Mk 8:34 pp Lk 9:23; Lk 14:27; Heb 12:2

Endurance of suffering 1Pe 2:21–23 *See also* Mt 10:24–25; Jn 15:20; 1Th 2:14–15; Heb 12:3

Service Mt 20:25–28 pp Mk 10:42–45; Jn 13:13–17

Faithfulness Heb 3:1–2

Love Eph 5:1–2,25; 1Jn 3:16

Patience 1Ti 1:16

Forgiveness of others Eph 4:32; Col 3:13

Gentleness and humility Mt 11:29

Purity 1Jn 3:3

Prayer Lk 11:1

God wants his people to follow Jesus Christ's example and be conformed to his image
Ro 8:29; 1Co 15:49

Those who followed Jesus Christ's example
1Co 11:1 *Paul;* 1Th 1:6 *the converts in Thessalonica;* Ac 7:60 *Stephen is following the example set by Jesus Christ in Lk 23:34.*

See also

2030 Christ, holiness	8120 following Christ
2036 Christ, humility	
2048 Christ, love of	8206 Christlikeness
2327 Christ as servant	8428 example
	8449 imitating
2570 Christ, suffering	8453 obedience
	8475 self-denial
6652 forgiveness	

2342
Jesus Christ, Holy Spirit in life of

See 3269 Holy Spirit, in life of Jesus Christ

2345
Jesus Christ, kingdom of

The present and future realm in which Jesus Christ exercises full authority, and through which he triumphs over all opposition.

Jesus Christ's kingdom is a heavenly kingdom
It is not of this world Jn 18:36 *See also* Rev 5:6; 7:10; 21:1,3

The kingdom was given to him by God Da 7:14 *See also* Ps 72:1; Da 2:44; Mt 28:18; Jn 16:15

The kingdom is his by right Col 1:15–16 *See also* Heb 1:8; Ps 45:6; Rev 22:13

Jesus Christ inherits the kingdom promised to David
Lk 1:32 *See also* Ro 15:12; Isa 11:10; Rev 2:27; Ps 2:9

Jesus Christ reveals God's kingdom on earth

Jesus Christ brought in God's kingdom
Mt 4:17 *The expressions "kingdom of heaven" and the "kingdom of God" are interchangeable. See also* Mt 3:2; 10:7; 12:28 pp Lk 11:20; Mk 1:15; Lk 17:20–21

Miracles are a sign of the kingdom
Jn 6:14–15 *See also* Mt 8:26–27 pp Mk 4:39–41 pp Lk 8:24–25 *authority over the created world;* Mt 11:2–5 pp Lk 7:19–22 *authority to heal* Authority *over life and death:* Lk 7:11–15; Rev 1:17–18

Parables are a sign of the kingdom
Mt 13:1–52 *See also* Mk 4:1–34; Lk 8:4–15; 13:18–21

Jesus Christ exercises kingdom authority today

Believers enter Jesus Christ's kingdom immediately Lk 23:42–43 *See also* Mt 5:3 pp Lk 6:20; Mt 11:11

Believers are redeemed from the kingdom of darkness Col 1:12–13 *See also* Eph 5:5

Believers enjoy the blessings of Jesus Christ's kingdom now Mt 16:19 *See also* Da 7:22,27; Lk 12:32; 22:29–30; Jas 2:5; Rev 1:5–6,9; 3:21

Jesus Christ rules over every authority now 1Pe 3:22 *See also* Eph 1:20–23; Php 2:9; Col 2:10; Heb 12:2; Rev 12:10; 19:16

Jesus Christ's kingdom will be fully established at his return

His kingdom will come with power at a specific moment Mt 25:31 *See also* Zec 9:10; Mt 24:30–31 pp Mk 13:26–27 pp Lk 21:27; 2Ti 4:1

His kingdom will replace all earthly authority Rev 11:15 *See also* 1Co 15:24–25,50–52; Php 3:20–21

All creation will acknowledge Jesus Christ's kingship Php 2:10–11 *See also* Ps 2:6–8; Rev 5:13

His kingdom lasts for ever Lk 1:33 *See also* Isa 9:7

See also
2051 Christ, majesty of	2375 kingdom of God
2069 Christ, pre-eminence	2565 Christ, second coming
2215 Christ, Son of David	5369 kingship, divine
2233 Son of Man	7950 mission of Christ
2312 Christ as king	9145 Messianic age
2351 Christ, miracles	
2357 Christ, parables	

2348

Jesus Christ, life of

See 2500 Jesus Christ, history of

2351

Jesus Christ, miracles of

Supernatural acts of Jesus Christ, revealing and confirming his Messianic credentials, and the coming of God's kingdom. The miracles of Christ are to be seen as an integral part of his ministry.

Examples of the kind of miracles Jesus Christ performed

Authority over natural forces Mt 8:27 pp Mk 4:41 pp Lk 8:25 *See also* Mt 14:19–20 pp Mk 6:41–43 pp Lk 9:16–17 pp Jn 6:11–13 *the feeding of 5,000;* Mt 14:25 pp Mk 6:48 pp Jn 6:19 *Jesus Christ walks on water;* Mt 17:27; Lk 5:4,6; Jn 2:9 *Jesus Christ turns water into wine.*

Healing the sick Mt 4:24 *See also* Mt 8:13 pp Lk 7:10; Mt 8:15 pp Mk 1:31 pp Lk 4:39 *Simon's mother-in-law;* Mt 9:22 pp Mk 5:29 pp Lk 8:44 *the woman with the issue of blood;* Mt 9:29–30; 12:13 pp Mk 3:5 pp Lk 6:10 *the man with a shrivelled hand;* Mk 7:35; Lk 17:14; Jn 4:52–53; 5:8–9; 9:6–7

Casting out demons Mk 1:34 pp Mt 8:16 pp Lk 4:41 *See also* Mt 9:33; 12:22 pp Lk 11:14; Mt 17:18 pp Mk 9:25–26 pp Lk 9:42

Raising the dead Lk 7:14–15 *See also* Mt 9:25 pp Mk 5:41–42 pp Lk 8:54–55; Jn 11:43–44

The purpose of Jesus Christ's miracles

To bring healing and wholeness Lk 8:35 *See also* Mt 15:28; Lk 17:14–15; Jn 9:38

To reveal God's kingdom Mt 12:28 pp Lk 11:20 *See also* Mt 11:4–5 pp Lk 7:22

To fulfil God's word Mt 8:16–17 *See also* Isa 53:4; Mt 12:15–17; Lk 4:18–19; Isa 61:1–2; Lk 4:21

To bring glory to God Jn 11:4 *See also* Mt 15:31; Jn 2:11

To show Jesus to be the Messiah Ac 2:22 *See also* Mt 11:3–5 pp Lk 7:19–22; Jn 5:36; 10:25,37–38; 11:42

Varying responses to Jesus Christ's miracles

Terror and fear Mk 4:41 pp Lk 8:25 *See also* Mt 8:34; Mk 5:15 pp Lk 8:35

Wonder and amazement Lk 4:36 pp Mk 1:27 *See also* Mt 9:33; 12:23; Lk 9:43; 11:14

Faith and gratitude Lk 19:37 *See also* Mk 5:18–20 pp Lk 8:38–39; Lk 17:15–16; Jn 9:38; 14:11; 20:30–31

Opposition and hatred Jn 15:24 *See also* Mt 11:20–21 pp Lk 10:13; Mt 12:24 pp Mk 3:22 pp Lk 11:15; Jn 12:10–11,37–38

Limitations on Jesus Christ's miracles

Jesus Christ restricted his miracles because of superficial faith Jn 2:23–24 *See also* Mt 12:38–39 pp Lk 11:29; Mt 16:1–4 pp Mk 8:11–12; Jn 2:18; 6:30

Miracles require faith Mt 13:58 pp Mk 6:5 *See also* Mt 14:28–31; 17:14–20

Jesus Christ's miracles performed through others

Through the disciples during Jesus Christ's lifetime Mt 10:1 pp Mk 3:14–15 pp Lk 9:1–2; Mk 9:38 pp Lk 9:49; Lk 10:17

Through the apostles after Jesus Christ's ascension Ac 3:6,16; 4:10; 5:12; 6:8; 8:6–7; 16:18; 19:11; 2Co 12:12

Through the church 1Co 12:10,28–29

See also
1045 God, glory of	2375 kingdom of God
1415 miracles	
1448 signs	5333 healing
2206 Jesus, the Christ	5784 amazement
	8020 faith
2345 Christ, kingdom of	8835 unbelief
	9310 resurrection

2354

Jesus Christ, mission of

The work that Jesus Christ was sent to do, including both his healing and preaching ministry, but particularly his work of salvation. Jesus Christ sends Christians to continue his work by proclaiming his message of salvation.

Jesus Christ was called to his mission from the beginning of time

Isa 49:1 *See also* Mic 5:2; 1Pe 1:20

Jesus' mission as Messiah was foretold

His mission to help and heal the poor Isa 61:1–3 *See also* Isa 11:3–5; 32:3–4; 35:5–6; 42:3,7

His mission to rule and establish the kingdom of God Isa 9:6–7 *See also* Ge 49:10; Ps 132:11; Jer 23:5–6; Da 2:44

His mission to establish justice and peace Isa 11:4–5 *See also* Isa 2:4; 9:4–7; 42:4

His mission to suffer and die Isa 53:3–10 *See also* Isa 50:6; 52:14; Da 9:26; Mk 8:31; Lk 24:26–27; Ac 8:32–35

His mission was fulfilled in humility and poverty Zec 9:9 *See also* Isa 42:2–3; 49:7

His mission was for all nations Isa 49:6 *See also* Isa 11:10; 42:1–6; 55:4–5

Aspects of Jesus Christ's mission

Preaching and teaching Lk 4:43 pp Mk 1:38 *See also* Mt 4:17; 5:2; Mk 1:21; Jn 8:2; 18:37

Sacrificial service Mt 20:28 pp Mk 10:45 *See also* Lk 22:27; Jn 13:13–16; Php 2:7

Healing Mt 4:23 *A healing ministry was one of the signs of the expected Messiah. See also* Mt 14:14; Mk 1:34; Lk 4:40; 5:15; Jn 9:4–7

Judgment Jn 9:39 *Jesus Christ does not come to condemn, but the response people make to him is the ultimate criterion of judgment. Those truly seeking God turn to faith in Jesus Christ; unbelievers, by their rejection of him, are confirmed in their unbelief. See also* Lk 12:49; Jn 3:17–18; 5:22; 8:10–11,26; 12:47–48

Criteria for the direction of Jesus Christ's mission
Obedience to his Father's will Jn 6:38
See also Mt 26:39 pp Mk 14:36
pp Lk 22:42; Jn 4:34; 14:31; 18:11

The fulfilment of the Law and the Prophets Mt 5:17 *See also* Mt 13:35;
26:54; Lk 4:18–21; 18:31; Ro 3:21

Jesus Christ's saving death is the supreme aspect and focus of his mission
Jesus Christ came to save and to give life Jn 10:10 *See also* Mt 1:21; Lk 19:10;
Jn 3:17; 1Ti 1:15; 2Ti 1:10

Jesus Christ came to suffer and to die
Mt 16:21   pp Mk 8:31 pp Lk 9:22 *See also*
Mt 20:28 pp Mk 10:45; Jn 12:27;
Ro 3:24–25; Col 1:20; 1Jn 4:10

Jesus Christ was aware of the personal cost of his mission Lk 12:50
See also Mt 26:38–39 pp Mk 14:34–36
pp Lk 22:42

The mission of Jesus Christ continues today
Jesus Christ's own work continues
Heb 7:24–25 *See also* Ro 8:34; 15:18;
2Co 4:10–11; Heb 6:20; 9:12,14; 13:21

Christians are called to share in Jesus Christ's mission Jn 20:21 *See also*
Mt 28:19–20; Mk 16:15; Jn 14:12

See also
1513 Trinity, mission of	2570 Christ, suffering
2230 Messiah, coming of	3212 Holy Spirit & mission
2324 Christ as Saviour	7027 church, purpose
2327 Christ as servant	7739 missionaries
2351 Christ, miracles	7950 mission of Christ
2525 Christ, cross of	8424 evangelism

2357
Jesus Christ, parables of

A central feature of Jesus Christ's teaching was the use of extended similes and short stories about the kingdom of God, based on human experience. Christ used them frequently to call for a response to his message.

Parables are a central feature of Jesus Christ's teaching
Mt 13:34–35 *See also* Ps 78:2;
Mk 4:33–34

Different characteristics of Jesus Christ's parables
They vary in complexity and length
Mt 7:6; 13:18–23 pp Mk 4:13–20
pp Lk 8:11–15; Mt 13:37–45,52

They vary in their use of metaphors, word pictures, objects and actions
Mt 5:13–16; 13:44; 18:2–3; 21:18–22
pp Mk 11:12–14, 20–24; Lk 15:8–10

They have different levels of meaning
Often the full impact of a parable may be lost if the Jewish context is not understood:
Lk 10:30–37; 15:11–32

They draw on human experience
Mt 13:33 pp Lk 13:20–21; Mt 18:12–14
pp Lk 15:4–7; Lk 7:41–43

The themes of Jesus Christ's parables
The kingdom of God Mk 4:30
pp Lk 13:18 *See also* Mt 13:31–32
pp Mk 4:31–32 pp Lk 13:19–21;
Mt 13:44–45; Mk 4:26–29

Relationship with God Lk 15:20 *See also*
Mt 7:9–11 pp Lk 11:11–13;
Mt 18:12–14 pp Lk 15:4–7; Lk 18:7–8

Right behaviour Lk 10:37 *See also*
Mt 7:24–27 pp Lk 6:47–49; Lk 13:6–9;
15:27

The time of the end Mt 25:34 *See also*
Mt 25:1,14–19 pp Lk 19:11–15;
Mk 13:35; Lk 12:35–36,40 pp Mt 24:44;
Lk 16:22–23

Jesus Christ speaks about himself
Mt 21:37   pp Mk 12:6 pp Lk 20:13 *See also* Mt 22:2; 25:10
The "I am" sayings of Jesus Christ are brief picture parables: Jn 6:35; 8:12; 10:14;
15:1

Understanding Jesus Christ's parables
Further explanation is sometimes needed Mt 13:36 *See also* Mt 13:18
pp Mk 4:13 pp Lk 8:11; Mt 15:15
pp Mk 7:17

The meaning is sometimes hidden
Lk 8:9–10 pp Mt 13:11–16
pp Mk 4:11–12 *The meaning of Jesus Christ's parables was concealed only from those whose hearts and minds were closed.*
See also Isa 6:9–10

Responses to Jesus Christ's parables
The parables demand action
Mt 5:14–16 *See also* Mt 4:24; 7:5–6;
13:43,45–46; 25:13,40,45;
Lk 12:21,32–33

Positive responses Mt 13:16 *See also*
Mt 7:28–29; 13:51

Rejection of Jesus Christ and his parables Lk 20:19   pp Mt 21:45–46
pp Mk 12:12 *See also* Lk 16:14

Examples of Jesus Christ's parables
Mt 13:1–23 pp Mk 4:1–20 pp Lk 8:4–15
parable of the sower; Mt 13:47–52
parable of the net; Mt 18:12–14
pp Lk 15:4–7 *parable of the lost sheep;*
Lk 10:25–37 *parable of the good Samaritan;* Lk 15:11–32 *parable of the lost son;* Lk 18:9–14 *parable of the Pharisee and the tax collector*

See also
1670 symbols	5409 metaphor
2363 Christ, preaching & teaching	5438 parables
	5660 bridegroom
2375 kingdom of God	8309 morality
	9105 last things
2565 Christ, second coming	9410 heaven
	9510 hell

2360
Jesus Christ, prayers of

Prayer was the essence of Jesus Christ's relationship with the Father. He prayed for himself and his

mission, and he continues to pray for all believers.

Jesus Christ's practice of prayer
He prayed regularly Lk 5:16 *Luke records more instances of Jesus Christ praying than any other Gospel writer.*

He often prayed alone Mk 1:35 *See also*
Mt 14:23 pp Mk 6:46; Lk 6:12; 9:18

Prayer at specific times in Jesus Christ's life
Before his death: Mt 26:36–46
pp Mk 14:32–41 pp Lk 22:39–46;
Jn 17:1–26
On the cross: Mt 27:46 pp Mk 15:34;
Lk 23:34,46
Lk 3:21–22 *at his baptism;* Lk 6:12–13
before choosing the apostles; Lk 9:28–29
before his transfiguration

Characteristics of Jesus Christ's prayers
Communion with his Father Mt 6:9
pp Lk 11:2; Mt 11:27 pp Lk 10:22

Submission to his Father Heb 5:7 *See also* Mt 6:10; 26:36 pp Mk 14:36
pp Lk 22:42

Giving praise and thanks to his Father
Mt 11:25–26 pp Lk 10:21 *See also*
Mt 14:19 pp Mk 6:41 pp Lk 9:16
pp Jn 6:11; Mt 15:36 pp Mk 8:6–7;
Mt 26:26–27 pp Mk 14:22–23
pp Lk 22:17–19 pp 1Co 11:24 *the Lord's Supper;* Lk 24:30; Jn 11:41–42

The scope of Jesus Christ's prayers
Mt 19:13–15 pp Mk 10:13–16
pp Lk 18:15–17 *for children*
For his disciples: Lk 22:31–32; Jn 14:16;
17:6–19
Lk 23:34 *for his persecutors*
For himself: Jn 12:27–28; 17:1–5
Jn 17:20–26 *for all believers*

Jesus Christ's continuing ministry of prayer
Heb 7:25 *See also* Ro 8:34; 1Jn 2:1

Jesus Christ's teaching about prayer
Mt 6:9–15 pp Lk 11:2–4 *See also*
Mt 5:44; 6:5–8; Lk 6:28; 18:1–8,9–14;
21:36

See also
2057 Christ, obedience	2570 Christ, suffering
2306 Christ, high priest	8352 thankfulness
	8602 prayer
2525 Christ, cross of	8658 Lord's Prayer
2530 Christ, death of	

2363
Jesus Christ, preaching and teaching of

A vital feature of Jesus Christ's ministry, focusing on his authoritative proclamation of the kingdom of God.

Jesus Christ's mission as preaching and teaching
Lk 4:43   pp Mk 1:38 *See also* Mt 11:5
pp Lk 7:22; Mk 6:6; Jn 7:16; Ac 1:1

Jesus Christ was regarded as a teacher and prophet

Jn 1:38 *"Rabbi" was an honorific title given to Jesus Christ unofficially by the people. See also* Mt 16:14 pp Mk 8:28 pp Lk 9:19; Mt 23:10; 26:25; Mk 9:5; 10:51; Jn 13:13

The sources of Jesus Christ's preaching and teaching

Jesus Christ's words were grounded in Scripture Lk 24:27 *See also* Mt 4:4 pp Lk 4:4; Dt 8:3; Mt 21:16; Ps 8:2; Mt 22:29–32 pp Mk 12:24–27 pp Lk 20:35–38

Jesus Christ's words came from God Jn 7:16 *See also* Jn 3:2; 8:28; 12:49–50

Jesus Christ spoke in the power of the Spirit Ac 1:2 *See also* Lk 4:14–15; Jn 3:34; 6:63

The content of Jesus Christ's preaching and teaching

The kingdom of God Lk 9:11 *See also* Mt 4:17,23; 6:33; 13:24; Mk 1:15; Jn 3:3

God as Father Jn 14:8–14 *See also* Mt 6:31–32 pp Lk 12:30–31; Mt 10:32–33; 18:10; Mk 11:25; Jn 5:17–23; 8:18–19

Jesus Christ's own identity Jn 4:25–26 *See also* Mt 16:13–17 pp Mk 8:27–30 pp Lk 9:18–21; Lk 4:20–21; 24:44; Jn 10:11; 14:6–7

Jesus Christ's mission Mk 9:31 pp Mt 17:22–23 pp Lk 9:44 *See also* Mt 20:17–19 pp Mk 10:32–34 pp Lk 18:31–34; Lk 19:9–10; 24:46; Jn 6:51; 10:14–15

How people should live Mt 5:48 *See also* Mt 5:20–22,43–44; 7:12; 19:21–24 pp Mk 10:21–25 pp Lk 18:22–25; Mt 22:35–40 pp Mk 12:28–31; Lk 6:35; Jn 13:34–35; 15:12–13

The future Mk 14:62 pp Lk 22:69 *See also* Mt 10:15 pp Lk 10:12; Mt 12:36–37; 24:1–2 pp Mk 13:1–2 pp Lk 21:5–6; Mt 24:36–44; 25:31–33; Lk 17:26–35

Jesus Christ criticised false teachings Mt 15:6–9 pp Mk 7:6–7 *See also* Isa 29:13; Mt 7:15–16; 16:12; 23:2–4; Mk 12:38–39 pp Lk 20:45–46

The results of Jesus Christ's preaching and teaching

Jesus Christ invited a response Mt 11:28–30 *See also* Mt 13:23 pp Mk 4:20 pp Lk 8:15; Mt 22:8–10; Lk 14:21–24; Jn 5:24

Jesus Christ looked for an obedient response Lk 11:28 *See also* Mt 7:24–27; 11:15; 13:23 pp Mk 4:20 pp Lk 8:15; Mt 28:20; Mk 4:9; Jn 14:23–24

People responded to Jesus Christ's preaching and teaching Jn 12:42 *See also* Mt 8:19–22 pp Lk 9:57–60; Mt 13:10–15 pp Mk 4:10–12; Jn 4:39; 6:68–69

Characteristics of Jesus Christ's preaching and teaching

It had authority Mt 7:28–29 *See also* Mt 21:23 pp Mk 11:28 pp Lk 20:2; Mt 22:22 pp Mk 12:17 pp Lk 20:26; Mk 1:22 pp Lk 4:32; Mk 1:27; Jn 7:15

Jesus Christ lived out what he preached and taught Jn 10:38 *The "miracles" (literally "works") conveyed the*

same message as Jesus Christ's words. See also* Mt 11:29; 16:24 pp Mk 8:34 pp Lk 9:23; Jn 13:15,34

Jesus Christ's preaching and teaching methods

His use of lessons drawn from people's experience Mt 9:16–17 pp Mk 2:21–22 pp Lk 5:36–37; Mt 12:11–12; 18:12 pp Lk 15:4; Lk 9:62; 13:15–16

His use of parables Mt 13:34 *See also* Mt 13:3 pp Mk 4:2 pp Lk 8:4

His use of everyday objects Mt 6:26–29 pp Lk 12:23–27; Mt 22:19–21 pp Mk 12:15–17 pp Lk 20:24–25

His use of questions Mt 6:25–28; 21:24–25 pp Mk 11:29 pp Lk 20:3–4; Lk 10:36–37

See also

1040 God, fatherhood	2357 Christ, parables
1660 Sermon on the Mount	2369 Christ, responses to
2012 Christ, authority	2375 kingdom of God
2318 Christ as prophet	3269 Holy Spirit in Christ
2333 Christ, attitude to OT	7420 Rabbi
	8114 discipleship

2366
Jesus Christ, prophecies concerning

The OT points ahead to the person and ministry of Jesus Christ. Christ's fulfilment of OT prophecy is often noted by NT writers as a demonstration of God's faithfulness to his promises of salvation and as confirmation of the divine authority of Jesus Christ.

Jesus Christ fulfils OT prophecy
He fulfils the OT as a whole Lk 24:27 *See also* Mt 5:17; Lk 24:44; 2Co 1:20

He fulfils God's promises to Abraham Gal 3:14 *See also* Lk 1:54–55,72–74; Gal 3:16

He fulfils God's promises through the prophets Ac 10:43 *See also* Mt 26:56; Ac 3:18,24; 13:27; Ro 1:2; 1Pe 1:10

Prophecies about Jesus Christ's birth
Mt 1:23 *See also* Isa 7:14; Mt 1:21; Lk 1:31–32; Isa 9:6; Mt 2:6–7; Mic 5:2; Mt 2:15; Hos 11:1

Prophecies about Jesus Christ's ministry
He brings good news Lk 4:17–19 *See also* Isa 61:1–2; Mt 4:13–16; Isa 9:1–2

He divides people and is rejected Lk 2:34–35 *See also* Mt 3:11–12 pp Mk 1:7–8 pp Lk 3:16–17; Mt 21:42 pp Mk 12:10–11 pp Lk 20:17; Ps 118:22–23; Jn 13:18; Ps 41:9

He teaches in parables Mt 13:35 *See also* Ps 78:2; Mt 13:13–15 pp Mk 4:11–12 pp Lk 8:10; Isa 6:9–10

Prophecies about Jesus Christ's death
The Lord's Supper Mt 26:28 pp Mk 14:24 pp Lk 22:20 *See also* Isa 53:12; Jer 31:34

The betrayal Mt 27:9–10 *Matthew brings together two prophetic passages fulfilled by this incident:* Jer 19:1–13; Zec 11:12–13 Jn 18:9; 6:39

The cross Mt 27:46 pp Mk 15:34 *See also* Ps 22:1; Mt 27:35 fn; Ps 22:18; Lk 23:46; Ps 31:5

Prophecies about Jesus Christ's resurrection and ascension
Mt 12:39–40 pp Lk 11:29–30 *See also* Jnh 1:17; Ac 2:25–28; Ps 16:8–11; Ac 2:31; 13:35; 2:34; Ps 110:1; Eph 4:8; Ps 68:18

Prophecies about Jesus Christ's titles
Jesus Christ as Son of God Ac 13:32–33 *See also* Ps 2:7; Heb 1:5; 5:5; Mt 22:44 pp Mk 12:36 pp Lk 20:42; Ps 110:1; Heb 1:8–9; Ps 45:6–7

Jesus Christ as Son of Man Mt 26:64 pp Mk 14:62 pp Lk 22:69 *See also* Da 7:13–14; Mk 8:31 pp Lk 9:22

Jesus Christ as Son of David Rev 22:16 *See also* 2Sa 7:12–16 pp 1Ch 17:11–14; Lk 1:32–33; Isa 9:7; Ac 13:34; Isa 55:3; Ro 15:12; Isa 11:1

Jesus Christ as the coming Messianic king Mt 26:31 pp Mk 14:27; Zec 13:7; Mt 21:4–5; Zec 9:9

Jesus Christ as the suffering servant Ac 8:32–35 *See also* Isa 53:7–8; Mt 12:17–21; Isa 42:1–4

Jesus Christ as the prophet who is to come Ac 3:22 *See also* Dt 18:18; Lk 4:18–19; Isa 61:1–2; Jn 6:14

Jesus Christ as priest Heb 7:21 *See also* Ps 110:4; Heb 5:5–6; 7:17

See also

2215 Christ, Son of David	2357 Christ, parables
2218 Christ, Son of God	2505 Christ, ascension
2221 Christ, Son of Man	2515 Christ, birth of
2230 Messiah, coming of	2525 Christ, cross of
2318 Christ as prophet	2530 Christ, death of
2327 Christ as servant	2560 Christ, resurrection

2369
Jesus Christ, responses to

The NT records a number of responses to Jesus Christ on the part of those who encountered him, both positive and negative.

Negative responses to Jesus Christ
Rejection Mt 21:42; Mk 7:5–8; Lk 4:28–30; 10:16

Lack of faith Mk 6:4–6 pp Mt 13:57–58

Questioning his authority Mk 11:27–33 pp Mt 21:23–27 pp Lk 20:1–8

Hardening of hearts Mt 13:10–17; Jn 12:37–41

Attributing his power to satanic forces Mt 9:33–34

Demanding his death Lk 23:20–24; Jn 10:22–40

Positive recognition of Jesus Christ's identity

As Messiah Jn 1:41 See also Lk 2:11; 9:20; Ac 5:42

As King Jn 1:49 See also Mt 2:1–2; 27:37

As Lord Jn 6:68 See also Jn 13:13

As Son of David Mt 15:22

As Son of God Ac 9:20 See also Mt 8:29; Jn 1:34,49

As Teacher Mt 19:16 pp Mk 10:17 pp Lk 18:18 See also Mt 23:10; Jn 11:28

Responses to Jesus Christ by those whom he healed

Faith Mk 10:52 pp Lk 18:42 See also Mt 8:13; 9:27–31; Jn 4:43–54

Thankfulness Lk 17:11–19

Witnessing to others Lk 8:38–39; Jn 1:40–42,45–46; 5:10–15; 9:13–34

Responses to Jesus Christ by those whom he met and taught

Amazement Mt 7:26–29 See also Mk 12:17

Delight Mk 12:37

Faith Mt 8:10; 9:2,22; 15:28; Jn 12:11,41–43

Repentance Lk 19:8 See also Mt 11:20; Mk 6:12; Lk 13:2–5

Obedience Mt 28:20; Jn 15:20; 17:6

Worship Mt 2:2; 14:33
Worship is a response to Jesus Christ which is especially associated with the period after his resurrection: Mt 28:9; Lk 24:52

Responses to Jesus Christ by those whom he redeemed

Faith Ac 16:31 See also Ro 10:9–10; 1Jn 3:23; 5:5

Obedience Ro 16:26; Php 2:12; Heb 5:8–9; 1Pe 4:17

Calling on his name Ac 9:14,21; Ro 10:13; 1Co 1:2

Giving thanks in his name Eph 5:20

Glorifying his name 2Th 1:12

Proclaiming him to the world Ac 5:42 See also Ac 8:5; 16:10; Ro 15:19; Col 1:28; 2Ti 1:8

See also
2012 Christ, authority	2545 Christ, opposition to
2218 Christ, Son of God	5932 response
2221 Christ, Son of Man	7757 preaching, effects
2321 Christ as redeemer	8020 faith
	8622 worship
2363 Christ, preaching & teaching	8712 denial of Christ
	8836 unbelief, response

2372
Jesus Christ, victory of

Jesus Christ triumphs over and disarms all the powers of evil arrayed

against him. Believers are able to share in this victory through faith in Jesus Christ.

The scope of Jesus Christ's victory

Over temptation Heb 4:15 See also Mt 4:1–11 pp Lk 4:1–13

Over sin Ro 5:20–21 See also 1Jn 3:5,8

Over Satan Jn 12:31 Satan is called "the prince of this world" in John's Gospel. See also Lk 10:18–19; Jn 14:30; 16:11; Heb 2:14–15

Over evil spirits Mk 1:23–27 pp Lk 4:33–36

Over all powers Col 2:15 "powers and authorities" include evil spiritual beings. See also Ro 8:38–39; 1Co 15:24–25; Eph 1:21–22; 4:8; Ps 68:18

Over the world Jn 16:33 Here, as elsewhere in John's Gospel, "world" refers to the human race in rebellion against God. See also 2Th 2:8 "the lawless one" represents the leader of human forces of evil; 1Jn 5:4–5; Rev 17:12–14; 19:11–21

Over death Ro 6:9 See also Ac 2:24; 1Co 15:26,54–57; 2Ti 1:10; Rev 1:18

The manner of Jesus Christ's victory

By the written word of God Mt 4:4–10 pp Lk 4:4–12

By his death on the cross Heb 2:14 See also Col 2:15; Rev 12:11

By God's authority Lk 11:20 pp Mt 12:28

By his spoken word Mt 8:16 See also Mt 8:8 pp Lk 7:7; Mt 8:13

Consequences of Jesus Christ's victory

Assurance for believers Jn 16:33; 1Th 4:13; Rev 5:5

Victory for believers 1Co 15:57 See also Ro 7:21–25; 8:37; 16:20

See also
2012 Christ, authority	2575 Christ, temptation of
2224 Christ, the Lord	4127 Satan, defeat of
2312 Christ as king	
2321 Christ as redeemer	5596 victory
2324 Christ as Saviour	8482 spiritual warfare
2525 Christ, cross of	9020 death
2560 Christ, resurrection	

2375

kingdom of God

Or, less frequently, "kingdom of heaven", the kingly rule of God in the lives of people and nations. It refers to the recognition of the authority of God, rather than a definite geographical area, and begins with the ministry of Jesus Christ.

2376
kingdom of God, coming of

The kingdom of God comes into being wherever the kingly authority of God is acknowledged. Although God is always sovereign, Scripture looks to a future "realm" or "reign" of salvation. This has come in Christ and yet will come in its fulness only when Jesus Christ returns.

God is sovereign over Israel and over the whole earth

Ps 47:7–8 See also Ex 15:18; 1Sa 12:12; 1Ch 16:31; 28:5; 29:11–12; Ps 9:7–8; 45:6; 93:1–2; 103:19; 145:11–13; Isa 37:16; Da 4:34–35

The coming reign of God

Its expectation Isa 51:4–5; Mk 15:43 pp Lk 23:51 See also Isa 2:2–4 pp Mic 4:1–3; Isa 32:1; Jer 3:17; Da 2:44; 7:18,21–22,27; Zec 8:22; 14:9; Mk 11:10

Its association with the coming of the Messiah Isa 9:6–7; Da 7:14 "Son of Man" was Jesus Christ's usual way of referring to himself. See also Isa 11:1–9; Jer 23:5–6; Mic 5:2

The kingdom of God was central in the preaching of Jesus Christ and the apostles

Mt 24:14; Lk 8:1; Ac 28:31 See also Mt 4:17,23; 9:35; 10:7 Jesus Christ's instructions to the Twelve; Mk 1:13–14; Lk 4:43; 9:2,11; 10:9; Ac 1:3,6–8; 8:12; 19:8; 20:25; 28:23

The kingdom of God has come in Christ: it is present

Mt 11:12 Following the Jewish convention of avoiding the use of the divine name, Matthew usually speaks of "the kingdom of heaven". See also Mt 3:1–2; 4:17; 13:31–32 pp Mk 4:30–32 pp Lk 13:18–19; Mt 13:33 pp Lk 13:20–21; Mt 16:28 pp Mk 9:1 pp Lk 9:27; Lk 11:20; 16:16; 17:20–21

The kingdom of God will come in its fulness only when Jesus Christ returns: it is future

Lk 22:18 pp Mt 26:29 pp Mk 14:25 See also Mt 6:10 pp Lk 11:2; Mt 25:31,34; Lk 22:16; 1Co 15:24; 2Ti 4:18; Rev 11:15; 12:10

See also
1130 God, sovereignty	5369 kingship, divine
2230 Messiah, coming of	7020 church, the
	7263 theocracy
2312 Christ as king	7754 preaching
2357 Christ, parables	9105 last things
2565 Christ, second coming	9145 Messianic age
	9610 hope

2377
kingdom of God, entry into

Entering or inheriting the kingdom of God is the privilege of those who acknowledge and live by the rule of God and have become part of the

new order of salvation and
righteousness in Christ.

Entry into the kingdom of God is of vital importance
It is costly Mt 13:44; Ac 14:22 *See also*
Mt 8:19–20 pp Lk 9:57–58;
Mt 13:45–46; Lk 18:29–30; 2Th 1:5;
Rev 1:9

It is a matter of urgency Lk 9:59–62
pp Mt 8:21–22

Conditions of entry into the kingdom of God
Childlike trust Mk 10:15 pp Lk 18:17
See also Mt 18:3

To be born again of God's Spirit Jn 3:3
See also Jn 3:5; 1Co 15:50

Obedience to God's will Mt 7:21

Warnings about entry into the kingdom of God
The way is narrow Lk 13:24–28 *See also*
Mt 7:13–14; 23:13

The wicked will not inherit the kingdom
1Co 6:9–10 *See also* Mt 5:20;
Mk 9:43–47; Gal 5:19–21; Eph 5:5

The need for readiness and
watchfulness Mt 24:42–44 *See also*
Mt 24:37–39 pp Lk 17:26–27; Mt 25:13;
Lk 12:35–40

Entry is not based on outward
appearances nor granted to all who
claim to know the Lord Mt 7:21–23 *See
also* Mt 13:24–30,47–50; Lk 13:25–27

The kingdom of God is a kingdom of grace
It belongs to those qualified by God
Col 1:12–13 *See also* Lk 12:32;
22:29–30

It belongs to the poor and the poor in
spirit Lk 6:20 pp Mt 5:3 *See also* Mt 11:5
pp Lk 7:22; Mt 19:23–24
pp Mk 10:23–25 pp Lk 18:24–25 *It is
hard for the rich to enter the kingdom of
God;* Jas 2:5; 5:1

It belongs to the childlike Mt 19:14
pp Mk 10:14 pp Lk 18:16

It belongs to sinners Mk 2:17
pp Mt 9:12–13 pp Lk 5:31–32 *See also*
Mt 21:31

It belongs to those who are persecuted
for Jesus Christ's sake Mt 5:10
pp Lk 6:22–23

It belongs to Gentiles as well as to
Jews Mt 8:11 *See also* Mt 21:43;
22:8–10 *those initially uninvited represent
the Gentiles;* Lk 14:21–24

See also
3230 Holy Spirit &	6728 regeneration
regeneration	7510 Gentiles
4841 narrowness	8154 righteousness
5703 inheritance	8205 childlikeness
6510 salvation	8207 commitment
6666 grace	8808 riches

2378
kingdom of God, characteristics of
Those who have entered the
kingdom must live according to its
values, anticipating the reign of

peace which will come when Jesus
Christ returns.

The kingdom of God does not conform to the standards of this world
Jn 18:36; Ro 14:17

Those who inherit the kingdom of God are to bear its fruit
1Th 2:12 *See also* Mt 25:34–36;
2Pe 1:10–11

The kingdom of God is and will be a kingdom of peace
Peace between people Isa 2:2–4
pp Mic 4:1–4; Jas 3:18 *See also* Isa 9:5;
19:24–25; Mic 5:4–5; Mt 5:9 *The
Sermon on the Mount (Mt 5:1–7:29) is
often thought of as a description of life in
the kingdom.*

The peace and prosperity of all
creation Isa 11:6–9 *See also*
Isa 35:1–2,9; 41:17–19; Eze 47:9,12;
Hos 2:21–22

The kingdom of God is a kingdom of forgiveness
Mt 6:12 pp Lk 11:4; Mt 18:21–35;
Lk 17:3–4

Status in the kingdom of God
Mt 18:1–5 pp Mk 9:33–37
pp Lk 9:46–48; Mt 20:25–28
pp Mk 10:42–45 pp Lk 22:25–27 *See
also* Mt 5:19; 11:11 pp Lk 7:28; Mt 19:30
pp Mk 10:31

See also
2345 Christ, kingdom	6652 forgiveness	
of	6700 peace	
3254 Holy Spirit, fruit	8206 Christlikeness	
of	8256 fruitfulness	
5498 reward	8276 humility	

2400
Jesus Christ, gospel of

2410
cross, the
An instrument of execution, used
especially by the Roman authorities
for putting criminals to death. The
sufferings of Jesus Christ on the
cross, foreshadowed in the OT, are
related in the NT gospel accounts.
Scripture sees the death of Christ as
central to the Christian faith.
Through the cross and resurrection
of Christ, God achieved the
redemption of believers.

2411
cross, predictions of
The death of Jesus Christ fulfils OT
predictions and was clearly
anticipated in his teaching.

The cross foreshadowed in the OT
Ps 22:1 *See also* Ge 3:15;
Ps 22:6–7,16–18; 31:5; 69:21;
Isa 52:12–13; Zec 12:10; 13:7

Jesus Christ predicts his death on the cross
Jesus Christ's first announcement of
his death Mt 16:21 pp Mk 8:31
pp Lk 9:22

Jesus Christ's second announcement
of his death Mt 17:22–23 *See also*
Mk 9:31

Jesus Christ's third announcement of
his death Mt 20:18–19
pp Mk 10:33–34 pp Lk 18:31–33

Other allusions to the cross
In the teaching of Jesus Christ
Mt 26:31 *See also* Mt 20:22 pp Mk 10:38;
Mt 26:2; Mk 2:19–20; 10:45; Lk 9:44;
22:42
*"lifted up" is used in John's Gospel as a
reference to the crucifixion:* Jn 3:14; 8:28;
12:32–33
Jn 18:11

In history Mt 17:9–13 *John the Baptist's
fate indicates what is to happen to Jesus
Christ.*

In the experience of Jesus Christ
Mt 26:12 pp Mk 14:8 *Jesus Christ's
reaction to the woman anointing him
seems to suggest that he will die the death
of a criminal.*

In the Lord's Supper Mt 26:26–28
pp Mk 14:22–25 pp Lk 22:19–20

God's perfect timing for Jesus Christ's death on the cross
Jn 2:4 *See also* Jn 7:6,8,30; 8:20; 13:1;
17:1

The curse of the cross
Dt 21:22–23 *To be nailed to a cross is the
equivalent of being hanged on a tree. See
also* Ac 5:30; Gal 3:10–13; 1Pe 2:24

See also
1315 God as	5560 suffering
redeemer	5827 curse
2221 Christ, Son of	6652 forgiveness
Man	7933 Lord's Supper
2233 Son of Man	
2366 Christ,	
prophecies	
concerning	

2412
cross, Gospel accounts of
Each of the four Gospels provides a
detailed account of Jesus Christ's
death on the cross.

The way to the cross
Simon is compelled to carry the cross
Mk 15:21 pp Mt 27:32 pp Lk 23:26

Women follow the cross and Jesus
Christ is offered relief from pain
Lk 23:27–31 *See also* Mt 27:34
pp Mk 15:23

The crucifixion of Jesus Christ
Jesus Christ crucified between two
criminals Mk 15:22–27
pp Mt 27:33–38 pp Lk 23:32–43
*"Golgotha" is a transliteration of the
Aramaic word for "a skull". Its actual
location is uncertain.*

The humiliation of Jesus Christ on the
cross Mk 15:29–32 pp Mt 27:39–44
pp Lk 23:35–39

The words of Jesus Christ on the cross
Jn 19:30 See also Mt 27:46 pp Mk 15:34;
Mt 27:50; Mk 15:37;
Lk 23:28–31,34,43,46; Jn 19:26–28

The death of Jesus Christ
Mk 15:33–37 pp Mt 27:45–50
pp Lk 23:44–46 See also Jn 19:28–35
According to John, Jesus Christ was on the cross while the Passover lambs were being sacrificed.

Supernatural events at the cross
Mk 15:38 pp Mt 27:51–53 pp Lk 23:45

Witnesses of the crucifixion
Mk 15:39–41 pp Mt 27:54–56
pp Lk 23:47–49

See also
2525 Christ, cross of   5281 crucifixion
2530 Christ, death of   9020 death
2545 Christ,   9310 resurrection
    opposition to
2570 Christ,
    suffering

2413
cross, of Jesus Christ
See 2525 Jesus Christ, cross of

2414
cross, centrality of

The death of Jesus Christ on the cross is central to the Christian faith. Through the cross and resurrection of Christ, God achieved the redemption of believers and brought hope to the world.

The gospel as the "message of the cross"
1Co 2:2 See also 1Co 1:17–18,23;
Gal 3:1

The cross redeems from the curse of the law
Gal 3:13 See also Ro 6:14; 7:4; 2Co 5:21;
Gal 2:19–21; Eph 1:7; 2:13–16;
Col 2:13–14; Tit 2:14; 1Pe 1:18–19

The cross brings reconciliation and justification
Ro 4:25; 5:10 See also Ro 5:8–9;
1Co 15:3–4; Eph 2:16; Col 1:20–22

The cross destroys the power of Satan
Col 2:13–15 See also Jn 12:31; 14:30;
Gal 1:4; Heb 2:14–15; 1Pe 3:21–22

The cross as a stumbling-block or offence
1Co 1:22–24 See also Gal 5:11; 6:12

The cross unites believers with Jesus Christ
Ro 6:4–7 See also Ro 6:2; 8:36;
1Co 15:30–31; 2Co 4:10–12; 5:14–15;
Gal 2:20; Eph 2:14–16; Col 2:20; 3:1–3;
2Ti 2:11

The cross as a symbol of discipleship
Mt 16:24 pp Mk 8:34 pp Lk 9:23–24;
Php 2:5–8 See also Mt 10:38; Lk 14:27;
Jn 12:23–25; Ro 8:13; Gal 5:24; 6:14;
Eph 5:25–26; Col 3:5; 1Pe 2:21,24

See also
2321 Christ as   6712 propitiation
   redeemer   6716 reconciliation
6510 salvation   6720 redemption
6614 atonement   6752 substitution
6676 justification   7317 blood of Christ
6684 mediator   8114 discipleship

2420
gospel

The good news of God's redemption of sinful humanity through the life, death and resurrection of his Son Jesus Christ.
This set of themes consists of the following:
2421 gospel, historical foundation of
2422 gospel, confirmation of
2423 gospel, essence of
2424 gospel, promises of
2425 gospel, requirements of
2426 gospel, responses to
2427 gospel, transmission of
2428 gospel, descriptions of

2421
gospel, historical foundation of

The gospel rests upon the history of Jesus Christ: his birth, obedient life, atoning death, physical resurrection from the dead and his ascension into heaven.

The incarnation of Jesus Christ
The historical facts Lk 2:4–7 See also
Lk 2:10–12; Mt 1:20–21; Lk 1:30–35

Its theological significance Jn 1:14 See also Jn 1:9; Ro 8:3; 2Co 8:9; Gal 4:4–5;
Php 2:6–7; 1Ti 3:16; Heb 2:14;
1Jn 1:1–2

The sinless life of Jesus Christ
1Pe 2:22 See also Isa 53:9; 2Co 5:21;
Heb 4:15; 7:26–28; 1Jn 3:5

The death of Jesus Christ
An historical event Php 2:8 See also
Mt 27:50 pp Mk 15:37 pp Lk 23:46
pp Jn 19:30

Its redemptive significance Ro 5:8–11
See also Lk 12:49–50; 24:26; Jn 17:4;
Ac 2:23; Ro 5:19; 1Co 1:23–24; 1Pe 2:24

The resurrection of Jesus Christ
Its historical reality 1Co 15:3–8 See also
Mt 28:1–8 pp Mk 16:1–8 pp Lk 24:1–10
pp Jn 20:1–9; 2Ti 2:8–10

Its implication for believers 1Co 15:14
See also Ro 4:25 in relation to justification;
Ro 6:1–14 in relation to sanctification;
1Co 15:21,42–49 in relation to the resurrection of believers

The ascension of Jesus Christ
Ac 1:9 See also Mk 16:19; Lk 24:50–51;
Ac 1:1–2; 2:33; Ro 8:34; Col 3:1;
1Ti 3:16; Heb 1:3; 12:2

See also
2075 Christ, sinless   2515 Christ, birth of
2375 kingdom of   2530 Christ, death of
   God   2555 Christ,
2505 Christ,   resurrection
   ascension   appearances

See also
2560 Christ,   5849 exaltation
   resurrection   6614 atonement
2595 incarnation   6720 redemption

2422
gospel, confirmation of

The trustworthiness of the gospel of Jesus Christ rests upon the fulfilment of OT prophecies concerning Jesus Christ, the apostolic witness to Jesus Christ and the divine witness to Jesus Christ during his ministry, culminating in his resurrection.

Prophecies of the OT concerning Jesus Christ
Fulfilment of prophecy recognised by Jesus Christ Mt 26:54–56 See also
Mt 26:24,31; Lk 4:21; 21:22;
24:25–27,44,46; Jn 13:18; Ps 41:9

Fulfilment of prophecy recognised by NT speakers and writers Ro 3:21 See also Lk 1:68–70; Ac 3:18; 10:43; 26:22;
Ro 1:2; 1Co 15:3–5; 1Pe 1:10–12
Particular prophecies fulfilled:
Mt 1:22–23; Isa 7:14; Mt 2:5–6;
Mic 5:2; Mt 2:15; Hos 11:1; Mt 2:17–18;
Jer 31:15; Mt 2:23; 4:14–16; Isa 9:1–2;
Mt 8:17; Isa 53:4; Mt 12:17–21;
Isa 42:1–4; Mt 21:4–5; Zec 9:9;
Mt 27:9–10; Jn 19:24; Ps 22:18;
Jn 19:28,36; Ex 12:46; Jn 19:37;
Zec 12:10; Ac 2:25–28; Ps 16:8–11

Realisation of types
The sign of Jonah: Mt 12:38–41
pp Lk 11:29–32; Mt 16:4
Jesus Christ as the bread of life:
Jn 6:31–35,48–51
Heb 3:1–6 Jesus Christ as the greater
Moses; Heb 6:20–7:10 Jesus Christ as the high priest after the order of Melchizedek

Fulfilment of ceremony and sacrifice
Jn 1:29 Jesus Christ fulfils all that the sacrificial system stood for. See also
Heb 9:6–14; 1Pe 1:18–19

Witness of the apostles to Jesus Christ
Jn 19:35 See also Lk 24:48; Jn 1:14;
15:27; 21:24; Ac 1:8; 2:32; 4:20; 5:32;
13:31; 1Pe 5:1; 1Jn 1:1–2; 4:14

Witness of God the Father to his Son
Mt 3:16–17 pp Mk 1:9–11
pp Lk 3:21–22 See also Jn 1:32–34;
Mt 17:5 pp Mk 9:7 pp Lk 9:35;
Jn 12:23–32; 2Pe 1:17–18

Jesus Christ vindicated by his resurrection
Ro 1:1–4 See also Ac 2:24–28;
Ps 16:8–11; Ac 13:30–35; 17:31;
Ro 8:11; 10:9; 1Co 15:14–15; 1Pe 1:21

Warnings against false gospels
Gal 1:6–9 See also 1Co 3:11; 1Jn 4:1–3

See also
1429 prophecy, OT   7915 confirmation
   fulfilment   9312 resurrection,
2366 Christ,   significance of
   prophecies   Christ's
   concerning
5624 witnesses to
   Christ

2423
gospel, essence of

The chief characteristic and fundamental doctrine of the gospel is that Jesus Christ is both Lord and Saviour.

Jesus Christ as Lord
The universal lordship of Jesus Christ Mt 28:18 *See also* Da 7:13–14; Lk 10:22; Jn 3:35; 17:2; Ac 10:36; Ro 14:9; 1Co 15:27; Eph 1:20–22; Php 2:9–10; Col 1:15–20

Personal implications of the lordship of Jesus Christ Lk 12:8–9; Ro 10:9 *See also* Mt 7:21–27 pp Lk 6:46–49; Jn 13:13–14

The lordship of Jesus Christ can only be acknowledged through divine inspiration and revelation 1Co 12:3 *See also* Jn 16:13–15; 1Jn 4:2–3

Jesus Christ as Saviour
Lk 2:11 *See also* Jn 1:29; 4:42; Ac 5:31; 1Ti 2:5–6; Tit 2:11–14; 1Jn 4:14

Jesus Christ is the promised Messiah Mt 1:20–23 *See also* Isa 7:14; Ps 130:8; Isa 53:11; Ac 13:23

Jesus Christ did everything that was required to save his people Jn 19:30 *He fulfilled all God's righteous requirements, made perfect atonement for sin and gained victory over death for all who believe in him. See also* Mt 3:15; Jn 4:34; 17:4; 1Co 15:20–22

Salvation comes only through Jesus Christ Jn 14:6 *See also* Ac 4:12; 10:43; 16:30–31; 1Ti 2:5

Jesus Christ will return to judge the world and bring his people to glory Mt 16:27 *See also* Jn 14:3; Ac 1:11; 17:31; 1Th 4:16–17; 2Ti 4:1; Rev 1:7; 22:7,12,20

See also

2206 Jesus, the Christ	5380 law and gospel
2224 Christ, the Lord	5396 lordship of Christ
2324 Christ as Saviour	5454 power, God's saving
2414 cross, centrality	6510 salvation
2565 Christ, second coming	6666 grace

2424
gospel, promises of

To all who believe and submit to its demands, the promises of the gospel include forgiveness of sins, new life in Jesus Christ and adoption into the family of God.

Forgiveness of sins
The sin of God's people is imputed to God's Son Jn 1:29 *See also* Isa 53:4–6; Lk 24:46–47; Ac 5:30–32; 13:38; Tit 2:13–14; Heb 9:28; 1Pe 2:24

The righteousness of God's Son is imputed to God's people Ro 1:16–17 *See also* Ro 3:21–26; 9:30; Php 3:7–9

Peace with God
Ro 5:1–2 *See also* Jn 14:27; Ro 8:1–4,31–35

New birth
1Pe 1:23–25 *See also* Jn 1:12–13; 3:5–8; Jas 1:18

Eternal life
Jn 3:14–16 *See also* Jn 1:4; 6:68–69; 10:10; 20:31; 1Jn 1:1–2; 5:12

The gift of the Holy Spirit
Ac 2:38 *See also* Joel 2:28–32; Jn 7:37–39; Ac 8:14–17; 19:1–7

Adoption into God's family
Ro 8:12–17 *See also* Jn 1:12–13; Gal 3:26; 4:4–6; Eph 1:5

See also

3257 Holy Spirit, gift of	6705 peace, experience
6606 access to God	6728 regeneration
6608 adoption	7115 children of God
6644 eternal life	8104 assurance
6652 forgiveness	8154 righteousness
6676 justification	

2425
gospel, requirements of

The gospel demands an obedient response to all that God has done for humanity in Jesus Christ. This includes faith in God, trust in the work of Jesus Christ, the repenting of sin, being baptised, and becoming like Christ through discipleship.

The requirement of faith
Belief in God Heb 11:6 *See also* Jn 10:38; 11:25–27; 14:8–11

Trust in Jesus Christ Jn 3:14–16 *See also* Jn 1:12–13; 3:36; 7:37–39; 20:31; Ac 13:38–39; 16:31; Ro 3:22

The requirement of repentance
A conscious change of mind and heart Ac 3:17–20 *See also* Ps 51:17; Jer 3:12–13; 6:16; Lk 18:13–14; Ac 17:30

Turning away from sin Ac 8:22 *See also* 2Ch 7:14; Ps 34:14; Isa 59:20; Jer 25:4–6

Turning towards God Ac 20:21 *See also* Dt 4:29–31; 30:8–10; Isa 44:21–22; 55:6–7; Hos 14:1–2; Jas 4:8–10

The requirement of baptism
Ac 2:38 *See also* Mt 28:18–20; Ac 8:12,36–38; 10:47–48; 19:1–5; 22:16

The requirement of public confession of Jesus Christ
Ro 10:9–10 *See also* Mt 10:32 pp Lk 12:8–9

The requirement of discipleship
Willingness to learn from Jesus Christ Mt 11:28–30 *See also* Jn 13:14–15; Php 2:5; 1Pe 2:21

Willingness to obey Jesus Christ Jn 14:15 *See also* Jn 14:21,23; 15:10; 1Jn 2:3–6; 3:21–24; 5:3; 2Jn 6

Willingness to suffer for the sake of Jesus Christ Mt 16:24 pp Mk 8:34 pp Lk 9:23 *See also* Ac 14:21–22; Php 1:29; 2Ti 3:10–12; Jas 1:2; 1Pe 3:14; 4:12–19

See also

5560 suffering	8207 commitment
6732 repentance	8407 confession of Christ
7903 baptism	
8020 faith	8454 obedience to God
8114 discipleship	
8120 following Christ	

2426
gospel, responses to

The gospel cannot be subscribed to half-heartedly or in part; it must be either accepted or rejected.

The gospel calls for a positive response
Ro 10:5–13 *See also* Ac 13:38–39; 16:29–32; Ro 3:21–26; Jn 6:41–52; 1Jn 5:1,5,10–12

The command to accept the gospel
Mt 11:28; Ac 17:30 *See also* Mt 6:19–24 pp Lk 11:34–36; Mt 7:7–12 pp Lk 11:9–13; Mt 7:24–27 pp Lk 6:47–49; Jn 4:13–14; 6:35–40; 8:31–32,36; 10:9–10; 11:25–26; 12:44–46

Examples of people who accepted the gospel
Mk 1:16–18 pp Mt 4:18–22 *See also* Mk 1:19–20; Mt 9:9 pp Mk 2:14 pp Lk 5:27–28 *Matthew was also known as Levi*; Ac 2:41; 11:19–21; 13:46–48; 16:13–15

Rejection of the gospel
Through lack of perception Jn 12:37–41 *See also* Mt 13:13–15 pp Mk 4:10–12 pp Lk 8:9–10; Isa 6:9; Ro 11:8; Eph 4:17–19

Through worldly distractions Mt 13:22 pp Mk 4:18–19 pp Lk 8:14 *See also* Mt 6:24 pp Lk 16:13; 2Ti 4:10; Jas 4:4; 1Jn 2:15

Through indifference Mt 12:30 pp Lk 11:23

Through hostility to God Ro 8:6–8 *See also* Jn 7:13–20; 10:24–33; Ac 4:15–18; 5:17–28; 7:51–53; 19:8–9; 21:27–32; 1Th 2:14–16

Warnings against rejecting the gospel
Heb 2:1–4 *See also* Mk 8:36–38; Lk 12:5,16–21; 13:22–30; Jn 12:47–50; Heb 6:4–6; 10:29–31; 12:25; 2Pe 2:17–22

Examples of people who rejected the gospel
Mt 19:16–22 pp Mk 10:17–22 pp Lk 18:18–23 *See also* Ac 5:29–33; 7:51–58; 17:32; 13:44–47; 19:23–28; 24:24–25; 26:24–28

The gospel evokes opposition
Jn 17:14; Ac 17:13 *See also* Ac 13:8; 17:5–9; 1Th 2:14–16

The gospel evokes persecution
Ac 8:1–3; 1Th 3:7 *See also* Ac 13:49–50; 2Th 1:4

2427
gospel, transmission of

The gospel has been passed down
through the NT witness to Jesus
Christ, through the proclamation of
the good news about Jesus Christ,
and through the providential
guidance of the Holy Spirit.

The NT witness to Jesus Christ
The events of Jesus Christ's life were
carefully recorded Lk 1:1–4 *See also*
Jn 21:24; Ac 1:1–2

The apostles bore witness to the gospel
1Co 15:3–8; 2Pe 1:16; 1Jn 1:1–4 *See
also* Lk 24:45–48; Jn 15:27;
Ac 1:8,21–22; 2:32; 4:1–20; 5:32;
13:30–31; Heb 2:3–4; 1Pe 5:1; 1Jn 4:14

The proclamation of the gospel
Ac 5:42; Ro 10:14–15; 1Co 15:1–2;
Eph 3:8–9 *See also* Ac 8:12; 1Co 1:21;
Gal 1:23; 2Ti 4:2; Heb 13:7

The guidance of the Holy Spirit in the transmission of the gospel
Jn 14:26; 15:26 *See also* Jn 16:12–15;
Ac 5:32; Heb 2:3–4; 1Jn 5:6

2428
gospel, descriptions of

The beauty, authority and
importance of the gospel can be seen
from the way it is described in
Scripture.

In the Gospels
As good and joyful news Mt 4:23 *See
also* Mk 1:14; 16:15; Lk 2:10–11

As being of heavenly origin
Jn 17:16–18 *See also* Jn 8:28; 12:49–50;
14:10,24

As words of life Jn 6:63 *See also*
Jn 3:11–15

As being complete and gloriously rich
Col 1:25–27 *See also* Ro 10:12–13;
Eph 3:8

In the OT
Isa 52:7–10 *See also* Isa 40:9; 41:27;
61:1; Na 1:15

In the NT
1Ti 1:11 *See also* Ac 20:24; Ro 1:16–17;
10:15; Isa 52:7; Ro 15:18–19; Eph 1:13;
Rev 14:6

2500
Jesus Christ, history of

This set of themes consists of the
following:

2505
Jesus Christ, ascension of

The return of Jesus Christ to his
Father in order to establish his
kingdom, having completed his
work on earth.

Jesus Christ's ascension described
Ac 1:9–11 *As in the OT, the cloud
symbolises God's presence. See also*
Mk 16:19; Lk 24:51; Ac 1:2; Eph 4:10;
1Ti 3:16; Heb 9:24; 1Pe 3:22; Rev 12:5

Predictions of Jesus Christ's ascension
In the OT Eph 4:7–8 *See also* Ps 68:18

Jesus Christ looks forward to his
ascension as his return to his Father
Jn 16:28 *See also* Jn 6:62; 7:33; 14:28;
16:5,10; 17:11,13; 20:17

Jesus Christ establishes his kingdom by his ascension
He ascended to send the Holy Spirit
Jn 16:7 *See also* Jn 7:39;
14:16–19,25–26; 15:26–27; Ac 2:33

He ascended to prepare a place for his
people Jn 14:2–4

He ascended to exaltation and glory
Lk 24:26; Ac 2:33; Eph 1:20–21;
1Pe 3:22

He ascended to exercise his high
priestly ministry Heb 4:14 *See also*
Heb 7:25; 9:24

He ascended so that believers may
follow him 1Th 4:17

Jesus Christ's ascension indicates the manner of his return
Ac 1:11 *See also* Mt 24:30 pp Mk 13:26
pp Lk 21:27; Rev 1:7

2510
Jesus Christ, baptism of

In obedience to God's will Jesus
Christ was baptised in the River
Jordan by John. The event was sealed
by the descent of the Holy Spirit and
the Father's voice of approval.

John tries to prevent Jesus Christ from being baptised
Mt 3:13–14 *John was baptising repentant
sinners but he knew that Jesus Christ was
sinless.*

The necessity of Jesus Christ's baptism
Mt 3:15 *See also* Mk 10:38; Lk 12:50

The events surrounding Jesus Christ's baptism
The baptism itself Mk 1:9 pp Mt 3:13
pp Lk 3:21

Jesus Christ prays while being
baptised Lk 3:21

The Holy Spirit descends on Jesus
Christ Mk 1:10 pp Mt 3:16 pp Lk 3:22
*The Holy Spirit came upon Jesus Christ to
equip him for his ministry which was
about to begin and to give him strength at a
time of temptation. See also* Jn 1:32–34

The voice of the Father is heard
Mt 3:17 pp Mk 1:11 pp Lk 3:22 *These
words, which are an allusion to Ps 2:7 and
Isa 42:1, were repeated at the
transfiguration. See also* Mt 17:5
pp Mk 9:7 pp Lk 9:35

2515
Jesus Christ, birth of

Jesus Christ was born to a poor
unmarried Jewish couple in the
village of Bethlehem. As Son of God,
he was conceived by the Holy Spirit
in the womb of his mother Mary.

Jesus Christ's birth is prophesied in the OT

The prophecy of a coming ruler
Isa 9:6-7

The prophecy of a virgin's son Isa 7:14

The prophecy concerning his birthplace Mic 5:2 *"Bethlehem Ephrathah" is the village where David grew up ("the town of David").*

Jesus Christ was conceived by the Holy Spirit and born of a virgin

Mt 1:18,23 *See also* Mt 1:20; Lk 1:34-35

Jesus Christ's incarnation

Jn 1:14; Gal 4:4 *See also* Ro 8:3; 2Co 8:9; Php 2:7-8; 1Ti 3:16; 1Jn 4:2

The circumstances of Jesus Christ's birth

An angel informs Mary that she is to be the mother of the Messiah Lk 1:26-38

Mary responds in praise Lk 1:46-55

An angel explains to Joseph why Mary's baby is so special Mt 1:18-25

The birth of Jesus Christ takes place Lk 2:1-7

Angels announce Jesus Christ's birth to some shepherds Lk 2:8-20

The Magi search for Jesus Christ's birthplace and Herod tries to kill him Mt 2:1-18 *These events could have taken place at any time in Jesus Christ's first two years.*

See also

2033 Christ, humanity	2421 gospel, historical
2036 Christ, humility	foundation
2215 Christ, Son of David	2540 Christ, genealogy
2218 Christ, Son of God	2595 incarnation
2230 Messiah, coming of	4110 angels
2312 Christ as king	5099 Mary, mother of Christ
2366 Christ, prophecies concerning	

2520
Jesus Christ, childhood of

As an infant Jesus Christ was consecrated in the temple, accompanied by prophetic utterances regarding his future ministry. His childhood was characterised by a growth in wisdom and grace and, in particular, a strong desire to learn of God his Father and to understand the Scriptures.

Jesus Christ was consecrated as an infant

Lk 2:22 *See also* Lk 2:23-24

Indications of Jesus Christ's future ministry were revealed

Through the words of Simeon
Lk 2:30-32 *See also* Lk 2:25-29,34-35

Through the words of Anna Lk 2:38

The visit of the Magi
Mt 2:1-12

The escape to Egypt
Mt 2:13-15

The return from Egypt
Mt 2:19-20 *See also* Mt 2:15; Hos 11:1; Mt 2:21

Jesus Christ lives in Nazareth
Mt 2:22-23 *See also* Lk 2:39

Jesus Christ grows up
Lk 2:40 *See also* Lk 2:52

Jesus Christ visited the temple

He celebrates the Passover there
Lk 2:41-42

He stays behind in the temple
Lk 2:43-45,48-50

He displays his understanding of the Scriptures there Lk 2:46-47

The obedience of Jesus Christ
Lk 2:51

Mary and Joseph remember the sayings and events of Jesus Christ's childhood
Lk 2:19,33,51

See also

1427 prophecy	2515 Christ, birth of
2033 Christ, humanity	2535 Christ, family of
2057 Christ, obedience	5099 Mary, mother of Christ
2081 Christ, wisdom	5669 children, examples
2218 Christ, Son of God	5688 firstborn
2333 Christ, attitude to OT	
2366 Christ, prophecies concerning	

2525
Jesus Christ, cross of

The death of Jesus Christ is of central importance to the Christian faith. Through Christ's death, sinners are reconciled to God and to their fellow human beings. Paul summarises the gospel as "the message of the cross".

Jesus Christ foretold his death on the cross
Mt 20:18-19 pp Mk 10:33-34 pp Lk 18:31-32 *See also* Mt 26:2; Jn 3:14-15; 8:28; 12:32-33; 18:32

The facts of Jesus Christ's death on the cross

Carrying Jesus Christ's cross Jn 19:17 *Though Jesus Christ began to carry his cross, the Romans soon forced Simon of Cyrene to continue with it. See also* Mt 27:32 pp Mk 15:21 pp Lk 23:26

Jesus Christ refused the comfort of wine, which would have lessened the pains of his suffering Mt 27:34 pp Mk 15:23

Jesus Christ was nailed to the cross Lk 23:33 pp Mt 27:35 pp Mk 15:24-25 pp Jn 19:18

Jesus Christ's words from the cross Lk 23:34,43; Jn 19:26-27; Mt 27:46 pp Mk 15:34; Ps 22:1; Lk 23:46; Jn 19:28-30

Signs accompanying Jesus Christ's death on the cross

Darkness over the whole land for three hours: Mt 27:45; Mk 15:33 pp Lk 23:44-45
The temple curtain torn from top to bottom: Mt 27:51 pp Mk 15:38 pp Lk 23:45; Mt 27:52-53 *the dead come back to life*

People at the scene of the cross

The Roman centurion and his men:
Mt 27:35-36,54 pp Mk 15:39 pp Lk 23:47
The two criminals crucified with Jesus Christ: Mt 27:38 pp Mk 15:27 pp Lk 23:32-33 pp Jn 19:18; Mt 27:44; Lk 23:39-43
Mt 27:39-43 pp Mk 15:29-32 pp Lk 23:35-37 *people who insulted and mocked Jesus Christ*
Jesus Christ's mother and other women: Mt 27:55-56 pp Mk 15:40-41 pp Lk 23:27-31 pp Jn 19:25; Lk 23:49
Jn 19:26-27 *John*

Responsibility for the cross

The cross as God's plan Ac 2:23 *See also* Isa 53:10; Mt 26:39 pp Mk 14:36 pp Lk 22:42; Mt 26:42; Jn 14:30-31; Ac 4:25-28; Ps 2:1-2; Rev 13:8

The crowd's call for Jesus Christ's crucifixion Mt 27:21-22 pp Mk 15:12-14 pp Lk 23:18-21 pp Jn 19:15; Mt 27:25; Ac 2:36; 1Th 2:14-15

Jewish and Roman leaders' responsibility Mt 27:1,20 pp Mk 15:11; Mt 27:26 pp Mk 15:15 pp Jn 19:16; Lk 23:24-25; Jn 19:6-7; Ac 4:10; 1Co 2:8

The triumph of the cross
Col 2:15

The cross brings glory to Jesus Christ
Jn 17:1 *Jesus Christ refers to his approaching death, the climax of his earthly life.* Jn 12:28; 13:31-32; 17:5; Php 2:8-11; Heb 12:2; Rev 5:8-14

The cross brings reconciliation
Eph 2:13-17 *See also* Ro 5:9-10; 2Co 5:18-19; Col 1:20

Identification with the crucified Christ releases believers from their old way of life
Gal 2:20 *See also* Ro 6:5-13; Gal 5:24-25; 6:14; Col 2:13-14

Jesus Christ's cross is central to the Christian message
1Co 2:2 *See also* Ac 2:23-24; 3:13; 5:30; 13:27-29; Gal 3:1

Jesus Christ's cross is the symbol of Christian discipleship
Mt 16:24 pp Mk 8:34 pp Lk 9:23 *See also* Mt 10:38; Jn 21:18-19

See also

2024 Christ, glory of	6214 participation in Christ
2057 Christ, obedience	6617 atonement in NT
2366 Christ, prophecies concerning	6652 forgiveness
2372 Christ, victory	6684 mediator
2410 cross, the	6716 reconciliation
2530 Christ, death of	7950 mission of Christ
2570 Christ, suffering	

2530
Jesus Christ, death of

The death of Jesus Christ by crucifixion is of central importance to the NT. Through the faithful, obedient death of Christ, God grants sinners forgiveness and eternal life. The Christian sacraments of baptism and the Lord's Supper focus upon the death of Christ.

Jesus Christ's death was foretold
In time and in eternity Rev 13:8 *See also* Isa 53:10–12; Zec 12:10; Jn 1:29,36

By Jesus Christ himself Mt 16:21 pp Mk 8:31 pp Lk 9:22 *See also* Mt 17:22–23; 26:12 pp Jn 12:7; Jn 16:16,28; 18:4

Jesus Christ willingly planned to give his life Jn 10:11 *See also* Jn 10:15,17–18; 13:1; 15:13; 1Jn 3:16

Plots to kill Jesus Christ
Mk 3:6 pp Mt 12:14 *See also* Mt 26:4 pp Mk 14:1; Lk 13:31; 19:47; Jn 5:18; 7:25; 8:37,40

The manner of Jesus Christ's death
Jesus Christ died by crucifixion Lk 23:33 pp Mt 27:35 pp Mk 15:24–25

The moment of death Mk 15:37 pp Mt 27:50 pp Lk 23:46 pp Jn 19:30 *See also* Jn 19:33

Events accompanying Jesus Christ's death Mt 27:45 *Darkness descended on the land;* Mt 27:51 *The curtain of the temple was split;* Mt 27:52–53 *The dead emerged from their tombs.*

Jesus Christ's burial Mt 27:58–60 pp Mk 15:43–46 pp Lk 23:51–53 pp Jn 19:38–42

The unique character of Jesus Christ's death
Jesus Christ's body did not decay Ac 2:31 *See also* Ps 16:10; Ac 2:27; 13:36–37

Jesus Christ descended to the dead Ro 1:4 *See also* 1Pe 3:18–22

Jesus Christ was raised bodily from the dead Lk 24:36–40 *See also* Jn 21:12–13; Ac 10:41; 25:19

Death had no power over Jesus Christ Ac 2:24 *See also* Ro 6:9–10; Rev 1:18

Jesus Christ's death was a unique sacrifice Heb 7:27 *See also* 1Co 5:7; Eph 5:2; Heb 9:26,28; 10:10,12; 1Jn 2:2; 4:10

Achievements of Jesus Christ's death
Jesus Christ's death establishes the new covenant Lk 22:20 pp Mt 26:28 pp Mk 14:24 pp 1Co 11:25 *See also* Heb 9:15; 13:20

Jesus Christ's death is a victory Col 2:14–15 *See also* Heb 2:9,14–15; Rev 12:11

Jesus Christ's death brings redemption Rev 5:9 *See also* Mk 10:45 pp Mt 20:28; Ac 20:28; Gal 3:13; Eph 1:7; Tit 2:14; 1Pe 1:18–19

Jesus Christ's death brings forgiveness and cleansing 1Jn 1:7 *See also* Heb 9:14; Rev 1:5; 7:14

Jesus Christ's death brings sanctification Heb 13:12 *See also* Heb 10:14; 1Pe 1:2

Believers identify with Jesus Christ in his death
Ro 6:3–8 *See also* 2Co 5:14–15; Gal 2:20; Col 2:11; 2Ti 2:11

See also

1352 covenant, the new	6020 sin
2315 Christ as Lamb	6510 salvation
2321 Christ as redeemer	6614 atonement
	6652 forgiveness
2410 cross, the	6684 mediator
2560 Christ, resurrection	7317 blood of Christ
	7933 Lord's Supper

2535
Jesus Christ, family of

Jesus Christ belonged to a human family and experienced family relationships during his earthly ministry. Such relationships underline the fact of Christ's humanity.

Jesus Christ was born into a family
He is placed in a family tree Mt 1:1–17; Lk 1:34–37; 3:23–38

His birth was a natural one Lk 2:5–7 *Jesus Christ's conception was miraculous, his birth natural. See also* Lk 2:21–22 *see* Lev 12:2–4 *for the instructions concerning purification after childbirth*

He grew up within a family Lk 2:48 *See also* Lk 2:51–52

Jesus Christ's family is mentioned during his earthly ministry
Mt 13:55–56 pp Mk 6:3 *See also* Mt 12:46–47 pp Mk 3:31–32 pp Lk 8:19–20; Jn 2:1,12

Jesus Christ's natural brothers
James Gal 1:19 *This verse gives support to the traditional view that James, elder at Jerusalem and writer of the NT letter which bears his name was the Lord's brother. (Other references to him include Ac 15:13; 21:18; 1Co 15:7; Jas 1:1.) See also* Mt 13:55 pp Mk 6:3

Jude Jude 1 *See also* Mt 13:55 pp Mk 6:3 *Jude is understood to be a variation of Judas.*

The nature of Jesus Christ's relationships with his family
He was obedient to and caring towards his parents Lk 2:51 *See also* Jn 19:26–27

The will of his heavenly Father took precedence over the wishes of his natural family Jn 2:3–4 *In John's Gospel, Jesus Christ's "time" (or "hour") is his cross. Here Christ insists that only his heavenly Father can dictate the course of his ministry. See also* Mt 12:48–50 pp Mk 3:33–35; Lk 2:48–49; Jn 7:6–8

His family did not fully understand his ministry Jn 7:3–5 *See also* Mk 3:21

Jesus Christ's natural family were among the first Christians Ac 1:14 *See also* 1Co 9:5

See also

2033 Christ, humanity	2540 Christ, genealogy
2057 Christ, obedience	5099 Mary, mother of Christ
2515 Christ, birth of	5680 family
2520 Christ, childhood	

2540
Jesus Christ, genealogy of

Jesus Christ's human ancestry is traced back in two separate lines to David and thence back to Adam. Jesus' descent from David is of importance for his Messianic claims.

Jesus Christ is descended from Adam
Lk 3:23–38

Jesus Christ is descended from Abraham
Gal 3:16 *See also* Ac 3:25–26

Jesus Christ is descended from Isaac
Ge 21:12; 26:2–4; Gal 3:16

Jesus Christ is descended from Jacob
Ge 28:13–14; Mt 1:2; Lk 3:34

Jesus Christ is descended from the tribe of Judah
Heb 7:14 *See also* Ru 4:18–22

Jesus Christ is descended from Jesse
Isa 11:1; Ro 15:12

Jesus Christ is descended from David
Jesus Christ's human lineage Mt 1:1–17; Lk 2:4 *See also* 1Ch 3:10–19; Lk 3:23–31

Jesus Christ as the Son of David Rev 22:16 *See also* Mt 1:20; 20:30–31 pp Mk 10:47–48 pp Lk 18:38–39; Mt 21:9,15; Lk 1:27,32; Jn 7:42

Jesus Christ is greater than David Mt 22:41–45 pp Mk 12:35–37 pp Lk 20:41–44 *See also* Ps 110:1; Rev 5:5; 22:16

Jesus Christ is greater than Solomon Mt 12:42 pp Lk 11:31

Jesus Christ as the son of Joseph and Mary
Mt 13:55 pp Mk 6:3; Jn 6:42 *See also* Mt 1:16; Lk 4:22; Jn 1:45

See also

2033 Christ, humanity	2312 Christ as king
2078 Christ, sonship of	2535 Christ, family of
2215 Christ, Son of David	5078 Abraham, significance
2218 Christ, Son of God	5083 Adam, and Christ
2230 Messiah, coming of	5089 David, significance
	7248 patriarchs

2545
Jesus Christ, opposition to

Jesus Christ encountered criticism, grumbling and plotting because he was seen as a threat to the religious and political hierarchy, and because he exposed sin.

Opposition by different groups
By family and friends Lk 4:24–29 *See also* Mt 13:55–57 pp Mk 6:3–4; Mk 3:21; Jn 7:3–5

By religious leaders Mt 12:14 pp Mk 3:6 pp Lk 6:11 *See also* Jn 11:47–53

By political leaders Mt 2:13–14; Lk 13:31

Opposition through criticism and accusation
Criticism of Jesus Christ's choice of company Mt 9:11 pp Mk 2:16 pp Lk 5:30 *See also* Lk 7:39; 19:7

Criticism for breaking with tradition Mt 15:1–2 pp Mk 7:5 *Though criticism is directed at the disciples, it is really against Jesus Christ;* Lk 10:16; 11:38

Accusations of Sabbath-breaking Jn 5:16 *See also* Mt 12:2 pp Mk 2:24 pp Lk 6:2; Mt 12:10 pp Mk 3:2 pp Lk 6:7; Lk 13:14; 14:1

Accusations of blasphemy Jn 10:33 *See also* Mt 9:3 pp Mk 2:6–7 pp Lk 5:21; Mt 26:65 pp Mk 14:64; Jn 5:18; 10:36

Accusations of being demon-possessed Jn 10:20 *See also* Mt 12:24 pp Mk 3:22 pp Lk 11:15; Jn 7:20; 8:48

Reasons for opposing Jesus Christ
Because of hatred Jn 15:23–25 *See also* Jn 7:7; 8:40; 15:18

Because people's minds are closed Jn 8:43–44 *See also* Jn 8:37; 2Co 4:4

Jesus Christ knew where opposition would lead
Mt 16:21 pp Mk 8:31–32 pp Lk 9:22 *See also* Mt 17:22–23 pp Mk 9:31; Mt 20:17–19 pp Mk 10:32–34 pp Lk 18:31–32; Lk 9:44

Unsuccessful opposition before the crucifixion
Early attempts to arrest Jesus Christ Jn 10:39 *See also* Jn 7:30,32,44

Attempts on Jesus Christ's life Jn 8:59 *See also* Lk 4:28–30; Jn 7:19; 10:31

Opposition that led to the crucifixion
Plots by the Jewish leaders Mt 26:3–4 pp Mk 14:1–2 pp Lk 22:2 *See also* Mt 21:46 pp Mk 12:12 pp Lk 20:19; Jn 11:57

The chief priests stirred up the crowd Mt 27:20–23 pp Mk 15:11–14 pp Lk 23:21 *See also* Jn 19:15

Rejection by political authorities Mt 27:26 pp Mk 15:15 pp Lk 23:24–25 *See also* Lk 23:7–12; Jn 19:16; Ac 4:25–27; Ps 2:1–2

The mockery of the Roman soldiers Mt 27:27–31 pp Mk 15:16–20

The betrayal by Judas Iscariot Mt 26:14–16 pp Mk 14:10–11 pp Lk 22:3–6; Mt 26:47–50 pp Mk 14:43–45 pp Lk 22:47–48; Jn 18:2–5

Opposition at the crucifixion
Mt 27:39–44 pp Mk 15:29–32 pp Lk 23:35–39; Jn 19:21

Opposition to Jesus Christ in apostolic preaching
Ac 3:13–15 *See also* Ac 2:23; 4:10; 5:30; 7:52–53; 10:39; 13:27–29

Saul of Tarsus opposes Jesus Christ
Ac 9:4–5 *See also* Ac 22:7–8; 26:14–15

See also

2369 Christ, responses to	7505 Jews, the attitudes to Christ
2410 cross, the	7552 Pharisees,
2426 gospel, responses	8729 enemies of Christ
2570 Christ, suffering	8785 opposition
2585 Christ, trial	8797 persecution, attitudes
5798 betrayal	
7464 teachers of the law	

2550
Jesus Christ, pre-existence of
See 2018 Jesus Christ, divinity of

2555
Jesus Christ, resurrection appearances of

Jesus Christ appeared to various groups and individuals on several occasions after his death, prior to his ascension into heaven.

The resurrection appearances of Jesus Christ on the third day
To Mary Magdalene Jn 20:10–18 *See also* Mk 16:9–11

To the women at the tomb Mt 28:1–10 pp Mk 16:1–8 pp Lk 24:1–12

To Peter Lk 24:34; 1Co 15:5

To the two travellers to Emmaus Mk 16:12–13; Lk 24:13–16,30–32

To the disciples in the upper room Mk 16:14 pp Lk 24:36 pp Jn 20:19

Further appearances of Jesus Christ
To the disciples in the upper room Jn 20:26; 1Co 15:5

Other appearances Jn 21:1 *See also* Mt 28:16–17; 1Co 15:6–7

Jesus Christ appears at his ascension Mk 16:19; Lk 24:50–51; Ac 1:9

Jesus Christ's resurrection body
It was different from his pre-crucifixion body Jn 20:26 *This suggests that the resurrected body of Jesus Christ was not restricted by natural laws: closed doors provided no barrier to Jesus Christ's bodily appearance to his disciples. See also* **Mk 16:12** *The failure to recognise Jesus Christ may be an indication of his changed appearance but also might emphasise the*

disciples' own sorrow and lack of faith; Jn 20:14,19 pp Lk 24:36

It was a body of flesh and blood Lk 24:39 *See also* Lk 24:42–43; Jn 20:20

Jesus Christ foretold his resurrection appearances
Jn 16:16

Responses to Jesus Christ's resurrection appearances
Fear and alarm Lk 24:37 *See also* Mt 28:10

Doubt and disbelief Mk 16:11 *See also* Mt 28:17; Mk 16:13–14; Lk 24:11–12; Jn 20:9,13–14,25

Belief and joy Mt 28:8 *See also* Lk 24:31–32,41; Jn 20:16,18,27–29

Understanding and worship Mt 28:9 *See also* Lk 24:8,45–47; Jn 2:22; Ac 2:31–33

The significance of Jesus Christ's resurrection appearances
They gave proof of Jesus Christ's deity Jn 20:28–29 *See also* Lk 24:31–34; Jn 20:8; Ac 10:41–42

Christian life and faith depend on the trustworthiness of the witnesses' testimony 1Co 15:17 *See also* Jn 20:31; Ac 3:15; Ro 1:4; 1Co 15:1–58; 1Th 4:14; 1Pe 1:3

See also

2505 Christ, ascension	5624 witnesses to Christ
2560 Christ, resurrection	9311 resurrection of Christ

2560
Jesus Christ, resurrection of

True Christian preaching is centred on the fact that God raised Jesus Christ from the dead so that believers may have victory over sin and death and receive the blessings of eternal life.

The resurrection of Jesus Christ is foretold
In Scripture 1Co 15:3–4 *See also* Ps 16:10; 49:15; Isa 53:10–12; Hos 6:2; Lk 24:46; Ac 2:29–31; 26:22–23

By Jesus Christ Mt 16:21 pp Mk 8:31 pp Lk 9:22 *See also* Mt 12:40 *the sign of Jonah;* Mt 17:9 pp Mk 9:9 *the transfiguration;* Mt 17:22–23 pp Mk 9:31; Mt 20:18–19 pp Mk 10:33–34 pp Lk 18:31–33; Mt 26:32 pp Mk 14:28; Jn 2:19–22 *Jesus Christ clears the temple;* Jn 16:16

The resurrection is preached by the apostles
Ac 4:33 *See also* Ac 2:24–32; 10:40–41; 17:2–3,18,31

The certainty of the resurrection
Ac 1:3 *See also* 1Co 15:3–8 *These verses particularly stress the physical reality of the risen Christ:* Lk 24:36–43; Jn 20:26–28

The necessity of the resurrection
1Co 15:17 *See also* Jn 20:9

The results of Jesus Christ's resurrection

God's power is demonstrated Eph 1:19-20 *See also* Ac 2:24; 1Co 6:14

The sonship of Jesus Christ is declared Ro 1:4 *See also* Ac 13:33

The lordship of Jesus Christ is declared Ro 14:9
The lordship of Jesus Christ is seen in that he was raised to the right hand of God: Ac 5:30-31; Eph 1:20-22 2Co 5:15

The destruction of death's power is declared Rev 1:18 *See also* Ac 2:24; Ro 6:9

The benefits of Jesus Christ's resurrection for believers

It is the foundation of salvation Ro 4:25 *See also* Jn 11:25-26; Ro 10:9; 1Pe 1:21; 3:21

It provides the power to live for God Ro 6:4 *See also* Ro 7:4; 8:11; Eph 2:4-7; Php 3:8-11; Col 2:12; 3:1; Heb 13:20-21

The intercession of Jesus Christ depends upon it Ro 8:34 *See also* Heb 7:25

It brings assurance of resurrection to eternal life 1Co 6:14 *See also* Ro 6:5; 1Co 15:20-22; 2Co 4:14; 1Th 4:14; 1Pe 1:3-4

See also

2218 Christ, Son of God	2505 Christ, ascension
2224 Christ, the Lord	2530 Christ, death of
2324 Christ as Saviour	2555 Christ, resurrection appearances
2363 Christ, preaching & teaching	3278 Holy Spirit, indwelling
2366 Christ, prophecies concerning	6744 sanctification 9311 resurrection of Christ
2372 Christ, victory	

2565
Jesus Christ, second coming of

Jesus Christ will return visibly and in glory at the end of history to raise the dead, judge the world, destroy all evil and opposition to God and consummate his kingdom. Believers are encouraged to be prepared for his return, waiting with eagerness and joy.

The second coming is foretold

In the OT Da 7:13-14 *See also* Ps 72:2-4; Isa 2:2-4 pp Mic 4:1-3; Isa 11:4-9; 40:5

By Jesus Christ Mt 24:30 pp Mk 13:26 pp Lk 21:27 *See also* Mt 16:27; 25:31; Mk 14:62; Lk 12:40; Jn 14:3,28

By the angels at Jesus Christ's ascension Ac 1:11

By the apostles Php 3:20 *See also* Ac 3:20-21; 1Co 1:7; 11:26; 1Th 1:10; 3:13; 4:16; 2Th 1:7-10; Heb 9:28

NT terms for the second coming

"Parousia"
Meaning literally "presence" or "coming", the term was used in the NT world of a

royal visit: Mt 24:3; Jas 5:7-8; 2Pe 3:4; 1Jn 2:28

"Apocalypsis"
Meaning literally "unveiling", "apocalypsis" suggests that the second coming will make visible that which is already true of Jesus Christ but presently hidden from human sight: Lk 17:30; 1Co 1:7; 2Th 1:7; 1Pe 1:7; 4:13

"Epiphaneia"
Meaning literally "appearing" or "manifestation", the term suggests coming out into view from a hidden background: 2Th 2:8; 1Ti 6:14; 2Ti 4:1; Tit 2:13

Events that will precede the second coming

The universal preaching of the gospel Mt 24:14 pp Mk 13:10 *See also* Mt 28:19-20; Ac 1:7-8

The persecution of believers Mt 24:9 pp Mk 13:9 pp Lk 21:12 *See also* Mt 24:21 pp Mk 13:19; Mt 24:22 pp Mk 13:20; Mk 13:12-13 pp Mt 24:12-13 pp Lk 21:16-17; 2Ti 3:1; Rev 7:14

Apostasy, nominal religion and godlessness 1Ti 4:1 *See also* Mt 24:10; 2Ti 3:1-5; 2Pe 3:3-4

The revelation of the antichrist 1Jn 2:18 *The antichrist is a name given to the one who will lead opposition to God's kingdom. It appears to refer to an individual but may denote a corporate movement. See also* Da 7:20-22; 2Th 2:3-4; 1Jn 4:3; Rev 13:1-10

The appearance of false Christs and false prophets Mt 24:24 pp Mk 13:22 *See also* Mt 7:15; 24:5 pp Mk 13:6 pp Lk 21:8; Mt 24:11; Lk 17:23; 2Jn 7

Wars and rumours of wars Mt 24:6-7 pp Mk 13:7-8 pp Lk 21:9-10

Famines and earthquakes Mt 24:7-8 pp Mk 13:8 pp Lk 21:11

Cosmic changes Mt 24:29 pp Mk 13:24 pp Lk 21:25-26

The timing of the second coming

At God's appointed time Ac 3:20-21 *See also* Mt 24:36 pp Mk 13:32; Lk 17:20-30; Ac 1:7; 2Pe 3:9

Unexpectedly 1Th 5:1-2 *See also* Mt 24:27 pp Lk 17:24; Mt 24:43-44 pp Lk 12:39-40; 2Pe 3:10; Rev 3:3; 16:15

After a delay Mt 25:5 *Part of a parable concerning the coming of Jesus Christ who is represented by the bridegroom. See also* Mt 25:19; 2Pe 3:3-9

Imminently Mt 24:30-34 pp Mk 13:26-30 pp Lk 21:27-32 *See also* Jn 21:22; Ro 13:11-12; Jas 5:8-9; Rev 3:11; 22:7,20

The manner of the second coming

Jesus Christ's personal return Ac 1:11 *See also* Ac 3:20; 1Th 4:16; Heb 9:28

A visible and glorious return Rev 1:7 *See also* Mt 24:30 pp Mk 13:26 pp Lk 21:27; Mt 26:64; Ac 1:9

With the sound of a trumpet Mt 24:31; 1Co 15:52; 1Th 4:16

With angels Mt 16:27; 24:31; 2Th 1:7

The purpose of the second coming

To raise the dead 1Co 15:22-23 *See also* Jn 5:28-29; 1Co 15:52; 1Th 4:16

To judge all people Ps 96:13 *See also* Ps 98:9; Mt 16:27; 25:31-32; 2Ti 4:1; Rev 20:11-15; 22:12

To judge the wicked 2Th 1:7-10 *See also* Mt 24:51; Ro 2:5; 2Pe 3:7; Jude 15

To separate the wicked from the righteous Mt 25:31-32 *See also* Mt 24:40-41 pp Lk 17:34-35

To destroy all evil and opposition to God's kingdom 2Th 2:8 *See also* 1Co 15:24-26; Rev 20:10,14

To reward believers Mt 24:46-47; Lk 12:37; 2Ti 4:8; 1Pe 5:4; 1Jn 3:1

To gather the church together Jn 14:3; 1Th 4:17; 2Th 2:1

To bring final salvation Lk 21:28; Heb 9:28

To transform the saints into his likeness 1Co 15:51-52; Php 3:20-21; Col 3:4

To end the present age Mt 24:3; 1Co 15:24; 2Pe 3:10,12

To restore and renew all things Ac 3:21; 2Pe 3:13; Rev 21:1-5

Reactions at Jesus Christ's second coming

Mt 24:30 *all peoples will mourn*; 2Th 1:10 *His people will marvel.*

Present implications of the second coming for believers

They must always be watchful and ready Mt 24:42-44 *See also* Mt 25:10; Mk 13:35; Lk 12:35-36

They must be faithful stewards Mt 25:14-30 pp Lk 19:12-27

They must eagerly expect his coming 1Co 1:7 *See also* Lk 21:28; Php 3:20; Tit 2:13

They must endure suffering with patient endurance Mt 24:13; 1Pe 1:6-7

They must wait patiently 1Th 1:10; Jas 5:7-8

It is an incentive to holiness 1Jn 3:2-3 *See also* Col 3:4-5; 1Ti 6:14; 2Pe 3:11; 1Jn 2:23,28

It is an incentive to mission 2Ti 4:1-2 *See also* 2Pe 3:12

See also

7774 prophets, false	9105 last things
8318 patience	9115 antichrist, the
8424 evangelism	9140 last days
8490 watchfulness	9220 day of the LORD
8746 false Christs	9240 last judgment
8794 persecution	9610 hope

2570
Jesus Christ, suffering of

Jesus Christ's life was characterised by suffering, though the worst experiences were reserved for his final days. His sufferings are both redemptive and an example to believers.

Jesus Christ's sufferings foretold

In the OT Ps 22:6-8,16-18; Isa 50:6; 52:13-53:12; Zec 9:9-10; 12:10; 13:7; 1Pe 1:11

In Jesus Christ's predictions Mt 16:21 pp Mk 8:31 pp Lk 9:22 *See also* Mt 20:17–19 pp Mk 10:32–34 pp Lk 18:31–32; Jn 12:32–33

Jesus Christ's suffering during his lifetime

As a child Mt 2:13–15

Because of his family Mk 3:20–21 *See also* Jn 7:3–5

Because of the crowds' unbelief Mk 9:19 pp Mt 17:17 pp Lk 9:41 *See also* Mt 12:39 pp Lk 11:29; Mk 8:11–12

Because of the disciples' slowness Mk 8:17–21 pp Mt 16:8–11

Because of the religious leaders Mt 12:14 pp Mk 3:6 pp Lk 6:11 *See also* Jn 5:18; 7:1; 8:48

Because of human suffering Lk 19:41 *See also* Mk 7:34; Lk 7:13; Jn 11:33–35

Jesus Christ's suffering at the time of his death

He was inwardly troubled Jn 12:27 *See also* Mt 26:36–42 pp Mk 14:32–39 pp Lk 22:40–44; Jn 13:21

He was betrayed Mt 26:21–25 pp Mk 14:17–21 pp Lk 22:21–23; Mt 26:47–49 pp Mk 14:43–45 pp Lk 22:47–48 pp Jn 18:2–5; Jn 13:18–30

He was humiliated Mt 27:27–30 pp Mk 15:16–19 *See also* Mt 26:67–68 pp Mk 14:65 pp Lk 22:63–65; Mt 27:26 pp Mk 15:15 pp Lk 23:22; Lk 23:11; Jn 18:22; 19:1

He was crucified Lk 23:33 pp Mt 27:35 pp Mk 15:25 pp Jn 19:18

He suffered separation from God Mt 27:46 pp Mk 15:34 pp Lk 23:46 *See also* Ps 22:1

Jesus Christ's attitude to his suffering

He did not retaliate in his suffering 1Pe 2:23 *See also* Mt 27:12–14 pp Mk 15:3–5; Lk 23:34

He grew through the experience of suffering Heb 5:8 *See also* Heb 2:10

Jesus Christ's sufferings were necessary for salvation

Lk 24:26–27 *See also* Lk 24:46–47; Ac 3:18; 17:3; 26:23

Jesus Christ suffered as a unique sacrifice Heb 7:27; 9:25–26

The Christian experience of suffering

Believers share in Jesus Christ's sufferings 2Co 1:5 *See also* Mt 25:34–40; Ac 9:4–5 pp Ac 22:7–8 pp Ac 26:15; Ro 8:17; Php 3:10; 1Pe 4:13

Jesus Christ's sufferings are an example for believers 1Pe 2:21 *See also* Jn 16:18–20; Php 2:5–7

See also
1135 God, suffering of	2525 Christ, cross of
2015 Christ, compassion	2545 Christ, opposition to
2033 Christ, humanity	5564 suffering of Christ
2327 Christ as servant	5879 humiliation
2339 Christ, example of	6230 rejection

2575
Jesus Christ, temptation of

Repeated yet unsuccessful efforts made by Satan and by human beings to deflect Jesus Christ from his Father's will.

The wilderness temptations

Mk 1:13

Tempted to turn stones into bread Mt 4:2–3 pp Lk 4:2–3

Tempted to abuse miraculous power Mt 4:5–6 pp Lk 4:9–11 *See also* Mt 12:38; 16:1 pp Mk 8:11; Lk 11:16; Jn 2:18

Tempted by the offer of an easy route to power Mt 4:8–9 pp Lk 4:5–7

Tempted to doubt he was God's Son Mt 4:3 pp Lk 4:3 *See also* Mt 4:6 pp Lk 4:9; Mt 27:40

Temptation continued throughout Jesus Christ's life

Lk 22:28 *Trials can include temptations.*

Opponents tempted Jesus Christ with trick questions Mt 22:15 pp Mk 12:13 pp Lk 20:20

Jesus Christ tempted to sidestep the cross Mt 16:21–23 pp Mk 8:32–33 *See also* Mt 26:39–44 pp Mk 14:35–41 pp Lk 22:41–44; Mt 27:40 pp Mk 15:30

Jesus Christ steadfastly resisted temptation

Jesus Christ resisted temptation by trusting God's word Mt 4:4 pp Lk 4:4 *See also* Mt 4:7 pp Lk 4:12; Mt 4:10 pp Lk 4:8

Jesus Christ resisted temptation by obeying his Father Heb 5:7–8 *See also* Mt 26:39 pp Mk 14:36 pp Lk 22:42; Mt 26:42

Results of Jesus Christ's temptations

Satan left Jesus Christ alone Mt 4:11 pp Lk 4:13

Jesus Christ remained sinless Heb 4:15 *Refers to Jesus Christ as high priest and as sacrificial lamb. See also* Jn 8:46; 1Pe 2:22

Jesus Christ helps those who are being tempted Heb 2:18 *See also* Heb 4:14–16

See also
2075 Christ, sinless	6252 temptation &
2372 Christ, victory	Christ
4122 Satan, tempter	8453 obedience
5379 law, Christ's attitude	

2580
Jesus Christ, transfiguration of

The revelation of the glory of Jesus Christ, shortly before his death, at which his disciples caught sight of him in his full majesty. The transfiguration brought home to the disciples that Jesus Christ is the Son of God.

The glory of Jesus Christ is revealed at the transfiguration

Jesus Christ prepares for his glory to be revealed Lk 9:28 pp Mt 17:1 pp Mk 9:2

Jesus Christ is visibly transfigured Mt 17:2 pp Mk 9:2–3 pp Lk 9:29 *The transfiguration was a glimpse of Jesus Christ's glory whereby his physical appearance was visibly changed.*

The disciples are eye-witnesses of Jesus Christ's glory Mt 17:6 *See also* Mk 9:9; Lk 9:32; Jn 1:14; 2Pe 1:16

Moses and Elijah appear at the transfiguration

Lk 9:30–31 pp Mt 17:3 pp Mk 9:4 *"departure" refers to Jesus Christ's death.*

God's voice is heard at the transfiguration

Mt 17:5 pp Mk 9:7 pp Lk 9:35 *God the Father's voice is heard authenticating Jesus Christ's ministry. See also* Mt 3:17 pp Mk 1:11 pp Lk 3:22; 2Pe 1:17–18

The disciples' response to the transfiguration

Peter's wish to build shelters Mt 17:4 pp Mk 9:5–6 pp Lk 9:33

Fear Mt 17:6–7; Mk 9:6; Lk 9:34

Questioning and confusion Mt 17:10 pp Mk 9:10–11

They keep to themselves what they have seen and heard Lk 9:36 pp Mt 17:9–10 pp Mk 9:9–10 *These verses reiterate that Jesus Christ's full glory was hidden from the world until his resurrection.*

See also
1040 God, fatherhood	2218 Christ, Son of God
1403 God, revelation	2510 Christ, baptism of
2024 Christ, glory of	
2051 Christ, majesty of	5092 Elijah
2063 Christ, perfection	5101 Moses
2078 Christ, sonship of	5196 voice

2585
Jesus Christ, trial of

Jesus Christ, falsely accused of blasphemy towards God and treason towards Rome, humbly endured his trial as a fulfilment of the purposes of God.

The preliminary hearing before Annas

Jn 18:12–14 *Annas, though deposed from office by the Romans, was probably still regarded by many as the true high priest;* Jn 18:19–23

The trial before Caiaphas and the Sanhedrin

Jesus Christ is sent to the ruling high priest Mt 26:57 pp Mk 14:53 pp Jn 18:24; Lk 22:54

False evidence is sought Mt 26:59–60

pp Mk 14:55–56 *The Sanhedrin was the high court of the Jews and consisted of 71 chief priests, elders and teachers of the law, including the high priest who presided.*

False accusations are made
Mt 26:60–61 pp Mk 14:57–59 *A person could only be convicted on the evidence of two or more witnesses.*

Jesus Christ's trial centres upon his Messianic claims
Jesus declares himself to be the Christ
Mt 26:63–64 pp Mk 14:61–62 *See also* Lk 22:66–70

Jesus Christ is charged with blasphemy Mt 26:65–66
pp Mk 14:63–64; Mt 27:1 pp Mk 15:1 *The Sanhedrin decided that Jesus Christ deserved death but charged him with treason rather than blasphemy.*

Jesus is mocked as the Christ
Mt 26:67–68 pp Mk 14:65
pp Lk 22:63–65

The trial before Pilate
The Sanhedrin hand Jesus Christ over to Pilate Mt 27:2 pp Mk 15:1; Lk 23:1; Jn 18:28–32

Jesus Christ accepts the title of king
Jn 18:36–37 *See also* Mt 27:11
pp Mk 15:2; Lk 23:2–3; Jn 19:9–12; 1Ti 6:13

Pilate decides Jesus Christ is innocent
Lk 23:4 *See also* Lk 23:14–15,22; Jn 18:38; 19:4–6; Ac 13:28

Pilate sends Jesus Christ to Herod
Lk 23:5–10

Herod sends Jesus Christ back to Pilate Lk 23:11–12

Pilate seeks to release Jesus Christ
Jn 19:12 *See also* Mt 27:15–18
pp Mk 15:6–10 *Pilate appeals to the crowd on the basis of Jesus Christ's kingship;* Mt 27:19 *Pilate is warned by his wife not to get involved;* Lk 23:16,20,22; Jn 18:38–39; 19:6,15

The crowd demand the release of Barabbas and the crucifixion of Jesus Christ Mt 27:20 pp Mk 15:11 *See also* Mt 27:21–23 pp Mk 15:12–14; Lk 23:18,21,23; Jn 18:40; 19:6–7,12,15

The crowd's demands prevail
Mk 15:15 pp Mt 27:26 *See also* Mt 27:24 *Pilate denies responsibility;* Mt 27:25; Lk 23:23–25; Jn 19:16; Ac 3:13–14 *The emphasis is on the people's responsibility.*

Jesus Christ is mocked as king
Jn 19:2–3 *See also* Mt 27:27–31
pp Mk 15:16–20; Jn 19:15

Jesus Christ's response to his trial
Isa 53:7 *See also* Mt 26:62–63
pp Mk 14:60–61; Mt 27:12,14
pp Mk 15:5; Lk 23:9; Jn 19:9;
Ac 8:32–35; 1Pe 2:23

Jesus Christ's trial confirms he is God's servant
Ac 4:27–28 *See also* Isa 53:10;
Jn 19:8–11; Ac 2:23 *The outcome of the trial fulfilled God's declared purpose.*

See also
1115 God, purpose of	2218 Christ, Son of God
2206 Jesus, the Christ	2312 Christ as king
	2315 Christ as Lamb

See also
2327 Christ as servant	5593 trial
2525 Christ, cross of	5950 silence
2530 Christ, death of	8815 ridicule
2570 Christ, suffering	

2590
Jesus Christ, triumphal entry of

Jesus Christ rode into Jerusalem on a colt, royally yet humbly, to the rejoicing of his followers, but provoking opposition from the Jewish religious leaders.

The colt used in Jesus Christ's entry into Jerusalem
Jesus Christ's instructions to his disciples Lk 19:29–31 pp Mt 21:1–3 pp Mk 11:1–3

The obedience of the disciples Mt 21:6 pp Mk 11:4–6 pp Lk 19:32–34

Jesus Christ's entry into Jerusalem
Jn 12:14–15 pp Mt 21:4–5 *See also* Isa 62:11; Zec 9:9

The response of the crowd to Jesus Christ's entry into Jerusalem
Proclamation of Jesus Christ's kingship Mt 21:8 pp Mk 11:8
pp Lk 19:36; 2Ki 9:13 *Spreading cloaks on the road was an act of royal homage.*

Proclamation of Jesus' messiahship
Mt 21:9 pp Mk 11:9–10
pp Lk 19:37–38 *See also* Ps 118:26

Proclamation of Jesus Christ's victory
Jn 12:13 *Palm branches were used in celebration of victory. See also* Lev 23:40; Ps 118:27; Rev 7:9

The response of the Pharisees to Jesus Christ's entry into Jerusalem
Lk 19:39–40

See also
2036 Christ, humility	2324 Christ as Saviour
2051 Christ, majesty of	2345 Christ, kingdom of
2206 Jesus, the Christ	2372 Christ, victory of
2215 Christ, Son of David	2545 Christ, opposition to
2221 Christ, Son of Man	7240 Jerusalem, history
2312 Christ as king	8664 praise

2595
incarnation

The assuming by God of human nature in the person of Jesus Christ. The incarnation is the fixed and permanent physical dwelling of God in his world, as opposed to the temporary manifestation of the divine presence and power in a theophany.

God the Son assumed human nature
Jn 1:14 *See also* Jn 1:9; 8:56; 1Ti 3:16; 1Jn 1:1–2; 4:2; 2Jn 7

Jesus Christ's incarnation involved a supernatural conception
Lk 1:35 *See also* Isa 9:6; Mt 1:18; Jn 14:9 *The incarnation was such that the Son was the exact representation of the Father;* Ro 1:4; Col 1:15,19; Heb 1:2–3

Jesus Christ's incarnation involved a virgin birth
Mt 1:22–23 *See also* Isa 7:14; Lk 1:34; Ro 1:3; Gal 4:4; Php 2:8; Heb 2:14

The cost of the incarnation
Php 2:6–7 *See also* 2Co 8:9; Heb 2:10 *The incarnation involved Jesus Christ's suffering.*

The necessity of the incarnation
Ro 8:3 *See also* Ro 5:17–19; 2Co 5:19; Col 1:22; 1Ti 2:5 *Only a person who is fully human and fully divine can be the effective mediator between God and humanity;* Heb 2:17–18; 4:15

See also
1454 theophany	2515 Christ, birth of
1690 word of God	5020 human nature
2033 Christ, humanity	5099 Mary, mother of Christ
2036 Christ, humility	6614 atonement
2218 Christ, Son of God	6684 mediator
	6752 substitution

3000
Holy Spirit

3005
Holy Spirit, qualities of

3010
God, the Holy Spirit

The co-equal and co-eternal Spirit of the Father and the Son, who inspired Scripture and brings new life to the people of God. The Spirit of God is often portrayed in Scripture in terms of "breath", "life" or "wind", indicating his role in sustaining and bringing life to God's creation. This set of themes consists of the following:

3015 Holy Spirit, divinity of
3020 Holy Spirit, joy of
3025 Holy Spirit, personality of
3030 Holy Spirit, power of
3035 Holy Spirit, presence of
3040 Holy Spirit, promise of
3045 Holy Spirit, sovereignty of
3050 Holy Spirit, wisdom of

3015
Holy Spirit, divinity of

The Holy Spirit's attributes and activities are always those of God. The titles used of the Holy Spirit identify him as part of the triune nature of the divine being.

The Holy Spirit possesses the attributes of God

He is present everywhere Ps 139:7–8
See also Jn 14:17

He knows all things Isa 40:13 *NIV footnote. See also* Jn 16:13; 1Co 2:10–11

He has infinite power Zec 4:6 *See also* Lk 1:35

He is eternal Heb 9:14 *See also* Jn 14:16

He is unique Eph 4:4–6 *See also* 1Co 12:4

He is holy Ro 1:4 *See also* Ro 5:5; 1Co 6:19 *The Christian's body is also holy because it is the place where God dwells by his Spirit;* 2Co 6:6
The Holy Spirit is the seal of ownership marking those who belong to God:
Eph 1:13; 4:30
1Th 1:5; 2Ti 1:14; Tit 3:5; Heb 2:4; 9:8;
1Pe 1:12; 2Pe 1:21; Jude 20

The Holy Spirit performs divine works

He creates Ps 104:30 *See also* Ge 1:2; Job 26:13; 33:4; Ps 33:6

He gives life Eze 37:14 *See also* Ge 2:7; Ro 8:2,11

The Holy Spirit is identified with the person and activity of the Godhead

"Holy Spirit" and "God" are used interchangeably Ac 5:3–4 *See also* 1Co 3:16

The Spirit is called "Lord"
2Co 3:17–18

It is possible to blaspheme the Spirit Mt 12:32; Mk 3:29; Lk 12:10

The Spirit is sent by the Father and the Son Jn 15:26 *See also* Jn 16:14–15

The Spirit is identified with the Father and the Son Mt 28:19–20 *in commissioning;* 2Co 13:14 *in benediction;* Eph 2:18 *in access to God*
In believers' lives: Gal 4:6; 1Pe 1:1–2

The Holy Spirit is given divine titles

The Spirit of God 2Ch 15:1 *See also* Ex 31:3; Nu 24:2; 1Sa 10:10 *Saul prophesies at Gibeah;* 1Sa 19:20; 2Ch 24:20; Eze 11:24; Mt 3:16 *at Jesus Christ's baptism;* 1Co 2:11,14; 2Co 3:3; Php 3:3; 1Pe 4:14

The Spirit of the Lᴏʀᴅ Jdg 3:10; Isa 61:1 *See also* Jdg 6:34; 1Sa 16:13–14; 2Sa 23:2; 1Ki 22:24; 2Ki 2:16; 2Ch 18:23; Isa 11:2; 63:14; Eze 11:5; 37:1

The Spirit of the Lord Lk 4:18; 2Co 3:17

The Spirit of Christ Ro 8:9 *See also* Gal 4:6; Php 1:19; 1Pe 1:11

The Spirit of Jesus Ac 16:7

See also

1080 God, living	3245 Holy Spirit,
1170 God, unity of	blasphemy
1510 Trinity, the	against
2018 Christ, divinity	3266 Holy Spirit in
3030 Holy Spirit,	creation
power	3290 Holy Spirit,
3045 Holy Spirit,	life-giver
sovereignty	8314 orthodoxy
3110 Holy Spirit,	8750 false teachings
titles of	

3020
Holy Spirit, joy of

The Holy Spirit brings joy to believers, giving them an inner contentment and happiness which is not dependent upon external circumstances.

The Holy Spirit enables the Messiah to bring joy
Isa 61:1–3 *See also* Isa 9:2–3

The Holy Spirit gives joy

To those anticipating Jesus Christ's birth Lk 1:41–45 *See also* Lk 1:67–68

To Jesus Christ Lk 10:21 *See also* Heb 1:9

To disciples even in the face of opposition Ac 13:52 *See also* Ac 16:25; 1Th 1:6; 1Pe 4:13–14

The Holy Spirit's fruit includes joy
Gal 5:22 *See also* Ro 14:17; 15:13

Evidence of the Holy Spirit's work prompts believers to rejoice
Ac 11:15–18 *See also* Ac 11:23–24

See also

1070 God, joy of	3269 Holy Spirit in
2039 Christ, joy of	Christ
3218 Holy Spirit &	5874 happiness
praise	8283 joy
3254 Holy Spirit, fruit	
of	

3025
Holy Spirit, personality of

The Holy Spirit is not an impersonal power but a real person with his own personality.

The Holy Spirit is involved in personal relationships
He is in relationship with the Father and the Son Mt 28:19 *See also* Jn 16:14–15; 2Co 13:14; 1Pe 1:2; Jude 20–21

He is in relationship with Christians Ac 15:28

The Spirit can be treated in personal ways Ac 5:3 *See also* Ac 5:9; Heb 10:29

Personal characteristics of the Holy Spirit
The Spirit is wise Isa 11:2; Eph 1:17 *See also* Jn 14:26; Ro 8:27

The Spirit can experience emotion and pain Eph 4:30 *See also* Isa 63:10; Heb 10:29

Grammatical indications of the Holy Spirit's personhood
Jn 14:16 *See also* Jn 14:26; 15:26; 16:7

Examples of the Holy Spirit's actions
He teaches: Lk 12:12; 1Co 2:13
Ro 8:16 *He testifies;* Ro 8:26 *He intercedes;* Ac 20:23 *He warns*
He speaks: 2Sa 23:2; Ac 8:29; 10:19; 11:12; 13:2; Rev 2:7
1Co 2:11 *He knows;* Gal 4:6 *He calls out;*
Jn 16:13 *He hears*

The Holy Spirit's own personality is seen by the gifts he gives and the attitudes he promotes
Gal 5:22–23 *See also* Lk 10:21; Ac 9:31; Ro 5:5; 8:6; 14:17; 15:13; 2Co 13:14; 1Jn 1:6; 5:6

See also

1510 Trinity, the	3215 Holy Spirit &
3015 Holy Spirit,	peace
divinity	3254 Holy Spirit,
3020 Holy Spirit, joy	fruit of
of	3263 Holy Spirit,
3110 Holy Spirit,	guidance
titles of	3284 Holy Spirit,
3140 Holy Spirit,	resisting
teacher	
3209 Holy Spirit &	
love	

3030
Holy Spirit, power of

The Holy Spirit equips and empowers believers so that the reign and reality of God is revealed through them in the world.

The power of the Holy Spirit is witnessed to in the OT
Isa 11:2–3 *See also* Isa 42:1

The Spirit will show his power on the earth Isa 32:15

The Spirit's power will enable people to serve God Eze 36:26–27 *See also* Jer 31:33

The Spirit's power will prompt prophecy and visions Joel 2:28–29 *See also* Ac 2:17–18

The Holy Spirit's power is described by OT imagery
Oil: 1Sa 10:1; 16:13
Isa 63:11–12 *the arm of God*
The hand of God: Eze 3:14; 37:1

The Holy Spirit's power is demonstrated in the OT
In creation Ge 1:2; Job 33:4; Ps 104:30

In acts of judgment and war Jdg 14:19 *See also* Jdg 3:10; 6:34; 11:29; 14:6; 15:14; 1Sa 11:6; 16:13

In the lives of his servants Mic 3:8 *See also* Nu 11:17; 1Sa 10:6,10

The Holy Spirit's power is seen in the life of Jesus Christ
In his conception Lk 1:35

In his teaching and ministry
Mt 7:28–29; 12:28; Mk 1:22,27;
Lk 4:14; 5:17; Ac 10:38

In his resurrection Ro 1:4 *See also* Ro 8:11; 1Ti 3:16; 1Pe 3:18

The Holy Spirit's power is seen in the church's mission
In the church's witness and preaching Ac 1:8 *See also* Lk 24:49; Ac 6:10; 16:7; 1Co 2:4; 1Th 1:5

In the apostolic ministry of signs and wonders Ro 15:18–19 *See also* Heb 2:4

In miraculous works in the church Gal 3:5 *See also* 1Co 12:28

The Holy Spirit's power builds Christian character
Ro 15:13 *See also* 2Ti 1:7

The Holy Spirit's power strengthens the church

Eph 3:16 *See also* Ro 1:11; 1Co 1:7–8

See also

1105 God, power of	3251 Holy Spirit,
1415 miracles	filling with
2066 Christ, power of	3266 Holy Spirit in
3224 Holy Spirit &	creation
preaching	3269 Holy Spirit in
3233 Holy Spirit &	Christ
sanctification	5452 power
3242 Holy Spirit,	9310 resurrection
baptism with	

3035

Holy Spirit, presence of

Present throughout the world, the Holy Spirit convicts the world of sin and brings peace and comfort to believers through his refreshing and restoring presence.

The Holy Spirit is present and active in creation

Ge 1:2 *See also* Job 33:4; Ps 104:30

The Holy Spirit is present everywhere

Ps 139:7 *See also* Ac 20:23

He is equated with God's presence Ps 51:11

He is present with God's people Hag 2:5 *See also* Isa 59:21; 63:10–14; Eze 36:27; 37:14; 1Co 3:16; Eph 2:22

He is present in Jesus Christ's ministry Lk 4:14,18; 5:17; 6:19; 10:21; Ac 10:38

He is present with Jesus Christ's disciples Jn 14:16–17 *See also* Jn 14:26; 15:26–27

The consequences of the Holy Spirit's presence in the church

He convicts of sin Jn 16:7–11; 1Th 1:5

He gives direction Ac 13:2; 15:28

He transforms experience Php 1:19

He encourages Ac 9:31

He empowers Christians for witness Ac 1:8; 6:10

He sanctifies 2Co 3:18 *See also* Ro 15:16; 2Th 2:13; 1Pe 1:2

The Holy Spirit's presence has observable effects

2Co 3:3 *See also* Jn 3:21; Ac 11:23

He brings blessing and fellowship 2Co 13:14 *See also* Php 2:1; 1Pe 4:14

He brings freedom and peace 2Co 3:17 *See also* Ro 8:2,5–9

He brings life Ro 8:10–11

See also

1110 God, present	3269 Holy Spirit in
everywhere	Christ
3130 Holy Spirit,	3278 Holy Spirit,
Counsellor	indwelling
3215 Holy Spirit &	3290 Holy Spirit,
peace	life-giver
3233 Holy Spirit &	3296 Holy Spirit in
sanctification	the world
3263 Holy Spirit,	6717 reconciliation,
guidance	world to God
3266 Holy Spirit in	8495 witnessing
creation	

3040

Holy Spirit, promise of

The OT foretold and Jesus Christ reaffirmed that the Holy Spirit would be poured out on God's people, transforming, empowering and gifting them.

OT promises of the Holy Spirit fulfilled in the OT

The promised Spirit enables prophecy 1Sa 10:6 *See also* 1Sa 10:10

The Spirit fulfils the promised presence of the LORD Ex 33:14 *See also* Isa 63:11,14; Hag 2:5

OT promises of the Holy Spirit fulfilled in the NT

The Spirit implements the promised new covenant Jer 31:33–34 *See also* Ro 8:2,9–10; 2Co 3:3,6; Heb 8:10–11

The promised Spirit will renew Israel Eze 36:26–27 *See also* Eze 11:19; 37:14

The promised Spirit is the guarantee for Israel's future Isa 44:3 *See also* Isa 32:15; 59:21; Eze 39:29

The promised Spirit will empower the life and work of the Messiah Isa 61:1–2 *See also* Isa 11:2; Lk 4:18–19

The Spirit is promised for all people Joel 2:28–29 *See also* Ac 2:17–18

Promises of the Holy Spirit in the NT

The promise that Jesus Christ would baptise with the Spirit Mt 3:11 pp Mk 1:8 pp Lk 3:16 *See also* Jn 1:33; Ac 1:5; 11:16

The Spirit is promised by Jesus Christ Lk 24:49 *See also* Jn 15:26; 16:7–15; Ac 1:5–8

The Spirit is promised for the time after Jesus Christ's resurrection and ascension Jn 7:39 *See also* Ac 2:4,33

The promised Spirit fulfils God's word to Abraham Gal 3:14

The promised Spirit guarantees to believers their future inheritance Eph 1:13–14

See also

1352 covenant, the	3257 Holy Spirit, gift
new	of
3035 Holy Spirit,	3269 Holy Spirit in
presence of	Christ
3230 Holy Spirit &	3272 Holy Spirit in
regeneration	OT
3233 Holy Spirit &	3281 Holy Spirit,
sanctification	inspiration
3242 Holy Spirit,	3290 Holy Spirit,
baptism with	life-giver
3251 Holy Spirit,	5467 promises,
filling with	divine

3045

Holy Spirit, sovereignty of

The Holy Spirit has supreme power and acts in accordance with divine purposes, exercising authority and control in the world and over God's people.

The Holy Spirit is Lord

2Co 3:17–18 *See also* Jdg 3:10

The Holy Spirit is sovereign in bringing spiritual life

Jn 3:1–8 *See also* Eze 37:14; Jn 6:63; Ro 8:2; Tit 3:5; 1Pe 1:2

The Holy Spirit's will is sovereign

He determines the distribution of spiritual gifts 1Co 12:11 *See also* 1Sa 10:6,10; 19:20,23; Heb 2:4

He controls the appointment of leaders Ac 13:2 *See also* Ac 20:28

The Holy Spirit demonstrates his sovereignty over creation

He participates in the work of creation Job 33:4 *See also* Ge 1:2; Ps 104:30

He performs miraculous deeds Ac 8:39 *See also* 1Ki 18:12; 2Ki 2:16; Mt 12:28–38 pp Mk 3:22–30 pp Lk 11:14–23

The Holy Spirit exercises his rule in the lives of individuals

Jesus Christ is led by the Spirit Mt 4:1 pp Mk 1:12 pp Lk 4:1

God's people are led by the Spirit Gal 5:18 *See also* 1Ch 28:12; Ps 143:10; Mt 10:20; Lk 2:27; Jn 16:13; Ac 8:29; 20:22

God's people are restrained by the Spirit Ac 16:6–7

God's people are given victory by the Spirit Jdg 3:10 *See also* Jdg 14:6,19; 15:14

The Holy Spirit's sovereignty is confirmed by the greatness of his attributes

Ps 139:7 *His presence*; 1Co 2:4 *His power*; 1Co 2:10–11 *His knowledge*

See also

1020 God, all-	3230 Holy Spirit &
knowing	regeneration
1110 God, present	3251 Holy Spirit,
everywhere	filling with
1130 God,	3263 Holy Spirit,
sovereignty	guidance
1469 visions	3266 Holy Spirit in
3015 Holy Spirit,	creation
divinity	3290 Holy Spirit,
3030 Holy Spirit,	life-giver
power	7966 spiritual gifts

3050

Holy Spirit, wisdom of

The quality of being discerning and perceptive which is a characteristic of the Holy Spirit. The Holy Spirit is the source of human wisdom.

Those who knew and can know the wisdom of the Holy Spirit

Joshua Dt 34:9 *Either a wise human spirit or the Spirit of God who gives wisdom (NIV footnote).*

The Messiah Isa 11:2

Jesus Christ Lk 2:40 *See also* Col 2:9 *"fulness" includes wisdom.*

Christians Eph 1:17

The Holy Spirit is the source of wisdom

Job 32:6–9; Ac 6:9–10; 1Co 2:12–14 *These references to the wisdom of Solomon*

*make it clear that it was a gift from God.
As the Spirit of God came upon other OT
characters to equip them for office (e.g.,
Saul in 1Sa 10:10) it is not unreasonable to
conclude that Solomon's wisdom was also
imparted through the Holy Spirit:*
1Ki 3:8–9,12; 4:29–34; 10:1,23–24
Pr 2:6; Da 5:10–16 *Daniel's wisdom;*
Ac 6:3 *the choosing of the Seven;* Ac 15:28;
1Co 2:11; 12:8; Col 1:9

The Holy Spirit as teacher
Jn 14:26 *See also* Ne 9:20; Mt 10:19–20
pp Mk 13:11 pp Lk 12:12; 1Jn 2:27

See also

1180 God, wisdom of	8226 discernment
2081 Christ, wisdom	8281 insight
3140 Holy Spirit, teacher	8319 perception, spiritual
7966 spiritual gifts	8361 wisdom

3100

Holy Spirit, titles and descriptions of

3110

Holy Spirit, titles and names of

The names and terms for the Holy
Spirit relate to his power, activity
and presence in the world, often
indicating the nature of his actions
or the gifts which he conveys to
believers.

Titles relating the Holy Spirit to God
The Spirit of God Ge 1:2 *See also*
Ge 41:38; 1Sa 10:10; 19:20,23; Ro 8:9;
1Co 6:11; 2Co 3:3; Eph 4:30; Php 3:3

The Spirit of the LORD
*The Spirit empowered the judges to deliver
the people:* Jdg 3:10; 6:34; 11:29; 13:25;
14:6,19; 15:14
1Sa 10:6; 16:13; 2Sa 23:2
*The Messiah will be empowered by the
Spirit:* Isa 11:2; 61:1
2Co 3:17

Forms of reference to the Spirit of God
My Spirit Ge 6:3; Isa 30:1; 59:21;
Joel 2:28–29; Hag 2:5; Zec 4:6; 6:8;
Mt 12:18

His Spirit Isa 34:16; 63:10–11; Zec 7:12;
Ro 8:11; Eph 2:22

Your Spirit Ne 9:20,30; Ps 51:11; 139:7;
143:10

The Spirit of your Father Mt 10:20

The promised Holy Spirit Ac 2:33;
Eph 1:13

**The Spirit of him who raised Jesus
from the dead** Ro 8:11

The spirit of the gods
Seen from a pagan viewpoint:
Da 4:8–9,18; 5:11,14

Titles relating the Holy Spirit to God the Son
Gal 4:6 *See also* Ac 16:7; Ro 8:9;
Php 1:19; 1Pe 1:11

Titles revealing the Holy Spirit's essential nature
The Spirit of truth Jn 16:13 *See also*
Jn 14:17; 15:26; 1Jn 4:6

The Spirit of holiness Ro 1:4

The Spirit of life Ro 8:2

The Spirit of glory 1Pe 4:14

The eternal Spirit Heb 9:14

Titles showing the nature of the Holy Spirit's activity
The Counsellor Jn 14:26; 15:26

**The Spirit of wisdom and
understanding** Isa 11:2 *See also*
Dt 34:9 fn; Eph 1:17

The Spirit of grace and supplication
Zec 12:10 fn

The Spirit of sonship Ro 8:15

The Spirit of judgment and fire
Isa 4:4 fn

See also

1235 God, the LORD	3269 Holy Spirit in Christ
1460 truth	
1510 Trinity, the	3281 Holy Spirit, inspiration
3015 Holy Spirit, divinity	
3120 Holy Spirit, descriptions	3290 Holy Spirit, life-giver
3130 Holy Spirit, Counsellor	5042 name of God, significance
3233 Holy Spirit & sanctification	6608 adoption

3120

Holy Spirit, descriptions of

Though himself invisible, the Holy
Spirit may appear in symbolic form
and his activities may be described
metaphorically.

The dove
Mt 3:16 pp Mk 1:10 pp Lk 3:22 *See also*
Jn 1:32

The wind or breath
Ac 2:2 *This phenomenon accompanied the
filling with the Spirit. See also*
Eze 37:9–14 *The same Hebrew word is
here translated "breath", "wind" and
"spirit";* Jn 3:8; 20:22

The fire
Ac 2:3–4 *See also* Isa 4:4; Mt 3:11–12
pp Lk 3:16–17; 1Th 5:19

The oil of anointing
Isa 61:1; Ac 10:38

Water
Jn 7:37–39 *See also* Isa 44:3; Jn 4:14;
1Co 12:13

A seal
Eph 1:13 *See also* Eph 4:30

A deposit
2Co 1:21–22; Eph 1:14

A guide or shepherd
Isa 63:14 *See also* Isa 34:16

A voice
Heb 3:7–11 *See also* Eze 2:2;
Mt 10:19–20 pp Mk 13:11; Jn 16:13

God's gift
Ac 2:38 *See also* Ac 1:4; 8:20; 10:45;
11:17

The power of God
Lk 1:35 *See also* Lk 5:17; 6:19; 24:49

See also

1105 God, power of	4293 water	
3110 Holy Spirit, titles of	4636 dove	
	4826 fire	
3239 Holy Spirit, anointing	4860 wind	
	5329 guarantee	
3269 Holy Spirit in Christ	5518 seal	
3287 Holy Spirit, sealing of	7784 shepherd	

3130

Holy Spirit, as Counsellor

The Holy Spirit is the one who
comforts, advises and strengthens
Christians, drawing them closer to
Jesus Christ.

The Holy Spirit is Counsellor in addition to Jesus Christ
Jesus Christ is a Counsellor 1Jn 2:1
*One Greek word "Parakletos" underlies
this phrase which is primarily a legal term.
It can also bear the meaning "comforter".*

The Spirit is another Counsellor
Jn 14:16–17 *The word "another" means
"another of the same kind". After the
ascension, the Spirit is to assume the
ministry of Jesus Christ.*

The Counsellor is the gift of the exalted
Christ Jn 16:7 *See also* Jn 7:38–39;
Ac 2:33

The Counsellor comforts and reassures believers
Jn 14:16–18; Ac 11:12 *Peter is reassured
about going to the house of Cornelius;*
Ro 8:16 *Believers are reassured that they
are God's children.*

The Counsellor strengthens and equips the church
Eph 3:16 *See also* Ac 4:31 *The Jerusalem
church is strengthened in the face of
opposition;* Ac 9:31 *the church in Judea,
Galilee and Samaria;* Ro 8:26

The Counsellor teaches and instructs believers
**The Spirit reminds the disciples of
Jesus Christ's teaching** Jn 14:26 *See
also* Jn 16:14; 1Jn 5:6–8

**The Spirit teaches the church further
truth** Jn 16:13 *See also* 1Co 2:9–10;
1Jn 2:27

The Counsellor helps the church in its mission
**The Spirit testifies to Jesus Christ and
helps the church to do likewise**
Jn 15:26–27 *See also* Ac 1:8

**The Spirit convicts the unbelieving
world** Jn 16:8–11; 1Co 14:24–25

**Examples of the Spirit's help in witness
and mission** Ac 4:8 *Peter before the
Sanhedrin;* 1Co 2:3–4 *Paul in Corinth;*
1Th 1:5 *Paul and Silas in Thessalonica*

**The Counsellor draws believers closer
to Jesus Christ** Eph 3:16–17 *See also*
Jn 14:23; Ro 8:9–11

3140
Holy Spirit, as teacher

Having instructed God's people in the OT and Jesus Christ's disciples in the NT, the Spirit of truth continues to reveal the truth of God to believers.

The Holy Spirit as teacher in the OT
The Spirit teaches on practical matters
1Ch 28:12–13 *See also* Ex 31:2–6 pp Ex 35:30–35; 1Ch 28:19

The Spirit teaches the ways of God
Ps 143:10 *See also* Ne 9:20,30; Isa 48:16–17

The Spirit teaches about the salvation which is to come in Jesus Christ
1Pe 1:10–11 *See also* Heb 9:8; 10:15–17

The Holy Spirit empowers Jesus Christ's teaching
Lk 4:14–15 *See also* Jn 3:34; Ac 1:2

The Holy Spirit teaches Jesus Christ's disciples
The Spirit will teach the disciples what to say when persecuted Mt 10:19–20 pp Mk 13:11 pp Lk 12:11–12 *See also* Ac 4:8; 6:10

Jesus Christ promises the Spirit's teaching ministry Jn 14:26 *See also* Jn 14:16; 16:13–15

The Spirit continues to teach believers
1Jn 2:20 *See also* 1Jn 2:27

The Spirit teaches the churches
Rev 2:7,11,17,29; 3:6,13,22

The Spirit teaches within believers' hearts, in contrast to the written code
Eze 36:27; Ro 2:29; 2Co 3:7–8

The Holy Spirit's teaching centres on Jesus Christ
Jn 16:14–15

The Holy Spirit inspires Scripture for teaching
2Ti 3:16

3200

Holy Spirit, ministry and work of

This set of themes consists of the following:

3203
Holy Spirit, and assurance

The Holy Spirit assures believers of their standing in Christ and their eternal salvation.

The Holy Spirit makes an individual a member of Christ
Ro 8:9 *See also* 1Co 2:12; 6:11,17; 1Th 4:8

The Holy Spirit assures believers that they have been born anew
Ro 2:29 *The true sign of belonging to God is not any outward mark on the body, but the regenerating power of the Spirit within.* *See also* Jn 3:5–6; Ro 7:6; 2Co 3:6; Gal 4:29; Tit 3:5–7

The Holy Spirit assures believers that they are God's children
Ro 8:14–16 *See also* Gal 4:6

The Holy Spirit assures believers that God loves them
Ro 5:5

The Holy Spirit assures believers that Jesus Christ lives in them and they in him
1Jn 4:13 *See also* 1Co 12:13; 1Jn 3:24

The Holy Spirit assures believers that God's power is within them
Gal 3:5 *See also* 1Co 2:4–5

The fruit of the Spirit is evidence of the believer's standing in Christ
Mt 7:15–20 *Spiritual gifts alone are not a sufficient basis for assurance. See also* Ac 13:52; Ro 8:6; 14:17; 2Co 6:6; Gal 5:16–25; 1Th 1:6

The Holy Spirit assures believers of the significance of Jesus Christ
1Co 2:10–12 *See also* 2Co 3:14–17; Eph 3:5

The Holy Spirit is the first instalment of the believer's inheritance in the kingdom of God
2Co 1:21–22 *See also* Eph 1:13–14; 4:30

The Holy Spirit assures believers of their final victory in Christ
2Co 5:5 *See also* Ro 8:11,15–17,23; Eph 1:14

3206
Holy Spirit, and grace

See 6670 grace, and Holy Spirit

3209
Holy Spirit, and love

Heartfelt concern and steadfast practical care is part of the evidence of the Holy Spirit's presence in the lives of believers.

The Holy Spirit's work and fruit includes the characteristic of love
Gal 5:22 *See also* Ac 9:31; Ro 15:30; Col 1:8; 1Th 4:8–10

The Holy Spirit fills believers with the love of God
Ro 5:5 *See also* Eze 11:19; Eph 3:16–19

The Holy Spirit enables believers to live with one another in love
Eph 4:2–3 *See also* 2Co 6:6; Gal 5:14–16,25–26; Php 2:1–2

The gift of the Holy Spirit results in practical love
Ac 4:31–35

Love is essential in the exercise of the gifts of the Holy Spirit
1Co 13:1–13 *See also* 1Co 14:1,12,26

See also

1085 God, love of	6652 forgiveness
2048 Christ, love of	7028 church, life of
3254 Holy Spirit, fruit of	7921 fellowship
	8292 love
5015 heart & Holy Spirit	8463 priority of faith, hope & love

3212
Holy Spirit, and mission

The Holy Spirit directs and empowers believers in their missionary tasks, bearing witness to Jesus Christ and preparing the hearts of men and women to respond to him in faith.

The Holy Spirit equips God's people
He inspired the prophets Ne 9:30; Job 32:8; Isa 48:16; Mic 3:8; Heb 1:1

He empowered Jesus Christ as Messiah Isa 11:2; 42:1; Mt 3:16 pp Mk 1:10 pp Lk 3:21–22 pp Jn 1:32–34; Ac 10:38

He empowered the first Christians Ac 1:8; 2:16–17; 8:17; 10:44; 11:15; 19:6 *The outpouring of God's Spirit begins to extend beyond the Jews.*

He empowers God's people today Jn 14:16; Ro 8:26–27; 1Co 12:3–7

The Holy Spirit accomplishes the mission of God
He convicts of sin Jn 16:8 *See also* Ac 2:37; 1Co 14:24–25

He directs mission Ac 13:2 *See also* Ac 8:29; 10:19–20; 13:4; 16:6–10

He inspires witnesses and speakers Ac 6:9–10 *See also* Mt 10:19–20 pp Mk 13:11 pp Lk 21:14–15; Ac 2:14; 4:31; 11:15; 13:9–10; 1Th 1:5; 1Pe 1:12

He gives signs and wonders Ro 15:18–19 *See also* Jn 1:50; Ac 5:13; 2Co 12:12; Gal 3:5; Heb 2:4

The Holy Spirit's missionary activity is ongoing
He cares for God's people involved in mission Jn 16:13,7; Ac 15:28; 1Pe 5:7

He sanctifies God's people Ro 8:10,14; 15:16; 2Th 2:13

He encourages God's people Ro 8:16,27; 2Th 2:17; 1Jn 3:24; 4:13

See also

1449 signs, purposes	3281 Holy Spirit, inspiration
3030 Holy Spirit, power	3293 Holy Spirit, witness of
3224 Holy Spirit & preaching	7948 mission
3248 Holy Spirit, conviction	8420 equipping
	8424 evangelism
3263 Holy Spirit, guidance	8495 witnessing

3215
Holy Spirit, and peace

The Holy Spirit brings a sense of well-being, contentment and wholeness to believers whatever their outward circumstances. Peace

---

is therefore an indication of the Holy Spirit's presence.

Peace is part of the nature of the Holy Spirit
The Spirit is likened to a dove, the symbol of peace Mt 3:16 pp Mk 1:10 pp Lk 3:22 pp Jn 1:32

As part of the Godhead the Spirit is the God of peace Php 4:9; 1Th 5:23; Heb 13:20

Peace is a resource that the Holy Spirit gives to believers
Ro 14:17 *See also* Jn 14:15–19 *The Greek word "parakletos" means "one called alongside", hence "comforter" or "advocate"; Ro 15:13*

The fruit of the Spirit includes peace
Gal 5:22–25 *See also* Ro 8:6

The Holy Spirit brings peace to God's people concerning their circumstances
He changes situations to bring peace Isa 32:14–18 *See also* Isa 63:14; Ac 9:31

He brings peace of mind to those facing difficult situations Php 1:19 *See also* Hag 2:5; Jn 16:5–21; 20:21–22

The Holy Spirit brings peaceful relationships
Between believers Eph 4:3

Between believers and God the Father Ro 8:1–2 *See also* Ro 8:11,14–17 *The result of the Spirit's work is contrasted with fear, the opposite of peace.*

See also

1110 God, present everywhere	3130 Holy Spirit, Counsellor
2424 gospel, promises	3254 Holy Spirit, fruit of
3035 Holy Spirit, presence of	3269 Holy Spirit in Christ
3120 Holy Spirit, descriptions	5058 rest, spiritual
	6700 peace

3218
Holy Spirit, and praise

The Holy Spirit inspires believers to extol, worship and thank God. His aim is to glorify the Father and the Son.

The promise that the Holy Spirit will bring praise
Isa 61:1–3

The Holy Spirit inspires praise
True praise must be inspired by the Spirit Jn 4:23–24 *See also* Php 3:3

The Spirit prompts praise 2Sa 23:1–2 *See also At Jesus Christ's coming:* Lk 1:67–68; 2:27–28 Lk 10:21 *The Spirit prompts Jesus Christ to praise the Father.*

Evidence of the Holy Spirit's work inspires praise
The Spirit's convicting work inspires praise 1Co 14:24–25

The Spirit's converting work inspires praise Ac 11:15–18 *See also* 2Th 2:13

The Holy Spirit activates the church's praise
Eph 5:18–20 *See also* Ac 10:44–46; Col 3:16–17

See also

3221 Holy Spirit & prayer	8352 thankfulness
	8602 prayer
3275 Holy Spirit in the church	8622 worship
	8646 doxology
3281 Holy Spirit, inspiration	8660 magnifying God
7028 church, life of	8664 praise
8297 love for God	

3221
Holy Spirit, and prayer

The Holy Spirit intercedes for God's people and also prompts their petitions, supplications and thanksgivings.

The Holy Spirit enables God's children to address him as "Abba"
Ro 8:15 *See also* Gal 4:6

The role of the Holy Spirit in prayer
He prompts supplication Zec 12:10 *"a spirit" (NIV text) or "the Spirit" (NIV footnote).*

He inspires prayers of praise Lk 10:21 *See also* Eph 5:18–20

He inspires praying in tongues Ac 2:4 *See also* Ac 10:44–46; 19:6; 1Co 14:14–18

He intercedes for believers Ro 8:26–27

The evidence of the Holy Spirit's work prompts praise and thanks
1Th 1:2–5 *See also* Ac 11:15–18

Believers are exhorted to pray in the Spirit
Eph 6:18–20 *See also* Jude 20

The love of the Holy Spirit is a motive for prayer
Ro 15:30–32 *See also* Lk 11:13; Ac 8:14–17

See also

1040 God, fatherhood	7972 tongues, gift of
2360 Christ, prayers of	8221 courage, strength from God
3218 Holy Spirit & praise	8352 thankfulness
3281 Holy Spirit, inspiration	8602 prayer

3224
Holy Spirit, and preaching

True Christian preaching is grounded in the word of God and applied by the Holy Spirit to its audience.

The Holy Spirit is identified with the proclaimed word of God
Eph 6:17 *See also* Jn 6:63

The Holy Spirit sends God's messengers
Ac 13:4–5

The Holy Spirit equips, inspires and instructs God's messengers
He inspires the OT prophets Mic 3:8
See also Isa 61:1–2; Eze 2:2–5; 2Pe 1:21

He inspires Jesus Christ's teaching ministry Lk 4:18–21 *See also* Isa 61:1–2; Mt 12:18; Isa 42:1; Jn 3:34

The apostles preach in the Spirit's power 1Co 2:4–5 *See also* Lk 24:45–49; Ac 4:8–12 *Peter;* Ac 6:10 *Stephen;* Ac 13:4–5 *Paul and Barnabas;* 1Th 1:5; 1Pe 1:12

The Holy Spirit teaches and applies the preached word of God to its hearers
Jn 14:26 *See also* Jn 16:15; 1Co 2:13

See also

1432 prophecy in NT	3269 Holy Spirit in
1611 Scripture,	Christ
inspiration &	3281 Holy Spirit,
authority	inspiration
1690 word of God	3293 Holy Spirit,
2363 Christ,	witness of
preaching &	5842 eloquence
teaching	7754 preaching
3140 Holy Spirit,	7773 prophets, role
teacher	
3239 Holy Spirit,	
anointing	

3227
Holy Spirit, and prophecy

See 1427 prophecy

3230
Holy Spirit, and regeneration

God's Spirit works to bring the gift of new birth and renewal to those who have been called to faith.

The Holy Spirit's work is promised
Eze 36:26–27 *See also* Eze 37:14

Jesus Christ proclaims the Holy Spirit's work
Jn 3:5–8

The Holy Spirit's work brings salvation
Tit 3:5–6 *"washing" (apparently a reference to baptism) signifies regeneration. See also* Eph 5:25–27

Regeneration is a creative work of God's Spirit alone
It cannot be achieved by human means
Jn 6:63 *See also* Jn 1:13; 3:6

It cannot be achieved through the works of the law 2Co 3:6 *See also* Ro 2:29; 7:6; 8:2; Gal 3:2

See also

2424 gospel,	5065 spirit, fallen &
promises	redeemed
3248 Holy Spirit,	5655 birth
conviction	6728 regeneration
3290 Holy Spirit,	6745 sanctification,
life-giver	nature & basis
3296 Holy Spirit in	7903 baptism
the world	8144 renewal
5016 heart, fallen &	8150 revival,
redeemed	personal

3233
Holy Spirit, and sanctification

The work of the Holy Spirit in enabling believers to lead holy lives, dedicated to the service of God and conformed to his likeness.

The Spirit of holiness is promised
Mt 3:11 pp Lk 3:16 *"fire" implies the Holy Spirit's work of purification and judgment.*

Sanctification is a special work of the Holy Spirit
Ro 15:16 *See also* 1Co 6:11; Gal 5:5; 1Pe 1:2

The Holy Spirit requires believers to be sanctified
2Th 2:13 *Sanctification is a necessary part of being a Christian. See also* 1Co 6:18–19

The Holy Spirit enables believers to be sanctified
Ro 8:4 *See also* Ro 8:13; Eph 5:18

The Holy Spirit produces sanctification
Gal 5:22–23 *See also* Ro 14:17; 2Ti 1:7

The process of sanctification
The Holy Spirit makes believers more like Jesus Christ 2Co 3:18

The Holy Spirit helps mortify sinful human nature Ro 8:13 *See also* Gal 5:17

The Holy Spirit is opposed to natural desires Gal 5:16–17 *See also* Ro 8:5–9; Jude 19

Examples of people sanctified by the Holy Spirit
Joshua: Nu 27:18 fn; Dt 34:9 fn
Lk 2:25 *Simeon*
The deacons in Jerusalem: Ac 6:3,5
Ac 11:24 *Barnabas;* 2Co 6:6 *Paul and his companions*

See also

1065 God, holiness	6744 sanctification
of	8206 Christlikeness
2030 Christ, holiness	8217 conformity
3242 Holy Spirit,	8272 holiness,
baptism with	growth in
3254 Holy Spirit, fruit	8348 spiritual
of	growth
4018 life, spiritual	
5023 image of God	
6670 grace & Holy	
Spirit	

3236
Holy Spirit, and Scripture

The Holy Spirit inspired the original writing of all the Scriptures, and illumines their meaning to believers.

The Holy Spirit inspired the writing of Scripture
The Spirit inspired the writers of the OT
2Sa 23:1–2 *See also* Ne 9:30; Eze 2:2; 11:24–25; Mic 3:8; Zec 7:12

The NT recognises OT writings as inspired by the Holy Spirit 2Ti 3:16 *"God-breathed" means "breathed out by God" rather than "inspired";* 2Pe 1:20–21 *See also* Mt 22:43

pp Mk 12:36; Ac 1:16; 4:25; 28:25–27; Heb 3:7–11; 10:15–17; 1Pe 1:11

The Spirit inspired the writers of the NT
Eph 3:4–5 *This revelation by the Spirit probably includes the apostles' understanding of the gospel and their preaching as well as the writings of the NT. See also* 1Co 7:40; Rev 2:7,11,17,29; 3:6,13,22

The Holy Spirit illumines the meaning of Scripture
1Co 2:12–16 *"what God has freely given" refers to "God's secret wisdom" (verse 7), the "deep things of God" (verse 10) and the "thoughts of God" (verse 11). See also* Jn 14:26; 16:13–15; 2Co 3:14–17; Heb 9:8; 1Jn 2:20,27

The relationship between the word and the Holy Spirit
The association of God's Spirit and breath with his word(s) Ps 33:6; Isa 59:21; Jn 3:34; 6:63; Eph 6:17 *"word" here probably means "the gospel" rather than Scripture as a whole.*

The Spirit is essential for obeying God's law Ro 2:29 *Reliance on the letter of the law alone is useless. See also* Ro 7:6; 2Co 3:6; Gal 3:2,5; 5:18

The Spirit enables believers to fulfil the law Ro 8:4 *See also* Gal 5:4–5

See also

1427 prophecy	3272 Holy Spirit in
1439 revelation	OT
1610 Scripture	3281 Holy Spirit,
1690 word of God	inspiration
3140 Holy Spirit,	4018 life, spiritual
teacher	5375 law
3224 Holy Spirit &	8124 guidance
preaching	
3233 Holy Spirit &	
sanctification	

3239
Holy Spirit, anointing of

"Anoint" means to set someone apart, to authorise and equip him or her for a task of spiritual importance. Jesus Christ is set apart by the work of the Holy Spirit for his ministry of preaching, healing and deliverance. The Holy Spirit sets Christians apart for their ministry in Christ's name.

Jesus Christ anointed by the Holy Spirit
The Messiah's anointing is predicted
Isa 61:1–3 *"Messiah" means "anointed one"*

The Spirit anoints Jesus Christ at the start of his ministry Mt 3:16
pp Mk 1:10 pp Lk 3:22 pp Jn 1:32; Ac 10:38

Jesus Christ declares his anointing
Lk 4:18–21 *See also* Isa 61:1–2

The first Christians declare Jesus Christ's anointing Ac 4:26–27

Evidence pointing to the Spirit's anointing in Jesus Christ's ministry
Mt 4:23–25; 7:28–29; 12:28; Lk 4:14–15; 5:17; 6:19; 7:14–15

Believers anointed by the Holy Spirit

The Spirit anoints God's chosen people 2Sa 23:1–2 *Samuel*

Anointing enables Christians to stand firm 2Co 1:21–22

Anointing guards Christians against falsehood 1Jn 2:20,27

See also

2206 Jesus, the Christ	3257 Holy Spirit, gift of
3030 Holy Spirit, power	3269 Holy Spirit in Christ
3242 Holy Spirit, baptism with	3272 Holy Spirit in OT
3251 Holy Spirit, filling with	7304 anointing
	8420 equipping

3242
Holy Spirit, baptism with

A divine act, promised by John the Baptist and by Jesus Christ, whereby the Holy Spirit initiates Christians into realised union and communion with the glorified Jesus Christ, thus equipping and enabling them for sanctity and service.

Baptism with the Holy Spirit promised
John the Baptist anticipates baptism with the Spirit Jn 1:33 pp Mt 3:11 pp Mk 1:8 pp Lk 3:16

Jesus Christ promises baptism with the Spirit Ac 1:4–5 *See also* Lk 24:49; Ac 1:8

The gift of the Holy Spirit followed Jesus Christ's glorification
Ac 2:33 *See also* Jn 7:39

Instances of baptism with the Holy Spirit
Ac 2:2–4 *at Pentecost*
On subsequent occasions: Ac 8:15–17; 10:44–47; 19:6
A work of God recognised by Jewish Christians as experienced by Gentiles: Ac 10:46–47; 11:15–17; 15:8

The gift of the Holy Spirit is for all believers at the outset of their Christian lives
Ac 2:38–39 *See also* Ac 2:16–18; Joel 2:28–29; Gal 3:2–5

This gift of the Holy Spirit links believers together in the one body of Christ
1Co 12:13

See also

3040 Holy Spirit, promise of	5098 John the Baptist
3239 Holy Spirit, anointing	6754 union with Christ
3251 Holy Spirit, filling with	7903 baptism
3257 Holy Spirit, gift of	8422 equipping, spiritual
3269 Holy Spirit in Christ	

3245
Holy Spirit, blasphemy against

The denial of the action of the Holy Spirit in the ministry of Jesus Christ, or the attribution of his works to demonic influence.

Jesus Christ warns against blasphemy
Mk 3:29 pp Mt 12:31–32 pp Lk 12:10 *See also* 1Jn 5:16

Blasphemy as erroneously attributing the work of the Holy Spirit to demonic influence
Jesus Christ is accused of being possessed by demons Mk 3:22 pp Mt 12:24 pp Lk 11:15 *See also* Mt 10:25; Jn 7:20; 8:48,52; 10:20

Jesus Christ is accused of casting out demons by demonic power Mt 9:34 *See also* Mt 12:24 pp Mk 3:22 pp Lk 11:15

Jesus Christ refutes these charges Mt 12:25–29 pp Mk 3:23–27 pp Lk 11:17–22

Blasphemy as acting in ways which deny the Holy Spirit's work
Ac 5:3 *See also* Isa 63:10; 1Th 5:19; Heb 10:26–31

See also

2372 Christ, victory	4165 exorcism
3284 Holy Spirit, resisting	5800 blasphemy
	6020 sin
3293 Holy Spirit, witness of	6652 forgiveness
4130 demons	8843 unforgivable sin

3248
Holy Spirit, conviction of

The Holy Spirit convinces human beings of sin and of the reality of forgiveness through Jesus Christ.

The Holy Spirit convicts the world of sin and its consequences
Jn 16:8–11

Ways in which the Holy Spirit brings conviction
Through preaching Ac 2:37 *See also* Ac 16:14; 1Th 1:5

Through the exercise of spiritual gifts 1Co 14:24–25

The reality of the Holy Spirit's conviction in the lives of believers
He brings illumination Eph 1:17–18 *See also* 1Co 2:8–10,14–16

He gives assurance about their new relationship with God Ro 8:15–16 *See also* Gal 4:6

He convicts of the need for constant change Ro 8:5–9 *See also* Gal 5:16–23

See also

3203 Holy Spirit & assurance	6124 condemnation
3224 Holy Spirit & preaching	6172 guilt
	6632 conviction
	6732 repentance
3233 Holy Spirit & sanctification	8104 assurance
	8154 righteousness
3293 Holy Spirit, witness of	9210 judgment, God's
3296 Holy Spirit in the world	

3251
Holy Spirit, filling with

To be filled with the Holy Spirit is to be energised and controlled by the third person of the Godhead in such a way that under the acknowledged lordship of Jesus Christ the full presence and power of God are experienced. Spirit-filling leads to renewal, obedience, boldness in testimony and an arresting quality in believers' lives.

People filled with the Holy Spirit before the ministry of Jesus Christ
In the OT Ex 31:3 *Bezalel filled with the Spirit for artwork on the tabernacle;* Dt 34:9 fn *Joshua filled with the Spirit to succeed Moses*

In the events surrounding the birth of John the Baptist Lk 1:15 *John the Baptist filled with the Spirit from birth;* Lk 1:41 *Elizabeth filled with the Spirit and speaks words of praise;* Lk 1:67 *Zechariah prophesies about the life of John and God's salvation*

Jesus Christ is full of the Holy Spirit
Lk 4:1 *See also* Lk 10:21; Jn 3:34; Ac 10:38

NT terminology
Ac 1:5; 2:4; 10:47 *While these terms are virtually synonymous when used of initial experiences of the Spirit, "filled" is also used to designate subsequent experiences and renewings of the same divine power, while the other terms are not.*

"Be filled with the Spirit": an apostolic command Eph 5:18 *The present tense of the verb implies the need to be regularly filled and re-filled with the Spirit.*

"Filled with the Spirit": a conscious experience of God's power Ac 2:4 *See also* Ac 4:31; 9:17

"Full of the Spirit": a consistent quality of Christian character Ac 6:3–5 *See also* Ac 11:24; 13:52

"Filled with the Spirit": the inspiration to speak words of witness, challenge or rebuke Ac 4:8 *Peter testifying before the Sanhedrin;* Ac 7:55 *Stephen testifying to the Sanhedrin, seeing the glory of God;* Ac 13:9 *Paul rebuking Elymas*

Characteristics of the Spirit-filled life
The Spirit of Christ should rule believers' lives Ro 8:4–6 *See also* Gal 5:16,25

The Spirit produces fruit of Christlike character Ro 15:13; 2Co 6:6; Gal 5:22–23

The Spirit brings liberty Ro 7:6 *See also* 2Co 3:17; Gal 5:1

Being filled with the Spirit often leads to words of praise Ac 2:4 *See also* Ac 4:31; 10:44–46; 19:6; Eph 5:18–20

Characteristics linked with the fulness of the Spirit

Skill: Ex 31:3; 35:31
Wisdom: Dt 34:9 fn; Ac 6:3
Joy: Lk 10:21; Ac 13:52
Faith: Ac 6:5; 11:24

See also

3030 Holy Spirit, power	3278 Holy Spirit, indwelling
3218 Holy Spirit & praise	3293 Holy Spirit, witness of
3242 Holy Spirit, baptism with	4018 life, spiritual
3254 Holy Spirit, fruit of	5452 power
3257 Holy Spirit, gift of	6744 sanctification
	8144 renewal
	8453 obedience

3254
Holy Spirit, fruit of

The living presence of the Holy Spirit in believers leads to Christlike virtues within them, just as a living tree will bear good fruit.

God expects his people to bear spiritual fruit

Isa 5:4 *See also* Mt 7:12–20 *"fruit" is a term used to indicate the produce or outcome of a person's life;* Jn 15:8

The fruit of the Spirit leads to believers becoming Christlike

The gift of the Spirit begins this lifelong process 2Co 3:18

Christlike qualities are contrasted with sinful ones Gal 5:16–17 *See also* Ro 8:5–14; 1Co 12:7; Gal 6:8; Eph 5:8–16; Col 3:1–17

The fruit of Spirit-filled living

Gal 5:22–23 *"fruit" is singular, emphasising that these qualities are mutually dependent aspects of Christian living. See also* Eph 5:9

Examples of the fruit of the Spirit

Love Ro 5:5; 1Co 13:1–13

Joy Php 1:18–19; 1Th 1:6

Peace Ro 8:6; 14:17

Patience Heb 6:12; Jas 5:7–11

Kindness 2Co 6:6; Col 3:12; 2Pe 1:7

Goodness Ro 15:14; 2Pe 1:5

Faithfulness 1Co 10:13 *God's faithfulness is also here presented as the reason for faithfulness;* 3Jn 3

Gentleness Mt 11:29–30 *Jesus Christ displays such gentleness;* 1Th 2:7

Self-control 2Ti 3:3; 2Pe 1:6

Other evidence of the Holy Spirit's activity

Ro 14:17 *righteousness*
Hope: Ro 15:13; Gal 5:5
Eph 1:17 *wisdom;* Eph 5:18 *temperance*

The evidence of the fruit of the Spirit is a result of divine activity, not of human effort

1Co 3:9,16; Gal 2:20

See also

1035 God, faithfulness	3215 Holy Spirit & peace
2339 Christ, example of	3233 Holy Spirit & sanctification
2378 kingdom of God, characteristics	3278 Holy Spirit, indwelling
	7966 spiritual gifts
3020 Holy Spirit, joy of	8206 Christlikeness
	8255 fruit, spiritual
3209 Holy Spirit & love	8258 fruitfulness, spiritual

3257
Holy Spirit, gift of

In the OT the gift of the Holy Spirit was restricted to individuals for particular tasks, but at Pentecost and on subsequent occasions, the Holy Spirit is given to all believers.

The gift of the Holy Spirit in the OT

The Spirit is given to individuals for specific tasks 1Sa 10:6 *to Saul, for kingship;* Ex 31:2–5 *to Bezalel, for craftsmanship*

The gift of the Spirit can be withdrawn 1Sa 16:14; Ps 51:11 *See also* Jdg 16:20; 1Ki 22:24

The gift of the Holy Spirit is foretold

He is promised by John the Baptist Mt 3:11 pp Mk 1:8 pp Lk 3:16 pp Jn 1:33

He is promised by Jesus Christ Lk 24:49; Jn 7:37–39; 14:16,26; 15:26; 16:7; Ac 1:4–5,8; 11:16

The gift of the Holy Spirit before Pentecost

Individuals filled with the Spirit Lk 1:15 *See also* Lk 1:41,67; 2:25–27

Jesus Christ receives the gift of the Spirit Mt 3:16 pp Mk 1:10 pp Lk 3:22 pp Jn 1:32

Jesus Christ bids his disciples receive the Holy Spirit Jn 20:22

The gift of the Holy Spirit at Pentecost and after

At Pentecost Ac 2:2–4 *See also* Ac 2:33

The Spirit was given on later occasions Ac 10:44 *See also* Ac 8:15–17; 9:17; 19:6; Gal 3:5; Heb 2:4

The gift of the Spirit is for all believers Ac 2:38–39 *See also* Ac 2:17; 5:32; 10:45; 11:17; 15:8; Ro 8:9; Gal 3:14; 1Th 4:8; Heb 2:4

God's willingness to give the Spirit Lk 11:13 *See also* Jn 3:34

God's purposes require the gift of the Holy Spirit

To give assurance of acceptance by God Ac 15:8 *See also* Ac 10:47; 11:17; 1Jn 3:24; 4:13

To convict the world of sin Jn 16:7–8; Ac 2:37

To provide spiritual gifts Ac 2:4; 10:45–46; 19:6; 1Co 12:4–11

To work miracles, signs and wonders Ro 15:18–19; Gal 3:5; Heb 2:4

To give boldness in preaching and witnessing Ac 1:8 *See also* Ac 4:31; 5:32

To cultivate the fruit of the Spirit Ro 14:17 *See also* Ro 5:5; 15:13; Gal 5:16

To sanctify the believer 2Th 2:13; 1Pe 1:2

See also

3035 Holy Spirit, presence of	3251 Holy Spirit, filling with
3203 Holy Spirit & assurance	3272 Holy Spirit in OT
3212 Holy Spirit & mission	3278 Holy Spirit, indwelling
3239 Holy Spirit, anointing	4018 life, spiritual
3242 Holy Spirit, baptism with	7408 Pentecost
3248 Holy Spirit, conviction	7966 spiritual gifts

3260
Holy Spirit, gifts of

See 7966 spiritual gifts

3263
Holy Spirit, guidance of

The Holy Spirit gives guidance to groups and individuals facing challenges, decisions and difficulties. Such guidance, however given, effectively specifies the will of God in situations of choice within the biblically established guidelines of righteousness.

Knowing divine guidance is associated with the presence of the Holy Spirit

Isa 63:11–14 *See also* 1Ki 18:12; Ps 139:7–10

The Holy Spirit guides Jesus Christ in his ministry

Lk 4:1 pp Mt 4:1 pp Mk 1:12 *See also* Ac 10:37–38

The Holy Spirit guides the church in its corporate decisions

Ac 13:2 *See also* Ac 15:28

The Holy Spirit's guidance of believers

The Holy Spirit guides individual believers Ro 8:14 *See also* Gal 5:18

He guides through the word of God, spiritually understood and kept before the mind Isa 59:21

He guides in prayer Ro 8:26–27

He guides through spiritual gifts 1Co 12:7–11

He guides in Christian living Ro 8:14; Gal 5:25

He guides in witness and evangelism Mk 13:11 pp Mt 10:19–20 pp Lk 12:11–12; Ac 8:29 *See also* 1Co 2:13

He guides in ministry Ac 16:6–7; 20:22

He guides into a knowledge of truth Jn 16:13

See also

1175 God, will of	3269 Holy Spirit in
1436 reality	Christ
2427 gospel,	8124 guidance
transmission	8409 decision-
3140 Holy Spirit,	making &
teacher	providence

3266

Holy Spirit, in creation

The Holy Spirit was active with the Father and the Word in creation. He is the active power of God present within creation.

The Holy Spirit is involved in creative activity

Ge 1:2 *See also* Job 26:13; Ps 33:6 *The word translated "breath" is the same word that is used for "Spirit".*

The Holy Spirit is the breath of life throughout creation

Ge 2:7 *See also* Job 12:10; 32:8; 33:4; 34:14–15; Ps 104:30

The Holy Spirit is present everywhere in creation

Ps 139:7–8

The Holy Spirit controls nature and history

Isa 34:16 *See also* Isa 40:7

The Holy Spirit enables creative achievement

Ex 31:1–5 *See also* Ex 35:30–35

See also

1110 God, present	3120 Holy Spirit,
everywhere	descriptions
1325 God, the	3272 Holy Spirit in
Creator	OT
2303 Christ as	3290 Holy Spirit,
creator	life-giver
3035 Holy Spirit,	4005 creation
presence of	5081 Adam, life of
3045 Holy Spirit,	
sovereignty	

3269

Holy Spirit, in the life of Jesus Christ

From the moment of his conception Jesus Christ was empowered by the Holy Spirit. Christ's possession of the Holy Spirit was demonstrated publicly at several points in his ministry. After his resurrection the Holy Spirit demonstrated him to be the Son of God.

OT prophecies of the Holy Spirit in Jesus Christ's life

Isa 11:2 *See also* Ps 45:2; Isa 42:1; 61:1; Zec 12:10

Jesus Christ was conceived by the Holy Spirit

Lk 1:35 *See also* Mt 1:18,20

The Holy Spirit at Jesus Christ's baptism

Mt 3:16 pp Mk 1:10 pp Lk 3:22 pp Jn 1:32

Jesus Christ lived by the Holy Spirit

Lk 10:21 *See also* Mt 4:1 pp Mk 1:12 pp Lk 4:1; Lk 1:80; 1Pe 3:18

Jesus Christ's ministry was empowered by the Holy Spirit

Heb 9:14

In preaching Lk 4:18 *See also* Isa 61:1; Mt 12:18; Lk 4:14–15,21; Jn 3:34; Ac 1:2

In working miracles Ac 10:38 *See also* Mt 12:15–18,28 pp Lk 11:20; Lk 5:17

Jesus Christ was vindicated by the Holy Spirit

Ro 1:4 *See also* 1Ti 3:16; 1Pe 3:18

Jesus Christ promises the Holy Spirit to his disciples

Lk 11:13 *See also* Mt 10:20 pp Mk 13:11; Lk 12:12; Jn 7:39; 14:16–17,26; 15:26; 16:13–15

Jesus Christ gives the Holy Spirit to his disciples

Jn 20:22 *See also* Ac 2:33

See also

1250 Abba	3040 Holy Spirit,
2066 Christ, power of	promise of
2351 Christ, miracles	3239 Holy Spirit,
2363 Christ,	anointing
preaching &	3242 Holy Spirit,
teaching	baptism with
2510 Christ, baptism	3257 Holy Spirit, gift
of	of
2515 Christ, birth of	3278 Holy Spirit,
2560 Christ,	indwelling
resurrection	

3272

Holy Spirit, in OT

The OT portrays the Holy Spirit as being active in creation, in equipping individuals for skilled tasks and in inspiring prophecy and revelation.

The Holy Spirit as the presence of God

He is active in creation Ge 1:2 *See also* Job 33:4; Ps 104:30

He is present everywhere Ps 139:7

His sovereignty Isa 34:16 *See also* Eze 36:27; 37:14

All life is dependent on the Spirit Job 34:14–15 *NIV footnote at verse 14. See also* Ge 6:3

He is present with God's people Isa 63:11–14 *See also* Ne 9:20; Hag 2:5

The Holy Spirit equips individuals

For leadership Jdg 3:10 *See also* Nu 11:17,25–29 *The gift of prophecy was given temporarily to the elders in order to establish them as leaders of God's people;* Nu 27:18 fn; Dt 34:9 fn; Jdg 6:34; 11:29; 13:25; 1Sa 10:6; 11:6; 16:13

In bringing revelation Ge 41:38–39 *See also* Da 4:8–9,18; 5:11,14

By empowering the prophet Eze 2:2; 3:12,14,24; 8:3; 11:24; 43:5

By giving special strength Jdg 14:6,19; 15:14

By guidance Ps 143:10

In planning 1Ch 28:12

In craftsmanship Ex 31:3–5; 35:31–35

In building Zec 4:6

The Holy Spirit inspires

Prophecy 2Ch 24:20 *See also* Nu 24:2; 1Sa 10:6,10; 19:20,23; 2Ch 15:1; 20:14; Isa 48:16; Eze 11:5; Mic 3:8; 2Pe 1:21

Teaching Ne 9:20,30

Praise 2Sa 23:1–2

A declaration of allegiance 1Ch 12:18

Examples of the awareness of the Holy Spirit's activity

1Ki 18:12; 2Ki 2:16

Examples of grieving the Holy Spirit

Isa 63:10 *See also* Ge 6:3; 1Sa 16:14; Ps 51:11; 106:33–48; Isa 30:1; Mic 2:7; Zec 7:12

Promises of the Holy Spirit for the future

The Spirit and the Messiah Isa 11:2 *See also* Isa 42:1; 61:1

The outpouring of the Spirit
Joel 2:28–29 *See also* Isa 32:15; 44:3; 59:21; Eze 36:27; 37:14; 39:29

See also

1427 prophecy	3140 Holy Spirit,
1443 revelation, OT	teacher
2366 Christ,	3218 Holy Spirit &
prophecies	praise
concerning	3266 Holy Spirit in
3015 Holy Spirit,	creation
divinity	3284 Holy Spirit,
3035 Holy Spirit,	resisting
presence of	3290 Holy Spirit,
3040 Holy Spirit,	life-giver
promise of	
3045 Holy Spirit,	
sovereignty	

3275

Holy Spirit, in the church

The church depends upon the activity of the Holy Spirit, without which its effective and faithful service is impossible.

The Holy Spirit forms the church

1Co 12:13 *See also* Ac 2:1–4,16–18; Joel 2:28–29; Ac 10:44–48; Eph 2:21–22

The Holy Spirit indwells the church

1Co 3:16 *"you" here is plural and refers to the whole church. See also* Eze 10:4; Jn 16:14; 1Co 6:19; 2Co 6:16; 1Pe 4:14

The Holy Spirit enables the church to function as the body of Christ

1Co 12:7 *See also* Ex 31:1–5; Nu 11:24–27; 1Sa 10:5–11; Ro 12:5; 1Co 12:8–11

The Holy Spirit enables Christian unity

Eph 4:3–4; Php 2:1

The church worships, serves and speaks by the Holy Spirit

The church worships by the Spirit
Ac 2:11 *See also* Jn 4:24; Ac 10:45–46; Ro 8:15; 1Co 14:26–33; Php 3:3

The church serves by the Spirit
Ro 12:6–8 *See also* 1Co 12:7–11;
Eph 4:7–13

The church speaks by the Spirit
Ac 6:10 *See also* Ac 4:8; 1Co 14:24–25

**The Holy Spirit communicates
Jesus Christ's message to the
church**
Rev 2:7 *See also* Jn 14:26; 16:13;
Rev 2:11,17,29; 3:6,13,22

**The Holy Spirit and the church's
mission**
The church fulfils its mission by the
Spirit Ac 1:8 *See also* Jn 15:26–27;
20:21–23; Ac 4:31; Gal 3:3

The Spirit directs the church's
missionary enterprise Ac 13:2–3;
15:28; 16:6

See also
1610 Scripture	3242 Holy Spirit,
3035 Holy Spirit,	baptism with
presence of	3263 Holy Spirit,
3140 Holy Spirit,	guidance
teacher	7020 church, the
3212 Holy Spirit &	7030 unity
mission	7966 spiritual gifts
3224 Holy Spirit &	8622 worship
preaching	
3239 Holy Spirit,	
anointing	

3278
Holy Spirit, indwelling of

The Holy Spirit dwells within Jesus
Christ and his disciples.
Recognisable results in believers'
lives include Christlikeness and the
fruit of the Spirit.

**The indwelling of the Holy Spirit
in the OT**
Ge 41:38; Ex 35:31 *See also* Nu 27:18;
1Sa 10:6–7; Isa 59:21; Hag 2:5

**The Holy Spirit indwells Jesus
Christ**
Isa 11:2; Mt 12:18; Isa 42:1; Lk 4:18;
Isa 61:1; Ac 10:38

**The indwelling of the Holy Spirit
is promised to believers**
Jn 14:17 *See also* Eze 36:27; 37:14

The Holy Spirit indwells believers
2Ti 1:14
*Believers are described as the temple of the
Holy Spirit:* 1Co 3:16; 6:19
Eph 2:22; 1Jn 2:27; 3:24

**Results of the Holy Spirit's
indwelling in believers**
The Holy Spirit guarantees life Ro 8:11
See also Eze 37:14; Jn 7:38–39

The Holy Spirit assures believers that
they belong to God Ro 8:14–16 *See also*
2Co 1:21–22; Gal 4:6; Eph 1:13–14;
1Jn 4:13

Wisdom and insight are received
Ge 41:38; Dt 34:9 fn; Da 4:8–9,18;
5:11,14

Strength is received Eph 3:16

Preaching and public testimony is
aided Mt 10:20 pp Mk 13:11
pp Lk 12:12; Ac 4:8–12; 5:29–32

The moral law is obeyed Eze 36:27;
Ro 8:4–5,13; Gal 5:16

The fruit of the Spirit is displayed
Gal 5:22–23 *See also* Ro 5:5; 14:17;
15:13,30

**Those without the Holy Spirit's
indwelling are not Christlike**
Gal 5:17; Jude 18–19

See also
3035 Holy Spirit,	3287 Holy Spirit,
presence of	sealing of
3251 Holy Spirit,	3290 Holy Spirit,
filling with	life-giver
3254 Holy Spirit, fruit	4018 life, spiritual
of	6744 sanctification
3257 Holy Spirit, gift	7115 children of God
of	8104 assurance
3269 Holy Spirit in	8206 Christlikeness
Christ	

3281
Holy Spirit, inspiration of

The Holy Spirit inspires prophecy
and gives knowledge of God, insight
and wisdom. Scripture declares itself
to have been inspired by God.

**The Holy Spirit inspired the
writers of Scripture**
2Ti 3:16 *See also* Mt 22:43 pp Mk 12:36;
Ac 1:16; 4:25; 28:25; Heb 3:7; 9:8; 10:15

**The Holy Spirit inspires believers
to honour Jesus Christ**
1Co 12:3 *See also* 1Jn 4:2

**Purposes of the Holy Spirit's
inspiration**
Eph 1:17 *See also* 2Ti 3:16–17

The Holy Spirit inspired prophecy
Nu 24:2–3; 2Pe 1:21 *See also*
Nu 11:25–29; 1Sa 10:6,10; 19:20,23;
2Sa 23:2; 1Ch 12:18; 2Ch 15:1; 20:14;
24:20; Ac 11:28; 19:6; 1Pe 1:11–12

**People aware of the Holy Spirit's
inspiration**
2Sa 23:2 *See also* Isa 48:16 *Isaiah;*
Mic 3:8 *Micah;* Ac 15:28 *the Council of
Jerusalem
Paul:* 1Co 2:13; 7:40

The Holy Spirit gives revelation
God's purposes revealed 1Co 2:10–13
See also Eph 1:17; 3:3–6; 1Jn 2:27
The Messiah revealed to Simeon
Lk 2:25–27

Visions given Ac 7:55 *See also* Joel 2:28;
Ac 2:17; Rev 1:10; 4:2

Visions interpreted Ac 10:19–20

Dreams interpreted Ge 41:38–39;
Da 4:8–9,18; 5:11,14

David's plans for the temple 1Ch 28:12

Wisdom and knowledge are given
1Co 12:8 *See also* Isa 11:2; Ac 6:10;
Eph 1:17

God's fatherhood revealed to believers
Ro 8:15–16; Gal 4:6

**Speech is inspired by the Holy
Spirit**
Testifying to God Mt 10:20
pp Mk 13:11 *See also* Lk 12:12;
Ac 4:8,31; 13:9

Instruction Ne 9:20 *See also* Ne 9:30;
Ac 1:2; 1Ti 4:1

Speaking in tongues Ac 2:4; 10:44–46;
19:6

Prayer Ro 8:26–27; Eph 6:18

See also
1403 God, revelation	3221 Holy Spirit &
1409 dream	prayer
1428 prophecy, OT	3224 Holy Spirit &
inspiration	preaching
1469 visions	3272 Holy Spirit in
1611 Scripture,	OT
inspiration &	7972 tongues, gift of
authority	8281 insight
3140 Holy Spirit,	8366 wisdom,
teacher	source of

3284
Holy Spirit, resisting

The work of the Holy Spirit can be
resisted through disobedience and
unbelief.

**Scriptural images of resisting the
Holy Spirit**
Grieving the Spirit Isa 63:10; Eph 4:30

Resisting the Spirit Ac 7:51 *See also*
Ge 6:3; Ac 6:9–10

Blaspheming against the Spirit
Mk 3:29 pp Mt 12:31 pp Lk 12:10 *See
also* Heb 10:29

Quenching the Spirit 1Th 5:19

Lying to the Spirit Ac 5:3

Testing the Spirit Ac 5:9

**Ways in which the Holy Spirit is
resisted**
Through sin Gal 5:17 *See also*
Eph 4:30–31

Through rebellion Ps 106:33 *See also*
Isa 63:10

Through hardness of heart Zec 7:12
See also Ac 7:51

Through spiritual blindness 1Co 2:14

See also
3025 Holy Spirit,	6222 rebellion
personality	against God
3245 Holy Spirit,	6245 stubbornness
blasphemy	7966 spiritual gifts
against	8718 disobedience
5931 resistance	8834 unbelief

3287
Holy Spirit, sealing of

Based on the practice of sealing
letters, documents and property, the
Holy Spirit is described as being a
seal on the lives of God's people,
affirming their Christian character,
marking them out as belonging to
God and guarding them from the
world and the devil.

**The Holy Spirit's seal on the life
of Jesus Christ**
Jn 6:27 *The Greek implies a once-and-for-
all sealing at a particular time in the past
and probably alludes to the baptism of
Jesus Christ when the Holy Spirit came
upon him. See also* Isa 42:1; 61:1

The seal of the Holy Spirit in the life of believers

The seal marks God's ownership
2Co 1:21–22 See also Rev 7:3–4; 9:4; 14:1; 22:4

The seal acts as a guarantee of redemption Eph 1:13–14 See also 2Co 5:5; Eph 4:30; 1Pe 1:5

See also
1511 Trinity, relationships in	3242 Holy Spirit, baptism with
2510 Christ, baptism of	3257 Holy Spirit, gift of
3110 Holy Spirit, titles of	3269 Holy Spirit in Christ
3120 Holy Spirit, descriptions	5518 seal
3239 Holy Spirit, anointing	7903 baptism

3290
Holy Spirit, the life-giver

Through the Holy Spirit, God gives birth to and supports both natural and spiritual life. For this reason, Scripture likens the Holy Spirit to life-giving water.

The creating Spirit (or breath) of God gives and sustains life
Ge 1:2 See also Ge 2:7; Job 26:13; 27:3; 32:8 fn; 33:4; 34:14 fn; Ps 33:6; 104:30

The Holy Spirit gives new life
Eze 37:1–14 See also Eze 36:26–28

The Holy Spirit is the life-giver in the conception of Jesus Christ
Mt 1:18 See also Mt 1:20; Lk 1:35

The Holy Spirit gives resurrection life to Jesus Christ
1Pe 3:18 See also Ro 1:4

The Holy Spirit brings new spiritual life
Jn 3:5 See also Jn 3:6,8; 6:63

The Spirit sets believers free from bondage to works that lead to death
Ro 8:2 See also Ro 8:6,13; Gal 6:8

The Holy Spirit is described as life-giving water
Jn 7:37–39 Words spoken by Jesus Christ at the Feast of Tabernacles. See also Isa 32:15; 44:3–4; Eze 36:25–27; 39:29; 47:1–12; Zec 14:8; Jn 4:10,14; Rev 22:1–2,17

See also
2424 gospel, promises	3266 Holy Spirit in creation
2595 incarnation	4018 life, spiritual
3120 Holy Spirit, descriptions	4278 spring of water
3230 Holy Spirit & regeneration	5655 birth
3233 Holy Spirit & sanctification	6644 eternal life
	6728 regeneration

3293
Holy Spirit, witness of

The Holy Spirit bears witness to the person and work of Jesus Christ, and enables believers to bear effective witness to him.

The Holy Spirit bears witness to Jesus Christ

The Spirit's testimony 1Jn 4:2–3 See also Ac 5:32; 1Co 12:3

At Jesus Christ's baptism Jn 1:32–34 See also Mt 3:16 pp Mk 1:10 pp Lk 3:22

After Jesus Christ's ascension
Jn 15:26 See also Jn 14:26; 16:13–14; 1Jn 5:6

The Holy Spirit's witness enables believers to be effective
He brings assurance to believers
1Jn 3:24 See also 1Jn 4:13; 5:7–10

He gives assurance of the finality of Jesus Christ's saving work
Heb 10:14–17

He gives believers confidence in their status as children of God Ro 8:15–16 See also Gal 4:6

See also
2422 gospel, confirmation	3224 Holy Spirit & preaching
3030 Holy Spirit, power	5624 witnesses to Christ
3203 Holy Spirit & assurance	6608 adoption
3212 Holy Spirit & mission	8104 assurance
	8498 witnessing & Holy Spirit

3296
Holy Spirit, work in the world

The Holy Spirit, active in the created world, works to show the futility and sinfulness of life without God, and brings a conviction of the presence of God, his righteousness and coming judgment.

The Holy Spirit is active in the created world
In creation itself Job 33:4; Ps 33:6 See also Ge 1:2; Job 26:13; Ps 104:30

In ordering the natural world
Isa 34:11–17

The Holy Spirit is present everywhere in the world
Ps 139:7

The unbelieving world will not recognise the Holy Spirit
Jn 14:17 John uses "the world" to describe those who live apart from God. See also 1Co 2:14

The Holy Spirit testifies to the truth
Jn 15:26 See also Ro 8:16; 1Co 2:11–14

The Holy Spirit convicts the world
Jn 16:7–11 See also 1Co 14:24–25

The Holy Spirit empowers the church to serve the world in mission
Ac 1:8 See also Jn 15:26–27

See also
1110 God, present everywhere	3248 Holy Spirit, conviction
1225 God as Spirit	3266 Holy Spirit in creation
3212 Holy Spirit & mission	4025 world, the

4000
Creation

4005
creation

The created order, established as a sovereign decision on the part of God. The creation is dependent upon and under the authority of its Creator. Scripture affirms the role of both Jesus Christ and the Holy Spirit in the work of creation.

4006
creation, origin of

The free act of God based on his own wisdom and power, forming the whole natural order by his word.

God is Creator of the universe and everything in it
Ne 9:6 See also Ge 1:1; 2:1; Ps 24:1–2; Pr 8:22–31; Ecc 3:11; 11:5; Isa 66:1–2; Jer 10:16; 51:19; Jn 1:3; Ac 4:24; 7:50; 14:15; 17:24

Light and darkness Ge 1:3–5 See also Isa 45:7

The heavens Ps 136:5 See also Ge 1:6–8; Ps 33:6; 96:5; Am 5:8; Rev 14:7

The land Ge 1:9–10 See also Ps 95:5; 102:25; 104:5–6; Ge 1:14; Ex 20:11; Ps 74:17; 118:24

The sea and sea creatures Ps 95:5 See also Ge 1:20–22

Birds Ge 1:20–22

Land animals Ge 1:24–25 See also Job 40:15

The human race Ge 1:26–27 Genesis witnesses to order and progression in God's creative activity. The creation of Adam and Eve is not merely the end point, but the climax to the sequence. See also Ge 2:7,21–22; 5:1–2; Dt 32:6; Ps 100:3; 139:14; Pr 14:31; 17:5; 22:2; Ecc 12:1,7

The role of Jesus Christ in creation
Jn 1:3 See also Jn 1:10; 1Co 8:6; Col 1:16; Heb 1:2

The role of the Spirit in creation
Job 33:4 See also Ge 1:2; Ps 104:30; Isa 40:12–13

The creation of the world
Ge 1:1; Heb 11:3 See also Ps 33:9; 148:5; Ro 4:17

The original creation was complete and perfect
Its completion Ge 2:1 See also Ge 2:2–3; Ex 20:11; Isa 48:12–13; Heb 4:3

Its perfection Ge 1:31 See also Ge 1:10,12,18,21,25; Ecc 7:29; Isa 45:18; 1Ti 4:4

The witness of creation
Creation should cause people to worship God Rev 4:11 See also Ne 9:6; Ps 19:1–4; 95:6; 148:5,13; Ro 1:20 God's power and deity is witnessed through the created order.

Sinners refuse the witness of creation
Ro 1:18–20

Believers receive the witness of creation by faith Heb 11:3 *See also* Ge 6:6

See also

2303 Christ as creator	4060 nature
3266 Holy Spirit in creation	4203 earth, the
	4241 Garden of Eden
4015 life	4603 animals
4026 world, God's creation	4909 beginning
4045 chaos	5002 human race & creation
	5273 creativity

4007
creation, and God

The natural world is sustained by God and speaks of God.

God sustains the creation
He upholds the natural order Heb 1:3 *See also* Job 38:33–37; Ps 104:1–35; 135:6–7; 145:16–17; Mt 10:29–30; Col 1:17

He sustains humanity Ac 17:28 *See also* Job 33:4; Ps 36:6; Da 4:34–35; 1Co 8:6

Creation is upheld for the good of humanity Ge 8:22 *See also* Ge 9:12–16; Mt 6:11

God's sustaining power reserves the world for judgment 2Pe 3:7 *See also* 2Pe 3:9–12 *Time is being given for sinners to repent.*

God has given humanity responsibility to preserve creation
Ge 1:28 *See also* Ge 2:15; 9:1–3; Ps 8:6–8; 115:16; Heb 2:8; Jas 3:7

Creation is spoilt by sin
Ge 3:17–19 *See also* Ro 8:20–22; Heb 6:8

Creation speaks of God's nature and character
His revelation of himself Job 12:7–10 *This is not to suggest that animals can talk to human beings, rather it is a poetic device to stress what can be learnt from created things.*

His eternal power and divine nature Ro 1:20 *See also* Jer 32:17

His authority Job 38:4–39:30; Jer 33:2

His glory and majesty Ps 19:1–2 *See also* Ps 8:1–9

His love and faithfulness Ps 36:5 *See also* Mt 6:30

His power Isa 40:25–28

His wisdom Ps 136:5 *See also* Pr 8:27–29

His unchangeableness and eternity Ps 102:25–27 *See also* Ps 90:1–2; Heb 1:11

His spiritual work in believers' lives Mt 13:3–43

See also

1035 God, faithfulness	1330 God, the provider
1045 God, glory of	1355 providence
1180 God, wisdom of	1440 revelation, creation
1325 God, the Creator	

See also

3296 Holy Spirit in the world	6020 sin
4903 time	8321 perfection, divine
5053 responsibility for world	

4008
creation, and Jesus Christ

See 2303 Jesus Christ, as creator

4009
creation, and Holy Spirit

See 3266 Holy Spirit, in creation

4010
creation, renewal of

God's creation, spoilt by sin, will one day be completely renewed. The old order will pass away and a new everlasting order established.

The renewal of creation
The passing away of the old order 2Pe 3:10–12 *See also* Ps 102:25–26; Isa 34:4; 51:6; Mt 5:18; 24:35; Rev 6:14; 21:4

The expectancy of nature Ro 8:19–22 *See also* Ge 3:17–19; 5:29

Jesus Christ's destruction of all his enemies 1Co 15:24–28 *See also* Ps 110:1; Ac 2:34–35; Heb 1:13; 10:13

The new heavens and new earth Rev 21:1–2 *See also* Isa 65:17; 66:22; Ac 3:21; Heb 11:10,16; 12:22; 2Pe 3:13; Rev 3:12; 21:3–5,10

The purity of the new creation Rev 21:27 *See also* Ps 37:20; Isa 52:1; Joel 3:17; Rev 20:10; 22:14–15

The creation of the new humanity
The new birth 2Co 5:17 *See also* Jn 3:3,5–8; Ro 6:4; Gal 6:15; Eph 2:15; Tit 3:5

Renewal in God's image Col 3:10 *See also* Eph 4:24

A new heart and a new spirit Eze 36:26 *"new" refers to the work of the Holy Spirit in renewing Christians as they believe in Jesus Christ. This renewing will be complete in the new creation. See also* Ps 51:10; Jer 31:33; Eze 11:19; 18:31; 2Co 4:16; Col 3:1

A new mind Eph 4:23 *See also* Ro 12:1–2

A new song Rev 5:9–10 *See also* Ps 33:3; 40:3; 144:9; 149:1; Isa 42:10; Rev 14:3; 15:3–4

The future glorification of humanity
The desire for a new body Ro 8:23–25 *See also* Ro 8:17–18; 2Co 5:1–5

The resurrection of a new body Ro 8:11 *See also* Job 19:25–27; Da 12:2–3; Jn 5:28–29; Ac 24:15

The nature of the resurrection body 1Co 15:42–54 *See also* Php 3:21

The absence of sorrow and pain Rev 21:4 *See also* Isa 25:7–8; 35:10; 51:11; 60:20; 65:19; Rev 7:17

A new name Isa 56:5 *See also* Isa 62:2; 65:15; Rev 2:17; 3:12

A new home Jn 14:2 *See also* 2Co 5:1

God will dwell with his people Rev 21:3 *See also* Eze 48:35; Zec 2:10

See also

5977 waiting	9160 new heavens & new earth
6698 newness	
6720 redemption	9165 restoration
6728 regeneration	9310 resurrection
8144 renewal	9410 heaven
9020 death	9610 hope
9121 eternity	

4015

life

The state of being alive, characterised by vitality, growth and development.
This set of themes consists of the following:
4016 life, human
4017 life, animal and plant
4018 life, spiritual
4019 life, believers' experience of
4020 life, of faith

4016
life, human

Seen by Scripture as the climax of the work of creation, life is a gift of God and is to be treated with reverence and respect.

Life is from God
Ge 2:7; Ac 3:15; 17:25 *See also* 1Sa 2:6; Job 33:4; Ps 139:13; Da 5:23; Ac 17:28; Jas 4:14–15

The ultimate duration of life is unknown to people
Ps 39:4 *See also* Ge 27:2; Jas 4:13–14

Life is precious
Mt 10:31 *See also* Ge 1:26–27 *Since all people are made in the image of God they are of value to him and should be so to each other;* Ge 9:5–6; Ps 49:7–9; 139:14; Mt 16:26 pp Lk 9:25

God's presence in life
Dt 30:16; Ps 23:6 *See also* Ps 71:5–6,9

Life is to be lived for God
Ecc 12:13; Jer 10:23; Mic 6:8; Mt 10:39; Php 1:21

The span of human life
Ecc 11:8–12:8 *See also* Ps 90:10

Life is temporary 2Co 5:1 *See also* Ps 49:12; 103:15–16; Isa 38:12; 2Pe 1:13–14

Life is short 1Ch 29:15; Job 14:1; Jas 4:14 *See also* Job 7:6–7; 8:9; 9:25; 14:2; Ps 39:4–6; 89:47; 90:12; 102:11; 144:4; Ecc 6:12; Isa 40:6–8

The termination of life by death is due to sin Ro 5:12 *See also* Ge 2:17; 1Co 15:22

Examples of long life Ge 5:3–32; 9:29; 11:10–32

A full span of years Pr 3:16 *See also*
Ex 20:12 pp Dt 5:16; Ex 23:25–26;
1Ki 3:14; Job 5:26; Pr 3:2; 9:11; 10:27

Attitudes to life
Life loved 1Pe 3:10 *See also*
Ps 34:12–13; Job 8:21; Ps 91:16

Life despised Ecc 2:22–23 *See also*
Job 7:16; 10:1; Ecc 2:17; Jnh 4:8

See also

1050 God, goodness	4903 time
of	5061 sanctity of life
1080 God, living	5785 ambition
1325 God, the	7346 death penalty
Creator	8224 dependence
1330 God, the	9020 death
provider	

4017
life, animal and plant

All living creatures and plants were
made by God and are sustained by
him.

Animal life
Animals were created by God Ge 2:19;
Ps 104:24 *See also* Ge 1:20–25

Animals are cared for by God
Ps 145:15–16; Mt 6:26 pp Lk 12:24
See also Dt 22:7;
Ps 104:10–12,14,17–18,21,27; 136:25;
147:9; Jnh 4:11; Mt 10:29

Animal life is controlled by God
Da 6:22 *See also* Nu 22:28; Jnh 1:17;
Heb 11:33

**Animal life has been placed under
human care** Ge 1:26 *See also* Ge 1:28;
2:19; 9:2; Ps 8:6–8; Da 2:38; Heb 2:8;
Jas 3:7

Animals serve human needs Ge 3:21;
Mt 21:1–3 pp Mk 11:1–3
pp Lk 19:29–31

**Animal life saved by Noah from the
flood** Ge 6:19–22

**Animals subsequently given to
humanity for food** Ge 9:3–4;
Dt 12:20–25

Clean and unclean animals Ge 7:2–3;
Lev 11:47

Animals used in sacrifice Ge 4:4 *See
also* Ge 8:20; Lev 17:11; Heb 9:22

Animal life glorifies God Ps 148:7; 150:6

Plant life
Plants were created by God
Ge 1:11–12

Plant life is often short-lived Mt 6:30
pp Lk 12:28 *See also* Ps 90:5–6;
103:15–16; Isa 37:27; 51:12; 1Pe 1:24;
Isa 40:6–8

Plants are provided for food
Ge 1:29–30 *See also* Ge 2:16–17; 3:2;
9:3; 1Ki 18:5; Job 28:5; Ps 104:14;
147:8–9; Da 4:32; Joel 2:22

Plant life glorifies God Ps 96:12–13

See also

1105 God, power of	4603 animals
4005 creation	5375 law
4241 Garden of Eden	6614 atonement
4402 plants	7314 blood
4404 food	8664 praise
4528 trees	

4018
life, spiritual

Life embraces more than physical
existence; it includes humanity's
relationship with God. Human
beings come to life spiritually only
through faith in the redeeming work
of God in Jesus Christ. This spiritual
life is a foretaste of the life which
believers will finally enjoy to the full
in the new heaven and earth. Life in
the Spirit means keeping in step with
the promptings and guidance of the
Holy Spirit, and always being open
to his gifts and empowerment.

The nature of spiritual life
It is new life Ac 5:20 *See also* Ac 11:18;
2Pe 1:3; 1Jn 3:14

It is true life 1Ti 6:19

It is eternal life Ro 5:21 *See also*
Da 12:2; Mt 19:29; Jn 6:27; 1Jn 5:11,20

It is abundant life Ps 16:11; Jer 17:8 *See
also* Ps 1:3; Jn 10:10

The origins and nature of
spiritual life
**Spiritual life is the work of the Holy
Spirit** Jn 3:6,8 *See also* Eze 36:26;
Jn 3:3,5–7; Ro 8:11; Tit 3:5–7

**Spiritual life unites believers to Jesus
Christ** Eph 2:4–5 *See also* Ro 6:3–5;
8:10; 1Co 12:13; Col 2:13; 1Jn 5:12

**Spiritual life makes believers the
children of God** Jn 1:12–13 *See also*
Dt 30:20; Mt 6:9; Ro 8:15; Jas 1:18;
1Jn 4:7; 5:1

**Spiritual life brings people to know
God** Jn 17:3 *See also* Mt 11:27

Spiritual life brings about faith Jn 3:15;
20:31 *See also* Jn 3:16,36; 5:24; 6:40;
11:25

Keeping in step with the Spirit
A new way of life is made possible
Gal 5:25 *See also* Ro 8:5–6,9–16;
Gal 5:16–18,22–24

Bondage to the written law is ended
Ro 2:29 *See also* Ro 7:6; 8:2; 2Co 3:6;
Gal 5:17–18

Obedience to God is made possible
Ro 8:4 *See also* Eze 36:27; Ro 8:13;
Gal 5:16; 1Th 4:7–8

Deepening unity is encouraged
Eph 4:3 *See also* Col 2:13; Php 2:1–4

**Strength and encouragement are
received** Ac 9:31

Gifts for those living in the Spirit
**Gifts are given for building up the
church** 1Co 12:4–11 *See also*
Ro 12:6–8; 1Co 12:27–30

Visions are given Ac 2:17; Joel 2:28;
Rev 1:10,12–13; 4:2; 17:3; 21:10

Miracles are worked Mt 12:28 *See also*
Ac 10:38; Ro 15:19; Gal 3:5

Ministry is enhanced 2Co 3:6 *See also*
2Co 3:7–9

Those living in the Spirit receive
revelation and guidance
God is revealed as Father Gal 4:6 *See
also* Ro 8:14–16

God's purposes are revealed
1Co 2:9–10 *See also* Ro 15:13;
2Co 5:2–5; Gal 5:5; Eph 1:17–18

Guidance is given to believers Ac 8:29
See also Ac 10:19; 11:12; 13:2; 16:6–7;
20:22–23

Help is given to pray Ro 8:26–27;
Eph 6:18; Jude 20

The Holy Spirit sanctifies those in
whom he lives
**Through the Spirit, Jesus Christ lives in
believers** Eph 3:16–17

The Spirit transforms believers
2Co 3:18 *See also* Ro 15:16; 2Th 2:13;
1Pe 1:2

**The fruit of the Spirit is seen in
believers' lives** Ac 13:52; Ro 5:5; 8:6;
14:17; 15:30; Gal 5:22–23; Col 1:8;
1Th 1:6

Examples of life in the Holy Spirit
Jesus Christ Mt 4:1 pp Mk 1:12
pp Lk 4:1; Mt 12:18,28; Lk 4:14,18;
10:21; Ac 10:38

Simeon Lk 2:25–27

Peter Ac 4:8; 10:19,44

Stephen Ac 6:5,10; 7:55

The first Christians Ac 4:31; 6:3–5;
11:24,27–29; 13:1–3; 15:28

See also

2354 Christ, mission	3290 Holy Spirit,
3230 Holy Spirit &	life-giver
regeneration	5197 walking
3233 Holy Spirit &	5442 pilgrimage
sanctification	6644 eternal life
3254 Holy Spirit, fruit	6728 regeneration
of	7030 unity
3263 Holy Spirit,	7966 spiritual gifts
guidance	8134 knowing God
3269 Holy Spirit in	8162 spiritual vitality
Christ	8164 spirituality
3275 Holy Spirit in	8453 obedience
the church	9310 resurrection
3278 Holy Spirit,	
indwelling	

4019
life, believers' experience of

God is at work in all that happens to
believers, whether to warn them, to
draw them to himself or to do them
good.

God has a purpose in all the
experiences that believers have
in life
Ro 8:28; Eph 1:11 *See also* Ge 21:22;
28:16; 39:20–21; 45:5–8; 1Sa 2:6–9;
1Ch 29:11–12; Job 42:10–13;
Ps 75:6–7; Ac 17:28; 1Pe 4:12

**Rejection of this conviction leads to
despair** Ecc 1:1–2,16–17

God uses every experience in the
lives of believers for good
To warn and correct Ps 119:67 *See also*
Ge 12:17; 2Ch 7:13–14; Job 5:17;
Isa 38:17; 48:9–10; Am 4:10–11;
Ro 2:4; Heb 12:5–11; Rev 9:20–21

To test and exercise believers' trust in God Dt 8:15–16 *See also* Ex 15:22–25; Jdg 2:21–22; Ps 23:1–6; 81:7; Isa 43:1–2; Na 1:7; Ro 8:35–39; Php 4:12; Heb 11:17–19; 13:6

To purify and prepare believers for glory 2Co 4:16–17 *See also* Job 23:10; Ps 66:10; Isa 48:10; Jer 9:7; Zec 13:8–9; Ro 5:3–5; 8:28–30; 1Pe 1:6–7

To benefit others Est 4:14; 2Co 1:3–6; 4:15; Php 1:12–14; 2Ti 2:10

In all of life's experiences believers should be thankful and trusting Php 4:6 *See also* Ge 8:20 *Noah's sacrifice would, among other things, express his thankfulness;* Dt 8:18; Job 1:20–21; Ps 103:1–2; Pr 3:5–6; Ac 16:25; Eph 5:20; 1Ti 4:4–5

Believers do not merit the blessings they receive Ps 103:10 *See also* Ge 32:10; 50:19–21; Ezr 9:13; La 3:22; Lk 7:6; Ro 6:23

See also

1130	God, sovereignty
1180	God, wisdom of
1190	glory
5596	victory
6248	temptation
6705	peace, experience
8206	Christlikeness
8230	discipline
8347	spiritual growth
8352	thankfulness
8459	perseverance

4020
life, of faith

The way by which believers journey through this world and into the life to come. Jesus Christ himself is the way to life.

Life seen as travelling with God
Walking with God Ge 17:1 *See also* Ge 5:22,24; 6:9; 48:15; Ps 56:13; 89:15; Mic 4:5; Zec 10:12

Journeying from the old to the new Isa 43:19 *See also* Ex 18:8; Isa 40:3–5; Mic 2:13

God's guidance along the way Ex 13:21 *See also* Ex 23:20; Dt 1:32–33; 8:2; Ne 9:12,19; Ps 25:9; Jer 2:17; Gal 5:25

God's ways
Walking in God's way Isa 35:8; 1Jn 2:6 *See also* Ge 18:19; Ex 18:20; Dt 10:12–13; 13:5; 28:9; Jos 22:5; Job 23:10–12; Ps 1:1–2; 18:30; 2Ti 3:10

God teaches believers his way Isa 48:17 *See also* 1Sa 12:23; 1Ki 8:35–36 pp 2Ch 6:26–27; Ps 25:8–9,12; 86:11; 119:30; Pr 6:23; Isa 2:3; 30:20–21
Characteristics of the way of life include holiness, obedience, trust, humility, joy and peace: Ps 16:11; 23:2; Pr 8:20; Jer 6:16; Mic 6:8; Gal 5:22–23

Sinners refuse to follow God's way Isa 53:6 *See also* Isa 56:11; Ac 14:16; 2Pe 2:15

All other routes end in death Pr 14:12 *See also* Dt 11:28; 31:29; Jdg 2:17; 2Ki 21:22; Ps 1:6; Pr 15:10; 16:25

Those who travel God's way are blessed Pr 4:18 *See also* Dt 5:33; 1Ki 8:23; Pr 11:5; Isa 26:7–8; Mt 5:3–12

Jesus Christ is the way to life
Jn 14:6; Col 2:3 *See also* Jn 8:12; Heb 12:2
"the Way" was an early designation of Christianity, suggestive of the content of the church's message that Jesus Christ is the way to life: Ac 9:2; 19:9,23; 22:4; 24:14,22

Entrance to the way to life
Entrance is restricted Mt 7:13–14 *See also* Jn 10:9; 14:6

Entrance is by faith Heb 11:8–10 *See also* Jn 3:15–16; 2Co 5:7; Heb 11:6,13–16

See also

1220	God as shepherd
1315	God as redeemer
2324	Christ as Saviour
2339	Christ, example of
2363	Christ, preaching & teaching
3140	Holy Spirit, teacher
5953	stability
8020	faith
8107	assurance & life of faith
8168	way, the
8837	unbelief & life of faith

4025

world, the

Scripture understands "the world" in a number of senses. It initially refers to the world as God's good creation. However, that same world has now fallen into sin, with the result that it can be a threat to believers. Believers are called to live in the world, maintaining contact with it, while remaining distinct from it, and avoiding being contaminated by it.
This set of themes consists of the following:
4026 world, as God's creation
4027 world, as fallen
4028 world, as redeemed
4029 world, human beings in
4030 world, human behaviour in

4026
world, as God's creation

The heavens and the earth were created by God, and ordered by him and for him.

The world was created out of nothing
By the will of God Ge 1:1 *See also* Ps 96:5; 102:25; 148:5; Isa 40:28; Heb 11:3; Rev 4:11; 10:6

By the word of God Jn 1:1–3 *Jesus Christ as the eternal Word is creator of all things. See also* Ge 1:3; Jn 1:10; 1Co 8:6; Heb 1:2; 2Pe 3:5

By the Spirit of God Ge 1:2 *See also* Job 26:13; 33:4; Ps 33:6

By the hand of God Heb 1:10 *See also* Ps 8:3

By the mind of God Ps 136:5 *See also* Ps 104:24; Pr 3:19–20

The world God created was perfect
Ge 1:31 *See also* 1Ti 4:4

God created the world for a purpose
For his glory Ps 19:1–2 *See also* Ps 50:6; 148:1–4; Ro 1:20; 11:36

That people might worship and revere him Ps 147:4–5 *See also* Ge 15:5; Ne 9:6; Job 22:12; Isa 40:25–26; Jer 31:35

For his possession and use Dt 10:14; Col 1:16–17 *See also* Ps 24:1–2; 50:12; 89:11; Ac 7:49 *God reigns within the world he has made.*

See also

1045	God, glory of
1115	God, purpose of
1130	God, sovereignty
1180	God, wisdom of
1325	God, the Creator
1690	word of God
2303	Christ as creator
3266	Holy Spirit in creation
4005	creation
4055	heaven and earth
4203	earth, the
8355	understanding

4027
world, as fallen

The world has fallen into sin and rebellion against its Creator. As a result, it has come under the power of Satan.

The world is under the power of Satan
He is prince of this world Jn 14:30 *See also* Jn 12:31; 2Co 4:4; 1Jn 4:4

He holds the world in his grasp 1Jn 5:19 *See also* Eph 2:1–4

The world is opposed to God
It is evil Jn 7:7 *See also* Jn 3:19–20; Gal 1:4; 1Jn 2:15–16

Evil extends to the unseen world of the heavenly realms Eph 6:12

It is opposed to God's wisdom 1Co 1:21 *See also* 1Co 1:25; 2:6–8; 3:19

It is opposed to the life of faith Jn 15:18–19 *See also* Jn 1:10–11; 17:6,9,14–18,25; Jas 2:5; 4:4; 1Jn 3:1

It is opposed to Jesus Christ's kingdom Jn 18:36 *See also* Isa 40:23; Mt 4:8–10 pp Lk 4:5–8; Mt 24:14; Lk 12:30; Jn 8:23; 14:17; 2Co 10:3; Heb 11:38; 1Pe 2:11

The world is under judgment
It is condemned 1Co 11:32 *See also* Ge 6:5–7; 7:4,21; Isa 13:11; Zep 3:8; Mt 18:7; Jn 12:31; 16:11; 1Jn 2:17

It will be judged in righteousness Ps 9:8 *See also* Ps 96:13; Isa 26:9; Na 1:5–6; Ac 17:31; Ro 3:19

It will be judged by the saints 1Co 6:2

See also

1075	God, justice of
1310	God as judge
2345	Christ, kingdom of
4120	Satan
5875	hatred
6020	sin
6124	condemnation
6142	decay
8482	spiritual warfare
8734	evil
8785	opposition
9210	judgment, God's

4028
world, as redeemed

Though fallen, the world is offered the hope of redemption and restoration through Jesus Christ.

This world has an end
It is temporary 1Pe 1:24 See also Isa 40:6-7; Mt 5:18; 24:35 pp Mk 13:31 pp Lk 21:33; 1Co 7:31; Heb 1:10-12; 12:26-27

It is under God's judgment Isa 13:13 See also Isa 34:4; 51:6; Joel 2:30-31; 2Pe 3:10; 1Jn 2:17; Rev 20:11

Through Jesus Christ there is redemption and renewal for the world
For humanity 1Jn 2:2 See also Mt 1:21; Jn 1:29; 3:16-17; Ro 5:18; 2Co 5:18-19

For creation Ro 8:19-21 See also Mt 24:7-8 pp Mk 13:8 pp Lk 21:10-11; Col 1:20

The promise of a new heaven and a new earth 2Pe 3:13 See also Isa 65:17; 1Co 15:24-28; Eph 1:10; Rev 21:1-4

See also

2321 Christ as redeemer	4826 fire
2324 Christ as Saviour	5295 destruction
4010 creation, renewal	6510 salvation
4809 darkness	6720 redemption
	9160 new heavens & new earth
	9410 heaven

4029
world, human beings in

The world is intended to be the dwelling-place of humanity, as the height of God's creation. Human beings are organised within the world into groupings and nations and have a God-given authority to rule.

The responsibility of human beings to rule
Over the earth Ge 2:15-16 See also Ge 1:25-26,29; Ps 8:4-6

Over the animal kingdom Ge 1:28 "subdue" and "rule" do not give liberty to exploit and abuse but responsibility for caring for and bringing the best out of God's world. See also Ge 9:1-5; Dt 22:6-7; Pr 27:23-27; Mt 6:25-26; Ac 10:11-13

The response of human beings to God's commission to rule
Failure through abuse Hos 4:2-3 See also Ge 3:12; 6:11-12; Dt 28:15-21

Refusal to fill the earth Ge 11:5-7 See also Ge 4:17

Obedience and blessing Dt 28:4-5 See also Ge 49:25

The ordering of nations within the world
By language Ge 11:8-9 See also Ge 10:5; Ne 13:24; Est 1:22; Ac 2:6-8; Rev 14:6

By race Rev 7:9 See also Rev 5:9; 13:7

By territory Ac 17:26 See also Ge 13:11-12; Nu 13:27-29

By their rise and fall Jer 18:7-10 See also 2Ch 15:6; Isa 19:2; Jer 1:10; Da 7:17-18; Mt 24:7 pp Mk 13:8 pp Lk 21:10-11

By government Ro 13:1 See also Da 2:21; 4:17; 1Pe 2:13-14

The world as the object of the gospel proclamation
God sent Jesus Christ to this world Jn 3:16 See also Isa 45:22; Jn 1:10,29; 1Jn 2:2; 4:9

Believers are commanded to evangelise this world Mt 28:18-19 See also Mk 16:15; Lk 24:46-47; Ac 1:8

See also

2354 Christ, mission	5080 Adam
2420 gospel	5326 government
3296 Holy Spirit in the world	5367 kingdoms
5001 human race, the	5374 languages
5051 responsibility	5475 property
	5540 society
	8424 evangelism

4030
world, human behaviour in

Human behaviour in the world is now characterised by self-centredness as a result of sin. Believers are called upon to renounce such sinful behaviour.

Human passion in the world is expressed in various ways
In physical desires 1Jn 2:15-16 See also Ex 20:17; Pr 27:20; Lk 12:15; 21:34; Jas 4:4; 2Pe 2:18-20

In indulgence Jas 5:1,5 See also Job 21:7-13; Ps 73:2-3; 2Ti 4:10

In intellectual pursuits Col 2:8 See also Gal 4:3-5; Eph 2:3

In a weak will Ex 23:2 See also Job 31:34; Ro 6:17-19

Though remaining in the world, believers are not of the world
Jn 17:6-19

Believers are to renounce the passions of the world
Through a renewed mind Ro 12:2 See also Gal 1:4; Eph 4:23; Col 3:5-10

Through obedience 1Pe 1:14-15 See also 2Co 10:2-5; Gal 5:24; 6:15; Eph 5:17; Tit 2:12; Jas 1:27; 2Pe 1:4

Through having spiritual priorities Lk 12:29-31 pp Mt 6:31-33 See also Mt 10:39; Lk 14:26-27; 17:33; Jn 12:24-26; 1Ti 6:6

Through growing to maturity 1Co 3:1 See also Heb 5:12; 6:1-3

The futility of worldly pursuits
They bring no lasting material gain 1Ti 6:7 See also Job 1:21; Ps 49:17; Ecc 5:15; 1Ti 6:17-19

They bring no spiritual gain Mk 8:36-37 pp Lk 9:25 See also Job 20:4-5; Ps 17:14; Lk 16:25-26

See also

5038 mind, the human	8300 love & the world
5769 behaviour	8341 separation
5902 maturity	8453 obedience
8114 discipleship	8461 priorities
8154 righteousness	8730 enemies of believers
8211 commitment to world	8848 worldliness

4035
abundance

A state of plenty. Since Israel was often restricted in resources, abundance was an important feature of her future hope, and became a symbol of spiritual well-being.

Examples of material abundance
Rain Dt 32:2 See also 1Ki 18:41,45; Job 36:28; Ps 68:9; Joel 2:23

Water, streams and rivers Ps 78:20 See also Nu 24:7; 2Ch 32:4; Ps 1:3; Isa 44:4; Eze 47:5

Luxuriant growth and fruitfulness Eze 47:12 See also Eze 19:10; 31:2-9; Da 4:12,21; Rev 22:2

Harvest, food, milk and wine Am 9:13 See also 2Ch 31:10; Ps 4:7; 23:5; 37:19; Pr 3:10; Isa 7:22; Jer 44:17; Joel 3:13; Mic 2:11

Spaciousness Ps 31:8 See also Ge 26:22; Ps 66:12

Wealth and possessions Ge 24:35 See also Ge 30:43; 36:7; 2Sa 19:32; 2Ch 1:15; 9:22; Job 1:3

Canaan Ex 3:8 See also Nu 13:27; Dt 8:8; Jer 2:7

Material abundance a reward for obedience
Lev 26:5 See also Dt 30:9; Job 42:12; Ps 132:15

Obedience not always rewarded in this way Job 1:12; 2:6; Php 4:12

Examples of spiritual abundance
The abundance of divine power Dt 9:26; Ps 93:4; Joel 2:29-32; Eph 1:18-20; 3:20

The abundance of divine grace Ro 5:20; 2Co 9:8-14; Eph 1:7; 2:6-7; 1Ti 1:14; 1Pe 1:2; 2Pe 1:2

The abundance of human thanksgiving 2Co 4:15 See also Ps 119:171

The abundance of God's future blessing 2Co 4:17 See also Ps 36:8; Isa 64:4; Jn 10:10; 1Co 2:9; 2Pe 1:11; Rev 14:3

See also

1055 God, grace & mercy	5850 excess
1335 blessing	6666 grace
4293 water	8256 fruitfulness
5475 property	8809 riches

4040
beauty

A physical or spiritual quality which brings pleasure to those who behold it. Scripture stresses the beauty of

God himself and his creation, while noting that the beauty of the creation can lead away from God or become idolised.

Beauty in nature
Job 38:31; Ecc 3:11 *See also* Ge 49:21; Eze 20:6; 31:7–9

Beautiful people
Women Ge 29:17; Est 1:11 *See also* Ge 6:2; 12:11,14; 24:15–16; 26:7; Dt 21:11; 1Sa 25:3; 2Sa 13:1; 14:27; 1Ki 1:3–4
Esther: Est 2:7,17
Job 42:15; Ps 45:11; SS 2:14; 4:7; 7:1

Men Ge 39:6 *See also* 1Sa 16:12; 17:42; 2Sa 14:25; 1Ki 1:6; SS 1:16; 5:10; Eze 23:6,23

An enhanced quality Est 2:2–3 *See also*
Est 2:9,12; Isa 3:24; Eze 7:20

Beauty and lack of beauty as external impressions Isa 53:2 *See also* Pr 11:22; 31:30; 1Pe 3:3

May lead to pride and lust Pr 6:25–26;
Eze 28:17 *See also* Ge 12:11–12; 39:7; 2Sa 11:2–4; Eze 23:12

Beautiful artefacts
Lk 21:5 *See also* Jos 7:21; Eze 27:3–4,11,24; Ac 3:2

The beauty of Jerusalem
Ps 50:2 *See also* Ps 48:2; Jer 6:2; La 2:15; Eze 16:10–15,25; Da 11:45; Rev 21:2

The beauty of God as the joy of believers
Ps 27:4 *See also* 1Ch 16:29; Ps 29:2; Isa 4:2; 33:17; 52:7; 61:3; Jer 11:16; Ro 10:15

See also
1190 glory	5171 nose
4342 jewels	5778 adorning
4472 lily	6133 coveting
4496 perfume	8322 perfection,
5141 cheeks	human
5163 legs	

4045
chaos

A state of complete disorder or confusion. The first stage of creation where, having brought something out of nothing, God had not yet brought order to the universe. This primeval chaos, often symbolised by surging waters, threatens to disrupt God's order at any time. God sometimes allows a return to chaos as judgment.

God creates order out of chaos
God creates something out of nothing
Ge 1:1–2 *See also* Ps 33:9; 148:5–6; Ro 4:17; Heb 11:3

God brings order to his creation
Isa 45:12 *See also* Ge 1:14–19; Job 9:8; Ps 8:3; Isa 48:13

Chaos threatens God's order
Life and order in creation must be sustained by God Ps 104:29; Col 1:16–17 *See also* Job 12:10;

Job 34:14–15; Isa 42:5; Heb 1:2–3

The raging sea as a symbol of chaos
Ps 46:2–3 *The raging sea is a frequent symbol of the chaos from which the world was created and to which it could return. Yet those whose confidence is in the God who brought order out of chaos have nothing to fear;* Ps 104:7–9 *See also* Ex 15:8; Ps 69:2,15; 77:16; Pr 8:29; Zec 10:11; Mt 8:23–27 pp Mk 4:36–41 pp Lk 8:22–25

Threatening nations are likened to the raging seas as bringers of chaos
Isa 17:12–13 *See also* Ps 46:6; Jer 46:7

Spiritual and political chaos Jdg 17:6 *A period of anarchy, when no spiritual or political authority was recognised in Israel;* Eph 4:14 *See also* Gal 1:7

God uses chaos as a judgment
Isa 34:11 *See also*
Isa 24:1,3–4,10–12,17–21; 27:10; 32:14; Zep 1:14–15; Rev 6:15–17

Floodwaters as a symbol of the chaos of judgment Jnh 2:3 *See also* Ge 6:17; Job 20:28; 22:16; Isa 8:7

Panic and destruction characterise the chaos that follows judgment Zec 14:13 *See also* Jdg 7:22; 1Sa 14:20; 2Ch 20:22–23; Isa 19:2; Eze 38:21; Hag 2:22

See also
3296 Holy Spirit in	4809 darkness
the world	5815 confusion
4005 creation	9140 last days
4065 orderliness	9210 judgment,
4266 sea	God's

4050
dust

Human beings were created from the dust by God and will return to it at death. Dust is therefore taken as a symbol of poverty, lowliness and humility. In Scripture dust is shaken off the feet to warn of future judgment, and is also used as a means of expressing grief.

Human beings were created from the dust by God
Ge 2:7 *See also* Ge 18:27; Ps 103:14; 1Co 15:47

We will all return to dust when we die
Ge 3:19 *God's curse upon Adam affected all humanity;* Ps 90:3 *See also* Job 10:9; 34:15; Ecc 12:7

Dust as a symbol of poverty, lowliness and humility
1Sa 2:8 *See also* Ge 18:27; 1Ki 16:2; Job 30:19

Dust as a simile for a multitude
Ge 13:16 *See also* Ge 28:14; Ps 78:27

Dust is shaken off the feet as a warning of judgment
Mk 6:11 pp Mt 10:14 pp Lk 9:5 *See also* Lk 10:10–11; Ac 13:51

Dust is used in expressing grief and repentance
Job 42:5–6; La 2:10 *See also* Jos 7:6; Job 2:12; Eze 27:30; Rev 18:19

See also
1670 symbols	6735 repentance,
4006 creation, origin	examples
4315 clay	7454 sprinkling
5081 Adam, life of	8276 humility
5419 mourning	9021 death, natural
5446 poverty	9210 judgment,
5952 sorrow	God's

4055
heaven and earth

An expression which in the original Hebrew refers to the whole of creation. It is frequently used in relation to God both as Creator and Lord in order to emphasise his power and authority.

Heaven and earth in relation to God
He is the Creator of heaven and earth
Isa 37:16 pp 2Ki 19:15 *See also* Ge 14:18–23; 2Ch 2:12; Ps 115:15; 121:2; 124:8; 134:3; 146:5–6; Ac 14:15; 17:24

He is Lord of heaven and earth
Mt 11:25 pp Lk 10:21 *See also* 1Ch 29:11–12; Ezr 5:11; Jer 23:23–24; 33:25–26

The personification of heaven and earth
Dt 31:28 *See also* Dt 4:26; 30:19; Ps 69:34; Jer 51:48

Allusions to the end of heaven and earth
Mt 24:35 pp Mk 13:31 pp Lk 21:33 *See also* Mt 5:18; Lk 16:17

The expression "between heaven and earth"
1Ch 21:16 *See also* Zec 5:9

See also
1110 God, present	4005 creation
everywhere	4287 universe
1230 God, the Lord	9160 new heavens &
1325 God, the	new earth
Creator	9410 heaven

4060
nature

God's creation, often with special reference to plant and animal life.

Nature is God's creation
Ps 89:11 *See also* Isa 45:12; Jer 27:5; Ac 4:24; 14:15; 17:24; Rev 4:11; 10:6

Plants Ge 1:11–12 *See also* Ge 2:4–9; Ps 104:14–16

Land and sea Ps 24:1 *See also* Ge 1:9–10; Job 38:4–11; Isa 40:12; Am 5:8; Jnh 1:9

The sun, moon and stars Job 9:9 *See also* Ge 1:14–18; Ps 8:3; 148:3–5; Jer 31:35

Animals Ge 1:20–22 *See also* Job 12:7–10; Ps 104:25

Human beings Ex 4:11; Isa 45:12
The Genesis creation accounts put human beings at the height of God's creation:
Ge 1:26–27; 2:7
Ps 95:6; 100:3; Pr 22:2; Jer 27:5

The distinction between humanity and the rest of nature

God created human beings alone in his image Ge 1:26–27; Col 3:9–10 *See also* Ge 5:1; 9:6; Jas 3:9

Humanity is the steward of nature Ps 115:16 *See also* Ge 1:26–30; 2:15; Ps 8:5–8

God is active in nature

In sustaining nature Mt 10:29 pp Lk 12:6 *See also* Ps 147:1–17; Ac 17:24–28; Col 1:17; Heb 2:10

In providing for plant life Lev 26:4; Mt 6:28–29 pp Lk 12:27 *See also* Job 38:25; Ps 104:14–16; Jnh 4:6–10

In the elements and seasons Ps 135:7 *See also* Ge 8:22; Job 5:10; 36:27; 37:11–13; Jer 10:13

God makes himself known through the natural order

Job 36:24–26 *See also* Ps 8:1–4; 19:1–3; Ac 14:15–17; 17:24–28; Ro 1:18–21

See also

1325 God, the Creator	4025 world, the
1330 God, the provider	4402 plants
1440 revelation, creation	4603 animals
4005 creation	4969 seasons
4016 life, human	5001 human race, the
4017 life, animal & plant	5556 stewardship

4065

orderliness

In his creating, sustaining and saving work, God reveals himself as a God of order. Likewise, the life of his people and of society as a whole should be orderly.

Orderliness in creation

Isa 45:12 *See also* Ge 1:31; Job 26:7–10; 38:4–11; Ps 8:3; 19:1; 104:5–9; Isa 40:26; Ac 17:26

Orderliness in providence

Ge 8:22 *See also* Ps 65:9; 104:14–27; 145:15; Ac 14:17

Orderliness in salvation

Salvation was planned by God Ro 8:29 *See also* 1Co 2:7; Eph 1:4–5; 2Ti 1:9; Tit 1:2; 1Pe 1:2; Rev 13:8

Jesus Christ's coming was prepared in advance Lk 24:26–27 *See also* Jn 5:46; Ac 2:23; 3:18; Gal 4:4

Orderliness in the life of God's people

Corporate worship must be orderly Ex 25:9; 1Co 14:40 *See also* 1Ch 28:12; Ac 7:44; 1Co 14:32–33

Personal devotion includes orderliness 1Th 5:6 *See also* Pr 25:28; Ro 13:13; 1Co 7:17; Eph 5:16; 1Ti 3:2–5

Respect for leaders as part of God's order Ex 22:28; Heb 13:17 *See also* 1Sa 24:6; 1Ti 5:17; Heb 13:7

Order in pastoral care 1Co 12:28; Tit 1:5 *See also* Ac 6:3; 14:23; Ro 12:4–8; Eph 4:11; 1Pe 4:10; 5:1–3

Orderliness in society

God gives responsibility in his administration to men and women Ps 82:6; Da 6:2–7; Ro 13:1; Tit 3:1; 1Pe 2:13–14

Governing authorities are ordained by God Ro 13:1 *See also* Jn 19:11; Ro 13:6

Those in authority are to be honoured Tit 3:1 *See also* Mt 22:21 pp Mk 12:17 pp Lk 20:25; 1Ti 2:1–2; 1Pe 2:13

Order in the home and workplace 1Ti 3:4 *See also* Ex 6:14; 20:12; 1Sa 3:13; Job 1:5; Eph 6:1,5; 1Ti 3:4,12; 6:1; Tit 1:6; 2:4–5,9–10; 1Pe 2:18

See also

1325 God, the Creator	5680 family
4005 creation	7026 church, leadership
4025 world, the	
4045 chaos	8490 watchfulness
5215 authority	8625 worship, acceptable attitudes
5326 government	
5359 justice	
5542 society, positive	

4100

Supernatural beings

4110

angels

Spiritual beings who assist God, especially in his work of salvation, conveying his word to human beings and attending to the needs of God's people.
This set of themes consists of the following:
4111 angels, as God's servants
4112 angels, as God's messengers
4113 angels, as agents of God's judgment
4114 angels, and praise of God
4115 angel, of the Lord
4116 angels, opposed to God

4111

angels, as God's servants

Angels have specific yet limited roles to play in declaring God's will and purposes for humanity.

Angels are God's servants

Ps 103:20 *See also* Heb 1:7; Ps 104:4

Named angels

The archangel Michael: Da 10:13; 12:1; Jude 9; Rev 12:7
Gabriel: Da 8:16; 9:21; Lk 1:19,26

Angels as agents of God's salvation

Heb 1:14 *See also* Ex 23:23; 32:34; 33:2; Nu 20:16; Isa 63:8–9

Angels do not fully understand God's salvation 1Pe 1:10–12

Angels deliver God's people from their enemies 2Ki 19:35 pp 2Ch 32:21 pp Isa 37:36; Ac 5:19; 12:6–11

Angels as mediators

Ac 7:53 *The law was mediated by angels to Moses and Israel. See also* Job 33:22–26; Ac 7:38; Gal 3:19; Heb 2:2

Angels as revealers of God's will

Zec 1:8–10 *See also* Da 7:15–16; Zec 4:11–14; Rev 17:1; 21:9

Angels convey and fulfil God's instructions Zec 3:6–7; Mt 2:13; Nu 22:21–35; Zec 3:6–7; Mt 2:13; Gal 1:8; Rev 7:2

Angels attend to the needs of God's people

Angels provide food at special times 1Ki 19:5–7 *See also* Ps 78:23–25

Angels provide protection Ps 91:11–12 *See also* Ge 19:15; 48:16; Ps 34:7; Da 3:28; 6:22; Mt 18:10; Ac 27:23–24

Angels give guidance

Ex 23:20 *See also* Ge 24:7,40; Ac 8:26

Angels serve Jesus Christ

Angels care for Jesus Christ's needs Mt 4:11 pp Mk 1:13 *See also* Lk 22:43

Angels are ready to protect Jesus Christ Mt 26:53 *See also* Mt 2:13,19–20; 4:6 pp Lk 4:10; Ps 91:11–12

Angels are inferior to Jesus Christ Heb 1:5–13

See also

1355 providence	7939 ministry
1439 revelation	8124 guidance
4145 archangels	9412 heaven, worship & service
4834 light, natural	
5480 protection	
5698 guardian	
6634 deliverance	
7160 servants of the Lord	

4112

angels, as God's messengers

Spiritual messengers with the special role of making known God's work of salvation.

Angels give hope through the words of the prophets

Isa 40:3–5 *The voice in this passage may be that of an angel.*
Isaiah: Isa 40:1–2,6–8
Daniel: Da 8:15–16; 10:12,14–21; 12:8–13
Zechariah: Zec 1:12–21; 2:3–5; 4:1–7

Angels and the coming of the Messiah

An angel foretells the birth of John the Baptist Lk 1:11–13 *See also* Lk 1:14–19

Angels foretell Jesus Christ's birth Mt 1:20–21 *See also* Lk 1:26–38

Angels announce Jesus Christ's birth Lk 2:8–11 *See also* Lk 2:12–20

Angels announce Jesus Christ's resurrection

Mt 28:5–7 pp Mk 16:5–7 *See also* Lk 24:4–7,23; Jn 20:10–14

Angels foretell Jesus Christ's second coming

Ac 1:10–11

Angels reveal the gospel for the Gentiles
Ac 11:13 See also Ac 10:1–5,30–33; Rev 14:6–7

Angels foretell God's final triumph
Rev 1:1 See also Rev 19:9; 22:1,6,16

See also
1454 theophany	5098 John the
2505 Christ, ascension	Baptist
	5408 messenger
2515 Christ, birth of	7772 prophets
2555 Christ, resurrection appearances	9105 last things
	9610 hope
2565 Christ, second coming	

4113
angels, as agents of God's judgment

Spiritual beings who assist God in carrying out his judgments. Angels will be especially active when Jesus Christ returns for the last judgment.

Angels as agents of earthly judgments
Ps 78:49

Against Sodom and Gomorrah
Ge 19:13,24–25

Against opponents of God Ex 12:23;
2Ki 19:35 pp 2Ch 32:21 pp Isa 37:36; Ps 35:4–6

Against Israel Ex 32:35; 2Sa 24:16–17
pp 1Ch 21:15–16; 1Co 10:10

Against Herod Antipas Ac 12:18–23

Angels restrained by God's mercy
1Ch 21:15–16 pp 2Sa 24:16–17 See also Ge 18:20–32

Angels and final judgment
Angels proclaim God's sovereignty Rev 12:10–12 See also Rev 10:1–4; 11:15

Angels announce God's final invitation
Rev 14:6–7 See also Rev 14:9–13; 19:9

Angels hold back the final judgment
Rev 7:1–3

Angels carry out preliminary warning judgments Rev 8:1–13; 9:1–16; 10:5–7

Angels accompany Jesus Christ when he returns to judge 2Th 1:7 See also
Mt 16:27; 25:31; Mk 8:38 pp Lk 9:26; 1Th 3:13

Angels gather everyone for the final judgment Mt 13:37–41 See also
Mt 13:49–50; 24:31; Rev 14:15–19

Angels announce the final judgment
Rev 14:15 See also Rev 10:8–11; 17:1–3,7,15; 18:1–2,4

Angels enact the final judgment
Rev 15:1 See also Rev 14:16–19; 15:6–8; 16:1–21; 18:21; 19:17–18; 20:1–3

Angels are subject to judgment
1Co 6:3 See also 2Pe 2:4; Jude 6

See also
1025 God, anger of	5484 punishment by God
1055 God, grace & mercy	5978 warning
1310 God as judge	9210 judgment, God's
2309 Christ as judge	9240 last judgment
4508 sickle	
4843 plague	

4114
angels, and praise of God

Spiritual beings who praise God in a manner that is beyond human capacity.

Angels worship God in his presence
Rev 7:11 See also Rev 3:5; 8:2

Angels praise God for his works
Angels praise God's work of creation Job 38:4–7 See also Ps 148:1–5; Ne 9:6

Angels praise God's work of redemption Lk 2:13–14 The angels are praising God for Jesus Christ's birth. See also Isa 44:23; 49:13; Lk 15:10; Heb 1:6; Dt 32:43 fn

Angels praise God's kingdom
Ps 103:19–21 See also Ps 96:10–11 pp 1Ch 16:30–31; Ps 145:10–11; Rev 11:15

Angelic beings praise God
Isa 6:2–4 See also Rev 4:8; 5:8–10; 7:11–12

Thousands of angels worship God
Heb 12:22 See also Dt 33:2; Ps 68:17; Da 7:10; Rev 5:11–12

Images of angelic beings decorate Israel's sanctuaries
1Ki 6:23–29 pp 2Ch 3:7 pp 2Ch 3:10–13 See also Ex 26:1; Eze 41:18–20,25 The images of the cherubim represent the angels who worship God in heaven.

Angels are not to be worshipped
Rev 22:8–9 See also Mt 4:9–10 pp Lk 4:7–8; Ro 1:25; Col 2:18

See also
1130 God, sovereignty	6720 redemption
2378 kingdom of God, characteristics	7396 Most Holy Place
	7458 tabernacle, the
4005 creation	7470 temple, significance
4150 cherubim	8622 worship
4170 host of heaven	8664 praise
4180 seraphim	

4115
angel, of the Lord
See 4140 angel of the Lord

4116
angels, opposed to God

Spiritual beings who fell with Satan. They are under God's judgment and are subject to the authority of believers.

Spiritual authorities led by Satan
2Co 11:14 See also Jn 12:31; 16:11; Eph 6:12; Rev 9:11

Angels opposed to God will be judged
Jude 6 See also Job 4:18; 15:15; Mt 25:41; 2Pe 2:4; Rev 20:10

Jesus Christ has defeated Satan and his angels
Col 2:15 See also Ge 3:15; Eph 1:19–21

Satan's angels are resisted by God's faithful angels
Rev 12:7–9 See also Da 10:13,20 The princes of Persia and Greece appear to be spiritual powers who resist God's rule over these regions.

Jesus Christ gives authority over Satan and his angels to believers
Lk 10:18–19 See also Ro 8:38–39; 16:20; 1Co 6:3; Eph 6:10–13; Jas 4:7

See also
2372 Christ, victory	4135 demons, Christ's authority over
2525 Christ, cross of	
4124 Satan, kingdom of	6157 fall, of Satan
4126 Satan, resistance to	8484 spiritual warfare, enemies
4127 Satan, defeat of	
4131 demons, kinds of	

4120
Satan

The one who opposes the person and purposes of God. Satan is especially associated with deceit, temptation and testing, through which he attempts to deflect believers from obeying God.
This set of themes consists of the following:
4121 Satan, as the enemy of God
4122 Satan, as tempter
4123 Satan, as deceiver
4124 Satan, kingdom of
4125 Satan, agents of
4126 Satan, resistance to
4127 Satan, defeat of

4121
Satan, as the enemy of God

Scripture provides numerous examples of ways in which Satan opposes the presence and purposes of God in his world.

Satan and God's people
Satan opposes believers 1Ch 21:1 See also Job 2:1–7; Zec 3:1–2; 1Th 2:18

Satan accuses believers Rev 12:10 See also Job 1:8–11; Zec 3:1–2

Satan slanders believers 1Ti 5:14

Satan tests believers and causes their suffering Rev 2:10 See also Eph 6:11–13,16

Satan opposes the work of the archangel Michael Jude 9 See also The implication of these verses is that

Michael's work is in direct opposition to that of Satan. Michael is the protector of God's people while Satan is their opponent: Da 10:13,21; 12:1; **Rev** 12:7

Satan opposes God
Satan opposes God's purposes
Mt 16:23 pp Mk 8:33

Satan opposes God's word
Mt 13:3–19 pp Mk 4:3–16 pp Lk 8:4–12 *the parable of the sower;* **Mt** 13:24–39 *the parable of the weeds and its explanation;* Ac 13:8–10 *Elymas, the sorcerer, acts on Satan's behalf to oppose Barnabas and Paul.*

Satan opposes God's righteousness
1Jn 3:7–10

Satan blasphemes God Rev 13:6

Satan's opposition to God's work will not succeed
Zec 3:2 *God rebukes him;* Lk 10:19 *His reign is temporary.*

Satan's role as adversary earns him varied titles
The devil
He is the adversary because he deceives: Rev 12:9; 20:2–3

Belial
He is the adversary because he is the troublemaker or scoundrel (the same Hebrew word is used in the OT passages as in 2Co 6:15 to describe Satan's work): Dt 13:13; 1Ki 21:10; Pr 6:12; 2Co 6:15

The dragon
He is the adversary because he is the enemy: Rev 12:4,13–14

The serpent
He is the adversary because he thwarts spiritual insight: Ge 3:1–5,13; 2Co 11:3

The prince of this world
He is the adversary because his rule is temporary, not absolute: Jn 12:31; 14:30; 16:11

The angel of the Abyss Rev 9:11 *He is the adversary because he is the destroyer.*

See also

1115 God, purpose of	8739 evil, examples of
4145 archangels	8785 opposition
5214 attack	8787 opposition to God
6157 fall, of Satan	
8727 enemies	8802 pride

4122
Satan, as tempter

God's people are incited to evil by Satan. He seeks to exploit their weaknesses in order to deflect them from obedience to God.

Satan incites God's people to evil
Satan exploits human weaknesses
Ge 3:1–5 *Rev 12:9 identifies the serpent with Satan. See also* Job 2:4–5; Eph 4:26–27

He tempts Christians to fall away
1Th 3:5 *See also* Lk 22:31; 1Ti 3:7; 2Ti 2:26

He inspires people to put God to the test Ac 5:3–9 *See also* Ps 78:18,41; 106:14; Ac 15:10; 1Co 10:9

He makes sin attractive
Lack of integrity: Mt 5:37; Ac 5:3
Sinful desires: 1Co 7:5; 1Ti 5:14–15
2Co 2:10–11 *unforgiveness;* Jas 3:14–16 *envy and selfish ambition*

Jesus Christ is tempted by Satan
In the wilderness Mt 4:1–11
pp Mk 1:13 pp Lk 4:1–13

Through Simon Peter Mt 16:23
pp Mk 8:33

Jesus Christ identifies with believers
Heb 4:15 *See also* Heb 2:8

Satan tests Christians
Rev 2:10 *See also* Lk 22:31; Rev 3:10

Satan's temptations can be resisted
By being alert 1Pe 5:8

By prayer Mt 26:41 pp Mk 14:38
pp Lk 22:40 *See also* Mt 6:13 pp Lk 11:4; Lk 22:32,46

By relying on God's faithfulness
1Co 10:13 *See also* 2Pe 2:9; Rev 3:10

By Jesus Christ's service as high priest
Heb 2:18; 4:15

See also

2306 Christ, high priest	5201 accusation
	5530 sifting
2575 Christ, temptation	6248 temptation

4123
Satan, as deceiver

Satan's character is deceitful, devious and cunning as in a variety of guises he seeks to influence people for his own ends.

Satan's deceitful character
He is evil Mt 6:13 *See also* Mt 5:37; 13:19; Jn 17:15; 2Th 3:3; 1Jn 2:13–14; 3:8,12; 5:18

He is a liar Jn 8:44 *See also* Ge 3:4–5; Job 1:11; 2:5; Rev 3:9

He is devious 2Co 11:14 *See also* 2Co 11:3; Eph 6:11; 2Th 2:9; 1Ti 3:7; 2Ti 2:26

He is scheming Eph 6:11 *See also* 2Co 2:10–11

He is a slanderer Job 1:9–11 *See also* 1Ti 5:14–15; Rev 2:9

Satan's deceitful work
He deceives individuals 1Ti 2:14 *Eve was deceived by Satan the serpent. See also* Da 8:25; 2Ti 3:13; Rev 12:9; 20:3,10

He works counterfeit miracles
2Th 2:9–10 *See also* Ex 7:11–12,22; Dt 13:1–2; Mt 24:24 pp Mk 13:22; Rev 13:13–14; 19:20

He appoints false prophets Mt 7:15 *See also* Dt 13:5; Jer 23:26; 28:15; 29:21; Eze 13:6–10; 2Pe 2:1–3,18–19

He misuses Scripture Mt 4:6 pp Lk 4:10

He blinds unbelievers 2Co 4:4

See also

1415 miracles	8735 evil, origins of
6145 deceit	8776 lies
7774 prophets, false	

4124
Satan, kingdom of

Satan is depicted as the prince of this world, having power over demons and over godless people. He is, however, subject to God's sovereignty and therefore his power is limited and his rule temporary.

Satan's power
He has power in the world 1Jn 5:19 *See also* Jn 7:7; 8:44; 14:17; 15:18–19; 16:20; 17:14; Ac 26:18; 2Co 4:4; Eph 2:2; Col 1:13; 1Jn 2:15–16; 4:4–5; Rev 13:12

He claims power over this world
Mt 4:8–9 pp Lk 4:6

He is called the "prince" or the "god" of this world Jn 12:31 *See also These titles indicate the temporary nature of Satan's rule:* Jn 14:30; 16:11; 2Co 4:4

He is responsible for some illnesses
Lk 13:16 *See also* Job 2:7; Ac 10:38; 2Co 12:7 *Paul's "thorn in the flesh" may or may not have been a physical illness.*

He is responsible for death Heb 2:14

Satan's kingdom
He has a kingdom Mt 12:26
pp Lk 11:18; Col 1:13 *See also* Ac 26:18; Eph 2:2

He has a throne Rev 2:13

He is the prince of demons Mt 9:34 *The name Beelzebub is used elsewhere to name the prince of the demons. This name was used also to identify Satan. See also* Mt 12:24 pp Mk 3:22 pp Lk 11:15

Satan's authority is limited
He cannot do more than God allows
Job 1:12 *See also* Job 2:6; 1Co 10:13; Rev 12:12; 20:3

His rule is temporary Ro 16:20; Rev 20:10

See also

1130 God, sovereignty	4025 world, the
	5347 injustice
2345 Christ, kingdom of	5459 prince
2375 kingdom of God	

4125
Satan, agents of

Satan works in this world through people and through those spiritual beings who acknowledge his authority. His agents oppose God's will and purposes.

Satan works through people
Satan's human agents pursue his evil desires Jn 8:44 *Jesus Christ speaking of the relationship of some unbelieving Jews to Satan. See also* Ac 13:10; 1Jn 3:8–10,12

Satan works through people to oppose God's purposes Ac 5:1–9 *Ananias and Sapphira;* Mt 16:23 pp Mk 8:33 *Simon Peter*
Judas Iscariot: Lk 22:3; Jn 6:70; 13:2,27
Ac 13:8–10 *Elymas, the sorcerer*

Examples of people doing Satan's work
False prophets Dt 13:5; Jer 23:26–27; 28:15; 29:21; Eze 13:6–9; Mt 7:15; 24:24; 2Pe 2:1–3

Others who lead people away from God Dt 13:13; 2Ki 21:9–26 *Manasseh and his son, Amon;* Pr 7:21 *the adulteress;* Isa 3:12; Jer 50:6; 2Pe 2:18–19

Satan works through his spiritual agents
Satan's angels Mt 25:41 *See also* 2Pe 2:4; Rev 12:7 *"angel" and "messenger" are the same word in Greek*

Satan's demons Lk 13:11–16 *See also* Mt 12:22; Lk 11:14–15

Satan's agents are identified by various images and titles
The little horn Da 8:9–12 *This probably represents Antiochus Epiphanes.*

The prince of Persia Da 10:13 *probably representing a demon with influence over the Persian kingdom*

The king of the North Da 11:28 *probably representing Antiochus Epiphanes*

The antichrist 1Jn 4:1–4; 2Jn 7

The man of lawlessness 2Th 2:3–10

The beast Rev 11:7; 13:1–8,11–18; 14:9–11; 16:13; 17:8; 19:20; 20:10

The false prophet Rev 16:13; 19:20

The prostitute or Babylon the Great Rev 14:8; 16:19; 17:1–18; 18:1–10,18; 19:2

See also

4116 angels opposed to God	4195 spirits
4131 demons, kinds of	4609 beast, the
	7774 prophets, false
	9115 antichrist, the

4126
Satan, resistance to

Jesus Christ resisted Satan in his ministry, and believers are commanded to follow his example in this respect. God assists believers in this struggle.

Satan can be resisted
His power is limited Job 1:12; 2:6; 1Co 10:13; Rev 12:12; 20:3

Jesus Christ resists Satan Mt 4:1–11 pp Lk 4:1–13; Jn 1:5; Heb 2:18; 4:15

Christians can resist Satan Jas 4:7 *See also* Lk 10:19; Ro 6:13; Eph 4:26–27; 6:11–13; 1Pe 5:8–9; 2Pe 3:17; 1Jn 2:13–14

God protects his people from Satan
2Th 3:3 *See also* 1Jn 5:18

God's protection is to be sought in prayer
Jn 17:15 *See also* Mt 6:13; Lk 22:31–32; Eph 6:11,18

Jesus Christ has the victory over Satan
Jesus Christ's defeat of Satan on the cross Col 2:15 *See also* Jn 12:31; Rev 12:11

Jesus Christ's name is powerful against Satan Php 2:10 *See also* Isa 45:23; Ps 118:10–12; Mk 16:17–18; Lk 10:17; Ac 16:18

God's love cannot be thwarted Ro 8:38–39

Resisting Satan brings reward
2Ti 4:7–8 *See also* Jas 1:12; Rev 2:7,17,26; 3:5,12,21

See also

1320 God as Saviour	8482 spiritual warfare
2372 Christ, victory	8490 watchfulness
5498 reward	8602 prayer
5596 victory	8737 evil, responses to
6030 sin, avoidance	
6213 participation in sin	
6251 temptation, resisting	

4127
Satan, defeat of

Though defeated on Jesus Christ's cross, Satan is still active in this world, but his final overthrow by God is certain.

Satan is defeated by Jesus Christ
Jesus Christ is stronger than Satan Jn 14:30 *See also* Mt 12:28; Lk 13:16; Ac 10:38; Gal 1:4

Jesus Christ came to destroy Satan's work 1Jn 3:8 *See also* Heb 2:14–15

Satan is defeated on the cross Col 1:13; Tit 2:14; Rev 3:21

Satan's defeat is foreseen by Jesus Christ Jn 12:31 *See also* Mt 25:41; Lk 10:18; Jn 16:11

Satan's agents are also defeated Col 2:15 *See also* Ro 8:38–39

Satan is defeated by Christians
Rev 12:11 *See also* Ac 5:40–42; 1Jn 2:13–14

Satan's final overthrow
Satan and his agents will be destroyed Ro 16:20 *See also* Rev 17:14

Satan's final destiny 1Ti 3:6 *judgment Torment:* Rev 20:1–3,10

Death, the result of Satan's work, will be defeated 1Co 15:26; Rev 20:13–14

See also

2066 Christ, power of	8738 evil, victory over
2351 Christ, miracles	9021 death, natural
2372 Christ, victory	9105 last things
2410 cross, the	9240 last judgment
4135 demons, Christ's authority over	9511 hell, place of punishment
5290 defeat	
5454 power, God's saving	

4130

demons

Evil spiritual forces; Scripture stresses the reality of demonic forces and recognises a number of categories to which they may be assigned. Jesus Christ's authority over such demonic forces is seen at work in his ministry and in that of his disciples.

This set of themes consists of the following:
4131 demons, kinds of
4132 demons, malevolence of
4133 demons, possession by
4134 demons, exorcism of
4135 demons, Jesus Christ's authority over

4131
demons, kinds of

Scripture uses a number of terms to refer to demonic forces, stressing both their reality and hostility to God.

Demons
Dt 32:17; 1Co 10:20–21 *See also* Ps 106:37; Mt 8:16; Mk 7:26; Ro 8:38; Jas 2:19; Rev 9:20

Evil spirits
Mt 10:1; Ac 5:16; 8:7 *See also* Mt 12:43–45; Mk 1:23–26; 3:11; Rev 18:2

Other terms for demons
Spirits Ac 16:16 *See also* Mk 9:17

Spirits of demons Rev 16:14

Deceiving spirits 1Ti 4:1

Authorities, powers and forces Eph 6:12; Col 2:15; 1Pe 3:22

See also

4116 angels opposed to God	4195 spirits
4125 Satan, agents of	

4132
demons, malevolence of

Demons are opposed to the person and work of God and seek to lead human beings, including believers, away from him. For this reason, believers are forbidden to be involved with them.

Demons harm individuals
Demons cause torment and pain *Saul's torment:* 1Sa 16:14–16,23; 18:10–11; 19:9–10
Mt 15:22; 17:15 pp Mk 9:18–20 pp Lk 9:39–42 *the boy with an evil spirit;* Mk 5:5; Lk 6:18; 13:11; Ac 5:16; 19:16 *the seven sons of Sceva*

Demons cause dissension Jdg 9:23–25

Demons cause illness and handicaps Mk 9:17–27 pp Mt 17:14–18 pp Lk 9:37–42 *See also* Mt 9:32–33; Lk 11:14; 13:11

Demons are deceitful
Demons inspire false prophets 1Ki 22:21–23 pp 2Ch 18:21–22

Demons incite war Rev 16:13–14

Demons lead people away from God 1Jn 4:1–6 *See also* 1Ti 4:1–2; Rev 16:13–14

The inspiration of pagan religions by demons
Pagan gods are identified as demons 1Co 10:20–21 *See also* Dt 32:16–17; Ps 106:36–39; Rev 9:20

Demons inhabit ruins of pagan cities
Rev 18:2

All involvement with spirits and mediums is forbidden
Lev 19:31 See also Ex 22:18;
Lev 20:6,27; Dt 18:10–14; Jer 27:9

Witchcraft is identified as a work of the sinful nature Gal 5:19–20

Involvement with sorcery or witchcraft is futile Isa 47:9 See also
1Sa 28:7,14–20; Isa 8:19–22; 19:3–4;
47:12–15; Na 3:3–4

Examples of renunciation of the work of demons
Ac 19:19 See also 1Sa 28:9; 2Ki 23:24

See also
4155 divination	6145 deceit
4175 mediums	8734 evil
4185 sorcery and	8768 idolatry
magic	8776 lies
5560 suffering	

4133
demons, possession by

A recognised condition in Jesus Christ's lifetime in which an individual is dominated by the influence of a demon. In his ministry, Jesus Christ encountered and delivered many people in such a condition. Many of Christ's critics unsuccessfully sought to ascribe his authority and powers to demonic possession.

Unfounded accusations of demon-possession
Against John the Baptist Mt 11:18
pp Lk 7:33

Against Jesus Christ Jn 10:20–21 See also Mt 9:34; 12:24 pp Mk 3:22
pp Lk 11:15; Jn 7:20; 8:48–52

Unfounded accusations of demon-possession against Jesus Christ are refuted Mt 12:25–28 pp Mk 3:23–30
pp Lk 11:17–20; Jn 10:21

Demon-possession arising from sin
1Sa 18:9–10

The consequences of demon-possession
Irrational behaviour 1Sa 18:10–11 See also 1Sa 19:9–10

Unnatural physical strength Mk 5:4
pp Mt 8:28 pp Lk 8:29 See also Ac 19:16

Self-harm Mk 5:5

Violent behaviour Mk 9:18 pp Lk 9:39
See also Mt 8:28 pp Mk 5:3–5
pp Lk 8:27–29

The impairment of faculties Mt 12:22
pp Lk 11:14 See also Mt 9:32; Mk 9:17;
Lk 13:11

Suffering Mt 15:22 pp Mk 7:25–26 See also 1Sa 16:14–16; Mt 17:15 pp Mk 9:18
pp Lk 9:39; Lk 6:18

Jesus Christ delivers from demon-possession
Mt 8:16 pp Mk 1:32 pp Lk 4:40 See also

Mt 4:24; 9:32; 12:22; 15:22
pp Mk 7:25–26

Multiple demon-possession
Jesus Christ encounters cases of multiple demon-possession and is able to deliver Mk 16:9 See also
Mk 5:1–17 pp Lk 8:26–35; Lk 8:2

Further evidence of the possibility of multiple demon-possession
Mt 12:43–45 pp Lk 11:24–26

Demons recognise divine authority and their own limited powers
Jas 2:19

Demons know Jesus Christ's identity
Mk 1:24 pp Lk 4:34 See also Mt 8:29
pp Mk 5:7 pp Lk 8:28; Mk 1:34
pp Lk 4:41; Mk 3:11; Ac 19:15

Demons recognise Jesus Christ's disciples Ac 16:16–17

Jesus Christ's disciples have power to release from demon-possession by calling on Jesus' name Ac 5:16;
19:13–16

See also
2018 Christ, divinity	3245 Holy Spirit,
2545 Christ,	blasphemy
opposition to	against

4134
demons, exorcism of

Jesus Christ drove out many demons during his earthly ministry and he delegated this authority to his disciples.

Jesus Christ understood exorcism as part of his ministry
Lk 13:32 See also Lk 4:18

He drove out demons from individuals brought to him Mt 8:16 pp Mk 1:32–34
pp Lk 4:40–41 See also Mt 4:24

He drove out demons from individuals whom he encountered Mk 1:23–26
pp Lk 4:33–35 See also Mk 1:39

Jesus Christ had power over demons
He was able to drive demons out at a distance Mt 15:22–28 pp Mk 7:25–30

He used words of rebuke to drive out demons Mt 17:18 pp Mk 9:25
pp Lk 9:42 See also Mk 1:25 pp Lk 4:35;
Lk 4:41

Jesus Christ identifies the spiritual resources needed for exorcising demons
The Spirit of God Mt 12:28 pp Lk 11:20

Faith Mt 17:19–20

Prayer (and fasting) Mk 9:28–29

The ministry of exorcism was an indication of the kingdom's presence
Mt 12:28 pp Lk 11:20

The results of being delivered from demon-possession
Visible transformation and healing
Mk 5:15 pp Lk 8:35 See also Mt 9:33;
Lk 11:14; 13:13

Devotion to Jesus Christ Lk 8:1–2 See also Mk 5:18 pp Lk 8:38

Loss of supernatural faculties
Ac 16:16–19

Demons seek to return Mt 12:43–45
pp Lk 11:24–26

The impact of exorcism on those who observe it
Amazement Mt 9:33; 12:23; Mk 1:27
pp Lk 4:36; Lk 11:14

Fear Mt 8:34 pp Mk 5:17 pp Lk 8:37

See also
2066 Christ, power of	5784 amazement
2351 Christ, miracles	6634 deliverance
2375 kingdom of	6658 freedom
God	8226 discernment
4160 driving out	8482 spiritual
4165 exorcism	warfare

4135
demons, Jesus Christ's authority over

Demons are subject to the authority of Jesus Christ during his ministry and subsequently in the ministry of the church.

All spiritual powers are subject to Jesus Christ who has supreme authority
Eph 1:19–22 See also Ro 8:38; Eph 3:10;
Col 1:16; 2:10,15

Demons are powerless before Jesus Christ
Demons can only do what he permits
Mt 8:31–32 pp Mk 5:12–13
pp Lk 8:32–33

Demons obey his command Mt 17:18
pp Mk 9:25–26 pp Lk 9:42 See also
Mt 9:33–34; Mk 1:34; 16:9; Lk 11:14

Demons disperse at his word Mk 9:25
See also Mk 1:25 pp Lk 4:35

The name of Jesus Christ has power against demons
Jesus Christ's name is used by his disciples Mk 16:17 See also Mk 9:38–39
pp Lk 9:49–50; Lk 10:17; Ac 16:18

Jesus Christ anticipates the misuse of his own name Mt 7:22–23 See also
Ac 19:13–16 an example where Jesus' name is used in cases of demon-possession—but not by Jesus Christ's disciples, and not successfully

Jesus Christ's disciples have delegated power over demons
In Jesus Christ's own lifetime Mt 10:1
See also Mt 10:7; Mk 3:14–15; 6:7
pp Lk 9:1; Mk 6:13; Lk 10:17,19

In the ongoing ministry of the church
Mk 16:17 See also Ac 5:16; 8:7; 16:18;
19:12

Others will attempt to drive out demons
Mt 12:27 pp Lk 11:19; Mk 9:38
pp Lk 9:49; Ac 19:13–15

The final punishment of demons
2Pe 2:4; Jude 6

See also
2012 Christ,
  authority
2372 Christ, victory
3275 Holy Spirit in
  the church

4127 Satan, defeat
  of

4140

angel of the Lord

A title given to those angelic servants of God who are given specific tasks in furthering God's purposes among humanity. These tasks include the giving of revelations, guidance, encouragement, warnings and the execution of judgment on those who oppose God's purposes.

The status of the angel of the Lord

He is identified with the Lord Ex 3:2–6
The angel of the Lord here speaks for God and is recognised as God and as a messenger from God. This may indicate that the angel speaks on God's behalf (compare with the role of the prophets) or, as some believe, this may be a manifestation of the pre-incarnate Jesus Christ. See also Ge 16:7,13; 31:11–13; Jdg 2:1–2; 6:11–12,14; 13:19–22; Zec 3:1–2

He is distinguished from the Lord 2Sa 24:16 pp 1Ch 21:15 See also Zec 1:12–13; Lk 1:19; Heb 1:4

The angel of the Lord is active in various ways

He calls and speaks Ge 16:7–8; 21:17; 22:11,15; 2Ki 1:3,15

He has physical contact with people 1Ki 19:5,7; Ac 12:7

He appears in human likeness Ge 18:2,16,22; 19:1; Jdg 6:11–12; Ac 27:23

He appears in supernatural form, often evoking fear Ex 3:2; Nu 22:22–24,31; 1Ch 21:16; Lk 1:11–12; 2:9

He appears in dreams and visions Ge 31:11; Zec 1:8,11; 3:1,5; Mt 2:13,19; Ac 10:3

Functions of the angel of the Lord

He reveals information, often about forthcoming births Jdg 13:3 See also Mt 1:20; Lk 1:11,13

He gives guidance and instruction Ac 8:26 See also Ge 16:9; 22:11–12; 24:7,40; Ex 23:23; Nu 22:35

He comforts those in need Ge 21:17 See also 1Ki 19:5–7; Ac 27:23–25

He affirms promises and gives blessing Ge 22:15–18 See also Lk 1:26–28,30–33; 2:10–11

He leads, delivers and protects Israel Ps 34:7 See also Ex 14:19; Isa 63:9

He rebukes sinful Israel Jdg 2:1–4

He rolls back the tombstone Mt 28:2

He rescues those in prison Ac 5:19; 12:8–9

He executes judgment on sin Ac 12:23 See also 2Sa 24:15–16 pp 1Ch 21:14–15; 2Ki 19:35 pp Isa 37:36; Ps 35:4–6

See also
1210 God, human
  descriptions
1409 dream
1454 theophany

1469 visions
4110 angels
5174 prostration
5408 messenger

4145

archangels

The archangel associated with the second coming
1Th 4:16

The archangel Gabriel
Gabriel as an interpreter of visions Da 8:15–26 See also Da 9:20–27

Gabriel as a messenger of God Lk 1:11–20 See also Lk 1:26–38

The archangel Michael
Michael described as a prince Da 10:12–13 See also Da 10:21

Michael depicted as a warrior and protector Da 12:1 See also Rev 12:7

Associated with the death of Moses Jude 9

See also
1469 visions
4110 angels
4120 Satan
5102 Moses, life of

5174 prostration
5408 messenger
9310 resurrection

4150

cherubim

Winged, heavenly creatures represented in the tabernacle and the temple.

Description of the cherubim
Eze 10:12–14 See also
Eze 1:4–14,22–24; 10:5,8,21–22; 41:18–19; Rev 4:6–8

Cherubim represented in the tabernacle and the temple
Cherubim as decorations Ex 26:1 See also Ex 36:8; 1Ki 6:29 pp 2Ch 3:7; 1Ki 7:29,36

Cherubim at the entrance to the inner sanctuary Ex 26:31–33; 36:35; 1Ki 6:32,35; 2Ch 3:14

Cherubim over the ark of the covenant Heb 9:5 See also Ex 25:17–22; 37:7–9; Nu 7:89; 1Ki 6:23–28 pp 2Ch 3:10–13; 1Ki 8:6–7 pp 2Ch 5:7–8; 1Ch 28:18

Cherubim represented in Ezekiel's vision of the temple
Eze 41:18,20,25

Cherubim represent the place of God's throne
1Sa 4:4 See also 2Sa 6:2 pp 1Ch 13:6; 2Ki 19:15 pp Isa 37:16; Ps 80:1; 99:1; Eze 10:1; Rev 4:6; 5:6

Cherubim as guardians
Ge 3:24 See also Eze 28:14,16

Cherubim as God's chariot
2Sa 22:11 pp Ps 18:10 See also 1Ch 28:18

Cherubim as agents of judgment
Cherubim remove God's glory Eze 9:3; 10:3–4,15–19; 11:22–23

God's judgment poured out Eze 10:2,6–7; Rev 6:1–8 *the living creatures release the four horsemen of God's judgment on earth;* Rev 15:7

See also
1045 God, glory of
1065 God, holiness
  of
4114 angels and
  praise
4180 seraphim
4627 creatures
4690 wings
5252 chariots

5581 throne
5698 guardian
7306 ark of the
  covenant
7459 tabernacle, in
  OT
7467 temple,
  Solomon's

4155

divination

Attempts to discover the unknown or the future by supernatural means, involving communication with the spirit world. It is expressly forbidden by God and has disastrous consequences.

Divination was part of early beliefs and practices
Ge 41:24; Ex 7:11; Isa 31:1–2; 47:9; Jer 27:9; Eze 21:21; Da 2:2; 5:7

Examples of divination in NT times
Ac 8:9–13,18–24; 13:6–12; 16:16–18

The reality of a supernatural spirit world
The spirit world is real and alluring Ac 8:11 See also Ge 44:5,15; 1Sa 6:2; Ac 8:9–10

The spirit world is powerful and dangerous 2Ki 9:22 See also Nu 22:6–7,12; 2Ki 17:17; Zec 10:2; Eph 6:12; 2Th 2:9–10; Rev 18:23

Deliberate involvement with divination forbidden
Lev 19:31 See also Ex 22:18; Lev 19:26; Dt 18:10–14; 2Ki 21:6; Isa 8:19–20; Eze 13:23; Mic 5:12; Mal 3:5; Gal 5:20

It is God's divine privilege to reveal or conceal things
Dt 29:29 See also Pr 25:2

Examples of the evil of divination
1Sa 28:7 See also 1Sa 28:3–15

Casting lots to make decisions
Divination is clearly forbidden but some practices such as casting lots seem acceptable ways of discovering God's will in particular circumstances:
1Ch 26:13–16; Ne 11:1; Ac 1:26

See also
1412 foreknowledge
4175 mediums
4185 sorcery and
  magic
4190 spiritism

4195 spirits
7392 lots, casting of
8124 guidance
8734 evil
9130 future, the

4160

driving out

Driving out demons
In Jesus Christ's ministry Mk 1:34 *See also* Mt 8:16; 9:32–33 pp Lk 11:14; Mk 1:39; Lk 13:32

Jesus Christ accused of using satanic power to drive out demons
Mt 12:24–28 pp Mk 3:22–26 pp Lk 11:15–20 *See also* Mt 9:34

Jesus Christ commissioned his disciples to drive out demons Mt 10:1 pp Lk 9:1 *See also* Mt 10:8; Mk 3:15; 6:13

The failure of the disciples to drive out demons Mk 9:18

Others attempted to use Jesus Christ's authority Lk 9:49; Ac 19:13

Driving out demons is no substitute for obedience to the will of God Mt 7:22

Driving out demons and Satan as an aspect of Jesus Christ's overall ministry Jn 12:31

Driving out people
Nu 33:51–52 *See also* Ex 10:11; Ps 44:2; Pr 19:26; 22:10; Jer 29:2; Mt 21:12

See also
2351 Christ, miracles	4134 demons,
2375 kingdom of	exorcism
God	4165 exorcism

4165

exorcism

The expulsion of an evil spirit or spirits from a person. Jesus Christ has unique authority as an exorcist. He delegated this authority to the disciples.

Exorcism was practised with varying degrees of success by Jews and pagans
Mt 7:22; 12:27 pp Lk 11:19; Ac 19:13–16

Jesus Christ had unique authority as an exorcist
Mk 1:27 pp Lk 4:36; Mt 12:25–28 pp Lk 11:17–18 *The authority Jesus Christ exercised over evil spirits demonstrated that God's kingly authority was present in him. See also* Mt 12:29 pp Mk 3:27 pp Lk 11:21–22 *Jesus Christ is the "strong man". His power over evil spirits shows that Satan is defeated.*

Jesus Christ had a general ministry of exorcism
Mt 8:16 pp Mk 1:34 pp Lk 4:41; Mk 1:39; Lk 6:17–18; 7:21

Jesus Christ gave the apostles power to cast out evil spirits
Mt 10:1 pp Mk 6:7 pp Lk 9:1; Mk 3:14–15; 16:17; Lk 10:17

After the ascension the apostles cast out evil spirits
Ac 5:16; 19:12

Various symptoms associated with the need for exorcism
Violent or self-destructive behaviour Mk 5:1–5 pp Lk 8:27–29

Deafness and muteness Mt 9:32; Mk 9:17; Lk 11:14

Seizures Mt 17:14–15 pp Mk 9:17–18 pp Lk 9:38–39

Various components of exorcism
A word of command Mk 1:25 pp Lk 4:35 *See also* Mt 8:32; Mk 9:25; Ac 16:18

The demons recognise the source of the authority addressing them Mk 1:24 pp Lk 4:34 *See also* Mt 8:29 pp Mk 5:7 pp Lk 8:28; Ac 16:17

Exorcism was often accompanied by an element of violence or trauma
Mk 1:26 *See also* Mk 9:26; Mt 8:32 pp Mk 5:13 pp Lk 8:32–33; Ac 19:16

Exorcism changes the behaviour or condition of the person delivered
Mk 5:15 pp Lk 8:35 *See also* Mt 9:33 pp Lk 11:14

An exorcised person may be "repossessed" Mt 12:43–45 pp Lk 11:24–26

Methods of exorcism other than the word of command
Exorcism may be achieved at a distance Mt 15:21–28 pp Mk 7:24–30; Ac 19:12

On rare occasions an object is used
Ac 19:12 *This was an unusual demonstration of power in a city noted for magic.*

David's music brought relief to Saul
1Sa 16:14–16,23

Intensive prayer is sometimes necessary Mk 9:29

See also
2012 Christ,	4120 Satan
authority	4134 demons,
2066 Christ, power of	exorcism
2351 Christ, miracles	4160 driving out
2354 Christ, mission	6634 deliverance
2375 kingdom of	8226 discernment
God	

4170

host of heaven

God's angelic attendants
Ps 148:2 *See also* 1Ki 22:19–22 pp 2Ch 18:18–21; Ps 103:21; Lk 2:8–15

The stars in the sky
Created by God Ps 33:6 *See also* Ne 9:6; Isa 40:26; 45:12

Objects of worship 2Ki 23:4–5 *See also* 2Ki 17:16; 21:3–5 pp 2Ch 33:3–5; Jer 19:13; Zep 1:4–5

Portrayed symbolically Da 8:10 *See also* Isa 34:4

See also
1325 God, the	4281 stars
Creator	8646 doxology
4114 angels and	8769 idolatry, in OT
praise	9410 heaven

4175

mediums

People who claim to be channels through whom the spirits of the dead speak to the living.

God's people must not be mediums
Dt 18:10–12

God's people must not consult mediums
Isa 8:19–20 *See also* Lev 19:31; 20:6; 2Ki 23:24; Jer 27:9

Examples of those who turned to mediums
King Saul 1Sa 28:3–16; 1Ch 10:13

King Manasseh 2Ki 21:6 pp 2Ch 33:6

The Egyptians Isa 19:3

See also
1025 God, anger of	7141 people of God,
1690 word of God	OT
4185 sorcery and	8021 faith
magic	8460 pleasing God
4190 spiritism	8754 fear
5288 dead, the	

4180

seraphim

An order of angels, mentioned only in one OT passage. Seraphim (the plural is also rendered seraphs) have a physical appearance and a moral and spiritual nature; they understand and use speech. Their functions include the worship of God and the communication of the assurance of forgiveness.

Their appearance
Isa 6:2 *The covering of faces and feet expresses reverence, humility and awe before God.*

Their functions
Worship of God Isa 6:3 pp Rev 4:8

Communication with the prophet
Isa 6:6–7

See also
4114 angels and	8625 worship,
praise	acceptable
4150 cherubim	attitudes
6653 forgiveness,	
divine	

4185

sorcery and magic

The attempt to discover or influence the future by means forbidden by God, including the use of divination, astrology or witchcraft. Such practices are strongly condemned in Scripture.

Examples of magic and sorcery
Magic practices Rev 18:23 *Babylon, here, represents the world as the centre of seduction.*

Divination Zec 10:2

Spiritism Isa 8:19–20 *See also* 2Ch 33:6

Astrology 2Ch 33:3–5 pp 2Ki 21:3–5

Examples of those who practised sorcery
Egyptian magicians: Ex 7:11; 8:18
Balaam: Nu 22:6; 23:23
2Ki 21:6 *Manasseh, king of Judah;*

Isa 47:9–13 the Babylonians; Ac 8:9–11 Simon of Samaria; Ac 13:6–8 Bar-Jesus of Cyprus; Ac 19:19 people in Ephesus

All sorcery and magic is strongly forbidden
Dt 18:9–12 *See also* Lev 19:26,31; Jer 27:9–10; Eze 13:18,20

God is stronger than sorcerers and magicians
Ex 7:11–12; 8:16–19; Isa 44:24–25

God's judgment comes upon sorcerers and magicians
Lev 20:6; Mic 5:12; Ac 13:6–11; Rev 21:8; Gal 5:19–21

God made participation in occult practices punishable by death
Ex 22:18; Lev 20:27

King Saul was judged for occult practices 1Ch 10:13–14

Jesus Christ can deliver from occultism
Ac 16:16–18; 19:18–19; Ro 8:38–39

See also

1025 God, anger of	8160 seeking God
1310 God as judge	8709 astrology
1409 dream	8829 superstition
4155 divination	8846 ungodliness
4175 mediums	9210 judgment,
4190 spiritism	God's
7392 lots, casting of	

4190

spiritism

The use of mediums or other spiritual intermediaries to communicate with the dead. Scripture forbids such practices, which are inconsistent with obedience to a living God.

Spiritism forbidden by God
Lev 19:31 *See also* Dt 18:10–12

Punishment for spiritism
Lev 20:27 *See also* Lev 20:6

Spiritism practised in Israel
2Ki 21:6 pp 2Ch 33:6 *See also* 1Sa 28:4–20

Spiritists expelled from Israel
2Ki 23:24 *See also* 1Sa 28:3

The futility of spiritism
Isa 8:19 *See also* Isa 19:2–3

See also

1025 God, anger of	6218 provoking God
4132 demons,	8648 enquiring of
malevolence	God
4155 divination	8744 faithlessness
4175 mediums	as
4185 sorcery and	disobedience
magic	
5484 punishment by	
God	

4195

spirits

Intelligent beings which exist separately from bodies. God is spirit and he has given human beings a spiritual entity. He has also created a

---

realm of spiritual beings—some have remained good, others have become evil. Evil spirits seek to control and destroy people, but Jesus Christ has the victory over them.

God is spirit
Jn 4:24 *See also* Ge 1:2; Job 33:4; Rev 1:4 fn; 3:1 fn; 4:5 fn; 5:6 fn

Other spirits
The spirit of human beings Pr 20:27 *See also* Job 32:8; Ecc 12:7; Lk 8:55; 23:46; Jn 3:6; Ac 7:59; Jas 2:26

The spirits of the dead Isa 26:14 *See also* Pr 2:18; Isa 14:9; Heb 12:23

Angels Heb 1:14 *See also* Jdg 6:21–22; 13:20–21; Zec 6:5; Ac 23:8

Satan Job 1:6 *See also* Job 2:1; 2Co 11:14; Eph 6:11–12

Demons Rev 16:13–14 *See also* Lk 6:18; 7:21; Ac 23:8; 1Pe 3:19; Rev 18:2

The role of spirits
As instruments of punishment
1Sa 16:14 *See also* Jdg 9:23; 1Sa 18:10; 19:9; 1Ki 22:20–22 pp 2Ch 18:19–21

As instruments of testing to inspire faith in believers 1Pe 5:8–9 *See also* Job 1:8–12,22; 2:3–6,10; Mt 4:1 pp Mk 1:13 pp Lk 4:2; Jas 4:7–8

Evil spirits and humanity
Possession by spirits Mk 9:17–18 pp Lk 9:39 *See also* Mt 8:28 pp Lk 8:27; Mt 15:22 pp Mk 7:25; Mk 1:23 pp Lk 4:33

Casting out spirits Mt 8:16 pp Mk 1:34 pp Lk 4:40 *See also* Mt 12:28 pp Lk 11:20; Mt 17:18 pp Mk 9:25–26 pp Lk 9:42; Ac 5:16; 8:7

Consultation with spirits forbidden
Dt 18:10–11 *See also* Lev 19:31; 20:6; 1Sa 28:8–9; 2Ki 21:6 pp 2Ch 33:6; Isa 8:19; 19:3

Discernment and testing of spirits
1Jn 4:1 *See also* 1Co 12:10; 1Jn 4:2–6

Jesus Christ has supremacy over all created spirits
Col 2:10 *See also* Mk 1:24–27,34 pp Lk 4:41; Lk 4:33–36; 10:17–19; Col 2:15

See also

1225 God as Spirit	4165 exorcism
2012 Christ,	4190 spiritism
authority	5062 spirit
3010 God, the Holy	8228 discernment,
Spirit	examples
4110 angels	8734 evil
4120 Satan	8832 testing
4130 demons	

4200

Places

4203

earth, the

Created and sustained by God, the world is both his possession and the dwelling-place of his creatures. As

---

such, it should bring him glory, and will one day be judged by him.

God created the earth from nothing
Ex 20:11; Ne 9:6; Ac 14:15 *See also* Ge 1:1–2; Ex 31:17; 2Ki 19:15; Job 26:7; Ps 74:17; 115:15; 119:90; Isa 44:24; 45:12; 48:13; Jer 10:12; 27:5; 32:17; 33:2; Am 4:13; Jn 1:3; Ac 4:24; Heb 11:3; 2Pe 3:5; Rev 10:6; 14:7

The earth belongs to God
Dt 10:14; Ps 24:1; 95:4–5 *See also* Ex 9:29; Jos 3:13; 1Sa 2:8; 1Ch 29:11; Ps 47:9; 89:11; 1Co 10:26

God controls and sustains the earth
Ps 135:6–7 *See also* Ge 9:16–17; Job 5:10; 28:5; Ps 104:13–14; 147:8; Jer 10:13; 33:25; Hos 6:3; Col 1:17; Heb 1:3

God's character seen on earth
Ps 33:5 *See also* Ps 85:11; 119:64; Isa 6:3; 11:9; Jer 9:24

The earth should resound to God's glory and praise
Ps 96:1; Isa 44:23 *See also* Ps 47:2; 66:4; 72:9; 108:5; 148:7; Isa 49:13; Hab 3:3; Rev 5:13

The earth is the habitation of human beings and the animals
Ps 115:16 *See also* Ge 1:22,26,28–30; 8:17; 9:1; Ac 17:26

God judges the earth
1Ch 16:14; Na 1:5 *See also* Ge 18:25; Dt 32:22; 1Sa 2:10; 2Sa 22:16; Job 9:6; Ps 46:6; 77:18; Isa 2:21; 26:9; Jer 10:10

God will destroy the earth one day
Ps 102:25–26; 2Pe 3:10–12 *See also* Isa 24:1–6; 51:6; Jer 4:23–26; Mt 24:35 pp Mk 13:31; 2Pe 3:7; Rev 20:11

God will create a new earth
2Pe 3:13 *See also* Isa 65:17; 66:22; Rev 21:1

See also

1110 God, present	4005 creation
everywhere	4025 world, the
1193 glory,	4055 heaven and
revelation of	earth
1325 God, the	4206 land
Creator	4287 universe
1330 God, the	8472 respect for
provider	environment
2303 Christ as	9160 new heavens &
creator	new earth

4206

land

Areas of territory, the possession of which was regarded as a sign of security and prosperity. The land of Israel was regarded as the land promised by God to his people and a sign of his covenant faithfulness.

4207
land, as a divine gift

God's gift of the land of Israel is fundamental to the covenant promises made to Abraham and his descendants.

Land as part of God's creation
Ge 1:9–10

The land (Canaan) promised to Abraham
Ge 12:7 See also Ge 12:1; 13:15–17; 17:8; 24:7

The boundaries of the promised land
Ge 15:18–21 See also Ex 23:31; Nu 34:1–12

God's promise and its gradual fulfilment
The promise made to the patriarchs Ge 26:3–4 See also Ge 23:17–20; 28:13; 35:12; 48:3–4; 50:24–25 The patriarchs maintained only a very small part of the land. But Genesis closes with the prospect of much more.

The promise confirmed during the wilderness wanderings Ex 3:7–8 See also Ex 6:4,8; 13:5,11; 32:11–14; 33:1–3; Nu 11:10–12

Exploration of the promised land Nu 13:1–2 See also Nu 13:21–25

Entry delayed because of unbelief and rebellion Nu 13:27–33 See also Nu 14:1–4,26–35,40–45

Critical importance of obedience in the promised land Dt 5:32–33 Moses, at the end of his life, urges all the Israelites always to remember the LORD and his commands; enjoyment of the land is dependent upon the people's obedience. See also Dt 6:10–12

Invasion of the land Jos 1:2 The theme of the book of Joshua is the land: chapters 1–12 its invasion and conquest, chapters 13–21 its division among the Israelite tribes. See also Jos 2:1

Gradual conquest of the land Jos 13:1 See also Jos 7:2; 8:1; 9:1–2; 10:29–30; 13:2–6; 14:12; 17:12–18

The promise fulfilled Jos 21:43–45

Division of the land Jos 23:4–5

Conflict with the Philistines over the land 1Sa 7:7–14 Philistine aggression had imperilled the prospect of a full possession of the land until David overpowered them. See also Jdg 2:21–22; 13:1; 15:11; 1Sa 4:10–11; 13:17–19; 17:1–2; 31:1,7

Jerusalem captured by David 2Sa 5:6–7

The land at rest and prosperous
Under David 2Sa 7:1 See also 2Sa 8:1–6,14; 10:15–19

Under Solomon 1Ki 5:4 See also 1Ki 4:20–21

The exile and subsequent return to the land
Losing the land Lev 26:14,32–33 See also Dt 28:63–65; Jer 16:13; 17:4; 25:11; 44:22; La 5:2

Return to the land Jer 23:7–8 See also Isa 14:1; 35:10; 43:5–6; Eze 20:41–42; 34:11–13; Am 9:14–15

See also

1025 God, anger of	6700 peace
1035 God, faithfulness	7135 Israel, people of God
1348 covenant with Abraham	7215 exile, the
5078 Abraham, significance	7257 promised land
5477 property, land	8744 faithlessness as disobedience
5605 warfare	9165 restoration

4208
land, as a divine responsibility

Israel's land is a gift from God, though ultimately it remains under divine ownership. Life in the land is therefore characterised by both privilege and responsibility.

The land is a gift from God
Dt 26:5–9

It is Israel's inheritance Dt 26:1 See also Ex 32:13; Dt 4:21,38; 15:4; 19:10

Eleven full tribes share the inheritance Nu 26:52–55

Inherited land east of Jordan allotted by Moses Nu 32:33 See also Jos 12:6; 13:8,15,24,29

Inherited land west of Jordan allotted by Joshua and others Nu 34:17–29 See also Jos 14:1,13; 15:1,20; 16:4; 18:11; 19:1,10,17,24,32,40,51

Levi receives no inheritance of land Nu 26:62; Dt 18:1; Jos 13:14,33

Israelite households to hold their inheritance in perpetuity Nu 36:7–9 See also 1Ki 21:3; Eze 46:18

The land remains under divine ownership
Lev 25:23

Responsibility to God for the land
Mt 21:33–46

The tithe Lev 27:30 The tithe of the land's produce given to the LORD, is a kind of rent, a way of acknowledging his ownership.

Harvest festivals Ex 23:16 See also Lev 23:15–21,33–43

Sabbath rest Lev 25:1–7

The Year of Jubilee Lev 25:8–13

Responsibility to fellow Israelites in the land
Individual property rights to be respected Dt 19:14 See also Dt 27:17; Pr 15:25; 22:28; 23:10; Hos 5:10

Violation of these rights severely condemned Isa 5:8 See also 1Ki 21:17–19; Job 20:19; Eze 45:8–9; Mic 2:2,9

Responsibility to the poor in the land
The fallow (sabbath) year Ex 23:10–11 See also Lev 25:6–7; Dt 15:1–3 Debts probably include the labour of a debtor's dependants, working to pay off his debt.

The Year of Jubilee Lev 25:8–13

Harvesting conventions Lev 19:9–10 See also Lev 23:22; Dt 24:19–22; Ru 2:2–3

The land reflects God's blessing and curse
Blessing Dt 28:1–6,11–12 See also Lev 25:18–19; Dt 11:13–15; Ps 65:9–13; 67:5–6

Curse Dt 28:15,18,21 See also Lev 18:24–28; 20:22–24; 26:42–45; 1Ki 17:1

See also

1335 blessing	7429 Sabbath, in OT
4464 harvest	7482 Year of Jubilee
5446 poverty	8260 generosity
5704 inheritance, material	8488 tithing
5827 curse	8790 oppression
7354 feasts and festivals	

4209
land, spiritual aspects of

Scripture presents land in a spiritual perspective. The whole earth, once perfect but now contaminated by the fall, will one day be renewed. There will be a new heaven and earth where life is abundant and God's presence is experienced for ever.

Eden: the original good land
Ge 2:8–9

Paradise lost: expulsion from the garden
Ge 3:17–19 See also Ro 8:19–20

The promised land: an echo of Eden
Dt 8:7–10 See also Ex 3:8,17; 13:5; Lev 20:24; Nu 13:27; Dt 6:3; 11:8–12; 26:9; 27:3

The land of Israel after the exile
Promise of a return to the land Am 9:14–15 See also Isa 14:1; 35:1–10; Eze 20:41–42; 34:11–13; Am 9:11–12; Ac 15:16–17

Promise of a restored environment Isa 51:3 See also Zec 8:12–13

The final restoration of the land
Isa 65:17 See also Isa 66:22; Ro 8:21

Jesus Christ will reign eternally over new heavens and a new earth Zec 9:9–10 See also Mt 21:5; Jn 12:15; 2Pe 3:13; Rev 21:1–4; 22:1–5

Vision of life on the new earth Isa 11:6–9 See also Hos 2:18–23; Mic 4:2–4

The new Eden: the Christian's inheritance
Heb 11:13–16 See also Ps 37:11; Mt 5:5; Ro 8:17; 2Pe 3:13; Rev 2:7; 21:7 "paradise" is a Persian word taken over into the Greek, meaning "park" or "garden". In Ge 2:8 it refers to Eden: Lk 23:43; 2Co 12:1–4

4212

astronomy

The study of the stars and planets, with a view to understanding their movements and their use in fixing the time of significant events.

Astronomy as a study
It demonstrates the greatness of God and his creation Job 9:7–9; Isa 40:26 *See also* Ge 2:1; Dt 10:14; 1Ch 16:26; Ne 9:6 *Nehemiah's prayer reviews God's grace and power in creation*; Job 22:12; 25:5; 26:9; Ps 19:1–6; 33:6; 74:16; 89:5,11; 96:5; 104:2; 136:5,7–9; 148:3; Pr 3:19 *Divine wisdom permeates the whole creation*; Isa 38:8 *the LORD's sign to Hezekiah*; Isa 45:12; Jer 31:35; Mt 5:45; Heb 1:10 *credited to Jesus Christ*

It demonstrates the humility of the human race Ps 8:3–4

The use of astronomy to determine dates
Ge 1:3–5; Ps 81:3; 104:19

The mysteries of astronomy are beyond human understanding
Job 38:31–33

God's judgment and astronomical disturbances
Joel 2:31; Mt 24:29 pp Mk 13:25 pp Lk 21:25 *See also* Isa 13:10; 24:23; 30:26; 34:4; 51:6; 60:9–20 *the glory of Zion*; Eze 32:7–8; Joel 2:10; 3:15; Am 8:9; Ac 2:20; 2Pe 3:10; Rev 8:12

Lessons from astronomy
The stars as symbols of plenty Ge 15:5

The regularity of the heavens as a symbol of the bleakness of life Ecc 1:5

The differing splendour within the creation 1Co 15:41

Wandering stars as a symbol of lostness Jude 13

4215

Babylon

In OT times, the commercial, religious and political capital of Babylonia, which was the dominant power in the Near East in the sixth century B.C. In the NT, "Babylon" signifies the world and its forces in opposition to God. It is often

contrasted with "the new Jerusalem", in which God will finally reign supreme.

The founding of Babylon
Ge 10:8–10 *Shinar was an alternative name for Babylon.*

Biblical events prior to the exile in Babylon
Inhabitants of Babylon exiled to Samaria 2Ki 17:24–33

Envoys from Babylon visit Hezekiah 2Ki 20:12–19 pp Isa 39:1–8 *Hezekiah's reception of the envoys was designed to lead to a coalition against Assyria, but in the end it brought about the very opposite of what he had hoped for.*

Manasseh, king of Judah, exiled to Babylon 2Ch 33:10–11

Jehoiakim, king of Judah, becomes a vassal of Nebuchadnezzar, king of Babylon 2Ki 24:1–2 pp 2Ch 36:6–7

Nebuchadnezzar lays siege to Jerusalem 2Ki 24:10–17 pp 2Ch 36:9–10

Nebuchadnezzar conquers Jerusalem and deports the population 2Ki 25:1–21 pp 2Ch 36:17–20 pp Jer 39:1–10 pp Jer 52:4–27

Exile in Babylon
The people of Judah exiled in Babylon 1Ch 9:1 *See also* 2Ch 36:20; Ps 137:1–9; Da 1:1–7

Advice for those exiled in Babylon Jer 29:4–14

Cyrus king of Babylon decrees that the Jerusalem temple should be rebuilt
Ezr 5:13–16 *See also* 2Ch 36:22–23 pp Ezr 1:1–4

Exiles return from Babylon Ezr 2:1–2 pp Ne 7:6–7

Babylon, an instrument of divine judgment
2Ki 24:2–4 *See also* Jer 20:4–6; 21:10

The fall of Babylon
Predictions of Babylon's fall Jer 51:59–64 *See also* Isa 14:3–23; 47:1–15; Jer 50:1–10

Babylon conquered by Darius Da 5:30–31

Babylon used figuratively
By Peter 1Pe 5:13 *Babylon is traditionally interpreted as Rome, but may also mean Mesopotamian Babylon, Egyptian Babylon, or Jerusalem.*

Of the world opposed to God Rev 14:8 *See also* Rev 17:3–6; 18:1–24

4218

cave

A natural cavity in a rock face, often used as a place of refuge.

Caves as places of refuge
Jdg 6:2; 1Sa 22:1–2 *See also* Ge 19:30; Jos 10:16–18,22–23,27; Jdg 15:8,11; 1Sa 13:6; 24:2–22 *Saul comes to David's cave, but David spares his life*; 2Sa 17:9; 23:13 pp 1Ch 11:15; 1Ki 18:4,13; 19:9; Ps 57:1 Title; 142:1 Title; Isa 2:19–21 *a place of refuge in the face of divine judgment*; Jer 48:28; 49:8; Eze 33:27; Heb 11:38 *a place of refuge for those being persecuted for their faith*; Rev 6:15

Caves used as graves
Jn 11:38 *See also* Ge 23:8–20; 25:9; 49:29–32; 50:13

4221

cistern

A reservoir for storing water collected from rainfall or from a spring. When empty, it was used for a variety of purposes. The word is also employed in a figurative sense.

Cisterns were used to collect water
2Ch 26:10 *See also* 2Ki 18:31 pp Isa 36:16; Jer 14:3

Other uses for cisterns
Jer 38:6–13 *See also* Ge 37:19–24,28–30; Jer 41:4–7,9; Zec 9:11

Cisterns used as symbols
Cisterns as symbols of spiritual well-being Jer 2:13

Cisterns as symbols of physical well-being Pr 5:15–19

4224

cities of the plain

The cities of the plain of the River Jordan, chosen by Lot as a place of residence
Ge 13:10–12

Abraham rescues their inhabitants Ge 14:1–24

Abraham prays for their inhabitants Ge 18:17–33

Judgment on their sin Ge 19:1–29

The cities of the plain as symbols of sin and judgment
Dt 29:23; Lk 17:28–29

4227

deep, the

Unfathomed waters, sometimes seen as existing under the earth, held back by God's power. The term is also used of deep seas, and in metaphorical contexts.

Unfathomed waters
Ge 1:2; Ps 104:6–9 See also Ge 7:11; 49:25; Dt 33:13; Job 38:16; Ps 95:4; 139:15; Pr 3:20; 8:27–28; Isa 7:11; Ro 10:7

Deep seas
Ex 15:5; Jnh 2:3 See also Job 7:12; 38:30; Ps 42:7; Isa 44:27; 51:10; Hab 3:10; Mt 18:6; Lk 5:4

The deep used metaphorically of a desperate situation
Ps 18:16 See also 2Sa 22:17; Ps 30:1; 69:2,15; 130:1

See also
4203 earth, the   4813 depth
4266 sea   9520 Abyss, the
4293 water

4230

desert

The desert as a harsh place
Jer 2:6 See also Isa 25:4–5; 49:10; Jer 4:26; 22:6; Hos 13:5

The desert as a place of human activity
Living in the desert Ge 21:21 See also Jdg 1:16; Pr 21:19; Jer 25:24; Eze 34:25; Lk 1:80

Grazing livestock in the desert Ex 3:1 See also Ge 36:24; 1Ch 5:9; Job 24:5

Hiding in the desert 1Sa 23:14–15 See also 1Sa 23:25

Dying in the desert
Ex 14:11–12; Jn 6:49 See also Ex 16:3; Nu 3:4; 14:29; 32:13; 1Co 10:5; Heb 3:17

God leading and caring for his people in the desert
Dt 2:7; Ne 9:19–21; Ps 78:52 See also Ex 13:18; 17:1,5–6; Dt 1:19; 8:2; 29:5; 32:10; Jos 24:7; Ps 136:16; Am 2:10; Ac 7:36; 13:18

John the Baptist in the desert
Mk 1:4 See also Mt 3:3 pp Mk 1:2–3 pp Lk 3:4; Isa 40:3

Jesus Christ in the desert
Mt 4:1 pp Mk 1:12–13 pp Lk 4:1

Specific deserts
Ge 21:14 Beersheba; Ex 15:22 Shur; Ex 16:1 Sin; Ex 19:1–2 Sinai; Nu 12:16 Paran; Nu 13:21 Zin; Nu 33:8 Etham; Dt 2:26 Kedemoth; Jos 18:12 Beth Aven; 1Sa 23:24 Maon; 1Sa 24:1 En Gedi; 1Sa 26:2 Ziph; 1Ki 19:15 Damascus; 2Ki 3:8 Edom; 2Ch 20:16 Jeruel;

2Ch 20:20 Tekoa; Ps 29:8 Kadesh; Ps 63:1 Title Judah; Mt 3:1 Judea; Ac 8:26 the desert road from Jerusalem to Gaza

Deserts used figuratively
Jer 2:31 See also Isa 35:6; 40:3; Jer 50:12; La 4:3; Hos 2:3

See also
2575 Christ,   5098 John the
     temptation   Baptist
4299 wilderness   7221 exodus, the
4360 sand

4233

field of blood

The field purchased by Judas Iscariot in which he subsequently died
Ac 1:18–19 See also Mt 27:3–10

4236

fountain

A source of natural spring water. Figuratively, it symbolises a place of cleansing, tears or sexual fulfilment. Significantly, God is pictured as a fountain of life.

The fountain as a source of spring water
Pr 18:4

Figurative use of fountains
A place of cleansing Zec 13:1

Tears of inconsolable grief Jer 9:1

Sexual fulfilment SS 4:12 See also Pr 5:15–18; SS 4:15

A source of life Pr 14:27 See also Ps 36:8–9; 87:7; Pr 10:11; 13:14; 16:22; Joel 3:18

See also
3120 Holy Spirit,   4260 rivers &
     descriptions   streams
3290 Holy Spirit,   4278 spring of water
     life-giver   4293 water
4018 life, spiritual   4296 wells
4227 deep, the   5198 weeping

4239

garden

A piece of land where flowers, fruit and vegetables may be grown. The Garden of Eden was the garden entrusted to the care of Adam and Eve.

4240

garden, natural

A place of leisure for growing flowers, fruit and vegetables.

General references to gardens
1Ki 21:2; Ecc 2:5 See also SS 4:12; 5:1; 6:2; Isa 5:7; Jer 29:5; La 2:6; Am 4:9; 9:14
References to garden plants: Mt 13:32; Lk 11:42; 13:19

Gardens require irrigation
Dt 11:10; Isa 1:30 See also Nu 24:6; Job 8:16; Isa 58:11; Jer 31:12

Gardens attached to palaces
Est 1:5–6 See also 2Ki 21:18,26; Ne 3:15; Est 7:7; Jer 39:4

Idolatrous worship in gardens
Isa 65:3 See also Isa 1:29; 66:17

Jesus Christ betrayed in a garden
Mt 26:36 pp Mk 14:32 Gethsemane was a garden

Jesus Christ buried in a garden tomb
Jn 19:41–42

See also
4402 plants   4528 trees
4446 flowers   4532 vegetables
4450 fruit   4538 vineyard
4468 horticulture

4241

Garden of Eden, the

The garden created by God and entrusted to the care of Adam and Eve.

The "garden of the LORD"
Ge 2:8; 13:10 See also Ge 2:9–14; Isa 51:3; Eze 31:9,18 Ancient Egypt is likened to Eden; Eze 36:35; Joel 2:3

The place of fellowship with God
Ge 3:8

Where God spoke to Adam Ge 2:16–18

Where Adam was to work Ge 2:15,19

Where God made Eve and gave her to Adam Ge 2:18 See also Ge 2:20–24

Where Adam and Eve lived in innocence Ge 2:25; 3:7,11

Where God abundantly provided for Adam and Eve Ge 2:9–17 The trees of Eden are important. They are both the evidence of God's love and one is the focus of Adam's test.

The paradise that humanity has lost
Where Adam and Eve disobeyed God Ge 3:6 See also Ge 2:17; 3:1–7,11

Where humanity came under God's curse Ge 3:16–19

The place from which Adam and Eve were banished Ge 3:23 See also Ge 3:22,24

The picture of God's blessing
Isa 51:3 See also Isa 58:11; Jer 31:12

Where God first promised Satan's destruction Ge 3:14–15

Where God first provided a covering for sinners Ge 3:21

Eden as an anticipation of heaven
Lk 23:43 The word "paradise" (which means "park" or "walled garden") clearly refers back to the idea of Eden. See also 2Co 12:3,4; Rev 2:7; 22:1–3; Eze 28:12–13 the former glory of the king of Tyre likened to that of Adam in the Garden of Eden

See also

4122 Satan, tempter	6248 temptation
4209 land, spiritual aspects	7922 fellowship with God
4526 tree of life	8154 righteousness
5634 work & the fall	8718 disobedience
6021 sin, nature of	9410 heaven
6155 fall of Adam & Eve	9430 paradise

4245

hills

The promised land was a place of hills
The high ground to the east of Jordan
Dt 3:12 *See also* Ge 31:21

The high ground of Judah in the south
Jos 11:21 *See also* Jos 12:8; Lk 1:39

The high ground of Judah includes
Jerusalem Joel 3:17 *See also* Ps 2:6;
Isa 10:32; Da 9:16

The high ground to the north Jdg 3:27
See also Jos 20:7; 2Ki 5:22

Topics associated with hills
Plenty Joel 3:18 *See also* Dt 8:7–9;
Ps 50:10; 72:3,16; Isa 7:25; Am 9:13

Age Job 15:7 *See also* Ge 49:26;
Dt 33:15; Pr 8:25; Hab 3:6

Hiding Jos 2:16; 1Sa 23:14

Grazing 1Ki 22:17; Jer 33:13; Eze 34:6;
Mt 18:12

Idolatrous worship Dt 12:2 *See also*
1Ki 11:7; 14:23; 2Ki 17:10; 23:13;
Jer 13:27; Hos 4:13

Hills used metaphorically
Mt 5:14 *See also* Ps 114:4; Isa 40:12;
55:12

See also

4035 abundance	7257 promised land
4254 mountains	7269 Zion
4830 height	7312 Baal
5511 safety	7374 high places
5611 watchman	8769 idolatry, in OT

4248

islands

Used of the islands and coastlands of the eastern Mediterranean and, especially by Isaiah, as a more general term indicating distant nations that are called upon to respond to God. Several specific islands are mentioned in the NT.

The islands and coastlands of the Mediterranean
Isa 11:11 *See also* Isa 42:10; 60:9;
Jer 2:10–11; 31:10; Eze 26:15–18;
27:3–7; Da 11:18,29–30

Islands as a symbol of human insignificance before God
Isa 40:15–17

Islands as a symbol of distant nations
Nations who do not know God
Isa 66:19 *See also* Isa 41:1; 49:1

Nations who are not beyond God's law
and judgment Isa 59:18 *See also*

Eze 25:16–17; 39:6; Rev 6:12–14;
16:17–20

Nations called to respond to God
Isa 42:10–12 *See also* Isa 24:15; 42:4;
51:4–5

Islands mentioned in the NT
Cos Ac 21:1

Crete Ac 27:7–26; Tit 1:5,12

Cyprus Ac 4:36; 11:19–21; 13:4–12;
15:39; 21:16

Kios Ac 20:15

Malta Ac 27:39–28:11

Patmos Rev 1:9

Rhodes Ac 21:1

Samos Ac 20:15

Samothrace Ac 16:11

Sicily Ac 28:12 *Syracuse was the leading city of Sicily.*

See also

4266 sea	7510 Gentiles
5107 Paul	7948 mission
5517 seafaring	

4251

moon

The moon created by God
Ps 8:3 *See also* Ps 74:16

The moon listed among the heavenly bodies
Ge 37:9; Ps 148:3; Ecc 12:2; 1Co 15:41

The moon as a basis for the calendar
The moon governs the night
Ge 1:16–18 *See also* Ps 136:7–9;
Jer 31:35

Seasons marked by the moon
Ps 104:19 *See also* Ge 1:14

Months marked by the new moon
Nu 28:14; 1Ch 23:31; Isa 66:23

The moon as a symbol of permanence
Ps 89:37 *See also* Ps 72:5,7
The moon will not be needed in the new Jerusalem: Isa 60:19–20; Rev 21:23

Idolatrous worship of the moon
Dt 4:19 *See also* Dt 17:3; 2Ki 23:5;
Job 31:26; Jer 8:2

Signs in the moon indicating divine intervention
At the close of history Isa 13:10; 30:26;
Joel 2:10,31; Ac 2:20; Mt 24:29
pp Mk 13:24–25; Rev 6:12; 12:1

Other examples Jos 10:12–13; Eze 32:7

The moon thought to affect the mind
Ps 121:6 *The moon is indicated as a source of danger;* Mt 4:24 *The Greek expression translated "having seizures" originally meant "moonstruck".*

See also

2565 Christ, second coming	4970 seasons of year
4281 stars	7398 New Moon festival
4284 sun	8768 idolatry
4809 darkness	9220 day of the LORD
4951 month	
4957 night	

4254

mountains

These natural features of Palestine are often used as poetic symbols when describing God or his dealings with his people. Specific mountains are remembered because of their association with important events in the history of Israel. Some of the key events in the life and ministry of Jesus Christ take place on mountain sites.

Mountains and the character of God
Mountains and the steadfastness of
God Ps 125:2 *See also* Ps 11:1; 90:2;
Isa 54:10

Mountains tremble at God's awesome
presence Jdg 5:5 *The violent physical response to the presence of the holy God evokes a sense of his might and majesty.*
See also Ex 19:16–19; Ps 97:5; Isa 64:1;
Mic 1:3–4; Hab 3:3–6

Mountains cannot stand before the
anger of God Ps 18:7 *See also*
Jer 4:23–26; Na 1:5–6; Rev 6:12–14;
16:19–20

Mountains as places of encounter with God
Ex 34:1–3 *See also* 1Ki 19:11–13;
2Pe 1:16–18

Specific mountains as the sites of important events in Israel's history
The mountains of Abarim: site of
Israel's camp Nu 33:47–48

Mount Ararat: resting place of Noah's
ark Ge 8:1–5

Mount Carmel: scene of Elijah's defeat
of the prophets of Baal 1Ki 18:16–40

Mount Ebal: site of cursing; Mount
Gerizim: site of blessing Dt 11:29;
27:12–13; Jos 8:30–35

Mount Gilboa: place of Saul's suicide
1Ch 10:1–12 pp 1Sa 31:1–13
pp 2Sa 1:4–12

Mount Hermon: a boundary of Israel
Dt 3:8; Jos 11:16–17; Ps 42:6–7; 89:12

Mount Hor: place of Aaron's death
Nu 33:37–39 *See also* Nu 20:22–29

Mount Moriah: testing place of
Abraham Ge 22:1–3

Mount Moriah: site of Solomon's
temple 2Ch 3:1

Mount Nebo: place of Moses' death
Dt 32:48–52 *See also* Dt 34:1–5

Mount Sinai: God gives Moses the law
Ex 24:12 *See also* Ex 31:18; Ne 9:13–14

Mount Tabor: scene of Sisera's defeat
Jdg 4:12–16

Mountains as the sites of significant events in the NT
On the Mount of Temptation the devil
offers Jesus Christ the kingdoms of
the world Mt 4:8–9 pp Lk 4:5–7

In the Sermon on the Mount Jesus Christ teaches about life in the kingdom of God Mt 5:1–2

On the Mount of Transfiguration Jesus Christ's glory is revealed Mt 17:1–8 pp Mk 9:2–8 pp Lk 9:28–36

On the Mount of Olives Jesus Christ teaches about the destruction of the temple and the last things Mt 24:3 pp Mk 13:3–4

See also

1025 God, anger of	2580 Christ,
1090 God, majesty of	transfiguration
1140 God, the eternal	4245 hills
1660 Sermon on the	4269 Sinai, Mount
Mount	4290 valleys
2575 Christ,	7269 Zion
temptation	7374 high places

4257

pit

A hole in the ground
Mt 15:14 *See also* Ex 21:33–34; 2Sa 18:17; 23:20; Mt 12:11; Mk 12:1; Lk 6:39

A pit used as a trap
Ps 35:7–8 *See also* Ps 7:15; 9:15; 57:6; 94:13; Pr 26:27; Ecc 10:8; Isa 24:17–18; Jer 18:20–22; 48:43–44; Eze 19:4,8

A pit as a symbol of distress or grief
Ps 40:2 *See also* Job 9:30–31; Ps 88:6; Pr 22:14; 23:27; La 3:53–55; Zec 9:11

The pit as a term for the grave
Isa 14:15 *See also* Job 33:18,22,24,28,30; Ps 28:1; 30:3,9; 55:23; 69:15; 88:4; 103:4; 143:7; Pr 1:12; Isa 14:19; 38:17–18; Eze 26:20; 28:8; 31:14,16,18; 32:23–25,29–30; Jnh 2:6

The pit as a symbol of judgment
Isa 30:33

See also

4813 depth	9240 last judgment
5241 burial	9510 hell
5589 trap	9530 Hades
9020 death	9540 Sheol
9040 grave, the	

4260

rivers and streams

The term river is used to refer to all kinds of watercourses, including wadis (dried-up desert river beds) and permanent rivers. It is also used symbolically to refer to things which threaten or overwhelm people and nations, such as invading nations, the peace of God and the Holy Spirit.

Different kinds of rivers and streams
Wadis 1Ki 17:7 *Wadis were dry river beds in summer but became raging torrents in the rainy season. See also* Ge 32:22 *The Jabbok was a wadi, here in full flow;* Nu 21:13–15; Job 6:15–17; Jer 15:18

Springs Ps 104:10 *See also* Ge 16:7; Ex 15:27; Jdg 1:14–15; 2Ki 2:19–22

Permanent rivers Ge 2:10–14 *See also* Ge 41:1–3; Nu 22:1; Dt 1:7; Isa 18:1

Canals Da 8:2 *See also* Ex 7:19; Ezr 8:21; Eze 1:1 *Although called a river here, the Kebar was a canal of the Euphrates.*

Some significant rivers and streams in Scripture
River Arnon
The Arnon flowed through Moab to the mid point of the Dead Sea: Nu 21:13–15; Jdg 11:18; Isa 16:2; Jer 48:20

Rivers of Damascus 2Ki 5:12 *The Abana flowed through the city of Damascus and the Pharpar just to the south of it.*

River Euphrates
The Euphrates flowed through Mesopotamia for some 1,700 miles (2,700 km) from its source in eastern Turkey to the Persian Gulf: Dt 1:7; 2Ki 23:29 pp 2Ch 35:20; Isa 11:15; Jer 51:63–64; Rev 16:12

River Habor 2Ki 17:6 pp 2Ki 18:11 *The Habor was a tributary of the Euphrates.*

River Jabbok
The Jabbok flowed westward through Gilead into the Jordan about 20 miles (32 km) north of the Dead Sea: Ge 32:22; Nu 21:23–24; Dt 3:16; Jdg 11:13

River Jordan
The Jordan flowed from the slopes of Mount Hermon through Lake Huleh and the Sea of Galilee, and on into the Dead Sea, providing a fertile basin on either side of the river: Ge 13:10–11; 32:9–10; Nu 22:1; Jos 3:14–4:9; 2Ki 5:8–14; Mk 1:4–5 pp Mt 3:5–6

River Kebar
The Kebar was a canal of the Euphrates in Babylon where the exiles gathered to pray: Eze 1:1; 3:15; 43:1–3

River Kerith 1Ki 17:2–7 *The exact location of this wadi is uncertain, but it ran from the east into the Jordan or one of its tributaries.*

River Kishon
The Kishon flowed north-west across the Plain of Megiddo and could quickly flood as a result of storms: Jdg 4:6–7,13; 5:21; 1Ki 18:40; Ps 83:9

River Nile
The Nile flowed north some 3,500 miles (5,600 km) from Lake Victoria to the Mediterranean, providing a natural irrigation system in the desert through its annual floodings: Ex 1:22–2:10; 7:17–21; Isa 19:5–8; Eze 29:3–5

River Tigris
The Tigris flowed from the Armenian mountains through Mesopotamia to join the Euphrates some 40 miles (65 km) north of the Persian Gulf: Ge 2:14; Da 10:4–5; Na 2:6–8

The crossing of rivers and streams
Rivers crossed by fords Jos 2:7; Jdg 3:28; 12:5–6; 2Sa 17:16

Rivers crossed by miraculous intervention from God Jos 3:14–17; 2Ki 2:7–8,13–14

Human uses of rivers and streams
As boundaries Ge 15:18 *See also* Jos 1:2; 12:2; 1Ki 4:21

For irrigation Dt 11:10 *The reference may be to a machine operated by foot, or to the foot breaking through the mud walls of the irrigation channel to let the water flow into the fields. See also* Eze 17:5–8; 19:10

As places of prayer Ac 16:13 *See also* Ps 137:1–3; Eze 3:15

For ritual washing and baptism 2Ki 5:10 *See also* Mk 1:5 pp Mt 3:6; Ac 8:36–38

God as sovereign Creator is ruler and judge over all rivers and streams
Ps 74:15 *See also* Ps 78:13–16; 107:33–35; Isa 19:5–8; Rev 8:10–11; 16:12

The symbolic use of rivers and streams
A symbol of threatening circumstances Ps 124:1–5 *See also* Ps 32:6; 88:16–17

A symbol of invading nations Jer 47:2 *See also* Isa 8:7–8; Jer 46:7–8

A symbol of God's judgment on his enemies 2Sa 5:20 *"Baal Perazim" means "the lord who breaks out". The picture is of a river bursting its banks. See also* Job 20:28–29; Isa 59:19; Na 1:7–8

A symbol of God's peace Isa 48:18 *See also* Isa 66:12

A symbol of God's sustaining power Ps 46:4–5 *See also* Isa 8:6

A symbol of God's provision and blessing Joel 3:18 *See also* Ps 1:3; 36:8–9; Isa 30:25

A symbol of renewal and life Isa 41:18 *See also* Eze 47:1–12; Rev 22:1–2

A symbol of the Holy Spirit Jn 7:37–39 *See also* Isa 44:3; Jn 4:13–14

See also

3215 Holy Spirit &	4296 wells
peace	4844 rain
4236 fountain	4849 snow
4266 sea	5580 thirst
4293 water	

4263

Rome

The city state at the heart of the great world empire of NT times, pictured in the book of Revelation as the embodiment of corrupt earthly power. A large church had been established in Rome long before Paul arrived there, towards the end of his life and his mission. His letter to the believers in Rome includes a comprehensive explanation of the gospel.

Rome and the mission of Paul
Paul plans to visit Rome Ac 19:21 *See also* Ro 1:13–15; 15:23–29

Jesus Christ confirms that Paul will preach the gospel in Rome Ac 23:11

Paul is sent for trial in Rome
Ac 25:10–12 *See also* Ac 27:1–2

Paul arrives in Rome Ac 28:14–16

Paul preaches in Rome Ac 28:30–31
See also Ac 28:23–24; Php 1:12–13

The church in Rome existed long before Paul's arrival
Ro 15:23–24 *See also* Ac 28:15; Ro 1:8;
16:3–16 *Although Paul had never been to Rome, he seemed to be personally acquainted with 26 people associated with the church there, so its overall size was probably quite considerable.*

Paul's letter to the church in Rome presents the whole gospel
Ro 1:16–17 *The gospel is God's offer of salvation to all.*

Sin and the universal need for salvation Ro 3:23 *See also* Ro 3:10; 6:23

God's "rescue" through Jesus Christ available to all Ro 3:22 *See also* Ro 1:16

Peace with God through believing in Jesus Christ Ro 5:1–2 *See also* Ro 4:23–25; 5:8–10

Gentiles obtain salvation Ro 10:11–13

Rome is pictured as the embodiment of corrupt earthly power
Rev 17:1–18 *Verse 9 clearly identifies the city as Rome, widely known then as the city built on seven hills. See also* Rev 14:8 *Babylon was the great godless city of the OT and here is taken by most commentators to depict Rome, which in turn represents corrupt worldly power in general. However, some believe that only a general reference to the world system is in mind, and others that a literal reference to the actual city of Babylon is intended;* Rev 16:19; 18:1–24

See also

2420 gospel	5541 society,
4215 Babylon	negative
5107 Paul	6615 atonement,
5256 city	necessity
5305 empires	6676 justification
5457 power, human	

4266

sea

The sea created and controlled by God
Ge 1:9–10; Jer 5:22 *See also* Ps 95:5; 107:29; 146:6; Isa 50:2; Am 5:8; 9:6; Ac 4:24; 14:15

Creatures of the sea
Ps 104:25 *See also* Ge 1:21; Ps 8:8; Eze 38:20; Hos 4:3; Hab 1:14

Sea monsters sometimes represented spiritual forces Ps 74:13 *See also* Job 26:12; Isa 27:1; Rev 13:1

The sea represented hidden depths
Am 9:3 *See also* 2Sa 22:16; Job 38:16; Mic 7:19; Mt 18:6

Named seas
The Red, or Reed, Sea Ex 10:19 *See also* Heb 11:29

The Dead, or Salt, Sea Ge 14:3 *See also* 2Ki 14:25

The Sea of Galilee Nu 34:11; Jn 6:1

The Great, or Mediterranean, Sea Nu 34:6–7 *See also* Eze 47:10

The Adriatic Sea Ac 27:27 *In NT times referring to an area extending south of the present Adriatic Sea.*

The Sea before the temple
1Ki 7:23–26,39; 2Ki 16:17; 25:13

The sea before the throne
Rev 4:6; 15:2

Metaphorical references to the sea
Isa 17:12; Jas 1:6 *See also* Job 7:12; 11:9; 14:11–12; Ps 93:4; Isa 5:30; 11:9; 48:18; 57:20; Jer 6:23; 49:23; 50:42; 51:42; La 2:13; Eze 26:3; Zec 10:11; Jude 13

No more sea
Rev 21:1

See also

4227 deep, the	5300 drowning
4260 rivers &	5407 merchants
streams	5517 seafaring
4293 water	7222 exodus, events
4357 salt	of
4627 creatures	7467 temple,
4642 fish	Solomon's
4813 depth	

4269

Sinai, Mount

The mountain in the Sinai peninsula (probably present-day Jebel Musa), also called Horeb in the OT, where God made a covenant with Israel, establishing them as his people and giving them his laws. In the NT Sinai is seen as symbolising the old covenant.

Mount Sinai and the call of Moses
Ex 3:1–10 *Most scholars agree that the names Horeb and Sinai are used interchangeably of the same mountain, although some see them as referring to separate peaks within the same range. See also* Ac 7:30–34

God reveals himself to Israel at Mount Sinai
The people of Israel arrive at Mount Sinai three months after leaving Egypt Ex 19:1–2

God promises to make Israel his people Ex 19:3–6

God calls for holiness among his people Ex 19:10–15,20–24

God appears in a theophany Ex 19:16–19 *See also* Dt 4:10–12; Heb 12:18–21

God gives his laws to Israel on Mount Sinai
God gives Israel the Ten Commandments Ex 20:1–17
pp Dt 5:6–21

Israel responds with fear to God's revelation Ex 20:18–21; Dt 5:23–27; 18:16

God gives Israel the Book of the Covenant Ex 20:22–23:19 *These laws, largely an expansion and exposition of the Ten Commandments, are called "the Book of the Covenant" in Ex 24:7.*

God establishes the covenant with Israel on Mount Sinai
Moses performs the ceremony establishing the covenant Ex 24:4–8

Moses and other leaders ascend Mount Sinai to seal the covenant with a meal before God Ex 24:9–11

Moses ascends Mount Sinai further to receive the stone tablets and the requirements of covenant worship Ex 24:12–18 *During Moses' 40 days on Mount Sinai, God revealed to him the requirements of covenant worship, as outlined in Ex 25:1–31:18. See also* Lev 7:37–38; 26:46

Moses descends Mount Sinai and discovers Israel's idolatry
Ex 32:19 *See also* Ex 32:1–6,21–35; Dt 9:8–21; Ps 106:19–23

God commands Israel to move on from Mount Sinai
Ex 33:1–6,15–16

God calls Moses up Mount Sinai again
Moses is commanded to prepare new stone tablets Ex 34:1–4

God reveals his nature and name to Moses Ex 34:5–7

God renews his covenant with Israel Ex 34:10–28

Moses descends Mount Sinai, his face radiant Ex 34:29–35

The people of Israel prepare to move on from Mount Sinai
God commands Moses to take a census of Israel in the Desert of Sinai Nu 1:1–4; 3:14–16

The Israelites celebrate the Passover at Mount Sinai Nu 9:1–5

The Israelites leave Mount Sinai Nu 10:11–13 *The Israelites had been at Mount Sinai for almost a year (see also Ex 19:1);* Dt 1:6–8

Later generations look back to God's revelation on Mount Sinai
Jdg 5:5 *Ascribing the title "the One of Sinai" to God, Deborah acknowledges the great importance of his revelation at Mount Sinai. See also* 1Ki 19:8–9 *Elijah's return to Horeb, the mountain of God, shows his need to hear God clearly again;* Ne 9:13–14; Ps 68:7–8; 106:19–23; Mal 4:4; Ac 7:37–38

Mount Sinai seen by NT writers as a symbol of the old covenant
Gal 4:24–31 *Hagar, Mount Sinai and the present city of Jerusalem stand for the old covenant and bondage to the law, while Sarah and the new heavenly Jerusalem stand for the new covenant and living by faith;* Heb 12:18–29

4272

sky

The sky demonstrating God's creative power and providence

Ps 19:1; Jer 14:22 *See also* Ge 1:8–9; Job 26:7; 37:15–18; Ps 36:5; 68:34; 71:19; 77:16–18; 78:23; 147:8; Isa 50:3; Hos 2:21–22

The sky associated with heavenly bodies

Ge 1:14–15; Dt 4:19 *See also* Ge 22:17 *a promise repeated many times in the OT;* Job 37:21; Ps 89:37

The sky associated with birds

Ge 1:20; Pr 30:19; Jer 4:25; 8:7; La 4:19

The sky associated with rain and hail

Ge 8:2 *See also* Ex 9:22–23; Jos 10:11; 2Sa 22:12; 1Ki 18:45; Ps 147:8; Lk 4:25; Rev 11:6; 16:21

The sky associated with unusual phenomena

Isa 34:4; Mt 24:29–30 *See also* Ex 20:21–22; Jos 10:13; Jer 10:2; Joel 2:10; 3:16; Mk 13:25; Rev 6:13–14; 8:10; 9:1–2; 12:4; 20:11

The sky used figuratively

Mt 16:2–3 *See also* Ex 24:10; Dt 1:28; Pr 23:5; Jer 51:53; Mt 11:23; Lk 17:24

4275

Sodom and Gomorrah

Two neighbouring cities, probably located at the eastern or south-eastern end of the Dead Sea, noted for their sinfulness. God's response in wrath and judgment serves as a warning to subsequent generations.

Sodom and Gomorrah's location

Ge 10:19; 13:10–12

Sodom became Lot's home

Ge 13:10–12

Sodom and Gomorrah at war

Sodom and Gomorrah, with other cities of the plain, defeated by the alliance of four kings Ge 14:1–12

Abram rescues Lot and is honoured by the king of Sodom and his allies Ge 14:13–24

The wickedness of Sodom and Gomorrah

Ge 13:13 *See also* Ge 18:20–21; 19:1–9

Abraham pleads for the righteous in Sodom and Gomorrah

Ge 18:16–32

God's judgment against Sodom and Gomorrah

Ge 19:13 *See also* Ge 19:23–29; Dt 29:23; Lk 17:29

The story of Sodom and Gomorrah becomes a picture of human sinfulness and divine judgment

Jude 7 *See also* Isa 3:9; 13:19; Jer 23:14; La 4:6; Eze 16:44–58; Am 4:11; Mt 10:15 pp Lk 10:12; Mt 11:23–24; Lk 17:28–30; 2Pe 2:6–9

4278

spring of water

Springs of water were important to the life of Israel, providing fresh water for the people. Both God and the gospel are often compared to springs of living water, on account of their life-bringing and refreshing qualities.

The symbolic importance of springs of water to Israel

Living water as a sign of hope and prosperity Zec 14:8 *See also* Isa 12:3; 49:10; Jer 31:9

Living water as a source of fertility Jer 17:8 *See also* Ps 1:3

Living water as a sign of God's presence and power Ex 17:1–7; Nu 20:1–11

God as a spring of water

Jer 2:13 *See also* Jer 17:13

The gospel as a spring of water

Jn 4:13–14 *See also* Ps 42:2; Isa 55:1; Jn 7:37; Rev 21:6; 22:17

Other biblical uses of the image of a spring

Pr 25:26 *spoiling what is good;* Jas 3:9–11 *the tongue compared to a spring;* 2Pe 2:17 *a dry spring as a symbol of sterility*

4281

stars

Heavenly luminaries other than the sun and moon, often worshipped as gods by pagan nations. Scripture stresses that the stars were created by God, and are subject to him. Stars are often treated as symbols of the generosity of God, and his faithfulness to his promises.

The relationship between God and the stars

God is the creator Ps 33:6 *See also* Ge 1:16; Ne 9:6; Ps 136:7–9; 148:3–6

The stars demonstrate the power of their maker Isa 40:26 *See also* Job 9:7–9; 38:31–33; Ps 147:4–5; Isa 45:11–12; Am 5:8

Worship of the stars

Prohibited by God Dt 4:19 *See also* Dt 17:3; 2Ki 23:4–5

God's judgment of star worshippers Jer 8:2 *See also* Jer 19:12–13; Am 5:25–27; Zep 1:4–5; Ac 7:42–43

Examples of star worship 2Ki 17:16; 21:3–5; 2Ch 33:5; Ac 28:11

Reading the stars

Isa 47:13 *See also* Da 2:2–5; 4:7

Signs in the stars

Isa 34:4 *See also* Eze 32:7–8; Rev 6:13

The star of Bethlehem

Mt 2:9–10 *See also* Mt 2:2,7

The stars illustrating God's promise to Abraham

Ge 15:5 *See also* Ge 22:17; Dt 10:22; 1Ch 27:23; Ne 9:23; Jer 33:22; Heb 11:12

Metaphorical references to the stars

A coming ruler Nu 24:17

The morning star Rev 22:16 *See also* Isa 14:12–13; 2Pe 1:19; Rev 2:28

Wandering stars Jude 13

Stars representing angels Rev 1:16,20

God's people shining like stars Php 2:15 *See also* Da 12:3

4284

sun

Created as a source of light and heat and an indicator of time and direction. The sun is also used as a metaphor for the splendour and light of God himself and the righteousness of his people.

Natural functions of the sun

A source of light Ge 1:16–18 *See also* Ps 136:7–8

A marker of time Ge 1:14 *See also* Ge 29:7; Ex 22:26; Jdg 9:33; 1Sa 11:9

An indicator of direction Nu 21:11 *See also* Ex 27:13; Dt 11:30; Jos 19:12; Ps 113:3; Isa 45:6

A blessing, necessary for life Ecc 11:7 *See also* Dt 33:13–14; Job 8:16; Mt 5:45

The scorching heat causing discomfort and harm Jnh 4:8 *See also* Ps 121:6; Isa 49:10; Mt 13:6; Jas 1:11; Rev 7:16

Worship of the sun
Forbidden to God's people Dt 4:19 *See also* Dt 17:2–5; Job 31:26–28

Practised in Israel and Egypt Eze 8:16 *See also* 2Ki 23:5,11; Jer 8:1–2; 43:13

Sunlight and God's judgment
Joel 2:31; Mt 24:29–30 pp Mk 13:24 pp Lk 21:25–26 *See also* Ex 10:21–23; Isa 13:9–10; Jer 4:28; Eze 32:7–8; Joel 3:14–15; Am 5:20; Mt 27:45 pp Mk 15:33 pp Lk 23:44 *the crucifixion*; Ac 2:20; Rev 6:12–17

God and the sun
God as creator and controller Job 9:7; Ps 74:16 *See also* Jos 10:12–13; 2Ki 20:8–11; Ps 19:1–6; 148:3,5; Isa 38:8; Jer 31:35–36; Hab 3:11

God likened to the sun Lk 1:78–79 *See also* Ps 84:11; Isa 9:2; Hab 3:4; Mal 4:2; Mt 17:2; 2Co 4:6; Rev 1:16

God's glory outshines the sun Rev 21:23 *See also* Isa 24:23; 60:19–20; Ac 26:13; Rev 22:5

Metaphorical allusions to the sun
In Paul's conversion experience Ac 26:13

As righteousness Ps 37:6; Mt 13:43 *See also* 2Sa 23:3–4; Pr 4:18; Isa 58:8,10; 62:1; Da 12:3

As constancy and dependability Hos 6:3 *See also* Ps 72:5,17; 89:36

The setting sun signifying a premature end Jer 15:9; Am 8:9; Mic 3:6

Miracles and signs concerning the sun
Darkening of the sun: Isa 5:30; 24:23; Am 8:9

The sun standing still or reversing: Jos 10:12–13; 2Ki 20:11; Isa 38:8; Hab 3:11

See also
4272 sky	4846 shadow
4281 stars	4857 west
4809 darkness	4903 time
4821 east	4918 dawn
4829 heat	4921 day
4834 light, natural	4960 noon

4287

universe

All existing things, including the earth and its creatures and all the heavenly bodies. The universe was made by God and is sustained by Jesus Christ.

God as the Maker of all things
Ps 115:15; Jer 10:16; Rev 4:11 *See also* Ge 14:19; 2Ki 19:15; Ecc 11:5;

Isa 37:16; 44:24; Ac 14:15; Ro 11:33–36; 1Co 8:6; Eph 3:9; Heb 11:3

God as the ruler of the universe
1Ch 29:12; Ac 17:24 *See also* Ps 119:91; Jer 33:25; Mt 11:25

Jesus Christ, the one through whom the universe was made, now sustains all things
Jn 1:3; Col 1:15–17 *The title "firstborn" implies that Jesus Christ is the heir, that everything belongs to him*; Heb 1:2–3 *See also* Jn 13:3; 1Co 8:6; Eph 1:22; 4:10

The universe is temporary
Mt 24:35; 2Pe 3:10–12 *See also* Mt 5:18; 24:29; Lk 21:26

Future renewal of the universe
Eph 1:10; 2Pe 3:13 *See also* Isa 65:17; 66:22; Mt 19:28; Ro 8:19–22; Eph 1:10

Other references to the universe
Dt 4:25–26; 30:19; Php 2:15

See also
1325 God, the Creator	4055 heaven and earth
1355 providence	5215 authority
2303 Christ as creator	8146 renewal, natural order
3266 Holy Spirit in creation	9120 eternity
4005 creation	9160 new heavens & new earth
4025 world, the	

4290

valleys

Valleys used as places of permanent settlement
Ge 26:17 *See also* Nu 14:25; Jos 17:16; Jdg 18:28; 1Ch 12:14–15

Valleys as places for camp-sites
Jdg 6:33 *See also* Nu 21:10–12; Dt 3:29; Jdg 7:8–12; 1Ch 11:15

Valleys used for pasture and crops
1Ch 4:39–40 *Palestine was noted as a dry land, but valleys provided the necessary moisture for pastures and crop growth. See also* 1Ch 27:29; Ps 65:13

Valleys used for battles
Ge 14:8 *See also* Jos 11:7–8; 1Sa 17:1–3; 2Sa 8:13; 2Ch 25:11–12 pp 2Ki 14:7

Valleys as places of worship and sacrifice
2Ch 28:3 *See also* Dt 21:1–9; 2Ch 20:25–26; Jer 2:23–25; 32:35

Valleys on the day of the LORD
Isa 22:5; Mic 1:3–4; Zec 14:3–5

The metaphorical use of valleys
The valley of death Ps 23:4 *See also* Job 21:32–33

The valley of decision Joel 3:14 *See also* Joel 3:1–2,12

The valley of dry bones Eze 37:1–14

The levelling of valleys as a preparation for the coming of the Lord Lk 3:4–5 *See also* Isa 40:3–4

The Valley of Hinnom
The Valley of Hinnom as part of the boundary between Judah and Benjamin, lying to the south of Jerusalem Jos 15:8; 18:16

The Valley of Hinnom as a place of child sacrifice 2Ch 28:3 *See also* Jer 32:35

The Valley of Hinnom as a place of God's judgment Jer 7:30–32 *See also* Jer 19:1–15

The Kidron Valley
The Kidron Valley as a boundary of Jerusalem 1Ki 2:36–37 *See also* 2Sa 15:23; Jer 31:38–40; Jn 18:1

The Kidron Valley as a place for the destruction of pagan cult objects 1Ki 15:11–13; 2Ki 23:4–6 pp 2Ch 34:3–4 *See also* 2Ki 23:12

The Kidron Valley in prophetic visions Eze 47:1–8; Joel 3:1–2 *See also* Zec 14:8

See also
4245 hills	7435 sacrifice, in OT
4254 mountains	9220 day of the LORD
4406 agriculture	9510 hell
5605 warfare	

4293

water

The colourless, odourless liquid that is essential for sustenance of life in human beings and animals. God is described as the spring of living water, being the source of life and salvation to those who come to him.

Water for drinking
For human beings 2Sa 23:15–16 pp 1Ch 11:17–18 *See also* Ge 21:14–19 *God provides water for Hagar and Ishmael;* Ex 15:22–27; 17:1–3; Nu 20:1–11; Dt 2:28; Jdg 4:19; 5:25; 1Sa 30:11–12; 1Ki 17:10 *Elijah asks for water at Zarephath for a drink of water;* 2Ki 6:22; 2Ch 18:25–26; Ne 9:20; Job 6:19; Isa 33:16; Da 1:8–16 *Daniel's resolve to live on vegetables and water;* Hos 2:5; Mt 10:42 pp Mk 9:41; Jn 4:7; 1Ti 5:23

For animals 2Ki 3:9 *See also* Ge 24:13–19; 29:1–10; Ex 2:15–16; 17:3; 2Ki 3:17; Ps 104:10–11; Isa 43:20; Lk 13:15

Water as a general descriptive term for liquid
Ex 23:25 *See also* 1Sa 25:11; 1Ki 13:6–22; 18:4; Job 22:7; Pr 25:21

Abstention from water during fasting
Dt 9:9 *See also* Ex 34:28; Dt 9:18; Ezr 10:6

Water for washing
For general hygiene Ge 18:4 *See also* Ge 24:32; 43:24; Lk 7:44; Jn 13:1–17

For ritual cleansing Lev 17:15 *See also* Ex 30:17–21; Lev 1:3–9; 16:20–24; Nu 17:9–21; Jn 2:6; Heb 10:22

Water for cooking
Ex 12:9–10 *See also* Eze 24:3–5

Rainwater
Jdg 5:4 *See also* Ge 7:11–12;

Job 5:10; 37:13; 38:25–28,37; Ps 77:17;
Ecc 11:3; Hos 6:3

Sources and stores of water
Wells Ge 26:19–20 *See also* Ge 21:19;
24:11; Isa 37:25; Jn 4:6

Springs Jas 3:11–12 *See also*
Jos 15:15–19 pp Jdg 1:11–15;
Rev 8:10–11; 14:7; 16:4

Cisterns Jer 2:13 *See also* Lev 11:36;
2Ki 18:31 pp Isa 36:16; Pr 5:15–16;
Jer 14:3; 38:6

Abundance of water as a sign of blessing
Dt 8:7 *See also* Nu 24:7; Dt 10:7;
Ps 1:1–3; Jer 17:7–8; Eze 17:5–6;
19:10–11

Baptism in water
Mt 3:11 pp Mk 1:8 pp Lk 3:16 *See also*
Mt 3:13–17 pp Mk 1:9–11
pp Lk 3:21–22 pp Jn 1:31–34;
Jn 1:26–27; 3:23; Ac 1:5; 8:36–39;
10:47; 11:16; 1Pe 3:20–22

Living water
Jer 17:13 *See also* Zec 14:8–9;
Jn 4:4–26; 7:37–39; Rev 7:13–17;
21:6–8; 22:1–2,17

Metaphorical references to water
As a symbol of affliction 2Sa 22:17;
Ps 69:1; Isa 30:20; 43:2

As a symbol of salvation Isa 12:3;
49:10; 55:1; Eze 36:25; Jn 7:38

As a symbol of life Jn 4:14; 7:37–39;
Rev 21:6; 22:17

Other metaphorical references SS 4:15;
Isa 30:20; 35:6; 44:12; Jer 9:1;
Eph 5:25–26; 2Pe 2:17

See also

3120 Holy Spirit, descriptions	4296 wells
4236 fountain	4844 rain
4260 rivers & streams	5580 thirst
4266 sea	7342 cleanliness
4278 spring of water	7416 purification
	7478 washing
	7903 baptism

4296

wells

Artificial openings to tap
underground water supplies. They
were very important for life in a
settled urban society and this is
reflected in their symbolical use in
Scripture.

The importance of wells in urban life
Ne 9:25 *See also* Dt 6:10–11

Women drew water for domestic use
Ge 24:11–20 *See also* 1Sa 9:11; Jn 4:7–9

Livestock were watered at wells
Ge 29:2–3 *See also* Ge 29:7–10;
Ex 2:15–17

Wells were sometimes a source of contention
Ge 21:25 *See also* Ge 26:12–22;
Nu 20:17; 21:22

Wells as landmarks
Ge 16:7 *Verse 14 refers to this spring as a
well. See also* Ge 16:14; 21:31
*"Beersheba" means either "well of seven"
or "well of the oath"*; Ge 26:20–22; Jn 4:6

Figurative use of wells
Associated with God and his goodness
Isa 12:3; Jer 17:13 *See also* Jer 2:13;
Jn 4:14; Rev 7:17

Associated with human love Pr 5:15

**In warnings against and judgment of
sin** Jer 6:7 *See also* Pr 23:27; Jer 51:36

See also

3290 Holy Spirit, life-giver	4278 spring of water
4221 cistern	4293 water
4236 fountain	5621 wheel
4260 rivers & streams	

4299

wilderness

Wilderness as a wild, uncultivated area of land, frequently interchangeable with "desert"
Jer 2:6 *See also* Jer 50:12

Good news for the wilderness
Isa 35:1–10 *See also* Isa 40:3–5; Mt 3:3
pp Mk 1:3 pp Lk 3:4

See also

2575 Christ, temptation	7206 community
4230 desert	7358 Feast of Tabernacles
5098 John the Baptist	7459 tabernacle, in OT
5101 Moses	7474 Tent of Meeting
5694 generation	

4300

Metals and minerals

4303

metals

Gold, silver, bronze, iron, copper, tin
and lead are all mentioned in
Scripture. Prized for their value, they
were used in a variety of ways.
Scripture uses as an image a metal
refiner's fire for the purification of
the lives of believers.

Gold
Job 23:10 *See also* Ex 25:10–22;
38:21–24; 1Ki 6:27–35; 7:48–50;
10:14–21; Ps 19:7–11; Rev 3:18; 17:4

Silver
Ps 12:6 *See also* Ge 37:26–28;
Ex 38:25–28; 2Ch 9:26–27; Ps 119:72;
Mt 27:3–10

Bronze
Ge 4:22 *See also* Ex 27:1–7; 38:29–31;
Nu 16:31–40; 2Ch 4:9–18

Iron
Dt 3:11 *See also* Dt 8:7–9; Jdg 4:2–3;
Job 40:15–18; Eze 27:19

Copper
Job 28:2 *See also* Mk 12:41–44
pp Lk 21:1–4

Tin
Eze 27:12 *See also* Eze 22:18

Lead
It was an exceptionally heavy metal
Ex 15:10 *See also* Zec 5:5–8

It was refined before use Jer 6:29 *See
also* Nu 31:21–23; Eze 22:18–20

Inscriptions were sometimes made on
lead Job 19:23–24

It was traded between nations
Eze 27:12

The value of metals
All metals were of value Jos 22:8 *See
also* 1Ch 18:10; 22:14; 29:1–7;
Rev 18:11–12

The relative value of metals Isa 60:17
See also 1Ki 10:21 pp 2Ch 9:20;
1Ki 14:25–28

Trade with metals
1Ki 10:22 pp 2Ch 9:21 *See also*
Ge 37:28; 1Ki 10:11,14–15
pp 2Ch 9:13–14; 1Ki 22:48;
Eze 27:13,22; Zep 1:11

Idols were often made from various metals
Lev 19:4 *See also* 1Ki 14:9; Ps 106:19;
Isa 48:5; Da 5:22–23; 11:8

The refining of metals as an image of purification
Isa 48:10; Mal 3:2 *See also* Ps 12:6;
Zec 13:9

See also

4306 minerals	4351 refining
4312 bronze	4363 silver
4321 copper	4372 tin
4333 gold	5587 trade
4336 iron	7416 purification
4345 metalworkers	8768 idolatry

4306

minerals

Material mined from the earth,
especially metal ores and other
substances of neither animal nor
vegetable origin.

Bitumen
Ge 11:1–4

Chalk
Isa 27:9

Crystal
Job 28:17; Rev 4:6

Flint
Eze 3:9 *See also* Job 28:9; Zec 7:12

Lime
Am 2:1 *See also* Isa 33:10–12

Marble
Est 1:6 *See also* 1Ch 29:2; SS 5:15;
Rev 18:11–12

Pitch
Ge 6:14 *See also* Ex 2:3; Isa 34:9

Salt
Lev 2:13 *See also* Dt 29:23; Job 39:5–6; Eze 47:6–11

Soda
Pr 25:20 *"soda" in this instance is probably sodium carbonate, which would react violently with vinegar. See also* Job 9:30–31; Jer 2:22

Sulphur
Ge 19:24 *See also* Dt 29:23; Lk 17:29; Rev 19:20

Tar
Ge 14:10 *See also* Ex 2:3

Precious stones
Eze 28:13 *See also* Ex 28:15–21; Job 28:5–6; Isa 54:11–12; Eze 27:16; Rev 21:18

Metals
Isa 60:17 *See also* Nu 31:21–23; Dt 8:7–9; Job 28:2; Ps 119:72; Eze 27:12

Stone
Pr 27:3 *See also* Jos 7:3–5; Job 6:12; 38:29–30; Jer 5:3

Sand
Mt 7:24–27

See also

4303 metals	4357 salt
4309 bitumen and tar	4360 sand
4327 flint	4366 stones
4342 jewels	4369 sulphur
4348 mining	

4309

bitumen and tar

Tar
Ge 14:10 *See also* Ex 2:1–3 *the infant Moses placed in a basket coated with tar*

Bitumen
Ge 11:1–4

See also

4306 minerals	4318 coal

4312

bronze

A metal highly prized for its strength and durability. It had a variety of uses in biblical times and was employed extensively in both the tabernacle and temple.

Bronze as a material used by craftsmen
Ge 4:22 *See also* Ex 31:1–6 pp Ex 35:30–34; 1Ki 7:13–14; 1Ch 22:15–16; 2Ch 2:7,13–14; 24:12

Characteristics of bronze
It was renowned for its strength
Jer 15:12 *See also* Lev 26:18–19; Dt 28:23; Job 6:12; 37:18; 40:18; 41:27; Isa 48:4; Jer 1:18; 15:20; Da 7:19; Mic 4:13

It was noted for its brilliance
Da 10:5–6 *See also* Eze 40:3; Rev 1:15; 2:18

The monetary value of bronze
It was an expensive metal
Rev 18:11–12 *See also* 1Ch 18:8–10; Ezr 8:26–27; Eze 27:13

It was less valuable than gold or silver
Isa 60:17 *See also* 1Ki 14:25–28 pp 2Ch 12:9–11

Offerings of bronze were made at various times
Ex 35:24 *See also* Ex 25:1–7 pp Ex 35:4–9; Ex 38:29–31; 1Ch 18:9–11; 22:14; 29:6–7

Bronze was used in the tabernacle
For the altar and its utensils 2Ch 1:5–6 *See also* Ex 27:1–6 pp Ex 38:1–6; Ex 35:16 pp Ex 39:39; Nu 4:13; 16:39–40

For the laver Ex 30:18 *See also* Ex 35:16; 38:8

For the tent and the framework of the tabernacle Ex 27:17–19 pp Ex 38:17–20 *See also* Ex 26:10–11,36–37; 27:9–11 pp Ex 38:9–11; Ex 36:18,37–38

Bronze was used extensively in the temple
2Ch 4:18 *See also* 1Ki 7:23–33,38–45 pp 2Ch 4:9–16; 1Ki 8:64; 2Ki 16:17; 25:13–17 pp Jer 52:17–23; 1Ch 18:8; 29:2; 2Ch 4:1

Other uses of bronze
For armour 1Sa 17:5–6 *See also* 1Sa 17:38

For weapons 2Sa 21:16 *See also* 1Sa 17:6; 2Sa 22:35 pp Ps 18:34

For shackles Jdg 16:21 *See also* 2Ki 25:7 pp Jer 39:7 pp Jer 52:11; 2Ch 33:11; 36:6; Da 4:15,23

For gates Ps 107:16 *See also* Dt 33:25; 1Ki 4:13; 1Ch 22:3; Isa 45:2

For the bronze snake Nu 21:9 *See also* 2Ki 18:4

For idols Da 5:4 *See also* Da 5:23; Rev 9:20

For mirrors Ex 38:8 *See also* Job 37:18

For cooking utensils Lev 6:28

For tools Ge 4:22

For musical instruments 1Ch 15:19

For statues Da 2:32,35,45

Bronze as booty in war
Jos 22:7–8 *See also* Nu 31:21–23; Jos 6:24; 2Sa 8:8 pp 1Ch 18:8

The metaphorical use of bronze
Da 2:39 *See also* Lev 26:19; Dt 28:23; Job 40:18; Jer 1:18,18; Zec 6:1

See also

4303 metals	5612 weapons
5209 armour	7452 snake, bronze
5212 arts and crafts	7459 tabernacle, in OT
5260 coinage	
5268 cooking	7467 temple, Solomon's
5421 musical instruments	8768 idolatry
5583 tools	

4315

clay

Clay was a basic building material in biblical times and clay pottery was widely used.

Clay pottery
Moulded by potters Jer 18:3–4 *See also* Isa 29:16; 41:25; 45:9

Used to make pots Lev 6:28 *See also* Lev 11:33; 14:5,50; 15:12; La 4:2

Used to make jars Jer 19:1–3 *See also* Nu 5:17; Jer 32:14; 2Co 4:7

Other uses of clay
To make idols Da 2:31–35 *See also* Da 2:41–45

To make moulds 1Ki 7:46 pp 2Ch 4:17

To make bricks Na 3:14 *See also* Jer 43:9

In plastering Lev 14:42

To make furnaces Ps 12:6

To seal documents Job 38:14

Clay tablets were used for writing on Eze 4:1

Clay was a relatively weak material
Job 13:12 *See also* Job 4:18–19

Clay was a very common material
Job 27:16 *See also* 2Ti 2:20

God and his people compared to a potter and the clay
Isa 64:8 *See also* Job 10:9; 33:6; Jer 18:6; Ro 9:19–21

See also

5222 baking	5574 tablet
5239 bricks	5591 treasure
5445 potters & pottery	8768 idolatry

4318

coal

Carbonised vegetable material of wood, woody matter or charcoal, used for burning.

Coal used to burn incense
Lev 16:12–13 *See also* Nu 16:16–18,35–38

Coal burned in the Most Holy Place
Isa 6:4–7

Coal used for baking and cooking
1Ki 19:6 *See also* Isa 44:19; Eze 24:9–11; Jn 21:9

Coal used for domestic fires
Isa 47:14 *See also* Isa 30:12–14

Coal used by blacksmiths
Isa 44:12 *See also* Isa 54:16

Burning coal associated with divine punishment
Ps 11:6 *See also* Ps 120:3–4; 140:9–10

Burning coal in descriptions of God
In poetic passages 2Sa 22:8–9 pp Ps 18:7–8

4321

In visions Eze 1:4–14 *See also*
Eze 10:1–2

Metaphorical use of coal
2Sa 14:7 *See also* Pr 6:27–29; 25:21–22;
Ro 12:17–21

See also

4306 minerals	5268 cooking
4345 metalworkers	5482 punishment
4826 fire	7308 Atonement,
4829 heat	Day of
4833 light	7386 incense
5222 baking	

4321

copper

The mining of copper
Dt 8:7–9 *See also* Job 28:2–10

The smelting of copper
Eze 22:20–21 *See also* Eze 22:18; 24:11

Coins made of copper
Mt 10:9 *See also* Mk 12:41–42
pp Lk 21:1–2 *Coins of various
denominations were made of copper in late
OT and in NT times.*

See also

4303 metals	4345 metalworkers
4306 minerals	4348 mining
4312 bronze	4351 refining
4333 gold	4363 silver
4336 iron	5260 coinage

4324

dross

Impurities removed from molten
metal during refining. In a spiritual
sense, wicked people whom God
removes in judgment, and also
impurities in believers which are
removed by discipline and trials.

God removes the wicked like dross
Ps 119:119 *See also* Isa 30:28;
Jer 6:28–30; Eze 22:19–22

Dross as a metaphor for impurity in God's people
Eze 22:18 *See also* Isa 1:21–23;
Eze 24:11–13; 36:25; Am 9:8–10;
Jas 1:21

God purges the dross from his people
Isa 1:25–26 *See also* Pr 17:3; 25:4;
Da 12:10; Mal 3:2–3; 2Co 7:1; 1Pe 1:7

By the blood of Jesus Christ Zec 13:1;
Heb 9:14; 1Jn 1:7

By the work of the Holy Spirit
Eze 36:25–27; Mt 3:11–12
pp Lk 3:16–17

By testing and affliction Ps 66:10–12;
Isa 48:10; Jer 9:7; Zec 13:9

See also

3233 Holy Spirit &	5979 waste
sanctification	6744 sanctification
4303 metals	7416 purification
4345 metalworkers	8324 purity
4351 refining	8832 testing
5321 furnace	9210 judgment,
5593 trial	God's

4327

flint

Flint tools
Jos 5:2–3 *See also* Ex 4:25; Jer 17:1

Flinty rock
Job 28:9 *See also* Dt 32:13–14

Metaphorical use of flint
Eze 3:9 *See also* Isa 5:28; 50:7; Zec 7:12

See also

4306 minerals	4508 sickle
4354 rock	5583 tools

4330

glass

A substance remarkable for its
transparency. Two phenomena seen
by John in his vision in the book of
Revelation are likened to glass.

The sea of glass
Rev 15:2 *See also* Rev 4:2–6

The gold in the new Jerusalem likened to glass
Rev 21:21 *See also* Rev 21:15–18

See also

4312 bronze	5411 mirror

4333

gold

The most valuable of all metals, gold
was indicative of wealth and
prosperity in biblical times. It had a
wide variety of uses and was
employed extensively in both the
tabernacle and the temple.

Gold was of great value
Isa 60:17 *See also* Jos 6:18–19,24;
1Ki 20:1–6; 2Ki 7:8; 14:14; 2Ch 21:3;
Job 28:12–19 *Wisdom cannot be bought
with gold*; Ps 45:9,13; 72:15; 105:37;
Pr 20:15; Eze 28:13; Da 11:8,38;
Joel 3:4–5; 2Ti 2:20; Rev 21:18,21 *The
streets of the new Jerusalem are to be paved
with gold.*

Gold was indicative of wealth
Ge 13:2 *See also* Ge 24:35; Dt 8:12–14;
17:17; Jos 22:8 *Joshua sends the eastern
tribes home*; 2Ki 20:13 pp Isa 39:2;
2Ch 1:15; 32:27; Job 3:15; 31:24–28;
Ecc 2:8; Isa 2:7; Eze 16:13 *The
adornments of unfaithful Jerusalem*;
Eze 28:4; Zep 1:18; Zec 9:3; 14:14;
Jas 2:2; Rev 18:16

Gold was relatively rare
Isa 13:12

Gold was mined from the earth
Job 28:5–6 *See also* Ge 2:11–12

Gold was refined by fire
Rev 3:18 *See also* Nu 31:21–23;
Job 28:1; Pr 17:3; 27:21; Zec 13:9;
Mal 3:3; 1Pe 1:7

Gold was obtained through trade
1Ki 10:22 pp 2Ch 9:21 *See also*
1Ki 9:26–28 pp 2Ch 8:17–18; 1Ki 10:11

pp 2Ch 9:9; 1Ki 22:48; Isa 60:6; Jer 10:9;
Eze 27:22; Rev 18:11–13

Gold was worked by goldsmiths
Isa 46:6 *See also* 1Ch 29:4–5;
2Ch 2:7,13–14; Jer 10:9

Gold was presented as offerings to God
Ex 35:22 *See also* Ex 25:1–7; 35:5;
Nu 7:84–86; 31:50–54; 2Sa 8:11;
Ezr 1:1–11; 2:69; 7:12–18; 8:24–34;
Ne 7:70–72

Gold was given to rulers as tribute and bribes
1Ki 10:14–15 pp 2Ch 9:13–14 *See also*
1Ki 10:24–25 pp 2Ch 9:23–24;
2Ki 12:18; 16:7–9; 18:13–16; 23:33–35
pp 2Ch 36:3; 2Ch 16:2–3

Gold was given as gifts
Job 42:11 *See also* Ge 24:53; 2Sa 8:9–10
pp 1Ch 18:9–10; 1Ki 10:10 pp 2Ch 9:9;
2Ki 5:5; Mt 2:11

The use of gold in the tabernacle
Ex 38:21–24 *See also*
Ex 25:11–13,17–18 *the atonement cover
and cherubim*; Ex 25:28–29,31,36,38;
26:6,29,32,37; 30:1–5 *the altar*;
Ex 39:37–38; 40:5; Lev 24:4; Nu 8:4

The use of gold in priestly vestments
Ex 28:4–5 *See also*
Ex 28:11–15,22–27,33–38;
39:15–20,25–26,30–31

The use of gold in the temple
1Ch 22:14 *See also* 1Ki 6:28,30,32,35;
7:48–51; 2Ki 18:16; 1Ch 28:14–18;
29:1–7; 2Ch 3:4–10; 4:7–8,19–22

Gold symbols of office
Crown 2Sa 12:30 pp 1Ch 20:2 *See also*
Est 8:15; Ps 21:1–3; Zec 6:11; Rev 4:4;
14:14

Throne 1Ki 10:18–20 pp 2Ch 9:17–19

Sceptre Est 4:11 *See also* Est 5:2; 8:4

Chain Da 5:7 *See also* Ge 41:42;
Da 5:16,29

Other uses of gold
Jewellery Ex 35:22 *See also*
Ge 24:53,22; Ex 3:22; 11:2; 12:35;
32:2,24 *used to make the golden calf*;
Nu 31:50; Jdg 8:24–26 *used to make
Gideon's ephod*; 2Sa 1:24; Pr 11:22;
25:11; SS 1:11; Jer 4:30; Da 10:5; 1Pe 3:3

Idols Ex 20:23 *See also* Ex 32:31;
Dt 7:25; 29:17; Ps 115:4; 135:15;
Isa 2:20; 30:22; 31:7; 40:19; 46:6;
Jer 10:3–5; Eze 16:17; Da 3:1
Nebuchadnezzar's image of gold;
Da 3:4–7,14; 5:4,23; Hos 8:4; Hab 2:19;
Ac 17:29; Rev 9:20

Currency Mt 10:5–10 *See also* Nu 22:18;
24:13; 2Sa 21:4; 1Ch 21:25; Ps 119:72;
Eze 7:19; Da 11:43; Ac 3:6; 20:33;
1Pe 1:18

Models 1Sa 6:4 *See also*
1Sa 6:8,11,15,17–18

Shields 1Ki 10:16–17 pp 2Ch 9:15–16
See also 2Sa 8:7; 1Ki 14:26 pp 2Ch 12:9

Goblets 1Ki 10:21 pp 2Ch 9:20 *See also*
Est 1:7; Jer 51:7; Da 5:2–3,23; Rev 17:4

Couches Est 1:6

Metaphorical and proverbial use of gold

Job 22:23–25 *See also* Job 23:8–10; Ps 19:9–10; 68:13; Pr 3:13–14; 16:16; 22:1; 25:11; SS 5:10–15; La 4:1–2; Da 2:37–38

See also

4303 metals	5437 palaces
4306 minerals	5615 weights
4345 metalworkers	7306 ark of the
4351 refining	covenant
4363 silver	7459 tabernacle, in
5260 coinage	OT
5272 craftsmen	8809 riches

4336

iron

Iron ore is mined from the earth

Job 28:2 *See also* Dt 8:7–9

Iron ore is refined by smelting in a furnace

Such imagery is often used of God's testing of his people Eze 22:20 *See also* Nu 31:21–23; Jer 6:27–29; Eze 22:18

Egypt is described as an iron-smelting furnace Dt 4:20 *See also* 1Ki 8:51; Jer 11:4

Iron was a valuable metal

Rev 18:11–12 *See also* Jos 22:6–8; Isa 60:17; Eze 27:12,19

Iron was prized for its great strength

Da 2:40–43 *See also* Lev 26:19; Dt 28:23
The great strength of certain animals is conveyed through the imagery of iron: Job 40:15–18; 41:27
Iron is symbolic of the strength of the LORD's rule: Ps 2:9; Rev 2:27; 19:15
Isa 48:4; Jer 1:18; 15:12; Da 2:31–35
Daniel's dream of four beasts: Da 7:7,19
Mic 4:13

Iron objects were taken as booty in war

Jos 6:24 *See also* Jos 6:15–19; 22:8

Iron was used in the construction of the temple

1Ch 29:2 *See also* 1Ch 22:14–16; 29:7; 2Ch 2:7,13–14; 24:12

Other uses of iron

For tools Ge 4:22 *See also* Dt 27:5; Jos 8:30–31; 2Sa 12:31 pp 1Ch 20:3; 2Sa 23:7; 1Ki 6:7; 2Ki 6:5–6; Job 19:23–24; Jer 17:1; Am 1:3; 1Ti 4:2

For chains, shackles and fetters Ps 105:18 *See also* Ps 107:10; 149:6–9; Da 4:15,23; Mk 5:1–4

For chariots Jdg 1:19 *See also* Jos 17:15–18; Jdg 4:2–3,12–13

For gates and gate fittings Ac 12:10 *See also* Dt 33:25; 1Ch 22:3; Ps 107:15–16; Isa 45:2

For weapons and armour 1Sa 17:7 *See also* Nu 35:16; Job 20:24; Rev 9:9

For idols Da 5:4 *See also* Da 5:23

For yokes Dt 28:48 *See also* Jer 28:13–14

For horns 1Ki 22:11 pp 2Ch 18:10

For cooking utensils Eze 4:3

For a bed Dt 3:11

See also

4303 metals	5251 chains
4345 metalworkers	5252 chariots
4348 mining	5323 gate
4351 refining	5461 prisoners
4696 yoke	5583 tools
5209 armour	5612 weapons

4339

ivory

Ivory, a semiprecious substance derived from elephant tusks, was procured through trade

1Ki 10:22 pp 2Ch 9:21 *See also* Eze 27:15; Rev 18:11–13

Articles inlaid with ivory were a sign of wealth

1Ki 10:18 pp 2Ch 9:17 *See also* 1Ki 22:39; Ps 45:8; Eze 27:6; Am 3:15; 6:4

The metaphorical use of ivory

SS 5:14 *See also* SS 7:4

See also

4342 jewels	5574 tablet
5211 art	5587 trade
5437 palaces	

4342

jewels

Precious stones, prized for their beauty and value are mentioned frequently in Scripture.

The breastpiece of the high priest was set with twelve jewels

Ex 28:15–21 pp Ex 39:8–14

The king of Tyre is depicted as having been adorned with jewels

Eze 28:11–13

The new Jerusalem is described as being constructed of jewels

Rev 21:18–21

Jewels in royal crowns

2Sa 12:30 pp 1Ch 20:2 *See also* Zec 9:16

Jewels acquired through trade

Eze 27:22 *See also* 1Ki 10:2 pp 2Ch 9:1; 1Ki 10:10–11 pp 2Ch 9:9–10; Rev 18:11–12

Wisdom is said to be more precious than jewels

Pr 8:10–11 *See also* Job 28:12–19; Pr 3:13–15; 20:15

Jewels mentioned elsewhere in Scripture

Carnelian Rev 4:3 *See also* Rev 21:20

Chrysolite Eze 10:9 *See also* SS 5:14; Eze 1:16; Da 10:6

Coral Eze 27:16

Emeralds Rev 4:3

Jasper Rev 4:3

Onyx Ex 28:9–14 pp Ex 39:6–7 *See also* Ge 2:10–12; Ex 25:1–7 pp Ex 35:4–9; Ex 35:27; 1Ch 29:2

Pearls Mt 7:6 *See also* Mt 13:45–46; 1Ti 2:9–10; Rev 17:4; 18:11–12,15–17

Rubies Pr 31:10 *See also* Isa 54:11–12; La 4:7; Eze 27:16

Sapphires Isa 54:11 *See also* Ex 24:9–10; Job 28:5–6; SS 5:14; La 4:7; Eze 1:26; 10:1

Turquoise Eze 27:16 *See also* 1Ch 29:2; Isa 54:11

See also

4306 minerals	5915 ornaments
4333 gold	7320 breastpiece
4363 silver	8361 wisdom
4366 stones	

4345

metalworkers

The work of goldsmiths

Making idols Isa 40:19 *See also* Isa 41:6–7; 46:6; Jer 10:8–10,14–15; 51:17–18

Rebuilding the wall of Jerusalem Ne 3:31–32 *See also* Ne 3:8

The work of silversmiths

Making idols Jdg 17:4 *See also* Ac 19:23–41

Working with refined silver Pr 25:4

The work of blacksmiths

Making idols Isa 44:9–12

Manufacturing weapons Isa 54:16–17 *See also* 1Sa 13:19

The work of other metalworkers and craftsmen

Making idols Dt 27:15 *See also* Hos 8:4–6; 2Ti 4:14–15

The construction of the tabernacle Ex 31:1–6; 35:30–36:2; 39:2–3

The construction of the temple 1Ch 22:14–16; 29:1–5; 2Ch 2:7,13–14

See also

4303 metals	4363 silver
4312 bronze	4372 tin
4321 copper	5212 arts and crafts
4333 gold	5272 craftsmen
4336 iron	8768 idolatry
4351 refining	

4348

mining

Metal ores and precious stones mined from the earth

Job 28:1–11 *See also* Dt 8:7–9; 1Ki 7:13–50

See also

4303 metals	4336 iron
4306 minerals	4342 jewels
4312 bronze	4345 metalworkers
4318 coal	4351 refining
4321 copper	4363 silver
4333 gold	4372 tin

4351

refining

The process of heating metals to high temperatures in order to burn away impurities. It is often used in a metaphorical sense to depict God refining his people to get rid of impurities in their faith.

Precious metals produced by refining
Ps 12:6 *See also* 1Ch 28:14–18; 29:3–5; Job 28:1–2; 1Pe 1:7; Rev 3:18

God refines his people
Refining involves suffering
Ps 66:10–12 *See also* Isa 48:9–11; Jer 9:7–9

Refining for purging and purification
Zec 13:8–9 *See also* Jer 6:27–30; Da 11:35; 12:10; Mal 3:2–4

See also

4303 metals	4363 silver
4324 dross	4826 fire
4333 gold	7416 purification
4345 metalworkers	8325 purity
4348 mining	8832 testing

4354

rock

A symbol of strength and permanence and a place where people in danger often took refuge. God is depicted as the Rock of Israel, being the strength, security and deliverance for his people.

Rock as a symbol of strength, stability and permanence
Zec 12:3 *See also* Job 18:4; 19:23–24; 41:24; Na 1:6

Rocks as places of refuge and shelter
1Sa 13:6; 23:25 *David's hiding-place from Saul;* Job 24:8; 30:6; Ps 27:5; 40:2; SS 2:14; Isa 2:10,19,21; 32:2; Jer 4:29; 16:16; 48:28; 49:16 pp Ob 3; Rev 6:15–16

God as a rock
Symbolising his strength and faithfulness Isa 26:4 *See also*
Ge 49:23–25; Dt 32:3–4; 1Sa 2:2; 2Sa 23:2–4; Ps 28:1; 42:9; 62:6; 92:14–15; Isa 44:8; Hab 1:12

Symbolising safety and refuge in him
Ps 71:3 *See also* Dt 32:30; 2Sa 22:31–32 pp Ps 18:30–31; Ps 31:2–3; 61:1–3; 62:7; 94:22; 144:1–2; Isa 17:10

Associated with salvation and deliverance Dt 32:15–18; 2Sa 22:47 pp Ps 18:46; Ps 19:14; 62:2; 78:35; 89:26; 95:1

Associated with judgment and punishment Isa 8:13–15; Ro 9:33; 1Pe 2:8

Other gods as rocks
Dt 32:31 *See also* Dt 32:36–38

Water from the rock
Nu 20:8 *See also* Ex 17:6; Nu 20:10–13; Dt 8:15; Ne 9:15; Ps 78:15–16,20; 105:41; Isa 48:21; 1Co 10:3–4

Rocks as foundations
Mt 7:24–25 pp Lk 6:47–48 *See also* Mt 16:13–20

Rocks in mining, quarrying and building
Dt 8:9; Job 28:5–6,9–10; Isa 51:1–2; Jer 23:29; 51:26; Da 2:34–35,45

Rocks used as altars
Jdg 6:20–21; 13:19–20

Rock and burial places
Rocks erected over graves Jos 7:26; 8:29; 2Sa 18:17

Tombs quarried in rock Lk 23:53 pp Mt 27:59–60 pp Mk 15:46 *See also* Isa 22:16

Rocks used to seal caves and tombs
Jos 10:17–18,27; Mt 27:59–60 pp Mk 15:46; Mt 27:66; 28:2; Mk 16:2–4 pp Lk 24:2 pp Jn 20:1

Rocky soil in the parable of the sower
Mt 13:20–21 pp Mk 4:16–17 pp Lk 8:13 *See also* Mt 13:5 pp Mk 4:5 pp Lk 8:6

Rocks in place-names
Jdg 7:25; 15:8–13; 20:45–47; 21:13; 2Sa 20:8; 1Ch 11:15

See also

1240 God, the Rock	5240 building
4218 cave	5317 foundation
4327 flint	5490 refuge
4348 mining	5511 safety
4366 stones	5953 stability
5113 Peter, disciple	9050 tombs

4357

salt

A basic commodity, used for seasoning and preserving food in biblical times.

The importance of salt in the sacrificial system
Lev 2:13 *See also* Ex 30:34–35 *The addition of salt to incense was probably to make it burn more easily and quickly;* Ezr 6:6–10; 7:21–23; Eze 43:22–24

The covenant of salt
Nu 18:17–19 *See also* Lev 2:13; 2Ch 13:4–5

Believers as the salt of the earth
Mt 5:13 *This teaching reflects the importance of salt as a preservative and seasoning. See also* Mk 9:50; Lk 14:34–35

Salt as a symbol of desolation
Zep 2:9 *See also* Dt 29:23–25; Job 39:5–6; Ps 107:33–34; Jer 17:5–8

Salt sown on arable land to render it worthless
Jer 48:8–9 *See also* Jdg 9:42–45

Lot's wife turned into a pillar of salt
Ge 19:23–26

The Dead Sea an important source of salt
Eze 47:11

Salt water
Jas 3:9–12 *See also* Eze 47:7–9

Salt herbs
Job 30:4

Practical uses of salt
Salt used as a seasoning Job 6:6–7

Salt rubbed on newborn infants
Eze 16:4

Symbolic use of salt
2Ki 2:19–22

Figurative use of salt
Mk 9:49 *See also* Ezr 4:14 *The literal translation of the Hebrew phrase used here is "... we eat the salt of the palace ...";* Col 4:6

Salt in place-names
The Dead Sea Jos 12:3 *The Dead Sea was known as "the Salt Sea" or "the Sea of the Arabah" in biblical times. See also* Ge 14:3; Nu 34:3–4,10–12; Dt 3:16–17; Jos 3:15–16; 15:2–3,5–6; 18:19

The Valley of Salt 2Sa 8:13 *See also* 2Ki 14:7 pp 2Ch 25:11; 1Ch 18:12

The City of Salt Jos 15:62

See also

1350 covenant with Israel's priests	5655 birth
4293 water	6130 corruption
4306 minerals	7322 burnt offering
4466 herbs and spices	7368 grain offering
5546 speech	7386 incense
	7435 sacrifice, in OT

4360

sand

A fine granular substance formed by the erosion of rocks, and found especially in the deserts and by the sea. It is often used as a symbol of innumerability and occasionally as a symbol of instability.

Sand as a fine granular substance
In the desert Ex 2:12 *See also* Job 39:13–15; Isa 35:6–7

At the sea Jer 5:22 *See also* Dt 33:18–19; Ac 27:39

Sand-bars Ac 27:41 *See also* Ac 27:17

The weight of sand Job 6:2–3 *See also* Pr 27:3

Sand representing innumerability
God promised that Israel would be as innumerable as sand Ge 22:15–18 *See also* Ge 32:9–12; 1Ki 4:20; Isa 10:20–22; 48:17–19; Jer 33:19–22; Hos 1:8–10; Ro 9:22–27; Heb 11:11–12

Armies described as being as innumerable as sand 1Sa 13:5 *See also* Jos 11:1–5; Jdg 7:12; 2Sa 17:11; Rev 20:7–8

Other comparisons with the innumerability of sand Ge 41:49 *See also* 1Ki 4:29; Job 29:18; Ps 78:27–29; 139:17–18; Jer 15:8; Hab 1:8–9

The instability and impermanence of sand
Mt 7:24–27 pp Lk 6:46–49

See also

4281 stars	4354 rock
4306 minerals	5891 instability

silver

A precious metal often surpassed in value only by gold. It had a variety of uses and by NT times was common in coinage.

Silver mined
Job 28:1–4

Silver acquired through trade
1Ki 10:22 pp 2Ch 9:20 See also Jer 10:9; Eze 27:12; Rev 18:11–12

Silver refined
Ps 66:10 See also Pr 17:3; 27:21; Isa 48:10; Eze 22:20–22; Zec 13:9; Mal 3:3

Silver worked by silversmiths
Pr 25:4 See also 2Ch 2:7,13–14; Ac 19:24

Possession of silver a sign of wealth
Ge 13:2 See also Ge 24:35; Nu 22:18; Dt 8:13; 17:17; Jos 22:8; 2Ch 32:27 Hezekiah's riches; Job 3:13–15; 27:16; Ps 105:37; Ecc 2:8; Isa 2:7; 60:17; Eze 16:13 the adornments of unfaithful Jerusalem; Eze 28:4; Da 11:43; Hos 2:8; Zec 9:3; 14:14

Silver given as offerings to God
Ex 25:1–3 See also Ex 35:5,24; Nu 7:84–85; 2Sa 8:11 pp 1Ch 18:11; 1Ch 29:7; Ezr 1:1–11; 2:68–69; 7:13–16; 8:24–30; Ne 7:71–72

Silver in the tabernacle
Ex 38:17 See also Ex 26:18–25 pp Ex 36:23–30; Ex 26:31–32 pp Ex 36:35–36; Ex 27:9–11 pp Ex 38:9–12; Ex 27:17; 38:18–19,25–28; Nu 10:2

Silver in the temple
1Ch 22:14 See also 1Ki 7:51 pp 2Ch 5:1; 1Ki 15:15 pp 2Ch 15:18; 2Ki 25:15 pp Jer 52:19; 1Ch 28:14–17; 29:2–5; 2Ch 24:14; Da 5:2

Silver abundant in Jerusalem in Solomon's time
1Ki 10:27 pp 2Ch 1:15 pp 2Ch 9:27 See also 1Ki 10:21 pp 2Ch 9:20

Silver as currency
Ge 37:28 See also Ge 20:16; 23:15–16; 33:19; 42:35; Ex 21:32; 38:25; Lev 5:15; 27:6,16; Nu 3:50; 18:16 the redemption of firstborn males; Dt 2:6,28; 14:22–26; 22:19,28–29; Jos 24:32; Jdg 9:4; 16:5 The rulers of the Philistines offer to pay Delilah for the secret of Samson's great strength; Jdg 17:10; 1Sa 9:8; 2Sa 18:11; 24:24 David buys Araunah's threshing-floor and oxen; 1Ki 10:29 pp 2Ch 1:17; 1Ki 16:24; 20:39; 2Ki 6:25; 1Ch 19:6; 2Ch 25:6; Ezr 7:21–22; Ne 5:15; Est 3:9 Haman promises to pay those who destroy the Jews; Job 42:11; Isa 7:23; Jer 32:9–10,44; Hos 3:1–2; Am 2:6; 8:5–6; Zep 1:11; Zec 11:12–13; Mt 10:9; 26:15; 27:3–10 Judas returns the thirty silver coins; Lk 10:35; Ac 3:6

Silver as tribute
2Ki 23:33–35 pp 2Ch 36:3 See also 1Ki 15:18–19 pp 2Ch 16:2–3; 2Ki 16:8; 18:14–15; 2Ch 9:13–14,23–24; 17:11; 27:5

Silver as plunder
Jdg 5:19 See also Ex 3:22; Nu 31:21–23; Jos 6:18–19,24; 7:21; 2Ki 14:14 pp 2Ch 25:24; Eze 38:13; Na 2:9

Silver idols or statues
Ex 20:23 See also Dt 7:25; 29:17; Jdg 17:1–4; Ps 115:4; Isa 2:20; 30:22; 31:7; 40:19; 46:6; Jer 10:3–4,8–9; Da 2:32 the statue in Nebuchadnezzar's dream; Da 5:4,23; Hos 8:4; 13:2; Hab 2:19; Ac 17:29; 19:24; Rev 9:20

Silver jewellery
Ge 24:53 See also SS 1:11; Eze 16:17

Silver referred to metaphorically
Job 22:23–25 See also Ps 12:6; 68:13; 119:72; Pr 2:1–5; 3:13–14; 8:10,19; 10:20; 16:16; 22:1 Esteem is better than silver or gold; Pr 25:11; Ecc 12:6; Isa 1:22

See also

4303 metals	5412 money
4333 gold	5594 tribute
4348 mining	5615 weights
4351 refining	5915 ornaments
5260 coinage	7402 offerings
5272 craftsmen	8768 idolatry

stones

Pieces of rock, used extensively for building.

Stones used in building
The temple in Jerusalem 1Ki 5:17–18 See also 1Ki 6:14–18,36; 7:9–12 King David's preparations for the building of the temple: 1Ch 22:2,14; 29:2 2Ki 22:3–7 pp 2Ch 34:8–11 repairing the temple; Ezr 6:1–4 rebuilding the temple after the exile; Mt 24:1–2 pp Mk 13:1–2 pp Lk 21:5–6 Jesus Christ prophesies the temple's destruction.

Other references to building with stone
Ge 11:1–3; Lev 14:39–45; 2Ch 16:6; Ne 4:1–3; Isa 9:10; Am 5:11

Boundary stones
Dt 19:14 See also Dt 27:17; Job 24:2; Pr 22:28; 23:10–11; Hos 5:10

Stones covering openings
Wells Ge 29:1–10

The lions' den Da 6:16–17

Tombs Mk 15:42–46 pp Mt 27:57–60 See also Mt 27:62–28:4 pp Mk 16:1–5 pp Lk 24:1–3; Jn 11:38–44; 20:1

Stone jars
Ex 7:19 See also Jn 2:1–10

Stones as weapons
Jdg 20:16 See also Nu 35:17; 1Sa 17:38–50; 1Ch 12:2; 2Ch 26:15

Stones in religious use
Stone altars Ex 20:24–26 See also Dt 27:1–8; Jos 8:30–32; 1Ki 18:30–38

Memorial stones 1Sa 7:12 See also Ge 28:10–22; 31:43–53; 35:14–15; Ex 24:3–4; Dt 27:1–8; Jos 4:1–24; 24:26–27

Ten Commandments written on stone
Ex 31:18 See also Ex 24:12; 34:1–4; Dt 4:13; 5:22; 9:9–11; 10:1–3; 1Ki 8:9; Heb 9:3–4

Sacred stones 1Ki 14:22–23
Commands to destroy idolatrous stones in Canaan: Ex 23:24; 34:13; Dt 7:5; 12:3; 16:22
2Ki 3:2; 10:26–27; 17:10; 18:4; 23:14; 2Ch 31:1; Isa 27:9; Hos 3:4; 10:1–2; Mic 5:13

Stone idols Hab 2:19 See also Dt 4:28; 28:36,64; 29:17; 2Ki 19:18 pp Isa 37:19; Ac 17:29; Rev 9:20

Stonecutters and stonemasons
1Ki 5:15 pp 2Ch 2:2 See also 2Sa 5:11; 2Ki 12:11–12; 1Ch 22:2,15; 2Ch 2:18

Death by stoning
Lev 24:10–16 See also Ex 19:12–13; 21:28–32; Lev 20:2,27; Nu 15:32–36; Dt 13:6–11; 17:2–5; 21:18–21; Jos 7:25; 1Ki 12:18 pp 2Ch 10:18; 1Ki 21:1–13
Stoning the prophets: Mt 21:33–35; 23:37 pp Lk 13:34
Stoning of Stephen and Paul: Ac 7:54–60; 14:19; 2Co 11:25

Jesus Christ described as a stone
1Pe 2:4–8 See also Ps 118:22; Isa 8:14; 28:16; Mt 21:42–44 pp Mk 12:10–11 pp Lk 20:17–18; Ac 4:8–12; Ro 9:33

Believers described as living stones
1Pe 2:5

Metaphorical references to stones
Eze 36:26 See also Ex 15:5,15–16; 1Ki 10:27 pp 2Ch 1:15 pp 2Ch 9:27; Ne 9:11; Job 6:12; 38:29–30; Eze 3:9; 11:19

See also

4306 minerals	5403 masons
4354 rock	5557 stoning
4482 millstones	5583 tools
5235 boundary	5612 weapons
5240 building	7302 altar
5269 cornerstone	9050 tombs

sulphur

A yellow, crystalline substance, also known as brimstone, which ignites and burns readily. It is invariably associated with divine punishment in Scripture.

Burning sulphur causes desolation
Dt 29:23 See also Job 18:12–17

Divine punishment by means of burning sulphur
Ps 11:5–6 See also Isa 30:31–33; 34:8–10; Eze 38:21–23; Rev 9:13–19; 14:9–11

Sodom and Gomorrah destroyed by burning sulphur
Ge 19:24–25 See also Lk 17:28–29

The lake of burning sulphur
Rev 21:8 *See also* Rev 19:19–21;
20:7–10

See also
4275 Sodom and   5482 punishment
     Gomorrah   9511 hell, place of
4306 minerals   punishment
4826 fire

4372

tin

Tin smelted in furnaces
Eze 22:20 *See also* Nu 31:21–23;
Eze 22:18

Tin traded by merchants
Eze 27:12

See also
4303 metals   5321 furnace
4306 minerals   5407 merchants
4345 metalworkers   5587 trade
4351 refining

4400

Vegetation and food

4402

plants

Plants are an important aspect of
God's creation, and a major source of
food and materials. Scripture refers
to many plants, with their various
uses.

Plants as a source of food
Ge 1:29–30 *See also* Ge 1:11–12;
3:17–19; 9:3; Ps 104:14

**Growth of plants dependent upon
soil, sun and irrigation**
Dt 32:2 *See also* Ge 2:4–5; 2Ki 19:26
pp Isa 37:27; Job 8:16–19; Isa 61:11;
Zec 10:1; Mt 13:3–8 pp Mk 4:3–8
pp Lk 8:5–8; Jas 1:11

Individual plants
Aloes Nu 24:5–6 *See also* Ps 45:8;
Pr 7:17; SS 4:13–14

Calamus Jer 6:20 *See also* SS 4:12–14;
Isa 43:24; Eze 27:19

Crocus Isa 35:1–2

Hyssop 1Ki 4:33 *See also* Ex 12:22;
Ps 51:7; Jn 19:29

Lily Lk 12:27 pp Mt 6:28–29 *See also*
SS 2:1–2; Hos 14:5

Lotus Job 40:21–22

Mandrake SS 7:13 *See also* Ge 30:14–16

Mustard Mt 13:31–32 pp Mk 4:30–32
pp Lk 13:18–19

Myrtle Isa 55:13 *See also* Isa 41:18–20;
Zec 1:8–10

Reed Ex 2:3 *See also* Job 8:11;
Isa 19:6–7

Rose SS 2:1

Rush Isa 19:6–7

See also
4017 life, animal &   4494 papyrus
     plant   4502 reed
4444 flax   4504 roots
4466 herbs and   4534 vine
     spices   4540 weeds
4470 hyssop   8257 fruitfulness,
4472 lily   natural
4484 mustard seed

4404

food

Scripture contains references to
varied foodstuffs, which comprised
the diet of the people of the Near
East in biblical times.

**God made provision for food in
creation**
Ge 1:29–30

Flour
Flour the main ingredient in bread
Ge 18:6 *See also* Ex 29:2; Jdg 6:19;
1Sa 28:24; Mt 13:33 pp Lk 13:21

Flour figured largely in the staple diet
1Ki 17:12–16 *See also* 2Sa 17:27–29;
1Ki 4:22–23; 2Ki 4:41; 7:1,16;
1Ch 12:40

**Fine flour more refined and more
expensive than the common variety**
Eze 16:13 *See also* Eze 16:19;
Rev 18:11–13

Flour in grain offerings Lev 2:1–10 *See
also* Lev 6:14–23; 14:8–11;
Nu 5:11–15; 6:13–15; 15:1–4; 28:9;
29:7–11; 1Ch 23:29; Eze 46:14

Flour in other offerings Lev 5:11 *See
also* Ex 29:1–3,22–25; Lev 7:12;
8:25–28; 23:15–17

Honey
Honey a sweet delicacy Ge 43:11 *See
also* Ex 16:31; Dt 32:13; Jdg 14:8–9;
1Sa 14:25–26; 2Sa 17:27–29;
1Ki 14:1–3; 2Ki 18:31–32
*Honey's sweetness and the sweetness of
God's law:* Ps 19:10; 119:103
Ps 81:13–16; SS 4:11; 5:1; Isa 7:22;
Jer 41:8; Eze 16:13

**The promised land described as
flowing with milk and honey** Ex 3:7–8
See also Ex 3:17; 13:5; 33:3; Lev 20:24
*The spies confirm the goodness of the
promised land:* Nu 13:27; 14:8
Nu 16:12–14; Dt 6:3; 11:8–9; 26:9;
31:20; Jos 5:6; Jer 32:22; Eze 20:6,15

**Prohibition against burning honey on
the altar** Lev 2:11

Raisins
2Sa 16:1 *See also* Nu 6:1–4; 1Sa 25:18;
30:11–12; 2Sa 6:19 pp 1Ch 16:3;
1Ch 12:40; SS 2:5; Hos 3:1

Lentils
Ge 25:29–34 *See also* 2Sa 17:27–29;
23:11–12; Eze 4:1–10

Cheese
1Sa 17:17–18 *See also* 2Sa 17:27–29;
Job 10:8–11

**Believers should not eat food
offered to idols**
Ac 15:19–20 *See also* Ac 21:25;
1Co 8:1–13; Rev 2:14

See also
4418 bread   4480 milk
4438 eating   4532 vegetables
4450 fruit   4612 birds
4474 manna   4642 fish
4476 meals   7402 offerings
4478 meat   8770 idolatry, in NT

4406

agriculture

The science of cultivation. The task,
given to humanity, of cultivating the
land is a reflection of God's own care
for his creation.

A major activity for humanity
Ge 2:15 *See also* Ge 3:23; 4:2,12; 9:20;
47:19; Dt 8:7–8; 1Ki 19:19; 2Ch 26:10;
Isa 37:30

**Growth is according to the
sovereign will of God**
He has established the seasons
Ge 8:22; Ac 14:17 *See also* Lev 26:4;
Jer 5:24

**He provides for the growth of the
crops** Ps 65:9 *See also* Ps 104:14;
107:37–38; 147:8; Eze 34:26–27;
Zec 8:12; Mt 6:30; 2Co 9:10

**OT laws for agriculture showed how to
co-operate with God** Lev 19:19 *See also*
Lev 19:23; 25:3–4; Dt 22:10

**Harvest festivals were for thanking
God for his provision** Ex 34:22 *See also*
Lev 23:10,39–41; Dt 16:10,13

**Cultivation was affected by the
fall**
Ge 3:17 *See also* Ge 3:18–19; 4:12; 5:29;
Ro 8:20

**Agricultural images of God's
action among his people**
Isa 5:7; Mt 9:37; Jn 12:24 *See also*
Isa 17:5–6; 24:13; Jer 8:20; 50:16;
51:33; Hos 6:11; Mt 13:3–8
pp Mk 4:3–8 pp Lk 8:5–8; Mt 13:18–23
pp Mk 4:13–20 pp Lk 8:11–15;
Mt 13:24–30; Mk 4:26–29; Jn 4:35–38

See also
1325 God, the   4498 ploughing
     Creator   4510 sowing &
4017 life, animal &   reaping
     plant   4522 threshing
4430 crops   4538 vineyard
4454 gleaning   4550 winnowing
4464 harvest   4970 seasons of
4468 horticulture   year

4408

balm

**Balm was a herb valued for its
healing properties**
Jer 8:22 *See also* 2Ch 28:15; Jer 46:11;
51:8

**Balm was exported from Israel to
other nations**
Ge 43:11 *See also* Ge 37:25; Eze 27:17

See also
4466 herbs and   5333 healing
    spices   5587 trade
4490 ointment

4410

banquets

Grand, celebratory meals consisting usually of rich food and flowing wine. Banquets usually accompanied weddings, religious festivals and other celebrations. Prophecies of the Messianic age refer to a banquet to which the righteous will be invited.

Characteristics of banquets
They were usually held in a hall SS 2:4
See also Est 7:8; Da 5:10

Honoured guests were given special places Lk 14:7–11 *See also* Pr 25:6–7; Mt 23:6 pp Mk 12:39 pp Lk 20:46

Guests reclined on couches Est 1:6; Mt 26:7 pp Mk 14:3 pp Lk 7:36; Jn 12:2

Invitations were sent out Lk 14:17 pp Mt 22:3

Occasions for holding banquets
To celebrate weddings Mt 22:2 *See also* Ge 29:21–22 *a feast celebrates Jacob's wedding;* Jdg 14:10 *Samson gives a wedding feast;* Est 2:18 *Xerxes celebrates Esther's choice as queen with a banquet;* Mt 25:10; Lk 12:36; Jn 2:8–9; Rev 19:9 *the marriage supper of the Lamb*

To celebrate birthdays Ge 40:20; Mk 6:21

To celebrate other events Ge 21:8 *Abraham celebrates Isaac's weaning. Jews celebrate their deliverance from Haman in what became the Feast of Purim:* Est 8:17; 9:17–19 Lk 15:23 *The father celebrates the prodigal son's return.*

Religious celebrations Ps 22:29 *See also* 2Ch 30:21–22; 35:13; Zec 7:6

Activities at banquets
Good food and drink Isa 25:6 *See also* Job 1:4; Zec 7:6; Mt 22:4; Lk 15:23

Drunkenness and revelry 1Sa 25:36 *See also* Est 1:7–8,10; Ecc 10:19; Jer 51:39; Da 5:3–4

Music and dancing Isa 5:12 *See also* Mt 14:6 pp Mk 6:22; Lk 15:25

Further examples of banquets
Ge 26:30 *Isaac holds a feast for Abimelech;* Ge 43:34 *Joseph feasts with his brothers;* 2Sa 3:20 *David holds a feast for Abner;* 1Ki 3:15 *Solomon gives a feast for all his court. Xerxes gives a banquet for his nobles and officials:* Est 1:3,5 Est 1:9 *Queen Vashti holds a banquet for the women of the palace. Esther prepares banquets for the king and Haman:* Est 5:4–5,8 Da 5:1–2 *Belshazzar has a banquet for 1,000 nobles;* Lk 5:29 pp Mt 9:10 *Levi holds a banquet for Jesus Christ;* Lk 14:1 *Jesus Christ is the guest of a leading Pharisee.*

An invitation to a banquet seen as a sign of God's grace
Lk 14:12–14 *See also* 2Ki 6:23 *The king of Israel prepares a banquet for captured Aramean troops;* Mt 22:8–10 pp Lk 14:21–23

The Messianic banquet
Mt 8:11 *See also* Lk 13:29; 14:15

See also
4404 food   5742 wedding
4434 drinking   5878 honour
4438 eating   7354 feasts and
5231 birthday   festivals
5355 invitations   8642 celebration
5699 guests   9150 Messianic
5710 marriage,   banquet
    customs

4412

binding corn

Binding corn as a feature of agricultural life
Ge 37:7 *See also* Lev 19:9 *the law of the gleaner;* Lev 23:10,22; Dt 11:14; 24:19; Ru 2:16; Isa 17:5

Metaphorical usage
Ps 126:6 *See also* Job 5:26; Pr 10:5; Jer 9:22; Mic 4:12; Mt 9:37–38; 13:30; Lk 10:2

See also
4406 agriculture   4464 harvest
4428 corn   4510 sowing &
4430 crops   reaping
4454 gleaning   4542 wheat

4416

branch

The limb of a tree. The term is used literally, symbolically and metaphorically in Scripture. Branches are personified at times and the Messiah is referred to as the Branch.

Branches of various trees
Vine branches Ge 49:22 *See also* Nu 13:23; Isa 18:5; Jer 5:10; 6:9; 48:32; Eze 17:5–8; 19:10–14; Jn 15:5–6

Olive branches Dt 24:20 *See also* Ne 8:14–16; Jer 11:16; Zec 4:12

Palm branches Rev 7:9 *See also* Ne 8:15; Isa 9:14; 19:15

Branches of other trees Jer 1:11 *See also* Ge 30:37–39; Ne 8:15; Eze 17:22–23; 31:3; Heb 9:19

Branches cut down for Jesus Christ's triumphal entry into Jerusalem
Mt 21:7–9 pp Mk 11:7–10 pp Jn 12:12–13

Branches providing shelter
Mt 13:31–32 pp Lk 13:18–19 *See also* Eze 31:3–14; Da 4:10–14,20–22

The symbolic use of branches
Jer 1:11–12 *See also* Isa 9:14–15; 19:13–15

Branches in visions
Ge 40:9–13 *See also* Zec 4:1–14

The metaphorical use of branches
Job 29:19 *See also* Ge 49:22; Job 15:32–35; 18:5–16

The personification of branches
In general Jn 15:5–6 *See also* Ro 11:11–24

The Messiah as the Branch Jer 23:5 *See also* Isa 4:2; 11:1–5; Jer 33:15–16; Zec 3:8; 6:12–13

The branches of the lampstand in the tabernacle
Ex 25:31–32 *See also* Ex 25:35–36; 37:17–22

See also
2203 Christ, titles of   4534 vine
2230 Messiah,   4552 wood
    coming of   5373 lamp &
4492 olive   lampstand
4528 trees

4418

bread

The basic component of the staple diet in biblical times. Consecrated bread was continually laid out in the Holy Place of the tabernacle and temple. Jesus Christ called himself the bread of life.

Bread the basic component of the diet
Mt 6:11 pp Lk 11:3 *See also* Ge 14:18; 18:3–6 *Abraham entertains the three angels;* Ge 25:34; 27:17; 45:23; Dt 8:7–9; 23:4; Jdg 8:5–6 *Gideon asks for bread for his troops;* Jdg 19:19; Ru 2:14; 1Sa 2:36; 17:17; 21:2–3; 25:7–11 *Nabal refuses bread to David's men;* 1Ki 13:7–22; 17:10–16 *The widow at Zarephath feeds Elijah and is rewarded;* 1Ki 19:5–6; Job 23:12; Ps 104:14–15; Pr 30:8; Isa 33:16; 51:14; 55:2; Jer 37:21 *Jeremiah's rations in prison;* Jer 42:14; La 5:6; Eze 4:9; Dt 8:3; Mt 4:3–4 pp Lk 4:3–4 *the temptation of Jesus Christ;* Mk 6:8; 2Co 9:10

A diet consisting solely of bread was indicative of deprivation
1Ki 22:27 pp 2Ch 18:26 *See also* Pr 6:26; La 1:11; 2:12; 4:4

Kinds of bread
Unleavened bread Ex 12:39 *See also* Ex 12:8,14–20; 13:3–7

Manna Ex 16:31–35 *See also* Ex 16:4–8,11–12,14–19; Ne 9:15; Ps 78:23–25; 105:40

Gifts of bread
Ge 45:23 *See also* 1Sa 10:3–4; 16:20; 25:18; 2Sa 6:19 pp 1Ch 16:3; 2Sa 16:1–2; 1Ki 14:3; 2Ki 4:42

Offerings of bread
Lev 7:11–14 *See also* Ex 29:2,32–34; Lev 2:11; 8:31–32; 23:20; Nu 6:17–20; Jdg 6:19–21

The bread of the Presence
Lev 24:5–8
The table for the bread of the Presence: Ex 25:23–30; 35:10–13; 39:33–36; 40:22–23; Nu 4:4–8

4420

1Sa 21:1–6 *David and his men eat the consecrated bread*; 1Ch 9:31–32; 23:29; 2Ch 2:4; 13:11; Ne 10:32–33; Mt 12:1–8 pp Mk 2:23–28 pp Lk 6:1–5 *Jesus Christ and his disciples in the cornfields on the Sabbath*; Heb 9:1–2

Jesus Christ as the bread of life
Jn 6:25–35 *See also* Jn 6:41–59

Miracles of multiplication of bread
Mt 14:13–21 pp Mk 6:32–44 pp Lk 9:10–17 pp Jn 6:1–13 *See also* Mt 15:32–38 pp Mk 8:1–10

The breaking of bread as a symbol of the death of Jesus Christ
Mt 26:26–29 pp Mk 14:22–25 pp Lk 22:17–20 pp 1Co 11:24–25 *See also* Lk 24:28–35; Ac 2:42,46; 20:6–7,11; 27:35; 1Co 10:16–17

See also

2351 Christ, miracles	5341 hunger
4404 food	5573 table
4432 dough	7360 Feast of
4474 manna	Unleavened
4530 unleavened	Bread
bread	7402 offerings
4554 yeast	7933 Lord's Supper
5222 baking	

4420

breakfast

Breakfast is the first meal of the day
Jn 21:1–13 *See also* Jdg 19:5–10

See also

4404 food	4476 meals
4438 eating	

4422

brier

Prickly vegetation, painful to the touch, often seen as a symbol of dereliction.

A brier as prickly vegetation
Eze 28:24 *See also* Isa 7:23–25; Eze 2:6; Mic 7:2–4

A brier as a symbol of dereliction
Isa 5:6 *See also* Job 31:38–40; Isa 32:11–13; 55:13; Hos 9:6

Briers are destroyed by fire
Isa 10:17 *See also* Isa 9:18; 27:4

Briers as an instrument of punishment
Jdg 8:16 *See also* Jdg 8:4–7

See also
4520 thorns

4424

cedar

A tall, majestic tree, native to Lebanon. In OT times it was highly prized for its wood, which was used extensively in the construction of Solomon's temple.

Cedar trees associated with Lebanon
1Ki 4:33 *See also* Jdg 9:15; 2Ki 14:9 pp 2Ch 25:18; 2Ki 19:23 pp Isa 37:24; Ps 29:5; 92:12; 104:16; SS 5:15; Isa 14:8; Jer 22:23; Eze 27:5; Hos 14:5–6; Zec 11:1–2

The cedar as a tall, majestic tree
Eze 31:3 *See also* Job 40:17; Ps 80:10; Isa 2:12–13; Eze 17:22–23; 31:7–8; Am 2:9

Cedar trees indicating a fertile, well-watered land
Nu 24:5–6 *See also* Ps 92:12–15; Isa 41:17–20

Cedar used allegorically
Eze 17:1–4 *prophecy of a Davidic king being taken into captivity*; Eze 17:22–23 *prophecy of the Messiah coming from David's family*

Cedar as a costly and valued wood
1Ki 10:27 pp 2Ch 1:15 pp 2Ch 9:27 *See also* SS 8:8–9; Isa 9:8–10

Cedar wood used in ritual purification
Lev 14:48–53 *See also* Lev 14:1–7; Nu 19:1–6

Cedar wood imported from the north
Ezr 3:7 *See also* 2Sa 5:11; 1Ki 5:1–11 pp 2Ch 2:3–16; 1Ki 9:11; 1Ch 22:4

Cedar wood used in the construction of buildings
Royal palaces and great houses
1Ki 7:2–3 *See also* 2Sa 5:11; 7:2; 1Ki 7:7,11–12; SS 1:17; Jer 22:11–15

The temple 1Ki 6:18 *See also* 2Sa 7:7; 1Ki 6:9–10,20,36; 7:12

See also

4528 trees	7416 purification
4552 wood	7467 temple,
5437 palaces	Solomon's

4426

chaff

Husks of wheat or other cereal. It was separated from the grain by threshing, whereupon it usually blew away, as it was lighter than the grain. Sometimes however, it was burned as fuel. The wicked are frequently likened to chaff in Scripture.

Grain was threshed on outdoor threshing-floors to separate the chaff
Da 2:31–35 *See also* Hos 13:3

Characteristics of chaff
It is blown by the wind Job 13:25
It is light Job 41:28
It is useless Isa 33:11

The wicked are compared to chaff
They will disappear as chaff is blown away Ps 1:1–6 *See also* Job 21:17–18;

Ps 35:4–6; 83:13–15; Isa 17:13; 29:5; 40:24–25; Jer 13:24

Their punishment is compared to threshing Isa 41:15–16 *See also* Isa 41:2

Their end will be like chaff which is burned Mt 3:11–12 pp Lk 3:16–17

See also

4456 grain	4524 threshing-floor
4522 threshing	4550 winnowing

4428

corn

A cereal crop cultivated for food use. An important agricultural crop in biblical times, it is mentioned frequently in Scripture.

The importance of corn
It was a basic foodstuff Ps 65:9 *See also* 2Ki 4:42–44; Eze 36:24–31; Mt 12:1–8 pp Mk 2:23–28 pp Lk 6:1–5

It was an important cereal crop Ps 72:16 *See also* Jdg 15:1–6; Ps 65:11–13; Isa 36:16–17

Harvesting corn
Mk 4:26–29 *See also* Dt 16:9–10; Job 24:22–24; Isa 17:4–6; Jer 9:22

Legislation relating to corn
Dt 23:25 *See also* Ex 22:6

Corn featuring in dreams
Ge 37:5–8 *See also* Ge 41:5–7,22–32

The metaphorical use of corn
Hos 14:5–7 *See also* Jer 50:11–13

See also

4404 food	4456 grain
4406 agriculture	4464 harvest
4412 binding corn	4542 wheat
4430 crops	

4430

crops

Crops represent God's provision and are regulated by the Mosaic law. Their failure is associated with disobedience.

Crops related to the law of Moses
Dt 7:12–13 *See also* Ex 23:10–11,16; Lev 23:39; 25:3,15–16,20–22; 26:3–4; Dt 14:28–29; 16:13 *the Feast of Tabernacles*; Dt 22:9; 26:12; 28:11; 30:8–9; Ne 10:35–37; Pr 3:9–10; Mal 3:10–11

Crops representing God's goodness
Ps 65:9–10; Ac 14:17 *See also* Ge 26:12; Jer 2:7; Eze 34:27–29; 36:30; Zec 8:12; Jas 5:17–18

The failure of crops as a result of disobedience
Dt 11:16–17 *See also* Ge 4:10–12; Dt 28:18,42,49–51; Jdg 6:3–4; Job 31:5–8; Ps 78:46; 105:34–35; Am 7:1; Hag 1:9–10

Crops used metaphorically
Jas 5:7 *See also* Isa 5:1–2; Mt 13:8,23; 21:40–41; Lk 12:16–17; Jn 4:36; 2Ti 2:6; Heb 6:7–8; Rev 22:1–2

See also
1355 providence	4464 harvest
4404 food	4510 sowing &
4406 agriculture	reaping
4428 corn	4540 weeds
4450 fruit	4542 wheat
4456 grain	5903 maturity,
4458 grape	physical

4432

dough

A mixture of flour and water to which yeast is added and which is then baked to produce bread. Scripture makes several comparisons with it to teach spiritual lessons.

Dough and the process of making bread
Yeast was normally added and the dough left to rise Ex 12:33–34 See also Ex 12:39

Dough was kneaded before baking Jer 7:18 See also 2Sa 13:8; Hos 7:4

Spiritual lessons from comparisons with dough
The dough offered as firstfruits Ro 11:13–16

The influence of yeast on the dough Mt 13:33 pp Lk 13:20–21 See also 1Co 5:1–8; Gal 5:1–10

See also
2375 kingdom of	5222 baking
God	5435 ovens
4418 bread	7222 exodus, events
4554 yeast	of

4434

drinking

Scripture lays down no general prohibition of the consumption of alcohol, but warns against its abuse.

4435
drinking

Wine as a gift of God
A sign of his blessing Dt 7:13 See also Ge 27:28; Dt 33:28; Pr 3:9–10; Joel 2:18–19,22–24; 3:18; Am 9:13–14

Drinking wine has God's approval Dt 14:26 See also Jn 2:1–10; 1Ti 5:23 approval implicit in the advice given

Withdrawal of wine is evidence of divine judgment
Isa 24:6–7 See also Jer 48:32–33

Drinking used extensively as a metaphor
Of suffering God's judgment Job 21:20; Ps 75:8; Isa 29:9; Jer 25:15–17; Eze 23:31–34; Hab 2:16; Rev 18:3

Of love Pr 7:18

Of Jesus Christ's destiny of suffering Mt 26:42 See also Mt 26:39 pp Mk 14:36 pp Lk 22:42; Mt 20:22–23 pp Mk 10:38–39; Jn 18:11

Of spiritual satisfaction Jn 4:13–14

Of the Christian experience of the Holy Spirit Jn 7:37

Jesus Christ's symbolic use of wine
Mt 26:27–29 pp Mk 14:23–25 pp Lk 22:17–18, 20 See also Jn 6:53–56 the believer's participation in Jesus Christ

See also
2570 Christ,	5580 thirst
suffering	7350 drink offering
4293 water	7933 Lord's Supper
4480 milk	8102 abiding in
4536 vinegar	Christ
4544 wine	9210 judgment,
5167 mouth	God's
5283 cup	

4436
drinking, abstention from

Scripture indicates that the abuse of drinking, such as drunkenness, is unacceptable. It also indicates the advantages of abstention from drinking in certain situations.

For some, at certain times, total abstinence is right
Lev 10:8–9; Eze 44:21 priests; Nu 6:1–4,20 Nazirites; Jdg 13:2–5,7,13–14; Pr 31:4–5; Isa 22:12–13; Jer 35:1–14; Da 1:5–16 John the Baptist: Mt 11:18; Lk 1:15 Mt 27:34 Jesus Christ; Ro 14:21 the Christian who does not want to give offence

Warnings against the abuse of alcohol
Isa 5:11 See also Pr 20:1; Isa 5:22; Hab 2:15; Lk 21:34; Ro 13:13; 1Co 6:9–10; 11:20–21; Gal 5:19–21; Eph 5:18; 1Th 5:7–8; Tit 2:3

Christian leaders are to be sober
1Ti 3:2–3 See also 1Ti 3:8; Tit 1:7

Examples of drunkenness
Ge 9:20–21; 19:30–35; 1Sa 25:36; 2Sa 11:12–13; 1Ki 16:9; 20:16; Est 1:10; Isa 28:7; 56:10–12; Mt 24:49 pp Lk 12:45

Some accusations of drunkenness were unfounded
1Sa 1:13–15; Mt 11:19 pp Lk 7:34; Ac 2:13–15 the disciples on the day of Pentecost

See also
5850 excess	8339 self-control
5947 shame	8430 fasting
6106 addiction	8821 self-indulgence
7734 leaders,	
spiritual	

4438

eating

The consumption of food, necessary for survival. Scripture cites enjoyment of eating as a gift of God but emphasises that it is not the main priority in life, for God will provide abundantly for his children.

Eating for survival
Ne 5:1–2 See also Ge 28:20–22; 1Ki 17:12; 19:3–8; 2Ki 25:3

Eating as a sign of life and health
Dt 4:28 See also 2Sa 13:5–10; Ps 102:4; Mk 5:35–43 pp Lk 8:49–56; Lk 24:36–43; Jn 6:48–58

Enjoyment of eating as a gift of God
Ecc 3:13 See also Ge 27:1–25; Ecc 2:24–25; 5:18; 8:15; 9:7

God blesses his people with sufficient food
Ps 37:25 See also Lev 26:3–5,23–26; Dt 8:16; 11:15; 12:7; Jos 24:11–13; Ps 22:26; 78:23–29; 127:2; 128:1–2; Pr 13:25; Isa 1:19; 7:22; 65:13,21–22; Joel 2:26; Am 9:14; Mic 6:9–16; Hag 1:5–11

Eating should not be one's chief priority
Mt 4:1–4 pp Lk 4:1–4 See also Dt 8:3; Nu 11:4–34; Mt 6:25–34 pp Lk 12:22–31; Lk 12:16–20; Col 2:13–17

Eating as a religious observance
Sacrificial meals Ex 18:12 See also Ex 29:32–33; 32:6; Lev 6:14–7:10; 8:31; 21:21–23; Nu 18:8–13; Dt 15:19–20; 1Sa 1:1–5; 9:11–13; 20:24–29; Eze 44:3; Hos 8:13; Heb 13:9–10

Sacrificial meals for pagan gods Ex 34:15 See also Eze 18:5–6,14–15; 22:9; 1Co 8:4–13; 10:23–28

The Passover and Feast of Unleavened Bread Ex 12:1–11 See also Ex 12:14–20; Lev 23:4–8; Nu 28:16–25; Dt 16:1–8; Mt 26:17–19 pp Mk 14:12–16 pp Lk 22:7–13

The Lord's Supper Mt 26:26–29 pp Mk 14:22–25 pp Lk 22:17–20 See also 1Co 11:23–34

Restrictions on eating
Ge 9:1–4 See also Ge 2:15–17; 3:1–7 Eve and Adam eat the fruit of the tree; Ge 3:22; 32:22–32; 43:32; Ex 22:31; Lev 7:19,22–27; 11:1–47 pp Dt 14:3–20 clean and unclean food; Lev 22:4–8; 23:6; Nu 6:1–4; Dt 12:23–25; Eze 44:31; Mk 7:14–19; Ro 14:1–3,19–21

Eating and hospitality
Eating at a royal court 1Ki 2:7 See also 2Sa 9:1–13; 1Ki 18:19; Da 11:26

Eating as a guest in another's home Ge 18:3–5 See also Ge 19:3; 43:16; Ex 2:18–20; Jdg 19:5–9; 2Ki 4:8; Pr 23:6–7; Mt 9:9–13 pp Mk 2:14–17 pp Lk 5:27–32; Mt 26:6–7 pp Mk 14:3; Lk 14:1–14

Fasting
Est 4:16 See also 2Sa 3:35; Mt 4:1–2 pp Lk 4:1–2

Cannibalism
Dt 28:53 See also 2Ki 6:24–29; Jer 19:9

Metaphorical references to eating
Jn 6:50 Coming to faith in Jesus Christ; Rev 3:20 Having fellowship with Jesus Christ. See also Ps 14:4 pp Ps 53:4;

Ps 141:4; Pr 1:29–31; 4:17; 18:21;
31:27; SS 5:1; Isa 55:1–2; Eze 3:1–3;
Mic 3:1–3; Rev 2:7; 10:9; 17:16;
19:17–19

See also

4293 water	7406 Passover
4404 food	7435 sacrifice, in OT
4410 banquets	7933 Lord's Supper
4476 meals	8432 fasting,
5312 feasting	practice
7326 cannibalism	8445 hospitality
7354 feasts and	
festivals	

4440

fig-tree

A tree common in the Near East,
with soft, sweet fruit which can be
eaten fresh or dried. The fruit was an
important part of the diet in biblical
times and the tree was symbolic of
peace and security.

Figs
Figs prized as a sweet, pleasant fruit
Jdg 9:10–11 *See also* Nu 13:21–23

**Figs a significant part of the diet in
biblical times** Nu 20:5 *See also* Dt 8:7–9;
1Sa 30:11–12; Ne 13:15

Figs given in gifts of food 1Sa 25:18 *See
also* 2Sa 16:1; 1Ch 12:40

Other uses of figs and fig leaves
2Ki 20:1–7 *See also* Ge 3:6–7; Isa 38:21

Judah likened to figs Jer 24:1–10;
29:15–19

The fig-tree as a symbol of peace
and security
1Ki 4:25 *See also* 2Ki 18:28–32
pp Isa 36:13–18; Mic 4:1–5 *See also*
Zec 3:10

Destruction of fig-trees
By God Hos 2:12 *See also* Ps 105:33;
Am 4:9

By enemies Joel 1:6–7 *See also* Jer 5:17

Descriptions of the fig-tree and
its fruit
Early figs Hos 9:10 *See also* SS 2:13;
Isa 28:4; Mic 7:1; Na 3:12

Late figs Rev 6:12–13

Failure of the crop Jer 8:13 *See also*
Joel 1:12; Hab 3:17–18; Hag 2:19

Fig-trees in the teaching of Jesus
Christ and the apostles
In parables and object lessons
Jas 3:9–12 *See also* Mt 7:15–20
pp Lk 6:43–45; Lk 13:6–9

The lesson of the fig-tree Mt 24:32–35
pp Mk 13:28–31 pp Lk 21:29–31

Jesus Christ curses a fig-tree
Mt 21:18–22 pp Mk 11:12–14, 20–24

See also

1670 symbols	4528 trees
4450 fruit	
4518 sycamore-fig	
tree	

4442

firstfruits

Offerings of the produce of the land,
being the first and best of the crops,
given in acknowledgment of God's
abundant blessings. The term is also
used metaphorically to indicate the
first of a much larger group that is to
follow, such as those who will be
raised from the dead.

Offering firstfruits
Ex 23:19 *See also* Ex 34:26;
Lev 2:11–16; Dt 26:1–11; Ne 10:35–39;
13:31; Pr 3:9–10; Ro 11:16

Firstfruits given to priests and
Levites
Nu 18:8–13 *See also* Dt 18:1–5;
2Ch 31:2–5; Ne 12:44–47;
Eze 44:28–30

Firstfruits offered at feasts
The Feast of Firstfruits Lev 23:9–14

The Feast of Weeks (Harvest) Ex 23:16;
34:22; Lev 23:15–20; Nu 28:26

Firstborn of human beings and
animals regarded as firstfruits
Ps 78:51 *See also* Ex 13:1–2,11–16;
Nu 18:14–19; Ps 105:36

Metaphorical use of firstfruits
Firstfruits of God's harvest Jer 2:1–3

**Jesus Christ the firstfruits of the
resurrection** 1Co 15:20–28 *See also*
Ac 26:22–23

Firstfruits of salvation Jas 1:18 *See also*
Ro 8:23; 2Th 2:13 fn; Rev 14:1–5

See also

4456 grain	7390 Levites
4544 wine	7402 offerings
5688 firstborn	7766 priests
6510 salvation	8488 tithing
7357 Feast of	9310 resurrection
Firstfruits	

4444

flax

**Flax is the linum plant from which
linen is made**
Ex 9:31; Jos 2:6; Jdg 15:14

Making flax into linen
Pr 31:13; Isa 19:9

See also

5258 cloth	5392 linen

4446

flowers

The blossoming part of plants and
trees, from which the seeds or fruit
develop. Often admired for their
beauty, Scripture uses their fleeting
existence as an illustration of the
transience of human life.

Carvings of flowers
In the tabernacle Ex 25:31–36
pp Ex 37:17–22

In the temple 1Ki 6:18 *See also*
1Ki 6:29,31–35; 7:15–22,25–26
pp 2Ch 4:4–5

Metaphorical depictions of
people as flowers
Isa 28:1–6 *See also* Isa 5:18–25

Human existence is likened to
the short life cycle of flowers
1Pe 1:24–25 *See also* Isa 40:6–8;
Job 14:1–2; Ps 103:13–18; Jas 1:9–11

Flowers and the changing
seasons
SS 2:11–13 *See also* Isa 18:5–6

The lily
Its beauty Lk 12:27–28 pp Mt 6:28–30
See also SS 2:1–2; Hos 14:4–7

Lilies in psalm titles Ps 45:1 Title *See
also* Ps 60:1 Title; 69:1 Title; 80:1 Title

Their metaphorical use SS 4:5 *See also*
SS 2:16; 5:13; 6:2–3; 7:2

The crocus
Isa 35:1–2

The rose
SS 2:1

See also

4240 garden, natural	4528 trees
4402 plants	4540 weeds
4466 herbs and	7459 tabernacle, in
spices	OT
4468 horticulture	7467 temple,
4472 lily	Solomon's

4448

forests

Forests the source of timber
Ne 2:8 *See also* Dt 19:5; Isa 44:13–14;
Jer 10:3; Eze 39:10

Forests the habitat of wild
animals
Ps 50:9–11 *See also* Ps 80:13;
104:20–22; Isa 56:9; Jer 5:6; 12:8;
Eze 34:25; Mic 5:8; 7:14

Destruction of forests
As punishment Jer 21:14 *See also*
Isa 10:18–19,33–34; Zec 11:1–3

As a demonstration of power Jer 46:23
See also 2Ki 19:22–24 pp Isa 37:23–25;
Eze 20:46–48

**To render land suitable for human
habitation** Jos 17:14–18

Forest fires
Jas 3:5 *See also* Ps 83:14–15; Isa 9:18;
Jer 21:14

The Palace of the Forest of
Lebanon
1Ki 7:2 *See also* 1Ki 10:17 pp 2Ch 9:16;
1Ki 10:21 pp 2Ch 9:20

Location of forests
1Sa 22:5 *See also* 2Sa 18:6–17;
Eze 20:46–48

Poetic references to forests
SS 2:3 *See also* 1Ch 16:33; Ps 29:9; 96:12;
Isa 7:2; 44:23

4450

fruit

Edible produce of trees, usually sweet and pleasant-tasting. The climate of the Near East is particularly suitable for a wide range of fruit and several varieties are mentioned in Scripture.

Apples
Sweet, pleasant-tasting fruit SS 2:3 *See also* Pr 25:11; SS 2:5; 7:8

Apple trees Joel 1:12 *See also* SS 2:3; 8:5 *Figurative use: the apple of the eye:* Dt 32:10; Ps 17:8; Pr 7:2; Zec 2:8

Dates
2Sa 6:19 pp 1Ch 16:3

Figs
Nu 13:23 *See also* Nu 20:5;
1Sa 25:18–20; 30:11–12; 2Sa 16:1;
1Ch 12:40; Mk 11:13

Grapes
Dt 32:3–14 *See also* Ge 40:9–11;
Nu 13:23–24; 20:5

Melons
Nu 11:5 *See also* Isa 1:8; Jer 10:5

Pomegranates
Pleasant-tasting fruit Dt 8:7–8 *See also* Nu 13:23; 20:5; SS 6:11; 7:12; 8:2

Pomegranate trees 1Sa 14:2 *See also* Joel 1:12; Hag 2:19 *Use in similes:* SS 4:3,13; 6:7

Representations of pomegranates in the tabernacle and temple
2Ki 25:16–17 pp Jer 52:20–23 *See also* Ex 28:31–35 pp Ex 39:22–26;
1Ki 7:15–20,40–42 pp 2Ch 4:11–13;
2Ch 3:16

Fruit and the fall
Ge 3:12 *See also* Ge 3:1–7

General references to fruit
Am 8:1–2 *See also* Ge 1:11–12,29;
Lev 19:23–25; Ecc 2:5; Eze 47:12;
Mic 7:1; Rev 22:1–2

Fruit as a symbol of spiritual growth
Mt 3:10; 12:33

4452

gall

Gall is a bitter herb
Pr 5:3–4 *See also* Ps 69:19–21;
La 3:13–15,19–20

Gall was offered to Jesus Christ at the crucifixion
Mt 27:33–34

Gall is a secretion of the liver
Job 16:12–13

4454

gleaning

Picking up grain or fruit left by the harvesters.

Commands concerning gleaning
Lev 19:9–10 *See also* Lev 23:22

People involved with gleaning
Ru 2:2–3,7–8,15–23; Job 24:6

Gleaning used figuratively, to mean something insignificant
Isa 17:5–6 *See also* Jdg 8:2; Isa 24:13;
Jer 6:9; Mic 7:1

4456

grain

The seed of cereals. Together with wine and oil, it was one of the three basic commodities in biblical times. Grain offerings were central to Israelite religion and tithes and firstfruits of grain were also given to God.

Grain was a basic foodstuff
Dt 7:12–13 *See also* Dt 11:13–15;
28:49–51; 33:28; Ru 2:14; 1Sa 17:17;
25:18; 2Sa 17:27–29; Ne 5:1–3,10–11

Harvesting and threshing grain
Dt 25:4 *See also* Lev 19:9–10; Dt 24:19;
Jdg 6:11; Ru 2:2–9,15–17; 3:2

Storing grain
Ge 41:47–49 *See also* Ge 41:33–36;
2Ch 32:27–28; Pr 11:26; Jer 50:26;
Joel 1:17; Lk 12:16–21

Tithes and firstfruits of grain
Lev 27:30 *See also* Lev 23:9–11;
Dt 12:17; 14:23; 18:1–5; 2Ch 31:4–5;
Ne 10:37–39; 13:12

The grain offering
Lev 2:1–16 *See also* Lev 6:14–23;
23:15–16; Nu 5:11–28; 15:1–12;
1Ki 8:64

Barley as grain
The cultivation of barley 2Sa 14:30 *See also* Ex 9:31; Lev 27:16; Dt 8:7–9;
Ru 1:22; 2:17–18,23; 3:2; 2Sa 21:9;
1Ch 11:13; Job 31:38–40; Isa 28:24–25;
Joel 1:11

Trade in barley Hos 3:2 *See also* 2Ki 7:1,16–18; 2Ch 2:10,15–16; 27:5;
Eze 13:19; Rev 6:6

The consumption of barley Eze 4:9–12 *See also* Jdg 7:13; Ru 3:15–17;

2Sa 17:27–29; 1Ki 4:28; 2Ki 4:42–44;
Jer 41:8; Jn 6:5–13

Offerings of barley Eze 45:13 *See also* Nu 5:11–15

Other kinds of grain
Corn Ps 72:16 *See also* Ge 37:7; Ps 65:13;
Hos 14:7

Millet Eze 4:9

Spelt Isa 28:24–25 *See also* Ex 9:22–32;
Eze 4:9

Wheat Eze 27:17 *See also* Jdg 6:11;
2Ch 27:5; Ps 147:14; Jn 12:24

Allusions to grain in the teaching of Jesus Christ
Mk 4:26–29 *See also* Mt 13:1–9
pp Mk 4:3–8; Mt 13:18–23
pp Mk 4:14–20; Mt 13:24–30,36–43;
Lk 12:13–21; 16:1–9; 17:35; Jn 12:24

4458

grape

Fruit which grows in clusters on a vine. It was very widely cultivated in the Near East in biblical times and was used mostly for making wine.

The cultivation of grapes indicative of rich and fertile land
Nu 20:2–5 *See also* Nu 13:21–25

The failure of the grape harvest indicative of misfortune or disaster
Isa 32:10–13 *See also* Jer 8:13; Mic 7:1;
Hab 3:16–19

Grapes used to make wine
Dt 28:39 *See also* Ge 40:9–11;
49:10–12; Mic 6:15

Treading grapes
Am 9:13 *See also* Jdg 9:27; Ne 13:15;
Jer 25:30

Harvesting grapes
Jer 49:9–10 pp Ob 5 *See also* Lev 26:5;
Nu 13:20; Isa 62:8–9

Regulations concerning the grape harvest
Lev 19:10 *See also* Lev 25:1–7; Dt 23:24;
24:21

Dried grapes: raisins
1Sa 30:11–12 *See also* 1Sa 25:14–19;
2Sa 6:17–19 pp 1Ch 16:1–3;
2Sa 16:1–2; 1Ch 12:38–40; SS 2:5;
Hos 3:1

Nazirites were forbidden to consume grapes or grape products
Nu 6:1–4 *See also* Jdg 13:2–14

The metaphorical use of grapes
Jer 6:9 *See also* Dt 32:32–33; Jdg 8:2;
Job 15:32–34; Ps 80:8–19; Isa 5:1–7;
24:5–13; 65:8; Jer 48:32; Hos 9:10;
Joel 3:12–13; Rev 14:17–20

The proverbial use of grapes
Mt 7:15–16 pp Lk 6:43–45 *See also*
Jer 31:29–30; Eze 18:1–2; 1Co 9:7;
Jas 3:12

See also
4404 food	4538 vineyard
4450 fruit	4544 wine
4454 gleaning	4546 winepress
4464 harvest	8257 fruitfulness,
4534 vine	natural

4460

grass

Green vegetation, which grows
rapidly after rainfall, and serves as
good food for many animals. The
withering of grass in hot weather is
often used in Scripture as a symbol of
the frailty and brevity of human life.

Grass is food for animals
1Ki 18:5 *See also* Nu 22:4; Dt 11:15;
Job 6:5; 40:15; Ps 104:14; 106:20;
Jer 14:5; Da 4:25,32–33; 5:21

**Rain is essential for the growth of
grass**
Job 38:25–27 *See also* Dt 32:2; 2Sa 23:4;
Ps 147:8; Pr 19:12; Mic 5:7

**Grass grows quickly and
abundantly**
Isa 44:3–4 *See also* Job 5:25; Ps 72:16;
92:7; Isa 35:7; 66:14

**Grass withers, dies and burns
easily**
Isa 15:6 *See also* Ps 102:4,11; Isa 5:24;
Jer 12:4; Rev 8:7

The life cycle of grass is short
Ps 129:6 *See also* Isa 37:27; Mt 6:28–34
pp Lk 12:27–31

**The brevity of human life is
compared to that of grass**
Isa 40:6–8 *See also* 2Ki 19:25–26;
Job 8:11–13; Ps 37:1–2; 90:5;
103:13–19; Isa 51:12; 1Pe 1:24–25

See also
| 1670 symbols | 4402 plants |
| 4016 life, human | 4528 trees |

4462

grinding

Grinding using a hand mill
Ex 11:5; Mt 24:41 pp Lk 17:35 *See also*
Nu 11:8; Jdg 16:21 *Samson doing a
woman's work*; Isa 47:2

Grinding grain into flour
Nu 15:20 *See also* Nu 15:21; 2Ch 2:10;
Ne 10:37; Job 31:10; Isa 28:28;
Eze 44:30

Grinding incense
Ex 30:36; Lev 16:12

Grinding as an act of destruction
Dt 9:21 *See also* 2Ki 23:15

Grinding used figuratively
Isa 3:15 *See also* Pr 27:22

See also
| 4456 grain | 5282 crushing |
| 4482 millstones | |

4464

harvest

The gathering of mature crops from
the land. The successful culmination
of the agricultural year was evidence
of God's goodness and consequently
marked with festivity. Harvest is also
used widely in a metaphorical sense.

**The harvest is evidence of God's
goodness**
Ge 8:22; 2Co 9:10 *See also*
Lev 26:5,9–10; Ps 67:6; 85:12; 107:37;
Isa 62:8–9; Jer 5:24

Laws relating to the harvest
Ex 23:10–11; 34:21; Lev 19:9,23–25;
23:22; 25:4–5,11–12,18–27;
Nu 18:12–13; Dt 24:19–21

Harvest festivals
Ex 23:16; 34:22; Lev 23:10–16,33–43;
Dt 16:13–15

Harvest marked times of the year
Ru 1:22 *See also* Jos 3:15; Jdg 15:1;
1Sa 6:13; 12:17; 2Sa 21:9–10; 23:13;
Jer 8:20

Characteristics of harvest
Rejoicing Isa 9:3 *See also* Ps 126:5–6;
Isa 16:9

Hard work Pr 10:5 *See also* Pr 14:4; 20:4

**Failed harvests are a sign of
God's judgment**
Poor harvests Jer 12:13 *See also*
Isa 17:10–11; 32:10; Jer 8:13; Joel 1:11;
Am 4:7; Mic 6:15; Hag 1:6

Others eating the harvest Jer 5:17 *See
also* Ne 9:37; Job 5:5; 31:12

The metaphorical use of harvest
Joel 3:13; Mt 9:37–38; Gal 6:9;
Rev 14:15–16 *See also* Pr 18:20; 25:13;
26:1; Isa 17:5; 18:4–5; 24:13; 28:4; 33:4;
Jer 2:3; 51:33; Hos 6:11
*The parable of the weeds and its
explanation:* Mt 13:30,39
Mt 25:24; Mk 4:29 *the parable of the
growing seed;* Mk 12:1–9 *the parable of
the tenants;* Lk 10:2; Jn 4:35–36;
Ro 1:13; 1Co 9:10–11; Heb 12:11;
Jas 3:18

See also
1050 God, goodness	4522 threshing
of	4550 winnowing
1355 providence	7357 Feast of
4406 agriculture	Firstfruits
4430 crops	7358 Feast of
4454 gleaning	Tabernacles
4510 sowing &	7361 Feast of Weeks
reaping	7402 offerings

4466

herbs and spices

Plants whose leaves or seeds are used
as food or flavourings and sometimes
for medicine. The rich variety of
such plants in the Near East results in
numerous references in Scripture.

Aloes
Jn 19:39–40 *See also* Nu 24:5–6;
Ps 45:6–8; Pr 7:17–18; SS 4:12–14

Balm
Ge 43:11 *See also* Ge 37:25; Jer 8:22

Bitter herbs
Ex 12:5–8 *See also* Nu 9:9–11; La 3:15

Caraway
Isa 28:27 *See also* Isa 28:25

Cassia
Ps 45:8 *See also* Ex 30:22–25; Eze 27:19

Cinnamon
Rev 18:11–13 *See also* Ex 30:22–25;
Pr 7:17–18; SS 4:12–14

Coriander
Ex 16:31 *See also* Nu 11:7

Cummin
Isa 28:25,27; Mt 23:23

Dill
Mt 23:23

Henna
SS 1:14 *See also* SS 4:13

Mint
Mt 23:23 pp Lk 11:42

Myrrh
Est 2:12 *See also* SS 1:13; Mt 2:11;
Jn 19:38–39

Rue
Lk 11:42

Saffron
SS 4:13–14

Salt herbs
Job 30:1–5

Other spices
Given as gifts or as tribute 1Ki 10:10
pp 2Ch 9:9 *See also* 1Ki 10:1–2
pp 2Ch 9:1; 1Ki 10:25 pp 2Ch 9:24

Traded between countries Ge 37:25 *See
also* Eze 27:22; Rev 18:11–13

Used in burial customs 2Ch 16:14 *See
also* Mk 16:1 pp Lk 23:56–24:1; Jn 19:40

Used for perfume or flavouring
Ex 30:34–35 *See also* Ps 75:8; SS 4:10;
Eze 24:10

Stores of spices 2Ch 32:27 *See also*
2Ki 20:13 pp Isa 39:2; 1Ch 9:29–30

See also
4402 plants	5241 burial
4408 balm	5303 embalming
4486 myrrh	5407 merchants
4490 ointment	5587 trade
4496 perfume	5594 tribute
4528 trees	7406 Passover

4468

horticulture

The art of garden cultivation, first
practised in the Garden of Eden.

**Horticulture in the Garden of
Eden**
**The man and woman tended the
garden** Ge 2:15–23

The fall brought about a change in human priorities from horticulture to agriculture Ge 3:17–19 *See also* Ge 4:2

Egyptian agriculture is likened to horticulture
Dt 11:10–11

Horticulture is totally dependent on good irrigation
Isa 58:11 *See also* Ge 2:4–14; 13:10; Nu 24:5–7; Job 8:16; SS 4:12,15; Isa 51:3; Jer 31:12

Those who practised horticulture
Kings Ecc 2:5–6 *See also* 1Ki 21:2; 2Ki 21:18,26; 25:4 pp Jer 39:4 pp Jer 52:7; Ne 3:15; Est 1:5–6; 7:7–8; SS 8:13

Common people Jer 29:28 *See also* Jer 29:1–7; Jn 19:41

Gardeners Jn 20:15 *See also* Isa 5:7; Jn 15:1

Kinds of horticulture
Vegetable gardens 1Ki 21:2

Fruit gardens Am 9:14 *See also* Ge 2:16–17; 3:1–3

Herb gardens Lk 11:42 *See also* SS 6:2; Mt 13:31–32 pp Mk 4:31–32 pp Lk 13:19

Horticultural diseases and pestilence
Am 4:9

See also
4239 garden	4528 trees
4406 agriculture	4532 vegetables
4450 fruit	4538 vineyard
4466 herbs and spices	4540 weeds
	6154 fall, the

4470

hyssop

A plant closely associated with cleansing in the OT, being used extensively in rituals for purification.

Hyssop associated with cleansing
Ps 51:2–7 *See also* Heb 9:19–22

Hyssop in religious ritual
At the Passover Ex 12:21–25

At the slaughter of the red heifer Nu 19:1–10

In rites of cleansing Nu 19:17–20 *See also* Lev 14:1–7,48–53

Hyssop as a well-known plant
1Ki 4:33

Hyssop at the crucifixion
Jn 19:28–30

See also
4402 plants	7416 purification
7342 cleanliness	7478 washing

4472

lily

Lilies admired for their beauty
Lk 12:22–31 pp Mt 6:25–34 *See also* SS 2:16; 4:5; 6:2–3

The metaphorical use of lilies
SS 2:1–2 *See also* SS 5:13; 7:2; Hos 14:5

Ornamental representations of lilies adorned Solomon's temple
1Ki 7:19 *See also* 1Ki 7:22,25–26 pp 2Ch 4:4–5

Lilies mentioned in some titles of tunes in the Psalms
Ps 69:1 Title *See also* Ps 45:1 Title; 60:1 Title; 80:1 Title

See also
4402 plants	7467 temple,
4446 flowers	Solomon's

4474

manna

The source of food provided miraculously for the children of Israel during their desert wanderings. The NT sees this heavenly food as a symbol of Jesus Christ as the bread of life.

Manna provided by God
Ex 16:31; Jos 5:12 *See also* Ex 16:32–35; Nu 11:6–9; Ne 9:15; Ps 78:24–25; Jn 6:31,49; Heb 9:4

Manna as a type
A type of the word of God Dt 8:3 *See also* Dt 8:16; Ne 9:20; Mt 4:4

A type of Jesus Christ Jn 6:50–51 *See also* Jn 6:32–35,47–48,52–58

A symbol of future blessing Rev 2:17

See also
1330 God, the provider	5222 baking
2203 Christ, titles of	7221 exodus, the

4476

meals

Food eaten at set times, on special occasions or following significant events. Sacrificial meals formed part of Israelite worship in the OT, as does the Lord's Supper for worship by believers in the NT.

Regular daily meals
Breakfast Jn 21:12

Lunch Lk 14:12–14 *See also* Ge 43:16,31–34; Ru 2:14; Ac 10:9–10

Evening meal Lk 17:7–8 *See also* Mt 9:10–13 pp Mk 2:15–17 pp Lk 5:29–32; Mk 14:3 pp Lk 7:36 pp Jn 12:1–2; Lk 14:12–14

Royal meals
Ge 40:20 *See also* 1Sa 20:18–34; 2Sa 9:9–13; 1Ki 4:22–28; 18:19; Est 1:1–12; 2:18; 7:1–10; Mt 14:6–11 pp Mk 6:21–28

Meals of the poor
Pr 15:17 *See also* 1Ki 17:10–16

Sacrificial meals
Ge 31:53–54 *See also* Ex 12:1–11; 29:31–34; Lev 6:14–29; 7:1–6; 8:31; 10:12–15; Dt 16:1–8; 1Sa 1:3–8; 9:11–24; 20:28–29

Symbolic meals
Mt 26:20–29 pp Mk 14:17–25 pp Lk 22:14–22 *See also* 1Co 11:17–34

Wedding and funeral meals
Mt 22:1–14 pp Lk 14:16–24 *See also* Jer 16:5; Jn 2:1–10; Rev 19:6–9

Meals and hospitality
2Ki 4:8 *See also* Ge 18:1–8; 19:1–3; Jdg 5:24–25; 13:15–16; 1Sa 28:24–25

Meals as occasions of fellowship
Rev 3:20 *See also* Pr 15:17; Lk 5:29–32; 7:36

See also
1345 covenant	5742 wedding
4404 food	7355 feasts &
4410 banquets	festivals
4420 breakfast	7435 sacrifice, in OT
4438 eating	7933 Lord's Supper
5320 funeral	8445 hospitality

4478

meat

The flesh of animals, consumed as food. In biblical times it was a luxury, eaten on special occasions, usually in the context of sacrificial worship.

Meat a luxury food
Ex 16:3 *See also* Nu 11:4–5; 1Sa 25:11; Isa 22:12–13; Da 10:3

Meat served to honoured guests
1Sa 28:21–25 *See also* Ge 18:1–8; Jdg 6:11–21; 13:9–16; 1Sa 9:22–24; 2Sa 12:1–4; 1Ki 19:19–21; Pr 9:1–6; Isa 25:6; Lk 15:20–24

Meat provided by God
1Ki 17:2–6 *See also* Ex 16:1–14; Nu 11:4–34; Ps 78:17–31

Restrictions on eating certain types of meat
Unclean meat Lev 11:1–47 pp Dt 14:3–20 *See also* Isa 65:2–5

Other prohibited meat Ge 9:4 *See also* Ex 21:28; 22:31; Lev 19:26; Dt 12:23; 14:21; 1Sa 14:33–34; Eze 4:14; 33:25; Ac 15:20,29; 21:25

Eating meat in worship
The Passover lamb Ex 12:1–11 *See also* Ex 12:43–49; Dt 16:1–8

Other sacrifices Ex 29:31–34 *See also* Lev 7:11–18; Nu 18:14–19; Dt 12:27; 1Sa 1:3–8; 2:12–16; Jer 7:21; Hos 8:13

Non-consecrated meat
Dt 12:4–25

Allegorical and metaphorical references to meat
Mic 3:1–3 *See also* Eze 11:1–12; 24:1–13

Varying convictions about eating meat
Ro 14:1–23

See also

4404 food
4476 meals
4530 unleavened
    bread
4618 calf
4663 lamb

5773 abstinence,
    discipline
7340 clean and
    unclean
7406 Passover
7435 sacrifice, in OT

4480

milk

A common source of food and nourishment, associated with rich and productive land. The term is also used figuratively as a form of spiritual food suitable for those who have yet to reach maturity in the Christian faith.

Milk as a source of nourishment

Dt 32:13–14 *See also* Ge 18:8; Jdg 4:19; 2Sa 17:29; Pr 27:27; Eze 25:4; 1Co 9:7 *illustrating the support of the ministry*

Milk as an indication of prosperity and well-being

Dt 6:3 *A frequent description of the promised land;* Isa 55:1 *See also* Ex 3:8; Lev 20:24; Nu 13:27; Isa 7:22; 60:16; Eze 20:6; Joel 3:18

Laws concerning milk

Ex 23:19; 34:26; Dt 14:21

Elementary Christian teaching likened to milk

Heb 5:12–13 *See also* 1Co 3:2; 1Pe 2:2

Milk used figuratively

Pr 30:33 *See also* Ge 49:12; Job 10:10; SS 4:11; 5:12; La 4:7

See also

4404 food
5881 immaturity

7257 promised land

4482

millstones

Pairs of upper and lower millstones were used for grinding grain in the ancient East. Millstones were common features of the daily life of ordinary people.

Millstones as a means of earning a living

Dt 24:6 *See also* Isa 47:1–2; Jer 25:10; Rev 18:22

Millstones were heavy and burdensome

Mt 18:6 pp Mk 9:42 pp Lk 17:2

Millstones as potential weapons

Jdg 9:50–53 *See also* 2Sa 11:21

Millstones in figurative use

Job 41:24

Millstones as symbols of destructive force

Rev 18:21

See also

4456 grain
4462 grinding

5295 destruction

4484

mustard seed

A very small seed which grew rapidly into a substantial plant. It was used in parables by Jesus Christ to encourage the faith of the individual and to illustrate the growth of the kingdom of God.

The mustard seed and the faith of the individual

Lk 17:5–6 *See also* Mt 17:14–20

The mustard seed and the kingdom of God

Mt 13:31–32 pp Mk 4:30–32 pp Lk 13:18–19

See also

2375 kingdom of
    God
4402 plants
4506 seed

4528 trees
5438 parables
8020 faith
8443 growth

4486

myrrh

A resinous substance derived from certain trees and bushes native to the Near East. It was a valuable commodity and had a variety of uses.

Myrrh was traded by merchants

Ge 37:25 *See also* Rev 18:11–13

Myrrh was presented as a gift

Mt 2:11 *See also* Ge 43:11

Uses of myrrh

In the sacred anointing oil Ex 30:22–28

As a perfume SS 1:13 *See also* Ps 45:8; Pr 7:10–18; SS 3:6

In beauty treatments Est 2:12 *See also* SS 5:5

As a painkiller Mk 15:22–23

In embalming Jn 19:38–40

The metaphorical use of myrrh

SS 5:13 *See also* SS 4:1–7,12–14; 5:1

See also

4466 herbs and
    spices
4496 perfume
4528 trees
5241 burial

5325 gifts
5407 merchants
5587 trade
7386 incense

4488

oil

Normally olive oil, which was in plentiful supply in Israel and in general household use. Its ritual uses included the anointing of priests and kings and ceremonial cleansing; in the NT oil was used to anoint the sick. As a sign of God's provision for his people, oil was associated with prosperity and gladness, and was a mark of spiritual blessing.

The production of oil

Job 24:11 *Olives were pressed either with a pestle and mortar or in a stone press;* Mt 26:36 *"Gethsemane" means "oil press", named after the stone presses associated with the Mount of Olives.*

General uses of oil

As a necessary provision 1Ch 12:40; 2Ch 11:11

As a fuel for lamps Ex 27:20 pp Lev 24:2 *See also* Ex 35:14 pp Ex 39:37; Nu 4:9; Mt 25:1–10

Mixed with flour in baking 1Ki 17:12–16 *See also* Ex 29:23; Nu 11:8

As an ointment Isa 1:6 *See also* Ps 55:21; Lk 10:34

Oil for use in the sanctuary

Ne 10:39 *See also* Ex 25:6 pp Ex 35:8; Nu 4:16; 1Ch 9:29; Ezr 6:9

Oil used for ceremonial anointing

Instructions for making and using the anointing oil Ex 30:23–33 *See also* Ex 31:11; 37:29

Holy objects were consecrated by anointing with oil
Jacob twice anoints a pillar at Bethel: Ge 28:18; 31:13; 35:14
God's command to anoint the tabernacle and its furnishings: Ex 40:9–11; Lev 8:10–11

Priests were ordained by anointing with oil Lev 8:12 pp Ex 29:7 *See also* Ex 29:21 pp Lev 8:30; Lev 10:7; 21:10–12; Ps 133:2; Zec 4:12–14

Kings were anointed with oil 1Sa 10:1 *Saul*
David. Anointing with oil is associated with the gift of the Holy Spirit: 1Sa 16:13; Ps 89:20
1Ki 1:39 *Solomon;* 2Ki 9:1–6 *Jehu*

Further ceremonial uses of oil

In ceremonial cleansing
Lev 14:15–18,24–29

In offerings
At the consecration of priests: Ex 29:2; Nu 8:8
At the daily sacrifice: Ex 29:40; Nu 28:5
With the grain offering: Lev 2:1–7; 6:20–21; Nu 7:13
Lev 7:12 *with the thank offering;* Nu 6:15 *at the completion of the Nazirite's vow*
With the burnt offering: Nu 28:9,28; Eze 46:4–5

Oil was excluded from certain offerings Lev 5:11; Nu 5:15

Oil used to anoint the sick

Jas 5:14 *See also* Mk 6:13

God's provision of oil

Oil as a sign of God's blessing Dt 32:13 *See also* Dt 7:13; 8:7–8; 11:14; Hos 2:8

Oil withdrawn as a sign of judgment Dt 28:40 *See also* Dt 28:51; Joel 1:10; Mic 6:15; Hag 1:11

Renewed provision of oil following restoration Jer 31:12 *See also* Hos 2:22; Joel 2:18–19,24

The firstfruits of the oil harvest Nu 18:12; Dt 18:4; 2Ch 31:5; Ne 10:37

Tithes of oil Dt 12:17; 14:23; Ne 13:12

Oil as a commodity for trade 1Ki 5:11 pp 2Ch 2:10; Ezr 3:7; Eze 27:17; Hos 12:1

Oil as a sign of prosperity Job 29:6 *See also* Dt 33:24; 2Ki 20:13 pp Isa 39:2; Pr 21:20; Isa 57:9; Eze 16:18–19

Oil associated with celebration Ps 45:7 *The joy with which God anoints his servants is likened to the oil which anoints the bridegroom in preparation for his wedding. See also* Ps 104:15; Ecc 9:8; Isa 61:3; Mt 6:17 *Oil draws attention away from the fact that a person is fasting;* Heb 1:9

Oil as a sign of honour Ps 23:5 *Oil was used to anoint the heads of honoured guests at a meal. See also* Ps 141:5; Lk 7:46

See also

3239 Holy Spirit, anointing	5373 lamp & lampstand
4404 food	5617 measures, liquid
4490 ointment	
4492 olive	7304 anointing
4496 perfume	7368 grain offering
5222 baking	8283 joy

4490

ointment

A liquid blend of aromatic substances, usually spices, used as a cosmetic and also as a medicinal balm. Lotions were applied to the body to refresh, to improve appearance and to give a pleasing fragrance. Balm, especially from Gilead, was used to soothe pain and to heal wounds.

Preparation of ointment Job 41:31 *One way of making ointment was to crush solid ingredients and boil them together in olive oil.*

Preparation of the holy anointing oil Ex 35:28 *See also* Ex 25:6 pp Ex 35:8; Ex 30:23–25,33 *The holy anointing oil was to be prepared only by those authorised to do so.*

Ointments made from blended spices 2Ch 16:14; SS 3:6; Lk 23:56

Containers for ointment Isa 3:20 *Ointments kept in alabaster boxes increased in quality, and so in value, with age:* Mt 26:7 pp Mk 14:3 Lk 7:37

Uses of ointment

As a cosmetic lotion Ru 3:3 *See also* Est 2:12; SS 1:12; Eze 16:9 Ps 104:15 *See also* 2Sa 12:20; 14:2; Ecc 9:8; Da 10:3; Mt 6:17; Ex 30:32

To anoint the heads of guests Ps 23:5 *See also* Ps 133:2 *This may reflect the custom of anointing a guest with perfumed ointment which melted and ran down the face and clothes to produce a pleasing fragrance;* Lk 7:46

To anoint the dead Mt 26:12 pp Mk 14:8 *See also* Jn 12:7; Ge 50:2–3,26; Mk 16:1 pp Lk 24:1; Jn 19:39–40

Expensive ointments Mt 26:8–9 pp Mk 14:4–5 *(Spike)nard*

was an expensive import from India. See also Pr 21:17; SS 4:13–14; Am 6:6 *The use of expensive ointments was a mark of luxury;* Jn 12:5

Ointment used in healing

Oil used to soothe and heal Isa 1:6 *See also* Ps 55:21; Lk 10:34

Medicinal balm Jer 8:22 *Gilead was famous for its healing balsam. See also* 2Ch 28:15; Jer 46:11; 51:8

See also

4408 balm	5241 burial
4466 herbs and spices	5285 cures
	5333 healing
4486 myrrh	5405 medicine
4488 oil	7304 anointing
4496 perfume	7386 incense
5234 bottle	

4492

olive

An evergreen tree native to the Near East. Also the fruit of this tree, for which it is cultivated. The fruit can be eaten or pressed to produce oil for food or other uses.

Olive oil

Olives pressed to produce oil Mic 6:15 *See also* Ex 29:40; Lev 24:2; Nu 28:5

Olive oil in food use Eze 16:13 *See also* Nu 18:11–13; Dt 8:6–9; 1Ch 27:28; 2Ch 11:5–11; Job 29:4–6

Olive oil used in the tabernacle Lev 24:2 *See also* Ex 25:1–7; 30:22–33; 35:4–9,28

Offerings of olive oil Ex 29:38–41 *See also* Nu 18:12–13; 28:3–8; Ezr 7:21–23; Eze 16:19

Payment, tribute and trade in olive oil 1Ki 5:10–11 *See also* 2Ch 2:8–10,15–16; Hos 12:1; Lk 16:1–8; Rev 18:11–13

Olive trees

Olive trees cultivated for their fruit Hag 2:19 *See also* Ge 8:11; Dt 28:38–40; 2Ki 18:31–32; Isa 41:19; Am 4:9

Wild olive trees Ne 8:15 *See also* Ro 11:24

Olive trees in visions Rev 11:3–6 *See also* Zec 4:1–14

Metaphorical references to olive trees Ps 52:8 *See also* Jdg 9:8–9; Job 15:33; Ps 128:3; Isa 17:4–6; 24:10–13; Jer 11:16–17; Hos 14:5–6; Ro 11:1–36 *the grafting of olive trees*

Olive groves Ex 23:10–11 *See also* Dt 6:10–11; Jos 24:13; Jdg 15:4–5; 1Sa 8:11–14; Ne 5:9–11; 9:25; Jn 18:1–3

Olive wood 1Ki 6:23–28 *See also* 1Ki 6:31–35

See also

4450 fruit	4528 trees
4488 oil	4552 wood

4494

papyrus

A large plant growing in marshland, sometimes to a height of six metres.

Papyrus was used for making boats Ex 2:3; Job 9:26; Isa 18:2

Papyrus indicates an ample water supply Job 8:11–13; Isa 35:7 *Papyrus growing in what was once desert depicts the blessing coming on God's redeemed people.*

See also

4402 plants	5515 scroll

4496

perfume

Substances used to make perfumes

By blending ingredients Ex 30:23–24,34

Substances used as perfumes SS 4:13–14 *See also* SS 1:12–14; 3:6; 5:13; Mk 14:3; Jn 12:3

Perfume ingredients as traded commodities Ge 37:25; Eze 27:19; Rev 18:13

The attractive fragrance of perfume

Its tempting allure Pr 7:17 *See also* Isa 57:9; Eze 23:40–41

Its pleasing fragrance Pr 27:9; SS 1:3; 4:10

Fragrance used metaphorically 2Co 2:14–16 *See also* Eph 5:2; Php 4:18

Examples of the use of perfume

As a cosmetic Est 2:12 *See also* Ru 3:3

To give fragrance to clothes Ps 45:8 *See also* SS 4:11

In burying the dead Mt 26:12 pp Mk 14:8 *See also* 2Ch 16:14; Mk 16:1 pp Lk 23:56–24:1; Jn 12:7; 19:39–40

Perfumers

Commissioned to make oil and incense for the sanctuary Ex 37:29 *See also* Ex 30:25,33 *The manufacture of the sacred anointing oil by unauthorised persons was forbidden;* Ex 30:35; 1Ch 9:30

Other references to perfumers 1Sa 8:13 *perfumers in the service of the king;* Ne 3:8 *Hananiah*

See also

4466 herbs and spices	5234 bottle
	5241 burial
4486 myrrh	6241 seduction
4488 oil	7304 anointing
4490 ointment	7386 incense
5183 smell	

4498

ploughing

Cutting up the furrows in soil and turning it up before work can be done on the land.

Ploughing as a way of life
1Ki 19:19–21; Lk 17:7 *See also* 1Sa 8:12; 13:19–21; Job 1:14; Pr 20:4; Isa 28:24; Eze 36:9; Am 9:13

Rules concerning ploughing
Ex 23:10–11; 34:21; Dt 22:10

Ploughing used figuratively
Job 4:8; Lk 9:62 *See also* Jdg 14:18; Ps 129:3; 141:7; Isa 2:4; Jer 4:3; Hos 10:11–12; Am 6:12; 1Co 9:10

See also

4208 land, divine responsibility	4970 seasons of year
4406 agriculture	5056 rest
4464 harvest	7482 Year of Jubilee
4510 sowing & reaping	

4500

poison

A substance obtained from plants or animals that can cause illness, pain, disability or death. It is often used symbolically to refer to distress or bitterness.

Kinds of poison
Poison from plants, water or food
Ex 15:23; Dt 32:32; 2Ki 2:19–22; 4:39–40; Hos 10:4

Poison from animals or reptiles
Nu 21:6; Dt 32:24,33

Poison used symbolically
To refer to distress
In these incidences God himself is portrayed as the one who brings such bitter experiences: Job 6:4; Jer 8:14; 9:15; 23:15

To refer to evil and its effects
Job 20:12–16 *See also* Dt 29:18; 32:32–33; Ps 58:4; Pr 23:32; Isa 14:29; Jer 8:17; Am 6:12; Ac 14:2; Ro 3:13; Ps 140:1–3; Jas 3:8; Rev 9:5

See also

4687 snake	9210 judgment, God's
5799 bitterness	
8734 evil	

4502

reed

A plant that grows in water
Job 8:11 *See also* Ge 41:1–4,17–21; Ex 2:1–6; 1Ki 14:15; Job 40:21; Isa 19:6; 35:7

Reeds are weak and fragile plants
Mt 11:7 pp Lk 7:24 *See also* 2Ki 18:21 pp Isa 36:6; Isa 58:5; Mt 12:20; Isa 42:3

Uses of reeds
For fuel Job 41:20

As measuring rods Rev 11:1

The metaphorical use of reeds
Isa 9:14–15 *See also* Isa 19:14–15; Eze 29:6–7

See also

4402 plants	8357 weakness
5801 brokenness	

4504

roots

The source and foundation of a tree or plant, anchoring it to the soil, usually found beneath the surface of the ground. Scripture contains literal, metaphorical and figurative references to roots.

Roots of trees and plants
Job 30:4 *See also* Job 14:7–9; Mt 13:3–6 pp Mk 4:2–6; Mk 11:20–21

Jesus Christ as the "Root of David"
Rev 22:16 *See also* Isa 11:1–5,10–12; 53:1–3; Ro 15:8–12; Rev 5:5

The metaphorical use of roots
Individuals and nations depicted as trees or plants with roots Job 29:18–20 *See also* Jdg 5:14; Job 8:11–19; 18:5–17; Ps 1:3; 80:14–15; Isa 5:22–24; 14:30; 37:30–32 *the LORD's sign to Hezekiah;* Jer 17:7–8; Eze 17:1–10; 31:3–9 *Nebuchadnezzar's dream of a tree:* Da 4:13–16,23–26 Hos 9:16; 14:5; Mal 4:1; Mt 3:10 pp Lk 3:9; Mt 13:18–21 pp Mk 4:13–17 pp Lk 8:11–13 *the parable of the sower;* Mt 15:13; Ro 11:13–21

Sources and foundations described as roots 1Ti 6:10 *See also* Job 19:28; 28:9; Pr 12:12; Isa 14:29; Am 2:9; Jnh 2:6

Bitter roots Heb 12:15 *See also* Dt 29:18

Roots as a symbol of stability and growth
Taking root Col 2:6–7 *See also* 2Ki 19:30; Job 5:3; Ps 80:8–9; Isa 27:6; 40:24; Jer 12:2; Eph 3:14–19

Being uprooted Job 19:10 *See also* 1Ki 14:15; Ps 52:5; Pr 10:30; 12:3; Jer 1:10; 12:14–15; 31:28; 45:4; Eze 17:9; 19:12; Jude 12

See also

2203 Christ, titles of	5317 foundation
4402 plants	5953 stability
4416 branch	8443 growth
4528 trees	

4506

seed

The means of propagating life from one generation to another. Figuratively, the term illustrates principles of spiritual life and growth, especially in later parts of the OT and throughout the NT.

How seed was used
Seed for eating Ge 1:29; 42:1–2; Ne 5:1–2; Isa 28:28; Ecc 11:6

Seed as an offering Lev 23:15–21 pp Nu 28:26–31; 2Ch 31:5

Seed to measure value Lev 27:16

How seed was appreciated
The presence of seed was a blessing Zec 8:12 *See also* Ge 8:22; Ps 67:6; 85:12

The absence of seed was a curse Joel 1:16–17 *See also* Dt 28:38–42

Regulations in the law concerning seed
Dt 22:9 pp Lev 19:19 *See also* Lev 11:37–38; 27:30

Seed used figuratively to illustrate kingdom life
To illustrate those ready to enter the kingdom of God Jn 4:35–38

To illustrate birth into eternal life 1Pe 1:23 *See also* 1Jn 3:9

To illustrate the growth of the kingdom of God Mt 13:31–32 pp Mk 4:30–32 pp Lk 13:18–19; Mk 4:26–29 *See also* Mt 13:24–30,36–43

To illustrate the growth of the church 1Co 3:6–7

To illustrate God's word and people's response to it Mt 13:1–23 pp Mk 4:1–20 pp Lk 8:4–15 *the parable of the sower*

To illustrate faith Mt 17:20

To illustrate the principle that death comes before life Jn 12:23–25 *See also* 1Co 15:36

To illustrate the resurrection body 1Co 15:35–38

God calls his people to sow seeds of righteousness
Jas 3:18 *See also* Ps 126:5–6; Pr 22:8; Jer 4:3–4; Hos 10:12; 2Co 9:6,10; Gal 6:7–9

See also

2357 Christ, parables	5724 offspring
2375 kingdom of God	6728 regeneration
4015 life	8020 faith
4446 flowers	8160 seeking God
4464 harvest	8256 fruitfulness
4484 mustard seed	8443 growth

4508

sickle

A cutting tool with a short handle used in harvesting grain. Early blades were made of wood lined with flint teeth; these were later replaced with curved iron blades. The cutting down of grain at harvest with a sickle is used as a symbol of God's judgment.

Sickles used to harvest grain
Mk 4:29 *See also* Dt 16:9; 23:25 *Sickles were not to be used in another person's field;* 1Sa 13:19–21; Jer 50:16

Cutting down grain as a symbol of judgment
Joel 3:13; Rev 14:14–19 *See also* Isa 17:5; Jer 51:33; Mic 4:12; Mt 13:30

See also

4406 agriculture	5583 tools
4428 corn	9210 judgment, God's
4456 grain	
4464 harvest	
4510 sowing & reaping	

4510

sowing and reaping

OT references are mainly agricultural

with regulatory laws covering crop production and festivals of thanksgiving. God's blessing was reflected in the harvest. The NT refers more to the spiritual sowing and reaping that takes place in the kingdom of God.

Regulations concerning the sowing and reaping of crops
Laws of purity related to planting Lev 19:23–25; Dt 22:9

Reapers are to leave gleanings for the poor Lev 19:9–10; 23:22; Dt 24:19; Ru 2:2–3,15–16

Harvest celebrations Ex 23:16 *See also* Lev 23:9–11,39–41; Dt 16:9–10,13–15

The Sabbath-rest for the land and its cultivators Ex 23:10–11; 34:21; Lev 25:3–5,11

Reaping a good harvest is a blessing from God
It is a consequence of obedience Ge 26:12; Lev 25:18–22; 26:3–5,10

It is a promise to the remnant of God's people Am 9:13–14 *See also* Isa 30:23; 62:8–9; 65:21–22; Jer 31:5; Zec 8:11–12

God's judgment on Israel is reflected in reaping a poor harvest
A poor yield of crops Lev 26:18–20; Dt 28:15,38–40; Isa 5:10; 17:10–11; Jer 8:13; 12:13; Hag 1:6,10–11

The harvesting of one's crops by others Lev 26:15–16 *See also* Ne 9:36–37; Job 31:7–8; Jer 5:17; Mic 6:15

Proverbs and poems of sowing and harvest
Pr 10:5; 20:4; Isa 28:23–29

Moral and spiritual sowing and reaping
Good and evil Job 4:8 *See also* Pr 11:18; 22:8; Hos 8:7; 10:12–13; Gal 6:7–8; Jas 3:18

Sowing and reaping in the kingdom of God Mk 4:3–8 pp Mt 13:3–8 pp Lk 8:5–8 *See also* Mt 13:18–23 pp Mk 4:14–20 pp Lk 8:11–15; Mt 13:24–30,37–39; Mk 4:26–29

The certainty of reaping Ps 126:5–6; Gal 6:9

Reaping where others have sown Jn 4:35–38; Ro 1:13; 1Co 3:5–9

Reaping a material harvest from spiritual sowing 1Co 9:9–11

People and nations are reaped for judgment
Joel 3:13 *See also* Jer 51:33; Hos 6:11; Rev 14:15–19

Metaphorical use of sowing and reaping
Isa 5:1–7; 17:4–6; Jer 2:3,21; 1Co 15:35–44; 2Co 9:6–11

See also

4406 agriculture	4508 sickle
4412 binding corn	5903 maturity,
4430 crops	physical
4454 gleaning	7354 feasts and
4464 harvest	festivals
4468 horticulture	8257 fruitfulness,
4498 ploughing	natural
4506 seed	

4512

staff

The staff was a basic item of personal property
It was carried at most times 1Sa 14:27 *See also* Ge 47:31; Jdg 6:21; Heb 9:4

It was carried by travellers Ge 32:10 *See also* Ex 12:11; Mt 10:5–10 pp Mk 6:7–13 pp Lk 9:1–6

It was carried by shepherds Mic 7:14 *See also* Ps 23:4; Zec 11:7,10–14

The staff was sometimes a symbol of authority
Ge 49:10 *See also* Ge 38:18,25; Nu 21:17–18; Jdg 5:14; 2Ki 18:21 pp Isa 36:6; Mt 27:28–30 pp Mk 15:19

God's miraculous power was manifest through Moses' and Aaron's staffs
Ex 4:2–5,15–17; 7:8–12,14–20 *the plague of blood;* Ex 8:5–6 *the plague of frogs;* Ex 8:16–17 *the plague of gnats;* Ex 9:22–24 *the plague of hail;* Ex 10:12–14 *the plague of locusts;* Ex 14:15–16 *the parting of the Red Sea;* Ex 17:5–13

The budding of Aaron's staff: Nu 17:1–10; Heb 9:4 Nu 20:7–13

See also

5071 Aaron	5513 sceptre
5101 Moses	7784 shepherd

4514

stick

Literal uses of a stick of wood
For fuel Am 4:11 *See also* 1Ki 17:8–12; Zec 3:1–2

For beating Isa 28:27 *See also* 1Sa 17:41–44

To extend one's reach Mk 15:33–36 pp Mt 27:45–49

Elisha and the axe-head that floats 2Ki 6:1–7

As an expression of contempt Hos 4:10–12 *See also* Eze 21:8–12

Sticks used figuratively
Symbolic use Eze 37:15–28

Dry as a stick La 4:8

See also

4416 branch	4528 trees
4512 staff	4552 wood

4516

straw

Uses of straw
As animal bedding and fodder Ge 24:32 *See also* Ge 24:22–25;

Jdg 19:16–19; 1Ki 4:27–28; Isa 11:7; 65:25

In brickmaking Ex 5:6–7 *See also* Ex 5:10–13,15–18

The lightness and fragility of straw
Job 21:18 *See also* Job 41:26–29; Isa 5:24

Straw is of little value
Isa 33:11 *See also* Isa 25:10; Jer 23:28; 1Co 3:10–15

See also

4426 chaff	5239 bricks

4518

sycamore-fig tree

Sycamore-fig trees were plentiful in Judea
1Ki 10:27 pp 2Ch 1:15 pp 2Ch 9:27 *See also* Lk 19:4

The cultivation of sycamore-fig trees
Am 7:14 *See also* 1Ch 27:28; Ps 78:47

See also

4440 fig-tree	4528 trees
4450 fruit	

4520

thorns

Thorns and thistles as the result of the curse of the fall
Ge 3:17–19 *See also* Nu 33:55; Jos 23:12–13; Isa 5:5–6; 7:23–25; 55:8–13; Jer 12:13; Hos 9:6

Thorns and thistles as worthless weeds
Heb 6:7–8 *See also* 2Sa 23:6; 2Ki 14:9 pp 2Ch 25:18; Mt 7:16 pp Lk 6:44; Mt 13:1–8 pp Mk 4:1–8 pp Lk 8:4–8; Mt 13:22 pp Mk 4:18–19 pp Lk 8:14

Thorns unpleasant and to be avoided
2Sa 23:6–7 *See also* Pr 15:19; 22:5; SS 2:2; Hos 2:6

Thorns associated with burning
Isa 33:12 *See also* Ex 22:6; Ps 118:12; Ecc 7:6; Isa 9:18; 10:17; 27:4

Thorns used as instruments of punishment
Jdg 8:16 *See also* Jdg 8:4–7

Thorns indicative of desolation and dereliction
Hos 10:8 *See also* Pr 24:30–31; Isa 32:11–15

Jesus Christ crowned with thorns
Mt 27:28–29 pp Mk 15:16–18 pp Jn 19:2–6

Metaphorical use of thorns
Mic 7:4 *See also* Eze 2:6; 28:24; 2Co 12:7

See also

4402 plants	5280 crown
4422 brier	5482 punishment
4540 weeds	5827 curse

4522

threshing

The process of beating out or separating grain from harvested stalks.

Threshing and the harvest
Lev 26:5 *See also* Jdg 6:11; 1Ch 21:20; 1Co 9:9; Dt 25:4; 1Ti 5:18 *Paul is adapting a humane OT law to the support of Christian workers.*

Threshing implements
2Sa 24:22 pp 1Ch 21:23 *A threshing-sledge was a board studded underneath with sharp stones which was dragged by oxen over the wheat ears in order to separate the kernels. See also* Job 41:30; Isa 28:27–28; 41:15

Threshing used figuratively
Isa 27:12; Hos 10:11 *See also* 2Ki 13:7; Pr 20:26; Jer 50:11; Mic 4:13

See also
4426 chaff	4524 threshing-floor
4456 grain	4550 winnowing
4464 harvest	5530 sifting
4510 sowing &	5621 wheel
reaping	

4524

threshing-floor

The place where winnowing and threshing took place at harvest time.

The threshing-floor and agriculture
Ge 50:10–11; Jdg 6:37; Ru 3:2–14; 1Sa 23:1; 2Sa 6:6 pp 1Ch 13:9; 1Ki 22:10 pp 2Ch 18:9; Job 39:12

The threshing-floor as a symbol of harvest
Dt 16:13 *See also* Nu 15:20; 18:27,30; Dt 15:14; 2Ki 6:27; Hos 9:1–2; Joel 2:24

The threshing-floor as a symbol of judgment
Isa 21:10; Hos 13:3 *See also* Jer 51:33; Da 2:35; Mic 4:12; Mt 3:12 pp Lk 3:17

A threshing-floor was the site of the Jerusalem temple
2Ch 3:1 *See also* 2Sa 24:16–25 pp 1Ch 21:15–26

See also
4406 agriculture	7467 temple,
4426 chaff	Solomon's
4464 harvest	9210 judgment,
4522 threshing	God's
4550 winnowing	

4526

tree of life

One of two trees situated in the centre of the Garden of Eden. It is also mentioned in Revelation, where it symbolises life and salvation.

The tree of life in the Garden of Eden
Ge 2:8–17 *See also* Ge 3:22–24

The tree of life in Revelation
Rev 22:1–2 *See also* Rev 2:7; 22:14–15,18–19

The tree of life as a metaphor
Pr 15:4 *See also* Pr 3:13–18; 11:30; 13:12

See also
4241 Garden of Eden	5033 knowledge of
4528 trees	good & evil

4528

trees

Large, woody plants with trunk, branches, leaves and roots, noted for their long lives. Scripture refers to many different varieties of tree.

God's creation of trees
Ge 1:11–12

Acacia
Ex 37:1–5 *See also* Ex 25:1–16,23; 26:15,26; 27:1,6; 30:1; 36:36; 37:25; 38:1; Dt 10:3; Isa 41:19

Almond tree
Jer 1:11–12 *See also* Ge 30:37–39; Ex 25:31–34 pp Ex 37:17–20; Ecc 12:5

Almug-wood
1Ki 10:11–12

Balsam tree
2Sa 5:22–25 pp 1Ch 14:13–16

Broom tree
Job 30:4 *See also* 1Ki 19:3–4; Ps 120:4

Cedar tree
Eze 31:3 *See also* 1Ki 4:33; 10:27; Ps 92:12–15

Cypress tree
Isa 44:14 *See also* Ge 6:14; Isa 41:19; 60:13; Eze 27:6

Fig-tree
Mic 4:4 *See also* Dt 8:7–9; Lk 21:29–31

Fir tree
Isa 41:19–20 *See also* Isa 60:13

Myrtle
Isa 55:13 *See also* Isa 41:19; Zec 1:8–11

Oak tree
Jos 24:26 *See also* Ge 35:4,8; Jdg 6:11–19; 2Sa 18:9–14; 1Ki 13:13–14; Ps 29:9; 56:1; Isa 1:29–30; 2:12–13; 6:13; 44:14; 57:5; 61:3; Eze 6:13; 27:6; Hos 4:13; Am 2:9; Zec 11:2

Olive tree
Ps 52:8 *See also* Jdg 9:8–9; Zec 4:1–14; Ro 11:24

Palm tree
Nu 33:9 *See also* Ex 15:27; 1Ki 6:29,35; 2Ch 3:5; Ps 92:12; SS 7:8; Eze 40:16; 41:17–20

Pine tree
Isa 60:13 *See also* 1Ki 6:15; 9:11; 2Ki 19:23 pp Isa 37:24; Isa 14:8; 41:19; 55:13; Eze 27:5; 31:8; Hos 14:8; Zec 11:2

Plane trees
Ge 30:37 *See also* Eze 31:8

Poplar tree
Isa 44:4 *See also* Ge 30:37; Hos 4:13

Sycamore-fig tree
1Ki 10:27 pp 2Ch 1:15 pp 2Ch 9:27

Terebinth tree
Isa 6:13 *See also* Hos 4:13

Willow tree
Eze 17:5–6

Great trees
Ge 13:18 *See also* Ge 14:13; 18:1; Dt 11:30

Symbolic use of trees
As a symbol of permanence or long life
Isa 65:22

As a symbol of well-being Ps 1:3; Jer 17:8

As a means of execution Dt 21:23; Ac 5:30; Gal 3:13; 1Pe 2:24

As bearers of fruit Mt 3:10; 7:17–19; 12:33; Lk 6:43–44

The trees of life and knowledge Ge 2:9; Rev 2:7; 22:2,14

As an example of distorted vision Mk 8:24

See also
4402 plants	4492 olive
4404 food	4504 roots
4416 branch	4518 sycamore-fig
4424 cedar	tree
4440 fig-tree	4526 tree of life
4448 forests	4552 wood
4450 fruit	

4530

unleavened bread

Bread baked without yeast, often made because of insufficient time to prepare bread in the conventional manner. It was also eaten at the Passover Feast and was presented with sacrifices and offerings.

Unleavened bread prepared in haste
Ex 12:39 *See also* Ge 19:1–3; Ex 12:8–11; Jdg 6:17–19; 1Sa 28:21–25

Unleavened bread eaten to commemorate the Passover
Ex 12:1–20; 13:3–7; 23:15; 34:18; Lev 23:5–6 pp Nu 28:16–17; Nu 9:9–11; Dt 16:1–4,8; Eze 45:21

Unleavened bread presented to God as an offering
Lev 2:11 *See also* Ex 29:2–4 pp Lev 8:1–3; Ex 29:22–25 pp Lev 8:25–28; Lev 2:4–5; 6:14–17; 7:11–12; Nu 6:13–20

Symbolism of unleavened bread
1Co 5:6–8

See also
4404 food	7364 fellowship
4418 bread	offering
4432 dough	7368 grain offering
4554 yeast	7406 Passover
7360 Feast of	7745 ordination
Unleavened	
Bread	

Offerings of wheat
Ex 34:22 *See also* Ex 29:2–3; Ezr 6:9;
7:21–23; Eze 45:13

Trade in wheat
Eze 27:17 *See also* Am 8:4–6;
Rev 18:11–13

Wheat as payment or tribute
2Ch 2:8–10 pp 1Ki 5:11 *See also*
2Ch 2:15–16; 27:5; Lk 16:1–7; Rev 6:6

Metaphorical references to wheat
Mt 3:11–12 pp Lk 3:16–17 *See also*
SS 7:2; Lk 22:31–32

See also

4404 food	4522 threshing
4426 chaff	4524 threshing-floor
4428 corn	4540 weeds
4430 crops	5282 crushing
4456 grain	7368 grain offering
4464 harvest	
4510 sowing & reaping	

4944

wine

Drink made from fermented grape
juice, often drunk instead of water in
biblical times. Scripture recognises
the richness of wine and its value in
bringing joy to people; however, it
condemns the excessive drinking of
wine, and recommends total
abstinence in some situations.

Offerings of wine
Nu 15:5 *See also* Ex 29:40;
Lev 23:12–13; Nu 28:14; Dt 32:37–38;
1Sa 1:24; Ezr 6:8–10

Tithes and firstfruits of wine
Ne 13:12 *See also* Nu 18:11–12;
Dt 12:17; 14:23–26; 18:4–5;
2Ch 31:4–5

Wine as a sign of blessing
Ge 27:28 *See also* Dt 7:13; 11:13–14;
33:28; 2Ki 18:31–32; 1Ch 12:40; Ps 4:7;
Pr 3:9–10; Jer 31:12; Joel 2:18–24; 3:18;
Am 9:13–14

Lack of wine as a sign of God's displeasure
Jer 48:33 *See also* Dt 28:38–51;
Isa 24:7–9; Joel 1:10; Hag 2:14–16

Wine as an alternative to water
1Ti 5:23 *See also* Ge 14:17–18;
Jdg 19:19; La 2:12; Mt 27:48
pp Mk 15:36 pp Lk 23:36
pp Jn 19:28–29

Wine with meals
Ge 27:25 *See also* Ru 2:14; Job 1:18–19;
Pr 9:1–6; Isa 22:13

The pleasant taste and effects of wine
Isa 25:6 *See also* Jdg 9:12–13;
Ps 104:14–15; Ecc 9:7; 10:19; SS 1:2–4;
4:10; 7:8–9

The dangers of drinking wine
Pr 20:1 *See also* Ge 9:20–27 Noah;
Ge 19:30–38 Lot and his daughters;

1Sa 1:13–15; 2Sa 13:28; Est 1:10–12;
Isa 28:1,7; Hos 7:3–5; Joel 1:5;
Na 1:9–10; Ac 2:1–21; Eph 5:18

The irresponsibility of wine drinkers
Pr 21:17 *See also* Pr 23:19–21,29–35;
31:4–7; Ecc 2:3; Isa 5:11–12,22–23;
22:13; 56:12; Mic 2:11

Abstinence from wine
Lev 10:9 *See also* Nu 6:1–21;
Jdg 13:2–7; Jer 35:1–19; Eze 44:21;
Da 1:3–16; 10:1–3; Am 2:11–12;
Lk 1:11–17; 7:33

Stores of wine
2Ch 32:28 *See also* 1Ch 9:29; 27:27;
2Ch 11:11–12; Ne 10:37–39

Wine stewards
Est 1:7–8 *See also* Ge 40:1–13;
Ne 1:11–2:1

Trade in wine
Joel 3:3 *See also* Rev 18:11–13

Jesus Christ's miracle of water turned into wine
Jn 2:1–11

Drugged wine
Mt 27:34 pp Mk 15:23

Metaphorical use of wine
Ps 75:8 *God's wrath is often pictured as a
cup of wine to be drunk. See also*
Ge 49:11–12; Job 32:19; Ps 60:3; 78:65;
Pr 4:17; Isa 55:1 *quenching spiritual
thirst*; Jer 23:9; 25:15; 48:11; 51:7
*illustrating judgment and the moral
decadence of Babylon the Great*;
Rev 14:8–10; 16:19; 17:1–2; 18:3

Wine as a symbol of the suffering and death of Jesus Christ
Lk 22:20 pp Mt 26:27–28
pp Mk 14:23–24 pp 1Co 11:25–26

See also

4410 banquets	4538 vineyard
4435 drinking	4546 winepress
4458 grape	4548 wineskin
4534 vine	7350 drink offering
4536 vinegar	7933 Lord's Supper

4546

winepress

The vat in which grapes were
trodden to produce juice for making
wine. Scripture sometimes uses the
image of treading grapes at the
winepress to depict scenes of divine
wrath and punishment.

Winepresses were widely used
Dt 15:12–14 *See also* Nu 18:25–27,30;
Jdg 6:11; 2Ki 6:24–27

Treading grapes at winepresses
Literal references Ne 13:15 *See also*
Job 24:11; Isa 16:10; Jer 48:33

Metaphorical references La 1:15 *See
also* Isa 63:1–6; Joel 3:13;
Rev 14:17–20; 19:11–16

The association of winepresses with harvest
Rev 14:18–19 *See also* Dt 16:13–15

Winepresses in vineyards
Isa 5:1–2 *See also* Mt 21:33–34
pp Mk 12:1

Winepresses in place-names
Jdg 7:25 *See also* Zec 14:10

See also

1025 God, anger of	4534 vine
4435 drinking	4538 vineyard
4458 grape	4544 wine
4464 harvest	4548 wineskin

4548

wineskin

A container or sack, made from
animal skin to hold wine. Jesus
Christ used the image of old and new
wineskins to explain the differences
between himself and John the
Baptist.

Wineskins used to store or carry wine
1Sa 10:2–4 *See also* 1Sa 1:24; Ps 119:83;
Jer 13:12–14; Hab 2:15–16

Old and new wineskins
Job 32:17–20 *New wine was stored in
new wineskins, which expanded with the
wine as it fermented. See also* Jos 9:3–13

Wineskins as gifts
2Sa 16:1–2 *See also* 1Sa 16:14–20;
25:14–20

The parable of old and new wineskins
Mt 9:14–17 pp Mk 2:18–22
pp Lk 5:33–39

See also

4544 wine	5234 bottle
4546 winepress	5325 gifts

4550

winnowing

The exposing of grain to the air by
either tossing or fanning so that the
loose outer part is blown away. It is
also used figuratively to refer to
God's judgment.

Winnowing took place at the threshing-floor
Ru 3:2

Winnowing used figuratively
Jer 15:7; Mt 3:12 pp Lk 3:17 *See also*
Pr 20:8,26; Isa 41:16; Jer 4:11; 51:2

See also

4426 chaff	4522 threshing
4456 grain	4524 threshing-floor
4464 harvest	5530 sifting

4552

wood

Trunks and branches of trees used as
raw material for various objects and
as fuel for burning. Acacia wood was
used extensively in the tabernacle
and olive wood in the temple.

Various kinds of wood

Acacia wood Ex 27:1 *See also*
Ex 25:10–13,23; 26:15–17,26–27; 27:6;
30:1–5; 35:4–7,24; 37:1–4; 38:1;
Dt 10:1–3

Cedar wood Lev 14:48–53 *See also*
Lev 14:1–7; Nu 19:1–8

Olive wood 1Ki 6:23 *See also*
1Ki 6:31–35

Cypress wood Eze 27:3–6

Items made from wood

Ex 7:19 *See also* Lev 11:29–32;
15:11–12; Nu 31:19–20; 35:16–18;
Ne 8:4; Isa 10:15; Jer 28:13; Eze 15:2–3;
41:22,25; 2Ti 2:20

Wooden idols

Dt 29:16–18 *See also* Dt 28:36,64;
Jdg 6:26; 2Ki 19:18 pp Isa 37:19;
Isa 40:18–20; 44:13–20; 45:20; 48:5;
Jer 2:26–28; 3:9; 10:6–8; Eze 20:32;
Da 5:1–4,23; Hos 4:12; 10:5–6;
Hab 2:19; Rev 9:20

Carpentry

Ex 31:1–5 pp Ex 35:30–33 *See also*
2Ch 2:13–14

Wood for burning sacrifices

Ne 10:34 *See also* Ge 22:3–13;
Lev 1:3–17; 3:1–5; 1Sa 6:14;
2Sa 24:22–23 pp 1Ch 21:23;
1Ki 18:22–24,30–38

Wood as fuel

Eze 24:3–5 *See also* Pr 26:20–21;
Isa 44:13–20; Eze 15:1–8

Chopping and gathering wood

Dt 19:5 *See also* Nu 15:32–36;
Dt 29:10–11; Jos 9:3–27; 2Ki 6:1–7

Metaphorical references to wood

Zec 12:6 *See also* Job 41:27; Jer 5:12–14

Symbolic use of wood

Eze 37:15–28 *See also* Ex 15:23–26

See also

4416 branch	5247 carpenters
4448 forests	5272 craftsmen
4514 stick	5322 gallows
4528 trees	5583 tools
4696 yoke	5621 wheel
5210 arrows	

4554

yeast

A raising agent commonly used in
bread. Bread that was required
quickly was baked without yeast, as
at the first Passover, commemorated
annually in the Feast of Unleavened
Bread. Although some non-meat
offerings contained yeast, it could
not be burned on the altar.

Unleavened bread was made without yeast

Ex 12:39 *See also* Ge 19:3;
Ex 12:8–11,34; Jdg 6:17–19;
1Sa 28:24–25

The consumption of yeast was prohibited during the Feast of Unleavened Bread

Ex 12:14–15 *See also* Ex 12:17–20;

13:3,6–7; 23:15,18; 34:18; Lev 23:6;
Nu 28:17; Dt 16:1–4; Eze 45:21

Sacrifices burned on the altar were not to contain yeast

Lev 2:11 *See also* Ex 29:1–3,22–24;
34:25; Lev 2:4–5; 6:16–17; 7:12–13;
8:2–3,26; 10:12; Nu 6:14–15,19

Some offerings contained yeast

Lev 23:17

Yeast as an image of the kingdom of God

Mt 13:33 pp Lk 13:20–21

Metaphorical references to yeast as something evil

1Co 5:6–8 *See also* Mt 16:5–12
pp Mk 8:14–21; Lk 12:1–3; Gal 5:2–12

See also

2375 kingdom of God	7360 Feast of Unleavened
4418 bread	Bread
4432 dough	7402 offerings
5345 influence	

4600

Living beings

4603

animals

A category of living creatures that
dwell mainly on the land,
distinguished from fishes, birds and
insects. Scripture stresses that all
animals are created by God and are
subordinate to human beings.

4604

animals, nature of

As a class within the created order,
their variety reflects God's generous
giving. He makes human beings
their stewards, though they
themselves come into the category
of creatures.

Animals in their profusion

Ge 1:24–25 *See also* Ge 7:1–3,13–16;
8:15–19; Ps 50:9–11; 148:7–10;
Isa 43:20; Eze 36:11

Animals as illustrated by their variety

Isa 11:6–8 *See also* Ex 23:12 *Ox, donkey*;
Ex 25:3–5 *Goat, sea cow*; Lev 11:4–7
Rabbit, pig; Lev 11:29–30 *Weasel, rat*;
Nu 19:2 *Heifer*; Dt 14:4–5 *Deer, gazelle,
antelope*; 1Sa 17:34–35 *Sheep, bear, lion*;
Job 40:15–24 *possibly the hippopotamus*;
Job 41:1–34 *possibly the crocodile*;
Ps 58:4 *Snake*; Ps 105:30 *Frog*; SS 2:15
Fox; Isa 13:21–22 *Jackal, wild goat,
hyena*; Isa 51:8 *Worm*

Human beings within the animal creation

As part of creation Ge 2:7;
Ecc 3:18–21 *See also* Ps 49:12

Significantly different from the rest of creation Ge 1:26–27

Human beings as stewards of the animal kingdom

Ps 8:6–8 *See also* Ge 1:26–28; 2:19–20;
9:1–2; Heb 2:6–8; Jas 3:7–8

Animals as the objects of divine, and therefore human, care

Ge 9:8–10 *See also* Ge 8:1; Ex 9:4–6;
2Ki 3:17; Job 5:23; 38:39–41; 39:1–30;
Ps 104:20–21; Pr 12:10; 27:23;
Joel 2:22; Jnh 4:11

Animals and Noah's ark

Ge 7:13–23

See also

4017 life, animal & plant	4657 horse
4618 calf	4666 lion
4621 colt	4687 snake
4624 cow	5001 human race, the
4627 creatures	8472 respect for environment
4630 dog	
4633 donkey	

4605

animals, religious role of

Central to the OT sacrificial system,
they were governed by strict laws
within the Mosaic code.

Animals as defined by the Law of Moses

Animals for food Lev 20:25–26 *See also*
Ex 22:31; Lev 22:8; Dt 12:15–16,21;
14:3–8; Eze 4:14; 44:31; Ac 10:9–14;
11:6; 15:19–20

Animals dedicated to the Lord
Ex 13:1–2 *See also*
Lev 27:9–13,26–28,32–33; Nu 18:15

Domestic animals Ex 21:33–36;
22:10–15; Lev 24:18–21

Relationships with animals forbidden
Ex 22:19; Lev 19:19

Animal carcasses Lev 11:39

Animals in the context of Israel's sacrificial system

Used in various sacrifices Lev 1:1–2;
Ps 66:15 *See also* Ge 8:20; Lev 3:1;
Nu 7:87–88; Dt 16:2; 2Ch 29:32–33;
35:10–13

Animals forbidden as sacrifices
Mal 1:8 *See also* Lev 22:24–25;
Dt 15:21; Mal 1:13–14

Animals in the context of judgment

Involved in judgment Zep 1:3 *See also*
Ge 6:7; 7:20–23 *the flood*
The plagues of Egypt: Ex 9:22–25; 13:15;
Ps 135:8
Jer 9:10; 12:4; 50:3; Eze 25:12–13;
Joel 1:19–20; Hab 2:17; Zec 14:15

As agents of judgment Lev 26:21–22
See also Eze 33:27; 39:4,17–18;
Da 4:31–32; Hos 2:12

See also

4615 bull	7340 clean and unclean
4651 goat	
4663 lamb	7402 offerings
4681 ram	7435 sacrifice, in OT
4684 sheep	9210 judgment, God's
5375 law	
5858 fat	
7316 blood, OT sacrifices	

4609

beast, the

In apocalyptic literature, symbol of the ultimate adversary of God in the great final spiritual battle.

Beasts represent rulers and nations opposed to God
Da 7:3–7,11–12,17,19–23

The beast represents the antichrist in the final spiritual battle
The emergence of the beast Rev 11:7; 13:1,11; 17:3

The power and authority of the beast Rev 13:2–7,12–15

Those who will worship the beast, and those who will not Rev 13:8,16–18; 14:9–11; 16:2; 20:4

The defeat of the beast and the fulfilment of God's purposes
Rev 16:10–11; 17:7–14,16–17; 19:19–20

See also
2372 Christ, victory	9105 last things
4121 Satan, enemy of God	9115 antichrist, the
8704 apostasy	9240 last judgment

4612

birds

Part of the created world, used for food. In OT times they were also used in sacrifices. In Scripture, birds are used in many metaphors.

Part of creation
Ge 1:21 *See also* Ge 1:20–30; 2:20; 1Co 15:39; Jas 3:7

Cared for by God Lk 12:24 pp Mt 6:26 *See also* Job 38:41; Ps 50:11; 147:9

To be cared for by humanity Dt 22:6–7

Specific varieties of bird
Raven Ge 8:7; 1Ki 17:4; SS 5:11

Eagle Ex 19:4; Job 39:27; Pr 23:5; Isa 40:31; Jer 49:16; Eze 17:3; Da 4:33; Hos 8:1

Hen Mt 23:37

Cock Pr 30:31; Mt 26:74

Ostrich Job 39:13–18; La 4:3

Owl Ps 102:6; Isa 34:11,15; Jer 50:39; Mic 1:8; Zep 2:14

Quail Ex 16:13; Nu 11:31–32; Ps 105:40

Sparrow Ps 84:3; Pr 26:2; Mt 10:29–31

Stork Ps 104:17; Jer 8:7; Zec 5:9

Vulture Job 15:23; Pr 30:17; Mic 1:16; Hab 1:8; Mt 24:28

Birds of prey Dt 28:26; 1Sa 17:46; 1Ki 16:4; Isa 18:6; Jer 12:9; Rev 19:17–18

Protected at the flood
Ge 6:20 *See also* Ge 8:17–19

Used in sacrifice
Ge 8:20 *See also* Ge 15:10; Lev 1:14; 12:8; 14:3–7,49–53; Lk 2:22–24

Used as food
Dt 14:11 *See also* Lev 17:13–14

Some not to be eaten
Lev 20:25 *See also* Lev 11:13–19 pp Dt 14:12–18

Not to be used as an object of worship
Dt 4:15–17 *See also* Ro 1:23

Appearing in dreams and visions
Ge 40:17; Ac 11:6; Rev 4:7; 12:14

Used metaphorically
Of freedom Ps 55:6 *See also* Ps 11:1

Of isolation Ps 102:7

Of powerlessness Hos 11:11

Of being trapped Ps 124:7 *See also* Pr 6:5; 7:23; Jer 5:26; La 3:52; Eze 13:20; Hos 7:12; Am 3:5

Of cruel invaders Isa 46:11 *See also* Dt 28:49–50

Of an object of hatred Jer 12:9

See also
1325 God, the Creator	4675 nest
	4678 pigeon
1330 God, the provider	4690 wings
	7340 clean and unclean
1409 dream	
4603 animals	7435 sacrifice, in OT
4627 creatures	8769 idolatry, in OT
4636 dove	

4615

bull

Bulls were particularly prized as sacrifices on account of their considerable value. The sacrifice of a bull was especially associated with the sin offering.

Bulls offered as sacrifices
Ex 29:36; 2Sa 6:12–13; Ac 14:13 *Also used in pagan sacrifices. See also* Nu 23:1–4; Job 42:7–8; Ps 66:15; Heb 9:13

Instructions for the offering of a bull Lev 4:13–21 *See also* Lev 1:3–9

Bulls sacrificed on significant occasions Nu 28:16–20 *The Passover. See also* Ex 24:4–5 *the covenant confirmed*; Ex 29:10–14; Lev 9:2; 16:11–14 *the Day of Atonement*; Nu 8:5–12; 29:12–13; 1Sa 1:24; 1Ch 15:25–26; 29:21–22; 2Ch 29:20–24; Ezr 6:9–10; 8:35; Eze 43:19–27; 45:18–24

Godly sacrifices in contrast to pagan ones 1Ki 18:22–24 *See also* Jdg 6:25–28

Even the sacrifice of bulls invalid without the spiritual conditions being fulfilled
Ps 69:30–31; Isa 1:11 *See also* Ps 50:9,13; Isa 66:3; Hos 12:11

Provisional nature of the OT sin offering of a bull
Heb 10:4

The bull as a symbol of strength
Dt 33:17 *See also* Ps 22:12; 68:30

Laws concerning bulls
Ex 21:28–36

Bulls in the design of the temple
1Ki 7:25–29 pp 2Ch 4:3–4; 2Ki 16:17; Jer 52:20

Bulls in the setting of judgment
Isa 34:6–7; Jer 50:27

Bulls and idolatry
Ps 106:20

See also
4605 animals, religious role	7316 blood, OT sacrifices
4624 cow	7324 calf worship
4654 horn	7435 sacrifice, in OT
6614 atonement	7444 sin offering

4618

calf

A young animal prized as the source of tender meat, suitable for celebrations. However, it also had associations with both the OT sacrificial system and idolatry.

The association of the calf with idolatry
Ex 32:2–8; 1Ki 12:28–29 *See also* Ex 32:19–24; Dt 9:16–21; 2Ki 10:28–29; 17:16; 2Ch 11:15; Ne 9:16–18; Ps 106:19–20; Hos 8:5–6; 10:5; 13:2; Ac 7:41

The sacrifice of calves
Mic 6:6 *See also* Lev 9:1–4,8–11; 2Sa 6:12–13; 1Ki 1:9–10; Heb 9:11–12,19–20

The flesh of the calf as a prized food
Pr 15:17; Lk 15:22–23 *See also* Ge 18:6–8; 1Sa 14:31–32; 28:24–25

The metaphorical use of calves
Jer 31:18; Mal 4:2 *See also* Ps 29:6; 68:30; Jer 34:18; 46:20–21

See also
4404 food	7316 blood, OT sacrifices
4476 meals	
4605 animals, religious role	7324 calf worship
4615 bull	7435 sacrifice, in OT
4624 cow	8768 idolatry

4621

colt

A young, untrained horse or donkey, associated in Scripture with humility or peace.

A colt is a young donkey
Job 11:12 *See also* Ge 49:11

The use of a colt by the coming king
Zec 9:9 *See also* Mt 21:2–7 pp Mk 11:2–7 pp Lk 19:30–35; Jn 12:15

See also
2036 Christ, humility	4633 donkey
2590 Christ, triumphal entry	4657 horse

4624

cow

Cows, in OT times, often symbolised wealth and material well-being.

Cows as evidence of prosperity
Job 21:10 *Part of Job's complaint about the prosperity of the wicked. See also* Ge 12:16; 24:35; 32:5,13–15; 41:1–4,17–21,25–27; 2Sa 12:2; 2Ch 32:27–28; Ps 50:10 *evidence of God's wealth;* Hab 3:17–18 *the believer's joy despite the absence of prosperity*

In the history of Israel
1Sa 6:7–14

Cows in God's new earth
Isa 11:7 *See also* Isa 30:23; 32:20

Cows as a source of nourishment and fuel
2Sa 17:29; Eze 4:15

Laws concerning cows
Ex 22:30; Lev 22:28

Cows in metaphors
Of stupidity Job 18:3

Of godless women Am 4:1

See also
1050 God, goodness	4480 milk
of	4615 bull
4406 agriculture	4618 calf

4627

creatures

Generally, living beings within God's creation, especially the exotic animals seen in visions, which often have a deep symbolic significance.

Creatures representing angelic beings who worship God
Eze 1:5–6; Rev 4:6–8 *The strange creatures of Ezekiel and Revelation seem to stand for the fulness and variety of God's creation. See also* Eze 1:7–25; 3:12–13; 10:15–22 *The creatures are here identified as cherubim;* Rev 4:9–11; 5:6–14; 6:1–3,5–6; 7:11; 14:3; 15:7; 19:4

Creatures representing kings or kingdoms
Da 7:17; 8:20–21 *The "beasts" here are unnatural, and represent the hostility of human empires to the rule of God. The horns represent individual kings within an imperial dynasty.*

Creatures representing Satan
The beast here represents Satan, with the horns representing royal authority at a time of Roman persecution of the church: Rev 12:3–4,7–9; 13:1
Da 7:2–8,19–26; 8:3–12; Rev 11:7; 13:2–8,11–18; 17:3,7–13

See also
1469 visions	4603 animals
1670 symbols	4609 beast, the
4110 angels	9105 last things
4150 cherubim	

4630

dog

Although used by shepherds and occasionally kept as pets, in Bible times most dogs were semi-wild scavengers.

The animal
Ex 11:7; Jdg 7:5; Job 30:1

Dogs as scavengers Ex 22:31; 1Ki 14:11; 16:4; 21:19,23; 22:38; 2Ki 9:10,36; Ps 59:6,14; 68:23

Dogs as dangerous and bloodthirsty
Jer 15:3; Ps 22:16,20; 2Pe 2:22

Dogs in the teaching of Jesus Christ
Mt 7:6; 15:26–27 pp Mk 7:27–28 *See also* Lk 16:21

Dogs in proverbs
Pr 26:11,17; Ecc 9:4

Dogs used as a term of abuse or low esteem
1Sa 17:43; 24:14; 2Sa 9:8; 16:9; 2Ki 8:13; Isa 56:10–11; Php 3:2; Rev 22:15

See also
4604 animals   7512 Gentiles, in NT

4633

donkey

A beast of burden, used to carry both goods and people.

Used for carrying goods
1Sa 16:20 *See also* Ge 22:3–5; 42:27; Ex 23:12 pp Dt 5:14 *As beasts of burden they were afforded rest on the Sabbath.*

Used for personal transport
1Sa 25:20; Mt 21:7 *See also* Ex 4:20 *Balaam's talking donkey:* Nu 22:22; 2Pe 2:16
Jos 15:18; Jdg 19:28; 2Sa 17:23; 19:26; 1Ki 13:23–29; Zec 9:9; Mt 21:5; Lk 10:34; Jn 12:14

The value of donkeys
Ex 22:4 *See also* Ex 20:17 pp Dt 5:21; Ex 22:9; Nu 16:15; Dt 22:3–4; 1Sa 12:3; Job 24:3; Lk 13:15

Mistreatment of donkeys
Nu 22:23 *See also* Dt 22:10

Sometimes found in the wild
Job 39:5 *See also* Job 6:5; Jer 2:24; Hos 8:9

Figurative use of the donkey
Ge 16:12 *See also* Ge 49:14; 2Ki 6:25; Isa 1:3; Jer 22:19

Samson and the donkey's jaw-bone
Jdg 15:15–16

See also
2590 Christ,	4621 colt
triumphal entry	4672 manger
4604 animals	5590 travel

4636

dove

A common species of bird. In Scripture the dove symbolises the Spirit of God, and also certain kinds of human behaviour.

A kind of bird
Ge 8:8–12; SS 2:12; Jer 8:7

Doves as sacrifices for those who were poor
Lev 5:7 *See also* Ge 15:9; Lev 1:14; 5:11; 12:6–8; 14:22,30; 15:14,29; Nu 6:10; Mt 21:12 pp Mk 11:15; Lk 2:24; Jn 2:14

"Dove" as a term of endearment
SS 2:14; 5:2; 6:9

Israel as God's "dove" Ps 68:13; 74:19

"Dove" used figuratively
Ps 55:6; SS 1:15; 4:1; 5:12; Isa 38:14; 59:11; Jer 48:28; Eze 7:16; Hos 7:11; 11:11; Na 2:7; Mt 10:16

The dove as a symbol of the Spirit of God
Mt 3:16 pp Mk 1:10 pp Lk 3:22 pp Jn 1:32–34

See also
1670 symbols	4612 birds
2510 Christ, baptism	4678 pigeon
of	7435 sacrifice, in OT
3120 Holy Spirit,	8264 gentleness
descriptions	8277 innocence
3269 Holy Spirit in	8299 love in
Christ	relationships

4639

dung and manure

Human dung is considered unclean
Dt 23:12–14; Eze 4:12–14

The Dung Gate of Jerusalem Ne 2:13; 3:13–14; 12:31

Uses of manure
As fertiliser Lk 13:8; 14:35

As fuel Eze 4:15

Symbolic references to dung
As fuel 1Ki 14:10

As something perishable Job 20:7

As something trampled down Isa 25:10

As something worthless Php 3:8

See also
4406 agriculture	6151 dirt
5268 cooking	7340 clean and
5979 waste	unclean

4642

fish

A basic ingredient of diet in biblical times. Fishing was regarded as a trade rather than a recreation.

Fish as part of God's creation
Ge 1:20–22 *See also* Ge 1:26; 9:2; 1Ki 4:33; Ps 8:8; 1Co 15:39

Fish as food

Mt 7:9–10　pp Lk 11:11; Mt 14:17
pp Mk 6:38 pp Lk 9:16 pp Jn 6:9 *See also*
Nu 11:5; Ne 13:16; Mt 15:34 pp Mk 8:7;
Lk 24:42; Jn 21:13

Rules about eating fish

Lev 11:9–12; Dt 14:9–10

Fish related to judgment

Ex 7:18; Isa 19:8 *See also* Ps 105:29;
Isa 50:2; Hos 4:3; Zep 1:3

Fish as the object of pagan worship

Dt 4:15–18 *See also* Jdg 16:23 *Dagon was the fish god.*

Fish involved in miracles

Jnh 1:17; Lk 5:4–7 *See also*
Mt 14:19–21 pp Mk 6:39–44
pp Lk 9:14–17 pp Jn 6:10–13;
Mt 15:35–38 pp Mk 8:7–9;
Mt 17:24–27; Jn 21:5–6

Figurative uses of fish

Fish as a symbol of entrapment
Ecc 9:12 *See also* Eze 29:4–5;
Hab 1:14–17

Fish as a symbol of the kingdom of God Mt 13:47–48 *See also* Eze 47:10

Fish as a symbol of the resurrection
Mt 12:40

Fishermen as the first disciples

Mt 4:18　pp Mk 1:16

Figurative use of fishermen

Jer 16:16; Mt 4:19 *Describing the disciples' evangelistic role.*

See also
2351 Christ, miracles　5433 occupations
5425 net　　　　　　　8747 false gods

4645

fleece

The woolly covering of a sheep used as an article of clothing or for warmth

Job 31:20; Heb 11:37

Used by Gideon for reassurance that he was doing God's will

Jdg 6:36–40

See also
4684 sheep　　　　8124 guidance
4693 wool

4648

goad

A spike used to drive animals on. The term is also figuratively applied to prompting and guiding people into action.

The goad as a farming implement

Used with animals 1Sa 13:21

Used as a weapon Jdg 3:31

Goading as a symbol of discipline

God's word as a goad Ecc 12:11 *See also* Ac 2:37

Conscience as a goad

Ac 26:14 *See also*
Ex 25:2; Job 20:2; Ro 2:15

Encouragement as a goad

Heb 10:24
See also 1Th 1:3 *The promptings of love and faith may be seen as symbolic goads.*

People goaded into doing wrong

Ge 3:1,12; Ex 32:1,23; Job 15:5; Jn 13:2

See also
1690 word of God　　8230 discipline
5008 conscience　　 8414 encourage-
6248 temptation　　　　　ment
8124 guidance

4651

goat

A common animal used both for food and within the sacrificial system.

The economic importance of goats

For food Ge 27:9; Jdg 13:15 *See also*
Dt 14:4,21; Jdg 6:19; Pr 27:27; Lk 15:29

For fabric Ex 35:26 *The tabernacle curtains were spun from goat hair, the ordinary material for making tents. See also* Ex 26:7; 36:14; Rev 6:12

As a measure of wealth and payment
Ge 30:32; 1Sa 25:2 *See also*
Ge 32:5,13–14; 47:17; Pr 27:26;
Eze 27:21

Goats used in sacrifice

For worship Ge 15:9; Jdg 13:19;
Ps 66:13–15

For atonement for sin Lev 4:23;
Ezr 8:35 *See also* Lev 3:12; 4:28; 5:6; 9:3;
Nu 7:16,22,28; 15:27

As a fellowship offering Nu 7:17,23,29

At the dedication of the temple
1Ki 8:63　pp 2Ch 7:5 *See also* 2Ch 30:24;
Ezr 6:17

Flawless goats were required Ex 12:5
See also Lev 1:10; Eze 43:22

The sacrifice of goats is unable to actually remove sins

Isa 1:11 *In spite of their many sacrifices there was no evidence of repentance;*
Heb 9:12–14; 10:3–4

Goats are symbolic of sinful humanity

Mt 25:32

See also
4603 animals　　　　7435 sacrifice, in OT
4654 horn　　　　　 7440 scapegoat
5155 hair　　　　　　7459 tabernacle, in
6614 atonement　　　　　OT
6750 sin-bearer

4654

horn

The hard, pointed growth on the heads of certain animals; a projection resembling such a growth. The horns of animals were regarded as symbols of strength. In apocalyptic writings, horns may denote various powers and enemies

of God. Altars were made with horn-like corner projections.

Horns of animals

Ge 22:13
Some species of owls have "horns" (or "tufts"): Lev 11:16; Dt 14:15
Ps 22:21; 69:31

Uses of animal horns

As musical instruments Ex 19:13;
Jos 6:4; 1Ch 15:28; 2Ch 15:14; Ps 81:3;
98:6; Da 3:5,7,10,15; Hos 5:8

As oil containers 1Sa 16:1,13; 1Ki 1:39

Uses of imitation horns

As projections at corners of altars
Ex 27:2; 29:12; 30:2–3,10; 37:25–26;
38:2; Lev 4:7,18,25,30,34; 8:15; 9:9;
16:18; 1Ki 1:50–51; 2:28; Ps 118:27;
Jer 17:1; Eze 43:15,20; Am 3:14;
Rev 9:13

As prophetic signs 1Ki 22:11
pp 2Ch 18:10

Horns as symbols of strength

Describing God's saving power
2Sa 22:2–3　pp Ps 18:2 *See also* Lk 1:69

Describing human strength Dt 33:17
See also 1Sa 2:1,10; Ps 75:10; 89:17,24;
92:10; 112:9; 132:17; 148:14; Jer 48:25;
La 2:3,17; Eze 29:21; 34:21; Mic 4:13

Symbolising the power of world rulers and enemies of God Da 7:7–25;
8:3–4,5–11,19–22; Zec 1:18–21;
Rev 12:3–9; 13:1–6,11–14;
17:3–8,12–17

Symbolising the power of Jesus Christ
Rev 5:6

See also
1427 prophecy　　　5595 trumpet
1670 symbols　　　　5954 strength
2315 Christ as Lamb　6510 salvation
4488 oil　　　　　　 7302 altar
4615 bull　　　　　　7304 anointing
4681 ram
5421 musical
　　 instruments

4657

horse

The animal most commonly associated with war and battle, the horse also appears figuratively in poetic and prophetic literature. Its domesticated usage was mainly for personal travel and the haulage of heavy loads.

The military use of horses

Ex 15:1; Jos 11:4; 2Ki 6:14–15
Pharaoh's army: Ex 14:9,28; Dt 11:4;
Isa 43:16–17
The battles between Israel and Aram:
1Ki 20:1,20–21
Job 39:19–25; Ps 76:6; Isa 5:28; Jer 4:13;
46:9; 51:21; Eze 38:4; Hab 1:8

Disabling horses in wartime

Jos 11:6 *See also* Jos 11:9; 2Sa 8:4
pp 1Ch 18:4; Mic 5:10

Warnings against reliance on horses
Isa 31:1 *See also* Dt 17:16; Ps 20:7; 33:17; 147:10

The ritual use of horses
Est 6:7–9 *See also* 1Sa 8:11; 2Sa 15:1; Jer 22:4

Horses as a means of exchange and a measure of wealth
Ge 47:17; 1Ki 4:26 *See also* 1Ki 9:19; 10:25–26 pp 2Ch 1:14; 2Ch 9:28; Isa 2:7

Horses as a means of transport and for the haulage of loads
2Ki 5:9 *See also* 2Ki 14:20 pp 2Ch 25:28; Est 8:10,14; Isa 21:7,9; 66:20

Harness and tackle for horses
Ps 32:9 *See also* 2Ki 19:28; Job 41:13; Isa 30:28; 37:29; Rev 14:20

The figurative and prophetic use of horse imagery
Jas 3:2–3; Rev 19:11 *See also* 2Ki 13:14; Isa 28:28; Joel 2:4; Zec 1:6–8; Rev 6:1–8; 9:17; 19:14

Heavenly horses
2Ki 2:11 *See also* 2Ki 6:17; 7:6

See also

4621 colt	5252 chariots
4633 donkey	5590 travel
4852 thunder	

4660
insects
A wide variety of insects are mentioned in Scripture. Some are useful in the provision of food, while others are viciously destructive. Their behaviour is used figuratively in the poetic and prophetic literature.

Regulations concerning insects as food
Lev 11:20–23 *See also* Dt 14:19

Kinds of insect
The ant Pr 6:6 *See also* Pr 30:25

The bee Jdg 14:8 *See also* Dt 1:44; Ps 118:12; Isa 7:18

The flea 1Sa 24:14; 26:20

The fly Ex 8:24 *See also* Ex 8:21–22,29–31; Ps 78:45; Ecc 10:1; Isa 51:6

The gnat Ex 8:16; Mt 23:24 *See also* Ex 8:17–18; Ps 105:31

The grasshopper Isa 40:22 *See also* Nu 13:33; 1Ki 8:37 pp 2Ch 6:28; Ps 105:34; Ecc 12:5; Na 3:15

The hornet Ex 23:28; Dt 7:20; Jos 24:12

The locust Joel 2:25; Mt 3:4 pp Mk 1:6 *See also* Ex 10:12–14; Ps 78:46; Pr 30:27; Jer 46:23

The moth Job 13:28; Mt 6:19–20 *See also* Job 4:19; 27:18; Ps 39:11; Isa 50:9; 51:8; Hos 5:12; Lk 12:33; Jas 5:2

The spider
Although not strictly an insect the spider is most conveniently included under this category: Job 8:14; Isa 59:5

See also

4404 food	4690 wings
4669 locust	4843 plague

4663
lamb
A common source of clothing and meat, this animal was given heightened significance by its place in the Jewish sacrificial system and was used figuratively of Jesus Christ.

The economic importance of lambs
As food 2Sa 12:4 *See also* Dt 28:4; Am 6:4

As a means of exchange Ge 30:32 *See also* 2Ki 3:4

The sacrificial significance of lambs
Their general use Ge 22:7 *See also* Ex 29:38; Lev 3:7; 14:12,24; 1Sa 7:9

The Passover lamb Ex 12:21 *See also* Ex 12:3,7; 2Ch 30:15–17; Ezr 6:20; Lk 22:7

The best had to be chosen Nu 6:14 *See also* Lev 4:32; 23:12; Nu 28:3–4,11; Eze 46:4

They were costly Lev 12:8 *See also* Ex 34:20

The figurative use of lambs
In general Ps 114:4; Lk 10:3 *See also* Isa 40:11; 65:25; Jer 11:19; Jn 21:15

Describing Jesus Christ and his work Jn 1:36; 1Pe 1:18–19 *See also* Ac 8:32; Isa 53:7; 1Co 5:7; Rev 5:12; 22:3

See also

1670 symbols	4693 wool
2315 Christ as Lamb	7406 Passover
4681 ram	7435 sacrifice, in OT
4684 sheep	7784 shepherd

4666
lion
An important animal in the natural history of Palestine; a symbol of power and strength.

Lions seen as a threat to life
Da 6:7 *See also* Jdg 14:5; 1Ki 13:24–28; 20:36; Da 6:24

God's deliverance from lions
Da 6:22 *See also* 1Sa 17:34–37; 2Ti 4:17; Heb 11:33

The figurative use of lions
As powerful Job 10:16 *See also* Ge 49:9; Ps 22:13,21

As cunning Ps 10:9 *See also* Ps 17:12; La 3:10

As fearsome Jer 12:8; 51:38

As voracious Ps 7:2 *See also* Ps 35:17; 57:4; Jer 2:30; Zep 3:3

They are not invincible Ps 34:10 *See also* Job 4:10–11; Ps 58:6; 91:13

Jesus Christ is likened to a lion Rev 5:5

Satan is likened to a lion 1Pe 5:8

The lion in God's new creation
Isa 11:6 *See also* Isa 65:25

Lions as a decoration
1Ki 7:29,36; 10:20

Samson's riddle concerning a lion
Jdg 14:12–18

See also

4603 animals	4627 creatures

4669
locust
The most destructive of all biblical insects, also used figuratively as a devouring pest.

There was no defence against locusts
Joel 2:4–5 *See also* Pr 30:27

Locusts were frequently a sign of God's judgment
Dt 28:38; Am 4:9
The eighth plague on Egypt:
Ex 10:4,12–14,19
Dt 28:42 *curses for disobedience;* 1Ki 8:37 pp 2Ch 6:28; 2Ch 7:13–14; Ps 78:46; 105:34; Joel 1:4; 2:25; Am 7:1

Locusts were a source of food
Lev 11:22 *See also* Mt 3:4 pp Mk 1:6

Locusts used figuratively
Of numerous and destructive invaders Jdg 7:12; Isa 33:4 *See also* Jdg 6:5; Jer 46:23; 51:14,27; Na 3:15–17

Of terrifying end-time activity Rev 9:3 *See also* Rev 9:7

See also

1670 symbols	9105 last things
4660 insects	9210 judgment,
4843 plague	God's

4672
manger
A feeding trough in a stable or stall, filled with fodder for donkeys, oxen, etc. The term is also used to refer to the stall in which animals were kept. The newborn Jesus was laid in a manger because there was no room at an inn.

A feeding place for livestock
Recognised by the animals of the household Isa 1:3 *Israel is like a wild animal which does not recognise or accept God's provision. See also* Job 39:9

Provision for farm animals Pr 14:4 *See also* Pr 12:10; Isa 30:24

Provision for beasts of burden Ge 24:32 *See also* Ge 24:25; 42:27; Jdg 19:19

Jesus Christ laid in a manger
Lk 2:7 *See also* Lk 2:12,16

Farm animals kept in stalls
Cattle kept in stalls 1Ki 4:23 *See also* 2Ch 32:28; Ps 50:9; Hab 3:17; Mal 4:2

Other animals kept in stalls 1Ki 4:26 pp 2Ch 9:25; Lk 13:15

See also
2036 Christ, humility   4406 agriculture
2515 Christ, birth of   4603 animals

4675

nest

The nest as the home of a bird rearing its young
Ps 84:3 *See also* Dt 22:6–7;
Job 39:27–30; Ps 104:12,17;
Isa 34:11,15; Jer 48:28; Eze 17:23

The nest as a place of security
Mt 8:20 pp Lk 9:58 *See also*
Dt 32:10–11; Pr 27:8; Hab 2:9

The nest may not always be safe
Isa 10:14 *See also* Nu 24:21–22; Isa 16:2;
Jer 49:16; Ob 4

The nest as the home of the viper
Isa 11:8

See also
4612 birds   5942 security

4678

pigeon

A bird used, along with doves, for sacrifices, especially by those who could not afford lambs.

A pigeon offered as sacrifice
Lev 1:14 *See also* Ge 15:9; Lev 1:15–17;
14:21–22; 15:14,29; Nu 6:10

Pigeons offered as a sacrifice by the poor
Lev 5:7 *See also* Lk 2:22–24

See also
4612 birds   7402 offerings
4636 dove   7435 sacrifice, in OT
7340 clean and
     unclean

4681

ram

The male sheep, part of an agrarian economy and used in sacrifice. Its skin had value and its horn was used in worship.

Rams as part of an agrarian economy
Ge 31:38 *See also* Ge 32:14; Dt 32:14;
2Ki 3:4; Eze 27:21; 34:17

Rams were used for religious purposes
As sacrificial victims Ge 22:13 *See also*
Nu 23:2; 1Sa 15:22; 1Ch 15:26; Mic 6:7

In the making of a covenant
Ge 15:9–10

For guilt offerings Lev 5:15 *See also*
Lev 5:16–19; 6:6; 19:21–22; Nu 5:8;
2Ch 29:21; Ezr 10:19

For fellowship or burnt offerings
Lev 9:4 *See also* Lev 9:1–3; 16:3–5;
Nu 6:14–17; 7:17; 15:6–7; 28:11; 29:2;
Eze 43:23–24; 46:4

For Aaron's ordination
Lev 8:22 *See also* Ex 29:1–34;
Lev 8:23–30

The ram's skin brought as an offering for the construction of the tabernacle
Ex 26:14 *See also* Ex 25:5; 35:7; 36:19

The ram's horn
Ps 81:3 *See also* Ex 19:13; Jos 6:4;
1Ch 15:28; Ps 98:6

Daniel's vision of the ram
Da 8:3 *See also* Da 8:4–8,20

See also
4406 agriculture   7435 sacrifice, in OT
4654 horn   7459 tabernacle, in
4684 sheep   OT
4693 wool   7745 ordination
7402 offerings

4684

sheep

Sheep were a major feature of ancient Israel's rural economy. Although they were of importance as a source of food and wool, they also symbolise helplessness and the need for guidance.

The economic importance of sheep
As a measure of wealth and God's blessing 1Sa 25:2; Ps 144:13 *See also*
Ge 12:16; 30:43; Ex 9:3; 22:1;
Dt 22:1–2; Jos 6:21; 2Sa 12:2–3;
Job 1:3; 42:12

As a source of food 1Sa 25:18 *See also*
Lev 7:23; Nu 18:17–18; 1Sa 14:32;
2Sa 17:29; 1Ch 12:40

As a source of wool 2Ki 3:4 *See also*
Ge 31:19; 38:12–13; Dt 18:4; 1Sa 25:7;
2Sa 13:23–24; Eze 27:18

Sheep were used in striking a bargain
Ge 21:27 *See also* Ge 20:14; 30:25–43

The care of sheep was a recognised occupation 1Sa 16:11 *See also*
Ge 29:2–3; 37:13; 1Sa 17:34–35; SS 1:7;
Hos 12:12

Sheep were used in sacrifice
Ex 20:24 *See also* Lev 1:10; 22:19,23;
Nu 22:40; Dt 18:3; 1Ki 1:9; 8:5; Jn 2:14

The symbolic importance of sheep
Israel without a leader 1Ki 22:17 *See also* Nu 27:16–17; 2Sa 24:17; Zec 10:2;
13:7; Mt 26:31

Helplessness Isa 53:7; Mt 9:36 *See also*
Ps 44:11; 49:14; Jer 12:3; Mt 10:16;
Ro 8:36; Ps 44:22

Judgment Mt 25:32–33 *See also*
Eze 34:17

Sin Isa 53:6; 1Pe 2:25 *See also*
Ps 119:176; Eze 34:16; Mt 18:12

The people that belong to God Ps 100:3
See also Ps 74:1; 78:52; 79:13; Jer 23:1;
50:6; Eze 34:11–15; Mic 2:12

Jesus Christ's care for his own
Lk 12:32; Jn 10:1–16,26–30 *See also*
Jn 21:16–17; Heb 13:20

A picture of God's future blessings
Isa 5:17

See also
1220 God as   4663 lamb
     shepherd   4681 ram
2330 Christ as   4693 wool
     shepherd   5611 watchman
4478 meat   7130 flock, God's
4645 fleece   7784 shepherd
4651 goat

4687

snake

A reptile, often associated with cunning and danger, or occasionally with satanic temptation.

Snakes as crawling reptiles
Ge 3:14 *See also* Isa 65:25; Mic 7:17

Snakes are dangerous
Both to animals and human beings
Ge 49:17 *See also* Ge 3:15; Ex 4:3;
7:9–13; Pr 23:32; Ecc 10:8,11; Isa 30:6;
Ac 28:3–6

Some are poisonous Isa 14:29 *See also*
Dt 8:15; 32:33; Job 20:14,16; Rev 9:19

They were sometimes used to bring God's judgment 1Co 10:9 *See also*
Nu 21:4–6; Am 5:19; 9:3

They may be overcome Ps 91:13 *See also* Mk 16:18; Lk 10:19

One day they will be rendered harmless Isa 11:8

Snakes used symbolically
Of Israel's enemies *See also* Isa 27:1;
Jer 46:22; 51:34

Of cunning and intelligence Mt 10:16

Of something harmful Mt 7:9–10
pp Lk 11:11

Of the ungodly Ps 58:4–5 *See also*
Ps 140:3; Mt 3:7; 12:34; 23:33; Ro 3:13

Of Satan Rev 12:9 *See also* Ge 3:1–13;
2Co 11:3; Rev 20:2

Of salvation Jn 3:14–15 *See also*
Nu 21:7–9; 2Ki 18:4

See also
1670 symbols   7452 snake, bronze
4122 Satan, tempter

4690

wings

Limbs which enable flight. In Scripture these are mainly used either of angelic beings or in various symbolic senses, especially of God's protection.

Wings of birds or insects
Ge 7:14; Lev 1:17; Job 39:13,26; Isa 18:1

Clean and unclean winged creatures
Lev 11:13–25; Dt 14:11–20;
Ac 10:12–15

Wings of angelic beings

Cherubim Ex 25:20 *See also* Ex 37:9;
1Ki 8:6–7 pp 2Ch 5:7–8; 1Ch 28:18;
2Ch 3:11–13; Eze 1:5–25; 3:13;
10:5–22

Other angelic beings Isa 6:2 *See also*
Isa 6:6; Rev 4:8

Wings as a metaphor of protection

Birds protect their young Dt 32:11;
Isa 34:15; Mt 23:37 pp Lk 13:34

**God's protection likened to a bird's
wings** Ps 91:4 *See also* Ex 19:4; Ru 2:12;
Ps 17:8; 36:7; 57:1; 61:4; 63:7; Isa 31:5

**Egypt's protection likened to an
eagle's wings** Eze 17:7 *Zedekiah's
fruitless appeal to Egypt for help against
Babylon*

Wings as a metaphor for God's judgment

Judgment on Israel Dt 28:49 *See also*
Isa 8:7–8; Eze 17:3–4; Hos 8:1; Hab 1:8;
Zec 5:9

Judgment on others Jer 48:40; 49:22;
Rev 9:9

Other figurative uses of wings

God rides on the wings of the wind
2Sa 22:11 pp Ps 18:10 *See also* Ps 104:3

God renews his people's strength
Isa 40:31

Israel described as a winged bird
Ps 68:13; Isa 10:14

Wings symbolise the ability to escape
Ps 55:6 *See also* Rev 12:14

Wings symbolise instability Pr 23:5 *See
also* Ecc 10:20

Wings symbolise strength Da 7:6 *See
also* Da 7:4

Wings of the dawn Ps 139:9

Wings of the sun Mal 4:2 *God is likened
to the rays of the sun.*

See also

4110 angels	7306 ark of the
4150 cherubim	covenant
4180 seraphim	7340 clean and
4612 birds	unclean
4660 insects	7396 Most Holy
4860 wind	Place
5126 arm	9210 judgment,
5480 protection	God's

4693

wool

Wool used for clothing
Eze 34:3 *See also* Lev 13:47–48;
Dt 22:11; Pr 31:13; Isa 51:8; Eze 44:17

Wool used in sacrificial ritual
Nu 19:6; Heb 9:19

Wool as a valuable commodity
2Ki 3:4 *See also* Dt 18:4; Eze 27:18;
Hos 2:5,9

Figurative use of wool
Isa 1:18 *See also* Ps 147:16; Da 7:9;
Rev 1:14

See also

4645 fleece	5145 clothing
4684 sheep	5258 cloth

4696

yoke

The wooden collar which joins two
animals, usually oxen, to enable
them to pull together. Used
metaphorically the term may denote
the partnership of those who share a
yoke or, more usually, the subjection
of those under a yoke. As his
covenant partners God's people are
yoked to him and he will break the
oppressive yoke of their enemies.

Literal references to yokes
1Sa 6:7; 1Ki 19:19 *See also* Job 1:3;
42:12; Lk 14:19
*Cows that have never been yoked are
offered as sacrifices:* Nu 19:2; Dt 21:3
*Ox yokes are used to burn slaughtered
animals:* 2Sa 24:22; 1Ki 19:21

God's yoke
Jer 2:20 *See also* Jer 5:5
Mt 11:29–30

The yoke as a symbol of partnership
Partnership in Jesus Christ's service
Php 4:3

Unsuitable partnerships 2Co 6:14–16
Marriage to unbelievers: Ge 24:3–4;
1Ki 11:4; 1Co 7:39
Involvement with pagan gods: Nu 25:2–3;
Ps 106:28; 1Co 10:18–21
1Co 5:9–10 *too close association with the
immoral*

The yoke as a symbol of subjection
The yoke of the law Ac 15:10 *See also*
Mt 23:4; Gal 5:1

Israel under the yoke of enemies
Dt 28:47–48; Jer 27:2 *Jeremiah
symbolically portrays the coming
Babylonian exile. See also* Isa 47:6;
Jer 27:8,11–13
*Hananiah's prophecy of an early end to
Babylonian oppression will be proved false:*
Jer 28:2–4,10–14
La 1:14; 3:27; Hos 10:11

The yoke of other masters Ge 27:40
*Esau will throw off the yoke of Jacob.
The people's complaint about harsh
servitude under Solomon is ignored by
Rehoboam:* 1Ki 12:4 pp 2Ch 10:4;
1Ki 12:9–11 pp 2Ch 10:9–11; 1Ki 12:14
pp 2Ch 10:14
*God's people are urged to lift the yoke of
injustice and oppression from their fellows:*
Isa 58:6,9
1Ti 6:1 *Slaves are to respect their masters.*

God breaks the yoke of oppression
Eze 34:27; Hos 11:4
Egypt's yoke broken: Ex 6:6–7; Lev 26:13;
Eze 30:18
Assyria's yoke broken: Isa 9:4; 10:27;
14:25; Na 1:13
Jer 30:8 *Babylon's yoke broken*

See also

4406 agriculture	5347 injustice
4498 ploughing	6634 deliverance
4603 animals	6658 freedom
4624 cow	7140 people of God
5205 alliance	7446 slavery
5246 captivity	8790 oppression

4800

Natural and supernatural phenomena

4801

black

A dark colour often associated with
impending judgment or with evil.

Black as descriptive of colour
Mt 5:36 *See also* Ex 10:15 *the plague of
locusts;* Lev 11:13–14 pp Dt 14:12–13
unclean food; Lev 13:31; Dt 4:11;
1Ki 18:45; Job 28:3; 30:28,30; SS 5:11;
La 4:7–8
Black horses: Zec 6:2,6; Rev 6:5
Rev 6:12

Black as the opposite of light
Job 3:5 *Job cursing the day of his birth. See
also* Isa 5:30; 45:7; Am 5:8

Black in the setting of impending judgment
Joel 2:2 *See also* Am 8:9; Zep 1:15

Black as a symbol of evil
Job 34:22 *See also* Jn 3:19; 2Pe 2:17;
Jude 13

See also

4807 colours	6169 godlessness
4809 darkness	8734 evil
4846 shadow	9105 last things
4859 white	9210 judgment,
4957 night	God's
6020 sin	

4802

blight

A disease ruinous to crops. In the OT
blight was seen as evidence of God's
judgment.

Blight as punishment from God
Dt 28:22 *See also* Hos 9:16; Am 4:9;
Hag 2:17

Deliverance from blight
1Ki 8:37–39 pp 2Ch 6:28–30

Blight as a symbol of sorrow
Ps 102:4

See also

4430 crops	5568 suffering,
4468 horticulture	causes
4839 mildew	5952 sorrow
5297 disease	6223 rebellion of
5484 punishment by	Israel
God	8256 fruitfulness

4803

breadth

Breadth as a measurement
Isa 40:12 *See also* Ge 6:15 *Noah's ark
The tabernacle:* Ex 25:10; 27:1,12–13;
37:25
Dt 3:11 *Og's bed;* 1Ki 6:2
The temple and its furnishings: 1Ki 7:2;
2Ch 3:3; 4:1; Ezr 6:3

Ezekiel's vision of a temple: Eze 40:7,42;
41:9–12
Land set aside for the LORD: Eze 45:1–3;
48:13–15
Zec 2:2 *Jerusalem;* Zec 5:2 *the flying
scroll;* Rev 21:16 *the new Jerusalem*

Breadth indicating large areas
Ge 13:17 *See also* 2Sa 22:37 pp Ps 18:36;
Job 37:10; Isa 8:7–8; 30:23; 33:21;
Mt 7:13–14

Breadth of understanding
1Ki 4:29

Breadth of Jesus Christ's love
Eph 3:14–19

See also
2048 Christ, love of	5618 measures,
4813 depth	linear
4830 height	5619 distance & area
4832 length	8355 understanding
4841 narrowness	

4804

breath

The imagery of breath is often used
to convey spiritual essence and
power, unseen except in its effects,
including aspects of the person and
work of the Holy Spirit. The main
Hebrew and Greek words translated
as "breath" in the NIV are also
translated as "spirit" and "wind".

The breath of life
Life imparted by God Ge 2:7; Ac 17:25
See also Ge 1:30; 6:17; 7:15,22; Job 27:3;
33:4; Ps 104:30; Isa 42:5; 57:16;
Jer 38:16; Rev 11:11

Life recalled by his sovereign will
Ecc 12:7 *See also* 1Ki 17:17;
Job 34:14–15; Ps 104:29; Isa 40:7

The breath of God
An emblem of the Holy Spirit
Jn 20:21–22 *See also* Eze 37:5,14

God's creative breath Ps 33:6 *See also*
Ge 1:2; Job 26:13; 33:4

God's enlightening breath Job 32:8 *See
also* Jn 14:26; 16:13–15; 2Ti 3:16–17;
2Pe 1:20–21

God's regenerating breath
Eze 37:4–14 *See also* Jn 3:5–8;
1Th 1:4–5; Tit 3:5

God's empowering breath Ac 2:1–4 *See
also* Isa 11:2; 61:1; Joel 2:28–29;
Jn 20:21–22; Ac 1:8

God's destroying breath 2Th 2:8 *See
also* Ex 15:10; 2Sa 22:16 pp Ps 18:15;
Job 4:9; 15:30; Isa 11:4; 30:28,33; 40:24;
59:19; Eze 21:31

See also
1305 God, activity of	3266 Holy Spirit in
3030 Holy Spirit,	creation
power	3281 Holy Spirit,
3120 Holy Spirit,	inspiration
descriptions	3290 Holy Spirit,
3230 Holy Spirit &	life-giver
regeneration	4015 life
3239 Holy Spirit,	4860 wind
anointing	5062 spirit
3242 Holy Spirit,	
baptism with	

4805

clouds

A natural feature of the sky, often
associated with God's judgment,
presence and glory.

Clouds as a natural phenomenon
Rain clouds 1Ki 18:44–45 *See also*
Ge 9:13–16; Job 36:28; Ecc 11:3;
Lk 12:54

Clouds representing the sky Job 20:6;
35:5; Isa 14:14; Jer 51:9

**Clouds subject to God's sovereign
control** Job 37:13 *See also* Jdg 5:4;
Job 26:8; Ps 135:7; 147:8; Pr 3:20; 8:28;
Isa 5:6; Jer 10:13; 51:16; Zec 10:1

**Clouds expressing the mystery of
God's world** Job 37:15–16 *See also*
Job 22:14; 26:9; 36:29; 38:9,37; Ecc 11:4

Clouds of smoke Lev 16:13; Jdg 20:38

Clouds as symbols of spiritual truths
A symbol of judgment Eze 30:3 *See also*
Eze 30:18; 34:12; Joel 2:2; Zep 1:15

A symbol of blessing Isa 45:8

A symbol of impermanence Job 7:9 *See
also* Job 30:15; Pr 16:15; Hos 6:4; 13:3

Other positive symbolic uses Isa 25:5;
44:22; Heb 12:1

Other negative symbolic uses Pr 25:14;
Ecc 12:2; Jude 12

Clouds as a symbol of God's presence and glory
Revealing God's majesty Na 1:3 *See
also* Job 37:11; Ps 97:2; Isa 30:27,30
The clouds as God's chariot: Dt 33:26;
Ps 68:4; 104:3; Jer 4:13

The cloud of God's presence
Ex 13:21–22
Guiding Israel in the wilderness:
Nu 9:15–22; 10:11–12,34; 11:25; 14:14;
Dt 31:15; Ne 9:12,19; Ps 78:14; 99:7;
105:39
Saving Israel from her enemies:
Ex 14:19–20,24; 1Co 10:1–2; Rev 14:14

The cloud of God's awesomeness
Lev 16:2 *See also* Ex 19:9,16; 34:5;
Nu 12:5,10; Dt 4:11; 5:22

The cloud of God's glory 1Ki 8:10–12
pp 2Ch 5:13–6:1 *See also* Ex 16:10;
24:15–18; 33:9–10; 40:34–38;
Nu 16:42; Eze 1:28

Clouds revealing Jesus Christ's glory
Mt 17:5 pp Mk 9:7 pp Lk 9:34 *Jesus
Christ's transfiguration;* Ac 1:9 *Jesus
Christ's ascension;* Rev 1:7 *See also*
Da 7:13
Heralding Jesus Christ's return: Mt 24:30
pp Mk 13:26 pp Lk 21:27; Mt 26:64
pp Mk 14:62; 1Th 4:17

See also
1045 God, glory of	2580 Christ,
1330 God, the	transfiguration
provider	4844 rain
1454 theophany	4848 smoke
1670 symbols	4853 weather
2024 Christ, glory of	7251 pillar of cloud
2505 Christ,	& fire
ascension	8124 guidance
2565 Christ, second	
coming	

4806

cold

Cold as part of the seasonal rhythm of the year
Ge 8:22 *See also* Job 37:9

Cold as an aspect of the night
Ge 31:40 *See also* Job 24:7; Jer 36:30

Cold as a source of discomfort
2Co 11:27 *See also* Pr 25:20; Jn 18:18;
Ac 28:2

Cold as a source of refreshment
Pr 25:25 *See also* Pr 25:13; Mt 10:42

See also
4827 frost	4970 seasons of
4829 heat	year
4849 snow	5132 biting
4853 weather	

4807

colours

A wide range of colours are
mentioned in Scripture, some being
used symbolically.

Colours mentioned in Scripture
White Ge 49:12; 2Ki 5:27

Blue Est 1:6; Eze 27:24 *See also* Ex 26:1;
39:22

Yellow Rev 9:17 *See also* Lev 13:30

Green Mk 6:39 *An indication as to the
season; the grass is green in Galilee in
spring.*
All the references are to plants or foliage:
Ge 1:30; Ps 23:2; Jer 17:8; Rev 8:7

Red 2Ki 3:22; Mt 16:2 *See also* Ge 25:30;
Ex 36:19; Rev 12:3

Purple Mk 15:17
All the references are to rich or royal cloth:
Nu 4:13; Pr 31:22; Da 5:7; Ac 16:14

Scarlet Isa 1:18 *See also* Ge 38:28;
Ex 35:23 *Purple, scarlet, crimson and red
are closely related and sometimes
interchangeable in Scripture;* Nu 4:8;
SS 4:3; Mt 27:28; Rev 17:4

Crimson Isa 63:1 *See also* 2Ch 2:7

Black SS 5:11 *See also* Rev 6:12

The whole spectrum Eze 1:28 *See also*
Rev 4:3; 10:1

Colours used symbolically
Rev 6:2 *White here symbolises conquest;*
Rev 17:3 *See also* Rev 6:4 *bloodshed and
war;* Rev 6:8 *death*
Blessedness and purity: Rev 7:9; 19:14,11
Rev 20:11 *holiness*

See also
4801 black	4845 rainbow
4808 crimson	4859 white

4808

crimson

A deep red colour used
interchangeably with scarlet and

sometimes with purple. It has associations with blood and richness.

The richness of crimson used for ornamentation

Ex 25:3–4; 28:6 *It was used extensively in the construction of the tabernacle;* 2Ch 2:7 *See also* 2Ch 2:14; 3:14

Crimson associated with splendour and prosperity

2Sa 1:24; Rev 18:16 *See also* Pr 31:21; Jer 4:30; Na 2:3; Mt 27:28 pp Mk 15:17; Rev 18:12

Crimson associated with blood and sin

Isa 1:18 *See also* Lev 14:3–6,49–53; Nu 19:6; Isa 63:1–3; Heb 9:19; Rev 17:3–4

Everyday use of the colour crimson

Ge 38:28; Jos 2:17–18; SS 4:3

See also

4807 colours	7459 tabernacle, in
5258 cloth	OT

4809

darkness

The absence of light. Often used figuratively as a symbol of sin, chaos or the absence of God.

4810
darkness, natural

Scripture stresses that God is able to be present and known, even in the darkest aspects of the world.

Darkness as a symbol of the terrifying majesty of God

Ex 20:18–21; Ps 97:2 *See also* Dt 4:11–12; 5:22–24; Heb 12:18–21

God is the source of natural darkness

Isa 45:7 *See also* Ge 1:2–5,16–18; Job 26:10; Ps 74:16; 104:19–20

God's eye penetrates the darkness

Job 34:21–22; Ps 139:11–12 *See also* Da 2:22; Am 5:8–9; 2Co 4:6

Miracles involving natural darkness

Mt 27:45 pp Mk 15:33 pp Lk 23:44–45 *See also* Ex 10:21–23; 14:19–20; Jos 24:6–7; Ps 105:26–28; Isa 50:3; Ac 2:19–20; Joel 2:30–32; Ac 13:9–12

Natural darkness used poetically

2Sa 22:10–12 pp Ps 18:9–11; Job 3:1–10

See also

1020 God, all-knowing	4005 creation
1090 God, majesty of	4801 black
1415 miracles	4833 light
	4957 night

4811
darkness, as a symbol of sin

Darkness is often used in Scripture as a symbol of sin and its effects. It is often contrasted with light, as a symbol of forgiveness and the presence of God.

Darkness as a symbol of sin

Jn 3:19–20 *See also* Job 24:16–17; Pr 2:12–15; 4:19; Isa 5:20; 29:15; Mt 6:23; Lk 22:53 *Jesus Christ arrested;* Ro 1:21

Paul encourages believers to live in the light: Ro 13:12; 2Co 6:14; Eph 5:8–12 1Jn 1:5–6

Darkness as a symbol of the effects of sin

Darkness symbolising ignorance of the truth 2Co 4:4 *See also* Ps 82:5; Isa 8:20; 2Co 3:14–15; Eph 4:18

Darkness symbolising the inability to find the right way Jn 12:35 *See also* Job 12:24–25; Isa 59:9–10; Mt 5:14; 1Jn 2:9,11

Darkness symbolises times of trial Job 3:3–6; 19:8; 23:16–17; 30:26; Ps 107:10; 143:3; Ecc 11:8

Darkness symbolises death and the grave Job 10:20–22 *See also* Ps 49:19; 88:10–12

God's provision for the darkness of sin

God himself is a remedy for darkness 2Sa 22:29 *See also* Ps 18:28; 30:5; 91:4–7; Isa 42:16; 50:10; Mic 7:8

God will deliver from darkness Isa 9:2 *See also* Mt 4:16; Ps 107:13–14; Isa 29:18; 49:8–9; Lk 1:78–79; Ac 26:17–18; Col 1:13; 1Th 5:4–5; 1Pe 2:9

God's Son saves believers from darkness Jn 8:12 *See also* Jn 1:4–5; 12:46; 1Co 4:5; 2Co 4:6; Ge 1:3; Eph 5:8; 2Pe 1:19; 1Jn 2:8

God's people rescue others from darkness Isa 42:6–7 *See also* Isa 60:1–5

See also

4027 world, fallen	6181 ignorance
4846 shadow	6184 imagination
5560 suffering	8718 disobedience
5831 depression	8734 evil
6020 sin	9020 death
6139 deadness, spiritual	9210 judgment, God's

4812
darkness, and God's judgment

Darkness is used figuratively of God's present and final judgment upon individuals, unfaithful Israel and the heathen nations.

Darkness as a symbol of judgment upon ungodly individuals

Mt 25:30 *See also* 1Sa 2:9–10; Job 5:13–14; 12:25; 15:22–23,30; 18:5–6,18; 20:24–26; 22:10–11 *Eliphaz reasons on the assumption that Job's suffering proves his wickedness;*

Ps 35:5–6; Isa 8:22; Jer 23:11–12; Mt 22:13; 2Pe 2:17; Jude 13; Rev 16:10–11

Darkness as a symbol of judgment upon unfaithful Israel

Dt 28:28–29; Isa 5:29–30 *This will be fulfilled at the time of Israel's captivity. See also* Isa 59:9–10; Ro 11:10; Jer 4:27–28; 13:16; La 3:2,6; Mt 8:12

Darkness as a symbol of judgment upon heathen nations

Isa 47:5–7; Eze 30:18; 32:7–8; Na 1:8

Darkness as a symbol of judgment at the day of the Lord

Joel 2:31 *See also* Isa 13:9–10; 34:4; Joel 2:1–2,10; 3:14–15; Am 5:18–20; 8:9; Zep 1:14–15; Zec 14:6; Mt 24:29; Ac 2:19–20; 1Th 5:1–3; Rev 6:12–17

See also

1310 God as judge	9220 day of the LORD
9210 judgment, God's	9240 last judgment

4813

depth

Depth as a literal measurement

Ge 7:20 *See also* 1Ki 7:31,35; Eze 40:6,9,30; 43:13; Ac 27:28

Depth indicating the strength of human emotions

2Co 2:4 *See also* La 3:60

Depth as a characteristic of wisdom

Ro 11:33; Php 1:9

Depth representing the immeasurability of God

Ro 11:33

Depth used to express the love of God

Ro 8:38–39 *See also* Eph 3:16–19

See also

1085 God, love of	4832 length
1180 God, wisdom of	5618 measures, linear
2048 Christ, love of	
4227 deep, the	5619 distance & area
4266 sea	5844 emotions
4803 breadth	8281 insight
4830 height	

4814

dew

The nightly condensation of moisture from the atmosphere

SS 5:2 *See also* Jdg 6:36–40 *Gideon's sign Nebuchadnezzar's judgment:* Da 4:25; 5:21

Dew as a sign of God's blessing and provision

Dt 33:13 *See also* Ge 27:28; Job 38:28; Pr 3:19–20; Hos 14:5; Zec 8:12

Dew associated with manna

Ex 16:13–14; Nu 11:9

Lack of dew a sign of God's judgment

1Ki 17:1 *See also* Ge 27:39; 2Sa 1:21; Hag 1:10

4815

Dew used metaphorically
Dt 32:2; Ps 110:3; Isa 26:19 *See also*
2Sa 17:12; Job 29:19; Ps 133:3; Pr 19:12;
Isa 18:4; Hos 6:4; 13:3; Mic 5:7

See also

1335 blessing	9210 judgment,
4844 rain	God's

4815

drought

A severe long-term absence of water
or drink of any kind, leading to
disaster for the people affected in
this way. Scripture provides
examples of such droughts, while
also indicating the possibility and
dangers of long-term spiritual thirst
arising through disobedience or lack
of faith.

4816
drought, physical

Drought arises through the absence
of rain, leading to severe hardship
for those who are affected by it.

**Drought may be a sign of God's
displeasure**
Dt 11:17 *See also* Dt 28:22–24; 2Sa 1:21;
1Ki 17:1; Ps 107:33–34; Isa 5:6,13;
Jer 2:2–3; 14:1–6; 50:38; Eze 22:23–24;
Am 4:7; Hag 1:11; Jas 5:17

**The response of believers to
drought**
It tests their faith 1Ki 17:7;
Hab 3:17–18 *See also* Dt 8:15; Isa 41:17;
48:20–21; Jer 2:5–6; Hos 13:5

It gives opportunity to help others
Ac 11:28–29 *See also* Ge 41:56–57;
1Ki 17:9; 18:1–4

**Rain is a sign of God's general
favour or of his forgiveness**
His general favour Ac 14:17 *See also*
Ge 27:28; Job 5:10; 38:25–28;
Ps 65:9–10; 147:8; Jer 5:24; 14:22;
Mt 5:45

His response to repentance
Joel 2:12,23 *See also* Mal 3:10

His response to obedience
Dt 11:13–14 *See also* Lev 26:3–4

His response to prayer Jas 5:18 *See also*
1Ki 8:35–36; 18:36–46; Zec 10:1

See also

1330 God, the	5569 hardship
provider	8358 weakness,
4293 water	physical
4819 dryness	9210 judgment,
4822 famine	God's
4844 rain	

4817
drought, spiritual

Scripture indicates that believers,
both as individuals and
communities, may go through
periods in which they fail to
experience the refreshing and life-
giving presence of God. One cause of

such spiritual thirst is unbelief.
Scripture also indicates ways in
which this thirst may be relieved.

Spiritual drought in unbelievers
Ps 68:6 *See also* Isa 29:7–8

The remedy for spiritual drought is to
be found in Jesus Christ Jn 7:37–39 *See
also* Isa 45:8; 55:1; Jn 4:13–14;
Tit 3:5–7; Rev 22:17

**The experience of spiritual
drought in believers**
Ps 63:1 *See also* Ps 143:6; Eze 19:10–14

**The cause of spiritual drought in
believers**
Unconfessed sin Ps 32:3–4 *See also*
Ps 66:18; Isa 1:28–30

Spiritual depression Ps 42:1–2

Self-reliance Jer 2:13 *See also*
Jer 17:5–6

God's judgment Am 8:11

**The remedy for spiritual drought
in the lives of believers**
Through confession 1Jn 1:8–9 *See also*
Ps 32:5; 51:12; 1Jn 3:19–22

Through Scripture Ps 1:2–3 *See also*
Dt 32:1–2; Isa 55:10–11

Through Jesus Christ Jn 6:35 *See also*
Jn 7:37–39; Jas 5:7–8

Through the Holy Spirit Isa 44:3 *See also*
Isa 32:13–15; Ro 15:13

Finally in heaven Rev 7:16–17

See also

1610 Scripture	8027 faith, testing of
3120 Holy Spirit,	8148 revival
descriptions	8359 weakness,
4971 seasons of life	spiritual
5580 thirst	8656 longing for
5831 depression	God
6024 sin, effects of	8835 unbelief
6624 confession of	
sin	

4819

dryness

A lack of moisture, often due to lack
of rain or a period of drought,
leading to vegetation drying up.
Dryness is often used as a symbol of
hopelessness or of the absence of
God's blessing.

The dryness of river beds
Evaporation and recession of
floodwaters Ge 8:13–14 *See also*
Ge 8:1–11

God's drying up of rivers to allow his
people to cross Jos 4:23 *See also*
Ex 14:10–31; Jos 2:10; 3:1–17; 5:1;
Ps 106:7–11; Isa 11:15; 51:10

Other instances of rivers drying up
1Ki 17:7 *See also* 2Ki 19:24 pp Isa 37:25;
Ps 74:15; Isa 15:6; 19:4–10; 42:15;
44:24–27; 50:2; Jer 48:34; 51:36;
Eze 30:12; Joel 1:20; Na 1:4

The dryness of vegetation
Ps 37:2 *See also* Job 8:11–12,19; 14:2;
15:30; Isa 34:4 *on the day of the* Lord;
Isa 40:7–8; Jer 8:13; 12:4;
Eze 19:10–14; Hos 9:16; Mt 13:3–6

pp Mk 4:2–6 pp Lk 8:4–6 *the parable of
the sower*; Mt 21:19–20 pp Mk 11:20–21
the fig-tree withers

Physical dryness
Eze 37:11 *See also* Ps 102:4,11; Pr 17:22;
Zec 11:17

**Dryness indicative of desolation
and hopelessness**
Joel 1:12 *See also* Isa 24:7; 33:9;
Jer 23:10; Joel 1:10,17; Zec 9:5; 10:11

**Dryness indicating God's
withholding of moisture due to
sin**
Dt 28:22–24; 1Ki 8:35–36

See also

4230 desert	4844 rain
4293 water	5580 thirst
4815 drought	7221 exodus, the
4823 famine,	7227 flood, the
physical	

4820

earthquake

Earthquakes as natural events
Am 1:1 *See also* 1Sa 14:15; Zec 14:5;
Ac 16:26

**Earthquakes remain under God's
sovereignty**
Ps 75:3 *See also* Ps 46:2–3

**Earthquakes as a demonstration
of God's power**
Ps 77:18 *See also* Ex 19:18;
Nu 16:31–32; Jdg 5:5; 2Sa 22:8
pp Ps 18:7; Isa 29:6; Na 1:5; Ac 16:26;
Rev 11:19

**Elijah and the earthquake on
Mount Horeb**
1Ki 19:11–12

**The earthquake accompanying
Jesus Christ's death and
resurrection**
Mt 28:2 *See also* Mt 27:54

**Earthquakes among the signs of
the end time**
Mt 24:7 pp Mk 13:8 pp Lk 21:11 *See also*
Isa 24:19–20; Eze 38:19–20; Rev 6:12;
8:5; 11:13; 16:18

See also

4203 earth, the	9140 last days
9105 last things	

4821

east

The geographical direction often
identified by the position of the
rising sun. Many of Israel's invaders
came from the east, often giving the
term a negative association in OT
writings.

East as a point of the compass
Ge 2:8; Mt 2:1–2 *See also* Ge 4:16;
13:11,14; Dt 3:27; Ps 107:3; Lk 13:29;
Rev 21:13

**East and west used to
demonstrate vast extent**
Ge 28:14; Isa 43:5 *See also* 1Ch 12:15;

Job 23:8; Ps 75:6; 103:12; Zec 8:7;
Mt 8:11; 24:27; Lk 13:29

East identified by the rising sun

Nu 2:3 *See also* Jos 1:15; 19:12; Ps 50:1;
113:3; Isa 41:25; 45:6

The east wind

Job 15:2 *The east wind blows straight out
of the desert*; Ps 48:7 *See also* Ge 41:6;
Ex 10:13; Isa 27:8; Jer 4:11; 18:17;
Eze 17:10; 27:26; Hos 13:15; Jnh 4:8

Military threat from the east

Jdg 6:33 *See also* Jdg 10:8; 1Ch 5:10;
Isa 9:12; 46:11

See also

4284 sun	4850 south
4842 north	4857 west

4822

famine

A severe long-term absence of food,
leading to disaster for the people
affected in this way. Scripture
provides examples of such famines,
while also indicating the possibility
and dangers of spiritual famine
arising through disobedience or lack
of faith.

4823
famine, physical

A serious shortage of food caused by
drought, war or natural disasters.
Famine is seen as a sign of God's
judgment on Israel.

Examples of famines

In the days of Abraham Ge 12:10 *See
also* Ge 26:1

In the days of Joseph Ge 41:53–57;
Ac 7:11

In the days of Ruth Ru 1:1

In the days of David 2Sa 21:1

In the days of Elijah 1Ki 18:1–5; Lk 4:25

In the days of Elisha 2Ki 4:38; 6:25

In the days of the prophets Isa 51:19;
Jer 44:13; Eze 7:15; Joel 1:10–12

In the days of Claudius Ac 11:28

In the last days Mt 24:7 pp Mk 13:8
pp Lk 21:11

Natural causes of famine

Dt 28:22 *crop disease*
Drought: 1Ki 18:1–2; Jer 14:1–6
War: 2Ki 6:24–25; 25:1–3
Joel 1:4 *locusts*

Spiritual causes of famine

The disobedience of God's people
Dt 28:15–18 *See also*
Dt 28:22–24,38–40,42,51,53; 32:24;
Jdg 6:1–5; 2Sa 21:1; 24:13
pp 1Ch 21:11–12; Isa 51:19–20;
Jer 5:17; 11:22; 14:11–18; 18:21;
29:17–18; 32:24; Eze 5:16–17;
6:11–12; 14:13

God's judgment on the ungodly
Ge 41:28–30; Isa 14:29–30; Rev 6:8;
18:8

The effects of famine

Desperation and death La 4:9 *See also*
Ge 47:13,20; Dt 28:53; 2Ki 7:3–4;
Ne 5:3; Jer 52:6; Lk 15:14–16; 23:28–29

**God's people seek him and return to
him** Jdg 6:6 *See also* 2Sa 21:1;
Lk 15:17–18

God's provision in famine

He gives warnings beforehand
Ge 41:25–27; 1Ki 17:1; 2Ki 8:1;
Ac 11:28

He gives wisdom to men Ge 41:33–36;
42:1–2; 45:11; 47:4; Ps 105:16–22;
Ac 7:10–11

He provides for his people Job 5:20 *See
also* Ge 26:1–3; 1Ki 17:2–16 *Sometimes
he provides miraculously*; Ps 33:18–19;
37:19; Eze 34:29; 36:29–30

He sends deliverance 2Ki 7:1–9,16;
Jer 32:36–37

Responses to famine

Accepting God's chastisements
Jer 27:12–13; 38:2–3; 42:13–17; 44:27

Caring for one's family Ge 45:11;
Ru 1:1; 2Ki 8:1–2

Helping those in need Ac 11:29–30

Praying 1Ki 8:35–40 pp 2Ch 6:26–31

Trusting in the Lord Ro 8:35–37

See also

1030 God,	5605 warfare
compassion	6732 repentance
1355 providence	7326 cannibalism
4464 harvest	8358 weakness,
4816 drought,	physical
physical	8718 disobedience
5341 hunger	9210 judgment,
5529 sieges	God's

4824
famine, spiritual

A state of spiritual hunger arising
from a failure to experience the
presence and joy of God. Scripture
describes such experiences, indicates
one ultimate cause to be unbelief
and points to ways in which this
famine can be relieved.

The experience of spiritual
famine

God's word is withheld Am 8:11–12
See also 1Sa 3:1; Ps 74:9; La 2:9;
Eze 7:26; Lk 23:8–9

God's Spirit is withheld Ps 51:11 *See
also* Ps 107:33–34

Causes of spiritual famine

Sin Isa 59:2

Unbelief Ac 13:46 *See also* Ac 28:25–28

Worldliness Isa 55:2

False beliefs Isa 8:19–22

Self-satisfaction Rev 3:17 *It is possible
to be well-fed physically but famished
spiritually.*

Testing God Ps 78:18–19,29–31

God testing his servants Job 23:3,8–10

Consequences of spiritual
famine

Spiritual weakness Ps 119:81 *See also*
Ps 84:2

Loss of hope and joy Joel 1:16 *See also*
Ps 51:12

Relief of spiritual famine

Relief is promised to God's people
Ps 107:9 *See also* Ps 85:8–13; Isa 58:11;
65:21; Am 9:13–15

Relief comes through Jesus Christ
Jn 6:35 *See also* Isa 9:1–3; Lk 1:53;
Jn 6:32–33,48,50,58; 1Co 10:3–4

Relief comes by the word Isa 55:10–11
See also Mt 4:4 pp Lk 4:4; Dt 8:3

Relief comes by the Spirit Ac 2:17 *See
also* Joel 2:28; Ps 107:35–38;
Isa 35:1–10; 44:3

Final relief is found in heaven Rev 7:16
See also Isa 49:9–10; Ps 16:11; Rev 21:6

Conditions of relief from spiritual
famine

It is offered freely Isa 55:1 *See also*
Jn 7:37; Rev 22:17

It is for those who desire it Mt 5:6 *See
also* Lk 6:21

It is for those who pray Ps 107:4–9;
Jas 5:16

It is for those who repent Ps 81:8–10;
Isa 64:9–10; Hos 14:1–8; Joel 2:13–14

It is for those who have patience
Jas 5:7 *See also* Ps 126:4–6; Ecc 11:1;
Jn 4:35; Jas 5:16–18

See also

4817 drought,	6020 sin
spiritual	8318 patience
5450 poverty,	8359 weakness,
spiritual	spiritual
5580 thirst	8832 testing
5939 satisfaction	8834 unbelief
5943 self-deception	

4826

fire

Scripture shows fire being used in a
variety of ways in this world. Fire is
often mentioned as a symbol,
denoting God's presence and power,
his judgment or his purifying work.

Domestic uses of fire

Isa 50:11; Jer 36:22; Mt 5:15; Mk 14:67
pp Lk 22:55 pp Jn 18:18; Jn 21:9; Ac 28:2

Cremation

1Sa 31:12 *See also* Jos 7:25; Am 6:10

Fire as an instrument of
punishment

Lev 20:14 *See also* Ge 38:24; Lev 20:14;
21:9; Jdg 9:49; Da 3:6

Fire as an instrument of divine
judgment

In general terms 2Pe 3:10 *See also*
Ge 19:24; Lev 10:2; Nu 11:1; 16:35;
2Th 1:7–8

Eternal fire Rev 20:10 *See also* Isa 33:14;
66:24; Mt 3:12 pp Lk 3:17; Mt 18:8
pp Mk 9:43; Mt 25:41; Rev 14:10–11

Fire used in worship
Nu 28:2 *See also* Lev 24:7; 1Sa 7:9;
2Ch 13:11; Ezr 3:3

Prayers answered by fire
1Ch 21:26 *See also* 1Ki 18:38; 2Ki 1:10;
2Ch 7:1

Symbolic significance of fire
God's presence and power Ex 3:2;
Ac 2:3 *See also* Ex 13:21; 19:18;
Lev 9:24; Dt 4:36; Jdg 6:21; 13:20;
2Ki 2:11; Ps 50:3; 97:3; Jer 23:29

Judgment Mal 4:1 *See also* Dt 4:24;
Isa 66:15–16; Jer 5:14; 48:45; Eze 22:20;
Am 1:4; 1Co 3:15

Purification or refinement 1Pe 1:7 *See
also* Nu 31:23; Isa 48:10; Zec 13:9;
Mal 3:2; 1Co 3:13; Rev 3:18

Zeal Jn 2:17 *See also* Ps 69:9; Jer 20:9;
Lk 24:32; 2Ti 1:6

The power to destroy Jas 3:6 *See also*
Pr 6:27–29; 16:27; Isa 9:18; 43:2

See also

1065 God, holiness of	7251 pillar of cloud & fire
3120 Holy Spirit, descriptions	7322 burnt offering
4318 coal	8326 purity, moral & spiritual
4351 refining	9210 judgment, God's
4848 smoke	9510 hell
5222 baking	
5482 punishment	

frost

A covering of the ground with fine
particles of ice, characteristic of cold
weather.

Frost is under God's control
Ps 147:16 *See also* Job 38:29

**Frost will be absent on the day of
the LORD**
Zec 14:6

See also

4806 cold	4970 seasons of year
4849 snow	
4853 weather	

hail

Hail as destructive
Jos 10:11; Eze 13:11–13

Hail as a sign of the power of God
Job 38:22–23; Ps 105:32; 147:17–18;
Isa 28:2; Hag 2:17

**Hail as one of the ten plagues of
Egypt**
Ex 9:18–33

**Hail as an aspect of the final
divine judgment**
Rev 8:7; 11:19; 16:21

See also

4272 sky	4852 thunder
4838 lightning	4853 weather
4843 plague	9210 judgment, God's
4844 rain	
4851 storm	

heat

The heat of the sun
Isa 4:6 *See also* Ge 8:22; 18:1; 31:40;
Dt 28:22 *Scorching heat was a curse for
disobedience;* 1Sa 11:11; 2Sa 4:5; Ne 7:3;
Job 24:19; Ps 19:6; Isa 18:4; 49:10 *relief
from heat in the promised restoration of
Israel;* Jer 36:30; Hos 13:5; Jnh 4:8;
Mt 20:12; Lk 12:55 *Jesus Christ on
interpreting the times;* Jas 1:11; Rev 7:16

Artificial heat
Ac 28:3 *See also* 1Ki 19:6; Eze 24:11;
Da 3:22; Hos 7:7; 1Ti 4:2

Bodily heat
La 5:10

**Heat associated with action in
battle**
1Sa 14:22; Isa 21:15

Heat associated with anger
Isa 25:4–5 *See also* Ex 11:8; 2Ki 23:26;
Ps 39:3; 78:49; Eze 38:18

Heat associated with judgment
2Pe 3:12; Rev 16:9

**Heat referring to animals
entering period of fertility**
Ge 30:41–42; Jer 2:24

See also

4284 sun	4960 noon
4351 refining	5435 ovens
4826 fire	5789 anger
4855 weather, God's judgment	

height

Height as a measurement
1Ki 6:10 *See also* Ge 6:15; Ex 27:1;
1Ki 6:2,26; 2Ch 4:1–2; Ne 4:6; Est 5:14;
Jer 52:21–22; Eze 43:13; Rev 21:16

**Height in relation to physical
stature**
1Sa 16:7 *See also* Eze 19:11; 31:10,14;
Da 4:10

**Mountain peaks described as
heights**
Jdg 6:26 *See also* Nu 23:3; Isa 22:16

Height equivalent to zenith
Da 8:8

Height used as a metaphor
Rev 2:5

**Height used to express the love
of God**
Ro 8:38–39 *See also* Eph 3:16–19

See also

1085 God, love of	5173 outward appearance
2048 Christ, love of	5585 towers
4254 mountains	5618 measures, linear
4803 breadth	
4813 depth	5619 distance & area
4832 length	

largeness

Large flocks and herds
Job 1:3 *See also* Ge 30:43; Ex 12:38;
Nu 32:1; Jos 22:8; 2Sa 12:1–3; Jer 49:32

Large cities
Dt 9:1 *See also* Nu 13:28; Dt 1:28; 6:10;
Jos 10:2; 14:12; 1Ki 4:13; Ne 7:4

Large armies
Jos 11:4 *See also* Nu 20:20; 2Ki 18:17;
2Ch 24:24; Eze 17:15; Da 11:11–13,25;
Joel 2:2

Large crowds of people
Mt 4:25 *See also* 2Ch 15:9; 30:5,13;
Ezr 10:1; Mt 8:1; 20:29 pp Mk 10:46;
Mt 26:47; Mk 4:1; 6:34; Lk 5:29;
7:11–12; 23:27; Jn 12:9

See also

4841 narrowness	8701 affluence
4847 smallness	

length

Length as measurement
Lev 19:35 *See also* Ge 6:15; Ex 26:12;
2Sa 8:2; 2Ch 3:8
Ezekiel's vision of a temple:
Eze 40:5,11,20; 41:4,8,12,15; 42:10–11
Ac 12:10; Rev 21:16

Length of land
Ge 13:17 *See also* Eze 48:8,13,18,21

Length of life
Ps 90:10 *See also* Ps 21:4; Pr 10:27

Length of time
Ex 12:40 *See also* 2Sa 2:11

Length of Jesus Christ's love
Eph 3:14–19

See also

2048 Christ, love of	5618 measures, linear
4016 life, human	
4803 breadth	5619 distance & area
4813 depth	7257 promised land
4830 height	8275 honesty

light

The brightness that enables sight in
the darkness. Scripture often uses
light as a symbol of the saving
presence of God in a fallen world,
with darkness being used as a symbol
of sin or the absence of God.

4834
light, natural

Scripture stresses that every source of
light (sun, moon and stars) is created
by God, and subject to him.

God is the source of natural light
Ge 1:3–5 *See also* Ge 1:14–18;
2Sa 22:13–15; Job 41:18–21;

Ps 8:3–4; 74:16; 97:4; 136:7–9; Isa 45:7; Jer 31:35; Jas 1:17

God controls natural light
Ps 104:19 *See also* Job 9:7; 36:30–32; Ps 121:5–6; Mt 5:45; 2Co 4:6

Miracles involving natural light
The pillars of cloud and fire
Ex 13:21–22; 14:20; Dt 1:31; Ne 9:12,19; Ps 78:14; 105:39

Other miracles Ex 9:23–24; 10:23; Isa 38:8; Hab 3:11; Lk 23:44–45; Ac 9:3; 22:6,9,11; 26:13

Natural light associated with angels
Mt 28:3; Lk 24:4; Ac 12:7

Natural light used figuratively
The sun Rev 1:16 *See also* Isa 30:26; Lk 21:25; Rev 12:1

Lightning Lk 9:29 pp Mt 17:2 pp Mk 9:2 *See also* Eze 1:4; Da 10:6; Hos 6:5; Lk 10:18; 17:24

Light Ps 104:2 *See also* Eze 1:26–28

See also

1415 miracles	4838 lightning
4005 creation	4918 dawn
4251 moon	4921 day
4281 stars	4954 morning
4284 sun	5373 lamp &
4810 darkness,	lampstand
natural	

4835
light, spiritual

Light is often used in Scripture as a symbol of the presence of God in the world. It is often especially associated with the word of God, the salvation brought about by God, or the person of Jesus Christ.

Light as a symbol of God
God's purity 1Jn 1:5 *See also* Job 25:4–6; Isa 5:20; 1Jn 1:7

God's glory Rev 21:23 *See also* Ps 76:4; 84:11; Isa 60:19–20; Hab 3:4; 1Ti 6:15–16

God's knowledge Ps 90:8; 139:11–12; Da 2:22; 1Co 4:5

God's unchangeability Jas 1:17

God's vengeance Ps 94:1; Isa 10:17

Satan as an imitator of light 2Co 11:14

Light as a symbol of God's favour towards his people
Ezr 9:8 *See also* Nu 6:25; Job 3:20; 29:2–3; Ps 4:6; 31:16; 44:3; 67:1; 80:3,7; Mic 7:8–9; Rev 22:5

Light as a symbol of God's word
As perceived by believers Ps 119:105 *See also* Ps 19:8; 119:130; 2Pe 1:19

As perceived by unbelievers Jn 3:20 *See also* Job 24:13–17; Jn 1:5

Light as a symbol of salvation
1Pe 2:9 *See also* Isa 9:2; 51:4; Ac 26:23; Eph 5:14; Col 1:12; 1Jn 2:8

Light as a symbol of Jesus Christ
Foretold in the OT Nu 24:17 *See also* Isa 9:2; 42:6–7; 49:6; 53:11; Mal 4:2

Revealed in the NT Jn 8:12 *See also* Mt 4:16; 17:2; Lk 1:78–79; 2:32; Jn 1:4–9; 9:5; 12:35–36,46; Ac 13:47; 2Co 4:6; Heb 1:3; Rev 1:16; 22:16

See also

1020 God, all-knowing	1130 God, sovereignty
1025 God, anger of	2206 Jesus, the Christ
1035 God, faithfulness	5149 eyes
1045 God, glory of	6510 salvation
1065 God, holiness of	8419 enlightenment

4836
light, and the people of God

Scripture often uses light as a symbol of the people of God, and especially the manner in which believers are able and required to reflect the glory of God in a dark world of sin.

The people of God as the light of the world
Mt 5:14–16 *See also* Ps 37:5–6; Pr 4:18; 13:9; Isa 58:8–10; 60:1–5; 62:1; Da 12:3; Lk 2:32; Ac 13:47

Examples of believers acting as light to the world
Moses on Mount Sinai: Ex 34:29–30,35 2Sa 23:3–4 *the righteous ruler, fully realised in Jesus Christ;* Job 29:21–25 *Job as a counsellor;* Jn 5:35 *John the Baptist;* Ac 6:15 *Stephen;* Php 2:15 *the Philippian church*

God is the source of the light of his people
God and his law as the source of light
Ps 27:1; 118:27 *See also* Jdg 5:31; Job 11:13–17; 22:27–28; Ps 19:8; 34:5; 56:13; 97:11; Pr 6:23; Ecc 8:1; Isa 60:19–20; Jn 1:5

The gospel of forgiveness as a source of light Ac 26:17–18 *See also* Job 33:28–30; Ps 112:4; Isa 9:2; 29:18; Mt 4:16; Jn 3:19–21; Eph 1:18; 5:27; Heb 6:4; 10:32

The people of God are called to live in his light
Eph 5:8–14; 1Jn 1:7 *See also* Ps 36:9; 89:15; Isa 2:5; Lk 16:8; Jn 9:4; 12:35–36; Ro 13:12; 1Th 5:5–6; 1Jn 2:8–10

See also

5622 witnesses	7115 children of God
6610 adoption, descriptions	7140 people of God
6744 sanctification	8266 holiness
	8495 witnessing

4838
lightning

Lightning as an aspect of heavy rain storms
Ex 9:23–24

Lightning as a symbol
A symbol of the power of God
Job 36:30–33 *See also* 2Sa 22:13,15; Job 37:3,11,15

The LORD speaks to Job: Job 38:24,35 Ps 18:12–14; 77:18

The plagues on Egypt: Ps 78:48; 105:32 Ps 97:4; 135:7; 144:6; Jer 10:12–13; Rev 16:18

A symbol of brightness Mt 28:3; Lk 9:29 *See also* Eze 21:10,15,28; Da 10:6; Hab 3:11; Zec 9:14; Lk 24:4

Lightning as "fire from heaven"
Job 1:16 *See also* 2Ki 1:10–12; Lk 9:54; Rev 20:9

Lightning as a sign of the presence of God
Ex 19:16 *At Mount Sinai;* Rev 4:5 *See also* Ex 20:18; Eze 1:4,13–14; Rev 8:5; 11:19

Lightning used metaphorically
Mt 24:27 pp Lk 17:24 *See also* Hos 6:5; Na 2:4; Lk 10:18

See also

1105 God, power of	4834 light, natural
1670 symbols	4852 thunder
2580 Christ, transfiguration	4854 weather, God's sovereignty
4110 angels	

4839
mildew

A fungal plant disease, often seen as a sign of God's judgment
Dt 28:22; Am 4:9 *See also* 1Ki 8:37 pp 2Ch 6:28; Hag 2:17

Regulations concerning mildew
Lev 13:47–59; 14:34–57

See also

4802 blight	9210 judgment,
4843 plague	God's

4840
mist

Mist is a natural phenomenon
Mist as a source of water Ge 2:5–6 *NIV footnote at verse 6*

Mist as a barrier to effective vision
Ac 13:11

Mist as a symbol
Of a lack of substance or permanence
Hos 6:4; Jas 4:14 *See also* Hos 13:3; 2Pe 2:17

Of God's forgiveness Isa 44:22

See also

4844 rain	4853 weather

4841
narrowness

A state in which something is confined and restricted, lacking in breadth. It usually has pejorative implications, but Jesus Christ described the way of salvation in terms of narrowness.

Narrowness equated with no escape
Nu 22:24–26 *See also* Pr 23:26–28

4842
Narrowness associated with discomfort
Isa 28:20

The narrow gate
Mt 7:13–14 *See also* Lk 13:22–30

Narrowness in the architecture of the temple
1Ki 6:4 *See also* Eze 40:16,25; 41:16,26; 42:5

See also
4803 breadth	5323 gate
4831 largeness	7467 temple,
4847 smallness	Solomon's

4842
north

The geographical direction opposite to south, often used to demonstrate the vast extent between the two.

North as a point of the compass
Job 37:22 *See also* Ge 13:14; Dt 2:3; Jos 18:5; Ecc 11:3; Isa 14:31; Jer 1:13–15; 3:18 *Although geographically situated to the east of Israel, invaders from Mesopotamia had to enter the country from the north, following the land route around the desert areas;* Jer 46:6; Eze 8:5; 26:7; Am 8:12; Zep 2:13

North and south used to demonstrate vast extent
Ge 28:14 *See also* Job 23:9; Isa 43:6; Eze 20:47; 21:4; Da 8:4; Zec 6:6

The north wind
Pr 25:23 *See also* Ecc 1:6; SS 4:16; Eze 1:4

See also
4821 east	4857 west
4850 south	

4843
plague

Affliction with disease, destruction or environmental disaster as an expression of divine judgment, usually resulting in death. The purpose may be as a punishment or to encourage repentance.

The nature of plague
Eze 6:11–12 *See also* 2Ch 20:9; Jer 14:12; 27:8; Eze 14:21; Rev 6:8

Plagues sent upon Egypt
Plagues described Ex 7:17–18; 8:5–6,16–17,21,24; 9:6,9–10,22–25; 10:4–6,13–15,21–23; 11:4–6; 12:29–30

Plagues withdrawn in answer to prayer Ex 8:12–13,29; 9:29,33; 10:18–19

Plagues recalled and celebrated Ps 78:41–51; 105:26–36; 135:8–9; Am 4:10; Ac 7:36

Plagues sent upon Israel
Plagues threatened for breaking God's covenant Lev 26:23–26 *See also* Lev 26:14–16; Dt 28:20–24

Plagues experienced in fulfilment of God's covenant Ex 32:33–35; Nu 11:31–34; 14:36–38; 16:41–50; 25:3–9; 2Sa 24:11–17 pp 1Ch 21:9–17; Joel 1:2–12; Am 4:6–11

Plagues withdrawn after intercession or obedience Nu 14:10–20; 16:46–48; 21:6–9; 25:6–11; 2Sa 24:18–25 pp 1Ch 21:18–26; 1Ki 8:37–40 pp 2Ch 6:28–31; Ps 106:23,28–31

Plagues announced by prophets as God's judgment Jer 21:5–10 *See also* Jer 24:10; 29:17–19; 34:17; 44:13; Eze 5:12,17; 33:27

Plagues sent upon other nations
1Sa 5:6–12; Isa 19:22; Jer 28:8; Eze 28:22–23; Hab 3:5–6; Zec 14:12–15

Apocalyptic visions of plague as God's judgment
Lk 21:11 pp Mt 24:7 pp Mk 13:8 *See also* Rev 6:8; 11:6; 15:1,6–8; 16:1–21; 18:4–8; 22:18

Divine protection from plague
Ps 91:3–8 *See also* Ex 8:22–23; 9:4,6,26; 10:23; 11:7; 12:13,23,27; 2Ch 20:9

See also
4669 locust	5297 disease
4815 drought	7222 exodus, events
4822 famine	of
4828 hail	9020 death
5295 destruction	

4844
rain

Rain as a natural phenomenon
2Sa 21:10; 1Ki 18:41,44; Ezr 10:9; Ecc 11:3; Isa 4:6; Lk 12:54; Heb 6:7

Associated with cold weather Ac 28:2

God controls the rain
Ge 2:5; Jer 51:16 *See also* 1Ki 18:1; Job 5:10; 28:26; 37:6; 38:25; Ps 68:8; 135:7; 147:8; Jer 10:13; 14:22

God's bounty in giving rain to Israel Dt 28:12 *See also* Lev 26:4; Dt 11:14

God's bounty in giving rain to all humanity Mt 5:45; Ac 14:17 *See also* Zec 10:1

God's punishment through rain and flood Ge 7:4 *See also* Ex 9:33–34; 1Sa 12:17–18; Eze 38:22

God's punishment through drought Dt 11:17 *See also* 1Ki 8:35–36 pp 2Ch 6:26–27; 1Ki 17:1; Isa 5:6; Am 4:7; Zec 14:17–18; Jas 5:17; Rev 11:6

Rain as a symbol of spiritual truth
God's power to save Isa 55:10–11 *See also* 2Sa 23:4; Isa 45:8

God's powerful anger Eze 13:11–13 *See also* 2Sa 22:12; Job 20:23; Isa 28:2

Power of circumstances Mt 7:27 *See also* Mt 7:25

Rain in other imagery
Ability to satisfy: Dt 32:2; Job 29:23; Ps 72:6; Pr 16:15
Clouds without rain: uselessness: Pr 25:14; Jude 12
Pr 25:23; 26:1

The rainbow
Ge 9:14–16 *a sign of God's covenant;* Eze 1:28; Rev 4:3; 10:1

See also
1050 God, goodness	4838 lightning
of	4845 rainbow
1325 God, the	4851 storm
Creator	4854 weather, God's
4272 sky	sovereignty
4293 water	5454 power, God's
4816 drought,	saving
physical	7227 flood, the
4819 dryness	

4845
rainbow

An arch of colours in the sky, formed by the sun's rays passing through raindrops. It was the sign of God's covenant with Noah, established in the aftermath of the great flood.

The rainbow as a sign of God's covenant with Noah
Ge 9:12–17

The rainbow as a sign of God's glory
Eze 1:28; Rev 4:3; 10:1

See also
1045 God, glory of	4807 colours
1347 covenant with	4844 rain
Noah	5106 Noah
1670 symbols	7227 flood, the

4846
shadow

Primarily a symbol of protection, of the brevity of life and of the experience of death, in contrast to God's character and work.

Shadow as a general symbol of protection
Isa 30:2–3 *See also* Jdg 9:15; Jer 48:45; Hos 14:7; Jnh 4:5–6; Mk 4:32

A symbol of God's protection Ps 91:1 *See also* Ps 17:8; 36:7; 57:1; 63:7; 121:5; Isa 4:5–6; 25:4–5; 49:2; 51:16

A symbol of the protection given by God's chosen one Isa 32:2; La 4:20; Eze 17:22–23

Shadow as a symbol of life
Of the brevity of life Ps 144:4 *See also* 1Ch 29:15; Job 8:9; 14:2; Ps 102:11; 109:23; Ecc 6:12; 8:13

Of life's sadness and despair Isa 59:9 *See also* Job 3:3–5; 7:2–3; 16:16; 17:7

Shadow as a symbol of the experience of death
Job 38:17; Ps 23:4 *See also* Job 10:21–22

Shadow in contrast to God
Shadow contrasts with God's unchanging nature Jas 1:17

God's light pierces all shadow Job 12:22 *See also* Job 34:22; Ps 139:11–12; Da 2:22

God's salvation reaches to those whose life is in shadow Mt 4:16 *See also* Isa 9:2; 60:1–2; Lk 1:79

OT ceremonies as a shadow of the reality in Jesus Christ
Col 2:16–17 *See also* Heb 8:5; 10:1

Real shadows
Jdg 9:36; Ne 13:19; SS 2:17; 4:6; Jer 6:4

Real shadows involved in miracles
2Ki 20:9–11 pp Isa 38:8; Ac 5:15

See also

1160 God, unchangeable	1460 truth
1320 God as Saviour	4809 darkness
1403 God, revelation	4833 light
1416 miracles	5480 protection
1436 reality	5490 refuge
	9020 death

4847

smallness

Smallness with regard to size
Jas 3:4–5 *See also* Ge 19:20; Ex 12:4; Jos 17:15; 1Ki 17:13; 18:44; 20:27; 2Ki 4:10; 6:1; Pr 30:24–28 *smallness equated with wisdom*; Ecc 9:14; Isa 49:19–20; Mic 5:2; Mt 7:14; 17:20; Lk 17:6; Ac 27:16

Smallness with regard to importance and social standing
Dt 1:17 *See also* 1Ki 22:31 pp 2Ch 18:30; 2Ch 15:13; Job 3:16–19; Ps 115:13; Jer 49:15 pp Ob 2; Ac 26:22; Rev 11:18; 13:16; 19:5,18; 20:12

Smallness with regard to insignificance
1Sa 18:23 *See also* 1Sa 15:17; 20:2; 1Ki 2:20; Isa 49:6; Lk 19:17

Smallness with regard to weakness
Am 7:2–5

See also

4484 mustard seed	5671 clan
4831 largeness	7145 remnant
4841 narrowness	8357 weakness
5601 village	

4848

smoke

Smoke associated with the divine presence
Ex 19:18; Isa 6:4 *See also* Ex 20:18; Ps 104:32; 144:5; Isa 4:5; Rev 15:8

Smoke associated with divine judgment
Isa 9:18–19 *See also* Ge 15:17; 19:28 *the destruction of Sodom and Gomorrah*; 2Sa 22:9 pp Ps 18:8; Isa 30:27; 34:10; Joel 2:30; Na 2:13; Ac 2:19; Rev 14:11; 18:9,18; 19:3

Smoke associated with the offering of incense
Lev 16:13 *See also* Rev 8:4

Smoke associated with warfare
Jos 8:20–21; Jdg 20:38,40

Smoke used poetically
For something insubstantial Hos 13:3 *See also* Ps 37:20; 68:2; Isa 51:6

In various other ways Pr 10:26 *See also* Job 41:20; Ps 119:83; SS 3:6; Isa 14:31; 65:5; Rev 9:2–3,17–18

See also

1670 symbols	4805 clouds
4318 coal	4826 fire

4849

snow

Snow in winter
2Sa 23:20 pp 1Ch 11:22 *See also* Pr 31:21

Snow all year round on Mount Lebanon
Jer 18:14

Melting snow forms temporary streams
Job 6:16; 24:19

Snow under divine control
Ps 148:8 *See also* Job 37:6; 38:22; Ps 147:16; Isa 55:10–11

Snow as a symbol of whiteness
Ex 4:6; Rev 1:14 *See also* Nu 12:10; 2Ki 5:27; La 4:7; Da 7:9; Mt 28:3

Snow as a symbol of purity
Ps 51:7; Isa 1:18

See also

4806 cold	4859 white
4827 frost	4969 seasons
4828 hail	8324 purity
4853 weather	

4850

south

The geographical direction opposite to north, often used to demonstrate the vast extent between the two.

South as a point of the compass
Job 9:9; Mt 12:42 pp Lk 11:31 *See also* Ge 13:14; Nu 10:6; Dt 33:2; 1Sa 23:19; Job 39:26; Da 8:9; Ac 21:3

South and north used to demonstrate vast extent
Isa 43:6 *See also* Ge 28:14; Job 23:9; Eze 20:47; 21:4

See also

4821 east	4857 west
4842 north	

4851

storm

Storms and bad weather
Ex 9:24; Mt 8:24 pp Lk 8:23; Ac 27:15 *See also* Job 36:33; Isa 4:6; Ac 27:18,20; 2Pe 2:17

The storms of life
Job 30:22; Pr 1:27 *See also* Job 9:17; Ps 55:8; Pr 10:25; Isa 25:4; 32:2; 54:11; Jer 25:32; Eze 38:9; Mt 7:24–27; Jas 1:6

God controls storms
Jnh 1:4; Na 1:3; Zec 10:1 *See also* Ps 83:15; 107:29; Jer 11:16; 23:19; 30:23

Jesus Christ stills the storm
Lk 8:24 pp Mt 8:26 pp Mk 4:39

See also

2351 Christ, miracles	4858 whirlwind
4838 lightning	4860 wind
4844 rain	4971 seasons of life
4852 thunder	5300 drowning
4853 weather	

4852

thunder

Thunder as an aspect of violent weather
Job 28:26 *See also* Job 36:29,33; Ps 93:4; Jer 10:13; 51:16

Thunder as a sign of the presence of God
Ex 19:16 *See also* Ex 20:18; 1Sa 12:17–18; Job 26:14; 37:4–5; 40:9; Ps 18:13; 29:3; 68:33; 81:7; Jn 12:29; Rev 4:5; 6:1; 8:5; 10:3–4; 11:19; 14:2; 19:6

Thunder as an expression of the judgment of God
1Sa 2:10 *See also* Ex 9:23,28–29,33–34; 1Sa 7:10; 2Sa 22:14; Ps 77:17–18; 104:7; Isa 29:6; 30:30; 33:3; Jer 25:30; Joel 2:11; 3:16; Am 1:2; Rev 16:18

The thunder of horses' hoofs
Jdg 5:22 *See also* Rev 9:9

The Sons of Thunder
Mk 3:17

See also

1670 symbols	4853 weather
4838 lightning	9210 judgment, God's
4851 storm	

4853

weather

Patterns of climatic conditions, such as wind and rain, which were of major importance to the rural economies of the Near East. Scripture stresses the sovereignty of God over the weather and sees it as a possible means of judgment or reward.

4854

weather, God's sovereignty over

The weather is under the control of God, who alone is able to direct it.

The weather is under God's control
Job 28:25–27; Mt 8:26–27 pp Mk 4:39–41 pp Lk 8:24–25 *See also* Job 5:10; 26:8–9,13; 37:1–18; Ps 135:7; 147:8,16–18; 148:8; Jer 10:13

God alone understands the mysteries of the weather
Pr 3:19–20; Jn 3:8 *See also* Job 36:26–33; 38:22–30,34–35,37; Ecc 11:3–5

4855
Israel's economy was dependent on the weather
Lev 26:4 *See also* Dt 11:10–15; 28:12; Jer 5:24; Hos 6:3

The weather demonstrates God's goodness and mercy
Ge 8:22; Mt 5:45; Ac 14:17 *See also* Ge 9:14–16; Dt 33:13–14; Ps 68:7–9; Isa 30:23; 49:10; Joel 2:23; Zec 10:1

The weather as a demonstration of God's direct intervention
Jnh 1:4 *See also* Ex 14:21; Nu 11:31; Ps 78:26; Jnh 4:8

The weather as an answer to prayer
Jas 5:17–18 *See also* 1Sa 12:17–18; 1Ki 8:35–36 pp 2Ch 6:26–27; 1Ki 18:41–44

The weather can cause suffering
Ge 31:40; Ac 28:2 *See also* Ezr 10:9; Job 1:16,18–19; Mt 20:12; Jn 18:18; Ac 27:15

See also
1050 God, goodness of	4844 rain
	4860 wind
1130 God, sovereignty	4970 seasons of year
1330 God, the provider	8602 prayer

4855
weather, as God's judgment

The weather can be seen as an expression of God's judgment and grace, as well as providing insights concerning human nature.

The weather as an expression of God's judgment
Judgment in battle Jos 10:11 *See also* 2Sa 22:10–15; Isa 30:30; Eze 38:22

Judgment in general 1Ki 17:1; Hag 1:10–11 *See also* Ge 7:11–12; Ex 9:22–26; Lev 26:18–19; Dt 11:17; 28:22–24; Jer 3:3; 14:1–6; Eze 22:24; Am 4:7; Zec 14:17–19

The weather as a source of spiritual insight
About the shortness of life Jas 4:14 *See also* Job 7:9; 24:19; 30:15; Hos 13:3; Jas 1:11

About empty profession Hos 6:4 *See also* Job 6:15–17; Pr 25:14; 2Pe 2:17

About God's judgment Jer 23:19 *See also* Jer 4:11; Hos 8:7

About God's salvation Isa 55:10–11 *See also* Isa 44:22; 45:8

About righteous rule 2Sa 23:3–4 *See also* Ps 72:6; Pr 16:15; Isa 25:4–5

About wholesome teaching Dt 32:2 *See also* Job 29:23

About the troubles of life Mt 7:24–27

About the signs of the times Mt 16:2–3 *See also* Lk 12:54–56

See also
4284 sun	4829 heat
4805 clouds	4840 mist
4806 cold	4849 snow
4814 dew	4851 storm
4815 drought	4852 thunder
4827 frost	

4857
west

The geographical direction often identified by the position of the setting sun.

West as a point of the compass
Ex 10:19; Lk 12:54 *See also* Ge 13:14; Ex 27:12; Nu 34:6; Dt 3:27; Jos 5:1; 2Sa 13:34; 1Ki 4:24; 7:25; Job 18:20; Isa 24:14; 49:12; 59:19; Hos 11:10; Rev 21:13

West and east used to demonstrate vast extent
Ps 103:12; Mt 24:27 *See also* Job 23:8; Ps 75:6; Isa 43:5; Zec 8:7; 14:4; Mt 8:11

West identified by the setting sun
Dt 11:30; Ps 113:3 *See also* Ps 50:1; Isa 45:6; Mal 1:11

See also
4284 sun	4842 north
4821 east	4850 south

4858
whirlwind

A violent wind, often associated with the presence and activity of God.

The presence of God in whirlwinds
In replying to Job Job 38:1

In the forces of nature Ps 77:18

In taking Elijah up to heaven 2Ki 2:11 *See also* 2Ki 2:1; Na 1:3

Whirlwinds as symbols of disaster or divine judgment
Isa 40:24; Jer 23:19 *See also* Pr 1:27; Isa 5:28; 21:1; 66:15; Jer 4:13; Hos 4:19; 8:7; Zec 7:14

See also
4851 storm	4860 wind
4853 weather	

4859
white

A symbol of purity and regeneration reflecting godliness, and also a symbol of victory.

White used symbolically
Of purity and holiness Mt 17:1–2 pp Mk 9:2–3 *See also* Da 7:9; Mt 28:2–3 pp Mk 16:5; Jn 20:12; Ac 1:10; Rev 1:12–14; 4:4; 6:1–2; 19:11–14; 20:11

Of forgiveness and regeneration Isa 1:18 *See also* Ps 51:7; Rev 3:4–5,18; 6:11; 7:9,13–14

Of superficial righteousness Mt 23:27 *See also* Eze 13:10–15; 22:28; Ac 23:3

Of joy Ecc 9:7–8

White used descriptively
Est 1:6; La 4:7 *See also* Ge 30:37; 49:12; Ex 16:31 *the manna*; Lev 11:18 *Skin diseases:* Lev 13:3–4,38–39; 2Ki 5:27

Jdg 5:10–11; Est 8:15; Job 6:6; 41:32; Joel 1:7

White horses: Zec 1:8; 6:1–6 Mt 5:36; Rev 2:17

See also
2063 Christ, perfection	6652 forgiveness
	7342 cleanliness
4801 black	7416 purification
4807 colours	8324 purity
4849 snow	8767 hypocrisy
5145 clothing	

4860
wind

In Hebrew the same word can denote "breath", "wind" or "spirit". Scripture describes the powerful effect of wind, and uses the image figuratively to speak of God's power and presence in the world.

The origins of the wind
Ex 14:21–22; Ps 78:26; Am 4:13 *See also* Ge 8:1 *A wind caused the flood waters to recede;* Ex 10:13–14 *An east wind brought the plague of locusts on Egypt;* Ex 10:19; Nu 11:31 *A wind brought quail to feed the Israelites;* Job 28:25; Ps 107:25; 135:7; 148:7–8; Isa 11:15; Jer 10:13; Eze 13:13; Jnh 1:4; 4:8

The effects of the wind
1Ki 19:11; Eze 27:26; Ac 27:13–15 *See also* Ge 41:5–6; Job 1:18–19; 37:9,17–18; Da 7:2; Mt 14:24; Lk 12:55; Jn 6:16–18; Jas 3:4

Wind used figuratively
As an image of the Holy Spirit Jn 3:8 *The Greek word for "Spirit" is the same as that for "wind", allowing Jesus Christ to play on the double meaning of the word.*

As an image of spiritual instability Jas 1:6

As an image of destruction Ps 103:15–16; Mt 7:24–27 *See also* Job 21:17–18; Ps 1:4; 48:7; Isa 17:13; 32:2; Jer 4:11–12; 22:22; Eze 19:12; Da 2:34–35; Hos 8:7; Am 1:14; Hab 1:9; Eph 4:14; Jude 12; Rev 6:12–13

As an image of something insubstantial Ecc 1:14 *See also* Job 6:26; Pr 11:29; 27:15–16; Isa 26:18; Jer 5:13; Hos 12:1

See also
1670 symbols	4858 whirlwind
3120 Holy Spirit, descriptions	5062 spirit
	5864 futility
4804 breath	9210 judgment, God's
4851 storm	

4900
Time

4903
time

A creation of God which marks the duration of life and which is measured by changes in the created order. The flow of time is directed by God who appoints particular "times" within his unfolding purposes. Because human life is brief, time should be used properly, making the most of every opportunity.

Time as a creation of God
Time began at creation Ge 1:5 *See also* 1Co 2:7

Time is marked by change in the created order Ge 1:14 *The main divisions of time were based upon the phases of the sun and moon. See also* Ps 104:19; Jer 33:20

The timelessness of God Ps 90:2 *See also* Ge 1:1; Ps 93:2; Pr 8:22–26; Hab 1:12; Jn 1:1–2

God's perception of time 2Pe 3:8 *See also* Ps 90:4

Measurement of time
Divisions of time Ge 1:8 *A day was marked by the regular cycle of evening and morning;* Nu 28:14 *Months were determined by the regular phases of the moon;* 1Ki 4:7 *The year consisted of twelve lunar months;* Jn 11:9 *An hour was one twelfth of the period of daylight.*

Indefinite periods of time 1Sa 1:22; Jer 32:14; Lk 20:9; Ac 14:28; 18:23

Recurring times and seasons
God's seasonal provision Dt 11:14 *See also* Lev 26:4; Dt 28:12; Ps 145:15–16; Jer 5:24; Ac 14:17

Appointed times for festivals Lev 23:4 *See also* Ex 13:10; 23:15 pp Ex 34:18; Nu 9:2–3

A right time for every activity Ecc 3:1–8 *See also* Ecc 3:11; 8:6; Jer 8:7

Times of human life in God's hands Ps 31:15; 139:16 *See also* Job 14:5; Da 2:21; Ac 17:26

Appointed times within God's unfolding purpose
The time of fulfilment of promise *The time of Isaac's birth:* Ge 21:2; Ro 9:9 Lk 1:20 *the time of John the Baptist's birth;* Ac 7:17 *the time of Israel's possession of the land*

The time of Israel's deliverance Ps 102:13 *See also* Hab 2:3; 3:16

The time of Jesus Christ's coming Gal 4:2–4 *See also* Mk 1:15; Lk 19:44; 1Ti 2:6; Tit 1:3

The time of Jesus Christ's death Jn 12:23 *See also* Mt 26:18; Jn 2:4; 8:20; 13:1; Ro 5:6; 1Pe 1:11

The time of Jesus Christ's return 1Co 4:5 *See also* Mt 24:36; Eph 1:10; Heb 9:28; 1Ti 6:15

The time of God's judgment Ps 75:2; Eze 7:7–8; 24:14; Zep 2:2; Mt 8:29; Rev 11:18

The appointed time of the end Da 8:19; 11:27,29; Mk 13:32; Ac 1:6–7

The time between Jesus Christ's first and second coming
The time of salvation 2Co 6:2 *The time of salvation lies between the two comings of Jesus Christ. See also* Isa 49:8; Heb 11:13

The end times Ac 2:17; Heb 1:2; 1Pe 1:20; 1Jn 2:18

Proper use of time
Recognising the brevity of human life Ps 90:12 *See also* Ps 39:4–6; Pr 27:1; Jas 4:14

Seeking God Isa 55:6 *See also* Ps 32:6; 69:13; 95:7–8; Ecc 12:1,6–7

Looking to eternal realities 1Co 7:29–31 *See also* Ps 10:6; Isa 56:12; Lk 12:16–21; Ro 13:11–12; Jas 5:7–9

Making the most of opportunities Col 4:5 *See also* Gal 6:10; Eph 5:16

See also
1115 God, purpose of	4978 year
4016 life, human	5046 opportunities
4921 day	5385 leisure
4945 history	8438 giving time
4948 hour	9120 eternity
4951 month	9155 millennium

4906

abolition

The final ending and elimination of practices or states of affairs. Scripture looks forward to God's final abolition of the present order, through the inauguration of the new Jerusalem.

Things to be abolished in the kingdom of God
War and destruction Hos 2:18 *See also* Ps 46:9–10; Isa 9:5; Zec 9:10

Illness and suffering Ex 23:25–26 *See also* Ex 15:26; Dt 7:15; Isa 53:4; Mt 8:16–17 pp Mk 1:32–34 pp Lk 4:40–41

Sin Ro 6:6 *See also* Eze 36:25–26 *God speaks here of his abolition of sinful, human hard-heartedness;* Ro 8:3–4; Heb 9:26

Death and mourning 1Co 15:24–26; Rev 21:1–4 *See also* Isa 25:7–8; 65:17–20; 1Co 15:54–55; 2Ti 1:10; Rev 20:13–14

The abolition of idolatry in Israel
Israel was commanded to abolish Canaanite worship Ex 23:24 *See also* Ex 34:13; Nu 33:50–52; Dt 12:2–3

The abolition of mediums and spiritists Dt 18:9–12; 1Sa 28:3–9; 2Ki 23:24

In Asa's reign 1Ki 15:11–13 pp 2Ch 14:2–3

In Hezekiah's reign 2Ki 18:4 pp 2Ch 31:1

In Josiah's reign 2Ki 23:4–20 pp 2Ch 34:3–7 pp 2Ch 34:33

The abolition of the temple
Sacrifice in the temple abolished Da 11:31 *Antiochus Epiphanes abolished the daily sacrifice in the temple in 168 B.C., thereby attacking the symbolic centre of Israel's life. See also* Da 12:11

Jesus Christ was accused of seeking to abolish the temple Mt 26:61 pp Mk 14:58 *See also* Mt 21:12–13 pp Mk 11:15–17 pp Lk 19:45–46 *Jesus Christ's action may have been understood as a symbolic abolition of a defiled sacrificial system;* Mt 27:39–40 pp Mk 15:29–30; Ac 6:14

The final abolition of the temple in the new Jerusalem Rev 21:22

Abolition and the law
The law has not been abolished Mt 5:17–19 *See also* Ro 3:31

The law has been abolished as an instrument of condemnation Col 2:13–14 *See also* 2Co 3:6–17; Eph 2:14–16; Heb 10:1–10

The law does not abolish God's promises Gal 3:17–18 *God did not abolish his promise of righteousness to Abraham when he gave the law, because the promise was not conditional upon keeping the law but is received by faith. See also* Ro 4:14

The offence of the cross is abolished by accepting circumcision Gal 5:11 *Jews found offensive the Christians' claim that salvation did not come through keeping the law, but instead through faith in a crucified Messiah, whom the law had cursed. Paul regarded "the offence of the cross" as central to the gospel, and refused to make salvation conditional upon circumcision and obedience to the law. See also* 1Co 1:22–24; 2:2; Gal 3:13; 5:2; 6:14–15

See also
4175 mediums	7466 temples
5297 disease	8768 idolatry
5333 healing	9020 death
5375 law	9115 antichrist, the
7334 circumcision	9160 new heavens &
7374 high places	new earth

4909

beginning

A starting point, origin or source. The beginning often refers to the time of or before the creation of the world. God is described as the Beginning and the End, denoting the eternity of his existence. Jesus Christ's coming marks a new beginning both for God's people and, finally, for all creation.

Beginning as the starting point
As the source Ps 111:10 *See also* Pr 1:7; 9:10; Mic 1:13 *the source of Israel's sin;* Col 1:18 *Jesus Christ as the source of the church's life*

As the origin Job 8:7; Ac 26:4; Heb 7:3

As the commencement Lev 23:5; Jdg 7:19; 1Ki 6:1 pp 2Ch 3:1; Lk 23:54; 1Jn 2:7; 2Jn 5

The beginning: before the creation
Pr 8:22–23

Jesus Christ's existence predates the creation Jn 17:5 *See also* Jn 1:1–2; 8:58; Col 1:15–17; 1Jn 1:1; 2:13–14

Salvation planned before the creation Eph 1:3–4 *See also* 1Co 2:7; 2Th 2:13; 2Ti 1:9; Tit 1:2

The beginning: the creation
Ge 1:1; Heb 1:10 *See also* Ps 102:25; Isa 40:21; Da 12:1; Mt 24:21 pp Mk 13:19

Marriage ordained from the beginning
Mt 19:4–6 pp Mk 10:6–9 *See also*
Ge 1:27; 2:24

The beginning of Israel's nationhood
Ex 12:2 *See also* 2Sa 7:10 pp 1Ch 17:9;
Isa 52:4; Jer 2:2–3

New beginnings for God's people
For Israel Hos 2:14–15 *See also* Isa 1:26;
43:18–19; 44:26; 61:4; Jer 33:7–9

For believers 2Co 5:17 *See also* 2Co 4:6;
Eph 2:10

A new creation Isa 65:17 *See also*
Isa 66:22; 2Pe 3:13; Rev 21:1

Beginnings of significant events
The rebuilding of Jerusalem Ne 2:18;
Hag 1:14

Jesus Christ's ministry Mt 4:17 *See also*
Mk 1:1,15; Lk 3:23; Ac 1:1

The beginning of signs of the end
Mt 24:7–8 pp Mk 13:8; Lk 21:28

The beginning and the end
Implying all-inclusiveness Ge 44:12;
Dt 31:24; 1Sa 3:12; Mt 20:8

The beginning and end contrasted
Pr 20:21; Ecc 7:8; 2Pe 2:20

Completing what is begun Php 1:6 *See
also* 2Co 8:6; Gal 3:3; Heb 3:14;
Rev 2:5,19

God as the Beginning and the End
Isa 44:6; Rev 21:6 *See also* Isa 41:4;
48:12; Rev 1:17; 2:8; 22:13

Satan as sinful from the beginning
Jn 8:44 *See also* 1Jn 3:8

See also

1140 God, the eternal	6698 newness
4005 creation	6730 reinstatement
4915 completion	9120 eternity
4918 dawn	9160 new heavens &
4930 end	new earth
5655 birth	9165 restoration

4912

chance

The occurrence of events at random,
as undesigned happenings. While
people may perceive events as
random, in Scripture all events are
subject to God's sovereignty.

Chance in human life
Chance events 2Ch 18:33–34
pp 1Ki 22:34–38 *See also* 1Sa 6:7–9;
Pr 26:10

Human life seems to be governed by
chance, not merit Ecc 9:11 *See also*
Ecc 2:17–19

Providence at work through apparent
chance Jnh 1:17 *See also* Ru 2:3;
Lk 23:44–45 pp Mt 27:45, 51
pp Mk 15:33, 38; Ac 16:26

Chance events overruled by God's sovereignty
The casting of lots and the element of
chance Pr 16:33 *See also* Nu 33:53–54;
Jdg 20:8–10; Ne 10:34; 11:1; Lk 23:34
pp Mt 27:35 pp Mk 15:24; Ac 1:23–26

**Urim and Thummim, seeming to be
dependent on chance** Ex 28:29–30 *The
Urim and Thummim were used by the high
priest to declare God's will. It was a form of
casting lots showing either an affirmative
or negative response to an enquiry. See also*
Nu 27:21; 1Sa 28:4–6; Ezr 2:62–63
pp Ne 7:64–65

See also

1130 God,	4937 fate, fatalism
sovereignty	7392 lots, casting of
1355 providence	8124 guidance

4915

completion

The bringing to fulfilment of a work,
such as the work of creation or
redemption.

Creation was completed by the seventh day
Ge 2:1–2; Dt 32:4 *See also* Ge 1:3–4
*Genesis chapter 1 records the creation
completed on each successive day as being
"good"*; Ex 20:11; Jn 1:3; Col 1:16;
Heb 1:2; 4:3; 11:3

All things are completed in God's time
Gal 4:4 *See also* Ge 15:16; Da 9:24;
Mk 1:15; Ro 5:6; Eph 1:10

The work of redemption is a completed work
Jesus Christ brought his earthly work
to completion Jn 17:4; 19:30 *See also*
Jn 4:34; 5:36

Jesus Christ will present his church
complete to his Father Jn 6:37–40,45;
17:24

Jesus Christ makes his people
complete in himself Eph 3:19; Php 1:6;
Col 2:10 *See also* Jn 15:11; 16:24;
Ro 15:14; Col 2:2; Jas 1:4

Believers are to complete their God-given work
Ac 20:24 *See also* Ac 14:26; Ro 15:28;
Col 4:17; 2Ti 4:7

The completion of the age
This world will come to an end
Isa 65:17 *See also* Isa 66:22; Mt 19:28;
Eph 1:9–10; Heb 1:11–12;
2Pe 3:10–12; Rev 21:1–5

There will be a final separation of the
righteous and wicked
Mt 13:36–43,47–50; 25:32–41;
2Th 1:8–10

See also

1429 prophecy, OT	4942 fulness
fulfilment	5596 victory
1439 revelation	7436 sacrifice, NT
4005 creation	fulfilment
4903 time	8320 perfection
4930 end	9105 last things

4918

dawn

The time marked by the rising of the
sun. It signals the end of night and
relief from its attendant concerns,
and the approach of daylight with
the opportunity for renewed daily
activity. The light of dawn following

---

darkness is a symbol of hope and
vindication, fulfilled especially in
the coming of the Messiah through
whom God's new age dawns.

Dawn as the end of the night
It ends the darkness of the night
Am 5:8 *See also* 2Sa 23:4; Job 41:18

It signals the end of nightly activity
Ge 32:22–26; Jdg 19:25–26; 1Sa 14:36;
25:36; 2Sa 2:32; 17:22; SS 2:16–17

Waiting for the dawn to bring relief
Ps 130:6 *See also* Job 7:3–4; Ps 46:5;
Isa 21:12; 38:13; Ac 27:29

Dawn as the beginning of a new day
It provides the earliest opportunity of
the day Da 6:19 *First light provides the
earliest opportunity for action and implies
urgency. See also* Ge 19:15; Jos 6:15 *Dawn
was a common time for military
campaigns to begin*; Jdg 9:33; 16:2;
1Sa 19:11; Mt 28:1 pp Mk 16:2
pp Lk 24:1 *Women visit Jesus Christ's
tomb at dawn*; Mk 1:35 pp Lk 4:42 *Jesus
Christ prays at dawn*; Lk 22:66; Jn 8:2;
Ac 27:33

Important activity begins at dawn
Ne 4:21 *See also* Ne 8:3

Dawn as a symbol of blessings to come
The Messiah brings a new dawn
Isa 9:2; Rev 22:16 *See also* Nu 24:17;
Mt 4:16; Lk 1:78–79; Jn 1:4–5; 8:12

A symbol of hope and vindication
Ps 37:6; 112:4 *See also* Jdg 5:31; Ps 57:8
pp Ps 108:2; Pr 4:18; Isa 58:8; 60:1–3;
62:1

A symbol of God's coming in glory
Hab 3:3–4 *See also* Mal 4:2

A symbol of renewal Ps 110:3

Dawn as a symbol of God's revelation
1Jn 2:8 *See also* Isa 8:20; 2Pe 1:19

Dawn as a time of reckoning
Darkness at dawn as a picture of
judgment Isa 13:10–11 *See also* Job 3:9;
Am 4:13

The light of dawn exposes the wicked
Job 38:12–13; Jn 3:19–20; Eph 5:11–13

See also

1439 revelation	4954 morning
4284 sun	4957 night
4809 darkness	8154 righteousness
4821 east	8419 enlightenment
4833 light	9165 restoration
4921 day	9610 hope

4921

day

A period of 24 hours or, as distinct
from night, the period of daylight.
The term may also be used more
generally to refer to a point in time.
Daylight is used figuratively to
describe the illumination afforded to
believers, who are urged to use the
opportunities it presents and to

avoid the evil usually associated with darkness.

Day and daylight

Day as a period of 24 hours Ge 1:8; Mt 20:19; Jn 4:43; 11:6

Day as the period of daylight Ge 1:5 *See also* Ge 1:14–18; 8:22; Ps 74:16; Jer 33:20

Daylight gives opportunity for activity

A time for human endeavour Jn 11:9–10 *See also* Jos 10:12–13; Ac 27:29

A time of spiritual opportunity Jn 9:4–5 *See also* Jn 12:35–36

Daylight allows things to be seen

Daylight activities are seen by all 2Sa 12:11–12; Eze 12:3–4; Mt 10:27 pp Lk 12:3

Examples of those avoiding daylight Jdg 6:27 *Gideon;* Jn 3:2 *Nicodemus*

Daylight activities should be decent Ro 13:12–13 *See also* Eph 5:8–14; 1Th 5:5–8; 2Pe 2:13

Six working days ordained

Ex 20:8–11 pp Dt 5:12–15

Particular days of the week

The Sabbath (Saturday) Ex 20:8–10 pp Dt 5:12–15 *The Sabbath was reckoned from sunset on Friday to sunset on Saturday. See also* Lk 4:16; Col 2:16; Heb 4:4

The Day of Preparation for the Sabbath (Friday) Mk 15:42 pp Lk 23:54; Jn 19:31

The first day of the week (Sunday) Ac 20:7 *See also* Mk 16:2 pp Lk 24:1 pp Jn 20:1; Mk 16:9; 1Co 16:2; Rev 1:10

Festival days

Lev 23:5–6 *Passover and Unleavened Bread;* Lev 23:27–28 *the Day of Atonement The Feast of Tabernacles:* Lev 23:34–36; Jn 7:37 Nu 28:26 *the day of firstfruits*

Day as a point in time

The day of salvation 2Co 6:2 *See also* Isa 25:9; 49:8

God sends the day of disaster Dt 32:35; Jer 17:18; 51:2; Mk 13:19

God helps on the day of distress Ps 86:7 *See also* Ge 35:3; 2Sa 22:19 pp Ps 18:18; 2Ki 19:3–4 pp Isa 37:3–4; Ps 94:13; Jer 17:17

The final days of time

The last days Ac 2:17–18 *See also* Joel 2:28–29; Isa 2:2 pp Mic 4:1; Hos 3:5; 1Ti 4:1; 2Ti 3:1; Heb 1:2; 1Pe 1:20

The day of the LORD Isa 13:9–11 *A day of salvation for God's people:* Jer 30:7–9; Zep 3:16–17; Php 1:6; 2Ti 1:12 *A day of wrath and judgment:* Joel 2:1–2; Ob 15; Zep 1:14–15 *The day will come unexpectedly:* 1Th 5:2; 2Pe 3:10

The last day Jn 6:39–40 *See also* Jn 11:24; 12:48

References to specific periods of days at the end of history

Da 12:11–12; Rev 11:3; 12:6

God's different perception of time

2Pe 3:8 *See also* Ps 90:4

See also

4833 light	7354 feasts and
4903 time	festivals
4918 dawn	7428 Sabbath
4957 night	7930 Lord's Day, the
5046 opportunities	9140 last days
5231 birthday	9220 day of the LORD
7308 Atonement, Day	
of	

4924

delay

A postponement or pause, which can result from a deliberate decision or a failure to achieve the intended objective in the time available. Scripture stresses that apparent delays on the part of God are due to his love and wisdom, especially to give sinners time for repentance.

4925
delay, divine

Delays by God do not result from any failure on his part, but reflect unrealistic human expectations concerning his actions. God delays his vengeance in order to give time for human repentance.

God delays to allow for repentance

To give time for repentance Lk 13:6–9; Ro 2:4; 2Pe 3:8–9 *See also* Mt 3:7–11 pp Lk 3:7–10; 1Ti 2:4; Jas 5:7; Rev 2:21

In response to repentance 1Ki 21:29 *See also* 1Ki 21:21–28

Where there is no repentance, God does not delay Eze 12:25 *See also* Eze 21:24–26; Rev 2:16

God delays judgment for the sake of his name

Isa 48:9 *See also* Ne 9:30–31

Jesus Christ delayed visiting Lazarus for God's glory

Jn 11:1–6 *See also* Jn 11:11–23, 38–44

The giving of the Holy Spirit was delayed until Pentecost

Lk 24:49 *See also* Ac 1:4; 2:1–4

God acts when he wants and nothing can delay him

Heb 10:37 *Referring to the second coming of Jesus Christ. See also* Hab 2:3 *Referring to the LORD's delay in sending the Babylonians to conquer Judah and take her inhabitants into exile;* Rev 22:20

Other examples of delay

Ex 32:1

See also

2565 Christ, second	4903 time
coming	5558 storing
3257 Holy Spirit, gift	5977 waiting
of	6732 repentance

4926
delay, human

Human delay is often the result of fear, indecision or disobedience to God. Scripture indicates that delay is to be avoided.

Examples of delay as a result of fear

Israel entering the promised land Nu 13:31–32 *See also* Nu 13:1–3, 17–20, 27–30; 14:33–35

Gideon responding to God's call Jdg 6:36–40

Examples of delay as a result of disobedience

Lot escaping from Sodom Ge 19:16 *See also* Ge 19:12–15

Jonah going to Nineveh Jnh 1:3 *See also* Ps 119:60; Jnh 1:1–2; 3:1–3 *Jonah obeyed the second time.*

Nothing should delay believers from following Jesus Christ

Mt 8:21–22 pp Lk 9:59–60 *See also* Mt 9:9; Mk 1:20; Lk 14:15–24; 19:5–6

People should not delay in the matter of salvation

Isa 55:6 *See also* Am 6:3; Ac 24:24–26; 2Co 6:2; Heb 2:3

Believers are not to delay in fulfilling their vows to God and obligations to others

Ecc 5:4 *See also* Lev 19:13; Dt 23:21; Ps 61:8

Examples of human responses to delay

Sarah's wrong response brought trouble Ge 16:1–6

Saul's wrong response cost him the kingship 1Sa 13:11–12 *See also* 1Sa 13:8–10, 13–14

Jacob responded with patience Ge 29:20–30

Paul responded by giving instructions to Timothy 1Ti 3:14–15

Daniel responded by praying Da 9:19 *See also* Da 9:1–23; 10:10–13 *Gabriel explains the reason for the delay.*

David responded by calling on the LORD Ps 13:1; 40:17; 141:1

See also

5877 hesitation	8318 patience
6510 salvation	8489 urgency
8114 discipleship	8602 prayer
8120 following Christ	8718 disobedience
8160 seeking God	8754 fear

4930

end

A limit in time or space, or the outcome of a sequence of actions or events. God knows the end from the beginning. He is without limit: he exercises control over the furthest reaches of the world, and will bring to an end earthly powers, human life and the present age. Those who persevere to the end will be saved.

God is without limit
Heb 1:12 *See also* Ps 102:26–27; Da 6:26; 7:14; Mt 24:35 pp Mk 13:31 pp Lk 21:33; Lk 1:33

God is the Beginning and the End
Rev 21:6 *See also* Isa 44:6; Rev 22:13

God brings earthly powers to an end
Isa 13:11; Da 2:44 *See also* Ps 89:44; Isa 21:16; 23:9; Jer 48:2 *Moab;* Jer 49:37 *Elam;* Eze 7:2–6 *Israel;* Eze 26:21 *Tyre;* Eze 30:18 *Egypt;* Da 5:26 *Babylon*

Persevering to the end
Mt 10:22; 24:13; Php 1:6; Heb 3:14; 10:36

See also

1115 God, purpose of	5235 boundary
4909 beginning	8459 perseverance
4915 completion	9020 death
4918 dawn	9105 last things
4938 fate, final destiny	9120 eternity

---

evening

The time between the fading of daylight and nightfall. The onset of darkness marks the end of the working day and is a time for rest and refreshment. It is an assigned time for sacrifice and an opportunity for reflection and prayer. The evening also brings dangers.

Evening marks the end of the day
Evening and God's work of creation Ge 1:5

The onset of darkness Pr 7:9
Evening shadows soon disappear in the darkness: Ps 102:11; 109:23 Jer 6:4

Days reckoned from evening to evening Ex 12:18; Lev 23:32 *The Sabbath began at sunset on Friday.*

Ritual uncleanness lasts until evening Lev 11:39–40; 17:15; Nu 19:7–8; Dt 23:11

Waiting on God until evening Jos 7:6 *See also* Jdg 20:23,26–27; 21:2–3

Mourning until evening 2Sa 1:12

City gates shut at evening Jos 2:5; 2Ki 7:9–11; Ne 13:19; Eze 46:2

Executed criminals to be buried by evening Dt 21:22–23; Jos 8:29; 10:26; Mt 27:57–58 pp Mk 15:42–43 pp Lk 23:52–54; Jn 19:31

Evening as a time for refreshment
A time to rest from labour Ps 104:23; Lk 21:37 *See also* Jdg 19:16; Ru 2:17; Job 7:2; Zep 2:7; Mt 20:8; Mk 4:35–38 pp Mt 8:23 pp Lk 8:22–23

A time to rest from travel Jdg 19:9 *See also* Ge 19:1–2; Nu 9:21; Lk 24:29

A time to return home Mt 21:17 *See also* Ge 30:16; Mk 11:11,19; Jn 6:16–17

A time to eat Ex 16:12; 1Ki 17:6; Mt 14:15; Jn 13:2

A time for reflection and prayer Ge 24:63 *See also* Ps 55:17; 141:2; Mt 14:23 pp Mk 6:46

Evening religious duties
The evening sacrifice Ex 29:38–41 *See also* Nu 28:8; 1Ch 16:40; Ezr 3:3 *The time of the evening sacrifice, probably about 3 p.m.:* 1Ki 18:29; Ezr 9:4–5; Da 9:21

Lighting the lamps in the sanctuary Ex 30:8 *See also* Ex 27:21 pp Lev 24:3

The Passover sacrifice Ex 12:6 *See also* Lev 23:5; Nu 9:2–5; Dt 16:6; Jos 5:10; Mt 26:20 pp Mk 14:17–18; Lk 22:14

Adulterous behaviour in the evening
2Sa 11:2–4; Job 24:15; Pr 7:14–20

Other evening activities
Mt 8:16 pp Mk 1:32 pp Lk 4:40 *People came to Jesus Christ after sunset, when the Sabbath was over. See also* Ge 24:11 *Water collected in the evening, the coolest time of the day;* Mt 16:2 *Red sky in the evening as a sign of fair weather*

The dangers of the evening .
Isa 17:14; Zep 3:3 *Israel's rulers are likened to wolves who prowl in the evening looking for food. See also* 2Ki 7:7; Ps 59:6; Hab 1:8

See also

4438 eating	5056 rest
4809 darkness	5339 home
4833 light	5533 sleep, physical
4921 day	5628 work
4954 morning	7402 offerings
4957 night	7435 sacrifice, in OT

---

fate

A hidden power which some believe to control and determine everything that happens in such a way that it is impossible to prevent or change things. Scripture stresses both the sovereignty of God and human responsibility and has no place for this pagan notion. The term is also used in a looser sense, to mean "end" or "destiny".

4937
fate, and fatalism

The belief that all things are predetermined, especially by the stars, removing human freedom and responsibility. Scripture affirms human freedom and responsibility and declares that the sun, moon and stars are all part of God's creation and are subject to him.

The heavenly bodies subject to God's authority
The heavenly bodies are created by God Ge 1:14–18; Job 9:9; Ps 8:3; 74:16; 148:3–5; Am 5:8

The heavenly bodies are subject to the rule and providence of God Isa 40:26 *See also* Job 38:31–32; Ps 104:19; Jer 31:35; Mt 5:45

The biblical rejection of fatalism in human choice
Human beings are free to choose between right and wrong Dt 11:26–28 *See also* Dt 30:15–19; Eze 18:21–23

Human beings are free to call upon the name of the Lord Joel 2:32; Ac 2:21; Ro 10:11–13

Human beings are free to seek the Lord 1Ch 28:9; Isa 55:6

Human beings are free to come to the Lord Rev 22:17 *See also* Mt 11:28

See also

1115 God, purpose of	6209 pagans
1130 God, sovereignty	6622 choice
	6658 freedom
1355 providence	8160 seeking God
4005 creation	8640 calling upon God
5051 responsibility	8709 astrology

4938
fate, and final destiny

The final destiny or predetermined end of individuals, groups or nations.

Death, the fate of humanity
Ecc 7:2 *See also* Ecc 2:14–16; 3:19–22; 9:2–6; Heb 9:27

The fate of the ungodly
Isa 65:11–12 *See also* Job 8:11–19; Ps 49:13–20; 73:17; Eph 5:5–6; 2Pe 2:4–9

The fate of the godly
The fate of the godly in terms of God's rewards 2Pe 1:10–11 *See also* Mt 5:3–10; 25:34; Lk 6:20–22; 1Co 2:7; Jas 1:12; 2:5

The fate of the godly in terms of present suffering 2Ti 3:12 *See also* Jn 15:20; 1Th 3:1–4; 1Pe 4:12–14

The fate of individuals
Lk 2:34–35 *See also* 1Ki 20:37–42; 21:17–26; Lk 22:22 pp Mt 26:24 pp Mk 14:21

The fate of human regulations, institutions and earthly realms
Da 7:27 *See also* Job 12:23–25; Isa 34:1–4; Da 2:21; Mt 24:35 pp Mk 13:31 pp Lk 21:33; Col 2:20–22; Rev 18:1–3

See also

2375 kingdom of God	6203 mortality
	6696 necessity
4930 end	6708 predestination
5006 human race, destiny	9020 death
	9105 last things
5482 punishment	9130 future, the
5705 inheritance, spiritual	9210 judgment, God's

---

fulness

The totality of something, as it is brought to completion by being filled. Jesus Christ is seen as expressing the full nature and purposes of God, so that believers may rest assured that, through Christ, they know God as he really is. Believers are also being brought to fulness through the gospel, although the final fulness of joy and understanding will take place only in the future kingdom of God.

Jesus Christ, the fulness of God
Jesus Christ, the fulness of God's nature Col 2:9–10 See also Col 1:19
Jesus Christ, the fulness of God's attributes Jn 1:14 See also Jn 1:16

Christians and the church enjoy fulness through Jesus Christ
Eph 4:11–13 See also Jn 10:10; Eph 1:22–23; 3:14–19; Col 2:9–10

Believers receive fulness of joy from God
1Pe 1:8–9 See also Ps 16:11; Jn 17:13; Ac 16:29–34; Ro 15:13

The fulness of knowledge and understanding
Fulness of understanding comes through Jesus Christ Col 2:2–3 See also Ro 15:14; Col 1:9; Phm 6

Fulness of understanding is only fully realised when believers see God face to face 1Co 13:12

Believers should be constantly filled with the Holy Spirit
Eph 5:18 See also Ac 2:1–4; 4:31; 6:3–4; 13:52

Believers receive the fulness of God's love through Jesus Christ
1Jn 4:12 See also 1Jn 4:16–18

God works out his purposes in the fulness of time
Eph 1:9–10 See also Lk 21:24 Whatever the precise meaning of the phrase "the times of the Gentiles", it clearly indicates the sovereignty of God over times and events; Gal 4:1–5

Fulness indicating the completion of God's saving activity amongst both Jews and Gentiles
Ro 11:25 See also Ro 11:11–12

See also
2018 Christ, divinity	4915 completion
3242 Holy Spirit,	5026 knowledge
baptism with	7020 church, the
3251 Holy Spirit,	8283 joy
filling with	8292 love
4903 time	8355 understanding

4945

history

In Scripture, more than a record of and reflection on past events, but a process under God's control which has as its goal the eventual fulfilment of his purposes and through which he makes himself known. The goal of history is realised in Jesus Christ, through whom the age of salvation is inaugurated. Both the OT and NT

point to the importance of faith rooted in historical events.

God is active in history
God's control over historical events Da 2:21; Ac 17:26 See also Ge 45:5–8; 1Ki 12:15 pp 2Ch 10:15; Da 4:25; 7:25; Am 9:7

God's saving purposes worked out through history Eph 1:11 See also Isa 14:24–27; 37:26; 41:4; 46:10–11; Ac 1:7; 2:23

God is known through his people's history
God is known to his people Isa 46:9 See also Ex 10:2; Dt 4:32–35; Ps 77:11–15; Isa 43:10–13; 44:6–8; Mic 6:5

God is revealed to the nations Ps 126:2 See also 1Ki 8:56–60

The Israelites were called to remember their history
The past was recalled in festivals Lev 23:42–43; Dt 16:1–6

The past was recounted to successive generations Ps 78:2–7 See also Dt 32:7–9; Jdg 6:13; Ps 44:1–3

Jesus Christ as the centre of the history of salvation
He is its beginning and end Rev 22:13 See also Rev 1:8,17; 2:8

God's saving purposes in history fulfilled in Jesus Christ Eph 1:9–10 See also Ro 5:6; Gal 4:4; Col 1:17

Jesus Christ inaugurates God's new age Col 1:18 See also Da 7:13–14; Mk 1:15; Mt 12:28 pp Lk 11:20; Eph 2:7

The Christian faith is based on the historical facts of salvation
Testimony passed on by eye-witnesses Lk 1:1–4 See also Heb 2:3; 1Pe 5:1; 2Pe 1:16; 1Jn 1:1–3

Remembering Jesus Christ's death 1Co 11:23–25 pp Lk 22:19–20

Jesus Christ's resurrection as historical fact Ac 1:3 See also Lk 24:1–3,39; Jn 20:27; 1Co 15:3–8

Historical references in the NT Lk 1:1–2; Mt 2:1; Lk 3:1–2; Mt 14:3–4 pp Mk 6:17–18; Ac 5:37

Landmarks in salvation history
The creation Ge 1:1; 2:7

The fall Ge 3:6–7; Ro 5:12

The call of Abraham Ge 12:1–3; Heb 11:8

The exodus from Egypt Ex 13:3; 19:4–6

The birth of Jesus Christ Jn 1:14; Heb 1:1–2

Jesus Christ's death and resurrection 1Co 15:3–4; Php 2:6–11; Heb 1:3–4

See also
1115 God, purpose	2421 gospel,
of	historical
1130 God,	foundation
sovereignty	4963 past, the
1439 revelation	7140 people of God
2230 Messiah,	7240 Jerusalem,
coming of	history
2348 Jesus Christ,	7258 promised land,
life of	early history
2375 kingdom of	8670 remembering
God	

4948

hour

One twelfth of the period of daylight between sunrise and sunset. Measurement of time in biblical days was often approximate, referring most frequently to the broad divisions of time marked by the third, sixth and ninth hours. The term also denotes a significant or appointed moment or period of time, especially the hour of Jesus Christ's suffering and his return.

Hour as a period of time
A measured interval Jn 11:9 See also Mt 20:9–12 The working day lasted twelve hours; Lk 22:59; Ac 19:34; Rev 8:1

Symbolising a brief time Mt 6:27 pp Lk 12:25 See also Mt 26:40 pp Mk 14:37 God's judgment will come quickly: in a single hour: Rev 17:12; 18:10,17,19

Symbolising a significant period Ecc 9:12 See also Lk 22:53 Darkness provides an hour of opportunity for the powers of evil.

Hours denoting specific times of day
Mt 20:3–5 The third, sixth and ninth hours marked the principal divisions of the day.

The third hour: 9 a.m. Mk 15:25 See also Ac 2:15

The sixth hour: noon Jn 4:6 See also Ge 43:16; 1Ki 18:27; Job 5:14; Mt 27:45 pp Mk 15:33 pp Lk 23:44

The ninth hour: 3 p.m. Mt 27:46 pp Mk 15:34 See also Ac 3:1; 10:30

Midnight Ex 11:4 See also Ps 119:62; Mt 25:6; Mk 13:35; Ac 16:25

Other hours of the day Jn 4:52 the seventh hour: 1 p.m.; Jn 1:39 the tenth hour: 4 p.m.; Mt 20:6 the eleventh hour: 5 p.m.

A particular unnamed time of day Mt 8:13 See also Mt 15:28; Lk 22:14; Ac 16:33; Rev 11:13

Hour as an appointed time in God's purpose
The hour of Jesus Christ's suffering Jn 12:23–24 See also Mt 26:45 pp Mk 14:41; Mk 14:35; Jn 12:27

The unexpected hour of Jesus Christ's return Mt 24:36 pp Mk 13:32 See also Mt 24:42–44 pp Lk 12:39–40; Mt 25:13

The time before Jesus Christ's return Ro 13:11 See also 1Jn 2:18

The hour of God's judgment Rev 14:7

See also
2530 Christ, death of	8490 watchfulness
4903 time	8602 prayer
4921 day	9140 last days
4969 seasons	9210 judgment,
5046 opportunities	God's

month

A thirty-day period of the year measured from one new moon to the next. There were twelve months in the year, with a thirteenth inserted periodically to bring the lunar calendar into line with the solar year. Early month names may have been linked with the seasons. After the exile, Babylonian names were adopted.

Months marked by the new moon
Nu 28:11-14 *Special sacrifices marked the first day of each month. See also* Ps 81:3; Isa 66:23; Eze 46:6; Am 8:5 *No work was done on the first day of the month.*

Months as periods of 30 days
Dt 21:13 *The prescribed period of mourning was 30 days (a month). See also* Nu 20:29; Dt 34:8

The first month: Abib/Nisan
Ex 12:2 *Abib, meaning "young head of grain" was the Canaanite name for Israel's first month. Modern equivalent: March-April. See also* Ex 40:2; Nu 9:1

Feasts in the month of Abib Dt 16:1 *Passover celebrated on 14th Abib. See also* Ex 13:4; 23:15 *the Feast of Unleavened bread (15th-21st);* Lev 23:5-6 pp Nu 28:16-17; Lev 23:10-11 *The first sheaf of barley was brought to the priest on 16th Abib.*
Nisan was the post-exilic name for the first month: Ne 2:1; Est 3:7

The second month: Ziv
1Ki 6:1 *Ziv was the pre-exilic name; the post-exilic name, Iyyar, does not appear in the Bible. Modern equivalent: April-May. See also* 1Ki 6:37; Nu 9:11 *A late Passover might be held on 14th Ziv;* 2Ch 30:13-15 *Hezekiah's celebration of the Passover was in the second month.*

The third month: Sivan
Est 8:9 *Modern equivalent: May-June. See also* Ex 19:1; Eze 31:1

Pentecost celebrated in the month of Sivan Lev 23:15-16 *on 6th Sivan*

The fourth month: Tammuz
Eze 1:1 *Modern equivalent: June-July;* Eze 8:14 *Tammuz was a fertility goddess; her annual death was mourned in the month named after her.*

The fifth month
Nu 33:38 *The name of the fifth month, Ab, does not appear in the Bible. Modern equivalent: July-August;* 2Ki 25:8

The sixth month: Elul
Ne 6:15 *Modern equivalent: August-September. See also* Eze 8:1; Hag 1:1; Lk 1:26

The seventh month: Ethanim
1Ki 8:2 *Ethanim is the pre-exilic name; its Babylonian equivalent, Tishri, does not appear in the Bible. Modern equivalent: September-October.*

Feasts and sacred days in the month of Ethanim Lev 23:23-24 pp Nu 29:1 *The Feast of Trumpets (1st). This is celebrated today as the Jewish New Year (Rosh Hashanah);* Lev 23:27 pp Nu 29:7 *the Day of Atonement (10th);* Lev 23:34 pp Nu 29:12 *the Feast of Tabernacles (15th-21st);* Lev 23:36 *Solemn Assembly (22nd)*

The eighth month: Bul
1Ki 6:38 *Bul's post-exilic equivalent, Marcheshvan, is not mentioned in the Bible. Modern equivalent: October-November. See also* 1Ki 12:32-33 *Jeroboam offset Israel's religious calendar by one month. This is the alternative Feast of Tabernacles (15th);* Zec 1:1

The ninth month: Kislev
Zec 7:1 *Modern equivalent: November-December. See also* Ne 1:1; Hag 2:18

Hanukkah celebrated in the month of Kislev Jn 10:22 *the Feast of Dedication of the Temple (25th)*

The tenth month: Tebeth
Est 2:16 *Modern equivalent: December-January;* Jer 39:1

The eleventh month: Shebat
Dt 1:3 *Modern equivalent: January-February;* Zec 1:7

The twelfth month: Adar
Est 8:12 *Modern equivalent: February-March. See also* Est 3:13; 9:1

Purim celebrated in the month of Adar Est 9:20-22 *the Feast of Purim (14th-15th)*

See also
4251 moon	7398 New Moon
4442 firstfruits	festival
4464 harvest	7400 New Year, the
4970 seasons of year	7406 Passover
4978 year	7408 Pentecost
7308 Atonement, Day	7418 Purim
of	
7354 feasts and	
festivals	

4954

morning

The period of time roughly between dawn and noon. Morning was an assigned time for worship, sacrifice and prayer. The morning light uncovers events of the night and provides opportunity for renewed daily activity. God's blessings are received new every morning, and the start of a new day symbolises renewal and hope.

Morning as the start of a new day
The period of time created by God Ge 1:5 *See also* Ge 1:8; Ex 18:13-14 *The working day is reckoned from morning till evening;* Ex 27:21 *The night is reckoned from evening till morning;* Job 38:12

The transience of morning mist Isa 44:22; Hos 6:4; 13:3

Morning as a symbol of renewed hope Ps 30:5 *See also* Ps 130:6; Isa 21:11-12; 26:19

The Messiah brings a new morning Mal 4:2; 2Pe 1:19 *See also* Lk 1:78-79; Ro 13:12; 1Jn 2:8; Rev 2:28; 22:16

The sky in the morning Mt 16:3

Morning as an opportunity for activity
A time for travel Ge 19:2; 22:3; 31:55; Nu 9:21; 22:21; Jos 3:1; 1Sa 17:20

A time for battle Jos 8:10-14; Jdg 9:33; 2Ki 3:21-23; 2Ch 20:20

A time to begin daily labour Ru 2:7 *See also* Ecc 11:6; Mt 20:1

A time to begin important activity Ex 9:13; 34:2-4 *See also* Ex 7:15; 8:20; 1Ki 18:26; Ac 23:12; 28:23

A time to respond to nightly revelation Ge 20:8; 28:18; 41:8

A time to administer justice Jer 21:12; Zep 3:5

Morning as a time of revelation
A time of discovery Ge 29:25; 2Ki 19:35 pp Isa 37:36 *See also* Ge 19:27-28; Jdg 6:28; 1Sa 5:4; Isa 17:14; 1Ki 3:21; 2Ki 6:15; Ac 12:18; 1Co 4:5

Morning brings God's revelation Ex 16:7-8 *See also* Nu 16:5; Jos 7:14; 1Sa 9:19; Isa 50:4; Eze 12:8

Morning devotions
A time for offering sacrifices Eze 46:13-15 *See also* Ex 29:38-40; 36:3; Nu 28:3-5; 1Ch 16:40; 2Ch 2:4; 13:11; 29:20-21; Job 1:5

A time for prayer Ps 88:13 *See also* Ps 5:3; 55:17; Mk 1:35

A time to praise God Ps 92:1-3 *See also* 1Ch 23:30; Ps 59:16; 65:8

Priestly duties each morning Ex 30:7 *burning incense;* Lev 6:12 *making the burnt offering*

God's blessings are received new each morning
La 3:22-23 *See also* Ex 16:12-15 *God's provision of manna in the desert;* 1Ki 17:6 *God supplies Elijah with food;* Ps 90:14; Isa 33:2

See also
1439 revelation	4933 evening
4281 stars	4957 night
4833 light	4960 noon
4918 dawn	6698 newness
4921 day	8144 renewal

4957

night

The period of darkness between evening and morning. It is generally a time for the cessation of daily activity and for sleep, but, because darkness also gives an opportunity for evil, there is need to be watchful. The term may also be used figuratively to refer to evil or to a period of distress. Night-time also provides opportunity for contemplation and for prayer.

Night distinguished from day
Ge 1:5 *See also* Ge 1:14-18; Ps 74:16

Night as a time for rest and sleep
Rest from daily activity Jdg 19:9;
Ecc 2:23; Jn 9:4; 11:9–10

Sleep Ge 15:12; 28:11; Job 4:13

Activity day and night implies continuity and commitment
Weeping Ps 42:3; Jer 9:1; 14:17

Prayer Ne 1:6; Ps 88:1; Lk 18:7;
1Th 3:10

Meditation Jos 1:8; Ps 1:2

Worship Lk 2:37; Ac 26:7; Rev 4:8; 7:15

Work 1Ch 9:33; 1Th 2:9; 2Th 3:8

The watches of the night
In OT times: three watches La 2:19 *the
first watch: sunset to midnight;* Jdg 7:19
the second watch: midnight to 3 a.m.;
Ex 14:24 *the last watch: 3 a.m. to dawn*

In NT times: four watches Mk 13:35 *See
also* Mt 14:25 pp Mk 6:48; Lk 12:38

Night associated with evil
The period when evil is at work
Jn 13:30 *Night symbolises the darkness in
Judas' soul, and denotes, too, the time of
activity of the powers of darkness. See also*
Job 30:26; Pr 4:19; Lk 22:53

Opportunity for evil 1Co 4:5 *Evil
flourishes under cover of darkness. See also*
Pr 2:13; Jn 3:19–20; Job 24:14 *Murder;*
Pr 7:8–9 *Adultery;* 1Th 5:7 *Drunkenness;*
Jer 49:9 pp Ob 5 *Theft*

Believers do not belong to the night
1Th 5:5 *See also* Jn 12:35–36; Ro 13:12;
Eph 5:8; Col 1:13

Believers are to remain watchful
1Th 5:6 *See also* Mt 24:42–44; 25:13;
Mk 13:36–37

Night associated with distress
Gloom caused by distress
Ps 107:13–14; Isa 9:2; 59:9

Night as a time of weeping Ps 6:6; 30:5;
La 1:2

Night as an opportunity to seek God
In prayer Lk 6:12 *See also* 1Sa 15:11;
Ps 22:2; 119:62

In worship Ac 16:25 *See also* Job 35:10;
Ps 42:8; 77:6; 139:1–2; 149:5; Isa 30:29

In contemplation Ps 63:6 *See also*
Ps 119:55; Isa 26:9

Night as an opportunity to receive revelation
God's voice at night 1Sa 3:4

God's revelation through visions
2Ch 7:12; Da 2:19; 7:2; Zec 1:8; Ac 18:9;
23:11

God's revelation through dreams
Ge 20:3; 31:24; 1Ki 3:5; Job 33:15

No night in heaven
Rev 21:25; 22:5

See also

1409 dream	5056 rest
4806 cold	5533 sleep, physical
4810 darkness,	8493 watchfulness,
natural	believers
4918 dawn	8602 prayer
4921 day	8662 meditation
4933 evening	8734 evil

---

noon
The mid-point between sunrise and
sunset when the sun is at its
brightest. Noon is a time to seek
shelter from the heat of the day. The
darkening of the midday sun and the
surprise attack of the enemy at noon
are signs of God's judgment. The
brilliance of the noonday sun is
likened to the glory of Jesus Christ
and to the vindication of God's
people.

Noon as a time of severe heat
Shelter from the noonday heat
Isa 4:5–6 *See also* Isa 16:3 *Moab likens
asylum sought from Judah to shelter from
the noonday sun;* Isa 25:4

Time to rest from the sun's heat
2Sa 4:5; SS 1:7 *See also* Ge 18:1; Ru 2:7
Ruth rests from her gleaning at noon;
1Sa 11:11 *Saul's army halts its destruction
of the Ammonites at midday;* 1Ki 20:16
*Israel's enemies relax at midday, unaware
of the imminence of battle;* Mt 20:12
*Workers in the vineyard might have been
expected to rest during the hottest part of
the day;* Jn 4:6 *Jesus Christ rests from his
journey by the well of Sychar.*

Noon as a natural break in the day
1Ki 18:26–29; Ne 8:3

Noon as a time for prayer
Ps 55:16–17 *The devout Jew prayed three
times daily. See also* Da 6:10; Ac 10:9

Noon as a time of God's judgment
A time of unexpected destruction
Jer 15:8 *Armies usually attacked at dawn;
a noon raid would take the people by
surprise. See also* Jer 6:4; 20:16; Zep 2:4

**Darkness at noon is a sign of God's
judgment** Job 5:14; Am 8:9 *See also*
Dt 28:29; Isa 59:9–10

Mt 27:45 pp Mk 15:33 pp Lk 23:44–45
*The noonday sun is darkened following the
crucifixion.*

The noonday sun as a symbol of glory
The glory of Jesus Christ Rev 1:16 *See
also* Mt 17:2

The vindication of God's people
Jdg 5:31 *See also* Job 11:17; Ps 37:6;
Isa 58:10; Mt 13:43

Events that occurred at noon
*Joseph invites his brothers to eat with him
at noon:* Ge 43:16,26
Jos 10:12–13 *The sun stops in the middle
of the sky, allowing Joshua to defeat the
Amorites;* 2Ki 4:18–20 *The Shunammite
woman's son dies at noon.*
*Paul's encounter with the risen Christ
about noon:* Ac 22:6; 26:13

See also

1193 glory,	4954 morning
revelation of	5056 rest
4284 sun	5295 destruction
4829 heat	8602 prayer
4918 dawn	9210 judgment,
4921 day	God's

---

past, the
Jesus Christ transforms the past and
sets people free to live in a new way.
God's people should remember
former blessings but not return to
former sins.

Recalling God's work in the past
Remembering God's work of creation
Ex 20:11; Ps 104:5–9; 136:1–9

Remembering God's saving works
Ps 105:5 pp 1Ch 16:12 *See also* Dt 8:2;
Jos 24:2; 1Sa 12:6; Ne 9:7; Ps 106:6;
114:1; 136:10; 143:5; Isa 51:1–2;
Mic 6:5

**Remembering God's work in Jesus
Christ** 2Ti 2:8 *See also* 1Co 11:23–26
*One of the purposes of the Lord's Supper is
to remember Jesus Christ and his death on
the cross.*

Learning from the past
Ro 15:4 *See also* Dt 4:9; 32:7; Zec 1:4;
1Co 10:6,11; Heb 12:16; 1Pe 3:5–6;
1Jn 3:12

Rediscovering God's word from the past
2Ki 22:8–13 pp 2Ch 34:15–21 *See also*
2Ki 23:1–3 pp 2Ch 34:29–31;
2Ki 23:21–23

Leaving the past behind
**Jesus Christ sets believers free from
the past** 2Co 5:17 *See also* Isa 65:16;
Gal 4:3–5; Col 1:13–14

**Warnings not to rely on or be
preoccupied with the past** Isa 43:18
*This can mean either that God is not to be
restricted to his past actions or that Israel
should forget their former sins. See also*
Php 3:13–14

Dangers of the past
The danger of ignoring the past
Ps 78:11 *See also* Ex 1:8; Dt 32:18;
Ps 106:13,21; Hos 2:13

The danger of lapsing into past sins
Gal 4:8–9 *See also* Heb 6:4–6; 2Pe 1:9;
Rev 2:4–5; 3:3

Jesus Christ supersedes God's revelation in the past
**Jesus Christ supersedes earlier
expectations** Ac 17:30 *See also*
Ac 14:15–16

**Jesus Christ supersedes earlier
covenants** Heb 7:22 *See also* Heb 1:1–2;
8:13; 9:14–15; 10:15–18; Jer 31:33–34;
Heb 12:24

**Jesus Christ reveals God's past
mystery** Col 1:26–27 *See also*
Ro 16:25–26; 1Co 2:7; Eph 1:9; 3:2–6,9

See also

1020 God, all-	6227 regret
knowing	6728 regeneration
1345 covenant	7933 Lord's Supper
4945 history	8670 remembering
4966 present, the	8763 forgetting
5694 generation	9130 future, the
5854 experience of	
God	

4966

present, the

God's blessings are available now and are to be received in faith and contentment. It is dangerous to live only for current blessings and pleasures.

Blessings promised for the present
The blessing of God's presence now
Hag 1:13 *See also* Dt 31:6; 1Ki 8:57

The blessing of Jesus Christ's presence now Mt 1:23 *See also* Isa 7:14; 8:8,10; Mt 18:20; 28:20; Jn 14:18; Ac 18:10

The blessing of the Spirit's presence now Jn 14:16–17 *See also* Jn 14:25–27; 16:7,13–16

Other blessings given in the present
Mk 10:29–30 pp Mt 19:29
pp Lk 18:29–30 *See also* Ex 23:25; 1Ki 3:13 pp 2Ch 1:12; Ps 121:3–8; Mt 6:33; 1Ti 4:8; 1Pe 1:9

Future blessings are partially fulfilled in the present
Eph 1:13–14 *See also* Ro 8:23,30; 2Co 1:22; 5:5; Eph 1:3; Heb 12:22–24

Prayer for present provision and blessing
Lk 11:3 pp Mt 6:11
Prayers for physical provision: Ge 28:20; Pr 30:8

Mt 6:13 pp Lk 11:4 *prayers for spiritual provision*

The secret of contentment in the present
Php 4:10–13 *See also* 1Ti 6:6–8

The dangers of living for the present
Ecc 3:12–13 *Ecclesiastes in particular reflects upon the emptiness of life without God. Though the good things of the present life are a gift from God and to be valued as such, they cannot bring ultimate fulfilment;* Lk 12:15–20 *See also* Ecc 2:24; 5:18; 8:15; 9:7,9; Isa 22:13; 1Co 15:32; Php 3:19; 1Ti 6:9–10; Jas 4:13–17; 1Ti 6:17

The challenge of the present
The challenge to respond to God now
2Co 6:2 *See also* Dt 4:39–40; 5:1; 7:11; 10:13; 30:15–16; Ps 95:7–8; Isa 55:6; Hos 10:12; Heb 3:7

The challenge to serve God now
Eph 5:15–16 *See also* Gal 6:10; Col 4:5

See also
3035 Holy Spirit, presence of	5939 satisfaction
3296 Holy Spirit in the world	8102 abiding in Christ
4963 past, the	8489 urgency
5046 opportunities	8610 prayer, asking God
5204 age	9130 future, the
5846 enjoyment	

4969

seasons

The main periods of the year which each have their own distinctive

weather. In life, the varied periods of human experience.

4970

seasons, of the year

Distinctive periods of the year marked by certain climatic conditions. Seasons are examples of God's perfect order in the world. They represent the balanced cycle of creation which is sustained by God and through which his provision and mercy are made known.

Seasons are appointed by God
Seasons are created by God
Ps 74:16–17 *See also* Ge 1:14; 8:22; Ps 104:19

Seasons are sustained by God Jer 5:24
See also Job 38:32–33; Eze 34:26; Ac 14:17

The agricultural seasons of Palestine
The dry and rainy seasons Joel 2:23
The rainy season, accounting for over 90 per cent of the national rainfall, runs from October to March/April. Its beginning is marked by the autumn rains in October/ November; the lighter spring showers in April/May announce the coming of the dry season. See also Ezr 10:13; Hos 6:3; Jas 5:7
Israel's continued enjoyment of seasonal blessings was conditional upon her obedience: Lev 26:3–4; Dt 11:13–14; 28:12

Seedtime and harvest Pr 20:4 *Ploughing and sowing take place from October to December when the autumn rains have begun to soften the ground. Most crops are harvested between April and June. See also* Ex 34:21; Nu 13:20; Job 5:26; Ps 1:3

Spring
Spring rain as a sign of blessing
Job 29:23 *The gentle spring rains signal the approach of harvest;* Pr 16:15; Jer 3:3; Zec 10:1

Spring as a time of growth SS 2:11–13
Spring marks a pleasant interval between the heavy winter rains and the onset of the dry season. See also Pr 27:25; Joel 2:22; Mt 24:32 pp Mk 13:28 pp Lk 21:29–30

Spring as a time for war 2Sa 11:1
pp 1Ch 20:1 *The time following the spring harvest (May/June), when agricultural commitments are reduced;* 1Ki 20:26; 2Ki 13:20

Festivals celebrated in spring
Lev 23:5–6 pp Nu 28:16–17 *Passover and Unleavened Bread;* Lev 23:10 *offering the firstfruits of the barley harvest;* Lev 23:15–16 pp Dt 16:9–10 *The Feast of Weeks celebrated the ingathering of the grain harvest.*

Summer
A period of intense heat Ps 32:4 *See also* Job 6:17

A time for harvesting summer fruit
Jer 8:20 *See also* Pr 10:5; Jer 40:10–12 *Grapes, olives and figs are harvested in July/September;* Mic 7:1

A time to store harvested grain Pr 6:8; 30:25

Autumn
The breaking of the summer drought
Ps 84:6 *Autumn is the start of the rainy season and corresponds to the time of ploughing and sowing.*

Festivals celebrated in autumn
Lev 23:24 pp Nu 29:1 *the Feast of Trumpets;* Lev 23:27 pp Nu 29:7 *the Day of Atonement;* Lev 23:34 pp Nu 29:12 *the Feast of Tabernacles*

Winter
A time of inclement weather
Job 37:6–10 *See also* Isa 55:10; Jer 36:22

A time when travelling is difficult
Mt 24:20 pp Mk 13:18; 2Ti 4:21; Ac 27:12; 1Co 16:6; Tit 3:12

Celebration of the Feast of Dedication
Jn 10:22 *The Feast of Dedication (Hannukah) commemorates the rededication of the temple by Judas Maccabeus in 165 B.C.*

See also
1035 God, faithfulness	4844 rain
1325 God, the Creator	4849 snow
	4951 month
4406 agriculture	4975 week
4464 harvest	5607 warfare, examples
4806 cold	
4829 heat	7354 feasts and festivals

4971

seasons, of life

Appropriate or appointed periods of time which are part of the variety and development of human life and experience and which influence human affairs. The times and seasons for individuals and nations are set by God, who works all things together towards the final fulfilment of his purposes.

The seasons of life are appointed by God
The seasons of individual lives
Ecc 3:1–8; Ps 31:15 *See also* Job 14:5; Ps 139:16; Ecc 3:11; Ro 8:28; Jas 4:13–15

The seasons of nations and the world
Da 2:21; Ac 17:26 *See also* Da 4:17; 7:25; Ac 1:7

A time to die
The transience of human life
Ps 103:15–16 *See also* Job 7:6–8; 14:1–2; Ps 37:2; 102:11; Ecc 6:12

Death comes at its appointed time
Job 5:26 *See also* Ge 47:29; 1Ki 2:1; Lk 12:20

Times of sadness and joy
A time to mourn Jer 27:41; 37:34; 50:3–4; Dt 34:8; Jer 4:28

A time to rejoice Jn 16:21–22 *See also* Dt 28:47; Est 9:22; Isa 61:2–3

A time to speak
Pr 15:23; 25:11; 2Ti 4:2 *Christians are to be always ready to share the gospel.*

Times appointed for the world

The rise and fall of nations Da 2:37–45; 8:19–25; 11:2–4,24–27; Lk 21:24

The time to receive God's salvation 2Co 6:2 See also Isa 49:8; 55:6; Heb 4:7

The time of God's judgment Dt 32:35; Eze 30:3; Zep 2:2; Ac 17:31

Times appointed for God's people

Times for worship Lev 23:4 See also Ex 34:18; Nu 9:2–3; 10:10

Times of blessing Ps 102:13 See also Eze 34:26; Ac 3:19; 7:17

A time of vindication Da 7:21–22 See also Ac 1:6; Ro 8:18; 1Pe 5:6

Times of testing Ps 66:10; Eze 21:3; Mt 13:21 pp Mk 4:17 pp Lk 8:13; 1Pe 1:6–7; Rev 2:10

Times for withdrawal or solitude Mk 1:35 See also 1Ki 17:2–6; Mk 6:30–32; Gal 1:17

Waiting for God's appointed time Hab 2:3 See also Ro 8:23–25; Heb 9:28; 11:13

Times appointed for Jesus Christ

The appointed time of his birth Gal 4:4

The appointed time of his death Jn 12:23 See also Mt 26:18; Mk 14:41; Lk 9:51; Jn 2:4; 7:6–8; 12:27; 13:1

The appointed time of his return Lk 21:8; Ac 3:20–21; 17:31; 1Co 4:5; Rev 1:3

See also
1115 God, purpose of	8124 guidance
1130 God, sovereignty	8678 waiting on God
4016 life, human	9021 death, natural
4817 drought, spiritual	9140 last days
4903 time	9210 judgment, God's
	9220 day of the LORD

week

The pattern of weeks provides a useful framework for marking time in agricultural and religious life. The story of creation is described in terms of seven days and illustrates a cycle of work and rest. Feasts and other rituals last for a certain number of weeks.

The seven days of creation
Ge 2:1–3 See also Ge 1:5,8,13,19,23,31

The Sabbath-rest
Dt 5:12–14 pp Ex 20:8–11 See also Ex 34:21; 35:2; Heb 4:3–4,8–10

Seven-day intervals or periods
After building the ark Noah had seven days' notice of the flood Ge 7:4

Noah sent out the dove at seven-day intervals Ge 8:8–12

Marching round Jericho Heb 11:30 See also Jos 6:12–15

Other examples of seven-day intervals or periods Ex 7:25; 29:30; 1Sa 10:8; 11:3; 13:8; 1Ki 20:29; 1Ch 9:25; Ac 20:6; 21:4; 28:14

Rituals lasting seven days

Menstrual impurity Lev 15:19

Initial period of uncleanness after childbirth Lev 12:1–2 This would be fourteen days if the child were a girl (Lev 12:5).

Mourning Ge 50:10 See also 1Sa 31:13 pp 1Ch 10:12; Job 2:13; Eze 3:15

The Feast of Weeks
Dt 16:9–10 See also Ex 34:22; Lev 23:15–21; Nu 28:26–31

Feasts lasting seven days

Wedding feasts Ge 29:27 See also Jdg 14:10–12

The Feast of Unleavened Bread Ex 34:18 See also Lev 23:5–8; 2Ch 30:21–23; 35:17; Ezr 6:22

The Feast of Tabernacles Lev 23:34 See also Lev 23:36; Ne 8:18

Dedication of the temple 1Ki 8:65 pp 2Ch 7:8–9

Daniel's "weeks"
Da 9:24 "sevens" may also be translated "weeks". See also Da 9:25–27

God promises that times and seasons will always continue
Jer 5:24 See also Ge 8:22

See also
1653 numbers, 6–10	7354 feasts and festivals
4005 creation	
4903 time	7361 Feast of Weeks
4921 day	7408 Pentecost
4970 seasons of year	7428 Sabbath
5056 rest	

year

A period of twelve months, with additional periods inserted to bring the lunar year into line with the solar year. Certain calendar years have special significance. The term also denotes an indeterminate time when God will intervene to restore his people and punish his enemies.

The year made up of 12 months
1Ki 4:7 See also 1Ch 27:1–15; Est 2:12; Da 4:29; Rev 22:2

The start of the year

The start of the religious year Ex 12:2 The exodus from Egypt in Abib (March–April) marked a new beginning in the life of God's people. See also Lev 23:5 pp Nu 28:16 Abib is referred to as the first month; 2Ch 35:1; Ezr 6:19

The start of the agricultural year Ex 23:16 The Feast of Ingathering (or Tabernacles) was celebrated in the seventh month. See also Ex 34:22; Lev 23:23–24 pp Nu 29:1

God's blessing through the year
Ps 65:9–13 See also Dt 11:11–15; 28:12

A thousand years as one day
Ps 90:4; 2Pe 3:8

Special years
The sabbatical year Lev 25:1–7 See also Ex 23:10–11; Lev 25:20–22 God's

provision for the seventh year Dt 15:1 See also Dt 15:9; Ne 10:31; Dt 31:10–13 the law of God to be read every seventh year at the Feast of Tabernacles

The Year of Jubilee Lev 25:8–10 The Year of Jubilee began in the seventh month. See also Lev 25:11–12 The Year of Jubilee is a sabbath year; Lev 25:13 Each Hebrew is to return to his family property; Lev 25:28 Land is returned to its original owner; Lev 25:40 Hebrew slaves are to be released; Lev 25:54

Hebrew slaves released in the seventh year Ex 21:2 pp Dt 15:12 See also Jer 34:14

The year of the LORD's favour
Isa 61:1–3 This has echoes of the Year of Jubilee and points to the time when God will restore his people. See also Lk 4:18–21; Isa 49:8–9; 2Co 6:2 Isa 63:4 Salvation for God's people is accompanied by judgment on his enemies.

The year of punishment
Jer 11:23; 23:12; 48:44

See also
4406 agriculture	7447 slavery, in OT
4951 month	7482 Year of Jubilee
4970 seasons of year	9155 millennium
5204 age	9165 restoration
5725 old age	9210 judgment, God's
7400 New Year, the	
7431 sabbatical year	

5000

Humanity

human race, the

Human beings are the high point of God's creation. They alone are created in his image. As a result of sin they are alienated from God and from one another, and are unable by themselves to alter this situation. The salvation of humanity rests totally upon the atoning sacrifice of Jesus Christ, received by grace through faith.

This set of themes consists of the following:
5002 human race, and creation
5003 human race, and God
5004 human race, and sin
5005 human race, and redemption
5006 human race, destiny of

5002

human race, and creation

Although the human race is the pinnacle of God's creative work, it shares the inherent limitations of the physical realm. Human beings are nevertheless given responsibility to manage and steward the world.

The human race is an integral part of the physical creation

The human race was created from the ground Ge 2:7 *The Hebrew word for man, "adam" sounds like the Hebrew word for ground "adamah". See also* Ge 3:17–19; Job 10:8–9; Ps 103:13–14

The human race was created on the same day as the animals Ge 1:24–27

The human race was created from dust like the animals Ge 2:7,19

The human race is set apart from the rest of creation

The human race is uniquely created in God's image Ge 5:1–2 *See also* Ge 1:26–27; 9:6; Jas 3:9

The human race is given authority to take care of creation Ge 1:26–28 *See also* Ge 2:15; 9:1–3; Ps 8:3–8; Heb 2:5–8

The human race is created with the power of choice Ge 2:16–17 *See also* Ge 2:19

Human beings are created accountable to God for their actions Mt 12:36 *See also* Eze 18:20; Jn 3:18–19; Ro 2:14–15; Rev 2:23

The human race is created dependent upon God Mt 4:4; 2Co 3:5 *See also* 2Ch 20:12; Jer 10:23; Jas 4:13–15

The human race comprises two complementary genders

Ge 2:18–24 *See also* Ge 1:26–27; 5:1–2

The human race is one entity with a common ancestry in Adam

Ac 17:26 *See also* Ge 9:18–19; 10:32–11:1

See also

1325 God, the Creator	5093 Eve
4005 creation	5664 children
4029 world, human beings in	5700 headship
5023 image of God	5707 male and female
5082 Adam, significance	5708 marriage
	5714 men
	5745 women

5003
human race, and God

Though vastly superior to the human race, God nevertheless loves, sustains and governs it, sending his Son as a human being to redeem humanity.

God is incomparably superior to the human race

Isa 40:15–22 *See also* Job 25:1–6; 38:1–7; Ps 8:3–4; Isa 31:1–3; Ac 17:24–25; 1Co 1:20–25

The human race is dependent upon God

Job 34:14–15 *See also* Job 12:10; Ps 36:5–6; Ac 17:24–28

The human race is valued and loved by God

The human race is the object of God's care and compassion Ps 103:13 *See also* Ps 10:17–18; La 3:31–33; Mt 6:25–33 pp Lk 12:22–31

God wants to bless the human race Ge 12:1–3; Ro 10:12

God wants to save the human race Jn 3:16–17 *See also* 1Ti 2:1–4; 2Pe 3:8–9

God highly values the human race and human life Ge 9:6 *See also* Ex 20:13; Mt 16:26 pp Mk 8:36–37 pp Lk 9:25; 1Pe 1:18–19

God is sovereign and watches over the human race

Ps 33:10–15 *See also* Ps 9:7–8; Pr 5:21; Da 5:18–21

God will judge and punish the wickedness of the human race

Isa 2:12–17 *See also* Mt 13:40–43; Ac 17:29–31; Ro 2:5–11

God is to be feared and worshipped by the entire human race

Ps 33:8; Ro 1:20–25 *See also* 1Ch 16:28–31; Ps 96:7–10

See also

1055 God, grace & mercy	5027 knowledge, God's of humanity
1085 God, love of	
1320 God as Saviour	5061 sanctity of life
1330 God, the provider	6510 salvation
	6614 atonement
2033 Christ, humanity	6720 redemption
2410 cross, the	8471 respect for human beings

5004
human race, and sin

As a result of the fall, human beings have become separated from God through sin, and are divided amongst themselves. All are in a condition of spiritual blindness, slavery and death, and are incapable of saving themselves from this situation.

All the human race is sinful

Ro 3:9–12 *See also* Ps 14:1–3; 53:1–3; Ge 6:5–13; Job 15:14–16; Ecc 7:20; Ro 1:18–32; Rev 18:1–5 *Babylon symbolises human society which in its opposition to God has become thoroughly corrupt.*

The human race is estranged from God

Isa 59:1–2 *See also* Ge 3:8–10,22–24; Ps 5:4–5; Eph 2:12; 4:17–18; Col 1:21

The human race is spiritually callous, blind, enslaved and dead

Eph 2:1–3; 4:17–19 *See also* Ro 1:21; 5:12–14; 6:16–20; 2Co 4:4; 1Jn 5:19

The human race is divided

The human race is divided individual against individual Ge 4:3–9; Ro 1:28–29

The human race is divided man against woman Ge 3:8–12,16; Pr 21:9

The human race is divided nation against nation Ge 11:1–9; Mt 24:6–7

The human race is divided Jew against Gentile Ac 10:27–28; Eph 2:11–12

The human race is divided rich against poor Am 8:4–6; Jas 2:1–7

The human race has been weakened by sin

The human race has become subject to death Ge 2:16–17; Ro 6:23 *See also* Ro 5:12; 1Co 15:21; Jas 1:15

Human beings have become weak and frail Isa 40:6–7 *See also* Job 14:1–12; Ps 90:3–6; 103:13–16; Ecc 12:1–7; 1Pe 1:24–25

See also

4809 darkness	6173 guilt, and God
5347 injustice	6203 mortality
5450 poverty, spiritual	6222 rebellion against God
5541 society, negative	7449 slavery, spiritual
6023 sin, universality	8341 separation
6156 fall of humanity	8357 weakness

5005
human race, and redemption

Through Jesus Christ's death on the cross and his redemption, human beings are offered a salvation that will give them spiritual life and freedom, reconcile them to God, and unite them to one another as part of a new humanity.

Salvation is offered to the human race through Jesus Christ

Jn 3:14–17 *See also* Mt 28:18–20; Lk 24:45–47; Ac 2:38–39; 10:34–35,44–48; 1Ti 2:1–7; Tit 2:11–14; Rev 14:6–7

The Saviour was himself a human being

Gal 4:4; 1Ti 2:5–6 *See also* Mt 1:1; Ro 1:3–4; 8:3; Php 2:8; Heb 2:17

The human race is reconciled to God through Jesus Christ's death on the cross

2Co 5:18–21 *See also* Ro 5:1–2; Eph 2:14–18; Col 1:19–22; Heb 2:17; 10:19–22

The human race is united in Jesus Christ

Gal 3:26–28 *See also* Jn 10:14–16; 1Co 12:12–13; Eph 2:13–22; Col 3:9–11; Rev 5:9–14

The human race is renewed in Jesus Christ

Eph 2:15 *See also* 1Co 15:47–49; 2Co 5:17

In Jesus Christ the human race is given spiritual life and freedom

Eph 2:4–5 *See also* Ro 5:17–18; 8:1–2,9–11; 2Co 3:13–17

See also

2033 Christ, humanity	6614 atonement
2221 Christ, Son of Man	6676 justification
	6712 propitiation
2410 cross, the	6716 reconciliation
2530 Christ, death of	6720 redemption
6510 salvation	7020 church, the
	7140 people of God

5006
human race, destiny of

All human beings must face judgment, when God will reward them according to their attitude towards him.

The human race will face final judgment
Mt 16:27; 1Co 4:5 *See also* Da 12:1–2; Mal 3:16–18; Mt 13:40–43; Jn 5:24–29; Ro 2:5–11

Unbelievers will be separated from God
2Th 1:8–10 *See also* Mt 25:31–46; Mk 9:42–48; Lk 13:22–28; 2Pe 3:7; Rev 20:11–15

Those who have faith will live in God's presence
Rev 21:1–3; Jn 14:1–3 *See also* Zec 2:10–13; Rev 7:13–17; 22:3–4

United in the praise of God Rev 7:9–10
See also Isa 2:2–4 pp Mic 4:1–3; Mt 8:11 pp Lk 13:29; Rev 5:9–10; 21:22–27

Delivered from suffering, pain and death Rev 21:3–4 *See also* Isa 25:6–8; 65:17–25; Rev 7:16–17; 22:1–3

Sharing in the glory of Jesus Christ
Col 3:4; 1Pe 5:4 *See also* 2Ti 4:8

See also

1310 God as judge	9020 death
2315 Christ as Lamb	9105 last things
2330 Christ as shepherd	9120 eternity
5482 punishment	9210 judgment, God's
5498 reward	9410 heaven
6644 eternal life	9510 hell

5008
conscience

An innate ability to discern the difference between right and wrong, which Scripture describes as having its origin in God himself.

5009
conscience, nature of

The faculty, given to every individual, that is capable of producing guilt, or reassurance in the case of innocence. Though never wholly reliable, the conscience is cleansed when the individual turns to God for forgiveness. It is possible for the conscience to become deadened through lack of use.

The natural conscience
Ro 2:14–15 *Human beings have a built-in ability to know what is right and wrong.*

Guilty consciences
Ge 42:21 *See also* Ex 9:27; 1Sa 24:5; 2Sa 24:10; Ezr 9:6; Ps 40:12; Jn 8:7–11

Clear consciences
Before God Ac 24:16 *See also* Job 27:6; Ac 23:1; Ro 9:1; 2Ti 1:3

Before others 2Co 1:12 *See also* Ge 20:5–6; 2Co 4:2; 1Th 2:10; 1Ti 1:5; 3:9; Heb 13:18; 1Pe 3:16; 1Co 4:4 *Conscience is not an infallible guide and a clear conscience does not necessarily imply innocence before God.*

Consciences cleansed by the death of Jesus Christ
Heb 9:14 *See also* Ps 51:10; Heb 9:9; 10:2,22; 1Pe 3:21

Bad or corrupted consciences
Tit 1:15–16 *See also* Ge 6:5; Ex 7:14; 8:15; Jer 6:15; 17:9; Ac 5:2; Ro 2:5; Eph 4:19; 1Ti 1:19; 4:2

See also

2530 Christ, death of	6130 corruption
5031 knowledge of sin	6178 hardness of heart
5191 thought	6652 forgiveness
5769 behaviour	8226 discernment
6020 sin	8275 honesty

5010
conscience, matters of

Scripture gives guidance on matters of conscience, particularly in cases where believers may reach different conclusions on certain matters of moral or spiritual choice.

Having a right attitude to Christians with different opinions
Consciences may differ Ro 14:2

Different conscientious decisions must not be condemned Ro 14:1 *The gospel dispenses believers from all prohibitions concerning food. Those who are strong in faith realise this, and joyfully accept this liberty. Yet others are hindered from accepting this, on account of scruples about food inherited from their past life. Paul asks those with a clearer grasp of the gospel to respect anyone whose "faith is weak", so that, in their own time, they may come to share the fulness of the liberty of the children of God. See also* Ro 14:10,13; 1Co 10:29–30

God accepts and supports people who reach different conscientious decisions Ro 14:3–4

God alone must judge whether decisions of the conscience are right or wrong Ro 14:12–13 *See also* Col 2:16

Decision-making
Decisions should honour Jesus Christ Ro 14:6 *See also* Ro 14:7–9,22; 1Co 10:31; Col 2:20–23

Decisions should arise from convictions Ro 14:5 *See also* Ro 14:23

Decisions should be based on good doctrine 1Co 10:25–26

Consideration of others
Regard for another's position 1Co 10:23–24 *See also* Ro 14:14

Restraint of freedom for the sake of another 1Co 8:9 *"The weak" are Christians who have yet to grasp the full implications of the gospel. At this stage, they are likely to be scandalised by the full public exercise of Christian freedom on the part of those who are more mature in their faith. Paul's advice is to respect the sensitivities of the weak, and wait for these fellow believers to become spiritually mature. Paul is not suggesting that Christians should cease to exercise the liberty of faith. Rather, he is asking for pastoral sensitivity. See also* Ro 14:15,19–21; 15:1–3; 1Co 8:10–13; 10:27–29

Appeals to conscience
1Ki 12:1–15; Ac 10:9–16; 15:6–11 *Peter argues against circumcision for Gentile believers*; 1Co 8:4–8; Phm 8–21; Gal 2:11–16 *Consciences are not infallible.*

See also

5051 responsibility	8020 faith
5802 care	8292 love
5881 immaturity	8408 decision-making
5902 maturity	
6658 freedom	8469 respect

5012
heart

A vital bodily organ. The term is used in Scripture of the inner life of God or a person. The entire inner person, though fallen, may be changed by the Holy Spirit, in which case it should show evidence of renewal. This set of themes consists of the following:

5013 heart, divine
5014 heart, human
5015 heart, and Holy Spirit
5016 heart, fallen and redeemed
5017 heart, results of renewal in

5013
heart, divine

The inner thoughts, feelings, will and desires of God, as they are revealed in Scripture and in Jesus Christ.

Aspects of the heart of God
His joy Zep 3:17 *See also* Dt 30:9; Ps 147:11; 149:4; Isa 42:1; Jer 9:24; Lk 3:22

His compassion Hos 11:8 *See also* Ge 8:21; Ex 33:19; 34:6–7; Ps 78:38–39; 103:8–11; 106:44–45; Isa 54:10; Mt 5:44–45; Jn 3:16; Ro 9:15; 2Co 1:3; Jas 5:11

His affection Dt 7:7–8 *See also* 1Ki 9:3 pp 2Ch 7:16; Ps 148:14; Isa 40:11; Jer 31:3; 32:41

His intentions Ps 33:11 *See also* 1Sa 2:35; Job 10:13; Isa 63:4; Jer 23:20; 29:11; 30:24; Ac 13:22

His inner pain Ge 6:6 *See also* Isa 63:9–10; Hos 11:8; Eph 4:30

The heart of Jesus Christ
His joy Jn 15:11 *See also* Lk 10:21; Jn 17:13

His compassion Mt 9:36 *See also* Mt 14:14; 15:32; 20:34; 23:37; Lk 7:13; 19:41; Jn 11:35–36

His affection Jn 13:1 *See also*
Mt 11:28–29; Mk 10:21; Jn 21:20;
Php 1:8

His inner pain Mk 3:5 *See also* Lk 22:44;
Jn 11:35–36,38; 12:27

God's people are to reflect God's heart
Col 3:10 *See also* 1Sa 13:14; Ac 13:22;
Jer 3:15; Lk 6:27–36; Ro 8:29;
1Co 15:49; 2Co 3:18; Eph 4:24;
1Jn 3:2,17

See also

1025 God, anger of	2027 Christ, grace &
1030 God,	mercy
compassion	2039 Christ, joy of
1055 God, grace &	2048 Christ, love of
mercy	5023 image of God
1085 God, love of	8265 godliness
1210 God, human	8440 glorifying God
descriptions	
2015 Christ,	
compassion	

5014
heart, human

A vital bodily organ. The word also
refers to anything that is central or
essential, such as the inner life of a
person.

The heart as a vital bodily organ
2Ki 9:24 *See also* Ex 28:29–30;
2Sa 18:14; Hab 3:16

The heart as a central position
Ps 46:2 *See also* Ex 15:8; Dt 11:3;
Eze 27:26; Jnh 2:3

The heart as the inner person
The intellect Lk 2:19 *See also* Ge 6:5;
1Ki 2:44
Solomon's wise and discerning heart:
1Ki 3:9,12; 10:24
Job 22:22; Pr 14:30,33
The making of plans: Pr 16:1,9; 19:21;
20:5; 24:2

The desires Mt 6:21
The love of women: Ge 34:3,8; Dt 17:17;
Job 31:9; Mt 5:28
Nu 15:39
The love of God: 1Ch 29:18; Job 19:27;
Jn 5:42
Job 17:11; Ps 62:10 *the love of riches;*
Lk 12:29

The emotions
Fear and anxiety: Ge 42:28; Dt 1:28;
28:65; Jos 2:11; 1Sa 4:13; 17:32; 25:37;
Ps 18:45; Pr 12:25; Isa 13:7; 19:3; 21:4
Terror: Lev 26:36; Dt 28:67; Jos 7:5;
1Sa 28:5
Despair: Dt 28:65; Ecc 2:20
Sadness and anguish: Ne 2:2; Ps 22:14;
55:4; Pr 15:13
Cheerfulness, joy and pleasure: Ps 104:15;
Pr 15:13,15; 17:22; 27:9,11; Ecc 2:8,10;
5:20; SS 3:11; Ac 14:17
Courage and hope: Pr 13:12; Mt 9:2,22;
Jn 14:1; 16:33

The will 2Ch 29:31 *See also* Ex 25:2;
Dt 29:18; 1Sa 10:26; 2Ch 36:22
pp Ezr 1:1; Ezr 7:27; Ne 4:6; Ps 84:5

Affection 2Sa 14:1 *See also* Ex 4:14;
1Sa 14:7; SS 3:1–4; 4:9; 5:4

See also

5024 inner being	5874 happiness
5038 mind, the	5908 motives
human	6184 imagination
5062 spirit	8361 wisdom
5832 desire	8754 fear
5844 emotions	9610 hope
5847 enthusiasm	

5015
heart, and Holy Spirit

The Holy Spirit comes to dwell
within believers, renewing them and
directing their hearts towards a
greater love for God.

The renewal of the heart by the Holy Spirit
Ps 51:10; Eze 36:26 *See also*
Ps 51:12–17; Isa 57:15; Jer 24:7;
Eze 18:31

The heart as the residence of the Holy Spirit
Ro 8:9 *See also* Jn 7:37–39; Ro 5:5;
2Co 1:22; Gal 4:6; Eph 3:16–17;
Col 1:27

The heart bears the fruit of the Spirit
Gal 5:22–23

Love for God Mk 12:30 pp Mt 22:37
pp Lk 10:27 *See also* Ex 25:2; Dt 6:5;
11:13; 30:6; 1Ki 15:14

Faithfulness to God Ps 44:18 *See also*
1Ki 2:4; 1Ch 29:18; Ne 9:8; Ac 11:23

Other results of the Holy Spirit's indwelling of the heart
Heartfelt worship of God Col 3:16 *See
also* 1Sa 2:1; 2Ch 11:16; 29:31;
Job 11:13; Ps 9:1; 33:21; 86:12; 138:1;
Ro 15:6; Eph 5:18–19; Php 3:3

Heartfelt prayer to God Ps 119:145 *See
also* Ge 24:45; 1Sa 1:13; 1Ch 22:19;
Ps 21:2; 27:8; 63:1; 84:2; Ro 8:26–27

Wholehearted obedience to God
Ps 119:34 *See also* Dt 26:16; 30:14–17;
32:46; 1Ki 14:8; 2Ki 23:3,25; Ne 2:12;
Ps 40:8; 119:2,69,112; Ro 6:17

Wholehearted trust in God Pr 3:5–6 *See
also* Ps 62:8; Mk 11:23; Lk 24:25;
Heb 10:22

Wholehearted service for God Ro 1:9
See also Dt 10:12; Jos 22:5; 1Sa 12:20,24

See also

3233 Holy Spirit &	7966 spiritual gifts
sanctification	8251 faithfulness to
3254 Holy Spirit, fruit	God
of	8297 love for God
3278 Holy Spirit,	8453 obedience
indwelling	8602 prayer
4018 life, spiritual	8632 adoration
6658 freedom	
7336 circumcision,	
spiritual	

5016
heart, fallen and redeemed

The inner thoughts and feelings of
an unregenerate person are opposed
to God, making that person reject
God and his love. At conversion the
renewing work of the Holy Spirit

transforms the human heart,
enabling it to love and obey God.

The unregenerate heart
Hostile to God Ps 14:1 pp Ps 53:1 *See
also* 1Ki 15:3; 2Ch 12:14; Pr 19:3;
Jn 5:42; Ac 8:21–22; Ro 1:31; 8:7;
Heb 3:12

Hardened against God Jer 18:12
Pharaoh's hard heart: Ex 4:21;
7:3,14,22–23; 8:15,32; 14:8
Dt 2:30; Isa 6:10; 42:25; Jer 16:12;
Da 5:20; Mt 13:15; Ac 28:27; Ro 2:5;
Rev 16:9,11

Spiritually ignorant Eph 4:18 *See also*
2Sa 6:16 pp 1Ch 15:29; Ro 1:21;
2Co 3:15; 4:4

Proud Ps 73:7 *See also* Pr 18:12; 21:4;
Jer 48:29; 49:16; Eze 28:2,17; Ob 3;
Rev 18:7

Deceitful Jer 17:9 *See also* Job 31:33–34;
Ps 5:9; 28:3; 62:4; Pr 6:14; 23:7; 24:12;
26:23–25; Isa 44:20; Jer 22:17; 2Ti 3:13

Sinful Ge 6:5 *See also* Job 36:13; Ps 10:3;
41:6; 55:21; Pr 6:18; 20:9; Isa 1:5; Mt 9:4
pp Mk 2:8 pp Lk 5:22; Mt 15:18–19
pp Mk 7:20–23

Condemned Pr 11:20 *See also*
Ps 101:4–5; Pr 16:5; 17:20; Ecc 11:9;
Isa 10:12; Jer 17:10; Eze 25:6–7; Ro 1:24

Conversion: the changed heart
Convinced of need Jn 16:8 *See also*
Jer 29:12–14; Ac 2:37; 16:30; Ro 7:7;
1Co 14:25

Changed by the Holy Spirit
Eze 36:25–27 *See also* Jer 4:14; 24:7;
Eze 11:19; 18:31; Jn 3:5–6; Ro 2:29;
Tit 3:4–5

Given faith 2Co 4:6 *See also* Ac 5:31–32;
15:9; 16:14–15; Ro 10:8–10; Eph 2:8

Spurious conversion
A less-than-saving change 1Sa 10:9 *See
also* Mt 13:5–6 pp Mk 4:5–6 pp Lk 8:6;
Mt 13:20–21 pp Mk 4:16–17
pp Lk 8:13; Heb 6:4–8; 10:26–29

See also

3230 Holy Spirit &	6178 hardness of
regeneration	heart
3248 Holy Spirit,	6185 imagination,
conviction	desires
3284 Holy Spirit,	6626 conversion
resisting	8020 faith
5799 bitterness	8777 lust
6026 sin, judgment	8802 pride
on	8834 unbelief

5017
heart, results of renewal in

An individual, if renewed and led by
the Holy Spirit, will be aware of new
spiritual experiences and desires, and
also of the Holy Spirit's work of
restoring character. These things
provide evidence of the grace of God
at work in the life of a believer.

Inward experiences of the renewed heart
Assurance 1Jn 3:19–21 *See also*
Ps 112:7–8; Ro 8:14–16; Eph 1:18–19;
1Jn 5:10

Love for God's word Ro 7:22 *See also* Dt 4:9; Ps 37:31; 119:11,30,111; Pr 6:21; Jer 15:16; 31:33

Desire for holiness Mt 5:8 *See also* 2Ch 17:6; Ps 19:14; 24:3–4; 73:1; Pr 7:25; Ecc 10:2; Col 3:1–2; 2Ti 2:22; 1Pe 3:15
Circumcision as a symbol of being set apart for God: Dt 10:16; Jer 4:4

Desire to seek God 1Ki 8:38–39 *See also* Ps 119:10,58,145

Encouragement Ps 27:14 *See also* 2Ch 16:9; Ps 73:26; Jer 51:46
The peace of Jesus Christ as a source of encouragement: Jn 14:1,27; Col 3:15 2Co 4:1,14; Php 4:7; Col 2:2; 4:8; Phm 20; Heb 12:3,5; 13:9

Joy Ps 105:3 pp 1Ch 16:10 *See also* 1Ki 8:66 pp 2Ch 7:10; Ps 4:7; 16:9; Isa 65:14; Zep 3:14; Lk 24:32; Ac 2:46–47

Desire for the salvation of others Ro 9:1–3 *See also* Ro 10:1

Various kinds of distress Ps 143:4 *See also* Ps 38:8; 69:20; Jer 4:19; 8:18–19; 23:9; La 1:20; 2:11
Concern for others: Ac 21:13; 2Co 2:4; Php 3:18

Love for the church 1Pe 1:22 *See also* Zec 7:10; Jn 13:14–15; Ac 4:32; 2Co 6:11–13; 7:2–3; Php 1:7–9; 1Ti 1:5; 1Jn 3:11–18

The renewed heart and the restoration of character
Sincerity and integrity towards God and other people Ps 86:11 *See also* 1Ki 3:6; 9:4; Job 33:3; Ps 15:2; 78:72; Mt 18:35; 2Co 5:12; Eph 6:5–6; Col 3:22–23; Jas 4:8

Humility Ps 131:1 *See also* Dt 8:14; 2Ki 22:19; 2Ch 32:25–26; Mt 5:3; Php 2:3–5

Wisdom Pr 2:10 *See also* Job 38:36; Ps 90:12; Pr 2:2; 3:1,3; 23:15

The possibility of the renewed heart becoming faithless
The importance of self-examination before God Ps 139:23–24 *See also* Dt 8:2; 13:3; Jdg 5:15–16; 1Sa 16:7; 1Ch 28:9; 2Ch 32:31; Ps 7:9; 26:2; Pr 17:3; Jer 20:12; Ac 1:24

Backsliding Hos 5:4 *See also* 1Ki 11:4,9; Ps 78:8,37; Isa 29:13; 57:11; Jer 12:2; Hos 10:2; Mal 2:2; Ac 5:3

Restoration after backsliding Joel 2:12–13 *See also* Dt 4:29; 30:2–3; Jos 24:23; 1Ki 8:46–51; Ps 51:10; Isa 57:15; Jer 3:17

See also

4018 life, spiritual	8160 seeking God
7925 fellowship among believers	8266 holiness
	8276 humility
	8283 joy
8104 assurance	8477 self-examination
8144 renewal	
8150 revival, personal	8704 apostasy
	9165 restoration

5019

human nature

Scripture declares that human nature was created by God in his image and

likeness, and set above all other creatures.

5020
human nature

Human nature was created by God, is corrupted by sin and can only be renewed and recreated through the grace of God. Redemption was achieved by Jesus Christ taking upon himself sinful human nature on the cross, so delivering from the power and penalty of sin.

Human nature is created by God
God created humanity Ex 4:11; Isa 45:12 *See also* Ge 1:26–27; Ps 95:6; 100:3; Pr 22:2; Jer 27:5

God created human beings as male and female Ge 1:27; 5:2 *See also* Mk 10:6 pp Mt 19:4

God created human beings in his image and likeness Col 3:9–10 *See also* Ge 1:26–27; 5:1; 9:6; Jas 3:9

Human nature is created inferior to God himself Ps 8:3–5 *See also* Nu 23:19; Ps 144:3; Hos 11:9

Human nature is given life by the Spirit of God Ge 2:7 *See also* Job 12:10; 27:3; Isa 42:5; 57:16; Jer 38:16

Human beings are dependent upon God Jer 10:23 *See also* 2Ch 20:12; Ps 16:2; Mt 4:4; 2Co 3:5

Human beings have freedom to choose between good and evil Dt 11:26–28 *See also* Dt 30:15–16,19; Jos 24:15; 1Ch 28:9; Jer 26:3; Eze 18:21–23

The components of human nature
The soul Ps 116:7 *The Hebrew and Greek words for "soul" are translated in various ways by the NIV, including "breath" and "life". It refers chiefly to the principle of life.* *See also* Mk 8:35–37; Lk 1:46; 1Pe 1:9; 2:11

The spirit Jas 2:26 *The Hebrew and Greek words for "spirit" are translated in various ways by the NIV, including "breath", "heart" and "mind". It often refers to the identity-giving aspect of human nature. See also* Job 34:14; Ps 77:3; 142:3; Mt 26:41; Lk 8:55; Ac 7:59; Ro 8:16; Heb 4:12

The flesh Jer 17:5 *The Hebrew and Greek words for "flesh" are translated in various ways by the NIV, including "body", "flesh" and "human nature". The term can refer specifically to the frailty of human nature or to human nature in opposition to God. See also* Ge 6:3; Job 10:4; Ps 78:39; Mt 26:41; Php 3:3–5

Human nature became corrupted by sin
Sin has its origins in the disobedience of Adam and Eve Ge 2:16; 3:1–6; Ro 5:12–19; 2Co 11:3; 1Ti 2:14; Jas 1:13–15

Sin affects human nature universally Isa 64:6 *See also* Job 25:4; Jer 17:9; Jn 3:19; Ro 3:23

Human nature is trapped in its sinful condition Ro 7:24 *See also* Ge 6:5;

Jn 8:34–36; Ro 6:16–17; 7:5; Eph 2:3; 2Pe 2:18–19

Sin hardens human nature 1Sa 6:6 *See also* Ex 8:15,32; Ps 95:8; Pr 28:14; Heb 3:8,15; 4:7

Human nature is mortal on account of sin Ro 5:12; 8:10 *See also* Ge 6:5–7; Job 14:1–5; 1Co 15:22; 2Co 5:1; 2Ti 1:10

Human nature can be redeemed through Jesus Christ
Jesus Christ took human nature upon himself Jn 1:14

Jesus Christ mediated between God and humanity in his human nature 1Ti 2:3–6 *See also* Heb 8:6; 9:15; 1Jn 2:1

Jesus Christ makes possible the reversal of Adam's disobedience Ro 5:19 *See also* Ro 5:12–17

Jesus Christ makes possible a sharing in God's nature 2Pe 1:4

See also

2321 Christ as redeemer	5062 spirit
	6022 sin, causes of
4005 creation	6166 flesh, sinful nature
4018 life, spiritual	
5014 heart, human	8442 good works
5023 image of God	8735 evil, origins of
5038 mind, the human	8848 worldliness

5021
humanity, of Jesus Christ

See 2033 Jesus Christ, humanity of

5023

image of God

Humanity is created in the image or likeness of God. This image of God, given in creation, was damaged in the fall, but may be restored through Jesus Christ.

Humanity created in God's image
Ge 1:26–27 *Image and likeness are probably synonymous terms in Hebrew parallelism. No physical likeness between God and humanity is intended. See also* Ge 5:1–2

Paul implies that the divine image is associated in the first place with men *Although Paul at points seems to imply that the image of God is especially associated with males, he does not imply that this involves male supremacy:* 1Co 11:7,11–12

Respect for human life in God's image Ge 9:6; Jas 3:9

The divine image implies partnership with God in the stewardship of creation Ge 1:26 *See also* Ps 8:3–8

The divine image includes imitating God's love and justice Mt 5:48 *See also* Dt 10:17–19

The image of God disfigured, though not totally destroyed, in the fall
Ro 3:23

Fallen humanity in contention with creation Ge 3:17–19

Fallen humanity and the exploitation of nature Dt 22:6–7; Isa 7:23–25

Jesus Christ the image of God
Php 2:6; Col 1:15 *See also* 2Co 4:4

He is the exact representation of God Heb 1:3

He reveals God Jn 1:18

Jesus Christ is the perfect human being
Jn 1:4 *See also* Jn 1:9,14; Php 2:7; Heb 2:17

Restoration of the divine image through Jesus Christ
The divine image is renewed in all who are united with him by faith Ro 8:29 *See also* 2Co 3:18; Eph 1:13–14; 4:22–24; Col 3:9–10

The promise of complete restoration in the future 1Co 15:49; 1Jn 3:2 *See also* 1Co 15:42,45–48; Php 3:21

The Christian life as a process of transformation 2Co 3:18

See also

1325	God, the Creator
2063	Christ, perfection
3233	Holy Spirit & sanctification
5034	likeness
5081	Adam, life of
5700	headship
6156	fall of humanity
6728	regeneration
6756	union with Christ, significance
8206	Christlikeness
8322	perfection, human
8471	respect for human beings

5024

inner being

The deepest aspects of human nature, known completely by God, to be contrasted with the outward appearance or public image of a person.

The contrast of the inner being with the outward person
The desires of the inner being Ro 7:14–25 *See also* Ps 51:3–6

The inner being is not subject to physical constraints 2Co 4:7–18

The inner being should take priority over the outward person
1Pe 3:3–4 *See also* 1Sa 16:7; Eph 3:16–19

See also

4018	life, spiritual
4813	depth
5008	conscience
5012	heart
5062	spirit
5173	outward appearance
5844	emotions
5940	searching
5965	temperament
6166	flesh, sinful nature
8162	spiritual vitality
8164	spirituality

5025

killing

Depriving another person or animal of life, usually by physical force. Scripture identifies various types of killing. While forbidding murder, killing of human beings is permitted

in the form of execution and war. Animals may be killed for food or sacrifice, provided that the blood is ritually disposed of.

Murder
Murder prohibited by the sixth commandment Ex 20:13 pp Dt 5:17

Murder prohibited from the time of Noah *See also* Ge 9:5–6; Lev 17:11

The life of the murderer is forfeit Ge 9:6

Judicial killing
Judicial killing permitted for capital crimes Ex 21:12 *See also* Ex 22:18–20; Dt 17:8–13; 21:18–21; 22:21–27

Executed criminals are under the curse of God Dt 21:23

Unintentional killing (manslaughter)
The accidental killing of a fellow human being Ex 21:13 *See also* Dt 4:41–42

The provision of cities of refuge to avoid blood revenge Dt 19:2–13 *Blood revenge, based on Ge 9:6, refers to the judicial revenge of a family or clan against a man who accidentally kills one of their members.*

Killing in war
Killing in a holy war Jos 6:17,21

Killing in other wars Dt 20:10–15

The killing of animals
Regulations for disposal of blood Lev 17:3–7,11

Animals may be killed at a distance from the sanctuary Dt 12:15–16

Limitations on the killing of animals Dt 22:6–7 *This limitation appears to be an attempt to preserve the balance of nature.*

See also

5040	murder
5493	retribution
5495	revenge & retaliation
5605	warfare
5975	violence
7338	cities of refuge
7346	death penalty

5026

knowledge

A state of awareness and understanding, resulting from information which has been obtained or revealed concerning people or objects. Scripture stresses God's total knowledge of his creation and also the importance of his people knowing his will and purposes for them.

This set of themes consists of the following:

5027

knowledge, God's of humanity

God knows all people comprehensively, their nature, their deeds and their thoughts. He understands every aspect of their lives, past, present and future.

God knows all people
1Ki 8:39 pp 2Ch 6:30 *See also* Job 34:21; Ps 7:9; Jer 17:10; 23:24; 32:19; Ac 1:24

God knows his own people
2Ti 2:19 *See also* 1Co 8:3; Gal 4:9

He knows them by name Isa 43:1 *See also* Ex 33:17; Isa 45:3–4

He knows them individually and intimately Jer 1:5 *See also* Ps 119:168; 139:1–16; 1Co 13:12

He knows their needs and troubles Mt 6:31–32 *See also* Ps 34:15; 142:3; Jer 18:23; Mt 6:7–8

He knows their sin Heb 4:13 *See also* Isa 48:8; Jer 29:23; Hos 5:3; Am 5:12

The knowledge of Jesus Christ
He knows all people Jn 2:25 *See also* Mt 12:25 pp Lk 11:17; Mk 2:8 pp Mt 9:4 pp Lk 5:22

He knows them by name Jn 10:3 *See also* Jn 10:14

He knows their needs and troubles Rev 2:9 *See also* Rev 2:13

He knows their sins Rev 3:15–16 *See also* Rev 3:1–2

He knows their past and future Jn 4:16–18 *See also* Jn 1:47; 4:39 Mt 26:33–34 pp Mk 14:29–30 pp Jn 13:37–38

See also

1020	God, all-knowing
1030	God, compassion
2015	Christ, compassion
2330	Christ as shepherd
6221	rebellion
6638	election

5028

knowledge, God as source of human

All knowledge proceeds from God, although many do not acknowledge it. The pursuit of knowledge apart from God is futile and leads to pride.

God is the source of all knowledge
Pr 2:6 *See also* Job 28:28; Pr 1:7; 9:10

Pursuit of knowledge apart from God led to the fall
Ge 3:1–7 *See also* Ge 3:22–24

Pursuit of knowledge apart from God is futile
Ecc 12:11–12 *See also* Ecc 1:16–18; 1Co 8:1

Pursuit of the knowledge that proceeds from God merits divine approval
Pr 3:13–18 *See also* Pr 2:3–5; 4:5; 15:14; 2Pe 1:5

God bestows knowledge on certain individuals
Da 1:17 *See also* Ex 31:1–5; 35:30–36:1; 1Ki 3:10–12; 2Ch 1:10–12; 1Co 12:8

See also
1180 God, wisdom of	6154 fall, the
5302 education	8226 discernment
5531 skill	8281 insight
5864 futility	8355 understanding
5894 intelligence	8361 wisdom

5029
knowledge, of God

Human knowledge of God may be a purely intellectual phenomenon, as when one knows about God through observing the results of his actions, but God's people know him in a personal way because of their relationship with him.

Knowledge of God through his actions
God acts in creation Ro 1:20 *See also* Ps 19:1–4; Ac 14:17

God acts in judgment Eze 38:22–23 *See also* Ex 7:5; 14:4; Ps 83:9–18; Eze 6:13; 39:6,23

God acts in saving his people Isa 52:9–10 *See also* 1Sa 17:46–47; Isa 37:20; 49:26

God's people know him through his dealings with them
God delivers his people Ex 6:6–7 *See also* Ex 10:2; 16:6; Dt 4:32–35; Jos 3:10; 4:23–24; 1Ki 20:13,28

God provides and cares for his people Ex 16:8 *See also* 1Ki 8:56–60; Isa 41:17–20; 45:4–6; Eze 37:26–28

In giving them his law Eze 20:19–20 *See also* Ex 31:13; Eze 20:11–12

God judges and restores his people Eze 11:10–12 *See also* Nu 14:34; Jer 24:5–7; 31:33–34; Eze 6:2–10; 7:4; 12:15–16; 20:38; 36:11; 37:14

Knowledge of God leads to confidence in him
Ps 9:10 *See also* Ge 22:7–8; Job 19:25; Ps 18:2; 37:25; 71:5–6; Isa 12:1–2; Da 11:32

See also
1150 God, truth of	6181 ignorance
1310 God as judge	7140 people of God
1320 God as Saviour	7221 exodus, the
1325 God, the Creator	8134 knowing God
1330 God, the provider	8213 confidence
	8319 perception, spiritual
1400 God, knowledge of	

5030
knowledge, of Jesus Christ

The believer's understanding and experience of Jesus Christ, which arises from a personal relationship established through faith.

Jesus Christ is the supreme revelation of God
Jn 14:6–10 *See also* Mt 11:27; Jn 1:1–2; 8:19; 17:26; Col 1:15–20; Heb 1:3

Knowledge of Jesus Christ acquired through a personal relationship with him
Jn 4:42 *See also* Mt 9:4–8 pp Mk 2:8–12 pp Lk 5:22–26; Jn 10:38; 14:11

Knowledge of Jesus Christ acquired through the work of the Holy Spirit
Jn 15:26 *See also* 1Co 12:3; 1Jn 5:6–9

Knowledge of Jesus Christ is associated with knowing God
Jn 17:26 *See also* Jn 8:19; 10:14–15,27–30; Jn 14:6–11; 15:15

Knowledge of Jesus Christ should increase consistently
Php 3:10; 2Pe 3:18 *See also* 2Pe 1:5–8

Consequences of knowing Jesus Christ
Reconciliation with God 2Co 5:19–20; Eph 2:16

Access to God Ro 5:1–2; Eph 2:18

Becoming like Jesus Christ Php 3:10

Peace Jn 14:1; 16:33; Ro 5:1–2; Eph 2:14–18

Hope Eph 1:17–18

Eternal life Jn 17:3 *See also* Jn 10:27–28; 1Jn 5:13,20

Renewal Eph 4:19–22

Unity among believers Jn 17:21

Rejection by the world Jn 15:18–21; 16:2–3; 17:14

Knowledge of Jesus Christ is to manifest itself in obedience
1Jn 2:3–6 *See also* Mt 7:21–23; 25:31–46; Jn 14:15,21,23; 15:4–5

See also
2018 Christ, divinity	6644 eternal life
2045 Christ, knowledge of	6666 grace
	6700 peace
2595 incarnation	6716 reconciliation
3293 Holy Spirit, witness of	8256 fruitfulness
	8453 obedience
6606 access to God	

5031
knowledge, of sin

Originating with the fall, it is revealed by conscience, the law and the Holy Spirit.

Knowledge of sin as a result of the fall
Ge 3:1–13 *See also* Ge 2:16–17; 3:22

Knowledge of sin through conscience
Ro 2:14–15 *See also* 1Sa 24:5–6; 2Sa 24:10; Heb 10:22

Knowledge of sin through the law
Ro 3:20 *See also* Ro 5:13; 7:7

The law was taught to all in Israel
Lev 10:11 *See also* Dt 4:1; 5:31; 6:6–9

Knowledge of sin through the convicting power of the Holy Spirit
Jn 16:7–11 *See also* 1Th 1:5

See also
3248 Holy Spirit, conviction	6172 guilt
	6614 atonement
5008 conscience	6624 confession of sin
5033 knowledge of good & evil	6632 conviction
5375 law	6733 repentance
6020 sin	

5033
knowledge of good and evil

Every human being has some innate knowledge of good and evil. The full knowledge of good and evil derives from God and is revealed in Scripture. The human desire of Adam and Eve to know good and evil, and thus gain independence from God, brought about the fall.

The human quest for knowledge of good and evil
Ge 3:22 *See also* Ge 2:9; 3:5–6; 2Sa 14:17; 19:35; Eze 28:2–7

The consequences of the attempt to attain this knowledge
Ge 2:17 *See also* Ge 3:7–19; Eze 28:13–19; Ro 1:28–32

God as the source of full knowledge of good and evil
Ps 119:66 *See also* Job 28:28; Ps 34:11–14; 111:10; Ro 7:7

The natural knowledge of good and evil
Given in the human conscience
Ro 2:14–15 *See also* Job 27:6; Eze 36:31; Jn 3:20; Ac 24:16; Ro 9:1; 2Co 1:12; 1Ti 1:5,18–19; 1Pe 3:15–16

Conscience and moral decisions
1Sa 25:30–34; 1Ch 21:6–7; Ps 37:27; Am 5:14–15; Eph 4:25–32

A natural knowledge of good and evil will not necessarily empower anyone to do good Ro 7:15–25

See also
5008 conscience	6154 fall, the
5031 knowledge of sin	8226 discernment
	8357 weakness
5080 Adam	8361 wisdom
5093 Eve	8734 evil
6020 sin	8755 folly

5034
likeness

The similarity between objects or persons. Humanity is created in the likeness of God. Jesus Christ possesses a likeness to both God and humanity, which is expressed and safeguarded by the doctrine of the incarnation.

Human beings are created in the likeness of God
Ge 1:26–27 *See also* Ge 5:1; 9:6; Col 3:9–10; Jas 3:9

Redemption includes being conformed to God's likeness

The likeness of God the Father Mt 5:48
See also Eph 4:20–24

The likeness of God the Son Ro 8:29
See also 1Co 2:16; 2Co 3:18;
Eph 4:11–13

Jesus Christ was in the likeness of God and humanity

Jesus Christ is like God Col 1:15 *While stating that Jesus Christ is like God, Scripture also insists that this likeness is grounded in the fact that Jesus Christ is God. See also* 2Co 4:4; Php 2:6; Heb 1:3

Jesus Christ is like human beings Ro 8:3 *While stating that Jesus Christ is like humanity Scripture also insists that this likeness is grounded in the fact that Jesus Christ is human. Yet Christ did not share human sinfulness* 2Co 5:21; Heb 4:15. *See also* Php 2:6–7

See also

2018 Christ, divinity	2221 Christ, Son of
2033 Christ,	Man
humanity	5023 image of God
2218 Christ, Son of	5308 equality
God	

5035

mind

The seat of human consciousness, thought and desires. Scripture stresses that the minds of believers must be shaped by the knowledge and love of God, as their ways of thinking and acting become more like the pattern set out in Jesus Christ.

5036
mind, of God

God's pattern of thought and attitude of heart is holy, righteous and good. It is expressed in his law and his word, and also in the outworking of his mercy, but it is, ultimately, beyond human understanding.

God's mind is expressed in his law and his word

Ex 20:1–17 *See also* Dt 4:1–2;
6:1,24–25; Ps 119:4,34,66,89,105,130

The mind of God is holy, righteous and good

Ro 7:7 *See also* Dt 4:8; Nu 23:19;
1Sa 15:29; 2Sa 22:31 pp Ps 18:30;
Pr 30:5; Ps 19:7–10;
119:68,75,137–138,142; Jn 17:17;
Ro 7:12

The mind of God is also expressed in his merciful acts

Eph 2:4–5 *See also* Ne 9:31; Ps 123:2;
Isa 55:7; Da 9:18; Hos 11:8; Mic 7:18;
Lk 1:78; Ro 9:18; 11:32; 12:1; 1Pe 1:3;
2:10

The constancy of the mind of God

Nu 23:19 *See also* 1Sa 15:29; Ps 110:4;
Eze 24:14

God changes his mind

Drawing back from threatened actions Jer 26:13 *The idea of God "relenting" does not mean a capricious change of mind, but the considered decision on God's part not to proceed with a threatened course of action in response to repentance on the part of individuals or the people. See also* Ex 32:12–14; Jer 18:5–10; 26:3,19; Joel 2:13–14; Am 7:3,6; Jnh 3:9–10; 4:2

Grieving over past actions 1Sa 15:11
See also Ge 6:6–7; 1Sa 15:35

The mind of God is, ultimately, beyond human understanding

Because of God's greatness Isa 55:8–9 *See also* Isa 40:13–14,28; 44:6–7; Ro 11:33–36; 1Co 2:16

Because of human lowliness Ecc 5:1–2
See also Ecc 7:23–25

See also

1065 God, holiness of	1690 word of God
1090 God, majesty of	5001 human race, the
1115 God, purpose of	5378 law, OT
1120 God, repentance of	6687 mercy, God's
1175 God, will of	8306 mercifulness
1180 God, wisdom of	8355 understanding

5037
mind, of Christ

The mind of Christ reveals the essence of God's nature. Jesus Christ desires that his followers adopt his attitudes; this comes about through the work of the Holy Spirit.

The mind of Christ discloses the mind of God

In relation to righteousness, holiness and the law Jn 14:9–11 *See also* Mt 5:17; Jn 15:10; 1Co 1:30

In mercy 1Ti 1:15–16 *See also* Mt 9:12–13 pp Mk 2:17 pp Lk 5:31–32; Hos 6:6; Mt 23:23; Jude 21

The mind of Christ is made known to believers by the Holy Spirit

Jn 14:26 *See also* Jn 16:12–15; Ro 8:9;
1Co 2:11–13

The plans and purposes of Jesus Christ are made known to the first Christians by the Spirit Ac 16:6–7 *See also* Ac 8:29; 10:19; 11:12,28; 13:2; 15:28

Knowledge of the mind of Christ leads to holiness

1Co 2:14–16 *See also* Php 2:5–11;
1Pe 4:1–2

See also

2054 Christ, mind of	8226 discernment
3263 Holy Spirit, guidance	8272 holiness, growth in
5135 blindness, spiritual	8347 spiritual growth
5766 attitudes to life	
8128 guidance, receiving	

5038
mind, the human

On account of its inner orientation the fallen human mind is in conflict with the mind of God. It is nevertheless capable of knowing God, and of being changed and renewed by him.

The human mind is the seat of reason and decision-making

Job 12:1–3 *See also* 1Ch 17:2; 2Ch 7:11;
Ne 5:7; Ps 19:14; 49:3; Pr 15:28; 19:21;
Ecc 2:3; 8:16; Da 4:16; 5:12; 7:1;
Ro 10:10; 14:5; 1Co 14:14–15; 1Pe 1:13;
Rev 17:9

The fallen human mind

The human mind is fatally flawed by sin Jer 17:9 *See also* Ge 6:5; 8:21; 2Ch 12:14;
Ps 5:9; 64:6; 73:7; Isa 32:6; Jer 17:1;
Ro 8:5–8; Eph 4:17–18

Even the fallen mind can know something of God through creation Ro 1:19–20

The fallen mind tends to confuse the Creator with his creation Isa 44:16–18
See also Ro 1:21–25

Consequences of the human mind's sinfulness

Sinful attitudes lead to sinful words and actions Mt 15:19 pp Mk 7:21–22
See also Ro 1:28–32; Eph 4:17–19;
Col 2:18; 1Ti 6:5; 2Ti 3:8

Sinfulness leads to death Ro 2:5 *See also* Ro 6:23; Col 1:21

Doubt and instability Jas 1:6–8

God can change the attitudes of the sinful human mind

The mind can be convicted of sin Ps 51:3 *See also* 1Ki 2:44; Jn 16:8–11

The mind can be changed 1Th 1:9 *See also* 2Ch 32:26; Job 42:6; Ps 119:36;
Ac 2:37; 26:17–18

It is God who enlightens the mind 2Co 4:6 *See also* Dt 29:4 *God may withhold understanding;* 1Sa 10:9;
Job 38:36; Isa 32:4; Jer 24:7; 31:33;
32:39; Eze 11:19; 18:31; 36:26–27;
Ro 2:4; 2Co 3:14

It is God who renews the human mind Ps 51:10 *See also* Tit 3:3–7

The renewed mind of the believer

Ro 12:1–2

Renewal brings knowledge of God Col 1:9–10

Renewal brings peace Php 4:7 *See also* Isa 26:3

Renewal leads to obedience Ro 8:5 *See also* Ro 7:25; 12:1–2; Col 1:10; 3:1–2;
1Pe 1:13; Heb 8:10; 10:16; Jer 31:33

The believer's mind needs growth and renewal 2Co 11:3 *See also* Ro 7:22–23;
Eph 1:17; Col 1:9

See also

1409 dream	6178 hardness of heart
1441 revelation, necessity	6181 ignorance
5894 intelligence	6733 repentance
5904 maturity, spiritual	8145 renewal, people of God

See also
8361 wisdom   8419 enlightenment
8408 decision-   8777 lust
     making

5040

murder

The unlawful killing of individual human beings, forbidden by God and carrying the threat of severe punishment.

Murder forbidden by the law
Ex 20:13 pp Dt 5:17 See also Mt 5:21; 19:18 pp Mk 10:19 pp Lk 18:20; Ro 13:9; 1Ti 1:9; Jas 2:11–12

Murder is to be punished
Punishment by death Ex 21:12 See also Ge 9:6; Lev 24:17,21; Nu 35:16–21,31; Dt 19:11–13

Punishment by banishing Ge 4:13–14 See also Pr 28:17

Punishment by exclusion from the kingdom Rev 21:8; 22:15

Unintentional murderers are protected from avengers
Nu 35:11 See also Nu 35:22–29,32; Jos 21:13,21,27,32,38

Witnesses are required before murder is proven
Nu 35:30 See also Dt 17:6; 19:15; Heb 10:28

Unpremeditated murder
Nu 35:22–24 See also Ex 21:13; Dt 4:41–44; 19:4; Jos 20:1–3

Premeditated motives of murder
Jealousy Ge 4:8 See also 1Jn 3:12

Lust 2Sa 12:9–10 Many motives contributed to David's plan to remove Uriah. It began with lust. See also 2Sa 11:1–17

Rebellion and power 2Ki 12:20 See also Jdg 3:21; 2Ki 9:14,24; 19:36–37

To remove opponents 1Ki 2:25 See also Jdg 9:1–6; 2Sa 20:9–10; 2Ch 21:4

To take revenge 2Sa 13:28–29 See also Ex 2:11–13; 2Sa 3:27; 4:1–8

Robbery Pr 1:11–13 See also Lk 10:30

Persecution Mt 24:9 pp Lk 21:12–17 See also 2Ch 21:13; Job 24:14; Pr 29:10; Mt 14:6–11; 23:30–37; Mk 3:6; Ac 2:23; 7:54–60; 2Ti 4:6

Murder as an attitude as well as an action
Mt 5:21–22 See also Mt 15:19; Jn 8:44; 1Jn 3:15

Murderers can be pardoned
Unjustly Lk 23:25 pp Mt 27:15–17 pp Mk 15:6–11 pp Jn 18:39–40 See also Ac 3:14

Justly—through God's grace
2Sa 12:9–13; Ac 26:10; 1Ti 1:13–15 See also Ex 2:12–3:12; Ac 7:58; 8:3; 9:1,13; 22:4; 1Co 15:9; Eph 3:8

See also
1055 God, grace &   5789 anger
     mercy   7318 blood, symbol
5025 killing   of guilt
5482 punishment   7346 death penalty
5494 revenge   8794 persecution
5622 witnesses

5041

name

The title given to a person or object by one who is in a position of authority or ownership. Names often reflect the characteristics of a person or the aspirations or wishes for that person of the one bestowing the name.

5042

name of God, significance of

God's name is synonymous with his person, his presence and his power, and is therefore held in the highest honour.

God is referred to as the Name
Ac 5:41 See also Lev 24:10–16; 2Sa 6:2 pp 1Ch 13:6; 3Jn 7

God's person is revealed in his name
Ex 34:5–7 See also Ge 14:18–20; 17:1; 21:33; 32:29–30; Ex 3:13–15; 6:3; 33:19; Jdg 13:17–18; Jer 16:21

God's name is synonymous with his presence
Nu 6:22–27 See also Dt 12:5–7; 1Ki 8:15–21 pp 2Ch 6:4–11; Ne 1:9; Ps 20:1; 54:1; 74:7; 75:1; Isa 30:27; Jn 17:11–12

The name of God identifies his people
Dt 28:10 See also 2Ch 7:14; Isa 43:6–7; Mic 4:5; 5:4

Dishonouring God's name is a serious offence
Ex 20:7 See also Lev 19:12; 22:2,32; Ps 74:10,18; 139:20; Eze 43:7–8; Mal 1:6

The righteous honour God's name
Ps 29:2 See also Ne 1:11; Ps 86:11–12; Isa 26:13; Mal 2:5; 3:16–4:2

The name of Jesus Christ
Supplication is to be made in the name of Jesus Christ Jn 14:13–14 See also Mt 18:19–20; Jn 15:16; 16:23–24

Healing and other miracles performed in the name of Jesus Christ Ac 3:6–8 See also Ac 3:16; 4:30

Baptism in Jesus Christ's name Ac 2:38 See also Mt 28:19; Ac 8:12,15–16; 10:48; 19:5

Salvation is in the name of Jesus Christ Ac 4:12 See also Jn 14:6; 20:31; Ac 2:21; Joel 2:32; 1Co 6:11; 1Jn 2:12; Php 2:9–11

See also
1205 God, titles of   6510 salvation
1415 miracles   7903 baptism
2203 Christ, titles of 8334 reverence &
3110 Holy Spirit,   God's nature
     titles of   8607 prayer, God's
5333 healing   promises
5429 oaths   8807 profanity
5800 blasphemy

5043

names, significance of

Labels that identify individuals. They may also denote aspects of character or reputation.

A name may reflect an individual's nature
1Sa 25:25 See also Ge 17:5 "Abraham" means "father of many"; Ge 32:27–29 "Israel" means "he struggles with God"; Ex 34:14; Mk 5:9 pp Lk 8:30

Additional names or nicknames
Mk 3:17 In NT times an additional name or surname reflecting someone's character was sometimes appended to the given name. See also Lk 6:15; Jn 1:42 "Cephas" and "Peter" mean "rock" in Aramaic and Greek respectively; Ac 4:36

A name may indicate an individual's reputation and standing in the community
A good name indicates a good reputation Pr 22:1 See also Pr 3:4; 10:7; Ecc 7:1; SS 1:3

A bad name indicates a bad reputation Ne 6:13 See also Dt 22:13–19; Pr 25:9–10

Survival of one's name is important
Ru 4:9–10 See also Ge 48:15–16; Nu 27:1–4; Dt 25:7–9; 2Sa 18:18; Job 18:17–19

Preservation of a name indicates divine blessing Isa 56:4–5 See also Ge 12:1–3; 2Sa 7:9 pp 1Ch 17:8; 1Ki 1:47; Isa 66:22

Obliteration of a name is associated with death
Jer 11:19 See also Dt 7:24; 9:14; 2Sa 14:7; 2Ki 14:27

Obliteration of a name is often linked with divine judgment
Ps 9:5–6 See also Dt 29:20; Ps 109:13; Isa 14:22–23; 48:18–19; Na 1:14

Bearing someone's name indicates ownership or identification
Rev 22:3–4 See also Ex 23:21; 2Ch 7:14; Dt 28:10; Isa 43:6–7; Jer 14:9; Da 9:18–19; Rev 3:12; 14:1; 22:4

God knows his people by name
Isa 43:1 See also Ex 33:12,17; Isa 45:3; 49:1; Jn 10:3

See also
1040 God,   5827 curse
     fatherhood   6608 adoption
1335 blessing   7140 people of God
5082 Adam,   8203 character
     significance   8332 reputation
5680 family

5044
names, giving of

Scripture contains many examples of the naming of people and places. Personal names, usually given at birth by parents, were sometimes changed at a later date.

Names may reflect personal experiences
Ge 41:51–52 See also Ge 29:31–35; 30:6–8,18–20,23–24; 35:18; Ex 2:10,21–22; 18:3–4; 1Sa 1:20; 1Ch 4:9

Names may reflect national experiences
1Sa 4:21 See also Ge 10:25 pp 1Ch 1:19; Isa 8:3–4; Hos 1:2–11

Names may indicate future destiny
Mt 1:21 See also Lk 1:31–33

The giving of a name reflects the authority of the giver
Ge 1:5–10; 2:19–20 See also Ge 2:23; 35:18; 2Ki 23:34 pp 2Ch 36:4; 2Ki 24:17; Lk 1:62–63

The changing of names
On divine instruction Ge 17:3–8 See also Ge 17:15–16; 35:9–10; Jn 1:42

In relation to salvation Isa 62:2 See also Isa 65:15; Rev 2:17

In the light of past experience Jdg 6:32 See also Ru 1:20

In the future Zec 8:3 See also Isa 1:26; 44:5; 58:12; 62:4,12; Jer 7:32; 20:3–6; Mal 1:4

In a new culture Ge 41:45 See also Da 1:7

The instance of Paul Ac 13:9 The occasion of and reason for the change from "Saul" to "Paul" are not clear.

Place-names may reflect events or experiences
Ge 11:8–9; 16:13–14; 19:21–22; 21:31; 26:32–33; 28:18–19; 31:45–50; 32:1–2,30; 33:17; 35:7–8

See also
1065 God, holiness of
1105 God, power of
1348 covenant with Abraham
5215 authority
5655 birth

5046
opportunities

Events or moments at which actions of importance or significance can be achieved. God provides opportune moments both for his people to serve him and to proclaim the gospel and for those outside the church to respond to the gospel.

5047
opportunities, in life

Scripture views life as divinely ordained to include occasions when certain forms of behaviour are appropriate.

The need to discern opportune moments
Ecc 3:1

Every possible opportunity should be taken to do good
Gal 6:10 See also Lk 10:33; Jn 9:4; Eph 5:16; Col 4:5; 2Ti 4:2

Examples of individuals who seized opportunities to serve God
Rahab saved the spies and her household: Jos 2:8–14; 6:23
2Ki 5:1–3 Naaman's wife's maid helped Naaman by telling her mistress about Elisha; Ne 2:2–5 Nehemiah gained permission to rebuild the walls of Jerusalem.
Esther saved the Jews from Haman's plot: Est 4:14; 7:3–6
Da 2:14–16 Daniel offered to interpret Nebuchadnezzar's dream; Ac 18:24–26 Priscilla and Aquila taught Apollos.

Some opportunities should be rejected
1Sa 24:3–4,10; 26:6–11

Opportunities to do evil may have appalling consequences
Ge 4:8 Cain made an opportunity to murder Abel; Ge 25:29–31 Jacob took the opportunity to "buy" Esau's birthright. Joseph's brothers seized the opportunity to capture and sell him: Ge 37:18–20,27
Da 6:4–5 Daniel's enemies sought and found an opportunity to lay a charge against him.
Judas sought an opportunity to betray Jesus Christ: Mt 26:16 pp Mk 14:11 pp Lk 22:6

Giving others an opportunity to do wrong must be avoided
1Ti 5:14

See also
1355 providence
4903 time
4918 dawn
4921 day
4933 evening
4954 morning
4957 night
5299 door
5861 favour, human
8493 watchfulness, believers
8754 fear

5048
opportunities, and salvation

God chooses the right moment in his work to save humanity. It is important to seize the opportunities he offers, both in receiving salvation and in working with him to offer it to others.

Israel had opportunities of salvation
At Sinai Ex 19:4–8 God had saved Israel from slavery in Egypt. Now they accepted the opportunity to become his covenant people.

At Shechem Jos 24:14–15 After Israel entered Canaan, Joshua challenged them to forsake idolatry and renew the covenant with the LORD.

The coming of Jesus Christ offers a new and urgent opportunity to respond to God
Mt 3:1–2; Gal 4:4 See also Mt 10:7; Mk 1:15; Ro 5:6

The message of opportunity continues after the resurrection of Jesus Christ
For Israel Ac 3:24–26

For the Gentiles Ac 17:30 See also Ac 17:23,31

God in his mercy gives opportunity to repent and believe
Ro 2:4; 2Pe 3:8–9

The urgency of the need to respond to God's opportunity of salvation
2Co 6:2; Heb 4:7 See also Ps 95:7–8; Isa 49:8; 55:6–7

God will judge evil at an opportune time
Rev 14:18 See also Rev 14:7

It is possible to refuse the opportunity of salvation, with sad consequences
The lesson of Israel Nu 14:8–10; Ps 95:7–11; 2Co 6:1–2; Heb 4:3,7 Hebrews warns Christians not to miss their chance of blessing.

The seriousness of rejecting the good news Mt 10:14 pp Mk 6:11 pp Lk 9:5; Lk 19:41–42 Jesus Christ wept over Jerusalem because the city didn't recognise its opportunity; Ac 13:46–51; 28:25–28

Christians should take every opportunity to tell others the good news
Jn 4:35 See also Lk 10:2; 1Co 16:9; Col 4:5; 1Pe 3:15

See also
1055 God, grace & mercy
1095 God, patience of
2377 kingdom of God, entry into
2426 gospel, responses
5051 responsibility
6232 rejection of God, results
8489 urgency
9210 judgment, God's
9240 last judgment

5050
reason

The human capacity to think logically and intelligently, thereby discovering truth or persuading others. But human reason is limited and cannot arrive at a true and full knowledge of God without divine assistance and revelation.

The human power of reason
1Co 13:11

Human reason is limited
Job 32:11–12 See also Job 32:3

Human reason is far inferior to divine reason
1Co 1:18–31 See also Job 12:20,24–25; Isa 29:14; 55:8–9

Human reason may point people towards God

Ro 2:14–15 *See also* Isa 1:18–20; Ac 17:22–23,27–28; Ro 1:19–20; Heb 11:17–19

Paul reasons with unbelievers

Ac 17:2–4 *See also* Ac 17:17; 18:4,19

Believers are to give reasons for their faith

1Pe 3:15

God reasons with his rebellious people

Isa 1:18–19

See also
1440 revelation,   5191 thought
      creation   5441 philosophy
2054 Christ, mind of   5894 intelligence
5008 conscience   7703 apologetics
5029 knowledge of   7751 persuasion
      God   8361 wisdom
5038 mind, the
      human

5051

responsibility

An obligation, especially to give account of one's actions. Scripture stresses that the responsibilities which believers and the church have arise from their special and privileged relationship to God.

5052

responsibility, to God

Even though God is sovereign, all people everywhere are accountable to him for everything they do, say or think.

People are responsible for their own sins

God is not responsible for human sin Dt 24:16; Eze 18:4 *See also* Job 19:4; Ps 51:4–5; Jer 31:30; Eze 18:20; 33:1–20; Ro 6:23

Death is the result of sin Ro 5:12; 6:23 *See also* Ge 3:1–7; Isa 43:27; Eze 18:4; 1Co 15:21–22

The law heightens human responsibility for sin

It brings knowledge of sin Ro 5:20 *Because the law brings knowledge of sin, it prevents people from claiming ignorance of the nature and seriousness of that sin. See also* Ro 7:7–9; Gal 3:19

It applies not only to actions but also to words and thoughts Mt 5:22,28 *See also* Jer 17:9–10; Mt 15:18–19

It brings judgment Ecc 12:14; Mt 12:36–37; 1Co 4:5 *See also* Job 15:5–6; Ro 2:16; 14:12; 2Co 5:10; 1Pe 4:5; Jude 15

Ignorance does not remove responsibility

Lev 5:17 *See also* Lk 12:48; Ac 3:17–19; Ro 1:20

The responsibility of humanity to repent and believe

It is commanded by God Ac 17:30 *See also* Eze 18:30; Mt 4:17; Mk 1:15; 6:12; Lk 24:46–47

Jesus Christ's life and ministry heightens the responsibility to repent Jn 3:18; 15:22 *See also* Mt 11:20–24; 12:41–42 pp Lk 11:31–32; Jn 12:48

See also
5376 law, purpose of   6732 repentance
5667 children,   7760 preachers,
      responsibilities   responsibilities
      to God   7967 spiritual gifts,
6020 sin   responsibility
6611 adoption,   8403 commands
      privileges &   8495 witnessing
      duties
6641 election,
      responsibilities

5053

responsibility, for God's world

All humanity has a moral obligation under God to one another, whether as national leaders, ministers, spouses, parents, children, believers or simply as human beings. This moral obligation is shown in the Scriptures to also include the animal kingdom and the environment.

The responsibility of national leaders

To reward good and punish evil Ro 13:3–4 *See also* Pr 16:12

To administer justice Pr 31:4–5,8–9 *See also* Dt 27:19; Pr 14:31; 17:5; 29:4,14

The responsibility of Christian leaders

To care for believers 1Pe 5:2 *See also* Jn 21:15–17; Ac 20:28

To preach, teach and handle the Scriptures properly 2Ti 2:15; 4:2 *See also* Eze 33:6

The responsibility of those who are married

To love each other Eph 5:25; Tit 2:4

To mutually honour each other Eph 5:22; 1Pe 3:7 *See also* 1Pe 3:1

The responsibility of parents to their children

Eph 6:4 *See also* Dt 6:7; Pr 13:24; 22:6; 1Ti 3:4; Tit 2:4

The responsibility of children to honour their parents

Eph 6:1–3 *See also* Dt 5:16

The responsibility of every believer to represent Jesus Christ in the world

Mt 5:13,14; 28:19–20 *See also* Mk 16:15; Ac 1:8

The responsibility of every human being to love God and others

Lk 10:27 pp Mt 22:37–39 pp Mk 12:29–31 *See also* Dt 6:5; Lev 19:18; 1Sa 20:17; Pr 14:31; Mt 5:43–45; Lk 10:28–37

The responsibility to exercise dominion over the animal kingdom and creation

Ge 1:26; Pr 12:10 *See also* Ge 9:2; Ex 23:5; Dt 22:4,6–7; 25:4; Ps 8:6–8

See also
4005 creation   5731 parents
4029 world, human   5744 wife
      beings in   7939 ministry
4603 animals   7948 mission
5001 human race,   8242 ethics,
      the   personal
5366 king   8472 respect for
5702 husband   environment

5054

responsibility, examples of

Scripture provides examples of individuals and situations in which responsibility is accepted, delegated or denied.

Examples of responsibility accepted

Noah to build the ark Ge 6:13–14,22 *See also* Heb 11:7

Joseph over Potiphar's household Ge 39:4 *See also* Ge 39:1–6

Joseph over the other prisoners Ge 39:22 *See also* Ge 39:20–23

Joseph over the whole of Egypt Ge 41:39–41 *See also* Ge 41:55–57; 45:8–9

Levites to be priests Nu 3:5–7 *See also* Nu 8:5–26

Solomon, not David, to build the temple 1Ch 22:2–10

Ezekiel to be a watchman Eze 3:16–21

Jesus Christ in dying on the cross Php 2:8 *See also* Mt 26:39; Jn 10:18; Ro 5:19

Examples of delegation of responsibility

Moses chose leaders to judge Ex 18:24–26 *See also* Ex 18:13–23

The apostles delegated responsibility to seven men Ac 6:3 *See also* Ac 6:1–6

Responsibility delegated to elders Ac 14:23

Examples of denial of responsibility

Adam and Eve in eating the fruit Ge 3:11–13 *God held them both responsible.*

Aaron after making the golden calf Ex 32:19–24

Saul after not destroying everything belonging to the Amalekites 1Sa 15:3,7–9,15

Pilate after ordering Jesus Christ to be crucified Mt 27:24

Judas after betraying Jesus Christ Mt 27:3–5

See also
4208 land, divine   5685 fathers,
      responsibility   responsibilities
5216 authority   5716 middle age
5668 children,   5719 mothers,
      responsibilities   responsibilities
      to parents   5851 excuse

5056

rest

Scripture recognises the need for physical and spiritual relief and stresses that the true resting-place of humanity lies in God, the Creator and Redeemer.

5057

rest, physical

The need for physical rest is recognised in Scripture, and provision is made for ensuring that people are allowed time for rest.

Jesus Christ needed physical rest

Jn 4:6 *See also* Mk 4:38; 6:31; Lk 9:58

The provision of rest

The need for rest Mk 6:31 *See also* Ps 23:2–3; Pr 17:1; Ecc 4:6; Mt 11:28–30

Provision of sleep for rest Ps 4:8 *See also* Ps 127:2; Ecc 5:12

Provision of a Sabbath-rest Ex 34:21; Mk 2:27 *See also* Ex 20:8–11 pp Dt 5:12–15; Ex 31:15; 35:2; Lev 23:3; Ne 13:15; Isa 58:13–14

The purpose of rest

To renew strength La 5:5 *See also* Isa 40:29–31

To know peace Mt 6:25–34 *See also* Job 11:18–19; Ps 3:5; 16:8; Pr 3:24; Php 4:6–7

The character of rest

The absence of war Jos 11:23 *See also* Jos 14:15; 1Ki 5:4; 1Ch 22:9; Ps 46:9–10; Pr 1:33; Isa 14:3

The absence of social strife 2Co 13:11 *See also* Ecc 10:4; 1Co 1:10; 1Th 4:11; Heb 12:14; Jas 3:17–18; 1Pe 3:8

The absence of fear Mk 4:37–38 pp Mt 8:24–25 pp Lk 8:23–24 *See also* Ge 32:11; Ps 127:2; Mic 4:4; Mt 6:31 pp Lk 12:29

The absence of anxiety 1Pe 5:7 *See also* Mt 6:25; Php 4:6

The presence of God Ex 33:14 *See also* Dt 33:27; Mt 11:28

The experience of security Dt 33:12 *See also* Pr 19:23

The experience of peace in death Rev 14:13 *See also* Dt 31:16; Job 3:13–17

The destruction of rest

By business Ps 39:6 *See also* Ge 31:40; Ecc 1:13; 2:23; 8:16; Lk 21:34

By conflict 2Co 7:5 *See also* La 5:5; 2Co 6:5; 11:27

By grief Ler 45:3 *See also* Job 3:26; Ps 77:4; Da 6:18

By unconfessed guilt Ps 32:3–5 *See also* Ge 4:12; Dt 28:65–67; Isa 48:22; 57:20–21; Rev 14:11

By sickness Job 30:17 *See also* Job 7:4–5

5058

rest, spiritual

To be at rest spiritually is to find peace with God through Jesus Christ. This rest is promised to all who put their trust in God and obey him.

The human desire for spiritual rest

La 5:19–22 *See also* Ps 55:4–8; La 3:25–26; 1Ti 2:2

Spiritual rest is to be found in God alone

Mt 11:28–30 *See also* Ex 33:14; Ps 23:2; 51:12; 62:1–2,5–8; 91:1–13; Isa 26:3–4; Jn 14:27; Ro 5:1; Gal 1:3; 5:22; Col 1:20

God promises his people spiritual rest

Heb 4:9–11 *See also* Ps 1:3; 37:7; 116:7; 119:165; 125:1; 131:1–3; Pr 29:25; Isa 30:15; 32:17–18; 58:11; Jer 6:16; 17:7–8; Jn 14:1; Ro 8:6; 1Pe 3:4

Spiritual rest is not for the wicked

Ps 1:4–5 *See also* Ps 112:10; Ecc 2:23; Isa 48:22; 57:20–21

God's offer of rest rejected by a faithless people

Isa 28:12; Jer 6:16

5059

rest, eternal

Eternal rest consists of peace with God, an absence of toil and tribulation and a final deliverance from pain, sorrow and death. It is promised as the inheritance of the people of God.

Eternal rest foreshadowed in the OT

In God's rest after creation Heb 4:3–4 *See also* Ge 2:2–3

In the rest promised to Joshua Heb 4:8 *See also* Dt 31:7; Jos 22:4; Ps 95:7–11

The eternal state described as rest

Heb 4:9 *See also* Job 3:11–19; Rev 14:13

Aspects of eternal rest

Being in the presence of God Lk 23:43 *See also* Jn 14:3; Php 1:23; 1Th 4:17–18; Rev 3:4; 7:15

Happiness 2Co 5:8 *See also* Mt 25:23; Lk 13:29

Refreshment and satisfaction Rev 7:17 *See also* Ps 16:11; 17:15; Eze 47:1–12; Rev 22:1–2

The absence of trouble 2Th 1:6–7 *See also* Rev 6:10–11; 7:14

The absence of labour Rev 14:13 *See also* Job 3:17; Isa 57:2; 65:22–23; Heb 4:1–11

The absence of pain, sorrow and death Rev 21:4 *See also* Isa 25:8; 65:19; Lk 20:36; Ro 8:23; 1Co 15:24; Rev 7:16–17

The absence of conflict and harm Isa 65:25 *See also* Isa 11:6–9; Hos 2:18

The absence of the curse Rev 22:3

Eternal rest is conditional upon faithful obedience

Heb 4:11,1–2

5061

sanctity of life

Scripture treats human life as a divine gift and something for which humans are responsible. It is thus to be valued and respected. No human being has the right to take the life of another.

The sanctity of all human life

It proceeds from God Ge 2:7; Ac 17:25

It is precious to God Ge 1:27 *See also* Ge 4:10–11; 2Sa 18:12–13; Mt 6:25–26

It is protected by God Dt 22:8 *See also* Ge 4:15; Nu 35:11–12; Jer 22:3

Death is by God's appointment Heb 9:27 *See also* Job 14:5; Ps 90:3,5

God prohibits unlawful taking of life Ex 20:13 pp Dt 5:17 *See also* Mt 19:18; Ro 13:9 *So precious is human life that some situations which required the death penalty in the OT are dealt with differently in the NT (e.g., Jn 8:5,11).*

God punishes unlawful taking of life Ge 9:6 *See also* Ex 21:14; 2Sa 12:9; 2Ki 21:16

The sanctity of children's lives

Children are planned by God Ge 18:10; Jdg 13:3–4; 1Ki 13:2; 2Ki 4:16–17; Jer 1:5; Lk 1:13–17,24–25,31–33,35

Children are precious and to be treasured Ps 127:3–4 *See also* Ge 33:5; 48:9; Ps 113:9; 128:3

Child sacrifice is opposed Ge 22:10–12; Lev 18:21; Dt 12:31; 2Ki 3:27; 16:3 pp 2Ch 28:3; Ps 106:38; Isa 57:5; Jer 7:30–31; 19:5; Eze 16:20–21

Warnings against murder of children Ex 1:16–17; Ac 7:19

Antenatal life is fully human Job 31:15;
Ps 22:9; 119:73; 139:13–16; Isa 46:3–4;
49:1,5; Jer 1:5
*Luke uses the same words here of an
unborn child as he does in 2:12,16 of a
newborn child and in 18:15 of little ones:
Lk 1:41,44*

Injury to a pregnant woman is serious
Ex 21:22–25; Am 1:13

The sanctity of old age
The old are to be respected Pr 23:22
See also Lev 19:32; Job 32:6; Ps 71:18;
1Ti 5:1–2

The old are to be cherished 1Ti 5:4 *See
also* Ge 47:12–13; 1Sa 22:3;
Jn 19:26–27

See also

5023 image of God	7332 child sacrifice
5040 murder	7346 death penalty
5067 suicide	8273 holiness,
5664 children	ethical aspects
5725 old age	8469 respect
5731 parents	9020 death
5766 attitudes to life	

5062

spirit

In Scripture the innermost aspect of
human nature. The three-fold
division of spirit, soul and body is
sometimes used to refer to this
distinction between the physical and
spiritual aspects of human existence.

5063
spirit, nature of

The life-giving principle of human
nature, to be distinguished from the
purely physical aspects of life.

The human spirit as distinct from
the body
Mt 26:41 pp Mk 14:38; 1Th 5:23 *See
also* Ro 8:10; 1Co 5:3–5; 7:34; 2Co 7:1;
Col 2:5; Heb 4:12 *"spirit" and "soul"
may be two names for the inner being
penetrated by the word of God, or they may
distinguish the inner person in relation to
God ("spirit") from their relation to the
world ("soul"); Jas 2:26; Rev 18:13*

The human spirit vitalises the
body
Jas 2:26 *See also* Ge 2:7; Job 34:14;
Lk 8:55; 1Co 15:45; Rev 13:15 *"breath"
is the same word as "spirit" in Greek.*

The human spirit as the seat of
thought and feeling
The seat of perception Eze 13:3;
Mk 2:8; Ro 8:16; 1Co 2:11

The seat of feeling 2Sa 13:39;
Job 32:18; Isa 54:6; 57:15; 66:2;
Eze 3:14; Da 7:15; Mt 5:3; Lk 1:47;
Jn 11:33; 13:21

The seat of volition Mt 26:41
pp Mk 14:38; 2Co 12:18; Php 1:27

The human spirit survives
physical death
2Co 5:1–5 *See also* 1Sa 28:13–14;
Mt 10:28; Ac 7:59; Ro 8:23; Heb 12:23;
1Pe 3:19; 4:6

Jesus Christ had a human spirit
Jn 13:21 *See also* Mt 27:50 pp Lk 23:46
pp Jn 19:30; Jn 12:27

See also

2033 Christ,	8319 perception,
humanity	spiritual
4804 breath	8355 understanding
5024 inner being	8408 decision-
5026 knowledge	making
5058 rest, spiritual	9024 death, spiritual
5136 body	9135 immortality
5191 thought	

5064
spirit, emotional aspects of

A human being is made up of a
variety of emotions and attitudes.
Sometimes one trait is or becomes so
dominant as to make it characteristic
of the entire personality.

Examples of a bad spirit
Pride Pr 16:18

Jealousy Nu 5:14

Fear 2Ki 19:7 pp Isa 37:7

Unfaithfulness Hos 4:12; 5:4

Despair Isa 61:3

Spiritual dullness Ro 11:8; Dt 29:4;
Isa 29:10

Examples of a good spirit
Humility Pr 29:23 *See also* Nu 12:3;
Isa 57:15

Submission Nu 14:24 *See also*
Nu 14:6–9

Wisdom Dt 34:9; 1Ki 3:11–12; Job 32:8;
Da 4:9

Steadfastness Ps 51:10,12

Strength Lk 1:17; Mal 4:5

Zeal Ro 12:11; Jn 2:17

Gentleness 1Co 4:21; 1Pe 3:4

Trust 2Co 4:13

God can effect a change of spirit
Eze 36:26 *See also* Eze 11:19; 18:31;
Hag 1:14; Zec 12:10

See also

3230 Holy Spirit &	5965 temperament
regeneration	6744 sanctification
5015 heart & Holy	8164 spirituality
Spirit	8203 character
5761 attitudes	8255 fruit, spiritual
5844 emotions	

5065
spirit, fallen and redeemed

Every aspect of the human
personality, including the spirit, was
affected by the fall. At regeneration
the human personality is
transformed by the Holy Spirit.

The human spirit is directly
created by God
Nu 16:22 *See also* Isa 42:5; Zec 12:1;
Heb 12:9 *"human fathers" is literally
"fathers of our flesh (bodies)", i.e., there is
an antithesis between those who are the
fathers of people's bodies and God, who is
the Father of their spirits. Thus bodies are
derived from parents but souls from God.*

The human spirit was affected by
the fall
Jer 17:9 *See also* Ge 6:5; Ps 64:6; 78:37;
Mt 15:19 pp Mk 7:21; Eze 18:31

The human spirit is renewed by
the Holy Spirit at regeneration
Eze 36:26–27 *See also* Ps 51:10;
Jer 31:33; Eze 11:19; Jn 3:6; Ro 8:10;
Gal 5:22–23

The regenerated human spirit
beyond death
It is perfected in heaven Heb 12:22–23
See also 2Co 5:8

It is incomplete without a resurrection
body Ro 8:23 *See also* 2Co 5:1–4

See also

3233 Holy Spirit &	6154 fall, the
sanctification	6626 conversion
4018 life, spiritual	6644 eternal life
4195 spirits	6728 regeneration
5135 blindness,	8320 perfection
spiritual	9410 heaven
6020 sin	
6139 deadness,	
spiritual	

5067

suicide

The deliberate taking of one's own
life, a rare occurrence in Scripture.

Psychological causes of suicide
A sense of guilt leads to suicide
Mt 27:5 *See also* Ac 1:18–19

Defeat leads to suicide 1Sa 31:4 *See
also* 1Sa 31:5–6 pp 1Ch 10:4–5; 2Sa 1:9;
17:23; 1Ki 16:18

Defiance leads to suicide
Jdg 16:26–30; 2Sa 17:23

Failure leads to attempted suicide
Ac 16:27

Desire for death is more
frequently expressed in the Bible
than actual suicide
The desire for death in a prophet's
depression 1Ki 19:3–4 *See also*
Jer 15:10; 20:14–18; Jnh 4:1–3 *A desire
for death does not lead to taking of one's
own life, but to entrusting the place and
time of one's death to the Lord.*

The desire for death arising from grief
and pain Job 10:1 *See also* Job 3:1–4;
7:15–16

The desire for death because of
judgment Rev 9:6 *See also* Hos 10:8;
Rev 6:16

Life hated because of its
apparent futility
Ecc 2:17 *See also* Ps 90:8–10; Ecc 4:1–3

Suicide usurps God's sovereignty
over life
God is Creator, and thus has authority
over his creation Job 10:12 *See also*
Ge 2:7,17; Ps 90:1–10; 139:13–15

God controls life and death Job 1:21 *See
also* Ex 23:25–26; Dt 32:39; Job 30:23;
Ecc 8:8; Lk 12:22–25; Heb 9:27

Taking life, including one's own,
is sin
Ex 20:13

God's command that believers love themselves is violated by suicide
Lev 19:18; Mt 22:39; Eph 5:29

God's command that believers should love others is violated by suicide
Mt 7:12 *Relatives and friends are hurt when a loved one commits suicide.*

See also
5040 murder	6172 guilt
5331 hanging	9020 death
5831 depression	

5070

Individuals in OT and NT

5071

Aaron

The elder brother of Moses and Miriam. He served as a spokesman for his brother in the confrontation with Pharaoh, which eventually led to the exodus from Egypt. He was later consecrated as high priest.

5072
Aaron, spokesman for Moses

He was called by God to speak for his brother Moses in the confrontation with Pharaoh and to lead the Israelites out of Egypt. Negligence of the LORD's express command cost him the privilege of entering the promised land.

Aaron's genealogy and family
Ex 6:20; Lev 10:1–3; Nu 3:1–2; 1Ch 6:3

Aaron was spokesman for Moses in Egypt
His call Ex 4:14–16

The brothers meet and confront Pharaoh Ex 5:1 *See also* Ex 4:27–28

The command to lead the Israelites out of Egypt Ex 6:13

Aaron's staff Ex 7:8–12,19–20; 8:5–6,16–17

Pharaoh's hardness of heart Ex 11:10

Subsequent events in Aaron's life
The LORD's instructions for the Passover Ex 12:43 *See also* Ex 12:1–3

The Israelites grumble against Moses and Aaron Ex 16:2–3,9

Aaron commemorates the LORD's provision of manna Ex 16:33

The meeting of Aaron and Jethro Ex 18:12

Aaron as census-taker Nu 1:3; 4:34,46

Aaron as prayer partner Ex 17:10,12

Aaron's jealousy and subsequent repentance Nu 12:1–2,5,11

Aaron makes the people a golden calf Ex 32:4 *See also* Ex 32:1–3,5; Ac 7:40

Moses rebukes him Ex 32:21–24,35; Dt 9:20

Rebellion against Moses and Aaron Nu 14:2; 16:3,11,20–22,39–48

Aaron's authority vindicated Nu 17:8
See also Nu 17:10

The LORD prevents Aaron and Moses from entering the promised land Nu 20:2,7–12

The death of Aaron
Nu 20:25–26,28–29; 33:38–39

See also
4512 staff	7257 promised land
5101 Moses	7324 calf worship
5265 complaints	8768 idolatry
7221 exodus, the	

5073
Aaron, as model priest

Aaron was made high priest and charged with the responsibility of making offerings for the sins of the people and ensuring that the LORD was worshipped in the proper manner. His priesthood was to pass to his descendants, thus ensuring its continuity.

Aaron was high priest
His call to the priesthood Nu 3:10 *See also* Ex 28:1; 1Sa 12:6; Ps 99:6; Heb 5:4

His anointing, ordination and consecration Ex 28:41; 29:7–9; Lev 8:12,14,22,27,30

His priestly garments Ex 28:2 *See also* Ex 28:4,36,42; Lev 8:7–9

The significance of the priestly garments Ex 28:9–12,30,34–35,36–38

Skilled craftsmen were employed in the making of the priestly garments Ex 31:6,10

Fellow Levites were to help Aaron in ministry Nu 18:2

Aaron's priestly privileges
In sacrificial offerings
Ex 29:27–28,32–33; Lev 2:3; 7:35–36; Nu 18:8–9,11–13

In tithes Nu 18:28; Ne 10:37

In cities allotted to his descendants Jos 21:19

Aaron's priestly responsibilities
Respect for the holiness of the LORD and his sanctuary Lev 10:3 *See also* Lev 10:1–2; 22:1–2; Nu 18:7

Keeping ritually clean Lev 21:10–12

Tending the lamps in the Tent of Meeting Ex 27:21; 30:7

Obeying the LORD's commands about sacrificial ritual and offerings Lev 6:8–9,14,24–25; 7:1,11,37; 9:22; Nu 18:8

Taking responsibility for the offences against the sanctuary and the priesthood Nu 18:1

The future of Aaron's priesthood
The LORD's requirements are to stand for all time Ex 30:8; Lev 7:36; 22:3

The priesthood continues through Aaron's descendants Nu 20:28

Aaron's priesthood compared with Melchizedek's Heb 7:11

See also
1350 covenant with Israel's priests	7376 high priest
	7390 Levites
2306 Christ, high priest	7412 priesthood
	7435 sacrifice, in OT
4681 ram	7766 priests
6616 atonement in OT	8266 holiness
	8488 tithing

5075

Abraham

The OT patriarch born in Ur and called by God to live in Canaan. God promised to make his descendants into a great nation, a promise fulfilled initially in Israel, and subsequently in the Christian church. His trust in God is seen as exemplary by NT writers.

5076
Abraham, life of

God called Abraham to live as a nomad in Canaan and promised the land to his descendants, naming him "father of many", although he had no heir until his old age.

Abraham's ancestors, marriage and descendants
The line of descent from Shem to Abraham 1Ch 1:24–27

Abraham's marriage to Sarah Ge 11:29–30

Abraham's descendants 1Ch 1:28–34

Abraham was called to live in Canaan
His migration from Ur to Canaan Ge 11:31–12:5 *See also* Jos 24:2–3; Ac 7:2–4; Heb 11:8–9

His nomadic way of life in Canaan Heb 11:9 *See also* Ge 12:6–10; 13:1–4

God gives Abraham his new name Ge 17:5 *The giving of a new name signifies a new relationship to God. "Abram" has the sense of "revered father", whereas "Abraham" means "father of many people". See also* Ge 17:15

Abraham buys a burial site for Sarah Ge 23:3–4 *This is his only acquisition of land in Canaan. See also* Ge 23:17–20; 49:29–32

Abraham's dealings with his nephew, Lot
Ge 12:4–5 *Abraham is accompanied to Canaan by Lot;* Ge 13:5–12 *Abraham and Lot separate;* Ge 14:8–16 *Abraham rescues Lot from five local kings. Abraham's intercession for Sodom saves Lot:* Ge 18:20–33; 19:29

Significant encounters in Abraham's life
With Melchizedek: Ge 14:18–20; Heb 7:1–10
Ge 18:1–22 *with three angels*

God's covenant with Abraham
God makes a covenant with Abraham Ge 15:1–21 *See also* Ac 7:5–7

God gives Abram the name Abraham, as a sign of the covenant Ge 17:1–8

God gives Abraham the gift of circumcision as a sign of the covenant Ge 17:9–27 See also Ac 7:8; Ro 4:11

Abraham's family

Abraham and Sarah were childless Ge 11:30 See also Ge 15:2–3; 17:17; 18:11–13

Abraham's pretence that Sarah is his sister Ge 12:10–20; 20:1–18

The birth of Ishmael Ge 16:1–4,15–16

The birth of Isaac Ge 21:1–7

Abraham dismisses Hagar and Ishmael Ge 21:8–14

God tests Abraham over Isaac Ge 22:1–19 See also Heb 11:17–19; Jas 2:21

Abraham's wife Sarah dies Ge 23:1–2

Abraham makes arrangements for a wife for Isaac Ge 24:1–9

Abraham marries Keturah and has children by her Ge 25:1–2 pp 1Ch 1:32

The death of Abraham Ge 25:7–11

The time span of Abraham's life

Ge 12:4 Abraham leaves Haran at the age of 75.
Ishmael is born when Abraham is 86: Ge 16:3,16
Ge 17:1 Abraham renamed and circumcised at the age of 99; Ge 21:5 Isaac born when Abraham is 100; Ge 23:1 Sarah dies when Abraham is 137. Ge 17:17 indicates that Sarah was ten years younger than Abraham; Ge 25:7 Abraham dies at the age of 175.

See also
1335 blessing	5225 barrenness
1348 covenant with Abraham	5467 promises, divine
4207 land, divine gift	5590 travel
4275 Sodom and Gomorrah	5672 concubines
5094 Jacob	6620 calling
5100 Melchizedek	8832 testing

5077
Abraham, character of

Despite some shortcomings as a husband and father, his obedience, faith, hospitality and effective intercession were exemplary. Such qualities led to his being called "friend of God".

Abraham, the friend of God

He was blessed by God Ge 14:18–19 See also Ge 21:22; 24:1,35

He worshipped God Ge 21:33 See also Ge 12:8; 13:4,18

He had faith in God Ge 15:6 See also Ro 4:18–22; Heb 6:15 Abraham's faith is seen in the length of time (25 years) that he waited for the realisation of the promise; Heb 11:8–12,17–19

He was obedient Ge 22:1–19 See also Ge 12:4; 26:5; Jas 2:20–22

He was a prophet and intercessor Ge 20:7 See also Ge 18:16–33 As a prophet, God reveals his will to Abraham; as an intercessor, Abraham brings the

revelation back to God and pleads for him to change his mind.

He was called the friend of God Jas 2:23 See also Ge 15:6; 2Ch 20:7; Isa 41:8

Abraham's weaknesses as head of his household

He was held responsible by God for his family Ge 18:19 As the following references show, Abraham did not discharge this responsibility well.

He exploited his wife in a cowardly way Ge 12:10–20; 20:1–18

He fathered Ishmael as a result of wavering faith Ge 16:1–4

He allowed Sarah to mistreat Hagar Ge 16:4–6; 21:9–14

Abraham's strengths as a member of society

He was well-respected outside his household Ge 21:22; 23:6

He sought to resolve disputes amicably Ge 13:5–12; 21:25–31

His wealth was a source of prestige Ge 24:35 See also Ge 13:2; 24:1

He was honoured for his military prowess Ge 14:13–21

He was concerned to maintain his independence from the Canaanites Ge 14:22–24 See also Ge 23:7–16; 24:1–4

He showed hospitality to strangers Ge 18:1–8

See also
5714 men	8445 hospitality
7772 prophets	8453 obedience
8122 friendship with God	8602 prayer

5078
Abraham, significance of

Whereas Jews see Abraham as the father of their nation on account of God's covenant with him, Christians see Abraham as the father of all who believe in Jesus Christ.

The significance of Abraham for nations other than Israel

Abraham was the father of many nations Ge 17:3–6 See also Ge 17:20; 25:1–4,12–18 Muslim Arabs trace their ancestry through Ishmael to Abraham.

Abraham was to be a means of blessing to many nations Ge 12:3 See also Ge 18:18; 22:17–18; Ac 3:25

The significance of Abraham for the people of Israel

Israel traces its origins back to God's call of Abraham Ge 12:1–2 See also Jos 24:2–3; Ac 7:2–3; Heb 11:8–10

God promises the land of Canaan to Abraham's descendants Ne 9:7–8 See also Ge 15:1–21; 17:1–8; Ex 6:8; Dt 9:5; Ac 7:4–5

God is subsequently known in Israel as the God of Abraham 1Ki 18:36 See also Ge 24:26–27; 26:24; 31:53; Ps 47:9; Ac 7:32; Ex 3:6

Abraham is seen as the father of the Jewish nation Jn 8:39 See also Ps 105:5–6; Isa 41:8; 51:1–2; Lk 1:54–55; Jn 8:33; Ac 13:26; Ro 11:1

God deals with Israel on the basis of his covenant with Abraham 1Ch 16:14–18 pp Ps 105:7–11 See also Ex 2:23–25; 2Ki 13:22–23; Ps 105:42–45; Lk 1:68–75

Circumcision was the sign of participation in God's covenant with Abraham Ge 17:9–14 See also Lev 12:3; Jn 7:22; Ac 15:1

The significance of Abraham for Christians

Abraham was an ancestor of Jesus Christ Mt 1:1 pp Lk 3:34

Jesus Christ attacks Jewish confidence in mere physical descent from Abraham Mt 3:9–10 pp Lk 3:8–9 See also Jn 8:33–41

Jesus Christ makes a point of identifying outcasts as children of Abraham Lk 19:7–9 See also Lk 13:10–16

God's promise to Abraham is not inherited by those who obey the law Gal 3:15–18 See also Ro 4:13–16; Gal 4:21–31

God's promise to Abraham is fulfilled in Jesus Christ, who is Abraham's seed Gal 3:16 See also Ge 12:7; 13:15; 24:7; Gal 3:19,29

Abraham is the father of those who are justified by faith Gal 3:6–9 See also Ge 15:6; Ro 4:1–25

Abraham's obedience to God shows that faith must lead to good works Jas 2:20–24

Fellowship with Abraham is a symbol of salvation

Mt 8:11–12 See also Lk 13:28–29; 16:19–26

See also
1035 God, faithfulness	7140 people of God
1245 God of the fathers	7248 patriarchs
	7258 promised land, early history
5375 law	7334 circumcision
6676 justification	7505 Jews, the
7135 Israel, people of God	7510 Gentiles
	8020 faith

5080

Adam

The Hebrew word "adam" is used both for "man" in general and also as the personal name of the first man that God created. It sounds like the word "adamah", meaning "ground".

5081
Adam, creation and life of

Adam is portrayed as the height of God's creation, made in the image and likeness of God, and entrusted with the stewardship of creation.

The creation of Adam

As a unique event Ge 2:7

In the image of God Ge 1:26–27 *See also* Ge 5:1; 1Co 11:7; Jas 3:9

His commission from God Ge 1:28; 2:15 *See also* Ge 1:26; Ps 8:4–8; 115:14–16

His incompleteness without Eve Ge 2:18–24 *See also* Ge 1:27; 5:1–2; Mt 19:4–6 pp Mk 10:6–9

His position and privileges Ge 1:28–29; 2:19–20

The limitations of his freedom Ge 2:16–17 *See also* Ge 3:1–3

The fall of Adam
The nature of his sin Ge 3:6 *See also* Ge 2:16–17; 3:12,17; Hos 6:7

Immediate results of his sin Ge 3:7–10

God's curse upon Adam and the earth Ge 3:17–19 *See also* Ge 5:29; Job 7:1; 10:9; Ps 90:3; Ecc 2:17–23; 3:20; Ro 8:20

The life of Adam after the fall
His expulsion from the garden Ge 3:21–24

His children Ge 4:1–2 *See also* Ge 4:25; 5:3–4; 1Ch 1:1

His lifespan and death Ge 5:5

See also

1325 God, the Creator	5093 Eve
4050 dust	5628 work
4241 Garden of Eden	5714 men
5002 human race & creation	6112 banishment
5023 image of God	6154 fall, the
5033 knowledge of good & evil	8718 disobedience

5082
Adam, significance of

Throughout the NT, Adam is seen as a real historical figure, from whom all humanity is descended and by whose sin all humanity is affected.

Adam as the original member of the human race
Ac 17:26; 1Co 15:45–49 *See also* Ge 2:7; Lk 3:23–38 *The genealogy of Jesus Christ is traced back to Adam.*

Adam's relationship with Eve
Adam as one flesh with Eve Mt 19:3–6 pp Mk 10:2–9 *See also* Ge 2:24; 1Co 6:16; Eph 5:31

Adam as the head of Eve
1Co 11:3,8–12; 1Ti 2:12–15

The reality and results of Adam's sin
Sin spread to all the human race Ro 5:19 *See also* Ge 4:3–16; Ps 51:5; Pr 20:9; Ro 3:23

Death was introduced into the world Ro 5:12 *See also* Ro 5:14–17; 6:23; 1Co 15:21–22

Condemnation for the human race resulted Ro 5:16,18

See also

5004 human race & sin	5708 marriage
5215 authority	5959 submission
5556 stewardship	6023 sin, universality
5700 headship	

5083
Adam, and Jesus Christ

Paul presents Jesus Christ as both the last Adam, succeeding where the first Adam failed, and the second man, standing at the head of a new humanity.

The contrast between the first and second Adam
Ro 5:14 *By his sin Adam brought universal misery on humanity. In this he is the foreshadower and prototype of Jesus Christ, who through his righteous act brings the universal hope of redemption.*

The contrast in nature of the first Adam and the second Adam
Adam was a living being; Jesus Christ is a life-giving being 1Co 15:45

Adam was natural, Jesus Christ is spiritual 1Co 15:46

Adam was earthly, Jesus Christ is heavenly 1Co 15:47

The contrast in the consequences of the actions of the first Adam and the second Adam
Adam brought death, Jesus Christ brings life Ro 5:15,17; 1Co 15:21–23

Adam brought judgment, Jesus Christ brings justification Ro 5:16,18–19

The assurance this doctrine brings 1Co 15:48–49 *See also* Php 3:20–21

See also

1680 types	6676 justification
4015 life	9020 death
5110 Paul, teaching of	9310 resurrection
6124 condemnation	9410 heaven

5085
David

The youngest son of Jesse and great-grandson of Ruth and Boaz, who became Israel's greatest king. Born in the town of Bethlehem, he probably lived c. 1040–970 B.C.

5086
David, rise of

David rose from humble origins to become Israel's greatest king. His rise to power is seen by OT writers as evidence of God's guiding hand upon both David and Israel.

David was the great-grandson of Ruth and Boaz
Ru 4:13–22

David was anointed king by Samuel
1Sa 16:1–13

David was a member of Saul's court
1Sa 16:17–23 *See also* 1Sa 18:2,5

David's defeat of Goliath
1Sa 17:50–51 *See also* 1Sa 17:4–11,17–26,32–54

David's friendship with Jonathan
1Sa 18:1 *See also* 1Sa 19:1–7; 20:1–42; 23:16–18; 2Sa 1:25–27

The relationship between David and Saul
Saul's jealousy of David 1Sa 18:9–12 *See also* 1Sa 18:15,28–29; 19:1,9–17; Ps 59:1–4

His flight from Saul 1Sa 23:14 *See also* 1Sa 21:10; 22:1–5; 27:1–6; Ps 52:1; 54:1–7; 56:1–2; 57:1–6

His refusal to harm Saul 1Sa 24:3–7 *See also* 1Sa 26:7–25

His reaction to Saul's death 2Sa 1:11–12 *See also* 2Sa 1:17–27

See also

5691 friends, good	8304 loyalty
7784 shepherd	8773 jealousy

5087
David, reign of

David reigned over Judah for seven and a half years and over all Israel for 33 years. He extended the kingdom to the boundaries promised by God to Joshua.

David reigned over Judah in Hebron
2Sa 2:4 *See also* 2Sa 2:8–11; 3:1,12–21

David reigned over Israel in Jerusalem
2Sa 5:3–10 pp 1Ch 11:1–9

David extended the boundaries of the kingdom
2Sa 8:6 *See also* 2Sa 5:17–25 pp 1Ch 14:8–17; 2Sa 8:1–14 pp 1Ch 18:1–13; 2Sa 10:1–19

David's kingship
He ruled justly 2Sa 8:15 *See also* 2Sa 9:1–11; 23:3–4

His problems with his children 2Sa 13:1–21

Absalom's conspiracy 2Sa 15:10 *See also* 2Sa 15:13–18; 18:1–17,28–33; 19:4–8; Ps 3:1–8

David's mightiest warriors were called "the Thirty" 2Sa 23:13–17 pp 1Ch 11:15–19 *See also* 2Sa 23:24–39 pp 1Ch 11:26–47; 2Sa 23:20–23 pp 1Ch 11:23–25; 1Ch 12:4,16–18; 27:5–6

The struggle against the northern supporters of Saul 2Sa 3:1

The revolt led by Sheba 2Sa 20:1–22

The census of Israel and Judah 2Sa 24:1–17

Solomon succeeds David despite the claims of Adonijah
1Ki 1:5–53

The death of David
1Ki 2:10–12 pp 1Ch 29:26–28 *See also* 2Sa 23:1–7; 1Ki 2:1–9

5088
David, character of

David, although not perfect, is portrayed as a man and a king after God's own heart.

David's appearance and attributes
1Sa 16:18 *See also* 1Sa 16:12

David's characteristics
His dependence upon God 1Sa 13:14 *See also* 1Sa 23:2,4,9–13; Ps 23:1–6; 34:1–7; 54:1–4; 62:1–2; 142:1–7

His trust in God 1Sa 17:34–37 *See also* 1Sa 17:40–51

His loyalty to others 1Sa 20:41–42 *See also* 2Sa 9:1,6–7

His respect for those in authority 1Sa 24:1–7 *See also* 1Sa 26:1–25

His deep humanity is evident in his paternal grief 2Sa 18:32–33 *See also* 2Sa 13:38–39; 18:5; 19:1–7

David's abilities
He was a strategist and courageous commander 2Sa 8:3–6 *See also* 1Sa 17:34–47; 2Sa 5:6–10,17–25; 8:1,13–14; 1Sa 27:5–11

He was a musician and poet 2Sa 23:1 *He played the harp:* 1Sa 16:18,23; 18:10; 19:9–10
2Sa 22:1 pp Ps 18:1 Title *He sang:* 1Ch 16:7; Ps 3:1 Title; 34:1 Title; 51:1 Title; 52:1 Title; 54:1 Title; 63:1 Title

He was a wise leader 2Sa 8:15 *See also* 2Sa 7:18–29; 15:14,25–29,32–36; 16:5–12; 19:18–29; 21:1–9

His military activities prevented him from building the temple 1Ki 5:3; 1Ch 22:7–8

David's sin and repentance
His adultery with Bathsheba and murder of Uriah 2Sa 11:2–4; 12:7–10 *See also* 2Sa 11:14–17,26–27

His repentance 2Sa 12:13–23; Ps 51:1–19

5089
David, significance of

David was instrumental in the establishment of Jerusalem as the centre of Israel's worship. Through David's personal rule, God exercised his own kingship over his people. David thus foreshadowed the Messiah, who would spring from his royal line.

The historical significance of David
The establishment of Jerusalem as the centre of worship 2Sa 6:1–11 pp 1Ch 13:1–14; 2Sa 6:12–15 pp 1Ch 15:25–28

Preparations for building the temple
1Ch 28:2–9 *See also* 2Sa 7:1–7 pp 1Ch 17:1–6; 1Ki 8:17–19 pp 2Ch 6:7–9; 1Ch 22:1–19; 23:4–5; 25:1; 26:12; 29:1–5

The spiritual significance of David
The son of God and chosen king Ps 2:6–7

An eternal priest Ps 110:4

A sign of God's final victory Ps 2:8–11; 110:1–3

God's covenant with David
2Sa 7:11–16 pp 1Ch 17:10–14 *See also* 1Ki 11:11–13; 2Ki 8:19 pp 2Ch 21:7; Ps 89:1–37; 132:12; Isa 55:3; Jer 33:17; Eze 37:21–28; Ac 13:22–23,32–37

David as a type of Jesus Christ
Jesus Christ as the Son of David Jer 23:5; Eze 34:23–24 *See also* Isa 16:5; Mt 1:1; 12:23; 15:22; 20:30 pp Mk 10:46–47 pp Lk 18:35–38; Jn 7:41–42; Rev 22:16

Jesus Christ's kingship is linked with David's kingship
Lk 1:32–33 *See also* Isa 9:7; 16:5; Jer 23:5–6; Mt 22:41–46 pp Mk 12:35–37 pp Lk 20:41–44; Ps 110:1

5091
Deborah

An outstanding leader in Israel when the nation faced a crisis of resurgent Canaanite power in the time of the judges. Her name means "bee".

Deborah's calling
As a judge Jdg 4:4–5; 5:7 *She was probably called upon to settle intertribal disputes, "mother in Israel" meaning one who promotes the unity of God's family.*

As a prophetess Jdg 4:4,7,9,14

Deborah's response to the Canaanite threat
She was petitioned by the people Jdg 5:11–12

She appointed Barak commander-in-chief Jdg 4:6

She accompanied the army into battle Jdg 4:8–10

She led the people in victory celebration Jdg 5:1–3,28–31 *In this*

respect she is like Moses and Miriam (Ex 15:1,20).

Deborah's character
She was wise, decisive, courageous, inspiring and bold Jdg 4:5–9,14; 5:9,15–17 *Her confidence was in God's word and promise and she did not shrink from rebuking God's people.*

She gave credit to others Jdg 5:14–15,18–19,24–27

She gave glory to God Jdg 5:20–23 *These verses are a poetic acknowledgment that God has fought on Israel's behalf.*

She was God's person for the hour
Jdg 5:31 *See also* Est 4:14

5092
Elijah

Living in Israel, his ministry as a prophet was to oppose the worship of Baal in Israel, and the sin, injustices and idolatry of Ahab, Jezebel and Ahaziah. He came, probably, from Tishbe in Gilead, but his parentage is not certain. His name means "the LORD is God".

Elijah's special standing as a prophet
His prophecies and prayers were fulfilled and attested by miracles *Drought prophesied and experienced:* 1Ki 17:1,7; 18:1–6; Jas 5:17 1Ki 17:14 *provision of flour and oil prophesied Rain prophesied:* 1Ki 18:41,44–45 1Ki 17:17–24 *The widow's son is restored to life. Fire falls from heaven at Elijah's prayer:* 1Ki 18:36–38; 2Ki 1:10,12 *The death of Ahab and Jezebel, and of Ahab's line prophesied and fulfilled:* 1Ki 21:20–24; 22:37–38; 2Ki 9:30–37

The word of the LORD came to him 1Ki 19:9–18 *See also* 1Ki 17:8; 18:1; 21:17,23,28; 22:38

Elijah's ministry to Israel
He confronts Ahab, king of Israel 1Ki 18:16–18 *See also* 1Ki 21:20–22

He challenges the people of Israel 1Ki 18:21

He challenges Baal and his prophets 1Ki 18:20–29,36–38

The prophets of Baal are sentenced to death and executed 1Ki 18:40

Elijah calls down fire on Ahaziah's messengers 2Ki 1:1–14

He predicts Ahaziah's death 2Ki 1:16–17

He appoints successors to continue the fight against Baal worshippers 1Ki 19:15–17 *See also* 1Ki 19:19–21 *Elisha is called;* 2Ki 8:13–15; 9:1–13 *Jehu is anointed by one of Elisha's assistants.*

5093

He does not die, but is taken up to heaven
2Ki 2:11–12

Elijah's lifestyle and character
It was one of simplicity 1Ki 17:2–6; 19:4–5; 2Ki 1:8

He was a man of action and physical endurance 1Ki 17:1,3,9

Parallels between Elijah and Moses
2Ki 2:8 *See also* Ex 14:21–22; Jos 3:14–17; 2Ki 2:14

Elijah's return is awaited by Israel
Some Jews believed John the Baptist was Elijah returned Lk 1:17 *See also* Mal 4:5–6
Jesus Christ recognises John as Elijah: Mt 11:14; 17:9–13 pp Mk 9:9–13
Jn 1:21 *John the Baptist denies being Elijah.*
Similarities of lifestyle and dress between Elijah and John: 2Ki 1:8; Mt 3:4
pp Mk 1:6

Elijah appears at the transfiguration of Jesus Christ
Mt 17:1–8 pp Mk 9:2–8

See also
1431 prophecy, OT methods	5582 tiredness
2580 Christ, transfiguration	5831 depression
	7312 Baal
4815 drought	7773 prophets, role
5098 John the Baptist	7775 prophets, lives
5101 Moses	8752 false worship
	8768 idolatry

5093

Eve

The wife of Adam and the first woman created. Her significance lies in being the first to be deceived and become disobedient to God. She is only given her name (which resembles the word for "living") by Adam after the expulsion from Eden.

Eve was created in the image of God
Ge 1:27

Eve was a companion for Adam in Eden
Ge 2:18

Eve was deceived
Ge 3:1–7 *See also* Ge 3:13; 2Co 11:3; 1Ti 2:13–14

Events in Eve's life
Her creation Ge 1:26–27; 2:21–23

Her shame Ge 3:8–13

The curse upon her Ge 3:16

Adam names her Ge 3:20

The LORD clothes her Ge 3:21

She becomes a mother Ge 4:1–2

See also
1325 God, the Creator	5081 Adam, life of
4123 Satan, deceiver	5663 childbirth
4241 Garden of Eden	5718 mothers
5002 human race & creation	5744 wife
	5745 women
5023 image of God	6154 fall, the
	8718 disobedience

5094

Jacob

The grandson of Abraham, and one of the two twin sons of Isaac. As the firstborn son of Isaac, Esau was entitled to inherit all of Isaac's property. However, he sold this to his brother Jacob to satisfy his immediate physical hunger. Through subsequent deception, Jacob was able to gain Isaac's blessing, and inherit all that was rightly Esau's. Despite such major faults, Scripture regards Jacob as further confirmation of God's promises to Abraham, and a model of faith and obedience.

5095

Jacob, life and character of

The grandson of Abraham and son of Isaac, who was chosen by God, despite his personal faults and shortcomings, to be the recipient of the promises made to Abraham. His name means "he grasps the heel", an allusion to the circumstances of his birth (Ge 25:25–26).

Jacob's birth
Ge 25:21–26

Jacob obtains the rights of the firstborn son
Ge 27:36 *See also* Ge 25:29–34; 27:1–29; Heb 12:16–17

Jacob inherits the promises made to Abraham
Ge 28:10–15 *See also* Ge 12:1–3; 15:5; 27:29; 28:3–4; 35:11–13

Jacob flees to Haran
As the result of Esau's enmity
Ge 27:41–45 *See also* Ge 28:5

He encounters God at Bethel
Ge 28:10–22 *The encounter with God at Bethel confirms that Jacob has received the promise made to Abraham, and that Jacob has accepted his role as bearer of that promise to future generations.*

He marries Leah and Rachel Ge 28:1–2
See also Ge 29:16–30 *Jacob is deceived by Laban into marrying Leah before Rachel.*

He accumulates wealth Ge 30:29–43
See also Ge 31:4–9,14–16,36–42

Jacob returns to Canaan
His flight from Haran Ge 31:1–3 *See also* Ge 31:10–13,17–24,44–55

His encounter with God Ge 32:24–30
The change of his name from "Jacob"

(meaning "he grasps the heel", figuratively, "he deceives") to "Israel" (meaning "he struggles with God") confirms Jacob as the recipient of the Abrahamic blessings. See also Ge 35:1–5,9–15

His reunion with Esau Ge 33:1–17

Jacob's children
His twelve sons Ge 35:22–26 *See also* Ge 29:32–35; 30:3–13; 35:16–18

The rape of his daughter Ge 34:1–2 *See also* Ge 34:5,7,13–31

His favouritism towards Joseph and Benjamin Ge 37:3–4 *See also* Ge 37:31–35; 42:1–4; 44:20,22,27–31

His reunion with Joseph Ge 46:29–30
See also Ge 45:27–28; 46:1–4; 47:11

Jacob blesses his descendants
Heb 11:21 *See also* Ge 48:15–20; 49:1–28

Jacob's death and burial
Ge 47:28–30 *See also* Ge 49:29–33; 50:2–3,12–13

See also
1335 blessing	6145 deceit
1409 dream	7266 tribes of Israel
1469 visions	8753 favouritism
5075 Abraham	8773 jealousy
5948 shrewdness	

5096

Jacob, the patriarch

God's covenant promises to Abraham were inherited by Jacob, through his father Isaac, and so it was through his line of descent that the promised Messiah was to come.

Jacob was one of the three patriarchs
Ex 3:6 *See also* Nu 32:11; Dt 1:8; Mt 8:11; 22:32; Ac 3:13

Jacob received the Abrahamic promises
God's promise to Abraham Ge 12:1–3

Jacob chosen in preference to Esau
Ro 9:11–13 *See also* Ge 25:23; Mal 1:2

The promises given to Jacob and his descendants Ge 28:3–4 *See also* Ge 28:13–15; 35:11–12; Lev 26:42; 1Ch 16:17 pp Ps 105:10; Heb 11:9

Jacob's descendants
He fathered the twelve tribes Ex 1:1–5 *See also* 1Ki 18:31; 1Ch 2:1–2

He was the father of the nation
Ps 22:23 *See also* Ps 77:15; Isa 45:19

Jacob as a symbol for the nation
Jacob and Israel were linked together as equivalent terms for the nation
Ps 14:7 *See also* Nu 23:7; 24:5; 1Ch 16:13; Ps 78:5; 114:1; 135:4; Isa 9:8; 43:28

The nation is described as the house of Jacob Ex 19:3 *See also* Isa 2:6; 8:17; Jer 5:20; Am 9:8; Lk 1:33

Other descriptions of the nation
Dt 33:4; Ps 87:2; Isa 27:9; 59:20; 41:21; Jer 30:18; La 2:2; Mal 2:12; Ro 11:26

National and patriarchal references merged Ps 46:7 *See also* Ps 20:1; 24:6; 75:9; 94:7; 99:4; Jer 10:16

5098

John the Baptist

The forerunner of Jesus Christ, born to elderly parents of the Aaronic line. His public ministry began in the Judean wilderness with a call to repentance and baptism. His ministry is seen as a fulfilment of OT prophecy, in preparation for the ministry of Jesus Christ. He was executed by Herod.

John's birth and early years
His birth and naming Lk 1:57–60 *See also* Lk 1:5–13,61–66

Prophetic words over his life Lk 1:14–17 *See also* Lk 1:76–79

He was related to Jesus Christ Lk 1:36

His early years Lk 1:80

John's ministry
His simple lifestyle Mt 3:4 pp Mk 1:6; Mt 11:18 pp Lk 7:33; Lk 7:24–25

His call for repentance Lk 3:3 pp Mt 3:1 pp Mk 1:4

He fulfilled Isaiah's prophecy Mt 3:3 pp Mk 1:2–3 pp Lk 3:4–6 *Just as roads were improved in the ancient world in preparation for the visit of a king, so John calls for people to prepare spiritually and morally for the imminent coming of the Messiah. See also* Isa 40:3; Jn 1:23

His practice of baptism Mk 1:4–5 pp Mt 3:5–6 *See also* Jn 3:23; 10:40

His challenge to established religion Mt 3:7–10 pp Lk 3:7–9 *See also* Lk 3:10–14

The contrast of his own baptism with that which the Messiah would bring Lk 3:15–17 pp Mt 3:11–12 pp Mk 1:7–8

His testimony to Jesus Christ Jn 1:15 *See also* Jn 1:6–8,21–27; 10:41

He recognises that his own ministry must decrease, while that of Jesus Christ will increase Jn 3:27–30

John's baptising of Jesus Christ
Mt 3:13–15 pp Mk 1:9 pp Lk 3:21 *John's reluctance to baptise Jesus Christ lay in his recognition of who Jesus was and the apparent inappropriateness of such a baptism;* Jn 1:29–34

John and his disciples
John had disciples Jn 1:35–37; 3:25; 4:1

He taught them to pray Lk 11:1

His disciples become envious of Jesus Christ Jn 3:25–26

He sends his disciples to question Jesus Christ Mt 11:2–6 pp Lk 7:18–23

Locked up in prison, John needed reassurance that his expectations about Jesus Christ had been well-founded.

John's disciples and the first Christians Ac 18:24–19:7

John's imprisonment and death
His confrontation with Herod leads to his imprisonment Lk 3:19–20 *See also* Mt 14:3–5 pp Mk 6:17–20

His execution Mt 14:6–12 pp Mk 6:21–29

Some thought Jesus Christ to be John risen from the dead
Mk 8:27–28 pp Mt 16:13–14 *See also* Mt 14:1–2 pp Mk 6:14–16 pp Lk 9:7–9

Jesus Christ's estimation of John
Jesus Christ honours him Mt 11:11 pp Lk 7:28

Jesus Christ sees him as marking the end of the old covenant and the arrival of the kingdom Lk 16:16 *See also* Mt 11:12–13

Jesus Christ sees him as the promised Elijah Mt 11:14 *On the basis of Malachi's prophecy (Mal 4:5), it was widely accepted that Elijah must come before the Messiah could appear. This identification would have been reinforced by John dressing like Elijah (see 2Ki 1:8). See also* Mt 11:10; Mal 3:1; Mt 17:11–13 pp Mk 9:11–13

See also
1427 prophecy   4230 desert
2510 Christ, baptism   5092 Elijah
       of   5225 barrenness
3242 Holy Spirit,   7772 prophets
       baptism with   7903 baptism

5099

Mary, mother of Jesus Christ

Mary, the mother of Jesus Christ, provides Christians with an example of obedience to God and trust in Christ. She shared in the sufferings of her son, and took her place alongside the other disciples.

Mary's background
She was from Nazareth Lk 1:26; 2:39,51

She was related to Elizabeth, a descendant of Aaron Lk 1:5,36

Possibly descended from David Lk 1:32

She was betrothed to Joseph Lk 1:27

She was a virgin Lk 1:34 *The Greek word translated "virgin" means "young", "unmarried" and implies virginity. Betrothal might take place as early as 12 years old and lasted usually for a year, being as binding as a marriage contract, though without sexual relations. See also* Isa 7:14; Mt 1:23

The events in Mary's life leading up to the birth of Jesus Christ
The annunciation Lk 1:30–31

Mary's response of submission and obedience Lk 1:38

The Magnificat expresses Mary's wonder and joy Lk 1:46–55

Elizabeth's response to Mary Lk 1:42–45

Mary, the mother
The birth of Jesus Christ Lk 2:4–16

Her memories Lk 2:51

Jesus Christ's circumcision and presentation Lk 2:21–24 *Joseph and Mary were poor and they could not afford to offer a lamb (see Lev 12:8).*

The flight to Egypt Mt 2:14

Her other children Mt 13:55–56 pp Mk 6:3

Her anxieties Lk 2:48

Her doubts about Jesus Christ Mk 3:20–21,31

She could not dominate Jesus Christ Mk 3:34–35 pp Mt 12:48–50 pp Lk 8:19–21; Jn 2:4

Mary, the disciple
Mary acknowledges Jesus Christ's authority Jn 2:5 *At the wedding at Cana.*

Mary at the cross Jn 19:25 *Many Christians see this as the poignant fulfilment of Simeon's prophecy in Lk 2:35.*

Mary in Jesus Christ's family Jn 19:26–27

Mary praying with other disciples Ac 1:14

See also
2515 Christ, birth of   2595 incarnation
2520 Christ,   5740 virgin
       childhood   7334 circumcision
2525 Christ, cross of
2535 Christ, family of

5100

Melchizedek

"King of Righteousness": king and priest of Salem, who blessed Abraham. David assumed Melchizedek's role as king and priest of Jerusalem for himself and his descendants. Jesus Christ succeeded to this role and became a high priest in the order of Melchizedek.

Melchizedek was both king and priest
As a king, Melchizedek entertained Abraham Ge 14:18 *See also* Heb 7:1

As a priest, Melchizedek blessed Abraham Ge 14:18–19

Abraham acknowledged Melchizedek as a priest of the LORD Ge 14:20,22 *Melchizedek here points ahead to Jesus Christ, who is also priest and king.*

The status of Melchizedek
David appropriates Melchizedek's office and authority for himself and his descendants Ps 110:1–2,4 *The word "order" here means "in succession to", meaning that Christ assumes the status and function of Melchizedek.*

The Davidic Messiah (Christ) inherits the office of Melchizedek Mt 22:41–44 pp Mk 12:35–37 pp Lk 20:41–44 *Jesus Christ was at that time being acclaimed as the "Son of David" and by implication here claims to be the Messiah. See also*

Mt 20:30 pp Mk 10:47 pp Lk 18:35–39;
Mt 21:9 pp Mk 11:10; Mt 21:15; Ac 2:34

Jesus Christ as high priest after the order of Melchizedek
Heb 5:8–10; 6:19–20 *Only the high priest could sacrifice for the sins of the nation in the inner sanctuary behind the curtain.*

The characteristics of the order of Melchizedek
Heb 7:2–3 *Melchizedek's order of priesthood was one of kingship, peace and righteousness; it did not depend on genealogical descent (unlike the Levitical priesthood); it is eternal, without known beginning or end. See also* Ps 110:4; Heb 5:6; 6:20; 7:21

The uniqueness of Jesus Christ's high priesthood in the order of Melchizedek
Heb 7:6–7 *Melchizedek was superior to Abraham and therefore to the Levitical priesthood descended from Abraham;* Ps 110:4 *The priesthood is secured by God's oath. See also* Heb 6:17–20; 7:16,20–22,26–27; 8:1–2

Jesus Christ's high priesthood makes the Levitical priesthood obsolete
Heb 8:13 *See also* Heb 7:11,18–19; 8:7–13

See also

1205	God, titles of
2206	Jesus, the Christ
2215	Christ, Son of David
2306	Christ, high priest
5075	Abraham
5085	David
5368	kingship
7376	high priest
7412	priesthood
7766	priests
8445	hospitality
8488	tithing

5101

Moses

One of the most important figures in the OT. Moses was called by God to lead Israel out of captivity in Egypt through the Sinai wilderness to the brink of the promised land. He was the mediator of the old covenant, and in several major respects anticipates the person of Jesus Christ.

5102
Moses, life of

The life of Moses sets the scene for the great events of the exodus from Egypt, and the showing forth of the power of the LORD, culminating in the giving of the covenant at Sinai and the preparations for entry into the promised land.

The meaning of the name Moses
Ex 2:10

Moses' birth and early life
Ex 2:1–3,5–6; Ac 7:20–22

Moses kills an Egyptian
Ex 2:11–15; Ac 7:23–29

The calling of Moses
God reveals himself to Moses at the burning bush Ex 3:1–5

He is called to deliver his people Ex 3:10 *See also* Ex 3:7–9

Moses learns the divine name Ex 3:14

Moses protests his inadequacy Ex 3:11 *See also* Ex 3:13; 4:1,10–13,16 *Moses is given Aaron as spokesman.*

Moses' confrontation with Pharaoh
Moses and Aaron speak to Pharaoh Ex 7:6–7

Pharaoh's disobedience leads to the plagues Ex 7:1–5

The death of the firstborn in Egypt Ex 11:4–9

The institution of the Passover Ex 12:26–27

Moses leads Israel in the exodus from Egypt
The crossing of the Red Sea Ex 14:29 *See also* Ex 14:26–28; Jos 2:10; 4:23; Heb 11:29

Thanksgiving for deliverance from Egypt Ex 15:1

The establishment of the covenant with Moses
Moses is given the Ten Commandments Ex 31:18

He smashes the tablets because of the people's idolatry Ex 32:19; Dt 9:16–17

He puts the new stone tablets in the ark Dt 10:3–5

Moses leads Israel in the wilderness
He asks to see the glory of the LORD Ex 33:18,22–23; Lk 9:30–32

The LORD promises his presence on the journey Ex 33:14

The construction of the tabernacle Ex 39:32; Heb 8:5

Moses inaugurates the Aaronic priesthood Lev 8:30; Nu 6:22–27

Moses on the brink of the promised land
He takes a census before the entry into Canaan Nu 1:2

He sends spies ahead Nu 13:1–3

He is vindicated against the grumblers Nu 16:28–32; 21:4–9

He is prohibited from entering the promised land Nu 20:12 *See also* Dt 3:23–26; 34:4

Joshua succeeds Moses
Nu 27:18,22

The death of Moses
Dt 34:4–5 *See also* Dt 34:6; Jude 9

See also

1349	covenant at Sinai
1406	burning bush
1630	Book of the Covenant
1640	Book of the Law
4269	Sinai, Mount
5072	Aaron, spokesman
5377	law, Ten Commandments
7222	exodus, events of
7258	promised land, early history
7412	priesthood
8768	idolatry

5103
Moses, significance of

Moses performed a number of major roles in the history of Israel. Many of these roles later found their perfection in Jesus Christ.

The roles of Moses
As teacher Ex 18:20; Mt 23:10; Jn 1:38

As intercessor Ex 17:11; 32:11; Nu 12:13; 21:7; Ps 106:23; Jn 17:9; Heb 7:25

As servant of the LORD Jos 1:1–2; 2Ch 24:6; Ac 3:13; Heb 3:5; Rev 15:3

As prophet Nu 12:6–8; Dt 18:15; 34:10; Ac 3:22

As deliverer Ex 3:10; Ac 7:35; Gal 5:1

As judge Ex 18:13

As writer Ex 24:4; Dt 31:9; Lk 24:27; Jn 1:45; 5:46

As shepherd Ex 3:1; Ps 77:20; Jn 10:11

As the friend of God Ex 33:11 *See also* Ex 33:17; Mt 17:5; Jn 5:20

As the mediator of the law and the covenant Ex 19:5–6; Dt 6:1–3; 31:9; Jos 23:6; 2Ki 18:12; Gal 3:19; Heb 9:15; 12:24

Characteristics of Moses
He was a man of faith Ex 14:13–14; Heb 11:24–28

He was not eloquent Ex 4:10

He understood that the law meant life Dt 32:46–47 *See also* Mt 5:17–19; 19:17; Ac 7:38

He was passionate in his defence of the LORD's holiness Ex 32:19; Nu 16:30; Lk 19:45–46

He worked miracles that brought glory to God Ex 14:15–18; Jn 2:11

Institutions established by Moses
He fathers, and is identified with, the Judaic legal system Jos 1:7–8; 1Ki 2:3; Ezr 3:2; Ne 13:1; Jn 5:45; 7:23; 1Co 9:9

He inaugurates the ritual slaughter of the Passover lamb Ex 12:21 *See also* Jn 1:29

He sprinkles the people with the blood of the covenant Ex 24:8; Lev 17:11; Mt 26:28; Heb 9:13–14; 11:28

He orders the atonement sacrifice Nu 16:46; Ro 3:25

Moses enters the glory of the LORD
Ex 24:17–18; 34:29; Mt 17:2; 2Co 3:7; Rev 15:3–4

Moses present at the transfiguration
Mk 9:4 pp Mt 17:3 pp Lk 9:30

Jesus Christ is superior to Moses
Heb 3:3,5–6

5104
Moses, foreshadower of Jesus Christ

Moses foreshadows Jesus Christ in his role as a lawgiver, as a mediator between God and his people and as a prophet who declared the will of God. In these matters, Jesus Christ brought to perfection the work begun through Moses.

Parallels between the infancies of Moses and Jesus Christ
Their births Ac 7:20 See also Lk 2:11

Moses' mother hid him to escape the slaughter decreed by Pharaoh Ex 1:22; 2:2

Herod's attempt to slaughter Jesus Christ Mt 2:12,16

Moses, the Israelite exile in Egypt and Midian Ex 2:11,15,22; Dt 34:4

Joseph takes Jesus Christ to Egypt for safety Mt 2:13; 8:20 Moses, like Jesus Christ, had no settled home in his own country.

Supernatural signs confirmed the callings both of Moses and Jesus Christ
Ex 4:5–9; Mt 3:17

Parallels between Moses and Jesus Christ
As mediators of covenants Heb 9:15 See also Ex 19:3–9; Jn 1:17; Heb 8:6–7

As those intimate with God Ex 33:11; Jn 5:20 See also Dt 34:10; Mt 17:3–5; Jn 14:9–11

As prophets Dt 34:10; Ac 3:22; Jn 6:14 See also Dt 18:15–18; Lk 24:19; Jn 4:19; Ac 7:37

As priests Heb 9:11–12 See also Heb 10:11–12

As those who reveal the glory of God Ex 34:33–35; 2Co 3:18 See also Jn 1:17

Moses as servant; Jesus Christ as Son Heb 3:1–6

5106
Noah

A figure of major importance in the early chapters of Genesis, with whom God established a covenant,

---

the sign of which was the rainbow. The life of Noah (whose name means "rest" or "comfort") demonstrates God's ability to save the righteous and destroy the ungodly.

Noah's righteousness
Noah walked with God Ge 6:8–9 See also Eze 14:14,20

Noah enjoyed God's protection 2Pe 2:5

Noah illustrates God's restoring grace after judgment Isa 54:7–10

The history of Noah
Noah's family Ge 5:22–29; 1Ch 1:1–3

Noah built the ark at God's command Heb 11:7 See also Ge 6:11–21

Noah had three sons Ge 5:32 See also Ge 9:18–19; 1Ch 1:4 The earth was repopulated after the flood, by the descendants of Noah's sons: Ge 10:1,32

Noah saved his family and animals from the flood Ge 7:7–9 See also Ge 8:18–19; 1Pe 3:20

Noah worshipped the LORD Ge 8:20

God established a covenant with Noah, the sign of which is the rainbow Ge 8:21–22 See also Ge 9:8–9,12–17

Noah lived to a great age Ge 9:28–29

Noah's character
Noah was obedient Ge 6:22 See also Ge 8:15–19

Noah was reverent Ge 8:20

Noah was a man of the soil Ge 9:20

Noah was subject to human frailty Ge 9:21 Nakedness was seen as shameful by OT writers.

Noah blessed and cursed his sons in a prophetic way Ge 9:24–27

Jesus Christ was a direct descendant of Noah
Lk 3:23,36

The last days are likened to the time of Noah
Mt 24:37–39 pp Lk 17:26–27

5107
Paul

The "apostle to the Gentiles". Converted from Judaism by an encounter with the risen Christ, Paul planted and corresponded with churches through much of the Mediterranean. In his letters, Paul stresses the universality of the gospel, which knows no distinction between Jew and Gentile, and the effects of Christian faith upon life and conduct.

5108
Paul, life of

Paul, previously known as Saul, had been a zealous persecutor of the church, but an encounter with the risen Christ (c. A.D. 35) led to his becoming the apostle to the Gentiles, with a mission to proclaim the gospel throughout the Gentile world. He was probably martyred during the persecutions of Nero, possibly in A.D. 67.

Paul's early life
His Jewish heritage Php 3:4–5

His citizenship Ac 22:27–28

His place of birth and education Ac 22:3 See also Ac 21:39

His trade as a tentmaker Ac 18:1–3

Paul's conversion
His persecution of the church Php 3:5–6 See also Ac 7:59–8:3; 9:1–2; 22:19–20; Gal 1:13

His conversion on the road to Damascus and his apostolic calling Ac 9:1–19 pp Ac 22:3–16; 26:9–18

Paul's early Christian activity
His journey to Arabia Gal 1:15–17 Acts makes no mention of this trip, but it seems that Paul went to Arabia immediately after he met Ananias and then subsequently returned to preach in Damascus.

His return to Damascus 2Co 11:32–33 See also Ac 9:19–25

His visit to Jerusalem (c. A.D. 38) Gal 1:18 See also Ac 9:26–28

His return to his home town of Tarsus Ac 9:29–30 See also Gal 1:21 Tarsus was in Cilicia.

His stay in Antioch Ac 11:25–26

Paul's first missionary journey and his partnership with Barnabas (c. A.D. 46–48)
Ac 13:1–6,13–14,49–51; 14:1,5–7,21–28

Paul and the Council of Jerusalem (c. A.D. 49)
The similarities between Paul and Luke here suggests that both writers are referring to the same events in these passages. Some, however, prefer to equate the meeting recorded in Gal 2:1–10 with the journey to Jerusalem mentioned in Ac 11:30: Ac 15:1–6,22–35; Gal 2:1–10

Paul's second missionary journey (c. A.D. 50–52)
His disagreement with Barnabas and his new partnership with Silas Ac 15:36–41

In Asia Minor Ac 16:6–8

In Macedonia Ac 16:9–12; 17:1,10

In Greece Ac 17:15; 18:1 It was from Corinth that Paul wrote to the Thessalonians.

His return to Antioch Ac 18:18–22

5109
Paul's third missionary journey (c. A.D. 53–57)
His general purpose in making his journey Ac 18:23

At Ephesus Ac 19:1–12; 1Co 15:32; 16:8–9

His visit to Corinth
2Co 1:15–16,23–2:4; 13:2 *Most scholars believe that Paul wrote 1 Corinthians from Ephesus, and that he also visited Corinth during this period. This visit, however, proved to be such a painful experience for him that he abandoned plans for a third visit, and instead wrote the Corinthians a "tearful" letter, calling them to repent of their sinful behaviour.*

His journey to Greece Ac 20:1–6; 2Co 2:12–13 *Paul had hoped that Titus would bring him news from Corinth. They finally met in Macedonia, and Titus brought good news about the Corinthians' change of heart. Paul then wrote 2 Corinthians before visiting Corinth for a third time.*

His return to Jerusalem with the collection Ac 20:6,13–16; 21:1–8,15,17–19; Ro 15:25–26 *Paul wrote Romans at this point in his travels. There is a considerable degree of uncertainty as to precisely when Galatians, Ephesians, Philippians, Colossians and Philemon were written.*

Paul under arrest
His life threatened in Jerusalem Ac 21:27–34; 23:12–21

In Caesarea (c. A.D. 57–59) Ac 23:23–35; 24:23–27

His appeal to Caesar Ac 25:1–12

His shipwreck Ac 27:1–28:10

His visit to Rome (c. A.D. 60) Ac 28:11–16,30–31

The latter part of Paul's life
These verses from the Pastoral Epistles may indicate that Paul was ultimately released and undertook further journeys in the Eastern Mediterranean before his death: 1Ti 1:3; 2Ti 4:13,20; Tit 1:5; 3:12

See also

5109
Paul, apostle to the Gentiles
Paul saw his encounter with the risen Christ as a call to apostleship, with a special mission to proclaim the gospel to the Gentile world. Paul's complete dedication to Jesus Christ made his own personal weaknesses a vehicle for the power of God.

Paul's calling as an apostle: origins and implications
His calling began with his encounter with the risen Christ Gal 1:15–16 *See also* Ac 9:3–19 pp Ac 22:6–16; 26:12–18; 1Co 9:1

His calling involved his being sent to the unevangelised Gentile world Gal 2:9 *See also* Ac 22:21; Ro 15:18–21; 2Co 10:13–16; Eph 3:7–9

His calling put him under an obligation to preach the gospel 1Co 9:16 *See also* Ro 1:14–15; 2Co 5:11–14

Paul's commitment to his apostolic calling
He supported himself in order to present the gospel free of charge 1Th 2:6–9 *See also* 1Co 9:3–18; 2Co 12:13

He put the gospel before everything else 2Co 4:5 *See also* Ro 9:1–3; 1Co 9:19–23; Php 1:12–26

He boasted in his weaknesses 2Co 12:7–10 *See also* 2Co 4:7–10; 6:3–10; 11:21–29

He experienced God's power at work through him 2Co 12:11–12 *See also* Ac 13:6–12; 19:11–12; Ro 15:18–19; 1Co 2:4–5; 1Th 1:4–5

He had a confident attitude to death Php 3:10–11 *See also* 2Co 5:6–10; Php 1:20–24; 2Ti 4:6–8

Paul and the example of Jesus Christ
His appeal to Jesus Christ as an example to the churches 2Co 8:9 *Paul here uses the example of Jesus Christ in order to encourage the Corinthians in their giving. See also* Ro 15:1–3; Php 2:5–11

His own exemplary imitation of Jesus Christ 1Co 11:1 *See also* 1Co 4:14–17; Php 3:12–17; 4:8–9; 2Th 3:6–9

His sharing of Jesus Christ's sufferings Col 1:24 *Paul is not suggesting here that there is any deficiency in Jesus Christ's atoning sacrifice. Rather, there are some aspects of suffering which Christ could not experience because they arose only as a result of people preaching the message of the cross and suffering because of it. See also* 2Co 1:5–9; 4:7–12; Gal 6:17

Paul and the churches
His integrity in dealing with the churches 2Co 1:12 *See also* Ac 20:17–21; 2Co 2:17; 4:1–2; 1Th 2:10–12

His love for the churches Php 1:8 *See also* 2Co 11:7–11; 12:14–15; 1Th 3:12

His prayers for the churches 1Th 1:2 *See also* Ro 1:8–10; Eph 1:15–19; 2Th 1:11–12

His dependence on the prayers of the churches 1Th 5:25 *See also* Ro 15:30–32; Eph 6:19–20; Phm 22

Paul's imagery of apostleship
As Jesus Christ's ambassador 2Co 5:20; Eph 6:19–20

As a builder Ro 15:20; 1Co 3:10

As a farmer 1Co 3:5–9

As a father 1Co 4:15; 1Th 2:11–12

As a mother Gal 4:19; 1Th 2:6–7

As God's captive 1Co 4:9; 2Co 2:14–16 *Paul portrays God as a victorious Roman general, with himself as a captive, bringing up the rear of the triumphal procession.*

As Jesus Christ's slave *The word translated "servant" in these verses commonly meant "slave":* Ro 1:1; 2Co 4:5; Php 1:1; Tit 1:1

Paul's successors were to safeguard the truth of the gospel after his death
2Ti 2:1–2 *See also* 2Ti 1:13–14; 3:10–4:8

See also

5110
Paul, teaching of
Paul's understanding of the Christian life was dominated by the importance of Jesus Christ's death and resurrection, by means of which he saw God as having acted decisively to redeem the world. Paul emphasised that Jews and Gentiles alike are justified by faith, and share together in the glorious new era of the Holy Spirit, which is to be consummated at Christ's return.

The redeeming work of Jesus Christ
God's work of redemption in Jesus Christ's death and resurrection Ro 3:25 *See also* Ro 8:3–4; 2Co 5:18–19; Col 1:21–22

Jesus Christ as substitute, exchanges places with the sinner 2Co 5:21 *See also* Gal 3:13–14; 4:4–5

Jesus Christ reverses the effects of Adam's sin 1Co 15:21–22 *See also* Ro 5:12–19

The death and resurrection of Jesus Christ mark the beginning of God's new order
New life comes through the death and resurrection of Jesus Christ Gal 2:20 *See also* 2Co 5:16–17; Eph 2:4–7; Col 2:13

Jesus Christ's death and resurrection are the basis for a new moral life Ro 6:11–13 *See also* Ro 6:1–7; 2Co 5:15; Col 2:20–3:11

Those who participate in God's new order are "in Christ" 1Co 1:30 *See also* Ro 8:1–2; Eph 1:3–14 *Paul extends the scope of the phrase "in Christ" to include believers, their activity, and the salvation they have received.*

Both Jews and Gentiles are justified by faith
Paul stresses that salvation is by grace through faith alone Eph 2:8–9 *See also* Ro 3:21–26; 4:16; 5:1–2

Jewish works of the law have no role in salvation Gal 2:15–16 *See also* Ro 4:13–15; 9:30–10:4; Gal 3:6–14; Php 3:8–9

Both Jews and Gentiles are united in the one body of Christ 1Co 12:13 *See also Gal 3:26–28; Eph 2:14–18; 3:6*

The Holy Spirit
His indwelling is an integral part of Christian experience Ro 8:9 *See also* Ac 19:1–7; Gal 3:2–5 *Paul's questions suggest that he identifies receiving the Spirit with becoming a Christian.*

He equips the church with gifts 1Co 12:1–11 *See also* 1Co 14:1–33

He enables believers to relate to God as Father Gal 4:6–7 *See also* Ro 8:14–17; Eph 2:18

He guides believers into a right understanding of the law Ro 7:6 *See also* Ro 2:29; 8:3–4; 2Co 3:3,6

He overcomes believers' sinful human nature Ro 8:13 *See also* Ro 8:5–8; Gal 5:16–25; 6:8

He is the guarantee of eternal life Ro 8:11 *See also* Ro 8:23; 2Co 5:4–5; Eph 1:13–14

The return of Jesus Christ
Paul lived in the hope of the forthcoming personal return of the risen Christ Php 3:20–21 *See also* 1Co 15:22–28; 1Th 4:14–17; 2Th 1:6–10

Believers are to be raised with Christ upon his return 1Th 4:14 *See also* 1Co 15:12–23

The whole created order will be renewed at the return of Jesus Christ Ro 8:19–21 *See also* Eph 1:9–10

See also
2321 Christ as redeemer	3278 Holy Spirit, indwelling
2410 cross, the	5375 law
2565 Christ, second coming	6020 sin
3233 Holy Spirit & sanctification	6666 grace
3275 Holy Spirit in the church	6676 justification
	7110 body of Christ
	8020 faith

5112

Peter

The foremost of the disciples of Jesus Christ during his lifetime and of the apostles after the resurrection.

5113
Peter, the disciple

The son of Jonas or John, he was called Simon until Jesus Christ gave him the name Peter meaning "rock".

Peter's background and family
He lived in Capernaum Mt 8:14 pp Mk 1:29 pp Lk 4:38; Jn 1:44 *He originally came from Bethsaida.*

He was a fisherman by trade Lk 5:10

Peter as Jesus Christ's disciple
He was called by Jesus Christ Mt 4:18–20 pp Mk 1:16–20; Lk 5:10; Jn 1:40–42

He witnessed Jesus Christ perform many miracles Mt 8:14–15

pp Mk 1:30–31 pp Lk 4:38–39; Mt 17:24–27; Lk 5:4–8; Jn 21:2–6

He was chosen to be with Jesus Christ on certain occasions Mt 17:1–2 pp Mk 9:2 pp Lk 9:28–29 *at the transfiguration of Jesus Christ;* Mt 26:36–37 pp Mk 14:32–33 *in the Garden of Gethsemane;* Mk 5:37 pp Lk 8:51

He sometimes acted as spokesman for the other disciples
He asked Jesus Christ to teach them: Mt 15:15; 18:21
He confessed Jesus as Messiah and Son of God: Mt 16:15–16 pp Mk 8:29 pp Lk 9:20; Jn 6:69
Mt 17:4 pp Mk 9:5 pp Lk 9:33 *He asked Jesus Christ to prolong the transfiguration experience;* Mt 19:27 pp Mk 10:28 pp Lk 18:28; Mk 1:36–37; Lk 5:4–5; Jn 6:68

His impetuous nature interacted with his devotion to Jesus Christ
Mt 14:28–29 *He wanted to walk to Jesus Christ on the water;* Mt 16:22 pp Mk 8:32 *He tried to prevent Jesus Christ from going to his death;* Mt 26:35 pp Mk 14:31 pp Lk 22:33 pp Jn 13:37 *He vowed that he was willing to die for Jesus Christ;* Jn 13:6–8; 18:10

He was the subject of both special commendation and rebuke
Mt 16:17–19 *He was commended for his confession of faith in Jesus Christ;* Mt 16:23 pp Mk 8:33 *He was rebuked for his opposition to Jesus Christ's prediction of his suffering;* Mt 26:34 pp Mk 14:30 pp Lk 22:34 pp Jn 13:38 *He was warned that he would disown Jesus Christ;* Mt 26:40–41 pp Mk 14:37–38 *He was rebuked for falling asleep in the Garden of Gethsemane;* Jn 18:10–11; 21:20–22

Peter's denial of Jesus Christ and his reinstatement
He denied that he knew Jesus Christ Mt 26:69–74 pp Mk 14:66–71 pp Lk 22:54–60 pp Jn 18:15–18, 25–27

He repented of his denial Mt 26:75 pp Mk 14:72 pp Lk 22:61–62

The risen Christ appeared to him on his own Lk 24:33–34; 1Co 15:4–5

He was reinstated by Jesus Christ in front of other disciples Jn 21:15–17

See also
6730 reinstatement	7620 disciples
7024 church, nature of	7630 Twelve, the
	8712 denial of Christ

5114
Peter, the apostle

As a result of the coming of the Holy Spirit, Peter was transformed into a dynamic apostle and witness to Jesus Christ.

Peter's credentials as an apostle
Mt 10:2; Ac 2:37; 5:29; 1Pe 1:1; 2Pe 1:1

Peter as an apostle to the Jews Gal 2:8

Peter's leadership
Ac 1:21–22; 2:14; 3:12; 4:8; 5:29; 8:20

Peter and the Gentiles
He was the first to baptise Gentiles who had not been circumcised Ac 10:47–48

He defended this action against critics Ac 11:17; 15:7–11

He later wavered in his attitude to the Gentiles Gal 2:11–14

The miraculous power of the Holy Spirit at work in Peter
Ac 3:2–7; 5:9–10,15–16; 9:34,40; 12:1–11 *Peter himself experienced a miracle when imprisoned by Herod Agrippa.*

Peter's missionary travels
1Co 1:12 *He visited Corinth;* 1Co 9:5 *He took his wife with him;* 1Pe 1:1 *He visited northern Asia Minor;* 1Pe 5:13 *One interpretation of this verse is that Peter was writing from Rome and was using the name "Babylon" symbolically to refer to Rome.*

See also
7378 high priest, NT	7739 missionaries
7512 Gentiles, in NT	8619 prayer in church
7706 apostles	
7733 leaders	

5115
Peter, preacher and teacher

Peter preached mainly to the Jews. He taught both through his preaching and his letters.

Peter's commission
Jn 21:17

Peter quoted from the OT in his teaching
Referring to the death of Judas: Ac 1:16,20
On the day of Pentecost: Ac 2:16–20,25–28,34–35
Ac 3:22–23; 4:11
Writing to Christians in Asia Minor: 1Pe 1:15–16,24–25; 2:6–8; 3:5–6,12,14,20; 4:18; 5:5; 2Pe 2:5–9

Peter taught about Jesus Christ
About the life and miracles of Jesus Christ Ac 2:22 *See also* Ac 10:36–39; 2Pe 1:17–18

About Jesus Christ's suffering and death Ac 2:23 *See also* Ac 3:13–15; 4:10; 5:30; 10:39; 1Pe 2:22–23; 3:18

About the resurrection of Jesus Christ Ac 2:24 *See also* Ac 2:31–32; 3:15; 4:10; 5:30; 10:40–41; 1Pe 1:3,21; 3:18

About the ascension and exaltation of Jesus Christ Ac 5:31 *See also* Ac 2:33,36; 3:13; 1Pe 1:21; 3:22

About the second coming of Jesus Christ 1Pe 5:4 *See also* 1Pe 1:7,13; 4:13; 2Pe 3:10–13

Peter taught about salvation through repentance and faith in Jesus Christ
Ac 4:12 *See also* Ac 2:38; 3:19; 10:43

Peter taught that God cared for all people
Ac 10:34; 15:7–9

Peter wrote his first letter to encourage Christians
1Pe 1:1; 5:12 *See also* 1Pe 2:1 *He exhorted*

them to live holy lives; **1Pe** 2:13–14 *They must obey authority;* **1Pe** 3:16
They must endure suffering and injustice as Jesus Christ did: **1Pe** 4:12–16,19
1Pe 5:10 *God will vindicate and save his people.*

Peter wrote his second letter to strengthen Christians who were at risk from false teaching
2Pe 1:12 *See also* **2Pe** 1:16 *He reminded them of the truth of the gospel;* **2Pe** 2:3 *He warned them of the judgment awaiting false teachers;* **2Pe** 3:13 *They must keep alive their hope in the coming day of the Lord.*

See also
7754 preaching   8414 encourage-
7797 teaching   ment
                   8749 false teachers

5117

Ruth

A young Moabite widow, who, because of her selfless devotion to her mother-in-law Naomi, and to Naomi's God, gained a husband and a child, a place in Jewish history and became the great-grandmother of David and an ancestor of Jesus Christ.

Ruth faces the problems of widowhood
Ru 1:3–5 *See also* **Ru** 1:6–13

Ruth commits herself to Naomi
Ru 1:16–17 *See also* **Ru** 1:18,22; 2:11

Ruth and Boaz
Boaz allows Ruth to glean in his fields
Ru 2:8–9 *See also* **Ru** 2:14–23

Ruth asks Boaz to be her "kinsman-redeemer" **Ru** 3:9 *The kinsman-redeemer was the closest male relative who had responsibility to marry a widow within the family and thereby protect the interests of needy members of the extended family.*

Boaz negotiates with a nearer relative of Ruth's **Ru** 4:1–8

Boaz marries Ruth **Ru** 4:9–10 *See also* **Ru** 4:11–13

She has a son who is presented to Naomi **Ru** 4:13 *See also* **Ru** 4:17

Ruth is included in the genealogy of Jesus Christ
Mt 1:5–6

See also
2540 Christ,   5743 widows
    genealogy   7388 kinsman-
5086 David, rise of   redeemer
5720 mothers,
    examples

5118

Solomon

The son of David and Bathsheba, who succeeded David as king of Israel. Noted for his great wisdom, Solomon was responsible for the building of the temple of the Lord.

In his latter years, influenced by his many foreign wives, he turned to idolatry.

5119
Solomon, life of

Solomon succeeded his father David as king and secured Israel's stability through treaties with foreign powers.

Solomon's birth
1Ch 3:1–9 *See also* **2Sa** 12:24–25

Solomon's accession
Adonijah's rivalry **1Ki** 1:5 *See also* **1Ki** 1:11–14,24–25; 2:13–25

David's approval **1Ki** 1:30
pp **1Ch** 29:23 *See also* **1Ki** 1:32–35; 2:1–4

The coronation **1Ki** 1:38–40
pp **1Ch** 29:21–22 *See also* **1Ki** 2:12

Solomon's administration of Israel
1Ki 4:7 *See also* **1Ki** 4:20–25,27; 10:25–27

Solomon's building projects
The temple **2Ch** 3:1 pp **1Ki** 6:1 *See also* **1Ki** 5:5–6,10–11; 6:14,37–38; 8:63

The palace **1Ki** 7:1–3

Other building projects
1Ki 9:15–19; **2Ch** 9:20; **Ecc** 2:6
Solomon's Pools
Solomon's Colonnade: **1Ki** 7:7–8; **Jn** 10:23; **Ac** 3:11

Solomon's many wives
1Ki 11:1–5 *See also* **1Ki** 3:1

Solomon's death
1Ki 11:42–43 pp **2Ch** 9:30–31

See also
5366 king   7467 temple,
5368 kingship   Solomon's
5937 rivalry
7236 Israel, united
    kingdom

5120
Solomon, character of

Solomon was a man of outstanding gifts and abilities. Initially he was approved by God, but the latter years of his reign were marred by idolatry and apostasy.

Solomon's abilities
Wisdom **1Ki** 4:29 *See also* **1Ki** 3:7–12 pp **2Ch** 1:8–12; **1Ki** 3:16–28; 10:6–7 pp **2Ch** 9:5–6; **Mt** 12:42

Political shrewdness **1Ki** 3:1 *See also* **1Ki** 4:21; 10:13

Dealing with individuals **1Ki** 2:35 *See also* **1Ki** 2:24,27

Poetry and writing **1Ki** 4:32 *See also* **Ps** 72:1 Title; 127:1 Title; **Pr** 1:1; 10:1; 25:1

Solomon's righteousness
1Ki 8:62–63 pp **2Ch** 7:4–5 *See also* **1Ki** 3:6–15; 8:54–61,65–66

Solomon's sin
Ne 13:26 *See also* **Dt** 17:16–17; **1Ki** 10:26,28; 11:1,4,9–13

Solomon's splendour was renowned
Mt 6:29 pp **Lk** 12:27

See also
5205 alliance   8704 apostasy
5732 polygamy   8768 idolatry
8361 wisdom

5125

Parts of the body and clothing

5126

arm

Used as a symbol of strength and as a means of expressing affection and relationship. Some ornaments are worn on the arm.

Everyday uses of arms
Nu 11:12 *carrying;* **Nu** 20:11 *hitting;* **2Sa** 22:35 pp **Ps** 18:34 *archery*
Support: **2Ki** 5:18; 7:2,17
Harvesting: **Ps** 129:7; **Isa** 17:5
Isa 44:12 *craftsmanship;* **Hos** 11:3 *teaching to walk*

The arm as a symbol of human strength
Of physical strength in general
Ge 49:24; **Jdg** 15:14; 16:12; **Pr** 31:17; **Isa** 44:12

Of strength for battle **Eze** 30:24–25 *See also* **Job** 35:9

The arm as a symbol of human weakness
A broken arm expresses defeat
Jer 48:25 *See also* **Job** 38:15; **Ps** 10:15; **Eze** 30:21–22,24–25; **Zec** 11:17

Restrained arms **Jer** 40:4; **Ac** 12:7

Feeble arms need to be strengthened
Job 26:2 *See also* **Heb** 12:12

Human arms are weak compared with God's strength **Job** 40:9 *See also* **2Ch** 32:8

The arm of God as a symbol
Of the might of God **Ps** 77:15 *See also* **Ps** 89:10,13; **Isa** 63:12; **Jer** 27:5

Of the power of God to save **Nu** 11:23 *See also* **Ex** 6:6; **Dt** 9:29; 33:27; **2Ch** 6:32; **Isa** 53:1; 59:1,16

Of the eternity of God **Dt** 33:27

Of the holiness of God **Ps** 98:1; **Isa** 52:10

Arms as an expression of affection and greeting
Used to embrace in greeting **Ge** 45:14 *See also* **Ge** 29:13; 33:4; 46:29; 48:10; **Lk** 15:20; **Ac** 20:37

Used to embrace a wife or lover **SS** 2:6 *See also* **Ge** 16:5; **2Sa** 12:8; **Pr** 5:20; **SS** 8:3; **Mic** 7:5

Used to embrace the young **Mk** 10:16 *See also* **Nu** 11:12; **2Sa** 12:3;

1Ki 17:19,23; 2Ki 4:16; Isa 49:22;
La 2:12; Mk 9:36; Lk 2:28; Ac 20:10

Open arms express generosity
Pr 31:20

**Used in phrases expressing the
adoption of false gods** 1Ki 9:9
pp 2Ch 7:22

The beauty of the arm
SS 5:14

Objects worn on the arm
Ornaments Ge 24:30,47; Nu 31:50;
2Sa 1:10; Isa 3:18–19; Eze 16:11; 23:42

Identification marks Ge 38:28,30

Magic charms Eze 13:18,20

See also

1065 God, holiness of	5139 bracelet
1105 God, power of	5156 hand
1140 God, the eternal	5865 gestures
1210 God, human descriptions	5915 ornaments
	5956 strength, human
1320 God as Saviour	8358 weakness,
1670 symbols	physical

5127

back

As the part of the body used for
bearing loads it is used both literally
and metaphorically.

**The human back used for
carrying**
Jesus Christ carried his cross on his
back Jn 19:17 *See also* Mt 27:32
pp Mk 15:21 pp Lk 23:26 *The shape of the
cross necessitated it being carried across the
shoulders and back. It appears that Jesus
Christ started to carry his own cross but
Simon of Cyrene took over as Christ
weakened.*

Weapons carried on the back 1Sa 17:6

**Animals carry people and goods
on their backs**
Isa 30:6 *See also* Ex 15:1,21; 2Sa 13:29;
16:1–2; 18:9; 19:26; 2Ki 18:23
pp Isa 36:8; Isa 21:7; 30:16; Jer 6:23;
Hag 2:22; Rev 9:17

**Riding on the backs of animals may
indicate royalty or privilege** Zec 9:9 *See
also* 1Ki 1:33,38,44
Nobility and wealth: Jdg 5:10; 10:4;
12:14
Authority: Rev 6:1–8; 19:11–21

**Jesus Christ mounted a donkey for his
triumphal entry into Jerusalem**
Mt 21:7–9 pp Mk 11:7–11
pp Lk 19:35–38 *See also* Jn 12:13–15

**Carrying a burden on the back
represents bearing suffering and
trials**
Ps 66:11 *See also* Ps 38:4; Ecc 1:13; 3:10;
Mt 11:28–30

Injury to the back
Jdg 3:22; 2Sa 2:23; Job 20:24–25

Pain in the back causing anguish
Ps 38:7

The back endures punishment
Bending of the back indicates loss of
physical strength Ps 69:23 *See also*
Ro 11:10

Beating on the back is a punishment
Pr 10:13; 14:3; 19:29; 26:3

**Beating on the back may be an unjust
punishment for God's servants** Isa 50:6
See also Isa 53:4–5; Mt 21:35 pp Mk 12:3
pp Lk 20:11 *The servants in the parable
represent the OT prophets.*

Jesus Christ endured flogging
Mt 27:26 pp Mk 15:15 pp Jn 19:1 *Jesus
Christ becomes the suffering servant of
Isaiah's prophecies.*

The apostles endured flogging
2Co 11:23–25 *See also* Ac 5:40;
16:22–23,37; 21:32; 2Co 6:5,9

**Jesus Christ's disciples should expect
similar flogging** Mt 10:17 *See also*
Mt 23:34; Mk 13:9

**Whipping on the back used figuratively
in a warning** Jos 23:12–13

**Walking over the back used
figuratively to indicate defeat** Isa 51:23

**Turning one's back means
desertion**
God makes the enemies of his people
flee Ex 23:27 *See also* 2Sa 22:41
pp Ps 18:40; Ps 21:12

Israel flees from her enemies Jos 7:12

God's people desert him Ne 9:29 *"To
turn one's back", in these verses and the
following verses, also implies a lack of
respect and reverence for God and his ways.
See also* 2Ch 29:6; Isa 1:4; 59:12–13;
Jer 2:27; 32:33–34; Eze 8:16

God's people desert his instruction
Zec 7:11; 2Pe 2:21

**Thrusting behind one's back
means discarding**
Isa 38:17 *God forgives sins, putting them
out of sight;* Eze 23:35 *See also* 1Ki 14:9;
Ne 9:26

God turns his back in his grace
Ex 33:22–23 *To see God's face would
bring death.*

**God turns his back against
disobedient people**
Jer 18:17

See also

1055 God, grace & mercy	2366 Christ, prophecies concerning
1065 God, holiness of	
1075 God, justice of	2570 Christ, suffering
1210 God, human descriptions	4633 donkey
1255 face of God	4657 horse
2230 Messiah, coming of	5313 flogging
	8794 persecution

5128

baldness

Loss of hair on the head as the result
of natural causes or deliberate action.
Baldness may be used to signify
judgment, mourning or shame.

**Instructions regarding baldness
within Jewish law**
Associated with idolatrous practice
Lev 21:5; Dt 14:1; Jer 16:6 *In pagan
Canaan mourners shaved their foreheads.*

Regarding sores on bald heads
Lev 13:40–42

**Cleansing may involve shaving the
head** Lev 14:8–9; Nu 6:9,18; Dt 21:12

Vows that involve shaving the head
Jdg 13:5; 16:17–19; Ac 18:18 *based on
the Nazirite rule recorded in Nu 6:1–21*

**Baldness may signify God's
judgment**
Eze 5:1 *Ezekiel instructed to shave his
head to symbolise this*

Judgment on Jerusalem and Judah
Isa 3:17,24; 7:20

**Baldness as a symbol of
mourning**
Job 1:20 *Job here mourns the loss of his
children, household and livestock. See also*
Isa 15:2; 22:12; Jer 48:37; Eze 27:31;
Am 8:10; Mic 1:16

**Used figuratively to indicate the
mourning of a nation** Jer 47:5

Baldness as a symbol of shame
2Ki 2:23; Eze 7:18; 1Co 11:5–6

Examples of baldness
Eze 29:18 *baldness caused by the rubbing
of leather helmets in warfare;* Jdg 16:19
Samson; 2Ki 2:23 *Elisha*

See also

5154 forehead	5419 mourning
5155 hair	5947 shame
5157 head	9210 judgment,
5158 head-covering	God's
5180 shaving	

5129

bathing

**Bathing as an act of ritual
cleansing**
Lev 14:8–9 *See also* Lev 15:4–11;
16:26–28; Nu 19:7–8

**Bathing as a means of cleansing
or refreshing the body**
Ex 2:5; 2Sa 11:2; 1Ki 22:38

**Bathing referred to
metaphorically**
Dt 33:24; Ps 58:10; Isa 34:5–6; Eze 16:9;
23:40

See also

4293 water	7416 purification
6151 dirt	7426 ritual washing
7342 cleanliness	7478 washing

5130

beard

References to the beard
Eze 5:1 *See also* Jdg 16:17; 1Sa 21:13;
2Sa 20:9; Ps 133:2

Cutting or pulling the beard
In grief Jer 48:37 *Moab is in mourning.
See also* Isa 15:2; Jer 41:5

In dismay Ezr 9:3

In the ceremony of cleansing Lev 14:9

As an extreme insult 2Sa 10:4–5
pp 1Ch 19:4–5; Isa 7:20; 50:6

**Cutting the edges of the beard was
forbidden** Lev 19:27 *This is a prohibition
still adhered to by some Jews today;*
Lev 21:5

See also

5128 baldness	5893 insults
5150 face	7340 clean and
5155 hair	unclean
5180 shaving	7422 ritual
5419 mourning	

5131

belt

An item of clothing, worn round the
waist, used for gathering clothes and
holding weapons or money.

The belt as an item of clothing
1Ki 18:46 *See also* 2Sa 20:8; 1Ki 2:5;
2Ki 4:29; 9:1; Ps 109:19; Isa 5:27;
Jer 13:1–11; Da 10:5; Mt 10:9
pp Mk 6:8; Ac 21:11

**Part of the battledress of a
warrior**
1Sa 18:4 *See also* 2Sa 18:11; Eze 23:15

**A leather belt was a sign of rough
living**
2Ki 1:8 *See also* Mt 3:4 pp Mk 1:6

**The belt symbolises truth and
righteousness**
Isa 11:5; Eph 6:14

See also

5144 cloak	8154 righteousness
5145 clothing	8486 spiritual
5177 robes	warfare,
5612 weapons	armour

5132

biting

The use of teeth to harm, threaten or
express frustration. It is illustrative of
the effect of slander, cold wind,
excessive wine or of God's judgment.

Biting used literally
An effect of demon-possession
Mk 9:18

Biting by reptiles and animals Nu 21:6
See also Ecc 10:8,11; Da 6:24

**Reptiles and animals prevented from
biting** Da 6:21–22 *See also* Mk 16:18;
Ac 28:4–5; Heb 11:33

Biting used metaphorically
Of God's judgment on the wicked
Jer 8:17 *See also* Joel 1:6; Am 5:19; 9:3

Of the wicked against God's people
Ac 7:54 *See also* Ps 35:16; 37:12; La 2:16;
1Co 15:32 *A fulfilment of the prophecy of
Isa 22:13, indicating that the devouring of
God's people is a part of the greed of the
wicked;* 2Ti 4:17

Of Satan and demons 1Pe 5:8; Rev 9:8

Of the frustration of the wicked
Lk 13:28 *See also* Ps 112:10; Mt 8:12;
13:42; 22:13; 24:51; 25:30; Rev 16:10

Of quarrelling, slander and treachery
Gal 5:15 *See also* Ge 49:17; Ps 57:4; 58:4;
140:3; Ro 3:13–14; 2Co 12:20

Of a cold wind Job 37:9–10 *See also*
Isa 28:2

Of penetrating sarcasm Mt 23:27–28
See also Ps 115:3–7; Isa 46:5–7; 1Co 4:8;
2Co 12:11–13

Of the effect of excessive wine
Pr 23:31–32

See also

4130 demons	5951 slander
4603 animals	5969 treachery
4687 snake	8794 persecution
4860 wind	9210 judgment,
5189 teeth	God's
5546 speech	9510 hell
5924 quarrel-	
someness	

5133

blindness

The inability on the part of someone
to see properly. Blindness is often
used in Scripture as a symbol of
human sin.

5134

blindness, natural

The inability to see properly. The
healing of such physical blindness
was one of the many miracles
performed by Jesus Christ, who
restored sight to the blind at several
points during his ministry. Scripture
often treats blindness as a symbol of
the human inability or refusal to
realise the importance of God and
the gospel. The restoration of sight
can thus be treated as a symbol of
coming to faith.

The causes of blindness
A natural affliction Ex 4:11 *See also*
Ge 27:1; 29:17; 1Sa 3:2; 4:15; Jn 9:1–3;
Ac 22:11; Gal 4:15

A consequence of sin Ge 19:11;
Dt 28:28–29; 2Ki 6:18; Ps 69:23;
Ac 13:9–11

A result of human cruelty Nu 16:14;
Jdg 16:21; 2Ki 25:7 pp Jer 39:7; 52:11

Directions to care for the blind
Lev 19:14; Dt 27:18; Job 29:15; Jer 31:8

The healing of blindness
Lk 14:13

The Lord makes blind eyes see
2Ki 6:17,20; Ps 146:8; Isa 35:5; 61:1 fn

**The healing of the blind by Jesus
Christ** Lk 4:18 *See also* Mt 9:27–30; 11:5
pp Lk 7:21–22; Mt 12:22; 15:30–31;
20:29–34 pp Mk 10:46–52
pp Lk 18:35–43; Mk 8:22–25; Jn 9:6–7;
Ac 9:17–18 *through Ananias*

Blindness as a symbol
Of moral defect Lev 20:4; Dt 16:19;
1Sa 12:3; Pr 28:27; Mt 5:29; 6:23; 18:9;
Lk 6:39

Of grief Ge 21:19; 1Sa 2:33; Job 17:7;
Ps 6:7; 31:9; 38:10; 88:9; Isa 38:14

Of the powerlessness of idols Ps 115:5
pp Ps 135:16

See also

1466 vision	5296 disabilities
2351 Christ, miracles	5359 justice
5149 eyes	5823 cruelty

5135

blindness, spiritual

An inability or unwillingness to
perceive the truth of the gospel.

Unbelievers are spiritually blind
1Co 2:14 *See also* Ps 32:9; 92:6–7;
Pr 4:19
*The blindness both of idols and those who
worship them:* Isa 44:9,18–19
Eze 12:2; Mic 4:12
*Jesus Christ speaks in parables because of
the spiritual dullness of the people:*
Mt 13:13–15; Lk 8:10; Isa 6:9–10
Mt 15:16; Lk 24:25; Jn 1:5; 9:40–41 *the
spiritual blindness of the Pharisees;*
Ro 3:11; 1Co 14:23,24

**Spiritual blindness is a result of
sin**
La 4:14; Zep 1:17; 2Co 4:4 *See also*
Mk 9:32; Lk 18:34; Jn 3:19–20;
12:39–40; Eph 4:17–19

**The consequences of spiritual
blindness**
Ro 1:18–23 *See also* Dt 28:28–29 *lack of
success, oppression and robbery;* Ps 82:5;
Isa 42:25 *the violence of war;* Isa 59:10;
La 4:14; Mt 6:23; Ac 28:26–27;
Isa 6:9–10; 2Co 4:4; 1Jn 1:6
Hatred and darkness: 1Jn 2:9,11

**The removal of spiritual
blindness**
2Co 4:6 *See also* Nu 24:4; 2Ki 6:17 *Elisha
asks the Lord to open his servant's eyes;*
Ps 119:18,130; 146:8; Isa 32:3; 35:5;
42:16–18; Lk 4:18; Isa 61:1 fn;
Lk 24:31; Jn 3:3 *No-one can see the
kingdom of God without being born again;*
Jn 8:12 *Jesus Christ is the light of the
world;* Jn 9:39; Ac 26:18; 2Co 3:16;
Eph 1:18; 5:8; 1Pe 2:9

The spiritual blindness of Israel
Isa 1:3 *See also* Dt 29:4; 32:28; Isa 29:10;
Jer 4:22; 5:21; Mic 4:12; Ro 11:7–8,25;
2Co 3:14–15

The spiritual blindness of leaders
Mt 15:14 *See also* Isa 29:9–12; 56:10;
Mt 23:16–19,24–26; Lk 6:39; Jn 3:10;
8:27; 9:40–41; 10:6; Ro 2:19–21;
2Pe 2:12

**The spiritual blindness of
believers**
Jn 14:9 *See also* Job 42:3; Da 12:8;
Mt 15:16 pp Mk 7:18; Mt 16:9
pp Mk 8:21; Lk 2:50; 9:45; 24:25;
Jn 12:16; 2Pe 1:9

**The spiritual blindness of a
church**
Rev 3:17–18

5136

body

Used in Scripture in both a physical and metaphorical sense, the body is susceptible to sin and suffering, but may be offered to God in worship and will finally be transformed by resurrection.

The body is formed by God
Ps 139:15–16 *See also* Ge 2:7,22; Job 10:8–11; Ecc 11:5

The body's appearance
The beauty and strength of the body 1Sa 16:12 *See also* 1Sa 9:2; 2Sa 11:2; SS 5:10–16; 7:1–9; Da 10:6

Clothing for the body Ex 22:27; 28:42; Lev 16:4; 2Ki 6:30; Isa 20:2

Diseases affecting the body
Bodily pain Job 2:7 *See also* Ge 3:16; 2Ch 21:19; Job 7:5; 14:22; 17:7; 30:30; Ps 38:7; 2Co 12:7

Leprosy Lev 13:2–17; Nu 12:10; 2Sa 3:29; 2Ki 5:1–2,6–7; 2Ch 26:19–21; Mt 8:2–3 pp Mk 1:40–42 pp Lk 5:12–13; Lk 17:12–13

Boils Ex 9:9–11; Lev 13:18–23; Dt 28:27,35; 2Ki 20:7 pp Isa 38:21

The marks of suffering Jn 20:25,27; Gal 6:17

Healing of the body
Mk 5:25–29 pp Mt 9:20–22 pp Lk 8:43–44 *See also* Ex 4:7; 2Ki 5:10,14; Job 33:25; Mt 8:3–4 pp Mk 1:41–42 pp Lk 5:13

Certain actions and attitudes affect the health of the body
The body's response to godliness Pr 14:30 *See also* Pr 3:7–8; 4:20–22

Godliness is no guarantee of bodily health Job 21:23–26; Ps 73:4

The body's response to sin Ps 38:3
Suffering and death are the result of sin in general, but specific experiences of suffering cannot usually be traced to specific sin. See also Ps 32:2–3; 38:4–11; 109:18; Pr 5:11

The body's response to distress Ps 31:9–10 *See also* Ps 44:25; Na 2:10

The body's response to fear Job 4:14–15; 21:6; Isa 21:3; Da 10:15–17

Life here and now in the body
"In the body" meaning "in this life" 2Co 5:6 *See also* 2Co 5:8–10; Gal 2:20; Php 1:20,22,24; 2Pe 1:13

"Body" meaning "self" Ps 63:1 *See also* Ge 47:18; Ne 9:37; 2Co 7:5

Bodily relationships
Parenthood Ge 15:4 *See also* Ge 35:11; 2Sa 7:12; Mic 6:7; Ro 4:19; Heb 7:10

Kinship 2Sa 5:1 pp 1Ch 11:1 *See also* Ge 2:23; 29:14; Jdg 9:2; Ne 5:5; Isa 58:7

Marriage 1Co 7:4 *See also* Mt 19:5 pp Mk 10:7–8; Eph 5:28–29,31; Ge 2:24

Rituals performed on the body
Circumcision: Ge 17:13–14; Jer 9:25; Eph 2:11
Ceremonies for cleansing the body: Lev 15:16; Nu 8:7
Prohibition of pagan mourning customs: Lev 19:28; 21:5

The believer's body as a temple of the Holy Spirit
1Co 6:19–20 *See also* Jn 2:19–22 *Jesus Christ also likens his body to a temple;* Ro 8:10–11

Believers are to devote their bodies to God
2Co 7:1 *See also* Ro 6:13; 8:13; 12:1; 1Co 9:27; 1Th 4:4; 5:23; Jas 3:2

Sin at work in the body
The body is subject to sinful desires Mt 26:41 pp Mk 14:38 *See also* Ro 6:6; 7:23–24

Bodily temptation is to be resisted Ro 6:12 *See also* Ro 1:24; 6:19; 1Co 6:13–16,18; Jude 8

Undue concern for the body is to be avoided 1Ti 4:8 *See also* Mt 6:25–32 pp Lk 12:22–30; Mt 10:28 pp Lk 12:4–5

The resurrection of the body
Dead bodies restored to this life 1Ki 17:20–22; 2Ki 4:32–36; 13:21; Mt 9:25 pp Mk 5:41–42 pp Lk 8:54–55; Lk 7:14–15; Jn 11:43–44

The resurrection body of believers Php 3:21 *See also* Ps 16:9–10; Isa 26:19; Ro 8:11,23; 1Co 15:35–54

Bodies other than human
Idols of pagan gods 1Sa 5:4; Ps 115:4–7; 135:15–17

Angelic beings Isa 6:2; Eze 1:11,23; 10:12

Heavenly bodies Mt 24:29 pp Mk 13:25 pp Lk 21:26; Ac 7:42; 1Co 15:40–41

Body in a metaphorical sense
A body of people: Ezr 8:20; 1Ti 4:14
A body of laws: Dt 4:8; Ro 2:20

5137

bones

Associated in Hebrew thought with both death and life. A symbol of the whole person, and also the state of one's well-being.

Bones represent dead bodies
Human remains to be treated with respect 1Sa 31:13 pp 1Ch 10:12 *See*
also 2Sa 21:12–14; 1Ki 13:31; 2Ki 23:18; Eze 39:15

Non-burial as a sign of disrespect Am 2:1–2

Non-burial as a sign of God's judgment Ps 53:5 *See also* 2Ki 9:34–37; Ps 141:7; Jer 8:1–2; Eze 24:4–5,10

Bones were considered to be unclean
Bones made anyone who touched them unclean Nu 19:16 *See also* Nu 19:18; Mt 23:27

Bones used to desecrate objects of pagan worship 2Ki 23:14 *See also* 1Ki 13:2; 2Ki 23:16,20; 2Ch 34:5; Eze 6:5

Bones as a sign of hope
The hope of God's promise Ge 50:25 *See also* Ex 13:19; Jos 24:32; Heb 11:22
The presence of Joseph's bones among the Israelites was a constant reminder of God's promise to Joseph concerning the promised land.

The hope of life after death Eze 37:1–14 *See also* 2Ki 13:21

The hope of the Passover lamb Jn 19:36 *See also* Ex 12:46; Nu 9:12; Ps 34:20 *Jesus Christ fulfilled the symbolism of the unbroken bones of the Passover lamb.*

Bones represent living individuals
Bones indicate a living body Lk 24:39

Bones represent a whole person Ps 35:10 *"My whole being" is literally "my bones". See also* Job 2:4–5; 10:11; Ps 6:2; 51:7–8; Isa 66:14

Bones represent kinship Ge 2:23 *"flesh and blood" in these passages is literally "bone and flesh":* Ge 29:14; Jdg 9:2; 2Sa 5:1 pp 1Ch 11:1; 2Sa 19:12–13

Bones represent physical health
Bones associated with good health Pr 15:30 *See also* Pr 3:7–8; 16:24

Bones symbolise strength and vigour Job 21:23–24 *See also* Job 20:11; 40:18; Pr 25:15

Bones associated with God's protection Ps 34:19–20 *See also* ˣ Jn 19:36

Mere skin and bone represents bad health Job 19:20 *See also* Job 33:21; Ps 102:5; La 4:8

Broken bones symbolise defeat or oppression Nu 24:8 *See also* Isa 38:13; Jer 50:17; La 3:4; Da 6:24; Mic 3:2–3

Health can be damaged by negative attitudes Pr 14:30 *See also* Job 4:14; Pr 12:4; 17:22; Hab 3:16

Health can be damaged by sin Ps 38:3 *See also* Ps 32:3; 109:18; La 1:13

Repentance brings restoration Ps 6:2 *See also* Ps 51:18

Health can be damaged through obedience to God's will Jer 23:9 *See also* Job 30:17; 33:19; Ps 22:14,17; 31:10; 42:10; Jer 20:9

See also

1670 symbols	6732 repentance
5241 burial	8230 discipline
5297 disease	9030 dead bodies
5334 health	9210 judgment,
5560 suffering	God's
6020 sin	9610 hope

5138

bowing

An act of submission before something or someone deemed worthy of honour.

Bowing as an act of submission
Ge 42:6; 2Sa 1:2; Ps 72:9 *See also*
Ge 33:3; 43:26–28; 49:8; Ex 11:8; 18:7;
Ru 2:10; 1Sa 2:36; 24:8; 25:23; 2Sa 15:5;
18:28; 1Ki 1:16; 1Ch 21:21; Isa 49:23

Bowing before angels
Ge 18:2 *See also* Ge 19:1; Nu 22:31;
Lk 24:5

Bowing before God
Ex 4:31; 2Ch 20:18; Ps 95:6 *See also*
Ge 17:3; 24:26; Ex 12:27; 34:8; Dt 26:10;
33:3; 1Ki 1:47; 2Ki 17:36; 1Ch 29:20;
2Ch 29:28; Ne 8:6; Ps 22:27; Isa 66:23

Bowing before the temple
Ps 5:7 *The temple represented God's presence. See also* Ps 138:2

Bowing before idols
Ex 32:8; 2Ki 17:16; Isa 2:8 *See also*
Nu 25:2; Dt 29:26; 2Ki 21:3; 2Ch 25:14;
Isa 44:17,19; Eze 8:16; Mic 5:13

Bowing before Jesus Christ
Mt 2:11; Php 2:10 *See also* Mt 8:2; 9:18;
15:25; 27:29; Mk 5:6; 10:17; Lk 17:16

Bowing as an expression of sorrow
Ps 35:14; 145:14 *See also* Ps 38:6; 57:6;
146:8; La 2:10

See also

5161 kneeling	8305 meekness
5163 legs	8333 reverence
5174 prostration	8469 respect
5878 honour	8622 worship
5952 sorrow	8768 idolatry
5959 submission	

5139

bracelet

An expensive ornamental armlet usually worn by women.
Eze 16:10–13 *See also*
Ge 24:22–31,47–48; Nu 31:50;
2Sa 1:10; Isa 3:18–23; Eze 23:42

See also

4342 jewels	5915 ornaments
5126 arm	8808 riches
5778 adorning	

5140

breasts

On a woman, the bosom; on a man the upper part of the chest. Female breasts are primarily referred to as a means of feeding young and as a

figurative description of Israel and God as nursing mothers. Beating of the breast is a sign of remorse. The breast is protected in physical and spiritual warfare.

Breasts as a symbol of fertility
Ge 49:25

Breasts as the means of feeding young
See also
1Sa 1:23 *until they are weaned;* 1Ki 3:20;
Job 3:12; Ps 22:9; SS 8:1; Joel 2:16;
Lk 11:27 *"Nursing" includes breast-feeding.*

Nursing mothers and their children experience acute distress Lk 23:29 *See also* Job 24:9; Mt 24:19 pp Mk 13:17 pp Lk 21:23 *The implication is that children nursing at their mothers' breasts are completely vulnerable and defenceless.*

Other creatures breast-feed their young La 4:3

Female breasts are attractive
SS 8:10 *See also* Pr 5:19; SS 4:5; 7:3,7–8

Breasts are a source of temptation
Pr 5:20

Undeveloped breasts are a sign of youth SS 8:8

The figurative breasts of Israel
Jerusalem as a breasted woman
Eze 16:7

Jerusalem as a nursing mother
Isa 66:10–12

Jerusalem as a prostitute Eze 23:3 *The two sisters are Samaria and Jerusalem. See also* Eze 23:8,21; Hos 2:2 *Gomer's unfaithfulness is likened to that of Israel.*

Dry breasts are a sign of God's punishment Hos 9:14

God's care exceeds that of nursing mothers
Isa 49:15 *See also* Isa 49:23; 60:16 *The Gentiles will be used by God to provide nursing for Israel.*

Beating of breasts
As a sign of grief Na 2:7 *See also*
Isa 32:12–13; Eze 21:12; 23:34;
Lk 23:48

As a sign of contrition Lk 18:13 *See also*
Jer 31:19

Protection of the breast
The high priest's breastpiece Ex 25:7;
28:15–30; 29:5; 35:9,27; 39:8–21;
Lev 8:8

Breastplates worn for protection in confrontations Rev 9:9,17

Figurative breastplates as spiritual armour Eph 6:14 *See also* Isa 59:17;
1Th 5:8

Animal breasts used in sacrificial offerings
Ex 29:26–27; Lev 7:30–31; 8:29;
9:20–21; 10:14–15; Nu 6:20; 18:18

See also

1215 God, feminine	5664 children
descriptions	5718 mothers
4480 milk	5733 pregnancy
5199 womb	6239 prostitution
5237 breastplate	7239 Jerusalem
5428 nurse	7320 breastpiece
5652 babies	

5141

cheeks

Literally, the parts either side of the face. Striking the cheek is an extreme form of insult.

Cheeks as features of beauty
SS 1:10 *See also* SS 5:13

Cheeks can bear symbols of grief
La 1:2

Striking the cheek is a form of insult or challenge
Job 16:10; Mt 5:39 *See also* La 3:30;
Mic 5:1; Mt 26:67; Jn 18:22–23; Lk 6:29

Plucking the beard from the cheek is a form of insult
Isa 50:6 *See also* 2Sa 10:4–5
pp 1Ch 19:4–5

See also

2570 Christ,	5150 face
suffering	5865 gestures
5130 beard	5893 insults
5149 eyes	

5142

clapping

Applauding with one's hands, as an expression of delight. Scripture portrays even the creation sharing in this delight at the majesty of its Creator.

Clapping as an expression of delight
At a coronation 2Ki 11:12

Expressing praise Ps 47:1

Expressing the delight of the creation in its Creator Ps 98:8 *See also* Isa 55:12

Clapping as an act of derision
La 2:15 *See also* Job 27:21–23; 34:37;
Eze 25:6; Na 3:19

See also

5156 hand	8283 joy
5830 delight	

5143

climbing

Physical climbing
Dt 32:49–50 *See also* Nu 27:12;
1Sa 14:8–13; 1Ki 18:42; 2Ki 19:23;
2Ch 20:16; Isa 40:9; Jer 4:29; Lk 19:4

Climbing associated with worship
Ps 24:3 *Because Jerusalem was built at a high elevation, going to worship there usually involved ascent. See also*
Ps 122:3–4; Isa 2:3; 30:29; Zec 14:17

Figurative climbing

Ps 139:8; Jer 9:21 *See also* Ge 28:12;
49:22; Dt 30:12; SS 7:8; Isa 14:13–14;
24:18; Am 9:2; Jn 1:51

See also

4245 hills	5553 stairways
4254 mountains	8622 worship

5144

cloak

A protective outer garment, often
treated as a symbol of authority.

The cloak used as a garment

Ac 12:8 *See also* Ge 39:12,18; 1Ki 19:13;
SS 5:7; Mt 5:40 pp Lk 6:29; Mt 9:20–21
pp Mk 5:27–28 pp Lk 8:44 *A woman's
bleeding is stopped;* Mt 14:36 pp Mk 6:56;
Mt 24:18 pp Mk 13:16; Ac 22:22–24;
2Ti 4:13

The cloak used as a covering or blanket

Ex 22:26–27 *See also* Dt 24:13,17

Symbolic use of the cloak

Royal symbolism 2Ki 9:13 *This
constituted an act of royal homage. See
also* Mt 21:7–8 pp Mk 11:7–8
pp Lk 19:35–36

Prophetic symbolism 1Ki 19:19 *See also*
1Ki 11:30; 2Ki 2:8,13–14

The cloak torn as a symbol of mourning Ezr 9:3 *See also* Ezr 9:5

Figurative use of cloaks

Ps 109:29 *See also* Ps 109:18–19;
Pr 30:4; Isa 59:17

See also

5145 clothing	5216 authority
5146 covering	5259 coat
5177 robes	7462 tassel
5188 tearing of clothes	

5145

clothing

Garments were originally provided
by God for Adam and Eve. Kings and
priests were given special garments.
God's people should neither be
unduly anxious about how they
dress, nor judge others by what they
wear. Inner clothing is more
important than outer adornment.

The origin of clothing

Ge 3:21

Various regulations regarding clothing

Lev 15:1–27; Dt 22:5,11–12

Special clothing for priests

Ex 28:1–5; 29:5–6; 39:1; Lev 8:7–9;
Eze 44:17–19

Rich clothing a sign of wealth or status

Ge 41:42; 2Sa 13:18; Est 6:8–9; 8:15;
Ps 45:13–14; Da 5:7; Lk 16:19; Ac 12:21

The Israelites' clothing did not wear out in the desert wanderings

Dt 8:4; 29:5; Ne 9:21

Clothing as a symbol of fragility and perishability

Isa 51:8 *See also* Isa 50:9

Symbolic actions involving clothing

The hem or corner of a garment Ru 3:9
*The corner of a garment spread over a
person denotes protection and possession.
Touching or taking hold of the corner of a
garment indicates putting oneself under the
control or domination of another:*
Zec 8:23; Mt 9:20 pp Lk 8:44; Jn 20:17
*Cutting or tearing off the corner of someone
else's garment indicates rebellion or a
desire to break away from their control or
authority:* 1Sa 15:27; 24:4–5
*Tearing one's own garments is a sign of
mourning or distress:* Ge 37:29,34; 44:13;
Lev 10:6
2Sa 3:31

Provision of rich clothing a picture of God's love

Eze 16:10–13; Lk 15:22

Examples of unusual clothing

Joseph's richly ornamented robe
Ge 37:3,23,32

**The dress of Elijah and John the
Baptist** 2Ki 1:8; Mt 3:4 pp Mk 1:6

**Isaiah's lack of clothing a prophetic
sign** Isa 20:2–4

The mock robing of Jesus Christ
Mt 27:28 pp Mk 15:17 pp Jn 19:2;
Lk 23:11

**Gambling at the cross for Jesus
Christ's clothing** Mt 27:35 pp Mk 15:24
pp Lk 23:34 pp Jn 19:23–24; Ps 22:18

Women and clothing

Women praised for making clothing
Pr 31:21,24; Ac 9:39

Women urged to dress modestly
1Ti 2:9 *See also* 1Pe 3:3

Believers not to be unduly anxious about clothing

Mt 6:28–30 pp Lk 12:27–28

Believers not to discriminate because of clothing

Jas 2:1–4

Inner clothing more important than outer adornment

1Pe 3:3–4 *See also* 1Sa 16:7; Pr 31:25;
Isa 52:1; 61:3; Col 3:12; 1Ti 2:9–10;
1Pe 5:5

The robe of righteousness

Isa 61:10 *See also* Job 29:14;
Ps 132:9,16; Zec 3:3–5; Mt 22:1–14;
2Co 5:2–4; Rev 3:17–18; 19:8

White clothing, the clothing of heaven

The transfiguration of Jesus Christ
Mt 17:2 pp Mk 9:3 pp Lk 9:29

The angels at the tomb Mt 28:3
pp Mk 16:5 pp Lk 24:4; Jn 20:12

The vision of the redeemed Rev 3:4–5
See also Rev 3:18; 4:4; 6:11; 7:9

The vision of the exalted Christ

Rev 1:13; 19:13

See also

4645 fleece	5188 tearing of clothes
4807 colours	
5131 belt	5258 cloth
5144 cloak	5915 ornaments
5158 head-covering	6742 sackcloth & ashes
5177 robes	
5179 sandal	7478 washing

5146

covering

That which literally or
metaphorically hides from the
human or divine eye what should
not be seen.

Covering for the human body

Ge 3:7; Eze 16:8 *See also* Ge 9:23;
Ex 22:26–27; 28:42; Isa 47:3; 57:8;
Eze 16:10; Hos 2:9; Jnh 3:6; Rev 3:18

Covering as a sign of submission or humility

Isa 6:2 *See also* Ge 24:65; 1Co 11:5–15
*Some suggest that this passage refers either
to a woman's modesty or to her dignity
considering her new Christian status of
equality with man.*

The covering of human sin through atonement

Ps 32:1–2 *See also* Ge 20:16; Lev 4:20
*The word translated "atonement" literally
means "covering";* Ne 4:5; Job 14:17;
Ps 32:5; 85:2; Pr 17:9; Ro 4:7–8;
Jas 5:20; 1Pe 4:8

Natural phenomena as God's covering

Ps 18:11 *See also* Ex 19:18; Nu 9:15–16;
Ps 105:39

See also

5145 clothing	5258 cloth
5158 head-covering	5812 concealment
5169 nakedness	6614 atonement
5195 veil	

5147

deafness

The condition of being wholly, or
partly, without hearing. It can be
expressed in physical or spiritual
terms and is often used to depict
spiritual rebellion.

God's control of deafness

Ex 4:11 *See also* Ps 94:9; Pr 20:12;
Lk 1:20,62

Physical aspects of deafness

Compassion for the deaf Lev 19:14

Deafness sometimes caused by Satan
Mk 9:25

Healed by Jesus Christ Mt 11:5
pp Lk 7:22 *See also* Mk 7:32–37;
Lk 22:49–51

Spiritual aspects of deafness

God deaf to a rebellious people Dt 1:45
See also Ps 28:1; 38:13; 39:12

Rebellious humanity deaf to God
Jer 6:10 *See also* Pr 28:9;

Isa 6:10; 42:19–20; Eze 33:32; 37:4; Mic 7:16; Zec 7:11; Mt 13:15; Mk 4:9–12; Lk 8:10; Jn 12:40; Ac 28:26–27; 2Ti 4:4; Rev 2:7 *Sin brings spiritual deafness.*

The deafness of idols
Dt 4:28 *See also* Ps 115:6; 135:17; Da 5:23; Rev 9:20

Release from deafness
Through repentance Isa 29:18 *See also* Isa 35:5; 42:18

Through the coming of Jesus Christ
Lk 7:22 pp Mt 11:5 *See also* Mk 7:32–37

See also

2351 Christ, miracles	6178 hardness of
5148 ear	heart
5159 hearing	6222 rebellion
5165 listening	against God
5168 muteness	8351 teachableness
5333 healing	8768 idolatry
5806 compassion	

5148

ear

The organ of hearing; the ear is referred to in various OT rites and is a symbol of attention, alertness or readiness to hear.

The ear in the OT rites
Piercing the ear: a symbol of servanthood Ps 40:6 *See also* Ex 21:5–6; Dt 15:16–17

Blood applied to the ear: a symbol of cleansing and ordination Lev 8:23 *See also* Ex 29:20; Lev 14:14

God's ear as a symbol of his alertness to humanity
Ps 116:1–2 *See also* 2Ki 19:16; 2Ch 7:15; Ne 1:6
God's ear is especially alert to the poor and the oppressed, as well as to the righteous: Job 34:28; Jas 5:4
Ps 5:1; 31:2; 34:15; 88:2; 130:1–2; Da 9:18

God's ear may be turned away from humanity
Ps 28:1 *The refusal to turn an ear towards someone was a symbol of refusing to listen. See also* Dt 1:45; La 3:56; Eze 8:18 *God's attending ear is partly dependent on human attitudes to him.*

The human ear used symbolically
Human ears should be open to God Isa 50:4–5; 55:3 *See also* Job 42:5; Ps 81:8; Isa 30:21; 32:3; Mt 13:9 pp Mk 4:9 pp Lk 8:8 *"He who has ears" implies a potential willingness to listen;* Mt 13:16; Mk 9:7; Rev 2:7

Human ears may be closed against God Zec 7:11–13 *See also* Ps 58:4–5; Isa 6:10

The human ear should also be open to others Isa 48:8; Jer 6:10; Eze 12:2; Ac 7:51,57; 2Ti 4:4
Pr 21:13

A discerning ear brings knowledge and understanding
Job 12:11; 13:1; 34:3; Pr 18:15

See also

1210 God, human	5806 compassion
descriptions	5865 gestures
1670 symbols	5946 sensitivity
5147 deafness	7745 ordination
5159 hearing	8226 discernment
5165 listening	8342 servanthood

5149

eyes

The part of the body designed for seeing. In Scripture eyes are often associated with light, watchfulness or spiritual understanding, whereas blindness may be a metaphor for darkness, ignorance of God or rebellion against him. The eyes of God watch over all his creation.

Eyes are part of the physical body
Dt 28:65; Job 11:20; 31:16; Ps 69:3

Eyes may represent the whole person Lk 10:23; Rev 1:7

Eyesight is a vital sense Mt 6:22 *See also* Ps 54:7; Pr 20:12; La 4:17; Mt 11:5 pp Lk 7:22; Mt 20:33 pp Mk 10:51 pp Lk 18:41; Ac 28:27; 1Co 12:17

Eyes may have a powerful emotional effect SS 4:9

Eyes reflect character, feelings and emotions
Malice: Ps 35:19; Pr 6:13; 10:10; 16:30
Haughtiness: Ps 101:5; Pr 21:4
Mk 3:5 *anger;* Mk 10:21 *love*
Sorrow: Ps 88:9; Jn 11:33–35
Desire: 2Pe 2:14; 1Jn 2:16

God's eyes are upon all his creation
God is aware of everything Job 34:21 *See also* 1Sa 16:7; Ps 94:9; 139:16; Pr 15:3; Am 9:8; Hab 1:13; Zec 3:9; 4:10; Heb 4:13

God watches over his people with care Ps 34:15 *See also* Dt 11:12; 1Ki 8:29; 9:3; Ps 1:6; 121:3–5; Pr 22:12; 1Pe 3:12

God's eyes symbolise his assessment of human behaviour Ge 6:8 *See also* Ex 15:26; Jdg 2:11; 1Ki 15:5; 2Co 8:21

Human eyes may symbolise spiritual vision
God opens eyes in a spiritual sense Ps 119:18 *The "opening of eyes" is an important biblical metaphor for revelation;* Eph 1:18 *See also* Nu 24:3–4; 2Ki 6:17; Ezr 9:8; Isa 35:5; 61:1; Mt 6:22–23 pp Lk 11:34–36; Ac 26:18; Heb 11:27

Human eyes should be directed towards God Ps 34:5; 123:1–2 *Lifting one's eyes towards God is an important biblical image of prayer.* 2Ch 20:12; Ps 25:15; 27:4; Isa 40:26; Jn 17:1; Ac 7:55; 2Co 3:16; Heb 12:2

Human eyes will ultimately see God
Job 19:25–27 *See also* Isa 33:17; Jn 17:24; 1Co 13:12; 1Jn 3:2; Rev 22:4

Eyes are a channel of temptation
Mt 4:8–9 pp Lk 4:5–7 *See also* Ge 3:6; Nu 15:39; Jos 7:21; 2Sa 11:2; Ps 119:37; Ecc 2:10; 6:9; Mt 5:28–29; 1Jn 2:16

Eyes should be guarded against evil
Job 31:1; Pr 4:25 *See also* Ps 101:3; Isa 33:15–16 *The direction of human eyes is a matter of choice.*

Closing one's eyes may symbolise indifference to God and his will
Mt 13:15 *See also* Isa 6:10; Pr 28:27; Eze 22:26; Mt 23:16–17; Jn 9:41

See also

1020 God, all-knowing	5865 gestures
1466 vision	6248 temptation
1670 symbols	7781 seer
4811 darkness, symbol of sin	8226 discernment
5135 blindness, spiritual	8474 seeing God
	8490 watchfulness
	9410 heaven

5150

face

The main visual characteristic of a person. Facial features are recognisable as uniquely those of a particular person. The face also indicates mood and attitude. The showing or directing of the face towards someone or something may indicate regard, approval or determination, while hiding or turning away of the face indicates the opposite.

The face is the main recognisable feature of a person
Examples of facial recognition Mt 26:71 pp Mk 14:66–67 pp Lk 22:56 *See also* Est 5:2,9; Mt 13:55 pp Mk 6:3; Mt 14:35 pp Mk 6:54; Jn 1:36,47–48

Examples of failure to recognise faces Ge 42:8 *See also* Ge 38:15; Lk 24:16; Jn 20:14 *There is no evidence to suggest that Jesus Christ's post-resurrection face was different.*

The face may be used symbolically to represent the whole person Dt 7:10

The physical appearance of faces
Attractive faces SS 1:15–16 *See also* 1Sa 16:12; Ecc 8:1; Da 1:4

Disfigured faces Isa 52:14 *See also* Job 2:12; Mt 27:29–30 pp Mk 14:65 pp Lk 22:63; Jn 18:22

Facial expressions
The face expresses a person's mood Ge 4:5 *See also* Ge 21:6; 1Sa 1:18; Job 29:24; Da 5:6,9; Lk 24:17; Jn 20:15

Averting the face may express worship, respect, modesty or shame Ex 3:6 *See also* Ge 24:65; Ru 2:10; 1Sa 5:3–4; 1Ki 18:42; 1Ch 21:21; Job 11:15; Ps 83:16; Isa 6:2; Jer 13:26; Lk 5:12

Setting the face expresses determination Lk 9:51 *the literal translation is "set his face to go"*

Other gestures involving the human face
Hiding the face from someone as a sign of loss of favour Dt 31:17–18; Job 13:24

Raising the face as a sign of lack of shame Job 11:15

Slapping someone's face as a challenge or insult 1Ki 22:24; Jn 18:22

Spitting in someone's face as an insult Dt 25:9; Mt 26:67

Seeing someone's face
An indicator of acceptance Ge 33:10 *See also* Ge 43:3–4; 44:23–26; Dt 34:10

Indicating confrontation Gal 2:11 *See also* 2Sa 14:24–32; 2Ki 14:8

Not seeing someone's face may indicate rejection Ex 10:28

Examples of supernatural facial appearance
Mt 17:2 pp Mk 9:2–3 pp Lk 9:29 *See also* Ex 34:30; Mt 28:3 pp Mk 16:5 pp Lk 24:4; Ac 6:15; 2Co 3:7–8,18; Rev 1:14,16

The face of God
As a symbol of blessing Nu 6:25–26 *See also* 2Sa 21:1; 1Ch 16:11; Ps 4:6; 31:16; 67:1; 80:19; 105:4; 119:135; Eze 39:29

Seeking the LORD's face means seeking his will 2Ch 7:14; Ps 27:8; Hos 5:15

God's face may be turned away, hidden or set against people as a sign of opposition or removal from favour Dt 31:17 *See also* Lev 17:10; 2Ch 30:9; Ps 44:24; Isa 1:15; 59:2; 64:7; Eze 14:8; 39:23; Mic 3:4; 1Pe 3:12; Ps 34:15–16

People cannot normally see God's face Ex 33:20 *See also* Ge 32:30; Dt 34:10; Job 13:15; 19:26–27; 1Co 13:12; Rev 22:4 *In the end all human beings will see God face to face.* Isa 50:7

"Face of the earth" indicates the earth's total area
Ge 6:7; 7:4; Dt 6:15; 14:2; Ps 104:30; Zep 1:2–3; Lk 21:35

See also

1255 face of God	5164 lips
5141 cheeks	5167 mouth
5148 ear	5865 gestures
5149 eyes	5947 shame
5154 forehead	8469 respect

5151

feet

The part of the body associated with moving and with foundation, direction and chosen path. Feet may symbolise the response to God's direction. The feet of God and of Jesus Christ are mentioned symbolically to describe some divine characteristics.

Feet as part of the physical body
Human feet Ex 30:19–21; Lev 8:23; Dt 8:4; Jos 14:9; 2Sa 4:4; 1Ki 15:23; SS 7:1; Eze 6:11; 25:6; Lk 7:44; Ac 3:7

The feet of creatures and objects of worship Ge 8:9; Ex 37:3; Eze 1:7; Da 2:33

A whole person may be represented by the foot
Job 28:4; Ps 36:11; Pr 6:18; Isa 59:7

Symbolic references to human feet
In relation to guidance, direction and following Ps 17:5 *See also* Ps 37:31; 44:18; 56:13; 119:101,105; Pr 3:6; 4:26–27; Lk 1:79

In relation to disobedience and waywardness Ps 1:1 *See also* 2Ki 21:22; Job 31:5; Pr 1:15–16; 4:14; 6:18; Isa 59:7; Mt 18:8 pp Mk 9:45

In relation to a secure standing with God Ps 40:2 *See also* 2Sa 2:9; 2Sa 22:34 pp Ps 18:33; Ps 31:8; 66:9; Pr 4:26; Hab 3:19; 1Co 15:58; Eph 6:13

In relation to bringing the gospel Isa 52:7 *See also* Na 1:15; Ro 10:15; Eph 6:15

In relation to expressing attitudes and emotions Jos 10:24 *defeat and humiliation*; Ru 3:4–8 *requesting marriage and redemption*; 1Sa 25:24 *supplication and homage Hospitality and servanthood:* 1Sa 25:41; Lk 7:44; Jn 13:5 *Defeat and subservience:* 2Sa 22:39–40 pp Ps 18:38–39; Eze 24:17 *mourning;* Mt 10:14 pp Mk 6:11 pp Lk 9:5 *scorn and a warning to those who reject God's message Worship and reverence:* Ac 4:35; 10:25 Heb 10:29 *rejection*

"Jesus' feet" symbolises the source and place of God's grace
Worshippers come to Jesus Christ's feet Lk 8:35 *See also* Mt 28:9

The sinful come to Jesus Christ's feet Lk 7:37–38 *See also* Jn 12:3

The suffering come to Jesus Christ's feet Mt 15:30 *See also* Mk 5:22–23 pp Mt 9:18 pp Lk 8:41; Mk 7:25 pp Mt 15:25; Jn 11:32

People sit at Jesus Christ's feet to learn Lk 10:39 *It was common practice for disciples to gather around their teacher in this way. See also* Jn 8:2

Ultimately all will come to Jesus Christ's feet in worship Ro 14:11; Isa 45:23; Php 2:10

"Feet of God" symbolises his majestic presence
Zec 14:4 *See also* Ex 24:10; Isa 66:1; Na 1:3; Mt 5:35; Zec 7:49; Rev 10:2

God's feet are referred to in relation to worship Ps 99:5; 110:1; 132:7; Rev 1:17

"Beneath/under the feet" to denote the defeat and subservience of enemies
Jos 10:24; 2Sa 22:39; 1Ki 5:3; Ps 8:6; 45:5; 47:3; Isa 49:23; La 3:34; Mal 4:3; Mt 22:42–45; Ps 110:1; Ac 2:34–36; Ro 16:20; 1Co 15:25–28; Eph 1:22–23; Heb 10:13; Rev 3:9

See also

2420 gospel	5865 gestures
4050 dust	7342 cleanliness
5153 foot-washing	8120 following
5163 legs	Christ
5179 sandal	9125 footstool
5197 walking	

5152

fingers

Parts of the hand used in various kinds of activity, both good and bad. They were prominent in the OT sacrificial ritual, and were also used as a symbol for authority, accusation and minimum effort.

Regular activities using the fingers
Ps 144:1; Pr 31:19; SS 5:5

Fingers used in sacrificial ritual
In the consecration of priests Ex 29:12 *See also* Lev 8:15

In the ritual for the sin offering Lev 4:6 *See also* Lev 4:17,25,30,34; 9:9

In the ritual of the Day of Atonement Lev 16:14,19

In cleansing rituals Lev 14:16; Nu 19:4

The finger as a unit of measurement
Jer 52:21

Deformed fingers
2Sa 21:20 pp 1Ch 20:6

Jesus Christ's fingers
Jesus Christ heals with his fingers Mk 7:32–35

Jesus Christ writes with his fingers Jn 8:6 *See also* Da 5:5

Proving Jesus Christ's resurrection
Jn 20:25 *See also* Jn 20:27

Evil done with the fingers
Idolatrous worship Isa 2:8 *See also* Isa 17:8; 59:3

Making accusations Isa 58:9 *See also* Pr 6:12–13

Doing harm Job 1:12

Fingers used in symbolic actions
The finger ring as a sign of authority Ge 41:42 *See also* Est 3:10; 8:2; Lk 15:22

The finger as a symbol of minimal effort Mt 23:4 *See also* 1Ki 12:10 pp 2Ch 10:10 *Rehoboam refusing to lift the burdens placed on the people by his father Solomon;* Lk 11:46

The finger as a visible reminder Pr 7:2–3 *See also* Dt 6:8; 11:18

See also

1260 finger of God	5865 gestures
2351 Christ, miracles	7308 Atonement,
5156 hand	Day of
5192 thumbs	7422 ritual
5194 touch	8768 idolatry
5201 accusation	
5618 measures,	
linear	

5153

foot-washing

A practice of hospitality used by Jesus Christ to express his servanthood.

5154

Foot-washing as a sign of courteous hospitality
Ge 18:4 *See also* Ge 19:2; Jdg 19:21; 1Sa 25:41; Lk 7:44

Jesus Christ washes his disciples' feet
Jn 13:3–5 *The washing of feet was a lowly task normally performed by a servant.*

As an example of servanthood for his followers Jn 13:14 *See also* Mt 20:26–27 pp Mk 10:44–45; Lk 22:26–27; 1Ti 5:10

As a symbol of spiritual cleansing Jn 13:6–10

See also

2327 Christ as servant	6652 forgiveness
2339 Christ, example of	7342 cleanliness
	7478 washing
5151 feet	8342 servanthood
	8445 hospitality

5154

forehead

The front of the head between the eyes. Often used figuratively in phrases denoting a stubborn or persevering attitude. The forehead is the place where symbols of remembrance or allegiance can be placed. Such symbols may particularly represent allegiance to God or Satan.

Literal use of the forehead
Lev 13:41–43; 2Ch 26:19–20
In the following verses the forehead is used as a symbol of a person's strength. Injury to the forehead is associated with the end of life: Nu 24:17; 1Sa 17:49; Jer 48:45; Eze 3:9

The forehead used figuratively to denote stubbornness
Isa 48:4

The forehead as a place for symbols which prompt remembrance
Ex 13:9 *See also* Ex 13:16
Some Jews take these words literally and tie phylacteries, small boxes containing Scripture verses, to their foreheads: Dt 6:8; 11:18

The forehead as a place for symbols of dedication and allegiance
To God and his purposes Ex 28:36–38 *See also* Eze 9:4; Rev 7:3; 9:4; 14:1; 22:4
The receipt of this symbol of allegiance provides protection in judgment and a reminder of the Passover where God's marked people escaped judgment.

To Satan and his ways Rev 13:16; 14:9; 17:5; 20:4

See also

5150 face	8207 commitment
5157 head	8467 reminders
6245 stubbornness	8670 remembering
7410 phylactery	

5155

hair

Various conditions, both physical and spiritual, are indicated in Scripture by human hair. Animal hair is used for a variety of purposes.

Physical qualities of human hair
A woman's hair is attractive SS 7:5 *See also* 2Ki 9:30; SS 4:1; 1Co 11:15

A man's hair shows vigour Jdg 16:17–22 *See also* 2Sa 14:26; SS 5:11

Grey hair shows the glory of old age Pr 16:31 *See also* Lev 19:32 *"aged" may be translated "grey-haired";* Pr 20:29

Greying hair as a sign of declining strength Hos 7:9

White hair as a sign of age and wisdom Rev 1:14 *See also* Da 7:9

Hair as indicating physical or spiritual conditions
Unharmed hair speaks of protection Mt 10:30 pp Lk 12:7 *See also* 1Sa 14:45; 2Sa 14:11; Da 3:27; Lk 21:18; Ac 27:34

Hair standing on end indicates fear Job 4:15

Baldness may indicate God's judgment Isa 3:24 *See also* Isa 3:17

Hair colour may indicate skin disease Lev 13:3 *See also* Lev 13:10–11,26,30–37,40–45

Rituals and customs involving the hair
Rules concerning hair for those under a vow Nu 6:5 *See also* Nu 6:9,18–19; Jdg 13:5; 16:17; 1Sa 1:11; Ac 18:18; 21:23–24

Rules concerning hair for those being cleansed Lev 14:8–9

Mourning customs affecting hair Mic 1:16 *See also* Lev 10:6; Dt 21:12–13; Job 1:20; Jer 16:6; 47:5; 48:37; Am 8:10

Grief signified by tearing or cutting one's hair Ezr 9:3 *See also* Isa 22:12; Jer 7:29

Humiliating others by shaving or pulling out the hair 2Sa 10:4 pp 1Ch 19:4 *See also* Ne 13:25; Isa 7:20

Pagan customs to be avoided Lev 19:27 *See also* Dt 14:1–2

Customs concerning hair and public worship 1Co 11:6,13–15; 1Ti 2:9; 1Pe 3:3

Animal hair
Animal hair used in tabernacle furnishings Ex 26:7 *See also* Ex 25:4; 35:26; 36:14

A prophet's clothing made from animal hair 2Ki 1:8 *See also* Zec 13:4; Mt 3:4 pp Mk 1:6

Animal hair as a disguise Ge 27:16 *See also* 1Sa 19:13,16

Hair used to wipe Jesus Christ's feet
Jn 12:3 *See also* Lk 7:38,44; Jn 11:2

Nazirite vows forbade the cutting of hair
The reason for taking a Nazirite vow, separation to the Lord Nu 6:1–2 *While attention is often focused on Nazirite prohibitions, it is important to note that the primary reason was for separating oneself to God. Both men and women could make the vow;* Nu 6:8

The requirements of the Nazirite vow Nu 6:2–4 *Nazirites must abstain from all produce of the vine;* Nu 6:5 *Nazirites must not cut their hair;* Nu 6:6–7 *Nazirites must not touch a dead body.*

The rules for re-establishing a broken Nazirite vow Nu 6:9–12

The regulations for completing the Nazirite vow Nu 6:13–17 *The Nazirite vow is completed, first, through prescribed sacrifices;* Nu 6:18 *The Nazirite vow is completed, second, through cutting off one's hair and burning it on the altar;* Nu 6:19–20 *The Nazirite vow is completed, third, through ritual acts performed by the priest.*

Examples of people dedicated to being lifelong Nazirites
Samson was a lifelong Nazirite: Jdg 13:2–7; 16:1–22
1Sa 1:10–11 *Samuel was a lifelong Nazirite;* Lk 1:13–15 *John the Baptist was possibly a Nazirite.*

Examples of temporary Nazirite vows Ac 18:18; 21:20–26

Nazirites to be seen as gifts from God to his people Am 2:11–12

Expressions involving hair
Jdg 20:16; Rev 6:12

See also

1670 symbols	5725 old age
5098 John the Baptist	5741 vows
5128 baldness	5879 humiliation
5130 beard	6742 sackcloth & ashes
5158 head-covering	7340 clean and unclean
5180 shaving	
5419 mourning	

5156

hand

Associated in Scripture with various activities, the hand symbolises particularly power and strength. Jesus Christ's hands often bring healing and blessing.

The hand as part of the physical body
Hands used for physical work 1Th 4:11 *See also* Ge 31:42; Ex 35:25; Dt 2:7; Job 1:10; Ps 90:17; Ecc 2:11; Ac 20:34

Hands used for praying Ex 9:29 *See also* 1Ki 8:38 pp 2Ch 6:29; 2Ch 6:12–13; Ezr 9:5; Ps 77:2; 88:9; 1Ti 2:8

Hands used in clapping 2Ki 11:12
Clapping as a sign of approval or support: Ps 47:1; 98:8; Isa 55:12
Clapping as a sign of derision or mockery: Job 27:23; La 2:15; Eze 25:6; Na 3:19

Hands used for carrying weapons Jer 21:4 *See also* Nu 22:29; 35:17; Jos 5:13; 1Sa 18:10; 2Ki 11:11 pp 2Ch 23:10; Eze 9:1–2

Hands used for writing Gal 6:11 *See also*
1Ch 28:19; Da 5:5,24; Ro 16:22;
Col 4:18; 2Th 3:17; Phm 19

Hands as a means of assistance
Mt 9:25 pp Mk 5:41 pp Lk 8:54 *See also*
Ps 109:31; Isa 63:12; La 4:6; Mk 9:27;
Ac 3:7; 9:41

Hands used in making idols 2Ch 32:19
See also Dt 31:29; 2Ki 19:18; 22:17;
2Ch 34:25; Ac 7:41

Idle hands Ecc 10:18 *See also* Pr 6:10;
10:4; 21:25; 24:33; Ecc 4:5; 11:6

Right and left hands
Right hand as the place of honour
1Ki 2:19 *See also* Ge 48:13–14;
1Ch 6:39; Ps 45:9; Jer 22:24;
Mt 25:33–34

Significant uses of the left hand
Jdg 20:16 *See also* Ge 48:13–14;
Jdg 3:15,21; 1Ch 12:2; Eze 39:3; Mt 6:3

Symbolic uses of the hand
The hand as a symbol of power
Job 30:2 *See also* Dt 32:39–40;
1Ki 11:12; Isa 47:6; Da 9:15

The hand as a symbol of violence
Ps 58:2 *See also* Job 16:17; 31:21;
Pr 6:17; Isa 1:15; 59:3,6; Eze 23:45

Clean hands as a symbol of innocence
Ps 24:3–4 *See also* Dt 21:6–7; 2Sa 22:21
pp Ps 18:20; Job 17:9; 22:30; Ps 26:6;
73:13; Mt 27:24; Jas 4:8

Limp hands as a symbol of paralysing
fear Eze 21:7 *See also* Ne 6:9; Job 4:3;
Isa 13:7; 35:3; Jer 47:3; Eze 7:17–18;
Zep 3:16

Hands as a symbol of temptation
Mt 18:8 *See also* Ge 3:22; Eze 18:8,17;
Mt 5:30; Mk 9:43

**Hands used in making
agreements**
Striking hands in pledge Ezr 10:19;
Pr 6:1; 11:15; 17:18; 22:26

Symbolic actions in oath taking
Ge 14:22; 24:2,9; 47:29

Joining hands in partnership or
fellowship 2Ki 10:15; Isa 2:6; Hos 7:5;
Gal 2:9

Figurative use of hands
1Sa 19:5 *See also* Jdg 12:3; 1Sa 28:21;
Job 13:14; Ps 119:109; Isa 2:8

Hands of Jesus Christ
Jesus Christ's hands used in healing
Lk 4:40 *See also* Mt 8:3 pp Mk 1:41
pp Lk 5:13; Mt 9:18 pp Mk 5:23; Mk 6:5;
7:32–33; Lk 13:13

Jesus Christ's hands used in blessing
Mk 10:13–16 pp Mt 19:13–15 *See also*
Lk 24:50

Jesus Christ's hands were pierced
Jn 20:27 *See also* Ps 22:16; Isa 53:5;
Zec 12:10; Jn 19:37; Lk 24:40; Jn 20:25;
Ac 2:23

Hands of angels
Eze 10:7–8 *See also* 1Ch 21:15–16
pp 2Sa 24:16; Isa 6:6; Eze 1:8

Significant examples of hands
In Jacob's life: Ge 25:26; 27:16,22–23
Moses' miracles: Ex 10:22; 14:21,27
Ne 4:17 Nehemiah's defences; Mt 26:23
Judas' betrayal

See also

5157

head

The position of the head often
expresses an attitude or emotion.
Figuratively head may mean
"chief", "first" or "top".

The head as part of the body
Heads of people Ge 28:11,18; 48:14,17;
Jdg 5:26; SS 2:6; Jnh 2:5

Heads of animals Ex 12:9; Lev 1:4;
2Ki 6:25
*"head of cattle" refers to the number of
cattle:* Ex 22:1; 1Ki 4:23; 2Ch 15:11;
35:9

Heads of idols 1Sa 5:4; 19:13,16

**The head as the uppermost part
of the body**
Lev 13:12; 2Sa 14:25; Job 2:7; Isa 1:6;
Hab 3:13; Jn 13:9

A measure of height 1Sa 9:2; 10:23

A crown worn on the head 2Sa 1:10;
Est 2:17; Ps 21:3; Jer 13:18; La 5:16;
Zec 6:11

A turban worn on the head Lev 8:9;
Eze 23:15; Zec 3:5

Death and decapitation Ge 40:19;
1Sa 17:46,51; 2Sa 4:7; 16:9; Mt 14:8–11
pp Mk 6:24–28

**Head used figuratively in various
expressions**
"Be it on one's own head": personal
responsibility that is inescapable
Lev 20:9,11–13,27; Jos 2:19; 1Sa 25:39;
2Sa 1:16; 1Ki 2:33; Eze 9:10; 33:4–5

"To come back on one's own head": a
wrongdoer suffering the very wrong he
or she has committed 1Ki 8:32
pp 2Ch 6:23; Ne 4:4; Est 9:25; Ps 7:16;
140:9; Joel 3:4,7; Ob 15

"To heap burning coals on his head":
generosity towards an enemy in the
hope of causing a change of heart
Pr 25:22; Ro 12:20

"Not a hair on one's head will be lost":
absolute safety 1Sa 14:45; 1Ki 1:52;
Da 3:27; Lk 12:7; Ac 27:34

"To keep one's head": staying calm
2Ti 4:5

"Making it up out of one's head":
imagining something Ne 6:8

"Blessing resting on your head"
Ge 49:26; Dt 33:16; Pr 10:6; Isa 35:10;
51:11

Rituals concerning the head
Cleansing after infectious skin diseases:
Lev 14:9,18,29
*Provisions connected with the Nazirite
vow:* Nu 6:9; Jdg 13:5; 16:17; 1Sa 1:11
Dt 21:12

The anointing of the head Ex 29:7;
Lev 8:12; Mt 26:7 pp Mk 14:3

**Covering or uncovering the head
in Christian worship**
1Co 11:4–7,10,13–15

**Expressions of grief involving the
head**
Bowing the head Ps 35:14; La 2:10

Shaving the head Dt 14:1; Isa 15:2;
Jer 47:5; 48:37; Eze 7:18; 27:30–31;
44:20; Am 8:10; Mic 1:16

Putting dust on the head Jos 7:6;
1Sa 4:12; 2Sa 1:2; 15:32; Ne 9:1;
Job 2:12

Covering the head 2Sa 15:30; Est 6:12;
Jer 14:3–4

**Various attitudes expressed with
the head**
Lifting up the head in joy and
expectation Ps 3:3; 27:6; 110:7;
Lk 21:28

Bowing the head in humility Isa 58:5;
Lk 18:13

Hanging the head in shame and
dejection Jdg 8:28; Job 10:15

Shaking the head in scorn 2Ki 19:21
pp Isa 37:22; Job 16:4; Ps 109:25;
Jer 18:16; 48:27; La 2:15; Mt 27:39
pp Mk 15:29; Ps 22:7

Rearing the head in rebellion Ps 83:2

Head meaning "chief" or "first"
Jesus Christ as the head 1Co 11:3;
Eph 1:10,22; 5:23; Col 1:18; 2:10,19

The head of a family, tribe or kingdom
Ex 6:14,25; Nu 1:4; 17:3; Jdg 11:8–9;
Isa 7:8–9; 9:14–15

Man as the head 1Co 11:3; Eph 5:23

Head meaning "top"
Head of a street Pr 1:21; Isa 51:20;
La 2:19; 4:1; Eze 16:25; Na 3:10

Head of a valley Isa 28:1,4

Head of a table 1Sa 9:22

Head of a stalk of grain Lev 2:14;
Hos 8:7

Head of an axe Dt 19:5; 2Ki 6:5

Head meaning "front"
2Ch 20:21; Joel 2:11

See also

5158

head-covering

A form of clothing worn on the
head, often as a sign of status or
rank.

Priestly head-coverings
Ex 29:6 *See also* Ex 28:4 pp Lev 8:9;
Lev 16:4; Zec 3:5

Royal head-coverings
Eze 21:25–26 *See also* 2Sa 1:10;

2Ki 11:12 pp 2Ch 23:11; Est 1:10–11; 2:17; Ps 21:1–3; SS 3:11; Rev 14:14

Military head-coverings
1Sa 17:5 See also 2Ch 26:14; Eze 23:15,24; 27:10; 38:5

Head-coverings in mourning
2Sa 15:30 See also Est 6:12; Eze 24:17

Head-coverings in worship
1Co 11:4–7 NIV footnote gives an alternative translation for these verses, taking hair as the head-covering.

Metaphorical use of head-coverings
Job 29:14 See also Eph 6:17

See also
1670 symbols	5195 veil
5144 cloak	5209 armour
5145 clothing	5259 coat
5157 head	5280 crown
5177 robes	5419 mourning

5159

hearing

In Scripture, both physical hearing and spiritual apprehension. God hears the prayers of his people and the cry of the oppressed. People must hear and respond to God's word.

Divine hearing
God hears the prayers of his people
2Sa 22:7 See also Ps 3:4; Isa 65:24; Jn 11:41–42; 1Pe 3:12; Ps 34:15

God hears the grumbling of his people
Nu 11:1 See also Ex 16:7–9,11–12; Nu 12:1–2; 14:27

God hears the cry of the oppressed
Jas 5:4 See also Ex 3:7; Ps 94:9

God does not hear the unrighteous
Isa 59:1–2 See also Ps 66:18; Isa 1:15; Jer 11:11,14; Eze 8:18; Am 5:23; Jn 9:31

Other gods cannot hear 1Ki 18:26–27; Ps 115:6; 135:17; Isa 46:7

Hearing the word of God
The importance of hearing God's word
Dt 5:1; Eph 1:13 See also Dt 4:1; Jer 2:4; 7:2; Mic 1:2; Mt 13:16–17 pp Lk 10:23–24; Jn 5:24; Ro 10:17

Having ears to hear Mt 11:15 See also Mt 13:9; Mk 4:9,23; Lk 8:8; Rev 2:7,11,17,29; 3:6,13,22

The gospel must not only be heard but accepted and acted on Heb 4:2 See also Mt 7:24–27; Mk 4:14–20 pp Mt 13:19–23 pp Lk 8:11–15; Ro 2:13; Gal 3:2,5; 1Th 2:13; Jas 1:22–24

It is God who grants effective hearing
Ac 16:14 See also Pr 20:12; Isa 50:5; 2Th 2:13–14

Some people refuse to hear God's word Jer 6:10 See also Isa 42:18–20; Eze 12:2; Ac 7:51; 2Ti 4:4

God denies the effective hearing of his word to those who stubbornly resist him Mt 13:10–15 pp Mk 4:10–12 pp Lk 8:9–10 See also Isa 6:9–10; Jn 8:43; Ac 28:26–27; Ro 11:8; Dt 29:4; Isa 29:10

The first Christians witnessed to what they had heard
Ac 22:14–15 See also Ac 4:20; Heb 2:3; 1Jn 1:1

Physical hearing was restored by Jesus Christ
Mk 7:35–37 See also Mt 11:5 pp Lk 7:22

The dead will hear the voice of the Son of God
Jn 5:25 See also Jn 5:28–29; 11:43–44

See also
1210 God, human descriptions	5147 deafness
	5148 ear
2351 Christ, miracles	5165 listening
2426 gospel, responses	8319 perception, spiritual
3224 Holy Spirit & preaching	8453 obedience
	8602 prayer

5160

heel

The heel as a vulnerable part of the body
Ge 3:15; Job 18:9

"Lifting up one's heel" as a metaphor of betrayal
Ps 41:9; Jn 13:18

Jacob grasps Esau by the heel at birth
Ge 25:26 Jacob's name means "he grasps the heel" which, figuratively, means "he deceives"; Hos 12:3

See also
5095 Jacob, life	5865 gestures
5151 feet	6145 deceit
5798 betrayal	

5161

kneeling

A bodily posture which expresses an attitude of humility, especially in worship, prayer or submission to the authority of another person.

Kneeling in worship
Ps 95:6 See also 2Ch 7:3; 29:29

Kneeling in submission
To God Isa 45:23 See also Ro 14:11; Ps 22:29

To Jesus Christ Php 2:9–11 See also Mt 27:29 kneeling in mock submission; Mk 5:6; 10:17; Lk 5:8

To other people Est 3:2 See also 1Ki 1:16; 2Ki 1:13; Mt 18:26

Kneeling in prayer
Da 6:10; Mt 9:18; Eph 3:14 See also 1Ki 8:54; 2Ch 6:13; Ezr 9:5; Mt 8:2; 15:25; 17:14; 20:20; Lk 22:41; Ac 7:60; 9:40; 20:36; 21:5

See also
2069 Christ, pre-eminence	5865 gestures
	5959 submission
2369 Christ, responses to	8276 humility
	8602 prayer
5138 bowing	8622 worship

5162

lameness

A physical condition impairing leg movement.

Causes of lameness
Congenital Ac 3:2; 14:8

Accidental 2Sa 4:4 See also 2Sa 9:3,13

Care for the lame
General care Job 29:15 See also Jer 31:8; Lk 14:13–14

Healing Mt 11:5–6 pp Lk 7:22 See also Mt 4:23–24; 8:6–7; 9:2–8 pp Mk 2:1–12 pp Lk 5:17–26; Mt 15:30–31; 21:14; Ac 3:6–10; 8:7–8; 9:33–34; 14:8

The spiritual significance of lameness
Relative importance of lameness
Mk 9:45

Parallel to weakness 2Sa 5:6–8; Isa 35:2–3; Heb 12:12–13

As a parallel to fools' words Pr 26:7

Ultimate healing in heaven Isa 35:6

Lameness in animals
Dt 15:21; Mal 1:7–8,13

See also
5151 feet	5296 disabilities
5163 legs	5297 disease
5197 walking	5333 healing
5278 cripples	5876 helpfulness

5163

legs

The legs of an animal were among the choice parts offered in sacrifices. In a human being legs provide strength. Bowing the knee symbolises the submitting of one's human strength to God's control.

Choice parts of a sacrificial animal
Eze 24:4 See also Ex 12:9
Entirely burnt up on the altar in the burnt offering: Ex 29:17–18; Lev 1:9,13; 8:21; 9:13–14
Lev 4:11–12 burnt outside the camp in the sin offering

Legs of human beings are objects of beauty
SS 5:15; 7:1

Legs of human beings symbolise strength
Rev 10:1 See also 1Sa 17:6; Ps 147:10; Da 2:33,40; 10:6

God's judgment saps human strength
Da 5:5–6 See also Eze 7:17; 21:7; Na 2:10; Hab 3:16

God's judgment brings pain and disgrace Dt 28:35
Shaven or bare legs were a sign of disgrace: Isa 7:20; 47:2

God gives strength to the weak
Heb 12:12–13 See also Job 4:4; Isa 35:3

The legs of Jesus Christ were not broken at his death

Jn 19:31–36

See also

1310 God as judge	5190 thigh
2530 Christ, death of	5197 walking
5151 feet	5956 strength,
5161 kneeling	human
5178 running	5959 submission
5184 standing	7435 sacrifice, in OT
5186 stumbling	

5164

lips

Lips as part of the human body

As a vehicle of speech 1Sa 1:13; Job 15:6; 33:3

As a means of eating and drinking SS 7:9; Da 10:3; Joel 1:5; Jn 19:29

As an object of beauty SS 4:3,11; 5:13

Lips attributed to God

Job 11:5 *See also* Job 23:12; Ps 17:4; 89:34; Isa 30:27

Lips associated with various kinds of speech

Praising lips Ps 34:1 *See also* Ps 51:15; 63:3,5; 119:171; Isa 57:19; Mt 21:16; Ps 8:2; Heb 13:15

Praying lips Ps 21:2 *See also* Job 13:6; Ps 17:1

Lips that speak God's word Ac 15:7 *See also* Ex 13:9; Lk 4:22

Lips that speak promises and vows Ps 66:14 *See also* Nu 30:6,12; Dt 23:23

Lips that give testimony Ps 40:9; 119:13; Lk 22:71

Encouraging lips Job 16:5; Pr 10:21

Lips expressing different moods

Joyful lips Job 8:21; Ps 71:23

Lips that express hesitancy Ex 6:12,30

Apprehensive lips Hab 3:16

Lips that speak rashly Ps 106:33

Lips associated with wrong values

Perverse and sinful lips Job 6:30 *See also* Ps 59:12; 140:9; Pr 4:24; 16:30; 19:1; Isa 6:5

Lips can tempt into sin Pr 5:3 *See also* Pr 14:7; 17:4; 18:6–7

Deceitful lips Pr 24:28 *See also* Ps 31:18; 34:13; 120:2; Pr 10:18; Isa 59:3

Flattering lips Ps 12:2–3

Hypocritical lips Ps 50:16; Pr 26:23–24; Jer 12:2; Mt 15:8 pp Mk 7:6; Isa 29:13

Lips associated with positive values

Lips that speak truth Pr 12:19 *See also* Pr 8:6–7; 16:13; 23:16; Jer 17:16; Mal 2:6–7

Lips that speak wisdom Pr 10:32 *See also* Ps 40:9; Pr 10:13; 15:7; 20:15; 22:17–18

Wise lips are profitable

Pr 12:14 *See also* Pr 13:2; 18:20

Foolish lips are disastrous

Ecc 10:12 *See also* Pr 14:3; 18:7

Lips must be watched over by God

People must guard their own lips
Ps 141:3 *See also* Ex 23:13; Pr 13:3; 1Pe 3:10; Ps 34:12

Lips must be purified Isa 6:7 *See also* Hos 2:17; Zep 3:9; Col 3:8

Lips need God's touch Ps 45:2; Da 10:16

See also

1210 God, human	5865 gestures
descriptions	6145 deceit
1460 truth	6248 temptation
5167 mouth	8361 wisdom
5193 tongue	8767 hypocrisy
5546 speech	8776 lies

5165

listening

People are called upon to listen attentively to God's word, to his Son and also to words of wisdom. Christians must not only listen to God's word but also put it into practice. Those who refuse to listen to God's word or to correction are condemned.

The importance of listening

To God's word and his spokesmen
1Sa 3:10 *See also* 2Ch 20:15; Ps 81:8; Jer 26:3–6; Mic 1:2; Ac 2:14; 13:16; 28:28

To Jesus Christ Mt 17:5 pp Mk 9:7 pp Lk 9:35; Jn 10:27 *See also* Mt 15:10 pp Mk 7:14; Lk 10:16,39; Jn 10:8,16

To words of wisdom Pr 19:20; Jas 1:19 *See also* Ps 34:11; Pr 5:7; 7:24; 8:32–34; 12:15; 13:1; 15:31; Lk 2:46; Jas 2:5

Believers should not listen to false prophets or ungodly suggestions

Jer 23:16 *See also* Dt 13:1–3,6–8; Jer 27:9,14–17; 29:8–9; Eze 13:19; 1Jn 4:1,5–6; 2Jn 10

The wicked refuse to listen to God

Eze 3:7 *See also* Ex 7:13 *Pharaoh's refusal to listen;* 2Ki 17:14,40; 18:12; Ne 9:17; Ps 81:11; Isa 65:12

It is a particular emphasis of the prophecy of Jeremiah that the people have refused to listen to God's voice: Jer 7:13,26–27; 12:17; 13:11; 17:23; 22:21; 25:3,7; 29:19; 32:33; 34:14; 35:15,17; 37:2; 38:15; 44:5,16

Eze 20:8; Zec 7:11–12; Mal 2:2; Lk 16:29–31

Those who refuse to listen to correction are condemned

Mt 18:15–17

God's people must not only listen to God's word but also put it into practice

Lk 11:28; Jas 1:22–24 *In Hebrew and Greek the verb "listen" is related to the verb "to obey". See also* Eze 33:32; Mt 7:24–27 pp Lk 6:47–49; Ro 2:13

Examples of people listening

Ge 18:10 *Sarah at the tent entrance;* Ge 27:5 *Rebekah to Isaac;* 1Sa 3:9–10

Samuel to God; Pr 19:27 *a son to instruction;* Lk 2:46 *Jesus Christ to the teachers of the law*
The crowds to Jesus Christ: Lk 5:1; 20:45
Lk 10:39 *Mary to Jesus Christ*
People to the apostles: Ac 16:14,25; 26:29

See also

1690 word of God	7797 teaching
2363 Christ,	8361 wisdom
preaching &	8403 commands
teaching	8453 obedience
5147 deafness	8749 false teachers
5159 hearing	

5166

liver and kidneys

The liver and kidneys as vital internal organs of the body

Pr 7:23 *See also* Job 16:13; 20:24–25

The liver and kidneys are symbolic of human emotions and the conscience

Ps 73:21 *The Hebrew words for liver and kidneys are occasionally translated as "heart", "spirit" or "inmost being". See also* Job 19:27; Pr 23:16; Jer 12:2; La 2:11; 3:13

God examines the innermost being as symbolised by the kidneys Ps 26:2 *See also* Ps 7:9; Jer 11:20; 17:10; 20:12

God is concerned for the innermost being as symbolised by the kidneys Ps 139:13 *See also* Ps 16:7

The liver and kidneys as offered in animal sacrifice

Liver and kidneys offered in various sacrifices Lev 3:3–5 *The liver and kidneys are associated with the fat as the choice parts of the animal. See also* Lev 3:9–11,14–16; 4:8–10; 7:3–6

Liver and kidneys had a central role in the ordination services for priests Ex 29:13,22–25; Lev 8:16–17,25–28; 9:8–10,19–21

Divination by inspection of the liver

Eze 21:21 *Divination by inspection of the liver (hepatoscopy) was a common practice. The future was predicted from the colour and configuration of the liver of a sacrificial animal, usually a sheep.*

See also

1020 God, all-	5172 offal
knowing	5844 emotions
4155 divination	5858 fat
5008 conscience	7402 offerings
5014 heart, human	7435 sacrifice, in OT
5024 inner being	
5038 mind, the	
human	

5167

mouth

In addition to its normal physical functions, it has great potential for good and evil. The words of God's mouth are always effective. Mouth is also used in the sense of an entrance or opening.

The words of God's mouth

They are always effective La 3:38 *See also* Isa 55:11

They are creative and life-giving Dt 8:3 *See also* Ps 33:6; Mt 4:4

They bring judgment Hos 6:5 *See also* Job 15:30; 2Th 2:8; Rev 2:16

They are reliable Nu 23:19 *See also* 1Ki 8:15 pp 2Ch 6:4; 1Ki 8:24 pp 2Ch 6:15; Heb 6:13–18

They are to be treasured Ps 119:72 *See also* Jos 1:8; Job 23:12; Ps 119:13–14,103

God puts his words into the mouths of his people

Dt 18:18 *See also* Ex 4:12,15; Nu 22:38; 1Ki 17:24; Isa 49:2; Jer 1:7,9; Eze 3:1–4; Ac 4:25,31

The mouth used for eating and drinking

Pr 18:20 *See also* Jdg 7:5–6; Ps 78:29–30; Pr 19:24; 30:20; Ecc 6:7; Eze 4:14; Na 3:12; Ac 11:8

The mouths of animals

The danger they represent 1Sa 17:35; Job 41:14,19,21; Am 3:12

Enemies described as dangerous animals Ps 22:13 *also* Ps 22:21; 2Ti 4:17

God controls the mouths of dangerous animals Da 6:22 *See also* Nu 22:28–30; Heb 11:33; 2Pe 2:16; Rev 12:15–16; 16:13

The mouth used for speaking

To speak what is good Pr 10:11 *See also* Job 16:5; Ps 19:14; Pr 8:7

To praise Ps 71:8 *See also* Ps 51:15; 63:5; 89:1; Ro 15:6

To testify about God Ps 71:15 *See also* Ps 71:18; Ro 10:10

To teach God's wisdom Ps 49:3 *See also* Ps 37:30; Pr 10:31; Mal 2:6–7; Mt 13:35; Ps 78:2

To speak what is bad Ps 10:7 *See also* 1Sa 2:3; Job 20:12; Ps 5:9; 36:3; 50:19; Pr 5:3; 7:21; 11:9; 15:28; 26:28; Isa 9:17; 29:13; Lk 6:45; Rev 13:5–6

Gestures involving the mouth

Job 3:1 *Opening the mouth signifies declaration;* Job 21:5 *Clapping the hand over the mouth signifies keeping silent from fear or astonishment;* Ac 23:2 *Striking the mouth signifies rebuke.*

God fills mouths

With good things Ps 81:10

With joy Ps 126:2 *See also* Ezr 3:13; Job 8:21; 35:10; Ps 40:3; 132:16; 149:6; Isa 35:6; Lk 1:64

With food Ps 145:15 *See also* Ne 9:20; Ps 78:27–30; 81:16; 104:27–28; Lk 1:53

Mouth meaning entrance or opening

The mouth of a well Ge 29:2–3,8–10

The mouth of a sack Ge 42:27; 43:12,21; 44:1–2,8

The mouth of the grave Ps 141:7; Isa 5:14 *"the grave" is literally "Sheol", the shadowy abode of the departed.*

The mouth of a cave Jos 10:18,22,27; 1Ki 19:13; Jer 48:28

The mouth of a river Jos 15:5; 18:19; Isa 19:7

The mouth of the earth Ge 4:11; Nu 16:30,32; 26:10; Dt 11:6

Mouth likened to a sword

Job 5:15; Isa 49:2

See also

1210 God, human descriptions	5187 taste
1690 word of God	5193 tongue
4404 food	5627 word
4438 eating	5865 gestures
4804 breath	7754 preaching
5164 lips	7772 prophets

5168

muteness

The inability to speak or to make sounds comprehensible as speech.

Physical muteness

A disability, sometimes associated with demon-possession, healed by Jesus Christ Mt 9:32–33 *See also* Mt 12:22 pp Lk 11:14; Mt 15:30–31; Mk 7:31–37; 9:14–29

Healing as a Messianic sign Mt 12:22–23 *See also* Isa 32:4; 35:6; Mt 4:23; 9:33

God and muteness

God gives and withholds speech Ex 4:11–12 *See also* Ex 4:10

God may impose muteness in judgment Lk 1:20 *See also* Lk 1:64

God may silence his prophets Eze 3:26 *See also* Eze 24:27; 33:22

The muteness of idols

1Co 12:2 *See also* 1Ki 18:26; Ps 115:5 pp Ps 135:16; Isa 41:26,28; 46:7; Jer 10:5; Hab 2:18–19

Spiritual aspects of muteness and silence

Evil silenced by God Job 5:16; Ps 63:11; 107:42; Eze 16:63; Mk 3:4; Ro 3:19

Evil silenced by godliness 1Pe 2:15

Silence on earth Hab 2:20

Silence in heaven Rev 8:1

God opens believers' mouths in praise Ps 40:3

Voluntary muteness

Of David Ps 38:13–14 *See also* Ps 39:1–3,9

Of Jesus Christ Isa 53:7 *See also* Ac 8:32; Ps 38:13; Mt 26:62–63 pp Mk 14:60–61; Mt 27:12–14 pp Mk 15:5 pp Jn 19:9; Lk 23:8–9

See also

2351 Christ, miracles	5333 healing
4130 demons	5950 silence
5147 deafness	8768 idolatry

5169

nakedness

Nakedness was innocent before the fall

Ge 2:25

The shame of nakedness a result of the fall

Ge 3:7–11

Public exposure of nakedness is indicative of shame or humiliation

Rev 3:18 *See also* Ge 9:22–23; Ex 20:26; Isa 47:3; Eze 16:8,35–37; Hos 2:9–10; Am 2:16; Na 3:5; Hab 2:15; Rev 17:16

Exposure of nakedness is symbolic of adultery and prostitution

Eze 23:18 *See also* Isa 57:8; La 1:8; Eze 16:36

Nakedness is symbolic of dire poverty

Rev 3:17 *See also* Dt 28:48; 2Ch 28:15; Job 1:21; 24:4–10; Isa 58:6–7; Mic 1:8,11; Ro 8:35; 2Co 11:27

See also

5446 poverty	6239 prostitution
5947 shame	6243 adultery,
6155 fall of Adam &	spiritual
Eve	8277 innocence

5170

neck

The neck may express human pride

"Stiff-necked" as a term for obstinacy Ex 32:9 *See also* Ex 34:9; Dt 9:6; 31:27; 2Ki 17:14; Ne 9:16–29; Pr 29:1; Jer 19:15; Ac 7:51

An outstretched neck as a sign of pride Isa 3:16 *See also* Ps 75:5

Placing the foot on the neck as a sign of conquest Jos 10:24

Ornaments were hung around the neck

Pr 3:3; 6:20–21

A millstone placed around the neck as punishment

Mt 18:6 pp Mk 9:42

See also

1095 God, patience	6245 stubbornness
of	7135 Israel, people
5331 hanging	of God
5865 gestures	8802 pride

5171

nose

The nose as part of the human body

Human life is given and sustained through the nostrils Ge 2:7 *See also* Ge 7:22; Nu 11:20; Job 27:3; Isa 2:22

The nose and the sense of smell

Ge 27:27 *See also* Job 39:25; SS 4:11; Da 3:27; Am 4:10; 1Co 12:17

Animals snort and sniff through their noses

Job 39:20; 41:18,20; Jer 2:24; 8:16

The nose and sneezing

2Ki 4:35

The nose as an object of beauty
SS 7:4

The nose may be adorned with rings
Eze 16:12 *See also* Ge 24:22,30,47;
Isa 3:21

The nose is vulnerable to attack
Pr 30:33 *See also* Eze 23:25

Captives are led by rings or hooks in the nose
2Ki 19:28 pp Isa 37:29 *See also*
2Ch 33:11; Am 4:2

Contempt is communicated by means of the nose
Ps 10:5; Isa 57:4; Mal 1:13; Lk 16:14;
23:35; Ac 17:32

Offence is taken, metaphorically, by the nose
People take offence 2Sa 16:21 *See also*
Ge 34:30; Ex 5:21; 2Sa 10:6 pp 1Ch 19:6

God takes offence Isa 65:5

God's power is indicated by the blast of his nostrils
Ex 15:8 *See also* 2Sa 22:9 pp Ps 18:8;
2Sa 22:16 pp Ps 18:15

Lifeless idols have noses
Ps 115:6 *See also* Dt 4:28

See also

1095 God, patience of	4496 perfume
1105 God, power of	4804 breath
1325 God, the Creator	5183 smell
4016 life, human	5246 captivity
	5818 contempt
	6206 offence

offal

The internal organs of an animal, traditionally regarded as being inferior to meat, and used as a symbol of disgrace.

Offal is symbolic of disgrace
Mal 2:3 *See also* Na 3:6

In animal sacrifices the offal was removed and burnt outside the camp
Ex 29:14 *See also* Lev 4:11–12; 8:17;
16:27; Nu 19:3–5,5

Jesus Christ bears the believer's disgrace
Heb 13:11–13

See also

2324 Christ as Saviour	5836 disgrace
2525 Christ, cross of	6027 sin, remedy for
5166 liver and kidneys	6752 substitution
	7435 sacrifice, in OT

outward appearance

That which is visible on the outside may sometimes reveal the true person, but is sometimes misleading. Judging by it and boasting in it are typical of sinful humanity. God sees the inner reality.

Outward appearance can reveal the truth
Spiritually Mt 7:16–20 pp Lk 6:43–45
See also Mt 5:16; 12:33–37; Jn 15:8;
Jas 2:17–18

Emotionally Pr 15:13 *See also*
1Sa 1:16–18; Pr 17:22; Ecc 8:1;
Da 5:5–6; Mk 10:22

Outward appearance can be deceptive
Mt 23:25–28 *See also* Isa 29:13; 53:2–3;
Mt 7:15; Lk 11:39–41; 2Co 11:13–15;
Col 2:23; Heb 13:2

While people may judge by outward appearance, God does not
People take note of outward appearance Jn 7:23–24 *See also*
Lk 16:14–15; Jn 8:15; 2Co 10:7;
Jas 2:1–4; Rev 3:17

God looks at the heart 1Sa 16:6–7 *See also* 1Ki 8:39 pp 2Ch 6:30; Ps 139:1–2;
Pr 16:2; 21:2; Isa 11:3–5; Lk 16:15;
Gal 2:6; Rev 2:23

The folly of boasting in outward appearance
Lk 20:45–47 *See also* Mt 6:2,5,16;
2Co 5:12; Gal 6:12

What is unseen is more important than outward appearance
2Co 4:16–18 *See also* Ps 51:6;
147:10–11; Ro 2:28–29

Beautiful physical appearance
Examples of the problems and opportunities caused by beautiful outward appearance Ge 12:11–15
Sarah's beauty led to Abraham's folly;
Ge 39:6–7 *Joseph's handsome appearance led to his being tempted by Potiphar's wife;*
1Sa 9:2; 16:12; 25:3; 2Sa 11:2–3
Bathsheba's beauty tempted David;
2Sa 14:25–26; Est 1:10–11; 2:7 *Esther's beauty was an opportunity for God.*

The cultivation of inner beauty encouraged 1Pe 3:3–5; 1Ti 2:9–10

See also

1020 God, all-knowing	5145 clothing
4040 beauty	5840 eagerness
5012 heart	6145 deceit
5024 inner being	8784 nominal religion

prostration

The act of falling down upon one's face in front of someone, as a gesture of fear or reverence before God or a person of high rank.

Prostration before God
In reverence or fear Nu 20:6;
1Ch 29:20; Rev 7:11 *See also* Ge 17:3;
Lev 9:24; Nu 24:4; 1Sa 5:3; 1Ki 18:39;
Ne 8:6; Eze 1:28; Mt 2:11; 17:6; 26:39;
Lk 5:12

As an expression of grieving over sin
Dt 9:18,25; Jos 7:6; Isa 15:3; Eze 9:8

Prostration before God's messenger
Nu 22:31 *See also* Jos 5:14; Jdg 13:20;
1Ch 21:16; Da 8:17; Lk 24:5

Prostration before other people
1Sa 24:8; Isa 51:23 *See also* Ru 2:10;
1Sa 25:23; 28:14; 2Sa 14:4; 19:18;
Isa 49:23; Da 2:46

See also

1065 God, holiness of	5865 gestures
1090 God, majesty of	5899 lament
2224 Christ, the Lord	5959 submission
5150 face	8333 reverence
5161 kneeling	8469 respect
5801 brokenness	8622 worship

reading

The gaining of information through written documents. The Law was read regularly in the synagogue. Jesus Christ expected the Scriptures to be read. NT letters were read in the churches to which they were sent.

Reading of the Law to Israel
By Moses Ex 24:7 *See also* Dt 31:10–11

By Joshua Jos 8:34–35

By Josiah 2Ki 23:2 pp 2Ch 34:30

In Ezra's time Ne 8:2–3,18; 9:3; 13:1

Reading of the Law in the synagogue
Ac 15:21 *See also* Lk 4:16; Ac 13:15,27;
2Co 3:14–15

Other examples of reading
Dt 17:18–20
Jeremiah's words were to be read in public:
Jer 36:6–8; 51:61
Da 9:2 *Daniel foresaw the end of the exile through reading the Scriptures.*

Jesus Christ expected the Scriptures to be read
Mt 12:3–5 pp Mk 2:25–26 pp Lk 6:3–4
See also Mt 19:4; 21:16,42
pp Mk 12:10–11 pp Lk 20:17; Mt 22:31;
24:15 pp Mk 13:14

Reading of NT letters
Col 4:16 *See also* Ac 15:31; 1Th 5:27

Reasons for reading the Scriptures
They are God-breathed 2Ti 3:16

God's word is true Jn 17:7

To understand the truth about Jesus Christ Lk 24:26–27; Eph 3:4

To believe and be saved from God's wrath Jn 20:31; 2Ti 3:15

To learn how to serve and please God Ps 119:105,130; 2Ti 3:16; Rev 1:3

They teach Christians and give them hope Ro 15:4; 1Jn 2:1,12–14,21

They enable Christians to discern truth from error Ac 18:28 *See also* Ac 17:11;
Gal 1:6–9; 2Pe 3:14–16; 1Jn 2:26; 4:1

See also

1610 Scripture	5232 book
1640 Book of the Law	5375 law
	5391 letters
2363 Christ, preaching & teaching	5393 literacy
	5514 scribes
	5515 scroll

5176

See also
5638 writing   8627 worship,
7939 ministry   elements

5176

ring

An ornament or a status symbol, sometimes used in sacred furnishings or as a charm.

Rings worn as jewellery

Gold nose rings, worn especially by women
These were often given by a suitor as a symbol of betrothal: Ge 24:22,30,47; Pr 11:22; Isa 3:21; Eze 16:12

The signet ring as a sign of authority
Ge 41:42; Nu 31:50; Est 3:10,12; 8:8; Da 6:17
People are sometimes symbolically referred to as God's signet ring, having his seal of ownership and authority: Jer 22:24; Hag 2:23

Gold ear-rings, worn by men and women
Ear-rings were sometimes used as charms or amulets: Ge 35:4; Ex 32:2–3; 35:22; Jdg 8:24–25

Rings as indications of wealth or status
Job 42:11; Hos 2:13; Lk 15:22; Jas 2:2

Rings used in sacred furnishings
On the ark of the covenant
Ex 25:12–15

On the table Ex 25:26–27

In the tabernacle Ex 26:24–29

On priestly garments Ex 28:23–24

For carrying altars Ex 27:4–7; 30:4; 37:27

See also
1670 symbols   5708 marriage
4333 gold   5778 adorning
5139 bracelet   5915 ornaments
5171 nose   7306 ark of the
5215 authority   covenant
5518 seal   7459 tabernacle, in
5654 betrothal   OT

5177

robes

A formal style of clothing, often indicating priesthood, royalty or elevated social status.

Priestly robes
Aaron's priestly robes Ex 28:4 *See also*
Ex 28:31–34; 29:5; 39:22–26; Lev 8:7; Ps 133:2

Other wearers of priestly robes
1Sa 2:19; 1Ch 15:27

Royal robes
The majestic robes of God Ps 93:1; Isa 6:1; 63:1

Robes for kings and queens Est 5:1 *See also* 1Ki 22:10 pp 2Ch 18:9; 1Ki 22:30 pp 2Ch 18:29; Est 8:15; Jnh 3:6; Ac 12:21

Jesus Christ robed as a king and mocked Mk 15:17 pp Mt 27:28 *See also* Jn 19:2,5

Robes indicating office, favour or wealth
Ge 41:42 *See also* Ge 37:3; Jos 7:21; 1Sa 18:4; 2Sa 13:18; 1Ki 10:25; Est 6:7–11; Isa 3:18–23; 22:21; Mic 2:8; Mk 12:38; Lk 20:46; 15:22

Robes associated with righteousness and purity
Isa 61:10 *See also* Rev 6:11; 7:9,13–14; 22:14

Tearing of robes to show mourning or repentance
Job 2:12 *See also* 2Ch 34:27

See also
1090 God, majesty of   5778 adorning
2570 Christ,   6732 repentance
   suffering   7767 priests, OT
5131 belt   institution
5145 clothing   8154 righteousness
5188 tearing of   9414 heaven,
   clothes   community of
5419 mourning   redeemed
5742 wedding

5178

running

Scripture gives pictures of running in both its literal and metaphorical senses, the image of the Christian life as a race being particularly significant.

Running away
Fleeing in battle Ex 23:27 *See also* Lev 26:36–37; Jos 7:12; 8:3–19; 1Sa 14:20–22

Escaping from danger Pr 18:10 *See also* Ge 19:12–22; Ne 6:10–11; Isa 10:1–3; Jer 17:16; 48:4–6; 51:6,44–45; Am 2:14–16; Jn 10:12–13

Running away from individuals
1Sa 19:11–12 *See also* Ge 16:6–8; 31:20–21; 39:11–15; Jn 10:2–5

Running away from God Jnh 1:1–10

Running away from evil 2Ti 2:22 *See also* 1Co 6:18; 10:14; 1Ti 6:11

Running after people or things
Ps 16:4 *See also* Ru 3:10; Isa 5:11; Jer 2:23–25; Eze 16:32–34; Mt 6:28–34 pp Lk 12:27–31

Running in eagerness
Jn 20:1–4 *See also* 2Ch 23:12; Mk 9:25; Lk 17:22–23; Ac 3:11; 21:30

Running swiftly
Job 9:25 *See also* Job 39:13–18; Ecc 9:11; Jer 12:5

Heralds running ahead of a dignitary
1Sa 8:11 *See also* 2Sa 15:1; 1Ki 1:5; 18:46

Messages carried by runners
2Sa 18:19 *See also* 2Sa 18:21–32; 2Ki 4:25–31; 5:20–23; 9:1–3; Ps 147:15; Jer 23:21; Hab 2:2; Zec 2:3–5

The life of the believer likened to running a race
Gal 2:2 *See also* Ps 119:32; Pr 4:10–12; Isa 40:30–31; Ac 20:24; 1Co 9:24–27; Gal 5:7; Php 2:14–16; 2Ti 4:6–8; Heb 12:1; 2Jn 9

See also
5197 walking   5342 hunting
5280 crown   5408 messenger
5319 fugitives   8110 athletics
5335 herald   8140 prize

5179

sandal

A form of open shoe worn in warm climates, and the only form of foot-covering to be of major importance in Scripture. Both the wearing and the removal of sandals is often seen as symbolic; to go barefoot was often a sign of shame, mourning or poverty.

Sandals were normally worn by an official, soldier or messenger
1Ki 2:5; Eph 6:15

Untying and carrying sandals was the task of a servant
Mt 3:11 pp Mk 1:7 pp Lk 3:16 pp Jn 1:27
John considers himself unworthy to be a slave of Jesus Christ. See also Ac 13:25

The removal of sandals as a gesture
As a mark of respect in the presence of God Ex 3:5 *See also* Jos 5:15; Ac 7:33

To show rejection of any claim to property Dt 25:9–10; Ru 4:7–8; Ps 60:8 pp Ps 108:9

To predict the defeat and disgrace of Egypt and Assyria Isa 20:2–4

As a sign of mourning and repentance 2Sa 15:30; Eze 24:17,23; Mic 1:8

The symbolic use of sandals
As symbols of readiness for action Ex 12:11

As symbols of oppression and injustice Am 2:6; 8:6

Fine sandals as a status symbol Eze 16:10; Lk 15:22

Sandals as an example of the need for minimum possessions in God's service
Mt 10:10 pp Mk 6:9 pp Lk 10:4; Lk 22:35

See also
5145 clothing   5197 walking
5151 feet

5180

shaving

The removal of hair with a razor or other sharp implement. Both male and female Israelites allowed their hair to grow long. Barbers trimmed, but did not crop, men's hair, so giving special significance to the shaving of the head or whole body.

These actions indicated shame or grief.

Personal toilet
Ge 41:14; 2Sa 14:26

Symbolic shaving
Shaved head a sign of grief Job 1:20 *See also* Dt 21:10–14; Isa 15:2; Jer 47:5; 48:36–37; Eze 27:31; Am 8:10; Mic 1:16; Jer 7:29; 41:5

A shaved head a sign of shame 2Sa 10:4 pp 1Ch 19:4 *See also* Ezr 9:3; Isa 7:20; 50:6; Jer 2:16; Eze 7:18; 1Co 11:5–6

Shaving in ritual cleansing
Lev 14:8–9; Nu 8:7; Ac 21:24

Shaving as a visual aid
Eze 5:1–4

After a period of dedication
Nu 6:18

Shaving forbidden
As a pagan practice Lev 19:27; 21:5 *See also* Dt 14:1 *Pagans shaved the front of their heads as a sign of mourning. God's people should have a different attitude to bereavement from those who have no hope;* Eze 44:20

For the sake of a Nazirite vow Nu 6:5 *See also* Jdg 16:17; 1Sa 1:11

See also

1670 symbols	5947 shame
5128 baldness	5952 sorrow
5155 hair	7342 cleanliness
5372 knife	7424 ritual law
5836 disgrace	8218 consecration
5938 sadness	8223 dedication

5181

sitting

A bodily posture associated with resting, eating or instruction. When used of God, the image often conveys the idea of kingly authority over creation.

Sitting to rest
Ge 18:1; Jn 4:6 *See also* Ex 2:15; 17:12; 1Ki 19:4; Mt 26:36

Sitting to eat
Ex 32:6; Lk 17:7 *See also* Jdg 19:6; Ru 2:14; 1Sa 20:24; Pr 23:1; Jer 16:8; Mt 14:19; 1Co 10:7

Sitting to teach or to learn
Mt 5:1–2 *See also* Mt 13:2; Mk 9:35; Lk 2:46; 10:39; Jn 8:2

Sitting for prayer
Jdg 21:2 *See also* 2Sa 7:18

Sitting as a sign of authority
Human authority Ex 11:5 *See also* 1Ki 1:13; 3:6; 2Ki 10:30; Zec 6:13; Mk 10:37

Divine authority Ps 29:10 *See also* 1Ki 22:19; Ps 47:8; 80:1; Isa 6:1; Mt 26:64; Lk 20:42; Heb 1:3; 10:12; 12:2; Rev 3:21; 4:10; 7:10

Sitting to judge
Ex 18:13; Mt 25:31 *See also* 2Sa 19:8;

Pr 20:8; Isa 28:6; Jer 38:7; Da 7:26; Joel 3:12; Mt 27:19; Lk 22:30; Ac 23:3

Sitting as a sign of possession and peace
Mic 4:4 *See also* Zec 3:10

Jesus Christ seated at God's right hand
Lk 22:69; Eph 1:20; 2:6; Col 3:1

See also

1090 God, majesty of	5184 standing
1310 God as judge	5219 authority,
2309 Christ as judge	human
2363 Christ,	institutions
preaching &	5358 judges
teaching	5581 throne
4438 eating	7797 teaching

5182

skin

The outer covering of the body. Diseased skin is often subject to pain and regarded as unclean.

Skin as the outer covering of the body
Job 10:10–11 *See also* Ge 3:21; 27:11; Eze 37:6,8

Violence against the skin
Mic 3:2–3 *See also* Job 2:4–5

Skin and bones
Ps 102:5 *To be reduced to skin and bones is a mark of severe suffering. See also* Nu 4:8–14 *animal skins used for covering the ark of the Testimony;* Job 19:20; La 3:4; 4:8

Skin diseases
Skin diseases are painful Job 30:30 *See also* Job 7:5; 18:13; La 5:10

They can be defiling Nu 5:2–3 *See also* Lev 13:1–11,43–46; 22:4

As God's punishment for sin Nu 12:10–11 *Miriam;* 2Ki 5:26–27 *Naaman;* 2Ch 26:19–20 *Uzziah*

Healed by Jesus Christ Mt 8:2–3 pp Mk 1:40–42 pp Lk 5:12–13; Lk 17:12–14

Skin cannot be changed
Jer 13:23

A person can know God even when the skin has been destroyed
Job 19:26–27

See also

5136 body	5560 suffering
5137 bones	7340 clean and
5146 covering	unclean
5297 disease	7348 defilement
5333 healing	9210 judgment,
5390 leprosy	God's
5436 pain	9310 resurrection

5183

smell

An aroma; God is pleased by the aroma of sacrifice, whether a literal sacrifice or the figurative offering of Christian service is a picture of its

acceptability to him. Bad smells can indicate physical decay or the results of judgment. To be a stench to someone is to be held in contempt or hated by that person.

The aroma of sacrifice
Ge 8:21 *See also* Lev 1:9; 2:2; 3:5; 4:31; 6:15,21; 8:21; 23:13,18; Nu 15:14,24 *offerings to be made for unintentional breaking of the LORD's commandments;* Nu 18:17; 28:2; 29:2

Substances to create a pleasing smell
Ex 30:7–8 *See also* Ex 30:22–29,34–38; 35:28; 37:29; 40:26–27; Nu 4:16; 2Ch 2:4; 13:11

The aroma of sacrifice is not always pleasing to God
Lev 26:31; Eze 8:11–13; 20:27–29

Jesus Christ was the supreme fragrant offering
Eph 5:2

God accepts his people as fragrant incense
Eze 20:41 *See also* Hos 14:5–6

A pleasing aroma depicts acceptable Christian service
2Co 2:14–16 *See also* Php 4:18

Fragrance associated with the expression of love
SS 1:2–3; 4:16–5:1 *The beloved's garden is an image of her body. See also* Ps 45:8; SS 1:12–13; 3:6; 4:10–11; 5:13; 7:8; Jn 12:3

A bad smell
Indicating decay Jn 11:39 *See also* Ex 16:20 *Manna soon smelled bad if kept. This meant the Israelites had to trust God afresh for each day's supply.*

As the result of God's judgment *The first plague on Egypt, which made the Nile smell bad:* Ex 7:18,21 Isa 34:3; Am 4:10

As a picture of the results of judgment Isa 3:24; 19:6; Joel 2:20

As a figurative cause of contempt or hatred Ge 34:30; Ex 5:21 *The word "offence" is from a Hebrew root-word meaning "to smell bad":* 1Sa 13:4; 2Sa 10:6 pp 1Ch 19:6; 2Sa 16:21

Idols cannot smell
Ps 115:4–6 *See also* Dt 4:28

See also

4490 ointment	7386 incense
4496 perfume	7402 offerings
5171 nose	7434 sacrifice
6142 decay	8768 idolatry
6206 offence	

5184

standing

The bodily posture of being in a stationary upright position.

Standing as a sign of authority
Ac 7:55

Standing merely to wait or rest
Ex 33:21 *See also* Jos 3:8; 1Ki 20:38; Mt 12:47; 20:3; 26:73; Lk 19:24; Jn 8:9

Standing ready for action
Nu 22:23; Ac 5:23 *See also* Dt 10:8;
Jos 5:13; 1Sa 17:16; 1Ch 21:16; Lk 1:11;
Ac 16:9; Rev 7:1

Standing to show respect or honour
Da 2:2 *See also* 1Ki 10:8; 22:19; 2Ch 6:3;
Ne 8:4; Jer 36:21; Da 10:11

Standing in the presence of God
In heaven Lk 1:19 *See also* Zec 6:5;
Rev 7:9; 8:2

On earth Ge 19:27; Ex 3:5; Ne 9:5 *See also* Ex 33:10; Dt 4:10; 29:10; 1Sa 1:26;
1Ch 23:30; 2Ch 20:9; Ps 24:3; Jer 28:5;
Mt 6:5; Mk 11:25; Lk 18:11; Ro 14:4

Standing for trial or judgment
Ex 18:13; Ro 14:10 *See also* Nu 5:16;
35:12; Dt 19:17; 1Sa 12:3,7; Zec 3:1;
Mt 27:11; Lk 11:32; Ac 23:6; 25:10;
Rev 20:12

Standing firm as a believer
Pr 10:25; 1Co 15:58 *See also* Lk 21:28;
Ro 5:2; 11:20; 1Co 15:1; 16:13;
2Co 1:21,24; Gal 5:1; Php 4:1; Col 4:12;
2Th 2:15; Jas 5:8; 1Pe 5:12

Against evil and temptation 1Co 10:13;
Eph 6:11–14

Against enemies and opposition
Ps 94:16 *See also* Ex 14:13; 2Ch 20:17;
Isa 7:9; Jer 1:17; Eph 6:11–14; Php 1:27

Other metaphorical uses of standing
God's purpose will stand Isa 46:10 *See also* Isa 14:24

Standing in the gap Eze 22:30 *See also* Ps 106:23

See also
1065 God, holiness of	8334 reverence & God's nature
2336 Christ, exaltation	8611 prayer for others
5181 sitting	8727 enemies
5767 attitudes in prayer	8737 evil, responses to
5878 honour	
6251 temptation, resisting	

5185

stomach

As well as the physical stomach, the term is used in association with God's judgment or in a figurative sense.

Stomach as part of the physical body
1Co 6:13 *See also* Job 40:16; SS 7:2;
Da 2:32

Jonah in the stomach of a huge fish
Mt 12:40 *See also* Jnh 1:17–2:1

Ritual laws concerning the stomach
Mk 7:18–19 pp Mt 15:17 *See also* Lev 11:41–45

Afflictions of the stomach
Lk 15:16 *hunger*; 1Ti 5:23 *illness*

Fatal wounding in the stomach
Jdg 3:21; 2Sa 2:23; 3:27; 4:6; 20:10

The stomach and God's judgment
Severe stomach pain Jer 30:6–7 *See also* Nu 5:20–22,27

Crawling on one's stomach as a sign of submission Ge 3:14 *Part of God's curse upon Satan. See also* Ps 72:9; Isa 49:23;
65:25; Mic 7:17

Hunger as a result of God's judgment
Mic 6:14 *See also* Job 20:12–15,20–23;
Pr 13:25; Isa 9:20; Eze 7:19

An empty stomach as a warning
Am 4:6

The stomach and God's blessing
In the OT a full stomach was one sign of God's blessing: Ps 34:9–10; 37:19,25;
Pr 10:3

Figurative uses of the stomach
Stomach as a symbol of inner thoughts
Eze 3:3 *See also* Pr 18:8; 26:22;
Rev 10:9–10

Stomach as a symbol of worldliness
Php 3:19 *See also* Ro 16:18

Stomach as something to be filled
Pr 18:20 *See also* Job 15:2; Jer 51:34

See also
4120 Satan	5792 appetite
5012 heart	5869 greed
5024 inner being	7424 ritual law
5040 murder	8848 worldliness
5136 body	9210 judgment,
5199 womb	God's
5341 hunger	

5186

stumbling

Faltering or falling in the course of running or walking. The term is also used metaphorically to refer to failure, hesitation or difficulty.

Physical stumbling
Lev 19:14
Through fear: Lev 26:37; Isa 21:4
Isa 28:7 *through drunkenness*
In battle: Na 2:5; 3:3

God protects his people from stumbling
Ps 56:13 *See also* 1Sa 2:4; Job 4:4;
Ps 37:24; 116:8

The enemies of God's people will stumble
Jer 20:11 *See also* Ps 9:3; 27:2

God's people will stumble if they sin
Isa 8:14; Jer 13:16

Avoiding stumbling by keeping God's law
Ps 119:165 *See also* Pr 3:23,26; 4:11–12;
Isa 26:7–8; 40:30–31

The wicked stumble because they reject God's way
Pr 4:19; Hos 14:9

Causes of stumbling
Dishonesty Isa 59:14

Arrogance Jer 50:32; Hos 5:5

False teaching by religious leaders
Hos 4:5; Mal 2:8

Idolatry Jer 18:15

Trust in riches Eze 7:19

Trust in secular political alliances
Isa 31:3

Stumbling as a consequence of sin and divine judgment
Making one's own stumbling-block
Eze 14:3–4,7

Stumbling over obstacles sent by God
Jer 6:21; 13:16; Eze 3:20

Some stumbling is educative or disciplinary Da 11:35; Ro 9:32–33

Jesus Christ as the light that prevents believers from stumbling
Jn 9:5; 11:9–10

Jesus Christ as a stumbling-block for unbelievers
1Co 1:23 *See also* 1Pe 2:8

Stumbling and sin
All sin and stumble Jas 2:10; 3:2

None should feel superior to others
Pr 24:17; 1Co 10:12

None should cause others to stumble
Ro 14:20; 1Co 10:32

See also
2414 cross, centrality	6206 offence
4833 light	6738 rescue
5133 blindness	8714 dishonesty
5480 protection	8741 failure
5605 warfare	8749 false teachers
5877 hesitation	8754 fear

5187

taste

The act of tasting is used figuratively of experiencing the goodness of God and his word and of a variety of experiences: misery, sin, wisdom, love, death and blessing.

The taste of food or drink
Ex 16:31 *See also* Ge 25:28;
27:4,7,9,14,17,31; Nu 11:7–8;
2Sa 19:34–35; Jn 2:9

Legalistic prohibitions against tasting certain foods are condemned by Paul
Col 2:20–22

Taste used figuratively
Of the experience of misery Job 6:6–7
In his complaint against God, Job compares the unacceptability of his lot to inedible food. See also Job 27:2

Of the experience of the goodness of God Ps 34:8 *See also* Heb 6:4–5; 1Pe 2:3

Of the experience of the goodness of the word of God Ps 119:103 *See also* Ps 19:10; Jer 15:16; Eze 3:3;
Rev 10:9–10

Of the experience of sin Pr 20:17

Of the experience of wisdom
Pr 24:13–14

Of the experience of love SS 2:3 *See also* SS 4:11,16

Of the effectiveness of Christian influence Mt 5:13 pp Lk 14:34–35

Of the experience of death Heb 2:9 *See also* Mt 16:28 pp Mk 9:1 pp Lk 9:27; Jn 8:52

Of the blessings of the kingdom of God Lk 14:24; 22:29–30

To determine not to taste food until a task was completed was commonly used as an oath
1Sa 14:24–46; 2Sa 3:35; Jnh 3:7; Ac 23:14

See also

1050 God, goodness of	5284 cupbearer
4357 salt	5429 oaths
4404 food	5792 appetite
4544 wine	5832 desire
5167 mouth	5852 experience
	8774 legalism

5188

tearing of clothes

Primarily associated with mourning, such action was an expression of deep sorrow and heartfelt grief. It was also a natural reaction at times of great distress and in cases of sincere repentance.

The tearing of clothes was a sign of mourning
It was a demonstration of grief 2Sa 1:11–12 *See also* 2Sa 13:30–31; 2Ki 2:11–12; Job 1:20; 2:12

It was often associated with wearing sackcloth Ge 37:34 *See also* 2Sa 3:31–32

The high priest was forbidden to tear his clothes in mourning Lev 21:10–12 *See also* Lev 10:1–7

The tearing of clothes indicated deep distress
Jdg 11:34–35 *Jephthah had vowed to sacrifice whatever came out of the door of his house to meet him. See also* Ge 37:29; 44:12–13; Nu 14:1–9; Jos 7:3–6; 2Ki 6:26–30; 18:28–19:4 pp Isa 36:13–37:4; Est 3:13–4:1; Ac 14:8–18

Repentance was sometimes accompanied by the tearing of clothes
1Ki 21:20–27 *See also* Jer 36:21–24 *an indication of the lack of repentance;* Joel 2:12–14 *God requires that the tearing of clothes should express genuine repentance.*

Other references to the tearing of clothes
As an expression of anger Mt 26:63–65 pp Mk 14:61–63

To stop the spread of mildew Lev 13:53–58

As a symbol of the dividing of the kingdom 1Sa 15:27–28

See also

1670 symbols	6732 repentance
5177 robes	6742 sackcloth &
5198 weeping	ashes
5419 mourning	7376 high priest
5795 bereavement	8429 fasting
5899 lament	9020 death

5189

teeth

Scripture often uses teeth symbolically, to refer to the power of individuals or to human rage (as in the "gnashing of teeth").

Teeth in a literal sense
In eating Nu 11:33 *See also* Da 7:5,7,19; Zec 9:7; Rev 9:8

As an object of beauty SS 4:2 *See also* Ge 49:12; SS 6:6

As an object of fear Job 41:14 *See also* Dt 32:24; Job 20:16; Joel 1:6

Teeth used symbolically
To represent offensive weapons Ps 57:4; Pr 30:14

To symbolise military power Isa 41:15 *See also* Joel 1:6; Am 1:3; Hab 3:12

God rescues his people from the teeth of their enemies Ps 124:6 *See also* Job 4:10; Da 6:20–21

Breaking the teeth of the wicked ends their power Ps 3:7 *See also* Job 29:17; Ps 58:6 *Enemies are often described as dangerous animals.*

Gnashing of teeth
In rage Ac 7:54 *See also* Job 16:9; Ps 35:16; 37:12

In frustration Ps 112:10

In anguish Mt 8:12; 13:42,50; 22:13; 24:51; 25:30; Lk 13:28

In gloating La 2:16

Under demonic influence Mk 9:18

Proverbial sayings about teeth
Job 19:20; Pr 10:26; Jer 31:29–30; Eze 18:2

See also

4040 beauty	5132 biting
4508 sickle	5481 proverb
4522 threshing	5789 anger

5190

thigh

The human thigh
A symbol of strength Job 40:17; Da 2:32

Weapons strapped to the thigh Jdg 3:16,21

The hand is placed under the thigh when taking an oath Ge 24:2,9; 47:29

The priests' undergarments covered the thigh Ex 28:42–43 *See also* Ex 20:26; Lev 6:10; 16:3–4; Eze 44:17–18

The wasting of the thigh
The wasting away of the thigh is part of the judgment on an unfaithful wife: Nu 5:21–22,27

The thigh as a place of identification Rev 19:16

The right thighs of animals used in sacrificial offerings
Ex 29:22,27; Lev 7:32–34; 8:25–26; 9:21; 10:14–15; Nu 6:20; 18:18

See also

5136 body	5612 weapons
5145 clothing	5865 gestures
5163 legs	5954 strength
5169 nakedness	7435 sacrifice, in OT
5429 oaths	8839 unfaithfulness

5191

thought

The human ability to reason and reflect. Believers are called to reflect upon the words and works of God as they are made known through Scripture and to avoid speculation based purely upon human reason.

Human thought and God
God's thoughts are infinitely higher than human thoughts Isa 55:8–9 *See also* Ps 92:5; 139:17–18; 1Co 2:10–11

God knows all human thoughts 1Ch 28:9 *See also* Ge 6:5; Ps 94:11; 139:1–4; Mt 9:4; 12:25 pp Lk 11:17; Lk 9:47; Heb 4:12

Meditating on God's words Ps 1:1–2 *See also* Dt 6:6–7; 11:18; Jos 1:8; Ps 119:15,23,78,97

Meditating on God's works Ps 77:12 *See also* 1Sa 12:24; Ps 106:7; 107:43; 119:27; 143:5; 145:4–5; Isa 1:18

Warnings against founding faith on speculative thought or human wisdom
Col 2:8 *See also* Isa 29:14; 1Co 1:20; 2:6; 3:19–20; 2Co 10:5; Jas 3:13–15

Believers are to give thought to others
To think about their needs Php 2:4 *See also* Zec 7:10; Lk 10:36–37; Ro 12:13; 1Co 12:26; 14:11–12; 1Ti 5:3; 1Jn 3:17

To think about their abilities Php 2:3 *See also* 1Co 12:24–25; 14:26–33; Heb 10:24

To think about, and learn from, their shortcomings Gal 6:1 *See also* Ac 8:20–21; Ro 1:21; Eph 4:17–19

Believers are to give thought to themselves
To think accurately about themselves and their God-given abilities Ro 12:3 *See also* 1Co 1:26; 3:18; 10:12; 14:20,37; 2Co 11:5–6; Gal 6:3; Php 2:3; 1Ti 4:4

To think about their shortcomings and temptations 2Co 10:12 *See also* Pr 6:6; Mt 15:19; Ro 2:15; 1Co 13:11; 2Co 10:7; Eph 2:3; Php 3:13; Col 1:21

To think about their needs Php 3:7–9 *See also* Mt 6:31–34; Php 2:4

To think rightly about their plans and ambitions 1Pe 1:13–14 *See also* Dt 15:9; Pr 5:6; 14:8,15; Isa 55:7; Hag 1:5; Lk 14:31 *Jesus Christ wanted his followers to consider carefully the cost of being a disciple;* Ac 5:35; Ro 13:14; Php 4:8; Col 3:1–2; Heb 3:1; 11:15; Jas 1:2; 1Pe 4:1; 2Pe 3:1–2

See also

1020 God, all-knowing	5050 reason
5012 heart	5063 spirit, nature of
5035 mind	5441 philosophy

See also
5761 attitudes   8361 wisdom
5864 futility   8477 self-
6185 imagination,   examination
     desires   8662 meditation

5192

thumbs

The role of the thumb in sacrificial ritual
Ex 29:20; Lev 8:23–24; 14:14,17,25,28

Thumbs cut off
Jdg 1:6–7

See also
5152 fingers   7435 sacrifice, in OT
5156 hand

5193

tongue

The organ of speech, which Scripture stresses can be the source of both praise and blame. The tongue is to be kept under control, on account of its capacity for evil words.

The tongue as a bodily organ
As part of the body Jas 3:5 *See also* Jdg 7:5; Job 41:1; Mk 7:33; Lk 16:24; Rev 16:10

Used for eating Nu 22:4; Job 12:11; 34:3; Ps 68:23

Used for drinking Jdg 7:5

Used for licking 1Ki 21:19; 22:38; Lk 16:21

Parched with thirst Ps 22:15; 137:6; Isa 41:17; La 4:4

The tongue as an organ of speech
It is God-given Ex 4:10–11 *See also* Eze 3:26; Lk 1:20–22,62–64

God is able to loose the tongue of the mute Mk 7:33–35 *See also* Isa 32:4; 35:6; Mt 15:30–31; Lk 1:64

Reasons for holding one's tongue
To restrain sin Pr 10:19 *See also* Pr 11:12; 17:27–28; 21:23; Jas 1:26; 1Pe 3:10

As a mark of respect and awe Job 29:9–10; Hab 2:20

The tongue's potential for good
Right use of the tongue requires an act of the will Job 27:4 *See also* Ps 39:1; 141:3

The tongue can praise God Ps 35:28 *See also* Ps 16:9; 45:1; 51:14; 66:17; 71:24; 119:172; 126:2; Ac 2:26; Jas 3:9

The tongue can speak God-given words 2Sa 23:2 *See also* Pr 16:1; Isa 50:4; Mic 3:8; Lk 21:14–15

Every tongue will acknowledge God Isa 45:23 *See also* Ro 14:11; Php 2:10–11

The tongue can speak wisdom Ps 37:30 *See also* Pr 10:19–20; 12:18; 15:23; 31:26

The tongue can bring healing Pr 15:4 *See also* Pr 12:18

The tongue's potential for evil
The tongue's power needs to be controlled Pr 18:21; Jas 3:3–10 *See also* Job 27:4; Ps 34:13; Pr 11:12; Jas 1:26

The tongue can speak deceitfully Ps 5:9 *See also* Ps 50:19; 52:4; 120:2–3; Pr 15:4; 17:20; Jer 9:8; Mic 6:12; Ro 3:13

The tongue can speak lies Jer 9:3 *See also* Pr 6:17; 21:6; 26:28

Other evil uses of the tongue Ps 10:7 *See also* Ps 12:3–4; 52:2; Pr 6:24; Isa 57:4; 59:3; Jer 18:18

The punishment for a perverse tongue Pr 10:31

Tongue in the sense of language
As a foreign language Ac 2:8–11 *See also* Est 1:22; Ps 114:1; Isa 28:11; 33:19; 66:18; 1Co 14:10

As a language given by the Holy Spirit Ac 2:4 *See also* Mk 16:17; Ac 10:46; 19:6; 1Co 12:10,28,30; 13:1,8; 14:2–23

Metaphors used to describe the tongue
The tongue as a dangerous weapon Ps 57:4; 64:3; Jer 9:3,8

Other metaphors Ps 140:3; Pr 10:20; Isa 5:24; Ac 2:3; Jas 3:6

See also
1690 word of God   5196 voice
5164 lips   5546 speech
5167 mouth   5950 silence
5168 muteness   7972 tongues, gift of
5187 taste

5194

touch

God prohibits physical contact in certain circumstances and warns of serious consequences of violating the ritual law in this respect. Great significance is attached to the touch of God, Jesus Christ and angels and the disciples' touching of the risen Christ.

God's prohibits touch in certain circumstances
At Mount Sinai Ex 19:12–13 *See also* Heb 12:18–24

With the furnishings and articles of the tabernacle Nu 4:15 *See also* 2Sa 6:6–7

The law concerning touching certain articles
Anyone or anything touching what is ritually unclean also becomes unclean Nu 19:21–22 *See also* Lev 5:2–3; 7:19–21; 11:8,24–40; 12:4; 15:5–12,19–27; 22:4–6; Nu 19:11–16 *the law concerning dead bodies;* Dt 14:8 *Pigs are unclean;* Isa 52:11; Hag 2:10–14

Touching what is purified confers consecration Ex 29:37; 30:29; Lev 6:18,27

Man-made rules against touching certain things are condemned by Paul
Col 2:20–22

The touch of God
Upon Jacob, to humble him Ge 32:25,32

Upon those he calls to be prophets Jer 1:9 *See also* Isa 6:7; Eze 2:8–3:4; Da 10:16

Upon the world he has made, to display his glory Ps 104:32 *See also* Ps 144:5; Am 9:5

The touch of Jesus Christ
To heal Mt 8:3 pp Mk 1:41–42 pp Lk 5:13 *See also* Mt 9:29–30; 20:34; Mk 7:33; 8:22–25; Lk 22:51

To raise the dead Mt 9:18–25 pp Mk 5:22–42 pp Lk 8:41–55 *In touching the dead, Jesus Christ shows his willingness to become unclean so that others can be healed. See also* Lk 7:14

To bring reassurance and show acceptance Mt 17:6–7; Mk 10:13 pp Mt 19:13 pp Lk 18:15

The touch of angels
1Ki 19:5,7; Da 8:18; 10:10,18

The reality of Jesus Christ's incarnation and resurrection is confirmed by touch
1Jn 1:1; Jn 20:24–27

The figurative use of touch
To mean harming people Eze 9:6 *See also* Ge 20:6; Jos 9:19; 1Ch 16:22 pp Ps 105:15; Pr 6:29; Zec 2:8–9; Heb 11:28

To mean separation from sin 2Co 6:17 *See also* Isa 52:11

See also
1265 hand of God   7340 clean and
2351 Christ, miracles   unclean
2515 Christ, birth of   7348 defilement
2555 Christ,   7372 hands, laying
     resurrection   on
     appearances   7424 ritual law
5156 hand   8774 legalism
5333 healing   9030 dead bodies

5195

veil

Generally, an item of female dress worn by an unmarried woman in the presence of her future husband and also by a prostitute. Head-coverings were worn by men and women as a sign of mourning. The term is also used metaphorically to indicate a lack of understanding of God's truth. Scripture uses the imagery of "removing a veil" to refer to God's final self-revelation at the end of the age, or the making known of God's will and nature through Jesus Christ or other means.

The veil as an item of female dress
Worn by women in general SS 4:1 *The veil covered the lower part of the face, so focusing attention on the eyes and temples. See also* Ge 24:65 *Rebekah veils herself in the presence of her future husband, Isaac;* SS 4:3; 6:7

Worn by prostitutes Ge 38:14–15 *See also* SS 1:7

Worn by female sorcerers Eze 13:18,21

Worn as a sign of wealth and status
Isa 3:19; 47:2 *Babylon's veil will be removed as a mark of her humiliation.*

Veils worn as a sign of grief
Faces covered in sorrow and dismay
2Sa 15:30 *See also* Lev 13:45 *A veil worn by the ceremonially unclean signifies grief at separation from God;* Jer 14:4

Veils customarily worn by mourners
2Sa 19:4 *See also* Eze 24:17,22

Faces covered as a sign of disgrace
Est 6:12; 7:8; Mic 3:7

Head-coverings in worship
1Co 11:4 *A man's uncovered head in worship signifies submission to his spiritual head, i.e., Jesus Christ;*
1Co 11:5–6 *A woman's covered head signifies proper submission to her husband. See also* 1Co 11:7,13

God's sight of humanity is not veiled
The wicked foolishly boast that God does not see them Job 22:12–14 *See also* Ps 10:11; 94:7; Isa 29:15

God's people complain that God does not see their suffering Ps 44:24 *See also* Job 13:24; Ps 69:17; 88:14

God sees all humanity Job 28:24 *See also* Ge 16:13; Job 34:21; Ps 33:13; 139:1–3

People's deeds will be made known
1Co 4:5 *See also* Job 28:11; Isa 26:21; Mt 10:26 pp Lk 12:2; 1Co 3:13

The truth about God is sometimes veiled
The veil worn by Moses 2Co 3:13 *After speaking with God, Moses' face was radiant; the veil, possibly a loose part of his clothing pulled over his face, prevented the Israelites from seeing that the radiance did not last. See also* Ex 34:29–35

Lack of understanding of God's truth
2Co 3:14–15 *See also* Isa 44:18; La 3:65; 1Co 2:14; 2Co 4:3; Eph 4:18

The unveiling of God's truth
God's hidden truth is revealed to believers 1Co 2:7–10; Col 1:26 *See also* Isa 64:4; Ro 16:25–26; 2Co 3:16–18; Eph 1:9; 3:3–6; 2Ti 1:10; Tit 3:1–3

God's self-revelation at the end of the age Da 12:2–4 *See also* Isa 25:7–8; Ro 8:19; 1Jn 3:2

See also

1020 God, all-knowing	5150 face
1110 God, present everywhere	5158 head-covering
1439 revelation	5419 mourning
5135 blindness, spiritual	5952 sorrow
5145 clothing	6694 mystery
	7344 curtain
	8419 enlightenment

---

voice

The organ of speech; someone's voice expresses a person's character,

thoughts and emotions, and attracts attention by its tone and volume.

The human voice
The sound of familiar voices Ac 12:14
See also Ge 27:22; Jdg 18:3; 1Sa 24:16; 26:17; SS 2:14; 8:13

Groups of people speaking in unison
Ex 24:3 *See also* 1Sa 10:24; 2Ch 5:13; 23:11; Ezr 10:12; Ac 12:22; 19:34; 22:22

Voices communicate in various ways
Voices expressing defiance 1Sa 17:8
See also 2Ki 19:22 pp Isa 37:23

Voices that give a battle cry 1Sa 17:20; 2Ch 13:15; Isa 8:9; Jer 4:16,19

Festive voices 2Sa 19:35; Jer 7:34; 16:9; 25:10; 33:11

Voices expressing distress Jdg 21:2 *See also* Ge 27:34; Nu 14:1; 2Sa 22:7 pp Ps 18:6; 1Ki 22:36; Jer 4:31; Eze 27:30; Da 6:20; Mt 2:18; Jer 31:15

Voices of varying volume
God's loud voice Job 37:5 *See also* Dt 5:22; Isa 33:3; Eze 43:2; Jn 12:28–29

Loud human voices 1Sa 28:12; 2Ch 20:19; Ezr 10:12; Isa 40:9; Lk 4:33; Ac 7:57

God's quiet voice 1Ki 19:12–13 *See also* Job 26:14

Quiet human voices Job 4:16; Ecc 9:17; Isa 42:2

Voices addressed to God
In praise Lk 17:15 *See also* Jdg 5:11; 1Ki 8:55; Ezr 3:11; Ps 47:1; 100:1–4; Isa 24:14; Lk 19:37

In prayer Ps 27:7 *See also* Dt 33:7; Ps 64:1

Assurance that God hears his people's voice Ps 5:3 *See also* Ex 22:23; Dt 24:15; Ps 55:17; Isa 19:20

God's response to his people's voice
Ne 9:9 *See also* Ge 21:17; Ex 2:23–25; 3:9; Nu 20:16

God sometimes refuses to hear his people's voice Eze 8:18 *See also* Isa 1:15; 59:1–2; Jer 14:12; Am 5:23

The futility of lifting up one's voice to an idol
Jdg 10:14; 1Ki 18:26,28; Jer 11:12

Voices that proclaim God's word
Ro 10:18 *The original sense of the voice of the heavens is reapplied to all who proclaim the gospel. See also* Isa 58:1; Mic 3:8; Ac 2:14

The voice of God
God's voice addresses individuals
Ge 3:9 *See also* Ex 3:4; 1Sa 3:4; Isa 6:8; Jer 1:4; Eze 1:28

God's voice is awe-inspiring Ps 29:3–9
See also Dt 5:26; 18:16; Job 37:2; Ps 46:6; 68:33; Isa 30:30–31; 42:13; Eze 1:24; Heb 12:19,26

God's voice demands obedience
Ex 15:26; Dt 30:20; 1Sa 15:22; Isa 30:21; Heb 3:7–8

God's voice affirms his Son Mt 3:17
pp Mk 1:11 pp Lk 3:22 *at Jesus Christ's baptism;* Mt 17:5 pp Mk 9:7

pp Lk 9:35–36 *at the transfiguration;*
Jn 12:28; 2Pe 1:17–18

The voice of Jesus Christ
His voice is recognisable
Jn 10:1–5,14–16,27

His voice calls people to him Jn 7:37
See also Ac 9:4–7 pp Ac 22:7–9; 26:14–16; Rev 3:20

His voice raises the dead Jn 5:25,28; 11:43

His voice cries out Mt 27:46
pp Mk 15:34; Mt 27:50 pp Lk 23:46

Other voices
The voices of angels Job 38:7; Da 10:6; Mt 1:20–21; 2:13; Rev 5:2,11–12; 14:7–9; 18:2

The voice of wisdom Pr 1:20; 8:1–4

The voices of the natural world
Ps 19:1–4 *See also* Job 38:41; Ps 93:3; Ro 10:18

See also

5159 hearing	5528 shouting
5164 lips	5546 speech
5167 mouth	5627 word
5168 muteness	7754 preaching
5193 tongue	7960 singing
5198 weeping	8602 prayer

---

walking

The action of travelling on foot at a normal pace. The image of walking with God is used in Scripture to represent the behaviour of believers in their relationship with God.

The physical activity of walking
For travel Ge 13:17; Dt 6:7 *See also* Jdg 5:10; 1Ki 18:7; Am 3:3; Mt 4:18; Lk 24:17

As a miracle Mt 11:5; 14:25–26 *See also* Ac 3:6–8; 14:10

God walking Lev 26:12 *See also* Ge 3:8

Walking used figuratively of human behaviour
Walking in sin and darkness 1Ki 15:26; Pr 2:12–13 *See also* Ps 1:1; 82:5; Pr 2:12–13; 1Jn 1:6

Sometimes darkness represents depressing circumstances La 3:2 *See also* Ps 23:4; Isa 9:2; 59:9

Walking with God Ge 5:22–24; 17:1; Rev 3:4 *See also* Ge 6:9; Dt 8:6; 10:12; 1Ki 2:3–4; Isa 2:3; Jer 7:23; Mic 4:5; 6:8; Zec 3:7; Mal 2:6

Walking in the truth or in the light
Dt 5:33; 1Jn 1:7 *See also* Ps 15:2; 26:2–3; 56:13; 86:11; 89:15; Pr 4:12; Isa 2:5; 2Jn 4–6; 3Jn 3–4; Rev 21:24

Walking as a way of living or behaving
Eph 2:1–2 *See also* Ro 8:1; 2Co 5:7; Eph 4:1; 5:2; Col 1:10

See also

4020 life of faith	5505 roads
4809 darkness	5590 travel
4833 light	5769 behaviour
5178 running	6754 union with Christ
5186 stumbling	
5333 healing	8102 abiding in Christ
5336 highway	

weeping

The physical act of shedding tears as the result of sadness or joy or in recognition of sin.

Weeping in personal grief
Ge 23:2; Ps 42:3; Rev 5:4 *See also* Ge 27:38; 37:35; Jdg 11:37; Ru 1:9; 1Sa 11:4; 20:41; 2Sa 3:16; 13:19; 15:30; 18:33 *David weeps for Absalom*; 2Ki 8:11; 13:14; 20:3; Job 16:16,20; Ps 39:12; 56:8; 102:9; Jn 11:33; 20:11

Weeping in shared grief
Dt 34:8; Ps 137:1 *See also* Nu 14:1; 1Sa 11:4–5; 20:41; 30:4; 2Sa 1:12 *David and his men mourn for Saul and Jonathan*; 2Sa 1:24; 3:34; Job 2:12; Ps 80:4–5; Isa 15:2–3; 33:7; Mk 5:38; Ac 21:13

Weeping in personal remorse over failure and sin
Mt 26:75 pp Mk 14:72 pp Lk 22:62 *See also* 1Sa 2:33; Lk 7:38; Heb 12:17

Weeping in group response to sin
Ne 8:9; Jer 3:21; Jas 5:1 *See also* Nu 25:6; Dt 1:45; Jdg 20:26; 21:2; Ezr 3:12–13 *the people's response to the rebuilding of the temple*; Isa 22:12–13; Jer 25:34; 31:9; 50:4; La 1:2; 2:18; Joel 2:12; Am 5:16–17; 8:10; Zec 12:10–11; Mt 8:12

Weeping in response to others' sin and judgment
Ps 119:136; Jer 13:17; 2Co 2:4 *See also* Ezr 10:1; Ne 1:4; Isa 16:9; Jer 9:1; 14:17; 22:10; La 1:16; 3:48; Eze 27:31; Mic 1:8; Lk 19:41 *Jesus Christ weeps over Jerusalem*; Lk 23:28; Ac 20:31; Php 3:18; Rev 18:15–16

Divine weeping
Isa 16:9

Jesus Christ's weeping
Jn 11:35 *See also* Heb 5:7

Weeping for joy
Ge 29:11; 42:24; 45:14–15

False weeping
Mal 2:13

Comfort promised to those who weep
Ps 126:5–6; Rev 21:4 *See also* Ps 30:5; 116:8; Isa 25:8; 30:19; 65:19; Jer 31:16; Lk 6:21; Jn 16:20

See also
3248	Holy Spirit, conviction
5398	loss
5419	mourning
5795	bereavement
5801	brokenness
5805	comfort
5938	sadness
5952	sorrow
6227	regret
6624	confession of sin
6732	repentance

womb

The part of the female body where offspring are conceived and developed. A barren womb can be indicative of God's displeasure or a test of faith, while a fruitful womb may be a sign of his favour. It is God who creates within the womb. In ancient Israel, the first offspring of every womb belonged to God.

The womb as the place of conception and gestation
Ps 139:13–16 *See also* Ge 25:23–24; 38:27; Dt 28:53,57; Job 3:10–12; 10:18–19; 31:15; Ps 22:9–11; Ecc 11:5; Isa 44:2,24; 49:5; 66:7–9; Jer 1:5; 20:14–18; Hos 12:3; Lk 1:41–45; Jn 3:4; Ro 4:19–21

The barren womb
Indicating divine displeasure Ge 20:18 *See also* Ge 29:31; Hos 9:11,14

As a test of faith Lk 1:6–25 *See also* Ge 30:22–23; 1Sa 1:5–6

A blessing in times of persecution Lk 23:29–31 *See also* Mt 24:19 pp Mk 13:17 pp Lk 21:23

A fruitful womb may indicate God's favour
Dt 7:13 *See also* Ge 29:31; 30:22–23; 49:25; Dt 28:4,11; 30:9; Ps 127:3–5; 128:3–4

The first offspring of every womb belonged to God
Ex 13:1–2 *See also* Ex 13:12,15; Nu 18:15

Proverbial use of the womb
Job 1:21 *See also* Job 15:34–35; 24:20; 38:8,29; Ps 110:3; Pr 30:15–16; 31:2; Ecc 5:15; Hos 13:13

Spiritual life beginning in the womb
Ps 22:9–10 *See also* Ps 51:5; 58:3; 71:6

See also
5061	sanctity of life	5715	menstruation
5225	barrenness	5718	mothers
5652	babies	5733	pregnancy
5655	birth	5744	wife
5663	childbirth	5745	women
5664	children	8256	fruitfulness

Human civilisation

accusation

A charge brought against a person in a legal, ecclesiastical or spiritual context.

In legal affairs in general
In the OT legal systems Dt 19:15–21 *See also* Dt 17:2–7; 1Ki 21:8–13; Ezr 4:6; Ne 5:6–7; Da 6:4–5

In the NT legal systems Ac 19:38–41 *See also* Ac 7:1; 18:12–13; 23:23–30; 24:1–9; 25:1–2; 28:19

In God's covenant dealings with his people
Mic 6:1–2 *See also* Jer 2:5–9; Hos 4:1–3; 11:12–12:6

In the earthly experience of Jesus Christ
Jn 19:6 *See also* Mt 27:12–14,37 pp Mk 15:26 pp Lk 23:38 pp Jn 19:19–22; Lk 23:4; Jn 18:29; 19:4

In the experience of God's people
In the context of justification Ro 8:33 *See also* Isa 50:8–9; Col 1:22

In their standing in the eyes of the world Eph 5:3–4 *See also* Mt 5:16; 1Th 3:13

In the conduct of church affairs
Christian involvement in litigation Mt 5:25–26 pp Lk 12:58–59 *See also* 1Co 6:1–8

In the qualification for church leaders 1Ti 3:2 *See also* Tit 1:6

In church disputes 1Ti 5:19 *See also* Mt 18:15–20

In the character and activity of Satan
Zec 3:1–2 *See also* Job 1:9–11; Ps 109:6; Rev 12:9–10

See also
1345	covenant	5625	witnesses, false
4120	Satan		
5270	court	6676	justification
5383	lawsuits	7733	leaders
5401	madness	7772	prophets
5472	proof, evidence		
5623	witnesses, legal		

accusation, false

Scripture expressly forbids making false accusations, but God's people have often been subjected to them and many false accusations were made against Jesus Christ.

False accusation forbidden
Ex 23:7 *See also* Ex 23:1; Lev 19:16; Lk 3:14

Satan associated with false accusation
Zec 3:1 *Although taken as a proper name in English, "Satan" is in fact simply the Hebrew word meaning "accuser". See also* Job 1:6–12; Rev 12:10

Examples of false accusation
In the OT Ps 41:5–6 *See also* Ge 39:7–18; 2Sa 10:1–3; 1Ki 21:7–14; Ezr 4:6–16; Ne 6:5–7; Ps 35:19–20

In the experience of Jesus Christ Mt 26:59–61 pp Mk 14:55–59 *See also* Mt 9:34; 12:24 pp Mk 3:22 pp Lk 11:15; Lk 23:2

In the experience of the first Christians Ac 16:19–21 *See also* Mt 5:11–12; Ac 6:11–14

See also
2585	Christ, trial	6126	condemnation, human
4120	Satan		
5347	injustice	6145	deceit
5440	perjury	8776	lies
5625	witnesses, false	8782	mockery
5800	blasphemy	8794	persecution
5951	slander		

5203

acquittal

The declaration of innocence and release from custody. It may be literal, in the context of human courts of justice, or figurative, God being portrayed as the judge of all the earth.

Divine justice
Acquittal of the innocent Mt 12:33–37 *See also* 1Ki 8:31–32 pp 2Ch 6:22–23; Job 4:7; Pr 10:16; Da 6:16–22; Mt 12:5

Punishment of the guilty Ex 23:6–7 *See also* Ex 34:5–7; Job 4:8–9; Mic 6:9–16; Na 1:1–6

The acquittal of sinners in justification Ro 5:1–2 *See also* Ro 4:23–25

Human justice
Dt 25:1–3 *See also* Ex 22:2; 23:7–8; Dt 19:15–19; 2Ki 10:1–9; Isa 29:20–21

Unjust acquittal of the guilty
Pr 17:15 *See also* Pr 18:5; 24:23–25; Isa 5:22–23

Examples of acquittal of the innocent
Ac 18:12–17 *See also* Ac 16:35–39

Instances when the innocent were not acquitted
Jesus Christ was not acquitted because of pressure from the chief priests and the elders Mt 27:11–26 pp Mk 15:2–15 pp Lk 23:2–3, 18–25 pp Jn 18:29–19:16

Paul was not acquitted because he had appealed to Caesar Ac 26:30–32 *See also* Ac 25:1–12, 23–26:25

See also
1075 God, justice of	5383 lawsuits
1310 God as judge	6172 guilt
5347 injustice	6676 justification
5359 justice	8277 innocence

5204

age

The number of years reached or expected to be reached in a human life. The span of life is determined by God and may be divided into distinct phases, each with its own characteristics. The term may also refer to an era of history, particularly in contrasting the present age with the coming age to be inaugurated at Jesus Christ's return.

The span of life
In God's hands Mt 6:27 pp Lk 12:25 *See also* 1Sa 2:6; Ps 139:16; Ecc 8:8; Jas 4:14–15

Longevity in the OT Ge 5:5 *See also* Ge 5:27; 9:29
After the flood the length of human life is gradually reduced: Ge 6:3; 25:7; 47:28

The present-day span of life Ps 90:10 *See also* 2Sa 5:4–5 *David lives to be 70;* 2Sa 19:34–35 *Barzillai, aged 80, expects to die soon;* Isa 23:15

Its apparent brevity Ps 39:4–6 *See also* Ge 47:9; Job 7:6; Ps 89:47; 90:3–6

Long life is a blessing from God Pr 10:27 *See also* Ps 91:16; Pr 3:1–2

Phases of human life
Importance associated with age Ge 43:33; 1Sa 16:6–11; Lk 22:26

The age of discretion Jn 9:21–23 *See also* Lk 2:42

The age of maturity: 20 years Lev 27:3 *Adulthood reckoned from the age of 20;* Nu 26:2–4 *See also* Nu 1:3,45; 14:29; 32:11; Jos 5:4
The age of serving Levites reduced to 20: 1Ch 23:24; 2Ch 31:17; Ezr 3:8

Full maturity reckoned from the age of 30 Lk 3:23 *See also* Nu 4:3 *Levites assumed their duties at the age of 30;* Nu 8:24 *From the ages of 25 to 30, Levites may have served an apprenticeship.*

Old age Lev 27:7
Levites retired from duty at the age of 50: Nu 4:47; 8:25–26

Mountains as symbols of age
Hab 3:6 *See also* Ge 49:26; Job 15:7; Ps 90:2; Pr 8:25

Ages of history
Before Jesus Christ was revealed Eph 3:9 *See also* Ro 16:25–26; 1Co 10:11; Col 1:26; Heb 1:1–2

The present evil age Gal 1:4 *See also* 1Co 1:20; 2:6–8; 2Co 4:4; Eph 2:2; Tit 2:12

The end of this age Mt 13:49 *See also* Mt 13:39–40; 24:3,10

The age to come Mt 19:28–29 *See also* Mk 10:30 pp Lk 18:30; Lk 20:34–36; Eph 2:7; 1Ti 6:19

Blessing in the present age Heb 6:5 *See also* Mt 28:20; Mk 1:15; Eph 1:21; Heb 9:26

See also
4903 time	5746 youth
4945 history	5853 experience of
4971 seasons of life	life
4978 year	5887 inexperience
5694 generation	5902 maturity
5716 middle age	9140 last days
5725 old age	

5205

alliance

The coalition of two or more parties in order to achieve a particular aim. Political alliances might be formalised in a treaty or sealed by marriage. Human rebellion against God is demonstrated in hostile alliances against his people culminating in the rejection of Christ and the final gathering and overthrow of the nations outside Jerusalem. Because God's people are to depend on him alone, unholy alliances are condemned; however God does work in partnership with human allies and encourages his people to work together.

Political alliances
General examples Ge 14:1–3,13; 1Sa 27:2

Alliances formalised in a treaty Ge 21:27; 26:31; 1Ki 5:12; 15:19 pp 2Ch 16:3

Alliances sealed by marriage 1Ki 3:1; 2Ch 18:1; Da 11:6,17

Alliances against God and his people
Surrounding nations against God's people Ps 83:5–8 *See also* Jos 10:5–6; 11:4–5; 2Ch 20:1; Isa 7:1–2; Ne 4:8

The nations against Jesus Christ Ac 4:25–27 *See also* Ps 2:1–2

The nations against Jerusalem Zec 14:2; Rev 20:8–9

The wicked against the righteous Ps 31:13 *See also* Ps 56:6; 59:3; 71:10

The rich and powerful against the weak Mic 7:3 *See also* Ps 94:20–21

God is greater than human alliances Ps 48:4–5; Na 1:12 *See also* 2Ch 20:22; Isa 7:4; Eze 30:6; 31:17; Ob 7; Na 3:8–10

Unholy alliances condemned by God
God's people forbidden to ally with the unrighteous Ex 34:12; 2Co 6:14–16 *See also* Dt 23:6; Jos 9:7; 23:12

Examples of alliances condemned by God 2Ki 16:7 pp 2Ch 28:16 *Ahaz's proposed alliance with Assyria;* 2Ch 20:35–37 *Jehoshaphat's alliance with Ahaziah of Israel*
Judah's alliance with Egypt: Isa 30:1; 31:1
Hos 12:1 *Israel's vacillation between Egypt and Assyria*

The futility of trust in human allies Isa 31:3 *See also* Jer 13:21; 22:20–21; La 1:19

God works with human allies
God uses Cyrus to deliver Israel Isa 48:14 *See also* Isa 13:4; 41:2; Jer 50:9; 51:20–23

Fellow-workers with God 2Co 6:1 *See also* 1Co 3:9; 2Co 5:20

Believers allied in God's service
Working together Ezr 5:2; Ne 4:6; 1Co 15:10

Paul's fellow-workers Php 4:3 *See also* Ro 16:3,21; 2Co 8:23; Php 2:25; Phm 24

See also
1345 covenant	7030 unity
5592 treaty	7921 fellowship
5708 marriage	9220 day of the LORD
5817 conspiracies	

5206

archers

Those armed with arrows, whether for hunting or warfare. Archers were particularly valued on account of their accuracy.

Men who were archers
Ishmael Ge 21:20

Esau Ge 27:3 *See also* Ge 25:27

Jonathan 1Sa 20:18–23 *See also*
1Sa 20:35–38; 2Sa 1:22

Archers in the army of Israel and Judah
From the tribe of Reuben 1Ch 5:18

From the tribe of Benjamin 1Ch 8:40; 12:1–2

In Asa's army 2Ch 14:8

In Uzziah's army 2Ch 26:14

Archers in the armies of other nations
The Philistines 1Sa 31:1–3

The Assyrians 2Ki 19:32

The Medes Isa 13:17–18; Jer 50:9,14; 51:11

The Lydians Isa 66:19

The Babylonians Jer 4:29 *a prophecy of Babylon besieging Judah*

Men shot by archers
Saul 1Sa 31:3

Uriah 2Sa 11:24 *See also* 2Sa 11:14–17

Ahab, king of Israel 1Ki 22:34

Joram 2Ki 9:24

Josiah 2Ch 35:23

God likened to an archer
La 3:12–13 *See also* Ps 7:12–13; La 2:4; Eze 5:16; Zec 9:13

See also

5208 armies	5488 quivers
5210 arrows	5605 warfare
5236 bow and arrow	5612 weapons
5342 hunting	

5207

architecture

The design of buildings, for religious or secular use. Building designs were often regarded in Scripture as embodying spiritual truths, and capable of being divinely inspired.

Examples of architecture
The tabernacle Heb 8:5 *See also* Ex 25:8–9; 26:1–37

The temple 1Ch 28:11–12 *See also* 1Ki 6:1–10,15–38; 1Ch 28:19; 2Ch 3:1–17; 4:1–22

Altars Jos 8:31 *See also* Ex 20:25; 2Ki 16:10–11 *Adopting the design of a pagan altar indicated both idolatry and submission to Assyria.*

Ordinary dwellings Dt 22:8

Ezekiel's vision of a restored temple Eze 40:1–49; 41:1–26; 42:1–20; 43:10–17

Other structures Ge 11:4; 1Ki 7:1–12; Pr 24:3–4 *implies that a house must be more than bricks and mortar;* Jer 22:13–14

Divinely dictated design
The ark Ge 6:14–16 *the earliest recorded example of naval architecture*

Building design as a spiritual metaphor
The prophecy of the rejected stone Ps 118:22; Mt 21:42 pp Mk 12:10

pp Lk 20:17; 1Pe 2:7; Mt 7:24–27 *the two foundations* pp Lk 6:48–49; 1Co 3:10–13 *the work of Christian ministers;* Eph 2:19–22 *the church;* 1Pe 2:4–7; Isa 54:11–12 *the heavenly city;* Heb 11:10; Rev 21:9–22

God as the architect of creation
Job 38:4–5

See also

4841 narrowness	5437 palaces
5212 arts and crafts	5443 pillars
5240 building	5778 adorning
5256 city	7459 tabernacle, in
5269 cornerstone	OT
5317 foundation	7467 temple,
5340 house	Solomon's

5208

armies

An organised military force for the defence or expansion of national borders. Israel's national life was characterised by many battles with foreign nations such as Egypt, Philistia, Assyria and Babylon and by Roman occupation.

Examples of armies in conflict with Israel
The Egyptian army when Israel left Egypt Ex 14:5–9,23–25

The inhabitants of Canaan when Israel entered the promised land Jos 3:10; 12:1,7; 23:9; Jdg 3:1–3

The Philistines, a constant enemy 1Sa 13:5; 14:20–23; 17:1–3; 31:1,7 pp 1Ch 10:7

Assyria, defeating the northern kingdom of Israel 2Ki 15:29; 17:5–6; Isa 36:1

Babylon, defeating the southern kingdom of Judah 2Ki 24:1; 25:1; Jer 39:1 pp Jer 52:4; 2Ki 25:10–11 pp 2Ch 36:17

Palestine occupied by the Roman army in NT times
Roman law in force at the time of Jesus Christ Lk 2:1; Jn 18:28

Roman military personnel in the life of Jesus Christ and in the lives of the first Christians Mt 8:5 pp Lk 7:3; Mt 27:54 pp Lk 23:47; Ac 10:1; 21:31

Development of Israel's army from the time of the exodus to the reign of Solomon
A military census taken after the exodus Nu 1:3; 26:2

Fighting men to possess the promised land Dt 7:1–2; Jos 1:10–11; 12:1

The army as a tribal militia assembled in times of crisis Jdg 4:1–6

Certain tribes gaining reputations for proficiency in particular forms of combat Jdg 20:16; 1Ch 12:2,8,24–37

Saul and David having regular contingents of special forces 1Sa 13:2; 2Sa 15:18; 23:8–12 pp 1Ch 11:10–14

Forces divided into twelve battalions, each serving for a month at a time 1Ch 27:1

Chariot forces hardly known in David's time, but much used by Solomon 2Sa 8:3–4; 1Ki 4:26; 10:26

God's sovereignty over the armies of Israel and over his spiritual armies
Jos 5:13–15; 1Sa 17:45; 1Ki 22:19; 2Ki 6:17

In the final battle between good and evil, Jesus Christ appearing as the leader of the armies of heaven Rev 19:14,19

God as the commander of armies
Ps 89:8 *The term here, and in the following verses, translated as "L*ORD *God Almighty" may also be translated "L*ORD *God of hosts" or "L*ORD *God of armies". See also* 1Ki 19:10; Jer 5:14; Hos 12:5; Am 4:13

See also

5206 archers	5544 soldiers
5209 armour	5545 spear
5261 commander	5605 warfare
5266 conscription	5612 weapons
5406 mercenaries	8482 spiritual
5434 officer	warfare
5529 sieges	

5209

armour

Protective covering worn by soldiers to prevent injury in battle. However, those who wore it were not impregnable. Christians are to be equipped with spiritual armour.

Coat of armour
The breastplate 2Ch 26:14 *See also* 1Sa 17:5,38; 2Sa 20:8; Eph 6:14

The belt 2Sa 20:8 *The belt was an essential item of armour as it held the protective parts of the tunic in place. See also* 1Sa 18:4; 2Sa 18:11; Eph 6:14

The helmet 1Sa 17:5 *See also* 1Sa 17:38; 2Ch 26:14; Jer 46:4; Eze 38:5

The shield Jer 46:3 *See also* 2Ch 11:12; 32:5; Ne 4:16; Eph 6:16

Armour worn by soldiers
2Ch 26:14 *See also* Nu 31:3–5; 32:20–21,27; Jos 4:13; Jer 46:3–4

Armour-bearers
1Sa 16:21 *Armour-bearers were sometimes used to carry the shield and additional weapons for a military leader or outstanding warrior. See also* Jdg 9:54; 1Sa 14:1,6–14; 17:7

Those wearing armour were not impregnable
1Ki 20:11; 22:34 pp 2Ch 18:33 *See also* 1Sa 17:48–49; 31:3–4; Lk 11:21–22

Christians are to be equipped with spiritual armour
Eph 6:11 *See also* Eph 6:13–17; Ro 13:12; 2Co 6:7; 1Th 5:8

See also

5131 belt	5612 weapons
5237 breastplate	7320 breastpiece
5259 coat	8486 spiritual
5480 protection	warfare,
5527 shield	armour
5605 warfare	

5210

arrows

Pointed pieces of wood, shot from a
bow, used in hunting and warfare. In
the hands of skilful archers they are
accurate and deadly weapons.
Figuratively, they represent
conviction and judgments from
God, or the hurtful words of men
and women.

Characteristics of arrows
Deadly Ps 64:3 *See also* Dt 32:42;
Ps 7:13; Eze 5:16

Accurate 2Ki 9:24

Sharp and piercing Ps 45:5 *See also*
2Ki 9:24; Job 20:24; Ps 120:4; Isa 5:28

Arrows used as a sign
To warn David 1Sa 20:19–22

Of victory over Aram 2Ki 13:17–19

Of divination by the Babylonians
Eze 21:21

Arrows referred to figuratively
To describe conviction from God
Ps 38:2 *See also* Job 6:4; 34:6;
La 3:12–13

To describe judgment from God
Ps 64:7 *See also* Dt 32:23,42; Ps 45:5;
Eze 5:16

To describe false accusations
Ps 64:3–4 *See also* Ps 11:2; 57:4

To describe false testimony Pr 25:18
See also Pr 26:18–19; Jer 9:3,8

To describe attacks of Satan Eph 6:16

As lightning Ps 77:17 *See also* 2Sa 22:15;
Ps 144:6; Zec 9:14

As sons as a blessing from God
Ps 127:3–5

See also
1670 symbols	5488 quivers
4120 Satan	5612 weapons
5206 archers	8486 spiritual
5236 bow and arrow	warfare,
5342 hunting	armour

5211

art

Skilful, creative work, carried out
using a variety of materials. Purposes
included decoration, ornamentation
and representation of objects of
worship, the last of which Scripture
firmly condemns.

Painting
Eze 8:10 *See also* Eze 23:11–15

Decorative panelling
2Ch 3:5–7 *See also* 1Ki 6:14–15;
Ps 74:3–6; Jer 22:14

Decoration and ornamentation in gold
1Ki 6:21–22 pp 2Ch 3:4–7 *See also*
1Ki 6:31–35; 10:14–21 pp 2Ch 9:13–20

Decoration and ornamentation in ivory
SS 5:14 *See also* 1Ki 10:18 pp 2Ch 9:17;
1Ki 22:39; Ps 45:8; Am 3:15; 6:4

Carving and sculpture
1Ki 6:18 *See also* 1Ki 6:29–35; 2Ch 3:7;
Ps 144:12; Eze 41:15–26

Engraving
As an artistic skill 1Ki 7:34–37 *See also*
Ex 28:9–12,15–21,36–38;
39:6–7,8–14,30–31; 1Ki 7:31,36;
2Ch 2:5–7,13–14

Metaphorical references to engraving
Job 19:23–24 *See also* Isa 49:16;
Jer 17:1; Zec 3:9

Art in the tabernacle
Ex 26:1 *See also* Ex 25:18–21;
36:8,35–38; 37:7–9

Art in the temple
1Ki 7:48–50 pp 2Ch 4:19–22 *See also*
1Ki 7:13–22,27–37,40–45
pp 2Ch 4:11–16; 2Ch 3:15–17

Art associated with idolatry
Forbidden Dt 27:15 *See also* Ex 20:3–6
pp Dt 5:7–10; Ex 20:22–23; 34:10–17;
Lev 19:4; 26:1; Dt 4:16–19,23–24;
29:16–18

Examples of idols and images 2Ki 21:7
pp 2Ch 33:7 *See also* Ex 32:1–4;
Jdg 17:1–6; 18:11–31; Isa 46:1–2;
Jer 50:1–2; Eze 8:9–12

Condemned Hab 2:18 *See also*
Ex 34:10–14; Nu 33:51–52;
Dt 7:25–26; 2Ch 34:1–4; Isa 44:9–20;
Eze 7:20–22; Hos 13:1–3; Mic 5:13–14;
Na 1:14

See also
4312 bronze	5516 sculpture
4333 gold	5531 skill
4339 ivory	7459 tabernacle, in
5212 arts and crafts	OT
5247 carpenters	7467 temple,
5272 craftsmen	Solomon's
5273 creativity	8768 idolatry

5212

arts and crafts

Artistic skills, usually practised by
craftsmen and passed on from
generation to generation, of which a
wide variety are mentioned in
Scripture.

Metalwork
Ex 39:2–3 *See also* Ex 31:1–5
pp Ex 35:30–33; 1Sa 13:19–21;
1Ki 7:13–14; Isa 41:7; Jer 10:9;
Ac 19:23–41

Stonework
1Ki 5:17–18 *See also* 1Ki 6:36; 7:9–12;
2Ki 22:3–6 pp 2Ch 34:8–11; 1Ch 22:2;
2Ch 2:13–14; Eze 40:42

Building
1Co 3:10–15 *See also* 2Ch 34:11;
Ezr 3:10; Isa 9:8–10; Am 5:11;
Heb 3:3–4

Pottery
Isa 41:25 *See also* 2Sa 17:27–29;

1Ch 4:21–23; Isa 29:16; 45:9; 64:8;
Jer 18:1–10; 19:1; Ro 9:19–21

Carpentry
Isa 44:13 *See also* Ge 6:14; 2Sa 5:11
pp 1Ch 14:1; 1Ki 6:31–33;
2Ki 12:10–12 pp 2Ch 24:11–12;
Mt 13:54–55 pp Mk 6:2–3

Engraving
Ex 28:9–12 pp Ex 39:6–7 *See also*
Ex 28:36–37 pp Ex 39:30–31;
1Ki 7:30–36; 2Ch 2:13–14

Dyeing
Ex 36:19 pp Ex 26:14 *See also*
Ex 35:22–23

Weaving and embroidery
Ex 35:34–35 *See also* Ex 28:39–40
pp Ex 39:22–29; 2Ki 23:7; 1Ch 4:21;
Isa 19:9–10; 38:12

Tanning
Ac 9:43 *See also* Ac 10:5–6,32–33

Making idols
Lev 26:1 *See also* 2Ki 17:14–16;
Isa 40:18–20; 41:5–7; 44:9–20

See also
4345 metalworkers	5306 engraving
5211 art	5403 masons
5240 building	5433 occupations
5247 carpenters	5445 potters &
5272 craftsmen	pottery
5301 dyeing	8768 idolatry
5304 embroidery	

5213

assembly

Assemblies of the Israelites
Lev 23:1–2 *See also* Ex 35:1; Lev 4:14;
8:1–5; Nu 10:1–7; 15:35–36; 16:45–47;
1Sa 7:5; 1Ki 8:22; 1Ch 15:3; 2Ch 29:28;
Ezr 3:1; Ps 22:25; 40:9–10; 149:1;
Am 5:21

Assembling armies for war and groups for self-protection
Jdg 20:2 *See also* Jdg 10:17; 1Sa 7:6;
13:5; 17:2; Est 8:11; 9:16

Assemblies of the Christian church
Ac 14:27 *The Greek word for "church" can
also be translated "assembly". See also*
Mt 16:18; Ac 13:1–2; 14:23; 1Co 11:18;
14:23; 16:19

Assemblies for other purposes
Ac 19:39 *See also* Lk 23:1; Ac 19:32,41;
23:7

See also
5208 armies	7209 congregation
5279 crowds	7565 Sanhedrin
5338 holiday	7610 Council of
7020 church, the	Jerusalem
7206 community	7930 Lord's Day, the

5214

attack

A violent act of aggression often
associated with intent to invade,
sometimes as an act of retribution
and occasionally as a strategic act of
self-defence. Scripture also

recognises the possibility of spiritual aggression through attack by evil forces.

Examples of God's people attacking others

Ge 14:14–16 *Abraham attacks the captors of the king of Sodom;* **Jdg** 7:19–21 *Gideon attacks the Midianites;* **1Sa** 14:13–14 *Jonathan attacks the Philistines;* **2Sa** 5:6–7 pp 1Ch 11:4–5 *David attacks the Jebusites;* **Dt** 20:1–20 *Moses gives detailed instruction on going to war.*

The Israelites attack the inhabitants of Canaan Jos 6:2,20 *See also*

Jos 8:1–3,21–22; 10:9–10,29–42; 11:7–8,16–23

Examples of God's people attacked by others

By the Amalekites Ex 17:8–13

By the Midianites Jdg 6:1–6

By the Ammonites Jdg 10:9; 11:4–6; 2Sa 10:8 pp 1Ch 19:9; 2Ch 20:1

By the Philistines 1Sa 7:7 *See also* 2Sa 5:17,22 pp 1Ch 14:8,13; Ps 56:1–2

By Syria (Aram) 1Ki 20:1 *See also* 1Ki 20:26; 2Ki 3:21–27 *the Moabites seek to attack Israel but are routed;* 2Ki 5:2; 6:24–25; 12:17; 2Ch 16:1–4; 28:5

By the Egyptians 2Ch 12:1–4,7–9

Attacks on God's people resulting in exile

Israel attacked by the Assyrians 2Ki 17:3–6 *See also* 2Ki 18:9–12

Judah attacked by the Babylonians 2Ch 36:5–7 pp 2Ki 24:1 *See also* 2Ki 24:10–16; 25:1,8–11 pp 2Ch 36:15–20; Jer 32:24; Eze 33:21

God's people attack each other

Intertribal warfare Jdg 9:22–23,39–45; 20:18–48

The north (Israel) and south (Judah) attack each other 2Ki 14:11–14

pp 2Ch 25:20–24 *See also* 2Ch 13:1–3

Attacks within the church Jas 4:1–2 *See also* Php 3:2; 1Th 5:15; Jas 4:11–12; 1Pe 3:9

Examples of individuals who were attacked

Ge 4:8; Ac 16:22 *See also* Ex 21:12–20; 1Sa 19:9–10; 24:7

The danger of attack by Satan and his agents

1Pe 5:8–9 *See also* Mt 4:1–11 pp Lk 4:1–13; Eph 6:12; Rev 11:7

God provides protection against both physical and spiritual attack

Eph 6:13–18 *See also* Ps 7:10; 18:1–3; 138:7; 2Ti 4:18

See also

5290 defeat	5605 warfare
5291 defence	5612 weapons
5354 invasions	5814 confrontation
5527 shield	5975 violence
5529 sieges	8482 spiritual
5572 sword	warfare
5596 victory	

5215

authority

The right to act or speak in certain ways, in accordance with the authorisation of a higher power. All human authority derives from God, and is to be exercised in a responsible manner.

This set of themes consists of the following:

5216 authority, nature of
5217 authority, in the church
5218 authority, in the home
5219 authority, of human institutions
5220 authority, abuse of

5216
authority, nature of

The God-given freedom of action expressed in rightful power to control the actions of others.

Ultimate authority belongs to God, who does as he pleases

Ps 115:3 *See also* 2Ch 20:6; Job 9:12; 23:13; 42:2; Ps 135:6; Isa 14:27; 43:13; 45:9; 46:10; Da 4:35 *Nebuchadnezzar acknowledges God's authority;* Ro 9:19–21; Eph 1:11 *God's authority is demonstrated in election.*

Human authority

All human authority is given and established by God Ro 13:1 *See also* Da 2:21; 4:17; 5:18–21; Jn 19:11

It involves the rightful freedom to give orders Mt 8:9 pp Lk 7:8 *The centurion to Jesus Christ. See also* Ge 41:35; Nu 27:20; Dt 1:15 *Moses delegates authority;* Jdg 9:29; Ezr 7:24; Ne 3:7; Est 9:29; Isa 22:21; Jer 38:10; Mt 25:23 pp Lk 19:17 *the parable of the talents;* Mk 13:34; Lk 20:20; 23:7; Jn 19:10 *Paul had the authority of the chief priests to arrest believers:* Ac 9:14; 26:10,12 1Pe 2:13

It is limited, unlike God's authority Jn 19:10–11

Responsibilities of those with authority

They are to act as servants, not lording it over people Mt 20:25–28 pp Mk 10:42–45 *See also* Jn 13:4–15

Their authority is to be used for the benefit of others 2Co 10:8 *See also* 2Co 13:10

It is sometimes necessary to withhold exercising authority for others' good 1Co 9:4–18 *See also* 1Co 6:1–7; 8:8–13; 10:23–24

Examples of the authority of believers

Authority over possessions Ac 5:4 *Peter to Ananias regarding the land he sold.*

Authority over the will 1Co 7:37 *Paul on marriage.*

Authority to become children of God Jn 1:12

The authority of the law over believers during their lifetime

Ro 7:1

See also

1130 God,	4110 angels
sovereignty	4120 Satan
1610 Scripture	5452 power
2012 Christ,	6658 freedom
authority	7706 apostles
2345 Christ, kingdom	7733 leaders
of	
3045 Holy Spirit,	
sovereignty	

5217
authority, in the church

The exercise of freedom under Jesus Christ's authority for the good of the church.

Supreme authority belongs to Jesus Christ as head of the church

Eph 5:23 *See also* Eph 1:22; 4:15; 5:24; Col 1:18

Spiritual authority under Jesus Christ in the church is possessed by elders

As shepherds who teach and care for the flock Ac 20:28 *See also* Jn 21:15–17; Eph 4:11–13; 1Ti 3:2; 5:17; Tit 2:1–10; 1Pe 5:2

As overseers ruling the church Ac 20:28 *See also* Ro 12:8; 1Th 5:12 *Those serving as overseers must rule their own homes well;* 1Ti 5:17

The response of the church to the authority of elders

Elders are to be obeyed Heb 13:17

Elders are to be honoured and respected 1Th 5:12–13 *See also* 1Ti 5:17

Paul limits the authority of women in the church

1Ti 2:12 *Some believe Paul's restriction to apply to the women in the Ephesian church who were seizing authority rather than having been granted it. Others believe Paul is prohibiting women from being official teachers in the assembled church. See also* 1Co 11:5–6,10; 14:33–37

The reason for this prohibition derives from God's order of creation 1Ti 2:13–14 *See also* 1Co 11:3,7–10

Kinds of authority within the church

Authority to preach the gospel Mt 28:18–19; Mk 16:15

Authority to excommunicate Mt 18:15–18; 1Co 5:1–5 *"hand this man over to Satan" here means "send back into the world ruled by Satan";* 1Co 5:9–13

Authority to forgive sins Mt 18:18; Jn 20:23

See also

2212 Christ, head of	7784 shepherd
church	7943 ministry in
7026 church,	church
leadership	
7720 elders in the	
church	

5218

authority, in the home

The exercise of God-given authority within the husband-wife and parent-child relationships.

A husband is given headship over his wife
Eph 5:23

The basis for this headship
God's headship over Jesus Christ 1Co 11:3

Jesus Christ's headship over the church Eph 5:23

God's order of creation 1Co 11:8–9 See also Ge 2:20–22

This headship has been affected by the fall
Ge 3:16

How this headship is to be exercised
Lovingly and sacrificially Eph 5:25 See also Eph 5:28,33; Col 3:19; 1Pe 3:7

As Jesus Christ rules as head of the church Eph 5:25–29

Regarding his wife as part of himself Eph 5:28–29 See also 1Pe 3:7

Christian wives are to submit to their husbands
Eph 5:22 pp Col 3:18

They are to follow the example of the submission of the church to Jesus Christ Eph 5:24

Fathers are heads of their families
Ge 18:19 See also Ge 35:2; Jos 24:15; Eph 6:4; 1Ti 3:4,12; Tit 1:6

Fathers' authority is to be exercised reasonably
Eph 6:4 See also Col 3:21

The response of children to parental authority
Obedience Eph 6:1 pp Col 3:20 See also Pr 6:20; 23:22

Respect Eph 6:2–3 See also Dt 5:16; Ex 20:12; 21:15,17; Dt 27:16; Pr 19:26; 20:20; Mt 19:19 pp Mk 10:19 pp Lk 18:20

Kinds of authority within the family
Authority to discipline Pr 19:18 See also Pr 23:13; 29:17

Authority to teach Pr 1:8 See also Pr 3:1; 13:1

Authority to command Col 3:20 pp Eph 6:1 See also Pr 6:20–23

See also
5664 children	5708 marriage
5680 family	5718 mothers
5684 fathers	5731 parents
5700 headship	

5219

authority, of human institutions

The exercise of God-established freedom to regulate society for the good of its members.

Without authority sin is unrestrained
Ro 1:24–26 See also Ge 6:5 This was before the giving of the law; Jdg 21:25; Ro 13:4

All human authorities are instituted and established by God
Ro 13:1–2 See also Ge 9:5–6; Da 2:21,37–38; 4:17; 5:18–21,26; Jn 19:11; 1Pe 2:13

Rulers are God's servants to do good and restrain evil
Ro 13:4 See also Isa 45:1; Jer 25:9; 27:6; 43:10; Ro 13:6; 1Ti 2:2; 1Pe 2:14

The proper response to human authorities
They are to be obeyed by everyone Ro 13:1 See also Ecc 8:2; Mt 22:17–21 pp Mk 12:14–17 pp Lk 20:22–25; Ro 13:5–7; Tit 3:1; 1Pe 2:13–14

They are to be honoured and respected Pr 24:21 See also Ro 13:7; 1Pe 2:17

They are not to be obeyed if their demands conflict with the law of God Ac 4:19 See also Ex 1:17; 1Ki 21:3; Da 3:18; 6:12; Mt 22:21 pp Mk 12:17 pp Lk 20:25; Heb 11:23

They are to be prayed for 1Ti 2:1–2 See also Jer 29:7

Christians are to use rights granted by the authorities Ac 16:35–39; 22:22–29; 25:1–12

See also
5008 conscience	5605 warfare
5257 civil authorities	5959 submission
5404 masters	7446 slavery
5504 rights	8240 ethics
5509 rulers	8456 obedience to
5520 servants	authorities
5577 taxation	

5220

authority, abuse of

The misuse of a person's freedom of action in order to exploit, oppress or treat other people in a way that is not for their good.

Warnings against the abuse of authority
By employers over employees Eph 6:9 See also Lev 25:43; Dt 24:14

By fathers over children Eph 6:4 pp Col 3:21

By husbands over wives Col 3:19

By elders over the church 1Pe 5:2–3 See also Eze 34:2–7

By those mistreating foreigners Ex 22:21 See also Ex 23:9

By leaders over those who are led Mt 20:25–27 pp Mk 10:42–44 See also Lk 22:25–26

By those taking advantage of the helpless or poor Ex 22:22 See also Pr 22:22; Eze 22:29; Zec 7:10

By those who oppress others Jer 22:17 See also Ps 73:8; 119:134; Eze 22:7

Examples of the abuse of authority
Ge 16:6 See also Ex 1:11; 1Ki 12:14; Jas 2:6

See also
5310 exploitation	5448 poverty,
5347 injustice	attitudes to
5395 lordship,	8790 oppression
human & divine	8827 selfishness

5221

baking

Cooking in an oven or over an open fire. Bread baked in this way was the staple diet of the population in biblical times. Bricks were also sometimes produced by baking.

Baking bread
In ovens Lev 26:26 See also Ex 8:3; Lev 7:9; 11:35

Over open fires 1Ki 19:6 See also Isa 44:14–19; Eze 4:9–15; Jn 21:9

Unleavened bread Ex 12:39 Bread was usually baked with yeast, but where there was insufficient time for kneading and proving, the raising agent was omitted. See also Ge 19:1–3; Lev 6:14–17; 1Sa 28:24

Baking of offerings
Lev 2:4–10 See also Lev 6:14–18; 7:9–10; 23:15–18; 24:5–6; 2Ki 4:42

Baking of manna
Ex 16:21–23

Baking of clay
Da 2:32–33 See also Ge 11:3; Da 2:41–43

Bakers
At home Ge 18:6 See also Lev 26:26 Women baked at home or in communal ovens; 2Sa 13:6–8

At royal courts 1Sa 8:13 See also Ge 40:1–22; 41:10

In the temple 1Ch 9:31 See also 1Ch 23:28–29; Eze 46:20

As tradesmen in towns Jer 37:21 See also Hos 7:4

See also
4315 clay	5268 cooking
4318 coal	5435 ovens
4418 bread	5445 potters &
4474 manna	pottery
4554 yeast	7402 offerings
5239 bricks	

5223

banner

Generally, a standard raised in battle as a rallying point for armies. God is described as Israel's banner in recognition of his powerful defence of his people. The Messiah will raise a banner to rally the scattered exiles of Israel.

Israel's tribes identified by banners
Nu 2:2 See also Nu 1:52; 2:17,34; 10:14

Banners carried into battle

Battle standards carried by armies
Ps 20:5 *See also* Ps 74:4; SS 6:4; Isa 30:17 *Banners to rally armies were often set up on the top of a hill*; Jer 4:21

The LORD as Israel's banner
Ex 17:15–16 *The LORD is the rallying point for Israel and the source of the nation's confidence in battle. See also* Ps 60:4–6

God's banner raised against his people
Isa 5:25–26 *God raises a banner to rally nations to battle against Israel. See also* Jer 4:6; 6:1

God's banner raised against the nations
Isa 13:2–5 *See also* Isa 18:3; 31:9; Jer 50:2; 51:12,27–28

The Messiah as a banner to the peoples
Isa 11:10–12 *See also* Isa 49:22; 62:10; Zec 10:8; Jn 12:32

Other references to banners
SS 2:4 *The king's love is like a banner, displayed for all to see*; Eze 27:7 *a banner made from embroidered linen*

See also
1205 God, titles of	5208 armies
1448 signs	7215 exile, the
2230 Messiah, coming of	9210 judgment, God's

---

barn

Barns were associated with industry and prosperity
Full barns were a sign of blessing
Pr 3:9–10 *See also* Dt 28:8; Ps 144:12–15

Empty barns were a sign of poverty
Hag 2:15–19

The priority of spiritual over material prosperity Lk 12:15–21 *See also* Mt 6:25–26; Lk 12:23–24

God's barn is a metaphor for the kingdom of heaven
Lk 3:16–17 pp Mt 3:11–12 *See also* Mt 13:24–30

See also
4035 abundance	4524 threshing-floor
4406 agriculture	5446 poverty
4456 grain	5558 storing
4464 harvest	

---

barrenness

A lack of fertility, especially the inability of a woman to conceive.

Barren land
Barrenness describes waste and unproductive land Jer 2:6 *See also* Dt 32:10; Joel 2:20

Barren land as a sign of God's disfavour Ge 3:18 *Thorns and thistles are often used to designate barren or unproductive land. See also* Hos 10:8; Heb 6:8

Fertility, as opposed to barrenness, as a sign of God's blessing

Ex 23:25–26 *Consequently, the inability to conceive was regarded as a sign of God's displeasure. See also* Dt 7:13–14; 11:14–15; Ps 113:9; Isa 41:18 *God's end-time blessings:* Isa 54:1; Gal 4:27

The barren woman
Her desire for children Ge 30:1–2 *See also* Pr 30:16

Examples of barren women Ge 16:1 *Sarah*; Ge 29:31 *Rachel*; Jdg 13:3 *Manoah's wife*; 1Sa 2:5 *Hannah*; Lk 1:7 *Elizabeth*; Lk 1:36–37 *The ability to bear a child in these circumstances, especially in old age, was seen as a sign of God's blessing and his miraculous power.*

Barrenness was sometimes seen as a sign of God's disfavour Ge 16:1–4; 20:17–18; 29:31–34; 1Sa 1:1–20; Isa 4:1; Lk 1:5–25

Childlessness was not always the result of barrenness Dt 28:41

Barrenness might be an advantage in some circumstances Lk 23:29 *Referring to the disasters about to come upon Jerusalem.*

Metaphorically, barrenness may describe an unproductive or desperate condition
Heb 6:7–8 *See also* Job 3:7; Lk 13:6–9

See also
4206 land	5733 pregnancy
5199 womb	5836 disgrace
5664 children	8845 unfruitfulness
5680 family	

---

basin

A receptacle for liquids, often used for washing or purification rites.

Basins used as receptacles
Ex 12:22 *A basin is used to collect the blood of sacrifices. See also* Ex 24:6; Lev 14:5,50

Basins used for ritual washing
Between the altar and the Tent of Meeting Ex 30:18; 40:11,30; Lev 8:11

In Solomon's temple 2Ch 4:6 *See also* 1Ki 7:30,38 pp 2Ch 4:14; 2Ki 16:17 *Basins and bowls used in the temple:* 1Ki 7:40; Jer 52:17–18

A basin used for ritual washing
Jn 13:5

See also
5153 foot-washing	7426 ritual washing
5445 potters & pottery	7467 temple, Solomon's
7342 cleanliness	7478 washing
7416 purification	7766 priests

---

basket

Flat, open baskets to carry bread
In the chief baker's dream Ge 40:16–18

For offering unleavened bread
Ex 29:23 pp Lev 8:26 *See also* Ex 29:2–3 pp Lev 8:1–2; Nu 6:15–17

Baskets used to hold food
To store household provisions Dt 28:5 *Signifying the continued provision of food for the household. See also* Dt 28:17

To collect food Mt 14:20 pp Mk 6:43 pp Lk 9:17 pp Jn 6:13 *See also* Mt 13:48; 15:37 pp Mk 8:8; Mt 16:9–10 pp Mk 8:19–20

Baskets used to carry fruit
Jer 24:1–2 *See also* Dt 23:24; Ps 81:6; Am 8:1–2

Other uses of baskets
Ex 2:3–5 *Moses is put into a papyrus basket*; Dt 26:2–4 *firstfruits presented in a basket*; 2Ki 10:7 *the heads of Ahab's sons sent to Jehu in baskets*; Zec 5:6–11 *The wickedness of Jerusalem is removed, figuratively, to Babylon in a basket. Paul is lowered from the wall of Damascus in a basket:* Ac 9:25; 2Co 11:33

See also
2351 Christ, miracles	4440 fig-tree
4404 food	4642 fish
4418 bread	5222 baking

---

battering-rams

Battering-rams used to make breaches in the walls of besieged cities
Historic references to the breaking down of walls 2Sa 20:15 *The wall of Abel Beth Maacah. References to breached or broken walls are evidence that the use of battering-rams was common;* 2Ki 14:13 pp 2Ch 25:23; Jer 39:2 pp 2Ch 36:19 pp Jer 52:7; Ne 1:3

Figurative references to the breaking down of walls Ps 89:40 *referring to God's displeasure with David's dynasty*

Prophetic references to the breaking down of walls as a picture of the LORD's power Isa 22:5; 24:12; Eze 21:22; 26:9; Mic 2:13

Peace is symbolised by no breaching of walls Ps 144:14

Model battering-rams were part of the symbolic representation of the siege of Jerusalem
Eze 4:2

See also
5214 attack	5605 warfare
5529 sieges	5612 weapons
5604 walls	

---

bed

A household item of furniture set aside for sleep, rest and quietness.

Various kinds of bed
Dt 3:11; Am 6:4; Ac 9:34 *See also* Mt 9:6 pp Mk 2:11–12 pp Lk 5:18–19; Mk 2:4 pp Mt 9:2 pp Lk 5:24; Ac 5:15

The bed as a place of rest
2Ki 4:10 *See also* 1Sa 3:2; 2Sa 4:5,7;

11:13; Est 7:8; Job 33:15; Ps 139:8;
Pr 7:16–17; 26:14; Isa 28:20 *Beds were
not always comfortable*; Da 4:5; 7:1;
Lk 11:7

The bed as a place of recuperation

Ps 41:3; Ac 28:8 *See also* Ge 48:2;
Ex 21:18; 2Sa 13:5; 1Ki 17:19; 2Ki 1:4;
4:21; Job 7:13–14; 33:19; Da 8:27;
Mt 8:14 pp Mk 1:30; Rev 2:22

The bed as a place in which to be alone

Ps 4:4; Mic 2:1 *See also* 1Ki 21:4;
2Ki 6:12; 11:2; Ps 6:6; 63:6; Ecc 10:20

The bed representing sexual union

Dt 22:30; Heb 13:4 *See also* Ge 39:7;
Dt 27:20; 2Sa 13:11; 1Ch 5:1; Eze 22:10;
23:17

Unusual places used as beds

Ge 28:11; 1Ki 19:5; Jnh 1:5; Mk 4:38

Bed associated with a description of apostasy

Isa 57:7

See also

1409 dream	6237 sexual sin
5056 rest	6243 adultery,
5297 disease	spiritual
5533 sleep, physical	8704 apostasy

5230

beggars

People in great need who appeal for help, both from others and from God.

Appeals for material help

2Ki 6:26 *During a time of famine*; Lk 16:3
See also 2Ki 8:3–5; Job 19:16; 24:4–5;
29:11–12; Ps 37:25 *never having to beg
seen as God's blessing*; Ps 109:10 *begging
seen as God's judgment*; La 4:4

Appeals for mercy from others

Est 8:3 *See also* 1Sa 15:25; 2Sa 14:4;
2Ki 1:13; Est 4:8; 7:7; Job 30:28;
Mt 18:26–32

Examples of beggars

Mk 10:46 pp Lk 18:35 *blind Bartimaeus*;
Lk 16:20–21 *Lazarus*; Jn 9:8 *the man
born blind*; Ac 3:2–3 *the crippled man at
the temple gate*

Care for the destitute commended

Isa 58:6–7; Mt 26:11 pp Mk 14:7
pp Jn 12:8 *Jesus Christ implies that we
should care for them. See also* Dt 15:11;
Pr 19:17 *kindness to the poor rewarded*;
Pr 21:13; 22:9; 28:27; 31:9,20 *the
behaviour of the wife of noble character*;
Zec 7:10; Mt 5:42 pp Lk 6:30; Mt 19:21
pp Mk 10:21 pp Lk 18:22 *Jesus Christ and
the rich young man*; Lk 12:33; 14:13

Pleas for God's help

From the Israelites Ex 2:23 *In the OT
there are many examples of the Israelites
begging God for his help in times of dire
need. See also* Jos 24:7; Jdg 4:3; 6:6;
2Ch 14:11; Am 7:5

From individuals Ps 18:6 *See
also* 2Sa 24:10 pp 1Ch 21:8; Ps 28:2;
Jnh 2:2; Hab 1:2; Lk 16:27

People begged Jesus Christ for help

Mt 14:35–36 pp Mk 6:56 *See also*
Mt 8:31 pp Mk 5:12 pp Lk 8:32;
Mt 15:22 pp Mk 7:26; Mk 7:32; 10:47;
Lk 5:12 pp Mk 1:40; Lk 8:28; 9:38–40;
Jn 4:47

See also

4822 famine	8306 mercifulness
5289 debt	8434 giving
5446 poverty	8614 prayer,
5806 compassion	answers
8260 generosity	

5231

birthday

Birthday celebrations

Mk 6:21 pp Mt 14:6 *See also* Ge 40:20

Cursing the day of birth

Job 3:1–4 *See also* Jer 20:14–15

See also

2515 Christ, birth of	5663 childbirth
4410 banquets	5699 guests
5655 birth	8642 celebration

5232

book

Used most frequently to refer to a particular book of the Bible being written, another book of the Bible or a source no longer available. It is used occasionally of books in general or metaphorically of God's record of events.

References to books being written

Jer 25:13; 30:2; Na 1:1; Jn 20:30;
Rev 22:7,9–10,18–19

References to other books of Scripture

2Ch 35:12; Ezr 6:18; Ne 13:1; Mk 12:26;
Lk 3:4; 20:42; Ac 1:1 *Luke's Gospel*;
Ac 1:20; 7:42; 8:28

References to books no longer available

The Book of the Wars of the Lord
Nu 21:14 *This was probably an ancient
collection of war songs in praise of God.*

The Book of Jashar Jos 10:13 *An early
account of Israel's wars, possibly in poetic
form, but never a part of canonical
Scripture. See also* 2Sa 1:18

The book of the annals of the kings of
Israel and Judah 2Ch 16:11 *These
sources were probably records of the reigns
of the kings of Israel and Judah, compiled
by the succession of Israel's prophets
spanning the kingdom period (see e.g., 1Ch
29:29; 2Ch 12:15; 20:34; 26:22; 32:32).
See also* 1Ki 11:41; 14:19,29; 2Ki 1:18;
8:23; 1Ch 9:1; 27:24; 2Ch 24:27; 27:7

The book of the annals Ne 12:23 *This
was probably the official temple chronicle,
containing various lists and records
(compare with Ne 7:5).*

*Similar annals were kept by the Persian
kings:* Est 2:23; 6:1; 10:2

References to books in general

Ecc 12:12 *See also* Jn 21:25; Ac 19:19 *as
sources of magical knowledge*

Books used metaphorically of God's infallible record of events

Rev 20:11–12 *See also* Da 7:10; 10:21;
12:1

See also

1610 Scripture	5393 literacy
1630 Book of the	5514 scribes
Covenant	5515 scroll
1640 Book of the	5638 writing
Law	9420 book of life
5175 reading	

5233

borrowing

Asking for and receiving money or goods for temporary use as a neighbourly kindness.

Believers should respond to requests to borrow

Mt 5:42 *See also* Dt 15:7–11; Lk 6:35;
11:5–8

God's blessing on Israel made borrowing unnecessary

Dt 28:12 *See also* Dt 15:6

The responsibilities of those who borrow

Repayment Ps 37:21; Ro 13:8

Restitution Ex 22:14–15; 2Ki 6:5–7

Borrowing can bring debt and servitude

Pr 22:7 *See also* Mt 18:23–25

Security for borrowing

Warnings against putting up security
Pr 11:15 *See also* Pr 6:1–5; 17:18;
22:26–27

Security may be required Pr 20:16;
27:13

Security must be just Dt 24:6 *See also*
Job 22:6; Ne 5:3–13

Jesus Christ was willing to borrow

Examples of borrowing
Lk 5:3 *See also* Mt 21:1–3 pp Mk 11:1–3
pp Lk 19:30–31; Mt 26:17–19
pp Mk 14:12–16 pp Lk 22:10–12

Other examples

Ex 3:21–2; 11:2–3; 12:35–36; 2Ki 4:3;
Ne 5:3

See also

5274 credit	5389 lending
5289 debt	5492 restitution
5353 interest	8434 giving

5234

bottle

Bottles made from animal skins

Holding wine Jos 9:4,13; 1Sa 1:24; 10:3;
16:20; 2Sa 16:1; Job 32:19; Mt 9:17
pp Mk 2:22 pp Lk 5:37–38

Holding water Ge 21:14–15,19;
Ps 56:8 fn

Holding milk Jdg 4:19

Earthenware bottles
1Ki 14:3; Job 38:37; Ps 33:7; Jer 19:1,10

Bottles for oil and ointment
1Sa 10:1; 2Ki 9:1; Isa 3:20; Mt 26:7
pp Mk 14:3 pp Lk 7:37

See also
4293 water	4544 wine
4330 glass	4548 wineskin
4488 oil	5445 potters &
4490 ointment	pottery
4496 perfume	

5235

boundary

The agreed limits to the lands of an individual or people. Designated by God and protected by law, both national and local boundaries could be subject to dispute.

The importance of boundary marks
Dt 19:14; Pr 23:10 *See also* Dt 27:17; Pr 22:28

Examples of significant boundaries
Boundaries of the promised land
Ex 23:31; 1Ki 4:21 *See also* Nu 34:1–12; Dt 3:12–17; Jos 13:1–33; 15:1–63; 16:1–10; 17:1–18; 18:11–28; 19:1–48; Isa 26:15; Eze 47:15–20; 48:1–8

Boundaries of other nations
Ac 17:26 *See also* Ge 10:18–19; Nu 21:13; 33:37,44; Dt 32:8; Jos 12:2–5; Jdg 1:36; 11:18; Eze 29:10

City boundaries Nu 35:26

Religious boundaries Ex 19:12 *See also* Ex 19:23

Boundary problems and disputes
Job 24:2 *See also* Jos 22:25; Hos 5:10; Am 1:13; Mic 5:6

God establishes other boundaries
Job 26:10 *See also* Job 38:9–11; Ps 104:9; Pr 8:29; Jer 5:22

Metaphorical boundaries
Ps 16:6

See also
4207 land, divine gift	5619 distance & area
4366 stones	7257 promised land
5256 city	9120 eternity

5236

bow and arrow

A weapon used for hunting and in warfare. In the Scriptures the tongue is likened to a bow and unfaithful Israel to a faulty bow. The bow is also symbolic of military power.

The bow and arrow used for hunting
Ge 27:3 *See also* Isa 7:24

The bow and arrow used in warfare
Ge 48:22; 1Ki 22:34 pp 2Ch 18:33 *See also* Jos 24:12; 1Sa 2:4; 18:4; 2Sa 1:22; 22:35 pp Ps 18:34; 2Ki 9:24; 2Ch 14:8

Asa's army; 2Ch 26:14; Ne 4:13,16; Isa 5:28; 13:18; Jer 6:23; 50:14,29

The tongue likened to a bow
Jer 9:3 *See also* Ps 64:2–4

Unfaithful Israel likened to a faulty bow
Ps 78:57 *See also* Hos 7:16

The bow as a symbol of power and strength
Of military power Ps 44:6–7; 60:4 *See also* Ge 49:24; Ps 46:9; Hos 1:5,7; 2:18; Zec 9:10

Of God's power in judgment
Ps 7:11–12 *See also* Ps 21:11–12; La 2:4; 3:12; Hab 3:9; Zec 9:13; Rev 6:2

Of personal strength and vigour
Job 29:20 *See also* Job 30:11

See also
5193 tongue	5608 warfare,
5206 archers	strategies
5210 arrows	5612 weapons
5342 hunting	9210 judgment,
5488 quivers	God's

5237

breastplate

A coat of armour comprising one or more pieces of bronze, iron or chain mail covering the chest and back to protect the heart and other vital organs. Used figuratively it refers to righteousness, faith and love.

Breastplates were coats or tunics of armour
They were part of military dress
2Ch 26:14 *See also* 1Sa 17:5,38; 2Sa 20:8

They were worn by soldiers 2Sa 20:8 *See also* Ne 4:16; Jer 46:4; 51:3

Bronze breastplates 1Sa 17:5

Iron breastplates Rev 9:9

Those wearing breastplates were not impregnable
1Ki 22:34 pp 2Ch 18:33 *See also* 1Sa 31:3; 1Ki 20:11

The breastplate was often referred to figuratively
As a picture of righteousness
Isa 59:17; Eph 6:14

As a picture of faith and love 1Th 5:8

As a picture of invincibility Rev 9:9

See also
4312 bronze	7320 breastpiece
4336 iron	8020 faith
5145 clothing	8154 righteousness
5209 armour	8292 love
5480 protection	8486 spiritual
5544 soldiers	warfare,
5605 warfare	armour

5238

bribery

The practice of offering an incentive, usually money, in order to dishonestly or illegally procure a

decision or action in favour of the giver.

Bribery is sin
It is forbidden by God on the grounds of truth and justice Ex 23:8; 2Ch 19:7 *See also* Dt 10:17; 16:18–20; Job 36:18

The prevalence of the sin Pr 17:8 *See also* Pr 6:32–35; 21:14

The seriousness of the sin Job 15:34 *See also* Dt 27:25; Isa 1:23–24; 5:22–23; 33:15; Am 5:12; Mic 3:9–12

The results of bribery
Personal corruption Ecc 7:7 *See also* Ps 26:9–10; 1Ti 6:10

The perversion of justice Pr 17:23 *See also* Ex 23:8; Dt 16:19

The decay of society Pr 29:4 *See also* Eze 22:12 *Corruption, violence and decay render society subject to God's judgment.*

Examples of bribery
Balak and Balaam: Nu 22:16; 2Pe 2:15
Jdg 16:5 *Delilah*
Samuel and his sons: 1Sa 8:1–3; 12:2–3
1Ki 15:18–19 *King Asa;* 2Ki 16:7–9 *King Ahaz;* Est 3:9 *Haman;* Mt 26:14–16
pp Mk 14:10–11 pp Lk 22:4–6 *Judas;*
Mt 28:11–15 *the soldiers at the tomb;*
Ac 24:26 *Governor Felix*

See also
1075 God, justice of	5347 injustice
1125 God,	5413 money,
righteousness	attitudes
1185 God, zeal of	6130 corruption
1310 God as judge	6604 acceptance,
5253 cheating	human
5311 extortion	8790 oppression
5318 fraud	

5239

bricks

Bricks used in construction
The tower of Babel Ge 11:3–4

Altars Isa 65:3

Pavements Jer 43:9

Bricks were cheaper than stone
Isa 9:10

Repair of brickwork Na 3:14

Making bricks as a punishment
Ex 1:14; 2Sa 12:30–31 *See also* Ex 5:7–19

See also
4315 clay	5240 building
4366 stones	5269 cornerstone

5240

building

The construction of something together with the skilled people involved. Scripture also uses the term figuratively.

Building materials
Ge 11:3; 1Ki 5:17; Hag 1:8 *See also* Ex 27:1; 1Ki 6:9; 2Ch 2:3; Isa 54:11

Building skills
1Ki 5:18 *See also* Ex 36:1; 1Ki 6:7; 2Ki 12:11; 22:5–6; 1Ch 22:1–2

The variety of building projects
Towns and cities 1Ki 16:24 *See also* Ge 4:17; Jdg 1:26; 1Ch 11:8

Houses Ecc 2:4 *See also* Jer 35:8–9

Temples Ac 17:24 *See also* 1Ki 6:2; 8:13; Ezr 3:10

Altars Jos 8:30–31 *See also* Ge 8:20; Ex 24:4; 2Sa 24:25

Palaces 2Sa 5:11 *See also* 1Ki 3:1; 7:2; Hos 8:14

Walls Ps 51:18 *See also* Ne 2:17–18; Mic 7:11

The tower of Babel Ge 11:4–5

Building used figuratively
Mt 16:18; 2Co 5:1; 1Th 5:11; 1Pe 2:4–5 *See also* 1Ki 11:38
Jesus Christ as the capstone of a building:
Ps 118:22; Mt 21:42 pp Mk 12:10
pp Lk 20:17; Ac 4:11; 1Pe 2:7
Pr 9:1 *the house of wisdom;* Mt 7:24–26
pp Lk 6:48–49 *the wise and foolish builders;* Ro 15:20; 1Co 3:9–15;
2Co 10:8; Eph 2:20–22; 4:12,29;
Col 2:7; Heb 3:3–4; 11:10

See also
4366 stones	5604 walls
5207 architecture	5778 adorning
5212 arts and crafts	7254 plumb-line
5272 craftsmen	7467 temple,
5317 foundation	Solomon's
5403 masons	8413 edification
5506 roof	

5241

burial

The burying of a dead body, usually in a family tomb. The lack of a proper burial was regarded as a great misfortune and disgrace. Burial was usually accompanied by mourning.

Burial in a family tomb
Ge 49:29–31 *See also* Ge 23:19–20; 25:9–10; 50:13; Jdg 8:32; 16:31; 1Sa 25:1 *"at his home" probably refers to the family tomb, but could mean more literally under the floor of the house or yard;* 2Sa 2:32; 17:23

Other places of burial
Ge 35:8,19–20

Burial of criminals hung on a tree
Dt 21:22–23 *See also* Jn 19:31 *The request of the Jews was probably not only to avoid desecrating a special Sabbath, but also to identify Jesus Christ as one cursed by God.*

Burial of an executed criminal or enemy under a heap of stones
Jos 7:26; 8:29; 10:27; 2Sa 18:17

Lack of a proper burial
Jer 22:18–19 *See also* Dt 28:26; 2Sa 21:12–14; 1Ki 13:22; Ecc 6:3; Jer 7:33; 16:4; 25:33

Common burial-grounds
2Ki 23:6; Jer 26:23; Mt 27:7

Burial accompanied by mourning
Ac 8:2 *See also* Dt 34:5–8

Preparation of Jesus Christ's body for burial
Jn 19:39–40 *See also* Mt 26:12
pp Mk 14:8; Mk 16:1 pp Lk 24:1
pp Jn 12:7

See also
4354 rock	9020 death
5275 cremation	9030 dead bodies
5303 embalming	9040 grave, the
5320 funeral	9050 tombs
5419 mourning	
7908 baptism, significance	

5242

buying and selling

Buying and selling are an integral part of the everyday life of the world. Scripture makes it clear that God expects moral dealings by his people in this area of life as in every other.

Some biblical transactions
The first recorded transaction
Ge 23:3–4 *Many other transactions had obviously taken place before this, from the earliest times.*

Transactions in land Ge 47:20–22; Ru 4:3; Pr 31:16; Jer 32:9–10; Mt 27:7; Lk 14:18; Ac 4:34

Buying animals Lk 14:19

Buying food and drink Ge 41:57; Dt 2:28; Jn 6:5; 13:29; Rev 6:6

Transactions in other goods Rev 18:11–13

Buying of slaves Ge 17:12; Ex 21:2; Lev 25:44–45; Hos 3:1–2

The labour market Lev 25:39–40; Mt 20:1–2

God's standards in buying and selling
Fairness Ge 23:5–13; 2Sa 24:24

Honesty Lev 19:35–36 *See also* Ge 23:14–16; Dt 25:13–16; Pr 11:1; 16:11; 20:10,23

Sins to avoid in buying and selling
Dishonesty Pr 20:14; Am 8:5; Mic 6:10–11

Greed Pr 11:26

Exploitation Lev 25:14 *See also* La 5:4; Am 8:6

Extravagance Lk 15:13

Desecration of the Sabbath Ne 10:31; 13:15–22; Am 8:5

Desecration of the temple Mt 21:12–13 pp Mk 11:15–17 pp Lk 19:45–46 *The merchants were operating within the outer court of the temple, itself consecrated as a place of prayer and worship. See also* Jn 2:14–16

Worldliness Eze 7:12; 1Co 7:29–31; Jas 4:13

Oppression through the control of buying and selling
Rev 13:16–17

Spiritual transactions
Sinners sold to sin 1Ki 21:20; Ro 7:14

Israel sold and redeemed Jdg 2:14; Ps 44:12; Isa 43:1; 50:1; 52:3

Jesus Christ has bought his people
Ac 20:28 *See also* 1Co 6:20; 7:23; 1Pe 1:18–19; 2Pe 2:1

Spiritual wealth to be bought Pr 23:23
See also Isa 55:1; Mt 13:44–46; 25:9; Rev 3:18

Gifts money cannot buy Job 28:12–19; Ps 49:7–8; Mk 8:37; Ac 8:20

See also
5310 exploitation	5613 weights &
5337 hiring	measures
5402 market	5913 negotiation
5407 merchants	6721 redemption in
5412 money	life
5587 trade	7446 slavery
5603 wages	8275 honesty

5243

byword

Individuals become a byword
As a punishment for idolatry
Eze 14:7–8

As a trial of faith Job 17:6 *See also* Job 30:9

God's people become a byword
As a punishment for disobedience
Dt 28:37 *See also* 1Ki 9:6–9
pp 2Ch 7:19–22; Jer 24:8–10; Eze 23:1–10; Joel 2:17

As a trial of faith Ps 44:9–26

See also
5482 punishment	8782 mockery
5593 trial	8819 scoffing
8428 example	

5244

camp

A dwelling-place in the desert, often linked with the idea of a wandering people.

Camps and the nomadic lifestyle of early Israel
At the time of the patriarchs Ge 25:16 *See also* Ge 26:17; 31:25; 32:21; 33:18

During Israel's wanderings in the wilderness Nu 1:52; 9:17–18 *See also* Ex 13:20; 16:13; 19:16–17; 32:26–27

During the entry into the promised land Jos 4:19

The camp as a symbol of God's holy presence
All that was unclean was put outside the camp Lev 13:46; Dt 23:14 *See also* Ex 29:14; Lev 24:14; Nu 5:2–4; Heb 13:11–13 *a picture of Jesus Christ's rejection*

The camp and God's protection
Ge 32:2 *See also* Ps 34:7

The camp as a military base
1Sa 17:1 *See also* Jdg 7:8–11,13–15; 2Ki 3:24; Jer 50:29; Eze 4:2

See also
5427 nomads	7221 exodus, the
5578 tents	7474 Tent of
5605 warfare	Meeting

5245

captain

A senior military officer, usually in charge of a ruler's personal guards or bodyguards, the temple guard or a group of soldiers. The word is also used to refer to the commander of a ship's crew.

Captains in charge of a ruler's personal guards or bodyguards
Potiphar, captain of Pharaoh's guard Ge 37:36; 39:1; 40:3–4; 41:10,12

David, captain of Saul's bodyguard 1Sa 22:14

The captain of the guard arrests Jeremiah Jer 37:13

Captains in charge of the temple guard
Ac 4:1 See also Ac 5:24,26

Captains in charge of soldiers
King Ahaziah sends a captain with fifty men to Elijah 2Ki 1:9–14

Captains come to the help of Deborah Jdg 5:14

Solomon's captains were Israelites 1Ki 9:22 pp 2Ch 8:9

God will remove captains in judgment Isa 3:1–3

Captains in charge of a ship's crew
The ship's captain orders Jonah to call on his god Jnh 1:6

Sea captains will bemoan the fall of Babylon Rev 18:17–19

See also
5208 armies
5250 centurion
5261 commander
5330 guard
5434 officer
5489 rank
5544 soldiers

5246

captivity

The state of individuals, communities or nations held in bondage by a foreign power. Such captivity may be punishment from God who, nevertheless, hears the cry of his captive people. God will punish those who, in their arrogance, take others captive. The term is sometimes used metaphorically of the bondage of sin. Jesus Christ alone can free people from such a state.

Individuals and communities taken into captivity
1Sa 30:1–3 See also Ge 14:11–14

Nations taken into captivity
Jer 48:46 See also Ex 6:9; Nu 31:9–12; Isa 20:3–4

The captivity of Israel
As a punishment from the LORD
Ps 106:39–43 See also Ps 78:58–61

The LORD hears the cry of his people
Ex 2:23 See also Ex 6:5–6; 1Ki 8:46–51; Ps 69:33; 106:44–46

The Israelites were never to forget their captivity in Egypt Dt 5:15 See also Ex 13:3,14; Dt 6:12,20–21; 15:12–15; 16:11–12; 24:17–18,21–22; Jos 24:17; Jer 34:12–14

God will punish those who take others into captivity
Am 1:6–7 See also 2Ch 28:9–15; Ne 4:4; Am 1:9–10; Ac 7:6–7

Captivity used metaphorically
Of the bondage of sin Jn 8:34 See also Ac 8:23; Ro 7:14,25; 2Ti 2:26; 2Pe 2:19

Jesus Christ alone can free from such sin 2Co 10:5 See also Isa 42:6–7; 61:1; Lk 4:18; Jn 8:36; Gal 2:4–5; 5:1; Eph 4:8; Ps 68:18

See also
5251 chains
5344 imprisonment
5460 prison
5507 rope and cord
6020 sin
6634 deliverance
6658 freedom
6714 ransom
6720 redemption
7215 exile, the
7446 slavery
8790 oppression

5247

carpenters

Examples of carpenters at work
In the building of the ark Ge 6:14–16

In the construction of the tabernacle Ex 31:2–5 See also Ex 35:30–33

In the building of David's palace 2Sa 5:11 pp 1Ch 14:1

In the building of the temple 1Ki 5:18 See also 1Ch 22:15; 2Ch 2:13–14

In the restoration of the temple 2Ki 12:11 See also 2Ki 22:6; 2Ch 24:12; 34:11

In rebuilding the temple Ezr 3:7

In boatbuilding Eze 27:5–6

Carpenters among the exiles in Babylon
2Ki 24:16 Carpenters are literally "craftsmen in wood". See also Jer 24:1; 29:2

Joseph as a carpenter
Mt 13:55

Jesus Christ as a carpenter
Mk 6:3

See also
4552 wood
5212 arts and crafts
5240 building
5272 craftsmen
5306 engraving
5433 occupations
5516 sculpture
5531 skill
5583 tools

5248

cart

General description of carts
Nu 7:3; 1Sa 6:7,14 *made of wood*;
Isa 5:18 *pulled by ropes*; Isa 28:27–28 *equipped with heavy wheels*

Carts as a means of transport
Carts used to transport people Ge 46:5 See also Ge 45:19–21,27; Isa 66:20

Carts used as military transport
Eze 23:24 See also Eze 26:10

Carts used to transport grain Am 2:13 See also Ps 65:11

Carts used to transport the tabernacle
Nu 7:6–8 *The heavier items of the tabernacle and its furniture were carried on covered carts drawn by oxen.*

A new cart to transport the ark of the LORD 1Sa 6:8 *The Philistines send the ark back to Israel. See also* 1Sa 6:10–11; 2Sa 6:2–3 pp 1Ch 13:7 *The ark is started on its journey to Jerusalem.*

See also
4406 agriculture
5252 chariots
5621 wheel
7306 ark of the covenant
7459 tabernacle, in OT

5249

census

The counting of individuals, usually for the purpose of war or taxation.

Motivations for a census
To count the number of fighting men available Nu 1:1–4; 26:1–4 See also Nu 1:5–49; 26:5–65

For ascertaining those qualified to be included in the Jewish community Ezr 2:1–65 pp Ne 7:6–67

For purposes of taxation Lk 2:2; Ac 5:37 See also Ex 30:12

God's anger at David's unauthorised census
2Sa 24:1–9 pp 1Ch 21:1–6 *David's sin in taking this census was probably that he did so from a motive of self-sufficiency rather than trusting in God.*

See also
5577 taxation
5605 warfare
7230 genealogies

5250

centurion

A Roman military officer in charge of one hundred soldiers.

The centurion who asked Jesus Christ to heal his servant
Mt 8:5–9 pp Lk 7:2–8

The centurion present at the death of Jesus Christ
Mt 27:54 pp Mk 15:39 pp Lk 23:47 See also Mk 15:44–45

The centurion Cornelius
Ac 10:1–48; 11:1–18

The centurions involved in guarding Paul
Ac 22:25–26; 23:17–18,23; 24:23; 27:1,3,6,11,31,43

See also
5245 captain
5261 commander
5330 guard
5434 officer
5489 rank
5544 soldiers

5251

chains

Used to hold people in captivity, both physically and spiritually, but also an emblem of honour and public office.

Chains as a means of physical restraint
Mk 5:4 pp Lk 8:29 Ac 12:6–7 *See also* 2Ki 23:33; Jer 40:1–4; Ac 16:26; 21:33; 22:29; 26:29; 28:20; Eph 6:20; Php 1:7,13–17 *Paul in chains for Christ*; Col 4:3,18; 2Ti 1:16; 2:9; Phm 10,13; Heb 11:36

Chains as a metaphor of captivity
Political bondage Isa 45:14 *See also* Job 36:8–9; Ps 2:3; 107:10–14; Isa 28:22; 52:2; Eze 7:23; Na 3:10

Spiritual bondage to sin Ps 116:16 *See also* Isa 58:6–10; La 3:7

God's binding of sinful angels Jude 6 *See also* Rev 20:1–2

The domination of others Ecc 7:26

Chains as a form of ornament
As emblems of honour or rank Da 5:29 *See also* Ge 41:42; Da 5:7,16

As a form of jewellery Pr 1:9 *See also* Ex 28:22–25 *the high priest's breastplate*; Ex 39:15–18; Jdg 8:26; Isa 3:20

As adornment of idols Isa 40:19

As adornment of places of worship 2Ch 3:16 *See also* Ex 28:13–14; 1Ki 6:21; 7:17; 2Ch 3:5

See also
4696 yoke	5878 honour
5246 captivity	5915 ornaments
5344 imprisonment	6658 freedom
5482 punishment	6720 redemption
5507 rope and cord	7446 slavery

5252

chariots

Horse-drawn vehicles used for carrying important people when travelling or on ceremonial occasions, and in war for carrying warriors. The chariot is used as a symbol of military power, the power of God and as a picture of God's angelic army.

Chariots used for travelling
Ge 46:29 *See also* Ge 50:9; Jdg 4:15; 2Sa 15:1; 1Ki 12:18; 18:44; 20:33; 2Ki 5:21; 9:16,21; 10:16; Ac 8:28

Chariots used on ceremonial occasions
Ge 41:43 *See also* Ge 50:9; Jer 17:25

Chariots used for carrying warriors
Ex 14:6–7 *See also* Dt 11:4; 20:1; Jos 11:4; 17:16; Jdg 1:19; 4:13; 1Sa 8:11; 13:5 *the Philistines prepare for battle*; 2Sa 1:6; 8:4 pp 1Ch 18:4; 1Ki 10:26 pp 2Ch 1:14; 1Ki 20:1; 2Ki 6:14; 8:21; 10:2; 1Ch 19:6 *the Ammonites hire*

chariots and charioteers; 2Ch 12:3; 14:9; Eze 23:24; 26:7,10; Na 2:4

The chariot as a symbol of military might
Ps 20:7 *See also* 2Ki 19:23 pp Isa 37:24; Isa 2:7; 22:7,18; 31:1; 36:9; Jer 50:37; 51:21; Mic 5:10; Na 2:13; Hag 2:22

The chariot as a symbol of God's mighty power
Ps 104:3 *See also* 2Ki 2:11; Ps 68:4,33; Isa 19:1; Eze 1:15–21; Zec 6:1–8

God's mighty angelic army depicted by chariots
2Ki 6:17 *See also* Ps 68:17; Isa 66:15; Jer 4:13; Hab 3:8

See also
4110 angels	5590 travel
4657 horse	5605 warfare
5208 armies	5621 wheel

5253

cheating

Cheating is condemned
Lev 6:1–5 *See also* 1Co 6:7–8; 1Th 4:6

Examples of cheating
Not paying fair wages Ge 31:6–9; Jas 5:4

Using dishonest weights or scales Dt 25:13–16; Hos 12:7–8; Am 8:5

Charging excess taxes Lk 19:8

Offering blemished animals for sacrifice Mal 1:12–14

Moving boundary stones Dt 19:14; 27:17

Samuel as an example of someone who did not cheat
1Sa 12:3–4

See also
5310 exploitation	6145 deceit
5318 fraud	8714 dishonesty

5254

citadel

An especially secure city, or part of a city, where soldiers were often based.

Examples of citadels
Ps 48:12–13 *See also* 2Sa 12:26; 1Ki 16:18; 2Ki 15:25; Ne 1:1–2; 2:8; 7:2; Est 1:2,5; 3:15; 9:6; Ps 48:1–3; 122:7; Isa 34:13; Da 8:2

Proverbial use of citadel
Pr 18:19

See also
5256 city	5437 palaces
5315 fortifications	7270 Zion, as a place
5316 fortress	

5255

citizenship

The privilege of belonging to a city or country. Scripture portrays believers as living in two realms, being members of both human society and of the heavenly city. In

both realms there are duties as well as privileges.

Dual citizenship
Mt 22:21 pp Mk 12:17 pp Lk 20:25 *See also* Ezr 7:26

Earthly citizenship
Privileges and duties of citizens Ro 13:1–7 *See also* Ecc 8:2; Mt 17:27; Tit 3:1; 1Pe 2:13–17

Privileges and duties of Roman citizenship Ac 16:37; 22:25–29; 23:27; 25:10

Heavenly citizenship and the Christian hope
Php 3:20; Heb 13:14 *See also* Lk 22:29–30; Jn 14:2; 1Pe 1:4; Rev 21:2,27; 22:3–5

Gentiles are included in the citizenship of heaven Eph 2:19 *See also* Eph 2:12–13

See also
2375 kingdom of God	5577 taxation
	5611 watchman
4263 Rome	6710 privileges
5219 authority, human institutions	7105 believers
	7512 Gentiles, in NT
	7530 foreigners
5256 city	9410 heaven
5540 society	

5256

city

A large walled centre of population providing security for its inhabitants. The OT often uses the term as a symbol of the security of heaven.

Types of city
Ancient cities Ge 4:17; 10:10–12

Fortified cities Nu 32:34–36; Dt 9:1; Jos 10:20; 14:12

Royal cities Jos 10:2; 1Sa 27:5; 1Ch 11:7

Cities of refuge Dt 4:41–43; 19:1–13

Cities were frequently large
Dt 1:28; Jnh 3:2–3 *See also* Dt 6:10; 9:1; Ne 7:4; Jnh 4:11

Cities were surrounded by walls
Dt 3:5; Ezr 4:12; 2Co 11:32–33 *See also* Dt 28:52; Jos 2:15; 1Ki 3:1; 4:13; 2Ch 33:14

Cities were places of security
Nu 32:17 *See also* Jos 10:20; 2Ch 11:5–12; 14:6; 17:2; Jer 4:5

Cities could fall
2Sa 5:7; Ne 1:3; Jer 51:58 *See also* Dt 20:12,19–20; 1Ki 16:17–18; 2Ki 25:1–4; Isa 13:19; Jer 32:24–25; Am 5:9

The holy city
Ps 48:1–2 *See also* 1Ki 11:36; 14:21; 1Ch 11:5; Ne 11:1; Isa 52:1; Jer 25:29; Da 9:16; Mt 5:35

City law
Lev 25:29–30

The city as a symbol
Of strength Jer 1:18

Of heaven Heb 11:10 *See also*
Heb 11:16; 12:22; 13:14;
Rev 21:2,20–27; 22:1–5

See also

4224 cities of the plain	5604 walls
5255 citizenship	5942 security
5315 fortifications	7239 Jerusalem
5529 sieges	7269 Zion
5540 society	7338 cities of refuge
5586 town	9410 heaven

5257

civil authorities

Divinely appointed servants and
agents of God exercising their God-
given authority for the good of those
they govern and punishing those
who do wrong, and to whom all
must submit.

Civil authorities are divinely appointed

Jn 19:11; Ro 13:1 *See also* 1Sa 9:17;
16:1; Ps 78:70–71; Pr 8:15–16; Jer 27:6;
43:10; Da 2:21,37–38; 4:17,32;
5:18–21,26–28

Civil authorities are God's servants and agents

Ro 13:4 *See also* Isa 45:1; Jer 25:9; 27:6;
43:10; Ro 13:6

Civil authority exercised for the good of all and in order to punish wrongdoers

Pr 21:15; 1Pe 2:13–14 *See also* Ge 9:6;
Ezr 7:26; Ps 72:12–14; 78:72; Pr 19:12;
29:4,14; Ac 25:11; Ro 13:3–4; 1Ti 2:2

Everyone must submit to civil authorities

Pr 24:21–22; Tit 3:1 *See also* Ecc 8:2–5;
Mt 17:24–27; 22:15–21
pp Mk 12:13–17 pp Lk 20:20–25;
Ro 13:1,5–7; 1Pe 2:13–14,17

Civil authorities are only to be obeyed in what is lawful according to Scripture

Ac 5:29 *See also* Ex 1:17; 1Ki 21:2–3;
Da 1:8; 3:28; 6:7–10; Mt 22:21
pp Mk 12:17 pp Lk 20:25; Ac 4:19;
Heb 11:23

See also

4065 orderliness	5464 proconsul
5219 authority, human institutions	5485 punishment, legal aspects
5326 government	5509 rulers
5358 judges	5577 taxation
5366 king	5959 submission
5375 law	8456 obedience to authorities

5258

cloth

A woven material from which
garments or coverings were made.
Different kinds of material are
associated with different ranks and
social positions.

Cloth for daily wear

Pr 31:22 *See also* Nu 15:38; Jdg 5:30;

14:12; 2Sa 1:24; 1Ch 15:27; Ps 45:14;
Eze 16:10,13; Mt 9:16; Jn 19:23; Ac 9:39

Cloth for general coverings

1Sa 21:9 *See also* 2Sa 17:19; Pr 7:16

Cloth for special uses

For religious garments Ex 28:6 *See also*
Ex 28:8,31,39,42; 35:19; 39:1,5,22,41

For the tabernacle Ex 26:1 *See also*
Ex 26:4; 36:8; 2Ch 3:14

To cover religious objects Nu 4:5–13

Sackcloth as a sign of mourning
Ge 37:34 *See also* 2Sa 3:31; 1Ki 21:27;
2Ki 19:1; Ne 9:1; Ps 35:13; Isa 3:24;
Jer 4:8; Joel 1:13

For burials Mt 27:59 pp Mk 15:46
pp Lk 23:53 *See also* Jn 11:44; 20:7

To wrap babies in Eze 16:4 *See also*
Lk 2:7,12

Rules relating to cloth

Lev 13:47–49; 19:19

See also

4693 wool	5578 tents
4807 colours	6742 sackcloth & ashes
5145 clothing	
5212 arts and crafts	7352 ephod
5241 burial	7459 tabernacle, in OT
5301 dyeing	
5392 linen	
5551 spinning & weaving	

5259

coat

Various objects were given an outer
coating to fit them for their
particular purpose.

An outer coating given to various objects

**An outer coat of pitch made wood and
papyrus waterproof** Ge 6:14 *See also*
Ex 2:3

**An outer coat of plaster made stone
suitable for writing on** Dt 27:2–4

**An outer coat of glaze rendered
earthenware suitable for food use**
Pr 26:23

Coats of armour for protection

2Ch 26:14 *See also* 1Sa 17:4–7,38

Coat used metaphorically

Job 41:13–17

See also

5144 cloak	5209 armour
5145 clothing	5237 breastplate
5177 robes	

5260

coinage

Coinage was not used until the late
7th century B.C. Weights of silver
and gold were earlier used as
"currency". By the later exile a
variety of minted coinage, made
from gold, silver, bronze or copper,
gradually replaced the method of
reckoning currency by weighing out
precious metals. Israelite, Persian,

Greek and Roman coins are
mentioned in Scripture.

The talent

A unit of weight 1Ki 10:14 pp 2Ch 9:13
See also Ex 38:25,29; 1Ki 9:28
pp 2Ch 8:18; 1Ki 10:10 pp 2Ch 9:9;
1Ch 22:14

**A weight for precious metals used as
currency** 1Ki 20:39 *See also* 1Ki 9:14;
16:24; 2Ki 5:5,22–23; 15:19; 18:14;
23:33 pp 2Ch 36:3; 1Ch 19:6;
2Ch 25:6,9; 27:5; Est 3:9

Adopted as the name of a coin
Mt 18:23–35 *See also* Mt 25:14–30

The shekel

Its value Eze 45:10–12 *See also*
Ex 30:13; 38:25–26; Lev 27:25;
Nu 3:46–47; 18:16

Used as currency Isa 7:23 *See also*
Ex 30:15; Lev 27:1–8; Dt 22:19,29;
Jdg 9:4; 16:5; 17:10; 1Sa 13:21;
2Sa 18:12; 2Ki 6:25; 7:1,16,18;
1Ch 21:25 *David's payment for the
threshing-floor as the temple site*;
2Ch 1:17; Ne 5:15; 10:32; Jer 32:9;
Hos 3:2

The denarius

Referred to in Jesus Christ's parables
Mt 20:1–16 *One denarius was the average
worker's daily wage. See also*
Mt 18:21–35; Lk 7:41–47

**As the unit for the payment of taxes to
Rome** Mt 22:15–21 pp Mk 12:13–17
pp Lk 20:20–26

The penny

Mt 10:29 pp Lk 12:6 *The "penny" was
not a coin in use in biblical times, but the
term is employed in the NIV for two
different copper coins, the "assarion" and
the "quadrans", which were of relatively
little value. See also* Mt 5:25–26
pp Lk 12:58–59; Mk 12:42

The gerah

Lev 27:25 *See also* Ex 30:13; Nu 3:47;
18:16; Eze 45:12

The drachma

Ac 19:19 *See also* Ezr 2:69; Ne 7:70–72

The four-drachma coin

Mt 17:24–27

The daric

1Ch 29:7 *See also* Ezr 8:27

Unnamed coins

General references to coins
Jn 2:13–16 *See also* Mt 27:6

Silver coins Mt 26:14–15 *See also*
Mt 27:3–10; Zec 11:12–13;
Lk 10:30–35; 15:8–10 *Although
translated simply as "silver coins", it is the
"drachma" which is referred to here.*

Copper coins Mk 12:41–42
pp Lk 21:1–2 *The Greek coin "lepton" is
translated as "copper coin" in these
passages.*

See also

4303 metals	5412 money
4321 copper	5577 taxation
4333 gold	5615 weights
4363 silver	

commander

A general term referring to a senior military officer in charge of soldiers.

Commanders of various ranks

Supreme commander 2Ki 18:17

Field commander Isa 36:2

Provincial commander 1Ki 20:14

Commander of captains 2Ch 8:9

Commander of the citadel Ne 7:2

Commanders over various numbers of men

Dt 1:15; Nu 31:14

Commanders serving under various rulers

Ge 21:22 *Abimelech*; Jdg 4:2 *Jabin*; 1Sa 14:50 *Saul*; 2Ki 5:1 *the king of Aram*; 2Ki 11:4 *Jehoiada*; 2Ki 25:8 *Nebuchadnezzar*
David: 1Ch 11:6; 12:8,14; 15:25; 25:1; 28:1
2Ch 1:2 *Solomon*; Mk 6:21 *Herod*

The commander of the Roman troops

Ac 21:31–34; 22:26–30; 23:10,17–23; 24:22

The commander of the army of the Lord

Jos 5:13–15

Commanders in spiritual warfare

2Ti 2:4

See also
5208 armies	5434 officer
5245 captain	5489 rank
5250 centurion	5544 soldiers

commendation

The act of speaking favourably of someone. Scripture commends those who are faithful and obedient to God.

Commendation as speaking favourably of others

Pr 15:2 *See also* Ps 145:4; Ecc 8:15

Examples of those commended by God

Mt 26:10; Lk 7:9 *See also* Mt 15:28 *a Canaanite woman*; Mt 16:17–18 *Simon Peter*; Lk 21:3 *a poor widow*; Heb 11:4 *Abel*; Heb 11:5 *Enoch*

Commendation for obedience and faith

Ps 40:4; Heb 11:1–2 *See also* Ps 119:1; Pr 16:20; Isa 56:2; Jer 17:7; Mt 25:34; Ro 14:18; 2Co 8:18; Heb 11:39

Commendation for perseverance

Isa 30:18 *See also* Jas 1:12; 5:11; 1Pe 2:19–20

Examples of human commendation of others

2Sa 14:25; 2Co 10:18 *See also* Ge 12:15; 49:8; Ne 11:2; Est 2:17; Job 29:11;

Pr 12:8; 27:2,21; 28:4; 31:28,30–31; Ecc 8:10; SS 6:9; Da 10:11; Lk 16:8; Jn 5:41,44; 12:43; Ac 18:27; Ro 2:28; 13:3; 16:1; 1Co 11:2,17,22; 2Co 3:1; 12:11; 1Th 2:6; 1Pe 2:14

Self-commendation is to be avoided

2Co 5:12 *See also* 2Co 6:4–10

See also
8369 worthiness	8460 pleasing God
8458 peacemakers	8664 praise

communication

The effective conveyance of a message. God has communicated with humanity, especially through his Son. Christians are encouraged to communicate God's word effectively to others.

God communicates with people

Through his creation Ps 19:1–4 *See also* Ro 1:20

Through the Scriptures 2Pe 1:20–21 *See also* Jer 36:2; Eze 1:3; Zec 7:12; 2Ti 3:16

Through his Son Jn 1:18; Heb 1:1–3 *See also* Jn 1:14; Col 1:15; 2:9

Through the human conscience Jn 8:9; Ro 2:14–15

Through the providential ordering of life Ac 14:16–17; 17:26–27

Through angelic appearances Jdg 6:11–12; 13:3; Zec 1:9; Mt 1:20; Lk 1:11–13,28; 2:9–11; Ac 8:26; Rev 1:1

Through dreams 1Ki 3:5; Da 7:1; Mt 2:13

Through visions Isa 1:1; Eze 11:24–25; Da 8:1; Ob 1–21; Ac 10:3,9–17

Through a donkey Nu 22:27–31

Through miracles Jn 11:25,43–44; Ac 2:22 *The miracles of Jesus Christ were not merely wonderful occurrences; they were also signs that conveyed spiritual truth.*

God has communicated directly with individuals

Ex 3:2–6 *See also* Ex 33:9,21; 1Ki 19:12–13

Jesus Christ and communication

Jesus Christ communicated his Father's will Jn 12:49 *See also* Jn 14:9–10,24; 15:15; 17:8

Jesus Christ used parables in order to communicate with some but not with others Mk 4:10–12 pp Mt 13:10–15 pp Lk 8:9–10; Isa 6:9–10; Jn 9:39

The Holy Spirit and communication

Jn 16:15 *See also* Jn 14:26; 15:26; 16:8,13; Ro 8:16; Gal 4:6; 1Jn 3:24

Christians are to communicate the good news to other people

Lk 24:46–48 *See also* Mt 10:7; 28:19–20; Mk 6:12; 16:15,20; Ac 1:8; 4:20; 20:27; 26:17–20; Ro 10:14–15; 1Th 1:8

The failure of communication

Inadequate perception of the truth Mk 8:16–21 *See also* Mk 4:13; Jn 1:10; 8:27; 10:6; 13:22; 14:9; 16:18

Wilful rejection of the truth Eph 4:18 *See also* Jn 8:44,47; Ro 1:21–25; Heb 3:12–13

See also
1416 miracles	4112 angels,
1439 revelation	messengers
1690 word of God	5546 speech
2357 Christ, parables	7754 preaching
2420 gospel	8424 evangelism
3140 Holy Spirit,	8495 witnessing
teacher	
3275 Holy Spirit in	
the church	

compensation

Compensation under the law of Moses

For personal injuries Ex 21:26–27 *See also* Ex 21:32

For the loss of an animal Ex 21:33–34 *See also* Ex 21:35–36

For theft Ex 22:1,3–4 *See also* Ex 22:7–9

For damage to property Ex 22:5–6

For breach of trust Ex 22:10–15; Lev 6:1–7; Nu 5:5–7 *Compensation was only paid when someone was at fault. Similar laws apparently existed in patriarchal times: see Ge 31:39.*

Compensation later in the OT

The law applied by David 2Sa 12:4–6

Sevenfold compensation for theft Pr 6:30–31 *presumably "sevenfold" here means "manifold"; he will pay in full*

Adultery beyond compensation Pr 6:32–35

Compensation a mark of repentance Eze 33:15

Compensation in the NT

For losses inflicted Lk 19:8 *In his zeal, after being converted, Zacchaeus goes beyond the requirements of the law. See also* Phm 18–19

For losses sustained for the gospel Mt 19:29 pp Lk 18:29–30 *God is far more generous under grace than he required wrongdoers to be under law.*

See also
5276 crime	5492 restitution
5375 law	5555 stealing
5398 loss	5679 dowry
5482 punishment	

complaints

The expression of a grievance or displeasure, usually against the actions and attitudes of others including God himself.

Complaints against God

Israel in the wilderness Nu 11:1; 14:26–27 *See also* Ex 16:8,12; Nu 21:5; 1Co 10:10–11

Moses Ex 5:22–23 *See also*
Nu 11:11–15

Elijah 1Ki 19:4

Job Job 10:1–2 *See also* Job 7:11–21;
9:27–28; 21:4; 23:2; 33:13

The psalmists Ps 64:1 *See also*
Ps 73:13–21; 77:7–9; 88:3–18; 142:2

The prophets Jer 20:7–8 *See also*
Jer 12:1–4; Jnh 4:1–3;
Hab 1:2–4,12–17

Complaints against Jesus Christ
Mt 9:11 pp Mk 2:16 pp Lk 5:30 *See also*
Mt 12:2 pp Mk 2:24 pp Lk 6:2; Mt 15:2
pp Mk 7:5; Mk 2:7 pp Mt 9:3; Lk 15:2;
Jn 6:41–43

Examples of justified complaints
Ac 6:1 *See also* Ge 21:25; 2Sa 15:2–4

**Examples of unjustified
complaints**
Ex 17:3 *See also* Ex 14:11–12; 15:24;
16:2–3; Ac 18:14–15

**Scripture denounces unjustified
complaints**
Php 2:14 *See also* Isa 40:27; La 3:39;
Jas 5:9; 1Pe 4:9

See also

5201 accusation	5839 dissatisfaction
5761 attitudes	8765 grudge
5821 criticism among believers	

conscription

The compulsory calling up of people
to service, especially military service.
The OT refers to men being
conscripted to serve in the army, or
in major building projects.

**Men conscripted to serve in the
army**
**Moses drew up lists of potential
fighting men for the conquest of
Canaan** Nu 1:2–3 *See also*
Nu 1:17–19,45–46
*Moses took a second census, after the
generation which had come out of Egypt
had died:* Nu 26:2,3–4,63–65

**Deborah called up troops to attack
Jabin, a Canaanite king** Jdg 4:4–7

**God restricted the number of men
conscripted by Gideon** Jdg 7:1–8 *The
purpose of this was to make clear that
Israel's victory was in God's strength alone.*

**The Benjamites raised a tribal militia to
fight the rest of Israel** Jdg 20:15–17

**King Saul chose men to fight the
Philistines** 1Sa 13:2; 14:52

King David maintained a regular army
1Ch 27:1–15

The conscription of labourers
Those in charge of conscription
2Ki 25:19 pp Jer 52:25

**Solomon used conscripts to build the
temple and other projects** 1Ki 5:13–15
pp 2Ch 2:2; 1Ki 9:15,20–21
pp 2Ch 8:7–8

See also

5208 armies	5605 warfare
5249 census	5628 work
5519 secretary	

control

The exercise of authority and
restraint over individuals and events.
Scripture stresses that God is in
sovereign control over his creation.
A limited degree of control over
creation is delegated to humanity.

God controls the whole world
Ge 1:1,3 *See also* Ne 9:6; Ps 102:25;
Ac 17:24; Heb 11:3

**God controls the affairs of
heaven and earth**
Dt 4:39; Da 4:35

He gives wealth Dt 8:18 *See also*
1Ch 29:12

**He appoints and deposes earthly
rulers** Ps 75:6–7; Da 2:21; 4:17,32;
5:18,21,26

He controls human hearts Pr 21:1

He controls times and seasons Ge 8:22
See also Ps 31:15; Da 2:21; Am 4:9;
Ac 1:7

He controls the weather Am 4:7;
Mt 5:45

He saves those whom he wills
Ro 9:11–16

He fixes human destiny Mt 25:34,41

Human control over creation
Ge 1:26–28 *See also* Ge 2:15,19–20;
3:16–19 *After the fall it became difficult
for human beings to control creation.*

**Human control over earthly
territories**
Jos 18:1; 2Sa 8:1,3; 2Ch 17:5; Da 11:43

**Both the godly and ungodly
should control themselves**
Pr 16:32; 29:11; 1Co 7:9,37; 2Co 10:5;
1Th 4:4

**Prophecy should be under the control
of the prophets** 1Co 14:32

The evil one has limited control
1Jn 5:19 *See also* Job 1:6–7; Eph 6:12;
Col 1:13

**Jesus Christ will have final
control over all things**
Php 3:21 *See also* 1Co 15:24–28 *Jesus
Christ himself will be finally made subject
to God.*

See also

1130 God, sovereignty	5326 government
4120 Satan	5452 power
4945 history	5509 rulers
5051 responsibility	5700 headship
5215 authority	5934 restraint
5261 commander	8339 self-control

cooking

Scripture contains much evidence of
methods of cooking and types of

food cooked in biblical times.
Cooking was an essential part of
sacrificial worship, as well as being a
domestic necessity.

Cooks
1Sa 8:10–13 *See also* 1Sa 9:23–24

Cooking utensils
1Sa 2:13–14 *See also* Lev 2:7; 6:28; 7:9;
11:35; Nu 11:8; Eze 11:3; Zec 14:20–21

Cooking methods
Baking Ge 19:3; Ex 16:23; Lev 26:26;
1Sa 28:24; Eze 46:20

Boiling Ex 16:23 *See also* Nu 6:19;
1Sa 2:13

Roasting 1Sa 2:15 *See also* Ex 12:8–9;
Dt 16:5–7; Pr 12:27; Isa 44:16,19

Food cooked
Meat Eze 24:10 *See also* Ge 27:3–19;
Ex 29:31; Lev 8:31; 1Ki 17:6; Mic 3:3
*Injunctions against cooking a goat in its
mother's milk:* Ex 23:19; 34:26; Dt 14:21

Grain 1Sa 17:17 *See also* Jos 5:11;
Ru 2:14; 1Sa 25:18; 2Sa 17:27–28;
1Ki 17:10–16

Stew Ge 25:29 *See also* 2Ki 4:38–41

Human flesh La 4:10 *See also*
2Ki 6:26–29

Cooked offerings
Lev 2:7 *See also* Lev 2:14; 7:9; 8:31;
2Ch 35:13; Eze 46:20,24

See also

4293 water	4478 meat
4318 coal	5222 baking
4404 food	5435 ovens
4456 grain	7340 clean and unclean
4466 herbs and spices	7402 offerings

cornerstone

A stone that can be in the
foundation, above ground level or at
the summit of the roof (the
"capstone"). The cornerstone of a
large building gives it a reliable and
firm foundation, leading to the
cohesion and stability of the whole
building. In Scripture, such
foundation-stones are taken as
symbolic of the basis of faith in Jesus
Christ and the church. Jesus Christ is
thus represented as both the
foundation upon which the church
is built, and the capstone which
crowns the whole.

**The place of the cornerstone in
buildings**
Job 38:4–6 *See also* Jer 51:26; 1Pe 2:4–8

**The cornerstone is prominent,
indispensable and should be
reliable**
Isa 28:16 *See also* Ps 118:22; Isa 19:13

Jesus Christ is the cornerstone of the church
Eph 2:19–22 *See also* 1Pe 2:5–6; Isa 28:16

The cornerstone is a sure foundation for believers, but a stumbling-block for unbelievers
Rejection of the cornerstone leads to stumbling and rejection Mt 21:42–44 pp Mk 12:10–11 pp Lk 20:17–18 *See also* Ps 118:22–23; Isa 8:13–15; Ro 9:33; Isa 28:16; 1Pe 2:7–8

Reliance on the cornerstone gives security to believers 1Pe 2:6–7 *See also* Isa 28:16; Ac 4:10–12; Eph 2:20–22

The capstone as the crowning glory of a building
Ps 118:22

For all the following NT references, NIV footnote is "cornerstone": Mt 21:42–44 pp Mk 12:10 pp Lk 20:17–18; Ac 4:10–12; 1Pe 2:4–8

See also

1670 symbols	5604 walls
2212 Christ, head of church	7024 church, nature of
5317 foundation	

5270

court

Usually, a legal body dispensing justice, but the word may also refer to a royal court, the original function of which was the dispensation of justice by the monarch.

Courts of law
Provision for and procedures of courts Ex 18:25–26; Dt 1:15–17; 17:9; Ru 4:2–5; 1Ch 26:29; 2Ch 19:8–11

Justice dispensed by the court Dt 25:1 *See also* Job 11:10; Am 5:15; Zec 8:16–17

Disputes settled in court Jdg 4:4–5 *See also* Ex 21:22; Job 5:4; 9:32–35; Pr 25:7–8; 29:9; Mt 5:25–26 pp Lk 12:58–59; Ac 18:12–17; 19:38–39; 25:1–26:27

Provision for a court of appeal Dt 17:8–13

Corruption in the court Pr 22:22–23 *See also* Ex 23:1–3,6–8; Job 31:21–22; Isa 29:20–21; Am 5:7–15; Jas 2:6

The divine lawcourt Da 7:9–10 *See also* Isa 3:13–17; Da 7:23–27; 1Co 4:2–5

Royal courts
Egyptian Ge 50:4–7

Israelite Jer 29:2 *See also* 1Ki 3:15; Jer 34:19–20; 41:16

Babylonian Da 2:48–49 *See also* Da 1:3–5

Persian Est 4:11 *See also* Est 5:1–2

The divine courts Ps 84:10 *See also* Ps 65:4; 84:1–2; 92:12–13; 96:8; 100:4

See also

1075 God, justice of	5366 king
5203 acquittal	5375 law
5271 courtyard	5383 lawsuits
5305 empires	5509 rulers
5358 judges	7565 Sanhedrin
5359 justice	9230 judgment seat

5271

courtyard

An enclosed, uncovered area within the precincts of large buildings such as temples, palaces and houses. The wilderness tabernacle also incorporated a courtyard.

The courtyard of the tabernacle
Ex 27:9–19 *See also* Ex 38:9–20

The courtyard of the temple
1Ki 7:12 *See also* 1Ki 8:64 pp 2Ch 7:7; 2Ch 4:9; 23:5; 24:21; Jer 26:2; 36:10; Eze 40:14

Courtyards of palaces
Est 2:11 *See also* Jer 32:2; 39:15

Courtyards of private houses
Ne 8:16 *See also* 2Sa 17:18; Mt 26:69 pp Mk 14:66 pp Lk 22:55; Jn 18:15

See also

5340 house	7469 temple, Herod's
5437 palaces	
7459 tabernacle, in OT	

5272

craftsmen

Skilled workers and artisans. God is sometimes compared to a master craftsman in his work of creation. Scripture also identifies God as the giver of talent and ability to certain individuals, in particular those employed in the construction of the tabernacle and the temple.

God the Creator seen as a master craftsman
Pr 3:19–20 *See also* Ge 1:1–31; Job 38:4–38 *inanimate creation*; Job 38:39–39:30 *animate creation*; Pr 8:22–31

Craftsmen employed in the construction of the tabernacle and its furnishings
Ex 31:1–11 *See also* Ex 26:1,31; 28:6–8,15; 35:30–36:3,8–38:11; 39:1–3

Craftsmen employed in the construction of the temple and its furnishings
1Ki 7:13–45 pp 2Ch 4:2–6 pp 2Ch 4:10–16 *See also* 1Ki 5:17–18; 1Ch 22:14–16; 29:3–5; 2Ch 2:5–7,13–14

Craftsmen employed in the manufacture of idols
Isa 40:19–20 *See also* Isa 41:5–7; 44:9–20; Jer 10:3–10; Hos 8:4–6; 13:2; Ac 19:23–41

Carpenters
2Sa 5:11 pp 1Ch 14:1 *See also* 2Ch 24:12; Isa 44:13; Eze 27:9; Mt 13:55 pp Mk 6:3

Gem cutters
Ex 28:11

Masons
2Ch 24:12 *See also* 1Ch 22:14–16; Ezr 3:7

Goldsmiths
Isa 46:6 *See also* Ne 3:31–32; Jer 51:17

Silversmiths
Pr 25:4 *See also* Jdg 17:4; Ac 19:24

Potters
Ro 9:21 *See also* 1Ch 4:23; Isa 64:8; Jer 18:2–4

Weavers and embroiderers
Skilled craftsmen Ex 35:35 *See also* Ex 26:1,31; 28:6,15; 39:22,27; Isa 19:9–10; 38:12

A weaver's shuttle Job 7:6

A weaver's rod 1Ch 20:5 *See also* 1Sa 17:7; 2Sa 21:19; 1Ch 11:23

Craftsmen taken into exile
2Ki 24:10–17 *See also* Isa 3:1–3; Jer 24:1; 29:2; 52:12–16

Craftsmen in place-names
1Ch 4:14 *See also* Ne 11:31–35

Metaphorical references to craftsmen
Pr 8:22–31 *See also* Isa 41:25; 64:8; Jer 18:6; Zec 1:20–21; 1Co 3:10

See also

1325 God, the Creator	5445 potters & pottery
4040 beauty	5531 skill
4345 metalworkers	7459 tabernacle, in OT
5211 art	
5212 arts and crafts	7467 temple, Solomon's
5247 carpenters	
5403 masons	8768 idolatry

5273

creativity

Imagination and skill used in the expression of visual or performing arts. Human creativity has its source in God, but may be used either to his honour or dishonour.

God's creativity
Isa 64:8 *See also* Job 38:1–41; Ps 139:13–16; Ecc 3:11; Isa 45:7–12,18; Eph 2:10 *Redemption may be described in terms of re-creation.*

God is the source of human creativity
Ex 35:30–35 *See also* Ex 31:1–6; 36:1–2

Creativity for its own sake
Ecc 2:4–6

Creativity used in the service of God
Building the tabernacle and temple Ex 36:8 *See also* 1Ch 22:15–16; 2Ch 2:5–7,13–14

Music and dancing Ps 149:3 *See also* 1Ch 6:31–32; 25:1–7; Ps 92:1–3; 98:5; 144:9

The abuse of human creativity
Hab 2:18 *Human creativity, like all of God's gifts, can be abused by sinful human beings, and used to dishonour him rather than serve him. See also* Dt 27:15;

2Ki 19:18; Isa 40:19–20; 44:10–13;
Ac 19:23–26

See also

1325 God, the	5272 craftsmen
Creator	5445 potters &
4005 creation	pottery
5211 art	5531 skill
5212 arts and crafts	6184 imagination
5240 building	

5274

credit

Money or goods lent under pledge of repayment (with or without interest). In the spiritual sense, Jesus Christ's righteousness is credited to believers.

Credit in Israel: charitable, not commercial
Dt 23:19–20 *See also* Ex 22:25; Ps 15:5; Eze 18:7,16–17

The pledge (security): laws protecting the borrower
Dt 24:10–13 *See also* Ex 22:26–27; Lev 25:39–40,42; Dt 24:6

Standing security for another may be hazardous
Pr 22:26–27 *See also* Pr 6:1–5; 11:15; 17:18 *The binding nature of the commitment cautions against a hasty and unwise engagement.*

Violations of Israel's "credit controls" roundly condemned
Ne 5:1–12; Job 22:6; 24:3,9; Eze 18:12; Am 2:8

The credit system not condemned by Jesus Christ
Mt 25:27 pp Lk 19:23

Christians to view this subject in the light of God's grace
Lk 6:34–35 *See also* Mt 18:23–27 *God is a model creditor.*

Creditors demanding a pledge to assure repayment
A personal effect Dt 24:6,10–13; Job 24:3; Pr 22:26–27

Mortgage of property Ne 5:3

The surety of a guarantor Pr 6:1–5; 11:15; 17:18; 22:26; 27:13

Creditors exacting repayments cruelly
2Ki 4:1 *See also* Job 22:6; 24:3,9; Ps 109:11; Isa 50:1; Eze 18:12–13; 22:12; Am 2:6,8; Mt 5:25–26; 18:25–26,34

Creditors to be considerate in their demands
Dt 24:6 *See also* Ex 22:26–27; Lev 25:35–43; Dt 24:10–13

Creditors perhaps remitting the debt entirely
Mt 18:27 *See also* Ne 5:10–12; Mt 6:12; Lk 7:41–43

Under Mosaic law creditors to cancel debts eventually
Dt 15:1–3 *See also* Dt 31:10; Ne 10:31

Spiritual aspects of credit
Faith credited as righteousness
Ro 4:1–11 *See also* Ge 15:6; Ps 32:2; 106:31; Eze 18:20; Ro 4:22–24; Jas 2:23

Jesus Christ's righteousness credited to believers 2Co 5:21 *See also* Ro 3:22; 1Co 1:30; Php 3:9

Moral aspects of credit
Php 4:17 *See also* Mt 10:40–42; 25:34–36; Lk 6:32–35; 2Co 5:10; Eph 6:7–8 *Good deeds will be remembered and rewarded in heaven.*

See also

5233 borrowing	5806 compassion
5289 debt	6652 forgiveness
5310 exploitation	6674 imputation
5353 interest	8154 righteousness
5389 lending	8790 oppression
5465 profit	
5500 reward, God's	
people	

5275

cremation

The burning of a dead body. Cremation was not practised by Israel or the first Christians. In difficult circumstances a corpse might be burnt and the remains buried.

Cremation of corpses
1Sa 31:12–13 *This was done to prevent any further abuse of the bodies by the Philistines. David later reburied the remains in a family grave (see 2Sa 21:12–14).*

Burning a body as a punishment
Lev 20:14; 21:9; Jos 7:15,25; 2Ki 23:20

Funeral fires for the kings of Judah
These were not for the purpose of cremating the king's corpse, but public demonstrations in his honour: 2Ch 16:14; Jer 34:5

See also

4826 fire	5482 punishment
5241 burial	9030 dead bodies
5320 funeral	

5276

crime

An offence against the established laws of society including murder, adultery, theft, perjury and treason. Scripture contains both warnings and teaching to help young people avoid a life of crime.

Crime in Israel
Dt 6:1–2 *Crime in Israel was the breaking of laws given by God.*

Examples of crimes covered by Israel's laws
Ex 20:13 *murder*; Ex 20:14 *adultery*; Ex 20:15 *theft*; Ex 20:16 *perjury* Treason: Jos 1:16–18; 2Sa 15:7–10; 1Ki 16:15–18; 2Ki 11:1–3 pp 2Ch 22:10–12

Examples of crime in the NT
Murder Mt 2:16; Ac 7:58

Adultery Jn 8:3–4; 1Co 5:1

Theft Jn 12:6

Perjury Mt 26:59–60 pp Mk 14:55–56; Ac 6:13; 25:7

Scripture warns young people that temptation may lead to crime
Violence Pr 1:10–19

Sexual immorality Pr 5:1–23; 6:20–29; 7:6–27

Scripture teaches parents to discipline their children
Pr 13:24; 19:18; 22:6,15; 23:13

See also

5040 murder	6206 offence
5277 criminals	6236 sexual sin
5375 law	6632 conviction
5440 perjury	8232 discipline,
5483 punishment	family
5555 stealing	8718 disobedience
6020 sin	

5277

criminals

Individuals who are guilty of crimes such as murder, adultery, theft, perjury or treason. Scripture refers to and gives examples of young law-breakers (delinquents).

Criminals guilty of murder
Cain Ge 4:8

Abimelech Jdg 9:5

Doeg the Edomite 1Sa 22:18

David 2Sa 11:14–17

Absalom 2Sa 13:23–29

Herod the Great Mt 2:16

Barabbas Mk 15:7 pp Lk 23:19

Criminals guilty of adultery
David 2Sa 11:2–5

Gomer (Hosea's wife) Hos 3:1

Criminals guilty of theft
Rachel Ge 31:19,30

Achan Jos 7:21

Judas Iscariot Jn 12:6

Criminals guilty of perjury
Joel and Abijah (sons of Samuel) 1Sa 8:3

Two who gave false evidence against Naboth 1Ki 21:13

Examples of criminals guilty of treason
Zimri 1Ki 16:15–18

Athaliah 2Ki 11:1–3 pp 2Ch 22:10–12

Examples of delinquents
Those who break the fifth commandment as minors may have been treated as criminals Ex 20:12

Manasseh, king of Judah 2Ki 21:1–2

Youths who jeered Elisha 2Ki 2:23–24

Those who ignore the wise counsel of Solomon Pr 1:1–4 *It seems that sections of Proverbs were written with young people in mind. Those who choose to act upon its wisdom will please God and keep themselves out of the troubles common to youth.*

Those who succumb to the evil desires of youth 2Ti 2:22 *Young people are warned that the strength of their desires can easily get them into trouble. Young Christians are, with God's help, able to control such desires.*

The punishment of criminals

By hanging Dt 21:22–23 *See also* 2Sa 21:9; Ezr 6:11; Est 7:9–10

By stoning Dt 22:23–24 *See also* Lev 20:1–2; Jos 7:24–25

By beating Dt 25:2–3 *See also* Ac 16:20–23; 2Co 11:24–25

By confiscation of property Ezr 7:26 *See also* Ezr 10:8

By crucifixion Lk 23:32–33 pp Mt 27:38 pp Mk 15:27 *See also* Lk 23:40–41

See also

2410 cross, the	5482 punishment
5040 murder	5555 stealing
5276 crime	6242 adultery
5344 imprisonment	7346 death penalty

5278

cripples

People whose walk, physical or spiritual, is hindered by deformity, permanent or temporary.

Physically crippled from birth

Ac 3:2 *See also* Ac 14:8

Physically crippled in life

By accident 2Sa 4:4 *See also* 2Sa 9:3,13

By God Ge 32:24–25 *God had a purpose in the crippling of Jacob: it was a mark of his meeting with God. See also* Ge 32:31–32; Heb 11:21

By Satan Lk 13:11 *See also* Lk 13:16

Cripples healed

By Jesus Christ Lk 7:22 pp Mt 11:4–5 *See also* Mt 15:30–31; Jn 5:1–9

By others Ac 3:7 *See also* Ac 4:9–10; 8:7; 14:9–10

Cripples and OT sacrifice

Lev 21:18–19 *A man must be without defect. Physical disability is a defilement to holiness. See also* Lev 21:6

Crippled animals Mal 1:8 *Animals, like people, must be holy, without defect, when brought to the Lord. See also* Ex 12:5; Lev 3:1; 4:3; 22:18–25; Nu 6:14; 28:3; Dt 15:21; 17:1; Mal 1:13–14

Spiritual aspects of being crippled

Physical crippling preferable to spiritual lameness Mt 18:8 *See also* Mk 5:29–30; 9:43

Cripples disadvantaged in life but welcome in the kingdom of God Mic 4:6–7 *See also* Jer 31:8; Eze 34:16; Lk 14:13,21

Spiritual cripples healed Isa 35:6 *See also* Heb 12:13

See also

2351 Christ, miracles	5162 lameness
4120 Satan	5296 disabilities
5094 Jacob	

See also

5333 healing	7413 priesthood, OT
5346 injury	7435 sacrifice, in OT
5378 law, OT	

5279

crowds

Multitudes of people feature prominently in the narrative parts of Scripture, particularly in the Gospels and Acts. The attitudes of the crowds to Jesus Christ throw light on his ministry, as do his attitudes to them.

Crowds tend towards evil

Ex 23:2; Ps 64:2; Isa 53:6; Jer 9:2; Eze 23:42; Mk 15:8–15

Crowds and worship

Ps 42:4 *See also* Ezr 10:1

God's judgment is pronounced on crowds of people

Joel 3:14 *See also* Eze 7:11–14

Multitudes are seen by John in his vision

Rev 7:9 *The redeemed in heaven;* Rev 17:15 *Sinful people on earth.*

Crowds played a large part in Jesus Christ's ministry

Gathering round him: Mt 13:2 pp Mk 4:1 pp Lk 8:4; Mk 3:20; 5:21; Lk 12:1 *Following him:* Mt 8:1; Mk 3:7; Lk 14:25; Jn 6:2

Mk 9:25 *running to the scene of his healings;* Lk 8:42 *almost crushing him;* Lk 3:7 *coming to him to be baptised;* Mt 15:30 *bringing people to him to be healed;* Lk 5:29 *eating with him;* Jn 12:34 *questioning him;* Jn 12:17 *spreading news of him;* Jn 7:12 *whispering about him*

Jesus Christ often taught crowds

Mk 2:13 *See also* Mt 4:25–5:2 pp Lk 6:17–20; Mt 11:7 pp Lk 7:24; Mt 13:1–3 pp Mk 4:1–3 pp Lk 8:4–5; Mt 13:34; 15:10 pp Mk 7:14; Mt 23:1; Mk 6:34; 10:1

Jesus Christ had compassion on the crowds

Mt 9:36 *See also* Mk 6:34

He healed them Mt 14:14 *See also* Mt 19:2

He fed them Mt 14:15–21 pp Mk 6:35–44 pp Lk 9:12–17 pp Jn 6:5–13; Mt 15:32–38 pp Mk 8:1–10

Jesus Christ's other contacts with crowds

Mt 26:55 pp Mk 14:48 *questioning them Being hindered by them:* Mt 9:23–25; Mk 2:4 pp Lk 5:19

Mt 14:22 pp Mk 6:45 *dismissing them;* Lk 4:30 *passing through them;* Mk 4:36 *leaving them;* Jn 5:13 *slipping away from them;* Mk 7:33 *leading a man away from the crowd to heal him*

Individuals mentioned in connection with a crowd

Mk 9:17 pp Lk 9:37–40 *the man with a demon-possessed son;* Mk 5:21–34 *Jairus and the woman with a haemorrhage;* Lk 7:12 *the widow with a dead son;*

Lk 19:2–3 *Zaccheus, unable to see Jesus Christ because of the crowd;* Mk 10:46–48 pp Lk 18:35–39 *blind Bartimaeus, rebuked by the crowd and healed by Jesus Christ;* Lk 11:27 *the woman who blessed Jesus Christ;* Jn 5:3–9 *the man, in the crowd of disabled people by the pool, whom Jesus Christ healed The crowd present at the raising of Lazarus:* Jn 11:42; 12:17

The crowds' varied reactions to Jesus Christ's teaching

Awe, amazement, delight and faith Mt 9:8; Mk 1:22; 12:37; Jn 7:31

Accusation, confusion and questioning Jn 7:20; 12:29,34

Crowds played a large part in the final events of Jesus Christ's life

Mt 21:46 pp Mk 12:12 pp Lk 20:19 *Fear of the crowds restrained the Jewish leaders. See also* Mt 21:8–11 *Crowds demonstrated on Jesus Christ's entry into Jerusalem;* Mk 15:8–15 *The crowd, stirred up by the chief priests, asked for the release of Barabbas;* Mt 27:24 *Pilate washed his hands in front of the crowd;* Mt 26:47 pp Mk 14:43 pp Lk 22:47 *A crowd came with Judas to Gethsemane.*

A crowd gathered in Jerusalem at Pentecost

Ac 2:6 *See also* Ac 2:14

Crowds featured prominently in the ministry of the apostles

Ac 5:16 *bringing the sick to be healed;* Ac 8:6 *listening to Philip's preaching in Samaria;* Ac 13:44–45 *listening to Paul and Barnabas in Pisidian Antioch;* Ac 14:11–19 *attempting to worship Paul and Barnabas in Lystra;* Ac 16:22 *attacking Paul and Silas in Philippi;* Ac 17:5–13 *being stirred up against Paul in Thessalonica and Berea;* Ac 19:30–35 *rising up against Paul in Ephesus;* Ac 21:27–40 *rising up against Paul in Jerusalem;* Ac 22:22 *giving Paul a limited hearing in Jerusalem*

Crowds as the source of loud noise

Isa 13:4 *See also* Da 10:6; Rev 19:1,6

See also

2015 Christ, compassion	2590 Christ, triumphal entry
2351 Christ, miracles	5110 Paul, teaching of
2363 Christ, preaching & teaching	5923 public opinion
2369 Christ, responses to	5936 riots
2545 Christ, opposition to	8622 worship
	8787 opposition to God

5280

crown

An encircling ornament for the head, worn by monarchs as a symbol of royal authority. Also a wreath, worn on joyful occasions or presented to the winner of a race. Used figuratively, the word indicates honour and blessing, the reward awaiting believers in heaven.

A crown as an ornament worn by monarchs

By kings 2Ki 11:12 pp 2Ch 23:11
Crowns worn by the kings of Israel and Judah signified their consecration to God.
See also 2Sa 1:10; Ps 89:39; 132:18; Pr 27:24; Zec 9:16

By queens Est 1:11; 2:17

A crown as a symbol of royal authority

2Sa 12:30 pp 1Ch 20:2 *See also* Ps 21:3; Isa 23:8; Jer 13:18; Eze 21:26; Zec 6:11,14; Rev 12:3; 13:1; 19:12

A crown as a symbol of honour

Est 8:15; Job 19:9; 31:36; Eze 23:42

A crown as a wreath

Worn on joyful occasions, such as a wedding *See also* SS 3:11 *See also* Pr 4:9; Isa 61:3; Eze 16:12; 23:42

A wreath of laurel leaves, worn by the winner of a race 1Co 9:25 *See also* 2Ti 2:5

The mock crown (wreath) of thorns put on Jesus Christ's head

Mt 27:29 pp Mk 15:17 *See also* Jn 19:2,5

Crown is used figuratively to indicate honour and blessing

Isa 62:3 *See also* Pr 4:9; 12:4; 14:24; 16:31; 17:6; Isa 28:5; 61:3; La 5:16; Rev 6:2; 9:7; 12:1; 14:14

Paul's joy and crown 1Th 2:19 *See also* Php 4:1

Crown represents the honour and blessing that await believers in heaven

1Co 9:25 *See also* 2Ti 4:8; Jas 1:12; 1Pe 5:4; Rev 2:10; 3:11; 4:4,10

See also
2312 Christ as king
2570 Christ, suffering
4342 jewels
4520 thorns
5216 authority
5366 king
5500 reward, God's people
5878 honour
6644 eternal life
8110 athletics
8140 prize
9413 heaven, inheritance

crucifixion

A most painful, cruel and protracted form of execution which involved the victim being roped or nailed to an elevated wooden cross. This form of execution was favoured by the Romans, who regarded it as a deterrent to political rebellion against the authority of Rome at the time of Jesus Christ.

The method of crucifixion

The victim was scourged before crucifixion Jn 19:1 pp Mt 27:26 pp Mk 15:15 pp Lk 23:22 *See also* Lk 23:16

The victim carried his cross Jn 19:17
Jesus Christ, having already been scourged, was probably too weak to continue carrying the cross: Mt 27:32–33; Mk 15:21–22; Lk 23:26

The victim was fixed to the cross Lk 23:33 pp Mt 27:35 pp Mk 15:24 pp Jn 19:23 *See also* Jn 20:25

A charge board was fixed to the cross Mt 27:37 pp Mk 15:26 pp Lk 23:38 pp Jn 19:19

The victim's sufferings were protracted Mt 27:54 pp Mk 15:39 pp Lk 23:47; Jn 19:32–33,34 *See also* Mk 15:25,33,37

OT prophecies concerning Jesus Christ's crucifixion

Ps 22:16–18
None of Jesus Christ's bones will be broken: Ex 12:46; Nu 9:12; Ps 34:20; Jn 19:36
Ps 22:1,7–8; 69:21; 109:25; Isa 50:6; 53:5,9; Am 8:9–10; Zec 12:10; 13:6–7

Jesus Christ's predictions concerning the manner of his death

Jn 12:32–33 *See also* Jn 3:14; 8:28; 18:31–32

Responsibility for the crucifixion ascribed to Jews and Gentiles alike

1Co 2:8 *See also* Jn 19:15; Ac 2:23

The crucifixion involved a curse

Dt 21:22–23 *See also* Ge 2:17; Ac 5:30; 10:39; 13:29; Gal 3:13; 1Pe 2:24

The crucifixion involved shame

Heb 12:2 *See also* 1Co 1:23; Php 2:8; Heb 13:13

Believers are united with Jesus Christ in his crucifixion

Gal 2:20 *See also* Ro 6:6

Crucifixion illustrates discipleship

Mk 8:34 pp Mt 16:24 pp Lk 9:23 *See also* Mt 10:38; Lk 14:27; Gal 5:24; 6:14

The crucifixion is remembered in glory

Rev 5:6 *See also* Rev 1:7

See also
2412 cross, accounts of
2525 Christ, cross of
2530 Christ, death of
2545 Christ, opposition to
5827 curse
5947 shame
6614 atonement
6716 reconciliation
6744 sanctification
6754 union with Christ
7346 death penalty
8451 mortification

crushing

Crushing as physically breaking in pieces

Dt 9:21 *See also* 2Ch 34:7; Job 39:14–15; Isa 27:9; Da 2:40

Crushing in the preparation of food and drink

Lev 2:14,16; Nu 11:8; Job 24:11; Mic 6:15

Crushing denoting physical violence

2Sa 22:38–39; Ps 110:5–6; Isa 53:5 *See also* Lev 22:24; Dt 23:1; Job 6:8–9; Isa 3:15; Am 2:13; Mal 1:4

Crushing used metaphorically

Ge 3:15 *Widely regarded as being the earliest prediction of Jesus Christ's triumph over Satan;* Pr 18:14; 2Co 4:8 *See also* Job 19:2; Pr 15:4; Mt 21:44 pp Lk 20:18; Ro 16:20

See also
5347 injustice
5801 brokenness
5975 violence

cup

A drinking vessel, usually made of pottery but sometimes, in wealthy households especially, of gold or silver. Cups might take the form of goblets or of shallow bowls large enough for several people to share, as a sign of fellowship. The word is also used figuratively to refer to the portion of blessing or judgment divinely allotted to individuals or nations.

General references to drinking vessels

Jer 35:5 *See also* Ge 40:11; 44:2–5; Pr 23:31; SS 7:2; Da 5:2–3; Mt 10:42 pp Mk 9:41

Golden goblets as a sign of wealth

1Ki 10:21 pp 2Ch 9:20 *See also* Est 1:7

Sharing a cup as a sign of fellowship

2Sa 12:3

The shared cup at the Lord's Supper

Mt 26:27 pp Mk 14:23 pp Lk 22:17 *See also* 1Co 11:25
1Co 10:16 *See also* 1Co 10:21

Cups symbolising corrupt lives

Mt 23:25–26 *The Pharisees observed ceremonial washings but neglected the need for inward cleansing. See also* Lk 11:39; Rev 17:4

The cup of God's wrath

The cup drunk by the nations Jer 25:15–17 *See also* Ps 75:8; Jer 51:7; Zec 12:2–3; Rev 14:10
God's wrath against Edom: Jer 49:12; La 4:21
God's wrath against Babylon: Hab 2:16; Rev 16:19; 18:6

The cup drunk by God's people Eze 23:32–34; Isa 51:17 *Following judgment, God promises to restore his people. See also* Isa 51:22

The cup drunk by Jesus Christ Jn 18:11 *See also* Mt 20:22–23 pp Mk 10:38–39
Mt 26:42 *The cup of God's wrath may pass from guilty humanity only if Jesus Christ drinks it. See also* Mt 26:39 pp Mk 14:36 pp Lk 22:42

The cup of God's blessing

Ps 16:5 *See also* Ps 23:5; 36:8; 116:12–13

See also
1310 God as judge
1335 blessing
2570 Christ, suffering
4333 gold
4410 banquets
4435 drinking
5284 cupbearer
5445 potters & pottery

See also
5493 retribution
7340 clean and
  unclean
7933 Lord's Supper
9210 judgment,
  God's

5284

cupbearer

One who served a king with wine, often having himself first tasted it for quality and as a safety measure. Some cupbearers became favourites of the king and so wielded considerable political influence.

Pharaoh's cupbearer
Imprisoned Ge 40:1,5

His dream Ge 40:9–11

Dream interpreted by Joseph Ge 40:12–14

Restored to court Ge 40:21

Forgetful of Joseph Ge 40:23

Remembers Joseph Ge 41:9

Solomon's cupbearers
1Ki 10:4–5 pp 2Ch 9:4

Artaxerxes' cupbearer, Nehemiah
Ne 1:11; 2:1

See also
1409 dream
5118 Solomon
5270 court
5283 cup
5344 imprisonment
5345 influence
5460 prison
5523 servants, good
8670 remembering
8763 forgetting
9165 restoration

5285

cures

The removing of illness or other disorder, either mental or physical. Scripture describes the curing of various diseases and conditions. It also points to humanity's area of spiritual need, its sinful condition, declaring Jesus Christ to be the only effective cure.

God's curing of illness
Job 5:17–18 See also Ps 30:2; 103:2–5; 147:3; Jer 33:6

Illnesses and conditions cured by Jesus Christ
Mt 11:4–5 pp Lk 7:21–22 See also Isa 35:5–6

Demon-possession Mt 15:22–28; Mk 5:1–20 pp Lk 8:26–39

Deafness and muteness Mt 12:22 pp Lk 11:14; Mk 7:31–37

Paralysis and lameness Mt 9:2–8 pp Mk 2:3–12 pp Lk 5:18–26; Jn 5:1–14

Bleeding Mk 5:25–34

Blindness Mk 8:22–26; Jn 9:1–7

Leprosy Mt 8:2–4 pp Mk 1:40–44 pp Lk 5:12–14; Lk 17:11–19

Death itself is cured by Jesus Christ
Jn 11:1–44 See also Mk 5:35–43; Lk 7:11–16

Illnesses and conditions cured by the apostles
Ac 5:12–16 See also Ac 3:1–10; 19:11–12

Illnesses cured by the grace of God
Php 2:26–27 Epaphroditus, Paul's fellow-worker; Jas 5:15–16 the importance of prayer in curing illness

Illnesses cured in the name of Jesus Christ
Mk 9:39; Ac 3:6,16; 4:10,30

Humanity's sinfulness cured by Jesus Christ
Sinfulness affects all humanity Ro 3:23

Prophecy of healing through Jesus Christ's death Isa 53:5

Jesus Christ's mission to cure humanity Mt 9:12–13 pp Mk 2:17 pp Lk 5:31 See also Lk 19:10

See also
1055 God, grace &
  mercy
2015 Christ,
  compassion
5001 human race,
  the
5333 healing
5334 health
5405 medicine
6027 sin, remedy for
6510 salvation

5286

custom

An established way or rule (often unwritten) of behaviour, either for an individual or in a society.

Examples of the customs of individuals
1Sa 27:11; Job 1:5; Mk 10:1; Lk 4:16; Ac 17:2

Examples of group customs
1Sa 2:13; 1Ki 18:28; Lk 1:9; Ac 16:20–21

Examples of social customs
Ge 29:26 The older daughter is married before the younger; Jdg 8:24 The Ishmaelites wore gold ear-rings; Jdg 14:10 wedding feasts; Ru 4:7 exchanging sandals as symbol of closing deals; 1Sa 20:25 Court customs; 2Ki 11:14; Est 1:13 Mourning customs; Eze 24:17,22 Mt 27:15 pp Mk 15:6 pp Jn 18:39 release of prisoners at Passover Mary and Joseph obey the customs of the law: Lk 2:27,42 Jn 19:40 burial customs; Ac 25:16 Roman legal customs

A custom can commemorate a particular event
Jdg 11:39–40; Est 9:27

God's people are not to follow improper customs
Lev 18:30 See also Lev 20:23; 2Ki 17:7–8,19,33,40–41; Est 3:8; Ps 106:34–35,40–41; Jer 10:2–3

The issue of whether or not Gentile Christians should follow Jewish customs
Gal 2:14–16 See also Ac 6:11–14; 15:1–2,28–29; 21:21,24; 28:17; Gal 4:9–10; Col 2:8

See also
5155 hair
5303 embalming
5540 society
5588 traditions
5699 guests
5710 marriage,
  customs
5769 behaviour
5873 habits
7328 ceremonies
7394 memorial
7422 ritual
8217 conformity

5287

dance

Movement, usually in response to music, which is often a spontaneous expression of joy and delight in the Lord.

Dance as an expression of joy
Ex 15:20; Ps 30:11 See also Jdg 11:34; 21:21–23; 1Sa 18:6–7; 21:11; 29:5; Ecc 3:4; SS 6:13; Jer 31:4,13; La 5:15; Mt 11:17 pp Lk 7:32; Mk 6:22 The daughter of Herodias dances for Herod; Lk 15:25

Dance as an expression of praise
Ps 150:4 See also Ps 149:3; 2Sa 6:14,16; 1Ch 15:29

Dance as an aspect of pagan worship
1Ki 18:26 See also Ex 32:19

See also
5273 creativity
5420 music
8283 joy
8627 worship,
  elements
8666 praise, manner
  & methods

5288

dead, the

Human beings who have died. Scripture provides illustrations of the manner in which the dead are to be buried, as well as explaining the doctrines of resurrection and judgment.

Preparation of the dead for burial
Washing Ac 9:37 A custom common to both Jews and Greeks.

Embalming Mt 26:12 See also Ge 50:2,26; 2Ch 16:14

Grave clothes Jn 11:44 See also Mk 15:46 pp Mt 27:59 pp Jn 19:40; Jn 20:7; Ac 5:6

Provision for the dead
Burial Ge 49:29–30 It was the normal practice for the people of God to be buried. See also Jos 24:30; Ru 1:17; 1Ki 11:15; Ac 8:2

Cremation Jos 7:25 Cremation was not a Hebrew practice, except in cases of difficulty. See also 1Sa 31:12; Am 6:10

The plight of the unburied dead
Ps 79:2 To be unburied was a disgrace, a mark of judgment. See also Ecc 6:3; Isa 14:19; Jer 7:33; 16:6

Personal contact with a dead body conferred uncleanness
Nu 19:11 See also Lev 21:11; Nu 6:6

The place of the dead
Sheol and Hades Eze 31:16 *Sheol is the OT term for the place of the dead; a grave, an underworld, a pit. Hades is the NT equivalent. See also* 2Ki 21:26; Ps 88:3–4; 89:48; 116:3; Ecc 9:10; Isa 14:9–10; Ac 2:31

A place of judgment Ps 49:13–14 *See also* Ps 31:17; 88:3–5; Na 1:14; Mt 5:22; 11:23 pp Lk 10:15; Mt 16:18; Rev 1:18; 20:13–14

A place of deliverance Ps 139:8 *See also* Ps 16:10; 30:3; 86:13; 107:20; Hos 13:14; Jnh 2:2; Ac 2:27

The plight of the dead outside of Christ
Physical death is the result of sin Ro 6:23 *See also* Ge 2:17; Eze 18:20; Ro 1:32; 5:12; 8:6; Jas 1:15

Final judgment will follow resurrection Rev 21:8 *The "second death" is the throwing of the lost into the lake of fire. See also* Mt 10:28; 25:41; 1Jn 5:16–17; Jude 12

Promises to the dead in Christ
Death is but a sleep 1Th 4:13–14 *See also* Jn 11:11–14; 1Co 15:17–22,51–53

Death has no hold on believers Jn 8:51 *See also* Jn 11:25–26; Ro 8:38–39

Believers will be delivered from the second death Rev 2:11 *See also* Rev 20:6

See also

5241 burial	9210 judgment,
5303 embalming	God's
6510 salvation	9310 resurrection
9020 death	9510 hell
9030 dead bodies	9530 Hades
9040 grave, the	9540 Sheol
9050 tombs	

5289

debt

God is the Maker and sustainer of all things and therefore all creatures owe everything to him. Scripture provides guidance concerning both debt and debtors.

Everyone is in debt to God as Creator
1Co 4:7 *See also* Dt 8:17–18; 1Ch 29:11–13; Ps 24:1–2; Ecc 5:19; Ac 14:17; 17:25; 1Ti 6:17

Everyone is in debt to God as lawgiver
Ro 3:19; Jas 2:10 *See also* Dt 27:26; Ps 49:7–8; Mal 3:8–10; Lk 7:41–42; Gal 3:10; 5:3

Believers are in debt to God as Redeemer
He has paid their debt Gal 3:13 *See also* 2Co 8:9; 1Pe 1:18; Rev 5:9

A sense of debt inspires devotion to God Ps 116:12 *See also* Lk 7:41–47; Ro 8:12; 1Co 6:20

Indebtedness to God affects attitude to others Mt 10:8 *See also* Mt 6:12 pp Lk 11:4; Mt 18:21–35; 1Jn 3:16; 4:11

Examples of people in debt
1Sa 22:2; 2Ki 4:1; Ne 5:4; Mt 5:25–26; 18:23–35; Lk 16:1–8; Ro 4:4; Jas 5:4

Debts must be paid
Lev 19:13; 2Ki 4:7; Ps 37:21; Ro 13:7–8

Social ills result from debt
Ne 5:3–5; Job 24:3,9; Ps 109:11; Eze 18:12–13; 22:12; Am 2:6

OT laws sought to minimise debt
By commanding generous lending to the poor Ex 22:25; Lev 25:35–36; Dt 15:7–11; Ps 15:5; Pr 19:17

By curbing exploitation of debtors Lev 25:37–43; Dt 24:6

By cancelling debts every seventh year Dt 15:1–3; 31:10; Ne 10:31

Preventatives against needless debt
Keeping short accounts Mt 5:25; Ro 13:8

Remembering the evil consequences Pr 22:7; Mt 5:26

Debts to the state
Paying taxes Mt 22:17–21 pp Mk 12:14–17 pp Lk 20:22–25 *See also* Ro 13:6–7

Civic honour Ro 13:7

Debts to employees
Ro 4:4 *See also* Lev 19:13; Jas 5:4

Debts within the church
Towards Christian workers Phm 18–19 *See also* 1Co 9:7–12; Gal 6:6

Towards the unsaved Ro 1:14

The indebtedness of the Gentile church towards the Jerusalem church Ro 15:26–27

Debts to be cancelled
Mt 6:12 pp Lk 11:4 *See also* 1Co 13:5

Debts one should never pay
Ro 12:17 *See also* 1Pe 3:9

A debt one can never cease paying
Ro 13:8–10

See also

5233 borrowing	5577 taxation
5274 credit	6652 forgiveness
5353 interest	6714 ransom
5389 lending	6720 redemption
5404 masters	8224 dependence
5446 poverty	8292 love

5290

defeat

The overcoming of or being overcome by a physical, spiritual or circumstantial enemy. Those humbled before God by such a defeat eventually come to see it as a positive experience, leading to increased spiritual maturity. The way to avoid being defeated is to trust in God and to wear the spiritual armour he provides.

Defeat as the overcoming of enemies
Physical enemies such as armies Ge 14:5–6 *See also* Ge 14:15; 36:35; Dt 1:4; 4:46; 7:1–2; 29:7; Jos 10:33; 11:1–9; Jdg 7:19–22; 1Sa 7:10; 11:11; 14:48; 17:50; 2Sa 2:17; 5:17–25 pp 1Ch 14:8–17; Ps 92:11; Jer 37:10; Zec 9:15; Heb 7:1; 11:34

Spiritual enemies such as Satan Ge 3:15 *See also* Lk 10:19; Jn 12:31; 14:30; Ro 16:20; Col 2:15; 2Th 2:8; Heb 2:14; 1Jn 2:13–14; 3:8; Rev 12:11; 15:2; 17:14; 20:10

The world as the realm of sin Jn 16:33 *See also* Ro 8:37; 12:21; 1Jn 4:4; 5:4–5; Rev 2:7,11,17,26; 3:5,12,21; 5:5; 21:7

Defeat as being overcome by enemies
By physical enemies Lev 26:17 *The Israelites were often defeated by their enemies as a punishment for disobeying God. See also* Nu 14:41–43; Dt 1:42; 28:25; Jos 7:4; Jdg 2:15; 3:12–14; 1Sa 4:1–11; 1Ki 8:33 pp 2Ch 6:24; Ps 13:4; 44:9–12; 78:62; Jer 19:7–9; 21:7

By spiritual enemies Jas 1:13–15 *See also* Ge 3:6–22; 2Sa 11:2–17; 1Co 6:7; 1Th 2:18; 3:5; 1Ti 5:11; 2Pe 2:20

By circumstances Ps 39:10 *This refers to God's chastisement through affliction;* Ps 116:3 *See also* Ps 32:4; 38:2; 2Sa 22:5–6 pp Ps 18:4–5; 1Ki 19:1–4; Job 36:8–9; Jer 23:9; Da 10:16; Lk 8:37; Ro 12:21

Defeat as a positive experience
Jas 4:10 *See also* 2Ch 7:14–15; Ps 119:67,71; 2Co 12:7–10; Heb 12:9–11; 1Pe 5:6

Defeat can be avoided
By trusting in God Ps 25:1–3 *See also* 2Ch 13:18; Ps 22:5; 31:1–4 pp Ps 71:1–3; Ps 112:6–8; 125:1; Isa 26:3; Ro 9:33; 10:11; 1Pe 2:6

By wearing the spiritual armour God provides Eph 6:10–18 *See also* Ro 13:12; 1Th 5:8

See also

4127 Satan, defeat of	8276 humility
4160 driving out	8482 spiritual
5482 punishment	warfare
5597 victory, act of	8727 enemies
God	8738 evil, victory
5605 warfare	over
6248 temptation	9020 death
8030 trust	

5291

defence

A means of protection and security against the attacks of others. Scripture insists that the most reliable form of defence for believers is trust in the Lord.

5292
defence, divine

God defends his people, especially the most vulnerable. Because of

God's defence, although Christians sometimes face trials and persecutions their eternal security is never threatened.

God defends his people
Isa 41:10–12 See also Ex 23:20,27; 1Sa 2:9; 2Ki 6:16–17; Ps 34:7; 144:10; Isa 19:20; 51:16,22; 54:16–17; Jer 50:34; 51:36; Zec 9:8; Mt 16:18; Jn 10:28–29; 2Ti 4:16–18

God defends especially the most vulnerable of his people
Ps 10:17–18 See also Dt 10:17–18; Ps 68:5; 146:9; Pr 23:10–11

God defended the city of Jerusalem
2Ki 19:32–34 pp Isa 37:33–35 See also 2Ki 20:6 pp Isa 38:6; Ps 48:3; Isa 31:5; Zec 2:4–5; 12:8

God's defence of his people is pictured in various ways
As a hiding-place Ps 32:7 See also Ps 17:8; 27:5; 31:20

As a refuge Ps 57:1 See also Dt 33:27; Ps 46:1; Pr 14:26; 18:10; Joel 3:16; Na 1:7

As a shield Ps 115:9–11 See also Ge 15:1; Ps 84:11; 119:114; Pr 30:5

As a combination of images 2Sa 22:1–4 pp Ps 18:2–3 See also Ps 71:3; 91:1–4; 144:1–2; Isa 25:4

The most reliable defence for God's people is to trust only in him
Isa 31:1 See also 2Ch 16:7–9; Ps 20:6–8; 37:16–19; 125:1–2; Isa 17:7–8; Da 3:16–18; Hos 14:3

Examples of prayers for God's defence
Ps 25:20 See also 2Ki 19:14–19 pp Isa 37:14–20; 2Ch 20:10–12; 32:17,20; Ps 35:23; 74:22; 86:2

Because of God's defence the eternal security of believers is never threatened
1Pe 1:3–5 See also Mt 10:28–31 pp Lk 12:4–7; Jn 10:28–29; 17:15; Ro 8:31–39; 2Ti 4:18; Heb 11:32–39; 1Pe 5:8–10; Jude 24; Rev 2:10; 7:13–17

See also
1240 God, the Rock	5490 refuge
1320 God as Saviour	5527 shield
4126 Satan,	5698 guardian
resistance to	8459 perseverance
5315 fortifications	8486 spiritual
5316 fortress	warfare,
5330 guard	armour
5480 protection	

5293
defence, human

God's people are to defend the needy and those in their care. They are also to defend the truth entrusted to them.

Defence of the needy
God commands his people to defend the needy Pr 31:8–9 See also Isa 1:17; 10:1–2; 58:6–7,9–10

Examples of those who defended the needy Ps 72:4
Moses: Ex 2:17; Ac 7:24
Ru 2:15–16 Boaz

Neglect of the cause of the needy is condemned Ps 82:2–4 See also Job 5:4; Isa 1:23–24; 29:20–21; Jer 5:26–29; 22:15–17

Church leaders are to defend the flock of God
Ac 20:28–31 See also Jn 21:15–17; 1Ti 4:6; Tit 1:10–11; Heb 13:17; 1Pe 5:2

Christians are urged to defend the faith
It is the responsibility of all believers Jude 3 See also Php 1:27–28; 2Th 2:15

It is the responsibility of Christian leaders in particular 2Ti 1:13–14 See also 1Ti 1:3–10; 6:20–21; Tit 1:12–14

Examples of leaders who defended the faith Php 1:16 See also Ac 6:8–10 Stephen; Ac 18:27–28 Apollos Paul: Gal 1:6–9; 2:11–14; Php 1:7

See also
1460 truth	5944 self-defence
5051 responsibility	7703 apologetics
5208 armies	7733 leaders
5448 poverty,	8292 love
attitudes to	8313 nurture
5607 warfare,	8822 self-
examples	justification

5295

destruction

The demolition or eradication of buildings, peoples or individuals. Since God is the Creator and sustainer of all things, wanton ruin is contrary to his will as his original purposes cannot be fulfilled. God will bring about the final destruction of all that is evil in the last judgment.

God disapproves of wanton destruction
Of human life Ex 20:13 pp Dt 5:17 See also Ge 4:8–12; 9:5–6; 2Sa 12:7–10

Of the world in general Rev 11:18
As God's representatives on earth human beings are to be good stewards of the creation. They are not to exploit or waste the world, but to care for it: Ge 1:28; 2:15; Dt 20:19–20

Of spiritual life Ro 14:15 See also 1Co 8:9–11; 2Ti 2:17–18; 2Pe 2:1

Agents of destruction
Satan Job 1:12–19; Jn 8:44; 10:10

The wicked Ps 55:11; Pr 1:10–12; Lk 13:1–3

Nature Mt 6:19; Lk 13:4–5

God himself brings destruction on the wicked
God decrees destruction for sinners Ps 37:38 See also Ge 6:5–7; Ps 5:6; 46:8; Isa 34:2; Am 1:3–8; 2:1–3; Lk 3:9; 1Jn 3:8

By the forces of nature Ge 7:4 See also Ge 19:24–25; Dt 28:15–24; Ps 48:7; Eze 5:16; 13:13; Lk 17:29; Rev 6:12–14

By means of angels 1Co 10:10 See also Ex 12:23; 2Sa 24:15–17

pp 1Ch 21:14–17; 1Ch 21:12; 2Ki 19:35 pp 2Ch 32:21 pp Isa 37:36; Ac 12:23; Rev 7:2–3

By means of human beings Dt 7:16 See also Nu 21:3; Dt 2:34; 3:6; 28:47–48; Jos 6:21; 8:26; 11:20; Jer 25:9

Destruction in the final judgment
2Th 1:8–9 See also Mal 4:1; 2Th 2:8; Rev 17:8,11; 18:21; 20:10,14

Destruction is sudden 1Th 5:3 See also Pr 6:15; 24:21–22; 29:1; Ecc 9:12; Isa 30:13; 47:11; Jer 15:8; 2Pe 3:10

Warnings against the way of destruction Mt 7:13 See also Jos 6:18; 1Ti 6:9

God keeps his people from destruction
Ex 12:13 See also Ps 91:9–10; Ro 8:35–39

God's kingdom is indestructible
Heb 12:28 See also Ps 46:5; 125:1; Da 2:44

There will be no destruction in the world to come
Isa 11:9 See also Da 7:27; Rev 21:3–5; 22:15

See also
1310 God as judge	5605 warfare
2375 kingdom of	5979 waste
God	6142 decay
4110 angels	6510 salvation
4120 Satan	6702 peace,
5359 justice	destruction
5508 ruins	9510 hell

5296

disabilities

Physical incapacities resulting from physical or spiritual causes.

Examples of disabilities
Barrenness Ge 11:30; 25:21; Mt 19:12

Blindness Mt 12:22; 15:30; 20:30; Mk 8:22; Jn 9:1

Deafness Ps 38:13; Mk 7:32

Muteness Ps 38:13; Mt 12:22; Lk 11:14

Lameness Lev 21:18; 2Sa 5:6; Mt 15:31; 21:14; Ac 14:8

Causes of disabilities
God's judgment Dt 28:28

Accident 2Sa 4:4; 2Ki 1:2

Old age Ge 27:1; 1Sa 4:15; 2Sa 19:35; Ps 71:9; Ecc 12:3–4; Zec 8:4; Heb 11:21

Congenital defects Mt 19:12; Jn 9:1; Ac 14:8

Cruelty Jdg 1:6–7; 16:21; 1Sa 11:2; 2Ki 25:7; Eze 23:25

Illness 1Ki 15:23 pp 2Ch 16:12; Gal 4:13–15

Acts of God Ge 19:11; 32:25,31–32; Lev 26:16; 1Ki 13:4; 2Ki 6:18; 15:5; 2Ch 21:18–19; 26:19–21; Lk 1:20; Ac 9:8 Saul's blindness; Ac 13:11; 22:11

Acts of evil spirits Mt 9:32–33; 12:22; Mk 9:17,25–26; Lk 11:14; 13:11,16

Unfavourable aspects of disability

Unfair advantage taken of the disabled
Lev 19:14; 2Sa 19:26; Jn 5:7

Disabilities restrict service for God
Lev 21:16–23; 2Sa 19:31–37

Favourable aspects of disabilities

Prayer to the Lord Ge 25:21; 1Sa 1:10; Mt 9:27; 20:30; Mk 7:32; 8:22; 2Co 12:8

Prevention of overconfidence 2Co 12:7

Proof of God's grace 2Co 12:9–10

Demonstration of God's power
Jn 9:2–3

Disability and God's people

God's blessing may prevent or remove disability Ge 25:21; Ex 23:25–26; Ps 113:9; Isa 49:21; 54:1; Lk 1:36; Heb 11:11

God's providence Ex 4:11

God protects his servants by disabling their enemies 2Ki 6:18

Human attitudes to disabilities

Bitterness 1Sa 1:10

Contempt Ge 16:4; 1Sa 1:6; 2Ki 2:23; Pr 17:5

Inertness Jn 5:6

Rejoicing 2Co 12:9–10

God's compassion towards those with disabilities

Revealed in the precepts of the law
Lev 19:14; Dt 27:18

Revealed in the promises of the prophets Isa 42:16; Jer 31:8; Mic 4:6–7; Zep 3:19

Revealed in the deeds of Jesus Christ
Mt 9:27–33; 15:29–31 pp Mk 7:31–37; Mt 21:14; Lk 7:21–23

Responsibilities towards those with disabilities

To treat them with respect Lev 19:14

Not to take advantage of them
Dt 27:18

To provide help for them Job 29:15; Pr 31:8; Lk 14:13–14

See also
1030 God, compassion	5225 barrenness
	5278 cripples
1310 God as judge	5297 disease
5133 blindness	5333 healing
5147 deafness	5726 old age,
5162 lameness	attainment
5168 muteness	5823 cruelty

disease

An illness or other condition which prevents people or animals from achieving their full potential or adversely affects their abilities.

General and specific examples of disease

General references Mt 8:17; Mk 3:10 *See also* Ex 15:26; Dt 7:15; 2Ch 16:12; Jn 5:3; Ac 28:9

Blindness Jn 9:1

Boils and sores Ex 9:9; Job 2:7; Isa 38:21; Lk 16:20

Depression Pr 13:12

Dropsy Lk 14:2

Dysentery Ac 28:8

Epilepsy Mt 17:15 *See also* Mt 4:24; Mk 9:17–18

Fever Job 30:30 *See also* Mt 8:14 pp Mk 1:30 pp Lk 4:38; Ac 28:8

Haemorrhaging Mt 9:20 pp Mk 5:25 pp Lk 8:43

Inflammation Dt 28:22

Insanity 1Sa 21:13; Da 4:33–35

Leprosy Nu 12:10; 2Ch 26:21; Mt 11:5; Lk 17:11–19

Paralysis Mt 4:24; 8:6; 9:2 pp Mk 2:3 pp Lk 5:18; Lk 13:11; Ac 3:2; 8:7; 9:33

Sunstroke 2Ki 4:18–19; Ps 121:5–6; Isa 49:10; Jnh 4:8

Tumours Dt 28:27; 1Sa 5:6

Voluntary starvation 1Sa 1:7; 28:20; Ps 102:4; 107:18

Wasting Lev 26:16; Dt 28:22

Even the righteous suffer disease

Job 2:3,7 *See also* Ps 38:2–3; 41:7–8

Examples of the righteous suffering

2Ki 20:1 pp 2Ch 32:24; Da 8:27; Lk 7:2; Jn 11:1; Ac 9:36–37; Gal 4:13; Php 2:25–27; 1Ti 5:23; 2Ti 4:20

Causes of disease

Jn 9:2

Original sin Ge 3:16–17

Accident 2Ki 4:39–40

Judgment Ps 107:17–18 *See also* Ex 9:8–10; Lev 26:14–16; Nu 16:41–49; 2Ki 5:27; Jer 14:12; 1Co 11:29–30

Testing Job 2:5

Response to sickness and disease

The compassion of God Mk 1:32–34 *See also* Ps 41:3; Mt 8:17

Compassion Eze 34:4; Mt 25:36; Lk 9:2; 10:30–37

Humble submission Job 13:15 *See also* 2Co 12:8–10

Prayer Jas 5:14 *See also* Ge 20:17; 2Co 12:8

Spiritual disease

Isa 1:5–6 *See also* Jer 8:22; 30:12; Mic 1:9; Mt 9:12–13 pp Lk 5:31–32

Salvation and healing from disease

Salvation achieved through the cross of Jesus Christ Isa 53:4–5

Salvation made perfect in heaven
Rev 22:1–3 *See also* Eze 47:12; Rev 7:17; 21:1–4

See also
4843 plague	5333 healing
5133 blindness	5334 health
5162 lameness	5390 leprosy
5182 skin	5405 medicine
5285 cures	5568 suffering,
5296 disabilities	causes
5298 doctors	

doctors

People who are qualified in medicine and treat those who are ill. Doctors do not feature extensively in Scripture; rather God is portrayed as the source of health and healing for his people. Prophets were sometimes intermediaries in healing and priests were responsible for diagnosing certain diseases in accordance with the law. Luke, the author of the Gospel of that name and Acts, was a doctor.

God as the source of physical health and healing
Ex 15:26 *See also* Nu 12:10–15; 21:4–9; Dt 32:39; Ps 6:2

God as the source of spiritual healing
Job 5:18 *See also* Isa 53:5; Jer 33:6; Hos 6:1

Jesus Christ as a healer
Mt 8:16–17 pp Mk 1:32–34 pp Lk 4:40 *See also* Isa 53:4; Mt 4:24; 14:14 pp Lk 9:11

Prophets as intermediaries in healing
2Ki 5:1–14; 20:1–7 pp 2Ch 32:24 pp Isa 38:1–5; Isa 38:21

Priests in a medical role
Lev 13:1–46; 15:1–33

Medical treatments mentioned in Scripture
Use of oils and emollients on wounds
Isa 1:6 *See also* Jer 46:11

Splinting and bandaging of broken limbs Eze 30:21

Poultices 2Ki 20:7 *See also* Isa 38:21

Human doctors mentioned in Scripture
Their limited ability contrasted with God's power 2Ch 16:12–13 *See also* Job 13:4; Mk 5:25–29 pp Lk 8:43–44

Non-Israelite doctors Ge 50:2 *These were Egyptian physicians. See also* Col 4:14 *Luke was a Greek.*

Figurative use Mk 2:17 pp Mt 9:12 pp Lk 5:31 *See also* Lk 4:23

See also
2351 Christ, miracles	5334 health
4490 ointment	5405 medicine
5285 cures	5410 midwife
5296 disabilities	5428 nurse
5297 disease	5571 surgery
5333 healing	

door

A point of entry, especially to a house. The door-frame was given special significance within the law of Moses, and temple doorkeepers had a special status. Used figuratively, it relates to opportunity, and Jesus

Christ used it of himself as the means of access to God.

The function of doors: gaining or barring entry

Ps 24:7 See also Ge 19:6,9–11; Ex 12:22; 2Sa 13:17–18; 2Ki 4:4–5 Elisha and the widow's oil; Ne 13:19; Ps 24:9; Pr 5:8 warning against adultery; Mt 6:6 Jesus Christ advocates secret prayer; Mk 1:33; Lk 11:7; Jn 18:15–16; Ac 5:19; Rev 3:8

The status and role of temple doorkeepers

Ps 84:10 See also 2Ki 25:18 pp Jer 52:24; 1Ch 15:23–24; 2Ch 23:19; 34:13

The door and its surroundings as a symbol of a household

Ex 12:22–23 See also Ex 12:7; 21:6; Dt 6:9; 11:20; 15:16–17; 22:21; Isa 57:8; Eze 45:19

Figurative use of opening a door
The door as a symbol of opportunity
1Co 16:8–9 See also Ge 4:7; Hos 2:15; Ac 14:27; Col 4:3; Rev 3:7–8

Opening the door as a symbol of allowing Jesus Christ into one's life
Rev 3:20 See also Lk 12:35–36

The door opened in answer to prayer
Mt 7:7–8 pp Lk 11:9–10

Jesus Christ as the means of access to God Jn 10:7 "Door" is sometimes used as a synonym for "gate". See also Jn 10:9

The door is indicative of imminent arrival Mt 24:33 pp Mk 13:29

The door as the entry to the coming kindgom Mt 25:10–12; Lk 13:23–25

See also
5046 opportunities	5340 house
5323 gate	5364 key
5324 gatekeepers	6606 access to God

drowning

The Egyptians pursuing Israel drowned in the Red Sea
Heb 11:29 See also Ex 14:21–28; 15:1–5

Jonah was delivered from drowning
Jnh 2:2–7

The demon-possessed herd of pigs drowned in the Sea of Galilee
Mk 5:1–13 pp Mt 8:28–32 pp Lk 8:26–33

Jesus Christ's disciples feared they would drown in a storm
Mk 4:35–41 pp Mt 8:23–27 pp Lk 8:22–25

Drowning in the teaching of Jesus Christ
Mt 18:6

Metaphorical use
Job 10:15

See also
4266 sea	6634 deliverance
4851 storm	7222 exodus, events
5517 seafaring	of
5569 hardship	9020 death
6022 sin, causes of	

dyeing

Dyeing cloth or animal skin
Ex 26:14 See also Ex 25:5; 35:7,23; 36:19; 39:34

See also
4807 colours	5258 cloth
5212 arts and crafts	

education

The imparting of spiritual, intellectual, moral and social instruction, the basis for which is the fear of the LORD. People continue learning throughout the whole of life. The education of children in the OT was centred on the home and synagogue and was largely of a religious and ethical nature. In the NT, children were included in the community of the church, but the home was still the main sphere of their education.

The fear of the LORD is the basis for all education
Ps 111:10 See also 2Ch 26:5; Ps 25:12; Pr 1:7; 2:1–8; 9:10; 15:33; Isa 11:1–3

Faith is an essential element of Christian education
Heb 11:3 See also 2Ti 3:15

Education should not oppose the truth about God
2Co 10:5 See also Mt 18:6; 1Ti 6:20–21

Education should emphasise that the world has a richness and coherence derived from God
Ps 24:1; Jn 1:3 See also Job 12:7–10; Ps 104:5–26; 1Co 10:26; Col 1:17; Heb 1:3

Education in the home
Through parental instruction Dt 6:4–9; Ps 78:4–6 See also Dt 4:9–10; 6:20–25; 11:18–21; Pr 22:6; Isa 38:19; Eph 6:4; Col 3:21

Examples of parents teaching their children Ge 18:19; Pr 31:1–9; 2Ti 3:14–15

Through parental example 2Ti 1:5 See also 2Ch 20:31–32; 26:3–4

Through discipline Pr 29:15 See also Pr 1:7; 2Ti 4:2; Tit 1:13

Education through religious worship
Jos 8:34–35 See also 2Ch 20:13; Ezr 8:21; Ne 12:43; Mt 21:15–16

Education through religious festivals
Dt 31:9–13 See also Ex 12:24–27; 13:6–8

See also
3140 Holy Spirit,	7756 preaching,
teacher	content
5664 children	7793 teachers
5685 fathers,	7797 teaching
responsibilities	8232 discipline,
5731 parents	family
7354 feasts and	8365 wisdom,
festivals	human

embalming

The Jewish custom of preparing a body for the grave. However, the technically correct use of the term describes the removal of the internal organs of the dead and filling the cavity with spices. This originated with the Egyptians but was not practised by the Jews. Biblical teaching concerning life after death makes embalming unnecessary.

Jacob and Joseph were embalmed in Egypt
Ge 50:2–3 See also Ge 50:26

Jesus Christ was embalmed
Jn 19:39–40 pp Mt 27:59 pp Mk 15:46 pp Lk 23:53

Further embalming of Jesus Christ was planned
Mk 16:1 pp Lk 24:1

See also
2530 Christ, death of	6644 eternal life
5241 burial	9030 dead bodies

embroidery

Examples of embroidery
The entrance curtain to the tabernacle
Ex 26:36 See also Ex 27:16; 36:37; 38:18

Aaron's sash Ex 28:39 See also Ex 39:29

Costly robes Ps 45:14 See also Eze 16:10,13,18; 26:16

An expensive sail Eze 27:7

Embroidery was important in trade
Eze 27:16,24

Embroidered garments were the spoils of war
Jdg 5:30

The developing human embryo is likened to God's embroidery
Ps 139:15

See also
5145 clothing	5531 skill
5212 arts and crafts	7344 curtain
5258 cloth	7459 tabernacle, in
5433 occupations	OT

empires

Spheres of influence of major powers in the ancient world. The most important empires to relate to the history of the people of God are those of Assyria, Babylon and Rome. Scripture stresses that the grandeur and power of such empires are temporary; only God remains.

Empires of biblical times
The Hittite empire Jos 1:4 *Canaan was still known as "the land of the Hittites" for centuries after the Hittites withdrew to the north. See also* Ge 23:10; 49:29–30; 50:13; 2Sa 11:3–24 *Hittites continue to feature in the OT histories, despite the earlier withdrawal of the Hittites to Anatolia. The Hittite most commonly referred to in the OT is Uriah, husband of Bathsheba.*

The Egyptian empire Ge 12:10; Ex 12:40–41; Dt 6:21; 2Ch 35:20; 36:3

The Assyrian empire 2Ki 15:19–21; 16:7–18; 17:3–6,23–27; 2Ch 32:1–22; Isa 7:17–20; 36:1–18; Hos 11:5; 14:3

The Babylonian empire Ezr 5:12–17; Ne 7:6; Est 2:6; Ps 137:1; Isa 39:1–7; Jer 20:4–6; 21:2–7; 27:6–22; 29:10

The Roman empire Ac 16:37; 18:2; 19:21; 22:25 *Roman citizenship brought considerable privileges to those who possessed it;* Ac 23:11; 25:25; 28:16

The transience of human empires
Da 2:44 *See also* Isa 13:1–22; 40:6–8; Jer 51:37–40; Da 2:31–45
The references to "Babylon the Great" in Revelation are probably meant to be understood as references to the Roman empire, at a time when Christians were being persecuted by the Roman authorities for their faith: Rev 14:8; 18:1–8

See also
1105 God, power of	4945 history
4215 Babylon	7216 exile in Assyria
4263 Rome	

---

engraving

Engraving on the high priest's equipment
Ex 28:9–12,21,36; 39:6,14,30

Engraving in the temple
2Ch 2:7 *See also* 1Ki 7:31,36; 2Ch 2:14

Engraving on stone
Job 19:24; Zec 3:9

The Ten Commandments engraved on tablets
Ex 32:15–16 *See also* 2Co 3:7–8

Figurative use of engraving
Isa 49:16; Jer 17:1

See also
5211 art	5516 sculpture
5212 arts and crafts	5574 tablet
5272 craftsmen	5638 writing
5352 inscriptions	

---

envoy

An official representative sent on behalf of a king or government to

other kings or nations. Believers are God's envoys to his world, bearing the good news of salvation on his behalf.

Envoys sent to other kings or governments
Ps 68:31; Pr 13:17; Isa 30:4

To continue or promote good relations 1Ki 5:1 *See also* 2Sa 10:2 pp 1Ch 19:2; 2Ki 20:12–13 pp Isa 39:1–2; Isa 30:6; 57:9 *in this instance with godless nations*

To deceive Jos 9:4

To ask for military help 2Ki 17:4; Eze 17:15

To make enquiries 2Ch 32:31; Isa 14:32

With a message to prepare for war Isa 18:2; Jer 49:14 pp Ob 1

To negotiate for peace Isa 33:7; Lk 14:32

With a message of God's judgment to the nations Jer 27:3

With a message of rebellion Lk 19:14

Believers are God's envoys to his world
2Co 5:20 *See also* Mt 28:19; Jn 17:18; 20:21; Ro 10:15; Isa 52:7; 2Co 2:17; Eph 6:20

See also
5408 messenger	7739 missionaries
7105 believers	7754 preaching
7706 apostles	8424 evangelism
7724 evangelists	

---

equality

Scripture declares that all people are equal in the sight of God, and that all are equally in need of the redemption achieved through the saving death of Jesus Christ. All believers have equal status before God, despite differences in their social standing and background.

The equality of Father and Son
Jesus Christ claims equality with God Jn 5:18 *See also* Jn 10:30; Mt 11:27; Jn 17:10–22

The apostles treat Jesus Christ as equal with God 2Th 2:16–17 *See also* Ac 2:38; Gal 1:3; Php 2:6; 1Th 3:11; 1Jn 5:20

The equality of all people before God
God is the maker of all people, whatever their status Pr 22:2 *See also* Ac 17:26

All people have sinned, whatever their origin or status Ro 3:22–24

God shows no partiality in his dealings with people Dt 10:17 *See also* Job 31:13–15; Ro 2:11; Eph 6:9; 1Pe 1:17

The gospel is proclaimed equally to all Ac 10:34

All believers are one, whatever their origin, status or gender Gal 3:28

Equality among believers
1Co 12:25; 2Co 8:13–14; 11:12

Believers must not give preferential treatment to the rich Jas 2:2–4 *See also* Lev 19:15

Believers must not show favouritism Jas 2:9 *See also* 1Ti 5:21; Jas 2:1

See also
1512 Trinity, equality of	5707 male and female
2420 gospel	5769 behaviour
5001 human race, the	5838 disrespect
5034 likeness	7105 believers
5554 status	8753 favouritism
	8800 prejudice

---

eunuchs

Castrated men. In the Bible eunuchs are usually portrayed as having positions of responsibility in royal courts. Though eunuchs were excluded from certain privileges under the old covenant, they were at no disadvantage under the new.

Eunuchs as royal servants
Est 1:10–11 *See also* 2Ki 20:16–18 pp Isa 39:5–7; Est 2:1–3,15; 4:4–11; Jer 38:7 fn; Ac 8:27

Eunuchs among the people of God
Exclusions of eunuchs from the assembly and the priesthood Dt 23:1 *See also* Lev 21:16–23

Eunuchs not excluded from God's blessings if obedient Isa 56:3–5

Eunuchs could become Christians like anyone else Ac 8:26–39 *the Ethiopian eunuch*

Eunuch as an image for celibacy
Mt 19:10–12 *Jesus Christ teaches that castration is not the only legitimate reason for celibacy. Some men may be called to voluntary celibacy because of the demands of their role in the kingdom of heaven.*

Paul suggests that a dogmatic demand for circumcision might lead to a demand for emasculation
Gal 5:12

See also
5736 singleness	8468 renunciation
7334 circumcision	

---

exploitation

Taking advantage of weak and vulnerable groups within society, especially financially; a practice that is prohibited in Scripture. Rather, such groups of people should be treated with special care and concern.

Exploitation is forbidden

Pr 22:23 *See also* Job 22:5–9; Pr 23:10;
Isa 5:8; 59:12–15; Eze 45:9–10;
Mic 2:1–3; Zec 7:10

God protects those who are liable to exploitation

Dt 10:18; Ps 12:5 *See also* Dt 10:17;
Ps 10:17–18; 68:5; Isa 25:4

God provides for those liable to exploitation

Ex 23:10; Dt 14:28–29; 26:12–13;
Ps 22:26; 68:10; 132:15

Examples of groups of people who must not be exploited

The poor Pr 17:5; Isa 3:14–15;
Am 2:6–7; 5:11; Zec 7:10

Orphans and the fatherless Ps 10:17;
Isa 1:23; Jer 5:27–29; 22:3

Widows and aliens Ps 94:1–6; 146:9;
Jer 22:3; 49:11; Zec 7:10

The weak Ps 41:1; 72:13; 82:3

Believers' responsibilities towards those vulnerable to exploitation

To pray for them Ps 82:3

To care and provide for them Jas 1:27

Particular responsibilities towards the weak Ac 20:35 *See also* 1Th 5:14

Particular responsibilities for widows
Ac 6:1–6; 1Ti 5:3–16; Jas 1:27

Particular responsibilities towards orphans Jas 1:27

Particular responsibilities towards the poor and needy Pr 22:9 *See also*
Mt 6:2–3; 19:16–21; Lk 19:8;
Ac 4:34–35; 9:36; 10:2; Ro 15:25–27

Examples of exploitation

2Sa 23:15–17 *David*; Mt 23:15 *the Pharisees*; Ac 8:18–23 *Simon Magus*

See also

1330 God, the	5446 poverty
provider	5730 orphans
5220 authority,	5743 widows
abuse	7530 foreigners
5253 cheating	8790 oppression
5318 fraud	
5349 injustice,	
examples	

5311

extortion

Literally "twisting out"; obtaining money, etc., by violence, threats or unreasonable demands.

Extortion condemned

Ps 62:10 *See also* Ecc 7:7; Isa 10:1–2;
Eze 22:13; 1Co 6:9–10

Extortioners can be saved

1Co 6:9–11

What God requires from extortioners

Repentance Lk 3:12–14

Restitution Lev 6:4–5; Lk 19:8

Curses upon those who are guilty of extortion

Jer 22:17–19 *See also* Eze 18:18;
22:12–14; Am 5:11; Hab 2:6

Blessings upon those who avoid extortion

Isa 33:15–16

Examples of extortion

1Sa 2:12–17 *Eli's sons*; 1Sa 8:11–18 *the wicked king foretold by Samuel*;
1Sa 13:19–21 *the Philistines*; Ne 5:1–5
the Jews in Nehemiah's day; Eze 22:29
Israel under the kings; Mt 18:28 *the servant in the parable*; Mt 23:25 *the Pharisees*; Lk 18:11 *sinners in the eyes of the Pharisee*; 1Co 5:9–11 *some Christians before conversion*

See also

5347 injustice	5576 tax collectors
5353 interest	5577 taxation
5412 money	5869 greed
5465 profit	8714 dishonesty
5492 restitution	8790 oppression
5555 stealing	

5312

feasting

Taking part in festive meals that were often a feature of Israel's celebrations of religious festivals.

Feasting on special occasions

To mark a covenant Ge 31:54 *The sacrifice and the meal were important elements in the covenant-making process.*
See also Ge 26:28–31; Ex 24:11;
1Co 11:25–26

Weddings Jdg 14:10 *See also* Ge 29:22;
Est 2:18; Mt 22:2; Jn 2:1–10; Rev 19:9

Family celebrations Ge 21:8 *See also*
Lk 15:23–24

National celebrations 1Ki 1:25 *See also*
Est 9:17

Israel's religious feasts

Passover (or the Feast of Unleavened Bread) to celebrate the exodus
Ex 23:15; Dt 16:1–3; Lev 23:4–6;
2Ch 35:17; Mt 26:17; Lk 2:41

Pentecost, to celebrate the early harvest Ex 34:22 *Pentecost was also known in the OT as "the Feast of Weeks" or the "Feast of Harvest". See also*
Ex 23:16; Nu 28:26

The Feast of Tabernacles, to celebrate the autumn harvest Ex 23:16 *See also*
Lev 23:34; Dt 16:13; Ezr 3:4; Ne 8:14;
Zec 14:16

The Feast of Dedication, to celebrate the rededication of the temple
Jn 10:22

The Feast of Purim, to celebrate deliverance Est 9:17 *See also* Est 9:22,26

Feasting amongst God's people

Ne 8:10; Ac 2:46 *See also* 1Ki 3:15;
Est 8:17; 9:17; Job 1:4

Feasting amongst the heathen

Examples of pagan feasts 1Sa 30:16;
Da 5:1; Mk 6:21–28

Warnings and instructions to Christians regarding pagan feasts
1Co 10:27–28; 1Pe 4:3–4

Feasting as an occasion to sin

1Co 10:7 *See also* Ex 32:6; 1Sa 25:36;
2Sa 13:28; Hab 2:15; 1Co 10:28

Feasting as an evangelistic occasion

Lk 5:29 *See also* Mk 2:16–17; Lk 15:2

Feasting defended by Jesus Christ

Mt 11:19 pp Lk 7:34–35 *See also*
Mt 9:14–15 pp Mk 2:18–20
pp Lk 5:33–35

Feasting as a symbol of spiritual blessings

Mt 22:2 *See also* Pr 9:1–6; Isa 25:6;
55:1–2; Lk 14:15; Rev 3:20

Feasting in heaven

Rev 19:9 *See also* Mt 8:11

See also

4410 banquets	7408 Pentecost
5355 invitations	7418 Purim
5710 marriage,	7921 fellowship
customs	7936 love feast
7354 feasts and	8642 celebration
festivals	9150 Messianic
7406 Passover	banquet

5313

flogging

Physical beating inflicted as punishment.

Flogging and beating in the law

Dt 25:2–3 *See also* Ex 21:20

Justified flogging

Pr 19:25; 1Pe 2:20 *See also* Ne 13:25;
Pr 17:10; 18:6; 19:29; Lk 12:47–48

Unjustified flogging

Isa 50:6; Heb 11:36 *See also* Ex 5:14;
Pr 17:26; Jer 20:2; 37:15

Jesus Christ flogged

Mk 15:15 pp Mt 27:26 pp Jn 19:1 *See also* Isa 53:5; Mt 20:19 pp Mk 10:34
pp Lk 18:32

The apostles flogged

Mt 10:17; Ac 5:40 *See also* Mt 23:34;
Mk 13:9; Ac 16:22–23,37; 18:17;
22:19,24–25; 2Co 6:5; 11:24–25

Flogging used figuratively

2Sa 7:14 *See also* Job 5:21; Ps 89:32;
Isa 10:26; 54:11

See also

2570 Christ,	5584 torture
suffering	8230 discipline
5482 punishment	8794 persecution

5314

flute

Early origin of the flute

Ge 4:19–21 *Jubal was descended from Cain and was in the seventh generation after Adam.*

The flute used in worship

In Israelite worship Ps 150:1–6 *See also*
1Sa 10:5; Ps 5:1 Title; Isa 30:29

In pagan worship Da 3:7 *See also*
Da 3:5,10–11,15

The flute played at celebratory events
1Ki 1:38–40 *See also* Job 21:12; Isa 5:12; Mt 11:17 pp Lk 7:32; Rev 18:22

The flute used in mourning
Mt 9:23–24 *See also* Job 30:31; Jer 48:36

The flute used metaphorically by Paul
1Co 14:6–10

See also

5420 music	5422 musicians
5421 musical instruments	8627 worship, elements

5315

fortifications

Structures erected as part of a defence policy. Fortifications protected the inhabitants and their possessions, and also guarded the trade routes. Scripture sees God as the secure fortification of his people in times of danger.

City fortifications
Fortified cities Nu 13:28 *See also* Nu 32:17; Dt 3:4–5; 28:52; Jos 14:12; 19:35–38; 2Ki 18:13; 2Ch 8:5; 11:5–12,23; Ne 9:25; Isa 36:1; Jer 4:5; 34:7; Eze 21:20; Zep 1:16

Walled cities Jos 6:5 *See also* Dt 1:28; 9:1; Jos 6:20; 1Sa 31:10,12; 1Ki 3:1; 2Ch 36:19; Ne 1:3; 2:8,17; Jer 49:27; 51:44; Eze 26:4

Fortification systems
Garrisons 2Sa 8:6 *See also* 2Sa 8:14; 23:14; 1Ch 11:16; 18:6,13; 2Ch 1:14; 8:6; 9:25; 17:2

Towers 2Ch 26:10 *See also* Jdg 9:46,50–52; 2Ki 9:17; 2Ch 27:4

Regional outposts 1Ki 9:17–19 pp 2Ch 8:3–6 *See also* 1Sa 22:4; 23:14; 2Sa 5:17; 23:14; 2Ch 1:14; 9:25; 17:2; 27:3–4

Peoples at risk without fortifications
Eze 38:11 *See also* Jer 49:31

God and fortresses
God as a fortress for his people Ps 18:2 pp 2Sa 22:2–3 *See also* Ps 9:9; 37:39; 46:1; 61:3; 71:3; 73:28; 91:2,9–10; Pr 14:26

God warns against trusting in human fortifications Dt 28:52 *See also* Isa 2:12–18; Jer 5:17; Hos 8:14; Joel 2:7–9; Zep 1:14–16

God's judgment against fortresses Am 5:9–10 *See also* Isa 17:3; 25:2,12; La 2:2; Hos 10:14; Am 1:3–2:5; Mic 5:11

See also

5254 citadel	5480 protection
5256 city	5490 refuge
5291 defence	5529 sieges
5316 fortress	5585 towers
5323 gate	5604 walls
5437 palaces	
5454 power, God's saving	

5316

fortress

A secure dwelling-place, often a city, protected by walled defences. God is seen as the fortress of his people, their security and divine protector.

Fortresses were places of security
Jer 4:5–6 *See also* 1Sa 23:14; 2Sa 5:9 pp 1Ch 11:7–8; 2Sa 20:6; 24:7; 1Ki 15:17

Examples of fortified cities
Nu 32:34–36 *See also* Dt 3:4–5; Jos 19:35–38; 2Sa 5:6–7 pp 1Ch 11:4–5; 1Ki 4:13; 12:25

Fortresses were symbolic of self-reliance
Dt 28:52 *See also* Pr 10:15; Eze 24:21; Da 11:38–39

Fortresses cannot withstand the judgment of God
Jer 51:53 *See also* Isa 2:12–18; 17:1–3; 25:2,12; Jer 48:1; La 2:2
Judgment on Israel's neighbours:
Am 1:4,7,10,12,14; 2:2,5
Hos 10:13–14 *punishment for Israel;*
Na 3:12 *judgment on Nineveh*

God is the secure fortress of his people
Ps 9:9 *See also* 2Sa 22:2–3 pp Ps 18:2; Ps 31:2–3; 59:9,16–17; 144:2; Pr 14:26; Isa 17:10; 25:4; Na 1:7

See also

5256 city	5942 security
5315 fortifications	7240 Jerusalem, history
5323 gate	
5324 gatekeepers	7270 Zion, as a place
5490 refuge	7338 cities of refuge
5604 walls	8030 trust
5611 watchman	

5317

foundation

The solid base on which a secure structure may be built; used chiefly for the base of the temple. It is used figuratively of Jesus Christ and the apostles and prophets as the secure foundation on which the church is built. Obedience to the teaching of Jesus Christ is the true foundation of Christian living.

The place of foundations in building
1Ki 5:17
Jericho rebuilt: Jos 6:26; 1Ki 16:34
Solomon builds the temple: 1Ki 6:37; 7:10; 2Ch 3:3; 8:16
Ezr 3:3,11–12; 4:12 *restoring the walls of Jerusalem;* Ezr 5:16; 6:3; Job 4:19; Isa 44:28; Eze 41:8; Hag 2:18; Zec 4:9; 8:9; Ac 16:26

Destruction of foundations is an indication of divine judgment
La 4:11 *See also* Dt 32:22; 2Sa 22:16; Jer 51:25–26; Eze 13:14; 30:4; Mic 1:6

The foundation of the church
Jesus Christ 1Co 3:11 *See also* Isa 28:16

The apostles and prophets Ro 15:20; 1Co 3:10; Eph 2:19–20

The church as the foundation of God's truth
1Ti 3:14–15 *See also* 2Ti 2:19

Obedience as a secure foundation
Mt 7:24–27 pp Lk 6:46–49 *See also* Job 22:15–18; 1Co 3:12–15; 1Ti 6:18–19

The foundation of the earth
Ps 102:25 *See also* 1Sa 2:8; Job 38:4; Ps 18:7,15; 24:1–2; 82:5; Pr 8:22–31; Isa 48:13; 51:13,16; Mic 6:2; Zec 12:1; Heb 1:10

The foundations of the city of God
Heb 11:10 *See also* Rev 21:14,19

Figurative use of foundation
God himself as the foundation
Isa 33:5–6

The foundation of God's throne
Ps 89:14 *See also* Ps 97:2

The need for a firm foundation in the Christian life
Mt 7:24–27; 16:18; Eph 2:19–22; Heb 6:1–2; 1Pe 2:4–5

See also

1155 God, truthfulness	5340 house
2421 gospel, historical foundation	7024 church, nature of
4354 rock	7467 temple, Solomon's
5207 architecture	7706 apostles
5240 building	7772 prophets
5269 cornerstone	8241 ethics, basis of

5318

fraud

The obtaining of goods or money by deception. Scripture condemns this practice, requiring believers to be honest in their dealings with one another.

Fraud of all kinds is forbidden
Lev 19:11 *See also* Lev 19:13; Mk 10:19; 1Co 6:8

The importance of integrity in public life
2Ki 12:15 *See also* Nu 16:15; 1Sa 12:4; 2Sa 18:12; 1Ki 13:8; 2Ki 5:16

Kinds of fraud
Stealing Ex 20:15 pp Dt 5:19 *See also* Dt 23:24; Eph 4:28; Tit 2:12; 1Pe 4:15

Breach of trust Lev 6:2; Eze 16:17; Lk 16:12

Not repaying loans Ps 37:21

Not paying fair wages Ge 31:6–9; Jas 5:4

Using dishonest weights or scales Lev 19:35–36; Pr 20:23 *See also* Dt 25:13–16; Hos 12:7–8; Am 8:5

Charging excess taxes Lk 19:8

Moving boundary stones Pr 23:10 *See also* Dt 19:14; 27:17

Extortion Hab 2:6 *See also* Isa 10:2; Eze 22:12; Am 5:11; Mt 18:28

See also

5253 cheating	5948 shrewdness
5310 exploitation	6145 deceit
5512 scales &	8714 dishonesty
balances	8790 oppression
5555 stealing	
5613 weights &	
measures	

5319

fugitives

People fleeing, especially from persecution or punishment and seeking refuge. The OT makes special provision for the needs of such people.

Fugitives are those in flight

From family Ge 35:1 *See also* Ge 35:7; Jdg 9:21; 2Sa 13:34; 15:13–15

From war 2Sa 24:13; Ob 14 *See also* Lev 26:36; Nu 21:29; Jos 8:20,22; 2Sa 10:14; Jer 46:22; 48:19; Eze 17:21; 24:26

From other people Ex 2:15; Mt 2:13 *See also* Ex 14:27; 1Sa 22:17; 1Ki 2:39; 11:40; Isa 15:5,9; 45:20; Jer 48:6,45; Mt 24:15–20 pp Mk 13:14–17 pp Lk 21:21–23; Ac 8:1

From vengeance Jer 50:28 *See also* Ge 4:14; Job 15:22; Pr 28:17; Jer 44:14; 48:19

Comfort for the fugitives

Isa 21:14 *See also* Nu 35:6; Dt 23:15; Isa 16:3–4

See also

5347 injustice	5605 warfare
5490 refuge	7338 cities of refuge
5491 refugees	

5320

funeral

Funerals were times for expressing grief

Ge 50:10; Ac 9:36–39

Hired musicians sometimes played a funeral dirge

Mt 9:23

The funeral bier

2Sa 3:31–32; Lk 7:14

Funeral fires lit in honour of worthy kings of Judah

2Ch 16:14; 21:19; Jer 34:5

Funerals often concluded with burial in a family tomb

Ge 49:29–31

Jesus Christ had no funeral ceremony

Lk 23:53 pp Mt 27:59 pp Mk 15:46 pp Jn 19:40–42

See also

5241 burial	5795 bereavement
5275 cremation	9020 death
5303 embalming	9030 dead bodies
5419 mourning	

5321

furnace

A closed fireplace made of brick or stone for domestic or industrial usage. Used figuratively, it represents God's presence, testing and judgment.

Everyday use of furnaces

As a stove or oven Ne 3:11; 12:38; La 5:10; Da 3:6

As a kiln Ex 9:8

For smelting metals Ps 12:6; Pr 27:21

Figurative use of furnaces

As a symbol of God's majestic presence Ge 15:17; Isa 31:9

As a symbol of affliction and testing Isa 48:10 *See also* Dt 4:20; 1Ki 8:51; Pr 17:3; Jer 11:4

As a symbol of God's wrath Mt 13:42 *See also* Ge 19:28; Ps 21:9; Eze 22:17–22; Mal 4:1; Mt 13:50; Rev 9:2

See also

4336 iron	4829 heat
4345 metalworkers	5435 ovens
4351 refining	5560 suffering
4372 tin	8832 testing
4826 fire	9510 hell

5322

gallows

A wooden structure, sometimes a tree, used to impale or display a body after death, or for execution by hanging. Those hanged on gallows were deemed to be under God's curse.

A gallows used for impalement and display of bodies

Ezr 6:11 *See also* Jos 8:29; 10:26; 2Sa 4:12

A gallows used for execution

Est 7:9–10 *See also* Est 2:23; 9:13

Those hanged on gallows are under God's curse

Gal 3:13 *See also* Dt 21:23

See also

4528 trees	5482 punishment
5281 crucifixion	5827 curse
5331 hanging	7346 death penalty

5323

gate

A point of entry to a walled city or walled-off area, such as the temple. It was a place where business was transacted and where justice and punishment were dispensed. It is used figuratively of the entry to death and also of the starting-point of the Christian life.

The purpose of gates as defended points of entry

Dt 3:5

The gates of Jericho: Jos 2:5,7
Jdg 5:8; 1Sa 23:7; 2Ch 8:5; 14:7;
Ps 107:16; 147:13; Isa 22:7; 45:1–2
The destruction of Babylon's gates foretold:
Jer 51:30,58
Eze 38:11; 46:9; Hos 11:6; Lk 7:12 *Jesus Christ approaches Nain;* Ac 9:24; 12:10; 16:13
The new Jerusalem: Rev 21:25; 22:14

Examples of gates

The gates of Jerusalem Ne 2:13–15 *See also* 2Ki 14:13 pp 2Ch 25:23; Ne 1:3; 2:3,8
The Sheep Gate: Ne 3:1,32; Jn 5:2
Ne 3:3,6,13–15 *the Valley Gate, Dung Gate and Fountain Gate;* Ne 3:26 *the Water Gate;* Ne 3:28–29,31; 6:1; 7:3; 11:19; 12:39; Ps 122:2; Isa 60:11; Jer 1:15

The gates of the temple Ac 3:2 *See also* 2Ch 23:19; 24:8; 31:2; Jer 20:2; Eze 44:11; Ac 3:10

Other examples of gates Jos 6:26 *See also* Ge 28:17; 1Sa 17:52; 1Ki 16:34; Mt 16:18; Jn 10:1–3; Ac 10:17

Uses of the area around the gate

A place of (sometimes false) worship 2Ch 31:2 *See also* 2Ki 23:8; Ps 9:14; 118:19–20; Eze 46:2; Ac 14:13

A place of business Ge 23:10–11 *See also* Ru 4:1,11; 2Ki 7:1,18; Ne 13:19–22

A place where decisions are made and justice dispensed Ge 34:19–20 *See also* Dt 21:19; 22:13–19; 25:7–10; Jos 20:4; 2Sa 15:2; 1Ki 22:10; Est 2:19,21; 3:2–3

A place of punishment, banishment and begging Dt 17:5 *See also* Dt 22:23–24; Jos 8:29; 2Ki 7:3; Jer 20:2; Eze 21:15; Lk 16:20; Heb 13:12; Rev 22:14–15

A place of counsel Pr 1:20–21; 8:1–3

Figurative use of the gate

Coming to worship Ps 24:7–10; 100:4

The entrance to death Isa 38:10 *See also* Job 17:16; 38:17; Ps 9:13; 107:18

The entrance to the Christian life Mt 7:13–14 *See also* Jn 10:7–10

The entry to the heavenly city of God Rev 22:14 *See also* Eze 48:30–34; Rev 21:12–15,21,25

See also

2377 kingdom of	5299 door
God, entry into	5315 fortifications
4841 narrowness	5316 fortress
5256 city	5324 gatekeepers

5324

gatekeepers

Levite temple servants, responsible for protecting the palace and the temple from those who would desecrate it or steal its treasures. City gatekeepers also existed.

The ancestry of gatekeepers

1Ch 9:17–22 *See also* 1Ch 26:1–13; Ezr 2:42; Ne 7:45

The special status of gatekeepers
Ezr 7:24 See also Ezr 2:70; Ne 7:73; 12:47; 13:5

The functions of gatekeepers
1Ch 9:23–27 See also 2Ch 8:14; Ne 11:19

Examples of gatekeepers
2Ch 35:15 See also 1Ch 15:16–18; 16:37–38; 23:3–5; 26:14–19; Ne 10:28–29,39; 12:25,45

City gatekeepers
2Ki 7:10–11 See also Ne 7:1–3

See also

5323 gate	7467 temple,
5330 guard	Solomon's
5611 watchman	8490 watchfulness
7390 Levites	

5325

gifts

Presents, given freely and without payment. Scripture lays considerable emphasis on salvation as a gift given by God to sinful, undeserving men and women.

Gifts given by God
His one and only Son, Jesus Christ Jn 3:16 See also 2Co 9:14–15

Salvation and eternal life Ro 6:23 See also Jn 4:10; Ro 5:12–17; 11:25–32; 1Pe 3:7; Rev 22:17

Grace Eph 2:8–9 See also 2Co 9:8–11,14–15; Eph 3:7; 4:7–8

Holy Spirit Ac 2:38 See also Lk 11:13; Ac 1:4; 8:18; 10:44; 11:15; Heb 6:4

Spiritual gifts 1Co 12:1–11 See also Ro 12:4–8; 1Co 1:4–7; 12:27–31; 13:2; 14:1; 1Ti 4:14; 2Ti 1:6; Heb 2:4; 1Pe 4:10

Other gifts from God Jas 1:17 *Children:* Ge 30:20; 1Sa 1:27 Jas 1:5 *wisdom;* 1Co 7:1–7 *Satisfaction in work:* Ecc 3:13; 5:19

Gifts given to God
Ps 68:18 See also Nu 7:3; 18:9; 31:52; Dt 12:11; 16:16–17; 2Ch 31:12–14; Ps 68:29; 76:11; Isa 18:7; Eze 20:39; Mt 5:23–24; 15:3–6 pp Mk 7:9–13 *condemnation concerning the Corban oath;* Lk 21:1–4

Gifts given to false gods
Da 11:38 See also Eze 20:25–26,30–31

Gifts given by kings
To their subjects Est 2:18 See also 2Sa 6:19 pp 1Ch 16:2–3; 2Sa 11:8; Eze 46:16–17; Da 2:6,48; 5:13–17

To other kings 2Ki 16:8 See also 1Ki 15:18–19; 2Ki 12:17–18; 20:12 pp Isa 39:1; Ps 72:10

Gifts given to kings
2Ch 17:11 See also 1Sa 10:27; 1Ki 10:25 pp 2Ch 9:24; 2Ch 17:5; 32:23; Isa 1:23; Mic 7:3

Gifts given to the poor and needy
Ac 11:29–30 See also Est 9:20–22;

Ps 112:9; Ac 10:4; 24:17; 1Co 16:1–3; 2Co 8:16–21; 9:5

Gifts given by fathers
Ge 25:6 See also Mt 7:7–11 pp Lk 11:9–13

Gifts given at marriage
1Ki 9:16 See also Ge 24:53; 34:11–12; Ex 22:16–17; Dt 22:28–29; 1Sa 18:24–27

Gifts given to assuage anger
Pr 21:14 See also Ge 32:13–21; 43:1–26; 1Sa 25:4–35

See also

1050 God, goodness of	6510 salvation
	6646 eternal life, gift
3257 Holy Spirit, gift of	7402 offerings
	7966 spiritual gifts
4207 land, divine gift	8261 generosity,
5594 tribute	God's
5654 betrothal	8434 giving
5889 ingratitude	

5326

government

God's gracious rule over the nations, particularly Israel. Also, the divinely established ruling of people by God's appointed authorities for the good of society and to prevent anarchy.

God governs the nations
Ps 22:28 See also 1Ch 29:12; 2Ch 20:6; Ps 9:7–8; 47:2,7–8; 66:7; 67:4; 103:19; Da 4:32,35; 1Ti 6:15

Jesus Christ also governs the nations
Isa 9:6 See also Ps 72:8–11; 110:2; Zec 6:13; 9:10; Rev 2:27; Ps 2:9; Rev 12:5; 19:15

The manner of God's government of Israel was unique
Jdg 8:23 See also 1Sa 8:7; 12:12

God governs individuals
Pr 21:1 See also Pr 16:1,9; 19:21; 20:24; Jer 10:23; La 3:37; Da 5:23; Ac 17:26; Jas 4:13–15

God has established human agencies for the government of people
Ro 13:1 See also Ge 9:5–6; Pr 8:15–16; Da 2:37–38; 4:17,32; 5:21; Mt 22:17–21; Jn 19:11; 1Ti 2:2–3; 1Pe 2:13

Government is for the good of society Ro 13:4 See also Ps 72:12–14; 82:3–4

Government is established to prevent anarchy Ro 13:2–3 See also Ge 9:6; Ezr 7:26; Pr 21:15; 28:2; 29:4; Ac 25:11; Ro 13:4; 1Pe 2:14

See also

1355 providence	5375 law
4065 orderliness	5395 lordship,
5219 authority,	human &
human	divine
institutions	5509 rulers
5257 civil authorities	5540 society
5267 control	7263 theocracy
5327 governors	8453 obedience

5327

governors

Those who ruled with an authority delegated to them by a higher ruler to whom they were responsible.

Joseph as governor of Egypt
Ge 42:6 See also Ge 41:41,43,55; 45:8,26

Governors of Judah
Gedaliah had a short period in office 2Ki 25:22–23 See also Jer 40:7,11; 41:2,18

Sheshbazzar laid the temple foundations Ezr 5:14 See also Ezr 1:8

Zerubbabel *Zerubbabel is possibly the same person as Sheshbazzar:* Hag 1:1,14; 2:2,21

Nehemiah rebuilt the walls of Jerusalem Ne 5:14 See also Ne 8:9; 10:1; 12:26

Governors before Nehemiah Ne 5:15

Persian governors
Tattenai Ezr 5:3 *"Trans-Euphrates" (literally "beyond the river", i.e., the Euphrates River) to the Persians included the areas of Aram, Phoenicia and Palestine. See also* Ezr 5:6; 6:6,13

Other governors of Trans-Euphrates Ezr 8:36 See also Ne 2:7,9; 3:7

Other Persian governors Est 3:12 See also Est 8:9; 9:3; Da 3:2–3,27; 6:7

Satraps *Satraps were Persian provincial governors:* Ezr 8:36; Est 3:12; 8:9; 9:3; Da 3:2–3,27; 6:1–4,6,7

Other OT references to governors
Jdg 9:30; 1Ki 4:7 *Solomon's twelve district governors;* 1Ki 4:19; 2Ki 10:5; 23:8; 2Ch 9:14; Jer 51:23,28,57; Eze 23:6,12,23; Mal 1:8

Roman governors
Quirinius, governor of Syria Lk 2:1–2

Pilate, governor of Judea Mt 27:2,11,14,15,21,27; 28:14; Lk 3:1; 20:20; Jn 18:28

Felix, governor of Judea Ac 23:24,26,33–34; 24:1,10

Festus, governor of Judea Ac 26:30–32 *Festus did not understand Paul but might well have released him but for his (Paul's) appeal to Rome.*

The governor of Damascus
2Co 11:32

Other NT references to governors
Mt 10:18; Mk 13:9 pp Lk 21:12; 1Pe 2:14

Standards of performance of governors
Some were good Ge 41:39–40; 1Ki 4:27; 2Ki 10:1; Ezr 5:16

Some were bad Ne 5:14–15; Ac 24:26

5328

greeting

Spoken greetings
Formal greetings 2Sa 8:9–10 pp 1Ch 18:9–10 *See also* Ge 14:17–20; 47:7 fn; 1Sa 25:14; Mt 10:11–15; 23:7 pp Mk 12:38 pp Lk 20:46; Lk 11:43

Less formal greetings Ex 18:7 *See also* Ge 33:4; 46:29; Jdg 18:15; 1Sa 10:3–4; 13:10; 17:22; 30:21; 2Ki 10:12–15; Isa 14:9; Mt 5:47; 26:49 *Judas betrays Jesus Christ*; Mt 28:9; Mk 9:15; Lk 1:39–41 *Mary visits Elizabeth*; Ac 18:22; 21:7,19

Examples of spoken greetings Ru 2:4 *See also* 1Sa 25:4–6

Written greetings
Greetings at the beginning of letters 1Th 1:1 *See also* Ezr 4:17; 5:7; 7:12; Ac 15:23; 23:26; Ro 1:1–7; 1Co 1:1–3; 2Co 1:1–2; Gal 1:1–5; Eph 1:1–2; Php 1:1–2; Col 1:1–2; 2Th 1:1–2 1Ti 1:1–2; 2Ti 1:1–2; Tit 1:1–4; Phm 1–3; Jas 1:1; 1Pe 1:1–2; 2Pe 1:1–2; 2Jn 1–3; 3Jn 1; Jude 1–2

Greetings at the close of letters Eph 6:23–24 *See also* Ro 16:3–27; 1Co 16:19–24; 2Co 13:12–14; Php 4:21–23; Col 4:10–18; 1Th 5:25–28; 2Th 3:16–18; 2Ti 4:19–22; Tit 3:15; Php 1:23–25; Heb 13:24–25; 1Pe 5:13–14; 2Jn 12–13; 3Jn 13–14

Messengers forbidden to greet fellow travellers
2Ki 4:29 *See also* Lk 10:1–4

5329

guarantee

A pledge given that a promise will be fulfilled; a deposit or down payment making fulfilment obligatory. All God's promises are guaranteed in and through Jesus Christ.

Laws relating to guarantees
Promises must be kept Nu 30:2 *See also* Ps 15:4–5

The poor must not be oppressed Ex 22:26–27 *See also* Dt 24:6,10–12,17

Special laws relating to women Nu 30:3–16

Guarantees could be written or spoken Nu 30:2; Ezr 10:19

Examples of guarantees
Judah's pledge to bring Benjamin back Ge 43:8–9 *See also* Ge 44:32

The people's pledge to keep the law 2Ki 23:3; 2Ch 34:32

Other examples of guarantees Job 17:3 *Job's need of a pledge*; Job 22:6 *Eliphaz' accusation against Job*; Job 24:3 *Job's complaint against the wicked*; Est 8:8 *the king's seal*; Eze 17:18 *Zedekiah's broken pledge*; Am 2:8 *the priests taking pledges*; Mic 7:20 *God's pledge to his people*; 1Pe 3:21 *Baptism understood as a pledge*

God's promises are guaranteed in Jesus Christ
Jesus Christ, the guarantee of salvation for believers Heb 7:22 *See also* 2Co 1:18–20

The Holy Spirit, the guarantee of believers' inheritance 2Co 1:21–22; Eph 1:13–14 *See also* 2Co 5:5

Salvation guaranteed to all who believe Ro 4:16 *See also* Rev 7:2–3; 9:4; 14:1

The oath of God is unbreakable Nu 23:19 *See also* Tit 1:2; Heb 6:17–20

5330

guard

A watchman, sentinel or bodyguard for a king or ruler. The word is also used metaphorically.

Bodyguards for kings
1Sa 22:14 *See also* 1Sa 26:14–15; 28:2; 2Sa 16:6; 23:23 pp 1Ch 11:25; 1Ki 1:8,10; 2Ki 11:7–8; 2Ch 12:11

Guards at the tomb of Jesus Christ
Mt 27:65–66 *See also* Mt 28:4

Other examples of human guards
Ne 4:9,23; Lk 22:4 *See also* Ge 37:36; 2Ki 25:11 pp Jer 39:9; Jer 51:12; Mt 27:54; Lk 2:8; 11:21; 22:52,63; Ac 4:1; 12:4,6,10,19; 16:23; 22:20; 23:35; 24:23; 28:16; Php 1:13

Angelic guards
Ps 91:11–12 *See also* Ge 3:24; 1Co 4:15

The Lᴏʀᴅ guards his people himself
Dt 32:9–11; Ps 97:10 *See also* Ge 28:15; 1Sa 2:9; 2Sa 22:31 pp Ps 18:30; Ps 1:6; 121:3–8; Pr 2:7–8; 30:5; Isa 27:3; 31:5; 52:12; 58:8

Figurative references to guarding
Guarding one's conduct Pr 4:23; 1Ti 4:16 *See also* Dt 4:9; Pr 7:2; 16:17; 19:16; Ecc 5:1; Mal 2:15–16 *Jesus Christ warns his disciples against the Pharisees and Sadducees*: Mt 16:6,11–12

Ac 20:28; 1Co 16:13; Php 4:7; 2Pe 3:17; 2Jn 8

Guarding one's tongue Ps 141:3 *See also* Pr 13:3; Jas 3:3–8

Christians are to guard the gospel
2Ti 1:14 *See also* Ac 20:30–31; 1Ti 6:20; 2Ti 4:14–15

Church leaders are to guard those in their care
Ac 20:28–31 *See also* Heb 13:17; 1Pe 5:2

5331

hanging

Death by suspension from the neck or impaling on a pole, or the suspension of a body after execution by another means.

Suicide by hanging
2Sa 17:23; Mt 27:5

Execution by hanging or impaling
Ge 40:18–22 *The crucifixion of Jesus Christ is described as hanging on a tree*: Ac 5:30; 10:39 *Impalement*: Ezr 6:11; Est 2:23 fn; 7:9–10; 9:12–13

Hanging after execution
Dt 21:22; Jos 8:29; 10:26; 2Sa 4:12; 21:9–10

Anyone hung on a tree was under God's curse
Dt 21:23; Gal 3:13

5332

harp

Early origins of the harp
Ge 4:19–21 *Jubal was descended from Cain and was in the seventh generation after Adam.*

The harp used in worship
In joyous religious celebrations 2Sa 6:2–5 pp 1Ch 13:6–8 *See also* 1Ch 15:28; 2Ch 20:27–28; Ne 12:27; Ps 49:4; 137:1–4; Isa 30:32; Am 5:23; Rev 14:2–3

In temple worship 2Ch 5:12 *See also* 1Ki 10:12 pp 2Ch 9:11; 1Ch 15:16,21; 16:5; 25:1,3,6; 2Ch 29:25

Associated with praising God Ps 43:4 *See also* Ps 33:2; 57:7–8; 71:22; 81:1–2; 92:1–4; 98:4–6; 108:1–2; 147:7; 149:3; 150:3; Rev 5:8–10; 15:2–4

In pagan worship Da 3:7 *See also* Da 3:5,10,15

The harp used to elicit divine inspiration
2Ki 3:15–19 *See also* 1Sa 10:5–6; 18:10

The harp used to relieve depression
1Sa 16:23 *See also* 1Sa 16:16; 19:9–10

The harp in secular use
In joyous celebrations Ge 31:27 *See also* Job 21:12; Isa 5:12; 14:11; 24:8; Eze 26:13; Am 6:5–6; Rev 18:22

At times of mourning Isa 16:11 *See also* Job 30:31

By prostitutes Isa 23:16

See also
5085 David	5422 musicians
5314 flute	5433 occupations
5420 music	8627 worship,
5421 musical	elements
instruments	

5333

healing

The bringing about of a state of physical or spiritual health. Scripture recognises a close link between physical and spiritual health, with healing often being seen as an image of salvation in Christ.

God as the author of healing
Ex 15:26; Ps 103:2–3 *See also* Lk 5:15

General aspects of healing
Requests for healing 2Ki 20:1–11 pp 2Ch 32:24–26 pp Isa 38:1–8 *See also* 2Ki 1:2; Jas 5:14

Quarantine regulations Lev 12:1–4; 13:4,26,46; 14:8; Nu 5:2; 31:19; 2Ki 15:5; Lk 17:12

Healing results in discipleship Mk 10:52 *See also* Jn 6:2

Healing results in praise Ac 3:8–9 *See also* Mk 2:12; Jn 9:30–33,38

Miraculous healing
By Jesus Christ Mt 8:2–3 ; Lk 4:18 *See also* Mt 9:27–30; 14:34–36 pp Mk 6:53–56; Mt 15:21–28 pp Mk 7:24–30; Mk 1:32–34 pp Lk 4:40; Lk 6:17–19; 8:48; 9:11; 17:19

Through the prophets 1Ki 17:17–24; 2Ki 4:29–37; 5:10–14

Through the apostles Mt 10:1 pp Lk 9:1–2; Ac 3:6–8; 5:15–16; 9:34; 14:8–10; 19:11–12; 28:8–9

In the church 1Co 12:8–9 *See also* Mk 16:17–18; 1Co 12:28,30

Healing of fever
Mt 8:15 pp Mk 1:31 pp Lk 4:39; Jn 4:46–54

Healing of demon-possession
Mt 9:32–33; 12:22; Mk 5:1–20; 9:17–27 pp Lk 9:38–43; Ac 16:16–19; 19:11–12

Healing withheld
2Co 12:8–9; 2Ti 4:20

Medical treatments to bring healing
Consulting doctors 2Ch 16:12 ; Mt 9:12 *See also* Jer 8:22; Col 4:14

Taking medicine 1Ti 5:23

Disinfecting the house Lev 14:41–42

Using splints Eze 30:21

Using bandages and oil Isa 1:6 *See also* Lk 10:34

The spiritual significance of healing
As an image of salvation Ps 41:4; 103:2–5; 147:3; Jer 3:22; 14:19; 17:14; Eze 47:12; Hos 6:1; Mal 4:2; Mt 8:17; Isa 53:4–5

Heaven is the place of ultimate healing Rev 21:4 *See also* Ro 8:18; Rev 22:2

See also
1415 miracles	7027 church,
2351 Christ, miracles	purpose
4408 balm	7372 hands, laying
5136 body	on
5297 disease	7966 spiritual gifts
5298 doctors	8614 prayer,
5334 health	answers
5405 medicine	

5334

health

A state of physical and spiritual well-being, which Scripture declares to be possible only through faith in Jesus Christ.

Salvation as spiritual health
The need for salvation Ps 38:3,7; . Mt 9:12–13; Lk 5:31–32

The promise of salvation Ex 15:2; Ps 32:4–5; 149:4; 1Th 5:9; Tit 2:11; 2Pe 3:15; Rev 12:10

The experience of salvation Ps 13:5–6; 91:16; 118:14; Isa 12:1–3

The importance of health
Health is to be sought after 3Jn 2 *See also* Jer 8:15; Jn 5:6,9; 1Th 5:23

Health as a wish in greeting people 1Sa 25:6; 2Sa 20:9

Health promised by God to his people Jer 33:6

A cause for praise Mt 15:31 *See also* Ac 4:9–12

The pursuit of health
Hygiene Dt 23:13

Care of the body 1Co 6:18–20 *See also* Pr 4:20–22; Ac 27:34; Ro 6:13; 1Co 9:24–27; Eph 5:29; 1Ti 4:7–8

The balance of work and rest Ex 34:21 *See also* Ex 20:8–11

Mental health
State of the natural mind Ro 8:6–7 *See also* Col 2:18

Mental disorder Dt 28:28; 1Sa 16:14–15; Da 4:28–37; Jn 10:20; Ac 26:25

An anxious mind Job 10:1; Jer 15:10; Lk 10:41; 21:34; 24:17

Anxiety resulting from judgment Dt 28:65 *See also* Dt 28:34; Zec 12:4; Ro 1:28

The healthy mind Ps 42:6; Pr 12:25; Ro 12:2 *See also* Mt 22:37 pp Mk 12:30 pp Lk 10:27; Php 4:6–8; 1Pe 5:7

See also
4438 eating	5333 healing
5038 mind, the	5401 madness
human	5405 medicine
5056 rest	6510 salvation
5136 body	7342 cleanliness
5137 bones	8162 spiritual vitality
5297 disease	8849 worry
5298 doctors	

5335

herald

One who proclaims a message or paves the way for a promised event. In Scripture both angels and human beings are employed as heralds, and on occasions even specific events may herald future happenings.

Heralds in human affairs
2Ki 18:28 *See also* Ex 5:10; 1Sa 11:7; 2Sa 18:19; 1Ki 21:12; 2Ki 10:20; 11:12; 2Ch 30:6; Est 1:19–22; 6:11; Da 3:4; Jnh 3:7

To preach is to act as a herald
Pronouncing judgment Jnh 3:4 *See also* Jer 4:5; 46:14

Bringing good news Isa 40:9 *See also* Isa 48:20; 52:7–8; Na 1:15

Preaching the gospel Mt 24:14; Ac 5:42; 1Ti 2:7 *See also* Ac 4:2; 8:5 *Philip proclaims the gospel*; Ac 9:20; 10:42 *Peter at Cornelius' house*; Ac 15:7; 17:3; 28:31 *Paul preaches at Rome*; 1Co 1:23; 2Co 1:19; Gal 2:2; Col 1:23; 1Ti 3:16; 2Ti 1:11

John the Baptist as a herald
Mt 11:10 pp Mk 1:2 pp Lk 7:27 *See also* Mal 3:1; Mt 3:1–3; Isa 40:3; Lk 1:17,76; Jn 1:15; 3:28

Angels as heralds
Lk 2:10 *See also* Jdg 6:12; Mt 1:20–21; 28:5–6 pp Mk 16:5–6 pp Lk 24:4–6; Lk 1:13,30–31; 2:13–14; Rev 14:6

Events heralding what is to happen
Mt 24:32–33 pp Mk 13:28–29 pp Lk 21:29–31; 2Th 2:3

Jesus Christ as a herald
Lk 4:43 pp Mk 1:38 *See also* Mt 4:17 pp Mk 1:14–15 pp Lk 4:18–19; Isa 61:1–2; Lk 8:1

See also
2363 Christ,	5178 running
preaching &	5408 messenger
teaching	7706 apostles
4110 angels	7724 evangelists
5098 John the	7754 preaching
Baptist	7772 prophets

5336

highway

A major road through Edom and Moab
Nu 20:17 *Moses to the king of Edom. See*

also Nu 20:19; 21:22 pp Dt 2:27;
Nu 21:33 pp Dt 3:1; Dt 2:8

Main roads deserted in time of trouble and war
Isa 33:8

Highways for the large-scale movement of people
Isa 19:23 *Isaiah prophesies the future harmony that will exist between former enemies, who will then worship the* LORD *together. See also* Isa 11:16; 35:8–10; 49:11; 62:10; Jer 31:21

The "highway for our God"
Isa 40:3–4 *Isaiah foresees how God will bring his people home from exile in Babylon. See also* Mk 1:2–4 pp Mt 2:1–3 pp Lk 3:2–6 *John the Baptist's call to repentance is seen as the necessary preparation for the coming of the Messiah.*

Used metaphorically
Pr 15:19 *See also* Pr 7:27; 16:17

See also

2230 Messiah, coming of	5505 roads
5357 journey	5590 travel
5442 pilgrimage	6734 repentance, importance

5337

hiring

Laws relating to hiring
Hired workers must be paid on time
Lev 19:13 *See also* Dt 24:14–15; Jas 5:4

Regular rates of pay must be established Lev 25:50

Hired workers are to be treated with kindness Lev 25:6,39–40,53

Hired foreigners were excluded from the Passover Ex 12:43–45

Hired workers must be carefully chosen Pr 26:10

Loss of a hired animal is covered by the price Ex 22:15

Various kinds of hiring
A hired husband Ge 30:16

A hired prophet Dt 23:4 *See also* Ne 6:12–13; 13:2; Jude 11

A hired priest Jdg 17:10; 18:4

Hired soldiers Jdg 9:4; 2Sa 10:6; 2Ki 7:6; 1Ch 19:6–7; 2Ch 25:6; Jer 46:21 *No hired mercenary army was ever approved by the* LORD *(see 2Ch 25:7–10).*

Other hirings 1Sa 2:5 *hirings for food;* 2Ch 24:12 *masons and carpenters;* Ezr 4:5 *counsellors;* Isa 7:20 *a razor, symbolising the judgment to be brought by the king of Assyria;* Isa 23:17 *prostitutes;* Isa 46:6 *goldsmiths;* Mk 1:20 *fishermen*

Teachings illustrated by hired workers
The brevity and hardness of life
Job 7:1–3 *See also* Job 14:6

Christian workers Mt 20:1–15 *This parable teaches that believers should not serve in a mercenary spirit but recognise that God's reward is based upon grace.*

The severity of the world and the kindness of God Lk 15:15–19

The difference between hired and good shepherds
Jn 10:11–13 *See also* 1Pe 5:2

See also

5212 arts and crafts	5520 servants
5272 craftsmen	5603 wages
5311 extortion	5628 work
5404 masters	6720 redemption
5406 mercenaries	8342 servanthood
5433 occupations	8790 oppression

5338

holiday

A day or period of time during which regular work is suspended. In Israel, the Sabbath provided a weekly break from everyday labour, giving opportunity for rest and religious assembly, and was the pattern for set days of rest and annual festivals. The NT records events in the life of Jesus Christ which are marked by Christian holidays.

The Sabbath day
Ge 2:2–3 *See also* Ex 31:13–17 *Their observance of the Sabbath marked Israel out as the distinctive people of God;* Jer 17:24; Mk 2:27; Heb 4:4

The purpose of holidays
For rest and refreshment Ex 23:12 *The Sabbath provided a rest period each week. See also* Ex 20:8–11 pp Dt 5:12–14; Ex 34:21

To restore society Lev 25:2–5 *The sabbath year allowed the land to be rested;* Lev 25:10 *The restoration of family property in the Year of Jubilee;* Dt 15:12 *The sabbath year marked the release of Hebrew slaves.*

To assemble for worship Lev 23:3 *Release from the ties of everyday labour gives opportunity for the people of God to meet together in worship;* Nu 29:12 *See also* Lev 23:27 pp Nu 29:7; Dt 16:8; Isa 1:13
Ps 42:4 *See also* Ps 68:24–27; 118:27

To recall God's deliverance Dt 5:15 *See also* Dt 16:3,12; Heb 4:11

Israel's seven annual holidays
Ex 12:16 pp Lev 23:7–8 *the first and seventh days of the Feast of Unleavened Bread;* Lev 23:21 pp Nu 28:26 *the day of firstfruits (Pentecost);* Lev 23:24–25 pp Nu 29:1 *the Feast of Trumpets;* Lev 23:28–32 pp Lev 16:29–31 *the Day of Atonement;* Lev 23:34–36 *the first and eighth days of the Feast of Tabernacles*

Christian holidays linked with the life of Jesus Christ
The Lord's Day Ac 20:7 *See also* Mk 16:9 *The church meets together on the first day of the week: the day of Jesus Christ's resurrection;* 1Co 16:2; Rev 1:10

Christmas Day Lk 2:7 *See also* Jn 1:14

Epiphany Mt 2:1–2,9–11

Lent Mt 4:1–2 pp Mk 1:12–13 pp Lk 4:1–2

Good Friday Mt 27:45–50 pp Mk 15:33–37 pp Lk 23:44–46; Jn 19:28–30

Easter Sunday Mk 16:5–6 pp Mt 28:5–6 pp Lk 24:4–6

Ascension Day Lk 24:50–51; Ac 1:9

Pentecost (Whit Sunday) Ac 2:1–4

See also

1325 God, the Creator	7354 feasts and festivals
5056 rest	7428 Sabbath
5213 assembly	7482 Year of Jubilee
5312 feasting	8642 celebration
5385 leisure	8670 remembering
5628 work	

5339

home

The place of origin or residence, to which people feel attached and where they belong. The term is used of houses, towns, lands and in various figurative and spiritual senses.

Divine blessing upon homes
It brings peace and security Isa 32:18 *See also* 2Ki 13:5; Ps 127:1–2

It is promised to the righteous Pr 3:33 *See also* Pr 12:7; 14:11; 15:6; 24:3–4

It is granted because of a godly presence 2Sa 6:11 pp 1Ch 13:14 *See also* Ge 30:27–30; 39:4–5

Human affection for homes
2Sa 19:37 *See also* Ge 31:30; Nu 10:29–30; Ru 1:6–18 *Ruth's loyalty to Naomi is stronger than her attachment to her homeland;* 1Sa 7:17; Job 29:18; Ps 102:13–14; 137:1–6

Instructions for home life
Dt 6:6–9; 20:5–8; 24:5; Eph 6:1–4; Col 3:18–4:1; 1Ti 5:4,8,11–14; Tit 2:4–5

Homes as places of hospitality
Ge 29:13–14; Jdg 19:18–21; 2Ki 4:8–10; Jn 19:25–27; Phm 22; Heb 13:2

Israel's home in Canaan
It is promised to them 2Sa 7:10–11 pp 1Ch 17:9–10 *See also* Ex 6:8; Nu 14:30; Ps 78:55

It was taken from them 2Ki 17:22–23; 25:21 *See also* 2Ki 17:5–6; 18:10–11; 2Ch 36:20–21; Ps 79:6–7; Joel 3:6

It was restored to them Zep 3:20 *See also* Eze 36:8

Homes for animals
Job 39:5–6; Ps 84:3; 104:17–18; Pr 30:26–28

Homes in Jesus Christ's ministry
Lk 9:58 *Jesus Christ had no permanent home.*
Jesus Christ was welcomed into people's homes and ministered there: Lk 10:38–42; 14:1
Mk 5:18–20 pp Lk 8:38–39 *The healed demoniac is sent back to his home town and family to be a witness.*
Jesus Christ's instructions on sending out the Twelve: Mt 10:11–14 pp Mk 6:10–11 pp Lk 9:4–5; Lk 10:5–7

Mt 19:29 pp Mk 10:29–30
pp Lk 18:29–30

Homelessness
1Co 4:11 *Paul had no permanent home;*
Job 24:1–12 *the suffering of the homeless;*
Heb 11:8–10 *People of faith do not see
this world as their final home.*

Home in a spiritual and figurative sense
Jn 14:2,23 *See also* Job 17:13–15;
Ecc 12:5; Lk 16:9; 2Co 5:1–10; 2Pe 3:13

See also

5015 heart & Holy	5680 family
Spirit	8300 love & the
5218 authority in	world
home	8313 nurture
5302 education	8445 hospitality
5340 house	8626 worship,
5478 property,	places
houses	9410 heaven
5491 refugees	

5340

house

The place where someone lives. Its
extended use includes a household
and dynasty and its figurative use
includes the house of God and
heaven.

The construction of houses
Foundations 1Ki 5:17; Ezr 6:3–4;
Jer 51:26; Eze 41:8

Building materials Ge 11:3–4;
Ex 1:11–14; Lev 14:40–45; 1Ki 5:18;
7:9–12; SS 1:17; Isa 9:10

Rooms and decoration Ge 43:30;
Jdg 3:20,23–25; 1Ki 7:6 *Solomon's
palace;* 1Ki 17:19 *Elijah stays with the
widow at Zarephath;* 1Ki 22:25; 2Ki 1:2;
4:10 *Elisha's room at the Shunammite's
house;* Ne 8:16; Jer 22:14; Eze 8:10;
Da 5:5; Am 3:15; Ac 20:8–9

Roofs Jos 2:6; 1Sa 9:25–26; Mk 2:4
pp Lk 5:19

Regulations regarding houses
Lev 14:33–53; 25:29–34; 27:14–15;
Dt 22:8

Various uses for houses
House arrest Jer 37:15 *See also*
Ge 40:2–3; 2Sa 20:3; Ac 28:16,30–31

Church gatherings Col 4:15 *See also*
Ac 1:13–14; 2:1–2; 5:42; 12:12;
Ro 16:5; 1Co 16:19; Phm 1–2

Parables and proverbs about houses
Pr 21:20 *See also* Pr 9:1–4 *the house of
wisdom;* Pr 9:13–18 *the house of folly;*
Pr 14:1; 17:13; 21:9; 24:27; 25:17;
Ecc 10:18; SS 8:7; Mt 12:29 pp Mk 3:27
pp Lk 11:21–22 *plundering the strong
man's house;* Mt 12:43–45
pp Lk 11:24–26 *the return of evil spirits to
an unoccupied house;* Mt 13:52;
24:42–51 pp Lk 12:39–46

The house of God
God's heavenly dwelling Isa 66:1–2 *See
also* 1Ki 8:30 pp 2Ch 6:21; 1Ki 8:39
pp 2Ch 6:30; 1Ki 8:43 pp 2Ch 6:33;
1Ki 8:49–50 pp 2Ch 6:39; Isa 57:15;
Jn 14:2

The earthly tabernacle and temple
Ex 25:8 *See also* Ex 15:17; 29:44–46 *the
Tent of Meeting;* Dt 12:5,11; 2Sa 7:1–7
pp 1Ch 17:1–6 *David's desire to build a
permanent house for God to dwell in;*
Ezr 5:13–16; Ps 23:6; 26:8; 27:4;
84:1–4,10; Hag 1:2–3,8–9,14

The household
Household affairs 2Sa 17:23 *See also*
2Ki 20:1 pp Isa 38:1; Pr 31:21,27;
1Ti 3:4–5,12

**Examples of how God relates to
households** Ge 17:12–14,23–27;
Lev 16:6,11,17; Nu.16:31–33; Jn 4:53;
Ac 16:15,31–34; 1Co 16:15

The church as God's household
Eph 2:19–22 *See also* Nu 12:7;
1Ti 3:14–15; Heb 3:1–6; 1Pe 2:4–5

House in the sense of a dynasty
2Sa 7:16 pp 1Ch 17:14 *"house" is used
here in the sense of "royal house" or
"dynasty". See also* Ex 40:38;
Jos 21:43–45
The house of Eli: 1Sa 2:27–36; 3:11–14
The house of Saul: 2Sa 3:1; 9:1
2Sa 3:28–29
The house of David: 2Sa 7:25–29
pp 1Ch 17:23–27; 1Ki 2:31–33
1Ki 21:21–22,28–29; Zec 12:10–14

See also

5240 building	7384 household
5269 cornerstone	gods
5317 foundation	7459 tabernacle, in
5339 home	OT
5478 property,	7467 temple,
houses	Solomon's
7020 church, the	8626 worship,
7382 house of God	places

5341

hunger

A state of emptiness, reflecting a lack
of physical or spiritual food.
Scripture recognises the physical
aspects of human hunger which can
only be met by the living God.

Kinds of hunger
Physical Dt 8:3

Spiritual Mt 5:6 *See also* Ps 63:1,5;
107:9; Am 8:11; Lk 6:21; Jn 6:35;
1Pe 2:2

Causes of hunger
Famine Ge 41:55; 2Ki 6:25–29;
Ne 5:1–2

Fasting Mt 4:2 pp Lk 4:2

Fatigue 1Sa 21:3; 2Sa 17:29; Mt 12:1–4;
Mk 6:35–36; 8:2–3

Folly Pr 19:15; 20:4; Lk 15:14

God's action Lev 26:26; Dt 28:48;
Isa 5:13; 9:20; Eze 7:19

The hardships of gospel work
1Co 4:11; 2Co 6:5; 11:27; Php 4:12

Effects of hunger
Physical deterioration Job 30:3;
La 2:19; 4:9

Mental preoccupation Isa 29:8;
Ac 10:10–13 *Peter's consciousness was*

*supernaturally heightened to receive a
vision from God.*

Moral degradation Lev 26:29; Dt 28:53;
2Ki 6:28–29; Jer 19:9; La 2:20; 4:10;
Eze 5:10

An occasion for temptation Ge 3:6 *Eve;*
Ge 25:29–34 *Esau;* Pr 6:30–31; Isa 8:21;
Mt 4:3 pp Lk 4:3 *Jesus Christ*

An opportunity for proving God Dt 8:3;
Ne 9:15; Php 4:12

God satisfies hunger
He provides food for all creation
Ps 107:9; 145:15–16 *See also*
Dt 32:13–14; Ps 17:14; 37:25;
104:21,27–28; 111:5; 132:15; 136:25;
146:7; 147:9; Isa 49:10

**He provides through supernatural
means** Ps 78:24–25 *See also*
Ex 16:12–15; 1Ki 17:4–16; Ne 9:15;
Mt 14:19–21 pp Mk 6:41–44
pp Lk 9:16–17 pp Jn 6:11–14 *the feeding
of the 5,000;* Mk 8:7–8

He provides through natural means
Ge 3:17–19; Jos 5:12; Pr 16:26; Isa 58:7;
Mt 25:35; 2Th 3:10

He provides completely in heaven
Rev 7:16

Jesus Christ was hungry
Mt 4:2 pp Lk 4:2; Mt 21:18 pp Mk 11:12;
Jn 4:31

See also

2033 Christ,	5580 thirst
humanity	5792 appetite
4404 food	5845 emptiness
4438 eating	5939 satisfaction
4822 famine	8429 fasting
5185 stomach	8656 longing for
5560 suffering	God

5342

hunting

Hunters who pursue a prey, literally or figuratively
Human beings Ge 10:9; Ps 91:3 *See also*
Ge 25:27; 27:3; 49:9,27; Lev 17:13;
1Sa 24:11; Ps 124:7

Lions Job 38:39 *See also* Nu 23:24;
Job 4:11; Ps 17:12; 22:13; 104:21;
Isa 5:29; Eze 19:6; 22:25; Am 3:4;
Na 2:12

Eagles Job 9:26 *See also* Job 39:27–30

God Am 9:3 *See also* Job 19:22;
Jer 16:16; Eze 12:13

People being hunted by their enemies
Ps 10:2; Jer 5:26 *See also* Ge 31:36;
1Sa 23:23; 26:20; Job 18:8–10;
Ps 119:110; 140:5,11; 141:9; Pr 6:5;
Ecc 9:12; Isa 10:2; 13:14; 59:15; La 3:52;
Mic 7:2

See also

4642 fish	5319 fugitives
5206 archers	5425 net
5210 arrows	5488 quivers
5236 bow and arrow	5589 trap

5343

idleness

Laziness or unproductiveness. As work is hallowed by God's working, idleness is regarded as a sin against oneself and society.

Idleness reproached
In terms of daily labour 1Th 5:14 *Paul to the Christians at Thessalonica. See also* Pr 19:24; 10:4; 22:13; 26:13–16; 2Th 3:6–15; 1Ti 5:13; Tit 1:12

In matters of faith Heb 6:11–12 *To Christians who were tempted to give up.*

Idleness discouraged by examples of industriousness
Pr 6:6–8 *See also* Pr 31:27 *the good wife*; Ecc 11:6; 2Th 3:7–9 *Paul referring to his practice of not depending on others for his living*

The results of idleness
Pr 6:9–11 *See also* Pr 10:26; 12:24; 13:4; 15:19; 19:15; 20:4; Ecc 10:18

See also

5446 poverty	5628 work
5524 servants, bad	5833 diligence
5534 sleep, spiritual	5868 gossip
5539 sluggard	8783 neglect
5575 talk, idle	

5344

imprisonment

Being confined in prison is used both literally and figuratively in Scripture. Release from prison is used as a picture of freedom from spiritual bondage.

The anticipation or threat of imprisonment
Mt 5:25–26 pp Lk 12:58 *See also* Ac 20:23; Rev 2:10

Imprisonment for law-breaking
Ezr 7:26 *See also* Ge 40:3; 2Ki 17:4; Jer 52:11; Mt 18:30

Imprisonment while on remand
Nu 15:33–34 *See also* Lev 24:12; Mt 27:16 pp Mk 15:7 pp Lk 23:19

Imprisonment of the innocent, often with malicious intent
Jer 38:28; Lk 21:12 *See also* Ge 39:20–22; 40:14–15; 42:16–17 *Joseph planning the welfare of his brothers*; 1Ki 22:27 *Ahab orders Micaiah's imprisonment*; 2Ch 16:10; Jer 32:2–3; 37:15; Mt 14:3 *John the Baptist imprisoned by Herod*; Ac 8:3; 16:23–24 *Paul and Silas in prison*; Ac 22:4,19; 23:29; 24:27; 26:10,31; 2Co 6:5; 11:23; Heb 11:36

Release from imprisonment
By earthly rulers Ge 41:14; 2Ki 25:27 pp Jer 52:31; Jer 39:13–14

By divine intervention Ps 146:7 *See also* Ps 68:6; 102:20; 107:10–14; 142:7; Isa 42:7; 49:9; 51:14; 61:1; Ac 12:1–11

Imprisonment used in a figurative or poetic sense
Lk 4:18 *See also* Isa 61:1; Job 11:10; 12:14; Ps 66:11; Ecc 4:14; Ro 7:23; Gal 3:22–23; 1Pe 3:19; Rev 20:7

See also

2321 Christ as redeemer	5482 punishment
5098 John the Baptist	5507 rope and cord
	6020 sin
5246 captivity	6658 freedom
5364 key	6723 redemption, NT
5460 prison	7449 slavery, spiritual
5461 prisoners	

5345

influence

The ability to affect others or events. Also, the experience of being affected by someone or something else. Scripture recognises the wide-ranging power of influence for both good and evil.

Teaching on influence
Exhortations to be influenced by good and to influence others for good
Mt 5:13–16 *See also* Pr 1:8–9; 7:1–5; 25:15; Php 4:8–9

Exhortations to resist evil influence and not to be a bad influence
Dt 4:15–19; Pr 5:1–14; 6:20–26; Mt 18:5–6; Ro 12:2; 14:13; 1Co 5:6–8; 8:9–13; 2Co 6:14–18; 2Ti 2:14; Jas 4:7

Good influence in its various contexts
The influence of the Holy Spirit
Ac 2:1–13; 8:26–40; 16:6–10; Ro 8:5–17, 26–27; 1Co 2:10–16; 12:3

People of good influence 2Ti 1:5 *See also* Ge 41:41–43; 1Ki 10:1–9; 15:11–14; 2Ki 18:1–8; 23:1–25

Evil influence in its various contexts
People of evil influence 2Ki 9:22 *See also* Mt 15:1–14; 16:5–12; 23:13–15; 27:20; 2Co 11:3–4,13–15; 2Pe 2:1–3

Corrupting influence of evil cultures
Jos 23:6–8,12–13; Jdg 2:10–13; 1Ki 11:1–6; Ezr 9:1–2; Ne 13:15–27; 1Co 12:1–2; 15:33

The influence of Satan Mt 16:23 *See also* Mk 1:23–26 pp Lk 4:33–35; Mk 4:15 pp Mt 13:19 pp Lk 8:12; Lk 22:3–4; Jn 13:27–30; 2Co 12:7

Further aspects of influence
The influence of prayer Ge 18:20–33; Ex 32:9–14; 2Ch 7:13–15; Da 9:1–23; Jnh 3:3–10

The influence of words Pr 12:18 *See also* Pr 15:4; 16:23–24; 28:23; Jas 3:5–6

The influence of parents Pr 1:8–9 *See also* 2Ch 22:2–3; Pr 4:1–4; 6:20–22; 2Ti 1:5

See also

1610 Scripture	5690 friends
3130 Holy Spirit, Counsellor	7751 persuasion
	7797 teaching
3263 Holy Spirit, guidance	8124 guidance
	8412 decisions
5452 power	8602 prayer
5547 speech, power of	8739 evil, examples of

5346

injury

Physical or mental hurt, usually resulting from the deliberate actions or words of others.

Physical injury
Jdg 1:6 *See also* Ge 32:25; Lk 10:30; 2Co 11:23–25

Reparation must be made for physical injury Ex 21:19,22; Lev 24:17–22

Jesus Christ suffered physical injury Mt 16:21; Jn 19:1

God's people may suffer physical injury for his sake Jer 38:6; Gal 6:17; Col 1:24; 1Pe 2:19

Mental injury
Injury by slander Lev 19:16; Pr 30:10; Mt 5:11; Tit 3:2; Jas 4:11; 1Pe 2:1

Injury by injustice Ps 58:1–2; Ecc 3:16; Isa 59:4–6; Eze 34:4

Jesus Christ suffered mental injury Mt 26:59–60; 1Pe 2:20–23

God's people may suffer mental injury for his sake Mt 5:11 *See also* Ps 38:20; Jer 15:15; 1Th 2:2; 1Pe 2:19

All deliberate injury ruled out by love
Ro 13:10

Spiritual injury suffered by God's people
Isa 1:5–6; Jer 10:19; 30:12; Hos 6:1 *Sometimes this is God's judgment.*

See also

5025 killing	5372 knife
5061 sanctity of life	5494 revenge
5209 armour	5560 suffering
5210 arrows	5951 slander
5333 healing	5975 violence
5348 injustice	6221 rebellion

5347

injustice

The unnecessary and unjustified ill treatment of others, through false accusation or through the inflicting of pain or punishment. Having its origin in Satan, it works through the sinful human heart and shows itself in every sphere of life. It merits the wrath of God.

5348

injustice, nature and source of

Characterised by deception, dishonesty and heartlessness, injustice is the oppression of the needy and the weak. Its origin is Satan and it works through the sinful hearts of men and women.

The nature of injustice

Injustice seen in false accusation *See also* Ge 39:19–20; 1Ki 21:8–10

Injustice seen in dishonesty 1Sa 8:3; Isa 59:14; Mt 26:59–61; Ac 24:26–27

Injustice seen in pain inflicted on the innocent Mt 2:16–18; 27:26; Ac 4:3; 23:3

Injustice seen in oppression of the poor, the needy and the helpless Ex 1:11–14; 1Sa 8:11; 2Ch 10:14; Job 31:13–14; Ps 10:2,8–11; 105:17–18; Pr 22:16; Isa 5:8; Jer 22:13; Am 5:11; Mk 12:38–40; Jas 5:4–6

The sources of injustice

The devil 1Jn 3:10 *The word "devil" means "slanderer". See also* Jn 8:44; Rev 2:10; 2Th 2:9–11 *The word "Satan" means "adversary"—the same person as the devil;* Jas 3:14–15; Rev 2:13

The world 1Jn 2:16 *"the world" here means society without God and hostile to him. See also* Ex 23:2; Ps 69:4; Pr 31:4–5; Eze 22:12; Mt 5:11–12; Jn 15:18–19

Sinful hearts Mt 15:19 *See also* Ps 64:6; 140:2; Jer 6:13–15; Mic 2:2; Gal 5:19–21

See also

4025 world, the	5831 depression
4120 Satan	6020 sin
5012 heart	6145 deceit
5446 poverty	8277 innocence
5562 suffering,	8714 dishonesty
innocent	8790 oppression
5823 cruelty	

5349
injustice, examples of

Injustice can be found, in varying degrees of intensity, in every area of human relationships. It produces exploitation and suffering, both mental and physical.

Injustice occurs in family life
Mk 7:9–13 pp Mt 15:3–6 *See also* Ge 27:35; Lev 20:9–10; Mal 2:13–14; 1Co 7:4–5; Eph 6:4; Col 3:19,21

Injustice occurs in the community
Isa 59:14–15 *See also* Lev 19:16; Dt 19:14; 23:24–25; 24:6–7; Ps 101:5; Pr 3:28–30; 22:28; 23:10–11; Jer 17:11

Injustice occurs in the business world
Hos 12:7 *See also* Lev 19:35; Pr 11:1; 1Ti 6:10

Injustice occurs in courts of law
Pr 24:23–24 *See also* Ps 26:10; Pr 14:5; 28:21; Isa 5:22–23; 29:21; Hos 10:4; Am 5:12; Hab 1:4; Mal 2:9; Ac 16:36–37

Injustice can be caused by rulers and governments
Isa 10:1–2 *See also* Ex 1:10–11; Ps 58:1–2; 94:20–21; Pr 29:4; 31:4–5; Ecc 5:8–9; Isa 1:21; Mic 3:8; Hab 2:9 Lk 23:4–25 pp Mt 27:15–26 pp Mk 15:6–15 pp Jn 18:38–40 *See also* Ro 13:1–4 *the proper role of governing authorities*

See also

5202 accusation,	5680 family
false	6126 condemnation,
5215 authority	human
5310 exploitation	6130 corruption
5383 lawsuits	8452 neighbours,
5412 money	duty to
5452 power	8751 false witness
5512 scales &	
balances	

5350
injustice, hated by God

God's hatred of injustice is seen in his vindication of its victims, his solemn warnings, his penalties against the guilty and his commands to his people to renounce it.

God hates injustice
Pr 6:16–19 *See also* Pr 11:1; 12:22; 17:15

God will vindicate the victims of injustice
They cry for justice Ps 43:1 *There are some OT passages where vengeance upon persecutors is called for (e.g., Ps 35:1–8; Ps 69:22–28; Jer 11:18–20; 18:19–23). These are called "imprecatory". They arose from zeal for God's honour and from the desire for moral stability in society. They reflect an under-developed view of God's ultimate judgments and the failure to distinguish between the guilty and their innocent families. In the light of the NT the motives behind these prayers may be applauded but it is recognised that now they are best expressed in the denunciation of injustice accompanied by gospel witness, through which the hearts of oppressors are changed, leaving the matter of judgment as God's prerogative alone. See also* Ne 4:4–5; Ps 94:1–7; Rev 6:10; Job 19:25 *In OT times a redeemer was a near relative responsible for securing the just rights of a poor kinsperson.*

God will answer their cry Lk 18:1–8 *See also* Ps 12:5; 94:20–23; 2Th 1:6–7; 2Ti 4:14; 2Pe 2:9; Rev 18:20; 19:2

God condemns injustice Isa 10:1–3 *See also* Dt 16:19; Am 1:3–4

God will punish the unjust Mic 2:1–3 *See also* Dt 27:17,19; 1Ki 21:19; Pr 19:5; 21:28; Am 5:11–12; 8:4–7; Na 3:1; Mal 3:5; Lk 12:45–46 *Possibility of injustice among believers:* 1Co 6:6–8; 1Th 4:6 Jas 5:1–6; Rev 1:7

The apparent present success of the unjust Ps 37:1–2 *See also* Ps 73:3–11,15–17; Isa 26:10–11; Hab 1:12–13

God's people must hate injustice
Injustice forbidden by God Pr 22:22 *See also* Ex 20:16; 22:21–22; 23:6–8; Lev 19:13,15,35; Dt 24:14–15,17; Eze 45:9; Zec 7:10; Eph 6:9

Injustice should be renounced by God's people Ps 119:163 *See also* Dt 24:7; Ps 82:2; Pr 29:27; Col 3:21

Injustice displaced by love Mk 12:31; Ro 13:10; Col 3:19

God's people must bear injustice patiently Jas 5:7–8 *See also* Mt 5:39,44–45; 1Co 6:7

See also

1075 God, justice of	5834 disagreement
1125 God,	6218 provoking God
righteousness	8318 patience
1310 God as judge	8807 profanity
5359 justice	9210 judgment,
5375 law	God's
5482 punishment	
5614 weights &	
measures, laws	

5352
inscriptions

An inscription can signify ownership or jurisdiction
Mt 22:20–21 pp Mk 12:16–17 pp Lk 20:24–25; Ac 17:23

The inscription on objects set apart for God
Zec 14:20–21 *See also* Ex 39:30

An inscription can be symbolic of permanence
Of a person's words Isa 30:8 ; 2Ti 2:19 *See also* Job 19:23–24

Of the effect of sin Jer 17:1

Inscriptions written by the finger of God
Ex 31:18 *See also* Ex 32:15–16; Dt 9:10; Da 5:5,22–28; Zec 3:9

See also

1260 finger of God	5306 engraving
1690 word of God	5638 writing

5353
interest

The charge for the lending of money on a commercial or private loan. The practice of charging interest (known as usury) is treated with caution by OT writers on account of its potential for exploitation.

Usury forbidden among the Israelites
Ex 22:25 *See also* Lev 25:35–37; Dt 23:19

Lending without interest: a characteristic of the righteous Ps 15:5; Eze 18:8,17; Lk 6:30,31

Exacting interest: a characteristic of the wicked Pr 28:8; Jer 15:10; Eze 18:13; 22:12; 1Ti 6:9,10

Lending: a charitable, not a commercial, activity Dt 15:8; Ps 112:5; Lk 6:35

Example of oppression through usury Ne 5:6–11

Usury permissible for commercial transactions involving "outsiders"
Dt 23:20 *This legislation permits rather than encourages usury and remains subject to considerations protecting the poor. See also* Dt 15:1–11; Mt 25:27 pp Lk 19:23

5354

invasions

A hostile incursion into the territory of another tribe or nation, often with the object of its permanent annexation.

The Israelites' invasion of Canaan
Their success had been preordained Dt 7:22; Lev 20:23–24 *See also* Ex 12:25; Lev 14:34; 23:10; Dt 6:10–12; 7:17–24

Moses gave instructions on how to proceed Dt 7:1–5; 20:10–20

Joshua followed Moses in leading the invasion Jos 11:23 *See also* Jos 6:20; 8:18–19; 10:29–43

The invasion continued under other leaders Jdg 1:4; 4:23–24; 11:21–22,32–33; 2Ki 3:24; 1Ch 4:41–43

Invasion of the Israelites' land
By the Philistines Jdg 10:6–10; 1Ch 14:9; 2Ch 21:16–17

By other nations Jdg 6:3–5 *See also* Jdg 2:14; 2Ki 13:20; 2Ch 20:1; 24:23

Israel taken into captivity by Assyrian invaders 2Ki 17:5–6 pp 2Ki 18:9–11

Judah taken into captivity by Babylonian invaders 2Ki 25:1 pp Jer 39:12Ki 25:10–11 pp Jer 39:8–9; 52:4

Invasion of the promised land was a cause of great sadnesss Ps 79:1 *See also* Ne 1:1–4; La 1:1–3; Da 9:4–6

Examples of non-human invasion
By locusts Ex 10:14

By evil spiritual forces Mt 12:43–45 pp Lk 11:24–26Lk 22:3 *See also* Mk 9:17–18 pp Mt 17:14–16 pp Lk 9:38–40; Ro 5:12–14; Eph 6:12

5355

invitations

A request for attendance, often to a celebration or feast. Invitations to the blessings of the gospel are sometimes presented as requests to attend a banquet. In a negative sense one can be invited to sin.

Invitations to receive hospitality
Ac 16:15 *See also* Ge 24:31–33 *Laban*

shows hospitality to Abraham's servant and his animals; Ge 31:54; Ex 2:20; Nu 10:29–32; 1Sa 9:22–24 *Saul dines with Samuel*; 1Ki 13:7; Job 1:4; Jer 35:2 *Jesus Christ invited to eat with Pharisees*: Lk 7:36; 11:37
Jn 21:12; Ac 10:23; 1Co 10:27

Invitations to a wedding or a banquet
Lk 14:8–14 *See also* Est 5:4,12; Jn 2:2

Invitations requesting help
Ac 16:9 *See also* Jdg 1:3; 11:6; 2Ki 16:7; Ac 8:30–31

Invitations of the lovers in the Song of Solomon
SS 2:13; 4:8; 7:11; 8:14

Invitations to join in worshipping God
Ps 34:3 *See also* Ps 66:5–6,16; 95:1–2,5–6

Invitations of the Lord Jesus Christ to follow him
Mt 4:19 pp Mk 1:17 pp Lk 5:10 *See also* Mk 10:21 pp Mt 19:21 pp Lk 18:22

Invitations to the blessings of the gospel
Invitations given in varied terms Mt 11:28–30 *See also* Isa 1:18; Zec 3:10 *"to sit under his vine and fig-tree" refers to the peaceful security of the kingdom of God. See* 1Ki 4:25; Mic 4:4; Mt 25:34; Jn 4:29; Rev 3:20; 22:17

Invitations using the imagery of a banquet Lk 14:16–17 *See also* Isa 55:1–3; Mt 22:1–14; Rev 19:7–9

Invitations given with deceitful motives
2Sa 15:10–12 *See also* 2Sa 13:23–29; 1Ki 1:5–10; Ne 6:1–8

Invitations to do what is sinful
Ge 39:7 *See also* Ge 3:1–4; 39:12; Ex 34:15–16; Nu 22:6,11,17; 23:7; 25:1–2; Pr 1:10–11

5356

irony

Irony directed against idolaters
1Ki 18:27 *See also* Isa 44:12–19

Irony in the speeches of Job and his friends
Job 12:2 *See also* Job 16:2–3

Irony in declarations of impending punishment
Jer 34:17 *See also* Jdg 9:1–21

Irony used for instruction
1Co 4:7–14

Other examples of irony
2Sa 6:20; Mk 2:17; 15:17–19; Ac 26:28

5357

journey

People going on journeys
Nu 33:1–2; Ro 15:24 *See also* Ge 29:1; 45:21; Nu 9:10; Jos 9:11–13; 1Ki 19:4; Ne 2:6; Pr 7:19; Ac 9:3; 1Co 16:3

Journeys of Jesus Christ
From Egypt to Nazareth Mt 2:19–23
Journeys in Galilee Mk 6:1–56
Journeys in Judea Mt 20:17–21:11
Journeys in Samaria Lk 9:51–56; Jn 4:6

God's guidance on journeys
Ge 24:27; Dt 1:33 *See also* Ge 28:20; Dt 2:7; Jos 24:17; Jdg 18:5; Ezr 7:9; 8:21

The disciples' evangelistic journeys
Mt 10:5–15 pp Mk 6:7–11 pp Lk 9:1–5

Journeys used figuratively
Job 16:22 *See also* Mt 21:33 pp Mk 12:1; Mt 25:13–14; Lk 11:6

5358

judges

Individuals responsible for the administration of justice and/or the operation of government. In the OT the term "judge" is also used in a special sense meaning a leader of Israel. God is portrayed in Scripture as the judge of all the earth; in the NT Jesus Christ is presented as the judge appointed by God.

Judges as leaders of Israel
1Sa 7:15 *See also* Jdg 2:16–19; 3:9–11; 4:4–10; Ru 1:1; 2Ki 23:22

The role of judges
Judicial and punitive Dt 25:1–2 *See also* Ge 19:6–9; Ex 18:13–26; 22:7–9; Nu 25:5; Dt 1:16; 19:16–21; 21:1–2; 2Ch 19:5–7; Eze 44:24; Lk 12:14; 1Co 6:2–5; Rev 20:4

Administrative Ex 21:2–6; Ezr 10:14; Ac 24:10

The status of judges in ancient Israel
Jos 8:33 *See also* Jos 23:1–24:1; 2Ki 23:22; 2Ch 1:2–3

The jurisdiction of judges
Local judges Dt 16:18 *See also* 2Ch 19:5

Judges with national authority 1Sa 7:15–17 *See also* Dt 17:8–9; 2Sa 15:4

Regulations relating to judges
Dt 1:16 *See also* Dt 17:12; 25:2–3

Corrupt judges
Mic 7:3 *See also* Lk 18:2–8

Levitical judges
Eze 44:24 *See also* 1Ch 23:3–4; 26:29

Judges during periods of foreign rule
Under the Babylonian empire Da 3:2–3

Under the Medo-Persian empire
Ezr 7:25 See also Ezr 4:9

Under the Roman Empire Mt 27:19 See also Mt 5:25 pp Lk 12:58; Jn 19:13; Ac 24:10

God as judge
Isa 33:22 See also Jdg 11:27; 1Sa 24:12,15; 1Ki 8:31–32; 1Ch 16:33; Job 9:15; Ps 58:11; 94:2; Jn 8:50; 12:48; Heb 12:23

The righteousness of God's judgment
Ge 18:25 See also Ps 7:11; 50:6

Jesus Christ appointed as judge
Ac 10:42 See also Jn 5:22,27,30; Ac 17:31; 2Co 5:10; 2Ti 4:1,8

See also

1125 God, righteousness	5326 government
1310 God as judge	5359 justice
2072 Christ, righteousness	6130 corruption
2309 Christ as judge	7135 Israel, people of God
4065 orderliness	7733 leaders
5091 Deborah	9210 judgment, God's

5359

justice

A concern to act rightly, and to be seen by others to act rightly. Divine justice embraces every aspect of the right ordering of human society according to the will of God, its creator.

5360
justice, of God

The moral righteousness of God is revealed in his laws and expressed in his judicial acts. God's commands and judgments meet perfect standards of justice, and his apportioning of punishments and rewards is also perfectly just. God's justice is impartial. Special praise is his for vindicating the penitent and the needy who have no human champions. Ultimately, all God's ways will be seen as just and equitable.

God's justice declared
God the Father Ps 92:15; 1Pe 1:17 See also Ge 18:25; Job 36:3; Ps 11:7; 25:8; 33:5; 51:4; Isa 61:8; Jer 9:24; Zep 3:5; Rev 15:3

God the Son 1Jn 2:1 See also Ps 45:6; Heb 1:8–9; Ps 72:1–4
The righteousness of the coming Messiah: Isa 9:7; 11:3–5; 42:1,3; Mal 3:1–3 Ac 3:14; 1Co 1:30; Rev 19:11

God the Spirit Jn 16:8–11 See also Ac 5:3,9; Eph 4:1,28,30

God's justice described
As impartial 1Pe 1:17 See also Dt 10:17;

2Ch 19:7; Job 34:19; Da 5:27; Ac 10:34; Ro 2:5,11; Gal 2:6; Eph 6:9; Col 3:25

As inescapable Ro 2:3 See also Ps 68:21–23; Jer 11:11; 16:16–18; 51:53; La 2:22; Am 9:1–4; Ob 4; Heb 2:2–3

As infallible Heb 4:13 See also 1Sa 2:3; 1Ch 28:9; Pr 16:2; 21:2; 24:12; Lk 16:15; Ro 2:2,16

God's justice desired
By the oppressed Ps 9:19 See also Jdg 3:9; Ps 7:6; 10:12–14

By those who are misrepresented Ps 26:1 See also 1Sa 24:15; Ps 35:23–24

God's justice doubted
Mal 2:17 See also Job 6:29; 27:2; 34:5; Ps 73:2–14; Ecc 8:11,14; Isa 40:27; Ro 9:14,19–20

God's justice demonstrated
In his demands for social justice
Mic 6:8 See also Dt 16:18,20; Isa 1:16–17; Am 5:21–24; Mal 3:5; Mt 23:23; Lk 20:46–47

In his defence of the oppressed
Ps 103:6 See also Ps 72:2; 140:12; Pr 22:22–23; Isa 11:4; Eze 34:16; Lk 18:7–8

In his vindication of the righteous
Ro 8:33 See also Ps 17:1–2; 24:5; Isa 50:8–9; 54:17; 61:8

In the cross Ro 3:25–26 See also 2Co 5:21; Gal 3:13

In the resurrection Ac 17:31

On the day of judgment Ro 2:5 See also Ps 9:8; Ac 17:31; Rev 16:5,7; 19:2

See also

1075 God, justice of	6674 imputation
1310 God as judge	6712 propitiation
2042 Christ, justice of	8721 doubt
2309 Christ as judge	9210 judgment, God's
2410 cross, the	9230 judgment seat
6614 atonement	9240 last judgment

5361
justice, human

God created the world in justice, and expects that his creatures will deal fairly and justly with one another as a result. Sin brings injustice into the world, by disrupting the justice established by God at creation. As a result, human justice often falls short of God's standards.

God shows his concern for human justice
By commanding it Isa 56:1; Mic 6:8 See also Ex 23:1–9; Dt 24:17; Ps 82:3; Pr 21:3; Hos 12:6; Ro 13:7

By commending its maintenance
Ps 106:3 See also Ge 20:5–6; 1Ki 3:11–12,28; Job 1:8; Ps 37:37; 112:5

By condemning its neglect Mal 3:5 See also Dt 27:19; Job 31:13–14; Isa 3:14,15; 10:1; Jer 7:5–8,14
destruction follows ignored warnings: Eze 22:29–31

Justice in relationships within the family
Parents and children Ex 20:12 pp Dt 5:16 See also Mt 15:4; Eph 6:1–3; Col 3:20–21; 1Ti 3:4

Brothers and sisters Ge 4:9–10

Husband and wife Mal 2:14; 1Co 7:4–5; Col 3:18–19

Justice in the community
Pr 29:7; Jas 1:27 See also Job 29:16; Ps 82:3; Pr 29:14; 31:8–9; Isa 1:17; Jer 22:16

Justice in the business world
Col 4:1 See also Lev 19:35–36; Dt 25:15; Eph 6:9; Jas 5:1–4

Justice in courts of law
Ex 23:6–8 See also Lev 19:15; Dt 1:16; 16:18–20; 17:6; 25:1–3; 27:25; 2Ch 19:5–7; Pr 12:17
Partiality condemned: Pr 18:5; 24:23–25; 28:21
Pr 18:17; Jn 18:23; Ac 23:3

Justice in rulers and governments
Pr 8:15 See also 1Ki 10:9; 1Ch 18:14; Pr 16:12–13; 29:26–27; 31:8–9; Jer 22:13–16 judgment against the son of King Josiah; Eze 45:9; Ro 13:1–4; 1Pe 2:13–14,17

Justice in the community of faith
Am 5:21–24; Lk 11:42 See also Isa 58:6–7; Hos 6:6; 12:6; Mt 23:23; 1Co 6:1–8; Jas 2:1–4,12–13

Justice in a believer's life
Mic 6:8 See also Pr 21:3; Php 4:8; Tit 2:12; 1Pe 3:16

See also

5347 injustice	5680 family
5375 law	5743 widows
5404 masters	6172 guilt
5446 poverty	7733 leaders
5482 punishment	8275 honesty
5520 servants	8790 oppression

5362
justice, in believers' lives

God requires justice to be evident in the lives of his people. Through justification, believers are granted the status of being righteous in his sight, and are called upon to live out that righteousness in their lives.

God's law demands justice
The law is written on the conscience
Ro 2:14–15 See also Ge 20:5–6; Pr 20:27 Isa 51:7 See also Ecc 8:5

The law in the OT Ex 20:1–3; Dt 6:4–5 See also Ex 20:4–17 pp Dt 5:6–21; Ps 119:1,165 pp Mt 22:37–40

The law in the NT Mt 5:17 See also Ro 7:7,12,22; 13:10; 1Ti 1:8–11

Justification is by faith
Ro 1:17 See also Hab 2:4; Ge 15:6; Ro 3:21–24; 4:24–25; 5:1; 9:30; Gal 3:6,24; Php 3:9

The marks of the just person
Jas 2:17 Although justification is by faith alone it is always to be accompanied by

righteous behaviour. See also
Mt 25:34–36; Eph 2:10; 1Jn 3:7, 9

Thinking justly Ps 1:2 *See also* Ps 24:4;
40:8; 119:111–112; Mt 5:8; Php 4:8

Speaking justly Ps 141:3 *See also*
Pr 4:24; 8:6–8; Eph 4:25; 1Pe 3:10

Behaving justly Mic 6:8 *See also* Dt 6:25;
Ps 106:3; Pr 21:3; Isa 33:15–16;
Ac 24:16

Examples of just people
Job 1:8 *See also* 2Sa 8:15; 1Ki 3:11–12,
28; Lk 23:50–51; Ac 25:8,11

The vindication of the just
2Ti 4:8 *See also* Ps 86:17; Da 12:3;
Rev 7:9–17

See also
5008 conscience	6676 justification
5596 victory	8154 righteousness

5364

key

A tool for opening a locked door.
Used mainly symbolically in
Scripture to speak of Jesus Christ's
victory over death and his authority
over believers, or of the need of
deliverance from the imprisonment
brought to human nature by sin and
the law.

Keys for opening doors
Jdg 3:23–25; 1Ch 9:27; Lk 3:20; 11:7;
Jn 20:19,26; Ac 5:23

The symbolic use of keys
**As a symbol of Jesus Christ's
complete authority** Rev 3:7 *See also*
Isa 22:22

**As a symbol of Jesus Christ's ultimate
victory over death and hell** Rev 1:18

As a symbol of Satan's ultimate defeat
Rev 20:1–3 *See also* Rev 9:1

**As a symbol of Jesus Christ's
authoritative ministry through his
church** Mt 16:19 *Usually understood as
illustrating how God's forgiveness is made
effective through preaching the gospel.*

As a symbol of living faith Isa 33:6 *See
also* Mt 13:52

**Being locked up as a symbol of
obstacles to faith** Gal 3:23 *See also*
Lk 11:52

See also
5215 authority	5375 law
5299 door	8020 faith
5344 imprisonment	

5365

kidnapping

The abduction of a person, normally
for the purpose of selling into
slavery.

Examples of kidnapping
Joseph Ge 37:23–28; 40:15; 45:3–5

The girls at Shiloh Jdg 21:16–23

The penalty for kidnapping
Ex 21:16 *See also* Dt 24:7; 1Ti 1:9–10

See also
7346 death penalty   7446 slavery

5366

king

The ruler or monarch of a country or
realm. God is king of all the earth
and human kings are called to rule in
accordance with his will. The failure
of kings in Israel and Judah after
David led to the expectation of a
coming king like David. This was
fulfilled in Jesus Christ: the true King
of Israel and all the world.

God is king of his people and of
all the earth
Ps 47:8 *The Hebrew refers to the rule of a
king;* 1Ti 6:15–16 *See also* Ex 15:18;
1Sa 12:12; 2Ch 20:6; Ps 24:10;
47:2,6–7; 93:1; 96:10; 97:1; 99:1;
Isa 6:5; 44:6; 1Ti 1:17; Rev 15:3; 19:6

Significant kings
Melchizedek, king of Salem Ge 14:18;
Heb 5:6,10; 6:20–7:17; Ps 110:4

The Pharaohs, the kings of Egypt
Ge 12:14–20; 41:39–40; Ex 12:30–32;
14:4; 1Ki 3:1; 2Ki 23:29,33–34;
Eze 32:1–10; Ro 9:17

Saul
*Israel's demand for a king is seen as a
rejection of God's rule:* 1Sa 8:4–9,19–22;
10:17–19; 12:12–15
*The king is seen as a gracious gift from
God:* 1Sa 9:1–2; 10:1,24; 11:14–15;
13:1,11–14; 15:17,26
Saul's death: 1Sa 31:1–4 pp 1Ch 10:1–4;
1Ch 10:13–14

David 1Ch 29:26–28 pp 1Ki 2:10–12
See also 1Sa 16:13; 2Sa 5:3–5
pp 1Ch 11:3; 2Sa 8:1–14
pp 1Ch 18:1–13; 1Ki 11:38; Ps 18:50;
78:70–72
God's covenant with David: 2Sa 7:8–16
pp 1Ch 17:7–14; 1Ki 9:4–5;
2Ch 7:17–18; Ps 132:11–12

Solomon 2Sa 12:24–25; 1Ki 2:12
pp 2Ch 1:1; 1Ki 4:29–34; 6:1 pp 2Ch 3:1
Solomon began to build the temple;
1Ki 10:23–25 pp 2Ch 9:22–24;
1Ki 11:1,4,42–43 pp 2Ch 9:30–31
Solomon's death

Nebuchadnezzar, king of Babylon
2Ki 24:1 pp 2Ch 36:6–7
*Nebuchadnezzar laid siege to Jerusalem in
588 B.C.:* 2Ki 25:1 pp 2Ch 36:17
pp Jer 39:1; 52:4; Da 1:1
Jer 21:7; 27:6,8; Eze 29:18–19
*Nebuchadnezzar besieged Tyre for 15
years;* Da 2:1,46–47; 3:1 *the image of
gold;* Da 3:28–29; 4:28–37

Cyrus, king of Persia 2Ch 36:22–23
pp Ezr 1:1–4; Ezr 5:13–6:5;
Isa 44:28–45:1,13; Da 6:28

The Herods, rulers in Palestine
Herod the Great: Mt 2:1–3,16
Herod Antipas: Mt 14:1–2
pp Mk 6:14–16 pp Lk 9:7–9; Mk 8:15;
Lk 3:19–20; 13:31; 23:7–12; Ac 4:27
Herod Agrippa I: Ac 12:1–4,19–23

5366

The kings of the united kingdom
Saul 1Sa 10:20–24; 11:12–15

David 1Sa 16:13; 2Sa 2:1–4; 5:1–5;
1Ki 2:11; 1Ch 11:1–29:30

Solomon 1Ki 1:39; 2Ch 1:1–9:31

The kings of Israel, the northern
kingdom
Jeroboam I 1Ki 12:20,25–14:20

Nadab 1Ki 15:25–31

Baasha 1Ki 15:32–16:7

Elah 1Ki 16:8–14

Zimri 1Ki 16:15–20

Tibni 1Ki 16:21–22

Omri 1Ki 16:23–28

Ahab 1Ki 16:29–22:40

Ahaziah 1Ki 22:51–53; 2Ki 1:1–18

Joram (Jehoram) 2Ki 3:1–8:15

Jehu 2Ki 9:3–10:36

Jehoahaz 2Ki 13:1–9

Jehoash (Joash) 2Ki 13:10–25;
14:8–16

Jeroboam II 2Ki 14:23–29

Zechariah 2Ki 15:8–12

Shallum 2Ki 15:13–15

Menahem 2Ki 15:16–22

Pekahiah 2Ki 15:23–26

Pekah 2Ki 15:27–31

Hoshea 2Ki 17:1–6

The kings and queen of Judah,
the southern kingdom
Rehoboam 1Ki 12:1–24
pp 2Ch 10:1–11:4; 2Ch 11:5–12:8;
1Ki 14:21–31 pp 2Ch 12:9–16

Abijah 1Ki 15:1–8 pp 2Ch 13:1–14:1

Asa 1Ki 15:9–24 pp 2Ch 14:2–16:14

Jehoshaphat 1Ki 22:41–50
pp 2Ch 20:31–21:1; 2Ch 17:1–21:3

Jehoram (Joram) 2Ki 8:16–24
pp 2Ch 21:4–20

Ahaziah 2Ki 8:25–29 pp 2Ch 22:1–6;
2Ki 9:21–29 pp 2Ch 22:7–9

Queen Athaliah 2Ki 11:1–21
pp 2Ch 22:10–23:21

Joash (Jehoash) 2Ki 11:2–12:21
pp 2Ch 22:10–24:27

Amaziah 2Ki 14:1–22 pp 2Ch 25:1–28

Azariah (= Uzziah) 2Ki 14:21–22;
15:1–7 pp 2Ch 26:1–23

Jotham 2Ki 15:32–38 pp 2Ch 27:1–9

Ahaz 2Ki 16:1–20 pp 2Ch 28:1–27

Hezekiah 2Ki 18:1–20:21
pp 2Ch 29:1–32:33 pp Isa 36:1–39:8

Manasseh 2Ki 21:1–18
pp 2Ch 33:1–20

Amon 2Ki 21:19–26 pp 2Ch 33:21–25

Josiah 2Ki 22:1–23:30
pp 2Ch 34:1–35:27

Jehoahaz 2Ki 23:31–34 pp 2Ch 36:2–4

Jehoiakim 2Ki 23:36–24:6
pp 2Ch 36:5–8

Jehoiachin 2Ki 24:8–17
pp 2Ch 36:9–10

Zedekiah (= Mattaniah) 2Ki 24:18–25:7
pp 2Ch 36:11–21 pp Jer 52:1–11

5367
The expectation of a future king like David
Jer 23:5-6 *See also* Isa 9:6-7; 11:1-5; 16:5; Jer 30:8-9; 33:15; Eze 34:23-24; 37:24-25; Am 9:11; Mic 5:2-5; Hag 2:20-23

The duties of the king
To fear God 2Sa 23:3-4; Pr 20:28 *See also* Dt 17:14-20; 1Sa 10:25; Ps 2:10-11

To maintain righteousness and administer justice Pr 29:4,14 *See also* 1Ki 3:28; Pr 16:12-13; 20:8,26; 31:4-5,8-9; Isa 11:4; Jer 33:15; Ro 13:4

To read the law of God and ensure it was obeyed Dt 17:18-20 *See also* 1Ki 2:1-4; 9:4-5; 2Ki 11:12

The coronation of the king
His anointing by the prophet of God 1Sa 10:1; 16:1-13

His proclamation as king before the people 2Ki 11:12 pp 2Ch 23:11 *See also* 1Sa 10:17-25; 11:15; 2Sa 2:4; 5:1-3 pp 1Ch 11:1-3; 2Sa 15:10; 1Ki 1:28-40; 12:1 pp 2Ch 10:1; 1Ki 12:20

Royal Psalms
These Psalms, although used in honour of the king of the day, possibly at his coronation, share the expectation of a greater king. The NT regards them as fulfilled in Jesus Christ: Ps 2:6-9; 45:1; 72:1; 110:1; 132:10

Jesus Christ is the true King of Israel and of the world
Mt 27:37 pp Mk 15:26 pp Lk 23:38 Jn 1:49 *See also* Mt 21:5; Mk 15:2 pp Mt 27:11 pp Lk 23:3; Jn 18:36-37; Ac 17:7; 1Co 15:25; Heb 1:8; Ps 45:6; Rev 17:14; 19:16

Jesus Christ fulfils the expectation of a son of David who will be a king like David
Lk 1:32-33 *See also* Lk 1:69; Ac 13:22-23; Ro 1:3; 2Ti 2:8; Rev 5:5; 22:16

See also
1130 God, sovereignty	5085 David
2215 Christ, Son of David	5118 Solomon
2230 Messiah, coming of	5367 kingdoms
2312 Christ as king	5368 kingship
2375 kingdom of God	5487 queen
	5581 throne

5367
kingdoms
Realms or reigns of kings. The kingdoms of this world have power under the sovereignty of God. They are ultimately judged by God and will be superseded by the kingdom of God. The phrase "the kingdom of the air" is used to describe the spiritual realm in which Satan operates.

Israel and the kingdoms around her
1Ki 4:21 *See also* Dt 3:21-22; 28:25;

Jos 11:10; Jdg 2:20-3:4; 1Sa 10:18; 2Ch 17:10; 20:29; Ne 9:22; Jer 34:1

The kingdoms of this world
God is sovereign over the kingdoms of this world 2Ki 19:15 pp Isa 37:16 *See also* 2Ki 5:1; 19:19; 2Ch 20:6; 36:23 pp Ezr 1:2; Ps 46:6; Pr 21:1; Isa 45:1

The kingdoms of this world will honour and worship God Ps 102:21-22 *See also* Ps 68:32; Rev 21:24-26

Under the sovereignty of God a succession of kingdoms will rule the earth Da 2:36-43; 7:17,23-25; 8:19-22

The kingdom of God will supersede and be greater than the kingdoms of this world Rev 11:15; Jn 16:33 *See also* Da 2:44-45; 6:26; 7:13-14,18,27

God's judgment on the kingdoms of this world Zep 3:8 *See also* Ps 79:6; Isa 10:10-11; 13:19; Jer 28:8; Da 7:26; Hag 2:22; Rev 6:15-17

God's people will be given sovereignty over the kingdoms of this world Da 7:27 *See also* Jer 1:10; Rev 2:26-27

In this world God enables his people to overcome "kingdoms" by faith Heb 11:32-33; 1Jn 5:4

The devil tempts Jesus Christ by offering him the kingdoms of this world if he will worship him Mt 4:8-10 pp Lk 4:5-8

The kingdom of the air
Eph 2:1-2

The kingdom of Satan
Mt 12:26 pp Lk 11:18

The kingdoms of the sea
Isa 23:11 *The Phoenicians, who were great sailors, appeared to have dominion over the sea (see Isa 23:1-4), but in reality it belongs to God.*

See also
1130 God, sovereignty	5366 king
2345 Christ, kingdom of	5368 kingship
	5596 victory
2375 kingdom of God	8024 faith & blessings
4027 world, fallen	8482 spiritual warfare
4124 Satan, kingdom of	9210 judgment, God's

5368
kingship
The sovereignty and rule of a king. Scripture stresses that all human authority derives ultimately from God, and that human kings are required to acknowledge and respond to this divine authority.

5369
kingship, divine
God is sovereign over all the earth. Jesus Christ is the true King of Israel and David's greater son.

The kingship of God
God is sovereign over all the earth 1Ch 29:11-12 *See also* Ex 15:18;

1Ch 16:31; Ps 9:7-8; 45:6; 103:19; Isa 37:16

God is called king Ps 29:10; 47:6-7 *See also* 1Sa 12:12; Ps 47:2; 95:3; Isa 6:5; 44:6; 1Ti 1:17; 6:15; Rev 15:3

God rules as king Ps 96:10 *See also* Ps 47:8; 93:1; 97:1; 99:1

The kingdom of God Mk 1:14-15 *See also* Ps 145:11-13; Mt 4:17,23; 11:12; Lk 4:43; 11:20; 16:16; 1Co 15:24; Rev 11:15

The kingship of Jesus Christ
Jesus Christ is the true king of Israel and of the world Jn 1:49 *See also* Mt 21:5; Zec 9:9; Mk 15:2 pp Mt 27:11 pp Lk 23:3; Jn 18:36-37; Ac 17:7; Heb 1:8; Ps 45:6; Rev 17:14; 19:16

Jesus Christ is David's greater son Lk 1:32-33; Ac 13:36-37 *Jesus Christ is not only David's son but he is greater than David. See also* Mt 1:1; Mk 12:35-37 pp Mt 22:41-45 pp Lk 20:41-44; Lk 1:69; Ac 2:29-36; 13:22-23; Ro 1:3; 2Ti 2:8; Rev 5:5; 22:16

The kingship of believers
2Ti 2:12 *See also* Eph 2:6; 1Pe 2:9; Rev 2:26-27; 3:21; 5:10

See also
1130 God, sovereignty	2312 Christ as king
	2375 kingdom of God
2206 Jesus, the Christ	
2215 Christ, Son of David	

5370
kingship, human
Human kings are to be respected. Israel demanded and received a king from God but the failure of kings after David led to the expectation of a coming great king in succession to David.

Human kingship
Human kingship is to be respected as ordained by God Ro 13:1-7 *See also* 1Ti 2:1-2; 1Pe 2:13,17

Allegiance to God is greater than allegiance to human kings Da 2:47; Ac 5:29; Heb 11:23,27

Kingship in Israel
Israel is ruled by God and his appointed leader Jdg 8:22-23; 19:1; 21:25; 1Sa 7:15-17; 12:12

Israel demands and receives a king from God 1Sa 8:4-9 *See also* Dt 17:14-20; 1Sa 8:19-22; 10:1,17-19,24; 11:14-15; 12:12-15 *The demand for a king is seen as a rejection of God's rule but at the same time the king is seen as a gracious gift from God;* Hos 13:10-11

David is Israel's greatest king 1Ch 29:26-28 pp 1Ki 2:10-12 Ps 78:70-72 *See also* 1Sa 16:13; 2Sa 5:3-5 pp 1Ch 11:3; 2Sa 8:1-14 pp 1Ch 18:1-13; 1Ki 3:14; 11:6,38; 2Ki 14:3; Ps 18:50

God's covenant with David 2Sa 7:8-16 pp 1Ch 17:7-14 *See also* 1Ki 9:4-5 pp 2Ch 7:17-18; Ps 132:11-12

The failure of the kingship after David leads to the expectation of a future king like David

Jer 33:15 *See also* Isa 9:6–7; 11:1–5; 16:5; Jer 23:5–6; 30:8–9; Eze 34:23–24; 37:24–25; Am 9:11; Mic 5:2–5; Mk 11:10

Royal Psalms

These Psalms, although used for the king of the day, share the expectation of a greater future king. The NT regards them as fulfilled in Jesus Christ: Ps 2:6–9; 45:1; 72:1; 110:1; 132:11

See also

2230 Messiah, coming of	5487 queen
5085 David	5581 throne
5118 Solomon	7233 Israel, northern kingdom
5219 authority, human institutions	7236 Israel, united kingdom
5366 king	7245 Judah, kingdom of

5372

knife

The knife as a domestic cutting implement

Used for general purposes Pr 23:2; 30:14; Jer 36:23 *cutting a scroll*

Knives used for shaving

Lev 19:27; 21:5; Jdg 16:17; Isa 15:2; Eze 7:18; Mic 1:16

Knives used in religious ceremonies

In circumcision

Flint rather than metal knives were used because of their sharpness: Ex 4:25; Jos 5:2–3

In sacrifice Ge 15:10; 22:10; Ex 29:17; Lev 8:20

Knives used for wounding

For self-mutilation

This practice was associated with pagan worship, sometimes as an expression of mourning: Lev 19:28; 21:5; Dt 14:1–2; 1Ki 18:28; Jer 16:6; 41:5; 47:5; 48:37

In mutilation of others

As a punishment: Ex 21:23–25; Lev 24:17–20; Dt 25:12

Against prisoners of war: Jdg 1:6; 16:21

As a threat: 1Sa 11:7

Knives used in figures of speech

For self-discipline Pr 23:2; Mt 5:29–30; 18:8–9; Mk 9:43–47

As a symbol of pruning Isa 18:5; Jn 15:1–2

As a symbol of wickedness Pr 30:14

See also

4327 flint	5571 surgery
5130 beard	5572 sword
5155 hair	5583 tools
5346 injury	7334 circumcision
5419 mourning	7402 offerings
5482 punishment	7435 sacrifice, in OT

5373

lamp and lampstand

A device to give light, especially in buildings, and the stand on which it

was placed. They were both used as symbols of the gospel or of churches which resulted from the preaching of the gospel.

Domestic lamps

Pr 31:18 *See also* 2Ki 4:10; Jer 25:10; Da 5:5; Lk 15:8; Ac 20:8; Rev 18:23

Lamps in the tabernacle and temple

2Ch 4:7; Heb 9:2 *See also* Ex 25:31–40; 26:35; 30:27; 31:8; 35:14; 37:17–24; 39:37; 40:4,24–25; Nu 4:9–10; 8:1–4; 1Ki 7:49; 2Ch 4:19–21; Jer 52:19

Tending the lamps

Ex 27:20–21 *See also* Ex 30:7–8; Lev 24:2–4; Nu 3:31; 1Sa 3:3; 2Ch 13:11; 29:7

Lamps used metaphorically

2Sa 21:17 *The lamp of Israel represents the king;* Ps 119:105; Mt 5:15–16 *See also* Mk 4:21; Lk 8:16; 11:33

Jn 5:35; Rev 1:12–13 *The lampstands represent the seven churches. See also* 2Sa 22:29; Job 18:5–6; 29:2–3; Ps 18:28; Pr 13:9; Zep 1:12; Zec 4:2; Mt 6:22 pp Lk 11:34–36; Mt 25:1–13 *the parable of the ten virgins;* Lk 12:35; Rev 11:4; 22:5

See also

1670 symbols	7467 temple, Solomon's
4488 oil	
4833 light	
7459 tabernacle, in OT	

5374

languages

The means of communication shared in common by groups of people. Scripture teaches that the diversity of languages in the world is a result of sin, but the outpouring of the Holy Spirit in Acts broke down the barriers of language and nationality.

The origin of different languages

Ge 11:1–9 *See also* Ge 10:2–5,20,30–31

The close relationship between language and national identity

Isa 19:18 *See also* Ne 13:23–27; Zec 8:23; Rev 5:9; 7:9; 10:11; 11:9; 13:7; 14:6; 17:15

Language barriers

Ne 13:23–24 *See also* Dt 28:49–50; Ps 81:5; Jer 5:15; Eze 3:5–6; Da 1:4; 1Co 14:10–11

The diversity of languages in the Persian empire

Est 8:9 *See also* Ezr 4:7; Est 1:22; 3:12

God's revelation not limited to any single language

Ac 2:1–11 *See also* Ps 19:1–4; Ac 10:44–48

Aramaic

Aramaic in the OT 2Ki 18:26 pp Isa 36:11 *Aramaic is a language related to Hebrew, known from Assyrian times. Under the influence of the Persian empire*

Aramaic was the diplomatic language in later OT times. In Palestine, by the time of the NT, it was spoken widely, having largely displaced Hebrew as the everyday language of the Jews. See also Ezr 4:7 *The text of Ezr 4:8–6:18 and 7:12–26 is in Aramaic;* Jer 10:11 *The text of Jer 10:11 is in Aramaic;* Da 2:4 *The text of Da 2:4–7:28 is in Aramaic.*

By NT times Aramaic had become the common language of Palestinian Jews Jn 20:16 *See also* Jn 5:2; 19:13,17,20; Ac 21:40–22:2; 26:14

Aramaic expressions found in the NT Mt 27:46 pp Mk 15:34 *See also* Mt 5:22; Mk 5:41; 7:34; 14:36; Jn 20:16; Ro 8:15; 1Co 16:22 fn; Gal 4:6

Hebrew

2Ki 18:26 pp Isa 36:11 *Hebrew was the language of Israel in the period of the OT. By the time of the NT, it had been partially displaced in everyday use by Aramaic. See also* 2Ki 18:28 pp 2Ch 32:18 pp Isa 36:13; Rev 9:11; 16:16

Greek

Jn 19:20 *Greek was the major cultural and commercial language of the eastern Mediterranean world. The NT was written in this language, ensuring the rapid spread of the gospel in this region. See also* Ac 21:37–39; Rev 9:11

See also

1440 revelation, creation	5547 speech, power of
3242 Holy Spirit, baptism with	5585 towers
3251 Holy Spirit, filling with	5627 word
3257 Holy Spirit, gift of	7972 tongues, gift of

5375

law

The God-given regulation of the life of the people of God in relationship with him. As the command of God, it enables and gives shape to the relationship between God and human beings on the one hand, and between fellow human beings on the other.

This set of themes consists of the following:

5376 law, purpose of
5377 law, Ten Commandments
5378 law, OT
5379 law, Jesus Christ's attitude to
5380 law, and gospel
5381 law, letter and spirit of

5376

law, purpose of

The law covers and regulates every area of life of the covenant people of God in accordance with the commands of God. Although the laws may be divided into categories of civil, criminal, social and cultic (or ritual) law, these distinctions are not clear-cut, and occasionally overlap with one another.

The origins of the law
Law as God's command is found in the story of creation Ge 2:16–17

The law expresses the covenant relation between God and his people Dt 4:44–45; 5:1 See also Ex 20:1–17 pp Dt 5:6–21; Dt 10:12–13; 30:1–16

The purpose of the law
The law shows the proper response to the holiness of God Lev 19:2

The law ensures that the people continue to receive the blessings of the covenant promises Dt 6:24–25 See also Ge 22:17–18; Ex 20:12; Dt 6:3–7

Breaking the law leads to forfeiting the covenant blessings Jer 11:9–11 See also Ex 32:1–4

The law deepens the believer's knowledge of God through meditation Ps 1:1–2 See also Dt 6:2; Ps 19:7–14; 119:25–32,105–120

The law will finally be written on believers' hearts Jer 31:33 See also Eze 11:19–20

The general principles underlying the law
Justice Dt 16:20

Righteousness Dt 16:18

Holiness Lev 19:2

Love Lev 19:18–19

See also

1075 God, justice of	5276 crime
1125 God, righteousness	5359 justice
1345 covenant	5482 punishment
5051 responsibility	8154 righteousness
5215 authority	8266 holiness
	8453 obedience

5377
law, Ten Commandments

The basic laws given to Israel through Moses following the exodus from Egypt (Ex 20:1–17; Dt 5:6–21). The first four commandments safeguard Israel's special relation to God; the remaining six protect individuals within the community and promote their well-being.

The Ten Commandments are to govern the life of Israel as the people of God
Israel should obey God alone Ex 20:2–3 pp Dt 5:6–7 See also Dt 6:13–15

Idolatry forbidden Ex 20:4–6 pp Dt 5:8–10 See also Ex 32:1–8; Lev 19:4; 1Co 10:7

God's name should not be misused Ex 20:7 pp Dt 5:11 See also Mt 7:21

A day of rest is commanded Ex 20:8–11 pp Dt 5:12–15 See also Ex 16:23; Lev 19:3; Isa 56:2; Jer 17:21–22

Parents are to be honoured Ex 20:12 pp Dt 5:16 See also Mt 15:4; Eph 6:1–3

Murder is forbidden Ex 20:13 pp Dt 5:17 See also Ge 4:8–16; Mt 5:21

Adultery is forbidden Ex 20:14 pp Dt 5:18 See also Lev 18:20; 2Sa 11:2–5; Mt 5:27; Heb 13:4

Stealing is forbidden Ex 20:15 pp Dt 5:19 See also Lev 19:11,13

False witness is forbidden Ex 20:16 pp Dt 5:20 See also Lev 19:11

Coveting is forbidden Ex 20:17 pp Dt 5:21 See also Lev 19:17–18; Job 31:9–12; Ro 7:7

The circumstances surrounding the giving of the Ten Commandments
The Ten Commandments written on stone tablets Ex 24:12 See also Dt 4:13; 9:9–10

The stone tablets broken Ex 32:19 Moses broke the stone tablets when he saw that the Israelites had sinned by making the golden calf. See also Dt 9:16–17

A second set of stone tablets made Ex 34:1,28 See also Dt 10:1–2

The second set of stone tablets put in the ark of the covenant Ex 40:20 See also Dt 10:1–2

See also

5040 murder	5800 blasphemy
5061 sanctity of life	6133 coveting
5104 Moses, foreshadower of Christ	6242 adultery
	7221 exodus, the
5555 stealing	7428 Sabbath
5731 parents	8751 false witness
	8768 idolatry

5378
law, OT

OT laws and legal traditions govern every aspect of the life of the covenant people of God.

Kinds of OT law
Criminal law Ex 21:12–14 Criminal law deals with crimes against persons punishable by a court.

Civil law Dt 16:18–20 Civil law deals with the upholding in court of legally established rights against possible abuse. See also Dt 15:12–18

Social law Ex 22:21–22 Social law deals with behaviour or standards of behaviour which are not strictly enforceable in the courts. See also Dt 24:19–22

Cultic law Cultic law deals explicitly with the ritual or religious life of the people of God. Leviticus chapters 1–7 are totally devoted to this kind of law: Lev 1:10–13; 4:13–21; 7:11–18

Examples of OT law
Conditions for freeing servants Ex 21:2–6 pp Dt 15:12–18 See also Ex 21:3–11; Lev 25:39–55

Dealing with injuries Ex 21:23–25 See also Mt 5:38

Property is to be protected Ex 22:1 See also Lev 6:1–7; Lk 19:8

The rights of aliens must be respected Ex 22:21 See also Lev 19:33; Dt 10:19

Justice must be universally respected Ex 23:2–3 See also Lev 19:15

The Sabbath must be observed by all Ex 23:12 See also Ex 20:8–11

Three annual festivals are to be celebrated Ex 23:15–16 See also Ex 12:17; Dt 16:16

Worship must be in accordance with God's will and must be kept pure Dt 12:1–7; 13:6–8

Certain foods are declared to be unclean Lev 11:1–23 pp Dt 14:3–20

A tenth of all produce must be given to God Dt 14:22 See also Lev 27:30

Cultic laws are grounded in the holiness of God Lev 11:44; 19:1–2 See also 1Pe 1:16 Full details were given for each type of offering: burnt, grain, fellowship, sin and guilt offerings. Only perfect animals were to be offered: Lev 1:3; 2:1–2; 3:1–2; 4:27–28; 5:17–18

Rules governing infectious or contagious diseases Lev 13:2; 15:13

There must not be unlawful sexual relations Lev 18:6

A Day of Atonement must be held See also Lev 23:26–32 pp Lev 16:2–34 pp Nu 29:7–11

See also

5475 property	7424 ritual law
6614 atonement	7434 sacrifice
7340 clean and unclean	7446 slavery
	8488 tithing
7402 offerings	8622 worship

5379
law, Jesus Christ's attitude to

Jesus Christ accepted the authority of the OT law and saw himself as coming to fulfil its purpose.

Jesus Christ's disputes with the Pharisees and teachers of the law
The Pharisees and teachers of the law accuse Jesus Christ's disciples of not following tradition Mk 7:5 pp Mt 15:2

Jesus Christ accuses the Pharisees and teachers of the law of hypocrisy Mk 7:6–8 pp Mt 15:7–9 See also Isa 29:13

Jesus Christ gives examples where human tradition is observed rather than God's law Mk 7:10–13 pp Mt 15:3–6; Mt 23:1–36 pp Mk 12:38–39 pp Lk 20:45–46

The Pharisees accuse Jesus Christ of breaking the Sabbath Mk 2:23–24 pp Mt 12:1–2 pp Lk 6:1–2

Jesus Christ demonstrates his authority over the Sabbath Mk 2:27–3:4 pp Mt 12:8–10 pp Lk 6:5–7

Jesus Christ challenges the religious leaders to think about principles not rules Mk 3:4 pp Lk 6:9 pp Mt 12:11–12 See also Lk 13:10–17

Jesus Christ came to fulfil the law
Mt 5:17,21–22 Jesus Christ went beyond

the literal rules of the law, to the thought behind the act. See also Ex 20:13 Mt 5:27–28 *See also* Ex 20:14

Jesus Christ asserts the continuing validity of the law
Mt 5:18–19; Lk 10:25–28 pp Mt 22:37–39 pp Mk 12:29–34 *See also* Lk 10:29–37; 16:16

Jesus Christ himself was obedient to the law and its commands
In honouring his parents Lk 2:41–51

In being baptised Mt 3:13–15

In resisting temptation Lk 4:1–13

In observing the Passover Lk 22:7–8

In submitting to the will of God Mt 26:39 pp Mk 14:35–36 pp Lk 22:41–42

See also

2057 Christ, obedience	7464 teachers of the law
2333 Christ, attitude to OT	7550 Pharisees
2545 Christ, opposition to	8767 hypocrisy

5380
law, and gospel

The law, which bears witness to the grace of God, points ahead to its fulfilment and climax in the gospel of Jesus Christ. The gospel does not abolish the law, but fulfils it, by allowing it to be seen in its proper light.

Human beings cannot fulfil the law by their own efforts
Ro 3:20 ; Gal 2:15–16 *See also* Ac 13:39; Ro 4:13–15

The law brings knowledge of human sin and the need for redemption
Ro 3:20; 5:20 *See also* 1Ti 1:9–10; 1Jn 3:4

The law points to the coming of Jesus Christ
Gal 3:24

Believers are not justified by works of the law, but through faith in the blood of Jesus Christ
Ro 3:28 ; Gal 3:11 *See also* Hab 2:4; Ro 4:1–5; Gal 3:10–14; Eph 2:15

The relationship between believers and the law
Dying to the law through Jesus Christ Gal 2:19

The law remains valid for believers Ro 7:11–12; 1Ti 1:8; 1Pe 1:15–16 *See also* Lev 11:44–45; 19:2; 20:7; Ro 7:7–11; 13:8–10; Jas 2:8–11

The Holy Spirit enables believers to fulfil the law through Jesus Christ Ro 8:3–4 *See also* Jer 31:31–34; Eze 11:19–20; Gal 5:13–18

See also

2324 Christ as Saviour	6020 sin
2420 gospel	6661 freedom and law
4018 life, spiritual	

6669 grace & salvation	8292 love
6676 justification	8311 morality & redemption
8158 righteousness of believers	
8241 ethics, basis of	

5381
law, letter and spirit of

A rigid adherence to the letter of the law often masks hypocrisy and neglect of its spirit, namely having God at the centre of one's life and putting others before oneself, or recognising that the law points to Jesus Christ.

The letter of the law
Overemphasis on keeping some parts of the law Mk 7:1–8 pp Mt 15:1–2 *See also* Isa 29:13; Mt 9:10–13 pp Mk 2:15–17 pp Lk 5:29–32

Hypocrisy with regard to keeping the law Mk 7:9–13 pp Mt 15:3–6 *See also* Mt 23:1–33; Lk 11:37–52; 18:9–14; Jn 9:1–16; Ro 2:17–24; Isa 52:5

The spirit of the law ·
Jesus Christ and the law Mt 5:17–6:19 *See also* Mt 19:16–30 pp Mk 10:17–30 pp Lk 18:18–30

Jesus Christ's attitude to the Sabbath Mk 2:23–3:6 pp Mt 12:1–14 pp Lk 6:1–11 *See also* Mk 1:21–28 pp Lk 4:31–37; Lk 13:10–17; 14:1–6; Jn 5:1–16; 7:21–24

Jesus Christ's treatment of the woman taken in adultery Jn 8:2–11

The greatest commandment Mt 22:34–40 pp Mk 12:28–34 *See also* Mt 25:31–46

The importance of obedience and right attitudes outweighs that of outward actions Ro 2:25–29 *See also* 1Sa 15:22–23; Ps 51:16–17; Pr 21:3; Isa 1:11–17; Jer 7:21–23; Hos 6:6; Am 5:21–24; Mic 6:6–8; Gal 3:1–5

The spirit of the law is embodied in the new covenant 2Co 3:3–6 *See also* Jn 4:19–24; Ro 7:4–6; 8:1–11; 1Co 15:45–46; 2Co 3:13–18; Gal 5:18; Heb 7:18–22; 8:1–13; Jer 31:31–34

See also

1352 covenant, the new	6020 sin
	7428 Sabbath
2324 Christ as Saviour	8154 righteousness
	8403 commands
2333 Christ, attitude to OT	8703 antinomianism
3140 Holy Spirit, teacher	8774 legalism
	8775 libertinism
5173 outward appearance	

5383

lawsuits

Legal trials in which the court decides between two opposing parties. OT law makes provision for such trials, insisting on justice for all, regardless of social status.

Regulations relating to lawsuits
Warnings against discrimination on the basis of social status Ex 23:6 *See also* Ex 23:3; Lev 19:15; Dt 1:17; Pr 22:22–23

Warnings against false testimony Ex 23:1–2 *See also* Ex 20:16 pp Dt 5:20; Dt 19:15–21; Zec 8:16

Provision for a court of appeal Dt 17:8–13 *See also* Dt 1:15–18

Lawsuits to judge between two parties
Dt 25:1 *See also* Ex 18:16; 21:22; Job 9:32–35; Pr 25:7–10; 29:9; Mt 5:25–26; Jas 2:5–7

Believers should not bring lawsuits against each other
1Co 6:1–8

Injustice in lawsuits
Am 5:15 *See also* Isa 29:20–21; Am 2:7; 5:7–12

Excess of lawsuits a symptom of social disorder
Hos 10:4

Examples of lawsuits
2Sa 15:1–4 *See also* 2Sa 14:1–20; 1Ki 3:16–27; 2Ki 6:26–29; Ac 18:12–16; 19:35–41

See also

5270 court	5504 rights
5358 judges	5593 trial
5361 justice, human	5622 witnesses
5375 law	8800 prejudice
5384 lawyer	

5384

lawyer

A lawyer as a person skilled in the Mosaic law
Mt 22:35; Lk 7:30; 10:25,37; 11:45–46,52; 14:3; Tit 3:13

A lawyer as a person trained in rhetoric
Ac 24:1 *The word translated "lawyer" means literally "orator": a person trained in rhetoric who served as an attorney-at-law in a court trial.*

See also

5375 law	7464 teachers of the law
5383 lawsuits	

5385

leisure

Time for rest and recreational activities. Economic conditions in biblical times did not allow ordinary people much free time for leisure. However Scripture does give principles which apply to leisure.

5386
leisure, nature and purpose of

Scripture affirms that periods of rest and leisure are part of God's creation order. These periods of rest are to be used wisely.

5387

The need for leisure

The Sabbath rest Ge 2:2; Ex 20:8–10
pp Dt 5:12–15 See also Ex 23:11 During
the sabbath year, the labourers presumably
also rested; Lev 23:3

Rest commanded by Jesus Christ
Mk 6:31–32

Leisure a gift of God

Ps 23:2 See also Mt 11:28; Mk 2:27;
Rev 14:13

Loss of leisure a judgment Isa 48:22
See also Ecc 2:23; 5:12; Isa 57:20–21;
Rev 14:11

Responsible use of leisure

Work must come first Pr 10:5;
Lk 17:7–8

Remember God's presence 1Co 10:31
See also Ecc 9:7–10

Use time wisely Eph 5:15–16

The dangers of leisure

Idleness 1Ti 5:13 See also Pr 6:9–11;
24:30–31; 26:14; Ecc 10:18; 2Th 3:11;
Heb 6:12

Preoccupation with pleasure Lk 8:14
See also Pr 21:17; Isa 5:11; Lk 15:13;
1Ti 5:6; 2Ti 3:4; Jas 5:5

Susceptibility to sin 1Ti 5:13 See also
2Sa 11:1–5; Est 1:10–11; Am 4:1

Spiritual complacency Am 6:1,4–7 See
also Isa 5:11–13; Lk 12:16–21; 21:34

See also
5056 rest	5810 complacency
5343 idleness	5918 pleasure
5532 sleep	7428 Sabbath
5537 sleeplessness	8808 riches
5539 sluggard	

5387

leisure, and pastimes

Scripture gives examples of many
different kinds of leisure activity.

Necessary leisure activities

Sleeping
Ps 127:2; Ecc 5:12 See also Ps 4:8;
Mk 4:38; Ac 12:6

Eating and drinking Ge 24:54; Ecc 3:13

Pleasurable pastimes

Hospitality Ge 18:3–5; 1Pe 4:9

Feasting 1Ki 3:15; Ne 8:10; Est 8:17;
Job 1:4

Music 1Sa 16:23 See also 1Sa 16:16–18;
2Ki 3:14–15

Dancing Ecc 3:4
Dancing for joy: Ex 15:20; Jdg 11:34;
1Sa 18:6; Job 21:11; Jer 31:4
Dancing on festive occasions:
Jdg 21:19–21
Mk 6:22 dancing in revelry
Dancing in worship: 2Sa 6:14–16,21;
Ps 149:3; 150:4

Physical recreation 1Ti 4:8 See also
1Co 9:24–27 Although Paul never
mentions Christians taking part in the
games (which were often associated with
pagan festivals), he does show an
appreciation of the discipline necessary;
2Ti 2:5

Gardening Ecc 2:5–6 See also Ge 2:15

Enjoyment of nature Ps 8:3; 104:10–14

Sightseeing Mk 13:1; Ac 17:16

Education and literature Ecc 1:13 See
also 1Ki 4:32–34; Est 6:1; Pr 1:5;
Ecc 12:12; Ac 17:21; 2Ti 4:13

Children's games Zec 8:5 See also
Mt 11:16–17 pp Lk 7:32

Harmful pastimes

Licentious amusements 1Pe 4:3 See
also Ge 9:20–21; Ex 32:19; Pr 23:29–30;
Ro 13:13; Eph 5:4,12

Cruel amusements Jdg 16:25; 2Sa 2:14

See also
4434 drinking	6237 sexual sin
4438 eating	7921 fellowship
5287 dance	8110 athletics
5312 feasting	8445 hospitality
5420 music	8602 prayer
5664 children	8622 worship

5389

lending

Freely giving the temporary use of
property or possessions at no
personal advantage. Scripture lays
down conditions for lending and
emphasises the responsibilities that
it brings.

The motivation for lending

Generosity Ps 37:25–26 See also
Dt 15:11; Pr 3:27–28; Mt 5:42

Pity Dt 15:7–8 See also Lev 25:35–36;
Mk 14:7

Not necessarily expecting repayment
Lk 6:34–36

The dangers of lending

Domination Pr 22:7 See also Dt 15:6;
28:12–13,43–44; Ne 5:4–5

Loss Ex 22:14; 2Ki 6:5; Isa 24:1–2

Exploitation Lev 25:36–37

Usury Ex 22:25 See also Dt 23:19;
Ps 15:5; Eze 18:8,12–13

Safeguards for the lender

Under the old covenant Ex 22:14 This
specific case probably represents a general
principle of restitution governing all kinds
of lending.

Under the new covenant Lk 6:30–31
Generosity may be risky but brings its
reward Pr 19:17 See also Ps 112:5;
Mt 5:7

Jesus Christ was lent a donkey

Mt 21:3 pp Mk 11:3 pp Lk 19:31;
Lk 19:34

See also
5233 borrowing	5492 restitution
5274 credit	5806 compassion
5289 debt	8260 generosity
5310 exploitation	8291 kindness
5353 interest	8434 giving
5446 poverty	8790 oppression

5390

leprosy

An infectious skin disease. The
leprosy mentioned in Scripture,

---

however, covers a wider range of
dermatological conditions than that
now referred to as the modern
Hansen's disease, known
colloquially as leprosy.

Regulations for the control of leprosy

Sufferers are banned from society
Nu 5:2 See also Lev 13:1–46; Dt 24:8–9;
2Ki 7:3

**Sufferers are banned from Levitical
service** Lev 22:4

**Sufferers are to report to a priest on
being cured** Mt 8:4 See also Lk 17:14;
Lev 14:1–9

The healing of leprosy

2Ki 5:1,14; Mt 8:2–3 pp Mk 1:40–41;
Lk 17:12–15

Spiritual significance of leprosy

As a validating sign from God Ex 4:6–7

As a judgment from God Nu 12:10–15;
2Ki 5:27; 2Ch 26:19–23

See also
2351 Christ, miracles	8341 separation
5182 skin	9210 judgment,
5297 disease	God's
5333 healing	
7340 clean and	
unclean	

5391

letters

A form of written communication
often used for the transfer of
instruction, information and advice
or important news.

Letters of encouragement or exhortation

Est 9:30; 2Th 2:15; Heb 13:22 See also
2Ch 2:11; 21:12; Isa 39:1; Jer 29:1;
Ac 15:23–31; 1Co 5:9; 2Co 10:9–11;
Col 4:16; 1Th 5:27; 2Pe 3:1

Malicious, threatening or devious letters

2Sa 11:14–15; 2Th 2:1–2 See also
1Ki 21:8; 2Ki 19:14 pp Isa 37:14;
2Ch 32:17; Ezr 4:7; Ne 6:5,19; Ac 9:1–2;
22:5

Letters of authorisation or identification

Ezr 7:11; 1Co 16:3 See also 2Ki 5:5–6;
Ne 2:7–9; Ac 23:25,33–34; 2Co 3:1

Affairs of state conducted by letter

Est 1:22 See also 2Ki 10:1–3,6–7;
Ezr 5:6–7

Letters as invitations to worship

2Ch 30:1,6; Est 9:20,26,29

Letters attributed to specific authors

Paul Ro 1:1; 1Co 1:1 with Sosthenes
With Timothy: 2Co 1:1; Php 1:1;
Col 1:1; Phm 1
Gal 1:1; Eph 1:1
With Silas and Timothy: 1Th 1:1; 2Th 1:1
1Ti 1:1; 2Ti 1:1; Tit 1:1; 2Pe 3:15–16

James Jas 1:1

Peter 1Pe 1:1; 2Pe 1:1

Jude Jude 1

Jesus Christ Rev 2:1,8,12,18; 3:1,7,14

Letters written by a secretary
Ro 16:22; 1Pe 5:12

Letters of the alphabet
The letter of the law Mt 5:18

Paul writing in large letters Gal 6:11

See also

5263 communication	5408 messenger
5352 inscriptions	5426 news
5355 invitations	5439 pen
5381 law, letter &	5514 scribes
spirit	5519 secretary
	5638 writing

5392

linen

Fine cloth woven from flax used in clothing and curtains. It was also used in burials.

People dressed in linen
Linen clothing Jdg 14:12–13 *See also* Jer 13:1; Hos 2:5,9; Mk 14:51

It expressed prosperity Ge 41:42 *See also* Est 8:15; Isa 3:23; Eze 16:10,13; Lk 16:19; Rev 18:16; 19:8

It was worn by priests Lev 16:23 *See also* Ex 28:39,42; Lev 6:10; 16:4,32; 1Sa 2:18; 22:18; 2Sa 6:14; 1Ch 15:27; 2Ch 5:12; Eze 44:17–18

It was worn by angelic visitors
Rev 15:6 *See also* Eze 9:2–3,11; 10:2,6–7; 40:3; Da 10:5; 12:6–7; Rev 19:8,14

Linen as an offering
Ex 25:3–4; 35:5–6,23

Linen used to make things
In the tabernacle Ex 26:1 *See also* Ex 26:31,36; 27:9,16,18; 28:5,8,15; 38:9,16,18

Other products Pr 31:22 *See also* Est 1:6; Pr 7:16; Eze 27:7

People skilled in working with linen
1Ch 4:21 *See also* Ex 35:25,35; 36:8,35,37; 38:23; 39:2,5,8,24,27–29; 2Ch 2:13–14; 3:14; Isa 19:9

Regulations for wearing linen
Dt 22:11

Linen as merchandise
Eze 27:16 *See also* Pr 31:24; Rev 18:12

Contaminated linen
Lev 13:47–48,52,59

Linen used as grave clothes
Mt 27:59 pp Mk 15:46 pp Lk 23:53 pp Jn 19:40 *See also* Lk 24:12; Jn 11:44; 20:5–7

See also

4444 flax	5587 trade
5145 clothing	7412 priesthood
5241 burial	7459 tabernacle, in
5551 spinning &	OT
weaving	

5393

literacy

Literacy in the OT
2Ki 19:14 *See also* 2Ki 5:7; 23:2; Ne 8:2; Jer 29:29; 51:61

Literacy in the NT
Lk 4:16; Ac 8:28; Rev 1:3 *See also* Ac 13:15; 2Co 1:13; Eph 3:4; Col 4:16; 1Th 5:27; 1Ti 4:13

The use of secretaries for reading and writing
2Ki 22:8–10; Ezr 4:18,23; Est 6:1; Jer 36:4; Ro 16:22

Examples of literacy in Scripture
Ne 9:38; Jn 8:8 *See also* Dt 31:24–26; Jos 18:9; 1Ch 28:19; Lk 1:63; Jn 19:20; Ac 15:27

Examples of illiteracy in Scripture
Isa 29:12

See also

5175 reading	5515 scroll
5232 book	5519 secretary
5439 pen	5638 writing
5514 scribes	

5394

lordship

The exercise of power and authority. Lordship belongs to God by nature but may be delegated to human beings. The lordship of Jesus Christ over humanity rests upon his divine nature.

5395
lordship, human and divine

Scripture recognises that human beings exercise authority in various capacities and ways. However, it insists that all human authority derives ultimately from God himself.

Human lordship within society
Lk 12:42

The lordship of masters over their servants Ps 123:2; Mt 18:25; 25:19; Lk 12:36; 16:3; Eph 6:5,9; Col 3:22

The lordship of owners over their possessions Jdg 19:23; Mk 12:9 pp Mt 21:40 pp Lk 20:15; Lk 19:33; Gal 4:1

The use of Lord (NIV "Sir") as a title of respect Mt 27:63; Lk 13:8; Jn 12:21; 20:15; Ac 16:30; 1Pe 3:6

Human lordship within the church
Mk 10:42–45 pp Mt 20:25–28 pp Lk 22:25–27

Christian lordship as a pastoral responsibility 1Pe 5:2–3

The lordship of God
"Lord" as a title for God Ex 3:14–15 *In the NIV, "Lord" indicates a person with*
authority (this can be used of God) and "Lord" indicates Yahweh, the special Israelite name for God, revealed here to Moses.
In the OT "Lord" is by far the most frequently used word for God (over 6,500 times): Ex 6:3,6; Isa 6:1–5; 45:5–8,18; Hos 2:20
Lk 1:32; 2:9; Rev 11:15; 16:7

God is Lord of heaven and earth
Ps 135:5–6 ; Mt 11:25 pp Lk 10:21 *See also* Ps 2:2–4; 57:11; 97:9; Da 2:47; Ac 17:24; 1Ti 6:15

The revelation of the lordship of God
The word of the Lord is the authoritative revelation of God's lordship Eze 3:11; 1Pe 1:25 *See also* Isa 40:8; 1:2; 45:19; Jer 1:2,9; Eze 1:3; 2:4
God revealed as having the prerogative to avenge: Ro 12:19; Dt 32:35
God revealed as the God and Father of his people: 2Co 6:16–18; Lev 26:12; Isa 52:11; Eze 20:34,41; 2Sa 7:14; Jas 5:10
In Acts "the word of the Lord" refers to the gospel: Ac 8:25; 13:49; 15:36; 16:32; 19:10,20

God's lordship will be revealed to all on the day of the Lord Isa 2:11–12,17; Zep 1:14–18 *See also* Isa 13:6,9–11; Joel 2:1–2; Am 5:18–20; 1Co 5:5; 1Th 5:2; 2Th 2:2; 2Pe 3:10
Believers and the day of the Lord Jesus Christ: 1Co 1:8; 2Co 1:14

See also

1130 God,	1439 revelation
sovereignty	1610 Scripture
1205 God, titles of	5215 authority
1230 God, the Lord	5457 power, human
1235 God, the Lord	7734 leaders,
1310 God as judge	spiritual
1427 prophecy	9220 day of the Lord

5396
lordship, of Jesus Christ

Jesus Christ has authority and dominion over the church and the world on account of his divine status, which was publicly demonstrated through his resurrection from the dead and exaltation to the right hand of God.

Lord as a title for Jesus Christ
Ro 10:9 *In view of the OT background to the word "Lord" it is clear that this confession was not just of Jesus Christ's authority but also of his divinity;* 2Co 4:5 *See also* Mk 2:28 pp Mt 12:8 pp Lk 6:5; Jn 13:13; 20:28; Ac 9:17; 1Co 8:6; 12:3; Eph 4:5

Jesus Christ is the Lord of the church
Col 1:18 *See also* Ro 14:8; 1Co 5:4–5; 2Co 10:8; 13:10; Eph 1:22; Col 2:6

Jesus Christ is Lord over all
Mt 28:18; 1Pe 3:21–22 *See also* Ac 10:36; 1Co 15:24–25; Eph 1:10; Col 2:10

The lordship of Jesus Christ is grounded in his resurrection from the dead
Ac 2:36; Ro 14:9 *See also* Jn 13:3; Ro 1:4; Eph 1:20–22; Php 2:6–11; Heb 1:3–4

The exaltation of Jesus Christ to God's right hand Heb 1:13 *See also* Ps 110:1; Mk 12:36 pp Mt 22:44 pp Lk 20:42–43; Mk 14:62 pp Mt 26:64 pp Lk 22:69; Ac 2:33–35; 1Co 15:25; Eph 1:20; Col 3:1; Heb 1:3; 8:1; 10:12–13; 12:2

The coming of the Lord Jesus Christ will reveal his lordship
Php 3:20; Jas 5:7–8 *See also* 1Co 1:7; 4:5; Php 4:5; 1Th 3:13; 4:15–17; 2Th 2:1; 1Ti 6:14

Believers look forward to the Lord's coming 1Co 16:22 *See also* Rev 22:20

See also
2012 Christ, authority	2565 Christ, second coming
2212 Christ, head of church	8407 confession of Christ
2224 Christ, the Lord	8632 adoration
2312 Christ as king	
2336 Christ, exaltation	

5398

loss

In a fallen world, believers are always liable to lose those things that they hold precious. Whilst offering comfort, Scripture urges believers to set their hearts upon eternal treasures, which cannot be lost.

Loss is part of a fallen world
Mt 6:19

Loss of property
Through theft *See also* Job 1:15,17

Through accident Ge 31:39; Ex 21:33–34; 22:15; 2Ki 6:5

Through disaster Job 1:16; Ac 27:10,18–21

Through one's own fault Pr 6:10–11; 24:33–34; 13:11,18; Lk 15:13

Through the judgment of God Jer 17:4; Mal 1:4

Loss of family and friends
Through bereavement Ge 23:2; 37:34; 50:3; Nu 20:29; Dt 34:8; Ru 1:21 *Naomi had lost her husband and her two sons*; 2Sa 12:18–23; 2Ki 4:18–21; Eze 24:15–18; Lk 7:11–13

Through violence and disaster 2Sa 1:12; Job 1:18–19; Isa 47:8–9

Through alienation Job 19:13–22; Ps 31:11–12; 1Co 7:10–15

Losses in warfare
Ge 14:11–12; 1Sa 4:17; 23:5; 30:1–2; 1Ki 20:21; 2Ch 13:17; 36:17–20; Lk 21:24

Other kinds of loss
Health and strength Ps 31:9–10; 32:3–4; 102:3–5,11

Reputation Ps 102:8; 2Co 6:8

Dignity Job 30:15

Power Da 4:31; 7:26

Employment Lk 16:1–3

Time Ex 21:19; Ac 27:9

Spiritual loss
Of the ungodly Pr 6:12–15; 2Th 1:8–10

Of the worldly Mt 16:26 pp Mk 8:36 pp Lk 9:25 *See also* Lk 12:20–21; Heb 12:16–17

Of the disobedient Mt 7:26–27 pp Lk 6:49

Of the Jewish nation Jer 50:6; Mt 21:43

Of the lazy servant Mt 25:26–30

Of the careless worker 1Co 3:12–15

Of the apostate Heb 6:4–6

Voluntary loss
By Jesus Christ for the salvation of humanity Php 2:6–11

For Jesus Christ Mt 16:25 pp Mk 8:35 pp Lk 9:24; Php 3:7–9 *See also* Mt 10:39; 19:12; 1Co 4:9–13; Heb 10:34; 11:24–26

Losses made good
By restitution Ex 21:19,34

By recovery Lk 15:4,8,20

By God's goodness Job 42:10; Mt 19:29 pp Mk 10:29–30 pp Lk 18:29–30; Ro 11:12

God seeks the lost soul
Lk 19:10 *See also* Lk 15:4,8,20

Comfort in loss
God's comfort Ps 146:9; 2Co 1:3–4

The comfort of others Job 2:11; Jn 11:19; Ac 11:28–29; Jas 1:27

Treasures that cannot be lost
Mt 6:20 *See also* Lk 12:33; Jn 16:22; 1Pe 1:3–5

See also
1030 God, compassion	5795 bereavement
5264 compensation	5805 comfort
5295 destruction	6142 decay
5492 restitution	6510 salvation
5605 warfare	8808 riches
5703 inheritance	8848 worldliness

5399

luxury

Opulence or grandeur of lifestyle which may be associated with wealth or status, especially royalty. Scripture warns of the dangers of unnecessary displays of luxury but encourages the right kind of splendour to reflect the glory and honour due to God.

Examples of luxurious lifestyles
The opulence of Solomon's court 1Ki 10:21 pp 2Ch 9:20 *See also* 1Ki 4:22–24 *Solomon's daily provisions*; 1Ki 7:1 *Solomon's palace Solomon's throne*: 1Ki 10:18–20 pp 2Ch 9:17–19

Luxury enjoyed by other kings Lk 7:25 pp Mt 11:8 *See also* 1Sa 8:11–17 *Samuel warns Israel about what a king will demand of them*; 2Sa 7:2 *David*;

2Ch 32:27–29 *Hezekiah*; Est 1:4–7 *Xerxes*; Da 4:30 *Nebuchadnezzar*

Luxury enjoyed by the wealthy
Lk 16:19 *The rich man in Jesus Christ's parable. See also* Isa 3:18–23 *upper-class women of Zion*; Am 6:4–6 *the wealthy of Israel*

Luxury accompanying high status
Ge 41:41–43 *Mordecai*: Est 6:7–8; 8:15 Da 5:29 *Daniel*

Luxury enjoyed by a bride Ps 45:13–15 *See also* Isa 61:10; Jer 2:32; Rev 21:2

Luxury and poverty
Luxury at the expense of the poor Jas 5:4–5 *See also* Jer 22:13–14 *King Jehoiakim*; Eze 34:3 *the leaders of Israel*

Luxury brings responsibility to the poor 1Ti 6:18 *See also* Jer 22:15–16; Lk 16:20–21; 19:8; Ac 4:34–35

The perils of luxury
Luxury brings a false sense of security Lk 12:19 *See also* Job 31:24–25; Pr 11:28; 1Ti 6:17

Luxury distracts from God Dt 32:15 *also* Dt 8:13–14; Mt 13:22 pp Mk 4:19 pp Lk 8:14; Mt 19:21–24 pp Mk 10:21–23 pp Lk 18:21–24; 1Ti 6:10

Earthly luxury does not last Mt 6:19 *See also* Pr 23:5; 27:24; Isa 13:22 *The luxurious lifestyle of the wicked will be swept away by God's judgment*; Jas 5:1–3; Rev 18:7–9

The right attitude to luxury
Php 4:11–12 *See also* 1Sa 2:7; Job 1:21

The true source of beauty
1Pe 3:3–4 *See also* 1Ti 2:9–10

Luxury reflecting God's glory
Ex 25:3–9 pp Ex 35:5–9 *materials for the tabernacle*; Ex 28:4–5 *the priestly garments*; 1Ki 6:14–35 pp 2Ch 3:4–14 *the splendour of Solomon's temple*; Mk 13:1 pp Lk 21:5 *the magnificence of Herod's temple*; Rev 21:15–21 *the glory of the new Jerusalem*

See also
4333 gold	7467 temple, Solomon's
5118 Solomon	8622 worship
5145 clothing	8778 materialism
5412 money	8808 riches
5446 poverty	8821 self-indulgence
5856 extravagance	

5400

lyre

The lyre used in Israelite worship
In joyful religious celebrations 2Sa 6:2–5 pp 1Ch 13:6–8 *See also* 1Sa 10:5; 1Ch 15:25–28; Ne 12:27

In temple worship 2Ch 5:12 *See also* 1Ki 10:12 pp 2Ch 9:11; 1Ch 15:16,20; 16:5–6; 25:1,6; 2Ch 29:25

In praising God Ps 71:22 *See also* Ps 33:1–3; 57:7–8; 81:1–2; 92:1–4; 108:1–2; 144:9; 150:3

The lyre used in pagan worship
Da 3:7 *See also* Da 3:5,10,15

The lyre in secular use
Isa 5:12

See also

5332 harp	5422 musicians
5420 music	8627 worship,
5421 musical	elements
instruments	8664 praise

5401

madness

A term used in two different senses. The OT suggests that God may occasionally inflict a state of insanity upon individuals as a punishment. The term may also be used of someone whose words or actions are difficult to understand or easy to reject, as with Jesus Christ's preaching and healing.

Madness as a punishment
Jer 25:15–16 *See also* Dt 28:28,32–34; Jer 50:35–38; 51:7; Da 4:28–37; Zec 12:4

Madness linked with folly
Ecc 7:25 *See also* Pr 26:18; Ecc 1:17; 2:12; 9:3; 10:13; 2Pe 2:16

Accusations of madness against God's servants
Jn 10:19–21 *See also* 2Ki 9:1–11; Jer 29:25–26; Hos 9:7–8; Mt 12:24 pp Mk 3:20–22 pp Lk 11:15; Ac 26:24–25; 2Co 5:13

David feigned madness to save his life
Ps 34:1 Title *See also* 1Sa 21:10–15

See also

1025 God, anger of	5482 punishment
2351 Christ, miracles	6230 rejection
4130 demons	8756 folly, examples
5086 David, rise of	

5402

market

The market was a central feature of life in biblical times. Some of the biblical terms for redemption are drawn from the market-place.

Ancient market-places
1Ki 20:34 *Ahab's treaty with Ben-Hadad suggests that by the 9th century B.C. there was a highly developed system of international trade.*
International trade in Tyre: Isa 23:3; Eze 27:24

The market as a place of commerce
Methods of trading
Cash: Ge 23:10–18; Jn 2:14–16
Bartering: Ge 47:17; Hos 3:2

Sealing transactions Ru 4:7 *with a sandal;* Jer 32:11–12 *by signature*

Other activities in the market-place
It was where children played
Mt 11:16–17 pp Lk 7:32

It was where labourers waited for hire
Mt 20:3

It was where meat was sold 1Co 10:25
Some of this meat had come from pagan sacrifices.

It was where magistrates were present
Ac 16:19

God's work in the market-place
Jesus Christ healed the sick Mk 6:56

Paul preached Ac 17:16–17

Sins in the market-place
Greed, dishonesty and materialism
Hos 12:7; Am 8:5; Mic 6:11

The hypocrisy of the Pharisees Mt 23:7
pp Mk 12:38 pp Lk 20:46; Mk 7:4 *the problem was ritual defilement;* Lk 11:43

Rough crowds Ac 16:22; 17:5

The temple courts become a market
Jn 2:14–16 pp Mt 21:12–13 pp Mk 11:15–17 pp Lk 19:45–46

Markets will be destroyed in judgment
Zep 1:11; Rev 18:11–13

Biblical terms for redemption are drawn from market language
In the gospel call Pr 8:3–5 *The city gates were often places for business deals;* Isa 1:18; 55:1,2; Mt 13:45–46

God's people have been bought
Ac 20:28 *See also* Ex 15:16; Ps 74:2; 1Co 6:20; 7:23; 2Pe 2:1; Rev 5:9; 14:4

God's people have been redeemed
Gal 4:4–5 *The Greek word "exagorazo" means "to buy" and was used, for example, of the buying of slaves. See also* Gal 3:13–14; Rev 14:3 *The Greek "agorazo", translated here as "redeemed", may also be translated as "bought". Elsewhere (e.g., Tit 2:14; 1Pe 1:18), "lutro" meaning "to release" is used, conveying a similar idea.*

Redeeming the time
The Greek "exagorazo" here translated as "make the most of": Eph 5:16; Col 4:5

See also

1315 God as	5587 trade
redeemer	6720 redemption
5242 buying &	7140 people of God
selling	7754 preaching
5407 merchants	

5403

masons

Building projects on which masons were employed
David's palace 2Sa 5:11 pp 1Ch 14:1

Solomon's palace 1Ki 7:9–12

The temple 1Ki 6:7; 1Ch 22:14–15 *See also* 1Ki 5:15–18 pp 2Ch 2:2; 2Ch 2:18

The repair of the temple 2Ki 12:11–12 pp 2Ch 24:12; 2Ki 22:5–6 pp 2Ch 34:11

The rebuilding of the temple Ezr 3:7

Herod's temple Mk 13:1–2

The work of masons
Skilled work 2Ch 2:13–14

Dressed stone was superior Isa 9:10
The arrogant boast of the inhabitants of Samaria.

Dangerous work Ecc 10:9

Masons could make mistakes
Ps 118:22 *See also* Mt 21:42 pp Mk 12:10 pp Lk 20:17 *Jesus Christ interprets the saying as referring to his rejection by the Jews;* Ac 4:11; 1Pe 2:7

God is described as a mason
1Pe 2:4–6 *See also* Job 38:6; Isa 28:16

See also

4366 stones	5272 craftsmen
5207 architecture	5516 sculpture
5239 bricks	7467 temple,
5240 building	Solomon's
5269 cornerstone	

5404

masters

Those who obtain work from others, whether in the capacity of unpaid service or paid employment. Scripture sets out both the obligations and rights of masters in relation to those who work for them.

Masters have obligations to their servants
To deal fairly with them Job 31:13–14 *See also* 2Ki 22:7; Job 31:38–40; Mt 10:10–11 pp Lk 10:7; 1Ti 5:18

To be generous Dt 15:12–15,18 *See also* Phm 12–16

To make provision for rest and worship
Dt 5:12–15 pp Ex 20:8–11 *See also* Ex 12:43–44; Dt 16:11–16

Not to defraud them Lev 19:13 *Day labourers were paid in the evening (see Mt 20:8). Delaying payment could cause great hardship to a poor man. See also* Dt 24:15; Mal 3:5; Jas 5:4

Not to exploit them Dt 24:14 *See also* Ge 31:7,41; Isa 58:3; Jer 22:13; Ac 16:16,19

Not to neglect them Dt 12:19 *See also* Dt 14:27

Not to oppress them Eph 6:9 *See also* Ge 16:6; Ex 1:11–14; 21:20–21,26–27; Lev 25:39–55; 1Ki 12:4,10–14; Isa 30:12–13

God is the heavenly Master over earthly masters
Col 4:1 *See also* Eph 6:9; Mt 25:14–30 pp Lk 19:12–26

Blessings promised to good masters
Pr 19:17 *See also* Dt 15:10; Pr 28:27

Examples of good and bad masters
Good masters Ge 18:19 *Abraham;* Job 31:13–15 *Job;* Lk 7:2 *a Roman centurion*

Bad masters Ge 16:6 *Sarah;* Ge 31:7 *Laban;* Ge 39:7–20 *Potiphar's wife*

See also

5056 rest	5972 unkindness
5347 injustice	7446 slavery
5359 justice	8260 generosity
5522 servants, work	8291 kindness
conditions	8783 neglect
5823 cruelty	8790 oppression

5405

medicine

The means that God has given for the cure of physical troubles. Medicine often symbolises the application of the gospel of God's grace in Jesus Christ for the healing of moral and spiritual ills.

Preventative medicine
A cheerful disposition Pr 17:22

Disinfection Lev 14:41; 15:5

Salt Eze 16:4

Physical exercise 1Ti 4:8

Curative medicine
Balm Jer 51:8 *An example of medicine used as a picture of the gospel. The nation had the cure for its ills in the mercy of God if only it would repent and turn to him. See also* Jer 8:22; 46:11

Leaves Eze 47:12 *See also* Rev 22:2

Mud Jn 9:6 *The connection between the medium and the cure is not always clear. For example, the use of mud, spittle, oil and water appears sometimes to be more symbolic than practical.*

Oil Mk 6:13; Lk 10:34; Jas 5:14

A poultice 2Ki 20:7 *See also* Isa 38:21

Spittle Mk 7:33

Water Lev 15:5; 2Ki 5:10; Jn 9:7

Wine 1Ti 5:23 *See also* Lk 10:34

Eye salve Rev 3:18

Music
The music was intended to cure moods of depression in Saul's case, and extreme agitation in Elisha: 1Sa 16:23; 18:10; 2Ki 3:14–15

Spiritual surgery Mt 5:27–30; Ro 8:13

Soothing medicine
Myrrh Mk 15:23

Oil *See also* Isa 1:6

Wine Pr 31:6; Mt 27:48; Lk 23:36

Medicine cannot cure everything
Dt 28:27; Jer 17:9; 30:12–13; 46:11; Mk 5:25–26

Application of the gospel as medicine
Mt 11:28 *See also* Lk 5:31–32

Resurrection as the ultimate medicine for all ills
1Co 15:42–44 *See also* Php 3:20–21

See also

1415 miracles	5297 disease
4408 balm	5298 doctors
4488 oil	5333 healing
4490 ointment	5334 health
4544 wine	7342 cleanliness
5285 cures	

5406

mercenaries

Soldiers who offers their services for money, irrespective of the nationality of the army in question.

Mercenaries in the Egyptian army
Jer 46:20–21 *These mercenaries were drawn from Cush to the south of Egypt, Put to the west of Egypt and Lydia in north Africa.*

Mercenaries in the Ammonite army
2Sa 10:6 pp 1Ch 19:7

Mercenaries hired by Jehoiada the priest
2Ki 11:4,19 *The Carites were from Caria in south-west Asia Minor.*

Mercenaries in the army of Judah
2Ch 25:6

Fear of mercenary attack
2Ki 7:6–7

See also

5208 armies	5544 soldiers
5337 hiring	

5407

merchants

Traders who bought and sold goods and articles of value, often transporting their wares from one country to another according to the demands in different localities.

Some merchants transported their goods by caravan
Ge 37:25–28 *See also* Job 6:15–21

Some merchants traded by sea
Pr 31:14 *See also* 1Ki 9:26–28 pp 2Ch 8:17–18; 1Ki 10:11–12 pp 2Ch 9:10–11; 1Ki 22:48 pp 2Ch 20:35–37; Ps 107:23; Isa 23:2–3; Eze 27:25

Merchants often lived close to one another
Zep 1:11 *See also* Ne 3:31–32; Eze 17:4

Merchants set the standards for weights and measures
Ge 23:16 *See also* Hos 12:7; Am 8:4–6

Ordinary citizens sold goods to merchants
Pr 31:24 *See also* Ge 37:28; Pr 31:18–19

Merchants were credited with wisdom and shrewdness
Mt 13:44–46

Goods traded by merchants
Rev 18:11–13 *See also* SS 3:6; Eze 27:12–24

Merchants flourished during Solomon's reign
1Ki 10:14–15 pp 2Ch 9:13–14 *See also* 1Ki 10:21–22 pp 2Ch 9:20–21; 1Ki 10:26–29 pp 2Ch 1:14–17

Foreign merchants in Jerusalem
Ne 13:15–22

Cities famed for their merchants
Tyre Eze 27:1–36

Tarshish Eze 38:13; Jnh 1:3

Babylon the Great Rev 18:2–24

See also

5242 buying &	5587 trade
selling	5613 weights &
5402 market	measures
5517 seafaring	5948 shrewdness

5408

messenger

An individual whose task is to convey information from one person to another. The word "angel" derives from the Greek word for "messenger". The word "apostle" comes from the Greek work meaning "sent".

Messengers conveying information from one person to another
Pr 13:17; 25:13 *There are many references to messengers in this sense. See also* Ge 32:3; Nu 20:14; Jdg 6:35; 1Sa 23:27; 2Sa 11:22; 15:13; 1Ki 19:2; 22:13; 2Ki 1:3 *Elijah intercepts the messengers of Ahaziah;* 2Ki 5:10 *Elisha sent a messenger with instructions for Naaman's healing;* 2Ki 6:32; Job 1:14; Isa 37:9 *Sennacherib sends messengers to Hezekiah;* Jer 51:31; Da 3:4; Php 2:25

Messengers from God to humanity
The OT prophets Nu 16:28; Isa 6:8 *See also* Dt 18:18; Jdg 6:8; 2Sa 12:25; 1Ki 16:7; 2Ki 17:13; Ecc 5:6; Isa 41:27; 42:19; 48:16; Jer 1:5 *the call of Jeremiah Jeremiah faithfully repeated the* LORD's *message to no avail:* Jer 7:25; 25:4; 26:4–6; 44:4
Eze 38:17; Hab 2:2; Hag 1:13; Zec 4:9; Mal 1:1 *"Malachi" means "my messenger".*

The priests Mal 2:7

John the Baptist Mt 11:10 pp Lk 7:27 pp Mk 1:2; Jn 1:6; Mal 3:1

Apostles and teachers Gal 1:1 *See also* Mt 23:34; Mk 3:14; Lk 11:49; Ro 1:5; 11:13; 1Ti 1:1; 2:7; 2Ti 1:11

Angelic messengers Da 4:13; Lk 1:19 *See also* Jdg 6:11–12; 1Ki 19:5; Zec 1:14; 3:6
Angels appeared to Joseph in dreams: Mt 1:20; 2:13,19
Lk 1:11,28; 2:9–10 *The shepherds at Bethlehem heard God's message through an angel;* Ac 8:26; 10:3 *Cornelius receives instructions from an angel;* Gal 1:8; Heb 2:2–3; Rev 1:1; 22:16

Jesus Christ as God's ultimate messenger
Jn 7:28–29 *See also* Jn 8:42; 9:4; 10:36; 13:16; 17:8; Heb 1:1–2; 3:1

A messenger of Satan
2Co 12:7

See also

2354 Christ, mission	5335 herald
4110 angels	7706 apostles
5098 John the	7754 preaching
Baptist	7772 prophets

5409

metaphor

An image which suggests similarities between two different ideas, without implying that they are identical. Scripture uses metaphors extensively, as a way of illustrating aspects of its teaching.

Examples of metaphors for God
Father Dt 32:6; Isa 64:8; Mal 2:10; Eph 4:6

Rock Dt 32:4 *See also* 1Sa 2:2; 2Sa 22:2; Ps 62:2; 78:35

Shepherd Ps 23:1 *See also* Ps 28:9; 80:1; Eze 34:11–16

Examples of metaphors for Jesus Christ
Bread of life Jn 6:35–51

Good shepherd Jn 10:11,14

Light of the world Jn 8:12; 9:5

Examples of metaphors for the Holy Spirit
Counsellor Jn 14:16,26; 15:26; 16:7

Breath Ge 2:7; Job 32:8; 33:4; 34:14

Wind Jn 3:8

Examples of metaphors for the church
Bride Rev 19:7; 21:2–9; 22:17

Household of God Eph 2:19; 1Ti 3:15

Body of Christ Ro 12:4; 1Co 12:12–27; Eph 1:22–23; Col 1:24

See also

1040 God, fatherhood	2203 Christ, titles of
1215 God, feminine descriptions	2315 Christ as Lamb
	2330 Christ as shepherd
1220 God as shepherd	3110 Holy Spirit, titles of
1240 God, the Rock	5438 parables
1670 symbols	7020 church, the

5410

midwife

Midwives assist at childbirth
Ge 35:17 *See also* Ge 38:28

Midwives ordered to kill all newborn boys
Ex 1:15–21

See also

5428 nurse	5663 childbirth
5652 babies	

5411

mirror

Actual mirrors
Job 37:18 *Mirrored glass was unknown in ancient times. Metal mirrors gave an adequate though imperfect reflection. See also* Ex 38:8; Isa 3:23

Mirrors illustrating human attitudes
Jas 1:23–25 *See also* Pr 27:19; 2Co 3:18

Mirrors illustrating an imperfect human view of God
1Co 13:12

See also

4293 water	4330 glass
4303 metals	6199 imperfection
4312 bronze	8474 seeing God

5412

money

Scripture stresses the positive and negative aspects of money, making it clear that the pursuit or love of money can easily lead to spiritual decay.

5413
money, attitudes to

Money can be a blessing or a snare according to one's attitude.

Money as a gift from God
Dt 8:18 *See also* 1Sa 2:7; 1Ki 3:13; Pr 8:18–21; 1Ti 6:17

The dangers of money
Being ruled by money Mt 6:24 pp Lk 16:13 *See also* Eph 5:5

Loving money 1Ti 6:10 *See also* Ecc 5:10; Lk 8:14; 16:14; 1Ti 3:3,8; 2Ti 3:2; Tit 1:7; Heb 13:5; 1Pe 5:2

Trusting in money 1Ti 6:17 *See also* Dt 8:12–14; Job 31:24; Ps 52:7; 62:10; Pr 11:4,28; 27:24; Isa 10:3; Jer 48:7; Lk 12:16–21 *the parable of the rich fool*; Jas 1:11; 5:1–3; Rev 18:14

Boasting in money Ps 49:5–6 *See also* Jer 9:23–24; Hos 12:8; Jas 4:13–16

Examples of those led astray by the love of money
Balaam: Dt 23:4; 2Pe 2:15
Jos 7:20–21 *Achan;* 2Ki 5:19–27 *Gehazi;* Mt 19:22–23 pp Mk 10:22–23 pp Lk 18:23–24 *the rich young ruler;* Mt 26:14–15 pp Mk 14:10–11 pp Lk 22:4–5 *Judas Iscariot*

Gifts and qualities that are better than money
Redemption Ps 49:7–9 *See also* Isa 52:3; Mt 16:26 pp Mk 8:37 pp Lk 9:25; 1Pe 1:18–19

Wisdom Pr 4:7 *See also* Ps 49:20; Pr 3:13–16; 8:10–11; 16:16; 17:16; 20:15

A good reputation Pr 22:1

A good wife Pr 31:10

Healing Ac 3:6

Spiritual power Ac 8:19–20

Spiritual riches Isa 55:1 *See also* Rev 3:18

See also

5311 extortion	8302 love, abuse of
5869 greed	8361 wisdom
6133 coveting	8701 affluence
6714 ransom	8768 idolatry
7734 leaders, spiritual	8778 materialism
	8808 riches
8030 trust	8848 worldliness

5414
money, stewardship of

The righteous handling of money is an important practical test of godliness.

Money must be obtained honestly
Not by theft Ex 20:15 pp Dt 5:19 *See also* Pr 10:2; 19:26; Mk 10:19

Not by fraudulent practices Lev 19:13 *See also* Pr 11:1; 13:11; 20:10; Eze 28:18

Not by usury Ex 22:25 *See also* Ps 15:5; Pr 28:8

Not at the expense of justice Ex 23:8 *See also* Pr 15:27; 16:8; Jer 17:11

Not by extortion Lk 3:13 *See also* Eze 22:12

Not by oppression Jas 5:4 *See also* Pr 22:16; Eze 18:7–8; Am 5:11; Mal 3:5

Not at the expense of health Pr 23:4

Not at the expense of witness Ge 14:22–23; 3Jn 7

Not at the expense of spiritual well-being Mt 16:26 pp Mk 8:36 pp Lk 9:25; Lk 12:16–21; 1Ti 6:9

By work, trade, investment or inheritance 2Th 3:12 *See also* Ge 15:2; 34:21; Pr 13:11,22; 14:23; 19:14; Mt 25:27 pp Lk 19:23

Money must be cared for diligently
Personal money Pr 27:23–24

Money held on trust 2Ki 22:4–7; Mt 25:14–27; Lk 16:10–12; 1Co 4:2

Money must be used in a God-honouring way
For the support of the family 1Ti 5:8 *See also* 1Ti 5:16

For benefiting the poor, especially God's people Gal 6:10 *See also* Pr 19:17; 28:27; Mt 6:3–4; Lk 12:33; Jn 13:29; Ac 2:45; Ro 15:26; Gal 2:10; 1Ti 6:18

For the work of God's kingdom Gal 6:6 *See also* Pr 3:9–10; Mal 3:10; Lk 8:3; 16:9; Php 4:14–19; 1Ti 5:17–18

Examples of godly people who have used their money well
Those who were wealthy but godly Ge 13:2; 26:14; 30:43; 2Sa 19:32; 2Ch 9:22; Job 1:3; Mt 27:57; Ac 4:34–36

Those who had little but gave much Mk 12:41–44 pp Lk 21:1–4; 2Co 8:1–4

See also

5446 poverty	7784 shepherd
5475 property	7939 ministry
5556 stewardship	8260 generosity
5628 work	8434 giving
5703 inheritance	8488 tithing

5415
money, uses of

Monetary transactions have taken place from the earliest biblical times. Originally precious metals were weighed out; coins were introduced later.

The first mention of money
Ge 17:12

The use of money
For the purchase and sale of land
Ge 23:14–15 See also Jer 32:9–10; Mt 27:7; Ac 4:34; 5:1–2; 7:16

For the purchase and sale of food
Ge 41:57; 42:5,35; 2Ki 7:16; Jn 6:5,7; Rev 6:6

For other merchandise Rev 18:11–13 See also Ge 37:25; Jas 4:13

For religious offerings Ex 30:11–16 See also Nu 3:44–48; Dt 12:4–6; 2Ki 22:4–6 pp 2Ch 34:9–11; Ezr 7:15–17

For gifts to the poor Mt 26:9 pp Mk 14:5 pp Jn 12:5 See also Ac 3:3

For wages Mt 20:2 See also Jas 5:4

For investment and moneylending
Mt 25:27 pp Lk 19:23 See also Ex 22:25; Ne 5:10–11; Lk 6:34–35

For provision for the future Ecc 7:12

For the settlement of disputes
Ex 21:8–11,35; 22:15

For taxes Mt 17:24 See also 1Ki 10:15; Ne 5:4; Mt 22:17–19 pp Mk 12:15 pp Lk 20:22–24

For tribute money 2Ki 15:19–20

For the purchase of slaves Lev 22:11

For bribery Est 3:9; Mt 28:12–13; Ac 24:26

Fortune-telling for money Mic 3:11; Ac 16:16

Blood money Mt 27:6

Money changers
Mt 21:12 pp Mk 11:15 pp Jn 2:14

See also
5233 borrowing	5389 lending
5242 buying &	5577 taxation
selling	5613 weights &
5260 coinage	measures
5274 credit	7446 slavery
5353 interest	

monotony

The sameness that arises through dull and wearisome routines, and which cause individuals to feel bored. Scripture often portrays monotony as a cause of sin, in that individuals, in seeking excitement, often fall into sinful practices.

Monotony can give rise to sin
Discontent in the desert Nu 11:4–6 See also Ex 16:2–3,35; Nu 14:33 The monotony of 40 years in the desert was a judgment on Israel's unbelief.

At Sinai impatience leads to idolatry
Ex 32:1 See also Ex 32:23; Ac 7:40

Situations which give rise to monotony
Desert Ps 107:4–5 See also Dt 1:19; Isa 40:30; Mk 1:12–13

Prison Ps 107:10 See also Jdg 16:21; Ps 66:11; Jer 38:6; Mt 4:12; Rev 2:10

Illness Ps 107:17–18 See also Lev 26:15–16; Job 30:16–17; Ps 6:3; Lk 13:11; Jn 5:5

Storm at sea Ps 107:25–26 See also Jnh 2:3; Ac 27:27

Darkness Ps 143:3 See also Ex 10:22; Ps 130:6; Mk 15:33; Lk 2:8

Work Ge 3:17–19 See also Job 7:2; Ecc 2:11; Gal 6:9; Rev 2:2–3

Siege 2Ki 6:25 See also 2Ki 25:2; Isa 36:12

Slavery Ex 2:23 See also Job 7:2; 1Ti 6:1; 1Pe 2:18

Sleeplessness Job 7:4 See also Est 6:1; Job 30:17; Ecc 5:12; Da 6:18; Heb 12:3

Monotony arising from difficult human relations
A nagging wife Pr 19:13 See also Pr 27:15

Unhelpful counsellors Job 6:6 This refers to the useless advice of Job's friends. See also Col 4:6 This, by contrast, is how the conversation of Christians is to be characterised.

See also
2575 Christ,	5537 sleeplessness
temptation	5628 work
5297 disease	7221 exodus, the

mourning

The expression of grief at a time of bereavement or repentance, often accompanied by weeping, tearing of clothes and wearing sackcloth.

Regulations for the mourning of priests after bereavement
Lev 21:1–4,10–11

Mourning of God's people after bereavement
Israel for Aaron Nu 20:29

Israel for Moses Dt 34:8

David for Saul and Jonathan
2Sa 1:11–12 See also 2Sa 1:17–27

David for Absalom 2Sa 18:33

Job for his children Job 1:20–21

Other examples See also Ge 37:34–35; 50:11; 2Sa 13:31; 14:2; 2Ch 35:23–25; Mt 2:18; Jn 11:31,33; Ac 8:2

Examples of heathen mourning after bereavement
Isa 15:2–3; Jer 47:5; 48:37; Eze 27:30–32

Mourning as an expression of repentance
Ex 33:4; Ezr 9:3–6

Mourning because of misfortune
2Sa 13:9; Job 2:12–13

The employment of professional mourners
Jer 9:17–18; Am 5:16; Mt 9:23 pp Mk 5:39 pp Lk 8:52

Mourning spoken of metaphorically
Jer 7:29 See also Isa 3:18–24; Eze 7:18; Joel 1:8; Am 8:10; Mic 1:16

As a sign of repentance for sin
Joel 2:12–13 See also Isa 22:12

See also
5198 weeping	5952 sorrow
5241 burial	6732 repentance
5320 funeral	6742 sackcloth &
5795 bereavement	ashes
5899 lament	9020 death

music

Music played a major role in the lives of people in biblical times. It was used in both sacred and secular activities and was most often associated with joy and celebration.

Music comes from God
God's presence inspires music
Ps 96:13 See also Ps 98:4

It is a gift of God Job 35:10

Music was closely associated with praise and worship
Ps 33:2 See also Jdg 5:3; Ne 12:27; Ps 27:6; 57:7; 81:1–2; 87:7; 92:3; 95:2; 98:4; 108:1; 144:9; 147:7; 149:3; 150:1–6; Eph 5:19–20; Col 3:16

Music was employed extensively in the tabernacle and the temple
1Ch 25:6–7 See also 1Ch 6:31–32; 25:1; 2Ch 5:12–14; 35:15; Ezr 2:65

Music and the psalms
Many psalms are dedicated to the "director of music" Ps 11:1 Title See also Ps 13:1 Title; 31:1 Title; 42:1 Title; 49:1 Title; 77:1 Title; 139:1 Title; Hab 3:19

The titles of some psalms probably give an indication of melody
Ps 9:1 Title See also Ps 22:1 Title; 45:1 Title; 56:1 Title; 57:1 Title; 58:1 Title; 59:1 Title; 60:1 Title; 69:1 Title; 75:1 Title; 80:1 Title

The titles of some psalms indicate specific musical accompaniment
Ps 4:1 Title See also Ps 5:1 Title; 6:1 Title; 54:1 Title; 55:1 Title; 61:1 Title; 67:1 Title; 76:1 Title; Hab 3:19

Uses of music
To celebrate victory 2Ch 20:27–28 See also Ex 15:1–21; Jdg 5:1–31; 1Sa 18:6–7; Isa 30:32

At times of celebration Ge 31:27 See also Job 21:12; Isa 16:10; La 5:14; Eze 26:13; Lk 15:25; Rev 18:22

At banquets
Isa 5:12 See also Am 6:4–6

As an expression of joy 1Sa 18:6–7 See also 2Sa 6:5; 1Ki 1:40; Job 21:12; Jas 5:13

For pleasure Ecc 2:8 See also 2Sa 19:35

For divine inspiration 2Ki 3:14–15; 1Sa 18:10

To relieve depression 1Sa 16:23 See also 1Sa 16:16–18

At times of mourning 2Sa 1:17–18 ;
Mt 9:23 *See also* Job 30:31; 35:10;
Jer 48:36

**Prophets sometimes prophesied
to musical accompaniment**
1Sa 10:5–6 *See also* 2Ki 3:14–19

**Lack of music is a sign of
judgment**
Isa 24:8 *See also* Rev 18:22

Music in pagan worship
Da 3:5 *See also* Da 3:7,10,15

Music played by prostitutes
Isa 23:16

The misuse of music
Ps 69:12 *See also* Ps 137:3; Da 3:4–7;
Am 5:23; 6:5

See also

5273 creativity	7960 singing
5421 musical	8283 joy
instruments	8627 worship,
5422 musicians	elements
5595 trumpet	8664 praise

5421

musical instruments

Scripture names a large number of
musical instruments, particularly in
the OT, reflecting the importance of
music in Israelite worship and
culture.

Wind instruments
Trumpets Ex 19:16; 20:18; Lev 25:9;
Jdg 3:27; 1Ki 1:39; Ps 150:3; Rev 8:7–13

Flutes Ge 4:21; Job 21:12; Ps 150:4;
Da 3:5–15; Mt 9:23; 11:17

Horns Ps 98:4–6 *The NIV translates
several different Hebrew words as "ram's
horn" or "horn", including "shophar" (Ps
81:3) which is translated elsewhere as
"trumpet". The horn was a very similar
instrument to the trumpet, being made
from the horn of an animal, usually a ram.
See also* Ex 19:13; 2Ch 15:14; Ps 81:3

Stringed instruments
Harps Ge 4:21; 1Sa 16:18; Job 30:31;
Ps 43:4; 81:2; 149:3; 150:3; Da 3:5–11;
Rev 5:8

Lyres Ps 33:2; 71:22; 81:2; 108:2; 144:9;
Da 3:5–10

**Several of the psalms were intended to
be sung to the accompaniment of
stringed instruments** Ps 4:1 Title *See
also* Ps 6:1 Title; 54:1 Title; 55:1 Title;
61:1 Title; 67:1 Title; 76:1 Title

Percussion instruments
Tambourines Ps 149:3; Isa 5:12 *See also*
Ge 31:27; Ex 15:20–21; Jdg 11:34;
1Sa 10:5; 18:6–7; 2Sa 6:5 pp 1Ch 13:8;
Job 21:12; Ps 68:24–25; 81:1–2; 150:4;
Isa 24:8; 30:32; Jer 31:4

Cymbals Ps 150:1–6; 1Co 13:1 *See also*
2Sa 6:5 pp 1Ch 13:8
*David's appointment of the Levites to
sound the cymbals in the temple worship:*
1Ch 15:16,19; 16:5,42; 25:1,6
1Ch 15:28; 2Ch 5:12–13; 29:25;
Ezr 3:10; Ne 12:27

Sistrums 2Sa 6:3–5

Babylonian instruments
Da 3:4–5 *See also* Da 3:7,10,15;
Rev 18:21–22

See also

4654 horn	5422 musicians
5314 flute	5595 trumpet
5332 harp	8627 worship,
5400 lyre	elements
5420 music	

5422

musicians

Players of musical instruments.
Levitical musicians played an
extensive role in Israelite worship.
Other musicians are also mentioned
in Scripture, in both sacred and
secular contexts.

**Levitical musicians in the
tabernacle**
Appointed by David 1Ch 6:31–47 *See
also* 1Ch 15:16–17; 25:1–5

Responsibilities 1Ch 15:19–21 *See also*
1Ch 15:16; 25:6–7

Allocation of duties 1Ch 25:8–31

Levitical musicians in the temple
2Ch 5:12–13 *See also* 1Ch 9:33;
2Ch 35:15

Other musicians
Jubal was the first musician
Ge 4:17–21

King David was a renowned musician
1Sa 16:15–18 *See also* 1Sa 16:23;
18:10–11; 19:9–10; 2Sa 6:5; 23:1

Unidentified musicians Ps 68:24–25
See also 2Ki 3:11–19; Ps 137:1–3;
Rev 18:21–22

See also

5420 music	7467 temple,
5421 musical	Solomon's
instruments	7960 singing
7459 tabernacle, in	8627 worship,
OT	elements

5423

myths

Stories that are made up and which
are contrary to right doctrine or holy
living.

Some prefer myths to truth
2Ti 4:3–4

**Myths are harmful to the body of
Christ**
1Ti 1:3–4 *See also* 1Ti 4:6–8

**Sound teaching by God's
servants dispels myths**
Tit 1:13–14 *See also* 1Ti 4:1–6;
Tit 1:9–11

See also

1462 truth, in NT	8750 false teachings
7230 genealogies	8766 heresies
7748 false religion	8829 superstition

5424

nationalism

A concern to preserve or proclaim
the distinctive features of a nation or
people.

**The recognition of different
national groups**
Ge 10:32 *Ge 10:32 is the summary
conclusion of the table of nations which
begins in Ge 10:1. See also* Ge 17:4–6;
19:36–38; Ex 3:8; 1Ki 9:20 pp 2Ch 8:7

**Israel was to be a special nation
set apart for God**
The choosing of the nation of Israel
Ex 19:5–6 *See also* Ge 12:1–3; Ex 33:13;
Dt 7:6–8; 14:2; 2Sa 7:23 pp 1Ch 17:21;
Ps 33:12; Ro 9:4–5

The mission of Israel to the nations
Ex 34:10 *See also* Dt 4:6

Examples of nationalism
Positive examples Ru 1:16–17 *See also*
Ex 8:23; 34:24; Dt 26:5; Isa 10:6

Negative examples Isa 1:4 *See also*
Nu 13:31–32; 24:14; 1Ki 22:4; Pr 14:34;
Isa 14:1–2; Jer 49:31; Eze 36:5; Joel 1:6;
3:2

**The people of God transcend all
national boundaries**
The church is God's holy nation
1Pe 2:9–10 *See also* Eph 2:19

People of all nations are included
Mt 8:11 *See also* Mt 28:19;
Ac 11:18,20–21; Rev 5:9; 7:9; 14:6

Christian unity is greater than
nationalism Gal 3:26–29 *See also*
Ro 9:6–8; Eph 2:11–13

See also

7020 church, the	7236 Israel, united
7030 unity	kingdom
7135 Israel, people of	7510 Gentiles
God	7515 anti-semitism
7140 people of God	

5425

net

Instruments of meshed string, used
for fishing or hunting. The term can
also be used in a symbolic manner,
to refer to the way in which people
are ensnared by sin or by their
enemies.

Nets used in fishing and hunting
Isa 51:20; Eze 47:10; Mt 4:18 *See also*
Pr 1:17; Isa 19:8; Eze 26:5; Mt 4:21
pp Mk 1:19; Mt 13:47; Mk 1:18;
Lk 5:2–4; Jn 21:6

Nets used metaphorically
To describe people being caught by
others Pr 29:5; Hab 1:15–17 *See also*
Job 18:8; Ps 9:15; 10:9; 25:15; 35:7;
57:6; 140:5; 141:10; Ecc 9:12; Eze 19:8;
Hos 5:1; Mic 7:2

To describe being caught by the Lord
Job 19:6; Hos 7:12; Lk 5:10 *See also*
La 1:13; Eze 12:13; 17:20; 32:3

Networks used in design
Ex 27:4–5; 1Ki 7:17; Jer 52:22

See also

4642 fish	5433 occupations
5342 hunting	5589 trap

5426

news

Information on significant or recent events conveyed through a variety of official or unofficial means. The ministry of Jesus Christ centred on the good news of the kingdom. The Greek word for "gospel" means "good news".

Political news reported by official and self-appointed messengers
1Sa 31:8–9 *See also* 2Sa 1:1–10; 15:13; 18:19–32; 2Ki 7:8–11

Personal news conveyed through friends, relatives and by letter
Col 4:7–9 *See also* Ge 29:11–13; Php 2:19–20

Divine news announced by angels
Lk 1:19 *See also* Ge 19:1; Lk 1:26–33; 2:8–12

The effect of good news
Pr 25:25 *See also* Ge 45:16; Pr 15:30; Na 3:18–19; Jn 4:51–53; 1Th 3:6–10

Reactions to bad news
Jer 49:23 *See also* 1Sa 4:12–22; 2Sa 4:10; Job 1:14–21; Jnh 3:1–10; Jn 11:1–6

The good news of Jesus Christ
Foretold Nu 24:17; Isa 7:14; 9:7; 11:2; 53:3–12; 61:1–3; Mic 5:2; Zec 9:9; 11:12–13

Announced and demonstrated by Jesus Christ Mt 4:23 *See also* Mt 11:5; Mk 1:15; Lk 4:17–19,43

Proclaimed by apostles and preachers Ac 14:21 *See also* Mk 16:15; Ro 10:14–15; 2Ti 1:11

Spread by word of mouth Ac 11:19–20 *See also* Mt 4:24

Receiving the good news Ac 8:12

Rejecting the good news Ro 10:16

See also

2375 kingdom of God	5391 letters
2420 gospel	5408 messenger
5048 opportunities & salvation	5510 rumours
5263 communication	7740 missionaries, call
5307 envoy	7754 preaching
5335 herald	8424 evangelism

5427

nomads

People who moved about from place to place, having no settled abode. They lived in tents and frequented desert places.

Examples of nomads
The patriarchs Ps 105:12–13; Heb 11:8–9 *See also* Ge 12:8;

13:3,15,18; 26:25; 31:25; 35:21; Dt 26:5; 1Ch 16:18–20

Israel during her desert wanderings
Nu 32:13 *See also* 1Ch 17:5–6 *The Tabernacle was designed as a place of worship during this nomadic existence.*

Other nomadic peoples Ge 4:20 *Jabal*; Jdg 4:17 *the Kenites The Midianites*: Jdg 6:3; Hab 3:7 *Kedar*: Ps 120:5; Jer 49:28–29; Eze 25:4 Isa 13:20 *Arabs*; Jer 35:1–11 *The Recabites retained their nomadic ways long after Israel had settled in the land of Canaan.*

Desert tracks followed by nomads
Jdg 8:11; Jer 3:2

The nomadic life as a spiritual symbol
1Pe 2:11 *See also* Heb 11:13–16; 1Pe 1:17

Jesus Christ as a nomad
Mt 8:20

See also

5076 Abraham, life of	7221 exodus, the
5244 camp	7459 tabernacle, in
5578 tents	OT
5590 travel	7530 foreigners

5428

nurse

A woman who breast-feeds an infant.

The child's mother as nurse
Ge 21:7 *See also* 1Ki 3:21

A servant as nurse
Ex 2:7 *See also* Ex 2:9

Often wet-nurses remained in the family after the child was weaned
Ge 24:56–59 *See also* Ge 35:8; 2Sa 4:4; 2Ki 11:2–3 pp 2Ch 22:11

Metaphorical use
Nu 11:12 *See also* Isa 66:9–13; La 4:3

See also

5140 breasts	5664 children
5520 servants	5718 mothers
5652 babies	8313 nurture

5429

oaths

Solemn, binding promises, the truth of which are affirmed by appeal to God as witness. God himself makes solemn oaths to individuals. Scripture makes clear that oaths should be made wisely and not be broken.

5430

oaths, human

Solemn, binding statements made in God's name. The OT forbids the making of oaths in the name of other gods and the NT suggests that it is best to refrain from making oaths.

Oaths are considered binding
Nu 30:2 *See also* Dt 23:21; Mt 23:16–22

Oaths to be taken only in God's name
Dt 6:13 *See also* Ps 24:3–4; Jer 12:16

False oaths forbidden
Lev 19:12 *See also* Ex 20:7 pp Dt 5:11; Lev 6:3–5; Zec 5:3–4

Examples of oaths
In bearing witness Ex 22:11; Nu 5:19; 1Ki 8:31

In showing allegiance 2Ki 11:4; Ecc 8:2; Jer 38:16; Eze 17:13

In covenants Ge 21:22–31; 26:26–31; 31:44–53; Jos 9:3–21

As a curse Jos 6:26; Mt 26:71–74 pp Mk 14:70–71

As assurance that a promise will be kept Ge 14:22–23 *See also* Ge 24:3–9,37–41; 47:28–31; 50:24–25; Ps 132:1–5

Unwise or thoughtless oaths
Ge 25:33 *See also* Lev 5:4; Mt 14:6–7 pp Mk 6:22–23

Advice against taking oaths
Jas 5:12 *See also* Mt 5:33–37

See also

1345 covenant	5741 vows
5440 perjury	8650 hands, lifting
5444 pledges	up

5431
oaths, divine

Solemn promises made by God to individuals and their offspring. He swears by himself because there is nothing greater to swear by.

God swears by himself
Heb 6:13–14 *See also* Ge 22:16; Ps 89:35; Isa 45:23; 62:8; Heb 6:16–18

Examples of God's promises by oath
To Abraham Ge 22:15–18 *See also* Ge 24:7; 26:3; Ex 33:1; Dt 6:18; 7:8; Lk 1:72–73

To David Ps 132:11–12 *See also* 2Sa 3:9–10; 7:11–16; Ps 89:3–4,35–37; Ac 2:30

To his anointed one Ps 110:4 *See also* Heb 7:17–28

To the generation in the wilderness Dt 1:34–36 *See also* Nu 14:20–35; Heb 3:10–11; Ps 95:10–11

To Israel Dt 29:12–15 *See also* Eze 16:8

See also

2306 Christ, high priest	5466 promises
5100 Melchizedek	7915 confirmation
	9411 heaven

5433

occupations

Professions, trades and means of employment. A great variety of occupations, both secular and religious, are mentioned in Scripture.

Builders
Ps 127:1 *See also* Ps 118:22; Mt 21:42

pp Mk 12:10 pp Lk 20:17; Ac 4:11;
1Co 3:10–15; Heb 3:3; 1Pe 2:7

Embroiderers
Ex 38:23

Weavers and spinners
Ex 39:22; Pr 31:19

Stonemasons
2Ki 12:12; 22:5–6

Carpenters and woodworkers
2Ki 22:5–6; Mt 13:55

Musicians
1Ch 15:19–22; 16:42; Hab 3:19

Tanners
Ac 9:43 See also Ac 10:6,32

Linen workers
1Ch 4:21

Washermen
Isa 7:3 See also 2Ki 18:17 pp Isa 36:2

Blacksmiths
Isa 44:12 See also 1Sa 13:19–21;
Isa 54:16

Merchants
Ne 3:31–32 See also
1Ki 10:14–15,28–29 pp 2Ch 1:16–17;
Ne 13:19–21; Hos 12:7; Mt 13:45–46

Tentmakers
Ac 18:1–3

Soldiers
2Ki 5:1 See also Mt 8:5–13
pp Lk 7:1–10; Lk 3:14; Ac 10:1–8;
2Ti 2:3–4

Priests
Ge 46:20 See also Ge 14:18; Ex 18:1;
28:3; 40:13; Jdg 17:12–13; 1Sa 2:27–29;
1Ki 4:2–5; Mal 2:7; Mt 8:4

Levites and temple servants
Nu 1:50–51 See also 1Ch 15:16,22; 16:4;
Ezr 2:70; Ne 12:44–47; Lk 10:32

Watchmen
Ps 127:1 See also 2Sa 18:24–27;
SS 3:1–4; 5:7; Isa 21:11–12; 56:10;
Eze 33:2–6; Jn 10:1–3

Shepherds
Ge 47:3 See also Ge 29:1–10; 46:31–34;
Ex 2:16–17; 1Sa 17:20; 21:7; Am 1:1;
Lk 2:8–18; Jn 10:2–4

Farmers
Zec 13:4–5 See also Isa 28:24–25;
Jer 31:5; Joel 1:11; Mt 13:3–9
pp Mk 4:3–8 pp Lk 8:5–8; Mt 21:33
pp Mk 12:1 pp Lk 20:9; 2Ti 2:6; Jas 5:7

Fishermen
Mt 13:48 See also Isa 19:8; Jer 16:16;
Eze 47:10; Mt 4:18–19 pp Mk 1:16–17;
Lk 5:2

Doctors
Mk 5:25–26 pp Lk 8:43 See also Mt 9:12
pp Mk 2:17 pp Lk 5:31; Col 4:14

Lawyers
Ac 24:1 See also Tit 3:13

See also
4345 metalworkers　　5544 soldiers
4406 agriculture　　　5576 tax collectors
5240 building　　　　　5611 watchman
5272 craftsmen　　　　7766 priests
5298 doctors　　　　　7785 shepherd,
5384 lawyer　　　　　　　occupation
5407 merchants

5434

officer

A person holding a position of
authority (serving others), in a
government, an army or navy, the
church or other organisation.

Examples of officers
Government officers 1Ki 4:5 See also
1Ki 4:7–19,27–28; 20:14; 2Ki 15:25;
18:24 pp Isa 36:9; Ezr 4:8; Ne 11:9;
Isa 33:18

Army officers Ex 14:7 See also Ex 15:4;
Dt 20:8–9; 2Sa 8:7; 2Ki 6:8;
1Ch 27:16–22; Isa 21:5; Jer 38:17–18;
Eze 23:15; Ac 21:32; 25:23

Navy officers 2Ch 8:18

Church officers Php 1:1 See also
Ac 20:17,28; 1Ti 3:1,8–10; 5:17;
Tit 1:5,7

Other kinds of officer
**The officer in charge of the king's
palace** 1Ki 4:6; 18:3; 2Ki 18:18; 19:2

The officer in charge of the treasuries
1Ch 26:24; 2Ch 24:11

**The priest in charge of punishing
troublemakers in the temple court**
Jer 20:1–2

The commander of the king's guard
Da 2:14–15

A court attendant Mt 5:25 pp Lk 12:58

A member of the temple guard
Lk 22:4,52; Ac 5:22,26

The attendant of a Roman magistrate
Ac 16:35,38

See also
5208 armies　　　　　7715 deacons
5245 captain　　　　　7719 elders as
5250 centurion　　　　　leaders
5261 commander　　　7748 overseers
5358 judges　　　　　7766 priests
5489 rank　　　　　　7939 ministry
5509 rulers

5435

ovens

**Ovens were a common feature of
domestic life and activity**
Ex 8:1–4

Uses for ovens
For baking bread Lev 26:23–26

For baking grain offerings Lev 2:4; 7:9

Ovens could be rendered unclean
Lev 11:35

**Ovens were characterised by
great heat**
La 5:10; Hos 7:4,6–7

**The Tower of the Ovens was a
place in Jerusalem in
Nehemiah's day**
Ne 3:11; 12:38

See also
4418 bread　　　　　5321 furnace
5222 baking　　　　　7368 grain offering
5268 cooking

5436

pain

A sense of physical suffering,
anguish or distress, which has a
number of causes. Scripture indicates
the sources of pain and its potential
spiritual implications and results.

Pain is universal
Ro 8:22 See also Ge 3:16–17; Job 5:7

The origins of pain
Satanic activity Ge 3:15 See also
Job 1:12; 2:6–7; Lk 13:16; 2Co 12:7

Human activity Ps 37:14 See also Ge 4:8;
Ex 1:10–11; Na 3:1–4; Hab 2:6,8,10,12

God's judgment and glory Jn 9:2–3 See
also Ex 9:11; Nu 12:10–11;
2Ch 26:19–20; Ps 38:3–5; Pr 5:11;
Ac 12:23; 13:11; 2Co 12:9

Kinds of pain
Physical pain Ps 38:7 See also Job 30:17;
Mt 10:28; Lk 23:33; 2Co 4:16–18;
11:23–27

Mental pain Jer 15:18 See also
Ps 42:5–6,11; Jer 12:6; Mt 26:38;
2Co 2:13; 2Pe 2:8

Bereavement Jn 11:33–35 See also
Ge 35:18; 50:1; 2Sa 12:22–23; Php 2:27;
1Th 4:13

Spiritual pain
Conviction of sin Jn 16:8 See also
Ps 32:3–5; 51:1–2; Lk 7:38; Ac 26:14

The anguish of hell Mk 9:47–48 See also
Mt 5:22; 8:12; Lk 13:28; Rev 6:16

Perplexity Isa 50:10 See also Job 23:8–9;
Ps 22:1; 88:1–3; Jer 20:7

Concern for others Gal 4:19 See also
Ac 20:19; 2Co 2:1–5; 11:28; Php 3:18;
Col 1:28–2:1; Heb 5:7

The failure of others Mt 26:56 See also
Mt 26:40; Jn 13:21; Gal 4:16;
2Ti 4:10,16; 3Jn 10

Fruitful results of pain
It draws believers to God 1Pe 4:19 See
also Jn 14:1,18; Ro 8:26; 2Co 7:5–6;
Heb 4:15–16; 5:8

It equips believers to help others
2Co 1:4 See also Ro 5:3–5; 12:15;
Heb 2:18; 12:11

**It helps believers to anticipate the
resurrection** 1Co 15:54–57 See also
Ro 8:19; 2Co 4:17; 1Th 4:14

It points believers to heaven Rev 21:4
See also Ro 8:18; Rev 7:15–17

See also
1135 God, suffering　5782 agony
　of　　　　　　　　5823 cruelty
5281 crucifixion　　　5893 insults
5297 disease　　　　5952 sorrow
5482 punishment　　9020 death
5560 suffering

5437

palaces

Fortified, luxurious residences for kings. They normally served as the seat and symbol of royal authority.

David's palace on Mount Zion
1Ch 14:1 *See also* 2Sa 5:6–11 pp 1Ch 11:4–8; 2Sa 7:1–2 pp 1Ch 17:1

Solomon's palace in Jerusalem
1Ki 10:4–5 pp 2Ch 9:3–4 *See also* 1Ki 7:1–12; 10:16–21 pp 2Ch 9:15–20; 2Ch 8:11

Gold and valuable items were stored in the palace in Jerusalem
1Ki 15:18–19 pp 2Ch 16:2–3 *See also* 1Ki 14:25–26 pp 2Ch 12:9; 2Ki 12:17–18; 14:13–14 pp 2Ch 25:23–24; 2Ki 16:7–8 pp 2Ch 28:20–21; 2Ki 18:14–15; 24:13; 2Ch 21:16–17; Jer 27:18–22

The royal palace in Jerusalem was destroyed by the Babylonians
2Ki 25:9 pp 2Ch 36:19 pp Jer 52:13 *See also* Jer 22:1–6; 39:8

Other palaces
The kings of Israel had palaces in Samaria 1Ki 21:1 *See also* 1Ki 16:18; 20:5–6,43; 2Ki 15:25

Foreign palaces
Pharaoh's palace in Egypt: Ge 12:15; 41:40; 47:14; Ex 8:3
The royal palace in Babylon: Da 4:29–30; 5:5
Est 1:9 *King Xerxes' palace in Persia and Media*

Summer palaces Jdg 3:20–21

Palaces in NT times
Mt 26:3–4; Jn 18:28; Ac 23:35; Php 1:12–13

Features of palaces
Palace gardens 2Ki 21:18 *See also* 2Ki 21:25–26; Est 1:5–6

The luxury of palaces
1Ki 22:39 *See also* Nu 22:18; Ps 45:8–9; Isa 13:22; Jer 22:13–17; Mt 11:8 pp Lk 7:25

Palaces were administered by royal officials
2Ki 10:5 *See also* 1Ki 4:6; 18:3; 2Ki 15:5; 2Ch 28:7; Isa 22:15

See also

4410 banquets	5366 king
5254 citadel	5399 luxury
5271 courtyard	5487 queen
5316 fortress	5591 treasure

5438

parables

Stories told to convey a general truth or spiritual message, often requiring explanation or interpretation. They were used by the prophets and

featured extensively in Jesus Christ's ministry.

Parables in the OT
Told by prophets Hos 12:10 *See also* 2Sa 12:1–10; 1Ki 20:35–42; Eze 17:1–18; 20:49; 24:3–13

Told by others Ps 78:1–2 *See also* Jdg 9:7–20; 2Sa 14:4–14; 2Ki 14:9–10 pp 2Ch 25:18–19; Pr 1:5–6

Parables in the ministry of Jesus Christ
Reasons for Jesus Christ's use of parables Mt 13:10–15 pp Mk 4:10–12 pp Lk 8:9–10 *See also* Isa 6:9–10

Examples of parables told by Jesus Christ Mt 13:3–8 pp Mk 4:3–8 pp Lk 8:5–8 *See also* Mt 7:24–27 pp Lk 6:47–49 *the wise and foolish builders*; Mt 13:24–30,31–32 pp Mk 4:30–32 pp Lk 13:18–19 *the mustard seed*; Mt 13:33,44–50; 18:12–14 pp Lk 15:4–7 *the lost sheep*; Mt 18:23–35; 20:1–16; 21:33–41 pp Mk 12:1–9 pp Lk 20:9–16 *the tenants*; Mt 22:1–14; 25:1–13,14–30; Mk 4:26–29; 7:14–15; Lk 10:25–37; 12:16–21,35–48; 14:16–24; 15:8–32; 18:9–14; 19:12–27

Interpretations of parables given by Jesus Christ Mk 4:33–34 *See also* Mt 13:18–23 pp Mk 4:14–20 pp Lk 8:11–15; Mt 13:36–43; Mk 7:17–23

See also

1431 prophecy, OT methods	5409 metaphor
	5481 proverb
2357 Christ, parables	7756 preaching, content
2363 Christ, preaching & teaching	7757 preaching, effects

5439

pen

The pen as an implement for writing
Isa 8:1 *See also* 3Jn 13

By extension, refering to what is written
Jer 8:8 *This means that what they wrote was untrue. See also* Mt 5:18; Lk 16:17

Used symbolically
Ps 45:1

Sharpened with a penknife
Jer 36:23

See also

5514 scribes	5638 writing
5515 scroll	

5440

perjury

Swearing falsely, usually in a legal context, either by taking a false oath or by breaking one's oath later. God hates perjury.

God hates perjury
Zec 8:16–17 *See also* Ps 24:3–4;

Isa 48:1; Jer 5:2; 7:9–10; Hos 10:4; Zec 5:3–4; Mal 3:5; 1Ti 1:9–10

The Law forbade perjury
Ex 20:16 pp Dt 5:20; Ex 23:1–3; Lev 19:12; Nu 30:2

Punishment for perjury
Lev 6:1–7; Dt 19:16–21

Examples of perjury
Against Naboth 1Ki 21:1–19

Against Jesus Christ Mt 26:59–61 pp Mk 14:55–59

Against Stephen Ac 6:12–14

See also

1461 truth, nature of	5444 pledges
5276 crime	8751 false witness
5277 criminals	8776 lies
5361 justice, human	8828 spite
5430 oaths, human	

5441

philosophy

An ideology or system of values which seeks to understand and, through rational argument, to investigate the nature and meaning of reality. Scripture exposes the emptiness of philosophy based purely upon human wisdom, while affirming that, at its best, human wisdom points towards God, and can serve as a preparation for the gospel.

The gospel represents the height of human reason
Ac 17:18–23

The quest for understanding
Ecc 7:25; Ac 17:18–21 *See also* Job 34:2–4; Ecc 1:13; 7:27,29–8:1; 12:12

The benefit of received wisdom
Job 15:17–18; Pr 1:2–4; Ecc 12:9–11

The limits of human enquiry
Job 11:7–9; Ecc 8:16–17 *See also* Job 38:36–37; Ps 145:3; Ecc 3:11; Isa 40:28; 55:8–9; Ac 17:23; Ro 11:33–34; Isa 40:13; 1Co 1:20–21

The danger of philosophical speculation
Col 2:8; 1Ti 6:20–21 *See also* Gal 4:3; Col 2:20; 1Ti 1:4; 6:4; Tit 3:9

True insight is given by God
Job 12:13; Ecc 2:26; Mt 13:11 pp Lk 8:10; 2Ti 3:7

True meaning is found in relationship with God
Ac 17:24–28 *See also* Ecc 12:1; Rev 4:11

Epicureanism
Paul meets some Epicureans in Athens Ac 17:16–18 *Followers of the Greek philosophy founded by Epicurus (341–270 B.C.). In strong contrast to the Stoics, they taught that pleasure, and the avoidance of all disturbance, pain and fear, was the chief goal of life.*

Epicureans' assessment of Paul and his message Ac 17:18 *Paul's listeners mistook the Greek word for "resurrection"* *("anastasis") for the name of a strange god. While Epicureans did not deny the existence of gods, they believed they had no interest in the lives of human beings, and that therefore everything in life was the result of mere chance.*

Epicurean and Stoic philosophers bring Paul to the Areopagus
Ac 17:19–20

The response of Epicureans and others to Paul's preaching Ac 17:32

Docetism

Docetism questions the reality of the incarnation 2Jn 7 *Docetism is a denial of the physical reality of Jesus Christ's incarnation that may have been prompted by the typically Greek perception of physical matter as evil. See also* 1Jn 2:22–23
Scripture affirms the physical incarnation of Jesus Christ: Jn 1:14; 1Ti 3:16; Heb 2:14
Scripture emphasises the physical death of the Son of God: Ro 8:3; Php 2:6–8; 1Jn 4:10

Docetic views are identified as heretical 1Jn 4:1–3 *See also* Jn 6:53–56

Gnosticism

Contrary to the teaching of Gnosticism, the world is not inherently evil 1Ti 4:4 *Gnosticism was a religious philosophy whose fundamental belief in the inherent evil of the created realm led to a number of heretical teachings about creation, human nature, the person of Jesus Christ, salvation and ethics.*
Creation is God's work and is therefore good: Ge 1:31; Ne 9:6; Ps 19:1; Ac 17:24; Col 1:15–17; Rev 4:11
Creation, though fallen, will be redeemed and reconciled to God through Jesus Christ: Ro 8:20–21; Eph 1:9–10; Col 1:19–20

Contrary to the teaching of Gnosticism, human beings are not sparks of divinity trapped in evil, fleshly bodies Ac 17:26
Human beings are a good creation of God: Ge 1:26–27; 2:7; Ps 8:3–8
Human beings can know bodily redemption and use their bodies to serve God: Ro 6:12–13; 8:22–23; 12:1; 1Co 6:12–18,19–20; 1Th 5:23
The future existence of glorified human beings will be a bodily existence, not just a spiritual one: Ro 8:10–11; 1Co 15:35–44; 2Co 5:1–4; Php 3:20–21; 2Ti 2:16–18

Contrary to the teaching of Gnosticism, Jesus Christ did not merely appear in human form Jn 1:14
The Son of God became a real flesh-and-blood human being: Lk 24:36–43; Col 2:9; Heb 2:14; 1Jn 1:1–3; 4:2–3; 2Jn 7
As a man, the Son of God experienced death on the cross: Jn 19:33–34; 1Co 2:8; Php 2:6–8; Col 1:19–22; 1Jn 5:6

Contrary to the teaching of Gnosticism, salvation is not found simply in a divine revelation of special knowledge
Salvation is by faith in the crucified Christ: 1Co 3:18–20; Col 2:8,18–19; 1Ti 6:20–21
All knowledge and wisdom needed for full salvation are to be found in Christ:

1Co 1:18–25; Col 1:19–20; 2:2–4,8–10; 2Pe 1:3

Contrary to the teaching of Gnosticism, Christian behaviour is not to be marked by licence and ritualistic self-denial
There is no value in empty ceremonial observance or ritualistic self-denial: Mt 15:10–11 pp Mk 7:14–15; Ro 14:5–6; Col 2:16–17,20–23; 1Ti 4:1–5
Christian behaviour is to be marked by liberty, not by licence: 1Co 6:12–20; Gal 5:13; Col 3:5–14; Tit 1:15–16; 1Pe 2:16; 1Jn 1:5–6; 2:3–6; 3:3–10; Jude 4

Stoicism

Paul encounters the Stoics in Athens
Ac 17:16–18 *The Stoics were a leading philosophical group based, like their rivals the Epicureans, in Athens. Stoics held that God was the inner reason of the universe and that salvation lay in accepting one's place in the established order.*

Stoics ridicule Paul Ac 17:18

Stoics misunderstand Paul's message
Ac 17:18

Paul presents a view of God very different from that of the Stoics
Ac 17:24–25 *In contrast to Stoic belief God is the Creator;* Ac 17:26–27 *In contrast to Stoic belief God is a personal being.*

Response of the Stoics to Paul's message Ac 17:32–34

See also

2033 Christ, humanity	8355 understanding
4005 creation	8361 wisdom
5002 human race & creation	8748 false religion
5026 knowledge	8750 false teachings
6510 salvation	8766 heresies
8237 doctrine, false	9311 resurrection of Christ

pilgrimage

A journey made to a holy or revered place as an act of devotion or duty. As well as Jerusalem, there were several such holy places in Israel.

The annual pilgrimages
Ex 34:23–24; Lk 2:41–42 *See also* Ex 23:14,17; Dt 16:16; 31:11; 2Ch 5:2–3; 30:1,13; La 1:4; Eze 46:9; Zec 14:16–19; Jn 5:1; 7:14

Pilgrimages to Jerusalem
Ps 122:1–4 *See also* Ps 84:5; Isa 2:3; 30:29; Mic 4:2; Ac 2:5–11

Accompanying sacrifices
1Ki 12:27–28; Isa 1:12

Other centres of pilgrimage
1Sa 1:3; 1Ki 3:4; 12:26–30

Used metaphorically
Ge 47:9 *See also* Heb 11:13–16

See also

4020 life of faith	7266 tribes of Israel
5312 feasting	7354 feasts and festivals
5357 journey	
5590 travel	8288 joy of Israel
5976 visiting	8622 worship
6606 access to God	8769 idolatry, in OT

pillars

Supports or decorations in buildings and free-standing memorial monuments. The word is also used figuratively, with reference to strength and beauty.

Pillars in the temple
1Ki 7:21

Pillars erected as memorials
Ge 28:18–22 *See also* Ge 31:45–53; 35:14–15,19–20; Ex 24:4; Dt 27:2–6; Jos 4:1–9; 2Sa 18:18

The pillar of cloud and fire
Ex 13:21–22 *See also* Ex 33:9; Ne 9:12

The figurative use of pillars
Jer 1:18 *See also* Job 9:6; 26:11; Ps 75:3; 144:12; SS 5:15; Gal 2:9; Rev 3:12; 10:1

Kings were sometimes crowned beside a pillar
Jdg 9:6 *See also* 2Ki 11:12–14 pp 2Ch 23:11–13

Other notable incidents connected with pillars
Lot's wife and the pillar of salt
Ge 19:24–26

Samson's destruction of a temple
Jdg 16:25–30

See also

5366 king	7394 memorial
7251 pillar of cloud & fire	7467 temple, Solomon's

pledges

A solemn, binding promise, often involving the deposit of valuable items or property as a guarantee that the promise will be kept. To break a pledge is to sin against God.

Pledges were binding
Nu 30:2 *See also* Nu 30:3–15 *In certain cases pledges made by daughters or wives could be nullified by fathers or husbands respectively.*

Pledges were solemn promises
2Ki 23:3 pp 2Ch 34:31–32 *See also* 1Ch 29:24; Ezr 10:19; Eze 17:16–18; Mic 7:20; 1Pe 3:21

Pledges were guarantees that a promise would be kept
Items deposited to secure a pledge
Ge 38:17–18 *See also* Ex 22:26–27; Dt 24:10–13; Pr 20:16; 27:13

Unjust exaction of pledges condemned Dt 24:17 *See also* Job 22:4–6; 24:2–3; Am 2:6–8

Warning against making pledges on behalf of others

Pr 11:15 *The foolishness of making a pledge as security for someone else's debt.* See also Pr 6:1–5; 17:18; 22:26–27

Pledges and betrothal

Mt 1:18–19 *Betrothal was a pledge to marry and as such was much more binding than the modern Western practice of engagement. It could only be broken by divorce and the betrothed woman was already described as a wife. See also Ex 22:16; Dt 22:23–25; Lk 1:27*

See also

1346 covenants	5466 promises
1690 word of God	5518 seal
3040 Holy Spirit,	5654 betrothal
promise of	5708 marriage
5329 guarantee	5741 vows
5429 oaths	5925 rashness
5440 perjury	

5445

potters and pottery

Pottery was in common use for both household and ceremonial utensils, though for sacred use precious metals were often preferred. Broken pottery symbolises worthlessness and judgment. The potter formed clay with his hands on a wheel which he turned with his feet. The descriptions of God as a potter and of his people as clay emphasise God's sovereignty and also his concern for what he has made.

Potters in Scripture

Examples of potters Jer 18:2 *See also* 1Ch 4:23; Jer 19:1; Zec 11:13 *Potters may have been associated with the temple, possibly because of the continuing need for new vessels to be used in religious ceremonies;* Mt 27:7

Description of the potter's work Pr 26:23; Jer 18:3–4

God depicted as a potter

God's authority over what he has made Jer 18:6 *See also* Isa 29:16; 45:9–10; Ro 9:20–21

God's concern for what he has made Isa 64:8–9 *See also* Ge 2:7–8 *"Formed" commonly describes the action of the potter. God "formed" both individuals and the nation;* Job 10:8–9; Ps 103:14; 119:73; Isa 43:1

Broken pottery

Contaminated pottery to be broken Lev 11:33–35; 15:12

Broken pottery as a symbol of judgment Jer 19:10–11 *See also* Ps 2:9; Rev 2:7; Isa 30:14; Jer 25:34; 48:12

Broken pottery as a symbol of worthlessness Ps 31:12 *See also* Jer 22:28; 19:2 *The Potsherd Gate was so called because it overlooked the dump for broken pottery.*

Pottery of little value

La 4:2 *See also* Ps 60:8 pp Ps 108:9; 2Co 4:7 *Valuables were often concealed in*

apparently worthless clay jars which did not attract attention.

Examples of items of pottery

2Sa 17:28; 2Ti 2:20

Cooking pots Jdg 6:19; 1Sa 2:14; 2Ki 4:38–41; Job 41:20; Mic 3:3

Pitchers to carry water Ge 24:17–20; Jdg 7:16; Mk 14:13 pp Lk 22:10; Jn 4:28

Water jugs 1Sa 26:11–12; 1Ki 17:10; 19:6

Drinking vessels Jdg 5:25; Jer 35:5; Mt 26:27–28 pp Mk 14:23–24 pp Lk 22:20 pp 1Co 11:25

Other pottery containers 1Ki 14:3; 2Ki 4:3–4; 21:13; Jer 32:14 *Documents could be kept intact in clay jars for many years;* Mt 26:23; Jn 13:5

Household lamps 2Ki 4:10; Mt 5:15

Pottery used in religious rituals

Basins to hold the blood of sacrifices Ex 12:21–22 *See also* Ex 24:6; Lev 14:5,50

Utensils to cook or bake offerings Lev 6:28 *The sin offering was cooked in a pot which was then broken. See also* Lev 2:5 *The grain offering might be baked on a clay griddle;* Lev 6:21; 7:9

Clay water jars Nu 5:17; 19:17

Lamps Ex 25:37 *A clay lamp was held on each of the golden lampstand's seven branches. See also* Ex 27:21; 30:8; Lev 24:3–4; 1Sa 3:3; 1Ki 7:49

See also

1130 God,	5373 lamp &
sovereignty	lampstand
4315 clay	5621 wheel
5222 baking	5959 submission
5226 basin	7478 washing
5234 bottle	9210 judgment,
5268 cooking	God's
5283 cup	

5446

poverty

The state of being without material possessions or wealth. Scripture indicates that poverty is contrary to God's intention for his people, and that those who are poor and destitute are to be treated with special consideration and compassion.

5447

poverty, causes of

To want for the necessities of life is ultimately the result of human sin.

Poverty arises from human sin

Ge 3:17–19 *Compare this with the description of Eden in Ge 2:9–14.*

Causes of poverty

Divine retribution brings poverty Dt 28:47–48 *See also* Pr 22:16; Isa 3:1; Am 4:6; 5:11

Idleness brings poverty Pr 6:10–11 *See also* Pr 10:4; 14:23; 20:13; 24:33–34

Dissolute living brings poverty Pr 21:17 *See also* Pr 6:26; 28:19; Lk 15:14

Lack of discipline brings poverty Pr 13:18; 21:5

Rash promises bring poverty Pr 22:26–27

Debt brings poverty Mt 18:23–25

Neglect of God's law of giving brings poverty Pr 11:24; 28:22; Ac 20:35

Neglect of God's work brings poverty Hag 1:9

Oppression brings poverty Jdg 6:6; Job 20:19; Pr 13:23; Isa 1:7; Jas 5:4

Famine brings poverty Ge 45:11; 47:20–21

Misfortune brings poverty Job 1:13–21 *These trials were inflicted by Satan but allowed by God as a test of Job's faith.*

Poverty affects good as well as evil people

The righteous often escape poverty Dt 8:7–9; Ps 34:9–10; 37:25

Many of the godly have been poor 2Ki 4:1; Lk 16:20; Ro 15:26

Jesus Christ was poor Mt 8:20

Results of poverty

Poverty results in ruin Pr 10:15

Poverty results in shame Pr 13:18; Lk 16:3

Poverty results in misery Pr 31:7

Poverty results in crime Pr 6:30; 30:8–9

Poverty need not lead to ungodliness Ps 119:71; Mk 12:44 pp Lk 21:4; 2Co 8:2; Jas 2:5; Rev 2:9

Voluntary poverty

Jesus Christ's example of voluntary poverty 2Co 8:9

Voluntary poverty commanded of some Mt 19:21–22 *Jesus Christ did not say this to everyone.*

Voluntary poverty experienced by others *See also* Heb 10:34

Love essential in voluntary poverty 1Co 13:3; 2Co 6:10

See also

1175 God, will of	5353 interest
4822 famine	5399 luxury
5169 nakedness	5493 retribution
5230 beggars	5605 warfare
5289 debt	8260 generosity
5348 injustice	8790 oppression

5448

poverty, attitudes towards

The plight of those in need calls for compassionate action of which Jesus Christ is the great example and in which the early church was faithful. Such compassion will be rewarded.

The treatment of the poor

They are not to be neglected Dt 15:7–8 *See also* Pr 17:5; Ro 12:13; Gal 6:10; Jas 2:15–16; 1Jn 3:17

They are not to be unjustly treated Ex 23:6 *See also* Lev 25:35–37; Dt 24:14–15; 2Sa 12:1–4 *Nathan rebukes David in the parable about the rich man and the poor man;* Job 24:1–4;

Pr 22:22; 29:7; Jer 22:2–3,16; Eze 18:10–13; Am 2:6–7; Zec 7:10; Jas 2:2–4 *favouritism forbidden in Christian meetings*

They are to have special rights and privileges Dt 14:28–29 *See also* Ex 23:11; Lev 19:9–10; 25:5–6; Pr 19:17

They are to be cared for Ps 82:3–4 *See also* Job 29:11–17; Lk 3:11; Ac 9:36

They are to be helped generously Dt 15:9–11 *See also* Dt 14:29; Ru 2:14; Ps 112:9; Jer 39:10; Lk 19:8; Ac 10:2; 2Co 9:7

They are to be helped without ostentation Mt 6:2

Jesus Christ's compassion for the poor
Mt 15:32 pp Mk 8:1–3 *See also* Lk 4:18–19; Jn 13:29; Ac 10:38

The attitude of the first Christians towards poverty
Ac 2:44–45 *See also* Ac 4:32–35; 11:29–30; 20:35; 24:17; Ro 15:25–27; 2Co 8:13–15; Gal 2:10

Compassion for the poor will be rewarded
Ps 41:1 *See also* Pr 19:17; 28:27; Mt 19:21; 25:34–36; Mk 9:41; Heb 13:16

Examples of the poor who need help
Orphans Dt 10:18; 14:28–29; Ps 10:14; 146:9; Pr 23:10; Isa 10:2

Widows Dt 14:29; 16:11; Ru 4:5; 2Ki 4:1; Job 22:9; Mal 3:5; Ac 6:1; 1Ti 5:3,9,16; Jas 1:27

See also

2015 Christ,	5802 care
compassion	5806 compassion
2048 Christ, love of	8260 generosity
5293 defence, human	8434 giving
5359 justice	8611 prayer for
5730 orphans	others
5743 widows	
5765 attitudes to	
people	

5449
poverty, remedies for

Although poverty can never be totally eliminated from this sinful world, it can be alleviated. Scripture provides guidance concerning how this may be done.

Poverty will always exist in this world
Mt 26:11 pp Jn 12:8 *See also* Dt 15:11

God's concern over poverty
God cares for the poor Ps 35:10; 68:10 *See also* Dt 15:4–5; Job 5:16; Ps 14:6; 113:7; 140:12; Isa 25:4

The law made concessions for poverty Lev 5:7,11; 12:8; 14:21–22; 27:8

God judges those who oppress the poor Eze 18:12–13; Am 4:1–2

The poor should be encouraged to help themselves
Mosaic law enabled the poor to help themselves Ex 23:11; Lev 19:10; 23:22; 25:25,28,39,41 *The jubilee helped*

towards release from the poverty trap; Dt 23:25

Paul exhorts the poor to work
1Th 4:11; 2Th 3:10

Paul sets the poor an example
Ac 20:34; 1Th 2:9; 2Th 3:8

The relatives of the poor should help
1Ti 5:4 *See also* Ge 45:9–11; Lev 25:25; 1Ti 5:8,16

Those better off should help the poor
The poor can be helped by means of gifts Ac 10:4 *See also* Dt 15:7–8; Ps 112:9; Pr 31:20; Mt 19:21 pp Mk 10:21 pp Lk 18:22; Lk 19:8; Ac 9:36; Eph 4:28; 1Ti 6:17–18

The poor can be helped in practical ways Mt 25:34–40; Lk 11:41; 14:13; Ac 9:36,39; 1Ti 5:9–10; Jas 2:15–16; 1Jn 3:17

The poor can be helped by others upholding justice Ps 82:3 *See also* Dt 24:12–15; Pr 22:22; 29:7,14; 31:9; Isa 10:1–2; Jer 22:16

The church should help the poor
Gal 2:10 *See also* Ac 24:17; Ro 15:26; 1Ti 5:16

God's greatest gift to the poor is the good news of Jesus Christ
Lk 4:18 *See also* Isa 61:1; Mt 11:5 pp Lk 7:22; Lk 14:21 *Scripture regards spiritual and social welfare as closely connected.*

See also

1030 God,	5325 gifts
compassion	5680 family
1075 God, justice of	5976 visiting
1330 God, the	6714 ransom
provider	

5450
poverty, spiritual

The lack of spiritual riches and gifts is seen by Scripture as an especially distressing cause of poverty. Awareness of spiritual poverty leads to a turning towards God in order to receive the riches he graciously offers through the gospel.

The ungodly are spiritually poor
They lack faith Mt 13:58 pp Mk 6:6

They lack understanding Pr 10:21; Isa 5:13; 56:10–11; Jer 5:4; Hos 4:6; 1Ti 6:5

They lack God Eph 2:12

They lack eternal life Mt 16:26 pp Lk 9:25; Lk 12:20–21; 16:22–23; Jas 5:1–6

They lack knowledge of their spiritual poverty Rev 3:17

Spiritual poverty may be a judgment
Am 8:11 *See also* Ps 51:11; 74:9; La 2:9; Eze 7:26; Mt 13:14–15; Rev 2:5

The godly are aware of their poverty
David recognised that he was poor and needy Ps 40:17 *See also* Ps 34:6; 35:10; 70:5; 86:1; 109:22

Others recognise their spiritual poverty Ro 7:18 *See also* Job 42:6; Ps 8:3–4; Lk 5:8; 7:6; Ro 7:24

Those who know that they are poor will be blessed by God
God will satisfy the poor in spirit Mt 5:3 pp Lk 6:20–21 *See also* Mt 5:6

God will save the poor in spirit Ps 116:6

God will accept the poor in spirit Ps 51:17; Isa 66:2

God will be close to the poor in spirit Ps 34:18; Isa 57:15

God will hear the prayers of the poor in spirit Ps 102:17

God will give grace to the poor in spirit Jas 4:6,10; 1Pe 5:5–6; Pr 3:34

God will meet the needs of the poor in spirit Isa 61:1; Lk 1:53

Spiritual riches are better than material riches
Poverty with righteousness is better Ps 37:16; Pr 15:16–17; 16:8; 19:1,22; 28:6

Poverty with wisdom is better Pr 16:16; 19:1,22; 28:6

Poverty with humility is better Pr 16:19

Poverty with peace and quiet is better Pr 17:1

Spiritual riches exalt the poor Jas 1:9

Spiritual riches endure Heb 10:34; 11:37–40; 1Pe 1:4

Spiritual riches more than compensate for material poverty 2Co 6:10; Jas 2:5; Rev 2:9

See also

1620 beatitudes, the	8276 humility
5580 thirst	8808 riches
5801 brokenness	

5452

power

The quality which enables individuals to achieve their aims. Scripture stresses the power of God, demonstrated in Jesus Christ's resurrection and bestowed through the Holy Spirit. Scripture also stresses the relative powerlessness of humanity in God's sight.

5453
power, of God

See 1105 God, power of

5454
power, God's saving

God has power to save and protect and through his power he will defeat those who oppose him.

God's power to save
Ps 20:6 *See also* 2Ch 20:12,15;
Isa 40:9–10; 2Pe 1:3–4

Jesus Christ's power to perform miracles
Lk 6:19 *See also* Mt 13:54; 14:2
pp Mk 6:14; Mk 5:30 pp Lk 8:46;
Lk 4:36; 5:17; Ac 10:38

God's power to protect
1Pe 1:3–5 *See also* Da 6:26–27;
Jn 17:11; Ro 8:38–39

God's people pray for God to act in power
2Ch 14:11 *See also* 2Ch 20:12;
Ps 68:1–2,28; Jer 14:9; Ac 4:23–31;
2Co 10:4

The power of the gospel
Ro 1:16 *See also* Ro 4:21 *God has power to fulfil his promises*; Ro 5:6; 8:3; 1Co 1:18

The power of God's kingdom
Mt 6:13 fn; Mk 9:1; 1Co 4:19–20

Preaching and power
1Co 2:4–5 *See also* Ac 4:33; 9:22;
Ro 15:18–19; 1Co 1:17–18; Eph 3:7;
1Th 1:5; 2Ti 1:7–8

The powers that oppose God will be defeated
1Co 15:24; Col 2:15 *See also* Isa 24:21;
59:15–20; Da 7:26–27; 8:25; Eph 6:12;
Rev 12:10; 18:10

The power of God over death
Ps 89:48; Ecc 8:8; Isa 25:8; Hos 13:14;
1Co 6:14; 15:26,42–44,54–57;
Heb 2:14–15

See also

1105 God, power of	3224 Holy Spirit &
1265 hand of God	preaching
1320 God as Saviour	8424 evangelism
2066 Christ, power of	8727 enemies
2372 Christ, victory	9020 death
2420 gospel	9310 resurrection
3030 Holy Spirit, power	

5455
power, of Jesus Christ
See 2066 Jesus Christ, power of

5456
power, of Holy Spirit
See 3030 Holy Spirit, power of

5457
power, human

All human power and authority comes from God. God also gives special power to his people.

All human power comes from God
Dt 8:17–18; Ro 13:1 *See also* Jdg 3:12;
2Ki 13:3,5; 2Ch 25:8; Da 2:37; 4:29–32;
Jn 19:10–11; Ac 4:28; Col 1:16;
1Pe 2:13–14

God gives power to his people
God's power is at work in believers
Ps 68:35 *See also* Isa 40:29–31; 2Co 4:7;

10:4; 12:9; Eph 3:20; 6:10; Col 1:11;
2Th 1:11

Examples of God giving power to believers
Moses: Ex 4:21; Dt 34:12; Ac 7:22
2Sa 5:10 pp 1Ch 11:9 *David*; 1Ki 18:46
Elijah; 2Ch 27:6 *Jotham*; Da 2:23 *Daniel*;
Lk 1:17 *John the Baptist*
Jesus Christ gives power to his disciples:
Lk 9:1 pp Mt 10:1 pp Mk 6:7; Lk 10:19
Christians heal by God's power: Ac 4:7,10;
6:8; 1Co 12:10

God gives resurrection power to believers
Eph 1:19–20 *See also*
2Co 13:4; Php 3:10; Col 1:29; 2:12

The Holy Spirit equips individuals for special tasks
Jdg 3:10 *Othniel*
Samson: Jdg 14:6,19; 15:14
Saul: 1Sa 10:6,10; 11:6
1Sa 16:13 *David*; Isa 61:1 *the Messiah, fulfilled in Jesus Christ (Lk 4:18)*; Mic 3:8
Micah; Lk 1:35 *Mary*; Lk 4:14 *Jesus Christ*

The Holy Spirit gives power to believers
Ac 1:8 *See also* Lk 24:49;
Ro 15:13; Eph 3:16

Human power derives from wisdom
Ecc 7:19 *See also* Pr 3:27; 8:14; 24:5;
Ecc 9:13–18

The abuse of human power
Pr 28:28 *See also* Jdg 6:2; Job 21:7;
Pr 28:12; Ecc 4:1; Jer 5:27–28; 23:10;
Eze 22:6; Mic 2:1; 7:3

The absence of human power
Dt 28:32; 2Ch 14:11; Ne 5:5;
Job 5:15–16; 6:11–13

The power of the wicked is temporary
Ps 37:16–17 *See also* Est 9:1;
Ps 37:32–33; Pr 11:7; Eze 13:20–21

See also

1105 God, power of	5215 authority
3239 Holy Spirit,	5347 injustice
anointing	5367 kingdoms
3269 Holy Spirit in	5785 ambition
Christ	5954 strength
4215 Babylon	8361 wisdom
4263 Rome	8790 oppression

---

prince

The son of a king, or a very important official, leader or ruler. The title is given to Jesus Christ and also to angelic spirits (in particular Michael and Satan).

A prince as the son of a king
2Ch 11:22 *See also* 2Sa 13:32;
2Ki 10:6–8; 11:2; Ps 45:16

A prince as someone occupying a very important position
Ge 49:26 pp Dt 33:16 *See also* Ge 23:6;
1Sa 2:8; 2Sa 3:38; Ps 113:8

A prince as a very important official, leader or ruler
Est 1:3 *See also* Nu 21:18; 22:8,13–15;
Jos 13:21; Jdg 5:15; 2Ch 21:4; 22:8;
Ezr 1:8; Est 6:9; Ps 68:27; Pr 8:16;
Eze 21:12

Princes of Israel oppress the people:
Eze 22:6; 45:8–9
Eze 38:2–3; Da 9:6; Hos 3:4

The Messiah is described as a prince
Isa 9:6 *See also* Eze 34:24; 37:25; 44:3;
Da 8:11,25

Angelic spirits (whether good or evil) are described as princes
Da 10:13 *The prince of the Persian kingdom was possibly a demon, exercising influence in the interests of Satan. See also*
Da 10:20–21; 12:1

Satan is described as a prince
Mt 9:34 *See also* Mt 12:24 pp Mk 3:22
pp Lk 11:15; Jn 12:31; 14:30; 16:11;
Eph 2:2

The splendour of the princess
Ps 45:13 *See also* Ps 45:9

See also

2203 Christ, titles of	5327 governors
2230 Messiah,	5366 king
coming of	5457 power, human
4124 Satan, kingdom	5487 queen
of	5509 rulers
4145 archangels	7735 leaders,
4195 spirits	political

---

prison

A place of confinement, such as a jail or dungeon, used to imprison individuals.

Irregular prisons
Ge 37:22 *A cistern was usually a plaster-coated underground rock cavity used for storing water. See also* Nu 12:14–15
Miriam's confinement may have been as much isolation as punishment; Jer 38:6,13

Houses used as prisons
Jer 37:15 *See also* 2Sa 20:3; Lk 22:54;
Ac 28:16

Legally established prisons
Ge 39:20; Ac 5:18 *See also* Ge 42:16–19;
Jdg 16:21; 1Ki 22:27; 2Ki 17:4; 25:27;
2Ch 16:10; Mt 14:3; Lk 21:12; Ac 4:3;
12:4–7; 16:37

Barracks or guardhouses as prisons
Jer 32:2; Ac 22:24; Php 1:12–13

Figurative and poetic use of prisons
Isa 42:7 *See also* Job 11:10; Ps 88:8;
142:7; Isa 24:22; Lk 12:58; 1Pe 3:19;
2Pe 2:4; Rev 1:18
The restriction of Satan's activity is pictured as his binding and imprisonment:
Rev 20:1,7

See also

5246 captivity	5461 prisoners
5344 imprisonment	6660 freedom
5364 key	through Christ

---

prisoners

People who have been deprived of their liberty and confined against their will.

People imprisoned out of anger, envy or jealousy

Ge 37:24; Jer 52:11 *See also* Ge 39:19; 40:3; 41:14; 42:16
Samson: Jdg 16:21,25
2Ki 17:4 *Hoshea, king of Israel*;
2Ki 25:18; 2Ch 28:5,17; 33:11
Manasseh: Isa 14:17; 20:4; Hab 1:9

People imprisoned for lawlessness

Ezr 7:26; Mt 27:16 pp Mk 15:6–7
pp Lk 23:19 *See also* Ex 12:29;
Isa 42:22–24

People imprisoned for their faithfulness to God

Micaiah 1Ki 22:27 pp 2Ch 18:26

Hanani, seer to Asa 2Ch 16:10

Jeremiah Jer 32:2; 33:1; 37:15,18,21; 38:6,9; 39:15

John the Baptist Mt 4:12 pp Mk 1:14;
Mt 11:2; 14:3 pp Mk 6:17; Mt 14:10
pp Mk 6:27; Lk 3:20

The apostles Ac 5:18

Simon Peter Ac 12:5

The early Christian believers Ac 8:3;
9:21; 22:4,19; 26:10; Heb 10:34

Paul Ac 12:4; 22:27; 23:29; 28:17;
2Co 6:5; 11:23; Eph 3:1; 4:1; Phm 1

Paul and Silas Ac 16:23–24

Aristarchus Col 4:10

Epaphras Phm 23

The saints of old Heb 11:36

Figurative and poetic use of imprisonment

Gal 3:22–23 *See also* Ps 142:7; Isa 24:22;
42:6–7,22; Eze 19:9; Zec 9:11–12;
Mt 18:30

The LORD does not abandon prisoners

Ps 79:11 *See also* Ge 39:21; Ps 68:6;
69:33; 102:20; 107:10; 146:7;
Isa 49:8–9; 61:1; La 3:31–36

Christians should show concern for prisoners

Heb 13:3 *See also* Mt 25:36,39,43

See also
5098 John the Baptist	5482 punishment
5108 Paul, life of	5560 suffering
5246 captivity	6658 freedom
5344 imprisonment	8116 discipleship, cost
5460 prison	

5463

proclamations

Edicts or public declarations issued by the civil or religious authorities.

Examples of proclamations in biblical times

Ex 1:15–22 *Pharaoh's edict that all Hebrew boys were to be drowned*; Ex 32:5 *Aaron's proclamation of a festival to the LORD*; 1Ki 21:9–10 *Jezebel's proclamation to ensnare Naboth*; 2Ki 10:20 *Jehu's proclamation of an assembly in honour of Baal*; 2Ch 24:9 *Joash's proclamation of a*

tax for the LORD; 2Ch 30:1–10 *Hezekiah's invitation to celebrate the Passover*
Cyrus' decrees concerning the rebuilding of the Jerusalem temple: Ezr 1:1; 5:13; 6:3; 7:13
Ne 8:14–15 *the Levites' proclamation of festival arrangements*
Xerxes' decrees in the time of Esther: Est 1:20; 2:8; 3:14; 4:3; 8:11
Darius' decrees in the time of Daniel: Da 6:7,15
Jnh 3:7 *the king of Nineveh's proclamation of a fast of repentance*;
Lk 2:1 *Caesar Augustus' proclamation of a census*

See also
2427 gospel, transmission	7354 feasts and festivals
5219 authority, human institutions	7754 preaching
	8424 evangelism
5335 herald	8489 urgency

5464

proconsul

The ex-consul who ruled the Roman province of Asia was a proconsul

Ac 19:38

The governor of a Roman senatorial province was a proconsul

The proconsul of the province of Cyprus Ac 13:7–8,12

The proconsul of the province of Achaia Ac 18:12

See also
5257 civil authorities	5509 rulers
5327 governors	

5465

profit

In the financial sense, gain through trading. The word is also used in Scripture of spiritual gain.

Legitimate profit

As the result of hard work Pr 14:23;
21:5 *See also* Pr 31:18

As the reward of generosity Pr 11:24;
Lk 6:38

As the gift of God Dt 8:18

It is withheld by God in judgment
Dt 28:15–20; Jer 12:13; Hag 1:9

It is for this life only Ecc 1:3–4; 1Ti 6:7

Profiting by oppression

A common practice of the wicked
Ecc 5:8–9

It is often cloaked in hypocrisy *See also*
Eze 33:31

It is against God's law Lev 25:37

It is of little worth *See also* Pr 11:16; 16:8

It is short-lived Job 20:18–19;
Isa 23:17–18; Jer 17:11

It is judged by God Pr 1:18–19;
Eze 22:12–14; Mic 4:13; Hab 2:9

Its avoidance is rewarded Pr 28:16;
Isa 33:15–16

Profiting by dishonesty

It is common amongst the wicked
Jer 22:17

It is forbidden to God's servants
Ex 18:21; 1Sa 8:3; 1Ti 3:8; Tit 1:7

Profiting selfishly

It is common amongst the wicked
Isa 56:11

It is avoided by the godly Ps 119:36

Using religion for profit

In the OT *See also* Nu 22:16–17;
1Sa 2:12–16; Jer 6:13; 8:10

In the NT 2Co 2:17 *See also* Ac 8:18–23;
1Ti 6:5; Tit 1:11; Jude 11

Profiting spiritually

Through the Scriptures 1Ti 4:13–15;
2Ti 3:16–17

Through wisdom Pr 3:13–14

Through doctrine Tit 3:8

Through godliness and contentment
1Ti 6:6 *See also* 1Ti 4:8

Through chastening Heb 12:10

Through spiritual gifts 1Co 12:7

Through service Mt 25:14–30;
Lk 19:11–27

Through sacrifice Mt 19:29
pp Mk 10:29–30 pp Lk 18:29–30;
Heb 11:35

Through death Php 1:21 *See also*
Php 1:23

Doubts expressed about profiting spiritually Job 9:29–31; 21:15; 34:9;
35:1–3; Ps 73:13; Ecc 2:15; 6:8;
Mal 3:14

It is better than worldly wealth
Mt 16:26 pp Mk 8:36 pp Lk 9:25

Unprofitable things

Ecc 6:11 *mere words*; Ecc 10:11 *delayed action*; Isa 44:10 *idolatry*; Php 3:7 *legalistic works*; 1Co 13:1–3 *zeal without love*; 1Co 14:6 *speech without understanding*; Heb 4:2 *hearing without faith*; Tit 3:9 *needless controversy*

See also
5310 exploitation	7774 prophets, false
5311 extortion	8260 generosity
5587 trade	8714 dishonesty
5628 work	8767 hypocrisy
5833 diligence	8790 oppression
5869 greed	8827 selfishness

5466

promises

Binding offers or commitments on the part of one person or people to another. The value of such promises depends upon the reliability and trustworthiness of the person who makes the promises. Scripture stresses the total reliability of God, including his promise to bestow his Spirit and urges believers to demonstrate the same trustworthiness in their dealings with one another.

5467
promises, divine

The promises of God reveal his particular and eternal purposes to which he is unchangeably committed and upon which believers can totally depend. These promises are, however, conditional upon obedience on the part of believers.

God's promises are irrevocable
He is absolutely trustworthy Nu 23:19 *See also* Tit 1:2; Heb 6:13–18

He is unchanging Ps 110:4; Mal 3:6–7; Jas 1:17–18

He has the power and will to fulfil his promises Isa 55:11 *See also* Ro 4:21

He is faithful in keeping all his promises Jos 21:45; 23:14–15; 1Ki 8:56; Ps 145:13; Heb 10:23

His promises stem from his goodness and glory 2Pe 1:3–4

God may confirm his promises with an oath Ge 22:15–18 *See also* Ge 26:3; Isa 45:23; Am 6:8; 8:7

Examples of God's promises through covenant relationship
Ge 9:8–17 *with Noah*
With Abraham: Ge 15:9–21; 17:1–22; Heb 11:8–9,17–19
Ge 26:3–4 *with Isaac*
With Jacob: Ge 28:13–15; 46:2–4
With Moses and the Israelites: Ex 19:1–6; 24:1–8
Nu 25:10–12 *with Phinehas*
With David: 2Sa 7:5–16
pp 1Ch 17:4–14; 1Ki 8:15,24
Jer 31:31–34 *with Jeremiah*

The grounding of God's promises in Christ
God's promises are fulfilled in Jesus Christ 2Co 1:18–20 *See also* Mt 5:17; Lk 4:16–21; Ac 2:29–31; 3:21–26; 7:37; Dt 18:15–18; Ac 13:23,32–34; 26:6–7; Ro 1:2–3; 15:8; Heb 9:15

Jesus Christ brings superior promises through the new covenant Heb 8:6–8 *Jesus Christ mediates a covenant of inner transformation, willing obedience, intimate relationship with God and forgiveness of sins for ever. See also* Eph 1:13–14; Heb 7:22; 11:13,39–40; 2Pe 1:1–4

Jesus Christ has the right to make promises on God's behalf Jn 3:34–35 *See also* Jn 1:1–2,14; 8:25–29; Heb 1:1–3

God's promises must be received by believers
They are received by faith Gal 3:22 *See also* Jn 1:12; Ro 4:13–16

They are received by perseverance and obedience Heb 10:36 *See also* Ro 4:19–24; 2Co 7:1; Heb 6:12

God's promises unite believing Jews and Gentiles Eph 3:6 *See also* Ac 2:38–39; Ro 9:8; Gal 3:29; 4:28; Eph 2:11–18; Heb 11:39–40

Disaster awaits those who reject God's promises Jos 23:12–16;

Jn 3:18–20,36; 2Ti 2:11–13; Heb 6:4–12; 2Pe 3:3–10

Particular promises of God in Christ
The gift of the Holy Spirit Lk 24:49; Ac 1:4; 2:33; Eph 1:13

The fulness of life and eternal life 2Ti 1:1; Heb 12:26–28; Jas 1:12; 2:5; 1Jn 2:25

Resurrection Jn 5:29; 11:25–26; 1Co 15:48–57; 2Co 4:14; 1Th 4:16

The forgiveness of sins 1Jn 1:9

The presence of God Ex 3:12; 33:14; Jos 1:9; Isa 58:9; Mt 28:20; Heb 13:5

The peace of God 1Ch 22:9; Ps 85:8; Isa 9:6–7; Ro 5:1; Php 4:4–9

Joy in God Ps 16:11; 132:16; Jn 16:20–24

The knowledge of God Jer 31:33–34; Jn 17:25–26; 1Jn 5:20

See also

1035 God, faithfulness	6644 eternal life
1345 covenant	6652 forgiveness
2366 Christ, prophecies concerning	6700 peace
	8020 faith
	8125 guidance, promise
2424 gospel, promises	8453 obedience
3040 Holy Spirit, promise of	8607 prayer, God's promises

5468
promises, human

Believers must be faithful in keeping promises made to others and to God, because they have been called to live in integrity and truth. False or broken promises are considered as sin.

Examples of promises between people
Ge 14:22–24 *Abraham and the king of Sodom*; Ge 21:22–24 *Abraham and Abimelech*; Ge 47:29–31 *Jacob and Joseph*; Nu 30:1–16 *in family life*; Jos 2:12–21 *Rahab and the spies*

Examples of people making promises to God
Ge 28:20–21 *Jacob*; Jdg 11:29–40 *Jephthah*; 1Sa 1:11–20 *Hannah*; 2Sa 15:7–12 *Absalom*; Ne 10:28–29 *returning exiles*

Accompaniments to human promises
Taking an oath Dt 6:13 *See also* Ge 14:22; 21:24; 47:31; Jos 2:12–14; Ne 10:29

Declaring a curse 2Sa 3:35 *See also* Ru 1:17; 1Sa 14:24; 2Sa 3:9–10; 1Ki 2:23; Mt 26:73–75 pp Mk 14:70–72

Instructions regarding human promises
The importance of keeping promises Nu 30:1–2 *See also* Ps 50:14; Pr 5:18–23; Mal 2:14–16; Mt 19:4–9

The sin and peril of false promises Lev 19:12 *See also* Ex 20:7; Dt 23:21; Jer 8:11–12; Eze 13:1–7,10–12; Zec 8:17; 2Pe 2:17–19

The danger of making promises rashly, lightly or in ignorance Ecc 5:1–7 *See also* Pr 20:25; Mt 14:1–11 pp Mk 6:21–28; Mt 23:16–22

The call of Jesus Christ to integrity and truth in making promises
Mt 5:33–37 *See also* Dt 23:22–23; Ecc 5:2,5

See also

1460 truth	5827 curse
5329 guarantee	8248 faithfulness
5430 oaths, human	8751 false witness
5444 pledges	8807 profanity
5741 vows	8839 unfaithfulness
5800 blasphemy	

5469
promise, of Holy Spirit
See 3040 Holy Spirit, promise of

5471
proof

A confirmation and verification of a belief, such as belief in the existence of God, in the trustworthiness of a witness or in the resurrection of Jesus Christ.

5472
proof, as evidence

In the judicial sense, evidence is required to confirm the testimony of a witness. In the lives of believers, practical evidence should be obvious as proof of the reality of their faith.

The Mosaic law required proof to be offered in various legal contexts
In giving testimony Dt 19:15 *See also* Ex 23:2; Lev 5:1; Dt 17:6

In accusations of immorality Dt 22:13–21 *See also* Nu 5:11–31

In accusations of idolatry Dt 13:12–15

Evidence offered as proof of the gospel
The evidence of witnesses 2Pe 1:16–18 *See also* Ac 1:3; 1Co 15:5–7; Heb 2:3–4; 1Jn 1:1–3

Believers' lives are to prove the reality of their faith Jn 15:8 *See also* Mt 25:31–46; Ac 26:20; 1Co 4:2; 2Co 8:24

Evidence and signs given as proof
Looking for signs of the will of God Jdg 6:36–38

The signs of Jesus Christ as a basis of faith Jn 2:11

Jesus Christ's criticism of those who demanded other signs Mt 16:4 *The "sign of Jonah" is a reference to the resurrection of Jesus Christ.*

See also

1416 miracles	2366 Christ, prophecies concerning
1461 truth, nature of	
2351 Christ, miracles	

See also
2422 gospel,   5624 witnesses to
     confirmation   Christ
2560 Christ,   5625 witnesses,
     resurrection   false
5359 justice   7915 confirmation
5440 perjury   8112 certainty

5473
proof, through testing

God seeks proof of genuine love, faith and growth in the lives of his people. To this end, he tests them in various ways. However, when people test him, it is often a symptom of lack of trust.

Reasons for God's testing of Israel
To refine them Zec 13:8–9 *See also* Ps 66:10–12; Pr 17:3; Isa 48:10; Jer 6:27–30; 9:7

To prove their obedience Ex 16:4 *See also* Ex 15:25–26; Dt 8:2–5,15–16; Jdg 2:22; 3:1–4; 1Ch 29:17

To prove their love for him Dt 13:1–3

God tests individuals
1Pe 1:6–7 *See also* Ge 22:1–18 *Abraham*; Job 23:10 *Job*; 2Ch 32:31 *Hezekiah*; Jn 6:5–6 *Philip*; Jas 1:2–3,12

Those who test God are usually motivated by lack of trust
Ps 78:18–22 *See also* Ex 17:1–7; Nu 14:22–23; Dt 6:16; Ps 78:40–44,56–57; 106:13–15; 1Co 10:9; Heb 3:7–11; Ps 95:7–11

God may invite certain people to test him
Mal 3:10 *See also* Isa 7:10–14

God's people are to seek proof through testing in certain areas
Believers are to test themselves 2Co 13:5 *See also* Gal 6:4

Believers are to test what they hear 1Th 5:21 *See also* 1Co 14:29; 1Jn 4:1–3

See also
4351 refining   8020 faith
5560 suffering   8453 obedience
5593 trial   8477 self-
6020 sin   examination
7416 purification   8794 persecution
7774 prophets, false   8832 testing

5475

property

The ultimate source of all property is God. While property is entrusted to human beings, they have responsibilities towards God as a result of their stewardship.

5476
property, nature of

Possessions are a gift from God to be used for his glory, for human pleasure and in benefiting others.

Possessions are a cause for thanksgiving
Ecc 5:19 *See also* Ge 39:2–4; Dt 8:18; 1Ch 29:12; 2Ch 31:21; Hos 2:8

Owning possessions is open to abuse
They can be coveted Ex 20:17 *See also* 1Ki 21:1–4; Jer 6:13; Mic 2:2; Lk 12:15; 1Co 7:29–31

They can cause deceit Ac 5:1–9

They can cause pride and forgetfulness Pr 30:9 *See also* 2Ki 20:13–17; Da 4:30; 5:20; Hos 13:6; Mt 19:24; Lk 12:13–21

Abuse of ownership leads to judgment Isa 3:16–24; 5:8; Hab 2:6–9

Property is for benefiting others
It is to be used to help others Ac 2:44–45; 4:32–35; Gal 6:6,10; Eph 4:28; 1Ti 6:17–18; Jas 2:15–16; 1Jn 3:17–18

It is to be used to assist strangers Lev 25:35; Nu 35:15; Dt 10:19; Mt 5:42

Property provides no lasting satisfaction
Ecc 2:26 *See also* Job 27:16–17; Ps 39:6; Ecc 2:21; Eze 28:4–7; Hag 1:6; Mt 6:19–21; Lk 12:20–21; Jas 5:3

Laws governing the inheritance of property
Nu 27:3–11; Dt 21:15–17; Eze 46:16–18

Godly men of property
Ge 13:2 *Abraham*; Ge 26:14 *Isaac Jacob*; Ge 30:43; 32:5; 36:7 2Sa 19:32 *Barzillai*; 1Ch 29:28 *David Solomon*; 2Ch 1:15; 9:22 2Ch 32:27–29 *Hezekiah*; Job 1:3 *Job*; Mt 27:57 *Joseph of Arimathea*; Ac 4:36–37 *Barnabas*

See also
5556 stewardship   8260 generosity
5703 inheritance   8434 giving
5839 dissatisfaction   8701 affluence
5960 success   8763 forgetting
6133 coveting   8802 pride
6145 deceit   8808 riches

5477
property, land

All land belongs to God, and he allows people to care for it and use it for their own needs and the needs of others. The land promised to Israel is a special case illustrating the spiritual inheritance of all believers and God's ultimate purpose for the world.

All land belongs to God
It is in his possession and care Ps 24:1 *See also* Ex 9:29; Ps 33:5; 1Co 10:26

It is given to human beings to manage Ge 2:15 *All exploitation of land is therefore contrary to God's purpose. See also* Ps 8:6; 115:16

The land promised to Israel
It was promised on oath Ge 12:6–7 *See also* Ge 13:14–17; 15:7,18; 17:8; 50:24; Ex 6:8; Dt 6:10–11; 31:20–21; Jdg 2:1

It was a fruitful land Ex 3:8 *See also* Lev 20:24; Nu 14:7–8; Jos 5:6

The distribution of the land Lev 25:34; Nu 33:53–54; 35:2–5

Individual land rights
Legitimate purchase or sale Ge 23:15–16; 33:19; 47:20; 2Sa 24:24; Pr 31:16; Jer 32:6–15 *Jeremiah's purchase was an act of faith. Judas bought land with blood money:* Mt 27:7–10; Ac 1:18

Examples of renting SS 8:11; Mt 21:33–41 pp Mk 12:1–9 pp Lk 20:9–16

Laws of inheritance Nu 36:6–9; Mic 2:2

Encroachment was forbidden Dt 19:14 *Land boundaries were marked out by stones, the removal of which was a serious offence;* Dt 27:17; Job 24:2; Pr 22:28; 23:10; Hos 5:10

Redemption of land Lev 25:23–28; Ru 4:2–9

God's ultimate purpose for the world
The heavenly land Heb 11:13–16 *See also* Heb 11:8–10

A new heaven and earth Isa 65:17 *See also* Isa 66:22; Rev 21:1–2

The inheritance of the righteous Mt 5:5 *See also* Ps 37:11,29; 2Pe 3:13

See also
1325 God, the   5701 heir
     Creator   5802 care
4206 land   6720 redemption
5001 human race,   7257 promised land
     the   9160 new heavens &
5075 Abraham   new earth
5310 exploitation   9410 heaven
5657 birthright

5478
property, houses

From at least the time of the flood people have built houses to live in and these have been a major part of their property; the temple was seen as God's house.

Houses are a major part of people's property
Ex 12:22; Hag 1:4; Mt 7:24–27; Heb 3:3

The homeless have no property
1Co 4:11 *See also* Job 24:8; La 4:5; Lk 9:58

Property has no lasting value
Heb 10:34 *See also* Dt 6:11–12; Mt 19:29

Materials used in house building
Clay Job 4:19

Brick Ex 1:11–14; Isa 9:10

Stone and wood Lev 14:40,42; Hab 2:11

Luxurious building materials 1Ki 22:39; Est 1:6; Am 3:15

Houses are protected by God
Ps 127:1 *See also* Ex 12:27

Houses as dwellings
For sinners Jos 2:1; Pr 7:27; 21:9

For friends Zec 13:6; Lk 10:38; Jn 12:1–2

Other uses for houses
For work Jer 18:2
For hospitality Lk 10:5–7 pp Mt 10:11 pp Mk 6:10 See also Ge 19:3; Mt 25:35; Ac 16:15; 1Ti 5:10; Heb 13:2
For church gatherings Ac 20:20 See also Ro 16:5; 1Co 16:19; Col 4:15; Phm 2
As palaces 2Sa 7:2; 1Ki 7:1–2; 22:39; Da 4:29–30; Mt 11:8

Legislation concerning houses
Respecting the houses of others Ex 20:17; Mic 2:2
Redemption of property Lev 25:29–33

The LORD's house
God's promise to David 2Sa 7:11; 1Ki 5:5
Solomon's building 1Ki 6:1,2,7,12,14
Ezra's rebuilding Ezr 3:9–10
It was a place to meet God Ps 23:6; 27:4; 84:10; 122:1; Isa 56:7; Joel 3:18; Jn 2:16–17; Ps 69:9
It is a picture of the church Eph 2:19–20 See also 1Co 3:9–11

See also
5239 bricks	7025 church, unity
5240 building	7382 house of God
5339 home	7467 temple,
5340 house	Solomon's
5437 palaces	8445 hospitality

5480

protection

Defence from attack, hurt or exploitation. The ultimate protector is God but he also uses others in defending the weak and needy.

Protection from oppression
Ps 72:4 See also Dt 10:18; Ps 12:5; 35:10; Lk 1:51–53

Protection from exploitation
Job 24:3–4 See also Pr 30:14; Eze 18:10–13; Am 4:1; 8:4–6; Mk 12:38–40; Jas 5:1–6

Means of protection against physical attack
Armour 1Sa 17:38; 1Ki 20:11; Jer 46:4
Shields Jer 46:3
Helmets 1Sa 17:38; Jer 46:4

Spiritual protection
Jn 17:11–12 See also Jn 10:28–29; 1Co 10:13; Php 1:6; 4:7; 2Ti 1:12; 1Pe 1:5; Jude 24

Believers need protection from spiritual dangers
From Satan 1Pe 5:8 See also Job 1:9; Mt 6:13; Jn 17:15; Eph 6:11–12; 2Th 2:9; 3:3
From Satan's agents in the world Jn 15:18–19 See also Ps 27:2; 31:15; 109:1–3,31; Mic 7:2–3; Mt 10:28–29,36; Lk 1:68–74; Ro 8:36; 1Jn 3:13; 4:4

God protects his people
By watching over them and helping them Ps 121:5 See also 1Sa 2:9; Ps 1:6; 34:15; 37:40; 40:17; 140:1; 2Co 1:10

By his presence with them Heb 13:5 See also Jos 1:5; Ps 119:116,170; Isa 43:1–3; Jn 16:33; Ac 18:10

By sending angels to protect them
Ps 34:7 See also Ge 21:17; Ex 23:20; Nu 22:22,24,26,31,34; 2Ki 6:17; Ps 91:11; Mt 18:10; Heb 1:14

By using people to defend them
Pr 31:8–9 See also Nu 35:25; Isa 1:17; 58:6; Jer 5:28; 22:16; Lk 10:33–35; Jas 1:27

Conditions of God's protection
Prayer Ps 72:12 See also Job 6:23; Ps 59:1; 82:3; 145:19; Jn 17:11
Right attitudes Ps 91:14 See also Dt 23:14; Ps 116:6; Pr 2:7–8,11; 11:6; 14:3; 1Co 13:7

See also
2330 Christ as	5454 power, God's
shepherd	saving
4110 angels	5490 refuge
4126 Satan,	5527 shield
resistance to	8421 equipping,
5209 armour	physical
5291 defence	8727 enemies
5315 fortifications	8794 persecution

5481

proverb

A popular saying, regarded as conveying wisdom. Scripture records a great number of didactic proverbs and also preserves some popular sayings.

Proverbs identified with wisdom
Pr 26:7 See also Ps 49:1–4; Pr 1:1–6; 26:9; Ecc 12:9–11

Solomon's many proverbs
1Ki 4:29–34 See also Pr 1:1; 10:1; 25:1; Ecc 12:9–10

Kinds of proverb
On wisdom Pr 15:33 See also Pr 10:13; 11:2; 12:8; 13:10; 14:8; 16:16; 18:4; 19:8; 21:30; 23:4,9; 28:26; 29:15
On righteousness and wickedness Pr 10:3 See also Pr 10:16,28–32; 11:10; 12:3,10,21,26; 13:9; 14:32; 16:31; 18:10; 21:15; 25:26; 29:2
On wealth and poverty Pr 10:22 See also Pr 11:4,28; 15:16; 22:1–2,4; 23:4–5; 28:6,11; 29:3
On speech and silence Pr 10:19 See also Pr 11:12; 12:18–19; 15:4; 17:20,28; 18:21; 21:6,23; 25:15; 28:23
Longer discourses Pr 1:10–19 See also Pr 3:1–10,13–18; 5:1–23; 7:1–5; 30:15–16,21–31; 31:10–31
Popular sayings 1Sa 24:12–13 See also 1Sa 10:9–12; 19:23–24; Eze 12:21–25; 16:44–48; 18:1–4; Lk 4:23–30; 2Pe 2:17–22

See also
5118 Solomon	5923 public opinion
5438 parables	5935 riddles
5503 rich, the	7150 righteous, the
5546 speech	8365 wisdom,
5779 advice	human

5482

punishment

A form of physical pain or deprivation, generally in proportion to the offence which gives rise to it. Scripture stresses the reality of punishment by God for sin, while urging that human punishment should be humane.

5483

punishment, nature of

Punishment is the inevitable and equitable consequence of breaking the law of God. In keeping with God's justice and righteousness, punishment is administered by him or by human beings as his agents.

God warned Adam and Eve of the punishment for disobedience
Ge 2:16–17 See also Ge 3:1–5

Adam and Eve's original disobedience brought inevitable punishment
Upon the serpent Ge 3:14–15 See also Col 2:15; Rev 12:9; 20:1–3,10
Upon the woman Ge 3:16 See also Ps 48:6; Isa 13:8; 21:3; Jer 4:31; 1Ti 2:14–15
Upon the man Ge 3:19 See also Job 5:7; 7:1; Ps 90:5,7,8; Ecc 1:3; Isa 40:2
Upon creation Ge 3:17 See also Ge 5:29; Jer 12:4; Ro 8:19–22

The punishment of death
Ro 6:23 See also Eze 18:4; 33:8; Ro 5:12; 6:21; 1Co 15:21–22

Banishment as punishment
Ge 3:23 See also Ge 4:10–16; Dt 29:27,28; 2Ki 25:21; Mt 8:12

Punishment must be appropriate to the crime
Ge 9:6 See also Ex 21:23–25; Lev 24:17–22; Jdg 9:24

Punishment reflects the obligations of the offenders towards their victims
Ex 22:3 See also Ex 21:2,26–27; 22:4–9

Divine punishment is always totally just
Ge 18:25 See also Ge 20:4; Ex 34:7; Dt 32:35; 2Ch 6:23; Isa 3:11; Mt 16:27; 1Co 3:12–15; 1Th 4:6

God appoints human agents to administer his punishment
Ro 13:4 See also Isa 45:1,14; Jer 51:20; Mic 4:13; 1Pe 2:13–14

See also
1075 God, justice of	6020 sin
5436 pain	6112 banishment
5493 retribution	6154 fall, the
5495 revenge &	6652 forgiveness
retaliation	8718 disobedience
5560 suffering	9020 death

5484
punishment, by God

God's chastening of his children and his judgment on impenitent sinners and supernatural evil powers.

God's punishment of his children
Through the discipline of suffering and hardship Heb 12:5 – 7 *See also* Pr 3:11 – 12; Dt 4:36; 8:5; 2Sa 7:14; Job 5:17
Elihu's response to Job's suffering: Job 33:19; 36:10
Ps 32:3–4; 94:12–13; 118:18; 119:75; Zep 3:7; Jas 1:12; Rev 3:19

Through death 1Co 11:30 – 32 *See also* Lev 10:1 – 3; Nu 11:1 – 3; 1Sa 4:17 – 21; 2Sa 6:6 – 8 pp 1Ch 13:9 – 11

God's punishment of the ungodly
Their punishment is certain Ro 1:18 *See also* Pr 10:24; Isa 13:11; 26:21; 66:16; Jn 5:28 – 29; Eph 5:6; Col 3:6; 1Th 5:3; Heb 2:2 – 3

Their punishment is just Ps 96:13 *See also* Ge 18:25; Ex 9:27; Ps 98:9; Jn 5:28 – 30; Ro 3:5 – 8; 1Pe 2:23; Rev 16:5 – 7

Their punishment involves destruction in hell Lk 12:5 pp Mt 10:28 *See also* Mt 5:29 – 30

Fire as an image of destruction Mt 5:22 *See also* Isa 33:14; 66:15; Na 1:6; Mal 4:1; Mt 13:40 – 43; Mk 9:43,48; Lk 16:22 – 24; Jude 7,23; Rev 20:14 – 15

Their punishment will involve exclusion from God's presence Mt 7:23 *See also* Mt 22:13; 25:41; Lk 13:24 – 28; Rev 21:27

Their punishment will be eternal 2Th 1:8 – 9 *Interpreters differ over whether "everlasting destruction" implies an experience which continues for ever, or annihilation that is everlasting in the sense of being irreversible. See also* Da 12:2; Mt 25:46; Rev 14:11

The punishment of the second death Rev 2:11 *The "second death" refers to the final state of the unrepentant. See also* Rev 20:6; 21:8

There will be degrees of punishment Mk 12:40 pp Lk 20:47 *See also* Mt 11:22,24; Lk 12:47 – 48

The punishment of God's spiritual enemies
Satan Rev 20:2 *See also* Isa 14:12 – 15; 1Ti 3:6; Heb 2:14; Rev 12:9; 20:10

Fallen angels 2Pe 2:4 *See also* Isa 24:21 – 22; Mt 25:41; Jude 6

See also
1025 God, anger of	8231 discipline,
4116 angels opposed	divine
to God	9210 judgment,
4127 Satan, defeat of	God's
4826 fire	9240 last judgment
5295 destruction	9511 hell, place of
5926 rebuke	punishment

5485
punishment, legal aspects of

The law sets out details of penalties which may be imposed upon people as a result of their committing of offences.

Just punishments
Banishment Ge 3:23 *See also* 2Sa 14:13 – 14; Ezr 7:26; Job 18:18; Jer 16:15; 23:8; 29:14; Zec 5:3

Beating Dt 25:2 – 3

Burning Ge 38:24 *See also* Lev 20:14; 21:9; Da 3:6

Confiscation of property Est 8:1 *See also* Ezr 10:8

Hanging Jos 8:29 *See also* Dt 21:22 – 23; Jos 10:26; 1Sa 31:8 – 10; 2Sa 4:12
Hanging is sometimes a self-inflicted punishment: 2Sa 17:23; Mt 27:5
2Sa 21:9 – 10; Gal 3:13

Impaling Ezr 6:11 *See also* Ge 40:19 – 22
Hanging was by impaling among the Persians: Est 2:23 fn; 5:14

Stoning Ex 19:12 – 13 *See also* Ex 21:29; Lev 20:2,27
The punishment for blasphemy: Lev 24:14,16,23
Nu 15:36; Dt 13:10; 17:5; 21:21; 22:21,24; Jos 7:25; 1Ki 21:13 – 15

Unjust punishments and persecutions
Banishment Ac 18:2

Beating Mt 27:26 pp Mk 15:15 pp Jn 19:1 *See also* Isa 53:5; Ac 16:37; 2Co 11:24

Beheading Mt 14:9 – 10 pp Mk 6:27 *See also* Mk 6:16; Ac 12:2; Rev 20:4

Being thrown to wild animals Da 6:16; 1Co 15:32

Hanging Ac 5:30 *See also* Ac 10:39

Imprisonment Ac 5:18 *See also* Ge 39:20 – 22; 1Ki 22:27; Jer 37:15; 38:6; Ac 12:4; 16:23; 23:35; 26:10; 2Co 11:23; Heb 11:36

Stoning Ac 7:59 *See also* 1Ki 12:18 pp 2Ch 10:18; La 3:53; Mt 21:35; Ac 14:19; 2Co 11:25; Heb 11:37

Confiscation of property 1Ki 21:15 – 16 *See also* 2Sa 16:4

See also
5257 civil authorities	5375 law
5275 cremation	5475 property
5277 criminals	5557 stoning
5313 flogging	7346 death penalty
5331 hanging	8794 persecution
5344 imprisonment	

queen

In OT times the chief wife of a king's harem or a female monarch. A queen mother, as a king's widow and the mother of the reigning king, would have held a position of some authority and influence.

A queen as the wife of a king
A chief wife among several Est 2:17 *See also* Est 1:9 – 12; 2:4

Enjoying a position of some influence Est 1:15 – 18; 2:22; 5:12; 7:5 – 8

Enjoying the king's special favour Est 5:2 – 3 *See also* Est 7:1 – 3; 8:1,7; 9:12; SS 6:8 – 9; Ne 2:6; Ps 45:9

Sometimes granted considerable authority Est 9:29 *See also* Est 9:31

A queen as a female monarch
The queen of Sheba 1Ki 10:1 pp 2Ch 9:1 *See also* 1Ki 10:2 – 10 pp 2Ch 9:1 – 9; 1Ki 10:13 pp 2Ch 9:12; Mt 12:42 pp Lk 11:31

Queen Athaliah of Judah 2Ki 11:1 – 21 pp 2Ch 22:10 – 23:21

Queen used figuratively
Of Jerusalem La 1:1; Eze 16:13

Of Babylon Isa 47:5,7; Rev 18:7

Queen of Heaven: a title for the Babylonian goddess Ishtar
Jer 7:18; 44:17 – 19,25

A queen mother as a king's widow and mother of the reigning king
1Ki 2:19 *See also* 1Ki 15:13 pp 2Ch 15:16; 2Ki 10:13; 24:8,12,15; Jer 13:18; 22:26; 29:2; Da 5:10; Ac 8:27

See also
4215 Babylon	5457 power, human
5215 authority	5509 rulers
5280 crown	5581 throne
5345 influence	8747 false gods
5366 king	

quivers

A case for carrying arrows on hunting expeditions or in battle.

Quivers used on hunting expeditions
Ge 27:3

Loaded quivers taken into battle
Job 39:23; Isa 22:6

Quivers referred to figuratively
To depict the deadly fire-power of an enemy Jer 5:16

As a symbol of a man's many sons Ps 127:5

To depict the LORD's concealment of his servant Isa 49:2

As an instrument of the LORD's discipline La 3:13

See also
5206 archers	5236 bow and arrow
5210 arrows	

rank

A person's seniority and/or status, especially in military, government or priestly positions. Christians should not be concerned about rank or status.

Differences in rank amongst those in charge of both military and civil affairs
Emperor Lk 2:1; 3:1

King 2Sa 5:3 – 5; 1Ki 4:1

Judge Jdg 2:16 – 19 *The book of Judges calls individual judges "deliverers" e.g., 3:9, 15.*

Prince Jdg 5:15; 2Sa 3:38

Leader Nu 2:3–7,10–12; Jdg 4:4; 1Sa 10:1

Military ranks

Commander 2Sa 2:8; Ac 24:22

Captain Ge 39:1; Jdg 5:14; 2Ki 1:9–13; Isa 3:3

Officer 1Ki 4:5; 9:22; 1Ch 27:1; Ac 25:23

Centurion Mt 8:5; Ac 27:43

Civil ranks

Noble Est 1:3; 2:18

Official 1Ch 28:1; Jer 52:10

Governor 1Ki 4:7–19; Hag 1:1; Ac 23:24

Tetrarch Lk 3:1

Heads of clans/tribes Jos 14:1; 1Ki 8:1

Heads of families Nu 7:2; Jos 2:12–13

Division of labour involving different degrees of responsibility Ex 18:20–23

Rank was conferred as a reward
1Sa 18:5

Rank within the priesthood

The high priest Lev 21:10; Nu 35:25,28,32; Hag 1:1; Zec 3:1; Lk 3:2

Priests Ex 28:1–2; Lev 8:5–12; Nu 4:16; Jos 22:31; 2Ki 11:9

Levites Ex 32:26; Nu 1:50; Dt 12:18–19; 2Ch 11:13–14

Officers in the NT church
In contrast to the priesthood, offices within the NT Church are according to gifts; individuals with different gifts are listed but do not form a hierarchy: Ro 12:4–8; 1Co 12:28–30; Eph 4:11
Even where there is a hint of rank, the qualities of both classes are very similar: Php 1:1; 1Ti 3:1–13

Some individuals are worthy of double honour 1Ti 5:17 *Comparison between verses 17 and 28 of Acts 20 shows that the same individuals could be called "elders", "overseers" or "shepherds" (pastors).*

All believers are called priests 1Pe 2:5,9; Rev 1:6; 5:10; 20:6

Jesus Christ taught his disciples not to seek rank or status
Mt 18:1–4 pp Mk 9:33–37 pp Lk 9:46–48

See also

5245 captain	5434 officer
5250 centurion	5509 rulers
5257 civil authorities	5554 status
5261 commander	5723 nobles
5327 governors	7376 high priest
5358 judges	7766 priests

5490

refuge

A safe retreat; a place of healing and renewal; also a stronghold from which to launch a counter-attack.

False refuges
Flight Ge 3:8–9; Ps 139:7–12 *See also* Isa 28:15,17

Idolatry Isa 44:9 *See also* Dt 32:31,37–38

Human support Jer 17:5 *See also* Ps 20:7–8; 142:4; Isa 30:1–2; Zec 4:6; Php 3:3

False confidence Jer 6:14 *See also* Eze 13:10–12; Mt 7:26–27; Rev 6:15–17

God alone is the true refuge of believers
Dt 33:27 *See also* 1Sa 2:2; 2Sa 22:32; Ps 18:31; 46:1; 62:6–7; Jn 10:28–29; Ro 8:31–32,38–39; Php 4:7

Pictures to describe God as a refuge

A fortress Ps 46:7 *See also* Ps 28:8; 48:3; 59:16; 62:2; 71:3; 91:2; 144:1–3

A rock 2Sa 22:2–3 pp Ps 18:2 *See also* Ge 49:24; Dt 32:4,15; 2Sa 22:47; Ps 31:2; 94:22; Isa 26:4; Hab 1:12

A shade Ps 91:1 *See also* Ps 121:5; SS 2:3; Isa 25:4–5

Sheltering wings Ps 57:1 *See also* Dt 32:10–11; Ru 2:12; Ps 17:8; 36:7; Mt 23:37

A shield Ge 15:1 *See also* Dt 33:29; 2Sa 22:31; Ps 3:3; 28:7; 84:11; Pr 30:5; Eph 6:16

A tower Pr 18:10 *See also* Ps 61:3

Cities of refuge
Nu 35:11 *See also* Dt 4:41–43; 19:1–13; Jos 20:1–9

See also

1240 God, the Rock	5585 towers
4218 cave	5942 security
4354 rock	5954 strength
5316 fortress	6510 salvation
5491 refugees	7338 cities of refuge
5511 safety	7438 sanctuary

5491

refugees

Fugitives driven from home because of personal, political or religious persecution, or because of physical danger.

Examples of refugees
Ge 16:6–8 *Hagar*; Ge 46:1; Ex 12:37–39; Ru 1:1; Mt 2:13–15 *Mary, Joseph and Jesus Christ*; Ac 18:2

Refugees are to be treated kindly
Dt 23:15–16; Mt 25:35; Phm 10:16

Refugees from legal accusation are to be provided for
Nu 35:6; Jos 20:1–6

The LORD is a place of spiritual refuge
Dt 33:27; 2Sa 22:3; Ps 9:9; 59:16; Isa 25:4; Jer 16:19; Na 1:7

See also

1320 God as Saviour	5590 travel
5319 fugitives	5689 friendlessness
5446 poverty	6687 mercy, God's
5480 protection	7338 cities of refuge
5490 refuge	

5492

restitution

The return of something lost or stolen so that the original situation is restored. This central theme of the

OT law is supremely fulfilled through Jesus Christ making restitution for Adam's sin, thus restoring fellowship with God and hope of eternal life.

Reasons for restitution
For crimes committed Ex 22:2–3 *See also* Ex 22:7,16–17; Lev 6:1–6; 24:17–21; Nu 5:6–7; Eze 33:14–15

For accidental loss Ex 22:5–6 *See also* Ex 21:33–34; 22:10–15

For unintentional sin Lev 5:14–16

As part of confession Nu 5:5–7

In cases of misplaced accusation Ps 69:4

The basis of decisions regarding restitution
Arbitration Ex 22:8–9

The amount of restitution is to exceed the amount stolen Ex 22:1 *See also* Ex 22:4; Lev 6:5; 2Sa 12:5–6; Pr 6:31

Land should belong to its rightful owners 2Sa 9:7

Examples of restitution
1Sa 6:17 *The Philistines make restitution for desecrating the ark of God;* 1Ki 20:34 *Ben-Hadad makes restitution for the cities his father had taken from Israel;* 2Ki 8:1–6 *The king makes restitution to the Shunammite by returning her house and land;* Ne 5:10–12 *Nehemiah orders restitution to be made to the poor;* Lk 19:8–9 *Zacchaeus makes restitution to those he had cheated.*

The act of restitution is to be motivated by love
Ro 13:8–10 *See also* Mt 5:23–24,44; Col 3:13–14

God promises physical restitution
Isa 57:18; 61:3–4; Jer 30:17–18

Jesus Christ makes restitution for sin
He restores fellowship with God Ro 5:19 *See also* 2Co 5:21; Heb 9:28

He restores the hope of eternal life 1Co 15:21–22 *See also* 1Co 15:45–49

Restitution is made to Jesus Christ
Php 2:8–9 *Here God's exaltation of Jesus Christ is seen as restitution to his position of glory. See also* Isa 53:10–12

Restitution is made to those who make sacrifices for the gospel
Mt 19:21 pp Mk 10:21 pp Lk 18:22 *See also* Mt 19:29 pp Mk 10:29–30 pp Lk 18:29–30; Mk 8:35 pp Mt 16:25 pp Lk 9:24; Jn 12:24–25; Php 3:8–10

See also

2321 Christ as	6716 reconciliation
redeemer	6730 reinstatement
2336 Christ,	6732 repentance
exaltation	7370 guilt offering
5493 retribution	8154 righteousness
6029 sin, forgiveness	9165 restoration
6676 justification	

5493

retribution

Recompense for evil. In Scripture this is the prerogative of God and of the authorities ordained by God, and never of individuals.

The principle of retribution
Ex 20:5–6; Ro 12:19; Heb 10:30 *See also* Dt 32:35; Ex 32:33–34; Lev 26:23–25; Dt 7:9–10; 32:41–43; Job 34:11; Pr 24:12; Isa 1:24; Na 1:2

Divine retribution is just
Ge 18:25 *See also* Dt 32:3–4; 2Ch 12:1–6; Ps 58:10–11; Jer 5:7–9,26–29; Hos 4:6

Retribution is often built into the nature of wrongdoing
Ps 7:15–16 *See also* Ps 37:14–15; Pr 1:18; 26:27; 28:10; Ecc 10:8; Mt 26:52; Gal 6:7–8

Retribution is placed in the hands of governments
Ge 9:6; Ex 21:23–25 *This "lex talionis" (law of exacting like for like) was not for private retribution. It insisted that justice be fair and not out of proportion to the crime;* Ro 13:4 *See also* Lev 24:17–22; Nu 35:16–25; 1Pe 2:14

Private retribution is forbidden
Pr 24:29 *See also* Mt 5:38–39; Ro 12:19

Prayer for retribution
Ps 28:4 *Christians can agree with these prayers, hating all that opposes the Lord and goodness, and gladly anticipating the ultimate vindication of God's glory. Christians leave judgment in God's hands, but nonetheless grieve over the world's pain and over the death of every unrepentant sinner;* 2Th 1:6–10 *See also* Ps 79:10; 94:1–2; 137:8–9; La 3:64–66

The final retribution
Rev 20:15 *See also* Ps 62:11–12; Jn 5:28–29; Ro 2:5–11

Examples of direct divine retribution on people
In the fall Ge 3:14,17 *See also* Ge 3:15–16,18–19

In the flood Ge 6:5–7

At the Tower of Babel *See also* Ge 11:5–7

On Sodom and Gomorrah Ge 19:24

In the ten plagues on Egypt Ex 7:16–17; 11:1; 12:29

On the Israelites in the wilderness Ex 32:35 *See also* 1Co 10:6–10

On the heathen nations Lev 18:25; Dt 9:4

On the rebellious nation of Israel Lev 18:28; Dt 28:47–48

On idolatrous Judah Isa 65:6–7; 66:6; Eze 5:11–13

On Babylon Jer 51:6,24,56

Upon all the nations Ob 15–16

On Jerusalem Mt 23:35–36 *This judgment came on Jerusalem in* A.D. *70.*

Upon persecutors and unbelievers 1Th 2:14–16

Examples of divine retribution on individuals
Ac 12:23 *See also* Nu 16:30; 2Sa 6:7; 12:10; Jer 23:2; Ac 5:3–5,9; 1Co 11:29–30

Examples of divine retribution through human beings
Jdg 1:7; 9:56–57; 2Sa 18:17 *Through Jehu upon the house of Ahab:* 2Ki 9:7,24,30–33

Natural retribution
Ro 1:27; 2Ti 3:13

Examples of retribution by the state
Jos 7:25; 1Ki 2:31–32; Est 7:10; Lk 23:40–41

National retribution
Jos 10:13–14; Jdg 11:36; Est 9:5 *The special case of God's dealings with the nation of Israel and her enemies is not a basis on which to argue for a concept of a war, just or otherwise. A just war has to be in defence of the nation or of the defenceless, and involve a minimum of suffering.*

Warnings of future retribution
Ac 17:31 *See also* Mt 25:31–32

See also
1075 God, justice of	5494 revenge
1310 God as judge	8450 martyrdom
5214 attack	9105 last things
5215 authority	9210 judgment,
5359 justice	God's
5482 punishment	9510 hell

5494

revenge

The returning of injury or insult. Scripture insists that human revenge is unacceptable and is to be left in the hands of God.

5495

revenge, and retaliation

Scripture teaches that it is wrong to strike back or to return evil for evil, whether by immediate retaliation or by taking revenge later. Justice must be done, but this must be left in the hands of God, or of the authorities ordained by God.

OT teaching about revenge
Revenge forbidden in the OT Ge 4:15; Lev 19:18; Dt 32:35; Pr 20:22 *See also* Dt 19:5–7,11–13; 23:7; Pr 24:29; Jer 29:7

The "lex talionis" (law of exacting like for like) Ex 21:23–25 *This was not a rule for personal revenge but to ensure that judicial punishments were neither unjust nor malicious. See also* Lev 24:17–21; Dt 19:18–21

Personal revenge forbidden in the NT
By Jesus Christ Mt 5:38–45 *See also* Lk 6:27–36

By the apostles Ro 12:17; 1Th 5:15; 1Pe 3:9 *See also* 1Co 13:4–5

The evil effects of revenge illustrated in the life of Samson
Jdg 15:1–8,9–10,11–12

Alternatives to revenge
Avoiding the problem Ro 12:18; 1Pe 4:8

Evading the attack Mt 10:23; Lk 4:29–30

Accepting the injury 1Co 6:7; Heb 10:32–34

Using the law Ac 22:25; 1Co 6:1–6 *going to law*

Forgiving and setting an example Lk 23:34; Ac 7:59–60 *Ashes on the head were a sign of repentance. Doing good to one's attackers may lead them to a change of heart:* Ro 12:19–21; Pr 25:21–22

God will avenge his people
Lk 18:7–8 *See also* Dt 32:43; 1Sa 24:12; 2Ki 9:7; Ps 18:47; Rev 6:10; 19:2

See also
5359 justice	7346 death penalty
5493 retribution	7438 sanctuary
5944 self-defence	8292 love
6652 forgiveness	9105 last things
7310 avenger of	
blood	

5496

revenge, examples of

Ungodly people are often vengeful, and even Christians are not always exemplary in this respect. However, each case should be considered on its merits, and the claims of justice taken into account.

Revenge among the ungodly
Lk 6:11 pp Mt 12:14 pp Mk 3:6 *See also* Ge 4:24 *Compare Lamech's words with those of Jesus Christ in* Mt 18:21–22; 1Ki 19:2 *Jezebel;* 1Ki 22:27 *Ahab;* Est 3:6 *Haman;* Eze 25:15 *the Philistines Herodias:* Mk 6:19,24 Ac 5:33 *the Sanhedrin;* Ac 23:12 *unbelieving Jews*

Revenge among God's people
Jdg 8:4–9; Est 9:1,5 *See also* Ge 16:5–6; Gal 4:30; Jdg 16:28–30 *Samson;* 1Sa 25:10–13; 2Sa 10:4–7 *David did not retaliate at once, but only when a military threat appeared;* 2Sa 3:27 *Joab;* Lk 9:51–56 *James and John;* Jn 18:10–11 *Peter;* Ac 23:2–5 *Paul*

Examples of non-retaliation
By Jesus Christ 1Pe 2:23 *See also* Isa 50:6–7; 53:7; Lk 23:34

By David 1Sa 24:1–12; Ps 35:11–14,17; 38:12–15

By others Ge 50:15–21 *Joseph;* 1Sa 12:23 *Samuel;* 1Ki 22:24–25 *Micaiah;* Job 31:29 *Job;* Ac 7:59–60 *Stephen*

Expressions of desire for revenge
Ps 28:4; 109:8–14; 137:8–9; Jer 15:15; 18:21; Gal 1:8–9; 5:12; Rev 6:10; 16:5–7; 18:6,20

See also

2315 Christ as Lamb	8794 persecution
8450 martyrdom	8828 spite

5498

reward

Recompense in recognition of services rendered. Scripture stresses that while salvation is a gift of God, believers will be rewarded according to their deeds. Believers should be honest in rewarding others for their work.

5499
reward, divine

God's dealings with people are always in harmony with his grace and his justice, hating evil and loving good. No gift of God is on the basis of merit, but on the basis of his faithfulness to his promises.

God's reward is in harmony with his character

His graciousness Ro 4:4–5 *See also* Ps 103:10; Mt 20:14–15; Lk 17:7–10; Ro 11:6–7; Eph 2:8–10

His justice Ro 2:6–11 *See also* Dt 28:1–2 *blessings for obedience;* Dt 28:15 *curses for disobedience;* Ps 19:9–11; 62:12; Pr 13:21; 14:14; Jer 17:10; 32:19; 1Co 3:8; 2Co 9:6; Gal 6:7–9; Eph 6:8; Col 3:25

The reward of the ungodly

Ro 6:23 *See also* Ex 20:5; Dt 7:9–10; Pr 22:22–23; Isa 13:11; 26:21; 59:18; 65:6–7; 66:6; Eze 7:4; 9:10; 11:21; Hos 9:7; Zep 1:12; 2Th 1:6; Heb 2:1–2

The reward of the godly

God's treatment of the righteous
Ro 8:17–18 *See also* Ex 19:5; Ru 2:12; 2Sa 22:25 pp Ps 18:20, 24; 1Ki 3:14; 2Ch 15:7; Ps 19:9–11; 58:11; Pr 11:18,28; 13:21; 19:17; 31:31; Isa 62:10–12; Jer 31:16; Mt 5:12; Lk 6:34–35; 1Co 2:9–10; Jas 1:25

The example of Jesus Christ
Php 2:8–11 *See also* Heb 12:2–3

Apparent unfair treatment of the godly
Ps 73:13–14 *See also* Job 1:1; 2:11–13; 9:29–31; Isa 49:4; Hab 1:12–13; Mt 5:10; 2Ti 3:12

See also

1055 God, grace & mercy	5522 servants, work conditions
1075 God, justice of	5882 impartiality
2057 Christ, obedience	8265 godliness
2336 Christ, exaltation	8437 giving talents
2339 Christ, example of	8454 obedience to God
5482 punishment	9413 heaven, inheritance

5500
reward, for God's people

God gives blessings to his people who serve him faithfully and who suffer for him. God himself is his people's greatest reward. The fulness will be theirs at the coming of Jesus Christ.

God promises to reward his people

For faithful service 1Co 3:12–15; Col 3:23–24 *See also* Ex 32:28–29; Nu 14:30; 25:10–13; Isa 40:10; 62:11; Da 12:3; Mt 10:41–42; 25:28–29; Mk 9:41

In and through self-denial Mt 19:29 pp Mk 10:29–30 *See also* Mt 16:24–26; 19:21; Lk 18:28–30; 1Co 9:26–27; Heb 10:33–34; 11:36–40

At the coming of Jesus Christ
Mt 19:27–28 *See also* Mt 16:27; 25:31–36; Lk 14:12–14; 2Ti 4:7–8; 1Pe 5:4; Rev 22:12

God himself is his people's greatest reward

Ge 15:1 *See also* Dt 32:9; Ps 73:26; Rev 21:3

The certainty of future reward is an incentive to holiness

Php 3:12–14 *See also* Heb 10:35; 11:6,24–26; 2Jn 8; Rev 2:10

See also

1335 blessing	8110 athletics
2375 kingdom of God	8117 discipleship, benefits
2565 Christ, second coming	8248 faithfulness
5280 crown	8266 holiness
6644 eternal life	8342 servanthood
6744 sanctification	9310 resurrection

5501
reward, human

Honest reward for services rendered is commended. Even though such reward is often deserved, it is not always given.

Reward for services rendered

Payment for work done Col 4:1 *See also* Ge 29:28–29; 2Sa 19:32–36; Pr 13:13; Mt 20:1–2; 25:23; Ro 4:4; 1Co 9:24–25; 1Ti 5:17–18

Favour for help received 1Sa 17:23–25 *See also* Ge 41:41–45; Jos 2:14; Est 6:1–3,6–10; Da 2:46–49

Unjust treatment and reward

Ac 10:37–39
In a sinful world, good is often unrewarded, or even repaid with evil: Ge 29:22–25; 39:19–20; 40:23; Nu 14:1–4; 1Sa 25:21; 2Sa 15:1–4; Ps 41:9; 55:12–14; Jer 38:4–6; Jn 13:18

Dishonest reward forbidden

Dt 16:19 *In a fallen world there are many opportunities to gain by wrongdoing. See also* Nu 22:7,16–17; 24:11; 1Ki 13:7–8; 2Ki 5:20–24; Job 17:5; Isa 1:23;

Mic 3:11; 7:3; Mt 26:14–15 pp Mk 14:10–11; Ac 1:18

Rewarding the undeserving

Ro 12:20 *See also* Ge 47:11–12; 1Sa 12:23; 24:16–19; Mt 5:38–41,44–47

See also

5238 bribery	5798 betrayal
5347 injustice	5861 favour, human
5404 masters	5876 helpfulness
5489 rank	6145 deceit
5603 wages	8442 good works
5628 work	

5503

rich, the

It is hard but not impossible for rich people to enter God's kingdom. They must put their hope in God, not in their riches. Rich people who live selfishly, abuse their position and fail to repent and live for Jesus Christ, are in peril.

Parables concerning rich people

2Sa 12:1–10; Mt 13:44–46; 18:23; 22:2 pp Lk 14:16; Mt 25:14 pp Lk 19:12; Lk 12:16; 15:11–13; 16:1; 18:10

Rich people have received blessing

1Ti 6:17 *See also* Ps 1:3; 112:1–3

They have friends Pr 14:20; 19:4

They have power Pr 22:7

They have security Pr 10:15; 18:11

Warnings to rich people

They should recognise that God is the giver of riches Dt 8:17–18 *See also* Dt 32:13–15; Hos 2:8

They should not be arrogant or complacent on account of their riches Jer 9:23–24 *See also* Ps 49:5–6; Jer 49:4; Hos 12:8; 1Ti 6:17; Rev 3:17

They should not trust in their riches Pr 11:28 *See also* Ps 49:6; 52:7; 62:10; Jer 48:7

They face disaster if they lack wisdom Ps 49:20 *See also* Pr 28:11; Jer 9:23–24

They must live moral lives Pr 28:6 *See also* Pr 22:16; Jer 5:27–28; 17:11; Mic 6:12

Wealth can bring anxiety Ecc 5:12 *See also* Mt 6:25–34 pp Lk 12:22–31

Riches are of fleeting value Lk 12:16–21 *See also* Ps 49:5–12; Pr 27:24; Ecc 5:15; Isa 10:3; Mt 6:19; 1Ti 6:7; Job 1:21; Jas 1:10–11

Ultimate security is found in God alone Ex 15:2; 2Sa 22:33; 1Ch 16:11; Ps 28:7; 29:11; 46:1; 52:6–7; Isa 12:2; Hab 3:19

It is hard for rich people to enter God's kingdom Mt 19:23–26 pp Mk 10:23–27 pp Lk 18:24–27 *See also* Mt 13:22 pp Mk 4:18–19 pp Lk 8:14; Mt 19:16–22 pp Mk 10:17–22 pp Lk 18:18–23

Rich people will be judged for their behaviour

Zec 11:5–6; Lk 1:53

If they exploit, oppress or kill the poor
Jas 5:1–4 See also Pr 14:31; 22:16; 28:3;
Eze 18:12–13; 22:29–31; Jas 2:6; 5:6

If they hoard wealth and live selfishly
Jas 5:5 See also Lk 12:16–21; 16:19–31

If they slander the name of Jesus Christ Jas 2:7

Commands to rich people
To seek God's kingdom as first priority
Mt 6:19–21,31–33 pp Lk 12:29–31;
1Ti 6:19

To repent from sin Rev 3:17,19

To be generous towards the needy
1Ti 6:18 See also Mt 19:21 pp Mk 10:21
pp Lk 18:22; Lk 3:11; 11:41; 12:33–34;
14:12–14; 16:9; 19:8; 2Co 8:1–5,9 Jesus
Christ's example the motivation for
generosity; 2Co 8:13–15; 9:6–15

Incorrect attitudes to the rich
Ecc 10:20 cursing them; Ps 49:16–17
living in awe of them; Ps 49:5–6 fearing
them
Showing favouritism to them:
Job 34:18–19; Pr 22:2; Jas 2:1–4

God brings good news for rich people
Ps 22:29–31; Mt 9:9–10 pp Mk 2:14–15
pp Lk 5:27–29; Mt 27:57 pp Mk 15:43
pp Lk 23:50–51; Lk 19:1–10

Examples of rich people
Abraham: Ge 12:10–16; 13:2
Ge 26:1–14 Isaac
Jacob: Ge 27:19,28; 30:29–43; 35:11–12
The Israelites, who entered a fertile
promised land with an abundance of
wealth plundered from the Egyptians:
Ge 15:14; Ex 3:22; 12:36; Ps 105:37
1Ki 10:23 pp 2Ch 9:22 Solomon
Hezekiah: 2Ki 20:13; 2Ch 32:27–29
Joseph of Arimathea; Mt 27:57–60
pp Mk 15:43–46 pp Lk 23:50–53;
Jn 19:38–42

See also
2339 Christ, example	6732 repentance
of	8260 generosity
5412 money	8790 oppression
5446 poverty	8808 riches
5810 complacency	8827 selfishness
5890 insecurity	8849 worry
5942 security	

rights

The basis of a claim to respect, and
just and fair treatment. God has
rights over his creation as a result of
his sovereignty and authority.
Through being the height of his
creation, human beings also have
rights, which are to be respected.

The rights that God gives
God gives rights to the poor and needy
Ex 22:22 See also Ex 22:25–27;
Lev 19:9–10; Job 36:6

God gives rights to slaves Lev 22:11
See also Ex 21:2–6 pp Dt 15:12–18;
Ex 21:7–11,26–27

God gives rights to strangers
Lev 19:33–34 See also Ex 22:21;
Lev 19:10

**God gives rights to those who commit
manslaughter** Nu 35:9–12 See also
Dt 4:41–42; Jos 20:1–6

God gives rights in marriage
1Co 7:3–5 See also Ex 21:7–11;
Dt 22:13–21; Eph 5:22–33

God gives rights to parents Col 3:20
pp Eph 6:1 See also Ex 20:12 pp Dt 5:16;
1Ti 5:4

God gives rights to children Heb 12:16
See also Ge 25:29–34; Dt 21:15–17;
1Ch 5:1–2; Eph 6:4

God gives rights to Christians Jn 1:12
See also Gal 3:26–4:7; Rev 2:7; 3:21;
22:14

God gives rights to leaders 1Co 9:18
See also 1Co 9:1–17; 1Ti 5:17–18

Why God gives rights
**God gives rights to keep an orderly
society** Lev 19:29 See also Dt 15:1–6

God gives rights to protect people
Dt 19:15 See also Lev 25:23–43,47–55

The defence of rights
God, the defender of rights Mic 7:8–10
The implied speaker here is Israel. See also
Dt 10:18; Ps 68:5; Pr 23:10–11

Abuse of rights punished by God
Isa 10:1–4 See also Jer 5:26–29;
Am 2:6–8

**Leaders are to protect the rights of
others** Ps 72:1–4 See also Pr 31:4–9;
Ecc 5:8

The rights which God has
God has a right to be worshipped
2Ki 17:36 See also Mt 4:10 pp Lk 4:8;
Dt 6:13; Jn 4:24

God has a right to be obeyed
Dt 10:12–13 See also Dt 26:16–18;
30:16

See also
5051 responsibility	5520 servants
5215 authority	5657 birthright
5359 justice	5738 sons
5375 law	5743 widows
5404 masters	6710 privileges
5477 property, land	8402 claims

roads

Recognised routes for travellers, or
streets in towns and cities. In biblical
times travelling by road was
recognised as dangerous.

Kinds of road
In the open country Ex 13:17–18;
Ac 19:1 See also Ge 16:7; Nu 20:17;
Dt 1:2; Jos 10:10–11; Jdg 21:19;
1Sa 17:52; Isa 15:5

In towns and cities Ac 9:11 See also
Est 6:9; Jer 37:21

Activities associated with roads and streets
Travelling Jdg 5:10; 2Ki 2:23; Lk 9:57;
10:30–33; Ac 8:36

Talking Lk 24:32 See also Dt 6:7;
Mk 9:33; Lk 10:4; 13:26

Waiting 1Sa 4:13; 2Sa 15:2; 1Ki 20:38

Helping others Dt 22:4; 27:18;
Lk 10:30–33

Leisure and play Zec 8:4–5

Begging Lk 18:35

Living on the streets Mt 22:9–10
pp Lk 14:21–23 See also Job 31:32

Prayer Mt 6:5

Idolatry 2Ch 28:24; Jer 44:17; Eze 16:25

Injustice and dishonesty Isa 59:14 See
also Jer 5:1

Dangers of the road
Ezr 8:31 See also 1Ki 13:24; Ezr 8:22;
Ecc 12:5; Pr 22:13; Hos 7:1;
Lk 10:30–33

Troubled times affecting roads and streets
Ps 55:11; Na 2:4 See also Jos 2:19;
Jer 6:25; Hos 6:9; Isa 5:25; 33:7–8;
51:20; Am 5:16

Roads and streets deserted Jdg 5:6 See
also Jer 9:21; 33:10; La 1:4; Zep 3:6

Escape Jer 48:19

The road back from exile
Isa 40:3 See also Isa 11:16; 35:8; 57:14

Roads used figuratively
Mt 7:13–14 See also Ge 49:17; Pr 15:19;
Isa 59:8; Jer 3:2; 18:15; 31:21; Lk 3:5;
Rev 22:2

Roads of special importance in the NT
The road to Emmaus Lk 24:13–32

The road to Damascus Ac 9:3–9,17;
22:6; 26:13

See also
5197 walking	5586 town
5256 city	5590 travel
5263 communication	5828 danger
5336 highway	8168 way, the

roof

Most buildings in biblical times had
flat roofs. With the hot climate, they
had a wider range of uses than
merely providing shelter for the
building.

Uses of roofs
**Shelter erected on the roof to make an
extra room** 2Ki 4:10 See also 2Sa 16:22;
Pr 21:9; 25:24

Guests lodged on the roof Jos 2:8 See
also 1Sa 9:25–26

**The roof used as a place for leisure and
relaxation** 2Sa 11:2 See also Da 4:29;
Mt 24:17 pp Mk 13:15 pp Lk 17:31

**The roof used as a place of religious
observance** Ne 8:16 See also 2Ki 23:12;
Jer 19:13; 32:29; Zep 1:5; Ac 10:9

In cities, some roofs were open, public places
Isa 15:3 See also Jdg 9:50–52; 2Sa 18:24;
Jer 48:38; Mt 10:26–27 pp Lk 12:2–3

Roofs were usually constructed with a thick layer of clay
Mk 2:4 pp Lk 5:19

Roof as a synonym for house
Mt 8:8 pp Lk 7:6 See also Ge 19:8

See also

5207 architecture	5340 house
5240 building	5553 stairways
5269 cornerstone	

5507

rope and cord

Items normally used in domestic and military situations, but also used in Scripture in a symbolic sense to refer to bondage or constraint.

Various uses for rope and cord

In clothes and furnishing Ex 28:28,37; Nu 15:38; 1Ki 20:31; Est 1:6; Eze 27:24

For tents Ex 35:18; 39:40; Nu 3:37; 4:32; Isa 54:2

In sailing Ac 27:17,32,40

In military use 2Sa 17:13
Stringing the bow is a symbolic expression which also reflects actual practice: Ps 7:12; 11:2; Jer 51:3

For rescue and escape Jos 2:15; 1Sa 19:12; Jer 38:6,13; Ac 9:25; 2Co 11:33

To restrain animals Job 39:5; 41:1–2; Ps 32:9; Mt 21:2 pp Mk 11:2 pp Lk 19:30

To restrain people Jdg 15:13–14; Eze 3:25; 4:8; Mt 14:3 pp Mk 6:17

Rope and cord as symbols of bondage

Of evil Pr 5:22 *See also* Ps 129:4; 140:5; Isa 5:18; 58:6; Ro 7:6

Of suffering Lk 13:16 *See also* Job 16:8; 36:8; Ps 119:61; Da 3:21; Mt 14:3 pp Mk 6:17; Mk 15:1; Jn 18:12,24

Of death Ps 18:4–5 pp 2Sa 22:6 *See also* Ps 116:3

Rope and cord as symbols of spiritual and emotional ties

Symbols of loving relationships
Hos 11:4 *See also* Ecc 4:12; Jer 10:20; Ro 7:2

Symbols of obedience Pr 7:2–3 *See also* Dt 6:8; 11:18; Pr 3:3; 6:20–21

Symbols of life Ecc 12:6 *See also* Ps 16:6

See also

5236 bow and arrow	5934 restraint
5251 chains	6658 freedom
5344 imprisonment	6720 redemption
5517 seafaring	7254 plumb-line
5578 tents	7921 fellowship
5690 friends	8790 oppression

5508

ruins

The remains of a city, town or building after destruction or neglect. In Scripture it mainly describes the aftermath of divine judgment.

Israel's reduction to ruins

As a covenant curse for disobeying God Lev 26:27–33 *See also* Dt 13:16; 28:49–52

The ruin prophesied Jer 9:11; Mic 1:6–7 *See also* Isa 5:5–7; 6:11–13; Jer 4:7,20,23–26; 22:5; Eze 6:6–7,14; 21:27; Am 3:13–15; 7:9

The ruin described 2Ki 25:8–15 pp 2Ch 36:17–19 pp Jer 39:8–10 pp Jer 52:12–19

The ruin lamented Ps 89:39–41 *See also* Ps 74:3; 80:12–16; Isa 64:8–12; La 2:5–9

The ruin explained Jer 44:2–6 *See also* Eze 33:23–29

Restoration of Israel's ruins

Restoration of the ruins prophesied Isa 51:3; 61:4 *See also* Isa 44:24–26; 58:12; Jer 30:18–19; 31:27–28; Eze 36:8–12,33–36; Am 9:11–12

Restoration of the ruins fulfilled at the return from exile Ezr 3:1–13; Ne 1:3–4; 2:11–20; Hag 1:1–15

Ruins through God's judgment on Israel's enemies

Assyria
Nineveh was the capital of Assyria: Na 3:7; Zep 2:13–15

Babylon Isa 13:19–22; 23:13; Jer 51:37

Edom Eze 35:1–4,9; Mal 1:2–4

Egypt Jer 46:19; Eze 29:8–12

Moab Jer 48:1,18

Philistia Zep 2:4–6

Tyre Eze 26:3–4,11–14,19–21

Towns and sites ruined

In warfare Jos 8:24–29; 1Ch 20:1

In natural disaster Joel 1:6–12,16–17

Apocalyptic prophecies of ruin

Isa 24:1–13; 27:9–10; Rev 16:17–21; 18:21–23

Repairs to the ruined temple, altar and defences

1Ki 18:30 *See also* 2Ki 12:1–12 pp 2Ch 24:4–13; 2Ki 22:3–7 pp 2Ch 34:8–13

Proverbial references to ruins

Pr 25:28 *See also* Job 3:13–14; 15:27–28; Ps 102:6; Pr 24:30–31

See also

1025 God, anger of	9165 restoration
5295 destruction	9210 judgment,
7468 temple,	God's
rebuilding	

5509

rulers

Officials who, acting as God's servants, govern others and exercise authority over them. Also the originators of the laws of their realms. In the NT, rulers are also spiritual powers.

Officials exercising authority over people

Mt 20:25 pp Mk 10:42 *See also* 2Ch 23:20; Ps 2:2; Pr 28:2; Isa 16:1; Da 5:7; Hos 13:10; Lk 1:52; 12:11; Ac 7:27; Ex 2:14; 1Co 2:6–8

Godly rulers in foreign lands
Ps 105:16–22; Da 2:48

Importance of submitting to civil authorities Ro 13:3; Tit 3:1

Examples of rulers

Rulers of areas apart from Israel
Ge 25:16; 34:2; 41:41; 45:8; 2Ch 32:31; Eze 28:2; 31:11; Da 9:1; Ac 7:10,18

The five Philistine rulers Jos 13:3 *The Hebrew word translated "rulers" is related to the word "tyrant" and is only used of Philistine rulers. See also* Jdg 3:3; 15:11; 16:18; 1Sa 5:8; 6:16; 29:2; 1Ch 12:19

The king of Israel is referred to as a ruler 2Sa 5:1–2 pp 1Ch 11:1–2 *See also* 1Ki 1:34–35; 11:34; 1Ch 5:2; Mic 5:1

Other rulers of Israel (or parts of it)
1Ki 22:26 pp 2Ch 18:25; Ne 3:9; Isa 1:23; Jer 30:21; Mic 3:1; Mt 2:6; Lk 18:18

One of three groups that made up the Sanhedrin Ac 4:5 *See also* Lk 23:13; 24:20; Jn 7:48; Ac 4:8; 13:27

Jesus Christ is described as a ruler
Rev 1:5 *See also* Mt 2:6; Mic 5:2; Rev 3:14

God the Father is also called a ruler
1Ti 6:15

A ruler as the originator of the laws of his realm

Pr 8:15

Rulers are appointed by God

Ro 13:1–2 *See also* 2Sa 6:21; 7:7–8 pp 1Ch 17:6–7; 1Ki 11:34; Ps 2:7 fn; Isa 44:28; Jer 27:6; Da 2:38; 4:17; Jn 19:11; Ro 9:17; Ex 9:16

Rulers are God's servants

Ro 13:4 *See also* Isa 45:1; Jer 25:9; 43:10

Rulers are God's representatives

Ps 58:1 *The Hebrew word translated "rulers" literally means "gods", a title given to those whose position called for them to act as earthly representatives of God's heavenly court. See also* Ps 82:1; Jn 10:34–35; Ps 82:6; Ac 23:5; Ex 22:28

Rulers as spiritual powers

Eph 3:10 *See also* Eph 1:21 *In the NT, rulers are spiritual powers, some of whom exercise a Satanic authority;* Eph 6:12; Col 1:16

Synagogue rulers

Mk 5:22 pp Mt 9:18 pp Lk 8:41 *The ruler of a synagogue looked after the building and supervised the worship in it. See also* Mk 5:35–36 pp Lk 8:49–50; Mk 5:38; Lk 13:14; Ac 13:15; 18:8,17

See also

5219 authority,	5457 power, human
human	5459 prince
institutions	5464 proconsul
5257 civil authorities	7456 synagogue
5326 government	7733 leaders
5361 justice, human	8482 spiritual
5366 king	warfare
5434 officer	

5510

rumours

Insubstantial information, frequently not factual and leading to groundless fears.

Rumours can give rise to fear
Jer 51:46 ; Mt 24:6 pp Mk 13:7 *See also*
Job 28:22; Eze 7:26; 1Ti 4:7

Rumours can come from misunderstanding what has been said
Jn 21:23

Rumours are sometimes maliciously spread
Pr 17:4 ; 3Jn 10 *See also* Pr 16:28; 26:24;
1Ti 3:11; 5:13; 6:11

See also

5193 tongue	5868 gossip
5426 news	8830 suspicion
5575 talk, idle	

5511

safety

Being free from danger or harm. God
promises to keep his people from all
lasting spiritual and physical danger;
he requires, however, that his people
act responsibly.

God promises safety
To his people Dt 12:10 *See also*
Dt 33:12,26–29; Ps 48:8; Jer 32:37–38;
Zec 14:11; Ro 8:31

To those who trust in him Ps 91:9–10
See also Job 11:13–19; Ps 37:3; Pr 18:10;
29:25

To those who obey him Lev 25:18–19
See also Lev 26:5; Pr 1:33; 3:21–26;
28:26

To those in need Job 5:11,15; Isa 14:30

But not to the wicked Job 5:4; Pr 28:18;
Jer 12:12

Safety from enemies
Heb 13:6 *See also* Jos 10:21; Ps 3:5–6;
12:7; 31:20; 78:53; Eze 28:26; Rev 3:10

Safety from dangers
Isa 43:2 *See also* Ps 23:4; Eze 34:25,28

Spiritual safety
1Jn 5:18 *See also* Ro 8:35–39; 2Ti 4:18;
Rev 2:11

Safety in God alone
Ps 4:8 *See also* Zec 8:10

Safety in Jesus Christ Jn 17:12 *See also*
Jer 23:5–6 pp Jer 33:15–16;
Jn 10:11–15,28–30

Angels providing safety
Mt 4:6 pp Lk 4:10–11 *See also* Ge 19:16;
48:15–16; Ex 23:20; Ps 91:11–12;
Da 3:28; 6:22; Ac 5:19; 12:11; Rev 7:2–3

Human responsibility for safety
Personal Pr 11:15; Jer 4:6; 6:1;
Mt 24:15–16 pp Mk 13:14
pp Lk 21:20–21; Ac 2:40; 27:44

Family Ge 4:9; 43:9; 44:32; Mt 2:13

Friends 1Sa 20:12–13; 22:22–23

Neighbours Ex 22:5–15

Officials Ne 2:7; Ac 23:24

Kings 1Ki 4:25; 2Ch 15:5,15; Pr 20:28

Pastors Heb 13:17 *See also*
Jn 10:11–15; Ac 20:28; Php 3:1

Concern for safety
David for Absalom 2Sa 18:29,32

Mephibosheth for David 2Sa 19:24,30

Father for son Lk 15:27

Prayers for safety
Ps 16:1 *See also* Ex 33:15; Ezr 8:21–23;
Job 30:15,20; Ps 17:8–9; 19:13; 27:4–5;
119:29; 140:1–4; 141:8–10; Mt 6:13

Possible dangers inherent in safety
False security 1Th 5:3 *See also* Dt 29:19;
1Ki 22:27–28 pp 2Ch 18:26–27;
Job 21:9,16–18; Eze 39:6; Da 8:25;
Ob 3–4; Zep 2:15

Complacency Pr 1:32; Lk 12:16–21

Wickedness Jer 7:9–10; Eze 39:26

Perfect safety in God's kingdom
Isa 11:6–10 *See also* Isa 2:4; 65:25;
Hos 2:18; Mic 4:3–4; Rev 7:16;
Isa 49:10

See also

1320 God as Saviour	5942 security
2324 Christ as Saviour	6510 salvation
	6634 deliverance
4354 rock	6738 rescue
5480 protection	8104 assurance
5490 refuge	8131 guidance, results
5828 danger	

5512

scales and balances

Weighing devices designed to ensure
fair dealing. The terms are also used
metaphorically in Scripture.

Scales and balances were used in business transactions
Jer 32:10

Scales and balances should not be used dishonestly
Exhortations to honest dealing
Lev 19:35–36 *See also* Eze 45:10

The Lord hates dishonest dealing
Pr 20:10 *See also* Pr 11:1; 16:11; 20:23

**Dishonest dealing was one of the
reasons for God's judgment on his
people** Jer 5:1 *See also* Hos 12:6–7;
Am 8:4–8; Mic 6:10–13

Scales and balances used metaphorically
To emphasise Job's distress Job 6:2

To highlight God's greatness Isa 40:15
See also Isa 40:12

Of God's judgment Da 5:25–30 *See also*
Eze 5:1–2; Rev 6:5–6

See also

5347 injustice	8714 dishonesty
5614 weights & measures, laws	9210 judgment, God's

5513

sceptre

A staff, generally ornate, held as a
symbol of sovereign authority.

God's own authority is symbolised as a sceptre
Ps 45:6 *See also* Ge 49:10; Nu 24:17;
Ps 60:7 pp Ps 108:8; Isa 30:31

The sceptre is a symbol of Jesus Christ's reign
Heb 1:8 *See also* Ps 45:6; Ge 49:10;
Nu 24:17; Ps 110:2; Rev 2:27; Ps 2:9;
Rev 19:15; 12:5

Earthly rulers had sceptres as symbols of authority
Their description Est 4:11; Eze 19:11
See also Est 5:2; 8:4; Eze 19:14

OT examples Nu 21:18 *See also*
Ps 125:3; Isa 14:5; Jer 48:17;
Eze 19:11,14; 21:10,13; Am 1:5,8;
Zec 10:11

The extension of a ruler's sceptre to one of his subjects was a sign of favour
Est 5:2 *See also* Est 4:11; 8:4

Jesus Christ's tormentors gave him a mock sceptre
Mt 27:29

See also

1130 God, sovereignty	4512 staff
1670 symbols	5215 authority
2570 Christ, suffering	5368 kingship
	5509 rulers

5514

scribes

Experts in the understanding and
study of the law of Moses. Scribes
had political power in NT times, and
sat on the Sanhedrin. They were also
referred to as lawyers and teachers of
the law. They opposed Jesus Christ,
who condemned their hypocrisy.

The duties of scribes
**Writing records, legal contracts,
letters and accounts** *See also* 2Sa 8:16
pp 1Ch 18:15; 1Ki 4:3; 2Ki 12:10
pp 2Ch 24:11; Jer 32:12; 36:26

Advising the king 2Ki 18:18 pp Isa 36:3;
2Ki 19:2; 1Ch 27:32

Conscripting people to the army
2Ki 25:19 pp Jer 52:25

Examples of scribes who are mentioned by name
Shaphan 2Ki 22:8 pp 2Ch 34:18

Baruch Jer 36:4–32

Ezra
*After the exile, scribes became copyists and
interpreters of the law:* Ezr 7:6;
Ne 8:1–4,9

Clans or families of scribes
1Ch 2:55

The office of priest and scribe
*Up to the time of the Babylonian exile only
priests were allowed to be scribes:* Ezr 7:6;
Ne 8:9; 12:26

Scribes had political power in NT times and sat on the Sanhedrin
*By this time, scribes were also referred to as
"teachers of the law" and "lawyers":*

Mt 16:21 pp Mk 8:31 pp Lk 9:22;
Mt 26:3 pp Mk 14:1 pp Lk 22:2

Scribes opposed Jesus Christ
Mt 21:15; Lk 19:47 pp Mt 21:15
pp Mk 11:18

Jesus Christ condemned the scribes' hypocrisy
Mt 23:27–28 See also Mt 23:1–7
pp Mk 12:38–39 pp Lk 20:45–46

See also
2545 Christ,	5779 advice
opposition to	5780 advisers
5266 conscription	7464 teachers of the
5384 lawyer	law
5391 letters	7565 Sanhedrin
5638 writing	8767 hypocrisy

5515

scroll

A long strip of leather or papyrus on which people wrote.

Writing on a scroll
Ex 17:14; Nu 5:23; Dt 17:18; Ezr 6:2;
Ps 40:7; Isa 30:8; Jer 36:2,4,18; Lk 4:17;
Heb 10:7; Rev 1:11

With a pen Isa 8:1

In ink Jer 36:18

In columns Jer 36:23

A scroll written on both sides was unusual
These references indicate a saturation of the scroll with words of God's judgment:
Eze 2:9–10; Zec 5:2–3; Rev 5:1

A scroll was often sealed to protect its contents
Isa 29:11; Da 12:4; Rev 5:1–2,9

Scrolls were of various sizes
Isa 8:1; Rev 10:2

Unrolling and rolling up a scroll
Eze 2:9–10; Lk 4:17,20
The rolling up of a scroll is used metaphorically of the final judgment:
Isa 34:4; Rev 6:14

A scroll may represent the word of God
Rev 10:2
The image of "eating the scroll" points to the need to become totally immersed in the word of God: Eze 2:9–3:4; Rev 10:8–10

A scroll may represent the revelation of God's purposes
Rev 5:1–5

See also
1630 Book of the	5391 letters
Covenant	5439 pen
1640 Book of the	5514 scribes
Law	5518 seal
4494 papyrus	5638 writing
5175 reading	9420 book of life
5232 book	

5516

sculpture

Sculpture created by carving
1Ki 6:29 pp 2Ch 3:7 See also
1Ki 6:32,35; 2Ki 21:7; Eze 41:17–18,25

Sculpture created out of metal
1Ki 7:23 See also Ex 25:18;
1Ki 7:24,30,37; 2Ch 4:3; 28:2

Sculpture used in the setting of idolatry
Ex 32:4; Ac 19:24 See also Dt 4:15–18;
2Ki 17:16; Isa 40:19–20; 44:12–13;
48:5; Da 3:1; Hab 2:18; Ac 17:29

See also
4303 metals	5247 carpenters
4315 clay	5272 craftsmen
4345 metalworkers	5403 masons
4552 wood	5445 potters &
5211 art	pottery
5212 arts and crafts	8768 idolatry

5517

seafaring

Ideas and images drawn from seafaring are used in Scripture to illustrate important aspects of the Christian life. Although Israel was not a seafaring nation, ships and sailing played a part in her history, as they did in the spreading of the gospel in the NT.

Israel's harbours
Ge 49:13 See also Jdg 5:17

The art of shipbuilding
Eze 27:3–9

Ships used for various purposes
Deliverance from danger: Noah's ark
Ge 6:1–9:17

Trade 1Ki 9:27–28 pp 2Ch 8:18
Eze 27:25 See also 1Ki 10:11,22
pp 2Ch 9:21; 1Ki 22:48–49
pp 2Ch 20:35–37

Slavery Dt 28:68; Rev 18:11–13

Invasion Nu 24:24 See also Eze 30:9;
Da 11:30,40

To carry refugees Isa 60:9

To carry passengers Jnh 1:3; Mt 9:1 ;
Ac 13:4 See also Mt 14:13; 15:39;
Mk 3:9; Ac 13:13; 14:26; 15:39; 16:11;
18:18 Paul sails for Syria with Aquila and
Priscilla; Ac 18:21; 20:3,6,13–16;
21:1–3,6–7; 27:1–8; 28:11–13

Seafarers
Ps 107:23–30; 2Co 11:25 See also
1Ki 22:48 pp 2Ch 20:37; Jnh 1:3–15;
Mt 8:23–27 pp Mk 4:35–41
pp Lk 8:22–26; Mt 14:22–33
pp Mk 6:45–53 pp Jn 6:16–21;
Ac 27:9–44

Judgment on seafarers
Isa 23:1 See also Isa 2:16; 23:14;
33:21–23; 43:14; Eze 27:26–36;
Rev 18:17–19

Metaphorical references to ships and seafaring
Spiritual immaturity as a ship tossed at sea Eph 4:14

Abandoning sound teaching as shipwreck 1Ti 1:19

Faith as an anchor Heb 6:19

Other seafaring analogies Jas 3:4–5 See
also Ps 48:7; Pr 31:14; Jas 1:6

Noah's ark as a symbol of Jesus Christ
1Pe 3:20

See also
4227 deep, the	5245 captain
4248 islands	5587 trade
4266 sea	5590 travel
4642 fish	7203 ark, Noah's
4851 storm	

5518

seal

A personalised design used to produce an imprint in clay or wax which was then attached, usually to documents and letters as a mark of ownership, authenticity and authority. A seal might also refer to what is given as a pledge or guarantee or be used to keep something secure.

The nature and use of a seal
Seals engraved on precious stone
Ex 28:11 pp Ex 39:6 See also Ex 28:21
pp Ex 39:14; Ex 28:36 pp Ex 39:30

Seals used to imprint soft clay
Job 38:14

Ways of carrying a personal seal
Figuratively used SS 8:6

Worn round the neck Ge 38:18 The seal
took the form of an engraved cylinder
pierced from end to end and worn on a cord
round the neck. See also Ge 38:25

Worn as a signet ring Jer 22:24 See also
Nu 31:50; Isa 3:21

A seal as a mark of authority
Given to signify delegation of authority
Ge 41:42; Est 3:10; 8:2; Rev 7:2

God's seal validates his servants'
ministry Jn 6:27; 1Co 9:2

A seal authenticates documents
Est 8:8–10 See also 1Ki 21:8; Est 3:12

A seal used to keep something secure
Da 6:17 See also Dt 32:34; Job 14:17;
Ps 40:9; SS 4:12; Mt 27:65–66; Rev 20:3

Documents sealed to prevent alteration
Binding agreements Ne 9:38–10:1 See
also Jer 32:10–11,14,44

The words of prophecy Da 12:4 See also
Isa 8:16–17; 29:10–11; Da 8:26; 9:24;
12:9; Rev 10:4; 22:10

The scroll and its seals Rev 5:1–4,9 See
also Rev 5:5; 6:1–12; 8:1

A seal as a pledge or guarantee
Dt 29:12; Hag 2:23; Ro 4:11

A seal as a mark of belonging
The mark of the beast Rev 13:16–17;
14:9–11

God's seal of ownership 2Ti 2:19;
Rev 7:3–8 See also Eze 9:4; Gal 6:17;
Rev 9:4

The Spirit as a pledge of final
redemption 2Co 1:21–22 The Holy
Spirit both seals believers as belonging to
God and guarantees their future
inheritance. See also Eph 1:13–14; 4:30

5519

secretary

A secretary was a royal official often responsible for correspondence
2Sa 8:17; 20:25; 1Ki 4:3; 2Ki 18:18,37; 19:2; 22:12; 2Ch 34:13,15–18 *Shaphan takes the Book of the Law to King Josiah;* Ezr 4:8–9,17,23; Est 3:12; 8:9; Jer 36:10

A secretary collected the temple repair money
2Ki 12:10–12; 2Ch 24:11

A secretary was in charge of conscripting soldiers
2Ki 25:19 pp Jer 52:25; 2Ch 26:11

Secretaries to writers of NT letters
Tertius and Silas acted in the capacity of secretary, writing down what the apostles told them to: Ro 16:22; 1Pe 5:12

5520

servants

Someone who serves another. Scripture provides guidance concerning the roles of servants, noting in particular that Jesus Christ chose to be a servant and commands believers to serve one another.

5521
servant, Jesus Christ as
See 2327 Jesus Christ, as servant

5522
servants, working conditions of

Those who serve are to be treated fairly and with respect. Jesus Christ himself chose to be a servant and lays responsibility of service on those who follow.

Servants are to be treated fairly
They are not to be exploited Eph 6:9 *See also* Lev 25:39–40,53

They are to be paid fairly and promptly Dt 24:14–15 *See also* Ge 29:15; Lev 19:13; Nu 18:29–31; 1Ki 5:6; Job 7:1–2; Jer 22:13; Mt 20:4,8; Ro 4:4; Col 4:1; 2Th 3:10

Examples of servants treated unfairly
Jas 5:4 *See also* Ge 31:7,41; Ex 2:23–24; Job 24:10–11; Mal 3:5

Jesus Christ as a servant
Mt 20:28 *See also* Php 2:7

Believers follow Jesus Christ's example as servants
They are servants of Jesus Christ and his church Ro 1:1 *See also* Lk 1:38; 1Co 12:5; 16:15; Eph 4:12; Col 1:23; 3:24

They work to please God Eph 6:5–6 *See also* Col 3:22–24; Tit 2:9–10

Christian workers should be paid honourably
1Ti 5:17–18 *See also* Lk 10:7; 1Co 9:7–11; Gal 6:6

God rewards his servants
Eph 6:8 *See also* Job 34:10–11; Pr 10:16; Mt 6:3–4; 25:23; Jn 4:36; 2Ti 4:8

Service of sin has its reward
Ro 6:23 *See also* Pr 11:18; Hos 9:1; 2Pe 2:15

5523
servants, good

Scripture identifies certain qualities which are found in good servants and requires that these qualities should be found in believers' service of God.

Qualities found in good servants
Diligence Ecc 9:10 *See also* 1Ki 11:28; Pr 10:4; 22:29; Mt 25:14–23 pp Lk 19:12–19

Faithfulness 1Co 4:2 *See also* Ex 21:5–6; 2Sa 15:21; 2Ch 34:11–12; Ne 13:13; Pr 25:13; Da 6:4

Honesty 2Ki 22:7 *See also* Ge 39:6; 2Ki 12:15; Tit 2:9–10

Obedience Eph 6:5 *See also* Lk 17:10; Col 3:22

Perseverance Ge 31:40–41 *See also* 2Th 3:12–13

Respect 1Ti 6:1–2 *See also* Mal 1:6; 1Pe 2:18

Willingness Eph 6:6–7 *See also* 1Ch 28:21; Tit 2:9

Examples of good servants
Abraham's servant: Ge 24:9,49 *David's servants:* 2Sa 12:18; 23:13–17 2Ki 5:13 *Naaman's servants;* Mt 8:9 *a centurion's servants*

Good servants are often rewarded by their employers
They are advanced by them Ge 39:4–5; Pr 27:18; Mt 25:21,23

They have their confidence Ge 24:2–4,10

Good servants often bring blessings on their employers
Ge 30:27–30; 39:2–4

Good servants have God with them
Ge 24:7,27; 31:7,42; 39:3,21; Mt 24:46; Ac 7:9–10

5524
servants, bad

Bad servants are characterised by disobedience, idleness and dishonesty.

Characteristics of bad servants
Idleness 2Th 3:11 *See also* Pr 18:9; Mt 25:24–30 pp Lk 19:20–26

Dishonesty Lk 16:12 *See also* Ge 21:25; Lev 6:2; 2Ki 5:20–25; Eph 6:6; Col 3:22

Disloyalty Lk 16:13 *See also* 2Sa 19:24–27; Jn 10:13; Ac 27:30

Quarrelsomeness Mt 24:48–49 *See also* Ge 13:7; 26:20; Mt 18:23–30

Discontentment Lk 3:14 *See also* Mt 20:9–15

Refusing correction Pr 29:19

Examples of bad servants
Ziba: 2Sa 16:1–4; 19:26–29 1Ki 2:39 *Shimei's slaves;* 1Ki 16:9–10 *Zimri;* 2Ki 5:19–27 *Gehazi;* Job 19:16 *Job's servants;* Phm 8–16 *Onesimus was a bad servant who became good.*

5526

shibboleth

"Shibboleth" a Hebrew word meaning "flood" or "ear of corn"
Ps 69:15 *See also* Ps 69:2; Isa 27:12 *"Shibboleth" is here translated as flowing.*

Dialectal variation in the pronunciation of "shibboleth"
Jdg 12:6

The pronunciation of "shibboleth" featured in a civil war between Gilead and Ephraim
The Gileadites had defeated the Ammonites Jdg 10:7–9,17–18; 11:4–11,32–33

This victory led to civil war between Gilead and Ephraim Jdg 12:1–4

Ephraimites were identified on the basis of their pronunciation of "shibboleth" Jdg 12:5–6

5527

shield

A piece of armour used to fend off blows or missiles such as arrows. God is described as the shield of his people; protecting, giving help, strength and favour. Faith is the shield with which believers are to ward off spiritual attack.

Shields are pieces of armour
2Ch 11:11–12; 32:5; Ne 4:16; Na 2:5 *A number of shields were used to make a wall of defence.*

Kinds of shield
Large and small shields Jer 46:3 *See also* 1Ki 10:16–17 pp 2Ch 9:15–16; 2Ch 14:8

Gold shields 2Sa 8:7 pp 1Ch 18:7 *See also* 1Ki 10:16–17; 14:26

Bronze shields 1Ki 14:27

Shields made of combustible materials Eze 39:9

Shields covered with leather Isa 21:5 *Leather shields were rubbed with oil to preserve them and to deflect blows from swords or arrows.*

Shields in warfare
As part of an army's equipment 2Ch 14:8 *See also* 1Ch 12:23–24; 2Ch 11:12; 26:14; Ne 4:16

Their use in battle 1Ch 5:18 *See also* 1Sa 17:7; 2Ki 19:32; Jer 46:3,9; 51:11; Eze 23:24

The figurative use of shields
God is called a shield of his people Ge 15:1 *See also* 2Sa 22:3; Ps 7:10; 18:2; Pr 2:7

God acts as a shield Ex 14:19–20 *See also* Isa 52:12; 58:8

God protects his people Isa 31:5 *See also* Ps 3:3; 12:7; 32:10; 125:2; 140:7; Zec 2:5; 12:8

God is a refuge for his people Ps 144:2 *See also* Ps 18:30; 119:114; Pr 30:5

God is the help and strength of his people Ps 28:7 *See also* Dt 33:29; Ps 33:20; 115:9–11

God gives victory to his people 2Sa 22:36 pp Ps 18:35

God's favour is compared to a shield Ps 5:12 *See also* Ps 3:3; 32:10; 84:9–11

God's faithfulness is compared to a shield Ps 91:4

A shield is used as a picture of defiance towards God Job 15:25–26

Faith is given to the believer to act as a shield Eph 6:16 *See also* 1Pe 1:5

See also
1035	God, faithfulness
4126	Satan, resistance to
5209	armour
5237	breastplate
5291	defence
5480	protection
5490	refuge
5596	victory
5605	warfare
5954	strength
8020	faith
8486	spiritual warfare, armour

5528

shouting
A loud cry of joy, excitement or distress. Scripture often speaks of praise in terms of shouting,

---

reflecting both the joy of the speaker and the greatness of God.

Shouting to be heard
1Sa 17:20; Lk 23:21; Ac 22:23–24 *See also* Jdg 7:20; 15:14; 2Ki 9:27; 2Ch 13:15; Job 39:25; Ps 60:8; Zep 1:14; Mt 20:30–31; Jn 19:12; Ac 16:17; 17:6; 21:36

Shouting in distress
Nu 16:34; Lk 4:41 *See also* 1Ki 18:26–28; Lk 8:28; Ac 14:14; 19:28; 21:28; 25:24

Shouting for joy
Ezr 3:11–13; Jn 12:13; Rev 19:6 *See also* Ex 32:17; Lev 9:24; Nu 23:21; 1Sa 4:6; 2Sa 6:15; 1Ki 1:39; 1Ch 15:28; 2Ch 15:14; Job 3:7; 8:21; 33:26; 38:7; Ps 20:5; 33:3; 42:4; 65:13; Pr 11:10; Isa 16:9–10; 26:19; Mt 21:15; Lk 17:15; Rev 5:12; 19:1

Joyful shouting commanded
Jos 6:5; Ps 47:1; Zep 3:14 *See also* Ps 66:1; 95:1; 100:1; Isa 40:9; 44:23; 58:1; Jer 31:7; Zec 9:9

See also
5196	voice
5283	joy
8622	worship
8664	praise

5529

sieges
Sustained battle against fortified cities, preventing renewal of supplies; a common tactic in OT times. Samaria and Jerusalem both fell to sieges.

Sieges used by and against Israel
Dt 20:12,19–20; Jdg 9:50; 1Sa 11:1; 2Sa 11:1; 20:15

Ben-Hadad II twice besieged Samaria, unsuccessfully
1Ki 20:1 *See also* 1Ki 20:15–20; 2Ki 6:24; 7:3–7

Shalmaneser V besieged Samaria
2Ki 17:5–6 *See also* 2Ki 18:9–12

Sennacherib besieged Jerusalem, unsuccessfully
2Ki 18:17,35–36; 2Ch 32:1–5; Isa 29:5–8; 37:36–37

Nebuchadnezzar besieged Jerusalem
2Ki 25:1 *See also* 2Ki 25:2–11 pp Jer 39:1–10; 2Ch 36:17–20 pp Jer 52:4–15

Jesus Christ warned that Jerusalem would be besieged and destroyed
Lk 19:43 *The Roman army destroyed Jerusalem in A.D. 70 using an embankment to besiege the city. See also* Lk 21:20–24

Sieges caused great suffering and people adopted desperate measures for survival
Dt 28:51–57; 2Ki 6:24–29; 18:27

See also
5208	armies
5214	attack
5228	battering-rams
5244	camp
5246	captivity
5344	imprisonment
5354	invasions
5605	warfare
7215	exile, the
7239	Jerusalem
9220	day of the LORD

5530

sifting
The process of separating different substances, especially grain and chaff, normally by passing them through sieves. It is used as a symbol of judgment in which the good are separated from the evil.

Sifting as an act of separation
Jdg 7:4

Sifting as a symbol of judgment
Isa 30:28 *See also* Am 9:9; Lk 22:31

See also
4426	chaff
4456	grain
4550	winnowing
9210	judgment, God's

5531

skill
A trade or craft acquired by training or practice, or a special ability or expertise that may be an endowment of the Holy Spirit. Scripture lists many skills and abilities, particularly used in the building of the tabernacle and temple.

Skill offered in God's service
Ex 35:10; 1Ch 22:15–16 *See also* 1Ch 28:21

Skill in particular crafts
In working metal 2Ch 2:7 *Skill with silver:* Jdg 17:4; Ac 19:24 1Ki 7:14–15,41–45 pp 2Ch 4:12–16 *Skill with gold:* 2Ch 3:5–7; Isa 46:6 2Ti 4:14

In working stone 1Ch 22:2 *See also* 1Ki 5:15–18 pp 2Ch 2:2; 1Ki 6:36; 7:9–13

With timber 1Ki 5:6 pp 2Ch 2:8–9 *See also* 1Ki 6:14–36

With fabrics Ex 38:23 *Skill in embroidery:* Ex 26:1,36; 28:39 *Skill in weaving:* Ex 29:5; 39:1–5 Ex 35:25 *skill in spinning*

With music 1Ch 15:22; 2Ch 34:12–13; Ps 33:3

Other skills Ge 25:27 *hunting Seamanship:* 1Ki 9:27; Eze 27:8 Job 32:22 *flattery;* Ps 45:1 *writing Enchanting:* Ps 58:5; Isa 3:3 Ps 78:72 *leadership;* Jer 2:33 *love;* Jer 9:17 *Mourning: professional mourners were a feature of life in Bible times;* Jer 50:9 *fighting;* Eze 28:5 *trading*

Undesirable skills
In constructing idols Isa 44:13 *See also* Isa 40:19–20; 41:7; Jer 10:9; Hos 13:2; Ac 17:29

Doing evil Jer 4:22 *See also* Isa 25:11; Eze 21:31; Mic 7:3

Acquiring skill

Through training 1Ch 5:18; 2Ch 2:13–14

Military skill: Ge 14:14; 2Ch 26:11 1Ch 25:7 *musical skill;* Lk 6:40 *teaching abilities;* 1Co 9:25 *Athletic prowess requires strict training;* Heb 5:14 *distinguishing good from evil through proper training*

Skills given by God Ex 31:1–6

pp Ex 35:30–35 *These skills may well have been developed through training, but they are recognised as gifts from God. See also* Ex 36:1–2; Dt 33:11 *Moses prays for Levi's skills to be blessed by God;* Isa 50:4 *Skill in the right use of words comes from God;* Ro 12:6–8 *Special abilities are given by God to believers.*

See also

3272 Holy Spirit in OT	5433 occupations
5212 arts and crafts	5551 spinning & weaving
5240 building	7960 singing
5273 creativity	7966 spiritual gifts
5304 embroidery	8421 equipping, physical
5403 masons	

5532

sleep

A state of slumber or rest, reflecting tiredness and the need for refreshment. Although sleep is a natural physical process, Scripture also uses the term in a number of important spiritual senses.

5533
sleep, physical

A gift from God providing necessary rest, usually at night, for the restoration of mind and body. It is sometimes denied, sometimes used by God for his purposes and sometimes abused by people.

Sleep is a gift from God
It is pleasant and refreshing Ecc 5:12
See also 1Ki 19:5; Jer 31:26; Jn 11:12–13

It is God's gift to his faithful people Ps 127:2 *See also* Pr 3:21–24

It is often denied to the wicked Isa 48:22

Sleep as a nocturnal activity
It is associated with night-time 1Th 5:7
See also Lk 17:34; Jn 9:4; Ro 13:11–12

It is associated with dreams Ge 28:11–12; 41:1,5; Isa 29:7–8; Da 2:1; 4:5; 7:1

It is associated with sexual activity Ge 30:15–16; 2Sa 11:4 *Abraham and Hagar:* Ge 16:2,4 Ge 26:10; 30:3–5; 35:22; 38:18; 39:14; Ex 22:16; Dt 22:22; 2Sa 3:7; Heb 13:4

Blessings in sleep
Peace Ps 4:8 *See also* Mt 8:24 pp Mk 4:38 pp Lk 8:23; Ac 12:6

Protection Ps 121:3–4 *See also* Ps 3:5–6; 68:13; Eze 34:25

Deep and light sleep
Deep sleep for the creation of Eve Ge 2:21

Deep sleep for revelation Ge 15:12; Job 4:12–13; 33:14–18; Da 7:2,13; Ac 16:9

Deep sleep as a judgment 1Sa 26:12; Isa 29:10 *The sleep in this instance is symbolic.*

Light sleep SS 5:2

Sleeping at the wrong time
While on duty Pr 19:15; Mt 28:13; Mk 13:36

During harvest Pr 10:5

Instead of praying Jnh 1:5–6; Mt 26:40 pp Mk 14:37 pp Lk 22:45–46

During a sermon Ac 20:9

At the transfiguration Lk 9:32

Amidst danger Jdg 16:13–14,19; Pr 6:1–5; 23:34; Mt 13:25

Excessive sleep
Pr 6:9–11 *See also* Pr 20:13; 23:21; Isa 56:10

See also

1409 dream	5571 surgery
4957 night	5582 tiredness
5056 rest	5802 care
5229 bed	6700 peace
5343 idleness	8328 quietness
5537 sleeplessness	

5534
sleep, spiritual

Scripture often uses sleep as an image of spiritual laziness or a lack of alertness towards God.

Sleep as an image of spiritual laziness
Lack of watchfulness Isa 56:10 *See also* Mt 24:43–44 pp Lk 12:39–40; Mk 13:35–36

Spiritual dullness Ac 28:25–27 *See also* Isa 6:9–10; Pr 23:34–35 *As a result of God's judgment:* Ro 11:8; Isa 29:10

God's call to awake from sleep
The need to arise Ro 13:11–12 *See also* Isa 51:17; 52:1; 60:1; Eph 5:14; Rev 3:2

The command to be alert Rev 16:15 *See also* Mt 26:41; Mk 13:32–34; Lk 12:35; Eph 6:18; 1Th 5:6–8; 1Pe 5:8

The plea for revival Ps 80:18; 85:6

The image of God awaking from sleep
From his past judgments Ps 78:65

Prayers for God to rise up against his enemies Ps 7:6 *See also* Ps 35:23; 44:23–24; 73:20; 80:1–2; Isa 51:9

The contrast between God who never sleeps and false gods
Ps 121:3–4 *See also* 1Ki 18:27; Hab 2:19

See also

5611 watchman	8148 revival
6139 deadness, spiritual	8490 watchfulness
	8602 prayer

5535
sleep, and death

Scripture often uses sleep as an image of death, indicating that believers will be awakened to resurrection on the last day.

Death described in the imagery of sleep
The sleep of death for human beings in general Ps 90:3–6 *See also* Job 7:21; 14:10–12; Ps 13:3; Da 12:2; Mt 9:24 pp Mk 5:39 pp Lk 8:52–53

Death as resting with the ancestors 1Ki 2:10 *See also* Dt 31:16; 2Sa 7:12; 1Ki 11:43 *Solomon;* 1Ki 14:20,31; 16:6; 22:50 *Jehoshaphat;* 2Ki 14:16; 15:7; 16:20; 20:21 *Hezekiah;* 2Ki 21:18 *Manasseh*

Those who fall asleep in Christ Rev 14:13 *See also* Jn 11:11–14; Ac 7:60; 1Co 15:6,17–19

Death is not the end of existence
Jn 5:28–29 *See also* Job 14:13–15; Ps 17:15; Isa 26:19; Da 12:3; Lk 16:22–23; 1Co 15:20,51–57; 1Th 4:13–18

Sleep denoting the finality of judgment for the lost Jer 51:57 *See also* Ps 7:3–5; 76:5; Jer 51:39

See also

5482 punishment	9240 last judgment
6644 eternal life	9310 resurrection
9020 death	9410 heaven
9210 judgment, God's	9510 hell

5537

sleeplessness

The absence of or inability to sleep. Scripture suggests that sleeplessness will sometimes result from divine intervention. Scripture also provides examples of deliberate sleeplessness in order to seek God.

Anxiety and sorrow as causes of sleeplessness
Ecc 2:22–23 *See also* Pr 6:1–4; Ecc 5:12; Jer 45:3

Other causes of sleeplessness
Work Ps 127:2

Pain and sickness Job 30:17 *See also* Job 7:4–5; 33:19; Rev 14:11

Evil deeds Pr 4:14–16 *See also* Isa 5:27

Concern for God's cause Ps 132:4–5 *See also* Isa 62:6; Lk 2:37; 6:12; Ac 12:12

People who experienced sleeplessness
Jacob Ge 31:40

Saul 1Sa 16:14 *Loss of sleep probably among the troubles of Saul alleviated by David's playing. See also* 1Sa 16:15–23

Xerxes Est 6:1

Job Job 7:4 *See also* Job 7:11–15

Darius Da 6:18

Paul 2Co 11:27 *See also* 2Co 6:5

5538

God deprives sinners of rest
Isa 48:22 pp Heb 3:11; 4:1–5

Restlessness because of judgment on sin Rev 14:11 *See also* Dt 28:67;
1Sa 16:14; Isa 21:4; 23:12; 57:20–21;
La 5:5

Sleeplessness allows people to receive messages from God
Da 2:1; Zec 4:1 *See also* 1Sa 3:1–10;
Da 2:29; Mt 27:19

A challenge to abandon sleep
Abandoning actual sleep Lk 6:12 *See also* Mt 26:36–46 pp Mk 14:32–42
pp Lk 22:47–53; Lk 2:37; Rev 16:15
Abandoning spiritual lethargy Ps 57:8
See also Pr 6:10; Ecc 5:2; Isa 51:9

God's watchfulness
Ps 121:3–4; Isa 40:28–31

The blessing of sleep
Ps 4:8 *See also* Lev 26:6; Ps 3:5; 127:2;
Pr 3:24

See also

1409 dream	5933 restlessness
1469 visions	8490 watchfulness
5482 punishment	8734 evil
5532 sleep	8849 worry
5831 depression	

5538

sling

Used by shepherds to defend their flocks, it consisted of a strip of leather broad enough to contain a stone. A string was attached to each end of this strip. It was swung around fast and when one string was released the stone could be hurled out with great force and accuracy.

David felled Goliath with a stone from his sling
1Sa 17:40,49–50

Slings were also used by soldiers as weapons
Jdg 20:16; 2Ki 3:25; 1Ch 12:2;
2Ch 26:14

Slings were known for their destructive power
Job 41:28; Zec 9:15

Slings used metaphorically
1Sa 25:29; Pr 26:8; Jer 10:18

See also

4366 stones	5612 weapons
5210 arrows	7784 shepherd
5544 soldiers	

5539

sluggard

Someone characterised by a settled attitude of slothfulness and idleness. Such people are consistently condemned throughout Scripture.

Sluggards are characterised by slothfulness and idleness
They are lazy and refuse to work
Pr 6:6–8 *See also* Pr 12:27; 15:19; 19:24;
20:4; 21:25; 24:30–31; 26:15

They love to stay in bed when they should be up and active Pr 6:9 *See also* Pr 26:14

They make excuses to avoid work
Pr 22:13 *See also* Pr 26:13

Their desires are not met Pr 13:4 *See also* Pr 20:4; 21:25–26

Their laziness leads to poverty
Pr 6:10–11 *See also* Pr 10:4–5; 12:24;
18:9; 19:15; 20:13; 24:33–34; Ecc 4:5;
10:18

Their attitude is irritating to others
Pr 10:26

They are conceited Pr 26:16

Sluggards condemned throughout Scripture
In the book of Proverbs Pr 10:4 *See also*
Pr 6:6–11; 12:11,24,27; 13:4; 14:23;
18:9; 28:19

By Jesus Christ Mt 20:3,6; 25:24–30

In the epistles 1Th 5:14 *See also*
2Th 3:6,10–11; 1Ti 5:13; Tit 1:12; 3:14;
Heb 6:12

See also

5343 idleness	5803 carelessness
5446 poverty	5833 diligence
5524 servants, bad	5978 warning
5533 sleep, physical	6125 condemnation,
5629 work, ordained	divine
by God	8755 folly

5540

society

The network of relationships, institutions and shared values that together make up the corporate aspect of human life. Though often regarded as hostile to God and threatening to faith, society can be viewed positively as capable of redemption and an object of God's saving activity.

5541

society, negative aspects of

Often pictured as an immoral city or a world of evil, it is regarded as corrupt and godless, hostile to true faith and therefore destined for judgment.

The city as a symbol of corrupt society
Rev 18:2–3 *Babylon stands for the corrupt Roman state and also for godless society in general. See also* Ge 11:1–9; 19:1–13;
Eze 22:1–5; Mt 23:37–39
pp Lk 13:34–35; Rev 14:8

"The world" as a description of society alienated from, and hostile to, both God and his people
Gal 3:22 *The Greek word translated "world" often means not the physical world, but the world of human life. See also* Jn 15:18; Eph 6:12; 1Jn 5:19; Rev 12:9

Fallen society becomes pluralistic
Israel was continually threatened by the pluralism of the surrounding societies Jos 23:6–8 *See also*
Ex 23:32–33; Jos 24:14–23; 1Ki 11:1–6;
18:16–40 *Baal was a name used for a variety of local Canaanite deities;*
Ezr 9:1–2; Isa 2:6–8; Da 3:1–12

Pluralism was also a feature of the societies of the NT Ac 17:16–23 *See also* 1Co 8:4–6; 2Ti 4:3–4; 1Jn 5:21

Pluralism is to be resisted and faith in one God and Saviour maintained
1Ti 2:5 *See also* Isa 43:10–11; Jn 14:6;
Ac 4:12

Fallen society becomes secular
Life in a godless society becomes spiritually futile and morally depraved
Ro 1:21 *See also* Ro 1:18–32; 2Ti 3:1–5;
Rev 18:1–3

Israel ignores warnings about becoming a society which has forgotten God Ps 81:11–12 *See also*
Jer 3:19–21; Heb 3:7–11

Israel became an example of a society which, though outwardly religious, lived without reference to God
Am 5:21–24 *Amos here summarises, and rejects, current religious practices in Israel in the 8th century B.C. See also* Am 2:6–7;
5:4–15 *Bethel and Gilgal were popular national shrines, where religion had taken the place of righteousness and relationship;*
Am 8:4–10

See also

4030 world,	5256 city
behaviour in	6169 godlessness
4215 Babylon	8710 atheism
4263 Rome	8768 idolatry
5001 human race,	8848 worldliness
the	

5542

society, positive aspects of

The object of God's love and the sphere of God's blessing. God's people should adopt a positive but critical attitude to, and involvement in society, and should seek to influence it for good, while guarding against its corrupting influence.

Society is the object of God's redeeming love and the sphere of his blessing
The city as a positive image of society
Isa 1:26–27 *See also* Ps 122:6–9;
Isa 54:11–14; Heb 11:10,15–16;
Rev 21:1–4,22–22:5

The world as the object of God's love
Jn 3:16–17 *See also* Jn 6:33; 2Co 5:19;
1Jn 4:14; Rev 11:15

God's people are to be positively involved in society
They are to seek to be a positive influence Jn 17:15–18 *See also* Jer 29:7
God's people, in exile in Babylon, are to seek the welfare of that society, rather than simply long to return home; Mt 5:13–16;
1Co 5:9–10

They are to avoid being corrupted by society's worldliness Jas 1:27 *See also* Ro 12:2; Jas 4:4; 1Jn 2:15–17

They do not owe society their ultimate loyalty Jn 17:16 *See also* Jn 15:19; Heb 13:14; 1Pe 2:11

They are to adopt a positive attitude to society's properly instituted authorities Ro 13:1–7; Tit 3:1 *See also* Mt 22:17–21 pp Mk 12:14–17 pp Lk 20:22–25; 1Pe 2:13–17

While being submissive, they are not to give absolute obedience to any merely human authority in society Ac 4:18–20 *See also* Ac 5:27–29

Examples of those positively involved in society

Da 2:48–49 *See also* Ge 41:41–49 *Joseph*; Est 10:1–3 *Mordecai*; Da 1:1–21 *Daniel and his friends*

See also

4029 world, human	5359 justice
beings in	5577 taxation
4065 orderliness	5587 trade
5219 authority,	5680 family
human	5709 marriage,
institutions	purpose
5255 citizenship	7446 slavery
5326 government	8243 ethics, social

soldiers

Active members of an army, whatever their rank. Paul uses the term frequently in his letters to draw attention to the fact that believers are engaged in spiritual warfare.

Armies of soldiers under different commanders

Moses' soldiers Nu 31:27–28,32

Joshua's soldiers Jos 8:10–19

Abimelech's soldiers Jdg 9:34–35

Benjamin's soldiers Jdg 20:14–16

Philistine soldiers 1Sa 13:5

Saul's soldiers 1Sa 13:22; 15:4,15,21; 26:7

Hadadezer's soldiers 2Sa 8:4

Aramean soldiers 2Sa 10:6

Jehoahaz' soldiers 2Ki 13:7

David's soldiers 2Sa 3:23 *David's soldiers under Joab*; 2Sa 23:8–39 pp 1Ch 11:10–47 *David's mighty men*; 2Sa 24:1–9 pp 1Ch 21:1–16 *David displeased the LORD by counting his fighting men*; 1Ch 12:23–38; 27:1–22

Zedekiah's soldiers 2Ki 25:5

Babylonian soldiers Jer 41:3

Individual soldiers

2Ki 5:1 *See also* 1Sa 14:28; 2Ch 17:17; Da 3:20–22

Soldiers came to John the Baptist

Lk 3:14

Soldiers involved in the last events of Jesus Christ's life on earth

In his arrest and trial Lk 23:11,36; Jn 18:3,12; 19:2

In his crucifixion Mt 27:27; Jn 19:16,23–24,32–34

After his crucifixion Mt 27:65–66

After his resurrection Mt 28:2–4,12,15

Soldiers involved in the lives of the apostles

Peter Ac 12:4,6,18

Paul Ac 21:32,35,37

Soldiers used metaphorically

Eze 27:27; 39:20; Joel 2:7; Am 2:15–16

Paul draws parallels between a soldier and a Christian

1Co 9:7 *An apostle has a right to be supported in material things by those to whom he preaches.*

Christians are called fellow-soldiers Php 2:25; Phm 2

Christians must put Jesus Christ first 2Ti 2:3–4

God as the commander of an army of soldiers

Ps 89:8 *The term here translated "LORD God Almighty" can be translated "LORD God of hosts" or "LORD God of armies". See also* 1Ki 19:10; Jer 5:14; Hos 12:5; Am 4:13

See also

5206 archers	5406 mercenaries
5208 armies	5434 officer
5209 armour	5489 rank
5245 captain	5605 warfare
5250 centurion	8482 spiritual
5261 commander	warfare
5266 conscription	

spear

A weapon of warfare for stabbing or throwing. God promises a time when they will be changed into instruments of peace.

People killed by spears

Nu 25:6–8; 2Sa 2:23; 18:14; 23:21 pp 1Ch 11:23

Jesus Christ pierced by a spear

Jn 19:34 *See also* Isa 53:5; Zec 12:10; Jn 20:27; Rev 1:7

Armies of Judah armed with spears

2Ch 11:12; 14:8; 25:5; 26:14; Ne 4:13

Armies of other nations that used spears

The Philistines 1Sa 17:7

The Babylonians Jer 6:22–23

The Egyptians 2Sa 23:21 pp 1Ch 11:23; Jer 46:2–4

The Romans Jn 19:34

God's people are not to trust in spears but in God

1Sa 17:47 *See also* 1Sa 17:45–46

King Saul and his spear

Used against David 1Sa 18:10–11 *See also* 1Sa 19:9–10

Used against Jonathan 1Sa 20:33

David takes Saul's spear 1Sa 26:5–24

Joshua's spear used as a sign of victory

Jos 8:18 *See also* Jos 8:19,25–26

Goliath's spear symbolises his strength

1Sa 17:7,45–47; 2Sa 21:19; 1Ch 20:5

Spears will be turned into pruning hooks

Isa 2:4 pp Mic 4:3 *Some believe that the peace described in Isa 2:1–4 has been inaugurated with the coming of Jesus Christ. Others maintain that it refers to conditions that will obtain during a future reign of Jesus Christ on earth. The details are generally taken to be figurative rather than literal. See also* Ps 46:9

Pruning hooks will be turned into spears

Joel 3:10

See also

2412 cross, accounts	2530 Christ, death of
of	5612 weapons

speech

The human capacity to express oneself and communicate with others through the spoken word. God addresses humans through the spoken word, and supremely in and through Jesus Christ.

5547

speech, power and significance of

A person's speech has an enormous influence for good or ill and is a sure guide to character.

The impact of speech

It has the power of life and death Pr 18:21; Jas 3:1–12 *See also* Pr 15:2,4

It can bring ruin or joy to the speaker Pr 12:13–14 *See also* Ps 140:9; Pr 10:14; 13:3; 14:3; 18:6–7,20; 21:23; Ecc 10:12–14

It can destroy others Pr 11:9 *See also* Job 19:2; Ps 55:20–21; 57:4; 64:3–4; 140:3; Pr 11:11; 12:6,18; 16:27

It can bring life to others Pr 10:11 *See also* Pr 10:20–21,31–32; 16:21,23–24; 25:12; Isa 50:4; Eph 4:29

The timing of speech

There is an appropriate time for speaking Ecc 3:1–8 *See also* Pr 15:23,28; 25:11–12

There is an appropriate time for silence Pr 11:12–13 *See also* 1Sa 10:27; Pr 10:19; 17:27–28; 21:23; 26:4; Ecc 5:2–3; Am 5:13; Hab 2:20; Zep 1:7; Jas 1:19

Spoken witness produces faith

Ro 10:17 *See also* Isa 50:4; Ac 2:40–41; 28:23–24; 1Pe 3:15

5548
Jesus Christ was silent before his accusers
1Pe 2:22–23 *See also* Mt 26:63 pp Mk 14:61; Mt 27:14 pp Mk 15:5; Lk 23:9; Jn 19:8–9

Speech is an expression of a person's character
Mt 12:34–37 *See also* Ps 5:9; 15:1–5; Mt 15:10–20 pp Mk 7:14–23; Lk 6:45; Jas 1:26; Rev 14:5

See also

2315 Christ as Lamb	5196 voice
3281 Holy Spirit, inspiration	5356 irony
	5374 languages
5164 lips	5842 eloquence
5167 mouth	5950 silence
5168 muteness	7754 preaching
5193 tongue	

5548
speech, divine

Scripture assumes and affirms that God has spoken to many different people throughout the ages in a variety of ways.

Speech as a synonym for revelation
Heb 1:1–2 *See also* Dt 8:3; 1Sa 3:1,7; Ps 147:19; Jn 17:6–8,14; 1Co 2:6–10

Different modes of divine speech
The voice of nature Isa 30:30–31 *See also* Ps 29:3–9; Job 37:1–5 *God's voice is depicted as thunder, the most awesome sound in nature;* Isa 33:3

A literal, audible voice Mt 17:5 pp Mk 9:7 pp Lk 9:34 *See also* 1Ki 19:9–13; Da 4:31; Jn 12:28–29; Ac 9:3–7

Visions Ge 46:2 *See also* Isa 6:8–13; Jer 1:11–14; Eze 1:28–2:1; Ac 18:9–10; 22:17–18

Dreams Ge 31:24 *See also* Ge 20:3–7; 1Ki 3:5–14; Job 33:15–18; Mt 1:20–21; 2:13; 1:19–20

Divine speech through human messengers
Jesus Christ Jn 14:10 *See also* Jn 7:16; 8:28; 12:49–50; 14:24

Prophets 2Pe 1:21 *See also* 1Sa 8:7–9; 1Ki 17:24; 2Ch 36:15; Isa 38:4–8; Eze 3:10–11; Zec 7:4–12

Apostles 1Th 2:13 *See also* Gal 1:11–12; 2Pe 3:2; 1Jn 1:1–3

Divine speech through angels
Ac 8:26 *See also* Da 9:20–23; Lk 1:11–20,26–38

Examples of divine communication
Dialogues between individuals and God Ge 4:9–15 *See also* Ge 18:16–33; Ex 3:3–4:17; Ac 9:10–16

Messages received by people Ge 35:1 *See also* Ge 12:1–3; Jos 1:1–9; 2Sa 7:4–16; 1Ki 6:11–13

Descriptions of divine speech
The sound of God's voice Eze 43:1–2 *See also* 1Ki 19:12; Rev 1:15

The effect of God's word Isa 55:10–11
See also Ps 119:105; Jer 23:29; Zec 1:13; Heb 4:12; Rev 19:15

The character of divine speech Ps 12:6
See also Ps 18:30; 19:7–11; 119:89,160; 1Pe 1:24–25; Isa 40:6–8

God's word is recognised and loved by his people
Ps 119:103 *See also* Eze 3:1–3; Jn 10:3–5,27; Ac 13:48

God's word is supremely revealed in Jesus Christ
Jn 1:14 *See also* Heb 1:2

See also

1210 God, human descriptions	2363 Christ, preaching & teaching
1403 God, revelation	4110 angels
1409 dream	5263 communication
1428 prophecy, OT inspiration	7706 apostles
1439 revelation	7773 prophets, role
1469 visions	
1690 word of God	

5549
speech, positive aspects of

The way in which believers speak should reflect their calling as Christians. Christian speech should be sincere, godly and honouring to God.

The desire for godly speech
In oneself Ps 19:14 *See also* Ps 17:3; 39:1; 141:3

In others Eph 4:29–31 *See also* Pr 4:24; Ecc 5:6; Eph 5:4; Col 3:8–10; 1Pe 3:9–10; Ps 34:12–13

Characteristics of godly speech in relation to God
It gives glory to God Heb 13:15 *See also* Ps 34:1; 35:28; 51:15; 1Pe 2:9

It gives thanks and praise to God Col 3:17 *See also* Dt 8:10; 1Ch 16:4,7–8,34–36; Ps 100:4; 118:1,19,21,28–29; Joel 2:26; Mk 8:6–7; Col 2:7; 1Th 5:18; Jas 3:9–10

It confesses Jesus Christ as Lord Ro 10:9–10 *See also* Mt 10:32–33 pp Lk 12:8–9; Mt 16:16; 1Co 12:3

Characteristics of godly speech in relation to others
It is gentle, gracious and tactful Col 4:6 *See also* Jdg 8:1–3; Pr 10:32; 15:1; 16:24; Ecc 10:12; Da 2:14–16; 1Pe 3:15

It is kind Pr 12:25 *See also* Ge 50:19–21; Job 4:3–4; 1Co 4:13; 2Ti 2:24–25

It is instructive and edifying Col 3:16 *See also* Pr 12:18; 15:2,4,7; 20:15; 25:11–12; 31:26; Mal 2:7; Eph 4:15,29

It is prudent and restrained Pr 17:27 *See also* Pr 15:28; 18:13; Ecc 5:2; 9:17; Jas 1:19

It is honest and unadorned Mt 5:37 *See also* Ps 15:2–3; 141:5; Pr 24:26; 27:5–6,9; 28:23

It is truthful and sincere Zec 8:16 *See also* Ex 20:16 pp Dt 5:20; Pr 12:17,19,22; Mal 2:6; 2Co 2:17; 4:2; 6:7; Eph 4:25

It is wise Ps 37:30 *See also* Pr 10:13,31; 13:14; Ac 6:10

It will speak of God and his works
Dt 6:6–9 *See also* Ps 40:9–10; 145:7; Mal 3:16

Jesus Christ's speech was perfect and unique
Jn 7:46 *See also* Mt 7:28–29; 13:54 pp Mk 6:2; Lk 4:22; 1Pe 2:22–23; Isa 53:9

Speech as a means of blessing people
Nu 6:22–27 *See also* Ge 1:22,28; Dt 21:5; 1Ch 23:13

See also

1335 blessing	8291 kindness
1460 truth	8352 thankfulness
5922 prudence	8361 wisdom
7797 teaching	8407 confession of Christ
8252 faithfulness, relationships	8413 edification
8275 honesty	8664 praise

5550
speech, negative aspects of

The sinfulness of fallen human nature can express itself in speech, provoking God's displeasure and causing enmity and division amongst people.

Evil speech comes from a corrupt heart
Mt 12:33–35 *See also* Pr 2:12–15; 24:1–2; Mt 15:10–11 pp Mk 7:14–15; Lk 6:43–45

Evil speech is a feature of a corrupt society
Mic 6:12–13 *See also* Isa 6:5; 59:1–4,12–15; Jer 9:1–9; Ro 1:29–32; 2Ti 3:1–5

Evil speech provokes God's displeasure
Pr 12:22 *See also* Pr 6:16–19

Kinds of evil speech
Profaning God's name Ex 20:7 pp Dt 5:11 *See also* Ex 22:28; Lev 19:12; Ps 139:19–20

Lies and deceit Ps 5:9 *See also* Ps 36:3; 52:1–4; 62:4; Pr 14:5,25; 15:4; 17:20

Foolish boasting Ps 94:4 *See also* Ps 10:2–6; 12:3–4; Isa 10:12–14; 2Th 2:3–4; Jas 4:13–16; 2Pe 2:17–18

Ridicule and insults Pr 11:12 *See also* 1Sa 17:41–44; 2Ki 2:23–24; Ne 2:19; Pr 9:7; La 2:15–16; Mt 5:22; 27:39–44 pp Mk 15:29–32 pp Lk 23:35–39; Jn 9:28–29

Criticism and complaint Nu 12:1–15 *See also* Nu 16:1–50; 1Sa 17:28; Pr 19:13; 21:9,19; 25:24; Ac 11:2–3; Php 2:14–15

Slander Lev 19:16 *See also* 1Ki 21:1–14; Pr 10:18; Jas 4:11

Cursing Ex 21:17 *See also* 2Sa 16:5–8; Pr 20:20; Jas 3:9–10

Gossip Pr 16:28 *See also* Pr 11:13; 17:9; 20:19

Obscenity Eph 5:4 *See also* Col 3:8

Evil speech is silenced

By God's actions Ps 107:41–42 *See also* Ps 63:11; Eze 16:63

By believers' blameless lives 1Pe 2:15 *See also* Tit 2:7–8

See also

5575 talk, idle	5925 rashness
5800 blasphemy	6121 boasting
5803 carelessness	6145 deceit
5820 criticism	8760 fools,
5827 curse	characteristics
5868 gossip	8815 ridicule
5893 insults	

5551

spinning and weaving

Spinning as the process of making thread
Pr 31:19; Mt 6:28 pp Lk 12:27

Weaving as the process of making cloth
Ex 28:39

Weavers and spinners
Isa 19:9 *See also* Ex 35:25,35; 39:22,27; 2Ki 23:7

The figurative use of spinning and weaving
Job 7:6; Isa 38:12 *See also* Jdg 16:13; 1Sa 17:7; Isa 59:5

See also

4444 flax	5272 craftsmen
5145 clothing	5392 linen
5212 arts and crafts	5433 occupations
5258 cloth	

5552

spies

Spies were used to collect information, usually of a military nature
Joseph's brothers accused of being spies: Ge 42:9–11,14–16,30–34
Spies sent to reconnoitre the promised land: Nu 13:1–20; 21:32; Jos 2:1–3
Rahab hides the spies: Jos 6:17,22,25; Heb 11:31; Jas 2:25
Jos 7:2; Jdg 1:23–24; 18:2,14,17; 2Sa 10:3 pp 1Ch 19:3

Spies were used to incriminate Jesus Christ and the first Christians
Lk 20:20–22 pp Mt 22:15–16 pp Mk 12:13–14; Gal 2:4

See also

5202 accusation,	5941 secrecy
false	5969 treachery
5605 warfare	

5553

stairways

Steps which provide access to upper levels, usually of buildings. The term is also used figuratively as a means of ascent from earth to heaven.

Stairways relating to places of worship
In Solomon's temple 1Ki 6:8

Used by the Levites Ne 9:4

In Ezekiel's vision of the new temple Eze 40:49 *See also* Eze 40:6,22,26,31,34,37,49; 41:7; 43:17

Steps forbidden for the altar Ex 20:26

Stairways relating to royalty
1Ki 10:19–20 pp 2Ch 9:18–19 *See also* 2Ki 9:13; 20:11 pp Isa 38:8

Stairways in city walls and fortresses
Ne 3:15 *See also* Ne 3:19; 12:37; Ac 21:35,40

Stairways in houses
For access to upper floors and basements Ac 9:39 *See also* 2Sa 18:33; 1Ki 17:19; Ac 1:13; 9:37; 10:20; 20:8,11

Figurative use of stairways
Ge 28:12 *See also* Jn 1:51

See also

1670 symbols	5506 roof
5340 house	5604 walls

5554

status

A person's standing in society in the sight of others. The status of individuals in the sight of the world often differs radically from their status in the sight of God, but it is the latter that really matters.

Factors contributing to high social status
High status associated with a position of secular authority Da 2:37–38 *See also* 2Sa 15:1–6; 1Ch 29:26–28

High status based upon a position of domestic authority Mal 1:6 *See also* Ps 123:2; Lk 17:7–10; 1Co 11:3

High status owing to recognition of religious authority Ac 5:34 *See also* Mt 23:1–2,8–10; Ac 23:1–5

High status owing to pious conduct Mt 23:5–7 pp Mk 12:38–39 pp Lk 20:45–46 *See also* Mt 6:2,5,16; Lk 7:4–5

High status based on wealth Pr 19:4 *See also* 1Ki 10:4–7 pp 2Ch 9:3–6; Job 1:1–3; Jas 2:1–4

Factors contributing to low social status
Low status on account of occupation Mt 9:11 pp Mk 2:16 pp Lk 5:30 *See also* Lk 15:1–2; 18:11

Low status through sickness Lev 13:45–46 *See also* Mt 20:29–31 pp Mk 10:46–48 pp Lk 18:35–39; Lk 17:12–13

Low status through poverty Am 5:11–12 *See also* Job 24:1–12; Lk 16:20; Jas 2:1–4

Status in God's kingdom
The reversal of human status Mt 5:3–6 pp Lk 6:20–21 *See also* Mt 19:13–15 pp Mk 10:13–16 pp Lk 18:15–17; Mt 19:16–30 pp Mk 10:17–31

pp Lk 18:18–30; Lk 1:52–53; 16:19–26; 1Co 1:26–29

Believers must take the lowest status Mt 18:1–5 pp Mk 9:33–37 pp Lk 9:46–48 *See also* Mt 20:20–28 pp Mk 10:35–45; Lk 14:7–11; Jn 13:12–15; Php 2:3–5

All believers enjoy equal status before God Gal 3:28 *See also* 1Co 7:22; 11:11–12; Phm 15–17; Jas 1:9–10

See also

2378 kingdom of	6610 adoption,
God,	descriptions
characteristics	8276 humility
5308 equality	8342 servanthood
5446 poverty	8767 hypocrisy
5489 rank	8802 pride
5509 rulers	8810 riches, dangers
5700 headship	

5555

stealing

Theft is always condemned in Scripture, though the possibility of mitigating circumstances is recognised. Converted thieves must show their repentance, if possible, in a practical way.

Stealing is condemned as a sin
It is prohibited Ex 20:15 pp Dt 5:19 *See also* Lev 19:11; Ps 62:10; Mk 10:19 pp Lk 18:20; Ro 2:21; 13:9

Punishment for stealing 1Co 6:9–10 *See also* Ex 21:16; 22:1–4; Lev 6:2–5

The disgrace of thieves Jer 2:26

The company of thieves is to be avoided Pr 29:24; Isa 1:23

Stealing is denied Ge 44:8; 1Sa 12:3–5

Mitigating circumstances for stealing
Poverty Pr 6:30–31 *See also* Pr 30:7–9

Stealing is commonplace in this world
It is part of life in a sinful world Hos 4:2; Mt 6:19 *See also* Mt 15:19

Roadside robbery Lk 10:30 *See also* Pr 1:10–15; 2Co 11:26

Sheep stealing Job 24:2; 2Sa 12:4

Dishonesty in trade Jer 22:17; Eze 28:18; Hos 12:7; Am 8:5

Dishonest tax collectors Lk 3:13; 19:8

Theft in the temple Mt 21:12–13 pp Mk 11:15–17 pp Lk 19:45–46; Jer 7:11

Theft in the family Ge 31:19; Jdg 17:1–2

Wife stealing 2Sa 11:3

Kidnapping 2Ki 11:2 pp 2Ch 22:11

Temple robbers Ac 19:37; Ro 2:22

Body stealing Mt 27:64

Examples of stealing
Ge 31:19 *Rachel*
Achan: Jos 7:11,20–21
Jdg 17:1–2 *Micah the Ephraimite*
Two crucified thieves: Mt 27:38 pp Mk 15:27; Mt 27:44; Lk 23:32
Jn 12:6 *Judas*

Stealing as an image
Of forbidden pleasures Pr 9:17

Of a captivated heart 2Sa 15:6; SS 4:9

Of unexpected loss Pr 6:10–11;
24:33–34

Of God's judgment 1Th 5:2 *See also*
Jer 49:9–10 pp Ob 5–6; Mt 24:42–44;
2Pe 3:10

Spiritual stealing
Stealing from God Mal 3:8–9

Lying prophets *See also* Jer 23:30

False shepherds Jn 10:1 *See also*
Jn 10:8,10

Converted thieves
Lk 23:39–43 *the thief on the cross;*
1Co 6:9–11 *some of the Corinthians*

Repentance must be borne out in
practical actions Eph 4:28 *See also*
Eze 33:15; Lk 19:8 *Zacchaeus;* Tit 2:10

There is no stealing in heaven
Mt 6:20

See also

5253 cheating	5492 restitution
5277 criminals	6626 conversion
5311 extortion	6732 repentance
5365 kidnapping	8488 tithing
5377 law, Ten	8714 dishonesty
Command-	8790 oppression
ments	

5556

stewardship

The careful use, control and
management of the possessions of
another that have been entrusted to
one. The term is also used to refer to
the responsible use of wealth and
possessions by Christians.

Individuals acting as stewards
Adam in the Garden of Eden Ge 2:15

Joseph in Potiphar's household
Ge 39:4–6

Daniel as administrator in Babylon
Da 6:1–3

Groups acting as stewards
The priests serving in the tabernacle
Lev 22:9; 1Sa 2:15

The seven chosen by the Jerusalem
church Ac 6:1–6

Household stewards
Ge 43:16; 44:1–12; 2Sa 16:1; 19:17;
Est 1:8

Jesus Christ's teaching on
stewardship
Using parables to emphasise
accountability Lk 16:1–12 *See also*
Mt 25:14–30; Lk 19:12–27

Emphasising each individual's
responsibility Lk 12:48 *See also*
Mt 12:36

The apostles continued this
teaching
Ro 14:12 *See also* 1Pe 4:4–5

To be a good steward is an
honourable thing
1Ti 3:13 *See also* Pr 27:18

Christians are entrusted with the
stewardship of the gospel
1Co 4:1–2 *See also* 1Co 9:17;
2Co 5:19–21; Gal 1:15–16; 2:7;
1Th 2:4; 1Ti 1:11; 4:14; 6:20; 2Ti 1:14;
Tit 1:3,7

Christians are to be wise
stewards of their God-given gifts
1Co 4:7

They are to use their gifts to benefit
others 1Pe 4:10–11

They are to develop their gifts
1Ti 4:14–15

They are to care for their bodies
1Co 6:18–20

Believers are to be wise
stewards of their material
possessions
Dt 8:17–18

Jesus Christ's teaching on sharing
possessions Mt 19:21 pp Mk 10:21
pp Lk 18:22 *See also* Mt 6:1–4,19–21;
Lk 6:38; 21:1–4; Ac 20:35

Sharing of possessions among the first
Christians Ac 4:32–35 *See also*
2Co 8:1–5

The apostle Paul's teaching on sharing
possessions Ac 20:35; 2Co 9:6–11

See also

4903 time	7966 spiritual gifts
5002 human race &	8345 servanthood &
creation	worship
5052 responsibility	8354 trust-
to God	worthiness
5414 money,	8438 giving time
stewardship	8472 respect for
5475 property	environment
5520 servants	
5704 inheritance,	
material	

5557

stoning

To strike an offender with stones
until he or she is dead. Stoning
normally took place outside the city
walls. The prosecution witnesses, of
whom there must be at least two,
had to throw the first stones,
followed if necessary by the
spectators.

Stoning was the punishment for
certain offences under the
Mosaic law
Lev 20:1–2,27; 24:13–14; Dt 13:6–10;
17:2–7; 22:23–24

Examples of stoning in upholding
the Mosaic law
Lev 24:23; Nu 15:32–36; Jos 7:24–25;
1Ki 21:13–15; Jn 8:1–11

Examples of the threatened or
actual stoning of God's servants
Nu 14:10 *Joshua and Caleb;* 1Sa 30:6
David; 2Sa 16:6; 2Ch 24:20–21
Jesus Christ; Jn 8:59; 10:31–33
Ac 7:58–59 *Stephen*
Paul; Ac 14:19; 2Co 11:25
Heb 11:37

See also

5025 killing	7346 death penalty
5482 punishment	8450 martyrdom
5493 retribution	8794 persecution
5975 violence	9020 death

5558

storing

A laying up of surpluses for times of
scarcity. It includes such facilities as
store cities and storehouses and also
refers to hoarding treasures.
Figuratively the word is used of the
accumulation of human sin and
God's consequent judgment.

Store cities
Ex 1:11 *See also* Ge 41:35,48; 1Ki 9:19;
2Ch 8:4–6; 16:4; 17:12–13

Storehouses
Ge 41:56 *See also* 1Ki 4:7; 7:51
pp 2Ch 5:1; 2Ki 14:14; 18:15; 24:13;
1Ch 26:15; 27:25; 2Ch 8:15; 16:2;
31:10–11; 32:27–28; Ezr 2:69; Est 3:9;
Pr 24:4; Mal 3:10; Mk 12:41–44
pp Lk 21:1–4

The contents of storehouses
Materials kept in storage Ge 6:21 *See
also* Ge 41:34–35,49; 1Ki 7:51
pp 2Ch 5:1; 2Ch 11:11; 31:5,11–12;
32:27–28; Ezr 4:15; 5:17; 6:1–2,5;
Ne 10:37–39; Isa 10:28; Jer 41:8

Empty storehouses a disaster Joel 1:17
See also Ge 41:35–36; 1Ch 27:25

Roofs and watchtowers provided
storage space
Jos 2:6

God's storehouse
Ps 135:7 *See also* Dt 28:12; 32:34;
Job 14:17; 38:22–23; Ps 33:7; 104:13;
Pr 2:7 *victory held in store for the
righteous;* Jer 10:13; 51:16; Col 1:5;
2Ti 4:8; 1Pe 1:3–5

Warnings against storing up
selfishly or thoughtlessly
Mt 6:19 *See also* Job 20:20; 31:24–28;
Lk 12:15–21; 19:20–23

Storing up treasure in heaven
Mt 6:20 *See also* Mt 19:21; Lk 12:33–34;
1Ti 6:17–19

Storing up sin and judgment
Hos 13:12 *See also* Ro 2:5

God's judgment is stored up
2Pe 3:7 *See also* Job 38:22–23; Isa 26:11;
2Pe 2:17; Jude 12–13

See also

4221 cistern	5591 treasure
4456 grain	5869 greed
5224 barn	5907 miserliness
5506 roof	8778 materialism
5585 towers	8808 riches

5559

stress

A state of personal anxiety, strain or
tension resulting from the pressures
of human life. Scripture indicates a
number of causes and means of
dealing with stress.

The experience of stress
Ps 38:8 ; Mk 14:33–39 pp Mt 26:37–44 pp Lk 22:39–46; 2Co 1:8 *See also* Job 6:2; Ps 77:2; Jer 4:19; Jn 12:27; 13:21; Heb 5:7

Possible causes of stress
Disobedience to God's will Dt 28:65 *See also* 2Sa 24:14 pp 1Ch 21:13; Ps 38:4; Mt 14:9 pp Mk 6:26

Family ties 1Co 7:33 *See also* Ge 21:11; 43:6; 1Sa 1:6–16

The burdens of leadership 2Co 11:28 *See also* Nu 11:14; 2Co 2:4; Heb 13:17

Threats of injury or violence La 1:20 *See also* Ge 32:7; 1Sa 28:5; 1Ki 19:1–2; Est 7:4; Ps 56:1–2; Jer 19:9

Unjust leaders Ex 5:19; Ne 9:37

The wickedness of others 1Ki 19:14 *See also* Ro 9:2–3; 2Pe 2:7–8

Academic study Ecc 1:13

The effects of stress
Pr 12:25; Mt 13:22 pp Mk 4:18 pp Lk 8:14 *See also* 1Ki 19:3–4; Ps 31:9–10; Lk 10:40–41

Appeals to God in stressful situations
Ps 102:2; Jnh 2:2 *See also* 2Sa 22:7 pp Ps 18:6; 2Ch 20:9; 33:12; Ps 4:1; 25:17; 106:44; 120:1

God comforts believers under stress
Ps 94:19; Mt 11:28; 1Pe 5:7 *See also* 1Sa 30:6; Ps 107:6; 119:143; Jn 14:1,27; 16:33; 2Co 4:8–10; Php 4:6

See also

5056 rest	5831 depression
5537 sleeplessness	5890 insecurity
5567 suffering,	5901 loneliness
emotional	8713 discourage-
5582 tiredness	ment
5628 work	8754 fear
5805 comfort	8849 worry

5560

suffering

The experience of pain or distress, both physical and emotional. Scripture is thoroughly realistic about the place of suffering in the world and in the lives of believers. To become a Christian is not to escape from suffering, but to be able to bear suffering with dignity and hope. This set of themes consists of the following:
5561 suffering, nature of
5562 suffering, of the innocent
5563 suffering, of God
5564 suffering, of Jesus Christ
5565 suffering, of believers
5566 suffering, encouragements in
5567 suffering, emotional aspects of
5568 suffering, causes of
5569 suffering, hardship

5561

suffering, nature of

Since the fall, human beings have suffered in various ways. Scripture provides insights into the nature and place of suffering both in the world and in the lives of believers.

Suffering began with the fall
Ge 2:17; 3:16–19; Ro 5:12

Suffering is universal
Job 5:7; 14:1

Different kinds of suffering
Physical pain and illness Ge 48:1 *See also* 2Ki 20:1 pp 2Ch 32:24 pp Isa 38:1; Job 2:7; Ps 42:10; Mt 8:6; 17:15; Lk 4:38; Ac 28:8; 2Ti 4:20; Jas 5:14

Emotional stress Ps 55:4–5 *See also* Ge 35:18 *"Ben-Oni" means "son of my trouble"*; Pr 12:25; Jn 11:32–35; Php 2:27

Spiritual suffering Ps 22:1 *See also* Mt 27:46 pp Mk 15:34

The prospect of death Ge 3:19 *See also* Ecc 12:7

Major causes of suffering
The disorder in creation Ge 3:17 *See also* Ge 12:10; Joel 1:4; Mt 24:7 pp Lk 21:11; Ro 8:22; Rev 11:13

Human cruelty Ps 54:3
Murder: Ge 4:8; Ex 1:16,22; 1Ki 21:19; Mt 2:16
Ge 49:5–7
Oppression: Ex 1:11; Am 2:6–7; 4:1; Mal 3:5
2Ki 6:25; 19:17 *warfare;* 2Ch 10:13–14; Job 1:14–15,17; Am 1:3,13; Jas 5:4–6; Rev 6:4

Family troubles Ps 27:10 *See also* 1Sa 1:7; 2Sa 16:11; Job 19:14–19; Mal 2:14; Mt 10:36; Jas 1:27

Old age Ps 71:9 *See also* Ecc 12:1–7

Satan's activity 1Jn 5:19 *See also* Job 1:12; 2:6–7; Lk 13:16; 2Co 12:7; Rev 2:10; 20:7–8

Aggravations to suffering
Memories Job 29:2

Fears Job 3:25; Heb 2:15

Resentment Job 2:9

Sin and suffering
They are not necessarily related Jn 9:3 *See also* Job 2:3; Lk 13:2

They are sometimes closely related Ro 1:18 *See also* Ge 6:5–7; Nu 14:33; Dt 28:15; Ps 107:17; Eze 23:49; Ac 5:5,10; Ro 1:27; 1Co 11:29–30; Jude 7; Rev 2:22

God's final judgment Mt 25:41 *See also* Da 12:2; Mt 8:12; Mk 9:48; Isa 66:24; Rev 20:15

Effects of suffering
Hardness of heart Rev 16:9 *See also* Ex 7:22; Rev 9:20–21

Repentance 2Ch 33:12; Lk 15:17–18

Blessing Ps 119:71 *See also* Isa 38:17

See also

5436 pain	5972 unkindness
5605 warfare	6020 sin
5782 agony	6142 decay
5823 cruelty	6154 fall, the
5952 sorrow	9020 death

5562

suffering, of the innocent

Scripture does not teach that the wicked will suffer, whereas the innocent and blameless will prosper. It offers insights into the place of suffering in the lives of the innocent, and the apparent injustice of this situation.

The apparent injustice of suffering
Hab 1:13 *See also* Job 19:7; 24:1,12; Ps 59:3–4; 74:1,11; 88:5,14

The wrong answers to suffering
The concept that those who suffer must be sinners: Job 4:7; Jn 9:2–3
Eze 18:25 *the idea that God is unjust*

The wrong reactions to suffering
Job 2:9–10 *resentment against God;* Job 23:13–15 *being terrified of God;* Job 40:2 *arguing with God;* Ps 73:3 *envying the wicked;* Ps 73:13 *disillusionment*

The right reactions to suffering
Reverent submission Job 1:21 *See also* Job 28:28; 34:12; 36:26; 37:19; 40:4; La 3:40,49–50; Mt 10:28

Trust in God Ge 18:25; Ps 55:22–23 *See also* Ex 2:23; Ps 56:3–4; 59:16; 62:5; 70:2; 107:6,13,19,28
Ps 119:50,153; Da 3:17–18 *the trust shown by Shadrach, Meshach and Abednego;* Hab 3:17–18; 1Pe 2:23 *the example of Jesus Christ;* 1Pe 4:19; 5:7

God's reaction to suffering
Concern for those who suffer Ps 9:12 *See also* Ex 2:25; 2Ki 14:26; Ps 1:6; 33:18–19; Jas 5:4

Anger at the wicked Ps 11:5; 59:8; Eze 36:6–7; Hab 2:9,12

God's response to suffering
Deliverance for those who suffer Ps 34:19 *See also* Job 42:10–12; Rev 7:16; 21:4

Judgment for the wicked Mal 3:5 *See also* Ex 3:19–20; Ps 73:16–18; 141:10; Am 1:3; Na 3:1,19; Hab 2:16; Mt 25:41–46; Jas 2:13; 1Pe 4:18; Rev 18:6–7

See also

1030 God,	1320 God as Saviour
compassion	5347 injustice
1075 God, justice of	5959 submission
1085 God, love of	8020 faith
1125 God,	8030 trust
righteousness	8333 reverence
1310 God as judge	

5563

suffering, of God

See 1135 God, suffering of

5564
suffering, of Jesus Christ

Jesus Christ suffered on behalf of his people, showing both the reality of his human nature, and the extent of his love for humanity. Those sufferings reached their climax in the sufferings of Jesus Christ upon the cross, through which God chose to redeem the world.

The OT foretold Jesus Christ's suffering
NT references to the OT Scriptures Lk 24:25-26 See also Lk 24:46; Ac 3:18; 17:2-3; 26:22-23; 1Co 15:3

Types and foreshadowings of Jesus Christ's suffering Ge 22:2,8,13; Ex 12:22-23; 1Sa 19:5; 2Sa 16:11-12; 1Ki 21:15; Ps 55:12-14; 57:4; Heb 13:11-12

Prophetic statements of Jesus Christ's suffering Ge 3:15; Ps 2:2; 22:1,7-8,12-18; 69:21; Isa 53:3-12

Jesus Christ himself foretold his suffering
Mt 16:21 pp Lk 9:22 See also Mt 17:12 pp Mk 9:12; Mt 20:18-19 pp Mk 10:33-34 pp Lk 18:31-32; Mk 9:31; Lk 17:25; 20:13-15 compare with Naboth (1Kings chapter 21); Lk 22:15; Jn 12:27

Aspects in Jesus Christ's suffering
The enmity of Satan Ge 3:15 In the temptation of Jesus Christ: Mt 4:1-3 pp Lk 4:1-3; Mt 4:5 pp Lk 4:9; Mt 4:8 pp Lk 4:5 pp Mk 1:13 Mt 16:23 In entering Judas Iscariot: Lk 22:3; Jn 13:27 Jn 14:30; Rev 12:4

The hatred of the world Jn 7:7 See also Mt 2:13; Jn 1:10; 3:20; 15:18-20; 1Co 2:8

Rejection by his own people Jn 1:11 See also Isa 53:1; Mt 23:37; Lk 19:41-42; 24:20; Jn 18:40; Ac 2:36; 3:13; 4:10; 1Th 2:14-15

The failure of his disciples Mk 14:50 pp Mt 26:56 See also Mt 16:22; 26:40,74-75; Lk 18:34

Betrayal by Judas Mt 26:23 pp Mk 14:18 pp Lk 22:21 pp Jn 13:21

God's judgment of his Son for the sins of the world Mt 27:46 pp Mk 15:34 See also Ps 22:1; Isa 53:5-6,10; Lk 22:42; Ro 3:25-26; 2Co 5:21; Gal 3:13; Heb 2:10,14; 1Pe 2:24

Jesus Christ's willing submission to suffering
Mt 26:42 pp Mk 14:36 pp Lk 22:42 See also Isa 53:7,11; Lk 23:46; Heb 5:7-8; 12:2; 1Pe 2:23

See also
1135 God, suffering of	2410 cross, the
2033 Christ, humanity	2570 Christ, suffering
2324 Christ as Saviour	4025 world, the
2339 Christ, example of	5798 betrayal
	5827 curse
	6614 atonement
	6720 redemption

5565
suffering, of believers

Believers ought to expect to suffer as an inevitable part of their calling. To believe is not to evade suffering; it is to face it with new confidence and hope. Rightly approached, suffering develops the character of believers, equips them for more effective service, draws believers closer to Jesus Christ and prepares them for eternal life.

Believers must expect suffering
Jesus Christ foretold it Mt 10:22 pp Mk 13:13 See also Mt 10:17; 23:34; 24:9; Lk 21:16-17

The apostles foretold it Ac 14:22; 2Ti 3:12 See also Php 1:29; 1Jn 3:13; Rev 2:10

The experience of the OT shows it Ro 8:36; Heb 11:25-26,32-38

The experience of the NT shows it Ac 4:3; 5:40; 9:29; 12:1-3; 2Co 11:23-29; Gal 3:4; 1Th 2:2,14; 1Pe 4:4; Heb 10:32-34

Suffering for Jesus Christ is commendable
Mt 5:10-12 pp Lk 6:20-23 See also Ac 5:41; 2Ti 1:8; 1Pe 2:19; 3:17; 4:12-16

Suffering is profitable
It affirms believers' adoption Heb 12:7 See also Jn 15:19; 17:14; Ro 8:17; Gal 6:17; 2Th 1:4-5

It is the price of godliness Heb 12:11 See also Ps 119:67,71; Isa 38:17; Jn 15:2; 1Pe 1:6-7

It is a condition of service 2Co 4:10; Col 1:24 See also Ps 126:5-6; Ac 9:16; 20:23-24; 1Co 4:9-13; 2Co 1:3-5; Gal 4:19; Php 3:18; Col 2:1; 2Ti 1:11-12; 2:3,10

It develops trust 2Co 1:9 See also 1Pe 4:19

It develops character Ro 5:3-4 See also Heb 5:8; Jas 1:3

It deepens fellowship 1Co 12:26 See also Ro 12:15; 2Co 1:7; 8:2; Gal 4:14-15; 6:2

It draws believers to the Lord Php 3:8,10 See also Job 42:5; 2Co 4:8-10; 12:9-10; 1Pe 4:13

It prepares believers for heaven 2Co 4:16-5:4

See also
1040 God, fatherhood	8347 spiritual growth
6608 adoption	8450 martyrdom
8206 Christlikeness	8794 persecution
8266 holiness	8832 testing
8342 servanthood	

5566
suffering, encouragements in

Believers are encouraged by the loving care and faithful promises of God and by the example, support

and prayers of fellow believers. The prospect of heaven helps them to endure.

The encouragement of God's love
The care of the Father Ps 103:13 See also Ps 86:17; Isa 50:10; 64:8-9; Lk 18:6-7; Jn 16:27; 17:11,15; Ro 8:32; 2Co 1:3

The sympathetic understanding of Jesus Christ Heb 2:18 See also Isa 40:11; 42:3; 53:5; Lk 4:18; Isa 61:1; Jn 14:27; 16:22; Ro 8:35-39; Heb 4:15; 7:25; 12:3

The comfort of the Spirit Jn 14:16-17 See also Lk 11:13; Ro 5:5; 8:26; Gal 5:22-23; Eph 3:16; 1Pe 4:14

The promises of God Ps 119:50; Ro 8:28; 2Co 12:9 See also Isa 41:10; 43:2-3; Mt 6:31-33; Ro 15:4; Php 4:7; 1Pe 5:10

The encouragement of the fellowship of believers
Examples from the past Heb 12:1 See also Ps 102:17-18; Jer 20:11; Php 4:11; Heb 11:25-26; Jas 5:10-11

Support from other believers 1Th 5:11 See also Ru 2:13; Ac 28:15; Ro 16:4; 2Co 7:6-7; Php 4:14; Col 4:11; 1Th 2:11-12; 4:18; 2Ti 4:9,11; Phm 13; Heb 10:25

The encouragement of looking ahead
The assurance of victory Ro 8:37 See also Ro 16:20; 1Co 15:20,25,55-57; 1Th 4:16-17

The prospect of glory Ro 8:18 See also Job 19:25-26; Isa 65:17; 2Co 4:17-5:1; 2Th 1:6-7; 2Pe 3:13; Jude 24-25; Rev 7:16-17; 21:1-4

See also
1035 God, faithfulness	5805 comfort
1190 glory	5963 sympathy
2015 Christ, compassion	6705 peace, experience
2048 Christ, love of	7921 fellowship
3130 Holy Spirit, Counsellor	8414 encouragement
5596 victory	9310 resurrection

5567
suffering, emotional aspects of

Suffering gives rise to inner distress, on account of a sense of injustice, frustration, loss or anger. Christ himself provides an example of such suffering to believers.

Causes of emotional suffering
A sense of injustice Ps 119:53 See also Job 19:7; Ps 82:2

Frustration Job 19:8 See also Job 23:8-9; 1Th 2:18

Loss Ge 27:34 See also Ru 1:20-21; Pr 5:11-14; La 1:12

Bereavement 2Sa 18:33 See also Ge 23:1-2; 37:34-35; 50:1-3; Ex 12:30; Dt 34:8; 2Sa 19:4; Mt 2:16-18; Jer 31:15; Jn 11:32-35

Childlessness Ge 30:1 *See also* 1Sa 1:4-8

Parting from loved ones Ac 20:38 *See also* 1Sa 20:41; 2Ki 2:12; SS 5:6-8

Spiritual loss Lk 13:28 *See also* Jdg 2:4; Mt 25:11

Great fear Ge 45:3 *See also* Ge 20:8; 32:7-8; Ex 20:18-19; 1Sa 17:24; 1Ki 19:3-4; Isa 21:2-4; Da 5:8-9; Lk 21:26

Guilt Mt 27:3-4 *See also* Ge 3:8; Jn 16:8; Ac 2:37; Heb 10:2,22

Emotional suffering in the Lord's work

Jesus Christ's suffering Isa 53:3 *See also* Mt 26:38 pp Mk 14:34

The apostles' suffering 2Co 11:28-29 *See also* Ro 9:1-4; 1Co 15:31; 2Co 1:8-9; Gal 4:19

Expressions of emotional suffering

Sadness Ne 2:1-3; Ps 107:39; 116:3; Mt 26:22 pp Mk 14:19

Weeping and groaning Jer 9:1 *Joseph wept as he saw his brothers again:* Ge 42:24; 43:30; 45:1-2 2Sa 15:30 *Covering the head and going barefoot were also signs of sorrow:* Ezr 3:12-13; Ne 1:4; Ps 6:6-7; 32:3-4; 137:1; Isa 15:5; Jer 14:17; Mt 26:75 *Peter wept bitterly after disowning Jesus Christ;* Jn 11:35

Anger Jnh 4:1 *See also* Ex 32:19-20; 2Sa 6:8; Rev 16:10-11

Bitterness Ex 17:3; 1Sa 30:6; Job 3:1; 7:11; Jnh 4:3; Ro 3:14

God's response to the emotional suffering of believers

He comforts them 2Co 1:3-4

He has delivered them through Jesus Christ Isa 53:4

Jesus Christ gives them rest Jn 14:1 *See also* Mt 11:28-30; Jn 14:27

There is no suffering in heaven Rev 21:4 *See also* Isa 35:10; Rev 7:17

The proper response of believers to emotional suffering

Assessing the problem before God Ps 73:16-17; 119:78; Ro 8:28

Controlled emotion before God Jdg 20:23; Ps 22:1-2; 62:8; 74:1

Prayer Heb 5:7 *See also* Ge 18:22-25; 32:9-11; Nu 16:22; 2Sa 12:15-17; Ps 38:9; 77:1-9; Jnh 2:1; Mk 5:22-23; Jas 5:13

Continuing to do what is right Job 1:20-22; Eph 4:1; Php 1:27

See also

5056 rest	5879 humiliation
5198 weeping	5945 self-pity
5795 bereavement	6172 guilt
5799 bitterness	8602 prayer
5831 depression	8754 fear

5568
suffering, causes of

The ultimate cause of suffering is sin, which has brought violence, disease and death into the world. All

suffering, however, is under the sovereign purpose of God, who is able to use it for his glory.

The ultimate cause of suffering is sin

Ge 3:14-19 *It need not be the result of particular sins:* Job 1:1; Jn 9:1-3 Job 5:6-7; Ro 5:12-14

Suffering as a result of human wickedness

Murder Ge 4:8 *See also* Ge 49:5-7; 1Sa 18:10-11

Injury Mt 26:67

Cruelty Ps 71:4 *See also* Jdg 1:7; Ps 54:3; Am 1:13; Mt 2:16-18; Lk 10:30

Rioting 2Ki 7:17; Ac 16:22

Warfare Jer 50:22 *See also* Ge 14:1-2,11-12; Ex 13:17; Jos 6:20-21; 10:22-26; Jdg 1:4-7; 1Ki 22:35; 2Ki 17:5-6; Zec 14:2; Lk 21:20-24; Rev 6:4

Injustice Eze 9:9 *See also* Ge 39:19-20; 1Ki 21:11-14; 2Ki 21:16; Ps 58:1-2; 64:6

Oppression Ecc 4:1 *See also* Ex 1:11; 1Ki 12:1-4,12-14; Ps 12:5; Jas 5:1-6

Adultery 2Sa 12:9; Mal 2:14

Theft Mt 6:19 *See also* Ge 31:19; Job 1:14-15,17; 24:2

Broken relationships Job 19:14-19; Ps 27:10; Pr 16:28; Ac 15:39

Hatred Ps 109:3 *See also* 2Sa 13:15; Tit 3:3

Jealousy Ge 37:4 *See also* Ge 4:4-5; 16:6; 21:8-10; 1Sa 18:8-9; Mt 27:18

Persecution Jn 15:20 *See also* Jer 38:6; Da 3:4-6; 6:7; Mt 5:10-12; 10:35-36; Rev 6:9-11

Suffering as a result of misfortune

Accidents 2Sa 4:4; 2Ki 1:2; Lk 13:4

Sickness Ge 48:1 *See also* 2Ki 20:1; Job 2:7; Ps 42:10; Mt 8:6; Ac 28:8; Php 2:27; 2Ti 4:20; Jas 5:14

Hunger and want Ge 12:10; Job 30:3; Isa 5:13; Mt 25:42-43

Natural disasters 1Ki 22:48; Job 1:16,18-19; Isa 29:6; Joel 1:4; Zec 14:5; Mt 24:7; Ac 27:18-20

Suffering through old age and death

Ageing 2Sa 19:34-35; Ps 71:9; Ecc 12:1

Bereavement Ge 23:1-2; Job 1:18-19; Lk 7:11-13; Jn 11:33-35; Jas 1:27

Suffering through anxiety

Pr 12:25 *See also* Dt 28:65-67; Lk 21:26

Suffering through foolishness

Ps 107:17 *See also* Jdg 11:34-36; Pr 10:1; 11:15; 14:1; 23:29-30; Lk 15:17

Suffering through Satanic activity

The influence of Satan Ge 3:1 *See also* Job 1:12; 2:6-7; Lk 13:16; 1Jn 5:19; Rev 2:10; 20:7-8

Demon-possession Mt 8:28; 12:22; 15:22

Suffering brought about by God himself

All suffering comes within his will Jn 9:3; Eph 1:11

Some suffering is for his immediate glory Jn 21:19

Jesus Christ's suffering produces salvation Isa 53:10 *See also* Ac 2:23

Christian suffering produces good fruits Ro 5:3-4; 2Co 1:9; Heb 12:11; Jas 1:2,3

God's people must be disciplined Heb 12:7 *See also* Ex 32:35; 2Sa 12:13-14; Ps 119:67,71; Pr 3:11-12; Heb 12:8-11

The wicked must be punished Ro 6:23 *See also* Ge 6:5-7; Jn 5:14; 2Th 1:8; Rev 9:4; 20:15

Suffering accepted voluntarily

By Jesus Christ 1Pe 2:21 *See also* Isa 53:3-5,10; Lk 9:22

By his people 2Co 12:15 *See also* 2Co 4:10-12; Php 3:10; Heb 11:35

For the good of others Jn 15:13 *See also* Ro 5:7; Phm 18

See also

1045 God, glory of	5297 disease
1130 God, sovereignty	5346 injury
4120 Satan	8230 discipline
4822 famine	8755 folly
	8790 oppression

5569
suffering, hardship

Scripture provides examples of types of hardship which people may expect to encounter.

Different kinds of hardship

Poverty Pr 10:15 *See also* Dt 15:11; Job 24:5-11; Mt 26:11 pp Mk 14:7; Jn 12:8

Hunger and thirst Ps 107:4-5 *See also* Ge 41:53-57; Ex 15:22-24; 16:2-3; 17:1-3; Nu 11:4-6; 1Ki 17:7-12; Ne 5:1-5; Mt 4:2 pp Lk 4:2

Hard labour Ge 3:17-19 *See also* Ge 31:38-42; 2Ch 10:3-4; Ecc 2:21-22; 1Th 2:9

Oppression Job 35:9 *See also* Ex 1:11; 2:23; 5:8-9; 2Ki 4:1; Ps 12:5; 31:9-13; Ecc 4:1; Jer 6:6; Am 3:9; Jas 5:4

Danger Ne 4:21-23 *See also* Ex 18:8; 1Ki 1:26; 1Ch 11:15-19; Ac 27:27-44

Examples of those who suffered hardship

Israel Dt 28:47-48 *God's people suffered under his chastisement. See also* Dt 8:15 *their suffering in the wilderness;* Dt 26:6-7 *their suffering in Egypt*

David was oppressed by his enemies Ps 132:1

Paul suffered in serving the Lord 2Co 6:4-5

God's people must endure hardship

The example of Jesus Christ 2Co 8:9

The suffering of believers Ac 14:21-22 *See also* 1Co 4:11-13; 2Co 1:8-9;

11:23–29; Php 4:11–14; 2Ti 2:3;
Heb 10:34; 11:37–38; 12:7; Rev 2:3

The need for faith, courage and endurance 2Co 1:9; Heb 3:6; 10:36;
Jas 1:12; Rev 1:9; 14:12

God helps his people through hardship
He provides for them Dt 8:16;
1Ki 17:2–9; 2Co 1:10; Php 1:19; 4:19

He comforts them with his love
Ro 8:35–39; 2Co 1:3–4; Heb 13:5

He sets heaven before them
Rev 7:16–17

See also

1085 God, love of	5580 thirst
1330 God, the	5628 work
provider	5828 danger
5341 hunger	8219 courage
5446 poverty	8418 endurance

5571

surgery

The physical removal of part of the human body, either in response to severe illness or as a form of punishment.

Medical surgery
Eze 30:21

Punitive surgery
Dt 25:12; Jdg 1:6–7; 1Sa 17:51; 31:9;
2Sa 4:7,12; 2Ki 25:7

Ritual or cultural surgery
Castration
The primary meaning of "eunuch" in the OT is "court officer" and need not always imply castration; similarly with the NT counterpart: 2Ki 20:18; Est 2:3; Isa 56:3;
Mt 19:12; Ac 8:27

Circumcision Ge 17:10–14; Ex 4:25;
Lev 12:3; Jos 5:8; Lk 2:21

Dismemberment
A solemn call to the nation to act:
Jdg 19:29; 1Sa 11:7

Ear piercing Ex 21:5–6 *There may be a reference to this in Ps 40:6.*

Pagan mutilation Lev 19:28; Dt 14:1;
1Ki 18:28

Animal sacrifices Ge 15:10; Ex 29:17;
Lev 1:6,12; 3:9

Miraculous surgery
Ge 2:21–22; Lk 22:50–51

Spiritual surgery
Heart transplant Eze 36:26

Amputation Mt 5:29–30 *Jesus Christ is using hyperbole (deliberate exaggeration) to stress the need at times for radical action.*
See also Mt 18:8–9; Mk 9:43–47

Grafting Ro 11:17–24

Pruning Isa 18:5; Jn 15:1–2

Felling Isa 10:33–34; Lk 3:9

See also

5012 heart	6728 regeneration
5285 cures	7332 child sacrifice
5309 eunuchs	7334 circumcision
5372 knife	7346 death penalty
5405 medicine	7422 ritual
5482 punishment	7435 sacrifice, in OT

5572

sword

A hand-wielded blade in common use throughout biblical times as a weapon of war and in OT times as an instrument of execution. The sword is also a symbol of aggression, authority and power.

The sword as the principal weapon of war
It was in common use Ex 17:13 *See also*
Nu 21:24–35; Jos 11:10–12; 19:47

Swordsmen fought and fell in great numbers Jdg 3:28–30 *See also*
Jdg 20:17; 2Sa 24:9

Some swordsmen showed great strength and ability 2Sa 23:10 *See also*
1Sa 21:8–9; 2Sa 23:12

The sword used for other purposes
As an instrument of execution and decapitation 2Sa 1:14–16 *See also*
1Sa 15:33; 17:51; 22:18–19; 1Ki 19:1;
Ac 12:2; Ro 8:35

For murder 2Ki 19:37 *See also* Jos 6:21;
1Ki 2:34; Ac 12:2

For committing suicide 1Sa 31:4–6
pp 1Ch 10:4 *See also* Ac 16:27

Metaphorical use of the sword
To symbolise God's opposition to the sinful Ge 3:24 *See also* Nu 22:21–23,31;
Dt 33:29

To symbolise warfare Lev 26:6–8

To symbolise temporal power
Eze 32:11–12 *See also* Ps 45:3; Mic 5:6

To symbolise suffering Lk 2:34–35

To symbolise judgment Ex 5:3;
Mt 10:34 *See also* Jdg 7:20–22;
2Ch 20:9; Ps 7:12; Isa 31:8;
Jer 50:35–37; Eze 11:8–10; 21:3; 33:2

To symbolise the word of God
Eph 6:17 *See also* Heb 4:12; Rev 1:16;
2:12

See also

1690 word of God	5605 warfare
5025 killing	5612 weapons
5040 murder	7346 death penalty
5067 suicide	8482 spiritual
5131 belt	warfare
5214 attack	9210 judgment,
5360 justice, God	God's

5573

table

An item of furniture used principally for putting food on. Sharing at the same table was a mark of fellowship and to eat at the table of rulers was deemed a great privilege. In the tabernacle and temple a special table held the bread of the Presence. Tables were also used for business transactions.

Tables used for eating
A table as household furniture 2Ki 4:10

Reclining at table Lk 7:36 *See also*
Mt 26:7 pp Mk 14:3; Lk 11:37; Jn 12:2

Tables set for meals Ps 23:5; Isa 21:5
See also Job 36:16; Ps 69:22; 78:19 *The people of Israel doubted God's ability to provide;* Pr 9:2; Eze 23:41

Giving thanks for food at the table
Lk 24:30 *See also* Mt 26:26–27
pp Mk 14:22–23 pp Lk 22:17–19;
1Co 11:23–24

Dogs eat scraps from the table
Mt 15:27 pp Mk 7:28 *See also* Jdg 1:7;
Lk 16:21

Eating at the table of rulers
Rulers were required to entertain
Ne 5:17–18 *See also* 1Ki 4:27; 10:4–5
pp 2Ch 9:3–4

A bestowal of authority Lk 22:29–30
See also Mt 22:2–3; Lk 14:15

A mark of honour and favour Ge 43:34;
2Sa 9:11; 1Ki 2:7; 18:19; 2Ki 25:28–29
pp Jer 52:32–33; Lk 14:7 *Jesus Christ criticises those who seek the most prestigious places at the table.*

Sharing at the same table was a mark of fellowship
A sign of participation 1Co 10:16–20

Unacceptable table fellowship
Da 1:5–8; 1Co 10:21 *See also* 1Sa 20:34
Jonathan refuses to eat with Saul;
1Ki 18:19; Isa 65:11; Jer 7:18

Betrayal of table fellowship Ps 41:9 *See also* 1Sa 20:29–31 *Saul wishes to kill David while inviting him to share his table;* Da 11:27; Mt 26:20–21
pp Mk 14:18 pp Lk 22:21

Serving at table
Lk 22:27 *See also* Lk 12:37; Ac 6:2 *The first Christians recognised the importance of practical service by appointing deacons to "wait on tables".*

Tables used in business
Jn 2:14–15 *See also* Mt 21:12
pp Mk 11:15

Tables used in worship
The table in the tabernacle
Ex 25:23–30 *The table was for the bread of the Presence: an offering of twelve loaves, one from each of the twelve tribes.*
See also Ex 37:10–16; 26:35; 30:27 *The table was anointed for use;* Ex 35:13
pp Ex 39:36; Ex 40:4
The Kohathites were responsible for the table: Nu 3:31; 4:7
Heb 9:2

The tables in Solomon's temple
2Ch 4:8 *See also* 1Ki 7:48 pp 2Ch 4:19;
1Ch 28:16; 2Ch 13:11; 29:18

The tables in Ezekiel's temple
Eze 40:39–43; 41:22; 44:16

Tables in worship after the exile
1Ch 9:31–32; Ne 10:33
Probably references to the altar, defiled by the people's substandard offerings:
Mal 1:7,12

See also

4410 banquets	7467 temple,
4418 bread	Solomon's
4476 meals	7921 fellowship
6212 participation	7933 Lord's Supper
7302 altar	8342 servanthood
7459 tabernacle, in	8445 hospitality
OT	

5574

tablet

A flat, usually rectangular, surface used for writing. Stone tablets, symbolising permanence, were usually engraved with an iron tool. Tablets of moist clay and writing boards of wood or ivory containing a layer of wax were inscribed with a stylus. The term is also used figuratively to refer to the human heart.

Tablets engraved with an iron tool
Job 19:23–24 *See also* Jer 17:1

The Ten Commandments were inscribed on stone tablets
The tablets were inscribed by God
Dt 9:9–11 *In keeping with ancient Near Eastern practice, the two tablets may have been duplicates of a single covenant document. See also* Ex 24:12; 31:18; Dt 4:13; 5:22

The tablets were broken Ex 32:15–19 *See also* Dt 9:15–17

New tablets were inscribed by God Dt 10:1–4 *See also* Ex 34:4,28–29

The new tablets were put into the ark Dt 10:5 *See also* 1Ki 8:9 pp 2Ch 5:10; Heb 9:4

God's commands were copied onto altar stones Dt 27:2–8 *See also* Jos 8:30–32

Writing tablets
Tablets of unspecified material Hab 2:2 *See also* Isa 30:8; Lk 1:63

Other surfaces used for writing
1Ki 7:36 *The bases of the bronze lavers in Solomon's temple were engraved;* Isa 8:1 *Isaiah's inscription is with a pen on a scroll;* Eze 4:1 *Ezekiel draws a plan of Jerusalem on a clay tablet. This was a common medium for plans in Babylon.*

Tablets of the heart
The commands and teachings of Proverbs Pr 3:3 *See also* Pr 6:21; 7:3

The new covenant Jer 31:33 *Under the new covenant God's law will be inward, written on human hearts rather than on tablets of stone. See also* Eze 36:26–27; 2Co 3:3; Heb 8:10; 10:16

See also

1260 finger of God	5377 law, Ten
1349 covenant at	Command-
Sinai	ments
1352 covenant, the	5439 pen
new	5638 writing
4366 stones	7306 ark of the
5012 heart	covenant
5306 engraving	7410 phylactery
5352 inscriptions	

5575

talk, idle

Loose or careless speech, often motivated by curiosity, which can lead to unacceptable consequences. Scripture emphasises the importance of avoiding careless talk, and considering one's words with care.

Unfounded boasting is idle talk
2Pe 2:17–19 *See also* Ps 10:3; 49:6; 52:1; Pr 25:14; 27:1; Ac 8:9–10; Jas 4:16

Human questioning of God is idle talk
Ro 9:20–21 *See also* Isa 29:16; 45:9

Flattery is idle talk
Ro 16:18 *See also* Pr 7:21

Meaningless conversation is idle talk
Job 27:11–12 *Job referring to the words of his comforters.*
These criticisms of Job by his companions are unjustified: Job 8:2; 11:2; 35:16
Pr 20:14

Examples of idle talk
1Ki 20:10–11 *See also* Nu 12:1–2; Jdg 9:26–41; 1Sa 17:41–44

Idle talk is folly
A mark of the fool Job 15:2–3 *See also* Pr 14:3,23; Ecc 10:12–14; 1Ti 1:6–7

Talking too much Ecc 5:7 *See also* Pr 10:19; 17:28; 21:23; Ecc 5:3

Speaking rashly Pr 20:25 *See also* Ecc 5:6; Jas 1:19

Idle talk is combated by upright living
1Pe 2:15

Idle talk has no place in the church
1Co 4:20 *See also* Eph 4:29; 5:4; Tit 1:10–11

All idle talk will be judged
Mt 12:36–37

See also

5193 tongue	5868 gossip
5510 rumours	5951 slander
5546 speech	6121 boasting
5803 carelessness	8755 folly
5838 disrespect	8830 suspicion
5863 flattery	8847 vulgarity

5576

tax collectors

Governments have a right to collect taxes, but those who collect them have often been unpopular, not least because they seem to have demanded more than they were entitled to. Jesus Christ welcomed such people, as he did other sinners, and many repented as a result of his affirming attitude.

Honest tax collectors deserve respect
Ro 13:6–7

Temple taxes collected by Levites 2Ch 24:6,9

Temple tax paid by Jesus Christ Mt 17:24–26

Tax collectors often unpopular
In NT times Lk 18:11 *Tax collectors were widely suspected of corruption.*

Tax collectors despised as collaborators with Rome
Jesus Christ recognises this popular contempt Mt 5:46; 18:17; Lk 18:11

Many tax collectors come to John
Lk 3:12–13 *See also* Mt 21:31–32; Lk 7:29

Many tax collectors flock around Jesus Christ
Lk 15:1 *See also* Mt 9:10 pp Mk 2:15 pp Lk 5:29

Jesus Christ criticised for eating with tax collectors Lk 15:2 *See also* Mt 9:11 pp Mk 2:16 pp Lk 5:30; Mt 11:19 pp Lk 7:34; Lk 19:1–7

Jesus Christ defends his concern Mt 9:12–14 pp Mk 2:17 pp Lk 5:31 *See also* Lk 15:3–4 *The parables in Luke chapter 15 are in part a defence of Jesus Christ's concern for tax collectors and sinners.*

Tax collectors converted
In the parable Lk 18:13–14

Matthew Levi Mt 9:9 pp Mk 2:13–14 pp Lk 5:27–28

Zacchaeus Lk 19:1–9

See also

2048 Christ, love of	5691 friends, good
2545 Christ,	6040 sinners
opposition to	6130 corruption
4263 Rome	6626 conversion
5098 John the	7903 baptism
Baptist	7912 collections
5577 taxation	

5577

taxation

Any form of payment levied on people by a supervising authority.

Taxation exacted from subject nations
Tribute to Moab Jdg 3:15,17–18

Tribute to David 2Sa 8:2 pp 1Ch 18:2; 2Sa 8:6 pp 1Ch 18:6

Tribute to Solomon 1Ki 4:21

Tribute to Assyria 2Ki 17:3; Hos 10:6

Tribute to Egypt 2Ki 23:33 pp 2Ch 36:3

Tribute to Judah 2Ch 17:11; 26:8; Isa 16:1

Tribute to Persia Est 10:1

Universal tribute Ps 72:10 *Universal tribute means universal reign. This psalm is widely regarded as Messianic.*

Refusal to pay tribute was a sign of rebellion 2Ki 17:4; Ezr 4:13

Taxation for the support of the state
Land tax 2Ki 23:35 *See also* Ge 41:34; Ne 5:4

Census tax
Ex 30:11–16; Lk 2:1

Trade tax 1Ki 10:14–15 pp 2Ch 9:13–14

Such levies may be unjustly burdensome 1Sa 8:10–18 *See also* Da 11:20

Covenantal taxation: the tithe
Tithing prescribed Lev 27:30–33 *As part of their covenantal obligations the Israelites were commanded to offer a tenth of their income to the LORD. See also* Ge 14:20

The tithe supported the priests and the poor Nu 18:21 *See also* Dt 14:28–29

The tithe often seems to have been neglected Mal 3:8–10 *See also* 2Ch 31:4

Taxation for the support of the temple
Mt 17:24–26 *See also* 2Ch 24:4–12 pp 2Ki 12:4–5

Jesus Christ and taxation
Jesus Christ was falsely accused of opposing taxation Lk 23:1–2

He himself paid tax Mt 17:24–27

He commanded others to pay taxes Mt 22:15–22 pp Mk 12:13–17 pp Lk 20:20–26

Believers and taxation
Paying taxes demonstrates submission to God Ro 13:1,5–6; 1Pe 2:13

Paying taxes should silence unjust criticism Ro 13:3; 1Pe 2:15

Paying taxes is reimbursement for services rendered Mt 22:15–22 *"Give" in verse 21 means "give back as in settlement of a debt"; Ro 13:7*

See also
4206 land	5576 tax collectors
5215 authority	5594 tribute
5249 census	7766 priests
5289 debt	8453 obedience
5347 injustice	8488 tithing
5446 poverty	8790 oppression

5578

tents

A portable structure made of cloth or skins used mainly by nomads or semi-nomads. God's tent or tabernacle is a meeting-place with him.

Tents as portable dwellings used especially by semi-nomadic peoples
They were living quarters for God's people Ge 4:20 *See also* Ge 12:8; 13:12; 18:1; 25:27; Nu 11:10; 1Sa 4:10; 2Sa 20:1; 1Ki 12:16

Sometimes women of distinction had their own tents Ge 24:67 *See also* Ge 31:33; Jdg 4:17–18

A tent housed the ark of God 2Sa 6:17 pp 1Ch 16:1 *See also* 2Sa 7:2; 1Ch 15:1; 2Ch 1:4

Tents associated with other peoples Jdg 6:5 *See also* Ge 9:27; Jdg 7:13; Hab 3:7

Kings and armies camped in tents Jdg 7:13 *See also* Nu 31:10; 2Ki 7:7–8

Tents for storage
1Sa 17:54 *See also* Jos 7:21–23

Tents were illustrative of a nomadic life
Jer 35:7; Heb 11:9–10 *See also* Ge 12:8; 13:5,18; 18:1–6; 20:13; Ex 16:16; 33:8,10; Nu 1:50

Tents sometimes associated with sin
Job 8:22 *See also* Ge 9:21 *Noah's drunkenness;* Nu 16:26 *the rebellion of Korah, Dathan and Abiram;* Jos 7:21–23 *Achan's sin;* 1Ki 20:16; Job 4:21; 11:14; 12:6; 15:34; 18:6; 21:28; 22:23; Ps 84:10

The construction of tents
Tentmakers Ac 18:3

The materials used Ex 26:7 pp Ex 36:14 *See also* Ex 26:14–29 pp Ex 36:19–34

Tent pegs and ropes Ex 27:19 *See also* Ex 35:18; 38:20,31; 39:40; Nu 3:26,37; 4:32; Jdg 4:21; Isa 22:25; Zec 10:4

Colours of tents SS 1:5 *See also* Ex 26:14

Pitching tents Jer 10:20 *See also* Ge 26:25; 33:19; Jdg 4:11; 2Sa 16:22

The metaphorical use of tents
As an image of creation Ps 104:2 *See also* Ps 19:4

As a metaphor for death 2Co 5:1; 2Pe 1:13–14

God's tent is a meeting-place with him
The tabernacle Ex 25:8–9 *See also* Ex 26:1–37; 39:32

The Tent of Meeting Ex 27:21; 33:7 *See also* Ex 28:43; 29:10–11,30,44; 33:11; Lev 1:1; Nu 1:1; Dt 31:14–15

God "tenting" with his people
Jn 1:14 *See also* Ex 25:8; 29:45–46; 40:34–38; Lev 26:11–12; Nu 5:3; Dt 12:11; Eze 37:27; 2Co 6:16; Rev 21:3

See also
5340 house	7344 curtain
5427 nomads	7459 tabernacle, in
6606 access to God	OT
7306 ark of the	7474 Tent of
covenant	Meeting

5579

tetrarch

A ruler over one quarter of a region; a son of Herod the Great who ruled one quarter of the area originally ruled by his father.

Herod Archelaus, governor of Judea, Idumea and Samaria
Mt 2:22 *The tetrarchy system had been started by Philip of Macedon and adopted by the Romans.*

Herod Antipas, tetrarch of Galilee and Perea
Mt 14:1,9 *Sometimes a tetrarch would be given the courtesy title of king;* Mk 6:14 pp Lk 9:7; Lk 3:1,19; 23:7; Ac 13:1

Herod Philip, tetrarch of Iturea and Traconitis
Lk 3:1

Lysanias, tetrarch of Abilene
Lk 3:1

See also
5219 authority,	5509 rulers
human	7735 leaders,
institutions	political
5327 governors	8456 obedience to
5361 justice, human	authorities
5366 king	

5580

thirst

Water is basic to human life. In Scripture the physical need to drink is often used as a picture of human spiritual need that only God can satisfy.

Physical thirst quenched
Ex 17:1–6 *See also* Nu 20:2–11; Dt 8:15; Jdg 15:18–19; Ne 9:15,20; Ps 78:15–16; 105:41; 107:4–9,33,35; 114:8; Isa 48:21

The satisfaction of spiritual thirst
It is to be found in God Isa 41:17–18 *See also* Ps 23:1–2; Isa 12:2–3; 35:6–7; 58:11

It is experienced through Jesus Christ 1Co 10:3–4 *See also* Jn 4:7–14; 6:35

It is known by the indwelling of the Holy Spirit Jn 7:38–39

The blessing is mediated through believers to others Isa 32:2; Jn 7:38

There is no satisfaction of spiritual thirst apart from God
Jer 2:13 *See also* Isa 65:13; Jer 2:17–18; 2Pe 2:17 *False teachers promise blessing and refreshment to others, but prove to be empty and worthless.*

Invitations to seek satisfaction for spiritual thirst in God
Isa 55:1 *See also* Jn 7:37; Rev 22:17

Those seeking satisfaction for spiritual thirst in God
Examples of seekers Ps 42:1–2 *See also* Ps 38:9; 63:1; 143:6; Isa 26:9

They will be rewarded Mt 5:6

Heaven is their final reward Rev 7:16–17 *See also* Eze 47:1–12; Zec 14:8–9; 2Co 5:2; 2Ti 4:8; Heb 11:16; Rev 21:6–7; 22:1–3

See also
3290 Holy Spirit,	5839 dissatisfaction
life-giver	5939 satisfaction
4293 water	8160 seeking God
4434 drinking	8429 fasting
4815 drought	8656 longing for
5341 hunger	God
5832 desire	9410 heaven

5581

throne

An elevated seat occupied by a person with authority (e.g., a king). It symbolises the dignity, honour, sovereignty and the kingdom of the king whose seat it is. Supremely, these things belong to God himself.

A throne as an elevated seat
1Ki 10:18–19 pp 2Ch 9:17–18

A throne is occupied by a person with authority (usually a king)
Pr 20:8; Isa 14:9; Lk 1:52

Thrones of the kings of Israel 1Ki 1:46
See also 1Ki 2:19; 7:7; 22:10
pp 2Ch 18:9; 2Ki 11:19 pp 2Ch 23:20;
Jer 13:18; Ac 12:21

Thrones of the kings of the nations
Ex 11:5; 12:29; Est 1:2; 5:1; Jer 1:15;
Eze 26:16; Jnh 3:6

A throne symbolises dignity and honour
Ge 41:40 *See also* 1Sa 2:8; 2Ki 25:28
pp Jer 52:32; Isa 22:23

A throne also symbolises sovereignty
The royal power of earthly kings
1Ki 1:13 *"Sit upon a throne" means "to exercise royal power". See also* Dt 17:18
King Solomon established on his father's throne: 1Ki 1:17–35; 2:4,12,24; 3:6; 5:5;
8:20 pp 2Ch 6:10; 1Ki 8:25 pp 2Ch 6:16;
1Ki 9:5; 10:9 pp 2Ch 9:8; 1Ch 28:5;
29:23
1Ki 16:11; 2Ki 10:3
King Jehu established on the throne of Israel: 2Ki 10:30; 15:12
Ps 122:5; 132:11–12; Jer 22:2,30; 29:16;
33:17 *This verse is fulfilled ultimately in Jesus Christ (Lk 1:32);* Jer 43:10

Satan's throne on earth Rev 2:13 *Satan is seen as "ruling" from Pergamum, the official centre of emperor worship in the province of Asia.*

The beast's throne Rev 13:2 *See also* Rev 16:10

The twenty-four elders are enthroned
Rev 4:4 *The elders are thought to be representative of either the whole company of believers in heaven or an exalted angelic order. See also* Rev 11:16

Jesus Christ reigns from his eternal throne Isa 9:7 *See also* Zec 6:13;
Mt 25:31; Lk 1:32–33

Almighty God is seated in majesty on his holy throne Ex 17:16 *See also*
Ps 47:8; Heb 8:1; 12:2
Visions of God enthroned in heaven:
1Ki 22:19 pp 2Ch 18:18; Eze 1:26; 10:1;
Da 7:9; Rev 4:2–10; 5:1,7,13; 7:10,15;
19:4; 21:5
God's throne as the judgment seat:
Ps 9:4–10; 11:4; Jer 49:38; Rev 6:16;
20:11–12
God's throne as the focus of worship:
Rev 7:11; 8:3; 14:3
God's throne as a metaphor for God's presence: Rev 1:4; 4:5; 7:9; 12:5; 16:17;
21:3; 22:1,3

A throne symbolises a kingdom
The kingdoms of earthly kings 2Sa 3:10
See also 1Ki 1:37,47; Pr 20:28; 25:5;
29:14; Da 4:36; 5:20; Hag 2:22
God's covenant with David that his throne would be established for ever: 2Sa 7:13–16
pp 1Ch 17:12–14; 1Ki 2:33,45; 9:5
pp 2Ch 7:18; 1Ch 22:10; Ps 89:4,29,36

The unseen kingdom of God's righteous rule Ps 89:14 *See also* Ps 93:2;
97:2; 103:19; La 5:19

The ark of the covenant seen as God's throne
1Sa 4:4 *God was understood to be enthroned between the cherubim (i.e., upon the lid, or "mercy seat") of the ark of the covenant. See also* 2Sa 6:2; 2Ki 19:15
pp Isa 37:16; Ps 80:1; 99:1; Jer 17:12

Jerusalem is also called God's throne
Jer 3:17

Heaven described as God's throne
Ps 2:4 *See also* Ps 123:1; Isa 40:22;
Mt 5:34; 23:22; Ac 7:49; Isa 66:1

God's throne is a throne of grace
Heb 4:16

Believers share in the heavenly reign of Jesus Christ
Mt 19:28 *See also* Lk 22:30; 2Ti 2:12;
Rev 3:21; 20:4,6

See also
1090	God, majesty of
1130	God, sovereignty
2312	Christ as king
2375	kingdom of God
2565	Christ, second coming
5181	sitting
5216	authority
5366	king
5368	kingship
9125	footstool
9230	judgment seat
9411	heaven

5582

tiredness

A natural outcome of work and stress for which God has provided relief, rest and renewal. Scripture recognises that tiredness may have spiritual, as well as physical, causes.

Causes of tiredness
Work Mt 8:24 pp Mk 4:38 pp Lk 8:23
See also Ecc 10:15; 12:12

Afflictions and stress Job 16:7 *See also*
2Sa 17:29; 1Ki 19:3–5; Ps 69:3;
2Co 12:15

Concern and anxiety Ps 31:9–10 *See also* Ps 6:6; 32:3–4; 119:28; Jer 45:3;
Lk 22:45

Desire for money and possessions
Pr 23:4

Travelling Dt 25:18; Jdg 8:4; 2Sa 16:14;
Jn 4:6

Old age Ecc 12:3

Zeal for the Lord's work Ps 119:139

Battles Jdg 4:21; 1Sa 14:31; 2Sa 21:15;
23:10; Jer 51:30

Sin and rebellion Isa 57:10; Jer 9:5;
Eze 23:43

Foolishness Ecc 1:8; Isa 46:1; 47:13;
Jer 12:13

Help from God to deal with tiredness
God's promises of help and rest
Isa 40:28–31 *See also* Isa 46:4; 2Co 9:8

Jesus Christ offers rest and encouragement Mt 11:28–30;
Rev 2:2–3 *See also* Mk 6:31

Trusting God as the antidote to anxiety and sorrow Mt 6:25–27
pp Lk 12:25–27 *See also* Ps 119:28

God's provision of times for rest
Ge 1:5; 2:2 pp Ex 20:8–11
pp Dt 5:12–15; Ps 127:2; Jer 31:25

Help from others to deal with tiredness
Encouragements to be strong in the Lord and to persevere Ps 27:14;
1Co 15:58 *See also* Gal 6:9; 2Th 3:13;
Heb 12:1–3

God's help channelled through others
Isa 50:4 *See also* 2Co 1:3–4

Physical help from others 2Sa 16:2 *See also* Ex 17:12; Jdg 8:15; 2Sa 17:28–29;
1Ki 19:5–6

Advice about lifestyle Ex 18:17–23

See also
5056 rest	7428 Sabbath
5532 sleep	8020 faith
5628 work	8102 abiding in
5922 prudence	Christ
5954 strength	8357 weakness
6666 grace	8602 prayer

5583

tools

Implements used for agricultural or mechanical purposes. Early tools were of wood, flint or stone. The development of ironworking brought iron-bladed tools and farm implements into common use. Axes were used to fell trees; hammers, chisels and saws were used by both carpenters and masons. Assyria and Babylon are depicted as tools in God's hand.

Tools made from iron and bronze
General references Ge 4:22 *See also*
2Sa 12:31 pp 1Ch 20:3 *saws, iron picks and axes*; 2Sa 23:7 *iron tools*

Iron axe-heads 2Ki 6:4–5 *Axes comprised an iron head fitted to a wooden shaft. See also* Dt 19:5

Sharpening iron tools 1Sa 13:19–21 *A ploughshare is the cutting blade of a plough. A mattock is a large pick with a flat edge used for loosening soil and cutting. See also* Ecc 10:10

Tools used in specific tasks
Axes used for felling trees Jdg 9:48 *See also* Dt 20:19–20; Ps 74:5–6
Mt 3:10 pp Lk 3:9 *Felling trees with an axe as a symbol of judgment. See also*
Jer 46:22–23

Woodworking tools Isa 44:13 *See also*
Ex 21:6 pp Dt 15:17 *awl;* Jer 10:3–4
chisel, hammer and nails

Metalworking tools Job 19:24 *See also*
Ex 28:36 pp Ex 39:30; Jer 17:1
Isa 41:7 *See also* Ex 32:4; Isa 44:12;
Jer 10:9

Stoneworking tools 1Ki 6:7; 7:9 *Saws were used in both carpentry and stonemasonry. See also* Ex 34:1; Dt 10:3;
Isa 22:16; Jer 23:29
No tools were to be used on stones for an altar: Ex 20:25; Dt 27:5; Jos 8:31

Agricultural tools Isa 2:4 pp Mic 4:3 *A pruning hook is a curved blade used in*

pruning. See also Joel 3:10; Isa 18:5
pruning knives; Isa 30:24 *fork and shovel
A winnowing fork is a wooden pitchfork
used to toss grain into the wind:* Jer 15:7;
Mt 3:12 pp Lk 3:17

The nations as tools in God's hand

Isa 10:15 *Assyria is used by God to punish
his people. See also* Isa 10:5; Jer 50:23
Babylon is a hammer in God's hand.

See also

4327 flint	5247 carpenters
4336 iron	5306 engraving
4406 agriculture	5364 key
4508 sickle	5372 knife
4648 goad	5403 masons
5212 arts and crafts	7254 plumb-line

5584

torture

The torture of people

Jer 52:10–11 *See also* Dt 28:29–35;
Jdg 8:16; 16:21; Job 19:2; Ps 137:3;
Isa 13:15–18; 51:23; La 5:11–13;
Eze 23:10; Mt 18:34; Ac 16:22–24;
Heb 11:35–38; Rev 9:5,10

The torture of Jesus Christ

Lk 22:63 *See also* Mt 27:27–31
pp Mk 15:16–20; Jn 19:2–3
Jn 19:18 pp Mt 27:35 pp Mk 15:24
pp Lk 23:33 *Crucifixion was essentially
death by torture.*

Torture in the setting of judgment

Mt 8:29 pp Mk 5:7 pp Lk 8:28;
Rev 20:10 *See also* Mt 25:46; Lk 16:23;
Rev 14:11; 18:7

See also

2570 Christ,	5782 agony
suffering	5823 cruelty
5281 crucifixion	8450 martyrdom
5313 flogging	8796 persecution,
5436 pain	forms of
5482 punishment	9210 judgment,
5557 stoning	God's
5560 suffering	

5585

towers

Tall structures, normally constructed
of brick or stone. They were chiefly
used for observation of the
surrounding countryside in order to
warn of the approach of enemies or
robbers.

Examples of watchtowers

Isa 32:14 *See also* Jdg 8:17; 9:51–52;
1Ch 27:25; 2Ch 14:7; 26:9–10,15; 32:5;
Ne 3:25–27

Destruction of towers synonymous with defeat

Eze 26:4 *See also* Isa 30:25;
32:14; Jer 50:15; Eze 26:9

Watchmen stationed in towers

2Ki 9:17–20 *See also* Isa 21:6–9; La 4:17

Towers built as protection against thieves

Mt 21:33 pp Mk 12:1 *See also*
Isa 5:1–2

Towers of Jerusalem

2Ch 26:9; 32:5; Ne 3:1,11,25–26;
12:38–39; Jer 31:38; Zec 14:10; Lk 13:4

Towers as place-names and landmarks

Ge 11:4–5 *See also* Ge 35:21 *"Migdal
Eder" means "tower of the flock"*;
Jdg 8:17; 9:46,51

Parable of building a tower

Lk 18:28–29

Figurative use of towers

Symbolic of the security found in God
alone Pr 18:10 *See also* Ps 48:3; 61:3

Symbolic of God's judgment Eze 26:4
See also Jer 50:15; Zep 1:15–16

Associated with human beauty SS 4:4
See also SS 7:4; 8:9–10

The tower of Babel

The building of the tower of Babel
Ge 11:1–4 *The attempt to build the city
and the tower is the result of human pride.
God responds by confusing people's
language and by scattering them:*
Ge 11:5–9; Ps 55:9

**The confusion of Babel reversed at
Pentecost** Ac 2:5–11

See also

4538 vineyard	5435 ovens
5240 building	5558 storing
5254 citadel	5604 walls
5315 fortifications	5611 watchman
5316 fortress	

5586

town

A large concentration of dwellings,
often walled, to be distinguished
from the larger cities.

A town was a large concentration of dwellings

1Sa 23:7 *See also* Jos 19:50; Mk 6:10;
Ac 16:4

Town officials

Dt 16:18; Jdg 8:14–16 *See also* Dt 19:12;
21:3,19; 22:15; 25:7; Ru 4:2; 1Sa 16:4;
Ezr 10:14; Lk 18:2–3

Town records

Ru 4:10 *See also* Lk 2:3–4

Laws concerning towns

Lev 25:33; Nu 35:4–5

Town celebrations and worship

Dt 16:5 *See also* 1Sa 9:10–14; 20:29;
2Ch 28:25

The town was a close-knit community

Ru 1:19 *See also* 1Sa 4:13

Towns associated with Jesus Christ

Mt 13:54 *Nazareth, his home town*;
Lk 4:31 *Capernaum in Galilee*; Lk 8:1,4;
Jn 4:5 *Sychar in Samaria*

Wickedness in towns

Dt 13:13 *See also* Jdg 6:30; 2Ki 2:23;
2Ch 30:10; Mt 23:34

Judgment on towns

Dt 13:15; Isa 25:2 *See also* 2Ki 3:19;
Mt 10:11

See also

2363 Christ,	5315 fortifications
preaching &	5505 roads
teaching	5601 village
5256 city	7206 community

5587

trade

Fair business transactions are
essential to distribute the benefits of
God's goodness between individuals
and nations. Scripture insists on
honesty in trade and warns against
abuses.

Trade in ancient Israel

Lev 25:14 *Land transactions required the
approval of the ruler of the state*; 2Ki 4:7;
7:1; Ne 3:31–32
The good wife's trade: Pr 31:13–18,24
Zep 1:11; Mt 21:12 pp Mk 11:15–16
pp Lk 19:45 pp Jn 2:14–16 *trade in
Jerusalem in Jesus Christ's day*

International trade

Under Solomon 1Ki 9:26–28
pp 2Ch 8:17–18 *See also* 1Ki 10:14–15
pp 2Ch 9:13–14 *Transit taxes were
imposed on inter-state trade. Also some
taxes were owed to the state by merchants
for some kinds of trade*; 1Ki 10:28–29
pp 2Ch 1:16–17; 2Ch 9:21; SS 3:6–7

Under Jehoshaphat 1Ki 22:48
pp 2Ch 20:35–37 *Soon afterwards the
port of Ezion Geber passed back into the
hands of Edom (see 2Ki 8:20).*

In the Psalms Ps 107:23

Trade among the nations

Hittites Ge 23:16

Shechemites Ge 34:10,21

Ishmaelites Ge 37:25

Midianites Ge 37:28

Egypt Ge 42:34; Isa 45:14

Sheba Job 6:19; Jer 6:20

Damascus 1Ki 20:34

Tyre and the surrounding nations
Isa 23:8 *See also* Eze 27:1–36

Tarshish Eze 38:13; Jnh 1:3–5

Nineveh Na 3:16

Ancient Babylon Eze 16:29; 17:4

Babylon the Great Rev 18:9–24 *See also*
Rev 18:2–3

Honesty is essential in trade

Lev 19:35–36 *See also* Dt 25:13–16;
Pr 11:1; 16:11; 20:10,23

Warnings against abuses in trade

Dishonesty Am 8:4–5 *See also*
Eze 28:18; Hos 12:7; Mic 6:10–11

Oppression Job 20:18–19; Eze 28:16

Overconfidence Jas 4:13–16

Pride Eze 28:5 *See also* Isa 2:12,16;
23:17–18

Sabbath trading Ne 10:31; 13:15–22

The slave trade Ge 37:26–28,36; 39:1;
Am 2:6; 8:6; 1Ti 1:10; Rev 18:13

Sacrilegious trade Jn 2:14–16

Immoral trade Joel 3:3

The imagery of trade applied to spiritual matters

Mt 13:45–46 *See also* Pr 23:23;
Mt 25:14–18; Lk 19:13; 1Co 6:20

See also

5242 buying & selling	5517 seafaring
5310 exploitation	5614 weights & measures,
5361 justice, human	laws
5402 market	7428 Sabbath
5407 merchants	8275 honesty
5433 occupations	8714 dishonesty
5512 scales & balances	

5588

traditions

Beliefs or customs handed down
from previous generations. Believers
are to hold to the traditions of the
Christian faith. Human traditions
can be contrary to God's word and
thereby come into conflict with the
Christian faith.

Examples of human traditions

Ru 4:7; 2Ch 35:25; Eze 24:17,22;
Mk 7:3–4; Lk 2:42; Jn 19:40

Believers are to hold to and hand on the traditions of the Christian faith

1Co 11:2; 1Th 5:21; 2Ti 2:2 *See also*
Dt 4:9–10; 6:6–7; 11:19; 1Co 11:23;
Eph 2:20; 2Th 2:15; 3:6

Human traditions can be contrary to God's word

Mt 15:3–6 pp Mk 7:9–13; Col 2:8 *See
also* Mic 6:16; Col 2:20–22; Tit 1:13–14

The Christian faith is in conflict with traditions of purely human origins

Mk 2:18–22 pp Mt 9:14–17
pp Lk 5:33–39; 1Pe 1:18–19 *See also*
Mt 15:2 pp Mk 7:5; Gal 2:11–16; 4:9–11

See also

5286 custom	8142 religion
5376 law, purpose of	8429 fasting
5873 habits	8748 false religion
7328 ceremonies	8767 hypocrisy
7430 Sabbath, in NT	8774 legalism
7550 Pharisees	
7770 priests, NT tasks	

5589

trap

A device used as a snare in hunting
or warfare to capture animals or
people; a tactic, plot or scheme
designed to deceive someone into
trouble or sin.

Traps used in hunting and warfare

Job 40:24; Isa 42:22; Eze 19:4; Am 3:5

Kinds of traps

Words Jdg 12:5–6; Pr 6:2; 12:13;
Isa 29:21; Jer 9:8; Mk 12:13,15

Actions Ge 27:6–12; 37:23–24;
1Sa 28:9; 2Sa 21:5; 2Ki 21:24; La 1:19;
Hab 2:9–11; Lk 22:48

Temptation 1Ti 6:9 *See also* Ex 23:33;
34:12; Dt 7:16,25; Jos 23:12–13;
Jdg 2:3; 8:27; 16:15–16; Pr 11:6; 20:25;
22:24–25; Ecc 7:26; Eze 13:18; Hos 5:1

Evil times Ecc 9:12

Fear of other people Pr 29:25

Wisdom is alert to traps 1Ch 12:16–17;
Pr 13:14

Those who trap others have evil hearts

Isa 32:7 *See also* Ps 36:3–4; 64:6;
Pr 6:14; 12:20; 16:27–30

Traps prepared by sinners

Against innocent people Ps 38:12 *See
also* Ge 4:8; 2Ch 24:21; Ne 6:1–4;
Est 2:22; 9:25; Job 30:11–12; Ps 10:2;
31:13; 35:4; 119:110; 140:5; 142:3;
Jer 5:26; 9:8; 18:22; La 3:60–61; 4:20;
Da 6:4–7; Ac 23:19–21

Against God Ps 2:1–2 *See also* Ac 4:25;
Ps 21:11; 83:5; Hos 7:15; Na 1:11

Against Jesus Christ Mt 22:15 *See also*
Mt 22:18 pp Mk 12:15; Mt 26:21,25;
Mk 3:6; Lk 20:26; Jn 8:6; 18:3–4

Against the truth Hos 9:8 *See also*
Ac 14:5; 20:3; Eph 4:14

The wicked caught in their own traps
Pr 28:10 *See also* Est 7:10; Job 18:7–10;
Ps 9:16; Pr 1:18; 5:22; 12:13; 18:7; 29:6;
Jer 8:9; Da 6:24

The devil sets traps

1Ti 3:7 *See also* Ac 13:10; 2Co 2:11;
Eph 6:11; 2Ti 2:26

God sets traps for the wicked

Jer 50:24 *See also* Isa 8:14; 28:13; Jer 8:9;
48:43–44; Eze 12:13; 17:20; Ob 7;
Lk 21:34; Ro 11:9; Ps 69:22

God frees his people from traps

Ps 91:3 *See also* 2Sa 22:5–7; Ne 4:7–9;
Job 5:13; Ps 31:4; 124:6–8; 141:9;
Pr 3:26

God forbids the trapping of the innocent Zec 8:17

The gospel does not trap people by deception

1Th 2:3 *See also* 2Co 4:2; 2Pe 1:16

See also

2545 Christ, opposition to	5817 conspiracies
4257 pit	5969 treachery
5342 hunting	6145 deceit
5425 net	6248 temptation
5546 speech	8277 innocence
5798 betrayal	8754 fear

5590

travel

Whole communities travelled

The exodus Ex 17:1

The exile 2Ch 36:20

The return from exile Ezr 2:1–2

Nomadic travelling

Ge 12:6

Military forces travelled

Ex 14:4; 2Sa 10:16; 2Ki 25:1

Officials travelled

Ge 41:46 *See also* 2Ki 5:1–5 *Naaman*;
Ne 2:5 *Nehemiah*; Ac 8:27 *the Ethiopian
eunuch*

Refugees travelled

2Ki 25:26; Mt 2:13–14

Business travel

Jas 4:13 *See also* Lk 10:33

Travelling on pilgrimage

Lk 2:41–44

Missionary travels

The Jews Mt 23:15

Jesus Christ and his disciples Mk 1:39;
8:27; Lk 8:1; 14:25

The apostles Ac 8:40; 11:19; 13:6; 15:3;
18:23

Modes of travel

Ge 37:25 *in caravans*; Lk 24:13–15 *on
foot*; Ac 8:28–29 *by chariot*; Ac 23:23 *on
horseback*; Rev 18:17 *by ship*

The dangers of travel

2Co 11:26 *See also* 2Ch 15:5;
Ezr 8:21–23; Job 6:15–20; Lk 10:30;
Ac 27:14–44

Guidance while travelling

Ge 24:26–27; Ex 13:21; Ac 16:6–7

See also

4020 life of faith	7215 exile, the
5197 walking	7222 exodus, events of
5357 journey	
5427 nomads	7740 missionaries, call
5442 pilgrimage	
5491 refugees	8124 guidance
5505 roads	8168 way, the

5591

treasure

Highly valued objects or
accumulated riches. Treasure has at
best only short-term benefit but can
bring spiritual dangers. Spiritual
treasure is of eternal value and comes
from knowing and serving God.

The limitations of accumulated treasure

It is easily lost Isa 64:11 *See also*
2Ki 24:13; Jer 15:13; 17:3; 20:5;
La 1:10–11; Hos 13:15; Ob 6; Mt 6:19;
Jas 5:2–3; Rev 18:14

It is no security against God's
displeasure Pr 11:4 *See also* Job 20:20;
Jer 51:13; Eze 7:19; Hos 9:6; Zep 1:18;
Lk 12:16–21

It does not satisfy Ecc 5:10 *See also*
Ps 39:6; Hag 1:6

The spiritual dangers of accumulated treasure

It can lead to pride 1Ti 6:17 *See also*
Dt 8:13–14; Eze 7:20; 28:4–5; Da 4:30

It can lead a person away from God
Rev 3:17 *See also* Job 31:24–25,28;
Pr 11:28

It can lead to greed Lk 12:15 *See also*
1Ti 6:9–10

Acquiring it can lead to dishonesty
Jos 7:21; Ps 62:10; Pr 21:6

It can lead to idolatry Ex 32:2–4;
Isa 2:7–8; Eze 7:20; 16:17

Spiritual treasure
Treasure consists in knowing God and
his wisdom Col 2:2–3 *See also*
Job 28:12–19; Pr 2:4; 3:13–15;
8:10–11; 24:3–4; Isa 33:6

God's word is supreme treasure
Job 23:12; Ps 19:9–10; 119:72,127

The kingdom of God is supreme
treasure Mt 13:44 *See also*
Mt 13:45–46,52

Spiritual treasure is more important
than material possessions Heb 11:26
See also Job 22:23–25; Mt 13:44–46

It is of eternal value Lk 12:33 *See also*
Mt 6:20; 1Pe 1:4

It is gained through generosity and
wisdom Mt 19:21 pp Mk 10:21
pp Lk 18:22 *See also* Pr 8:21; 15:6;
1Ti 6:18–19

Treasure reveals true commitment
Mt 6:21 pp Lk 12:34 *See also* Mt 6:24
pp Lk 16:13

Believers willingly give God their treasures
Mt 2:11 *See also* Ex 35:22; Jos 6:24;
1Ch 29:3–5

God's people are his treasured possession
Dt 7:6 *See also* Ex 19:5; Dt 14:2; 26:18;
Ps 135:4; Mal 3:17

The gospel as treasure in clay jars
2Co 4:7

See also

2375 kingdom of God	5558 storing
4333 gold	5703 inheritance
4342 jewels	5869 greed
4363 silver	7140 people of God
5412 money	8361 wisdom
5475 property	8808 riches

5592

treaty

A formal agreement between
individuals or nations, promising
commitment to each other's
interests. Israel was forbidden to
enter into such agreements with
other nations in the promised land.

Treaties between individuals
1Sa 18:3–4 *See also* Ge 21:22–32;
26:26–31; 1Sa 20:8,16–17; 22:8; 23:18;
2Sa 3:12–13

Treaties between individuals acting on behalf of their nation
1Ki 5:12–18; 15:18–19; Isa 33:8
*Probably the agreement made when
Hezekiah paid large sums to Sennacherib
(2Ki 18:14); Eze 17:12–14*

Treaties between cities or nations
Jos 9:3–16; 10:1; 11:18–19; 1Sa 11:1–2;
Hos 12:1

Treaties entered into should be honoured
Eze 17:15–18 *See also* Jer 34:8–20;
Da 11:22–24 *"he will act deceitfully"
(verse 23), is a reference to Antiochus
Epiphanes (of the Seleucid dynasty) who
reneged on the friendship shown to Egypt;*
Hos 10:4; Am 1:9–10; Gal 3:15

Israel forbidden to enter into treaties with other nations in the promised land
Dt 7:1–2 *See also* Ex 23:31–32;
34:11–12,15–16; Dt 23:6;
1Ki 20:34,42–43; Ezr 9:12

See also

1346 covenants	5690 friends
5205 alliance	5783 agreement

5593

trial

A process of testing or investigation,
which may be legal, as in a court
case, or spiritual, as in a testing of
faith or power. Scripture makes
reference to both.

Legal trials
The need for legal trials Dt 16:18–20;
Jn 7:50–51; Ac 16:37–39

Trials concerning accidental killings
Jos 20:9 *See also* Nu 35:9–12; Jos 20:1–6

Unjust trials Mk 13:9–13
pp Mt 24:9–11 pp Lk 21:12 *See also*
1Ki 21:1–14; Ps 37:32–33; Ac 12:1–4;
16:37

The trial of Jesus Christ Mt 26:57–68
pp Mk 14:53–65 pp Jn 18:19–24 *See also*
Mt 27:11–26 pp Mk 15:2–15
pp Lk 23:2–25 pp Jn 18:28–19:16

The trial of Paul Ac 27:23–24 *See also*
Ac 22:30–23:11; 24:1–23;
25:1–12,23–26:32

Trials of faith
Through testing or temptation
Jas 1:2–3 *See also* Ge 22:1; Lk 22:28;
2Co 8:1–2; 1Th 3:2–4; 2Th 1:4;
Jas 1:12; 1Pe 1:6; 4:12–16; 2Pe 2:4–9;
Rev 3:10

Through burdensome responsibilities
Gal 4:14

Trials of strength or power
Dt 7:19 *See also* Ex 7:8–24; Dt 29:2–3;
1Ki 18:16–40

See also

2585 Christ, trial	7330 chief priests
5347 injustice	8027 faith, testing of
5359 justice	8794 persecution
5383 lawsuits	8832 testing

5594

tribute

Gifts and honours paid as a mark of
respect and submission to kings and
others in authority; also, praise given
to those to whom it is due.

Tribute required by God
The spoils of war Nu 31:28 *See also*
Nu 31:29,36–41

The glory due to his name Ps 96:7–9;
Heb 13:15

Tribute paid to kings
Eglon, king of Moab Jdg 3:15,17–18

David, from the Moabites 2Sa 8:2
pp 1Ch 18:2

David, from the Arameans 2Sa 8:6
pp 1Ch 18:6

Solomon, from all the lands 1Ki 4:21
See also Ezr 4:20

Ben-Hadad's demands from Ahab
1Ki 20:2–9

Ahab, from the king of Moab 2Ki 3:4

Isaiah's advice to Moab Isa 16:1–2

Jehoshaphat, from the Philistines and
Arabs 2Ch 17:11

Uzziah, from the Ammonites 2Ch 26:8

Jotham, from the Ammonites 2Ch 27:5

The Assyrian kings, from Israel
2Ki 15:19–20; 17:3–4; Hos 10:5–6

Pharaoh Neco, from Jehoiakim
2Ki 23:35

Babylonian plunder 2Ki 24:13;
2Ch 36:18

Artaxerxes, from the Jews Ezr 4:13;
7:24

Xerxes, from the whole empire Est 10:1

Roman taxes Mt 22:17 pp Mk 12:14
pp Lk 20:22

Tribute paid to those in authority
David 2Sa 9:6

Daniel Da 2:46

Haman Est 3:2

Herod Ac 12:21–23

Tribute in the form of praise
David, of Saul and Jonathan
2Sa 1:23–27

Paul, of faithful friends Ro 16:3–13;
2Co 8:22–24; Php 2:19–30;
Col 4:7–14; 2Ti 1:16–18

John, of Demetrius 3Jn 12

Christian principles on paying tribute
OT teaching Pr 24:21–22

Jesus Christ's teaching Mt 22:21
pp Mk 12:17 pp Lk 20:25

Apostolic teaching Ro 13:7 *See also*
1Pe 2:17

Tribute due to Jesus Christ
Prophesied in the OT Ps 72:10–11 *See
also* Ps 89:22; Isa 52:15

Due because of his exaltation
Php 2:9–11 *See also* Isa 45:23

Fulfilled in the New Jerusalem
Rev 21:24,26

See also

2336 Christ, exaltation	5325 gifts
	5577 taxation
2375 kingdom of God	5878 honour
	8488 tithing
4215 Babylon	8622 worship
4263 Rome	8664 praise
5085 David	

5595

trumpet

A musical instrument with a loud, piercing sound, used as a signal, both in times of war and of peace. It was also used extensively in Israelite worship and was frequently associated with divine activity.

Trumpets used to summon the Israelites
Nu 10:1–7 *See also* Isa 27:13

Trumpets sounded to announce religious festivals
Lev 25:8–12 *See also* Lev 23:24; Nu 10:10; 29:1; Ps 81:3–4 *The NIV usually translates the Hebrew word "shophar" as "trumpet", but in this instance it is translated "ram's horn";* Joel 2:15

Trumpets sounded to attract public attention
2Sa 20:1 *See also* 1Sa 13:3; Mt 6:2

Trumpets blown to announce the accession of a king
1Ki 1:39 *See also* 2Sa 15:10; 1Ki 1:34,41–43; 2Ki 9:13; 11:14 pp 2Ch 23:13

Trumpets used to warn of impending danger
Joel 2:1 *See also* Jer 4:5; 6:1,17; Eze 33:1–6; Hos 8:1; Am 3:6

Use of the trumpet in war
As a call to arms Jdg 6:33–35 *See also* Jdg 3:27–28; Ne 4:16–20; Isa 18:3; Jer 51:27; Eze 7:14; 1Co 14:8

As a battle cry 2Ch 13:12 *See also* Jos 6:2–20; Jdg 7:8,16–22; 2Ch 13:14–15; Job 39:24–25; Jer 4:19–21; 42:14; Hos 5:8; Am 2:2; Zep 1:15–16

To signal retreat 2Sa 2:28 *See also* 2Sa 20:22

Use of the trumpet in worship
Played by priests 2Ch 29:26 *See also* Ezr 3:10; Ne 12:31–36,40–42

Played in the tabernacle 1Ch 16:6 *See also* 1Ch 15:24; 16:42

Played in the temple 2Ch 5:12–13 *See also* 2Ki 12:13; 2Ch 7:6; 29:27–28

Played to praise God Ps 150:3 *See also* 1Ch 13:8; 2Ch 15:14–15; 20:28; 29:26; Ne 12:40–41; Ps 98:4–6

Accompanying the ark of the covenant 1Ch 15:28 pp 2Sa 6:14–15 *See also* Jos 6:4,8,13

The trumpet associated with divine activity
In visible manifestations of God Ex 19:16–19 *See also* Ex 20:18; Zec 9:14; Heb 12:18–21

At the second coming of Jesus Christ 1Th 4:16 *See also* Mt 24:31; 1Co 15:51–52

In metaphorical use Rev 4:1 *See also* Isa 58:1; Rev 1:10

The trumpet associated with angelic activity
Rev 8:2 *See also* Rev 8:6–8,10,12–13; 9:1,13–14; 10:7; 11:15

Trumpets sometimes made from silver
Nu 10:2

Trumpets sometimes made from animal horn
Jos 6:4 *See also* Ex 19:13; Ps 81:3

The trumpet in non-Israelite use
Rev 18:22 *See also* Jer 51:27

See also
1454 theophany
5213 assembly
5420 music
5421 musical instruments
5422 musicians
5605 warfare
5611 watchman
5978 warning
7306 ark of the covenant
7359 Feast of Trumpets
8622 worship
8664 praise

5596

victory

The conquest of, or gaining a decisive advantage over, an enemy. The gospel proclaims the victory of God in Christ over the forces of evil in the world.

5597

victory, as an act of God

God is the source of all victory, which he grants to those who obey his commands and put their confidence in him. This principle holds true in all believers' conflicts, whether physical or spiritual.

God is the source of all victory
Dt 20:1–4 *See also* 2Ch 20:15; Ps 18:35; 1Co 15:57; 2Co 2:14

Victory is achieved by God, not people
Ps 20:7–8 *See also* 1Sa 17:45–47; Ps 44:3–7; 60:11–12; 146:3; Pr 21:31

Victory should be ascribed to God
Ps 118:15 *See also* Ex 15:1; Ps 21:1; 1Co 15:57; Rev 19:1–2

Victory depends on faithfulness
God grants victory to those who are faithful to him 1Ch 22:13 *See also* Ex 23:20–23; Ps 112:8; Pr 2:7

Unfaithfulness to God brings defeat Nu 14:41–43 *See also* Dt 28:15,25; 2Ch 24:20

Examples of God giving victory
Ex 17:8–15 *to Israel over the Amalekites To Joshua at Jericho:* Jos 6:2–5,20 *·* Jdg 7:15–22 *to Gideon over the Midianites;* Jdg 15:12–19 *to Samson over 1,000 Philistines;* 1Sa 7:7–12 *to the Israelites at Mizpah;* 1Sa 17:38–50 *to David over Goliath;* 1Ki 18:36–39 *to Elijah at Mount Carmel;* 1Ch 11:4–9 *when David conquered Jerusalem*

God is able to work through defeat
Ge 50:20 *See also* Jdg 16:24,30; Ro 8:28; 2Co 4:7–12; 12:7–10

God is able to fulfil his purposes through the victory of unbelievers
Isa 44:28–45:4 *See also* Isa 41:25; 45:13; Eze 33:27–29 *This is how Ezekiel is to explain Babylon's victory over Jerusalem;* Ac 2:36; 3:17–18

See also
1115 God, purpose of
1130 God, sovereignty
1230 God, the Lord
5290 defeat
5605 warfare
5960 success
8727 enemies

5598

victory, over spiritual forces

In spiritual warfare victory is assured since Jesus Christ has already won it on the cross and in the resurrection. Christians will eventually share in Christ's complete victory and through him overcome their spiritual enemies.

The victories won by Jesus Christ
Over sin and temptation Heb 4:15 *See also* Mt 4:1–11; Heb 2:18; 1Pe 2:22

Over the world Jn 16:33 *See also* Rev 3:21; 17:14

Over the devil 1Jn 3:8 *See also* Mt 12:29 pp Mk 3:27 pp Lk 11:22; Lk 10:18; Jn 12:31; Col 2:15; Heb 2:14

Over death Ac 2:24 *See also* Ro 5:17; 6:9–10; 1Co 15:54–57; 2Ti 1:10

Over every enemy 1Co 15:24–25 *See also* Isa 42:13; Php 2:9–11; Heb 10:13

Believers have victory through Christ
Over the power of sin Ro 7:24–25 *See also* Ro 6:11–14; Col 3:9–10

Over temptation 1Co 10:13 *See also* Mt 6:13 pp Lk 11:4; Heb 2:18; 4:15–16

Over the world 1Jn 5:4–5 *See also* Jn 15:19; Tit 2:11–13; 2Pe 1:3–4

Over the devil Rev 12:10–11 *See also* Ro 16:20; Eph 6:12–13; 1Jn 2:13–14; 4:4

Over death 1Co 15:22–23 *See also* Jn 11:25–26; 1Co 15:54–57; 1Th 4:13–17

Believers share in Christ's victory
Ro 8:37; 1Co 15:57; 1Jn 5:4–5 *See also* Jn 11:25; Ro 6:5; 1Co 15:20; 2Co 2:14; Php 4:13; Heb 11:33–34 *Victory is received by faith.*

The final victory
The vision of final victory in Jesus Christ Rev 2:26; 3:5

It will be complete at the end of the age 1Co 15:24 *See also* Rev 21:1–3,7

Although certain it has not yet been fully realised Heb 2:8 *See also* Ac 3:21; Ro 8:24–25; Eph 1:10; Php 3:20–21; 2Th 2:8

5599
victory, of Jesus Christ

See 2372 Jesus Christ, victory of

5601
village

Villages were small rural settlements without walls
Lev 25:31 *See also* Dt 3:5; 1Ch 5:16; 2Ch 32:27–29; Est 9:19; SS 7:11; Mt 14:15

Villages associated with neighbouring towns and cities
Jer 19:15 *See also* Jos 10:37; 13:23; 1Sa 6:18; Ne 12:28

Villages were particularly vulnerable to invasion
Eze 38:11 *See also* Jdg 5:7; 2Ch 14:14

Village records and teachers
1Ch 4:32; 9:22; Lk 5:17

Villages as the scene of gospel preaching
Mk 6:6 *See also* Ac 8:25

5602
vomit

The literal act of vomiting
Jnh 2:10

Proverbial references to vomiting
Pr 26:11 *See also* Pr 23:6–8; 25:16–17; 2Pe 2:17–22

Metaphorical references to vomiting
An illustration of exile and destruction
Lev 18:24–28 *See also* Lev 20:22–24

An illustration of punishment
Isa 19:13–14 *See also* Jer 25:15–29; 48:26

An illustration of corruption Isa 28:7–8

An illustration of the fate of the wicked
Job 20:12–15

5603
wages

Payment by an employer for workdone; all labourers should be paid fairly and regularly.

Laws relating to wages
Payment should be made regularly
Dt 24:14–15 *See also* Lev 19:13

Regular rates of pay Lev 25:50; Mk 6:37 pp Jn 6:7; Mk 14:5 pp Jn 12:5

Labourers should not be defrauded
Mal 3:5; Jas 5:4 *See also* Jer 22:13

A fair wage should be paid Mt 20:2–4
A normal day's pay for a labourer in NT times was one denarius. See also Col 4:1

A fair day's work should be done
2Th 3:10–12 *See also* Eph 6:7–8; Col 3:23

Labourers should be content with a fair wage Lk 3:14

Wage earners suffer in times of trouble
Egypt under judgment Isa 19:10

Jerusalem under judgment Hag 1:6 *See also* Zec 8:10

The world under judgment Rev 6:6

The example of Jacob as a wage earner
Hos 12:12 *See also* Ge 29:15 *He agreed his wages beforehand;* Ge 29:18 *He was paid in kind;* Ge 29:25–27 *He was cheated by Laban;* Ge 30:28–34 *He makes an arrangement he can turn to advantage;* Ge 31:6–7 *He accuses Laban of dishonesty;* Ge 31:8–9 *He protests his own honesty;* Ge 31:38–42 *He looks back on his experience.*

The wages of God's servants
The Levites Nu 18:30–31; Ne 12:44; 13:10–13

Temple workers 1Ki 5:6; 2Ki 12:11–15; 22:3–7 pp 2Ch 34:8–11; 2Ki 22:9 pp 2Ch 34:16–17

Zechariah's derisory pay
Zec 11:12–13; Mt 27:3–10

Labourers in the parable of the workers in the vineyard Mt 20:1–16

Ministers of the gospel 1Ti 5:17–18 *See also* Dt 25:4; Lk 10:7; Jn 4:36–38; 1Co 9:7–14; Gal 6:6

The apostle Paul
It was Paul's choice to work freely:
1Co 9:15; 2Co 11:7–9
Php 4:18 *He expressed gratitude for gifts he received.*

Spiritual lessons from wages
Life's rewards are hard-earned
Job 7:1–3; Gal 6:7–10

The wages of sin Ro 6:21–23 *See also* Job 15:31–32; Isa 65:7; Jer 51:6; 2Pe 2:13

The freeness of God's grace Ro 4:4–5

The generosity of God Mt 20:9–16

The rewards of righteousness Pr 10:16; 11:18; 31:31; Mt 10:42 pp Mk 9:41; 1Co 3:14; Heb 6:10; 2Jn 8

5604
walls

Kinds of wall
Walls of houses and palaces La 2:7 *See also* 1Sa 18:10–11; 20:25; Isa 38:2; Da 5:5

Walls of towns 2Ch 14:7 *See also* Nu 35:4; 1Sa 31:10; 2Sa 18:24

Walls of cities Dt 3:5; Ne 2:17 *See also* Jos 2:15; 6:5,20; 1Ki 3:1; 2Ki 3:27; 2Ch 27:3; Ps 55:10; Isa 58:12; Ac 9:25

Walls of the temple 1Ki 6:27; 7:12

Walls of vineyards Mt 21:33 *See also* Nu 22:24–25; Ps 80:12

The fragility of walls
Walls broken down by enemies
Dt 28:52 ; Pr 25:28 ; Jer 50:15 *See also* 2Sa 20:15; 2Ki 14:13; 25:4 *the fall of Jerusalem to the Babylonians;* 2Ch 26:6; 36:19; Ne 1:3; Ps 89:40; Isa 5:5; 22:5; La 2:8; Eze 26:4; Am 4:3

Walls collapsing of their own accord
Isa 30:13 *See also* 1Ki 20:30; Ps 62:3; Eze 13:10–16

The figurative use of walls
Denoting protection Isa 25:4 *See also* 1Sa 25:16; Ezr 9:9; Isa 26:1; Zec 2:5

Denoting separation and impregnability Eph 2:14 *See also* Pr 18:11; Isa 59:10; Jer 1:18; Eze 22:30; Ac 23:3

The walls in the new Jerusalem
Rev 21:12–19

5605
warfare

The state of being at war with an opposing nation or people. Scripture neither condemns nor glories in warfare, but recognises it as a continuing aspect of this fallen world. In particular, the NT stresses the importance of spiritual warfare in the life of faith.

5606
warfare, nature of

Warfare is characteristic of a fallen world. Scripture describes how some wars are justified and others are not.

Warfare is characteristic of a fallen world

It is an aspect of life in a fallen world
Ex 17:16; 2Sa 3:1; 1Ki 14:30

It is caused by sin Jas 4:1–2 See also
Ps 140:1–2; Pr 10:12; 29:22; 1Co 3:3

It is horrific in nature Na 3:3 See also
2Ch 25:12; Zec 14:2

Warfare as a sign of the end times

Mt 24:6–7 pp Mk 13:7–8
pp Lk 21:9–10

Sometimes God forbids war

Dt 1:41–42 See also 1Ki 12:24;
1Ch 22:8; Ps 68:30; 120:7

Sometimes God commands war

Jos 8:1 See also Nu 31:7; Dt 20:1–4;
Jos 10:40; Jdg 6:16; Ps 144:1; Isa 13:3–4

Warfare is sometimes a means of judgment

1Sa 15:2 See also 2Ki 21:10–15; 24:2–4;
Isa 10:12–19; Jer 4:14–18

God's will that warfare will finally cease

Ps 46:9; Isa 2:4; Mic 4:3

See also
5025 killing	8482 spiritual
5814 confrontation	warfare
5975 violence	9105 last things
6020 sin	9210 judgment,
6154 fall, the	God's

5607
warfare, examples of

From the time of entering the
promised land, Israel was obliged to
engage in warfare against other
nations. Success is attributed to
Israel's trust in the LORD and failure
to lack of faith and disobedience.

Israel had to engage in warfare to enter Canaan

It was commanded by God Dt 7:1–2
See also Ex 23:27–31; Dt 9:1–5;
20:16–18

Joshua conquers the land Jos 11:23 See
also Jos 6:2; 8:1–2; 10:40–42; Ne 9:24;
Ps 44:1–3

Israel failed to drive out the remaining
Canaanites Jdg 1:19 Judah distrusted
God's power to destroy their enemy's iron
chariots. See also Jdg 1:28; 2:1–3,14–15

Israel was obliged to engage in warfare to defend the land

When unfaithful they were defeated
Jdg 3:12–14 See also Lev 26:14–17,33;
Dt 28:15,25; Jdg 3:7–8; 6:1–3;
2Ch 12:1–4; 24:23–24

When faithful they were victorious
2Ch 20:20 See also Dt 28:1,7;
1Sa 7:7–14; 11:1–11; 2Ch 20:15–24

Israel's internal struggles

2Sa 3:1; 1Ki 12:21 See also 2Sa 2:8–17;
15:14; 1Ki 15:6–7,16; 2Ki 13:12;
14:9–15

Israel's constant unfaithfulness led to the exile

1Ch 5:25–26 See also 2Ki 17:5–8,22–23

Judah's constant unfaithfulness led to the Babylonian captivity

2Ch 36:16–17 See also 2Ki 25:1
pp Jer 52:4–5; 2Ki 25:8–11
pp Jer 52:12–15; 2Ki 25:21 pp Jer 52:27;
Jer 1:13–16

See also
5214 attack	5960 success
5223 banner	6221 rebellion
5246 captivity	7212 exile
5290 defeat	7215 exile, the
5291 defence	8741 failure
5596 victory	8839 unfaithfulness

5608
warfare, strategies in

Scripture describes the strategies
employed by Israel in warfare.
Although recognising the
importance of military preparation,
Scripture stresses that Israel's trust is
to be in God, rather than military
might or prowess.

Preparations for warfare

Holding a council of war Pr 20:18 See
also Pr 11:14; 24:6; Lk 14:31–32

Assembling an army 2Sa 18:1 See also
Nu 1:2–3; 1Sa 11:6–8; 2Ch 25:5–6;
26:11–14; Da 11:10–13

Reconnaissance Nu 21:32 See also
Dt 1:22; Jos 2:1; 7:2–3; Jdg 7:9–11;
18:2,5–10

Avoiding warfare

Making a treaty Jos 9:15 See also
Ge 26:28–29; Jos 10:1; 1Sa 11:1;
1Ki 5:12

Representative combat 1Sa 17:8–10
See also 2Sa 2:12–17

Strategies employed in warfare

Dividing into groups Jdg 9:43–44 See
also Ge 14:14–15; 32:7–8; Jdg 7:16–21;
1Sa 11:11; 2Sa 18:1–2

Attacking by night Jdg 7:19 The Hebrews
divided the night into three watches. See
also Ge 14:14–15; 1Sa 14:36; Jer 6:5

Setting an ambush 2Ch 13:13–14 See
also Jos 8:4–7; Jdg 9:34,42–44;
20:29–44

Swiftness of action Jos 8:19 See also
Jos 10:6–9; 11:7; 2Sa 5:22–25

Trusting in God in warfare

Of greater importance than military
might or prowess Dt 20:1; Ps 20:7 See
also 1Sa 17:45–47; Ps 33:16–17;
147:10–11; Zec 4:6

Demonstrated by seeking God before
a battle Jdg 1:1 See also Jdg 20:27–28;
2Sa 5:18–19,22–25

Strengthened by seeing God fighting
for Israel Ex 14:29–31; Jos 10:10–14;
2Ki 19:35

See also
4657 horse	5544 soldiers
5208 armies	5552 spies
5209 armour	5592 treaty
5252 chariots	5611 watchman
5266 conscription	5917 plans
5529 sieges	8727 enemies

5609
warfare, spiritual

See 8482 spiritual warfare

5611
watchman

A person stationed on the highest
part of a city wall to warn
inhabitants of an approaching
enemy or messenger; also a person
who kept watch over pastures,
vineyards and sheep. The OT
prophets were spiritual watchmen,
warning the people of Israel of God's
judgment.

Watchmen stationed on the highest part of a city wall

To warn inhabitants of an approaching
enemy 2Ki 9:17 See also 1Sa 14:16;
2Sa 13:34; Ps 127:1; 130:6; SS 3:3; 5:7;
Jer 51:12

To give notice of approaching
messengers 2Sa 18:24–27 See also
2Ki 9:18,20; Isa 21:6,8; 52:8

Watchmen stationed on towers in pastures and vineyards to guard against thieves

2Ch 26:10; Isa 27:3; Mic 4:8

Watchmen stationed on hills

Jer 31:6 This was to give notice of the
various phases of the moon in order to fix
the times for the most important festivals.

Watchmen who guarded sheep

Jn 10:3

The OT prophets were spiritual watchmen warning the people of Israel of God's judgment

Jer 6:17 See also Isa 21:11–12; 56:10;
62:6; Eze 3:17; 33:2,6–7; Hos 9:8;
Hab 2:1

See also
4538 vineyard	5978 warning
5330 guard	7772 prophets
5408 messenger	8490 watchfulness
5585 towers	

5612
weapons

Instruments of warfare. God's people
are to trust in him rather than in
weapons. Scripture speaks of a day
when weapons will become
instruments of peace. The term is
also used metaphorically.

Weapons of warfare

1Ch 12:23,33; Ne 4:16–18 See also
Ge 49:5; 1Sa 8:12; 17:45,54; 21:8;
2Sa 1:27; 2Ki 11:8 pp 2Ch 23:7;
2Ki 11:11 pp 2Ch 23:10; 1Ch 12:34–37;
2Ch 32:5; Ne 4:23; Eze 26:7–11; 32:27;
Jn 18:3

Trust in God rather than in weapons

Ps 20:7–8; Isa 31:1 See also Dt 1:41–44;
20:1; 1Sa 17:45–47; 2Ch 20:20–24;

32:7–8; Ps 33:16–19; 76:3; 147:10–11; Pr 21:31; Ecc 9:18; Isa 22:8–11; 54:16–17; Zec 4:6

A day when weapons of war will become instruments of peace
Isa 2:4 pp Mic 4:3 See also Ps 46:9; Isa 9:5; Eze 39:7–10; Hos 2:18; Zec 9:10

Weapons used metaphorically by God
Isa 59:15–18; Jer 50:25 See also Ps 7:11–13; Isa 13:5; Jer 51:20; Eze 9:1–8

Weapons used metaphorically by Christians
2Co 10:4; Eph 6:11–17 See also Ro 13:12; 2Co 6:7; 1Th 5:8

See also
4366 stones	5527 shield
5131 belt	5538 sling
5209 armour	5545 spear
5210 arrows	5572 sword
5228 battering-rams	8486 spiritual
5236 bow and arrow	warfare,
5252 chariots	armour

5613
weights and measures

The peoples of the ancient Near East used a variety of standards of weights and measures, so that modern equivalents can only be approximate. The focus of Scripture is on the importance of keeping just weights and measures, and the prophets denounced those who used false balances and deceitful measures.
This set of themes consists of the following:
5614 weights and measures, laws concerning
5615 weights and measures, weights
5616 weights and measures, dry
5617 weights and measures, liquid
5618 weights and measures, linear
5619 weights and measures, distance and area

5614
weights and measures, laws concerning

God expects his people to use accurate weights and measures, and to use just balances. This is underlined in the Law, the Prophets and the wisdom literature.

The law demanded honesty in using weights and measures
Lev 19:35–36 Cheating by falsifying weights and measures was common in a culture where there was no standardisation or regulatory authority. See also Dt 25:13–16

The prophets called for the right use of weights and measures
A call for honesty Eze 45:9–10

Condemnation of dishonesty
Am 8:4–6 See also Hos 12:7–8; Mic 6:10–14

Instruction from Proverbs on weights and measures
Pr 20:10 See also Pr 11:1; 16:11 Merchants carried stones of different sizes in a pouch for weighing silver for payment; Pr 20:23; 22:28 To move a boundary stone was in effect to steal land.

See also
5242 buying & selling	5407 merchants
5253 cheating	5512 scales & balances
5318 fraud	8275 honesty
5347 injustice	8714 dishonesty

5615
weights and measures, weights

Ancient weights were usually made of stone or metal, often inscribed with their weight and standard, the shekel being the basic weight of all Semitic nations. Weights of gold and silver served as currency, since coinage was not invented until the seventh century B.C. Weights are given in ascending order, with their approximate imperial and metric equivalents.

Gerah (1/20 shekel): about 1/50 ounce (about 0.6 gram)
Lev 27:25 See also Ex 30:13; Nu 3:47; 18:16; Eze 45:12

Beka (10 gerahs): about 1/5 ounce (about 5.8 grams)
2Ch 9:15–16 pp 1Ki 10:16–17 See also Ge 24:22; Ex 38:25–26

Pim (2/3 shekel): about 1/4 ounce (about 7.7 grams)
1Sa 13:21 The Hebrew word translated "two thirds of a shekel" is "pim", its only mention in Scripture.

Shekel (2 bekas): about 2/5 ounce (about 11.5 grams)
The shekel in relation to other weights Eze 45:12

The shekel as a weight of metal objects 1Sa 17:5 See also 1Sa 17:7; 2Sa 21:16

The shekel as a weight of food Eze 4:10

The shekel as a weight of gold or silver objects 2Ch 3:9 See also Ge 24:22; Nu 7:13–14; Jdg 8:26

The shekel as a weight of gold or silver Ge 23:14–16 The phrase "the weight current among the merchants" reflects the local variation in standards. See also Ge 37:28; Dt 22:28–29; Jos 7:20–21; Jdg 17:1–4; 2Sa 18:11–12; 1Ki 10:29 pp 2Ch 1:17; 2Ki 5:4–5; Ne 5:15; Jer 32:9; Da 5:25–27 "Tekel" can mean "weighed" or "shekel".

The royal shekel 2Sa 14:26 The royal shekel, also known in Babylonia, was slightly heavier (at about 13 grams) than the standard shekel and reflects David's attempts to bring some standardisation to this weight.

The sanctuary shekel Nu 18:15–16 The sanctuary shekel was more precisely regulated than the common shekel, weighing exactly 20 gerahs. The common shekel may have weighed slightly less as a result of greater handling and wider circulation. See also Ex 30:13–15,22–25; 38:24–26; Lev 5:15; 27:1–7; Nu 3:46–50

Mina (50 shekels): about 1 1/4 pounds (about 0.6 kilogram)
Eze 45:12 Although the mina is valued here at 60 shekels, there is some evidence that in the pre-exilic period it was valued at 50 shekels. See also 1Ki 10:17; Ezr 2:69; Ne 7:71–72; Da 5:25–26 "Mene" can mean both "numbered" and "mina"; Lk 19:11–27 By NT times the mina had become coinage rather than simply a weight of silver, and was worth about three months' wages.

Talent (3,000 shekels, 60 minas): about 75 pounds (about 34 kilograms)
1Ch 29:7 See also Ex 25:39; 2Sa 12:30 pp 1Ch 20:2; 1Ki 10:14 pp 2Ch 9:13; 1Ki 16:24; 2Ki 18:14; Ezr 8:26; Est 3:9; Mt 18:24–25 By NT times the talent had become coinage, and ten thousand talents would have been the equivalent of millions of pounds sterling; Mt 25:14–30

Other minor weights
Kesitah Ge 33:19 The price in the original Hebrew is "one hundred kesitahs", a unit of unknown weight and value.

Litra
The word translated "pint" in Jn 12:3 and "pound" in 19:39 is "litra", a loanword from the Latin "libra", meaning "pound" and weighing 12 ounces (327 grams): Jn 12:3; 19:39

Peres Da 5:28 "Peres" means "division" and denotes a half-shekel.

See also
4303 metals	5412 money
5260 coinage	

5616
weights and measures, dry

These terms derive originally from the containers used, which held a fixed amount. Measures are given in ascending order, with their approximate imperial and metric equivalents.

Cab (1/18 ephah): about 2 pints (about 1 litre)
2Ki 6:25 This is the only mention in Scripture of this measure.

Omer (1/10 ephah): about 4 pints (about 2 litres)
Ex 16:16–22 This incident records the only mention in Scripture of this measure. See also Ex 16:32,36

Seah (1/3 ephah): about 13 pints (about 7.3 litres)
Ge 18:6 The seah was a measure used for flour and cereals. See also 1Sa 25:18; 1Ki 18:32; 2Ki 7:1

Ephah: about 3/5 bushel (about 22 litres)
Ru 2:17 The ephah was used only for flour

and cereals, and had subdivisions of 1/6 and 1/10. See also **Lev** *5:11; 24:5;* **Nu** *15:4–9;* **Jdg** *6:19;* **1Sa** *17:17;* **Eze** *45:10–11;* **Zec** *5:6–8 The word for "measuring basket" in the Hebrew is "ephah".*

Lethek (5 ephahs or 1/2 homer): about 3 bushels (about 110 litres)

Hos *3:2 Possibly a Phoenician measure, this is the only mention in Scripture of this measure.*

Cor (10 ephahs): about 6 bushels (about 220 litres)

1Ki *4:22 The cor was used for measuring flour and cereals, and also appears to have been used for measuring oil. See also* **1Ki** *5:11;* **2Ch** *2:10; 27:5;* **Ezr** *7:22;* **Eze** *45:14*

Homer (10 ephahs): about 6 bushels (about 220 litres)

Lev *27:16 The homer is an older word than the cor, but is equivalent to it. It originally meant "a donkey load" and was widely used throughout the ancient Near East from the second millennium B.C. as a measure for cereals. See also* **Nu** *11:32;* **Isa** *5:10;* **Eze** *45:11,13–14;* **Hos** *3:2*

Other dry measures found in the NT

Quart (choinix): about 1 1/2–2 pints (about 1 litre) **Rev** *6:6 The word translated "quart" is "choinix", a Greek measure.*

Saton (equivalent to the OT seah) **Mt** *13:33 pp* **Lk** *13:21 The "large amount" referred to is "three sata" in the Greek.*

Bowl (modius): about 15 1/2 pints (about 8.75 litres) **Mt** *5:15 pp* **Mk** *4:21 pp* **Lk** *11:33 The word translated "bowl" is the Roman measure "modius".*

Koros (equivalent to the OT cor) **Lk** *16:7 The measure translated as "a thousand bushels" is "one hundred korous" in the Greek.*

See also

4456 grain	5558 storing
4542 wheat	7435 sacrifice, in OT

5617
weights and measures, liquid

These terms derive originally from the containers used, which held a fixed amount. There is some uncertainty about the capacity of the bath, and therefore of other liquid measures dependent upon it. Measures are given in ascending order, with their approximate imperial and metric equivalents.

Log (1/72 bath): about 1/2 pint (about 0.3 litre)

Lev *14:10 This is the only mention in Scripture of the log, as a measure of oil used in the ritual for cleansing infectious skin diseases. See also* **Lev** *14:12–18,21–22*

Hin (1/6 bath): about 7 pints (about 4 litres)

Ex *29:38–41 The hin was used as a measure of oil, wine and water. See also*

Lev *23:12–13;* **Nu** *15:4–10;* **Eze** *4:11; 46:5–7*

Bath (1 ephah): about 5 gallons (about 22 litres)

Eze *45:11 The bath was the equivalent liquid measure of the ephah, and was used to measure oil, wine and water. See also* **1Ki** *5:11; 7:38;* **2Ch** *2:10;* **Ezr** *7:21–22;* **Isa** *5:10;* **Eze** *45:14;* **Lk** *16:6 The measure translated as "eight hundred gallons" is "one hundred batous" in the original ("batos" being the Greek form of the Hebrew "bath");* **Jn** *2:6 The measure translated as "twenty to thirty gallons" is "two to three metretas" in the original, a Greek measure roughly equivalent to the bath.*

See also

4293 water	4544 wine
4488 oil	

5618
weights and measures, linear

These terms were based on natural units of measurement that could be easily applied. Measures are given in ascending order, with their approximate imperial and metric equivalents.

Finger (1/4 handbreadth): about 3/4 inch (about 1.85 centimetres)

Jer *52:21 The finger was 1/4 handbreadth and was the smallest subdivision of the cubit. This is its only mention in Scripture.*

Handbreadth (4 fingers): about 3 inches (about 8 centimetres)

Ex *25:25 pp* **Ex** *37:12 The handbreadth was the width of the hand at the base of the four fingers. See also* **1Ki** *7:26 pp* **2Ch** *4:5;* **Ps** *39:5 The handbreadth is here used figuratively of the shortness of human life;* **Eze** *40:5*

Span (half a cubit): about 9 inches (about 23 centimetres)

Ex *28:16 pp* **Ex** *39:9 The span was the width of the outstretched hand from thumb to little finger. See also* **1Sa** *17:4 Goliath's height is given in the Hebrew as "six cubits and a span";* **Ps** *90:10 The span is here used figuratively of the shortness of human life;* **Eze** *43:13*

Cubit (2 spans): about 18 inches (about 0.5 metre)

Ex *25:10 pp* **Ex** *37:1 The cubit was the distance from the fingertip to the elbow, and was used to measure height, size, depth and distance. See also* **Ge** *7:20 The Hebrew describes the depth of the water as "fifteen cubits";* **Ex** *27:9–18 pp* **Ex** *38:9–15;* **1Ki** *6:2–3 pp* **2Ch** *3:3–4;* **1Ch** *11:23 The Hebrew describes the man as "five cubits tall";* **Eze** *40:5; 45:1–6; 47:3–5;* **Jn** *21:8 The Greek text describes the distance as "about two hundred cubits";* **Rev** *21:17*

Reed (6 cubits): about 10 feet (about 3 metres)

Eze *41:8 Originally a measuring instrument, the reed became a recognised measure of six cubits (the rod). See also* **Eze** *40:3,5–7;* **Rev** *11:1; 21:15–16*

Mile

Mt *5:41 The Greek word for "mile" here is "milion", a transliteration of the Roman measurement "mille passuum", "a thousand paces". See also* **Lk** *24:13 The measurement in the Greek is "sixty stadia". Eight stadia were about one mile (about 1480 metres);* **Jn** *6:19 The measurement in the Greek is "twenty-five or thirty stadia";* **Jn** *11:18 The measurement in the Greek is "fifteen stadia".*

See also

4803 breadth	4847 smallness
4813 depth	4903 time
4830 height	5152 fingers
4832 length	7254 plumb-line
4841 narrowness	

5619
weights and measures, distance and area

Diverse expressions were used for these measurements, their being determined in the most practical way possible, reckoned by known averages.

Expressions of distance

A bow-shot **Ge** *21:15–16*

Some distance **Ex** *33:7 A variety of distance often lies behind this expression, as can be seen in the examples that follow. See also* **Ge** *35:16; 36:6;* **Nu** *2:2; 1Sa 26:13; 2Sa 15:17;* **Mt** *8:30*

A Sabbath day's journey **Ac** *1:12 While this is the only mention of this phrase in Scripture, it was in fact a popular expression, indicating the distance a devout Jew could walk on the Sabbath. It was based on the rabbinical interpretation of* **Ex** *16:29 in the light of* **Nu** *35:5, and was limited to 2,000 cubits.*

A day's journey **1Ki** *19:3–4 See also* **Nu** *11:31*

A three-day journey **Ge** *30:36 See also* **Ex** *3:18;* **Nu** *10:33;* **Ezr** *10:7–9;* **Jnh** *3:3*

Far away **Dt** *28:49 See also* **1Ki** *8:46 pp* **2Ch** *6:36;* **Isa** *6:12;* **Eze** *11:15–16;* **Joel** *3:8;* **Zec** *6:15;* **Ac** *22:21*

Expressions of area

Area expressed by the yoke **1Sa** *14:14 The area translated "about half an acre" in the Hebrew means "half a yoke". The yoke was the area of land ploughed by a yoke of oxen in one day, approximately one acre. See also* **Isa** *5:10 The Hebrew describes the area as "ten-yoke", that is, the land ploughed by ten yoke of oxen in one day.*

Area expressed by the amount of seed required to sow the land **Lev** *27:16*

Area expressed by its constituent measurements **Eze** *40:47 See also* **Ex** *28:16 pp* **Ex** *39:9;* **1Ki** *7:23;* **Eze** *45:1–6*

See also

4206 land	5357 journey
4406 agriculture	5590 travel
5235 boundary	

5621

wheel

Early wheels were solid wooden discs. These were replaced around 1500 B.C. by lighter, spoked wheels. The most common use of wheels is on chariots and carts; they were also used by potters and in machinery for drawing water from a well. The chariot throne of God has wheels which are vividly described.

Chariot wheels

Ex 14:25; Na 3:2 *The sound of chariot wheels announces the approach of the enemy. See also* 2Ki 7:6; Isa 5:28; Jer 47:3; Joel 2:5; Rev 9:9

Wagon wheels

The Hebrew word for "wheel" is here used for "wagon": Eze 23:24; 26:10

Threshing wheels

Pr 20:26 *Threshing was carried out by driving a sledge or a cart with heavy wheels over the grain. See also* Isa 28:27–28

Other examples of wheels

1Ki 7:32–33 *The stands for basins in Solomon's temple were mounted on wheels. See also* 1Ki 7:30; Ecc 12:6 *A wheel formed part of the machinery for drawing water from a well;* Jer 18:3 *Potters turned their clay on a wheel.*

The wheels of God's chariot throne

Eze 11:22–23; Da 7:9 *See also* 2Ki 2:11; Isa 66:15; Eze 1:15–21; 3:12–13; 10:1–19

See also

4150 cherubim	5252 chariots
4296 wells	5445 potters &
4522 threshing	pottery
5248 cart	5581 throne

5622

witnesses

Individuals who, having observed something take place, are able to give an accurate and full account of what has happened. Witnesses were of central importance to OT law. The theme of giving account is also of major importance to evangelism, which rests upon believers explaining the impact of Jesus Christ upon their lives.

5623

witnesses, legal

God gave detailed instructions about the conduct of witnesses in the legal processes of Israel and also in the affairs of the church.

God himself as a witness

Ge 31:50; Mal 2:14

General legal requirements about witnesses

A witness to a crime was required to give evidence Lev 5:1 *See also* Pr 29:24

Two or more witnesses were required to prove someone guilty Dt 19:15 *See also* Dt 17:6; Mt 18:15–16; 2Co 13:1

The role of witnesses in capital cases

At least two witnesses were required Nu 35:30 *See also* Dt 17:2–6; Heb 10:28

Witnesses were required to participate in the execution Dt 17:7 *See also* Lev 24:13–16; Dt 13:6–11; Ac 7:57–58

The role of witnesses in other legal matters

Land transactions Jer 32:9–12 *See also* Ge 23:10–18; Ru 4:1–9; Jer 32:25,44

Levirate marriage Ru 4:9–11

The role of witnesses in disputes concerning believers

Mt 18:15–17 *See also* 2Co 13:1; 1Ti 5:19

See also

1020 God, all-knowing	5471 proof
	5834 disagreement
1461 truth, nature of	7346 death penalty
5270 court	8331 reliability
5277 criminals	

5624

witnesses, to Jesus Christ

The NT identifies a variety of witnesses to Jesus Christ, who confirm his identity and importance. It also stresses the importance of believers bearing witness to Christ in the world.

The witness of the OT

Ac 26:22–23 *See also* Lk 24:27; Jn 5:39–40; Heb 12:1–2

The witness of John the Baptist

Jn 1:6–8 *See also* Mt 3:1–3; Isa 40:3; Mt 3:11–12 pp Mk 1:7–8 pp Lk 3:15–18; Jn 1:15,19–31; 3:26–30; 5:33–35

The witness of the Holy Spirit

Jn 15:26 *See also* Ac 5:32; Ro 8:16; 1Jn 5:6–9

The witness of the Father

Jn 8:18 *See also* Mt 3:17 pp Mk 1:11 pp Lk 3:22; Mt 17:5 pp Mk 9:7 pp Lk 9:35; Jn 5:37–38

The witness of Jesus Christ to himself

Jn 5:36; 8:14 *See also* Jn 13:13; 14:11

The witness of Jesus Christ's miracles

Jn 14:11 *See also* Jn 10:25; 15:24

The witness of the first Christians

Commissioned by Jesus Christ Ac 1:8 *The cost of being a witness to Jesus Christ:* Mt 10:17–20; Lk 21:12–13; Ac 4:18–21 Lk 1:1–2; 24:48; Jn 15:27; Ac 1:21–22; 2:32; 4:33; 13:31 *The commissioning of Paul:* Ac 9:5–6; 22:14–15; 23:11; 26:16 Heb 2:3; 1Pe 5:1; 2Pe 1:16; 1Jn 1:1

The witness of converts

1Pe 3:15–16 *See also* 2Ti 1:8

See also

1690 word of God	7706 apostles
2351 Christ, miracles	7915 confirmation
2422 gospel,	7948 mission
confirmation	8424 evangelism
3293 Holy Spirit,	8495 witnessing
witness of	8787 opposition to
5098 John the	God
Baptist	
5565 suffering of	
believers	

5625

witnesses, false

Scripture prohibits individuals from bearing false witness against their neighbours.

False testimony forbidden

Ex 20:16 pp Dt 5:20 *See also* Ex 23:1–2; Lev 19:12; Pr 6:16–19; 24:28; Lk 3:14; Mt 15:19; 19:18 pp Mk 10:19 pp Lk 18:20

The effect of false witnesses on other people and society

Pr 25:18 *See also* Ps 27:12; 35:11; Pr 12:17; 14:5,25; 18:5; 19:28

False witnesses will be punished

Dt 19:16–21 *See also* Lev 6:1–7; Pr 19:5,9; 21:28; Isa 29:20–21; Zec 5:3–4

Examples of false witnesses

1Ki 21:8–13; Mt 26:59–61 pp Mk 14:55–59; Mt 28:12–15; Ac 6:11–14

See also

5202 accusation,	6145 deceit
false	8734 evil
5347 injustice	8751 false witness
5361 justice, human	8776 lies
5493 retribution	8828 spite
5951 slander	

5627

word

Jesus Christ is described as God's word. The word encompassed the promise of God and the gospel and is a help in trial and temptation. Human beings should use words wisely.

Jesus Christ and God's word

Jesus Christ described as the Word Jn 1:1–3 *See also* Jn 1:14; Heb 1:1–2; 1Jn 1:1–2; Rev 19:13

Jesus Christ preaches the word Mk 2:2 *See also* Mt 7:24–29 pp Lk 6:47–49; Mt 13:20–23 pp Mk 4:13–20 pp Lk 8:11–15 *the parable of the sower;* Lk 11:28; Jn 3:34; 5:24; 6:63–68; 8:31–32,47,52; 12:47–50; 14:10–24; 15:3; 17:6–8

The word and the gospel

Ac 4:31 *See also* Ac 4:29; 13:44–46; 19:10; 20:24; Dt 30:14; Ro 10:8–10; Col 1:5; 2:2; 1Th 1:5; Heb 4:2

God's word is a promise and help in trial and temptation

Ps 119:9–11 *See also* Ps 33:4–5; 119:105,133; Dt 8:3; Mt 4:4; Jn 14:23–24; 17:17; Eph 6:17; Heb 4:12; 1Jn 5:3

Words should be used wisely

Mt 12:36–37 *See also* Jdg 8:1–3; 2Ch 10:13–14; Pr 10:19; 12:18,25; 15:1; 16:24; 25:15; Ecc 12:11; Jas 3:1–12

See also

1150 God, truth of	5193 tongue
1690 word of God	5243 byword
2203 Christ, titles of	5263 communi-
2363 Christ,	cation
preaching &	5408 messenger
teaching	5547 speech, power
2420 gospel	of
3266 Holy Spirit in	7793 teachers
creation	

5628

work

Work was ordained by God as a means of fulfilment, service and praise. It is to be supplemented by rest, following the pattern of God's creation of the world. Despite the effects of sin, work can still be honouring to God.

This set of themes consists of the following:

5629 work, as ordained by God
5630 work, divine and human
5631 work, of God
5632 work, of Jesus Christ
5633 work, of Holy Spirit
5634 work, and the fall
5635 work, and redemption
5636 work, and rest

5629

work, as ordained by God

God ordained work as the normal routine of living. Every legitimate human task, therefore, is of intrinsic worth, however menial it may seem, and is potentially a means of glorifying God.

Work is ordained by God

Ge 1:27–28 *See also* Ex 20:9 pp Dt 5:13; Ps 104:23 *Work is part of the rhythm of life.*

God's purposes in ordaining work

That people should be self-supporting
Ge 3:19 *See also* Ps 128:2; 1Th 4:12

That people should find self-fulfilment
Ecc 2:24 *See also* Pr 14:23; Ecc 3:22; 5:19

That people should serve others
Eph 4:28 *See also* Pr 31:15; 1Th 2:9; 1Ti 5:8

That people should glorify God
Col 3:17 *See also* 1Co 10:31; Eph 6:5–8 pp Col 3:22–24

Consequences of viewing work as God's ordinance

Work is seen as a moral duty Tit 3:14 *See also* Pr 6:6; Ecc 9:10; 1Th 4:11; 2Th 3:7–12

Any legitimate work may be seen as God's calling Ge 2:15 *See also*

Ex 31:1–6; 35:30–35; Ps 78:70–71; Mt 13:55 pp Mk 6:3; Ro 13:6; 1Co 7:17,20–24

Work is seen as a stewardship from God himself Col 3:23–24 *See also*

Mt 25:14–30 pp Lk 19:12–27; Eph 6:5–8

Criticism of those who will not work

2Th 3:10–11

See also

4005 creation	5520 servants
5051 responsibility	5603 wages
5273 creativity	5785 ambition
5404 masters	5908 motives
5433 occupations	5939 satisfaction
5498 reward	8440 glorifying God

5630

work, divine and human

God has ordained that some of his purposes be fulfilled through the co-operation (conscious or unconscious) of human beings.

God works in co-operation with people's work

Human labour is futile apart from God
Ps 127:1 *See also* Ge 11:8; Jn 15:5

God often works through human means Ps 77:20 *See also* Ac 9:15; Ro 13:6; 2Co 7:6

God gives the gifts needed for work
Ex 31:3,6; Lk 12:48; 1Pe 4:11

Human workers should acknowledge their dependence upon God Dt 8:18 *See also* Ps 90:17; Ne 6:9,16; 2Co 3:5

The apostles as God's fellow-workers
1Co 3:9; 2Co 6:1 *See also* Mk 16:20

Examples of divine and human co-operation in work

Php 2:12–13

God creates and people cultivate
Ge 2:15; Isa 28:23–29; 1Co 3:7

God gives and people are generous
1Ki 17:9; 2Co 8:1–5

God speaks through prophets' words
Dt 18:15–18; 2Sa 12:25; Jer 37:2; Hos 12:13; Mt 1:22; 2Pe 1:21

See also

1115 God, purpose	7772 prophets
of	8224 dependence
1305 God, activity of	8260 generosity
1427 prophecy	8347 spiritual
1439 revelation	growth
5583 tools	8420 equipping
6671 grace &	8434 giving
Christian life	

5631

work, of God

See 1300 God, work of

5632

work, of Jesus Christ

See 2300 Jesus Christ, ministry and work of

5633

work, of Holy Spirit

See 3200 Holy Spirit, ministry and work of 3296 Holy Spirit, work in the world

5634

work, and the fall

Human work, which was once a pleasure, became a burden only on account of human disobedience.

Work is under God's judgment

Ge 3:17–19 *See also* Ge 5:29

Work is often frustrating

Ecc 2:22–23 *See also* Ecc 2:11,18; 4:8; 5:16–17

Work may exploit rather than enhance society

Through dishonesty Lev 19:35; Dt 25:13; Hos 12:7

Through oppression Ex 1:11–14; 1Ki 12:4,10–14

Work may be undervalued or overvalued

Some people avoid work to their cost
Pr 6:6–11; 13:4; 19:15; 24:30–34; Ecc 10:18; 2Th 3:10–11

Some people overwork to their cost
Ex 18:17–18; Ps 127:2; Lk 10:41–42; 12:15–21

See also

5343 idleness	8714 dishonesty
5418 monotony	8718 disobedience
5864 futility	8778 materialism
6154 fall, the	8790 oppression
7446 slavery	
8713 discourage-	
ment	

5635

work, and redemption

Although human activity cannot merit eternal redemption, work done in this life may, with God's enabling, substantially reflect the divine ideal, in anticipation of the perfect service of heaven.

Human work cannot merit redemption

Eph 2:8–9; 2Ti 1:9; Tit 3:4–5

Jesus Christ's finished work secures redemption

Jn 17:4 *See also* Jn 4:34; 19:30; Heb 9:12

Faith leads believers to perform good works

Jas 2:14 *See also* Mt 7:16–20; 12:33; Lk 3:8–9; Ro 2:13; Heb 6:10–12; Jas 2:17–26

Redeemed workers fulfil God's purpose in work

By applying biblical virtues in employment Pr 10:4; 14:23; Gal 6:9; Col 4:1

By the pursuit of excellence Ecc 9:10; Tit 2:7–8; 3:8; 1Pe 2:12,15

By doing their work as those responsible to God Ro 12:1; 1Co 7:24; 10:31; Eph 6:7; Col 3:23

Work done, as for the Lord, will be rewarded by the Lord
Col 3:23–24 See also 2Ch 31:21; Mt 25:21; 1Co 15:58

Work will continue in the life to come
Rev 22:3 See also Mt 25:21,23; Lk 19:17,19

See also
2321 Christ as redeemer	8345 servanthood & worship
5840 eagerness	8442 good works
6669 grace & salvation	8459 perseverance
6720 redemption	8774 legalism
7160 servants of the Lord	9412 heaven, worship & service
8275 honesty	

5636
work, and rest

In creation, God has established a pattern of work and rest that is to be a model for believers.

Work and rest built into creation
Ex 20:11 See also Ge 2:1–3; Ps 104:19–23

The pattern of work and rest confirmed in the OT
By Sabbath observance Ex 20:10 pp Dt 5:14; Lev 23:3

By observing holy festivals Ex 12:16; Lev 16:29; 23:6–8 pp Nu 28:17–18; Lev 23:28–31 pp Nu 29:7; Lev 23:35–36,39 pp Nu 29:12; Est 9:17–19

Work and rest in the ministry of Jesus Christ
Mk 6:30–32 See also Jn 4:6

Wisdom needed to balance work and rest
To avoid idleness Pr 6:9–11; 10:4–5; 14:23; 20:13; 24:30–34

To avoid overwork Ex 18:13–24; Ps 127:2; Lk 10:38–42

Work and rest are both potential means of glorifying God
1Co 10:31 See also Ecc 2:24; Col 3:17

Work and rest will be perfectly fulfilled in heaven
Rev 14:13; 22:3

See also
2033 Christ, humanity	5533 sleep, physical
2339 Christ, example of	5582 tiredness
	5922 prudence
5057 rest, physical	7354 feasts and festivals
5386 leisure	7428 Sabbath
5447 poverty, causes	8361 wisdom

---

writing

A form of communication, including the writing of books, letters and scrolls. Many kinds of materials have

been written on. Figuratively speaking, the heart can be written on.

Uses of writing
Books Jer 30:2 See also Lk 1:3

The law Dt 31:24 See also Jos 24:26; 2Ki 23:21

Annals and records 1Ki 11:41 See also 2Ki 12:19; 1Ch 29:29; 2Ch 35:25

Agreements Ne 9:38

Legal documents Dt 24:1; Mk 10:4

Letters 2Sa 11:14; Ro 16:22; Col 4:18 In those days the sender would add a few words to a letter dictated to and written by a secretary. See also 1Ki 21:8–11; Est 3:12; Gal 6:11; 2Pe 3:1

Writing materials
Stone Ex 32:15–16 See also Dt 27:2–3; Job 19:24

Wood Nu 17:2–3; Dt 6:9

Metal Zec 14:20

Walls Da 5:5–8

Writing tablets Hab 2:2; Lk 1:63

Scrolls Dt 17:18; Rev 1:11 See also Ex 17:14; Nu 5:23; Job 19:23; Isa 8:1; Jer 36:18; 51:60

Writing kits
Eze 9:2–3 See also Eze 9:11; 2Jn 12; 3Jn 13

God writes
The law Ex 31:18; 32:15–16; 34:1

Figurative writing of God Ps 139:16 See also Ps 87:6; Lk 10:20

Jesus Christ writes
Jn 8:6

Writing on the heart
Jer 31:33 See also Heb 8:10; 10:16 Ro 2:15 See also Pr 3:3; 7:3; Jer 17:1; 2Co 3:2

General references to writing
Ge 5:1; Dt 31:19; Jos 18:4; 2Ch 35:4; Ps 102:18

See also
1610 Scripture	5391 letters
4494 papyrus	5393 literacy
5175 reading	5439 pen
5232 book	5514 scribes
5352 inscriptions	5515 scroll
5377 law, Ten Command-ments	5519 secretary

Human relationships

ancestors

The ancestors of Israel
Abraham, Isaac and Jacob Lev 26:45 See also Jas 2:21

More immediate forebears Am 2:4 See also 1Ki 19:3–4; Ac 28:17

Ancestors of specific groups of people
Jos 17:1 See also Ge 10:21

Ancestors of individuals
Ro 9:5 See also Heb 7:10

The figurative use of ancestors
Eze 16:3

See also
1245 God of the fathers	5680 family
	5694 generation
2540 Christ, genealogy	6160 fathers, sin of
	7230 genealogies
5076 Abraham, life of	7248 patriarchs
5096 Jacob, patriarch	

---

babies

The gift of young children from God is usually seen as a blessing. The term is also used figuratively of those who are young or immature in the faith.

Babies as a blessing from God
Ps 127:3 See also Ge 1:28; 17:16; 24:59–60; Pr 17:6; Lk 1:41–42

The promise of a baby
Ge 17:15–19 See also Ge 18:10–14; 2Ki 4:14–17; Lk 1:11–24

Examples of biblical characters as babies
Ge 21:1–7 Isaac; Ge 25:21–26 Esau and Jacob; Ex 2:1–10 Moses; Jdg 13:2–25 Samson; Ru 4:13–17 Obed, the father of Jesse; 2Sa 12:24–25 Solomon; Lk 1:57–66 John the Baptist

Babies as prophetic signs
Isa 7:14 See also Isa 8:3–4; 9:6–7; Hos 1:2–11; Lk 2:8–12

OT laws concerned with the birth of babies
Lk 2:21–24 See also Ge 17:9–12; Ex 13:1–2; Lev 12:1–8; Lk 1:59

A mother's love for her baby
Isa 49:15 See also 1Ki 3:16–28; Isa 66:12–13

Babies are sinful from birth
Ps 51:5 See also Ps 58:3; Jn 9:34

The death of babies
Ex 1:15–22 See also Ex 11:4–5; 2Sa 12:13–23; La 2:11–12; Mt 2:16–18; Ac 7:17–19

Jesus Christ and babies
Jesus Christ's own birth and babyhood Mt 1:18–23 See also Isa 7:14; Mt 2:1–23; Lk 1:26–38; 2:1–40

Jesus Christ's response to babies Lk 18:15–17 pp Mt 19:13–15 pp Mk 10:13–16

Babyhood used as a spiritual image
1Co 3:1–2 See also Ps 8:2; Mt 21:16; 11:25; Ro 2:20; 1Co 14:20; Eph 4:14; Heb 5:11–14; 1Pe 2:2–3

See also
2515 Christ, birth of	5718 mothers
5061 sanctity of life	5724 offspring
5225 barrenness	5731 parents
5663 childbirth	5881 immaturity
5664 children	8313 nurture

5654

betrothal

The period of engagement preceding marriage; betrothal was a binding contract established between two families and sealed by the exchange of gifts. During this period the couple did not live together; sexual relations with each other at this stage was regarded as equivalent to adultery. Betrothal describes the relationship between God and his people and between Jesus Christ and the church.

Betrothal and the choice of a spouse

Wives were often chosen by parents for their sons Ge 21:21 *It was usual practice for the groom's parents to choose his wife and arrange the wedding. See also* Ge 24:4; 38:6

Suitable husbands were sought by parents for their daughters Ru 3:1–4 *Naomi, in the role of parent, assumes responsibility to find a husband for Ruth. See also* Jdg 1:12–13; 1Sa 18:17,21

Betrothal following the couple's wishes Jdg 14:1–4 *Sometimes the man chose a prospective bride and his parents negotiated the marriage. See also* Ge 34:1–4; 24:57–58; 26:34–35 *Esau chose a bride against his parents' wishes.*

Betrothal preceded marriage

Ge 29:21; Dt 20:7 *A betrothed soldier was exempted from military service until after his marriage;* Mt 1:24; 1Co 7:36–38

An exchange of gifts accompanyed betrothal

The bride-price Ge 34:11–12 *This gift, which was given by the groom to the bride's family as compensation, sealed the marriage contract. See also* Ge 24:53; 29:18,27; Ex 22:16–17; Dt 22:28–29; 2Sa 3:14

The dowry 1Ki 9:16 *The dowry was a gift from the bride's father to the bride and/or groom.*
Servants were given to the bride as a dowry:
Ge 24:59; 29:24,29
Jdg 1:14–15

Betrothal was treated as marriage

Dt 22:23–24 *Though there were no sexual relations within the betrothal period, the commitment was regarded almost as seriously as marriage and infidelity of a betrothed partner was treated as adultery. See also* Ge 19:14 *The men betrothed to Lot's daughters are described as his "sons-in-law";* Mt 1:18–20 *Mary's pregnancy during betrothal left her open to the charge and consequences of unfaithfulness.*

Betrothal portrays the relationship between God and his people

Hos 2:19–20; 2Co 11:2 *See also* Jn 3:29; Eph 5:25–27; Rev 19:7–9; 21:2

See also
5444 pledges	5710 marriage,
5659 bride	customs
5660 bridegroom	5740 virgin
5679 dowry	5742 wedding
5680 family	5744 wife
5702 husband	6236 sexual sin

5655

birth

The beginning or origin of life, in which a living creature comes into the world. Scripture draws a distinction between physical and spiritual birth, insisting that a person must be not only physically but also spiritually born in order to have life to the full.

Physical birth

God creates all life Job 10:8–12; Ps 71:6; 139:13

Human beings are sinful from the moment of birth Ps 51:5 *See also* Job 15:14; 25:4; Ps 58:3; Jn 3:6; 9:34; Ro 5:12,17–19

The necessity of spiritual birth

Being born again Jn 3:3

Being born of the Spirit Jn 3:5–8 *See also* Ps 87:4–6; Mt 18:3; Jn 1:12–13; 1Pe 1:3; 2:2

The agents of the new birth: word and Spirit

1Pe 1:23 *See also* Lk 10:21; Jn 3:5,7–8; Tit 3:5; Jas 1:18

The fruit of the new birth: holiness and love

1Jn 3:9; 4:7 *See also* Mt 18:4; 1Jn 2:29; 5:3–4,18

Spiritual birth and the nation of Israel

Dt 32:18 *See also* Nu 11:12 *Moses implies that God himself gave birth to the people.*

Birth seen as entry into a condition or status

Ethnic identity from birth Ex 12:48; Eze 16:3; Ac 17:26; 22:27–28; Gal 2:15; 4:4; Eph 2:11; Php 3:4–5

Physical or mental disability from birth Jn 9:1; Ac 3:2; 14:8

See also
2515 Christ, birth of	5733 pregnancy
5199 womb	5739 twins
5231 birthday	6023 sin,
5652 babies	universality
5657 birthright	6728 regeneration
5663 childbirth	7334 circumcision
5688 firstborn	

5657

birthright

The right of the firstborn son in ancient Israel to inherit his father's estate. Where the property was divided, the firstborn received a double share.

Birthright was recognised amongst the patriarchs

Ge 25:5–6,34

Birthright and the law

It was guaranteed under the law Dt 21:15–17 *See also* 1Ch 26:10 *some ignored this law*

Daughters and others could inherit if there were no sons Nu 27:1–11

Only sons of a lawful marriage qualified Ge 21:8–13; Jdg 11:1–2

Birthright and kingship

Succession was normally to the firstborn 2Ch 21:1–3 *See also* 2Ch 11:18–22 *favouritism could intrude here also*

Transfer of the birthright

Through misconduct 1Ch 5:1 *See also* Ge 49:3–4

By transaction Ge 25:29–34 *See also* Heb 12:16–17

The Christian birthright

Ro 8:17 *Jesus Christ is the firstborn over all creation; by the grace of God Christians share in his inheritance. See also* Gal 4:7; Col 1:15; Heb 1:2

See also
5368 kingship	5701 heir
5672 concubines	5703 inheritance
5674 daughters	5738 sons
5681 family	6608 adoption
5684 fathers	9413 heaven,
5688 firstborn	inheritance

5658

boys

As those who would continue the family line boys were seen as a great blessing from God. Circumcised on the eighth day, as they grew towards maturity they were to be taught by their fathers. In the story of God's people, Israelite boys are seen serving God, being ministered to by men of God and suffering at the hands of ungodly kings.

Boys in general are seen as a blessing from God

Ps 127:3–5 *See also* Ru 4:13–17; Ps 128:3–4

Particular boys who are seen as a special gift from God

The boy Isaac, a gift to Abraham and Sarah Ge 17:15–22 *See also* Ge 21:1–7

The boy Samson, a gift to Manoah and his wife Jdg 13:2–5 *See also* Jdg 13:24–25

The boy Samuel, a gift to Elkanah and Hannah 1Sa 1:1–20

The boy John, a gift to Zechariah and Elizabeth Lk 1:5–25 *See also* Lk 1:57–66

The boy Jesus, a gift to Mary and Joseph Lk 1:26–38 *See also* Mt 1:20–21

Boys were circumcised on the eighth day

Ge 17:9–14 *See also* Lev 12:3; Lk 1:59; 2:21

Boys were taught by their fathers
Pr 4:1–4 *While examples of fatherly instruction in Scripture are confined to wisdom literature and liturgical material, other sources indicate that the education provided was more wide-ranging, and would include the teaching of a trade. See also* Ex 13:8; Dt 6:20–25; Pr 4:10–13

Israelite boys who served God
The boy Samuel served God in the temple 1Sa 3:1–21

The boy David served God by killing Goliath 1Sa 17:20–51

The boy King Joash served God 2Ch 24:1–2 pp 2Ki 12:1–2

The boy King Josiah served God 2Ch 34:1–2 pp 2Ki 22:1–2

The boy Jesus had a conscious relationship with God Lk 2:41–50

Boys who are ministered to by men of God
Through Elijah, God restored the life of a widow's son 1Ki 17:17–23

Through Elisha, God restored the life of a Shunammite's son 2Ki 4:32–37

Jesus Christ healed a demon-possessed boy Mt 17:14–18 pp Mk 9:14–27 pp Lk 9:37–43

Both Herod and Pharaoh ordered that Israelite boys be killed
Mt 2:16 *See also* Ex 1:15–22

See also

2520 Christ, childhood	5664 children
5098 John the Baptist	5695 girls
5225 barrenness	5731 parents
5302 education	5738 sons
	7334 circumcision

bride

A woman who is about to be married or who has just got married. In the NT the church is described as the bride of Christ.

Jewels and ornaments worn by a bride at her wedding
Isa 61:10 *See also* Ps 45:9,14; SS 4:9; Isa 49:18; Jer 2:32

Joy and happiness associated with a bride
Jer 33:10–11 *See also* Jer 7:34; 16:9; 25:10; Rev 18:23

The bride as the object of the bridegroom's love and affection
Isa 62:5 *See also* SS 4:8–15; 5:1

The bridegroom as the object of the bride's love and affection
Jer 2:2–3

Exemptions for a newly married bride
Joel 2:16 *A newly married bride would normally be excused from certain civic and religious duties. See also* Dt 24:5

The bride price
Ge 34:11–12 *A bridegroom was required to pay a bride-price to the father of his*

bride. *See also* Ge 29:18–30; 1Sa 18:20–27

Proof of a bride's virginity was required in certain circumstances
Dt 22:13–21

The church depicted as the bride of Christ
Eph 5:25–27 *See also* Rev 19:7–9; 21:1–2,9–27; 22:17

See also

4342 jewels	5744 wife
5660 bridegroom	7024 church, nature of
5679 dowry	
5702 husband	7241 Jerusalem, significance
5708 marriage	
5740 virgin	8283 joy
5742 wedding	8292 love

bridegroom

A man who is to be married or who has just got married. In the NT Jesus Christ is portrayed as a bridegroom and the church as his bride.

The bridegroom and the wedding ceremony
The bridegroom wore special clothing Isa 61:10

The bridegroom took part in the procession to the bride's home Mt 25:1–12

The bridegroom had a group of companions Jdg 14:10–11

The bridegroom had a special friend as an attendant Jn 3:29 *See also* Jdg 14:20–15:2; Jn 2:7–10 *The "master of the banquet" was probably the friend who attended the bridegroom.*

The bridegroom was sometimes responsible for giving the wedding banquet Jdg 14:10 *See also* Jn 2:9–10

The bridegroom led his bride to a specially prepared bridal chamber Joel 2:16 *See also* Ps 19:4–5

Bridegrooms were associated with happiness and rejoicing
Jer 7:34 *See also* Isa 62:5; Jer 16:9; 25:10; 33:11; Rev 18:23

Bridegrooms were excused from military service and certain other duties
Dt 24:5 *See also* Dt 20:1–7

Jesus Christ is portrayed as a bridegroom
Mt 9:14–15 pp Mk 2:18–20 pp Lk 5:33–35 *Jesus Christ refers to himself as the bridegroom. See also* Eph 5:22–33

The future coming of Jesus Christ compared to the sudden arrival of the bridegroom
Mt 25:1–10

See also

2212 Christ, head of church	5744 wife
	7020 church, the
5659 bride	8283 joy
5702 husband	9150 Messianic banquet
5708 marriage	
5742 wedding	

brothers

The son of one's parents, or of either mother or father. God's people may be referred to collectively as brothers, all being children of one heavenly Father.

Close relationship between brothers
Lev 21:1–3 *See also* Nu 6:6–7; Dt 28:54; Pr 18:24; Eze 44:25

Duties of brothers
Levirate marriage Dt 25:5–10 *See also* Ge 38:6–11; Mt 22:23–30 pp Mk 12:18–25 pp Lk 20:27–36

Participation in arrangement of marriages for sisters Ge 34:11–17 *See also* Ge 24:50–60

Protection of sisters 2Sa 13:1–33 *See also* Ge 34:24–31; Lev 21:3

Younger brothers taking news of older brothers to their father 1Sa 17:17–18 *See also* Ge 37:12–17

The priority of the eldest brother
Dt 21:15–17 *See also* Ge 43:33; 44:12; 1Sa 20:29; 1Ch 5:1–2; 2Ch 21:1–3; Ps 89:27; Heb 12:16

Examples of younger brothers superseding their elder brothers
Ge 25:21–23 *See also* Ge 48:8–20; Dt 33:13–17; 1Sa 16:6–13; 1Ki 2:22

Brothers as heirs
Nu 27:8–11 *See also* Ecc 4:8

Twin brothers
Ge 25:24–26 *See also* Ge 38:27–30; Mal 1:2–3

Half-brothers
Jdg 11:1–2 *See also* Ge 21:8–9; Jdg 8:30–31; 9:1–6

Brothers-in-law
Nu 10:29–32 *See also* Ge 38:8; Dt 25:5,7; Jdg 4:11

Examples of brothers failing to live up to expectations of them
Ge 4:8–12 *See also* Ge 37:3–4,12–33; 38:6–10; Jdg 9:1–5; 2Ch 21:4

Application of the term "brothers"
To siblings Ge 42:32 *See also* Ge 16:9–12; 25:18; Jdg 16:31; 1Sa 17:17–22; 22:1; 2Ch 21:13; Ne 1:2; 5:14; Job 19:17; 42:11; Pr 17:17; Mt 10:21 pp Mk 13:12 pp Lk 21:16; Mt 13:55 pp Mk 6:3; Jn 7:3–5

To relatives Ru 4:3 *See also* Nu 36:2; Pr 27:10

To members of the same tribe 2Sa 19:11–12 *See also* Nu 8:26

To Israelites Dt 3:18 *See also* Dt 10:9; 17:15; Jdg 20:23; 2Sa 19:41; 1Ch 13:2; Jer 7:15

To descendants of a common ancestor Nu 20:14 *See also* Dt 2:4; 23:7

To equals and fellow-citizens

Lev 19:17 See also Dt 1:16; 15:3; 22:1; 23:19; 2Sa 2:26; Mt 5:22–24; 7:3–5 pp Lk 6:41–42

Love for God must exceed love for brothers

Lk 14:26 See also Dt 33:9; Mt 19:29 pp Mk 10:29–30 pp Lk 18:29–30

Jesus Christ calls his disciples his "brothers"

Mt 12:49–50 pp Mk 3:34–35 pp Lk 8:21 See also Mt 25:34–40; 28:10; Jn 20:17; Heb 2:11

The fraternal relationship among God's people

Fellow Christians called brothers Mt 23:8 See also Ac 15:23; 28:14; 1Co 5:11; 2Co 1:1; 9:3; 11:9; 12:18; 2Th 2:13; Phm 1

Believers urged to love each other 1Th 4:10 See also Ro 12:10; Jas 2:14–17; 1Pe 2:17; 2Pe 1:5–9

The church referred to as "the brothers" Ac 14:2 See also Ac 9:30; 11:1,29; 15:3; 16:2; 17:14; 21:17

Brother as an honorific term

Equals called "brothers" Ge 29:4 See also 1Sa 30:22–23; 2Sa 1:26; 20:9; 1Ki 13:29–30; Ac 1:16; 2:37; 3:17; 7:2; 22:1; 28:17

Fellow Christians called "brothers" 1Co 1:10 See also Ac 9:17; 22:13; Ro 8:12; 11:25; 1Co 2:1; 7:24; 2Co 8:1; Gal 4:31; 1Th 2:14; Heb 3:1; Jas 1:16; 5:10

See also

2212 Christ, head of church	5738 sons
5680 family	6610 adoption, descriptions
5688 firstborn	7115 children of God
5704 inheritance, material	7120 Christians
5711 marriage, restrictions	8298 love for one another
5737 sisters	8452 neighbours, duty to

5662

certificate of divorce

A certificate of divorce was required under Mosaic law

Mk 10:4 pp Mt 19:7 *The certificate provided a divorced wife with some legal protection and permitted her to remarry. See also Dt 24:1–4; Hos 2:2 These words may have been adapted from a divorce bill; Mt 5:31*

God gave his unfaithful people a certificate of divorce

Jer 3:8 See also Isa 50:1 *Unlike Israel, Judah had been given no certificate of divorce. The exile is thus portrayed as only a temporary separation.*

See also

5675 divorce	5744 wife
5711 marriage, restrictions	6242 adultery

5663

childbirth

Seen by Scripture as a token of God's favour, and used figuratively to picture a number of central biblical themes.

Childbirth in the OT

Childbirth as a blessing Ge 1:28 See also Dt 7:14; Ps 127:3–5

Childlessness a cause of shame in Israel Ge 30:1 See also 1Sa 1:6,10–11; Lk 1:24–25

The nature of human childbirth

The pain of childbirth a consequence of the fall Ge 3:16

The need for ceremonial purification after childbirth Lev 12:1–8 *Under the old covenant, unsanctioned contact with blood was ceremonially defiling; Lk 2:24*

The role of midwives in childbirth Ex 1:15–21

The joy of childbirth Ge 21:6; Jn 16:21

Childbirth and salvation

The birth of a Saviour Ge 3:15 *Although childbirth is a focus of judgment, through it the human race continues, and the Messiah comes into the world. See also* Ge 12:2–3; 15:3–6; Isa 7:14; 9:6–7; Mt 1:18–25; Lk 1:35; 2:4–7; Gal 3:16; 4:4; Rev 12:5

Salvation in childbearing 1Ti 2:15 *A Christian mother fulfils her calling in childbearing; some take it to mean she will be kept safe in childbirth. Some, however, take this verse as a reference to Ge 3:15, and the coming of Jesus Christ, as above.*

Childbirth used figuratively

To describe weakness and vulnerability Eze 16:4–6

To describe weakness under judgment 2Ki 19:3 pp Isa 37:3 See also Ps 48:6; Isa 23:4; 26:17–18; Jer 4:31; Hos 2:3; 13:13; Mic 4:10

To describe troubles prior to God's final triumph Mt 24:7–8 pp Mk 13:8 See also Ro 8:22

To describe love and compassion Isa 49:15

To describe regeneration Jn 3:6–7 See also Jn 1:12–13; Jas 1:18; 1Pe 1:23

To describe pastoral concern Gal 4:19

To describe the disciples' joy Jn 16:21–22

To describe triumph and salvation Isa 54:1 See also Gal 4:27; Isa 26:19; 66:7–11

God's sovereignty in childbirth

All children are God's gift Ps 127:3

God controls the events of childbirth Ge 25:22–23; Ps 139:13,16

Childbirth in old age Ge 17:16–19; Lk 1:5–13,18–20,23–25

Childbirth as an answer to prayer Ge 25:21; 1Sa 1:20; Lk 1:13

Childbirth for the barren woman Ps 113:9 See also Ge 25:21; Jdg 13:2–5; 1Sa 2:5; Isa 54:1

Jesus Christ born of a virgin Isa 7:14 *See also* Mt 1:22–23,18; Lk 1:30–31,34–37 *"impossible" births demonstrate God's power and grace and show that salvation comes from the Lord.*

See also

1320 God as Saviour	5410 midwife
2230 Messiah, coming of	5655 birth
2366 Christ, prophecies concerning	5668 children, responsibilities to parents
2515 Christ, birth of	5719 mothers, responsibilities
5093 Eve	6154 fall, the
5225 barrenness	

5664

children

Scripture indicates that children are a gift from God and are to be loved, disciplined and cared for. The term "children of God" is used to describe Christian believers, who must grow up in the faith which they have accepted.

This set of themes consists of the following:

5665 children, attitudes towards
5666 children, needs of
5667 children, responsibilities to God
5668 children, responsibilities to parents
5669 children, examples of

5665
children, attitudes towards

Christians must welcome children as Jesus Christ did. They are used by Christ as an example of how believers should receive the kingdom, and as an example of immaturity by Paul.

Children as a gift from God

Ps 113:9; 127:3 See also Ge 33:5; 48:9; Jos 24:3

Jesus Christ welcomes children

Mt 19:13–14 pp Mk 10:13–16 pp Lk 18:15–17

Those who enter the kingdom must be like children

God's truth is revealed to the childlike Mt 11:25 pp Lk 10:21 See also 1Co 1:26–29

Children as people welcomed by Jesus Christ Mt 18:2–5 pp Mk 9:36–37 pp Lk 9:47–48 See also Mt 10:40–42 pp Mk 9:41; Mt 18:10,14

Children as a picture of immature Christians

1Co 14:20; 1Pe 2:2–3 See also 1Co 13:11; Heb 5:13

Promises to children

Dt 5:16; Ac 2:39 See also Pr 8:32; Eph 6:2–3

Warnings relating to children

Warnings to those who cause children to stumble Mt 18:6 pp Mk 9:42

Warnings to Israel, the disobedient child Isa 30:1 *See also* Isa 30:9

See also

2375 kingdom of God	5881 immaturity
5730 orphans	8205 childlikeness
	8276 humility

5666
children, needs of

Children need love, affection, discipline and guidance from their parents. This is shown through teaching, training, discipline, the meeting of material needs and the provision of a personal example of faith.

Teaching children
Dt 6:6–7 *See also* Ex 10:2; 12:26–27; 13:14–15; Dt 4:9; 6:20–21; 11:19; Pr 1:8; Isa 38:19; Joel 1:3

Training children
Pr 22:6; Eph 6:4 *See also* Dt 31:12–13; Jos 8:35; 2Ki 12:2; Ps 34:11; 78:5; Pr 3:1

Disciplining children
Pr 13:24; Heb 12:7–11 *See also* Pr 19:18; 22:15; 23:13; 29:15,17; 1Ti 3:4,12

Lack of discipline 1Sa 3:13; 1Ki 1:6

Good examples set for children by parents
David: 1Ki 9:4; 2Ch 17:3
2Ch 26:4 *Amaziah*
Lois and Eunice: 2Ti 1:5; 3:15

Bad examples set for children by parents
Ahab and Jezebel: 1Ki 22:52; 2Ch 22:3; Jer 9:14
Mt 14:8 *Herodias*

Provision and care for children
Mt 7:9–11 pp Lk 11:11–13 *See also* 1Sa 2:19; Pr 31:15,21; 2Co 12:14

Love for children
Tit 2:4 *See also* Ge 37:3 *Jacob's special love for Joseph*
Jacob's love for Benjamin:
Ge 44:20,29–31
2Sa 18:33 *David's love for Absalom;*
Lk 15:20 *the father's love for the prodigal son*

See also

5218 authority in home	7797 teaching
5680 family	8230 discipline
5731 parents	8313 nurture
	8753 favouritism

5667
children, responsibilities to God

The responsibilities of children to God as their heavenly Father include honouring and obeying him.

The responsibilities of children to their heavenly Father
To honour and obey him in reverent fear Ps 34:11 *See also* Pr 2:5; 9:10

To seek wisdom Pr 4:5–7 *See also* Pr 1:1–4; 8:32–33; 10:1

To listen and learn Pr 1:8–9 *See also* Pr 4:1–4; 23:22

To praise God Ps 8:2 *See also* Mt 21:15–16

To join in worship Ne 12:43 *See also* Jos 8:35

Relationship to Jesus Christ transcends the child-parent relationship
Lk 18:29–30 pp Mt 19:29
pp Mk 10:29–30

See also

1040 God, fatherhood	8361 wisdom
	8444 honouring God
5052 responsibility to God	8460 pleasing God
8120 following Christ	8664 praise

5668
children, responsibilities to parents

Children owe their parents certain important responsibilities, including the duty to honour and obey them.

The duties of children towards their parents
They are to honour their parents
Ex 20:12 pp Dt 5:16 *See also* Pr 17:6; Mk 7:10; Eph 6:1–3

They are to obey their parents
Col 3:20–21 *See also* Eph 6:1

They are to behave well Pr 20:11

Children as a blessing and source of joy to their parents
Ps 127:4–5; Pr 23:24 *See also* Ps 128:3; Pr 15:20; 27:11; 29:3; Lk 15:23–24

Children born to barren mothers bring special joy
Sarah: Ge 18:11; 21:2
Rachel: Ge 29:31; 30:22
Manoah's wife: Jdg 13:2,24
Hannah: 1Sa 1:5,20
Elizabeth: Lk 1:7,24,57

Children as a source of grief and disappointment to their parents
Pr 17:25 *See also* 1Sa 8:3; Pr 17:21; 19:13,26; 28:7; 29:15

The punishment of children
The punishment of wicked children
Ex 21:15; Lev 20:9; Dt 21:18–21; Pr 30:17; 2Ti 3:2

The punishment of children for the sins of their fathers
Ex 20:5–6; Nu 14:18; Jer 31:29–30
Jeremiah here stresses the importance of individual responsibility in the present crisis without denying the notion of corporate responsibility; Jer 32:18

See also

5225 barrenness	5719 mothers, responsibilities
5663 childbirth	
5685 fathers, responsibilities	6160 fathers, sin of
	8453 obedience

5669
children, examples of

In Scripture specific children are

marked out as belonging to the Lord. Mention of others is made in association with miracles or notable situations.

The child Jesus Christ
Mt 1:23 *See also* Mt 2:11; Lk 2:34,49–51

Other notable children
Ex 2:7–8 *Moses;* Jdg 11:36 *Jephthah's daughter*
Samuel: 1Sa 2:18,26
David: 1Sa 16:11; 17:33,41–42
2Ki 5:2 *the young girl who helped Naaman;* Lk 1:80 *John the Baptist;*
2Ti 3:15 *Timothy*

Children in the miracles of Jesus Christ
Jairus' daughter: Mt 9:18 pp Mk 5:22–23 pp Lk 8:41–42; Mt 9:23–25 pp Mk 5:38–43 pp Lk 8:49–55; Mt 15:21–28 pp Mk 7:24–30 *Canaanite woman's daughter;* Mt 17:14–18 pp Mk 9:17–27 pp Lk 9:38–43 *boy with epilepsy;* Lk 7:11–15 *widow's son at Nain;* Jn 4:46–52 *official's son at Capernaum*
Jn 6:9 *the boy who gave his lunch to help feed the crowd*

See also

2078 Christ, sonship of	5652 babies
	5661 brothers
2515 Christ, birth of	5674 daughters
2520 Christ, childhood	5688 firstborn
	5737 sisters
5098 John the Baptist	5738 sons
	6608 adoption
5101 Moses	

5671
clan

A social unit, larger than a family but smaller than a tribe.

Membership of a clan
Jdg 6:15 *See also* Lev 25:10; Jos 7:14–18; Ru 2:1; 1Sa 9:21; 10:17–21; 18:18

Marriage and the clan
Jdg 12:9 *See also* Ge 24:34–41; Nu 36:1–12

Inheritance within the clan
Nu 27:8–11

The responsibility of the clan for protection and revenge
Lev 25:47–49 *See also* Ru 3:7–12; 4:1–12; 2Sa 14:5–7

The clans of Israel listed
Nu 26:1–61

The land allocated to the clans
Jos 13:15–33; 15:1–19:48

Non-Israelite clans
Ge 10:5 *See also* Ge 10:15–20,31–32; 36:40–43

See also

5680 family	7266 tribes of Israel
5704 inheritance, material	7388 kinsman-redeemer
7135 Israel, people of God	

5672

concubines

A woman, often a servant or slave, with whom a man had regular sexual relations, but to whom he was not married. A concubine did not have the rights of a wife and her children were not rightful heirs, though a wife might offer a servant to her husband as a concubine to have children on her behalf.

Concubines and wives
Concubines were distinguished from wives 1Ki 11:3 *Having concubines alongside wives was accepted in a polygamous society. See also* Jdg 8:30–31; 2Sa 5:13; 19:5; 2Ch 11:21; Da 5:2–3

Concubines were sometimes called wives Ge 16:3 *Hagar was Abraham's "wife" only in a secondary sense. See also* Ge 25:1 *Keturah was one of Abraham's concubines;* Jdg 19:1–4

Concubines did not have the rights of a wife Ge 21:8–14 *They were more easily dismissed;* Ex 21:7–11 *They did have some legal protection.*

Maidservants were given as concubines Ge 30:3–6 *Bilhah's sons would be regarded by Rachel as her own and would thus share the inheritance with Jacob's other sons. See also* Ge 30:9; 16:1–2; Gal 4:22–23

The tension between concubines and wives Ge 16:4–6 *Though Abraham's concubine, Hagar's status was still that of servant. See also* Ge 21:9; Pr 30:23; Gal 4:29

Children born to concubines were not rightful heirs Ge 21:10–12 *See also* Ge 25:5–6; Jdg 9:18; Ro 9:7; Gal 4:30; Heb 11:18

Concubines were a symbol of possession
By taking Jacob's concubine, Reuben laid premature claim to his father's estate Ge 35:22 *See also* Ge 49:3–4; 1Ch 5:1

Taking the concubine(s) of a king was tantamount to laying claim to the kingdom 2Sa 3:7 *Abner is accused here of trying to usurp Ish-Bosheth's inheritance. See also* 2Sa 12:8; 16:21–22; 1Ki 2:21–22

Further examples of concubines
Ge 22:23–24 *Nahor's concubine, Reumah;* Ge 36:12 *Eliphaz' concubine, Timna;* Jdg 19:1 *a Levite's concubine;* 2Sa 15:16 *David's concubines;* 1Ch 1:32 *Abraham's concubine, Keturah;* 1Ch 2:46–48 *Caleb's concubines, Ephah and Maacah;* 1Ch 7:14 *Manasseh's concubine;* Est 2:14 *Xerxes' concubines;* Da 5:23 *Belshazzar's concubines*

See also
5703 inheritance	5732 polygamy
5708 marriage	5744 wife
5717 monogamy	7446 slavery

5673

cousins

Marriage to cousins
Nu 36:11 *See also* 1Ch 23:22

Family responsibilities undertaken by cousins where there were no closer relatives
Est 2:7 *See also* Lev 25:47–49; Jer 32:6–12

Cousins mentioned in Scripture
Col 4:10 *See also* Lev 10:4

See also
5681 family	5711 marriage, restrictions

5674

daughters

The female offspring of parents. Daughters lived in their father's house, under his protection, until marriage. Usually they became his heirs only if he had no sons to inherit his estate. Normally they shared in the inheritance of their husbands.

Protection of daughters
Fathers were responsible for protecting their daughters Ge 31:50 *See also* Ge 19:12–13,15–17; Nu 30:3–5

Examples of fathers who failed to protect their daughters Ge 19:8 *See also* Jdg 19:24; 2Sa 13:6–14

Marriage of daughters
Fathers were responsible for arranging marriages for their daughters Ge 34:8–9 *See also* Ge 29:26; Jos 15:16–17 pp Jdg 1:12–13; Jdg 12:9; 21:1; 1Sa 18:17–21; 25:44

Fathers received a bride-price from their daughters' husbands 1Sa 18:25 *See also* Ge 29:16–27

Fathers gave a dowry to their daughters 1Ki 9:16 *See also* Jos 15:17–19 pp Jdg 1:13–15

Sometimes the marriage of a daughter was the basis of a political alliance 1Ki 3:1 *See also* Da 11:6,17

In cases of dispute, parents were expected to prove their daughter's virginity Dt 22:13–21

Inheritance of daughters
If a man had no sons, the inheritance went to his daughters Nu 27:1–11 *See also* Jos 17:3–6

Daughters who inherited their father's property were obliged to marry within his clan Nu 36:1–12

Job allocated his daughters an inheritance Job 42:13–15

Priests' daughters
Lev 10:14 *See also* Lev 21:1–2,9; 22:12–13; Nu 18:11,19; Eze 44:25

Slavery of daughters
In dire circumstances fathers

sometimes sold their daughters into slavery Ne 5:5 *See also* Ex 21:7

A slave girl married to a son was to be accorded the rights of a daughter Ex 21:9

Immorality of daughters
Prostitution of daughters forbidden Lev 19:29 *See also* Lev 21:9

Incest of Lot's daughters Ge 19:30–38

Daughters-in-law
Sexual relations with daughters-in-law forbidden Lev 18:15 *See also* Lev 20:12; Eze 22:11

Examples of daughters-in-law Ru 4:14–15 *See also* Ge 38:6–26; Ru 1:3–17

Daughters in a spiritual role
Ac 21:9 *See also* Joel 2:28; Ac 2:17

An adopted daughter
Est 2:7

Daughter in a non-literal sense
Of an area, town or country or its population Mt 21:5 pp Jn 12:15 *See also* 2Ki 19:21; Ps 137:8; Isa 10:30; 23:12; 52:2; Jer 6:23; 48:18; 51:33; La 1:15; 2:10; Mic 4:8; Zep 3:14; Zec 2:7; 9:9

Of the female inhabitants of an area, town or country Lk 23:27–29 *See also* Ge 24:3,13; 2Sa 1:24; SS 3:5; 5:8; Isa 32:9–11; Eze 13:17; 32:18

Of the female descendants Lk 13:16 *See also* 1Pe 3:5–6

As an honorific term Mt 9:22 pp Mk 5:34 pp Lk 8:48

Daughters in a theological sense
God's people are his sons and daughters 2Co 6:18 *See also* Jer 14:17; 31:21–22

Family relationships must be subservient to one's relationship with God Mt 10:37 *See also* Mt 10:35 pp Lk 12:53

See also
5664 children	5708 marriage
5679 dowry	5724 offspring
5680 family	5737 sisters
5684 fathers	5738 sons
5695 girls	6239 prostitution
5701 heir	7115 children of God

5675

divorce

The legal dissolution of a marriage. Though not part of God's original intention for marriage, divorce is permitted under certain circumstances, especially marital unfaithfulness. In general, properly divorced parties are free to remarry.

5676

divorce, in OT

Usually initiated by the husband who issued his wife with a certificate of divorce and sent her from his home, divorce broke the marriage bond and allowed parties to remarry. It was not part of God's original purpose for marriage, and is permitted only because of human sinfulness. God is depicted as taking divorce proceedings against adulterous Israel.

The nature of divorce
Divorce dissolves a marriage Mk 10:4 pp Mt 19:7 *The certificate of divorce was a legal document ending the marriage. See also* Lev 22:12–13 *Divorce ends the restrictions on a priest's daughter which were the result of her marriage;* Nu 30:9 *Following divorce a husband is no longer responsible for his wife;* Dt 24:1–2 *Divorce properly entered into allows the parties to remarry;* Hos 2:2; Mt 5:31

Divorce was not God's original intention Mal 2:10–16 *God's displeasure at those of his people who divorced their Jewish wives to marry foreigners, thus breaking faith with their partners and with God;* Mt 19:4–8 pp Mk 10:5–9 *The Law of Moses did not command divorce, but regulated an existing practice, particularly to protect the wife. See also* Ge 1:27; 2:24

Circumstances permitting divorce
Displeasure Dt 24:1 *See also* Dt 21:13–14; Mt 19:3

Returning exiles were required to divorce their foreign wives Ezr 10:10–11 *See also* Ezr 10:2–3

Circumstances where divorce was not allowed
Dt 22:13–19 *where a husband makes false accusations about his wife's virginity;* Dt 22:28–29 *where the marriage is contracted following the rape of a virgin*

Restrictions on remarriage after divorce
Former partners who marry others Dt 24:3–4 *See also* Jer 3:1

Priests could not marry divorcees Lev 21:7,14; Eze 44:22

The divorce between God and Israel
It was due to Israel's unfaithfulness Jer 3:6–10 *See also* Isa 50:1; Jer 31:32

God's desire for reconciliation Isa 54:4–8 *See also* Isa 62:4–5; Eze 16:60–63; Hos 2:14–16

See also
5375 law	6243 adultery,
5662 certificate of	spiritual
divorce	8248 faithfulness
5708 marriage	8839 unfaithfulness
5740 virgin	

5677
divorce, amongst believers

Jesus Christ challenged the liberal approach to divorce taken by some rabbis of his day, and upheld the idea of marriage as a lifelong commitment. Remarriage after divorce is generally classed as adultery and, where possible,

---

divorced parties should seek reconciliation. There are circumstances, however, where remarriage is permissible.

The liberal attitude to divorce
Mt 19:3 *See also* Dt 21:14; 24:1

The undesirability of divorce
God's plan for marriage Mt 19:4–6 pp Mk 10:6–9 *See also* Ge 1:27; 2:24; Mal 2:15; Eph 5:31

Divorce is permitted because of human sinfulness Mt 19:8 pp Mk 10:5

Christians should not seek divorce 1Co 7:10 *This command, echoing Jesus Christ's words, applies where both parties are believers. See also* 1Co 7:12–14

Remarriage after divorce
Believers should seek reconciliation 1Co 7:11 *See also* Dt 24:2–4 *Marriage to another after divorce prevents reconciliation.*

Remarriage after divorce is classed as adultery Lk 16:18 pp Mk 10:11–12 *This is a general rule, though there may be exceptions (see below). See also* Ro 7:2–3; 1Co 7:39

Remarriage may be permissible 1Co 7:27–28 *"unmarried" means literally "freed from a wife" and thus may be applied to those widowed or properly divorced. It is no sin for them to (re)marry.*

Possible grounds for divorce and remarriage Mt 19:9; 1Co 7:15 *See also* Jer 3:8 *God divorced Israel because of her adultery;* Mt 1:18–19; 5:32

See also
6242 adultery	6718 reconciliation,
6658 freedom	believers

5679
dowry

A present given by a woman's father on her marriage. At betrothal the bridegroom gave a compensatory gift, known as the bride-price, to the woman's family.

The bride-price
Ex 22:16–17 *See also* Ge 34:12

Usually it consisted of payment in kind Ge 24:53 *See also* Ge 29:16–28; 31:41; 1Sa 18:25; 2Sa 3:14

The dowry given by the bride's father
1Ki 9:16 *See also* Ge 24:59–61; 29:24,29; Jdg 1:14–15

See also
5325 gifts	5660 bridegroom
5654 betrothal	5708 marriage
5659 bride	5742 wedding

5680
family

People who are linked by marriage or physical descent. The western idea of a "nuclear" family represents a narrow definition of the scope of the family. The ancient Near East had a

---

broader and more extended understanding of family, which is often reflected in the Scriptural material.

5681
family, nature of

A unit ordained by God for the comfort and protection of its members. It is usually a group of relatives, but the people of God are also seen as a family.

The scope of the family in Scripture
The family unit Ge 43:7 *See also* Ex 1:1; 12:3; Jdg 11:2; 1Sa 1:21; 27:3; 2Sa 2:3; 1Ki 17:15; 1Ch 13:14 *The family of Obed-Edom is blessed by the presence of the ark;* Pr 27:27; 31:15 *The wife of noble character provides for her family;* Mk 3:21; Lk 12:52; Ac 16:33–34 *The Philippian jailer and his family are baptised;* 1Ti 5:8

The extended family or clan Ge 24:37–38 *See also* Ge 24:40; 46:27; 50:22; Nu 2:2; 18:1 *the priesthood of Aaron and his family;* Dt 25:5 *Levirate marriage provides for the continuity of the family;* Jos 2:17–18; 6:23,25; 1Sa 22:22; 1Ki 14:14; 2Ki 11:1 pp 2Ch 22:10 *Athaliah destroys the royal family of Judah;* Ezr 10:16; Jer 35:3; 38:17; Da 1:3

The descendants of any individual Jn 7:42 *See also* Dt 25:10; Jos 13:29; 1Sa 2:31–32,36; 3:11–13; Da 11:7

The people of God Heb 2:10–15 *See also* Ps 22:22; Am 3:1; Gal 6:10; 1Pe 4:17

Marriage obligations and restrictions within the family
Marriage within the wider family circle was preferable in early times Jdg 14:3 *See also* Ge 24:1–9,37,40; 27:46–28:2,6–9; Ex 2:1

Incestuous marriage was forbidden Lev 18:6–18 *See also* Lev 20:17,19–21; Dt 27:20–23; Mt 14:3 pp Mk 6:17; 1Co 5:1–5

The obligation to marry the widow of a dead brother Dt 25:5–10 *See also* Ge 38:8–10; Ru 2:19–20; 4:1–10; Mt 22:23–32 pp Mk 12:18–27 pp Lk 20:27–38

Laws of inheritance kept property within the family
Nu 27:1–11 *See also* Lev 25:25–28; Job 42:13–15

Examples of family solidarity
Ge 14:8–16 *Abraham and Lot;* 2Sa 18:31–33 *David and Absalom;* Ru 1:11–18 *Naomi and Ruth;* Ne 4:13; Ac 23:12–24; 1Ti 5:3–4 *Family solidarity is encouraged.*

See also
2535 Christ, family of	5732 polygamy
5671 clan	5736 singleness
5688 firstborn	6608 adoption
5701 heir	7140 people of God
5703 inheritance	7388 kinsman-
5708 marriage	redeemer
5717 monogamy	

5682
family, significance of

God created the family and is deeply concerned for its welfare. Scripture uses family metaphors to describe the relationship between God and his people.

God created the family
Ps 68:6 See also Ge 1:26–27; 2:23–24

God cares for the families of those who honour him
Ge 7:1 See also Ge 6:18 pp Dt 5:8–10; 2Sa 6:11; Jer 35:18–19; 38:17–18

God judges families who disobey him
Ex 20:4–5 See also Nu 16:23–32; Dt 11:6; Jos 7:24–26; 1Sa 3:12–14; 2Sa 24:17

Families in Israel
The extended family was the basic social unit Ne 7:5 See also Lev 25:10; 27:16; Nu 2:32; 4:40

Family heads were community leaders Nu 36:1 See also Nu 1:4; 31:26; 1Ki 8:1; 2Ch 1:2

Families had religious obligations Dt 12:7 See also Ex 12:22–23; Dt 12:11–12; 1Sa 1:21

Families were to teach their children God's law Ps 78:5–7 See also Ge 18:19; Ex 12:26–27; Dt 4:9; 6:6–7; Pr 1:8–9

The relationship between God and his people described in family metaphors
They are his family Gal 6:10 See also Am 3:1; Eph 3:15; 1Pe 4:17

They are his children Jn 1:12–13 See also Dt 14:1; Isa 63:16; Hos 11:1–4; Ro 8:15–17; Gal 4:4–7; Eph 1:5

They are brothers and sisters in God's family Heb 2:11 See also Ps 22:22; Isa 8:17–18; Mt 12:50 pp Lk 8:21; Mk 3:31–34; Heb 2:12–17

The salvation of families
Ac 16:34 See also Ac 11:14; 18:8; 1Co 1:16

Good family management as a qualification for church office
1Ti 3:4–5 See also 1Ti 3:12

Christians are to support their families
1Ti 5:8 See also 1Ti 5:4

The urgent demands of the kingdom of God should take priority over family responsibilities
Lk 9:59–60 pp Mt 8:21–22 See also Mk 3:31–34; Lk 9:61–62; Mt 10:34–38 pp Lk 12:51–53; Mic 7:6

See also
1040	God, fatherhood
5218	authority in home
5661	brothers
5664	children
5696	grandchildren
5697	grandparents
5700	headship
5702	husband
5731	parents
5737	sisters
5744	wife
8232	discipline, family

5684
fathers

The male parent of children. Scripture indicates the role and responsibilities of fathers, and shows how God can be thought of as a loving father, who directs and guides his children.

5685
fathers, responsibilities of

Fathers have a responsibility to love, instruct and discipline their children in the ways of the Lord. In return they are to be honoured and obeyed by their children.

The role of fathers
To love and care for their children Ps 103:13 See also Dt 1:31; Job 1:4–5; Mt 7:9–11 pp Lk 11:11–13; Col 3:21

To discipline their children Pr 13:24 See also Dt 8:5; 21:18–21; Pr 3:11–12; 15:5; 19:18; 22:15; 23:13; 29:15; 1Ti 3:2–5,12; Heb 12:7–11

To instruct their children Ps 78:2–8 See also Dt 4:9; 6:6–7,20–24; 11:18–21; 31:13; Pr 13:1; 22:6; Eph 6:4

The rights of fathers
To be honoured by their children Ex 20:12 pp Dt 5:16 See also Lev 19:3; Mt 15:4 pp Mk 7:10; Ex 21:17; Mt 19:17–19 pp Mk 10:18–19 pp Lk 18:19–20; Eph 6:2–3

To be obeyed by their children Col 3:20 See also Dt 21:18–21; Pr 6:20; 8:32; Lk 2:51; Eph 6:1

To be heeded by their children Pr 23:22 See also Pr 1:8; 4:1,10; 13:1

The joy of fathers
Pr 23:24 See also Ps 127:3–5; 128:3–4; Pr 10:1; 28:7; 29:3

The sorrow of fathers
Pr 17:21 See also Pr 10:1; 17:25; 19:13

The roles of fathers-in-law
Ge 29:21–23; 31:39–42; Ex 3:1; 18:14–27; Jdg 19:3–9; 1Sa 4:19–21; Jn 18:13

Children's responsibility to honour their parents
Ex 20:12 pp Dt 5:16 *"Honour" implies respect, obedience and care for the parents' needs.* See also Lev 19:3; Mt 19:19 pp Mk 10:19 pp Lk 18:20; Eph 6:1–3

Penalties for disobeying parents
Ex 21:15,17; Dt 21:18–21; Pr 20:20; Mt 15:4–6; Mk 7:10–13

The ministry of Jesus Christ may produce conflict within families
Lk 12:53 pp Mt 10:35–36

Following Jesus Christ involves a commitment to him even deeper than love of one's parents
Mt 10:37 See also Lk 14:26

See also
5218	authority in home	5738	sons
5664	children	6160	fathers, sin of
5674	daughters	7796	teaching
5680	family	8120	following Christ
5696	grandchildren	8232	discipline, family
5697	grandparents		
5702	husband		

5686
fathers, examples of

The ideal father, from a biblical perspective, is one who loves God, is obedient to him and reflects this in his daily living and in the care and upbringing of his children.

Fathers who followed divine principles within their families
Abraham Ge 18:19 See also Ge 17:1–7,18–20; 21:1–5,8–13; 22:1–18

Zechariah Lk 1:5–20 See also Lk 1:62–80

The father of the prodigal Lk 15:11–31

Fathers who acted wrongly
Through favouritism Ge 37:3–4 See also Ge 25:28

Through lack of discipline 1Sa 2:22–25 See also 1Sa 2:27–36; 3:11–18

The intercession of fathers for their children
Abraham Ge 17:18–22

David 1Ch 29:10–19 See also 2Sa 12:15–23

Job Job 1:4–5

The father of the demoniac Mt 17:14–15 pp Mk 9:17–18 pp Lk 9:38–39

The royal official Jn 4:46–49

See also
1040	God, fatherhood	5718	mothers
1245	God of the fathers	5730	orphans
1250	Abba	5731	parents
5700	headship	7718	elders
		8753	favouritism

5688
firstborn

The firstborn male in a family; as in many cultures, in an Israelite family the eldest son had unique privileges, including the right of inheritance. The title "firstborn" was therefore a title of honour.

The privileges of the firstborn
The place of honour in the family Ge 10:15 *In this and other lists, the firstborn is specially noted;* Ge 43:33 See also Ge 22:21; 25:13; 35:23; 36:15; 46:8; Dt 33:17

The right of inheritance Dt 21:15–17; 2Ch 21:3

The right to a blessing Ge 27:19,30–39

The sin of despising these privileges Ge 25:31–34 See also Heb 12:16–17

These privileges could be transferred
Ge 48:14 *See also* Ge 48:18–19; 49:3–4;
1Ch 2:3; 5:1–2; 26:10

The death of the firstborn a great tragedy
Ex 4:23 *See also* Ex 11:4–6; 12:12,29;
Nu 33:4; Jos 6:26; 1Ki 16:34; Ps 78:51;
105:36; 135:8; 136:10; Heb 11:28

Repentance likened to grief over the
death of a firstborn Zec 12:10

God's claim upon the firstborn
In ancient times Ge 4:4 *See also*
Ge 22:1–2,12

After the exodus Ex 13:1–2 *See also*
Ex 13:11–15; 22:29; 34:19–20;
Nu 18:15,17; Dt 14:23; 15:19; Ne 10:36

The Levites consecrated in place of the
firstborn Nu 3:11–13,39–51; 8:15–18

The offering of a firstborn insufficient
to redeem from the consequences of
sin Mic 6:7

Heathen sacrifice of the firstborn
2Ch 28:3; Eze 20:26

Jesus Christ the "firstborn"
The firstborn of Mary Lk 2:7,22–23

The firstborn of God Ro 8:29 *"firstborn"
here means that Jesus Christ is above
creation, rather than part of it. The title
"firstborn" has strong Messianic
associations;* Col 1:15 ; Heb 1:6

The "firstborn from the dead" Col 1:18
See also Rev 1:5

God's people honoured as his "firstborn"
Israel Ex 4:22

David Ps 89:27 *prophetic of Jesus Christ*

Ephraim Jer 31:9

The church Heb 12:23

See also

1335 blessing	5701 heir
2069 Christ, pre-eminence	5703 inheritance
	6710 privileges
2218 Christ, Son of God	7024 church, nature of
4442 firstfruits	7222 exodus, events of
5095 Jacob, life	
5657 birthright	8218 consecration

5689

friendlessness

The bitter experience of the absence
of friendship, leading to a sense of
isolation and despair. It is often
blamed on the faithlessness of others
or even on God himself.

The experience of friendlessness
The darkness of being alone Ps 88:18
See also Ps 88:8; 102:7; 142:4

Contempt and rejection Ps 31:11–12
See also Ps 38:11

Hatred and loathing Job 19:13–19 *See
also* Job 30:10

Slander and conspiracy Ps 31:13 *See
also* Jer 20:10

Examples of friendlessness
Elijah 1Ki 19:10

Jesus Christ Mk 14:50 *See also* Isa 53:3;
Mt 26:56; Jn 16:32

The prodigal son Lk 15:16

The lame man at the pool of Bethesda
Jn 5:7

Paul 2Ti 4:16 *See also* 2Ti 4:10–11

The undesirability of friendlessness
Ge 2:18; Ecc 4:9–12

Cultivating true friends is the way to avoid friendlessness
1Sa 18:1; Ps 119:63 *See also* Lk 16:19

See also

5398 loss	5805 comfort
5690 friends	5901 loneliness
5734 relationships	7921 fellowship
5770 abandonment	8727 enemies

5690

friends

Those to whom one is close.
Scripture stresses that friendship is
often but not always a positive thing:
where good friends can be invaluable
in the life of faith, bad friends can be
obstacles to the faith of believers, or
even lead them astray totally.

5691
friends, good

Those whose commitment from the
heart is shown in practical, often
sacrificial, care, love and service.
They are a source of encouragement,
sympathy, comfort and support in
time of need. Such relationships are
to be cultivated, especially among
believers.

Examples of good friends
David and Jonathan 1Sa 18:1–3 *See
also* 1Sa 20:17,42; 2Sa 1:26

Job's friends Job 2:11

Ruth and Naomi Ru 1:16–17

Paul's friends in ministry Ro 16:3–5 *See
also* 2Co 2:12–13 *Titus;* Php 2:25
Epaphroditus; Col 4:7 *Tychicus;* Col 4:14
Luke; 2Ti 1:2–4 *Timothy;* Phm 1
Philemon

Other examples 1Sa 22:23 *David and
Abiathar;* 2Sa 10:2 *David and Nahash;*
2Sa 15:19–21 *David and Ittai;*
2Sa 15:32–37 *David and Hushai;* 1Ki 5:1
David and Hiram; 2Ki 2:2 *Elijah and
Elisha;* 2Ki 10:15 *Jehonadab and Jehu;*
Mk 2:3–4 *the friends who brought the
paralysed man to Jesus Christ*

The benefits brought by good friends
Comfort and sympathy Job 2:11–13 *See
also* Pr 17:17

Support and encouragement
1Sa 23:16–17; Pr 18:24; Ecc 4:9–10 *See
also* Pr 27:10; Ecc 4:11–12; Am 3:3;
Mt 27:55–56; 28:1; Ro 1:11–12

Sacrificial service Jn 15:13 *See also*
Ro 5:7

Shared joy and sorrow Lk 15:5;
Ro 12:15

Loving rebuke Pr 27:6,9; Eph 4:15

Encouragement in good works
Ro 14:13; Heb 10:24

Challenge Pr 27:17

Good friendship among believers
Unity in the love and fear of the LORD
Ps 119:63 *See also* Mal 3:16; Php 4:1

Worshipping together Ps 55:13–14;
133:1; Ac 2:42–43,46–47

Sharing possessions Ac 2:44–45;
4:32–35; 11:29

Serving together Gal 2:8–9; Php 1:3–5

Praying for one another Job 42:10;
2Th 1:11–12; Jas 5:16

Living peaceably Ro 12:18; Php 4:2–3

Covering sins Pr 10:12; 16:28; 17:9 *A
friend does not stir up trouble by spreading
details of wrongs suffered, but rather seeks
reconciliation;* 1Co 13:6; 1Pe 4:8

Restoring from sin Gal 6:1–2;
Jas 5:19–20

Jesus Christ is the friend of sinners
Mt 11:19 pp Lk 7:34

See also

5086 David, rise of	8287 joy, experience
5108 Paul, life of	8292 love
5874 happiness	8304 loyalty
5895 intimacy	8414 encouragement
8122 friendship with God	8445 hospitality
8252 faithfulness, relationships	8475 self-denial

5692
friends, bad

Those who are close or who exercise
influence, who prove to be
unreliable or deceptive or who lead
astray. Scripture provides numerous
instructive examples of the negative
effects of bad friends upon believers.

Friends who lead astray
From worship Dt 13:6–8 *See also*
Dt 23:6; 1Ki 11:2

From good character 1Co 15:33 *See
also* Pr 12:26; 22:24–25

From friendship with God Jas 4:4 *See
also* Isa 52:11; Jer 9:4–5; Mic 7:5;
2Co 6:14–18; 7:1

Friends who are unreliable
In their commitment Job 6:14–17

In their trustworthiness Ps 41:9 *See also*
Ps 38:11; 55:20–21; Ob 7; Mt 26:14–15;
Jn 13:18 *Jesus Christ is speaking about his
betrayal by Judas.*

In their support 2Ti 4:16 *See also*
2Ti 4:10

Examples of bad friends
Those who lead astray Ge 3:12 *See also*
1Ki 12:8–11; Est 5:14

Those who are inconstant Job 19:19
*Presumably these friends are not merely the
ones who attempted to comfort him. See
also* Mt 26:31,33–34; 2Ti 4:10,16

See also

5798 betrayal	8755 folly
5835 disappointment	8759 fools
5863 flattery	8767 hypocrisy
5868 gossip	8773 jealousy
5973 unreliability	8841 unfaithfulness
6145 deceit	to people
8729 enemies of	
Christ	

5694

generation

The population as a whole at any one time, or the interval of time separating parents and children.

All the contemporaries of an individual
Ge 7:1 See also Ex 1:6; Jdg 2:10; Ps 24:6; 78:8; 112:2; Jer 2:31; 7:29; Mt 11:16 pp Lk 7:31; Mt 24:32–34 pp Mk 13:28–30 pp Lk 21:29–32; Ac 2:40; 13:36; Php 2:14–16

The everlasting kingdom of God
La 5:19 See also Ps 72:5; 145:13; Da 4:3; Eph 3:20–21

The passing of time expressed in terms of generations
Ex 3:15 See also Ge 9:12; 17:12; Ex 12:17; 20:5 pp Dt 5:9 the enduring consequences of rebellion; Ex 31:16; Lev 23:41; Nu 15:38; 35:29; Dt 29:22; Jos 22:27; Est 9:28; Ps 72:5 traditionally taken as referring to the Messiah; Ps 105:8; Isa 34:10; Jer 50:39; Lk 1:46–50

Past generations
Isa 51:9 See also Dt 32:7; Job 8:8; Isa 41:4; 61:4; Eph 3:4–5; Col 1:25–26

The requirement to teach the next generation
Dt 4:9 See also Dt 6:6–7; 32:7; Ps 22:30; 71:18; 78:1–8; 79:13

Time references by specific numbers of generations
Mt 1:17 See also Ex 34:6–7; Nu 14:18; Dt 7:9; 23:2–3,7–8; 2Ki 10:30; 15:12; 1Ch 16:15; Job 42:16

The generation that died in the wilderness
Nu 32:13 See also Dt 1:34–36; 2:14; 32:5,20; Heb 3:7–11; Ps 95:7–11

Jesus Christ's comments concerning his own wicked generation
Mk 8:38 See also Mt 12:39–42 pp Lk 11:29–32; Mt 12:43–45; 16:4 pp Mk 8:12; Mt 17:17 pp Mk 9:19 pp Lk 9:41; Mt 23:33–36; Lk 11:47–51; 17:22–25

See also

1140 God, the eternal	6178 hardness of
5664 children	heart
5724 offspring	7230 genealogies

5695

girls

Scripture provides insights into, and examples of, the way in which girls

have a place in the purposes of God. Although the OT tends to portray girls mainly as potential wives or sexual partners, Jesus Christ's raising of Jairus' daughter can be seen as a symbol of the positive value placed on them.

The portrayal of girls in the OT
As potential wives Jdg 21:21–25 See also Ge 24:12–51; Jdg 11:29–40; 1Sa 18:17–27

As sexual partners Jdg 19:24 This way of treating girls as mere sexual objects illustrates the moral corruption of the men of Gibeah. Though not condemned in this passage, such behaviour was totally contrary to OT law. See also Ge 19:1–8; 34:1–4

Chaste girls were to be protected but promiscuous girls were to be punished Dt 22:13–21

Girls undertaking various kinds of work
As slaves or servants Ex 21:7–9 See also Ru 2:8–9; 1Ki 1:1–4; Ac 12:13–14

Drawing water and tending animals Ex 2:16 See also Ge 24:15–20; 1Sa 9:11

Repairing the walls of Jerusalem Ne 3:12

In domestic service 1Sa 8:13

The place of girls in serving the purposes of God
Girls receive ministry from Jesus Christ and the apostles Mk 5:35–43 pp Mt 9:23–25 pp Lk 8:49–56 See also Mt 15:21–28 pp Mk 7:24–30; Ac 16:16–18

Girls receive and use spiritual gifts Ac 2:16–17 See also Joel 2:28; Ac 21:8–9

Examples of girls serving the purposes of God 2Ki 5:2–6 The example of this servant girl, instrumental in Naaman's healing, shows that girls have a value and a status before God not generally acknowledged in OT culture; Est 2:1–18 Having become queen under the providence of God, Esther, chosen while a young virgin, is later able to use her influence to save the Jews from fierce persecution; Lk 1:26–33 Mary should be regarded as a girl, as she is a virgin betrothed and not a woman married.

See also

5652 babies	5731 parents
5664 children	5735 sexuality
5674 daughters	5740 virgin
5707 male and	5744 wife
female	5745 women
5708 marriage	6240 rape

5696

grandchildren

Grandchildren mentioned in Scripture
Terah's grandson, Lot Ge 11:31

Nahor's grandchildren Ge 29:5 See also Ge 24:47–48

Laban's grandchildren Ge 31:55 See also Ge 31:26–28

Zibeon the Hivite's granddaughter, Oholibamah Ge 36:2 See also Ge 36:14

Esau's grandchildren Ge 36:12–13 See also Ge 36:16–17

Jacob's grandchildren Ge 46:7 See also Ge 45:10

Gideon's grandson Jdg 8:22

Abdon's grandsons Jdg 12:13–14

Saul's grandson, Mephibosheth 2Sa 19:24 See also 2Sa 9:9–10; 16:3

Omri's granddaughter, Athaliah 2Ki 8:26 pp 2Ch 22:2

The grandsons of the sons of Ulam 1Ch 8:40

Nebuchadnezzar's grandson Jer 27:6–7

Grandchildren as representative of descendants
Ex 10:1–2 See also Dt 4:25–26; 2Ki 17:41

Believing grandchildren have a responsibility to care for their grandparents
1Ti 5:4

See also

5664 children	5697 grandparents
5680 family	5724 offspring

5697

grandparents

Grandparents mentioned in Scripture
Saul, the grandfather of Mephibosheth 2Sa 9:7 See also 2Sa 16:3; 19:26–28

Maacah, the grandmother of Asa 1Ki 15:9–10 See also 1Ki 15:13 pp 2Ch 15:16

Lois, the grandmother of Timothy 2Ti 1:5

Believers have a responsibility to support their grandparents
1Ti 5:4

See also

5680 family	5725 old age
5696 grandchildren	5731 parents

5698

guardian

Human guardianship
Responsibility for people Gal 4:2 See also Ru 3:9–13; 2Ki 10:1; 1Co 4:14–15

Responsibility for other things Ge 1:28 See also Ge 9:5,12; Lev 25:23; Ps 8:6–8

God's guardianship of people
He loves and cares Jer 31:3 See also Ps 103:13–14; 139:14; Mt 6:32; Lk 12:7; Eph 2:4–5; 1Pe 5:7

He defends and protects Ps 125:2 See also 2Ch 32:8; Ps 41:2; 57:1; Isa 25:4; Mt 23:37; Jn 17:11; 2Th 3:3; 1Pe 1:5

He teaches and guides Ps 25:9 See also Dt 1:33; 8:2; Ps 139:10; Pr 3:5–6; Isa 30:21; 42:16; Jn 16:13

He keeps and provides Ps 23:1 See also Ps 28:15; Dt 8:18; Ps 121:4; Mal 3:10; 1Ti 6:17; 2Ti 1:12; Jude 24

God's guardianship of other things

He is guardian of his word Mt 24:35 See also Dt 29:29; Mt 5:18; Mk 13:32

He is guardian of the world Ps 24:1 See also Ps 33:6–7; 50:10; 89:9; 93:1

Christians are guardians of God's truth

2Th 2:15 See also Dt 6:6–7; Gal 2:11; Eph 4:1,3; Php 1:27; 1Th 2:12

Angelic guardianship

Ps 91:11–12 See also Ge 3:24; Ex 14:19; Jdg 2:1; 2Ki 6:17; Ps 34:7; Isa 63:9; Ac 8:26; 12:15; 27:23; Gal 3:19

See also

1040 God, fatherhood	5291 defence
1085 God, love of	5316 fortress
1220 God as shepherd	5330 guard
	5480 protection
1330 God, the provider	5490 refuge
	5527 shield
4110 angels	5731 parents

5699

guests

People who receive hospitality, especially at others' homes. Guests are often invited to special celebrations such as weddings or birthdays. God invites all people as guests at his feast but many refuse.

Occasions for inviting guests

Weddings Ge 29:21–22 See also Est 2:17–18; Jn 2:1–10

Birthday celebrations Ge 40:20; Mt 14:6 pp Mk 6:21–22; Mt 14:9 pp Mk 6:26

Other special occasions 1Sa 9:22–24; 1Ki 1:41,49; Est 1:8

Receiving guests

Receiving Jesus Christ as a guest Lk 19:7 See also Mt 9:10 pp Mk 2:15 pp Lk 5:29; Mt 26:6–7 pp Mk 14:3 pp Jn 12:1–3; Lk 7:36,49; 10:38; 14:1; 24:29; Jn 2:2; Rev 3:20

God's people give hospitality Ac 10:32 See also 2Ki 4:8–10; Mt 10:11 pp Mk 6:10 pp Lk 9:4; Lk 10:33–37; Ac 16:34; 21:8; 28:7

Customs associated with receiving guests

Anointing them with oil Ps 23:5 Anointing with oil was a customary treatment for honoured guests. See also Ps 92:10; Lk 7:46; Jn 12:3

Washing their feet Ge 18:4–5 See also Ge 19:2; 24:32; 43:24; 1Sa 25:41; Lk 7:44; Jn 13:1–17 It was usually the slave's duty to wash away dirt accumulated in travelling.

Guests treated badly Jdg 19:20–23; 2Sa 15:11; Jer 41:1–2; Lk 7:44–46

Guests rejecting their hosts

1Ki 1:49; Job 19:15

Advice given to guests

Do not promote yourself Pr 25:6–7 See also Lk 14:7–11

Do not criticise the food 1Co 10:27 See also Lk 10:7

Do not outstay your welcome Pr 25:17

God invites people to be his guests

Rev 19:9 See also Isa 55:1; Mt 11:28; Jn 7:37; Rev 22:17

Some refuse God's invitation Lk 14:24 See also Mt 22:1–7; Lk 14:16–20

Some accept God's invitation Mt 22:8–10 See also Mt 9:15 pp Mk 2:19 pp Lk 5:34; Lk 14:21–23

Guest rooms

Mk 14:14 pp Mt 26:18 pp Lk 22:11; Phm 22

See also

2375 kingdom of God	5742 wedding
	5976 visiting
4404 food	8260 generosity
4410 banquets	8445 hospitality
5153 foot-washing	8642 celebration
5231 birthday	9150 Messianic banquet
5355 invitations	

5700

headship

The quality of being in a position of leadership or guidance. Headship has to do with God's relation to this created world, and to his ordering of relationships within it. Headship among human beings does not necessarily signify superior status, but rather a role of leadership and care. Scripture sees it as involving servanthood, and views Jesus Christ as the supreme model of this.

God as head over all things

1Ch 29:11 See also Isa 45:23; Da 4:34–35; Ro 9:14–21; 1Co 15:24–28

Headship within the Godhead

The Father's eternal headship 1Co 11:3 See also 1Co 15:24–28; Php 2:6

The Father's headship in the Son's earthly life and ministry Jn 6:38 See also Mt 26:39 pp Mk 14:36 pp Lk 22:42; Php 2:6–8; Heb 5:7–8

Jesus Christ as head of all creation

Head of the created order Col 1:15–17 The description of Jesus Christ as the firstborn does not imply he is part of creation, but rather stresses his rights of inheritance over it. See also Heb 1:2–4

Head of all earthly and spiritual powers Eph 1:20–22 See also Col 1:15–18; 2:10; Heb 2:8

Head of the church Eph 4:15–16 See also Eph 5:23; Col 1:18; 2:19

Head over all things at the end Eph 1:9–10 See also 1Co 15:25–27; Rev 19:11–16

Delegated headship in God's world

Headship of humanity over creation Ge 1:28 See also Ps 8:1–9; Heb 2:5–8

Headship of rulers over their nations Ps 18:43 See also 1Sa 15:17; Isa 7:8–9; Da 2:31–38; Ro 13:1–6; 1Pe 2:13–14

Headship of chiefs over their tribes and families Jos 22:13–14 See also Nu 1:1–16; Jdg 10:17–11:11; 1Ch 5:15

Headship of the husband over his wife Eph 5:22–24 See also 1Co 11:3–16 Women, including wives, were told to cover their heads when praying or prophesying in public as an acknowledgment, apparently, that headship attaches to males; Col 3:18; 1Pe 3:1–6

Headship of leaders over the people of God 1Th 5:12 See also 1Sa 24:1–7; Isa 3:1–7 The removal of headship and leadership is seen as a mark of God's judgment; Heb 13:17

Humility, love and respect are to be the framework for delegated headship 1Pe 5:1–3 See also Eph 5:21,25–30

See also

1510 Trinity, the	5744 wife
2212 Christ, head of church	5959 submission
	7026 church, leadership
5218 authority in home	7733 leaders
5702 husband	7748 overseers

5701

heir

Property and power in biblical times normally descended from father to son. Jesus Christ is therefore called God's heir, and believers are said to inherit in him.

The heir in ancient Israel

The heir of property Ge 15:3–4 See also Pr 13:22; 19:14

The heir of power 1Ki 2:12 pp 1Ch 29:28 See also 1Ki 11:43; 14:31; 15:3

Lack of an heir regarded as a very serious matter Dt 25:5–6; Jdg 21:17; 2Sa 14:4–7 The woman of Tekoa was interceding indirectly for Absalom, David's heir, who had been banished.

Daughters and other relatives could be heirs if there were no sons Nu 27:1–11

Property could be inherited before death Lk 15:11–12 The prodigal son's request of inheritance before death could perhaps be regarded as an insult, but graciously the father complied out of love.

An heir must not give up his inheritance Heb 12:16 See also Ge 25:29–34; Nu 36:6–7; 1Ki 21:3; Jer 49:1

The firstborn son was heir to a double share Dt 21:17

Jesus Christ as the heir of God

Heb 1:2 See also Mt 28:18; Lk 19:12; Jn 3:35

Jesus Christ is heir as the Father's firstborn Heb 1:6

Envy of Jesus Christ as heir Mt 21:37–39 pp Mk 12:6–8 pp Lk 20:13–15

God's people as heirs

God himself as his people's inheritance Jos 18:7; Ps 73:26; 119:57; 142:5; Jer 51:19

Israel as heirs to land Ex 32:13 *See also* Ps 105:44

Noah, heir of righteousness Heb 11:7

Abraham, heir of promise Ge 17:4–8; Lk 1:54–55; Heb 11:8–9

David, heir of a kingdom 2Sa 7:8–16

Israel, heirs of the prophets Ac 3:25; Ro 3:2

All believers are heirs by faith Gal 3:29 *See also* Ro 4:13–17

Heirs under the covenant Heb 6:17 *See also* Heb 9:15

Heirs through God's grace Gal 3:18 *See also* Col 1:12

Co-heirs with Jesus Christ Ro 8:17

The privileges of God's heirs

Believers are heirs to the full rights of sons Gal 4:1–7

Believers are heirs as the firstborn Heb 12:23

Believers are heirs of salvation Heb 1:14

Believers are heirs of eternal life Tit 3:7; 1Pe 1:3–4

Believers are heirs of the earth Mt 5:5; Ps 37:11

Believers are heirs of the kingdom Mt 25:34

Believers are heirs of all things 1Co 3:21–22; 2Co 6:10; Rev 21:7

Believers are heirs of life 1Pe 3:7

Believers as heirs share Jesus Christ's throne Lk 22:29–30; Rev 3:21

God's inheritance is his people

Dt 32:9; Zec 2:12

See also

1055 God, grace & mercy	2375 kingdom of God
1345 covenant	5368 kingship
2012 Christ, authority	5657 birthright
2069 Christ, pre-eminence	5688 firstborn
2078 Christ, sonship of	5703 inheritance
	5738 sons
	6608 adoption

5702

husband

The male partner in a marriage relationship. The origin of this God-ordained institution is traced back in the Bible to the Garden of Eden. Scripture stresses that marriage is a God-ordained institution, within which the husband is pledged to love and care for his wife. Scripture contains many examples, both good and bad, of how husbands behaved. The ultimate examples of a good husband in Scripture are God as the husband of Israel and Jesus Christ as the bridegroom of the church.

God's pattern for marriage

Husband and wife are one flesh Ge 1:27 *See also* Ge 2:23–24; Mal 2:15; Mt 19:4–6 pp Mk 10:6–9

The husband is head of the wife Eph 5:23 *See also* 1Co 11:3

Duties of a husband

To leave his parents and be united to his wife Mt 19:5 pp Mk 10:7–8 *See also* Ge 2:24

To love his wife Eph 5:25 *See also* Dt 24:5; Pr 5:18; Ecc 9:9; Eph 5:28–33; Col 3:19; 1Pe 3:7

To fulfil his marital duty 1Co 7:3–5 *See also* Ex 21:10–11

To be faithful to his wife Ex 20:14 pp Dt 5:18 *See also* Lev 20:10; Dt 22:22; Mal 2:14; Mt 5:27–28; 1Co 7:14–16

Adam, the first husband

Ge 2:20–24

Behaviour which is commended in husbands

1Sa 1:3–8 *See also* Ge 24:67; 29:20; Ru 3:7–4:11; Est 5:1–3; Hos 3:1–3; Mt 1:18–25

Behaviour which is condemned in husbands

2Sa 12:7–10 *See also* Ge 29:30–31; 38:8–10; Jdg 19:16–29; Mal 2:13–16

God as a husband

Isa 54:5 *See also* Jer 3:14; 31:32; Eze 16:8

Jesus Christ as a bridegroom

Eph 5:25–27 *See also* Mt 9:14–15 pp Mk 2:18–20 pp Lk 5:33–35; 2Co 11:2; Rev 21:2

See also

5660 bridegroom	6243 adultery, spiritual
5675 divorce	7020 church, the
5708 marriage	7135 Israel, people
5729 one flesh	of God
5732 polygamy	8299 love in
5744 wife	relationships
6242 adultery	

5703

inheritance

A birthright or endowment, often in the form of goods or land, passed down from one generation to another. Scripture treats eternal life and other privileges of faith as an inheritance from God.

5704
inheritance, material

Family property was normally handed down in biblical times through sons, with a special place for the firstborn. The land of Israel was regarded as the nation's inheritance.

Inheritance of family property

It was normally handed down through sons Ge 15:3–4 *See also* Ge 25:5; Jer 49:1; Eze 46:16–17; Mt 21:38 pp Mk 12:7 pp Lk 20:14; Gal 4:30; Ge 21:10

The absence of a son as a male heir was seen as a serious disadvantage Ge 25:21; Dt 25:5–6; Jdg 21:17; 1Sa 1:10–11; 2Sa 14:4–7

Other relatives could inherit Nu 27:8–11 *See also* Nu 27:1–7; 36:2–4; Ru 4:1–4; Job 42:15

Servants could inherit Ge 15:2–3

Inheritance before death Lk 15:11–12 *The son's asking for his inheritance is perhaps to be seen as an insult.*

The rights of the firstborn Dt 21:15–17 *See also* Ge 27:19,32; 2Ch 21:3

Stewardship of one's own inheritance

It must be preserved 1Ki 21:2–3 *See also* Pr 13:22

It must not be squandered Heb 12:16 *See also* Ge 25:29–34; Lk 15:13

It must not be fought over Lk 12:13–15

Respect for the inheritance of others

Mic 2:2–3 *See also* Eze 46:18

The land as Israel's inheritance

It was promised to Abraham Ge 12:6–7 *See also* Ge 13:14–15; 15:7,18–21; 17:8; Ac 7:3–5; Heb 11:8

It was confirmed to Moses and the patriarchs Ex 6:2–4,8

Entry was denied because of sin Nu 14:22–23; Dt 4:21

It was entered by faith Heb 11:8–9,30

It was conquered by Joshua Jos 1:1–4; 11:23

It was allotted to the tribes Jos 14:1–5

It was a land for the godly Ps 37:9,11,22,29,34

It was a good inheritance Ex 3:8 *See also* Lev 20:24; Nu 13:21–27; Dt 8:7–8; 11:10–12; Ps 65:9–10; Jer 2:7

The LORD's inheritance in the land Ex 15:17; Jos 22:19; Zec 2:12

The inheritance was lost through sin Jer 17:4 *See also* Ps 79:1; La 5:2

God's judgment on the nations Jer 12:14–17

The land was regained through grace Ezr 1:1–2; Jer 29:10–11

God renewed his promises Ps 69:34–36 *The Jews did return to the land; some look, however, for a further fulfilment of these promises in the future; others see them as fulfilled in Jesus Christ. See also* Isa 57:13; 58:13–14; 61:7; 65:9; Zec 8:12

See also

1345 covenant	5680 family
4206 land	5688 firstborn
5476 property	5701 heir
5556 stewardship	5738 sons
5657 birthright	7258 promised land,
5674 daughters	early history

5705
inheritance, spiritual

Believers are privileged to receive a spiritual inheritance from their heavenly Father as a result of their adoption into the family of God through faith.

Believers have an inheritance in Christ

Jesus Christ as God's heir Heb 1:2 *See also* Mt 21:37–39 pp Mk 12:6–8 pp Lk 20:13–15; Mt 28:18; Lk 19:12; Jn 3:35; Heb 1:4–6; Ps 2:7–8

Believers are co-heirs with Christ Ro 8:17 *See also* Eph 3:6

Believers are heirs under the covenant Heb 6:17; 9:15

Believers are heirs by grace Gal 3:18 *See also* Ac 20:32; Col 1:12

Believers are heirs through faith Gal 3:29 *See also* Ro 4:13–17; Heb 11:7–10

The nature of the spiritual inheritance of believers

They inherit salvation Heb 1:14

They inherit eternal life Mt 19:29; Lk 10:25; Tit 3:7; 1Pe 3:7

They have the full rights of sons Gal 4:4–7

They have the rights of the firstborn Heb 12:22–23 *See also* Ex 4:22; 2Ki 2:9

They inherit the earth Mt 5:5 *See also* Ps 37:11

They inherit the kingdom Mt 25:34 *See also* Lk 22:28–30; Rev 3:21

They inherit all things Lk 15:31; 1Co 3:21–22; Rev 21:7

Their inheritance is the word of God Ps 119:111

They inherit the Lord himself Ps 73:26 *See also* Nu 18:20; Dt 10:9; Ps 142:5; Jer 10:16; 51:19

It is a good inheritance Ps 16:6

The permanence of believers' spiritual inheritance

It has been prepared from the creation Mt 25:34

It is guaranteed for eternity 1Pe 1:3–5 *See also* Ps 37:18; Da 12:13

It is sealed with God's promise Eph 1:13–14 *See also* Rev 7:3; 9:4

The conditions of spiritual inheritance

It is conditional upon continuing obedience and faith 1Pe 3:9–12 *See also* Ps 34:12–16; 25:12–13; 37:11,29,34; 61:5; Pr 28:10; Mt 5:5; Col 3:24; Heb 6:12; Jas 2:5

It is denied to the ungodly Eph 5:5 *See also* Ps 37:9,22; 1Co 6:9–10; 10:1–5; Gal 5:19–21; Heb 3:12–19; Rev 21:27

See also

5707

male and female

God created humanity as male and female. Although gender differences are evident in behaviour and role,

---

Scripture teaches the equality and complementarity of the sexes.

The creation of male and female
Ge 1:27 *See also* Ge 2:20–24; 5:2

The fall disrupted relationships between male and female
Ge 3:14–19 *See also* 2Sa 13:1–19; Pr 5:3–14; Mt 5:28; Ro 1:26–27

The equality of male and female
Equality under many old covenant regulations Nu 5:5–7 *See also* Lev 20:10–12; Nu 5:1–4; Dt 15:12–15; 23:17–18

Equality in religious observance Ex 35:22 *See also* Nu 6:1–4; Dt 31:12; 2Sa 6:19

Equality of accountability La 2:21 *See also* Lev 20:27; 2Ch 36:15–17; Ac 5:1–11

Equality in Christ Gal 3:26–28 *See also* Ac 2:17–18; Joel 2:28–29; 1Co 11:11–12

Variations in the treatment of male and female

In OT patriarchal society Lev 27:1–7 *See also* Ge 17:9–14; Ex 13:1–2,14–15; Nu 3:14–15; 5:11–31; 18:8–10

In legislation protecting women under the old covenant Nu 27:1–7 *See also* Nu 36:1–12; Dt 22:13–19,25–29

In roles within the NT church community 1Co 14:33–35 *See also* 1Co 11:3–10; Eph 5:22–24 *The idea of "headship" is complex, but is generally regarded as including the ideas of responsibility and authority within a relationship*; 1Ti 2:11–15; Tit 2:1–5

In behaviour within the NT church community 1Ti 2:8–10 *See also* 1Co 11:3–16; 1Ti 5:1–2

Male and female roles within marriage
1Co 7:1–7 *See also* Pr 31:10–31; Eph 5:22–33; Col 3:18–19; 1Pe 3:1–7

Male and female imagery used of God

Female imagery Mt 23:37 pp Lk 13:34 *See also* Pr 8:1–11; Isa 66:12–13

Male imagery Ps 47:2 *See also* Ex 15:3; Ps 23:1; Mt 6:6; Lk 11:11–13 pp Mt 7:9–11

See also

5708

marriage

The union of a man and a woman in a permanent relationship. Though a lifelong monogamous commitment is presented as the ideal, polygamous marriages were occasionally known in OT times and carried the same legal and moral rights and

---

responsibilities. God's relationship with his people is described in terms of the marriage bond.

5709

marriage, purpose of

Marriage is part of God's intention for humanity from creation and forms the basis for the family which is the primary unit of society. Where marriage flourishes it blesses both the couple and the wider community.

Marriage is part of God's plan for the human race
From creation Mt 19:4 pp Mk 10:6 *See also* Ge 1:27; 1Co 11:11–12 *Man and woman are not independent of each other.*

It is to provide companionship Ge 2:18 *See also* Ge 2:20–22; 3:12; Pr 31:10–12

It is to be a committed, exclusive relationship Ge 2:23–24 *See also* Mt 19:5 pp Mk 10:7–8; 1Co 7:2; Eph 5:31

It is a lifelong partnership Mt 19:6 pp Mk 10:9 *See also* Ro 7:2; 1Co 7:39

It is the intended context for raising children Mal 2:15 *See also* 1Co 7:14

It will not exist in the life to come Mt 22:30 pp Mk 12:25 pp Lk 20:34–35; 1Co 7:29–31

Marriage as a covenant relationship
Mal 2:14 *See also* Pr 2:17; Eze 16:8

Sex and marriage
Sex belongs within marriage 1Co 7:9 *See also* Ge 29:21 *Men who violated virgins were expected to marry them:* Ex 22:16–17; Dt 22:28–29 *Dt 22:13–21 A woman was expected to be a virgin when she married.*

The sexual relationship is exclusive SS 2:16 *See also* Dt 22:22–24 *Marital unfaithfulness is condemned;* Pr 5:15–19; 1Co 6:16; 7:3–5

Love and submission in marriage
Falling in love prior to marriage Ge 29:20 *See also* Ge 34:3–4; 1Sa 18:20

Husbands are to love their wives Eph 5:25 *See also* Ge 24:67; 1Sa 1:5; Ecc 9:9; Hos 3:1; Eph 5:28–29,33; Col 3:19

Wives are to submit to their husbands Ge 3:16; Eph 5:22–24 *See also* Col 3:18; Tit 2:4–5; 1Pe 3:1–6

Celibacy as a calling from God
1Co 7:7–8 *See also* Jer 16:2; Mt 19:10–12; 1Co 7:36–38 *Whilst Paul commends the unmarried state, for those not so called it is no sin to marry;* 1Ti 5:11–14

See also

5710

marriage, customs concerning

Marriage between two individuals united their families and involved the whole community. Parents, particularly fathers, took an active part in selecting partners for their children. There was often a long period of betrothal; wedding celebrations were usually elaborate and might last a week or more.

The choice of a marriage partner
Parents usually chose a suitable partner Ge 38:6 *See also* Ge 24:2–4; 21:21 *Occasionally mothers made the wedding arrangements.*

The wishes of the couple Ge 24:57–58 *Rebekah is consulted about her proposed marriage to Isaac. See also* Ge 34:4,8–9; Jdg 14:2; 1Sa 18:20

The bride-price
Daughters were "given" by their fathers Ge 29:28; Ex 2:21; 1Sa 18:21

Fathers often received payment Ge 29:18; 34:12 *See also* Ge 29:30; Ex 22:16–17; Dt 22:28–29; 1Sa 18:17,27

Daughters were given as a reward Jdg 1:12–13 pp Jos 15:16–17 *See also* 1Sa 18:25

The exchange of wedding gifts
Gifts from the bridegroom's family Ge 24:53

Gifts from the bride's father *Servants given to the bride as a dowry:* Ge 24:59; 29:24,29 *Cities and land given as a dowry:* Jdg 1:14–15 pp Jos 15:18–19; 1Ki 9:16

The period of betrothal
Betrothal followed payment of the bride-price 2Sa 3:14 *See also* Ge 29:19–20 *Jacob worked for Laban during his period of betrothal to Rachel.*

A betrothed couple were regarded as husband and wife Ge 19:14; Dt 22:23–24 *Unfaithfulness during the period of betrothal is treated as adultery;* Mt 1:18–20 *Divorce is required to break a betrothal.*

Sexual relationships took place only after the wedding Ge 29:21 *Betrothed women were referred to as virgins:* Joel 1:8; Lk 1:27 Mt 1:25; 1Co 7:36–38

Soldiers and marriage
Dt 20:7 *Engaged soldiers were to marry before going into battle;* Dt 24:5 *Recently married soldiers were exempted from military service for a year.*

The wedding celebrations
The bride wore an elaborate dress and jewellery Eze 16:9–13 *An allegorical description of God dressing Jerusalem as a bride. See also* Ps 45:13; Isa 61:10; Jer 2:32; Rev 21:2

Attendants on the bride and groom Ps 45:14; Jn 3:29 *See also* Jdg 14:11,20; Mt 9:15 pp Mk 2:19 pp Lk 5:34; Mt 25:1–10

The wedding banquet Ge 29:22; Jdg 14:10; Mt 22:2; Rev 19:9

Wedding festivities Ps 78:63; Isa 62:5; Jer 7:34; 33:11

The invitation to a wedding Mt 22:3–4 *Invited guests were called when the feast was ready.* *It was an insult to the host to refuse to attend:* Mt 22:5–7; Lk 14:18–21 Mt 22:11–12 *Guests were expected to dress appropriately.*

See also

4410 banquets	5679 dowry
5654 betrothal	5684 fathers
5659 bride	5731 parents
5660 bridegroom	5742 wedding

5711

marriage, restrictions concerning

The OT law forbade intermarriage with people who worshipped idols because it threatened the covenant relationship with God and his people. Marriage with close relations was also forbidden. Remarriage is permissible following the death of a spouse and, in certain circumstances, following divorce.

Intermarriage with foreigners
Examples of marriages to foreigners Ge 38:2; 41:45; Ex 2:21; Lev 24:10; Ru 1:4; 1Ch 2:34–35; Ezr 10:18–44

Warnings against marrying foreigners Ex 34:16 *See also* Dt 7:3–4; Jos 23:12–13

Intermarriage with foreigners led to idolatry Jdg 3:5–6; 1Ki 11:1–8 *Royal marriages to foreigners brought disastrous consequences. See also* 1Ki 16:31; Mal 2:11 *Intermarriage among returning exiles was a major problem facing Ezra and Nehemiah:* Ezr 9:1–2,14; 10:1–2; Ne 13:23–27

Parents sought to avoid their children marrying foreigners Ne 10:30 *See also* Ge 24:3–4 *Abraham seeks a bride for Isaac from among his own people. Esau's foreign wives are a source of grief to his parents:* Ge 26:34–35; 27:46 Ge 28:1–2 *Isaac forbids Jacob to marry a Canaanite woman;* Jdg 14:3 *Samson's parents encourage him to marry an Israelite.*

Marriage to foreigners may be permissible Ru 4:13 *Boaz' marriage to Ruth the Moabitess was acceptable because Ruth embraced the Israelite faith. Restrictions were on the grounds of religion not of race.*

Foreign wives were put aside after the exile Ezr 10:3 *See also* Ezr 10:10–17

Marriages between Christians and unbelievers
Christians should not marry unbelievers 1Co 7:39; 2Co 6:14

Christians should not leave an unbelieving spouse 1Co 7:12–16

Restrictions on marriage to close relatives
Sexual relations with close relatives is forbidden Lev 18:6–18 *See also* Lev 20:11–12,14,19–21; Dt 22:30;

Eze 22:10–11; Mt 14:3–4 pp Mk 6:17–18

Examples of marriage to close relatives Ge 20:12 *Abraham was married to his half-sister;* 2Sa 13:13 *Tamar suggests marriage with her half-brother, Amnon.*

Levirate marriage
The levirate law was instituted to preserve the dead father's name Dt 25:5–10; Ru 4:10 *Levirate marriage refers to the legal obligation of a brother-in-law to produce heirs for his dead brother by marrying his widow. When there was no brother-in-law responsibility fell to a near relative, also described as a "kinsman-redeemer". See also* Ge 38:8,11; Ru 1:11–13; 3:9; 4:5; Mt 22:24–26 pp Mk 12:19–22 pp Lk 20:28–31

Unwillingness to fulfil the levirate law Ge 38:9,14,26; Ru 4:6

Regulations governing seduction and rape
Ex 22:16; Dt 22:28–29

Remarriage
Widows are free to remarry Ro 7:2–3 *See also* Ru 1:9; 1Co 7:8–9; 1Ti 5:14

Remarriage after divorce may be adultery Lk 16:18 pp Mt 19:9 pp Mk 10:11–12 *See also* 1Co 7:10–11

Remarriage after divorce permissible in certain circumstances Dt 24:1–4; Mt 5:32; 1Co 7:15,27–28

See also

5661 brothers	6240 rape
5672 concubines	6241 seduction
5675 divorce	7388 kinsman-
5703 inheritance	redeemer
5732 polygamy	7530 foreigners
5743 widows	

5712

marriage, between God and his people

Marriage is used to describe the relationship between God and Israel in the OT and between Jesus Christ and the church in the NT. Contemplating marriage deepens understanding of God's love for his people; examining God's covenant love for his people similarly enriches an understanding of marriage.

God's marriage relationship with Israel
God's marriage covenant with Israel Eze 16:8–14 *The covenant at Sinai was seen as a form of marriage. See also* Jer 31:32; Eze 16:59–60

God as Israel's husband Isa 54:5 *See also* Hos 2:7; Joel 1:8

Israel's early devotion Jer 2:2 *See also* Eze 16:43; Hos 2:15

The breakdown of God's marriage to Israel
Israel's adultery Jer 3:20 *See also* Jer 2:32; Eze 16:32–34; Hos 1:2; 9:1

Israel's alienation from God is likened to a divorce Hos 2:2 *Israel's unfaithfulness led to a form of divorce between God and his people. This was sometimes identified with the exile. See also* Isa 50:1; Jer 3:6–10

The renewal of God's marriage to Israel
God calls his bride to return Jer 3:12–14; Hos 3:1–3 *See also* Isa 54:6–8; Hos 2:14

The renewed relationship Isa 62:4–5 *See also* Jer 31:31–33; Eze 16:62; Hos 2:16,19–20

Jesus Christ's marriage relationship with the church
Jesus Christ's love as a model for marriage Eph 5:25–33

Jesus Christ is described as a bridegroom Jn 3:29 *John the Baptist describes Jesus Christ as the bridegroom and himself as the best man. See also* Mt 9:15 pp Mk 2:19–20 pp Lk 5:34–35; Mt 22:2; 25:1–13

The church as Christ's bride 2Co 11:2; Rev 19:7–8 *See also* Rev 21:2,9–10; 22:17

See also
1030 God, compassion	6740 returning to God
1035 God, faithfulness	7020 church, the
1085 God, love of	8251 faithfulness to God
1349 covenant at Sinai	8840 unfaithfulness to God
1680 types	
6243 adultery, spiritual	

5714

men

God created both men and women in his image and likeness. Scripture portrays men in both their strengths and weaknesses, their successes and failures. While noting that they are incomplete without women, and share equally in the privileges and tasks entrusted to them by God, men have nevertheless been given specific responsibilities by God.

The place of men
Men are equal with women in creation Ge 1:27 *See also* Ge 5:2

Men are incomplete without women Ge 2:18 *See also* Ge 2:21–25; 1Co 11:11–12

Absence of men in society seen as a curse Isa 3:1–3 *See also* La 5:14; Eze 17:11–14

Men are equal with women in redemption Gal 3:28 *See also* Ac 2:17–18; Joel 2:28–29

The role of men
As leaders in marriage and family life Eph 5:22–24 *See also* 1Co 11:3; Col 3:18–21

As leaders in Israelite society and worship Nu 1:16 *See also* Ex 34:23–24; Nu 3:10–15; Dt 1:9–15; 1Sa 8:1; Ezr 10:16–17

As leaders in the early church 1Ti 3:2 *See also* Ac 6:2–6; 1Ti 2:12 *The role of teaching and exercising authority is here restricted to men. Interpretations vary as to whether Paul is reflecting cultural circumstance or establishing theological principle;* 1Ti 3:8

The character requirements of men
To be prayerful and godly 1Ti 2:8 *See also* Da 6:10–11; 1Ti 4:7–8; 6:11–12

To be courageous 1Co 16:13 *While courage can be exercised by all, it is identified here as a specifically male characteristic. See also* Ac 4:13; 27:21–25

To be determined and decisive Mt 11:12 *See also* 1Ch 12:38

To be humble 1Pe 5:5 *See also* Nu 12:3; Da 10:12; Mt 11:29

To love their wives Col 3:19 *See also* Pr 5:15–19; Eph 5:25–33

To be good fathers to their children Eph 6:4 *See also* Ge 37:3–4 *Jacob's favouritism was the cause of resentment developing in the family;* 1Sa 3:12–13 *Eli is rebuked for having failed to father his sons properly;* Col 3:21

To exercise proper sexual restraint 1Th 4:3–7 *That Paul is particularly thinking of men here seems apparent from the NIV footnote at verse 4. See also* Lev 18:1–22; Pr 6:23–29; Mt 5:27–28; 1Co 5:1–2; 7:2–5

Examples of godly men
Ge 6:9 *Noah;* Ge 22:1–12 *Abraham;* Ex 32:30–32 *Moses;* 1Sa 24:1–7 *David;* 2Ki 18:1–7 *Hezekiah;* Job 1:1–8 *Job;* Da 6:10 *Daniel;* Ac 4:13–20 *Peter and John;* Ac 7:54–60 *Stephen;* Heb 11:4–28 *OT heroes of faith;* Jas 5:17–18 *Elijah*

Examples of godly men who had moments of failure
Ge 20:1–3 *Abraham was deceitful;* Nu 20:2–12 *Moses and Aaron showed unbelief;* 2Sa 11:1–27 *David committed adultery with Bathsheba and plotted Uriah's death;* 1Ki 19:1–5 *Elijah became fearful and wanted to die;* Jnh 1:1–3 *Jonah ran from God's call on his life;* Mt 26:69–75 pp Mk 14:66–72 pp Lk 22:55–62 pp Jn 18:16–18, 25–27 *Peter denied Jesus Christ;* Ac 16:36–40 *Paul and Barnabas fell into sharp disagreement.*

Examples of ungodly men
Ge 19:4–5 *The ungodliness of the men of Sodom lay in sexual immorality;* Ge 38:8–10 *Onan's ungodliness lay in failing to fulfil his obligations to his brother's wife;* Nu 16:1–35 *Korah's ungodliness lay in rebellion against God's leaders;* 1Sa 2:12 *Eli's sons' ungodliness lay in their abuse of the sacrifices;* 1Ki 16:29–33 *Ahab's ungodliness lay in intermarriage and idolatry;* 2Ki 21:1–9 pp 2Ch 33:1–9 *Manasseh's ungodliness lay in idolatry, divination and human sacrifice;* Mt 2:16 *Herod's ungodliness lay in the wholesale slaughter of infants;* Mt 14:3–11 pp Mk 6:17–28 *Herod the tetrarch's ungodliness lay in immorality and murder;* Ac 8:9–23 *Simon's ungodliness lay in the practice of magic;* Jude 4–19 *The ungodliness of men in the*

church lay in their rejection of apostolic doctrine and lifestyle.

Examples of fearful men
Ge 26:7–9 *Isaac's fear of the Philistines led him to lie;* Nu 13:26–33 *The spies' fear led them to give a bad report;* 1Sa 28:5–7 *Saul's fear of the Philistines led him to enquire of a medium when the* LORD *did not answer him;* 2Sa 3:7–11 *Ish-Bosheth's fear of his brother led him to stay silent concerning sin;* Jn 19:4–16 pp Mt 27:19–26 pp Mk 15:9–15 pp Lk 23:13–25 *Pilate's fear of the crowd led him to condemn Jesus Christ, even though he knew he was innocent;* Ac 24:24–25 *Felix' fear arose from the message of the gospel.*

Examples of weak men
Lev 26:36–39 *Men who are disobedient to God will be weak;* 1Sa 3:12–13 *Eli's weakness lay in failing to restrain his sons;* 1Ki 21:1–16 *Ahab's weakness lay in his allowing his wife to rule his life and his kingdom.*

See also
2033 Christ, humanity	5700 headship
5001 human race, the	5702 husband
5020 human nature	5707 male and female
5658 boys	5745 women
5680 family	6238 homosexuality
5684 fathers	7733 leaders

5715

menstruation

A woman was considered ceremonially unclean during menstruation
Lev 15:19–23 *See also* Lev 12:1–5; 15:25–30; Isa 30:22

Sexual intercourse during menstruation forbidden
Lev 18:19 *See also* Lev 20:18; Eze 18:5–6; 22:10

The discomfort of menstruation
Ge 31:35

See also
6236 sexual sin	7426 ritual washing
7424 ritual law	

5716

middle age

The period between youth and old age. Middle age is marked by physical strength and experience and should bring maturity and stability. Many of God's servants began ministry in middle age, often after having been prepared in their youth. Middle age may also bring complacency and the temptation to leave the devotion and commitments of youth.

Middle age defined
Adulthood reckoned from age 20 Nu 1:2–3 *See also* Ex 30:14; 38:26; Nu 26:2–4

1Ch 23:24 *See also* 2Ch 31:17; Ezr 3:8

Full maturity reckoned from age 30
Lk 3:23 *See also* Nu 4:30,43

Characteristics of middle age
Physical strength Lev 27:3–7 *Strength is greatest between 20 and 60. See also* Nu 1:45 *Men served in the army from age 20;* Jos 14:10 *Caleb, in his prime at 40, is still strong at 85.*

Growth in wisdom and experience
Ecc 1:16 *See also* 1Sa 17:33; 2Sa 17:8; 2Ch 17:13
1Ch 22:5 *See also* 1Ch 29:1; Pr 7:7

Maturity and stability Eph 4:13–14 *See also* 1Co 2:6; Heb 5:11–14; Jas 1:4

The responsibilities of middle age
The need to be prepared for these responsibilities Pr 22:6 *See also* Pr 4:1–4 *Solomon passes on wisdom learned from his father.* Lk 1:80 *See also* 1Sa 2:26; Lk 2:40

The need to train for service Nu 8:24 *The period from 25 to 30 (see Nu 4:3) may have been a period of apprenticeship. See also* 1Ch 23:27 *In later years the apprenticeship may have started at 20;* Nu 11:28

The start of service in middle age
Nu 4:3 *See also* Ac 7:23 *Moses showed concern for his fellow Israelites at age 40;* Jos 14:7 *Caleb was 40 when he explored Canaan;* 1Sa 7:3–4 *Samuel became judge over Israel in his thirties;* Lk 3:3 *John the Baptist began his public ministry at about 30;* Jn 8:57 *Jesus Christ had not achieved the status of wisdom and authority associated with old age in Israel;* 1Ti 3:1–13 *The mention of families in the instructions to elders and deacons suggests that these leaders were of middle age.*

Rulers coming to office in middle age
Ge 41:46 *Joseph;* 1Sa 13:1 *Saul;* 2Sa 5:4 *David;* 2Sa 2:10 *Ish-Bosheth;* 2Ch 12:13 pp 1Ki 14:21 *Rehoboam;* 2Ch 20:31 *Jehoshaphat*

Temptations of middle age
Complacency 2Sa 11:1; Isa 32:9–11; Am 6:1

Worldly distractions 2Sa 11:4; 1Ki 11:3–4; Ecc 2:1–8; Lk 12:18–19

Turning from the commitment of youth
Pr 2:16–17; Mal 2:14

See also

4971 seasons of life	6248 temptation
5051 responsibility	8203 character
5204 age	8207 commitment
5810 complacency	8344 servanthood in
5853 experience of	believers
life	8370 zeal
5902 maturity	
5956 strength,	
human	

5717

monogamy

The practice of having and remaining faithful to only one marriage partner at one time. It is set out as God's ideal for human relationships; an ideal demonstrated in the use of the marriage bond to

---

portray the relationship between God and his people.

Monogamy as God's original intention for marriage
Ge 2:22–24 *See also* Mal 2:15; Mt 19:4–6 pp Mk 10:6–9; Eph 5:31

Monogamy is shown in God's relationship with his people
God's marriage with Israel Eze 16:8 *See also* Isa 54:5–8; Jer 2:2–3; Hos 2:16–20; 3:1; Eph 5:32–33

God's exclusive commitment to Israel Dt 14:2; Am 3:2 *See also* Ex 19:5–6; Dt 26:18; 32:8; Ps 135:4

Monogamy in marriage
The commitment to a lifelong, loving companionship Ge 2:18; Pr 5:15–19 *The satisfaction that may be found in marriage makes marital unfaithfulness and polygamy unnecessary. See also* Pr 2:17; Ecc 9:9; Mal 2:14

Polygamy undermines full commitment Dt 21:15 *Favouritism within polygamous relationships undermines the close companionship which should characterise marriage. See also* Ge 29:30; 1Sa 1:1–8; 2Ch 11:21–22

Monogamy is implicit in teaching about divorce
Mt 19:9 pp Mk 10:11 *See also* Lk 16:18

Monogamy is commanded
1Co 7:2–4 *This is an implicit, but clear prohibition of polygamy;* 1Ti 3:12 *Monogamy is obligatory in leaders. See also* 1Ti 3:2; Tit 1:6

See also

5675 divorce	5732 polygamy
5680 family	5744 wife
5702 husband	6242 adultery
5708 marriage	

5718

mothers

The female parent of children. The role and influence of mothers are frequently stressed in Scripture, and their care for children is used as a picture of God's care for his people.

5719
mothers, responsibilities of

The fundamental importance of motherhood is recognised throughout Scripture.

Motherhood and childbirth
God plans happiness for women in motherhood Ps 113:9

The need for a mother's cleansing after childbirth Lev 12:1–8; Lk 2:22–24

A mother's relationship with her children
A mother loves and cares for her children 1Th 2:7 *Paul's statement assumes that a mother's normal attitude towards her child is one of love and care. See also* Lk 2:48

A mother's role as teacher Pr 1:8 *See also* Pr 6:20; 2Ti 1:5

The responsibility to discipline children Pr 29:15

The joy or sorrow of parents at their children's conduct
Pr 10:1 *See also* Pr 23:25

The negative influence of some mothers upon their children
2Ch 22:3 *See also* Ge 27:5–17; 1Ki 22:52; Mt 14:6–8; 20:20–22

Children's reponsibility to honour their parents
Ex 20:12 pp Dt 5:16 *"Honour" implies respect, obedience and care for the parents' needs. See also* Lev 19:3; Mt 19:19 pp Mk 10:19 pp Lk 18:20; Eph 6:1–3

This honour is due especially to mothers in old age Pr 23:22

Penalties for disobeying parents
Ex 21:15,17; Dt 21:18–21; Pr 20:20; Mt 15:4–6 pp Mk 7:10–13

Sexual relations with one's mother or mother-in-law are forbidden
Lev 18:7; Dt 27:23

Upon marriage the mother-child relationship becomes secondary
Ge 2:24 *See also* Mt 19:5 pp Mk 10:7; Eph 5:31

Care for a mother-in-law
Ru 2:11 *See also* Mt 8:14–15 pp Mk 1:29–31 pp Lk 4:38

The ministry of Jesus Christ may produce conflict within families
Lk 12:53 pp Mt 10:35–36

Following Jesus Christ involves a commitment to him even deeper than love of one's parents
Mt 10:37 *See also* Lk 14:26

Jesus Christ regards those who do God's will as his own family
Mt 12:49–50 pp Mk 3:31–35 pp Lk 8:19–21 *See also* Mt 19:29 pp Mk 10:29 pp Lk 18:29–30

See also

5218 authority in	5684 fathers
home	5731 parents
5428 nurse	5802 care
5652 babies	8209 commitment to
5663 childbirth	Christ
5668 children,	8287 joy, experience
responsibilities	8299 love in
to parents	relationships

5720
mothers, examples of

Examples are given in Scripture of notable mothers, mothers-in-law and grandmothers.

Eve, the mother of all the living
Ge 3:20 *See also* Ge 3:16

Hagar, the mother of Ishmael
Ge 16:1–4,15

5721

Sarah, the mother of Isaac
Ge 21:1–3 *See also* Ge 17:15–19;
18:10–14

Rebekah, mother of Esau and Jacob
Ge 25:21,24; 27:5–17

Rachel, mother of Joseph and Benjamin
Ge 30:22–24; 35:16–18

Jochebed, mother of Moses
Ex 2:1–2; 6:20; Heb 11:23

Naomi, Ruth's mother-in-law
Ru 1:15; 4:13–17

Hannah, mother of Samuel
1Sa 1:2,11,20

Jezebel, who taught her sons to worship Baal rather than the LORD
1Ki 22:52; 2Ki 9:22

The Shunammite woman
2Ki 4:16–22,32–37

Elizabeth, mother of John the Baptist
Lk 1:5–7,13,24–25,57

Mary, mother of Jesus Christ
Lk 2:6–7 *See also* Mt 1:18;
Lk 1:26–31,38; 2:19; Jn 2:1–5;
19:25–27; Ac 1:14

Herodias, a treacherous mother
Mt 14:8 pp Mk 6:24–25

Rufus' mother, a mother to Paul
Ro 16:13

Lois and Eunice, a godly grandmother and a mother
2Ti 1:5

See also

1130	God, sovereignty
2515	Christ, birth of
5093	Eve
5099	Mary, mother of Christ
5101	Moses
5117	Ruth
5225	barrenness
5345	influence
5467	promises, divine
5655	birth
5688	firstborn
5697	grandparents

5721
mothers, as a symbol

Motherhood is used in Scripture to illustrate the relationship between God and his people, to describe certain aspects of Israel and also to explain the difference between the two covenants.

God's tender care for his children is like a mother's
God's care like that of a mother bird
Dt 32:11; Mt 23:37 pp Lk 13:34

God never forgets his children
Isa 49:15

Becoming a Christian is like birth
Jn 3:5–6

The believer trusts God as a weaned child trusts his or her mother
Ps 131:1–2; Isa 66:13

Israel pictured as a mother
Eze 16:44–45 *See also* Isa 50:1; 54:1;
66:7–13; Eze 16:3; 19:2,10; Hos 2:2–13

Mothers as symbols of the old and new covenants
Gal 4:21–28

See also

1040	God, fatherhood	7135	Israel, people of God
1215	God, feminine descriptions	7241	Jerusalem, significance
1345	covenant	8031	trust, importance
6728	regeneration		

5723

nobles

People of high rank who therefore had great power and importance.

Nobles were of high rank
Est 1:14; Pr 25:6–7 *See also* Jdg 5:25;
1Ki 21:8,11; 2Ki 24:12; 2Ch 23:20;
Ne 4:14,19; 7:5; Est 5:11; Jer 27:20;
Lk 19:12; 1Co 1:26

Nobles had great power and importance
Da 5:1–3 *See also* Jdg 5:13; 2Sa 10:2–3
pp 1Ch 19:2–3; Est 1:3,11,16,21; 2:18;
9:3; Ps 47:9; Pr 8:15–16; Jer 14:3;
Jnh 3:7

Nobles' abuse of their rank and power
Ne 5:6–7,12 *See also* Ne 3:5; 13:17;
Eze 34:2

God's judgment of nobles who abused their power
Job 34:18–19 *See also* Job 12:20–21;
Ps 107:40; 149:6–8; Isa 5:13–14; 34:12;
Eze 17:12; Na 3:10

See also

5347	injustice	5878	honour
5395	lordship, human & divine	7735	leaders, political
5457	power, human	8790	oppression
5489	rank	9210	judgment, God's
5509	rulers		

5724

offspring

Literally, physical descendants, and figuratively, the recipients of a spiritual inheritance.

Physical offspring
Offspring as physical descendants
Ge 12:7 *See also* Ge 13:15–16; Nu 18:19;
Ru 4:12; Isa 61:9

Offspring as a blessing to parents
Ps 127:3–5 *See also* Ge 21:6–7; Dt 7:14;
Lk 1:41–45

Offspring as a blessing to others
Ge 28:14 *See also* Ge 22:17–18;
2Sa 7:12–13 pp 1Ch 17:11–12;
Lk 1:76–79

Absence of offspring seen as a sadness or curse Ge 15:2–3 *See also*
Lev 20:20; Ps 109:9; Jer 22:30

Steps to be taken to provide offspring under the law Dt 25:5–6 *See also*

Ru 4:10,13; Mt 22:24 pp Mk 12:19
pp Lk 20:28

Offspring as a result of God's special intervention Heb 11:11 *See also*
Ge 21:1–2; 25:21; Jdg 13:2–3;
Lk 1:11–13; Ro 4:18–21

God's claim on the firstborn offspring
Ex 13:1–2 *See also* Ex 13:11–16;
34:19–20; Nu 3:11–13; 8:15–18;
Lk 2:22–24

Offspring can inherit parents' blessing or punishment Ex 20:5–6 pp Dt 5:9–10
See also Lev 26:39; Jer 22:28–30;
Hos 9:15–17

The fate of the offspring of the wicked
Job 27:13–14 *See also* Ps 37:28;
Isa 14:20–22

Spiritual offspring
Human beings, the offspring of God through creation Ac 17:26–29

The offspring of Abraham Gal 3:29 *See also* Jn 8:31–41; Ro 4:13–17; 9:6–8

Believers, spiritual offspring through new birth 1Pe 1:23 *See also* Jn 3:3–8;
1Jn 3:9; Rev 12:17

See also

4506	seed	5694	generation
5075	Abraham	5696	grandchildren
5199	womb	5705	inheritance, spiritual
5225	barrenness	5731	parents
5652	babies	7115	children of God
5664	children		
5688	firstborn		

5725

old age

Living for a relatively long time was regarded as a blessing from God and the aged in society are to be respected. Advancing years can bring greater wisdom and in both the OT and NT elders are given authority and leadership. Old age brings physical weakness and Scripture recognises this but states God's ability to strengthen and sustain the aged.

5726
old age, attainment of

Attaining old age is regarded as a blessing from God, often as a reward for obedience. The physical weakness brought by old age is recognised; so too is God's ability to strengthen and sustain the aged. Old age is often accompanied by a growth in wisdom and discernment.

Life expectancy in the OT
Before the flood Ge 5:5,8,11,27
Methuselah died in the year of the flood;
Ge 9:29

After the flood Ge 6:3 *See also*
Ge 11:10–25 *Following the flood, the span of life gradually reduces;* Ge 25:7–8
Abraham's death at 175 is considered "a good old age".

In later generations Ps 90:10 *See also* 2Sa 5:4–5; 19:34–35

Attaining old age is a blessing from God
Long life as a reward for obedience Dt 5:33 *See also* Ex 20:12 pp Dt 5:16; Dt 4:40; Pr 3:1–2; 16:31; Ecc 8:13

Reaching old age is a mark of God's favour Ge 15:15 *See also* Ge 24:1; 35:29 *Isaac;* Jdg 8:32 *Gideon;* 1Ch 29:28 *David, like Abraham and Gideon is described as dying at "a good old age";* 2Ch 24:15 *Jehoiada;* Job 42:17 *Job*

People reaching old age indicates God's blessing on society Zec 8:4 *See also* Isa 65:20

Seeing grandchildren is a sign of blessing Pr 17:6 *See also* Ge 48:11; 50:22–23; Ru 4:15; Job 42:16; Ps 128:5–6; Isa 53:10

Failure to reach old age is a result of God's judgment 1Sa 2:31–33

The disabilities of old age
Its frailties Ps 71:9 *See also* Ge 27:1; 48:10; 1Ki 1:1; 15:23; Ecc 12:2–7 *an allegory portraying physical decline*

The progressive inability to have children Ge 18:11–13 *See also* Ge 17:17; 37:3 *Children born in old age were rare and therefore special;* 2Ki 4:14; Lk 1:18

The approach of death Ge 27:2; 1Ki 1:15; 1Ch 23:1

God's provision for the aged
God strengthens and sustains them Isa 46:4 *See also* Dt 34:7; Jos 14:10–11; Job 5:26; Ps 92:14

God gives them children Ge 21:7 *Abraham and Sarah;* 2Ki 4:16–17 *the Shunammite woman;* Lk 1:36 *Elizabeth*

Wisdom and self-control should accompany old age
Job 12:12 *See also* Job 15:10; Pr 20:29; Jn 8:9; Tit 2:2

See also

1335 blessing	5724 offspring
4015 life	5795 bereavement
5296 disabilities	8357 weakness
5446 poverty	8361 wisdom
5498 reward	8453 obedience
5696 grandchildren	9020 death

5727
old age, attitudes to

Old age is generally held in honour and the aged in society are to be respected. Because of the wisdom associated with their advancing years elders had an important role of authority and guidance in Israelite society and the NT speaks of the leadership of elders within the church.

Old age is to be held in honour
Respect for the aged Lev 19:32; 1Pe 5:5 *See also* Job 29:8; Pr 16:31; 20:29; 1Ti 5:1

Respect for parents Lev 19:3; Pr 23:22 *See also* Ex 20:12; 21:17; Lev 20:9;

Dt 27:16; Pr 30:17; Mt 15:4 pp Mk 7:10; Eph 6:1–3; Col 3:20

Old age is associated with wisdom
Deferring to the wisdom of the aged Job 32:6–7 *See also* 1Ki 12:6–8 pp 2Ch 10:6–8 *Rehoboam rejected the advice of elders and rebellion ensued;* Job 12:12; 15:10; Phm 9 *Paul refers to his age to add authority to his words.*

Learning from the previous generation Ps 71:18 *See also* Job 8:8; Ps 37:25–26

Old age does not necessarily bring superior wisdom Ecc 4:13 *See also* Job 32:9; Ps 105:22

Showing disrespect for the elderly is a sign of evil days
Isa 3:5 *See also* Dt 28:50; Job 30:1; Isa 47:6; La 5:12

The role and status of elders
Elders of non-Israelite nations Ge 50:7; Nu 22:7

Elders in Israel
Israel's elders were probably the heads of families, qualified to lead by virtue of age and experience: Ex 3:16–18; 4:29–31; 19:7
Nu 11:25 *The number of elders is reduced to 70 who are anointed by the Spirit for leadership alongside Moses. Town elders were responsible for apprehending murderers and settling matrimonial disputes:* Dt 19:11–12; 22:15–18; 25:7
2Sa 5:3 *Israel's elders accept David as king;* Mt 26:57 pp Mk 14:53 *Jewish elders were among those who tried Jesus Christ. By NT times they had become involved with religious as well as civil affairs and their title related more to their role than to age.*

Elders in the church 1Ti 5:17 *See also* 1Ti 3:1–7; Tit 1:5–9; Jas 5:14; 1Pe 5:1–2

God as the "Ancient of Days"
God as one "advanced in years" Da 7:9 *This description of God as the "Ancient of Days" implies that he possesses the respectability, authority and wisdom to judge that accompanies age. It also points to his eternity. See also* Da 7:13,22; Rev 1:14

The eternity of God Ps 9:7 *See also* Ps 29:10; 90:2; Isa 41:4; 44:6

See also

1140 God, the eternal	5853 experience of
1205 God, titles of	life
5358 judges	7718 elders
5731 parents	7733 leaders
5746 youth	8469 respect
5838 disrespect	

5729
one flesh

A sign and expression of the inseparable union between husband and wife. This is not only physical but emotional, mental and spiritual. It is also used to describe the union between Jesus Christ and the church.

One flesh describes the inseparable union between husband and wife
Ge 2:22–24 *See also* 1Co 6:16; Eph 5:28–29,31

One flesh refers to sexual union which Scripture describes in various ways
To lie with Ge 4:1,17,25; 19:31–35; 29:21,23,30; 1Sa 1:19; 2Sa 11:11; 12:24; 16:21

To come together Mt 1:18; 1Co 7:5

To have union or unite with 1Co 6:15–16 *See also* Ge 2:24; Mt 1:25; 19:5 pp Mk 10:7; Eph 5:31

Natural relations Ro 1:26–27

One flesh expresses an intimacy encouraged by God
Only within heterosexual marriage Mt 19:4–6 pp Mk 10:6–9 *See also* Ge 1:27; 2:24; Ex 20:14 pp Dt 5:18; Lev 20:10; Mt 5:27–28; 1Co 5:9–11; 6:9; 7:4

Intimate relations between members of the same sex are unnatural and wrong Lev 18:22 *See also* Ro 1:26–27; 1Co 6:9

One flesh describes the union between Jesus Christ and the church
Eph 5:31–32 *See also* Ge 2:24; 1Co 6:16–17

See also

5229 bed	6754 union with
5708 marriage	Christ
5735 sexuality	7020 church, the
6236 sexual sin	7155 saints

5730
orphans

Children whose parents are dead; a vulnerable group of people to whom God shows special kindness. He expects his people to do the same. Those who exploit them incur God's judgment.

Orphans as symbols
Of weakness Ps 82:3 *See also* Job 29:12; Isa 9:17

Of disgrace La 5:1–3 *See also* Ps 109:9,12

God cares for orphans
Dt 10:18 *See also* Ps 10:14,17–18; 68:5; 146:9; Jer 49:11; Hos 14:3

God expects his people to care for orphans
They are not to be oppressed Zec 7:10 *See also* Dt 24:17; 26:12–13; Jer 22:3

Caring for them brings blessing Dt 24:19 *See also* Dt 14:28–29; Isa 1:17; Jer 7:5–7; Jas 1:27

Exploitation of orphans is a mark of wickedness
Ps 94:5–6 *See also* Job 6:27; 22:9; 24:3,9; 31:17,21; Isa 1:23; Jer 5:28; Eze 22:7

God punishes those who oppress orphans
Dt 27:19 *See also* Ex 22:22–24; Pr 23:10–11; Isa 10:1–4; Mal 3:5

Orphans are included among God's people
Dt 16:11,14

Jesus Christ includes those who are spiritually fatherless
Jn 14:18 *See also* Gal 4:5,7

Examples of orphans
Ge 11:27–28 *Lot;* Nu 27:1–5 *the daughters of Zelophedad;* Est 2:7 *Esther*

See also

1030 God, compassion	6608 adoption
1040 God, fatherhood	7115 children of God
1310 God as judge	7140 people of God
5310 exploitation	8291 kindness
5666 children, needs	8790 oppression
5797 bereavement, comfort in	9210 judgment, God's

5731

parents

Scripture stipulates that children should show respect and concern for their parents.

Honouring parents
Ex 20:12 pp Dt 5:16 *See also* Lev 19:3; Pr 23:22; Mt 19:16–19 pp Mk 10:17–19 pp Lk 18:18–20; Eph 6:1–3; Col 3:20; 1Ti 5:4

Dishonouring parents
2Ti 3:1–2 *See also* Ex 21:15–17; Dt 21:18–21; Eze 22:7; Mt 15:1–6 pp Mk 7:1–13; Ro 1:28–32

Love between parents and children can be suppressed
Lk 21:16–17 pp Mt 10:21 pp Mk 13:12 *See also* Zec 13:2–3

Love for God must surpass love for parents
Lk 14:26 *See also* Dt 33:8–11; Lk 18:28–30 pp Mt 19:27–29 pp Mk 10:28–30

Divine love surpasses parental love
Ps 27:10

The belief that children were punished for their parents' sins
Jn 9:1–3 *See also* Ex 20:5–6 pp Dt 5:9–10; Job 21:19–21; Eze 18:1–4

Parents caring for their children
2Co 12:14 *See also* Pr 19:14; 23:24–25; Heb 11:23

Children caring for their parents
1Sa 22:3–4 *See also* Jos 2:8–20; 6:22–23; Pr 17:6

Mourning for parents
Lev 21:1–2 *See also* Lev 21:10–11; Nu 6:2–7; Dt 21:10–13; Eze 44:25

Parents and the marriage of their children
A man leaves his parents to marry his wife Ge 2:21–24 *See also* Mt 19:3–6

pp Mk 10:2–9; Eph 5:25–33

Parents were responsible for vindicating their daughter's reputation
Dt 22:13–19

Sometimes parents jointly arranged their children's marriages Jdg 14:1–3

See also

2078 Christ, sonship of	5696 grandchildren
5218 authority in home	5697 grandparents
5664 children	5708 marriage
5674 daughters	5718 mothers
5684 fathers	5738 sons
	6160 fathers, sin of

5732

polygamy

The practice of having more than one wife at one time. Although not explicitly forbidden in Scripture as a general practice, it is presented as problematic and monogamy is the clearly preferred option.

Monogamy is God's intention for marriage
Ge 2:24 *See also* Jer 2:2; Hos 2:19–20; Eph 5:31

Early examples of polygamy
Ge 4:19 *See also* Ge 26:34; 28:9; 29:28

Reasons for the practice of polygamy
Sealing foreign treaties 1Ki 3:1 *See also* 1Ki 16:31

Producing offspring Ge 16:1–3; 2Ch 13:21 *A large family, and especially numerous progeny, was regarded as a sign of divine blessing. See also* Ge 30:3–5,9; Jdg 8:30; 2Sa 3:1–5; 1Ch 7:4; 2Ch 11:23; 24:2–3

Problems associated with polygamy
Being led away from God Dt 17:17 *It was common for kings to cement foreign alliances by marriage. Israel's king is warned against the practice;* 1Ki 11:1–8 *See also* Ne 13:25–26; Mal 2:11

Conflicts within families Ge 29:30; 30:1; Dt 21:15–17 *See also* Ge 16:4–6 *Sarah and Hagar;* 1Sa 1:4–7 *Hannah and Peninnah;* 2Ch 11:21–22; 1Ki 1:11–13 *the conflict over the succession to David's throne*

Further examples of polygamy
2Sa 5:13 pp 1Ch 14:3 *See also* 1Sa 25:40–43; 2Sa 12:8–9; 1Ki 20:5 *Ahab;* 2Ki 24:15 *Jehoiachin;* 1Ch 4:5 *Ashhur;* Da 5:2 *Belshazzar*

Restrictions on polygamous relationships
Ge 31:50; Ex 21:10; Lev 18:18

Polygamy forbidden
1Co 7:2; 1Ti 3:2 *Polygamy is expressly forbidden for church leaders.*

See also

5672 concubines	5717 monogamy
5680 family	5744 wife
5702 husband	8252 faithfulness,
5708 marriage	relationships

5733

pregnancy

Pregnancy regarded as a blessing from God
Ge 4:1 *See also* Ge 4:17; 16:4; 20:17–18; 29:32; 30:1–2,4–6,17,23

Pregnancy after barrenness
Ge 25:21 *See also* Ge 30:22–23; 1Sa 1:1–20; 2Ki 4:11–17; Lk 1:24–25

Pregnancy in old age
Lk 1:36–37 *See also* Ge 18:9–15; 21:1–7

Ritual uncleanness after pregnancy
Lev 12:1–7

Pregnancy outside marriage
As a result of incest Ge 19:30–38

As a result of prostitution Ge 38:24–25 *See also* Ge 38:13–19

As a result of adultery 2Sa 11:2–5

Pregnancy in troubled times sometimes a misfortune
Because of atrocities committed in war 2Ki 15:16 *See also* 2Ki 8:12; Hos 13:16; Am 1:13

Because of additional hardship in harsh circumstances Mt 24:15–21 pp Mk 13:14–19 pp Lk 21:20–24

Premature birth
Ex 21:22–25 *See also* 1Sa 4:19

Labour pains
1Th 5:3 *See also* Ge 3:16; 1Sa 4:19; Rev 12:2

Miscarriage
Ex 23:25–26 *See also* Ge 31:38; Job 21:10; Hos 9:14

Figurative use of pregnancy
Ps 7:14 *See also* Hos 9:11

See also

5061 sanctity of life	5652 babies
5199 womb	5655 birth
5225 barrenness	5663 childbirth
5410 midwife	5724 offspring
5428 nurse	5739 twins

5734

relationships

God created people to be in relationship with himself and with one another in friendship, marriage, family, society and the church.

Human beings are created to be in relationship
With God Rev 21:3 *See also* Isa 43:6–7; Hos 11:1; 2Co 6:18

With one another Ge 2:18 *See also* Ps 127:4; Pr 17:6,17; 18:24; 27:10; Ecc 4:9–12

Relationship with God
Is entered by faith Jn 1:12–13 *See also* Mt 12:50 pp Mk 3:35 pp Lk 8:21; Jn 17:3; Gal 3:26

Is expressed through covenant Ex 6:7 *This is often known as the covenant formula. See also* Ge 17:7; 2Sa 7:14–15 pp 1Ch 17:13–14; Lk 22:20 pp Mt 26:28 pp Mk 14:24; 2Co 6:16; Lev 26:12; Heb 10:15–18; Jer 31:33–34

Relationships between believers
Believers are to be in relationship with one another in the church Gal 3:28 *See also* Eph 2:14–16,19

Believers are to maintain good relationships Eph 4:3 *See also* Ro 12:18; 14:19; Heb 12:14

Believers are to restore broken relationships Mt 18:15 *See also* Mt 5:23–24; Eph 4:26

See also

1040 God, fatherhood	7025 church, unity
1511 Trinity, relationships in	8252 faithfulness, relationships
5361 justice, human	8299 love in relationships
5680 family	8603 prayer, relationship with God
5690 friends	
5708 marriage	
6608 adoption	
6672 grace in relationships	

5735

sexuality

Men and women are intended to complement one another and to take pleasure in one another. God has provided for the full and glad expression of this in marriage.

Sexuality comes from God
It was created by God Ge 1:27

God intended men and women to complement one another 1Co 11:11 *See also* Ge 2:18–22

Sexual differences
In strength 1Pe 3:7

In role 1Co 11:3–5; 14:34–35; Eph 5:22–25; Col 3:18–19; 1Ti 2:12–14; 1Pe 3:1

In dress Dt 22:5 *See also* 1Co 11:14–15

Sexual activity
It was ordained by God Ge 1:28 *This command was made before the fall, and no guilt attaches to it.*

Marriage in its proper context Ge 2:23–24 *"one flesh" implies both bodily union and an inseparable intimate relationship. See also* Mt 19:4–6 pp Mk 10:6–9; 1Co 7:2–4; Eph 5:31–33

Sexual desire SS 4:3–15 *"Song of Songs" celebrates the beauty of sex in a loving context. It contains much delicate and intimate imagery that applies directly to human lovers and can also be applied to Jesus Christ and the church. See also* Ge 3:16; SS 1:2–4; 4:16; 7:11–13; 8:10

Abstinence is possible Mt 19:12; 1Co 7:1,5

Perversions of sexuality
Adultery Ex 20:14 pp Dt 5:18 *See also* Heb 13:4

Lust Mt 5:28 *Lust may also lead to other sexual sins. See also* Eph 4:19; 5:3; Col 3:5; 1Pe 4:3

Promiscuity Dt 22:13–21; Ro 1:24

Prostitution Lev 19:29

Homosexuality Ro 1:26–27 *See also* Ge 19:4–7; Lev 18:22

Bestiality Ex 22:19

Sexual perversion will be punished 1Co 6:9–10; Rev 21:8; 22:15

Sexual perversion can be cleansed 1Co 6:11

Sexuality is transcended in heaven
Mt 22:30

See also

5707 male and female	5832 desire
5708 marriage	6236 sexual sin
5729 one flesh	6652 forgiveness
5773 abstinence, discipline	8339 self-control
	8777 lust
	9410 heaven

5736

singleness

Not being married; the state prior to betrothal or following separation or the death of a spouse. In Scripture, an unmarried woman generally lives with, and is the responsibility of, her family. Whilst the unmarried are freer of worldly concerns and may devote themselves more fully to God, those already married should not separate, and those without the gift of celibacy should not remain single.

Responsibility for an unmarried woman
An unmarried woman is responsible to her father Dt 22:16 *See also* Ex 2:21; Nu 30:3–5; Jdg 1:12–13; 1Sa 18:17,21

An unmarried woman is dependent on her brothers Lev 21:3 *See also* Ge 24:51; 34:14–15; Eze 44:25

Widowed or divorced women could return to their parents' home Ru 1:8–13 *See also* Ge 38:11; Lev 22:13; Jdg 19:2

Regulations relating to the unmarried
Dt 20:7; 22:20–21,28–29

The unwelcome prospect of remaining unmarried
Jdg 11:37–39; Isa 54:6 *See also* Ge 19:31–32; Isa 49:20–21; 62:4; Hos 2:2; Gal 4:27; Isa 54:1

Celibacy
Celibacy is a calling from God 1Co 7:7 *See also* Jer 16:2; Mt 19:10–12 *It is better to marry than to burn with passion:* 1Co 7:9,36; 1Ti 5:11–14

Believers should remain as they are when called 1Co 7:25–28 *See also* 1Co 7:10,12–13,17,24

Sexual abstinence within marriage is strictly limited 1Co 7:2–6 *See also* Ex 19:15; 1Sa 21:4–5

The desirability of being unmarried 1Co 7:8 *See also* 1Co 7:1,11,37–38

The unmarried may devote themselves to God 1Co 7:32–35 *See also* Lk 14:20,26; Ac 21:9; 1Ti 5:5

Marriage belongs to a passing order Mt 22:30 pp Mk 12:25 pp Lk 20:35 *See also* 1Co 7:29–31

See also

5309 eunuchs	5743 widows
5675 divorce	5744 wife
5702 husband	6236 sexual sin
5709 marriage, purpose	8204 chastity
	8225 devotion
5740 virgin	

5737

sisters

The daughter of one's parents, or of either mother or father. The relationship with a sister is a close one, especially with an unmarried sister.

The relationship with a sister was a close one
Eze 44:25 *See also* Lev 21:1–3; Nu 6:6–7; Job 1:1–4

A brother had some measure of responsibility for his sister
SS 8:8–9 *See also* Ge 24:28–60; 2Sa 13:19–20

Sexual relationships with sisters
Marrying a sister was permissible in pre-Mosaic times Ge 20:12

Sexual relationships with a sister were later forbidden in Mosaic law Lev 18:9 *See also* Lev 18:11–13,18; 20:17; Dt 27:22; Eze 22:11

Rape Ge 34:1–31 *Dinah's rape was avenged by her brothers;* 2Sa 13:1–19 *Tamar was raped by her half-brother;* 2Sa 13:23–36 *Absalom avenged Tamar's rape.*

Sometimes the wives of the patriarchs posed as their sisters
Ge 20:13 *See also* Ge 12:10–20; 20:1–7; 26:1–10

Examples of the behaviour of sisters
Jealousy Ge 30:1 *See also* Ge 30:7–8

Criticism Lk 10:38–42 *See also* Nu 12:1–15

Kindness and concern 2Ch 22:11 pp 2Ki 11:2 *See also* Ex 2:1–8; Job 42:11; Jn 11:1–3,17–32

Sisters-in-law
Marriage to a sister-in-law was allowed in specific circumstances Dt 25:5–10 *See also* Ge 38:6–11

Sexual relationships with sisters-in-law were forbidden under normal circumstances Lev 18:16 *See also* Lev 20:21; Mk 6:17–20; Lk 3:19–20

Sister used as a term of affection
By a husband SS 4:9–10 *See also* SS 4:12; 5:1–2

In the church Ro 16:1 *See also* 1Ti 5:1–2; Phm 1–2; Jas 2:15–17; 2Jn 13

The metaphorical use of sister
Of death Job 17:13–16

Of wisdom Pr 7:1–5

Of nations Jer 3:6–10 *See also*
Eze 16:44–63; 23:1–49

Sister as a theological term
Describing the relationship of
believers to Jesus Christ Mt 12:46–50
pp Mk 3:31–35

**Jesus Christ requires his followers to
put him before family ties** Lk 14:26 *See
also* Mt 19:29 pp Mk 10:29–30

See also

5661 brothers	5744 wife
5674 daughters	5745 women
5680 family	6236 sexual sin

5738

sons

The male offspring of parents. While
sharing in the general privileges and
responsibilities of children, sons had
special claims to inheritance from
their parents. To refer to Christians
as "sons of God" is to identify both
their relationship to God and also
their rights as heirs of God. A
significant number of titles for Jesus
Christ make use of the term "Son",
stressing the close relationship
between the Father and Son.

Privileges of sonship
Inheritance Pr 13:22; Gal 4:7; Heb 1:2

Being disciplined
*Discipline is here seen as a loving means of
enabling a child to grow to maturity:*
Dt 8:5; Pr 19:18; 29:17; Heb 12:5–11;
Rev 3:19

Being loved and provided for
Lk 11:11–13 pp Mt 7:9–11

Being prayed for Ge 17:18–20;
2Sa 12:16; Job 1:5

Examples of good sons
Ge 9:23 *Shem and Japheth;* Ge 22:6–12
Isaac
Joseph: Ge 45:8–11; 47:11–12
Lk 2:51 *The voluntary obedience of the
child Jesus towards Mary and Joseph is
widely regarded as setting an example for
believers.*
Timothy: 2Ti 1:5; 3:14–15

Examples of bad sons
Ge 37:1–35 *Jacob's eleven sons;*
Lk 15:11–32

Christians as sons of God
Heb 12:5–6 *See also* Ro 8:14; 9:26;
2Co 6:18; Heb 12:7

Adopted sons
Ex 2:10 *See also* Ge 48:5

Sons-in-law
Ge 19:12–14; Jdg 19:5; 1Sa 18:18–27

Family relationships must be
subservient to one's relationship
with God
Mt 10:35 pp Lk 12:53; Mt 10:37

Son as an honorific term
Mt 9:2 pp Mt 9:5; Lk 15:31

Sons in a spiritual role
1Ti 1:18 *See also* Joel 2:28; Ac 2:17;
2Ti 1:1

Son in a non-literal sense
Mt 23:15; Mk 3:17; Jn 12:36; Ac 4:36;
1Th 5:5

Titles of Jesus Christ as Son
Son Isa 9:6 *See also* Ps 2:7,12; Mt 3:17;
Jn 3:35

Son of Joseph
*Jesus Christ is described in this way by
those who have yet to understand the
circumstances of his conception and birth:*
Lk 3:23; Jn 1:45; 6:42

Son of Mary Mk 6:3

Son of David Mt 15:22 *See also*
Mk 10:47–48 pp Lk 18:38–39

Son of God Ac 9:20 *See also* Mt 4:3;
Lk 1:35; Jn 1:34; 19:7; Ro 1:3–4; 1Jn 5:5

Son of the living God Mt 16:16

Son of the Most High Lk 1:32

Son of Man Lk 19:10 *See also* Mt 8:20;
17:22; Mk 9:12; Lk 17:22; Jn 5:27;
Ac 7:56

See also

2078 Christ, sonship of	5701 heir
	5703 inheritance
5658 boys	5708 marriage
5661 brothers	5731 parents
5664 children	6608 adoption
5674 daughters	7115 children of God
5680 family	

5739

twins

Two children born of the same
parents at the same time.
Figuratively used to describe a
matching pair.

Examples of twins
Ge 25:21–26 *Although Jacob and Esau
were twins, their very different characters
indicate that God deals with and relates to
people individually. See also* Ge 38:27–30;
Jn 20:24 *Didymus means "twin". It is not
known who his twin was;* Jn 21:2;
Ac 28:11 *the mythical twin sons of Zeus
regarded as special protectors of sailors*

Twins used to illustrate God's
election
Ro 9:10–16

Twins used figuratively for
matching pairs
SS 4:2,5; 6:6; 7:3

See also

5094 Jacob	5664 children
5661 brothers	5737 sisters

5740

virgin

Generally a young person, especially
a female, who has not had sexual
intercourse. Virginity is an
important quality in a bride, and its
surrender or violation prior to
marriage is sternly condemned. In
the miracle of the incarnation, Mary

was still a virgin when Jesus Christ
was conceived. Virginity is also used
metaphorically to denote purity and
innocence.

Virginity is important in a bride
Virgins were sought as brides
Ge 24:14–16; SS 4:12 *See also*
Ge 24:42–45 *The word translated
"maiden" might also refer to a virgin;*
Lev 21:13–14; Dt 22:13–19; Est 2:2,17;
Isa 62:5; Eze 44:22

The church presented as a virgin bride
2Co 11:2 *See also* Eph 5:25–27;
Rev 19:7–8

The loss of virginity before
marriage
Of a virgin not pledged in marriage
Ex 22:16–17 *See also* Dt 22:28–29;
2Sa 13:12–16

Of a virgin pledged in marriage
Dt 22:20–21 *See also* Dt 22:23–24
*Betrothal was as serious a commitment as
marriage itself; consorting with another
person during this period was tantamount
to adultery;* Dt 22:25–27; Mt 1:18–19

**Some fathers surrendered their
daughters' virginity** Ge 19:8 *See also*
Jdg 19:24

Particular roles involving virgins
Maidens in victory processions
Ps 68:25; Jer 31:4 *See also* Ex 15:20–21;
Jdg 11:34; 1Sa 18:6

Virgins as bridesmaids Ps 45:14 *See also*
Mt 25:1

A virgin looked after King David
1Ki 1:1–4

Virginity as a sign of purity and
innocence
**Virgins were spared after military
victories** Nu 31:17–18 *See also*
Jdg 21:11–12

Israel's virgin purity lost Jer 18:13 *See
also* Jer 31:21–23; Eze 23:3–8

Virginity as a metaphor for
(apparent) inviolability
2Ki 19:21 pp Isa 37:22; Isa 47:1

Lost opportunities of virgin
youthfulness
Am 5:2 *See also* Jdg 11:36–40; Isa 23:12;
Jer 46:11; La 1:15–16; 2:13; Joel 1:8

Paul's advice about virgins
A virgin is freer to serve God
1Co 7:32–35 *The unmarried have fewer
responsibilities and worldly cares and so
may offer undivided devotion to God. See
also* 1Co 7:25–28

**Remaining unmarried is a preferred
option** 1Co 7:8,37–38

**Marriage is the proper outlet for sexual
passion** 1Co 7:9 *Though Paul urges
abstinence, sexual passion is not wrong;
however, sexual relationships must be
confined to marriage;* 1Co 7:36

Mary's virginity at Jesus Christ's
conception
Mt 1:20–25 *See also* Isa 7:14;
Lk 1:27,34–35

Parable of the ten virgins
Mt 25:1–13

5741

VOWS

Promises made to God, usually in the context of worship or religious practice. There was no requirement on any Israelite to make vows, but once made, they were binding and had to be kept.

Vows were binding
Dt 23:21–23 *See also* Nu 30:2,9; Pr 20:25; Ecc 5:4–6; Mal 1:14

Exceptions to keeping vows
Nu 30:3–8 *In certain cases vows made by daughters or wives could be nullified by fathers or husbands respectively. See also* Nu 30:10–15

Vows made to God in the context of worship
To offer sacrifices Lev 22:17–19 *See also* Lev 7:16; 22:21; 27:9; Nu 15:2–4,8–10; Dt 12:6,11; Ps 50:14; 66:13; Pr 7:14; Jnh 2:9

To dedicate people, animals or property to God Lev 27:1–25

To give money 2Ki 12:4–5 *See also* Dt 23:18

Motives for making vows
To elicit God's help 1Sa 1:11 *See also* Ge 28:20–22; Nu 21:2; Jdg 11:30–40; 2Sa 15:7–8; Ps 66:13–14

To express thanksgiving Ps 116:12–14 *See also* Ps 50:14; 56:12; 116:17–18; Jnh 1:16; 2:9

To praise God Ps 22:25 *See also* Ps 61:8; 65:1

Vows of Nazirites
Nu 6:1–21; Jdg 13:2–5 *Samson was set apart as a Nazirite from birth;* 1Sa 1:11 *Samuel may have been a Nazirite.*

Examples of vows made to God
By David Ps 132:2–5

By Paul Ac 18:18 *See also* Ac 21:24–26

Abuse of vows
Mt 15:5–6 pp Mk 7:11–13

Vows made to idols
Jer 44:25–28

5742

wedding

The public acknowledgment and celebration of a couple's marriage.

The wedding followed betrothal and was a preliminary to sexual union. The occasion was marked by feasting, singing and rejoicing. The bride wore a wedding dress, jewellery and ornaments and both she and the groom were waited on by attendants.

Wedding garments
The bride's wedding dress Ps 45:13 *See also* Ge 24:65; Eze 16:10; Rev 19:7–8; 21:2

The bride's jewellery and ornaments Isa 49:18 *See also* Isa 61:10; Jer 2:32; Eze 16:11–12

Wedding festivities
Weddings were occasions for rejoicing Jer 33:11
Wedding festivities might last for a week or two: Ge 29:27–28; Jdg 14:12 SS 3:11; Isa 62:5; Jer 7:34

Wedding songs Ps 45:1 Title; 78:63

The wedding banquet Jdg 14:10 *See also* Ge 29:21–22 *A feast celebrates Jacob's wedding;* Mt 22:2 *a wedding banquet given by a king for his son;* Jn 2:3–10 *Jesus Christ changes water into wine at a wedding feast;* Rev 19:9 *the marriage supper of the Lamb*

Guests and attendants at weddings
Wedding guests Jn 2:1–2 *See also* Mt 22:3–10,11–12 *Wedding guests were expected to wear appropriate clothes;* Lk 14:8–10

Attendants on the groom Jn 3:29 *See also* Jdg 14:11,20; Mt 9:15 pp Mk 2:19 pp Lk 5:34

Bridesmaids Ps 45:14 *See also* Mt 25:1–10

Wedding gifts
1Ki 9:16 *See also* Ge 24:59; 29:24,29; Jdg 1:14–15

Elements in the wedding ceremony
Covering the bride
Sometimes the groom would cover the bride with his cloak as a symbol of protection: Ru 3:9; Eze 16:8

A covenanted commitment Pr 2:17; Mal 2:14

Blessing the couple Ge 24:60; Ru 4:11

Consummating the marriage Joel 2:16 *See also* Ge 29:23; Ps 19:5

5743

widows

God's tender concern for bereaved wives is declared throughout the whole of Scripture. He defends their rights and expects his people to do the same.

God is the protector of widows
Ps 68:5 *See also* Dt 10:18; Ps 146:9; Pr 15:25; Jer 49:11

Jesus Christ's concern for widows
Mk 12:41–44 pp Lk 21:1–4; Lk 7:11–15; 18:1–5

Widows are to be treated justly
Dt 27:19 *See also* Ex 22:22–24; Job 24:21–22; Ps 94:6; Isa 10:1–4; Jer 22:3–5; Eze 22:25

Widows are not to be exploited
Ex 22:22 *See also* Isa 10:1–2; Eze 22:7; Mal 3:5; Mk 12:38–40 pp Lk 20:45–47

The law requires God's people to provide for widows
Dt 24:19 *See also* Dt 14:28–29; 16:11; 24:17,20–21; 26:12; Isa 1:17 *The prophet encourages God's people to return to the law.*

The Christian community are to care for widows
1Ti 5:3 *See also* 1Ti 5:4–16; 1Co 7:8–9; Jas 1:27

Examples of widows and their treatment
Dt 16:14; Ru 1:16–17; 1Ki 17:13–14; Job 24:3; 29:13; Lk 2:36–38 *Anna;* Lk 4:25–26; 7:11–17 *the widow of Nain;* Ac 6:1; 9:36–41 *Dorcas*

Women widowed because of God's judgment
Ex 22:22–24 *See also* Ps 109:9; Isa 9:17; Jer 15:8; La 5:3

Laws governing the remarriage of widows
The people generally Dt 25:5–10 *The OT emphasises continuity of the family line. See also* Ge 38:8; Ru 3:12 *Boaz refers to the law which gave the nearest male relative the duty of marrying the widow;* Ru 4:10; Mk 12:19 pp Lk 20:28

The priests Lev 21:13–14 *See also* Eze 44:22

Widowhood as the personification of a city
La 1:1 *A lament for desolate Jerusalem. See also* Isa 54:4–5 *a prophecy of the restoration of Jerusalem;* Rev 18:7 *the boasts of Babylon*

5744

wife

The female partner in a marriage relationship. The origin of this God-ordained institution is traced back in the Bible to the Garden of Eden. Scripture stresses that marriage is a God-ordained institution, within which the husband should love and care for his wife, just as the wife should obey, honour and care for her husband. A good wife is portrayed as a great blessing, but a bad wife influences her husband for evil. In the OT, Israel is sometimes portrayed as God's wife; in the NT, the church is described as Christ's bride.

God's pattern for marriage
Husband and wife are one flesh
Ge 1:27 *See also* Ge 2:23–24; Mal 2:15; Mt 19:4–6 pp Mk 10:6–9

The wife as helper and companion
Ge 2:18 *See also* Ge 2:20–22

The husband is head of the wife
Eph 5:23 *See also* 1Co 11:3

The wife is the weaker partner 1Pe 3:7 *See also* Ge 3:16

The Israelites were forbidden to take foreign wives
Dt 7:3–4 *See also* Ex 34:16; Jos 23:12–13

Duties of a wife
To submit to and respect her husband
Col 3:18 *See also* Eph 5:22–24,33; 1Pe 3:1–6

To care for her husband and household Pr 31:10–31 *See also* Tit 2:4–5

To be faithful to her husband Ex 20:14 pp Dt 5:18 *See also* Nu 5:11–31; Pr 23:27; Mt 14:3–4 pp Mk 6:17–18; Mk 10:12; Lk 3:19

Advice on widows remarrying
1Co 7:39–40 *See also* 1Co 7:8–9

Childless wives
Ge 25:21 *See also* Ge 18:9–15; Jdg 13:2–5; 1Sa 1:9–20; Lk 1:5–25

Good wives
Pr 31:10–31 *See also* 1Sa 19:11–17; 25:14–35; Pr 12:4; 18:22; 19:14; Tit 2:3–5; 1Pe 3:1–6

Wives giving good counsel
Mt 27:19 *See also* Jdg 13:22–23; Da 5:10–12

Bad wives
Pr 12:4 *See also* Pr 19:13; 21:19; 25:24

Wives influencing their husbands for evil
Ge 3:8–12 *See also* 1Ki 11:3–4; 21:20–26; Est 5:9–14; Job 2:9

Israel as the wife of God
Jer 3:20 *Israel's relationship with God was at times comparable to that of an unfaithful wife;* Eze 16:8 *See also* Isa 62:5; Jer 2:2; Eze 16:32; Hos 1:2; 2:2

The church as the bride of Christ
Rev 21:2 *See also* Eph 5:25–27; Rev 19:7

See also
5093 Eve	5732 polygamy
5225 barrenness	5743 widows
5659 bride	6242 adultery
5675 divorce	6243 adultery,
5702 husband	spiritual
5708 marriage	7135 Israel, people
5729 one flesh	of God

5745

women

God created both women and men in his image and likeness. Scripture shows women in a variety of roles, playing an important part in God's salvation plan. In Christ, there is no fundamental distinction between believers on account of gender, race or social status. Women played a significant part in the life of Jesus Christ and in the early church. The NT both records their role and faces the questions thereby raised.

The creation of women
Ge 2:20–24 *See also* Ge 1:27; 5:1–2; 1Ti 2:13

Women and the fall
1Ti 2:14 *See also* Ge 3:1–16; 2Co 11:3

Examples of godly women
Ru 1:16–17 *Ruth;* 1Sa 1:9–28 *Hannah;* 1Sa 25:2–35 *Abigail;* Est 4:15–16 *Esther;* Lk 1:41–45 *Elizabeth;* Ac 9:36–42 *Tabitha*

Examples of women who are condemned or judged
2Sa 6:16–23 *Michal;* 1Ki 21:1–25 *Jezebel;* Pr 5:1–6 *the adulteress* *The women of Jerusalem:* Isa 3:16–4:1; Eze 13:17–23

OT laws concerning women
Ex 21:22–25; Lev 12:1–8; 15:19–30; Dt 22:5

Women in office in the OT
As a judge or leader Jdg 4:4–5

As a prophetess Ex 15:20–21 *See also* Jdg 4:4; 2Ki 22:14–20; Isa 8:3

As a queen 2Ki 11:1–3 *See also* 1Ki 10:1–13 pp 2Ch 9:1–12; Est 1:9–21; 2:17

Women as wives and mothers in the OT
Pr 12:4 *See also* Ge 2:24; 21:11–12; Pr 18:22; 31:10–31

Women in the life of Jesus Christ
In the birth narratives Lk 1:26–56; 2:16–19,36–38

In the ministry of Jesus Christ
Lk 8:1–3 *Jesus Christ respected women and talked to them as individuals with spiritual understanding. This was a considerable deviation from the cultural conventions of the time. See also* Mt 9:20–22 pp Mk 5:25–34 pp Lk 8:43–48; Mt 15:21–28 pp Mk 7:24–30; Mk 12:41–44 pp Lk 21:1–4; Lk 10:38–42; Jn 4:7–30; 11:17–44

In the passion narratives Mt 27:55–56 pp Mk 15:40–41 pp Lk 23:49 *See also* Mt 26:6–13 pp Mk 14:3–9 pp Lk 7:37–38 pp Jn 12:1–8; Mt 27:61 pp Mk 15:47 pp Lk 23:55–56; Mt 28:1–10 pp Mk 16:1–11 pp Lk 24:1–11

Women's ministry in the early church
As prophets Ac 21:8–9 *See also* Ac 2:17–18; Joel 2:28–29; 1Co 11:5

As teachers Tit 2:3–5 *See also* Ac 18:24–26

As deacons Ro 16:1–2 *NIV footnote at verse 1. See also* 1Ti 3:11 fn

As hostesses Col 4:15 *See also* Ac 16:15; 1Co 16:19

As workers in the church Ro 16:12 *See also* Ro 16:6; Php 4:2–3

As an apostle Ro 16:7 *Interpreters disagree over whether Junias was a man or a woman, and also over whether Paul meant these two were notable in the ranks of the apostles or were well-known to the apostles.*

Instructions to women in the early church community
Their role in the church meetings
1Co 11:5–16; 14:33–35; 1Ti 2:11–12

Their behaviour as Christians
1Ti 2:9–10; 5:11–16; Tit 2:3–5; 1Pe 3:1–6

The care of women in the early church community
Ac 6:1; 1Ti 5:1–10

Women as the weaker sex
1Pe 3:7 *See also* 1Ti 2:13–14

Women and their relationships
Their relationship to God through Jesus Christ Gal 3:26–29

Their relationship to their husbands
Ro 7:2–3; 1Co 7:1–5,10–16,39–40; Eph 5:22–24,33; Col 3:18; Tit 2:4–5; 1Pe 3:1–6

Their relationship to men 1Co 11:3 *Some interpret this as referring to a husband, rather than to men generally. See also* 1Co 11:7–12; 1Ti 2:11–12

Feminism and the Bible's teaching on women
The equality of the sexes and rejection of female subordination 1Co 11:11–12; Gal 3:28

Examples of the abuse of women by men Jdg 11:30–40; 19:22–30; 2Sa 13:1–20; Ac 16:16–21

Women who are strong role models
Jdg 4:4 *Deborah;* 2Ki 22:14–20 *Huldah;* Pr 31:10–31 *the wife of noble character;* SS 3:1–5 *the beloved;* Ac 16:13–15 *Lydia*

See also
5093 Eve	5708 marriage
5659 bride	5718 mothers
5674 daughters	5743 widows
5680 family	5744 wife
5695 girls	6240 rape
5700 headship	
5707 male and	
female	

5746

youth

Scripture characterises youth as a time of vigour and strength. It speaks, too, of the pressures and expectations of youth, warns about the temptations facing young people, and instructs the young about what is expected of them.

The vigour of youth
Pr 20:29 *See also* Job 33:25; Ps 103:5; 144:12; SS 2:3; Ecc 11:9–10
Isa 40:30 *Even youthful strength and vigour may fail. See also* Job 20:11; Ps 78:31; Am 8:13

The duties of youth
To remember God Ecc 12:1 *See also* 1Ki 18:12; Ps 71:5; La 3:25–27
Ps 119:9 *See also* Ps 71:17; Eze 4:14

To respect the elderly Lev 19:32 *See also* Job 29:8; 32:6; 1Ti 5:1; 1Pe 5:5

To honour parents Ex 20:12 pp Dt 5:16 *See also* Eph 6:2–3; Lev 19:3; 1Ti 5:4

To obey parents Pr 1:8 *See also* Pr 6:20; 23:22; Eph 6:1; Col 3:20

To remain faithful to one's partner Pr 5:18 *See also* Pr 2:17; Mal 2:14–15

Examples of godly young people
Godly young men 1Sa 2:18 *Samuel*; 1Sa 17:33 *David, fighting Goliath*; 2Ch 24:1–2 pp 2Ki 12:1–2 *Joash became king at the age of seven*; 2Ch 34:1–2 pp 2Ki 22:1–2 *Josiah became king at the age of eight*; Lk 2:42–52 *Jesus Christ at the age of twelve*; 2Ti 1:5 *Timothy*

Godly young women Jdg 11:36 *Jephthah's daughter*; Ru 1:16–17 *Ruth*; Est 4:15–16 *Esther*; Lk 1:38 *the virgin Mary*; Ac 21:9 *Philip's daughters*

The promise of youth
Israel's youthful devotion Jer 2:2 *See also* Jer 3:4; Eze 16:22,43
Hos 2:14–15 *See also* Isa 54:4; 62:5; Eze 16:60

Dying young as a sign of judgment Ps 89:45 *See also* Job 36:14; Ps 78:63; Isa 13:12; Jer 9:21 *The death of children and young people symbolises loss of hope for the future*; Jer 11:22

Particular pressures of youth
The inexperience of youth 1Ki 3:7; 1Ch 22:5; 29:1; 2Ch 13:7; Jer 1:6; 1Ti 4:12

Temptations facing the young 2Ti 2:22 *See also* Pr 7:7; Lk 15:13,30; Mt 19:22 pp Mk 10:22 pp Lk 18:23; Tit 2:6

Troubles faced from the time of one's youth 2Sa 19:7; Ps 88:15; 129:1–2

The sins of youth
Ps 25:7 *See also* Job 13:26

Disrespect for older people
2Ki 2:23–24; Job 30:1; Isa 3:5; La 5:12

Dishonouring parents
Dt 21:18–20; Pr 15:20; 30:11; 2Ti 3:2

Persistent sinfulness
Jer 3:24–25; 22:21; 32:30

The sinfulness of Israel's youth
Eze 23:3,8,19–21; Hos 11:1–2

Examples of sinful young men
1Sa 2:17 *the sons of Eli*; 1Sa 8:2–3 *the sons of Samuel*; 2Sa 15:6 *Absalom*; 1Ki 12:8–14 pp 2Ch 10:8–11 *Rehoboam*; 2Ki 21:1–2 pp 2Ch 33:1–2 *Manasseh*

See also
5276 crime	5887 inexperience
5664 children	5949 shyness
5716 middle age	5954 strength
5725 old age	6020 sin
5731 parents	6248 temptation
5740 virgin	8453 obedience

5760
Human attitudes and behaviour

5761
attitudes

The ways in which people think or feel about something or someone and which affect their behaviour. This set of themes consists of the following:
5762 attitudes, God's to people
5763 attitudes, positive to God
5764 attitudes, negative to God
5765 attitudes, to other people
5766 attitudes, to life
5767 attitudes, in prayer

5762
attitudes, God's to people

Scripture indicates the ways in which God relates to people, often suggesting that these illustrate the ways in which believers should behave.

God's love
Jn 3:16 *See also* Ps 36:5–7; 107:1; 136:1; Jn 13:1; Ro 5:5; 8:35–39; Eph 5:2; 1Jn 4:8–10,16

God's compassion
Ps 116:5 *See also* Isa 54:8; Jer 9:24; Hos 11:4; Mt 9:36; Ro 2:4; 11:22; 2Co 1:3; Eph 2:7; Tit 3:4; Jas 5:11

God's grace and mercy
Jn 1:14 *See also* Dt 4:31; Da 9:9; Ro 5:15; 2Co 8:9; Eph 2:4,7; 1Ti 1:14; 1Pe 5:10

God's jealousy
Ex 20:5 pp Dt 5:9 *See also* Dt 4:24; Jos 24:19; Na 1:2

God's patience
2Pe 3:9 *See also* Ne 9:30; Ro 9:22; 1Ti 1:16; 1Pe 3:20

God's faithfulness
Ps 117:2 *See also* Ex 34:6; Dt 7:9; Ps 25:10; 36:5; 119:90; La 3:22–23; 1Co 10:13; 1Jn 1:9

See also
1030 God, compassion	5379 law, Christ's attitude
1035 God, faithfulness	5825 cruelty, God's attitude
1055 God, grace & mercy	6025 sin & God's character
1085 God, love of	8773 jealousy
1095 God, patience of	8792 oppression, God's attitude

5763
attitudes, positive to God

Scripture identifies a range of positive attitudes towards God, which believers are encouraged to adopt.

Trust
Pr 3:5 *See also* Ps 20:7; 25:1–2; 40:4; 56:11; Jn 14:1; Ro 15:13

Faith
Mt 8:10 pp Lk 7:9 *See also* Mt 9:2 pp Mk 2:5 pp Lk 5:20; Heb 11:1–39

Hope
Job 13:15 *See also* Ps 25:5; Isa 40:31; Mic 7:7; Ro 4:18

Love
Dt 6:5 *See also* Dt 30:6; Ps 18:1; 116:1; Jn 21:15–17

Holiness
Heb 12:14; 1Pe 1:15–16 *See also* Dt 7:6; 14:1–2; Ro 12:1–2; 1Co 5:7–8; Col 3:2

Awesome respect
Ecc 12:13 *See also* Dt 10:12–13; Pr 1:7; 9:10; Jer 5:22; Ac 9:31; Rev 14:7

Repentance
2Co 7:10 *See also* Job 42:6; Eze 14:6; Ac 2:38; 17:30

Humility
Isa 66:2 *See also* Ezr 8:21; Jas 4:10; 1Pe 5:6

Self-denial
Mt 16:24 pp Mk 8:34 pp Lk 9:23

Submission
Jas 4:7 *See also* Job 22:21; Ro 8:7; 10:3

Thankfulness
1Th 5:18 *See also* 1Ch 16:34; Ps 35:18; 100:4; Mt 14:19; Eph 5:20; Php 4:6; Col 2:7

Praise
Heb 13:15 *See also* Ezr 3:11; Ps 148:1–5; 150:1–6; Isa 42:10; 61:3; Ac 2:46–47; Jas 5:13

Prayerfulness
Jas 5:13 *See also* Mt 14:23; 26:41; Ro 8:26; 1Th 5:17

Reverence
Ps 5:7 *See also* Ne 5:15; Mal 2:5; 4:2; Eph 5:21; Heb 12:28; 1Pe 3:1–2

Watchfulness
Col 4:2 *See also* Lk 12:37–38; 1Th 5:6–8; 1Pe 5:8

See also
5959 submission	8352 thankfulness
6732 repentance	8475 self-denial
8020 faith	8490 watchfulness
8266 holiness	8618 prayerfulness
8297 love for God	8664 praise
8333 reverence	9612 hope, in God

5764
attitudes, negative to God

Scripture identifies a range of negative attitudes towards God, which believers are encouraged to avoid.

Rejection
Isa 53:3 *See also* Lev 26:15–16; 1Sa 8:7; Eze 5:6; 20:15–16; Jn 1:11

Lack of faith
Mk 4:40 pp Mt 8:26 pp Lk 8:25 *See also* Mt 13:58 pp Mk 6:6

Pride
Dt 8:14 *See also* Lev 26:19; Lk 1:51; Jas 4:6; 1Pe 5:5; Pr 3:34

Stubbornness
Jer 5:23 *See also* Ps 78:8; Isa 48:4; Mk 3:5; 16:14; Ro 2:5

Rebellion
Ps 78:40 *See also* Dt 1:26; Isa 1:2; Jer 2:29; Eze 2:3; Hos 7:13; Tit 1:10; Heb 3:16

Hostility
Ro 8:7 *See also* Lev 26:21,23–24,27–28; Hos 9:7

See also

5818 contempt	8719 distrust
5838 disrespect	8744 faithlessness
5885 indifference	as
6178 hardness of	disobedience
heart	8802 pride
6222 rebellion	8822 self-
against God	justification
6231 rejection of God	8834 unbelief
6245 stubbornness	

5765
attitudes, to other people

Scripture illustrates a range of attitudes towards other people, some of which are commended, while others are condemned.

Love
Jn 13:34–35 *See also* Mt 22:39 pp Mk 12:31 pp Lk 10:27; 1Co 13:1–13; Eph 5:2; 1Th 4:9; 1Jn 3:11; 4:7

Forgiveness
Col 3:13 *See also* Mt 6:14; Mk 11:25; Lk 6:37; 17:3; Eph 4:32

Helpfulness
Ac 9:36 *See also* Eze 16:49; Mt 25:44; Ac 20:35; 1Co 12:28; 2Co 9:2; 1Ti 5:9–10; Heb 6:10

Hospitality
Ro 12:13 *See also* Ge 18:1–8; Lk 10:38; Heb 13:2

Generosity
2Co 8:2 *See also* Ps 37:21,26; Mt 10:8; Ac 10:2; 2Co 9:6–7; 1Ti 6:18

Kindness
Eph 4:32 *See also* Pr 14:31; 1Co 13:4; Col 3:12; 2Ti 2:24; Tit 2:4–5

Humility
1Pe 5:5 *See also* Pr 3:34; Mt 20:26–28 pp Mk 10:43–45; Php 2:3–8; Tit 3:1–2; Jas 3:13

Patience
1Th 5:14 *See also* Pr 16:32; 1Co 13:4;

Gal 5:22; Eph 4:2; Col 1:11; 2Ti 4:2; Jas 5:7–11

Submission
Eph 5:21
Submission to governing authorities:
Ro 13:1,5; 1Pe 2:13
Submission of wives to husbands:
Eph 5:22–24; Col 3:18; 1Ti 2:11; 1Pe 3:1,5–6
Jas 3:17; 1Pe 2:18 *submission of slaves to masters;* 1Pe 5:5

Gentleness
Php 4:5 *See also* Gal 5:23; Eph 4:2; Col 3:12

Unselfishness
Php 2:4 *See also* Pr 18:1; Gal 5:19–20; Php 1:17; Jas 3:14,16

Pride
Ro 12:16 *See also* Pr 8:13; 2Co 12:7; Gal 5:26

Jealousy
Pr 27:4 *See also* Ge 30:1; 37:11; Ac 5:17; 7:9; 1Co 3:3; 2Co 12:20

Judgment
Lk 6:37 pp Mt 7:1 *See also* Jn 8:3–7

Anger
Eph 4:31 *See also* Ge 4:3–5; 2Ki 5:11; Mk 3:5; Eph 4:26; 1Ti 2:8

Hatred
1Jn 3:15 *See also* 1Jn 2:9,11; 4:20

Partiality
Ge 37:3 *See also* Ge 25:28; Ex 23:3; Lev 19:15; 1Ti 5:21; Jas 2:1–4

See also

5789 anger	8260 generosity
5813 conceit	8291 kindness
5875 hatred	8298 love for one
5876 helpfulness	another
5897 judging others	8356 unselfishness
5959 submission	8445 hospitality
6655 forgiveness,	
application	

5766
attitudes, to life

The way in which people think or feel about human life is of major importance to morality. Scripture declares the sanctity of life, and the attitudes towards life which should follow.

The sanctity of life
Ps 49:7–8; Mt 16:26 pp Mk 8:37

Fear
1Jn 4:18 *See also* Ps 23:4; 91:5; 112:7–8; Isa 35:4; 41:10; 1Pe 3:6

Courage
1Co 16:13 *See also* Jos 1:6–7; 1Sa 17:32,37; Ac 4:13

Rejoicing
Ps 118:24 *See also* Ro 5:3; 12:15; 1Pe 4:13

Anxiety
Php 4:6 *See also* Ps 94:19; Pr 12:25; Ecc 11:10; Mt 6:25–34 pp Lk 12:22–31; Lk 10:41; 1Pe 5:7

Being forward-looking and positive
Php 3:12–14 *See also* Lk 9:62; 2Ti 1:7; 2:3–6

See also

4020 life of faith	5769 behaviour
5061 sanctity of life	5914 optimism
5413 money,	5916 pessimism
attitudes	8219 courage
5448 poverty,	8283 joy
attitudes to	8754 fear
5727 old age,	8849 worry
attitudes	

5767
attitudes, in prayer

Attitudes in prayer include both the postures people adopt while praying and the hopes that they have concerning its outcome. Scripture points to the need for humility and expectation on the part of those who pray.

Positions adopted for prayer
Bowing down and kneeling Ps 95:6 *See also* Ge 24:26; Ex 4:31; Isa 45:23; Da 6:10; Lk 22:41; Ac 7:60; Eph 3:14; Php 2:10

Falling on one's face before God Mt 26:39 *See also* Nu 20:6; Jos 5:14; 2Ch 20:18

Standing Mk 11:25 *See also* 1Ki 8:22; Lk 18:11

Attitudes in the spiritual life
Standing for warfare Eph 6:13–14 *See also* 2Th 2:15; Jas 5:8

Walking with God Mic 6:8 *See also* Isa 40:31; 1Jn 1:7

Running Heb 12:1 *See also* Isa 40:31

See also

5161 kneeling	8482 spiritual
5174 prostration	warfare
5178 running	8620 prayer,
5181 sitting	practicalities
5184 standing	8625 worship,
5197 walking	acceptable
8432 fasting, practice	attitudes

5769
behaviour

A person's actions or way of life. Good behaviour will not earn salvation, but believers must practise good behaviour in accordance with Scripture as evidence of their conversion. Scripture stresses that bad behaviour is inconsistent with Christian faith and urges believers to mend their ways.

Examples of good behaviour
Ge 6:22; Lk 1:6 *See also* Ge 5:24; 2Ki 18:3; Job 1:8; Jn 1:47; 3Jn 3,5–6,12

Examples of bad behaviour
1Ki 16:30 *See also* Ge 4:8; 6:5; 1Sa 25:3; 2Ti 4:14; 3Jn 9–10

Good behaviour towards God is commanded
Ex 20:2–11 pp Dt 5:6–15

Obedience to God's word Ps 1:2 *See also* Ps 19:7–11; 119:1–4

Good behaviour towards other people is commanded
1Pe 2:12 *See also* Ex 20:12–17 pp Dt 5:16–21; Ps 15:1–5; Pr 12:2 *Pr 10:1–31:31 contains much wisdom concerning good and bad behaviour;* Mt 5:21–24

Good behaviour does not earn salvation
Ro 3:20; Tit 3:5 *See also* Gal 2:15–16; Eph 2:8–9; Php 3:9

Good behaviour confirms a believer's profession of faith
Jas 2:14–19; 2Pe 1:5–11 *See also* Mt 7:16–20 pp Lk 6:43–45

Obedience to Jesus Christ and his teachings Mt 7:24–25 pp Lk 6:47–48 *See also* Jn 14:15,23; 15:10; Col 3:16

A believer has died to sin and is alive to God
Ro 6:11–14 *See also* Ro 6:2,19; Gal 5:16,24–25; Eph 4:22–24; Col 3:1,5,9–10; 1Th 5:5–8

See also

4030 world, behaviour in	8158 righteousness of believers
5286 custom	8217 conformity
5377 law, Ten Command- ments	8240 ethics
	8309 morality
	8337 reverence & behaviour
5761 attitudes	8442 good works
5873 habits	
6020 sin	

5770

abandonment

The state and experience of being forsaken, shared by God as well as by human beings.

God is abandoned
God's people deliberately abandon him Jer 2:13 *See also* Dt 32:15; Jdg 2:12; 1Ki 9:9 pp 2Ch 7:22; 2Ch 13:11; Isa 1:4; Jer 17:13

God's people abandon his law Jer 9:12–14 *See also* 1Ki 18:18; 2Ch 12:1; Ps 89:30; 119:53; Pr 4:2,6; Heb 10:28

God's people abandon his covenant Dt 29:25 *See also* Jer 22:9; 31:32; Da 11:30

God's people abandon his temple 2Ch 24:18; 29:6

Those who abandon the gospel 1Ti 4:1 *See also* Heb 10:26,29; Rev 2:4

God abandons those who forsake him
2Ch 24:20 *See also* Nu 32:15 *Moses warns the Transjordan tribes;* Dt 31:17 *Israel's rebellion predicted;* Dt 32:30 *The LORD abandoned Saul:* 1Sa 18:12; 28:15
1Ki 9:7 pp 2Ch 7:20; 1Ch 28:9; Ne 9:28; Isa 2:6; Jer 12:7; La 2:7

God shows mercy to those who have been justly abandoned
Isa 54:7 *See also* Ne 9:19,28,31; Jer 51:5

Those who feel abandoned by God
God's people La 5:20 *See also* Ps 22:1; 43:2; 71:11; 74:1; 89:38

Their prayers Ps 38:21–22 *See also* 1Ki 8:57; Ps 27:9; 71:9,18; 119:8; Jer 14:9

Jesus Christ's feelings of abandonment Mt 27:46 pp Mk 15:34 *See also* Ps 22:1; Ac 2:27; Ps 16:10

God promises never to abandon his people
Dt 31:8 *See also* Lev 26:44; Dt 4:31; 31:6; 1Sa 12:22; Ps 37:25,28; 94:14; Isa 49:14–16; Mt 28:20; 2Co 4:9; Heb 13:5

Examples of people who were abandoned
Ge 16:7–8 *Hagar;* 1Sa 30:13 *a slave;* Isa 49:15 *a newborn baby;* Eze 16:3–6 *Jerusalem;* Ac 14:19 *Paul*

See also

1035 God, faithfulness	5901 loneliness
1055 God, grace & mercy	6233 rejection, experience
2570 Christ, suffering	8602 prayer
	8704 apostasy
5689 friendlessness	8743 faithlessness
5831 depression	9614 hope, results of absence

5771

abstinence

The deliberate decision to do without something, especially as a form of spiritual discipline expressing commitment or repentance.

5772
abstinence, from drinking
See 4436 drinking, abstention from

5773
abstinence, as a discipline

Israel's abstinence from certain sorts of meat
Lev 7:22–27; 11:1–47; Dt 14:1–21; Ac 10:9–14 *God used the food laws to teach Peter a spiritual lesson.*

Israel's abstinence from other things
Ex 19:14–15; Lev 16:29–31; Nu 6:1–4 *See also* Ex 31:16–17; Nu 29:7; Jdg 13:4; 1Sa 21:4

Abstinence from food
As an expression of repentance 1Sa 7:5–6; Ezr 10:6 *See also* 2Sa 1:11–12; Ne 1:3–4; Joel 2:12; Jnh 3:5

Expressing a seeking after God Ac 13:1–2 *See also* Mt 4:1–2 pp Lk 4:1–2; Mt 9:14–15 pp Mk 2:18–20 pp Lk 5:33–35; Lk 2:36–37; Ac 9:9; 14:23; Ro 14:6

Temporary sexual abstinence as a form of discipline
Ex 19:15; 1Sa 21:4–5; 1Co 7:5

Denial of selfish desires
Mt 16:24 pp Mk 8:34 pp Lk 9:23
1Pe 2:11 *See also* Ro 13:13

Voluntary abstinence for the sake of others
1Co 8:13 *See also* Ac 15:19–20,29; 21:25; Ro 14:21; 1Co 9:12,19–27; 10:15–31

Abstinence may be hypocritical
Mt 6:16 *See also* Isa 58:3–7; Jer 14:10–12; Zec 7:2–6; Lk 18:11–12; 1Ti 4:2–5

See also

4436 drinking, abstention	8204 chastity
4544 wine	8339 self-control
5794 asceticism	8429 fasting
5850 excess	8451 mortification
6732 repentance	8475 self-denial
7340 clean and unclean	8737 evil, responses to

5775

abuse

The deliberate misuse of gifts or privileges, and the insulting of individuals. Scripture stresses that neither God's gifts nor his people are to be abused.

The abuse of God and his people
Of God himself 2Ki 19:16

Of God's people Ne 4:1–4; 1Pe 4:4 *See also* Mt 5:11; Ac 2:13; 17:32; 18:6; Rev 2:9

Of God's servants Ac 2:13 *See also* 2Ch 36:16; Ps 22:6–8; 69:7–12; 123:3; Jer 20:7

Of Jesus Christ Lk 16:14 *See also* Lk 23:11

The abuse of Christian freedom is condemned
Believers are required to resist sin Ro 6:12 *See also* Ro 6:14; Heb 12:1–2; 1Jn 5:16–18

Grace does not give believers the freedom to sin Ro 6:1–2 *See also* Ro 6:15; 3:5–8; Gal 2:17–21

The dangers of abusing Christian freedom
1Co 8:9–12 *becoming a stumbling-block to others;* Gal 5:13 *indulging oneself;* 1Pe 2:16 *as means of covering up evil*

Examples of the abuse of Christian freedom
Sexual excesses 1Co 5:1–2 *See also* 1Co 6:12–20; Rev 2:20–22

Abuse of giving Ac 5:1–2

Abuse of the Lord's Supper 1Co 11:20–22

Falling back into sin Ro 6:1–2; Heb 12:1; 1Jn 1:8–10

Disobedience towards God Eph 5:6; 1Pe 2:8; 1Jn 2:3–4; 3:4

Abuse of spiritual gifts 1Co 14:1–20

Eating food sacrificed to idols 1Co 8:1–13; Rev 2:14,20

See also

4434 drinking	6236 sexual sin
5220 authority, abuse	6662 freedom, abuse
5457 power, human	8302 love, abuse of
5769 behaviour	8703 antinomianism
6106 addiction	8775 libertinism
6187 immorality	8815 ridicule

5776

achievement

Human beings can achieve many things, though any achievement which disregards God is futile. God always achieves what he intends. Anything of eternal value needs God-given resources.

Kinds of human achievement

Accumulation of wealth Est 1:4 *See also* 1Ki 10:23 pp 2Ch 9:22; 1Ki 10:26–27 pp 2Ch 9:27; Job 42:12; Ecc 2:4–9

Political power Ge 41:41–43 *See also* 1Ki 4:21 pp 2Ch 9:26; Est 1:1; 10:2–3; Da 2:37–38,48

Buildings 1Ki 7:1–12; Da 4:30; Mk 13:1

Great learning 1Ki 4:32–34; Ecc 1:13–16; Da 1:17

Military victory Ge 14:14–16; Ex 17:8–13; Jos 8:24–26; Jdg 4:14–16; 1Sa 18:7; 2Sa 22:35–43 pp Ps 18:34–42

Acts of courage 1Sa 14:6–14; 17:50; 2Sa 23:8–21 pp 1Ch 11:11–23

Spiritual achievements Ro 15:19 *See also* Lk 10:17; Jn 14:12; Ac 14:3; 20:26–27; 2Co 3:1–3; 1Jn 2:13–14; Rev 2:19

Limitations of human achievements

Human achievements can lead to pride Isa 10:12–15 *See also* Dt 8:10–18; 2Ch 26:16; Da 4:29–30

Human achievements can give false security Lk 12:16–20 *See also* 2Ki 19:11–13 pp Isa 37:11–13; 2Ki 19:21–28 pp Isa 37:21–29; Jer 48:7; 1Ti 6:17; Rev 18:7–8

Human achievements are ultimately futile Ecc 2:11 *See also* Ps 39:6; Ecc 2:17–23; Isa 40:6; Hab 2:13

Human achievements do not lead to justification Ac 13:39; Ro 5:1; 1Co 6:11; Gal 2:15–16,21

God can thwart human achievements

Ge 11:1–9 *God will overthrow all human achievement that is in opposition to him.* *See also* Job 5:12; Ps 33:10; Isa 13:19; Rev 18:10,16–19

God's achievements

God's purposes are always accomplished Isa 46:10 *See also* Job 42:2; Isa 14:24; 55:10–11; Jer 23:20; 30:24

Creation as God's achievement Ps 104:24 *See also* Ge 1:1,31; Ps 104:2–23; Isa 40:25–26

Salvation as God's achievement Heb 7:25 *See also* Jn 17:4; 19:28,30; Ac 4:12; Php 1:6; Heb 10:14; 12:2

Spiritual resources for human achievements

Achieving things with God's help Ps 127:1 *See also* 2Sa 22:30 pp Ps 18:29; 2Ch 26:5; Zec 4:6–9; Jn 15:5; Ac 1:8; Ro 15:18–19; 1Co 3:6; Php 2:13; 4:13

Achieving things by faith Mk 9:23 *See also* Mt 17:20; 21:21 pp Mk 11:22–23; Lk 17:6

Achieving things through prayer Jn 14:13–14 *See also* 1Sa 1:27; Jas 5:16–18

Achievements out of trials and sorrows 2Co 4:17 *See also* Ro 5:3–4; 2Co 7:10; 12:7–10; Jas 1:2–4

Achieving things with the help of fellow believers Gal 6:2 *See also* Ac 2:42–45; 4:32–37; 5:12–16; Php 4:13–14,18; Heb 10:24–25

See also

1130 God, sovereignty	5960 success
	8023 faith, necessity
2530 Christ, death of	8420 equipping
5785 ambition	8441 goals
5811 compromise	8610 prayer, asking God
5864 futility	
5954 strength	8802 pride

5777

admonition

A loving attempt to correct another's attitude or behaviour. Christians are to admonish fellow believers.

The prophets admonished Israel

2Ki 17:13; Ne 9:29–30 *See also* Jdg 6:7–10; Mal 2:1–4

Parents are to admonish their children

Pr 22:6; Eph 6:4 *See also* Ge 18:19; Dt 11:19; Pr 13:24; 19:18; 22:15; 23:13

Leaders are to admonish those in their care

2Ti 4:2 *See also* 1Co 4:14; Col 1:28; 1Th 5:12; Tit 2:15; 3:10

Christians are to admonish fellow believers

Col 3:16 *See also* Ps 141:5; Lk 17:3; Ro 15:14; 1Th 5:14; 2Ti 3:16

It is wise to accept legitimate admonition

Pr 13:18; 25:12 *See also* Pr 15:5; Ecc 7:5; Jer 2:30; 5:3; 7:28; Zep 3:1–2,7–8

See also

5664 children	7734 leaders, spiritual
5731 parents	
5926 rebuke	7773 prophets, role
5978 warning	7789 shepherd, church leader
6221 rebellion	
6245 stubbornness	8232 discipline, family
7105 believers	
7720 elders in the church	

5778

adorning

A form of ornamentation, using especially jewels and precious metals, to enhance the beauty of buildings or people.

Buildings were adorned with various materials

2Ch 3:6 *See also* Ps 45:8; Isa 60:13; Am 3:15

Objects of worship were adorned

Hos 10:1 *See also* Jer 10:3–4

Women adorned themselves with jewellery and fine clothes

Eze 16:11–12 *See also* 2Sa 1:24; Jer 4:30; Eze 16:13

Personal adornment should not be allowed to detract from worship

1Ti 2:9 *See also* 1Pe 3:3–4

Adorning used in a metaphorical sense

Isa 61:10 *See also* Job 40:10; Ps 93:5; 144:12; Pr 1:8–9; Isa 60:7; Rev 21:2

See also

4040 beauty	5211 art
4342 jewels	5915 ornaments
5145 clothing	8308 modesty
5207 architecture	8808 riches

5779

advice

Counsel is essential for gaining wisdom, though human advice is not always reliable. God's advice is necessary and trustworthy for guidance in life.

Human advice

A wise person seeks advice from others Pr 12:15 *See also* Pr 11:14; 13:10; 15:12,22; 19:20; 24:6; 27:9; Ecc 4:13

Rejecting good advice can lead to disaster Pr 1:30–31 *See also* 1Ki 12:8 pp 2Ch 10:8; 1Ki 12:13–15 pp 2Ch 10:13–15; Pr 1:25–26; Jer 18:18; Ac 27:11

Human advice can have unseen dangers Pr 12:5 *See also* Job 21:16; Ps 1:1; Isa 19:11; Eze 11:2

Examples of good human advice Ex 18:17–24 *Jethro;* 2Sa 17:5–16 *Hushai Persian experts;* Est 1:13–22; 2:1–4 *Da 4:27 Daniel;* Ac 5:38 *Gamaliel;* 2Co 8:10 *Paul*

Examples of bad human advice Nu 31:15–16 *Balaam Ahithophel;* 2Sa 15:31–34; 16:20–23; 17:1–4,21–23 1Ki 12:28 *Jeroboam;* Isa 19:11 *Egyptian advisers*

Seeking advice from false gods is futile

Lev 19:31 *See also* Dt 18:14; 2Ch 25:15–16; Isa 19:3; 41:28–29; 47:12–13

God needs no-one to advise him

Isa 40:13–14 *See also* Job 12:13; Pr 8:14; Isa 28:29

God gives advice

To his people Ps 32:8 *See also* Ps 16:7; 73:24; Rev 3:18

Through Jesus Christ and his Spirit Isa 11:2 *See also* Isa 9:6; Jn 14:26; 15:26; 16:13

Through his word 2Ti 3:16

God frustrates bad advice
1Co 1:19 *See also* 2Sa 17:14; Ps 33:10

Examples of receiving God's advice
David: 1Sa 23:1–4; 2Sa 2:1
Jehoshaphat: 1Ki 22:5 pp 2Ch 18:4

Examples of rejecting God's advice
Job: Job 38:2; 42:2–3
Israel: Ps 106:13; 107:11

See also
1180 God, wisdom of	6145 deceit
3130 Holy Spirit, Counsellor	8124 guidance
	8361 wisdom
3263 Holy Spirit, guidance	8408 decision-making
5780 advisers	8412 decisions

5780

advisers

Those who give advice and counsel. Human advice is desirable, but not always reliable. Only God's counsel is wholly dependable.

Human advisers
It is wise to consult advisers Pr 15:22
See also Pr 12:15; 13:10; 15:12; 19:20; 20:18; 24:6; Ecc 4:13

It is folly to reject wise advisers
Pr 11:14 *See also* 1Ki 12:8 pp 2Ch 10:8; 1Ki 12:13–15 pp 2Ch 10:13–15; Pr 1:25–26,30–31; Jer 18:18; Ac 27:11,21

Unwise advisers are dangerous Ps 1:1
See also Job 21:16; 42:7; Pr 12:5; Isa 19:11; Eze 11:2–4

Advisers who trust in false gods must be rejected Isa 8:19–20 *See also* 2Ch 25:15–16; Isa 19:3; 47:13–15

Examples of wise advisers
Ex 18:17–24 *Jethro*
Daniel: Da 2:23,48; 4:18,27; 5:11–12
Ac 5:38–39 *Gamaliel*; 2Co 8:10–12 *Paul*

Examples of bad advisers
Nu 31:16 *Balaam*
Ahithophel: 2Sa 15:31; 17:1,7
1Ki 12:28–30 *Jeroboam*; Isa 19:11
Egyptian advisers; Jn 11:49–53 *Caiaphas*

Examples of official advisers
Ge 26:26; 2Sa 15:12; 16:23; 1Ki 4:5; 1Ch 27:32–33

God as adviser
God is an adviser Ps 16:7 *See also*
1Ki 22:5 pp 2Ch 18:4; Ps 32:8; 73:24; Rev 3:18

The promised Messiah is an adviser
Isa 9:6 *See also* Isa 11:2

The Holy Spirit is an adviser Jn 14:26
See also Jn 14:16; 15:26; 16:13 *The Holy Spirit's counsel defends believers from every accusation and provides all necessary teaching and guidance.*

See also
1180 God, wisdom of	3140 Holy Spirit, teacher
2081 Christ, wisdom	
3130 Holy Spirit, Counsellor	3263 Holy Spirit, guidance

See also
4155 divination	8361 wisdom
5744 wife	8408 decision-making
5779 advice	
5917 plans	8412 decisions
8124 guidance	8755 folly

5781

affection

Positive feelings towards another, often expressed in terms of attachment and warmth.

People and things arouse affection
Whole churches Php 1:7 *See also* 2Co 7:13–15

Friends 1Sa 18:1 *See also* 1Sa 18:3; 20:41–42; Jn 11:36; Ro 16:5,9,12; Col 4:14; 3Jn 1

Strangers Lk 7:13

The temple Eze 24:21

Jerusalem Ne 1:3–4 *See also* Ps 137:6

Affection is sometimes expressed in familial terms
1Sa 3:16; 1Co 4:17 *See also* 1Sa 4:16; 24:11; 2Sa 18:22; 2Ki 2:12; Jn 13:33; 2Co 6:13; 2Ti 2:1; Phm 10; 1Pe 5:13; 1Jn 2:28

Emotions expressing affection
Tenderness Ge 34:3 *See also* Lk 7:38; Php 2:1

Longing Php 1:8 *See also* 2Sa 14:1; Mt 23:37 pp Lk 13:34; Ro 15:23; 2Co 7:11; Gal 4:20; Php 2:26; 4:1; 2Ti 1:4

Openness 2Co 6:11 *See also* 2Co 6:12–13

Compassion Mt 9:36 pp Mk 6:34 *See also* 1Ki 3:26; Isa 49:15; Lk 15:20; Eph 4:32; Col 3:12; 1Pe 3:8

Sorrow 2Co 2:4 *See also* Ps 35:14; La 2:11; Ro 9:2–3

Joy Phm 7 *See also* Pr 23:15; 27:11; Gal 4:14–15; 2Jn 12

Concern 1Co 4:14 *See also* Pr 1:8; 27:6; 31:2–3; Ecc 12:12; 2Co 7:7; 8:16; 12:19; Gal 4:11–12,19; Php 4:10; 1Ti 1:18

See also
2015 Christ, compassion	5898 kissing
	5952 sorrow
5690 friends	5966 tenderness
5806 compassion	8283 joy
5844 emotions	8292 love
5895 intimacy	8632 adoration

5782

agony

Intense suffering of body, mind or spirit, brought about by illness, death or the judgment of God.

Examples of agony
Agony of body Ps 6:2 *See also* Ps 31:10; 42:10; Isa 21:3; Jn 16:21; Rev 9:5; 16:10

Agony of heart Jer 4:19 *See also* Dt 2:25; 1Sa 1:16 *Hannah prays for a son*; Job 6:2; 7:11; Ps 6:3; 25:17; 31:7; 38:8; 55:4; Isa 65:14; Mt 26:38; Mk 14:33; Lk 22:44 *Jesus Christ prays on the Mount of Olives*; Ro 9:2; 2Co 2:4

Causes of agony
Illness Jer 15:18 *See also* Job 30:16–17; Ps 6:2–3; 38:7; 69:29

Death Ac 2:24 *See also* Job 26:5; Ps 18:4–6; 42:10; 55:4; 116:3

The judgment of God Lk 16:24–25 *See also* Jer 4:19; Eze 30:16; Mic 4:10; Zec 9:5; Mt 22:13; 24:51; 25:30

See also
1135 God, suffering of	5823 cruelty
	5879 humiliation
2570 Christ, suffering	5952 sorrow
	8794 persecution
5349 injustice, examples	9020 death
	9210 judgment, God's
5436 pain	
5560 suffering	

5783

agreement

Being of one mind with others, whether for good or evil purposes. Agreement among believers is commended as a means of enhancing unity and peace, and building up the people of God.

Agreements made by deliberate choice
Agreement to do good Job 2:11 *See also* Ne 5:9–13

Agreement to do wrong Da 6:7 *See also* Jer 7:18; Lk 22:5–6 pp Mk 14:11; Ac 5:1–2; 23:20–21

Legal agreements
Between witnesses Dt 17:6 *See also* Nu 35:30; Dt 19:15; Ru 4:9–11; Mt 18:16

Treaties 1Ki 15:19–20 pp 2Ch 16:3–4 *See also* Ge 21:27; 26:28–31; Jos 9:15; 11:19; 1Ki 5:12; 20:34

Ways of making agreements
By accepting terms offered Ge 23:16
See also Ge 30:31–34; 34:24; Jos 2:21; Jdg 15:12–13; 17:10–11; 1Sa 20:16–17

Through mutually acceptable terms
Ge 37:26–27 *See also* Ge 13:8–9; 26:19–22; Ac 15:28–29

Agreement reached by persuasion
Da 1:12–14

Agreement commended to believers
Agreement enhances unity Eph 4:3 *See also* 2Ch 30:12; Ps 133:1; Jn 17:11,21–23; Ro 15:5

Agreement avoids division 1Co 1:10
See also Ro 12:16; Php 2:1–3; 4:2

Agreements made before God
Agreement in prayer Mt 18:19 *See also* 1Ki 1:36; Ac 1:14; 4:24; 12:12; Ro 15:30–31

Agreement in praise Ne 8:6 *See also* 1Ch 16:36 pp Ps 106:48; Ps 41:13; 72:19; 1Co 14:16; Rev 5:13–14

Agreement with God's terms Ex 24:3
See also Nu 5:22; Dt 27:15–26; 2Ki 23:3 pp 2Ch 34:32; Jer 11:1–5

See also

1345 covenant	5834 disagreement
5205 alliance	6700 peace
5592 treaty	7025 church, unity
5623 witnesses, legal	7030 unity
5811 compromise	7206 community

5784

amazement

Astonishment and surprise are frequent responses to the actions and words of God and Jesus Christ.

Amazement at God's actions

His marvellous deeds Ps 98:1 *See also* Jos 3:5 *The LORD promises to do amazing things when his people cross the Jordan;* Jdg 13:19; 1Ch 16:24; Ps 71:17; 72:18; 86:10; 96:3; 118:23; Isa 25:1; Da 3:24 *Nebuchadnezzar is amazed at seeing four men in the furnace;* Rev 15:1,3

His creation Job 37:5

His judgment Isa 29:9; Hab 1:5; Jn 5:28

Throughout his life Jesus Christ inspired amazement

Mt 27:14 pp Mk 15:5; Lk 2:33,47; 4:22

Amazement at Jesus Christ's teaching

At his inherent authority Mt 7:28–29 *See also* Mt 13:54 pp Mk 6:2; **Mk 1:22** pp Lk 4:32; Mk 1:27 pp Lk 4:36; Jn 7:15

In debate with the Pharisees Mt 22:22 pp Mk 12:17 pp Lk 20:26

In theological debate with the Sadducees Mt 22:33

After talking with the rich young man Mt 19:25 pp Mk 10:26; **Mk 10:24**

After the cleansing of the temple Mk 11:18 pp Lk 19:47 *Here the crowds' amazement causes the chief priests and teachers of the law to fear Jesus Christ.*

Amazement at Jesus Christ's revelation of himself

Lk 24:41; Jn 5:20; 2Th 1:10

Amazement at Jesus Christ's miracles

Miracles of healing Mt 15:31 *See also* Mt 9:8 pp Mk 2:12 pp Lk 5:26 *at the healing of the paralytic;* Mk 5:42 pp Lk 8:56 *at the healing of Jairus' daughter;* Ac 3:10–11 *at the healing of the crippled beggar*

The casting out of demons Mk 1:27 *Demonised mutes:* Mt 9:33; Lk 11:14 Mk 5:20 *Legion;* Lk 9:43 *a boy with an evil spirit*

Miracles of nature Mt 8:27 pp Lk 8:25 *See also* Mt 21:20 *the withered fig-tree;* Mk 6:51 *Jesus Christ walking on the water;* Lk 5:9 *the miraculous haul of fish*

Amazement at the coming of the Holy Spirit and subsequent events

Ac 2:12 *See also* Ac 2:7; 8:13 *Simon's amazement at the miracles performed by Philip;* Ac 9:21 *amazement at the change in Saul;* Ac 10:45 *astonishment at the Holy Spirit being poured out on the Gentiles;* Ac 12:16 *amazement at Peter's release from prison;* Ac 13:12

Jesus Christ himself experienced amazement

Mk 6:6; Lk 7:9

See also

2012 Christ, authority	3257 Holy Spirit, gift of
2351 Christ, miracles	5962 surprises
2363 Christ, preaching & teaching	8333 reverence

5785

ambition

A powerful personal drive towards achieving goals which are regarded as being of importance to the individual. Ambition is viewed negatively when these goals are selfish or evil, and positively when they are directed towards building up the church or furthering the kingdom of God.

5786

ambition, negative aspects of

In its negative sense, ambition is the pursuit of personal status and fortune, which is contrary to the purposes of God as expressed in Scripture.

Selfish ambition: a desire for personal aggrandisement

Mk 10:36–37 *See also* Ge 11:4 *the men of Babel;* 2Sa 15:1–4 *Absalom;* 1Ki 1:5 *Adonijah;* Isa 14:13–14 *the king of Babylon;* Eze 28:2 *the ruler of Tyre;* Da 11:36–38; Mic 7:3; Hab 2:4–5; Mt 20:21; Lk 22:24; Php 1:17; 2Th 2:4–7 *the antichrist*

Selfish ambition arises from fallen human nature

Gal 5:19–21 *See also* Pr 6:18; Eph 2:3; 1Jn 2:16

The results of selfish ambition

Humiliation by God Mt 23:12

The believer becomes spiritually unproductive Mk 4:18–19; Jas 3:14–16

Warnings against selfish ambition

Php 2:3 *See also* Jer 45:5 *God's word to Baruch*

See also

5541 society, negative	8804 pride, examples
5869 greed	8827 selfishness
6133 coveting	8848 worldliness
8777 lust	

5787

ambition, positive aspects of

In its positive sense, ambition is a personal desire for spiritual progress or achievement.

A longing for God and for what he can do in the believer

Mt 5:6; Php 3:13–14 *See also* Php 3:10; Ps 40:8; Lk 13:24; Col 1:29; 1Th 4:11; 2Ti 2:15; Heb 12:1; 1Pe 2:2; 2Pe 3:14

The desire for spiritual gifts

1Co 14:12 *See also* 1Ki 3:10–14 pp 2Ch 1:11–12; 1Co 12:31; 14:1,39

The desire for a leadership role in the church

1Ti 3:1

The longing for communion with God

Ps 27:4 *See also* Ps 73:25; 84:2

The compelling desire to preach the gospel

Ro 15:20 *See also* 1Co 9:16; Php 1:15–18 *Jesus Christ can be proclaimed, despite selfish personal ambition.*

Focus on future rewards

1Co 9:24–27 *See also* 2Ti 4:8; Heb 10:35–36; 11:26

See also

5840 eagerness	8206 Christlikeness
5904 maturity, spiritual	8266 holiness
7754 preaching	8424 evangelism
7966 spiritual gifts	8441 goals
8114 discipleship	8461 priorities
8134 knowing God	8465 progress

5789

anger

A state of indignation and outrage, often resulting from distress caused by injustice or insult. Scripture affirms God's righteous anger against sin and urges moderation in regard to human anger.

5790

anger, divine

The anger of God is directed against all human sin, disobedience, rebellion and wickedness, which threaten to thwart his purposes for his creation and people.

Causes of divine anger

Disobedience Isa 5:24–25 *See also* Nu 22:22; Jos 7:1; 2Ki 22:13; Ps 78:21–22; Mic 5:15; Zec 7:12; Mk 3:5; Ro 2:5; Eph 5:5–6; Heb 3:7–12

Sinfulness Isa 57:17 *See also* 1Ki 8:46; 11:9; 2Ch 19:2; 32:25; Eph 2:1–3; Col 3:5–6

Apostasy and idolatry Nu 25:3 *See also* Dt 4:25; 9:8; Jos 22:18; 23:16; Jdg 2:19–20; 10:6–7; 1Ki 14:15; 2Ki 22:17; Ezr 9:14; Jer 7:17–18

The characteristics of God that provoke his anger

He is a holy God Ps 7:11 *See also* Jos 24:19–20; Jer 10:10

He is a jealous God Dt 6:15 *See also* 1Ki 14:22; Ps 79:5; Eze 16:38; Na 1:2

He is the universal judge Ps 79:6 *See also* Ezr 8:22; Isa 34:2; Zep 3:8

He is also compassionate and slow to anger Ps 103:8 *See also* Ex 34:6; Ne 9:17; Ps 78:38; 86:15; Jnh 4:2; Na 1:3

Consequences of divine anger

Death and destruction Dt 9:8 *See also*
Ex 15:7; 32:10–11; Nu 11:1–2; Job 4:9;
Isa 13:5; Jer 32:29

Present judgment La 2:2 *See also*
Nu 32:13; 2Ki 13:3; Isa 51:20; Eze 7:8;
Hab 3:12; Mt 21:12–13

Future judgment Isa 13:9 *See also*
Da 8:19; Mt 3:7; Ro 2:5

God's rejection of his people Jer 7:29
See also Dt 31:17; 2Ki 17:18; 23:25–27;
Ps 78:59; 89:38; La 2:6–7

Being saved from the anger of God

God's anger may be temporary Ps 30:5
See also Ps 103:9; Isa 54:8; 57:16; 60:10

**God's anger cannot be averted by
human means** Zep 1:18 *See also* Pr 11:4

Humility and repentance are required
Zep 2:3 *See also* Ge 18:30–32;
Dt 9:18–19; 2Ch 12:7,12; 30:8; Isa 64:9;
Joel 2:13

**God's anger is averted on account of
his love for believers** La 3:22 *See also*
Hos 11:9

**God's anger is averted on account of
the work of Jesus Christ** Ro 5:9 *See also*
Jn 3:36; 1Th 1:10; 5:9

See also

1025 God, anger of	1310 God as judge
1030 God, compassion	2009 Christ, anger of
1055 God, grace & mercy	5283 cup
	6125 condemnation, divine
1075 God, justice of	6218 provoking God
1125 God, righteousness	6712 propitiation
	8768 idolatry

5791
anger, human

Human anger arises for a number of
reasons, some of which are
acceptable and others which are not.
Scripture stresses the potentially
destructive aspects of human anger
and urges moderation.

Reasons for human anger
Jealousy Ge 4:4–5 *See also* 1Sa 17:28;
18:8; 1Ki 21:4; Lk 15:28

Pride Jnh 4:1 *See also* 2Sa 3:8; 6:8;
2Ki 5:11; 2Ch 26:19

The truth 2Ch 16:10 *Hanani had
prophesied against the king. See also*
Nu 24:10; Jer 37:15

Human anger is sometimes justified
Ex 32:19 *See also* Ex 11:8; 16:20;
Nu 16:15; Lev 10:16; 1Sa 11:6; 20:34;
2Sa 12:5; Ne 5:6; Mk 3:5; Lk 14:21

Results of human anger
Strife Ge 4:8 *See also* 1Sa 20:30;
Ps 124:2–3; Pr 29:22; 30:33

God's judgment Mt 5:22 *See also*
Ge 49:5–7

Sin Jas 1:20 *See also* Ps 4:4; Pr 14:17;
2Co 12:20; Eph 4:26

Dealing with anger
Becoming slow to anger 1Co 13:5 *See
also* Ecc 7:9; Tit 1:7; Jas 1:19

Not taking revenge Ro 12:19

Renouncing anger Eph 4:31 *See also*
Ps 37:8; Col 3:8; 1Ti 2:8

See also

5359 justice	6686 mercy
5494 revenge	8773 jealousy
5927 resentment	8802 pride
6020 sin	9210 judgment,
6666 grace	God's

5792
appetite

A hunger or desire for something.
Although the primary reference of
the term is to a hunger for food, it
can also refer to other human
desires. Scripture distinguishes
between healthy and unhealthy
appetites, indicating what it is
appropriate to seek after.

Appetite as physical hunger
Nu 11:4; Pr 6:30 *See also* Ps 107:5–9;
Pr 16:26; Ecc 6:7; Isa 29:8; Jer 31:25;
50:19; La 2:12

Appetite as a spiritual hunger
Ps 143:6; Pr 25:25; Mt 5:6 *See also*
Ps 119:20,131

The gospel satisfies human hunger and thirst
Jn 4:13–14; 6:35 *See also* Ps 42:2;
Isa 55:1; Jn 6:27,50–51; 7:37; Rev 21:6;
22:17

Lust as sexual appetite
Pr 6:25; Eze 23:11; Col 3:5; 1Th 4:3–5

See also

4404 food	5866 gluttony
4438 eating	5869 greed
4822 famine	8656 longing for
5341 hunger	God
5580 thirst	8777 lust
5832 desire	8821 self-indulgence
5839 dissatisfaction	

5793
arrogance

Proud and unpleasant behaviour
towards other people, based on a
belief in one's own superiority or
greater importance.

Arrogance characterises the wicked person
As an attitude of the heart Mk 7:21–22
See also Job 35:12; Ps 10:2–11; 73:3–12;
86:14; 94:3–7; Mal 3:15; Ro 1:28–31

Arising from self-confidence
Isa 9:9–10; Da 4:29–30; Rev 18:7 *See
also* Ex 15:9; 1Ki 20:11; 2Ki 14:10
pp 2Ch 25:19; Isa 28:15; Eze 16:49;
Hos 12:8; Hab 2:4–5; Lk 18:9;
Ac 8:9–10; 2Pe 2:10–12

Issuing in words Ps 17:10; 119:51;
Jas 3:5 *See also* 1Sa 2:3; Ps 31:18; 119:69;
123:4; Pr 17:7; 21:24; Jer 43:1–2

Arrogance is essentially rebellion against God
Dt 1:43; 1Sa 15:23 *See also*
Ne 9:16–17,29; Job 36:8–9; Ps 5:5;
119:85; Hos 5:4–5; 7:10; Zep 3:1–4

Arrogance may even be found in the church
2Co 12:20 *See also* 1Co 4:18; 1Ti 6:17

The godly should reject arrogance
Pr 8:13; Jer 9:23–24 *See also* Jer 13:15;
Ro 11:20; 1Co 1:28–31; 4:7; 13:4;
Eph 2:8–9

God punishes the arrogant
Isa 2:17–18 *See also* Ex 18:11; 1Sa 15:23
The LORD rejects Saul as king;
2Ch 36:15–16; Ne 9:10 *the arrogance of
Egypt punished;* Ps 75:2–4; 119:21,78;
Isa 2:11; 5:15; 13:11; Jer 48:29–30;
50:31–32; Eze 7:8–10; Da 5:20
Nebuchadnezzar deposed; Zec 10:11

See also

5546 speech	8276 humility
5813 conceit	8782 mockery
5956 strength,	8801 presumption
human	8802 pride
5961 superiority	8815 ridicule
6121 boasting	8819 scoffing
6221 rebellion	

5794
asceticism

Rigorous self-denial of bodily
pleasures and needs. This can be
motivated either by a praiseworthy
desire to dedicate oneself completely
to God, or by an erroneous belief
that the physical body is evil.

Types of ascetic practice
The ascetic practice of fasting
Est 4:15–16 *See also* Jdg 20:26;
2Sa 1:11–12; Jer 36:5–6; Lk 2:37

**The ascetic practice of wearing
sackcloth and ashes** Da 9:3 *See also*
1Ki 21:27; Ne 9:1; Est 4:3

The ascetic practice of celibacy
1Co 7:1 *See also* Ex 19:15; 1Sa 21:4;
1Co 7:8,36–38; Rev 14:4

People who practised asceticism
The Nazirites and asceticism
Nu 6:1–8; Jdg 13:4–5; 16:17

John the Baptist and asceticism Mt 3:4
pp Mk 1:6; Mt 11:18 pp Lk 7:33

**John's disciples, the Pharisees and
asceticism** Mt 9:14 pp Mk 2:18
pp Lk 5:33; Lk 18:12

**The Jews and the ascetic practice of
regular fasting** Lev 23:26–32;
Zec 7:1–5

Jesus Christ refuses to enforce ascetic practices
Mk 2:18–19 pp Mt 9:14–17
pp Lk 5:34–35

Ascetic practice symbolises separation from the world and dedication to God
Asceticism as a sign of repentance
Jnh 3:6–9 *See also* 1Sa 7:6; Ezr 10:6;
Joel 1:13–14

Asceticism accompanying prayer
Ezr 8:23 *See also* 2Sa 12:16; Ne 1:4;
Ac 14:23; 1Co 7:5

Ascetic dedication to God's service
1Co 9:27 See also Da 1:8; Mt 19:12;
1Co 7:32–35

False asceticism opposed
**Rejection of fasting without true
repentance** Isa 58:3–7; Joel 2:12–14

**Condemnation of ostentatious
asceticism** Mt 6:16–18

**Asceticism not necessary for right
worship and conduct** Col 2:20–23;
1Ti 4:1–5 Asceticism that is based on a
negative view of the material world is
rejected.

See also
8429 fasting	8703 antinomianism
8451 mortification	8750 false teachings
8475 self-denial	

5795

bereavement

The experience or status of suffering
the loss through death of a close
relative or friend.

5796
bereavement, experience of

Scripture gives many examples of
how people respond to the death of
those they love.

The experience of bereavement
Abraham Ge 23:1–2

Jacob Ge 37:35 See also Ge 42:38; 48:7

Joseph Ge 50:10

David 2Sa 18:33 See also 2Sa 1:11–12;
3:32; 12:15–21

Job Job 1:20 At the news of the deaths of
his sons and daughters. See also Job 17:7

Jesus Christ Jn 11:35 Because of the
death of his friend, Lazarus.

The early Christians Ac 8:2 See also
Ac 9:39

The expression of grief
Ge 37:34; Ps 31:9 See also Dt 34:8;
1Sa 2:33; 2Sa 1:17; 3:31–34; 14:2;
2Ch 35:25; Ps 35:14; Isa 16:7; La 3:48;
Eze 24:17; Zec 12:10 prediction of
mourning for the Messiah; Php 2:27

Grief passes with time
Ge 24:67; 38:12; 2Sa 12:24

See also
2530 Christ, death of	5945 self-pity
5398 loss	5952 sorrow
5419 mourning	5970 unhappiness
5560 suffering	6203 mortality
5831 depression	9020 death
5916 pessimism	

5797
bereavement, God's comfort in

God cares for the bereaved, and can
turn their mourning into joy and
hope.

**God comforts the bereaved and
the sorrowful**
La 3:32–33; 2Co 1:3–4 See also
Ps 116:8; Mt 5:4; Rev 7:17

Mourning turned into joy Ps 30:11 See
also Isa 61:1–3; Jer 31:13; Jn 16:20

Despair turned into hope 1Th 4:13–14
"Falling asleep" was a euphemistic way of
talking about dying.

Fear turned into assurance Ps 23:4;
Isa 25:8–9 In the OT, death was generally
feared because it meant the loss of
meaningful existence. However, like several
references, this one looks beyond the grave
and anticipates NT hope for all who trust
in God; Ro 8:38–39 Paul's conclusion
after working through the implications of
the gospel. See also Jn 11:25–26;
1Co 15:55–57; 2Co 5:6–8;
Php 1:21–24; Rev 21:4

**God's care for widows and
orphans**
Dt 10:18; Ps 10:14 See also Ps 68:5;
146:9; Jer 49:11; Hos 14:3

**Jesus Christ cared for the
bereaved**
Lk 7:11–13; Jn 11:33 At the grave of his
friend, Lazarus. See also Lk 8:49–56

Caring for the bereaved
Dt 24:19 Special provisions in the law for
the bereaved; Ro 12:15 See also Dt 26:12;
Jer 22:3; Ac 6:1–3 The early church
provided for widows in the fellowship with
a special fund; 1Ti 5:3; Jas 1:27

See also
1030 God,	5743 widows
compassion	5802 care
2015 Christ,	8291 kindness
compassion	9310 resurrection
5730 orphans	9610 hope

5798

betrayal

The treacherous exposing or
deceiving of people by those they
formerly trusted. It is usually
associated with an enemy
masquerading as a friend, or with a
broken or abused relationship.
Betrayal was suffered by Jesus Christ
and can be expected by his followers.

**Betrayal is part of human
experience**
**Examples of those experiencing
betrayal** Ps 41:9 See also Jdg 16:18;
1Sa 18:17; 2Sa 19:26–27; Ps 55:12–14
Betrayal carries acute feelings for its
victims; Jer 12:6; La 1:2,19

**Examples of those murdered through
betrayal**
The power struggles of Israel's early
kingship period gave rise to many bloody
betrayals: 2Sa 3:27; 4:6; 11:15;
13:28–29; 20:10; 1Ki 21:8–10

**Betrayal is seen as a particularly
wicked act**
Isa 33:1 See also 1Ch 12:17; Pr 25:9–10;
Isa 24:16–17; Mt 26:24 pp Mk 14:21
pp Lk 22:22

The betrayal of Jesus Christ
**Judas determines to betray Jesus
Christ** Mt 26:14–16 pp Mk 14:10–11
pp Lk 22:3–6

Jesus Christ's knowledge of events
Mt 26:21–23 pp Mk 14:18–20 See also
Mt 20:17–19 pp Mk 10:33–34;
Lk 22:21; Jn 13:11,18; Ps 41:9;
Jn 13:21–27

Jesus Christ is betrayed by a kiss
Mt 26:47–49 pp Mk 14:43–45
pp Lk 22:47–48 The kiss featured in
several betrayals as part of feigned
friendship (see e.g., 2Sa 20:9–10 and Pr
27:6).

The betrayer's remorse Mt 27:3–5

**Betrayal may be part of Christian
experience**
Mt 10:21 pp Mk 13:12 pp Lk 21:16 See
also Da 7:25; Mt 10:35–36; Mic 7:6

**Betrayal as a sign of the end
times**
Mt 24:10

**God never betrays those who
trust in him**
Ps 89:33 See also Ps 118:8; 125:1;
Pr 29:25; Isa 26:3–4; 2Ti 1:12

See also
1035 God,	6145 deceit
faithfulness	8032 trust, lack of
2570 Christ,	8794 persecution
suffering	8830 suspicion
5040 murder	8841 unfaithfulness
5494 revenge	to people
5817 conspiracies	9105 last things
5969 treachery	

5799

bitterness

A feeling of anger and resentment,
caused particularly by perceived
unfairness in suffering or by adverse
circumstances.

The causes of bitterness
Adverse personal circumstances
Job 10:1 See also Ge 27:34; Ru 1:20
"Mara" means "bitter"; 1Sa 30:6;
2Sa 13:36; 2Ki 4:27; Ps 55:4–14;
Pr 17:25; Jer 6:26

External circumstances Eze 3:14
Because of the exiles' hardness of heart. See
also Job 21:25; 27:2; La 3:1–20; Eze 21:6

Human failure Mt 26:75
pp Lk 22:61–62 See also Ezr 10:1;
Jer 2:19; 4:18; La 1:4

**Bitterness is evidence of a sinful
heart**
Ac 8:23 See also Ro 3:10–18

Bitterness is to be avoided
Heb 12:15 See also Eph 4:31; Jas 3:14

The remedy for bitterness
Forgiveness Ge 33:1–11; Lk 15:25–32;
Eph 4:31–32

**The causes of bitterness will pass
away** Ps 37:1–2

**Examples of bitterness in
people's lives**
Ru 1:19–21; 2Sa 13:22; Est 5:9;
Lk 15:30

5800

blasphemy

The profaning, desecration and taking in vain of the name of God, or the reviling of any of his works or deeds. It is strongly forbidden by God as dishonouring to his name.

Blasphemy strongly forbidden
Ex 20:7 pp Dt 5:11 See also Ex 22:28; Lev 18:21; 19:12; 22:32; Nu 15:30–31

Blasphemy against God punished
Lev 24:10–16,23; 2Ki 19:20–37 pp Isa 37:21–38

Blasphemy against the Holy Spirit is unpardonable
Mk 3:28–30 pp Mt 12:31–32 pp Lk 12:10 See also Heb 10:29

God blasphemed indirectly
Rejecting his word and his servants blasphemes God Ne 9:26 See also 2Ch 36:16; Ps 107:11; Isa 5:24

Defiling sacred things blasphemes God Lev 22:1–2 See also Eze 20:27–28; 22:26; Mal 1:6–13

Despising the poor blasphemes God Pr 14:31 See also Am 2:7; Jas 2:5–7

Speaking against his people blasphemes God Zep 2:8–11; Ac 9:4–5 To persecute the church is to persecute Jesus Christ; Ac 26:9; 1Ti 1:13; Rev 2:9

Slandering celestial beings blasphemes God 2Pe 2:10–12; Jude 8–10

The sins of God's people may cause others to blaspheme
1Ti 6:1 See also 2Sa 12:13–14 The phrase "you have made the enemies of the LORD show utter contempt" reflects a scribal tradition which avoided any reference to blasphemy. The underlying idea of blasphemy would have been obvious to the original readers; Eze 36:20–23; Ro 2:24; Isa 52:5

God's enemies blaspheme him
Ps 139:20 See also Ps 74:10–11,18; Da 7:25; 11:36; 1Co 12:3; 2Th 2:4; Rev 13:5; 16:9,11,21; 17:3

False accusations of blasphemy
Jesus Christ falsely accused of blasphemy Mk 2:6–7 pp Mt 9:3 pp Lk 5:21 See also Mt 26:65–66 pp Mk 14:63–64; Jn 10:33–36

God's servants falsely accused of blasphemy 1Ki 21:9–13; Ac 6:11–14

See also
2585 Christ, trial
3245 Holy Spirit, blasphemy against
5547 speech, power of
6121 boasting
8807 profanity
8843 unforgivable sin
8844 unforgiveness
9115 antichrist, the

5801

brokenness

God breaks the spirit of the proud and arrogant so that in their humility and brokenness they may come to repentance and restoration. A crushed heart or spirit may be caused by tragic circumstances or by God's judgment.

Brokenness before God
Ps 51:17 See also Ps 34:18; 51:8; Isa 57:15; 66:2; Zec 12:10

Brokenness of heart
Ps 147:3 See also Ps 34:18; 69:20; 109:16; Isa 61:1; Jer 23:9; Eze 21:6–7

Brokenness of spirit
Job 17:1 See also Job 30:24; 31:38–40

Brokenness as a result of God's judgment
On individuals Isa 1:28 See also Job 24:20; Isa 8:12–15; 65:14–15; Jer 22:24–30

On nations Eze 32:28 See also Jer 48:4–5,16–17,38–39; 50:23–24; 51:6–10

Brokenness as contrition
Isa 66:1–2 See also Ps 34:18; 51:16–17; Isa 57:14–21

See also
1060 God, greatness of
1065 God, holiness of
1310 God as judge
3248 Holy Spirit, conviction
5450 poverty, spiritual
5947 shame
6020 sin
6222 rebellion against God
6732 repentance
6740 returning to God
8276 humility
9165 restoration

5802

care

A practical outworking of loving vigilance, efforts and tenderness. Care is perfectly shown by God. People should imitate God's care, but human care is often limited, faulty or misplaced in self-centred ways.

Caring as part of God's character
God's care for his children Ps 121:3 See also Ps 8:4; 23:1; 65:9; 115:12; Mt 6:32 pp Lk 12:30; Mt 10:30–31 pp Lk 12:7; Lk 15:20 God is the father in this parable.

Human care should reflect God's nature Jn 15:12 See also Ge 37:14; 1Sa 10:2; 2Sa 18:29; Est 2:11; Lk 10:34–35; Ac 20:31; Php 4:10,14; 1Th 3:10

God's care contrasted with human care Isa 49:15 See also Ps 118:9; Eze 34:2–3,11–12; Zec 10:2–3; Jn 10:13–14; 1Ti 3:5

Care involves responsibility
Ge 2:15 See also Ge 39:4; Nu 1:50; Pr 29:7; Mt 21:33–34,41 pp Mk 12:1–2

pp Mk 12:9 pp Lk 20:9–10, 16; 1Ti 6:20

God's care reflected in human relationships
Eph 5:25 See also Ps 103:13–14; Ecc 11:5; Isa 49:15; Eph 6:1,4; 1Ti 5:8

To be careless or uncaring is wrong
Jer 48:10 See also Dt 8:14; 2Ch 24:5; Isa 47:8; Zec 7:9–10; Mt 12:36

Care for worldly things is wrong
Php 4:6 See also Ecc 5:12; Mt 6:31–32 pp Lk 12:29–30; Mt 13:22 pp Mk 4:18–19 pp Lk 8:14; Lk 10:40–42; 21:34; 1Co 7:32–34

God relieves his people of cares
1Pe 5:7 There is a vital distinction between "care" in the sense of "loving care" which Christians are to practise, and "worldly care" in the sense of "anxiety" which Christians should transfer to God, since they and their needs are his responsibility. See also Ps 37:25; 55:22; Pr 3:5–6; Isa 53:4; Mt 11:28–29; Lk 12:11–12; Jn 14:1

See also
1085 God, love of
1220 God as shepherd
1330 God, the provider
5051 responsibility
5556 stewardship
5803 carelessness
5806 compassion
5885 indifference
8291 kindness
8292 love
8490 watchfulness
8849 worry

5803

carelessness

A lack of attention to one's thoughts and deeds, or a failure to give adequate thought to the consequences of one's actions, often leading to distressing results.

Carelessness in speech
Lev 5:4 See also Pr 20:25; Ecc 5:2,6; Mt 12:36

Warnings against carelessness in actions
Ex 21:33–34 See also Ex 21:22–25,28–29,35–36; 22:5; Lev 5:2–3; Nu 35:22–24

Unintentional sins resulting from carelessness
By the nation Lev 4:13 See also Nu 15:22–26

By an individual Lev 4:27 See also Lev 4:2–3,22–23; Nu 15:27–28; 35:22–24

Examples of carelessness
Careless speech Jdg 11:30–35 See also Ge 25:29–34; Mt 14:6–11 pp Mk 6:21–28

Careless actions and omissions Mt 7:26–27 pp Lk 6:49 See also Mt 25:1–13

See also
5025 killing
5430 oaths, human
5444 pledges
5575 talk, idle
5741 vows
5802 care
5810 complacency
5925 rashness
8755 folly
8783 neglect

5804

charm

The gracious effect of attracting and captivating others or the subtle ability to deceive and mislead them.

Charm to attract and captivate others

King Xerxes by Esther Est 2:17

A husband by his wife Pr 5:18–19

The lovers in the Song of Solomon SS 1:15–16 *See also* SS 2:14; 4:9–10; 5:16; 6:4–5; 7:6

Charm to deceive people

Pr 26:24–25 *See also* Pr 6:25–26; 31:30

The devil subtly seeks to deceive people 2Co 11:3,14 *See also* Ge 3:1–5,13; Mt 4:1–11 pp Mk 1:12–13 pp Lk 4:1–13

Absalom deceived others 2Sa 15:1–6

False teachers use charm to deceive others

For their own gain Ro 16:18 *See also* Jude 16

To draw people away from Jesus Christ 2Pe 2:18 *See also* 2Co 11:13–15

Christians must not be deceived by such charm Eph 4:14; 5:6; Col 2:4

See also

4040 beauty	6241 seduction
4185 sorcery and magic	6248 temptation
5863 flattery	7751 persuasion
6145 deceit	8749 false teachers
	8750 false teachings

5805

comfort

The consolation and reassurance of those who are in distress, anxiety or need. Such comfort is an essential aspect of human relationships. Scripture declares that God comforts his people in times of distress.

The comfort of friends and relations

Job 2:11; Jn 11:19 *See also* Ge 5:29; 24:67; 37:35; Ru 2:13; 2Sa 12:24; 1Ch 7:22; Job 16:5; 29:25; 42:11; Jn 11:31; Ac 20:12

Parental comfort

Isa 66:13; 1Th 2:11–12 *See also* Isa 66:11; Jer 31:15; Mt 2:18

God's comfort

Isa 49:13; 2Co 1:3–4 *See also* Ps 23:4; 71:20–21; 119:50,76; Isa 12:1; 40:1; 51:3,12; 52:9; 57:18; 61:2; Jer 8:18; 31:13; Zec 1:3,17; Mt 5:4; Lk 16:25; Php 2:1

Comfort as a specific work of the Holy Spirit

Jn 14:16–17 *The title "Counsellor" may be translated "Comforter". See also* Isa 11:2–3; Jn 15:26; 16:7

Comfort within the fellowship of believers

2Co 1:5–7 *See also* 1Co 14:3; 2Co 2:7; 7:6–7; Col 4:11; Heb 12:12

Promises of comfort

When worried Isa 43:1–13; Mt 6:25–34; Php 4:4–7; 1Pe 5:7

When lonely Ps 73:23–24; Isa 41:10; 49:14–16; Jn 14:15–21

When tired or weary Isa 40:28–31; Mt 11:28–30; 2Co 4:16–18; Php 4:12–13

When discouraged Ps 34:18; 42:5; La 3:20–23; Ro 8:28–39

False comfort

Lk 6:24 *See also* Job 16:2; Zec 10:2

Lack of comfort

Jer 16:7 *See also* Ps 69:20; Ecc 4:1; Isa 51:19; 54:11; La 1:2,16–17,21

See also

3130 Holy Spirit, Counsellor	5963 sympathy
5797 bereavement, comfort in	8104 assurance
	8357 weakness
	8414 encouragement
5876 helpfulness	
5952 sorrow	9610 hope
5955 strength, divine	

5806

compassion

A quality of care and sympathy, characteristic of God and Jesus Christ, usually shown in acts of kindness and consideration towards those in any kind of difficulty or crisis.

5807

compassion, of God

See 1030 God, compassion of

5808

compassion, of Jesus Christ

See 2015 Jesus Christ, compassion of

5809

compassion, human

An attitude of care and concern, grounded in pity and sympathy towards others. Christian compassion towards others should reflect the compassion of God for his people.

Compassion is a vital requirement in Christian character

Eph 4:32; Col 3:12 *See also* 2Co 1:3–5; 1Pe 3:8

Compassion needs to be shown in actions

1Jn 3:17 *See also* Isa 58:6–7; Mt 10:42 pp Mk 9:41; Mt 25:35–36; Ac 20:35

Examples of compassionate behaviour

To the oppressed and needy Job 29:12–17; 30:25; Pr 14:31; Lk 10:33–35; Ac 28:2

To the bereaved Ge 37:35; Ru 2:1–20; 2Sa 10:1–2; 1Ch 7:22; Jn 11:19

To children Ex 2:6; 1Ki 3:26; Isa 49:15

To prisoners 2Ch 28:15; 30:9; Ac 16:33–34; Heb 13:3

To forgiven sinners 2Co 2:7–8; Gal 6:1

To the sick Job 2:11–13; Ps 35:13

To the solitary Ecc 4:10–11

To widows and orphans Zec 7:9–10; Jas 1:27

To Jerusalem Ps 102:14

God inspires human compassion

Da 1:9 *See also* Ex 3:21; Ps 106:46; Jer 42:12

God rewards compassion

Pr 14:21 *See also* Ps 112:4–5; Pr 19:17

Lack of compassion

2Sa 12:6; Ps 69:20; 109:16; Eze 16:5; Am 1:11

Limits of human compassion

Dt 28:53–57; Isa 13:18; Jer 21:7; La 4:10

See also

1030 God, compassion	6686 mercy
	8264 gentleness
5802 care	8291 kindness
5963 sympathy	8292 love
6652 forgiveness	8306 mercifulness

5810

complacency

A self-satisfied state of negligence or carelessness, especially in relation to one's personal situation.

Spiritual complacency

Zep 1:12; Lk 12:19 *See also* Dt 8:14; 2Ch 20:33; Ps 10:4; Isa 43:22; 64:7; Jer 10:21; Eze 33:31; Da 9:13; Hos 7:7; Zep 1:6; Heb 6:12; 12:25

Examples of complacency

Jer 6:14; Ob 3; 1Co 5:1–2 *See also* Pr 30:20; Isa 16:6; Eze 28:2; Hag 1:2; Mal 1:6–14; Mt 7:26; 22:5; 26:33; Lk 12:47–48; 14:18; 1Co 4:8; Rev 3:15–17

Warnings against complacency

Am 6:1; 2Co 13:5 *See also* Pr 1:32; 10:4; 12:27; Ecc 10:18; Isa 32:9,11; 47:8–9; Eze 30:9; 1Co 10:12; Heb 2:3

See also

5135 blindness, spiritual	8704 apostasy
	8783 neglect
5343 idleness	8802 pride
5539 sluggard	8823 self-righteousness
5803 carelessness	
5885 indifference	

5811

compromise

Usually a combination of contrasting values, practices or persons incurring God's disapproval, but it can also be a positive way to achieve a greater good.

God forbids compromising associations

Israel was not to associate with paganism Ex 20:3 pp Dt 5:7 *See also* Ex 23:32–33; 34:12–16; Dt 7:2–4; 1Ki 18:21

Christians must not compromise their allegiance Jas 4:4 *See also* Mt 6:24 pp Lk 16:13; Ro 13:14; 2Co 6:14–16; Gal 1:6–9; Jas 4:8

Israel's compromises with paganism

In worship 1Ki 12:28–30 *The LORD's action in bringing Israel up out of Egypt is here attributed to the golden calves representing Baal. See also* Ex 32:2–6; Jdg 2:11–12; 8:27; 2Ki 1:2–3; 16:10–16; 17:32–33,41; 2Ch 28:22; Rev 2:20–23

In foreign alliances Isa 30:1–2 *See also* 2Ch 19:2; 20:35–37; 28:16–21; Isa 31:1; Hos 5:13; 7:8–9,11

In marriage 1Ki 11:1–11 *See also* 1Ki 16:31; 2Ch 18:1; Ezr 9:2; Ne 13:23,25–26

Motives for compromise

Fear Ge 26:7–9 *See also* Ge 12:11–13,18–19; 19:18–20; 20:2,11; Gal 2:12–13

Lack of faith Ge 16:1–2 *See also* Ge 15:2–3; 1Ki 12:26–33

Desire for material things Jos 7:21 *See also* Hag 1:2–4; Mt 13:22 pp Mk 4:18–19 pp Lk 8:14; Ac 5:1–4; 2Ti 4:10

Examples of those who refused to compromise

Est 3:4 *See also* Ge 39:7–12; 1Ki 22:13–14; Da 3:18; 6:7–10; 2Co 4:2

Compromise as a mutually acceptable solution

For the sake of the gospel 1Co 9:19–23 *See also* Ac 15:19–20,28–29; 21:20–26; Ro 14:19–22; 15:1–2

As an act of wisdom 1Ki 3:24–25; 12:6–7 pp 2Ch 10:6–7; Jer 40:9–10

As a means to peace Ge 13:8–9; 26:19–22; 37:26–27; Pr 25:8; Mt 5:25 pp Lk 12:58

See also

5205 alliance	8361 wisdom
5708 marriage	8702 agnosticism
5913 negotiation	8767 hypocrisy
6243 adultery,	8768 idolatry
spiritual	8831 syncretism
6716 reconciliation	
8217 conformity	
8269 holiness,	
separation from	
worldly	

5812

concealment

The deliberate hiding from view of a person, object or action. Those who sin against God often attempt to hide from him. The Bible teaches the need to confess sin and receive God's

forgiveness. Nothing is concealed from him and all secrets will ultimately be revealed.

Attempted concealment of sin from God

Ge 3:1–10 *See also* Nu 32:23; Jos 7:21; 2Ki 17:9; Job 24:13–17; Eze 8:12

Such attempts are foolish Pr 28:13 *See also* Isa 29:15

No sin can be concealed from God Heb 4:13 *See also* Job 13:9; 10:14; Ps 44:20–21; 69:5; Jer 16:17; Eze 11:5–6

Concealed sins will be exposed Ecc 12:14 *See also* Job 20:27; Mt 10:26 pp Lk 12:2; Ro 2:16; 1Co 4:5

Sins should be confessed to God and not concealed 1Jn 1:8–9 *See also* Ps 32:5–6

Believers should not conceal their light

Mt 5:14–16

God may conceal matters

Col 2:2–3; 3:3 *Christ is the mystery of God, which has now been made known. Through faith, believers share in this mystery. See also* Pr 25:2; Dt 29:29; Mt 13:11,35; Mk 13:32; Ac 1:7; Ro 16:25; Col 1:26

The concealment of people

Of Moses Heb 11:23 *See also* Ex 2:2

Of Israelite spies Jos 6:25 *See also* Jos 2:4–6; 6:17

See also

1439 revelation	6155 fall of Adam &
4809 darkness	Eve
4833 light	6624 confession of
5146 covering	sin
5837 disguise	6652 forgiveness
5941 secrecy	6694 mystery

5813

conceit

A state of pride arising out of an overestimation of one's own ability, possessions or importance.

The definition of conceit

Gal 6:3

Examples of conceit

In military strength 2Ki 18:33–35 *See also* Ex 15:9; 1Sa 17:42–44

In the power of idols Da 3:15 *See also* Ac 8:9–10

In personal abilities Mt 26:33 pp Mk 14:29 *See also* Ge 16:4; 1Ki 20:11; Est 5:10–12

In false teaching 1Ti 6:3–4

In possessions Hos 12:8

In intellectual ability Ps 73:7–9

In national status Isa 47:6–8 *See also* Isa 16:6; Jer 48:29

God's response to conceit

2Sa 22:28; 1Co 1:27–29 *See also* Isa 2:12; 23:9; 47:8–11; Ob 3–4

Warnings against conceit

Php 2:3 *See also* Pr 3:7; Isa 5:21; Jer 9:23–24; Ro 12:3,16; 1Co 3:18–21; 4:7; 8:2; Gal 5:26; 2Ti 3:4

The folly of conceit

Pr 26:12 *See also* Pr 28:26; Isa 16:6; Hos 10:13–14; Jas 3:5; 4:16

The danger of conceit for Christians

1Co 10:12 *See also* Ro 11:25; 2Co 12:7; 1Ti 3:6; 1Jn 2:16

Remedies for conceit

Being aware of one's sin Lk 18:9–14

Being prepared to mix with the lowly Ro 12:16

Considering others as being superior Php 2:3

See also

5764 attitudes,	8276 humility
negative to God	8755 folly
5793 arrogance	8802 pride
6121 boasting	8820 self-confidence
8224 dependence	

5814

confrontation

Confrontation in battle

Between armies Jdg 20:20; 2Ch 14:11 *See also* Jdg 20:25; 1Sa 4:1; 17:2; 31:1; 2Sa 10:17; 2Ch 13:3

Between individuals 1Sa 17:45 *See also* 2Sa 23:21; 1Ki 11:14; 2Ki 14:11

Personal confrontation

Between individuals Gal 2:11 *See also* Ex 8:20; 2Sa 22:19 pp Ps 18:18; 1Ki 22:24; 2Ch 26:18; Jer 28:10; Jn 18:26; Ac 13:8; 23:2

Between individuals and groups Nu 16:3; Ac 18:6 *See also* 1Sa 12:7; Eze 16:2; Ac 5:28–29; 6:9

Between believers and a sinner Lk 17:3 *See also* Lev 19:17; Mt 18:15; Gal 6:1; Jas 5:19–20

Confrontation between Jesus Christ and the Pharisees

Lk 11:53–54 *See also* Mt 16:1; 22:15; Mk 2:16; 7:5; Lk 6:2; 19:39; Jn 8:13

Confrontation with God

Job 9:32; Ac 9:4–5 *See also* Ge 32:24; Ex 15:7; Nu 22:22; 2Ch 35:21; Job 23:13; 31:14; 33:5; Ps 17:13; Isa 30:11; Jer 50:24; Ac 11:17

See also

2545 Christ,	8401 challenges
opposition to	8785 opposition
5605 warfare	8794 persecution
5924 quarrel-	
someness	

5815

confusion

A state of perplexity, bewilderment or disorder. Confusion may be brought about by God to cause the schemes of the wicked to fail and opposition to his people to prove ineffective. Confusion over spiritual truth is the natural state of humanity; believers, too, may be perplexed by God's purposes or thrown into confusion by false teaching.

Examples of people in confusion
2Sa 18:29; Est 3:15; Lk 21:25–26; Ac 17:8; 19:32

God sends confusion as judgment
The righteous ask God to confuse their enemies Ps 35:26 *See also* Ps 40:14; 55:9; 70:2

God sends confusion on Israel's enemies Ex 23:27 *See also* Dt 7:23; Ps 71:24

Israel, too, may experience confusion Dt 28:20 *See also* Dt 28:28; 2Ch 15:5–6; Jer 51:34

Examples of God sending confusion Ge 11:7–9 *at the tower of Babel*; Jos 10:10 *on the Amorites*; 1Sa 14:20 *on the Philistines*; 2Ch 20:22–23 *on Jehoshaphat's enemies*

Spiritual confusion is humanity's natural state
Isa 57:20–21 *See also* Isa 41:29; 1Co 1:18; 2:14; 2Co 4:3–4

Confusion relating to Jesus Christ
Confusion among the Jews Jn 6:52; Ac 2:6–7 *See also* Mt 12:23–24 pp Mk 3:22 pp Lk 11:15; Lk 9:7–9 pp Mt 14:1–2 pp Mk 6:14–16; Jn 3:4; Ac 2:12; 2Co 3:14

Confusion among Jesus Christ's disciples Mt 8:27 pp Mk 4:41 pp Lk 8:25 *See also* Mk 9:5–6 pp Mt 17:4 pp Lk 9:33–34; Mk 16:8; Lk 24:22–25; Jn 6:60; 16:17–19

Further examples of believers in confusion
Confusion over God's purposes 2Co 4:8 *See also* Ps 73:12–14; Ecc 7:15; Isa 21:3–4; Da 4:19; Hab 1:2–4; 2Co 7:5; Gal 4:19–20

Confusion over doctrine Gal 1:6–7 *See also* Gal 4:9,17; 5:10

Remedies for confusion
Confusion dispelled by asking God for understanding Jer 33:3 *See also* Jas 1:5

Confusion dispelled by the enlightenment of the Holy Spirit Jn 14:26 *See also* Jn 16:13; 1Co 2:9–10,13

Confusion combated by the teaching of wise leaders Ac 20:28–30; 2Ti 2:24–25; 4:2–3; Heb 13:17

Confusion dispelled by the instruction of Scripture Ps 119:103–105; 2Ti 3:16

Confusion goes as believers grow to spiritual maturity Eph 4:13–14 *See also* Php 1:9–10; Heb 5:14

See also

1310 God as judge	8314 orthodoxy
4045 chaos	8355 understanding
4065 orderliness	8361 wisdom
5135 blindness, spiritual	8615 prayer, doubts
5585 towers	8722 doubt
6020 sin	8726 doubters

5816

consciousness

The state of being aware, especially of one's actions and motivations, or of the existence and concerns of others. All people have a general awareness or consciousness of God and of sin, but it is often suppressed or destroyed.

Consciousness of sin
Through the law Ro 3:19–20 *See also* Ro 7:7–13; Jas 2:9–10

Through the convicting power of the Holy Spirit Jn 16:8 *See also* 1Co 14:24–25; Jude 14–15

Through comparison with God's righteousness Ps 143:2 *See also* Job 25:2–6; Ps 130:3–4

Consciousness of God
Through an innate knowledge of the creator Ro 1:28 *See also* Ac 17:22–31; Ro 1:28; Eph 4:17–19

Through the revelation of God in nature Ac 14:17 *See also* Ps 19:1–6; 50:6

Through observation of divine judgment Eze 6:13 *See also* Ps 83:16–18; Eze 29:6–9; 39:6

Through observation of divine blessing Jos 4:23–24 *See also* Ex 7:5; Dt 4:35; Isa 52:9–10

Lack of consciousness
Job 14:10–12 *See also* Ps 6:5; 30:9; 31:17; 88:10–12; 115:17–18; Ecc 9:5–6,10; Isa 38:18–19

See also

1440 revelation, creation	5031 knowledge of sin
3248 Holy Spirit, conviction	5035 mind
5008 conscience	8134 knowing God
5026 knowledge	9020 death
5029 knowledge of God	

5817

conspiracies

Malicious plots or plans to harm or to kill, which may be directed against other people, or even against God. Conspiracies are sometimes motivated by political aspirations, but may be simply an outlet for wrongdoing.

Conspiracies to sin
Mic 7:3 *See also* Ps 52:2; 64:6; Pr 16:27,30; Jer 11:9–10; Eze 22:25

Conspiracies to murder
Jer 18:23 *See also* Ge 37:17–23; 2Sa 11:2–17; 2Ch 24:20–21

Conspiracies to commit genocide
Est 9:24–25 *See also* 2Sa 21:1–6; Est 3:5–9

Conspiracies to hinder the work of God
Ne 4:7–8 *See also* Ne 4:11,15

Conspiracies against kings
Conspiracies to overthrow the king 2Ki 15:10 *See also* 1Ki 15:25–28; 16:8–10,15–18; 2Ki 9:14–24; 10:9–11; 12:19–21 pp 2Ch 24:25–26 *the assassination of Joash*; 2Ki 14:17–19 pp 2Ch 25:27 *the assassination of Amaziah*; 2Ki 15:15,23–25,30; 21:23–24 pp 2Ch 33:24–25 *the assassination of Amon*; Est 2:21–22; 6:2

Conspiracies against King David 2Sa 15:10–12 *See also* 1Sa 23:7–13,15,19–23; 2Sa 15:31; 1Ki 1:5–10; 2:28

False accusations of conspiracy against kings Am 7:10–11 *See also* 1Sa 22:6–8,13–16; Ne 6:5–9; Da 2:9

Conspiracies against cities and nations
Jer 48:2 *See also* Isa 7:5–6; Jer 49:30–33; Eze 11:2–3; Da 11:24–25; Hab 2:10

Conspiracies against God
Ps 2:1–3 *See also* Ps 21:11; 83:5–8; Hos 7:11–16; Na 1:9–11

Conspiracies against God's servants
2Ch 24:20–21 *See also* Ps 31:13; 35:4; 36:4; 37:12; 38:12; 52:2; 56:5; 59:3; 64:2; 71:10; 83:3; 105:24–25; Jer 11:18–19 *a plot against Jeremiah*; Jer 18:23; La 3:60–61

Conspiracies against Jesus Christ
Mt 12:14 pp Mk 3:6 pp Lk 6:11 *See also* Mt 26:3–4 pp Mk 14:1 pp Lk 22:1–2; Jn 11:53; Ac 4:27

Conspiracies against Paul
Ac 23:12–16 *See also* Ac 9:20–25; 14:1–7; 18:12; 20:3,19; 23:30

Conspirators condemned
Isa 33:15–16 *See also* 2Sa 12:1–12; Pr 3:29; 6:12–15; 12:20; 14:22; 24:1–2,8; Isa 8:12; Mic 2:1; Zec 8:16–17

See also

2545 Christ, opposition to	6224 rebellion against authority
5040 murder	
5589 trap	8751 false witness
5917 plans	
6222 rebellion against God	

5818

contempt

An attitude of scorn and derision. Examples are given of the way in which a rebellious and fallen world treats its creator with contempt.

Contempt of some people for others
Eliab for David 1Sa 17:28

Nabal for David 1Sa 25:10–11,14

King Hanun for David's men 2Sa 10:4–5

Sanballat, Geshem and Tobiah for Nehemiah's men Ne 2:19; 4:3

Contempt for parents
Pr 15:5,20; 23:22

Contempt from the godless
Job 16:10; Ps 31:18 *See also* Job 19:18; 30:1; Ps 35:21; 42:10; 69:19–20; 119:22; Isa 28:9–10,14; Jer 20:7

God's contempt for the godless
Ps 2:4 *See also* Job 12:21; Pr 1:26; Na 3:6

God will bring contempt on his people
Jer 18:16 *See also* Jer 25:9,18; Eze 22:4; Da 9:16; Mic 6:16

Human contempt for God
For God himself Nu 14:11 *See also* Nu 14:23; 16:30; Ps 14:1; 73:11

For his law Ps 78:10 *See also* Lev 22:9; Isa 30:9; Hos 4:6; Mk 7:9 pp Mt 15:3; Heb 10:28

For his prophets 2Ch 36:16 *See also* Am 7:12–13; Mt 5:12

For his works Zec 4:10 *See also* Hab 1:5; Ac 13:41

For his day Ne 13:15–21; Am 8:5

For his worship and service Mal 1:6–8,12–13; 2:11; 3:8–9,14

For his gospel Mt 7:6

For his kindness Ro 2:4

For his authority 2Pe 2:10

For his patience 2Pe 3:3–4,9

Jesus Christ as the object of contempt
Anticipated in prophecy Ps 22:6–8 *See also* Mt 27:43

Ps 69:19–21 *See also* Isa 53:3

During his earthly ministry Mt 13:54–57 pp Mk 6:1–4 *See also* Mt 9:24; Lk 16:14; Jn 9:34

While on the cross Mt 27:39 pp Mk 15:29 *See also* Mk 15:32; Lk 23:39

Contempt will be punished
Pr 1:26 *See also* Pr 3:34; 19:29; 22:10; Eze 25:3–7; 36:2–5

Final punishment is contempt
Da 12:2

See also
1670 symbols	8721 doubt
5838 disrespect	8782 mockery
5893 insults	8815 ridicule
5900 laughter	8819 scoffing
6151 dirt	
6222 rebellion against God	

5819

cowardice

An unwillingness to act in a situation of danger or opposition, because of fear. Avoiding the source of one's anxiety or fear, rather than dealing with it directly.

Cowardice prevents people from acknowledging Jesus Christ publicly
Jn 12:42–43 *See also* Jn 7:13; 9:22–23 *parents of the man born blind*; Jn 19:38; 20:19

Cowardice inhibits bad as well as good behaviour Mt 14:5; 21:26,46

Cowardice leads to avoidance of the difficulty Mt 26:56 *See also* 1Sa 13:6–7

---

the Philistine threat; 1Sa 17:24 *Goliath*; 1Ki 19:2–3; Jnh 1:10; Mt 26:69–74 pp Mk 14:66–71 pp Lk 22:57–60 pp Jn 18:15–18, 25–27; Lk 8:37 *after the destruction of the pigs*; Gal 2:12 *Peter*

Cowardice can spread within a group
Dt 20:8

Caleb and the other spies: Nu 13:30–33; Jos 14:8

Jdg 7:2–3; Jer 38:4

God can work through cowardice
In humbling disobedient people Lev 26:36–39; Isa 30:15–17

In routing the enemy *Rahab and the Israelite spies:* Jos 2:8–11,24

1Sa 14:15–16 *the Philistines*

God gives hope to the cowardly or fearful
Pr 29:25 *See also* Dt 1:27–31; Jdg 7:10–11; Ps 56:3–4; Isa 51:12–15; Lk 21:12–19

The Holy Spirit gave the disciples a supernatural boldness: Ac 4:5–10,13,29–31

Judgment on cowards
Rev 21:8 *Where cowardice meant rejecting the gospel and denying Jesus Christ.*

See also
5798 betrayal	8712 denial of Christ
8202 boldness	8754 fear
8219 courage	8839 unfaithfulness

5820

criticism

The judgment or evaluation of others. The word often has negative associations, implying a harsh or disapproving estimate of people or their actions.

5821

criticism, amongst believers

Harsh criticism is out of place among believers, who are urged to see each other in the best possible light. Criticism of God arises from a failure to understand his actions and purposes.

Criticism forbidden among believers
Jas 5:9 *See also* Mt 7:1–5 pp Lk 6:37–42; Ro 14:1–4,10–13; 1Co 10:10; Gal 5:15; Php 2:14–16; Jas 4:11–12

Reacting to criticism
Some criticism can be disregarded Ecc 7:21–22 *See also* 1Co 4:2–5; Col 2:16–18

Criticism can be dealt with by settling the dispute Mt 18:15 *See also* Pr 15:1

Integrity is a defence against criticism
Da 6:4 *See also* 2Co 8:20–21; Tit 2:7–8

Criticism can be constructive
Ps 141:5 *See also* Pr 10:17; 15:5; 27:6,9; 28:23

Criticism and complaint directed against God
Criticism of God for his apparent injustice Dt 1:26–27 *See also* Jer 20:7–9; Jnh 4:1–4; Hab 1:1–4,12–17; Mal 3:13–15; Ro 9:19–21; Isa 29:16; 45:9

Criticism of God for his apparent disregard of his people's plight Isa 40:27 *See also* Ps 10:1; 13:1–2; 22:1–2; 42:9–10; 44:23–24; 74:10–11; 80:4–6; 108:11–12

See also
5265 complaints	6115 blame
5897 judging others	

5822

criticism, against believers

Many notable servants of God were subject to criticism, which was sometimes vicious and severe. This was particularly true of Jesus Christ, who was constantly subject to complaint and criticism.

Examples of criticism directed against believers
The patriarchs criticised Ge 31:25–30 *See also* Ge 12:17–20; 16:5; 20:9–10; 30:1–2

Moses criticised Ex 17:3 *See also* Ex 2:11–14; 5:19–21; 14:11–12; 15:24; 16:2; Nu 12:1–2; 16:1–3,12–14,41

David criticised 1Sa 17:28 *See also* 2Sa 6:16–23; 15:1–4

Job criticised Job 8:1–2 *See also* Job 11:1–6; 15:1–6

The prophets criticised Jer 20:8 *See also* 1Ki 18:17; 22:24–27; Am 7:10–12

Criticism directed against Jesus Christ
Jesus Christ criticised by his family Mk 3:20–21 *See also* Lk 2:48; Jn 7:2–5

Jesus Christ criticised by his disciples Mk 4:38 *See also* Mt 16:21–23 pp Mk 8:31–33; Lk 10:40; Jn 6:60–61; 13:6–9

Jesus Christ criticised by the Pharisees Mt 9:10–11 pp Mk 2:15–16 pp Lk 5:29–30 *See also* Mt 12:1–2 pp Mk 2:23–24 pp Lk 6:1–2; Lk 15:1–2

Jesus Christ criticised for his teaching Jn 6:41–42 *See also* Mt 9:3 pp Mk 2:6–7 pp Lk 5:21; Jn 8:52–53

Paul criticised
Ac 21:27–28 *See also* Ac 18:12–13; 2Co 10:10

See also
2545 Christ, opposition to	9210 judgment, God's
8794 persecution	

5823

cruelty

Behaviour in which pain or suffering is deliberately inflicted on others, especially the weak and defenceless.

5824
cruelty, examples of

Scripture condemns cruelty, and gives examples of situations in which it was practised.

Cruelty is an expression of wickedness
Ps 71:4; Ro 1:28–31 See also Ps 35:16; 86:14; Pr 17:5; Ecc 4:1; Am 5:12

Forms of cruelty
The cruel nature of war 2Ki 8:12 See also 2Ki 15:16; Isa 13:15,18; Hos 10:14; 13:16; Na 3:10

The cruel nature of rape Ge 34:2 See also Jdg 19:25; 2Sa 13:14; Zec 14:2

The cruel nature of words Job 17:1–2; Ps 42:10; Mk 15:31 See also 1Sa 1:6–7; Job 11:3; Ps 22:7; 35:11; 89:50–51; 102:8; Jer 20:7; La 3:14

Particular examples of cruelty
Ge 37:23–24 Joseph's brothers; Ge 49:5–7 Simeon and Levi; Ex 1:22 Pharaoh; Jdg 1:6 Judah's cruelty to a local king; Jdg 4:2–3 Sisera; Jdg 10:6–8 the Philistines and Ammonites; 2Ch 16:10 Asa; Pr 5:8–9 the adulteress Nebuchadnezzar; Jer 21:7; Da 3:13–20 The officials at Jerusalem; Jer 37:15; 38:6–7
Eze 22:29 Israel; Na 3:18–19 the king of Assyria; Mt 2:16 King Herod Jesus Christ's torturers: Mt 27:26–31 pp Mk 15:15–20 pp Jn 19:15 Jesus Christ's executioners: Lk 23:33–39 pp Mt 27:35–44 pp Mk 15:24–32 pp Jn 19:18

See also
5040 murder	5789 anger
5281 crucifixion	5972 unkindness
5347 injustice	6178 hardness of
5436 pain	heart
5446 poverty	8790 oppression
5560 suffering	8794 persecution
5782 agony	

5825
cruelty, God's attitude to

God condemns cruelty. As part of the work of redemption, God suffers cruelty from the world in order to redeem believers.

God reproves cruelty
Dt 23:15–16; Pr 14:31; Isa 10:1–2; Eze 45:9 See also Ex 22:21; 23:9; Lev 25:42–43,46,53; Pr 12:10; Isa 13:11; Jer 22:3; Zec 7:10

God allows cruelty as part of his judgment
Isa 13:9; Jer 30:14; La 2:17 See also Dt 28:15–42 The LORD promises cruel judgment on those who disobey his laws; Isa 19:4; Jer 6:22–23; 13:14; 20:16; La 2:2,21; Hab 1:5–2:1

God delivers from cruelty
Ex 3:7–9; Ne 9:27; Ps 12:5 See also Jdg 2:18; 6:9; 1Sa 10:18; 2Sa 7:10; Ps 72:4,14; Isa 9:4; 25:4–5; 29:20

See also
5359 justice	6510 salvation
5482 punishment	6686 mercy
5493 retribution	8291 kindness
5560 suffering	8734 evil
5806 compassion	

5827
curse

An expression of contempt or malediction for someone. To be cursed is to suffer various kinds of misfortune, sometimes to the extent of being cut off from one's family or community, or of suffering death itself.

Divine curses
Divine curses came into effect after the fall Ge 3:14–19 See also Ge 5:29; 8:21 This curse refers to the flood; the curse of Ge 3:17 is not revoked here.

Divine curses come from disobeying the law Dt 28:15–19 See also Lev 26:14–39; Dt 11:26–28; 27:9–26; 28:20–68; 29:18–21; Jer 11:2–4,8; Da 9:11–14; Gal 3:10

Human curses
Human curses upon other human beings 2Ki 2:23–24 See also Ge 9:24–25; Jos 9:22–23; 1Sa 14:24–28; Ne 13:25

Human curses upon God Job 2:9; Rev 16:9 See also Isa 52:5; Eze 20:27

Human beings are forbidden to curse God and others Lev 24:15–16
Cursing rulers: Ex 22:28; 1Ki 21:13
Cursing one's father or mother: Ex 21:17; Mt 15:4 pp Mk 7:10; Lev 20:9
Lev 19:14 cursing the deaf

People can curse the day they were born
Jer 20:14 See also Job 3:1–10

Paul wishes himself cursed for the sake of Israel
Ro 9:3–4

Jesus Christ took the curse of the law upon himself
Gal 3:13–14 See also Dt 21:22–23

Christians are exhorted to bless those who curse them
Lk 6:27–28 See also Mt 5:39–42 pp Lk 6:29–30; Ro 12:14; 1Co 4:12–13

See also
1335 blessing	5800 blasphemy
2525 Christ, cross of	5893 insults
5281 crucifixion	6154 fall, the
5331 hanging	8734 evil
5375 law	8819 scoffing
5429 oaths	9030 dead bodies

5828
danger

A condition of threat, physical or spiritual, in which evil, malice, accident or destruction looms.

Physical danger
In nature Lk 8:23 pp Mt 8:24 pp Mk 4:37 See also 1Ki 19:11–12;

Ps 83:14–15; 107:23–28; Ac 16:26–30; 2Co 11:26; Rev 11:13

From human violence Ps 140:1 See also Ge 27:41–43; Ex 2:15; 1Sa 19:1–2; 2Sa 22:3; 1Ki 19:1–3; Ne 4:7–9; Ps 7:9; 64:1; 74:20; Ecc 12:5; Lk 4:28–29; Ac 21:35

Through foolishness Pr 22:3 See also Pr 27:12; Ecc 2:13–14

Spiritual danger
From the devil 1Pe 5:8 See also Ge 3:1–5; Job 1:6–12; 2:1–6; Mt 4:1–11 pp Lk 4:2–13; Jn 13:2; Heb 2:14; 1Jn 3:8; Rev 2:10; 20:10

Danger of hell through disobedience Mt 5:22 See also Lk 12:4–5; 1Co 5:4–5; Heb 6:4–6; 2Pe 2:4–10

Danger of loss through unfaithfulness 1Co 3:13–15 See also Ro 6:21,21; 1Co 9:26–27; 1Ti 6:9–10

Danger does not overcome the faithful Ro 8:35 See also 2Ti 3:10–11

Examples of those endangered
Israel by her enemies Ex 13:17–22; Est 3:1–6

Joseph, through betrayal Ge 37:18–28

Prophets, because of persecution Jer 38:1–11

Jonah, through disobedience Jnh 1:4–17

Jesus Christ, through betrayal Mt 26:3–4,14–16

Paul, through shipwreck Ac 27:13–20,42–44

See also
4120 Satan	6738 rescue
5511 safety	8493 watchfulness,
5589 trap	believers
5969 treachery	8727 enemies
5975 violence	8736 evil, warnings
5978 warning	against
6248 temptation	8833 threats

5829
defiance

Open refusal to obey any authority. Defiance is seen in the Bible as evil when authority is legitimate but good when authority is ungodly.

Defiance of God is condemned
Jer 50:29 See also 1Ki 13:21–22,26; Ps 139:19–22; Isa 3:8; 65:7; Jer 48:26,42

To defy God's people is to defy God
1Sa 17:10,23,25–26,36,45

Defiance of legitimate authority
Ro 13:2 See also Nu 15:30; 1Pe 2:13

Defiance of ungodly authority
Da 3:28 See also Da 6:13; Ac 4:19; 5:29; 17:7; Rev 20:4

See also
5215 authority	6193 impenitence
5257 civil authorities	6221 rebellion
5326 government	8718 disobedience
5457 power, human	

5830

delight

A sense of joy and pleasure, experienced especially through achievements or relationships.

God as the source of delight
Delight in the person of God Isa 61:10 *See also* Ne 1:11; Job 22:26; Ps 22:8; 37:4; 43:3–4; Isa 58:13–14

Delight in the word of God Ps 119:16; Ro 7:22 *See also* Ps 1:2; 19:7–14; 119:24,47; Jer 15:16

Delight in the works of God 1Sa 2:1; Ps 35:4–10; Ac 11:23

God expresses delight
Over his world Ps 104:31 *See also* Ge 1:31; Pr 8:30–31

Over his people Dt 30:9–10 *See also* 2Sa 22:20; Ps 147:10–11; 149:4; Isa 62:4; 65:18–19; Jer 31:20; 32:41; Mic 7:18

Over justice Pr 11:1 *See also* Pr 11:20; 12:22; Jer 9:24

Over his Messiah Mt 3:17 pp Mk 1:11 pp Lk 3:22 *See also* Isa 42:1; Mt 12:18–21; 17:5 pp Mk 9:7 pp Lk 9:35; 2Pe 1:17

God's delight is absent when something is viewed unfavourably 1Sa 15:22 *See also* Lev 26:31; Ps 51:16; 147:10

Natural delight in parenthood
Pr 3:12 *See also* Pr 23:24; 29:17; Mic 1:16

Sexual delight
SS 1:4 *See also* Ge 34:19; Pr 5:18; SS 2:3; 4:1; 7:10

Delight in the created order
In God's gifts Dt 26:11 *See also* Isa 55:2; Jer 31:12; Joel 2:23

In one's work Ecc 2:10 *See also* Dt 12:7; Ecc 3:22; 5:19; 8:15

In the achievements of others Col 2:5 *See also* Ex 18:9; Est 6:9; Pr 14:35; 1Th 2:13–14

The delight of believers in their relationship with God
Ps 9:2 *See also* 1Sa 2:1; Ne 1:11; Job 22:26; Ps 9:14; 13:5; 31:7; 35:9; 37:4; 89:16; 149:2; Lk 1:46–47

Delight in wrongdoing
Ps 62:4; 1Co 13:6 *See also* Ps 68:30; Pr 2:12–15; 18:2; Isa 66:3; Col 2:18; 2Th 2:12

See also

1070 God, joy of	5900 laughter
4040 beauty	5918 pleasure
5287 dance	5939 satisfaction
5841 ecstasy	7960 singing
5846 enjoyment	8283 joy
5874 happiness	8460 pleasing God

5831

depression

A deep sense of despondency, discouragement and sadness, often linked with a sense of personal powerlessness and a loss of meaning in and enthusiasm for life. Many biblical characters show evidence of such behaviour which originates in a number of different ways.

Some causes of depression
External circumstances 2Co 1:8 *See also* 1Ki 19:3–4; Job 9:23; Ps 42:1–11; 88:1–18; Joel 1:11

Physical illness or exhaustion 1Ki 19:5–8 *See also* Ge 21:15–16; Ps 6:1–7; 22:14–17; 31:9–12; Isa 38:1–2; Jnh 1:5

Fear of others 1Ki 19:1–3

Fear of failure 1Ki 19:4 *See also* Ex 4:1; Nu 11:11–15

Serious sin Mt 27:3–4 *See also* Ps 25:16–18; Jer 14:2–3,7; 16:9–10; Eze 4:16–17; 7:26–27; 12:19; Rev 16:10–11

A sense of the futility of life Ecc 2:17–20

Loss of sense of God's presence Ps 22:1–2 *See also* Mt 27:46; Mk 15:34

Symptoms of depression
A loathing of life and a desire to end it Nu 11:15 *See also* 1Ki 19:4; Job 10:1; Ecc 2:17; Jer 20:15–18; Jnh 4:8

Deep sorrow Ge 21:16 *See also* Jdg 21:2; 1Sa 1:10,16; Ps 42:3; Ne 1:4; 2:2; Est 4:1–3; Job 16:16; La 2:11

Loneliness 1Ki 19:10 *See also* Nu 11:14; 1Ki 19:14

Perplexity Ps 42:5 *See also* Hab 1:2; Lk 24:17; Jn 16:6

Despair Job 17:1 *See also* Ps 88:3–9; 2Co 1:8–9

Escapism Ps 55:6–8 *See also* 1Ki 19:1–3; Jer 8:22

Feeling forsaken by God Ps 22:1 *See also* Ps 27:9; 38:21; Isa 49:14; Jer 15:18; La 3:1–20

Examples of spiritual depression
Jdg 6:13; 1Ki 19:9–18; Ps 22:1–2,6–8; 42:1–7,9–11; 43:1–5

Remedies for depression
Renewed vision of God and being centred upon him 1Ki 19:11; Isa 26:3 *See also* Jer 17:7–8; Ro 8:6

Hope and trust in God Ps 42:11 *See also* Ps 22:9–11,22–31; Hab 3:16–18

Praise Ps 30:1 *See also* Ps 42:5; 107:1–43; Isa 61:1–3; 2Co 4:8–12

Reviewing what God has done Ps 77:11–12 *See also* Ps 42:6; 143:5; La 3:19–26; 2Co 7:6

Prayer Php 4:6–7 *See also* Ps 139:23

See also

5560 suffering	8283 joy
5770 abandonment	8713 discourage-
5799 bitterness	ment
5901 loneliness	8741 failure
5952 sorrow	8754 fear
5970 unhappiness	9614 hope, results
8104 assurance	of absence

5832

desire

A sense of longing for or wanting something. It may be a positive or negative force in the human character, but sinful desire is characteristic of human nature and must be overcome by the believer. God also expresses desires in Scripture.

Righteous desire
Desire for God Ps 73:25 *See also* Ps 42:1–2; 63:1–8; 143:6; Isa 26:8–9

Desire for right living Ps 40:8 *See also* Ps 119:174; Pr 22:1; Heb 13:18

Desire for wisdom 2Ch 1:7–12 pp 1Ki 3:5–14 *See also* Jas 1:5

Desire for spiritual gifts 1Co 14:1–5 *See also* 1Co 12:27–31

Desire for church office 1Ti 3:1

Sinful desire
Dt 5:21 pp Ex 20:17 *See also* Pr 11:6; Ro 1:24; 7:8; 1Ti 6:9–10; Jas 1:13–15; 2Pe 3:3; Jude 16–18

Sinful desire is inherent in human nature Eph 2:3 *See also* 2Pe 2:10,18

Following Jesus Christ means putting to death sinful desires Gal 5:24 *See also* Ro 8:5–14; 13:11–14; Eph 4:22–24; Col 3:5; 2Ti 2:22; 1Pe 1:14–15; 2:11; 4:1–5

The tension in believers between the desires of the old and new natures
Gal 5:16–17 *See also* Ro 7:18; Jas 4:1

Sexual desire
Ge 3:16 *See also* SS 7:10; 1Ti 5:11

Sinful lust condemned Mt 5:28 *See also* Ro 1:26; 1Th 4:3–4; 1Pe 4:3; 2Pe 2:18

God's desires
God desires true worship Mt 12:7 *See also* Hos 6:6; Mt 9:13; Am 5:21–24; Jn 4:21–24; Heb 10:5–14; Ps 40:6–8

God desires right living Ps 51:6 *See also* Jas 1:19–20

God's desires for his people 2Ch 9:8 *See also* Ps 132:13

See also

5785 ambition	7966 spiritual gifts
5792 appetite	8361 wisdom
5840 eagerness	8441 goals
6133 coveting	8656 longing for
6166 flesh, sinful	God
nature	8777 lust
6185 imagination,	8821 self-indulgence
desires	

5833

diligence

Conscientious hard work and perseverance, particularly with regard to a relationship with God. In Scripture diligence is highly commended. It may, however, be misguided.

Diligence and its results are commended

Pr 21:5 *See also* 1Ki 11:28; 2Ch 24:13; Ezr 5:8; 6:12; 7:23; Pr 12:14; 14:23; 31:17 *characteristic of the wife of noble character;* Ecc 3:13; Jer 31:16; 2Co 8:11 *regarding the collection for the poor Christians in Jerusalem;* 1Ti 5:17; 1Pe 5:2

Diligence contrasted with laziness

Pr 10:4 *See also* Pr 12:24,27; 13:4; 2Th 3:10

Diligence is important in the outworking of one's relationship with God

1Co 15:58; 1Ti 4:15–16

Examples of diligence *See also* 2Ch 15:15; 29:34 *the Levites;* Isa 62:6–7; Zec 6:15; Lk 8:15; Ac 17:11 *the Bereans The apostle Paul:* Ro 1:15; 1Co 4:12; 9:24–26; 2Co 6:5; 11:27; 1Th 2:9; 2Th 3:8; 2Ti 4:7
Ro 12:8; 16:12; 1Co 12:31; 14:1; 2Co 8:5 *the Macedonian churches;* Php 2:12–13; 1Th 5:12; Heb 6:11–12; 2Pe 1:10; Rev 2:2–3,19

Diligence was a characteristic of Jesus Christ's mission

Lk 9:51 *See also* Heb 12:1–2

Misguided diligence

Jn 5:39–40 *See also* Ps 127:2; Pr 28:20; Ecc 1:3; 2:11,19; 4:8; Mt 21:15,23–24; 1Ti 6:10

See also

5343 idleness	8207 commitment
5414 money, stewardship	8230 discipline
	8239 earnestness
5628 work	8248 faithfulness
5840 eagerness	8370 zeal
7939 ministry	8459 perseverance
8206 Christlikeness	

5834

disagreement

A failure to be of one mind, which should be avoided whenever possible within the church, the family and other areas of everyday life. Christians are urged to maintain the unity of the church and avoid damaging division.

Disagreement within the church

Between individuals Php 4:2 *See also* Mk 9:33–34 pp Lk 9:46; Ac 15:36–40 *these differences later reconciled; see* 1Co 9:6; 2Ti 4:11; 1Co 1:11–12; 3:3–4; 2Co 12:20

About doctrine Ac 15:1–2 *See also* Ac 15:11–14,19–20; Gal 2:11–14

Disagreement in the family

May cause estrangement Mic 7:6 *See also* Ge 27:41–45; 37:4

Is unpleasant to live with Pr 19:13; 21:9,19; 25:24; 27:15

Disagreement among witnesses

Mk 14:56 *The background to this statement is Dt 19:15, which demands that conviction can only take place on the testimony of two or three agreed witnesses.*

The wisdom of avoiding disagreement

2Ti 2:14 *See also* Pr 17:14; 20:3; 26:17,21; Ro 16:17; 2Ti 2:23

To prevent division Mt 12:25 pp Mk 3:24–25 pp Lk 11:17 *See also* 1Ki 12:16–17 pp 2Ch 10:16–17

Sin provokes disagreement

Gal 5:19–20 *See also* Pr 6:12–14; 17:19; Tit 3:9–11; Jas 3:16

Examples where disagreement is inevitable

1Sa 11:1–2 *Nahash's suggestion to the men of Jabesh Gilead;* 1Ki 20:8 *Ben-Hadad's demands on Ahab*

Examples of resolved disagreement

Ge 13:5–9 *Abraham and Lot resolve their disagreement over land and livestock;* Ge 26:19–22 *Isaac settles a disagreement about the water supply;* 1Ki 3:16–27 *Solomon resolves a disagreement between two prostitutes.*

Ways to resolve disagreement

Settlement out of court Mt 5:25 pp Lk 12:58 *See also* 1Co 6:1

Accepting weaknesses Ro 14:1

Striving for harmony 1Co 1:10 *See also* Ro 14:19; 15:5; 2Co 13:11; Eph 4:3; Php 2:2–3; Col 3:13–15; 1Th 5:13; 2Ti 2:23–24; 1Pe 3:8

Appointing wise leaders Dt 1:12–13 *Moses realised that he was unable to deal with all the people's disputes alone. See also* Mt 18:15–17; 1Co 6:5–6

Being of sound doctrine 1Ti 1:3–4 *See also* Tit 3:9–10

Those who seek to resolve disagreement are blessed

Mt 5:9 *See also* Jas 3:18

See also

5270 court	5811 compromise
5359 justice	5814 confrontation
5375 law	7025 church, unity
5383 lawsuits	7032 unity, God's
5675 divorce	people
5681 family	8458 peacemakers
5783 agreement	

5835

disappointment

The sadness experienced when people or circumstances do not fulfil expectations.

Disappointment caused by people or circumstances

Job 6:19–21; Jer 8:15 *See also* Ps 10:1; Pr 10:1; 13:12; 17:21; 29:21; Ecc 6:2; Isa 49:4; Jer 2:36; 14:19; La 4:17; Eze 37:11

Disappointment as a result of not understanding God's purposes

Lk 24:21 *See also* Job 30:26; Ps 73:13; Jer 15:18

Disappointment as the result of sin

Pr 11:7; Hag 1:9 *See also* Job 11:20; Pr 10:28; La 3:18; Hos 13:15; Joel 1:10; Zec 9:5

Examples of disappointment

Ru 1:20 *Naomi at her losses;* 1Sa 1:10 *Hannah with her childlessness;* 1Sa 15:11 *Samuel with Saul;* 1Sa 30:3–6 *David and his men at Ziklag;* 1Ki 19:4 *Elijah with his own performance;* Mt 19:22 pp Mk 10:22 pp Lk 18:23 *the rich young man;* 2Co 12:21 *Paul's possible disappointment with the Corinthians;* Gal 1:6 *Paul with the Galatians*

God's disappointment with people

Ge 6:6; 1Sa 15:35 *See also* Ps 78:40; Isa 63:10; Eze 6:9

God does not disappoint his faithful people

Jos 21:45; Ro 5:5 *See also* Jos 23:14; 1Ki 8:56; Ps 22:5; 25:3; 119:116

See also

5799 bitterness	5970 unhappiness
5831 depression	8713 discourage-
5839 dissatisfaction	ment
5938 sadness	8741 failure
5952 sorrow	9610 hope

5836

disgrace

Shame and dishonour that can arise from sin and idolatry. The exile of Israel brought disgrace upon God's name. God's people may suffer disgrace for the sake of Jesus Christ.

Examples of disgrace

Brought on Israel
As the result of Achan stealing what was dedicated to God: Jos 7:1–5,11–15
1Sa 17:23–26 *as the result of Goliath's boasting;* Ps 44:9–19 *when God no longer acted on Israel's behalf*

Brought on Israel's enemies Ps 6:10; 35:4,26; 40:14; 44:15; 70:2; 71:13; 83:17–18

Sin brings disgrace

Ge 3:8–10 *See also* Ps 52:1; Pr 13:5; 14:35; 18:3; Jer 3:25; Da 9:7–8; Hos 4:7; Ro 2:23–24

False prophets disgraced Jer 23:38–40

Idolaters disgraced Isa 45:16 *See also* Ex 32:25; Isa 1:29; Jer 2:26–28; Hos 10:6

The sexually immoral disgraced

Pr 6:32–33 *See also* Ge 34:1–7; Lev 20:17; Dt 22:21; Jdg 19:22–24; 20:4–7; 2Sa 11:2–5; 12:14; 13:12–14,22

Barrenness could bring disgrace

Ge 30:22–23; 1Sa 1:6; Lk 1:25

The exile brought disgrace upon God's name

Eze 36:20–21 *See also* Ne 1:3; 2:17; Jer 22:22; 51:51; La 5:1–2

God's people may suffer disgrace for the sake of Jesus Christ

Heb 11:26 *See also* Mt 5:11–12 pp Lk 6:22–23; Ac 5:41; Heb 13:13; 1Pe 2:21; 4:1,13; 5:10

See also

5225 barrenness	5947 shame
5838 disrespect	6020 sin
5843 embarrassment	6236 sexual sin
5878 honour	7215 exile, the
5879 humiliation	

5837

disguise

The hiding of one's personal identity for a variety of reasons
2Ch 35:20–24 *See also* Ge 38:13–26;
1Sa 28:4–12; 1Ki 14:1–6; 20:35–43;
22:29–37 pp 2Ch 18:28–34

See also

4123 Satan, deceiver	6145 deceit
5920 pretence	

5838

disrespect

The attitude of heart that leads people to treat God and others in ways that demonstrate a lack of esteem.

Causes of disrespect for God and Jesus Christ
Disrespect caused by a wrong view of God and Jesus Christ Ro 1:21–23 *See also* Lk 23:8–11

Disrespect caused by disobedience to God Ne 9:26 *See also* 2Ch 24:17–20;
2Ti 3:1–5

Disrespect caused by Satan Ac 5:3 *See also* Mt 8:28–29 pp Mk 5:1–7
pp Lk 8:26–28

Causes of disrespect for others
Disrespect for others caused by a wrong view of people Mt 19:13–14
pp Mk 10:13–14 pp Lk 18:15–16 *The lack of respect for the children arose from the erroneous belief that they were not important enough for Jesus Christ to bother with. See also Lk 10:25–37 Those who passed by failed to heed God's command to love their neighbours as themselves;*
Jas 2:1–4

Disrespect for others caused by seeking power and wealth Ecc 4:1 *See also* Jas 5:1–6

Disrespect for others caused by envy Mic 2:1–2 *See also* Ge 37:3–4

Disrespect for others caused by pride and contempt Ps 31:18 *See also*
Mt 27:27–31 pp Mk 15:16–20

Disrespect shown in speech
Jas 3:9 *See also* Mt 27:39–44
pp Mk 15:29–32 pp Lk 23:35–39;
1Ti 6:3–5

The development of disrespect
Disrespect can grow insidiously
1Ki 11:4 *See also* Jer 2:1–11
The temple area had been gradually invaded by commerce; Mk 11:15–17
pp Mt 21:12–13 pp Lk 19:45–46
pp Jn 2:13–17

Disrespect can spread infectiously
Dt 1:27–28 *See also* Est 1:16–18;
Mk 15:9–15 pp Mt 27:17–26
pp Lk 23:13–25; Ro 2:24

Disrespect can end fatally Lev 10:1–2
See also Ex 32:25–28; Dt 21:18–21;
Jer 25:4–11

See also

1025 God, anger of	5896 irreverence
1090 God, majesty of	8469 respect
2530 Christ, death of	8718 disobedience
5727 old age,	8782 mockery
attitudes	8790 oppression
5818 contempt	8839 unfaithfulness
5878 honour	

5839

dissatisfaction

The human feeling of emptiness and unfulfilment, at either a physical or spiritual level.

Hunger and thirst are never permanently satisfied
Ecc 6:7 *See also* Ps 59:15; Isa 55:2;
Jn 4:13–14

Dissatisfaction as a result of divine judgment
Lev 26:26 *See also* Isa 9:19–21;
Eze 7:19; Mic 6:14

Death is never satisfied
Pr 27:20 *See also* Pr 30:15–16; Hab 2:5

Dissatisfaction is characteristic of the unrighteous
Pr 13:4 *See also* Est 5:9–13; Ecc 5:10;
Eze 16:28–29; 3Jn 9–10

See also

4822 famine	5869 greed
5341 hunger	5939 satisfaction
5580 thirst	5970 unhappiness
5835 disappointment	9020 death
5853 experience of	
life	

5840

eagerness

A willingness, zeal or longing to accomplish a task or fulfil an ambition.

Eagerness to perform a task
1Ch 12:8; Ne 3:20 *See also* Ezr 5:8;
Pr 31:13; Ac 20:16; 1Th 2:17

Eagerness to fulfil personal ambitions
Zep 3:7; 1Ti 6:10 *See also* Ps 56:6;
Pr 1:11–12; 28:20; Mk 6:25;
Gal 4:17–18; Php 3:6

Eagerness for personal godliness
2Ch 15:15; 2Pe 1:10 *See also* 1Ch 28:9;
Ps 27:4; 42:1–2; 63:1; Pr 23:17; Ac 26:7;
1Co 14:1; 2Co 7:11; Heb 4:11; 6:11;
1Pe 2:2; 2Pe 1:5

Spiritual eagerness may be superficial and unreal
Isa 58:2 *See also* Ps 78:34–37; Isa 48:1

Believers should be eager to follow and serve their Lord
Eager to do good works Tit 2:14 *See also* 2Co 8:7,22; Tit 3:1,8,14; 1Pe 3:13

Eager to serve Ro 12:11; 1Pe 5:2 *See also* Ps 110:3; Ro 12:8; 1Co 14:12;
Eph 4:3; Tit 3:8

Eager to share the truth Ro 1:15;
2Pe 1:15 *See also* Ac 18:25; 21:13;
Ro 15:20; Php 1:20; Jude 3

Eager to receive or understand the truth Mk 12:37; Ac 10:33 *See also*
Mk 10:17 pp Mt 19:16 pp Lk 18:18;
Lk 2:15; 21:38; Jn 4:40; Ac 13:42; 17:11;
1Ti 4:15

Eager to give 2Co 8:7 *See also*
Ex 35:21–22; 1Ch 29:9; 2Co 8:11,19;
Gal 2:10; 1Ti 6:18

Eager to pray Col 4:2 *See also* Ro 15:30;
Php 1:3–4; Col 4:12

Eager for God's honour Nu 25:11 *See also* 1Ki 19:14; 2Ki 10:16; Jn 2:17

Eager to see Jesus Christ's return and the end of the world 1Co 1:7 *See also*
Mt 24:44 pp Lk 12:40; Ro 8:19 *Creation shares the same eager expectation;*
Ro 8:23; Gal 5:5; Php 3:20

See also

5046 opportunities	8207 commitment
5178 running	8239 earnestness
5785 ambition	8370 zeal
5847 enthusiasm	8495 witnessing
7755 preaching,	8656 longing for
importance	God
8114 discipleship	8767 hypocrisy

5841

ecstasy

An exalted condition of spiritual joy or rapture; usually reflecting the experience of the Holy Spirit.

Ecstasy in response to prophetic and visionary experiences
Nu 24:4; 2Co 12:3–4; Rev 1:10 *See also*
Nu 24:16; 1Sa 10:10–11; Isa 6:1 *Isaiah's vision of the Lord;* Eze 11:24–25;
Da 2:19–21; 10:7–8,16; Ac 9:10
Ananias' vision; Ac 10:3 *Cornelius' vision of the angel of God;* Ac 10:10–16; 11:5;
Rev 4:2; 17:3; 21:10

Ecstasy in response to the Holy Spirit
Ac 2:4 *See also* Ac 10:44–46; 13:52; 19:6

Ecstasy in response to Jesus Christ
Lk 10:21; 1Pe 1:8 *See also* Ps 4:7; 28:7;
Mt 28:8

Ecstasy as a corporate experience
Ezr 3:12 *See also* 1Ki 8:11 pp 2Ch 7:2;
Ezr 6:16

Transfiguration of appearance through ecstasy
Ex 34:29 *See also* Mt 17:2; Lk 1:22

Future ecstasy in response to God's coming kingdom
Isa 55:12; 1Co 2:9–10 *See also*
Isa 35:10; 51:11

See also

1409 dream	3281 Holy Spirit,
1427 prophecy	inspiration
1469 visions	4942 fulness
2039 Christ, joy of	5830 delight
3020 Holy Spirit, joy	7772 prophets
of	8283 joy

5842

eloquence

The ability to speak with fluency and persuasive power, using words appropriate to the circumstances.

Examples of lack of eloquence
Ex 4:10 *See also* Ex 6:12,30; 2Co 10:10; 11:6

Preaching the gospel does not rely on human eloquence
1Co 1:17 *See also* 1Co 1:19–21; 2:1; 13:1

Eloquence that comes from God
Ac 6:9–10 *See also* Ex 4:11,15–16; Isa 32:4; Mk 13:11; Lk 21:15; Ac 18:4; 19:8–10

Examples of eloquence in speeches
Ac 5:35–40; 17:22–23; 18:24–28

Eloquent words may lead to sin
Pr 7:21 *See also* Ps 12:3–4; 55:21; Pr 2:16; 5:3; 6:24; 29:5

Sayings concerning eloquence
Ps 45:1 *See also* Pr 10:31–32; 12:18; 22:11; Ecc 10:12

See also

2410 cross, the	5345 influence
2420 gospel	5547 speech, power
5101 Moses	of
5107 Paul	6020 sin
5193 tongue	7751 persuasion

5843

embarrassment

A state of discomfort and shame, caused by a sense of guilt over something that has been said or done.

Embarrassment may be a sign of misunderstanding or mistrust
Jn 13:6–8 *See also* Mk 2:16–17 *Jesus Christ's enemies approached the disciples knowing they would be embarrassed by the company he was keeping*; Mk 3:21 *The family of Jesus Christ were embarrassed by what they were hearing about him.*

Love includes not causing unnecessary embarrassment
Dt 24:10–11

Embarrassment caused by another person
2Ki 8:11 *Elisha's fixed gaze embarrassed Hazael who, as the following verses suggest, may already have had a guilty conscience.*

Embarrassment may motivate actions
Jdg 3:23–26; 2Ki 2:17

Doing right may be embarrassing
Ac 10:28–29

Embarrassment may motivate wrong behaviour Mk 6:26–27

See also

5836 disgrace	6172 guilt
5879 humiliation	8754 fear
5947 shame	

5844

emotions

Scripture portrays both human beings and God as having emotions. Human emotions and sentiments are of importance to the life of faith. Human feelings can be positive or negative and are subject to change and misinterpretation.

Emotions shown by God
Love Dt 7:7–8 *See also* Isa 43:4; Jer 31:3; Hos 11:1; Mk 10:21; Jn 13:1; 17:23; 1Jn 4:8,10,19

Compassion Ps 103:13 *See also* Ex 33:19; Dt 13:17; Jdg 2:18; Ps 116:5; Mt 9:36; 14:14; 15:32 pp Mk 8:2; Mt 20:34

Joy and delight Jer 32:41 *See also* Dt 30:9; Isa 62:4; Lk 15:32

Anger Ex 22:24 *See also* Dt 6:14–15; Jos 7:1; Jer 7:20; Eze 5:13; Mt 21:12–13 pp Mk 11:15–17 pp Lk 19:45–46 pp Jn 2:14–17

Human emotions experienced by God's people
Joy Isa 51:11 *See also* 1Sa 2:1; Ps 4:7; 28:7; 30:11–12; Lk 1:47; Ac 16:25

Love for God and one another Ps 116:1 *See also* Ps 18:1; Jn 21:17; 1Jn 4:11–12

Sorrow and pain Ps 6:6–7 *See also* 1Sa 1:7–8,10; 2Sa 18:33; 1Ki 19:3–4; Ps 88:15; 119:28; 137:1; Jer 15:18; Mic 7:1; Jn 11:19,31,33; Ro 9:2–3

Fear Ex 3:6 *See also* Ge 18:15; Jos 9:24; Isa 35:4; 41:10; Mt 8:26 pp Mk 4:40–41 pp Lk 8:25; Mt 28:8 pp Mk 16:8

God's people are to feel for one another Php 1:7–8 *See also* Ex 22:21; 23:9; 1Co 12:25–26; 2Co 6:11–13; 7:2–3; 11:29

Believers are to control their emotions
Gal 5:22–23 *See also* Pr 25:28; Eph 4:26; 5:18; Col 3:8; 1Ti 2:8; Jas 1:19–20

Emotions are changeable
Pr 14:13

The wicked may feel an unwarranted sense of security Am 6:1 *See also* Da 8:25; 11:21,24; Zec 1:15

See also

1025 God, anger of	5567 suffering,
1085 God, love of	emotional
1210 God, human	5874 happiness
descriptions	8283 joy
2009 Christ, anger of	8292 love
2048 Christ, love of	8754 fear
5014 heart, human	
5064 spirit,	
emotional	

5845

emptiness

Scripture stresses the emptiness of human life without God, and notes that Jesus Christ chose to empty

himself in order to redeem humanity.

Emptiness and creation
The world created to be filled
Isa 45:18; Hab 2:14 *See also* Ge 1:2

Emptiness as a symbol of judgment
Jer 4:23

Human life can be empty
Ru 1:21 *See also* Ecc 1:2; 3:19; 12:8

Human words can be empty
Job 35:13 *See also* Job 35:16; Isa 16:6; 36:5 pp 2Ki 18:20; Isa 59:4; Eph 5:6; 2Pe 2:18

Human attempts at fulfilment are empty
Work does not satisfy Isa 55:2 *See also* Ps 127:1–2; Ecc 2:17; 6:7; Hag 1:5–6

Pleasure does not last Job 20:5 *See also* Pr 21:17; Ecc 2:1–3,25

Wealth does not satisfy Ecc 5:10 *See also* Ecc 4:7–8; Lk 12:15; 1Ti 6:9–10

Material possessions are unreliable Lk 12:18–20 *See also* Job 8:13–15; 15:31; Ps 49:10,12,16–17; Pr 11:4; Ecc 5:15; 1Ti 6:7

False religion cannot save Isa 57:13 *See also* Jdg 10:14; Isa 44:17–18; 45:20; 46:7; Jer 11:12; Ac 14:15

Emptiness as the result of sin
Mic 6:13–14 *See also* Lev 26:14–16; Ps 78:32–33; Hos 4:10; Hag 1:7–9

God wants to remove the emptiness of people's lives
1Pe 1:18 *See also* Ps 81:10; Jn 1:16; 10:10; Eph 4:13; Col 2:10

Jesus Christ accepts emptiness in order to redeem humanity
Php 2:7 *See also* 2Co 8:9

See also

3251 Holy Spirit,	6644 eternal life
filling with	8366 wisdom,
4942 fulness	source of
5341 hunger	8748 false religion
5591 treasure	8778 materialism
5839 dissatisfaction	8808 riches
5864 futility	

5846

enjoyment

The ability to find pleasure and joy in life. Scripture sees the capacity for enjoyment as a gift from God, whose people are to find pleasure and happiness in him and the many blessings he has given to them.

Human capacity and opportunity for enjoyment is bestowed by God
Ecc 5:18–20; 1Ti 6:17 *See also* Ne 9:35; Ecc 2:24–26

People find enjoyment in a great diversity of things
Enjoyment of the land and its produce
Nu 14:31 *See also* Ge 45:17–18; Dt 20:6; 28:30; Isa 65:22; Jer 31:5

Enjoyment of long life and health
Ecc 11:8 *See also* Dt 6:1–2; 1Ch 29:28;
Pr 28:16; 3Jn 2

Enjoyment of peace and security
Ps 37:11 *See also* Jdg 8:28; Ps 37:3;
Jer 33:6–9; Ac 9:31; 24:2

Enjoyment of prosperity Ps 106:4–5 *See
also* Ps 37:18–19

Enjoyment of food and drink Ecc 8:15
See also Ne 8:9–12; Hab 1:16

Enjoyment of friendship and fellowship
Ro 15:24 *See also* Jdg 19:6,9,22;
Ps 55:12–14

Enjoyment of love Pr 7:18 *See also*
Ecc 9:9

**Enjoyment of the fruits of righteous
living** Isa 3:10 *See also* Pr 13:2

Enjoyment of good favour Ac 2:46–47
See also Ac 7:45–46

Enjoyment of work Ecc 3:22 *See also*
Ecc 3:13

Enjoyment of light of the world Jn 5:35
See also Job 33:28

Enjoyment of hospitality Ro 16:23

Enjoyment of rest Job 3:18

Enjoyment of fragrance Ex 30:38

**People also find unwholesome
enjoyment in sin**
Heb 11:24–25 *See also* Job 20:12–14

The land enjoying rest
2Ch 36:21 *See also* Lev 26:34,43

Lack of enjoyment
Ecc 4:8 *See also* Dt 28:30; Job 20:17–19;
21:23–25; Ecc 2:26; 6:1–6

See also
4015 life	5874 happiness
4438 eating	5918 pleasure
4942 fulness	6700 peace
5399 luxury	8283 joy
5830 delight	

5847

enthusiasm

A state of eagerness, leading to the
positive and committed
performance of actions.

Enthusiasm for doing good
1Pe 3:10–13 *See also* Tit 2:11–14

Enthusiasm for doing evil
Jer 8:6 *See also* Mic 2:1–2; Zep 3:7

Enthusiasm for work
Pr 31:10–19 *See also* Pr 6:6–11;
31:24,27

Enthusiasm for giving
2Co 9:2 *See also* 2Co 8:10–12; Gal 2:10

Enthusiasm for spiritual gifts
1Co 14:12 *See also* 1Co 14:39

Enthusiasm for serving God
2Co 8:16–17 *See also* 1Pe 5:2

See also
5539 sluggard	8345 servanthood &
5629 work, ordained	worship
by God	8370 zeal
5840 eagerness	8436 giving
6130 corruption	8442 good works
7966 spiritual gifts	
8239 earnestness	

5848

exaggeration

An overstatement of something,
usually relating to its importance or
value. People exaggerate because of
fear, envy, pride or self-pity.
Exaggeration can also be used
positively to good effect, for
example, in the teaching of Jesus
Christ.

**Exaggeration of difficulties
through fear**
Nu 13:32–33 *See also* Dt 1:28; 9:1

**Exaggeration of the lifestyle of
others through envy**
Job 21:7–10 *Job's complaint that the
wicked often appear to prosper is stated
with exaggeration in order to make his
point clear. See also Ps 73:3–12*

**Exaggerating one's status or
abilities through pride**
Eze 27:3 *See also* Eze 28:2; Hos 12:8;
Mt 8:19 pp Lk 9:57; Lk 22:33;
Ac 12:21–23; 1Co 4:8; Rev 3:17

**Exaggeration of the
achievements of others**
1Sa 21:11 *The reference to David as king
by the Philistines may be an exaggeration
reflecting the great success and popularity
of David among the Israelite people. See
also 1Sa 18:7; 29:5*

**Exaggeration of troubles through
self-pity**
1Ki 18:22 *See also* 1Ki 19:10,14,18;
Ps 12:1–2

**Exaggeration of the appearance
of others through admiration**
*These verses represent exaggeration typical
in poetic descriptive passages:* SS 5:10–16;
7:1–9

**Exaggeration used by Jesus
Christ as a teaching tool**
Mt 7:3–5 pp Lk 6:41–42 *See also*
Mt 5:29–30; 7:9–10 pp Lk 11:11–12;
Mt 13:33 pp Lk 13:20; Mt 19:24
pp Mk 10:25 pp Lk 18:25

See also
2357 Christ, parables	8302 love, abuse of
2363 Christ,	8733 envy
preaching &	8754 fear
teaching	8776 lies
6121 boasting	8802 pride
6145 deceit	

5849

exaltation

The lifting up or raising on high of a
person, in words or actions. The
exaltation of Jesus Christ, first on the
cross and then in his resurrection,
provides a model of how God exalts
the humble and obedient. God also
humbles those who exalt
themselves. Believers are called upon
to exalt God in their praise of him.

True exaltation comes from God
Ps 75:6–7 *See also* Ge 39:1–6;
1Sa 2:1–10; 2Sa 7:18–29

God exalts those who are humble
Jas 4:10 *See also* Mt 5:3–5; Lk 1:46–55;
1Pe 5:5–6; Pr 3:34

**Examples of God's exaltation of
his people**
God's exaltation of Joshua Jos 3:7

God's exaltation of David 2Sa 5:9–12
See also 2Sa 22:47–51 pp Ps 18:46–50;
Ps 89:19–29

God's exaltation of Solomon
1Ch 29:25 *See also* 1Ki 3:5–15
pp 2Ch 1:7–12; 1Ki 10:1–10
pp 2Ch 9:1–9

God's exaltation of Jesus Christ
**Prophecies of Jesus Christ's
exaltation** Isa 52:13 *See also* Ps 110:1–7

**The exaltation of Jesus Christ upon
the cross** Jn 3:14–15; 12:32 *See also* Jn 8:28

**God's exaltation of Jesus Christ in the
resurrection** Ac 2:32–36 *See also*
Ac 5:30–31; Php 2:9–11; Heb 7:26

Self-exaltation is wrong
Warnings against self-exaltation
Pr 25:6–7 *See also* Da 4:19–27;
Mt 23:5–12 pp Mk 12:38–39
pp Lk 20:45–47; Lk 14:7–11

Examples of self-exaltation
Isa 14:13–14 *See also* Ge 11:3–4;
Eze 28:1–2; Da 3:1–7; 2Th 2:3–4

Consequences of self-exaltation
Mt 23:12 pp Lk 14:11 *See also*
Ge 11:5–9; Isa 2:11–17; 14:12–20 *taunt
against the king of Babylon;* Da 4:28–33;
Lk 18:9–14

**The exaltation of God in his
people's praise**
Ex 15:1–2 *Rejoicing after the exodus from
Egypt. See also* Ps 34:1–3; 57:9–11; 99:5;
145:1–13; Isa 25:1; Da 4:36–37

See also
1190 glory	8276 humility
1270 right hand of	8440 glorifying God
God	8622 worship
2336 Christ,	8664 praise
exaltation	8802 pride
5878 honour	9410 heaven

5850

excess

A surplus of material or wealth,
especially food or drink. Scripture
criticises excessive consumption and
extravagance, which are seen as
exploiting the less fortunate and
leading to a lack of concern for God.

**Examples of excessive eating
and drinking**
The Israelites in idolatry Ex 32:2–6

**The Israelites' greed, after God's
miraculous provision** Nu 11:32

The Israelites in luxury Am 6:4–6

Other examples of excess
1Sa 25:36 *Nabal;* 1Sa 30:16 *the
Amalekites in victory;* Isa 56:12 *Israel's
wicked watchmen;* Da 5:1–4 *King
Belshazzar in pride;* Php 3:19 *the enemies*

of the cross of Christ; Rev 18:3 the godless
nations

Mentions of excess in Jesus Christ's parables
As a warning to the rich Lk 12:18–21

As a warning against ingratitude and
spiritual indifference Lk 15:13;
16:19–31

Excessive eating and drinking is never encouraged
Church leaders are not to overindulge
1Ti 3:2–3,8 See also Tit 1:7

It causes sickness Pr 25:16 See also
Pr 25:27

It brings poverty Pr 23:20–21 See also
Pr 21:17

It brings disgrace Pr 28:7

It is associated with laziness Tit 1:12

It shows a disregard for God
Isa 5:11–12 See also Hos 4:10–11;
Php 3:19

It leads the unwise man astray Pr 20:1

Commands for believers to abstain from such excesses
Gal 5:19–21; Eph 5:18 See also
1Co 6:10–13; 1Pe 4:3; 2Pe 2:13

The charging of excessive interest on loans is forbidden
Eze 18:8,13,17; 22:12

See also
4404 food	5856 extravagance
4435 drinking	5866 gluttony
4544 wine	5869 greed
5310 exploitation	8307 moderation
5353 interest	8339 self-control
5772 abstinence,	8768 idolatry
from drinking	

5851

excuse
The attempt to deny responsibility
for an action or for a lack of action.
There is no excuse for sin.

Examples of excuses given for wrong actions
Ge 3:12–13 by Adam and Eve for eating
the forbidden fruit; Ex 32:22–24 by Aaron
for making the golden calf; 1Sa 13:11–12
by Saul for acting as priest
By Saul for not fully obeying the LORD:
1Sa 15:20–21,24–25

Examples of excuses given for inaction
By Moses: Ex 3:11; 4:10
Jdg 6:15 by Gideon
By the lazy: Pr 22:13; 26:13
Jer 1:6 by Jeremiah
By the fearful: Mt 25:14–30;
Lk 19:12–27
Mt 25:41–45 by the ignorant

Excuses given by those unwilling to follow Jesus Christ
Lk 14:16–24 See also Mt 22:2–3;
Lk 9:59–62

There is no excuse for sin
Ro 1:20 See also Jn 9:41; 15:22; Ro 2:1;
3:19–23; 5:12; 1Jn 1:8,10

See also
4924 delay	6183 ignorance, of
5051 responsibility	God
5877 hesitation	8712 denial of Christ
6020 sin	8768 idolatry
6154 fall, the	

5852

experience
The direct personal knowledge of
people and situations which comes
from a firsthand encounter with life.
To experience God is to encounter
and know him directly, rather than
merely to know facts about him.

5853
experience, of life
Experience of life comes with
increasing age and through
observation, reflection and the
application of lessons learned.
Experience in a craft or profession
comes through training and practice.

Experience associated with advancing years
Job 12:12 See also Job 32:6–7;
1Ki 12:6–7 pp 2Ch 10:6–7; Ps 37:25;
Pr 4:1–4

Dissatisfaction with life's experiences
Ecc 2:11 See also Ecc 3:11 People are
made for eternity and cannot be fully
satisfied with the things of this world;
Ecc 1:13–17 application to study;
Ecc 2:1–3 devotion to pleasure; Ecc 2:4–6
pursuit of great projects; Ecc 2:7–8 a life of
materialism; Ecc 2:24–26 Human
experiences find fulfilment only in relation
to God. See also Ecc 3:12–14; 12:13–14

Learning from life's experiences
Pr 24:32 See also Job 4:8–9; 5:3;
Ps 107:43

Sympathy resulting from personal experience
Ex 23:9 See also Ex 22:21;
Dt 15:12–15; 2Co 1:3–4; Heb 10:32–34

Growing through experiences
Ro 5:3–4 See also Heb 5:8; Jas 1:2–4

Learning from everyday experiences
Mt 24:32 pp Mk 13:28 See also
Mt 16:2–3; Lk 12:54–55; Mt 6:28–31
pp Lk 12:27–29

Jesus Christ shared human experience
Heb 4:15 See also Heb 2:17–18; Php 2:8;
Heb 2:9

Experience in a craft or profession
Skilled craftsmen 2Ch 2:7 See also
2Ch 2:13–14; 1Ki 7:13–14; Ex 36:1–2;
1Ch 22:15–16

Experienced soldiers 2Ch 17:12–13
See also 1Sa 17:33; 2Sa 17:8; 1Ch 12:33;
SS 3:7–8

Other competent people 1Sa 12:2
Samuel's experience in leadership; Est 1:13
Xerxes consults experts in law and justice;
Mt 2:4 Herod consults teachers of the law;

Ac 18:2–3 Paul and Aquila were
experienced tent makers.

See also
2033 Christ,	5887 inexperience
humanity	6233 rejection,
4019 life, believers'	experience
experience	8281 insight
5026 knowledge	8287 joy, experience
5531 skill	8355 understanding
5725 old age	8361 wisdom
5844 emotions	

5854
experience, of God
Scripture stresses the importance and
also the possibility of a true
experience of the living God. This is
contrasted with the more academic
knowledge about him. Experiential
knowledge of God comes through
personal encounter, through the
witness of the Holy Spirit, through
reflection on his past goodness and
through the shared experiences of
others.

Personal experience of God
Contrasted with academic knowledge
Job 42:5 See also Jer 31:34; Jn 4:42;
5:39–40; Jas 2:19

Experience of God's blessing Ps 34:8
See also 1Pe 2:3; Heb 6:4–5

Experiencing God through Scripture
Mt 22:29; Jn 5:39–40; Ac 17:11–12;
2Ti 3:15–17

Knowing God through the Spirit
Ro 8:15–16 See also Jn 14:16–17,26;
16:14–15; 1Co 2:9–10; Isa 64:4

Examples of personal encounter with
God Dt 11:2–7 See also Dt 5:3–4;
Ge 32:30 Jacob; Ex 3:3–4 Moses; Isa 6:1
Isaiah; Ac 9:3–6 Saul of Tarsus;
2Co 12:2–4 Paul; Rev 1:17 John

Sharing experience of God
Experience of God through his people
Zec 8:23 See also Isa 45:14;
1Co 14:24–25

Leaders with experience of God
Jos 24:31 See also Nu 12:8; Jdg 6:22;
Ac 1:21–22; 1Co 15:3–7; 2Pe 1:16–18

Speaking to future generations
Dt 4:9–10 See also Ex 10:2; Dt 6:20–21;
Job 8:8–9; Ps 71:18

Speaking from personal experience:
OT Dt 7:18–19 See also 1Sa 17:34–37
David's experience teaches him to trust
God.
The exiles' confidence is based upon God's
deliverance in the past: Isa 43:14–17;
51:9–11
Jer 16:14–15

Speaking from personal experience:
NT Jn 3:11 See also Jn 20:18; Ac 4:13;
1Jn 1:1–3
Jn 9:25 See also Mk 5:19–20 pp Lk 8:39;
Jn 4:28–29

Confidence based on past experience
Mt 16:9–10 pp Mk 8:18–20 The
disciples' experience of Jesus Christ's
provision should have taught them not to
worry about food; 2Ti 4:17–18

5856

extravagance

Exaggerated, excessive or immoderate behaviour often linked with wastefulness which may result in personal harm. God's people are called to be wise stewards of what has been entrusted to them. However, Scripture also points to a right kind of open-handedness and generosity of spirit which reflects love and worship towards God and concern for others.

Examples of sinful extravagance
Wastefulness Lk 15:13 *See also* Pr 21:20; 29:3

Drunkenness and gluttony Pr 23:20 *See also* Dt 21:20; Eph 5:18; Php 3:19

The results of sinful extravagance
Wastefulness leads to poverty Lk 15:14–17 *See also* Pr 13:18; 22:16; 23:21

Extravagant living leads to spiritual complacency Lk 12:19–20 *See also* Isa 5:11–12; 22:12–13; 56:11–12; Am 6:1–6; Zep 1:12–13

The alternative to sinful extravagance
Thankful enjoyment of God's gifts 1Ti 4:3–4 *See also* Ac 10:13–15; 1Co 10:30–31

Stewardship of God's blessings Eze 34:18–19 *See also* Ge 2:15; Ex 23:10–12; Dt 15:14–15; Pr 22:9

Discipline and self-control 1Co 9:25–27 *See also* Ge 2:16–17; Mt 6:16–18 *fasting;* Ro 14:6 *abstinence from certain foods;* 1Co 7:5 *temporary abstinence from sexual relationships*

Examples of commendable extravagance in worship
Mk 14:3–5 pp Mt 26:6–9 pp Jn 12:3–5 *See also* Ex 36:3–7 *gifts for the tabernacle;* 2Sa 6:14–15 *David dancing before the ark Gifts for the temple:* 1Ch 29:3–4; 2Ch 24:10
Extravagance in praise and thanksgiving: Ps 119:171; 2Co 4:15; Col 2:7
The widow's offering: Mk 12:41–44 pp Lk 21:1–4

Examples of extravagance not commended in worship
Mic 6:7–8 *Extravagant offerings are no substitute for doing what God requires. See also* 1Sa 15:20–22

Other examples of commendable extravagance
Extravagance in caring for others 2Co 8:2–4 *See also* Mt 5:39–42 pp Lk 6:29–30; 2Co 9:12–13; 1Th 3:12

Extravagance in forgiveness Mt 18:21–22 *See also* Lk 17:3–4; Mt 18:26 *the king's generosity in forgiving his servant's debt;* Lk 15:22–23 *celebrations at the return of the prodigal son*

Warnings against failing to be extravagant towards God and others
Stinginess cheats God: Isa 43:24; Mal 3:8–9; Ac 5:1–2
Stinginess denies others: Dt 15:7–8; Pr 23:6–8
Stinginess results in personal loss: Pr 11:24; 28:22,27; Mt 18:32–34

The extravagance of God's grace
The gift of his Son Jn 3:16; 2Co 9:15

The blessings of God's salvation Ro 8:32 *See also* Ro 5:5,15; Eph 1:8; Tit 3:5–6; 1Jn 3:1

The abundance of God's provision Ps 23:5; 65:11; Isa 66:11; Joel 2:24; Zec 1:17

God's blessings promised to the generous Mal 3:10 *See also* Pr 19:17; 22:9; Lk 6:38; 2Co 9:6–11

5857

fame

The reputation gained by individuals or groups of people as a result of their achievements. Scripture shows how God's fame among the nations rested upon his saving actions and, in the NT, how the miracles of Jesus Christ brought him widespread fame. God's people are to rejoice in his fame, without lapsing into arrogance.

God's acts of salvation have brought him renown
Jos 9:9–10 *See also* Ex 8:9–11; Nu 14:13–16; Ps 72:1–19; 135:13–14; Isa 55:13; 63:11–14; Jer 32:20; Hab 3:2

Jesus Christ's teaching and miracles brought him fame
Mt 4:24 *See also* Mt 8:32–34 pp Mk 5:14–17 pp Lk 8:34–37; Mt 9:27–31; Mk 1:27–28 pp Lk 4:36–37

Jesus Christ taught servanthood rather than the pursuit of status and fame
Mk 9:33–35 pp Mt 18:1–4 pp Lk 9:46–48; Mk 10:42–45 pp Mt 20:25–28

Israel's fame dependent on her obedience to God
Dt 26:18–19 *See also* Dt 2:24–25

Israel made famous in order to glorify God
Jer 13:11 *See also* Jer 33:9

Israel's abuse of her fame led to judgment
Eze 16:14–15 *See also* Eze 16:35–42

Glorious restoration promised by God
Hos 14:7 *See also* Isa 61:1–4

Local, national or international fame
Local 1Ch 12:30

National Jos 6:27 *See also* Est 9:4

International 1Ch 14:17 *See also* 1Ki 4:31; 10:1 pp 2Ch 9:1; 2Ch 26:8; Isa 45:1–7

God's judgment on the arrogance that may come with fame
Isa 23:8–9 *See also* Jer 48:16–18,29–30; Eze 26:15–18

Famous for doing wrong
Nu 16:40; 1Ki 15:34; Jude 11

5858

fat

Used to describe a successful person, fruitful land or healthy animals. It is often associated with the idea of prosperity and contentment. It also designates the part of an animal used in OT sacrifices.

Fat as a symbol of success
Isa 10:27; Jer 5:27–28 *See also* Dt 32:15; Job 15:27–28; Eze 34:16

Fat representing fruitful land
Ge 45:18

Fat animals
Ge 41:2 *See also* Ge 41:17–21; 1Sa 15:9; Ps 66:15; Eze 34:20

Fat people
Jdg 3:17 *See also* Jdg 3:18–22

Fat used in the context of judgment
Isa 17:4

The fat of animals
Not to be eaten Lev 3:17 *See also* Lev 7:22–25

To be offered to God in sacrifice Lev 3:16 *See also* Ge 4:4; Lev 3:3–5; Nu 18:17; Dt 32:37–38; 1Sa 2:15–16; 15:22; 1Ki 8:64; Isa 34:6–7; 43:24; Eze 39:19

5859

favour

Looking kindly upon someone or treating someone with special regard. Scripture stresses the kindness and graciousness of God and Jesus Christ, which is not the result of human merit or achievement.

5860

favour, divine

See 1055 God, grace and mercy of
2027 Jesus Christ, grace and mercy of

5861

favour, human

Looking kindly upon someone or treating someone with special regard. Favour can be gained by means of good character, gifts, service or through the intervention of God. Scripture warns against undue favouritism.

Examples of those who were regarded with favour by others
OT characters 1Sa 2:26 *Samuel* *David:* 1Sa 16:18,21–22; 18:6–7; 20:3 *Esther:* Est 2:15,17 Da 1:9 *Daniel*

Jesus Christ Lk 2:52

The first Christians Ac 2:47; Ro 14:18

Finding favour can lead to being treated with special regard
Ru 2:13–16 *See also* Pr 16:15; 19:12

Being held in favour can create an opportunity for a request to be made
Ne 2:5 *See also* Ge 30:27; 47:29–30; 50:4–6; Nu 32:5; Ru 2:2; 1Sa 20:28–29; 27:5; Est 7:3; 8:5

Finding favour with others
Through good character Pr 3:3–4 *See also* Pr 13:15; 28:23; Ecc 9:11; Phm 14

Through the giving of gifts Ge 32:5; 33:8–11,15; 34:11–12; Ps 45:12; Pr 19:6; Eze 16:33–34

Through service rendered Ge 39:3–4 *See also* 2Sa 14:19–22; Eph 6:6 pp Col 3:22

Through the intervention of God Ge 39:21; Ex 3:21; 11:3; 12:36; Ne 1:11

Warnings against favouritism
Lev 19:15; 1Ti 5:21 *See also* Ex 23:3; Dt 1:17; Job 13:10; Pr 24:23–25; Mal 2:9; Jas 2:1–4,9

See also
1055 God, grace & mercy	5919 popularity
2027 Christ, grace & mercy	6604 acceptance, human
5262 commendation	6672 grace in relationships
5325 gifts	8291 kindness
5863 flattery	8753 favouritism

5863

flattery

Insincere and undeserved praise or words of encouragement, used with the intention of gaining favour with others.

Flattery is deceitful
Ps 12:2–3 *See also* Ps 5:9; 55:20–21; 62:4; Pr 27:6; Jer 9:8

The results of flattery are ruinous
Pr 26:28 *See also* Pr 29:5

Flattery is rejected by godly people
Job 32:21–22 *See also* Gal 1:10; 1Th 2:5–6

Honesty is preferable to flattery
Pr 28:23 *See also* Pr 16:13; 27:9

False teachers use flattery
Ro 16:17–18 *See also* 2Ti 4:3–4; Jude 16–19

Examples of flattery
2Sa 14:17–20 *The woman from Tekoa flatters David;* 2Sa 15:2–6 *Absalom to Israelites;* Da 6:21 *Daniel flatters the king;* Mt 22:16 pp Mk 12:14 pp Lk 20:21; Lk 20:21 *The spies from the teachers of the law flatter Jesus Christ;* Ac 12:22 *The crowds flatter Herod. the Pharisees and Herodians to Jesus Christ*

See also
5164 lips	5820 criticism
5546 speech	6145 deceit
5575 talk, idle	8237 doctrine, false
5690 friends	8714 dishonesty

5864

futility

All human life and human systems are ultimately useless without God, because death comes to all. God wants to deliver people from their futile ways.

Human life is futile
The brevity of life Ps 89:47 *See also* Job 7:6–7; 14:1–2; Ps 39:4–5; Ecc 6:12; Isa 40:6–7; Jas 4:14

Death is the destiny of all Job 9:22; Ecc 3:19–20; 9:2

The dead are forgotten Ps 103:15–16; Ecc 1:11; 2:16; 9:5

Human endeavour is futile
Ecc 1:14 *The writer speaks of human life without reference to God. See also* Ps 39:6; 127:2; Ecc 2:10–23; Hab 2:13; Jas 1:11

Human thoughts are futile
Ps 94:11 *See also* 1Co 3:19–20; Ro 1:21; Eph 4:17–18

Human attitudes are futile
Self-confidence is futile Isa 16:6 *See also* Jer 48:29–30; Lk 1:51–52

Relying solely on human help is futile Jer 17:5 *See also* Ps 60:11 pp Ps 108:12; Ps 146:3–4; Isa 2:22; 30:1–5; 31:1–3; La 4:17

False religion is futile
Idolatry is futile 2Ki 17:15 *See also* 1Sa 12:21; Ps 31:6; Jer 2:5; 10:8,14–15; 16:19; Jnh 2:8

Divination is futile Isa 8:19–22; Eze 13:6–9; Zec 10:2

Human religious systems are futile 1Ki 18:29 *See also* Isa 16:12; Jer 10:5; Ac 5:36–38; Col 2:20–23

Nominal religion is futile
Religious observance without true faith is futile Isa 1:13 *See also* Mal 3:14; Mt 15:8–9 pp Mk 7:6–7; 1Co 3:1–3; Jas 1:26

Mere religious language is futile Tit 3:9 *See also* Jer 7:8; La 2:14; Eph 5:6; Col 2:18; 1Ti 1:6; 2Ti 2:14; 2Pe 2:18

Christian endeavour using only human strength is futile Jn 15:5; 1Co 3:12–15

Hearing God's word without responding to it is futile Heb 4:2 *See also* Mt 7:26–27; 13:19–22; Jas 1:22–24; 2:20

Sin is futile because it achieves nothing
Jer 13:10 *See also* Ps 2:1; 112:10; 119:118; Pr 10:28; 11:7; Jer 51:58; Eph 5:11

Faithfulness to God may seem to be futile
Ps 73:13 *See also* Job 34:9; Ecc 7:15; 8:14; Isa 49:4

God wants to deliver people from futile ways
1Pe 1:18 *See also* 2Ti 2:21

See also
4015 life	6203 mortality
4030 world, behaviour in	8032 trust, lack of
4190 spiritism	8748 false religion
5067 suicide	8768 idolatry
5839 dissatisfaction	8784 nominal religion
5845 emptiness	8820 self-confidence

5865

gestures

Significant acts, bodily movements or signals which carry meaning, evoke responses or convey positive or negative feelings. They may or may not be accompanied by words or other communications.

Gestures are part of human communication
They give weight to a contract Ru 4:7 *See also* 2Sa 24:22–24 pp 1Ch 21:23–24; Jer 32:10–12

They add force to words 1Sa 11:7 *See also* Jos 7:25–26; 1Sa 15:27–28; 2Sa 12:16; Mt 21:12–13 pp Mk 11:15–17 pp Lk 19:45–46 pp Jn 2:15–16 *Use of gestures illustrates the demonstrative nature of much communication in the cultures of biblical times.*

Gestures often convey more than words
Gestures of joy 2Sa 6:14 *There is a spontaneous and*

unpremeditated element in many gestures:
Ge 21:6; Lev 9:24; Ac 3:8

Gestures of love 1Sa 1:5 *See also*
Ge 37:3; 1Sa 2:19; Lk 7:46–47; 10:34;
15:20; Jn 15:13; Ro 5:8

Gestures of mercy Isa 6:6–7 *See also*
1Sa 24:10–11; 2Sa 9:1,7; Mt 18:27 *Mercy
itself is a gesture of love.*

Gestures of worship and reverence
Ex 3:5 *See also* Ex 3:6; Jos 5:14; Ne 8:6;
Ps 63:4; 134:2; Mt 2:11; Lk 5:8; Jn 11:32;
Rev 1:17

Gestures of repentance Job 42:6 *See
also* 1Ki 21:27; Ezr 10:1; Isa 22:12;
Joel 2:12; Jnh 3:6–8; Mt 11:21
pp Lk 10:13; Mt 27:3–5

Gestures of sorrow and mourning
2Sa 3:31 *Gestures of sorrow and mourning
are very similar to those of repentance and
remorse. See also* 2Sa 19:4; Est 4:1;
Ps 137:1; Joel 1:13; Am 5:16

Gestures of dedication Ac 22:16 *See
also* Ge 17:10; Ex 21:6; 1Sa 20:41–42;
Ne 10:35–37

Gestures of anger Lk 15:28 *See also*
Ex 32:19; Nu 22:27; 1Sa 20:33–34;
Mt 26:65 pp Mk 14:63; Ac 7:54,57;
Rev 3:16

Gestures of treachery Lk 22:47–48
pp Mt 26:47–49 pp Mk 14:43–45 *See
also* 2Sa 3:27; 20:9–10

Gestures of contempt
Shaking of the head: Ps 22:7; 64:8;
Mt 27:39 pp Mk 15:29
Spitting: Mt 26:67 pp Mk 14:65; Rev 3:16

Other examples of gestures
The gesture of washing hands
Mt 27:24 *See also* Dt 21:6–7; Ps 26:6;
73:13

**The gesture of shaking dust from the
feet** Mt 10:14 pp Mk 6:11 pp Lk 9:5 *See
also* Lk 10:11; Ac 13:51

**Jesus Christ's gesture of washing the
disciples' feet** Jn 13:4–5,12–15 *This
was a gesture of service and a lesson in
both serving and being willing to accept
service.*

See also

1345 covenant	5194 touch
1448 signs	5783 agreement
1670 symbols	5818 contempt
5150 face	5898 kissing
5167 mouth	8625 worship,
5174 prostration	acceptable
5179 sandal	attitudes

5866

gluttony

Scripture condemns an excessive
greed for food. Its unrestrained self-
indulgence often leads to deeper
iniquity and represents a rejection of
godly moderation.

**Gluttony is a form of idolatry and
therefore condemned as
offensive to God**
Eph 5:5; Php 3:19 *See also* Ps 10:3;
Isa 22:12–14 *Gluttony as escapism, trying
to avoid God's requirements;* Zec 7:4–6
Even their religious feasts were nothing but

self-indulgence; Mk 7:21–23;
1Co 6:9–10; 10:7; Col 3:5; Jas 5:5

**Gluttony is closely linked with
drunkenness**
Ex 32:6; Jdg 9:27; 1Sa 25:36

**The destructive consequences of
gluttony**
Pr 23:20–21; 28:7 *See also* Pr 15:27;
28:25; Ecc 6:7

Warnings against gluttony
Pr 23:1–2; Lk 12:15; Eph 5:3; Col 3:5
See also Lk 12:19–20; 21:34;
1Co 5:9–11; Gal 5:19–21; Tit 1:12–13;
1Pe 4:3–4

Examples of gluttony
Ge 25:29–34 *Esau putting food before his
birthright;* Nu 11:32 *the children of Israel
gorging on quail;* 1Sa 30:16 *an Amalekite
raiding party;* 1Ki 1:24–25 *Adonijah
feasting with his supporters;* Da 5:1 *King
Belshazzar;* Mt 11:19 pp Lk 7:34 *Jesus
Christ falsely accused of gluttony;*
Mt 23:25 pp Lk 11:39 *the Pharisees;*
Mt 24:49 pp Lk 12:45 *the irresponsible
servant;* Lk 15:13 *the prodigal son;*
2Pe 2:13–14 *false teachers*

See also

4404 food	5869 greed
4434 drinking	8307 moderation
5850 excess	8821 self-indulgence

5867

golden rule

**The command of Jesus Christ to
love others as ourselves**
Mt 7:12 pp Lk 6:31 *See also*
Mt 22:39–40 pp Mk 12:31; Ro 13:8–9;
Gal 5:14

See also

8298 love for one	8452 neighbours,
another	duty to
8405 commands, in	
NT	

5868

gossip

Idle talk which foolishly or
maliciously spreads rumours or facts.
The effects of gossiping are divisive
and destructive.

Examples of gossiping
Ne 6:5–8 *False rumours were used to
intimidate Nehemiah;* Ps 41:5–8;
Jn 7:12–13; 3Jn 9–10

Dangers of talking too much
Pr 10:19 *See also* Pr 18:6–7; 21:23;
29:11; Ecc 5:2–3; Mt 12:36–37

Gossip can result from idleness
1Ti 5:13

Gossip has disastrous effects
Pr 16:28 *See also* Pr 11:13; 17:9;
25:9–10; 26:20

**Gossiping condemned and
forbidden**
Lev 19:16 *See also* Ex 23:1; Ps 101:5;
Pr 10:18; Ro 1:29–30; 2Co 12:20

Advice on avoiding gossip
Ps 141:3 *See also* Pr 20:19

See also

5193 tongue	8452 neighbours,
5343 idleness	duty to
5510 rumours	8815 ridicule
5546 speech	8828 spite
5575 talk, idle	8830 suspicion
5951 slander	

5869

greed

An excessive appetite for further
goods or food, often linked with
selfishness and gluttony.

5870
greed, condemnation of

Greed is condemned by Scripture as
contrary to the purposes of God.

**Greed is a feature of the fallen
world**
Ps 10:3; Ro 1:29 *See also* 1Co 5:10

**Greed is an expression of sinful
human nature**
Mk 7:21–22 pp Mt 15:19–20 *See also*
Eze 33:31; Ro 7:8

Examples of greed
Of individuals Jos 7:21; Eze 22:12;
Da 5:23

Of false teachers Mt 23:25 *See also*
Jer 6:13; 8:10; Lk 11:39; 2Pe 2:3,14

**Greed invites God's judgment
both now and later**
Eph 5:5 *See also* Pr 15:27; 28:8,25; 29:4;
Eze 18:10–13; 28:5–7; Am 8:4–7;
Mic 2:1–3; Hab 2:5–6; 1Co 6:9–10

See also

5412 money	8733 envy
5792 appetite	8773 jealousy
5866 gluttony	8821 self-indulgence
6133 coveting	8827 selfishness

5871
greed, believers' response to

Greed should have no place in the
lives of God's people.

**The righteous are not to be
greedy**
Pr 28:6 *See also* Ex 20:17 pp Dt 5:21;
Pr 11:28; 22:1; 23:4; Eze 18:8,17;
Ro 13:9

**The Christian leader is not to be
greedy**
1Ti 3:2–3 *See also* Tit 1:7; 1Pe 5:2

The example of Paul Ac 20:33 *See also*
1Th 2:5

The antidotes to greed
Greed must be repented of Lk 3:14
*John the Baptist counselling soldiers on
how they must express their repentance.*

The need to be on guard against greed
Ps 62:10; Lk 12:15 *See also* Lk 12:16–21

The need to be separate from greed
and from the greedy 1Co 5:11; Col 3:5
See also Job 36:18; Eph 5:3

The need to be content Heb 13:5 *See also* Php 4:11–13; 1Ti 6:3–10

The need to seek God, not gain
1Ti 6:17–18 *See also* 1Ki 3:11–14;
Ps 119:14; Jer 9:23–24

See also

5353 interest	5934 restraint
5874 happiness	8808 riches

5873

habits

Set patterns of behaviour. These patterns can be helpful when they lead to spiritual discipline and a regular pattern of prayer and worship; others can be detrimental to faith.

Examples of good habits
Reading and obeying God's word
Ps 119:56; Heb 5:14 *See also* Ps 119:44,97

Private prayer Lk 5:16 *See also* Ps 5:3; Mt 6:5–6; 14:23 pp Mk 6:46; Mk 1:35 pp Lk 4:42; Lk 6:12; 9:18; 11:1

Attendance at public worship Lk 4:16; Ac 2:46; 14:1; 17:2

Examples of bad habits
Jer 22:21 *See also* Ex 21:29,36; Jdg 2:19; Eze 33:31

Warnings to avoid certain habits
Heb 10:25 *See also* 1Ti 5:13

The difficulty of breaking bad habits
Jer 13:23

See also

5286 custom	6106 addiction
5588 traditions	8217 conformity
5761 attitudes	8428 example
5769 behaviour	8476 self-discipline

5874

happiness

A state of pleasure or joy experienced both by people and by God, but subject to change according to circumstances. True happiness derives from a secure and settled knowledge of God and a rejoicing in his works and covenant faithfulness. God rejoices over his faithful people.

Happiness found in human relationships
Dt 24:5 *See also* Ge 30:13; 34:19; 1Ki 10:8; Ps 113:9; Pr 23:24; Ecc 9:9; SS 4:10; Ro 15:24; 2Co 7:13

Happiness found in people and things
1Ki 4:20; Lk 1:14; 1Ti 6:17 *See also* Dt 20:6
David and Jonathan: 1Sa 18:3; 20:17
Ps 127:3–5; Ecc 3:12; 5:19; 8:15; 11:9; Isa 65:22; Jnh 4:6; Lk 12:19; Jn 16:21; Php 2:25–30

Happiness found in God
In God's presence Ps 16:11 *See also* Ps 21:6; 43:4; 1Th 3:9

In God's word Ps 119:35 *See also* Isa 55:2; Jer 15:16; Mk 12:37; Ro 7:22

In God's actions Ge 21:6; Ac 11:23 *See also* Ex 18:9; 1Sa 2:1; 19:5; 1Ki 8:66; Est 8:16; Ps 16:6; 92:4; 111:2; Isa 61:10; Ac 13:48

God's happiness
In obedient people Dt 30:9–10 *See also* 1Sa 15:22; Ps 147:11; Isa 9:17; Mt 25:21

In the righteous Pr 11:20 *See also* Ps 147:11; Pr 11:1; Ecc 2:26; Jer 9:24

Jesus Christ's recipe for happiness
Mt 5:3–10 pp Lk 6:20–22

Happiness may not be permanent
Ecc 7:14 *See also* Est 5:9; Job 7:7; Ps 10:6; Pr 15:13; Ecc 11:9; Jer 16:9; La 5:15; Joel 1:12

Happiness for those who trust in God
Ps 84:12 *See also* Ps 2:12; 34:8; 40:4; 146:5; Pr 16:20; Jer 17:7; Lk 1:45; Jn 20:29; Gal 3:9

Happiness for those who obey God
Ps 89:15 *See also* Job 5:17; Ps 1:1–2; 94:12; 112:1; 128:1; Pr 28:14; 29:18; Isa 56:1–2; Lk 11:27–28; Rev 1:3; 22:7

Happiness for those who are forgiven
Ps 32:1–2 *See also* Ro 4:7–8; Rev 22:14

Happiness for those who suffer persecution
1Pe 3:14 *See also* Mt 5:11–12; 1Pe 4:14

Happiness for those who persevere
Mt 11:6 *See also* Jas 1:12; 5:11; Rev 16:15

See also

1070 God, joy of	5918 pleasure
1335 blessing	5939 satisfaction
4971 seasons of life	5970 unhappiness
5528 shouting	8117 discipleship,
5830 delight	benefits
5846 enjoyment	8283 joy
5900 laughter	

5875

hatred

Hatred for others or God is associated with human sin. Scripture also emphasises God's hatred of sin and evil. Believers are commanded to love those who hate them.

Hatred as evidence of corrupt human nature
2Sa 13:15; Tit 3:3 *See also* Ge 37:4; Dt 7:15; 19:11–12; Jdg 11:7; 2Sa 13:22; Ps 25:19; 38:19; Pr 10:12; Mt 24:10; Gal 5:19–20; 1Jn 2:9–11; 3:15; 4:20

Hatred of God himself
Ps 81:15; Ro 1:29–31 *See also* Ex 20:5; Dt 7:10; 32:41; 2Ch 19:2; Ps 50:17; Pr 1:29; Jn 3:20; 15:23–25; Jas 4:4

Hatred of Jesus Christ
Jn 7:7 *See also* Isa 53:3; Mt 12:14; 21:46; 26:3–4; 27:22; Lk 19:14; Jn 17:14

Hatred of the godly and upright
1Ki 22:8; Mt 10:22 *See also* Est 9:1; Ps 35:19; 69:4; 109:3–5; Pr 29:10; Isa 66:5; Am 5:10; Mt 24:9–10 pp Mk 13:13 pp Lk 21:16–19; Lk 1:69–71; 6:22; Jn 15:18; Ac 9:29; 23:12–15; 1Jn 3:13

Believers are to love those who hate them
Lk 6:27–28 *See also* Mt 5:43–44

God's hatred of evil
Ps 5:4–5; Pr 6:16–19; Isa 61:8 *See also* Dt 12:31; 16:21–22; Ps 11:5; Isa 1:14; Jer 12:8; Hos 9:15; Am 5:21; Zec 8:16–17; Mal 2:16

The godly should also hate evil
Pr 8:13; Ro 12:9 *See also* Ex 18:21; Ps 31:6; 97:10; 101:3; 119:104,113,128,163; 139:21; Pr 13:5; 15:17; Am 5:15; Heb 1:9; Ps 45:7; Rev 2:6

See also

5350 injustice, hated by God	8727 enemies
	8785 opposition
5820 criticism	8794 persecution
6020 sin	8815 ridicule
6230 rejection	
8301 love and enemies	

5876

helpfulness

God's help
God promises his help Isa 41:10 *See also* Ps 121:3–4; Mt 28:20; Jn 14:16

People value God's help Ps 118:6–7 *See also* Dt 33:29; 2Ch 25:8; Ps 28:7; 54:4; Isa 50:9; Ac 26:22

People need God's help Ps 94:17 *See also* Jos 14:12; Ps 22:11,19; 40:17; 116:6; Isa 59:16; 63:5; Mt 9:36; Heb 13:6; Ps 118:6–7

God's help can be withheld 2Sa 22:42 *See also* Job 19:7; Ps 107:11–13; Hos 13:9; Zec 7:13

God's help is not imposed Jer 29:12 *See also* 2Ki 5:11–12; 2Ch 16:12; 1Pe 5:6–7

People should imitate God's help by being helpful 2Sa 9:1; Lk 10:36–37; Gal 6:2; Eph 5:1; Jas 2:14–17

Examples of human helpfulness
Shown to those in need Lk 10:34 *See also* 2Ch 28:15; Job 29:15–16; Ac 2:44–45; 4:34–35

Shown by young people 1Sa 2:18; 17:15,17; 20:36; 2Ki 5:2–3; Jn 6:9

Shown within marriage Ge 2:18,22; Pr 18:22; 31:12,20; 1Pe 3:7

Shown to God's servants Ro 16:2 *See also* Jos 2:4,15; 1Ki 17:10–11; Lk 10:7; 1Co 16:15–16; 2Co 1:11; Php 4:3; Phm 11

Helpfulness is remembered and rewarded
Mt 25:34–36 *See also* Jos 6:17; 1Ki 17:14; Ro 16:2

See also

1055 God, grace & mercy	5806 compassion
2027 Christ, grace & mercy	5861 favour, human
	5954 strength
5498 reward	6666 grace
5765 attitudes to people	8291 kindness
5802 care	8292 love
	8445 hospitality

5877

hesitation

A delay in reaching a decision, or a reluctance to reach a decision, on account of uncertainty, caution or rebellion. Scripture provides examples of individuals who hesitate in the face of divine commands or promises, and indicates its dangers.

Examples of people who hesitated
Lot Ge 19:16

Lot's wife Ge 19:26 *See also* Ge 19:17; Lk 17:32

Moses Ex 3:11,13; 4:1,10,13; 6:12

Peter in obeying the Lord Ac 11:12 *See also* Ac 10:14–20

Other examples
Israel on approaching the promised land:
Nu 13:31–33; 14:1–4
Jdg 6:36–40 *Gideon;* 1Ki 18:21 *Israel in the time of Elijah;* Jer 1:6 *Jeremiah*

Examples of people who did not hesitate
Caleb Nu 13:30

Simon and Andrew Mt 4:18–20
pp Mk 1:16–18 pp Lk 5:10–11
pp Jn 1:40–42

Paul Ac 20:27 *See also* Ac 20:20

Believers should not hesitate to act when they know what is right
They should not hesitate to speak Isa 58:1

Jesus Christ commands immediate obedience Lk 9:62 *See also* Lk 9:57–60 pp Mt 8:19–22

God does not hesitate
To bring judgment Eze 24:14 *See also* Eze 12:25; Da 9:14

The delay in Jesus Christ's return is not due to hesitation 2Pe 3:9

See also

1310 God as judge	8120 following Christ
4924 delay	8453 obedience
5186 stumbling	8721 doubt
5884 indecision	
6221 rebellion	

5878

honour

Great respect; the creation is called upon to respect and revere God as its Creator. Since human beings are made in the image of God, they should respect one another.

The creation honours its Creator
All creatures honour God Isa 43:20 *See also* Rev 5:13

The people of God honour God
Ex 12:40–42; Ps 22:23 *See also*
Ps 50:14–15; Isa 25:1–3; Jer 3:17;
33:7–9; 2Th 3:1

How God wishes to be honoured
Honouring God by worshipping him
Rev 5:11–12 *See also* Ps 50:23;
Rev 4:9–11

Honouring God by obeying him
Eze 33:31 *These people honoured God with their words only, but this was not true honour for they failed to obey his commands. See also* Nu 25:10–13;
Isa 29:13

Honouring God with one's body
1Co 6:19–20 *See also* Ro 12:1;
2Co 4:10–11

Honouring God with one's possessions Pr 3:9 *See also* Isa 60:9;
2Co 8:19

Honouring God by caring for others
Pr 14:31 *See also* Mt 25:31–40; Jas 1:27

The consequences of not honouring God
Mal 2:2 *See also* Nu 20:12; Da 5:22–31

Jesus Christ and honour
Honour given to Jesus Christ Heb 2:9
See also Ac 19:17; 2Pe 1:17; Mt 17:5;
Mk 9:7; Lk 9:35

The relationship of honour between the Father and the Son Jn 5:23 *See also*
Jn 8:49–50

God brings honour to people
1Sa 2:30 *See also* Ps 62:7; Zep 3:19–20;
Jn 12:26; Ro 2:9–11

Honouring others as a duty to God
Honouring one's parents Ex 20:12;
Eph 6:2–3 *See also* Mal 1:6; Mt 15:1–6;
Lk 18:20

Honouring fellow believers Ro 12:10
See also Php 2:29; 1Ti 5:17

See also

2336 Christ, exaltation	5908 motives
5042 name of God, significance	8333 reverence
	8444 honouring God
5184 standing	8469 respect
5594 tribute	8622 worship
5838 disrespect	8632 adoration
	8664 praise

5879

humiliation

The act of being put to shame, often in a public manner. Jesus Christ was humiliated through his suffering, degradation and execution. Believers may expect to suffer humiliation on account of their faith.

Examples of humiliation
David's men at the hands of Hanun
2Sa 10:4–5 pp 1Ch 19:4–5

Michal, by David's dancing
2Sa 6:14,20–22

Joab and his men, by David's seemingly inappropriate mourning
2Sa 19:5–6

Haman, by his death on the gallows prepared for Mordecai Est 6:11–12;
7:10

Job Job 19:5

Peter, by his denial of Jesus Christ
Mt 26:69–75 pp Mk 14:66–72
pp Lk 22:55–62 pp Jn 18:16–18, 25–27

Warnings against presumption Pr 25:7;
Lk 14:7–11; 1Co 10:12

People are often humiliated as a punishment for sin
Ob 8–10 *See also* 2Ki 19:28; Ezr 9:7;
Ps 35:26; Isa 13:11; 22:19; 25:11; 26:5;
Jer 15:9; 23:40; 31:19; 49:16; Eze 28:8;
Mal 2:9

Jesus Christ suffered humiliation
Jesus Christ's humiliation prophesied in the OT Isa 53:9,12 *See also* Isa 50:6;
52:14; 53:2–4; Ac 8:32–33; Isa 53:7–8

Jesus Christ's humiliation in his incarnation Php 2:6–8 *See also* 2Co 8:9

Jesus Christ's humiliation in his humble birth Lk 2:7

Jesus Christ's humiliation through the words of others Mt 9:34; 11:19
pp Lk 7:34; Mk 3:21; Jn 7:20; 9:16

Jesus Christ's humiliation through the actions of others Lk 4:28–29; 7:44–46

Jesus Christ's humiliation at his trials
Mk 14:55–65; Mt 27:27–31 *See also*
Mt 26:59–68 pp Jn 18:19–24; Mt 27:26
pp Mk 15:15 pp Lk 23:25 pp Jn 19:16
pp Mk 15:16–20 pp Jn 19:1–3;
Lk 23:9–11

Jesus Christ's humiliation at his crucifixion Lk 23:33–43 *See also*
Gal 3:13; Dt 21:23; Lk 22:37; Isa 53:12;
Mt 27:33–44 pp Mk 15:22–32
pp Jn 19:17–24

Believers should be prepared to suffer humiliation from unbelievers
2Ti 3:12 *See also* Mt 5:11; 10:17–18;
Jn 15:20; 16:2; Php 1:28–30; 1Th 1:6;
Heb 10:33–34; 1Pe 2:19–21; Rev 2:10

Believers are not to humiliate others
Jas 2:2–4 *See also* Mt 5:22; 7:4–5;
1Co 11:20–22

See also

2570 Christ, suffering	5947 shame
5169 nakedness	6240 rape
5180 shaving	8754 fear
5281 crucifixion	8782 mockery
5560 suffering	8794 persecution
5843 embarrassment	8815 ridicule

5880

humour

A time and place for humour
Ecc 3:1–4

Touches of humour in Scripture
Things people found funny Ge 18:12
See also Ge 17:17

Humour at others' expense Job 12:4

OT writers found wordplay humorous
Mic 1:10–11

Some passages seem to have a humorous intent 1Ki 18:27
Jesus Christ's hearers would probably have found his exaggeration (or "hyperbole") funny: Mt 19:24; Lk 6:42
Ac 12:13–16

See also
5356 irony   5900 laughter

5881

immaturity

The result of insufficient growth, or a failure to develop to one's full potential.

Marks of physical immaturity
Pride 2Sa 15:1–4

Rejection of wise counsel Dt 21:18; 1Ki 12:8

Tactlessness 1Ki 12:13–14

Lack of respect 2Ki 2:23; Job 19:18

Weakness of character 2Ch 13:7

Foolishness Pr 22:15

Lack of understanding Dt 1:39; Pr 1:4; Jnh 4:11; 1Co 13:11

Lack of self-control Tit 2:6

Disgrace Pr 29:15

Waste Lk 15:13

Spiritual immaturity is to be avoided
1Co 14:20; Heb 6:1 *See also* 2Co 13:9,11 *The word "perfection" may be understood in terms of maturity;* Eph 4:13,15; Col 1:28; 4:12; Jas 1:4; 2Pe 3:18

Marks of spiritual immaturity
Backsliding Mt 13:20–21
pp Mk 4:16–17 pp Lk 8:13 *Jesus Christ to his disciples. See also* Gal 4:8–9

An over-sensitive conscience Ro 14:2

Lack of spiritual understanding
1Co 3:1–2 *See also* Mt 11:16–19
pp Lk 7:31–35; Heb 5:11–14

Divisiveness 1Co 3:3

Instability Eph 4:14 *See also* Jas 1:6–7

Pride 1Ti 3:6 *The church overseer must be a spiritually mature person. See also* 1Pe 5:5

Remedies for immaturity
Confession of sin Pr 28:13 *See also* Jer 3:13–22; Jas 5:16; 1Jn 1:9

Discipline Pr 3:11–12 *See also* Ps 119:67–71; 1Pe 4:1–2; Rev 3:19

Prayer and meditation Ps 119:97–99
See also Ps 119:27; Jn 17:17–19; Ro 8:26; Heb 4:16; Jas 1:25

See also
5652 babies	8230 discipline
5664 children	8320 perfection
5902 maturity	8339 self-control
5925 rashness	8347 spiritual
6199 imperfection	growth
8205 childlikeness	8755 folly

5882

impartiality

The ability to be unbiased towards any one race, class or person. This attitude is demonstrated by God and is to be emulated by the human race.

God is impartial
Dt 10:17 *See also* 2Ch 19:7

God treats people impartially Mt 5:45
See also Job 25:3; 34:19; Pr 22:2; Ro 2:11; Eph 6:9

God judges impartially Col 3:25 *See also* Job 34:11–12; Ps 62:12; Jer 17:10; Ro 2:9–11; 2Co 5:10; 1Pe 1:17; Rev 22:12

God does not distinguish between people on the basis of external appearance 1Sa 16:7 *See also* Ps 147:10–11; Jer 9:25; Lk 16:15; Gal 2:6; Rev 2:23

God does not discriminate against different races or classes Ac 10:34–35; Gal 3:28 *See also* Dt 10:18; Job 34:19; Ac 10:28; 15:7–9

The impartiality of Jesus Christ
Jesus Christ's teaching was impartial
Lk 20:21 pp Mt 22:16 pp Mk 12:14 *See also* Mt 20:1–16 *a parable of Jesus Christ about divine impartiality*

Jesus Christ showed impartiality in his dealings with people Jn 4:9 *Jesus Christ contravened accepted boundaries of partiality in this encounter. See also* Mt 9:10–12 pp Mk 2:15–17 pp Lk 5:29–31; Mt 15:22–28 pp Mk 7:26–29; Mt 20:20–23 pp Mk 10:35–40

Impartiality commended
Jas 2:1 *See also* Pr 28:21; 1Co 3:3–4; 4:6–7; 1Ti 5:21; Jas 2:9

Humanity should judge impartially
Pr 24:23–25 *See also* Ex 18:16; Dt 1:17; 16:19; 24:17; Pr 17:15; 18:5; Mal 2:9

Showing impartiality to all people is commanded
Impartiality to foreigners Ex 22:21 *See also* Ex 23:9; Lev 19:33–34; Nu 15:15–16; Ro 10:12

Impartiality to children Dt 21:15–17

Impartiality to the poor Ex 23:6 *See also* Ex 23:3; Lev 19:15; Pr 29:7; Jas 2:2–7

Ways to avoid partiality
By not accepting bribes Ex 23:8 *See also* Job 36:18; Pr 15:27; Isa 1:23

By not following the crowd Ex 23:2; Mk 15:15

Christians should be partial towards spiritual principles
Mt 6:24 pp Lk 16:13 *See also* Mt 12:30 pp Lk 11:23; Mt 7:13–14; Mk 9:39–40 pp Lk 9:49–50

Examples where impartiality is absent
Ge 25:27–28 *Isaac and Rebekah to Jacob and Esau;* Ge 29:30–32 *Jacob to Leah and Rachel;* Ge 37:3–4 *Jacob to Joseph and his brothers;* 1Sa 1:4–6 *Elkanah to Hannah and Peninnah*

See also
1020 God, all-	8207 commitment
knowing	8277 innocence
1075 God, justice of	8324 purity
2042 Christ, justice	8753 favouritism
of	8790 oppression
5347 injustice	8800 prejudice
5359 justice	
5448 poverty,	
attitudes to	

5883

impatience

A refusal to wait for people or developments, frequently displaying a lack of faith.

Examples of impatience
Ge 16:1–2 *Abraham and Sarah who did not wait for God to give them the son he had promised;* Ge 25:30 *Esau's impatience cost him his birthright;* Nu 20:9–11 *Moses Israel:* Nu 21:4; Ps 106:13; Isa 59:7 1Sa 13:6–12 *Saul made the offering without waiting for Samuel;* 2Sa 13:2 *Amnon with his half-sister, Tamar;* 2Sa 14:29 *Absalom with Joab;* 2Sa 18:14 *Joab with Absalom;* 2Ki 5:11–12 *Naaman;* 2Ki 6:33 *King Joram Job:* Job 6:11; 21:4
Job 32:16 *Elihu;* Mt 18:29–30 *the unforgiving debtor;* Lk 15:2 *The younger son could not wait for his inheritance;* Jn 21:3 *Peter;* Ac 20:16 *Paul;* 1Co 11:20–21 *the Corinthian Christians at their communal meal;* Rev 6:10–11 *the martyrs waiting for the Lord to avenge their deaths*

Warnings against impatience
Ps 37:7; Pr 19:2; Gal 6:9; Jas 1:19–20
See also Pr 6:18; 12:16; 14:29; 15:18; 16:32; 20:3
Haste leads to poverty: Pr 21:5; 28:22
Pr 25:8 *the need to exercise caution in disputes*
Warnings against hasty speech: Pr 29:20; Ecc 5:2
Ecc 7:9; 8:3; Hab 2:3

See also
1095 God, patience	8318 patience
of	8459 perseverance
2060 Christ, patience	8613 prayer,
of	persistence
5418 monotony	8718 disobedience
5925 rashness	8834 unbelief
5977 waiting	

5884

indecision

Uncertainty, hesitation and doubt reflect a failure of the basic human ability to choose. They reveal an internal debate and lack of conviction.

Indecision arising from doubt and hesitation
Jas 1:6–8 *See also* 1Ki 18:21; Mt 14:31; 21:21; Mk 11:23; Ro 14:23

Examples of indecisive behaviour
Ex 3:11 *See also* Ex 4:13; 14:10–15; Jos 7:10; Est 5:8; Mt 27:21–26 pp Mk 15:9–15 pp Lk 23:13–25

pp Jn 18:38–40; Mk 16:11–14; Jn 20:25;
Ac 24:25

Indecision may be indicative of divided loyalty
Mt 6:24 pp Lk 16:13 *See also* Mt 19:22
pp Mk 10:22 pp Lk 18:23

Indecision or uncertainty may be prompted by Satan
Ge 3:1 *See also* Ge 3:4; Jn 8:44; 2Co 11:3;
Rev 12:9

See also

4926 delay, human	8615 prayer, doubts
5186 stumbling	8702 agnosticism
5877 hesitation	8720 double-
6622 choice	mindedness
8124 guidance	8721 doubt
8329 readiness	8837 unbelief & life
8408 decision-	of faith
making	

5895

indifference

A neutral attitude to God that is as
dangerous as hostility. It is
condemned as a rejection of God's
love and of the needs of others.

Indifference towards God
No desire to seek God Ro 3:11 *See also*
Isa 42:20; Jer 5:21; Zep 1:6; Mt 13:15;
24:12; Ac 28:27; Rev 3:15–22

Refusal to heed God's word Jer 37:2
See also Ps 81:11; Jer 6:10; 7:13; 25:3–7;
35:15; Eze 3:7; Zec 1:4; 7:11–13

Refusal to respond to God's discipline
Jer 5:3 *See also* Jer 2:30; 7:27–28; 17:23;
32:33

Ignoring God is rebellion against him
Eze 12:2 *See also* Jer 2:19; 7:26; 36:24;
Eze 20:8

People ignore God and his warnings at
their peril Jer 12:11 *See also* Ex 9:21,25;
2Ch 33:10–11; Ne 9:30; Pr 1:24–27;
13:18; Jer 11:8; 36:31; 44:5–6;
Mt 22:5–7

For those who ignore God's salvation,
there is no hope Heb 2:3 *See also*
Jer 7:24; Mt 12:30 pp Lk 11:23

Indifference to God's declared intentions
Eze 22:30 *See also* Nu 32:6–7;
Jdg 5:15–17,23; 2Ch 24:5; Ps 22:11;
Isa 64:7; Jer 48:10

Indifference of religious leaders condemned
Eze 34:2–4; Zec 11:16–17; Jn 10:12–13

Indifference towards the needs of others
Indifference arises from sin Pr 29:7 *See
also* Job 21:21; Isa 32:6; Jas 2:15–16;
5:1–6

Examples of indifference towards
others Ge 40:23 *towards Joseph;*
1Sa 25:10–11 *towards David*
Towards Jesus Christ: Mt 26:40
pp Mk 14:37 pp Lk 22:45
Towards Paul: 2Ti 4:10,16

Jesus Christ condemns indifference
Mt 25:41–45 *See also* Lk 10:30–32;
16:19–21

Jesus Christ's apparent indifference
Mk 4:38 pp Mt 8:24–25 pp Lk 8:23–24
*Jesus Christ sometimes delayed responding
to cries for help in order to draw out faith.*
See also Mt 15:26 pp Mk 7:27; Lk 10:40;
Jn 11:6

See also

2015 Christ,	6139 deadness,
compassion	spiritual
2042 Christ, justice	6178 hardness of
of	heart
2048 Christ, love of	6193 impenitence
5147 deafness	6221 rebellion
5810 complacency	6245 stubbornness
5884 indecision	8616 prayerlessness

5886

individualism

The recognition of individuality, of
the differences between particular
people, and of their special gifts,
needs and character. In a negative
sense, the term can mean placing the
needs of individuals above those of
the church as a whole, which is
contrary to the biblical emphasis on
all believers sharing in the common
ministry of the body of Christ.

Individualism stresses the differences between people
Recognising people's special gifts
1Co 12:4–6 *See also* Ro 12:6–8;
1Co 12:8–11,28–30; Eph 4:11; Heb 2:4;
1Pe 4:10

Recognising people's abilities and
opportunities Mt 25:14–15 *See also*
Lk 19:12–13; 1Co 4:7

Individualism and the church
Recognising the parts people play in
the church, the body of Christ
1Co 12:12 *See also* Ro 12:4–5;
1Co 12:14,17–20,27

Individualism must not emphasise the
individual at the expense of the church
as a whole 1Co 12:21–26 *See also*
Ro 12:3,10,16; Php 2:3

Contrary to self-seeking individualism,
believers should share in the common
ministry of the body of Christ Ac 2:42
See also Ac 2:44; 4:34–35; 2Co 8:13–14;
9:13; Heb 13:16

See also

3275 Holy Spirit in	7110 body of Christ
the church	7206 community
5308 equality	7921 fellowship
5325 gifts	7943 ministry in
5937 rivalry	church
7025 church, unity	8437 giving talents
7032 unity, God's	8827 selfishness
people	

5887

inexperience

Lack of experience of life or a
particular aspect of life. Inexperience

is often associated with the young
who are thus vulnerable and who
should be taught by those older and
wiser. God sometimes calls the
inexperienced to leadership but
usually also provides encouragement
and support from more experienced
leaders.

The inexperience of youth
1Sa 3:4–7; Jer 1:6 *See also* Dt 1:39;
1Ki 3:7; 1Ch 29:1; 2Ch 10:8–11
pp 1Ki 12:8–11; 2Ch 13:7; Isa 7:15–16

The inexperienced may be led astray
2Ki 17:41 *Children often follow in the
ways of their parents;* Mt 18:6 *See also*
1Ki 22:53; 2Ki 24:9; Mk 9:42; Lk 17:2

God's call to the inexperienced
Jer 1:7–8 *See also* 1Sa 16:11–13 *David,
Jesse's youngest son, is chosen by God;*
1Sa 17:33 *David's inexperience in the face
of Goliath;* 1Ti 4:12 *Timothy was called to
pastor a church despite his youth. In
general, however, church leaders should be
people of experience (see* 1Ti 3:6).

Support for the inexperienced
Teaching the inexperienced Dt 4:9–10;
Job 8:8–9 *Each generation learns from the
wisdom and experience of those going
before. See also* Dt 11:2–7; 31:13;
Job 32:6–7; Ps 71:18; 78:3–5; Pr 5:1–2;
Eph 6:4

Examples of help given to the
inexperienced 1Ch 22:5 *See also* Dt 1:38
*Moses is to encourage his young successor,
Joshua;* Jdg 3:1–2 *teaching warfare to
those who have no experience of it;*
1Sa 3:8–10 *Eli instructs the inexperienced
Samuel;* 1Ki 19:19–21 *Elisha becomes
Elijah's attendant;* 1Ch 28:20 *David
encourages Solomon to build the temple;*
Pr 4:3–4 *Solomon recalls the instruction
given by his father;* Ac 15:39 *Barnabas
takes John Mark with him;* 2Ti 3:14–15
*Paul reminds Timothy of the example he
has been given.*

See also

5051 responsibility	5949 shyness
5664 children	6181 ignorance
5725 old age	8277 innocence
5731 parents	8414 encourage-
5746 youth	ment
5853 experience of	
life	

5888

inferiority

A discouraging sense of being of less
importance or value in comparison
with others.

Inferiority as a depressing lack of self-worth
Jdg 6:15; Ps 22:6; 1Co 2:3 *See also*
1Sa 18:23; Ne 4:4; 6:9; Ps 31:9–10; 70:5;
74:21; 86:1; 109:22; 119:25,141;
Ecc 9:16; Isa 33:8; Jer 22:28; La 1:11;
Mal 2:9

Inferiority as a healthy sense of unworthiness
Isa 6:5; Mt 5:3; Lk 5:8 *See also*

2Sa 12:13; Job 42:6; Ps 38:1–22;
51:3–5; Rev 1:17; 3:17

God's judgment will bring inferiority on on proud nations
Ob 2 See also Isa 16:14; Jer 49:15;
Eze 29:15

Refusing to be intimidated by a sense of inferiority
Job 12:3; 1Ti 4:12 See also Job 13:2;
2Co 11:5; 12:11; Tit 2:15

God values those regarded as inferior and uses them
Dt 7:7–8; 1Co 1:27–28 See also 1Sa 2:8;
Ps 12:5; 34:6; 35:10; 36:7; 40:17; 72:13;
136:23; 140:12; Isa 11:4; 25:4; 29:19;
41:14; 49:7; 61:1–3; Hos 11:1–4

Jesus Christ valued those traditionally regarded as inferior
Mt 8:2–4 the diseased and ritually
unclean; Mt 9:10–13 the morally
unacceptable; Mt 15:21–29 non-Jews;
Mt 19:13–14 children; Lk 18:13 those
who are ashamed of their sins; Jn 4:9
women

Believers are to help and encourage those who feel inferior
Lk 14:13; Ro 12:16 See also Ps 82:3–4;
1Th 5:14; Heb 12:12–13

See also
4050 dust	8340 self-respect
5916 pessimism	8357 weakness
5961 superiority	8713 discourage-
6151 dirt	ment
8276 humility	8741 failure
8305 meekness	

ingratitude

The absence of due thankfulness.
Scripture gives examples of human
ingratitude to God for all the
blessings and gifts which he provides
for them. It is especially important
for Christians to give thanks to God.

The ingratitude of human beings to one another
Examples of ingratitude Ge 40:23 the
chief butler towards Joseph; Nu 16:13–14
Dathan and Abiram to Moses
The Israelites to Gideon and his family:
Jdg 8:35; 9:18
1Sa 25:21 Nabal to David; 2Ch 24:22
King Joash to Jehoiada; Ecc 9:15 the
citizens to the wise man who delivered a
city

Returning evil for good Ps 35:12 See
also Ge 44:4; Ps 109:5; Pr 17:13;
Jer 18:20

Ingratitude to God
It was in evidence at the fall Ge 3:2–3
Eve showed ingratitude for God's provision
by not believing him.

It is part of fallen human nature Ro 1:21

It is a sign of the last days 2Ti 3:2

Israel's repeated ingratitude to the
Lord
For deliverance from Egypt: Ex 16:3,8;

Ex 17:7; Heb 3:7–9,15; Ps 95:7–9
Dt 32:6 They were rebuked by Moses for
the way they repaid God; 1Sa 8:7–8 They
rejected the Lord when they rejected
Samuel; Ne 9:26 They rejected God's law
and killed his prophets.

Ingratitude compared with other sins
Becoming like animals Isa 1:3

Becoming like prostitutes
Eze 16:17–19

Becoming like an adulterous wife
Hos 2:8; 4:12; 5:4; 9:1

Jesus Christ exposed ingratitude
Lk 17:15–18

God is kind even to the ungrateful
Lk 6:35

It is important for believers to show gratitude to God
Ps 100:4 See also Ps 107:22; Col 1:12;
3:15; 1Th 5:18

See also
1055 God, grace &	8676 thanksgiving
mercy	8764 forgetting God
8352 thankfulness	

insecurity

Lack of security, often in relation to
one's future or to one's present
position. All human life is insecure,
but the future of sinners is
particularly dangerous and real
security is found only in God.

The insecurity of human life
Isa 40:6–8 See also Job 1:13–21;
Ps 90:10; 146:3–6; Ecc 9:1,12; 10:8–9;
Jer 51:58; 1Th 5:1–3

The insecurity of the sinner's life
Ps 37:1–2 See also Ps 37:9–11;
Pr 6:12–15; 11:5; 24:19–22; 29:1;
Isa 30:12–14; 47:8–11; Jer 6:13–15;
15:5–9; 49:16–18; Am 8:14

The insecurity of the rich
1Ti 6:17 See also Pr 27:24; Lk 12:15–21;
1Ti 6:7–10

Examples of behaviour motivated by insecurity
Saul's vendetta against David
1Sa 18:6–12 See also 1Sa 18:17–29;
19:1,9–17; 20:30–31

Assassination of political rivals
2Ki 11:1 pp 2Ch 22:10 See also
Jdg 9:1–6

True security is to be found in God alone
Pr 14:26 See also Dt 33:12; 1Ki 2:45;
Ps 16:5; 48:8; Pr 3:5–6

See also
4015 life	5884 indecision
5398 loss	5942 security
5828 danger	6040 sinners
5839 dissatisfaction	8722 doubt
5877 hesitation	8808 riches

instability

The danger of instability in the Christian life
Eph 4:14; Jas 1:6–8 See also
Mt 7:26–27; 2Pe 2:14; 3:16

Firmness of faith as an antidote to instability
1Co 15:58 See also Mt 7:24–25;
Col 1:23; 1Pe 5:10

Political instability
Pr 29:4

See also
1160 God,	5953 stability
unchangeable	8331 reliability
4360 sand	8357 weakness
4690 wings	8459 perseverance
4860 wind	8704 apostasy
5844 emotions	8721 doubt
5881 immaturity	

instinct

An innate urge, rooted in natural
conditioning rather than reason.
Scripture likens sinners to creatures
of instinct.

Animals are creatures of instinct
2Pe 2:12 See also Jude 10

Sinners are likened to creatures of instinct
Jude 10

People without the Holy Spirit are likened to creatures of instinct
Jude 19

Believers ought instinctively to obey God
Isa 1:3 Just as the animals instinctively
know their masters, so Israel should know
and obey God. See also Jer 8:7

See also
4604 animals	6040 sinners
5050 reason	6257 unbelievers
5769 behaviour	7130 flock, God's
5800 blasphemy	8454 obedience to
5832 desire	God

insults

Expressions of an individual's
hostility or contempt for God and
his servants or fellow human beings.
Believers are to follow Jesus Christ's
example in not returning insults.

Insults to God
Insults to God coming from open
unbelief 2Ki 19:14–16,20–23
pp 2Ch 32:16–19 pp Isa 37:14–17
pp Isa 37:21–24; Heb 10:29

Insults to God coming through the
suffering of believers Ps 69:7–9 See also
Jer 20:7–8; Ro 15:3; Heb 13:12–13

Insults to God lamented by the psalmist Ps 74:18,22–23 *See also* Ps 10:3

Jesus Christ insulted
Lk 18:31–33 pp Mt 20:17–19 pp Mk 10:32–34 *See also* Mt 26:67–68 pp Mk 14:65 pp Lk 22:63–65; Mt 27:39–44 pp Mk 15:29–32 pp Lk 23:35–39; Jn 8:48–49; 18:22–23; 1Pe 2:23

Israel insulted
Jer 51:51 *See also* 1Sa 17:26; 2Sa 21:20–21 pp 1Ch 20:6–7; Eze 21:28–32; Zep 2:8–10

Kings, prophets and others insulted
1Sa 10:27; 25:9–11,14; 2Sa 10:1–5 pp 1Ch 19:1–5; 2Ki 2:23–24; Ne 4:1–5; Ecc 10:20

The poor insulted
1Co 11:20–22; Jas 2:1–7

Christians insulted
Ac 18:6; 1Pe 4:14 *See also* Ac 2:13; 17:32; 19:8–9; 1Pe 4:4

The pain of insult
Ps 55:12–14 *See also* Ps 22:6–8; Job 19:1–3; 20:2–3; Ps 44:16; 55:3; 89:50–51; 109:21–25; La 3:55–63; 1Th 2:2; Rev 2:9

Dealing with insults
Avoiding insults Pr 9:7; 22:10

Not repaying insults Pr 12:16 *See also* Mt 5:39 pp Lk 6:27–29; 1Pe 3:9

Rejoicing in reproach for Jesus Christ's sake Mt 5:11–12 pp Lk 6:22–23 *See also* Ac 5:41; 2Co 12:10; Heb 10:32–34; 1Pe 4:13–14

Insult supposed but not intended Lk 11:45; Ac 23:1–5

See also

2570 Christ, suffering	5836 disgrace
2585 Christ, trial	5879 humiliation
5494 revenge	5951 slander
5775 abuse	8782 mockery
5800 blasphemy	8807 profanity
5818 contempt	8819 scoffing

5894

intelligence

The natural ability to acquire knowledge and to learn skills. It is not emphasised in Scripture because wisdom is viewed primarily in spiritual and moral terms. Human cleverness proves ultimately futile; nevertheless, believers are called to develop and use their minds to the full in God's service and to dedicate gifts and abilities to him.

Wisdom is primarily spiritual and moral
Pr 9:10 *See also* Job 28:28; Ps 111:10; Jas 3:13

The spiritual and moral inadequacy of unaided human intelligence
Unaided human intelligence proves futile Ps 94:11 *See also* Ecc 9:11; 12:12; Da 12:4; Ac 17:21; 1Co 3:20

Human intelligence does not bring knowledge of God 1Co 1:20–21 *See also* Jn 5:39–40; Ro 1:22–23; Col 2:8

Human intelligence cannot promote godliness Col 2:23 *See also* 1Co 8:1–2; Jas 3:14–16

Reliance on human intelligence brings judgment Isa 29:14 *See also* Job 5:13; Isa 44:25; 1Co 1:19

Many of the first Christians were not intelligent
1Co 1:26–31 *See also* Ac 4:13

Believers are to use their minds
The mind to be used in serving God Mk 12:30 pp Mt 22:37 pp Lk 10:27 *See also* 1Co 7:37 *The mind is to be used in seeking to discern God's will*; 1Co 14:15–18 *The mind is to be used in worship.*

God wants to renew the mind Ro 12:2 *See also* Eph 4:23; Heb 10:16; Jer 31:33

The mind must be correctly focused Ro 8:5–6; Php 4:6–7; Col 3:2

Examples of intelligent people
1Sa 25:3 *Abigail*; 2Ch 2:12 *Solomon*; Da 1:4 *young men from Israel exiled in Babylon*; Da 1:17 *Daniel, Shadrach, Meshach and Abednego*; Ac 5:34 *Gamaliel*; Ac 7:22 *Moses*; Ac 13:6–7 *Sergius Paulus*; Ac 26:24 *Paul*

Examples of believers using their minds
Ecc 8:9 *See also* Ezr 7:10 *Ezra*; Ecc 7:25 *the Teacher*; Da 10:12 *Daniel*; Ac 17:11 *the Bereans*; 2Ti 2:15 *Paul's expectation for Timothy*

God uses intelligence dedicated to him
Ge 41:46–49 *God uses Joseph's administrative skill*; Ex 31:2–6 pp Ex 35:30–35 *Craftsmen use artistic expertise*; 1Ki 7:13–14 pp 2Ch 2:13–14 *Huram does work in bronze for Solomon's temple*; 2Ch 26:15 *Skilful men design machines for the defence of Jerusalem*; Da 5:13–14 *Daniel's intelligence aids his witness in the Babylonian court*; Lk 1:3–4 *Luke's thorough research owes something to his medical training.*

See also

5026 knowledge	7797 teaching
5035 mind	8135 knowing God
5050 reason	8355 understanding
5191 thought	8361 wisdom
5531 skill	8419 enlightenment
6181 ignorance	8674 study

5895

intimacy

Close relationships are part of God's will for human life. Scripture speaks of intimate relationships between Jesus Christ and the Father, between God and his people, and between various individuals.

Jesus Christ's intimate relationship with his Father
Mt 11:27 *See also* Mt 3:17 pp Mk 1:11

pp Lk 3:22; Jn 5:20; 10:30,38; 14:10–11; 17:21

God's intimate relationship with his people
Jn 17:3 *"know" speaks of close personal relationship rather than theoretical or academic knowledge. See also* 2Ch 7:15–16; Ps 148:14; Hos 6:6; Jn 14:21; 15:4,15

Images of God's desire for intimacy with his people
God as a father Jer 31:9 *See also* Ps 103:13; Jer 31:20; Hos 11:1–4; Ro 8:15; 1Jn 3:1

God as a husband Isa 62:5 *See also* Isa 54:4–8; Jer 3:14; Hos 2:19; Eph 5:25–27; Rev 19:7; 21:2

Intimate relationships between men and women
As God's good purpose Ge 2:18 *See also* Ge 1:27–28; 2:24; Mt 19:5 pp Mk 10:7; 1Co 6:16; Eph 5:28,31; 1Ti 4:3–4

Examples of such close relationships *Jacob and Rachel:* Ge 29:20,30 Ru 4:13 *Boaz and Ruth Elkanah and Hannah:* 1Sa 1:5,8 Est 2:17 *Xerxes and Esther*; SS 1:15–16 *Solomon and his beloved*

Intimacy in other relationships
Close friendships commended Pr 18:24 *See also* Pr 17:17; 27:10; Ecc 4:9–12; Jn 15:13

Examples of close friendships *David and Jonathan:* 1Sa 18:1,3 *Elijah and Elisha:* 2Ki 2:2,4 2Ti 1:16 *Paul and Onesiphorus*

Examples of intimate family relationships
Ge 37:3 *Jacob and his son Joseph*; Ru 1:16 *Ruth and her mother-in-law Naomi*; 2Sa 18:33 *David and his son Absalom*

See also

1040 God, fatherhood	5966 tenderness
1250 Abba	6754 union with Christ
5680 family	8102 abiding in Christ
5690 friends	8135 knowing God
5708 marriage	8622 worship
5729 one flesh	
5735 sexuality	

5896

irreverence

A complete absence of the proper sense of awe, respect and wonder that is inspired and demanded by the character and activity of the living God. Irreverence involves disrespect for the character, deeds, words, law and ministers of God. As such, it brings judgment upon those who behave in this way.

Irreverence as the root of sin
Ro 3:10,18 *See also* Ps 36:1; 10:4–5; 55:19; Ro 1:21

Rebellion leads to irreverence
Jer 5:23–24 *See also* Isa 29:13; Mt 15:3–9

Causes of irreverence
Arrogance Ps 10:4-5 *See also* Dt 17:19-20

Self-deception Ps 36:1-2

Prosperity Pr 30:9 *See also* Ps 10:4-5

Kinds of irreverence
Insulting God Ps 69:9 *See also* Ps 74:22-23; Heb 10:29

Misusing God's name Ex 20:7 *See also* Lev 19:12; 24:10-16

Insulting God's representatives 1Ki 21:10-13 *See also* Dt 17:12; Ac 6:11

Ignoring God's law Nu 15:30 *See also* Isa 63:17; Jer 44:10; Am 2:7; 1Th 5:20

Worshipping idols Eze 20:39 *See also* Lev 18:21; 20:1-3

Sacrificial worship Lev 22:2 *See also* Lev 21:6; 1Sa 2:17; Mal 1:6-8

Towards holy objects and places 2Sa 6:6-7 *See also* Ps 74:7-8; 79:1; Jer 7:30

Attacking God's people Ps 22:7-8 *See also* 2Ki 19:9-12,16; Ps 31:18; 35:15-16; 74:10,18; 89:50-51; Eze 35:12; Da 7:8,21-22; Zep 2:10-11 *The insults of unbelievers are sometimes prompted by the sins of God's people:* Eze 36:20-23; Ro 2:24

Blasphemy against the Holy Spirit Mt 12:31-32 pp Mk 3:29 pp Lk 12:10 *Jesus Christ's opponents were beyond hope, so long as they continued to say that the work of the Holy Spirit was the work of Satan (Mt 12:24). See also* 1Co 12:3 *Jesus Christ was accused of blasphemy:* Jn 10:33; Mt 26:63-65 pp Mk 14:63-64

Social consequences of irreverence
In family relationships Mt 15:4 *See also* Ex 21:17 pp Lev 20:9; Pr 20:20; 30:11

Oppression and cruelty Ps 10:9-11 *See also* Ps 73:2-11; 94:4-7; Pr 8:13

Social irresponsibility Pr 17:5 *See also* Pr 14:31; Jer 34:16; Eze 22:11-12; Lk 18:2; Ro 1:28-32; 1Co 11:20-22

Irreverence brings condemnation and judgment
Dt 17:12-13; Ps 55:19 *See also* Nu 14:23; 2Ch 26:5,16; 36:15-16; Pr 1:29-31; 3:34; 28:14; Hos 10:3; 12:14; Heb 10:29; Jude 15

Particular warnings about the consequences of irreverence 1Sa 12:14-15 *See also* Dt 28:58-59; Mal 2:1-2

See also

5800 blasphemy	8771 idolatry,
5818 contempt	objections
5829 defiance	8782 mockery
5838 disrespect	8807 profanity
5893 insults	9210 judgment,
8333 reverence	God's

5898

judging others

God's people are to exercise fairness and impartiality when called upon to exercise judgment in legal or church matters. However, the temptation to pass judgment upon

the life or testimony of other individuals is clearly warned against.

Judging others in a legal situation
Fairness and impartiality are required by God Dt 16:18-20 *See also* Ex 23:6-7; Lev 19:15; Dt 1:16-17; Pr 24:23; Eze 18:5-8

Judges are appointed by God 1Ki 3:28 *See also* Ex 18:13-16; 1Sa 7:15; 12:1-4

Jesus Christ refuses to judge others
Jn 8:3-11 *See also* Lk 12:13-14; Jn 7:24; 8:15-16

Judging others in the church
Judgmental attitudes condemned Mt 7:1-5 pp Lk 6:37-42 *See also* Ro 2:1-3; 14:1-13; Col 2:16; Jas 2:1-4; 4:11-12

A discerning attitude commended 1Co 5:12-13 *See also* 1Co 5:1-5; 6:1-6

Evaluation of ministries commended Mt 7:15-20 *See also* 2Co 11:10-15; Php 3:2

See also

2309 Christ as judge	5820 criticism
5202 accusation,	5951 slander
false	8226 discernment
5358 judges	8230 discipline
5359 justice	

5898

kissing

Kissing within the family
Ge 29:13 *See also* Ge 27:26-27; 33:4; 48:10

Kissing as an expression of love
SS 1:2 *See also* Ge 29:11; SS 8:1; 1Pe 5:14

Kissing as a sign of reconciliation
Lk 15:20 *See also* Ge 45:15; 2Sa 14:33

Kissing as a sign of homage
1Sa 10:1 *See also* 1Ki 19:18; Job 31:27; Ps 2:12; Hos 13:2; Lk 7:38,45

Greeting with a kiss
Ex 18:7 *See also* Ex 4:27 *The holy kiss symbolises sharing in the fellowship of Jesus Christ:* Ro 16:16; 1Co 16:20; 2Co 13:12; 1Th 5:26; 1Pe 5:14

Kissing good-bye
Ru 1:14 *See also* Ge 31:28,55; 50:1; Ru 1:9; 1Sa 20:41; 1Ki 19:20; Ac 20:37

Blessing with a kiss
2Sa 19:39

Kissing linked with treachery
2Sa 20:9-10 *See also* Pr 7:13,21; 27:6; Mt 26:48-49 pp Mk 14:44-45 pp Lk 22:47-48

See also

1335 blessing	5798 betrayal
5328 greeting	5895 intimacy
5680 family	5969 treachery
5690 friends	6241 seduction
5734 relationships	7921 fellowship
5781 affection	8292 love

5899

lament

A song of mourning or sorrow. Laments may be occasioned by bereavement, personal trouble, national disaster or the judgment of God.

Lamentation occasioned by bereavement
2Sa 3:33-34 *See also* Ge 50:10; Jer 31:15; Mt 2:16-18; 9:23 pp Mk 5:38 pp Lk 8:52; Lk 23:27; Jn 11:31-33

Lamentation occasioned by personal trouble
Ps 56:2,8; 102:1-2

Lamentation occasioned by national disaster
2Ch 35:25 *See also* 2Sa 1:17-27; Est 4:1; 9:31; Jer 8:21-9:1

Lamentation occasioned by the judgment of God on Israel
Am 5:1-2 *The call to lament is sometimes meant as a warning of impending judgment;* La 1:1 *The book of Lamentations is a series of laments after the fall of Jerusalem. See also* Isa 3:24-26; 29:1-2; Jer 4:7-8; 7:29; 9:10,17-21; La 2:5; Eze 2:9-10; 19:1-14

Lamentation occasioned by the judgment of God on other nations
Isa 16:9-11 *See also* Isa 15:5,8; 16:7; 19:8; Jer 48:36; Eze 26:17-18; 27:2-36; 28:12-19; 30:2-4; 32:2-16

Lamentation as a sign of repentance
La 1:5,8; 3:39-40; Eze 9:3-6

See also

5198 weeping	6732 repentance
5265 complaints	7963 song
5419 mourning	9210 judgment,
5795 bereavement	God's
5952 sorrow	9250 woe

5900

laughter

The act or sound of laughing, often associated with joy and delight, yet occasionally linked with ridicule and scorn.

People laughing
Out of pleasure Ge 21:6 *See also* Pr 31:25; Ecc 3:4; 10:19

In scorn and derision Mt 9:24 pp Mk 5:40 pp Lk 8:53 *See also* Job 39:18; 41:29; Ps 52:6; La 1:7; Hab 1:10

God laughing
Ps 2:4 *See also* Ps 37:13; 59:8; Pr 1:26

God helping people to laugh
Ps 126:2; Lk 6:21 *See also* Job 5:22; 8:21; Jer 51:39 *as a prelude to judgment*

Laughter qualified
Pr 14:13 *See also* Ecc 2:2; 7:3

Laughter rebuked
Lk 6:25 *See also* Ecc 7:6; Jas 4:9

See also
5818 contempt   8283 joy
5830 delight   8782 mockery
5874 happiness   8815 ridicule
5880 humour

5901

loneliness

God intends human beings to live together in harmony and to value one another, but Scripture recognises many reasons for individuals to feel unwanted and isolated.

Loneliness is not part of God's plan for human beings
Ge 2:18 *See also* Ps 68:5–6; Isa 49:15

God is with his people at all times and in all circumstances
Isa 41:10 *See also* Dt 31:8; Jos 1:9; Ps 27:10; Isa 43:2; Mt 28:20; Jn 14:18; Heb 13:5–6

Reasons why people may experience loneliness
Sin Isa 59:2 *See also* Ge 4:10–12; 1Sa 28:5–6; Ps 81:11–12; Isa 64:7; Hos 5:6; Eph 4:18

Remorse Mt 27:4–5 *See also* 1Ch 21:17; Mt 26:75

Lack of friends Ps 142:4 *See also* Jn 5:7; 14:18

Social ostracism Jn 4:9 *A moral outcast (see Jn 4:18), she was collecting water at the hottest part of the day, when she could do so alone. See also* Lk 19:7 *A Jew who worked for the Roman occupying power was considered a traitor.*

Public shame Jn 8:3 *See also* Mk 15:29–32

Desertion 2Ti 4:16 *See also* Ps 38:11; 88:18

Loss of family Lk 7:12 *See also* Ru 1:3–5; 2Sa 18:33; 2Ki 4:1; Job 1:20–21; Ps 27:10; Mt 2:17–18; Jer 31:15; 1Ti 5:5

Loss of identity Lk 8:27 pp Mk 5:2–3 *See also* Lk 8:30 pp Mk 5:9

Discontent Ecc 4:8 *See also* Ecc 2:10–11,18; Heb 13:5–6

Disability Ac 3:2 *See also* Lev 21:17–18; Mt 9:32; 12:22

Disease Lk 17:12 *Lepers were forbidden to mix with those not affected. See also* Lev 13:4; Nu 5:1–3; 2Ki 7:3; 2Ch 26:21

Insomnia Ps 102:7 *See also* Job 7:4; Da 6:18

Depression 1Ki 19:4 *See also* Dt 33:27; Job 7:16; Ps 43:5; 73:16–17; Jer 15:10; Mic 7:1

Poverty Pr 19:7 *See also* 1Ki 17:12; Pr 19:4; Lk 15:14–16

Old age Ps 71:9 *See also* 2Sa 19:34–35

Dying and the approach of death
Ps 23:4 *See also* Ps 18:4–6; Ro 8:38–39

Loneliness experienced as a consequence of God's calling
God's setting apart for service
1Ki 19:10 *See also* Jdg 6:14–15; Jer 1:5; 4:18–19; 15:16–17

Leadership Mk 10:32 *See also*
Ex 24:1–2; Jos 1:6–7; Mt 20:17–19

Responsibility Nu 11:14 *See also*
Ex 18:17–18; 2Co 11:28

Jesus Christ experienced loneliness
Mt 27:46 pp Mk 15:33–34 *See also*
Ps 22:1–2; Mt 4:1–2 pp Lk 4:1–2; Mt 14:23; Lk 4:28–30; Jn 6:67; 16:32

Positive aspects of loneliness
Solitude provides an opportunity for communion with God Mt 6:6 *See also* Ex 3:1–2; 33:9; 2Ki 4:32–33; Mt 26:39; Mk 1:35; 6:45–46; Rev 1:9

Engaging in spiritual warfare Ge 32:24

The opportunity for spiritual experiences away from the crowd Mk 9:2 *See also* Da 10:8; 2Co 12:2–4

Solitude as rest from the turmoil of everyday life Mk 6:31–32 *See also* Mt 11:28

See also
1110 God, present   5770 abandonment
     everywhere   5795 bereavement
2530 Christ, death of   7921 fellowship
5056 rest   8341 separation
5689 friendlessness   8482 spiritual
5690 friends   warfare
5734 relationships   8602 prayer

5902

maturity

The full development at the end of a process of growth, by means of which a human being reaches adulthood.

5903
maturity, physical

In the OT, reaching adulthood brought with it certain privileges and responsibilities.

Growth to physical and psychological maturity
Lk 2:52 *Jesus Christ's normal childhood is evidence of his full humanity. See also* 1Sa 2:26; Lk 1:80; 2:40; 1Co 13:11

The responsibilities of maturity in the Israelite community
The payment of atonement money
Ex 30:11–16; 38:25–26

Eligibility for military service
Nu 1:2–3,45; 26:2; 2Ch 25:5

Accountability for actions Nu 14:29; 32:11

Inheritance of the land Nu 26:52–54

Serving Levites Nu 8:24–25; 1Ch 23:24,27; Ezr 3:8

Maturity should produce wisdom
Job 12:12 *See also* Job 15:10; 32:6–9; Pr 7:7; Ecc 4:13

Respect should be shown to the mature
Lev 19:32 *See also* Job 32:4; Pr 23:22; 1Ti 5:1–2; 1Pe 5:5

Maturity of years seen as God's blessing
Ge 24:1; Ru 4:15; 1Ch 29:28

The maturity of crops for harvest used as a metaphor
Joel 3:13; Jn 4:35–36 *See also*
Am 8:1–2; Mt 9:37–38 pp Lk 10:1–2; Mk 4:26–29; Rev 14:15

See also
2520 Christ,   5725 old age
     childhood   8361 wisdom
4464 harvest   8443 growth
5051 responsibility   8469 respect
5716 middle age

5904
maturity, spiritual

The development of Christlike character and behaviour in the Christian through a renewed mind and tested faith.

Christlikeness as the goal and model for spiritual maturity
Eph 4:13–15 *See also* Col 2:6–7; Heb 12:2

Marks of spiritual maturity
Spiritual understanding Col 2:2 *See also* Ro 15:14; 1Co 2:6; 14:20; Eph 1:17–18; Heb 5:12–6:1

Discernment of God's will and changed behaviour Col 1:9–10 *See also* Ro 12:2; 1Co 3:1–3; Gal 5:22–23; Eph 4:22–23; Php 1:9–11; 2Th 1:3

Stability Col 4:12 *See also* Eph 4:14; 2Pe 3:17–18

Care for the weaker brother Ro 15:1 *See also* Gal 6:1–2

Maturity is to be the aim of the Christian
Php 3:13–15 *See also* Lk 8:14 *a reason for spiritual immaturity;* 2Co 7:1; 13:11; 1Ti 6:11

The process of maturity
God causes spiritual growth Php 1:6 *See also* Gal 3:3; Heb 10:14

Possessing gifts of ministry
Eph 4:11–13 *See also* Ro 1:11

Being equipped by the word of God
2Ti 3:16–17 *See also* Ro 15:4; 1Pe 2:2; 1Jn 2:5

Persevering through trials Ro 5:3–5 *See also* Heb 2:10; Jas 1:3–4; 1Pe 5:10

The concern of the pastor is to help others to maturity
Col 1:28–29 *See also* 2Co 13:9–10; Gal 4:19

See also
1613 Scripture,   8226 discernment
     purpose   8230 discipline
3233 Holy Spirit &   8258 fruitfulness,
     sanctification   spiritual
5881 immaturity   8320 perfection
6744 sanctification   8347 spiritual
7026 church,   growth
     leadership
8215 confidence,
     results

5907

miserliness

A reluctance to part with money, often associated with the hoarding of money or possessions. While Scripture censures the squandering of resources, it also regards the hoarding of money or possessions as potentially idolatrous.

Miserliness as a form of idolatry
Pr 18:11; Mt 6:24 *See also* Dt 15:9;
Pr 11:26; Hos 12:8; Mt 6:19–21;
Eph 5:3–5; Col 3:5; 1Ti 6:17

The foolishness of miserliness
Ecc 2:26; 1Ti 6:7 *See also* Ps 39:6,11;
49:10; Pr 22:16; 23:6; 28:8,22;
Ecc 4:7–8; 5:10–11,15; Lk 12:15–21

Miserliness leads to misery
Pr 11:24; 1Ti 6:9–10 *See also* Pr 11:16;
Ecc 5:12–14; Jas 5:1–6

Some examples of miserliness
1Sa 25:3; Am 3:10; Lk 16:19–31;
Ac 5:1–2

See also

5412 money	8260 generosity
5446 poverty	8434 giving
5503 rich, the	8768 idolatry
5869 greed	8808 riches
5967 thrift	8827 selfishness

5908

motives

The underlying reasons for a course of action. Scripture stresses the importance of doing things with the intention of honouring and glorifying God and building up his people.

5909

motives, importance of

God acts from the highest, purest motives and expects his people to do the same.

God's supreme motive is the honour of his name
Ps 106:8 *See also* Ex 9:16; Ps 23:3;
Isa 43:7; Eze 36:20–23; Eph 1:11–14

God's glory is to be the highest motive of his people
1Co 10:31 *See also* Nu 25:7–13; Isa 26:8;
Col 3:17; 1Pe 4:11

Purity of motive is essential for acceptable worship
Mt 6:1–18 *See also* Ps 51:6,10; 86:11;
Mt 5:8

Wrong motives hinder effective prayer
Jas 4:3 *See also* Ps 66:18; 1Jn 3:21–22

Motives for good moral behaviour
Wanting to please God Col 3:22–25 *See also* Eph 6:5–8

Compassion for others Dt 24:17–22

The experience of slavery and the exodus were to promote compassion for the poor and the alien. See also Ex 22:21–27;
Lev 25:35–42,54–55

Fear of punishment for sin Heb 13:4 *See also* Col 3:5–6; 1Th 4:3–6

God judges the motives of the heart
Pr 16:2 *See also* 1Ch 28:9; Pr 20:27

See also

1020 God, all-knowing	8242 ethics, personal
1310 God as judge	8324 purity
5012 heart	8477 self-examination
5761 attitudes	
6185 imagination, desires	

5910

motives, examples of

Scripture reflects the wide range of motives which influence human behaviour.

Right actions can result from wrong motives
Php 1:15–18 *See also* 1Sa 18:20–23

Right motives do not always produce right actions
1Ki 8:17–19 pp 2Ch 6:7–9 *See also* Mt 1:18–20

Examples of wrong motives
Malice and envy Ge 37:11 *See also*
Ge 37:18–28; Est 3:1–9; Eze 25:15–16;
36:5; Mt 2:7–13

Greed Jn 12:4–6 *See also* 2Ki 5:19–27;
Tit 1:10–11

Motives are sometimes misjudged
Jos 22:9–34 *See also* Nu 32:1–33;
2Sa 10:1–4 pp 1Ch 19:1–4; 2Ki 5:5–7

Jesus Christ's actions motivated by a desire to do God's will
Jn 8:29 *See also* Jn 4:34; 6:38;
Heb 10:5–7; Ps 40:6–8

Paul's motives
Paul rejected all base motives in ministry 1Th 2:3–6 *See also* 2Co 2:17

Paul was motivated by his knowledge of God 2Co 5:9–12

Paul was concerned for the spiritual growth of others Php 4:14–18 *Paul's motive in rejoicing in the gift from the Philippians was the spiritual benefit which they would gain as a result of it. See also* Php 1:22–26; Phm 8–14

See also

2057 Christ, obedience	8436 giving possessions
2339 Christ, example of	8733 envy
5869 greed	8767 hypocrisy
8120 following Christ	8796 persecution, forms of
8426 evangelism, motivation	

5913

negotiation

Negotiation between peoples
Ge 21:23; Lk 14:31–32 *See also* Jos 9:6;

10:4; 1Sa 11:2; 2Sa 3:12–13; 1Ki 15:19;
2Ki 18:23 pp Isa 36:8

Negotiation in the buying of land
Ge 23:8–9 *See also* Ru 4:4; 2Sa 24:24;
Jer 32:8

Negotiation in the setting of wages
Ge 29:15 *See also* Ge 29:27; 30:32;
Jdg 17:10–11; 1Ki 5:6; Mt 20:2;
26:14–15 pp Mk 14:10 pp Lk 22:4

Negotiation for personal safety
Jos 2:12–13 *See also* Jdg 15:12–13;
1Sa 20:8; 30:15

See also

5242 buying & selling	5783 agreement
5468 promises, human	5811 compromise
5587 trade	6682 mediation
5592 treaty	6684 mediator
	8458 peacemakers

5914

optimism

The ability to face the future with confidence. For believers this is possible because of their knowledge of God.

Optimism resulting from faith
Confidence in God Ps 52:8; 125:1 *See also* Ps 25:4–5; 56:4; 71:5; 91:2; Na 1:7

Confidence in what God can do 2Co 1:10–11 *See also* Ps 27:1–3;
Jer 17:7; Mic 7:7; Heb 13:6; 1Jn 5:14

Confidence in what God will do in the future 2Co 5:5–8 *See also* Ac 24:14–15;
Gal 5:5; Php 1:3–6

Confidence founded on God's grace Isa 12:1–2 *See also* Ezr 10:2; 2Co 3:4–5;
Eph 3:12; 2Th 2:16–17; 1Jn 3:21–22

Encouragements to be optimistic
Jn 14:1; Ro 15:13 *See also* Ps 9:10;
37:3–5; 42:5; 115:9–11; Jn 14:27;
16:33; Ro 12:12; 1Ti 6:17; Heb 4:15;
10:19–23; 1Pe 1:13; 1Jn 2:28

Examples of optimism
In the OT 2Ch 32:8; Pr 12:25; 31:11

The apostle Peter 1Pe 5:10

The apostle Paul 2Co 7:4 *See also*
1Co 1:8–9; 4:17; 2Co 1:7; 2:3; 8:22;
Php 2:2; Col 4:9,12–13; 2Ti 1:12;
Phm 21

The apostle John 3Jn 3–5

Misplaced optimism
Trusting in anyone or anything other than God Ps 146:3 *See also* Jdg 9:26;
1Sa 15:32; Job 6:20; 8:12–13; Pr 11:7;
Jer 7:4; 9:4; 12:6; 49:4,31; Eze 29:16;
Mic 7:5; 2Co 9:4

Presumption Eze 13:6 *See also* Isa 58:4;
Jer 7:9–10; Lk 18:9

See also

1035 God, faithfulness	5916 pessimism
1055 God, grace & mercy	8020 faith
5026 knowledge	8105 assurance, basis of
5854 experience of God	8214 confidence, basis of
	8289 joy of church

See also
8414 encouragement   9613 hope as
8820 self-confidence   confidence

5915

ornaments

The use of jewellery and other adornments is not forbidden in Scripture, but excessive use can indicate worldliness. Inner spiritual adornment is of greater value.

Possession and use of various ornaments show wealth
Ornaments used to beautify
SS 1:10–11 *See also* Ge 37:3,23,32;
2Sa 1:24; Jer 2:32

Rings, ear-rings and nose rings
Ge 35:4; Ex 32:2–3; Jdg 8:24; Est 8:8;
Pr 25:12; Isa 3:19,21; Eze 16:12;
Lk 15:22; Jas 2:2

Bracelets and gold chains Ge 24:22;
41:42; Pr 1:9; Eze 16:11; Da 5:29

Bells Ex 28:33–35

Ornaments plundered from Egypt
Ex 3:22

The misuse of ornaments for pride and seduction
Isa 3:16 *See also* Eze 23:40,42; Hos 2:13

Ornaments as gifts
Ge 24:53 *See also* Ge 24:22; Job 42:11

Adornment as a picture of God's love
Eze 16:11–13 *See also* Isa 61:10;
Lk 15:22

Ornaments as symbols of authority
Ge 41:42 *See also* 2Sa 1:10; Est 3:10;
Da 5:29

Ornaments discarded
In mourning Ex 33:4–6 *See also*
Eze 26:16

To make idols Ex 32:2–4 *See also*
Jdg 8:24–27

As offerings to God Ex 35:22 *See also*
Nu 31:50

Inner, not outer, adornment encouraged
1Pe 3:3–4

See also
4333 gold	5251 chains
4342 jewels	5280 crown
5139 bracelet	5659 bride
5145 clothing	5778 adorning
5170 neck	8808 riches
5176 ring	

5916

pessimism

A negative and hopeless attitude, resulting either from viewing the world as being without God or from loss of faith in God.

The world may appear to be meaningless
Ecc 1:14 *See also* Ecc 1:1–11

Wisdom may be pointless
Ecc 1:17–18 *See also* Ecc 2:12–16

Pleasures may be empty
Ecc 2:1

Work may be in vain
Ecc 2:17 *See also* Ecc 2:18–23; 4:4

The world may seem corrupt and oppressive
Ecc 4:1 *See also* Ecc 4:2–3; 5:8–9

Loneliness can be depressing
Ecc 4:8

Wealth is no answer
Ecc 5:10 *See also* Ecc 5:11–15; 6:1–6;
Lk 12:18–20

Life is short and often miserable
Ecc 6:12 *In the OT, before the resurrection hope was fully developed, this life seemed to be all that there was. See also*
1Ch 29:15; Job 7:6; 14:7–12,18–22;
17:13–16

Suffering may lead to pessimism
Job 6:11 *See also* Job 30:26; La 3:16–18;
Eze 37:11

Suffering may cause a sense of God's rejection
Job 14:18–19 *See also* Job 19:5–13

The godless have no grounds for optimism
Eph 2:12 *See also* Job 8:13–15; Pr 10:24;
11:7; 24:19–20; Isa 19:3; Jer 4:9;
Mt 7:26–27; 1Th 4:13

Examples of pessimism
The Israelites on hearing about the strength of the Canaanites
Nu 13:31–33; Dt 1:28

Israel's enemies Dt 2:25; Jos 2:9

Naomi on her return to Israel Ru 1:21

The Israelites threatened by the Philistines 1Sa 17:11; 13:6–7

Elijah at Mount Horeb 1Ki 19:9–10

The men with leprosy at the gate of Samaria 2Ki 7:4

Judah facing the threat from Aram and Israel Isa 7:2

The Philistine cities on seeing Tyre's destruction Zec 9:5

Thomas after the resurrection
Jn 20:24–25

Paul's shipboard companions during the storm Ac 27:20

The antidote to pessimism is faith in God
Ps 42:5; 2Co 4:13–16 *See also* Isa 41:10;
La 3:21–24; 2Co 4:7–9

See also
5067 suicide	8027 faith, testing of
5569 hardship	8713 discourage-
5799 bitterness	ment
5831 depression	8754 fear
5835 disappointment	8834 unbelief
5901 loneliness	9614 hope, results
5914 optimism	of absence

5917

plans

Designs or schemes, prepared in advance of doing something. Scripture indicates the sovereign plans of God and the varied plans of men and women.

God's plans
For judgment Jer 18:11 *See also*
Nu 33:55–56; 2Ki 19:25–26;
Job 23:14–16; Isa 25:1–2; 37:26–27;
Jer 26:3; La 2:17; Mic 2:3
Prophecies against the enemies of God's people: Isa 14:24–27; 19:12,17; 23:8–9;
Jer 49:20; 50:45; Mic 4:11–13

For salvation Eph 1:11 *See also* Ps 40:5;
Heb 11:40

For the tabernacle and the temple
Ex 26:30–37 *See also*
1Ch 28:11–12,18–19; Eze 43:10–11

God's plans are revealed to his people
Am 3:7 *See also* Ex 26:30; Jer 49:20–21

God's plans are always fulfilled
Job 42:2 *See also* Ps 33:11; Isa 5:18–19;
14:24–27; 46:11

God may sometimes reverse his plans
Jer 36:3 *See also* Jer 18:5–10; 26:3;
Jnh 3:10

Plans of the wicked
Ps 64:5–6 *See also* 2Sa 17:1–4;
2Ki 16:10–11; Ps 140:2; Pr 14:22; 30:32;
Isa 30:1; Jer 18:12; Mic 2:1;
Mt 28:12–13

Plans of the righteous
Pr 12:5 *See also* 1Ch 28:2; Ps 14:6;
Pr 14:22; 21:5; Isa 32:8; Ro 1:13; 15:24;
2Co 1:15–17

Plans and the role of counsellors
Pr 15:22 *See also* Ezr 4:4–5; Pr 20:18

Malicious plans
Against other people 1Sa 18:25 *See also*
1Sa 23:10; Est 8:3; Jer 49:30

Against God's servants Jer 18:18 *See also* Mt 22:15; Jn 12:10–11; Ac 9:23–24;
27:42–43

Human plans are subject to God's will
Jas 4:13–15; Ps 33:10 *See also* Ps 20:4;
140:8; 146:4; Pr 16:1–3,9; 19:21; 21:30;
Ecc 9:10; Isa 8:10; 19:3; Jer 19:7

See also
1115 God, purpose	2545 Christ,
of	opposition to
1120 God,	5817 conspiracies
repentance of	6510 salvation
1130 God,	6694 mystery
sovereignty	8124 guidance
1160 God,	8734 evil
unchangeable	9210 judgment,
1175 God, will of	God's

5918

pleasure

A gratifying emotion, used in Scripture to refer to both human and divine emotions. Believers are invited to take pleasure in every aspect of God's creation, while not allowing pleasure in the creation to overshadow pleasure in the Creator himself.

Divine pleasure

That which gives God pleasure
Ps 147:11; Jer 9:24 *See also* Ps 37:23; 149:4; Pr 11:20; 12:22; Mt 11:25–26 pp Lk 10:21; Mt 12:18; Isa 42:1; Eph 1:5,9

That which does not give God pleasure
Ps 5:4; Eze 18:23 *See also* Ps 51:16; 147:10; Isa 1:11; Eze 18:32; 33:11

Human pleasure

God provides everything for the enjoyment of life Ecc 8:15; 1Ti 6:17

Pleasure in human physical relationships SS 4:10 *See also* SS 1:2; 2:3; 7:6

Such pleasures are not satisfying in themselves Ecc 2:10–11 *See also* Ecc 2:1–2,24–25

True pleasure is found in the things of God Ps 16:11; 37:4; Ro 7:22 *See also* Ps 1:2; 35:9; 43:4; 111:2; 112:1; 119:16; Pr 10:23; 16:13; 18:2; Isa 55:2; Jer 6:10; 15:16

Pleasures may also be misleading or positively sinful Lk 8:14; Tit 3:3 *See also* Pr 1:22; 2:14; Ecc 7:4; Isa 66:3; 2Th 2:12; 1Ti 5:6; 2Ti 3:4; Heb 11:25; Jas 4:3; 2Pe 2:13–14

See also
1070 God, joy of	5846 enjoyment
4040 beauty	5874 happiness
5385 leisure	5939 satisfaction
5735 sexuality	8283 joy
5830 delight	8460 pleasing God
5844 emotions	8821 self-indulgence

5919

popularity

The state of being liked and admired. Scripture notes how the faithful preaching of the gospel will lead to hostility and unpopularity, not least on account of its demands on people and its proclamation of judgment.

The popularity of Jesus Christ during his early ministry
Crowds gathered round him Mk 2:2 *See also* Mk 3:10; 5:24; Lk 5:1; 8:19,45

Many people followed him Mt 4:25; 13:2; 15:30; Mk 1:33; 2:13; Lk 12:1

The popularity of David
1Sa 18:7; 21:11; 29:5; 2Sa 3:36

Popularity can result from seeking approval from human beings, rather than from God
Jn 12:43 *See also* Lk 6:26; Col 3:22

Actions carried out to gain popularity
2Sa 15:1–6 *Absalom's attempt to curry favour*; Ac 12:1–3 *Herod's arrest of Christians*; Ac 24:27 *Felix' imprisonment*

of Paul; Ac 25:9 *Festus' prosecution of Paul*

Causes of unpopularity for the gospel
Its appeal to those whom the world regards as weak and foolish
1Co 1:26–29; 2:6–7

Its insistence that people are sinful
Ro 7:7; 1Ti 5:20; 1Jn 1:8

Its challenge to vested interests
Jn 11:45–48 *the Pharisees' privileged position*; Ac 19:23–40 *the silversmith's trade*; Ac 5:17–41; 21:27–36

The high demands that the gospel makes of people Mk 10:17–23

The difficulty of some of Jesus Christ's sayings Jn 6:60–66

See also
2369 Christ, responses to	5923 public opinion
2426 gospel, responses	8116 discipleship, cost
5279 crowds	8460 pleasing God
5861 favour, human	8848 worldliness

5920

pretence

The deception of others by individuals, usually for the sake of their own interest, safety or pride. Scripture condemns such pretence and demands honesty from believers at every point.

Pretence practised by people for their own interests
The wearing of a disguise 1Ki 14:1–6 *See also* Ge 27:5–19,35–36; 29:16–25; 38:13–16; 2Sa 14:1–3

Other pretences Ge 42:7 *See also* Ge 34:13–15,25; 2Sa 13:1–11; 2Ki 10:18–19; Pr 13:7; Jer 9:6–9; Mt 22:15–22 pp Mk 12:13–17 pp Lk 20:20–26

Pretence practised by people for their own safety
The wearing of a disguise Jos 9:3–22 *See also* 1Sa 28:7–12; 1Ki 22:29–32 pp 2Ch 18:28–32

Other pretences 1Sa 21:10–13 *See also* 1Sa 19:11–17; Ps 34:1 Title; Ac 27:29–30

Examples of pretence
That practised by people because of their pride Pr 12:9 *See also* 2Ch 35:20–22; Pr 13:7; Mt 6:2,5,16; 23:27–28; 24:4–5 pp Mk 13:5–6 pp Lk 21:8

That practised by people in their approach to God Jer 3:10 *See also* Mt 15:7–8 pp Mk 7:6; Isa 29:13

That commanded by the LORD for his own purpose 1Ki 20:37–43

God's people must rid themselves of pretence
1Pe 2:1 *See also* Ps 119:29; Lk 12:1; 1Pe 2:21–22; Isa 53:9

The gospel demolishes pretence
2Co 10:5

See also
5173 outward appearance	6145 deceit
5318 fraud	7774 prophets, false
5347 injustice	8714 dishonesty
5625 witnesses, false	8746 false Christs
5837 disguise	8767 hypocrisy
5863 flattery	8776 lies

5921

privacy

Privacy to conduct conversations
Jer 37:17 *See also* 1Sa 18:22; 2Sa 3:27; Jer 40:15

Privacy to express emotions
Ge 43:30 *See also* Mt 14:9–13

Privacy to teach and to learn
Mt 17:19 pp Mk 9:28 *See also* Mt 24:3 pp Mk 13:3; Lk 10:23; Gal 2:2

Privacy to pray
Lk 9:18 *See also* Mt 6:5–6; 14:22–23 pp Mk 6:45–46; Mt 26:36 pp Mk 14:32 pp Lk 22:39–42; Lk 6:12

See also
2360 Christ, prayers of	8620 prayer, practicalities
5941 secrecy	

5922

prudence

Careful, wise discernment; the avoidance of rash behaviour or speech; the good management of talents and resources and the showing of tact and wisdom in relationships with other people.

The link between prudence and wisdom
Pr 8:12 *See also* Pr 1:1–6

Characteristics of prudence
Discernment Pr 14:15 *See also* Pr 12:16; 14:8; Lk 14:28–32

Foresight and caution Pr 22:3 *See also* Pr 23:1–3; Am 5:13

Wise use of knowledge Pr 12:23 *See also* Pr 14:18; Mt 7:6

Wise speech Pr 21:23 *See also* Ps 39:1; Jas 3:5–8

A teachable spirit Pr 15:5

Prudence involves good management of talents and resources
Good management commended
Pr 6:6–11 *See also* Ge 41:33–40; Pr 24:27; Mt 25:14–30

Warnings against unwise financial dealings Pr 22:26–27 *See also* Pr 6:1–5; Mt 5:25–26

Examples of prudent behaviour
In averting disaster 1Sa 25:14–35 *See also* Ge 32:3–21

In avoiding persecution Ac 14:5–7 *See also* Mt 12:14–16 pp Mk 3:6–7 *Jesus Christ*
Paul: Ac 9:23–25,29–30
Ac 12:17 *Peter*

Prudence in dealing with other people
Ge 26:26–31 *Abimelech makes a treaty with Isaac;* Ge 32:3–21 *Jacob prepares to meet Esau;* Ne 2:1–6 *Nehemiah petitions Artaxerxes;* Da 1:8–14 *Daniel's diplomacy in avoiding Nebuchadnezzar's food;* Da 2:10–16 *Daniel's wisdom and tact in the face of death;* Mt 22:15–22 *Jesus Christ's wisdom on the question of paying taxes to Caesar;* Ac 5:33–40 *Gamaliel's speech to the Sanhedrin*

See also
2081 Christ, wisdom	8226 discernment
5026 knowledge	8276 humility
5546 speech	8281 insight
5575 talk, idle	8361 wisdom
5913 negotiation	8755 folly
5948 shrewdness	

5923

public opinion

The concepts and views held by the majority of the population. Scripture urges personal, independent thinking, based on God's word, rather than adherence to popular beliefs.

God's people should not be concerned about public opinion
Ex 23:2 *See also* Job 31:33–34; Ecc 7:21–22

Examples of the impact of public opinion
1Sa 14:45 *Public opinion saved Jonathan's life;* 1Sa 15:24 *Public opinion led to Saul losing his kingdom;* Mt 27:15–26 *Public opinion led to Jesus Christ being crucified;* Ac 12:3 *Public opinion led to Peter being imprisoned.*

Public opinion is often contrary to divine standards
Hag 1:2–11 *See also* Nu 13:21–14:10; Dt 1:19–40; 1Sa 8:4–9; 1Ki 18:21; Jer 2:31–35; 26:7–16

Public opinion is sometimes in accord with divine standards
Dt 5:28–29 *also see* Jos 24:19–24

Public opinion of Jesus Christ was divided
Concerning his identity Mt 16:13–17 pp Mk 8:27–29 pp Lk 9:18–20 *See also* Jn 7:40–43

Concerning his teaching and ministry Lk 12:51; Jn 7:12,43; 9:16; 10:19

See also
2369 Christ, responses to	5279 crowds
	5919 popularity

5924

quarrelsomeness

The evil of quarrelling
Jas 4:1–2 *See also* Ex 21:18–19; Pr 10:12; 13:10; 15:18; 20:3; 21:9; 22:10; 26:20–21; 27:15–16; 30:33; 2Ti 2:23

Quarrelsomeness is unfitting for God's people
1Co 3:3; 1Ti 3:2–3 *See also* Pr 17:19;

Isa 58:4; Ro 13:12–14; 2Co 12:20; 1Ti 6:3–5; 2Ti 2:14,23–24

Examples of quarrelsomeness
1Co 1:10–12 *See also* Ge 13:7–8; 26:20–22; Ex 17:1–7 *NIV footnote at verse 7;* Nu 20:1–13 *NIV footnote at verse 13;* Dt 33:8; Ps 95:8 fn; 106:32; Mk 9:33–34 pp Lk 9:46; Lk 22:24; Php 4:2–3

See also
5789 anger	6221 rebellion
5834 disagreement	8828 spite
5964 temper	

5925

rashness

Acting without careful consideration of the possible consequences or risks.

Examples of rashness
Ge 34:25–31 *Jacob's sons*
Moses: Ex 2:11–12; Ac 7:24–25; Nu 20:8–12; Ps 106:32
Jos 8:14–17 *the king of Ai;* Jdg 11:30–31 *Jephthah;* 1Sa 14:24 *King Saul;* 2Sa 6:6 *Uzzah;* 2Sa 12:18 *fear for King David;* 1Ki 1:5 *King Adonijah;* 2Ki 5:20–21 *Gehazi;* 2Ki 10:16 *Jehu;* 2Ch 26:16–20 *King Uzziah;* 2Ch 35:21–22 *King Josiah;* Hab 1:6 *the Babylonians;* Mt 8:19–20 *a would-be disciple;* Mt 14:6–10 pp Mk 6:26 *King Herod*
Peter: Mt 26:33–34; Jn 18:10
Ac 19:36 *the Ephesian crowd;* Gal 1:6 *the Galatian Christians;* 2Ti 3:2–4 *a characteristic of the last days*

Warnings against rashness
Pr 14:16; Ecc 5:2 *See also* Pr 6:16–18; 12:18; 13:3; 19:2; 20:3,25; 21:5; 25:8; 29:20; Ecc 7:9; 8:3; Mt 5:22; Zep 3:7; Ac 19:35–36; 1Ti 5:22; 2Ti 3:1–5

Antidotes to rashness
Trust in the guiding presence of the Lord Isa 52:12

Appreciating the importance of considered actions Jas 1:19 *See also* Lk 14:28–33

See also
5575 talk, idle	5883 impatience
5802 care	5922 prudence
5803 carelessness	8361 wisdom
5810 complacency	8755 folly

5926

rebuke

A verbal expression of blame. Scripture gives examples of both divine and human rebuke. Sometimes God issues rebukes directly but more commonly he did so through the OT prophets. In the NT Jesus Christ and the apostles issue rebukes and teach the church how to address those who sin.

God has an absolute right to rebuke those who depart from his ways
He sometimes exercises this right directly Lev 26:23–24 *See also* Dt 28:20; Ne 9:30; Job 5:17;

Ps 39:11; 50:21; 94:12; 105:14; 119:21; Jer 2:19,30; Heb 8:8

His rebuke is powerful Job 26:11; Ps 80:16; 104:7; Isa 50:2

In the OT much rebuke came indirectly
Balaam's ass rebukes Balaam: Nu 22:28; 2Pe 2:16
1Sa 2:25 *Eli rebukes his sons;* 1Sa 15:12–26 *Samuel rebukes Saul;* 1Sa 24:5–7 *David rebukes his men;* 2Sa 12:1–12 *Nathan rebukes David;* 1Ki 18:18 *Elijah rebukes Ahab;* Ezr 10:9–11 *Ezra rebukes the men of Judah and Benjamin;* Isa 1:10–17 *Isaiah rebukes Judah and Jerusalem;* Hos 4:1–3 *Hosea rebukes the Israelites.*

Examples of Jesus Christ issuing rebukes
To evil spirits Mt 17:18 pp Mk 9:25 pp Lk 9:42 *See also* Lk 4:41

To his disciples Mk 8:33 pp Mt 16:23; Mk 16:14

Other examples of rebuke being administered in the NT
Inappropriate rebukes by Jesus Christ's disciples: Mt 16:22 pp Mk 8:32; Mt 19:13 pp Mk 10:13 pp Lk 18:15
Lk 3:19 *John the Baptist rebukes Herod;* Lk 23:40–41 *The repentant thief on the cross rebukes the other crucified criminal.*

Proverbs on the subject of rebuke
The importance of responding correctly to a rebuke Pr 1:23–26 *See also* Pr 6:23; 10:17; 12:1; 15:10,31–32; 17:10; 19:25; Ecc 7:5

Different responses to a rebuke Pr 9:7–8

Instructions to believers on giving and receiving rebuke
On giving a rebuke Lev 19:17 *See also* Mt 18:15; Lk 17:3; Gal 6:1; Col 1:28; 3:16; 1Ti 5:1 *advice on rebuking those who are older;* 1Ti 5:20 *disciplining elders;* 2Ti 3:16 *the usefulness of Scripture for rebuking;* 2Ti 4:2; Tit 1:9,13; 2:15; Jas 5:19–20

On receiving a rebuke Heb 12:5 *See also* 1Co 16:14

Believers thus follow the example of the Lord himself Heb 12:6 *See also* Pr 3:12; Rev 3:19

See also
1613 Scripture, purpose	6115 blame
5113 Peter, disciple	6163 faults
5193 tongue	7772 prophets
5777 admonition	8230 discipline
5900 laughter	8718 disobedience

5927

resentment

A feeling of bitterness towards someone, usually as a result of their actions or words. Resentment is possible against God or against other people.

5928

resentment, against God

Resentment against God or Jesus Christ is usually the consequence of a lack of faith or unbelief or as a response to adverse circumstances.

Israel's resentment against God expressed in constant grumbling
Resentment at hardships and lack of provisions Ex 15:24; 16:2–3; 17:3; Nu 20:2–5; 21:4–5

Resentment due to faithless fear Ex 14:10–11; Nu 14:2–3,36; Dt 1:27; Ps 106:25

God's response to Israel's resentment
Punishment Nu 11:1; 14:27–30,37; Ps 106:26–27; 1Co 10:10

Merciful provision Ex 16:4,8–9,11–12; Nu 17:5,10

Expressions of resentment
At suffering Job 10:1 See also Job 3:20–26; 7:11; 1Sa 1:10; Ps 77:1–3; 142:2; Jer 15:18

At apparently unjust treatment by God Ru 1:20–21 See also Job 23:2; Isa 40:27

At God's word Mk 6:18–19 See also 1Ki 20:42–43; 21:4; 2Ch 30:10; 36:16

The folly of resentment
Job 5:2 See also Ps 73:21–22; Pr 15:12; 19:3; La 3:39

The evil of resentment
Job 36:13 See also Jas 3:14–16; Jude 16

Resentment towards Jesus Christ
At his miracles Mt 13:54–58 pp Mk 6:1–6; Mt 21:15

At his teaching Mt 15:12; Jn 6:60–61

At his claims Jn 6:41–43

See also
2545 Christ,   5799 bitterness
    opposition to   8834 unbelief
5791 anger, human

5929

resentment, against people

A sinful, emotional response to others or to circumstances, frequently caused by envy or a sense of injustice.

Causes of resentment
Unwelcome instruction Pr 3:11–12 See also Pr 1:7; 5:12

Feelings of rejection Ge 4:2–5 See also Jdg 8:1; Mt 20:24

Feelings of injustice Ac 6:1 See also Ge 27:34; 50:15; Mt 20:10–11; Col 3:21

Hard circumstances 1Sa 30:6 See also 1Sa 22:2

Disappointment with leaders Jos 9:18

Resentment has no place in godly living
Eph 4:31; Php 2:14 See also Lev 19:18; Dt 15:10; 2Co 9:5; 2Ti 2:24; Heb 12:15; Jas 3:14–15; 5:9; 1Pe 4:9

Dealing with resentment
Not an easy task Pr 18:19

Through forgiveness Pr 17:9 See also Pr 19:11

Through God-given contentment Php 4:11 See also 1Ti 6:6–10; Heb 13:5

Through conciliation Jdg 8:1–3

See also
5265 complaints   6230 rejection
5347 injustice   8733 envy
5560 suffering   8765 grudge
5835 disappointment 8773 jealousy
5839 dissatisfaction

5931

resistance

Opposition to the demands of the state or other legitimate authorities. Individuals must not resist such demands unless they are contrary to God's requirements. God will himself judge unjust rulers. Christians should not resist the evil person but, following Jesus Christ's teaching and example, entrust themselves to God.

God should not be resisted
2Ch 35:21; Ac 7:51; 11:17; Ro 9:19

Individuals should not resist legitimate authorities
Civil authorities Ro 13:1–2 See also Dt 17:12–13; 1Sa 24:6; Tit 3:1–2; 1Pe 2:13–14,17

Religious authorities Heb 13:17 See also Ac 23:5

Parental authority Eph 6:1; Col 3:20; 2Ti 3:2

Resistance of unjust authorities
Resistance to human authorities is justified when they oppose God's requirements Ex 1:15–17 See also Ex 1:22–2:3; Da 3:13–18; 6:6–10; Ac 4:18–20; 5:27–29; Heb 11:23

God will enable Christians, unjustly brought before human authorities, to defend themselves Mk 13:11 pp Mt 10:19–20 pp Lk 12:11–12 See also Lk 21:14–15

God will vindicate those of his people who cannot resist unjust authorities Da 3:28–29 See also Ge 39:20–21; Ecc 8:12; Da 6:19–28

God will himself judge unjust rulers Hos 5:10 See also 1Ki 21:15–19; Isa 1:23–26; 3:11–15; 10:1–3; 59:14–20; Eze 22:27–31; Mic 7:2–4

Resisting evil
Christians should not resist the evil person Mt 5:38–41 See also Mt 5:43–48; 26:52; Lk 6:27–30; Ro 12:19–21

Christians should follow the teaching and example of Jesus Christ and entrust themselves to God 1Pe 2:20–23 See also Isa 53:7–9; 2Ti 4:14

See also
3284 Holy Spirit,   6251 temptation,
    resisting   resisting
4126 Satan,   8453 obedience
    resistance to 8482 spiritual
5215 authority   warfare
5257 civil authorities 8737 evil, responses
5829 defiance   to
6030 sin, avoidance 8785 opposition
6221 rebellion

5932

response

People are to respond to God in obedience, worship and repentance and in love for others. Lack of response from others can be a sign of death, disobedience and defiance.

The response of people to God
Obedience and love for others Ex 24:3; 1Jn 4:11 See also Ex 19:8; 24:7; 1Ch 29:6–9; Ro 15:7; Gal 2:2; Php 2:1–4; 1Jn 2:3–6; 3:16–17

Worship Ne 8:6; Ro 12:1 See also Ne 12:24; Da 4:34–37

Repentance 2Ki 22:18–20 pp 2Ch 34:26–28; Ac 2:37–38

Response to the preaching of the gospel Ac 16:14 See also Ac 16:31–34; 1Co 15:1–2; Eph 1:13; Col 1:6; 1Th 2:13

Inappropriate responses 2Ch 32:24–25 See also Da 4:24–32; Ro 1:21–23

The response of God to people
God responds to those who seek him in prayer Ps 102:17 See also Ps 3:4; 40:1–3; Isa 19:22; Da 10:12; Mt 7:7–11 pp Lk 11:9–13; Lk 11:5–8; Jn 14:13–14; 15:7; 16:24

Sometimes God appears not to respond to prayer Job 19:7; Ps 10:1; 13:1–2; 22:1–2; 42:9–10; Isa 1:15; 59:1–2

False gods do not respond to people
1Ki 18:26–29 See also Dt 4:28; Isa 44:18; Jer 10:5

The response of people to others
Believers should respond to others in kindness and forgiveness Eph 4:32 See also Ge 50:15,21; Mt 5:38–42 pp Lk 6:29–30

Harsh or aggressive responses 2Sa 19:43; Ro 12:19–21

Lack of response
As an indication of death 1Sa 4:20; 2Ki 4:31

As a sign of disobedience Jer 7:27–29 See also Pr 29:19; Jer 2:30; 17:23; 32:33

As a sign of defiance 2Ki 18:36 pp Isa 36:21

From not knowing what to say Job 32:15–16; 40:3–5; Mt 22:46; Lk 20:26

Jesus Christ made no response at his trial
Mt 27:14 pp Mk 15:5; Mk 14:61; 1Pe 2:22–23; Isa 53:9

5933

restlessness

A lack of peace, experienced physically, spiritually or mentally.

Causes of restlessness
Worry Ecc 5:12; Jer 49:23 *See also* Ge 41:8; Est 6:1; Pr 15:16; Da 2:1; 6:18–19

Illness Job 7:4–5 *See also* Ps 6:2–6; 32:3–4; 38:3–10; Isa 38:13–14

Lack of purpose Ecc 2:22–23 *See also* Ps 107:4–5

Uncompleted business Ru 3:18

Rebelliousness Ge 27:40

Demon-possession Mk 5:3–5 pp Lk 8:29; Mt 12:43 pp Lk 11:24

Sinfulness Isa 57:20–21; Jude 13 *See also* Job 3:17; Ps 59:15; Isa 48:22; Jer 14:10; 50:6; 1Ti 6:20–21; Jas 3:8; Rev 14:11

Restlessness as part of God's judgment against sin
Dt 28:65–67 *See also* Ge 4:11–14; Ps 107:40; 109:10; La 4:15; Am 8:12; Zec 10:2

Antidotes to restlessness
Trusting in God Ps 62:1; Isa 26:3; 30:15; Php 4:6 *See also* Ex 33:14; Ps 46:10; Isa 32:17; Jer 6:16; Mt 6:31–32

Trusting in Jesus Christ Mt 11:28–30

5934

restraint

The holding back of actions, emotions or forces, whether one's own or another's. God holds back the power and extent of evil in the world and restrains his anger. Believers are to show similar self-control in life, especially in speech.

Restraint as the holding back of actions
The example of Jesus Christ Mt 26:52–53

Other examples Ex 36:6 *God restrains the Israelites;* 1Sa 3:13 *Eli's failure to restrain his sons*

David spared Saul's life: 1Sa 24:1–22; 26:1–25

1Ki 1:6 *David's failure to restrain Adonijah;* Est 5:10 *Haman's self-restraint;* Jer 14:10 *Judah's lack of restraint;* 2Pe 2:16 *Balaam's donkey*

Restraint as the holding back of emotions
Jesus Christ's silence under suffering 1Pe 2:21–23 *See also* Mt 26:62–63 pp Mk 14:60–61; Mt 27:12–14 pp Mk 15:4–5

Restraint as the holding back of forces
God and the Red Sea Ex 14:21 *See also* Ex 15:8; Ps 78:13

Jesus Christ and the wind and the waves Mt 8:23–27 pp Mk 4:36–41 pp Lk 8:22–25

God restrains the power of evil
In the world Mk 13:20 pp Mt 24:22 *See also* 2Ki 19:28; Ps 76:10; 2Th 2:6–7; Rev 20:2

From the righteous Jn 17:15 *See also* 1Sa 25:39; 1Ch 4:10; Ps 19:13; 34:7; 141:3; Mt 6:13 pp Lk 11:4; Rev 7:3

God restrains his anger
Ps 78:38 *See also* Ex 34:6; Nu 14:18; Ne 9:17; Ps 74:11; 86:15; 103:8; 145:8; Isa 48:9; Joel 2:13; Jnh 4:2; 2Pe 3:9

Believers are to show restraint
In their speech Ps 141:3; Jas 1:26 *See also* Ps 39:1; Pr 13:3; 21:23; Jas 3:2–12; 1Pe 3:10; Ps 34:13

In their actions Ps 32:9 *See also* Ro 6:12

5935

riddles

Enigmatic or allegorical statements whose meaning must be searched for or revealed by God. They may be compared with other forms of obscure communication and contrasted with clear messages. Riddles are associated with proverbs and parables as means of teaching wisdom.

Samson's riddle
The riddle posed Jdg 14:5–14 *In the ancient world, riddles were popular at feasts and special occasions.*

The riddle solved Jdg 14:15–20

Further examples of riddles
Riddles and dreams Ge 37:5–9 *Joseph's dreams;* Ge 40:5–8 *dreams of Pharaoh's cupbearer and baker;* Ge 41:1–8 *Pharaoh's dreams;* Da 2:1–3 *Nebuchadnezzar's dream*

Four mysteries Pr 30:18–19

The eagles and the vine Eze 17:2–8, 11–15

The writing on the wall Da 5:5–9, 25–28

Riddles in the ministry of Jesus Christ
Jn 16:25 *See also* Jn 2:19 *the destruction of the temple;* Jn 16:16–19 *Jesus Christ predicts his death and resurrection in enigmatic form.*

The riddle of the number of the beast
Rev 13:18; 17:7–9

Riddles and prophetic communication
Riddles contrasted with clear messages Nu 12:6–8 *See also* Dt 34:10; 1Co 13:12; 1Pe 1:10–11

Messianic prophecies cast as riddles Ge 49:8–11; Isa 11:1; 53:2

Riddles as means of teaching wisdom
Riddles explained by the wise Ps 49:3–4 *See also* 1Ki 10:3 pp 2Ch 9:2; Da 5:12

Riddles and proverbs Pr 1:1–6 *See also* Pr 6:6–8; 26:1–2, 7–10

Riddles and parables Ps 78:2 *See also* Jdg 9:7–15; 2Sa 12:1–4; Isa 5:1–2; Jer 13:1–7; Mt 13:34–35

5936

riots

The hostile reactions of crowds who take the law into their own hands, frequently in opposition to a messenger of God.

Riotous responses to unpopular actions or teaching
Ge 19:4–11 *the hostility of the men of Sodom against Lot;* Jdg 6:30–31 *The men of Ophrah call for the death of Gideon;* Jer 26:8–11 *The people react to Jeremiah's message;* Lk 4:28–30 *The people of Nazareth expel Jesus Christ;* Ac 19:23–34 *the anger of the Ephesians over Paul;* 2Co 6:5

Riots stirred up intentionally
Mt 27:20–24 pp Mk 15:6–15; Ac 6:8–14; 17:5–9; 21:27–35

Riotous behaviour avoided or quelled
Mt 26:3–5 pp Mk 14:1–2; Ac 19:35–41; 24:5–12

5937

rivalry

Viewing other people as a threat to

oneself in the accomplishment of some aim, or being in active competition with others for recognition or achievement.

Examples of rivalry at a national level
Between Israel and Judah
1Ki 15:25–31 *This is typical of the conflict that existed for 80 years after the division of the kingdom.*

Within Israel 1Ki 16:21–22

Between Assyria and Judah
2Ch 32:13–22; Isa 37:10¬13 *Assyria claimed that behind the rivalry of the nations lay the rivalry of their gods. The* LORD *vindicated himself in answer to Hezekiah's prayer (see Isa 37:14–38).*

Examples of rivalry at an individual level
Between Esau and Jacob Ge 25:29–34; 27:41

Between Peninnah and Hannah 1Sa 1:6–7

Between Saul and David 1Sa 18:7–9 *See also* 1Sa 20:31

Between Absalom and David 2Sa 15:1–13

Between Rehoboam and Jeroboam 1Ki 12:26–27

Condemnation of rivalry at an individual level
By the Mosaic law Lev 18:18

By Jesus Christ Lk 9:46–48 pp Mt 18:1–4 pp Mk 9:34–37 *See also* Mt 20:20–24 pp Mk 10:35–41; Mt 23:8–11

By Paul 1Co 3:3–4 *See also* 1Co 1:12–13

Rivalry between individuals is overcome in Christ
Gal 3:26–28 *See also* Mk 10:42–45 pp Mt 20:25–28; Php 1:15–18

See also

5834 disagreement	8773 jealousy
7030 unity	8785 opposition

5938

sadness

Heaviness of heart brought about through disappointment, disillusionment, failure or sin. It can lead to depression of spirit, but this can be relieved.

Sadness caused by disappointment or disillusionment
Ne 2:1–3 *See also* Ge 40:6–7; 1Ki 21:4; Ecc 6:1–2; Isa 19:1–10; Mt 19:21–22 pp Mk 10:21–22 pp Lk 18:22–23; Mt 26:21–22; Lk 24:17

Sadness leading to depression of spirit
Nu 11:14–15 *See also* Jos 7:7; 1Ki 19:3–4; Ps 42:3–4; Jer 15:10

The relief of sadness
Ps 42:5–6 *See also* Pr 12:25; 15:30; 17:22; 31:6–7; Php 2:19

See also

4971 seasons of life	5874 happiness
5198 weeping	5952 sorrow
5354 invasions	5970 unhappiness
5805 comfort	6227 regret
5831 depression	7963 song
5835 disappointment	9250 woe

5939

satisfaction

A state of contentment or fulfilment. Only God brings true satisfaction and Scripture advocates that believers should cultivate satisfaction in every situation. Jesus Christ's atoning death was the unique means of satisfying the demands of the law.

Satisfaction of hunger and thirst
Literal Pr 6:30 *See also* Lev 26:26; Dt 14:29; 26:12; Job 38:39–41; Ps 22:26; 59:15; 105:40; 132:15; 147:14; Ecc 6:7; Jer 31:25; Hos 13:6; Joel 2:19; Mic 6:14

Metaphorical Ps 104:13 *See also* Job 38:25–27; Isa 66:11; Jer 46:10; 50:19

Satisfaction in one's work
Ecc 3:13 *See also* Ecc 2:24; 5:18

Satisfaction with one's situation
Heb 13:5 *See also* Lk 3:14; Php 4:10–13; 1Ti 6:6–8

Spiritual satisfaction
Found in God Ps 17:15 *See also* Ps 63:1–5; 81:13–16; 90:14; Pr 19:23; Isa 55:1–2; Lk 6:21; Jn 4:7–15

As a result of God's good provision Ps 145:16 *See also* Dt 8:10; 11:15; Ps 91:16; 107:8–9; Isa 58:9–11

Jesus Christ satisfies the hungry Mt 14:15–20 pp Mk 6:35–44 pp Lk 9:12–17 *See also* Mt 15:32–37 pp Mk 8:2–8

Dissatisfaction
Riches do not bring satisfaction Ecc 5:10 *See also* Est 5:10–13; Ecc 4:8; Eze 7:19; Lk 12:13–21; 1Ti 6:7–10; Heb 13:5

Death is never satisfied Pr 27:20 *See also* Pr 30:15–16; Hab 2:5

Jesus Christ's satisfaction of the demands of the law
2Co 5:21; Heb 7:26–28; 9:11–14,25–10:10,12–14; 1Pe 3:18

See also

1330 God, the provider	5580 thirst
	5628 work
2321 Christ as redeemer	5839 dissatisfaction
	5845 emptiness
2324 Christ as Saviour	5874 happiness
	8808 riches
3215 Holy Spirit & peace	8823 self-righteousness
5341 hunger	

5940

searching

Scripture points to several aspects of searching: the human search for satisfaction in the things of this

world, the human search for God and God's search for lost humanity.

The human search for security in the world
The search for material well-being Lk 12:16–19 *See also* Ge 42:1–3; Ru 3:1; Job 28:1–11; La 1:11

The search for comfort Ps 119:82 *See also* Ex 14:10–12; Nu 11:4–6; 1Ki 1:1–4

The search for success Ecc 2:1–11 *See also* 2Ch 18:9–12; Jer 45:5

The search for security Jos 9:22–24 *The Gibeonites resorted to deception in their eagerness to be secure. See also* Ex 16:2–3; Jdg 18:7; 2Ki 20:19 pp Isa 39:8

The search for love Pr 7:18 *See also* Jdg 14:1–3; 2Sa 13:1–14; 1Ki 11:1–3

The search for wisdom and understanding Ecc 8:16–17 *See also* Ecc 7:24–29

Instructions to search for God
Isa 55:6–7 *See also* 1Ch 28:9; 2Ch 7:14; Jer 29:13; Mt 7:7–8

God's search for lost humanity
Eze 34:11 *See also* Lk 15:1–10; 19:9–10

God searches a person's innermost being
Pr 20:27 *See also* 1Ch 28:9; Ps 139:1–4; Jer 17:10; Ro 8:27; Rev 2:23

See also

1020 God, all-knowing	6701 peace, search for
1220 God as shepherd	8160 seeking God
5935 riddles	8648 enquiring of God
5960 success	8778 materialism
6650 finding	

5941

secrecy

Behaving in a way designed to keep intentions or feelings hidden from others. In Scripture acting or speaking in secret is often linked with wrongdoing, although not in all cases. But nothing can be kept secret from God.

Secrecy as a cover for wrongdoing
Eph 5:11–12 *See also* Dt 13:6; 27:15,24; 2Sa 15:10 *Absalom's camp;* 2Ki 17:9 *high places, centres of pagan Canaanite worship;* Job 31:24–28; Ps 10:8; Pr 9:17; 17:23; Isa 65:4; Ac 6:11; 2Co 4:2; 2Th 2:7
Secret activity of false teachers: 2Pe 2:1; Jude 4

Secrecy associated with Satan and the black arts
Rev 2:24 *See also* Ex 7:11,22; 8:7,18; 2Th 2:7

Secrecy sometimes ensures safety
Jos 2:1 *See also* Jdg 3:15–26; 2Sa 21:12

Est 2:20 *See also* Jer 13:17; 38:16; Mk 7:24; Jn 7:2–10; 19:38

Nothing can be kept secret from God
Jer 23:24 *See also* 2Sa 12:7–12; Job 13:10; Ps 44:20–21; 90:8; 101:5; 139:1–15

God's truths are not made known in secret
Isa 45:19 *See also* Isa 48:16; Jn 18:20; Ac 26:26

Secrecy in worship
Mt 6:16–18 *See also* Mt 6:1–6

Secrets
Divine secrets Dt 29:29 *See also* Job 11:5–6; Eze 28:3; Mt 13:10–11 pp Mk 4:10–11; Lk 8:10; Isa 6:9; 1Co 2:7; 4:1

Human secrets Pr 11:13 *See also* Jdg 16:5–17; Ro 2:16; 1Co 14:24–25; Php 4:12

See also
1403 God, revelation	8115 discipleship
4155 divination	8209 commitment to
4185 sorcery and	Christ
magic	8354 trustworthi-
5146 covering	ness
5812 concealment	8622 worship
5837 disguise	8747 false gods
6694 mystery	

5942

security

Guaranteed safety, whether natural or spiritual, from danger or loss. Scripture stresses that ultimate security is to be found only in God himself.

The security of Israel
Their security was found in God himself Dt 33:27 *See also* Dt 33:26,28–29; Ezr 8:21–23; Jer 31:10–11

They were secure from danger and loss Isa 54:17 *See also* Eze 34:27–28

Their security was conditional upon obedience Ex 19:5 *See also* Dt 28:1–6,15–19

The security of believers is guaranteed
By the everlasting covenant 2Sa 23:5 *See also* Ro 8:29–30

In spiritual security in Jesus Christ Jn 10:28–29 *See also* Jn 17:12,15; Ro 8:35–39; Php 1:6; Heb 7:25

In the provision of needs Mt 6:33 *See also* Ps 23:1,4; Php 4:19; Heb 13:5–6; Ps 118:6–7

In safety from danger Ps 46:1 *See also* Ps 91:1–15; 121:3–5; Jude 24–25

In a sure hope 2Ti 1:12 *See also* Job 19:25–27; Heb 6:19; 1Pe 1:3–5

In prophecies of security Isa 2:4; 11:6–9; 65:21–25; Mic 4:3–4; Rev 21:4

Provision for the security of human beings
Protection for the weak Ru 2:8–9;

1Sa 11:1–6; 22:22–23; Ezr 6:6–7; Pr 3:29; Ac 23:10,23–24; Ro 13:3

Financial pledges Pr 6:1–5; 11:15; 17:18; 22:26–27; Lk 10:35; Phm 17–19

Pastoral protection Jn 21:16; Ac 20:28; Php 2:19–20; 1Pe 5:1–2

False security
In Israel Jer 22:21 *See also* Isa 28:17–18; 29:13–15; Da 11:21–24; Am 6:1; Lk 3:8; Jn 8:33

In the church Rev 3:17 *See also* Rev 2:4,14,20; 3:1–2

In professing Christians 1Co 10:12 *See also* Mt 7:21–23; 22:11–12; 25:41–46; Lk 18:9; Heb 10:26–27; 2Pe 2:21–22; 1Jn 1:8–10; Jude 4

In the world 1Th 5:3 *See also* Jdg 8:11; 18:7; 1Sa 24:3–4; Job 12:6; 18:14; 31:24; Pr 27:24; Zec 1:15; Lk 17:26–28; 1Ti 6:17

See also
1345 covenant	8106 assurance
4025 world, the	8215 confidence,
5466 promises	results
5480 protection	8767 hypocrisy
5490 refuge	8808 riches
5890 insecurity	9610 hope
8020 faith	

5943

self-deception

The state of individuals or nations who do not face up to their sin, their spiritual state or their future with any realism. It also describes those who presume upon their relationship with God or their own ability, or who have a misplaced trust in idols.

Those who are deceived over their sin
1Jn 1:8 *See also* Ps 36:1–4; Jer 2:34–35; 17:9–10; 1Co 6:9–10; 1Jn 1:10

Those who are deceived over their spiritual state
Rev 3:17 *See also* Mt 23:13–15,23–33 pp Lk 11:42–52; Jn 8:33–34,39–47; Jas 1:22–26

Those who are deceived concerning the future
Jas 4:13–16 *See also* Jer 5:31; 6:13–14 pp Jer 8:10–11; Jer 14:14–16; 23:16–18; Eze 13:7–9; Mic 3:5; Lk 12:16–20

Those who presume on their relationship with God
Jer 7:9–11 *See also* Dt 29:14–21; Jer 37:9–10; Mt 3:8–9 pp Lk 3:8; Mt 7:21–23 pp Lk 13:25–27; Mt 25:41–46; Jn 8:39–47

The value of circumcision Ro 2:17–29; 1Co 7:19; Php 3:2–7

Those who presume on their own ability
1Co 3:18–20 *See also* Pr 12:15; Jer 49:16 pp Ob 3–4; Mt 26:33–35 pp Mk 14:27–31 pp Lk 22:33–34 pp Jn 13:37–38; 2Co 10:12; Gal 6:3

Those who deceive themselves about the acceptability of their worship
Isa 1:11–17 *See also* Isa 58:2–7; Jer 7:2–8,21–29; Am 5:21–24; Mal 1:6–14; Mt 6:5,7

Those who have a misplaced trust in their own righteousness
Lk 16:15 *See also* Pr 30:12; Isa 65:2–5; Lk 18:9–14

Those who have a misplaced trust in idols
Ro 1:20–23 *See also* Isa 44:17–20

See also
5813 conceit	8776 lies
5920 pretence	8801 presumption
6145 deceit	8822 self-
7334 circumcision	justification
7774 prophets, false	8823 self-
8714 dishonesty	righteousness

5944

self-defence

The people of God in the OT defended themselves, but their ultimate defence was to be God himself. Paul, using the channels open to him, answered false charges against him in the church and before civil authorities. Christians are not to take personal revenge but, following Jesus Christ's example, are to entrust themselves to God.

Defence of one's property
Ex 22:2–3

Defence of one's person
The use of a stronghold Jdg 6:2; 1Sa 23:14; 2Sa 5:17

The strength of numbers Ecc 4:12

Trust in the Lord Da 3:16–18

The example of Jesus Christ in self-defence
1Pe 2:20–23 *See also* Isa 53:7; Mt 5:39 pp Lk 6:29; Mt 26:52; Jn 18:11; Ro 12:19; 2Ti 4:14

Defence against spiritual enemies
Ac 20:28; Eph 6:10–12 *See also* Eph 6:13–18

Self-defence in the face of false accusations
Paul to the Corinthian church 1Co 9:1–3; 2Co 12:17–19

Paul before the civil authorities Ac 21:39–22:1,3–21,30–23:5; 24:10; 25:6–8,13–16; 26:1–2; 2Ti 4:16

The promise of the help of the Holy Spirit Lk 12:11–12 pp Mt 10:19–20 pp Mk 13:11 *See also* Lk 21:14–15

See also
3281 Holy Spirit,	5495 revenge &
inspiration	retaliation
5209 armour	5605 warfare
5214 attack	8490 watchfulness
5291 defence	8822 self-
5315 fortifications	justification
5480 protection	

self-pity

Sorrow or despondency aroused by one's own suffering or misfortune. It can result from personal loss or suffering, hardship in God's service or the judgment of God. Its cure is to remember the goodness of God.

Examples of self-pity as a result of personal loss or suffering
The Israelites in the wilderness Ex 16:3 *See also* Ex 14:10–12; 17:3; Nu 11:4–6; 14:1–4; Dt 1:26–28; 1Co 10:10–11

Job Job 6:1–13; 10:1 *See also* Job 3:1–26; 12:1–6; 16:6–17:2; 30:9–31

Other examples Ge 27:34,38; 2Sa 15:30; 2Ki 20:2–3 pp Isa 38:2–3; Ps 10:1; 73:2–3,13–14; 74:1

Examples of self-pity as a result of hardship in the service of God
Moses Nu 11:11–15 *See also* Ex 5:22–23; 17:4

Elijah 1Ki 19:4 *See also* 1Ki 19:10,14

Jeremiah Jer 15:10 *See also* Jer 15:18; 20:7–10,14–18

Other examples Jer 45:3 *See also* Jnh 4:1–5

Examples of self-pity as a result of God's judgment
Ps 137:1–9; La 3:1–18; Rev 18:9–19 *The kings, merchants and sailors will be full of self-pity when they see the destruction of Babylon, because their opportunities for making wealth will be gone.*

People calling upon others to pity them
Job 19:21 *See also* Mk 9:22; Lk 17:13

Turning to God puts self-pity in its true perspective
Ps 43:5; 73:16–17 *See also* Ps 3:1–4; 13:1–6; 37:1–7; 73:23–28; 106:7; La 3:19–26,31–33; 2Co 1:5; 6:3–10; Jas 1:2–3; 1Pe 4:13

See also

1050 God, goodness of	5848 exaggeration
5265 complaints	5952 sorrow
5560 suffering	5970 unhappiness
	8821 self-indulgence

sensitivity

Deep feelings for others and sympathy for their needs, leading to appropriate action on their behalf. Spiritual sensitivity is the ability to perceive and respond to the call of God or the spiritual demands of the moment. Oversensitivity and lack of sensitivity are extremes to be avoided.

God's sensitivity to his people
Ex 3:7 *See also* Jdg 2:18; Isa 40:2; La 3:22; Hos 2:14; Lk 1:78

Sensitivity shown by Jesus Christ
Mt 12:20 *See also* Isa 42:3
Mt 23:37 pp Lk 13:34 *See also* Lk 7:12–13; 19:41; Jn 9:34–35; 11:33–35

Jesus Christ's own experience of temptation Heb 4:14–15 *See also* Heb 2:18

Sensitivity to others
Arises from an experience of God's compassion 2Co 1:3–4 *See also* Php 2:1

Believers urged to show sensitivity Ro 12:15 *See also* Isa 40:2; Eph 4:32; Col 3:12–13; 1Pe 3:8; Heb 13:3

Sensitivity to foreigners in Israel Ex 23:9 pp Ex 22:21 *See also* Lev 19:33–34

Sensitivity to those in distress Job 2:11–13 *See also* Mt 26:38–40 pp Mk 14:34–37; 2Co 7:5–7; Heb 10:33–34; Jas 1:27

Sensitivity to those weak in faith Ro 15:1 *See also* Ro 14:1–3,15; 1Co 8:9–12; 1Th 2:7

Sensitivity in speech Pr 15:23; 16:24; 25:11,15; 1Pe 3:15

Insensitivity to others
Examples of insensitivity to others Dt 28:53–57 *As a result of God's judgment, the most sensitive person will become insensitive even to the needs of family;* 1Sa 1:13–14 *Eli's insensitivity to Hannah;* Job 16:2 *the insensitivity of Job's "comforters";* Jnh 4:9–11 *Jonah's insensitivity to the people of Nineveh;* Mt 19:13 pp Mk 10:13 pp Lk 18:15 *the disciples' insensitivity towards children brought to Jesus Christ;* 1Co 11:20–21 *insensitivity to the needs of others;* Jas 2:2–4 *insensitivity towards poorer visitors to church*

The results of insensitivity Ps 69:20; Pr 25:17,20

Oversensitivity
Oversensitivity in the face of rejection 1Sa 25:11–13 *David's hasty reaction towards Nabal;* Lk 9:53–54 *James' and John's hasty reaction*

Oversensitivity of conscience Ro 14:2; 1Co 8:6–8

Spiritual sensitivity
Spiritual awareness 1Sa 3:8 *See also* Mt 24:32–34 pp Mk 13:28–29 pp Lk 21:29–30; Ac 16:9–10

Lack of spiritual sensitivity Eph 4:18–19 *See also* Pr 23:31–35; Ro 1:28–29; 1Ti 4:1–4 *Refusing to repent:* Isa 42:25; Jer 5:3 *Refusing to pay attention:* Eze 12:2; Zec 7:11–14

God hardens human hearts Ex 7:3; Ro 1:24–25

See also

1030 God, compassion	5966 tenderness
2015 Christ, compassion	6178 hardness of heart
5135 blindness, spiritual	8226 discernment
5805 comfort	8264 gentleness
5806 compassion	8281 insight
5963 sympathy	8319 perception, spiritual

shame

An uncomfortable feeling of guilt and humiliation, usually arising from sin or failure.

Shame is to be avoided
Ps 25:2 *See also* Ps 25:20; 31:1,17; 44:15; 119:31,80

Causes of shame
Military defeat 2Ki 19:26

Natural afflictions Lk 1:25 *See also* Ge 30:23; Isa 4:1; 54:4 *not only childlessness but widowhood*

Humiliation by an enemy Ps 69:19 *See also* Ps 69:6–7; 1Sa 11:2; 2Sa 10:4–5; Isa 3:17; Mk 12:4

Nakedness Rev 3:18 *See also* Ge 2:25; 3:10; 9:22–23; Isa 47:3; Eze 16:37; Rev 16:15

The sin of relations or associates Pr 14:34

Heathen gods as a source of shame
2Sa 2:10 *"Bosheth" means "shame". According to 1Ch 8:33 he was originally Ish-Baal, but the name "Baal", subsequently associated with a heathen god, was changed by later writers to "Bosheth". See also* Jer 3:24; 11:13; Hos 9:10

Shame as a divine judgment
Jer 23:40 *See also* Ps 44:9; Jer 46:24

Shame brought upon God's enemies Ps 6:10; 31:17; 35:26; 70:2; 71:13; 109:29; 129:5

Shame as guilt for sin
Ezr 9:6 *See also* Pr 6:32; Da 9:5–7; Ro 6:20–21

Shame may lead to repentance 1Co 6:5; 2Co 7:9–11; 2Th 3:14

Some people are without shame Jer 3:3; 6:15; Zep 3:5

Jesus Christ bore shame
Heb 12:2 *See also* Dt 21:23; Mt 27:39–44; Heb 6:6

The temptation of being ashamed of Jesus Christ and the cross Mk 8:38 pp Lk 9:26 *See also* Ro 1:16; Gal 6:14

Those who trust in God will not be put to shame
Ps 25:3 *See also* Ps 119:5–6; Isa 28:16; Ro 9:33; 10:11; 1Pe 2:6; 4:16

See also

5128 baldness	6172 guilt
5169 nakedness	6227 regret
5801 brokenness	6732 repentance
5836 disgrace	8451 mortification
5843 embarrassment	8754 fear
5879 humiliation	

shrewdness

Astuteness or craftiness in dealings with others, especially in using one's understanding and judgment to one's own advantage. Scripture commends it when it is seen in wise words and actions directed towards a worthy goal, but condemns it when it takes the form of cunning and deceitful scheming for sinful and selfish ends.

Shrewdness as astuteness

It is encouraged in believers Mt 10:16; Lk 16:8–9 *Jesus Christ explains the parable of the dishonest manager (Lk 16:1–7) and urges his disciples to be shrewd in their use of worldly wealth.*

Practical demonstrations of astuteness Mt 7:24–25 pp Lk 6:47–48 *See also* Pr 12:23; 14:15; 15:5; 18:15; Mt 24:45–47 pp Lk 12:42–44

Jesus Christ's wisdom in answering his enemies Mt 22:18–22 pp Mk 12:15–17 pp Lk 20:23–26 *on the matter of paying taxes to Caesar;* Mt 22:31–32 pp Mk 12:26–27 pp Lk 20:37–38 *on the question of the resurrection;* Jn 8:7 *regarding the woman caught in adultery*

Further examples of astuteness 1Sa 23:22–23 *David's shrewdness in fleeing from Saul;* 2Sa 14:1–3 *Joab's ruse to persuade David to call Absalom back from exile;* 1Ki 3:28 *Solomon's wise judgment;* 2Ch 11:23 *Rehoboam acts wisely to secure his kingdom;* Da 1:11–13 *Daniel avoids eating royal food and wine;* Mt 2:16 *Herod is outwitted by the Magi;* Mk 7:27–29 pp Mt 15:26–28 *the Syro-Phoenician woman's wise response*

Shrewdness as crafty and deceitful scheming

It demonstrates human sinfulness Ps 64:6 *See also* Ps 15:5; Ps 83:3; 140:1–3; Pr 7:10; Ac 13:10; Eph 4:14

It is condemned by God 2Sa 22:26–27 pp Ps 18:25–26 *God is shrewd in dealing with those who cleverly deceive others;* Job 5:12–13 *See also* Ps 94:11; Pr 6:12–15; 12:2; Isa 5:21; 44:24–25; 1Co 1:19; Isa 29:14; 1Co 3:19–20

Others dislike it Pr 14:17; 25:23

It is a characteristic of Satan 2Co 11:3 *See also* Ge 3:1; 2Co 2:11; 11:13–15

The craftiness of Jesus Christ's enemies Mt 22:15–17 pp Mk 12:13–15 pp Lk 20:20–22 *The Pharisees try to trap Jesus Christ over paying taxes;* Mt 26:3–4 pp Mk 14:1–2 pp Lk 22:1–2 *The religious leaders plot Jesus Christ's death.*

Further examples of crafty scheming Ge 25:31–33 *Jacob buys Esau's birthright;* Ge 27:15–16 *Isaac is tricked into blessing Jacob;* Ex 1:10 *Pharaoh plans to reduce the number of Israelites;* Jos 9:3–6 *The Gibeonites deceive Joshua;* 2Sa 13:3 *Jonadab plots for Amnon against Tamar;* Ne 6:2–13 *schemes against Nehemiah;* 2Co 12:16 *Paul sarcastically echoes the slander against him that he tricked people into giving him money.*

See also

2081 Christ, wisdom	6186 evil scheming
5407 merchants	8365 wisdom,
5922 prudence	human
6145 deceit	

---

shyness

Moses was shy of public speaking
Ex 4:10–15; 6:12,30

Shyness caused by youth and inexperience
Jeremiah Jer 1:6

Timothy 1Co 16:10–11; 1Ti 4:12; 2Ti 1:7

The woman subject to bleeding was shy of making herself known
Mk 5:25–28,33

Jesus Christ taught his disciples not to be shy of bearing witness to him
Mt 5:14–16

See also

5546 speech	5968 timidity
5746 youth	8202 boldness
5843 embarrassment	8219 courage
5887 inexperience	8754 fear
5947 shame	

---

silence

A stillness or absence of noise, often associated with the absence of life or people, but also associated with a sense of expectancy or reverence, especially in the presence of God. Scripture stresses that God is not silent, but has spoken his word to his creation. The silence of Jesus Christ before his accusers is seen as the fulfilment of OT prophecy.

The silence of God

His apparent silence in the face of sin Ps 50:21 *See also* Job 34:29; Isa 42:14; 57:11

God will not remain silent in the face of sin Ps 50:3 *See also* Isa 62:1; 65:6–7

Prayers that God will not be silent Ps 28:1 *See also* Ps 35:22; 39:12; 83:1; 109:1; Isa 64:12; Hab 1:13

God silences those who oppose him 1Sa 2:9 *See also* Ps 8:2; 63:11; 107:42; Isa 25:5; 47:5; Jer 47:5; 48:2; 51:55 *Jesus Christ's opponents were silenced by his miracles and wisdom:* Mt 22:34; Mk 3:4; Lk 20:26 Ac 4:14; Ro 3:19

The silence of Jesus Christ

It was foretold in the OT Isa 53:7 *See also* Ac 8:32

Its fulfilment in the NT Mt 26:63 pp Mk 14:61 *before the Sanhedrin;* Mt 27:14 pp Mk 15:4–5 pp Jn 19:9 *before Pilate;* Lk 23:9 *before Herod*

Jesus Christ commands silence as a sign of his authority
Mk 1:25–26 pp Lk 4:35 *Jesus Christ silenced evil spirits;* Mk 4:39 *Jesus Christ silenced the storm.*

There are times when it is appropriate for God's people to be silent
The silence of expecting God to act Jos 6:10 *See also* Ge 24:21; Ex 14:14–15; 2Ki 2:3,5; Rev 8:1

The silence anticipating the wisdom of another person Job 29:7–10,21

The silence of prudence Pr 10:19; Ecc 3:7 *See also* 1Sa 10:27; Job 13:5; 33:31–33; Pr 11:12; 17:28

The silence of suffering La 3:28 *See also* Ps 39:9

The silence of shame Eze 16:63

The silence of anger Ps 4:4 *The psalmist is warning against hasty action when angry.*

The silence of amazement at God's actions Lk 9:36; Ac 15:12

A tongues-speaker should be silent if no interpreter is present 1Co 14:28 *silence in the church;* 1Co 14:30 *A prophet should be silent if another receives a revelation.*

Christian women are sometimes exhorted to be silent 1Ti 2:11–12 *See also* 1Co 14:34–35; 1Pe 3:1–4

There are times when it is inappropriate for God's people to be silent
When there is good news to tell 2Ki 7:9; Ps 40:9

When much depends upon a person's words Est 4:14 *See also* Jer 4:19; 20:9; Ac 18:9–10

When God should be praised Ps 30:11–12 *See also* Lk 19:37–40

When sin is unconfessed Ps 32:3

When God's people feel they have a genuine complaint Ps 39:1–2 *See also* Job 7:11; 23:16–17

When prayer is urgently required Isa 62:6–7

God's people are sometimes brought to silence
Job 31:34 *Job fearing the crowd;* Eze 3:26 *Ezekiel as a judgment on Israel;* Mk 9:34 *the disciples when their pride was exposed;* Lk 1:20 *Zechariah because of his unbelief*

Silencing the wicked
Believers pray that the wicked will be silenced Ps 31:17–18; 1Pe 2:23 *See also* Ps 143:12

Believers so live that the wicked may be silenced Tit 2:8; 1Pe 2:15

False teachers must be silenced
Tit 1:10–11 *"the circumcision group" believed that in order to be saved it was necessary to be circumcised and keep the Jewish ceremonial law.*

Death is compared to silence
Ps 94:17; 115:17

See also

2585 Christ, trial	5784 amazement
5147 deafness	8328 quietness
5168 muteness	8333 reverence
5196 voice	8602 prayer
5546 speech	

5951

slander

False and malicious talk about others. It not only harms those against whom it is directed, but also brings ruin to those who propagate it.

Slander condemned

Slander is sinful Mk 7:21–23 pp Mt 15:19–20 See also Jer 9:4–6; Eze 22:9; Ro 1:29–31; 2Co 12:20; 2Ti 3:2–4

Slander is forbidden Lev 19:16 See also Ex 23:1; Pr 3:30; 10:18; 12:22; Eph 4:31; Col 3:8; Tit 2:3; 3:1–2; Jas 4:11; 1Pe 2:1

Slander is destructive Pr 16:27 See also Pr 11:9; 26:28; 30:10

Dealing with slander

Committing one's cause to God Ps 120:1–2 See also Ps 12:1–7; 31:14–20; 64:1–4; 69:6–21; 109:1–5

Maintaining one's integrity 1Pe 2:12 See also Ps 119:23; 1Pe 2:15; 3:9,15–17

Rejoicing in the Lord Mt 5:11–12 See also Ac 5:41

Not listening to slander 1Sa 24:9 See also Pr 17:4

Judgment upon slanderers

Pr 21:28 See also Dt 22:13–19; Pr 19:5,9; 21:28; Isa 29:20–21; 51:7–8; 1Co 6:9–10

Examples of slander

Jer 18:18 See also Ge 39:7–20; 1Ki 21:1–14 Naboth's vineyard; Ne 6:5–7; Ps 31:13; 35:15–16; 38:19–20; 41:5–9; Lk 23:2; Ac 6:13–14; 24:5–9; Ro 3:8; 3Jn 9–10

See also
5132 biting	8751 false witness
5575 talk, idle	8776 lies
5868 gossip	8843 unforgivable
5893 insults	sin

5952

sorrow

The human reponse to painful and distressing life situations, especially those involving loss.

Sorrow caused by the trials of life

Ps 90:10 See also Ps 13:1–2; 31:9; Ecc 1:18; 2:23; Jer 20:18

Sorrow caused by fulfilling God's will

1Pe 1:6 See also Mt 26:38; Php 2:27

Sorrow caused by illness

Isa 38:2–3 See also Ps 6:1–7

Sorrow caused by childlessness

1Sa 1:16

Sorrow caused by parting

Ac 20:37 See also Mt 17:23 the disciples' reaction to Jesus Christ predicting his death; Lk 22:45; Jn 16:6

Sorrow caused by bereavement

Ge 23:2; Jn 20:11 See also Ge 50:1; Dt 34:8; 2Sa 19:2; Lk 7:12–14; 8:52; Jn 11:33–35; Ac 8:2

Sorrow caused by national calamities

Ps 137:1 See also Isa 15:3; 22:4; Jer 22:10; 48:17; Eze 21:6; 27:30

God and sorrow

God is close to those who grieve Ps 34:18 See also Ps 10:14; Isa 53:4; Jn 11:35

God comforts the sorrowing Jer 31:13 See also Isa 35:10; La 3:32–33; Jn 16:20; 1Th 4:13–14; Rev 21:4

Sorrow in response to human sin

The result of sinning Ps 16:4 See also 1Sa 2:33

Grief over the failure of others 2Co 2:4–5 See also Ge 34:7; 1Sa 20:34; Ezr 10:6; Eze 9:4; Ro 9:2; 1Co 5:2

Grief over one's own shortcomings Mt 5:4 See also Mt 26:75; 2Co 7:9–11; Jas 4:9

Sorrow in response to God's judgment on human sin

La 1:5 See also Ne 1:4; Jer 8:21; 10:19; 13:17; 14:2; Eze 21:6,12; Am 5:16–17; 8:10; Mic 1:8; Zep 1:15; Zec 12:10; Mt 8:12; 24:30; Rev 1:7

Jesus Christ's sorrow in response to human sin

Lk 19:41–42

The promise of final deliverance from sorrow

Isa 35:10; Rev 21:4

See also
5198 weeping	5938 sadness
5419 mourning	5970 unhappiness
5795 bereavement	6227 regret
5799 bitterness	6732 repentance
5831 depression	8713 discourage-
5835 disappointment	ment

5953

stability

The state of being in a firm or unwavering situation, whether emotional, political or personal. Stability is an important element of a settled life before God.

Stability in the life of faith

Stability for the believer is based on God's unchanging nature Dt 32:4; Ps 103:19 See also 1Sa 2:2; 2Sa 22:32; Job 25:2; Ps 62:2; 89:2; 93:2; Isa 26:4; Mt 7:24–27

Stability gives resistance to spiritual assault 1Co 16:13; Col 1:22–23 See also Ps 20:7–8; 40:2; Pr 10:25; Mt 10:22; Ro 16:25; 1Co 15:58; 2Co 1:24; Gal 5:1; Php 1:27,27; Col 4:12; 1Th 3:8; 2Th 2:15; Heb 6:19; 10:23; Jas 1:23–25; 5:8; 2Pe 1:12

Stability depends upon firmness of faith Col 2:5–7 See also Ps 57:7; 119:5; Isa 26:3; Eph 3:17; Heb 3:14; 1Pe 5:9–10

Stability is an important aim of Christian ministry Eph 4:14 See also Col 1:28

Political stability

2Sa 7:16; Pr 29:4 See also 1Sa 13:13; 2Sa 5:12; 1Ki 2:12; Pr 16:12; Isa 16:5

See also
1160 God,	5891 instability
unchangeable	5902 maturity
1240 God, the Rock	8020 faith
4354 rock	8215 confidence,
5184 standing	results
5269 cornerstone	8418 endurance
5317 foundation	8459 perseverance

5954

strength

The quality of power and might which characterises God and his relationship to his creation. Human strength can lead to rebellion against God on account of a belief in human self-sufficiency.

5955

strength, divine

The strength of God is made known in creation and redemption and in his empowering of believers to live faithfully.

The revelation of the strength of God

In creation Ro 1:20 See also Job 38:4,8,12,31–33; Ps 68:34; 104:1–3,32; Isa 40:12,25–26; Jer 32:17; Heb 1:2–3

In providence Ps 135:6 See also Ps 46:8–10; 115:3; Isa 14:24; 40:23; Jer 27:5; Da 4:35; Ac 17:26; Eph 1:11

In redemption Ex 6:6; Eph 1:19–20 Deliverance from Egypt: Ex 3:19–20; Dt 4:34,37; Ps 77:13–15; Isa 51:10; Jer 32:21
Dt 3:24; 2Sa 22:2–3 pp Ps 18:1–2 David's song of praise for deliverance; Ps 98:1; Isa 59:1,16

In human weakness 2Co 12:9–10; 13:4 See also Jdg 7:4–7; 1Co 1:25–27; Heb 11:34

In judgment Rev 6:15–17 See also Ps 89:10; Isa 63:5–6; Eze 20:33–35; Hab 3:12; 2Th 1:8–9; 2Pe 3:7; Rev 6:12–14; 18:8

God's strength brings comfort to believers

Ps 27:1 See also Ps 27:3; Jn 10:28–29; Ro 8:28,31

See also
1105 God, power of	4354 rock
1265 hand of God	4654 horn
1315 God as	5443 pillars
redeemer	5454 power, God's
1325 God, the	saving
Creator	8357 weakness
3278 Holy Spirit,	
indwelling	

5956
strength, human

All human strength derives from God. Among non-believers, strength may become a source of arrogant self-confidence, the oppression of others or rebellion against God.

The strength of the ungodly
Physical prowess 1Sa 17:4–10 *See also* Nu 13:31–33

Intelligence 1Co 1:22 *The Gentile world relies on fallen reason rather than revelation. See also* Ac 17:19–21,32; Col 2:8

Political and military might Ps 20:7 *See also* Ge 10:8–12; Ps 33:16; Isa 31:1; 36:18–20

Prosperity Ps 49:6 *See also* Jer 49:4; Lk 12:18–19; 1Ti 6:17

The ultimate futility of human strength
1Co 1:25 *See also* 2Ch 32:7–8; Ps 49:17; 146:3; Ecc 5:15; Isa 30:1–3; Lk 12:20; 1Co 1:19–20; 2:6; 1Ti 6:7; Jas 1:11

Negative consequences of human strength
Arrogant self-confidence Ge 11:4 *See also* 1Sa 17:41–44; Ps 52:1 *Boasting betrays the source of people's confidence;* Isa 36:8–9; Da 4:30; Lk 18:9–12; Gal 6:13; Php 3:3

Violence and oppression Ps 52:7 *See also* Ge 4:23–24; Ex 1:11–14; 5:10–14; Jdg 6:2,6; Ps 37:14; 73:3–8; Isa 5:8; Jas 5:4–6

The physical strength of some godly men
2Sa 23:20 pp 1Ch 11:22 *Benaiah;* 1Ch 11:20–21 *Abishai;* Heb 11:32–34

See also

5441 philosophy	8203 character
5457 power, human	8219 courage
6121 boasting	8790 oppression
6221 rebellion	8794 persecution
8030 trust	8820 self-confidence

5957
strength, spiritual

In contrast to human strength, God is the source and supplier of all spiritual strength through which believers can do all that God asks.

God is the source of spiritual strength
God gives strength Eph 6:10 *See also* Jdg 16:3,6,18–20; Ps 68:35; Isa 40:29–31; Lk 24:49; Ac 1:8; Eph 3:16,20; 2Th 2:16–17; 1Ti 1:12; 2Ti 1:7

Strength comes from the promise of his presence Jos 1:9 *See also* Dt 31:7–8; Ps 119:28; Isa 41:10; Jer 1:8; Hag 2:4; 2Ti 4:17

Strength comes from the realisation of his grace 2Ti 2:1 *See also* Ac 20:32; 1Co 15:10; Heb 13:9

Strength comes through the Holy Spirit Zec 4:6–7 *See also* Jdg 14:6; Lk 4:14; Eph 3:7,16

Overcoming strength is often veiled in weakness 2Co 12:7–10 *See also* Ps 8:2; Ac 14:19–20; 2Co 4:8–12; Col 2:15; Heb 11:32–38

Aspects of spiritual strength
Profound dependence upon God 1Sa 17:45 *See also* Ps 27:1; 44:4–8; 118:6; Isa 40:29–31; Da 3:16–18; Mt 26:42; 1Co 1:31; Gal 6:14; Heb 13:6

Humility and gentleness Mt 11:29 *See also* Nu 12:3; 1Th 2:6–8,11–12

See also

2036 Christ, humility	6666 grace
2066 Christ, power of	7921 fellowship
2410 cross, the	8413 edification
3030 Holy Spirit, power	8482 spiritual warfare
3035 Holy Spirit, presence of	

5959
submission

A humble attitude where obedience is rendered within a relationship; whether it be to God, authorities or other people at work, in the church, in marriage or in the family.

God requires submission
From all people Ps 2:9–11 *See also* Job 22:21; 1Pe 5:6

From Christians especially Mt 6:9–10 *See also* Heb 12:9; Jas 4:7

The submission of Jesus Christ to his Father
Lk 22:42 pp Mt 26:39 pp Mk 14:36 *See also* Jn 5:19; 12:49–50; 1Co 15:27–28; Heb 5:7–8; 10:5–7

The submissive spirit required in the church
In believers' relationships with one another Eph 5:21 *See also* Php 2:5–7

To Jesus Christ Eph 5:24 *See also* Eph 1:22–23; Col 1:18 *As the body is subject to the head, so the church is subject to Christ.*

To the Scriptures Jos 1:7–8 *See also* Ps 119:133; Col 3:15; Jas 1:22–25; Rev 22:18–19

To church leaders Heb 13:17 *See also* Ro 13:1; 1Co 16:15–16; 1Th 5:12–13

In prophecy 1Co 14:32 *The implication is that individual prophecies must be submitted to the overall judgment of the church.*

The submission of all to civil government
Ro 13:1 *See also* Mt 22:21 pp Mk 12:17 pp Lk 20:25; Ro 13:2–7; Tit 3:1; 1Pe 2:13–14

Submission within other relationships
Of wives to husbands Eph 5:22–24 *See also* Col 3:18; Tit 2:4–5; 1Pe 3:1,5–6

Of children to parents Eph 6:1–3 *See also* Ex 20:12; Gal 4:2; Col 3:20

Of slaves to masters Eph 6:5–8 *See also* Col 3:22–24; Tit 2:9–10; 1Pe 2:18

Of young to old 1Pe 5:5 *See also* Lev 19:32

Reciprocal attitudes are commended to safeguard against abuse Eph 5:25–33; 6:4,9; 1Ti 2:1–2; 1Pe 5:1–4 *Those in authority have a responsibility to set an example.*

See also

2057 Christ, obedience	5734 relationships
	7446 slavery
5218 authority in home	7733 leaders
	8276 humility
5564 suffering of Christ	8342 servanthood
	8351 teachableness
5680 family	8453 obedience
5709 marriage, purpose	

5960
success

The achieving of objectives or personal fulfilment. For believers, success depends on faithfulness to God. Success can lead to dependence on one's own strength, instead of upon God.

Causes of success
The favour of God Ge 39:23; Jos 1:7; 2Ch 20:20; 26:5

Human skill Ecc 10:10

Many advisers Pr 15:22

Nothing can succeed that is against God
Pr 21:30 *See also* Ac 5:34–39

Examples of prayers for success
Ge 24:12–15 *success in personal relationships*
Success in battle: 1Ch 4:10; 2Ch 14:11
Ne 1:11 *success in personal achievement;*
Ac 4:18–31 *success in ministry*

The dangers of success
Pride 2Ch 25:19 *See also* 1Sa 2:3; Pr 11:2; 16:5; Mic 2:3

Boasting Eph 2:8 *See also* Jas 4:13–17; Ps 10:3–4; Isa 10:15–16

Forgetting God Dt 32:18 *See also* Dt 8:11–17; Jdg 3:7; 8:33–34

Lack of thankfulness Ro 1:21; 2Ti 3:2

See also

5597 victory, act of God	5889 ingratitude
	5917 plans
5607 warfare, examples	6121 boasting
	8441 goals
5776 achievement	8741 failure
5857 fame	8802 pride
5858 fat	

5961
superiority

A sense of being of greater importance or value in comparison with others, which can lead to arrogance and boasting.

Superiority is a characteristic of the wicked person
It is the product of human pride Pr 21:24; 3Jn 9 *See also* 2Ch 26:16;

Ps 73:3–9; Isa 3:16; 9:9–10; Ro 1:30;
2Ti 3:4; 2Pe 2:10

It involves looking down on others
1Sa 17:42; Lk 18:9–14 *See also*
Ge 16:4–5; 1Sa 10:27; 2Sa 6:16
pp 1Ch 15:29; Ps 31:18; 101:5; 123:3–4;
Pr 15:20; 23:22; Am 5:10

It gives rise to boasting Est 5:11; Ac 8:9
See also 1Ki 20:11; Isa 16:6; Eze 28:2;
Da 7:8; Hos 12:8; Mt 26:33–35; Jas 3:5;
Jude 16

**God hates superior behaviour
and will judge it**
Isa 2:11–12; 1Pe 5:5 *See also* 1Sa 2:3;
2Sa 22:28; Job 20:6–7; Pr 3:11; 16:5,18;
21:4; Isa 2:17; 10:12; 13:11,19; 23:9;
Jer 9:23–24; Ob 12–13; Mt 18:10;
Ro 11:17–18; 14:3,10; 1Co 1:20–25;
1Ti 3:6; 6:17; Rev 18:7–8

**The attitude of the godly is not
superior**
They demonstrate a proper humility
Ps 131:1; Php 2:3 *See also* Ro 12:16;
1Co 4:6–7; Php 2:4–8
Jesus Christ's advice to those who
aspire to greatness Mt 20:20–28
pp Mk 10:35–45 *See also* Jn 13:12–17

See also

2069 Christ, pre- eminence	8276 humility
5793 arrogance	8790 oppression
5813 conceit	8802 pride
5848 exaggeration	8815 ridicule
5888 inferiority	8824 self- righteousness
6121 boasting	

surprises

People are often taken unawares by
God's power, love and wisdom. The
actions of God and Jesus Christ are
often described as surprising those
who witnessed them.

God's actions surprise people
Surprise at the sudden appearance of
angels Lk 1:11–12 *See also* Da 8:16–17;
Lk 1:28–29; 2:9; Ac 10:3–4

Surprise deliverance Da 3:26–27;
Ac 5:19–24; 12:14–18; 28:6

Surprise at special births Lk 1:29–34
See also Ge 17:17; Lk 1:18

Surprise at the circumstances of Jesus
Christ's death Mt 27:54

Surprise at the coming of the Holy
Spirit Ac 2:6–7 *See also* Ac 10:45

Surprise at the change in people's lives
Ac 9:21 *See also* Mk 5:15 pp Lk 8:35

Surprise at the second coming
Mt 24:44 pp Lk 12:40 *See also* Mal 3:1;
Mt 24:50 pp Lk 12:46; Mt 25:6,13;
Mk 13:36; Lk 21:34; 1Th 5:4

Surprise at discernment
Mt 25:37–39,44; Lk 5:22; Jn 4:19;
Ac 5:5,11

Jesus Christ surprised people
Surprise at Jesus Christ's moral
requirements Mt 5:20 *See also* Mt 5:48;
18:21–22

Surprise at Jesus Christ's humility
Jn 13:6

**Surprise at Jesus Christ's control of
natural elements** Mt 8:27 pp Mk 4:41
pp Lk 8:25 *See also* Mt 14:25–26
pp Mk 6:49–50; Mt 21:20; Lk 5:9;
Jn 2:8–10; 6:14

Surprise at the company Jesus Christ
kept Mk 2:16 pp Mt 9:11 pp Lk 5:30 *See
also* Lk 7:39

Surprise at Jesus Christ's healings
Mk 7:37 *See also* Mt 9:6–8,33; 15:31;
Mk 5:42 pp Lk 8:56

Surprise at the requirements for entry
into the kingdom of heaven
Mt 19:13–15 pp Mk 10:13–16
pp Lk 18:15–17; Mt 19:24–25
pp Mk 10:23–26 pp Lk 18:25–26

Surprise at Jesus Christ's teaching
authority Mk 1:22 pp Lk 4:32 *See also*
Mt 7:28–29; 22:33; Mk 6:2–4
pp Mt 13:53–54; Mk 11:18; Jn 7:15

Surprise at the wisdom of Jesus Christ
Mt 22:22 pp Mk 12:17 pp Lk 20:26

Surprise at the expectations of Jesus
Christ Mt 14:16–17 pp Mk 6:37
pp Lk 9:13 pp Jn 6:7–9 *See also*
Mt 15:33–36 pp Mk 8:4–6

Surprise at Jesus Christ's authority in
the spiritual realm Mk 1:27 pp Lk 4:36
See also Mk 5:15–17 pp Mt 8:33–34
pp Lk 8:35–37

Surprise at Jesus Christ's disregard
for Jewish customs Lk 11:38 *See also*
Mk 7:5 pp Mt 15:2; Jn 4:27

Surprise at Jesus Christ's rejection of
religious words and actions
Mt 7:21–23; Lk 13:26–27

Surprise at Jesus Christ bringing back
the dead Lk 7:14–16 *See also* Mk 5:42
pp Lk 8:56

Surprise at the post-resurrection
appearance of Jesus Christ
Lk 24:36–37

**Jesus Christ is surprised by
people's reactions**
By the great faith of an unlikely person
Mt 8:10 pp Lk 7:9

By lack of faith among God's people
Mk 6:4–6 pp Mt 13:57–58

By the dullness of his followers
Mt 15:16 pp Mk 7:18 *See also*
Mt 16:9–11 pp Mk 8:17–18

By lack of spiritual insight Jn 14:9 *See
also* Jn 3:10

Surprises for believers
Surprise at suffering 1Pe 4:12 *See also*
1Jn 3:13

Surprise at divine revelation Lk 24:32
See also Ac 10:17; 11:15

Surprises caused by believers
Surprising courage Ac 4:13 *See also*
Da 3:13

Surprise at miracles Ac 3:11–12; 8:13;
14:11

Surprise at the teaching about Jesus
Christ Ac 13:12

See also

1416 miracles	5565 suffering of
2012 Christ,	believers
authority	5784 amazement
2081 Christ, wisdom	5932 response
2351 Christ, miracles	8164 spirituality
2565 Christ, second	8226 discernment
coming	8834 unbelief

sympathy

The ability to appreciate another's
condition, especially through shared
experience of pain or suffering. God
sympathises with his people in their
sufferings, as does Jesus Christ as the
sympathetic high priest.

God sympathises with his people
Ps 10:14; 2Co 1:3–4 *See also*
Ex 22:26–27; Dt 10:18; Jdg 2:18; Ps 9:9;
91:15; Isa 40:1–2; 66:13; Jer 8:18;
2Co 7:6

**God's apparent lack of sympathy
may be evidence of judgment**
Jer 16:5–6 *See also* Isa 27:11; 63:15

**Jesus Christ sympathises with
those in distress**
Jn 11:35; Heb 4:15 *See also* Mt 9:36;
Mk 1:41; Lk 7:34; Heb 2:14–18

**Sympathy as a characteristic of
friendship**
1Sa 20:34; Job 2:11 *See also* Jdg 11:37;
1Sa 20:41; 2Sa 10:2–3 pp 1Ch 19:2–3;
Job 16:4–5; 19:21; 29:16; 30:25;
Ecc 4:10; Da 1:9; Jn 11:18–19

**Sympathy expected from God's
people**
Ex 23:9; Ro 12:15; 1Pe 3:8 *See also*
Ex 22:21; Lev 19:33–34; Dt 10:19;
Isa 58:6–7; 2Co 1:4–7; 2:7; 11:29;
Php 1:7; 2:1; 4:14; Col 3:12;
1Th 2:11–12; 1Ti 5:9–10; Heb 10:34;
13:3

The absence of sympathy
Ps 69:20 *See also* Dt 15:7; Job 6:14–18;
Ps 31:11–12; 38:11; 41:9; Jer 20:10;
La 1:16; Ob 12; Mt 18:33

See also

3130 Holy Spirit,	5966 tenderness
Counsellor	6686 mercy
5560 suffering	8291 kindness
5691 friends, good	8292 love
5805 comfort	8414 encourage-
5806 compassion	ment
5946 sensitivity	

temper

A person's usual character or
temporary frame of mind. The term
often refers to a temporary state of
anger, which Scripture insists must
be brief and controlled.

**General references to good
temper**
Pr 16:32 *See also* Pr 15:1; Mt 5:39;
Eph 4:2; 1Ti 3:2–3; 2Ti 2:24; Jas 3:17

**People who kept their temper
under provocation**
Joseph Ge 50:15–21

David 2Sa 16:5–13

Jesus Christ Lk 23:33–34

Stephen Ac 7:59–60

General references to bad temper
Pr 14:17; Mt 5:22 See also Ps 37:8; Pr 19:11; Ecc 7:8–9; Gal 5:19–20

People who lost their temper
Cain Ge 4:5

King Saul 1Sa 20:30 See also 1Sa 18:8; 19:9–10

Nabal 1Sa 25:14–17

Naaman 2Ki 5:11–12

The people in the synagogue at Nazareth Lk 4:28–29

The Pharisees Lk 6:11

The people of Ephesus Ac 19:28–29

Others 1Ki 21:4; 2Ch 16:10; Est 3:5,6; Da 3:19; Am 1:11; Ac 7:57–58; 22:22–23

Christians must do all they can to control their temper
Pr 22:24–25; Eph 4:26–27 See also Php 4:8; Jas 1:19–20; 1Pe 1:13; 2Pe 1:5–7

God enables Christians to control their temper
Gal 5:16–18,22–23 See also Php 2:12–13; 2Ti 1:7

See also
5495 revenge & retaliation	5965 temperament
5789 anger	8203 character
5834 disagreement	8328 quietness
5934 restraint	8339 self-control

5965

temperament

A person's disposition, especially as shown in mental or emotional responses. God's people should be of an even temperament.

God's people should be of even temperament
Pr 16:32 See also Tit 2:1–14

Even temperament is a requirement for church leadership
1Ti 3:2–3 See also 1Ti 3:8–9,11; Tit 1:7–9

Examples of people who had an unpleasant temperament
Saul 1Sa 16:23 Violent mood swings and bad temper were signs of mental instability in Saul. See also 1Sa 16:14–16; 18:6–15; 20:4–7,24–33

Nabal the Carmelite 1Sa 25:17 See also 1Sa 25:2–11,36–38

See also
5789 anger	8203 character
5964 temper	8339 self-control
6023 sin, universality	8476 self-discipline
7632 Twelve, characters of	

5966

tenderness

Physically, the state of being soft or easily damaged. Tenderness in relationships is an expression of love and affection which, in the case of God, is often linked with compassion for his people.

Physical tenderness
Of new plant growth Eze 17:22 See also Dt 32:2; 2Ki 19:26; Isa 37:27; 53:2; Mt 24:32 pp Mk 13:28

Of meat Ge 18:7

Of the young and immature Pr 4:3 See also Ge 33:13; Isa 47:1

Tenderness in relationships
Human love and affection Ge 34:3 See also 2Sa 1:26; SS 7:10; Lk 15:20

God's tenderness Isa 40:1–2; Lk 1:78 See also Dt 32:10–14; Isa 30:18; 54:10; 63:15; Jer 31:3,20; Hos 2:14; 11:1–4; Zep 3:17

The tenderness of Jesus Christ Mk 10:16 See also Mt 9:36; 14:14; 23:37; Mk 1:41; Jn 11:33–36; 19:26–27

A mark of Christian behaviour Php 2:1–2 See also 1Co 4:21; Php 1:8; Col 3:12; 1Pe 3:8

See also
1030 God, compassion	2048 Christ, love of
1085 God, love of	5781 affection
2015 Christ, compassion	5806 compassion
2036 Christ, humility	5946 sensitivity
	8264 gentleness
	8292 love

5967

thrift

Saving by the careful use of resources. In general this is encouraged in Scripture, though the dangers of meanness, materialism and anxiety are recognised.

Encouragements to thrift
To provide for the future Pr 21:20 See also Pr 6:6–8; 10:5; 12:27; 27:23–27; 30:25

To provide for children Ps 17:14; Pr 13:22; 2Co 12:14

To provide for others Dt 14:28–29; 1Co 16:2; Eph 4:28

Examples of thrift
Noah Ge 6:21

Joseph Ge 41:48 See also Ge 41:28–36,53

Solomon 1Ki 9:17–19 pp 2Ch 8:4–6

Jehoshaphat 2Ch 17:12

Hezekiah 2Ch 32:27–29

The good wife Pr 31:13–16

Jesus Christ Jn 6:12–13

The dangers of thrift
Meanness Jn 12:4–6 pp Mt 26:8–9 pp Mk 14:4–5 See also Pr 3:27–28; 11:24,26; 23:6–8; 28:22; Ecc 5:13; 2Co 9:6

Materialism Lk 12:15 See also Ecc 4:8; Mic 6:14; Lk 12:16–21

Anxiety Lk 12:22–31 pp Mt 6:25–34

Lack of thrift
Lk 15:13 See also Pr 21:17,20; 23:20–21; 29:3; Lk 16:1

Spiritual thrift
Mt 6:19–21; Eph 5:15–16 See also Pr 10:14; 1Ti 6:19

The wicked store up judgment
Ro 2:5–6 See also Ro 2:7–10; Rev 18:6–7

See also
5475 property	5979 waste
5556 stewardship	8434 giving
5680 family	8778 materialism
5802 care	8808 riches
5907 miserliness	8849 worry
5922 prudence	9130 future, the

5968

timidity

People who were timid in accepting God's call
Moses Ex 3:11–14; 4:1–3,10–15; 6:12,30

Gideon Jdg 6:14–15,36–40

Saul 1Sa 9:21; 15:17

David 1Sa 18:18

Jeremiah Jer 1:6

Timothy's timidity
2Ti 1:7 See also 1Co 16:10–11

Paul's gentleness misunderstood as timidity
2Co 10:1

Christians are to encourage the timid
1Th 5:14 See also Ro 8:15; 2Ti 1:7

See also
5819 cowardice	8219 courage
5843 embarrassment	8264 gentleness
5888 inferiority	8276 humility
5947 shame	8305 meekness
5949 shyness	8308 modesty
8202 boldness	8754 fear

5969

treachery

A betrayal of trust by a close companion, often involving a preconceived plan. Those found guilty of treachery are severely punished by God.

Treachery against God
Zep 3:4 See also Lev 26:40; Isa 48:8; 59:13

Treachery against other people
2Sa 20:9–10 See also Jdg 16:19 Delilah against Samson; 1Sa 18:17 Saul against David; 2Sa 3:27 Joab against Abner; 2Sa 4:6 Recab and Baanah against Ish-Bosheth; 2Sa 11:15 David against Uriah; 2Sa 13:28–29 Absalom against Amnon; 1Ki 21:7–13 Jezebel against Naboth; Ne 6:2 Sanballat and Geshem against Nehemiah; Est 3:8 Haman against

Mordecai; Mt 26:49 pp Mk 14:45
pp Lk 22:47–48 *Judas against Jesus
Christ;* Ac 7:18–19 *Pharaoh against the
Israelites*

Punishment of the treacherous

Ac 1:18 *See also* 2Sa 18:14–15 *Absalom;*
1Ki 2:31–34 *Joab;* 2Ki 9:30–37 *Jezebel;*
Est 7:10 *Haman;* Ps 25:3; 59:5; Isa 33:1

Treachery in the purposes of God

Ac 4:27–28 *See also* Ge 50:20;
Jdg 9:22–24; 2Ki 9:23; 11:14
pp 2Ch 23:13

See also

1115 God, purpose	6145 deceit
of	6221 rebellion
5359 justice	8032 trust, lack of
5482 punishment	8830 suspicion
5494 revenge	8841 unfaithfulness
5589 trap	to people
5798 betrayal	9210 judgment,
5817 conspiracies	God's

5970

unhappiness

A sense of despondency or sadness,
often linked with disappointment or
loss. Scripture documents human
unhappiness in response to a
number of situations, while recalling
God's unhappiness over the folly
and rebelliousness of sinful
humanity.

Unhappiness as the result of adverse circumstances

Ps 90:10; Mt 26:21–22 pp Mk 14:19 *See
also* Ge 26:34–35; 40:6–7; 42:24;
1Sa 1:8,15; Ne 1:4; 2:1–3 *Artaxerxes
queries Nehemiah's sadness;* Job 17:7;
30:25; Ps 10:1; 13:2; 31:9; Pr 17:21,25;
Isa 19:8–10; Jer 45:3

Unhappiness caused by loss

2Sa 19:1; Jn 16:5–6 *Jesus Christ had just
foretold his departure. See also* Ge 38:12;
42:38; 48:7; 2Sa 1:26; 14:2; Joel 1:8;
Mt 17:23; Lk 22:45; 24:17; Jn 20:11
Mary weeps at Jesus Christ's tomb;
Ac 20:38; Php 2:27; 1Th 4:13

Unhappiness over failure and sin

Eze 9:4; 1Co 5:1–2 *See also* Nu 14:39;
Jdg 20:26; 21:6; 1Sa 2:33; Ne 8:9–11;
Ps 88:1–9; 107:39; La 1:4–5;
Eze 21:6–7; Zec 12:10; Mt 27:3 *Judas
seized with remorse at his betrayal of Jesus
Christ;* Lk 22:62; Ro 9:2; 2Co 2:2–5;
7:8–11

Unhappiness caused by a person's own selfishness

1Ti 6:10 *See also* 1Ki 21:4; Est 6:12;
Pr 23:29–30; Mt 19:22 pp Mk 10:22
pp Lk 18:23

Jesus Christ knew unhappiness

Jn 11:35 *See also* Mt 26:38 pp Mk 14:34;
Jn 11:33; 12:27; 13:21

God also grieves

Ge 6:6–7 *Prior to the flood;* Eph 4:30 *See
also* Ge 18:20; 1Sa 15:11,35; 2Sa 24:16;
Ps 78:40; Isa 63:10; Jer 42:10

God's remedy for unhappiness

La 3:32–33; 1Pe 1:6 *See also*

Ps 6:7–8; 10:14; 31:9; 116:1–6;
Isa 35:10; 51:11; 60:20; 61:1–3;
Jer 8:18; 31:12–13; Jn 16:20–22

See also

5198 weeping	5945 self-pity
5795 bereavement	5952 sorrow
5831 depression	8713 discourage-
5835 disappointment	ment
5839 dissatisfaction	9250 woe
5916 pessimism	9614 hope, results
5938 sadness	of absence

5971

uniqueness

The quality of being without an
equal. Scripture stresses the
uniqueness of God and of the
salvation that is available only from
him. Jesus Christ is the unique
mediator between God and
humanity.

The uniqueness of God

Isa 40:25 *See also* Ex 8:10; 1Sa 2:2;
Isa 40:18; 1Ti 1:17; 6:15–16; Jude 25

As a forgiver of sins Mk 2:7

The uniqueness of the Trinity

The three persons are distinct
All use the first person singular pronoun:
Jn 12:28; 17:4; Ac 13:2
1Co 12:4–6; Eph 4:4–5

God is one Dt 6:4 *See also* Isa 44:6;
45:5–6; Eph 4:6; Jas 2:9

There is plurality in the Godhead
Ge 1:26–27; 3:22; 11:5–7; Isa 6:8;
Mt 28:20; 2Co 13:14

The uniqueness of Jesus Christ

As God's Son Jn 3:16 *NIV footnote "only
begotten" indicates that Jesus Christ is the
unique Son of God, in origin, eternity and
nature. See also* Jn 1:18; Col 1:15;
Heb 1:1–3,8,9

**As the mediator between God and
humanity** 1Ti 2:5 *See also* Jn 1:14;
Heb 8:6

As the sacrifice for sin Heb 7:27 *See
also* Ro 6:10; Heb 9:12; 10:10,14,18

As the Saviour Ac 4:12; Jn 14:6 *See also*
1Jn 5:12

As the foundation 1Co 3:11

The uniqueness of Scripture

Jude 3 *See also* 2Ti 3:15–16; Heb 1:1–2;
Rev 22:18–19

Each human being is unique

Ps 139:13–16 *See also* Jer 1:5; Gal 1:15

Each believer is unique

Rev 2:17 *See also* Isa 43:1; Jn 10:3;
1Co 8:3; 12:21; Gal 4:9; 2Ti 2:19

See also

1060 God, greatness	2324 Christ as
of	Saviour
1165 God, unique	6684 mediator
1510 Trinity, the	8799 polytheism
1651 numbers, 1–2	
2033 Christ,	
humanity	

5972

unkindness

Unsympathetic or cruel behaviour. It
is contrary to God's character and is
condemned in Scripture.

Unkindness condemned

In general terms Pr 11:17 *See also*
Pr 17:5; 25:20; Eph 4:31–32

Treatment of enemies Mt 5:43–44 *See
also* Ex 23:4–5; Pr 25:21;
Lk 6:27–28,35; Ro 12:14

Treatment of the poor Pr 14:31;
1Jn 3:17 *See also* Dt 15:7; 24:14;
Pr 21:13; Isa 3:15; 10:1–2; Eze 22:29;
Zec 7:10

Treatment of animals Pr 12:10 *See also*
Lev 22:28; Dt 22:6; 25:4; Lk 13:15; 14:5

Inhospitality condemned 1Pe 4:9 *See
also* Dt 23:4; Mt 25:41–43; Lk 9:52–53;
Heb 13:2; 3Jn 10

Some examples of unkindness

1Sa 11:2; 2Sa 12:4; 2Ki 25:7; Ne 5:5–6;
Job 24:2–12; Ps 35:15; 69:20–21;
109:16; Eze 34:4; Am 1:11; 5:11;
Jas 2:15–16

God's kindness as a model for believers

Ru 2:20; Ezr 9:9; Isa 63:7; Ac 14:17;
Ro 2:4; 11:22; Eph 2:7

See also

4603 animals	8727 enemies
5584 torture	8783 neglect
5823 cruelty	8790 oppression
8291 kindness	

5973

unreliability

The quality of a person or thing that
cannot be trusted or relied upon.
Scripture notes the unreliability of
human nature, while stressing the
total reliability of God.

Human nature is unreliable

Ps 78:57 *See also* Isa 49:15; Hos 6:4;
2Co 1:9

Examples of unreliable people

Ge 40:23 *the chief cupbearer;*
1Sa 13:13–14 *King Saul;* Hos 5:13 *Israel
Jesus Christ's disciples:* Mt 26:40
pp Mk 14:37 pp Lk 22:45; Mt 26:56
pp Mk 14:50

Unreliable people are not to be trusted
Pr 25:19 *See also* Ps 146:3–4; Isa 2:22

False gods are unreliable

Isa 45:20 *See also* Dt 4:28; Ps 115:4–8;
Isa 40:20; Jer 10:5,10,14–15; 51:17–18;
Da 5:23; Hab 2:18; Mt 24:5 pp Mk 13:6
pp Lk 21:8

Human wisdom is unreliable

1Co 3:19–20 *See also* Jdg 20:36;
Job 5:13; Isa 30:12–13; 59:4;
Eze 28:6–7; Ro 1:22; 1Co 1:19–21,25;
Col 2:23

Military strength is unreliable

Ps 44:6 *See also* 1Sa 17:45; Ps 33:16–17;

Isa 31:1; 36:4–6; Eze 33:26; Hos 1:7;
Hag 2:22; Mt 26:52

Material wealth is unreliable
Pr 11:28 *See also* Ps 62:10; Jer 49:4;
Hag 1:9; 2:16–17; Zec 9:3–4; Mt 6:19;
13:22 pp Mk 4:19 pp Lk 8:14;
1Ti 6:9–10

The consequences of unreliability
Unreliable actions let God down
Hos 11:2–3 *See also* Isa 5:7; Jer 2:21;
Mt 26:34 pp Mk 14:30 pp Lk 22:34;
Lk 16:10–12

Unreliability leads to disappointment
Jas 1:7–8 *See also* Mt 21:30,43;
Lk 16:10–12; Ac 15:37–38

Trust in unreliable things
Leads to self-delusion Isa 44:20 *See
also* Isa 47:10; Lk 12:20; Rev 3:17

Leads to judgment Jer 17:5 *See also*
Ps 49:13–14; 52:5–7; Isa 20:5;
Jer 46:25; Am 6:1,7

Unreliable people are judged
Eze 13:9 *See also* Isa 20:6; Mal 2:7–9;
Mt 23:38; 25:26–27 pp Lk 19:22–23

God is never unreliable
Nu 23:19 *See also* 1Ki 8:56; Ps 71:6;
Jn 8:26; 2Co 1:20; Tit 1:2; Heb 6:18;
1Jn 4:13–16

See also

5020 human nature	8357 weakness
5798 betrayal	8361 wisdom
6145 deceit	8755 folly
8030 trust	8768 idolatry
8331 reliability	8778 materialism
8354 trustworthiness	8839 unfaithfulness

5974

value

God places inestimable value on the
human soul. He paid the redemption
price of the blood of his son Jesus
Christ to purchase his own people
who are precious to him. Everything
that achieves or maintains this
relationship is to be valued.

Redemptive values of people, animals and property
Lev 27:1–25 *These are the values for
recovering or buying back what has been
dedicated to God. They were designed to
teach the Israelites the great cost of
redemption.*

The value of Jesus Christ
The betrayal price Mt 26:14–15
pp Mk 14:10–11 pp Lk 22:3–6 *See also*
Jer 32:6–9; Zec 11:12–13; Mt 27:9

His true value Php 3:8 *See also*
Mt 13:44–46; 1Pe 2:4–7

The value of people
They are made in the image of God
Ge 1:26–27 *Being made in God's image
gives humanity intrinsic worth and dignity.
See also* Ps 8:3–8; Col 3:10; Heb 2:6–8

The inestimable value of a human soul
Ps 49:7–8 *See also* Mt 16:26 pp Mk 8:37

The redemptive price of a soul
1Pe 1:18–19 *See also* Mt 20:28

---

pp Mk 10:45; Ac 20:28; 1Co 6:20; 7:23;
Rev 5:9

The value of God's people to him
1Pe 2:4 *See also* Ps 116:15; Isa 43:3–4;
Mt 6:26 pp Lk 12:24; Mt 10:31
pp Lk 12:7; Mt 12:12

The value of Christian life and service
Godly character 1Ti 4:8 *See also* 1Ti 6:6;
1Pe 3:4

Spiritual wisdom Job 28:12–19;
Pr 3:13–15; 8:11,19; 16:16; Jas 3:13–17

Steadfast faith 1Pe 1:7 *See also*
Job 23:10

Faithful service Dt 15:18; Mt 10:10
pp Lk 10:7

Good leadership 2Sa 18:3; 1Ti 5:17–18

Friendship 2Sa 1:26 *See also* 1Th 2:8;
Phm 12,16

A good marriage Pr 31:10 *See also*
Pr 12:4; 18:22

See also

2321 Christ as redeemer	6720 redemption
2378 kingdom of God, characteristics	8020 faith
	8265 godliness
	8296 love, nature of
5061 sanctity of life	8361 wisdom
5412 money	8779 materialism
5776 achievement	8808 riches

5975

violence

Unrestrained physical or verbal force
designed to hurt others, or to gain
mastery over them.

The world is full of violence
Ge 6:11–13; Job 24:2–4; Ps 55:9; 74:20;
Pr 13:2; Isa 59:1–8; Eze 7:23; Mic 2:1–2

God hates violence
Ps 11:5; 139:19; Jer 22:3; Eze 45:9;
Mal 2:16

Jesus Christ was not violent
Isa 42:1–3; 53:9; 1Pe 2:23

Christians should not be violent
Gal 5:19–21; Eph 4:2,31; Php 4:5

Christian leaders should not be violent
1Ch 22:8–9; 1Ti 3:3; 2Ti 2:24; Tit 1:7

God helps the victims of violence
2Sa 22:3,49; Ps 18:48; 72:14; 140:1–4;
Mt 2:13; Lk 22:50–51

Christians should help the victims of violence
Ge 14:14; 2Ch 28:9–15; Jer 38:9–12;
Lk 10:30,33; Ac 23:15–16

See also

1075 God, justice of	5568 suffering,
5025 killing	causes
5040 murder	5584 torture
5214 attack	5605 warfare
5282 crushing	5823 cruelty
5311 extortion	8734 evil
5346 injury	

5976

visiting

Calling to see a person or place.
Examples include pilgrims to
Jerusalem and those visiting family
and friends. Visiting those in need,
especially the sick and bereaved, is
particularly important. Individuals
and churches are encouraged and
strengthened by visits from other
believers.

Visiting particular people or places
Pilgrims visit Jerusalem Lk 24:18 *See
also* Lk 2:41; Jn 5:1; 12:12; Ac 2:9–11;
8:27–28

Visiting family, friends, etc Lk 11:6
*Moses, raised in Pharaoh's palace, visits
his fellow Israelites:* Ex 2:11; Ac 7:23
Jdg 15:1
*Jesus Christ often visited the home of Mary
and Martha in Bethany:* Mt 21:17;
Mk 11:11; Lk 10:38–42; Jn 11:20
Jn 4:43–46 *Jesus Christ visits his home
region of Galilee.*

Visits from foreign dignitaries 2Ch 9:1
pp 1Ki 10:1–2 *See also* 2Ch 18:2
pp 1Ki 22:2; 2Ki 20:12–13
pp Isa 39:1–2; Jer 27:3

Further examples Ge 34:1; 42:2;
Ac 7:12–15; Nu 22:7–8; 1Sa 28:8

Visiting those in need
Job 2:11; Mt 25:36 *See also* Job 42:11;
Mt 25:39–40

The sick 2Ki 8:29 pp 2Ch 22:6;
2Ki 13:14; Jas 5:14

The bereaved Ge 37:34–35; 1Ch 7:22;
Jn 11:19,45

Visiting fellow believers
Official visits Ac 15:2 *See also* Ac 11:30;
15:22; Gal 2:1–2

Visiting churches Ac 9:32 *See also*
Ac 11:27; 1Co 16:10; 2Co 8:22–24;
Gal 2:11; Php 2:19; 2Jn 12

Paul visits the churches Ac 15:36–41
See also Ac 19:21; Ro 15:23–29;
1Co 16:5–6; 2Co 1:15–16; 2:1; 12:14;
1Th 2:1

Visiting individuals Tit 3:12 *See also*
Ac 28:15; Php 2:25; 3Jn 13–14

Visiting prisoners 2Ti 1:16–17 *See also*
2Ti 4:9–13; Phm 12–13; Heb 13:3

Divine visitors
Angels Heb 13:2 *See also* Ge 18:1–2;
19:1; Jdg 6:11–12; 13:3–22;
Lk 1:11,26–28

The day of God's visitation 1Pe 2:12 *See
also* Isa 10:3; Jer 46:21; Mic 7:4;
Lk 19:44

See also

4110 angels	5795 bereavement
4140 angel of the Lord	5963 sympathy
	7354 feasts and
5461 prisoners	festivals
5590 travel	7739 missionaries
5680 family	7921 fellowship
5699 guests	8445 hospitality

waiting

Being in readiness for service or for some future appointment or event. Wild animals and the wicked lie in wait to ambush the unsuspecting; servants wait on their masters; believers and the whole creation wait for their renewal by God. God, too, waits for sinners to repent.

Waiting for future events
Waiting to see what happens Ru 3:18; Jnh 4:5; Ac 28:6

Waiting for a period of time Ge 8:10–12; Lev 12:4–5; Eze 44:26

Waiting for people
Waiting to meet others Ex 5:20; 7:15; 2Sa 16:1; 1Ki 20:38

Waiting to be joined by others 1Co 11:33 *See also* Ex 24:14; Ac 17:16; 20:5–6; 1Co 11:21

Waiting for word from others Job 29:21–23 *See also* 1Sa 10:8; 20:19; 2Sa 15:28; Lk 3:15

Waiting for God
For God's instruction Nu 9:8; Ps 106:13; Hab 2:1

For God's promise Heb 6:15 *See also* Hab 2:3; Lk 24:49; Ac 1:4–5; Heb 11:13

For God's kingdom Lk 2:25; Mk 15:43 pp Lk 23:51

For vindication from God Hab 3:16 *See also* Ps 119:84; Isa 51:5; Zep 3:8; Rev 6:11

For Jesus Christ's return Jas 5:7–8 *See also* Lk 12:36; 1Co 1:7; 1Th 1:10; Heb 9:28

Believers and creation wait for renewal Ro 8:19–21,23 *See also* Isa 65:17; Ro 8:11; 1Co 15:42–43; 2Pe 3:13; 1Jn 3:2; Rev 21:1

Lying in wait to attack
Preparing for military assault Jos 8:9; Jdg 9:32–33

Criminals wait for victims Pr 1:11–13 *See also* Dt 19:11; Ps 10:8; Pr 23:27–28; 24:15; Jer 5:26

The wicked lie in wait for God's servants Ps 37:32 *See also* Jdg 16:2 *The Philistines lay in wait for Samson;* Ps 59:3; 71:10–11; 119:95; Jer 20:10 *Jeremiah's enemies were looking for an opportunity against him;* Ac 23:21 *Some Jews were waiting to kill Paul.*

Jesus Christ's enemies waited to trap him Lk 11:53–54; Jn 7:1 *See also* Mt 12:10 pp Mk 3:2; Mk 11:18 pp Lk 19:47; Mk 12:13; Lk 20:20

Animals lie in wait for prey Job 38:40; Ps 10:9; Jer 5:6; La 3:10

Waiting as delaying
Jos 18:3 *See also* Jdg 18:9; 2Ki 7:9; 9:3; Ecc 5:4; Jer 4:6; Ac 22:16

Waiting as a servant
Mt 8:15 pp Mk 1:31 pp Lk 4:39 *See also* 1Ki 1:4; Lk 12:37; 17:8; Ac 6:2

God waits for sinners to repent
2Pe 3:9 *See also* Lk 15:20; Ro 2:4; 1Ti 1:16; 1Pe 3:20

See also

2565 Christ, second coming	8318 patience
4924 delay	8329 readiness
5184 standing	8490 watchfulness
5877 hesitation	8613 prayer, persistence
6510 salvation	8678 waiting on God
6723 redemption, NT	9105 last things

warning

Telling someone of coming disaster or danger or of the consequences of their action or attitude. Scripture gives strong warnings against idolatry, sin and false teaching.

Warnings of coming disaster or danger
Ge 41:28–32 *See also* Ge 19:12–13; Est 4:12–17; Mt 24:6–7 pp Mk 13:7–8 pp Lk 21:9–11; Mt 24:15–22 pp Mk 13:14–20 pp Lk 21:20–24; Ac 21:10–11; 23:16–21

Warnings against idolatry
Dt 6:14–15; 8:19 *See also* Dt 7:25; 11:16; 29:18–21; Jer 7:9–15; 25:4–11; 1Co 10:7–11; 1Jn 5:21

Warnings against sin
2Ch 19:10; Mt 5:29–30 *See also* Ge 2:16–17; Isa 13:11; Jer 21:14; Eze 3:17–19; 33:7–9; Jn 5:14; Ac 2:40; Ro 2:8–9; 6:23; 1Co 6:9–10; 2Th 1:8–9

Warnings against false teaching
Gal 1:7–8; 2Pe 3:17 *See also* Mt 10:32–33 pp Lk 12:8–10; Mt 16:6; Lk 12:1; Php 3:2; Col 2:8; Tit 1:10–11; 2Jn 7–11; Jude 4

See also

5135 blindness, spiritual	8706 apostasy, warnings
5482 punishment	8749 false teachers
5611 watchman	8750 false teachings
5777 admonition	8768 idolatry
6020 sin	9210 judgment, God's
6732 repentance	
8489 urgency	

waste

The misuse and squandering of resources. God condemns the waste of resources which he provides, especially spiritual provisions such as grace and opportunity. Sometimes extravagance in God's service is mistaken for waste.

Waste of material resources
Squandering is folly Lk 15:13–16 *See also* Pr 21:20; 29:3; Lk 16:1; Jas 5:1–6; 1Pe 4:3–5

As a consequence of yielding to temptation Pr 29:3 *See also* Pr 5:7–14

Jesus Christ avoids waste Jn 6:12–13

Spiritual resources should not be wasted
God's grace Jnh 2:8 *See also* Jn 12:35–36; 2Co 6:1; Gal 4:9–11; Heb 10:26–29,35; 2Pe 2:21

God-given abilities Mt 25:14–30; Lk 19:12–27

Opportunities for service Eph 5:16 *See also* Jn 9:4; Gal 6:10; Col 4:5

Spiritual teaching Mt 7:6 *Spiritual teaching is wasted if inappropriate to the spiritual capacity of the hearers. See also* Pr 9:7; 23:9; 1Co 2:14

Examples of wasted lives
Esau
Esau lived for the pleasures of the moment and threw away his spiritual inheritance: Ge 25:29–34; Heb 12:16

Samson Jdg 16:18–21 *Though Samson did retrieve something at the end of his life, his spiritual gift of supernatural strength was largely wasted through his indulgence in sexual immorality.*

King Saul 1Sa 16:21; 2Sa 1:17–27 *Through natural strength and spiritual gifts Saul had the prospect of establishing a successful royal dynasty. The future was lost through disobedience and the end of his reign was wasted through jealousy.*

Judas Iscariot Mt 27:3–5 *Judas had the best of opportunities—three years with Jesus Christ. This was thrown away in a moment of personal ambition.*

Devotion to God is not waste
Mt 26:6–13 pp Mk 14:3–9 *See also* Jn 12:1–8

Waste as the destruction of life and land
The frailty of human beings Job 13:28 *See also* Job 33:21; Ps 32:3; La 4:9; 2Co 4:16

Waste as a result of the judgment of God Jer 34:22 *See also* Lev 26:31–33,39; Nu 5:21; Dt 28:22; 29:23; 32:24; Ps 106:43; Isa 24:1,3; Eze 4:17; Hos 5:9

See also

5046 opportunities	6142 decay
5398 loss	6248 temptation
5531 skill	6666 grace
5856 extravagance	8438 giving time
5907 miserliness	8808 riches
5967 thrift	8821 self-indulgence

Sin and salvation

Sin

sin

Primarily a wrong relationship with God, which may express itself in wrong attitudes or actions towards God himself, other human beings, possessions or the environment. Scripture stresses that this condition is deeply rooted in human nature, and that only God is able to break its penalty, power and presence. This set of themes consists of the following:

6021 sin, nature of
6022 sin, causes of
6023 sin, universality of
6024 sin, effects of
6025 sin, and God's character
6026 sin, God's judgment on
6027 sin, God's remedy for
6028 sin, God's deliverance from
6029 sin, accepting forgiveness of
6030 sin, avoidance of

6021
sin, nature of

Scripture portrays sin in terms of wrongness before God in a variety of different ways, such as uncleanness, guilt or rebellion.

The basic nature of sin
All sin is directed against God Ps 51:4 *See also* Ge 13:13; Ex 10:16; Jdg 10:10; Ps 41:4; Lk 15:18

Sin is essentially a lack of faith in God Ro 14:23 *See also* Heb 11:6

Descriptions of sin
Corruption of God's good purposes Dt 32:5 *See also* Ge 6:11–12; Dt 9:12; 31:29; Jdg 2:19

Doing evil in God's sight Jn 3:19–20 *See also* Jdg 2:11; Ps 34:12–16; Pr 8:13; Isa 59:6–7; Mt 12:35 pp Lk 6:45

Ungodliness Jude 14–15 *See also* Isa 9:17; 32:6; 1Ti 1:9

Rebellion against God's authority Isa 30:9 *See also* Dt 9:7; 1Sa 15:23; Ps 78:40,56; Jer 3:13; Hos 7:13

The breaking or transgression of God's laws 1Jn 3:4 *See also* 1Sa 13:13–14; 1Ch 10:13; Ne 9:29; Mic 1:5; 7:18; Ro 2:23; 4:15; 5:14–17; Jas 2:10–11

Straying from the right path Isa 53:6 *See also* Ps 58:3; 95:10; 119:10,21,118

Incurring a debt Mt 6:12 *See also* Mt 18:21–35

Falling short of a standard Ro 3:23 *The words most commonly used for "sin" in the OT and NT originally signified "missing the mark".*

Uncleanness Ps 51:2; Isa 1:16 *See also* Ps 51:7; Heb 9:14

Kinds of sin
Sins of omission Jas 4:17 *See also* Mt 23:23 pp Lk 11:42; Mt 25:45

Deliberate sins Lk 12:47 *See also* Nu 15:30–31; Dt 1:42–43; 17:12; Ps 19:13; Isa 57:17; Ro 1:32

Unintentional sins Lk 12:48 *See also* Lev 4:1–5; Nu 15:22–29; Dt 4:41–42; Ac 3:17; 1Ti 1:13

Sin against the Holy Spirit Mk 3:29–30 pp Mt 12:31–32 pp Lk 12:10 *See also* 1Jn 5:16

See also
3245 Holy Spirit, blasphemy against
4811 darkness, symbol of sin
5135 blindness, spiritual
5375 law
6040 sinners
6206 offence
6221 rebellion
6237 sexual sin
7422 ritual
8802 pride
8834 unbelief
8846 ungodliness

6022
sin, causes of

Sin is the result of the fall, at which the creation rebels against God its Creator.

Sin as a result of the devil's activity
The devil's instigation of the first sin Ge 3:13 *See also* Ge 3:1–6; 2Co 11:3; Rev 12:9

The devil's role as tempter 1Th 3:5 *See also* Mt 4:1–11 pp Mk 1:12–13 pp Lk 4:1–13; Mt 6:13

The devil as the source of sinful behaviour Jn 8:44 *See also* Jn 8:38,41; 1Jn 3:8,10

The sins of angels 2Pe 2:4 *See also* Jude 6

Sin as a power in the world
Sin's reign from the time of Adam Ro 5:12 *See also* Ge 4:7; Jn 8:34; Ro 5:21; 6:16

Sin uses the law to provoke sinful desires Ro 7:5 *See also* Ro 7:7–12; 1Co 15:56

The world is under sin's dominion 1Jn 2:16 *See also* Lk 21:34; Tit 2:12

Sin is rooted in human nature
The human heart is dominated by sin Jer 17:9 *See also* Mt 15:19 pp Mk 7:21–22; Ro 1:24; Heb 3:12

Human nature is fundamentally opposed to God Ro 8:5–8 *See also* Ro 7:14–25; Gal 5:17–21; Eph 2:3; 2Pe 2:10,18

The act of sinning
Sin results from giving in to evil desires Jas 1:14–15 *See also* Ro 13:13–14; Jas 4:1; Jude 16

Sin results from the human desire to be like God Ge 3:5 *See also* Isa 14:12–14; Eze 28:2

Sin results when the body is placed at sin's disposal Ro 6:13 *See also* Mt 5:29–30; 18:8–9 pp Mk 9:43–47

Sin results from the influence of others 1Co 15:33 *See also* Ex 23:33; 1Ki 11:3; Pr 1:10; 22:24–25

The seriousness of leading others into sin Mk 9:42 pp Mt 18:6 pp Lk 17:1–2 *See also* 1Co 8:9–13

See also
4025 world, the
4120 Satan
6154 fall, the
6166 flesh, sinful nature

6023
sin, universality of

All human beings sin and are guilty in the sight of God on account of an inherently sinful disposition, which can be traced back to Adam. Acts of sin thus arise from a sinful human heart. The basis of cleansing and cancellation of "original sin" is the atoning death of Jesus Christ.

Adam, the cause of universal sin
Ro 5:19 *See also* Ge 3:1–24; Ro 5:12; 1Co 15:22

The universe is in subjection to sin
Gal 3:22 *See also* Ro 5:21; 11:32

Sin is inherent in human nature
Sinfulness from birth Ps 51:5 *See also* Job 25:4; Ps 58:3

The sinful heart Ge 6:5 *See also* Ge 8:21; Ecc 9:3; Jer 17:9; Mt 15:19 pp Mk 7:21

The sinful nature Eph 2:3 *See also* Ro 8:6–8; Gal 5:19–21

The universality of sin
No-one is righteous Ro 3:9–19 *See also* Ps 5:9; 10:7; 14:1–3 pp Ps 53:1–3; Ps 36:1; 140:3; Isa 59:7–8

All have sinned Ro 3:23 *See also* Ge 6:11–12; 1Ki 8:46 pp 2Ch 6:36; Ecc 7:20; Isa 53:6; Ro 1:18–32; Jas 3:2

Everyone is sinful in God's sight 1Jn 1:8 *See also* Ps 130:3; 143:2; Pr 20:9; Isa 64:6–7; Mt 19:17 pp Mk 10:18 pp Lk 18:19; 1Jn 1:10

Some characters in Scripture are described as being blameless in comparison with their contemporaries
Ge 5:24 *Enoch;* Ge 6:9 *Noah;* 1Ki 15:5 *David*

Jesus Christ alone is sinless
Heb 4:15; 1Pe 2:22 *See also* Isa 53:9; Lk 23:47; 2Co 5:21; Heb 7:26; 1Jn 3:5

See also
2075 Christ, sinless
4005 creation
5020 human nature
5080 Adam
6115 blame
6160 fathers, sin of
8201 blamelessness

6024
sin, effects of

Sin affects every level of human existence, including the sinner's relationship with God, with other human beings and with the environment.

The effects of sin on individuals
Lack of peace of mind Isa 57:20–21 *See also* Job 15:20–35; Ps 38:5–8; Pr 13:15–22; La 1:20–21

Bondage to a continuing habit of sin Jn 8:34 *See also* Pr 5:22; Ro 6:16; 2Ti 2:16

Physical death 1Co 15:56 *See also* Ge 2:17; 3:19; Pr 21:16; Ro 5:12–14; 6:21–23; 1Co 15:22; Jas 1:15

The sinful life is equivalent to death Eph 2:1 *See also* Ro 7:9,13; 8:10; Col 2:13

The effects of sin on the sinner before God

Uncleanness Isa 64:6 *See also*
Ps 106:39; Isa 6:5; Jer 2:22; La 1:8;
Mt 15:18–20 pp Mk 7:20–23

Guilt Ezr 9:6 *The prayer of Ezra. See also*
Ge 3:10; Ps 38:3–4; 44:15;
Isa 59:12–13; Jer 3:25; 14:20

Separation from God Isa 59:2 *See also*
Dt 31:18; Isa 1:15; 64:7; Eze 8:6;
Hos 5:6; Mic 3:4; Eph 2:12

The effects of sin on Israel

Pr 14:34 *See also* Jos 7:1–16 *Achan's sin;*
1Ki 8:33–40 *the consequences of sin for
Israel;* Isa 1:4–9 *the plight of Judah;*
Ro 1:21–32 *the condition of humanity*

The effects of sin on the world

The ground cursed Ge 3:17–18 *See also*
Jer 12:13; Ro 8:20–22

The land polluted Lev 18:25 *See also*
Ge 4:10–12; Nu 35:33–34; Ps 106:38;
Isa 24:4–6; Jer 3:1

See also
5447 poverty, causes   7340 clean and
5493 retribution   unclean
5568 suffering,   7348 defilement
     causes   7449 slavery,
5947 shame   spiritual
5952 sorrow   8341 separation
6172 guilt   9020 death

6025
sin, and God's character

In his righteousness and holiness,
God detests sin and its effects upon
humanity. In his mercy and grace,
he makes available a means of
atonement, by the death and
resurrection of Jesus Christ.

God's character and sin

God himself is perfect Hab 1:13;
1Jn 1:5 *See also* Dt 32:4; Jos 24:19;
Ps 97:2; Isa 6:3

Jesus Christ is sinless 1Pe 2:22 *See also*
Isa 53:9; 2Co 5:21; Heb 1:9; 7:26–27;
1Jn 3:5

God's people are to be holy
1Pe 1:15–16 *See also* Lev 11:44,45; 19:2;
20:7; Mt 5:48; 1Th 4:7; 1Jn 3:3

God's attitude to sin

God knows all sin Jer 16:17 *See also*
Job 10:14; Ps 139:1–4; Jer 2:22; Hos 7:2;
Am 5:12; Heb 4:13

God grieves over sin Ge 6:6 *See also*
Isa 63:10; Eph 4:30

God hates sin Ps 11:5 *See also* Dt 25:16;
2Sa 11:27; Ps 5:5; Pr 6:16–19; Zec 8:17;
Lk 16:15

Sin provokes God's anger Ro 1:18 *See
also* 2Ch 36:16; Eze 20:8; Am 1:3;
Jn 3:36; Eph 5:5–6; Col 3:5–6

God is also merciful and gracious
Ex 34:6–7 *See also* Ne 9:17,31; Ps 78:38;
103:8–14; La 3:22–23; Mic 7:18–19;
Ro 11:32

God's patience with sinners 2Pe 3:9 *See
also* Ro 2:4; 9:22; 1Ti 1:16

Jesus Christ is the supreme revelation of God's love for sinners

Jesus Christ's ministry of forgiveness
1Ti 1:15 *See also* Mt 9:2 pp Mk 2:5
pp Lk 5:20–21; Lk 7:36–50; 15:1–10;
19:5–10; Jn 8:1–11

**God's love shown in Jesus Christ's
death** Ro 5:8 *See also* Jn 3:16–17;
Eph 2:4; 1Pe 3:18; 1Jn 4:9–10

**The risen Christ gives grace to sinful
people** 1Jn 2:1 *See also* Ro 8:34;
Heb 2:17–18; 4:15–5:2

See also
1020 God, all-   2015 Christ,
    knowing   compassion
1025 God, anger of   2063 Christ,
1055 God, grace &   perfection
    mercy   5790 anger, divine
1065 God, holiness   6103 abomination
    of   6666 grace
1085 God, love of   6688 mercy,
1125 God,   demonstration
    righteousness   of God's

6026
sin, God's judgment on

Sin comes under the judgment of
God, in that it contradicts his nature
and opposes his purposes.

God's judgment on sin

God is the judge of sin Isa 26:21 *See
also* Ps 99:8; Isa 13:11; Am 3:14;
Zep 1:12; 1Th 4:6

God's judgment is certain Ro 2:12 *See
also* Ps 37:38; Pr 11:21; Heb 9:27

**God's judgment is in proportion to the
seriousness of the sin** Jer 21:14 *See also*
Dt 25:2; Isa 59:18; Mt 7:1–5;
Lk 12:47–48; Ro 2:5–6

**God's judgment under the Sinaitic
covenant** Ex 20:5 pp Dt 5:9 *The Sinaitic
covenant makes references to the judgment
of future generations for the sins of their
parents but, as a principle, this is abolished
by later prophets.*
*Curses for disobedience formed part of
God's covenant with Israel:*
Lev 26:14–39; Dt 28:15–68
Jer 31:29–30; Eze 18:1–32

**John the Baptist and Jesus Christ
warn of judgment** Mt 3:10 pp Lk 3:9 *See
also* Mt 3:12; 7:19; 12:36–37;
Mk 9:42–49

Ways in which God judges sin

**God causes sin to bring evil to the
sinner** 2Ch 6:23 *See also* Dt 19:19;
Est 7:10; Ps 7:15–16; Isa 30:13

God abandons people Isa 64:7 *See also*
Dt 31:17–18; Jos 7:11–12; La 4:16;
Eze 39:23–24

**Unrepentant sinners to be expelled
from the church** Mt 18:17 *See also*
1Co 5:1–13

**God exercises judgment through a
country's legal system** 1Pe 2:14 *See also*
Ro 13:3–4

**Untimely death is God's judgment on
all sin** Ge 2:17 *See also* Lev 20:1–17;
1Ch 10:13; Pr 11:19; Ro 1:32;
1Co 11:29–30

Sinners are excluded from the kingdom of God Rev 22:15 *See also*
1Co 6:9–10; Gal 5:9–21; Rev 21:27

Occasions of God's judgment on sin

OT examples Ge 3:16–24 *expulsion from
Eden;* Ge 6:1–7:24 *the flood;*
Ge 18:20–19:29 *Sodom and Gomorrah;*
Dt 9:1–5 *The Canaanites (the Anakites
were earlier inhabitants of Canaan).
The exile of Israel and Judah:*
2Ki 17:7–23; 24:10–20

The destruction of Jerusalem
Lk 11:47–51; 13:34–35

God's final judgment of the world
Rev 21:8 *See also* Isa 66:24;
Mt 25:31–46; 2Th 1:8–9; 2Pe 3:7;
Jude 7

See also
1310 God as judge   9210 judgment,
1349 covenant at   God's
    Sinai   9240 last judgment
5482 punishment   9510 hell

6027
sin, God's remedy for

Under the old covenant, sin was
forgiven through sacrifice, pre-
figuring the atoning death of Jesus
Christ, which brings forgiveness of
sins under the new covenant.

Atonement for sins in the OT was through the shedding of blood
Lev 17:11

Kinds of sin offering in the OT

**The sin offering was for unintentional
sins** Lev 4:1–5:13 *See also* Nu 15:22–31

**The guilt offering was for unintentional
sins, where restitution was required**
Lev 5:14–6:7 *See also* Nu 5:5–10

**The annual Day of Atonement cleansed
the nation of sin** Lev 16:1–34 *See also*
Ex 30:11–16; Lev 23:26–32; Heb 9:7

**The priests made atonement on
occasions of deliberate national sin**
Nu 16:46–48 *Aaron stops the plague after
Korah's sin;* Nu 25:13 *Phinehas stops the
plague after Moab caused Israel to sin.*

Sacrifices of atonement needed to be accompanied by repentance and a willingness to obey

**Worshippers recognised the need for
repentance and obedience** Pr 21:3 *See
also* Ps 40:6–8; 51:16–17

**The prophets declared the need for
obedience** 1Sa 15:22 *See also*
Isa 1:11–17; Jer 7:21–23; Hos 6:6;
Mic 6:6–8

**The prophets warned of judgment to
bring people to repentance** 2Ki 17:13
See also Isa 31:6–7; Jer 4:1–4; 35:15;
Eze 3:16–19; Jnh 3:4–10

The death of Jesus Christ brings forgiveness for sin

**Jesus Christ died on behalf of sinful
humanity** Ro 5:6 *See also* Mt 26:26–28;
Jn 10:11; 15:13; Gal 2:20

The early church proclaimed that Christ died for the sins of others 1Co 15:3 *See also* Ro 4:25; Gal 1:4; 1Pe 3:18

Jesus Christ bore sin on the cross 2Co 5:21 *See also* Isa 53:10–12; Heb 9:28; 1Pe 2:24

Jesus Christ has redeemed people by taking their place Mt 20:28 pp Mk 10:45 *See also* Gal 3:13; 1Ti 2:6; Tit 2:14

Jesus Christ's death is sacrificial Ro 3:25 *See also* Ro 8:3; 1Co 5:7; Eph 5:2; Heb 7:27; 10:5–13; 1Jn 2:2; 4:10

The shedding of Jesus Christ's blood brings forgiveness 1Jn 1:7 *See also* Jn 1:29; Eph 1:7; Heb 9:12–22; 13:12; 1Pe 1:18–19; Rev 7:14

See also

2315 Christ as Lamb	6614 atonement
2321 Christ as redeemer	6648 expiation
	6652 forgiveness
2324 Christ as Saviour	6712 propitiation
2525 Christ, cross of	7314 blood
2560 Christ, resurrection	7402 offerings
	7435 sacrifice, in OT

6028
sin, God's deliverance from

The gospel reveals the purpose and power of God to deal with sin and all of its effects. Scripture uses a range of images to express the comprehensiveness of salvation.

God's removal of sin
Atonement for sin Isa 6:7 *See also* Ex 32:30; Lev 4:27–31; Pr 16:6; Ro 3:25; Heb 2:17

Forgiveness of sin Mic 7:18; Ac 13:38 *See also* 1Ki 8:35–36; 2Ch 30:18–20; Ps 103:2–3; Isa 33:24; 55:7; Joel 3:21; Mt 26:27–28; Lk 24:46–47; Eph 1:7; 1Jn 1:9

Cancellation of a debt Mt 6:12 *See also* Mt 18:21–35; Lk 7:41–50

A covering over of sin 1Pe 4:8 *There is a close relation between "covering over sin" and "atoning for sin". See also* Ps 32:1; 85:2; Jas 5:20

The taking away of sin Ps 103:12 *See also* 2Sa 12:13; Isa 6:6–7; Zec 3:4; Jn 1:29; Heb 9:28; 1Jn 3:5

Remembering sin no more Isa 43:25 *See also* Ps 25:7; Jer 31:33–34; 2Co 5:19

God's deliverance for the sinner
The salvation of the sinner 1Ti 1:15 *See also* Ps 28:8–9; Mt 1:21; Lk 19:9–10; Jn 3:17; Heb 7:25

The image of healing Lk 5:31–32 pp Mt 9:12 pp Mk 2:17 *See also* 2Ch 7:14; Isa 53:5; 57:18–19; Hos 14:4; 1Pe 2:24

The image of cleansing Ps 51:2 *See also* Lev 16:30; Eze 36:25; Jn 13:1–11; Ac 22:16; Heb 10:22; 1Jn 1:9

Redemption by God Ps 130:8 *See also* Isa 44:22; Tit 2:14; 1Pe 1:18–19

Justification before God Gal 2:16 *See also* Isa 53:11; Ro 3:24–26; 4:5,25; 5:16–19; 8:33

Freedom from condemnation Ro 8:1 *See also* Jn 3:18; 8:3–11; Ro 8:34

Peace with God Ro 5:1 *See also* Isa 53:5; Lk 2:14; Eph 2:17

Reconciliation with God 2Co 5:18 *See also* Ro 5:9–11; Col 1:19–20

Sanctification to God Heb 10:10 *See also* 1Co 6:11; Eph 5:25–26; Col 1:22

Freedom from sin and the sinful nature Ro 7:24; 1Pe 2:24 *See also* Ro 6:1–18; 8:1–9; Gal 5:24

A transition from death to life Col 2:13 *See also* Lk 15:22–24; Eph 2:4–5

Receiving eternal life Ro 6:23 *See also* Jn 3:16,36; 5:24

See also

1315 God as redeemer	6658 freedom
	6676 justification
6124 condemnation	6700 peace
6510 salvation	6716 reconciliation
6644 eternal life	6720 redemption

6029
sin, accepting forgiveness of

Sinners must respond to God's offer of forgiveness through faith in Jesus Christ.

The conviction of sin
La 1:20; Jn 16:8–9 *See also* 1Ki 8:38–40; Isa 6:5; Eze 33:10–11; Ac 16:29

The inward response of faith
Ac 16:31 *See also* Mk 1:14–15; Jn 3:36; 5:24; Ac 13:38–39; 16:25–34; Ro 3:22–26; 10:8–10; Eph 2:8

The outward response of baptism
Ac 22:16 *See also* Mk 1:4–5 pp Mt 3:1–6 pp Lk 3:2–6; Ac 2:38; 8:36; Col 2:11–12; 1Pe 3:21

Confession of sin
Pr 28:13; 1Jn 1:9 *See also* Lev 16:20–22; 26:40–42; 2Sa 12:13; Ps 32:3–5; La 3:40; Lk 15:17–20; Ac 19:18

Repentance
Turning towards God Ac 3:19 *See also* 2Ch 6:36–39; Isa 55:7; Eze 18:21; Mt 3:1–2 pp Mk 1:4 pp Lk 3:2; Ac 17:30; 2Co 7:10; 1Th 1:9

Turning away from sin Jn 8:11 *See also* Jer 4:3–4; Lk 19:1–10; Jn 5:14; Ro 6:11–14; 1Pe 2:11

The making of restitution
Lk 19:8 *See also* Lev 6:1–7; Nu 5:6–8; Pr 6:30–31; Eze 33:12–16

The forgiveness of others
Lk 11:4 pp Mt 6:12 *See also* Mt 6:14–15; 18:21–35; Mk 11:25; Eph 4:32; Col 3:13

See also

2420 gospel	6626 conversion
3248 Holy Spirit, conviction	6732 repentance
	7903 baptism
5031 knowledge of sin	8020 faith
	8843 unforgivable sin
5492 restitution	
6193 impenitence	
6624 confession of sin	

6030
sin, avoidance of

God calls his people to avoid sin, and through Jesus Christ gives them the inner power to be victorious over it.

God's people are to resist sin
1Pe 2:11 *See also* Ps 97:10; Pr 4:23–27; 1Co 15:34; Eph 4:25–5:20; Jas 1:21

The Christian life is a constant struggle against sin
Heb 3:13 *See also* Ac 20:28; Ro 7:14–25; Eph 6:10–18; 1Pe 5:8–9

God helps his people to resist sin
Release from sin through Jesus Christ's death 1Pe 2:24 *See also* Ro 6:1–7; Gal 2:20; 5:24; Col 2:11–12

The avoidance of sin through new life in Jesus Christ 1Jn 3:9 *See also* 2Co 5:17; 1Pe 1:23; 1Jn 3:6; 5:18

Believers co-operate with Jesus Christ to avoid sin
Php 2:12–13

Believers are to put to death what is sinful in them Col 3:5 *See also* Ro 6:11–14; 8:13

Believers are to exchange sinful for righteous behaviour Ro 13:12–14 *The words used here, and in similar passages, are those used for "taking off" old clothes and "putting on" new ones. See also* Eph 4:22–24; Col 3:7–10; 1Ti 6:11; 2Ti 2:22

Believers are to allow the Spirit to inform and direct their conduct Ro 12:2 *See also* Ro 8:5–8; Gal 5:16–25

Practical steps for overcoming sin and temptation
Meditation on Scripture Ps 119:11 *See also* Ps 18:22–23; Mt 4:1–11 pp Lk 4:1–13; 2Ti 3:16–17

Prayerful dependence upon God Mt 6:13 pp Lk 11:4 *See also* Ps 19:13; Mt 26:41; 1Co 10:13; Heb 4:15–16

Active seeking of the good Ro 6:19 *See also* Ps 34:14; Isa 1:16–17; Am 5:14–15; 1Th 5:22; 3Jn 11

Incentives for avoiding sin
The fear of God Pr 16:6 *See also* Ex 20:20; Pr 3:7; 8:13

The holiness of God 1Pe 1:15–16 *See also* Lev 11:44–45; 19:2; 20:7; 1Co 6:18–20; 1Th 4:7

The expectation of Jesus Christ's return 1Pe 4:7 *See also* 2Co 5:9–10; 1Th 5:4–6; 2Pe 3:10–14

A consideration of the consequences of sin Gal 6:7–8 *See also* Mk 9:42–48; Ro 6:21–23; Heb 6:7–8; 10:26–31

The need to be a good witness to unbelievers 1Pe 2:15 *See also* 1Pe 3:1–2,15–16

The role of others in avoiding sin
Bad company is to be avoided 1Co 15:33 *See also* Dt 7:1–4; Ps 1:1; Pr 1:10; 1Co 5:1–13

A good example is to be followed 1Co 11:1 *See also* Php 3:17; 4:9; Heb 12:1–3; 1Pe 4:1–3

Believers are to support one another
Jas 5:19–20 See also Mt 18:15–17;
Gal 6:1–2; 1Ti 5:20; Heb 3:12

See also
2030 Christ, holiness	6744 sanctification
2306 Christ, high priest	7921 fellowship
	8266 holiness
3233 Holy Spirit & sanctification	8451 mortification
6248 temptation	8490 watchfulness

6040

sinners

All who have sinned. The term tends
to be used in particular of those
regarded as outside God's covenant
of grace, whose sins are therefore not
forgiven.

The universality of sinful behaviour
Only Jesus Christ is sinless 1Pe 2:22
See also Isa 53:9; 2Co 5:21; Heb 4:15;
7:26; 1Jn 3:5

Everyone else has sinned Gal 3:22 See
also 1Ki 8:46; Ro 3:9–19,23; 5:12,19

God's mercy towards sinners
**God graciously extends mercy to
sinners within the covenant** Ps 25:8–10
See also 1Ki 8:30; Ps 86:5; 130:8; Da 9:9;
1Jn 1:9

Jesus Christ died for sinners Ro 5:8;
1Ti 1:15 See also Ro 8:3

Sinners as those whose behaviour excludes them from God's covenant
**Prostitutes, tax collectors, idolatrous
Gentiles and the ungodly** Lk 15:1 See
also Dt 23:17–18; 1Sa 15:18; Lk 3:12;
7:37–38; Gal 2:15; 1Th 4:5; 1Pe 4:18;
Pr 11:31; 2Pe 2:5–6

Such sinners shunned by the Jews
Lk 7:39 See also Ps 1:1; Pr 1:10–16

The judgment of sinners
Prayers seeking their judgment
Ps 104:35 See also Ps 109:6–20;
137:7–9; 139:19

They are cut off from God Isa 59:2 See
also Ps 66:18; Pr 15:29; Isa 1:15; Jn 9:31;
1Co 6:9–10

They receive their just reward
Pr 13:21–22 See also Ps 1:5; 34:16;
37:38; Ecc 2:26

Prophecies of their judgment Isa 1:28
See also Isa 13:9; 33:14; Jer 4:18;
Am 9:10

Their final judgment 2Pe 3:7 See also
Isa 66:24; 2Th 1:8–9; 2Pe 2:9; Jude 15

Jesus Christ's attitude towards sinners
Jesus Christ's association with sinners
Mt 9:9–13 pp Mk 2:14–17
pp Lk 5:27–32 Jesus Christ's attitude and
behaviour were radically different from
that of his contemporaries. See also
Lk 15:1–10; 19:5–10; Ro 5:8;
1Ti 1:15–16

**Jesus Christ extended God's
forgiveness to sinners and welcomed
them into his kingdom** Mt 21:31–32 See
also Mt 9:2–7 pp Mk 2:3–12

**Jesus Christ's behaviour led to
accusations that he himself was a
sinner** Jn 9:16,24

**Jesus Christ's refusal to accept sinful
behaviour** Jn 8:10–11 See also Mt 4:17;
18:8–9 pp Mk 9:43–48; Jn 5:14

**Jesus Christ's use of the example of
sinners to teach his disciples**
Lk 6:32–34 pp Mt 5:46–47 See also
Lk 16:1–9

Sinners in the church
**Those who fall into sin should be
restored** Jas 5:19–20 See also Ps 51:13;
Mt 18:12–15; Gal 6:1

**Unrepentant sinners should be
expelled** Mt 18:15–17 See also
1Co 5:9–11

See also
1055 God, grace & mercy	6257 unbelievers
1310 God as judge	6666 grace
2048 Christ, love of	6686 mercy
2354 Christ, mission	6712 propitiation
5576 tax collectors	6750 sin-bearer
6020 sin	7918 excommunication

6100

Aspects of sin

6103

abomination

That which is utterly detestable in
the sight of God, particularly sin and
idolatry. Daniel predicts the
establishment of an "abomination
that causes desolation" on the
temple mount and Jesus Christ
reiterates this prophecy.

Sin is an abomination
God detests it Lev 20:13; Pr 26:24–26
See also Lev 18:26–30; Pr 6:16–19; 28:9;
Isa 66:3–4

The abomination of Babylon the Great
Rev 17:3–6 See also Jer 51:6–8;
Rev 14:8; 19:1–2

Idolatry is an abomination
Jer 32:32–35
Moses warns the Israelites against the
idolatry of the Canaanites: Dt 7:25–26;
12:31; 18:9–13; 27:15; 29:17–18
Dt 32:15–16
The idolatry of Solomon's latter years:
1Ki 11:4–8; 2Ki 23:13
Isa 44:19; Jer 4:1–2; 7:30; 16:18;
Eze 5:9; 7:20; 8:5–18 idolatry in the
temple; Eze 11:17–21; 20:30; Hos 9:10;
1Pe 4:3

Unclean animals are an abomination
Isa 66:17 See also Lev 7:21;
11:13–20,41–42; Isa 65:2–5; Rev 18:2

The abomination that causes desolation
Da 9:25–27 See also Da 11:29–32;
12:11–12; Mt 24:15–21
pp Mk 13:14–19; Rev 13:14–15

See also
4215 Babylon	7340 clean and unclean
6025 sin & God's character	8771 idolatry, objections
6236 sexual sin	
7324 calf worship	9105 last things

6106

addiction

The devotion of a person to
something, whether sin in general or
food, alcohol or wealth in particular,
so as to become dependent upon it.
A person will never be satisfied in
such a state of slavery. The answer to
addiction is self-control through the
resources of the new life in Christ.

Addiction is the consequence of sin
2Pe 2:19 See also Jn 8:34

Addiction to food, alcohol or drugs is to become dependent upon them
Php 3:18–19 See also Isa 5:11; 28:7–8;
56:12; Tit 2:3

Addiction to wealth is to be controlled by it
Mk 10:21–22 pp Lk 18:22–23 See also
Mt 26:14–16 pp Mk 14:10–11
pp Lk 22:3–6; Ac 16:19; 24:26; 2Pe 2:15

Addiction never satisfies
**Addiction to sinful habits does not
satisfy** Ro 6:20–21

**Addiction to food, alcohol or drugs
does not satisfy** Ecc 6:7 See also Pr 20:1;
21:17; 23:20–21,29–35; Hos 4:10–11
pp Mt 19:21–22

Addiction to wealth does not satisfy
Ecc 5:10 See also 1Ti 6:9–10; Jas 5:1–3

The answer to addiction: self-control through the new life in Christ
Pr 23:1–4; Ro 6:6–7,11–14 See also
Pr 25:16; Ro 6:16–19; 8:12–15;
1Co 6:12; 9:27; Gal 5:22–23

See also
4434 drinking	7446 slavery
4544 wine	8224 dependence
5775 abuse	8339 self-control
5866 gluttony	8475 self-denial
5939 satisfaction	8808 riches
6020 sin	

6109

alienation

A state of being separate or apart
from something or someone, often
accompanied by an awareness of the
separation. Human beings are
alienated from God on account of
sin. Alienation is also encountered in
other areas of life, including
relations between believers, and
between believers and secular
society.

Alienation from God because of sin

Sin causes separation from God
Gal 5:4 *Those seeking to justify themselves cut themselves off from Jesus Christ's saving work;* Col 1:21 *See also* Isa 59:1-2; Eze 39:23-24

Seen in discomfort in God's presence
Ge 3:8-10 *See also* Isa 6:5; Lk 5:8

Seen in defeat in battle Dt 1:42 *See also* Nu 14:41-45; Jos 7:11-12; Jdg 2:11-15

Seen in unanswered prayer Isa 59:1-2
See also Dt 1:45; Ps 66:18; Pr 1:28-30; Isa 1:15

Seen in unaccepted worship
Isa 1:11-14; Am 5:21-23; Mal 1:10

Seen in lost closeness with God
Ge 3:23-24; Ex 33:3; Isa 64:7; Eze 8:6; Hos 5:6; Jnh 1:3

A sense of alienation from God
Feelings of alienation Ps 22:1; Isa 49:14 *See also* Ps 39:12; 42:3-4,9-10; 44:23-24; Isa 40:27; La 2:1; Mt 27:46 pp Mk 15:34 *Jesus Christ's alienation from God as he bore the consequences of human sin was felt and actual.*

The reassurance of God's concern
Isa 49:15-16 *See also* Isa 43:1-5; 44:21; 54:7; Jer 31:20

Alienation from others
Alienation caused by a third party
Pr 16:28 *See also* Pr 17:9; Gal 4:17 *False teachers in Galatia tried to drive a wedge between Paul and the church.*

Examples of alienation Ge 3:7 *Man and woman;* Ge 4:3-8 *Cain and Abel;* Ge 27:41 *Jacob and Esau;* 1Sa 18:8-9 *Saul and David;* Job 19:13-19 *Job and his family and friends;* Ps 69:8 *the psalmist and his family;* Jer 12:6 *Jeremiah and his family;* Ac 15:39 *Paul and Barnabas;* Eph 2:12 *Jew and Gentile*

Overcoming alienation
Being reconciled to God Col 1:22 *See also* Ro 5:11; 2Co 5:18-20; 1Pe 2:25

Reconciliation with others Col 3:13 *See also* Lev 19:18; Mt 5:23-24

Examples of reconciliation Ge 33:4 *Jacob and Esau;* Ge 50:19-21 *Joseph and his brothers;* Eph 2:14-16 *Jew and Gentile*

God's people are aliens in the world
Jn 15:18-19 *See also* Jn 17:16; Php 3:20; Heb 11:13-16; 1Pe 2:11

Responsibility to the alien
God's concern for the outsider
Ps 146:9 *See also* Dt 10:18; Jer 30:17

The example of Jesus Christ
Mt 9:10-11 pp Mk 2:15-16 pp Lk 5:29-30 *Jesus Christ welcomed those who had been alienated by the rest of society. See also* Mt 8:2-3 pp Mk 1:40-42 pp Lk 5:12-13 *Jesus Christ touched the "untouchable" man with leprosy;* Mt 11:19 pp Lk 7:34

Equal treatment for the alien Lev 19:34 *See also* Ex 12:48-49; Lev 24:22

Ensuring justice for the alien Dt 24:17
The weaker members of Israelite society are

of special concern. See also Ex 22:21; Jer 22:3; Zec 7:9-10

Special provision for the alien
Lev 23:22 *God makes special provision for the poor so that they will have a share in the blessings of the land. See also* Lev 19:10; Dt 24:20; 14:28-29 *The third year's tithe is shared with those without inheritance in the land.*

See also

5004 human race & sin	7344 curtain
5446 poverty	7530 foreigners
5491 refugees	7545 outsiders
5901 loneliness	8269 holiness,
6233 rejection, experience	separation from worldly
6716 reconciliation	8341 separation
	9024 death, spiritual

6112

banishment

A form of punishment in which the guilty party is expelled from a region and forbidden to return. An important example is the banishment of Adam and Eve from Eden as a result of their disobedience to God.

Banishment is a punishment for disobedience
Ezr 7:26 *See also* Ex 12:15; 31:14; Lev 7:20-21; Nu 15:30

Banishment by God
Adam and Eve were banished from Eden because of their disobedience
Ge 3:22-24

God banished kings as a punishment
Nebuchadnezzar was banished from every human being because of his sin:
Da 4:25,32-33
Eze 28:16-17 *The king of Tyre was banished from God's presence because of his sin.*

God punished the people of Judah by banishing them from their land
Jer 23:39 *God also promised their return (Jer 32:37). See also* Jer 8:3; 24:9; 25:10; 27:10

At the final judgment, God will banish all evildoers Mt 7:23 *See also* Mt 8:12; 22:13; 25:46

Kings used banishment as a punishment
Saul expelled all mediums and spiritists from the land: 1Sa 28:3,9
1Ki 15:12 *Asa banished all the shrine-prostitutes from the land.*

The psalmists recognised banishment as the severest of punishments
Ps 5:10; 31:22; 37:22,28,34,38; 51:11; 71:9; 125:5; Jnh 2:4 *This portion of the book of Jonah is written in the same manner as the Psalms, i.e., as Hebrew poetry.*

The church is to use banishment as a means of discipline
1Co 5:12-13 *See also* Dt 17:7; 19:19; 21:21; 22:21,24; 24:7

See also

1310 God as judge	7918 excom-
2309 Christ as judge	munication
5483 punishment	8230 discipline
6155 fall of Adam & Eve	8341 separation
	8734 evil
7212 exile	9210 judgment,
7215 exile, the	God's
7245 Judah, kingdom of	

6115

blame

The state of having been accused, correctly or incorrectly, of doing something wrong. Guilt is felt as a result of having been justly blamed for a crime or wrong against a person. Scripture portrays blaming others as a natural human reaction to events. Blame may often be apportioned by people on the basis of a misunderstanding, whereas God's blame of people is just. Christians should seek to lead blameless lives.

Blaming others: a basic human characteristic since the fall
Ge 3:12-13
Moses: Nu 20:5; 21:5; Jos 22:15-18
1Sa 22:13-15; 2Sa 3:8; 1Ki 18:17-18; Ne 5:4-5; Job 4:5-7; 8:6; 11:14-15; Jer 38:4; Jn 9:1-2; 11:21; Ac 6:1

Blaming God
Jer 15:16-18 *See also* Job 2:9; 3:23; Ps 13:1-2; 22:1-2; 44:9-26; 60:1-3; 74:1-23; 79:1-5; Isa 40:27

God justly blames his people for their sins
Heb 8:8 *See also* Ro 9:19

Warnings about falsely attributing blame
Pr 3:30 *See also* Ps 71:13; 109:18-20,29; Ro 14:1-4; 15:7

Dealing with blame
By confession Ps 32:5 *See also* Ps 51:3-7

By forgiveness Lk 23:34 *See also* Ge 50:19-21; Eph 4:31-32

By correcting misunderstandings Jos 22:13-34

God's people should deal gently with those who deserve blame
Mt 18:15 *See also* Jas 5:19-20

God's people should aim to live free from blame
Php 1:9-10 *See also* Ge 17:1; Ps 19:13; 1Co 1:8; Php 2:15; 1Th 3:13; 5:23

See also

1075 God, justice of	5926 rebuke
5193 tongue	6163 faults
5201 accusation	6172 guilt
5202 accusation, false	8201 blamelessness
	8277 innocence
5276 crime	8428 example

6118

blemish

A mark or stain which spoils something or lessens its value. The term is often used symbolically to refer to sin. The OT sacrificial system specified that only unblemished animals should be sacrificed.

A blemish is ritually unacceptable
In animals to be sacrified Dt 15:21; Mal 1:13–14 *See also* Ex 12:5; Lev 22:20–25; Dt 17:1

In priests offering sacrifices Lev 21:17–23

A blemish or stain as a symbol of sin
Jer 2:22 *See also* Isa 59:3; Jude 23

Sinful people represented as blemishes 2Pe 2:13 *See also* Jude 12

Without blemish: physical or moral perfection
Absalom 2Sa 14:25

Daniel and his companions Da 1:3–4

Jesus Christ 1Pe 1:18–19 *See also* Heb 9:12–14

The church Eph 5:27 *See also* Col 1:22

See also
2075 Christ, sinless	7402 offerings
2315 Christ as Lamb	7416 purification
6020 sin	7435 sacrifice, in OT
7027 church, purpose	8320 perfection
	8324 purity

6121

boasting

Negatively, conceitedly praising oneself. Positively, trusting and exulting in who God is, and what he has done.

Boasting condemned
1Jn 2:16 *See also* Ps 10:2–6; 12:3–4; 52:1; 94:4; Hab 1:10–11; Ro 1:29–30; 2Ti 3:1–2

Boasting exposed as folly
Pr 27:1 *See also* Jdg 9:38–40; Pr 25:14; 1Co 3:18–23; Jas 4:13–16

Salvation by faith means no-one can boast about human merit
Eph 2:8–9 *See also* Lk 18:9–14; Ro 2:17–24; 3:27; 11:17–21; Gal 6:14

Examples of foolish boasting
Isa 10:12–14 *See also* Isa 37:24–25; Da 4:28–30 *Nebuchadnezzar*; Da 7:8,11; 11:36; Ac 8:9–10 *Simon the sorcerer*; 2Th 2:3–4 *the antichrist*; 2Pe 2:17–18

Legitimate boasting
Boasting in God Jer 9:23–24 *See also* 1Sa 2:1–3; Ps 34:2; 44:8; 1Co 1:27–31; Jer 9:24; 2Co 10:7–18; Heb 3:6

Boasting in the results of ministry
1Th 2:19–20 *See also* Ro 15:17–19; 1Co 15:31; 2Co 8:24–9:3

Boasting in the conduct of ministry
2Co 1:12–14 *See also* 1Co 9:15; 2Co 11:7–12; 2Ti 3:10–11

See also
5173 outward appearance	5961 superiority
5550 speech, negative	8710 atheism
	8802 pride
5575 talk, idle	8824 self-righteousness
5793 arrogance	9115 antichrist, the
5813 conceit	

6124

condemnation

An act of judgment, in which someone rebukes and denounces the actions and motivations of others. Scripture stresses the righteousness and trustworthiness of divine condemnation but notes how human judgments are often tainted and distorted by sin.

6125
condemnation, divine

God's righteous condemnation is directed against human sin and wickedness.

God's wrath causes divine condemnation
Ro 1:18–20 *See also* Rev 16:1–7

The reality and certainty of divine condemnation
Mk 16:15–16; Jn 5:28–29 *See also* Mt 12:36–37; 25:31–33,41–45; 2Pe 2:4–9

People's awareness of being under divine condemnation
2Sa 24:10 *See also* Ps 32:3–5; 51:3–4; Da 9:7–14

Examples of divine condemnation
Condemnation of individuals
Ge 3:16–19; Ac 5:1–11; Rev 20:11–15

Condemnation of groups, cities and nations Ge 11:4–9; 19:23–25; Joel 3:1–8,12–13

Divine condemnation averted through the work of Jesus Christ
Jn 3:16–18; 5:24; Ro 8:1–4 *See also* Ro 8:31–34

See also
1025 God, anger of	6615 atonement, necessity
1310 God as judge	
2309 Christ as judge	6717 reconciliation, world to God
2324 Christ as Saviour	
	8022 faith, basis of salvation
5484 punishment by God	
5790 anger, divine	8154 righteousness
6173 guilt, and God	9250 woe

6126
condemnation, human

The passing of judgment on others. This is valid when authorised by God, but otherwise it is frequently

partial, godless and self-protecting, and therefore unacceptable.

Condemnation and the legal process: impartial judgment demanded
Ex 23:6–8 *See also* Dt 1:15–17; 17:2–7; 19:15; 2Ch 19:4–7; Pr 17:15

The perversity and injustice of human condemnation
Ro 2:1–5 *See also* 2Sa 12:1–10; Da 6:1–16

People's false condemnation of Jesus Christ
Ac 13:27–28 *See also* Mt 26:59–63 pp Mk 14:55–61

NT warnings against judgment and condemnation
Mt 7:1–5 pp Lk 6:37–38, 41–42 *See also* Lk 18:9–14; Jn 8:3–11; Ro 14:1–4,9–13

God's protection of his people from false condemnation
Isa 50:7–9; Ro 8:31–39

See also
2027 Christ, grace & mercy	5897 judging others
	6652 forgiveness
2585 Christ, trial	6676 justification
5347 injustice	6686 mercy
5359 justice	8767 hypocrisy
5375 law	8823 self-righteousness
5820 criticism	

6130

corruption

A state of spiritual decay and moral dishonesty, arising from the effects of sin, which expresses itself in disobedience towards God.

Corruption of nature as a result of the fall
Ge 6:11

Sinful humanity is corrupt
Isa 1:4; Ac 2:40 *See also* Dt 32:20; Job 15:16; Ps 14:1–3 pp Ps 53:1–3; Pr 4:24; 6:12; Hos 9:9; Php 2:15; Tit 1:15–16

The gospel breaks the power of corruption
2Pe 1:4 *See also* 2Co 7:1–2; 2Pe 2:20; Jude 23

Examples and causes of corruption
Corruption as injustice Ps 55:23 *See also* 2Ch 19:7; Job 5:16; Isa 58:6; Eze 9:9

Disobedience towards God Dt 31:29 *See also* Dt 32:5; Jdg 2:19

Denying the truth 1Ti 6:5

Paganism Ezr 9:11

Mocking justice Pr 19:28

Taking bribes Ecc 7:7

Bad company 1Co 15:33

Careless talk Jas 3:5–6 *See also* Pr 4:24; 6:12

See also
4263 Rome	8714 dishonesty
5020 human nature	8734 evil
6142 decay	
6185 imagination, desires	

6133

coveting

Desiring to possess something at the expense of the legitimate owner.

6134

coveting, prohibition of

Coveting is forbidden by God and can lead to terrible consequences. It occasionally refers to a commendable earnest desiring.

Coveting is forbidden by God
In the Ten Commandments Ex 20:17 pp Dt 5:21; Ro 7:7–8 *Coveting is provoked by the law that forbids it. See also* Ro 13:9–10

Through the prophets Isa 5:8; 57:17; Eze 33:31; Am 2:6; 5:11–12; 8:5–6; Mic 2:2

In Jesus Christ's teaching Mt 6:19–21 *See also* Lk 12:15

Coveting has some terrible consequences
2Sa 11:2–4 *adultery*; 1Ki 21:18–19 *murders*
Failure to enter the kingdom of heaven: Mt 18:1–3; Mk 9:33–35 pp Lk 9:46–48; 1Co 6:9–10
Ac 5:3–10 *God's judgment*

Further examples of coveting
Jos 7:21 *See also* Dt 7:25; Jos 22:20 *Achan*; 1Sa 2:12–15 *Eli's sons*; 1Sa 8:3 *Samuel's sons*; 1Sa 15:9–10 *Saul*; Pr 30:16; Jer 6:13; 8:10; Hab 2:5 *Israel's enemies are likened to the grave, always swallowing people and never satisfied*; Ac 8:13–23 *Simon the sorcerer*

Believers may pray to be free from coveting
Ps 119:36

Godly people claim not to have coveted
Samuel 1Sa 12:3–5

Paul Ac 20:33 *See also* 1Co 9:12; 2Co 7:2; 11:9; 12:14–18; 1Th 2:5

Coveting as a commendable earnest desiring
A desire for the greater spiritual gifts: 1Co 12:31; 14:1,39
1Ti 3:1 *a desire to serve in a leadership role in the church*

See also
5446 poverty	8262 generosity,
5832 desire	human
5869 greed	8808 riches

6135

coveting, and other sins

Covetousness is associated with other sins and brings trouble with it.

Coveting is linked with other sins
Idolatry Eph 5:5 *See also* 1Co 10:6–7; Col 3:5

Pride Ps 10:3

Sexual sin Mt 5:28 *See also* 1Th 4:5

Laziness Pr 21:25–26

Covetousness is one of many sins which pollute a person
Mk 7:21–23

Love of money is covetousness
It is a source of evil 1Ti 6:9–10 *See also* Pr 10:2; 22:16; 28:20,22; 30:8–9

Examples of those who love money Lk 16:14; Jn 12:5–6 *See also* Mt 23:25 pp Lk 11:39; 2Pe 2:3,14 *False teachers are "experts in greed".*

Believers must not be lovers of money Heb 13:5; 1Pe 5:2 *Elders must not be greedy for money. See also* Ex 18:21; Eph 5:3; 1Ti 3:1–3

Love of money characterises the last days 2Ti 3:1–2

Coveting brings trouble
Jas 4:1–2 *See also* Pr 15:27; 28:25; 29:4

Even a gift can be given covetously
2Co 9:5 *The gift translated as "one grudgingly given" literally means a "covetous gift".*

See also
5343 idleness	8768 idolatry
5412 money	8773 jealousy
6020 sin	8777 lust
6242 adultery	8802 pride
8714 dishonesty	

6139

deadness, spiritual

Being morally and spiritually without life, therefore without a relationship with God. This condition, being the result of original sin, brings wrath and judgment and can be changed only by the sovereign, intervening grace of God.

Spiritual deadness is humanity's condition by nature
It is linked to physical death Ge 2:17 *See also* Ge 3:3,19; Pr 11:19; Eze 18:20–31; Jn 8:21–24; Ro 1:32; 6:23

It is the universal consequence of sin Eph 2:1 *See also* Ge 8:21; 1Ch 10:13; Ps 51:5; 58:3; Pr 21:16; Jn 6:53; Ro 3:23; 5:12–13,17; Col 2:13

It is confirmed in the law Ro 5:20 *See also* Ro 7:4–12; 8:2–4; Gal 2:19

It is evidenced in the human mind Ro 8:6; 2Co 4:4; Col 1:21; Tit 1:15

It is evidenced in the human body Ro 7:24 *See also* Ro 6:12–14,16; 8:10; 1Co 15:50; 2Co 5:10; Gal 6:7–8; Eph 4:22; 1Ti 5:6; Jas 3:6

Spiritual darkness brings judgment
God's judgment is final Lk 16:26 *See also* Isa 66:24; Mt 8:12; 25:30–32; Mk 9:43–49; Lk 13:28; Heb 9:27; 1Pe 1:17

The second death Rev 20:14–15 *See also* Mt 25:41; 1Jn 5:16–17; Jude 12; Rev 2:11; 21:8

Rescue from spiritual deadness is initiated by God
He brings salvation Eph 2:4–5 *See also* Ps 103:12; Isa 26:19; Eze 37:1–14

He brings union with the death of Jesus Christ Ro 6:4 *See also* Ro 6:5–10; 2Co 4:10; 5:15–17; Gal 2:19–20; 5:24; 6:14; Php 3:10; Col 2:12

He brings union with the resurrection of Jesus Christ Col 3:1 *See also* Ro 5:21; 6:11; Rev 20:4–5

He brings ultimate physical resurrection Ro 8:10–11 *See also* 1Co 15:42–49

Concern for those who are spiritually sleepy
Eph 5:14 *See also* Ro 13:11; 1Th 5:5–7; Rev 3:1–3

See also
5004 human race &	6510 salvation
sin	8341 separation
5020 human nature	8768 idolatry
5135 blindness,	9024 death, spiritual
spiritual	9210 judgment,
6023 sin, universality	God's
6154 fall, the	9510 hell
6178 hardness of	
heart	

6142

decay

As a consequence of the fall, all created things have a tendency to waste away and spoil. Jesus Christ brings deliverance from this.

Decay was decreed as a result of the fall
In human beings Ge 2:17

In the world Ge 3:17–19 *See also* Ro 8:20

Decay is the common experience of humanity
Ps 90:3–10 *See also* Ps 49:8–9

A decaying world is not worth clinging to
Mt 6:19–20 *See also* Ps 102:26; Lk 12:33; 1Jn 2:15–17

Jesus Christ is free from decay
Ac 2:24–31 *See also* Ps 16:8–11; Ac 13:34–37; Heb 7:26; 13:8

Believers are redeemed from decay
2Co 4:16 *See also* Job 19:26; Jn 3:16

Christians are "salt" in a decaying world
Mt 5:13 *See also* Mk 9:50; Lk 14:34

The world to come is free from decay
1Pe 1:3–5 *See also* Ro 8:21; 1Co 15:42; Heb 12:28; 13:14; Rev 21:4

Examples of the link between sin and decay
Lev 26:14–16,39
The curse on the unfaithful wife: Nu 5:20–22,27
Curses for disobedience: Dt 28:22; 32:24 Job 18:13; Ps 32:3; 49:13–14;

106:15,43; 112:10; Isa 5:24; 10:16; 17:4;
24:16; 64:7; Jer 49:7
The destruction of Jerusalem lamented:
La 2:6,8
Eze 4:17; 24:23; 33:10
Punishment for Israel's sin: Hos 4:3; 8:10
Hab 3:16; Jas 5:2

See also

5482 punishment	6644 eternal life
5979 waste	6720 redemption
6130 corruption	9020 death
6154 fall, the	9310 resurrection
6199 imperfection	9410 heaven

6145

deceit

Behaviour, in words or actions,
which is deliberately intended to
make people believe things that are
not true.

6146

deceit, and God's nature

Deceit is totally contrary to the
nature and purposes of God. The
gospel is grounded in the complete
truthfulness and trustworthiness of
God, whereas sin is based upon self-
deception.

**God's nature and purposes are
not based on deception**
Deceit is contrary to the nature of God
Tit 1:2 *See also* Jn 16:13; 1Pe 2:22
God cannot be deceived 1Ch 28:9 *See
also* Ps 139:1; Ac 5:3; 1Co 4:5

Jesus Christ and deception
Jesus Christ does not deceive
Isa 53:9

Satan's power rests on deception
Jn 8:44 *See also* Ge 3:1–4; 2Co 11:3,14;
2Th 2:9–10

The coming antichrist will rely on
deception 2Jn 7 *See also* Mt 24:24
pp Mk 13:22; Rev 13:14

False prophets and false teachers rely
on deception 2Co 11:13 *See also*
Jer 14:14; 23:26; Eze 13:6; Ac 20:30;
Ro 16:18; Eph 4:14; 1Ti 4:2;
Tit 1:10–11; 2Pe 2:1–3

**Deception is at the heart of
human sin**
The fall took place through deception
Ge 3:1–4,13 *See also* 1Ti 2:14

Deception is a characteristic of fallen
human nature Jer 17:9 *See also*
Job 15:35
Deceptive speech: Ps 5:9; 10:7; 35:20;
36:3; Mic 6:12; Ro 3:13
Ps 38:12; 116:11; Pr 12:5; Jer 9:4–5
deceptive friends and brothers; Hos 11:12;
Na 3:1; Mt 15:19 pp Mk 7:21–22;
Ro 1:29; 2Ti 3:13; Tit 1:12

Examples of deceit Ge 4:9 *Cain
Abraham:* Ge 12:13; 20:2
Ge 26:7 *Isaac;* Ge 27:19 *Jacob;* Ge 31:7
Laban; Ge 37:31 *Joseph's brothers;*
Ex 8:29 *Pharaoh;* Jos 9:4 *the Gibeonites
David:* 1Sa 21:2,13
2Sa 13:6 *Amnon;* 1Ki 13:18 *the old
prophet;* 2Ki 5:22 *Gehazi;* Mt 2:8 *Herod*

The Pharisees: Mt 22:18 pp Mk 12:15
pp Lk 20:23

See also

1020 God, all- knowing	5943 self-deception
1460 truth	8751 false witness
4123 Satan, deceiver	8767 hypocrisy
	9115 antichrist, the

6147

deceit, practice of

Deceit is condemned by God as an
attempt to deny his sovereignty and
his revelation of himself.

Deceit is forbidden by God
Condemnation of deception in general
Lev 19:11 *See also* Pr 12:22; 24:28

False witnesses condemned Ex 20:16
pp Dt 5:20 *See also* Pr 12:17; 14:5; 19:9

False measures prohibited Lev 19:35
See also Dt 25:13; Pr 11:1; 20:10;
Mic 6:11

Spiritual deception condemned
Tit 1:16 *See also* Mal 1:14; Mt 23:27–28;
Lk 6:46; Ro 2:21

**Deception must not be found in
the people of God**
God's people must not practise deceit
1Pe 2:1 *See also* Job 27:4; Ps 24:3–4;
32:2; Zep 3:13; Jn 4:24; 1Co 5:8;
Eph 4:25; Col 3:9; 1Pe 3:10; Rev 14:5

Christian leaders in particular must not
deceive 2Co 4:2 *See also* 2Co 1:12; 2:17;
1Th 2:3–5; 1Ti 3:8; Tit 1:7

God's people warned against being
deceived Eph 5:6 *See also* Jer 29:8;
1Co 6:9–10; 15:33; Gal 6:7; Col 2:8;
2Th 2:3; 1Jn 3:7

Deceit results in God's judgment
Ps 5:6 *See also* Dt 25:16; Ps 55:23;
119:118; Pr 20:17; 21:6; Jer 9:8–9;
Eze 13:9; Ac 5:9–10; Rev 21:8,27; 22:15

See also

4132 demons, malevolence	5908 motives
	5920 pretence
5613 weights & measures	5948 shrewdness
	8714 dishonesty
5804 charm	8776 lies
5863 flattery	

6151

dirt

Throwing dirt to signify contempt
2Sa 16:13 *See also* Na 3:6

Bathing to remove dirt
1Pe 3:21

**Comparative use of dirt to
emphasise abundance**
Zec 9:3

**Metaphorical use of filth to
represent sin**
Isa 4:4 *See also* Pr 30:11–14; Isa 28:8;
Jas 1:21; Rev 17:4

Refuse indicating worthlessness
1Co 4:13 *See also* 2Ki 9:37; Ps 83:10;
Isa 5:25; Jer 8:2; 9:22; 16:4; 25:33;
La 3:45; Php 3:8–9

See also

7340 clean and unclean	7416 purification
7342 cleanliness	7426 ritual washing
7348 defilement	7903 baptism
	8324 purity

6154

fall, the

The departure by creation, including
human beings, from the patterns
and standards set for it by God.
Creation now exists at a lower level
of integrity and fulfilment than that
which God originally intended for it.

6155

fall, of Adam and Eve

The first human beings abused their
God-given freedom. Their original
disobedience and resultant
expulsion from the Garden of Eden
is usually referred to as "the fall".

**The first sin was the
disobedience of Adam and Eve to
God's command**
Ge 2:17; 3:1–7 *See also* Hos 6:7;
Ro 5:12,14; 2Co 11:3; 1Ti 2:14

Causes of the fall
Disobedience Ge 2:16–17; 3:1–3;
Isa 43:27; Hos 6:7

Through satanic deception Ge 3:4,13;
2Co 11:3; 1Ti 2:14

Evil desire Ge 3:6

**Adam and Eve tried to hide their
disobedience**
Ge 3:8–13 *See also* Job 31:33

**The disobedience of Adam and
Eve affected every relationship in
life**
Relationship with God Ge 3:22–23 *See
also* Ge 4:14; Ps 90:3–10; Ro 1:20–21

Relationships among human beings
Ge 3:16 *See also* Ge 4:1–8; Ro 1:18–32;
Eph 2:1–3,11–12

The relationship between human
beings and the creation Ge 3:17–19 *See
also* Ge 3:14–15; 4:10–12; Ro 8:19

**The consequences of the
disobedience of Adam and Eve**
It leads to death and punishment
Ro 5:12 *See also* Ro 1:18; 1Co 15:21–22;
1Th 1:10; 2:14–16

Sin springs from within the human
mind, will and emotions Jas 1:13–15
See also Jas 4:6–7; 1Jn 2:15–17

See also

5023 image of God	5634 work & the fall
5033 knowledge of good & evil	6024 sin, effects of
	6112 banishment
5080 Adam	6213 participation in
5093 Eve	sin
5169 nakedness	8718 disobedience
5482 punishment	9020 death

6156
fall, of humanity

On account of their relation to Adam, all human beings have an inherent bias towards evil due to sin. Individual acts of sin reflect this bias, often referred to as "original sin".

All human beings, except for Jesus Christ, are sinful
Ro 3:23; Heb 4:15 *See also* Ge 6:5,11–12; Ps 14:1–3; 51:5; Isa 64:6–7; Jn 8:7; Ro 3:9–20; 5:12–19; Eph 2:1–3

Every part of a person is affected by sin
The heart Jer 17:9 *See also* Ge 6:5; 8:21; 1Sa 17:28; 2Ch 12:14; Ps 66:18; Jer 5:23; Mt 5:28; 15:8,19

The body Ro 6:6 *See also* Ro 6:12–13; 1Co 6:13,19–20

Human nature Ro 8:5–8 *See also* Ro 7:5; 1Co 5:5 fn; Gal 5:19–21; 6:8; Eph 2:3 fn

Believers are warned not to fall from grace
Heb 3:12–14 *See also* Mt 24:12–13; 1Co 15:2; Gal 5:4; Heb 4:11; 12:15; 2Pe 3:17; Rev 2:4–5

God is able to keep believers from falling
Jude 24 *See also* Job 33:14–18; Ro 16:25; Eph 6:13; 1Jn 5:18

See also
4027 world, fallen	6142 decay
5004 human race & sin	6166 flesh, sinful nature
5019 human nature	6199 imperfection
5065 spirit, fallen & redeemed	6510 salvation
6023 sin, universality	8459 perseverance
6130 corruption	8704 apostasy

6157
fall, of Satan and his angels

Satan and his angels rebelled against God and were removed from their positions of authority. They are now destined for judgment.

The rebellion of Satan and his angels
Isa 14:12–15 *Written about a king in Isaiah's own time, this passage has been used by both Jews and Christians as a description of the fall of Satan;* Jude 6 *See also* Job 4:18; Eze 28:15; Lk 10:18; Rev 12:7–9,12

The results of the rebellion of Satan and his angels
Constant spiritual warfare on the earth Rev 12:17 *See also* Mt 16:23 pp Mk 8:33; Ac 13:10; 2Co 11:13–15; Gal 5:16–18; 1Ti 3:6–7; Jas 4:7; 1Pe 5:8–9

God's punishment 2Pe 2:4 *See also* Mt 25:41; Jude 6; Rev 19:20; 20:10

See also
4110 angels	8482 spiritual warfare
4120 Satan	8735 evil, origins of
4130 demons	8802 pride
6021 sin, nature of	9210 judgment, God's
6026 sin, judgment on	
6221 rebellion	

6160

fathers, sin of the

Children may suffer on account of the sins committed by their forebears, just as they may also be blessed for their sake. Nevertheless, Scripture teaches that each individual must take responsibility for his or her own sin.

Children suffer the ill-effects of their fathers' sins
Ex 34:6–7 *See also* Ex 20:4–6 pp Dt 5:8–10; Lev 26:39; Nu 14:18,31–33; Jos 7:24–25; 1Ki 16:34; Jos 6:26; Job 21:19; Isa 14:21; Jer 32:18

The exilic prophets emphasised individual responsibility for sin
Eze 18:20 *See also* Jer 31:29–30; Eze 18:1–20

Children share in the blessing of their fathers
Ge 17:4–7; 26:24; Dt 7:9 *See also* Ge 6:17–18; 15:18–19; Ex 2:23–25; 20:4–6 pp Dt 5:8–10; Nu 25:10–13; 2Sa 7:11–16; 1Ki 11:12–13,31–34; Lk 1:50; Ro 11:28–29

See also
5051 responsibility	5680 family
5482 punishment	5684 fathers
5651 ancestors	6020 sin
5664 children	

6163

faults

Human weaknesses and failings which are sinful in themselves, and may lead to further sin. It is common, often as a means of averting blame, to put undue focus on the faults of others. However, where necessary, faults should be exposed and responsibility properly attributed. Jesus Christ lived a faultless life and God's people are challenged to live lives that are above reproach. The church will one day be presented without fault before God.

The variety of human faults
A flawed human nature Ro 7:14–23 *See also* Gal 5:17; Eph 2:3; 2Pe 2:18

Human weaknesses and failings Ro 15:1 *See also* Ro 8:28; 14:1–2

Faults in thought, word and deed Ps 78:57 *disloyalty and unfaithfulness to God;* Pr 14:21 *not showing concern for others;* Isa 53:6 *selfishness in going one's own way;* Hos 7:16 *unwillingness to turn*

to God; Jas 3:2 *failure to control the tongue;* Jas 4:17 *failure to do what is right*

Finding fault with others
Passing blame to others Ge 3:12 *Adam blames Eve for his disobedience. See also* Ex 32:22–24 *Aaron blames the Israelites for the golden calf;* 1Sa 13:11–12 *Saul blames his troops' impatience and Samuel's late arrival for his disobedience;* 1Sa 15:20–21 *Saul blames his soldiers for the failure to carry out God's instructions;* Mt 25:24–25 *The man who buried his talent blames his action on his master's hardness.*

Criticising and judging others Mt 7:1–5 *See also* Jas 4:11–12; 5:9; Jude 16

Finding fault with God's appointed leaders Ex 17:3 *See also* Ex 15:24; Nu 14:2; Jos 9:18; Ac 11:2–3; 2Co 10:1

Finding fault with God's people Mt 5:11 pp Lk 6:22 *See also* Ex 5:16–17; Ps 41:6; 71:10; Da 6:24

Finding fault with God Ps 78:19 *See also* Ex 16:7; Nu 14:27; 21:5; Eze 35:13

Finding fault with Jesus Christ Lk 6:7 pp Mt 12:10 pp Mk 3:4 *See also* Mt 9:3 pp Mk 2:7 pp Lk 5:21 *Jesus Christ is accused of blasphemy because he claims to forgive sin;* Mt 9:11 pp Mk 2:16 pp Lk 5:30 *Jesus Christ is criticised for his association with "sinners";* Mt 15:2 pp Mk 7:5 *Jesus Christ is criticised for failure to conform to ceremonial cleansing traditions;* Mt 26:59–61 pp Mk 14:55–59 *false charges brought against Jesus Christ at his trial;* Jn 9:16 *Jesus Christ is accused of breaking the Sabbath.*

Confronting human faults
Accepting blame for one's own faults Ps 51:3–4 *See also* Jnh 1:12; Lk 15:18

God holds his people at fault Jer 17:4 *See also* Heb 8:8–9; Jer 31:31–32

Faults cannot be hidden from God Ps 19:12; 44:21; 90:8; Ecc 12:14; 1Co 14:25

Confronting others with their faults Mt 18:15–17; Gal 6:1 *See also* Lk 17:3; Jas 5:19–20

Examples of those confronted with their faults 2Sa 12:7 *David;* 1Ki 14:7–9 *Jeroboam;* 2Ch 16:9 *Asa;* Da 5:23 *Belshazzar;* Mt 14:3 pp Mk 6:18 *Herod;* Ac 5:3 *Ananias and Sapphira;* Gal 2:11–12 *Peter*

God can deal with human faults
Freedom from the power of sin Ro 6:11–12; 8:3–4; 2Co 5:17; Gal 5:16

Strength for service 2Co 12:9–10; Php 4:13

Forgiveness Ps 65:3; Eph 4:32; Col 2:13; 1Jn 1:9

Faultlessness
Faultlessness shown by Jesus Christ 1Pe 2:22 *See also* Isa 53:9; Jn 8:46; Heb 4:15; 1Pe 1:19; 1Jn 3:5

God's people are to be above reproach 1Pe 2:12 *See also* Ro 12:17–18; 2Co 8:20–21 *Paul ensures that his handling of money is above criticism;* Php 2:14–15

Leaders, in particular, must be above reproach: 1Ti 3:2; Tit 1:6 2Pe 3:14

The church will be presented faultless before God Jude 24–25 *See also* Eph 5:27; Col 1:22; 1Th 3:13; 5:23

See also

1030 God, compassion	6652 forgiveness
5820 criticism	6671 grace & Christian life
5851 excuse	8266 holiness
5897 judging others	8357 weakness
6020 sin	8741 failure
6115 blame	
6200 imperfection, influence	

6166

flesh, sinful nature

The physical aspect of human beings, which distinguishes them from God and is therefore frequently used in the NT as a symbol of human sinful nature in contrast with God's perfection. (The Greek word for "flesh" is sometimes translated by other words and phrases in the passages cited in this theme.)

Flesh as the bodily substance of human beings

As individuals or in relation to others Ps 84:2 *See also* Ge 2:23–24; 29:14; 1Co 15:39
The following two examples from Paul, where the normal word for "flesh" underlies the translation "body", make clear that to live "in the flesh" is normal human experience; the phrase does not necessarily imply that human nature is sinful, even though in many other instances a specific connection between "flesh" and "sin" is intended: Gal 2:20; Php 1:22–24

As the means by which Jesus Christ identified with the human race to bring salvation Jn 1:14 *See also* Eph 2:15; Heb 10:20; 1Jn 4:2

As subject to mortality Isa 40:6–7 *See also* Ps 78:39; Ac 2:31; 1Co 15:50

As subject to weakness 2Ch 32:8 *See also* Ps 73:26; Mt 26:41 pp Mk 14:38

Flesh as contrasting human nature with God's perfection
The powerlessness of human beings contrasted with God's eternal power Isa 31:3 *See also* Jn 3:6; 6:63

Human or worldly standards contrasted with God's standards Jn 8:15 *See also* 1Co 1:26; 2Co 5:16; 10:3–4

Flesh as denoting the sinful nature of human beings
The tendency to sin Ro 7:18 *Paul does not mean that no goodness at all exists in people; nor that the physical aspect of human beings is inherently evil. He means that humans are invariably infected by evil and subject to its power. See also* Jer 17:5

The conflict in human experience between the sinful nature and the Spirit of God Gal 5:17 *See also* Ro 8:4–9; Gal 5:19–25

The sinful nature is opposed to God and his will
This opposition finds expression in a range of acts and attitudes Gal 5:19–21 *See also* Ro 7:14–25; 8:7; 13:13–14; 1Co 6:9–11; Eph 5:5; Jas 1:14–15; 1Pe 2:11; 2Pe 2:10,18; 1Jn 2:16

Confidence in the law is futile Ro 8:3
Because of the sinfulness of human nature, God's law is powerless to bring people into relationship with God; Gal 3:3 *Even the attempt to find acceptance with God through keeping his law is an act of the sinful nature because it involves rejecting his offer of salvation through his grace. See also* Ro 7:25; Php 3:3–9

The sinful nature controls human behaviour in ways which run counter to God's purpose Ro 8:8 *See also* Ro 7:5

The sinful nature therefore makes people subject to God's judgment and to death
Ro 8:13; Eph 2:3 *See also* Gal 6:8

Believers are not controlled by the sinful nature
Through Jesus Christ's entering into human flesh, God delivers from the power and consequences of human sinfulness Ro 8:3 *See also* Eph 2:15

Believers have crucified the sinful nature Ro 7:5–6 *See also* Ro 8:8–9; Gal 5:24; Col 2:11

The power of God's Spirit enables believers to continue to resist the sinful nature Ro 8:13 *See also* Ro 13:14; Gal 5:13; Col 3:5–6; 1Pe 2:11

God's provision of church discipline in eliminating the sinful nature 1Co 5:5
The discipline of excluding a sinner from the church community is intended to bring him to repentance and so abandon his sinful course of action. Repentance provoked by physical suffering is possibly also in mind.

See also

2075 Christ, sinless	6203 mortality
5020 human nature	6213 participation in sin
5082 Adam, significance	6248 temptation
5136 body	6658 freedom
6020 sin	8451 mortification
6156 fall of humanity	9020 death

6169

godlessness

An outlook and lifestyle which does not acknowledge God. God frustrates the evil purposes of the godless and judges them. Believers are to guard against godlessness.

Godlessness is an outlook and lifestyle which does not acknowledge God
Ps 14:1–3 *See also* Job 35:9–10; Ps 10:4–11; 36:1–4; Pr 11:9; 30:8–9

Examples of godlessness
Judah's religious leaders: Jer 23:11–12,15–17
Heb 12:16 *Esau*

God frustrates the evil purposes of the godless
Job 8:11–19; 34:29–30; Ps 9:17–20

God judges godless people and nations
Ro 1:18
The book of Job was written against a background which made no allowance for the prosperity of the godless or the misery of the godly, so no attempt is made to reconcile these things with the justice of God (as it is, for instance, in Ps 73): Job 13:15–16; 15:34; 20:4–5; 27:8–10; 36:8–13
Ps 50:16–22; Isa 10:6; 33:13–14

Believers are to guard against godlessness
Jude 3–23 *See also* 1Ti 4:7; 6:20–21

Jesus Christ will turn godlessness away from Israel
Ro 11:26–27

See also

1095 God, patience of	8704 apostasy
6020 sin	8710 atheism
6154 fall, the	8712 denial of Christ
6231 rejection of God	8764 forgetting God
8265 godliness	8768 idolatry
8702 agnosticism	8846 ungodliness

6172

guilt

Primarily a state of being at fault, often accompanied by a feeling of being in the wrong. Scripture affirms that human guilt arises from sin before God, and can only be purged through accepting the forgiveness offered through the death of Jesus Christ.

6173
guilt, and God

All human beings are guilty in the sight of God, and all require forgiveness and expiation of their sin. Guilt can arise through failing to know what is right, through failing to do what is right and through giving in to temptation to do wrong.

Guilt as the objective condition of sinners
Guilt results from intentional sin Lev 6:1–7; Jas 2:10 *See also* Nu 5:5–7; Dt 24:14–15; Ezr 9:13–15; Eze 22:1–4; Jn 16:7–8

Guilt results from unintentional sin Lev 4:13 *See also* Lev 4:22,27; Ac 3:17–20

Guilt as an accumulation of sin Hos 13:12 *See also* Ezr 9:6; Isa 1:4; 24:20

God's knowledge of human guilt Ps 69:5 *See also* Ge 4:8–10; Jos 7:1–26; Jer 2:22; 1Co 4:4–5

God's anger at human guilt 2Ch 24:18 *See also* Nu 32:10–13; 2Ki 22:11–13; Hos 12:13–14; Ro 1:18; 2:5–8; Eph 5:6–7

God's determination to punish the guilty

God himself punishes the guilty
Nu 14:18 *See also* Ex 20:5; Jer 25:12; Na 1:2–3

Human judges are to punish the guilty
Dt 25:1–3 *See also* Pr 17:15; 24:23–25; Ro 13:1–5; 1Pe 2:13–14

See also

1020 God, all-knowing	6023 sin, universality
1025 God, anger of	6124 condemnation
1075 God, justice of	7318 blood, symbol of guilt
1310 God as judge	8277 innocence
5482 punishment	
5493 retribution	

6174
guilt, human aspects of

Scripture affirms that all are guilty in the sight of God, and explores the various ways in which guilt affects human life, before offering forgiveness of guilt through the death of Jesus Christ.

Human awareness of guilt
Ps 51:3–5 *See also* Ge 42:21; Ps 32:1–4; Jn 8:3–11; Heb 9:9; 1Jn 3:19–20

Human beings are held responsible for their guilt
Lev 5:17 *See also* Isa 24:5–6; Eze 18:19–20; Hos 10:1–2; 13:16; Mt 12:35–36; Ro 14:12; 2Co 5:10; Rev 20:12

Guilt defiles human life
Isa 59:1–3 *See also* Ps 51:1–7; Jer 2:22; Heb 10:22

Human experience of guilt
Feelings of guilt in general Heb 10:1–2 *See also* 2Sa 24:10 pp 1Ch 21:8; 2Co 7:10; Heb 10:22; 1Jn 3:19–20

Guilt produces feelings of anguish and despair Mt 27:3–5 *See also* Ezr 9:1–7; 10:1; Ps 40:11–12; Pr 28:17; La 1:20

Guilt produces feelings of shame and disgrace Ezr 9:6 *See also* Jer 23:38–40

Guilt produces feelings of fear and terror Isa 6:1–7 *See also* Ge 3:8–10; Isa 33:14

Guilt produces feelings of unworthiness Lk 15:21 *See also* Ezr 9:13–15; Ps 51:11 *The fear of being cast out of God's presence is the result of the psalmist's sense of guilt*; Lk 5:8; 1Co 15:9

See also

5009 conscience	6115 blame
5277 criminals	6163 faults
5831 depression	6632 conviction
5843 embarrassment	6740 returning to God
5947 shame	8754 fear
5970 unhappiness	
6024 sin, effects of	

6175
guilt, removal of

Through the death of Jesus Christ, God has provided a means of removing guilt, thus opening the way for believers to know the blessings of a right relationship with him.

The removal of guilt is God's work
Jer 2:22; 50:20; Ro 8:33 *"Justify" is a legal term which includes the meaning "to declare not guilty"*. *See also* 2Sa 24:10 pp 1Ch 21:8; Ps 32:1–5; Isa 6:1–6

The removal of guilt requires confession
Ps 32:5 *See also* 2Sa 24:10 pp 1Ch 21:8; Ps 51:14; Jer 3:12–13; Ac 11:21; Ro 2:4; 2Ti 2:25; 1Jn 1:8–9

The removal of guilt by the OT sacrificial system
Guilt removed by the guilt offering Lev 6:6–7 *See also* Lev 19:20–22; Ezr 10:18–19

Guilt removed by the sin offering Nu 15:27–28 *See also* Lev 5:5–6; Nu 6:9–11

Guilt removed by the Day of Atonement Lev 16:20–34

Animal sacrifices are ultimately ineffective in removing guilt Heb 10:1–4 *See also* Heb 9:9

The removal of guilt by Jesus Christ's sacrificial death
Isa 53:10–12 *This prophecy finds its ultimate fulfilment in the person of Jesus Christ*; Heb 9:14 *See also* Jn 1:29 *The point of John's image is that Jesus Christ will be sacrificed, as lambs were, to remove people's guilt*; Ro 5:9 *The blood of Jesus Christ referred to here is his shed blood, and therefore speaks of his (sacrificial) death*; 2Co 5:21 *Human guilt is transferred to Jesus Christ, in order that believers might become righteous before God*; Tit 2:14; Heb 9:28; 10:11–14; 1Jn 1:7

The results of guilt being removed
A clean conscience Heb 9:14; 10:22

Peace with God Isa 53:5; Ro 5:1; Col 1:19–20

Access into God's presence Ro 5:1–2; Eph 2:18

Joy Ps 32:1–11; Ro 5:1–2

Hope Ro 5:1–2

A desire to worship God Ps 51:14–15

A desire to serve God Isa 6:6–8; Jn 21:15–20

See also

1055 God, grace & mercy	6624 confession of sin
1320 God as Saviour	6653 forgiveness, divine
2315 Christ as Lamb	6676 justification
2414 cross, centrality	6720 redemption
5203 acquittal	7370 guilt offering
6510 salvation	
6614 atonement	

6178
hardness of heart

Primarily, in Scripture, a persistent inner refusal to hear and obey the word of God. Also, in a more general sense, an uncaring or unsympathetic attitude towards other people.

Kinds of hardness of heart
As disobedience towards God Ps 95:8–9 *Referring to the disobedience of the Israelites in their wilderness wanderings*. *See also* Heb 3:7–9 Eph 4:18 *See also* Pr 28:14; Zec 7:12; Ro 2:5; Heb 3:12–15; 4:5–7

As the work of God Ex 10:20 *God's judgment on Pharaoh was to confirm him in his stubbornness so that he might feel the full weight of his wrath*; Isa 6:10 *See also* Jn 12:40

As an uncaring attitude towards other people Dt 15:7 *See also* Ps 17:10; 73:7; 119:70; Mt 19:8 pp Mk 10:5; Jas 2:15–16; 1Jn 3:17

Examples of hardness of heart
Pharaoh Ex 7:13,22; 8:19,32; 9:7,34–35

Israel 1Sa 6:6; Jer 5:23; 9:14; 11:8; 13:10; 16:12; 18:12; 23:26

Zedekiah 2Ch 36:12–13

Jesus Christ's disciples Mk 6:51–52; 8:17

Jesus Christ's generation Mt 13:15; 19:8 pp Mk 10:5; Mk 3:5

Paul's hearers Ac 28:25–27

God's remedies for hardness of heart
Repentance Ps 51:17 *See also* 1Ki 8:46–49; 2Ch 34:27; Jer 3:17; Eze 18:31

A work of grace Eze 11:19 *God's promise to Israel*. *See also* 1Ki 8:58; Jer 31:33; Eze 36:26

See also

5764 attitudes, negative to God	6245 stubbornness
6021 sin, nature of	7223 exodus, significance
6185 imagination, desires	8718 disobedience
6193 impenitence	8802 pride
6221 rebellion	8834 unbelief

6181
ignorance

A state of lack of knowledge or information, including a failure to know the person, will and ways of God. Scripture emphasises the importance of a true knowledge of God and makes such knowledge available.

6182
ignorance, and human situation

Ignorance is part of the human condition: as finite creatures, human knowledge is incomplete, but human beings can trust God, whose knowledge is complete, to guide their steps.

Ignorance of God
Finite human beings cannot know God completely Ecc 11:5 *See also* Job 38:1–7; Ecc 3:11

This ignorance will be dispelled at Jesus Christ's return 1Co 13:9–12

Ignorance of the future
Human beings are ignorant of future events Ecc 8:7–8 *See also* Ecc 3:22; 9:12; 10:14; 11:2,6; Ac 20:22

Human beings are ignorant of the time of Jesus Christ's return Mk 13:32–36 pp Mt 24:36–44

Presumptious plans should therefore be avoided Jas 4:13–16 *See also* Ps 39:6; Pr 27:1; Lk 12:16–21

God's guidance is essential Pr 20:24 *See also* Pr 19:21; Jer 10:23

Ignorance of doctrinal matters
Within the church 1Th 4:13–18 *See also* 1Co 10:1–10; 12:1–11

God has established teachers to combat ignorance 1Co 12:28 *See also* Eph 4:11–13; 1Ti 4:13; 5:17; 2Ti 3:16–17

Ignorance may lead to death
Pr 9:17–18 *See also* Pr 4:19; 7:21–23

See also

2565 Christ, second coming	6020 sin
5026 knowledge	8124 guidance
5135 blindness, spiritual	8134 knowing God
5149 eyes	8355 understanding
	8702 agnosticism

6183
ignorance, of God

A lack of knowledge of God, regarded as inexcusable by Scripture. God has made his existence, nature and power known to all through creation. God himself is not ignorant of human sin, but is able to discern the real intentions of human minds and wills.

Ignorance of God is inexcusable
God is made known through creation Ro 1:18–20 *As God is made known to all through nature, human ignorance of God is inexcusable. See also* Ps 19:1–4; Ac 14:17; 17:24–28; Ro 2:14–15

God revealed himself to Israel Ne 9:13–14 *See also* Ex 19:10–11,16–19; Ps 103:7; 147:19–20; Eze 20:5

Ignorance of God is linked to sin and rebellion
Among the Gentiles Eph 4:18–19 *See also* Ex 5:2; Jn 4:22; Ac 17:23; 1Th 4:3–5

In Israel Isa 1:2–3 *See also* Isa 56:10; Jer 2:8–9; 4:22; 5:4–5; 8:7–12; 9:6; 10:21; Hos 4:1,6; Am 3:10

Ignorance of God in the ministry of Jesus Christ
Among the religious leaders Jn 8:13–19 *See also* Mt 22:23–32 pp Mk 12:18–27 pp Lk 20:27–38; Jn 8:54–55; 16:2–3

Among his disciples Jn 14:8–11 *See also* Lk 18:31–34; Jn 14:5–7

God is not ignorant of human sin and motives
Ge 6:5; Heb 4:13 *See also* Ex 3:7; Job 28:12–28; Ps 139:1–6; 147:5; Eze 11:5; Mt 6:8; Ac 1:24

Human ignorance of sin and the revelation of God
The fall brought knowledge of sin Ge 3:22 *See also* Ge 3:4–7

The OT law exposed the nature of sin Ro 7:7 *See also* Ro 3:20; 4:15; 5:13

Human ignorance does not excuse sin
By individuals Lev 5:17–19 *The law made provision for atonement of sins committed as a result of ignorance. See also* Lev 4:27–35; Nu 15:27–29; Eze 45:20

By the nation Lev 4:13–21 *See also* Nu 15:22–26; Heb 9:7

By leaders Lev 4:22–26 *See also* Lev 4:3–12

Sin committed in ignorance incurs a lesser judgment than other sin
Lk 12:47–48 *See also* Pr 24:12; Ro 2:14–15

Repentance of sin committed in ignorance brings forgiveness
Ge 20:1–18 *See also* Ac 3:17–20; 1Ti 1:13

Ignorance of God and salvation
There is no salvation outside Jesus Christ Ac 4:12 *See also* Jn 14:6; 1Ti 2:5–6

Believers have a responsibility to remove ignorance of the gospel Ro 10:14–17 *See also* Mt 28:19–20

Ignorance and God's judgment
The justice of God in salvation Ge 18:25 *See also* Dt 32:4; Ne 9:33; Pr 24:12; Da 4:37; Lk 12:47–48

God's judgment falls on all who do not know him 2Th 1:8–10 *See also* Ps 79:6; Jer 10:25; Ro 2:8

God's judgment falls severely on those who choose to disobey him Pr 1:28–32 *on Israel*
On those who have heard the gospel: Ac 17:29–31; Heb 2:2–3; 2Pe 2:20–22

See also

1020 God, all-knowing	5052 responsibility to God
1310 God as judge	6178 hardness of heart
1325 God, the Creator	6221 rebellion
1403 God, revelation	6652 forgiveness
2324 Christ as Saviour	8424 evangelism
5033 knowledge of good & evil	

6184
imagination

The human ability to form mental pictures, often used to refer to human desires or schemes which are inclined towards evil. Scripture often treats the human heart as the focus of the imagination.

6185
imagination, inward desires

The usually sinful inclinations of a heart which is by nature corrupt and stubborn, but which may be renewed by God, resulting in purified desires.

The heart is the source of human desires
Pr 4:23 *See also* Ps 10:3; Mt 12:34–35 pp Lk 6:45

God knows the human heart
1Ki 8:39; 1Ch 28:9 *See also* 1Sa 16:7 *God's choice of David;* Ps 7:9; 19:14; 26:2; 38:9; 44:21; 139:2,23; Pr 15:26; 21:2; Jer 11:20 *The plot of Jeremiah's enemies is revealed to him by the* Lord; Jer 20:12; Eze 11:5; Rev 2:23; Mt 9:4 pp Mk 2:8 pp Lk 5:22 *Jesus Christ knows the thoughts of others.*

The corruption of the heart
Its inclination towards evil Ge 6:5 *See also* Ge 8:21; Ps 14:1–3 pp Ps 53:1–3; Ps 94:11; Ecc 9:3; Jer 17:9–10; Mt 15:18–19 pp Mk 7:20–23

Corruption finds particular expression in sexual sin Ro 1:24 *See also* Mt 5:28; Ro 1:26–27; Gal 5:19

The stubbornness of the heart
It leads to disregard for God Isa 65:2

It produces false confidence Dt 29:18–19 *See also* Jer 23:17

It leads to idolatry Jer 9:14 *See also* Jer 13:10

It leads to disobedience Jer 7:24 *See also* Jer 16:12

It brings God's judgment Jer 11:8 *See also* Pr 28:14; 29:1; Jer 18:12–13; Ro 2:5; Heb 3:7–11; Ps 95:7–11

God allows people to continue in their stubbornness *God hardens Pharaoh's heart:* Ex 4:21; 7:3; 14:4,17 Ps 81:11–12; Ro 1:28

God's renewal of the heart
It results in purified desires Jer 24:7; Eze 36:26 *See also* Dt 6:6; Eze 11:19; Ro 12:2; 2Co 4:6; Eph 4:23; Php 4:8–9; Heb 8:10; Jer 31:33

Examples of renewed hearts 2Ch 11:16; Ne 9:8; Ps 51:10; 57:7; 86:11; Jer 3:17

God delights in a pure heart Ps 24:3–5 *See also* Dt 5:29; Ps 73:1; 125:4; Mt 5:8

God fulfils the desires of hearts devoted to him Ps 37:4 *See also* Ps 21:2; 145:19; Mt 6:21 pp Lk 12:34; Mt 6:33 pp Lk 12:31

God gives the desire to follow him 1Ch 29:18

The human ability to visualise in parables
Mt 13:11–17 pp Mk 4:10–12 pp Lk 8:9–10; Lk 10:23–24

See also

1020 God, all-knowing	5273 creativity
1352 covenant, the new	5909 motives, importance
2045 Christ, knowledge of	6178 hardness of heart
5017 heart, renewal	6245 stubbornness
5191 thought	8602 prayer
	8718 disobedience

6186
imagination, evil scheming

Human thinking, darkened by sin, expressed in plans which are in opposition to God and which seek to take advantage of others.

Human thought is darkened by sin
As a result of rejecting God's revelation Ro 1:21 *See also* Ps 10:2–4; 2Co 3:14; Eph 4:17–18; Tit 1:15
As a result of excessive alcohol Pr 23:33
As a result of Satan's activity 2Co 4:4; Eph 2:1–3

Sinful human thinking finds expression in evil ways
In evil schemes and plans Pr 6:16–18 *See also* Ge 11:6; Ps 36:4; 64:5–6; Pr 6:14; 12:20; 14:22; 24:8–9; Ecc 8:11; Ro 1:30
In scheming against God 2Co 10:5 *See also* Dt 31:21; Ps 2:1–2; Hos 7:15; Na 1:11
In scheming against others La 3:60–61 *See also* Dt 15:9 *warnings against evil thinking as the year for cancelling debts approaches;* Job 21:27; Ps 10:2–3; 37:7; 38:12; 41:7–8; 140:1–2; Isa 32:7; Zec 8:16–17; Mt 26:3–4 pp Mk 14:1–2 pp Lk 22:1–2 pp Jn 11:53 *Jewish religious leaders plot against Jesus Christ.*
Human plans are an expression of pride Jas 4:13–16 *See also* Pr 18:11; Isa 10:7–11; 30:1; Lk 12:16–20
Evil plans will fail Lk 1:51 *See also* Est 9:25; Ps 21:11–12; 33:10; Pr 19:21; Isa 8:10; 19:3; 66:18; Mic 2:1; Na 1:9

False prophecy comes from evil thinking
Eze 13:2–3 *See also* Dt 13:1–3; Jer 23:16–17; Eze 13:17

See also

1440 revelation, creation	5810 complacency
2545 Christ, opposition to	6020 sin
4120 Satan	7774 prophets, false
4811 darkness, symbol of sin	8734 evil
5038 mind, the human	8802 pride
	8827 selfishness

immorality

Behaviour which is contrary to the will of God for his people. Although the term may be used to refer to a wide range of immoral actions, it is used especially in relation to unacceptable sexual behaviour.

6188
immorality, nature of sexual

Sexual behaviour which is contrary to God's law.

Sexual immorality is widespread in the world
1Co 5:9–10 *See also* 1Co 7:1–2; Rev 9:21

The cause of sexual immorality
Gal 5:19 *See also* Mt 15:19–20 pp Mk 7:21–23; Eph 4:17–19

The folly of sexual immorality
Pr 6:32 *See also* Pr 5:3–5,20; 6:26

Sexual immorality brings punishment
Heb 13:4 *See also* Lev 20:10–21; Pr 2:16–19; 22:14; Eze 16:38; Ro 1:24–27; Eph 5:5; Col 3:5–6; 1Th 4:3–6; Jude 7; Rev 21:8; 22:15

Sexual immorality has no place in the Christian life
1Th 4:3,7 *See also* Ac 15:20,29; 21:25; Ro 13:13; 1Co 6:9–11,13–20; 10:8; Eph 5:3; Col 3:5; Heb 12:16

Forgiveness for sexual immorality
1Co 6:11 *See also* Lk 7:36–39; Jn 8:3–11

See also

5012 heart	6652 forgiveness
5375 law	7348 defilement
5482 punishment	8204 chastity
5708 marriage	8324 purity
6166 flesh, sinful nature	8339 self-control
6248 temptation	8821 self-indulgence

6189
immorality, examples of sexual

Prohibited sexual relationships
Incest Lev 18:6 *See also* Ge 19:33–36 *Lot's daughters;* Ge 35:22; 38:13–18; Lev 18:7–20; 2Sa 16:22; 1Co 5:1 *more likely referring to his stepmother*
Adultery 2Sa 11:4; Jer 23:14; 29:23; Hos 1:2; Jn 4:17–18
Prostitution 1Co 6:15–16 *See also* Jdg 16:1; 1Ki 3:16; Hos 4:13–15
Fornication Nu 25:1,6; 1Sa 2:22
Rape Ge 34:1–2; 2Sa 13:10–14
Homosexuality Ge 19:5 *the men of Sodom;* Jdg 19:22 *the men of Gibeah*

Sexual immorality among Christians
1Co 5:1; 2Pe 2:13–14; Jude 4; Rev 2:14,20

Sexual immorality as a picture of spiritual unfaithfulness
Among God's people Jer 3:20 *See also* Jer 13:26–27 *reflecting the immorality of the pagan religions in which Israel had indulged;* Eze 6:9; 16:15–17; Hos 2:1–10; 3:1; 4:10–12; 5:4; Mt 12:39; 16:4
In the world Rev 14:8; 17:1–2,4; 18:2; 19:2

See also

4263 Rome	6236 sexual sin
5674 daughters	7918 excommunication
5719 mothers, responsibilities	8273 holiness, ethical aspects
5735 sexuality	8839 unfaithfulness
5737 sisters	
6130 corruption	

impenitence

A deliberate and persistent refusal to repent or to submit to God's will.

6194
impenitence, warnings against

Scripture stresses the seriousness of impenitence. Despite the goodness of God, some sinners refuse to repent and turn to him in faith.

Impenitence is a refusal to turn from sin
Hos 7:10; Ac 7:51 *See also* Job 34:33; Isa 1:4; Jer 9:6; Hos 11:5

Impenitence in spite of God's invitations and warnings
Isa 66:4; Zec 7:11–12 *See also* 2Ki 17:14; Zec 1:4
Impenitence is a recurring theme in Jeremiah's prophecies: Jer 7:25–26; 11:7–8,10; 13:10; 17:23; 25:3–4; 32:33; 44:4–5,16

Impenitence in spite of God's dealings
Nu 14:11 *See also* Ne 9:17; Mt 11:20–24 pp Lk 10:13–15

Impenitence in spite of God's punishment
Ps 78:31–32; Am 4:6 *See also* Isa 9:13; Jer 2:30; 3:2–3; 5:3; 30:15; Zep 3:2; Hag 2:17

Impenitence in spite of God's goodness
Ro 2:4 *See also* Job 15:11 *Although inappropriate for Job, the advice is still valid;* Ro 10:21

There is no remedy for persistent impenitence
2Ch 36:16; 2Th 2:10 *See also* Heb 6:4–6; 10:26–27

See also

5764 attitudes, negative to God	6245 stubbornness
5829 defiance	6732 repentance
6178 hardness of heart	8718 disobedience
6230 rejection	8742 faithlessness
	8783 neglect
	8834 unbelief

6195
impenitence, results of

The seriousness of the failure to repent is frequently underlined in Scripture, which provides numerous examples of impenitence and its consequences.

Warnings against impenitence
Heb 12:25 *See also* 2Ch 30:6–9;

Jer 4:1; 18:9–10; Eze 14:6; Hos 14:1–2; Mal 3:7; Lk 13:1–5; Heb 3:7–19; Ps 95:7–8; Rev 2:5,16

Results of impenitence
Storing up wrath for the day of judgment Ro 2:5 *See also* 2Ch 24:20; 36:16–17; Job 36:12; Pr 1:24–26; Am 4:9; Ro 1:24; 2Pe 2:21

Condemnation Mt 11:20

Hardness of heart Mt 13:13–15 *See also* Heb 3:7–11

Spiritual blindness Jn 12:40 *See also* Ro 11:8; Rev 3:17

Being forsaken by God 2Ki 17:13–20; 2Ch 29:6–9

Examples of impenitence
Ex 8:15 *Pharaoh*
Israel: Jdg 2:19; 1Sa 8:19; Ne 9:26–29; Da 9:13–14
2Ch 33:23 *Amon;* 2Ch 36:13 *Zedekiah;* Jer 6:15 *inhabitants of Jerusalem;* Mt 21:31 *the elders and chief priests;* Lk 18:18 *the hard-hearted;* Ro 1:18–23 *the pagans;* Rev 2:21–27 *Jezebel, the false prophetess*
Human beings at the end times:
Rev 9:20–21; 16:8–11

See also
1025 God, anger of	6124 condemnation
5135 blindness, spiritual	9210 judgment, God's
5484 punishment by God	

imperfection

The state of incompletion or decay that characterises the fallen world. Although God created the world perfect, it lapsed into its present state of imperfection through human sin.

6200
imperfection, influence of

Scripture indicates that the world, including human beings and institutions, are imperfect because of the contaminating influence of sin. This influence extends to the household of faith: both Israel and the Christian church are portrayed as prone to sin and weakness.

The creation is imperfect because of sin
Ge 3:17–19 *See also* Ge 5:29; Ro 8:20–22

Imperfection is expressed in corruption and death
Ps 103:15–16; 2Pe 1:4 *See also* 2Sa 14:14; Ps 90:3–10; Ecc 12:1–7; Jas 1:10; 1Pe 1:24

The imperfection of the spiritual creation
Job 4:18; Jude 6 *See also* 2Pe 2:4

The universal imperfection of human beings
Ro 3:23 *See also* Ge 6:5; 1Ki 8:46

pp 2Ch 6:36; Ps 14:3; 130:3; Pr 20:9; Ecc 7:20; Isa 53:6; 64:6; Gal 3:22; Jas 3:2

The imperfection of the household of faith
Israel and her leaders Ne 9:34; Jer 2:21 *See also* Jdg 2:11–13; Ne 9:16; Ps 106:39; Isa 3:14; Jer 50:6; Eze 20:30; Mic 3:1–3

The Christian church and its leaders 2Co 12:20; Php 3:12 *See also* 1Co 3:1–3; 13:12; Col 2:20; Heb 5:12; 1Jn 1:8; Rev 3:2,17

See also
4005 creation	6154 fall, the
5411 mirror	6203 mortality
5801 brokenness	8357 weakness
6020 sin	8734 evil
6130 corruption	8741 failure
6142 decay	9020 death

6201
imperfection, and God's purposes

The unacceptable falling short of the God-given ideal must be resisted and overcome.

Imperfection is contrary to God's purpose
In creation Ge 1:31
For individuals Eph 1:4
For the church Eph 5:25–27

Imperfection is unacceptable in God's presence
Sacrificial animals must be unblemished Dt 15:21; Mal 1:8 *See also* Ex 12:5; Lev 22:20–25; Nu 28:31; Dt 17:1

The priests must be physically perfect Lev 21:17–23

Moral imperfection separates from God Isa 59:2 *See also* Ps 66:18; Isa 50:1; 64:7; 1Co 6:9–10; Eph 5:5; Heb 10:26–27; Rev 21:27; 22:15

God's people should strive against imperfection
Mt 5:48 *See also* Ge 17:1; Dt 18:13; Ps 34:14; Ro 12:9; 2Co 13:11; Col 1:28; 3:5; 1Th 5:22; 2Ti 2:19; Heb 6:1; 12:14; 2Pe 3:14

Imperfection will be dealt with at Jesus Christ's return
Creation will be remade Isa 65:17 *See also* Isa 66:22; Mt 19:28; Ro 8:19–21; 2Pe 3:13; Rev 21:1–5

God's people will be perfected 1Jn 3:2 *See also* Php 3:20–21

Evil will be removed Rev 21:4 *See also* Isa 25:8; 65:19; 2Th 2:8; Rev 20:10; 21:8

See also
2565 Christ, second coming	8144 renewal
	8201 blamelessness
6720 redemption	8320 perfection
6744 sanctification	9105 last things

mortality

The human state of being subject to death and decay. God did not create human beings to be like this;

mortality is the consequence of sin and is countered by the gospel promise of eternal life in Jesus Christ.

Mortality originated in the fall
Ge 2:16–17

It is the decree of God Ps 90:3,5 *See also* Ge 3:19; 6:3

It is universal Ecc 3:20 *See also* 1Co 15:22

It is inevitable 2Sa 14:14; Job 30:23; Ecc 3:2; Ro 6:23

It is a judgment from God Ro 5:12 *See also* Ro 5:15–19

It leads to judgment Heb 9:27 *See also* 2Co 5:10

Mortality extends to the creation
Ro 8:20–21

Human beings likened to the animals Ecc 3:19

Human beings likened to the grass Ps 90:5–6; 103:15–16; Isa 40:6–7; 1Pe 1:24; Jas 1:10

The natural reaction to mortality
A sense of oppression Job 10:8–9

Carefree abandon 1Co 15:32 *See also* Isa 22:13

The godly reaction to mortality
Humility Job 20:6–11; Ps 22:29; 89:48; Ecc 3:21–22

Trust Lk 12:25

The pursuit of wisdom Ps 90:12

Saving faith Isa 55:6 *See also* Ps 39:4–8; 2Co 6:2

The struggle with sin Ro 6:12; 7:14–25

Death is not the end
The spirit returns to God Ecc 12:7 *See also* Php 1:23

The body will be raised Da 12:2; 1Co 15:53–54 *See also* Isa 25:8; Ro 8:11; 1Co 15:42–44; 2Co 5:4

Eternal life through Jesus Christ Jn 11:25–26 *See also* Mt 25:46; 2Ti 1:9–10; 1Jn 5:11–12; Rev 22:3–5

Eternal punishment for the wicked Mt 25:46; Rev 14:11; 20:10,15

See also
1310 God as judge	6154 fall, the
2324 Christ as Saviour	6644 eternal life
	9020 death
2423 gospel, essence	9135 immortality
4460 grass	9240 last judgment
6020 sin	9315 resurrection of believers
6142 decay	

offence

A transgression or affront against the law or an individual. The gospel itself is seen as offensive by unbelievers, who are often unable to cope with its radical challenge to their unbelief.

Legal offence
Dt 21:22–23 *See also* Ex 21:15–25; 22:1–5; Dt 19:15–21

Moral offence

Eze 22:11 *See also* Ex 22:16–17;
Lev 18:6–23; Dt 22:13–30; 2Sa 3:8;
1Co 6:9–10

An offence to others

On a national level 1Sa 13:4 *See also*
2Sa 10:6 pp 1Ch 19:6; Jer 24:9

On a personal level 2Sa 16:21 *See also*
Ge 20:1–16; 40:1; 1Sa 25:14–28 *Abigail
seeks David's forgiveness for Nabal's
offence*; Job 19:17; Pr 17:9; 18:19; 19:11;
Mt 13:54–57 pp Mk 6:1–4 *The people of
Nazareth take offence at Jesus Christ*;
Mt 15:1–12; 17:24–27; Jn 6:53–66

Offence against God

1Ki 8:50–51 *Offence against God is
synonymous with sin. See also* Job 7:21;
10:14; 13:23 *"wrongs", "sins" and
"offence" are three important OT terms for
sin*; Job 14:16–17; 34:31–33; Ps 59:3;
139:24; Isa 43:24; 44:22; 59:12;
Eze 18:1–32 *Ezekiel warns that the soul
who sins will die*; Eze 33:10; 37:23;
39:24; Am 5:12

Offence against God's house

Nu 18:1 *See also* Nu 18:23

The things of God are an offence to sinful people

Jer 6:10; 1Co 1:22–24 *See also* Gal 5:11

A stumbling-block as an object of offence

A stumbling-block for others Ro 14:13
*The concept behind the English word
"offence" is one of striking against
something or someone. The image of a
stumbling-block conveys the idea of
tripping or falling as a result of striking
against such an object. See also* Lev 19:14;
Mt 16:23; Ro 11:9–10; Ps 69:22–23;
1Co 8:9; 2Co 6:3

A stumbling-block for oneself Eze 14:7
See also Eze 14:3–4

A stumbling-block set up by God
Eze 3:20

See also

2369 Christ, responses to	5276 crime
2414 cross, centrality	5375 law
2426 gospel, responses	5485 punishment, legal aspects
5042 name of God, significance	6020 sin
5171 nose	6237 sexual sin
	6248 temptation
	8309 morality

6209

pagans

OT use of the term "pagan"

**Used of foreign adherents of heathen
religions** Isa 2:6 *See also* 2Ki 23:4–7;
Zep 1:4–6

**Used of heathen religions, peoples and
countries** Isa 57:8 *See also* La 1:10;
Am 7:17

In the Gospels "pagans" is synonymous with "Gentiles"

Mt 6:7 *See also* Mt 5:47; 6:32
pp Lk 12:30; Mt 18:17

The term "pagans" is used to refer to people who were neither Jews nor Christians

Pagans as idolaters 1Co 12:2 *See also*
1Co 10:7; Ex 32:6; 1Co 10:20

Pagans as immoral 1Pe 4:3 *See also*
1Co 5:1

Many believers lived among the pagans

1Pe 2:12 *See also* 3Jn 7

See also

4132 demons, malevolence	7471 temples, heathen
4936 fate	7510 Gentiles
5811 compromise	8142 religion
6257 unbelievers	8768 idolatry

6212

participation

Sharing in actions or identifying
with actions or people. All human
beings share in Adam's fall and its
consequences; believers share in
Christ and his life.

6213

participation, in sin

The natural condition of all human
beings as a result of sharing in
Adam's fall. Believers are called not
to associate with, nor give approval
to wickedness but to stand apart
from evil as God's holy people.

Participation in Adam

In Adam's humanity Ge 3:20; 5:1–3;
Jn 3:6; Ac 17:26; 1Co 15:48–49

In Adam's sin Ro 5:12 *See also* Hos 6:7;
Ro 5:15–19; 1Co 15:21–22
*The creation also participated in Adam's
sin:* Ge 3:17; Ro 8:20–21

In a sinful nature Eph 2:3 *See also*
Ro 7:5,14–20

Ways of participating in evil

Associating with evildoers Ps 50:18 *See
also* Ge 49:6; Lev 15:31; Jos 23:12–13;
Job 34:8; Ps 141:4; Pr 22:24–25;
2Jn 10–11 *giving hospitality to evildoers*

Giving approval to evil Lev 19:17;
Ps 64:5; Ro 1:32 *See also*
2Sa 3:28–29,37; Ps 49:13; Eze 13:22;
Lk 11:48; Ac 7:60; 22:20; Ro 14:22;
Eph 5:11

Sacrifice and idolatry Nu 25:1–3 *See
also* 2Ki 17:33; Hos 4:17; 1Co 10:18–20

God's people are not to participate in evil

God's people are called to be holy
Lev 20:26 *See also* Lev 11:44–45; 19:2;
1Pe 1:15–16

Separation from foreign gods Jos 23:7
See also Dt 12:30; 29:18; 1Ki 11:2

Separation from the godless Ezr 10:11
*Too close an association with the nations
round about, particularly in marriage,
would cause Israel to compromise her
unique relationship with God;* 2Co 6:14
*Often related to marriage, this applies to all
close alliances with unbelievers. See also*
Ezr 4:1–3; 9:1–2
Rev 18:4 *See also* Ezr 10:2; Ne 2:20;

10:30; 13:26–27; Jer 51:45; 1Co 7:39;
2Co 6:17; Isa 52:11

Separation from evildoers 1Ti 5:22 *See
also* Ro 16:17; 1Co 5:9–11; 2Th 3:14

See also

5004 human race & sin	6154 fall, the
5020 human nature	6166 flesh, sinful nature
5080 Adam	7140 people of God
5711 marriage, restrictions	8266 holiness
6020 sin	8768 idolatry

6214

participation, in Christ

The joining of believers to Jesus
Christ, through faith, whereby they
are freed from participation in Adam
by sharing in Christ's death and
resurrection, his nature, sufferings
and glory and whereby, too, they
become part of his body. Believers
therefore share in the fellowship,
ministry and hope of God's people,
which is anticipated by the OT and
fulfilled in the church.

Believers are united with Christ

Eph 1:13 *See also* Jn 13:8; 1Co 1:9; 6:17;
Heb 3:14

Faith liberates from participation in sin

Ro 5:15; Gal 5:24 *See also* Ro 5:16–21;
1Co 15:21–22; Col 2:11

Participation in Christ

In Christ's death and resurrection
Ro 6:3–4; Gal 2:20 *See also* Ro 6:5–8;
7:4; Gal 3:27; Col 2:12–13; 2Ti 2:11

In Christ's nature 2Pe 1:4 *See also*
Ro 8:29; 1Co 15:49; 2Co 3:18; 5:17;
Col 3:10; Heb 12:10

In Christ's sufferings Php 3:10 *See also*
Mt 16:24 pp Mk 8:34 pp Lk 9:23;
2Co 1:5; 1Pe 4:13

In Christ's glory Ro 8:17 *See also*
Jn 17:22; Eph 2:6; 2Th 2:14; 2Ti 2:12

Participation in Christ's body

1Co 10:16–17 *See also* Ro 12:5;
1Co 12:27

Sharing unity through Christ Gal 3:28
See also 1Co 1:2; Eph 2:21–22; Col 3:11

Sharing a source of life Eph 4:16 *See
also* Jn 15:4–5; Ro 11:17; Col 2:19

Sharing an inheritance Gal 3:29 *See also*
1Sa 26:19; Ps 106:5; Ac 3:25; 20:32;
Col 1:12; Heb 6:17

Sharing spiritual blessings Eph 1:3 *See
also* Ro 15:27; Php 1:7; Heb 6:4; Jude 3

Sharing a hope 1Pe 5:1 *See also*
Lk 20:35; 2Th 1:10; Rev 20:6

Sharing in worship 1Co 14:26 *See also*
2Ch 5:12–13; Ne 12:24

**Accepting responsibility towards
others** 1Co 12:26 *See also* Gal 6:1–2;
Php 2:1–4

Sharing one another's sufferings
2Co 1:4,7; Php 4:14; 2Ti 1:8;
Heb 10:33–34; Rev 1:9

Sharing with those in need Eze 45:16;
Ac 4:32; 2Co 8:4; 9:13; 1Ti 6:18;
Heb 13:16

Sharing in God's work 2Co 6:1; Php 1:5
Paul thanks the Philippians for their active support of his ministry. See also Nu 8:24; 18:2; 1Ch 16:38; Ezr 3:2; Ro 15:30; 1Co 9:10–13; 2Co 5:20; Gal 2:7–9; Php 4:15–16

Participation in Christ demands holiness
1Co 10:21 *See also* 1Co 6:15; Eph 5:6–7; Col 3:1–5

Participation of the nations in God's salvation
Gentiles are included among God's people Eph 3:6 *See also* Ro 11:24; Gal 3:8–9; Ge 12:3; 18:18; 22:18; Gal 3:14

God's promise to include the nations
Zec 2:11 *See also* Isa 2:3 pp Mic 4:2; Isa 14:1; 19:23–25; Zep 2:11; Zec 14:16

See also

2410 cross, the	7921 fellowship
3233 Holy Spirit & sanctification	7933 Lord's Supper
	7957 sacraments
6754 union with Christ	8102 abiding in Christ
7110 body of Christ	8206 Christlikeness
7903 baptism	

6218

provoking God

The arousing of God's righteous anger in response to the sin of his people, particularly their idolatry.

God is provoked by sin and disobedience
Dt 9:7–8 *See also* Nu 32:9–13; Dt 31:29; Jos 7:1; 2Sa 6:6–7 pp 1Ch 13:9–10
Uzzah's disobedience in touching the ark cost him his life; 2Sa 24:1; 1Ki 15:30; 16:2–3,7; 21:21–22; 2Ki 21:14–15; Isa 65:1–5; Jer 32:30–33

God is provoked by the rejection of his chosen leaders and prophets
2Ch 36:15–16 *See also* Nu 12:1,9

God is provoked by injustice
Ex 22:22–24 *See also* Isa 59:15–18; Eze 8:17; Hos 12:14

God is provoked by complaining
Nu 11:1 *See also* Ex 4:10–14; Nu 11:4–10,33

God is provoked by idolatry
Dt 4:25–26; Eze 16:26 *See also*
Dt 9:16–19; Jdg 2:12–13; 3:5–8; 1Ki 14:9,15; 16:13,26,33; 22:53; 2Ki 17:11; 22:17; 23:25–27; 2Ch 28:25; Ps 78:58–59; 106:28–29; Jer 7:17–19; 8:19; 25:6–7; 44:3,8; Eze 20:28

God is provoked by human sacrifice
2Ki 17:17; 21:6 pp 2Ch 33:6

See also

1025 God, anger of	7135 Israel, people
1185 God, zeal of	of God
5347 injustice	8032 trust, lack of
5482 punishment	8704 apostasy
5789 anger	8718 disobedience
6020 sin	8768 idolatry
6173 guilt, and God	
6232 rejection of God, results	

6221

rebellion

A state of revolt against established divine or human authority. Scripture condemns rebellion against God and indicates the futility of Israel's frequent rebellions against him.

6222
rebellion, against God

The human race is in rebellion against God through its disobedience and unbelief.

Examples of rebellion against God
Ps 2:2 *See also* Nu 20:24; 27:14; 1Sa 15:22–23; Ps 66:7

Warnings not to rebel
1Sa 12:14–15 *See also* Nu 14:9; 17:10; Ps 2:10–12; Eze 2:8

Indignation expressed over rebellion against God
Ps 5:10

The fate of the rebellious
Isa 66:24 *See also* Dt 13:5; Ps 68:6; Jer 28:16; 29:32; La 1:18,20; 3:42; Hos 13:16

God is ready to forgive those who rebel against him
Jer 33:8 *See also* Da 9:5–9

The end times will be characterised by open rebellion against God
2Th 2:3 *See also* 1Jn 2:18

See also

1055 God, grace & mercy	6020 sin
	6157 fall, of Satan
4027 world, fallen	6183 ignorance, of God
5482 punishment	
5764 attitudes, negative to God	6231 rejection of God
5793 arrogance	8756 folly, examples
5818 contempt	8801 presumption

6223
rebellion, of Israel

Despite God's repeated mercy, Israel's history is seen as a history of rebellion against God.

The history of Israel is seen as a history of rebellion
Ps 78:40 *See also* Ps 78:8,17,56; Dt 31:27; Ps 105:28; 106:7; 107:11; Isa 63:10; Eze 20:8,13,21

God's compassion and readiness to deliver his people Ne 9:28 *See also* Ne 9:16–31; Ps 106:43

Examples of Israel's rebellion
Dt 1:26,43; 9:7,23

Prophetic condemnation of Israel's rebellion
Hos 7:13 *See also* Zep 3:1

Isaiah depicts Israel as a rebellious nation Isa 1:2–5 *See also* Isa 1:20,23,28; 30:1,9; 48:8; 65:2–3

Jeremiah denounces the Israelites as rebels Jer 6:28 *See also* Jer 2:29; 3:13; 4:17; 5:23

Ezekiel condemns Israel as a rebellious house Eze 2:5–8 *See also* Eze 3:9,26–27; 12:2–3,9,25; 17:12; 24:3; 44:6

The rebellion of Israel in the parables of Jesus Christ
Mt 21:33–44 pp Mk 12:1–11 pp Lk 20:9–18; Lk 13:6–9

Israel's rebellion is a warning to believers
1Co 10:6 *See also* 1Co 10:1–12; Heb 3:7–4:2; Ps 95:7–11; Jude 5,7

See also

1025 God, anger of	8718 disobedience
5978 warning	8742 faithlessness
6245 stubbornness	8834 unbelief
7135 Israel, people of God	8840 unfaithfulness to God
8428 example	

6224
rebellion, against human authority

Human authority is frequently defied and resisted. To rebel against God's chosen leaders is to defy God himself.

Examples of rebellion against human leaders
Ge 14:3–4 *See also* 2Ki 18:7; 24:1,20 pp 2Ch 36:13 pp Jer 52:3; 2Ch 13:6; Mk 15:7

Rebellion against parents Dt 21:18–21

The rebellion of nations 1Ki 12:19 pp 2Ch 10:19; 2Ki 1:1

Accusations of rebellion
Ne 2:19; 6:5–8

Rebellion against God's chosen leaders
Ex 23:21 *See also* Nu 16:1–3; 20:2–5; Jos 1:18; 2Sa 15:10

Rebellion against legitimate authority is condemned
Ro 13:2 *See also* 1Pe 2:13

See also

1090 God, majesty of	5829 defiance
5255 citizenship	5924 quarrel-someness
5257 civil authorities	
5326 government	5931 resistance
5457 power, human	7733 leaders
5509 rulers	

6227

regret

Deep feelings of sorrow arising from past events now seen as sins, mistakes or misfortunes. It can either lead to true repentance or destructive bitterness.

Examples and expressions of regret

1Sa 26:21 See also Ge 27:33–35; Nu 12:10–12 Aaron and Miriam when they had spoken against Moses; Nu 14:1–2; Jdg 11:34–35 Jephthah when he returned home from fighting the Ammonites David when he counted the fighting men: 2Sa 24:10 pp 1Ch 21:8; 2Sa 24:14 pp 1Ch 21:13 1Ki 21:27 Ahab after he murdered Naboth and seized his vineyard; Da 6:14; Mt 26:75 pp Mk 14:72 pp Lk 22:61–62 Peter when he disowned Jesus Christ; Mt 27:3–4 Judas after betraying Jesus Christ

Divine expressions of regret

Ge 6:6 See also 1Sa 15:10–11,35; 2Sa 24:16 pp 1Ch 21:15

Actions which may lead to regret

Pr 5:11–14; 1Ti 6:9–10

The bitterness of vain regrets

There is no remedy for bitter regrets Heb 12:16–17 See also Ge 27:41; 2Sa 18:33; Pr 28:17; Eze 7:16–18; Lk 13:24–28; Rev 1:7

The unending remorse of the lost

Da 12:2 See also Isa 66:24; Mt 8:12; 25:30; Mk 9:47–48; Lk 16:22–23; Rev 14:11

Regret is an element of true repentance

2Co 7:8–10 See also Nu 14:39–40; 2Sa 12:13–17; 2Ki 22:18–20 pp 2Ch 34:26–28 Josiah's response on finding the Book of the Law; Ezr 10:1,6; Ps 38:2–8; 51:3; Jer 3:21–25; Joel 2:12; Jnh 3:6–9 the repentance of Nineveh; Mt 5:4; Lk 15:17–19 the prodigal son; Ac 2:37

Absence of regret

Sinning without shame Jer 6:15; Zep 3:5; 1Co 5:1–2

When the wicked die 2Ch 21:20

At the end of life 2Sa 23:5; 2Ti 4:6–8

In God's new creation Isa 65:17–19 See also Isa 35:10; Rev 21:4

See also

1120 God, repentance of	5945 self-pity
	5947 shame
5188 tearing of clothes	5952 sorrow
5801 brokenness	6624 confession of sin
5899 lament	6732 repentance
5938 sadness	

6230

rejection

The deliberate and conscious act of turning away from someone, or refusing to accept something that is being offered.

6231
rejection of God

The deliberate rejection of God lies at the heart of human sin. It is seen in rebellion against God's authority, purpose and instruction and results

---

in the rejection of God's servants and, ultimately, in the rejection of his Son.

Rejection of God

Rejection of God's authority 2Ki 17:15 See also Isa 1:4

Rejection of God in favour of other gods Dt 32:15–18 See also Ex 22:20; Dt 31:20; 1Sa 8:8; Isa 1:28; 65:11; Jer 15:6; Eze 14:5

Rejection of God as king 1Sa 8:7 See also 1Sa 10:19

Rejection of God's ways Ps 95:10; Isa 30:15 See also Ex 16:7–8; Nu 11:18–20; 14:27; Ps 81:11–13; Isa 8:6; 30:1–2; Lk 7:30

Rejection of the covenant 1Ki 19:10 See also Lev 26:15; 1Ki 19:14; Hos 8:1

Rejection of the promised land Nu 14:1–4,31; Ne 9:30

Rejection of God's compassion Mt 23:37 See also 2Ch 36:15; Ne 9:30; Hos 11:1–4

Rejection of God's word

Rejection of God's instruction 1Sa 15:10–11; 1Th 4:8 See also 1Sa 15:23,26; Ps 50:17; Pr 1:24–25; 5:12

Rejection of God's law Lev 26:43; Hos 4:6 See also 2Ki 17:26; Isa 5:24; Jer 6:19; 8:8–9; Eze 5:6; 20:13,16,24; Am 2:4; Mk 7:13 pp Mt 15:6

Rejection of God's messages Isa 30:12 See also Isa 65:12; Jer 6:10; 7:13; 35:17; 36:23–24; Ac 13:46

Rejection of God's messengers 2Ch 36:16; Ac 7:52 See also 2Ch 30:10; Jer 20:8; Zec 7:12; Mt 21:33–39 pp Mk 12:1–8 pp Lk 20:9–15; Ac 7:35,39

Rejection of Jesus Christ

Jesus Christ's rejection was prophesied Ps 118:22; Isa 53:3 It is generally accepted that God's servant in Isaiah chapter 53 refers to Jesus Christ; Mk 8:31 pp Mt 16:21 pp Lk 9:22 See also Isa 49:7; 50:6; 52:14; 53:7–8 Jesus Christ as the stone the builders rejected (Ps 118:22): Mt 21:42 pp Mk 12:10 pp Lk 20:17; Ac 4:11; 1Pe 2:7 Mk 9:12 pp Mt 17:12; Lk 17:25; Ro 9:33; Isa 28:16

The rejection of his earthly ministry Jn 1:11 Jesus Christ is rejected in his home town of Nazareth: Mt 13:54–58 pp Mk 6:1–6; Lk 4:28–29 The rejection of Jesus Christ's claims about himself: Jn 5:40,43; 6:41–42; 8:59; 9:16; 10:31 The Jews' rejection of Jesus Christ culminates in his death: Mt 27:22–23 pp Mk 15:12–14 pp Lk 23:20–23; Jn 11:53; 19:6,15; Ac 2:23; 4:10; 7:52

See also

1429 prophecy, OT fulfilment	8710 atheism
	8712 denial of Christ
2366 Christ, prophecies concerning	8718 disobedience
	8768 idolatry
2545 Christ, opposition to	8836 unbelief, response
6193 impenitence	8840 unfaithfulness to God
6221 rebellion	
7135 Israel, people of God	

6232
rejection of God, results of

Rejecting God angers and grieves him. To reject God can be to reject all the benefits of the gospel, and can lead to judgment and punishment.

Rejection grieves God

God rejected as Creator Ge 6:6

God rejected as a husband Eze 6:9 See also Jer 2:2; 3:20; 31:32; Hos 1:2

God rejected as a father Hos 11:1–4 See also Dt 32:18; Jer 3:19; 31:20

God rejected by Israel, his vineyard Isa 5:4 See also Jer 2:21

Rejection angers God and brings his wrath

Ezr 8:22; Jn 3:36 See also Lev 26:27–28; 2Ch 36:16; Zec 7:12; Ro 2:8

The results of rejecting God

Judgment Jer 1:16; Jn 12:48 See also Lev 26:14–17; Ps 50:22; Pr 1:24–26; Isa 28:22; Jer 6:19; 15:6; 26:4–6; Am 2:4–5; Jn 3:18–19

God rejects his people Dt 32:19; Ps 78:59; 119:118; Jer 6:30; 7:29; Hos 9:7

God rejects those who reject him Hos 4:6; Mt 10:33 pp Lk 12:9 See also 1Ch 28:9; 2Ch 15:2; Lk 9:26

God hides his face Dt 31:17–18; 32:20; Ps 88:14; Isa 1:15; Mic 3:4

God rejects the sanctuary and its worship Jer 26:31; 1Ki 9:6–7 pp 2Ch 7:19–20; La 2:7; Eze 7:24; 10:18–19; 11:22–23

God's people are removed from his presence into exile 2Ki 17:18–20,23; 23:27; 24:3,20 pp Jer 52:3; Jer 7:15; 15:1

Examples of others rejected by God Esau: Ro 9:13; Mal 1:2–3 Saul: 1Sa 15:23,26; 16:1; 28:15–16 Jer 22:24–25 Jehoiachin

God's rejection is not final

Lev 26:44; Ro 11:15 See also 1Sa 12:22; 2Ch 7:14; Ps 66:20; Isa 41:9; 49:21; 54:5–8; Jer 31:37; 33:24–26; Zec 10:6; Ro 11:1,25–29

See also

1025 God, anger of	6628 conversion, God's demand
1120 God, repentance of	7215 exile, the
1310 God as judge	9165 restoration
2426 gospel, responses	9210 judgment, God's
5482 punishment	9511 hell, place of punishment
5779 advice	
6124 condemnation	

6233
rejection, human experience of

Feelings of rejection by God may be a result of alienation caused directly or indirectly by sin. God's people also experience rejection by a hostile world. Experiences and feelings of rejection are to be met with prayer, forgiveness and perseverance, together with confidence in God's commitment to and compassion for, his people.

Feelings of rejection by God
Feelings of national rejection Ps 74:1; Isa 49:14 *See also* Ps 44:9; 108:11; Isa 40:27; Jer 13:17; 14:9; La 1:2; 5:20; Eze 37:11

Feelings of personal rejection Ps 13:1; Mt 27:46 pp Mk 15:34 *Jesus Christ experiences separation from his Father as a consequence of bearing human sin. See also* Ps 22:1–2; 43:2; 88:14

God's servants experience rejection
Samuel 1Sa 8:5–7

Elijah 1Ki 19:10 *See also* 1Ki 18:22; 19:1–4

The psalmist Ps 41:7 *See also* Ps 22:6–8; 31:12–13; 69:20; 71:10

Jeremiah Jer 15:10 *See also* Jer 20:7–9,14–15,18

Jesus Christ Isa 53:5; Jn 1:11 *See also* Lk 23:18

Jesus Christ's disciples Jn 15:18 *See also* Mt 5:10–11 pp Lk 6:22; Jn 17:14; Ac 13:50; 14:19; 16:22; 2Ti 3:12; 1Pe 4:12

Responding to rejection
Appealing to God 2Ch 6:42; Ps 27:9; 71:12 *See also* Ps 22:9–11,19–21; 44:23–24; 51:11–12; 77:7–12; 132:10; Jer 15:15; 20:12; La 5:21–22

Offering forgiveness Lk 23:34 *See also* Ge 50:17; Ac 7:59–60; 2Ti 4:16

Rejoicing in suffering Mt 5:11–12 pp Lk 6:22–23; Ac 5:41; Ro 5:3; Jas 1:2–3

Persevering Ac 5:28–29,42

Encouragement for those experiencing rejection
God's commitment to his people Isa 49:15–16 *See also* Ps 27:10; 94:14; Jer 31:20; La 3:21–24; Hos 11:1–4; Mt 10:30–31 pp Lk 12:7

God's compassion and forgiveness La 3:31–32 *See also* Dt 32:36; Ps 130:7–8; Isa 12:1–2; 49:13; Eze 39:25; Hos 11:8–9; 2Co 2:7–8 *God's readiness to forgive is to be reflected in the attitude of his people towards one another.*

God's strengthening Isa 40:28–31; 2Ti 4:17

God's vindication of his people Ps 135:14; Isa 50:6–9; 54:17; Ro 8:18; 1Pe 4:13; Rev 2:10

Support from fellow believers 2Co 1:4 *See also* Ac 14:22; 2Co 6:6–7

See also
1030	God, compassion
1085	God, love of
1320	God as Saviour
5770	abandonment
5789	anger
5799	bitterness
5820	criticism
5927	resentment
6115	blame
6652	forgiveness
8602	prayer
8794	persecution

---

sexual sin

Sexual relations are to be seen as an aspect of God's good creation which can be corrupted and devalued through human sin.
This set of themes consists of the following:
6237 sexual sin, nature of
6238 homosexuality
6239 prostitution
6240 rape
6241 seduction
6242 adultery
6243 adultery, spiritual

6237
sexual sin, nature of

Any transgression of the limits that God has set for the enjoyment of sex. Such sins are often life-dominating, but may be broken through the power and grace of Jesus Christ.

The origin of sexual sin
Fallen human nature Gal 5:19 *See also* Ro 13:12–14; Col 3:5–6

The heart Mt 15:19 pp Mk 7:21–22

The offensiveness of sexual sin
It defiles the sinner Mt 15:20 pp Mk 7:23 *See also* Ro 1:24; 1Co 6:18

It defiles society Lev 18:24–25 *See also* 1Co 5:6; Rev 19:2

It offends other people 2Pe 2:7–8 *See also* Ge 9:22–25; 34:7; 38:24; 2Sa 13:21–22; 2Co 12:21

It offends God 2Sa 11:27 *See also* Jer 13:26–27; Mal 3:5

Sexual sin under the old covenant
Pre-marital sex Dt 22:13–21

Adultery Ex 20:14 pp Dt 5:18 *See also* Lev 18:20; Dt 22:22–24

Prostitution Lev 19:29; Dt 23:17–18

Rape Dt 22:25–29

Homosexual intercourse Lev 18:22 *See also* Lev 20:13

Bestiality Ex 22:19; Lev 18:23; 20:15–16; Dt 27:21

Incest Lev 18:6–18; 20:17,19; Dt 22:30; 27:20,22–23; Eze 22:11

Intercourse during menstruation Lev 18:19; 20:18

Sexual sin under the new covenant
The OT laws are confirmed and strengthened Mt 5:27–28 *See also* Mt 5:31–32; Ro 1:24–27; 1Co 6:15–16; 7:9; Heb 13:4

The need for holiness in the lives of believers 1Th 4:3–7 *See also* Ac 15:29; Eph 5:3; Heb 12:16; 1Pe 1:15–16; Lev 11:44; 1Pe 4:1–3

The church must be kept pure Rev 2:14–16 *See also* 1Co 5:1–5,9–11; Rev 2:20

God's judgment on sexual sin
In this life Rev 2:21–23 *See also* Ge 19:24; Nu 25:1–9; 2Sa 12:11–12; Pr 7:26–27; 1Co 10:8

In the world to come Rev 21:8 *See also* Eph 5:5–6; 2Pe 2:6; Jude 7; Rev 22:14–15

God's power over sexual sin
It can be forgiven Jn 8:10–11 *See also* 2Sa 12:13; Ps 51:1 Title; Mt 21:31–32; Lk 7:36–38,47–50; Rev 2:21

Hearts can be changed 1Co 6:9–11

Resisting sexual sin
By remembering God's word Ps 119:9 *See also* Pr 6:23–24; 7:5

By resisting temptation Ge 39:6–12; Pr 7:24–25

By mortifying lust Job 31:1 *See also* Mt 5:29–30

By living in the Spirit Gal 5:16

By living for holiness Ro 6:19

By enjoying sex within proper limits Pr 5:18–20; 1Co 7:2,9

See also
5375	law
5482	punishment
5735	sexuality
6166	flesh, sinful nature
6187	immorality
6248	temptation
6652	forgiveness
7348	defilement
8266	holiness
8324	purity
8339	self control
8821	self-indulgence

6238
homosexuality

Sexual relations between people of the same sex. The biblical emphasis upon the loving union of male and female, as an integral part of God's creation ordinance, establishes the context against which the censure of homosexual practice is to be set.

God's creation order for sexuality
Ge 1:27–28; 2:18–24 *Both Jesus Christ and Paul endorsed the creation order:* Mk 10:6–9 pp Mt 19:4–5; Eph 5:31

OT prohibitions of homosexual practice
Lev 18:22 *See also* Lev 20:13

Homosexual practice is incompatible with the kingdom of God
1Co 6:9–10 *The meanings of the Greek words for "male prostitutes" and "homosexual offenders" are disputed, but the terms are commonly associated with particular forms of homosexual behaviour. See also* 1Ti 1:9–11

Sexual disorder is one consequence of rejecting God
Ro 1:21–27 *Homosexuality associated with pagan religious beliefs and practices:* 1Ki 14:24; 15:12; 2Ki 23:7

Examples of homosexual practice
In Sodom and Gomorrah: Ge 19:4–8; Jude 7

Jdg 19:16–24 *in Israel in a time of moral decadence*

See also

4005 creation	5717 monogamy
5707 male and female	

6239
prostitution

Scripture condemns the offering of sex for money or favours. However, it also stresses the prospect of new life in Christ for prostitutes, and points to some prostitutes as examples of faith.

Prostitution among the heathen
For money Ge 38:15–16; Jos 2:1; Joel 3:3

Religious prostitution Ge 38:21–22; Job 36:14

Prostitution in Israel
It was forbidden under God's law Lev 19:29; Dt 23:17–18

Priests were forbidden to marry prostitutes Lev 21:7,14

The penalties for prostitution Ge 38:24; Lev 21:9

Efforts to remove the shrine-prostitutes 1Ki 15:11–12; 22:45–46

The lure of prostitution Pr 7:10 *See also* 1Co 6:9

The prevalence of prostitution 1Ki 14:24 *See also* 1Ki 3:16; Jer 5:7; Hos 4:13–14; 6:10; Mic 1:7

Warnings against prostitution
It has dire consequences Pr 6:25–27 *See also* Jdg 16:1–2; Pr 23:26–27; 29:3; Lk 15:30

Christians must avoid it 1Co 6:15–16

Prostitutes can be redeemed
Mt 21:31–32 *See also* Lk 7:37–50; 1Co 6:9–11; Heb 11:31; Jas 2:25; Jos 6:22–25

Prostitution as a metaphor
For worldly corruption Rev 17:1–5 *See also* Isa 23:15–17; Na 3:4

For apostasy Dt 31:16 *See also* Ex 34:15–16; Lev 20:5; Jdg 2:17; 8:27,33; 1Ch 5:25; Ps 106:39; Isa 1:21; Eze 16:16–17,26,28,33–34,41; 23:1–35; Hos 4:10–12; 5:4

See also

4030 world, behaviour in	5947 shame
5136 body	6720 redemption
5169 nakedness	8218 consecration
5195 veil	8466 reformation
5420 music	8704 apostasy
	8768 idolatry

6240
rape

The sexual violation of an individual (normally, though not necessarily,

female). This is a deeply traumatic and degrading experience for the victim and is an evil that Scripture condemns.

Lust is the motivation for rape
2Sa 13:1–15

Women and rape
Women are particularly vulnerable to male assault 2Sa 13:14 *See also* Zec 14:2

Women were protected under the law Dt 22:25–29

Women are to be loved and cared for Eph 5:25,28–29 *See also* Ge 12:18–20; 1Pe 3:7

The trauma of rape
Its psychological and emotional effects 2Sa 13:19–20 *See also* Ge 34:6–7

Its physical effects Jdg 19:26–28 *See also* Jdg 20:4–5

Avenging the victim of rape
Ge 34:7–31; 2Sa 13:22–32; Jdg 20:6–11; Ro 12:19; 13:3–4; Jas 1:20

Examples of rape
Female rape Ge 34:1–3; Jdg 19:24–25; 2Sa 13:2–13; Zec 14:2

Attempted male rape Ge 19:4–9; Jdg 19:22–23; Lev 18:22; 20:13

See also

5494 revenge	5832 desire
5695 girls	5844 emotions
5714 men	5975 violence
5740 virgin	8777 lust
5745 women	

6241
seduction

The deliberate enticement or persuasion of someone into the abandonment of godly principles. Scripture speaks of both sexual and spiritual seduction.

Sexual seduction
Warnings to avoid temptation Pr 7:1–22; 2Ti 2:22 *See also* Pr 1:10; 2:16–19

Examples of enticement Ge 39:6–12; Nu 25:1–3 *See also* Nu 31:15–16; Jdg 16:1,4–5; 2Sa 11:1–4; 1Ki 11:1–6; Rev 2:14–16,20–22

The law as a deterrent Ex 22:16–17 *See also* Heb 13:4

Resisting temptation Job 31:1 *See also* Mal 3:5; Mt 5:27–30; 1Co 7:2–3; Php 4:8; 1Th 4:3–6

Spiritual seduction
Through Satan Ge 3:1 *See also* Jn 8:44; 2Co 2:11; 11:3,14; Eph 6:11

Through lying spirits and false prophets 1Jn 4:1 *See also* 1Ki 22:19–23 pp 2Ch 18:18–22; 1Ti 4:1; Mt 24:24–25 pp Mk 13:22–23

Through false teachers 2Pe 2:1,14–15 *See also* 2Ti 3:6–7,13; 1Jn 2:18–19; 2Jn 7–8; Jude 10–12

The need for vigilance 1Th 5:21–22 *See also* Ac 20:28–31

The process of seduction
A thought planted Ge 3:2–3 *See also* Mt 4:3; Jas 1:14; 1Jn 2:15

An advantage promised Ge 3:4–5 *See also* Mt 4:6

Attraction Ge 3:6 *See also* 1Jn 2:16

Persistence on the part of the seducer Mt 4:8–9 *See also* Ge 19:9; Jdg 16:15–16

Yielding Ge 3:6 *See also* Jas 1:15

See also

4120 Satan	8482 spiritual warfare
5746 youth	
6145 deceit	8490 watchfulness
7751 persuasion	8749 false teachers
7774 prophets, false	8776 lies

6242
adultery

Sexual relations involving at least one partner who is married to someone else. Such relations break the marriage covenant and are condemned in Scripture. Jesus Christ extended the understanding of adultery to include inner lust.

Adultery is condemned by God
God's law forbids it Ex 20:14 pp Dt 5:18 *See also* Lev 18:20; Mt 19:18 pp Mk 10:19 pp Lk 18:20; Jas 2:11

It is listed with other evil practices Ps 50:18; Jer 7:9–10; Hos 4:1–2; Lk 18:11; 1Ti 1:9–10

The lure of adultery
It begins with lust Pr 6:25; Mt 5:27–28 *See also* 2Sa 11:2–3; Job 31:1,9; Jer 5:8; Mt 15:19

It is seductive Pr 7:14–21 *See also* Pr 5:3,20

It is secretive Job 24:15; Pr 7:8–10; 30:20

It is a snare to the unwary Pr 7:7; 22:14; Ecc 7:26

It is resisted by the wise Pr 2:16 *See also* Ge 39:7–12; Pr 7:4–5

Adultery breaks the marriage covenant
Pr 2:17 *See also* Hos 2:2; Mal 2:14

The consequences of adultery
It destroys individuals and society Pr 6:32–34 *See also* Pr 5:4–5,9–11; 6:26–29; 7:22–27; Job 31:11–12

It was punishable by death under OT law Lev 20:10 *See also* Dt 22:22,23–24; Jn 8:4–5

Adulterers face God's judgment Heb 13:4 *See also* 2Sa 12:11–12; Mal 3:5; 1Co 6:9; Rev 2:22

Remarriage after divorce may be adultery
Mt 19:9 pp Mk 10:11 *See also* Mt 5:32; Lk 16:18; Ro 7:3

Hypocrisy in relation to adultery
Ro 2:22 *See also* 2Sa 12:5–6; Hos 4:14; Jn 8:7–9

Examples of adultery
2Sa 11:1–4 *See also* Jer 5:7 *the people of Jerusalem;* Jer 29:23 *the exiles in Babylon;*

Hos 3:1–3 *Hosea's wife, Gomer*; Jn 8:3 *the woman caught in adultery*; 2Pe 2:14 *false teachers in the church*

Children born of adultery

Isa 57:3 *"offspring of adulterers" was a term of abuse. See also* 2Sa 12:15–18 *David and Bathsheba's child died when he was seven days old;* Hos 2:4–5; 5:7

See also

4933 evening	5729 one flesh
5276 crime	7346 death penalty
5277 criminals	8248 faithfulness
5654 betrothal	8841 unfaithfulness
5675 divorce	to people
5708 marriage	

6243
adultery, spiritual

In Scripture there is a close link between sexual sin and spiritual corruption and immorality as promoted by false teachers. Scripture frequently uses the language of sexual sin to expose the infidelity of God's people.

The link between sexual sin and spiritual adultery

In practice Nu 25:1–3 *See also* Ex 34:15; Hos 4:14

In false teaching Rev 2:20–25 *See also* Nu 31:15–16; 2Ti 3:6; 2Pe 2:13–15; Jude 4,8; Rev 2:14–16

Spiritual adultery and God's covenant relationship with his people

God as a husband to his people Eze 16:8 *The spiritual relationship between God and his people is defined in terms of the intimate and exclusive bond of marriage. See also* Isa 54:5; Jer 3:14; 31:32; Eph 5:31–32

God is jealous for his people's affections Ex 34:14 *Just as husband and wife are jealous for their relationship in love, so God is jealous for the affections of his people. See also* Ex 20:4–5; Dt 4:23–24; 6:13–15

The history of spiritual adultery among God's people

Before Israel's kings Dt 31:16 *See also* Lev 17:7–9; 20:4–6; Jdg 2:16–17; 8:27,33–34

In the northern kingdom of Israel Hos 1:2 *See also* 1Ch 5:25; Eze 23:1–8; Hos 2:2–3; 4:10–12; 5:3–4

In the southern kingdom of Judah Jer 3:1–3 *See also* 2Ch 21:10–11; Isa 57:3–8; Jer 2:20; 5:7–8; 23:13–14; Eze 16:15–22; 23:11–21

In Jesus Christ's generation Mt 12:38–39 *See also* Mt 16:4

God's judgment on spiritual adultery

Jer 19:3–5 *See also* Jer 3:6–10; 16:10–13; Eze 23:36–49

Believers are not to be drawn into spiritual adultery

1Jn 2:15–17 *See also* 1Co 10:6–11; Col 3:5; Heb 3:12–14; 10:26–31; Jas 4:4–5; 1Jn 5:21

See also

1345 covenant	8704 apostasy
5712 marriage, God	8773 jealousy
& his people	8840 unfaithfulness
7215 exile, the	to God
8207 commitment	9210 judgment,
8459 perseverance	God's

6245

stubbornness

Proud and disobedient resistance to God's will and rejection of his commands.

Stubbornness is an attitude of heart

Jer 7:24 *See also* Dt 9:27; Jdg 2:19; Ps 78:8; Isa 48:4; Jer 3:17; 5:3; 9:14; 16:12; 18:12; Hos 4:16; Zec 7:11

The practical consequences of stubbornness

Eph 4:18 *See also* Ex 13:15; 33:3; Lev 26:19; 2Ch 26:16; Ne 9:16–17; Job 20:6–7; Ps 10:4; Pr 1:24–31; 28:14; 29:1 *sudden destruction for the unrepentant;* Isa 2:11 *a humbling on judgment day;* Jer 5:3; 11:8; 13:10; Da 5:20 *King Nebuchadnezzar deposed;* Hos 13:6 *The people of Israel forget their God;* Zep 3:11; Mk 6:51–52 *Jesus Christ's disciples amazed;* Mt 18:15–17; Ro 2:5 *The self-righteous store up wrath for the day of judgment.*

Commands not to be stubborn

Ne 9:29 *See also* Ex 33:5; 2Ch 30:8; Ps 95:8; Mk 16:14

Stubbornness can be God's judgment on sin

Isa 63:17 *When people persistently refuse to obey God, he brings about a condition where they cannot obey him, and consequently cannot receive his blessing. See also* Ex 4:21; 14:17; Dt 2:30; Jos 11:20; Ps 81:11–12; Ro 9:18; 11:7–8

God's appeal to stubborn people

Isa 65:2 *See also* Ro 10:21; 2Ch 32:24–25; Job 33:16–18; Isa 46:12; Jer 7:22–24; Eze 2:4–5; Zec 7:11–12; Ac 19:8–9

See also

3284 Holy Spirit,	6663 freedom of will
resisting	7223 exodus,
5170 neck	significance
5931 resistance	8718 disobedience
6020 sin	8785 opposition
6178 hardness of	8802 pride
heart	8836 unbelief,
6193 impenitence	response

6248

temptation

Pressure to yield to influences that can lead people away from God and into sin.

This set of themes consists of the following:

6249
temptation, universality of

Scripture makes clear that all human beings are subject to temptation. It provides examples of individuals who have faced and yielded to such influences.

The inevitability of temptation to do wrong

1Co 10:13 *See also* Pr 7:21–23; Mt 13:20–21 pp Mk 4:16–17 pp Lk 8:13; Lk 17:1; Ro 7:15; 1Co 10:12; 2Co 11:3; 1Pe 1:6

Examples of those who were tempted

Adam and Eve tempted Ge 3:6–7 *Sin enters the world through temptation, which leads to the fall of humanity.*

Esau tempted Ge 25:29–34

Achan tempted Jos 7:21

Samson tempted Jdg 14:16–17

David tempted 2Sa 11:2–4

Solomon tempted 1Ki 11:1,4

Gehazi tempted 2Ki 5:20–23

Peter tempted Mt 26:69–75 pp Lk 22:55–62 pp Jn 18:16–18, 25–27

Help for those facing temptation

Ro 8:31 *See also* Jos 1:5; Ro 8:37–39; Heb 4:15–16; 13:5; 1Jn 2:1; 4:4; Rev 3:10

See also

5033 knowledge of	6155 fall of Adam &
good & evil	Eve
6023 sin, universality	8027 faith, testing of

6250
temptation, sources of

Temptation comes from a number of sources but not from God.

Temptation arising from sinful human nature

Eph 2:1–3; Jas 1:14 *See also* Mt 5:29–30 pp Mk 9:43–47; Mt 6:23; Ro 7:18–23

Temptation from other people

2Pe 2:18 *See also* Ge 3:6; Pr 5:3–6

Temptation from Satan

Ge 3:1 *See also* 1Ch 21:1; Mt 4:1 pp Mk 1:13 pp Lk 4:2; Mk 4:15 pp Lk 8:12; 1Co 7:5; 1Th 3:5

Temptation from the world

1Jn 2:16 *See also* Mt 13:22 pp Mk 4:19 pp Lk 8:14

Attractions which lead to temptation

Money 1Ti 6:9–10

Power Dt 8:17–18; 2Ch 26:16

Lust Pr 6:25; 7:21

Pride Pr 11:2

Temptation does not come from God

Jas 1:13 *See also* Mt 6:13 pp Lk 11:4

See also

4025 world, the	6166 flesh, sinful
4122 Satan, tempter	nature
5345 influence	6237 sexual sin
5418 monotony	6241 seduction
5593 trial	7751 persuasion
6022 sin, causes of	8832 testing

6251
temptation, resisting

Being tempted is not in itself a sin.
Sin arises when believers give in to
temptation. Scripture urges believers
to resist temptation, and gives them
encouragement to face it.

**Encouragement to those facing
temptation**
Jas 1:12 *See also* Ro 8:37; Heb 2:18;
4:15–16; Jas 1:2–3; 1Jn 4:4

**Finding in God and his word
resources to overcome
temptation**
Da 11:32 *See also* Pr 2:1–2,12–15;
Mt 6:13 pp Lk 11:4; 1Ti 6:11–12; Jas 4:7

**Practical suggestions for
overcoming temptation**
Overcoming temptation through
prayer Mt 26:41 pp Mk 14:38
pp Lk 22:40 *See also* Mt 18:8–9; 1Co 7:5

Overcoming temptation through
personal discipline Heb 12:4,7;
2Pe 3:17

**Encouragements to resist
temptation**
Gal 6:1; 1Th 5:22 *See also* Pr 1:10–15;
Ro 6:12–14

**Examples of those who did not
give in to temptation**
Job 1:22 *See also* Ge 39:7–10; Job 2:10;
Jer 35:5–6; Da 1:8

Jesus Christ resisted temptation
Mt 4:4 pp Lk 4:4 *See also* Mt 4:7
pp Lk 4:12; Mt 4:10 pp Lk 4:8

See also

4126 Satan,	8339 self-control
resistance to	8454 obedience to
5598 victory over	God
spiritual forces	8476 self-discipline
5627 word	8493 watchfulness,
6744 sanctification	believers
8326 purity, moral &	
spiritual	

6252
temptation, and Jesus Christ

Jesus Christ, like every other human
being, knew temptation. However,
he never yielded to it. The
sinlessness of Christ refers to his
obedient refusal to give in to
temptation. It does not mean that he
did not experience temptation
himself.

The temptation of Jesus Christ
Mk 1:13 pp Mt 4:1–10 pp Lk 4:1–13

The temptation to avoid the cross
Mt 16:21–23 pp Mk 8:31–33 *See also*
Mt 26:36–44 pp Mk 14:32–42
pp Lk 22:40–46; Mt 27:39–44
pp Mk 15:31–32 pp Lk 23:36–37, 39

**The temptation to please the
crowd**
Lk 11:16 *See also* Mt 12:38–39
pp Lk 11:29; Jn 2:18; 6:30

**The significance of the
temptation of Jesus Christ**
Believers can identify with Jesus
Christ in his temptation Heb 2:18

Believers can have confidence in the
face of temptation Heb 4:15–16

See also

2075 Christ, sinless	2575 Christ,
	temptation

6253
temptation, avoiding causing

Any behaviour which might cause
others to do wrong is to be avoided.

**Warnings not to cause
temptation**
Lk 17:1

**Special care is needed to avoid
tempting those whose faith is
young**
Mt 18:6 *See also* Mk 9:42; Lk 17:2

**Temptation is linked to passing
judgment on others**
Ro 14:13

**Allowance must be made to avoid
causing temptation to those
whose faith is weak**
Ro 14:15,21

**Avoiding causing temptation by
exercising Christian freedom
responsibly**
1Co 8:9–13

Examples of causing temptation
Nu 25:1–2; Pr 16:29 *See also* Hab 2:15;
Mt 18:6

**Examples of restraining sin or
temptation**
Ge 37:21–22; Ac 20:28–31;
Eph 6:10–13; Heb 12:1–3; 1Pe 5:8–9;
1Jn 3:7

See also

5897 judging others	6206 offence
6030 sin, avoidance	

6257
unbelievers

Those who are unwilling to believe
and trust in God, especially as he has
made himself known in and through
Jesus Christ.

Characteristics of unbelievers
A refusal to believe in God Nu 14:11;
Ps 78:32; Jn 5:38; Ac 14:2

A refusal to trust in God Ps 78:22;
Heb 4:2

A persistence in sin Ps 78:32

Descriptions of unbelievers
They are blind 2Co 4:4 *See also*
Jn 9:39–41

They are disobedient Heb 3:12,18–19

**Unbelievers can become
believers**
1Ti 1:13 *See also* Mk 9:24

**The effect of tongues and
prophecy on unbelievers**
1Co 14:22–25

**Relationships between believers
and unbelievers**
Believers should not marry unbelievers
2Co 6:14–15

An unbelieving husband or wife
1Co 7:12–16 *See also* 1Pe 3:1

Eating with unbelievers 1Co 10:27–29

**The consequence of remaining
an unbeliever**
Jn 3:18 *See also* Lk 12:46; Jn 8:24; 12:48;
Rev 21:8

Examples of unbelievers
Some Israelites: Nu 14:13–39;
Dt 1:34–35; 1Co 10:10
Mt 17:20 *the disciples*; Mk 8:11–12 *some
Pharisees*
Some Jews: Ac 14:2; 17:5

See also

5135 blindness,	8426 evangelism,
spiritual	motivation
6020 sin	8718 disobedience
6040 sinners	8834 unbelief
6125 condemnation,	9023 death,
divine	unbelievers
6178 hardness of	9210 judgment,
heart	God's
7105 believers	9510 hell

6260
uncircumcised

Those who are outside the covenant
of God.

**Circumcision marked the
covenant people of God**
God's covenant with Abraham
Ge 17:10–12,14 *See also* Jos 5:6–7

Uncircumcised aliens participating in
Jewish religious practices had first to
be circumcised Ex 12:48; Eze 44:6–7,9;
Ac 11:3; 21:21

The term "uncircumcised"
Used to describe Gentiles Jdg 14:3;
15:18; 2Sa 1:20; Eze 28:10; 31:18;
32:19,21,24–32

As a term of derision Isa 52:1 *See also*
Ge 34:14; 1Sa 14:6; 17:26,36; 31:4
pp 1Ch 10:4

**Uncircumcision represents a
wrong inner spiritual attitude**
Jer 9:25–26 *The tribes mentioned also
practised male circumcision. See also*
Ac 7:51; Ro 2:25–27; 3:29–30;
1Co 7:18–19; Gal 5:6; 6:15; Col 2:13

**In Christ the barrier between the
circumcised and uncircumcised
is overcome**
Eph 2:11–13 *See also* Ro 4:9–12;
1Co 12:13; Col 3:11

See also
1348 covenant with Abraham
5012 heart
5761 attitudes
7334 circumcision
7510 Gentiles

6500
Salvation

6510
salvation

The transformation of a person's individual nature and relationship with God as a result of repentance and faith in the atoning death of Jesus Christ on the cross. All humanity stands in need of salvation, which is only possible through faith in Jesus Christ.

6511
salvation, nature of

Salvation involves a change in the relationship between God and a person. Salvation includes God's adoption of believers into his family, his acceptance of them as righteous and his forgiveness of their sins. It also includes personal renewal and transformation through the work of the Holy Spirit.

Salvation as a change in status before God
Access to God Ro 5:1–2 *See also* Eph 2:13; Heb 4:16

Adoption into the family of God Jn 1:12; Ro 8:22–24; Gal 4:4–7

Forgiveness of sin Ac 5:30–31 *See also* Ps 32:1–2; Mt 26:28; Ac 10:43; 13:38; Eph 1:7; Col 2:13

Heavenly citizenship Php 3:20–21 *See also* Eph 2:19; Col 3:1–2; Heb 12:22–24

Inheritance from God Ro 8:17 *See also* Col 1:12; Rev 21:7

Peace with God Eph 2:13–17 *See also* Isa 53:5; Jn 16:33; Ro 5:1–2; Col 3:15

Righteousness in the sight of God Ro 1:17 *See also* Isa 61:10; Ro 3:22; 4:3–13,25–5:1 *The idea of being righteous in the sight of God lies at the heart of Paul's doctrine of justification by faith;* 1Co 1:30; 2Co 5:21; Php 3:8–9; 2Ti 4:8; Heb 11:7

Salvation as a change in a person's nature
Becoming a new creation 2Co 5:17 *See also* Ro 6:4; Gal 6:14–15; Eph 2:15

Deliverance from God's righteous condemnation Ro 8:1–2 *See also* Isa 50:8; Ro 5:15–17; 8:33–39; Col 1:22

Deliverance from the power of sin and evil Gal 1:3–4 *See also* Ro 6:14; 7:21–25; 8:2–4; 1Pe 2:24; Rev 1:5

Inner personal renewal 1Jn 1:7 *See also* Ps 51:1–2,7; Heb 1:3; 10:19–22

New birth Jn 3:3–7 *See also* Jas 1:18; 1Pe 1:23; 1Jn 3:9

The presence of the Holy Spirit
Ro 8:10–11 *See also* Gal 5:2–25

See also
3230 Holy Spirit & regeneration
3278 Holy Spirit, indwelling
6124 condemnation
6606 access to God
6608 adoption
6644 eternal life
6652 forgiveness
6669 grace & salvation
6676 justification
6700 peace
6744 sanctification
8154 righteousness

6512
salvation, necessity and basis of

Scripture stresses that fallen human beings are cut off from God on account of their sin. All need to be saved, if they are to enter into a new relationship with God as their Creator and Redeemer. Salvation is not the result of human achievement, privilege or wisdom, but depends totally upon the graciousness of a loving God, supremely expressed in the cross of Jesus Christ. People must respond in repentance and faith if they are to benefit from God's offer of salvation in Christ.

The necessity of salvation
The universal rule of sin in human nature Isa 64:6; Ro 3:19–23; 5:12–18; 7:24; Eph 2:3

Sin cuts humanity off from God Isa 59:1–2 *See also* Ge 3:22–24; Eph 2:1–5; 4:18

Sin enslaves humanity to evil Jer 13:23; Hos 5:4; Zec 7:11–12; Ro 7:14–20; 2Pe 2:13–19

Salvation is grounded in the love of God
Salvation is not based on human achievement Ro 3:28; Eph 2:8–9 *See also* Ac 15:7–11; Ro 4:1–3; 5:1–2; Gal 2:16,21; 2Ti 1:9

Salvation is grounded in God's love for his people Eph 2:4–5 *See also* Dt 7:1–8; Jn 3:16–17; Ro 5:8; 2Th 2:16; 1Jn 4:9–19

Salvation is grounded in God's grace Ro 3:22–24 *See also* Jn 1:16; Ac 15:11; Ro 5:15–17; 2Co 6:1–2; Eph 1:5–8; 2:4–10; 1Ti 1:14–15; Tit 2:11; 3:4–7; Heb 2:9

Salvation and the work of Jesus Christ
Salvation is grounded in the work of Jesus Christ Ac 5:30–31; 1Ti 1:15 *See also* Jn 4:42; Ac 4:10–12; Ro 5:9–10; Php 3:20–21; 2Ti 1:9–10; Tit 3:5–7; Heb 7:24–25; 1Jn 4:14

Jesus Christ's death was totally sufficient for salvation 1Pe 3:18 *See also* Jn 17:1–4; Ac 4:10–12; Gal 1:3–4; Eph 1:5–10; 1Ti 2:5–6; 2Ti 1:9–10; Heb 10:10; 1Jn 4:9–10; Rev 7:9–10

Salvation demands a human decision
Jn 3:36; Ac 3:19 *See also* Mk 1:15;

Lk 8:50; Jn 3:17–18; Ac 2:37–39; Heb 12:25; 1Pe 2:4–8; 1Jn 5:10

See also
1085 God, love of
2324 Christ as Saviour
2369 Christ, responses to
2410 cross, the
2420 gospel
5005 human race & redemption
6028 sin, deliverance from
6639 election to salvation
6732 repentance
8022 faith, basis of salvation
8442 good works
9024 death, spiritual

6513
Saviour, God as
See 1320 God, as Saviour

6514
Saviour, Jesus Christ as
See 2324 Jesus Christ, as Saviour

6600
Aspects of salvation

6602
acceptance

The favourable reception of someone or something. God in his grace accepts human beings, their worship and their offerings. People are called to accept Jesus Christ and the message of the gospel and to respond to being accepted by accepting one another.

6603
acceptance, divine

God's gracious favour shown both to Israel and to the Gentiles. God accepts people who respond to him, and worship that is offered sincerely and is accompanied by wholehearted commitment.

God's acceptance of human beings
God's gracious acceptance of Israel 2Ki 13:23 *See also* Eze 20:40–41; Ro 11:1

God's acceptance of those who respond to him Ge 4:7; Eze 43:27; Jn 6:37 *See also* Ex 28:38; Ro 14:3; Heb 12:6; 2Pe 1:10–11

God's acceptance of the Gentiles Ro 15:16 *See also* Isa 56:6–7; Ac 10:34–35; 15:7–8

Prayers for acceptance by God Dt 21:8; 2Sa 24:23

God's acceptance of human worship
Acceptable sacrifices Lev 22:19–21; 1Pe 2:5 *See also* Lev 1:3–4; 19:5–7; 22:27–29; Mal 3:3–4; Jn 4:23; Ro 12:1; Php 4:18; Heb 12:28; 13:16

Acceptance of gifts offered for the tabernacle Nu 7:5 *See also* Nu 31:51–54

Unacceptable offerings Jer 14:10–12 *See also* Lev 7:18; 22:25; Mal 1:8–10; 2:13

Acceptable service Pr 21:3; Jas 1:27 *See also* 1Sa 15:22; Ps 51:6–7; Jer 6:19–20; Am 5:21–24; 2Co 6:17–18; Isa 52:11

God accepts prayer and praise Ps 6:9; Heb 13:15 *See also* Job 33:26; 42:8–9; Ps 119:108; Lk 18:13–14

See also

1055 God, grace & mercy	7402 offerings
1085 God, love of	8453 obedience
6614 atonement	8602 prayer
6666 grace	8622 worship
	8664 praise

6604
acceptance, human

The response of human beings to the revelation and grace of God. It is seen in receiving Jesus Christ, his words and the message of the gospel, and in the acceptance of one another for his sake. Believers are called, too, to accept instruction and discipline and to submit to God's will for their lives.

Human beings are to accept Jesus Christ
Receiving Jesus Christ Jn 1:12 *See also* Col 2:6

Accepting Jesus Christ by accepting others Jn 13:20 *See also* Mt 10:40; 18:5 pp Mk 9:37 pp Lk 9:48; Lk 10:16; Jn 12:44

Accepting Jesus Christ's words Jn 17:8 *See also* Mt 11:14; 19:11–12; Jn 3:33–34

Refusing to accept Jesus Christ and his words Jn 1:11; 3:11,32; 5:43–44; 6:60

Acceptance of the gospel
The gospel is worthy of acceptance 1Ti 1:15; Jas 1:21 *See also* Mt 13:23 pp Mk 4:20 pp Lk 8:15; 1Co 15:3; 1Ti 4:9–10

Examples of those accepting the gospel Ac 2:41 *3,000 on the day of Pentecost*; Ac 8:14 *the Samaritans*; Ac 11:1 *the Gentiles*
Believers in Corinth: 1Co 15:1; 2Co 11:4
Gal 1:9 *believers in Galatia*
Believers in Thessalonica: 1Th 1:6; 2Th 2:13

Rejection of the gospel Ac 22:18; Ro 11:15; 1Co 2:14

Acceptance of one another
A right self-acceptance 1Co 15:10 *Paul accepts himself as a sinner saved by God's grace and entrusted with an important ministry;* Gal 5:14 *Loving others requires a proper self-love: the recognition that people are made in God's image and are the objects of his love. See also* Lev 19:18; Mt 22:39 pp Mk 12:31; Mk 12:33; Ro 13:9; 1Ti 1:12–14; Jas 2:8

Acceptance of one another because of God's example Ro 15:7 *See also* Jn 13:34; 15:12

Acceptance of those whom God has accepted Ro 14:1 *See also* Dt 10:18–19 *God's people should reflect his concern for the weak and defenceless;* Mt 19:13–14 pp Mk 10:13–14 pp Lk 18:15–16 *Jesus Christ rebukes his disciples for turning away children.*
Ananias' acceptance of Saul: Ac 9:11–17; 22:12–13
Ac 9:27 *Barnabas' acceptance of Saul*
Acceptance of the Gentiles:
Ac 10:15,28,47

Acceptance of outsiders who join God's people Lev 19:33–34 *See also* Eze 47:22–23

Acceptance of itinerant ministers Gal 4:14 *See also* 1Co 16:10–11; Php 2:29–30

Acceptance of things given
Acceptance of gifts 1Sa 25:35 *See also* Ge 33:10–11; 1Sa 10:4; 1Ti 4:3–4

Refusal to accept gifts Ge 14:23–24 *Abraham refuses gifts offered by the king of Sodom;* 2Ki 5:15–16 *Elisha refuses a gift offered by Naaman;* Est 4:4 *Mordecai refuses fine clothes from Esther.*

Acceptance of instruction
Job 22:22; Pr 4:10; 10:8; 19:20; Isa 29:24

Acceptance of discipline
Job 5:17 *See also* Dt 21:18; Ps 94:12; Pr 3:11–12; 10:17; Heb 12:5–7; Rev 3:19

Acceptance of God's will
Mt 26:39 pp Mk 14:36 pp Lk 22:42 *See also* Job 2:10; Ps 40:8; Isa 50:5; Ro 8:28

Acceptance of bribes forbidden
Ex 23:8
God is impartial and cannot be bribed:
Dt 10:17; 2Ch 19:7
Ps 15:5; Pr 17:23; Isa 33:15

See also

1175 God, will of	7742 missionaries, support
1690 word of God	7797 teaching
2426 gospel, responses	8292 love
6230 rejection	8351 teachableness
6510 salvation	8353 tolerance
6669 grace & salvation	8445 hospitality

6606

access to God

The privilege of entering into the presence of God through the work of Jesus Christ.

Only the pure have access to God
Ps 24:3–4; 1Jn 3:21–22 *See also* Ps 41:12; 66:18–19; 73:28; Mt 5:8; 1Pe 3:12; Ps 34:15–14

The wicked do not have access to God
Ps 101:7; Isa 59:2 *See also* Ge 4:14,16; Lev 22:3; Dt 31:18; Ps 5:5; Isa 1:15; 64:7; Jer 7:15; 15:1; 23:39; 52:3; Eze 39:23; Hos 5:6; Mic 3:4

Access to God through the priests and sacrificial system
Access to God by this means in the OT Ex 29:44–45 *See also* Ex 29:29–30,36,38–39

This OT access to God fulfilled in Jesus Christ Heb 4:14–16; 7:23–25 *See also* Heb 2:17; 7:18–19; 10:10–12; 12:18–24

Access to God by the priesthood of all believers 1Pe 2:5 *See also* 1Pe 2:9; Rev 1:6

Access to God through the Tent of Meeting and the tabernacle
Access to God by this means in the OT Ex 33:7–11 *See also* Ex 40:1–2,34–35; Nu 1:51; 3:10,38; 18:7,22; 2Ch 1:3

This OT access to God fulfilled in Jesus Christ Heb 9:23–24 *See also* Ac 7:44; Heb 8:1–2,5–6; 9:11

Access to God through the Most Holy Place
Access to God by this means in the OT Heb 9:7–8 *See also* Lev 16:2,12–17,32–33; 1Ki 6:16; 8:6 pp 2Ch 5:7; 1Ki 8:10–11 pp 2Ch 5:13–14; 2Ch 3:8

Access to God by this means fulfilled in Jesus Christ Heb 9:12; 10:19–22 *See also* Mt 27:51 pp Mk 15:38; Heb 6:19–20; Heb 9:3–5

Believers have access to God by grace
Ps 21:6 *See also* Ps 51:10–11; 145:18; Hos 6:1–2; Ac 17:27; 2Co 4:14; Jas 4:8; Jude 24

Believers have access to God through Jesus Christ
Ro 5:1–2; Eph 2:18; 3:12 *See also* Jn 10:9; 14:6

See also

1065 God, holiness of	6732 repentance
2306 Christ, high priest	7434 sacrifice
6020 sin	7458 tabernacle, the
6636 drawing near to God	7766 priests
6666 grace	8104 assurance
	8324 purity
	8602 prayer

6608

adoption

The deliberate action by which a family gives to a person all the privileges of being a member of that family.

6609
adoption, nature of

The giving by God of the status and privileges of being his children. God adopts those who believe in him and grants them the benefits of his salvation.

A family adopts a child
Ge 15:3 *See also* Ge 48:5; Ex 2:10; Est 2:7

God adopts the nation of Israel
Dt 14:2 *See also* Dt 7:7; Isa 63:16; Am 3:1–2; Ro 9:4

God is Israel's father Jer 31:9 *See also* Mal 1:6

Israel is God's son Hos 11:1 *See also* Dt 14:1

God adopts believers as his children
Jn 1:12–13

God is the Father of believers 2Co 6:18 *See also* Mt 6:9 pp Lk 11:2

Believers are adopted as an outcome of predestination Eph 1:5

Believers are adopted as an outcome of redemption Gal 4:5

Believers are adopted as an outcome of justification Gal 3:24–26 *See also* Jn 1:12–13

Believers are adopted by grace Eph 1:3–6 *See also* Eze 16:3–6; Ro 4:16; Eph 1:11

The final adoption of believers will occur at the resurrection Ro 8:23 *See also* Eph 1:13–14; 1Jn 3:2

See also

5895 intimacy	6716 reconciliation
6510 salvation	6720 redemption
6638 election	7105 believers
6676 justification	7115 children of God
6708 predestination	9105 last things

6610
adoption, descriptions of

The words used by the NT to describe believers point to their status and privileges as the adopted children of God.

Believers are no longer slaves but sons
Gal 4:7–9 *See also* Jn 8:34–36; Ro 8:15; Phm 16

Believers are children of God
1Jn 3:1–2 *The title "child of God" is thought by some to be distinct from that of "son of God": "child" is thought to emphasise God's fatherhood, whilst "son" is thought to emphasise the Christian's privileges. These terms are however, sometimes used interchangeably. See also* Lk 20:36; Ro 8:21; Php 2:15; 1Jn 3:2; 5:2

Believers are sons of God
Ro 8:14 *See also* Ro 9:26; Gal 3:26

Believers are children of the resurrection
Lk 20:36

Believers are children of light, sons of light
Jn 12:36; Eph 5:8; 1Th 5:5

Believers are heirs of God
Ro 8:17 *See also* Gal 3:29; 4:7; Tit 3:7; Heb 6:17

Believers are brothers of Jesus Christ
Heb 2:11–12 *See also* Mt 12:48–50; Ro 8:29; Heb 2:17

Believers are brothers of other believers
1Jn 3:14 *See also* 1Jn 4:19–20; Rev 12:10; 19:10

Believers are members of God's household, his family
Eph 2:19 *See also* Gal 6:10; Heb 3:2–6

See also

5680 family	7140 people of God
5705 inheritance, spiritual	8134 knowing God

6611
adoption, privileges and duties of

As adopted members of the family of God, believers receive both the privileges and responsibilities of being children of God.

The privileges received by believers through adoption
Believers are given the Spirit of adoption Gal 4:6 *See also* Ro 8:15

Believers have access to their heavenly Father Eph 2:18 *See also* Eph 3:12; Heb 4:16

Believers become heirs with Christ of heaven Ro 8:17 *See also* Gal 3:29; 4:7; Col 1:12; 1Pe 1:4

The benefits God gives to those he adopts
Believers are pitied by him Ps 103:13

Believers are protected Pr 14:26

Believers are provided for Mt 6:31–33

Believers receive loving discipline Heb 12:6

Believers are never forsaken Ps 94:14

Believers are assured by the Spirit Ro 8:16

The responsibilities of God's adopted children
Believers are to walk in the light Jn 12:35–36; Eph 5:8; 1Th 5:4–5

Believers are to shun evil 2Co 6:17–18; Php 2:15

Believers are to purify themselves 2Co 7:1; 1Jn 3:2–3

Believers are to live obediently Mt 12:50; 1Pe 1:14; 1Jn 5:2–3

Believers are to live in peace Mt 5:9; Ro 14:19

Believers are to live in love Gal 5:13; 1Pe 4:8; 1Jn 3:18

Believers are to be watchful 1Th 5:5–6

See also

6606 access to God	8453 obedience
8104 assurance	

6614

atonement

Reconciliation; sin has alienated humanity from God and provoked God's anger. God has responded by providing the means of restoring this broken relationship, bringing both

sides to a place where they are at one again ("at-one-ment").

6615
atonement, necessity and nature of

Scripture stresses the seriousness and reality of human sin, and that human beings are unable to atone for their own sins. In his grace, God provides a means by which the situation can be remedied.

Atonement is necessary because of human sinfulness
Atonement is necessary because sin cuts people off from God Isa 59:2 *See also* Isa 64:7; Eze 39:23; Hab 1:13; Jn 9:31

Atonement is necessary because sin provokes God's wrath Eph 2:1–3 *See also* Ge 6:5–7; Ex 32:30–35; Ro 1:18–20; 2:8

God's gracious nature is the basis for atonement
Atonement is grounded in God's reluctance to punish sinners Eze 18:32 *See also* Eze 33:11; 1Ti 2:1–4; 2Pe 3:9

Atonement is grounded in God's readiness to forgive sin Ex 34:6–7 *The punishment of subsequent generations makes God's abhorrence of sin quite clear, but the extension of his love and forgiveness "to thousands" puts the emphasis in these verses on God's grace and compassion. See also* Ps 145:8; Da 9:9; Jnh 4:2

Atonement is grounded in God's covenant love Nu 14:19 *The Hebrew word for "great love" means God's loving faithfulness to those within the covenant. See also* Ps 25:6–7; 103:8–12; Joel 2:13

God's provision of atonement is a means of dealing with sin
Atonement through sacrifice Lev 9:7 *See also* Ex 30:10; Nu 15:22–26

God's promised new covenant of forgiveness was fulfilled in Jesus Christ's atoning death Heb 10:16–17 *See also* Jer 31:33–34; Mt 26:28; Heb 9:15; 12:24

Images used to portray the at-one-ment, or restored relationship, between God and humanity
Atonement as forgiveness of sins Eph 1:7–8 *See also* Lev 19:22; Ac 13:38; Col 2:13–14

Atonement as cleansing and purification Lev 16:30 *See also* Isa 6:6–7; Tit 2:14; 1Jn 1:7; Rev 7:14

Atonement as reconciliation 2Co 5:19 *See also* Ro 5:9–11; Eph 2:14–16

Atonement as healing 1Pe 2:24 *See also* 2Ch 7:14; Ps 103:2–3; Isa 53:5

Atonement as God buying people back for himself Rev 5:9 *See also* Mt 20:28 pp Mk 10:45; Ac 20:28; 1Pe 1:18–19

Atonement as making holy: creating a relationship of consecrated nearness to God Heb 10:10 *See also* Col 1:22; Heb 13:12

See also

1055 God, grace & mercy	6717 reconciliation, world to God
6025 sin & God's character	6720 redemption
6510 salvation	7314 blood
6653 forgiveness, divine	8266 holiness

6616
atonement, in OT

The OT laid down complex regulations by which the guilt of sin could be removed through the sacrificial system. Particular emphasis was placed upon the role of the high priest, who was required to make annual atonement for the sins of the people.

The covenantal framework of atonement
As God's covenant partners, the Israelites undertook to keep his laws Ex 24:3 *See also* Dt 26:17; Jos 24:24

The sin offering made atonement for unintentional sins under the covenant Lev 9:7 *See also* Lev 4:13–14; Nu 15:22–26

The guilt offering atoned for sins where reparation was required Lev 19:20–22 *See also* Lev 6:1–7

Deliberate flouting of God's law could not be atoned for Nu 15:30–31 *See also* Nu 35:33; 1Sa 3:14

The Day of Atonement provided for the removal of the nation's sin Lev 16:34 *See also* Ex 30:10; Lev 16:1–33 *The nation's sin was atoned for by sprinkling the atonement cover in the Most Holy Place with the blood of the sacrificial goat; the removal of the people's sin was symbolised by the driving of the scapegoat into the wilderness; Heb 9:7*

The atonement cover Ex 25:17–22 *The locating of God's presence above the atonement cover in the tabernacle demonstrated that it was only on the basis of atonement that God could accompany his people. See also* Ex 30:6; Lev 16:2; Nu 7:89

Atonement was effected by the blood of the sacrifice Lev 17:11 *The blood signified that the life of the animal had been given in place of that of the worshipper. See also* Heb 9:22

The role of priests in making atonement
Priests were dedicated to God in order to make atonement for others Ex 29:44 *See also* Lev 8:22–30

The priests had to make atonement for their own sins Heb 5:1–3 *See also* Lev 9:8–11

The priests represented the people before God to atone for their sin Heb 5:1 *See also* Ex 28:36–38; Lev 10:16–17

The people had to constant reminders of the need for atonement
Rituals of cleansing included an atoning offering Lev 12:7–8; 14:18–22,53; 15:15

Atonement was a feature of Israel's festivals Nu 28:22,30; 29:5,11

Abuses of the system of atonement
The sinful conduct of the priests who made atonement Hos 4:7–8 *See also* 1Sa 2:12–17; Jer 6:13–14; Eze 22:26; Mal 1:6–8

The sinful conduct of the people who sought atonement without repenting of their sins Hos 8:11–13 *See also* Isa 1:10–17; 66:3; Jer 7:21–24; Am 4:4

The need for repentance for a relationship of atonement Pr 16:6 *See also* 1Sa 15:22; Ps 51:16–17; Mic 6:6–8

The prophets foretold a renewing of God's relationship with Israel, involving atonement for sin
Isaiah's message about the obedient servant Isa 53:4–12

Jeremiah's prophecy of a new covenant Jer 31:31–34

Ezekiel's vision of a new temple Eze 43:18–27

See also

1345 covenant	7412 priesthood
6172 guilt	7435 sacrifice, in OT
6648 expiation	7440 scapegoat
6712 propitiation	7444 sin offering
7308 Atonement, Day of	7454 sprinkling
7376 high priest	8622 worship

6617
atonement, in NT

In dying for the sins of the world, Jesus Christ fulfilled and replaced the OT sacrificial system, so that all who believe in him are restored to fellowship with God. Christ is the true high priest, who finally liberates his people from the guilt of sin, by offering himself as the supreme sacrifice.

The atoning purpose of Jesus Christ's death
Jesus Christ's death on behalf of others Jn 10:11 *See also* Jn 10:14–18; 2Co 5:15; Heb 2:9; 1Jn 3:16

Jesus Christ's atoning death for sin 1Co 15:3 *See also* Ro 4:25; 8:3; Gal 1:4; 1Pe 3:18

The atoning significance of Jesus Christ's death is expressed by references to his blood Ro 5:9; Rev 5:9 *See also* Eph 2:13; 1Pe 1:18–19; 1Jn 1:7; Rev 7:14

Jesus Christ's atoning death is commemorated in the Lord's Supper 1Co 11:23–25 *See also* Mt 26:26–28 pp Mk 14:22–24 pp Lk 22:19–20

Explanations of the atonement
Jesus Christ's death as an atoning sacrifice Ro 3:25 *See also* 1Co 5:7; Eph 5:2; 1Jn 4:10; Rev 5:6

Jesus Christ's atoning death as redemption Mk 10:45 pp Mt 20:28 *See also* Ac 20:28; Gal 3:13–14; Eph 1:7; Col 1:13–14

The atonement is effective because of Jesus Christ's sinlessness
2Co 5:21 *See also* Heb 4:15; 1Pe 2:22–24; 1Jn 3:5

Jesus Christ's death fulfils and replaces the Day of Atonement
Jesus Christ makes atonement as the new high priest Heb 7:26–28

Jesus Christ is the mediator of the new and better covenant Heb 8:6–7; 9:15

Jesus Christ has made atonement in the true heavenly sanctuary Heb 8:1–2; 9:24

Jesus Christ's atoning blood brings effective cleansing Heb 9:12–14

Jesus Christ's single sacrifice replaces the many required under the old covenant Heb 10:11–14

Access to the heavenly sanctuary is now open Heb 10:19–20

By dying with Christ, believers are released from this age into the life of the age to come
Ro 6:1–7 *See also* Ro 7:4–6; Gal 2:19–20; 6:14; Eph 2:6–7; Col 2:11–13

God the Father and the atoning death of his Son
God's sending of his Son to make atonement 1Jn 4:14 *See also* Jn 3:16; Ro 8:32; 2Co 5:18; Gal 4:4–5

God's grace displayed in making atonement for the ungodly Eph 2:4–5 *See also* Ro 5:6–8; Eph 2:8–9; Tit 3:4–5

The worldwide scope of Jesus Christ's atoning death
1Jn 2:2 *See also* Jn 1:29; 2Co 5:19; 1Ti 2:5

The appropriate response to the atonement
The response of repentance Ac 3:19 *See also* Ac 2:38; 17:30; 20:21

The response of faith Ac 10:43 *See also* Jn 3:14–15; Ac 16:31; Ro 3:22; Gal 2:16

The response of baptism Ac 22:16 *See also* Ac 2:38; 1Pe 3:21

See also

2306 Christ, high priest	6027 sin, remedy for
2315 Christ as Lamb	6676 justification
2410 cross, the	6728 regeneration
2530 Christ, death of	6754 union with Christ
5005 human race & redemption	8020 faith
5492 restitution	9165 restoration

calling

God's summoning of individuals and people to himself, so that they will belong to him and serve him in his world. The calling of a believer may involve a specific place, task or vocation in life.

God calls individuals to belong to him and serve him

God calls all people everywhere
Ac 17:30 *See also* Pr 8:4; Isa 45:22; 55:1; Mt 9:13; 11:28–30; 22:9; Jn 7:37; Ac 2:39; Ro 10:18; Ps 19:4

Few respond positively to God's call
Mt 22:14 *See also* Isa 65:12; 66:4; Jer 7:13; 35:17; Mt 22:2–10 pp Lk 14:16–24

Responding to God's call-results in salvation Heb 9:15; Jude 1 *See also* Jn 5:25; 10:3; Ro 1:6; 8:28–30; 11:29; 1Co 1:9,24–29; 7:18–22; Gal 1:6; Eph 4:1; Php 3:14; 2Th 1:11; 2:14; 1Ti 6:12; Heb 3:1; 1Pe 5:10; 2Pe 1:3,10; Rev 17:14

God calls Christians to live differently
2Ti 1:9; 1Pe 2:9
Living in peace: 1Co 7:15; Col 3:15
Gal 5:13 *serving one another*
Living in hope: Eph 1:18; 4:4; 1Pe 2:20–21; 3:9 1Th 4:7

God called particular individuals to do specific tasks at specific times
Abraham: Ge 12:1–3; Isa 51:2; Heb 11:8
Ex 3:4 *Moses;* 1Sa 3:4–10 *Samuel;* Isa 6:8 *Isaiah*
Cyrus: Isa 41:2; 45:4
The servant of the LORD: Isa 42:6; 49:1
Jer 1:4–5 *Jeremiah;* Hos 1:2 *Hosea;* Am 7:15 *Amos*
Jonah: Jnh 1:1–2; 3:1–2
The disciples: Mt 4:18–22 pp Mk 1:16–20; Lk 5:2–11; Jn 1:35–42
Ac 13:2 *Barnabas and Paul*
Paul: Ro 1:1; 1Co 1:1; Gal 1:15

God called a people, Israel, to serve him in a special way
Isa 43:1 *See also* Hos 11:1–2

The believer's place in life is understood to be a calling
1Co 7:17 *See also* 1Co 7:20,24

See also
1115 God, purpose of	6708 predestination
3263 Holy Spirit, guidance	7621 disciples, calling
5076 Abraham, life of	7631 Twelve, calling of
5102 Moses, life of	7944 ministry, qualifications
6510 salvation	9610 hope
6638 election	
6705 peace, experience	

6623

choice

A deliberate act of will or decision, in which God chooses individuals or peoples to be his or calls them to perform certain tasks or responsibilities. Human beings are also required to make choices, particularly between good and evil.

God's sovereign choice
Mal 1:2–3 *See also* Ro 9:10–15; Ex 33:19; 1Co 1:27–28; Jas 2:5

God's chosen people
Israel Dt 7:6 *See also* Ex 19:4–6; Dt 14:2; Ps 65:4; Isa 14:1; 41:9; Jer 3:14
NT believers Eph 1:4 *See also* Ro 8:28–33; 1Pe 2:9

God chooses people for special tasks
Ex 3:10 *See also* 1Sa 9:17; 16:1–13; Hag 2:20–23; Mk 3:13–19 pp Lk 6:13–16; Ac 9:10–15; Gal 1:15–16

God chose where he was to be worshipped
Dt 12:5 *See also* Dt 12:11,14,18,26; 14:23; 16:2,6–7,11,15–16; 26:2; 31:11

People must choose between good and evil
Jos 24:15; Pr 16:16 *See also* Ex 32:26; Dt 30:19; 1Ki 18:21; Pr 3:31; 8:10; Jn 7:17

Examples of bad choices
Jas 4:4 *See also* Pr 1:28–33; Isa 65:12; 66:3–4; Mt 27:21 pp Mk 15:9–11

Examples of wise choices
Heb 11:24–26 *See also* Jos 24:21–24; Ru 1:16; 1Ki 3:5–14

See also
1130 God, sovereignty	6638 election
	6663 freedom of will
1175 God, will of	8124 guidance
2057 Christ, obedience	8361 wisdom
	8408 decision-making
5051 responsibility	
5877 hesitation	8412 decisions
6620 calling	

6624

confession, of sin

An admission of sin on the part of individuals or groups of people. Genuine repentance and confession herald divine forgiveness.

Confession of sin leads to divine forgiveness
Under the old covenant Pr 28:13 *See also* Lev 16:21 *Part of the ritual of the Day of Atonement involved the high priest confessing the sins of the nation, while laying his hands on the head of a sacrificial goat;* Lev 26:40–42; 1Ki 8:33–36 pp 2Ch 6:24–27; 1Ki 8:46–52 pp 2Ch 6:36–39; Ps 32:3–5

Under the new covenant 1Jn 1:8–10 *See also* Jas 5:13–16

Confession of sin accompanied by acts appropriate to repentance
Nu 5:5–8 *See also* Lev 5:5–6; Ezr 10:10–11; Ne 9:1–3; Lk 19:8; Ac 19:18–19

Examples of confession of sin
On behalf of the nation Ne 1:5–7 *See also* Ezr 9:5–15; Isa 59:12–13; 64:6–7; Jer 14:7,20; Da 9:4–14

By the people as a whole 1Sa 7:5–6 *See*

also Ezr 9:4–7,10–15; Ne 9:33–35; Ps 106:6; Jer 3:24–25

By individuals Ps 51:1–5 *See also* 2Sa 24:10 pp 1Ch 21:10; 2Sa 24:17 pp 1Ch 21:17; Job 7:20; 42:5–6; Isa 6:5

Confession of sin to other people
Jos 7:20–21 *See also* Lk 15:17–24; Jas 5:16

See also
6020 sin	8607 prayer, God's promises
6652 forgiveness	
6732 repentance	8625 worship, acceptable attitudes
7903 baptism	
8407 confession of Christ	

6626

conversion

Turning or returning to God in repentance, faith and obedience by those who do not know God or who have turned from him. Although conversion can be seen as a human act or decision, Scripture stresses that the work of God lies behind this human decision, guiding and motivating it.

6627
conversion, nature of

True repentance results in a turning from sin and an inner renewal which can only be brought about by God, who draws people to himself and who, through Jesus Christ, gives forgiveness and new life.

Conversion as turning to God
Turning back to God Dt 4:30–31; Lk 1:16–17 *See also* Dt 30:2–3,10; Lk 22:32; Jas 5:19–20

Turning from idolatry Ac 14:15 *See also* 1Sa 7:3; Jer 3:12–13; 4:1–2; 1Th 1:9–10

Turning from sinful ways 2Ki 17:13–14; Isa 55:6–7 *See also* 2Ki 13:11; 14:24; 15:9; Jer 18:11; 25:5; Eze 18:23; Da 9:13

Conversion as a turning away from unbelief to faith
It is linked to repentance Ac 3:19 *See also* Eze 14:6; 18:30; Ac 26:20

It is linked to coming to faith Ac 11:21

Conversion brings new life
It results in a transformed life 2Co 5:17 *See also* Ro 12:2; 2Co 3:18; Gal 6:14–15

It is symbolised in baptism Ro 6:3–4 *See also* Col 2:12; 3:1–3

It demands a new lifestyle Hos 12:6; Mt 18:3–4 *See also* Gal 5:22–24; Eph 4:1; 5:8–11; 1Pe 2:11–12

Conversion brings a new relationship with God
It brings a new status Gal 4:7 *See also* Gal 3:26–29; 1Jn 3:1; 1Pe 2:9–10

It brings a new understanding 2Co 3:15–16 *See also* Jer 31:34; Heb 8:11

Conversion is a work of God

God turns people to himself Jer 24:7; La 5:21 *See also* 1Ki 8:58; Jer 31:18; Eze 36:26–27; Jn 6:44; 15:16; Eph 2:12–13

God gives new birth Jas 1:17–18 *See also* Jn 3:3–6; Tit 3:4–5; 1Pe 1:23

See also

1055 God, grace & mercy	6732 repentance
3230 Holy Spirit & regeneration	6740 returning to God
5016 heart, fallen & redeemed	7907 baptism, practice
6666 grace	8020 faith
6698 newness	8135 knowing God
6728 regeneration	8144 renewal

6628
conversion, God's demands for

Through his servants, God calls people to turn to him. He wants to save the world which is alienated from him, and to restore those of his backslidden people who return to him and renew their commitment to the covenant.

The need for conversion
The world is alienated from God Ro 1:21–23 *See also* Ro 1:28; 3:11–12; Ps 14:3

The world does not know God Gal 4:8 *See also* 1Co 1:21; 15:34; 1Th 4:5; 2Th 1:8

God's people have turned away from him Mal 3:7 *See also* Nu 14:43; Dt 9:12; 1Sa 15:11 *Saul*; 1Ki 11:9 *Solomon*; 2Ch 25:27 *Amaziah*; Jer 8:5; Eze 6:9; Da 9:11; Ac 7:39

God's demands for the conversion of all people
Isa 45:22; Ac 17:30 *See also* Ps 65:5; Jnh 4:11; Zec 9:10

God's demands for the conversion of his own people
God's desire to save his people Eze 33:11 *See also* Jer 3:22; Joel 2:12–13; Zec 1:3

God's faithfulness to his people Jer 3:14 *See also* Lev 26:40–42; 2Ch 30:9; Hos 3:5; 6:1–3

God's promise of restoration 2Ch 7:13–14 *See also* 1Ki 8:48–49 pp 2Ch 6:38–39; Ne 1:9

The call to conversion through God's servants
The encouragement of his leaders Jos 24:14–15 *Joshua*; 2Ki 11:17 *Jehoiada* *Josiah*: 2Ki 23:24–25; 2Ch 34:31–33 2Ch 15:11–15 *Asa*; 2Ch 19:4 *Jehoshaphat*; 2Ch 29:6–10 *Hezekiah*; Ps 51:13 *David*

The ministry of his prophets Jer 35:15 *See also* Jer 25:4; Hos 14:1–2; Jnh 3:2

The preaching of believers Ac 26:16–18 *See also* Ac 2:38; Ro 10:14–15; Isa 52:7

Rejection of God's call to conversion

Isa 9:13 *See also* Jer 3:10; Hos 5:4; 7:10; Am 4:6–11

See also

1035 God, faithfulness	7733 leaders
4811 darkness, symbol of sin	7739 missionaries
	7754 preaching
5135 blindness, spiritual	7772 prophets
6231 rejection of God	9165 restoration

6629
conversion, examples of

Scripture gives examples of individuals and peoples who have turned to God in conversion.

Examples of conversion in the OT
Peoples who turned to God Isa 19:22 *Egypt*; Jnh 3:5–10 *Nineveh*

Individuals who turned to God
2Ki 5:15 *Naaman*; 2Ch 33:12–13 *Manasseh*; Da 4:34–37 *Nebuchadnezzar*; Jnh 1:16 *sailors on board ship with Jonah*

Examples of conversion in the NT
Examples of people in general Jn 4:42 *people of Sychar*; Ac 2:41 *3,000 people on the day of Pentecost*; Ac 8:12 *Samaritans*; Ac 9:35 *people of Lydda and Sharon*; Ac 15:3 *Gentile converts*

Examples of individual converts
Lk 15:18 *the prodigal son*; Lk 19:8–9 *Zacchaeus*; Ac 8:35–38 *the Ethiopian eunuch* *Paul*: Ac 9:3–18 pp Ac 22:6–11; 26:12–18 Ac 10:44–48 *Cornelius*; Ac 13:12 *the proconsul, Sergius Paulus*; Ac 16:14–15 *Lydia*; Ac 16:29–34 *the Philippian jailer*

The prophetic vision of the future conversion of Israel and the nations
Israel's turning back to God Hos 3:5 *See also* Jer 50:4–5; Hos 11:10–11; Ro 11:26

The conversion of the nations Jer 16:19 *See also* Ps 22:27–28; Isa 2:3 pp Mic 4:2; Zec 14:16

See also

2426 gospel, responses	7510 Gentiles
5108 Paul, life of	7757 preaching, effects

6632

conviction

The proving of a person guilty of sin or a crime. Scripture stresses that God has declared the guilt, together with its consequences, of sinful humanity. The term can also refer to a state of being convinced; i.e., the holding of a strong belief, especially a conscious awareness of one's guilt and the atoning death of Jesus Christ as the means of remission of that guilt.

Conviction is proving a person guilty of sin or a crime

Proving someone guilty of sin Jn 8:46 *See also* Jn 16:8–9 *NIV footnote at verse 8*; 1Co 14:24; Jas 2:9; Jude 15

Proving someone guilty of a crime Dt 19:15 *See also* Ex 22:9; Lev 17:3–4 *The death penalty only to be on the testimony of two or three witnesses:* Nu 35:30; Dt 17:6 2Sa 14:13; Ps 5:10; 109:7; Pr 24:25 *Pilate found no basis for the charges against Jesus Christ:* Lk 23:4,14,22; Jn 18:38 *There was no proof for the charges against Paul:* Ac 24:13; 25:7

God's conviction of sinful humanity

He declares them to be guilty Ro 3:19–20 *See also* Ps 5:9; 10:7; 14:1–3 pp Ps 53:1–3; Ps 140:3; Ecc 7:20; Isa 59:7–8; Ro 3:10–18

He also declares the consequences of their guilt Ge 2:17; 3:17–19; Ro 1:32; 5:12,16–19; 1Co 15:22

Conviction as holding a strong belief

Ro 14:5 *See also* Ge 45:28; Mt 17:20; Lk 20:6 pp Mt 21:26 pp Mk 11:32 *The people were convinced that John was a prophet*; Lk 16:31 *The conversion of those who were convinced by Paul's preaching:* Ac 17:4; 19:26; 28:24 Ac 26:9,26; Ro 2:19; 4:21; 8:38–39 *Paul's conviction that it is impossible to be separated from God's love;* Ro 14:14 *Paul's personal convictions about food regulations;* Ro 15:14; 2Co 5:14; Php 1:25; 1Th 1:5; 2Ti 1:5 *Paul is convinced by Timothy's faith;* 2Ti 1:12; 3:14

Conviction as the conscious awareness of one's guilt

Examples of conviction not resulting in repentance Ex 9:27 *See also* Ex 10:16; Nu 14:40; 22:34; Dt 1:41; Jdg 10:10 *Saul:* 1Sa 15:24; 24:17; 26:21 Mt 27:3–4 *Judas Iscariot;* Ac 24:25 *Governor Felix*

Examples of conviction leading to repentance Ac 2:37 *David:* 2Sa 12:13; Ps 51:3–4 Mt 26:75 pp Mk 14:72 pp Lk 22:62 *Peter* *The prodigal son:* Lk 15:17–18,21 Ac 16:30 *the Philippian jailer;* Ro 7:9

See also

3248 Holy Spirit, conviction	6626 conversion
	6732 repentance
3296 Holy Spirit in the world	7712 convincing
	7751 persuasion
5031 knowledge of sin	8112 certainty
5210 arrows	8630 worship, results
6172 guilt	

6634

deliverance

God frequently rescues people from danger, suffering and sin, often through human agency.

The source of deliverance
Deliverance comes from God Ps 3:8

See also Ex 3:7–8; Ps 18:2; Da 3:16–17; Jnh 2:9

There is no deliverance by other gods
2Ki 18:33 pp Isa 36:18

There is no escape from God Isa 43:13

Deliverance may be declined
Mt 26:53–54; Jn 18:36; Heb 11:35

Different kinds of deliverance
From danger 1Sa 17:37 *See also*
Lk 8:23–24; 2Co 1:9–10; 2Ti 4:17

From illness Ps 103:3; Isa 38:16

From trouble Ps 34:17,19; 54:7

From slavery Ex 20:2

From enemies Jer 38:10–13;
Da 6:19–22; Lk 1:74; 2Th 3:2

From Satan Lk 13:16; 22:31–32

From the fear of death Heb 2:14–15

From all fears Ps 34:4; Rev 1:17

From sin Gal 1:4 *See also* Ps 32:7;
2Th 2:13; Rev 1:5

From the coming wrath Lk 3:7;
1Th 1:10; 5:9

Deliverance for God's people
God promises deliverance Jer 15:11 *See also* Da 12:1

God's people are to pray for
deliverance Mt 6:13 *See also* 2Ki 19:19
pp Isa 37:20; Ps 59:1–2

The means of deliverance
Direct intervention by God Ex 14:13;
2Ki 7:6

Deliverance by angels Ac 12:7

Deliverance by human agency
Ge 37:17–22; Jdg 2:16; Ac 23:16–24

God's people as deliverers
Abraham Ge 14:14–16

Moses Ac 7:35–36 *See also* Ps 77:20

Joshua Ex 17:8–13

The judges Jdg 2:16 *See also*
Jdg 3:9,15,31; 4:1–10,23; 6:12,16; 10:1;
11:32; 13:2–5,24–25

Samuel 1Sa 7:3–13

Saul 1Sa 11:9–13

Jonathan 1Sa 14:45

David 2Sa 8:1,14

Jesus Christ Lk 4:18–19 *See also*
Isa 61:1–2; 1Ti 2:5; Heb 2:14–15

Ministers and others through the
gospel Ac 26:17–18; 2Ti 2:25–26;
Jas 5:19–20

Gifted Christians Mt 10:1 pp Lk 9:1 *See also* Mk 16:17; Ac 3:6; 8:6–7; 16:16–18;
1Co 12:10

**The proper response to
deliverance**
Praise Lk 5:25; Ac 3:8

Delight 1Sa 2:1

Thanksgiving Ps 30:11–12; 106:47;
107:6–8,14–15,20–21,30–31;
Ro 7:24–25

Trust Ps 40:1–3

Obedience Ps 56:12–13; Lk 8:38–39;
Jn 5:14; 8:10–11

See also

1320 God as Saviour	5596 victory
2324 Christ as Saviour	6028 sin, deliverance from
4127 Satan, defeat of	6658 freedom
4134 demons, exorcism	6738 rescue
4165 exorcism	8727 enemies
5490 refuge	8754 fear

drawing near to God

Under the old covenant, coming
near to God was closely linked with
the sacrificial system, but under the
new covenant Jesus Christ's sacrifice
has given believers free access into
God's presence.

**Drawing near to God under the
old covenant**
Access to God was restricted
Ex 24:1–2 *See also* Ex 19:20–24;
20:18–19; Lev 21:21; Dt 5:22–27;
Ps 65:4

Priests drew near to God in order to
minister to him Eze 44:15 *See also*
Lev 10:1–3; Eze 40:46; 42:13; 43:19;
45:4

The people drew near to God to offer
worship Lev 15:13–15 *See also*
Lev 9:1–5; Ps 96:8; 100:2–4; Mic 6:6–8

**Drawing near to God under the
new covenant**
Heb 10:19–22 *See also* 1Co 8:8;
Heb 7:11–19; 10:1–10

**God prompts his people to draw
near to him**
Isa 55:1–3 *See also* Isa 55:6–7;
Jer 3:21–4:2

Some refuse to draw near to God
Zep 3:2 *See also* Jer 2:30–31

**All people will ultimately draw
near to God**
Israel Jer 31:6 *See also* Jer 30:21–22;
Hos 3:4–5

All nations Isa 66:22–23

**God draws near to those who
draw near to him**
Jas 4:8 *See also* Ps 145:18; Jer 3:22;
30:21–22; Zec 1:3; Mal 3:7; Heb 7:19

See also

1352 covenant, the new	6606 access to God
2306 Christ, high priest	6614 atonement
	7412 priesthood
	7766 priests

election

Scripture affirms that God chooses a
people as his own, not on account of
their numerical strength or moral
merits, but on account of his love for
them. Election is on the basis of
divine grace, not human merit.

6639
election, to salvation

God chooses to bring individuals to
salvation through faith in Jesus
Christ.

**Election is part of God's eternal
decree**
Election is from eternity Eph 1:4 *See
also* 2Th 2:13; 2Ti 1:9

Election is God's sovereign
prerogative Ro 9:15–24; 11:1–6 *See
also* Ex 33:19; Isa 65:1; Jer 18:1–12;
Jn 15:16; 17:6; Ro 9:10–13; Eph 2:10

God's election places individuals
within the covenant of grace Ne 9:7–8
See also Ge 15:7–8,18–21; 18:19;
Gal 3:29

Election is not on the basis of merit
1Co 1:26–31 *See also* Dt 7:7–8; 9:4–6;
Jas 2:5

**God's election of his people is the
foundation of his saving action**
Election does not suspend God's use
of the means of salvation 2Th 2:13–14
See also Mt 1:21; Eph 2:8–10; Jas 1:18;
1Pe 1:2

Election works in tandem with the
call of the gospel Mt 22:14 *See also*
Ro 8:29–30

Election is evidenced through a
positive response to the gospel
1Th 1:4–5 *See also* Jn 6:37–40

Election is a motive for praise
Ro 11:28–36; Eph 1:3–14 *See also*
1Th 1:2–4

**Election is a source of practical
comfort**
Ro 8:31–39 *See also* Jn 10:27–29; 17:2

**Election is an incentive for
righteous behaviour**
Col 3:12–14 *See also* Jn 15:16–17;
Php 2:12–13; 2Th 2:13–15; 2Pe 1:3–11

**Election is a stimulus to the
preaching of the gospel**
2Ti 2:10

See also

1055 God, grace & mercy	6669 grace & salvation
1130 God, sovereignty	6708 predestination
1175 God, will of	7125 elect, the
1412 foreknowledge	8104 assurance
	8424 evangelism

6640
election, privileges of

God chose a people to enjoy a
unique relationship with him which
entailed the privilege of belonging to
him, sharing in all his inheritance,
serving him, praising him and
proclaiming him.

**God elected Israel out of all the
nations of the world**
Dt 7:6 *See also* Dt 14:1–2; 1Ki 3:8;
1Ch 16:13; Ps 105:6,43; 135:4;
Isa 41:8–9; Eze 20:5–6

The election of the nation is anticipated in the election of the patriarchs Dt 4:37–38 *See also* Dt 10:15; Ac 13:17–19

Election was not based on merit
Dt 7:7–8 *See also* Dt 9:4–6; Eze 16:1–14

God conferred privileges on the people he elected
Election meant that God dwelled in their midst 2Ch 6:6 *See also* 1Ki 14:21 pp 2Ch 12:13; 2Ki 21:7 pp 2Ch 33:7; 2Ch 6:34–35; 7:12,16; Ne 1:9; Ps 132:13

Election meant that God showed divine favour Ps 33:12 *See also* Ps 65:4; 106:4–5; Isa 14:1; 43:1,20; 44:1–5; 45:4; Zec 1:17

God gave responsibilities to the people he elected
Election calls for obedient and holy living Lev 20:26 *See also* Ex 19:5–6

Election means increased accountability Am 3:2 *See also* 2Ki 23:26

God's choice of Israel does not automatically imply election to salvation
Ro 9:6–8 *See also* Ro 11:7–8

See also
1345 covenant	7020 church, the
5705 inheritance, spiritual	7135 Israel, people of God
6608 adoption	7145 remnant
6710 privileges	7334 circumcision

6641
election, responsibilities of

God's election lays responsibilities upon those who have been chosen. Election to salvation has the natural consequence of election to service.

Election to leadership
Jer 1:5 *See also* Jdg 13:2–5; Ps 105:26; 106:23

Election to religious service
Dt 21:5 *See also* Dt 18:3–5; 1Sa 2:27–28; 1Ch 15:2; 2Ch 29:11

Election to build the house of God
Election to build the tabernacle Ex 31:2–5 *See also* Ex 35:30–33; 31:6–11; 35:34–36:2

Election to build the temple 1Ch 28:6 *See also* 1Ch 28:10; 29:1

Election of foreign kings as instruments of discipline
Isa 45:1
Cyrus: Isa 44:28; 48:14–15
The king of Assyria: Isa 7:17,20
Nebuchadnezzar: Jer 25:9; 27:6; 43:10

Election to kingship
1Ch 28:4
David: 1Sa 16:1–13; Ps 78:70–71; 89:3–4
1Sa 10:20–24 *Saul;* 1Ch 28:5–7 *Solomon*

Election of the Messiah
The OT predicts the coming of a "chosen one" Isa 42:1–7 *See also* Isa 9:6–7; 49:5–7

The NT identifies Jesus Christ as God's chosen Messiah Lk 9:35 pp Mt 3:16–17 *See also* Mt 12:15–21; Isa 42:1–4; 1Pe 1:18–21; 2:4–6

Election to apostleship
Lk 6:13–16 pp Mk 3:14–19 *See also* Jn 6:70; 13:18; 15:16,19; Ac 1:2,21–26; 9:15–16; 22:14–15; Ro 1:1; 1Co 1:1

See also
2230 Messiah, coming of	7620 disciples
	7706 apostles
5051 responsibility	7733 leaders
5370 kingship, human	7766 priests
	8342 servanthood
6620 calling	

eternal life

The state of being in a permanent living relationship with God, through Jesus Christ, begun in this life and consummated at the resurrection of believers.

6645
eternal life, nature of

Triumph over death and infinitely extended life. It also means a unique quality of life, knowing God in this life and sharing the life of Christ. Its source is God himself.

Eternal life is knowing God and enjoying his eternal blessings
Jn 17:3; Ps 16:11 *See also* Ps 21:4–6; Eph 1:3–14

Eternal glory is the believer's inheritance 2Co 4:17 *See also* Da 12:3; 2Ti 2:10; 1Pe 5:4,10

Contrasted with eternal judgment and rejection Mt 25:46 *Interpreters differ over whether "eternal punishment" implies an experience that continues for ever, or annihilation which is eternal in the sense of being irreversible. See also* Da 12:2; Mt 25:46; Jn 3:16; 2Th 1:8–9

The work of helping others come to eternal life Jn 4:35–36

Eternal life as endless life
The guarantee of the resurrection 1Co 15:20–22 *"firstfruits" because the resurrection of Jesus Christ is seen as the beginning of a harvest. See also* Ps 49:15; Isa 26:19; 1Th 4:14

Death will be vanquished Rev 21:4 *See also* Isa 25:8; 1Co 15:26,50–57

Believers will live for ever Jn 11:25–26 *See also* Lk 20:34–36; Jn 6:51,54,58; 8:51; 1Jn 2:17

Eternal life as a quality of life
Jn 10:10 *See also* Jn 4:14

One of the blessings associated with the kingdom of God Mt 19:29 pp Mk 10:30 pp Lk 18:30; Lk 18:18

Life with Christ Jn 6:67–69; 15:5; Col 3:4; 1Th 5:10

Eternal life as experiencing Jesus Christ's life
Gal 2:20 *See also* 2Co 4:10–11; Ro 6:4,8; 8:10–11

God is the source and giver of eternal life
God the Father Jn 17:3 *See also* Dt 5:26; Ps 36:9; 42:2; 56:13; Mt 22:32 pp Mk 12:27; Lk 20:38; 1Ti 6:13

God the Son Jn 14:6 *See also* Jn 1:4; 11:25–26; 17:3; 1Jn 1:1–2; 5:20

God the Holy Spirit Jn 6:63 *See also* 2Co 3:6; Gal 6:8

See also
1080 God, living	4018 life, spiritual
2218 Christ, Son of God	5482 punishment
	6510 salvation
2375 kingdom of God	8134 knowing God
	9120 eternity
3290 Holy Spirit, life-giver	9135 immortality
	9310 resurrection

6646
eternal life, gift of

Eternal life cannot be earned or merited but must be received as a gift from God.

Fruitless attempts to earn eternal life
Jn 5:39–40 *It is possible to study the mere letter of Scripture while ignoring coming to its focus, Jesus Christ;* Gal 3:11–12 *See also* Ro 3:20,28

Jesus Christ is the source of eternal life
1Jn 5:11–12 *See also* Jn 11:25–26; 14:6; Ro 5:21; Heb 5:9; 9:12; 2Ti 1:1,10; 1Jn 5:20

Eternal life is a gift
Ro 6:23 *See also* Jn 6:27; 10:28; Ro 2:7; 5:15–17; Eph 2:8–9; 1Pe 3:7; 2Pe 1:3

Received by faith Jn 3:36 *Faith in Jesus Christ, God's son, is the only way to gain eternal life. See also* Jn 3:16; 5:24; 6:40; 20:31; 1Ti 1:16

The need for personal commitment Jn 12:25–26 *See also* Mt 7:14; Mk 8:37–38; Ac 11:18 *Repentance is the first step of commitment;* Ro 6:8–11

See also
2324 Christ as Saviour	5380 law and gospel
	6027 sin, remedy for
2420 gospel	6676 justification
2560 Christ, resurrection	6732 repentance
	8207 commitment
5325 gifts	

6647
eternal life, experience of

Eternal life is a present possession, to be experienced here and now, but it also offers rich and joyful future prospects.

Eternal life as a present possession
Jn 5:24 *See also* Ro 6:22; Gal 2:20; Eph 2:4–5; Col 2:13; 3:1–4; 1Ti 6:12

The Holy Spirit as a sign of new life Ro 8:9; 1Co 3:16; 6:19; Eph 1:13–14; 2Ti 1:14

Eternal life as a future hope 1Pe 1:3–5

Present experience the basis for future hope Col 1:27; 2Th 2:16–17

6648

Eternal life contrasted with present suffering Ro 8:18 See also Mt 5:11–12; Lk 18:28–30 pp Mt 19:29 pp Mk 10:29–30; Jas 1:12

The life to come 1Ti 4:8 See also Ro 2:7; 2Co 5:4; Col 1:5; Jude 21

Being with Christ for ever 2Co 5:8 See also Lk 23:43; Jn 14:2–3; 17:24; 1Th 4:15–17

Assurance of eternal life

The keeping power of God
Jn 10:28–29 See also Ro 8:38–39; 1Pe 1:3–5

The believer's confidence in God
Jn 17:2–3 See also Ps 73:26; Job 19:25; 1Jn 5:11–13

The sure and certain hope Tit 1:2; 3:5–7; 2Pe 1:10–11

See also
1055 God, grace & mercy
1105 God, power of
2021 Christ, faithfulness
5565 suffering of believers
5705 inheritance, spiritual
8104 assurance
9024 death, spiritual
9413 heaven, inheritance
9610 hope

6648

expiation

The removal of the guilt of sin in God's sight by the offering of a vicarious sacrifice which, in its death, bears the sin of the individual or nation concerned.

Expiation is necessary because sin is punishable by God
Ex 32:30 See also Nu 16:46–48; Dt 21:8; Ps 79:8–9

Expiation and the sacrificial system
Unintentional sins expiated by the sin offering Lev 4:1–5:6; Nu 15:22–29

Unintentional sins requiring restitution expiated by the guilt offering
Lev 5:14–6:7; 19:20–22

The nation's sins expiated on the annual Day of Atonement Ex 30:10 See also Lev 16:3–34; Heb 9:7

Blood as a symbol of substitutionary sacrifice Lev 17:11 See also Eze 45:19–20; Heb 9:22; 13:11

The rite of expiation administered by the priests Lev 9:7 See also Lev 7:7; 9:15; 10:17–18; Nu 6:11

Expiation and special provision for the poor Lev 12:7–8 See also Lev 5:7–13; 14:21–32

The sin offering as a constant reminder of the need for expiation
Sin offerings for occasions of dedication Ex 29:31–33 See also Lev 8:14–15; Nu 8:12; 2Ch 29:21–24; Ezr 6:17

Sin offerings for occasions of purification Lev 12:6–7; 14:19–20,49–53; 15:13–15,28–30; Nu 19:1–13

Sin offerings as part of the regular

---

cycle of worship Nu 28:15,22,30; 29:5,11,16

The death of Jesus Christ as the fulfilment and replacement of the old sacrificial system
The death of Jesus Christ as a substitutionary, expiatory sacrifice
1Jn 2:2 See also 1Co 15:3; Gal 1:4; Heb 1:3; 1Pe 3:18

God's provision of Jesus Christ as an atoning sacrifice Ro 3:25 See also Isa 53:10; Ro 8:3; 1Jn 4:10

The blood of Jesus Christ as an atonement for sin Heb 9:13–14 See also Mt 26:28; Eph 1:7; 1Jn 1:7; Rev 1:5

The sacrifice of Jesus Christ as final and unique Heb 7:27 See also Ro 6:10; Heb 9:25–10:14

See also
2315 Christ as Lamb
2324 Christ as Saviour
2410 cross, the
6027 sin, remedy for
6173 guilt, and God
6510 salvation
6614 atonement
6652 forgiveness
6712 propitiation
6752 substitution
7316 blood, OT sacrifices
7766 priests

6650

finding

Discovering something or someone that is being looked for. The whole of Scripture points to God seeking out lost human beings and finding them. The delight of people at finding things (such as lost coins or wayward sons) is seen as a parable of the joy of God over repentant sinners.

Finding by searching
People do not always find what they are searching for Pr 20:6 See also Ge 27:36–40; 2Sa 17:20

God is sometimes found without being sought Ro 10:20 See also Isa 65:1; Ro 9:30–31

Promises that God can be found
Dt 4:29; Mt 7:7–8 pp Lk 11:9–10 See also Jer 29:13–14

People's joy in finding God
Finding the kingdom Mt 13:44 See also Mt 13:45–46

Finding the infant Jesus Mt 2:9–11 See also Lk 2:10–12,16–18

Finding the Messiah Jn 1:41 See also Mk 1:36; Jn 1:45

Finding the risen Christ Jn 20:20 See also Mt 28:1–9; Lk 24:40–43

Results of finding God
Finding truth Jn 8:31–32 See also Ps 25:4–5; Jn 16:13; 1Ti 2:3–4

Finding rest and security Ps 36:7 See also Ps 91:4; Mt 11:28–29

Finding mercy Pr 28:13 See also Ps 6:9; Mt 5:7

Finding satisfaction Ecc 2:24–25

Finding success 1Sa 18:14 See also Ge 39:23

Finding life Pr 8:35 See also Mt 7:13–14; 10:39

God's joy in finding repentant sinners
Lk 15:3–7 See also Lk 15:8–32

Other aspects of finding in life
Finding things Dt 14:21; Mt 17:24–27

Finding people Ge 41:38; Ac 19:1; 2Ti 1:16–17

Finding a wife Ge 24:1–4; Pr 18:22

Finding wisdom Pr 3:13; 24:14; Jas 1:5

Finding God's will Nu 9:8; Jn 7:17; Ro 12:2

Sin finds people out Nu 32:23; 2Sa 12:1–14; Ac 5:1–11

See also
1070 God, joy of
5940 searching
8160 seeking God
8283 joy

6652

forgiveness

The freeing of a person from guilt and its consequences, including punishment; usually as an act of favour, compassion or love, with the aim of restoring a broken personal relationship. Forgiveness can involve both the remission of punishment and the cancellation of debts.

6653

forgiveness, divine

God forgives the sins of believers on the basis of the once for all sacrifice offered by Jesus Christ on the cross. Believers' sins are no longer held against them, on account of the atoning death of Jesus Christ.

God's nature and forgiveness
Ex 34:5–7 See also Nu 14:17–20; Ne 9:16–17; Ps 103:1–18; Isa 43:25; Mic 7:18–20; 1Jn 1:8–9

God's promise of forgiveness
Jer 31:31–34 See also 2Ch 7:14; Isa 55:6–7; Heb 8:8–12

People's need of forgiveness
1Jn 1:8–10 See also Ps 51:1–5; Isa 6:1–5; Ro 3:9,23

The means of forgiveness
Under the old covenant Heb 9:22 See also Lev 4:27–31; 5:17–18

Under the new covenant Mt 26:27–28 See also Jn 1:29; Eph 1:7–8; Col 2:13–15

The assurance of forgiveness
1Jn 1:8–9 See also Ps 51:7; 103:8–12; 130:3–4; Pr 28:13; Isa 1:18; Ac 2:38; Jas 5:13–16; 1Jn 2:1–2

See also
3248 Holy Spirit, conviction
5009 conscience
6027 sin, remedy for
6175 guilt, removal of
6614 atonement
6627 conversion
6666 grace
6686 mercy
6716 reconciliation
6732 repentance
7314 blood
8103 assurance

6654
forgiveness, Jesus Christ's ministry of

A central feature of Jesus Christ's ministry was his declaration that believers' sins were forgiven through their faith in him.

Jesus Christ's ministry of forgiveness was foretold
Mt 1:20–21; Jn 1:29

Jesus Christ's exercise of forgiveness
Lk 23:33–34 *See also* Jn 8:3–11

Jesus Christ has authority on account of his divinity to forgive sins
Mt 9:1–8 pp Mk 2:1–12 pp Lk 5:17–26 *Jesus Christ's authority to forgive is authenticated by his healing of the paralytic.*

People's offence at Jesus Christ's exercise of forgiveness
Mk 2:5–7 pp Mt 9:2–3 pp Lk 5:20–21

Parables of forgiveness
Mt 18:23–35 *the unmerciful servant;* Lk 7:36–50; 15:11–32 *the lost son*

The church's ministry of forgiveness in Jesus Christ's name
Jn 20:21–23 *See also* Ac 2:38; 13:38; 26:15–18

See also

1352 covenant, the new	2424 gospel, promises
2012 Christ, authority	2530 Christ, death of
2351 Christ, miracles	2545 Christ, opposition to
2357 Christ, parables	5438 parables

6655
forgiveness, application of

God's forgiveness of believers' sins leads them to pray for his forgiveness of others and to be forgiving in their dealings with other people.

Prayers for forgiveness on behalf of others
For God's own people Ex 32:30–32 *See also* Ne 1:4–11; Da 9:4–19; Am 7:1–6

For other human beings Ge 18:20–33

For one's persecutors Lk 23:33–34 *See also* Mt 5:43–44; Ac 7:59–60

Prayers for forgiveness for oneself
Lk 11:4 pp Mt 6:12 *See also* Ne 9:1–3; Ps 51:1–17

Examples of forgiveness given
Ps 32:1–5 *See also* Isa 6:1–7; Jn 8:3–11

The call to exercise forgiveness
As a principle of life Lk 6:37 *See also* Mt 5:38–48 pp Lk 6:27–36

Within the church Col 3:12–13 *See also* 2Co 2:5–11; Eph 4:32; 1Pe 3:8–9

Forgiving enemies Pr 24:17; 25:21–22; Mt 5:44; Ro 12:20

Being forgiven is dependent on forgiving others
Mk 11:25–26 *NIV footnote at verse 26. See also* Mt 6:12 pp Lk 11:4; Mt 6:14–15; 18:21–35; Lk 6:37

Forgiveness is to be without limits
Lk 17:3–4 *See also* Mt 18:21–22

Examples of human forgiveness
Ac 7:59–60 *See also* Ge 50:15–21; 2Sa 16:5–11

See also

5494 revenge	6624 confession of sin
5765 attitudes to people	8452 neighbours, duty to
5820 criticism	
5927 resentment	8611 prayer for others
6029 sin, forgiveness	
6115 blame	8727 enemies
6124 condemnation	8844 unforgiveness

6658

freedom

The state of liberty that results from not being oppressed or in bondage. Scripture stresses that human beings lack freedom on account of sin, but that faith in Jesus Christ brings freedom from the power of sin and the law.

This set of themes consists of the following:

6659 freedom, acts of in OT

6660 freedom, through Jesus Christ

6661 freedom, and the law

6662 freedom, abuse of Christian

6663 freedom, of the will

6659
freedom, acts of in OT

The OT provides many examples of God delivering his people from bondage, of which the greatest is the exodus. These acts of deliverance foreshadow and prepare the way for the redeeming work of God through Jesus Christ, revealed in the NT.

God's people regain their freedom
The exodus from Egypt as an act of deliverance Ex 20:2 *See also* Ex 12:42; 16:6,32 *The people of Israel were frequently reminded that God had delivered them from Egypt;* Jos 24:6; Jdg 6:8; 2Sa 7:6; 1Ki 8:16; 2Ch 7:22; Ps 80:8; Jer 2:6; 11:4; Hos 12:9; Am 2:10; Mic 6:4; Hag 2:5; Heb 8:9; Jude 5

The return from exile in Babylon as an act of deliverance Isa 35:3–10 *See also* Isa 43:14–45:5,14–17; 49:8–26; 51:22–52:12; 54:1–17; 61:1–62:12; Eze 36:24–36; 37:15–28

Freedom granted to individuals to reflect God's past deliverance
Dt 15:12–15 *the sabbath year: all servants to be freed after six years* *The Year of Jubilee: all servants and slaves to be freed every fiftieth year:* Lev 25:10,39–43

God's purposes in bringing about his people's freedom
God sets his people free to be his own Ex 19:4; Nu 15:41; Hos 13:4

God sets his people free to serve him Ex 19:3–6; Lev 25:55

God sets his people free to praise him Isa 43:21

God sets his people free to be holy Lev 11:45; Dt 28:9–10

God sets his people free to receive his promised gifts Ex 3:8 *The inheritance is the promised land of Canaan, which foreshadows the gospel inheritance of eternal life in the kingdom of God;* Nu 14:7–8; Dt 8:7–9; Eze 20:6

Freedom is conditional upon obedience
Israel is commanded to remember the exodus as a matter of obedience Ex 13:8–10

Israel's freedom depends upon continuing obedience to the LORD Dt 28:25,47–48

Examples of Israel forfeiting freedom through sin Jdg 2:14; 3:7–8,12; 4:1–2; 6:1; 2Ki 17:6–23; Ps 137:1–4

See also

1105 God, power of	7215 exile, the
1315 God as redeemer	7221 exodus, the
1320 God as Saviour	7418 Purim
4207 land, divine gift	7431 sabbatical year
6634 deliverance	7482 Year of Jubilee
7141 people of God, OT	8718 disobedience

6660
freedom, through Jesus Christ

Jesus Christ, the promised deliverer, sets his people free from the present effects of sin and from the power of sin and will finally deliver them completely from its presence.

The OT points ahead to a new and greater freedom and to a new deliverer
The OT predicts Jesus Christ as the deliverer Isa 61:1 *See also* Isa 42:6–7

The redemption of the exodus foreshadows the redemption achieved by Jesus Christ Col 1:13–14 *See also* 1Co 10:1–4

Jesus Christ fulfils the OT predictions of him as deliverer Lk 4:18–19 *See also* Ro 11:26; Isa 59:20

The freedom that comes through Jesus Christ
Jn 8:32–36 *See also* Mt 1:21

Jesus Christ sets his people free from the penalty of sin 1Th 1:10 *See also* Jn 3:36; Ro 8:1–2; Heb 9:15; Rev 1:5

Jesus Christ sets his people free from the spiritual death that accompanies sin Ro 6:1–7 *See also* Eph 2:1–5; Heb 9:14

Jesus Christ sets his people free from the fear of death Heb 2:14–15

Jesus Christ will finally set his people free from death itself 1Co 15:22–23 *See also* Ro 5:12–17; 7:24

Jesus Christ sets his people free from the power of sin Ro 6:11–14 *See also* Ro 6:22–23

Jesus Christ sets his people free from the pollution of sin 2Pe 1:2–4 *See also* Gal 1:3–4

Jesus Christ sets his people free from the power of Satan Col 1:13–14 *See also* Mk 3:27 *The strong man is, by implication, Jesus Christ;* Ac 26:17–18

Jesus Christ will set his people free from the presence of sin Php 3:21 *See also* Eph 5:27; Col 1:22; 1Th 3:13; 5:23; Rev 21:4

Freedom as the result of being rescued from trials by Jesus Christ
2Ti 3:11 *See also* Ac 26:17; 2Ti 4:18; 2Pe 2:9

See also

1429 prophecy, OT fulfilment	5246 captivity
2230 Messiah, coming of	5344 imprisonment
2321 Christ as redeemer	6028 sin, deliverance from
2565 Christ, second coming	6714 ransom
4811 darkness, symbol of sin	6720 redemption
	7449 slavery, spiritual
	9020 death

6661
freedom, and the law

Jesus Christ sets his people free from the condemnation and oppression of the law. Through the Holy Spirit, believers are able to fulfil the law obediently according to God's intentions.

Jesus Christ sets believers free from the law
Jesus Christ's life of perfect obedience to the law was the fulfilment of it Mt 5:17 *See also* Gal 4:4–5; 1Pe 2:22

Jesus Christ's death fulfils the demands of the law 2Co 5:21 *See also* Heb 7:27; 9:11,26–28; 10:11–14; 1Pe 2:24; 3:18

On account of Jesus Christ's death, believers can be righteous independently of the law Ro 3:21–26 *See also* Jn 1:17; Ro 10:4; Php 3:9

Believers are set free from the law's condemnation
Gal 3:21–25 *See also* Ro 6:1–14; 7:1–6; Gal 3:13; 4:5,21–31 *The lives of Abraham, Sarah, Hagar, Ishmael and Isaac are interpreted figuratively, to illustrate the believer's freedom from the law's condemnation;* Gal 5:1; Eph 2:14–15; Col 2:13–14

The freedom of believers rests on the power of the Holy Spirit
Ro 7:1–6; 2Co 3:17–18 *See also* Ro 8:1–17; Gal 5:16–18,22–26

The believer's freedom to obey the law voluntarily
Ps 119:32 *See also* Ps 37:31; 119:45,97; Jer 31:33; 2Co 3:3; Jas 1:25; 2:12

See also

1345 covenant	4018 life, spiritual
2530 Christ, death of	5375 law
3030 Holy Spirit, power	6752 substitution
3233 Holy Spirit & sanctification	7328 ceremonies
	7334 circumcision
3251 Holy Spirit, filling with	8454 obedience to God
3278 Holy Spirit, indwelling	

6662
freedom, abuse of Christian

Although Christians have been set free from condemnation by grace, they remain under an obligation to be obedient to God. Abuses of Christian freedom result from a failure to take responsibilities towards God seriously.

Christian freedom can be abused
Believers are freed from condemnation Ro 8:1 *See also* Isa 50:8–9; Ro 8:33–39; Col 1:22; Rev 1:5

Sin need not enslave believers Jn 8:34–36 *See also* Ro 6:16–18; 7:14–25; 1Co 7:22–23; 2Pe 2:19

Believers must resist sin Ro 6:12,14 *See also* Heb 12:1–2; 1Jn 5:16–18

The false idea that grace gives believers the freedom to sin
Ro 6:1–2,15 *See also* Ro 3:5–8; 1Co 10:23; Gal 2:17–21

The dangers of abusing Christian freedom
Becoming a stumbling-block to others 1Co 8:9–12 *See also* Ro 15:1–3

Indulging oneself Gal 5:13 *See also* Ro 14:1–18

Using freedom to cover up evil 1Pe 2:16

Examples of abuse of Christian freedom
Falling back into deliberate sin Ro 6:1–2; Heb 12:1; 1Jn 3:6; 5:16–18

Disobedience towards God 1Jn 3:4; 2Co 10:6; Eph 5:6

Selfishness 1Jn 3:17 *See also* Lk 6:32–34

Eating food sacrificed to idols 1Co 8:1–13; Rev 2:14,20

See also

5020 human nature	8459 perseverance
5220 authority, abuse	8482 spiritual warfare
5775 abuse	8703 antinomianism
6666 grace	8770 idolatry, in NT
8272 holiness, growth in	8775 libertinism
8298 love for one another	8827 selfishness

6663
freedom, of the will

The ability to make decisions without being coerced by external forces. Scripture stresses that people are confronted with free choices between good and evil and commands them to choose good. However, it also notes that limitations are placed upon human actions through the enslaving power of sin.

Freedom of the will
Freedom of the will to choose between good and evil Dt 11:26–28 *See also* Dt 30:15–16,19; Jos 24:15; 1Ch 28:9; Jer 26:3; Eze 18:21–23

Freedom of the will to seek and find God Isa 55:6 *See also* Am 5:4; Ac 2:21; Ro 10:11; Isa 28:16; Rev 22:17

The effect of sin upon freedom of the will
Sin prevents human beings from breaking free from its bondage Ro 7:14–20 *See also* Ro 6:16,22; 7:25 *Paul stresses that it is only through Jesus Christ that human beings can be freed from servitude to sin.*

Sin hardens human hearts Heb 3:13 *See also* Da 5:20; Ro 1:21; Eph 4:17–19

God hardens human hearts Ex 9:12 *See also* Ex 4:21; 10:20; 14:4,8; Dt 2:30; Jos 11:19–20; Ro 1:22–24; 9:17–18

Human beings harden their own hearts 1Sa 6:6 *See also* Ex 8:15,32; Ps 95:8; Pr 28:14; Heb 3:8,15; 4:7

See also

1130 God, sovereignty	7366 freewill offering
5051 responsibility	8207 commitment
6030 sin, avoidance	8408 decision-making
6253 temptation, avoiding causing	

---

grace

The unmerited favour of God, made known through Jesus Christ, and expressed supremely in the redemption and full forgiveness of sinners through faith in Jesus Christ. This set of themes consists of the following:

6667 grace, in OT
6668 grace, and Jesus Christ
6669 grace, and salvation
6670 grace, and Holy Spirit
6671 grace, and Christian life
6672 grace, in human relationships

6667
grace, in OT

In the OT, grace is evident in the special relationship between God and his people.

God's grace was expressed in the covenant relationship

Dt 7:7–9; 2Ki 13:22–23 *See also* Ge 9:8–11; 17:1–8; Ex 6:2–8; Dt 8:17–18; Ne 1:5–6; Isa 55:1–3; Eze 16:1–8

God's grace affirmed

God's grace shown in his compassion
Ps 86:15; La 3:22; Joel 2:13 *See also* Ex 33:19; Dt 13:17–18; 2Ch 30:9; Ezr 8:22; Ps 103:13; Eze 39:25; Hos 2:19; Jnh 4:1–2; Mic 7:18–20; Zec 10:6; Mal 3:17

God's grace shown in his readiness to forgive Isa 55:7; Jer 33:6–9 *See also* Da 9:9–10; Mic 7:18–20

God's grace shown in his favour, provision and healing Lev 26:9; Jer 32:40–41 *See also* Nu 10:29; Dt 13:17–18; 2Sa 22:28; Ps 30:4–5; Isa 49:8; Jer 9:23–24; 33:6–9; Na 1:7; Zec 12:10

God made his grace known to individuals

Ne 9:16–20 *The Israelites confess their sins;* Job 10:12 *See also* Ge 24:35–36 *Abraham;* Ge 32:9–10 *Jacob;* Ge 39:20–21 *Joseph;* Ex 33:12–13 *Moses;* Dt 33:23 *Naphtali;* Jdg 2:18 *in the period of the judges;* 1Sa 2:21 *Hannah;* 1Ki 3:6 *Solomon;* Ezr 7:27–28 *Ezra;* Ne 2:8 *Nehemiah;* Ps 6:9 *David;* Isa 26:10 *God's grace may be unavailing.*

God's grace implored

2Ch 33:12; Ps 51:1; Isa 33:2 *See also* Ge 24:12; Ex 32:11; 1Ki 8:28–30; 2Ki 13:4; Ne 9:32; Ps 25:16; 69:13; Da 9:17–19; Hos 14:2; Hab 3:2; Zec 1:12

See also

1030 God, compassion	1320 God as Saviour
1055 God, grace & mercy	1330 God, the provider
1085 God, love of	1345 covenant
1095 God, patience of	5856 extravagance
	8261 generosity, God's

6668
grace, and Jesus Christ

Grace is demonstrated pre-eminently in Jesus Christ and the work he came to do.

God's promise of grace has been fulfilled in Jesus Christ

Jn 1:14,16–17; 2Ti 1:8–10 *See also* Jn 3:16–19; Ac 13:38; Ro 1:1–5; 5:8,16–17; Eph 1:3–8; Tit 2:11–14; 3:4–5; 1Pe 1:3–5

Grace was expressed in Jesus Christ's life and ministry

Mt 9:36 pp Mk 6:34; 2Co 8:9 *See also* Mt 9:10–13 pp Mk 2:15–17 pp Lk 5:27–32; Mt 11:4–5; 19:13–15 pp Mk 10:13–16 pp Lk 18:15–17; Lk 2:40; 4:22; 19:9–10; 23:34; Jn 10:11; Ac 10:37–38; Heb 2:9; 1Jn 3:16

Grace is demonstrated in Jesus Christ's atoning death on the cross

Jn 1:16–17; Eph 2:4–5; 1Pe 2:10 *See also* Jn 3:16; Ro 3:22–24; 5:1–2; 8:32;

1Co 1:4–6; 2Co 5:18–19; Gal 2:21; Eph 4:7; 2Th 2:16–17; 1Ti 1:13–14; 1Pe 1:3–5; 1Jn 4:10

See also

1115 God, purpose of	6615 atonement, necessity
2015 Christ, compassion of	6654 forgiveness, Christ's ministry
2027 Christ, grace & mercy	6676 justification
2048 Christ, love of	6708 predestination
2525 Christ, cross of	

6669
grace, and salvation

Deliverance through Jesus Christ is the result of accepting God's undeserved favour.

Salvation is all God's doing

Ro 5:6–8; 9:14–16; Eph 1:7; 1Ti 1:15–16 *See also* Ex 33:19; Ac 4:12; 20:24; Ro 5:15–17; 2Co 6:2; Col 1:13–14; 2Th 2:16; Tit 2:11; Heb 7:23–25; Rev 7:10

There is nothing human beings can do to save themselves

Tit 3:4–7 *See also* Lk 18:9–14; Ro 11:5–6

Salvation is not by keeping God's law

Gal 5:4 *See also* Ro 5:20–21; 6:14; 8:1–4; Gal 2:21; 3:17–18; 1Ti 1:9

Salvation must be accepted as a free gift by faith

Eph 2:4–9 *See also* Ac 15:7–11; 16:30–31; Ro 3:21–24; 4:14–16; 5:1–2; Heb 4:16

See also

2530 Christ, death of	6634 deliverance
4018 life, spiritual	6644 eternal life
5375 law	6710 privileges
6510 salvation	6720 redemption
6606 access to God	8020 faith
6626 conversion	

6670
grace, and Holy Spirit

The Holy Spirit is both an expression of God's grace and the means by which it is experienced.

The Holy Spirit is himself a gracious gift of God

Ac 2:38; 6:5–8; Tit 3:4–7; 1Jn 3:24 *See also* Jn 6:63; 20:21–22; Ac 5:32; 11:15–17; 15:6–8; 1Co 2:12; Gal 3:14

Through the Holy Spirit God brings believers out of slavery and into his family Ro 8:15–16 *See also* Gal 4:6–7; Eph 2:17–18

Through the Holy Spirit God equips believers to serve him 1Co 12:4–7 *See also* Jn 7:37–39; Ac 1:8; 2:4; 4:31; Ro 5:5; Gal 3:5; Heb 2:4

The Holy Spirit in God's gracious work of redemption

Ro 8:1–2 *See also* 1Co 2:4–5,13; 1Th 1:4–5; 1Pe 1:12

The Holy Spirit in God's gracious work of sanctifying and sustaining his people

2Co 3:17–18; 2Th 2:13 *See also* Ac 9:31; Ro 8:26–27; 14:17–18; 15:13; Gal 5:4–5,22–23; 6:8; Eph 2:22; 3:16–20; Php 1:18–19; 2Ti 1:14; Heb 10:29; Jas 4:4–6

See also

3230 Holy Spirit & regeneration	6744 sanctification
	7115 children of God
3233 Holy Spirit & sanctification	7966 spiritual gifts
3251 Holy Spirit, filling with	8102 abiding in Christ
3254 Holy Spirit, fruit of	

6671
grace, and Christian life

The Christian life, from its beginning to its end, is totally dependent upon the grace of God.

God's grace compensates for human weaknesses

2Co 12:8–9; 1Pe 5:10 *See also* 1Co 2:1–5; 2Co 9:8; Heb 2:14; 4:15; 5:2; Jas 4:6; 2Pe 3:17–18

Believers are to pray for grace

Heb 4:16 *See also* Ps 25:16; Hos 14:1–2; Col 1:9; 4:12

Christian experience may be summed up in terms of grace

1Co 15:10 *See also* Ac 18:27; Ro 5:2; Gal 1:15; Php 1:7

Believers should go on to experience more of God's grace

Ac 20:32 *See also* Ac 13:43; Col 1:3–6; Heb 13:9; 1Pe 5:12; 2Pe 3:18

Believers are enabled to serve Jesus Christ by his grace

1Pe 4:10 *See also* Ac 15:39–40; Ro 5:17; 12:6; 15:15; 1Co 3:10; 2Co 12:9; Gal 2:9; Eph 3:7–9

God's grace is seen in Christian character, especially in generosity

2Co 8:6–7 *Referring to a collection being taken up for the poor Christians in Jerusalem. See also* Ac 4:33; 11:22–23; 2Co 9:13–14; Col 4:6

An ongoing experience of God's grace requires the believer's co-operation

2Co 6:1 *See also* Php 2:12–13; Heb 12:15; 1Pe 5:5; Jas 4:6

See also

5902 maturity	8357 weakness
5954 strength	8434 giving
8256 fruitfulness	
8347 spiritual growth	

6672
grace, in human relationships

Undeserved favour or kindness, mercy, compassion and generosity are to be found in human relationships and are strongly encouraged in Scripture.

6674
Examples of grace in human relationships
Ru 2:10; 2Sa 9:1–7; Ac 28:2 *See also* Ge 33:8–11; Jos 2:12–14; 1Sa 15:6; 24:18; 1Ki 2:7; Ps 37:25–26; Ac 4:8–10; 1Co 4:13

Grace in relationships encouraged
Lk 6:27–28 pp Mt 5:44 *See also* Pr 14:9; Ro 15:7; Phm 14

Grace in relationships expressed as mercy and compassion
Eph 4:32 *See also* 2Ch 10:7; Zec 7:9; Mt 9:13; Hos 6:6; Mt 18:32–33; Lk 10:36–37; 17:3–4; Ro 15:1–2; 1Pe 3:8; Jude 22

Grace in relationships expressed as generosity and kindness
Dt 15:10–11 *See also* 1Sa 25:8; Ps 112:5; Pr 11:25–27; 1Co 10:24; 2Co 9:11–13; Gal 6:9–10; 1Ti 6:18; 2Ti 2:24; Heb 13:16; 2Pe 1:5–7

See also

5446 poverty	8262 generosity,
5806 compassion	human
5972 unkindness	8264 gentleness
6655 forgiveness,	8291 kindness
application	8292 love
6686 mercy	8445 hospitality
8244 ethics and	
grace	

6674
imputation

The crediting by God to believers with righteousness on account of Jesus Christ. Paul argues that Abraham did nothing which earned him the status of being righteous in the sight of God. Rather, Abraham believed the promise of God, and for that reason was granted the status of being righteous before God. Likewise, all who trust in Jesus Christ have righteousness imputed to them—that is, reckoned as if it was theirs. Imputation should not be confused with impartation. Believers are not made right ethically (impartation), but put right relationally (imputation). What God changes is not the character of believers but their legal standing before him. From this new position, believers are called to co-operate with the Holy Spirit in sanctification so that their character increasingly reflects their new standing.

Righteousness imputed through faith not works
The example of Abraham Ro 4:1–3 *See also* Ge 15:1–6; Ro 4:9–22; Gal 3:6–9

The testimony of David Ro 4:6–8 *See also* Ps 32:1–2

The principle holds true for everyone Ro 4:4–5,23–24 *See also* 1Co 1:30; 2Co 5:19; Gal 3:7–9; Php 3:9

Believers' sins are imputed to Jesus Christ
2Co 5:21

Imputed righteousness expresses itself in good works
Jas 2:20–24 *James does not contradict, but complements Paul's teaching by showing that the person who has been credited with righteousness will always express this in works.*

See also

2410 cross, the	6744 sanctification
5274 credit	8020 faith
6028 sin, deliverance	8154 righteousness
from	8266 holiness
6678 justification,	
Christ's work	

6676
justification

The acquittal, or declaration of being righteous, before God as judge. It is a central aspect of Paul's understanding of what God achieved for believers through the death and resurrection of Jesus Christ.

6677
justification, necessity of

Sinful, law-breaking humanity needs a means of justification because of its failure to keep God's law and live up to God's requirements.

Justification in human relationships
The acquittal of the innocent Dt 25:1 *See also* Pr 17:15; Isa 43:9,26; Ro 8:33

Justification of oneself Job 32:2 *See also* Lk 10:29; 16:15; 18:9–14

The need for justification
The reality of God's righteousness Ps 11:7 *See also* Ps 33:5; 35:28; Jer 23:6; Mt 6:33; Jn 17:25; Ro 1:17; 3:22

The reality of God's justice Ps 9:8 *See also* Job 36:3; Ps 11:7; 33:5; Isa 5:16; Jer 9:24; Lk 18:7; Rev 19:11

The reality of God's judgment Ge 18:25 *See also* Jdg 11:27; Ps 51:4; Mic 6:2; Mt 12:36; Ro 2:16

The reality of God's law Jas 4:12 *See also* Ex 20:2–17 pp Dt 5:6–21; Ps 19:7; Isa 33:22; Ro 7:12,16; 8:3–4; 1Ti 1:8

Human guilt shows the need for justification
Ps 143:2 *See also* Ro 3:23; 1Jn 1:8,10

People are unable to justify themselves, even through the law
Isa 64:6; Ro 3:20–21; Gal 2:15–16 *See also* Am 4:4; Mt 5:20; Lk 10:29; 16:15; 18:9–14; Ro 1:17; 3:20; Gal 2:21; 3:2–3; 2:11 *Paul opposes Peter's position on circumcision;* Gal 5:4; Php 3:4–8

See also

1075 God, justice of	6020 sin
1125 God,	7334 circumcision
righteousness	8822 self-
1310 God as judge	justification
2321 Christ as	9210 judgment,
redeemer	God's
5375 law	

6678
justification, and Jesus Christ's work

On account of the death and resurrection of Jesus Christ, the demands of the law of God are met, and believers are granted the status of being righteous in the sight of God.

Justification is grounded in the death of Jesus Christ
Jesus Christ's death shields believers from God's wrath Ro 5:9 *See also* Ro 3:24; 4:25; 5:18; 1Pe 2:24

Jesus Christ's death fulfils the demands of the law of God Ro 8:3–4 *See also* Ro 3:25–26; Gal 3:13; 1Jn 2:2

Justification is grounded in the resurrection of Jesus Christ
Ro 4:25; 10:9–10 *See also* Ac 2:22–39; 4:10–12; 17:30–31; 1Pe 3:18–21

Justification means believers are reckoned as righteous through the death of Jesus Christ
Ro 5:19; 1Co 1:30; 2Co 5:21 *See also* 1Co 6:9–11; Php 3:8–9 *The term "imputation" is used to refer to the process by which God treats believers as being righteous in his sight on account of Jesus Christ's death.*

Justification is received by faith
Ro 1:17 pp Gal 3:11 *See also* Hab 2:4; Ro 5:1; Eph 2:8

The example of Abraham Ge 15:6 *See also* Ro 4:1–5,9–22; Gal 3:6–9,16–18

The example of David Ro 4:6–8; Ps 32:1–2

Apostolic teaching on the need of faith for justification Ac 13:39 *See also* Ro 3:22,25,27–30; 4:5; 5:1; 9:30–32; 10:10; 1Co 6:11; Gal 2:16; 3:8,14; Eph 2:8

Justification is a gift of God's grace
Ro 3:24 *See also* Ro 5:15–17; 8:33; Tit 3:7

Not by works or the law Gal 3:11 *See also* Ro 3:20; 4:5; Gal 2:16,21; 3:2–5,24; 5:4–6; Eph 2:8–9

See also

1025 God, anger of	6614 atonement
1055 God, grace &	6674 imputation
mercy	6716 reconciliation
2324 Christ as	6720 redemption
Saviour	7510 Gentiles
5075 Abraham	8020 faith

6679
justification, results of

Justification brings a changed relationship with God and a future hope. It will also bring a change in behaviour.

The results of justification
Peace with God, access to his presence and the hope of his glory Ro 5:1–2 *See also* Ro 8:30; Tit 3:7

Assurance of forgiveness Ro 5:9;
Eph 1:13–14

**Knowing Jesus Christ and
participating in his resurrection**
Php 3:10–11 *See also* Ro 6:5

Freedom from condemnation
Ro 8:31–34 *See also* Ro 8:1–4;
Gal 3:13–14

Freedom from domination by sin
Ro 6:14,17–18

Adoption into God's family Ro 8:15–17;
Gal 4:6–7

Righteousness in the sight of God
Ro 5:17; Php 3:8–9 *See also* Ro 3:20–22;
1Co 1:30

Justification must lead to good works
Jas 2:24 *See also* Ro 6:15–18;
Gal 5:13–16; Jas 2:14–26

See also

2420 gospel	8104 assurance
6606 access to God	8136 knowing God,
6608 adoption	effects
6652 forgiveness	8157 righteousness
6661 freedom and	as faith
law	8442 good works
6700 peace	9610 hope
6744 sanctification	

6682

mediation

The achieving of fellowship and
reconciliation between separated
parties. Scripture declares that Jesus
Christ is the only true mediator
between God and humanity.

**Jesus Christ is the only mediator
between God and humanity**
1Ti 2:5–6

Mediation through the covenants
Through the covenants of law Gal 3:19
See also Ps 119:29; Jn 1:17

Through the covenants of promise
Heb 12:24 *See also* Ge 12:3; 17:7,11;
Isa 59:21; Heb 8:6; 9:15

**Mediation through the prophetic
word**
Eze 3:4 *See also* Ex 4:15–16; Jer 1:9

Jesus Christ is the supreme mediator
of the prophetic word Jn 7:40 *See also*
Mt 11:27; 17:5; Jn 14:6,9–10; Rev 19:13

**Mediation through priestly
intercession and blessing**
Mediation by sacrifice 1Ch 21:26
pp 2Sa 24:25 *See also* Dt 33:10;
1Ki 18:30–38; Heb 9:22–23

Jesus Christ as both priest and
sacrifice Heb 7:27 *See also* Isa 53:10;
Heb 2:17; 9:11–15

Mediation by praying for others
1Sa 12:23 *See also* Ge 20:7;
Ex 32:30–32; Ps 106:23; Jer 9:1

Jesus Christ's continuing intercession
Ro 8:34 *See also* Isa 53:12; Heb 7:25;
9:24

Mediation through blessing Dt 21:5 *See
also* Ge 12:2–3; Nu 6:22–27; 2Sa 6:18
pp 1Ch 16:2

**Jesus Christ mediates overflowing
blessing** Gal 3:14 *See also* Ac 3:25;
Ro 15:29; Gal 3:8; Eph 1:3

**Mediation for suffering and guilty
believers**
Job 9:32–35 *See also* Job 16:19–21;
1Jn 2:1

Universal mediation
Col 1:20

**Mediation between people and
Jesus Christ**
Mt 12:22; 15:30; Mk 2:3–12; 5:23;
9:17–18; Lk 4:38–39; Jn 4:47–49

Mediation between individuals
Ge 37:21–22 *Reuben for Joseph*;
Ge 41:9–13 *the baker for Joseph*;
1Sa 19:1–7 *Jonathan for David*;
2Sa 14:1–24 *Joab for Absalom*;
Phm 10–21 *Paul for Onesimus*

See also

1335 blessing	6716 reconciliation
1345 covenant	7434 sacrifice
1427 prophecy	7921 fellowship
5913 negotiation	8611 prayer for
6684 mediator	others

6684

mediator

An intermediary who intervenes
between two separated or alienated
parties, with the aim of achieving
reconciliation and fellowship.
Scripture declares that Jesus Christ is
the only true mediator between God
and humanity.

**A person who brings together
those who are separated from
each other**
2Sa 14:14

**Mediators between God and
humanity before the time of
Jesus Christ**
Abraham Ge 18:22–32 *See also* Ge 20:7

Moses Dt 5:5 *See also* Ex 32:30–32;
Dt 5:27; 9:18

Prophets Dt 18:18 *See also* 2Ch 36:15;
Jer 7:25; Am 3:7; Mt 23:34

Priests Nu 3:10 *See also* Ex 19:6;
Lev 9:7; Nu 16:48; 18:7

The suffering servant Isa 49:6 *See also*
Isa 42:1,4; 53:4–6,10–12

Angels Ac 7:53 *See also* Job 5:1;
16:19–21; 33:23; Da 4:13,23

**Jesus Christ is the only true
mediator**
1Ti 2:5

Jesus Christ as greater than all OT
mediators Jn 1:17 *See also* Heb 1:3;
3:1–6; 7:26–28; 8:6; 9:23–24

Mediators between people
2Sa 14:1–33 *Joab*; Mt 5:9 *Christians*;
Ac 9:26–27 *Barnabas*
Paul: 1Co 1:10–12; Php 4:2–3;
Phm 17–21

See also

2075 Christ, sinless	5408 messenger
2306 Christ, high	6682 mediation
priest	6712 propitiation
2327 Christ as	6716 reconciliation
servant	7950 mission of
2414 cross, centrality	Christ
2525 Christ, cross of	8458 peacemakers
2530 Christ, death of	

6686

mercy

A quality of compassion, especially
as expressed in God's forgiveness of
human sin. Scripture stresses God's
forbearance towards sinners. In his
mercy, God shields sinners from
what they deserve and gives gifts
that they do not deserve.
This set of themes consists of the
following:
6687 mercy, nature of God's
6688 mercy, demonstration of God's
6689 mercy, of Jesus Christ
6690 mercy, response to God's
6691 mercy, human

6687
mercy, nature of God's

A central aspect of God's character,
expressed in his covenant
relationships with undeserving
people.

God is merciful
Da 9:9; Eph 2:4 *See also* 2Sa 24:14;
Ne 9:31; Ps 5:7; 25:6; Jer 3:12; Lk 1:78;
1Ti 1:2; Jas 5:11; 1Pe 1:3; 2Jn 3; Jude 2

**God's mercy is expressed in his
faithfulness to his covenant with
his people**
Mic 7:18–20 *See also* Dt 4:31; 7:9;
1Ki 8:23–24; Ne 1:5; 9:30–31; Ps 143:1;
Isa 63:9; Lk 1:54–55,69–75

**God's faithfulness and mercy are
never-ending**
Ps 103:17 *See also* Ps 25:6; 106:1;
119:132

**God's mercy and grace are seen
in Jesus Christ**
Jn 1:14 *See also* Ro 3:22–24; 5:15;
Eph 1:7; Heb 4:16; Jude 21

**God's mercy is not confined to
the Jewish nation**
Ro 3:29–30 *See also* Isa 49:6; Jnh 4:2;
Ro 10:12; 11:28–32; 15:8–12; Gal 3:14;
Eph 3:6–8; Col 1:27

**God chooses when and where to
exercise his mercy**
Ro 9:15–16 *See also* Ex 33:19; Dt 7:7–8;
Ps 33:12; Jn 15:16; 1Co 1:27–29

**God responds in mercy to those
who call to him**
Ps 6:9 *There are many appeals to God's
mercy in the book of Psalms. See also*
1Ki 8:28; 2Ch 6:19; Job 9:15; Da 9:18

6688

mercy, demonstration of God's

God demonstrates his mercy in his various dealings with his people.

God as a parent

Ps 103:13–14; Eph 1:4–6 *See also* Isa 49:15; 63:7–8; 66:13; Jer 31:20; Hos 11:1–4; Mal 3:17; 2Co 1:3

God's mercy and compassion to those in distress

Isa 49:13 *See also* Ex 2:23–24; Ps 91:14–16; 111:2–9; 113:7–9; 142:1–3; Isa 63:9; Jnh 2:2; 2Co 4:1; Heb 4:16

In judgment, God's mercy is just and true

Dt 32:36 *See also* Ps 143:1; Isa 11:3–5; 30:18; 54:7–8; 60:10; Hab 3:2; Rev 19:11

God may choose to show no mercy

Ps 59:5 *See also* Jos 11:20; Jer 21:7; Jas 2:13

God's mercy shown in his actions

The act of salvation Eph 2:4–5 *See also* Ex 15:13; Jdg 2:18 *In the OT, salvation was seen in physical, as much as in spiritual, terms;* Ps 13:5; 28:6–8; 31:21–22
David appeals to God's mercy:
Ps 40:10–11; 57:1; 69:16; 86:15–16 Ps 98:2–3; 116:4–6; Ne 9:27; 1Pe 1:3; 2:10; 2Pe 3:15

His forgiveness Ps 51:1–2 *See also* Nu 14:18–19; Ps 25:6–7; 79:8; 130:1–4; Isa 55:7; Hos 14:1–4; Mic 7:18–19; 1Ti 1:15–16; 1Jn 1:9

His blessing Dt 13:17–18 *Moses concerning idolatry. See also* Dt 7:12–13; 30:3

See also
1040 God, fatherhood	5359 justice
1075 God, justice of	6025 sin & God's character
1315 God as redeemer	6510 salvation

6689

mercy, of Jesus Christ

Jesus Christ displays the same attitude of grace and mercy towards men and women as his Father does.

Jesus Christ is merciful

Lk 4:16–21 *See also* Isa 61:1–2 Jn 15:12–13 *See also* 2Co 8:9; 13:14; Eph 4:7; Php 2:1; 1Ti 1:16; 2Ti 1:18; 2:1; Jude 21

Jesus Christ's concern for people in need

Mt 9:36 pp Mk 6:34 *See also* Mt 14:14; 15:32 pp Mk 8:2; Mt 23:37 pp Lk 13:34

Jesus Christ's response to appeals for mercy

Mt 20:30–34 *See also* Mt 8:2–3 pp Mk 1:39–40 pp Lk 5:12–13; Mt 8:5–13; 9:18–30; 15:22; 17:14–18; Jn 11:6; 2Co 12:8–9

Jesus Christ's mercy in response to judgment

Jn 12:47

Jesus Christ as high priest

Heb 2:17–18 *See also* Heb 4:15

Jesus Christ's mercy is shown in his actions

In salvation Eph 5:2 *See also* Lk 19:10; Gal 2:20; Eph 5:25; 1Ti 1:14–16; Tit 3:4–7

In forgiveness Lk 23:34 *See also* Mk 2:10

In blessing Mk 10:13–16 pp Mt 19:13–15

See also
2015 Christ, compassion	2078 Christ, sonship of
2027 Christ, grace & mercy	2306 Christ, high priest
2033 Christ, humanity	6654 forgiveness, Christ's ministry
2048 Christ, love of	

6690

mercy, response to God's

God's merciful dealings with believers should move them to show similar acts of mercy to others, as well as to rejoice in his graciousness and proclaim it to others.

The proper response to God's mercy

A self-giving faith Ro 12:1 *See also* Ps 13:5; 52:8; Eph 2:8; 1Ti 1:16; Heb 4:16; 1Pe 5:5; Jas 4:6

A merciful attitude towards others Lk 6:36 *See also* Mic 6:8; Zec 7:9; Mt 5:7; 9:13; Lk 10:27–37; Jas 2:12–13

A forgiving attitude towards others Mt 6:12 pp Lk 11:4 *See also* Mt 6:14; 18:21–35; Lk 6:37; 17:3–4; 2Co 2:7; Eph 4:32; Col 3:13

Mercy is to be a characteristic of daily living Heb 13:1 *See also* Mt 25:37–40; Ro 12:9–21; Jude 23

By God's mercy, believers can persevere 2Co 4:1 *See also* 2Th 3:3–5

Sharing God's grace and mercy with others 2Co 8:1 *See also* 2Co 5:14–20

See also
| 5765 attitudes to people | 5932 response |
| | 8424 evangelism |

6691

mercy, human

Believers are urged to show the same qualities of mercy and compassion towards one another as God demonstrates to them. A lack of mercy is regarded as characteristic of godless people.

The need for human mercy

Pr 18:23 *See also* Dt 28:49–50; 2Sa 12:6; 1Ki 3:26; Job 19:21; Pr 21:10; Isa 47:6; 49:15; Zec 7:9–11

Believers should be merciful

Mic 6:8; Mt 5:7; Lk 6:36 *See also* Zec 7:9; Jas 2:12–13; 1Pe 3:9; Jude 22

Lack of mercy characterises the godless

Isa 13:18 *See also* Jer 6:23; 21:7; 50:42; Am 1:11–12; Hab 1:13–17; Mt 23:23

Lack of mercy on Israel's part was sometimes obedience to God

Dt 7:2 *Concerning the peoples they were to displace in the promised land. See also* Dt 13:6–9; 19:11–13,21; 28:53–54; Jos 6:17–19; 1Sa 15:18–19

Mercy as a greeting and a blessing

As a greeting 1Ti 1:2 *See also* 2Ti 1:2; 2Jn 3; Jude 2

As a blessing Gal 6:16 *See also* 2Ti 1:16–18; Jude 21

See also
5494 revenge	6672 grace in relationships
5809 compassion, human	8291 kindness
5823 cruelty	8306 mercifulness

mystery

Normally, God's plan of salvation which, though once unknown to human beings, is now revealed by God.

God's character and purpose cannot be discerned by human reason

Job 11:7 *See also* Job 38:1–42:6

God reveals his plans through dreams, interpreted by his servant

Da 2:28 *Nebuchadnezzar's dreams require the interpretation that God discloses to Daniel before they can be understood as a revelation of divine purposes for Babylon and the surrounding nations. See also* Da 2:17–49; 4:9

God's mysteries are revealed to a man inspired by his Spirit Da 4:18 *See also* Am 3:7

The mystery of God's kingdom

Mt 13:11 pp Mk 4:11 pp Lk 8:10 *God's plan to establish his kingdom is revealed only to those chosen to receive it. To those "outside" it is hidden in parables.*

Mystery as God's plan of salvation

God's plan, now revealed, has been hidden for long ages Eph 3:9 *The use of "mystery" in this sense is found particularly in Paul's letters. See also* Ro 16:25; 1Co 2:7; Col 1:26

God's plan is fulfilled in Jesus Christ Eph 1:9 *See also* Eph 3:4; Col 2:2;

1Ti 3:16 The "mystery of godliness" is the revealed secret that produces godliness in people.

God's plan through Jesus Christ is for the salvation of Gentiles as well as Jews Eph 3:6 See also Ro 11:25; Col 1:27

Ultimately God's plan is for the transformation of the whole creation Eph 1:9–10 See also 1Co 15:51–53; Rev 10:7; 17:5–8

God's plan is revealed by his Spirit so that his servants may publicly proclaim it Eph 3:8–9 See also Eph 3:4–6; 6:19; Col 1:25–27; 4:3; Rev 10:7

Mystery as other aspects of God's purposes
2Th 2:7 Paul's reference to "the secret power (literally "mystery") of lawlessness" suggests that we know some things about evil only as God reveals them. See also 1Co 13:2; 14:2

Mystery as an allegorical understanding
Eph 5:31–32 Paul sees Ge 2:24 as symbolising the unity between Jesus Christ and his church; the unity of husband and wife is a human reflection of that relationship.

See also
1145 God, transcendent	4006 creation, origin
1403 God, revelation	5812 concealment
1409 dream	5941 secrecy
1439 revelation	6510 salvation
2375 kingdom of God	8226 discernment
	8281 insight
	8361 wisdom

6696

necessity

That which makes certain actions or events occur. Scripture relates it to particular events which must happen to bring about God's plan of salvation and also to the behaviour that believers are to adopt as a result of their commitment to Jesus Christ.

The necessity of Jesus Christ's death and resurrection
Lk 24:25–27 See also Mt 16:21 pp Mk 8:31 pp Lk 9:22; Lk 17:25; 24:44–47; Jn 3:14–15; 20:9

The necessity of Jesus Christ's obedience
Lk 4:42–44 See also Mt 3:14–15; Lk 2:49; 13:31–33; Jn 4:4 The necessity lay in Jesus Christ's mission not in geography; Jn 9:4

The necessity of the events leading to the end times
Rev 1:1 See also Mk 13:7–8 pp Mt 24:6–8 pp Lk 21:9–11; Mk 13:10 pp Mt 24:14; 1Co 15:50–55; 2Co 5:10; Rev 4:1; 20:1–3; 22:6

Necessity and the law
Gal 5:3 See also Jn 19:7; Heb 5:3; 9:16,22–23

Necessity in the life of the Christian
The necessity of conversion Jn 3:5–7

See also Mt 18:2–3; Jn 3:3; Ac 4:12; 17:30

The necessity of godly behaviour 1Jn 2:6 See also Ro 15:1–2; 1Ti 3:14–15; 4:7–8; 2Ti 2:22–24; Tit 2:11–14

Necessity in the life of Paul
The necessity of Paul's calling Ac 9:15–16 See also Ac 9:6

The necessity of Paul's preaching of the gospel Ac 13:46; 19:21; 23:11; 27:21–25; 28:19; Ro 1:14; 1Co 9:16–18

The paradoxes of necessity
Freedom and necessity Ro 6:18 See also 1Co 9:19–23; 2Co 9:7; Phm 14

Responsibility and his necessity Mt 18:7 pp Lk 17:1 See also Lk 22:22 pp Mt 26:24 pp Mk 14:21; Ac 2:23

See also
2560 Christ, resurrection	6733 repentance
	8023 faith, necessity
5051 responsibility	8408 decision-making
6615 atonement, necessity	8412 decisions
6622 choice	8454 obedience to God
6658 freedom	
6677 justification, necessity	

6698

newness

Through Jesus Christ, God has made possible a new relationship between himself and sinful humanity. This involves the renewal of human nature and eventually a renewal of creation itself.

The newness of the gospel
The teaching of Jesus Christ was acclaimed as something new Mk 1:27

The kingdom of God is like new cloth Lk 5:36 pp Mt 9:16 pp Mk 2:21

The kingdom of God is like new wine Lk 5:37–38 pp Mt 9:17 pp Mk 2:22

A new covenant has been established between God and his people Jer 31:31; Heb 9:15 See also 1Co 11:25; 2Co 3:6; Heb 8:1–13; 10:20; 12:24

The newness brought to believers through redemption
Believers are called by a new name Isa 62:2 See also Rev 2:17

Believers are born anew 1Pe 1:3 See also Jn 3:1–16

A new life is made possible for believers Ac 5:20 See also Ro 6:4; Col 3:10

Believers are a new creation 2Co 5:17 See also Gal 6:15; Eph 4:23–24

Believers are given a new commandment Jn 13:34–35 See also 1Jn 2:7–8

The newness of creation to come through God's redeeming action
Rev 21:1–2 See also Isa 43:19; 65:17; 66:22; 2Pe 3:13; Rev 3:12; 21:5

See also
1352 covenant, the new	4010 creation, renewal
3290 Holy Spirit, life-giver	4018 life, spiritual

See also
5005 human race & redemption	8148 revival
5017 heart, renewal	9160 new heavens & new earth
6728 regeneration	9165 restoration
8144 renewal	

6700

peace

The state of harmony that is available to believers through having a right relationship with God and others and is especially associated with the presence of the Holy Spirit. This set of themes consists of the following:

6701 peace, human search for
6702 peace, human destruction of
6703 peace, divine in OT
6704 peace, divine in NT
6705 peace, believers' experience of
6706 peace, and Holy Spirit

6701

peace, human search for

Scripture teaches that peace is only found in God, but people try to find it elsewhere. A person's desire for peace varies according to his or her circumstances.

The places where people search for peace
People search for peace in others Ge 5:28–29 See also SS 8:10

People search for peace in material possessions Ecc 4:8 See also Job 21:7–13; Da 4:4; Mt 19:16–22; Lk 12:16–19

People search for peace in God Ps 4:8 See also Job 22:21; Pr 19:23; Isa 26:3; Lk 7:37–50

The dangers in searching for peace
It can lead to greed Ecc 4:6 See also Mt 23:25

It can lead to suffering and bondage Ge 42:1–17; Jos 9:3–27; Mk 5:25–26

It can lead to destruction 1Th 5:3 See also 2Ki 20:12–19; Lk 16:19–26

People's search for peace varies according to their circumstances
The desire can increase in times of suffering and difficulties Ex 2:23 See also Jer 14:19; 47:2–6; La 3:7–24; Eze 7:23–27; Mk 5:24–34 pp Mt 9:18–22 pp Lk 8:42–48

The desire can diminish in times of comfort Ex 8:12–15 See also Job 12:5; Hos 10:1; Am 6:1

See also
5560 suffering	6166 flesh, sinful nature
5690 friends	8808 riches
5869 greed	8823 self-righteousness
5874 happiness	
5901 loneliness	
5970 unhappiness	

6702
peace, human destruction of

Because of human sinfulness, God's provision of peace is always under threat. Scripture shows that this breaking of peace has implications for the whole of creation.

Causes of the destruction of peace

Sin and self-centredness Isa 57:21 See also Ge 11:4-9; Isa 59:7-8; Lk 19:41-44

Idolatry Zec 10:2 See also Ex 32:7-10; 1Ti 6:9-10

Fear and anxiety Jn 20:19 See also Jos 7:3-5; Pr 29:25; Jer 30:10; 46:27; Mt 6:31-34 pp Lk 12:29-30

The sins of ancestors Lev 26:36-42 See also Ge 3:16-19; 2Ki 23:26-27; Jer 31:29; Eze 18:2

Friends Jer 20:10 See also La 1:1-2,19

Enemies Ps 35:19-20 See also 2Ki 9:14-28; La 1:16

The consequences of the human destruction of peace

Humanity suffers Dt 28:53-57; 1Ki 2:5-6; 2Ki 6:24-29; 25:2-3; Eze 13:10-16; Rev 6:3-8

Nations suffer Jer 49:31-32 See also Eze 38:14-23

The land suffers Jer 25:37 See also Ex 8:12-14; Lev 26:27-35; Isa 1:7; 36:16-20

The whole creation suffers Rev 6:3-4 See also Ge 6:5-7; Isa 24:1-5; Ro 8:22; Rev 8:7-13

See also
4030 world, behaviour in	8727 enemies
4120 Satan	8754 fear
5605 warfare	8768 idolatry
6020 sin	8827 selfishness

6703
peace, divine in OT

Providing peace for his creation is a characteristic of God. In the OT peace came through adherence to God's will as expressed in his spoken word, covenants and law. The Hebrew word "shalom" means "peace in all its fulness, in every aspect of life".

Peace provided for God's people

Through obedience to God's spoken word Ge 2:16-17 See also 2Ki 5:13-19; Job 22:21-22; Ps 85:8; Isa 54:13; Da 10:15-19

Through obedience to God's covenants Dt 29:9 See also Dt 30:15-16; Mal 2:1-6

Through obedience to God's laws Ps 119:165 See also Lev 26:3-12; Dt 28:1-7; 2Ch 14:2-7; Ps 37:34-38; Pr 3:13-17; Isa 48:18

Peace expressed in signs Ge 9:13-16 See also Ex 13:21-22; 40:36-38; Jdg 6:22-24

Peace provided for God's nation

Through provision of the land Ps 37:11 See also 1Sa 7:13-14; 1Ch 4:40; Ps 37:3

Through provision of a holy city Isa 33:20-24 See also Ps 122:6-8; Isa 66:10-13; Jer 33:6-9; Zec 1:16-17

Through provision of a house of God Hag 2:9 See also 1Ch 22:6-10; Eze 37:24-28

Through provision of the law Isa 48:18 See also Dt 6:1-3; 30:15-16

The benefits of peace

Peace and God's presence Isa 41:10 See also Nu 6:22-26; Jos 1:9; Ps 23:1-4; 29:11; Jer 30:10-11

Peace in captivity Jer 29:7 See also Ex 1:6-12; Jer 31:1-2

Peace in suffering Ps 119:50 See also Isa 61:1-4; Jer 34:1-5

Peace in poverty Isa 14:30 See also 1Sa 2:6-9; Ps 68:5-10; Pr 17:1

Peace with enemies Pr 16:7 See also 1Ch 22:7-9; Jer 29:4-7

See also
1345 covenant	5446 poverty
4206 land	7446 slavery
5375 law	

6704
peace, divine in NT

God's ultimate provision of peace is discovered in the person and work of Jesus Christ. It is only through Christ that peace with God can be achieved and maintained.

Provision of peace through the Father

Peace in a believer's relationship with the Father Ro 5:1 See also Ro 8:1,31-39; 1Co 1:2-3

Peace through the Father's provision for the believer 1Ti 6:17 See also Mt 6:25-34 pp Lk 12:22-31; Mt 7:7-11 pp Lk 11:9-13

Provision of peace through Jesus Christ

Through Jesus Christ's coming Lk 2:10-14
These OT prophecies are fulfilled in the coming of Jesus Christ: Isa 9:6-7; Mic 5:2-5; Zec 9:9-10 Lk 2:25-32; Eph 2:17

Through Jesus Christ's teaching Jn 16:33 See also Jn 14:23-27; 15:3

Through Jesus Christ's ministry Ac 10:36 See also Mk 4:35-41 pp Mt 8:23-27 pp Lk 8:22-25; Lk 4:33-35 pp Mk 1:23-25; Lk 4:38-41 pp Mt 8:14-17 pp Mk 1:29-34

Through Jesus Christ's death Col 1:19-20 See also Isa 53:5; Mt 26:26-28 pp Mk 14:22-24 pp Lk 22:19-20; Gal 6:14-16; Eph 2:13-17

Through Jesus Christ's resurrection Lk 24:36 See also Mk 16:4-6 pp Lk 24:1-8; Jn 20:19-21,26-29; 2Co 4:14; Heb 13:20-21

Through Jesus Christ's ascension Ro 8:34 See also Lk 24:51-53; Ac 2:33-39

Provision of peace through the Holy Spirit

Through the Holy Spirit's inner witness 2Co 1:21-22 See also Ro 8:14-17; Gal 4:6-7

Through the Holy Spirit's presence Ac 9:31 See also Jn 14:16-18; Gal 5:16-18; Rev 22:17

Peace as the Holy Spirit's fruit and gift Gal 5:22 See also Ro 14:17

See also
1040 God, fatherhood	2505 Christ, ascension
1330 God, the provider	2555 Christ, resurrection appearances
1620 beatitudes, the	
2378 kingdom of God, characteristics	3215 Holy Spirit & peace
2410 cross, the	6716 reconciliation
2424 gospel, promises	8458 peacemakers

6705
peace, believers' experience of

Peace is the birthright of every believer in all circumstances. It is found only in God and is maintained through having a close relationship with him.

Peace for believers in differing situations

In times of sickness, pressure and hardships Ps 41:1-3; Mt 11:28 See also Job 1:13-22; 2:7-10; Ac 16:22-25; 2Co 12:7-10; 2Ti 4:16-18

In times of death and grief Jn 14:1-3 See also Job 19:25-26; 2Ki 22:18-20; Isa 57:1-2; 1Th 4:13-18

The effects of peace for believers

Forgiveness Ac 7:60 See also Ro 12:17-19

Encouragement 2Co 1:3-6 See also Php 4:11-13

Health and healing Pr 14:30 See also Isa 57:18-19

Security Pr 1:33 See also Ac 27:21-26; Ro 8:28,35-39

Hope Ro 15:13 See also Ro 5:1-5

How believers maintain peace

Through remaining in Christ Jn 15:4-7 See also Jn 16:33; Ro 5:1-5

Through living by the Holy Spirit Ro 8:6 See also Ro 14:17-19; Gal 5:22

Through obedience to God's word Jos 1:8-9 See also Ps 119:165-167

Through prayer and meditation Php 4:6-9 See also Ps 1:1-3; Isa 26:3; 1Ti 2:1-2

Final peace in death for believers

Isa 57:2; Rev 14:13 See also 2Ki 22:19-20; Lk 2:29

Hope of future peace for believers

Peace in heaven 1Pe 1:4 See also Jn 14:1-3; 1Th 4:13-14; Rev 7:9-17

Peace in God's new creation
Rev 21:1–4 *See also* Isa 11:6–9;
Ro 8:18–23; Rev 22:3–5

See also

1610 Scripture	8102 abiding in
3251 Holy Spirit,	Christ
filling with	8104 assurance
3254 Holy Spirit,	8117 discipleship,
fruit of	benefits
4020 life of faith	8602 prayer
5783 agreement	8662 meditation
6652 forgiveness	9610 hope

6706
peace, and Holy Spirit
See 3215 Holy Spirit, and peace

6708
predestination

God's foreordination of all events
and circumstances for the good of
his people and the glory of his name.

**Predestination depends on God's
sovereignty**
He is the Creator of all things
Jer 32:17–19 *See also* Ge 1:1;
Job 38:1–4; Isa 44:24–28; 45:12–13;
48:12–14

He rules over nature and history
Pr 16:4 *See also* Ge 18:10–14; Ps 67:4;
Pr 16:9,33; 21:1; Mt 8:23–27
pp Mk 4:35–41 pp Lk 8:22–25;
Mt 10:29–30; Ac 17:26

His will is perfect Ge 18:25 *See also*
Ex 33:19; Dt 32:4; Job 8:3; Ps 119:137;
Da 4:37

**God's predestined purposes
cannot be thwarted**
Human beings cannot stand against
his will Ro 9:19–21 *See also* Ps 2:1–4;
Pr 19:21; 21:30; Isa 14:24–27;
46:10–12; Da 4:35

False gods are impotent before him
Ps 115:3–8 *See also* Isa 44:8–20; 45:20;
48:14

He brings good out of evil Ge 50:20 *See
also* Ge 15:13–16; 45:4–8

**Predestination undergirds
biblical prophecy**
It explains the prophets' confidence
1Ki 22:17–28 *See also* 1Pe 1:10–12

It is demonstrated in the fulfilment of
prophecy 1Ki 22:29–38 *See also*
Mt 1:22; 2:15,23; 4:14; 8:17; 12:17–19;
Ac 2:17–25; 3:22–25; 13:27–30;
15:15–18

**The life and ministry of Jesus
Christ was predestined**
In that it was predicted by the prophets
Isa 9:6–7 *See also* Isa 11:1–10;
52:13–53:12; Jer 23:5–6; Ac 3:18;
Gal 4:4–5

In his sufferings and death Ac 2:23 *See
also* Mt 16:21; Lk 18:31–32; 22:22;
24:25–27,44–45; Jn 13:1; Ac 4:27–30

In the outcome it achieved Ge 3:15

**God's purpose in predestination
is to bless his people**
In the path their lives follow Ro 8:28 *See
also* Ps 139:14–16; Jer 29:11;
Mt 10:29–31 pp Lk 12:6–7

In their salvation Ro 8:29–30 *See also*
Ge 12:1–3; Mt 11:25–27; Mk 4:11;
Jn 6:37–44; Ac 13:48; 1Th 5:9

In their assurance of salvation
Ro 8:31–39 *See also* Jn 10:27–29; 17:2;
Eph 1:3–14 *Predestination is basic to
Christian certainty.*

Regarding final perseverance Php 1:6
See also Ps 138:8; Jn 6:37–40;
Php 2:12–13; Jas 5:11

Regarding God's call to righteousness
Eph 2:10 *See also* Jer 1:4–5; Ac 22:10;
Gal 1:15–17

Regarding future inheritance
Jn 14:2–3 *See also* Mt 25:34; Ro 8:30

God predestines judgment
Isa 65:11–12 *See also* Ge 6:17 *the flood*;
Ex 7:13; 9:13–18; Jos 11:20;
2Ki 19:25–26; Isa 14:24–27 *judgment on
Assyria*; Isa 19:12–14; 23:9 *judgment on
Tyre*; Jer 49:20; 50:45 *judgment on
Babylon*; 1Pe 2:6–8; Isa 8:14–15

**Predestination does not set aside
human responsibility**
Php 2:12–13 *See also* Jn 6:37,40;
Ac 13:48

See also

1115 God, purpose	1412 foreknowledge
of	1427 prophecy
1130 God,	6638 election
sovereignty	7125 elect, the
1175 God, will of	8104 assurance

6710
privileges

Spiritual and material benefits
conferred upon people by God. They
are given, not because of human
merit, but because of God's
graciousness, and therefore carry
responsibilities with them.

**Privileges as the gift of God, not
the result of human merit**
1Co 4:7 *See also* Lk 1:26–38; Eph 2:8–9;
Php 3:4–9

**The privileged position of
humanity in creation**
Ps 8:3–6 *See also* Ge 1:26–28

The privileged position of Israel
Ro 9:4–5 *See also* Dt 7:7–9;
2Sa 7:22–24; Ro 11:1–12

**The privileged position of the
believer**
The privilege of forgiveness and new
life Eph 1:3–8 *See also* 2Co 5:17–21;
Eph 2:3–9; Col 1:13–14

The privilege of access to God
Eph 2:18 *See also* Ro 5:1–2;
Heb 10:19–22; 12:18–24

The privilege of knowing God Jn 17:3
See also Jn 12:44–46; 14:6–7

The privilege of being God's children
Gal 4:4–7 *See also* Ro 8:14–17;
Gal 3:26–29; Heb 12:5–11

**The privilege of becoming God's
people** 1Pe 2:9–10 *See also*
Eph 2:19–22

**The privilege of receiving divine
insights** Lk 10:23–24 *See also*
Mt 13:10–17 pp Mk 4:10–12
pp Lk 8:9–10; Jn 15:15; 1Co 2:6–12;
1Pe 1:10–12

**The privilege of being called to
serve God**
Jer 1:5 *See also* 2Sa 7:18–21;
Jn 15:15–16; 1Co 15:8–10

The privilege of giving
1Ch 29:14–16 *See also* Ac 20:33–35;
2Co 8:1–15; 9:6–11

Privileges bring responsibilities
1Co 4:1–2 *See also* Mt 24:45–51
pp Lk 12:42–48; 1Co 6:19–20;
Heb 13:17

Privileges can be abused
1Sa 2:12–17 *Eli's sons*; 2Sa 11:1–4 *King
David*; 1Ki 21:1–16 *King Ahab*;
Ac 16:35–39 *magistrates in Philippi*;
Ac 23:1–3 *Ananias, the high priest*

Privileges can be withdrawn
Mt 21:33–43 pp Mk 12:1–9
pp Lk 20:9–16 *parable of the tenants*;
Mt 25:14–30 *parable of the talents*;
Lk 19:12–27 *parable of the ten minas*

See also

1055 God, grace &	6640 election,
mercy	privileges
1335 blessing	6666 grace
5051 responsibility	7921 fellowship
5255 citizenship	8117 discipleship,
5504 rights	benefits
6606 access to God	9420 book of life
6611 adoption,	
privileges &	
duties	

6712
propitiation

The satisfaction of the righteous
demands of God in relation to
human sin and its punishment
through the sacrificial death of Jesus
Christ upon the cross, by which the
penalty of sin is cancelled and the
anger of God averted. (The NIV is
distinctive at this point, in that it
generally translates this term by
"atonement" and related words.)

**The need for propitiation: God's
anger against sin**
Ps 7:11; Ro 2:5 *See also* Ex 32:11–14;
Nu 32:8–15; Dt 6:14–15; 2Ki 23:26;
Ps 78:38; Isa 30:27–31; Da 9:16–19;
Hos 11:8–9; Mt 25:41–46; Jn 3:36;
Ro 1:18; Eph 5:6

**The provision of propitiation:
Jesus Christ the atoning
sacrifice**
The promise in the OT Isa 53:5–6 *See
also* Isa 53:10–12

The fulfilment in the NT Ro 3:21–26 *See
also* Ro 5:9–10; Col 1:21–22; Heb 2:17;
9:11–14; 1Jn 2:2

The motivation for propitiation: God's love
1Jn 4:10 *See also* Ps 85:2–3; 103:8–12; Mic 7:18–19; Ro 5:6–8; 2Co 5:19

See also

1025 God, anger of	6614 atonement
1065 God, holiness of	6648 expiation
	6686 mercy
1075 God, justice of	6716 reconciliation
1085 God, love of	6752 substitution
2410 cross, the	7317 blood of Christ
6020 sin	

6714

ransom

The price paid for redemption, that is, for setting something or someone free from some form of obligation or captivity.

Ransom paid for what has been devoted to the Lord
Ex 13:12–13; 30:11–16; 34:20; Lev 27:1–33; Nu 3:40–51; 18:14–17

Ransom of a person's life instead-of punishment
Ex 21:28–32

Ransom from poverty and misfortune, including widowhood
Lev 25:25–28,47–55; Ru 4:1–13; Pr 13:8

Limitations on ransom payments
Nu 35:31–32 *See also* Lev 27:29

Paying a ransom to God
Ps 49:7–8 *See also* Ex 30:12–16; Job 33:24

Promises of redemption for the Lord's ransomed people
Isa 51:11 pp Isa 35:10 *See also* Isa 40:2; 43:3–5; Jer 31:11; Hos 13:14

The death of Jesus Christ seen as a ransom
Mk 10:45 pp Mt 20:28 *See also* Ac 20:28; 1Ti 2:5–6; Tit 2:14; Heb 9:15; 2Pe 2:1

The priceless value of the ransom of Jesus Christ
1Co 6:19–20 *See also* 1Co 7:23; 1Pe 1:18–19; Rev 5:9

See also

1315 God as redeemer	6752 substitution
2321 Christ as redeemer	7140 people of God
	7314 blood
2410 cross, the	7388 kinsman-redeemer
6658 freedom	7446 slavery
6720 redemption	7482 Year of Jubilee

6716

reconciliation

The restoration of fellowship between God and humanity and the resulting restoration of human relationships. The NT affirms that the reconciliation of the world to

God is only possible on the basis of the work of Jesus Christ.

6717
reconciliation, of the world to God

On account of sin, people are alienated from God and cut off from fellowship with him. Through Jesus Christ, God reconciles the world to himself, breaking down the barriers of hostility and estrangement.

A broken relationship through sin brings alienation from God
Isa 59:2 *See also* Ge 3:23–24 *the expulsion from Eden*; Ge 4:13–14 *Cain's alienation from God*; Isa 48:22; 64:7; Jer 33:5; Lk 18:13 *the tax collector's prayer for mercy*; Ro 5:10; 8:7; Eph 2:1–3,12; 4:18; Col 1:21; Jas 4:4

God takes the initiative in bringing about reconciliation
2Co 5:18–19 *See also* Ro 5:6–8; Gal 4:4–5; Eph 2:4–5; 1Jn 4:10

The means of reconciliation is the death of Jesus Christ
Ro 5:6 *See also* 2Co 5:18–19,21; Eph 2:13,16; Col 1:20

The results of reconciliation are both personal and universal
Peace with God Ro 5:1 *See also* Ac 10:36–46; Eph 2:14–19; Col 1:21–22

Access to God Ro 5:2 *See also* Eph 2:18; 3:12; Heb 10:19–22

Adoption as God's children Ro 8:15–16; Gal 3:26; 4:4–6; 1Jn 3:1–2

Peacemaking throughout the universe Col 1:20 *See also* Ro 11:15; Eph 1:7–10,22–23

Believers are to be the ambassadors of reconciliation
2Co 5:18–20

See also

2530 Christ, death of	6510 salvation
4010 creation, renewal	6614 atonement
	6676 justification
4028 world, redeemed	6682 mediation
	6720 redemption
5005 human race & redemption	7317 blood of Christ
	8341 separation
6024 sin, effects of	

6718
reconciliation, between believers

True reconciliation between people is only possible after they have been reconciled to God through Jesus Christ. Believers are urged to settle differences among themselves in brotherly love.

The cause of the breakdown in relationships is sin
Ge 27:41
The division between Joseph and his brothers: Ge 37:4–5,18–20

1Sa 15:12–14 *Samuel and Saul*; 2Sa 14:28 *Absalom and David*; Ac 15:37–40 *Paul and Barnabas*; Gal 2:11 *Paul opposes Peter*

Believers should be reconciled to one another
Mt 5:23–24 *See also* Mt 5:9,25 pp Lk 12:58; Mt 5:44; 18:15–17,21–35; Jn 17:20–23; Ro 12:18–21; 2Th 3:14–15

The death of Jesus Christ should bring believers together in peace
Eph 2:14–22

The church should display reconciliation
Col 3:12–15 *See also* Ro 12:18–21; Eph 4:32; 2Th 3:14–15

Examples of reconciliation between people
Ge 33:4 *See also* Ge 45:1–5 *Joseph and his brothers*; Jos 22:10–34 *Israel, Reuben and Gad*; Lk 23:12 *Herod and Pilate*; Jn 21:15–17 *Jesus Christ and Peter*; Ac 9:26–28 *Paul and the apostles*; 1Co 7:11 *a wife and her husband*

See also

5690 friends	7921 fellowship
5799 bitterness	8292 love
5898 kissing	8727 enemies
6652 forgiveness	8839 unfaithfulness

6720

redemption

The buying back or release of an object or person. In Scripture redemption refers to God's ransoming of believers only through the death of Jesus Christ upon the cross and to all the benefits that this brings.

6721
redemption, in everyday life

The purchase of a person's freedom or the buying back of an object from the possession of another. Scripture provides illustrations of these everyday meanings of the word.

The OT redemption of property, animals and individuals
Redemption of property Lev 25:24–28 *See also* Lev 27:15–20; Ru 4:1–6; Jer 32:8

Redemption of animals Ex 13:13 *See also* Ex 34:20; Lev 27:13,27; Nu 18:14–17

Redemption of individuals Ex 30:12–16 *See also* Ex 13:12–13; 21:8,28–32; 34:19–20; Lev 25:47–55; Nu 3:44–51

The redemption of the nation of Israel
Ex 6:6 *See also* Dt 9:26; 2Sa 7:23–24 pp 1Ch 17:21–22; Ne 1:10; Ps 77:15; 78:35; 106:10; Isa 43:1–3; Mic 6:4

Redemption as release from sin
Ps 130:8 *See also* Isa 40:2

The role of the redeemer

In helping close relatives regain property or freedom Lev 25:25 *See also* Lev 25:47–49; 27:15–20; Ru 2:20; 3:9; 4:1–8

In avenging death Nu 35:12,19–21

See also

5005 human race & redemption	7388 kinsman-redeemer
5493 retribution	8311 morality & redemption
5635 work & redemption	9165 restoration
6714 ransom	
7310 avenger of blood	

6722
redemption, in OT

The act of God by which he delivered his people from bondage. The exodus of Israel from Egypt and the later deliverance of Jerusalem from exile in Babylon are seen as definitive examples of God's redeeming acts.

God is the Redeemer of his people

God redeems his people from captivity out of love Dt 7:8 *See also* Ex 6:6–8; 15:13; Ps 130:7–8; Isa 43:14; 47:1–4; 63:16; Jer 15:21; 31:11; 50:34

His redemption guarantees security Isa 43:1–4 *See also* Isa 44:21–28; 48:20; 49:7,22–26; 52:9–12

He redeems from death Ps 49:15 *See also* Job 5:20; 19:25–26; Hos 13:14

His redemption is associated with his holiness Isa 41:14 *See also* Isa 43:14; 47:4; 48:17; 49:7; 54:5

He redeems by his mighty arm Lk 1:51 *See also* Dt 11:2; Ps 89:10; 77:15; Isa 62:8

See also

1065 God, holiness of	6634 deliverance
1105 God, power of	6658 freedom
1315 God as redeemer	6738 rescue
1320 God as Saviour	7215 exile, the
1680 types	7221 exodus, the
	7446 slavery

6723
redemption, in NT

The culmination of the OT work of redemption is seen in the cross of Jesus Christ, by which believers are liberated from bondage to sin.

Redemption is achieved through Jesus Christ
Eph 1:7

Jesus Christ's teaching on redemption
Mk 10:45 pp Mt 20:28 *See also* Mt 26:26–28 pp Mk 14:22–25 pp Lk 22:20–22

Apostolic teaching on redemption
Jesus Christ is the redemption of believers 1Co 1:30 *See also* 1Ti 2:6; Tit 2:14

Redemption comes through the shedding of the blood of Jesus Christ
Gal 3:13 *See also* Ac 20:28; Ro 3:25; 1Co 6:20; 7:23; 11:23–25; 1Pe 1:18–19; Heb 9:12; Rev 1:5–6; 5:9

The results of redemption
Forgiveness of sin Col 1:13–14

Justification and freedom from the law Gal 3:8–10 *See also* Ro 3:23–25; Gal 4:5

Inclusion in the covenant Gal 3:14 *See also* Heb 9:15

Freedom to live a new life Gal 4:4–7 *See also* 1Co 6:19–20; 7:22–24; Col 1:13; Tit 2:14; Heb 9:14; Rev 1:5–6; 5:9–10

Creation and believers await final redemption
Ro 8:19–23 *See also* Lk 21:28; Ac 3:21; Eph 1:14; 4:30

See also

2321 Christ as redeemer	6652 forgiveness
2420 gospel	6676 justification
4028 world, redeemed	7317 blood of Christ
5016 heart, fallen & redeemed	7933 Lord's Supper
5065 spirit, fallen & redeemed	8144 renewal
	9414 heaven, community of redeemed

6724
redeemer, God as

See 1315 God, as redeemer

6725
redeemer, Jesus Christ as

See 2321 Jesus Christ, as redeemer

6728
regeneration

The radical renewal of a person's inner being by the work of God's Spirit.

The need for regeneration
Jn 3:3 *See also* Eph 2:1,5; Col 2:13

Regeneration is a work of God
It originates in God the Father
Jn 1:12–13 *Regeneration cannot be controlled by human actions or rituals; it is an act of God's sovereign will.*

It is made possible by the resurrection of Jesus Christ 1Pe 1:3 *See also* Eph 2:4–5

It occurs through the hearing of the Christian gospel Jas 1:18 *See also* 1Pe 1:23–25 *The "word of God" is the good news about Jesus Christ.*

It is effected by God's Spirit Jn 3:5–8 *See also* Jn 6:63; Tit 3:5

Regeneration is given to those who believe in Jesus Christ
1Jn 5:1

Baptism is the sign of regeneration
Jn 3:5 *Water here is seen by some, though not all, interpreters as a reference to baptism, administered by the church to new converts as a sign of their new birth and their entry into the Christian*

community. See also Ac 2:38–39; Eph 5:25–26; Tit 3:5

The results of regeneration
Entry into God's kingdom Jn 3:5

A new holiness of life 1Jn 3:9 *See also* 1Jn 5:18; 1Pe 2:1–2

Love for other people 1Jn 4:7 *See also* 1Jn 5:2

Victory over the world's sinful pattern of life 1Jn 5:4

See also

1130 God, sovereignty	6653 forgiveness, divine
3230 Holy Spirit & regeneration	6734 repentance, importance
5016 heart, fallen & redeemed	8022 faith, basis of salvation
5017 heart, renewal	8104 assurance
5065 spirit, fallen & redeemed	8144 renewal
6020 sin	8150 revival, personal
6627 conversion	

6730
reinstatement

Restoration to a previous state or position. It is demonstrated in human relationships and also by God in his love and grace restoring fallen humanity and lifting up his people to their former place within his service.

The basis of reinstatement
God does not remember sin Ps 103:12; Isa 38:17; 43:25; Eze 20:44

God's unfailing love Ps 89:28; La 3:22; Hos 11:8

God's reinstatement of fallen humanity
Humanity's unique calling Heb 2:6–8 *See also* Ps 8:4–6; Ge 1:26–27; Isa 43:7

Humanity's fall and reinstatement Ro 3:23–24; 2Th 2:14 *See also* Ro 5:15–19; 8:17; Eph 1:12; Heb 2:10; 1Pe 5:1

God's reinstatement of Israel
The promise of reinstatement Mic 4:8 *See also* Isa 1:26; 60:10; Hag 2:9; Zec 1:17; 10:6–8

Reinstatement as God's people Hos 2:23 *See also* Ro 9:25; 1Pe 2:10

Reinstatement as God's bride Isa 54:5–8 *See also* Jer 3:12–14; Hos 2:14–20

Reinstatement in the land Jer 33:10–16 *See also* 2Ch 30:9; Jer 31:16–17; Hos 11:10–11

God's reinstatement of his servants
Jdg 16:22 *Samson's hair begins to grow again, indicating his renewed call to serve God;* Jer 15:19 *God will continue to speak through a repentant Jeremiah;* Da 4:34–36 *Nebuchadnezzar's sanity and kingdom is restored;* Jnh 3:1–2 *God renews Jonah's commission;* Jn 21:15–17 *Jesus Christ reinstates Peter after his denial.*

6732

Further examples of reinstatement

Ge 40:13 *Pharaoh's cupbearer reinstated;* **1Sa** 19:6–7 *David reinstated by Saul;* **2Sa** 9:7 *Mephibosheth reinstated by David;* **2Sa** 14:33 *Absalom reinstated by David;* **Da** 3:30 *Nebuchadnezzar reinstates Shadrach, Meshach and Abednego;* **Hos** 3:2–3 *Gomer reinstated as Hosea's wife;* **Lk** 15:22–24 *the prodigal reinstated by his father;* **Phm** 10 *Paul asks Philemon to reinstate his slave Onesimus;* **Phm** 24 *John Mark, formerly rejected, has here been reinstated as Paul's companion.*

See also

1095 God, patience of	6652 forgiveness
2036 Christ, humility	6716 reconciliation
5113 Peter, disciple	7918 excom-
5492 restitution	munication
6603 acceptance, divine	8144 renewal
6614 atonement	8318 patience
	9165 restoration

6732

repentance

A change of mind leading to a change of action. It involves a sincere turning from sin to serve God and includes sorrow for, and confession of, sin and where possible restitution. At points, Scripture refers to God changing his plans in response to events.

6733

repentance, nature of

Scripture stresses the necessity of repentance from sin if individuals and communities are to have full fellowship with God. It also uses the term to refer to God's relenting of sending judgment on his people, usually in response to human repentance.

Repentance is a requirement for fellowship with God
2Ki 17:13; 1Th 1:9 *See also* Ps 34:14; Isa 55:7; Ac 14:15; Jas 4:7–10

Repentance involves turning from sin
Sorrow for sin Ps 51:17; 2Co 7:8–10 *See also* Job 42:6; Ps 34:18; Isa 57:15; 66:2; Joel 2:12–13; Lk 18:13

Confession of sin Lk 15:17–19 *See also* Lev 5:5; Ps 51:1–3; Pr 28:13; Hos 14:1–2

Forsaking specific sins Ezr 10:10–11; Eze 14:6; Ac 15:19–20

Making appropriate restitution Nu 5:6–7; Lk 19:8

Repentance involves turning to God
Faith in God Isa 30:15 *See also* Lk 22:32; Ac 11:21; 20:21; 26:18

Obedience Eze 18:21–23 *See also* Mal 3:7–10

Repentance demonstrated by actions Ac 26:20 *See also* Isa 1:16–17; Da 4:27; Mt 3:8 pp Lk 3:8; Lk 3:10–14

Repentance must be sincere

Jer 3:10; 24:7 *See also* 1Ki 8:46–50 pp 2Ch 6:36–39; Ps 78:34–37; Hos 6:1–4

The repentance of God

Jer 26:3 *See also* Ex 32:14; Ps 106:45; Hos 11:8; Joel 2:13; Am 7:1–6

See also

1025 God, anger of	6624 confession of
1070 God, joy of	sin
1120 God, repentance of	6650 finding
5492 restitution	6740 returning to
5801 brokenness	God
5952 sorrow	8020 faith
6020 sin	8453 obedience

6734

repentance, importance of

Repentance is of central importance because sin brings God's judgment and fellowship with God is only possible through full and sincere repentance. God, through his servants, calls people to repent as the only way to escape the judgment and receive the forgiveness and restoration which he offers.

The call to repentance
Lk 5:32; Jas 5:19–20 *See also* Jer 25:4–6; Eze 33:7–9; Mk 1:4 pp Lk 3:3; Lk 24:47; 2Ti 2:24–26

Repentance opens the way for blessing
It is the only way to escape God's judgment Eze 18:30–32 *See also* Job 36:12; Jer 18:7–8; 26:3; Hos 11:5; Jnh 3:10; Lk 3:8–9; Rev 2:5

It prepares the way for God's kingdom Mt 4:17 pp Mk 1:14–15 *See also* Mt 3:2

It brings forgiveness and restoration 2Ch 7:13–14; Isa 55:7 *See also* Dt 30:1–10; Ne 1:8–9; Job 22:23–25; 36:10–11; Isa 44:22; Ac 2:38–39; 3:19; 5:31; 11:18

God desires that all people should repent
He wants everyone to be saved Eze 18:23

His patience with the unrepentant 2Pe 3:9 *See also* Isa 65:2; Ro 2:4; Rev 2:21

His discipline encourages repentance Jer 31:18–20 *See also* Isa 10:20–21; 19:22; Hos 2:6–7; 6:1

Taking God's opportunity for repentance
Isa 55:6; Ac 17:30–31 *See also* Heb 3:13–15; 4:7; Ps 95:7–8

Refusing God's opportunity for repentance
Examples of those who refuse to repent Jer 35:15 *See also* Jer 5:3; Mt 11:20; 21:32; Rev 9:20–21; 16:9–11

God confirms those who refuse to repent in their hardness of heart Mt 13:14–15 pp Mk 4:11–12 pp Lk 8:9–10; Ac 28:25–27; Isa 6:10

Repentance may not remove the effects of human sin

Nu 14:39–45 *The Israelites' repentance could not prevent the wandering that resulted from their refusal to enter the promised land;* 1Sa 15:24–26 *Saul's repentance is too late to escape God's judgment on his kingship;* 2Sa 12:13–14 *Despite David's repentance the son of his adulterous relationship with Bathsheba still died;* Heb 12:16–17 *Esau's repentance could not bring back the birthright he had sold to Jacob.*

See also

1030 God, compassion	6124 condemnation
2375 kingdom of God	6178 hardness of heart
2425 gospel, requirements	6652 forgiveness
5048 opportunities & salvation	6686 mercy
5763 attitudes, positive to God	8653 importunity to God
	9165 restoration
	9210 judgment, God's

6735

repentance, examples of

Scripture provides examples to illustrate the importance of repentance for individuals and communities.

The repentance of individuals
The call to personal repentance Ac 2:38 *See also* 2Ti 2:19

Examples of individual repentance Nu 22:31–35 *Balaam;* 2Sa 24:10 pp 1Ch 21:8 *David, after taking a census;* 1Ki 21:27–29 *Ahab;* 2Ki 22:19 *Josiah;* Job 42:6 *Job;* Ps 51:1–17 *David, following his adultery with Bathsheba;* Lk 15:21 *the prodigal son;* Lk 18:13 *the tax collector in the temple;* Mt 26:75 pp Mk 14:72 pp Lk 22:61–62 *Peter's sorrow after denying Jesus Christ;* Jn 21:15–17 *Peter's confession and reinstatement;* Ac 8:22–24 *Simon the sorcerer's repentance may not have been genuine.*

Corporate repentance
Examples of corporate repentance Jer 18:7–8; Mt 3:1–6 pp Mk 1:1–6 pp Lk 3:1–6 *See also* Nu 21:7 *Israel in the desert;* Jdg 10:15–16 *Israel in the time of the judges;* 1Sa 7:3–4 *Israel, after asking for a king;* Isa 19:22 *Egypt turns to God in repentance;* Ac 9:32–35 *the people of Lydda and Sharon*

Leaders encouraged corporate repentance Ezr 10:1 *See also* 2Ki 23:1–7 *Josiah leads Judah in repentance;* 2Ch 15:8–15 *Asa leads Judah in repentance;* 2Ch 30:6–9 *Hezekiah leads Israel and Judah in repentance;* Ezr 10:10–12 *Following the exile, Ezra leads the Israelites in repentance;* Jnh 3:6–8 *The king of Nineveh leads the people in repentance.*

Corporate repentance within the church Rev 2:4–5 *See also* 2Co 7:9–11; Rev 2:14–16, 20–22; 3:3, 19–20

Symbols of repentance
1Ki 21:27; Jnh 3:5 *See also* 1Sa 7:6;

Ezr 8:21; Ne 9:1; Jer 36:9; Joel 1:13–14; 2:12

See also

3248 Holy Spirit, conviction	7733 leaders
5419 mourning	7757 preaching, effects
5952 sorrow	8148 revival
6626 conversion	8431 fasting, reasons
6742 sackcloth & ashes	8477 self-examination
7020 church, the	
7206 community	

6736
repentance, of God

See 1120 God, repentance of

6738
rescue

Deliverance from people or forces that are overwhelming. It implies a liberator with strength and wisdom to ensure true freedom. God's physical rescue of the Israelites points to the spiritual deliverance obtained by Jesus Christ.

When rescue is the only answer
Ps 35:10 *See also* Dt 22:27; 28:29; 1Sa 12:21; Isa 42:22; Da 8:4,7; Hos 5:14; Mic 5:8; Ro 7:24

God's power to rescue in times of need
Isa 41:10; 1Co 10:13; 2Co 12:9–10; Heb 13:6

God's people cry to him for rescue
Jdg 10:15 *See also* 1Sa 7:8; Ps 22:11; 35:17; 43:1; 69:13–14; 71:2; 107:19; 140:1; 142:6; 143:9; 144:7; Pr 24:11; Ro 15:31 *Paul's need for protection*

God's physical rescue of his people
From their enemies Ex 3:8 *See also* Jdg 6:14
The Israelites recognise God's rescue: Ex 18:10; 1Sa 11:13; 2Sa 22:17–20 pp Ps 18:16–19; 2Ki 13:5; 1Ch 11:14; 2Ch 20:15; 32:22; Ne 9:27; Est 4:14; Jer 20:13
2Ch 20:29 *Israel's enemies recognise God's rescue of his people.*

From trouble Da 6:27 *See also* Ge 45:7; Job 5:19; Ps 32:7; 91:14–15; 126:1; Pr 11:8; Joel 2:32; Jnh 2:10; 2Pe 2:9

From oppression Ps 72:12–14; 82:3–4

God's spiritual rescue of believers
From the guilt, penalty and power of sin Isa 61:1 *See also* Lk 4:18; Jer 29:11–14; Ro 8:21; 1Th 1:10; Jude 24

From the dominion of Satan Col 1:13 *See also* Mt 6:13; Lk 1:74; 9:1; 11:21–22; 13:16

From spiritual attack 2Ti 4:18

From fear and the fear of death
Heb 2:14–15 *See also* Ps 34:4; 1Co 15:54–57; 2Co 1:10; Rev 2:10

Rescuers sent by God
Ac 7:34 *Moses*
Judges: Jdg 3:9,15; 10:1

Examples of people rescued
Ac 7:10 *Joseph;* Jer 38:6–13 *Jeremiah Daniel and his friends:* Da 3:17,28; 6:21–23,27
Ac 12:11 *Peter*
Paul: Ac 23:27; 26:17; 2Ti 3:11

See also

1105 God, power of	6028 sin, deliverance from
1315 God as redeemer	6510 salvation
1320 God as Saviour	6634 deliverance
2324 Christ as Saviour	6660 freedom through Christ
4120 Satan	6720 redemption
5480 protection	9020 death

6740
returning to God

Scripture declares that all humanity has turned away from God, and must return to him. The term "repentance" is often used to refer to this process of returning to God and the inward and outward changes that it demands of people. Scripture also indicates that believers can wander away from God; they too must return to him.

All people have turned away from God
Isa 53:6; 64:6 *See also* Job 25:4; Jer 17:9; Jn 3:19; Ro 3:23

Wayward people must return to God
Isa 44:22; Hos 14:1; Zec 1:3 *See also* 2Ch 30:9; Ne 1:9; Job 22:23; Jer 24:7; La 3:40; Hos 6:1; 12:6; Joel 2:12

Means of returning to God
Realisation of estrangement from God La 3:40 *See also* 1Sa 24:5; 2Sa 24:10; 2Ch 6:29–31; Ro 3:20

Acknowledgment of sin Ps 51:3 *See also* Ex 9:27; Nu 14:39–40; 22:34; Jos 7:20; 1Sa 15:24–25; Mt 27:3–4

Sorrow for sin Ps 38:18 *See also* Ps 51:1–2; 2Co 7:9–10

A sense of guilt for sin 2Sa 24:10 *See also* Ezr 9:5–6; Ps 38:1–4,17–18; 51:3; Ac 2:37–38

Repentance Isa 1:27; Ac 2:37–38 *See also* Isa 59:20

A parable of returning to God
Lk 15:11–24

Examples of people returning to God
Israelites: Jdg 10:15; 2Ch 15:4
2Sa 12:13–14 *David;* Jnh 3:5–10 *the people of Nineveh*

See also
1055 God, grace & mercy	6636 drawing near to God
1070 God, joy of	6653 forgiveness, divine
5009 conscience	
5048 opportunities & salvation	6717 reconciliation, world to God
6624 confession of sin	6732 repentance
6626 conversion	8489 urgency
	9165 restoration

6742
sackcloth and ashes

Sackcloth is a coarse, black cloth made from goat's hair that was worn together with the burnt ashes of wood as a sign of mourning for personal and national disaster, as a sign of repentance and at times of prayer for deliverance.

Sackcloth and ashes worn as a sign of mourning for the dead
By Jacob for Joseph Ge 37:34

By David, Joab and the people for Abner 2Sa 3:31

Sackcloth and ashes worn as a sign of mourning for personal or national disaster
Job 16:15; 42:6 *See also* Est 4:1; La 2:10; Joel 1:8

Sackcloth and ashes worn as a sign of repentance for sin
By Ahab 1Ki 21:27

By David and the elders 1Ch 21:16

By the Israelites Ne 9:1

By the Ninevites and their king Jnh 3:5–9 *Even the animals were to wear sackcloth.*

By others Isa 15:3; Jer 49:3; Eze 27:31; Mt 11:21 pp Lk 10:13

Sackcloth and ashes worn at times of prayer for deliverance
By Hezekiah and his companions 2Ki 19:1–2

By Daniel Da 9:3

Sackcloth was worn in many different ways
1Ki 20:31; 2Ki 6:30; Isa 3:24; 58:5; Joel 1:13

Sackcloth used figuratively
Isa 50:3

See also
1670 symbols	6634 deliverance
4050 dust	6732 repentance
5145 clothing	8602 prayer
5419 mourning	

6744
sanctification

The process of becoming consecrated to God, which is an integral aspect of being a member of the people of

God. This process of being made holy through the work of the Holy Spirit ultimately rests upon the sacrificial death of Jesus Christ, which the OT anticipates and foreshadows.

6745
sanctification, nature and basis of

The process of renewal and consecration by which believers are made holy through the work of the Holy Spirit. Sanctification is the consequence of justification and is dependent upon a person being in a right relationship with God.

Sanctification is grounded in the holiness of God
God is holy Eze 39:7 *See also* Lev 22:32; Jos 24:19; Ps 30:4; Hos 11:9; Isa 6:3; Rev 6:10

God demands that his people should reflect his holiness Lev 19:2 *See also* Lev 11:44–45; 20:7–8; Heb 2:11; 1Pe 1:15–16

Sanctification is the will of God for his people 1Th 4:3 *See also* Eph 1:4; 2:10; 2Th 2:13; 1Pe 1:1–2

The basis for sanctification
God's election of his people 1Co 1:2; Eph 1:4–11; 1Th 5:9

The atoning death of Jesus Christ Heb 13:12 *See also* Ro 6:11; 7:4; 8:2; 1Co 1:30; 6:11; Eph 5:25–27; Heb 10:10–14; 1Pe 2:5

The grace of God Lk 1:69–75; Php 2:13; 2Ti 1:9; Heb 12:10

The work of the Holy Spirit Ro 15:16; 2Th 2:13; 1Pe 1:2

The word of God Jn 17:17; Eph 5:25–26; 2Ti 3:16

The need for sanctification
The universal sinfulness of humanity Isa 64:6 *See also* Job 15:14–15; Ps 51:5; Ro 5:12–19; Eph 2:3

Enslavement to evil can only be broken through the death of Jesus Christ Jn 8:34–36 *See also* Ro 6:16–18; 8:5–7; Eph 4:17–24

The need for renewal and growth 2Pe 3:18 *See also* Ro 12:1–2; Col 1:10; 1Th 4:3–6; Heb 6:1–3

The nature of sanctification
A process which has already been initiated 1Co 1:2; 6:11

A process of growth in holiness Ro 12:1–3; 2Co 3:18; Eph 4:15; 1Th 4:3–7; Heb 12:14; 1Pe 2:1–3; 2Pe 3:18

Consecration to God Ex 32:29; 1Ch 29:5; Pr 23:26; Ro 12:1

See also
1065 God, holiness of	8144 renewal
4018 life, spiritual	8154 righteousness
6670 grace & Holy Spirit	8240 ethics
7416 purification	8265 godliness
	8266 holiness
	8453 obedience

6746
sanctification, means and results of

Sanctification results from the renewing work of the Holy Spirit and leads to the renewal of believers and their being equipped for ministry in the world.

The means of sanctification
The work of the Holy Spirit 1Co 6:11 *See also* Ro 8:9–11; 15:15–16; 1Co 12:13; 2Co 1:21–22; Eph 1:13–14; 2Th 2:13; Tit 3:4–7; 1Pe 1:1–2

Meditation on the Scriptures 1Pe 2:2–3 *See also* Dt 11:18; Ps 119:12–18,48; 143:5–6; Jn 17:17; Col 3:16; Jas 1:25

The active pursuit of holiness and righteousness 1Ti 6:11–12 *See also* 2Co 7:1; Gal 5:24; Eph 4:1; 1Th 5:22; 1Pe 2:9–12; 3Jn 11

Obedience and self-denial Ro 6:19–22; 8:5–14; Gal 2:20; 5:16–24; 1Pe 2:11

Prayer Ps 145:18 *See also* Mt 7:7–8; Ac 4:31; 1Ti 4:4; Jas 5:16; Jude 20

Confession of sin 1Jn 1:9 *See also* Ne 1:6–9; Ps 32:5; 40:11–12; Pr 28:13; Isa 64:5–7; Jer 14:20–22; La 3:40

Obstacles to sanctification
A lack of faith Mt 5:13; Jn 15:6; 2Co 12:20–21; 1Ti 1:18–19

Rebellion against God Eze 18:24 *See also* Dt 32:15–18; Job 34:26; Isa 65:11–12; Gal 1:6–7; 5:7–9; Heb 12:15; Rev 2:4–5

Satanic temptation 1Pe 5:8–9 *See also* Ac 5:3; 2Co 2:8–11; Jas 4:7

Self-indulgence and greed Lk 12:15 *See also* Lk 21:34; Ro 13:13; 2Co 12:21; Eph 4:19

Yielding to sinful desires 1Pe 1:14 *See also* Mk 4:18–19; 1Co 10:6–8; 1Pe 2:11; 2Pe 2:14–18; 1Jn 2:16–17

The results of sanctification
Good works 2Co 9:8 *See also* Eph 2:10; Col 1:10; 3:15–17; 2Th 2:16–17; Heb 10:24–25; Jas 2:14–26

Becoming like Jesus Christ 1Pe 2:21 *See also* Jn 13:15; Ro 8:28–30; 1Co 11:1; 2Co 3:18; Gal 3:27; 1Jn 3:2–3

Becoming like God Mt 5:48; Eph 5:1–2; Col 1:21–22

Perfection Mt 5:48 *See also* 2Co 13:11; Col 1:28

Blamelessness in the sight of God 2Pe 3:14 *See also* Eph 1:4; Col 1:21–22; 1Th 5:23

Being able to see God Heb 12:14

See also
3233 Holy Spirit & sanctification	8114 discipleship
5902 maturity	8206 Christlikeness
6030 sin, avoidance	8211 commitment to world
6652 forgiveness	8218 consecration
6728 regeneration	8451 mortification
6754 union with Christ	8475 self-denial

6747
sanctification, and Holy Spirit
See 3233 Holy Spirit, and sanctification

6750
sin-bearer

A person or animal that acts in God's sight in a substitutionary capacity, to whom are transferred the sins of others, together with the corresponding penalty for those sins.

The principle of accountability necessitates a sin-bearer
All are held responsible for their own sin and its consequences Lev 5:17 *See also* Lev 5:1; 20:16–21; 24:15–16; Eze 18:19–20

Individuals and nations come under God's judgment for their sin Eze 4:4–6 *Ezekiel's behaviour foreshadowed God's judgment on the sin of Israel and Judah. See also* Eze 16:58; 18:4; Mt 11:21–24 pp Lk 10:12–15; Ro 1:18–32; 6:23

God's gracious provision of a sin-bearer in the OT
God takes away the sin of those who repent Isa 44:22 *See also* 2Sa 12:13; Ps 103:12; Zec 3:4

The sacrifice of an animal to remove sin Lev 5:5–6 *See also* Lev 4:1–35; 5:14–6:7

The Day of Atonement and the removal of sin Lev 16:8–10 *The sacrificial goat expiated the sins of the people in the sight of God; the driving away of the scapegoat into the desert symbolised the removal of the sin of the community. See also* Lev 16:15–19 *the sin offering;* Lev 16:20–22 *the scapegoat*

The function of the priests in the sin-bearing process
The priests were responsible for the sanctuary Nu 18:1–7

Strict regulations governed the performance of their service Lev 22:9 *See also* Ex 28:42–43; 30:17–21; Lev 16:3–4

The priests bore the sin of the people in a representative capacity Ex 28:36–38 *See also* Lev 10:17

Jesus Christ as sin-bearer
Jesus Christ bore the sins of the world on the cross Heb 9:28 *See also* Isa 53:4–6,10–12; Jn 1:29; Col 2:14; Heb 10:11–14; 1Pe 2:24; 1Jn 3:5

Jesus Christ's intercessory role as high priest 1Jn 2:1 *See also* Ro 8:34; Heb 7:25

See also
2306 Christ, high priest	6648 expiation
	6712 propitiation
2315 Christ as Lamb	6752 substitution
5051 responsibility	7440 scapegoat
6027 sin, remedy for	7766 priests
6614 atonement	

6752

substitution

Jesus Christ died as the substitute for sinful humanity, taking humanity's place on the cross.

OT images of substitution
Examples of substitution Ge 22:13 *See also* Nu 3:12–13,41,45; 8:18; 1Sa 17:9; 1Ki 20:42; La 5:7; Eze 4:4

Substitutes atoning for sin or acting as sin bearers Lev 1:4 *See also* Ex 28:38; Lev 16:21–22; 22:19–20

Anticipations of the substitutionary work of Jesus Christ Isa 53:4–6 *NT writers have interpreted the servant as Jesus Christ: see Mt 8:17 and 1Pe 2:23–25. See also* Ps 69:9

The substitutionary work of Jesus Christ
Jesus Christ died for believers Mk 10:45; Ro 5:6,8; 1Th 5:10 *See also* Jn 10:11; 11:50; Ro 14:15; 2Co 5:14; Gal 2:20; 3:13; 1Ti 2:6; Tit 2:14; Heb 2:9; 1Pe 2:21; 1Jn 3:16

Jesus Christ died for sin 1Pe 2:24; 3:18 *See also* 2Co 5:21; Heb 9:28

Jesus Christ's substitution as an example
2Co 5:15 *See also* 1Pe 2:21

Jesus Christ's substitution as an act of love
Jn 15:13 *See also* Ex 32:32; Ro 9:3

See also
2048 Christ, love of	2530 Christ, death of
2315 Christ as Lamb	6027 sin, remedy for
2339 Christ, example of	6750 sin-bearer
2410 cross, the	7390 Levites
	7440 scapegoat

6754

union with Christ

The sharing of believers in the life of Jesus Christ by faith, allowing them to share in all the benefits and riches that result from his person and work.

6755
union with Christ, nature of

The nature of the union of Jesus Christ with believers is explained using a number of central images. The NT stresses the reality, closeness and considerable benefits of this union.

A covenantal relationship
OT background Isa 54:5–8 *The marriage covenant is used to illustrate the intimacy of the relationship between God and his people. See also* Jer 3:14; 31:32; Hos 2:7,16

In the NT Eph 5:31–32

A relationship deepened through the incarnation
Jn 1:14 *See also* Ro 8:3; 2Co 5:21;

Gal 4:4; Php 2:7–8; 1Ti 3:16; Heb 2:14–18

A relationship personally entered through faith
Jn 3:16 *See also* Jn 1:12; 2:11; 7:38; Ac 16:31; Ro 3:22; 8:1; 10:9–10; 2Co 5:17; Gal 2:16

A relationship enriched through the sacraments
Baptism Ro 6:3–5; Gal 3:27 *See also* Mt 28:19; Ro 6:8; Col 2:11–12

The Lord's Supper Mt 26:26–28 pp Mk 14:22–24 pp Lk 22:17–20; 1Co 10:16; 11:23–29

A relationship that affects every aspect of life
1Co 6:17 *See also* Jn 15:1–8; 17:20–26; Ro 8:9–11; 1Co 6:19–20; Gal 2:20

It is a mysterious relationship
Col 1:27 *See also* Eph 5:32

See also
2369 Christ, responses to	7155 saints
2595 incarnation	7903 baptism
4018 life, spiritual	7933 Lord's Supper
6214 participation in Christ	8102 abiding in Christ
6676 justification	8206 Christlikeness
7115 children of God	8258 fruitfulness, spiritual

6756
union with Christ, significance of

The union between Jesus Christ and believers is the basis for all exhortation to faithful, holy living, as well as to sharing in all his benefits.

For the believer
Identification with Jesus Christ Mt 10:40 *See also* Mt 18:5; 25:40; Eph 1:1; Php 1:1

The experience of being in Christ Ro 8:10; 2Co 5:17 *See also* Jn 14:20; 2Co 13:5; Gal 2:20; Eph 3:14–19; Col 1:27

Conformity to Jesus Christ Col 3:1–4 *See also* Mt 16:24 pp Mk 8:34 pp Lk 9:23; Ro 6:5; 1Co 6:15–17; 2Co 4:10; Eph 2:6; Php 3:10–11; 1Pe 4:13; 1Jn 2:6,28; 3:24; 5:20

Righteousness in Christ Ro 4:23–25; 2Co 5:21 *See also* Ro 1:17; 1Co 1:30

Blessing in Christ Eph 1:3–14

For the church
In persecution Ac 9:3–5 *See also* Ac 22:6–8; 26:14

In service 1Co 12:12 *See also* Ro 12:4–8; 1Co 12:27; Eph 1:22–23; 5:28–30; Col 3:15

See also
1335 blessing	8114 discipleship
2048 Christ, love of	8154 righteousness
3278 Holy Spirit, indwelling	8209 commitment to Christ
6744 sanctification	8265 godliness
7024 church, nature of	8797 persecution, attitudes
8020 faith	8813 riches, spiritual

7000
God's people

7010
The church as the people of God

7020
church, the

The community of faithful believers, of whom Jesus Christ is the head, called out from the world to serve God down the ages. Scripture emphasises that the church is the body of Christ whose members are intended to be filled with the Holy Spirit. Scriptural understanding of the church is corporate, rather than solitary or individual.

This set of themes consists of the following:
7021 church, OT anticipations of
7022 church, and Jesus Christ
7023 church, and Holy Spirit
7024 church, nature and foundations of
7025 church, unity and fellowship of
7026 church, leadership of
7027 church, purpose and mission of
7028 church, life of

7021
church, OT anticipations of

As the people of God, the Christian church is continuous with Israel. The OT provides important anticipations of the church.

OT terms for the people of God
The descendants of Abraham 2Ch 20:7; Isa 41:8–9; Ro 4:16; Gal 3:7 *"children of Abraham" in the NT refers to those who, like Abraham, put their faith in God*

The saints
The term for "saints" means "set apart for God", "made holy", and is the most frequently used NT term for Christians: 1Sa 2:9; 2Ch 6:41 pp Ps 132:9; Ps 16:3; 31:23; Da 7:18

The assembly
"assembly" means "a community gathered together in response to God's call to serve and worship him". Its NT equivalents include the synagogue and the church: Ps 1:5; 107:32; 149:1

The scope of the OT people of God
Israel as God's people Ex 6:7 *See also* Ex 19:5–6; Lev 26:12; Jer 30:22; Eze 36:28; Hos 2:23

Not all Israelites are God's people Ro 9:6–7 *Even within Israel there are believers and unbelievers. See also* Ezr 9:8 *Those Israelites who believed were sometimes called "a remnant"*; Isa 1:9; 11:11,16; Jer 23:3; Eze 14:22; Mic 2:12

God's people included non-Israelites Isa 2:2–3 pp Mic 4:1–2 *See also* Ex 12:38, 48–49; Dt 31:12; Ru 4:10–11

7022

The formation of the OT people of God

God's people are formed through God's promises Ge 12:2 *See also* Ge 15:5; 17:5–6; 22:17–18; Ex 1:7

God's people are chosen and called Dt 7:6 *See also* 1Ch 16:13 pp Ps 105:6; Ps 33:12; Eze 20:5

God's people have been redeemed Dt 5:6 pp Ex 20:2 *See also* Ex 6:6; 19:4; Eze 20:6

God formed a covenant with his people Ex 24:8 *See also* Ex 19:5; 34:10,27; Dt 4:13; Jdg 2:1; Jer 31:31

OT images of the people of God

As God's bride Jer 2:2 *This OT image is taken up in the many references to Jesus Christ as the bridegroom and the church as his bride. See also* Isa 62:5; Hos 2:16,19–20; Eph 5:25–27; Rev 21:2

As God's vine Isa 5:1–7 *These passages form the background to Jesus Christ's claim to be the true vine (Jn 15:1):* Ps 80:8; Jer 2:21; Eze 17:5–6; 19:10; Hos 10:1

As God's flock Ps 95:7 *See also* Ps 74:1; 77:20; 100:3; Isa 40:11; Zec 9:16; Mt 26:31; Zec 13:7; Lk 12:32; Jn 10:16 *The NT church is also described as a flock:* Ac 20:28–29; 1Pe 5:2–3

As God's inheritance Dt 4:20 *See also* Ps 28:9; 33:12; Isa 19:25; Mal 3:17

As God's family Am 3:1–2 *See also* Ex 4:22–23 *Israel was sometimes called God's "firstborn son" as well as his children;* Dt 1:31; 32:6; Ps 103:13; Isa 1:2; 30:9; Hos 11:1; Mal 2:10

Requirements of the people of God

To obey God's word Dt 5:1 *See also* Ex 24:3; Dt 6:1–3; 13:4; Jos 1:7; 1Sa 15:22

To remember their redemption Dt 5:15 *See also* Dt 7:18; 15:15; 16:12; Ps 105:5

To commemorate their redemption Ex 12:25–27 *The focus of Israel's commemoration of their redemption was the Passover, which is one of the ceremonies lying behind the Lord's Supper. See also* Nu 9:2–3; Dt 16:1; Lk 22:14–20

To love God wholeheartedly Dt 6:5 *See also* Dt 10:12; 11:1; 19:9; Jos 23:11

The marks of the people of God

Circumcision as a mark of God's people Ge 17:10–14; Lev 12:3 *Circumcision had to be internal as well as external, as a sign of spiritual commitment to God:* Dt 10:16; 30:6; Jer 4:4; Ro 2:27; Col 2:11

The presence of God Ex 25:8; 33:15–16; 40:35; Nu 10:33–36; 2Ch 5:14

See also
1193 glory, revelation of	7130 flock, God's
1345 covenant	7135 Israel, people of God
5075 Abraham	7141 people of God, OT
5213 assembly	
5703 inheritance	7145 remnant
6720 redemption	7334 circumcision
7115 children of God	

7022

church, and Jesus Christ

See 2212 Jesus Christ, head of the church

7023

church, and Holy Spirit

See 3275 Holy Spirit, in the church

7024

church, nature and foundations of

The church is the people called by God, who are united by their faith in Christ and by their common life in him. Various descriptions and metaphors emphasise the continuity between the people of God in the OT and NT.

NT images of the church

The body of Christ Ro 12:4–5 *See also* 1Co 12:12,27; Eph 3:6; 5:23; Col 1:18,24; 2:19; 3:15

God's building or temple 1Co 3:16–17 *See also* 1Co 3:10; 2Co 6:16; Eph 2:21–22; Heb 3:6; 10:21; 1Pe 2:5

A plant or vine Jn 15:1–8 *See also* Ro 11:17–24; 1Co 3:6–8

Jesus Christ's flock Jn 10:14–16 *See also* Mt 25:33; Lk 12:32; Ac 20:28–29; 1Pe 5:2–4

The bride of Christ Rev 21:2 *See also* Eph 5:25–27,31–32; Rev 19:7; 22:17

God's household or family Eph 2:19 *See also* Jn 8:35–36; Gal 6:10; Eph 3:15; 1Ti 3:15; Heb 2:11; 1Pe 2:17; 4:17

NT descriptions of the church

Emphasising continuity with the OT church
Abraham's offspring: Ro 4:16; Gal 3:7,29
The people of God: Ro 9:25; 2Co 6:16; Heb 13:12; 1Pe 2:9–10
The new Jerusalem: Gal 4:26; Heb 12:22; Rev 3:12; 21:2,9–10
Gal 6:16 *the Israel of God*

Emphasising God's call and authority in the church
Sons of God: Mt 5:9; Jn 1:12; Ro 8:15–16; 2Co 6:18; Gal 3:26; 4:5–6; 1Jn 3:10
The elect: Mt 24:22; Ro 11:7; 2Ti 2:10; 1Pe 1:1
Heirs of God and God's inheritance: Ro 8:17; Gal 3:29; 4:7; Tit 3:7; Heb 1:14; 6:17; 1Pe 1:4
A priesthood: 1Pe 2:5,9; Rev 1:6; 5:10; 20:6

Descriptions applied to the church by outsiders
Followers of the Way: Ac 9:2; 19:9,23; 22:4; 24:14
Ac 11:26 *Christians;* Ac 24:5 *"the Nazarene sect" means people belonging to Jesus the "Nazarene" (Mt 2:23)*

Descriptions used by Christians
The believers. All these titles are seldom in the singular, emphasising the

corporateness of Christian life: Ac 1:15; 2:44; 5:12; Gal 6:10; 1Ti 4:12; 1Pe 2:17
The disciples: Ac 6:1–2; 9:19; 11:26; 14:22; 20:1
The "saints" is the most frequently used NT term for Christians. It means "set apart for God", "made holy": Ro 1:7; 15:25; 1Co 6:1; 14:33; Eph 1:1; Php 4:21; Col 1:12; Jude 3

Other NT descriptions of the church 1Ti 3:15 *the pillar and foundation of the truth;* Heb 12:23 *The church of the firstborn: "the firstborn" is plural, referring to Christians as those born again through their union with Christ, who is the firstborn.*

The foundation of the church

Jesus Christ as the church's foundation-stone 1Co 3:11 *See also* Mt 7:24–25; 21:42 pp Mk 12:10 pp Lk 20:17; Ac 4:11; Eph 2:20; 1Pe 2:6; Isa 28:16; 1Pe 2:7; Ps 118:22

Apostles and prophets as founders of the church Eph 2:19–20 *See also* Mt 16:18–19; Rev 21:14

The church as God's people

A people chosen by God 1Pe 2:9 *See also* Jn 15:16; Ro 8:33; Eph 1:4; Col 3:12; 2Th 2:13; Jas 2:5; 1Pe 1:2

A people called by God Ro 1:6 *See also* Ac 2:39; 1Co 1:2,9; Gal 1:6; 2Th 2:14; 2Ti 1:9; Jude 1

A people loved by God 1Pe 2:10 *See also* Eph 2:1–5; Tit 3:4–7

God's covenant people Heb 8:8–10 *See also* Ro 11:27; Isa 59:20–21; Heb 10:16; Jer 31:31–33

See also
3278 Holy Spirit, indwelling	7110 body of Christ
5269 cornerstone	7142 people of God, NT
5317 foundation	7155 saints
5659 bride	7382 house of God
6638 election	7412 priesthood
7105 believers	7620 disciples

7025

church, unity and fellowship of

The church is one in essence, because it is founded on one gospel, united to one Lord and indwelt by one Spirit. Its unity is under constant threat because of the tendency to division that is inherent in fallen humanity, and needs to be continually maintained and actively expressed in fellowship.

The unity of the church

The church is one Ro 12:5 *See also* 1Co 12:12,20; Eph 4:25

The church transcends all barriers Col 3:11 *See also* Jn 10:16; Ac 10:28–29,47; 15:8–9; Gal 3:28; Eph 2:14–16; 3:6 *The great divide threatening the first Christians was between Jew and Gentile, but the church was able to unite the two into one body in Christ.*

The church's unity reflects the unity within the Trinity Eph 4:4–6 *The unity of the church is built around the persons of* *the Trinity: one Spirit, one Lord, one Father. See also* Jn 17:11; Ro 3:29–30; 10:12–13; Gal 3:27–28

The church's unity is the work of the Trinity Eph 2:16–18 *See also* Jn 11:52; Ac 10:45–47; 1Co 12:13; Eph 2:22; 4:3

The purpose of the church's unity
To lead others to faith Jn 17:23 *See also* Jn 17:21

To lead believers to maturity Eph 4:13

The nature of the church's unity
Php 2:1–2 *Emphasis is placed on an inner unity of mind and spirit rather than external uniformity. See also* 2Co 13:11; Php 1:27; Col 2:2

Appeals for unity in the church
Eph 4:3 *See also* Ro 12:10; 15:5,7; 1Co 12:25; Col 3:14; 1Pe 3:8

The church's unity is expressed in fellowship
Fellowship with God 1Co 1:9 *See also* 2Co 13:14; Php 2:1; 2Pe 1:4; 1Jn 1:3,6–7

Fellowship expressed by meeting together Ac 2:46 *See also* Ac 2:1,42; 5:12; 6:2; 1Co 14:26; Heb 10:25

Fellowship expressed through sharing resources Ac 2:44–45 *See also* Ac 4:32,34–37; 11:27–30; Ro 15:26; 1Co 16:1–2; 2Co 8:2–5,13–14; 9:13; Php 4:14–18

Fellowship through suffering Rev 1:9 *See also* Ro 8:17; 2Co 1:7; Php 3:10; 4:14; Heb 10:33–34; 13:3

Fellowship through shared spiritual blessings 1Co 9:23 *See also* Ro 11:17; Php 1:7; 2Th 2:14; 1Pe 5:1; Jude 3

Specific actions which express fellowship and unity in the church
Sharing in the Lord's Supper 1Co 10:16–17 *See also* Ac 2:46; 20:7; 1Co 11:33

Baptism as an expression of unity Eph 4:4–6 *See also* 1Co 12:13

Extending hospitality Ac 28:7; Ro 12:13; 16:23; 1Ti 5:10; Tit 1:8; 1Pe 4:9; 3Jn 8

Greeting one another Ac 18:27; Ro 16:3–16; 1Co 16:19–20; Col 4:10; Phm 17

Welcoming former opponents Ac 9:26–27; Gal 2:9; 2Co 2:5–8

Divisions in the church
Causes of division in the NT church
Personal ambition: Mk 9:34; 10:35–41 pp Mt 20:20–24
Ethnic tension: Ac 6:1
Differences of opinion: Ac 15:37–40; Php 4:2
Troublesome heretical leaders: Ro 16:17; Jude 19
Partisan spirit: 1Co 1:11–12; 3:3–4
1Co 6:1–6 *litigation and disputes*
Greed: 1Co 11:18,20–21; Jas 4:1–3

Warnings against divisions in the church 1Co 1:10 *See also* Ro 12:16; 16:17; 2Co 12:20; Eph 4:31; Jas 4:11

Acceptable differences in the church
In secondary matters of conscience, Christians are to respect rather than judge

each other. These things need not impair the essential unity that is in Christ: Ro 14:1–3,5–6; 1Co 8:9–13
In varieties of spiritual gifts: 1Co 12:4–6,14–25; Gal 2:7

Necessary divisions in the church
Between the true gospel and heretical alternatives: 2Co 11:2–6,13–15; Gal 1:6–9; Col 2:8,16–19; 1Ti 4:1–6; 1Jn 2:18–19; 2Jn 9–11; Jude 18–20
Between those truly committed to Jesus Christ, and those apparently part of the church but living sinful lives: 1Co 5:9–10; 2Th 3:6; 1Ti 6:3–5; 2Ti 3:2–9; 2Pe 1:20–21; 2:1–3; Rev 2:20,24; 3:1,4
Over essential gospel principles: Ac 15:2,5–6,19; Gal 2:11

See also

1170 God, unity of	7921 fellowship
5008 conscience	8210 commitment to
5834 disagreement	God's people
6754 union with	8292 love
Christ	8341 separation
7030 unity	8766 heresies
7206 community	
7918 excomm-	
unication	

7026
church, leadership of

Jesus Christ is the absolute head of the church. He sets leaders in the church to enable the whole church to grow into maturity. Christ's authority in the church is acknowledged more by the church's obedience to God than through any particular form of government.

Jesus Christ alone is head of the church
Col 1:18 *See also* Mt 23:8–10; Eph 1:22; 4:15; 5:23; Col 2:19; Heb 3:3

The Holy Spirit directs the church
Ac 13:2 *See also* Ac 15:28; 16:6–7; 20:28; Ro 8:14; 1Co 12:11; Rev 2:7,11

The appointment of leaders in the church
God calls and equips leaders Eph 4:11 *See also* Mt 16:18; Ac 1:24–26; 9:15–16; 20:28; 26:16–18; 1Co 12:28; Gal 1:15–17

Delegated leadership Ac 6:3–6; 14:23; Tit 1:5

The appointment of apostles
Mk 3:13–19 pp Mt 10:1–4 pp Lk 6:12–16
As founders of the church: 1Co 9:1–2; 2Co 3:3; Eph 2:20; Rev 21:14
As leaders of the church: Ac 2:42; 15:6,22–23; 1Th 2:6; 2Pe 3:2; Jude 17

Prophets as leaders Ac 15:32 *Judas and Silas were leaders in the Jerusalem church (Ac 15:22). See also* Ac 11:27–30; 13:1–2; Ro 12:6 *The role of prophets as leaders is distinct from the gift of prophecy, which was in principle available to all;* 1Co 12:28; 14:29–30; Eph 3:5

Evangelists as leaders Ac 21:8 *See also* Eph 4:11; 2Ti 4:5

Pastors and teachers as leaders
Ac 20:28 *See also* Jn 21:15–17; Ac 13:1; Ro 12:7; 1Co 12:28; 1Ti 3:2; Tit 1:9;

Jas 3:1; 1Pe 5:2 *Pastors are also called "shepherds".*

Elders as leaders 1Ti 3:1 *"Elder" and "overseer" or "bishop" are more or less interchangeable. See also* Ac 11:30; 14:23; 15:2,22; 20:17; 1Ti 5:17; Tit 1:5; Jas 5:14; 2Jn 1

Deacons as leaders Php 1:1 *"Deacon" means "one who serves". See also* Ac 6:5–6; 1Ti 3:8

Qualifications for church leadership
The first apostles were witnesses of Jesus Christ's life and resurrection: Ac 1:21–22; 10:41; 1Co 9:1–2; 15:7–8; 2Pe 1:16
Qualifications for elders and deacons: Ac 6:3; 1Ti 3:1–12; 5:17; Tit 1:6–9; 1Pe 5:1–4

Responsibilities of church leaders
To preach the gospel Ro 1:15; 1Co 1:17; Gal 2:8; Eph 3:8; 1Ti 2:7

To teach sound doctrine 1Ti 4:6,13; 5:17; Heb 13:7

To give direction in church life Ac 15:2,6,22–23; 16:4; 20:28–31; 1Ti 5:17; 1Pe 5:2

To be an example in loving service Mt 20:26–28 pp Mk 10:43–45; Mk 9:35; Jn 13:13–15; Heb 13:7; 1Pe 5:3

To train and appoint other leaders Ac 14:23; 1Ti 4:14; 2Ti 2:2; Tit 1:5

To pray for the sick Jas 5:14

To exercise discipline in the church 2Co 13:10; 1Th 5:12; 1Ti 1:20; 5:20; Tit 3:10; 3Jn 10

The church's responsibilities to its leaders
To respect and submit to its leaders Ac 16:4; 1Th 5:12–13; 1Ti 5:19; Heb 13:17

To pray for its leaders Eph 6:19; 1Th 5:25

To support its leaders financially 1Co 9:7–14; Php 4:15–19; 1Ti 5:17–18

The corporate government of the church
In choosing leaders Ac 6:3–6

In implementing decisions Ac 15:22–29

In building up the church Ro 12:4–8; 1Co 12:4–12,27; Eph 4:3,7–16; 1Pe 4:10–11

In discerning true and false teachings 1Jn 4:1–3; 2Jn 10; Rev 2:2

In exercising discipline Mt 18:15–20; 1Co 5:4–5; 2Co 2:6–8; 2Th 3:14–15

The structure of the church
The pattern of church life Ac 2:42 *See also* Ac 2:46; 5:42

The house church Ac 1:13–14; 12:12; 16:40; Ro 16:5; 1Co 16:19; Col 4:15; Phm 2

The local church Ac 13:1; Ro 16:1; 1Co 1:2 *It is unknown whether there were subdivisions of the church in towns such as Corinth;* 1Th 1:1

Churches in a region Ac 9:31; 15:41; 1Co 16:1; 2Co 8:1; Gal 1:2,22; Rev 1:4 *Normally the NT speaks of "churches" in an area rather than of a unified regional structure.*

The universal church Mt 16:18
Referring to the local as well as the universal church: 1Co 12:28; Eph 1:22; 3:10; 5:25

See also

2212 Christ, head of church	7715 deacons
3035 Holy Spirit, presence of	7720 elders in the church
5217 authority in church	7734 leaders, spiritual
5326 government	7784 shepherd
5745 women	7797 teaching
7706 apostles	7939 ministry
	8342 servanthood

7027
church, purpose and mission of

The church is called to praise and glorify God, to establish Jesus Christ's kingdom, and to proclaim the gospel throughout the world.

God's purposes for the church
To praise God 1Pe 2:9 *See also*
Eph 1:5–6,11–12,14; Heb 13:15;
1Pe 2:5

To share God's glory Ro 8:29–30 *See also* Mt 13:43; Jn 17:24; Ro 9:23;
1Co 2:7; Php 3:21; Col 3:4; 2Th 2:14;
Rev 2:26–27; 3:4–5,21

God will build his church Mt 16:18–19 *See also* Mt 27:40 pp Mk 15:29;
Jn 2:19–22; 1Co 3:9; Eph 2:21–22;
4:11–13; Heb 3:3–6; 1Pe 2:5

To challenge Satan's dominion
Eph 3:10–11 *"rulers and authorities in the heavenly realms" refers to the powers of evil. See also* Mt 16:18; Eph 6:12;
1Jn 2:14

To go into the world in mission
2Co 5:18 *See also* Mt 5:13–16;
28:19–20; Mk 16:15; Lk 24:48;
Jn 20:21; Ac 1:8; Php 2:15–16; Col 1:27

The church's mission
To preach the gospel to the world
Mk 13:10 pp Mt 24:14 *See also*
Mt 28:19; Lk 24:47; Jn 10:16; Ac 13:47

To do good to all Gal 6:10 *See also*
Mt 25:37–40; Lk 6:35; Ac 9:36;
Eph 2:10; 1Ti 6:18; Jas 1:27; 1Pe 2:12

Images of the church's mission
Mt 5:13–16; Jn 15:5–8
A fruitful plant in a fruitless world:
Mt 7:18–19; Ro 7:4; Eph 5:9–10;
Php 1:11; Col 1:6,10; Jas 3:17
Salt in an insipid world: Mk 9:50;
Lk 14:34–35
Light in a dark world: Ro 13:12–14;
Eph 5:8; Php 2:15; 1Th 5:5–6

The growth of the church
Numerical growth among the first Christians Ac 11:21 *See also* Ac 2:41,47;
4:4; 5:14; 6:1,7; 9:31,42; 11:24; 12:24;
13:49; 16:5; 17:4; 18:8; 19:20

The church is to grow to maturity
Eph 4:12–13 *See also* Php 1:6; 3:13–15;
2Th 1:3

Aspects of growth
Growth in character: 2Co 9:10; 1Th 3:12
Growth into Christ: Eph 4:15; Col 1:10;
2Pe 3:18

Heb 6:1 *growth in understanding*

Prayers for the growth of the church
Eph 3:14–19 *See also* Eph 1:17–19;
Php 1:9–11; Col 1:9–12; 1Th 3:11–13;
2Th 1:11–12

Visions of the church's final destiny
Rev 7:9–10 *John's vision of the church in glory. See also* Mt 24:31; Jn 10:16;
Eph 1:10; 1Th 4:16–17; Heb 12:22–23;
Rev 21:2

See also

1045 God, glory of	8256 fruitfulness
1115 God, purpose of	8347 spiritual growth
2375 kingdom of God	8424 evangelism
5902 maturity	8442 good works
6716 reconciliation	8482 spiritual warfare
7754 preaching	
7953 mission of church	

7028
church, life of

The church lives its life in union with Christ and in the power of the Holy Spirit. It is called to mutual love, holy living, and to worship.

The church lives its life in union with Christ
The church lives in Christ and Christ lives in the church 1Co 1:30 *See also*
Mt 18:20; Jn 15:5; 17:21; 1Co 8:6;
Gal 2:20; Col 1:27; 2:6; 1Jn 4:13

Believers are united with Christ in baptism Gal 3:27 *See also* Ac 2:38; 19:5;
Ro 6:3–4; Col 2:12

The church lives its life in the power of the Holy Spirit
The church lives in the Spirit, and the Spirit lives in the church Ro 8:9–11 *The indwelling Spirit is identified with the presence of Jesus Christ. See also* 1Co 3:16;
Gal 5:16,25; Eph 2:22; 2Ti 1:14;
1Jn 2:27

The Spirit is given to the church
Ac 1:4–5 *See also* Jn 20:22; Ac 2:4; 15:8;
Ro 7:6; 15:16; 1Co 6:11; Gal 3:3;
1Pe 1:1–2

The Spirit seals the church Eph 1:13
See also 2Co 1:22; 5:5; Eph 4:30

The Spirit guides the church Rev 2:7
See also Ac 8:29; 10:19; 11:12; 13:2;
20:23; 21:4

The Spirit teaches the church 1Co 2:13
See also Jn 16:13; Eph 1:17

The Spirit sanctifies the church
Ro 15:16 *See also* 1Co 6:11; 2Th 2:13;
1Pe 1:2

The Spirit endows the church with gifts
1Co 12:7 *See also* Ro 12:6–8;
1Co 12:8–11,28; Eph 4:11

The church as a fellowship
As a fellowship of mutual love 1Th 5:11
See also Ro 15:2; 1Co 14:12; Gal 6:10;
1Th 4:18; Heb 10:25

As a fellowship of ordinary people
1Co 1:26–27 *See also* Lk 6:20; Jas 2:5

The distinctiveness of the church
The church as a chosen people 1Pe 2:9
See also Eph 1:4; Col 3:12

The church as a holy people Heb 12:14
See also Ro 11:16; 15:16; 1Co 1:2;
Eph 2:21; 5:3; 1Th 3:13; Heb 2:11;
1Pe 1:15–16; 2Pe 3:11

The church as a people set apart
2Co 7:1 *The repeated call to be separate from evil is the practical outworking of the church's sanctification. See also*
1Co 5:9–12; 2Co 6:14–18; Eph 5:7;
2Th 3:14; 2Ti 3:1–5; Tit 3:10–11

The church as a heavenly people
Jn 17:14–16 *See also* Lk 10:20;
1Co 15:48; Gal 4:26; Eph 2:6; Php 3:20;
Col 3:1–4; Heb 11:16; 12:22–23

The church and worship
Praise in the life of the church
Heb 13:15 *See also* Ac 2:47; 1Co 14:26;
Eph 5:18–20; Php 3:3; Col 3:16

Prayer in the life of the church
Corporate prayer in the church: Ac 1:14;
2:42; 4:24–31; 12:5,12; 20:36; 21:5
Prayer for church leaders: Ro 15:30;
Eph 6:19–20; Col 4:2–4; 1Th 5:25;
2Th 3:1; Heb 13:18
Eph 6:18 *prayer for all Christians;*
1Ti 2:1–2 *prayer for all, including secular leaders*

Baptism in the life of the church
Ac 2:38; 1Co 1:13; Gal 3:26–27;
Eph 4:4–5; Col 2:11–12; 1Pe 3:21

The Lord's Supper in the life of the church
1Co 10:16–17 *The breaking of bread was central to the church's worship and a vital expression of its fellowship. See also*
Ac 2:42,46; 20:7; 1Co 10:21; 11:17–34

The suffering of the church
Suffering persecution from a hostile world Jn 16:33 *See also* Mt 5:10–12;
1Co 4:12; 2Co 4:9; 1Th 3:4; 2Ti 3:12

Sharing in the sufferings of Christ
Php 3:10 *See also* Jn 15:20; Ro 8:17;
2Co 4:10–11; 1Pe 4:13

Suffering as the road to glory Jas 1:12
See also Ro 5:3; 8:18; 2Co 4:17;
2Ti 2:11–12; 1Pe 5:10

See also

1432 prophecy in NT	8266 holiness
3275 Holy Spirit in the church	8413 edification
4018 life, spiritual	8619 prayer in church
7404 ordinances	8622 worship
7957 sacraments	8664 praise
7966 spiritual gifts	8676 thanksgiving

7030

unity

The bringing together of separate or fragmented parts into a unified whole. It is God's ultimate goal to unite the whole of creation; his desire for unity is evident, too, in the life of his people. God himself acts as a unity in all his works.

7031
unity, God's goal of

God's purpose is to bring together and reconcile to himself the whole of creation. This desire for unity is a reflection of the unity within the Godhead; it is expressed in marriage, and demonstrated in the fellowship of the church.

Unity is a reflection of God's person
Dt 6:4; Jn 17:22 See also Mk 12:29,32; Jn 1:1; 17:11; Gal 3:20; 1Jn 5:7

Alienation is a result of sin
Alienation from God Ge 3:8,23–24; Isa 59:2; Eze 28:16; Jas 4:4

Alienation from one another Ge 4:7–9,23–24; 6:11; Jas 4:1–2; Jude 19

God's purpose in unity
To bring together all peoples Ps 133:1; Eph 1:9–10

To unite all peoples under his rule Zec 14:9 See also Ge 49:10; Ps 72:8–11; Isa 2:2–4 pp Mic 4:1–3; Jn 10:16; Php 2:9–11; Rev 11:15

To unite all peoples in worship Isa 19:23–25 See also Ps 86:9; Isa 56:6–8; Zec 8:20–23; 14:16; Mk 11:17; Rev 15:4

To bring reconciliation between Jew and Gentile Eph 2:11–19 See also Isa 14:1; Ro 10:12; Gal 3:28; Col 3:11

To bring reconciliation among his people Jer 50:4 See also Isa 11:10–13; Eze 37:21–24; Mic 2:12; Mt 5:24; Php 4:2

To reconcile humanity to himself Col 1:19–22 See also Ro 5:10–11; 2Co 5:18–19; Heb 10:19–20

Expressions of unity brought by God
Unity between husband and wife Ge 2:24 See also Mal 2:15; Mt 19:5–6 pp Mk 10:7–8; 1Co 6:16; 7:4,10–11

Marriage as an expression of unity between God and his people Jer 2:2; Eph 5:31–32 See also Isa 54:5; Jer 31:32; Hos 2:16; Jn 3:29; Rev 19:7; 21:2,9

Unity within the church Jn 17:21 See also Ac 2:1; 4:32; 1Co 1:10; 10:17; 12:12; Eph 4:13

See also
1170 God, unity of
1510 Trinity, the
2230 Messiah, coming of
5712 marriage, God & his people
5729 one flesh
6109 alienation
6716 reconciliation
9145 Messianic age

7032
unity, of God's people

A distinguishing characteristic of God's people, which derives from their common relationship with God, and is expressed in commitment to one another, mutual concern, concerted action and harmony within the believing community.

Unity in a common relationship with God
As children of God Mal 2:10 See also Ps 133:1; Mt 23:8–9; Ro 8:15–17; Col 1:2,12; 1Jn 5:1

As the people of God 1Pe 2:9–10 See also Ex 6:7; 19:5–6; Dt 7:6; 2Sa 7:24 pp 1Ch 17:22; Mal 3:17; Eph 1:14; Heb 11:25

Unity in a common union with Christ
1Co 10:16–17; 12:27 See also Jn 11:52; Ro 12:4–5; 1Co 12:12; Gal 3:26–28; Eph 2:17–19; 4:16; Col 3:11

Unity through common receiving of the Holy Spirit
1Co 12:13 See also Isa 34:16; Ac 10:45–47; 1Co 12:4–11; 2Co 13:14; Eph 2:22; Heb 6:4

Unity in a common faith
Eph 4:4–6 See also Eph 4:13; Tit 1:4; 1Jn 1:1–3; Jude 3

Expressions of unity among God's people
Commitment to one another 1Sa 18:1–4; Ru 1:16–17; 1Th 2:8

Sharing possessions Ac 4:32 See also Lk 3:11; Ac 2:44–45; Ro 12:13; 15:27; Gal 6:6; 2Ti 2:6

Giving support Jos 22:3 See also Dt 3:18; Heb 10:24–25

Sharing troubles 2Co 1:7; Php 4:14

Unity expressed in agreement with one another
Living in harmony Ps 133:1; Eph 4:3; 1Pe 3:8 See also Ro 12:16; 14:17; 1Co 10:24; Eph 4:25; Php 4:2; Col 1:12–14; 3:15

United in purpose Php 1:27 See also Jdg 20:11; 1Sa 14:7; Ezr 3:8–10; Ne 4:6; Mt 18:19–20

Of one mind 1Co 1:10 See also 2Ch 30:12; Php 2:2

Unity expressed in worshipping together
Ro 15:5–6 See also Ps 22:22; 68:26; 122:1; 1Co 14:26; Heb 2:12

Unity marks out God's people
Jn 17:21–23 See also Jn 13:34–35

See also
5783 agreement
6700 peace
7025 church, unity
7140 people of God
7921 fellowship
7933 Lord's Supper
8210 commitment to God's people
8292 love

7033
unity, of God
See 1170 God, unity of

Titles of the people of God

believers

Those who have faith in God. After Pentecost, the term came to be used specifically to refer to Christians, that is, to those who believe and trust in God, as he has made himself known through Jesus Christ. The NT stresses that Jesus Christ brings the faith of OT believers to perfection and to its proper fulfilment.

Believers as those who have faith in God
1Ki 18:3–4 See also Jn 4:39–42; Ac 16:15; Jas 2:1

OT believers looked forward to the NT faith
Heb 11:13 See also Heb 11:39; 1Pe 1:10–12

The church is referred to as the believers
Ac 5:12 See also Ac 1:15; 2:44; 4:32; 9:41; 1Ti 4:12

In the early church a distinction was sometimes made between Jewish and Gentile believers
Ac 15:23 See also Ac 10:45; 11:1–3; 15:5; 21:20–25

The term believer is synonymous with Christian
1Co 7:12–13 See also Ac 15:2; 16:1; 1Co 6:5; 14:22; 2Co 6:14–15; 1Th 1:7; 1Ti 5:16

Believers are members of God's family
Gal 6:10 See also 1Ti 6:2; 1Pe 2:17

See also
4019 life, believers' experience
5078 Abraham, significance
6257 unbelievers
6610 adoption, descriptions
6705 peace, experience
7020 church, the
7120 Christians
7155 saints
7512 Gentiles, in NT
7620 disciples
8020 faith
9315 resurrection of believers

body of Christ

The term refers both to the physical body of Jesus Christ, which was broken on the cross in order that redemption might be accomplished through him, and to the church.

Jesus Christ's physical body

His birth Jn 1:14 *See also* Ro 1:3; Gal 4:4; 1Ti 3:16

His bodily needs Mt 8:24 pp Mk 4:38 pp Lk 8:23; Mk 11:12 pp Mt 21:18; Lk 4:2 pp Mt 4:2; Jn 4:6; 19:28

His physical suffering Mt 27:26 pp Mk 15:15 pp Jn 19:1 *See also* Mt 27:28–30 pp Mk 15:17–19 pp Jn 19:2–3; Lk 22:44

His real physical death Jn 19:31–37 *See also* Mt 27:35 pp Mk 15:24–25 pp Lk 23:33 pp Jn 19:23; Ac 2:23

His burial Mk 15:43–46 pp Mt 27:58–60 pp Lk 23:52–53 pp Jn 19:38–42

His physical resurrection Lk 24:37–43 *See also* Mt 28:9; Jn 20:19–20,27

The body of Christ symbolised in the Lord's Supper

Mt 26:26 pp Mk 14:22 pp Lk 22:19 *See also* Jn 6:51–58; 1Co 10:16; 11:23–30

The church as the body of Christ

Believers as members of the body of Christ 1Co 12:27 *See also* Ro 12:4–5; 1Co 12:12; Eph 4:4; Col 1:24

Jesus Christ as the head of the body Col 1:18 *See also* Eph 1:22; 5:23

Jesus Christ's resurrection body is a new temple Jn 2:19–22 *See also* Eph 2:19–22

Life in the body of Christ

Baptism is into the body of Christ 1Co 12:13 *See also* Gal 3:27

Believers receive spiritual life through the body of Christ Col 2:19 *See also* 1Co 10:16–17; Eph 4:15–16

Believers care for each other in the body of Christ 1Co 12:25–26 *See also* Eph 4:25; 5:29–30; Col 3:15

Believers have different gifts in the body of Christ Ro 12:4–5 *See also* Ro 12:6–8; 1Co 12:12–31; Eph 4:11–13

See also
2212 Christ, head of the church	7020 church, the
2530 Christ, death of	7105 believers
2560 Christ, resurrection	7921 fellowship
3275 Holy Spirit in the church	7933 Lord's Supper
6754 union with Christ	7957 sacraments
	7966 spiritual gifts
	8347 spiritual growth

7115

children of God

Israel and the church are the chief objects of God's fatherly love. People become God's children through faith and are then encouraged by Scripture to imitate their heavenly Father in their daily living.

Human beings as God's children
Ge 1:27; 6:2,4; Ps 82:6; Mal 2:10; Lk 3:38; Eph 3:14

Israel as God's children
Hos 11:1 *See also* Ex 4:22–23; Ps 73:15; 80:15; Isa 43:6; 63:16; Jer 31:20; Ro 9:4

Israel as God's rebellious children
Isa 1:2 *See also* Dt 32:5,20; Isa 30:1,9; Jer 3:4–5; 4:22; Eze 20:21

God's son
Promises of God's son 2Sa 7:12–14 pp 1Ch 17:11–13 *These words referred originally to David's son, Solomon, but in the NT they are applied to Jesus Christ. See also* 1Ch 22:10; 28:6; Ps 2:7; 89:26–27

Jesus Christ as God's son Heb 1:5 *See also* Mt 3:17 pp Mk 1:11 pp Lk 3:22; Lk 1:32; Ac 13:33; Ro 1:4

Jesus Christ's followers as God's children
Mt 9:2 pp Mk 2:5; Mt 9:22 pp Mk 5:34 pp Lk 8:48

Becoming God's children through faith in Jesus Christ
Becoming God's children by new birth Jn 1:12–13 *See also* Jn 12:36; Ro 9:8; Gal 3:26; 1Jn 5:1

Becoming God's children by adoption Eph 1:5 *See also* Ro 8:23 *This adoption will be fully realised in the future;* Gal 4:4–5

Becoming God's children by the Spirit Ro 8:15 *See also* Gal 4:6

God's dealings with his children
God loves his children 1Jn 3:1 *See also* Dt 1:31; Ps 103:13; Eph 5:1

God disciplines his children Dt 8:5 *See also* Pr 3:11–12; Heb 12:5–10

God does not abandon his children Hos 1:10 *God had previously (Hos 1:9) announced his judgment that Israel would be his people no longer. See also* Dt 31:6,8; Jos 1:5; Heb 13:5; Jer 31:9; Mal 3:17; Lk 15:24; Ro 9:26

Behaviour expected of God's children
God's children imitate their heavenly Father Eph 5:1 *See also* Mt 5:48; Lk 6:36

God's children live by the Father's standards Php 2:15 *See also* Lev 11:44–45; Dt 14:1–2; Mt 5:9,44–45 pp Lk 6:35–36; Ro 8:14; 2Co 6:17–18; 1Pe 1:14–16; 1Jn 3:10

The privileges and blessings of being God's children
God's children are eternally secure Jn 8:35 *See also* Ro 8:16,21; 1Jn 5:19

The needs of God's children are always supplied Mt 7:9–11 pp Lk 11:11–13 *See also* Mt 6:25–32 pp Lk 12:22–30 *needs for the present life;* Lk 20:36; Ro 8:23 *promises for the life to come*

God's children have a sure inheritance Rev 21:7 *See also* Jer 3:19; Ro 8:17–19; Gal 4:7; 1Jn 3:2

See also
1040 God, fatherhood	6658 freedom
1085 God, love of	7140 people of God
2218 Christ, Son of God	8020 faith
	8104 assurance
5701 heir	8230 discipline
6608 adoption	8266 holiness
	8449 imitating

7120

Christians

Those who belong to Jesus Christ; other designations in Scripture are believers, disciples and the children of God. Originally a nickname, the term is only used three times in the Bible.

The use of the term
Disciples first called Christians Ac 11:26

Agrippa not persuaded Ac 26:28

Suffering as a Christian 1Pe 4:16

Other biblical designations of Christians
Christians described as believers Ac 2:44 *See also* Ac 4:32; 5:12; Gal 6:10; Jas 2:1; 1Pe 2:17

Christians described as brothers Heb 2:11 *See also* Ac 15:3; Col 1:2; 2Th 2:13; Rev 19:10

Christians described as disciples Mt 28:19 *See also* Ac 6:1,7; 13:52; 14:22

Christians described as children of God 1Jn 3:1 *See also* Jn 1:12; Ro 8:16,21; Gal 3:26–4:7

Christians described as the church Ac 12:5 *See also* Ac 5:11; 8:1; 15:3; Ro 16:5; 2Co 1:1; Col 1:18,24; 1Ti 3:15

Christians described as the elect 1Pe 1:1 *See also* Mt 24:22; Ro 11:7; 2Ti 2:10; Tit 1:1

Christians described as heirs of God Ro 8:17 *See also* Gal 3:29; 4:7; Eph 3:6; 1Pe 3:7

Christians described as members of God's household Eph 2:19 *See also* 1Ti 3:15

Christians described as the people of God 1Pe 2:10 *See also* Eph 2:19; Col 3:12; Rev 21:3

Christians described as saints Ro 1:7 *See also* Ro 15:25; 1Co 6:2; 2Co 1:1; 13:13; Eph 1:15,18; 1Ti 5:10; Jude 3

See also
5661 brothers	7155 saints
7020 church, the	7620 disciples
7105 believers	8120 following Christ
7115 children of God	
7125 elect, the	8168 way, the
7140 people of God	8206 Christlikeness

7125

elect, the

Those chosen by God, entirely of his grace, for the special privilege of experiencing salvation.

Israel as the elect
Dt 7:6 *See also* Ex 19:4–6; Ps 105:6,43; 135:4; Isa 41:8–9; 43:10; 44:1–2; 45:4; Am 3:2; Ro 11:1–18

The church as the elect
Eph 1:4–5; 1Pe 1:1–2 *See also* Jn 10:4–5; 1Th 1:4–5; 1Pe 2:9; 5:13 *The Greek words translated "chosen lady" in 2Jn 1 could be a personal name, but it is*

more likely that this phrase and the phrase translated "chosen sister" in 2Jn 13 refer to local churches: 2Jn 1,13

Individuals chosen by God as his elect

Abraham Ge 18:18–19

Moses Ps 106:23

David 1Ki 8:16; Ps 89:3–4

Rufus Ro 16:13

God's elect enjoy his presence and favour

The elect are assured of the presence of God Heb 13:5–6 *See also* Jos 1:1–9; Ps 23:1–6

The elect are assured of the protection of God Mt 24:22 pp Mk 13:20 *See also* Ro 8:33–39; Rev 17:14

The elect are assured of a place in the world to come Mk 13:26–27 pp Mt 24:30–31 *See also* Isa 65:17–25; Jn 14:1–3; Jas 2:5; 2Pe 1:10–11

The elect are assured of justice Lk 18:7–8

Responsibilities of the elect

Col 3:12–17 *See also* Dt 14:1–2

See also
1020 God, all-knowing	6708 predestination
6620 calling	7020 church, the
6638 election	7135 Israel, people of God

flock, God's

God's people are frequently portrayed as a flock of sheep, for whom he cares with the tenderness and concern of a loving shepherd.

The divine shepherd

God portrayed as a shepherd Ps 23:1 *See also* Ps 80:1

Jesus Christ portrayed as a shepherd Jn 10:11 *See also* Mt 26:31; Zec 13:7

God's people are his flock

Israel and Judah depicted as God's flock Ps 77:20 *See also* Ps 78:52; Isa 63:11; Jer 13:17; 31:10; 50:17; Mic 2:12; 7:14

NT believers depicted as God's flock Ac 20:28 *See also* Lk 12:32; Jn 10:14–16

God cares for his flock

Isa 40:11 *See also* Ps 95:6–7; Eze 34:11–16; Mic 5:4; Zec 9:16

God judges his flock

Eze 34:17–24 *See also* Zec 11:7–16

The under-shepherds of the flock

Many of Israel's leaders exploited God's flock Eze 34:2–3 *See also* Jer 10:21; Zec 11:4–5; Jn 10:12–13

God will judge the corrupt shepherds Eze 34:7–10 *See also* Jer 23:1–5; 25:34–36; Zec 10:3; 11:17

Church leaders are to care for God's flock 1Pe 5:2–3 *See also* Ac 20:28–29

See also
1220 God as shepherd	5611 watchman
2330 Christ as shepherd	7020 church, the
	7140 people of God
4684 sheep	7733 leaders
5293 defence, human	7784 shepherd

Israel, as the people of God

God called Israel out of Egypt to be his own treasured possession and his covenant faithfulness with them is maintained, despite their persistent disobedience.

God's election of Israel

The nation was founded upon God's promises to the patriarchs Ge 12:1–3 *See also* Ge 17:1–8; 35:9–13

Israel as God's chosen possession 1Ki 8:53 *See also* Ex 19:3–6; Dt 7:6; 32:7–12; Ps 135:3–4

God redeemed Israel from Egypt Ex 6:6–7 *See also* Ex 3:7–10; 2Sa 7:22–24 pp 1Ch 17:20–22

God enters into a special covenant relationship with Israel Ex 24:3–8

Israel's privileged status within the covenant Ro 9:4–5 *See also* Ro 3:1–2; Php 3:4–6

Israel's disobedience to the covenant

Israel provoked God in the wilderness Ps 78:40–41 *See also* Ex 32:1–10; Nu 11:1–6; 14:1–4

Israel's unfaithfulness in the promised land Isa 1:4 *See also* Jdg 2:10–13; Jer 11:9–10; Eze 20:27–28

Israel exiled for her sins 2Ki 18:11–12 *See also* 2Ki 25:8–12 pp Jer 39:8–10; 52:12–16

God's promise to restore Israel

God's promise not to abandon Israel completely Dt 4:31 *See also* Lev 26:44–45; Isa 6:11–13 *Though Israel will be destroyed, a holy remnant will be left;* Jer 31:35–37

God's promise to bring Israel back to the land Jer 30:3 *See also* Isa 43:5–7; Eze 37:11–14

God's promise to reunite Israel Jer 3:18 *See also* Eze 37:15–23; Hos 1:10–11

The promise of a restored relationship between Israel and God Jer 31:31–34 *See also* Isa 40:1–2; Eze 36:24–28

Israel returns from exile Ezr 1:1–5 pp 2Ch 36:22–23

Jesus Christ, the Saviour of Israel

Jesus Christ's ministry was specifically to the nation of Israel Mt 10:5–6 *See also* Mt 15:21–28 pp Mk 7:24–30

Jesus accepts the title "Christ" (Messiah), God's anointed deliverer for Israel Mt 16:16–17 pp Mk 8:29 pp Lk 9:20 *Although Jesus accepted the title "Messiah" (Christ), he did not fulfil*

contemporary Israelite hopes of a political deliverer.

Jesus Christ declares to Israel the good news of God's reign Mk 1:14–15 *Jesus Christ takes up Isaiah's message of good news, that God is coming in sovereign power to restore Israel (see Isa 40:9–10, 52:7). See also* Mt 4:23; 9:35; Lk 8:1

Israel's rejection of Jesus Christ

Israel warned that rejection of Christ means exclusion from the kingdom Mt 8:11–12 *See also* Mt 21:33–46 pp Mk 12:1–12 pp Lk 20:9–19; Mt 22:1–10 pp Lk 14:16–24; Lk 13:28–30

Israel's rejection of the gospel Ro 9:30–10:4 *See also* Ac 28:24–28; Isa 6:9–10; 1Th 2:14–16

God's faithfulness to Israel maintained

Membership of the true Israel is based on God's election, not merely on physical descent from Abraham Ro 9:6–18

A remnant of Israel has been elected by grace Ro 11:1–12

Paul declares that "all Israel" will be saved Isa 59:20–21; Ro 11:25–32 *The phrase "all Israel" is interpreted as either: (1) the total number of the elect (either Jews, or Jews and Gentiles) of every generation, or (2) the great majority of Jews of the final generation who will be saved when Jesus Christ returns.*

The new Israel

The church as the new Israel Gal 6:15–16; Php 3:3 *See also* 1Pe 2:9–10

The church described as the 12 tribes of Israel Jas 1:1 *See also* Rev 7:4–8 *Some see this as a reference to members of actual Jewish tribes, but others see it as symbolic of all the faithful believers who live through the time of tribulation;* Rev 21:12 *The number 12 emphasises the continuity of the NT church and the OT people of God.*

The apostles as the 12 leaders of the new Israel Mt 19:28 *See also* Lk 22:28–30; Rev 21:14

See also
1345 covenant	7233 Israel, northern kingdom
2206 Jesus, the Christ	7236 Israel, united kingdom
6638 election	7505 Jews, the
7020 church, the	7510 Gentiles
7140 people of God	9165 restoration
7145 remnant	
7215 exile, the	

people of God

Those called out to belong to God and serve him in his world. God called Israel to be his people in the OT, anticipating the calling of the church in the NT.

7141
people of God, in OT

The OT relates how God called Israel to be his people.

Chosen by God
Dt 7:6 See also Dt 4:37; 1Ki 3:8; Isa 41:8–9; 43:1; 44:1–2; Eze 20:5

Loved by God
Dt 7:7–8 See also Dt 4:37; 23:5; 1Ki 10:9; Ps 44:3

Sanctified by God
Dt 28:9 See also Ex 19:6; 22:31; Lev 11:44–45; Dt 14:2; Isa 62:12

God's possession
Ex 19:5 See also Dt 14:2; 26:18; Ps 135:4; Isa 43:1; Mal 3:17

God's inheritance
Dt 4:20 See also Dt 9:26,29; Ps 28:9; 33:12; 68:9; 74:2; Jer 10:16; Joel 3:2; Mic 7:14

God's servants
Dt 32:36 See also Ne 1:6,11; Ps 135:14; Isa 41:8–9

God's children
Ex 4:22 See also Dt 32:6; Isa 63:16; 64:8; Jer 3:19; 31:9; Hos 11:1

God's sheep
Ps 95:6–7; Eze 34:11–16 See also Ps 28:9; 74:1; 79:13; 80:1; 100:3; Isa 40:11; Jer 23:1; 31:10

See also
1030 God, compassion	6744 sanctification
1040 God, fatherhood	7021 church, OT anticipations
1220 God as shepherd	7125 elect, the
1345 covenant	7135 Israel, people of God
6640 election, privileges	7511 Gentiles, in OT
	8270 holiness, set apart

7142
people of God, in NT

The NT relates how the Christian church is the new people of God, assuming all the privileges and responsibilities of Israel in the OT, but with a universal mission to all the world, rather than any one nation.

NT believers are God's people
Ro 9:22–26 See also 1Pe 2:10; 2Co 9:12; Eph 5:3; Rev 22:21

Believers are the true children of Abraham
Gal 3:29 See also Mt 3:9 pp Lk 3:8; Ro 4:16–18; Gal 3:6–9; 4:22–31; 1Pe 3:6

The church is the people of God
God's chosen people 1Pe 2:9 See also Col 3:12; 1Th 1:4; 2Th 2:13

God's children Jn 1:12–13 See also Gal 3:26; 4:4–6; Eph 1:5; Php 2:14–15

God's possession Eph 1:13–14; Tit 2:14; 1Pe 2:9

God's servants 1Pe 2:16; Rev 1:1; 2:20

The temple of God 1Pe 2:5 See also Eph 2:19–22; Heb 3:6

The body of Christ Eph 1:22–23 See also Ro 12:4–5; 1Co 12:27; Eph 4:11–13

Jesus Christ sends believers into all the world
Ac 1:8 See also Mt 28:19; Mk 13:10; 16:15; Lk 24:47; Jn 17:20–24

See also
1040 God, fatherhood	6639 election to salvation
2212 Christ, head of church	6728 regeneration
4836 light & people of God	7024 church, nature of
5078 Abraham, significance	7105 believers
6608 adoption	7115 children of God
	7120 Christians
	7512 Gentiles, in NT

7145
remnant

A small group of people who remain faithful to God, despite widespread unbelief or faithlessness around them. God preserves a remnant in order to ensure a renewed and restored people in the future.

God preserves a remnant of his people
Noah and his family Ge 7:23 See also Ge 6:7–8,18; 7:1,7

Joseph and the sons of Israel Ge 45:7 See also Ge 50:20

Seven thousand faithful in Israel 1Ki 19:18

Survivors of Assyria's invasion of Judah 2Ki 19:4 pp Isa 37:4 See also 2Ki 18:13

Survivors of the destruction of Israel
People from the northern kingdom of Israel who had moved to Judah and so escaped its destruction by Assyria: 2Ch 11:14; 15:9; 31:6; 34:9

Judah as the remnant of God's people 2Ki 17:18
After the fall of the northern capital, Samaria, Judah was regarded as the remnant of all Israel: 2Ki 21:14; 2Ch 34:21

Survivors of the fall of Jerusalem
Those taken as exiles into Babylon: 2Ki 25:11; 2Ch 36:20
Those left behind in Judah: 2Ki 25:12 pp Jer 39:10; 2Ki 25:22–23; Jer 40:11–12,15; 42:2; 43:5

Those who returned after the exile Ezr 9:8 See also Ezr 2:1–2; 9:13; Ne 1:2; Hag 1:12–14

Those waiting for Jesus Christ's coming Lk 2:25,38; Jn 1:12

The remnant as the few who escape judgment
Dt 4:27 See also Isa 10:22; Ro 9:27; Jer 6:9; 44:14,28; Eze 5:12

Ezekiel prays that Israel's destruction will not be total: Eze 9:8; 11:13 Eze 17:21; Am 3:12; 5:3

God's promise of hope and restoration
Hope for a remnant seen in the coming of the Messiah Isa 11:1 See also Isa 6:13; Jer 23:5; Zec 3:8

God's promise that survivors will remain Isa 4:2–3 See also Isa 1:9; Ro 9:29; Isa 17:6; 37:31–32 pp 2Ki 19:30–31; Eze 14:22; Joel 2:32

Themes associated with the remnant
The land restored to the remnant of God's people Isa 27:12–13; Zep 2:7–10; Zec 8:6–12; 10:9

A second exodus Isa 4:5–6; 10:26; 11:11,15–16; 31:5; Jer 16:14–15

Restoration of the people Isa 10:20–21 See also Isa 11:12; 28:5; 35:8–10; 46:3–4; Jer 31:7
Jer 23:3 See also Mic 2:12

Further promises associated with the remnant
The promise of future hope Isa 60:21–22; 61:4–6; Joel 3:1; Mic 4:6–7; 5:7–9

God's promise of forgiveness to the remnant Jer 50:20 See also Isa 33:24; Jer 31:34; 33:7–8; Mic 7:18

A renewed relationship with God Jer 24:5–7; 32:37–40; Zep 3:12–17

The need for faithful obedience Isa 1:19; Jer 42:6–10; 44:7–8; Ezr 9:14

The remnant as heirs of God's new covenant
Jer 31:2 The promise of the new covenant is made to the surviving remnant of Israel; Jer 31:31–33

A faithful remnant among the Jews Ro 11:5 See also Lk 1:16; 12:32; Ro 11:7,15,23,25–26; Jas 1:1

A faithful remnant from among the Gentiles Isa 56:6–8; Zec 14:16; Jn 10:16 Jesus Christ's other sheep are believing Gentiles who will be gathered with the believers of Israel; Ac 15:17; Am 9:12; Ro 11:17; Eph 3:6

God's new Israel includes all believers Mt 19:28 pp Lk 22:30; Gal 6:16; 1Pe 1:1; 2:9

Other references to a surviving remnant
Og, king of Bashan, only survivor of the Rephaites: Dt 3:11; Jos 13:12 Jdg 20:46–47 survivors from the tribe of Benjamin; 2Ch 18:16 the scattered remains of Israel's army under Ahab; Isa 16:4 fugitives from Moab; Isa 21:16–17 few survivors from Kedar

See also
1352 covenant, the new	7223 exodus, significance
6653 forgiveness, divine	8145 renewal, people of God
7135 Israel, people of God	9165 restoration
7140 people of God	9210 judgment, God's
7215 exile, the	

7150

righteous, the

The designation, especially in the OT, of those who live and act in accordance with God's commands.

Characteristics of the righteous
Pr 20:7 *See also* Ps 37:21;
Pr 10:11,20–21,31–32; 12:5; 13:5;
15:28; 21:25–26; 29:7,27; Mt 25:31–40

God's dealings with the righteous
He loves them Ps 146:8 *See also*
Ge 18:20–32

He protects them Pr 18:10 *See also*
Ps 1:5–6; 37:16–17,39; 55:22; Pr 10:29;
11:8; 12:21

He provides for them Pr 10:3 *See also*
Ps 37:25; Pr 13:25

He blesses them Ps 5:12 *See also*
Job 36:7; Pr 3:33; 10:6–7

He hears their petitions 1Pe 3:12 *See
also* Ps 34:17; Pr 15:29

The faith of the righteous
Hab 2:4 *See also* Ro 1:17; Gal 3:11;
Heb 10:38

The righteous are secure
Pr 12:3 *See also* Pr 10:30; 11:28; 12:7;
28:1

The righteous can be corrupted
Eze 18:24 *See also* Ex 23:8; Dt 16:19;
Ps 125:3; Eze 3:20; 33:12–13

The oppression of the righteous
Ps 37:12–13 *See also* Ps 31:17–18;
94:21; La 4:11–13; Am 2:6–7; 5:12;
Hab 1:4

**The equality, in human terms, of
the righteous and the wicked**
Mt 5:45 *See also* Ecc 8:12–14; 9:1–2

The reward of the righteous
Pr 10:16 *See also* Ps 37:29; 58:10–11;
92:12–15; Pr 10:6–7,28; 11:23,30–31;
13:21–22; 15:6; Isa 3:10

The death of the righteous
Isa 57:1 *See also* Ps 116:15; Pr 14:32

The hope of the righteous
Lk 14:12–14 *See also* Ps 17:14–15;
Pr 14:32; Mal 3:17–18; Ac 24:14–16

See also
5498 reward	8154 righteousness
5942 security	8672 striving with
6744 sanctification	God
7105 believers	8734 evil
7155 saints	9020 death
8114 discipleship	9310 resurrection

7155

saints

The people of God, especially in relation to their being set apart from the world to serve him. Believers are called upon to lead holy lives worthy of their calling.

Saints are set apart for God
1Co 1:2 *To be holy is to be set apart. The
same Greek word is used in the NT for both
"holy" and, in the plural, "saints". See
also* Dt 7:6; 26:19; Ps 4:3; Ro 1:7;
Heb 10:10

**They are members of God's covenant
people** Ps 85:8 *See also* 2Ch 6:41
pp Ps 132:9; Ps 30:4; 34:9; 50:5; 79:1–2;
132:16

They are believers Ro 16:15 *See also*
Ro 8:27; 15:31; Php 4:21–22; Col 1:26;
1Ti 5:10

They make up the church 1Co 14:33
See also Ac 9:32; Eph 1:1; Col 1:2

**Saints are to live lives worthy of
their calling**
Eph 5:3–4 *See also* Ro 16:2; Eph 4:1–3;
2Pe 3:11; Rev 13:10; 14:12

**Saints have responsibility for one
another**
Ro 12:13 *See also* Ro 15:25–26; 1Co 6:1;
16:1–2,15; 2Co 9:1–2,12

**Saints have spiritual union with
Jesus Christ**
Heb 2:11 *See also* Jn 15:4–5; 1Co 1:2;
Eph 1:1; Php 1:1; 4:21; Col 1:2;
2Th 1:10

Saints may be persecuted
Jn 15:19 *See also* Da 7:21,25; 8:24;
Jn 17:14; Ac 9:13; 26:10; Rev 13:7; 16:6

Saints are precious in God's sight
Ps 16:3 *See also* Ps 116:15; 147:11;
149:4; Eph 1:18

They enjoy God's protection 1Sa 2:9
See also Ps 31:23; 37:28; 97:10; Pr 2:8

They experience exaltation Da 7:18 *See
also* Ps 149:6–9; Da 7:22,27; Mt 27:52;
1Co 6:2; Col 1:12

See also
1345 covenant	7140 people of God
5480 protection	7925 fellowship
5705 inheritance,	among
spiritual	believers
6620 calling	8206 Christlikeness
6744 sanctification	8266 holiness
7020 church, the	8794 persecution
7105 believers	

7160

servants of the Lord

A description of individuals, groups, and the nation of Israel. Isaiah portrays a unique servant whom the NT identifies as Jesus Christ.

**Individuals as servants of the
Lord**
The patriarchs as servants of the Lord
Ex 32:13 *See also* Ge 18:3; 32:10;
Dt 9:27; 1Ch 16:13; Ps 105:6

Moses as the servant of the Lord
Ex 14:31 *See also* Nu 12:7–8; Dt 34:5;
Jos 1:1–2; Ne 1:7–8; Mal 4:4

Other leaders as servants of the Lord
Nu 14:24; Jos 5:14; 24:29; Jdg 2:8; 15:18

David as the servant of the Lord
Ps 89:20 *See also* 1Sa 23:11; 2Sa 7:5
pp 1Ch 17:4; 1Ki 14:8

Other kings as servants of the Lord
1Ki 3:7–9; 2Ch 32:16

Individual prophets as servants of the
Lord 1Ki 14:18; 18:36; 2Ki 14:25;
Isa 20:3

Paul as the servant of the Lord
Ac 27:23 *See also* Ro 1:1; Eph 3:1

Other individual believers as servants
of the Lord 1Sa 1:11; Job 1:8; 2:3;
42:7–8; Hag 2:23; Lk 1:38,48; 2:29;
Jas 1:1; 2Pe 1:1; Jude 1; Rev 1:1

Pagan kings as servants of the Lord
Jer 25:9 *See also* Isa 45:1; Jer 43:10

Groups of servants of the Lord
The people of Israel as the Lord's
servants Isa 41:8–9 *See also*
Lev 25:42,55; Ne 1:6,10; Isa 43:10;
Jer 30:10–11 pp Jer 46:27–28; Lk 1:54

Failure of the people of Israel to serve
the Lord Isa 42:19 *See also* Jdg 10:6;
1Sa 12:10; Ne 9:35; Mal 3:14

Priests as the Lord's servants
Ex 28:1,41; Lev 7:35; Nu 18:7; Heb 8:5

Levites as the Lord's servants Dt 18:7;
1Ch 23:28–31; Ezr 6:18; Eze 44:11

Prophets as the Lord's servants
Jer 7:25 *See also* Jer 29:19; 44:4;
Eze 38:17; Da 9:6; Am 3:7; Zec 1:6;
Mt 21:34–36 pp Mk 12:2–5
pp Lk 20:10–12; Rev 10:7

Other nations as the Lord's servants
Ps 72:11 *See also* Isa 56:6; Zep 3:9

**The Lord's servants recognised
as such by pagans**
Da 3:26 *See also* Da 6:16,20; Ac 16:17

The unique servant of the Lord
Isaiah's vision of this servant
Isa 42:1–4 *See also* Isa 49:1–6; 50:4–9;
52:13–53:12

Jesus Christ's life identifies him as the
Lord's servant Mt 12:17–21 *See also*
Mt 8:16–17; 20:28 pp Mk 10:45;
Mt 26:28 pp Mk 14:24; Mt 27:12–14
pp Mk 15:2–5; Mk 9:12; Jn 1:29; 12:38

NT leaders proclaim Jesus Christ as
the Lord's servant Ac 8:30–35 *See also*
Ac 3:13,26; Ro 10:16; 15:21; Php 2:6–8;
1Pe 2:21–25

The Lord's service
An exclusive service Dt 6:13 *See also*
Dt 10:12,20; Jos 22:5; 24:14–24;
Mt 6:24 pp Lk 16:13

Serving the Lord as he requires
Col 3:23–24 *See also* Ps 2:11; Lk 1:74;
12:35–36; Ro 7:6; Eph 6:7; 2Ti 2:24;
1Pe 2:16

The Lord's care for his servants
Ps 35:27 *See also* Isa 54:17; 65:13–15;
Da 3:28

The reward of the Lord's servants
Rev 22:3–5 *See also* Lk 12:37–38; 19:17;
Jn 12:26; 15:14–15

See also
2230 Messiah,	7446 slavery
coming of	7510 Gentiles
2327 Christ as	7768 priests, OT
servant	function
5500 reward, God's	7939 ministry
people	8344 servanthood in
5520 servants	believers

History of God's people in OT

ark, Noah's

The craft built at God's command by Noah and his family as a means of escape from the flood. The ark is seen as corresponding to the redemption offered to believers through Jesus Christ.

The building of the ark
The command to build Ge 6:14 *See also* Ge 6:1–13,15–16

Its purpose for Noah and his family Ge 6:17–18

Its purpose for the animals Ge 6:19 *See also* Ge 6:20–22

The ark and the flood
Noah obeyed God Ge 7:5 *See also* Ge 7:1–4,6–16

The ark served its purpose Ge 7:17 *See also* Ge 7:18–24; 8:1–19; 9:1–17

The significance of the ark elsewhere in Scripture
An instance of judgment Mt 24:38–39 pp Lk 17:26–27 *Judgment clearly divides humanity into the saved and the lost. See also* 2Pe 2:5

An example of faith Heb 11:7 *Noah took God at his word in circumstances which must have appeared ridiculous.*

A symbol of salvation 1Pe 3:20–21 *The link between the ark and baptism is in the twin ideas of water and salvation.*

See also
1347 covenant with Noah	5106 Noah
1680 types	6510 salvation
4845 rainbow	7227 flood, the
	7903 baptism

community

A group, small or large, of people. In Scripture it denotes the people of Israel, especially in pre-monarchic times and particularly during the period of the wilderness wanderings.

The community of Israel in the wilderness
Ex 16:1 *See also* Ex 17:1; Nu 13:26; 20:22,29

Moses and Aaron communicate God's instructions to the wilderness community Ex 35:1,4,20; Nu 10:2–3

Rebellion, discontent and grumbling within the wilderness community Ex 16:2–10; Nu 14:1–2,27,35–36; 16:8–33,41; 20:1–4; 27:14

Responsibilities towards one another within the wilderness community Lev 10:6; Nu 1:53

Leaders and officials, under Moses, of the wilderness community Ex 16:22

See also Ex 34:31; Nu 26:9; 31:13,26–27; 32:1–5

Censuses of the wilderness community Nu 1:1–3 *See also* Ex 38:25; Nu 1:17–19; 4:34

The community identity of pre-monarchic Israel
The importance of a community identity in matters of worship Lev 4:13–21 *See also* Ex 12:3–19,47–49; Lev 16:5,32–33; Nu 3:6–7; 8:9–11,20–21; 15:22–26; 19:9

The importance of a community in legal matters Lev 20:1–5 *See also* Nu 15:15

God promised that the patriarchs' descendants would be a community of nations Ge 35:11 *See also* Ge 28:3; 48:4

The families of the priests and Levites described as a community 2Ch 31:14–18

The Jews referred to as a community in NT times Ac 25:24

See also
1115 God, purpose of	7435 sacrifice, in OT
4299 wilderness	7505 Jews, the
5213 assembly	7719 elders as leaders
5249 census	9414 heaven, community of redeemed
7020 church, the	
7141 people of God, OT	

congregation

A group of people gathered or called together for a purpose. In Scripture a congregation refers particularly to the Israelites gathered for worship; it is also used of Christians in the NT.

The congregation of the Israelites
For the giving of the Ten Commandments Ex 19:17; Dt 5:22

For hearing God's word Ne 8:1–9 *See also* Dt 5:1; Ne 8:18; 9:1–3

For praising God Ps 22:22 *See also* Ps 40:9–10; 68:26; Heb 2:12

To make a sin offering for the sin of the community Lev 4:13–14; Nu 15:24

For the ordination of priests and Levites Lev 8:3–4; Nu 8:9

For census, retribution and major events Lev 24:14; Nu 1:18; Jos 18:1; Jdg 20:1; 1Sa 10:17

Exclusion from the assembly Dt 23:1–8

In the NT
Jewish congregations in the synagogue Lk 4:20 *See also* Ac 13:5,14–15; 14:1

Christian congregations Ac 2:46–47 *See also* Ac 5:12; 11:26; 20:7; 1Co 14:33–34; Jas 2:2

See also
5213 assembly	7505 Jews, the
7025 church, unity	7610 Council of Jerusalem
7120 Christians	
7140 people of God	8622 worship
7456 synagogue	

exile

A period of absence from one's homeland, often imposed as a form of punishment. The OT regards Israel's exile in Babylon as a form of divine punishment for past sin and as an opportunity for renewal and rededication.

Exile commanded by God for his purposes
Ge 12:1 *See also* Ge 11:4,8–9; Ps 44:11; Zec 2:6; Mt 2:13–15

Exile imposed as a form of punishment
On individuals Ge 3:23 *See also* Ge 17:14; Lev 7:20; 18:29; 19:8; 20:17; Dt 28:36; 1Sa 12:25; 2Ki 24:15–16; 2Ch 36:4,10; Zec 5:3

On Israel Lev 26:33 *See also* Dt 4:25–27; 28:36,64; Isa 6:11–13; 11:12; 25:11; 1Ch 5:26; 2Ch 36:20; Isa 5:13; Jer 25:8–11; 27:10; Am 5:27

On other nations Am 1:5,15; 5:5

Exile through military defeat
2Ki 18:9–11 *See also* 2Ki 15:29; 24:16; 1Ch 8:6; Job 30:8; Jer 50:17; Joel 3:1–2; Mic 1:16

Exile through personal choice
To escape danger Ex 2:15 *See also* Ge 16:6–8; 35:6–7; 1Sa 19:18; 21:10; 2Sa 13:38–39; Rev 1:9

To escape natural disaster Ge 46:5–6 *See also* Ge 26:1–3; Ru 1:1

To support friends 2Sa 15:19–21

At the advice of others Ge 27:42–45; 1Sa 20:12–13

Those exiled because of their faith
1Pe 1:1 *See also* Ac 8:1; 11:19; Heb 11:8–9,14–15,27,38; Jas 1:1

God does not intend exile to be permanent
2Sa 14:14 *See also* Ge 46:4; Nu 35:25; 2Ch 36:21; Isa 51:11; 61:4–6; 63:17; Jer 16:14–15; 29:10–14; 30:3; 32:37

See also
4215 Babylon	7215 exile, the
5246 captivity	7446 slavery
5290 defeat	7530 foreigners
5482 punishment	8794 persecution
5607 warfare, examples	9165 restoration
6112 banishment	9210 judgment, God's

exile, the

The period of Israel's captivity in foreign lands, under Assyria in the eighth century B.C., and under

Babylon in the sixth. Such exile is regarded by biblical writers as a judgment upon Israel for her folly and unfaithfulness. It is also seen as a time of repentance and renewal leading eventually to restoration.

7216
exile, in Assyria

People of the northern kingdom of Israel were taken into exile after their defeat by the Assyrians and the fall of Samaria. The Israelites were transported to Assyria in stages, starting with the upper strata of society. They were replaced by immigrants from other parts of the Assyrian empire. The Israelites had to share their land with these people when they returned from exile after the downfall of the Assyrians. This was the origin of the Samaritan people.

Israel was warned of coming punishment for her misconduct
God warned his people Dt 28:62–66; Isa 5:12–13 See also Lev 26:27–28; Dt 28:49–57; Isa 10:5–6; Hos 8:1–8; 13:16; Am 3:2,11; 5:27; 9:4,7–9; Mic 1:6–7

Some prophecies referred specifically to Assyria as God's instrument
Isa 8:4–7; 10:5–6 See also Hos 8:9–10; Na 1:11–13

Warning through Solomon
1Ki 8:46–50

The history of Israel's capture
Tiglath-Pileser III invades Israel in 743 B.C. but withdraws upon payment of slave-indemnity 2Ki 15:19–20

A further attack takes place ten years later 2Ki 15:29; 1Ch 5:26

Shalmaneser V comes on the scene 2Ki 17:3–6 After a three-year siege, Samaria falls in 722 B.C.

Israelites are removed to Assyria under Sargon II 2Ki 17:5–7 See also 2Ki 17:23

Non-Israelites are settled in Israel 2Ki 17:24

God sees his people in their distress
Ps 69:33 See also Lev 26:40–46

Assyria to be punished eventually
Isa 10:5 Despite having been used as God's instrument, Assyria will come under God's judgment. See also Isa 10:12; Na 3:18–19

Nineveh will fall Na 1:14; 2:1–2 See also Na 3:1–5

God's people will be restored
Hos 1:10–11; Am 9:14–15

See also
5354 invasions	8755 folly
5560 suffering	8769 idolatry, in OT
6223 rebellion of	8840 unfaithfulness
Israel	to God
7233 Israel, northern	9165 restoration
kingdom	9210 judgment,
7560 Samaritans, the	God's

7217
exile, in Babylon

The southern kingdom of Judah was conquered by Babylon under Nebuchadnezzar. Before and after the destruction of Jerusalem in 587 B.C. the population was taken into exile in three stages.

The entire episode was within the purposes of God and under his control
The reason for the captivity
2Ki 21:11–15 See also 1Ch 9:1; Ezr 9:7

The captivity foretold by the prophets
Isa 39:5–7 See also Jer 1:14–16; 13:17,19; Eze 12:11; 21:24

Babylon the instrument of God's chastisement of Judah Jer 22:25; 25:8–11

A remnant would be spared Eze 12:16

The historical details
Nebuchadnezzar marches against Jerusalem Da 1:1–2 See also 2Ki 25:1–21 pp 2Ch 36:17–20; Jer 39:1–10; 52:4–27

The people of Judah are taken into exile in three stages Jer 52:27–30

God watches over his people during their captivity
The LORD hears and answers the prayers of his people in captivity
Ps 69:33; Da 9:17–23; 10:12–14

Babylon spares certain captives, and gives them some freedom and dignity
2Ki 25:27–30; Da 1:12–20; 2:48–49; 3:30; 6:28

God encourages his people during their captivity Ps 69:33; Jer 29:11; Eze 36:37–38

Promises of eventual restoration
Eze 36:8

The promise of return from exile
Jer 33:7–8 See also Jer 16:15; 23:3; 24:5–7; 27:22; 29:14; 30:3; 31:27–28; La 4:22; Eze 34:12–13; Zep 3:20

Restoration to be a demonstration of God's grace Eze 36:22

The promise of covenant renewal
Jer 31:31–34; Eze 34:25; 36:26–27

The promise of return fulfilled
2Ch 36:22–23 pp Ezr 1:1–3; Ne 7:6

Babylonian oppressors to be punished
Jer 25:12–14 See also Jer 30:16; 50:18; 51:49,55–56,64; Eze 36:7

See also
1055 God, grace &	5493 retribution
mercy	6026 sin, judgment
1352 covenant, the	on
new	6722 redemption,
1429 prophecy, OT	OT
fulfilment	7540 Judaism
4215 Babylon	8718 disobedience
5246 captivity	8790 oppression

exodus, the

The escape of the Israelites from slavery in Egypt under Moses' leadership. Despite their great deliverance, hardness of heart and disobedience towards God persisted. Divine deliverance in the exodus foreshadowed the act of salvation through Jesus Christ.

7222
exodus, events of

The escape of the Israelites from slavery in Egypt and their deliverance in the crossing of the Red Sea. The beginning of a long and difficult journey under Moses' leadership to Canaan, the promised land.

God's promise of deliverance
Ex 6:1–8 See also Ex 3:7–10

The LORD smites the Egyptians with ten plagues
Pharaoh refuses, despite the plagues, to let the Israelites leave: Ex 11:9–10; Ps 105:26–36

The plague on the firstborn and the Passover
Ex 12:31 See also Ex 12:23

The Israelites leave Egypt
Ex 12:37–41; Nu 33:3–5 See also Ps 105:37–38

The crossing of the Red Sea
Ex 14:29–31 See also Ex 13:17–14:28

The Israelites' travels: described in detail in Exodus, Numbers, Deuteronomy and Joshua
Nu 33:6–48

God's mighty deliverance remembered in confession
Ps 106:6–7; Da 9:15

Events of the exodus: remembered in the Passover Feast
Ex 12:24–28 See also Jos 5:10

See also
1085 God, love of	7135 Israel, people
4843 plague	of God
5102 Moses, life of	7251 pillar of cloud
6634 deliverance	& fire
6659 freedom, acts	7406 Passover
in OT	

7223
exodus, spiritual significance of

Scripture records the many instances of praise being given to God on account of the exodus. The events of the exodus, however, reveal the lack of faith, the hardness of heart and the spiritual stubbornness that can persist among believers. Scripture warns of the consequences of these things. In addition the exodus is seen as an act of divine deliverance which foreshadows the greater act of salvation through Jesus Christ.

How great God is: remember what he has done
The song of Moses and Miriam after the crossing of the Red Sea Ex 15:1–4

The psalmist praises God for his deliverance in the exodus Ps 77:19–20 *See also* Ps 78:12–14,51–53; 105:26–45; 106:7–12; 114:1–4; 136:13–16

Joshua compares the crossing of the Jordan to the crossing of the Red Sea Jos 4:23–24

Nehemiah leads the people in praise of God by reciting all his wonderful deeds Ne 9:9–12

God did great things in the past: he will do them again
Dt 7:17–19

Rahab recounts what the LORD did at the Red Sea Jos 2:10–11

Isaiah looks forward to a future deliverance as a second exodus Isa 43:16–19 *See also* Isa 11:15–16; 51:10

The exodus is remembered at the renewal of the covenant at Shechem
Jos 24:16–18 *See also* Jos 24:5–7

Warnings against hardness of heart
Heb 3:7–9,16; 1Co 10:1–5 *See also* Ps 95:7–11

The disobedience of the Israelites despite their knowledge of God's deliverance
1Sa 12:8–9 *See also* Jdg 6:7–10; 2Ch 7:22; Jer 2:5–6; 7:22–26; 11:1–8 Ac 7:36–39

A picture of the deliverance from sin won for believers by Jesus Christ
Heb 4:2 *See also* Heb 3:1–4:13

The exodus as a sign of God's love
Hos 11:1

The exodus as an example of faith
Heb 11:29

See also
1105 God, power of	8023 faith, necessity
1265 hand of God	8665 praise, reasons
2324 Christ as Saviour	8718 disobedience
6178 hardness of heart	8835 unbelief
7908 baptism, significance	8840 unfaithfulness to God

7227

flood, the

A universal catastrophe by means of which the world was overwhelmed by water as the judgment of God on sinful humanity. Only Noah, his family and the animals were saved.

Details of the flood
Its source Ge 7:4,11–12; 8:2

Its extent Ge 7:17–20

Its duration Ge 7:24

Its effect Ge 7:21–23

The flood was God's judgment on sinful humanity
Wickedness had become universal Ge 6:5,11–13

Judgment would be universal Ge 6:7,13,17; 7:4

Judgment was universal Ge 7:21–22

Those not destroyed by the flood
Noah, who was blameless in the midst of wickedness Ge 6:8–9

Noah and his family kept safe in the ark Ge 7:23 *See also* Ge 6:14,18; 7:1,7,13; 8:15–16,18; 2Pe 2:5,9

God kept the animals safe in the ark Ge 6:19–21; 7:2–3,8–9,14–16; 8:1,17,19

God promised never to send another universal flood
God decided this in his heart Ge 8:21–22 *See also* Isa 54:9

God established his covenant with Noah Ge 9:8–11

The rainbow as the sign and reminder of God's covenant Ge 9:12–17

The story of the flood used figuratively
Of the judgment to come Da 9:26; 2Pe 3:6–7

Of Jesus Christ's second coming Mt 24:36–44 pp Lk 17:26–27

Of baptism 1Pe 3:20–21

See also
1347 covenant with Noah	6169 godlessness
4612 birds	6221 rebellion
4845 rainbow	7203 ark, Noah's
5106 Noah	7908 baptism, significance
5482 punishment	8734 evil

7230

genealogies

In Scripture, lists of the descendants or forebears of an individual, or a record of the names of particular groups of people.

Genealogies as records of ancestors and lines of descent
Mt 1:1–17 pp Lk 3:23–38 *See also* Ge 10:1–32; 11:10–32; 36:10–43; 1Ch 1:1–6:30; 9:35–44; Heb 7:3

Kinds of genealogies
Population lists 1Ch 9:1 *See also* Ge 46:8–27; 1Ch 9:3–22; 2Ch 31:16; Ezr 2:1–67 pp Ne 7:5–69

Heads of families 1Ch 9:34 *See also* 1Ch 8:1–28; 9:7–9; 26:31

Men eligible for military service 1Ch 7:2 *See also* Nu 26:1–62; 1Ch 7:4–11,30–40

Some prophets may have been responsible for recording or maintaining genealogies
2Ch 12:15

Christians are urged to avoid fruitless discussions concerning genealogies
Tit 3:9 *See also* 1Ti 1:3–4

See also
2540 Christ, genealogy	5671 clan
5075 Abraham	5694 generation
5106 Noah	5724 offspring
5651 ancestors	7505 Jews, the

7233

Israel, as northern kingdom

The northernmost region of the two kingdoms, comprising the ten northern tribes which broke away from Judah in 930 B.C. and remained independent until the Assyrian conquest of 722 B.C., when the nation was exiled because of its sinfulness.

Origins of the division between Judah and Israel
Israelite settlement in Canaan had developed around two distinct regions in the north and south Jos 18:5

The northern Israelite tribes were less ready to transfer allegiance from Saul to David 2Sa 2:10 *See also* 2Sa 19:41–20:2 *Israel seems to have been ready to follow Sheba, because he came from the same tribe as Saul.*

Israel's separation from Judah was the result of disobedience under Solomon 1Ki 11:26–33

Rehoboam's folly provoked Israel's rebellion 1Ki 12:1–17 pp 2Ch 10:1–17

Israel's foreign affairs
Israel at war with Judah (c. 930–886 B.C.) 1Ki 14:30 pp 2Ch 12:15; 2Ch 13:2–3; 16:1 pp 1Ki 15:16–17

Israel's wars with Aram (c. 886–753 B.C.) 1Ki 15:18–20 pp 2Ch 16:2–4; 1Ki 20:1,26; 2Ki 6:24–25; 10:32–33; 13:3,24–25; 14:28

Israel's alliance with Judah against Aram and Moab (853 B.C.) 1Ki 22:1–4 pp 2Ch 18:1–3; 2Ki 3:4–7

Israel attacked by Assyria (c. 743–734 B.C.) 2Ki 15:19–20,29

Israel's alliance with Aram against Judah (c. 735/734 B.C.) 2Ki 16:5; Isa 7:1

Israel conquered by Assyria, and her inhabitants exiled (722 B.C.) 2Ki 17:3–6 pp 2Ki 18:9–11

Centres of worship in Israel
The calf idols in Bethel and Dan 1Ki 12:26–33 *See also* 2Ki 10:29

Worship of Baal and Asherah in the capital, Samaria 1Ki 16:32–33

Gilgal was also a centre of worship Hos 12:11

Condemnation of Israel's way of life
Israel's worship condemned Am 4:4–5

Amos' language here is full of irony. See also Hos 8:11–13; **Am** 5:21–24

The corruption of Israel's priests
condemned Hos 6:9 *See also* Hos 4:6–9

Israel's unfaithfulness to God
condemned Hos 5:7 *See also*
2Ki 17:7–23; Hos 4:10–13

Prophetic condemnation of sin in
Israel Hos 4:1–2 *See also* Hos 6:11–7:2;
Am 2:6–8; 5:12

Israel condemned for looking to
foreign nations for help instead of to
God Hos 11:12–12:1 *See also*
Hos 5:13–15; 7:8–11; 8:9–10

God's attitude to the northern
kingdom of Israel
God's call to Israel to repent
Hos 14:1–2 *See also* Hos 10:12;
Am 5:4–6

God's attempt to call Israel back
through hardship 1Ki 17:1 *See also*
Am 4:6–11

God's rejection of Israel Hos 1:6 *See*
also 2Ch 25:5–7; Hos 1:8–9

God's punishment of Israel
Am 5:26–27 *See also* Hos 10:5–8;
Am 3:11–12

God's intention to restore Israel
Hos 1:10 *See also* Hos 2:23; 14:4–8;
Am 9:11–15

See also

1350 covenant with	7236 Israel, united
Israel's priests	kingdom
5366 king	7245 Judah,
5370 kingship,	kingdom of
human	7259 promised land,
6223 rebellion of	later history
Israel	7266 tribes of Israel
7135 Israel, people of	7560 Samaritans,
God	the
7215 exile, the	9165 restoration

7236

Israel, as united kingdom

The 12 tribes proclaimed Saul as
their first king in 1050 B.C., and
remained united under David and
Solomon, until the rebellion of the
ten northern tribes in 930 B.C.

Israel's request for a king
Israel requested a king because she
had been governed by corrupt judges
1Sa 8:1–5

Israel requested a king to be like the
other nations 1Sa 8:19–20

Israel requested a king because of the
threat from Ammon 1Sa 12:12

Israel's request for a king seen as a
rejection of God 1Sa 8:6–7 *See also*
1Sa 10:19; 12:16–19

Israel under Saul (1050–1010
B.C.)
Israel oppressed by the Philistines
1Sa 13:19–20

Saul chosen as Israel's deliverer
1Sa 10:1 *See also* 1Sa 10:17–25;
11:14–15

Israel victorious under Saul
1Sa 14:47–48 *See also* 1Sa 11:11–13;
15:7–8

Israel's war with the Philistines
1Sa 14:52 *See also* 1Sa 13:5–7;
14:20–23; 17:51–53

The popularity of David in Israel
1Sa 18:30 *See also* 1Sa 18:6–9

Israel defeated by the Philistines, and
the death of Saul 1Sa 31:1–10
pp 1Ch 10:1–10

Israel under David (1010–970
B.C.)
Civil war in Israel between David and
Ish-Bosheth, Saul's son 2Sa 3:1 *See also*
2Sa 2:8–17

David appointed king over Israel
2Sa 5:1–3 pp 1Ch 11:1–3 *See also*
1Sa 16:1

David makes Jerusalem the capital of
Israel 2Sa 5:6–10 pp 1Ch 11:4–9

Israel victorious under David
2Sa 8:1–14 pp 1Ch 18:1–13

Officials in Israel under David
2Sa 8:15–18 pp 1Ch 18:14–17;
2Sa 20:23–26

Civil war in Israel between David and
his son Absalom 2Sa 15:10–12; 18:1–8

God's judgment on Israel during
David's reign 2Sa 21:1; 24:1–16
pp 1Ch 21:1–15

All Israel contributes in preparation for
the building of the temple 1Ch 29:6–9

Israel under Solomon (970–930
B.C.)
Officials in Israel under Solomon
1Ki 4:1–19

Prosperity of Israel under Solomon
1Ki 10:27 pp 2Ch 1:15 *See also*
1Ki 4:20–25

Israel's trade relations under Solomon
1Ki 10:22 pp 2Ch 9:21 *See also*
1Ki 5:8–12 pp 2Ch 2:11–16;
1Ki 10:11–12 pp 2Ch 9:10–11;
1Ki 10:28–29 pp 2Ch 9:28

Solomon's building programme in
Israel 1Ki 6:1–37 pp 2Ch 3:1–14;
1Ki 7:1–12; 9:17–19 pp 2Ch 8:1–5

Solomon puts Israelites to forced
labour 1Ki 5:13–18

Division in Israel (930 B.C.)
Opposition to Solomon 1Ki 11:14–26

Israel divided because of her apostasy
1Ki 11:29–33

Rebellion in Israel against forced
labour 1Ki 12:1–19 pp 2Ch 10:1–19

See also

5085 David	7240 Jerusalem,
5118 Solomon	history
5366 king	7245 Judah,
5424 nationalism	kingdom of
5597 victory, act of	7266 tribes of Israel
God	7269 Zion
5605 warfare	7467 temple,
7135 Israel, people of	Solomon's
God	
7233 Israel, northern	
kingdom	

7239

Jerusalem

The city in southern Palestine,
situated in the Judean hills, around
20 miles west of the Dead Sea.

Established as the Israelite capital by
David, it remained the capital of
Judah from the reign of Rehoboam
until its destruction by the Romans
in A.D. 70.

7240
Jerusalem, history of

Jerusalem was originally a Jebusite
city, occupied by Israel at the time of
David. At this stage, it became the
capital city of Israel. Following the
disintegration of the united
kingdom, the city became the capital
of the southern kingdom of Judah.

Pre-Israelite Jerusalem
Inhabited by Jebusites Jdg 19:9–12 *See*
also Ge 10:15–16; 15:18–21; Ex 3:7–8;
23:23; 34:11; Nu 13:29; Dt 7:1–2;
Jos 3:10; 9:1–2; 10:1–7; 15:7–8; 18:28

Israelites unable to occupy Jerusalem
Jos 15:63 *See also* Jdg 1:4–8 *Although the*
men of Judah defeated the Jebusites in this
battle, their victory was not sufficient to
conquer them nor to gain permanent
control over the city; Jdg 1:21

Jerusalem conquered by David
1Ch 11:4–9 pp 2Sa 5:6–10

Jerusalem as the site of the ark
2Sa 6:12–19 pp 1Ch 15:25–16:3

Jerusalem capital city of David
and Solomon
2Sa 5:4–5 *See also* 2Sa 9:13; 11:1;
12:29–31 pp 1Ch 20:1–3;
2Sa 14:23–24; 15:13–14;
1Ki 2:10–12,36–45; 3:1; 8:1;
10:1–5,26–27; 11:41–43

Jerusalem capital of the
southern kingdom
1Ki 14:21 *See also* 1Ki 12:16–19
pp 2Ch 10:16–19; 1Ki 12:25–27;
15:9–10; 22:42 pp 2Ch 20:31;
2Ki 8:16–17 pp 2Ch 21:5; 2Ki 12:1
pp 2Ch 24:1; 2Ki 15:1–2 pp 2Ch 26:3;
2Ki 18:1–2 pp 2Ch 29:1; 2Ki 18:13–35
pp 2Ch 32:9–19 pp Isa 36:1–22;
2Ki 21:1 pp 2Ch 33:1; 2Ki 23:31–33
pp 2Ch 36:2–3

Jerusalem conquered by the
Babylonians
2Ki 24:18–25:12 pp 2Ch 36:11–20
pp Jer 39:1–10; 52:1–16

The rebuilding of Jerusalem
2Ch 36:23; Ezr 1:1–4; Ne 2:1–6:19

Jerusalem capital of Persian
province of Judah
Ne 1:1–3 *See also* Ezr 3:1; 4:4–6; 10:7;
Ne 13:6–7,15–16

Jerusalem in NT times
Mt 2:1–3 *See also* Mt 3:1–6
pp Mk 1:3–5; Mt 4:25; 15:1 pp Mk 7:1;
Lk 2:22,41; 4:9; Jn 11:55; Ac 9:1–2;
25:1–3

Prophetic warning of the destruction of Jerusalem
Lk 21:20–24 *See also* Lk 23:26–31

See also

1351 covenant with David	7216 exile in Assyria
5085 David	7217 exile in Babylon
5256 city	7236 Israel, united kingdom
5437 palaces	
5529 sieges	7245 Judah, kingdom of
6222 rebellion against God	7610 Council of Jerusalem
7135 Israel, people of God	

7241
Jerusalem, significance of

Chosen by God as the location for his sanctuary, Jerusalem was his symbolic dwelling and became the only acceptable place for sacrificial worship. It retained its symbolic significance in NT times when it came to represent the hope of restoration and renewal for the people of God.

Jerusalem chosen by God
1Ki 11:32 *See also* 1Ki 8:44–51
pp 2Ch 6:34–39; 1Ki 11:36; 14:21
pp 2Ch 12:13; 2Ki 23:27; Ne 1:8–9

The ark of the covenant brought to Jerusalem
1Ch 15:1–3 *See also* 2Sa 6:1–19
pp 1Ch 15:25–16:3

The temple located in Jerusalem
2Ch 3:1 *See also* 1Ch 6:31–32;
2Ch 20:27–28; 33:7; 36:14,22–23
pp Ezr 1:1–3; Ps 68:28–29;
Mk 11:11,15–16; Lk 2:41–51; 4:9;
Ac 22:13–18

Jerusalem the only acceptable place for sacrificial worship
Dt 12:1–7 *See also* Dt 12:20–28;
1Ki 12:26–13:3; 14:22–24; 22:42–43
pp 2Ch 20:31–33; 2Ki 12:1–3; 16:1–4
pp 2Ch 28:1–4; 2Ki 23:1–20
pp 2Ch 34:29–32; 2Ch 30:1–31:1;
Isa 66:20; Hos 10:8; Jn 4:20–21

Jerusalem referred to as God's dwelling-place
Ps 135:21 *See also* Isa 24:23; 31:9;
Jer 3:17

Personification of Jerusalem
Isa 52:1–2 *See also* Ps 147:12; Isa 3:8;
40:2; 41:27; 52:9; 62:6–7; Jer 2:1–2;
4:14; 6:8; 13:9,26–27; 15:5; La 1:17;
2:13–15; Eze 5:8; 16:1–63; 23:1–49;
Zep 3:14–17; Zec 9:9–10; Mt 23:37–39
pp Lk 13:34–35

Jerusalem the place of Jesus Christ's triumphal entry
Lk 19:28–38

Jerusalem the place of Jesus Christ's death and resurrection
Lk 23:26–49; 24:1–12,13–33

The outpouring of the Holy Spirit in Jerusalem
Ac 1:4–9 *See also* Ac 2:1–21

Jerusalem the administrative centre of the church
Ac 8:1 *See also* Ac 8:14,25; 11:1–22,27;
12:25; 13:13; 15:1–29; 16:4;
1Co 16:1–3; Gal 1:15–19; 2:1–10

The new Jerusalem
Rev 21:1–5 *See also* Eze 48:30–35;
Gal 4:25–26; Heb 12:18–24;
Rev 3:11–13; 21:9–27

See also

2505 Christ, ascension	7020 church, the
2530 Christ, death of	7269 Zion
2560 Christ, resurrection	7306 ark of the covenant
2590 Christ, triumphal entry	7374 high places
	7466 temples
3242 Holy Spirit, baptism with	8704 apostasy
	9165 restoration

7245
Judah, kingdom of

The southernmost of the two kingdoms into which Israel split after the death of Solomon. It was ruled by a series of Davidic kings until the sixth century B.C., when it became a province of the Babylonian empire.

Origin of the kingdom of Judah
1Ki 12:1–24 pp 2Ch 10:1–11:4

Loss of the wealth amassed in Judah
1Ki 14:25–26 pp 2Ch 12:9 *See also*
1Ki 15:18–19 pp 2Ch 16:2–3;
2Ki 12:17–18; 14:14 pp 2Ch 25:24;
2Ki 16:8 pp 2Ch 28:21; 2Ki 18:14–16;
2Ch 24:23

Apostasy in Judah
1Ki 14:22–24 *See also* 2Ki 8:16–19
pp 2Ch 21:5–7; 2Ki 16:10–16; 21:2–16
pp 2Ch 33:2–10; 2Ch 28:22–23

Religious revival in Judah
2Ki 18:2–7 pp 2Ch 29:1–2; 31:1,
20–21 *See also* 2Ki 12:1–16
pp 2Ch 24:1–14; 2Ki 23:1–25;
2Ch 34:1–13,29–33; 29:1–31:1;
35:1–19

The reign of Athaliah in Judah
2Ki 11:1–16 pp 2Ch 22:10–23:21

Coalitions between Judah and Israel
2Ki 8:28–29 pp 2Ch 22:5–6 *See also*
1Ki 22:1–5 pp 2Ch 18:1–3; 2Ki 3:4–7

War in Judah
With Israel 1Ki 15:6 *See also* 1Ki 14:30
pp 2Ch 12:15; 1Ki 15:16–17
pp 2Ch 16:1; 2Ki 14:8–14
pp 2Ch 25:17–24; 2Ki 16:5

With other nations 2Ki 14:7 *See also*
2Ki 8:20–22 pp 2Ch 21:8–10;
2Ki 18:8,13–19:36 pp 2Ch 32:9–19
pp Isa 36:1–22; 2Ch 21:16–17;
25:11–12; 28:17–18

Judah's loss of independence and change of status from kingdom to province
2Ki 25:1–12 pp 2Ch 36:17–20

pp Jer 39:1–10 *See also* 2Ki 25:22–24
pp Jer 40:7–9

See also

5366 king	7240 Jerusalem, history
5605 warfare	
7217 exile in Babylon	7505 Jews, the
7233 Israel, northern kingdom	8466 reformation
	8704 apostasy

7248
patriarchs

The patriarchs: Abraham, Isaac, Jacob and his twelve sons
Heb 7:4 *See also* Jn 7:22; Ac 7:8–9;
Ro 9:5; 11:28; 15:8

David also called a patriarch
Ac 2:29

See also

1245 God of the fathers	5096 Jacob, patriarch
1348 covenant with Abraham	5737 sisters
	7206 community
1351 covenant with David	7258 promised land, early history
5075 Abraham	
5089 David, significance	

7251
pillar of cloud and fire

A physical manifestation of the presence of God among his people; a special form of theophany particularly associated with Israel being offered guidance on the exodus journey.

Functions of the pillar of cloud and fire
To lead Israel Ex 13:21–22 *See also*
Ex 40:36–37; Nu 9:17; 14:14;
Ne 9:12,19

To separate and protect Israel from the armies of Egypt Ex 14:19–20 *This was just before the crossing of the Red Sea.*

To represent God's presence, especially to Moses Ex 33:9 *See also*
Nu 12:5–6; Dt 31:15–16; Ps 99:7

Effects of the pillar of cloud and fire
It evoked worship Ex 33:10

It caused the nations to speak of God
Nu 14:14

Experiencing the cloud did not guarantee acceptance by God
1Co 10:1–5

See also

1454 theophany	7474 Tent of Meeting
1670 symbols	
7222 exodus, events of	8124 guidance

7254
plumb-line

A cord weighted with lead that is used in building to check that vertical structures are true. It is used symbolically to refer to the divine standard against which God, the builder of his people, tests and judges them. It also symbolises the standards by which God will rebuild his people.

The plumb-line as the measuring tool of a structure
Zec 1:16; 4:9–10 *Using the plumb-line Zerubbabel will carry out his God-given task of building the temple. See also* Jer 31:38–40; Zec 2:1–2

God's plumb-line reveals the nation's failure
Although built true, Israel has become corrupt Am 7:7–8 *See also* Isa 1:21–24; 5:1–2,7; 59:14

God's testing brings judgment 2Ki 21:13 *See also* Isa 34:11; La 2:8

God will rebuild his people
God's promise to rebuild Israel Jer 31:4 *See also* Ps 69:35–36; 147:2; Isa 54:11–12

They will be rebuilt true to God's plumb-line Isa 28:16–17 *See also* Ps 51:18–19; Isa 1:25–26; Ps 89:14; 97:2; 99:4; Isa 16:5

See also

1075 God, justice of	8832 testing
5240 building	9165 restoration
5359 justice	9210 judgment,
8154 righteousness	God's
8309 morality	

7257

promised land, the

The territory of the Canaanite nations given by God to Abraham and his descendants as part of his covenant with them.

7258
promised land, early history of

The promise of a homeland, made to Abraham, began to unfold through Moses and Joshua. Moses taught that the land was to be held in trust by God's people, obedience to God's ways bringing blessing in the land and disobedience bringing his judgment.

The location of the promised land
Ge 15:18–21 *See also* Nu 34:1–12; Dt 7:1

Traditional descriptions of the promised land
Ex 3:17 *See also* Nu 13:26–27; Dt 8:7–8; Jer 32:22; Eze 20:6

The promised land and Abraham
The covenant with Abraham Ge 15:7–21 *See also* Ge 13:14–17; 17:7–8

The promised land given to Abraham's descendants Ge 12:7 *See also* Ge 17:8; 24:7; Ex 33:1

A burial plot was Abraham's only earthly possession in the promised land Ge 25:9–10 *See also* Ge 23:3–20

The promised land and the patriarchs
Ge 26:2–5 *See also* Ge 28:12–15; 35:1–12; 50:24–25

Later generations look back to the promise made to the patriarchs
Dt 1:8 *See also* Ex 32:13–14; Dt 6:20–23; Ne 9:7–8; Ps 105:8–11 pp 1Ch 16:15–18

The promised land and Moses
Moses is called to lead Israel into the promised land Dt 10:11 *See also* Ex 3:16–17; 6:1–8; Nu 11:12

A whole generation is not permitted to enter the promised land Jos 5:6 *See also* Nu 14:20–38; 32:9–13; Ps 106:24–27

Moses and Aaron are not permitted to enter the promised land Nu 20:12 *See also* Nu 20:23–29; 27:12–14; Dt 32:48–52; 34:1–4

Moses' instructions to destroy the inhabitants of the land and their practices Dt 7:16 *See also* Nu 33:50–53; Dt 7:1–6; 12:2–3; 18:9–12

The instructions for distributing the promised land Nu 33:54 *See also* Nu 34:13–15; 36:5–9; Jos 14:1–5; Ps 78:55

Obedience to the law was a condition for enjoying the blessings of the promised land Dt 6:1–3 *See also* Ex 20:12 pp Dt 5:16; Lev 26:3–12; Dt 6:17–19; 7:12–15; 11:8–15; 28:1–8; Jer 11:1–5

Warnings not to forget God and follow Canaanite ways Dt 11:16–17 *See also* Ex 34:12–16; Lev 18:1–5; Nu 33:55–56; Dt 8:10–14; 28:15–19; Jos 23:14–16

Laws concerning the land Lev 25:23–24 *The promised land is seen as belonging to God. See also* Ex 23:10–11; Lev 25:1–7,8–13; Nu 35:33–34

The promised land and Joshua
Joshua is called to lead the Israelites into the promised land Dt 31:7–8 *See also* Dt 3:28; Jos 1:1–6

The Israelites enter the promised land and begin to possess it Jos 3:14–17; 11:16–23; 21:43

God's people are given rest Jos 21:44–45 *See also* Dt 12:10; Jos 1:13–15

See also

1345 covenant	7221 exodus, the
1680 types	7248 patriarchs
4206 land	8257 fruitfulness,
5075 Abraham	natural
5102 Moses, life of	8453 obedience
7135 Israel, people of	8718 disobedience
God	

7259
promised land, later history of

Established firmly in the land under David and Solomon, God's people ultimately began to neglect the terms of the covenant and were

warned by the prophets of the consequent judgment and exile.

Israel's failure to take full possession of the promised land under the judges
Jdg 1:19 *See also* Jdg 1:27–35; 2:1–3; 18:1

Israel was finally established in the promised land under David and Solomon
1Ch 22:18 *See also* 2Sa 7:10–11 pp 1Ch 17:9–10; 1Ki 4:21,25

The promised land and the prophets
The prophetic condemnation of the life of God's people in the promised land Jer 2:7 *See also* Jer 3:1–3; Eze 22:23–29; Hos 4:1–3

Prophetic warning of coming judgment on the land and exile from it Isa 13:9 *See also* Isa 8:6–8; Jer 10:17–18; 16:10–13; Eze 7:2–4; Am 7:17

Prophetic assurance of ultimate deliverance and restoration to the promised land Jer 30:3 *See also* Isa 14:1–2; 60:15–22; Jer 24:5–7; Eze 11:17; 37:11–14; Am 9:14–15; Zec 2:10–12

The desolation of the promised land
By Antiochus Epiphanes Da 8:9–14 *The growing horn is Antiochus Epiphanes who tried to wipe out the Jewish faith in 168 B.C., forbidding Jewish practices and defiling the temple with pagan sacrifices and prostitution. See also* Da 11:29–35 *The help that would be received by God's people probably refers to the Maccabean revolt and the cleansing of the temple in 165 B.C., although by NT times the land would be occupied by Rome.*

By Rome Lk 21:20–24 pp Mt 24:15–21 pp Mk 13:14–19 *Jesus Christ prophesies the desolation of the nation by Rome in A.D. 70.*

The promised land in the NT
Referred to by Stephen Ac 7:3–7,45–47

Referred to by Paul Ac 13:16–19

Referred to by Hebrews Heb 11:8–10 *Abraham was looking for a more permanent city than the promised land could ever provide;* Heb 11:13–16

The concept of spiritual rest Heb 3:18–4:11

The church looks beyond the promised land Ac 1:6–8 *The apostles' concern was for the deliverance of the promised land from Roman domination, but Jesus Christ shows God's concern to be far wider, to all nations. See also* Rev 5:9–10; 7:9–17; 21:9–27

See also

5056 rest	7239 Jerusalem
5085 David	7245 Judah,
5118 Solomon	kingdom of
7145 remnant	7269 Zion
7215 exile, the	7505 Jews, the
7233 Israel, northern	7772 prophets
kingdom	
7236 Israel, united	
kingdom	

theocracy

The form of government among the early Israelites in which God was their supreme ruler, and his laws their laws.

The covenant at Sinai established the theocracy
Ex 19:5–6 *See also* Ex 19:8; 24:3,7–8; Dt 5:27

Moses and Joshua renewed the theocratic covenant
Dt 26:16–19; 29:9–15; Jos 24:24–25

Under the theocracy God was the Israelites' supreme ruler
Dt 33:5 *"Jeshurun" means "the upright one", i.e., Israel. See also* Nu 23:21; Dt 33:26; Jdg 8:23; Ps 145:1

In the theocracy Israel was governed by God's laws
Ex 20:1–17 pp Dt 5:6–21; Ex 21:1; Dt 4:1–2,13–14; 17:18–19; 31:12–13; Jos 1:7–8

Israel rejected the theocracy
1Sa 8:7 *See also* 1Sa 8:19; 10:19; 12:12

See also
1130 God,	5326 government
sovereignty	5358 judges
1349 covenant at	5368 kingship
Sinai	5375 law
2375 kingdom of	
God	

tribes of Israel

The divisions of Israel on lines of kinship, according to descent from the twelve sons of Jacob. These divisions were most pronounced in the period before Saul became king of Israel but were maintained throughout Israel's history.

Origin of the tribes of Israel
Twelve sons of Jacob Ge 35:22–26 *See also* Ge 29:31–35; 30:3–13,17–24; 35:16–18

Increased in number while living in Egypt Ge 46:5–27 *See also* Ex 1:1–7

Blessings on the tribes of Israel
Ge 49:1–28; Dt 33:1–29

Association of the twelve apostles with the tribes of Israel
Mt 19:28 *See also* Mt 10:1–4 pp Mk 3:13–19 pp Lk 6:12–16; Lk 22:28–30; Ac 1:12–26; Rev 21:12–14

Other NT references to the tribes of Israel
Jas 1:1 *See also* Ac 26:6–7

The tribes of Israel in end-time prophecy
Rev 7:1–8 *See also* Eze 47:13–14; 48:1–35; Rev 21:9–14

The tribe of Asher
The genealogy of Asher Ge 46:17 *See also* Nu 26:44–47; 1Ch 7:30–40

The history of Asher
In the wilderness: Nu 1:40–41; 10:25–28 *In the land of Canaan:* Dt 27:12–13; Jos 19:24–31; Jdg 7:22–23 *After the division of the kingdom:* 2Ch 30:6–11; Lk 2:36–38

The tribe of Benjamin
The genealogy of Benjamin Ge 46:21 *See also* Nu 26:38–41; 1Ch 7:6–12; 8:1–40; 9:1–9

The history of Benjamin
In the wilderness: Nu 1:36–37; 2:18–23 *In the land of Canaan:* Dt 27:12; Jos 18:11–28; 1Ch 12:1–2 Jdg 19:1–21:23 *the war against Benjamin After the division of the kingdom:* 1Ki 12:21–24 pp 2Ch 11:1–4; 2Ch 11:5–12; Ezr 1:5

The tribe of Dan
The genealogy of Dan Nu 26:42–43

The history of Dan
In the wilderness: Nu 1:38–39; 2:25; 10:25 *In the land of Canaan:* Dt 27:12–13; Jos 19:40–47; Jdg 18:1–31

The tribe of Ephraim
The tribe of Ephraim was descended from Joseph's younger son Jos 14:4 *See also* Ge 48:1–20

The genealogy of Ephraim
Nu 26:35–37 *See also* 1Ch 7:20–29

The history of Ephraim
In the wilderness: Nu 1:32–33; 2:18 *In the land of Canaan:* Jos 16:1–10; 17:14–18; Jdg 1:29; 7:22–8:3 Jdg 12:1–6 *the war against Ephraim*

Later prophecies against Ephraim
Isa 7:2–9

The tribe of Gad
The genealogy of Gad Ge 46:16 *See also* Nu 26:15–18

The history of Gad
In the wilderness: Nu 1:24–25; 2:10–14 *Their allocation of land east of the Jordan:* Nu 32:28–36; Dt 3:12–17; 29:7–8; Jos 13:24–28 *The conquest of Canaan:* Jos 1:12–18; 4:10–13; 22:1–34; 1Ch 5:18–22 *Under the monarchy:* 1Ch 5:25–26; 12:37

The tribe of Issachar
The genealogy of Issachar Ge 46:13 *See also* Nu 26:23–25; 1Ch 7:1–5

The history of Issachar
In the wilderness: Nu 1:28–29; 2:3–6 *In the land of Canaan:* Dt 27:12; Jos 19:17–23; Jdg 10:1 *Under the monarchy:* 1Ch 12:38–40; 2Ch 30:10–20

The tribe of Judah
The genealogy of Judah Nu 26:19–22 *See also* Ge 46:8–12; 1Ch 2:1–4:23

The tribe of Judah in the wilderness
Nu 1:26–27 *See also* Nu 2:3–4; 13:1–6; 34:16–19; Dt 27:11–12; 33:7

Judah was prominent among the tribes Ge 49:8–12 *See also* Nu 2:1–9; 7:10–17; 10:11–14; Jdg 1:1–20

The territory of the tribe of Judah
Jos 18:5 *See also* Jos 11:21; 15:1–63 *the extent of the allotment for Judah;* Jos 20:1–7 *cities of refuge in Judah Towns for the Levites in Judah:* Jos 21:1–4,9–16 1Sa 17:1; 22:3–5; 23:21–23; 27:8–10; 30:11–16; 2Sa 2:1; 24:5–7

Early evidence of the distinction between Judah and the other tribes
2Sa 24:9 pp 1Ch 21:5 *See also* 1Sa 11:8; 17:52; 18:16 *David's reign over Judah:* 2Sa 2:8–11; 3:9–10; 5:5 2Sa 11:11; 12:8; 19:40–20:2 *Judah remained loyal to David when Israel rebelled;* 2Sa 21:2; 24:1 *Israel and Judah united under Solomon:* 1Ki 1:35; 4:20,25

The separation of Judah from the northern tribes 1Ki 12:1–24 pp 2Ch 10:1–11:4

The continuing tribal identity of Judah
2Ch 19:8–11 *See also* 2Ki 17:18–20; Ps 78:67–68; Eze 37:15–28; 48:1–8,30–31; Rev 7:1–8

The tribe of Levi
The genealogy of Levi Ex 6:16–25; Nu 3:17–20; 26:57–62

The tribe of Levi is set apart to God
Ex 32:25–29 *Their loyalty to the LORD set them apart.* *They were given the responsibility of caring for the tabernacle:* Nu 1:47–53; 3:38

They were claimed by God as a substitute for the firstborn males of Israel Nu 3:11–13 *See also* Nu 3:40–45; 8:15–18

The tribe of Levi received no allotment of land Dt 18:1–2 *See also* Nu 18:23; Jos 13:32–33; 14:3–4

The tribe of Levi lived in designated towns Nu 35:1–8 *See also* Lev 25:32–34; Jos 21:1–42 pp 1Ch 6:54–80

Tithes and offerings given by the rest of Israel supported the tribe of Levi
Nu 18:21–24 *See also* Dt 14:22–29; Ne 10:37–38; 13:4–13

Moses blesses the tribe of Levi
Dt 33:8–11

The tribe of Levi in the period of the monarchy 1Ch 12:26–28 *Their fighting men join David at Hebron;* 1Ch 23:2–24 *David divides them into three groups and organises their responsibilities;* 1Ch 27:16–17 *David sets an army officer over them.*

The tribe of Manasseh
The tribe of Manasseh was descended from Joseph's older son Jos 14:4 *See also* Ge 48:3–20; Nu 26:28–37; 1Ch 7:14–19

Manasseh in the wilderness
Nu 1:34–35 *See also* Nu 2:18–21; 27:1–11; 36:1–12

The division of Manasseh into two
The half-tribe of Manasseh was allocated territory in Gilead: Nu 32:33,39–42; Dt 3:13–15; 29:7–8; Jos 12:4–6; 13:29–31; 1Ch 5:23 *The remainder of Manasseh was allocated territory west of the Jordan:* Jos 13:6–7; 16:1–4; 17:1–13; Jdg 1:27 Jos 22:1–34 *the threat of war against the*

half-tribe of Manasseh and the other Transjordan tribes

Manasseh in the period of the judges
Jdg 7:23 *See also* Jdg 6:11–16,33–35; 11:1–11; 12:1–7

Manasseh under the monarchy
1Ch 5:26 *See also* 1Ch 12:19–20; 26:32; 2Ch 15:9; 30:1–20; 34:8–9

The tribe of Naphtali
The genealogy of Naphtali Ge 46:24 *See also* Nu 26:48–50

The history of Naphtali
In the wilderness: Nu 1:42–43; 2:25–30
In the land of Canaan: Dt 27:12–13; Jdg 1:33; 4:4–10; 6:33–35
Under the monarchy: 2Ki 15:29; 1Ch 12:38–40; 2Ch 34:1–7

The territory of Naphtali Isa 9:1 *See also* Jos 19:32–39; Mt 4:13–16

The tribe of Reuben
The genealogy of Reuben Nu 26:5–7 *See also* Ge 46:8–9; Ex 6:14; 1Ch 5:1–10

The history of Reuben
In the wilderness: Nu 1:20–21; 2:10–16; 16:1–3
Their allocation of land: Nu 32:1–38; Dt 3:12–17; 29:7–8; Jos 13:15–23
The conquest of Canaan: Jos 1:12–18; 4:10–13; 22:1–34; 1Ch 5:18–22
Under the monarchy: 1Ch 5:25–26; 11:42; 12:37; 26:32; 27:16

The tribe of Simeon
The genealogy of Simeon Ex 6:15 *See also* Ge 46:10; Nu 26:12–14; 1Ch 4:24–37

The history of Simeon
In the wilderness: Nu 1:22–23; 2:10–16
In the land of Canaan: Jos 19:1–9; 1Ch 4:38–43; 12:23–25
Under the monarchy: 2Ch 15:9; 34:1–7

The tribe of Zebulun
The genealogy of Zebulun Ge 46:14 *See also* Nu 26:26–27

The history of Zebulun
In the wilderness: Nu 1:30–31; 2:3–9
In the land of Canaan: Dt 27:12–13; Jdg 1:30; 4:6,9–10; 5:13–14,18; 6:33–35; 12:11–12
Under the monarchy: 1Ch 12:33,40; 2Ch 30:10–20

The territory of Zebulun Isa 9:1 *See also* Jos 19:10–16; Mt 4:12–16

See also
1245 God of the	7248 patriarchs
fathers	7390 Levites
1654 numbers,	7520 dispersion, the
11–99	7630 Twelve, the
5094 Jacob	9240 last judgment
7135 Israel, people of	
God	

7269

Zion

The geographical and spiritual centre of life among God's people.

7270
Zion, as a place

Originally the name of the southernmost hill on which the Canaanite fortress-city of Jebus was

located. It was conquered by David around 1000 B.C. and renamed Jerusalem. Situated on the borders of Judah and Israel, it became David's capital. As the city expanded, the name Zion came to be applied to the whole city.

The name of Zion
1Ch 11:4–5 pp 2Sa 5:6–7

The early history of Zion
Early mention of Zion Ge 14:18

Early attempts to take control of Zion
Jos 15:63 pp Jdg 1:21

Zion as the City of David
Considered an impregnable fortress in David's time 2Sa 5:6 pp 1Ch 11:4–5 *See also* 2Sa 5:8

Captured by David 2Sa 5:7 pp 1Ch 11:4

Zion, established by David as his new capital and renamed 2Sa 5:9 pp 1Ch 11:7

Further strengthened by David
1Ch 11:8 pp 2Sa 5:9

The location of David's palace 2Sa 5:11 pp 1Ch 14:1

The new resting place for the ark of the covenant 1Ch 15:1–16:6 pp 2Sa 6:1–23

Zion as the name of the extended city of Jerusalem
Isa 33:20 *See also* 2Ki 19:20–21 pp Isa 37:21–22; Isa 4:3; La 1:4–8; Joel 2:32; Zep 3:14–16

See also
5085 David	7239 Jerusalem
5100 Melchizedek	7306 ark of the
5256 city	covenant
5437 palaces	8642 celebration

7271
Zion, as a symbol

Central to the life of the nation of Israel, it became the symbol of the whole nation and was seen, especially by the prophets, as the focus of God's promises and his final victory. In the NT Zion is a symbol of the new Israel, the church.

Zion as the dwelling-place of God
Ps 135:21 *See also* Ps 76:2; 132:13–14; Joel 3:17

Zion as a symbol of God's people
A symbol of Jerusalem Ps 9:14 *See also* Isa 52:1–2; La 2:8–10; Mic 4:6–8; Mt 21:5 pp Jn 12:15; Zec 9:9

A symbol of Judah Ps 78:68 *See also* Jer 14:19

A symbol of Israel La 2:1 *See also* Isa 46:13

Zion as the object of God's attention
The object of God's love Ps 87:2 *See also* Ps 102:13–16

The object of God's blessing Ps 133:3
See also Ps 132:13–16; 147:12–14

The object of God's judgment Jer 26:18
See also Mic 3:12; Isa 1:8–9; Jer 6:2–5,22–23; Joel 2:1–2

Zion as the focus of God's presence and promises
The security of Zion because of God's presence Ps 46:4–7 *See also* Ps 48:1–14; 125:1–2; Isa 37:22–23 pp 2Ki 19:21–22; Joel 3:16

The restoration of Zion because of God's promises Jer 30:17–22 *See also* Ps 126:1–3; Jer 29:10–14; 31:38–40; Mic 4:6–7

The salvation of Zion because of God's coming king and Saviour Zec 9:9–10 pp Mt 21:5 pp Jn 12:15 *See also* Isa 62:11–12; Mic 4:8

Zion destined to be a city for all peoples Ps 102:21–22 *See also* Ps 87:4–6; Isa 2:2–4 pp Mic 4:1–3; Isa 56:3–7; Zec 14:16

Zion as a NT symbol of the new Israel, the church
Heb 12:22–23 *See also* Ro 9:33; 1Pe 2:6; Isa 8:14; 28:16; Heb 11:16; Rev 14:1

See also
1085 God, love of	7140 people of God
2312 Christ as king	8622 worship
2324 Christ as	8664 praise
Saviour	9165 restoration
4028 world,	9210 judgment,
redeemed	God's
7020 church, the	

7300

Institutions and culture of OT

7302

altar

A construction, usually of wood, stone or metal, for the offering of sacrifice. The conflict between true and false religion often focused on altars, which were of key significance in biblical times.

Early altars built to the LORD
Ge 8:20 *These early altars were erected at sites where God's presence or power had been experienced.*
By Abraham: Ge 12:7–8; 13:18; 22:9
Ge 26:25 *by Isaac*
By Jacob: Ge 33:20; 35:7
By Moses: Ex 17:15; 24:4
Jos 8:30 *by Joshua;* Jdg 6:24 *by Gideon;* Jdg 21:4 *by unnamed Israelites;* 1Sa 7:17 *by Samuel;* 1Sa 14:35 *by Saul;* 2Sa 24:25 pp 1Ch 21:26 *by David*

Solomon's temple altar
It was preceded by the tabernacle altar of burnt offering: Ex 27:1–8; 30:1–10; 37:25–28; 38:1–7; Heb 9:3–4
1Ki 8:22; 6:20

OT pagan altars
A symptom of decline in the northern kingdom 1Ki 16:32; 2Ki 23:15; Hos 8:11; 10:1

A symptom of decline in the southern kingdom 2Ki 16:10 *ignoring the command in Dt 12:2–3;* 2Ki 21:3; Isa 17:8; Jer 11:13; 19:13; Zep 1:5

Josiah's reform targeted illicit altars 2Ki 23:12 *See also* Dt 7:5; 12:8–14 *Josiah was implementing the law requiring sacrifice to be offered only on the altar at the sanctuary of God's choice;* 2Ki 23:15–20

The altar in the second temple
Ezr 3:2–3 *See also* Ezr 7:17

Laws concerning the altar of burnt offering
Its construction Ex 20:24–26 *An earlier more basic form than in the tabernacle. No human hand was to shape the stones. See also* Ex 27:1–8; 38:1–7

Its use for the daily sacrifice Ex 29:38–39 *See also* Ex 30:28; Nu 4:13; 7:10,84

Its use for asylum 1Ki 1:50–51 *See also* Ex 21:14; 1Ki 2:28; Am 3:14

Laws concerning the incense altar
Its construction Ex 30:1–5 *See also* Ex 37:25–28

Its use Ex 30:7 *See also* Ex 30:8–10; Nu 4:11

Altars in the NT
The Jerusalem temple altar Mt 5:23–24 *See also* Mt 23:18–20; 1Co 9:13; 10:18; Heb 7:13; 9:4

Pagan altars Ac 17:23

The cross as an "altar" Heb 13:10

Altars in heaven Rev 6:9 *The lives of martyred saints are compared to the blood of offerings poured out at the base of the altar;* Rev 8:3 *The prayers of God's people are like incense, offered to him on the heavenly altar. See also* Rev 9:13; 11:1; 14:18; 16:7

See also
2315 Christ as Lamb	7454 sprinkling
6614 atonement	7458 tabernacle, the
7314 blood	7466 temples
7386 incense	8626 worship,
7402 offerings	places
7412 priesthood	8752 false worship
7435 sacrifice, in OT	

7304

anointing

The application of oil was associated with times of rejoicing and celebration. It also possessed a deeper significance, including that of being singled out by God for special favour or responsibilities.

Anointing as a social custom
In personal grooming Ecc 9:8 *The associations here are of joy and well-being. See also* Ru 3:3; Ps 92:10; Isa 57:9; Am 6:6; Mt 6:17

Anointing guests as a mark of honour Ps 23:5 *See also* Lk 7:36–39,44–47; Jn 12:3

Anointing corpses as a burial preparation Mk 16:1 *See also* Mt 26:6–12; Jn 19:38–40

Anointing religious objects
Ex 40:9–11 *Anointed objects are set apart (consecrated), to be used only in the performance of religious ceremonies. See also* Ge 28:18; Ex 30:22–33

Anointing people for office
Priests Ex 40:12–15 *See also* Lev 4:16; 21:10–12; 1Ch 29:22

Kings 1Ki 1:39 *See also* 1Sa 10:1; 16:12–13; 2Sa 5:3; 2Ki 11:12

A prophet 1Ki 19:15–16 *the only reference to the anointing of a prophet*

Anointing people for other purposes
For purification Lev 14:15–18

For healing Mk 6:13 *It has been suggested that anointing in a healing context may be related to the use of oil for medicinal purposes. See also* Jas 5:14

The figurative use of anointing
Anointing by God 1Sa 26:9 *Israel's king is frequently referred to as "the* LORD's *anointed". His physical anointing is seen as symbolising a divine anointing. The word "Messiah" literally means "the anointed one";* Isa 45:1 *Cyrus, as God's agent for a specific task, is referred to as "his anointed". See also* 2Sa 23:1; Ps 2:2; 45:2; 89:20; Eze 28:14

God's people in the OT 1Ch 16:22 pp Ps 105:15

Christian believers 2Co 1:21–22 *See also* 1Jn 2:20,27 *This anointing is not received in an outward ceremony but by sharing in the Holy Spirit's anointing of Jesus Christ.*

Jesus Christ as God's Anointed One (the Messiah)
Ac 4:26–27 *Jesus Christ's receiving of the Holy Spirit at his baptism was his "anointing" for his Messianic work;* Ac 10:38 *Note the link between anointing and the Holy Spirit. See also* Da 9:25–26; Lk 4:18; Isa 61:1; Heb 1:9

See also
1670 symbols	4488 oil
2206 Jesus, the	5333 healing
Christ	5368 kingship
2230 Messiah,	7413 priesthood, OT
coming of	7745 ordination
3120 Holy Spirit,	8218 consecration
descriptions	8266 holiness
3239 Holy Spirit,	
anointing	

7306

ark of the covenant

A rectangular wooden box, overlaid with gold, measuring 3.75 x 2.25 x 2.25 feet (1.1 x 0.7 x 0.7 metres). It contains the Law tablets and symbolises God's presence with his people.

Descriptions of the ark
Ex 25:22; Lev 16:2; Nu 10:33; Jos 3:6; 4:5,9; 1Sa 4:11

The construction of the ark
Ex 25:10–16; Dt 10:1; Ex 31:1–7;

35:10–12; 37:1–5; Dt 10:3; Ex 39:33,35; 40:1–5,20–21

The construction of the atonement cover
Ex 25:17–21; 26:34; 30:6; 37:6–9; 39:35; 40:20

The care of the ark
Nu 3:30–32; 4:5; Dt 10:8; 31:9

Major events in the history of the ark
The ark is taken to the promised land Jos 3:3,6,15–16; 6:4–16; 8:33

The ark is the focus of the covenant renewal at Mount Ebal Jdg 20:26–28

The ark is captured by the Philistines 1Sa 4:1–11,17–22; 5:1–12

The ark is returned to Israel 1Sa 6:1–3,10–15,19; 7:1–2

The ark is brought to Jerusalem 2Sa 6:1–12 pp 1Ch 13:3–14; 2Sa 6:17 pp 1Ch 16:1; 1Ch 15:1; 16:37; 2Sa 7:2–7 pp 1Ch 17:1–6; 2Sa 15:24–25,29 *David is fleeing from Absalom.*

The ark is placed in the temple 1Ki 8:1–6 pp 2Ch 5:2–7

The ark in later Israelite history 2Ch 35:3 *The ark must have been moved from the temple.*

The function of the ark
To contain the tablets of the Law Dt 10:5 *See also* Ex 25:16,21; 40:20; Dt 31:24–26; 1Ki 8:9; Heb 9:4 *The jar of manna and Aaron's rod were originally placed beside the ark (Ex 16:34; Nu 17:10), and were probably put inside it at a later date.*

As the place where God reveals his commands to Moses Nu 7:89 *See also* Ex 25:22; 30:6,36

As a symbol of the presence of God Lev 16:2 *See also* Nu 10:33–36; Jos 7:6; Jdg 20:27; 2Sa 7:2 pp 1Ch 17:1; 2Ch 6:41 pp Ps 132:8

Used on the Day of Atonement Lev 16:13–15

The ark's holiness and effect
Irreverent treatment of the ark brings judgment 2Sa 6:6–7 pp 1Ch 13:9–10 *See also* Jos 3:4; 1Sa 5:1–4,8–12; 6:19

The presence of the ark brings blessing 2Sa 6:11 pp 1Ch 13:14

A restored Israel in which the ark has no place
Jer 3:16

The ark in John's revelation
Rev 11:19 *The ark here symbolises the presence of God and is open and visible, not hidden in the Most Holy Place.*

See also
1640 Book of the	7396 Most Holy
Law	Place
5071 Aaron	7458 tabernacle, the
5377 law, Ten	7467 temple,
Command-	Solomon's
ments	7768 priests, OT
5581 throne	function
7241 Jerusalem,	9230 judgment seat
significance	
7308 Atonement, Day	
of	

7308

Atonement, Day of

The most holy day of Israel's year (the tenth day of the seventh month) on which the high priest entered the Most Holy Place to offer sacrifices for the sins of the nation. Hebrews sees this day as symbolic of the achievements of Jesus Christ on the cross.

The priestly rituals on the Day of Atonement
The priest's own preparations Lev 16:4,6,11–14

The preparation of two male goats Lev 16:7–10
The sacrifice atones for the people's sins: Ex 30:10; Lev 16:15–19
The scapegoat symbolically carries away the people's sins: Lev 16:10,20–22

Concluding procedures Lev 16:23–28

Additional offerings on the Day of Atonement Nu 29:8–11

Features unique to the Day of Atonement
The priest entered the Most Holy Place Heb 9:7 *See also* Lev 16:2

Sacrifice was made for all the sins of all the people Lev 16:30 *See also* Ex 30:10; Lev 16:16–17,21–22,34

It was a festival requiring humility and fasting Nu 29:7 *This provides a contrast to all other religious festivals which were times of joyous celebration and feasting: "deny yourselves" includes the idea of fasting. See also* Lev 16:29,31; 23:27–32; Ac 27:9

The Day of Atonement is paralleled and contrasted with the achievements of Jesus Christ in his death
Jesus Christ entered the Most Holy Place Heb 9:24 *See also* Heb 6:19–20; 9:11–12

Jesus Christ's blood was offered in sacrifice Heb 9:12 *See also* Ro 3:25

Jesus Christ's sacrifice was outside the city gates Heb 13:11–12

Jesus Christ's sacrifice was once for all Heb 9:25–26 *See also* Heb 10:12

Jesus Christ's sacrifice gives inner rather than ritual cleansing Heb 9:13–14 *See also* Heb 9:9–10

Jesus Christ's sacrifice gives access to God Heb 10:19–20 *On the Day of Atonement no-one else was allowed to be in the Tent of Meeting, let alone in the Most Holy Place. Access into the intimate presence of God is now the right of all believers. See also* Lev 16:17; Mt 27:51; Eph 2:18; 3:12

See also

2306 Christ, high priest	6614 atonement
2315 Christ as Lamb	7314 blood
2324 Christ as Saviour	7376 high priest
2410 cross, the	7396 Most Holy Place
6020 sin	7440 scapegoat
6606 access to God	8266 holiness

7310

avenger of blood

The one responsible in OT law for carrying out the death penalty in the case of murder, usually, the murdered person's next of kin.

The responsibility of the avenger of blood
Nu 35:16–21 *See also* Nu 35:26–27; Dt 19:11–12

Protection from the avenger of blood
Nu 35:10–15 *See also* Nu 35:22–25; Dt 19:4–6; Jos 20:1–6

Examples of avenging of blood
Ge 4:24; 2Sa 3:27; 14:11

God as an avenger of blood
Dt 32:43 *See also* Jdg 9:23–24; 2Ki 9:7; Ps 9:12; 79:10; Rev 6:10; 19:2

See also

5040 murder	7338 cities of refuge
5493 retribution	7346 death penalty
5495 revenge & retaliation	7388 kinsman-redeemer
5711 marriage, restrictions	9210 judgment, God's
7318 blood, symbol of guilt	

7312

Baal

Literally "master", used to refer to a variety of local gods in the Near East, encountered by Israel in Canaan. In the later period, the word comes to refer especially to the local god of the city of Tyre (Baal Melgart), on account of the increasing importance of that city in the region.

The history of Baal worship
In the exodus period Nu 25:3–5 *A Moabite deity whose worship involved sexual immorality. See also* Nu 22:41; Dt 4:3; Ps 106:28; Hos 9:10

In the time of the judges Jdg 2:12–13 *Ashtoreth was the consort of Baal. See also* Jdg 3:7; 6:31–32; 8:33; 10:6; 1Sa 7:4; 12:10

In the time of Elijah 1Ki 17:1 *The proclamation of a drought and the contest on Carmel challenged the supposed power of Baal. See also* 1Ki 16:30–33; 18:18–19:1; 22:53; 2Ki 10:18–29; 11:17–18

During the later monarchy in the north Hos 2:2–13 *Lovers are gods such as Baal. See also* Hos 11:2; 13:1

During the later monarchy in the south 2Ch 28:1–2 *The Judean kingdom copied the idolatry in the north. See also* Jer 2:8; 7:9; Hos 3:3

See also

5092 Elijah	8748 false religion
7774 prophets, false	8752 false worship
8237 doctrine, false	8768 idolatry
8747 false gods	

7314

blood

The symbol of life, which thus plays an especially important role in the sacrificial system of the OT. The shedding of the blood of a sacrificial animal represents the giving up of its life. The "blood of Christ" refers to Jesus Christ's obedient giving of his life, in order to achieve redemption and forgiveness.

7315
blood, as basis of life

Scripture treats blood as the basis of life, and regards the shedding of blood as representing the end of life.

Blood symbolises life
Lev 17:10–14 *See also* Ge 9:4–6; Dt 12:20–25; 2Sa 23:15–17; Ps 72:14; Jer 2:34; Eze 33:1–6; Mt 27:3–4; Lk 11:50–51 pp Mt 23:35–36

Blood indicating violent death
Ge 4:8–11 *See also* Ge 9:6; Jdg 9:22–24; 1Ki 2:5–6,28–34; 2Ki 9:30–33

Shedding blood as a sin
Ex 20:13 pp Dt 5:17 *See also* Ge 42:21–22; Dt 21:1–9; 2Ki 21:16; Pr 1:10–19; Isa 26:21; Mt 15:18–19 pp Mk 7:20–21; Ro 1:28–29

The eating of blood forbidden
Lev 3:17 *See also* Lev 7:26–27; 17:10–14; Dt 12:23; 1Sa 14:31–34; Ac 15:19–20,29

See also

4015 life	7346 death penalty
4233 field of blood	8278 innocence, teaching on
5025 killing	9020 death
5040 murder	

7316
blood, and OT sacrifices

The pouring out of animals' blood in sacrifice was God's provision, under the old covenant, for the atonement of sin.

God's provision of blood sacrifice to establish the old covenant
Ex 24:4–8 *See also* Heb 9:18–20

God's provision of blood sacrifices within the old covenant
Blood sacrifices and the priesthood Ex 29:10–21 pp Lev 8:14–24; Lev 9:8–14; 16:1–14

Blood sacrifices and various offerings Lev 1:1–17 *the burnt offering, to gain favour or express devotion;* Lev 3:1–17 *the fellowship, or peace, offering, to express gratitude;* Lev 4:1–35 *the sin offering, to gain forgiveness;* Lev 5:14–19 *the guilt offering, where restitution was required;* Lev 16:15–22 *the Day of Atonement, for the cleansing of the nation from unintentional sin*

7317

Blood sacrifices and the Passover
Ex 12:1–14 See also 2Ch 30:15–20;
35:1–19; Ezr 6:19–21; Mk 14:12
pp Lk 22:7–8

Blood sacrifices must come from animals without defect
Lev 22:17–25 See also Ex 12:5; Lev 1:3;
3:1; 4:3; 5:15; Nu 28:9,11; Dt 15:21;
Eze 43:22–27

Blood sacrifices must not come from human beings
2Ki 23:10 See also 2Ki 17:17; 21:1–6;
Eze 20:25–26; Mic 6:7

The limited effect of blood sacrifices
They can become mere external ritual
Isa 1:11–13 See also Isa 66:2–4

They are worthless without obedience to God Hos 6:6 See also 1Sa 15:22–23;
Ps 40:6–8; Am 4:4–5; 5:21–27

They are unable to cleanse the conscience Heb 9:9–10 See also
Heb 10:1–4

See also
1345 covenant	7370 guilt offering
6020 sin	7402 offerings
6752 substitution	7406 Passover
7322 burnt offering	7416 purification
7364 fellowship offering	7435 sacrifice, in OT
	7444 sin offering

7317
blood, of Jesus Christ

The shedding of the blood of Jesus Christ is seen as representing the giving of his life as an atoning sacrifice for the sins of humanity.

The blood of Jesus Christ as part of his humanity
Jn 19:33–34 See also Lk 22:44; Ac 5:28;
1Jn 5:6

The blood of Jesus Christ as a sacrifice
Heb 9:12–14,23–26; 10:3–14;
13:11–12

The blood of Jesus Christ as a symbol of atonement
Ro 3:25 See also Eph 1:7; Rev 7:14

The effects of the blood of Jesus Christ
The institution of the new covenant
1Co 11:25 pp Mt 26:27–28
pp Mk 14:23–24 pp Lk 22:20 See also
Heb 9:11–15; 12:24; 13:20

Redemption Ac 20:28;
1Pe 1:1–2,18–19; Rev 5:9–10

Forgiveness and justification Ro 5:9 See
also Mt 26:28 pp Mk 14:24 pp Lk 22:20;
Ro 3:25–26

Victory over evil and Satan
Rev 7:14–17; 12:10–11

Liberation from sin Rev 1:5–6

The promise of total restoration
Col 1:19–20

The blood of Jesus Christ and believers
Believers are cleansed from all sin
Heb 9:14; 10:22; 13:12; 1Jn 1:6–9

Believers have a new confidence before God Eph 2:13; Col 1:19–22;
Heb 10:19–22

The blood of Jesus Christ and the Lord's Supper
Invitations to share in the blood of Jesus Christ 1Co 10:16 See also
Jn 6:53–57

Warnings about sinning against the blood of Jesus Christ 1Co 11:27 See
also Heb 10:28–31

See also
1352 covenant, the new	6614 atonement
2315 Christ as Lamb	6652 forgiveness
2410 Christ as Lamb	6676 justification
4127 Satan, defeat of	6700 peace
5596 victory	6720 redemption
6606 access to God	7933 Lord's Supper

7318
blood, as symbol of guilt

Blood is often used as an image of people's sin and guilt, and the judgment which follows. Blood-guilt is ascribed to those who are responsible for the shedding of innocent blood.

Blood as an image of sin and guilt
Isa 59:2–3 See also Lev 20:9–13,27;
2Sa 1:14–16; Isa 1:15–18; Na 3:1;
Ac 18:6

Blood as an image of judgment
Isa 34:5–6 See also Ex 7:14–21;
Ps 78:44; 105:29; Ac 2:19–20;
Joel 2:30–31

Blood as a sign of the end times
Ac 2:19–20 See also Joel 2:30–31;
Rev 6:12–15; 8:7–9; 16:3–6

Blood-guilt, the result of shedding innocent blood
Examples of blood-guilt Ge 4:8–11 See
also 2Sa 1:14–16; 4:5–12; Eze 35:5–9;
Hab 2:12; Mt 27:3–8,24; Ac 5:28

The right to avenge blood-guilt under the law Dt 19:11–13 See also
Nu 35:16–28

Restraint to avoid further blood-guilt
Dt 4:41–42 See also Ge 4:15;
Nu 35:6–34; Dt 19:4–10; Jos 20:1–9

Blood-guilt cannot be forgotten
Ge 9:5–6 See also Ge 4:10–16; 42:22;
1Ki 2:28–33; Isa 26:21; Mt 23:30–31

See also
6172 guilt	9105 last things
7310 avenger of blood	9210 judgment, God's
7338 cities of refuge	

7320
breastpiece

A pouch worn on the chest of the high priest.

The breastpiece was worn by the high priest
Lev 8:5–9 See also Ex 28:15–16,29;
39:8–9

It was adorned with twelve precious stones Ex 28:17–21 See also Ex 25:3–7;
39:10–14

It contained the Urim and Thummim
Ex 28:30 The Urim and Thummim were
used in decision-making. See also Lev 8:8

It was attached to the ephod
Ex 28:22–28 See also Ex 39:15–21

See also
4342 jewels	7392 lots, casting of
5237 breastplate	8408 decision-making
7352 ephod	
7376 high priest	

7322
burnt offering

Probably the earliest and most basic form of sacrifice. It is seen fundamentally as a gift to God, either in thanksgiving for his goodness or for atonement for sin.

Hebrew names for the burnt offering
Dt 33:10 The rarer Hebrew expression
means something whole or complete;
Ps 66:13 The commoner expression in
Hebrew means that which "goes up" to
God. See also 1Sa 7:9; Ps 51:19

Early examples of burnt offerings
Ge 8:20
Probably all these examples include an
element of propitiation: Ge 22:2–8,13;
Ex 10:25; 18:12; 20:24; 24:5; Job 1:5

Regulations concerning the burnt offering
How the offering is to be made
Lev 1:1–17; 6:8–13; 7:8 the entitlement
of the priest; Mal 1:8

Occasions for making the offering
Nu 28:9–10 It was an additional offering
on the Sabbath.
As a daily offering: Ex 29:38–42; Ezr 3:3
Lev 8:18–21 at the ordination of priests
On the Day of Atonement: Lev 16:3,24
Nu 28:11–14 on the first of the month, the
new moon
At Passover: Nu 28:19,23
At Firstfruits and the Feast of Weeks:
Lev 23:12,18; Nu 28:27
At the beginning of the seventh month:
Nu 29:2,6
At the Feast of Tabernacles: Nu 29:13
Lk 2:24 for purification after childbirth

Burnt offerings in idolatrous worship
Ex 32:6; 2Ki 10:25

Warnings about misplaced confidence in the burnt offering
1Sa 15:22 See also Isa 1:11–15;
Jer 7:21–22; Hos 6:6; Am 5:25;
Mic 6:6–8

NT references to the burnt offering
Jesus Christ endorsed the prophets' teaching Mk 12:33–34 See also Mt 9:13;
12:7

The holy life of Jesus Christ is the perfect burnt offering Heb 10:5–10 See
also Heb 10:14

See also

7316 blood, OT sacrifices	7361 Feast of Weeks
7357 Feast of Firstfruits	7402 offerings
7358 Feast of Tabernacles	7406 Passover
	7435 sacrifice, in OT

7324

calf worship

A heathen (notably Egyptian and Canaanite) practice, in which statues of bull calves were worshipped as symbols of fertility and physical strength. Contrary to the second commandment this was copied by the Israelites and by Jeroboam after the division of the kingdom, in both cases incurring God's wrath.

Aaron made a golden calf for the Israelites to worship

This act was born partly of impatience Ex 32:1–4 *See also* Ex 32:7–8; Ps 106:19–22; Ac 7:41

It was swiftly condemned Ex 32:19–20 *See also* Ex 32:35; Dt 9:16–21; Ps 106:23

King Jeroboam initiated calf worship

As a matter of expediency 1Ki 12:26–30 *See also* 2Ki 17:15–16; 2Ch 11:14–15; 13:8

Jeroboam's sin was one of the main reasons for the Assyrian captivity 2Ki 17:18–28 *See also* Hos 8:4–9; 10:5–6

Calf worship is detestable and useless

Dt 7:25; Isa 44:9–20; 46:6–7; Ro 1:21–23

See also

4615 bull	8718 disobedience
4618 calf	8747 false gods
5071 Aaron	8752 false worship
6103 abomination	8768 idolatry

7326

cannibalism

God warns his people about cannibalism

Dt 28:53; Lev 26:29; Jer 19:9

Cannibalism as a result of God's judgment on his disobedient people

2Ki 6:24–29; La 2:20; 4:10; Eze 5:10

See also

4438 eating	5569 hardship
4823 famine, physical	6223 rebellion of Israel
5484 punishment by God	9210 judgment, God's
5529 sieges	

7328

ceremonies

Formal outward practices and rituals symbolising or marking events of importance or spiritual significance. Although they had their place in biblical cultural life, they may become empty and hypocritical, losing their deep spiritual meaning. Ceremonies thus become symbolic of empty legalism which should be rejected.

Ceremonies marking important events

Different stages in life Ge 50:7,10–11; Ex 13:2; Jdg 14:10; Jer 34:5; Jn 2:1–2; 20:4

Temple worship Ne 13:9 *See also* 1Ki 9:25; 1Ch 16:40; 2Ch 8:13; 29:15 *Some psalms include excerpts from temple liturgy relating to parts of temple-based worship ceremonies:* Ps 5:7; 118:19–20; 138:2 Ac 3:1

Appointing leaders Ac 13:2–3 *See also* Lev 8:30; 1Sa 16:13; 1Ki 1:39; Ac 6:5–6; 9:17; 1Ti 4:14

Historical events Ru 4:7–8 *See also* Ge 35:14; Ex 12:14; 13:9; Jos 4:4–9; 1Sa 7:12; Lk 22:19 pp 1Co 11:24–25

Ceremonies as spiritual symbols of God's presence

Mt 18:20 *There is a sense in which any gathering of believers is ceremonially symbolic of God's presence. See also* Ex 30:25–29; Nu 4:4; 10:35–36 *The ark of the covenant was a symbol of God's presence among his people. It, and its location, the tabernacle and later, the Most Holy Place, were therefore centres of the most elaborate ceremonies;* 1Ki 8:3–6 pp 2Ch 5:4–7; 1Ki 8:29 pp 2Ch 6:20; 1Ch 6:49; Heb 9:1–7

Initiation ceremonies

Circumcision Lev 12:3 *See also* Ge 17:10; Jos 5:2; Lk 2:21–24

Baptism Mt 28:19 *See also* Ac 2:38; 16:33–34; 1Pe 3:21

Ceremonies relating to ritual cleansing

Ex 30:18–20 *See also* Lev 14:14–18; 16:26; 22:6; Nu 19:7; Heb 9:10 *Many aspects of ritual activity were added to the biblical ones in Jewish laws and regulations.*

Ceremonies relating to atonement

Lev 17:11 *See also* Lev 4:20; 8:30–35; 16:10; Heb 5:1

Ceremonies conveying spiritual realities

Passover: a ceremony symbolising salvation history Lk 22:15–16 *See also* 2Ki 23:21–22; Ezr 6:21–22; Mt 26:17 pp Mk 14:12 pp Lk 22:7–9

Baptism: a ceremony symbolising new birth Jn 3:5 *See also* Ac 10:48; 22:16; Gal 3:27; Col 2:12

Marriage: a ceremony symbolising faithful partnership Mt 19:6 pp Mk 10:9; Eph 5:25–28; Heb 13:4; Rev 19:7

Ceremonies which lapsed into hypocrisy

Washing ceremonies without accompanying inner cleanliness Mt 23:25 *See also* Mt 23:27–28; Mk 7:4

Sacrificial ceremonies without inner repentance Am 5:21–22 *See also* 1Sa 15:22; Ps 51:16–17; Isa 1:11–17; Hos 8:11–13; Mal 1:8

Initiation ceremonies without real commitment 1Co 7:19 *See also* Ac 15:1,8–10; Ro 2:28–29; Gal 5:6

Jesus Christ brings freedom from meaningless ceremonies

Gal 5:1 *See also* Gal 4:8–10; Eph 2:14–18; Col 2:13–23; Heb 7:18–19

See also

5173 outward appearance	7957 sacraments
5588 traditions	8142 religion
5742 wedding	8622 worship
7404 ordinances	8774 legalism
7422 ritual	8784 nominal religion

7330

chief priests

A group of individuals in charge of temple worship in Jerusalem, and regarded as leading representatives of the Jewish people, who came into conflict with Jesus Christ and plotted his death.

OT references to the chief priest

2Ch 19:11 *See also* 2Ki 25:18 pp Jer 52:24 *Seraiah* Jehoiada: 2Ch 24:6,11 2Ch 31:10 *Azariah;* Ezr 7:5 *Ezra was descended from Aaron the chief priest*

The chief priests were in charge of temple worship in Jerusalem

Mt 2:4 *They were expected to pronounce on matters of Jewish law and interpretation of Scripture;* Mt 21:15 *Temple discipline was their responsibility.*

Jesus Christ predicted his suffering at the hands of the chief priests and elders

Mt 16:21 pp Mk 8:31 pp Lk 9:22 *See also* Mt 20:18 pp Mk 10:33

The response of the chief priests to Jesus Christ

They were puzzled by Jesus Christ's teaching Mt 21:23 pp Mk 11:27–28 pp Lk 20:1–2 *See also* Mt 21:45–46 pp Lk 20:19; Jn 7:32,45; 11:47 *As official representatives of the Jewish people, they feared the political repercussions of Jesus Christ's popularity.*

They and the elders plotted Jesus Christ's death Mt 26:3–5 pp Mk 14:1 *See also* Mt 26:59 pp Mk 14:55; Mt 27:1

They collaborated with Judas Mt 26:14 pp Mk 14:10 pp Lk 22:4; Mt 26:47 pp Mk 14:43 pp Lk 22:52 pp Jn 18:3; Mt 27:3–6

The role of the chief priests in the trial of Jesus Christ

They made accusations against Jesus Christ Mt 27:12 pp Mk 15:3; Lk 22:66; 23:10

7332

They persuaded the crowd against Jesus Christ Mt 27:20; Lk 23:4,13; Jn 19:6

They mocked Jesus Christ Mt 27:41 pp Mk 15:31

They handed Jesus Christ over to Pilate Mk 15:10; Lk 24:20; Jn 18:35

They persuaded Pilate to have the tomb guarded Mt 27:62–66

They bribed the soldiers Mt 28:11–15

They rejected Jesus Christ as king Jn 19:15,21

The chief priests' attempt to prevent the preaching of the gospel

By silencing the apostles Ac 4:23; 5:24

By authorising Paul to arrest believers Ac 9:14,21; 26:10,12

The involvement of the chief priests in the arrest and trial of Paul

Ac 22:30; 23:14; 25:2,15

See also
2530 Christ, death of	7469 temple, Herod's
2545 Christ, opposition to	7550 Pharisees
2560 Christ, resurrection	7555 Sadducees
2585 Christ, trial	7565 Sanhedrin
5107 Paul	7718 elders

7332

child sacrifice

Child sacrifice is unconditionally condemned in Scripture. The few cases in which it is known to have taken place are probably due to the influence of Israel's pagan neighbours.

Laws forbidding child sacrifice
Lev 18:21 Molech was the god of the Ammonites. See also Ex 22:29 to be interpreted with reference to Ex 13:12–16 and Ex 34:19,22; Dt 18:10

Instances of child sacrifice
2Ki 3:27; 16:3 pp 2Ch 28:3; 2Ki 17:17,31; 21:6 pp 2Ch 33:6; 2Ki 23:10 Josiah's reforms involved desecrating Topheth, where child sacrifices were offered; Isa 57:5; Jer 7:31

Arguments against child sacrifice
Child sacrifice is the idolatrous practice of the nations Dt 12:31 See also Lev 20:2–5; Ps 106:35–38; Jer 32:35; Hos 13:2

It defiles God's people Eze 20:26 See also Eze 20:31

It defiles God's sanctuary Eze 23:37,39

It incurs God's anger Jer 19:4–5; Eze 16:20–21,36–37; Hos 13:2

God's unique command to Abraham to sacrifice Isaac
Ge 22:1–2 This was a test of obedience for Abraham. The following verses dispel any idea that God desires human sacrifice; Heb 11:17

These verses may allude to the story of Abraham and Isaac, especially Ge 22:16: Jn 3:16; Ro 8:32

See also
1025 God, anger of	8747 false gods
7435 sacrifice, in OT	8752 false worship
8466 reformation	8768 idolatry

7334

circumcision

The practice of cutting away the foreskin of male children, usually within a short time of birth. In the OT, the practice is seen as a sign of membership of the people of God. The NT makes it clear that Christians are under no obligation to be circumcised.

7335

circumcision, physical

In the OT, circumcision is seen as an outward sign of membership of Israel, the people of God.

The significance of circumcision in God's covenant with Abraham
Ge 17:10–14 See also Ac 7:8

Circumcision is also for Abraham's descendants Ge 17:7

Circumcision as a sign of national identity
Dinah's brothers and the Shechemites: Ge 34:8–9,14–17
Ex 4:24–26; Jos 5:4–8

Circumcision is integrated into the Mosaic law
Lev 12:3; Jn 7:22 It was later sometimes forgotten that circumcision predated the Mosaic law.

Circumcision as an important Passover restriction
Ex 12:44,48–49; Jdg 14:3 Some of Israel's neighbours practised circumcision, but not the Philistines.

Circumcision was not necessarily a sign of consecration to God
Jer 9:25–26

NT accounts of circumcision practised in obedience to the law
Lk 1:59 John; Lk 2:21 Jesus Christ; Jn 7:23 Circumcision was permitted on the Sabbath; Php 3:5 Paul refers to his own circumcision; Ac 16:3 Timothy

The subject of circumcision debated by the first Christians
Ac 10:45; 11:2; 15:5; Gal 2:3 That Titus, a Greek, was not required to be circumcised illustrates the change in the attitude of the church concerning the relevance of the law to Gentile believers; Eph 2:11; Col 3:11; Tit 1:10

See also
1348 covenant with Abraham	6260 uncircumcised
1680 types	7140 people of God
5378 law, OT	7422 ritual
	7957 sacraments

7336

circumcision, spiritual

On its own, the physical sign of circumcision is no guarantee of finding favour in the sight of God. It was intended to be the outward sign of inward consecration and should be accompanied by repentance, faith and obedience. Paul stresses that circumcision confers no special privileges upon individuals; it is faith in God, rather than any outward sign, that ensures that believers stand in a right relationship to God.

Physical circumcision has no value without the obedience of the heart
Dt 30:6 See also Dt 10:14–16; Jer 4:4 Ro 2:28–29 See also Ro 2:25–27; 1Co 7:19

Circumcision and faith
Gal 5:6 See also Ro 3:30

Abraham's righteousness depended on his faith, not on the covenant of circumcision Gal 3:6; Ge 15:6; Ro 4:9–12

Paul values the law as part of God's plan Ro 3:1–2

The sharp debate about circumcision for Christians
The Council of Jerusalem Ac 15:1–19

Jewish Christians in Jerusalem criticise Peter for accepting hospitality from Cornelius and his (uncircumcised) friends Ac 11:1–3

God's acceptance of uncircumcised Gentiles is clear from the outpouring of the Holy Spirit upon them Ac 10:44–46 See also Ac 10:34

Peter's misgivings about Gentile believers and the law Gal 2:11–16 the dispute between Paul and Peter

Imposing circumcision upon Gentile Christians denies the freedom of the gospel
Gal 5:1–6 To insist on circumcision is to nullify the work of Jesus Christ on the cross. See also Gal 2:3–5; 3:14

"Judaisers" should be resisted
Gal 5:7–12; 6:12–13,15; Php 3:2–3; Tit 1:10–11

To be "in Christ" is to be spiritually circumcised Col 2:11–12 See also Col 3:11

Paul's confidence in Jesus Christ
Php 3:4–9

The relationship between baptism and circumcision in the NT
Col 2:11–13 Both circumcision and baptism may each be described as a "seal". Baptism signifies entry into the new covenant in the same way that circumcision marked initiation into the old; Ro 4:11 Abraham the father of all believers; 2Co 1:21–22; Eph 1:13

See also

2321 Christ as redeemer	8020 faith
3287 Holy Spirit, sealing of	8154 righteousness
	8207 commitment
6658 freedom	8218 consecration
7908 baptism, significance	8239 earnestness
	8453 obedience

7338

cities of refuge

Cities set apart at the time of the conquest of Canaan as places of refuge for those who had killed people by accident.
Nu 35:6–34; Dt 4:41–43; 19:1–13; Jos 20:2–9

See also

5025 killing	5942 security
5040 murder	7310 avenger of
5490 refuge	blood
5491 refugees	7438 sanctuary
5511 safety	

7340

clean and unclean

The distinction between things which were ritually acceptable and unacceptable to God. Animals were classified as either clean or unclean, denoting their suitability or unsuitability for sacrifice and food. The motives and intentions of the heart were also sometimes judged to be clean or unclean, as uncleanness was often linked with sin.

The OT distinction between clean and unclean
The command to distinguish between clean and unclean Lev 15:31 *See also* Lev 10:8–11; 20:22–26; Eze 22:26; 44:23

The distinction between clean and unclean animals Ge 7:2 *See also* Ge 7:8–9; 8:20; Lev 11:1–47 pp Dt 14:3–20; Lev 27:11–13

The NT attitude to clean and unclean animals Mk 7:14–23 pp Mt 15:10–20; Ac 10:11–15; 11:5–9

Places and inanimate objects could be clean or unclean Lev 10:14 *See also* Lev 4:12; 6:11; 11:32–38; 14:33–57; 2Ch 13:11

Causes of uncleanness
Physical contact with anything unclean Lev 5:2–3 *See also* Lev 7:19; Hos 9:3–4; Hag 2:10–14

Contact with corpses Nu 19:11 *See also* Lev 21:1–4,10–12; Nu 6:5–8

Infectious skin diseases Lev 13:1–46 *See also* Lev 14:1–32; Mt 8:2–4 pp Mk 1:40–44 pp Lk 5:12–14

Certain bodily functions Lev 12:2 *See also* Lev 12:5; 15:1–33

Consequences of uncleanness
Exclusion from worship Nu 22:3–5 *See also* Lev 12:4; Nu 9:6–12; 1Sa 20:24–26; 2Ch 23:19; 30:17

Isolation from God's people Nu 5:2 *See also* Lev 7:20–21; Dt 23:10–11

Cleansing from uncleanness
Lev 16:29–30 *See also* Lev 12:6–8; 16:15–16; 22:4–7; Nu 6:9–12; 19:1–22; 31:21–24; Heb 9:13

Inner, spiritual cleanness and uncleanness
Job 33:9; Ps 51:7 *See also* Ge 20:5; Ps 24:3–4; Pr 20:9; Isa 1:15–16; 64:6; La 1:8; Eze 36:25; Mt 15:10–20 pp Mk 7:14–23; Mt 23:25–28; Ac 10:28

See also

4404 food	7416 purification
5008 conscience	7424 ritual law
5297 disease	7426 ritual washing
6103 abomination	7454 sprinkling
7342 cleanliness	7478 washing
7348 defilement	9030 dead bodies

7342

cleanliness

Careful, fastidious attention to personal hygiene, particularly important in the climate of the Near East. In Scripture, sin is associated with lack of cleanliness, whereas redemption and baptism are linked with washing.

Cleanliness through bathing
As part of general personal hygiene Ru 3:1–3 *See also* Jn 13:10

For cleansing from uncleanness Lev 17:15–16 *See also* Lev 14:8–9; 15:13; 2Ki 5:9–14

Cleanliness through washing feet
A customary practice after a journey Ge 19:1–2 *See also* Ge 18:1–5; 24:32; 43:24; 1Sa 25:40–42; 2Sa 11:6–8; Lk 7:36–47

As a sign of humility and love Jn 13:2–17 *See also* 1Ti 5:9–10

Cleanliness through washing clothes
As part of general personal hygiene Isa 7:3 *See also* 2Ki 18:17 pp Isa 36:2

For cleansing from uncleanness Lev 11:40 *See also* Ex 19:10–11,14–15; Lev 13:6; 16:26; Nu 8:7; 19:21

Cleanliness through washing faces and hands
Mt 6:16–18 *See also* Ex 30:18–21; 40:30–31; Mt 15:2

Cleanliness through washing infants at birth
Eze 16:4–5

Cleansing agents
Jer 2:22 *See also* Job 9:30–31; Mal 3:2

The Pharisees' concern with outer cleanliness to the exclusion of inner purity
Mk 7:1–23 pp Mt 15:1–20 *See also* Lk 11:37–41

Cleanliness used metaphorically
Lack of cleanliness associated with sin Zec 3:1–7 *See also* Isa 4:4; Mt 12:43–45 pp Lk 11:24–26

Cleanliness associated with righteousness and purity Rev 19:14 *See also* Jer 4:14; Eph 5:25–27; Tit 3:4–7; Jas 4:8; Rev 15:6; 19:8

Baptism compared to washing away sins Ac 22:16 *See also* 1Pe 3:21–22

See also

4293 water	7348 defilement
5129 bathing	7416 purification
5153 foot-washing	7426 ritual washing
5226 basin	7478 washing
5655 birth	8324 purity
6151 dirt	
7340 clean and unclean	

7344

curtain

Mentioned chiefly in relation to the construction of the tabernacle. The curtain which separated off the Most Holy Place symbolised the separation between God and humanity. The tearing of the curtain when Jesus Christ was crucified symbolised the end of this separation and gave access into God's presence for believers.

Curtains for the construction of the tabernacle
Ex 26:1–6 *See also* Ex 36:8–13
Ex 26:7–13 *See also* Ex 36:14–18
Ex 26:36–37 *See also* Ex 36:37–38
Ex 27:9–18 *See also* Ex 38:9–19;
35:10–17 pp Ex 39:33–40; Nu 3:25–26

The curtain in the Most Holy Place
The Most Holy Place shielded with a curtain Heb 9:2–4 *See also*
Ex 26:31–33; 40:2–3,21; Nu 4:5;
2Ch 3:14 *As in the tabernacle, the Most Holy Place in Solomon's temple was shut off with a curtain.*

The curtain symbolises separation from God Lev 16:2 *See also* Nu 18:7; Heb 9:6–9

The curtain indicates the hiddenness of God Ps 18:11 pp 2Sa 22:12 *See also* Ex 20:21; Dt 4:11; Job 22:14; Ps 97:2; 1Ti 6:16

The torn curtain symbolises access to God Mt 27:51 pp Mk 15:38 pp Lk 23:45; Heb 10:19–20 *See also* Heb 6:19–20

Other examples of tent curtains
SS 1:5; Isa 54:2

See also

2530 Christ, death of	7467 temple,
5211 art	Solomon's
5272 craftsmen	7469 temple,
5578 tents	Herod's
6606 access to God	7474 Tent of
7396 Most Holy	Meeting
Place	8266 holiness
7459 tabernacle, in OT	8341 separation

death penalty

The lawful taking of human life by the civil or military authorities. The death penalty was inflicted by all nations in the ancient world. In Israel, the main method was stoning, amongst other nations, other forms such as hanging, beheading and crucifixion were used.

The ultimate authority for the death penalty lies with God alone
Examples of God taking human life Ex 12:29 See also Nu 16:35; 1Sa 6:19; 25:38; 2Sa 6:7 pp 1Ch 13:10; Ac 12:23

God may delegate his authority to human beings Ge 9:6; Jos 7:15,25; 1Sa 15:3,32–33

The role of the civil authority Ac 25:11; Ro 13:1,3–4

Causes of the death penalty
Sacrilege Ex 19:12–13

Serious abuse of one's parents Ex 21:15,17; Dt 21:18–21; Mt 15:4

Adultery Lev 20:10; Dt 22:22; Jn 8:5

Blasphemy Lev 24:16; Jn 19:7

Idolatry Lev 20:2

Immorality Lev 20:11–16; Dt 22:21–25

Kidnapping Ex 21:16

Murder Ge 9:6; Ex 21:12

Rebellion Dt 17:12

Sabbath-breaking Ex 31:14–15; Nu 15:32–36

Witchcraft Lev 20:27; 1Sa 28:9

Rape of a betrothed virgin Dt 22:23–29

Bestiality Ex 22:19

Child sacrifice Lev 20:2–5

Means of executing the death penalty
Beheading Ge 40:19; Mk 6:27 pp Mt 14:9–10

Burning Da 3:6

Crucifixion Mt 27:26 pp Mk 15:15 pp Jn 19:16; Mt 27:38 pp Mk 15:27 pp Lk 23:33

Hanging Ge 40:22; Dt 21:22–23; Ac 5:30; Gal 3:13

Impalement Ezr 6:11; Est 2:23 fn; 5:14; 7:9–10; 9:12–13

Stoning Lev 24:23; Dt 21:18–21 *Stoning was the duty of the whole community:* Lev 20:2; 24:14; Nu 15:35 *Stoning carried out lawfully:* Lev 24:23; Nu 15:36; Jos 7:25 *Stoning carried out unlawfully:* 1Ki 21:11–13; 2Ch 24:21; Ac 7:54–59 *The attempted stoning of Jesus Christ:* Jn 8:58–59; 10:31–33 Jn 8:3–11 *Jesus Christ refuses to carry out a stoning.*

The sword Ex 32:27; 1Sa 15:33; 22:18–19; 1Ki 2:29,46; 2Ch 23:14–15; Da 2:5; Ac 12:2; Heb 11:37

Wild beasts Da 6:16

The commutation of the death penalty
Ge 4:15; Ex 21:13,29–30; Nu 35:6; Dt 4:42; 19:1–10

See also

5025 killing	5361 justice, human
5040 murder	5557 stoning
5276 crime	5572 sword
5281 crucifixion	8450 martyrdom
5322 gallows	9020 death
5331 hanging	

defilement

The result of making oneself or someone else unclean in God's sight. Outward, physical defilement comes from contact with someone or something unclean, whereas sin produces inner, spiritual defilement.

Defilement through contact with anything unclean
Lev 20:25 See also Lev 7:19–21; 11:41–45; 21:1–4; 22:4–5; Nu 5:1–3; 6:9,12; Eze 4:9–15; 44:25; Da 1:8; Hag 2:10–14; Mal 1:7

Defilement through bodily emissions
Lev 12:2–7; 15:1–17

Defilement by sin
Eze 14:11 See also Lev 19:31; Ps 106:34–39; Jer 2:23; La 4:14; Eze 20:1–44; 22:1–4; 23:28–30; 37:23

Defilement as a result of illicit sexual relations
Lev 18:20 See also Ge 34:1–5 *rape*; Ge 34:27; 49:3–4; Lev 18:23–30 *bestiality Prostitution:* Lev 21:7,9,13–15 Nu 5:19–22,27–30; Dt 24:1–4; 1Ch 5:1; Eze 18:6; 22:11 *incest*; Eze 23:7,17; 33:26 *adultery*; Rev 14:4

Defilement of God's house
Lev 15:31 *Through uncleanness:* Nu 19:13,20 2Ch 29:4–5; 36:14; Ps 74:4–7; 79:1 *Through setting up idols:* Jer 7:30; 32:32–35 Eze 5:11; 9:7; 23:38; Ac 21:27–28 *Paul was falsely accused of bringing Gentiles into the temple area.*

Defilement of God's name
Eze 43:7–8

Defilement of altars and offerings
Ex 20:25 See also Nu 18:30–32; 2Ki 23:16,19

Defilement of the land
Nu 35:34 See also Jos 22:19; Isa 24:5; Jer 2:7; 3:9; 16:18; Eze 36:17–18

See also

4639 dung and manure	7342 cleanliness
6021 sin, nature of	7416 purification
6151 dirt	7426 ritual washing
6236 sexual sin	7478 washing
7340 clean and unclean	

drink offering

A sacrificial offering of wine poured out at the foot of the altar, to accompany a burnt, fellowship or grain offering.

The drink offering was an ancient custom
Ge 35:14

Drink offerings were proportionate to the size of animal sacrificed
Nu 15:5,7,10

Drink offerings were required on feasts and sacred days
As part of the daily offerings: Ex 29:41; Nu 28:7–8 Lev 23:13 *Firstfruits Feast of Weeks:* Lev 23:18; Nu 28:31 *Feast of Tabernacles:* Lev 23:37; Nu 29:30–31 Nu 28:24 *Passover;* Nu 28:9–10 *Sabbath offerings;* Nu 28:14 *monthly offerings;* Nu 29:6 *Feast of Trumpets;* Nu 29:11 *Day of Atonement*

Occasions for making a drink offering
To accompany sacrifices for unintentional sins Nu 15:24

To mark special occasions Nu 6:17 *after taking a Nazirite vow;* 1Ch 29:21 *at the accession of a king;* 2Ch 29:35 *during a religious reformation;* Eze 45:17 *in Ezekiel's vision of restored worship*

God's displeasure when drink offerings were poured out to idols
Jer 7:18 See also Isa 57:6; Jer 19:13; 32:29; 44:17–19,25; Eze 20:28

Drink offerings as a symbol
Of restoration after a locust plague Joel 2:13–14

Of devotion and sacrifice Php 2:17 See also 2Sa 23:15–17; 2Ti 4:6–8

See also

4544 wine	7364 fellowship
7302 altar	offering
7322 burnt offering	7368 grain offering

ephod

A garment worn by priests and high priests
Ex 28:4 See also Ex 28:6–13; 39:2–7; Lev 8:7; Jdg 17:5; 18:17–20; 1Sa 2:28; 22:18; 23:9; Hos 3:4

Worn by people other than priests
2Sa 6:14 pp 1Ch 15:27 See also Jdg 8:27; 1Sa 2:18

See also

5158 head-covering	7412 priesthood
7320 breastpiece	7766 priests
7376 high priest	

7354
feasts and festivals

The OT makes reference to a number of feasts and festivals, which generally commemorate an event in Israel's history (e.g., the Feast of Passover) or some season of the year (e.g., the Feast of Weeks). In the NT, some of these festivals are given new meanings, such as Pentecost, which was originally a harvest festival, but which came to celebrate the coming of the Holy Spirit.
This set of themes consists of the following:
7355 feasts and festivals, nature of
7356 Feast of Dedication
7357 Feast of Firstfruits
7358 Feast of Tabernacles
7359 Feast of Trumpets
7360 Feast of Unleavened Bread
7361 Feast of Weeks

7355
feasts and festivals, nature of

Israel's feasts and festivals were to be times of religious and community celebration. Ordained by God, they were to be the outward expression of a right spiritual attitude.

Feasts and festivals were appointed by God
Ex 5:1 See also Ex 10:9; Hos 9:5

Israel's three annual festivals
The three pilgrim festivals
Ex 23:14–19; 2Ch 8:12–13
The Feast of Unleavened Bread/Passover:
Ex 12:14; Nu 28:17
The Feast of Weeks/Harvest:
Lev 23:15–21; Nu 28:26
The Feast of Tabernacles/Ingathering:
Lev 23:39–41; Nu 29:12; Jdg 21:19;
1Ki 8:65 pp 2Ch 7:8

They were a joyful response to God's blessings Zec 8:19 *Contrasting with fasts. See also* Na 1:15

They were celebrated with sacrifices and offerings Nu 29:39; Eze 46:11

Israel's other festivals
New Moon festivals: Nu 10:10; 1Sa 20:18;
1Ch 23:31; Hos 2:11
Unlawful festivals: Ex 32:5;
1Ki 12:32–33

Festivals should be the outward expression of a right spiritual attitude
Isa 1:14; 29:1; Hos 5:7; Mal 2:3; 1Co 5:8

OT festivals find their fulfilment in Jesus Christ
Col 2:16–17

See also
4951 month	7435 sacrifice, in OT
4975 week	8142 religion
5312 feasting	8283 joy
5338 holiday	8642 celebration
7406 Passover	8768 idolatry

7356
Feast of Dedication

This feast began on 25th Kislev (November/December) and lasted seven days. It celebrated the cleansing of the temple and altar by Judas Maccabeus after they had been defiled by Antiochus Epiphanes.

Jesus Christ was challenged to declare his messiahship at the Feast of Dedication
Jn 10:22–24

7357
Feast of Firstfruits

The date of the offering of firstfruits, a celebration of God's gift of the harvest, is not clear; it was probably held on 16th Abib.

Offerings made at the celebration of the firstfruits
A burnt offering and a grain offering
Lev 23:12–13

Other offerings Lev 23:19–20

See also
4442 firstfruits	7368 grain offering
4464 harvest	7480 wave offering
7322 burnt offering	

7358
Feast of Tabernacles

This feast began on 15th Tishri (September/October) and lasted seven days. It celebrated the first gathering of the fruit and grain harvests and also God's provision for his people during their wilderness journey from Egypt to the promised land.

Instructions for celebrating the Feast of Tabernacles
Ex 23:16 *See also* Ex 23:14; 34:22–23;
Lev 23:33–34,39; Nu 29:12;
Dt 16:13,14,16

People lived in booths for the duration of the Feast of Tabernacles
Lev 23:40,42–43

The offerings to be made on each day of the Feast of Tabernacles
Lev 23:37; Nu 29:13–38

The Feast of Tabernacles was celebrated throughout Israel's history
2Ch 8:12–13 *under Solomon*
After the return from exile: Ezr 3:4;
Ne 8:17–18
In NT times: Jn 7:2–3,37–38

See also
7322 burnt offering	7444 sin offering
7368 grain offering	

7359
Feast of Trumpets

This feast, which is not specifically mentioned as such in the OT, took place at the observance of the new moon in the month of Tishri (September/October). It signalled the end of the agricultural year.

It was to be a day of rest, commemorated with the sounding of trumpets
Lev 23:24–25; Nu 29:1

Offerings were made to God
Lev 23:25; Nu 29:2–5

Celebrated after the exile
Ne 8:2–6

See also
4406 agriculture	5056 rest

7360
Feast of Unleavened Bread

The feast was kept from 15th-21st Abib (March/April), to commemorate the haste with which the Israelites left Egypt. It was always celebrated in the calendar of feasts with the Feast of Passover.

Celebrating the Feast of Unleavened Bread
Ex 12:15–20 *See also* Ex 12:39; 23:15;
Lev 23:6; Nu 28:17; Dt 16:3

All use of yeast was forbidden during the Feast of Unleavened Bread
All leaven was to be removed from the home before the feast began Ex 12:19; 13:7; Dt 16:4

No yeast was to be used in the preparation of food Ex 12:18–20; 13:6–7; 23:15

Sacrifices made at the Feast of Unleavened Bread
Lev 23:8; Nu 28:19–24

The Feast of Unleavened Bread in NT times
Mk 14:1,12; Ac 12:3; 1Co 5:6–8

See also
4404 food	7402 offerings
4554 yeast	7406 Passover
7222 exodus, events of	

7361
Feast of Weeks

This feast, which took place seven weeks after Passover in Sivan (May/June), was also known as the Feast of Pentecost. It expressed joy and thankfulness to God for the harvest.

The Feast of Weeks was one of three compulsory feasts
Ex 23:16; 34:22

Offerings made at the Feast of Weeks

The firstfruits of the wheat harvest were offered to God Nu 28:26; Dt 16:10 *The offerings brought were to be in proportion to the harvest.*

Two loaves of bread were also offered Lev 23:17

Burnt offerings and sin offerings were made Lev 23:18–20 pp Nu 28:27–30

The Feast of Weeks (Pentecost) in the NT

Ac 2:1–4 *The term "Pentecost" refers to the 50 days that separate this feast from the Passover Sabbath.*

See also
4442 firstfruits	7408 Pentecost
4464 harvest	7444 sin offering
7322 burnt offering	8352 thankfulness
7402 offerings	

7364

fellowship offering

Sacrificial meals shared by offerer, people and priests. The name of these offerings is related to the Hebrew "shalom", meaning "wholeness" or "peace", and they are therefore also known as "peace offerings".

Fellowship offerings were required by God
Ex 20:24

Their purpose was thanksgiving, vow fulfilment or freewill offering Lev 7:11–18

Regulations for making a fellowship offering
The animal Lev 3:1,6,12

Its slaughter Lev 3:2,8,13; 17:5–6

All requirements must be fulfilled for the offering to be acceptable Lev 19:5; 22:21; Jos 22:29
A right attitude: Am 5:22,24

The fellowship offering was shared
God received the best Lev 3:3–5,9–11,14–16

The priests received their share as food Lev 7:29–34

The people ate the rest Lev 10:14

Fellowship offerings affirmed the covenant relationship
The Sinai covenant with Israel: Ex 20:24; 24:4–6; Jos 8:31–32
God's covenant with the king: 1Sa 10:8; 11:15; 1Ki 9:25

The celebration of fellowship offerings
At seasonal festivals Lev 23:19 *the Feast of Weeks;* Nu 29:39 *the Feast of Tabernacles*

On other religious and national occasions
At the completion of the time of separation of a Nazirite: Nu 6:14,17–18
Nu 10:10 *at New Moons and other festivals*

Numbers chapter 7 contains many examples of the offerings made at the dedication of the tabernacle: Nu 7:17,23,29
On entering the promised land: Nu 15:8; Dt 27:7
2Sa 6:17–18 *on bringing the ark to Jerusalem;* 2Sa 24:25 *on locating the site for the temple;* 1Ki 8:63–64 pp 2Ch 7:7 *at the dedication of the temple*
Re-establishing the ordinances of the temple: 2Ch 29:35; 30:22; 31:2; 33:16
Pr 7:14
Ezekiel's vision of the restored temple includes the re-establishing of offerings: Eze 45:15,17; 46:2,12

Fellowship offerings in idolatrous worship
Ex 32:6

See also
4603 animals	7476 thank-offering
5741 vows	7480 wave offering
7302 altar	8352 thankfulness
7366 freewill offering	8626 worship,
7435 sacrifice, in OT	places
7459 tabernacle, in OT	

7366

freewill offering

An offering that in some ways resembled the thank-offering or peace offering. It was completely voluntary, prompted by an occasion of celebration or spiritual significance. The animal offered was eaten at a festive banquet.

Instructions for presenting a freewill offering
The animal to be offered Lev 22:17–22,23 *Some slightly deformed animals were perhaps acceptable because the freewill offering was voluntary.*

Eating the offering Lev 7:16

Freewill offerings were associated with joy and celebration
Ps 54:6–7 *See also* Dt 16:9–12 *during the Feast of Weeks*

Occasions for making freewill offerings
In maintaining public worship and at times of religious renewal Ex 35:20–29
Building the temple. See also 2Ch 31:14 *Hezekiah's reformation*
The return from exile: Ezr 1:4–6; 2:68; 7:16; 8:28; Ne 7:70–72
Eze 46:11–12 *Ezekiel's visionary ideal temple*

As an additional offering at certain festivals Nu 29:39
The offering had to be made at the sanctuary to be acceptable: Dt 12:5–6,17–18

Prophetic criticism of bragging over freewill offerings
Am 4:5 *A sarcastic attack on the offering of freewill gifts as a way to gain prestige.*

See also
4605 animals,	7435 sacrifice, in OT
religious role	7476 thank-offering
7364 fellowship	8488 tithing
offering	8676 thanksgiving
7402 offerings	

7368

grain offering

An offering that was usually offered as an accompaniment to animal sacrifices, but in special circumstances was presented alone. It could be cooked in various ways or presented uncooked. The offering could be made for a variety of purposes, depending on the sacrifice it accompanied.

The Hebrew word for "grain offering" can also mean simply "gift"
Ge 4:4; 32:13; 1Sa 2:17; 1Ki 4:21; Mk 7:11

The ingredients of the grain offering
Flour, oil and incense Lev 2:1–2

Salt Lev 2:13 *Salt, which prevented corruption, was offered with all the offerings.*

No yeast or honey Lev 2:11

Roasted ears of corn Lev 2:14–16

The preparation of the grain offering
Lev 2:4 *oven-baked like bread;* Lev 2:5–6 *on a griddle or in a pan*

The presentation of the grain offering
By fire Lev 2:2 *See also* Lev 2:3 *It might be eaten, but only by the priests and in the sanctuary.*

Accompanying vow fulfilment or freewill offerings Nu 15:1–10

With an animal sacrifice Nu 15:6 *See also* Nu 15:8–9 *the larger the animal, the larger the grain offering*

With the two daily offerings Ex 29:38–41

Circumstances under which the grain offering was presented alone Lev 6:19–23 *when a priest was consecrated*
In the ritual for a jealous husband: Nu 5:15,25

The character of the grain offering
It is most holy Lev 6:17

It is an aroma pleasing to the LORD Lev 2:2,9

See also
4826 fire	7766 priests
7435 sacrifice, in OT	

7370

guilt offering

An offering that resembled the sin offering, but was offered especially in cases where restitution could be made for an unintentional sin.

Circumstances for making the guilt offering

Unintentional sin against God Lev 5:17 *See also* Lev 5:15

Sin against a neighbour where restitution can be made Lev 5:16 *Where restitution is possible it is a requirement;* Lev 6:1–5 *A surcharge of twenty per cent was to be added;* Nu 5:5–8 *Restitution must be made to God if the wronged person is not accessible.*

The nature of the guilt offering
A ram without defect Lev 5:18

Regulations governing the offering Lev 7:1–6; Nu 18:9

Other situations requiring a guilt offering
Lev 14:12–14 *cleansing from infectious diseases;* Lev 19:20–22 *wronging a man by intercourse with a slave girl promised to him;* Nu 6:12 *cleansing a Nazirite after contact with a dead body;* Ezr 10:19 *for returning exiles who had intermarried*

Guilt offerings in Ezekiel's vision of the temple
Eze 40:38–39; 42:13; 44:29; 46:20

The death of the "suffering servant" is interpreted as a guilt offering
Isa 53:10

See also

2327 Christ as servant	6682 mediation
5492 restitution	7160 servants of the Lord
6027 sin, remedy for	7402 offerings
6175 guilt, removal of	7444 sin offering

7372

hands, laying on of

An action of God or human beings, often understood to convey healing, blessing or the gift of the Holy Spirit. It also indicates the conferring of authority upon individuals for the purpose of ministry.

Laying on of hands and the communication of gifts
Laying on of hands communicates God's blessing Mk 10:16 pp Mt 19:15 *See also* Ge 48:14–20

Laying on of hands conveys God's healing Lk 4:40 *See also* Mt 8:3 pp Mk 1:41 pp Lk 5:13 *the man with leprosy;* Mt 9:18 pp Mk 5:23 *Jairus' daughter;* Mt 9:29–30; Mk 6:5; 7:32–35; 16:18; Lk 13:13 *the crippled woman;* Ac 28:8; Jas 5:14

Laying on of hands conveys the gift of the Holy Spirit Ac 8:17 *See also* Dt 34:9 fn; Ac 8:19; 9:17; 19:6

Laying on of hands conveys reassurance Rev 1:17 *See also* Mt 17:7

Laying on of hands in commissioning for service
Nu 27:18–23 *See also* Nu 8:10; Dt 34:9; Ac 6:6; 13:3; 1Ti 4:14; 5:22; 2Ti 1:6

Laying on of hands in the OT sacrificial system
Laying on of hands in sin offerings Lev 16:21 *See also* Ex 29:10; Lev 4:4,15; 8:14; 2Ch 29:23

Laying on of hands in other offerings Lev 1:4 *See also* Ex 29:15,19; Lev 3:1–2; 8:18,22

Laying on of hands without reference to God
Laying on of hands on people with intent to harm Ge 37:27; Jos 2:19; 1Sa 23:7; 26:9–11,23; Isa 11:14; Lk 21:12

Laying on of hands in punishment Lev 24:14; Ne 13:21

The metaphorical laying of God's hand on people
God's hand brings favour Ne 2:8 *See also* Ezr 7:6,28; 8:18; Ne 2:18

God's hand brings protection Ezr 8:31 *See also* Ezr 7:9

God's hand brings prophetic revelation Eze 1:3 *See also* Eze 3:14,22; 8:1; 33:22; 37:1; 40:1

God's hand brings judgment Ex 7:4 *See also* 1Sa 5:6–12; Jer 15:6; Eze 39:21; Ac 13:11

See also

1265 hand of God	5865 gestures
1335 blessing	7745 ordination
3257 Holy Spirit, gift of	7967 spiritual gifts, responsibility
5156 hand	9310 resurrection
5333 healing	

7374

high places

Natural heights were sometimes the sites of shrines devoted to the Lord. However, the term usually refers to the places where shrines were set up to foreign gods, especially shrines where the worship of the Lord was in rivalry with Jerusalem.

High places referring to mountainous areas
Hab 3:19 *See also* Dt 32:13; Ps 18:33 pp 2Sa 22:34

High places express divine lordship
Am 4:13 *See also* Mic 1:3

High places referring to shrines to the Lord
High places were the focus of worship before the building of Solomon's temple 1Ki 3:2–3

High places associated with Samuel 1Sa 9:12 *See also* 1Sa 9:13–14,19

Associated with other prophets 1Sa 10:5

High places referring to foreign shrines
In Canaan before the conquest Dt 33:29

Among Israel's neighbours Isa 15:2 *See also* Isa 16:12

Israelite use of high places condemned
The building of shrines on high places 1Ki 12:31

High places condemned by God Lev 26:30 *See also* Nu 33:52; Dt 12:2

High places condemned by the prophets Eze 20:28–29 *See also* Jer 17:3

High places associated with foreign gods
Jer 32:35 *Baal;* 1Ki 11:7 *Chemosh and Molech*

Worship at the high places
High places regarded as unsatisfactory places to worship the Lord 2Ch 32:12 *See also* 2Ki 18:4 *The presence of Asherah poles is evidence of a consort for the Lord, typical of Baal worship, but alien to the biblical concept of God;* 2Ch 31:1

Characteristics of worship at the high places 2Ki 17:11 *burning incense;* 2Ki 23:20 *the presence of priests;* 2Ch 28:25 *sacrifices;* Eze 43:7 *a site for the tombs of kings*

Removal of the high places
Lev 26:30; Nu 33:52; 2Ch 14:3; 17:6

Commended for the zeal shown 2Ki 23:5 *See also* 2Ki 23:8,15

Used as a test 1Ki 15:14; 22:43; 2Ki 12:2–3; 14:3–4; 15:3–4,34–35; 2Ch 20:32–33

See also

6209 pagans	8747 false gods
7442 shrine	8748 false religion
8622 worship	8768 idolatry

7376

high priest

One of the most important people in Israel, responsible for the spiritual welfare of the nation and, in particular, for making atonement for the sins of the people. The NT recognises Jesus Christ as bringing this role to fulfilment, making the perfect sacrifice for the sins of his people, as both high priest and the sacrificial victim.

7377
high priest, in OT

The OT emphasises the spiritual importance of the high priest, especially as the one who makes atonement for the sins of the nation. It also sets out his duties and responsibilities.

The role of the high priest
Making atonement on the Day of Atonement Lev 16:3 *See also* Lev 16:1–34

Teaching Dt 33:10 *See also* Ezr 7:12; Ne 8:2

Providing oracles Lev 8:8 *See also* Nu 27:21; Dt 33:8

Interceding Ezr 9:5

7378

Administering the sanctuary Nu 3:38

Anointing kings 2Ki 11:12

Supervising censuses Nu 26:1-2

Encouraging soldiers Dt 20:2

Titles used to refer to the high priest

The priest Ex 31:10

The anointed priest Lev 4:3 See also Ex 30:30; Lev 4:5,16; 16:32

The high priest Lev 21:10 See also Hag 1:12-14; 2:2-4; Zec 3:1-8; 6:11

Melchizedek, the king-priest

Ge 14:18; Ps 110:4 David's son, as king-priest, is appointed to the order of Melchizedek, a priesthood superior to that of Aaron; Heb 7:11

High priesthood in the law

Only certain people might be high priests Nu 3:10

Consecration of a high priest Lev 8:30

Dignity of the high priesthood Dt 17:12 See also Lev 21:10

Dress of the high priest Ex 28:4 See also Lev 8:7-9; 16:4

Other high priests mentioned in the OT

1Sa 1:9 Eli; 1Sa 21:2 Ahimelech; 1Ch 24:3 Zadok; 2Ki 16:10 Uriah; 2Ki 22:4 Hilkiah; 2Ki 25:18 Seraiah; Ne 3:1 Eliashib

See also

1350 covenant with Israel's priests	7413 priesthood, OT
5073 Aaron, priest	7422 ritual
6614 atonement	7434 sacrifice
7302 altar	7438 sanctuary
7390 Levites	7459 tabernacle, in OT
7396 Most Holy Place	7768 priests, OT function

7378
high priest, in NT

Under the Roman administration the high priest remained the senior Jewish leader, but his power was limited by Roman supervision.

High priests of the NT

Lk 3:2; Ac 23:2 Annas was high priest from A.D. 6 until deposed by the Roman official, Gratus, in A.D. 15. Though replaced by his son Eleazar and, in A.D. 18, by Caiaphas, his son-in-law, Annas retained his authority in Jewish eyes. Strictly, there could only be one high priest at a time. Ananias, the high priest of Ac 23:2, was not related to the family of Annas.

Grandeur of the high priest

Jn 18:10,15 The courtyard was within a palace; Ac 6:12; 7:1 The high priest was president of the Sanhedrin.

The high priest's connections with Jesus Christ

Prophesying Jesus Christ's death Jn 11:49-50 Words spoken by Caiaphas in a political sense were seen to be prophetic, pointing forward to the sacrificing role the high priest would play

in the death of Jesus Christ. See also Jn 11:51-52

Presiding at Jesus Christ's trial

Jn 18:19-24 See also Mt 26:57-59 pp Mk 14:53-55; Mt 26:62-65 pp Mk 14:61-64; Lk 22:54; Jn 18:28 Caiaphas, the necessary go-between, brought Jesus Christ before Pilate.

The high priest's encounters with Peter and John

Ac 4:7 The teaching of Jesus Christ's resurrection was particularly abhorrent to the Sadducees, the priestly party to which Annas and Caiaphas belonged. See also Ac 5:17,21,29

The high priest's encounter with Stephen

Ac 7:1 Stephen was thought to have threatened the temple, the focus of high priestly power. See also Ac 7:57-59

Encounters of the high priests with Paul

Commissioning Paul to persecute Christians Ac 9:1-2

Ordering that Paul be struck Ac 23:3 See also Jn 18:21-23

Taking charges against Paul to the Roman governor Ac 24:1 See also Jn 18:28

NT references to OT high priests

Abiathar Mk 2:26

Melchizedek Heb 5:6

Jesus Christ as high priest

Heb 4:14-16 See also Heb 8:1-2; 9:14

See also

1432 prophecy in NT	7555 Sadducees
2306 Christ, high priest	7565 Sanhedrin
2585 Christ, trial	7734 leaders, spiritual
5347 injustice	7770 priests, NT tasks
7330 chief priests	8773 jealousy
7414 priesthood, NT	
7505 Jews, the	

7379
high priest, Jesus Christ as

See 2306 Jesus Christ, as high priest

7382

house of God

The place where God was seen to dwell with his people, initially the tabernacle and subsequently the temple at Jerusalem.

Early references to the house of God

Ge 28:16-17 "house of God" was first used by Jacob to commemorate the place where he met with God; Ge 28:19 "Bethel" means "house of God". See also Ge 28:22

The tabernacle as the house of God

The tabernacle was referred to as such before its construction Ex 23:19 See also Ex 34:26

In the wilderness God said he would dwell with his people in the tabernacle Ex 25:8-9

God's presence came and dwelt in the tabernacle when it was completed Ex 40:33-34 See also Ex 40:35-38

The temple as the permanent house of God

David's desire to build the LORD a permanent house 2Sa 7:1-2

This was not the LORD's will for David 2Sa 7:5-7,12-13 See also Ac 7:45-47

Solomon builds the temple in Jerusalem 1Ki 5:4-5; 6:1-2

God's presence dwelt there but was conditional upon the faithfulness of the people 1Ki 8:10-13 pp 2Ch 5:11-6:2 See also 1Ki 9:6-9

Zerubbabel's temple referred to as the house of God

Ezr 1:5 The returning exiles begin rebuilding the temple: Ezr 2:68; 3:8-9,11; 4:24; 5:2,13,16-17 Ezra's reforms: Ezr 10:1,6,9 Ne 6:10; 8:16; 10:32,34-38; 11:11,22; 12:40 Nehemiah's reforms: Ne 13:9,11,14

Other names given to the house of God

Sanctuary Ex 25:8

House of prayer Mt 21:13 pp Mk 11:17 pp Lk 19:46; Isa 56:7

God's dwelling-place Ac 7:45-47

The need for due reverence in worship

Ecc 5:1

The house of God under the new covenant

In the hearts of God's people 1Co 3:16; Gal 4:6 See also Ac 7:48; 17:24; 1Co 6:19; 2Co 1:22; 6:16; Eph 3:17

In the church, the body of Christ Heb 3:6 See also Eph 2:19-22; 1Pe 2:4-5

See also

1065 God, holiness of	7271 Zion, as symbol
3278 Holy Spirit, indwelling	7459 tabernacle, in OT
5015 heart & Holy Spirit	7467 temple, Solomon's
5340 house	8370 zeal
6641 election, responsibilities	8626 worship, places
7140 people of God	9410 heaven

7384

household gods

Known in the Hebrew as "teraphim", miniature idols small enough for their owners to keep in their homes or to carry with them when travelling.

Examples of the use of household gods

Ge 31:19 See also Ge 31:34; Jdg 17:1-6; 18:18,30-31; 1Sa 19:13-16; Eze 21:21 Three methods of divination are described

*here, shaking the arrows (belomancy),
consulting the household gods
(necromancy) and the examination of the
liver of a sacrificed victim (hepatoscopy).*

The use of household gods was contrary to God's law
Dt 7:25–26 *See also* Ex 20:4–6
pp Dt 5:8–10

The removal and condemnation of household gods
2Ki 23:24 *See also* Ge 35:2–4;
Isa 44:9–11; Eze 18:5–6; Zec 10:2

See also
1080 God, living	7324 calf worship
4155 divination	8747 false gods
4363 silver	8752 false worship
5138 bowing	8768 idolatry
5212 arts and crafts	8807 profanity
6243 adultery,	8840 unfaithfulness
spiritual	to God

7386

incense

An expensive resin from southern
Arabia and the fragrant aroma it
emits when offered in worship ritual.
It is also called frankincense.

Regulations governing the offering of incense
**The priest was to keep incense
burning on the altar daily** 2Ch 13:11 *See
also* Ex 30:7–9; Nu 4:16; Dt 33:10;
1Sa 2:28; 1Ch 6:49; 9:29; Lk 1:9

Only the priests were to burn incense
Korah, Dathan and Abiram:
Nu 16:16–18,35,40,46–47
2Ch 26:16–19 *Uzziah's pride*

**Failure to burn incense is
disobedience** 2Ch 29:7–8

The blending of the incense
Ex 30:34–38 *See also* Ex 25:6
pp Ex 35:8; Ex 35:28

Occasions for offering incense
At the setting up of the tabernacle:
Ex 39:38; 40:5,26–27
To accompany sacrifices:
Lev 2:1–2,15–16; 6:15
Lev 5:11 *not to accompany a sin offering;*
Lev 16:12 *on the Day of Atonement;*
Lev 24:7 *to accompany bread and oil;*
Nu 7:86 *As part of the offerings at the
dedication of the tabernacle, each leader
presented a golden incense dish.*

The altar of incense
Ex 30:1 *See also* Ex 30:27; 31:8,11;
35:15; 37:25–29; 1Ch 28:18

Burning incense to foreign gods
**Incense offered to other gods will not
bring answers to prayer** Jer 11:12;
44:21

**Israel disobeyed the LORD's
commands** Jer 7:9–10 *See also*
Jer 18:15; 19:13; 32:29; 44:5;
Eze 16:18–19; 20:28; Hos 11:2

**The practice continued under
successive kings**
In the early days of Solomon's reign:
1Ki 3:3; 11:8
1Ki 22:43 *Jehoshaphat*; 2Ki 12:3 *Joash*;
2Ki 14:4 *Amaziah*; 2Ki 15:4 *Azariah*;

2Ki 15:35 *Jotham*; 2Ki 16:4 pp 2Ch 28:4
Ahaz

It provoked God's anger Jer 44:3 *See
also* 2Ki 22:17; Isa 65:3; Jer 1:16; 11:17;
44:5,8,21; 48:35; Hos 2:13

The destruction of pagan incense altars
**As part of God's punishment for
disobedience** Lev 26:30; Eze 6:4,6,13

**Their destruction in religious
reformations** 2Ki 18:4 *under Hezekiah
Under Josiah:* 2Ki 23:5,8; 2Ch 34:4,7
*Nehemiah restored the storage rooms for
incense:* Ne 13:5,9

**Their destruction brought God's
blessing and deliverance** Isa 27:9

The significance of incense
**A right heart attitude is more important
to God** Isa 66:3; Jer 6:20

**It both accompanies and symbolises
prayer** Ps 141:2; Rev 5:8; 8:3–4

It symbolises worship 2Ch 2:4;
Da 2:46; Mal 1:11; Mt 2:11; Heb 9:4

It brings pleasure Pr 27:9; SS 3:6; 4:6;
Eze 20:41

See also
1045 God, glory of	7302 altar
1065 God, holiness of	7308 Atonement, Day of
4466 herbs and spices	7328 ceremonies
4496 perfume	7422 ritual
4848 smoke	7435 sacrifice, in OT
5183 smell	7459 tabernacle, in OT

7388

kinsman-redeemer

The relative who restores or
preserves the full community rights
of disadvantaged family members.
The concept arises from God's
covenant relationship with Israel
and points to the redemption of
humanity in Jesus Christ.

Covenant rules for the kinsman-redeemer
**The kinsman-redeemer's obligation to
redeem the land** Lev 25:25–28;
Jer 32:6–9

**The kinsman-redeemer's obligation to
redeem the enslaved** Lev 25:47–55

**The kinsman-redeemer's obligation to
provide an heir** Ge 38:8–10;
Dt 25:5–10; Mt 22:23–28
pp Mk 12:18–23 pp Lk 20:27–33

**The kinsman-redeemer's obligation to
avenge death** Nu 35:16–21

**The kinsman-redeemer's obligation to
be a trustee** Nu 5:5–8

The kinsman-redeemer in the book of Ruth
Ru 2:20 *See also* Ru 3:1–4:17

The LORD as redeemer
Ex 6:6–7 *See also* 2Sa 7:22–24;
Isa 43:1–7; 54:5–8; Jer 50:33–34

The kinsman-redeemer reflects God's concern for the poor and oppressed
Pr 23:10–11 *See also* Ps 68:5–6; 72:2–4

God's provision of Jesus Christ as kinsman-redeemer
Gal 4:4–7 *See also* Gal 3:13–14;
Heb 2:11–18

See also
1115 God, purpose of	5680 family
1345 covenant	6714 ransom
2033 Christ, humanity	6717 reconciliation, world to God
2321 Christ as redeemer	6720 redemption
5446 poverty	7310 avenger of blood

7390

Levites

Assistants to the Aaronic priests,
they exercised an auxiliary ministry,
caring for the tabernacle. After the
ark was brought to Jerusalem by
David their role was re-ordered and
extended. They were reconsecrated
during the reforms of Josiah and
Hezekiah and recommissioned by
Ezra and Nehemiah when the
Israelites returned from captivity.

The Levites and the care of the tabernacle
**The Levites are to transport, erect and
guard the tabernacle** Nu 1:48–53 *See
also* Nu 2:17; Dt 10:8

**The Gershonite branch of the Levites
are to care for the coverings and
curtains of the tabernacle** Nu 3:25–26
See also Nu 4:24–27

**The Kohathite branch of the Levites
are to care for the furnishings of the
sanctuary** Nu 3:31 *See also* Nu 4:4–20

**The Merarite branch of the Levites are
to care for the frames of the tabernacle**
Nu 3:36–37 *See also* Nu 4:29–33

The Levites are to have an auxiliary ministry
Nu 3:5–10 *See also* Nu 8:19; 18:1–7

The Levites are set apart for their ministry
Nu 8:20–21 *See also* Nu 8:5–15

The Levites' period of service was between the ages of 25 and 50
Nu 8:23–26 *See also* Nu 4:1–3 *Some
suggest that the reason for the discrepancy
in ages between Numbers chapters 4 and 8
is that the Levites had to serve an
apprenticeship for the first five years.*

Occasions after the settlement when the Levites transport the ark
1Sa 6:15; 2Sa 15:24; 1Ki 8:3–5
pp 2Ch 5:4–6; 1Ch 15:1–16

David re-orders and extends the role of the Levites
1Ch 23:2–6 *See also* 1Ch 6:31–49;
16:4–6; 23:24–32; 25:1–26:32

Hezekiah and Josiah rededicate the Levites
2Ch 29:3–36; 35:1–6

Ezra and Nehemiah recommission the Levites after the return from exile
Ezr 6:16–18 See also Ne 12:22–26

Ezekiel prophesies a restored but restricted role for the Levites in the new temple
Eze 44:10–14

See also
5420 music	7768 priests, OT
7266 tribes of Israel	function
7306 ark of the	7960 singing
covenant	8622 worship
7413 priesthood, OT	8664 praise
7459 tabernacle, in	8676 thanksgiving
OT	
7467 temple,	
Solomon's	

7392

lots, casting of

A means of determining the will of God, prior to the giving of the Holy Spirit at Pentecost. The casting of lots was also used by pagans for the same purpose. Such use reflects the belief that nothing occurred by chance.

Casting lots to determine the will of God
Pr 16:33

In the ministry of the high priest
Ex 28:30 *The "Urim and Thummim" were sacred lots maintained for the purpose of determining God's will. See also* Lev 8:7–9; 16:6–10; Nu 27:21; Dt 33:8; 1Sa 28:6; Ezr 2:63 pp Ne 7:65

To apportion land Nu 33:54 See also Nu 26:54–56; Jos 14:2; 18:10

To select individuals 1Sa 14:41–42 See also Jos 7:14–18; Jdg 20:9–10; 1Sa 10:20–21; Jnh 1:7 Ac 1:15–26

To assign priestly duties 1Ch 24:5 See also 1Ch 26:12–13; Ne 10:34; Lk 1:8–9

To settle disputes Pr 18:18

Casting lots as a means of divination
Eze 21:21–22 See also Est 3:7; 9:24–27 *The word "purim" is the plural of "pur" and means "lots".*

Casting lots as a means of distributing plunder
Joel 3:2–3 See also Na 3:10
Mt 27:35 pp Mk 15:24 pp Lk 23:34 pp Jn 19:24 See also Ps 22:18

See also
1429 prophecy, OT	7376 high priest
fulfilment	7706 apostles
2366 Christ,	7766 priests
prophecies	8124 guidance
concerning	8408 decision-
4155 divination	making
4912 chance	

7394

memorial

An object, institution or custom established or founded as a reminder of an important person or event held

to be worth remembering in the life of the community.

Objects as a memorial
Stones Jos 4:4–7 See also Ex 28:9–12 pp Ex 39:6–7; Ex 28:29

Money or gold Ex 30:16 See also Nu 31:54

Incense Lev 24:7 See also Isa 66:3

A crown Zec 6:9–15

Offerings as a memorial
Lev 2:1–2 See also Lev 5:11–13; Nu 10:10

Meals as a memorial
The Lord's Supper 1Co 11:23–26 See also Mt 26:26–28 pp Mk 14:22–24 pp Lk 22:17–20

The Passover and the Feast of Unleavened Bread Dt 16:1–8 pp Ex 12:14–20 pp Lev 23:4–8 pp Nu 28:16–25

See also
4963 past, the	8467 reminders
5443 pillars	8644 commem-
7354 feasts and	oration
festivals	8670 remembering
7933 Lord's Supper	8763 forgetting

7396

Most Holy Place

The inner sanctuary of the tabernacle set up at Sinai and of Solomon's temple, where the ark of the covenant was kept. It is a symbol of the unapproachable presence of God.

Terms used to describe the Most Holy Place
Ex 26:33 *"the Most Holy Place" (or "Holy of Holies"), in contrast to the "Holy Place" where the altar stood. This superlative suggests increasing closeness to the presence of God. The distinction is not always observed, however. In Leviticus chapter 16 "Holy Place" is used regularly (translated in NIV as "Most Holy Place" in verses 2, 16, 17, 20, 27, and as "sanctuary" in verse 3, though it is the inner sanctuary that is referred to, as the phrase "behind the curtain" (verse 2) shows);* 1Ki 6:16 *the "inner sanctuary" in contrast to the outer;* Heb 9:7 *literally "the second (tabernacle)" in contrast to the first or outer*

The structure and design of the Most Holy Place
In the wilderness tabernacle
The only details concern the curtains forming the walls of the two sanctuaries, and in particular the dividing curtain which separates the Most Holy Place from the outer sanctuary: Ex 26:31–33; 36:35–36; 40:21

In Solomon's temple 1Ki 6:16,19–20 pp 2Ch 3:8; 1Ki 6:23–28 pp 2Ch 3:10; 1Ki 6:31–32; 2Ch 3:14

In the temple in Ezekiel's vision
Eze 41:4,15–21,23; 45:3 *In Ezekiel's vision a portion of the land was sacred to the LORD and called the Most Holy Place.*

The significance and function of the Most Holy Place
To house the ark of the covenant
Ex 26:33 See also Ex 40:3; 1Ki 6:19; 8:6–9 pp 2Ch 5:7–9

To house the incense altar (in Solomon's temple) 1Ki 6:22; Heb 9:3–4 *Ex 30:6 and 40:5 suggest that the incense altar was housed in front of the curtain, i.e., in the Holy Place, the outer sanctuary.*

To be a symbol of the presence of God
Ps 28:2 See also Ex 26:33 *The curtain veiling the Most Holy Place represents the unapproachable presence of the Holy God;* Lev 16:2

The Most Holy Place on the Day of Atonement
Heb 9:7 See also Lev 16:16–17

The NT understanding of the Most Holy Place as the place of God's heavenly presence
Jesus Christ enters the Most Holy Place as Mediator Heb 9:8 See also Heb 6:19–20; 9:11–12,24

Entry to the Most Holy Place is open to all believers Heb 10:19–22 See also Mt 27:51 pp Lk 23:45 *By Jesus Christ's death the dividing curtain has been torn in two.*

See also
1065 God, holiness	7308 Atonement,
of	Day of
2306 Christ, high	7344 curtain
priest	7459 tabernacle, in
2525 Christ, cross of	OT
6606 access to God	7467 temple,
7306 ark of the	Solomon's
covenant	

7398

New Moon festival

The festival which marked the consecration to God of each new month in the year.

New Moon festivals were required under the Mosaic law
Nu 28:11

New Moon festivals were times of celebration
They were marked by blowing of trumpets Nu 10:10 See also Ps 81:3

They were celebrated with offerings
Nu 28:11–15; 1Ch 23:30–31; 2Ch 2:4; 8:12–13; 31:3 *reformed temple worship under Hezekiah;* Ne 10:32–33 *New Moon festivals were restored on the return from exile;* Eze 45:17; 46:1,3,6

They were times when normal work ceased
David was to dine with Saul: 1Sa 20:5,18,24
2Ki 4:23 *the Shunammite woman and her husband;* Am 8:5 *Some saw them as a hindrance to business.*

A wrong inner attitude at New Moon celebrations incurs God's anger
Isa 1:13–14; Hos 2:11; 5:7

NT reference to the New Moon festival
Col 2:16–17

See also

4951 month	7402 offerings
5595 trumpet	7429 Sabbath, in OT
7354 feasts and festivals	8218 consecration
7359 Feast of Trumpets	

7400

New Year, the

With the exception of one reference (Ex 12:2) the New Year is never specifically dated. The religious calendar apparently began in the spring and the agricultural calendar in the autumn. Later Judaism began its calendar in the autumn.

Evidence that the autumn was regarded as the New Year
The dedication of Solomon's temple 1Ki 8:2 *Solomon waited 11 months after the completion of the temple (see 1Ki 6:38), before dedicating it, most likely because the great Feast of Tabernacles marked the beginning of the year.*

Instructions for celebrating the Year of Jubilee Lev 25:8–9 *The Year of Jubilee was to be proclaimed on the tenth day of the seventh month, which was also the Day of Atonement. See also Lev 16:29*

Ezekiel's vision of the new temple Eze 40:1 *This vision of the new temple takes place at the beginning of the year. The "tenth of the month" refers presumably to the seventh month.*

Jeroboam's institution of an autumnal festival 1Ki 12:32 *This autumn festival was clearly intended to be equivalent not only to the feast in Judah, but also to other pagan New Year festivals, in spite of the eighth month being distinctive. See also 1Ki 12:33*

Evidence that the spring was regarded as the New Year
The institution of the Passover Ex 12:2 *This clearly links the spring Feast of Passover to the New Year. See also Lev 23:5; Nu 9:2*

Ezekiel's vision of the worship of the new temple Eze 45:18–19 *This purification of Ezekiel's (ideal) temple resembles the Day of Atonement but takes place in the spring. See also Eze 45:21*

Occasions associating the New Year with the autumn
The sounding of trumpets Nu 29:1 *See also Lev 23:24*

The Day of Atonement Lev 23:27

The Feast of Tabernacles Dt 16:13 *See also Lev 23:34*

Occasions associating the New Year with the spring
Passover Lev 23:5 *See also Ex 12:11*

The Feast of Unleavened Bread Lev 23:6 *See also Ex 12:17*

The Feast of Firstfruits Lev 23:10–11 *This is also known as the Feast of Weeks (Ex 23:16; Lev 23:9–21).*

See also

4251 moon	7358 Feast of Tabernacles
4951 month	
4978 year	7360 Feast of Unleavened Bread
7308 Atonement, Day of	
7357 Feast of Firstfruits	7406 Passover

7402

offerings

Anything offered up to God by human beings, including sacrificial offerings. A distinction can be made between offerings which involve the taking of life and other gifts made to God.

Sacrificial offerings as a sign of gratitude or repentance
Ge 4:4; Ps 107:22

Tithes were a regular form of offering
Ge 28:20–22; Lev 27:30 *See also* Ge 14:20

Part of every harvest was given as a freewill offering to God
As firstfruits: Ex 22:29; Nu 18:12; Dt 18:4; Ne 10:35
Lev 19:23–25 *Fruit from a tree could not be eaten until the fifth year;* Lev 23:38 *Extra gifts were offered on the Sabbath.*

Offerings and the tabernacle
For its construction Ex 25:1–2
pp Ex 35:5

At its dedication Nu 7:2–3

Offerings and Solomon's temple
David's personal gift 1Ch 29:2–5

Offerings for upkeep and restoration
In the reign of Joash: 2Ki 12:4–5; 2Ch 24:8–12
In the reign of Josiah: 2Ki 22:4–6 pp 2Ch 34:9–11

Offerings and the second temple
Ezr 3:5; 7:16; 8:24–30

Offerings and Herod's temple
Mk 12:41–43 pp Lk 21:1–3 *The poor widow was participating in a regular practice;* Lk 21:5

Some offerings are not acceptable
Mt 5:23–24 *Offerings are unacceptable unless the worshipper is reconciled to God. See also* Ge 4:3–5 *Cain's offering was not accepted on account of his incorrect attitude.*
Boasting about offerings makes them unacceptable: Am 4:4–5; Lk 18:12
Mt 23:23 pp Lk 11:42 *Meticulous tithing, without mercy or justice, is unacceptable.*

Offerings in the future kingdom
From the Gentile nations Ps 76:11; Isa 18:7; Mal 1:11

From God's people Eze 20:40; 44:30

Gifts and offerings in the NT
To help the needy Ac 4:34–35; 11:29–30; 1Co 16:1–4 *In several of his letters Paul mentions the freewill offering*

he was organising for poor Christians at Jerusalem; Heb 13:16

To support God's servants
Php 4:10–18

Offerings of praise
Heb 13:15

God's people are themselves an offering to God
Jer 2:3; Jas 1:18; Rev 14:4

Offerings as "Corban"
Mk 7:9–13 *"Corban" is a technical Jewish religious term, meaning "something dedicated, especially on oath". What Jesus Christ says implies that once the children had donated the amount they would have spent on their ageing parents for religious purposes, they were no longer responsible for their upkeep.*

See also

4442 firstfruits	7370 guilt offering
7322 burnt offering	7434 sacrifice
7350 drink offering	7444 sin offering
7364 fellowship offering	7476 thank-offering
	7480 wave offering
7366 freewill offering	8488 tithing
7368 grain offering	

7404

ordinances

Specific acts of worship commanded by God, sometimes including the sacraments.

The ordinance of Passover and Unleavened Bread
Ex 12:14 *See also* Ex 12:17,24,43; 13:10; Nu 9:12

The ordinance of the Day of Atonement
Lev 16:34 *See also* Lev 16:29,31; 23:31

The ordinance of the red-heifer ritual
Nu 19:2,10,21

Other occasions of worship as ordinances
Lev 23:41; 24:3; Nu 31:21; 2Ch 2:4; Ps 81:4; Eze 46:14

Ordinances associated with the priesthood
The Aaronic priests Ex 29:9 *See also* Ex 28:43; 30:21; Lev 7:36; 10:9; Nu 10:8

The Levites Nu 18:23; 2Ch 8:14

Ordinances in Christian worship
1Co 11:24–25 pp Mt 26:26–28 pp Mk 14:22–24 pp Lk 22:17–20 *See also* Mt 28:19–20 *Jesus Christ's commands to observe baptism and the Lord's Supper makes them ordinances of Christian worship;* Ac 2:38; 16:15; 18:8; 22:16

Ordinances were to be permanent
Lev 3:17 *See also* Ex 27:21; Lev 23:14,21

Ordinances were to be obeyed
2Ki 17:37 *See also* 1Sa 30:25; 2Ki 17:34; 2Ch 19:10; 33:8; Eze 44:24

Ordinances were for Israelites and Gentiles alike
Nu 15:15 *See also* Nu 9:14

God's ordinances are of supreme value
Ps 19:9

See also
7308 Atonement, Day of	7406 Passover
7328 ceremonies	7766 priests
7354 feasts and festivals	7903 baptism
7390 Levites	7933 Lord's Supper
	7957 sacraments
	8403 commands

7406

Passover

One of the major OT feasts. It specifically commemorates the exodus from Egypt as an act of God's deliverance. In Israel's calendar of feasts it was always celebrated with the Feast of Unleavened Bread.

The institution of the Passover
Ex 12:25–27 *The Hebrew term "Passover" derives from a verb meaning "to pass over" with the sense of "to spare".*

Celebrating the Passover
Instructions concerning its observance Ex 12:2–11,46–47; Nu 9:1–5; Dt 16:1–8

Combined with the Feast of Unleavened Bread Ex 34:25

The need for ritual cleansing Jn 11:55

Provision for ritual uncleanness Nu 9:6–13

Provision for non-Jews Ex 12:43–45,48–49; Nu 9:14

Its observance in the OT
These occasions are times of spiritual renewal, when the nation remembered how the Lord had saved them: Jos 5:10; 2Ki 23:21–23; 2Ch 30:1–5,13–20; Ezr 6:19–21

Ezekiel's vision of the future observance of the Passover Eze 45:21–24

The Passover in the NT
Its observance Lk 2:41–42; Jn 6:4; Ac 12:4

It was celebrated by Jesus Christ Lk 22:15 *At Passover time Jesus Christ himself was sacrificed and he inaugurated the Lord's Supper. See also* Mt 26:17–19 pp Mk 14:12–16 pp Lk 22:7–13; Jn 2:23 *Jesus Christ observed the Passover like other Jews.*

Jesus Christ identified with the Passover lamb 1Co 5:7 *See also* Jn 1:29,36; 19:36 *This may refer to the Passover victim;* Ex 12:46; Rev 5:5–6

See also
1320 God as Saviour	7335 circumcision, physical
2315 Christ as Lamb	7354 feasts and festivals
2410 cross, the	
4554 yeast	
4663 lamb	7404 ordinances
6722 redemption, OT	7933 Lord's Supper
7221 exodus, the	7957 sacraments

7408

Pentecost

One of Israel's three major agricultural festivals, the second great feast of the Jewish year. It is a harvest festival, also known as the Feast of Weeks. The original Jewish significance of this festival has been overshadowed by the Christian celebration of the coming of the Holy Spirit at Pentecost.

Pentecost was one of Israel's three major agricultural festivals
It was also known as the Feast of Weeks Dt 16:9–10 *See also* Ex 34:22; Dt 16:16–17; 2Ch 8:13

It is also referred to as the Feast of Harvest Ex 23:16

Instructions for the celebration of Pentecost
Its timing and sacrifices Lev 23:15–21 *The "fifty days" (verse 16) gives rise to the term "Pentecost" which is derived from the Greek word for "fiftieth";* Nu 28:26–31; Jer 5:24

Its link with the deliverance from Egypt Dt 16:12 *Pentecost later became associated with covenant renewal and the giving of the Law.*

Pentecost in the NT
It was observed by Paul Ac 20:16; 1Co 16:8

Its association with the coming of the Holy Spirit Ac 2:1–4,16–21; 11:15 *See also* Joel 2:28–32

See also
1345 covenant	3275 Holy Spirit in the church
3040 Holy Spirit, promise of	4018 life, spiritual
3242 Holy Spirit, baptism with	4464 harvest
3257 Holy Spirit, gift of	4951 month
	7361 Feast of Weeks

7410

phylactery

A leather box containing four sections of the law (Ex 11:13–21) written on parchment, and which Jewish men tied to the forehead and left arm (close to the heart) before morning prayers. The practice of wearing phylacteries arose, probably after the exile, from a literal interpretation by pious Jews of passages such as Exodus 13:9.

The significance of wearing phylacteries
A reminder of God's deliverance Ex 13:11–16 *See also* Ex 13:1–10

A reminder of God's requirements Dt 11:13–21 *Phylacteries, when worn, were to be an outward sign of the importance of taking God's word into the heart;* Ps 119:11; Pr 3:1–3 *See also* Dt 6:4–9; 30:14; Ro 10:8; Dt 32:46; Ps 37:31; 40:8; Pr 6:21; 7:2–3; Jer 31:33

A sign of allegiance and belonging Isa 44:5; Rev 7:3 *See also* SS 8:6; Rev 9:4; 14:1

The practice of wearing phylacteries
Mt 23:5 *Jesus Christ condemns the Pharisees for wearing phylacteries for outward show.*

See also
1670 symbols	5375 law
5012 heart	7394 memorial
5035 mind	

7412

priesthood

The body of people responsible for priestly duties, especially in relation to worship and sacrifice. The OT identifies Aaron and his heirs as having special priestly duties. In the NT, all believers are understood to share in this priesthood. Jesus Christ fulfils the OT concept of priesthood by being both the high priest and sacrifice, through which forgiveness of sins is completely achieved.

7413
priesthood, in OT

The institution of the priesthood or the particular body of people responsible for priestly duties.

The priesthood as an institution
It was a perpetual institution Ex 40:15 *See also* Nu 18:1; 25:13

It was distinct from the laity Nu 3:10

It was subject to the king's authority 1Ki 2:27

It was a privilege Nu 18:7 *See also* Ex 29:9; Nu 16:10; Jos 18:7

The priesthood as the body of people responsible for priestly duties
The Aaronic priesthood Ex 28:41 *See also* 1Ch 6:49; Ne 10:38

The Shiloh priesthood Jos 18:1 *See also* 1Sa 3:14; 1Ki 2:27; Ps 78:60 *The Shiloh priesthood ended when the Philistines took Shiloh (see 1Sa 4:17);* Jer 7:12

The Melchizedek priesthood Ps 110:4 *See also* Ge 14:18; Heb 5:10; 7:11–17

The Anathoth priesthood Jer 1:1 *See also* Jos 21:18; 1Ki 2:27

The Zadokite priesthood Eze 40:46 *The priestly line of Zadok lasted until 170 B.C.*

The Levitical priesthood Dt 17:9 *The term "the priests, who are Levites" appears only in Deuteronomy. Some think it reflects a situation in which all Levites were priests. Not all passages support this view, however, and the phrase may simply distinguish the ministry of the Levitical priests from the priesthood of the king.*

See also
1680 types	7767 priests, OT institution
5073 Aaron, priest	
7320 breastpiece	7768 priests, OT function
7352 ephod	
7377 high priest, OT	8622 worship
7390 Levites	

7414
priesthood, in NT

Jesus Christ recognised the function of the OT priesthood, but the gospel belief in Christ as high priest and the priesthood of all believers superseded the earlier concept.

Jesus Christ acknowledged the role of the Jerusalem priesthood
Mt 8:4 pp Mk 1:44 pp Lk 5:14

Characteristics of the Levitical priesthood
It was equivalent to the order of Aaron Heb 7:11

It was incompatible with membership of the tribe of Judah Heb 7:14

It was not established by divine oath Heb 7:20

Characteristics of the Melchizedek priesthood
Heb 7:15–16

How Jesus Christ's priesthood resembled the OT priesthood
He fulfilled the requirement of humanity Heb 2:17 See also Heb 5:1

He was not self-appointed Heb 5:4–5

He resembled Melchizedek Heb 5:10

How Jesus Christ's priesthood contrasts with the Levitical priesthood
It involves a change in the applicability of the law Heb 7:12–13

It lasts for ever Heb 7:23–24 See also Heb 10:11–12

It was based on a once-for-all sacrifice, not of animals but of himself Heb 9:26 See also Heb 9:12

It is effective, not simply illustrative Heb 10:14 See also Heb 8:5; 10:1,4

It is not that of a mere man, but of the Son of God Heb 7:28 See also Heb 4:14; 7:26

Characteristics of the priesthood of all believers
1Pe 2:9

They are to reflect the holiness of their great high priest 1Pe 1:15 See also Heb 10:10

They are to offer spiritual sacrifices 1Pe 2:5 See also Ro 12:1; Php 4:18; Heb 13:15

They are to intercede for others before God 1Ti 2:1 See also Rev 5:8,10

They are to represent God before other human beings 2Co 5:20 See also Eph 3:7–11

See also
2075 Christ, sinless	7769 priests, NT
2306 Christ, high	types
priest	7770 priests, NT
5100 Melchizedek	tasks
6614 atonement	8266 holiness
7378 high priest, NT	

7416
purification

Cleansing from sin or uncleanness, by means of ritual washing under the old covenant, but through the blood of Jesus Christ under the new covenant.

Purification from uncleanness
After contact with something unclean Lev 11:39–40 See also Lev 15:1–12,19–23; 17:15–16; Nu 19:10–20

After disease Lev 15:13–15 See also Lev 14:1–32

After childbirth and menstruation Lk 2:22 See also Lev 12:1–8; 2Sa 11:2–4

Purification from sin
1Jn 1:7 See also Nu 19:1–9; Job 1:5; Heb 1:3; 9:16–24; 1Jn 1:9

Purification of people
Priests and Levites Ezr 6:20 See also Ex 30:18–21; Lev 16:24–28; Nu 8:5–22; 19:7; 2Ch 4:6; Ne 12:30; 13:22,30

Lay people Ac 21:24–26 See also Ge 35:1–2; Nu 19:20; 31:19; 2Ch 30:13–20; Isa 66:17

Purification of inanimate objects
The temple 2Ch 34:8 See also 2Ch 29:15–19; Ne 13:6–9; Eze 45:18–20

Sacred objects Ex 29:36 See also Lev 8:15; 1Ch 23:28

Other items Lev 14:48–53 See also Nu 31:19–24

Purification of precious metals
Ps 12:6 See also Mal 3:3

Purification of the inner person
2Co 7:1 See also Mk 7:2–8; Ac 15:5–11; Tit 2:11–14; Jas 4:8; 1Pe 1:22; 1Jn 3:3

See also
4303 metals	7342 cleanliness
4351 refining	7348 defilement
4826 fire	7390 Levites
5226 basin	7422 ritual
5297 disease	7426 ritual washing
5390 leprosy	7478 washing
5715 menstruation	7766 priests
6020 sin	7903 baptism
7340 clean and	8266 holiness
unclean	8324 purity

7418
Purim

A Jewish festival of rejoicing and feasting celebrated in the month of Adar (February–March) commemorating the deliverance of the Jews recorded in the book of Esther.

The origins of Purim
Esther's position as queen Est 4:14

Haman's death Est 7:10

The right of the Jews to avenge themselves on their enemies Est 8:11

Explanation of the name Est 9:26 The word "pur", meaning "lots", relates to the lots cast to determine the time set for the massacre.

The date for celebrating Purim
Est 9:17–19 those living in Susa celebrated on 15th Adar, those in rural towns on 14th

The establishment of Purim
Est 9:27; 3:7

See also
1355 providence	7505 Jews, the
4951 month	8794 persecution
6634 deliverance	
7354 feasts and	
festivals	

7420
Rabbi

An honorific title, best translated as "master" or "teacher", and used to refer to distinguished teachers of the Jewish law. Jesus Christ is called Rabbi in the Gospels, indicating that he was regarded as a respected teacher by his audiences.

John the Baptist addressed as Rabbi by his disciples
Jn 3:26

Jesus Christ addressed as Rabbi
By two of John the Baptist's disciples Jn 1:38

By his own disciples Jn 4:31 See also Jn 6:25; 9:2; 11:8

By Peter Mk 9:5 See also Mk 11:21

By Nathanael and Nicodemus Jn 1:49; 3:2

By Judas Iscariot Mt 26:25 At the Last Supper; Mt 26:49 pp Mk 14:45 In the Garden of Gethsemane.

Jesus Christ addressed as Rabboni, the Aramaic form of Rabbi
Mk 10:51; Jn 20:16

Jesus Christ taught that his disciples were not to be called Rabbi
Mt 23:7–8

See also
2203 Christ, titles of	7793 teachers
7464 teachers of the	
law	

7422
ritual

The regulations governing Jewish religious life and worship, especially sacrifices, ritual cleanliness and food laws. By the sacrificial death of Jesus Christ these rituals have been fulfilled and play no part in the new covenant.

The purpose of ritual sacrifices
To atone for sin Lev 5:12–13 See also Ex 29:38–43; Lev 1:3–13; 4:1–3,13–14,20–23,26–28,31–35; 5:13; 6:1–7; 7:1–7; 16:1–34

To maintain fellowship between God and his people Lev 3:1–5; 7:11–15 *The offering was part burnt and part eaten in a fellowship meal and expressed covenant relationship with God.*

To express worship and gratitude to God
The grain offering was the only bloodless offering but it accompanied the other offerings and was burnt whole to express gratitude to God for the harvest and for particular blessings: Lev 2:1–3,8–16; 6:14–23; 7:9–10; 9:4; Nu 6:14–17; 28:3–13

Rituals for purification from ritual uncleanness
Childbirth Lk 2:22–24 *See also* Lev 12:1–8

Unclean diseases Mk 1:40–44 pp Mt 8:2–4 pp Lk 5:12–14 *See also* Lev 14:2–7

Unclean discharges Lev 15:32–33

Touching dead bodies Nu 19:11–13

Rituals relating to food
Clean and unclean foods Lev 11:1–2 *See also* Lev 11:44–47

The eating of blood is forbidden Ge 9:4–5; Lev 17:11–12; Ac 15:20

Rituals relating to the priesthood
Lev 8:30 *See also* Ex 29:1–9

Rituals relating to the place of worship
2Ch 29:4–5 *See also* Lev 16:15–20; 1Ki 8:62–63 pp 2Ch 7:4–5; Ezr 6:16–17

Rituals relating to special days
Festivals Lev 23:37

The Sabbath Ex 31:12–17; Mt 12:2 pp Mk 2:24 pp Lk 6:2

The initiation ritual of circumcision
Ge 17:10–14

Ritual only has meaning when accompanied by obedience
Ro 2:25 *See also* Isa 1:11–17; Mt 15:16–20 pp Mk 7:18–23; Mt 23:25; Ro 2:28–29; 1Co 7:19; 8:8

Rituals of the old covenant are fulfilled by Jesus Christ
Col 2:17 *See also* Mk 2:27–28; Col 2:11; Heb 10:1–3,8–10

Old covenant rituals are abolished under the new covenant
Heb 9:10 *See also* Mk 7:19; Ac 10:9–15; Ro 7:6; 14:14,20; Gal 5:6; 6:15; Eph 2:15; Col 2:13–16

See also
2333 Christ, attitude to OT	7402 offerings
7314 blood	7412 priesthood
7328 ceremonies	7416 purification
7334 circumcision	7424 ritual law
7340 clean and unclean	7426 ritual washing
	7435 sacrifice, in OT
	8324 purity

7424
ritual law

The rules and regulations regarding the conduct of the priests and people of Israel in approaching God, especially in worship. They were to be holy as God is holy. The perfect sacrifice of Jesus Christ on the cross is seen by NT writers as fulfilling this demand for holiness and obedience.

The ritual law and the priesthood
The priests were to be careful to obey God's commandments Lev 22:9 *See also* Lev 10:10; 22:3

The priests had to avoid ceremonial uncleanness
Contact with the dead caused uncleanness and was forbidden to the high priest: Lev 21:1–3,11; Nu 19:11,14
Lev 21:16–23 *No-one with a physical defect could serve as a priest;* Lev 22:20–25 *The sacrifices offered by the priests also had to be without defect.*

The ritual law and the people of Israel
The people were called to holiness Lev 19:2; 20:26 *See also* Lev 11:44–45; 20:7; 21:8; 22:32

The ritual law stipulated what they could eat Lev 11:46–47 *See also* Ge 7:2; 8:20; Lev 11:1–23 pp Dt 14:3–20; Dt 14:21

The ritual law regarding childbirth Lev 12:1–5; Lk 2:22–24

Jesus Christ's obedience and perfect sacrifice on the cross fulfilled the demands of the ritual law
Heb 10:8–10 *See also* Eph 2:15; Col 2:14; Heb 7:11,18,27; 10:1–3,11–14

See also
1065 God, holiness of	7402 offerings
2057 Christ, obedience	7422 ritual
2306 Christ, high priest	7426 ritual washing
2530 Christ, death of	7434 sacrifice
5185 stomach	7550 Pharisees
5194 touch	7766 priests
5375 law	8269 holiness, separation from worldly
7340 clean and unclean	

7426
ritual washing

The act of washing for consecration or for purification from uncleanness. It involved washing all or part of the body or one's clothing. Jesus Christ's attitude to the Pharisees reflected, not a disavowal of ritual washing, but disapproval of their emphasis on the outward, rather than inward, forms of religion.

Ritual washing for consecration
Ex 19:10–11 *See also* Ex 19:14; 40:12–15; Nu 8:5–7,21–22

Ritual washing for cleansing
Lev 17:15 *See also* Lev 13:6,34; 15:16–18,21–23; Nu 19:10,19

Methods of ritual washing
Washing clothes Nu 31:24 *See also* Lev 6:27; 11:24–28,39–40; 13:58; 14:43–47; Nu 19:21; Rev 7:14; 22:14

Bathing Lev 14:8–9 *See also* Lev 15:4–13,27; 16:26–28; 17:15; Nu 19:7–8; Dt 23:9–11; 2Ki 5:9–14; Ps 51:7; Heb 10:19–22

Sprinkling with the water of purification Nu 19:17–19 *See also* Nu 8:5–7; 19:13; Eze 36:24–25

Washing hands and feet Ex 30:17–21 *See also* Ex 40:30–32; Dt 21:6–9; Jn 13:5–10; Jas 4:8

Consequences of the failure to perform ritual washing
Nu 19:20 *See also* Lev 17:15–16; Nu 19:13

The NT perception of ritual washing
It was practised in NT times Jn 2:6 *See also* Jn 3:25

The Pharisees over-emphasised its importance Mt 15:1–11 pp Mk 7:1–23 *See also* Lk 11:37–41

Jesus Christ's atoning work rendered it unnecessary Heb 9:6–14

See also
5226 basin	7422 ritual
7340 clean and unclean	7424 ritual law
7342 cleanliness	7478 washing
7348 defilement	7550 Pharisees
7416 purification	8218 consecration

7428
Sabbath

The day of rest laid down for the people of God. The OT treated the seventh day of the week (Saturday) as the Sabbath, a custom continued in modern Judaism. The Christian church, in recognition of the importance of the resurrection of Jesus Christ, observed a day of rest on the first day of the week (Sunday).

7429
Sabbath, in OT

The Sabbath of rest is grounded in God's work of creation. Observance of a Sabbath day is distinctive of the people of God.

The Sabbath grounded in creation itself
Ge 2:3 *See also* Ps 118:24

The purpose of the Sabbath
To remember God's work in creation Ex 20:8–11 *See also* Ge 2:2; Ex 35:2

To remember the exodus Dt 5:12–15 *The idea of rest relates the concept of the Sabbath to the ultimate conquest of Canaan under David and to the return from exile. See also* Ge 8:4; 2Sa 7:1,11; Ps 95:10–11; Heb 4:9; Rev 14:13

To be a sign of the relationship between Israel and God and to give refreshment Ex 31:17 *See also* Dt 5:12–14

The Law required the Sabbath to be a holy day free from work Lev 23:3 *See also* Ex 34:21; 35:3; Lev 23:38; Isa 56:2; 58:13

The Sabbath was linked with celebration of the New Moon 2Ki 4:23 *See also* Isa 1:13; Eze 46:3; Hos 2:11; Am 8:5

Abuses of the Sabbath Ex 16:27–28 *gathering manna*; Nu 15:32 *gathering wood*; Ne 13:15–18 *doing ordinary work Engaging in commerce:* Ne 10:31; Am 8:5 Jer 17:21 *carrying loads*

Punishments for infringing the Sabbath law The death penalty Ex 31:14; Nu 15:35

Disaster for Jerusalem Jer 17:27; Eze 20:13; 22:8,15

Sacrifices to be offered on the Sabbath Bread Lev 24:8; 1Ch 9:32

Burnt offerings Nu 28:9–10; 1Ch 23:31; 2Ch 2:4

Other offerings Eze 46:4

See also
4005 creation	5056 rest
4975 week	5378 law, OT

7430
Sabbath, in NT

The NT develops the OT teaching on the Sabbath in three important directions. It declares that the Sabbath should not be observed in a legalistic manner; the Sabbath-rest is treated as an important symbol of the Christian doctrine of salvation; and finally, the NT itself indicates how Sunday, rather than Saturday, came to be seen as the Christian Sabbath.

Gospel incidents connected with the Sabbath Exorcism Mk 1:21–25 pp Lk 4:31–35

Healing Mt 12:9–14 pp Mk 3:1–6 pp Lk 6:6–11; Mk 1:30–31 pp Lk 4:38–40; Lk 13:10–17; 14:1–6; Jn 5:5–18; 9:1–16

Teaching Mk 6:2 pp Mt 13:54; Lk 4:16

Other references Mt 28:1 pp Mk 16:1; Lk 23:55–56; Jn 12:2

Jesus Christ's teaching regarding the Sabbath Jesus Christ observes the Sabbath regulation Lk 4:16 *See also* Mt 24:20; Ac 1:12

Human well-being is more important than rigid observance of the Law Mk 2:27–28 *See also* Mt 12:3

Ceremonial observance must give way before any higher, or more spiritual, motive Mt 12:5–6 *See also* Lk 6:5

Sabbath reading of Scripture provided an opportunity for reaching the Jews Ac 17:2 *See also* Ac 13:14,27,42,44; 15:21; 16:13; 18:4

Sabbath observance was optional for Gentile Christians Col 2:16

The Lord's Day Rev 1:10 *At an early stage the Sabbath was replaced by Sunday (the first day of the week) as the day for rest and worship. See also* Jn 20:19,26; Ac 20:7; 1Co 16:2

The Sabbath-rest is seen as a symbol of the salvation of the people of God Heb 4:1 *The OT promise of rest was unfulfilled, on account of Israel's disobedience*; Heb 3:18–19; 4:9 *The OT promise of rest remains open.*

See also
1610 Scripture	7930 Lord's Day, the
2333 Christ, attitude to OT	8774 legalism
2545 Christ, opposition to	

7431
Sabbath, sabbatical year

Just as the seventh day was observed as a day of rest, so the OT regarded every seventh year as a sabbath year, to be set aside for rest.

The sabbath year As a time for leaving fields fallow Ex 23:10–11 *See also* Lev 25:4; 26:34; Ne 10:31 *An important feature was the opportunity for the poor to benefit from unharvested fields.*

As a time for cancelling debts Dt 15:1 *See also* Dt 15:9; 31:10; Ne 10:31

As a time for freeing slaves Dt 15:12 *See also* Jer 34:14

The Year of Jubilee as seven Sabbaths Lev 25:8–12

See also
1653 numbers, 6–10	7447 slavery, in OT
4206 land	7482 Year of Jubilee
6658 freedom	

7434

sacrifice

An important aspect of the relationship between God and humanity but whereas the OT describes many sacrifices, the NT announces the fulfilment of sacrifice in Jesus Christ.

7435
sacrifice, in OT

An act that involved offering to God the life of an animal. It expressed gratitude for God's goodness or

acknowledgment of sin. It was also associated with establishing a covenant.

Sacrifice was an integral part of worship Ge 46:1; Ex 10:24–26; Jdg 13:19; 1Sa 1:3; 1Ki 3:4

Sacrifices were a means of offering thanks to God Ge 4:4 *Abel*; Ge 8:20 *Noah delivered from the flood*; Ex 18:12 *Jethro after God had delivered the Israelites*; Jdg 11:31 *Jephthah*; 1Sa 6:15 *after the safe return of the ark The returning exiles:* Ezr 3:3; 8:35 *In response to God's deliverance from danger and sickness:* Ps 27:6; 54:6; 107:17–22

Sacrifices were offered at regular religious festivals Lev 23:5–8 *Passover*; Lev 23:18–20 *the Feast of Weeks*; Lev 23:23–25 *the Feast of Trumpets The Day of Atonement:* Lev 16:6–10; 23:26–32 Lev 23:33–36 *the Feast of Tabernacles*

Special occasions were marked by sacrifices 1Ki 8:63 *the dedication of Solomon's temple*; 2Ch 29:31–33 *after Hezekiah had purified the temple*; Ezr 3:2–3 *the Jews who returned from the Babylonian exile*; Ezr 6:17 *at the completion of the second temple*

Sacrifices as signs of individual and national penitence Lev 4:1–3,13–14; Jdg 2:1–5; 20:26; 1Sa 7:8–9; 2Sa 24:10–25

The place of sacrifice It was divinely chosen Dt 12:13–14 *See also* Lev 17:3–5; Dt 12:2–6

Rival places of sacrifice caused the Israelites to sin 1Ki 12:28–29,32; 2Ch 15:17; 31:1 *Under Hezekiah the high places were destroyed.*

God condemned certain sacrifices Sacrifices to other gods 1Ki 11:7–8 *See also* Nu 25:1–3; 2Ki 16:4,15; Ps 106:28; Isa 57:7; 65:3,7; Jer 19:4

Human sacrifices Lev 18:21; Dt 12:31; 1Ki 16:34; 2Ki 3:26–27; 16:3; 17:31; 21:6; Eze 20:31

Sacrifice to the LORD may be rejected If it is a substitute for obedience 1Sa 15:20–22; Jer 7:21–22; Hos 8:11–13; Am 4:4; Mk 12:33

If it is a substitute for justice and mercy Isa 66:2–3; Mic 6:7–8; Mt 9:13

If it is imperfect Mal 1:13–14

Blessing is promised when right sacrifices are offered Ge 22:15–18; Ps 4:5; 50:14–15,23; 51:17

7436
sacrifice, NT fulfilment of

For the people of the new covenant, sacrifice is fulfilled in Jesus Christ. Christians should have nothing to do with other sacrifices but are to bring their own "spiritual" offerings.

The OT points ahead to the fulfilment of sacrifice in Jesus Christ

A new sacrificial system Isa 56:6–7 See also Isa 19:21

The new people of God Jer 33:18; Eze 20:40

The vision of the new temple Eze 40:46

The perfect sacrifice of Jesus Christ

Jesus Christ perceived his death as a sacrifice Mt 26:28 pp Mk 14:24 pp Lk 22:20 pp 1Co 11:25 See also Heb 5:1

The contrast with the OT sacrificial system Heb 7:27 See also Heb 9:23–26; 10:1–3,12

Jesus Christ's sacrifice of a life dedicated to God makes believers holy Tit 2:14; Heb 10:8–10

The sacrifices of Christians

Christians offer themselves as living sacrifices Ro 12:1
Paul saw his own death as part of a sacrificial offering: Php 2:17; 2Ti 4:6

The sacrifice of praise and good works Heb 13:15–16

Christian attitudes to pagan sacrifice

1Co 10:18–22,25–26,27–29 Christians must not appear to compromise with idolatrous worship.

sanctuary

A place or structure set aside for the worship of God. In Scripture the word generally refers to the tabernacle or the Jerusalem temple. By extension the word signifies a

---

location or spiritual state providing refuge from hostile forces, human, spiritual or natural.

The tabernacle

Ex 25:8–9 See also Ex 36:1; Heb 8:2,5

Worship in the tabernacle was divinely ordained in great detail Ex 30:7–10; Lev 7:37–38; 23:44; Ex 39:1; Nu 3:30–31; Heb 9:1

The people gave generously for the tabernacle Ex 36:4–5

Approach to God's sanctuary was strictly regulated Lev 12:4 See also Lev 21:21–23; Nu 3:10,38; 8:19; 18:5; 19:20; 2Ch 26:18

A reverent attitude was commanded Lev 19:30 pp Lev 26:2

The Jerusalem temple

David made extensive preparations for Solomon to build the temple 1Ch 22:17–19 See also 1Ch 28:2–3,6

The inner sanctuary of the temple corresponded to the Most Holy Place in the tabernacle 1Ki 6:19 See also 1Ki 8:6 pp 2Ch 5:7; 1Ch 6:49; Heb 9:1–4

Some places were considered sacred because of God's presence and activity

Ex 15:17 See also Ge 28:16–17; Ex 3:1–5; Ps 15:1; 63:2; 73:16–17; Jer 17:12

Conduct that displeases God will lead to a nation's sanctuaries being destroyed

Disobedience to God Lev 26:31 See also 2Ch 30:8; Eze 7:24; La 2:7; Am 7:9; Mal 2:11

Dishonesty in dealings Eze 28:18

Idolatry Lev 20:3; Eze 8:6; 23:38–39

Profaning the sanctuary Eze 44:7–8; Zep 3:4

Sanctuary from vengeance: the cities of refuge

Jos 20:2–3 See also Nu 35:6,9–12

God himself is his people's sanctuary

Ps 31:20 See also Dt 33:27; Ps 17:7–9; 27:1; 32:7; 46:1; 64:1–2; 91:4; Isa 25:4; Eze 11:16; Ro 8:38–39; Php 4:7; Heb 6:19

Non-material "sanctuaries" of God

Heaven, where God is perfectly worshipped Ps 102:19 See also Heb 9:24

God's worshipping people, in whom God dwells Ps 114:2 See also 1Co 6:19; Eph 2:21; 1Pe 2:5

Jesus Christ himself as the "place" where God dwelt on earth Jn 2:19–21

---

scapegoat

A goat which was sent into the wilderness by the high priest, as a symbol of the removal of the sins of the people.

The scapegoat as part of an OT ritual

Lev 16:7–10,20–22 See also Lev 16:26; Isa 53:4

The scapegoat anticipates Jesus Christ's atonement

Jn 1:29; 2Co 5:21; Heb 9:11–14 Jesus Christ's death is here contrasted with the OT sacrificial system.

shrine

A local sanctuary, often dedicated to pagan worship. Before the building of the temple the Israelites worshipped at several divinely sanctioned shrines; afterwards, worship at a central sanctuary was required. True worship of God required that pagan shrines be destroyed. It was Israel's failure to abandon these religious sites that led to syncretism and apostasy.

Common features of pagan shrines

A location on high ground under trees Eze 6:13 Mountains were considered the dwelling-places of the gods, whilst trees were associated with fertility. See also 2Ki 17:10; Isa 1:29 sacred trees; Jer 2:20; Eze 18:11 mountain shrines; Eze 20:28

Idols and sacred symbols Isa 44:13 See also 2Ki 10:26–27; 17:29–31; 2Ch 34:3–4; Ac 19:24

A serving priesthood 2Ki 23:5,20

Sacrifice to the deity Jer 48:35 See also 1Ki 22:43; 2Ki 12:3; 16:4 pp 2Ch 28:4; 2Ch 28:25

Shrine-prostitution Ge 38:21–22; Dt 23:17; 1Ki 14:24; 15:12; Job 36:14

Pagan shrines were to be destroyed

On Israel's entry into Canaan Dt 12:2–3 See also Ex 34:13–14; Nu 33:52; Dt 7:5

As a sign of religious reformation Jdg 6:25; 2Ki 23:8–20 See also 2Ki 10:25; 2Ch 14:3; 17:6; 2Ki 18:4

Shrines in Israel for the worship of God

Worship at the high places 1Ki 3:2–3 Following Canaanite custom, Israel set up shrines on high ground possibly, against God's instruction, at old Baal sites.

Worship at these non-legitimate sites was condemned. See also 2Ch 33:17

Worship at sites sanctioned by God
Ex 20:24 *See also* Jdg 6:22–24;
1Sa 9:12–14; 10:5

Examples of shrines dedicated to God
Bethel: Ge 12:8; Jdg 21:2
Shiloh: Jos 18:1; Jdg 21:19
Mizpah: Jdg 20:1; 1Sa 7:6
Gibeon: 1Ki 3:4–5; 1Ch 16:39–40;
2Ch 1:13

A central place of worship was later required 2Ki 18:22 pp Isa 36:7
Following the building of the temple, worship in various scattered shrines was condemned, probably because of associations with pagan worship. See also Dt 12:4–7 *The central sanctuary was, initially, the place where the tabernacle was located. Eventually this was superseded by the temple;* 2Sa 7:13 pp 1Ch 17:12

Israel's failure to abandon worship at the shrines led to apostasy
Improper worship at shrines dedicated to God Jdg 17:5 *See also* Jdg 18:30–31;
1Ki 12:28–31; 13:32; 2Ki 17:32–33;
2Ch 11:15; Am 4:4

The corruption of temple worship
2Ki 23:4–7; Eze 8:14–16

Shrines dedicated to false gods
1Ki 14:23–24; Eze 8:12 *See also*
1Ki 11:7–8; 2Ki 21:2–3
Child sacrifice was amongst the syncretistic practices adopted by Judah:
Jer 7:31; 19:5; 32:35
Am 5:26; Ac 7:43

Israel's spiritual adultery Eze 16:24–25
See also Jer 3:6; Eze 16:39; 18:6;
Hos 4:12–13

God's judgment on false places of worship Eze 6:3–6 *See also*
Lev 26:30–31; Hos 10:8

See also
6239 prostitution	8704 apostasy
6243 adultery,	8747 false gods
spiritual	8752 false worship
7302 altar	8768 idolatry
7312 Baal	8799 polytheism
7374 high places	8831 syncretism
7438 sanctuary	

7446

sin offering

Offerings to make atonement for both moral and ritual offences. The NT sees them as foreshadowing the death of Jesus Christ as an offering for human sin.

Occasions when a sin offering was required
Unintentional sins against God's laws:
Lev 4:2; Heb 9:7
Lev 5:1–4; 4:20 *The consequence of the offering is atonement and forgiveness.*
Purification after childbirth: Lev 12:6–8;
Lk 2:24
Cleansing from infectious diseases:
Lev 14:13–31; Mk 1:44
Cleansing from a bodily discharge:
Lev 15:15,30

The form the sin offering took depended on who committed the sin
Lev 4:3 *a priest who sins;* Lev 4:14 *the sin of the community as a whole;*
Lev 4:22–23 *a leader who sins unintentionally*
An individual who sins: Lev 4:27–35;
5:5–6

The ceremony when presenting an animal as a sin offering
The guilty identify themselves with the offering before killing it Lev 4:4,15,24

Confession Lev 5:5

Blood, representing the victim's lifeblood, is put on the altar
Lev 4:25,30,34

The best parts, being burned on the altar, are offered to God
Lev 4:8–10,26,35

Male members of priestly families may eat what remains Lev 6:26,29;
10:16–20

Special procedures for the offerings of the poor Lev 5:7–13

The special ceremony for priests and the community presenting a sin offering
Blood is taken into the sanctuary and placed on the altar Lev 4:5–7,16–18

The rest of the animal is incinerated, not eaten Lev 4:11–12,21 *emphasising the identity between the victim and the sin of the community*

Significant occasions when sin offerings were made
Lev 8:14–17 *at the ordination of Aaron and his sons;* Lev 16:1–34 *on the Day of Atonement;* 2Ki 12:16 *during Josiah's reformation;* 2Ch 29:21–24 *at the beginning of Hezekiah's reign;* Ezr 6:17 *at the dedication of the second temple;*
Ezr 8:35 *when the exiles returned*
As part of Ezekiel's vision of restored worship: Eze 40:39; 42:13; 43:19,21

The NT perspective on the sin offering
Jesus Christ was the supreme sin offering Ro 8:3; 2Co 5:21 *NIV footnote.*

Animal sacrifices had limited value
Heb 9:7–10

The death of Jesus Christ brings full cleansing and forgiveness
Heb 9:11–14 *See also* 1Pe 1:18–19

Unlike earthly priests, Jesus Christ needed no sin offering Heb 7:27 *See also* Heb 5:1–3

See also
2306 Christ, high	7402 offerings
priest	7435 sacrifice, in OT
2530 Christ, death of	7768 priests, OT
6614 atonement	function
7314 blood	

7446

slavery

The state of being an unpaid servant, whether through forcible subjection or voluntary submission. Slavery was common in biblical times, and

Scripture lays down strict guidelines as to how slaves are to be treated by their masters, stressing the new status that slaves have as a result of being believers in Jesus Christ. The image of slavery is also used to describe the state of sinful human beings.

7447
slavery, in OT

Slavery in the OT occurs when someone either voluntarily or forcibly becomes completely subject to another person's control.

Reasons for slavery
War Dt 20:10–11 *See also* Ge 14:21;
Nu 31:9; 2Ki 5:2; 2Ch 28:8

Purchase Lev 25:44–45 *See also*
Ge 37:23–28

Debt 2Ki 4:1 *See also* Ex 22:2–3;
Lev 25:39,47–48; Dt 15:12; Ne 5:1–5

Birth Ex 21:4 *See also* Ge 17:12–13;
Ecc 2:7; Jer 2:14

Conscription of foreigners as forced labour 2Sa 12:29–31 *See also*
Ex 1:11–14; Jos 9:22–23; 16:10;
Jdg 1:28; 1Ki 9:20–21

Rights of slaves
Rights of protection against physical and sexual abuse Lev 25:43 *See also*
Ex 21:7–11,20–21,26–27

Rights to participate in religious feasts and festivals Ex 23:12 *See also*
Ex 20:9–10; Dt 12:11–12

Rights to inherit property Ge 15:3

Rights of asylum Dt 23:15

The release of slaves
Release in the Year of Jubilee
Lev 25:54–55 *See also* Lev 25:39–41

Release after six years of service
Ex 21:2 *See also* Ex 21:3–6;
Dt 15:12–18; Jer 34:8–20 *The six-year principle was being abused in the time of Jeremiah.*

Release through redemption by a near relative Lev 25:47–53

The status of slaves
Slaves as property Lev 25:46 *See also*
Ex 21:32; Lev 25:39–42 *Fellow Israelites were not to be regarded as property.*

Slaves as trusted advisors 1Sa 9:5–10

See also
1315 God as	5672 concubines
redeemer	5674 daughters
5246 captivity	7222 exodus, events
5266 conscription	of
5289 debt	7388 kinsman-
5475 property	redeemer
5605 warfare	7482 Year of Jubilee

7448
slavery, in NT

The NT does not condone slavery but recognises that slavery exists, and that many slaves have become believers. The status of slaves in the church is transformed by the work of Jesus Christ. Slaves were accorded greater respect because they were seen to be spiritually equal with others.

Examples of slavery in the NT
Ac 16:16–21 *Paul and Silas deliver a demon-possessed slave girl*; Phm 8–21 *Paul returns the runaway slave Onesimus to his master.*

The gospel transforms the status of slaves
1Co 12:13; Gal 3:26–28

Instructions concerning slavery
Instructions to Christian slaves
Eph 6:5–8 *See also* 1Co 7:20–24; Col 3:22–24; 1Ti 6:1–2; Tit 2:9–10; 1Pe 2:18–21

Instructions to Christian masters
Eph 6:9 *See also* Col 4:1; Phm 8–17

The immorality of trading in slaves
1Ti 1:9–10

See also
2327 Christ as servant	5520 servants
5308 equality	6754 union with Christ
5404 masters	8342 servanthood

7449
slavery, spiritual

Because of sin humanity is in a state of slavery. On account of the atoning work of Jesus Christ, believers can break free from slavery to sin and enter into the glorious liberty of the children of God.

Humanity is enslaved
To sin Jn 8:33–36 *See also* Ro 6:12–18; 7:7–25; Tit 3:3; 2Pe 2:19

To the law Gal 5:1 *See also* Gal 4:1–7

To fear Ro 8:15 *See also* Heb 2:14–15

Jesus Christ as the example of the true slave
Jn 13:1–17 *Washing feet was the responsibility of the slaves of the household. See also* Mt 20:25–28 pp Mk 10:42–45; Php 2:5–11

Believers as slaves of God
They are God's servants Ro 6:22 *See also* Mt 6:24 pp Lk 16:13; Ro 1:1; Col 3:23–24; Jas 1:1; 1Pe 2:16; 2Pe 1:1

They are sons and heirs Gal 4:1–7 *See also* Ro 8:12–17

They have friendship with Jesus Christ Jn 15:15 *See also* Jas 2:21–23

They have true freedom Jn 8:31–36 *See also* Gal 4:21–31

Believers as slaves of righteousness
Ro 6:15–23

Believers as slaves of others
Mt 20:25–28 pp Mk 10:42–45 *See also* 1Co 9:19; 2Co 4:5; Gal 5:13

The image of slavery in the teaching of Jesus Christ
Mt 24:45–51 pp Lk 12:42–46 *Slavery involves readiness for the Master's return*; Mt 25:14–20 pp Lk 19:12–17 *Slavery involves faithfulness to the Master's purpose*; Lk 17:7–10 *Slavery involves diligence for the Master's good.*

Creation is itself in slavery until Jesus Christ returns
Ro 8:19–22

See also
2363 Christ, preaching & teaching	6614 atonement
	6658 freedom
	6720 redemption
4005 creation	7939 ministry
5004 human race & sin	8154 righteousness
	8453 obedience
5703 inheritance	8754 fear
6020 sin	

7452

snake, bronze

The means of salvation for Israel in the wilderness, a parallel to be found in Jesus Christ.

Healing and salvation resulted from looking at the bronze snake
Nu 21:8–9 *See also* Nu 21:4–7

The bronze snake became an object of idolatrous worship
2Ki 18:4

The bronze snake parallels Jesus Christ's crucifixion
Jn 3:14–15

See also
1680 types	4687 snake
2321 Christ as redeemer	5104 Moses, foreshadower of Christ
2324 Christ as Saviour	8768 idolatry
4312 bronze	

7454

sprinkling

In the OT, the blood of a sacrificial animal was sprinkled against the altar as a sign of atonement or consecration to the LORD. The NT uses the same image to refer to the gaining of forgiveness through the sacrificial death of Jesus Christ.

Sprinkling of an animal's blood as a sign of atonement
On the altar Lev 7:2 *See also* Ex 24:6; Lev 1:5,11; 3:2,8,13; 5:9; 9:12,18; 17:6; Nu 18:17; 2Ki 16:13,15; 2Ch 29:22–24; 30:16; 35:11; Eze 43:18,20; Heb 9:21

In front of the inner curtain in the tabernacle Lev 4:6 *See also* Lev 4:17

Towards the front of the Tent of Meeting Nu 19:4

On the front of the atonement cover Lev 16:14–16

On the door-frames of the houses where the Passover lamb was eaten Ex 12:7 *See also* Ex 12:22; Heb 11:28

Sprinkling of blood as a sign of consecration
The consecration of people Ex 24:8 *See also* Ex 29:20–21; Lev 8:23; Heb 9:19

The consecration of the altar Lev 16:18–19

Sprinkling of oil as a sign of consecration
Lev 8:11 *See also* Lev 8:30; 14:15–16,27

Sprinkling (usually with water) as a sign of cleansing
Nu 8:7; Eze 36:25 *See also* Lev 14:7,51; Nu 19:13,18–21; Isa 52:15; Heb 9:13

Sprinkling as an image of forgiveness in Christ
1Pe 1:2 *See also* Heb 9:11–14,18–28; 10:22; 12:24

Sprinkling of dust as a visible sign of mourning
Jos 7:6 *See also* Job 2:12; La 2:10; Eze 27:30

See also
1448 signs	7302 altar
4050 dust	7314 blood
5419 mourning	7342 cleanliness
6614 atonement	7434 sacrifice
6652 forgiveness	8218 consecration

7456

synagogue

A word meaning literally "a gathering together". In the NT it sometimes refers to a group of Jews meeting for worship but most often to the building in which they met.

Synagogue worship may have begun during the exile
Eze 14:1 *Unable to sacrifice in the temple, the community met together with spiritual leaders. See also* Eze 20:1

A synagogue might be established anywhere
Mk 1:21 *See also* Ac 6:9 *In Jerusalem Where there were too few male Jews for a synagogue there would sometimes be a place of prayer:* Ac 16:12–13,16 Ac 17:1,10; 18:19

The role of the synagogue
It was a focus for prayer and the reading of Scripture Ac 13:15 *See also* Ne 8:2–8; 9:3; Lk 4:15–33

It was a centre for community affairs Mt 10:17; Mk 13:9; Lk 12:11

Exclusion from the synagogue was used as a punishment Jn 9:22; 12:42

The leading of synagogue worship
It was the responsibility of the synagogue ruler Mk 5:22; Ac 18:8

Qualified laymen were allowed to teach Lk 4:16 *See also* Ac 13:15

Attendance at the synagogue
It was the practice of Jesus Christ Mt 9:35 *See also* Mk 6:2; Lk 4:16; Jn 6:59

It was the practice of Paul and other Jewish Christians Ac 9:19–20 *See also* Ac 14:1–2; 17:2; 19:8

The first Christians continued to worship in the synagogues Lk 24:53; Ac 19:8–9

See also

2363 Christ, preaching & teaching	5509 rulers
	7505 Jews, the
	7793 teachers
5175 reading	8626 worship,
5302 education	places

7458

tabernacle, the

The tabernacle (tent) was a portable and temporary shrine used for worship before the temple was built. It denotes the temporary dwelling of God among his people.

7459
tabernacle, in OT

A prefabricated portable structure that was used for worship from the wilderness period until Solomon built the Jerusalem temple.

The tabernacle was the place of God's presence
Ex 33:9–10 *See also* Ex 25:8; 40:34–35

The construction of the tabernacle
It was built at God's command Ex 25:9 *See also* Ex 25:40; 39:32,43

The materials used in its construction
Ex 25:3–7 *Many of these materials were available in the desert. Others, such as gold, would have been obtained from the Egyptians (Ex 12:35–36);* Ex 35:21–24

The plan for its construction
Ex 26:1,7,14–15,26

The skilled labour employed in its construction Ex 31:1–6
pp Ex 35:30–35 *See also* Ex 35:10,26; 36:1–2

The tabernacle courtyard and its contents
Its dimensions and construction
Ex 27:9,12,18

The altar of burnt offering Ex 27:1

The laver Ex 30:17–18

The tabernacle's Holy Place and its contents
Its construction Ex 26:36–37

The incense altar Ex 30:1,5

The lampstand Ex 25:31

The golden table for the bread of the Presence Ex 25:23,30; 26:35

The tabernacle's Most Holy Place and its contents
It was separated from the Holy Place by a curtain Ex 26:31–33 *It was designed as a perfect cube with sides of 10 cubits (4.5 metres).*

It contained the ark of the covenant Ex 26:33–34

The Levites were responsible for the tabernacle
Nu 1:50–51

The non-religious functions of the tabernacle
As a reference point for locating the different tribes in camp Nu 2:1–2 *Symbolising that God was central to the life of the nation.*

The movement of the cloud of glory showed when it was time to make or break camp Ex 40:36–38

Places where the tabernacle was sited
The tabernacle was dedicated at Sinai: Ex 40:1–2,9–11
Shiloh: Jos 18:1; 1Sa 1:3; Ps 78:60
1Sa 21:1 *Nob;* 1Ch 16:39 *Gibeon;*
2Ch 5:2–6 *Jerusalem*

See also

6606 access to God	7396 Most Holy
7302 altar	Place
7306 ark of the covenant	7402 offerings
	7467 temple,
7308 Atonement, Day of	Solomon's
	7474 Tent of
7358 Feast of Tabernacles	Meeting
	7768 priests, OT
7382 house of God	function
7390 Levites	

7460
tabernacle, in NT

The NT sees the tabernacle and its ceremonies as symbolising the saving work of Jesus Christ in his incarnation and death and in the experience of believers.

Jesus Christ as the tabernacle where God dwells
Jn 1:14; 2:19–21

The tabernacle showed that God was not limited to one place
Ac 7:44–47

The spiritual significance of the tabernacle
Heb 9:1–5

The earthly tabernacle as a copy of the heavenly one
Heb 8:5 *See also* Heb 8:1–2

The altar Rev 6:9–10; 8:3–5

The ark of the covenant Rev 11:19

The atonement cover Ex 25:22; Heb 4:16

The curtain preventing access to the holiest place Mt 27:51; Heb 6:19–20; 9:8; 10:19–20

Jesus Christ as high priest
Cleansing the earthly tabernacle
Heb 9:21 *See also* Heb 9:6–8 *on the Day of Atonement;* Heb 9:25

Through the blood of the cross, Jesus Christ enters the heavenly sanctuary
Heb 9:24 *See also* Heb 9:28

See also

1680 types	7376 high priest
2306 Christ, high priest	7438 sanctuary
	7469 temple,
7020 church, the	Herod's
7344 curtain	8622 worship

7462

tassel

A fringe of twisted threads attached to the bottom edge of Israelite men's cloaks. The Pharisees lengthened the tassels on their cloaks to draw attention to their piety.

Tassels attached to outer garments
On the corners of garments Nu 15:38 *See also* Dt 22:12

On the cloak of Jesus Christ Mt 9:20
pp Mk 5:27 pp Lk 8:44 *The woman probably touched the tassels on Jesus Christ's cloak. See also* Mt 14:36 pp Mk 6:56

Tassels as a reminder of God's law
Nu 15:39–41 *The movement of the tassels would draw back wandering eyes to God and his law.*

Ostentatious tassels symbolise outward religious show
Mt 23:5–7 pp Mk 12:38–39
pp Lk 20:46 *See also* Mt 6:1–6

See also

1670 symbols	7550 Pharisees
4807 colours	8453 obedience
5144 cloak	8467 reminders
5375 law	8670 remembering
7394 memorial	8767 hypocrisy
7410 phylactery	

7464

teachers of the law

Those professionally trained to develop, teach and apply the OT law. In the application of the law the oral teaching of these people often assumed greater authority than the written law. Thus, by the time of the NT, the teachers of the law were in conflict with Jesus Christ and the apostles, who taught with authority and condemned the outward religious acts that the teachers had fostered.

Teachers of the law mentioned by name
Ezra Ezr 7:1–21; Ne 8:1–18 *Teachers of the law arose after the exile from amongst the earlier scribes whose duties were more strictly secretarial.*

Nicodemus Jn 3:10

Gamaliel Ac 5:34 *Teachers of the law belonged mainly to the Pharisees but as a body were distinct from them.*

Teachers of the law in conflict with Jesus Christ
Concerning righteousness Mt 5:20

Concerning Jesus Christ's authority
Mt 9:2–8 pp Mk 2:5–12 pp Lk 5:20–26 *See also* Mk 3:22–27; 11:27–33
pp Lk 20:1–8

Concerning the seeking of signs
Mt 12:38–39

Concerning hypocrisy Mt 23:2–33
pp Mk 12:38–40 pp Lk 13:34–35; 20:46
See also Mt 15:1–8 pp Mk 7:1–8;
Isa 29:13

Concerning the children's praise
Mt 21:15–16 *See also* Ps 8:2

Concerning Jesus Christ's mixing with
sinners Mk 2:16–17　pp Lk 5:30–32 *See*
also Lk 15:1–7

Concerning Jesus Christ's identity
Mk 12:35–37 *See also* Ps 110:1

Concerning the Sabbath Lk 6:7–11

The teachers of the law sought to
get rid of Jesus Christ
By falsely accusing him Lk 23:10 *See*
also Mt 26:57–60 pp Mk 14:53–56 *The*
teachers of the law were entrusted with the
administration of the law as judges in the
Sanhedrin; Jn 8:3–6

By looking for ways to arrest and kill
him Mk 11:18　pp Lk 19:47 *See also*
Mk 14:1 pp Lk 22:2; Mk 14:43; Lk 20:19
pp Mk 12:12

By sending him to be tried before
Pilate Mk 15:1 *See also* Lk 22:66–23:1

The teachers of the law, with
others, mocked Christ crucified
Mt 27:41–42　pp Mk 15:31–32

Jesus Christ foretold the
opposition of the teachers of the
law
Mt 16:21　pp Mk 8:31 pp Lk 9:22 *See also*
Mt 20:18–19 pp Mk 10:33–34

Teachers of the law in conflict
with the apostles
Ac 4:5–7; 6:12

Teachers of the law in a non-
confrontational setting
Mt 2:4; 8:19–20; 13:52; Lk 20:39;
1Ti 1:7 *See also* Mt 7:28–29; 17:10
pp Mk 9:11; Mk 1:22; Ac 23:9

See also

2012 Christ, authority	5588 traditions
2363 Christ, preaching & teaching	7550 Pharisees
	7565 Sanhedrin
	7718 elders
	7793 teachers
2545 Christ, opposition to	8767 hypocrisy
	8787 opposition to
5375 law	God
5514 scribes	

7466

temples

Buildings for the worship of local or
national gods. After settling in the
promised land, Israel felt the need
for a permanent building set apart
for worship of the LORD. Three
temples were built at different
periods in Jerusalem. In the NT the
individual believer (or the body of
the church) is seen as the true temple
or dwelling-place of God.
This set of themes consists of the
following:
7467 temple, Solomon's
7468 temple, rebuilding of
7469 temple, Herod's

7470 temple, significance of
7471 temples, heathen

7467
temple, Solomon's

From the exodus until the reign of
Solomon, the tabernacle located in
various places served as Israel's
"temple" and the ordained place of
sacrifice. Solomon built the first
temple in Jerusalem.

Centres for worship and sacrifice
before the temple was built
Jos 18:1; 1Sa 7:2

David's preparations for the
building and worship in the first
temple
The plan for its construction
2Sa 7:12–13; 1Ch 17:1 pp 2Sa 7:1;
1Ch 28:11–12,19

The gifts for its construction
1Ch 29:2–3,6

Arrangements for the temple worship
1Ch 23:3–5

Solomon's construction of the
temple
1Ki 5:1–13; 6:7; 2Ch 2:17–18

The completion of the temple and
its furnishings
2Ch 2:5 *Although it followed the basic*
pattern of the tabernacle, Solomon
intended the temple to reflect God's
greatness. See also 1Ki 6:20–22
pp 2Ch 3:4–9 *The inner walls were*
overlaid with gold; 1Ki 6:27
pp 2Ch 3:11–12 *The wings of the*
cherubim reached from wall to wall;
1Ki 6:38
Not one laver but a huge reservoir and a
number of bronze basins: 1Ki 7:23
pp 2Ch 4:2; 1Ki 7:26–27 pp 2Ch 4:5;
1Ki 7:30
1Ki 7:49 *not one golden lampstand but*
ten; 2Ch 4:8 *not one table for the bread of*
the Presence but ten

The dedication of the temple
At the Feast of Tabernacles 1Ki 8:2
pp 2Ch 5:3

The glory of the LORD filled the temple
1Ki 8:6 pp 2Ch 5:7; 1Ki 8:10–11;
2Ch 5:11,13–14

The offering of sacrifices 1Ki 8:62–63
pp 2Ch 7:5

Solomon's prayer 1Ki 8:27
pp 2Ch 6:18

The temple after the division of
the kingdom
1Ki 12:26–30; 2Ch 13:4–12

Later kings of Judah used the
temple treasures for political
purposes
1Ki 15:18–19 pp 2Ch 16:2–3 *Asa took*
silver and gold to persuade the king of
Aram to be his ally against Israel;
2Ki 12:17–18 *Joash sent money and*
treasures to prevent the king of Aram
attacking Jerusalem; 2Ki 16:7–8
pp 2Ch 28:21 *Ahaz used gold and silver to*

gain the support of the king of Assyria
against his enemies; 2Ki 18:14–15
Hezekiah used temple silver to placate the
king of Assyria.

Foreign kings pillaged the temple
1Ki 14:25–26 pp 2Ch 12:9 *Shishak king*
of Egypt; 2Ki 24:13; 2Ch 36:18
Nebuchadnezzar

Under certain kings the temple
was cleansed and repaired
Joash: 2Ki 12:4–5 pp 2Ch 24:5;
2Ch 24:13–14
2Ki 15:35 pp 2Ch 27:3 *Jotham*
Hezekiah: 2Ch 29:3–5,15–16,18–19,25
2Ki 22:3–7 pp 2Ch 34:8–11 *Josiah*

The destruction of the temple by
the Babylonians
2Ki 25:13–15 pp Jer 52:17–19;
2Ch 36:18

The temple and the ministry of
the prophets
Isaiah received his call in the temple
Isa 6:1–8

Ezekiel had a vision of the glory of God
departing Eze 10:18–19

Micah's prophecy concerning the
temple's fate Jer 26:18; Mic 3:12

Jeremiah's ministry was closely linked
to the temple Jer 7:2,4,14; 19:14

See also

4215 Babylon	7396 Most Holy
5118 Solomon	Place
5272 craftsmen	7402 offerings
5324 gatekeepers	7438 sanctuary
7239 Jerusalem	7459 tabernacle, in
7302 altar	OT
7382 house of God	8466 reformation

7468
temple, rebuilding of

Following the exile Solomon's
ruined temple was rebuilt and
became the focus of the Jewish faith
worldwide.

Preparations for rebuilding the
temple
Ezr 1:1–4 pp 2Ch 36:22–23 *Cyrus gave*
permission for the exiled Jews to return to
Jerusalem to rebuild the temple (538 B.C.);
Ezr 1:7 *He sent back the temple treasures.*

Rebuilding the temple under the
leadership of Jeshua and
Zerubbabel
Ezr 3:3–6,8–13; 4:1–3

Interruptions to the rebuilding
The Jews' enemies persuaded
Artaxerxes to order the work to cease
Ezr 4:8,12–15,17,20–21,24

The prophets Haggai and Zechariah
called Zerubbabel and the people to
restart work Hag 1:4 *See also*
Ezr 5:1–12; Hag 1:5–7,14–15

The rebuilding authorised by King
Darius Ezr 5:3,11,13; 6:3–5,7–8

The dedication and worship of the
rebuilt temple Ezr 6:16; 7:11–17

The post-exilic temple and its worship was regarded as the spiritual centre for Jews worldwide
Ps 87:1–7; 135:21

The temple is the place where God is to be praised
Ps 100:4; 134:1–2 *See also*
Ps 135:19–20; 138:2

Prophecies of restoration of the temple
Zec 1:16 *See also* Jer 31:6,23; 33:18;
Eze 40:1–43:27

See also
7766 priests	8622 worship
7772 prophets	8664 praise

7469
temple, Herod's

Herod's temple, familiar to Jesus Christ and his disciples and frequented by the first Christians, was destroyed by the Romans in A.D. 70.

The building of Herod the Great's temple
Jn 2:20

Jesus Christ visited the temple and taught in its courts
He was taken there as a baby
Lk 2:22,34,36–38

He stayed in the temple courts after his parents had returned home from the Passover Feast Lk 2:41–43,46

He cast out of the temple court those who used it for material profit
Mt 21:12–13 pp Mk 11:15–17
pp Lk 19:45–46; Jn 2:14–16

He taught in the temple
Mk 12:35,41–43 pp Lk 21:1–4; Jn 7:14
The temple guards ignored instructions to arrest him because they were impressed by his teaching: Jn 7:32,45–46
Jn 8:2–3; 10:22–24

The religious leaders challenged his authority Mt 21:23 pp Mk 11:27–28
pp Lk 20:1–2

He foretold the complete destruction of the temple buildings Mt 24:1–2
pp Mk 13:1–2 pp Lk 21:5–6

The crucifixion and the temple
One of the charges against Jesus Christ was that he had said he would destroy the temple Mt 26:60–61

The curtain of the temple was torn in two at Jesus Christ's death Mt 27:51
The curtain symbolised the barrier between God and his people caused by their sins.

Believers in Jerusalem met in the temple courtyards
Ac 2:46; 5:12 *Solomon's Colonnade was on the east side of the temple courtyard.*

Apostles taught and healed in the temple courtyards
Ac 3:1–26; 5:19–26

Stephen was stoned for allegedly speaking against the temple
Ac 6:12–14
Ac 7:48–49

Paul was accused of taking Gentiles into temple courtyards forbidden to them
Ac 21:27–28

See also
2012 Christ, authority	2530 Christ, death of
2363 Christ, preaching & teaching	2585 Christ, trial
	5271 courtyard
	5281 crucifixion
2366 Christ, prophecies concerning	7344 curtain
	7406 Passover
2520 Christ, childhood	

7470
temple, significance of

The temple was both idealised and spiritualised by OT and NT writers.

The OT concept of an ideal temple in the future age of salvation
Isa 2:3 pp Mic 4:2 *See also* Isa 56:4–7;
66:20; Jer 33:11; Eze 37:28; 40:2–4
Ezekiel received a vision of a rebuilt temple to which the glory of the LORD had returned. Chapters 40–48 describe this temple and its worship in detail;
Hag 2:6–8; Zec 14:16; Mal 3:1–3

The superstitious belief that the presence of the temple in Jerusalem safeguarded the city
The origin of such a belief
2Ki 19:32–36; Ps 132:13–18

The prophets knew that disobedience to God would be judged in spite of the temple Mic 3:12 *See also* Jer 7:4,12–14

The link between the earthly temple and heaven
Heaven is described as God's temple
Ps 11:4 *See also* Hab 2:20; Heb 8:5; 9:24;
Rev 11:19; 14:15–17; 15:5–8

The ultimate "city of God" needs no temple, since it is permeated by God's presence Rev 21:22 *See also* Rev 21:3

The risen Christ as the temple where God's glory is revealed
Jn 2:19–21

The church as the temple where God's presence dwells
The individual believer as the temple of the Holy Spirit 1Co 6:19

The local church as God's temple *See also* 1Co 3:16–17

The whole church as God's temple
Eph 2:21–22 *See also* 2Co 6:16; 1Pe 2:5
"house" here alludes to the temple. The church offers not animal sacrifices but "spiritual sacrifices" of praise and service.

See also
1680 types	8470 respect for God
7020 church, the	8626 worship, places
7110 body of Christ	
7241 Jerusalem, significance	9145 Messianic age
	9410 heaven

7471
temples, heathen

Other nations also built temples to their gods, and apostate kings of Judah and Israel were condemned for erecting heathen temples in their own countries.

Heathen temples
The temple of Dagon: Jdg 16:28–30;
1Sa 5:2–4
1Sa 31:8–10; 2Ki 5:18 *the temple of Rimmon;* Na 1:14

Idolatrous temples in Israel and Judah
1Ki 12:26–30 *Jeroboam's temples at Bethel and Dan*
The temple of Baal in Samaria, destroyed by Jehu: 1Ki 16:32; 2Ki 10:21,23–27
2Ch 23:17 *Athaliah's sons used temples destroyed in the reign of Joash.*

The command to destroy pagan places of worship in Israel
Dt 12:2–3

Holy things and holy places were used for pagan worship
Ahaz: 2Ki 16:10–13; 2Ch 28:23
Manasseh: 2Ki 21:4–5; 2Ch 33:5,7
2Ch 24:7 *Athaliah's sons used objects from the temple for the worship of the Baals;* Eze 8:12–16 *God showed Ezekiel a vision of people worshipping false gods in the temple;* 2Ch 26:16–20 *Uzziah incurred judgment by usurping the priestly task of offering incense in the temple.*

See also
4812 darkness, God's judgment	7442 shrine
	8625 worship, acceptable attitudes
5688 firstborn	
5947 shame	
6239 prostitution	8704 apostasy
7236 Israel, united kingdom	8747 false gods
	8752 false worship
7245 Judah, kingdom of	8768 idolatry

7474

Tent of Meeting

A tent pitched by Moses outside the Israelite camp in the wilderness. There Moses met with God and others would enquire of the LORD. God's presence was shown there by a pillar of cloud. It seems to predate the construction and setting up of the tabernacle, after which, the term became synonymous with the tabernacle.

Moses pitched the Tent of Meeting outside the Israelite camp
Ex 33:7 *The tent was outside the camp because of the LORD's estrangement from his people (Ex 33:3) following their making the golden calf. It was possibly a temporary structure used until the tabernacle was completed.*

The Tent of Meeting was where the faithful met with God
Moses Ex 33:9,11

Those who wished to enquire of the Lord Ex 33:7

Joshua Ex 33:11

The pillar of cloud at the Tent of Meeting
It indicated God's presence Ex 33:9

Those who saw the cloud worshipped the Lord Ex 33:10

The Tent of Meeting and the tabernacle
This Tent of Meeting may be distinct from the tabernacle Ex 25:8–9

The tabernacle was constructed (in accordance with detailed instructions) after the Tent of Meeting Ex 35:10–11; 39:32–43

The tabernacle was set up after the Tent of Meeting Ex 40:1–2,33

The Tent of Meeting as a synonym for the tabernacle
Ex 40:2 *Afterwards "Tent of Meeting" became a synonym for the tabernacle, especially the tent part of the whole complex. See also*
Ex 40:6–7,22,24,29–30,34–35; Lev 1:1; 24:3; Nu 1:1; 31:54; Dt 31:14–15; Jos 18:1; 19:51; 1Sa 2:22; 1Ki 8:4 pp 2Ch 5:5; 1Ch 6:32; 9:21; 2Ch 1:3

See also
5101 Moses	7459 tabernacle, in
5578 tents	OT
7251 pillar of cloud &	8626 worship,
fire	places
7306 ark of the	8648 enquiring of
covenant	God
7358 Feast of	
Tabernacles	

7478

thank-offering

Together with vows and freewill offerings this was one of the three kinds of fellowship offering.

Presenting a thank-offering
An animal sacrifice Lev 7:15 *See also* Lev 22:29

Accompanied by bread, wafers and cakes Lev 7:12–13 *Cakes made with yeast can be offered, since these are not to be burned on the altar.*

The priest shares the meal Lev 7:14; 22:29–30

The occasions for presenting thank-offerings
For deliverance from distress, death or sickness Ps 50:23; 107:21–22 *See also* Ps 56:12–13 *deliverance from death;* Ps 116:17 *Deliverance from sickness; the earlier verses show the psalmist has been ill.*

Following a vow Ps 7:17 *A vow to praise God in anticipation of an answer to prayer. See also* Ps 66:13–14

At times of religious renewal 2Ch 29:31 *Hezekiah's reformation;* 2Ch 33:15–16 *Manasseh's repentance*

Thank-offerings mark the time of renewal Jeremiah longs for: Jer 17:26; 33:11

See also
4554 yeast	7402 offerings
5741 vows	8352 thankfulness
7364 fellowship	8676 thanksgiving
offering	
7366 freewill offering	

7478

washing

The physical or ritual cleansing of part or all of a person's body, a person's clothing or certain vessels. Washing can be symbolic of purification from defilement or cleansing from sin. It can also be part of preparation for a special act of religious service.

Washing as the cleansing of the body, clothing or certain vessels
Ex 30:17–21; Lev 13:53–54 *See also* Ex 40:30–32; Lev 6:27; 14:8–9; 15:2–13; 16:24,26–28; Nu 31:24; 2Ch 4:6 pp 1Ki 7:38; Jn 2:6

Jesus Christ taught that inner purity was more important than ritual washing
Mt 15:17–20 pp Mk 7:20–23 *See also* Mk 7:1–9 pp Mt 15:1–3; Mk 7:14–15 pp Mt 15:10–11; Lk 11:37–41

Washing as a symbolic act
Of purification from defilement Lev 11:24–25 *See also* Lev 11:28,40; 13:6,34; 15:4–8; 17:15–16; Dt 23:10–11; 2Ki 5:10

Of cleansing from sin 1Co 6:9–11; Eph 5:25–27 *See also* Ps 51:2,7; Isa 1:16; 4:4; Jer 4:14; Ac 22:16; Tit 3:5; Heb 10:22; Jas 4:8; Rev 7:14; 22:14

Of personal cleansing before a special act of religious service Lev 16:24 *See also* Ex 19:10–11; 29:4; 40:12–13,30–32; Lev 8:6; Nu 8:6–7,21

Washing one's hands was used as a symbolic declaration of innocence Dt 21:6–7 *See also* Ps 26:6; 73:13; Mt 27:24

See also
4293 water	7342 cleanliness
5129 bathing	7416 purification
5153 foot-washing	7426 ritual washing
5226 basin	7903 baptism
6020 sin	8218 consecration
7340 clean and	8325 purity
unclean	

7480

wave offering

A gift specially dedicated to God. The term itself may not be intended to convey a particular action.

The wave offering was part of every fellowship offering
Lev 7:34 *Although given to the priests, the offering belonged to the Lord. See also* Lev 7:28–32; 9:21

The wave offering was eaten by the priests
Ex 29:26–28; Lev 10:15; Nu 18:11,18

Occasions for making a wave offering
As a cereal offering when priests were consecrated Ex 29:23–24; Lev 8:27–29

As a guilt offering sacrificed at a ceremonial cleansing Lev 14:12,21,24

As part of the ritual when a woman was accused of adultery Nu 5:25

When celebrating harvest
Lev 23:10–11 *the firstfruits of the harvest* At the Feast of Weeks: Lev 23:15–17,20

When presenting a gift to God
Materials given for constructing the tabernacle: Ex 35:22; 38:24,29

When dedicating the Levites to God
Nu 8:11 *The dedication to God of the Levites symbolised the consecration of the whole nation. See also* Nu 8:13,15,21

See also
4442 firstfruits	7370 guilt offering
7357 Feast of	7390 Levites
Firstfruits	7412 priesthood
7361 Feast of Weeks	
7364 fellowship	
offering	

7482

Year of Jubilee

Celebrated in the fiftieth year as the culmination of seven sabbatical years. During this year property was restored and Hebrew slaves were released. This year of liberation gave opportunity for a new start, and is alluded to as a type of the Messianic age.

The institution of the Year of Jubilee
Lev 25:8–10

Land was left fallow in the Year of Jubilee
Lev 25:11–12,20–22 *These instructions apply to the sabbatical year. The Year of Jubilee may have been an additional fallow year, or may have coincided with the seventh sabbatical year.*

The restoration of property in the Year of Jubilee
Lev 25:13

Regulating the value of property
Lev 25:15–16; 27:16–19,23

Underlining the fact that God is the true owner of the land Lev 25:23–24
The restoration of property to those to whom God had originally entrusted it is a reminder that the land belongs to him. See also Jos 21:43; 1Ch 29:15; Heb 11:13

A means of preserving the inheritance from God Lev 25:25–28 *Families are urged to buy back land assigned to them by God. As a last resort, land is restored in the Year of Jubilee. See also* Lev 25:32–33; 27:24; Nu 36:4,7–9; 1Ki 21:3; Eze 46:16–18

The release of Hebrew slaves in the Year of Jubilee

Dt 15:12–15 *The release of slaves reflects God's redemption and preserves the freedom he has given;* Lev 25:54–55 *The Israelites may not be held permanently as slaves because they belong to God. See also* Lev 25:39–43,50–52; Jer 34:8–9,13–14

The Year of Jubilee is the year of the Lord's favour

Lk 4:18–19 *Jesus Christ alludes to the Year of Jubilee in proclaiming spiritual release and restoration. See also* Isa 61:1–2

See also
1654 numbers,	6658 freedom
11–99	7431 sabbatical year
4206 land	7446 slavery
4978 year	9145 Messianic age
5703 inheritance	9165 restoration

7500
Jews and Gentiles

7505
Jews, the

A post-exilic designation for descendants of the people from the kingdom of Judah and also for adherents to their religion from other nations. The term is used extensively in the NT where it has a variety of nuances.

Early use of the term "Jews"
Pre-exilic and exilic use Jer 40:11–12 *See also* Jer 32:12; 34:8–9; 38:19; 40:15; 41:3; 43:8–9; 44:1,26–27; 52:28–30; Da 3:8–12

Used of the citizens of the province of Judah Ezr 5:1 *See also* Ezr 4:23; 5:5; 6:7–8,14; Ne 2:16; 4:1–2,12; 5:6–8,17; 6:5–7; Zec 8:23

Used of the descendants of the exiles from the southern kingdom Est 2:5 *See also* Ezr 4:11–12; 7:12–20; Est 3:1–6,13; 4:3,12–14; 6:12–13; 8:5–13; 9:1–3,30–31; 10:3

NT use of the term "Jews"
Jewish people in general Mk 7:3 *See also* Mt 28:15; Lk 7:3; Jn 2:6; 4:9,19–22; 8:31–32; 11:18–19,31–33,45; 12:9–11; 18:20

Those Jewish leaders who were hostile to Jesus Christ Jn 19:31 *See also* Jn 2:18–20; 5:1–18; 6:35–42; 7:1,11–15; 8:48–59; 9:1–34; 10:22–33; 18:12–14,28–31; 19:38; 20:19

Jesus Christ as "king of the Jews"
Mt 27:37 pp Mk 15:26 pp Lk 23:38 pp Jn 19:19–21 *See also* Mt 2:1–2; 27:11 pp Mk 15:2 pp Jn 18:33; Mt 27:27–31 pp Mk 15:16–20; Jn 19:1–6; Mk 15:6–14 pp Jn 18:38–40

The gospel first preached to the Jews
Ac 11:19; Ro 10:16–21 *See also* Ac 2:1–41; 10:23–48; 13:14–43; Ro 1:16; 15:8–9; Gal 2:7–9

Opposition of certain Jews to the gospel
Ac 20:19 *See also* Ac 6:8–14; 9:23–25,28–30; 12:1–3; 13:44–45,49–50; 14:1–6,19; 17:4–9,13; 18:1–6,12–17; 20:3; 2Co 11:23–25; Ac 21:27–36; 23:12–15; 24:1–9; 25:1–7; 26:19–21

Believers described as Jews and Gentiles
Ac 6:1 *See also* Ac 21:20–21,39; 22:1–3; Ro 9:23–24; 1Co 1:22–24; 12:13

Jews and Gentiles equal in Christ
Ro 11:25–32 ; Gal 3:26–29 *See also* Ro 3:27–30; 10:12–13; 1Co 12:12–13; Col 3:11

Jews and Gentiles equally in need of salvation
Ro 3:1–20

See also
2312 Christ as king	7245 Judah,
5107 Paul	kingdom of
5214 attack	7510 Gentiles
5279 crowds	8787 opposition to
7105 believers	God
7135 Israel, people of	8794 persecution
God	

7510
Gentiles

Those who are not physical descendants of Abraham and were therefore regarded as being excluded from the promise made to him and his descendants. The Gentiles are often referred to as "the nations" in OT writings.

7511
Gentiles, in OT

Under the OT, Gentiles were generally excluded from the worship of the synagogue and from all the privileges of being Jewish. However, the OT made provision for non-Jews who believed in the God of Israel.

Believing foreigners were permitted to participate in worship
Ex 12:48–49 *See also* Nu 9:14; 15:13–16; 1Ki 8:41–43; Isa 56:6–8

Foreigners living in Israel were to be treated kindly
Ex 23:9 *See also* Ex 22:21; Lev 19:9–10; 24:22; Dt 26:12–15; 27:19

Divine promises concerning the Gentiles
All people will be blessed through Abraham Ge 12:3 *See also* Ge 18:18; 22:18; Gal 3:8–9

All nations will bow before God Ps 22:27–28 *See also* Ps 86:9; Da 7:14; Am 9:11–12

The Gentiles will be enlightened Isa 49:6 *See also* Isa 9:1–2; 42:6; 60:1–3; Lk 2:30–32

The Messiah will bring justice to the Gentiles Mt 12:18–21 *See also* Isa 42:1–4

Gentiles will become God's people Ro 9:22–25 *See also* Hos 2:23; 1Pe 2:10

Gentiles will praise God Ro 15:9–12 *See also* Dt 32:43; 2Sa 22:50; Ps 18:49; Isa 11:10

See also
2230 Messiah,	7340 clean and
coming of	unclean
2375 kingdom of	7505 Jews, the
God	7530 foreigners
5075 Abraham	7545 outsiders
5359 justice	7754 preaching
7141 people of God,	8020 faith
OT	

7512
Gentiles, in NT

Although Jesus Christ initially preached to Israel, his mission was soon extended to the Gentiles. From the outset, the Christian church accepted Gentiles as full members, refusing to make any distinction between Jew and Gentile. Paul, "the apostle to the Gentiles", laid particular emphasis on their role in the purposes of God.

Gentiles in Jesus Christ's earthly ministry
Jesus Christ's contact with Gentiles Mt 8:5–13 pp Lk 7:1–10; Mt 15:21–28 pp Mk 7:24–30

Jesus Christ's teaching concerning Gentiles Mt 21:33–43 pp Mk 12:1–11 pp Lk 20:9–16 Lk 21:20–24

Jesus Christ's instructions to his disciples concerning Gentiles Mt 10:5–6 *Initially the disciples were commanded to preach to Jews, but after his resurrection, Jesus Christ commissioned them to preach the message of the kingdom of God to all nations.* Mt 28:19–20 *See also* Mk 16:15–16; Lk 24:46–47

Peter sent to Gentiles
Ac 10:28 *See also* Ac 10:9–20; 11:5–14 Ac 10:44–48 *See also* Ac 11:15; 15:7–8

Paul, apostle to the Gentiles
Gal 2:7–9 *See also* Ac 9:15; 22:21; 26:15–23; Ro 1:13–15; 11:13; 15:15–19; Gal 2:2; Eph 3:1; 1Ti 2:7; 2Ti 4:17

Rejected by Jews, Paul turns more to the Gentiles Ac 18:6 *See also* Ac 13:46; 28:28

Response of the Gentiles to Paul's preaching
Ac 13:48 *See also* Ac 14:1–2; 15:12; 21:19; 1Co 1:23–24

Difficulties concerning the acceptance of Gentiles into the church
The question of mixing with Gentiles Ac 11:2–3 *See also* Ac 11:15–18; Gal 2:12–13

The question of circumcision Ac 15:5–31 *See also* Gal 2:1–5; 5:1–6

NT teaching on Gentiles

Gentiles now share the inheritance of God's people Israel Eph 2:13 ; Rev 5:9–10 *See also* Ro 3:29; 11:11–21; Gal 3:29; Rev 7:9; 14:6

There is no distinction between Jews and Gentiles Gal 3:28 *See also* Ro 2:9–11; Eph 2:19–20; Col 3:11

God calls both Jew and Gentile

Jn 10:16; Ac 13:47–48 *See also* Ro 9:24–26; 1Co 1:24–25; 2Ti 4:17

Both Jews and Gentiles are justified by faith Gal 3:6–14 *See also* Ro 4:9–12,16; Gal 5:6

See also

1115 God, purpose of	7334 circumcision
3251 Holy Spirit, filling with	7560 Samaritans, the
5107 Paul	7610 Council of
5112 Peter	Jerusalem
6676 justification	7903 baptism
7020 church, the	8774 legalism
7142 people of God, NT	

---

anti-semitism

A modern term, used to refer to a hatred of Jews or Arabs. Traces of anti-semitism may be discerned in biblical times.

The development of anti-semitism

Ex 1:8–14 *Strictly speaking, this hostility towards the Israelites in Egypt after the death of Joseph was not anti-semitism as this word is now understood. See also* Ex 1:15–16,22; 3:9; 5:6–9

Anti-semitism under Persian rule

Est 3:1–14 *See also* Ezr 4:1–8,24

Anti-semitism under Babylonian rule

Da 3:8–23 *See also* Da 6:3–14

Anti-semitism under Roman rule

Ac 18:1–2

See also

5560 suffering	8292 love
5875 hatred	8794 persecution
7505 Jews, the	8800 prejudice

---

dispersion, the

A technical term used to refer to God's people as they are scattered throughout the world.

The dispersion of the Jews

Promised and predicted Dt 4:25–28; 1Ki 14:15 *See also* Dt 28:15–68; Lev 26:27–35; Ne 1:8–9; Jer 13:24; Eze 6:8–10; 20:23–24; 22:15

The prediction fulfilled Jer 50:17; Da 9:7 *See also* Est 3:8; Ps 44:9–16; La 4:16; Eze 36:17–20; Zep 3:10; Zec 1:19; Jn 7:35 *In NT times there were more Jews living outside Palestine than within.*

The promise of return Isa 11:12 *See also* Dt 4:29–31; Jer 31:10; Eze 11:16–17

The dispersion of Christians

Ac 8:1 *Christians scattered because of persecution*; 1Pe 1:1 *See also* Ac 8:4; 11:19; Jas 1:1

See also

1025 God, anger of	8768 idolatry
7145 remnant	8794 persecution
7215 exile, the	8839 unfaithfulness
8160 seeking God	9165 restoration

---

exclusiveness

The keeping of a distinctive group identity by drawing clear boundary lines, to separate those within the group from outsiders with whom they are unwilling to associate.

The practice of exclusiveness by God's people, grounded in God's claim to exclusive worship

Ex 20:3 pp Dt 5:7 *See also* Ex 34:14; Dt 6:14–15; 2Ki 17:35–39; Isa 42:8

Exclusiveness in Israel, a practical expression of being a people set apart

An expression of being set apart for God Lev 20:26 *See also* Lev 15:31; 20:23–24; Dt 7:1–6

An expression of being set apart from others Nu 23:9 *See also* Jos 23:7; Ezr 6:21; Ne 13:1–3; Eze 44:9

The practice of exclusiveness

Expressed in the avoidance of marrying outsiders Ne 10:30 *See also* Dt 7:3–4; Ezr 9:1–4; 10:9–17; Ne 13:23–27

Expressed in a refusal to eat with outsiders Mt 9:10–11 pp Mk 2:15–16 pp Lk 5:29–30 *See also* Lk 15:1–2; Gal 2:12

The marks of Jewish exclusiveness

Circumcision Ge 17:9–14 *See also* Ex 12:48; Lev 12:3; Ac 7:8

Festival observance Ex 12:14–16 *See also* Ex 12:17–20; Lev 23:26–29; Nu 9:13

Observance of food laws Lev 3:17 *See also* Lev 7:22–27; 11:1–47; 17:10–14; Ac 15:29 *While food restrictions were not a requirement of the gospel, Gentile believers are here asked to respect the scruples of Jewish Christians in those areas that were traditionally important to them.*

Sexual relations restricted Lev 18:6 *See also* Lev 18:7–30; 20:10–21; Dt 27:20–23

Effects of Jewish exclusiveness

Division between Jews and Samaritans Jn 4:9 *See also* Ezr 4:1–3; Mt 10:5–6 *Jesus Christ was here dealing with his priority for that time;* Lk 9:51–53

Division between Jews and Gentiles Ac 10:28 *See also* Mt 10:5; 15:21–28 pp Mk 7:24–30 *Jesus Christ restricted his earthly ministry in general to the people of Israel, but instigated a mission to the Gentiles after his resurrection;* Jn 18:28

The problem of Jewish exclusiveness among the first Christians

The negative evaluation of Gentiles Ac 11:1–18 *See also* Gal 2:11–13,15

The requirement that Gentile believers be circumcised Ac 15:1 *See also* Ac 15:5; Gal 5:2–6; 6:12; Tit 1:10

Jewish exclusiveness overturned

By God giving his Spirit to the uncircumcised Gentiles Ac 15:8 *See also* Ac 10:44–11:18; 1Co 12:13; Gal 3:2–5

By the argument of justification by faith Gal 2:15–16 *See also* Ac 15:9–11; Ro 3:28–30; 4:9–12

See also

1185 God, zeal of	7530 foreigners
1235 God, the LORD	7545 outsiders
1345 covenant	7560 Samaritans,
5424 nationalism	the
5711 marriage, restrictions	8269 holiness, separation
7334 circumcision	from worldly
7510 Gentiles	8341 separation

---

foreigners

Foreigners played a major role in the life of Israel. They surrounded her, and lived within her borders. In order to fulfil her mission as the bearer of God's law, Israel had to distinguish herself from foreign nations and individuals, especially with regard to their religious beliefs. A clear distinction is made between foreign nations and foreign individuals, who are to be allowed to live freely among Israelites within the land.

The origins of foreign nations

Ge 9:19 *See also* Ge 11:1–9

The foreign nations of Ammon and Moab Ge 19:30–38

The relation of Israel and Edom Ge 25:21–34

Israel's relationship with foreign nations

Israel's captivity in Egypt Ex 6:6 *See also* Am 1:3,6,9,11,13; Isa 10:24–25 *God's judgment on Assyria;* Isa 47:6 *the fall of Babylon prophesied;* Eze 25:3,8,12,15; 26:2; Na 1:14 *Nineveh's destruction foretold*

Foreign nations as a threat to Israel Dt 7:1–4 *See also* Ge 9:25; 15:16 *"Amorites" and "Canaanites" are both terms used to describe generically the races expelled by Israel from the land of promise, a fate brought on themselves by flagrant sin;* Lev 18:25; 20:23; Dt 18:12

The need for Israel to keep separate from foreign nations Lev 20:26 *See also* Nu 23:9; Dt 7:4; Jos 23:7; Jdg 2:2; 1Ki 11:1–2; 16:31; Ezr 4:3; 6:21; 9:12; 10:11; Ne 10:30; 13:3 *Foreign religious beliefs and practices were seen as a constant threat to faith in the LORD. The command that Israel keep apart from foreign nations partly reflects a concern that Israel might adopt religious beliefs which compromise her commitment to the LORD.*

Foreign nations are described as uncircumcised Isa 52:1 *Circumcision was a sign of being within God's covenant. But some foreigners were also circumcised (Jer 9:25–26). See also* Ge 34:14; Ex 12:48; Jdg 14:3; 15:18; 1Sa 14:6; 17:26; 2Sa 1:20; Eze 28:10; 32:26

Israel's relation with foreigners within her boundaries
Foreigners are to be treated graciously Lev 19:34 *See also* Lev 19:10; 23:22; Dt 10:19; 14:29; 24:19–21; 26:12–13

Foreigners must not be oppressed Lev 19:33 *See also* Ex 22:21; 23:9; Dt 24:14,17; 27:19; Ps 146:9; Jer 7:6; 22:3; Zec 7:10

Foreigners have a positive role to play in Israel Isa 14:1

The rights of foreigners within Israel
Foreigners are to share in Sabbath-rest Ex 20:10 pp Dt 5:14; Ex 23:12

Foreigners are to receive a fair trial Dt 1:16

Foreigners are to participate in festivals and ceremonies Dt 16:11,14; 26:11; 29:10–11; 31:12; 2Ch 30:25

Ultimately inheritance rights were envisaged for foreigners Eze 47:22–23

The obligations of foreigners are similar to those of native Israelites Nu 9:14 *See also* Ex 12:19,48–49; Lev 16:29; 17:8,12–13,15; 18:26; 20:2; 22:18; 24:16 *The penalties for blasphemy apply to Israelite and foreigner alike;* Lev 24:22; Nu 15:14–16 *The rules on the presentation of offerings are to be the same for both the Israelites and the foreigner;* Nu 19:10; 35:15; Eze 14:7

Occasional distinctions made for foreigners Lev 25:47–48; Dt 14:21; 28:43

See also

1345 covenant	7334 circumcision
5359 justice	7447 slavery, in OT
5375 law	7510 Gentiles
5711 marriage, restrictions	7545 outsiders
5882 impartiality	8266 holiness
6260 uncircumcised	8791 oppression

7535

Greeks

The inhabitants of Greece and her empire. The term is also used to describe non-Jews, so that "Greek", in the NT, is virtually synonymous with "Gentile". While distinctions between Greek and Jew on the one hand, and Greek and barbarian on the other, were important in the world at large, such divisions are to have no place within the church.

The cultural distinctiveness of Greeks in NT times
Jn 7:35 *See also* Mk 7:26; Ac 6:1; 9:29; Ro 1:14

"Greeks" used to describe non-Jews
Ac 21:27–28 *See also* Ac 16:1–3; 20:21; Gal 2:3

"Greeks" used to refer to God-fearers
Jn 12:20 *See also* Ac 17:4,12,17; 18:4

Greeks may reject the gospel as foolishness
1Co 1:22–23 *The high value placed by the Greeks upon human wisdom could hinder their response to the gospel. See also* Ac 17:18–34

In Christ there is no distinction between Greeks and Jews
Greeks and Jews share the same salvation Ro 10:11–13 *See also* Ro 3:28–30; 1Co 1:22–24

Greeks and Jews are united in Christ Col 3:11 *See also* 1Co 12:13; Gal 3:26–29

See also

5107 Paul	7105 believers
5374 languages	7336 circumcision,
5441 philosophy	spiritual
6209 pagans	7505 Jews, the
7025 church, unity	7512 Gentiles, in NT
7032 unity, God's	7545 outsiders
people	8361 wisdom

7540

Judaism

Derived from "Judah" (the southern kingdom of the divided monarchy) the term refers to the religion and culture of the Jews from the time of the exile (586 B.C.) onwards.

The exile and the beginnings of Judaism
The people of Judah become known as Jews Ezr 4:12; Ne 4:2; Est 3:6; Jer 32:12; Mt 2:2; Jn 2:6

Jewish communities were formed in many places Jer 44:1; Ezr 2:1 *many stayed in Babylon;* Jn 7:35; Ac 2:8–11

Far from the Jerusalem temple, the exiles had difficulty in knowing how to worship Ps 137:4 *See also* Hos 3:4 *This prophecy to Israel also expresses the dilemma of the Jerusalem exiles.*

New forms of religion after the exile, probably beginning in Babylon
Emphasis on the Scriptures Ne 7:73–8:3

Synagogue worship Lk 4:16–17 *Unable to sacrifice in the temple, the exiles would have focused their worship on the Scriptures, a practice which developed into synagogue worship.*

Carefully observing the law Ezra went from Babylon to Jerusalem with the express intention of seeing that God's law was observed: Ezr 7:11,14,25

The temple and sacrifice
The returning exiles recommence the sacrifices Ezr 3:1–6

The temple rebuilt Ezr 3:8; 6:14–15

The temple as a focus for pilgrims Jn 12:20; Ac 2:5 *They had probably come for Passover and were staying until Pentecost;* Ac 8:27

The temple regarded with great reverence Mt 26:59–61 pp Mk 14:57–58; Ac 6:13; 21:27–29

Studying and obeying the law
Studying Scripture Jn 5:39

Total obedience essential Mt 23:23; Jas 2:10

Human rules added to God's law Mt 23:16–18; Mk 7:1–13 pp Mt 15:1–9

High regard for the Sabbath and traditional rules associated with it Mt 12:1–2 pp Mk 2:23–24 pp Lk 6:1–2

Groups within NT Judaism
Pharisees Mk 7:3–4 *The Pharisees stressed the fulfilment of the law by individuals. See also* Lk 11:38; 18:10–12; Ac 26:5

Sadducees Ac 5:17 *A powerful minority group, politically astute whilst theologically conservative, they saw temple worship as the chief purpose of the law. See also* Mt 3:7; Mk 12:18 pp Mt 22:23 pp Lk 20:27

Teachers of the law (scribes) *They preserved, copied, taught and administered the law:* Mt 17:10; Mk 9:14; Lk 2:46; Ac 4:5

Zealots Lk 6:15 *They favoured a "holy war" to drive out the Romans.*

Non-Jewish converts Mt 23:15; Ac 2:11; 6:5; 13:43

Judaism and Christianity
Conflict between Jesus Christ and the Jewish authorities Mk 14:1 *See also* Jn 11:45–50

Conflict between the first Christians and Judaism Jn 16:2; Ac 4:1–3; 5:17–18; Gal 1:13–14

Conflict produced by Jewish influence among the first Christians Ac 15:5 *See also* Ac 15:1–2; Gal 2:11–16 *Judaism gave birth to Christianity. After an initial uneasy co-existence a total break finally ensued.*

See also

5375 law	7468 temple,
5514 scribes	rebuilding
7215 exile, the	7505 Jews, the
7245 Judah,	7550 Pharisees
kingdom of	7555 Sadducees
7428 Sabbath	7610 Council of
7456 synagogue	Jerusalem
7464 teachers of the	
law	

7545

outsiders

Israel recognised two general categories of outsiders: those who lived outside Israel, usually referred to as "the nations" or "the Gentiles", and foreigners resident within Israel's boundaries. The latter, usually referred to as "aliens", were given considerable privileges under the covenant between God and Israel.

Israel's attitude to the Gentiles as outsiders

The nations as outsiders Lev 20:26; Ne 1:8; Ps 2:1; 46:10; 106:35; Hos 7:8; Joel 2:17

The conversion of the Gentiles foretold Isa 60:3 See also Ge 22:18; Ps 22:27; Isa 9:2; Hos 2:23

Israel's mission to the Gentiles was fulfilled in Jesus Christ Ac 13:47 See also Isa 49:6; Lk 2:32; Ac 28:28; Ro 11:11; Eph 3:6

Jesus Christ calls both Jew and Gentile Jn 10:16 See also Ac 13:47–48; Ro 9:24–26; 1Co 1:24; 2Ti 4:17

Israel's attitude to aliens as outsiders

Aliens are to be treated as members of the people of God Ex 23:9 See also Dt 29:9–15; 31:12; Jos 8:33–35

Aliens are protected by God Ps 146:9

Aliens must not be oppressed Jer 22:3 See also Jer 7:2–7; Eze 22:29; Zec 7:9–10

Aliens may share in Israel's worship Ex 12:17–20,43–49; Lev 22:17–19; Dt 16:13–15

The Samaritans as outsiders in Israel in NT times

Jn 4:9 By including Samaritans in his ministry, Jesus Christ demonstrated his concern for those who were treated as outsiders by society. See also Lk 10:33; 17:16; Jn 4:7

Christians are compared to aliens in the world

1Pe 2:11

The witness of believers to outsiders

Col 4:5 See also Mk 4:11; 1Co 5:12–13; 1Th 4:11–12; 1Ti 3:7

See also
5540 society	7525 exclusiveness
5711 marriage, restrictions	7530 foreigners
6109 alienation	7560 Samaritans, the
7510 Gentiles	

7550

Pharisees

A Jewish religious party whose members required a very strict adherence to the ritual law and to the traditions of their predecessors. They were hostile to the teaching of Jesus Christ, which they regarded as compromising their interpretation of the law.

7551

Pharisees, beliefs of

The Pharisees placed considerable emphasis upon the rigorous

upholding of the law, particularly the traditional forms in which the law had been established by their predecessors.

Pharisaic interpretation of the law

Pharisees were the recognised custodians of the law Mt 23:1–3

Pharisees emphasised the traditions of the elders Mk 7:3–4 For the Pharisees the oral law, the traditions of their predecessors, had an authority equal to that of the written law. See also Mt 15:1–2 pp Mk 7:5; Gal 1:14

Pharisaic observance of the law

The Sabbath Mt 12:1–2 pp Mk 2:23–24 pp Lk 6:1–2 See also Lk 13:14

Fasting Mt 9:14 pp Mk 2:18 pp Lk 5:33 See also Lk 18:9–12

Tithing Mt 23:23 pp Lk 11:42

Pharisaic doctrine

Ac 23:6–9

Pharisaic proselytism

Mt 23:15

See also
2333 Christ, attitude to OT	8432 fasting, practice
5381 law, letter & spirit	8488 tithing
7430 Sabbath, in NT	8774 legalism
7464 teachers of the law	8802 pride
7555 Sadducees	8824 self-righteousness
7570 sects	9314 resurrection of the dead

7552

Pharisees, attitudes to Jesus Christ

Pharisees opposed Jesus Christ during his ministry and were among those who brought about his crucifixion. Some Pharisees, however, accepted Christ's teaching and believed in him.

Dialogue between Jesus Christ and Pharisees

They demanded a sign to prove his messiahship Mt 12:38–42 pp Lk 11:29–32 See also Mt 16:1–4 pp Mk 8:11–12

They questioned him on matters of the law Mt 19:3–9 pp Mk 10:2–9 See also Mt 22:15–22 pp Mk 12:13–17 pp Lk 20:20–26; Mt 22:34–40 pp Mk 12:28–34; Jn 8:3–11

They called him Teacher Mk 12:13–14 pp Mt 22:15–16 See also Mt 12:38; 22:34–36; Lk 7:39–40; 19:39; 20:21,28; Jn 3:2; 8:3–4

Jesus Christ questioned them Mt 22:41–46 pp Mk 12:35–40 pp Lk 20:41–44 See also Mt 12:9–14 pp Mk 3:1–6 pp Lk 6:6–11; Mt 21:24–27 pp Mk 11:29–33 pp Lk 20:3–8; Lk 14:1–6

Social contact between Jesus Christ and Pharisees

Lk 7:36 See also Mk 7:1–2; Lk 11:37; 13:31; 14:1

Jesus Christ criticised the Pharisees

Lk 12:1 See also Mt 5:20; 16:5–12 pp Mk 8:14–21; Mt 21:33–45 pp Mk 12:1–11 pp Lk 20:9–19; Mt 23:1–36 pp Mk 12:38–40 pp Lk 20:45–47; Lk 11:37–52; 16:1–15; 18:9–14

The Pharisees opposed Jesus Christ

Lk 11:53–54

Accusing Jesus Christ of blasphemy: Mt 9:2–7 pp Mk 2:3–12 pp Lk 5:17–26 Mt 9:10–13 pp Mk 2:15–17 pp Lk 5:29–32

Accusing Jesus Christ of being demon-possessed: Mt 9:32–34; 12:22–24; Mk 3:22

Accusing Jesus Christ's disciples of breaking the Sabbath: Mt 12:1–2 pp Mk 2:23–24 pp Lk 6:1–2

Opposition to Jesus Christ's healing on the Sabbath: Mt 12:9–14; Mk 3:1–6; Lk 6:7; 14:1–6; Jn 9:13–16

Lk 7:36–39; 15:1–2; 19:37–40; Jn 8:13; 9:39–41

The Pharisees were among those who engineered Jesus Christ's death

Mk 3:6 pp Mt 12:14 pp Lk 6:11 See also Mt 21:45–46 pp Mk 12:12 pp Lk 20:19; Mk 12:13 pp Lk 20:20; Mt 27:62–64; Jn 7:32–49

Some Pharisees believed in Jesus Christ

Php 3:4–11 See also Jn 3:1–2; 12:42; 19:38–40; Ac 15:5; 23:6–9; 26:5

See also
2009 Christ, anger of	5810 complacency
2351 Christ, miracles	5817 conspiracies
2357 Christ, parables	6178 hardness of heart
2545 Christ, opposition to	8767 hypocrisy
4135 demons, Christ's authority over	8785 opposition
	8800 prejudice

7555

Sadducees

An influential Jewish party that denied the existence of the spirit world and the possibility of resurrection. Its members are portrayed as opposing Jesus Christ and the first Christians.

Many priests were Sadducees

Ac 5:17

Sadducees rejected the concepts of resurrection and spirit world

Ac 23:8

Sadducees questioned Jesus Christ about the resurrection

Mt 22:23–32 pp Mk 12:18–27 pp Lk 20:27–38

Sadducees denounced by John the Baptist
Mt 3:7–10

Sadducees denounced by Jesus Christ
Mt 16:6–12 *See also* Mt 21:28–45 *The chief priests were probably Sadducees (see Ac 5:17).*

The Sadducees oppose the first Christians
Ac 4:1–3 *See also* Ac 5:17–18

See also

2363 Christ, preaching & teaching	7330 chief priests
	7550 Pharisees
	7570 sects
4110 angels	8787 opposition to God
4554 yeast	
5098 John the Baptist	9314 resurrection of the dead

7560
Samaritans, the

The people of the northern kingdom of Israel, named after its capital city established by Omri. At the time of the NT, Samaritans were despised by Jews, on account of their inter-marriage with Gentiles after the fall of the northern kingdom in 721 B.C. However, the NT presents them as generally responding favourably to the gospel.

Samaria as the name of the northern kingdom
1Ki 21:1 *The entire northern kingdom is represented by the name of its royal capital, just as Jerusalem often represents Judah. See also* 1Ki 18:1–6; 2Ki 17:24; 23:19; Jer 31:5

The fall of Samaria
2Ki 17:3–5

Samaria's population deported
2Ki 17:6–18 *Sargon II of Assyria completed the siege begun by Shalmaneser V, deporting (according to his own annals) over 27,000 of Samaria's inhabitants. See also* 2Ki 18:11–12

Samaria resettled by other peoples
2Ki 17:24 *This resettlement, the first of several, led to intermarriage, and is seen by many as the origin of the Samaritans of NT times. See also* Ezr 4:2,9–10

Religion in Samaria after its fall
Syncretism arises in Samaria
2Ki 17:25–41 *Those resettled brought their own gods with them, but also worshipped the* Lord *as the god of the land. Ultimately these inter-mixed peoples would abandon their polytheism and would accept the law of Moses.*

Some in Samaria remain faithful and still make pilgrimage to Jerusalem
2Ch 30:10–11 *See also* 2Ch 30:1; 34:9; Jer 41:4–5

Samaritans and the restoration of Jerusalem
Samaritans offer to rebuild the temple with the returning exiles but are rejected Ezr 4:1–5 *The response of the Samaritans to this rejection, based on the*

Jews' desire to keep the faith pure, reflects the double-mindedness of their offer.

Ongoing opposition from the Samaritans to the work of the returned exiles Ezr 4:6,7–23

Samaria's religious background by the time of the NT
Samaria had established its own temple Jn 4:20 *The Samaritans built their own temple on Mount Gerizim. It was later destroyed by the Jews, which led to a hardening of attitudes between the two groups.*

Samaritan Scriptures contained only the Pentateuch Jn 4:22 *Jesus Christ highlights the limited revelation of the Samaritans. Since their Scriptures contained only the Pentateuch, they were expecting a Messiah that they could know little about.*

Samaritan and Jewish attitudes to one another Jn 4:9 *Samaritans were seen as being very lax in their religious observance, and Jews would not therefore share drinking vessels with them. By NT times the gulf between Jew and Samaritan was quite wide and bitter. See also* Lk 9:51–56 *The three-day journey from Galilee to Jerusalem involved overnight accommodation, which the Samaritans generally refused, causing many Jews to travel on the eastern side of the Jordan.*

Samaritans and the ministry of Jesus Christ
Initially Jesus Christ instructs his disciples not to go to the Samaritans
Mt 10:5–6

Jesus Christ is opposed by some Samaritans *See also* Lk 9:51–56

Jesus Christ ministers to a Samaritan woman and many Samaritans believe in him Jn 4:4–30,39–42

Jesus Christ heals a Samaritan leper
Lk 17:11–19

Jesus Christ tells a parable about a good Samaritan Lk 10:30–37 *For the Jews, the concept of a "good" Samaritan would have seemed very strange; but Jesus Christ shows that love and faith is not restricted to Israel's boundaries.*

Samaria and the ministry of the early first Christians
The risen Christ includes Samaria in the church's mission Ac 1:8

The church takes the gospel to Samaria Ac 8:1 *See also* Ac 8:4–13,25

The apostles pray for the gift of the Spirit for the Samaritan converts
Ac 8:14–17 *The delay in their reception of the Spirit until the apostles came from Jerusalem may have been God's way of removing the old Jewish-Samaritan divide in the infant church.*

The Samaritan church grows Ac 9:31

See also

5529 sieges	7468 temple, rebuilding
5711 marriage, restrictions	8314 orthodoxy
7216 exile in Assyria	8452 neighbours, duty to
7233 Israel, northern kingdom	8799 polytheism
	8831 syncretism

7565

Sanhedrin

The Hebrew form of the Greek word "synedrion", a council. The high court of the Jews, presided over by the high priest. Its seventy-one members included chief priests, elders and teachers of the law.

Jesus Christ and the Sanhedrin
Herod called together the Sanhedrin on hearing of the birth of Jesus Christ
Mt 2:4 *This is probably a reference to the entire Sanhedrin.*

Jesus Christ acknowledged the authority of the Sanhedrin Mt 5:22

Jesus Christ foretold that he would suffer at the hands of the Sanhedrin
Mt 16:21 pp Mk 8:31 pp Lk 9:22 *See also* Mt 20:18 pp Mk 10:33

These prophecies were fulfilled
Mt 26:57–68 pp Mk 14:58–65

The Sanhedrin plotted to kill Jesus Christ after he had raised Lazarus
Jn 11:47-53

The Sanhedrin, powerless to execute anyone, brought Jesus Christ to Pilate
Jn 18:28–31

Nicodemus and Joseph of Arimathea were members of the Sanhedrin
Jn 3:1; Mk 15:43 pp Lk 23:50–52

The term Sanhedrin could also apply to local councils
Mt 10:17 pp Mk 13:9

Peter and John were brought before the Sanhedrin
Ac 4:5–21 *See also* Ac 5:21,27,34,41

Stephen appeared before the Sanhedrin
Ac 6:12,15

Stephen angered the Sanhedrin by his defence Ac 7:54,57–58

Paul and the Sanhedrin
Paul was commissioned by the chief priests to persecute the church
Ac 9:14 *Ac 22:5 makes it clear that the entire Sanhedrin was involved. See also* Ac 9:1–2,21; 26:10–12

Paul was brought before the Sanhedrin
Ac 22:30–23:1 *See also* Ac 23:6,28; 24:20

Conspirators plotted to bring Paul before the Sanhedrin again, but he escaped Ac 23:12–15,20

The Sanhedrin brought Paul to the Roman governor, Festus Ac 25:1–2,15

See also

2585 Christ, trial	7330 chief priests
5107 Paul	7464 teachers of the law
5313 flogging	
5514 scribes	7550 Pharisees
5817 conspiracies	7555 Sadducees
5875 hatred	8794 persecution

7570

sects

The Pharisees described as a sect

Ac 26:5 *The word "sect" in the NT does not have the same negative connotations as in modern society. The Greek word for "sect" is also translated as "party" in the NIV. See also* Lk 5:30; Ac 15:5

The Sadducees described as a sect

Ac 5:17

Christians described as a sect

Ac 24:14 *See also* Ac 24:5; 28:21–22

Sectarianism condemned

1Co 3:3–4; 2Co 12:20; Gal 5:20

See also

7120 Christians	8237 doctrine, false
7540 Judaism	8748 false religion
7550 Pharisees	8766 heresies
7555 Sadducees	

7600

History of God's people in NT

7610

Council of Jerusalem

The Council of Jerusalem was possibly the first "assembly" of the Christian church, held c. A.D. 49

The Council met to consider whether circumcision was necessary for salvation Ac 15:1 *See also* Ro 4:9; Gal 5:2–3

Paul and Barnabas came from Antioch to Jerusalem to meet with the apostles and elders Ac 15:2–12

The Council agreed not to make it difficult for Gentiles who turned to God Ac 15:19–21 *The Council was concerned to avoid forcing Gentiles to adopt Jewish customs (such as circumcision), and at the same time to require Gentiles to behave considerately towards their "weaker brothers" of Jewish birth, not all of whom could be expected to acquire immediately the emancipated outlook on food-laws and the like that Peter and Paul had.*

James showed how the decision had confirmed an earlier prophecy Ac 15:15–18; Am 9:11–12

The written judgment was taken to the Gentile believers by Paul, Barnabas, Silas and Judas Ac 15:23–29; 16:4

The Council's judgment proved to be a great encouragement to the Gentile believers Ac 15:30–31; 16:5

See also

5108 Paul, life of	7720 elders in the
5375 law	church
7334 circumcision	7733 leaders
7510 Gentiles	8414 encourage-
7540 Judaism	ment
7706 apostles	

7620

disciples

The group of people called to follow and serve Jesus Christ.

7621

disciples, calling of

The term is applied to Christians in general, not to the Twelve only. It emphasises the importance of Jesus Christ's followers learning from Christ as their teacher.

Disciples learning from their master

Isa 8:16; Am 7:14 *See also* 1Ki 20:35; Ne 3:8; Isa 19:11; Mt 10:24; Mk 2:18 pp Lk 5:33; Lk 6:40; Jn 1:35; 9:28

Those referred to as disciples in the NT

The disciples as the apostles Mt 10:1–2 *The apostles were uniquely appointed as founding pillars of the church, but in some respects they were also representative disciples.*

The disciples as believers in general Mt 28:19; Ac 19:1–2 *Christian believers, not fully mature. See also* Lk 6:13,17; Ac 6:2; 11:26

The disciples as an intimate circle of believers Mt 18:1; Mk 4:10

How disciples are called

It sometimes implies physically following Jesus Christ and leaving everything Mt 4:19 pp Mk 1:16–20; Mt 8:18–22 pp Lk 9:57–60; Mt 9:9 pp Mk 2:14

Calling in a more general spiritual sense Jn 21:19 *See also* Lk 9:23; 14:25–27; Jn 8:12; 12:26; 21:22

How disciples learn from Jesus Christ the teacher

By repeating the words of Jesus Christ Lk 11:1–4 *The rhythmical form of much of Jesus Christ's teaching suggests he intended his words to be remembered verbatim. See also* Mt 5:3–10

By signs Jn 2:11 *See also* Mk 5:37,40 pp Lk 8:51

By understanding the OT Scriptures Jn 1:45 *See also* Lk 18:31–33; 24:27,32,44–45

By understanding the parables Mk 4:11–12 pp Mt 13:10–11 pp Lk 8:9–10 *See also* Mk 4:34

By practical experience of mission Lk 10:23–24 *These words follow the sending out of the seventy-two. See also* Mk 6:6–11; Lk 9:1–2 pp Mt 10:1

In periods of being alone with Jesus Christ Mk 6:31 *See also* Mt 16:21

In spite of their faulty understanding Lk 24:25 *See also* Mk 9:32 pp Lk 9:45; Lk 18:34

See also

1416 miracles	7120 Christians
2363 Christ,	7630 Twelve, the
preaching &	7706 apostles
teaching	7948 mission
5113 Peter, disciple	8114 discipleship
5438 parables	8120 following
6620 calling	Christ

7622

disciples, characteristics of

The content of discipleship is most clearly seen in the Christian's relationship to Jesus Christ. But this also affects a person's relationship to God the Father, the cross, the church and the world.

Disciples and their relationship to Jesus Christ

Coming to Christ and following him Mt 4:19 *See also* Mt 11:28; Mk 10:21; Lk 18:16

Receiving him Rev 3:20 *See also* Jn 1:12

Learning from him Mt 11:29 *See also* Mt 24:32 pp Mk 13:28

Lovingly obeying him Jn 14:15

Trusting him Jn 14:1

Confessing him Mt 10:38 pp Lk 14:27 *See also* Mk 8:38 pp Lk 9:26

Imitating him 1Co 11:1; 1Pe 2:21

Reflecting him Mt 5:16

Abiding in him Jn 15:4 *See also* Jn 6:66–68

Disciples and their relationship to God the Father

True sons and daughters of God Mt 5:44–45

Discipleship and glorifying God Mt 5:16

Disciples and their relationship to the cross

Self-denial Mt 16:24 pp Mk 8:34 pp Lk 9:23

Disciples and their relationship to the church

Treating other Christians as family Mk 3:34–35 *See also* Mt 18:15–17; Jn 15:12,17

Disciples and their relationship to the world

They are to be active in the world but are to be distinct from it Mt 5:13 *See also* Mt 5:14–16; Jn 17:11–23

They are to make other disciples Mt 28:19 *See also* Ac 1:8

See also

1040 God,	8030 trust
fatherhood	8248 faithfulness
2410 cross, the	8407 confession of
4025 world, the	Christ
5680 family	8453 obedience
7105 believers	8475 self-denial

7630

Twelve, the

The inner circle of the twelve disciples, called by Jesus Christ to follow him and carry on his mission after his death and resurrection.

7631
Twelve, calling of

Jesus Christ's chosen companions, whom he called and trained to carry on his mission after his death and resurrection.

The calling of the Twelve
Their names Mt 10:1–4
pp Mk 3:14–19 *See also* Lk 6:12–16; Ac 1:12–13

Their selection was preceded by prayer Lk 6:12–13

As Jesus Christ's companions, they were to share in his mission
Mk 3:14–15; 6:7–13 pp Mt 10:1, 9–14 pp Lk 9:1–6; Lk 8:1

Jesus Christ promised them authority at the final judgment Mt 19:28
pp Lk 22:30

After Judas' death the Twelve became the Eleven
Mt 28:16; Mk 16:14; Lk 24:9,33; Ac 2:14

The Eleven became the Twelve again with the election of Matthias Ac 1:26

The ministry of the Twelve after the resurrection supplemented by the appointment of deacons
Ac 6:2–3

The symbolic significance of the Twelve
The twelve tribes of Israel Ge 49:28; Eze 47:13; Mt 19:28 pp Lk 22:30 *Twelve symbolises completeness and is associated with the rule of God.*

See also

1654 numbers, 11–99	7239 Jerusalem
2354 Christ, mission	7266 tribes of Israel
2555 Christ, resurrection appearances	7470 temple, significance
6620 calling	7620 disciples
7024 church, nature of	7706 apostles
	7948 mission

7632
Twelve, diverse characters of

The Twelve were men of varied background, gifts and character.

The varied backgrounds of the Twelve
Peter, Andrew, James and John were fishermen: Mt 4:18,21
Mt 9:9 *Matthew was a tax collector;*
Mt 10:4 *Simon was a political activist.*

The varied roles of the Twelve
Some took a prominent role in the group Gal 2:9

Some played minor but significant roles Jn 1:40–42 *Andrew brought Peter to Jesus Christ;* Jn 1:45–46 *Philip brought Nathanael;* Jn 12:20–22 *Philip and Andrew brought the Greeks to Jesus Christ.*

The varied temperaments of the Twelve
Mt 14:28 *Peter was impetuous;* Lk 9:54 *James and John were fiery;* Lk 22:4 *Judas Iscariot was a traitorous loner;* Jn 20:25 *Thomas was cautious.*

The Twelve had a common call to discipleship and witness
Ac 1:21–22

The fallibility of the Twelve
Mk 8:31–33 *Peter misunderstood;*
Mk 16:14 *Jesus Christ rebuked the Eleven for not believing reports of his resurrection;* Lk 9:12–13 *Jesus Christ tested their reaction to human need;* Jn 14:8–9 *Philip asked the way to the Father.*

Jesus Christ gave the Twelve special teaching
Mk 4:10–11 *about his parables;* Mk 9:35 *about power and position;* Lk 18:31 *about his destiny*

Jesus Christ spent his last days and hours with the Twelve
Mk 11:11 *after the triumphal entry into Jerusalem;* Mk 14:17 *at the Last Supper*

The Twelve failed Jesus Christ
Jesus Christ's concern that they would leave him Jn 6:67–70

Judas betrayed him Mt 26:14–16
pp Mk 14:10 pp Lk 22:3–4

They failed to support him in his final agony of prayer Mt 26:40–41
pp Mk 14:37–38 pp Lk 22:45–46

Peter disowned Jesus Christ
Mt 26:74–75 pp Mk 14:71–72
pp Lk 22:60–61

All abandoned Jesus Christ Mt 26:56 *the exception was "the disciple whom Jesus loved", present at the crucifixion (Jn 19:25–27)*

See also

2363 Christ, preaching & teaching	5107 Paul
	5112 Peter
2585 Christ, trial	8114 discipleship
2590 Christ, triumphal entry	

7700

Leadership and the people of God

7703

apologetics

The art of explaining the faith in such a way as to make a reasoned defence against its detractors. Paul's Areopagus sermon is a classic example of biblical apologetics, which can be of value to all who are called upon to defend the faith today.

Paul's Areopagus sermon, a classic example of biblical apologetics
Paul speaks to his listeners on their own ground, starting on their own terms Ac 17:22–23

Paul presents the Christian position Ac 17:24–27

Paul supports his argument in a culturally appropriate way Ac 17:28 *Paul quotes from two secular writers, first from the Cretan poet Epimenides, and secondly from the Cilician poet Aratus.*

Paul concludes his argument and calls for a response Ac 17:29–31

Apologetics as a regular feature of Paul's ministry
Ac 18:4 *See also* Ac 9:26–30; 18:19; 19:8–10; 28:17–31

Apologetics is part of the work of church leaders
Tit 1:9

All Christians share responsibility for the task of apologetics
1Pe 3:15

Other examples of Christians engaging in apologetics
Ac 18:28 *See also* Ac 2:14–41; 6:8–10

Apologetics alone is an inadequate way of presenting the gospel
1Co 1:17–25 *See also* 1Co 2:1–5

See also

2420 gospel	7751 persuasion
5038 mind, the human	7756 preaching, content
5050 reason	7760 preachers, responsibilities
5107 Paul	
5293 defence, human	8424 evangelism
5622 witnesses	8495 witnessing
7724 evangelists	

7706

apostles

Appointed representatives, deriving authority and responsibilities from the person or group represented. The word refers especially to Jesus Christ's twelve disciples and also to Paul. Scripture identifies the functions of apostles and their authority, which is derived directly from Jesus Christ.

7707
apostles, designation of

An apostle is one who is "sent" by Jesus Christ. The word is used to refer especially to the inner circle of Christ's twelve disciples, but is also used specifically to refer to Paul, who was commissioned as an apostle by the risen Christ. The term is also applied more loosely to certain other leading Christians in the NT period.

Jesus Christ as an apostle
Heb 3:1 *This is the only place where the word "apostle" is used of Jesus Christ, though many passages refer to him as "sent";* Jn 20:21 *Jesus Christ, as God's "sent one", sets the standard and pattern for all who are likewise "sent" (i.e., for all*

apostolic ministry). See also Mt 10:40; Mk 9:37; Jn 5:23–24; 12:44–45

The twelve apostles called by Jesus Christ

Their appointment Mk 3:13–19 pp Mt 10:1–4 pp Lk 6:12–16

Their number Jn 6:70 *"the Twelve" is frequently used to designate these specially chosen disciples. The number twelve evokes the twelve tribes of Israel. See also* Mt 19:28; 20:17; Mk 11:11; Lk 8:1; Ac 6:2; 1Co 15:5; Rev 21:14

Their commissioning by the risen Christ Mt 28:18–20

The replacement for Judas Ac 1:15–26 *The symbolic number (twelve) is thus preserved.*

The qualifications for being an apostle Ac 1:21–22

Paul as an apostle

His self-designation Gal 1:1 *See also* Ro 1:1; 1Co 1:1; 1Ti 2:7

His commissioning by Jesus Christ Ac 26:12–18 *Although not one of the Twelve, Paul saw the risen Christ and was directly commissioned by him, sent especially to the Gentiles;* 1Co 15:3–10; Gal 2:8

Paul's apostleship and the church 1Co 9:1–2 *In Paul's case the sense of title or office and the ministry and function virtually coincide. He is an apostle both because he has seen and been commissioned by the risen Christ and because he functioned as an apostle by founding churches.*

Other apostles

Barnabas *Here "apostles" may refer to their ministry as missionary evangelists or to their role as "sent" by the church at Antioch:* Ac 14:4,14

James, the Lord's brother 1Co 15:7 *The most natural meaning of the words is that James is an apostle. This interpretation is confirmed by other references to James;* Gal 1:19; 2:9

Andronicus and Junias Ro 16:7

Silas 1Th 2:6

"Apostles" of the churches 2Co 8:23 *"representatives" is the translation here for "apostles";* Php 2:25 *"messenger" is the translation here for "apostle"*

False apostles

2Co 11:5 *Paul ironically refers to his opponents as "super-apostles";* 2Co 11:13; 12:11; Rev 2:2

See also

2057 Christ, obedience	7160 servants of the Lord
2327 Christ as servant	7621 disciples, calling
2339 Christ, example of	7631 Twelve, calling of
5109 Paul, apostle	7739 missionaries
5114 Peter, apostle	

7708
apostles, function of

In the NT apostles are servants, first of Jesus Christ and then of the

church. Apostolic service embraces a wide range of specific functions.

The functions of apostles during the earthly life and ministry of Jesus Christ

Being with Jesus Christ Mk 3:14 *See also* Mt 17:1; Mk 6:30–32 pp Lk 9:10

Learning from Jesus Christ Mk 8:31 *See also* Mt 18:1–4; Mk 4:10–12; Ac 1:2

Being sent out on a mission by Jesus Christ Lk 9:1–6 pp Mt 10:5–10 pp Mk 6:7–13 *As Jesus Christ's representatives their ministry was an extension of his. See also* Mk 3:14–15

Being commissioned to witness to Jesus Christ Ac 1:8; 10:39 *See also* Mt 28:18–20; Mk 16:15; Lk 24:46–49; Jn 17:18; 20:21

Apostles in the early church

They were witnesses of the resurrection Ac 1:21–22 *See also* Ac 2:32; 3:15; 4:33; 13:31; 1Pe 5:1

They were servants of Jesus Christ 2Pe 1:1 *See also* Ro 1:1; 1Co 4:1; 2Co 11:23; Php 1:1; Tit 1:1

They were servants of the church 2Co 13:4 *See also* Ro 15:25; 2Co 4:5; 11:8; 1Pe 5:1–3

They were the foundations of the church Eph 2:20 *Probably a reference to the apostolic preaching. The absence of the article before "prophets" suggests that "the apostles and prophets" represents one group of people, not two. See also* 1Co 12:28; Gal 2:9; Jude 17 *the prophetic ministry of the apostles*

They preached the gospel Ro 1:1–5 *See also* Mk 16:20; Ro 15:19–20; 1Co 1:17; Gal 1:15–16

They were guardians and teachers of the truth Ac 2:42 *See also* Jn 16:13–15; Ac 5:42; 6:2; Eph 3:2–6; 2Th 2:15; 2Ti 1:11

They founded churches 1Co 9:1–2 *See also* 1Co 3:5–6,10

They were authority figures within the church Ac 6:2–6 *The apostles took the initiative. Whilst they did not themselves appoint the Seven, they confirmed their appointment.*

They were called to suffer 2Ti 1:11–12 *See also* Ac 5:18; 1Co 4:9; 2Co 11:23–29

They were empowered by the Spirit Ac 4:8 *See also* Jn 20:22; Ac 1:8; 2:4; Eph 3:4–5

They were able to bestow the Spirit Ac 8:14–18 *Peter and John officially induct Samaritans as members of the body of Christ;* Ac 19:6

See also

2351 Christ, miracles	3257 Holy Spirit, gift of
2363 Christ, preaching & teaching	4165 exorcism
	5333 healing
2375 kingdom of God	5622 witnesses
	7734 leaders, spiritual
3212 Holy Spirit & mission	8114 discipleship
3224 Holy Spirit & preaching	8342 servanthood

7709
apostles, authority of

Apostolic authority derives directly from Jesus Christ, who commissions apostles. It is rigorously upheld within the church.

Apostolic authority is based on divine commission

Ro 1:5 *See also* Ro 1:1; 2Co 1:1; Gal 1:1; Eph 1:1; Col 1:1; 1Ti 1:1; 2Ti 1:1

Apostolic authority derives from Jesus Christ

Mt 10:40 *See also* Mt 28:18–20; Mk 6:7; 2Pe 3:2

The authority of apostles is related to their ministry role

1Co 12:28 *There appears to be a definite order of priority with apostles at the head. See also* Eph 4:11

The exercise of apostolic authority within the church

In building up the body 2Co 13:10 *Paul had special authority as founder of this church. See also* 2Co 10:8

In general oversight Ac 4:34–35; 6:2–6; 15:6,22–23; 16:4

In teaching 1Th 4:2 *See also* Gal 1:11–12; 1Th 2:4; 4:8

In appointing leaders Ac 14:23

In church discipline Ac 5:3–4,7–9; 1Co 5:3–5

The right to be supported 1Th 2:6 *Paul did not demand such support (see* 1Th 2:9). *See also* 1Co 9:4,11–14; 2Co 11:7–9

The marks of a true apostle

False apostles exist 1Co 9:2 *See also* 2Co 11:4–5; 12:11

Fruit confirms apostolic ministry 2Co 3:1–3

Signs confirm apostolic authority 2Co 12:12 *See also* Mk 16:20; Ac 5:12; Ro 15:19

See also

1449 signs, purposes	7026 church, leadership
5215 authority	7939 ministry

7712
convincing

Persuading one's hearers of the truth of one's case. Scripture gives examples of people who have been convinced of the truth of God's word and of the gospel.

Examples of prophets convincing their hearers

Elijah at Mount Carmel 1Ki 18:20–39

Jonah at Nineveh Jnh 3:1–9

Hardness of heart can prevent individuals from being convinced of the truth

The ministry of the prophets Jer 6:10 *See also* 1Ki 22:15–28 pp 2Ch 18:14–27; Jer 35:15; Eze 2:4–5; Am 7:10–13

The ministry of Jesus Christ
Jn 12:37–40 *See also* Isa 53:1; 6:10;
Mt 13:13–15 pp Mk 4:10–12
pp Lk 8:10; Isa 6:9–10; Jn 7:25–43

Examples of individuals convinced of the truth of the gospel
The Ethiopian eunuch Ac 8:26–38

Paul Ro 8:38–39 *See also* 2Co 5:14–15;
2Ti 1:12

Paul sought to convince others of the truth of the gospel Ac 18:4 *See also*
Ac 17:2–4; 19:8; 26:28–29; 28:23–24;
2Co 5:11

See also

1460 truth	6178 hardness of
2363 Christ,	heart
preaching &	6632 conviction
teaching	7751 persuasion
2369 Christ,	7754 preaching
responses to	7773 prophets, role
2420 gospel	7775 prophets, lives
5050 reason	8800 prejudice

7716

deacons

Those who "serve" in the Christian community, assisting the elders or overseers (bishops). The Greek word which the NIV translates four times as "deacon" occurs a further 25 times in the NT, where it is translated as "servant". It seems that all Christians have a general servant role, whereas some (deacons) are called to a specific office of service within the church.

The Seven: assistants to the apostles
Why they were needed Ac 6:1–4 *The verb "wait" means "to serve".*

Their qualifications and selection
Ac 6:3

Their names and appointment
Ac 6:5–6 *Although the Seven are not actually called "deacons", they were probably the earliest example of Christians carrying out the tasks which came to be linked with deacons.*

Deacons were assistants to overseers in Philippi
Php 1:1 *All Christians are "saints" (that is, set apart for God), but overseers and deacons have specific roles assigned to them.*

Qualifications for men and women deacons
1Ti 3:8–13 *There is no NT description of the precise role of deacons (although Ac 6:1–4 may imply a certain role). These qualifications would be appropriate for people responsible for financial management, administration, and social service, such as that offered to widows;*
1Ti 3:11 *The women may be deacons' wives (NIV text), or deaconesses (NIV footnote).*

Phoebe, a deaconess
Ro 16:1 *NIV footnote.*

See also

2327 Christ as	7734 leaders,
servant	spiritual
5520 servants	7748 overseers
7026 church,	7784 shepherd
leadership	7939 ministry
7372 hands, laying	8342 servanthood
on	8492 watchfulness,
7706 apostles	leaders
7718 elders	

7718

elders

Senior figures within Israel and the Christian church who are given special responsibilities for their people.

7719
elders, as community leaders

Since older men act as responsible leaders in many communities, "elder" is used as the title for a recognised leader.

Elders in early Israel
Elders represented their people
Ex 19:7 *See also* Ex 3:16; 4:29;
12:21–28; 24:1

Elders assisted Moses Nu 11:16–17
See also Ex 18:21–26; Nu 11:24–25

Elders met in a national assembly
Jos 23:2; 24:1; Jdg 21:16

Elders functioned as judges, sometimes in the town gate
Dt 19:11–12; Jdg 8:14; Ru 4:1–12

Elders during the period of the monarchy
Tribal and town elders 1Sa 30:26–31;
2Ki 10:5; 23:1; Jer 19:1

Elders were local representatives at national functions 1Ki 8:1

Elders advised the king 1Ki 12:6–8

Elders functioned as judges at the town gate Pr 31:23 *See also* 1Ki 21:8–14

Elders in Israel during and after the exile
Ezr 10:8,14; Eze 8:1; 14:1; 20:1–3

Elders in NT Jewish society
Elders were local town and synagogue leaders Mk 5:22; Lk 7:1–5

Elders were members of the Sanhedrin
Mk 15:1 *See also* Mt 5:22

Elders were guardians of religious traditions Mt 15:1–2 pp Mk 7:5 *See also* Mk 7:3

The elders' rejection of Jesus Christ predicted by him Mt 16:21 pp Mk 8:31 pp Lk 9:22

The involvement of the elders in the trial and condemnation of Jesus Christ
Mt 27:1 pp Mk 15:1

The elders' involvement with the first Christians *See also* Ac 4:5,8,23; 5:21;
6:12; 23:14; 25:15

See also

2545 Christ,	5727 old age,
opposition to	attitudes
2585 Christ, trial	7330 chief priests
5358 judges	7464 teachers of the
5359 justice	law
5375 law	7565 Sanhedrin
5509 rulers	7733 leaders

7720
elders, in the church

In the NT a group of leaders responsible for managing and teaching a local church. As the name implies, they were normally men of experience and maturity. Although women played a very significant part in early Christian ministry, there is no specific NT evidence for women as elders.

Elders in the Jerusalem church
Ac 15:4 *See also* Ac 11:30; 15:2,6,22–23;
16:4; 21:18

Elders are also called "overseers"
Ac 20:28 *In Ac 20:17 they are described as "elders". Here they are "overseers". See also* Tit 1:6–7

Elders are appointed by apostles or their delegates
Ac 14:23 *Here, as always in the NT, people are appointed to a joint eldership. There is no NT example of a single elder leading a church. See also* Tit 1:5

Qualifications for elders
Tit 1:6–9 *As in Ac 20:17,28, "elder" is here synonymous with "overseer". See also* 1Ti 3:1–7

The role of elders
As leaders 1Ti 5:17 *See also* 1Ti 3:5

As teachers 1Ti 5:17 *See also* 1Ti 3:2

As pastors and guardians against false teaching Ac 20:28–31 *See also* Tit 1:9;
1Pe 5:1–4

In the healing ministry Jas 5:14

The remuneration and correction of elders
See also
1Ti 5:17–20

Elders are to receive respect and submission from church members
Heb 13:17 *"leaders" is an alternative term for "elders". See also* 1Th 5:12; Heb 13:7

The twenty-four elders in heaven
The elders are seated on thrones
Rev 4:4 *These elders may be angelic beings corresponding to the twenty-four orders of Levites (1Ch 24–25) or symbolise Israel and the church (compare Rev 21:12–14). See also* Rev 5:5–6; 11:16; 14:3

The elders worship God and the Lamb
Rev 4:10–11 *See also* Rev 5:8–14;
7:11–13; 19:4

See also
4110 angels
5217 authority in
church
7026 church,
leadership
7715 deacons
7733 leaders
7748 overseers

7784 shepherd
7789 shepherd,
church leader
7793 teachers
7939 ministry
8492 watchfulness,
leaders

7724

evangelists

Those called by God to announce good news and, especially, to proclaim the good news of Jesus Christ. The work was first committed to the apostles and then to other believers gifted by the Holy Spirit for the task.

7725
evangelists, identity of

Some OT figures announced good news, but most evangelists are seen in the NT. The task was first given by Jesus Christ to the apostles and then to other believers. All Christians have a part in evangelism; there is, too, a special role of evangelist within the church, fulfilled by those with a particular gifting from the Holy Spirit.

An evangelist as one who announces good news
God as an announcer of good news
Gal 3:8 *See also* Ge 12:2–3; 22:18; 26:4; Jer 31:3–4; Ac 10:36

OT messengers announce good news
Ps 96:2–3 pp 1Ch 16:23–24 Isa 40:9 *The good news of the end of the Babylonian exile. See also* 2Ki 7:9; Ps 40:10; Isa 40:1–5; 41:27; 52:7; Na 1:15 *the good news of the deliverance from Assyria;* Mt 12:41 pp Lk 11:32; Ro 10:15; 2Pe 2:5

Angels announce good news
Lk 2:10–11 *See also* Lk 1:19; Rev 14:6

John the Baptist announces good news Lk 3:18 *See also* Lk 3:3; 16:16

Jesus Christ as an evangelist
Lk 4:18–19 *See also* Isa 61:1–2; Mt 4:23; 9:35; Mk 1:14–15; Lk 4:43; 8:1

The disciples as evangelists
Jesus Christ sends out the Twelve
Mk 3:14 *See also* Mt 10:7–8; Lk 9:1–2,6

Jesus Christ commissions the apostles Mk 16:15 *See also*
Mt 28:18–20; Lk 24:47; Ac 1:8

The evangelism of the apostles Ac 5:42 *See also* Ac 8:25 *Peter and John preach the gospel in Samaria;* Ac 15:7 *Peter preaches the gospel to Cornelius.*

Other believers as evangelists
Evangelists are gifted by God Eph 4:11

Paul as an evangelist Ac 20:24 *See also* Ro 1:9; 15:19–20; 1Co 1:17; 2Co 2:12; Gal 2:7

Philip the evangelist Ac 21:8 *See also* Ac 8:5,12,35,40

Other evangelists Ac 8:4 ; 2Ti 4:5 *Timothy's calling includes that of an evangelist. See also* Mk 5:20 pp Lk 8:39; Jn 4:28–29; Ac 18:26 *Priscilla and Aquila;* 1Pe 3:15

Evangelists within the family Mk 5:19
Witnessing to unbelieving partners: 1Co 7:16; 1Pe 3:1–2
Parents are a witness to their children: Eph 6:4; 2Ti 1:5; Tit 1:6

See also
2354 Christ, mission
2363 Christ,
preaching &
teaching
2420 gospel
5109 Paul, apostle

5622 witnesses
7706 apostles
7739 missionaries
7966 spiritual gifts
8424 evangelism

7726
evangelists, ministry of

Evangelists proclaim the good news of Jesus Christ, calling those who hear to believe in him. This may be in the context of missionary journeys, often in partnership with others, or within a more settled ministry. Carrying out the task requires integrity and commitment in the face of hardships and danger; it also brings joy at seeing the church grow.

The task of evangelists
Announcing good news Isa 52:7;
Lk 4:43 *See also* Ac 5:42; 8:12; 11:20; Ro 10:15

Proclaiming the gospel
Ro 15:16,20–21 *See also* Ac 8:5; 15:7; 1Co 1:17; 9:16; 15:1–2; 2Co 10:15–16

Testifying to the truth about Jesus Christ Ac 10:42–43 *See also* Jn 1:35–36; 15:26–27; Ac 1:8; 2:32–33; 17:2–3; 1Jn 1:1–3

Calling people to believe in Jesus Christ Ro 10:13–14 *See also*
Mk 1:14–15; Ac 13:38–39; 16:30–34; 18:4; 26:28; Ro 1:5; 1Co 15:11; 2Co 5:11

The context of the evangelist's work
Missionary journeys Ac 13:4–5; 14:24–25; 16:9–10

In partnership with others Lk 10:1 *See also* Mk 6:7; Ac 10:23; 14:1; 16:6; 17:14–15; Php 1:5

Within a settled period of ministry 2Ti 4:5 *Timothy as a pastor is also to do the work of an evangelist. See also* Ac 18:9–11 *Paul spends a year and a half in Corinth;* Ac 28:30–31 *Paul preaches the gospel whilst under house arrest in Rome;* 1Ti 4:13–14; 2Ti 4:2

The evangelist's integrity
2Co 2:17 *See also* 2Co 1:12; 1Th 2:3–5

The evangelist's commitment
Working so as not to be a burden 1Th 2:8–9 *See also* Ac 20:33–34; 1Co 4:12; 9:6

Facing hardship and danger
2Co 11:23–29

Arrest and imprisonment: Ac 5:18; 20:23–24; 21:33; Eph 6:19–20
Flogging: Ac 5:40; 16:22–23
Stoning: Ac 7:58; 14:19
Physical attack: Ac 9:29; 21:30–31
Opposition: Ac 20:19; 1Th 2:2
Concern for unbelievers: Ro 9:1–2; 10:1

Financial support for evangelists
1Co 9:11–14 *See also* 1Ti 5:18

The evangelist's blessing
Joy at seeing the church grow
1Th 3:7–9 *See also* Ac 15:3; 1Th 2:19–20

The satisfaction of seeing new converts grow in their faith 1Co 1:4–7; Eph 1:15–16; Php 1:3–6; 1Th 1:2–3

See also
5357 journey
5560 suffering
7754 preaching
7924 fellowship in
service
7939 ministry
7953 mission of
church

8202 boldness
8207 commitment
8414 encourage-
ment
8495 witnessing
8794 persecution

7730

explanation

The provision of the understanding of a dream, vision, parable, teaching or other matter, the meaning of which is less than obvious.

Examples of the explanation of dreams
By Joseph Ge 40:6–19; 41:10–32

By Daniel Da 2:16,24,27–45; 5:12,17

By angels Da 7:15–18,23–27

Examples of the explanation of visions
By Gabriel Da 8:15–16

By an angel *See also* Zec 1:8–10,18–21; Rev 17:3–7,18

By Peter Ac 11:4–17

Jesus Christ gave his disciples explanations
Of his parables Mk 4:34 *See also* Mt 15:15–20 pp Mk 7:17–23; Mt 13:36–43

Of the Scriptures referring to himself and his relationship to his Father Lk 24:27 *See also* Jn 16:25,29–30

Of his suffering, death and resurrection Mt 16:21 pp Mk 8:31 pp Lk 9:22 *See also* Jn 4:25–26

The gospel was explained
By Peter, at Pentecost: Ac 2:14,16
By Philip: Ac 8:30–31,34–35
By Paul: Ac 17:2–3; 28:23
Ac 18:24–26 *by Aquila and Priscilla*

Examples of other explanations
Jdg 14:12–17 *The Philistines desperately wanted the answer to Samson's riddle. Samuel forewarned Israel of the consequences of having a king:* 1Sa 8:9; 10:25
Solomon's great wisdom enabled him to answer many questions and explain many things: 1Ki 4:29–34; 10:1–3 pp 2Ch 9:1–2; Ne 8:7–8

See also

1403 God, revelation	5441 philosophy
1409 dream	7703 apologetics
1469 visions	7754 preaching
1610 Scripture	7797 teaching
4110 angels	8355 understanding
5438 parables	8361 wisdom

7733

leaders

God calls individuals to positions of leadership, both spiritual and political. Such leadership is seen as carrying responsibilities towards both God and his people and is to be exercised with humility.

7734
leaders, spiritual

Under the old covenant God called priests and prophets as spiritual leaders. Later the Pharisees gave spiritual leadership. After Jesus Christ had inaugurated the new covenant, authority was given to the apostles, who in turn appointed leaders in the churches they founded.

Priests as spiritual leaders
They were called by God Heb 5:4 *See also* Ex 28:1; Dt 18:5

The high priest represented the people in the presence of God Heb 5:1 *See also* Ex 28:29–30; Nu 27:21; Heb 8:3

Priests taught and explained God's law Mal 2:7 *See also* Lev 10:11; Hag 2:11–13

Examples of priests as spiritual leaders 1Sa 4:18 *The priest Eli was described as leading Israel;* 1Sa 7:5–9 *Samuel acted as on behalf of the people;* 2Ch 24:14 *Jehoiada the priest influenced Joash to serve God.*

Prophets as spiritual leaders
They were called by God 2Pe 1:21 *See also* Isa 6:8–9; Jer 1:5

Examples of prophets as spiritual leaders
Samuel led the people from idolatry back to the worship of God: 1Sa 7:3–4; 12:20–24 1Ki 18:18–21 *Elijah;* Hag 1:7–9 *Haggai*

Spiritual leaders in NT times
Mt 2:4 *officially recognised teachers of the law;* Mt 16:1; 21:23 *At a local level, elders had social and religious authority in local councils. Nationally, they were included in the Sanhedrin;* Mt 23:2; 26:59

The failure of spiritual leaders
In the OT Isa 28:7; Jer 23:11,13–17, 25–32; Mal 2:1–2

In the NT Mt 23:4–15; Mk 10:42–45 *Jesus Christ taught his disciples the qualities required for spiritual leadership.*

Spiritual leadership in the church
The apostles delegated authority Ac 4:34–35; 6:2–3; 14:23; Tit 1:5

The qualifications for church leadership 1Ti 3:1–9; Tit 1:6–9

Advice to leaders Ac 20:28 *See also* Ac 20:31,35; 1Ti 5:17–20; 1Pe 5:2–3

See also

5217 authority in church,	7772 prophets
7026 church,	7786 shepherd, king & leader
leadership	7939 ministry
7706 apostles	8471 respect for
7720 elders in the church	human beings
7766 priests	8492 watchfulness, leaders

7735
leaders, political

Since God is the ultimate ruler of all things, earthly authority derives from him. Although political leadership was exercised in various ways in Israel, there was always some overlap between political and spiritual leadership.

Israel had a variety of political leaders
Judges Jdg 2:16; 4:4

Kings 1Sa 8:1–21; 10:1; 16:1–13; 2Sa 7:12; 1Ki 1:28–40

Tribal elders and judges Ex 19:7; Dt 21:1–2; Ru 4:1–2; Job 29:7–12

Foreign powers imposed rulers on Israel Lk 3:1

Examples of those who were both political and spiritual leaders
1Sa 7:15 *Samuel was both prophet and judge.*
Moses: Ex 34:1,27–28
Jdg 6:25–27 *Gideon;* 2Ki 18:4
pp 2Ch 31:1 *Hezekiah;* 1Ch 6:31 *David*

Political leaders, like spiritual ones, were called by God
1Ki 11:31 *The prophet Ahijah confers authority on the leader of a revolt. See also* Ex 3:10 *Moses;* Jdg 6:14 *Gideon David:* 1Sa 16:1,6–12
Isa 45:1–2 *Cyrus was a Persian king, yet he is described as God's "anointed".*

To reject God's leadership is to reject God
1Sa 8:6–8 *See also* 1Sa 8:5,19–20 *Israel wanted a human ruler so that they might be like the surrounding nations.*

Responsibilities of leaders
To protect the weak Ps 72:1–14

To administer justice Ps 72:2; Pr 20:8; 29:4,14; Isa 9:7; 11:3–4

To shepherd the people Ps 78:70–72; Eze 34:2–6

Attributes required in leaders
Isa 11:1–2 *Being anointed by the Spirit of God.*
Reverence: Dt 17:18–20; Isa 11:3
Isa 11:5 *trustworthiness;* Pr 8:15–16 *wisdom*

The failure of leaders
Through exploiting their subjects Mt 20:25 *See also* Dt 17:16–17; 1Sa 8:11–17; 1Ki 12:4; Jer 22:13

Through usurping religious authority 1Sa 13:8–13; 2Ch 26:16–18

Through apostasy 1Ki 11:7–8; 2Ki 21:1–6

Through trusting in alliances with heathen powers Isa 31:1 *See also* 2Ki 20:12,17–18; Isa 30:1–2; Hos 7:11

Godless leadership is evil Lk 13:32 *See also* Da 7:1–7; Rev 13:1–3

People must have a right attitude to political leaders
They are to be obeyed Ro 13:1 *See also* Ro 13:5; 1Pe 2:13–17

But obedience to God must come first Ac 5:29 *See also* Da 3:18; 6:13

Prayers are to be made for them 1Ti 2:1–2

See also

1130 God, sovereignty	5366 king
3272 Holy Spirit in OT	5368 kingship
5205 alliance	5509 rulers
5219 authority, human institutions	7719 elders as leaders
5358 judges	8337 reverence & behaviour
	8704 apostasy
	8741 failure

7739

missionaries

Those called and commissioned by God to fulfil specific tasks, especially that of taking the gospel to those who have not heard it. Missionaries may be sent to other towns, cities or nations, or may be called to fulfil their task closer to home.

7740
missionaries, call of

God calls and sends out his people into the world. All believers are called to share the good news of the gospel, though some are specially commissioned by God, confirmed by the church and compelled by the gospel message to missionary service.

The call to all God's people
Ps 96:2–3 pp 1Ch 16:23–24 Mt 28:19 *See also* Mk 16:15; Jn 20:21; Ac 1:8

Missionaries in the OT
Those sent to their own people Isa 6:8–10 *See also* 2Pe 2:5 *Noah;* Jer 2:1–4 *Jeremiah's ministry extended further but was primarily to his own people, Judah;* Eze 2:3 *Ezekiel*

Those sent to other peoples 2Ki 17:27–28 *A priest from Samaria returns to teach the resettled population about the* LORD.
God's servant is to bring salvation to the whole world: Isa 42:6; 49:6; Ac 13:47
Am 7:15 *Amos, from Judah, is sent to the northern kingdom of Israel.*
Jonah is sent to the city of Nineveh: Jnh 1:1–2; 3:1–2

Missionaries in the NT
John the Baptist Jn 1:6–7 *See also*

Mal 4:5–6; Mt 11:10 pp Lk 7:27;
Mk 1:2–4; Mal 3:1; Isa 40:3; Jn 1:33

Jesus Christ's disciples Lk 9:1–6
*Healing and deliverance accompanies
preaching as part of the disciples' mission.
See also* Mt 10:5–16 *During Jesus Christ's
earthly ministry the disciples' mission was
limited to Israel;* Mk 6:7–11; Lk 10:1

Other believers Ac 11:19–20 *See also*
Ac 8:5 *Philip;* Ac 18:24 *Apollos;*
Ac 26:15–18 *Paul*

Receiving the missionary call
The call given by God Jer 1:4–10 *See
also* Mt 4:19 *Peter and Andrew;* Ac 8:26
Philip; Ac 22:21 *Paul*

The call confirmed by the church
Ac 13:2–3 *See also* Ac 14:26–27; 15:40;
22:14–15 *Paul's call to be a missionary to
the Gentiles is communicated through
Ananias;* Gal 2:7–9 *Paul's mission to the
Gentiles is recognised by the other apostles.*

The call through circumstances Ac 8:4
*Persecution drove the early church to wider
mission. See also* Ge 45:4–5 *Joseph sold
into slavery in Egypt;* Da 1:3–6 *Daniel
among those taken into exile in Babylon;*
Ac 18:1–2 *Priscilla and Aquila left Rome
because of persecution.*

**Missionaries compelled by the
message** Ac 4:18–20 *See also* 1Co 9:16;
2Co 5:14

See also

5107 Paul	6620 calling
5112 Peter	7724 evangelists
5624 witnesses to	7772 prophets
Christ	8495 witnessing

7741
missionaries, task of

God commits various tasks to his
servants. A principal task of those
sent by God is to take the good news
of the gospel to those who have not
heard it, and so to be a means
through which others come to faith.

The need for missionaries
Ro 10:14–15 *See also* Isa 52:7;
Mt 9:37–38 pp Lk 10:2

The work of missionaries
Proclaiming good news Isa 61:1–2 *See
also* Lk 4:18–19
Lk 4:43 *See also* Mt 4:23; 9:35
Ac 11:20 *See also* Ac 5:42; 8:12,25;
14:6–7; Ro 15:16

Calling people to turn to God Ac 26:20
See also 2Ch 30:6–9; Mk 1:4 pp Lk 3:3;
2Co 5:19–20

Announcing judgment Jnh 3:4 *See also*
Jer 25:30–31; 26:12–13; Eze 21:2–3;
Ac 10:42

Teaching and baptising new believers
Mt 28:19–20 *See also* Ac 2:41–42;
8:12–13; 1Co 4:17

Taking the message further afield
2Co 10:15–16 *See also* Ro 15:18–20,28;
Mt 24:14; Lk 24:47; Ac 16:9–10; 23:11

**Strengthening newly established
churches** Ac 18:23 *See also* Ac 8:14–17;
14:21–23; 15:36–41; 16:4–5

Examples of other specific assignments
Ex 3:10 *Moses is sent by God to Pharoah;*
Jos 22:3 *The eastern tribes complete their
mission to help the others take possession
of Canaan;* Jdg 6:14 *Gideon is sent by God
against the Midianites;* 1Sa 15:18–20
*Saul is given the task of destroying the
Amalekites;* 1Sa 16:1 *Samuel is sent by
God to anoint David as king;* Isa 48:15
*Cyrus is appointed to bring deliverance
from Babylon.*
*Barnabas' and Saul's mission to deliver
money collected for the church in Judea:*
Ac 11:30; 12:25
Tychicus sent with news of Paul:
Eph 6:22; Col 4:7–8

See also

2420 gospel	7924 fellowship in
6717 reconciliation,	service
world to God	7948 mission
7027 church,	8413 edification
purpose	8424 evangelism
7754 preaching	9210 judgment,
7797 teaching	God's
7903 baptism	

7742
missionaries, support for

Though facing hardships,
missionaries receive strength from
God to enable them to carry out
their task. They are entitled, too, to
receive support, encouragement and
financial assistance from other
believers.

Missionaries face hardships
Physical and emotional stress
Mt 10:17–23 pp Mk 13:11–13
pp Lk 21:12–19; 2Co 7:5 *See also*
Ro 8:35–36; 2Co 4:11–13; 6:3–5,8–10;
11:23–29; Php 4:12

Opposition to the message 1Co 16:9
See also Ac 4:17–18; 6:9; 13:6–8;
1Th 2:2

Missionaries strengthened by God
The Holy Spirit gives power to witness
Jn 20:21–22 *See also* Lk 24:49; Ac 1:8;
Ro 15:18–19; 1Co 2:4–5

Jesus Christ promises his presence
Mt 28:20 *See also* Mk 16:20; Ac 18:10

Missionaries supported by the church
**Missionaries supported by the sending
church** Ac 14:26 *See also* Ac 13:3; 15:40

Missionaries supported by believers
Ac 18:27 *See also* Ro 15:24;
2Co 8:23–24; Tit 3:13

**Missionary work supported by church
leaders** Ac 8:14 *See also* Ac 11:22–23;
15:30–32; Gal 2:7–9

Missionaries given financial support
Php 4:14–18 *See also* Php 2:25;
1Co 9:11–14; 16:5–6; Gal 6:6;
1Th 2:6–8

Missionaries supported in prayer
Col 4:3 *See also* Eph 6:19–20; Php 1:19;
1Th 5:25; 2Th 3:1

**Missionaries encouraged by visits and
news** Ac 28:15 *See also* Php 2:19;
2Ti 4:9–11; Tit 3:12; Phm 12–13

See also

3030 Holy Spirit,	8434 giving
power	8611 prayer for
5559 stress	others
5955 strength, divine	8787 opposition to
5976 visiting	God
7924 fellowship in	8794 persecution
service	
8414 encouragement	

7745
ordination

The appointment to a public
ministry or office, including
investing with the authority
required for this ministry. The most
important biblical model of
ordination is provided by the OT
priesthood.

Ordination of the OT priesthood
The ceremony of ordination Ex 28:41
See also Ex 29:29–46; 30:30;
Lev 8:30,33; Nu 3:3

The role of the ordained priest
*To properly apply the blood of the
ordination offering:* Ex 29:20–21;
Lev 7:37; 8:18
Lev 16:32 *to make atonement;*
Lev 21:10–12 *to observe a strict code of
behaviour*

**Jesus is the Messiah, the
anointed one**
Mt 16:16 *The Greek word "Christos", like
the Hebrew word "Messiah", means
"anointed (by God)".*

Ordination in the NT
**Jesus Christ appointed disciples
without reference to a ceremony of
ordination** Mk 3:14–15 pp Lk 6:13

**The apostles commissioned people for
service by laying on of hands** Ac 6:6 *See
also* Nu 8:10–11; 27:18–23; Ac 13:3
*Barnabas and Saul were commissioned for
missionary work.*

The appointment of elders Ac 14:23;
1Ti 1:18; 4:14; 5:22; 2Ti 1:6; Tit 1:5,6–9
*Certain qualities are required in an
appointed elder or minister.*

See also

2206 Jesus, the	7715 deacons
Christ	7718 elders
5215 authority	7734 leaders,
6620 calling	spiritual
7304 anointing	7767 priests, OT
7372 hands, laying	institution
on	7943 ministry in
7412 priesthood	church
7706 apostles	

7748
overseers

In the OT a variety of supervisory
roles are mentioned. In the NT
"overseers" (traditionally translated
"bishops") describes the role of local
church leaders.

Overseers in the OT
In secular life Ex 5:6; Ru 2:5–6;
1Ki 5:16; 2Ch 2:2; Ne 3:5; Pr 6:6–7

In religious life Nu 8:22; 1Ch 25:2;
2Ch 23:18; Ezr 3:9; Ne 11:11; Jer 20:1

Overseers in the NT
In secular life Mt 20:8

In the church Php 1:1 *A title for local
church leaders.*

The role of local church "elders"
Ac 20:28 *Here, as elsewhere in the NT,
"elders" and "overseers" are virtually
synonymous. See also* 1Pe 5:1–4

Their qualifications 1Ti 3:1–7 *See also*
Tit 1:7

A title of Jesus Christ 1Pe 2:25

See also

2203 Christ, titles of	7734 leaders,
5051 responsibility	spiritual
7026 church,	7789 shepherd,
leadership	church leader
7715 deacons	7939 ministry
7720 elders in the	8422 equipping,
church	spiritual

7751

persuasion

Attempting to win others over to
one's own point of view. It can be
either positive, as with preaching the
gospel, or it can spring from a malign
intent to seduce people from the
truth.

Means of persuasion
The persuasiveness of argument
Ac 16:15 *See also* Jdg 19:3,7; 2Sa 3:35;
Ac 5:40; 19:32–41; 21:14

The persuasiveness of proof Ac 1:3 *See
also* Ge 45:25–28

The persuasiveness of experience
1Co 14:24–25

The first Christians were
**persuaded of the truth of their
faith**
2Ti 1:12 *See also* Ro 4:20–21; 8:38–39;
2Ti 3:14

The apostles tried to persuade
others of the truth of the gospel
Ac 18:4 *See also* Ac 17:2–4; 19:8;
26:26–29; 28:23–24; 2Co 5:11

Scripture advises patience when
**seeking to persuade those in
power**
Pr 25:15 *See also* Lk 18:1–5

Scripture warns against the
persuasiveness of evil
The persuasiveness of adulterers
Pr 7:21 *See also* Pr 5:3; 7:5

The persuasiveness of false prophets
Jer 28:15

Examples of God's servants
**suffering through the
persuasiveness of others**
Mt 27:20 pp Mk 15:11 *See also* Ac 14:19

See also

5472 proof, evidence	7774 prophets, false
5842 eloquence	8318 patience
6146 deceit & God	8459 perseverance
6241 seduction	8495 witnessing
7703 apologetics	8749 false teachers
7712 convincing	

7754

preaching

The announcing of the good news of
God by his servants through the
faithful revelation of God's will, the
exposition of God's word and the
proclamation of Jesus Christ, the Son
of God. Jesus Christ had an
important preaching ministry.
This set of themes consists of the
following:
7755 preaching, importance of
7756 preaching, content of
7757 preaching, effects of
7758 preachers, call of
7759 preachers, qualifications for
7760 preachers, responsibilities of
7761 preaching, and Holy Spirit
7762 preaching, of Jesus Christ

7755
preaching, importance of

Preaching has a central place among
God's people and is vital to their life
and growth. It is authorised by God,
empowered by the Holy Spirit and
expressed supremely by Jesus Christ.

Preaching has its origin in God
It is a divine command Mk 16:15
pp Mt 28:18–20 *See also* Jnh 1:1–2;
Mt 10:5–7 pp Mk 6:7–12 pp Lk 9:1–6

It is rooted in God's grace Eph 3:7–9
See also Isa 6:1–10; Ro 15:15–16

It is empowered by God's Spirit Ac 1:8
See also Isa 61:1–3; Lk 24:46–49;
Ac 2:1–11; 4:8–12; 10:44; 1Co 2:4–5

The importance of preaching and
Jesus Christ
Jesus Christ himself came to preach
Mk 1:38 pp Lk 4:43 *See also* Eph 2:17

Jesus Christ's own ministry involved
much preaching Mt 4:23 *See also*
Mt 11:1–5 pp Lk 7:18–22

Jesus Christ commissioned his
disciples to preach Mk 3:14–15 *See
also* Mt 10:5–7 pp Lk 9:1–2

The importance of preaching and
the church
It is a natural part of the church's life
Ac 8:4 *See also* Ac 3:11–26; 15:35

It is a trust from God Gal 2:7 *See also*
1Th 2:4; 1Ti 1:11; Tit 1:3

It is an integral aspect of key ministries
in the church 1Ti 3:2 *See also*
Eph 4:11–12; 2Ti 4:2–5; Tit 1:7–9

Its importance to Paul 1Co 1:17–18 *See
also* Ac 9:20–22; 18:5; Ro 1:14–15;
1Co 1:22–25

It is an apostolic command 1Ti 4:13 *See
also* 2Ti 4:2

The importance of preaching for
salvation
Ro 10:14–15 *See also* Isa 52:7; Ro 10:17;
1Co 1:21

The importance of preaching
**means preachers and teachers
will be judged more strictly**
Jas 3:1 *See also* Ro 2:17–24

See also

1427 prophecy	5107 Paul
1610 Scripture	5622 witnesses
1660 Sermon on the	7703 apologetics
Mount	7772 prophets
2363 Christ,	7793 teachers
preaching &	7797 teaching
teaching	8495 witnessing

7756
preaching, content of

Preaching is centred on the nature
and will of God and his claims on all
people. Expressed in prophecy,
declaration or teaching, it includes
the proclamation of the way of
salvation to unbelievers and
instruction about the faith to
believers.

Preaching and the revelation of
God's character, word and will
Ac 20:26–27 *See also* Ex 8:1;
1Ki 12:21–24; Jer 7:1–11; Eze 2:3–3:4

Preaching and the declaration of
the gospel
Declaring the kingdom Mk 1:14–15
pp Mt 4:17 *See also* Mt 4:23 pp Lk 8:1;
Ac 19:8; 20:25

Declaring the person of Jesus Christ
and his life Ac 2:22 *See also*
Ac 10:36–38; 28:31; 2Co 1:19

Declaring the facts of the cross and
the resurrection Ac 2:23–24 *See also*
Ac 5:30; 10:39–42; 13:28–31;
1Co 1:22–24; 15:12–17

Declaring the victory and exaltation of
Jesus Christ Ac 2:33–35 *See also*
Ac 5:31; 1Pe 3:18–22

Declaring that Jesus is both Messiah
(Christ) and Lord Ac 2:36 *See also*
Ac 5:42; 8:5; 9:20–22; 10:36; 18:5

Declaring the call to repent Ac 17:30
See also Mk 1:15 pp Mt 4:17; Ac 2:38;
3:19; 26:20

Declaring the promise of forgiveness
Ac 13:38 *See also* Lk 24:46–47; Ac 2:38;
5:31; 10:43

Preaching finds expression in the
teaching of believers
The central place of teaching in the
lives of the first Christians Ac 2:42 *See
also* Ac 6:2; 11:25–26; 15:35; 18:24–26;
20:20

Teaching from the Scriptures Ac 18:11
See also 2Ch 17:7–9; Ne 8:2–8

Teaching on how to live Mt 28:19–20
See also Eph 4:20–24; 1Th 4:1–2;
Tit 2:1–15

Preaching and the edification of
believers
2Ti 4:2 *See also* Ac 13:42–43; 14:21–22;
20:2; 1Co 14:26–31

Preaching and the continuation
of apostolic doctrine
Preaching should be rooted in
apostolic doctrine, which is to be
faithfully handed on 2Ti 2:2 *See also*
1Co 11:2; 2Th 2:15; 2Ti 1:13–14

Preaching that does not conform to apostolic doctrine is to be rejected
1Ti 1:3–4 *See also* Gal 1:6–9; 1Ti 4:1–7; Tit 1:9–14

Preaching and the rejection of merely human wisdom
1Co 2:1–5 *See also* 1Co 1:18–25

See also
1610 Scripture	3224 Holy Spirit &
2357 Christ, parables	preaching
2427 gospel,	7730 explanation
transmission	8234 doctrine
2560 Christ,	8424 evangelism
resurrection	8750 false teachings

7757
preaching, effects of

Faithful preaching leads to, through the grace of God, the repentance of sinners, the birth of faith and the nourishment of believers. It can also evoke hostility from unbelievers.

The basis of effective preaching
It depends upon the grace of God
Ac 4:33 *See also* Isa 55:10–11; Ac 14:26–27; 1Co 15:10–11

It depends upon the power of the cross, not human wisdom
1Co 1:17–25 *See also* 1Co 2:1–5

It depends upon the power of the Holy Spirit Lk 4:18–19 *See also* Isa 61:1–2; Ac 2:1–11; 10:44–48; 1Co 2:4–5

It requires effective, supporting prayer
Col 4:3–4 *See also* Ac 4:29–31; 6:2–4; 13:1–5; 2Th 3:1

It needs to be received with faith
Heb 4:2 *See also* 1Th 2:13

Preaching and the repentance of sinners
Mt 12:41 pp Lk 11:32 *See also* Jnh 3:1–10; Mt 3:1–6 pp Mk 1:3–5 pp Lk 3:3–6

Preaching and the birth of faith
Ac 4:4 *See also* Ac 2:38–41; 8:9–13; 17:11–12; 1Co 15:1–2

Preaching and the nourishment of believers
Ac 14:21–22 *See also* Ro 16:25–27; Eph 4:11–16; Col 2:6–7

Effective preaching and its authentication by miracles
Mk 16:20 *See also* Mt 4:23–25; Lk 9:1–6 pp Mt 10:5–14 pp Mk 6:7–11; Ac 4:29–30; 8:5–8; 14:1–3

Inappropriate responses to preaching
Amazement Mt 7:28–29 *See also* Lk 4:31–32 pp Mk 1:21–22; Ac 2:5–12; 4:13–14

Offence Mk 6:1–6 pp Mt 13:54–58 *See also* 1Co 1:22–23

Mere academic interest Ac 17:16–32 *Paul in Athens and before the Areopagus;* Ac 24:22–26 *Paul before Felix and Drusilla*

Mockery Ac 17:32 *See also* 2Ch 36:15–16; Ac 2:13

Hostility Ac 17:13 *See also* Ac 4:1–3; 5:27–40; 7:54–60; 13:49–51; 17:5–9

See also
2369 Christ,	6732 repentance
responses to	7020 church, the
3212 Holy Spirit &	7903 baptism
mission	8020 faith
3293 Holy Spirit,	8414 encourage-
witness of	ment
5454 power, God's	
saving	

7758
preachers, call of

God declares his word through called and anointed preachers. He overcomes their reluctance, helps their weakness, authorises their message and confirms the truth of what they declare.

God's call of preachers
It is not dependent upon background
Am 7:14–15 *See also* Jer 1:1–5; Mt 4:18–20 pp Mk 1:16–19 pp Lk 5:1–11; Ac 9:10–16

It is not dependent upon ability
Ex 4:10–12 *See also* Jer 1:6–9; Ac 4:13

It is not dependent upon willingness
Ex 4:13 *See also* Jnh 1:1–3; Ac 9:1–6

It is a matter of God's sovereign choice
Jer 1:4–5 *See also* Isa 49:1–6; Eze 2:1–5; Am 7:14–15; Lk 4:18–19; Isa 61:1–2; Gal 1:15

God's commissioning of preachers
They are commissioned to declare God's word Eze 3:1; Ro 10:13–15 *See also* Jer 1:9; Jnh 3:1–2; Mt 28:18–20

They are to declare God's word with authority Tit 2:15 *See also* Jer 1:9–10; Mk 3:14–15; Lk 9:1–2

They are to declare God's word without fear Jer 1:7–8 *See also* Eze 2:3–7; 3:7–9; Ac 5:27–29; 2Ti 1:6–8

God's constraint upon preachers
1Co 9:16 *See also* Jer 20:8–9; Ac 4:18–20; Ro 1:14–15

God's confirmation of his call upon preachers
Ac 14:3 *See also* Ex 4:1–9; 1Ki 17:17–24; Mk 16:20; Ac 4:29–31; 1Co 2:4

See also
1690 word of God	5335 herald
5107 Paul	6620 calling
5115 Peter, preacher	6666 grace
& teacher	7620 disciples
5215 authority	7724 evangelists

7759
preachers, qualifications for

Those entrusted with the task of preaching must ensure that their lives are in line with their message. They must be of good character and conduct, be consistent in all they teach and do and be accountable to others.

Preachers must be of good character
1Ti 4:12 *See also* 1Th 2:9–10; 1Ti 4:16; 2Ti 2:20–26; Tit 2:7–8; Jas 3:1 *That the judgment is based on character, and not just on teaching, seems clear from the references to guarding the tongue which follow.*

Preachers must practise what they preach
Mt 23:2–4 *See also* Ro 2:21–23; Gal 2:11–14

Preachers must be accountable to others and to God
Mk 6:30 pp Lk 9:10 *See also* Ac 14:26–27; 21:17–19; Gal 2:1–2

Preachers must not look for honour for themselves
Mk 12:38–40 pp Mt 23:5–12 pp Lk 20:45–47 *See also* Ac 14:11–15; 1Co 3:5–6; 1Th 2:3–6

Preachers must not look for personal gain
2Co 2:17 *See also* Ac 20:33–35; 2Co 11:7–9; 1Th 2:6–9

Preachers must be people of integrity
2Co 4:2 *See also* 2Co 1:12; 1Th 2:3–6

See also
3239 Holy Spirit,	7944 ministry,
anointing	qualifications
5714 men	8114 discipleship
5769 behaviour	8203 character
5842 eloquence	8265 godliness
7720 elders in the	8266 holiness
church	8276 humility
	8342 servanthood

7760
preachers, responsibilities of

Those entrusted with the responsibility of preaching are to discharge it faithfully, boldly and persistently in the power of the Holy Spirit. The Christian community should honour faithful preachers and challenge those who fail to honour their responsibility.

The responsibilities of preachers
They must be diligent in their preaching 2Ti 2:15 *See also* 1Ti 4:13–16; 2Ti 4:1–5

They must be faithful in their preaching
Ac 20:20 *See also* Jer 26:1–2; 42:4; Ac 20:25–27

They must be persistent in their preaching 2Ti 4:1–5 *See also* Ac 18:4–6; 20:31; 1Th 2:1–2

They must be bold in their preaching
Ac 28:31 *See also* Jer 26:7–15; Am 7:10–17; Ac 4:18–20; 5:27–29; 14:1–3

They must be encouraging in their preaching Ac 14:21–22 *See also* Ac 15:32; 1Co 14:3–5; 1Th 2:11–12; 2Ti 4:2

They must be filled with the Holy Spirit
Ac 1:8; 1Co 2:4 *See also* Ac 4:31–33; 1Th 1:5; 1Pe 1:12

They must be compassionate in their preaching Mk 6:34 *See also* Mt 9:35–38

The responsibilities of the church towards preachers
Faithful preachers should be honoured 1Ti 5:17 *See also* Mt 13:53–57 pp Mk 6:2–4; Lk 10:3–8; Heb 13:7

Unfaithful preachers are to be exposed and will be judged Gal 1:6–9 *See also* Jer 14:14–16; Eze 13:1–23; 1Ti 1:3–4; 4:1–7; Tit 1:10–11; 2Pe 2:1–3; Rev 2:14–16,20–23

See also

5806 compassion	7948 mission
5833 diligence	8202 boldness
7020 church, the	8248 faithfulness
7739 missionaries	8342 servanthood
7774 prophets, false	8459 perseverance
7939 ministry	8749 false teachers

7761
preaching, and Holy Spirit
See 3224 Holy Spirit, and preaching

7762
preaching, of Jesus Christ
See 2363 Jesus Christ, preaching and teaching of

7766
priests
A group of men charged with the responsibility of mediating between God and his people, ensuring proper worship, and maintaining the spiritual health of the people of God.

7767
priests, institution in OT times
Priests played an important role in the OT and were regarded as having a special status and place in the life of Israel.

Pagan priests in the OT
1Sa 6:1–2; 2Ki 23:5; Hos 10:5; Zep 1:4

The special status of priests
Ezr 1:5; Isa 24:2; Hos 4:9; Mic 3:11

Associated with the descendants of Levi through Aaron
The exclusive nature of the priesthood 1Ch 6:49 *Only God has the right to nominate those who mediate between him and humanity. See also* Ex 6:16–20 *This genealogy shows Moses and Aaron were both descended from Levi;* Ex 28:1; 29:44; 30:30; Nu 16:40
Not all Levites were priests: Dt 18:1; Jer 33:21

Micah's priest Jdg 17:13

The Shiloh priesthood 1Ch 24:3 *See also* 1Ch 6:27

The priests in Dan Jdg 18:30

Descendants of Zadok Eze 44:15–16 *See also* 2Sa 8:17; 1Ch 6:50–53; 24:3

Criticism of priestly appointments that were not Levitical
1Ki 12:31 *See also* 1Ki 13:33; 2Ch 11:13–14; 13:9

The appointment of priests
Their preliminary purification Ex 29:4 *See also* Ex 30:19; 40:12

Their anointing Ex 30:30–32 *See also* Lev 8:30; Nu 3:3 *Kings and priests also were anointed.*

Their consecration Ex 29:1 *See also* Ex 29:12–14,18,20–21; Lev 8:12

Their ordination Ex 29:35 *See also* Ex 29:9,29,33; Lev 8:22,33; Jdg 17:5,12

The dress of the priests
Ex 28:40 *See also* Ex 28:42; 39:27–29; Lev 8:13

See also

1350 covenant with Israel's priests	7390 Levites
7304 anointing	7413 priesthood, OT
7377 high priest, OT	7745 ordination
	8218 consecration

7768
priests, function in OT times
Priests had a unique role: administering the sanctuary, offering sacrifice and leading and teaching the people. Accordingly they were set apart by a special code of conduct.

The priests were set apart
They were consecrated to the Lord Lev 22:9 *See also* Ex 28:1,4,41; 29:1,44; 30:34; 31:10; 35:19; 39:41

They were not to incur uncleanness Lev 21:1 *Some exceptions to uncleanness by touching a corpse are listed in verses 2–3. See also* Eze 44:25

They were not to shave or mutilate themselves Lev 21:5 *See also* Eze 44:20

They were not to marry any but a virtuous Israelite Lev 21:7 *See also* Eze 44:22

They were not to drink wine before entering the sanctuary Lev 10:9 *See also* Eze 44:21

They were disqualified by physical defects Lev 21:17 *See also* Lev 21:18–22

They were not to allow outsiders to eat the sacred offerings Lev 22:15–16 *See also* Lev 24:9; 1Sa 21:4; Mt 12:4

They were not to own land in Israel Nu 18:20 *See also* Eze 44:28

They were not to offer unacceptable sacrifices Lev 22:20 *See also* Mal 1:7–9

They were to obey God's law meticulously Lev 22:31 *See also* Eze 44:24

The priests supervised the sanctuary
They only had access to holy things Nu 3:10 *See also* Nu 4:5; Eze 40:45–46; 44:16; Joel 2:17

They tended the sanctuary lamps Ex 27:21

They carried the ark Dt 31:9 *See also* Jos 3:8,15,17; 4:9,16; 6:12

The priests supervised the sacrifices
Lev 1:5 *See also* Lev 1:8; 2:2; 1Ch 9:30

The priests led the nation
As role models Mal 2:6

As teachers Eze 44:23 *See also* Lev 10:10; Dt 31:10–13; Ezr 7:6; Mal 2:7

As judges Dt 17:9 *See also* Dt 19:17; 21:5; 2Ch 19:8; Eze 44:24

As encouragers in battle Nu 10:8 *See also* Jos 6:4; 2Ch 13:12

Prophetic criticism of the priests
La 4:13 *See also* Jer 2:8; 6:13; Eze 7:26; 22:26; Hos 4:6–9; 6:9; Zep 3:4

See also

5358 judges	7424 ritual law
6682 mediation	7435 sacrifice, in OT
7340 clean and unclean	7464 teachers of the law
7404 ordinances	

7769
priests, types of in NT times
The NT points to the fulfilment of the OT priesthood in Jesus Christ, and develops the idea that all Christian believers can be seen as priests. It also records the continuing role of priests in the life of Israel and pagan nations at this time.

Pagan priests
Ac 14:13

Jewish priests
The chief priests Mt 16:21

The Sadducees Ac 5:17 *The Sadducees were a conservative party composed entirely of priests who were influential in the Sanhedrin.*

Zechariah Lk 1:5 *See also* 1Ch 24:10

Emissaries to John the Baptist Jn 1:19 *Levites were closely associated with priests as temple personnel, perhaps mentioned here because of their teaching function. See also* 2Ch 35:3; Ne 8:7–9; Lk 10:31–32

Jesus Christ as high priest
Heb 8:1–2 *See also* Heb 4:14–16

Christians as priests
Rev 1:5–6 *See also* 1Pe 2:5,9; Rev 5:10; 20:6

See also

2306 Christ, high priest	7414 priesthood, NT
6684 mediator	7555 Sadducees
7330 chief priests	7565 Sanhedrin
7378 high priest, NT	8266 holiness

7770
priests, tasks in NT times
The priests mentioned in the NT performed various functions, all of which are fulfilled in Jesus Christ and the church, which is his body.

Priests offered sacrifices

Sacrifices made by pagan priests
Ac 14:13

Jewish sacrifice Heb 10:11

The sacrifice of Jesus Christ Heb 9:14
Jesus Christ is both priest and victim: his own body takes the place occupied by sacrifices in the OT ritual. See also Heb 10:10

The Christian sacrifice of a surrendered life Ro 12:1 *See also* Heb 13:16

The Christian sacrifice of praise Heb 13:15

Priests made intercession

The burning of incense Lk 1:9 *See also* Ex 30:7–8

Christian intercession Rev 5:8 *See also* 1Pe 2:5; Rev 1:6; 5:10; 20:6

Priests were guardians of tradition

They were trained in the teaching and application of OT law Mt 2:3–6; Jn 1:19

The Christian "tradition" 1Co 15:1–5; 2Ti 1:13–14; 2:2; Jude 3

Priests declared people clean or unclean

They supplied ritual certification of cleansing Mt 8:4 pp Mk 1:44 pp Lk 5:14 *See also* Lev 13:2–3; 14:2; Lk 17:14

Christians pronounce forgiveness Jn 20:21–23; Jas 5:16

See also

5588 traditions	7939 ministry
7020 church, the	8611 prayer for
7719 elders as	others
leaders	

7772

prophets

Individuals called and empowered by God to declare his will to his people, including the disclosure of his future intentions to save and judge his people. The term refers particularly to the great OT prophets, such as Isaiah and Jeremiah, who were raised up to guide the people of God at critical moments in their history and whose ministries and teaching remain of continuing importance today. At several points in his ministry, Jesus Christ was acclaimed as a prophet.

7773

prophets, role of

As agents of God, prophets acted in various capacities, as was required of them, in order to carry out his will and fulfil his purpose.

Prophets as God's spokesmen

They heralded impending judgment
Jnh 3:4 *See also* 1Ki 16:7; 2Ki 22:15–17 pp 2Ch 34:23–25; Jer 1:14–16; 5:14–17; Eze 5:8–12; 38:17

They advocated repentance 2Ki 17:13 *See also* 2Ch 24:19; Jer 3:12–13; 35:15; 44:4; Zec 1:3–6

They conveyed messages from God to the nations Eze 25:8–11 *See also* Jer 46:13; 47:1; 49:34; 50:1; Eze 25:2,12–14; 26:3; Am 1:9; Eze 29:2; Am 1:3,6,13; 2:1

The supernatural activities of prophets

They revealed future events
Eze 17:16–21 *See also* 1Ki 11:29–31; 20:13; Isa 7:13–14 *the birth of Immanuel;* Jer 29:10; Da 2:38–44; 9:2; Mt 2:15; Hos 11:1
Herod's slaughter of the infants in Bethlehem: Mt 2:17–18; Jer 31:15 Mt 8:17; Isa 53:4; Ac 3:18; 11:27–29; 21:10–11

They received dreams and visions
Nu 12:6 *See also* Eze 7:26; Da 7:1; 8:1; Hos 12:10

They worked miracles 2Ki 5:3 *See also* 1Ki 17:13–24; 2Ki 4:3–6,15–17, 32–35,40–44; 6:5–6

Prophets as intermediaries

Between God and the people
Dt 18:16–18 *See also* Ex 6:30–7:1; 2Sa 7:4–7; 12:7–14,24–25; 24:11–12; 1Ki 20:42; 2Ki 20:1 pp Isa 38:1; 2Ch 12:5; 28:9–11

Between the people and God 1Sa 7:9 *See also* Ge 20:7; 2Ki 20:11; 2Ch 32:20; Jer 11:14; 27:18; Eze 14:7

Their responsibility as watchmen
Eze 3:17–21 *The intermediary role of the prophet is highlighted by the image of a watchman who receives messages from God and conveys them to the people. See also* Eze 33:1–7; Hos 9:8

Prophets as leaders in the community

They gave advice Zec 7:2–3 *See also* 1Sa 9:6; 1Ki 22:6; 2Ki 3:11; 6:8–10; 22:14 pp 2Ch 34:22; 2Ch 29:25; Isa 37:2

They gave encouragement Ac 15:32 *See also* Ezr 5:1–2; Jer 29:4–7; Eze 11:17–21; Hag 1:13; 2:4

They led the people Hos 12:13 *See also* Dt 18:15; 1Sa 7:6; 1Ki 18:40

They appointed kings and leaders
1Sa 10:1 *See also* 1Sa 16:13; 1Ki 1:34,38; 19:15–16; 2Ki 9:6

Prophets as writers

1Ch 29:29 *See also* 2Ch 9:29; 13:22; 26:22; 32:32; Isa 30:8; Jer 30:2; 36:4; 51:60; Eze 43:11; Hab 2:2

See also

1427 prophecy	7734 leaders,
1443 revelation, OT	spiritual
1690 word of God	7781 seer
5777 admonition	8611 prayer for
5926 rebuke	others
6223 rebellion of	9210 judgment,
Israel	God's
6732 repentance	

7774

prophets, false

Men or women who falsely claim to speak on God's behalf. They are denounced in the OT and NT for leading people astray. Scripture provides criteria by which true prophets may be recognised and distinguished from false prophets, who often speak from base motives.

Criteria for recognising true prophets

A true prophet's word will be fulfilled
Dt 18:21–22 *See also* Jer 28:8–9

A true prophet's teaching commends righteous behaviour Dt 13:1–4 *See also* Eze 13:17–23; 14:4–8; La 2:14

A true prophet's godly life will reflect his calling Mt 7:15–20 *See also* Isa 28:7; Jer 23:10–11,14; Zep 3:4

A true prophet will acknowledge Jesus Christ as divine 1Jn 4:1–6

The motivations of false prophets

Their messages originate with themselves Jer 23:16 *See also* Jer 14:13–14; 23:25–32,36; Eze 13:1–7

Their messages may be occasioned by popular demand Jer 29:8–9
God places a strict requirement upon his prophets that they should proclaim only what is divinely revealed: Nu 22:35,38; 23:12,26; 24:12–13; 1Ki 22:13–14 Isa 30:10–11; Jer 5:30–31; Mic 2:11

Their messages may be given for financial reward Ne 6:12–13 *See also* Jer 6:13–14; Eze 13:19; Mic 3:11; 2Pe 2:1–3

Their messages may be the result of deception Jer 22:19–23
pp 2Ch 18:18–22 *See also* Eze 14:9

Their messages may be inspired by divination Jer 14:14 *See also* Eze 13:6–7; 22:28; Ac 13:6

Examples of false prophets

In the OT Ne 6:10–13 *See also* 1Ki 22:1–28 pp 2Ch 18:1–27; Jer 27:9–10,14–18

False prophetesses Ne 6:14; Eze 13:17

Prophets of other gods Jer 23:13 *See also* 1Ki 18:19–40; 2Ki 10:19; Jer 2:8

In the NT Mt 24:24 pp Mk 13:22 *See also* Mt 24:10–11; Ac 13:6–11
False prophets feature as part of the symbolism of the book of Revelation: Rev 2:20; 16:13; 19:20; 20:10

The punishment of false prophets

Dt 18:20 *See also* Dt 13:5; Zec 13:3; Jer 14:15
God sometimes intervened to strike the false prophet down: Jer 28:15–17; 29:21–23,30–32
Jer 23:34–40; Eze 13:8–16; Mic 3:5–6

See also

4155 divination	8750 false teachings
5908 motives	8776 lies
6145 deceit	8846 ungodliness
8748 false religion	9105 last things
8749 false teachers	

7775

prophets, lives of

God called individuals from differing backgrounds to speak as prophets on his behalf, sometimes in difficult circumstances.

The backgrounds of the prophets
Ex 2:1–10 *Moses was brought up in the Egyptian royal court;* 1Sa 1:21–28 *Samuel was a temple servant at Shiloh;* 1Ki 19:19–21 *Elisha was a farmer;* Eze 1:3 *Ezekiel was a priest living in exile in Babylonia.*
It is not entirely clear whether Amos was a wealthy sheep breeder and land owner or a poor migrant worker before his call to be a prophet. The Hebrew word translated "shepherd" could equally well be translated "sheep breeder": Am 1:1; 7:14

The calling of the prophets
Their initial encounter with God
Isa 6:1–4 *See also* Ex 3:1–6; Eze 1:4–28

God communicating his call Jer 1:4–5
See also Isa 6:8–10; Eze 2:3–3:5; Jnh 1:1; 3:1

Their response to God's call Jer 1:6–10
See also Ex 3:11–12

The family life of the prophets
Jer 16:1–4 *See also* Isa 7:3; 8:1–4; Eze 24:15–24; Hos 1:2–11; 3:1–5

The hardships faced by prophets
Persecution Heb 11:32–38 *See also* Ac 7:52

Reviling and beating Lk 6:22–23 pp Mt 5:11–12 *See also* Jer 20:1–2; Jas 5:10

Imprisonment Jer 37:11–16 *See also* 1Ki 22:26–27 pp 2Ch 18:25–26; 2Ch 16:10; Jer 37:21; 38:6–13

Killing 1Ki 19:14 *See also* 1Ki 18:4,13; 19:2; Jer 26:8–11,20–23; Mt 23:29–31,37 pp Lk 13:34; Lk 11:47–49; 1Th 2:4–15

The death of prophets
Dt 34:1–8 *Moses;* 1Sa 28:3 *Samuel;* 2Ki 2:11–12 *Elijah did not die but was taken up in a chariot of fire.*

See also
1421 oracles	5893 insults
1450 signs, kinds of	6620 calling
2318 Christ as	7712 convincing
prophet	7778 school of
5344 imprisonment	prophets
5420 music	8794 persecution
5560 suffering	9020 death

7776
prophet, Jesus Christ as
See 2318 Jesus Christ, as prophet

7778
school of prophets

A company of prophets working and prophesying together under the instruction and leadership of a more experienced prophet. There were also similar companies of false prophets.

A school of prophets used by God to influence others
1Sa 19:19–24 *See also*
1Sa 10:5–6,10–13; 2Ki 9:1–3; Ezr 5:2

Schools of prophets associated with particular places
Bethel 2Ki 2:3

Jericho 2Ki 2:15

Leaders of schools of prophets
Samuel and a school of prophets
1Sa 19:20

Elisha and a school of prophets
2Ki 2:15 *See also* 2Ki 4:1,38; 6:1–4

A school of prophets in danger
1Ki 18:4 *See also* 1Ki 18:13

Schools of false prophets
1Ki 18:19,40; 22:6 pp 2Ch 18:5; 1Ki 22:10 pp 2Ch 18:9; 1Ki 22:12–14 pp 2Ch 18:11–13; 1Ki 22:19–23 pp 2Ch 18:18–22; Ne 6:14

See also
1427 prophecy	7734 leaders,
1443 revelation, OT	spiritual
7141 people of God,	7772 prophets
OT	8794 persecution

7781
seer

Seer as an alternative title for a prophet
1Sa 9:9 *Literally, a "seer" is "one who sees", especially one who claims to see into the future or to have insight into the will of God. See also* 2Sa 24:11 pp 1Ch 21:9

Seers used by people to enquire of God
1Sa 9:8–9

David had seers to enquire of God for him 1Ch 25:1–5 *See also* 2Sa 24:11 pp 1Ch 21:9; 2Sa 15:27; 2Ch 29:25; 35:15

Seers were used by God to bring his word to the people
2Ki 17:13

Seers were used by God to bring his word to the king
2Ch 16:7–10; 33:18

The words of a seer were sometimes unwelcome
2Ch 16:7–10; Isa 30:10; Am 7:12–13

Samuel was called a seer
1Sa 9:11–14,18–19; 1Ch 9:22; 26:28; 29:29

Asaph, the psalmist, called a seer
2Ch 29:30

Seers wrote Israel's history
2Ch 33:18–19 *See also* 1Ch 29:29; 2Ch 9:29; 12:15

God judges Israel by blinding the seers
Isa 29:10; Mic 3:7

See also
1175 God, will of	4945 history
1428 prophecy, OT	5085 David
inspiration	7773 prophets, role
1690 word of God	8281 insight
2318 Christ as	8648 enquiring of
prophet	God

7784
shepherd

The work of a shepherd was important and responsible in the rural world of ancient Palestine. Since it involved leading, protecting and feeding a flock, it is seen as a metaphor for the task of leadership. Scripture declares that God is the Shepherd of his people.

7785
shepherd, as occupation

The occupation of a shepherd was both humble and honourable. In the marginal hill country of Palestine it was particularly demanding.

A shepherd as a keeper of flocks of animals
Ge 46:32 *The Hebrew word refers to a keeper of goats and cattle as well as sheep.*

The tasks of a shepherd
Tending, feeding and watering Ps 23:2
See also Ge 29:3; 26:19–22; Ex 22:5; Lk 13:15; Jn 21:15–17

Keeping and protecting Jer 31:10 *See also* Ge 4:2; Ps 23:4 *The rod is a crook (for extracting sheep from difficulty) and the staff a club (for warding off wild animals);* 1Sa 17:34–37

Leading, not driving, sheep Jn 10:3–4
See also Ex 3:1; Ps 23:2; 77:20; Isa 40:11; Jer 50:6

Gathering animals together Jn 10:3 *See also* Ps 147:4; Isa 40:26; Mt 25:32

The shepherd's routine
The search for pasture Ge 37:17

The midday rest SS 1:7

The night-watch Lk 2:8; Jer 43:12

Shearing, an annual festival 1Sa 25:7–8

The use of pens and folds Ps 50:9; Hab 3:17; Jn 10:1,16

Breeding Ge 30:40

Rearing
Rebekah's ruse depended on a method used to get a ewe to accept an alien lamb: Ge 27:16,27

The problems faced by shepherds
Drought and dry winds Jer 12:4; Hos 4:3; 13:15; Joel 1:17–20; Am 1:2

With animals and thieves
1Sa 17:34–37; 25:15; Jn 10:1,12

Shepherds as employers
Job 1:3 *See also* 1Sa 25:2; 2Ki 3:4; Am 1:1

Shepherds as employees
The status of a shepherd 1Sa 16:11; 17:28; Lk 2:8

The responsibilities of a shepherd
Ge 31:39; Am 3:12 *A shepherd who lost an animal to wild beasts had to produce evidence;* Mt 18:12 pp Lk 15:4

See also

1220 God as shepherd	5480 protection
4603 animals	5802 care
4684 sheep	5828 danger
5433 occupations	8490 watchfulness

7786
shepherd, as king and leader

Shepherd was a standard term for a leader or king throughout the ancient world. In this sense it often appears in the Bible.

General term for a king or leader
Isa 44:28 *The prophet describes this non-Jewish king as God's shepherd;* Jer 6:3 *See also* 2Sa 7:7; Ps 77:20; Isa 31:4; Jer 12:10; 49:19; 50:44

The Lord as shepherd
Of Israel Ps 80:1 *See also* Ge 49:24; Ps 28:9; Isa 40:11

Of the individual Ps 23:1 *See also* Ge 48:15

David as the model of a good shepherd
Experience as a real shepherd Ps 78:70–71 *See also* 1Sa 17:34–37; 2Sa 12:1–7 *The king is brought to his senses by a "shepherd" story;* Ps 23:1–4

The shepherd faces death for his flock 2Sa 24:17 *See also* Ex 32:32; Jn 10:11,15,17

David as a model of the coming Messiah Eze 34:23 *See also* Jer 23:4–5; 30:9; Hos 3:5

A good shepherd as a leader "after God's own heart"
Jer 3:15 *See also* Isa 40:11; Jer 31:10; Eze 34:12

A bad shepherd
1Ki 22:17

Criticisms of the shepherds of Israel
Jer 23:1–2 *See also* Jer 10:21; 22:21–22; Eze 34:1–10

See also

2230 Messiah, coming of	7135 Israel, people of God
5085 David	7735 leaders, political
5366 king	
5509 rulers	

7787
shepherd, God the
See 1220 God, as shepherd

7788
shepherd, Jesus Christ as
See 2330 Jesus Christ, as shepherd

7789
shepherd, as church leader

Church leaders are likened to shepherds, on account of their pastoral responsibilities and tasks.

Jesus Christ, the archetypal shepherd
1Pe 5:4

Appointment of shepherds
Eph 4:11 *See also* Mk 3:14; Ac 14:23; 1Co 12:28

Shepherd responsibilities
Feeding the flock Jn 21:15 *See also* Mk 6:34; Jn 21:17; 1Co 3:2; Heb 5:12–14; Jude 12

Caring for the flock Jn 21:16 *See also* Mt 25:36; Ac 20:28; Php 1:1; 1Ti 3:1–2; 2Ti 1:17; Tit 1:7; Jas 1:27; 1Pe 5:2

Protecting, from false teachers Ac 20:29 *See also* Mt 7:15; Jn 10:1,10

Leading, not exploiting 1Pe 5:3

Being accountable *See also* Heb 13:17

Risking death Jn 10:15; Ac 12:1–4; 21:13

See also

2330 Christ as shepherd	7748 overseers
5806 compassion	7793 teachers
7026 church, leadership	7939 ministry
7130 flock, God's	8124 guidance
7734 leaders, spiritual	8354 trustworthiness
	8428 example
	8750 false teachings

7793
teachers

Those who have responsibility for instructing others, especially in relation to matters of faith and life: in the home, parents; in Israel, priests and teachers of the law and in the NT church, apostles, prophets, pastors and teachers. At a less formal level Christians should seek to teach one another. God is the supreme teacher of his people.

God is the supreme teacher
Heb 8:10–11 *See also* Jer 31:33–34; Dt 8:3; Ps 32:8; Jn 14:26; 1Th 4:9; Tit 2:11–12

Parents as teachers
Eph 6:4 *See also* Dt 4:9–10; 6:4–9; 11:18–19; Ps 78:5–6; 2Ti 3:14–15

Priests as Israel's teachers
Mal 2:4–7 *See also* Lev 10:11; 2Ki 12:2; 2Ch 35:3; Ne 8:7–8; Eze 44:23

The apostles and their helpers as teachers
The apostles generally Ac 5:42 *See also* Mt 28:19–20; Ac 4:2,18; 5:21,28

Paul Ac 20:20 *See also* Ac 11:26; 15:35; 18:11; 1Co 4:17; 14:19; 1Th 4:1–2; 1Ti 2:7; 2Ti 1:11

Timothy 1Ti 4:6–16; 2Ti 2:23–25

The gift of teachers in the church
Eph 4:11 *See also* Ac 13:1; 1Co 12:28–29; 14:29–34; Gal 6:6; 1Ti 2:12; 2Ti 2:2

Elders as teachers
Tit 1:9 *See also* 1Ti 3:2; 5:17

Christians as teachers of one another
Col 3:16 *See also* Ro 15:14; 1Co 14:26

See also

1690 word of God	7420 Rabbi
2363 Christ, preaching & teaching	7464 teachers of the law
3140 Holy Spirit, teacher	7718 elders
5115 Peter, preacher & teacher	7755 preaching, importance
5731 parents	7766 priests
	7797 teaching
	8749 false teachers

7796
teaching

The act of instructing someone in matters of faith and morals, especially in the home or church. Teaching was a major aspect of the ministry of Jesus Christ.

7797
teaching

The apostles' teaching formed the basis of the instruction given to the first Christians. Parts of the NT draw a distinction between preaching and teaching, seeing the former as a means of converting individuals, and the latter as a means of instructing them after conversion.

The importance of teaching
Ecc 12:11–12 *"goads" prod the sluggish to action, while "embedded nails" furnish a kind of mental anchorage. "Shepherd" is almost certainly a reference to God himself. See also* Pr 1:8–9; 3:1–2; 4:1–4; 6:20–23; Mt 5:19; 1Co 14:6; 2Ti 4:2–3

Teaching given by parents
Pr 22:6 *See also* Dt 6:6–9; 11:18–19; Eph 6:1–4

The apostles' teaching
Ac 2:42 ; Tit 1:9 *See also* Mt 28:19–20; Ro 6:17; 16:17; 1Th 4:8; 2Th 2:15; 1Ti 1:10–11; 4:6; 6:3; 2Ti 1:13–14; 4:3; Tit 2:1

The gift of teaching in the church
Ro 12:7 *See also* 1Ti 4:13–14

Ways of teaching believers
Through example 1Th 1:5–6 *See also* 1Co 4:17; 11:1; Php 4:9; 1Th 2:14; 2Ti 3:10; Tit 2:3–7

Through dialogue with the teacher Ac 20:7; 19:8–9

Through explanation of ceremonies Ex 12:26–27; 13:14–16

Through proverbs Pr 1:1–6,20–28

Through the law Dt 6:6–9; 11:18–19; 27:1–26; Ps 78:5–8

Through mutual edification Col 3:16 *See also* Ro 15:14; 1Th 5:11; Heb 5:12

Through the instruction of different groups within the church Eph 5:22–6:9; Col 3:18–4:1; Tit 2:1–10; 1Pe 2:18–3:7; 5:1–5

The distinction between teaching and preaching
Ac 15:35 See also Mt 4:23; 9:35; 11:1; Lk 20:1; Ac 4:2; 5:42; 28:31

Examples of major themes taught in the NT church
Righteousness from God through faith in Jesus Christ Ro 3:21–22 See also Gal 2:20–21

Freedom in Christ from the demands of the law Gal 5:1–3

The humility of Jesus Christ Php 2:5–8 See also Heb 13:12–13

The supremacy of Jesus Christ Col 1:18

The superiority of Jesus Christ Heb 3:3 Hebrews also shows Jesus Christ to be superior to the angels, the high priest and the sacrifices.

Godly behaviour Eph 4:22–24 See also Ro 12:1–2; 1Ti 6:1–2

See also
2363 Christ, preaching & teaching	7730 explanation
	7754 preaching
	7793 teachers
5115 Peter, preacher & teacher	8234 doctrine
	8313 nurture
5302 education	8351 teachableness
5731 parents	8750 false teachings

7798
teaching, of Jesus Christ
See 2363 Jesus Christ, preaching and teaching of

7900
The life of the church

7903
baptism

A washing with water, which symbolises the cleansing of believers from the stain and dirt of sin through the grace of God. Jesus Christ submitted to baptism as an example to believers. Through the work of the Holy Spirit, baptism is linked with union with the risen Jesus Christ.

7904
baptism, of Jesus Christ
See 2510 Jesus Christ, baptism of

7905
baptism, with Holy Spirit
See 3242 Holy Spirit, baptism with

7906
baptism, in the Gospels
In the Gospels baptising is based on the symbolic practice in the OT and Judaism of cleansing with water.

Washing was the means of achieving ritual purity
Ex 30:19–20; Mk 7:3–4 The Greek word here translated "wash" is "baptizo", from which the English "baptise" comes.

Sprinkling with water symbolises spiritual cleansing
Eze 36:25 See also Zec 13:1; Heb 10:22

Being baptised by John was a confession that cleansing was needed
Mt 3:11 See also Mt 3:6; Mk 1:4–5 pp Lk 3:3; Ac 19:1–4

John promised that the Messiah would cleanse with the baptism of the Holy Spirit
Mt 3:11 pp Mk 1:8 pp Lk 3:16 See also Isa 44:3; Eze 36:25–26

Baptism involves both water and the Holy Spirit
Jn 3:5

The disciples of Jesus Christ baptised like John's
See also
Jn 3:22–23; 4:1

Jesus Christ was baptised by John
Mt 3:13–17 pp Mk 1:9–11 pp Lk 3:21–22 pp Jn 1:32–33

See also
2375 kingdom of God	5098 John the Baptist
2510 Christ, baptism of	7416 purification
3242 Holy Spirit, baptism with	8324 purity

7907
baptism, practice of
Baptism is associated with repenting of sin, believing the gospel message and becoming a member of Christ's body.

Baptism is ordained by Jesus Christ himself
Mt 28:19 See also Ac 9:17–18; 16:14–15

Baptism is linked with repentance
Ac 2:38 See also Heb 6:1–2 The "baptisms" referred to here may imply teaching about Jewish rituals or the baptism offered by John the Baptist.

Baptism follows the decision to believe
Ac 2:41; 18:8 See also Ac 8:12–13; 16:31–33

Baptism in the name of God or Jesus Christ
Baptism in or into the name of Jesus Christ Ac 19:5 See also Ac 2:38; 8:16; 10:48

Baptism in the name of the Trinity Mt 28:18–20

Baptism was by immersion
Ro 6:4 The word "buried" implies immersion. See also Ac 8:38

Baptism is linked with the gift of the Holy Spirit
Mk 1:8 ; Ac 1:5 See also Ac 2:4; 11:16 1Co 12:13 All the Christians at Corinth had been spiritually baptised into Christ and thus united with him.

Manifestations of the Holy Spirit may follow or precede water baptism
See also
Ac 8:12–17; 9:17–18; 10:44–48

The person who baptises is of little importance
1Co 1:14 What matters is not who baptises but the Saviour in whose name it is done.

Baptism "for the dead"
1Co 15:29 It is not certain if there was a ceremony of baptism "for the dead" in the NT church, nor whether, if it existed, Paul approved of it.

Passages which may imply infant baptism
The "households" (not merely individuals) may well have included children:
Ac 16:15,33; 18:8; 1Co 1:16
Mk 10:13–16; 1Co 7:14; Col 2:11–12 If baptism is here equated with circumcision, this suggests baptism is the sign of the new covenant.

Passages apparently negating infant baptism
Ac 2:38–41 infants cannot repent and believe; Gal 3:7 Under the new covenant it is faith in Jesus Christ, not an outward sign, that makes a person a child of God.

See also
3257 Holy Spirit, gift of	6732 repentance
4293 water	7105 believers
	7957 sacraments

7908
baptism, significance of
The NT uses a variety of images to explain the meaning of baptism, such as dying and rising with Christ, sharing in his death and being cleansed from sin.

Baptism is a symbol of the death of Jesus Christ
Lk 12:50 Jesus Christ described his death as a baptism or a flood overwhelming him. See also Ps 42:7; 69:1–2; 88:7; Mk 10:38–39

Baptism is a symbol of the burial of Jesus Christ
Ro 6:3–4 Immersion in water symbolises how the old sinful life is buried with Christ. Dying to sin and sharing Jesus Christ's sufferings, symbolised by baptism, is a lifelong process: Ro 8:13; Col 3:5

Baptism is a symbol of being saved from the flood
1Pe 3:21 The flood/baptism symbolises both judgment (the death of sinners and the death of Jesus Christ) and salvation (those in the ark and those in Christ passing safely through judgment). See also Ge 7:6–7

Baptism is the gospel equivalent of circumcision

Col 2:11–12 *The "circumcision in Christ" may refer either to his death on the cross or to baptism. See also Dt 10:16*

Baptism recalls the exodus

1Co 10:1–2 *In and through the exodus experience Israel was united with and obedient to Moses, as Jesus Christ's people are to him. See also Ex 14:19–24*

Baptism symbolises washing from sin

Ac 22:16 *Baptism is an outward sign of cleansing from sin and from a defiled life and conscience. See also 1Co 6:11; Tit 3:5; 1Pe 3:21*

Baptism is a symbol of putting on Christ

Gal 3:27 *Baptism is seen as putting on Christ, as one might put on a coat or garment, and thus be "clothed with Christ".*

Baptism as a symbol of unity

Eph 4:5 *See also* 1Co 12:13

See also

1670 symbols	6754 union with
2410 cross, the	Christ
2530 Christ, death of	7221 exodus, the
6029 sin, forgiveness	7336 circumcision,
6728 regeneration	spiritual
	7478 washing

7912

collections

The financial burden of God's work has always been shared amongst God's people. In the OT, this was mainly by compulsory tithes; in the NT by voluntary contributions.

The collection of compulsory tithes and other religious taxes

Tithes Lev 27:30 *See also* Nu 18:21

Redemption money Ex 30:12; Nu 3:46–47

Temple taxes 2Ch 24:5; Mt 17:24

The collection of voluntary contributions

For the tabernacle Ex 36:3 *See also* Nu 7:2–3,84–88

For the temple 1Ch 29:1–9

For the rebuilding of the temple Ezr 1:4

For the teaching ministry of the church Gal 6:6 *See also* Lk 8:1–3; Php 4:15–16; 1Ti 5:17–18

For the relief of the poor Ro 15:26 ; 1Co 16:1 *See also* Ac 2:45; 4:34–35; 11:29–30

The aim of collections

To share burdens equally 2Co 8:13–15

To supply people's needs 2Co 9:12

To arouse thanksgiving 2Co 9:12–15

The right attitude to collections

Generosity Ex 36:4–6; 2Co 8:11; 9:6

Cheerfulness 2Co 9:7

Discipline 1Co 16:2–4

Humility Mt 6:2–4

A willing spirit 2Co 8:12

A sacrificial spirit Mk 12:41–44 pp Lk 21:1–4; 2Co 8:1–4

The faithful administration of collections

2Ki 22:7; Ac 11:30; 2Co 8:19–21

See also

5449 poverty,	8260 generosity
remedies	8434 giving
5576 tax collectors	8488 tithing
5577 taxation	

7915

confirmation

The act of publicly affirming something or someone, usually with a view to declaring trustworthiness. God confirmed his covenants, oaths and promises to emphasise his intention to fulfil them and he confirms the gospel to demonstrate its truthfulness.

Confirmation of covenants

Dt 4:31 *See also* Ge 17:1–22; Dt 8:18; 2Ki 23:3; 1Ch 16:17; Ps 105:10; Da 9:26–27

Confirmation of oaths

Ps 119:106 *See also* Ge 26:1–5

Confirmation of promises

Ro 15:8 *See also* Dt 29:12–13; 2Ch 1:9; Heb 6:17

Confirmation of the gospel

Mk 16:20 *See also* Ac 14:3; 1Co 1:4–6; Php 1:7; Heb 2:3

Confirmation of wisdom

Job 28:25–28

Confirmation of vows

See also

Nu 30:1–16 *A vow made by a woman could be either confirmed or nullified by her father or husband.*

Confirmation of a witness's testimony

Dt 19:15 *Evidence accepted in court required confirmation by more than one witness. See also* 1Ki 1:11–14; Mk 14:56–59 *The proper judicial procedure was not followed at the trial of Jesus Christ;* Ro 9:1–4 *Paul here invokes the Holy Spirit as a witness;* Heb 6:16

Confirmation of letters

Ac 15:27 *This constituted verification of the authenticity of a letter which could easily have been forged or tampered with. See also* Est 9:29–32

Confirmation of office or position

1Sa 11:15

See also

1345 covenant	5471 proof
1448 signs	5623 witnesses,
2422 gospel,	legal
confirmation	5741 vows
5391 letters	8634 amen
5429 oaths	8751 false witness
5466 promises	

7918

excommunication

The last but reversible step in church discipline, resulting in exclusion from the fellowship of believers. The grounds that Scripture suggests for excommunication include public sin and immorality.

Jesus Christ authorises the church to excommunicate a sinning brother

Mt 18:15–18 *The binding of sinners is thought to refer to their exclusion from God's people, and loosing, to their restoration after repentance (compare Mt 16:19).*

Paul exhorts the Corinthian church to excommunicate an immoral brother

1Co 5:1–6 *By "hand this man over to Satan" (see also 1Ti 1:20) Paul means to expel him, by putting him out into the devil's territory, in the hope that being officially ostracised, he might repent and forsake his wicked way. Such discipline was necessary not only for the reclaiming of the sinner but also for the safety and purity of the church (verse 6). See also* 1Co 5:11–13

Excommunicated offenders who repent are to be lovingly restored to fellowship

2Co 2:5–11 *This passage probably refers to the offender mentioned in 1Corinthians chapter 5.*

See also

6040 sinners	8230 discipline
6112 banishment	8341 separation
7020 church, the	

7921

fellowship

Association based upon the sharing of something in common. Believers have fellowship with one another on the basis of their common fellowship with God, their participation in the blessings of the gospel and their common task of mission. True fellowship is demonstrated in concern for, and practical commitment to, one another.

7922

fellowship, with God

The relationship with God, disrupted by sin yet established through Jesus Christ, which provides the only proper basis for true human fellowship. God's desire for fellowship with humanity is made known through his calling of a people to be his own and to reflect his holiness and love.

God's fellowship with his people is shown by his presence

God's fellowship with Israel Lev 26:12 *See also* Ex 33:14; Isa 63:9; Hag 1:13

God's presence in the tabernacle Ex 25:8 *See also* Ex 29:45–46; 40:34–36; Lev 26:11; Dt 12:11

God's presence in the temple 1Ki 6:12–13 *See also* 1Ki 8:29 pp 2Ch 6:20; 2Ch 7:1–2; Isa 6:1

God's presence in the new Jerusalem Zec 2:10–13 *See also* Eze 37:26–28; 43:4–7; 48:35; Rev 21:3

The church's fellowship with God

Fellowship with the Father, Son and Holy Spirit Jn 14:23 *See also* Jn 14:7,16–17 *fellowship with the Spirit*

Fellowship is made possible through Jesus Christ Eph 2:18–19 *See also* Ro 5:10; 2Co 5:18–19; Col 1:20–22; Heb 10:19–22

Fellowship with Jesus Christ 1Co 1:9 *See also* Mt 28:20 *Jesus Christ's presence with his disciples*; Jn 15:4–5 *abiding in Christ*; Ro 6:4–5 *united with Christ in his death and resurrection*; 1Co 10:15–16 *communion with Christ at the Lord's Supper*; Php 3:10 *sharing in Christ's sufferings*

Fellowship with God is inseparable from fellowship with one another 1Jn 1:3 *See also* Mt 18:20; Mk 9:37; Jn 17:21; 2Co 13:11

The demands of fellowship with God

Holiness Lev 20:26; 2Co 6:14–18 *See also* Ex 34:12–14; Ezr 6:21; 1Co 5:11; Eph 5:8–11; Jas 4:4

Obedience to God's will 1Jn 3:24 *See also* Isa 57:15; Mt 12:49–50 pp Mk 3:34–35 pp Lk 8:21; Jn 14:21

Sin separates people from fellowship with God

Isa 59:2; 1Jn 1:5–6 *See also* Ge 3:8; Eze 39:23

Examples of fellowship with God

Ge 5:22 *Enoch*; Ge 6:9 *Noah*; 2Ch 20:7 *Abraham*
Moses: Ex 33:11; Nu 12:3
Jos 1:9 *Joshua*; Mal 2:6 *Levi*

See also

1346 covenants	8122 friendship with
1510 Trinity, the	God
5895 intimacy	8266 holiness
6020 sin	8604 prayer,
6652 forgiveness	response to
6716 reconciliation	God
7364 fellowship	9414 heaven,
offering	community of
8102 abiding in	redeemed
Christ	

7923
fellowship, in the gospel

A mutual participation in the blessings of God's grace. Believers are united with one another on the basis of their common reception of the benefits of salvation.

Fellowship and the community of God's people

God calls out a community of people, for fellowship with himself Dt 7:6 *See also* Ex 19:5–6; 1Pe 2:5,9–11

God will bless a people united in fellowship Mt 18:19–20; 2Ch 7:14; Jer 31:23–25; 1Co 11:29–34 *Wrong relationships between God's people hinder the flow of his blessing.*

God will restore fellowship with his scattered people Mic 2:12 *See also* Isa 11:12–13; Jer 3:18; 31:1; 50:4–5

Sharing in God's grace

Fellowship in a common blessing Ps 106:4–5 *See also* Nu 10:32; Jos 22:19

Fellowship in a common salvation Jude 3 *See also* 1Co 9:23 *sharing in the blessings of the gospel*; Php 1:7 *sharing in God's grace*; Tit 1:4 *sharing a common faith*; Heb 3:1 *sharing a common calling*; 1Pe 5:1 *sharing a common hope*; 2Pe 1:4 *sharing the divine nature*; 1Jn 1:7 *sharing in sanctification*

Fellowship in a common inheritance Col 1:12 *See also* Ro 8:17; 1Pe 3:7

Fellowship in God's family Heb 2:11 *See also* Mal 2:10; Mt 6:9 pp Lk 11:2 *the family prayer in which believers together address God as Father*; Mt 12:49–50 pp Mk 3:34–35 pp Lk 8:21; Mt 23:8–9

Fellowship between Jew and Gentile Eph 3:6 *See also* Ro 11:17; 15:27; Eph 2:16–18

Fellowship in holding a common truth

2Th 2:15 *See also* Ps 119:63; 1Co 11:2; 15:2–3; 2Ti 2:2; 3:14; Tit 2:15

Fellowship in union with Christ

1Co 10:16–17; Eph 2:19–22 *See also* Ro 12:5; 1Co 12:12,27; Eph 4:4–5; Col 1:15; 1Pe 2:4–5

Fellowship through the Holy Spirit

1Co 12:13 *See also* Eze 36:27–28; 2Co 13:14; Eph 4:3; Php 2:1

See also

1460 truth	6744 sanctification
3215 Holy Spirit &	6754 union with
peace	Christ
4476 meals	7140 people of God
5703 inheritance	7206 community
6212 participation	7903 baptism
6510 salvation	7933 Lord's Supper

7924
fellowship, in Christian service

Partnership in a common enterprise. God's people are called to work together especially in the task of mission, to recognise one another's gifts and to give support to one another's ministries.

Fellowship in mission
Partnership in preaching the gospel Gal 2:9 *See also* Mk 10:7; Lk 10:1–2; Php 1:5

Supporting the work of others Ac 14:26 ; Php 4:14–16 *The Philippians share in Paul's work through their giving.*

See also Ac 13:2–3; 15:40; 2Co 11:9; 3Jn 5–8

Standing together in adversity Heb 10:32–34 *See also* 2Co 1:7; Php 1:27–30; 4:14; Heb 11:25

Fellowship between Paul and his co-workers Php 4:3
Barnabas: Ac 11:26–30; 13:42–50; 14:1–23; 15:22–29
Ro 16:3 *Priscilla and Aquila*; Ro 16:9 *Urbanus*; Ro 16:21 *Timothy*; 2Co 8:23 *Titus*; Php 2:25 *Epaphroditus*; Phm 1 *Philemon*; Phm 24 *Mark, Aristarchus, Demas and Luke*

In fellowship different gifts are combined for effective service
1Co 12:12 *See also* 1Co 12:4–6

Spiritual gifts are given to all to share 1Co 12:7 *See also* Ro 12:4–8; 1Co 12:14–20; 1Pe 4:10

Recognising one another's gifts 1Co 12:21–26

Accepting one another's ministries Gal 2:7–8 *See also* 1Co 12:27–31; 16:15–18; 2Pe 3:15–16

Examples of sharing in different roles Ne 4:16–22 ; 1Co 3:5–8 *See also* Ex 4:15–16; 17:10–13; 1Co 12:8–11

Examples of working together in fellowship
Ecc 4:9–12 *See also* Dt 3:18–20 *the Reubenites and the Gadites join with the rest of Israel to conquer Canaan*; Jdg 20:11 *all Israel unites against Gibeah*; Ezr 3:8–10 *Those returning from exile work together to rebuild the temple*; Ne 4:6 *The Israelites work together to rebuild the walls of Jerusalem*; Lk 5:7–10 *Peter and Andrew, James and John are business partners.*

See also

2420 gospel	7966 spiritual gifts
4696 yoke	8342 servanthood
5205 alliance	8424 evangelism
5886 individualism	8495 witnessing
7953 mission of	8794 persecution
church	

7925
fellowship, among believers

The fellowship that believers share as a result of their common union with God through Jesus Christ is expressed in life together. It is evident in worship together, in a love for one another which reflects God's own love and in a practical commitment to one another which is demonstrated in concern for the weak and readiness to share with the poor and needy.

Sharing in the fellowship of God's love
1Jn 4:10–12 *See also* Jn 13:34; 15:12; Eph 5:1–2; 1Jn 3:10

Sharing in the fellowship of a common devotional life
Ac 2:42

Worshipping together Ps 55:14 *See also* Ps 42:4; 1Co 14:26; Eph 5:19; Col 3:16

Praying together Ac 1:14 *See also* Ac 4:24; 12:12; Jas 5:16

Breaking bread together
1Co 10:16–17; 2Pe 2:13; Jude 12 *Love feasts accompanied the Lord's Supper though these were open to abuse.*

True fellowship means sharing with those in need
Heb 13:16 *See also* Ac 20:34–35; Eph 4:28

Showing hospitality Ro 12:13 *See also* Isa 58:7; Heb 13:1–2; 1Pe 4:9; 3Jn 8

Sharing money and possessions
Dt 15:10–11; Ac 2:44–45 *See also* Dt 10:18–19 *God's people are to reflect his concern for the needy in society;* Mt 25:35–36; Lk 3:11; Ac 4:32–35; 2Co 8:13–15; 1Ti 6:17–18; Jas 1:27; 2:15–16

Examples of sharing with the needy
Job 31:16–20 *Job's compassion for the needy;* Ac 6:1 *the daily distribution to widows;* Ac 9:36 *Tabitha's concern for the poor*
The collection for believers in Judea:
Ac 11:29–30; Ro 15:26; 2Co 8:3–4

Strengthening one another in fellowship together
Bearing with the weak Gal 6:1–2 *See also* Isa 42:3; Ro 14:1; 15:1; 1Th 5:14

Strengthening the weak Isa 35:3–4 *See also* Job 4:3–4

Encouraging one another
Heb 10:24–25 *See also* 1Sa 23:16; Ro 1:12; 1Th 5:11; Heb 13:3

Putting the needs of others first
Ro 15:2 *See also* 1Co 10:24,32–33

True fellowship means living in harmony
1Pe 3:8 *See also* Ro 12:16; Eph 4:2–3; Php 2:1–4; Col 3:12–14

Showing equal concern for all
Ac 10:34; 1Co 12:25; Jas 2:1–4

Examples of fellowship Nu 10:31–32 *Moses and Hobab;* 1Sa 18:3 *David and Jonathan;* 2Ki 10:15–16 *Jehu and Jehonadab*

Failure to exhibit true fellowship
1Sa 30:22 *Troublemakers in David's army are unwilling to share the spoils;* 1Co 1:11–12 *factions within the church at Corinth;* 1Co 11:17–22 *Selfishness at love feasts humiliates the poor.*

See also

3035 Holy Spirit, presence of	7025 church, unity
5566 suffering, encouragement, ments in	7028 church, life of
5680 family	7030 unity
5690 friends	8298 love for one another
6705 peace, experience	8304 loyalty
	8602 prayer
	8622 worship

hymn

Poetry sung to the praise of God and for the mutual encouragement of believers. Hymns and songs are not clearly distinguished in Scripture,

but the NT contains examples of possible early Christian hymns.

Hymns are sung to the praise of God's name
Ps 40:3 ; Ro 15:8–11 *Because of Jesus Christ the Gentiles are now called upon to join with God's people in praising God. See also* Dt 32:43; 2Sa 22:50; Ps 18:49; 117:1; Heb 2:12

Christians are to sing hymns together for mutual encouragement
1Co 14:26 *See also* Eph 5:19; Col 3:16 *"Psalms" refers to the OT psalms (see Lk 20:42; 24:44; Ac 1:20; 13:33) some of which may have been set to music by Christians. "Psalm" could also describe a song newly composed for Christian worship (see 1Co 14:26 where "hymn" translates Greek "psalmos").*

Examples of singing hymns
By Jesus Christ and his disciples
Mt 26:30 pp Mk 14:26

By Paul and Silas in prison Ac 16:25

Examples of hymns
The Benedictus: Zechariah's song of thanksgiving at the birth of his son, John the Baptist Lk 1:68–79

The Magnificat: Mary's song of praise as the future mother of the Lord Lk 1:46–55

The Nunc Dimittis: Simeon's response to seeing the child Jesus Lk 2:29–32

Other examples of possible early Christian hymns Ro 11:33–36; Eph 5:14; Php 2:6–11; Col 1:15–20; 1Ti 3:16

See also

7960 singing	8627 worship, elements
7963 song	
8414 encouragement	8646 doxology
8440 glorifying God	8664 praise
8609 prayer as praise & thanksgiving	

Lord's Day, the

As well as keeping the Sabbath, the first Christians assembled together on the first day of the week to commemorate Jesus Christ's resurrection through the Lord's Supper. The Lord's Day quickly became the focal point of the Christian week, eventually assuming the characteristics of the Jewish Sabbath, namely worship and rest.

The disciples continued to observe the Sabbath
Lk 23:56 *See also* Ac 13:14,42; 16:13; 17:2; 18:4

The Lord's Day commemorated Jesus Christ's resurrection
The resurrection took place on the first day of the week Mk 16:9 *See also* Mt 28:1–7 pp Mk 16:1–7 pp Lk 24:1–6 pp Jn 20:1

The disciples assembled together on the first day of the week Ac 20:7 *See also* Jn 20:19–20,24–26

The Lord's Day took over the role of the Sabbath
1Co 16:2 *See also* Rev 1:10

See also

2560 Christ, resurrection	7428 Sabbath
	7933 Lord's Supper

Lord's Supper

The commemoration and remembrance of Jesus Christ's last supper, and all the benefits that result to believers. Other terms have been used subsequently by Christians, including "Communion" and "Eucharist".

Terms for the Lord's Supper in the NT
Ac 2:42 *"breaking of bread" could mean both eating together and also celebrating the Lord's Supper;* 1Co 10:16 *The Greek word "koinonia", here translated "participation", is traditionally translated "communion": hence the term "Holy Communion";* 1Co 11:20 *the Lord's Supper;* 1Co 11:24 *Underlying "had given thanks" is the Greek "eucharisteo", from which comes the term "Eucharist".*

Jesus Christ's institution of the Lord's Supper
1Co 11:23–25 pp Mt 26:26–28 pp Mk 14:22–24 pp Lk 22:17–20

Celebrating the Lord's Supper in the NT
As part of an ordinary meal 1Co 11:21 *The church was not necessarily wrong to include the sacrament in an ordinary meal; this should have been conducted in a charitable way.*

On the Lord's day Ac 20:7 *See also* Jn 20:26

The fourfold formula for breaking bread: taking, giving thanks, breaking, giving Mt 26:26 pp Mk 14:22 pp Lk 22:19 *See also* Lk 24:30; Jn 6:11; 1Co 11:24

The sharing of the cup 1Co 11:25 pp Mt 26:27–28 pp Mk 14:23–24 pp Lk 22:20

Themes connected with the Lord's Supper
The Passover 1Co 5:7–8 *See also* Jn 11:50 *Caiaphas' words may have an unintended Passover significance;* Jn 13:1; 19:14,33,36; Ex 12:46; Nu 9:12

The new covenant 1Co 11:25 pp Mt 26:27–28 pp Mk 14:23–24 pp Lk 22:20 *The reference to the (new) covenant implies a personal relationship with God and sins forgiven.*

Remembrance 1Co 11:24 pp Lk 22:19

Thanksgiving, fellowship and unity 1Co 10:16 *See also* Mt 26:26–27 pp Mk 14:22–23 pp Lk 22:19; 1Co 11:20–21

The Lord's return 1Co 11:26 *See also* Mt 26:29 pp Mk 14:25 pp Lk 22:16; 1Co 16:22; Rev 22:20

Separation from sin 1Co 10:21 *Paul is referring to feasts in heathen temples. See also* 1Co 11:27–32

A foretaste of heaven Mt 26:29 pp Mk 14:25

See also

1352 covenant, the new	8341 separation
2565 Christ, second coming	8352 thankfulness
6652 forgiveness	8477 self-examination
7030 unity	8670 remembering
7921 fellowship	9150 Messianic banquet
7936 love feast	9410 heaven

7936

love feast

The first Christians generally celebrated the Lord's Supper with the accompaniment of a meal, called the "agape" or "love feast".

OT antecedents of the love feast
The Passover meal Ex 12:3–11,15–16; Mt 26:17–18 pp Mk 14:12–15 pp Lk 22:7–12; 1Co 11:23–25

Other festive occasions Dt 12:7; Ne 8:10

The NT practice of the love feast
It was linked with the Lord's Supper Ac 2:46 *See also* Ac 20:7; 1Co 11:17–34

The name "love feasts" Jude 12 *See also* 2Pe 2:13 fn; Jn 13:2,34 *It was at the Last Supper that Jesus Christ gave his new commandment to his disciples to love one another as he had loved them.*

The charitable distribution of food Ac 6:1

Abuses of the love feast
Selfishness, indulgence and ostentation 1Co 11:20–22 *See also* 1Co 11:33–34

Licentiousness 2Pe 2:13

Ungodly participants, especially false teachers Jude 4,12 *See also* 2Pe 2:1,13

The heavenly love feast
Foretold by Jesus Christ Mt 26:29 pp Mk 14:25

The marriage supper of the Lamb
Rev 19:9 *See also* Isa 25:6; Mt 22:2–14 *The parable of the marriage supper indicates the prerequisites for attendance at the supper.*

See also

4435 drinking	7406 Passover
4438 eating	7921 fellowship
5385 leisure	7933 Lord's Supper
5946 sensitivity	8821 self-indulgence
7354 feasts and festivals	

7939

ministry

Service of a general, as well as a religious, nature. In its broadest sense ministry refers to service rendered to God or to people. Its more restricted sense refers to the

official service of individuals, specially set aside by the church.

7940

ministry, of Jesus Christ

See 2300 Jesus Christ, ministry and work of

7941

ministry, of Holy Spirit

See 3200 Holy Spirit, ministry and work of

7942

ministry, nature of

All creatures owe their Creator a ministry of service to him and to humanity. The example and teaching of Jesus Christ illustrate this.

All human beings owe a ministry of service to God
The debt owed by the creature to the Creator Ro 1:25

The service of the nations and their rulers Ps 148:7–11 *See also* Jer 3:17; Joel 3:1–2; Rev 15:4

Examples of the service of rulers
Ezr 1:1–2 Cyrus of Persia Nebuchadnezzar: Jer 25:9; 27:6; 43:10 *The Roman emperor and other authorities:* Ro 13:4,6; 1Pe 2:13–14

The ministry of the people of God
In the OT Ex 19:6 *See also* Isa 61:6

In the NT 1Pe 2:5,9 *See also* Rev 1:6; 20:6 *resurrected martyrs*

The ministry of priests, kings and prophets in the OT
The priests
Aaron: Ex 28:35; Nu 18:2 Dt 17:12
The Levites: 1Ch 15:2; Jer 33:22 Ezr 2:63; Heb 9:6; 13:10

The rulers
David: 2Sa 3:18; Ps 78:70; Lk 1:69; Ac 4:25
Hag 2:23 *Zerubbabel, governor of Judah*

The prophets
Moses: Nu 12:7–8; Jos 12:6; 2Co 3:7; Heb 3:5
1Sa 2:18 the young Samuel Elijah: 2Ki 9:36; 10:10
1Ch 25:1; Isa 20:3 *Isaiah;* Isa 42:1–4; Jer 7:25; 25:4; 1Pe 1:12; Rev 10:7; 11:18

The ministry of those specially set aside by the church
1Co 12:28; 1Ti 3:10 *Deacons;* Tit 1:5 *Elders;* 1Pe 5:2 *Overseers;* Eph 4:11

Jesus Christ fulfils the OT understanding of ministry
His ministry as servant Mt 12:18 *See also* Isa 42:1; Mt 20:28 pp Mk 10:45; Ac 3:13,26; 4:27,30

His ministry as shepherd, teacher and prophet Jn 10:11; 13:13; Ac 3:22

His ministry as priest Heb 6:20 *See also* Heb 8:6

His ministry as king Jn 18:37

NT ministry follows the pattern of Jesus Christ
In servanthood Mt 20:26–28 pp Mk 10:43–45 pp Lk 22:26–27 *See also* Mt 23:11 pp Mk 10:43

In teaching Mt 28:20

In shepherding Jn 21:15–17

In priesthood by self-sacrifice and intercession in prayer Php 2:17; 1Ti 2:1 *See also* 1Pe 2:5

Jesus Christ's servants can expect the same response that he received Jn 15:20

The ministry of angels
Angels are both ministers to God's people and fellow-servants with them:
Heb 1:7,14; Rev 19:10; 22:9

See also

2306 Christ, high priest	5368 kingship
2312 Christ as king	5520 servants
2318 Christ as prophet	7160 servants of the Lord
2327 Christ as servant	7412 priesthood
2330 Christ as shepherd	7446 slavery
	7772 prophets
	8342 servanthood

7943

ministry, in the church

The regular ministry of officially appointed or recognised ministers is a particular instance of the duty and call of all God's people.

The responsibilities of those in recognised ministry
As shepherds Ac 20:28 *See also* 1Pe 5:2

As watchmen Heb 13:17 *See also* Ro 16:17; Php 3:2

As teachers 1Ti 3:2 *See also* 2Ti 2:2,24

As examples 1Ti 4:16 *See also* Ac 20:28; 1Pe 5:3

What believers owe to those with recognised ministries
Respect 1Th 5:12–13 *See also* Php 2:29; 1Ti 5:17

Obedience Heb 13:17 *See also* 1Co 16:15–16

Support 1Co 9:14 *Despite Jesus Christ's command, Paul did not claim his rights in this matter, but supported himself as a tentmaker. See also* Lk 10:7; Gal 6:6; 1Ti 5:18; Dt 25:4

Prayer Ro 15:30 *See also* Eph 6:19; Php 1:19; 1Th 5:25; Heb 13:18

Hospitality Php 2:29–30 *See also* Gal 4:14

Imitation Heb 13:7

Recognised ministers should encourage the ministries of other believers
Col 4:17 *See also* Ro 12:6–8; 1Co 12:4–11 *The Holy Spirit allocates gifts and enables ministries. No individual has all the gifts; ministry is shared and mutual;* Eph 4:7,11–13

The motivation of ministry is mutual love
Gal 5:13 *See also* Ro 12:10; 13:8;

Col 3:12–14; 1Th 3:12; Heb 13:1;
1Pe 1:22; 1Jn 3:23

How love is expressed in mutual ministry

In humility Eph 4:2 *See also* Ro 12:10,16;
Gal 5:26; 1Pe 5:5

In patience 1Th 5:14 *See also* Jas 5:9

In acceptance and forbearance
Ro 15:7 *See also* Col 3:13

**In kindness, compassion and
forgiveness** Eph 4:32 *See also* Col 3:13;
1Th 5:15

In burden-bearing Gal 6:2

In encouragement 1Th 5:11 *See also*
Heb 3:13; 10:24–25

In teaching and admonition Col 3:16
See also Ro 15:14; Eph 5:19; 1Th 5:14

In prayer and confession of sin Jas 5:16

In hospitality 1Pe 4:9

See also

3254 Holy Spirit, fruit of	7745 ordination
3275 Holy Spirit in the church	7924 fellowship in service
6652 forgiveness	7966 spiritual gifts
7020 church, the	8292 love
7622 disciples, characteristics	8414 encouragement
7733 leaders	8445 hospitality

7944
ministry, qualifications for

God, who calls his people to
minister, also equips his people. The
chief qualifications are a response to
God's call, faithfulness, godliness
and Christlikeness.

God calls people to minister

**Qualification is by call, not gifting or
achievement** Dt 7:7–8 *See also* Dt 9:4–5

**God calls those who the world regards
as weak or foolish** 1Co 1:27–29

**Feelings of inadequacy to God's call
are common** Ex 3:11 *Moses*; Jdg 6:15
Gideon; 1Sa 9:21 *Saul*; 1Sa 18:18 *David*;
1Ki 3:7 *Solomon*; Isa 6:5 *Isaiah*; Jer 1:6
Jeremiah

Responding to God's call to minister

Readiness and availability 1Sa 3:10;
Isa 6:8

**Faith, rather than natural talent or
moral perfection, is required**
Heb 11:1–2 *See also* Ge 27:19–24 *Jacob
was a deceiver*; Nu 27:12–14 *Moses and
Aaron disobeyed God.*
David committed adultery and murder:
2Sa 11:4,14–15
1Ki 11:9–13 *Solomon disobeyed God's
command.*

NT ministers are recognised by call rather than their achievement

The Twelve Mt 10:1–4 pp Mk 3:14–19
pp Lk 6:12–16 *The Twelve, including
Peter and Judas, failed Jesus Christ at
critical times.*

Paul Ac 9:15; 26:6; 2Co 4:7–12; 12:7
*Though greatly gifted, Paul was kept
humble by his sense of unworthiness,*

---

*difficulties and disappointments and his
"thorn in the flesh"; 1Ti 1:16*

Ministry in the NT is described as service

Serving God Ro 1:9; Jas 1:1

Serving Jesus Christ Ro 1:1; Jude 1;
Rev 1:1

Serving the gospel Eph 3:7; Col 1:23

Serving the church Ro 15:31; 16:1;
1Co 16:15; 2Co 9:1; Eph 6:21;
Col 1:7,25

Ministry is described in terms of its source, content or nature

Its source
It is of the Spirit: 2Co 3:6,8
2Co 4:1 *It is from God.*

Its content Ac 6:2–4 *the word of God*;
2Co 5:18 *reconciliation*

Its nature
Apostolic: Ac 1:25; Gal 2:8
Ro 15:16 *priestly*

Various ministries are equally linked by qualifications of character

Ac 1:21 *the replacement for Judas*; Ac 6:3
the Seven
Overseers: 1Ti 3:2–7; Tit 1:7–9
1Ti 3:8–13 *deacons*; 1Ti 6:11 *Timothy*

The personal qualifications for ministry

Faithfulness 1Ti 6:11–14 *Timothy*;
2Ti 4:7 *Paul's claim for his own ministry
"faithful" is the sole description of the
ministries of Epaphras and Tychicus:*
Col 1:7; 4:7

Godliness Ac 8:21 *Simon was not right
with God.*
Timothy: 1Ti 6:11,20–21

Christlikeness Ac 1:21–22 *The
replacement apostle for Judas had to have
been with Jesus Christ from the beginning.*

See also

5932 response	8206 Christlikeness
6620 calling	8248 faithfulness
7720 elders in the church	8265 godliness
8020 faith	8420 equipping

7948
mission

Specific actions that bear witness to
the good news of what God has done
for his people. Israel, Jesus Christ and
the church all in their different ways
bear witness to the saving acts of
God in history. Christian mission is
empowered by the Holy Spirit.

7949
mission, of Israel

God chose Israel to be his own
people, and bring the good news of
his salvation to the world. God's
mission through Israel is fulfilled in
the mission of his servant and
continues through the mission of
the church.

Israel as a channel of God's blessing

**Blessings for all people through
Abraham** Ge 18:18 *See also* Ge 12:2–3;
22:18; 26:4 *God's promise repeated to
Isaac*; Ge 28:13–14 *God's promise
repeated to Jacob*; Ac 3:25; Gal 3:8

Israel's call to be a nation of priests
Ex 19:5–6 *See also* Isa 61:6

God's desire to display his glory

God's glory is to fill the earth Hab 2:14
See also Nu 14:21; Ps 72:18–19; Isa 6:3

God's people display his glory
Isa 60:1–3 *See also* Isa 46:13; 49:3; 55:5

**God's people declare his glory among
the nations** Ps 96:3 *See also* Ps 57:9;
96:10; 105:1–2 pp 1Ch 16:8–9;
Ps 145:11–12

The nations will be drawn to God's people

**In recognition of God's presence
among his people** Zec 8:20–23 *See also*
1Ki 10:1 pp 2Ch 9:1; Isa 45:14;
Jer 16:19; Eze 37:27–28; 39:7

**To Jerusalem as the centre of
universal worship** Isa 2:2–4
pp Mic 4:1–3 *See also* Isa 11:9; 25:6–8;
27:13; 56:6–8; Zec 14:16

God made known through his mighty acts

God's deliverance of Israel Ex 7:5 *See
also* Ps 98:1–3; 102:15–16; Isa 49:26;
Eze 38:23

God's action on behalf of Israel
Ex 34:10 *See also* Ex 8:19; Jos 4:24;
1Ki 8:41–43 pp 2Ch 6:32–33;
Ps 67:1–4; 126:2

God's renewal of Israel Eze 36:23 *See
also* Eze 20:40–41; 28:24–25; 38:16

Israel as a witness to other nations

God's people sent to other nations
Isa 66:19 *See also* 1Ki 17:9; Jnh 1:2; 3:2;
Mt 23:15

**Examples of God's people bearing
witness to him** Ge 41:16 *Joseph*;
Ex 7:16–17 *Moses and Aaron*; 2Ki 5:3
Naaman's servant girl; Da 2:44–47
Daniel; Da 3:16–18 *Shadrach, Meshach
and Abednego*

Israel's failure in mission

Isa 26:18 *See also* Eze 36:20–21

The fulfilment of God's mission through Israel

The mission of God's Messiah
Isa 11:10 *See also* Ro 15:12; Ps 72:17
*God's promise to Abraham is fulfilled
through the Messianic king*; Gal 3:16

The mission of God's servant Isa 49:6
See also Isa 42:1–6; 52:15

The mission of the church 1Pe 2:9 *See
also* Ro 15:16

See also

1045 God, glory of	5075 Abraham
1190 glory	5622 witnesses
1403 God, revelation	7140 people of God
2230 Messiah, coming of	7412 priesthood
2327 Christ as servant	7510 Gentiles

7950
mission, of Jesus Christ

Jesus Christ came to reveal God, to announce the coming of God's kingdom and to redeem a fallen humanity through his death on the cross. Though he came first to the Jews, the scope of Christ's mission includes the whole human race and continues through the Spirit-empowered witness of the church.

Jesus Christ's mission originated with God
It was purposed by God 1Pe 1:18–20 *See also* Ac 2:23; Eph 1:4–5

The Father sent the Son Gal 4:4–5 *See also* Jn 5:37–38; 7:29; 8:42; 10:36; 17:8; 1Jn 4:14

Jesus Christ came in willing obedience to the Father Jn 6:38; Php 2:5–8

Jesus Christ's mission was motivated by God's love Jn 3:16 *See also* Ro 5:8; 1Jn 4:10

Jesus Christ's mission was to make God known
He reveals God in his own person Jn 1:18 *See also* Jn 14:9; 17:26; Col 1:15; Heb 1:1–3

He reveals God through his teaching Jn 18:37 *See also* Mt 7:28–29; Jn 3:11–13

Jesus Christ's mission was to announce God's kingdom
Lk 4:43 *See also* Mt 4:17; Mk 1:14–15; Mt 12:28 pp Lk 11:20 *Jesus Christ's miracles reveal the presence of God's kingdom.*

Jesus Christ's mission was to redeem humanity
He came to seek and save the lost Lk 19:10 *See also* Lk 15:1–10

He came to save from sin Mt 1:21 *See also* Ro 3:25–26; 1Ti 1:15

He came to break the devil's power 1Jn 3:8 *See also* Ge 3:15; Jn 12:31; Heb 2:14–15

He came to bring eternal life Jn 10:10 *See also* Jn 6:38–40; 17:2–3

He came to give access to God Eph 2:18; 3:12; Heb 10:19–20

He came to restore a fallen humanity Ro 5:17–18; 1Co 15:21–22

Jesus Christ's mission was to establish the church
Mt 16:18 *See also* Eph 2:17–19; 5:25–27; 1Pe 2:4–5,9–10

The scope of Jesus Christ's mission
Jesus Christ came first to Israel Mt 10:5–6; 15:24; Jn 1:11

Jesus Christ's mission extends to all peoples Isa 49:6; Mt 8:11; Jn 10:16; Mt 8:10 pp Lk 7:9 *Jesus Christ commends the faith of a Roman centurion*; Mt 15:28 pp Mk 7:29 *Jesus Christ grants the request of a Canaanite woman*; Ac 1:8 *Jesus Christ sends his disciples out into the whole world*; Ac 26:17–18 *Paul's commission to go to the Gentiles is received directly from Jesus Christ.*

Jesus Christ's mission made the cross necessary
Mt 20:28 pp Mk 10:45 *See also* Mt 16:21 pp Mk 8:31 pp Lk 9:22; Lk 12:50; Col 2:14–15; Heb 12:2

Jesus Christ's mission will be completed at his return
1Jn 3:2 *See also* Mt 24:31 pp Mk 13:27; Col 3:4; 1Th 4:16–17

Jesus Christ's mission continues through the church
Jn 20:21–22 *See also* Mt 28:18–20; Jn 15:26–27

See also

2321 Christ as redeemer	2410 cross, the
2324 Christ as Saviour	2525 Christ, cross of
2354 Christ, mission	6510 salvation
2363 Christ, preaching & teaching	6720 redemption
2376 kingdom of God, coming	7024 church, nature of
	8495 witnessing

7951
mission, of Holy Spirit
See 3257 Holy Spirit, gift of

7952
mission, and Holy Spirit
See 3212 Holy Spirit, and mission

7953
mission, of the church

The continuation of Jesus Christ's mission through his followers. Believers are empowered by the Holy Spirit and sent out by Christ to bear witness to him and to preach, heal, teach, baptise and make disciples of all peoples.

The power and authority of the church's mission
Believers are sent out by Jesus Christ Jn 15:16 *See also* Mt 9:37–38; Lk 10:1–3; Jn 4:36–38

Believers are given authority by Jesus Christ Lk 9:1 *See also* Mt 10:1; 28:18; Mk 6:7; 16:17–18; Lk 10:17–19

Believers continue Jesus Christ's mission Jn 20:21 *See also* Jn 17:18

Believers are empowered by the Holy Spirit Ac 1:8 *See also* Lk 24:49; Jn 20:22; Ac 4:31; Heb 2:4

The task of the church in mission
Making disciples Mt 28:19–20 *See also* Ac 2:41–42; 14:15; 16:14–15; 18:8; Ro 10:14–15; 1Jn 1:2–3

Preaching and healing Lk 9:2 *See also* Mt 10:7–8; Mk 16:20; Lk 9:6

Proclaiming the gospel Ac 20:24 *See also* Ac 8:40; Ro 1:9; 15:20; 2Ti 1:11

Bearing witness to Jesus Christ Ac 5:30–32 *See also* Lk 24:48; Jn 15:26–27; Ac 4:20

Bringing honour to God Eph 3:10–11 *See also* Jn 15:8; 1Pe 2:12

The universal scope of the church's mission
Lk 24:47 *See also* Mt 24:14 pp Mk 13:10; 16:15

The church reaching out in mission
To the Jews Mt 10:5–6 *The disiples' mission began with the Jews. See also* Mt 10:9–15 pp Mk 6:8–11 pp Lk 9:3–5; pp Lk 10:4–12; Ac 11:19 *The scattered believers at first preached only to Jews.*

To the Samaritans Ac 8:4–8 *See also* Ac 8:14–17, 25

To the Gentiles *Paul as the apostle to the Gentiles:* Ac 9:15; Ro 11:13; 15:16 Ac 10:34–35 *Peter preaches to Cornelius and his family*; Ac 11:20–21 *Scattered believers preach to the Gentiles*; Ac 13:1–3 *Paul begins his first missionary journey (with Barnabas)*; Ac 15:40–41 *Paul begins his second missionary journey (with Silas)*; Ac 16:9–10 *Paul is called to preach the gospel in Macedonia*; Ac 18:23 *Paul's third missionary journey*; Ac 28:31 *Paul preaches the gospel in Rome.*

Missions undertaken by church officials
Ac 11:22–23 *Barnabas is sent to Antioch to strengthen the new church.*
Paul and Barnabas take gifts to Jerusalem: Ac 11:30; 12:25
Ac 15:22–23 *Judas and Silas are sent to Antioch with a letter from the apostles and elders.*

See also

2012 Christ, authority	7620 disciples
2420 gospel	7724 evangelists
3212 Holy Spirit & mission	7739 missionaries
5333 healing	7754 preaching
5622 witnesses	7903 baptism
7027 church, purpose	8424 evangelism

7957
sacraments

The sacraments of baptism and the Lord's Supper were instituted by Jesus Christ as signs and seals of the covenant. They explain the basis of this covenant and apply its benefits to believers. They replace circumcision and the Passover which were the sacraments of the old covenant.

The sacraments as signs of the new covenant
Baptism Mt 28:19 *Baptism is one sign of being a disciple of Jesus Christ. See also* Ac 2:38,41

The Lord's Supper 1Co 11:23–25 pp Mt 26:26–28 pp Mk 14:22–24 pp Lk 22:17–20 *The new covenant was sealed by the blood of Jesus Christ.*

The sacraments as a participation in the body of Christ
Baptism Gal 3:27 *In the NT baptism*

immediately follows conversion and testifies to the individual's union with Christ. See also Ro 6:3

The Lord's Supper 1Co 10:16–17 *The "body of Christ" is a term which goes beyond Jesus Christ to the church. Those who partake of the bread in this way are declaring their membership of the church. See also* Mt 26:26 pp Mk 14:22 pp Lk 22:19 pp 1Co 11:24; Jn 6:32–35,48 *Jesus Christ likens himself to bread as he is the source of spiritual life and nourishment;* Jn 6:50–58 *The believer who eats the bread of the Lord's Supper is renewing his or her dependence on Jesus Christ for spiritual life.*

The sacraments as a participation in the death of Christ
Baptism Ro 6:3–4 *Through baptism individuals declare that they have applied to themselves the death of Jesus Christ which atones for sin. See also* Ac 2:38; 22:16 *Baptism does not accomplish the cleansing from sin but it is the outward sign that this has taken place by faith;* Ro 6:5–7; Col 2:12; Tit 3:5; 1Pe 3:21

The Lord's Supper 1Co 11:26 *In taking the emblems of Jesus Christ's broken body and shed blood individuals perpetually apply the merits of Christ's death (i.e., forgiveness of sins) to themselves. See also* Mt 26:27–28 pp Mk 14:23–24 pp Lk 22:20 pp 1Co 11:25; Jn 6:53–56; 1Co 10:16

The sacraments of the old covenant
Circumcision Ac 7:8 *Circumcision was the initiation rite under the old covenant. See also* Ge 17:10–14; Ro 2:28–29 *Circumcision was never meant as merely an outward rite. To be effective it required a right attitude of heart;* Ro 4:10–11 *Circumcision was the seal of Abraham's righteousness imputed to him by his faith;* Col 2:11–12 *Circumcision has now been superseded by baptism for the Christian as the rite of initiation.*

The Passover Ex 12:25–27 *The Passover meal was instituted as a regular commemoration of Israel's redemption from slavery in Egypt. See also* Lk 22:15–16 *The death of Jesus Christ is closely associated with the Passover by its timing and meaning. The Lord's Supper has superseded the Passover as the corporate meal commemorating the act of redemption;* 1Co 5:7

See also

1345 covenant	7110 body of Christ
2315 Christ as Lamb	7334 circumcision
2410 cross, the	7404 ordinances
4418 bread	7406 Passover
6754 union with	7903 baptism
Christ	7933 Lord's Supper
7028 church, life of	

and singers were set aside solely for this purpose.

The call to sing praise to God
Ps 33:1–3; 96:1–2 *See also* Ps 5:11; 9:11; 30:4; 47:6; 68:4,32; 81:1–2; 95:1; 98:1,4–5,8–9; 117:1; 147:7; 149:1; Isa 44:23; 49:13; 52:9; Ro 15:11

The resolve to sing praise to God
Ps 104:33 *See also* Ps 7:17; 9:2; 13:6; 57:8–9; 59:16–17; 89:1; 101:1; 147:1

Singing in response to God's deliverance from enemies and sin
Isa 35:10 *See also* Ps 18:47–49; 71:22–24; Isa 54:1; 55:12; Rev 5:11–14; 15:3–4

God sings of his delight and love for his people
Zep 3:17

Singing in Israel
Singing accompanied major events
1Ch 15:27–28 *the bringing of the ark to Jerusalem;* 2Ch 5:12–13 *the dedication of the temple;* 2Ch 20:21–22 *a march into battle;* 2Ch 23:11–13 *a coronation;* 2Ch 29:27–28 *the purification of the temple*
The celebration of the Passover and Feast of Unleavened Bread: 2Ch 30:21; 35:15
Ne 12:27–29 *the dedication of the wall of Jerusalem*

Part of day-to-day worship 2Ch 23:18; Ne 11:23

Accompanied by instruments
1Ch 15:16 *See also* 1Ki 10:12 pp 2Ch 9:11; Ps 137:1–4

Musicians and singers appointed to lead Israel's singing 1Ch 9:33; 15:22 *See also* 1Ch 6:31–32; 25:6–7; Ezr 2:41 pp Ne 7:44; Ezr 2:65; Ne 11:22; 12:46

Singing in the NT
Eph 5:19–20 ; Jas 5:13 *See also* Mt 26:30 pp Mk 14:26; Ac 16:25; 1Co 14:15; Col 3:16

Singing is not always appropriate
Pr 25:20 *See also* Ecc 7:5
Am 5:23 *God detests the songs of Israel that are not accompanied by obedience and justice. See also* Isa 24:14–17; 25:5; Eze 26:13; Am 6:5–7; 8:3,10

See also

5420 music	8627 worship,
5421 musical	elements
instruments	8666 praise, manner
5422 musicians	& methods
5742 wedding	
7927 hymn	
7963 song	
8609 prayer as praise	
& thanksgiving	

Different kinds of song
Songs of praise and thanksgiving
2Ch 5:13; Ps 69:30 *See also* Ne 12:8,46; Ps 28:7; 95:2; Jer 30:18–19; Jnh 2:9; Jas 5:13

Songs of joy and celebration Ps 98:4 *See also* 2Sa 6:5 pp 1Ch 13:8; 1Ch 15:16; Ps 100:2; 107:22; 126:2,6; Isa 52:9; 55:12

Songs of victory and deliverance
Ex 15:1–18 *The song celebrating God's spectacular victory over Pharaoh and his army (compare with Rev 15:3). See also* Jdg 5:1–3; 1Sa 18:6–7; 2Sa 22:1–4; Ps 18:2; 32:7; 42:8; 118:15; Isa 26:1; 44:23; 49:13

Psalms and hymns Col 3:16 *"psalms, hymns and spiritual songs" are not clearly distinguished from each other in Scripture. See also* 1Ch 16:7; Ps 40:3; 47:7; Mt 26:30 pp Mk 14:26; 1Co 14:26; Ac 16:25; Eph 5:19

Songs of ascent Ps 122:1 Title *Psalms 120–134, the so-called "Songs of Ascent", are thought to have been sung by pilgrims on their way to Jerusalem.*

Songs of love Ps 45:1 Title *The title to this psalm describes it as "a wedding song";* SS 1:1; Isa 5:1; Eze 33:32

Laments 2Sa 1:17–19 *See also* 2Sa 3:33–34; 2Ch 35:25; Ps 102:1–2; Jer 7:29; 9:10,20; La 2:5 *The book of Lamentations is a series of laments after the fall of Jerusalem;* Eze 19:1,14; 26:17–18; 27:2,32; 28:12; 32:16; Am 5:1

Songs of derision Job 30:9; Ps 69:12; La 3:14,63; Mic 2:4

God is described as the song of believers
Ps 118:14 *See also* Ex 15:2; Isa 12:2

Songs can teach and warn
Dt 32:44–46 *See also* Dt 31:19,22,30; Ps 119:54; Eph 5:19

A new song
Singing a new song to God expresses a renewed desire to praise him
Ps 40:1–3 *See also* Ps 33:3; 98:1; 144:9; 149:1; Isa 42:10

In heaven God's people will sing a new song Rev 5:9–10 *See also* Rev 14:3

See also

5420 music	8609 prayer as
5421 musical	praise &
instruments	thanksgiving
5422 musicians	8627 worship,
5442 pilgrimage	elements
7927 hymn	8642 celebration
7960 singing	8666 praise, manner
8283 joy	& methods
	8676 thanksgiving

7960

singing

The musical voicing of praise to God. On account of God's majesty and great acts of salvation singing was a regular part of the life of Israel and of the early church. In Israel musicians

---

7963

song

In Scripture, songs express praise, thanksgiving, joy, victory and love. They also express sadness and derision and can be used to teach and warn. In heaven believers will sing a new song to God.

7966

spiritual gifts

Although all believers have received the gift of the Holy Spirit, Scripture points to God giving individuals certain special gifts of a spiritual nature for the fulfilling of specific tasks.

7967
spiritual gifts, and responsibility

A spiritual gift may be intended to equip its recipient for a specific function or appointment. Those who are equipped in this way need the enabling power of God's spirit to carry out their appointed tasks.

OT examples of God's gifts or appointments
God appoints prophets Jer 1:5

God appoints Israel's kings 1Sa 15:11 See also 2Sa 7:8; 12:7

God appoints the Persian king Cyrus Isa 45:1 See also Isa 41:2

God empowers leaders and kings with his Spirit Nu 27:18 See also Jdg 3:10; 6:34; 11:29; 13:25; 14:6,19; 15:14; 1Sa 10:6,10; 11:6; 16:13–14

The Spirit is given to the servant of the LORD Isa 42:1 See also Isa 61:1

Jesus Christ is endowed with the Holy Spirit
Mt 3:16–17 pp Mk 1:10–11 pp Lk 3:21–22 See also Jn 1:32–33; Ac 10:38

The apostles are endowed with the Holy Spirit
Ac 1:8

Spiritual gifts given to the church
Eph 4:11 See also 1Co 12:28

Many functions within the church yet unity is preserved Eph 4:4–7 See also 1Co 12:4–11

All Christians are appointed to build up the church Eph 4:15–16 See also 1Co 12:12

The experience of spiritual gifts
Associated with the laying on of hands 2Ti 1:6–7 See also Nu 8:10; 27:18; Dt 34:9; Ac 6:6; 1Ti 4:14; 5:22

Associated with prayer and fasting Ac 14:23 See also Ac 13:3

Spiritual gifts must not be neglected
1Ti 4:14 See also Lk 19:11–26

See also
3040 Holy Spirit, promise of	3275 Holy Spirit in the church
3212 Holy Spirit & mission	5051 responsibility
3224 Holy Spirit & preaching	5333 healing
	5556 stewardship
3269 Holy Spirit in Christ	7724 evangelists
	7734 leaders, spiritual
3272 Holy Spirit in OT	7797 teaching

7968
spiritual gifts, nature of

In both the OT and the NT God graciously pours out gifts on his people. They are to be welcomed and used for the good of all.

OT examples of God giving special gifts
God's gracious provision from above Joel 2:23–24 This gracious provision of material needs from above can be seen as foreshadowing God's bestowal of spiritual gifts. See also Ex 16:4,8,13–14; Dt 11:14; 1Ki 17:6; Job 5:10; Isa 55:10

Distribution of land to tribes Jos 13:6–7 The Hebrew word for "give" often includes the sense of "apportion" or "assign". See also Eze 47:21

The future promise of spiritual gifts Joel 2:28–29 See also Ac 2:17–18

In his earthly ministry Jesus Christ offers supernatural gifts
Mt 11:28 See also Mt 16:19; Lk 10:19; Jn 4:14; 6:51

Spiritual gifts linked with grace
Ro 12:6 See also Mt 10:8; 1Co 4:7

Specific reference to spiritual gifts
1Co 12:1 See also Ro 1:11; 1Co 14:1,12,37

Diverse gifts, one giver
1Co 12:4–6 See also Ro 12:6–8; 1Co 7:7,17; 12:8–11,27; Eph 4:11; Heb 2:4; 1Pe 4:10–11

The purpose of spiritual gifts is to build up the church
1Co 14:12 See also 1Co 12:7; 14:2–5,17–19,26,31; Eph 4:16

The body of Christ benefits from these varied gifts 1Co 12:12 See also 1Co 12:14–31; Ro 12:4–6

Encouragement to aspire to the greater spiritual gifts 1Co 12:31; 14:1

The importance of love in exercising spiritual gifts
1Co 13:1 See also Ro 12:5–9; 1Co 14:1

Warnings about spiritual gifts
1Co 14:39 See also 1Co 14:37; 1Th 5:19–20

See also
1432 prophecy in NT	8025 faith, origins of
3030 Holy Spirit, power	8306 mercifulness
	8342 servanthood
3275 Holy Spirit in the church	8361 wisdom
	8413 edification
7789 shepherd, church leader	8414 encouragement
7972 tongues, gift of	8420 equipping

7972
tongues, gift of

The divine enabling of a believer to use a language, unknown to the speaker. The gift of tongues may be used to praise God or to utter a message from God that, supplemented by the gift of interpretation of tongues, edifies other believers. Note that "tongues" can simply mean "other languages" at times.

Tongues is a gift of the Holy Spirit
It is given to individual believers Ac 2:4

See also 1Co 12:11,30 it is not universal among Christians

It was foretold in the OT 1Co 14:21; Isa 28:11

It is a divine gift in response to faith Mk 16:17

It may be given through the laying on of hands Ac 19:6

It is a sign of the presence of the Holy Spirit Ac 10:44–46

Tongues in relation to other gifts
The need for love 1Co 13:1

The need for prophecy 1Co 14:4–6

The need for intelligibility 1Co 14:9,13,16–19,23

The need for interpretation 1Co 12:8–10; 14:12–13

The transience of tongues 1Co 13:8

The use of tongues within the church
In prayer and praise Ro 8:26; 1Co 14:14–15,26,28; Eph 6:18; Jude 20

For the benefit of believers 1Co 12:7–10 See also 1Co 14:5, 16–17,26

In public it needs to be augmented by the gift of interpretation 1Co 14:26–28 See also 1Co 12:30; 14:5,13

See also
3221 Holy Spirit & prayer	5374 languages
	6257 unbelievers
3257 Holy Spirit, gift of	7966 spiritual gifts
	8413 edification
5193 tongue	

8000
The life of the believer

8010
Faith

8020
faith

A constant outlook of trust towards God, whereby human beings abandon all reliance on their own efforts and put their full confidence in him, his word and his promises. This set of themes consists of the following:

8021 faith, nature of
8022 faith, as basis of salvation
8023 faith, necessity of
8024 faith, and blessings of God
8025 faith, origins of
8026 faith, growth in
8027 faith, testing of
8028 faith, as a body of beliefs

8021
faith, nature of

Confidence in and commitment to God and Jesus Christ. These attitudes remain sure even though the objects of faith are unseen. True faith is seen

in obedient action, love and
continuing good works.

The object of faith
God as the object of faith Heb 11:6 *See also* Ps 25:1–2; 26:1; Pr 29:25; 1Pe 1:21

Jesus Christ as the object of faith
Jn 14:1 *See also* Jn 3:16,18,36; 6:68–69

False objects of faith
Human resources: Ps 20:7; Hos 10:13
Ps 118:9 *other people;* Pr 28:26 *self;*
Isa 42:17 *idols*

Faith is personal trust in God
2Sa 22:31 *See also* Ps 18:2–6; 27:13–14;
1Pe 2:23

True faith cannot be second-hand
2Ti 1:5 *See also* Jn 4:42

Faith and assurance
Assurance accompanies faith
Heb 11:1 *See also* Ro 4:19–21; 1Ti 3:13;
Heb 10:22

Faith may be mixed with doubt
Mt 14:31 *Simon Peter;* Mk 9:24 *the father
of the boy with an evil spirit;* Jn 20:24–28
Thomas

Faith and sight
2Co 5:7

Faith as trust in what is unseen
Jn 20:29 *See also* 2Co 4:18;
Heb 11:1–3,7,27

Faith looks towards an unseen future
Heb 11:13–14 *See also* Heb 11:8–10
Abraham; Heb 11:20–22 *Isaac, Jacob and
Joseph;* Heb 11:24–26 *Moses*

Faith and obedience
**True faith is demonstrated in
obedience** Ro 1:5; Heb 4:2 *See also*
Ro 16:26; 2Co 9:13; 1Pe 1:2

Examples of obedient faith
Noah builds the ark: Ge 6:22; Heb 11:7
Abraham leaves Haran: Ge 12:4;
Heb 11:8
Abraham offers Isaac: Ge 22:1–10;
Heb 11:17
Ex 14:15–16 *Moses parts the sea.*
Caleb and Joshua: Nu 13:30; 14:8–9
*Jos 3:5–13 Joshua at the river Jordan
Joshua at Jericho;* Jos 6:2–5; Heb 11:30
Jn 21:4–6 *Jesus Christ's disciples, fishing;*
Ac 26:19 *Paul*

Faith and works
**True faith is demonstrated in good
deeds** Jas 2:14–26 *See also* Php 2:17;
1Th 1:3; Tit 1:1; 2Pe 1:5

True faith issues in love Gal 5:6 *See also*
Eph 1:15; 6:23; 1Th 3:6; 5:8; 1Ti 1:5,14;
4:12

True faith is constantly productive
Lk 8:15 pp Mt 13:23 pp Mk 4:20 *See also*
Jn 15:1–5

See also

2369 Christ,	8292 love
responses to	8354 trustworthi-
4020 life of faith	ness
8031 trust,	8442 good works
importance	8454 obedience to
8104 assurance	God
8207 commitment	8722 doubt
8213 confidence	9610 hope

8022
faith, as basis of salvation

Both in the OT and in the NT faith is
the only basis of salvation. Faith is
the means by which God's grace in
Christ, and with him the blessings of
salvation, is received. Paul's doctrine
of justification by faith emphasises
the centrality of faith in the
Christian life.

Salvation by faith in the OT
Hab 2:4

**The faith of Abraham and other
individuals** Ge 15:6 *See also* Ro 4:9–16
*Abraham, the father of those righteous by
faith;* Heb 11:4 *Abel;* Heb 11:5 *Enoch;*
Heb 11:7 *Noah*

Salvation by faith in the NT
Ro 1:16–17 *See also* 1Co 1:21;
Php 3:8–9

Salvation through faith alone
Eph 2:8–9 *See also* Ro 3:27–28; 4:1–8;
Ps 32:1–2; Ro 9:30–32; Gal 3:10–14;
Dt 27:26

Salvation is by faith in Jesus Christ
Jn 3:14–16 *Being "lifted up" is a reference
to Jesus Christ's death on the cross;*
Ro 10:9–10 *The necessity of outward
confession, as evidence of personal faith in
Jesus Christ. See also* Jn 8:24; Ac 8:37 fn;
13:38–39; Ro 3:21–26; 4:24;
2Co 4:13–14; Gal 3:22

Salvation is for all who believe Ro 10:4
*Jesus Christ is the "end of the law", in the
sense that he brings it to its goal and
fulfilment, and accomplishes its
intentions. See also* Ac 15:7–9;
Ro 3:29–30

**Salvation is for those who persevere in
their faith** Col 1:21–23 *See also*
Heb 3:14; 6:11–12

Saving faith shows itself in action
Jas 2:14

Blessings of salvation received
through faith
Justification and peace with God
Ro 5:1–2; Gal 2:15–16; 5:5

Forgiveness Lk 7:48–50; Ac 10:43

Adoption into God's family Jn 1:12;
Gal 3:26

The gift of the Holy Spirit Jn 7:38–39;
Gal 3:2; Eph 1:13

Jesus Christ in the heart Eph 3:17

Protection through God's power
1Pe 1:5

Access to God Eph 3:12; Heb 10:22

Sanctification Ac 26:17–18

New life Gal 2:20

Eternal life Jn 3:16,36; 5:24; 6:40,47

Victory over death Jn 11:25–27

See also

2530 Christ, death of	6644 eternal life
3257 Holy Spirit, gift	6652 forgiveness
of	6676 justification
6510 salvation	6728 regeneration
6608 adoption	6744 sanctification
6626 conversion	7105 believers
6632 conviction	8154 righteousness

8023
faith, necessity of

A fundamental duty for all people
and the necessary response to God's
self-revelation. The only channel
through which God's blessings may
be received, and the only means by
which life may be made meaningful,
in relationship with God.

The call to faith
In the OT Ps 37:3–5 *See also* Pr 3:5–6;
Isa 26:4; 50:10

In the NT Jn 6:28–29 *See also* Mk 1:15;
Ac 16:30–31; 19:4; 20:21; Ro 1:5;
1Jn 3:23

God's self-revelation leaves no
excuse for unbelief
Jn 14:8–11; Ro 10:17–18 *See also*
Ps 19:4; Jn 1:10–12; Ro 1:18–21; 3:1–4;
Ps 51:4; Ro 16:25–27

The need for faith in God
The LORD is the only true God
Hab 2:18–20 *See also* Ps 115:2–11

God alone can be trusted absolutely
Ps 9:10 *See also* Ps 91:1–4; Isa 12:2;
Na 1:7

Faith in God is the basis for peace
Isa 26:3 *See also* Ps 42:11; Jn 14:1;
Ro 15:13; 2Pe 1:1–2

**Faith is necessary to receive God's
blessing** Heb 11:6 *See also* Ps 40:4;
Jer 17:7–8; Jn 5:24

**Faith is necessary to avoid God's
judgment** Jn 3:36 *See also* Jn 3:18;
2Th 2:12; 1Pe 2:6–8; Isa 28:16;
Ps 118:22; Isa 8:14

Actions not springing from faith
are sinful
Ro 14:23 *See also* Ro 14:5–8,14

Unbelief challenged
Heb 3:12–18; Ps 95:7–8 *comparison
with the Israelites in the wilderness;* Isa 7:9
Ahaz, king of Judah; Jer 17:5–6 *the people
of Judah;* Mk 16:14 *Jesus Christ's disciples
after the resurrection*

See also

1055 God, grace &	6512 salvation,
mercy	necessity &
1165 God, unique	basis
1320 God as Saviour	6644 eternal life
1439 revelation	6732 repentance
2324 Christ as	8224 dependence
Saviour	8834 unbelief
2427 gospel,	
transmission	

8024
faith, and blessings of God

Confidence in the ability and
willingness of God to act in
supernatural power to advance his
kingdom, and a commitment,
expressed in prayer and action, to
being the means by which he does
so.

God's power is released through faith
Mt 17:20 *See also* Mk 9:23; Lk 17:6

Praying in faith Mt 21:21–22
pp Mk 11:22–24 *See also* Jas 1:5–7;
5:14–15

Praying in Jesus Christ's name
Jn 14:12–14

In the OT, faith in God's power
Heb 11:32–34 *See also* Heb 11:11–12
*Abraham's faith when promised an heir in
his old age;* Jos 14:6–14 *Caleb receives
Hebron;* 1Sa 14:6 *Jonathan's confidence in
God's power to defeat the Philistines;*
1Sa 17:32–47 *David's confidence in God's
power to overcome Goliath;* 2Ch 20:20
*Jehoshaphat's faith in God's power to give
success against Moab and Ammon;*
2Ch 32:7–8 *Hezekiah's faith in God when
threatened by the Assyrians under
Sennacherib;* Da 6:23 *Daniel's faith when
in the lions' den*

In the NT, healing in response to faith
Mt 9:22 pp Mk 5:34 pp Lk 8:48 *The
woman had exercised faith by touching the
edge of Jesus Christ's cloak. See also*
Mt 9:29–30 *Two blind men are healed;*
Mk 10:52 pp Lk 18:42 *Bartimaeus
receives his sight;* Lk 17:19 *One of the ten
men with leprosy who thanked Jesus
Christ;* Ac 3:16 *the crippled man at the
temple gate;* Ac 14:8–10 *the crippled man
in Lystra*

Powerful ministries marked by faith
Ac 11:24 *See also* Ac 6:5–10 *Stephen;*
1Co 12:9 *Exceptional faith to meet specific
needs is a special spiritual gift.*

Faith and spiritual warfare
Eph 6:16 *See also* 1Th 5:8; 1Jn 5:4–5

The importance of love accompanying faith
1Co 13:2

See also
1105 God, power of	8304 loyalty
1415 miracles	8482 spiritual
2351 Christ, miracles	warfare
3030 Holy Spirit,	8612 prayer & faith
power	8720 double-
5333 healing	mindedness
8162 spiritual vitality	8738 evil, victory
8207 commitment	over

8025
faith, origins of

Faith is a gift from God himself and
is not to be seen as the result of
human striving or achievement.
Faith is inspired by the word and
works of God.

Faith is a gift from God
Jn 6:63–65; Eph 2:8–9 *See also*
Mt 16:15–17; Mk 9:24; Lk 17:5;
Ac 3:16; 14:27; 18:27; Ro 12:3; 1Co 4:7;
12:9; Php 1:29; Jas 2:5

Faith comes through God's word
Faith following a direct word from God
Heb 11:29–30; Ex 14:15 *Moses receives
God's instructions at the Red Sea;*
Jos 6:2–5 *Joshua receives God's*

instructions concerning Jericho;
Ac 27:23–25

Faith through the Scriptures Jn 2:22;
20:30–31; 2Ti 3:15

**Faith comes through hearing God's
word preached** Ro 10:14–17 *See also*
Isa 52:7; 53:1; Jn 1:7; 4:41–42; 17:20;
Ac 11:19–21; 1Co 2:4–5

**Faith comes through a personal
encounter with Jesus Christ**
Jn 9:35–38; 20:26–28

**Faith comes through witnessing
miracles**
Jn 14:11 *See also* Jn 2:11 *the miracle at
the wedding feast;* Jn 4:53 *Jesus Christ
heals an official's son.*
The raising of Lazarus: Jn 11:45; 12:11
Ac 9:42 *the raising of Tabitha*

Faith based on knowledge of God
Knowledge of God's faithfulness leads
to faith Ps 46:1–3; La 3:19–24; Na 1:7;
Ac 2:25–26

Knowledge of God's achievements
leads to faith Dt 3:21–22;
1Sa 17:34–37; Jer 14:22

See also
1105 God, power of	7754 preaching
1416 miracles	8112 certainty
1610 Scripture	8825 self-
2351 Christ, miracles	righteousness
5467 promises,	& gospel
divine	
6669 grace &	
salvation	

8026
faith, growth in

Christians are called to have a
growing faith, built up by prayer and
the encouragement of others, and
also through testing.

Examples of growing faith
2Th 1:3 *See also* Ac 16:5; 2Co 10:15;
Rev 2:19

Weak faith
Weak faith rebuked Mt 6:28–30
pp Lk 12:27–28 *See also* Mt 8:26
pp Mk 4:40 pp Lk 8:25; Mt 14:31; 16:8;
17:20

Other examples of weak faith
Jn 12:42–43; 19:38; Ro 14:1–2;
1Co 8:1–13

Strong faith
Strong faith commended and
encouraged Heb 10:22 *See also* Mt 8:10
pp Lk 7:9; Mt 9:20–22 pp Mk 5:25–34
pp Lk 8:43–48; Mt 15:28 pp Mk 7:29

The faith of OT leaders 1Ki 18:3
Obadiah; 2Ki 18:5 pp 2Ch 31:20
Hezekiah

The faith of Christian leaders 1Ti 4:12 ;
Heb 13:7 *See also* Ac 6:5 *Stephen;*
Ac 11:24 *Barnabas;* 2Ti 3:10 *Paul
Paul's encouragements to Timothy:*
1Ti 6:11; 2Ti 2:22

Other examples of strong faith
Hab 3:17–18 *See also* Job 13:15;
19:25–27; Mt 14:35–36 pp Mk 6:56;
2Co 8:7; Col 2:5–7

The growth of faith
Praying for more faith Lk 17:5 *See also*
Mk 9:24

The encouragement of others
2Ch 32:7–8; 1Th 3:10 *See also*
Nu 14:6–9; Lk 22:32; Ac 14:22;
Ro 1:11–12; 1Th 3:2–3; Jude 20

Faith strengthened through testing
Ro 4:18–21 *See also* Ge 15:5; Jas 1:2–4;
1Pe 1:6–7

See also
5566 suffering,	8347 spiritual
encourage-	growth
ments in	8414 encourage-
5914 optimism	ment
5957 strength,	8459 perseverance
spiritual	8611 prayer for
8205 childlikeness	others
8219 courage	8839 unfaithfulness
8248 faithfulness	

8027
faith, testing of

The means through which the
genuineness of faith is proved and
Christian character developed. God
promises to help his people during
times of testing.

God allows faith to be tested
Testing proves the genuineness of
faith 1Pe 1:6–7 *See also* Mt 13:20–21
pp Mk 4:16–17 pp Lk 8:13

Testing develops Christian character
Jas 1:2–4 *See also* Ro 5:3–4

Testing purifies God's people Isa 48:10
See also Ps 66:10–12; Jer 9:7; Zec 13:9;
Mal 3:2–3; 1Pe 4:17

Examples of God testing faith
Abraham is told to sacrifice Isaac:
Ge 22:1–2; Heb 11:17–19
Dt 8:2–5 *God tested Israel in the desert;*
Jdg 7:1–8 *God reduces Gideon's army;*
Mt 15:21–28 pp Mk 7:24–30 *Jesus
Christ appears to discourage the Canaanite
woman;* Jn 11:1–6 *Jesus Christ delays
going to Bethany when Lazarus is ill.*

Means by which faith is tested
God allows Satan to test faith Job 2:7
See also Lk 22:31; 1Th 3:4–5; Rev 2:10

Difficult circumstances test faith
1Ki 17:17–18; 2Ki 4:1,27–28; Ac 14:22;
2Co 11:25–27

Persecution tests faith Da 6:10–12;
Ac 8:1–4; Heb 11:35–38

Discouraging people test faith
2Ki 18:19–25 pp 2Ch 32:10–15
pp Isa 36:4–10; Mk 5:35–36
pp Lk 8:49–50; Mk 5:40 pp Mt 9:24
pp Lk 8:53

God's promise of help during testing
Isa 43:2; Lk 22:32 *See also* Ps 91:14–15;
1Co 10:13; 2Co 12:7–9; 1Pe 5:10;
2Pe 2:9

God's help through the
encouragement of others 1Th 3:2–3
See also 2Co 7:5–7

The response to trials
Rejoicing at sharing Jesus Christ's
suffering 1Pe 4:12–13

Praying for God's help Heb 4:14–16; 1Pe 4:19

Persevering Jas 1:12 *See also* 2Th 1:4; Heb 12:1–3; Jas 5:11; Rev 2:3,19

Examples of faith victorious through testing
Ge 22:9–12 *Abraham*; 2Ki 6:15–17 *Elisha's servant*; Job 1:22 *Job*; Da 3:16–27 *Shadrach, Meshach and Abednego*; Ac 5:27–29 *the apostles*; Ac 7:59–60 *Stephen*; 2Co 4:7–9 *Paul*

See also
1030 God, compassion	6248 temptation
1035 God, faithfulness	8418 endurance
4351 refining	8610 prayer, asking God
5565 suffering of believers	8741 failure
	8794 persecution
	8832 testing

8028
faith, as a body of beliefs

That body of essential truth to which Christians hold. It is revealed by God and is to be passed on by faithful teachers. Believers are urged to remain true to the faith and to contend for it.

Faith as the truth that Christians believe
Gal 1:23; 1Ti 2:7 *See also* Ac 6:7; Eph 4:5; 1Ti 1:2; Tit 3:15

Terms equivalent to "the faith"
The truth: Jn 14:6; 1Ti 3:15; 3Jn 3
Ac 2:42 *the apostles' teaching*
The gospel: Gal 1:6–9; Php 1:7
2Ti 1:13–14 *the good deposit*

Aspects of "the faith" summarised
Ac 2:22–24,32–33; 1Co 15:1–4; Php 2:5–11; Col 1:15–20; 1Ti 1:15; 3:16; 2Ti 2:11–13; Heb 6:1–2

The source and transmission of the faith
The faith has been given by God
Gal 1:11–12 *See also* Jn 1:17; 8:40; 1Co 11:23; 2Ti 3:16; 2Pe 1:21

The faith is passed on by apostles and teachers Tit 1:9 *See also* Jn 15:20; Ac 4:20; 2Ti 2:2; 2Pe 1:16

Christians must remain true to the faith
Ac 14:21–22; 1Co 16:13 *See also* Heb 4:14–16

Being strengthened in the faith Php 1:25; Col 2:6–7 *See also* Eph 4:11–13; Jude 20

The danger of turning from the faith Mt 24:10; Heb 6:6 *See also* Ac 13:8; 2Co 13:5–6; 1Ti 5:8; 6:10,20–21; Heb 2:1; 3:12; 10:35; 12:25

Christians must contend for the faith
Php 1:27; Jude 3

Refuting false teachers *See also* 1Ti 4:1–6; 2Ti 3:6–8; Tit 1:10–13; 2Jn 7

Witnessing to the truth 1Pe 3:15

Contending for the faith is a responsibility of leaders
Apostles: Php 1:7,15–16; 2Ti 4:7
1Ti 3:2 *overseers, who must be able to*

teach; 1Ti 3:9 *deacons*; 1Ti 6:12 *Timothy, responsible for the church at Ephesus*

See also
1439 revelation	8482 spiritual warfare
1460 truth	
2423 gospel, essence	8496 witnessing, importance
7734 leaders, spiritual	
7797 teaching	8704 apostasy
8234 doctrine	8743 faithlessness
8316 orthodoxy, in NT	8766 heresies

trust

Reliance on and confidence in a person. Scripture affirms the total trustworthiness of God, especially in relation to his promises to his people. Christian faith is, essentially, trust in the person and character of God. While Scripture insists that believers should be able to trust one another, it also provides examples of false or misplaced trust.

8031
trust, importance of

Scripture emphasises the importance of putting one's trust in God. This trust, which is nurtured by an understanding of God's revealed truth, finds expression in a life lived according to his purpose. There are examples in Scripture of proper trust being placed in other people.

Grounds for trust in God
Trust in God's power and strength
Ex 14:31; 2Ti 1:12 *See also* 2Sa 22:1–3 pp Ps 18:2–3; Ps 9:9–10; 115:9–11; 144:1–2

Trust in God's unfailing love Ps 13:5 *See also* Ex 15:13; Ps 17:7; 21:7; 33:18; 52:8; 147:11

Trust in God's salvation Isa 12:2 *See also* 1Sa 17:37; Ps 22:4–5; 40:2–3; Isa 25:9

Trust nurtured by God's revealed truth
Pr 22:19–21 *See also* Ps 18:30; 119:42; Pr 30:5; Jn 12:36; 14:1–3

Expressions of trust in God
Praise and worship Ps 4:5; 28:7; 64:10; Da 3:28

Perseverance in faith Isa 7:4–7; Jer 51:46–47; 2Th 1:4; Heb 10:35–36; 12:2–3; Jas 1:12; 5:11

Holding on to God's promise
1Ki 8:56–57; Ps 130:5; Ac 26:7; Ro 4:20–21; Col 1:5

Jesus Christ's trust in the Father
Lk 23:46 *See also* Ps 31:5; 22:8; Mt 27:43; Heb 2:13; Isa 8:17

King Hezekiah's trust in God
2Ki 18:5–7 pp 2Ch 31:20–21 *See also* 2Ki 18:30 pp Isa 36:15; 2Ki 19:14–19 pp Isa 37:14–20; 2Ch 32:20

Further examples of trust in God
Ru 2:12 *Ruth*; 1Ch 5:20 *the tribes of Reuben, Gad and Manasseh*; Da 3:17 *Shadrach, Meshach and Abednego*; Da 6:23 *Daniel*; Zep 3:12 *the meek and humble*; Ac 14:23 *members of the NT churches*

The results of trusting in God
Peace Isa 26:3–4 *See also* Ro 15:13

Security Ps 37:3 *See also* Ps 32:10; 125:1; Ps 29:25; Isa 28:16; 57:13

Protection from danger Ps 25:1–3; 31:14–15; 32:7; 33:18–22; 91:1–4

Freedom from fear Ps 27:1 *See also* Ps 23:4; 34:4; 56:3–4,10–11; 112:7

Prosperity Pr 28:25 *In the OT material prosperity is often seen as a sign of the spiritual wealth that belongs to those who trust God*; Pr 16:20; Jer 17:7–8

Strength Isa 30:15; 40:29–31

Physical life Ps 25:20; Jer 39:18; 49:11

Trust in people
God's servants entrusted with responsibility 1Co 4:1–2 *See also* Lk 16:1–2; 1Th 2:4; 2Ti 1:14

Trust at home and work Pr 31:10–11 *A good wife gives her husband confidence*; Tit 2:10 *Employees should be trustworthy*.

Examples of trusting others Ge 39:4 *See also* Ge 41:39–40; Ex 19:9 *Moses to be trusted by Israel*; 1Ch 9:22 *the gatekeepers appointed by David and Samuel*; Ne 2:6 *Nehemiah is trusted by Artaxerxes to return to Jerusalem*; Da 5:29–6:2 *Daniel given responsibility*; Php 2:25 *Paul's confidence in Epaphroditus*; 2Ti 2:2 *Timothy to find others to be entrusted to teach the gospel*

Continued trust in those who fail Jnh 3:1–2 *God re-appoints Jonah despite earlier disobedience. See also* Jn 21:15 *Jesus Christ reinstates Peter after his denial*; Ac 15:37–39 *Barnabas gives John Mark a second chance.*

See also
1035 God, faithfulness	8104 assurance
	8213 confidence
1460 truth	8224 dependence
1690 word of God	8248 faithfulness
5051 responsibility	8354 trustworthi-ness
5467 promises, divine	8678 waiting on God
8021 faith	

8032
trust, lack of

Forsaking God and relying on other objects of dependence. This is futile and it provokes God's anger. Failure to trust others may be the result of a betrayal of trust in the past.

Failure to trust God
The nature of failure to trust God Jer 2:13 *See also* Dt 31:16; Isa 8:6; 65:11

Examples of failure to trust God Dt 1:32–33 *See also* Nu 9:23; Ps 78:21–22; Nu 20:12 *Moses and Aaron*; 1Ki 11:4 *Solomon*; 2Ch 16:7 *Asa*; Rev 3:17 *the church at Laodicea*

The consequences of failure to trust God Heb 10:38–39 *See also* Hab 2:4;

Lev 26:14–20; Jer 13:24–25; 46:25; Hos 10:13–14

Objects of misplaced trust

Trust in false gods Ps 40:4 *See also* Dt 31:20; Ps 4:2; Isa 42:17; 47:9–10

Trust in alliances, real or metaphorical Isa 31:1 *See also* Isa 28:15; 30:1–2; Jer 2:18

Trust in human strength and resources Jer 17:5 *See also* Ps 44:6–7; 146:3; Pr 3:5; 28:26; Isa 2:22; 22:8–11; 30:15–16; Eze 16:15

Trust in the outward form of religion Mic 6:6–8 *See also* Jer 7:14 *trust in the temple;* Jer 28:15 *trust in false prophecy;* Jn 8:33 *trust in descent from Abraham;* Ro 2:17 *trust in possession of the law*

Trust in one's own righteousness Ro 3:19–20 *See also* Eze 33:13; Lk 18:9

Trust in wealth 1Ti 6:17 *See also* Job 31:24–25; Ps 49:5–6; 52:7; 62:10; Pr 11:28; Jer 48:7; 49:4; Lk 12:18–20

The futility of misplaced trust

Job 15:31 *See also* Job 8:13–15

Futility of trust in false gods Dt 32:37–38; 1Ki 18:26–29; Ps 115:5–8; Isa 37:19; Hab 2:18

Futility of trust in human resources Isa 64:6 *human righteousness;* Mt 6:19–20 *wealth and possessions;* Col 2:8 *human philosophy;* Jas 4:13–14 *human planning*

Futility of trust in others Pr 25:19; Isa 31:3

Failure to trust others

Jdg 11:20 ; Jer 12:6 *See also* Nu 21:23; Jer 9:4; Mic 7:5–6; Mt 10:36; Mk 13:12; Ac 15:37–38; 2Ti 4:14–15

See also

1025 God, anger of	8747 false gods
1050 God, goodness of	8768 idolatry
5798 betrayal	8812 riches, ungodly use
8331 reliability	8834 unbelief
8719 distrust	8841 unfaithfulness to people
8744 faithlessness as disobedience	

8100

The life of faith

8102

abiding in Christ

The NT stresses the need for believers to remain in Christ. The reality of this close personal relationship with Jesus Christ is expressed in obedience to his word and is essential to effective discipleship.

Jesus Christ tells his disciples to abide in him

Jn 15:4–9 *See also* Mt 24:10–13; Lk 9:62; Jn 6:67

NT writers exhort believers to abide in Christ

Col 2:6 *See also* Gal 4:9; 5:5–6; Col 3:1–3; Heb 12:1–3

Abiding in Christ depends upon holding on to his teaching

1Jn 2:24 *See also* Jn 8:31; 2Th 2:15; 2Ti 3:14; 2Jn 9; 3Jn 3–4

It depends on obedience to him Jn 15:10 *See also* Mt 7:24–25; Jn 14:23; Jas 1:25; 1Jn 3:24

It requires living like Jesus Christ 1Jn 2:6

Aids to abiding in Christ

Eating his flesh and drinking his blood Jn 6:56 *Jn 6:35–40 gives the primary explanation of this verse as being a metaphor of the believer coming in faith to Jesus Christ, the "bread of life". But the verse also reflects the language of the Lord's Supper.*

The Spirit's anointing 1Jn 2:27 *See also* Jn 14:17,23; Ro 8:9; 1Jn 3:24

Jesus Christ abides in believers

Jn 15:4 *It is clear that the believer's "abiding in Christ" and Jesus Christ's "abiding in him" are closely connected, although the verse does not make their exact relationship clear. Because of Jesus Christ's indwelling by his Spirit, believers are able to continue to live as his disciples; as they do so, the reality of his indwelling presence is deepened. See also* Jn 17:23; Col 1:27; 1Jn 3:24; Rev 3:20

By his Spirit Jn 14:17; Ro 8:9–10; 1Co 3:16; 1Jn 2:27

By faith Eph 3:17–19; Gal 2:20

Results of abiding in Christ

Fruitfulness Jn 15:4–5 *The picture of "bearing fruit" may cover many aspects of Christian life but it includes that of developing Christian character, effective Christian service and mission. These result, not from human effort, but from abiding in Christ. See also* Gal 5:22–23

Answered prayer Jn 15:7,16

Freedom from persistent sin 1Jn 3:6–9 *John is not saying that Christians are absolutely sinless. He says elsewhere that to claim sinless perfection is to deceive oneself (1Jn 1:8). But when people are born again there is the real possibility of living lives in which sin is not the norm. As believers abide in Christ more deeply, the grip of sin upon their lives is lessened.*

Relationship with God the Father *See also* Jn 14:23; 2Jn 9

Confidence in the face of the last day 1Jn 2:28

Warnings to those who fail to abide in Christ

Mt 24:12–13; Jn 15:2,6; 1Co 15:2; Heb 6:4–6

See also

3254 Holy Spirit, fruit of	6754 union with Christ
3278 Holy Spirit, indwelling	8114 discipleship
	8162 spiritual vitality
6214 participation in Christ	8256 fruitfulness
	8453 obedience
6705 peace, experience	8459 perseverance
	8602 prayer

8104

assurance

Certainty of a present relationship with God through Jesus Christ and a secure future hope which is based upon divine revelation, centred on the person, promises and action of God and confirmed by the Holy Spirit.

8105
assurance, basis of

The assurance of believers is based upon the certain knowledge of God revealed in creation and his mighty acts in history, upon the certainty of his promises, the vindication and resurrection of Christ and the inward testimony and outward demonstration of the power of the Holy Spirit.

Assurance is based upon the certain knowledge of God

Assurance comes from knowing God through creation Ro 1:19–20 *See also* Ps 19:1–4; Ac 14:17

Assurance comes from knowing God through his mighty acts Ex 6:7; Eze 37:13–14 *See also* Ex 16:12; 29:46; Jos 3:10–13; 1Ki 20:13; Isa 49:23; 60:16; Eze 20:42; 28:26

Assurance is based upon the certainty of God's word

Jn 17:8; 1Jn 5:9–10

Assurance because of God's oath Heb 6:17 *See also* Ge 50:24; Dt 4:31; 7:7–9; Ac 2:30; Heb 7:21

Assurance because of God's promise Jos 1:9; Ro 4:20–21 *See also* Jos 23:10,14; 2Sa 7:25–26 pp 1Ch 17:23–24; 1Ki 8:56; Ps 145:13; Isa 33:6; Heb 13:5; Jas 1:12; 2:5

Assurance is based upon God's vindication of his Son

Assurance because of the resurrection of Jesus Christ Ac 2:32; 17:31 *See also* Ac 1:3,22; 10:39–41; 13:30–31; Ro 1:4; 1Co 15:3–7; 1Pe 1:3

Assurance because of the miracles of Jesus Christ Mt 11:2–6 pp Lk 7:18–23; Jn 4:48; 10:38; 14:11; 20:30–31

Assurance comes through the work of the Holy Spirit

The Holy Spirit assures believers by enabling outward demonstrations of God's power Heb 2:4 *See also* Mk 16:17–18; 2Co 3:2–3; 1Th 1:5

The Holy Spirit assures believers by giving inward conviction Ro 8:16; 1Jn 4:13 *See also* Jn 15:26; 16:8–11; Ac 5:32; Gal 4:6

The Holy Spirit assures believers by sealing God's promise Eph 1:13–14 *See also* Ac 15:8; Ro 5:5; 2Co 1:22; 5:5; Eph 4:30; 1Jn 3:24

Assurance based upon the testimony of God's people

Assurance because of the testimony of eye-witnesses 2Pe 1:16–19 See also Ex 10:2; Lk 1:2–4; Jn 1:32–34; 15:27; 19:35; Ac 1:22; 4:20; 1Pe 5:1

Assurance because of the testimony of the apostles Ac 22:14–15; 1Co 1:6; 2:1; 1Th 2:13; 1Ti 2:5–7; Rev 1:2

Assurance is based upon godly living

1Jn 2:3–5 See also 1Jn 2:23 right belief about Jesus Christ; 1Jn 2:29 righteousness Not continuing in sin: 1Jn 3:9; 5:18 1Jn 3:14–20 love for fellow believers; 1Jn 5:1 love for God the Father and God the Son

See also

1403 God, revelation	3287 Holy Spirit, sealing of
2351 Christ, miracles	
2555 Christ, resurrection appearances	3293 Holy Spirit, witness of
	5622 witnesses
3203 Holy Spirit & assurance	8112 certainty
3248 Holy Spirit, conviction	

8106

assurance, nature of

The God-given security which believers have in the blessings of divine grace. Believers are assured of the unfailing love of God and of their relationship with him as Father, the salvation and eternal life which he offers and the sure hope of one day sharing his glory.

Assurance of a relationship with God

Assurance of God's unfailing love Ps 13:5 See also Ex 15:13; Ps 51:1; 130:7–8; Isa 54:10; Jn 13:1; 1Jn 4:9

Assurance of acceptance by God Ac 15:8; Ro 5:1; 14:3; 15:7

Assurance of adoption as God's children 1Jn 3:1–3 See also Jn 1:12–13; Ro 8:14–17; Gal 4:6; Jas 1:18; 1Jn 4:7; 5:1

Assurance of God's presence Dt 31:8 See also Ge 28:15; Jos 3:7; Isa 41:10; Jer 1:8; Mt 28:20; Jn 14:18; Ac 18:10

Assurance of access to God Eph 3:12 See also Ro 5:2; Eph 2:8; Heb 4:16; 10:19–22

Assurance of salvation

Isa 12:2 See also Ps 69:13

Assurance of redemption Job 19:25; Ps 111:9; Ro 3:24; Eph 1:14; Heb 9:12

Assurance of justification Ro 3:26; 5:16; 8:33–34; 1Co 6:11

Assurance of forgiveness 1Jn 1:9 See also 2Ch 7:14; Ps 32:5; 103:12; Isa 43:25; Jer 31:34; 36:3; Mic 7:18–19; Lk 24:47; Ac 2:38; 3:19; Col 2:13–14

Assurance of election Isa 43:1; Eph 1:4 See also Isa 44:1–2; Ro 8:28–30; 11:29; 1Co 1:9; 2Ti 1:9; 1Pe 2:9–10

Assurance of preservation 2Ti 1:12; Jude 24 See also Jn 6:39; Ro 8:38–39; 2Co 4:14; Php 1:6; Heb 7:25; 2Pe 1:10

Assurance of eternal life

Jn 3:15–16; 1Jn 5:11–13 See also Mt 19:29 pp Mk 10:30 pp Lk 18:30; Jn 5:24; 6:40; 11:25–26; 17:2; 1Jn 1:2; 5:20

Assurance of a future hope

Assurance of confidence at Jesus Christ's return Mt 24:30–31 pp Mk 13:26–27 pp Lk 21:27–28; 1Th 4:13–17

Assurance on the day of judgment 1Co 1:8; 1Th 3:13; 1Jn 4:17

Assurance in the hope of resurrection Jn 6:40; 1Co 15:42–44; Php 3:21

Assurance in the hope of glory Ro 8:18 See also Ro 5:2; Col 3:4; 1Th 2:12; 1Pe 5:10; Rev 5:10

Assurance in the hope of an eternal inheritance Ro 8:17 See also Mt 25:34; Gal 4:7; Heb 9:15; 1Pe 1:3–5

Assurance in the hope of an eternal reward Mt 5:12 pp Lk 6:23; 2Ti 4:7–8; Jas 1:12

See also

1035 God, faithfulness	6652 forgiveness
	6708 predestination
1190 glory	6754 union with Christ
2565 Christ, second coming	
	8213 confidence
6510 salvation	8459 perseverance
6638 election	9310 resurrection
6644 eternal life	

8107

assurance, and life of faith

The completeness of conviction and confidence expressed in the life of the believer, worked by the Holy Spirit. It derives from a reliance upon God and his promises alone, and results in boldness and steadfastness in service and in the face of difficulties.

Assurance and faith

Dt 9:3; Heb 10:22 See also Dt 1:21; Jos 1:9; 2Ch 20:17; Jn 17:8; Heb 11:1; 12:5

Assurance and hope

Heb 6:11 See also Pr 23:18; Heb 6:19

Assurance expressed by believers

Assurance in adversity Heb 13:6 See also Ps 118:6–7; 3:6; 27:3–5; 46:1–3; 71:5–6; 73:26; Ro 8:38–39; 2Co 4:16

Assurance of God's promises Jos 23:14 See also 1Ki 8:56; Ro 4:20–21; 2Co 1:20

Assurance in ministry Ro 1:16; 1Ti 3:13 See also 2Co 3:4; 4:1; 5:14; 1Th 1:5; 2Pe 1:12

Assurance in prayer 1Jn 5:14 See also 1Jn 3:21–22

Assurance of God's will Ro 14:5 See also Ro 14:14,23; 1Co 8:9–11

Assurance may be strengthened

Examples of believers asking for assurance Ge 15:8 Abraham; Ex 33:16 Moses; Jdg 6:17 Gideon; Lk 1:18 Zechariah

Assurance through understanding

Col 2:2

Assurance through waiting on God

Ps 46:10 See also Ps 27:14; 33:20; Isa 30:15; 32:17–18 The revelation of God's righteousness among his people results in true peace.

Assurance strengthened by others

2Ch 32:6–8 by example; 2Ti 3:14 through teaching; Col 4:12 through prayer; 1Th 3:2–3 through encouragement amidst trials

False teaching weakens assurance

2Th 2:2; 2Ti 2:18

The delusion of false assurance

The danger of self-assurance Lk 18:9–14; 2Co 10:12; Php 3:3–4

Such assurance proved false by conduct 1Jn 1:6 See also 1Jn 2:9–11; 3:6; 4:20; 2Jn 9; 3Jn 11

See also

4020 life of faith	8224 dependence
6705 peace, experience	8453 obedience
	8724 doubt, dealing with
8020 faith	
8030 trust	8823 self-righteousness
8202 boldness	
8221 courage, strength from God	9610 hope

8108

assurance, and Holy Spirit

See 3203 Holy Spirit, and assurance

8110

athletics

Sports engaged in by athletes. Scripture uses the image of running in a race to represent the Christian life. Believers should show similar perseverance as they press on to their heavenly reward.

The Christian life is like running a race

Ac 20:24 See also Gal 2:2; 5:7; Php 2:16; 1Ti 1:18–19

Christians, like athletes, are to be single-minded

2Ti 2:4–5 See also 1Co 9:24–27

Christians, like athletes, are to persevere

Heb 12:1 See also Php 3:12–14; 1Ti 6:12; Rev 3:11

The reward at the end of the race of life

2Ti 4:7–8 See also 1Co 9:25; Jas 1:12; 1Pe 5:4; Rev 2:10 The "crown" referred to is the garland or wreath awarded to the winner in athletics contests.

The race is not necessarily won by the swiftest

Ecc 9:11

See also

5178 running	8140 prize
5280 crown	8207 commitment
5387 leisure, pastimes	8459 perseverance
	9410 heaven
5498 reward	

8112
certainty

A sure knowledge or conviction that what is believed is true and trustworthy. Christian certainty does not arise from the credulity of the believer, but is based on the faithfulness and trustworthiness of God.

Affirmations and statements of certainty
Job 19:25 *See also* Jos 23:14; Ps 27:3; Da 3:17; Mk 5:28 pp Mt 9:21; Lk 1:3–4; Ro 8:38–39; Php 3:8; 1Jn 5:18–20

Certainty in God
Because of his character Heb 6:18 *See also* Nu 23:19–20; Dt 7:9–10; 32:3–4; 2Sa 7:28; Ps 18:30–31; Isa 26:4

Because his promises are confirmed Heb 6:16–19 *See also* Ro 15:8

His intervention encourages certainty Jdg 6:36–40 *See also* Ex 16:6–8; 33:12–23; Jos 3:9–13; 1Ki 18:36–39

Jesus Christ's certainty about his identity and mission
Jn 13:3 *See also* Mk 8:31 pp Mt 16:21 pp Lk 9:22; Jn 10:14–18; 14:6–11

Certainty and the believer
Certainty about who Jesus Christ is 2Ti 1:12 *See also* Mt 16:16 pp Mk 8:29 pp Lk 9:20; Jn 11:27; 20:28–29; 21:24

Certainty of salvation 2Co 1:21–22 *See also* Ro 4:16; 8:31–39; Php 1:6; Heb 6:18–19; 1Jn 4:13

Certainty gained through obedience 1Jn 2:3–6 *See also* Mt 7:24–27 pp Lk 6:46–49

Certainty in prayer 1Jn 5:14–15 *See also* Mt 7:7–11 pp Lk 11:9–13; Mt 18:19–20; 21:21–22 pp Mk 11:22–24; Jn 14:13–14

An area of permissible uncertainty Mk 13:32–37 *See also* Ac 1:6–7; 1Th 5:1–2

See also
1035 God, faithfulness	6632 conviction
2565 Christ, second coming	8104 assurance
	8213 confidence
3203 Holy Spirit & assurance	8602 prayer
	8721 doubt
	9610 hope

8114
discipleship

The process of becoming a committed follower of Jesus Christ, with all the spiritual discipline and benefits which this brings.

8115
discipleship, nature of

The state of following Jesus Christ, and serving and obeying him. The NT stresses the privileges, joys and cost of this calling.

Discipleship involves learning
Learning from God Jn 6:45 *See also* Isa 54:13; Lev 11:44–45; 19:2; 20:7; Eph 5:1–2; 1Pe 1:15–16

Learning from Jesus Christ Mt 11:29 *See also* Jn 13:15; Eph 4:20–21; Php 2:5; 1Pe 2:21; 1Jn 2:6

Learning from the Holy Spirit Jn 14:26 *See also* Lk 12:12; Jn 16:13; 1Co 2:13; Eph 1:17; 3:16–19; 1Pe 1:12

Learning from other people Php 4:9 *See also* Dt 4:10; 5:1; 31:12; 1Co 4:6,16; 11:1; Php 3:17; 2Th 3:7,9; 1Ti 2:11; 5:4; 2Ti 3:14

Learning to do what is good Tit 3:14 *See also* Ps 34:14; 37:27; Isa 1:17; 26:9; 3Jn 11

Jesus Christ calls people to be his disciples
Mt 4:19 pp Mk 1:17 *See also* Mt 4:21 pp Mk 1:20 *Jesus Christ calls James and John*; Mt 8:21–22 pp Lk 9:59–60; Mt 9:9 pp Mk 2:14 pp Lk 5:27 *Jesus Christ calls Matthew*; Mt 19:21 pp Mk 10:21 pp Lk 18:22; Jn 1:43 *Jesus Christ calls Philip*; Jn 21:19

The consequences of discipleship
Following Jesus Christ Mt 10:38 *See also* Mt 16:24 pp Mk 8:34 pp Lk 9:23; Lk 14:27; Jn 10:27; 12:26; Rev 14:4

Serving Jesus Christ Col 3:24 *See also* Mt 20:25–28 pp Mk 10:42–45; Ro 12:11; 1Th 1:9

Obeying Jesus Christ Jn 8:31 *See also* Jn 14:21,23–24; 15:10,14; 1Jn 2:3; 3:22,24; 5:3

Responding immediately to Jesus Christ's commands Mt 8:21–22 *See also* Mt 4:20 pp Mk 1:18; Mt 4:22 pp Mk 1:20 pp Lk 5:11

Living for Jesus Christ and not for oneself 2Co 5:15 *See also* Ro 14:7–8; 1Pe 4:2

Loving others Jn 13:12–17 *See also* Jn 15:9–14; 1Jn 4:7–21

Total commitment is required of Jesus Christ's disciples
Mt 10:37–39 *See also* Mt 16:24–25 pp Mk 8:34–35 pp Lk 9:23–24; Mk 6:8; Lk 14:26–27; 17:33; Jn 12:25

The purpose of discipleship is to become Christlike
Eph 4:22–24 *See also* Mt 5:48; Lk 6:40; Ro 8:29 *God's purpose in election*; Ro 12:1–2; 13:14; 2Co 3:18; 7:1; Eph 1:4; Col 1:28; 3:12; 2Ti 3:17 *the purpose of Scripture*; 1Pe 1:14–15 *a call to holiness*; 2Pe 1:5–7; 1Jn 3:2–3

Examples of secret discipleship
Jn 3:1–2 *See also* Jn 7:50; 12:42; 19:38–39

See also
1660 Sermon on the Mount	8206 Christlikeness
4020 life of faith	8207 commitment
5941 secrecy	8266 holiness
6744 sanctification	8342 servanthood
7620 disciples	8453 obedience
8102 abiding in Christ	

8116
discipleship, cost of

The denial of self-interests and desires, and a total commitment to do the will of God, even to the point of death.

The cost of discipleship involves a denial of self-interests and desires
The cost involves self-denial Mt 16:24 pp Mk 8:34 pp Lk 9:23 *See also* Mt 10:38; Lk 14:27

Self-denial means not living for oneself Ro 14:7 *See also* 2Co 5:15; Gal 2:20; 1Pe 4:2

The cost of discipleship is to be carefully considered
Lk 14:28–32

The cost of discipleship means total commitment to the will of God
Total surrender is required Lk 14:33 *See also* Php 3:7–8

The security of the world is to be resisted Mt 8:19–20 pp Lk 9:57–58

Jesus Christ must have first priority Lk 9:59–60 pp Mt 8:21–22 *See also* Mt 19:16–21 pp Mk 10:17–21 pp Lk 18:18–22; Col 1:18

Jesus Christ must come before family ties Lk 9:61–62 *See also* Mt 10:37; Lk 14:26

The cost of discipleship is constant
Lk 9:23

The cost of discipleship includes persecution
Jn 15:20 *See also* Ac 14:22; 2Ti 3:12

The cost of discipleship includes willingess to suffer and die for Jesus Christ's sake
Mt 10:38–39 *See also* Mt 16:24–25 pp Mk 8:34–35 pp Lk 9:23–24; Jn 12:25

See also
8120 following Christ	8461 priorities
8248 faithfulness	8475 self-denial
8356 unselfishness	8481 self-sacrifice
8450 martyrdom	8794 persecution
8451 mortification	

8117
discipleship, benefits of

Joy, peace and happiness result from following Jesus Christ, together with the hope of being like him and with him in heaven. This is anticipated in the OT, which stresses the importance of obedience to the LORD.

Blessings result from obedient discipleship
Lk 11:28 *See also* Pr 8:32; Mt 7:24–25 pp Lk 6:47–48; Jn 13:17; 14:21; Jas 1:25

Joy results from discipleship
Jn 15:10–11 *See also* Ps 119:14;

Ac 13:52; 16:34 *the Philippian jailer*;
Ro 14:17; 15:13; Gal 5:22 *the fruit of the
Spirit*; Php 1:25; 1Th 1:6; Heb 10:34;
1Pe 1:6,8; Jude 24

Peace results from discipleship

Jn 14:27 *See also* Nu 6:26; Ps 4:8; 29:11;
37:11; Isa 26:3; Mt 11:28–29 *Jesus Christ
promises rest for the weary*; Lk 2:14 *the
angels' greeting to the shepherds at the
birth of Jesus Christ
Jesus Christ's greeting to his disciples when
he first appeared to them after his
resurrection*: Lk 24:36; Jn 20:19
Jn 16:33; 20:21,26; Ro 2:10; 5:1;
Php 4:7; Col 3:15

True happiness results from discipleship

Happiness flows from doing God's will
Ps 1:1; 119:1–2 *See also* Ps 94:12; 112:1;
128:1; Pr 29:18

Disciples are truly happy Mt 5:3–12
pp Lk 6:20–23 *See also* Rev 1:3; 22:14

Disciples are abundantly recompensed in this life

Mk 10:29–30 pp Mt 19:29
pp Lk 18:29–30 *See also* Pr 15:16; 16:8;
Mt 7:7–11 pp Lk 11:9–13; Jn 8:12;
10:27; 12:26; Ro 8:31–39; 1Ti 6:6

Disciples are blessed by being united with Jesus Christ in the family of God

Mt 12:46–50 pp Mk 3:31–35
pp Lk 8:19–21 *See also* Gal 6:10;
Eph 2:19; 3:15

Disciples will be blessed with eternal life

Mt 19:29 pp Mk 10:30 pp Lk 18:30 *See
also* Mt 25:46; Ro 2:7; Gal 6:8; 1Jn 1:2;
5:11,13,20

Disciples have the hope of being like Jesus Christ and being with him in heaven

1Jn 3:2 *See also* Jn 12:26; 14:3; Ro 8:29;
1Co 15:49; 2Pe 1:4

See also
3254 Holy Spirit, fruit
  of
5874 happiness
6644 eternal life
6700 peace
7115 children of God
7921 fellowship
8124 guidance

8134 knowing God
8258 fruitfulness,
  spiritual
8283 joy
8347 spiritual
  growth
9610 hope

8120

following Jesus Christ

The NT provides examples of
individuals who followed Jesus
Christ and of the implications of this
decision for their lives.

Examples of those who followed Jesus Christ

Crowds of people Mt 4:25 *See also*
Mt 8:1; 12:15 pp Mk 3:7; Mt 14:13
pp Lk 9:11 pp Jn 6:2; Mt 19:2; Mk 2:15;
5:24; Lk 7:9,11

Those who were healed Mt 20:34 *See
also* Mk 10:52 pp Lk 18:43

Those who were needy Mt 9:27

The disciples Mt 8:23 *See also*
Mk 14:51; 15:41; Jn 18:15

Examples of those who obeyed Jesus Christ's call to follow him

Peter and Andrew Mt 4:18–20
pp Mk 1:16–18 *See also* Lk 5:11

James and John Mk 1:19–20

Matthew Mt 9:9 pp Mk 2:14
pp Lk 5:27–28

Philip Jn 1:43–45

Examples of those who hesitated when called to follow Jesus Christ

Mt 19:21 pp Mk 10:21 pp Lk 18:22–23;
Lk 9:59–60

Wrong motives in following Jesus Christ

1Co 1:11–13

The cost of following Jesus Christ

Carrying one's cross Mt 16:24–26
pp Mk 8:34–37 pp Lk 9:23–25 *See also*
Mt 10:37–39; Lk 14:25–33;
Jn 12:23–25

Leaving security behind Mt 8:19–20
pp Lk 9:57–58 *See also* Lk 9:61–62

Those who failed to persevere in
following Jesus Christ Jn 6:66

Those who persevered under suffering in following Jesus Christ

Jn 13:12–17; 21:19; Ac 22:4; 24:14;
Ro 15:5; 1Co 11:1; 1Th 1:6;
1Pe 2:20–23; Rev 14:4; 17:14

The blessings of following Jesus Christ

Mt 19:27–30 pp Mk 10:28–31
pp Lk 18:28–30 *The reward is not on the
basis of merit but the free gift promised to
those who follow Jesus Christ. See also*
Jn 8:12; 12:26

The limits on following Jesus Christ

Jn 13:36

See also
2339 Christ, example
  of
4020 life of faith
5279 crowds
5498 reward
5919 popularity
7620 disciples

7706 apostles
8114 discipleship
8206 Christlikeness
8209 commitment to
  Christ
8449 imitating
8453 obedience

8122

friendship, with God

A relationship of love and
faithfulness into which God calls all
people through faith.

Examples of friendship with God

Abraham Jas 2:23 *See also* 2Ch 20:7;
Isa 41:8

Moses Ex 33:11 *See also* Nu 12:8;
Dt 34:10

Job Job 29:4–5 *See also* Job 16:20–21

Examples of friendship with Jesus Christ

Mary, Martha and Lazarus Jn 11:5 *See
also* Jn 11:3,11,35–36; 12:1–2

The beloved disciple Jn 13:23 *"the
disciple whom Jesus loved" is generally
thought to be John. See also* Jn 19:26;
20:2; 21:7,20

The disciples Jn 15:14–15

The ministry of Jesus Christ is an expression of friendship to sinners

In his life on earth Mt 11:19 pp Lk 7:34
See also Lk 7:39; 19:7

In his death on the cross Jn 15:13 ;
Ro 5:7–8 *See also* Lk 12:4; Jn 3:16;
1Pe 3:18

God's delight in friendship with those who he loves

Isa 5:7; Hos 11:1–4 *See also* 1Jn 1:3

The reliability of God as a friend

Isa 54:10 *See also* Dt 7:9; Jos 1:5;
Pr 18:24; Jn 13:1; Heb 13:5

God's invitation for people to know his friendship

Ps 145:18; Jas 4:8; Rev 3:20 *Sharing a
meal is a strong expression of friendship in
Scripture. See also* Zec 1:3; Mal 3:7;
Ac 17:27; Jas 4:4

See also
1035 God,
  faithfulness
2015 Christ,
  compassion
2033 Christ,
  humanity
2233 Son of Man

5077 Abraham,
  character
5690 friends
5895 intimacy
7922 fellowship with
  God

8124

guidance

God has purposes and plans for his
people, as individuals and
communities. Believers and
churches should seek his direction
and counsel in discerning these
purposes and plans in their lives.
This set of themes consists of the
following:

8125 guidance, God's promises of
8126 guidance, need for God's
8127 guidance, of Holy Spirit
8128 guidance, receiving God's
8129 guidance, examples of God's
8130 guidance, from godly people
8131 guidance, results of

8125

guidance, God's promises of

Scripture bears witness to God's
promises of guidance for his people.

All God's intentions will be realised

God has purposes Isa 14:27 *See also*
Job 36:5; Isa 55:10–11; Jer 23:20;
Ro 8:28; Eph 3:10–11; 2Ti 1:9; Heb 6:17

God has plans La 2:17 *See also* Ps 33:11;
40:5; Pr 16:9; Isa 14:24; 25:1; 37:26

God desires his purposes and plans to be fulfilled Lk 22:42 pp Mt 26:39 pp Mk 14:36; Ac 21:14 *See also* 1Ch 13:2; Ps 57:2; 138:8; Ac 18:21; Ro 1:10; 15:32; Jas 4:13–15

Examples of God working out his purposes
Ac 2:23
Babylon and Israel: Isa 46:10–11; 48:14
Jer 29:10–11 restoration of Israel after the exile; Ac 13:36 David; Ro 9:11–12 Esau and Jacob; Ro 9:17 Pharaoh

God promises to guide Israel and Judah
Ex 15:13 *See also* Ex 32:34; Ps 23:2–3; 48:14; Isa 30:21; 49:10; 58:11; Jer 31:8–9; Eze 34:11–16; Lk 1:76–79

Other promises of God's guidance
Ge 12:1; 26:2–3; 1Sa 16:3; Ps 32:8; 67:4; Isa 42:16; Rev 7:17

See also
1115 God, purpose of	4020 life of faith
1175 God, will of	5942 security
1220 God as shepherd	

8126
guidance, need for God's

God's guidance is needed because people are naturally ignorant and rebellious and there are many who lead others astray.

The need to know and do the will of God
Jer 10:23 *See also* Ezr 7:18; 1Th 4:3; Heb 13:20–21; 1Pe 2:15; 1Jn 2:17; Mt 6:10; 7:21; 12:50 pp Mk 3:35 pp Lk 8:21; Jn 7:17

The concern of Jesus Christ to do the will of God Jn 6:38 *See also* Jn 4:34

By themselves people are ignorant of the right way in life
Pr 14:12 *See also* Ecc 6:12; 8:7; Isa 53:6; 59:10 *blindness the result of disobedience;* Mt 9:36; 1Pe 2:25

Warnings against false guidance
False prophets and teachers
Jer 23:25–27; Lk 11:52 pp Mt 23:13 *See also* Isa 9:16; Jer 23:13; 27:9–10; Mic 3:5; 2Pe 2:1–3; Jude 17–19

False shepherds and guides Jer 50:6; Mt 24:24 *See also* Isa 3:12; Jer 10:21; 23:1–2; Eze 34:4–6; Mt 15:14; Ac 20:30

Idols and mediums Zec 10:2 *See also* Lev 19:31; Isa 41:22–24; Am 2:4; Hab 2:19

Other agencies 1Ki 11:3; 2Ki 21:9; 2Ch 21:11; Pr 16:29; 1Co 15:33; Rev 12:9; 18:23

Despite knowing God's will, sinners still rebel against him
Jer 18:11–12 *See also* Isa 30:9–11; Jer 6:16; 42:5–6,19–21; 2Ti 4:3

The adverse consequences of false guidance and disobedience
1Ch 10:13–14 *See also* Job 5:12; Ps 33:10–11; 146:3–4; Isa 19:3; 30:1;

Jer 19:7; Hos 11:5–7; Heb 3:7–11; Ps 95:7–11

See also
1310 God as judge	5917 plans
2057 Christ, obedience	5927 resentment
	6181 ignorance
4195 spirits	7774 prophets, false
5133 blindness	8749 false teachers
5494 revenge	8768 idolatry

8127
guidance, of Holy Spirit
See 3263 Holy Spirit, guidance of

8128
guidance, receiving God's

God's guidance is promised to those who genuinely desire it and seek it.

God's readiness to guide his people
Ps 25:4–5; Jas 1:5 *See also* Ex 33:12–16; Job 6:24; Ps 5:8; 27:11; 31:3; 61:1–2; 86:11; 143:8

Guidance is given through the truth and counsel of God
Ps 43:3 *See also* Ps 16:7–8; 73:23–24; 119:35,105,133; Jn 10:3–4,27

Guidance is given to the humble and penitent
Pr 3:5–6 *See also* 2Ch 6:26–27; Ps 25:9; 139:23–24; Isa 57:15,18–19; Jer 50:4–5; Eze 20:1–3,30–31

Guidance is given to those willing to obey God's will
Mt 26:39 pp Mk 14:35–36 pp Lk 22:42 *See also* Nu 14:8–9; Ps 32:8–9; Isa 48:17–18; Ro 12:1–2

The role of the Holy Spirit in guidance
Lk 12:11–12 *See also* Ps 143:10; Jn 16:13; Ac 10:19–20; 13:2; 16:6–7; Gal 5:18; 1Jn 2:26–27

Receiving guidance from Scripture
Ps 119:105,133 *See also* Ps 19:8; Isa 8:19–20; Ac 17:11; 2Pe 1:19

Means of being guided by God
The pillar of cloud and the pillar of fire Ex 13:21–22 *See also* Ex 14:19–20; Ne 9:19

The Urim and the Thummin Ex 28:29–30; Nu 27:21

The casting of lots 1Sa 14:36–42; Pr 16:33; Jnh 1:7; Ac 1:26

Dreams and visions Mt 2:19–20 ; Ac 9:10–11 *See also* Ge 40:5–8; Joel 2:28; Ac 10:3–6; 11:5–9

Angels Ac 8:26 *See also* Ac 5:19

See also
1460 truth	8408 decision-making
1610 Scripture	
6622 choice	8412 decisions
6732 repentance	8602 prayer
8160 seeking God	8648 enquiring of God
8226 discernment	
8276 humility	8678 waiting on God

8129
guidance, examples of God's

Scripture provides numerous examples of individuals who have realised their need of God's guidance and who have been given direction by him.

Examples of God taking the initiative to lead his people
God's guidance of Israel and her leaders at the exodus Ex 13:17–18; Dt 8:2,15; 32:12; Jos 24:2–3; Ps 77:19–20; 106:9; Ac 7:36; 13:17

God's guidance likened to that of a shepherd Ps 23:1–3 *See also* Ps 78:52–54; Isa 40:11; 63:11–14; Jer 23:3; Eze 34:12–13; Hos 11:3–4; Jn 10:3

God's guidance of Paul during his missionary journeys Ac 16:6–10

Examples of God responding to requests for guidance
Abraham's servant Ge 24:12–27

Balaam Nu 23:3–8

Gideon Jdg 6:36–40

Israel Jdg 20:23–28; Ps 107:4–7, 23–30

Saul and Samuel 1Sa 9:6–10,15–20; 10:20–24

David 1Sa 23:1–5; 30:7–8; 2Sa 2:1; 5:18–19,22–25

Ahab and Micaiah 1Ki 22:12–23

Josiah and Huldah the prophetess 2Ki 22:13–20

Jehoshaphat and Jahaziel the son of Zechariah 2Ch 20:15–17

Zedekiah and Jeremiah Jer 21:1–7

Examples of God's guidance being refused or disobeyed
Saul 1Sa 28:4–7

The people of Jerusalem Jer 2:13–17; 43:1–4

See also
2330 Christ as shepherd	3263 Holy Spirit, guidance
3130 Holy Spirit, Counsellor	5960 success
	7221 exodus, the

8130
guidance, from godly people

Scripture gives examples of God guiding his people through the example and witness of godly leaders and men and women of faith.

The guidance of godly leaders
Moses Ex 32:34; 33:12–17; Dt 10:11; 31:2

Joshua Nu 27:15–18; Dt 1:38; 3:28; Jos 1:6

Gideon Jdg 7:17

David 2Sa 5:1–2 pp 1Ch 11:1–2; Ps 78:70–72

Solomon 1Ki 3:5–13 pp 2Ch 1:7–12

Israel's priests Dt 17:9–10; Mal 2:6–7

Israel's shepherds Jer 3:15; 23:3–4

Pastors and teachers in the church
Eph 4:11–13; 2Ti 2:24–26

Godly parents
Ge 18:19; Pr 4:11–13; 6:20–23; 13:1;
22:6; Eph 6:4

Other godly people
Job 31:18; Pr 16:23; Da 5:12–17

See also
5731 parents   7784 shepherd
5780 advisers   8361 wisdom
7733 leaders

8131
guidance, results of

Wise counsel, advice and direction
from God or his servants, if carefully
followed, will enrich and benefit
those to whom it is given.

**Guidance resulting in military
victory**
2Sa 5:17–20 pp 1Ch 14:8–11 *See also*
Jos 6:1–21; 8:1–22; Jdg 6:33–7:25;
2Sa 5:22–25 pp 1Ch 14:13–16

Guidance resulting in safety
Mt 2:1–23

**Guidance resulting in personal
benefit**
2Sa 2:1–4 *See also* Ge 24:10–27;
41:1–49; 2Ki 5:1–14

**Guidance resulting in the
appointment of leaders**
Ac 13:1–3 *See also* 1Ki 19:15–21;
Lk 6:12–16; Ac 1:15–26

Guidance inspiring confidence
Ac 23:11 *See also* Ge 46:1–7;
Ac 18:9–11

**Guidance resulting in spiritual
growth**
Pr 9:9 *See also* Ex 16:1–30; 1Ki 19:3–18;
Ac 9:1–19

**Guidance eliciting praise and
worship**
Da 2:19–23 *See also* Ex 14:15–15:21;
2Sa 7:1–29; Ps 73:23–28

Guidance leading to obedience
Ge 12:1–5 *See also* Ge 6:9–22;
Jdg 6:11–27

Guidance disregarded
Mt 19:16–22 pp Mk 10:17–22
pp Lk 18:18–23 *See also* Ge 3:1–6;
1Ki 22:1–38

See also
1020 God, all-   8347 spiritual
    knowing   growth
1180 God, wisdom of   8453 obedience
5605 warfare   8622 worship
5779 advice   8664 praise
8281 insight   8718 disobedience

8134

knowing God

A faith-relationship and love-
relationship with God involving
mind, heart and will, and bringing

experience of his presence and
power. To know God is to worship
him and be transformed by him.
Human knowledge of God, which
begins with knowledge about him,
comes through God's self-revelation.

8135
knowing God, nature of

To know God is not merely to know
things about him, such as his
character, but also to experience his
presence and power. To know God is
to be transformed by him. Human
knowledge of God is as a result of
God's revelation of himself.

The origin of knowing God
Knowing God depends on revelation
Ro 11:33–36 *See also* Isa 40:13;
Dt 29:29; Nu 12:6; 23:3; Job 12:22;
Isa 40:5; 65:1; Eze 20:5; Da 2:20–23,28
Am 4:13; Mt 11:25–27 pp Lk 10:21–22
*Jesus Christ praises the Father for the
revelation the disciples receive;*
Ro 16:25–26; Gal 1:12; Eph 3:4–5

God gives knowledge of his reality
through creation Ro 1:20 *See also* Ps 8:1;
19:1–4; 97:6; Ac 14:17; 17:24–27

God gives knowledge of his mercy and
his will through Scripture, both law and
gospel Ro 1:17 *See also* Dt 31:13;
Ac 10:36; 1Co 1:20–21; Heb 8:10–11;
Jer 31:33–34

God gives knowledge of himself
through Jesus Christ Mt 11:27
pp Lk 10:22 *See also* Jn 3:2; 8:19; 10:32;
14:7; 16:30; 17:3; Col 2:2; 2Ti 1:9–10;
1Pe 1:20–21

God gives knowledge of himself and
his ways through the Spirit Eph 1:17
See also Isa 11:2; Jn 14:16–17,26; 15:26;
16:12–15; Ac 4:31; 1Co 2:9–11; 12:8;
Eph 3:16–19; 1Pe 1:12

God gives knowledge of his greatness
and grace through experience of him,
submission to him and in answer to
prayer Ps 56:9–11 *See also* Ex 9:29;
Ps 17:6–7; 66:19–20; Isa 41:19–20;
45:3–6; 50:4; 60:16; Jer 22:16; 24:7;
Eze 6:7

The nature of knowing God
Knowing his character Jnh 4:2 *See also*
Dt 7:9; Ps 9:10; 36:10; 135:5; 1Th 4:3–5;
1Jn 4:8,16

Knowing his words and works Am 3:7
See also Ge 41:25 *Pharaoh;* Ex 6:6–7;
7:5,17; 18:11; Dt 29:29
Samuel: 1Sa 3:7,21
David: 1Sa 17:46; 2Sa 7:21
pp 1Ch 17:19; 2Sa 7:27 pp 1Ch 17:25
2Ki 8:10 *Elisha;* 2Ki 19:19 *Hezekiah;*
Ps 147:19; Eze 20:9; Lk 2:26 *Simeon;*
Jn 17:8; Ac 2:22; 22:14

To know Jesus Christ is to know God
Jn 14:6; Col 1:15 *See also* Mt 16:16–17;
Jn 8:19; 15:15; 16:15; 17:26; Col 2:2–3;
1Jn 5:20

To know God is to experience his
salvation Jn 17:3 *See also* Ps 17:6–7;
Isa 25:9; 43:12; 52:10; 56:1; 1Jn 5:13,20

See also
1320 God as Saviour   4018 life, spiritual
1403 God, revelation   5029 knowledge of
1439 revelation   God
1610 Scripture   5375 law
3140 Holy Spirit,
    teacher

8136
knowing God, effects of

Knowing God has a transforming
effect on a person spiritually and
morally and makes that person bold
in actions for God. Not knowing
God in the present will result in
dissatisfaction and degeneration into
wickedness and in the future will
bring eternal alienation from him.

The effects of knowing God
Spiritual transformation: from death to
life Col 1:9 *See also* Jn 17:3; Gal 4:8–9;
Eph 1:17; 3:19; Col 2:2

Moral transformation: from evil to
good Pr 2:1–6; 2Co 10:5; 1Th 4:3–5 *See
also* Ro 16:26; Eph 4:17–24;
Php 1:9–11; Col 1:10; 1Jn 3:10; 4:8

Boldness of action for God
Jer 32:38–39; Da 11:32 *See also*
Ps 138:3; Pr 28:1; Ac 6:8–10; 2Co 3:12;
1Pe 1:13

Biblical images of knowing God
Like parent and child 2Sa 7:14
pp 1Ch 17:13 1Jn 3:1
God disciplines like a parent: Heb 12:6;
Pr 3:12; Dt 8:5
Ps 2:7; 27:10; 68:5; 89:26; 103:13;
Isa 49:15; 66:12–13; Hos 11:1;
Mt 5:45,48; 6:6–9,18,32; Lk 15:11–32
the parable of the lost son; Jn 14:21;
1Co 1:3

Like husband and wife Isa 62:5;
Jer 3:14 *See also* Isa 54:5; Jer 2:2; 3:20;
31:32; Hos 2:16; Eph 5:25; Rev 19:7;
21:2

Like king and subject Ps 97:1 *See also*
1Sa 8:7; Ps 5:2; 10:16; 29:10; 44:4; 84:3;
95:3; 99:1; 145:1; Mt 6:33 pp Lk 12:31
*Jesus Christ on seeking first his
kingdom;* 1Ti 1:17; 6:15

Like shepherd and sheep Ge 48:15;
Ps 23:1–2; Isa 40:11 *See also* Ps 28:9;
80:1; Eze 34:16; Mic 7:14; Jn 10:11;
Rev 7:17

The peril of not knowing God
Lack of satisfaction and degeneration
in the present Ro 1:21–32; Tit 1:15–16
See also Ex 5:2; Jer 4:22; Ro 10:2–3;
1Th 4:3–5

Eternal punishment in the future
Mt 7:22–23; Ro 1:18–19 *See also*
Ro 2:5; 2Th 1:8

See also
1040 God,   2312 Christ as king
    fatherhood   6020 sin
1210 God, human   7115 children of God
    descriptions   8202 boldness
1215 God, feminine   8347 spiritual
    descriptions   growth
1220 God as   9210 judgment,
    shepherd   God's

8138

monotheism

The central doctrine that there is one true God, who alone is the object of worship. There is none like the LORD; other gods and idols are nothing. Scripture also indicates that there is a network of relationships within the Godhead which is stated in terms of the doctrine of the Trinity.

The doctrine of monotheism

There is only one God Dt 6:4; Eph 4:6; 1Ti 2:5 *See also* Dt 4:35; 32:39; Ne 9:6; Ps 83:18; 86:10; Isa 43:10; 44:6; 45:18; Mk 12:29,32; Ro 3:30; 1Co 8:6; Jas 2:19

There is none like the LORD 1Ki 8:23 *See also* Ex 8:10; 2Sa 7:22 pp 1Ch 17:20; Ps 89:6; Isa 40:18,25

He alone is to be worshipped Ex 20:3–5 pp Dt 5:7–9Jer 25:6 *See also* Ex 20:23; 34:14; Dt 6:14; 13:6–8; 2Ki 17:38–39; Ps 81:9; Jer 1:16; 19:4; 35:15

He alone is to be served Mk 12:30 pp Mt 22:37 *See also* Dt 6:4–5,13; 13:4; 1Sa 7:3; Mt 4:10 pp Lk 4:8; 1Th 1:9–10

Other gods are nothing Isa 37:19; 1Co 8:4; 10:19–20 *Idols are nothing in themselves, but those worshipping them open themselves to demonic influence. See also* Dt 32:17; Ps 106:36–37; Isa 40:18–20; 44:9–11; Ac 14:15; Gal 4:8

Monotheism and plurality in the Godhead

In the OT Ge 1:26 *See also* Ge 1:2 *The Spirit of God is seen as God's agent;* Ge 3:22; 11:7; Ex 3:2–6 *The angel of the LORD is identified with, yet distinct from, God;* Jdg 13:20–22; Ne 9:20; Ps 139:7; Isa 6:8; 63:10–14

The Trinity in the NT Mt 28:19; 2Co 13:14 *See also* Mt 3:16–17; Jn 14:26; 15:26; Ac 2:32–33; Eph 2:18; 1Pe 1:2

See also

1060 God, greatness of	3015 Holy Spirit, divinity
1130 God, sovereignty	4140 angel of the Lord
1165 God, unique	8710 atheism
1510 Trinity, the	8768 idolatry
2018 Christ, divinity	8799 polytheism

8140

prize

Something of value given to those competing in a race, which the Christian life is likened to. Though believers must accept discipline and training, a prize is reserved for everyone who is committed to Jesus Christ.

A prize is reserved for all believers

2Ti 4:7–8 *The crown is the wreath given to the winner of a race. See also* Jas 1:12; 1Pe 5:4

Requirements for winning the prize

Total dedication to God Ac 20:24 *See also* Php 3:7–8

Perseverance Php 3:14 *See also* Php 2:16; Heb 12:1; Rev 2:10; 3:11

Keeping God's rules 2Ti 2:5

Self-discipline 1Co 9:25–27

Hindrances to winning the prize

Falling into sin Heb 12:1

Following false teaching Gal 5:7 *See also* Gal 2:2; Col 2:18

See also

5280 crown	8248 faithfulness
5498 reward	8453 obedience
5591 treasure	8459 perseverance
5596 victory	8476 self-discipline
8110 athletics	9413 heaven,
8207 commitment	inheritance
8223 dedication	

8142

religion

A set of beliefs, a form of worship, ritual, prayer and a code of moral behaviour. True faith in God, moral standards and good works are important in relation to a biblical understanding of true religion, which is contrasted with the false religion of paganism.

Belief

Heb 11:6 *See also* Ge 15:6 *Belief can easily be misdirected and become superstition:* 1Sa 4:3–8; 1Ki 20:23 Jnh 3:5; Jas 2:19 *Belief by itself is insufficient for salvation.*

Worship

Jnh 1:16 *See also* 2Ki 19:37 pp Isa 37:38; Jer 44:17–19; Ac 17:22–23

Ritual

Mk 7:3–4 *See also* Ex 32:2–6; 1Ki 18:22–29; Heb 10:11

Prayer

Isa 44:17 *See also* 1Ki 18:26; Isa 45:20; Lk 2:37; Ac 10:4

Code of behaviour

Ne 9:13–14 *See also* 2Ki 23:3 pp 2Ch 34:31; Mt 19:16–20 pp Mk 10:17–20 pp Lk 18:18–21; Mt 23:23 pp Lk 11:42 *Religious people do not always see the inconsistencies in their behaviour;* Lk 1:6; Jn 18:28; Jas 1:26

True religious practice

Jas 1:27

Moral standards 1Co 7:19 *See also* Mt 15:16–20 pp Mk 7:18–23; Mk 12:33; Lk 11:39–41; Ro 10:2–4; 14:17

Good works 1Ti 5:4 *See also* Mt 19:21 pp Mk 10:21 pp Lk 18:22; Eph 2:10; Jas 2:14–17

See also

7328 ceremonies	8240 ethics
7422 ritual	8309 morality
7435 sacrifice, in OT	8603 prayer,
8028 faith, body of	relationship
beliefs	with God

See also

8625 worship, acceptable attitudes	8784 nominal religion
8748 false religion	8799 polytheism
	8831 syncretism

8144

renewal

The regeneration or revitalisation that God brings to his people and creation, as part of the process of redemption.

8145

renewal, of people of God

The transformation by God of the lives of his people, whether corporately or individually, leading to the recovery of lost vitality and purity.

Individual renewal

Isa 40:30–31; Eph 4:22–24 *See also* Ps 23:3; 51:10–12; 103:1–5; Jn 7:37–39; Ro 12:2; 2Co 4:16; Col 3:9–10; 2Ti 1:6; Tit 3:5

Corporate renewal

The renewal of Israel Eze 37:1–14 *See also* Jer 31:31–34; La 5:21; Eze 11:17–20; 36:24–28; Joel 2:28–32

Examples of national renewal 2Ch 34:29–33 *See also* Jos 24:1,14–27; Ezr 10:1–4; Ne 10:28–29

The new Jerusalem Isa 65:17–19 *See also* Rev 3:12; 21:2–4,10

The church Mt 9:16–19 pp Mk 2:21–22 pp Lk 5:36–39*Jesus Christ here prophesies the great act of renewal by God whereby the church rather than Israel becomes the people of God. See also* Ac 2:1–4,42–47

See also

3230 Holy Spirit & regeneration	6511 salvation
5005 human race & redemption	6728 regeneration
	6744 sanctification
5012 heart	8148 revival
5038 mind, the human	8311 morality & redemption
5065 spirit, fallen & redeemed	8466 reformation
	9165 restoration

8146

renewal, of natural order

God's transformation of the natural order is part of his plan of redeeming the whole universe as well as humanity.

Cosmic renewal

Rev 21:1; Ro 8:19–21 *See also* Isa 65:17; 66:22; Mt 19:28; 2Pe 3:10–13; Rev 21:5

The renewal of nature

Isa 11:6–9 *See also* Ps 104:30; Isa 35:1–2,5–7; 43:18–21; 65:25; Eze 34:25–27

8148

revival

The sovereign activity of God whereby he renews his people individually and corporately in vigour, affecting both sincerity of belief and quality of behaviour.

8149

revival, nature of

Scripture indicates that a number of characteristics precede revival, including repentance, humility and obedience.

Characteristics which precede revival

God's people long for renewal of their lives Ps 80:18 *See also* Ps 74:22; 80:1–17,19; 85:6

God's people must repent 2Ch 7:14 *See also* 1Ki 8:46–50 pp 2Ch 6:26–27; Isa 64:1–7; Hos 5:15; Ac 3:19

God's people experience a new awareness of sin 2Ki 22:11 *See also* Ps 32:3–5

God's people need to be humble Isa 57:15 *See also* Ps 149:4; Isa 66:2; Mic 6:6–8

God's people are revived through God's initiative Isa 59:16 *See also* Jer 24:7; 33:6–9; Tit 3:5

Characteristic results of revival

People experience inward change Heb 8:10–12 *See also* Jer 31:33–34; Eze 11:19; Ac 2:42–47

People live obedient lives Eze 11:20 *See also* Eph 4:1–3; 1Th 1:7–8

People are zealous for God's work Ezr 5:1–2 *See also* Hag 1:12–15

People are generous in giving Ex 36:5 *See also* 1Ch 29:6–9; 2Ch 31:3–8; Ac 11:28–30

People delight in worshipping God Ezr 3:11 *See also* Isa 12:1–6

People are joyful Ac 13:49–52 *See also* Isa 35:1–10; Ac 8:5–8

8150

revival, personal

The bringing back of individuals to life or vigour both at the point of personal regeneration through the work of the Holy Spirit and at other times in believers' lives.

Aspects of individual revival

Physical revival Isa 38:16 *See also* Jdg 15:18–19; 1Sa 14:27; 30:11–12; 1Ki 19:7–8; Job 33:25; Ps 41:3; 116:8–9

Revival of hope Ge 45:27 *See also* Ru 4:14–15

Revival of sanity Da 4:26,34,36

Spiritual revival Ps 23:3 *See also* 1Ki 19:9–15; Jn 21:15–19

The Holy Spirit brings regeneration by giving spiritual life to those dead in sin

Eph 2:1–5; Tit 3:5–6

Preparation for personal spiritual revival

The Holy Spirit convicts Jn 16:8–11; Ac 2:37; 1Th 1:5

Individuals appeal to God Jer 17:14 *See also* Ps 51:7–12; 119:34–37

Individuals long for God Ps 42:1–2 *See also* Ps 63:1

Personal repentance is required Ps 51:1–4 *See also* 2Ch 32:26; 33:11–13; Job 22:23; Jer 15:19

The believer must take responsibility for personal revival

2Ti 1:6

God is active in bringing about personal revival

Isa 57:15 *See also* Ps 43:3–4; Isa 40:31; Hag 1:14

God's law may initiate personal revival Ps 19:7 *See also* Ps 119:130,162

The fruit of personal revival

God receives praise Ps 40:3 *See also* 2Sa 22:50 pp Ps 18:49; Ps 51:15; 59:16; 61:8

God is obeyed 2Ch 33:15–16 *See also* Ac 2:14 *Peter had denied Jesus Christ seven weeks before.*

8151

revival, corporate

The experience of God's people both in the OT and NT when prayer is answered and their growth and effectiveness are renewed.

The recurring pattern of apostasy and revival in the OT

Jdg 2:10–19

God is petitioned to revive his people

Ps 80:14–15 *See also* Ps 85:4–7; Jer 31:18; La 5:21; Hab 3:2

Repentance is necessary for revival

God's people are urged to repent 2Ch 30:6 *Hezekiah's appeal to all Israel.* *See also* Isa 55:1–3; Jer 3:22; La 3:40; Hos 12:6; 14:1–2; Zec 1:3; Mal 3:7; Rev 2:5,16; 3:2–3

Wholehearted repentance is required Joel 2:12–13 *See also* Dt 4:29; 30:2–3; Jer 24:7; 29:13–14; Ac 19:18–19 *Repentance should be evidenced by deeds.*

Repentance prepares for revival Isa 59:20 *See also* Jdg 10:9–16; Ezr 10:1,10–12; Ne 1:9; Eze 18:30–32

Revival is God's work

Hos 6:2 *See also* Ps 80:3,7,17–19; Isa 32:14–17

God promises revival

God promises to revive his people Eze 11:19 *See also* Jer 31:33–34; Eze 36:26; Zec 10:6

The nations are included in the promise of revival Isa 2:3 pp Mic 4:2 *See also* Isa 19:22–25; 45:22; 56:6–8; Zec 8:20–22

The revival of Israel

Under Hezekiah 2Ki 18:4–6; 2Ch 29:3–5; 30:1; 31:4,9–10,20–21

Under Josiah 2Ki 23:1–4 pp 2Ch 34:29–33; 2Ch 35:1–3

Revival in the NT

Crowds turn to the Lord Mk 1:5; Jn 3:26; 4:39; Ac 2:41,47; 4:4; 11:21

The Holy Spirit is active in the revival of believers Ac 4:31 *See also* Ac 13:9; 2Co 4:16; Eph 5:18

The response of believers in revival Ro 12:1–2 *See also* Eph 4:23–24; Php 3:13–14; Col 3:9–14

8154

righteousness

Scripture identifies a close link between righteousness and faith. Part of "being in a right relationship with God" is believing and trusting in him. The NT does not see faith simply in terms of moral righteousness, but also in terms of a living trusting relationship with God. Scripture affirms the righteousness of God and Jesus Christ in all their activity.

8155

righteousness, of God

See 1125 God, righteousness of

8156

righteousness, of Jesus Christ

See 2072 Jesus Christ, righteousness of

8157
righteousness, as faith

Full faith and trust make a person pleasing in the sight of God.

Human righteousness compared with God's righteousness
Human beings cannot by themselves achieve righteousness in the sight of God Ecc 7:20; Isa 64:6; Mt 5:20 *See also* Pr 21:2; Da 9:18; Mt 23:28; Lk 16:15; 18:9; Ro 3:10,20; Php 3:6–7

True righteousness is the result of the action of God
Ro 8:3–4; Eph 4:24; 1Jn 2:29 *See also* Ro 6:13,16–20; 8:10; 14:17; Gal 5:5; Eph 5:9; Php 1:11; Heb 12:11; Jas 3:18; 1Pe 2:24; 1Jn 3:10

Faith pleases God
Ge 15:6; Heb 11:6 *See also* 1Sa 26:23; Ps 32:10; 40:4; 84:12; 106:30–31; Jer 17:7; Hab 2:4; Heb 10:38; 11:4,7

Righteousness and faith in Jesus Christ
It is God-given and not the result of human effort Ro 1:17; Php 3:8–9 *Paul is contrasting this righteousness with his own previous efforts. See also* Ac 13:39; Ro 3:21,27–28 *It is apparent that faith is not regarded as another kind of "work" which earns salvation;* Ro 4:1–8; 5:17; 9:30–31; Gal 3:11–12

Faith is centred on Jesus Christ and what he has accomplished Ro 5:1–2 *"justified" means "declared righteous" in a legal sense. See also* Ro 3:21–26; 4:18–25; 10:6–10; Gal 3:6–9

Saving faith is not mere belief, but acting on the basis of that belief Jas 2:21–24

See also

1125 God, righteousness	5274 credit
2072 Christ, righteousness	6674 imputation
5145 clothing	6676 justification
5177 robes	8020 faith
5237 breastplate	8030 trust
	8255 fruit, spiritual

8158
righteousness, of believers

A sincere desire to please God by keeping his law is both commanded and approved by him. However, human fallibility means that true righteousness must be the product of the Holy Spirit's work in the believer.

Righteousness includes keeping the laws of God
Dt 6:25; Job 27:6; 1Jn 3:7 *See also* Ge 6:9 *Noah;* Ge 18:19 *Abraham;* Dt 6:17–18; 1Ki 3:6 *David;* 1Ki 15:11; 2Ch 31:20 *Hezekiah;* Ps 7:8; 15:1–5; 17:1; 32:11; 45:7; Isa 26:7–9; 48:18; 51:1; Hos 14:9; Lk 2:25 *Simeon;* Ac 4:19; 2Co 6:14; 2Ti 3:15–16

God requires righteousness of his people
Am 5:24; Mt 6:33 *See also* Isa 1:16–17;

56:1; Jer 22:3; Hos 10:12; Zep 2:3; Mt 5:6; Eph 6:14; 1Ti 6:11; 2Ti 2:22

God loves those who are righteous
Ps 146:8; Pr 15:9; Jas 1:20 *See also* Ps 1:5–6; 14:5; 33:5; 37:6,28–30; 106:3; Pr 10:16

The righteous receive blessing from God
Pr 12:28; Mt 13:43 *See also* Ps 5:12; 34:15 *the LORD watches over them;* Ps 37:16–17; 55:22; 92:12; 112:4; Pr 10:2–3,6–7,16,29–32 *they are secure;* Pr 11:4–6; Isa 3:10; 33:15–16; Da 12:3; Jas 5:16 *their prayers are effective*

The righteous may suffer for their faith
Mt 5:10 *See also* Ps 94:21; Isa 57:1; Am 2:6; 5:12; 1Pe 3:14

See also

1620 beatitudes, the	8201 blamelessness
3233 Holy Spirit & sanctification	8266 holiness
5380 law and gospel	8453 obedience
6744 sanctification	8460 pleasing God
7150 righteous, the	8794 persecution
7449 slavery, spiritual	8823 self-righteousness

8160

seeking God

God's desire is that all people should seek after him and find him. Those who seek God with all their heart are rewarded, but those who fail to seek him do so to their eternal loss.

God's heart is for people to seek him
God wants people to seek him Ac 17:27 *See also* 1Ch 16:11; 22:19; Ps 14:2; Ac 15:16–17; Am 9:11–12; Heb 11:6

God calls people to seek him Isa 55:6–7 *See also* Hos 10:12; Am 5:4–6

God promises that people will seek him Jer 50:4 *See also* Hos 3:4–5; 5:13–15; Zep 2:3; Zec 8:20–23

God promises to be found by those who seek him Pr 8:17 *See also* Dt 4:29–31; 1Ch 28:9; 2Ch 15:1–2; Isa 45:19; Jer 29:11–14; Mt 7:7–8 pp Lk 11:9–10

God's opportunity for seeking him is now and is restricted to this life 2Co 6:2 *See also* Lk 16:19–31

Seeking God is an issue of the heart
Seeking God begins in the heart Ps 27:8 *See also* 2Ch 11:16

Wholeheartedness in seeking God is required Jer 29:13 *See also* Dt 4:27–29; 1Ch 22:17–19; 2Ch 15:12–15; Ps 63:1

Seeking God and his kingdom is the priority of life
Mt 6:33 pp Lk 12:31 *See also* Ps 27:4; Mt 13:44–46

Examples of people seeking God
2Ki 22:11–20 *Josiah;* 2Ch 14:2–7 *Asa*

Jehoshaphat: 2Ch 17:3–6; 20:1–4 Ezr 8:21–23 *Ezra;* Ps 27:4–8; Da 9:2–3; Ac 13:1–3

The consequences of seeking God
It leads to life Am 5:4–6 *See also* Ps 69:32; Ro 2:7–8

It leads to forgiveness 2Ch 7:14 *See also* 2Ch 30:18–20; Isa 55:6–7; Jer 26:17–19

It leads to blessing Ps 119:2 *See also* Ps 24:3–6; Isa 65:9–10

It leads to provision Ps 34:8–10 *See also* Mt 6:31–33 pp Lk 12:29–31

It leads to protection Ps 27:4–5 *See also* Ezr 8:21–23

It leads to understanding and wisdom Pr 28:5 *See also* Da 2:17–23

It leads to renewed strength Isa 40:30–31 *See also* Lk 22:42–43

It leads to rejoicing 1Ch 16:10 *See also* Ps 40:16; 70:4; 105:3

Hindrances to seeking God
Unrighteousness Hos 10:12–13 *See also* Isa 59:1–2

Pride Ps 10:4 *See also* 2Ch 26:16–18

Trusting in human resources Isa 31:1 *See also* 2Ch 16:12; Hos 5:13–15

Idolatry Zep 1:4–6 *See also* Ro 1:21–23

Superficial religion Am 5:5–6 *See also* Isa 58:1–9

Seeking God through occult practices is forbidden
1Ch 10:13–14 *See also* Lev 19:31; 20:6; Dt 18:10–12; 1Sa 28:4–20; Ac 16:16–18

Consequences of not seeking God
Loss of life 2Ch 15:13 *See also* Dt 13:6–10

Loss of salvation Ps 119:155

See also

1403 God, revelation	6650 finding
2360 Christ, prayers of	6732 repentance
3221 Holy Spirit & prayer	8124 guidance
4018 life, spiritual	8618 prayerfulness
5012 heart	8648 enquiring of God
5940 searching	8656 longing for God

8162

spiritual vitality

The quality of possessing a living faith, which is commended by Scripture.

Spiritual vitality commended
2Th 1:3 *See also* Job 17:9; Ps 84:7; 92:12; Pr 4:18; 1Ti 4:15; 2Pe 1:5–7

The means of developing spiritual vitality
Abiding in Christ Jn 15:4

Seeking to imitate Jesus Christ Eph 4:15 *See also* Jn 13:15; Ro 12:1–2; 13:14; 1Co 11:1; Gal 3:27; Php 3:10; 1Th 1:6; 1Pe 2:21; 1Jn 2:6,28

Resisting temptation 1Jn 2:14 *See also*
Mt 26:41; 1Co 7:5; 10:13; 1Th 3:5;
Heb 2:18; Jas 1:2–3,12; Rev 3:10

Developing discipline 1Ti 6:12 *See also*
Heb 12:7–11; Rev 3:18–19

Exhorting others 1Ki 2:2; 2Ch 15:7;
Isa 35:4; Hag 2:4; 1Co 16:13; Eph 6:10;
2Ti 2:1

Being filled with the Holy Spirit
Eph 5:18 *See also* Gal 5:16–18; 1Th 1:5

Obstacles to spiritual vitality
Lack of sound teaching 2Ti 4:1–3

A failure to progress beyond basic
teachings Heb 5:12; 1Pe 2:2

**Examples of individuals with
spiritual vitality**
1Sa 2:26 *Samuel*; Lk 1:80 *John the Baptist*
The young Jesus Christ: Lk 2:40,52
Ac 9:22 *Paul*

**The consequences of spiritual
vitality**
Spiritual growth Gal 5:22–23; 2Pe 3:18
See also Ro 12:1–2; 2Co 3:18;
Eph 4:11–15; Php 3:12; Col 1:10;
1Th 4:3–7

Loving others 1Jn 3:23 *See also* Gal 5:6;
Eph 1:15; 6:23; Col 1:4–5; 1Ti 1:5

Rejoicing in the Lord Php 4:4–7 *See
also* Ps 5:11; 13:5; 33:21; Isa 35:10;
Ac 16:34; 1Pe 4:12–13

Spiritual perseverance Heb 6:12 *See
also* 1Th 5:8; 1Ti 3:9; 2Ti 1:13;
Rev 13:10

See also

3251 Holy Spirit, filling with	8230 discipline
	8283 joy
3254 Holy Spirit, fruit of	8347 spiritual growth
4018 life, spiritual	8449 imitating
8164 spirituality	8459 perseverance
8206 Christlikeness	

spirituality

The quality of life generated and
nourished by the Spirit of God, in
which believers experience the
power and presence of God in their
lives. True spirituality comes from
living under the control of the Holy
Spirit and is evidenced by the fruit of
the Spirit, spiritual maturity and
growth in holiness.

The foundations of spirituality
The need for spiritual renewal
1Co 2:14; Ro 7:14; Jude 19

Believers have been renewed
spiritually Jn 3:5–8 *See also* Ro 8:11;
Tit 3:5; 1Pe 1:3,23

Faith Heb 11:6 *See also* Jn 6:53–58;
14:1; 20:31; Ac 16:31; Ro 10:9–10

A longing for God Ps 27:8 *See also*
Ps 119:2; 143:5–6; Php 3:10–14

The nature of spirituality
Living under the Spirit's control
Ro 8:5–9 *See also* Ro 8:12–13;
Gal 5:16–17; Eph 5:18

Reflecting Jesus Christ's character
2Co 3:18 *See also* Ro 8:29; 1Jn 3:2–3

Intimacy with God through the Spirit
Ro 8:14–16 *See also* Gal 4:6

Evidence of spirituality
Bearing spiritual fruit Gal 5:22–23 *See
also* Mt 7:17; Jn 15:5–8; Ro 14:17;
Eph 5:8–9

Love for one another 1Jn 4:7 *See also*
Jn 13:34–35; 1Co 13:1–4; Col 3:12

Spiritual maturity 1Co 3:1–3 *See also*
1Co 14:20; Heb 5:13–14

Showing concern for weaker believers
Gal 6:1 *See also* Ro 14:1–3,19–21;
1Co 8:9–13

Understanding spiritual truths
1Co 2:9–13 *See also* Jn 14:17; 16:13–15;
1Co 2:15–16

Holiness Tit 2:12 *See also* Ro 12:1–2;
1Co 6:19–20; Gal 5:24; Col 3:1–2

Obedience Jn 15:10; 1Jn 2:2–6; 5:2–3

Aids to spirituality
Co-operation with the Spirit Gal 5:25
See also Ac 7:51; Eph 4:30; 1Th 5:19

Meditation on God's word Jos 1:8;
Jn 17:7; 2Ti 3:15–17

Spending time with God Lk 6:12;
Mk 1:35; Ac 4:13

Encouragement of others Heb 10:24
See also Col 3:16; 1Th 2:11–12

Tests and trials Jas 1:2–4 *See also*
Ro 5:3–4; 1Pe 1:6–7

Examples of spirituality
Ge 5:24 *Enoch*; Ge 6:9 *Noah*
Moses: Nu 12:3,6–8
David: 1Sa 13:14; Ac 13:22
Stephen: Ac 6:5,8
Ac 11:24 *Barnabas*

See also

3233 Holy Spirit & sanctification	8162 spiritual vitality
4018 life, spiritual	8206 Christlikeness
5904 maturity, spiritual	8258 fruitfulness, spiritual
6744 sanctification	8266 holiness
7922 fellowship with God	8347 spiritual growth
8160 seeking God	8656 longing for God

theology

The study of God, as he has revealed
himself in Jesus Christ and in
Scripture.

**Theology is based on God's self-
revelation**
2Ti 3:15–17 *See also* Ps 1:1–3;
Ro 1:1–3; 15:4; 1Co 15:1–4; 2Pe 1:19

The benefits of theology
A concern for right teaching in the
church Tit 2:1 *See also* Heb 6:1–3

A deepened understanding of God
Ps 119:169 *See also* Ps 119:24; Ro 15:4;
2Ti 3:14–16

Spiritual illumination Ps 119:130 *See
also* Ps 119:105; 2Pe 1:19; 1Jn 2:8

Access to the truth Ps 33:4 *See also*
Ps 119:43,160; Col 1:3–6; Rev 21:5

An inspiration to meditation and praise
Ps 119:15–16 *See also* Jos 1:8; Ps 48:9;
56:4,10; 119:27,97–98,148; 143:5

A life of obedience and holiness
Ps 119:9–11; Mt 7:24–27; Lk 11:28;
Jn 14:15; 17:6; 2Ti 3:16–17; Jas 1:22

See also

1403 God, revelation	8142 religion
1460 truth	8206 Christlikeness
1610 Scripture	8234 doctrine
1690 word of God	8266 holiness
7797 teaching	8314 orthodoxy
8138 monotheism	8453 obedience

way, the

A term used metaphorically to refer
both to the Christian faith
(especially in Acts) and to Jesus
Christ himself (especially in John's
Gospel). Faith in Jesus Christ is the
only way of salvation for sinful
human beings. The term is often
used with other expressions in
Scripture to describe aspects of the
life of the believer.

**The Way refers to the Christian
faith**
Ac 9:2 *See also* Ac 19:9,23; 22:4;
24:14,22

**The way refers to Jesus Christ
himself**
Jn 14:6 *See also* Jn 10:9; 14:4–6; 1Ti 2:5;
Heb 10:19–20

**Faith in Jesus Christ is the only
way of salvation for sinful human
beings**
Ac 4:12 *See also* Mk 16:16; Jn 1:12–13;
3:15–16; Ac 16:31; Ro 10:9; Eph 2:8;
1Pe 1:5

**Way used with other terms to
describe the life of the believer**
The way of righteousness Mt 21:32 *See
also* Mt 3:1–12; 2Pe 2:21

The way of God Mt 22:16 pp Mk 12:14
pp Lk 20:21 *See also* Ps 18:30; Isa 55:9;
Ac 18:25–26; Heb 3:10; Ps 95:10

The way of the Lord Ac 18:24–25 *See
also* Ge 18:19; Ps 27:11; 143:8; Pr 10:29

The way of salvation Ac 16:17 *See also*
Mt 7:14

The way of peace Lk 1:79 *See also*
Isa 26:3,12; 57:20–21; Ro 3:17; Isa 59:8

The way of holiness Isa 35:8 *See also*
Heb 9:8

See also

2324 Christ as Saviour	6510 salvation
	6732 repentance
4018 life, spiritual	7105 believers
4020 life of faith	8022 faith, basis of salvation
5505 roads	
5553 stairways	8154 righteousness
5590 travel	8266 holiness

8200

The character of the believer

8201

blamelessness

A quality of life apparent in an individual against whom no just charge can be made. This is exemplified supremely in the blameless life and death of Jesus Christ. Though believers remain imperfect in this life, they are counted blameless in God's sight on account of the atoning death of Jesus Christ.

Jesus Christ's human life was blameless
1Pe 2:22 *See also* Isa 53:9; Jn 8:46; 2Co 5:21; Heb 7:26; 1Pe 1:19; 1Jn 3:5

Jesus Christ's blameless life and death were the perfect fulfilment of the OT sacrifices
The lamb or goat sacrificed at Passover had to be unblemished Ex 12:5

All other animals used as sacrifices had to be without defect Lev 1:3; 6:6; Nu 6:14; 28:19; Dt 15:21; Eze 45:23; Mal 1:8,13–14

Jesus Christ's death was as the perfect lamb of God Heb 9:14 *See also* Jn 1:29; 1Co 5:7; 1Pe 1:19; Rev 5:6; 6:1

In the OT, the righteous were often described as blameless
Ge 6:9; Job 1:1 *See also* 1Sa 12:3; 2Sa 22:21–25; Ps 15:1–5; 37:37; Pr 11:20; 28:18; SS 4:7; Lk 1:6

God counts believers as blameless in his sight on account of Jesus Christ's death for them
Ac 13:39 *See also* Ro 3:28; 5:1; 1Co 6:11; Gal 3:6; Eph 1:4; Php 3:9

Believers should be blameless in their Christian lives
1Ti 5:7 *See also* 2Co 6:3; Php 1:10; 2:14–15; 1Pe 1:15; 2:12; 2Pe 3:14; Jas 1:27

Paul, Silas and Timothy could claim to have been blameless 1Th 2:10

Officers of the church are to be blameless 1Ti 3:2; 6:14; Tit 1:6–7

The administration of financial help is to be blameless 2Co 8:20

Believers will be presented blameless before God at the last day
1Co 1:8; Jude 24 *See also* Eph 5:27; Col 1:22; 1Th 3:13; 5:23

See also
2075 Christ, sinless	6676 justification
2315 Christ as Lamb	6744 sanctification
2530 Christ, death of	7434 sacrifice
5562 suffering,	8277 innocence
innocent	8320 perfection
6115 blame	9240 last judgment
6118 blemish	

8202

boldness

Courage and confidence in approaching God and also other people.

Boldness in approaching God
Heb 10:19–22 *See also* Ge 18:27,31 *Abraham prays for Sodom*

Boldness in proclaiming the gospel to others
Ac 4:29 *Persecuted Christians pray.: See also* Ac 4:13,31; 9:28; 13:46; 14:3; 18:26; 19:8; 28:31

Boldness in dealing with others
Inner confidence Ps 138:3 *See also* 1Sa 17:34–50; Pr 28:1; 2Co 3:12 *Paul concerning his ministry*

Confident authority Phm 8–9 *See also* Ro 15:15; 2Co 10:1–2

Courage Mk 15:43 *See also* Ex 14:8; Nu 33:3

Persistence Lk 11:8 *The friend at midnight.*

Misplaced boldness
2Pe 2:10 *The heretics' arrogance. See also* 1Co 8:10

See also
3251 Holy Spirit,	8219 courage
filling with	8414 encourage-
5954 strength	ment
5968 timidity	8630 worship,
7754 preaching	results
8020 faith	8652 importunity
8104 assurance	8801 presumption
8213 confidence	

8203

character

The moral and mental features that define a person, whether good or evil. The term also means moral strength, which Scripture regards as something to be highly valued.

The character of God
God is the Father of believers Eph 1:2 *See also* Gal 1:1; Col 1:12; 1Th 1:3; 3:13

God is good Ps 34:8 *See also* Ex 33:19; La 3:25; Mt 19:17 pp Mk 10:18; 2Pe 1:3

God is holy 1Sa 2:2 *See also* Lev 11:44–45; Isa 6:3; 43:15; Eze 39:7; 1Pe 1:15; Rev 4:8

God is faithful Ps 36:5 *See also* Dt 7:9; 1Ki 8:56; Ps 89:2; 146:6; La 3:23; 1Th 5:23–24

God is just and righteous Ro 3:25–26 *See also* 2Ch 12:6; Ps 33:5; Isa 30:18; Zep 3:5; Ac 17:31; Rev 16:5–6

God is loving Ps 145:17 *See also* Jn 3:16; Ro 5:8; Eph 2:4; Tit 3:4–5; Heb 12:6; 1Jn 4:7–10

God is merciful and compassionate Ps 86:15; Lk 1:50 *See also* Ne 9:31; Isa 63:7; La 3:22; Jnh 4:2; Lk 18:10–14; 2Co 1:3; Jas 5:11

The character of Jesus Christ
Jesus Christ possesses the exact likeness of God Heb 1:3 *See also* 2Co 4:4; Col 1:15

Jesus Christ is faithful Heb 3:6 *See also* 2Th 3:3; Heb 2:17; Rev 1:5; 3:14

Jesus Christ is holy Mk 1:24 pp Lk 4:34 *See also* Lk 1:35; Jn 6:69; Heb 4:15; Rev 3:7

Jesus Christ is loving 2Co 5:14 *See also* Jn 15:9; Ro 8:35–39; 1Jn 3:16

The character of the Holy Spirit
The Holy Spirit is holy Ro 1:4 *See also* Ro 15:16; 1Co 6:19; Tit 3:5

The Holy Spirit is powerful Lk 4:14 *See also* Mic 3:8; Ac 1:8; Ro 15:13,19; 2Ti 1:7

The Holy Spirit is eternal Heb 9:14

The Holy Spirit is the Spirit of truth, the Counsellor Jn 14:16–17 *See also* Jn 14:26; 15:26; 16:7

Character as a moral strength
Ro 5:3–4 *See also* Ru 3:11; Pr 12:4; 31:10; Ac 17:11; 1Co 15:33

The character of believers
Believers should be compassionate Col 3:12 *See also* Ps 112:4; 1Pe 3:8

Believers should be humble 1Pe 5:5 *See also* Isa 29:19; Php 2:3; Col 3:12; 1Pe 3:8

Believers should be joyful Php 4:4 *See also* Ro 12:12; 15:13; 1Th 5:16

Believers should be loving 1Jn 4:7 *See also* Gal 5:22; Col 3:14; 1Th 4:9

Believers should be content Php 4:11 *See also* 1Ti 6:6–8; Heb 13:5

Believers should be holy Dt 7:6; 1Pe 1:15–16 *See also* Ro 12:1–2; Col 3:12; Heb 12:14

Believers are to be poor in spirit Mt 5:3

Believers are to be meek Mt 5:5

Believers are to be merciful Mt 5:7 *See also* Lk 6:36; Ro 12:8; Jas 3:17

Believers are to be pure in heart Mt 5:8 *See also* 2Co 11:2–3; Php 1:10; 1Ti 5:22; 2Ti 2:22

See also
1010 God, nature and	7105 believers
qualities of	8114 discipleship
2003 Jesus Christ,	8206 Christlikeness
qualities of	8273 holiness,
3005 Holy Spirit,	ethical aspects
qualities of	8347 spiritual
5034 likeness	growth
5765 attitudes to	8428 example
people	
6025 sin & God's	
character	

8204

chastity

The state of sexual abstinence. Although Scripture commends marriage, it insists that celibacy should be honoured.

Condemnation of sexual immorality
Nu 25:1; Mt 15:19; Ac 15:20; 1Co 10:8; Rev 2:14,20; 9:21

The command to avoid sexual immorality
Ro 13:13 See also Ac 15:19–20;
1Co 6:18; 10:8; Eph 5:3; 1Th 4:3

Believers should not associate with those who are sexually immoral
1Co 5:9–11

Sexual purity is commended
1Co 6:18–20 See also Ps 51:10; 119:9;
2Ti 2:22; 1Pe 2:11; Rev 14:1–4

Chastity and marriage
Marriage commended for those incapable of remaining chaste 1Co 7:9

The sanctity of marriage See also
Mk 10:2–12

The condemnation of adultery
Lev 18:20 See also Lev 20:10; Ex 20:14
pp Dt 5:18; Mt 5:27–28; Ro 2:22

See also

3278 Holy Spirit, indwelling	6187 immorality
5136 body	6236 sexual sin
5708 marriage	6242 adultery
5736 singleness	8326 purity, moral & spiritual
5740 virgin	8339 self-control
5773 abstinence, discipline	

8205

childlikeness

An attitude of simple trust and faith, to be distinguished from childishness. It is commended by Scripture as an appropriate attitude for the believer to take towards God.

God treats his people like children
Ps 103:13 See also Nu 11:12; Isa 49:15;
66:13; Jer 31:20; Hos 11:1–4;
Ro 8:14–17; Gal 4:1–7

God's people should respond to God as children to a parent
In trust Ps 131:2

In obedience 1Pe 1:14

In humility Lk 9:46–48 pp Mt 18:2–5
pp Mk 9:33–37 See also 1Ki 3:7 Solomon

In innocence Mk 10:13–15
pp Mt 19:13–14 pp Lk 18:15–17 See also
Lk 10:21

In imitating a model Eph 5:1–2 See also
1Jn 3:10

Childlikeness is reflected in pastoral care
1Th 2:7 See also 1Jn 2:28

Childlikeness is to be distinguished from immature childishness
1Co 3:1–3 See also Heb 5:12–6:1

See also

1040 God, fatherhood	8276 humility
5664 children	8277 innocence
5902 maturity	8305 meekness
8020 faith	8330 receptiveness
8030 trust	8351 teachableness
	8453 obedience

8206

Christlikeness

The process by which believers are conformed to the likeness of Jesus Christ, especially in relation to obedience to and trust in God. Through the Holy Spirit, God refashions believers in the image of his Son, who is set before them as a model of the form of the redeemed life.

Believers are to become Christlike
1Co 11:1; Php 2:5 Paul is arguing that believers must allow God to make them Christlike, which is the natural goal of their process of growing in faith. Christlikeness is not achieved by people merely trying to imitate Jesus Christ, but by God making believers more like his Son in sanctification, through the Spirit. See also
Jn 13:15; Ro 8:29; Eph 4:11–13;
Php 3:8–11,20–21; 1Jn 2:6

The Holy Spirit makes believers Christlike
2Co 3:18 See also Ro 8:5–9;
Gal 5:22–23; 1Th 1:6

Christlikeness is the aim of discipleship
Mt 10:25 See also Lk 6:40; 1Jn 2:6

Christlikeness is based on total commitment to Jesus Christ
Lk 9:57–62 See also Mt 9:9 pp Mk 2:14
pp Lk 5:27; Mt 19:21 pp Lk 18:22;
Jn 1:43; 10:27; 12:26; 15:10; 2Jn 9

The demonstration of Christlikeness
In costly sacrifice Mk 8:34–35
pp Mt 16:24 pp Lk 9:23–24 1Pe 2:21–23
See also Mt 10:38; Lk 14:26–27;
Jn 12:26; 21:19; Php 3:10; 1Pe 4:1

In humility and service Mt 20:26–28
pp Mk 10:43–45 See also Mt 11:29;
Mk 9:35; Lk 22:24–26; Jn 13:14–15;
Php 2:4–5

In love for other believers Jn 15:12;
1Jn 3:16 See also Jn 13:34; 15:17;
Eph 5:2,25

In a readiness to forgive others
Col 3:13 See also Mt 6:12 pp Lk 11:4

In sharing Jesus Christ's mission to the world Mt 4:19 pp Mk 1:17 See also
Jn 20:21

By following godly examples that imitate Jesus Christ 1Co 11:1 See also
Eph 5:1; 1Th 1:5–6; 2:14; Heb 6:12;
13:7–8; 3Jn 11

Christlikeness is part of God's re-creation
Ge 1:26–27; 2Co 4:4; Eph 4:24;
Col 3:10

The process of becoming Christlike
It is the purpose for which believers are saved Ro 8:28–29 See also
Eph 2:10; 2Pe 1:4

It continues in the experience of believers 2Co 3:18

It will be complete when believers finally share Jesus Christ's glory
1Jn 3:2–3 See also Ps 17:15; Jn 17:24;
1Co 15:49–53; Gal 4:19; Php 3:20–21;
Col 3:4; 1Jn 4:17

See also

2339 Christ, example of	8114 discipleship
	8120 following Christ
3254 Holy Spirit, fruit of	8266 holiness
3278 Holy Spirit, indwelling	8342 servanthood
	8347 spiritual growth
5904 maturity, spiritual	8453 obedience
6744 sanctification	8461 priorities
8020 faith	8475 self-denial

8207

commitment

A state of personal dedication to something or someone, which results in actively promoting and working for their good and well-being.

8208
commitment, to God

Commitment to God arises from faith in his promises, is expressed in worship and adoration and leads to obedience to his commands.

Commitment to God commanded
Dt 27:10; Jos 24:14; Ro 12:1–2 See also
Dt 6:13; 10:12–13; 13:4; Jos 22:5 Joshua reiterates Moses' commands; Jdg 6:10;
1Sa 7:3; 12:24; 1Ch 28:9 David's instructions to Solomon; 2Ch 19:9;
Jer 38:20; 1Th 4:1; 2Ti 2:22

Obedience to God's commands as a sign of commitment
Dt 7:9; Jos 24:24; Ro 6:17 See also
Ex 19:8; Dt 11:22; 1Ki 8:61; Ne 10:29;
Ps 40:6–8 The reference may be to the ear-piercing that was a sign of slaves' voluntary commitment to their masters;
Jer 7:23; 11:3; 38:20; 42:6; Hag 1:12;
Zec 6:15
Jesus Christ equates obedience with love:
Jn 14:15; 15:10
Ac 5:29; Ro 2:13

Love for God and worship of him are hallmarks of commitment
Dt 30:6; Jn 21:15 See also Dt 6:5; 10:12;
11:1,13,22; Jos 23:11; Ne 1:5;
Isa 56:6–7; Jer 20:12; Da 9:4; Mt 6:24
pp Lk 16:13; Mt 22:37 pp Mk 12:30

Benefits of commitment to God
Dt 30:20; 2Ch 16:9; Pr 16:3; Rev 2:10
See also Ex 19:5–6; 20:6; Dt 28:1;
1Sa 12:14; 1Ki 2:2–4; Ps 97:10;
Pr 2:7–8; Isa 1:19; Jer 26:13

Examples of commitment to God
Abraham: Ge 22:17–18; Heb 11:8
Nu 12:7 Moses; Jos 22:2 the tribes settled in Transjordan; 1Ki 15:5 David;
1Ki 15:14 pp 2Ch 15:17 Asa
Hezekiah: 2Ki 20:3; 2Ch 31:20
2Ki 23:25 Josiah; Ne 13:14 Nehemiah;
Jn 13:37 Simon Peter's good intentions

God's commitment of gifts and tasks to his people
God's commitment of gifts 1Co 9:17

God's commitment of the faith to believers Jude 3

See also

1345 covenant	8225 devotion
5375 law	8248 faithfulness
8031 trust,	8292 love
importance	8403 commands
8223 dedication	

8209
commitment, to Jesus Christ

Commitment to Jesus Christ is grounded in the knowledge of his saving power and divinity, and expresses itself in adoration and obedience to Jesus Christ.

Jesus Christ commanded people to make the commitment to follow him
Mt 4:19 pp Mk 1:17; Mt 9:9 pp Mk 2:14 pp Lk 5:27 *See also* Mt 19:21–22; Jn 1:43; 21:19,22; Ro 15:5; 1Co 1:12 *There may have been a "Christ-party" at Corinth, or in contrast with the sectarianism, Paul may be asserting his own commitment to Jesus Christ.*

Jesus Christ frequently spelt out the cost of commitment to him
Mt 10:37–38 pp Lk 14:26–27 Mt 16:24 pp Mk 8:34 pp Lk 9:23; Jn 12:25–26 *See also* Mt 8:22; 10:39 pp Mk 8:35 pp Lk 17:33; Mt 19:21 pp Mk 10:21 pp Lk 18:22; Lk 14:28–33; 1Pe 2:21

Jesus Christ's demand for commitment was sometimes met with a refusal
Lk 9:59 *See also* Lk 9:61

Sometimes people followed Jesus Christ without being truly committed to him
Jn 6:2 *This would have been true for many in the crowds. See also* Jn 6:66

Some committed themselves wholeheartedly to his invitation
Mt 4:20 pp Mk 1:18; Mt 4:22 pp Mk 1:20; Mt 9:9 pp Mk 2:14 pp Lk 5:28; Jn 1:40

Secret commitment to Jesus Christ
Jn 12:42 *See also* Jn 3:1–2

True commitment to Jesus Christ is seen in love and obedience to him
Jn 14:21; Php 2:12 *In response to who Jesus Christ is and what he has done. See also* Jn 8:31; 14:15,23–24; 1Co 11:1; 16:22; Eph 6:5–6,24; 1Jn 2:3; 3:22–24; Rev 14:4

See also

2224 Christ, the Lord	8115 discipleship
5591 treasure	8120 following
7620 disciples	Christ
7706 apostles	8407 confession of
7726 evangelists,	Christ
ministry	8453 obedience
8102 abiding in	8459 perseverance
Christ	8475 self-denial

8210
commitment, to God's people

Commitment to God means a commitment to his people. Believers are meant to be nourished and supported by the church, and to work towards its edification.

Commitment to the church
Ac 2:42; Eph 4:3–4; Col 3:15 *Paul uses the picture of the body to describe the interdependence of believers:* Ro 12:4–10; 1Co 12:12–27

Commitment to other Christians is an expression of love made known in Christ
Jn 13:34–35; Col 3:13–14; 1Pe 1:22 *See also* Jn 15:12,17; Ro 12:10,16; 13:8; Gal 5:13; Eph 4:32–5:2; 1Th 3:12; 4:9; 2Th 1:3; Heb 13:1; 1Pe 2:17; 1Jn 3:11,23; 4:7,21; 5:2

Such commitment is expressed in mutual responsibility and concern
Gal 6:2; Heb 10:24–25; 1Pe 3:8 *See also* Ro 14:13; 15:7,14; 1Co 1:10 *Paul's concern for unity among believers;* Eph 5:21; Col 3:13 *the responsibility of believers to forgive one another;* Col 3:16; 1Ti 5:11; Heb 3:13; Jas 4:11; 1Pe 4:9; 5:5

For its leaders, commitment to the church may prove a joy and a burden
Ac 20:28 *Paul speaking to the elders of the church at Ephesus;* 2Co 11:28 *See also* Col 1:24; 1Th 2:8; 5:12–13; 1Ti 3:1; Heb 13:17; 1Pe 5:1–3

See also

5051 responsibility	7140 people of God
7020 church, the	7921 fellowship

8211
commitment, to the world

Though the world is fallen, God still loves the world and is committed to it. Commitment by believers to worldly pursuits and evil is to be avoided as they are called upon to be "in the world" but "not of the world".

Commitment to this world to be avoided because it is a fallen and sinful place
Gal 1:4; 1Jn 5:19 *See also* 2Co 4:4; Eph 2:2; 6:12; 2Pe 1:4; 1Jn 2:16–17; 3:1,13

Though the world is fallen, God still loves it
Jn 3:16 *See also* 2Co 5:18–20

Preoccupation with the things of this world is incompatible with holy living
Jas 4:4; 1Jn 2:15 *See also* Jn 17:14–16; Ac 2:40; Ro 12:2; 1Co 7:31; 2Co 6:14–17; Isa 52:11; Php 2:15; Col 3:2; Tit 2:12; Jas 1:27; 1Pe 1:14; 2:11; 4:3

Commitment to the world is seen especially in materialism
1Ti 6:17 *See also* Mt 6:19; 19:23 pp Lk 18:24; Lk 12:16–21

The outcome of worldly commitment
Spiritual loss Lk 9:25 pp Mt 16:26 pp Mk 8:36 *See also* Mt 13:22; 2Ti 4:10

God's judgment 1Co 11:32 *See also* Jn 12:31; 16:11; Eph 5:6

Carelessness with regard to Jesus Christ's return Lk 21:34 *See also* Mt 24:38–39; Lk 12:40,46; 1Th 5:1–9

See also

4025 world, the	8266 holiness
5811 compromise	8778 materialism
5869 greed	8848 worldliness
6744 sanctification	

8213
confidence

A state of self-assurance regarding one's status or ability, often grounded in human achievements. Scripture insists that Christian confidence is to be grounded in what God has done for believers, rather than in what they themselves have achieved.

8214
confidence, basis of

The confidence of believers, is grounded in God's character, actions and trustworthy promises, rather than human achievements.

Confidence originates with God
In his unchanging and faithful nature Nu 23:19; Tit 1:1–2 *See also* 1Sa 15:29; Ps 33:11; 102:27; Pr 3:26; Isa 49:23; Mal 3:6; 2Ti 1:12; Jas 1:17

In his covenant Jer 32:40; Heb 9:15 *See also* Ge 9:16 *with all living creatures;* Ge 17:7 *with Abraham;* 2Sa 7:13 *with the house of David;* 2Sa 23:5; Ps 89:34; Isa 54:10; 55:3; Eze 16:60; Ac 3:25

In election Dt 7:6; Ro 8:28 *See also* Isa 41:9–10; Jer 31:3; Ro 8:33; 1Co 1:9; 1Th 5:24; 2Ti 2:19

In his past deliverances Ps 22:4–5; Ro 8:31–32 *See also* Dt 7:18; 20:1; Jos 1:5; 1Sa 17:37; 1Ki 8:57; Ps 44:1–5; 78:2–4; 2Co 1:10

In his word Isa 55:10–11 *See also* Ps 89:34; 119:74; 130:5; Ro 15:4; 1Pe 1:25; 2Pe 1:19

In his promises Jos 23:14; Heb 10:23 *See also* 1Ki 8:20; Ps 119:140; 2Pe 1:4

Confidence is centred on Jesus Christ
Ro 8:38–39 *See also* Ac 17:31; Ro 8:1; 2Co 1:20; Col 1:27; 1Ti 3:13; Heb 7:22,25; 9:15; 1Pe 2:6; Isa 28:16

Confidence is mediated by the Holy Spirit
Ro 8:16 *See also* 2Co 1:21–22; 5:5; Eph 1:13–14

8215
confidence, results of

God-given assurance produces spiritual maturity and stability, so that believers may withstand the adverse conditions of life.

Confidence in God's protection removes fear of disaster
Ps 46:1–2 *See also* Ex 14:13–14; Ps 56:3–4; Ac 27:22–25

Confidence in God's purposes produces hope
Ps 130:7; 2Co 1:10 *See also* Ps 25:3–6; 62:5–8; 71:5–7; Pr 23:17–18; Ro 5:3–5; 1Ti 6:17–18; Heb 6:17–19

Confidence in God's presence makes his people bold
Isa 41:8–10 *See also* Jos 1:5–9; Ps 3:3–6; 20:7; 23:4; 27:1–4; 138:3; Isa 12:2; 44:8; Jer 1:8; Ac 4:13; 9:27; 18:9–11; Eph 6:10–11

Confidence in God enables believers to endure difficulties
Hab 3:17–19; 2Ti 3:10–11 *See also* Job 19:26; Ps 42:9–10; Eph 6:13; Heb 10:32–35; 11:35–39; 12:1–2; 1Pe 3:14; 4:12–19; Rev 3:10

Confidence in God leads to awareness of security
Ps 23:1; Eph 6:10 *See also* Dt 33:12; Ps 7:9; 28:7; 40:2; 46:1–3; 112:6–8; 121:1–2; Pr 14:26; Isa 32:17; 2Co 1:21; Eph 6:13; 1Ti 3:13; 2Ti 1:12

conformity

Correspondence in character or behaviour; believers are not to conform to the ways of this world but are to be conformed to the image of Christ.

Believers are not to conform to the ways of this world
Ro 12:2; 1Pe 1:14 *See also* Ex 23:2; Lev 20:23; Dt 18:9 *Israel was not to imitate the practices of surrounding nations;* 2Ki 17:15; Eze 11:12; Da 1:8 *Daniel refused to conform to the ways of Babylon;* Da 3:12; Eph 4:17; Col 3:7–8; 1Th 5:6; 1Ti 1:9–11; 1Pe 4:3; 3Jn 11

Christians will be conformed to the image of Christ
Ro 8:29 *See also* Jn 13:15,34; Ro 13:14; 1Co 11:1; Eph 5:1–2; Php 2:5

The means of being conformed to Jesus Christ
In being completely united with him
Ro 6:3–10; 2Co 4:10 *See also* Ro 8:10–11,17–18; Php 3:10–11; 1Pe 4:13

In his death Php 3:10 *See also* Gal 6:14; Col 1:24; 3:3; 1Pe 2:21; 4:1

In his resurrection Eph 2:4–6 *See also* 1Co 15:20–22; Col 3:1

consecration

The setting apart of people, things, times or places as sacred, for God to use.

Consecration is the requirement of a holy God
Lev 20:7–8 *See also* Lev 11:44; 22:32

The consecration of people
The importance of personal consecration Ro 6:13

Inward consecration to God is symbolised by outward cleansing Ro 12:1; 2Co 5:14–15; 1Pe 2:24; Ex 19:10,14; 1Sa 16:5; 2Ch 30:17; 35:6; Ps 50:5; Ro 12:1

The consecration of all firstborn males Ex 13:2; Lk 2:22–23 *See also* Ex 13:12–13; Nu 3:11–13; 8:17–18 *The Levites served in place of the firstborn males in Israel.*

The consecration of priests Ex 29:1 *See also* Ex 19:22; 1Ki 13:33; 2Ch 30:3,24

The consecration of the Aaronic priesthood Ex 30:30 *See also* Ex 28:41; Lev 8:30; 1Ch 23:13

The consecration of the Levitical priesthood 1Ch 15:12; 2Ch 23:6; 29:5; 35:3

Special consecration is marked by a vow Nu 6:8,11 *the Nazirite vow*

The consecration of things
Altars Ex 29:36–37 *See also* Ex 30:29 *The use of oil in consecration:* Ex 40:9–11; Lev 8:11–12

Offerings Ex 28:38; 29:27; Lev 22:2; 2Ch 30:17

Garments Ex 28:3; 29:21; 40:13; Nu 15:39–40

Bread 1Sa 21:4,6; Mt 12:4 pp Mk 2:25–26 pp Lk 6:3–4

Meat Hag 2:12 *The state of consecration could be transmitted;* Jer 11:15 *True consecration should involve a right spirit.*

Certain places are consecrated
Ex 19:23 *Mount Sinai;* Ex 29:43–44 *the Tent of Meeting*
The tabernacle: Lev 8:10; Nu 7:1
The temple: 1Ki 8:64 pp 2Ch 7:7; 1Ki 9:3 pp 2Ch 7:16; 2Ch 29:17–19

Certain times are specially consecrated
Lev 25:10 *the Year of Jubilee*
The Sabbath: Ge 2:3; Ex 20:8,11; Dt 5:12

The consecration of daily life
1Ti 4:4–5 *The reference may be to grace before eating. See also* Zec 14:20–21

Consecration as preparation for work and worship
Nu 11:18; Jos 3:5; 7:13

Consecration to other gods incurs God's displeasure
Isa 66:17 *See also* Jdg 17:3; 2Ch 13:9; 26:18; 30:17; 36:14; Hos 9:10

courage

The quality of being able to act bravely under difficulties or in the face of opposition; being prepared to do dangerous or risky things in obedience to God, in the belief that he will strengthen, guard and protect his people.

8220
courage, in facing enemies

In the OT, courage is shown principally in the leading of God's people against their enemies.

God commands his people to be courageous
Jos 1:6–9 *The LORD to Joshua as he was about to lead the Israelites into Canaan. See also* Jos 1:18; 8:1; 10:8; Jdg 7:9–11; 2Ch 20:15,17

Recommended by leaders
Dt 1:21 *See also* Dt 31:1–8; Jos 10:25; 23:6; 2Sa 10:12; 2Ch 32:7

Seen in the behaviour of people of God
1Sa 17:32; Ac 4:13 *See also* Jos 1:10–11; 14:12; 1Sa 14:6–7; 17:45–47; Ac 13:44–47 *Paul and Barnabas;* Ac 19:8–10 *Paul at Ephesus*

8221
courage, as strength from God

God gives strength to his people. He enables them to be courageous through his gift of faith. God proves himself faithful to his promises and enables his people to trust him in everyday life.

Courage through faithful obedience
1Ch 22:11–13 See also 1Ch 28:20; Ge 12:1–4; Heb 11:8; Ge 22:1–5; Heb 11:17–19; 2Ch 15:8; 19:8–11; Ezr 7:27–28; 10:1–4; Mt 26:39 pp Mk 14:35–36 pp Lk 22:41–42

Courage in the face of wrongdoing
2Sa 12:7–9 The prophet accuses the king of adultery and murder. See also 2Ch 26:16–18 Azariah and Uzziah; Mk 6:18 John the Baptist and Herod; Heb 11:7,24–27

Courage under pressure
Ps 46:1–3 See also Ps 10:17; 27:3; Isa 12:2 Isaiah's encouragement of the exiles of Israel; Ac 27:22; 1Co 16:13; 2Co 6:4–10; Heb 3:6; 11:32–39; Mt 14:27 pp Mk 6:50 pp Jn 6:20

Courageous witness
Ac 4:18–20 See also Mt 10:19–26 pp Mk 13:9–11 pp Lk 21:12–15; Ac 23:11; Php 1:14,20

Courage in prayer
Heb 4:14–16 See also Ge 18:27–28; 1Ch 17:25 pp 2Sa 7:27

See also
5622 witnesses	8495 witnessing
8020 faith	8754 fear

8223

dedication

The single-minded devoting of a person, object or action to the honour of God.

Personal dedication to God must be wholehearted
Jos 22:5 See also Dt 10:20; Jos 24:14–15; 1Ch 28:9; Ne 10:28–29; Ps 119:106; Mt 22:37 pp Mk 12:30 pp Lk 10:27; Dt 6:5

OT dedication to the worship and service of God
Dedication of individuals Nu 6:1–8 See also Jdg 13:5,7; 16:17; 1Sa 1:11; Pr 20:25

Dedication of property Lev 27:1–8 See also Lev 27:9–27

Dedication of animals Lev 1:1–4

Dedication of the priesthood Nu 18:6 See also Ex 28:41; Lev 21:10–12; Dt 10:8; 1Ch 15:2; 23:13

Dedication of the tabernacle and its furnishings Nu 7:1 See also Nu 7:10,84,88

Dedication of the temple and its contents 1Ki 7:51 pp 2Ch 5:1;

1Ki 8:63–64; 15:15; 2Ch 2:4; 7:9; Ezr 6:16–18; Lk 21:5

Dedication of particular items of value 1Ki 7:51 pp 2Ch 5:1 See also 1Ki 15:15; 1Ch 29:1–5; 2Ch 3:6

Dedication of the booty of war 2Sa 8:11–12 pp 1Ch 18:11 See also Nu 31:28; Jos 6:19; 7:1,10–13; 1Ch 26:27

NT dedication to God and his service
Dedication is more usually applied to people than things Ro 12:1 See also Mt 6:24 pp Lk 16:13; Mt 19:29; Ac 4:36–37; Ro 6:13,16,19; 1Co 16:1–2; 1Ti 5:11; 1Pe 1:15–16; Lev 11:44

Particular work and time may be given over to the service of God Ac 6:1–4 See also Ac 1:14; 13:2; Ro 1:1

Service for others is to be dedicated to God and done in his name Col 3:17 See also 1Co 10:31; Eph 5:21; 6:5–7

See also
5605 warfare	7467 temple,
5959 submission	Solomon's
7356 Feast of	8207 commitment
Dedication	8218 consecration
7402 offerings	8225 devotion
7412 priesthood	8476 self-discipline
7459 tabernacle, in	
OT	

8224

dependence

Reliance upon God or upon others. Dependence on God for help with spiritual and physical needs arises out of an awareness of human helplessness, though dependence may be wrongly directed. People may look to others for encouragement and support, but over-dependence is not commended.

Dependence arising from a sense of helplessness
Physical helplessness Ps 18:6 See also Ps 107:4–6; 116:6; Mk 4:38 pp Mt 8:25 pp Lk 8:24; Mk 5:25–26 pp Mt 9:20 pp Lk 8:43

Spiritual helplessness Isa 64:6; Mk 9:17–18 pp Mt 17:14–16 pp Lk 9:38–40; Ro 5:6; 7:18

Dependence on God encouraged
God is to be trusted Heb 4:16 See also Ex 14:31; Dt 8:3; Ps 4:5; 9:10; 20:7; 37:3; Pr 3:5–6; Na 1:7; Jn 15:4–5

God is a refuge Ps 46:1 See also Dt 33:27; Ps 62:8; 71:1

God can help those who depend on him Heb 13:6 See also Ps 118:6–7; 22:4–5; 33:18–20; 94:17–18

God will help those who depend on him Lk 11:13 pp Mt 7:11 See also Ps 121:2–4; 145:18–19; Jas 1:5

Examples of failure to depend on God Nu 20:12; Dt 1:32; 9:23; 2Ki 17:14; Ps 49:6,13; Isa 42:17

Dependence on God for physical help
2Ch 20:12 Jehoshaphat and the people of

Judah. See also 2Ki 19:14 pp Isa 37:14 Hezekiah; 2Ch 13:18 the men of Judah Asa: 2Ch 14:11; 16:8 Ps 22:9–10 David; Mt 9:27–28 two blind men; Jn 2:3–5 Mary; 2Co 1:8–10 Paul

Dependence on God for spiritual needs
Mk 10:14–15 pp Mt 19:14 pp Lk 18:16–17 Childlike dependence is necessary for those who would enter God's kingdom; Jn 3:27 See also Ru 2:12; Lk 23:40–42; 24:47–49; 2Co 3:4–5

Dependence on God expressed in prayer
Ps 5:2 See also Ps 22:24; 88:13; 102:1; 119:147; 130:1–2

Examples of those crying out in dependence on God
Ex 2:23 the Israelites in Egypt; Job 30:28 Job in his suffering; Isa 30:19 the people of Jerusalem; La 3:55 Jeremiah; Jnh 2:2 Jonah from within the fish; Lk 18:13 the tax collector in the temple; Ac 12:5 the church praying for Peter; 2Co 1:11 the Corinthians praying for Paul

Misplaced dependence
Dependence on surrounding nations Jer 2:18 See also 2Ki 18:20–21 pp Isa 36:5–6; Isa 31:1

Dependence on false gods and religions Ps 40:4 See also Dt 31:20; Isa 42:17; Col 2:8

Dependence on human strength and resources Jer 17:5; Ro 9:16 See also Ps 33:16–17; 118:8–9; 127:1–2; Eph 2:8–9

Dependence on sinful behaviour Isa 30:12; 59:4

The futility of misplaced dependence
Pr 25:19; Jer 2:13 See also Isa 8:6–8; 31:3; Hos 10:13–14; Ac 12:20; 1Th 4:11–12

A proper dependence on others is commended
Human help can strengthen Gal 6:2 See also Ecc 4:9–12

Examples of a right dependence on others Lev 21:3 a priest's support for an unmarried sister Support for the poor and needy: Dt 15:11; Mt 25:35–36 1Sa 29:6 Achish found David to be a reliable soldier; Isa 8:2 Uriah and Zechariah were reliable witnesses; 2Ti 2:2 Reliable teachers are a blessing to the church.

See also
1035 God,	8021 faith
faithfulness	8026 faith, growth in
1240 God, the Rock	8030 trust
1320 God as Saviour	8331 reliability
5691 friends, good	8354 trustworthi-
6106 addiction	ness
7921 fellowship	8602 prayer

8225

devotion

Wholehearted commitment to God, to another person or to a task. God's people are encouraged to show such commitment.

God's people are to be wholehearted in their devotion to him

Dt 6:5; Ro 12:1 *See also* Dt 30:1–3; Jdg 5:2; Ps 119:2; Jer 29:13

Examples of devotion to God

Ps 42:1; Php 3:7–8
Caleb and Joshua: Nu 14:6–9; 32:11–12; Jos 14:7–12
2Ki 23:1–3 pp 2Ch 34:29–32 *Josiah and his subjects;* 2Ch 15:12–15 *the people of Judah*
The psalmists: Ps 27:1–4; 40:7–8; 84:2; 119:57,135–136
Paul: 1Co 2:2; 9:26–27; 2Co 1:8–10; Php 3:13–14; Col 1:24,28–29

Examples of devotion to other people

Mt 26:35 pp Mk 14:31; Jn 6:68 *See also* Ru 1:15–17 *Ruth to Naomi*
Jonathan to David: 1Sa 19:4–5; 20:12–13,41–42
Spouses to each other:
Eph 5:22–23,28–29; Col 3:18–19
2Co 8:1–5 *the Macedonian churches to Christians in poverty*

Examples of devotion to a specific task

The leaders and people of Israel to building the temple
1Ch 28:2–3,6,9–10; 29:1–6,17–19

Nehemiah and the people of Judah to rebuilding the walls of Jerusalem
Ne 2:4–6,17–18; 4:13–18,21–23; 6:15

Jesus Christ devoted to his mission
Lk 9:51 *See also* Mt 16:23 pp Mk 8:33; Lk 4:1–12 pp Mt 4:1–10; Lk 4:16–21; 22:42 pp Mt 26:39 pp Mk 14:35–36; Jn 9:4; 19:30

The disciples devoted themselves to the ministry of the church Ac 2:42; 5:42; 6:1–4; 8:4

See also

2057	Christ, obedience
2354	Christ, mission
5708	marriage
7942	ministry
7948	mission
8114	discipleship
8207	commitment
8223	dedication
8248	faithfulness
8434	giving

8226

discernment

The sound judgment which makes possible the distinguishing of good from evil, and the recognition of God's right ways for his people. It is necessary for the understanding of spiritual realities and, on a practical level, for right government and the avoidance of life's pitfalls.

8227
discernment, nature of

Discernment is given by God, through his Holy Spirit. It is received through God's word and through the insight of a renewed mind.

Discerning believers seek to grow in their understanding and knowledge of God's truth.

Discernment as sound judgment

Judging the right course Pr 15:21; Php 1:9–10 *See also* Pr 3:21–23; 8:8–9; 10:21; 11:12; 18:1; 24:30; Hos 14:9

Distinguishing good from evil 2Sa 14:17 *See also* Ge 3:22; Job 6:30; 34:3–4; Isa 7:15

Distinguishing holy from common Lev 10:10; 11:47; Eze 22:26; 44:23

Seeing through outward appearances Pr 28:11 *See also* 1Sa 16:7; Isa 11:3

Understanding the significance of events Dt 32:29–30 *See also* 1Ch 12:32; Est 1:13; Mt 24:32–33 pp Mk 13:28–29; Lk 12:54–56

Exercising judgment to rule 1Ki 3:9 *See also* Pr 8:14–16; 28:2,16; Jer 23:5

Discernment as insight into spiritual realities

Distinguishing between spirits 1Co 12:10 *See also* 1Ki 22:19–23 pp 2Ch 18:18–22; 1Ti 4:1; 1Jn 4:1–3

Discerning true and false prophecy Dt 13:1–3; 18:21–22; 1Co 14:29

Characteristics of discerning people

The discerning grow in wisdom Pr 1:5 *See also* Pr 9:9; 10:14; 14:6; 15:14; 17:24; 18:15

The discerning accept rebuke Pr 17:10; 19:25

The discerning keep God's law 1Ch 22:12; Ps 119:34; Pr 28:7

The source of discernment

Discernment is given by God Da 2:21 *See also* Pr 9:10; Da 2:27–28; 1Co 2:12–15

Discernment through God's word Heb 5:14 *See also* Ps 19:7; 119:98–100,130; Ro 2:18

Discernment through a renewed mind Ro 12:2 *See also* Jer 31:33; 1Co 2:16

Asking for discernment Ps 119:66 *See also* Ps 119:27,125; Jas 1:5

See also

1175	God, will of
1690	word of God
5026	knowledge
5033	knowledge of good & evil
5897	judging others
5946	sensitivity
7966	spiritual gifts
8281	insight
8319	perception, spiritual
8355	understanding
8361	wisdom

8228
discernment, examples of

Perfect discernment is displayed by God and Jesus Christ. Evil spirits also have discernment, about the person and work of Christ. Discernment has been evident in the rulers and spiritual leaders of God's people, but Israel, like children and the foolish who lack judgment, failed to discern God's purpose and truth.

God's discernment

Ps 139:1–4 *See also* Job 31:4; 34:21; Heb 4:13; 1Jn 3:20; Ps 19:12 *God alone knows our hidden faults.*

Jesus Christ's discernment

Jn 2:25 *See also* Mt 9:4 pp Mk 2:8 pp Lk 5:22 *Jesus Christ discerns the thoughts of the teachers of the law;* Mt 16:23 pp Mk 8:33 *Jesus Christ discerns the source of Peter's words;* Mt 22:18 pp Mk 12:15 pp Lk 20:23 *Jesus Christ discerns the true motive of his questioners;* Jn 1:47 *Jesus Christ sees into the heart of Nathaniel;* Jn 8:16 *Jesus Christ has perfect discernment of right and wrong.*

Evil spirits' discernment

Mk 1:23–24 pp Lk 4:33–34 *See also* Mk 1:34 pp Lk 4:41; Ac 16:17

Discernment in those who govern

Joseph: Ge 41:39; Ac 7:10
Solomon: 1Ki 3:12; 2Ch 2:12
Job 12:20 *elders*

Examples of spiritual discernment

2Ki 4:9 *See also* Jn 4:19,42
1Ki 22:19–23 pp 2Ch 18:18–22 *Micaiah discerns that a lying spirit is responsible for false prophecy. See also* Jer 23:16–22 *Jeremiah knows that the false prophets' message is not from God;* Ac 5:3 *Peter is aware of the deception of Ananias and Sapphira;* Ac 8:23 *Peter discerns the true condition of Simon's heart;* Ac 16:18 *Paul discerns the spiritual source of a girl's fortune-telling ability.*

Futher examples of discernment

2Sa 14:18–20 *David sees through Joab's ruse;* 1Ki 3:24–28 *Solomon discerns a child's true mother;* Ne 6:12–13 *Nehemiah sees through the plot against him.*

Lack of discernment

Young children lack discernment Dt 1:39 *See also* Isa 7:15–16; Jnh 4:11

Israel's lack of discernment Dt 32:28; Lk 12:54–56 *See also* Isa 1:3; 5:13; 44:18–19; Eze 12:2; Ac 28:27; Isa 6:9–10

Those who lack judgment Pr 6:32; 10:21 *See also* Pr 7:7; 9:4; 12:11; 18:1; 24:30

Other examples of lack of discernment
Ps 82:5 *the "gods" in the heavenly assembly;* Mic 4:12 *the nations who fail to discern God's plan*

See also

1020	God, all-knowing
1439	revelation
2045	Christ, knowledge of
2081	Christ, wisdom
3050	Holy Spirit, wisdom
4195	spirits
5008	conscience
5948	shrewdness
6181	ignorance
8330	receptiveness
8477	self-examination
8759	fools

8230

discipline

Loving and corrective training that leads to maturity and responsibility on the part of those who experience it.

8231
discipline, divine

God disciplines his people through his word, through their experiences and through punishment, so that they may live in ways pleasing to him.

The nature of God's discipline
It is a sign of God's love Heb 12:6 *See also* Pr 3:12; Ps 119:75; Rev 3:19

It is a sign of belonging to God's family Heb 12:6 *See also* Pr 3:12; Dt 8:5; 2Sa 7:14; Heb 12:7

It trains God's people Heb 12:11

The means of God's discipline
The use of Scripture 2Ti 3:16 *See also* Dt 4:36; 29:29; Isa 8:11

The knowledge of God's grace Tit 2:11–12

Instructive experiences *See also* Dt 8:1–5; 11:2–7; Ps 90:12; Isa 48:17

Painful experiences Heb 12:7 *See also* 2Co 12:7–10; Heb 12:5,11; 1Pe 1:6–7

Punishment Heb 12:6 *See also* Pr 3:12; Lev 26:18,21,23–24,27–28; 2Sa 7:14; Ps 73:14; Jer 32:19; Hos 5:2; 7:15–16; 1Co 11:32

God disciplines all and only his children
Heb 12:8 *See also* Heb 12:6

The goals of God's discipline
Respectful submission to God Heb 12:9

The good of God's people Heb 12:10 *See also* Job 5:17–18; Ps 94:12; 119:67,71,75

Spiritual growth Heb 12:11 *See also* Pr 1:2–3

Preparation for heaven 2Co 4:17–18 *See also* Ro 8:18; Jas 1:12

Believers should not despise God's discipline
Job 5:17 *See also* Heb 12:5; Pr 3:11

Divine discipline in the church
By reproof 2Co 7:8; 13:2; 2Th 3:15

For the benefit of sinners Mt 18:15; 1Co 5:1–7; 2Th 3:14

As a warning to others 1Ti 5:20

To be exercised with kindness 2Co 2:6; Gal 6:1

The role of witnesses Mt 18:16; 1Ti 5:19

See also

1085 God, love of	8266 holiness
5484 punishment by God	8347 spiritual growth
5560 suffering	8414 encouragement
5773 abstinence, discipline	8713 discouragement
6744 sanctification	
7115 children of God	

8232
discipline, in the family

Parents' loving, corrective training of their children, by verbal instruction

and punishments, so that they grow up in the way God wants.

Parents are to discipline their children
Heb 12:7 *See also* Dt 8:5; Heb 12:9–11

Parents discipline out of love for their children
Pr 13:24 *See also* Pr 3:12

The means of parental discipline
Training Pr 22:6 *See also* Ge 18:19; Dt 6:7; Pr 29:17; Eph 6:4; Col 3:21

Correction Pr 22:15 *See also* Pr 19:18; 23:13–14; 29:15

Verbal instruction Eph 6:4 *See also* Dt 4:9; 6:7,20–25; 11:19; 31:13; Ps 78:5; Pr 1:8; 6:20; Pr 3:15

Punishment Pr 23:13–14 *See also* Pr 22:15; 29:15

The purpose of parental discipline is to impart wisdom
Pr 29:15 *See also* Pr 19:18; 22:15; 29:17; Heb 12:9,11

Examples of parents who neglected discipline
Eli 1Sa 3:13

David 1Ki 1:5–6

See also

5666 children, needs	5718 mothers
5680 family	5731 parents
5685 fathers, responsibilities	8476 self-discipline

8234

doctrine

The body of teachings of the Christian faith concerning its central beliefs. Doctrine is grounded in Scripture and aims to maintain the integrity of Christianity by distinguishing it from non-Christian beliefs. Doctrine is of central importance in Christian preaching and teaching in that it equips the people of God for effective and faithful service in his world.

8235
doctrine, nature of

The teachings of Scripture, especially as expressed as a formulation and summary of revealed truth.

Doctrine communicated
In the OT Ezr 7:10 *See also* Dt 33:10; Ps 78:1–4; 119:33–36; Pr 4:1–2; Mal 2:6

In the ministry of Jesus Christ Mt 4:23 *See also* Mt 9:35; Mk 6:6,34; Lk 6:6; 13:10,22; 19:47; 20:1; 21:37; Jn 6:59 *The authority of Jesus Christ's teaching causes amazement:* Mt 7:28–29; 13:54; 22:23–33; Mk 1:21–22 pp Lk 4:31–32

In the ministry of the apostles Ac 2:42 *See also* Ac 4:2; 5:42; 18:11 2Ti 1:13 *See also* 1Co 15:3–5;

Php 2:5–11; 1Ti 3:16; Tit 2:1–10; Heb 5:11–6:2

In the church Eph 4:11 *See also* Ac 13:1; Ro 12:7; 1Co 12:28; 14:26; 1Ti 5:17; Jas 3:1

True doctrine is from God
Jn 7:16 ; 2Ti 3:16–17 *See also* Jn 8:28; 12:49–50; 14:10,24; 2Pe 1:20–21

See also

1439 revelation	5375 law
1460 truth	7754 preaching
1510 Trinity, the	7793 teachers
1610 Scripture	7796 teaching
2012 Christ, authority	7966 spiritual gifts
2363 Christ, preaching & teaching	8314 orthodoxy

8236
doctrine, purpose of

Sound doctrine is intended to shape and mould the people of God for life and service in the world.

The purpose of doctrine for the individual
It leads to repentance 2Ti 2:25

It leads to salvation 1Ti 4:16 *See also* Jn 20:31; 1Co 1:21–24; 2Ti 3:14–15

It is necessary for Christian maturity and effective service 2Ti 3:16–17 *See also* Ps 19:7–8; Ac 2:42–43; Eph 4:11–14; Heb 5:13–14

It makes possible a defence of the faith 1Pe 3:15–16 *See also* Col 2:2–4; Jude 3

It leads to enrichment and blessing Dt 32:1–4 *See also* Ps 19:7–11; 119:97–104; Isa 55:10–13; Eze 3:1–3

It leads to perfection Col 1:28

Doctrine as the basis of faithful ministry in the church
Tit 1:9 *See also* 1Ti 4:6,13–16; 2Ti 1:13–14; 2:2; Tit 2:1

See also

2420 gospel	7703 apologetics
3140 Holy Spirit, teacher	7939 ministry
5902 maturity	8020 faith
6510 salvation	8104 assurance
6732 repentance	8283 joy
6744 sanctification	8347 spiritual growth

8237
doctrine, false

Teaching that distorts or contradicts the revealed truth of God, causing division and distress in the church by leading people away from the truth.

False doctrine deviates from the truth
It contradicts the gospel of Jesus Christ Jude 3–4 *See also* 1Co 3:10–13; 2Co 11:3–4; Gal 1:6–7; 1Ti 6:3–4; 2Jn 7

It may be of human origin Col 2:8 *See also* Col 2:20–23; Mt 15:8–9 pp Mk 7:6–7; Isa 29:13

It may be of demonic origin
1Ti 4:1–5 *See also* 1Jn 4:2–3

The dangers of false doctrine
It leads to instability and confusion
Eph 4:14 *See also* Ac 15:24; Gal 1:7;
1Ti 1:18–20; 2Ti 2:16–18; Tit 1:10–11;
Heb 13:9; 2Pe 3:17

It causes division Ro 16:17–18 *See also*
1Ti 1:3–4

It leads to severe punishment
Gal 1:8–9 *See also* 2Co 11:13–15;
2Pe 2:1,17; Rev 2:14–16

False doctrine is to be dealt with by the church
Tit 1:10–11 *See also* 1Ti 1:3;
Tit 1:13–14

False doctrine will be common in later times
1Ti 4:1 *See also* Mk 13:5–6 pp Lk 21:8;
2Th 2:3; 2Ti 4:3–4

See also

1460 truth	8710 atheism
2420 gospel	8749 false teachers
5441 philosophy	8750 false teachings
5794 asceticism	8766 heresies
7774 prophets, false	8774 legalism
8226 discernment	8775 libertinism
8703 antinomianism	

8239
earnestness

An attitude characterised by
seriousness and commitment.
Scripture commends earnestness in
believers' attitudes towards God and
in the concerns of the gospel.

The significance of earnestness
In repentance Joel 2:12 *See also*
1Sa 7:2–3; Rev 3:19

In seeking God Jer 29:13 *See also*
Ps 119:2; Heb 11:6

In salvation Lk 13:24 *See also*
Mt 7:24–27 pp Lk 6:47–49; Heb 2:3;
6:11; Jas 1:22; 2:14

In love for God Dt 6:5 *See also* Mt 22:37
pp Mk 12:30 pp Lk 10:27

In prayer 2Ch 7:14 *See also* Isa 62:6–7;
Mt 6:5–6

In trusting God Pr 3:5 *See also*
Isa 26:3–4

In spiritual progress Php 2:12–13 *See
also* 1Co 9:24; Heb 12:1; 2Pe 1:5–11

In serving God Mt 6:24 pp Lk 16:13 *See
also* Dt 18:6–7; Lk 9:57–62; 1Co 12:31;
14:1; 2Ti 2:15

Examples of earnestness
In seeking God Ps 63:1 *See also*
2Ch 15:15; Hos 5:15

In prayer Ac 12:5 *See also* 1Th 3:10;
Jas 5:17–18

In evangelism 1Co 9:19–22 *See also*
1Th 2:2–9

In Christian living Php 3:13–14 *See also*
1Co 9:25–27; 2Co 8:7–8

Regarding personal needs Mt 9:18
pp Mk 5:22–23 pp Lk 8:41–42; Lk 7:4

Jesus Christ's own earnestness
Mt 26:39 pp Mk 14:35 pp Lk 22:42 *See
also* Jn 2:17; 4:34

Earnest concern for the people of God
For Israel Lk 19:41; Ro 9:1–3 *See also*
Ne 1:2–4; Isa 22:4; 62:1; Jer 4:19–21;
8:21; 9:1; 13:17; La 3:48; Mic 1:8–9;
Mt 23:37 pp Lk 13:34; Ro 10:1

For the church 2Co 11:28–29 *See also*
Ac 20:31; Ro 1:11; 2Co 2:4; 11:2–3;
Gal 4:19–20; Col 1:24,28–29; 2:1;
1Th 2:17

Earnestness may be misdirected
Ro 11:7 *See also* Ac 26:7

See also

5840 eagerness	8370 zeal
5847 enthusiasm	8653 importunity to
8207 commitment	God

8240
ethics

Principles, both theoretical and
practical, for righteous living in the
sight of God. Scripture provides
detailed guidance concerning the
conduct of believers, as well as
examples of individuals whose lives
illustrate positive and negative
aspects of behaviour.
This set of themes consists of the
following:
8241 ethics, basis of
8242 ethics, personal
8243 ethics, social
8244 ethics, and grace
8245 ethics, incentives towards

8241
ethics, basis of

The ultimate foundation of ethics is
the character and will of God, which
is made known supremely through
Jesus Christ and in Scripture.

The foundation of ethics is the revealed righteousness of God
Ro 1:18–20 *See also* Ps 97:6; Ro 2:14–15

The basis of ethics revealed in Scripture
All Scripture 2Ti 3:16–17

The word of God Lk 11:28; Jas 1:22 *See
also* Ps 103:20; 119:17; Jn 17:6; Rev 3:8

The commandments of God
Dt 11:26–28; Jdg 2:17; 2Ch 34:29–31

The will of God Mk 3:35 *See also*
Ps 143:10; Col 4:12

The commandments of Jesus Christ
Jn 15:10 *See also* Jn 13:34; 14:15;
15:12–17; 1Co 14:37

The example of Jesus Christ Jn 13:15
See also Ro 15:2–3,7; 2Co 8:9;
Eph 5:1–2,25; Php 2:5; Col 3:13;
1Pe 2:21

The ethical teaching of Jesus Christ
In the Sermon on the Mount:
Mt 5:22,28,32,34,39,44; 7:29
Jn 1:9; 3:18–19; 5:19; 12:48–49; 13:34;
14:6; 15:22; 17:6

Areas of life in which ethical conduct is expected of believers
In sexual behaviour Ro 1:26–27 *See also*
Lev 18:22–23; 1Co 5:1

In government Ro 13:1 *See also*
Mt 22:21 pp Mk 12:17 pp Lk 20:25;
Jn 19:11; Ro 13:2–5; 1Pe 2:13–14

In rewarding individuals 1Co 9:7

In punishing individuals Gal 6:7

See also

1160 God,	4005 creation
unchangeable	5215 authority
1403 God, revelation	5326 government
1610 Scripture	5708 marriage
2339 Christ, example	6236 sexual sin
of	8309 morality

8242
ethics, personal

Scripture teaches that individuals
have a responsibility before God for
their conduct.

Ethical principles in relationships generally
Mt 7:12; 22:39 pp Mk 12:31 *See also*
Ex 20:13–17 pp Dt 5:17–21; Lev 19:18;
Lk 6:31; Ro 12:9–10; Gal 6:10; 1Ti 5:10;
1Pe 3:8

The importance of thoughts and motives
Mt 6:1–4 *See also* Ex 21:13–14;
Mt 5:22,28; Php 4:8; Jas 1:15

Personal ethics in relation to God
Idolatry prohibited Ex 20:4 pp Dt 5:8
See also Lev 26:1; Jos 24:14; Ac 14:15;
1Jn 5:21; Rev 22:9

God's name to be honoured Ex 20:7
pp Dt 5:11 *See also* Lev 19:12; Dt 28:58;
Mt 5:34; 6:9 pp Lk 11:2; Jas 5:12

Sabbath observance Ex 20:8
pp Dt 5:12 *See also* Ex 31:15; 34:21;
Lev 26:2; Ne 10:31; Isa 56:2

Obedience to God's commands
Ac 5:29 *See also* Dt 26:16; Mt 7:21

Personal ethics and human relationships
Wives and husbands Eph 5:22,25 *See
also* Ge 2:24; Dt 24:5; Mt 19:6
pp Mk 10:9; 1Co 7:10–11; Col 3:18–19;
1Pe 3:1,7

Children and parents Eph 6:1–4 *See
also* Ex 20:12; 21:15; Lev 20:9; Dt 6:7;
Pr 19:18; 22:6; 23:22; Col 3:20–21;
1Ti 3:4; 5:4

The extended family 1Ti 5:8 *See also*
Lev 25:10,25,49; Nu 36:8; Dt 25:5;
1Sa 20:29

Slaves and masters Col 3:22; 4:1 *See
also* Ex 21:2; Eph 6:5,9; 1Ti 6:1; Tit 2:9;
1Pe 2:18

Employers and employees Lev 19:13
See also Dt 24:14–15; Job 31:13–14;
Jer 22:13; Mal 3:5; Jas 5:4

See also

5191 thought	8266 holiness
5404 masters	8307 moderation
5520 servants	8452 neighbours,
5680 family	duty to
5908 motives	8768 idolatry
7446 slavery	

8243
ethics, social

Scripture sees ethics as embracing the life of society as a whole, and not simply individual relationships.

The benefits of social ethics

Pr 14:34 *See also* 2Sa 23:3–4; Ps 2:10–12; Pr 11:11; 16:12; 25:5; 28:2; 29:4; Isa 54:14

Believers are to behave ethically in society

Praying for rulers 1Ti 2:1–2 *See also* Ezr 6:10; Ps 20:9; 72:1

Submitting to the authorities Ro 13:1; Tit 3:1; 1Pe 2:13–14 *See also* Ex 22:28; Dt 17:12; 1Sa 24:6; 1Ki 21:10; Pr 24:21; Ecc 8:2; Ac 23:5; Ro 13:5; 1Pe 2:17

Paying taxes Mt 22:21 pp Mk 12:17 pp Lk 20:25 *See also* Lev 27:30; Dt 14:28; Ne 10:32; Mt 17:27; Ro 13:6–7

Specific areas of social concern

Promoting justice Dt 16:19–20; Mic 6:8 *See also* Ex 23:8; Lev 19:15; Dt 27:19; Pr 21:3; Isa 1:17; 10:1; 56:1; 1Ti 5:21

Helping the poor Dt 15:7–9 *See also* Lev 25:35,39; Dt 24:12; Pr 19:17; Mt 19:21 pp Mk 10:21 pp Lk 18:22; Lk 11:41; 12:33; Ro 12:13; Gal 2:10; Jas 2:3–4

Feeding the hungry Dt 26:12 *See also* Ex 23:11; Lev 19:9–10; 23:22; Isa 58:10; Mt 15:32 pp Mk 8:2–3; Lk 3:11; Ro 12:20; Pr 25:21

Protecting the vulnerable Ps 82:3–4; Jas 1:27 *See also* Ex 22:22; 23:9; Lev 25:25; Dt 24:17; Ps 41:1; Pr 23:10; Isa 58:7; Jer 22:3,16; Ac 20:35

Peacemaking Mt 5:9 *See also* Pr 12:20; Ro 12:18; 14:19; Heb 12:14; Jas 3:17

Showing concern for the environment Ge 2:15 *See also* Ge 1:26–28; Lev 25:2–5; Ne 10:31; Ps 115:16

See also

4203 earth, the	5376 law, purpose of
5255 citizenship	5446 poverty
5257 civil authorities	5577 taxation
5341 hunger	6700 peace
5359 justice	

8244
ethics, and grace

Ethical conduct on the part of believers rests upon both the grace of God and human obedience.

People are unable to fulfil the law of God without divine grace

Mt 15:19 pp Mk 7:21–22; Ro 7:14–15 *See also* Ge 6:5; 1Ki 8:46; Ps 51:5; 64:6; Isa 53:6; Ro 1:21; 3:23; Gal 3:22; 1Jn 1:8

Ethical conduct also depends on human obedience

Dt 26:16; Php 2:12 *See also* Dt 4:40; 6:17; Jos 1:8; 22:5; 1Ki 2:3; 11:38; 2Ki 17:13; Jer 7:23; Mt 5:48; 7:21; 19:17; Ro 6:19; 2Co 7:1; 1Ti 6:11; 2Pe 1:5–7; 3:14; 1Jn 3:3

God assists believers' ethical endeavours

He enlightens their minds Ps 119:130 *See also* Dt 4:1; Ps 119:144; Pr 6:23; Mic 6:8; Ro 7:7; 1Co 2:12–14

He gives them his Spirit Gal 5:16 *See also* Eze 36:27; Jn 14:15–17; Ro 8:3–5,9,13; Gal 5:22–23; 2Th 2:13; 1Pe 1:2

He gives them spiritual resources 2Pe 1:3 *See also* 1Ki 8:58; Ps 19:13; Jn 15:5; 1Co 10:13; Eph 6:11,13; Php 2:13; 2Ti 1:7; Heb 2:18; Jas 4:6

God will bring believers to ethical perfection

He will deliver them from the power of sin Ro 7:24–25 *See also* 1Co 1:8; Eph 4:24; Col 3:10; Php 1:6; 1Th 3:13; Jude 24

He will make them like Jesus Christ 1Jn 3:2 *See also* Ro 8:29; 2Co 3:18

He is preparing them for a righteous existence 2Pe 3:13 *See also* Mt 13:41–43; Rev 21:8,27; 22:15

See also

3233 Holy Spirit & sanctification	8206 Christlikeness
	8320 perfection
6020 sin	8453 obedience
6666 grace	9160 new heavens &
6744 sanctification	new earth

8245
ethics, incentives towards

God's ethical demands are reinforced by a variety of sanctions and incentives.

Sanctions promoting ethical behaviour

The authorities Ro 13:3–4 *See also* Dt 16:18; 17:11–12; 25:1; Ps 82:3–4; 1Ti 2:1–4; 1Pe 2:13–14

God treats people as they treat others Mt 6:14–15 *See also* 2Sa 12:9–10; Mt 5:7; 7:2; 18:35; Jas 2:13

Unethical behaviour renders worship unacceptable Isa 58:4 *See also* Isa 1:13–15; Eze 33:31; Zec 7:5,9–10; Mt 23:23 pp Lk 11:42; Tit 1:16

The withdrawal of God's fellowship Isa 59:2 *See also* Ps 51:11; 66:18; Hos 5:6; Mic 3:4; Eph 4:30

God's judgment Gal 6:8 *See also* Dt 28:15; Isa 1:23–24; 1Co 6:9; 2Co 5:10; Col 3:5–6; Heb 12:14

Incentives to correct ethical behaviour

A new life in Christ Eph 5:8 *See also* Ro 6:2,13; 2Co 5:15; Col 3:9–10

God's goodness and love Eph 5:1–2 *See also* Ex 20:2; Ro 12:1; 2Co 8:8–9; Tit 2:14; 1Jn 3:16

Pleasing God Heb 13:16 *See also* 2Co 5:9; Col 3:20; 1Th 2:3–4; 4:1; 1Jn 3:22

True worship is made possible Ps 24:3–4 *See also* Pr 21:3; Hos 6:6; Isa 58:6–7; Mk 12:33; Jas 1:27

God's fellowship Jn 14:23 *See also* Dt 10:12–13; Ps 15:1–5; Rev 21:7

God's blessing Dt 16:20 *See also*

Dt 28:2; Ps 1:3; 84:11; Isa 56:1–2; 58:9–14; Mt 6:18

Future reward Lk 14:13–14 *See also* Mt 10:42 pp Mk 9:41; Mt 25:34–36; Lk 6:35; Ro 2:10; Col 3:24; Rev 22:12

See also

5498 reward	8622 worship
7922 fellowship with God	9210 judgment, God's
8460 pleasing God	

8248

faithfulness

Commitment to a relationship with God or fellow human beings; seen in that loyalty, devotion and service which is a reflection of God's own faithfulness. Scripture points to the faithfulness of Jesus Christ as an example for believers.

8249
faithfulness, of God

See 1035 God, faithfulness of

8250
faithfulness, of Jesus Christ

See 2021 Jesus Christ, faithfulness of

8251
faithfulness, to God

The proper response to God by his covenant people; seen in a steadfast commitment which reflects God's own faithfulness to the covenant. Encouraged in all believers, it is especially important in leaders.

Faithfulness is the proper response to God by his covenant people

God's covenant with his people requires faithfulness 1Ki 2:3–4 *See also* Ex 19:5; Dt 5:32–33; 10:12–13; 29:9; Isa 1:26

Faithfulness to God seen as marital fidelity Hos 2:20 *See also* Isa 54:5; Jer 2:2; Eze 16:8; Eph 1:1; 5:22–25

Faithfulness to God reflects God's faithfulness Dt 7:9 *See also* 1Sa 2:35; 1Co 10:12–13; Heb 4:14–16; 10:23; 1Pe 4:19

Faithfulness is seen as steadfast commitment to God

In unwavering devotion Mic 4:5 *See also* Jos 24:14–15; Lk 9:62; Rev 2:10

In obedience Dt 11:13; Eze 18:9

In service 1Sa 12:24; 2Ch 19:9; 34:10–12 pp 2Ki 22:4–7; Eze 44:15; 48:11; 1Ti 1:12

In giving 2Ch 31:12 *Faithfulness to God is expressed in giving to him for the benefit of others*; 2Co 8:1–5

In prayer Ro 12:12; 1Th 5:17

In patient endurance 2Ti 2:11–13; Heb 10:36; Rev 13:10; 14:12

In fulfilling vows Nu 30:2; Dt 23:21–23; Ps 22:25; 61:8; Ecc 5:4; Jnh 2:9

Faithfulness is especially important in leaders
1Co 4:1–2; 3Jn 3 *See also* Ex 18:21; 1Ti 4:13–16; 6:20; 2Ti 1:13–14; 2:2,15; 4:1–2

Encouragements to faithfulness
The call to faithfulness 1Co 15:58 *See also* Ps 24:6; Isa 26:4; Jn 14:1; 1Co 16:13; Gal 5:1; Eph 6:13

God watches over the faithful Ps 97:10 *See also* Ps 31:23; 37:28; 86:2; Pr 2:8

God rewards faithfulness 1Sa 26:23; Mt 25:21 pp Lk 19:17 *See also* Ps 101:6; Pr 28:20; Mt 24:45–47 pp Lk 12:42–44; 2Ti 4:6–8; Rev 17:14; 20:4

Lack of faithfulness
Hos 4:1 *See also* Ps 12:1; 78:8,37; Hos 1:2; 5:7; 9:1

See also

1035 God, faithfulness	8114 discipleship
1345 covenant	8208 commitment to God
2021 Christ, faithfulness	8453 obedience
5498 reward	8459 perseverance
5712 marriage, God & his people	8742 faithlessness
7734 leaders, spiritual	8840 unfaithfulness to God

8252
faithfulness, in human relationships

Loyalty and commitment within human relationships is important in the life of God's people. It is seen particularly in fidelity within marriage, fulfilling family obligations, honouring vows, dutiful service and trustworthy speech and conduct.

Faithfulness within society
It is important in the life of God's people Hos 12:6 *The word translated "love" is the Hebrew word "hesed", which here expresses the loyalty and faithfulness that should characterise the life of God's people. See also* Mic 6:8; Mt 23:23 pp Lk 11:42

It is a reflection of God's faithfulness to his people Ps 89:14 *See also* Dt 32:4; Isa 11:4–5

Faithfulness in marriage
Heb 13:4 *See also* Mal 2:11,14–15; Mt 5:27–28; Ex 20:14; Eph 5:33; 1Ti 5:9

Faithfulness in family relationships
1Ti 5:4,8 *See also* Ge 24:47–51 *fulfilling family obligations in marriage arrangements;* Ge 47:28–31 *fulfilling family obligations regarding burial Ruth's faithfulness to Naomi:* Ru 1:16–18; 2:11–12

1Sa 2:19 *Hannah visits Samuel regularly. The wife of noble character provides for her family:* Pr 31:15,21,27–28

Jn 19:25–27 *Jesus Christ provides for his mother.*

Faithfulness to vows and covenants
Nu 30:2
Jacob and Laban: Ge 29:18,30
The sons of Israel and Joseph: Ge 50:25; Ex 13:19
The Israelites and Rahab: Jos 2:14; 6:25
Jos 9:15–20 *Joshua and the Gibeonites David and Jonathan:* 1Sa 18:3; 20:8,42; 23:16
1Ki 20:34 *Ben-Hadad and Ahab*

Faithfulness in speech
In carrying messages Pr 13:17 *See also* Pr 25:13

In telling the truth Pr 12:17; 14:5

In bringing God's word Jer 23:28 *See also* 2Co 2:17; 4:2; 2Ti 2:15

Faithfulness in conduct
In serving others 3Jn 5 *See also* Ro 16:1–2; Gal 6:10; 1Pe 4:10

In intercession Ro 1:9–10; Eph 6:18; Col 4:2–4

In giving 2Co 8:7–11 *See also* 2Ch 31:5–10; Php 4:15–18

In handling money 2Ki 12:13–15 *See also* 2Ki 22:7; 2Ch 31:12–15; Mt 25:21; Lk 16:10; 19:17

The rarity of true faithfulness
Pr 20:6 *See also* Ps 12:1–2; Isa 57:1; Jer 17:9

See also

5430 oaths, human	8275 honesty
5468 promises, human	8354 trustworthiness
5680 family	8434 giving
5708 marriage	8652 importunity
5717 monogamy	
8210 commitment to God's people	

8253
faithfulness, examples of

Those who show loyalty, reliability and devotion in their relationships with God and others.

Abraham
Ne 9:7–8 *See also* Gal 3:9; Heb 11:8–12

Moses
Heb 3:5 *See also* Nu 12:7; Heb 11:24–28

Caleb
Nu 14:24 *See also* Dt 1:36; Jos 14:8–9

Elijah
1Ki 19:10 *See also* 1Ki 19:14

David
1Sa 29:6 *David, fleeing from Saul, shelters with Achish, king of Gath. See also* 2Sa 9:6–7; 22:22–24

Hezekiah
2Ki 20:3 pp Isa 38:3 *See also* 2Ch 31:20; 32:1

Daniel
Da 6:4 *See also* Da 6:10

Paul
1Ti 1:12 *See also* 1Co 7:25; 2Ti 4:7

Timothy
1Co 4:17 *See also* 2Ti 1:5

Silas
1Pe 5:12 *See also* Ac 16:25

Christian martyrs
Rev 2:13 *See also* Rev 2:10; 12:11

Further examples
Enoch: Ge 5:22–24; Heb 11:5
Noah: Ge 6:9; Heb 11:7
Jos 24:14–15 *Joshua;* 1Ki 19:18 *7,000 in Israel*
Josiah: 2Ki 22:2 pp 2Ch 34:2; 2Ch 35:26
Ne 13:13–14 *Nehemiah*
Job: Job 23:11–12; 27:6
Reliable witnesses: Isa 8:2; 2Ti 2:2
Da 3:16–18 *Shadrach, Meshach and Abednego;* Ac 4:18–20 *Peter and John*
Tychicus: Eph 6:21–22; Col 4:7
Epaphras: Col 1:7; 4:12
Onesimus: Col 4:9; Phm 10–11

See also

1462 truth, in NT	8225 devotion
5691 friends, good	8304 loyalty
5734 relationships	8331 reliability
8026 faith, growth in	8450 martyrdom
8027 faith, testing of	
8122 friendship with God	

8255

fruit, spiritual

The spiritual life and growth of believers is likened to a fruit-bearing tree. As the fruit is evidence of the health and vigour of the tree, so the believer's life, attitudes and behaviour should reflect the presence of the Holy Spirit.

Believers should exhibit evidence of their conversion
Jas 3:13 *See also* Mt 3:8 pp Lk 3:8–9; Mt 7:15–20; 12:33; Jn 15:16; Ro 7:4–5; Tit 3:14; Jas 2:14–26

The nature of spiritual fruit
Gal 5:22–23 *See also* Ro 8:5–6; Php 1:9–11; Jas 3:17

The sources of spiritual fruit
Acceptance of the gospel Lk 8:15 pp Mt 13:23 pp Mk 4:20

The old way of life put to death
Jn 12:24 *See also* Ro 6:6,11–14; 8:13–14; Gal 5:24; Eph 4:22–24; Col 3:5–10

Actively living a new life in Jesus Christ
Gal 6:7–9 *See also* Ro 6:11–14; Gal 5:25; Eph 5:8–9; Col 1:10; 3:12–15; 2Ti 2:22; 2Pe 1:5–8; Tit 3:14; 1Jn 3:18

Remaining close to Jesus Christ
Jn 15:4–5

Submission to God's discipline
Heb 12:10–11 *See also* Jn 15:1–2

See also

1040 God, fatherhood	8154 righteousness
3254 Holy Spirit, fruit of	8164 spirituality
6698 newness	8256 fruitfulness
8102 abiding in Christ	8348 spiritual growth
	8443 growth

8256

fruitfulness

Fruitfulness is seen as a sign of blessing and closeness to God, just as barrenness may be seen as a sign of God's disfavour. Scripture stresses that faith is given in order that it may bear fruit.

8257
fruitfulness, natural

In the OT fruitfulness is often used as a way of referring to God's material and physical blessings.

God's blessing on creation generally
Ge 1:11–12,22 See also Ge 8:17

Fruitfulness in the promised land
Lev 25:18–19 God's blessing was seen in terms of material prosperity. See also Lev 26:3–4; Dt 32:13; 33:13–16; Eze 34:27; Am 9:14; Zec 8:12

Fruitfulness in family relationships
Such fruitfulness promised Ge 13:16 See also Ge 15:5; 17:6,20; 22:17; Lev 26:9; Dt 7:13; 28:4,11; 30:9; Ps 128:3; Jer 23:3; Eze 36:11

Such fruitfulness commanded Ge 1:28 See also Ge 9:1,7; 35:11; 48:3–4

Examples of such fruitfulness
Ps 105:24 See also Ge 41:52; 47:27; 49:22; Ex 1:7; Ps 107:37–38

See also
1050 God, goodness of	5225 barrenness
1330 God, the provider	5664 children
	5724 offspring
4005 creation	5858 fat
4035 abundance	5960 success
5075 Abraham	8808 riches
	8845 unfruitfulness

8258
fruitfulness, spiritual

Fruitfulness is used by Scripture as a symbol of spiritual maturity and well-being.

Spiritual fruitfulness described
Gal 5:22–23 The results of the Holy Spirit's activity in the life of a Christian believer. See also Ps 92:12; Pr 11:30; Isa 32:17; Jer 11:16; Eze 19:10; Eph 5:9; Col 1:10; Jas 3:17

Spiritual fruitfulness expected in God's people
Jn 15:16 See also Isa 5:1–2; Mt 7:16–20 pp Lk 6:43–44 Such fruitfulness, seen in a person's behaviour, is evidence of their true character; Ro 7:4

The conditions for spiritual fruitfulness
Spiritual fruitfulness through an intimate relationship with Jesus Christ Jn 15:4–5

Spiritual fruitfulness through a commitment to God's word Ps 1:1–3 See also Mt 13:23; Jn 15:2–3

Spiritual fruitfulness through a death to self-interest Jn 12:24 Although Jesus Christ is speaking here primarily of his own death, the principle remains true for Christian living.

See also
1610 Scripture	8102 abiding in Christ
3254 Holy Spirit, fruit of	8255 fruit, spiritual
5902 maturity	8347 spiritual
6744 sanctification	growth
6754 union with Christ	8356 unselfishness

8260

generosity

The free and liberal bestowal of wealth, possessions or food upon others. The generosity of God is shown in his free bestowal of grace upon undeserving sinners.

8261
generosity, God's

The generosity of God is evident in the way in which he deals with his creation, and supremely with sinners. God bestows his gracious gifts upon sinners in salvation, in sanctification and through the coming of the Holy Spirit.

God's generous heart
Eph 1:7–9 See also Ex 34:6–7; Ps 33:18–22; Mt 7:11; Lk 15:22–24; Ro 11:35–36

God's generosity evident in creation
Ps 65:9–13 See also Ps 33:5; 68:9

God's generosity evident in providence
Ac 14:17 See also Ge 24:35; Nu 14:8; Dt 28:11; 33:23; Ps 66:12; 78:15; 132:15; 145:7; 147:6; Jer 31:12–14; 33:6–9; Mal 3:10; 1Ti 6:17

God's generosity experienced in salvation
Eph 1:3 See also Jn 1:16; Ro 5:5; 10:12; Eph 2:7; 3:8; Col 2:10; 1Jn 3:1

His love and mercifulness towards sinners Ps 116:5; 130:7; Isa 55:7; Hos 14:4; Eph 2:7; 1Jn 3:1

Redemption through the death of Jesus Christ Ro 3:24; Eph 1:7; 1Ti 1:14–16; Tit 2:13–14; 1Pe 1:18–19

His gift of eternal life Jn 3:16; 10:28; Ro 3:23–24; 5:17; 6:23; 1Ti 1:14–16

God's generosity experienced in sanctification
2Pe 1:2–3 See also Ps 23:5; 36:7–8; Eze 47:1–12; Php 2:12–13; 4:19; Jude 2

The gift of the Holy Spirit Joel 2:28–29 See also Ac 2:17–18; Eze 39:29; Jn 3:34; Ac 10:45; Ro 5:5; Tit 3:6

Wisdom Jas 1:5 See also Col 2:2

Comfort, strength and encouragement 2Co 1:5 See also Eph 3:16; 2Th 2:16–17

God's generosity in heaven
Inheritance 1Co 2:9 See also Eph 1:18

Reward Pr 28:20 See also Heb 10:35; Rev 21:1–4

See also
1050 God, goodness of	5705 inheritance, spiritual
1055 God, grace & mercy	6510 salvation
	8291 kindness
1325 God, the Creator	8361 wisdom
1355 providence	8416 encouragement, promises
3257 Holy Spirit, gift of	8813 riches, spiritual
5500 reward, God's people	

8262
generosity, human

Believers should be generous in their dealings with others, following the example of God himself.

Motivations for generosity
God's example 2Co 8:7–9 See also 1Jn 3:16–18

God's dealings with believers Eph 4:32–5:2 See also Mt 10:7–8; 18:21–35

Demonstrations of generosity
In material giving Ac 4:32–37 See also Lev 25:35; Dt 15:7–8; Mt 5:42; 19:21; 2Co 8:3; 9:5

In support of God's work Php 4:16 See also Ex 36:5; Nu 7:13–17; 1Ch 28:14–18; 29:9; 2Ch 31:9–10; Mk 12:41–44 pp Lk 21:1–4; Gal 6:6; 1Ti 5:17–18

In worship Mt 26:6–7 See also Ex 35:22; 1Ki 3:4; 8:63; 2Ch 1:6; 5:6; Ezr 6:9; Ro 12:1–2; Php 2:17

In acts of mercy Lk 10:33–35 See also 2Ki 6:22; 2Ch 28:15

In giving presents 1Ki 10:13 See also Ge 24:53; 32:17–21; 45:21–23; 2Ki 5:5; 8:9

Meanness and covetousness the opposites of generosity
Ecc 5:13 See also 2Sa 12:2–4; Isa 43:23–24; Mic 2:2; Mal 3:8–9; Mt 25:45; Lk 12:15

Generosity rewarded
Mal 3:10 See also Ps 37:25–26; 112:5,9; Pr 11:24–25; 22:9; Isa 58:10; Lk 6:38; 2Co 9:6–9; Gal 6:9–10

See also
1335 blessing	6652 forgiveness
5446 poverty	6686 mercy
5765 attitudes to people	7402 offerings
	8292 love
5806 compassion	8434 giving
5856 extravagance	8445 hospitality
5907 miserliness	

8264

gentleness

An expression of compassion, seen in God's dealings with the frail and weak, and expected of believers in their dealings with others.

The gentleness of God

In dealing with the wayward
Isa 40:1–2; Lk 1:76–79 *See also*
Isa 30:18–19; 54:8; 63:15 *God's gentleness is not always evident;*
Hos 2:13–15; Ro 2:4 *God's gentle dealings are not always appreciated.*

In caring for the weak Isa 40:11 *See also* 1Ki 19:12

The gentleness of Jesus Christ

Mt 11:29 *See also* Zec 9:9; Mt 21:4–5;
12:18–21; Isa 42:1–3; 2Co 10:1;
Php 2:1; Heb 5:2

Examples of Jesus Christ's gentleness

Mk 1:40–42; 5:25–34; 10:13–16;
Jn 8:3–11

Gentleness as strength esteemed by God

Pr 15:1; Jas 3:17 *See also* Pr 25:15;
Mt 5:5; 1Pe 3:1–4

Gentleness as a mark of Christian character

Col 3:12 *See also* Gal 5:22–23;
Eph 4:1–2; 1Ti 6:11

Believers are to reflect God's gentleness in their dealings with people

In correcting the wayward Gal 6:1 *See also* 2Ti 2:24–25

In reasoning with unbelievers
1Pe 3:15–16

In nurturing new believers 1Th 2:7

In showing consideration to all
Tit 3:1–2 *See also* Eph 4:32; Php 4:5

See also

1030 God, compassion	5806 compassion
2015 Christ, compassion	6686 mercy
	8255 fruit, spiritual
3254 Holy Spirit, fruit of	8276 humility
	8291 kindness
5765 attitudes to people	8305 meekness
	8306 mercifulness
	8318 patience

8265

godliness

Reverence for or devotion to God, producing a practical awareness of God in every aspect of life.

Examples of godliness in the OT

Ge 5:24 *Enoch;* Ge 6:9 *Noah;* 1Ki 18:3–4
Obadiah; 2Ch 31:20–21 *Hezekiah;*
Job 1:1 *Job*

Examples of godliness in the NT

Lk 2:25 *Simeon;* Lk 2:37 *Anna;* Jn 1:47
Nathanael
Jesus Christ: Jn 8:29; Heb 5:7
Ac 2:5; 8:2
Cornelius and his family: Ac 10:2,7
Ac 11:24 *Barnabas;* Ac 22:12 *Ananias*

God has a special concern for the godly

Ps 4:3 *"the godly" (sometimes translated "the saints") is often used in the OT to refer to God's people. See also* Ps 32:6;
Jn 9:31

Godly living

Godliness should be seen in the lives of believers 2Pe 3:11 *See also* 1Ti 2:2;
6:11; Tit 2:12

Jesus Christ is the beginning and end of godliness 1Ti 3:16 *The model and the power for godly living derives from the incarnate Christ. See also* Heb 5:7;
2Pe 1:3

The basis for godly living is true teaching about Jesus Christ 1Ti 6:3–4
See also Tit 1:1

Godly living demands self-discipline
1Co 9:24–27; 2Co 10:5; 1Ti 4:7–8

Sorrow for sin is a sign of godliness
2Co 7:10–11

The benefits of godliness

Its value in both this world and the next
1Ti 4:8

Its present blessings Dt 4:40; 1Ti 6:6
See also Isa 3:10; Tit 3:8

The promise of future blessing
Tit 2:11–13 *See also* 2Pe 3:11–12

Godliness does not guarantee escape from suffering

Ps 12:1 *See also* Mic 7:2; 2Ti 3:12;
2Pe 2:9

Apparent godliness may not be genuine

1Ti 6:5; 2Ti 3:4–5

See also

5499 reward, divine	8225 devotion
6169 godlessness	8266 holiness
6744 sanctification	8333 reverence
8154 righteousness	8361 wisdom
8201 blamelessness	8476 self-discipline
8206 Christlikeness	8846 ungodliness

8266

holiness

The quality of God that sets him utterly apart from his world, especially in terms of his purity and sanctity. The holiness of God is also manifested in the persons and work of Jesus Christ and the Holy Spirit. Believers are called upon to become like God in his holiness.
This set of themes consists of the following:

8267 holiness, of God
8268 holiness, of Jesus Christ
8269 holiness, as separation from the worldly
8270 holiness, as set apart for God
8271 holiness, purpose of
8272 holiness, believers' growth in
8273 holiness, ethical aspects of

8267

holiness, of God

See 1065 God, holiness of

8268

holiness, of Jesus Christ

See 2030 Jesus Christ, holiness of

8269

holiness, as separation from the worldly

God's people are called to holiness, which involves being distinct from other people. In the OT, this is seen in the command to separate from other nations and from everything that can compromise commitment to the LORD. In the NT believers are called to distance themselves from the ways and values of the world, which can be dishonouring to God and destructive to obedience to him.

Israel is to be set apart from other nations

Lev 20:23–26 *See also* Ex 33:15–16;
Lev 15:31; 18:29–30; Dt 7:1–6;
23:9–14; Ezr 9:1–2,10–12; Isa 52:11

Common things are designated clean or unclean by ritual law

Clean and unclean animals
Lev 11:46–47 *See also* Lev 11:1–23
pp Dt 14:3–20; Mk 7:14–19; Ac 10:14

Infectious skin diseases Lev 13:2–3;
14:2

Mildew Lev 13:47–49; 14:33–36

Bodily discharges Lev 12:2; 15:2

Corpses Lev 5:2–3; 11:31–40; 21:1,11

What is holy must be kept separate

The Israelites must distinguish between the holy and the common
Lev 10:10–11; Eze 44:23

Contact with the profane desecrates the holy Ac 21:28 *See also* Jer 51:51

Unclean people and things must be removed Nu 5:1–3; Ezr 10:10–11 *See also* Lev 7:22–27; 13:45–46; 19:5–8;
Nu 19:13,20; Dt 23:10–14; 2Ch 26:21

Unclean people are not to approach what is sacred Lev 7:20–21; 22:3–6

The holy must be treated with respect

Unintentional defilement of the holy carries a penalty Lev 5:14–16

Warnings against contempt for the holy Lev 22:1–2 *See also* Ex 19:10–13;
28:42–43; 30:18–21; 31:14–15;
Nu 4:15,17–20; Heb 10:28–29

Examples of contempt for the holy
Lev 10:1–2; Nu 16:1–7,18–35;
1Sa 6:19–20; 2Sa 6:6–7; Eze 22:26,31;
Ac 5:1–10

Christians are called to be separate from the ways of the world

Jn 15:19; Jas 4:4; 1Pe 2:9–11 *See also*
Jn 17:14–16; 2Co 6:14–7:1; 2Ti 2:19;
Jas 1:27

See also

4025 world, the	7342 cleanliness
5763 attitudes, positive to God	7424 ritual law
	7426 ritual washing
5811 compromise	8207 commitment
7340 clean and unclean	8341 separation
	8848 worldliness

8270
holiness, as set apart for God

Believers are holy, in that they are called to be set apart from the world as God's own people. Likewise certain days and articles are holy because they are set apart for God alone.

Believers are called to be a holy people, set apart for God
The nation of Israel Dt 7:6 *See also* Ex 19:5–6; Lev 20:26; Dt 26:18–19

The priests 1Ch 23:13 *See also* Lev 21:5–8

The Nazirites Nu 6:1–8

The apostles and prophets Lk 1:70; Ac 3:21; Eph 3:5; 2Pe 3:2

Christians Eph 1:4; 1Pe 1:15–16 *See also* 1Co 1:2; Col 3:12; 2Ti 1:9; 1Pe 2:9

Consecration sets apart for holiness
God's people are consecrated Lev 20:7–8 *See also* Ex 19:10–11, 14–15; Lev 11:44–45; Jos 3:5; 7:13; 1Sa 16:5

Priests are consecrated for divine service Ex 30:30 *See also* Ex 40:12–15; 1Sa 7:1; 1Ch 15:14; 2Ch 23:6; 29:5; 35:3

Articles are consecrated for divine use Ex 40:9–11 *See also* Ex 29:36–37; 30:25–29

Days and occasions set apart for God
The Sabbath Lev 23:1–3 *See also* Ge 2:3; Ex 16:23–25; 20:11

The Passover Lev 23:4–8; Nu 28:16,25

The Feast of Weeks Lev 23:15–16,21; Nu 28:26

The Feast of Trumpets Lev 23:23–25; Nu 29:1; Ne 8:2,9–11

The Day of Atonement Lev 23:26–28,32; Nu 29:7

The Feast of Tabernacles Lev 23:33–36; Nu 29:12

The sabbath year Lev 25:1–5

The Year of Jubilee Lev 25:8–12

Places identified with the presence of God are made holy
Holy ground Ex 3:5; Jos 5:15

Holy mountains Ex 19:18–23; 2Pe 1:18

The tabernacle Ex 29:42–44; 40:9

The temple 1Ki 8:10–13 pp 2Ch 7:16 *See also* 1Ki 8:10–13; Eze 42:14,20; Mt 24:15; Ac 6:13; 21:28

Jerusalem and the holy land Joel 3:17; Zec 2:12; Mt 4:5; 27:53

Things associated with worship are holy
Bread Ex 29:32–33; 1Sa 21:3–6; Mt 12:3–4 pp Mk 2:25–26 pp Lk 6:3–4

Perfume Ex 30:34–38

Ritual offerings Lev 6:24–29 *See also* Lev 6:17; 7:1,6; 10:12–13,16–18

Offerings dedicated with a vow Lev 27:9,14,20–23,28

Tithes Lev 27:30–33

The firstborn Ex 13:2,11–12; Lk 2:22–23

See also

4269 Sinai, Mount	7458 tabernacle, the
5155 hair	7525 exclusiveness
7140 people of God	7745 ordination
7396 Most Holy Place	7766 priests
	8218 consecration
7412 priesthood	8324 purity
7428 Sabbath	

8271
holiness, purpose of

God in his holiness desires a holy people amongst whom he can dwell, and who can effectively worship, witness to and serve him as they prepare for a future with God and to be like God.

The goal of holiness is to be like God
Lev 19:2; Mt 5:48 *See also* Ro 8:29; Heb 12:10; 1Pe 1:15–16; 1Jn 3:2–3

God dwells with holy people
God dwelt with the people of Israel Dt 23:14 *See also* Ex 29:42–46; Nu 5:1–3; 1Ki 9:3; Eze 37:26–28; Zec 2:10–12

God dwells with Christians Eph 2:19–22 *See also* 1Co 3:16–17

Holiness is required for acceptable worship
Heb 10:19–22 *See also* Lev 22:17–22; 2Ch 29:15–31; Isa 56:6–7; Mt 15:7–9 pp Mk 7:6; Isa 29:13; Ro 12:1

Holiness is needed for effective witness
1Pe 2:9–12 *See also* Eze 20:41; 36:20; 39:7; 1Pe 3:1–2

Holiness is needed for godly service
Heb 9:13–14 *See also* Ex 28:41; Lev 21:6–8; 2Ch 35:3; Zep 3:9; Lk 1:74–75; 2Ti 2:20–21; Tit 2:14

Holiness leads to a future hope
Holy people will see God Heb 12:14 *See also* Mt 5:8; 1Th 3:13; 2Th 1:10

Holy people will receive eternal life Ro 6:22 *See also* 2Pe 3:11

Holy people will inherit the kingdom Col 1:12 *See also* Da 7:18,22,27; Eph 1:18; Rev 20:6

Holy people will judge the world 1Co 6:2

Believers' ultimate destiny is to share God's holiness for ever Eph 5:25–27; Rev 21:2–3

See also

7922 fellowship with God	8495 witnessing
	8622 worship
8154 righteousness	9160 new heavens & new earth
8206 Christlikeness	
8265 godliness	9410 heaven
8474 seeing God	9610 hope

8272
holiness, believers' growth in

Believers are enabled to grow in holiness on account of the sacrificial death of Jesus Christ, foreshadowed by the OT sacrificial system, and through the sanctifying work of the Holy Spirit.

Holiness begins with God's initiative
God chooses who and what is to be holy 2Ch 7:16 pp 1Ki 9:3 *See also* Ex 20:11; Nu 16:7; 2Ch 29:11; Zec 2:12

God chooses and calls his people to holiness Dt 7:6; Eph 1:4 *See also* Dt 14:2; Ro 1:7; Col 3:12; 1Pe 1:2,15

Holiness is conferred by the holy God
Holiness is conferred by the presence of God Ex 29:42–43 *See also* Ex 3:4–5; 19:23; 2Ch 7:1–2

Holiness is conferred through covenant relationship with God Ex 19:5–6 *See also* Dt 28:9; Eze 37:26–28; 1Pe 2:9

Holiness is conferred by the sovereign action of God 1Th 5:23 *See also* Lev 20:8; Isa 4:3–4; Eze 36:25; Zep 1:7; Ac 15:9; Heb 2:11

Holiness through the OT rituals
Cleansing from what is unclean Nu 8:6–7 *See also* Ex 19:14; Nu 19:9; Ne 12:30

Purification and atonement through sacrifice Nu 8:12–14 *The OT sacrificial system and holiness laws foreshadow the perfect sacrifice of Jesus Christ that enables believers to grow in holiness through faith. See also* Ex 29:35–37; Lev 8:14–15; 16:5–10,15–22,29–30

Consecration by anointing Lev 8:10–12 *See also* Ex 29:21; 40:9

Holiness through Jesus Christ
Through the sacrifice of Jesus Christ Heb 10:10 *See also* Eph 5:25–27; Col 1:22; Heb 1:3; 9:13–14,23–28; 10:14,19–22; 13:12; 1Jn 1:7; 2:2; 4:10

Through relationship with Jesus Christ 1Co 1:2 *See also* 1Co 1:30

Holiness through the sanctifying work of the Holy Spirit
2Th 2:13 *See also* Jn 3:5–8; Ro 15:16; 1Co 6:11; 1Th 4:7–8; Tit 3:5; 1Pe 1:2

The human response to holiness
Repentance 1Jn 1:9 *See also* Ezr 9:1–7; 10:1–4; Ps 51:1–10; Ac 2:38; Ro 6:11–13; Jas 4:8

Faith Gal 5:5 *See also* Ro 1:17–18; 2Th 2:13

Obedience 1Pe 1:22 *See also* Ps 119:9; Jn 17:17; Ro 6:16–19

See also

2030 Christ, holiness	6744 sanctification
3233 Holy Spirit & sanctification	7304 anointing
	7416 purification
3278 Holy Spirit, indwelling	8020 faith
	8347 spiritual growth
6606 access to God	8453 obedience
6614 atonement	
6732 repentance	

8273
holiness, ethical aspects of

Behaviour that reflects the holy character of God himself is to be expressed in both social and personal dimensions of life.

Holiness in practice is a reflection of God's own character
1Pe 1:15–16 See also Lev 11:44–45; 19:2; 20:7; Eph 4:24; 1Jn 3:3

Holiness demands a different way of life
Shunning practices that defile
Lev 18:1–3; Eph 5:11–12; 1Ti 5:22 See also Lev 18:21–24,29–30; 20:1–3,6–7, 23–26; 21:7; 2Co 6:17–7:1; Gal 5:19–21,24; Eph 5:3–7; Col 3:5–10
Obedience to God's law Lev 20:7–8 See also Lev 18:4–5; 19:37; Dt 6:25; 28:9; Ps 119:9; Ro 7:12; 1Pe 1:22

Holiness is expressed in social behaviour
Care for the disadvantaged
Lev 19:9–10 See also Lev 19:14,33–34; 1Ti 5:3–4,8; Jas 1:27
A concern for truth and justice
Lev 19:15–16 See also Lev 19:11–13,35–37
Loving one's neighbour Lev 19:18 See also Lev 19:16–17 Most of the OT law can be seen as an expression of holiness.

Holiness is expressed in family and sexual relations
1Th 4:3–7 See also Lev 18:5–20,22–23; 19:3; 20:9; Eph 5:3; 1Co 6:13–15,18–19

Holiness is seen in personal character
Col 3:12 See also Eph 4:23–24,32–5:2; 2Ti 2:22

See also
1065 God, holiness of	5769 behaviour
5016 heart, fallen & redeemed	8203 character
	8240 ethics
5448 poverty, attitudes to	8277 innocence
5540 society	8337 reverence & behaviour

8275

honesty

Behaviour, in action and words, that aims to convey truth. This quality is an essential aspect of God's own nature and purposes, and is required of those whom he calls to be his people.

Honesty is integral to the gospel
The honesty of God 2Sa 7:28 See also Ps 19:7; 33:4; 111:7; 119:142,151; Isa 45:19; Jer 10:10; Jn 7:28; Ro 3:4; 1Th 1:9; 1Jn 5:20; Rev 3:7; 15:2–3; 19:9

The honesty demanded of believers
Ps 15:1–2; 2Co 4:2 See also Ex 18:21
Dishonest dealing forbidden by God:
Lev 19:35–36; Dt 25:13–16

1Ki 9:4–5; Pr 11:1; Eze 45:10; Zec 8:16–17; Jn 4:23–24; Ro 1:18; 1Co 5:8
Paul commends truthful speech:
Eph 4:15,25
Php 4:8
Qualities essential in church leadership:
1Ti 3:8; Tit 1:7
Tit 2:7–8

The honesty of Jesus Christ
1Pe 2:22 See also Mt 22:16 pp Mk 12:14
Jesus Christ's opponents flattering Jesus Christ, but nevertheless speaking the truth.

Other examples of honest behaviour commended by Scripture
Jacob: Ge 30:33; 43:12
1Sa 12:3–5 Samuel; 1Ki 17:24 Elijah;
1Ch 29:17 David; Job 27:4 Job; Da 6:4 Daniel
Paul: Ac 24:16; 2Co 1:12; 2:17; 4:2

The cost of honesty
Jer 26:15 See also Pr 17:26; 29:10,27; Isa 59:14–15; Am 5:10; Jn 8:45–46; 18:23; Gal 4:16

See also
1065 God, holiness of	5429 oaths
1075 God, justice of	5546 speech
1125 God, righteousness	5587 trade
	6145 deceit
1460 truth	8239 earnestness
5414 money, stewardship	8714 dishonesty
	8767 hypocrisy

8276

humility

An attitude of lowliness and obedience, grounded in the recognition of one's status before God as his creatures.

God commands humility
Mic 6:8; Jas 4:10; 1Pe 3:8 See also Ex 10:3; Pr 16:19; Isa 57:15; 58:5; Zep 2:3; Lk 14:9–11; Ro 12:3 sober assessment of oneself; 1Co 1:28; Eph 4:2; Col 3:12; Tit 3:2; Jas 3:13; 1Pe 5:5

God exalts the humble
Lk 1:52 See also 2Sa 7:8; 1Ki 14:7

Believers should humble themselves before God
2Ch 7:14; 1Pe 5:6 See also 2Sa 22:28
Humility linked with repentance:
1Ki 21:29; 2Ki 22:19; 2Ch 12:6–7,12; 30:11; 33:12,19; 34:27
Humility linked with God's favour:
Ps 18:27; 25:9; 138:6; 147:6; 149:4; Pr 3:34; 18:12; Jas 4:6; Isa 29:19; 38:15; 57:15; Pr 15:33; 22:4
Ps 35:13; Jer 44:10 lack of humility linked with disobedience

God humbles his people to renew and restore them
Ps 44:9 See also Lev 26:41; Dt 8:2,16; 1Ki 11:39; 2Ch 28:19; Ps 107:39; Isa 9:1; 2Co 12:21

God humbles the proud
Lk 18:14 See also 1Sa 2:7; Isa 2:11,17; 5:15; 13:11; 23:9; 25:11; 26:5; Da 4:37

Examples of humble people
Outstanding individuals Ge 32:10 Jacob; Ge 41:16 Joseph; Nu 12:3 Moses; 1Sa 9:21 Saul
David: 1Sa 18:18; 2Sa 7:18
1Ki 3:7 Solomon; Da 2:30 Daniel; Mt 3:14 John the Baptist; Lk 1:43 Elizabeth; Lk 1:48 Mary, the mother of Jesus Christ
Paul: 1Ti 1:15; Ac 20:19

Other examples 2Sa 16:4; Pr 6:3; 11:2; 16:19; 29:23; Da 5:22; Mt 8:8; 15:27; 18:4

The example of Jesus Christ
Php 2:5–8
The humility of Jesus Christ foretold:
Isa 53:3–5,7–8; Zec 9:9 pp Mt 21:5 pp Jn 12:15
Mt 11:29; 20:28; Lk 22:26–27; Jn 13:4; 2Co 8:9

See also
2036 Christ, humility	5813 conceit
4050 dust	6121 boasting
5146 covering	8305 meekness
5161 kneeling	8308 modesty
5793 arrogance	8754 fear
5801 brokenness	8802 pride

8277

innocence

The state of being devoid of guilt, experience of sin or evil motives or thoughts. Scripture commends this state to believers.

8278
innocence, teaching on

A highly valued quality to be eagerly sought. The OT stresses that the innocent deserve justice rather than evil. In the NT believers are encouraged to attain innocence.

Exhortations to be innocent
Mt 10:16 See also Ps 32:2; Ro 16:19; Php 2:14–15; 1Th 3:13; 5:23; 2Pe 3:14

Ascribing innocence to people
Innocence is ultimately established by God 1Co 4:4 See also Col 1:21–22

The need to acquit the innocent
1Ki 8:32 See also Ex 23:7; Nu 5:29–31; Dt 25:1; Pr 17:15; 18:5

The danger of acquitting the guilty
Pr 17:15 See also Pr 24:23–24

The rewards of innocence
Ps 15:1–5 See also Rev 14:1–5

The characteristics of innocence
Pr 21:8 See also Php 2:14–15; 4:8

The shedding of innocent blood
Its prohibition Dt 19:8–10 See also Jer 22:3

The guilt associated with it Jer 26:15 See also Dt 19:11–13; 2Ki 21:16; Ps 106:38; Pr 6:16–17; Isa 59:7; Jer 7:2–8

The need to purge the guilt
1Ki 2:31–33 See also Dt 21:1–9

The right to be avenged 2Sa 4:9–11 *See also* Nu 35:16–28

Examples of those shedding innocent blood Mt 27:3–4 *See also* 2Ki 24:1–4; Jnh 1:14

See also

5009 conscience	7314 blood
5203 acquittal	7338 cities of refuge
5360 justice, God	8201 blamelessness
5740 virgin	8324 purity
6172 guilt	
7310 avenger of blood	

8279
innocence, examples of

Innocence is displayed most purely in Jesus Christ but is also ascribed to others.

Examples of innocence
Innocence before the fall Ge 2:25

The innocence of Jesus Christ 1Pe 2:22 *See also* Isa 53:9; Mt 27:19; Lk 23:41; Jn 8:46; 2Co 5:21; Heb 4:15; 1Jn 3:4–5

Innocence in others Job 9:21; Jn 1:47 *See also* Ge 6:9 *Noah;* Jdg 21:20–22 *the assembly of Israel;* 2Sa 11:6–13 *Uriah;* Job 9:15 *Job;* Da 6:22 *Daniel;* 2Co 7:10–11 *the Corinthians*

The varied experiences of innocence
Loss of innocence Ge 3:1–13

The innocent wronged Isa 5:22–23 *See also* 1Sa 19:4–5; 2Sa 13:1–14; Isa 29:20–21; Mt 2:16; 12:1–7; Jas 5:6

Admissions of lack of innocence 2Ki 10:9 *See also* Ge 44:1–16

Claims to innocence Job 34:5–6 *See also* Ge 20:1–5; 2Sa 3:26–28; Isa 50:8–9; Ac 20:25–27

False claims to innocence Jer 2:34–35 *See also* Mt 27:24

Washing hands to signify innocence Mt 27:24 *See also* Ps 26:6; 73:13

A distorted view of innocence Pr 16:2 *See also* Job 4:7; 9:23,28

See also

2063 Christ, perfection	6154 fall, the
2075 Christ, sinless	7478 washing
5347 injustice	8266 holiness
5562 suffering, innocent	

8281
insight

The spiritual quality that enables a person to appreciate God's mind and will in matters of behaviour, truth and providence, especially where right perception is not obvious. Insight is akin to wisdom and understanding. It is given by God and is to be sought by believers.

Insight is given by God
2Ti 2:7 *See also* Pr 2:6

Insight through angelic instruction Job 33:23; Da 9:20–22

Insight through Jesus Christ's teaching Lk 24:45–47 *See also* Lk 24:27; Mt 16:12

Insight through the Holy Spirit 1Co 2:9–13 *See also* Isa 64:4; Eph 3:4–5

Human insight cannot comprehend spiritual truth 1Co 2:14 *See also* Job 9:11; 1Co 1:20–21

Insight into spiritual truth
Insight into the truth about Jesus Christ Col 2:2–3 *See also* Jn 16:12–15

Insight into the believer's hope and power Eph 1:18–19

Insight into the make-up of the church Ac 10:34–35; Eph 3:2–6

Insight into the number of the beast Rev 13:18

Insight into the providence of God
Joseph's insight Ge 50:20 *See also* Ge 45:4–8

David's insight 2Sa 5:12 pp 1Ch 14:2

Job's insight Job 42:1–6 *Job does not learn why he has suffered, but reaffirms his trust in God's superior wisdom and power. See also* Job 15:9 *Human insight into Job's suffering did not bring enlightenment;* Job 26:3; 34:35

Insight into correct behaviour
Php 1:9–11 *See also* Pr 28:7; Col 1:9–10; Ps 19:12 *discerning one's own faults;* Ps 119:34 *understanding God's law;* Pr 5:1–4 *avoiding evil*

Insight into the truth about people
2Ki 4:8–9 *The Shunammite woman recognises Elisha as a man of God;* Ne 6:1–2 *Nehemiah discerns the motives of his enemies;* Mt 9:3–4 pp Mk 2:6–8 pp Lk 5:21–22 *Jesus Christ is aware of the evil thoughts of the Pharisees and the teachers of the law;* Jn 4:19 *The woman of Samaria understands some of the truth about Jesus Christ.*

Insight is to be sought
Pr 2:3–5 *See also* Pr 3:21; 18:15

Asking God for insight Jas 1:5 *See also* 1Ki 3:9–12 pp 2Ch 1:10–12

Insight through meditation on God's word Ps 119:98–100 *See also* Ps 119:104; Da 9:2; Mt 22:29 pp Mk 12:24

Examples of people of insight
1Ki 4:29–34 *Solomon;* 1Ch 27:32 *Jonathan, David's uncle;* Da 5:11 *Daniel*

Examples of lack of insight
Mt 16:9–11 pp Mk 8:17–21 *Jesus Christ's disciples;* Mt 16:22 pp Mk 8:32 *Simon Peter;* Lk 24:25 *Cleopas and his companion;* Jn 3:10 *Nicodemus;* Jn 20:2 *Mary Magdalene*

See also

1180 God, wisdom of	5149 eyes
1441 revelation, necessity	5191 thought
1466 vision	8226 discernment
1614 Scripture, understanding	8319 perception, spiritual
2045 Christ, knowledge of	8355 understanding
5026 knowledge	8361 wisdom
	8419 enlightenment
	8474 seeing God

8282
intolerance

Unwillingness to allow or permit something beyond certain levels. God's intolerance should be the model for God's people, but they should avoid becoming wrongly intolerant.

God is intolerant of evil
God is pure and cannot tolerate evil Hab 1:13 *See also* Nu 25:3; Jos 7:1; 2Sa 6:7 pp 1Ch 13:10; 2Ki 17:11; Ps 5:6; Ro 1:18; Rev 21:27

God demonstrates his intolerance as the last resort Jer 44:22 *See also* Ex 4:10–14; 34:6–7; Nu 14:18; Ne 9:30; Ac 17:30; Ro 2:3–5

Human intolerance should reflect God's attitudes
Human intolerance of God's enemies Jdg 5:31 *See also* 1Sa 17:26; Ps 69:9; Mt 26:51 pp Mk 14:47 pp Lk 22:50; Jn 18:10; Eph 5:6–7

Human intolerance of ungodliness Ex 32:19–20 *See also* Dt 6:13–15; Ps 119:115; 1Ti 4:7; 2Ti 2:16; 3:5; Tit 2:12

Human intolerance of error Tit 3:10 *See also* Ac 17:11; 20:30–31; Gal 5:11–12; Eph 5:6–7; Col 2:8; Heb 13:9

Human intolerance of evil and sinfulness Rev 2:20 *See also* Job 28:28; Ps 34:14; 101:4–5; Mt 5:30; Ro 6:12; 12:9; Eph 4:25; 2Th 3:6; Rev 2:2

Human intolerance can be misguided
It can be a form of hypocrisy Lk 6:41–42 *See also* Mt 23:29–30; Lk 13:14–15; Jn 12:5–6

It can amount to exclusiveness Mt 23:13 *See also* Ac 15:1

It can be a form of oppression *Intolerance of minority, afflicted or underprivileged groups oftens leads to oppression:* Ex 1:11–14; 23:9; Pr 14:31; 28:3; Ecc 5:8; Mt 20:31 pp Mk 10:48 pp Lk 18:39

It can be harshly condemnatory Jn 8:5 *See also* Nu 21:4–5; Est 3:8; Mt 23:34–35; Jn 7:45–51; 16:2

It can be a form of bigotry Jn 15:19 *See also* Nu 11:27–29; Jdg 12:5–6; Mt 21:15–16; 23:16,18

Intolerance is usually a matter of decision
Intolerance leading to a good decision Lk 18:4–5 *See also* Lk 11:7–8

Intolerance leading to a bad decision Mt 19:13–14 pp Mk 10:13–14 pp Lk 18:15–16 *The disciples' intolerance is counteracted by Jesus Christ's tolerance.*

See also

1025 God, anger of	8353 tolerance
1095 God, patience of	8734 evil
	8750 false teachings
1125 God, righteousness	8771 idolatry, objections
5883 impatience	8790 oppression
6020 sin	8800 prejudice
8326 purity, moral & spiritual	

8283

joy

A quality or attitude of delight and happiness, which is ultimately grounded in the work of God as Father, Son and Holy Spirit. Among the many situations in which joy is experienced, Scripture recognises as supreme being accepted in the presence of God.

8284

joy, of God

See 1070 God, joy of

8285

joy, of Jesus Christ

See 2039 Jesus Christ, joy of

8286

joy, of Holy Spirit

See 3020 Holy Spirit, joy of

8287

joy, and human experience

Joy is experienced naturally in many circumstances of life and in human relationships. It is especially important in the life of God's people, who experience joy in response to all that God has done for them.

Poetic images of joy in creation
Ps 96:11–13 pp 1Ch 16:31–33 *See also* Job 39:13; Ps 65:12–13; 89:12; 97:1; 100:1; Isa 35:1–2; 49:13

Joy arising from specific circumstances
Joy because of the birth of children Lk 1:13–15 *See also* Ge 30:12–13; Lk 1:58

Joy because of victory and deliverance Ex 18:9; 1Sa 18:6; Jer 41:13; Zec 10:7

Joy because of the behaviour of others Pr 15:30 *See also* Pr 23:24–25; Mt 14:6–7; Heb 13:17

Joy because of God's blessings in everyday life Ecc 5:19–20

Joy arising from relationships
Php 4:1 *See also* Pr 5:18; SS 1:4; 3:11; Ro 12:15; 15:26–27; 1Co 12:26; Php 1:4–6; Phm 7

God's people find their joy in him
Ps 4:7; 16:11; Hab 3:17–18; Php 3:1 *See also* 1Ch 16:10; Ps 43:4; Php 1:23–26 *knowing Jesus Christ;* Php 4:4

God himself gives joy to his people Ne 12:43; Job 8:21; Ecc 2:26; Isa 9:3; Ac 13:52; 14:15–17

Reasons for God's people to know joy 1Sa 2:1 *God's deliverance;* 2Ch 6:41 *God's*

goodness; Job 22:22–26 *repentance;* Ps 19:8 *the rightness of God's precepts;* Ps 94:19 *God's consolation;* Ps 122:1 *being in God's presence;* Isa 25:9 *God's salvation;* Isa 58:13–14 *honouring the Sabbath;* Jer 15:16 *God's words;* Jer 31:12 *God's generosity;* Lk 1:46–49 *recognition by God;* Ro 15:13 *trusting God*

See also
1070 God, joy of	5874 happiness
2039 Christ, joy of	5918 pleasure
5664 children	7921 fellowship
5690 friends	8292 love
5708 marriage	8414 encourage-
5830 delight	ment

8288

joy, of Israel

Joy is characteristic of Israel's corporate worship, especially the great festivals.

Joy expressed in and through Israel's life of worship
Ps 100:1–4 *See also* Nu 10:10; Dt 27:6–7; Ps 98:4–6; 132:6–9; 149:2–5; Isa 30:29; Zec 8:19 *Feast of Tabernacles:* Lev 23:39–41; Dt 16:13–15 *Hezekiah celebrates the Passover:* 2Ch 30:21–23,26–27

Joy expressed by the individual as a result of faith
Ps 16:8–9; 28:7 *See also* Job 6:10; 33:26; Ps 5:11; 21:1; 71:23; 92:4; 104:34; 119:14,174; Pr 10:28; Isa 61:10

Joy experienced by the nation as the people of God
Ps 20:5; Isa 51:11; Jer 31:12–13 *See also* Dt 26:11; Ps 53:6; 105:43; 145:7

Joy predicted in prophetic assurances of restoration and blessing Isa 51:3 *See also* Isa 52:8–9; 55:12; 60:4–5; 66:10–11; Jer 30:18–19; 31:4,7; Joel 2:21–23; Zep 3:14; Zec 9:9

Joy at times of national celebration
The anointing of kings 1Ki 1:39–40 *See also* 1Ch 29:21–22; 2Ch 23:12–13

The consecration of the temple 1Ki 8:64–66 pp 2Ch 7:1–10 *See also* 1Ch 29:9,17

Consecration of the temple in the reign of King Hezekiah 2Ch 29:36

Deliverance of the Jews through Queen Esther Est 8:15–17 *See also* Est 9:20–22

The rebuilding of the temple and Jerusalem Ezr 6:16 *See also* Ezr 3:10–13; 6:22; Ne 3:16–17; 12:27

Other nations encouraged to share Israel's joy
Ps 47:1; Isa 24:14–16 *See also* Dt 32:43; Ps 66:1–2; 67:4; Isa 42:10–11; Jer 51:48

See also
5420 music	8622 worship
7354 feasts and	8642 celebration
festivals	8664 praise
7467 temple,	8676 thanksgiving
Solomon's	

8289

joy, of the church

The church is to rejoice in the salvation brought about by Jesus Christ's faithful life and death, and by the power of his resurrection. Even in adversity, believers know the joy of Jesus Christ.

Joy at the coming of Jesus Christ
Lk 2:8–11 *See also* Jn 3:27–29; 8:56

Joy as the hallmark of the kingdom of God
Gal 5:22 *See also* Mt 13:44; Lk 10:17–21; 15:4–10 pp Mt 18:12–14; Jn 4:34–36; 16:20–24; 17:13; Ro 12:12; 14:17–18; 1Th 5:16–18

Jesus Christ promises joy to his disciples Jn 15:9–11 *See also* Mt 5:11–12 pp Lk 6:22–23; Jn 16:20–24; 17:13

Joy among believers Ac 2:46–47 *See also* Ac 15:1–3; Ro 15:31–32; 2Co 2:3; Php 2:17–18

Joy experienced in relationship with Jesus Christ
1Pe 1:8–9 *See also* Jn 15:7–11; Heb 12:22–24; Rev 19:7

Joy experienced through conversion Ac 16:33–34 *See also* Ac 8:38–39; Ro 5:11

Joy experienced even in adversity
Ac 5:41; 1Pe 4:12–13 *See also* Mt 5:11–12 pp Lk 6:22–23; 2Co 7:4; 8:1–2; 12:7–10; 13:9; Php 2:17–18; Col 1:24; 1Th 1:6; Heb 10:34; Jas 1:2–3; 1Pe 1:3–6

Joy experienced by the apostles
Joy because of the believers' faith and obedience Ro 16:19; 3Jn 3–4 *See also* 2Co 7:4; Php 1:23–26; 4:1; Col 2:5; 1Th 2:19–20; 3:9

Joy because of the believers' love and concern 2Co 7:7 *See also* 2Co 7:12–13; Php 2:1–2 *the Philippians' love for one another;* Phm 7

Joy because of the believers' partnership in the gospel Php 1:4–6

See also
2375 kingdom of	6716 reconciliation
God	7020 church, the
3020 Holy Spirit, joy	8102 abiding in
of	Christ
3254 Holy Spirit, fruit	8248 faithfulness
of	8794 persecution
5560 suffering	

8291

kindness

The quality of compassion and generosity, characteristic of God's dealings towards the weak and poor, and demanded of believers. The same kindness is also shown in the words and deeds of Jesus Christ.

The kindness of God

To all Ac 14:17 *Paul to the pagans at Lystra. See also* Jer 9:24; Lk 6:35

To his people Isa 63:7 *See also* Ezr 9:9; Isa 54:8; Hos 11:4

To the king 2Sa 22:51 *See also* 1Ki 3:6

To individuals Ge 19:19 *Lot*; Ge 24:27 *Abraham*; Ge 32:10 *Jacob*; Ge 39:21 *Joseph*; Ru 1:8 *Ruth*; Ru 2:20 *Naomi*; Job 10:12 *Job*; 2Sa 9:1–13 *Mephibosheth through David*

The kindness of Jesus Christ

Mt 9:36 *See also* Mt 14:14; 20:34; Mk 8:2–3; Lk 7:13; Ac 20:35; Heb 4:15

Its demonstration in the gospel
Tit 3:4–5 *See also* Ro 11:22 *God's grace extending to the Gentiles while the Jews are judged for their unbelief*; Eph 2:7

Failure to acknowledge God's kindness is a sin

Ps 106:7 *See also* 2Ch 32:24–25; Ro 2:4

Kindness encouraged in people

In the OT Pr 14:21; Da 4:27 *See also* Pr 11:16–17; 12:25; 14:31; 19:17; 28:8

In the NT Eph 4:32 *See also* 1Co 4:13; 13:4; 2Co 6:6; Gal 5:22–23 *seen as the result of the Holy Spirit's work in the believer*; Col 3:12; 1Th 5:15; 2Ti 2:24 *a necessary characteristic of a church leader*; Tit 2:5; 2Pe 1:7

Examples of human kindness

By unbelievers 1Sa 15:6 *the Kenites to Israel*; 2Ki 25:28 *the king of Babylon to Jehoiachin*; Ac 27:3 *the centurion Julius to Paul*; Ac 28:2 *the Maltese islanders to Paul and his companions*

By God's people Ge 21:23 *Abraham to Abimelech*; Ge 47:29 *Joseph to Jacob*; Ge 50:21 *Joseph to his brothers when he might have been expected to settle old scores*; Jos 2:12–14 *the spies to Rahab Between Ruth and Boaz*: Ru 2:13; 3:10 *Between David and Jonathan*: 1Sa 20:8,14 2Sa 2:5 *The men of Gilead have their kindness rewarded*; 1Ki 2:7 *Solomon to Barzillai*; Ac 4:9 *Peter to a beggar*

When kindness fails

The failure to show kindness
Ps 109:16 *See also* Jdg 8:35 *the Israelites to Gideon's family*; 2Ch 10:7–8 *Rehoboam to the Israelites*; Job 24:21 *evil men to needy women*

Failure to respond to kindness
2Sa 10:2–4

Failure to remember kindness
2Ch 24:22

See also

1030 God, compassion	3254 Holy Spirit, fruit of
1050 God, goodness of	5446 poverty
1055 God, grace & mercy	5806 compassion
1085 God, love of	6666 grace
2015 Christ, compassion	6686 mercy
	8260 generosity
	8292 love

8292

love

A caring commitment, in which affection and delight are shown to others, which is grounded in the nature of God himself. In his words and actions, and supremely in the death of Jesus Christ on the cross, God demonstrates the nature of love and defines the direction in which human love in all its forms should develop.

This set of themes consists of the following:

8293 love, of God
8294 love, and Jesus Christ
8295 love, and Holy Spirit
8296 love, nature of
8297 love, for God
8298 love, for one another
8299 love, in relationships
8300 love, and the world
8301 love, and enemies
8302 love, abuse of

8293
love, of God

See 1085 God, love of

8294
love, and Jesus Christ

See 2048 Jesus Christ, love of

8295
love, and Holy Spirit

See 3209 Holy Spirit, and love

8296
love, nature of

Scripture offers an understanding of the source, character and value of love, based on the nature and actions of God.

God is the source of love

His very character is love 1Jn 4:7–8 *See also* 1Th 3:12; 2Ti 1:7; 1Jn 4:16,19

The love of God is revealed in the cross of Jesus Christ 1Jn 3:16; 4:10 *See also* Jn 15:13; Eph 5:2,25

Love is part of the Holy Spirit's fruit Gal 5:22 *See also* Ro 5:5; 15:30; Col 1:8

The loving-kindness of God referred to in the OT

Jer 31:3 *See also* Ex 15:13; 34:6; 2Ch 6:42; Ps 6:4; 32:10; 51:1; 107:43; Isa 54:10; 63:7; La 3:22; Hos 2:19

The love of God in the NT

To describe God's love for humanity Jn 3:16 *See also* Jn 5:42; 15:10; Ro 8:39; 2Co 13:14; Eph 2:4; Heb 12:6; 1Jn 3:1

To describe love for God Lk 10:27; Jn 14:21; 21:15; Ro 8:28; 1Th 1:3; Jas 1:12; 1Pe 1:8; 1Jn 5:3

To describe brotherly love Jn 13:35; Ro 13:8; 1Co 16:24; 2Co 8:8; Gal 5:13; Eph 4:2; Php 1:9; Col 2:2; Phm 5

To describe love expressed by eating together 2Pe 2:13 fn; Jude 12

To describe love in a negative sense

Lk 11:43; Jn 3:19; 12:43; 2Ti 4:10; 2Pe 2:15; 1Jn 2:15

Characteristics of love

1Co 13:4–8 *See also* Ro 12:9; 1Ti 1:5; 1Pe 1:22; 1Jn 4:18

Love is shown by deeds

1Jn 3:17–18 *See also* Jn 14:15,23; Ro 5:8; 14:15; Gal 2:20; 1Jn 4:9; 5:2–3; 2Jn 6; 3Jn 5–6

The pre-eminence of love

1Co 13:13 *See also* Mt 22:37–39 pp Mk 12:29–31; Ro 13:9–10; 1Co 12:31–13:3; Gal 5:6; Eph 3:17–19; Col 3:14; 2Pe 1:7; 1Jn 2:10

See also

1085 God, love of	6512 salvation, necessity & basis
2048 Christ, love of	
3203 Holy Spirit & assurance	6638 election
3209 Holy Spirit & love	7115 children of God
	8106 assurance
3254 Holy Spirit, fruit of	8122 friendship with God
5762 attitudes, God to people	8463 priority of faith, hope & love

---

8297
love, for God

Scripture teaches believers to love God and shows how such love should be expressed in worship and practical service.

Believers' response to God's love

1Jn 4:19 *See also* Dt 7:7–8; Ps 116:1; Jn 15:16; Eph 2:4–5; 1Jn 4:10

Love for God is commanded

Mt 22:37–38 pp Mk 12:29–30 *See also* Dt 6:5; 10:12; 11:1; Jos 22:5; 23:11; Ps 31:23

Loving God involves loving Jesus Christ

Jn 8:42 *See also* Jn 5:42; 15:23

Expressing love for God

Delight in worship and in God's house Ps 27:4 *See also* Ps 26:8; 43:4; 65:4; 84:2; 122:1,6; Ac 2:46–47

Love for God's word Ps 119:97 *See also* Ps 1:2; 19:7–8,10; 119:16,35,72,163; Jer 15:16; Eze 3:3

Self-sacrifice Lk 14:33 *See also* Jn 21:15–17; Ro 12:1; Php 3:8

Giving 1Ch 29:3 *See also* Ex 25:2; 35:5; 1Ch 29:6,9; 2Co 8:4–5,8; 9:7

Obeying God 1Jn 5:3 *See also* Ps 40:8; Jn 14:15,23; 15:14; 2Jn 6

Loving others 1Jn 4:21 *See also* Jn 13:35; 15:12; 1Jn 4:11

The blessings of loving God

Jn 14:15–16 *See also* Jn 14:23; 16:27; 1Pe 1:8

Examples of love for God and Jesus Christ

Ps 18:1 *See also* Ps 73:25; Mt 26:7 pp Mk 14:3; Jn 12:3; Lk 2:37; 7:47; 24:53; Jn 11:16; 21:16; Ac 21:13; Heb 6:10

8298

8298
love, for one another

Scripture instructs God's people to love one another and illustrates what this means in practice.

Reasons for loving one another
God commands it Gal 5:14 *See also* Lev 19:18
Love for foreigners commanded: Lev 19:34; Dt 10:19
Mt 22:39 pp Mk 12:31 *the second greatest commandment;* Jn 15:12 *Jesus Christ commands his disciples to love one another;* Ro 13:10; 1Th 4:9; Heb 13:1; Jas 2:8; 1Pe 1:22; 2:17; 1Jn 3:23; 4:21; 2Jn 5

God has taken the initiative in showing love 1Jn 4:11 *See also* Mal 2:10; 1Co 8:11–13; 1Jn 3:16

God's people are known by their love Jn 13:35 *See also* 1Jn 2:10; 3:14; 4:7,16,20

Love maintains fellowship 1Pe 4:8 *See also* Pr 10:12; 17:9; Eph 4:2

Love promotes sacrificial service 1Th 2:8 *See also* Pr 17:17; 2Co 12:15; Gal 5:13; Php 2:30; 4:10; 1Th 1:3

Expressing love for one another
In caring for the sick Mt 25:36 *See also* Job 2:11; Gal 4:14

In meeting material needs Mt 25:35 *See also* Dt 15:7–8; 1Jn 3:17

In affectionate greetings 2Co 13:12 *See also* Ge 33:4; 45:14–15; Ac 20:37; Ro 16:16; 1Co 16:20; 1Pe 5:14

Examples of the demonstration of love for one another
Ge 14:14–16 *Abraham for Lot;* Ex 32:31–32 *Moses for Israel;* 1Sa 18:3 *Jonathan;* Lk 7:2–6 *the Roman centurion for his servant;* Lk 10:29–37 *the good Samaritan;* Ac 4:32; 16:33 *the Philippian jailer;* Ac 20:38; Ro 16:4; 2Co 2:4; Eph 1:15; Php 1:8; 4:1; 2Ti 1:16–17 *Onesiphorus;* Phm 12; 3Jn 6

Paul's love for his churches
Corinth: 2Co 1:3–6; 2:4
Gal 4:19 *Galatia*
Philippi: Php 1:3,7; 4:1
Thessalonica: 1Th 2:7–8; 3:7–10,12

8299
love, in relationships

Human love is ennobled by being patterned on God's love for his people. It is also safeguarded by God's commands.

The love between husband and wife
Conjugal love is commanded Col 3:18–19 *See also* Ge 2:24; Dt 24:5; Pr 5:18–20; Ecc 9:9; Eph 5:22,28,33; 1Pe 3:7

It is patterned on God's love for his people Isa 54:5; Eph 5:25–27 *See also* Isa 62:5; Jer 3:14; Eze 16:8; Hos 2:19; 2Co 11:2; Rev 19:7

The power of human love SS 8:6–7 *See also* Ge 29:20,30; Pr 6:34–35

Examples of love in courtship and marriage
Ge 24:67 *Isaac and Rebekah;* Ge 29:18 *Jacob and Rachel;* Jdg 16:4 *Samson and Delilah;* 1Sa 1:5 *Elkanah and Hannah;* Est 2:17 *Xerxes and Esther;* SS 1:2; 4:10; Hos 3:1; Mt 1:19 *Joseph and Mary*

Safeguards on human love
Sexual immorality is condemned 1Co 7:2 *See also* Lev 18:22 *homosexual acts forbidden;* Lev 19:29 *prostitution forbidden;* Dt 23:17–18; Mt 5:32; Ac 15:29; Ro 1:26–27; 1Co 5:1; 6:18; 10:8; Eph 5:3; Col 3:5; 1Th 4:3

Adultery is condemned Ex 20:14 *See also* Lev 20:10; Dt 5:18; Pr 6:24; 1Co 6:9; Heb 13:4

Restrictions on divorce Mt 19:9 *See also* Mal 2:16; Mt 5:32; Mk 10:11–12; Lk 16:18; 1Co 7:10–11

Lust is condemned Mt 5:28 *See also* Job 31:1; Pr 6:25; 1Co 7:9; Eph 4:19; 1Th 4:5

Polygamy is forbidden 1Ti 3:2 *See also* Dt 17:17; Mal 2:15; 1Ti 3:12; Tit 1:6

8300
love, and the world

Scripture promotes the love of family, home and country and contains many examples of such love.

Parental love
Aspects of parental love Pr 13:24; Eph 6:4 *See also* Dt 6:7; 2Co 12:14; Col 3:21; 1Ti 3:4; 2Ti 3:15

Examples of maternal love Ge 21:16 *Hagar;* Ex 2:3 *Moses' mother;* Jdg 5:28; 1Sa 2:19 *Hannah;* 2Sa 21:10; 1Ki 3:26; 17:18
The Shunammite: 2Ki 4:20,27

Mt 15:22 pp Mk 7:26; Lk 2:48; 7:12–13 *the widow of Nain;* Jn 19:25

Examples of paternal love Ge 22:2 *Abraham;* Ge 31:28; 37:35; 42:38 *David;* 2Sa 12:16; 13:39
Mk 5:23 pp Lk 8:41–42 *Jairus*

Love for parents
Ex 20:12; 1Ti 5:4 *See also* Ge 46:29 *Joseph;* Lev 19:3; Jdg 11:36; 1Sa 22:3 *David;* 1Ki 19:20 *Elisha;* Jer 35:8; Mt 15:4 pp Mk 7:10; Lk 2:51; Jn 19:26–27; Eph 6:1; Col 3:20

Other instances of family love
Ge 34:7; 45:14–15 *Joseph and his brothers;* Ru 1:16–17; 2Sa 13:22 *Mordecai and Esther.* Est 2:7,11

Love of home and country
Examples of love of home Ge 31:30; 49:29; 50:25; Nu 10:30; Ru 1:6; 2Sa 10:12; 19:37; 23:15; Ne 4:14

Exhortations to patriotism Ps 122:6; 137:5–6 *See also* 2Sa 1:20; Est 4:8; Jer 51:50

Examples of patriotism 1Sa 17:26; 27:8–10; Ne 1:3–4; 2:5; Est 8:6; Ps 137:1; Jer 51:51; Ro 9:3

8301
love, and enemies

God loves even those who oppose him and believers must follow his example in loving their enemies.

God's love for sinners
Isa 53:6; Jn 3:16; 2Pe 3:9 *See also* Ge 18:32; La 3:33; Eze 18:23; Mt 5:45; Ro 5:8; 8:32; 2Co 5:19; 1Jn 4:9–10

The example of Jesus Christ
Mt 23:37 pp Lk 13:34 1Pe 3:18 *See also* Isa 53:5; Mt 20:28 pp Mk 10:45; Lk 23:34; Ro 5:6; 2Co 5:14; 8:9; Heb 3:12; 1Pe 2:21,24; 1Jn 2:2

God's people must love their enemies
Lev 19:18; Lk 6:35–36 *See also* Ex 23:4; Pr 24:17; 25:21; Mt 5:44; Lk 6:27; Col 3:13; 1Th 5:15; 2Ti 2:25; 1Pe 3:9

Examples of love for enemies
Ge 50:20–21 *Joseph;* Nu 12:13; 1Sa 24:17; 26:21; 2Sa 19:23; 2Ki 6:22 *the king of Israel;* Ac 7:60 *Stephen;* Ac 9:17 *Ananias;* 1Co 4:12

8302
love, abuse of

Scripture warns that love can be misdirected and shows a number of examples.

Exaggerated love of self

Self-interest is condemned Php 2:3–4
See also Mt 16:25 pp Mk 8:35 pp Lk 9:24;
Ro 14:15; 15:1; 1Co 8:9; 10:24; Gal 5:26;
Jas 3:14–15

Examples of self-love Est 6:6 Haman;
Isa 5:8; Da 4:30 Nebuchadnezzar;
2Ti 3:2; Jas 5:5

Love of prestige

Pride in one's position or reputation is
condemned Pr 25:27; 1Co 13:4 See also
Pr 21:4; 25:6–7; Mt 23:12 pp Lk 14:11;
Ro 12:10; Jas 3:1

Examples of the love of prestige
2Sa 15:1 Absalom; 1Ki 1:5 Adonijah;
Isa 14:13 the king of Babylon; Jer 46:5;
Eze 28:2; Mt 20:21; 23:6–7 pp Lk 20:46;
Lk 14:7; 22:24; Jn 12:43 the man of
lawlessness; 2Th 2:4; 3Jn 9

Love of the world

Love of the world is condemned
1Jn 2:15 See also Ex 23:2; Mt 16:26
pp Mk 8:36–37 pp Lk 9:25; Ro 12:2;
Col 3:2; 2Ti 2:4; Tit 2:12; Jas 4:4

Examples of the love of the world
Mt 24:38; Lk 14:18 those invited to the
great banquet; 2Ti 4:10 Demas

Love of money

Love of money is condemned
1Ti 6:9–10 See also Ps 62:10; Pr 28:20;
Ecc 5:10; Lk 12:15

Examples of the love of riches Jos 7:21
Achan; 2Ki 5:20 Gehazi; Mic 3:11;
Mt 19:22 pp Mk 10:22 pp Lk 18:23 the
rich young man; Mt 26:15 Judas Iscariot;
Lk 16:14; Jn 12:6; Ac 16:19; 24:26 Felix;
2Pe 2:15

Love of sin

The love of sin is condemned 2Th 2:12
See also Job 15:16; Pr 2:14; 17:19;
Ro 1:32; 2Pe 2:10

Examples of the love of sinning
1Ki 21:25 Ahab and Jezebel; Jer 14:10;
Mic 3:2; 2Pe 2:13–14

Love of other gods

Idolatry is condemned Dt 6:13–14 See
also Ex 20:3; Lev 26:1; Dt 12:30;
Ac 17:29; 1Jn 5:21

Examples of the love of idols Ex 32:4
the golden calf; Jdg 2:11–12; 2Ki 17:15;
Da 5:4 Belshazzar; Ac 17:16 the city of
Athens; Ro 1:23

See also
5413 money, attitudes	8768 idolatry 8802 pride
5813 conceit	8821 self-indulgence
5869 greed	8827 selfishness
6020 sin	
6243 adultery, spiritual	

loyalty

A commitment to an ongoing
relationship and to the attitude and
behaviour demanded by it. It is
evident in human relationships and

also in the covenant relationship
between God and his people.

God's loyalty to his people

God's covenant loyalty Dt 7:9 See also
1Ki 8:23 pp 2Ch 6:14; Ne 1:5; Ps 25:10;
89:28; 103:17–18; 106:45; Isa 54:10;
55:3

God's faithfulness to his promises
Heb 10:23 See also 1Ki 8:56;
Ps 91:14–16; 1Co 1:9

Loyalty to God

The loyalty of God's people 1Ch 29:18;
Jer 2:2 See also 1Ki 8:61; 2Ch 32:32;
35:26; 17:6

Examples of those loyal to God Nu 12:7
Moses; Nu 14:24 Caleb; Jos 24:14–15
Joshua and his family; Job 23:11 Job;
Isa 38:3 Hezekiah; Ac 4:19 Peter and
John; Ac 20:24 Paul

Failure to show loyalty to God Hos 6:4
See also Ps 78:8,37

Divided loyalties 2Ki 17:33 See also
Mt 6:24; Lk 16:13; 1Co 10:21; Jas 1:8

Loyalty in human relationships

Loyalty and covenant 1Sa 20:8

The loyalty of friends 1Sa 20:42;
Pr 17:17 See also 2Sa 16:17; Pr 27:10

Loyalty within the family Ru 1:16–17
See also Ge 20:13; 38:8; 47:29; Dt 25:5;
Ru 3:9; 1Co 7:3

Loyalty to those in authority Ro 13:1 See
also Ezr 7:26; Ecc 8:2; Mt 17:27; 22:21;
Tit 3:1; 1Pe 2:13–14

Examples of loyalty to rulers 2Sa 15:21
See also 1Sa 22:14 David's loyalty to Saul;
2Sa 3:8 Abner's loyalty to Saul's family;
1Ki 12:20 the loyalty of Judah to David's
house; 1Ch 12:33 the men of Zebulun's
loyalty to David

The loyalty of believers

Ro 12:10; Php 4:3 See also 1Co 4:17
Timothy; 1Co 16:15–16 the household of
Stephanas; Col 1:7 Epaphras; Col 4:7
Tychicus; Col 4:9 Onesimus

See also
1035 God, faithfulness	8292 love 8354 trustworthi-
1345 covenant	ness
5215 authority	8453 obedience
5691 friends, good	8742 faithlessness
8207 commitment	8839 unfaithfulness
8225 devotion	
8252 faithfulness, relationships	

meekness

An attitude of humble, submissive
and expectant trust in God, and a
loving, patient and gentle attitude
towards others.

Meekness required by God

Zep 2:3 See also Pr 16:19; 1Pe 3:4

God's promises to the meek

Ps 37:11; Mt 5:5; 1Pe 5:5 See also
Ps 25:9; 69:32 In Scripture, "the poor"
frequently represent the humble, godly
poor; Ps 147:6; Isa 29:19; 66:2;
Zep 3:11–12; Jas 4:6

God acts to save the meek

Ps 34:5–6 See also 2Sa 22:28;
Ps 10:12,17; 18:27; 45:4; 76:9; 149:4;
Pr 3:34

Meekness is a correct attitude in prayer

Ps 40:17 See also Ps 70:5

Godly wisdom produces meekness

Jas 3:13

Examples of meekness

Moses Nu 12:3

David 2Sa 16:11–12

Ahab 1Ki 21:27

Job Job 1:21

Jeremiah Jer 11:19 See also Jer 26:14

Mary, the mother of Jesus Christ
Lk 1:38

Stephen Ac 7:60

Paul 2Ti 4:16

Meekness in the life of Jesus Christ

Mt 11:29; 2Co 10:1 See also Isa 53:7;
Mt 21:5; Mk 14:61; Lk 23:34; 1Pe 2:23

Meekness is expected in the life of the Christian

A necessary characteristic Eph 4:2 See
also Gal 5:23; Php 2:3; 4:5; Col 3:12;
Tit 3:2; 1Pe 3:8

Towards enemies Mt 5:39–41;
Ro 12:17–20

In leadership 1Ti 6:11

In witness 1Pe 3:15

In discipline Gal 6:1 See also 1Co 4:21;
2Ti 2:25; Heb 5:2

In the family Eph 5:22,24; 6:1;
Col 3:18–20

In society Ro 13:1–2,5; 1Ti 2:2

See also
1620 beatitudes, the	8030 trust
2036 Christ, humility	8264 gentleness
5446 poverty	8276 humility
5959 submission	

mercifulness

An attitude of compassion and care,
grounded in the nature of God
himself, made manifest in the life
and ministry of Jesus Christ, and
expected of believers.

The mercifulness of God

Dt 4:31; Ps 78:38; Jer 3:12 See also
Dt 7:7–8; Ne 9:31; Zec 1:16;
Lk 1:50–54; Jas 5:11

The expression of God's mercifulness

In the forgiveness of sins Ps 78:38 See
also 2Sa 24:14; 1Ki 8:50; Ps 26:11; 51:1;
Da 9:9

In response to prayer Ps 6:2; 27:7 See
also 1Ki 8:28; Ps 9:13

The mercifulness of Jesus Christ

Mt 9:36; Heb 2:17 See also Mt 8:16;
Heb 4:16

The mercifulness expected of believers

Lk 6:36 *See also* Mic 6:8; Zec 7:9; Mt 9:13; 18:21–35 *the parable of the unmerciful servant;* Mt 23:23; Lk 10:29–37 *the parable of the good Samaritan;* Ro 12:8; Eph 4:32–5:2; Jas 2:12–13; 3:17; Jude 22–23

The blessing promised to the merciful

Mt 5:7 *Jesus Christ to his disciples.*

See also

1030 God, compassion	2027 Christ, grace & mercy
1055 God, grace & mercy	2048 Christ, love of
1085 God, love of	5806 compassion
2015 Christ, compassion	6652 forgiveness
	6686 mercy

8307

moderation

The classic virtue of temperate conduct, especially the avoidance of extremes. Scripture commends moderation as a way of life for Christians, while stressing the need for total commitment to God.

The ideal of moderation

Ecc 7:16–18

Moderation in a legal context

Ex 21:23–25 *The purpose of this legislation was not to encourage vengeance but to moderate or restrain it. See also* Lev 24:17–22; Nu 35:9–15 pp Dt 4:41–43; 19:1–10 *One purpose of cities of refuge was to moderate the revenge of families of the murdered.*

Moderation in personal and social relations

Pr 17:27 *See also* Ge 43:29–31; Pr 12:16; 23:4; Gal 5:22–23

Moderation in personal ethics

Tit 2:11–12 *See also* Pr 15:16 *Moderation in matters of wealth is affirmed. Moderation in speech is commended:* Mt 5:33–37; Col 4:6 Eph 5:18; 1Th 5:6–8; 1Ti 3:2–3,8,11; Tit 1:7–8; 2:2–8

Moderation in religious activity

Ecc 7:16–17 *See also* Mt 23:23–26; 1Co 14:26–33

Moderation must not lead to being spiritually lukewarm

Rev 3:15–16 *See also* Rev 3:1–2

See also

5494 revenge	8207 commitment
5850 excess	8240 ethics
5856 extravagance	8307 moderation
5934 restraint	8339 self-control
7338 cities of refuge	8370 zeal

8308

modesty

An attitude of humility, avoiding improper self-exaltation or excessive flamboyance. Scripture urges modesty in personal behaviour,

forms of dress and forms of behaviour.

Modesty as an attitude of humility

Ro 12:3 *See also* Pr 25:6–7; 29:23; Lk 22:25–27 pp Mt 20:25–28 pp Mk 10:42–45; Ro 11:20–21; 2Co 10:13–16; 12:5–6; Php 2:5–8; 1Pe 5:5

Believers should dress modestly

1Ti 2:9–10 *See also* Isa 3:16–24; 1Pe 3:3

Examples of those who acted with modesty

Ge 32:9–10 *Jacob;* Ge 41:15–16 *Joseph;* Jdg 6:15 *Gideon;* 1Sa 9:19–21 *Saul;* 2Sa 7:18 *David;* Jer 1:6 *Jeremiah;* Da 2:27–30 *Daniel;* Mt 8:5–9 pp Lk 7:6–8 *a centurion*

See also

5145 clothing	8477 self-
5793 arrogance	examination
6121 boasting	8802 pride
8276 humility	

8309

morality

Conformity to the standards of right living, especially in the sight of God. Scripture stresses that morality is grounded in the nature of God himself, and provides practical guidance concerning moral living and decision-making.

8310

morality, and creation

Human beings have been created moral creatures in the likeness of God, who is the source and standard of all that is good.

Morality is grounded in the nature of God himself

Dt 32:4; Lk 18:18–19 *See also* Ex 33:19; 34:5–7; Ps 25:8–9; 119:68

Human beings are morally aware

They are created in God's image
Ge 1:26–27

They have a conscience Ro 2:14–15 *See also* 2Co 4:2

They have been given a moral law Ge 2:16–17; Mk 10:6–9; Ge 2:23–24 *Standards for marriage are implicit in the creation.*

They are capable of sharing moral ideals Jn 1:9; Ro 13:1–7; Eph 3:15 *"whole family" is literally "all fatherhood", implying that every understanding of fatherhood and family is derived from God;* Php 4:8 *referring to pagan virtues;* Tit 3:1; 1Pe 2:13–14

Immoral acts are unnatural Ro 1:26–27

God's judgment implies moral responsibility Jer 17:10; Eze 18:20–21; Am 1:6; Ro 2:5–11

Human beings are morally flawed

Ro 3:23 *See also* Ps 64:6; Isa 32:6; Jer 17:9; Ro 1:28–32; 8:7; 1Ti 4:2

See also

1050 God, goodness of	5008 conscience
1065 God, holiness of	5020 human nature
1075 God, justice of	5051 responsibility
4007 creation and God	6020 sin
5004 human race & sin	6187 immorality
	8321 perfection, divine

8311

morality, and redemption

The morality which is appropriate for God's own people is expressed in the OT law, and in the person and teaching of Jesus Christ.

Relationship with God is expressed in moral terms

In the moral standards God expects of his people Lev 11:44–45; Mt 5:48 *See also* Mt 5:43–44 pp Lk 6:27–28; Lk 6:35–36; Eph 4:31–5:3; 1Pe 1:15–16; 3Jn 11

In God's moral laws Isa 51:4; Ro 7:12 *See also* Ex 20:1–7; Dt 6:25; Ps 119:137–138; 147:19–20; Pr 29:18; Isa 51:7

In God's denunciation of immorality and religious hypocrisy Am 2:6–7 *See also* Isa 1:15–23; Am 5:21–24; Mic 6:8; Eph 5:5; Col 3:5–7

In the life and teaching of Jesus Christ Jn 1:14 *See also* Mt 5:17–20; Jn 1:17–18; 3:19; Heb 4:15

The incentive for moral change lies in what God has done in redemption

In the OT Dt 24:17–18 *See also* Lev 19:13–18,35–36; Dt 15:12–15; 24:21–22

In the NT 1Co 6:19–20 *See also* Ro 12:1–2

Moral change brought about by God's work of renewal

Eze 36:26–27; 1Co 6:9–11 *See also* Ro 8:3–4,11–14; Gal 5:19–24; Eph 4:22–24; Php 2:12–13; Col 3:8–12; Heb 8:10; Jer 31:33

See also

5375 law	8154 righteousness
5769 behaviour	8240 ethics
6720 redemption	8266 holiness
6744 sanctification	8324 purity

8313

nurture

The activity of caring for others and nourishing them in the life of faith. This is necessary not only for children in the home but also for new or weak believers in the church.

The nurture of children in the home

By parental instruction and example Dt 4:9–10 *See also* Dt 6:4–9; 11:18–21; Pr 22:6; Eph 6:4; Col 3:21; 2Ti 1:5; 3:15

Examples of parental care Pr 1:8–10

See also Pr 2:1–5; 3:1–2; 4:1–4; 5:1–2; 6:1–3,20–24

The nurture of young believers in the church

By the caring attitude of leaders
1Th 2:7–12 *See also* Jn 21:15–17; Ac 20:18–20; 1Co 4:14–15; 1Th 3:10; Tit 1:9; 1Pe 5:1–3

By the leader's pattern of life Tit 2:6–7 *See also* Ac 20:33–35; 1Co 4:16–17; 11:1; Php 4:9; 1Th 1:5–6

By the caring attitude of fellow believers 1Th 5:14–15 *See also* Ro 14:1; 1Co 8:9–13; Gal 6:1–2; 1Th 5:11; Tit 2:3–5

By appropriate teaching 1Pe 2:2 *See also* 1Co 3:2; 14:20; Heb 5:11–14

By encouraging spiritual growth
2Pe 3:18 *See also* 2Co 3:18; Eph 4:15; 2Th 1:3

See also

1613 Scripture, purpose	5802 care
	7130 flock, God's
4480 milk	7942 ministry
5664 children	8031 trust,
5682 family, significance	importance
	8292 love
5731 parents	8443 growth
5777 admonition	

8314

orthodoxy

The holding of religious beliefs that are in harmony with the accepted views of the community of faith. Right belief (orthodoxy) is to show itself in right practice (orthopraxis).

8315
orthodoxy, in OT

The acceptance of God's revelation of himself to his people that should lead to worship and obedience.

Foundational truths about Israel's God
God is one Dt 6:4

God is unique Dt 4:39 *See also* Dt 4:35; Ps 97:9; Isa 44:6–8

God is self-existent Ex 3:14

God is the Creator Isa 40:28 *See also* Ge 1:1; 2:7; Job 38:4

God will not tolerate rivals Ex 20:3–6 pp Dt 5:7–8; Dt 8:19–20; 13:6–8; Isa 42:8

God commands universal worship Ps 86:9–10 *See also* Isa 19:21; Zec 8:20–22

Right belief is passed on through the community of faith
Ps 145:4 *See also* Ex 12:24–27; Dt 6:6–8,20–25; Jos 4:20–24; Ps 78:2–6

Right belief demands right practice
Reverent fear Dt 10:12–13

Worship Dt 12:4–7; 2Ki 17:35–39; 1Ch 16:28–29 pp Ps 96:7–9; Ps 95:6–7

Observance of festivals
Dt 16:1–2,9–17

Offering acceptable sacrifices
Lev 1:2–4; 5:5–6; Mal 1:7–8

Faithfulness to the covenant
Dt 29:9–15; Ps 25:10

Devotion to God Dt 6:5 *See also* Dt 11:1; 1Ch 22:19; Ps 31:23; Hos 6:6

Trust in God's faithfulness Ps 4:5; 33:4 *See also* Ps 37:3–5; 115:9–11; 119:89–93

Obedience Dt 5:32 *See also* Dt 6:1–3; 26:16–19; 1Sa 15:22; Isa 30:21; Jer 7:21–23

Justice in society Mic 6:8 *See also* Ps 106:3; Pr 21:3; Isa 1:11–17; 56:1

Walking in God's ways

God's ways are right Hos 14:9 *See also* Pr 10:29

Walking in God's ways brings his blessing Ge 18:19; Dt 5:33; 28:9; 30:19–20

Examples of kings who walked in God's ways 2Sa 22:22 pp Ps 18:21 *David*; 2Ch 14:2–4 pp 1Ki 15:11–12 *Asa*; 2Ch 17:3–6 *Jehoshaphat*; 2Ch 26:4 pp 2Ki 15:3 *Uzziah (and Amaziah)*; 2Ch 29:2 pp 2Ki 18:3 *Hezekiah*; 2Ch 34:2 pp 2Ki 22:2 *Josiah*

See also

1349 covenant at Sinai	8207 commitment
	8225 devotion
5359 justice	8251 faithfulness to
7354 feasts and	God
festivals	8453 obedience
7435 sacrifice, in OT	8622 worship
8030 trust	8768 idolatry
8138 monotheism	

8316
orthodoxy, in NT

Acceptance of the truth, especially about Jesus Christ, that is revealed by the Holy Spirit in the gospel and is passed on through the teaching of sound doctrine.

Orthodoxy is based on Jesus Christ who is the truth
Eph 4:21 *See also* Jn 1:14; 14:6

Orthodoxy is revealed in the gospel
Gal 1:11–12; 2Ti 1:13–14 *See also* 2Co 11:3–4; Gal 1:6–9; 2:5,14; Col 1:5–6; 1Ti 1:9–11

Orthodoxy is expressed in simple summaries of faith
1Ti 3:16 *See also* Ro 1:3–4; 1Co 15:3–5; Php 2:5–11

Orthodoxy is maintained through God's true ministers
1Ti 2:7 *See also* 1Ti 4:6; 2Ti 2:2,15

Orthodoxy must be defended against error
Tit 1:9 *See also* 1Ti 6:20–21

Orthodoxy is shown by the attitude to the incarnation
1Jn 4:2–3 *See also* 1Jn 4:15; 5:1,10

Orthodoxy is revealed by the Holy Spirit
Jn 16:13 *See also* Jn 14:17, 26; 15:26; 1Jn 2:27

Orthodoxy is demonstrated in believers' behaviour
Walking as children of light Jn 3:19–21; Eph 5:8; 1Jn 1:7

Following Jesus Christ's example Jn 13:15; 1Co 11:1; 1Pe 2:21; 1Jn 2:6

Loving and obeying Jesus Christ Jn 14:15,21,23; 15:10; 1Jn 2:3–5

Right belief requires right action Jas 2:19 *See also* Jas 2:14–18,20–26

Signs of a fall from orthodoxy
False prophecy 1Jn 4:1 *See also* Mt 7:22–23; Mk 13:21–22 pp Mt 24:11

Empty religion Mt 15:9 pp Mk 7:7 *See also* Isa 29:13; Mk 7:8–9 pp Mt 15:3

False teaching 1Ti 4:1–2; 2Ti 4:3–4 *See also* 1Ti 1:6–7; 6:3–5; Tit 1:10–14; 2Pe 2:1–2

Examples of false teachings contrary to orthodoxy
Christians are obliged to obey the entire OT law Gal 5:1–12

Justification comes only through the OT law Gal 2:15–21

The resurrection has already taken place 2Ti 2:16–18

Christians do not sin 1Jn 1:8–10

See also

1462 truth, in NT	8234 doctrine
2420 gospel	8309 morality
7756 preaching, content	8750 false teachings
	8766 heresies
7797 teaching	8774 legalism
8028 faith, body of beliefs	8784 nominal religion
8217 conformity	

8318

patience

The quality of forbearance and self-control which shows itself particularly in a willingness to wait upon God and his will. Believers are called upon to be patient in their expectations of God's actions, and in their relationships with one another.

God's patience
Ex 34:6–7; Ro 2:4 *See also* Ne 9:30; Isa 48:9; 65:2; Joel 2:13; Jnh 4:2; Na 1:3; Ac 17:30; Ro 3:25; 9:22; 1Pe 3:20; 2Pe 3:9

The patience of Jesus Christ
1Ti 1:16 *See also* Mt 17:17 pp Mk 9:19 pp Lk 9:41; Jn 14:9; 2Pe 3:15; Rev 2:21

Other examples of patience
2Th 1:4 *the Thessalonian believers Abraham*; Heb 6:15; Jas 5:11 *Job The churches of Asia Minor*: Rev 1:9; 2:2

Patience is part of the fruit of the Spirit
Gal 5:22 *See also* Col 1:10–11

God's people should exercise patience

Pr 19:11; Col 3:12 *See also* Pr 14:29; 16:32; 25:15; Mt 6:14–15; 18:35

People who need particular patience

Christian leaders 2Ti 4:2 *See also* 2Ti 3:10

Christian masters Eph 6:9

Patience is necessary in church life

Eph 4:2 *See also* Ro 15:1; Col 3:13; 1Th 5:14

God's word is to be received with patience

Heb 13:22 *See also* Pr 2:1–5; 2Ti 4:3

Patience is a characteristic of love

1Co 13:4

Patience is an aspect of faith and hope

Ps 33:20; Jas 5:7–8
David waits for the LORD *to act on his behalf:* Ps 5:2; 27:14; 37:7,34; 38:15
Ps 119:166; 130:5–6; Pr 20:22; Isa 8:17; 30:18; La 3:24,26; Mic 7:7; Zep 3:8; Ac 1:4 *Jesus Christ's instructions to the apostles to wait for the Holy Spirit;* Ro 8:25; 12:12; Tit 2:13; Heb 6:12,15 *the example of Abraham;* Jas 5:10; Rev 6:11

See also

1095 God, patience of	5883 impatience
2060 Christ, patience of	5934 restraint
	5977 waiting
3254 Holy Spirit, fruit of	6686 mercy
	8339 self-control
5765 attitudes to people	8353 tolerance
	8418 endurance
	8459 perseverance

8319

perception, spiritual

The ability to see beneath the outward form to the underlying, often hidden, reality. It is a necessary gift in dealing with people, understanding spiritual teaching and interpreting events. Perception is important for effective service, though is often lacking, even among God's people.

Perception in dealing with people

God's knowledge of human hearts
Ps 139:1–4 *See also* Ps 17:3; 44:21; Pr 24:12

Jesus Christ's perception of those around him Jn 2:24–25 *See also* Isa 11:1–4; Mt 9:3–4 pp Lk 5:21–22; Jn 4:16–19; Rev 2:23

True understanding by God's servants Ne 6:1–2; Job 21:27; Ac 5:1–3

Perception of spiritual truth

Recognising God's ultimate authority
Rev 4:1–2 *See also* 2Ki 6:15–17; Da 7:8–14

Understanding Jesus Christ's teaching Mt 13:10–11 pp Mk 4:10–11 pp Lk 8:9–10 *See also* Mt 13·16–23 pp Mk 4:13–20 pp Lk 8:11–15 *The*

parable of the sower is about the way Jesus Christ's teaching in parables is received.

Understanding who Jesus Christ is Mt 16:15–17 pp Mk 8:29 pp Lk 9:20 *See also* Ac 8:30–35; Isa 53:7–8

Understanding about Jesus Christ's death and resurrection Lk 24:45–46 *See also* Lk 24:30–35; Jn 12:16

Perception to interpret events

2Sa 5:11–12 *The building of a palace in the newly captured Jerusalem confirms to David his election by God;* Isa 43:9–12 *Through his miraculous direction of his people's history, God is perceived as the one, true God. See also* Isa 41:18–20; 64:4; Jnh 1:12 *Jonah recognises God's hand in the storm;* Ac 10:34–35 *Through the circumstances of his guidance, Peter realises that God's salvation is for Gentiles too.*

Perception leading to effective service

1Ki 3:9 pp 2Ch 1:10 *See also* 1Sa 16:7–13 *Samuel perceives that David is to be king;* 2Ki 4:8–10 *A Shunammite's perception of Elisha leads her to extend hospitality to him;* Heb 11:27 *Moses' perception of the invisible God*

Lack of perception

By those in the OT Isa 43:19 *See also* Ex 5:2 *Pharaoh;* Nu 22:31–34 *Balaam;* Dt 32:28–29 *Israel in the wilderness;* Isa 29:10–12 *the people of Jerusalem;* Isa 42:20 *Israel*

By some Jews in the NT Mt 13:13–15 pp Mk 4:12 pp Lk 8:10; Isa 6:9–10; Lk 12:56; Jn 3:3–4; Ac 28:26

By Jesus Christ's disciples Mt 15:16 pp Mk 7:18 *not understanding what makes a person unclean;* Mt 16:9 pp Mk 8:17–18 *not understanding about the teaching of the Pharisees and Sadducees;* Mt 16:22 pp Mk 8:32 *Peter cannot accept that Jesus Christ must be crucified;* Jn 14:9 *Philip does not understand that Jesus Christ reveals the Father;* Jn 20:9 *not understanding about the resurrection*
Not recognising the risen Christ: Jn 20:14; 21:4

See also

5135 blindness, spiritual	8021 faith
	8226 discernment
5149 eyes	8281 insight
5159 hearing	8355 understanding
5894 intelligence	8361 wisdom
5946 sensitivity	8834 unbelief
6178 hardness of heart	

8320

perfection

The state of completion and total self-sufficiency, characterised by an absence of any flaw or fault. This perfection is found in God himself and is the ultimate goal of the Christian life.

8321

perfection, divine

The state of being whole, complete or without defect in any way.

Only God is absolutely perfect

In his nature and character Dt 32:4 *See also* Ecc 3:14; Mt 5:48; Ro 11:33–36

In his word Ps 12:6 *See also* Ps 19:7; Pr 8:8–9; 30:5; 2Ti 3:16–17; Jas 1:25

In his morality Hab 1:13 *See also* 2Sa 22:26–27; Job 4:17; 1Jn 3:3

In his will and providence 2Sa 22:31 pp Ps 18:30 *See also* Ro 12:2; Jas 1:17

In his knowledge Job 37:16 *See also* Ps 139:4; Isa 40:13–14; Heb 4:13

In his faithfulness Isa 25:1

God's perfect creation

In its original condition Ge 2:1–2 *See also* Ge 1:10,12,18,21,25,31; Isa 40:25–26; Mk 4:3

The coming new creation 1Co 13:10 *See also* 2Pe 3:13; Rev 21:1–5; 22:1–5

God's perfect self-revelation in Jesus Christ

Jn 14:9 *See also* Jn 1:14; 2Co 4:4; Col 1:15; Heb 1:3

The moral perfection of Jesus Christ as God's Son

1Pe 2:22 *See also* Isa 53:9; 2Co 5:21; Heb 2:10; 4:15; 5:9; 7:26; 1Jn 3:5

The perfect sacrifice of Jesus Christ

Heb 9:14
Foreshadowed in the OT: Lev 22:21; Nu 19:2
1Pe 1:19

See also

1065 God, holiness of	2218 Christ, Son of God
1100 God, perfection	4005 creation
1403 God, revelation	8201 blamelessness
2063 Christ, perfection	8266 holiness
2075 Christ, sinless	8324 purity

8322

perfection, human

Human wholeness in the image of God, given at creation and lost in the fall, is to be fully restored in Jesus Christ.

Humanity was created perfect

Ge 1:26–27 *See also* Ge 5:1; Eze 28:12–15 *The king of Tyre is described in terms of the creation and fall of humanity;* Jas 3:9

Perfection was lost through sin

Ro 3:23 *See also* Ge 2:17; 3:16–19,23; Job 15:14–16; Eze 28:15–17; Ro 1:21

The need for moral perfection

Dt 18:13 *See also* Ge 17:1; Job 25:4; Ps 24:3–4

Human inability to keep God's law perfectly

Heb 7:19 *See also* Heb 7:11; 10:1

Perfection and redemption

God's purpose for believers Col 1:22 *See also* Da 11:35; 12:10; Eph 5:27 *God's purpose for the church;* Heb 10:14; 11:40; 12:23; Jas 1:4; Jude 24

The aim of Christian ministry Col 1:28 *See also* 2Co 11:2

The aim of the Christian Php 3:12 *See also* 2Co 13:9–11; Eph 4:13; Heb 6:1; Jas 1:4

Characteristics of perfection

Perfect love Mt 5:48 *Jesus Christ patterning his disciples' love on the love God has for all people. See also* 1Jn 4:12,18

Perfect holiness 2Co 7:1 *See also* Php 1:10; 2:15; Jas 1:27; 2Pe 3:14

Perfect obedience 1Ti 6:14; 1Jn 2:5

Perfect speech Jas 3:2

Perfect unity with other believers Jn 17:23 *See also* 1Co 1:10; Col 3:14

Perfect joy Jn 15:11 *See also* Jn 3:29; 16:24; 1Jn 1:4; 2Jn 12

Perfect peace Isa 26:3 *See also* Ps 119:165; Php 4:7

Perfect knowledge 1Co 13:9–12 *See also* Ro 15:14 *Although complete knowledge is inaccessible here and now, believers have all they need to live the Christian life;* Col 2:2

Perfection in describing human physical beauty

2Sa 14:25–27; SS 4:7; 5:2; 6:9

False claims to perfection

Job 36:4; Ps 64:6; 119:96; Eze 27:3–4; Php 3:6

See also

3278 Holy Spirit, indwelling	6720 redemption
5902 maturity	6744 sanctification
6020 sin	8114 discipleship
6154 fall, the	8206 Christlikeness
6199 imperfection	8255 fruit, spiritual

purity

An absence of blemish or stain, especially sin. The state of being morally and spiritually pure, which is seen by Scripture as the result of being the people of God and also as an expected distinguishing mark of the church.

8325
purity, nature of

The OT recognises a close link between outer cleanliness and inner purity. In the NT, special emphasis is placed on inner purity resulting from spiritual renewal.

Physical cleansing from impurity by washing or refining

Ge 18:4; Job 9:30; Ps 12:6

Ritual impurity must be avoided or cleansed

Lev 10:10–11 *See also* Isa 35:8; 52:1,11; Mk 7:2,4

Sexual sources of ritual impurity

Childbirth Lev 12:2 *See also* Lev 12:5; Lk 2:22

Sexual intercourse Ex 19:15; Lev 15:18; 1Sa 21:4

Seminal emission Lev 15:16–17; Dt 23:10–11; 1Sa 20:26

Menstruation Lev 15:19–20; 2Sa 11:2–4; Eze 18:6

Abnormal discharge Lev 15:1–2,25–27; Mt 9:20 pp Mk 5:25 pp Lk 8:43

Other sources of ritual impurity

Dead bodies Nu 19:11–16

Unclean creatures Ge 7:2 *See also* Lev 11:24,46–47; Dt 14:3; Hos 9:3

Skin diseases Lev 13:45 *See also* Mt 8:2–4 pp Mk 1:40–44 pp Lk 5:12–14

Mildew Lev 14:36

Contact with a sin offering Lev 16:26

Cleansing from ritual impurity

Lev 14:8 *See also* Lev 16:26; Nu 19:17–21,9,17–21; 31:22–23 *Fire is also a purifying agent.*

Contact with God demanded purity

Ex 19:10 *See also* Ex 19:14–15; 30:18–21; Heb 10:22

Ritual purity is not required under the new covenant

Mt 15:11 pp Mk 7:15 *What concerns God is moral impurity, associated with actions, not ritual impurity, associated with food, etc. See also* Ac 10:12–15; 21:26 *Paul took part in Jewish purification rites in accordance with his Jewish heritage;* Ro 14:14; Gal 2:11–12 *Peter temporarily relapsed into the habit of treating Gentiles as unclean;* Gal 2:14–15; 1Ti 4:4

See also

1065 God, holiness of	7342 cleanliness
4351 refining	7416 purification
4859 white	7424 ritual law
6606 access to God	7426 ritual washing
7340 clean and unclean	7478 washing
	8201 blamelessness
	8204 chastity

8326
purity, moral and spiritual

Moral and spiritual purity is demanded by God of his people. God calls his people to be holy, just as he is holy.

Divine purity

The purity of God Hab 1:13 *See also* Job 4:17; Ps 18:26; 1Jn 1:5

The purity of Jesus Christ 1Jn 3:3 *See also* Mt 17:2; Heb 7:26

Fellowship with God demands purity

Ps 24:3–4; Mt 5:8 *See also* Ps 51:6; 73:1

God's people are to live pure lives

Col 3:5 *See also* Lev 18:30; Job 31:1;

Ps 51:10; 1Co 5:7–8 *Yeast is a symbol of sin;* 1Co 6:15–20; 1Th 4:3; Tit 1:15; 2:5; Heb 13:4; Jas 1:27; 4:8

Purity is unobtainable by human effort

Because of the sinful human nature Job 14:4 *See also* Job 15:14; 25:4; Ecc 7:20

Because of the tendency to idolatry Hos 8:5

Because of self-deception Pr 30:12 *See also* Pr 20:9

Because of an unwillingness to be cleansed Eze 24:13

Symbols of purification from sin

Ps 51:7 *See also* Isa 6:6 *fire;* Mk 1:4 *water baptism;* 2Co 11:2 *virginity;* 2Pe 3:14 *spotlessness*

God promises to purify his people

Eze 36:25 *See also* Zep 3:9; Zec 13:1

Purification through Jesus Christ

Through pardon offered in his death Heb 9:14 *See also* Heb 12:24; 1Jn 1:7

Through his word Jn 15:3 *See also* Jn 13:10

Through his presence in resisting temptation Jas 4:7–8 *See also* 1Pe 5:9

Through hope built on his promises Tit 2:12–13 *See also* 1Jn 3:3

Purification through judgment

In the OT Lev 18:28 *See also* Dt 13:5; 17:7,12; Jdg 20:13; Mal 3:2–4

In the NT 1Co 5:13

Symbols of purity

Whiteness Da 7:9 *See also* Ps 51:7; Isa 1:18; Mt 17:2 pp Mk 9:3; Mt 28:3; Mk 16:5; Jn 20:12; Rev 1:14

Light 1Jn 1:7 *See also* Job 25:5; Eze 1:27; 2Co 6:14; Eph 5:8–9

Washing Ps 26:6 *See also* Ps 51:2

Fire Da 7:9–10 *See also* Isa 33:14; Eze 8:2; Rev 1:14–15

See also

2054 Christ, mind of	6187 immorality
2063 Christ, perfection	6744 sanctification
4293 water	8145 renewal, people of God
4826 fire	8266 holiness
4833 light	8277 innocence
5740 virgin	

quietness

A calm, peaceful and restrained attitude to life and way of approaching God frequently commended in Scripture even in adverse circumstances. It is also a condition experienced by God's friends and enemies when confronted by his majesty.

Quietness of life

A quiet manner of life commended 1Ti 2:1–2 *See also* Ps 35:20; 131:1–2; Mt 12:19; Isa 42:2; 1Th 4:11; 2Th 3:12; 1Ti 2:11; 1Pe 3:1–4

A quiet temperament Ge 25:27

Quiet activity Mt 1:19 See also Jdg 4:21; Ru 3:7; Eze 24:17; Ac 16:37

The wisdom of being quiet Am 5:13 See also Ge 34:5; Jdg 18:19–20; Est 7:4; Pr 15:18; Ecc 9:17; Ac 19:35–36

Quietness in different circumstances
In peace and rest Ps 23:2 See also 1Ch 4:40; Pr 17:1; Isa 32:17; Mk 6:31

After conflict 1Ch 22:9 See also Jos 11:23; 14:15; Jdg 3:11; 5:31; 8:28; 2Ch 14:1; 20:30; Isa 14:7; Jer 30:10 pp Jer 46:27; Zec 1:11

When in distress 2Sa 13:20; Ne 8:9–11; Isa 7:4

Because of a sense of shame Ge 3:8; Ne 5:8; Mk 9:34

When before a higher authority Jdg 3:19; Mk 1:25 pp Lk 4:35

God's quiet voice 1Ki 19:12–13

Absence of quietness
Because of inner conflict Job 3:26 See also Ru 3:18; Job 6:24; Ro 7:21–24

Because of sin Isa 57:20–21

The quietness of God
God chooses quietness Isa 18:4 See also Job 34:29; Isa 42:14; Eze 16:42

God rejects quietness Isa 62:1

God brings quietness Ps 76:8 See also Ps 46:10; 65:7; 89:9; 107:29; Isa 24:8; 25:5; Zep 3:17; Mt 8:26 pp Mk 4:39 pp Lk 8:24

Quietness before God
Being quiet before God Ps 37:7; Isa 30:15 See also Ex 14:14; La 3:26; 1Co 14:28,34–35; Rev 8:1

Quietness in prayer Mt 6:6 See also Ne 2:4; Mk 6:46 pp Mt 14:23; Lk 5:16; 6:12; 9:18

Quietness as calmness
In contrast with the storm Mt 8:26 pp Mk 4:39 pp Lk 8:24 See also Ps 107:30; Jnh 1:11–15

In contrast with rashness Ecc 10:4 See also Pr 15:18

In contrast with unrest Isa 7:4 See also Ne 8:11

In contrast with anger Eze 16:42

See also
3215 Holy Spirit & peace	8030 trust
4851 storm	8339 self-control
5056 rest	8361 wisdom
5933 restlessness	8602 prayer
5950 silence	8662 meditation
6700 peace	8678 waiting on God

readiness

A state of preparedness for future needs or happenings, whether predictable or uncertain. God through Jesus Christ prepared all that was necessary for the salvation of sinners. God's people are exhorted to be ready for warfare (physical and spiritual), death and the second

coming of Jesus Christ. All humanity should be ready for future judgment.

God has prepared everything for the salvation of sinners
Mt 22:4 A wedding banquet is often used to portray the blessings of salvation and the gathering of Jesus Christ with the redeemed in heaven. See also Lk 14:16–17; 1Pe 1:5

Exhortations to and descriptions of readiness for war
Against earthly enemies Joel 3:9–10 See also 1Ki 20:12; 1Ch 12:23–35, 33–37; 2Ch 25:5; Jer 51:11–12; Da 11:10

Against spiritual forces of evil Eph 6:11–18

God's people should always be ready
To face temptation 1Pe 5:8 See also Ps 39:1; Mt 26:41 pp Mk 14:38 pp Lk 22:46; 1Co 10:12

To face death 2Ki 20:1 pp Isa 38:1 See also Ge 46:30; Ac 21:13

To serve Eph 4:11–12; 1Pe 1:13 See also Nu 8:11; 1Sa 25:41; Jn 9:4; 2Co 8:19; 9:2; 2Ti 2:21; Tit 3:1

To speak the truth 1Pe 3:15 See also Pr 22:17–18; Jer 1:17; 2Ti 4:2

For the second coming of Chirst 1Jn 2:28 See also Mt 24:42,44,45–51 pp Lk 12:42–46; Mt 25:1–12,13; Mk 13:33–37; Lk 12:35–40; 1Th 5:8; Rev 3:11; 16:15; 19:7

All humanity should be ready for future judgment
Lk 12:47–48 This is one of many parables that Jesus Christ taught about his second coming and the need to be ready when he returns. See also Am 4:12; 1Pe 4:5

See also
2565 Christ, second coming	8342 servanthood
5184 standing	8420 equipping
5546 speech	8490 watchfulness
5605 warfare	8757 folly, effects of
5977 waiting	9020 death
6248 temptation	9230 judgment seat

receptiveness

An openness to people and ideas which needs to be tempered by discernment. It is an attitude which God desires and which he shows to all who call to him.

Receptiveness as a human quality
It is characterised by an open attitude Mt 13:16–17 See also Pr 18:15; 20:12

It is an aspect of love Jn 19:26–27 See also Ru 4:3–5,13; Mt 18:5 pp Mk 9:37 pp Lk 9:48; Mt 25:35; Ac 2:44–45; 4:32; 1Co 13:6–7; Gal 4:14

Thoughtful receptiveness requires discernment 1Jn 4:1 See also 1Co 2:14; Php 1:10; 1Th 5:21; Heb 5:14

Thoughtless receptiveness is dangerous 2Co 11:3–4 See also

Dt 11:16; 1Ki 11:4; Pr 7:21; Col 2:8; Heb 13:9; 2Jn 10

Spiritual receptiveness is fruitful Jn 15:5 See also Ps 1:3; Pr 3:5–6; 6:20–22; Jer 17:7–8; Jn 20:29

God is receptive to human beings
To their needs Mt 9:36 See also 2Ki 14:26; Ps 103:13–14; Isa 63:9; Mt 6:8; 15:32 pp Mk 8:2–3; Lk 7:13; 1Pe 5:7

To their cries Ps 38:9 See also Ex 3:7; 1Ki 9:3 pp 2Ch 7:12; Ps 6:8–9; 40:1; Isa 65:24; 1Pe 3:12

To their repentance Hos 14:1–4 See also 2Sa 12:13; Eze 18:27–28; Joel 2:13; Jnh 3:10; 4:2; Lk 15:7,10; 18:13–14

God's receptiveness may be withdrawn Zec 7:13 See also Ps 66:18; Pr 21:13; Isa 59:2; Jer 11:11; Mt 7:23; 27:46 pp Mk 15:34; Ps 22:1; Jas 1:7

People should be receptive to God
Spiritual receptiveness begins by receiving Jesus Christ Jn 1:12–13 See also Mt 10:40; Ac 2:41; 16:14; Col 2:6

Spiritual receptiveness requires openness to God's Spirit 1Co 2:12–16 See also Ro 8:5,16; 1Co 7:40; Gal 5:16,25; Rev 2:7

Receptiveness involves seeking and listening Isa 50:4–5 See also Dt 4:29; 1Ch 28:9; Ps 119:11; Pr 8:34; Mt 7:8 pp Lk 11:10; Lk 10:39; Eph 1:18; Jas 1:19

Receptiveness involves accepting and learning Mk 10:15 pp Lk 18:17 See also Ps 1:2; Lk 11:1; Jn 3:27; 6:45; Ac 8:30–31; 17:11; 1Th 2:13; 1Jn 2:27

Receptiveness requires obedience and action Jn 14:23 See also 1Sa 15:22; Isa 58:6–7; Mt 7:21; Jn 5:17; 7:17; Jas 1:25; 2:14; 1Pe 4:10

Refusing to be receptive to God
Zec 7:11–12 See also 2Ch 24:19; Jer 32:33; Mt 10:14 pp Mk 6:11 pp Lk 9:5; Jn 1:11; Ac 7:51–53; Jas 1:7–8

See also
1030 God, compassion	6602 acceptance
5159 hearing	8160 seeking God
5165 listening	8205 childlikeness
6178 hardness of heart	8226 discernment
6245 stubbornness	8292 love
	8351 teachableness
	8453 obedience

reliability

The quality of consistency and dependability which is the basis for confidence and reliance. It is exemplified by God in his changelessness and is required of God's people in their service and witness. Scripture gives warning, too, of those things which may prove unreliable.

The reliability of God
God's character and nature are reliable Dt 32:4 See also 1Sa 2:2; Ps 18:2; 62:7; 78:35; Isa 26:4

God is faithful to his covenants Dt 7:9 *See also* Ge 9:15–16; Ps 105:8–11; 111:5; Isa 54:10; Eze 16:60

God's love is reliable Ps 89:1–2 *See also* Ex 20:6 pp Dt 5:10; Ex 34:6–7; Nu 14:18; Ps 103:17–18; La 3:22–24; 1Jn 4:16

God's promises are reliable 1Ki 8:56 *See also* Jos 21:44–45; 23:15; Jer 29:10; Heb 6:13–18

God's presence is reliable Dt 31:6 *See also* Ge 28:15; Isa 41:10; Mt 28:20; Ac 18:10

God's strength and protection are reliable Ps 46:1; 1Co 1:8–9 *See also* Jos 14:9; 2Ch 13:18; 16:8; Ps 71:5–7; Php 1:6; 2Th 3:3; Jude 24

God's words are reliable Jn 8:26 *See also* Ps 33:4; Eze 12:25; Mt 5:18; Lk 21:33; Ro 3:4

The reliability of times and seasons
Ge 8:22 *See also* Ge 1:14; Ps 104:19; Ecc 1:4–5

The reliability of God's people
Reliability in witness Isa 8:2 *See also* Pr 12:17; 14:5,25; Jn 19:35; Ac 4:20

Reliability in teaching Pr 22:20–21 *See also* Ecc 12:10; 2Ti 2:2

Reliability of character 1Ti 3:2–10; Tit 1:6–9

Examples of reliable people
Ge 21:23–24 *Abraham*
Moses: Nu 12:7; Heb 3:5
Caleb: Nu 14:24; Jos 14:9–12
2Ch 34:12 *men working on the temple;*
Ne 7:2 *Hanani;* Eze 44:15 *Priests;* Mal 2:6
Levi; 1Co 4:17 *Timothy;* Col 1:7
Epaphras; Col 4:7–9 *Tychicus and Onesimus;* 2Ti 4:11 *Luke*

Warnings against unreliability
Examples of unreliable people Ps 78:57 *See also* 1Sa 29:6 *David was trusted by Achish, but was secretly deceiving him;* Jer 2:21 *the people of Israel*
False prophets: Eze 13:9; Zec 10:2; Mt 7:15
Gal 2:4 *Judaisers;* Hos 10:4 *Israel's kings*

Examples of things proving unreliable Jer 17:5 *See also* 2Ki 18:21 pp Isa 36:6 *false dependence upon Egypt*
False dependence on military strength: Ps 33:16; Hos 10:13
Isa 30:12–13 *false dependence upon human scheming*
False dependence upon human effort to achieve salvation: Gal 3:18; Col 2:8

See also
1155	God, truthfulness
1240	God, the Rock
1340	consistency
1460	truth
2021	Christ, faithfulness
5466	promises
5973	unreliability
8224	dependence
8248	faithfulness
8275	honesty
8304	loyalty
8354	trustworthiness

reputation

The estimation of a person in the sight of God or other people. Scripture stresses the importance of believers having a good reputation with those outside the faith.

God's defence of his own reputation
God's actions in history to uphold his reputation Ex 9:13–16 *See also* Eze 20:9–10

God's rebukes his people for failing to uphold his reputation Mal 2:2 *See also* Mal 1:6–11

God's promises to uphold his reputation Eze 36:22–23 *See also* Isa 42:8

The reputation of believers
Believers must seek a good reputation with God Ac 24:16 *See also* 2Co 5:9–10; 1Th 4:1

Believers must have a good reputation with outsiders Ac 5:13–16 *See also* Ac 2:46–47; 24:16; 1Ti 3:7

Believers must not boast to improve their own reputation 2Co 10:17–18 *See also* 1Co 3:5–7; Php 3:4–9

Believers must not seek a good reputation through outward show Mt 6:16–18 *See also* Mt 6:1–8; 23:2–12

Believers may find that serving God leads to a bad reputation with unbelievers Ac 17:5–8 *See also* 1Ki 19:1–5; Lk 23:1–2

Good reputations
Examples of God-fearers with a good reputation Lk 7:3–5 *the centurion;* Ac 10:1–4 *Cornelius*

Examples of believers with a good reputation Da 6:3–5 *Daniel;* Ac 9:36–39 *Dorcas;* Ac 16:1–2 *Timothy;* Ac 22:12–13 *Ananias;* Ro 1:8 *the church at Rome*

The blessing of a good reputation Pr 22:1 *See also* Ecc 7:1

Bad reputations
The reputation of sinners is known to God Ge 18:20–21 *See also* Rev 3:1–2; 18:4–5

Examples of reputed sinners 1Ki 16:29–33; 21:25–26; 2Ki 21:16–17

Outward reputation cannot compare with a righteous heart
1Sa 16:7 *See also* 1Ch 29:14–19; Rev 3:1–3

See also
5017	heart, renewal
5041	name
5173	outward appearance
5857	fame
5859	favour
6121	boasting
8203	character
8276	humility
8444	honouring God
8460	pleasing God
8471	respect for human beings
8802	pride

reverence

The proper sense of awe, respect and wonder that is inspired and demanded by an encounter with, or meditation upon, the character and activity of the living God.

reverence, and God's nature

Reverence for God results from considering his nature and all that he has done.

Believers should revere God and meditate upon his deeds
1Sa 12:24 *See also* Jos 24:14; Job 25:2; 37:23–24; Jer 32:40–41; Mal 2:5

Reverence is to be reserved exclusively for God
Dt 6:13–14

Reverence for God's creative activity
Dt 10:20–21 *See also* 1Sa 12:18; 1Ch 16:25; Ps 33:8–9; Ecc 3:14; Jer 5:22–24; Hab 3:2

Reverence for God's eternal existence
1Ti 1:17 *See also* 1Ti 6:16

Reverence for God's name
Mal 4:2 *See also* Isa 59:19; Mal 1:14; Rev 11:18

Reverence for God's holiness
Isa 8:13 *See also* Ps 96:4; Isa 29:23; Jer 10:7; Rev 15:4

Reverence for God's word
Isa 66:2 *See also* Dt 4:10–11; Ezr 9:4; 10:3

Reverence for God's works
Ecc 3:14 *See also* Ex 14:31; Ps 64:9

Reverence for God's mercy and compassion
Ps 5:7; 22:23; 130:4

Reverence for God's intervention in healing
Mt 9:8 pp Mk 2:12 pp Lk 5:26

Reverence for God's judgment
Ex 14:31; Am 3:8; Jnh 1:16; Rev 14:7

Reverence for God's anger
Dt 6:14–15; Ps 2:11–12; 76:7

Gentile nations will also revere and fear God
Ps 67:7 *See also* Jos 4:24; 1Ki 8:43 pp 2Ch 6:33; 2Ch 20:29; Ps 76:11–12; 102:15; Isa 59:19; Jer 33:9

Reverent fear of God is not mere terror but includes trust
Ex 20:20 *See also* Ge 28:16–17 *Jacob feels reverent awe in the presence of the God who has just promised to bless him;* Ps 2:11; Ac 9:31

Reverent fear of God is a remedy against other fears
Ps 56:4; Lk 12:4–5; 1Pe 3:14–15

See also
1065	God, holiness of
5763	attitudes, positive to God
5896	irreverence
8361	wisdom
8444	honouring God
8470	respect for God
8608	prayer & worship
8622	worship
8632	adoration
8660	magnifying God
8664	praise
8754	fear

8335
reverence, and blessing

Reverence for God brings favour to individual believers, their families and the community to which they belong.

God's blessing is conditional upon reverence for him
Ps 128:1 *See also* Ps 115:1; Ecc 8:12; Jer 32:39

The characteristics of reverence
Wisdom is based on reverence for God Ps 111:10 *See also* Pr 1:7; 9:10

Reverence is pure and eternal Ps 19:9

Reverence will characterise the Messiah Isa 11:2–3

God responds to those who revere him
Ps 147:11 *See also* Ps 25:14; Mal 3:16–18; Ac 10:35

Reverence brings God's special attention and compassion Ne 1:11; Ps 33:18; 103:13,17; 145:19; Lk 1:50

God is good to those who revere him Ps 31:19; Isa 33:6

Reverence brings God's protection and deliverance Ps 34:7; 60:4; 115:11; Pr 14:26

God meets the needs of those who revere him Ex 1:21; Ps 34:9; 111:5; Jer 5:24–25

Reverence for God is rewarded
God rewards the reverent with prosperity Dt 6:24 *See also* Job 1:9; Ps 25:12–13; 85:9; 112:1; 128:4; Pr 22:4; Mal 4:2

Those who revere God avoid his judgment Dt 28:58–67

God rewards reverence with long life and future hope Pr 10:27; 14:27; 19:23; 23:17–18; Ecc 8:13

God's blessings on those who revere him are a witness to the nations
Jer 33:9

Reverence ensures success in leadership
2Sa 23:3 *David*; 2Ch 26:5 *Uzziah*; Ac 9:31

See also
1060 God, greatness   6510 salvation
    of   8265 godliness
1335 blessing

8336
reverence, and obedience

Reverence towards God expresses itself in the actions, as well as the words and worship of believers. True reverence for God leads to obedience towards him.

Reverent fear is expressed in worship
Jnh 1:16

Reverence in worship is expressed in bodily attitudes
Bowing: Ex 12:27; Ps 95:6

Prostration: Ge 17:3; Nu 14:5; Da 10:15; Rev 5:14
Ex 3:5 *removing shoes*; Ex 3:6 *covering the face*
Kneeling: Ezr 9:5; Da 6:10; Eph 3:14

Reverence can be learnt through religious observances
A shared meal in God's presence
Dt 14:23

Hearing God's word Dt 4:9–14; 31:12–13

Reading God's word Dt 17:18–19

Reverence motivates people to avoid doing wrong
Pr 16:6 *See also* Ex 20:20; 2Ch 19:9–10; Job 1:1; 28:28; Pr 3:7; 8:13; 14:16; 2Co 7:1

Reverence leads people to obey God's law
Ecc 12:13 *See also* Dt 10:12–13; 13:4; Ne 5:14–18 *generous treatment of dependants*; 2Co 5:11 *evangelism*; Eph 5:21 *mutual submission*; Col 3:22 *obedience to masters*

Reverence is characterised by fearing God
Ecc 8:12; Ac 2:5

Gentile believers were called "God-fearing" Ac 10:2; 13:26,50; 17:4,17

See also
6744 sanctification   8251 faithfulness to
8208 commitment to   God
    God   8453 obedience

8337
reverence, and social behaviour

Reverence for God leads to proper respect for others and right relationships among the people of God.

Reverence for God affects believers' attitudes
Reverence produces respect for others Eph 5:21 *See also* 1Pe 2:17

Reverence affects social attitudes Lev 19:14; 25:17; Eph 6:5; Lev 25:36,43

Attitudes to work are affected by reverence to God Ex 1:17 *a conflict of duty*; Ex 18:21 *appointments in administration*; 2Ch 19:7 *justice*; 2Ch 19:9

Reverence for God affects believers' behaviour
Lev 19:14,32; 25:14–17,35–36; Ps 15:4; Pr 31:30 *Reverence for God should be respected*; Col 3:22 *Reverence for God inspires a slave's respect for his master. Reverence affects lifestyle:* Tit 2:2–3; 1Pe 3:1–2

Reverence for God may reduce hostility
2Ch 17:10

Lack of reverence has an adverse effect on behaviour
Dt 25:18; Ne 5:7–9; Ps 36:1

Reverence can be shown to fellow human beings as God's representatives
Jos 4:14; Ac 10:25

See also
5765 attitudes to   8243 ethics, social
    people   8471 respect for
7140 people of God   human beings

8339
self-control

Physical and emotional self-mastery, particularly in situations of intense provocation or temptation.

Self-control is the mark of a wise person
Pr 29:11 *See also* Pr 1:1–5

Self-control is an aspect of Christian character
Gal 5:22–23; Tit 2:11–12 *See also* 1Ti 3:2; Tit 1:8; 2:2,5–6; 2Pe 1:5–9

Self-control affects the whole person
Physical self-control 1Co 9:26–27 *See also* 1Co 7:36–38; 1Th 4:3–7

A mental discipline 1Pe 1:13 *See also* 1Th 5:6–8; 1Pe 4:7; 5:8

Controlled speech Ps 141:3; Jas 1:19 *See also* Ps 17:3; Pr 16:23; 21:23; Ecc 5:2; Jas 3:1–12

Self-control in response to persecution
Mt 5:39–40 pp Lk 6:27–29 *See also* 1Pe 2:18–23

Examples of self-control
Ge 39:7–12 *Joseph*
David: 1Sa 24:1–7; 26:7–12; 2Sa 16:9–10
Job: Job 31:1,30
Jesus Christ: Isa 53:7 *the servant, understood in the NT as a prophecy concerning Jesus Christ*; Mk 14:61; Mt 27:27–30
Paul: 1Co 4:12–13; 9:24–27

The dangers of a loss of self-control
Pr 18:7; Jer 14:10 *See also* 1Sa 18:10–11 *Saul*; 2Sa 13:7–14 *Amnon*; Ps 106:32–33 *Moses*; Pr 6:1–3; 29:18; Ac 24:25; Ro 1:24–31; 1Co 7:5 *aimed at those who thought that abstaining from sexual relations in marriage was spiritual*; 1Co 7:9; Col 2:23
False teaching was leading to the throwing off of restraints in the name of the gospel: 2Pe 2:12–14,18–19; Jude 4

See also
3254 Holy Spirit, fruit   8230 discipline
    of   8305 meekness
5267 control   8318 patience
5925 rashness   8459 perseverance
5934 restraint   8475 self-denial
6106 addiction   8777 lust
6187 immorality

8340
self-respect

A sense of personal worth and dignity. Scripture points to the need for believers to ground their self-respect in God himself, rather than trusting in the opinion and valuation of other individuals or society as a whole.

Self-respect is often assumed
Mt 22:39 pp Mk 12:31 See also Mt 7:12; 19:19; Ro 12:3; Eph 5:29

Examples of those who had self-respect
Job 12:3 See also Job 10:16; Pr 31:25; Php 3:4

The basis of self-respect
A relationship with God Ps 139:13–14 See also Ps 30:6; 1Co 3:16–17; 6:12–20; 2Co 6:16; Eph 2:22; 1Ti 4:4

Equality in God's community Jas 1:9–10 See also 1Co 12:22–25

A clear conscience and faithfulness to God 2Co 1:12 See also Jn 7:18; Gal 6:4; Heb 13:18

God's strength is a source of self-respect
Da 10:19 See also Ex 15:2; 2Sa 22:33; Ps 71:5; 89:17; 118:14; 2Ti 4:17

Self-respect results from disciplined living
Job 4:6 See also Pr 20:3; 1Th 4:4; Tit 2:2

Self-respect can be lost through humiliation
Jer 31:19 See also 2Sa 10:1–5 pp 1Ch 19:1–5; 2Sa 13:1–22; Da 4:33

Self-respect can rest on wrong foundations
Gal 6:3 See also Dt 8:17–18; Job 20:6–7; Php 3:4–7

Ways in which self-respect can be undermined
By others Job 30:1–15

By the effects of sin and the work of Satan Mk 5:2–5 pp Lk 8:27–29; Mk 5:25–28 pp Mt 9:20–22 pp Lk 8:43–48; Lk 15:13–16; 17:12–13

By unwise spiritual zeal Gal 6:1; 1Ti 5:1–2; Jude 22

See also
5879 humiliation	8339 self-control
5888 inferiority	8369 worthiness
5947 shame	8469 respect
8213 confidence	8802 pride

8341

separation

A setting apart. Separation is at the heart of the biblical idea of holiness. God is separate from his creation and has set apart his people from the world. Sin causes alienation between God and humanity, making necessary the reconciling work of Jesus Christ. The end of the age will bring the final separation between the righteous and the wicked.

God is without equal Ex 15:11 See also Ps 89:6; Isa 40:25–26

God is separate from his creation Isa 40:22 See also Ge 1:1; Isa 29:16; 45:11–12; Ro 1:25

The separateness of God's people
Dt 7:6 See also Ex 19:5–6; Dt 14:2; Ps 135:4

1Pe 2:9 See also 1Co 6:19–20; Tit 2:14

Separation from the world Lev 20:26 See also Nu 23:9; Ne 9:2; 10:28 Jn 15:18–19 See also Jn 17:16; Php 3:20; 1Pe 2:11

Separation from sin 2Co 6:17 See also Isa 52:11; Lev 15:31; Ezr 6:21; 1Co 6:18; 15:34; 2Co 7:1

Avoidance of evil association
1Co 15:33 See also Pr 13:20 Israel forbidden to associate and intermarry with Canaanite peoples: Dt 7:2–3; Jos 23:7 Ezr 4:3; 10:11; Ps 119:115; 2Co 6:14

Excommunication
Israelites refusing to follow God's commands to be cut off from God's people: Lev 18:29; Nu 15:30; 19:20; Mt 18:15–17 separation from unrepentant believers; Ro 16:17 separation from false teachers; 1Co 5:9–13 separation from wilfully sinful believers; 2Th 3:6 separation from wilfully disobedient believers; Tit 3:9–11 separation from divisive people

Separation for service to God Nu 6:2–3 the Nazirites; Nu 16:9 the Levites; 1Ch 23:13 Aaron and his descendants; 1Ch 25:1 prophets; Jer 1:5 Jeremiah Paul: Ro 1:1; Gal 1:15

Separation of holy places Ex 26:33 the Most Holy Place separated by a curtain; Ex 33:7 the Tent of Meeting placed outside the camp; Eze 42:20 Ezekiel's temple separated by a wall

Separation caused by sin
Separation from God Isa 59:2 See also Hab 1:13; Eph 4:18; Col 1:21

Separation at the final judgment
Mt 25:32–33 See also Mt 13:40–42,47–50

Separation of people from one another
Ru 1:16–17 Ruth will not be separated from Naomi; 2Ki 2:11 Elisha separated from Elijah; Phm 15 Philemon separated from Onesimus; Jn 4:9 separation between Jews and Samaritans; Eph 2:11–12 separation between Jews and Gentiles

The pain of separation Ac 20:37–38 See also 1Sa 20:41; Jn 16:20 Jesus Christ foretells his death and resurrection; 2Ti 1:4

The pain of separation through death Ac 8:2 See also Ge 37:33–35; Jer 31:15; Mt 2:18

Husband and wife not to be separated Mt 19:5–6 pp Mk 10:7–9 See also Ge 2:24; 1Co 7:10–13

Reconciliation through Jesus Christ ends the separation from God
2Co 5:18–20 See also Mt 27:46 pp Mk 15:34; Ps 22:1 Reconciliation with God is possible because Jesus Christ bore the punishment of separation from God that human sin deserves; Mt 27:51 pp Mk 15:38 pp Lk 23:45; Ro 8:35–39

Nothing can separate believers from God's love shown in Christ; Eph 2:14–15 Jew and Gentile reconciled through mutual reconciliation to God

See also
1065 God, holiness of	7025 church, unity
5004 human race & sin	7344 curtain
5675 divorce	7922 fellowship with God
6026 sin, judgment on	8270 holiness, set apart
6109 alienation	9020 death
6717 reconciliation, world to God	9240 last judgment

8342

servanthood

The state of being the servant of others, especially of God. Scripture stresses the privileges and responsibilities of being a servant of God and points to Jesus Christ as the model of servanthood.

8343
servanthood, in society

Servants and slaves were an important feature of everyday life in biblical times. The idea of servanthood is used both literally and metaphorically throughout Scripture.

Laws of servanthood
Ex 21:2–6 pp Dt 15:12–18 The words "servant" and "slave" are the same in Hebrew, but according to OT law, an Israelite servant was to be accorded more rights than a foreign slave. See also Ge 17:13; Ex 12:44; 20:10 pp Dt 5:14; Lev 25:39–55; Dt 21:10–14; 29:10–11; 1Ch 2:34–35

Citizens referred to as servants of the king
1Sa 17:34 See also 2Sa 18:29; 2Ki 5:6; Ezr 4:11; Pr 14:35; Mt 18:23

Kings as servants of other kings
2Ki 16:7 See also 2Sa 10:19 pp 1Ch 19:19; 2Ki 17:3; 24:1; Isa 60:10

Servant as a self-designated title of respect
2Sa 9:2 See also Ge 19:2; 32:4; 1Sa 17:34; 2Sa 14:6; 2Ki 2:15–16; 4:1; 6:3; Da 1:12–13; 2:4

Servanthood in Proverbs
Pr 14:35 See also Pr 11:29; 12:9; 17:2; 29:19; 30:10,21–23

Servanthood in the NT
Mt 23:8–12 See also Mt 6:24; Lk 17:7–10; Jn 15:20; Ro 12:3–8

See also
5219 authority, human institutions	5404 masters
	5520 servants
	5700 headship
5257 civil authorities	7446 slavery

8344
servanthood, in life of believers

Servanthood as an expression of subservience is an integral aspect of a person's relationship with God.

Servants of God in the OT
Abraham Ge 18:5 *See also* Ge 26:24; Dt 9:27; Ps 105:6,42

Moses Ex 14:31 *See also* Nu 12:7–8; Dt 34:5; Jos 1:1–2,7,13,15; 8:31,33; 11:15; 22:2,4–5; 2Ki 18:12; 2Ch 1:3; Heb 3:5; Rev 15:3

Joshua Jdg 2:8 *See also* Jos 24:29

David 2Sa 3:18 *See also* 2Sa 7:5 pp 1Ch 17:4; 2Sa 7:8 pp 1Ch 17:7; 2Sa 7:18–20,25; 1Ch 21:8; Ps 78:70; 89:3,20; 132:10; Eze 34:23–24; Lk 1:69; Ac 4:25–26

Jesus Christ and servanthood
Jesus Christ's teaching on servanthood Mt 6:24 *pp* Lk 16:13 *See also* Mt 25:31–46; Jn 12:26; 13:13–17; 15:15,20

Parables on servanthood Mt 20:1–16; 24:45–51 pp Lk 12:42–46; Mt 25:14–30 pp Lk 19:12–27; Lk 12:35–40; 17:7–10

Servants of God in the NT
Ac 16:17 *See also* Ac 2:18; 4:29; 2Pe 1:1; Jude 1

Paul as a servant
A servant of God Ro 15:17 *See also* Ro 1:9; 2Co 6:4; 2Ti 1:3

A servant of Jesus Christ Ro 1:1 *See also* Gal 1:10; Php 1:1

A servant of the gospel Eph 3:7 *See also* Col 1:23

A servant of the church 2Co 4:5 *See also* 2Co 13:4; Col 1:24–25

Christian servanthood
Gifts of service 1Pe 4:10 *See also* Ro 12:7; 1Co 12:5; Eph 4:12; 1Pe 2:16

Examples of service Ro 12:11 *See also* 2Co 9:12–13; Eph 6:6–7; Col 3:22–24; Rev 2:19

Christian leadership entails service 1Pe 5:2 *See also* Ac 6:2–4
The office of deacon was seen as a serving role: 1Ti 3:10,12–13

See also
2036 Christ, humility	7708 apostles,
2327 Christ as	function
servant	7715 deacons
2339 Christ, example	7733 leaders
of	7939 ministry
5153 foot-washing	8114 discipleship
7160 servants of the	
Lord	

8345
servanthood, and worship of God

The biblical understanding of servanthood has its foundation in people serving God in worship. The terms for "service" and "worship" are often interchangeable.

Worship is a central aspect of serving God
Ex 3:12 *See also* Ex 4:23; 8:1,20; 10:8; Jos 22:27; Ps 100:2; 102:22; Lk 4:8

Worship entails total obedience, not merely correct religious observances
Dt 10:12–13 *See also* Am 5:22–24; Mic 6:6–8

Worship and service to God must be exclusive
Mt 4:10 *pp* Lk 4:8 *See also* Dt 6:13

Serving false gods
Worshipping false gods forbidden Ex 20:3–5 *pp* Dt 5:8–9 *See also* Ex 23:24; 34:14; Jos 23:7

Warnings against serving false gods 2Ch 7:19–20 *See also* Dt 7:3–4; Jos 23:16; 24:20

Examples of idolatrous service 1Ki 16:31 *See also* Jdg 2:11,13; 2Ki 17:33; Jer 2:20; 11:10; Ro 1:25

Refusal to serve false gods Da 3:12 *See also* Jos 24:16–18; Da 3:18,28–29

Judgment for serving false gods Jdg 10:11–13 *See also* Jdg 10:6–10; Eze 20:30–38

The service of the Levites and the priesthood
Consecration of the priesthood Ex 29:1 *See also* Ex 28:1,41; 29:44; 40:12–16; Nu 3:9–13

Service in the Tent of Meeting Nu 4:3,23,30,35,39,43; 18:7

Service in the temple 1Ch 23:2–5 *See also* 1Ch 23:24–32; 24:3,5,19; 25:1,6–8 *musicians and singers;* 1Ch 26:12 *gatekeepers;* 1Ch 26:20 *treasurers;* 1Ch 26:29–32; Ezr 7:7; 8:20; Ne 7:46,60

The promise of restored service in the new temple Eze 44:15 *See also* Eze 44:10–14,24; 45:5

Examples of priestly service Lk 1:5,8–10,23

The true service of Jesus Christ as high priest Heb 8:1–2 *Hebrews sees the OT priesthood and its services as superseded by Jesus Christ. See also* Heb 8:3–6

The Christian's life as an act of worship
Ro 12:1 *See also* Rev 1:6; 5:10

See also
2306 Christ, high	8453 obedience
priest	8622 worship
5977 waiting	8747 false gods
7390 Levites	8752 false worship
7412 priesthood	8768 idolatry

spiritual growth

Scripture uses a number of images to emphasise that believers are meant to grow in their faith, understanding, holiness and commitment. It also provides advice on how this may be achieved.

8348
spiritual growth, nature of

Having given spiritual life to his people, God expects them to grow to maturity.

God desires the spiritual growth of his people
Mt 5:48; Heb 6:1 *See also* 2Co 13:9–11; Eph 1:4; 2:10; 3:17–19; Php 3:12; 1Th 4:1,7; 2Ti 1:9

Christlikeness is the goal of spiritual growth
Ro 8:29 *See also* Eph 4:13–15; Php 2:5; 1Jn 3:2–3

Aspects of spiritual growth
Growth in grace 2Pe 3:18 *See also* Pr 4:18; 1Pe 2:1–3

Growth in faith 2Th 1:3 *See also* 2Co 10:15

Growth in love 1Th 3:12 *See also* Ro 5:5; 1Co 14:1; Php 1:9; 1Th 4:9–10; Heb 10:24; 1Jn 4:7–21; 5:1–3

Growth in understanding Ps 119:27 ; 1Co 14:20 *See also* Ps 119:97–99; Ro 12:2; 16:19; 1Co 13:11; Eph 1:17–19; Php 1:9–10; Col 1:9; Heb 5:14

Growth in holiness 2Co 7:1 *See also* Eph 5:25–26; Heb 2:11; 10:10–14; 12:14; 13:12; 1Pe 1:15–16

Growth in fruitfulness Jn 15:16 *See also* Mt 13:23 pp Mk 4:20 pp Lk 8:15; Jn 15:2,8; Php 1:11; Col 1:10

Growth in contentment Php 4:11–12 *See also* 1Ti 6:6; Heb 13:5

Examples of spiritual growth
In individuals 1Sa 2:26 *Samuel;* Lk 1:80 *John the Baptist*
Jesus Christ: Lk 2:40,52
Paul: Ac 9:22; 1Co 9:26–27; Php 3:12–14
Ac 18:26 *Apollos;* Phm 11 *Onesimus;* 3Jn 2–3 *Gaius*

In the church Ac 9:31; 11:26; 16:5; 2Co 10:15; Col 1:6; 1Th 2:13; 2Th 1:3

See also
4450 fruit	8114 discipleship
5904 maturity,	8164 spirituality
spiritual	8206 Christlikeness
6744 sanctification	8255 fruit, spiritual
7027 church,	8258 fruitfulness,
purpose	spiritual
8102 abiding in	8266 holiness
Christ	8320 perfection

8349
spiritual growth, means of

God has provided various means by which believers may grow spiritually.

God supplies the resources for spiritual growth
Php 2:13; 2Pe 1:3 *See also* Jn 1:16; 4:14; 15:2,5; 1Co 10:13; 2Co 3:18; 9:10; Gal 5:22–23; Php 1:6; Col 2:19; Jas 1:17; 4:6; Jude 24

God's people must make efforts to grow spiritually
Php 2:12; 2Pe 1:5–9 *See also* Ro 6:19; 2Co 7:1; Gal 5:16,25; Eph 5:15–16; 6:11–13; 1Ti 4:7; 6:11–12; 2Ti 1:6; 2Pe 3:14; 1Jn 3:3; Jude 20

Specific means of spiritual growth
Death to self-interest Col 3:5 *See also* Mt 16:24 pp Mk 8:34 pp Lk 9:23; Ro 6:6,12; 8:13; Eph 4:22; Col 3:9; 1Pe 1:14; 2:11

The Scriptures 2Ti 3:16–17 *See also* Jos 1:8; Ps 19:7–8; 119:9–11; Jn 17:17; Eph 6:17; Col 3:16; 1Pe 2:2; 1Jn 2:14

Prayer Mt 6:13 pp Lk 11:4 Col 4:2 *See also* 1Ch 16:11; Mt 7:11 pp Lk 11:13; Mt 26:41 pp Mk 14:38 pp Lk 22:46; Jn 16:24; Ac 4:29–31; Eph 6:18; 1Th 5:17; Jas 1:5

Focusing on Jesus Christ Heb 3:1 *See also* Mt 11:29; Jn 13:15; Ro 15:5; Php 2:5; Heb 12:2–3; 1Pe 2:21; 1Jn 2:6

The role of the Holy Spirit in spiritual growth
Eph 3:16–18 *See also* Eph 1:13–14,17; 2:19–22

Christian leadership Eph 4:11–13 *See also* 1Co 4:16; 11:1; Php 1:25; 3:17; Heb 13:7,17; 1Pe 5:2–3

Faith in God Eph 6:16 *See also* Heb 11:6; 1Jn 5:4

Suffering and testing Ro 5:3–4 *See also* Job 23:10; Ps 119:67; Zec 13:9; Heb 12:10–11; 1Pe 1:6–7; Jas 1:2–4

Perseverance Heb 12:1 *See also* Php 3:12–14; 1Ti 4:15

Cultivating wholesome thinking Php 4:8

God will bring the spiritual growth of believers to completion
1Jn 3:2 *See also* Eph 5:25–27; Php 1:6; Jude 24–25; Rev 21:2

See also
1613 Scripture, purpose	8020 faith
4480 milk	8131 guidance, results
5051 responsibility	8207 commitment
5840 eagerness	8459 perseverance
7966 spiritual gifts	8602 prayer

teachableness

A quality in those who desire to learn, present in the disciples of Jesus Christ and seen in Christ's relationship to his Father. Unwillingness to receive the truth leads to spiritual darkness.

The importance of teachableness
For spiritual growth Heb 12:5–12 *See also* Heb 5:11–14

For a life of obedience Php 4:9 *See also* Jas 1:25; Rev 3:3

For discerning God's guidance Pr 3:5–6 *See also* Ps 25:4–5; Ro 12:2

The requirements for teachableness
Eagerness to learn Pr 18:15; Isa 50:4–5 *See also* 2Ch 26:3–5; Ps 27:11; 43:3; 86:11; 119:9–11; 139:23–24; 143:8–10

Willingness to learn
From God: Ex 15:26; Dt 5:27
From God's representatives: Ex 20:18–19; Dt 18:15; 31:12; Ne 8:3,9
From godly parents: Ps 34:11; Pr 4:10–13,20–21; 8:32–33; 13:1; 23:22–23
From the wise: Pr 1:5; 19:20; 22:17; 25:12
From Jesus Christ: Mt 12:42 pp Lk 11:31; Mt 17:5 pp Mk 9:7 pp Lk 9:35; Jn 10:27
From the Holy Spirit: Lk 12:11–12; Rev 2:7

Readiness to ask for help Ac 8:30–31 *See also* Mk 4:10; 9:11,28; 10:10; 13:4; Lk 3:12; 11:1

Readiness to pray for wisdom Jas 1:5 *See also* 2Ch 20:12; Ps 143:8–10

Readiness to pray for spiritual insight Eph 1:17–19 *See also* Eph 3:16–19; Col 1:9

Humility 1Co 3:18–20 *See also* Job 6:24; Pr 11:2; Mt 11:29; 18:3–4; 1Co 8:1–2; Jas 1:21

Living by truth already known Jn 8:31–32 *See also* 2Pe 1:5–8

Jesus Christ was willing to be taught by the Father
Jn 15:15 *See also* Jn 5:30; 8:26–28

Hindrances to teachableness
The activity of the devil 2Co 4:4 *See also* 2Ti 2:25–26

Not having the Holy Spirit 1Co 2:14

Unwillingness to be taught Isa 48:17–18 *See also* Ps 32:9; 81:11–12; Mt 13:14–15 pp Mk 4:12 pp Lk 8:10; Isa 6:9–10; Lk 11:52 *The "key to knowledge" is the fulfilment of the OT Scriptures in Jesus Christ;* Lk 16:31; 19:41–44; Jas 1:22–24

Reliance on the wisdom of the world 1Co 1:19–20 *See also* Isa 29:14; Ro 1:21–23; 2Co 10:4–5

Being afraid to ask questions Mk 9:32 pp Lk 9:45

See also
4120 Satan	7793 teachers
5133 blindness	7797 teaching
5302 education	8313 nurture
6178 hardness of heart	8330 receptiveness
6604 acceptance, human	8361 wisdom

thankfulness

Heartfelt gratitude to God, expressed in response to his love and mercy.

Thankfulness for God's goodness
Ps 100:4–5 *See also* 1Ch 16:8,34–35; 2Ch 7:3–6; Ezr 3:10–11; Ps 68:19; 106:1; 116:12–14; 136:1–3,26; Isa 63:7; 1Th 5:18; Heb 12:28

Thankfulness for deliverance
From adversity Ps 35:9–10 *See also*

Ps 31:7–8,21–23; 44:6–8; 66:8–9,16–20; 103:1–5

From slavery in Egypt Ex 15:20–21 *See also* Ex 15:1–18; Ps 105:1–45; 136:1–26

From the power of death 1Co 15:53–57

Thankfulness for answered prayer
1Sa 2:1–10 *See also* Ps 30:1–12; 66:16–20; 138:1–5; Jn 11:40

Thankfulness for others
Phm 4 *See also* Ne 11:17; Ro 1:8; Php 4:6; Col 1:10; 4:2; 1Ti 2:1; 2Ti 1:3

Thankfulness for Jesus Christ
2Co 9:15 *See also* Lk 2:25–32,36–38; Col 2:6; 3:15–17

Thankfulness for God's provision
Mt 14:19 pp Mk 6:41 pp Lk 9:16 pp Jn 6:11 *See also* Mt 15:36 pp Mk 8:6; Mt 26:26–27 pp Mk 14:22–23 pp Lk 22:17–19; Lk 24:30; Ac 27:35; Ro 14:6; 1Ti 4:3

Means of expressing thankfulness to God
In song Eph 5:19–20 *See also* Ps 69:30; 95:2; 96:1; Isa 55:12

In music Ps 27:6; 92:1–3

In dance Ps 149:3

In worship Ps 95:2; 100:4; Heb 12:28

See also
4019 life, believers' experience	8614 prayer, answers
5287 dance	8627 worship, elements
5420 music	
5889 ingratitude	8644 commem- oration
7476 thank-offering	
7963 song	8664 praise
8445 hospitality	8676 thanksgiving

tolerance

The virtue of being prepared to accept people and their viewpoints. While commended within the church, Scripture insists that believers must have a vital concern for maintaining and defending the truth.

Toleration should be exercised for the benefit of those whose faith is weak
Ro 14:1 *See also* Ro 14:2–6,13–22; 1Co 8:8–13

Examples of tolerance
By Jesus Christ: Mt 19:13–14 pp Mk 10:13–14 pp Lk 18:15–16 *in contrast to the disciples' intolerance;* Mk 9:33–36 pp Lk 9:46–47; Mk 9:38–40 pp Lk 9:49–50 Php 1:17–18 *by Paul*

Limits to toleration
Evil cannot be tolerated Hab 1:13

Wickedness cannot be tolerated Rev 2:2

Serious doctrinal errors cannot be tolerated Gal 2:4; 2Th 2:1–3 *See also* 1Ti 6:3–5,20–21; 2Ti 4:3–4; 2Pe 2:1

Sexual sin should not be tolerated 1Co 5:1–5; 6:18–20; Rev 2:14

Idolatry should not be tolerated 1Co 10:7; 1Jn 5:21

See also

1095	God, patience of	6602	acceptance
1460	truth	8026	faith, growth in
5661	brothers	8282	intolerance
5762	attitudes, God to people	8298	love for one another
6237	sexual sin	8318	patience

8354

trustworthiness

That quality of truthfulness and dependability which rewards faith. God is trustworthy and his people are called to be trustworthy in their dealings with other people. Scripture warns against pinning one's hopes on people and things that will prove untrustworthy.

God is trustworthy
God's words are trustworthy 2Sa 7:28 *See also* Ps 19:7; 111:7; Da 2:45; 1Ti 1:15; 4:9–10; Rev 21:5

God rewards trust in him Ps 22:4–5 *See also* Ps 20:6–8; 21:7; 125:1; Isa 25:9; 2Ti 1:12

Qualities of those who are trustworthy
Integrity in business dealings Dt 25:13–16 *See also* Lev 19:36; Pr 11:1; 20:23; Hos 12:7; Mic 6:11

Honesty in handling money 2Ki 12:15 *See also* 2Ki 22:7; Lk 16:10–12

Not corrupted by greed Ex 18:21 *Qualities of the elders appointed by Moses. See also* 1Sa 8:3; Pr 13:11; Eze 28:18; 1Ti 3:8

Ability to keep confidences Pr 11:13 *See also* Pr 20:19; 25:9

Truthfulness Pr 12:17 *See also* Pr 16:13; Zec 8:16–17; Eph 4:15,25 Pr 13:17 *See also* Pr 24:26; 25:13; 27:6

Faithfulness with what is entrusted Lk 12:48 *See also* Mt 25:14–27 pp Lk 19:12–23 1Co 4:1–2 *See also* 1Co 9:17; 1Ti 6:20; 2Ti 1:14; Jude 3

Trustworthiness required in leaders
1Pe 5:2–3 *See also* 1Ti 3:11 *trustworthiness also required in wives of deacons (NIV text) or deaconesses (NIV footnote);* Tit 1:7

Examples of people considered trustworthy
Ge 39:6 *Joseph;* Nu 12:7 *Moses;* 1Sa 27:12 *David. Though trusted by Achish, David was deceiving him;* 2Ki 22:5–7 pp 2Ch 34:10–12 *those supervising work on the temple;* Ne 13:13 *Nehemiah's treasurers;* Da 6:4 *Daniel;* Ac 12:20 *Blastus, Herod's treasurer;* 1Th 2:4 *Paul, approved by God*

People proving to be untrustworthy
Isa 2:22; Jer 17:5; Eze 16:15

Oneself Ps 49:13; Pr 28:26

People in positions of power Ps 146:3; Isa 20:5

Friends and family Ps 27:10; 41:9; Jer 9:4; 38:22; Mic 7:5

Things proving to be untrustworthy
Job 15:31 *See also* Job 8:13–19

Fortifications Dt 28:52; Jer 5:17

Military strength Ps 20:7; 44:6; Isa 31:1; Lk 11:22

Wealth Job 31:24; Ps 52:7; Pr 11:28; Jer 48:7; Lk 12:15–20

Idols Isa 42:17; Jer 13:25; Hab 2:18

Deceptive words Ps 5:9; Jer 7:4,8; 28:15

See also

1035	God, faithfulness	8252	faithfulness, relationships
1460	truth	8275	honesty
5412	money	8304	loyalty
5556	stewardship	8331	reliability
5973	unreliability	8808	riches
8031	trust, importance		

8355

understanding

God-given perception of the nature and meaning of things, resulting in sound judgment and decision-making; in particular the ability to discern spiritual truth and to apply it to human disposition and conduct.

The source of understanding
Understanding belongs to God Job 12:13; Ps 136:5 *See also* Ps 147:5; Pr 3:19; Jer 51:15; 15:15 *God's understanding gives rise to compassion.*

Understanding is a gift from God Pr 2:6; Isa 29:24 *See also* 1Ki 4:29; Job 38:36; Isa 32:3–4; Da 1:17; 2:21,30; 9:22; Ro 15:21; Isa 52:15

Understanding spiritual truth
Understanding truth about God 1Jn 5:20 *See also* Pr 2:5; 9:10; Isa 40:21,28; 43:10; Jer 9:24; Jn 10:38; Ro 1:20

Understanding God's purposes Dt 9:6 *God's reason for choosing Israel;* 1Ch 28:19 *God's plans for the temple;* Job 34:10–11 *the reason for Job's suffering;* Ps 73:16–17 *God's dealings with the wicked;* Isa 57:1–2 *God's purpose in taking the righteous;* Jer 9:12–13 *the reason for the exile God's purpose in bringing judgment:* Jer 23:20; 30:24 Da 8:15–16 *God's purposes in history God's will regarding his people:* Eph 5:17; Col 1:9

Understanding God's word Ps 119:73; Lk 24:45 *See also* Ne 8:8,12; Ps 119:27,125; Mt 24:15 pp Mk 13:14; Lk 24:27; Ac 8:30–31; Jn 12:16

Understanding Jesus Christ's teaching Mt 13:11 pp Mk 4:11 pp Lk 8:10; Mt 16:12; 17:13; Mk 4:33; 8:17; Jn 2:22

Understanding God's salvation
Eph 1:18 *See also* Isa 41:20; Ro 13:11; Eph 1:9; 3:4,17–19; Col 2:2; Phm 6

Human understanding is limited
Job 36:26; 37:5; Pr 3:5 *See also* Job 26:14; 36:29; 42:3; Pr 20:24; Ecc 11:5; Isa 40:13–14; 55:8–9; 1Co 13:12

Gaining understanding
Through faith Heb 11:3 *See also* Mt 16:8–9

Through God's Spirit 1Co 2:12 *See also* 1Ch 28:12; Job 32:8; Isa 11:2; Jn 14:26; 16:13–15; 1Co 2:14; Eph 1:17

Through God's word Ps 119:130 *See also* Dt 4:6; Ps 111:10; Da 9:2; Jn 20:9

Through wise teaching Ps 49:3 *See also* Job 8:8–10; Pr 1:2; 4:1; 15:32; Ecc 12:9

Lack of understanding of spiritual truth
Not knowing God Isa 1:3 *See also* Dt 32:28–29; Isa 27:11; Jer 4:22; Ro 10:19; Dt 32:21

Lack of understanding due to hardened hearts Dt 29:4 ; Isa 6:9–10 *See also* Job 17:4; Isa 44:18; 48:8; Jer 5:21; Eze 12:2; Mt 13:13–15 pp Mk 4:11–12 pp Lk 8:10; Mk 6:52; Jn 12:40; Ac 28:26–27; Eph 4:18

Not understanding God's purposes Ps 82:5; 92:6–7; Isa 5:13; 19:12; Mic 4:12; Lk 12:56; 1Co 2:8

Not understanding Jesus Christ's teaching Mt 13:19 *By Jesus Christ's disciples:* Mk 4:13; 9:32; Jn 4:32–33; 8:27; 11:13; 16:18 Lk 2:50 *by Jesus Christ's parents By some Jews:* Jn 2:20–21; 6:51–52; 8:43 Jn 4:11 *by the Samaritan woman*

Understanding people and situations
1Ch 12:32; Est 1:13; Job 13:1; Pr 20:5; Jn 7:24

Understanding languages
Ge 11:7; Dt 28:49; Ps 81:5; Isa 36:11; Ac 2:6; 1Co 14:2

Those who have understanding
The wise Dt 32:29; 1Ki 4:29; Pr 8:14; Hos 14:9

Good leaders Jer 3:15 *See also* Dt 1:13; 1Ch 22:12; 2Ch 30:22; Pr 28:2 *Bad leaders, by contrast, lack judgment:* Pr 28:16; Isa 56:11

The results of understanding
Seeking God Ps 14:2 *See also* Ps 53:2; Ro 3:11

Obedience Ps 119:34 *See also* Ne 10:28; Ps 32:9; 119:100; Pr 28:7

Taking the right path Pr 2:9 *See also* Ps 119:104; Pr 15:21

Life Ps 119:144; Pr 16:22

Sensible living Job 28:28 *avoidance of evil;* Pr 11:12 *slowness to criticise;* Pr 12:11 *conscientious labour;* Pr 13:15 *winning favour;* Pr 17:27 *showing restraint and an even temper;* Jas 3:13 *good deeds and humility*

The results of a lack of understanding
Foolish behaviour Pr 6:32 *committing*

adultery; **Pr** 7:7 *being easily seduced;*
Pr 17:18 *making rash commitments;*
Pr 18:1–2 *selfishness and self-importance;*
Pr 24:30–31 *idleness leading to ruin;*
Hos 4:11 *Drunkenness clouds
understanding.*

Death Pr 10:21; 21:16; **Hos** 4:14

See also

1441 revelation,	8226 discernment
necessity	8281 insight
1614 Scripture,	8319 perception,
understanding	spiritual
5026 knowledge	8361 wisdom
5036 mind of God	8419 enlightenment
6694 mystery	8755 folly
7730 explanation	

8356

unselfishness

Putting the concerns and interests of
others before one's own. Jesus Christ
was the supreme example of this and
believers should follow his example,
denying themselves in order to serve
others.

The supreme example of selflessness is that of Jesus Christ himself

In his life and work **Jn** 5:30 ; **Ro** 15:3 *See
also* **Mt** 15:32; **Jn** 13:3–5; **2Co** 8:9

In his dying for others **Mt** 20:26–28
pp **Mk** 10:43–45 **Php** 2:5–8 *See also*
Isa 53:3–12; **Jn** 10:17–18; **Ro** 5:6–8;
1Co 15:3; **2Co** 5:14; **1Th** 5:10;
1Pe 2:22–24; 3:18; **1Ti** 2:6

Unselfishness is a result of a relationship with Jesus Christ

Christian discipleship begins with a
denial of self-interest **Mt** 16:24
pp **Mk** 8:34 pp **Lk** 9:23 **Mk** 10:45 *See also*
Ro 6:6; **2Co** 5:15; **Eph** 4:22; **Col** 3:9

It springs from an experience of life
with Jesus Christ **Php** 1:21–24 *See also*
Php 3:7–11

It is inspired by the example of Jesus
Christ **Php** 2:4–5 *See also* **Jn** 13:14–15;
1**Jn** 3:16; 4:19–21

It is the result of the Spirit's work in the
believer **Gal** 5:22–26

Putting others first is fundamental in Christian behaviour

Ro 12:10 ; **1Co** 10:23–24 *This was
particularly so when it came to the exercise
of personal scruples. See also* **Ro** 14:7;
15:1–2; **1Co** 8:9; **Eph** 4:32–5:2;
Col 3:13; **1Ti** 6:18

Unselfishness involves a proper attitude to one's own self-importance

Php 2:3 *See also* **Ro** 12:16; **Gal** 6:2–3;
Eph 4:2; 5:21; **1Pe** 3:8; 5:5

Unselfishness is expressed in Christian service

Lk 22:26; **Gal** 5:13 *See also* **1Pe** 4:10; 5:2

Examples of unselfish behaviour

Those who put others first **Ge** 13:8–9
Abraham; **Ex** 32:31–32 *Moses;*
Ru 1:16–17 *Ruth;* **1Sa** 12:3–5 *Samuel;*

Ne 5:14–18 *Nehemiah;* **Mk** 12:41–44 *a
poor widow;* **Mt** 15:21–28 *a mother;*
Mt 26:6–13 pp **Mk** 14:3–9 *a woman with
a jar of perfume;* **Jn** 3:27–30 *John the
Baptist;* **Ac** 4:32–37 *the first Christians;*
Ro 16:3–4 *Priscilla and Aquila;*
1Co 16:15 *the household of Stephanas;*
Php 2:20–21 *Timothy;* **Php** 2:29–30
Epaphroditus

Paul's ministry was motivated by the interests of others **1Co** 10:32–33; 11:1

See also **Ac** 20:33–35;
1Co 9:3–15,19–23; **2Co** 11:23–29;
13:4; **Php** 2:17; **1Th** 2:8–9,19–20

See also

2339 Christ, example	8292 love
of	8305 meekness
5959 submission	8342 servanthood
7733 leaders	8475 self-denial
8260 generosity	8481 self-sacrifice
8276 humility	8827 selfishness
8291 kindness	

8357

weakness

A lack of strength, whether physical
or spiritual. Scripture attributes
weakness to human sin and
foolishness and urges believers to
find their true strength in God alone.

8358
weakness, physical

Lack of human strength may have a
number of causes. Believers should
be caring and compassionate
towards the weak.

Causes of human physical weakness

Sin **Ro** 8:3 *See also* **Ps** 90:10; **Ro** 5:6;
Heb 5:2

Divine action **Ge** 32:25 *Through
wrestling with God, Jacob carried a
physical reminder for the rest of his life. See
also* **Ge** 32:32; **Heb** 11:21

Disobedience **Jdg** 16:20 *See also*
Jdg 16:7,11,13,17; **Job** 18:7; **Eze** 7:17;
21:7; **1Co** 11:30

Satanic action **2Co** 12:7 *See also*
Isa 14:12; **Mk** 9:17–18; **Lk** 13:11

Disease or disability **Ps** 6:2; 31:9–10;
Jn 5:7; **Gal** 4:13–14

Weakness from birth **Ac** 3:2

Weakness in old age **Ge** 27:1 *See also*
2Sa 19:34–37; **1Ki** 1:1

Persecution **2Co** 11:30 *See also*
Nu 11:14–15; **1Ki** 19:3–6; **Mt** 26:38;
27:32 *The physical weakness of Jesus
Christ after flogging led to Simon carrying
the cross;* **Ac** 14:19–20; **1Co** 2:3
Weakness and fear are often associated;
2Co 11:23–29

Being faced with opposition **Nu** 13:18;
2Sa 3:29; **Ne** 6:9

Corporate weakness

2Ch 20:12 *See also* **Lev** 26:36; **Jdg** 6:15;
2Sa 3:1; **La** 1:6

Believers' responsibility to the weak

Ac 20:35 *See also* **Ps** 41:1; **Eze** 34:4;
Ro 14:1; 15:1; **1Co** 8:9; 9:22; **1Th** 5:14

The weakness of God

2Co 13:4 *See also* **1Co** 1:25; **Heb** 4:15

See also

5296 disabilities	5725 old age
5297 disease	5956 strength,
5310 exploitation	human
5347 injustice	6154 fall, the
5480 protection	6163 faults
5582 tiredness	8754 fear

8359
weakness, spiritual

Human standards of strength and
weakness are overturned by God's
perspective and may be used for his
glory.

Spiritual weakness leads to increased reliance on God

2Co 12:10 *See also* **Mt** 26:41
pp **Mk** 14:38; **Ro** 4:19; **1Co** 1:27–29;
2:2–5

Weakness demonstrates the power of God

1Co 1:27 *See also* **Isa** 40:29–31; 50:4;
Jer 31:25; **2Co** 12:5–10

God helps those who are weak

Ro 8:26 *See also* **Isa** 40:29; **Eze** 34:16;
Joel 3:10; **Heb** 11:34

Spiritual weakness should not be despised

Ro 15:1 *See also* **Mt** 26:41 pp **Mk** 14:38;
Ro 14:1; **1Co** 4:10; 8:7–12; 9:22

Overcoming spiritual weakness

The importance of overcoming
weakness **Heb** 12:12 *See also* **Jos** 1:6–7;
Joel 3:10; **Mt** 6:28–33; **1Co** 16:13;
Heb 11:11

Weakness can be overcome by
trusting in God **Ro** 4:20 *See also* **Mt** 8:26;
14:30–31; **2Ti** 1:6–8; **Jas** 1:6

See also

1045 God, glory of	6671 grace &
1180 God, wisdom of	Christian life
3030 Holy Spirit,	8026 faith, growth in
power	8030 trust
3221 Holy Spirit &	8224 dependence
prayer	8353 tolerance
5450 poverty,	
spiritual	
6253 temptation,	
avoiding	
causing	

8361

wisdom

The quality of knowledge,
discernment and understanding
characteristic of God himself. True
wisdom, seen in the ministry of Jesus
Christ, is a gift of the Holy Spirit.
Scripture affirms that true human
wisdom is a gift from God and points
out the folly of trusting in mere
human wisdom.

8362
wisdom, of God
See 1180 God, wisdom of

8363
wisdom, of Jesus Christ
See 2081 Jesus Christ, wisdom of

8364
wisdom, of Holy Spirit
See 3050 Holy Spirit, wisdom of

8365
wisdom, nature of human

The human quality which enables
the planning and successful
achievement of a desired goal. It may
be expressed as technical skill,
practical instruction and astuteness
in political affairs. True wisdom
includes spiritual discernment and,
above all, the reverence and
knowledge of God.

Wisdom as human skill
For work on the tabernacle Ex 36:1 *See
also* Ex 28:3 *making the priestly robes;*
Ex 31:2–6 pp Ex 35:30–35
*craftsmanship and design in metalwork,
stone, wood, embroidery and weaving;*
Ex 35:25–26 *spinning;* Ex 36:8 *making
and hanging curtains*

For work on the temple 1Ch 22:15 *See
also* 1Ch 28:21; 2Ch 2:7,13–14
pp 1Ki 7:13–14 *Huram-Abi, skilled in
bronze work*

Other skills
Making idols: Isa 40:20; Jer 10:9
Jer 9:17 *professional mourning;*
Eze 27:8–9 *seamanship*

Wisdom as instruction in practical living
Pr 14:8; Ecc 12:11 *See also* Pr 6:6;
10:5,8–9; 19:11; 20:1; 21:20; 29:11;
Ecc 7:7; 10:12

Wisdom as political astuteness
Wisdom brings political success
Pr 21:22; Ecc 9:14–15; Isa 10:13;
Eze 28:4–5

Wisdom in giving political advice
Ge 41:8; Est 1:13; Isa 19:11; Jer 51:57;
Da 4:6; 5:8; Ob 8
David's counsellors: 1Ch 26:14;
27:32–33

Wisdom in government Ge 41:33–36;
2Sa 14:20; 1Ki 5:12; Da 2:48

Wisdom associated with mystic arts
Ge 41:8; Ex 7:11; Ps 58:5; Da 2:7; 5:7,11

Wisdom as spiritual discernment
Understanding the plan of God
Ge 41:39 *See also* Jer 9:12; Rev 13:18;
17:9

Understanding God's ways Hos 14:9
See also Job 11:6; Ps 107:43; Da 12:10

Wisdom expressed in a right relationship with God
**Wisdom as reverent submission to
God** Job 28:28 *See also* Ps 111:10; Pr 1:7;
3:7; 9:10; Ecc 12:13; Mic 6:9

Wisdom as the knowledge of God
Pr 30:3; Isa 11:2 *See also* Eph 1:17;
Col 1:9

**Wisdom as obedience to God's
command** Dt 4:6 *See also* Ps 119:34,73

Wisdom personified
Wisdom calls out an invitation
Pr 8:1–4; 9:1–6

Wisdom teaches what is right
Pr 8:5–21

Wisdom existed before creation
Pr 8:22–32

Human wisdom can be opposed to God
1Co 1:18–25 *See also* 1Co 4:10

See also

1020 God, all-knowing	5531 skill
4813 depth	5894 intelligence
5029 knowledge of God	5922 prudence
5033 knowledge of good & evil	5948 shrewdness
5481 proverb	8281 insight
	8319 perception, spiritual
	8355 understanding

8366
wisdom, source of human

True wisdom belongs to God and
may be given by him alone. It
cannot be received by those who put
confidence in worldly wisdom which
is based upon human cleverness and
insight without God's revelation and
which will come to nothing.

True wisdom comes from God
It is given by God alone Job 12:13 *See
also* Ex 28:3; Job 38:36; Ecc 2:26;
Jas 3:17

It is received through God's word
Ps 19:7 *See also* Ps 119:99–100,130;
Ecc 8:5; Jer 8:8–9; Hos 4:6; Mt 7:24;
Col 3:16; 2Ti 3:15

**It is received through submission to
God** Pr 15:33 *See also* Isa 33:6

It is imparted by God's Spirit Eph 1:17
See also Ex 31:3 pp Ex 35:31; Job 32:8;
Da 4:18; 5:14; Ac 6:3,10; 1Co 12:8;
Eph 3:5

It is given in response to prayer Jas 1:5
See also 1Ki 3:9 pp 2Ch 1:10; Pr 2:3–6;
Da 10:12; Col 1:9

The emptiness of worldly wisdom
Worldly wisdom is foolishness to God
1Co 3:19–20 *See also* Job 5:13; Ps 94:11;
Ro 1:21–23

**God cannot be known by worldly
wisdom** 1Co 1:21 *See also* Ecc 8:16–17;
Isa 55:9; Ro 11:33–34; 1Co 1:17;
2:4–5,11–13

**Worldly wisdom builds pride and false
hope** Isa 47:10 *See also* Pr 3:7; 26:12;
28:11; Isa 5:21; Jer 9:23; Col 2:23
*Paul uses irony to condemn the "wisdom"
in which the Corinthians take pride:*
1Co 4:10; 2Co 11:18–19

Worldly wisdom will be confounded
Isa 29:14 *See also* 1Co 1:19–20;
Job 5:12–13; Pr 21:30; Isa 19:11; 44:25;
Jer 51:57; Eze 28:6–7,17; 1Co 1:25

The revelation of divine wisdom
It is revealed in Jesus Christ
1Co 1:23–24 *God's wisdom, which is
hidden from those who rely on human
wisdom, is the message of Christ crucified.
See also* 1Co 1:30; 2:6–8; Col 1:15–17

It is rejected by the worldly-wise
1Co 2:14 *See also* 1Co 1:18,22–23

It is revealed to the unlearned Mt 11:25
pp Lk 10:21; 1Co 3:18 *God's wisdom
may be received only by those willing to
give up all reliance on their own human
insight and understanding. See also*
1Co 1:26–27

It is revealed through the church
Eph 3:10

**God-given wisdom is superior to
worldly wisdom** Lk 21:15 *See also*
Ge 41:15; Ex 7:11–12; 1Ki 4:30;
Da 1:20; 5:7; Ac 6:10

See also

1180 God, wisdom of	5118 Solomon
1439 revelation	5191 thought
2045 Christ, knowledge of	5441 philosophy
	5457 power, human
2081 Christ, wisdom	8674 study
3050 Holy Spirit, wisdom	8755 folly
3281 Holy Spirit, inspiration	

8367
wisdom, importance of human

True wisdom may bring material
reward but its value far exceeds
earthly riches. To those who receive
it, it opens a path to life and security
and equips for leadership and right
conduct.

The supreme value of true wisdom
It is priceless Pr 4:7 *See also* Pr 3:13;
8:10–11

It leads to life Pr 15:24 *See also* Pr 11:30;
13:14; 16:22; 24:14; Da 12:3

It brings prosperity Pr 8:18 *The benefits
of wisdom may include material prosperity,
but more important is the moral and
spiritual prosperity which it brings. See also*
Pr 3:1–2; 19:8,8; 21:20–21; 24:3;
Jer 10:21

It gives security Pr 4:6 *See also* Pr 1:33;
2:6–11; 14:3; 28:26; Ecc 8:5

The application of wisdom
It touches the whole person 1Ki 3:12 *In
Hebrew, the "heart" represents the centre
of human personality. See also* Job 38:36;
Ps 51:6; Pr 2:2; 16:23; 22:17

It results in right action Col 4:5;
Jas 3:13 *See also* Ps 119:34; Pr 1:3; 4:11;
15:21; 23:19; Jer 4:22; Hos 14:9;
Ro 16:19; Eph 5:15; Col 1:9–10;
Jas 3:14–17

It results in watchfulness Mt 25:1–10
See also Pr 14:8; 22:3 pp Pr 27:12

Wisdom is necessary for leaders
Wisdom to govern Pr 8:15–16; Ac 6:3
See also Dt 1:13; 1Ki 5:7; 1Ch 22:12;

Ps 2:10; 105:22; **Pr** 28:2; **Ecc** 1:16; Isa 56:11; **Jer** 3:15

Wisdom to administer justice 1Ki 3:28
See also 1Ki 3:9 pp 2Ch 1:10; Ps 37:30; Pr 20:26; 24:23; Mt 24:45 pp Lk 12:42; 1Co 6:5

The teaching of wisdom
The wise give instruction Ecc 12:9 *See also* Ps 37:30; 49:3; Pr 1:20–21; 5:1; 8:1; 16:21; 31:26; Da 11:33; 1Co 2:6–7; Col 1:28; 3:16

The wise listen to instruction Pr 1:5; 15:31 *See also* Pr 4:1; 9:9; 10:8; 13:20; 15:12; 19:20

Examples of those endowed with wisdom
Ac 7:10 *Joseph;* **Dt** 1:15 *the elders of Israel;* Dt 34:9 *Joshua*
David: 2Sa 14:20; Ps 78:72
Solomon: 1Ki 3:16–28; 4:29–34; 10:4–8 pp 2Ch 9:3–7; 1Ch 22:12–13; Mt 12:42 pp Lk 11:31
Ezr 7:25 *Ezra;* Isa 11:2 *the Messiah;*
Da 1:17 *Daniel and his three friends*
Daniel: Da 2:19–23,27–28; 5:11–12
2Pe 3:15 *Paul*

See also

5035 mind	8305 meekness
5725 old age	8463 priority of faith,
5852 experience	hope & love
5903 maturity,	8492 watchfulness,
physical	leaders
7733 leaders	8701 affluence
7793 teachers	8808 riches
8226 discernment	

8369

worthiness

Only God truly merits honour and praise but he graciously considers those who humbly serve him with wholehearted devotion to be worthy disciples.

God the Father is worthy of honour and praise
Ps 145:3 *See also* Ps 22:4 pp Ps 18:3; 1Ch 16:25 pp Ps 96:4; Ps 48:1; Rev 4:11

Jesus Christ is worthy of honour and praise
Rev 5:12 *See also* Mt 3:17 pp Mk 1:11 pp Lk 3:22; Mt 17:5 pp Mk 9:7 pp Lk 9:35; Php 2:9–11; Heb 2:9; 3:3; 2Pe 1:17; Rev 5:9

People are considered worthy by others
Lk 7:4–5 *Note that the centurion did not consider himself to be worthy (Lk 7:7). See also* Ge 39:4; 41:38–40; 1Sa 16:6; 1Ki 1:42; Da 1:18–20; 2:46–48; 3:28–30; Ac 14:11–13

God considers no person (other than Jesus Christ) to be worthy by nature
Rev 5:4 *See also* Ps 14:3; 143:2; Ecc 7:20; Ro 3:10–12,23

Worthiness, like righteousness, is credited to a person by God
2Th 1:11 *See also* Lk 20:35; Ro 2:29; 2Co 10:18

Examples of people who are considered worthy by God
Those who put God first and deny themselves Mt 10:37–38 *See also* 1Sa 2:30; Lk 9:62; Ro 12:1–2

Those who suffer persecution for the sake of Jesus Christ Ac 5:41 *See also* Mt 5:10–12; 2Th 1:5; 1Pe 2:19–20

Those whose lives show Christlike godliness Col 1:10 *See also* 1Sa 16:7; Eph 4:1–2; 1Th 2:12; 1Ti 3:8–9,11; Tit 2:2; Rev 3:4

Those who stand firm for the gospel Php 1:27; 1Th 2:4; 2Ti 2:15

Those who are faithful in the use of resources which God has given them Mt 25:21–23 *See also* Mt 24:45–47 pp Lk 12:42–44; Lk 19:17; 1Ti 5:17

Those who welcome God's people Mt 10:11 *See also* Mt 10:41–42; Ro 16:2; 3Jn 6

Examples of worthy people
Ge 6:8–9 *Noah;* **Dt** 1:36 *Caleb;* **Dt** 34:10 *Moses;* **Job** 1:8 *Job*
Daniel: Da 9:23; 10:19
Lk 1:28 *Mary;* **Jas** 2:23 *Abraham*

See also

5556 stewardship	8225 devotion
5560 suffering	8248 faithfulness
5878 honour	8354 trustworthi-
5974 value	ness
6603 acceptance,	8445 hospitality
divine	8622 worship
8154 righteousness	8664 praise

8370

zeal

A single-minded desire, characterised by enthusiasm and devotion. In Scripture it is often directed towards God, but God is also credited with zeal for his people and for the honour of his name. Misdirected or inappropriate zeal can degenerate into fanaticism.

Zeal for God
1Ki 19:9–10 *See also* Nu 25:1–13; 1Ki 19:13–14; 2Ki 10:15–28; Pr 23:17

Zeal for God's house
Ps 69:7–9 *See also* Jn 2:13–17

Zeal for God's service
Ro 12:11 *See also* Ne 3:20; 2Co 8:16–22

Zeal for God's law
Ac 21:20 *See also* Ps 119:137–144

Zeal for the nation
2Sa 21:2

God's zeal
Manifested in wrath against sin Isa 42:13 *See also* Nu 25:10–11; Dt 29:18–21; Isa 59:12–19; Eze 5:8–13; 36:5–7; 38:18–23

Manifested in concern for his people Isa 26:11 *See also* 2Ki 19:29–31 pp Isa 37:30–32; Isa 9:1–7; 63:15; Eze 39:25

Misdirected zeal
Pr 19:2 *See also* Ac 21:40–22:5;

Ro 10:1–4; 1Co 13:3; Gal 1:13–14; 4:17–18; Php 3:6

Zeal for national identity: the Zealots
Ac 1:13 *See also* Mt 10:2–4 pp Mk 3:16–19 pp Lk 6:14–16

See also

1185 God, zeal of	7467 temple,
5108 Paul, life of	Solomon's
5375 law	8207 commitment
5832 desire	8223 dedication
5840 eagerness	8239 earnestness
5847 enthusiasm	8248 faithfulness

8400

The tasks of the believer

8401

challenges

God makes demands on his people and, often through spiritual leaders, confronts believers with their sin. He also calls to account false gods and those who exalt themselves against him. The wicked vainly challenge God by questioning his authority, seeking to resist his power and opposing his people.

God's challenge to his people
The challenge to obedience Dt 30:15–18 *See also* Ex 19:5–6; Dt 29:9; Am 5:14–15

The challenge to serve him alone 1Ki 18:21 *See also* Jos 24:14–15; Jer 3:12–14

The challenge to discipleship Mt 16:24–26 pp Mk 8:34–36 pp Lk 9:23–25 *See also* Mt 19:21 pp Mk 10:21 pp Lk 18:22; Lk 9:57–62 pp Mt 8:19–22; Jn 21:17–19

Challenging one another's sin
The call to rebuke and admonish Lk 17:3; Col 3:16 *See also* Lev 19:17; 1Th 5:14; 2Th 3:14–15; 2Ti 4:2; Tit 2:15; 3:10

Sin challenged by spiritual leaders Ne 9:30 *See also* Ne 9:26

Examples of leaders who challenged the sins of others 2Sa 12:1–7 *The prophet Nathan challenges David;* 2Ch 26:18 *Azariah the priest challenges Uzziah;* Eze 16:2 *Ezekiel was called to confront Jerusalem;* Hos 2:2 *Hosea challenges the unfaithfulness of Israel;* Ac 5:3–4 *Peter confronts Ananias;* Gal 2:11–14 *Paul challenges Peter.*

God's sovereignty is unchallengeable
It cannot be questioned Isa 45:9–11 *See also* Job 9:12; Jer 18:6

His purposes cannot be thwarted Isa 14:27 *See also* Job 42:2; Isa 46:10; Da 4:35; 5:21

No-one can stand against him Jer 49:19 *See also* Jer 50:44; 2Ch 20:6; Job 41:10

God's challenge to the wicked
He challenges false gods
1Ki 18:22–24 *See also* Isa 41:1,21–23

He challenges human pride Isa 23:9 *See also* Isa 13:19; Eze 28:2; Da 5:20

Challenges to God and his people
To God Isa 14:13–14; Ac 4:26–27 *See also* Ps 2:2; Ge 3:4–5 *The serpent challenges God's word;* Isa 5:19 *Isaiah's opponents challenge God to do what he has announced.*
The challenge of the antichrist: Da 11:36; 2Th 2:4; Rev 13:5–6
Mt 4:1 pp Mk 1:12–13 pp Lk 4:1–2 *Jesus Christ is tempted by the devil;* Mt 16:22 *Jesus Christ is challenged by Peter;* Jn 8:13 *the Pharisees challenge Jesus Christ*

To God's people 1Sa 17:8–11; Ps 42:10 *See also* Ps 42:3; 79:10; Da 7:25; 8:11; Joel 2:17; Eph 6:10–12 *God's people are equipped to stand against the devil's attacks;* Rev 13:7

Further examples of challenges
Jdg 14:4; 2Ki 14:8 pp 2Ch 25:17

See also

1105 God, power of	5924 quarrel-
1130 God,	someness
sovereignty	5931 resistance
5777 admonition	8114 discipleship
5814 confrontation	8403 commands
5829 defiance	8832 testing

8402

claims

The assertion of rights and recognition due. God as Creator and Redeemer makes claims on his world and on his people. The claims of Jesus Christ about himself as God and Messiah call for a response. In human relationships, too, claims are made by individuals about themselves and, as a result, on others.

The basis for God's claims
God's ownership of the world
Ps 24:1–2 *See also* Dt 10:14; Job 41:11; Ps 47:9; 89:11; Eze 18:4

God owns his people as Creator
Dt 32:6; Isa 43:6–7,15

God owns his people as Redeemer
1Co 6:19–20 *See also* Ex 20:2–3 pp Dt 5:6–7; Lev 25:55; Isa 43:1; Ro 14:8

The priority of God's claims
God's claim to first place Mt 6:33 pp Lk 12:31

God's claim on the firstborn *See also* Ex 13:2; 34:19; Lev 27:26; Nu 3:13; Ne 10:36

God's claim to the firstfruits Dt 26:1–2; Ne 10:35; Pr 3:9

God's claim to the tithe Lev 27:30; Mal 3:8–10

Acknowledging God's claims on human life
Wholehearted devotion to God
Dt 6:4–5 *See also* Mt 22:37 pp Mk 12:30

Obedience to God's law Lev 18:4–5 *See also* Lev 19:37; 22:31; Eze 20:19

The call to holiness Lev 11:45 *See also* Lev 19:2; 20:7,26; 1Pe 1:15–16

Honouring God's name Lev 19:12; 22:32–33

Observing the Sabbath Lev 19:3,30; 26:2; Eze 20:20

Not worshipping idols Lev 19:4; 26:1; Jdg 6:10; Isa 42:8

The claims of Jesus Christ
Jesus Christ's claim to fulfil the OT
Mt 5:17 *See also* Lk 4:17–21; 24:27; Jn 5:39

Jesus' claim to be the Messiah Lk 23:2 *See also* Mt 23:10; Mk 9:41; Lk 22:67; Jn 4:25–26

Jesus Christ's claim to be king of the Jews Mt 27:11 pp Mk 15:2 pp Lk 23:3; Jn 19:12,21

Jesus Christ's claim to divinity
Jn 10:33; 19:7 *See also* Mt 26:63–64 pp Mk 14:61–62 pp Lk 22:70; Mt 27:43; Mk 2:7 pp Lk 5:21 *Forgiveness of sin was recognised as the prerogative of God alone. Jesus Christ's claim to forgive sin is thus a claim to be God;* Jn 10:30; 14:9

Jesus Christ's claim to universal lordship Mt 28:18 *See also* Mt 25:31–32; Lk 22:69; Jn 17:2

The "I am" claims of Jesus Christ
Jn 8:58 *See also* Jn 6:35 *the bread of life;* Jn 8:12 *the light of the world;* Jn 10:7 *the gate for the sheep;* Jn 10:11 *the good shepherd;* Jn 11:25 *the resurrection and the life;* Jn 14:6 *the way and the truth and the life;* Jn 15:1 *the true vine*

The need to acknowledge Jesus Christ's claims Jn 8:24–30 *See also* Jn 14:11

Human claims
Those making claims about themselves Ps 73:9 *the proud boasting of the wicked;* Jer 23:34 *false prophets claim to speak God's word;* Mt 24:5 pp Mk 13:6 pp Lk 21:8 *false Christs;* Ac 5:36 *Theudas;* Ac 8:9 *Simon the sorcerer claimed to be someone great;* Ro 1:22 *idolaters claim to be wise;* Jude 16 *false teachers in the church;* Rev 2:2 *false apostles*

Claims must be verified by actions
Jas 2:14 *See also* Pr 20:6; Tit 1:16; 1Jn 1:6; 2:6,9

Making claims on others 2Sa 15:3 *grievances brought for judgment;* 2Sa 19:43 *Israel's claim on David as their king;* Ne 2:20 *Nehemiah's enemies have no claim on Jerusalem.*

Claims made about others Ps 35:20 *false accusations made against the righteous;* Mt 5:11 pp Lk 6:22 *Believers will be slandered by their enemies;* Lk 11:18–20 pp Mt 12:26–28 *The Jews claim that Jesus Christ's powers are demonic;* Ro 3:8 *slanderous claims made against Paul*

See also

1315 God as	2224 Christ, the
redeemer	Lord
1325 God, the	2312 Christ as king
Creator	4442 firstfruits
2203 Christ, titles of	5688 firstborn
2206 Jesus, the	6121 boasting
Christ	7428 Sabbath
2218 Christ, Son of	8488 tithing
God	

8403

commands

Demands made of his people, or obligations laid upon his people, by God. Scripture stresses that being the people of God involves responsibilities as well as privileges, and sets out the demands which God justly makes of his people.

8404
commands, in OT

The OT sets out the commands of God to his people Israel, indicating both their extent and their importance.

The reason for God's commands: the need to be holy
Lev 11:44–45 *See also* Lev 19:2; 20:7–8,26; 21:8

God's commands to Israel
Dt 5:31–33 *See also* Ex 16:23–24; 17:1; 25:22; 34:32; Nu 9:18–20; Dt 15:11 *The LORD commands generosity and kindness to the poor;* Dt 15:15; 24:17–18,21–22; 2Ch 29:25–26; Ne 8:1; 9:13–14

Demands made by God upon individuals
Ge 2:16–17 *Adam;* Ge 7:16 *Noah;* Ge 21:4 *Abraham*
Aaron: Lev 6:9; Nu 33:38
Nu 24:13 *Baalam*
Joshua: Dt 31:23; Jos 4:16–17
2Sa 5:25 *King David;* 1Ki 3:14 *King Solomon;* 1Ki 18:36 *Elijah*
Jeremiah: Jer 1:7; 26:2
Eze 37:9–10 *Ezekiel*

God's commands to non-human agencies
The universe Ps 33:6–9; 148:4–6

The living creation 2Ch 7:13; Job 39:27; Am 9:3; Jnh 2:10

The non-living creation Job 37:11–12; Ps 78:23–24; Isa 5:6; Jer 31:35

The angels Ps 91:11; 103:20

The sword, symbolising the judgment of God Jer 47:6–7; Am 9:4

Commands of the leaders of God's people
Dt 31:24–26 *Moses;* Jos 1:16–18 *Joshua;* 1Ki 18:40 *Elijah;* Ne 13:22 *Nehemiah*

Commands given by kings
Over Israel and Judah 1Ki 2:46; 1Ch 28:20–21; 2Ch 14:4

Over heathen nations Ge 12:20; Ex 1:22; Ezr 4:3; Est 1:12,15; 2:8; 3:2,13; Da 3:20–22; 5:29

Parental commands
Dt 32:44–46; Pr 3:1; 6:20; 7:1–2

The nature of God's commands
Ps 19:7–10 *See also* 1Ch 16:15; Ps 119:86,96,151,172

God's commands are to be loved

Ps 119:47–48 *See also* 1Ki 8:61;
1Ch 29:19; Job 23:12; Ps 112:1;
119:16,35,127–128,131,143

God's commands are to be obeyed

God commands obedience Ecc 12:13
See also Dt 4:2; 26:16–18; Jos 22:5;
Jer 7:22–23

Warnings against and examples of
disobedience 2Ki 17:13–14 *See also*
1Sa 13:13–14; 1Ki 11:10–11; La 1:18;
Da 9:4–6

The consequences of obedience
Dt 6:1–3 *See also* Ge 26:4–5; Ex 15:26;
Dt 4:1; 8:1; 1Ki 11:38

The consequences of disobedience
1Sa 12:14–15 *See also* Dt 11:26–28;
30:1–3; 1Ki 9:4–9; Ne 1:7–9; Jer 22:4–5

See also

1065 God, holiness of	8453 obedience
5375 law	8718 disobedience
5377 law, Ten Commandments	

8405
commands, in NT

The NT sets out the commands of
God and Jesus Christ for the church.

Commands made by God

Mt 22:36–40 pp Mk 12:28–31 *See also*
Mt 15:3 pp Mk 7:9; Mk 7:8;
Ac 13:46–47; 17:30; Ro 1:32; 1Ti 1:1;
Tit 1:3; 1Jn 3:23; 4:21; 2Jn 4

Commands made by Jesus Christ

In the Gospels Jn 13:34 *See also*
Mt 8:26–27 pp Mk 4:39–41
pp Lk 8:24–25; Mt 28:19–20;
Mk 1:25–27 pp Lk 4:35–36; Mk 5:43
pp Lk 8:56; Mk 9:25; Jn 15:12,17

In the rest of the NT 1Co 9:14 *See also*
Ac 10:42; 1Co 7:10–11; 14:37;
1Th 4:2,16; 2Pe 3:2 *"the command" (see
2Pe 2:21) here refers to Christianity
considered as a body of ethical teaching*

Commands made by the apostles

1Jn 2:7–8 *They received the command to
love at the beginning of their Christian
experience. See also* Ac 10:48; 16:4 *The
Greek word translated "decisions" literally
means "decrees";* Ac 16:18;
2Th 3:4,6,11–12
Paul urged Timothy to command others:
1Ti 1:3–5; 4:11; 6:17–18
1Ti 6:13–14

Obedience to the NT commands

Obedience is a requirement 1Jn 2:3–4
See also Mt 5:19 *"these commandments"
probably refers to the OT law as fulfilled by
Jesus Christ (see Mt 5:17–18);* Mt 19:17;
Lk 17:10; Jn 15:10; 1Co 7:19; 2Pe 2:21;
1Jn 3:21–24; 2Jn 5–6; Rev 14:12

Obedience is an expression of love and
faithfulness Jn 14:21 *See also* Jn 14:15;
15:14; 1Jn 5:2–3; Rev 12:17

Commands given by secular authorities

Mt 8:9 pp Lk 7:8 *the Roman centurion;*
Mt 14:9–10 pp Mk 6:27 *Herod orders the
beheading of John the Baptist;*
Mt 27:64–65; Lk 2:1; Ac 12:19;

16:22–24; 18:2 *Claudius ordered all the
Jews to leave Rome;* Ac 21:34; 23:10,35;
25:6,17,21,23

Commands given by religious authorities

Jn 11:57; Ac 4:15; 5:28,40; 23:2–3

Commands that came through Moses referred to in the NT

Heb 9:19–20 *See also* Mt 8:4
pp Mk 1:44; Mt 19:7–8 pp Mk 10:3–4;
Jn 8:5; Ro 7:8–13; Heb 12:18–21

See also

2333 Christ, attitude to OT	8292 love
5215 authority	8453 obedience
5257 civil authorities	8496 witnessing, importance
6628 conversion, God's demand	

8407
confession, of Jesus Christ

A public declaration of faith in Jesus
Christ, acknowledging both his
divinity and his lordship. Without
such, salvation is impossible.

Confession of faith in Jesus Christ is necessary for salvation

Ro 10:9–10 *See also* Mt 10:32–33
pp Lk 12:8–9; Mk 8:38; 2Ti 2:12;
1Jn 4:15; 2:23

Confessing Jesus Christ as Lord is only possible by the Holy Spirit

1Co 12:3

Results of confessing faith in Jesus Christ

Baptism Ac 2:38–41 *See also* Ac 18:8;
22:16

A change in lifestyle Mt 7:21–23 ;
2Ti 2:19 *See also* Lk 19:8–9; 1Ti 6:12;
Heb 13:15; 1Jn 1:6; 2:4

Persecution Jn 9:22 *See also*
Jn 12:42–43; 2Ti 3:12

Demons confessed Jesus Christ's divinity

Lk 4:41 *See also* Mt 8:28–29 pp Mk 5:7
pp Lk 8:28

Ultimately all will confess Jesus Christ's lordship

Php 2:9–11

Notable confessions of faith in Jesus Christ

Jn 1:49 *See also* Mt 14:33; 16:16
pp Mk 8:29 pp Lk 9:20; Jn 6:69; 11:27;
20:28

The refusal to confess Jesus Christ

Mt 10:32–33 pp Lk 12:8–9 *See also*
2Ti 2:12

See also

2224 Christ, the Lord	6624 confession of sin
2545 Christ, opposition to	7756 preaching, content
3230 Holy Spirit & regeneration	8495 witnessing
6231 rejection of God	8712 denial of Christ
6510 salvation	8794 persecution

8408
decision-making

The ability to arrive at a decision
after due consideration of all the
factors involved. The Christian life
involves making decisions at many
levels. Scripture offers guidance
concerning how such decisions
should be made, and provides
examples of good and bad decision-
making.

8409
decision-making, and providence

People need guidance from God
about how they should make up
their minds on difficult issues. God
gives them this through the Holy
Spirit, the Scriptures, individuals,
groups and other external means.

Decisions should be grounded in a relationship with God

Pr 3:5–6 *See also* Ps 23:1–3;
25:4–5,8–9,12; Pr 9:10 *Wisdom involves
making right moral decisions;* Mt 6:31–33
pp Lk 12:29–31

God guides decision-making

Through Scripture 2Ti 3:16–17 *See also*
Ps 19:7–11; 119:9,11,98–100,
104–105,130
*The temptation of Jesus Christ is a good
example of how Scripture can inform
decision-making:* Mt 4:4 pp Lk 4:4;
Dt 8:3; Mt 4:7 pp Lk 4:12; Dt 6:16;
Mt 4:10 pp Lk 4:8; Dt 6:13

Through supernatural intervention
Ac 18:9 *See also* Ge 28:10–15;
1Sa 16:6–7,12; Isa 30:21; 58:11;
Jer 32:6–9; Ac 9:10–16; 10:9–16;
11:27–30; 21:10–11; 26:19;
1Co 14:29–30

Through prayer Jas 1:5–6 *See also*
1Ki 3:9–12; Pr 2:3–6; Mt 7:7–11
pp Lk 11:9–13; Mt 21:22; Eph 6:18

Through circumstances Ac 6:1–4 *See
also* Nu 13:1–3; Dt 32:28–29;
Jos 2:23–24; Ru 2:2–3; 1Ki 3:26–28;
Ac 15:19–22; 16:3; 20:3,16; 1Co 16:8–9

The work of the Holy Spirit in decision-making

Jn 14:16–17 *See also* Jn 14:26;
16:13–15; Ac 8:29; 10:19; 13:2; 15:28;
16:6–10; 1Jn 2:20,27

Motivation in decision-making

Mt 6:33; Col 3:17 *See also* Ps 139:23–24;
Mt 20:25–28; 23:23; Ro 12:1;
1Co 10:31; 2Co 5:9; Php 4:8–9;
1Th 4:1; 5:8; 1Pe 2:12; 4:11

Humility is essential for divine guidance

Ps 25:9 *See also* Dt 10:12–13; Ps 25:14;
34:9–10; 73:1; 84:11; Isa 58:9–11;
Da 9:20–23

The need to test guidance

1Th 5:19–22

See also

1355 providence	6622 choice
1469 visions	6663 freedom of will
3263 Holy Spirit,	8124 guidance
guidance	8276 humility
5010 conscience,	8412 decisions
matters of	8605 prayer & God's
6248 temptation	will

8410
decision-making, examples of

Scripture provides examples of good and bad decision-making, as well as offering guidance as to how decisions ought to be made.

Examples of good decision-making
Jos 24:15 *See also* Ge 13:8–9; 35:2–4; Ex 18:24–25; 32:26; Ru 1:15–16; 1Sa 14:6–7; 24:4–7; Ne 4:21–23; Est 4:15–16; Ps 27:4; Da 1:8; 3:18; Mt 4:19–20; Mk 2:14 Lk 10:38–42; 19:8; Ac 4:36–37; 5:35–39; Heb 11:25–26

Examples of bad decision-making
Ge 3:6 *See also* Ge 12:10–13; 13:10–11; 16:1–3; Ex 32:1–4; Nu 13:31; 16:1–3; Jos 7:21 *Achan disobeyed the Lord's instructions;* Jdg 8:23–27; 14:3; 16:1; 1Sa 13:8–9 *Saul made the offering in Samuel's absence;* 2Sa 11:2–4; 1Ki 12:8–15 *Rehoboam followed bad advice;* 2Ki 24:1; Hos 2:5; Jnh 1:1–3; Mk 10:22; Lk 15:13; Ac 5:1–2; 24:27; Mt 26:14–16 pp Mk 14:10–11 pp Lk 22:4–6 *Judas decided to betray Jesus Christ for money;* Mk 15:1 pp Mt 27:1–2 *the decision to put Jesus Christ to death*

The sovereignty of God in decision-making
Ge 50:19–20 *See also* Ge 45:8; Nu 24:13 *Balaam could only curse or bless at the Lord's bidding;* Jdg 6:39–40; 14:4; 1Sa 2:25; 2Ch 25:20; Ps 103:13–14; Joel 2:25–26; Mic 7:8–9 *It was God's will that Jesus Christ should suffer:* Ac 2:23–24; 4:27–28 Ro 8:28–30

Decisions have to be made
Dt 30:19–20 *See also* 1Ki 18:21; Eze 18:30; Mt 27:17,21; Mk 10:21; Ac 2:38–40; 16:30–31; 2Co 1:15–17; Gal 3:2

Good decision-making involves consideration for others
Mic 6:8 *See also* Job 31:16–23; Isa 1:17; Jer 22:3; Am 5:14–15; Mt 5:13–16; 25:35–36; Jas 1:27

All decision-making must be subject to the will of God
Jas 4:13–15 *See also* Ps 127:1; Mt 26:39,42; Lk 12:16–21

See also

1130 God,	8361 wisdom
sovereignty	8648 enquiring of
1175 God, will of	God
5925 rashness	8755 folly
8116 discipleship,	
cost	

8412
decisions

The end result of a process of reflection upon possible courses of action, informed and sustained by a concern to please God.

Factors that should affect believers' decision-making
Desire to know God's will Ps 25:4–5 *See also* Ps 143:8; Hos 4:6 *Ignoring God's will leads to destruction;* Jn 10:27; 14:15–17

Confidence in God's readiness to reveal his will Ps 25:8–9 *See also* Ps 16:7; 25:12–14; 48:14; 73:23–24; Pr 3:5–6; Isa 30:19–21; Jer 9:23–24

Belief in God's overall plan for his people Ro 8:28–30 *See also* Eph 1:3–14; Php 2:12–13; Heb 11:39–40

God's promise to guide believers in their decisions Isa 58:11 *See also* Ps 32:8–9; Isa 42:16; 48:17; Jn 14:26; 16:13

Knowledge of scriptural principles Mk 12:29–31 pp Mt 22:35–40 *See also* Dt 6:4–5; Lev 19:18; Ex 20:1–17 pp Dt 5:6–21; Mt 7:12 pp Lk 6:31; Ro 13:9–10; Gal 5:14; Jas 2:8

A willingness to trust God Heb 11:17–19 *See also* Ge 15:4–6; 2Ch 20:20; Ps 25:1–2; 31:5; 143:8; Isa 12:2; Lk 1:45; Ro 4:3,20–24; Gal 2:16,20; Heb 11:1–39

See also

1115 God, purpose	5884 indecision
of	5917 plans
1175 God, will of	6622 choice
2330 Christ as	8020 faith
shepherd	8031 trust,
3130 Holy Spirit,	importance
Counsellor	8124 guidance
3263 Holy Spirit,	8408 decision-
guidance	making

8413
edification

The building up and strengthening in the faith of believers and churches. Believers are strengthened by God and are urged, too, to build up one another. The church is edified through God's word, through the Holy Spirit and the proper use of spiritual gifts, through the church's appointed ministries and through the mutual love, support and encouragement of its members.

God edifies his people by strengthening them
Isa 40:29–31; Eze 34:16 *See also* Ps 29:11; 73:26; Isa 40:11; 41:10; 2Th 2:16–17; 3:3; Heb 13:9

The edification of believers
God builds up the community of faith 1Pe 2:4–5 *See also* Jer 24:6–7; 31:4; 42:10; Eph 2:19–22

Believers are to build themselves up Jude 20 *See also* Col 2:6–7

Believers are to build one another up Ro 15:2 *See also* Ro 14:19; Eph 4:29; Heb 3:13

The means of edification
God's word Ac 20:32 *See also* Ps 119:28; Ro 4:20 *Abraham was strengthened in his faith by his acceptance of God's promise;* Ro 15:4; 2Ti 3:15–17; 1Pe 2:2

The Holy Spirit Eph 3:16 *See also* Ac 9:31

Spiritual gifts 1Co 14:26 *See also* Ro 1:11; 1Co 12:7; 14:3–4,12

Appointed ministries Eph 4:11–12 *Pastors are to build up the flock in their care:* Jer 3:15; 23:4; Eze 34:4; Zec 11:16 *Paul's apostolic commission includes strengthening the churches:* Ac 15:41; 18:23; 2Co 12:19 Ac 16:4–5 *The message from the Jerusalem apostles results in believers being strengthened.* *Paul's apostolic authority is for the building up of the church:* 2Co 10:8; 13:10

Love and encouragement Eph 4:15–16; 1Th 5:11 *See also* Ro 1:12; 14:20–21; 1Co 8:1,10–13; 10:23–24; Heb 12:12–13; Isa 35:3–4

Examples of those who edified others
Dt 3:28 *Moses;* Job 4:3–4 *Job;* Isa 40:1–2 *Isaiah;* Lk 22:32 *Simon Peter;* Ac 14:22 *Paul and Barnabas;* Ac 15:32 *Judas and Silas;* 1Th 3:2 *Timothy;* Phm 7 *Philemon*

The goal of edification
Eph 4:13 *Edification results in spiritual discernment:* Eph 4:14; Php 1:9–10; Heb 5:14 1Th 3:13 *Edification results in right living.*

See also

5240 building	7942 ministry
5902 maturity	7968 spiritual gifts
5954 strength	8347 spiritual
7020 church, the	growth
7110 body of Christ	8414 encourage-
7706 apostles	ment
7756 preaching,	
content	
7925 fellowship	
among	
believers	

8414
encouragement

Giving someone confidence and courage to do something. Scripture encourages believers to trust in God and to rely on the enabling of the Holy Spirit.

8415
encouragement, examples of

Believers can encourage one another to have greater confidence in God and so to be bolder in living out their faith.

In the OT
2Ch 32:6–7 *King Hezekiah encourages his people. See also* Jdg 20:21–22; 1Sa 23:16; 1Ch 11:10; 2Ch 30:22; 35:2 *King Josiah;* Ne 9:26; Da 2:18; Zec 8:20–22; Mal 3:16

In the NT

Ac 11:22–23; 1Th 2:11–12 *See also*
Ac 4:36; 13:43; 14:21–22 *Paul and
Barnabas*; Ac 15:32; 16:40; 18:27–28;
20:1–2 *after Paul's ministry in Ephesus*;
Ro 1:11–12 *Paul to the church at Rome*;
2Co 7:4,13; Eph 6:21–22 *Paul's fellow-
worker, Tychicus*; Php 1:14 *Paul in prison*;
Col 4:8; 1Th 3:2 *Timothy*; 1Th 3:7;
Phm 7; Heb 13:22; 1Pe 5:12

Encouragement as exhortation in
the life of faith

Col 1:28 *Paul describes his ministry. See
also* Lk 3:18 *John the Baptist*; Ro 12:1;
15:30; 1Co 4:16; 16:15–16; 2Co 2:7–8
dealing with a repentant member; 2Co 6:1;
Eph 4:1; 1Th 4:10; Heb 13:19; 1Pe 2:11;
Jude 3

Commands to encourage others

Isa 35:3–4
To Moses: Dt 1:38; 3:28
2Sa 19:7 *to David*; Isa 1:17; Ro 12:6–8;
15:2; 1Co 14:12; Col 3:16; 1Th 4:18;
5:11,14; 1Ti 5:1; 2Ti 4:2; Tit 1:9 *the
church overseer*; Tit 2:15; Heb 3:13; 10:25

Failure to encourage

Eze 34:4 *Condemnation of Israel's leaders.
See also* Job 16:2; Ps 69:20; Ecc 4:1;
Eze 16:49; Zec 10:2

Refusing to be comforted

Ge 37:34–35 *See also* Ps 77:2; Jer 31:15;
Mt 2:18

Scripture censures those who
encourage others to do evil

2Ch 22:2–3 *See also* 2Sa 11:25 *after
David and Joab had arranged Uriah's
death*; Ps 64:5 *evildoers*; Isa 41:7 *makers
of idols*; Jer 23:14; 29:8; Eze 13:22–23;
1Co 8:9–10

See also

5391 letters	7943 ministry in
5566 suffering,	church
encourage-	8030 trust
ments in	8202 boldness
5805 comfort	8213 confidence
5914 optimism	8219 courage
5954 strength	8713 discourage-
7927 hymn	ment

8416

encouragement, promises of
God's

God promises continual support for
his people, particularly when they
become weary, depressed or
disillusioned.

God's encouragement affirmed

Ps 10:17–18 *See also* 1Ch 29:12;
Ps 89:20–21; Isa 41:10; 49:13; Jer 29:11;
Zec 1:17; Ac 20:32; 1Pe 5:10

Means by which God encourages
believers

Meditation on his law and word
Jos 1:8–9; Ro 15:4 *See also* Ps 1:1–3;
Heb 12:5

Experience of the Holy Spirit
Jn 14:16–17 *The word used for Spirit here
means "Counsellor" or "one who
encourages or comforts". See also* Ac 9:31;
Ro 8:18–27; Php 2:1

Experience of God's
encouragement

2Co 4:16–18 *See also* 1Sa 30:6; Ps 86:17;
Isa 52:9; Da 10:18–19; Ac 9:31; 23:11;
2Co 1:3–4; 2Ti 4:17; Heb 6:18; 12:5;
1Pe 1:3

God's encouragement experienced
through the words and actions of
others Jdg 7:11 *Gideon and the dream of
the Midianite soldier*; 2Ch 15:8; Ezr 6:22
*the returned exiles helped by the king of
Assyria*; Ac 28:15; 2Co 7:4,13

Commands to be encouraged

1Co 16:13 *See also* Dt 31:6–8;
Jos 1:6–8,18; 10:25; 1Ch 22:13; 28:20;
2Ch 19:11; 32:7 *King Hezekiah*; Ezr 10:4;
Ps 27:14; Isa 54:2 *growth of the nation of
Israel after the exile*; Mt 14:27 pp Mk 6:50
Paul to his shipmates: Ac 27:22,25,36

Effects of being encouraged

Isa 40:30–31 *See also* Ps 25:3; Ro 15:5;
1Co 14:3; 2Co 3:12; Php 2:1–2; Col 2:2;
1Th 2:11–12

Prayers for encouragement

2Th 2:16–17 *See also* Ne 6:9; Ps 119:28;
Isa 38:14; Ro 15:5–6; Col 1:10–12

See also

1449 signs, purposes	8413 edification
5691 friends, good	8602 prayer
8144 renewal	9610 hope

8418

endurance

The ability to persevere in a task or
calling. The Christian is called to
endure in the face of trial or
opposition, and his endurance
brings spiritual rewards.

Endurance commended as a
virtue for God's people

Jos 1:7; Gal 6:9 *See also* Dt 5:32;
Jos 23:8; Job 17:9; Ac 11:23; 13:43;
14:22; Eph 4:14; 1Ti 6:11; 2Ti 2:3;
1Pe 2:20; Rev 13:10

Endurance is a hallmark of true
Christian profession

Mt 10:22 pp Mk 13:13 Lk 9:62 *See also*
Ac 20:24; 2Ti 2:12

Christian endurance originates
with God

Ro 15:5 *See also* 2Co 1:8–9;
Col 1:10–11; 2Th 3:5

Christian endurance involves
standing firm

1Co 15:58; Php 1:27 *See also* Gal 5:1;
Php 4:1; 2Th 2:15; 2Ti 3:14; 4:5

The results of enduring

Salvation Heb 10:36; Jas 1:12 *See also*
Ro 2:7; 15:4; 1Ti 4:16; 2Ti 2:10;
Heb 12:7–9

Protection Rev 3:10 *See also* 2Th 3:3–4

Spiritual fruit Jas 1:4 *See also* Lk 8:15;
Ro 5:3–5

Encouragement for others 2Co 1:6 *See
also* 1Pe 5:9; Heb 12:1–3; Rev 1:9

Examples of endurance

Ps 123:3–4; 1Co 4:12; 1Th 1:3; 2Th 1:4;
2Ti 3:10–11; Jas 5:11; Rev 2:3

See also

1340 consistency	8207 commitment
5500 reward, God's	8248 faithfulness
people	8318 patience
5566 suffering,	8459 perseverance
encourage-	8704 apostasy
ments in	8713 discourage-
6251 temptation,	ment
resisting	8794 persecution
8115 discipleship	

8419

enlightenment

The illumination of the mind,
especially by the word of God,
leading to delight and increased
pleasure in God.

Enlightenment as God-given
understanding and insight

Ps 43:3; Mic 7:8–9; Jn 8:12; Eph 1:18
See also 2Sa 22:29; Ezr 9:8; Job 29:2–3;
Ps 18:28; 36:10; 97:11; Isa 9:2; 42:6,16;
49:6; 60:1; Da 2:22; Lk 2:32; Jn 1:9; 9:5;
12:46; Ac 13:47; 26:18,23; 2Co 4:6;
Heb 6:4; 10:32; 1Pe 2:9

Enlightenment through the word
of God

Ps 119:130 *See also* Ps 19:8; Pr 6:23;
Isa 51:4; 2Pe 1:19

God needs no enlightenment

Isa 40:14

See also

1441 revelation,	5026 knowledge
necessity	8281 insight
4811 darkness,	8355 understanding
symbol of sin	8361 wisdom
4835 light, spiritual	

8420

equipping

The providing of all necessary
facilities for achieving a task.
Scripture suggests that God does not
provide tasks for believers without
also providing the gifts which are
needed to equip believers for those
tasks.

8421

equipping, physical

Scripture provides illustrations of
situations in which people are
equipped to carry out physical
actions.

Manual workers are equipped for
their tasks

1Ki 5:13–14 *See also* Ge 4:22; 11:3;
24:15; Ex 25:1–9; 1Ki 5:10; 19:21;
Ezr 1:5–6; Ne 2:7–8

Musicians are equipped to play

Isa 30:29 *See also* Ge 4:21; Jos 6:4;
1Sa 16:16–18; 1Ch 25:6–7; Ps 150:3–5;
Rev 5:8; 15:2

8422

Travellers are equipped for their journeys
2Sa 12:4 *See also* Ge 42:25; 45:19–23;
Ne 2:7; Jer 9:2; Lk 11:6

Those equipped with signs of authority
Ge 41:42 *Joseph*; Ge 49:10; Ex 4:17
Moses; Est 3:10 *Haman*; Est 4:11; 5:2;
Mt 16:19; Ac 9:2

Equipping for burial
Ge 23:8–9; Mk 14:8; Lk 23:56;
Jn 19:38–42

Soldiers are equipped for battle
Israel's armies Ex 13:18 *See also*
Nu 31:5; 32:20–22; Jos 4:13; 6:8;
Jdg 7:16; 1Sa 17:36–39; 1Ki 4:26;
1Ch 12:2; 2Ch 14:8

David 1Sa 17:40 *See also* 1Sa 22:9–10;
2Sa 22:40 pp Ps 18:39

Israel's enemies Ex 14:6–7 *See also*
1Sa 17:5–7; 2Sa 21:16; Jer 6:23; 46:4;
50:42; Da 11:13; Mt 26:47 pp Mk 14:43

Those providing protection are equipped
Ne 4:16–18; Ac 23:23–25

See also

3272 Holy Spirit in OT	5422 musicians
5208 armies	5480 protection
5215 authority	5590 travel
5241 burial	5628 work

8422

equipping, spiritual

Scripture provides examples of
individuals who have been equipped
to carry out tasks or responsibilities
of a spiritual nature.

Jesus Christ was equipped for his work
Isa 61:1–2 *See also* Ps 72:1; Isa 50:4–7;
Mt 12:18; Isa 42:1; Lk 4:18–19; 19:31;
Jn 3:34; Ac 10:38; Heb 10:5

God's people are equipped for service
In the OT Ex 4:10–12
Bezalel and Oholiab: Ex 31:1–6;
35:30–36:2
Lev 8:7–9; Jdg 3:10
Gideon: Jdg 6:14,34
Jdg 11:29; 14:19 *Samson*; 1Sa 10:10
Solomon: 1Ki 3:7–9; 2Ch 2:12
2Ki 2:9 *Elisha*; Ne 13:9; Isa 6:6–7;
Jer 1:9; Eze 1:1; 3:23

In the NT 2Ti 2:20–21 *See also* Mt 4:19;
Lk 1:15 *John the Baptist*; Lk 1:41,67
Zechariah; Lk 12:33; Ac 4:8 *Peter*; Ac 6:3;
9:17 *Ananias*; Ac 11:24 *Barnabas*;
Ro 13:12; Eph 4:12; 6:11–18; Php 4:19;
2Ti 3:16–17; Heb 13:20–21; 1Pe 3:15

Believers are equipped for spiritual tasks
By the call of Jesus Christ Mt 4:19
pp Mk 1:17 *See also* Mk 10:24–31;
Lk 9:1–2; 10:1–3; Jn 1:35–42

By spiritual gifts 1Co 12:7 *See also*
Ac 6:3–6; Ro 12:6–8;
1Co 12:8–11,27–31; Eph 4:7,11–12

By the word of God 2Ti 2:15 *See also*

Col 3:16; 2Ti 3:16–17; 2Pe 1:19;
1Jn 2:14

By the empowering of the Holy Spirit
Ac 2:4; 4:31; 13:9; Eph 5:18

For spiritual conflict Eph 6:11 *See also*
Ro 13:12; Eph 4:20–24; 6:12–18;
Col 3:12–15; 1Th 5:8; 1Ti 6:12;
Heb 13:21; 1Pe 3:15

See also

1690 word of God	5209 armour
2033 Christ, humanity	6620 calling
	7966 spiritual gifts
2354 Christ, mission	8342 servanthood
3212 Holy Spirit & mission	8401 challenges
	8482 spiritual warfare
3239 Holy Spirit, anointing	
3251 Holy Spirit, filling with	

8424

evangelism

The proclamation of the good news
of Jesus Christ, which arises
naturally from believers' love for
God and appreciation of all that God
has done for them. The NT stresses
the importance of evangelism, and
provides guidance as to how it
should be carried out.

8425

evangelism, nature of

Evangelism focuses on the
proclaiming of the good news of the
coming of the kingdom of God in
Christ, including the forgiveness of
sins and the hope of eternal life,
through the death and resurrection
of Jesus Christ.

Evangelism as the proclamation of good news
Isa 52:7; Mk 16:15 *See also* 2Sa 18:31;
2Ki 7:9; Isa 40:9; 41:27; Na 1:15;
Ac 14:7,15; Ro 10:15; 15:16; 1Ti 2:7;
2Ti 1:11

Jesus Christ as the focus of evangelism
The gospel message is revealed by
God Gal 1:11–12 *See also* Ro 16:25–26;
Gal 1:15–16; Eph 3:3–6

The gospel message centres on Jesus
Christ Mk 1:1; Eph 3:8 *See also* Lk 1:19;
2:10; 3:16–18; Ac 11:20; Ro 1:9; 2Co 4:4

The announcement of God's kingdom
Ac 28:31 *See also* Mt 24:14;
Mk 1:14–15; Lk 4:43; 8:1; 9:2; Ac 8:12

God's promises are fulfilled in Jesus
Christ Lk 4:18–19 *See also* Isa 61:1–2;
Mt 11:3–5 pp Lk 7:20–22; Ac 5:42; 8:35;
9:22; 13:32–33; Ro 1:2–4

Jesus Christ's death and resurrection
1Co 15:3–4 *See also* Ac 2:22–24; 3:15;
17:18; 1Co 15:14; 1:23; 2Ti 2:8

The announcement of God's salvation
Ro 1:16–17 *See also* Ps 40:10; 96:2–3
pp 1Ch 16:23–24; 1Co 1:21; 15:1–2;
Eph 1:13; 2Th 2:13–14

The call to repentance for the
forgiveness of sins Lk 24:47 *See also*

Mt 4:17; 12:41 pp Lk 11:32; Mk 1:4
pp Mt 3:2 pp Lk 3:3; Ac 2:38

The announcement of peace with God
Ac 10:36 *See also* Eph 2:17–18; 6:15

Evangelism and miracles
Mt 4:23 *Miracles are part of the gospel
proclamation, demonstrating that the
kingdom of God has come;* 1Co 2:4–5 *See
also* Mt 9:35; 10:7–8; Lk 9:6; 11:20;
Ro 15:18–19; 1Th 1:5; Heb 2:3–4

See also

1416 miracles	3224 Holy Spirit & preaching
1439 revelation	
2375 kingdom of God	6510 salvation
2427 gospel, transmission	6652 forgiveness
	6700 peace
	7027 church, purpose
2530 Christ, death of	
2560 Christ, resurrection	7754 preaching

8426

evangelism, motivation for

Evangelism arises from a natural
response to the grace of God, a
concern for those who have yet to
hear the good news and a desire to be
faithful to the great commission to
bring the good news to the ends of
the earth. Evangelism is guided and
directed by the Holy Spirit.

Motives for evangelism
Recognising God's call 2Ti 1:11 *See
also* Isa 6:8–9; Jnh 1:1–2; Ac 22:14–15;
2Co 4:1; 1Ti 2:7

A divine compulsion 1Co 9:16–17 *See
also* Jer 20:9; Am 3:8; Ac 4:20

A God-given responsibility
Eze 3:17–20 *See also* Eze 33:7–9;
1Co 3:10–15; 2Co 5:10–11

A desire to win the lost Ro 10:1;
1Co 9:19–23 *See also* Ac 20:19–20;
Ro 1:14–15; 9:1–3; 11:14; 15:17–20;
2Co 5:20

A recognition of coming judgment
Jude 23 *See also* Jas 5:20; 2Pe 3:9

Responding to God's grace
2Co 5:14–15 *See also* 2Co 5:18–19;
Eph 3:7; 1Ti 1:12–16

Confidence in the gospel Ro 1:16–17
See also Isa 55:10–11; 1Co 1:17–18;
2Co 10:4–5; 2Ti 1:8–9

God directs and guides evangelism
Divine guidance in evangelism
Ac 8:26–29; 16:6–10 *See also*
Ac 5:19–20; 9:10–11; 10:19–20; 11:12;
13:2; 18:9–11

God opens the door for evangelism
2Co 2:12 *See also* Ac 14:27; 1Co 16:9;
Col 4:3; Rev 3:8

Areas of ministry assigned by God
Gal 2:7–9 *See also* Ac 9:15

The Holy Spirit empowers evangelism
Ac 1:8 *See also* Mt 10:19–20
pp Mk 13:11 pp Lk 12:11–12;
Jn 15:26–27; 1Th 1:5

Evangelism as a result of persecution

Ac 8:4–5 *See also* Ac 11:19–21; 13:50–51; 14:6–7; 18:2

See also

3030 Holy Spirit, power	7724 evangelists
3212 Holy Spirit & mission	8124 guidance
5046 opportunities	8239 earnestness
5806 compassion	8370 zeal
6620 calling	8489 urgency
	8495 witnessing
	8794 persecution

8427
evangelism, kinds of

Scripture recognises that evangelism takes place in a variety of contexts, and offers models for evangelism in today's church.

Public evangelism

Preaching in synagogues Ac 14:1 *Paul begins his evangelism in Gentile cities by building links within the Jewish community.*
In Pisidian Antioch: Ac 13:14–16,42–44
Ac 17:2 *in Thessalonica;* Ac 17:10 *in Berea;* Ac 17:17 *in Athens;* Ac 18:4 *in Corinth;* Ac 19:8 *in Ephesus*

Preaching in recognised meeting-places Ac 17:19–23 *See also* Ac 5:25; 10:27–28; 16:13; 19:9

Making a public defence to accusers Ac 21:37–22:1 *See also* Ac 4:7–12; 7:1–2; 24:10; 26:1

Personal evangelism

Giving personal testimony 1Jn 1:1–3 *See also* Mk 5:19; Jn 4:39; Ac 26:9–18; 1Co 7:16; 1Pe 3:1–2

Evangelism in homes Ac 10:24–25 *Peter visits Cornelius' home to speak to those assembled.*
Believers invite others into their homes: Lk 5:29; Ac 18:26; 28:30–31
Believers visit the homes of others: Ac 9:17 pp Ac 22:12; Ac 16:32–34

Evangelism in strategic areas

Going to major centres Ac 16:12
Philippi; Ac 17:1 *Thessalonica;* Ac 17:15
Athens; Ac 18:1 *Corinth;* Ac 18:19
Ephesus
Rome: Ac 23:11; 28:14

Going into new territories
Ro 15:20,23–24; 2Co 10:15–16

Evangelism among strategic people

Speaking to prominent people Ac 18:8
Though the gospel is for all people without distinction, evangelism among certain people and groups enabled the message to spead further. See also Ac 13:7 *Paul before Sergius Paulus, proconsul of Cyprus;*
Ac 24:24 *Paul before Felix and his wife;*
Ac 25:8–9 *Paul before Festus;*
Ac 25:11–12 *Paul appeals to Caesar;*
Ac 26:2–3 *Paul before King Agrippa;*
Ac 28:7–8 *Paul in the home of the chief official on Malta*

Evangelising households Ac 16:34 *The conversion of the head of the household was often accompanied by the conversion of the whole family group. See also* Jn 4:53;
Ac 11:14; 18:8

Using literature in evangelism

Jn 20:30–31 *See also* Lk 1:1–4; Ac 1:1–2

Appealing to Scripture in evangelism

Ac 26:22–23 *See also* Ac 8:35; 10:43; 13:22–23; Ro 1:2–3; 16:25–26; 1Co 15:3–4

Signs and wonders in evangelism

Miracles confirm the message Ac 8:6 *See also* Mk 16:17–20; Ac 4:14; 19:10–12; 1Co 2:4–5; Heb 2:3–4

Miracles give opportunity for preaching Ac 3:9–16 *See also* Ac 2:5–14; 14:8–11; 16:26–31

Miracles result in people believing Ac 9:40–42 *See also* Jn 7:31; 11:45; Ac 9:33–35; 13:10–12

The response to evangelism

Acceptance of the message Ac 2:37–41 *See also* Ac 4:4; 17:4,34; 19:17–20; 1Th 2:13

Rejection of the message Heb 4:2 *See also* Ro 10:16; Ac 13:50–51; 17:32; 18:6

See also

1448 signs	7456 synagogue
5340 house	7739 missionaries
5622 witnesses	7948 mission
5680 family	

example

A person who acts as an illustration or model. Scripture provides examples of both good and bad conduct for the guidance of believers.

Scripture provides examples to inform and warn believers

Israel is an example to believers 1Co 10:6 *See also* 1Co 10:11

Job as an example of perseverance and patience Jas 5:10–11

The example of Jesus Christ is of special importance to Christians
Jn 13:15; 1Co 11:1 *See also* Mt 11:29; 16:24; Php 2:5–11; 1Ti 1:16; Heb 3:1–2; 12:2; 1Pe 2:21

The apostles set an example for believers to follow Php 3:17 *See also* 2Th 3:7

Christian leaders are to provide examples to their people 1Pe 5:3 ; Tit 2:7 *See also* 1Ti 4:12

Examples drawn from everyday life Gal 3:15; Jas 3:4

Biblical examples to be imitated

Faith Mt 15:22 *a Canaanite woman;*
Jn 4:4–29 *a Samaritan woman;*
Jn 20:24–29 *doubting Thomas;*
Ro 4:18–21 *Abraham;* Heb 11:4–38
various OT figures

Forgiving one's enemies and assailants Ge 33:1–11 *Esau;*
Ge 45:5–15 *Joseph;* 1Sa 24:8–22 *David;*
Lk 23:34 *Jesus Christ;* Ac 7:59 *Stephen*

Generous giving Ru 2:15–19 *Boaz;*
Job 29:11–16 *Job;* Mk 12:41–44
a widow; Ac 10:2 *Cornelius*

Praise Ex 15:1–2 *Moses;* Ex 18:9–12

Jethro; 1Ch 29:10–13 *David;*
Da 2:19–23 *Daniel;* Lk 1:57–68
Zechariah

Biblical examples to be avoided

Lev 20:23; Pr 22:24–25; Eze 20:18; Heb 4:11; 2Pe 3:17

See also

1670 symbols	6744 sanctification
1680 types	8120 following
2339 Christ, example of	Christ
5034 likeness	8124 guidance
5409 metaphor	8206 Christlikeness
5769 behaviour	8265 godliness
5904 maturity, spiritual	8347 spiritual growth
	8449 imitating

fasting

Abstaining from food, and possibly drink, for a limited period of time as a mark of religious commitment and devotion or as an expression of repentance for sins.

8430
fasting, nature of

Scripture frequently refers to individuals fasting and describes the different kinds of fast which may be undertaken.

Kinds of fasting

Abstaining from food and drink Ezr 10:6 *See also* Da 9:3; Ac 23:12

Abstaining from food only 1Sa 1:7 *See also* Da 6:18

The duration of fasting

One day: the normal fast period Lev 23:32; Jdg 20:26; 2Sa 1:12

Three days Est 4:16; Ac 9:9

Seven days 1Sa 31:13 pp 1Ch 10:12; 2Sa 12:16–20

Forty days
These 40-day fasts are all in unique circumstances and are not prescribed:
Ex 34:28; 1Ki 19:8; Mt 4:2 pp Lk 4:2

Regular observances of fasting

Those prescribed by the Law
Lev 16:29–31 *NIV footnote at verse 29.*
See also Lev 23:26–32; Nu 29:7;
Ac 27:9 fn

Those observed in Jewish tradition
Zec 8:19 *See also* Est 9:30–31; Zec 7:2–5

Those observed by the Pharisees
Lk 18:11–12

Involuntary fasts

Those imposed by decree 2Ch 20:3 *See also* 1Sa 14:24
A special instance of an individual instructed by God to fast: 1Ki 13:8–9,16
1Ki 21:9; Jer 36:9

Those imposed by circumstances
Ac 27:33; 2Co 6:5; 11:27

Voluntary fasts

Ne 1:4 *See also* Lk 2:37

8431
fasting, reasons for

Scripture identifies a number of situations in which fasting is appropriate.

Situations in which fasting is appropriate
Bereavement 1Ch 10:11–12
pp 1Sa 31:11–13 *See also* 2Sa 1:11–12;
3:31–35

Distress Est 4:3 *See also* 1Sa 1:7; 20:34;
1Ki 21:4–6; Ps 109:24; Da 6:18;
Ac 27:33

Penitence 1Sa 7:5–6 *See also* Ne 9:1–3;
Da 9:3–6 *Daniel identifies himself with the sin of the people*; Da 9:20;
Joel 1:13–14; 2:12–15; Jnh 3:5–9

Seeking God's intervention
2Sa 12:15–17 *See also* 2Ch 20:2–4;
Ezr 8:21; Est 4:15–16; Ps 35:13–14

Seeking guidance Jdg 20:26–28 *See also* Dt 9:9 *Moses fasts before the revelation of the Law*; Da 9:1–3,20–23;
10:1–2,12; Ac 13:1–3 *The church receives direction through the Holy Spirit while fasting.*

Indicating earnestness Ac 23:12–13

8432
fasting, practice of

Although fasting is a negative practice, it is not an end in itself but is to be undertaken for a positive purpose.

Fasting is not an end in itself
Fasting as empty ritual is condemned
Jer 14:11–12 *See also* Isa 58:1–7;
Zec 7:4–7

Fasting as mere show is condemned
Mt 6:16–18 *See also* Mt 9:14–15
pp Mk 2:18–20 pp Lk 5:33–35 *Jesus Christ repudiated fasting for its own sake whilst granting that there is a time and a place for it.*

Fasting imposed for false motives
1Sa 14:24–30

Attitudes appropriate to fasting
Humility Ps 35:13 *See also* 1Ki 21:27–29;
Ezr 8:21; Ps 69:10

Repentance 1Sa 7:6 *See also* Ne 9:1–3;
Joel 1:13–14; 2:12–15

Fasting and prayer
Ne 1:4 *See also* Ezr 8:21–23; Ps 35:13;
Da 9:3; Mt 17:20 fn pp Mk 9:29 fn;
Lk 2:37; 5:33; Ac 13:3; 14:23; 1Co 7:3–5

The motivation here is similar to that in abstaining from food.

Fasting and worship
Ac 13:2 *See also* Lk 2:37

giving

Dedicating or offering something or oneself to others or to God. Scripture stresses the importance of giving. The generosity and love of God in giving his only Son to die for his people is understood to lead to an obligation, on their part, to love God and others in return.

8435
giving, of oneself

The submission of the self to the will of God, in thanksgiving and service.

Jesus Christ's self-giving as an example to believers
1Jn 3:16 *See also* Mt 16:24 pp Mk 8:34
pp Lk 9:23; Mk 10:45; Jn 15:13; Ro 15:3;
Gal 1:4; Eph 5:1–2,25; Php 2:5–8;
Tit 2:14

Why self-giving is reasonable service to God
God's people belong to him by creation Dt 32:6 *See also* Ps 100:3;
Rev 4:11

God's people belong to him by redemption 1Co 6:19–20 *See also*
Rev 5:9

All good things are given by God
1Ch 29:14 *See also* Dt 8:18; Ac 17:25;
1Co 4:7; 1Ti 6:17

God's people giving themselves
To God Ro 12:1 *See also* 2Co 8:5

To one another 2Co 8:5 *See also*
1Co 16:15

To holy living Ro 6:19 *See also* Pr 23:26;
Ro 12:1

To the service of God 1Co 15:58 *See also* Jdg 5:2; 1Ch 29:5; 2Ch 17:16;
Ps 40:7–8; Isa 6:8; Ac 6:4; Ro 1:9;
1Ti 4:15

To a life of self-denial Lk 14:33 *See also*
Mt 16:24 pp Mk 8:34 pp Lk 9:23;
Lk 14:26; Ro 12:1 pp Lk 8:13; 10:33;
2Co 12:15; Php 3:8

To martyrdom Da 3:28 *See also*
Ac 20:24; 21:13; Rev 12:11

Rewards of self-giving
Mt 10:39 *See also* Mt 19:27–29
pp Mk 10:28–30 pp Lk 18:28–30;
Mk 8:35 pp Lk 17:33

The giving of thanks
Ps 50:23 *See also* 1Ch 16:8; Eph 5:4;
Php 4:4–7; Col 2:7; 3:15; Heb 12:28

8436
giving, of possessions

Making one's possessions available for God's service in the way in which he directs, as a practical recognition that all possessions come from him.

Ministries that require the giving of material possessions
The relief of the poor Pr 28:27 *See also*
Lev 25:25; Dt 15:7–8; Isa 58:7; Mt 19:21
pp Mk 10:21 pp Lk 18:22; Lk 12:33;
Ro 12:13; Gal 2:10

The support of God's servants
1Ti 5:17–18 *See also* Nu 3:48; 5:9;
2Ki 4:8–10; Mt 10:10; Gal 6:6;
Php 4:15–18

The care of widows and orphans
Jas 1:27 *See also* Dt 26:12; Ru 2:5–12;
1Ti 5:3–4

Motives for the giving of material possessions
Obedience to God 2Co 9:7 *See also*
Ex 30:11–16; Lev 12:6–8; Dt 14:28;
Mal 3:8–10; Mt 22:21 pp Mk 12:17
pp Lk 20:25; Ro 13:6–7

Gratitude for God's generosity
1Ch 29:14 *See also* Ge 28:20–22;
Dt 26:9–10; 1Sa 1:27–28

Love for others 1Jn 3:17 *See also*
2Ch 28:15; Mt 7:9–11; Lk 10:33–35

The manner of giving material possessions
Willingly and cheerfully Mt 10:8 *See also*
Ex 25:2; 35:5,22; 2Ki 12:4;
1Ch 29:6,9,17; 2Ch 24:10; 35:7–9;
Ezr 8:28; 2Co 8:11–12

Unostentatiously Mt 6:1–4

Regularly 1Co 16:2

Generously Ex 36:5; Nu 7:13;
1Ch 29:3–4; Lk 6:38; 2Co 8:2–3;
1Ti 6:18

God measures his people's giving
With a reckoning different from the world's 2Ch 6:8; Mk 12:41–44
pp Lk 21:1–4

With regard for people's capacity to give Lev 14:30; 27:8; Dt 16:17; Ezr 2:69;
Ac 11:29; 2Co 8:12

God rewards the giver appropriately
Php 4:18–19 *See also* 2Ch 31:10;
Pr 11:25; 22:9; 28:27; Ecc 11:1
encouragement to be enterprising in giving;
Isa 58:10; Mt 10:42; 25:34–36; Lk 16:9;
Ac 20:35; 2Co 9:6

God's reward overwhelming the giver
Pr 3:9–10 *See also* Mal 3:10; Lk 6:38

God's giving: the model for his people's giving
Mt 10:8 *See also* 2Co 8:8–9; 9:15

See also

1330 God, the provider	7402 offerings
5325 gifts	8206 Christlikeness
5446 poverty	8260 generosity
5679 dowry	8488 tithing
5809 compassion, human	8676 thanksgiving
5909 motives, importance	8767 hypocrisy

8437
giving, of talents

All human abilities and skills derive from God and are to be dedicated to his glory and the good of others.

Talents are given and sustained by God
1Co 4:7
Skill, ability and knowledge given by God for the making of the Tent of Meeting:
Ex 28:3; 31:3–6; 35:31–35; 36:1–2
Dt 8:18; 2Sa 22:34–35; Ps 18:33–34;
Mt 25:15 pp Lk 19:13; Ac 7:10; Ro 12:6;
1Co 12:7–8; 2Co 3:5; Eph 3:7; 4:7

Talents differ
Mt 25:15 *See also* 2Ch 2:13–14; Ro 12:6;
1Co 7:7; 12:4–6; Eph 4:11

Talents need to be developed
2Ti 1:6 *See also* Mt 25:16–30
pp Lk 19:12–26; 1Ti 4:14

Talents are to be devoted to God
For his own glory 1Pe 4:11 *See also*
Ex 35:10,25; 1Ki 7:40; 1Ch 9:13;
Ps 33:2–3; 137:4–5; 1Co 10:31

For the good of others 1Pe 4:10 *See also*
1Co 12:7; 14:12; Eph 4:12

Talents are to be accounted for
Mt 25:19 pp Lk 19:15 *See also* Mt 21:34
pp Mk 12:2 pp Lk 20:10; Lk 12:48

Rewards according to use or misuse of talents
Mt 25:21 *See also* Mt 25:23–30
pp Lk 19:17–26

See also

3281 Holy Spirit, inspiration	7966 spiritual gifts
5051 responsibility	8248 faithfulness
5272 craftsmen	8256 fruitfulness
5840 eagerness	8342 servanthood
5889 ingratitude	8742 faithlessness
	8783 neglect

8438
giving, of time

People are stewards of a deposit of time given by God, and will be held responsible for the way in which they use it.

Time is governed by God
God determines every lifespan
Job 14:5 *See also* Ps 31:15; 74:16–17;
139:16; Ac 17:26

God will demand an account of how time has been spent Ecc 3:17 *See also*
Mt 12:36; 1Pe 4:3–5

Time may be squandered
In ungodly living 1Pe 4:3 *See also*
Joel 2:25; Eph 2:2–3; Col 3:5–7

By neglecting God-given opportunities
Jer 8:20 *See also* Pr 20:4; Mt 25:11–12;
Lk 13:25; 19:44; Ac 24:25; Rev 2:21

Time may be saved
By understanding its brevity Ps 90:12
See also Jn 12:35; 1Co 7:29–31

By remembering its uncertainty Jn 9:4
See also Ecc 8:5–7; Jas 4:13–15

By making the most of present opportunities Eph 5:16 *See also* Ps 32:6;
Ecc 12:1; Est 4:14; Mt 4:17; Mk 1:15;
2Co 6:1–2; Gal 6:10; Col 4:5;
Heb 3:7–13

By allocating it wisely 1Ch 12:32 *See also* Ex 18:13–26; Ac 6:1–4

Time is to be spent wisely
In worship and meditation Ps 119:164
See also Ps 4:4; 55:17; La 3:40;
Da 6:10,13; Mk 1:35; 1Co 11:28

In work Pr 104:23 *See also* Ex 20:9
pp Dt 5:13; Ro 13:6

In rest Ex 20:8–10 *See also* Lev 16:29;
Mk 6:31

With one's family Dt 24:5 *See also*
Dt 6:7; Ecc 9:9; 1Ti 3:4

In fellowship 1Co 16:7 *See also* Ac 2:42;
20:7; Heb 10:25

Time is to be allocated according to priorities
Lk 10:41–42 *See also* Ps 1:1–3;
Hag 1:2–4; Mt 6:33; Ac 13:46–47;
17:16–17

See also

1310 God as judge	7925 fellowship among believers
4903 time	
5047 opportunities in life	8361 wisdom
5057 rest, physical	8461 priorities
5385 leisure	8622 worship
5628 work	8755 folly
5680 family	

8440
glorifying God

The giving of glory to God through acts of praise and obedience. Believers are to glorify God in their lives, as Jesus Christ glorified him in his life.

Believers are to glorify God
Ps 96:1–9 pp 1Ch 16:23–29; Isa 42:12
See also Isa 43:5–7; 66:18–19; Hab 2:14

God is entitled to be glorified
Ps 96:4–9 pp 1Ch 16:25–29 *See also*
Ps 29:1–2; 115:1; Isa 24:14–15

Glorifying God is the believer's natural response to him Ps 118:28 *See also*
Ps 34:3; 69:30; 86:12

God is glorified in Jesus Christ
Jn 13:31 *See also* Jn 14:13; 17:4

Reasons for glorifying God
His holiness Ps 99:9 *See also* Rev 15:4

His great deeds Ps 86:8–10 *See also*
Isa 25:1; 2Co 4:13–15

His loving mercy Ps 63:3 *See also*
Ps 115:1; Ro 15:8–9

His righteous judgments Rev 14:7 *See*

also Eze 28:22–23; Ro 11:33–36;
Rev 11:13

Means of glorifying God
By praising God Rev 4:11; 7:12 *See also*
Lk 2:13; Ro 11:33–36; 16:27;
Heb 13:20–21; 1Pe 4:11; 2Pe 3:18;
Jude 25

By living for God 1Co 10:31 *See also*
Ro 4:20; 1Co 6:20; 2Ti 1:11–12;
1Pe 4:10–13

By doing good works and bearing fruit
Jn 15:8; Php 1:9–11 *See also* Mt 5:16;
Gal 5:22–26; Heb 13:20–21; 1Pe 2:12

Examples of glorifying God
1Ch 29:10–13 *David;* Da 4:34–37
Nebuchadnezzar; Lk 1:46 *Mary, the mother of Jesus Christ;* Lk 2:13 *the angels;*
Lk 2:20 *the shepherds*
Jesus Christ: Jn 13:31–32; 17:1–4
The redeemed in heaven: **Rev** 4:11; 7:12

See also

1065 God, holiness of	7027 church, purpose
1194 glory, divine & human	8444 honouring God
	8624 worship, reasons
3218 Holy Spirit & praise	8660 magnifying God
4114 angels and praise	8665 praise, reasons
5628 work	8676 thanksgiving
5908 motives	

8441
goals

Jesus Christ's basic aim was to do his Father's will. Believers have the same objective, which Jesus Christ and the Holy Spirit enable them to achieve.

God's goals
To live with his people Lev 26:11–12
See also Ps 23:6; Zec 2:10; Jn 14:23;
Rev 21:3

To build his church in Christ Mt 16:18
See also Eph 2:19–22; Rev 21:2

To perfect his church in Christ
Eph 5:26–27 *See also* Ps 138:8; Php 1:6;
Col 2:10

Jesus Christ's goals
To do his Father's will Jn 6:38 *See also*
Mt 26:39 pp Mk 14:36 pp Lk 22:42;
Jn 4:34; 5:30; Heb 10:7,9

To preach the gospel Lk 4:43
pp Mk 1:38 *See also* Lk 4:18–19;
Isa 61:1–2

To save the lost Lk 19:10 *See also*
Mt 15:21–28 pp Mk 7:24–30; Lk 15:7
pp Mt 18:14; Lk 15:10

Jesus Christ achieved his goals Jn 17:4
See also Lk 13:32; Jn 12:31; 19:28,30

Believers' goals
To please God 2Co 5:9 *See also*
Ro 14:18; Eph 5:10,17; Col 1:9–10

To know God Php 3:8 *See also* Jn 17:3;
Php 3:10; 2Pe 3:18

To be faithful to Jesus Christ Jn 15:4
See also Mt 10:22 pp Mk 13:13;
Mt 24:13; Php 3:14; 2Ti 4:7; Heb 12:2;
Rev 2:26

To love one another Jn 13:34 *See also*

8442

Mt 22:34–40 pp Mk 12:28–31
pp Lk 10:25–28; Jn 15:12; 1Co 13:13;
16:14; 1Ti 1:5; 1Jn 4:11–12

To live at peace Ro 12:18 *See also*
Mk 9:50; 2Co 13:11; 1Th 4:11

To spread the gospel Mt 28:19–20 *See
also* Ac 20:24; Ro 11:14; 15:20;
1Co 9:16; 2Ti 4:2

To grow to maturity Eph 4:13 *See also*
Mt 5:48; Ro 8:29; 2Co 3:18; 7:1; 13:11

Believers' final goal is heaven
Rev 7:9–10 *See also* Jn 6:40;
1Co 15:51–52; 2Co 5:4–5; 1Th 4:17;
1Jn 3:2

**God guarantees that believers will
reach their goal** Jn 14:2–3 *See also*
Jn 6:39; Ro 8:38–39; Eph 1:13–14;
Php 1:6; 2Ti 1:12; 2:11–13; Rev 3:5,21

See also
1115 God, purpose of	7031 unity, God's goal
2354 Christ, mission	8134 knowing God
5776 achievement	8206 Christlikeness
5785 ambition	8320 perfection
5904 maturity, spiritual	8460 pleasing God
7027 church, purpose	8465 progress

8442

good works

Acts designed specifically to benefit
others, which are characteristic of
God. He requires and enables his
people to do good, although such is
contrary to their sinful human
nature. Salvation does not depend
on good works, but leads to them.

**Good works are characteristic of
God**
Jer 32:36–40 *See also* Ps 119:17,65;
125:1–4; Jer 32:41; Mic 2:7;
Zec 8:14–15; Ac 10:37–38

**Good works are unnatural for
sinful human beings**
Jer 13:23 *See also* Ps 5:9; 10:7; 14:1–3
pp Ps 53:1–3; Ps 36:1–4; 140:3;
Ecc 7:20; Isa 59:7–8; Jer 4:22;
Ro 3:9–18; 7:13–23

**God's people are encouraged to
do good works**
Gal 6:9–10 *See also* Ps 37:3; Ecc 3:12;
Mt 5:38–48 pp Lk 6:27–36; 1Pe 3:8–13;
Ps 34:12–16; 1Pe 4:19

**God is pleased with the good
works of his people**
Heb 13:16 *See also* 1Pe 2:15, 20; 3:17

Good works will be rewarded
Jn 5:28–29 *See also* Lk 6:35; Ro 2:5–11;
Gal 6:9–10; 1Ti 6:17–19

**Good works as evidence of
repentance**
Ps 34:14 *See also* Ps 37:27; 2Ti 2:20–21;
Jas 2:14–21,26; 3:13; 1Pe 3:10–12

**Good works as evidence of God's
grace in the lives of believers**
2Co 9:8 *See also* Ac 9:36; Php 2:12–13;
Col 1:10–12

**Good works are the purpose of
the new creation**
Eph 2:10 *See also* 2Ti 2:21; 3:16–17;
1Pe 2:13–15

**Jesus Christ criticised for doing
good works on the Sabbath**
Mt 12:9–14 pp Mk 3:1–6 pp Lk 6:6–11
See also Lk 13:10–17; Jn 9:1–41

See also
1050 God, goodness of	6732 repentance
5381 law, letter & spirit	7428 Sabbath
6020 sin	8021 faith
6674 imputation	8142 religion
	8154 righteousness

8443

growth

The process of development and
maturing, used to refer to the
progress of the kingdom of God and
the spiritual development of
believers. Scripture uses images of
growth (such as seeds, plants and
infants) to stress the dynamic nature
of personal faith and the kingdom of
God.

Images of growth
Infancy to maturity Eph 4:13–15 *See
also* 1Co 3:1–2; 13:11; 14:20;
Heb 5:12–14; 1Pe 2:2

Seeds and plants Lk 8:14–15
pp Mt 13:22–23 pp Mk 4:19–20 *See also*
2Co 9:10

**The apostles worked and prayed
for growth in believers**
2Co 13:9 *See also* Col 1:28; 4:12

Dimensions of spiritual growth
In faith 2Co 10:15–16 *See also* 2Th 1:3

In knowledge 2Pe 3:18 *See also*
Eph 1:17–18; 3:16–19; Col 1:10;
2Pe 1:3,6

In love 1Th 4:10 *See also* Php 1:9;
1Th 3:12; 2Pe 1:7–8

Growth comes from God
Col 2:19 *See also* 1Co 3:6–7; 2Co 9:10;
Php 1:6

**Growth comes through
discipleship**
Putting away the sinful self 1Pe 2:1 *See
also* Ro 8:13–14; 2Co 7:1; Gal 5:24;
Eph 4:22–24; Col 3:5–10

Moving on from basic teaching
Heb 6:1–2 *See also* Heb 5:11–14

Maturing in thinking 1Co 14:20 *See also*
Ro 12:1

Persevering in faith Jas 1:4 *See also*
Php 2:12; 3:12; 2Pe 1:5–8

**Contributing to growth in the church
by exercising gifts** Eph 4:11–12 *See
also* 1Co 14:1–5; Eph 4:13–16

**Examples of spiritual growth in
some of God's servants**
1Sa 2:26; Lk 2:52 *See also* Lk 1:80;
Ac 9:22

**The growth of the kingdom of
God**
**God promises that his kingdom will
grow** Col 1:6 *See also* Mt 13:31–33
pp Mk 4:30–32 pp Lk 13:18–21;
Mk 4:26–29

**The early church experienced rapid
numerical growth** Ac 4:4 *See also*
Ac 2:41,47; 5:14; 6:7; 9:31; 11:21; 14:1;
16:5

See also
2375 kingdom of God	8026 faith, growth in
4015 life	8114 discipleship
4406 agriculture	8255 fruit, spiritual
4971 seasons of life	8256 fruitfulness
5726 old age, attainment	8347 spiritual growth
5902 maturity	8465 progress

8444

honouring God

Giving the reverence and respect to
God which is his due. All God's
people have a duty to honour him in
every aspect of their lives, while
unbelievers and even animals can
also honour him.

God's people must honour him
Ps 22:23 *See also* Mal 1:6; 2:1–2;
Jn 5:22–23

Ways of honouring God
By worshipping him Da 4:34 *See also*
Isa 43:22–24; 1Ti 1:17; 6:15–16;
Rev 4:8–11; 5:6–14; 7:9–12

By holy living 1Co 6:18–20 *See also*
Ro 12:1–2; 2Co 8:23; Eph 5:1–3;
1Th 4:7–8; 1Pe 1:15–16

**By keeping the Sabbath and religious
feasts** Lev 19:30 *See also* Ex 20:8–11
pp Dt 5:12–15; Ex 12:42; 31:12–17;
Lev 26:2; Isa 58:13–14

By showing kindness to others
Pr 14:31 *See also* Dt 26:12–15;
Mt 10:40–42

By honouring his name and his word
Ac 19:13–17 *See also* Jdg 13:17;
Isa 26:13; Mal 3:16; Ac 13:48; 2Th 3:1

By acknowledging him as God
Da 3:28–29 *See also* 1Sa 6:4–5;
Isa 43:20; Rev 14:7

By giving tithes and offerings to him
Pr 3:9–10 *See also* Dt 26:1–11;
Mal 3:6–12; 2Co 8:19–21

By proclaiming his deeds Isa 63:7 *See
also* 1Ch 16:23–26; Ps 145:3–7;
Isa 12:4–6; Da 4:1–3

By obeying him Nu 27:12–14 *See also*
Nu 20:7–12

**God honours those who honour
him**
1Sa 2:27–30 *See also* Lev 10:1–3;
2Ch 26:18; Jn 12:26

**God requires sincerity from
those who honour him**
Mk 7:5–13 pp Mt 15:1–9 *See also*
Isa 29:13; Ac 5:1–11

All people will ultimately honour God

Jer 3:17 *See also* Isa 60:9; Ro 14:9–12; Isa 45:23–24; Php 2:9–11

Jesus Christ is to be honoured as God

Mt 17:5 pp Mk 9:7 pp Lk 9:35 Jn 5:22–23 *See also* Rev 5:12–13

See also

5878 honour	8470 respect for God
7930 Lord's Day, the	8622 worship
8266 holiness	8632 adoration
8334 reverence & God's nature	8660 magnifying God
8440 glorifying God	8664 praise
8453 obedience	

8445

hospitality

Acts of generosity and friendship towards strangers. God's people are called to be hospitable as part of their duty to others and in gratitude for the salvation they have received from God. Showing hospitality includes the responsibility to protect those received as guests.

8446

hospitality, a duty of God's people

Hospitality is commanded by God

Heb 13:2 *See also* Isa 58:6–7; Jn 13:12–15; Ro 12:13; 1Pe 4:9

Hospitality is a responsibility of leaders

1Ti 3:2 *See also* 1Ti 5:9–10; Tit 1:8

Hospitality indicates true discipleship

Job 31:32 *See also* Mt 25:35

Hospitality crosses social barriers

Of race Lev 19:33–34 *See also* Ex 22:21; 23:9

Of class and status Lk 14:12–14 *See also* Jas 2:2–4

Hospitality is to be offered to Christian ministers

Ro 16:1–2 *See also* Col 4:10; 3Jn 5–10

Hospitality is to be refused to false teachers

2Jn 10–11

Hospitality as a picture of salvation

Ps 23:5–6; Rev 3:20 *Jesus Christ comes as a willing guest to the repentant, as a sign of renewed fellowship. See also* Isa 25:6; Mt 22:1–14; Lk 14:15–24; 19:1–10; Jn 14:2–3

Warnings against inhospitable behaviour

Dt 23:3–4 *See also* Mt 10:14 pp Mk 6:11 pp Lk 9:5; Mt 25:41–45

See also

5051 responsibility	7530 foreigners
5690 friends	7733 leaders
5699 guests	8260 generosity
5765 attitudes to people	8291 kindness
6672 grace in relationships	8434 giving
	9410 heaven

8447

hospitality, examples of

Scripture provides many examples of friendship and generosity towards strangers, and encourages believers to be hospitable in turn.

Examples of hospitality in the OT

Ge 18:2–5 *See also* Ge 19:1–3 *Lot entertains visitors from God;* Ge 24:22–25 *Abraham's servant is welcomed in Rebekah's home;* Ex 2:20 *Moses is welcomed by a priest of Midian;* Jdg 13:15 *Manoah receives the angel of the* LORD. *Shelter is given to a Levite:* Jdg 19:1–4,20–21 2Sa 17:27–29 *hospitality shown to David and his people;* 1Ki 17:7–16 *The widow of Zarephath cares for Elijah despite her poverty;* 2Ki 4:8–10 *a Shunammite provides for Elisha;* Ne 5:17 *Nehemiah shows hospitality to fellow Jews.*

Hospitality shown to Jesus Christ

Mt 9:10 pp Mk 2:15 pp Lk 5:29 *Jesus Christ received hospitality from people of all social backgrounds. See also* Mt 8:14–15 pp Mk 1:29–31 pp Lk 4:38–39 *at Peter's house Jesus Christ anointed at Bethany:* Mt 26:6–7 pp Mk 14:3; Jn 12:1–3 Lk 7:36 *at the house of Simon the Pharisee;* Lk 10:38 *at the home of Mary and Martha;* Lk 14:1 *at the house of a prominent Pharisee;* Lk 19:5–7 *at Zacchaeus' house;* Lk 24:29 *with disciples in Emmaus;* Jn 2:2 *at the wedding at Cana*

Hospitality assisted the mission of the apostles

Hospitality shown to the disciples Mt 10:11–12 pp Mk 6:10 pp Lk 9:4 *Jesus Christ sends out the Twelve. See also* Lk 10:5–7

Hospitality shown to Peter Ac 10:32 *at the home of Simon the tanner;* Ac 10:48 *with Cornelius and his family*

Hospitality shown to Paul and his companions Ac 16:15 *at the house of Lydia;* Ac 16:34 *at the house of the Philippian jailer;* Ac 18:2–3 *with Aquila and Priscilla in Corinth;* Ac 21:8 *at the house of Philip;* Ac 21:16 *at the home of Mnason in Jerusalem;* Ac 28:2 *on Malta;* Ac 28:7 *at the home of Publius;* Ro 16:23 *with Gaius;* Phm 22 *as a guest of Philemon*

Christians opened their homes for gatherings of believers

1Co 16:19 *See also* Ac 2:46; Ro 16:3–5; Col 4:15; Phm 2

Examples of inhospitable behaviour

1Sa 25:10–11 *See also* Nu 20:18 *Edom;* Nu 21:21–23 *Sihon;* Dt 23:3–4 *Ammonites and Moabites;* Jdg 19:15 *Gibeah;* Lk 9:52–53 *a Samaritan village*

See also

2339 Christ, example of	5355 invitations
	5976 visiting
2354 Christ, mission	7020 church, the
4438 eating	7948 mission
4476 meals	8342 servanthood
5339 home	

8449

imitating

Following the example or copying the actions of another person. Christians are called upon to become Christlike. Becoming like Jesus Christ is, however, the result, not the condition, of conversion.

The people of God are to imitate God

Lev 11:44–45 *See also* Lev 19:2; 20:7,26; 21:8; 1Pe 1:16; Eph 5:1

The people of God are to imitate Jesus Christ

Jesus Christ is the example for believers Mt 16:24 pp Mk 8:34 pp Lk 9:23; Jn 13:15 *See also* Mt 11:29; Jn 13:34; Ro 13:14; 1Co 11:1; Eph 5:2; Php 2:5; Col 3:13; 1Pe 2:21; 4:1

God works in believers making them like Jesus Christ Ro 8:29 *See also* 2Co 4:10–12; Col 3:9–10

Good examples to imitate

Paul's example 1Co 4:16 *See also* 1Co 11:1; Php 3:17; 4:9; 1Th 1:6; 2Th 3:7–9

Christians are to imitate the good example of other believers 2Co 9:2; 1Th 2:14; Heb 6:12

Christian leaders are to set examples which can be imitated 1Ti 4:12 *See also* Tit 2:7–8; Heb 13:7; 1Pe 5:3

Believers are to imitate the good example of those who have gone before Heb 12:1; Jas 5:10–11

God's people are not to imitate bad examples

Israel must not imitate other nations Lev 20:23; Dt 18:9; 2Ki 17:15

God's people must not imitate the ungodly Ex 23:2; Ps 1:1; Pr 1:10–15; Mt 23:2–3; 1Co 15:33; 2Pe 3:17; 1Jn 3:11–12; Rev 2:14

No-one can obtain salvation by imitating Jesus Christ

Jn 3:16–18 *Jesus Christ teaches that salvation (eternal life) is a consequence of faith in him. He never links salvation with imitating him or any other act or acts. See also* Eph 2:8–9; 2Ti 1:8–9

See also

2339 Christ, example of	7733 leaders
	8217 conformity
6510 salvation	8428 example

8450

martyrdom

The term "martyr" comes from the Greek word for "witness", reminding believers that the supreme act of witness for the gospel is to give up one's life for its sake.

Jesus Christ as martyr
Jesus Christ had to suffer and die
Mk 8:31 *In that Jesus Christ gives up his life, he may be thought of as a martyr. But the NT stresses that he is far more than this. Through his death alone come all the benefits of salvation, in which all believers can share. See also* Isa 53:10

Jesus Christ's life is given as a ransom for believers Mt 20:28 pp Mk 10:45 *See also* Lk 9:22; Jn 10:11; Ac 2:23

Other examples of martyrdom
Abel Ge 4:8; Mt 23:35 pp Lk 11:51; Heb 11:4; 12:24; 1Jn 3:12

Zechariah 2Ch 24:20–21; Lk 11:51

John the Baptist Mt 14:10–12 pp Mk 6:27–29

Stephen Ac 7:58; 22:20 *Stephen is the first martyr of the Christian church.*

James Ac 12:2

Peter Jn 21:18–19

Antipas Rev 2:13

Unnamed martyrs 1Ki 19:10; Ro 11:3; Ne 9:26; Mt 23:30–34; Lk 11:47–49; Ac 7:52; Ro 8:35–36; Heb 11:35,37; Jas 5:6; Rev 11:7; 13:15; 16:6; 17:6

Noble qualities of martyrs
Courage Da 3:16–18

Prayerfulness Ac 7:59–60

Self-denial Rev 12:11 *See also* Mt 16:24 pp Mk 8:34; Lk 9:24

Serenity Ac 7:55–56

Steadfastness Rev 2:10 *See also* Heb 11:35
Ac 21:13 *See also* Da 3:16–18

Martyrdom must be recognised as a possibility for all believers
Lk 21:16 *See also* Mt 10:21 pp Mk 13:12; Mt 24:9; Jn 16:2; 21:18–19

Reasons for martyrdom
Refusal to engage in false worship
Da 3:6 *See also* Da 3:16–18; 6:7; 11:30–33; Rev 13:15

Courageous confrontation Ne 9:26 *See also* Mt 14:2–12 pp Mk 6:17–29; Ac 7:51–58; Rev 11:7–10

Public confession of Jesus Christ Mt 24:9 *See also* Mk 13:12–13; Lk 21:16–17

A holy life 1Jn 3:12

Methods of martyrdom
Beheading Mt 14:10; Mk 6:16; Lk 9:9; Rev 20:4

Burning Da 3:11; 1Co 13:3

Mutilation Heb 11:37

Stoning Ac 7:58; Heb 11:37

The sword Ac 12:2; Heb 11:37

Torture Heb 11:35

Retribution for instigators of martyrdom
Rev 6:9–10 *See also* Mt 23:35; Ac 12:1–2,23

Rewards of martyrdom
Rev 2:10 *See also* Mt 10:39; Rev 20:4

See also

5040 murder	8253 faithfulness,
5347 injustice	examples
5498 reward	8794 persecution
5560 suffering	9020 death
5622 witnesses	9310 resurrection
5823 cruelty	9610 hope
7346 death penalty	

8451

mortification

The act of self-denial or the "putting to death" of sinful instincts in order to have freedom from sin and to live in the power of the Holy Spirit. The NT stresses that this act of humiliation comes about through the grace of God. It is the result of, not the condition for, conversion.

Examples of mortification through humility
2Sa 10:1–5 *See also* Mt 27:3–5

Examples of mortification through self-denial
Lev 16:29–31 *See also* Ex 19:15; Lev 23:27–32; Nu 29:7

Mortification as the basis for discipleship
Self-denial is essential Mk 8:34–35 pp Mt 16:24–25 pp Lk 9:23–24 *See also* 1Jn 3:16

The necessity of putting to death sinful human nature and the world's values Ro 8:13; Col 3:5 *See also* Mt 5:29–30; Gal 5:24; 6:14; 1Pe 2:11

Dying to self is a means of knowing freedom from sin
Ro 6:6–7 *See also* Eph 4:22–23

The importance of sharing in the death of Christ
Gal 2:20 *See also* Ro 6:3; 7:4; 2Co 4:11–12; Php 3:10; Col 2:20; 2Ti 2:11

The example of Paul
1Co 9:27 *See also* 2Co 11:23–33; Gal 6:17

Mortification is not the same as self-infliction
Col 2:23 *See also* Php 3:2–3; Col 2:20–22; 1Ti 4:1–5

See also

5879 humiliation	8114 discipleship
5947 shame	8429 fasting
6030 sin, avoidance	8475 self-denial
6166 flesh, sinful	8477 self-
nature	examination
6658 freedom	

8452

neighbours, duty to

Scripture defines the identity of neighbours in various ways, and indicates the nature and extent of believers' obligations to them.

Neighbours defined
Those who live nearby Pr 3:29 *See also*

Ex 3:22; 12:4; Dt 19:14; 2Ki 4:3; Pr 27:10; Lk 15:4–6

Those of the same race Lev 19:18 *See also* 1Sa 15:27–28; 28:17; 1Ch 12:38–40

Peoples of surrounding nations Dt 1:7 *See also* Jos 9:16; 1Sa 7:14; Ezr 9:1; Ne 9:30; 10:28,31; Ps 76:11; Eze 16:26

Those who show mercy to people in need Lk 10:29–37

Fellow Christians Eph 4:25 *See also* Ro 15:1–2; Gal 5:13–16; Jas 4:11–12

Duties to neighbours
Love Mt 22:34–39 pp Mk 12:28–34 pp Lk 10:25–28 *See also* Lev 19:18; Dt 6:5; Mt 19:19; Ro 13:8–10; Gal 5:14; Jas 2:8–9

Assistance Ex 23:4–5 *See also* Dt 22:1–4; Pr 14:21; Mt 25:34–40

Fair treatment Ex 22:14 *See also* Ex 20:17; Lev 6:2–5; 19:15; Dt 5:21

Honest dealings Lev 19:13 *See also* Zec 8:16–17; Eph 4:25

Forgiveness Eph 4:32 *See also* Mt 18:21–35; Lk 17:3–4; Ro 15:1–2; Col 3:13

Reproof Lev 19:17 *See also* Lk 17:3; Gal 6:1–2

Prohibition of negative actions towards neighbours
False witness Ex 20:16 pp Dt 5:20 *See also* Lev 19:16; Pr 24:28

Oppression Jer 22:13 *See also* Pr 3:28

Judgment Jas 4:12 *See also* Mt 7:1–2; Lk 6:41–42; Ro 14:13

See also

2363 Christ,	5051 responsibility
preaching &	5867 golden rule
teaching	

8453

obedience

A willingness to submit to the authority of someone else and to actually do what one is asked or told to do. Scripture lays particular emphasis upon the need for believers to obey God, stressing his trustworthiness. This obedience is especially clear in the life and death of Jesus Christ.

8454

obedience, to God

A willingness to submit oneself to the will of God and to put it into effect. Scripture emphasises the necessity for God's laws to be followed, gives examples and reasons, and describes the rewards.

Obedience is demanded of God's people
Lev 25:18; 1Sa 15:22 *See also* Dt 26:16; 32:46; Ro 6:16–18; 1Pe 1:14–16

Examples of obedience in the OT
Jos 11:15 *See also* Ge 6:22; 12:1–4; 22:2–3; Ex 40:16; Jnh 3:3

The example of Jesus Christ Mt 26:39
pp Mk 14:36 pp Lk 22:42; Jn 14:31 *See
also* Jn 17:4; Ro 5:19; Php 2:8; Heb 5:8

Jesus Christ is obeyed

By the wind and the waves Mt 8:26–27
pp Mk 4:39–41 pp Lk 8:24–25

By evil spirits Mk 1:27 pp Lk 4:36

Obedience and love

Jn 14:15; 1Jn 5:3 *See also* Ps 119:167;
1Jn 2:5; 3:10; 2Jn 6

Obedience and faith

Heb 11:8; Mt 7:21 *Obedience to the will
of God demonstrates the reality of a
person's faith in Jesus Christ. See also*
Ro 1:5; Jas 2:14–26

God rewards those who obey him

Ex 19:5; Jn 15:10 *See also* Dt 5:29;
1Ki 3:14; 2Ki 18:5–7; Mt 7:21,24–25
pp Lk 6:47–48; Mt 12:50 pp Mk 3:35
Heb 8:21; Jn 12:26; 14:21,23; 21:4–6;
1Jn 2:17

Obedience to the word of God

Mt 7:24–27; Jas 1:22 *See also*
Ps 119:9–11; Jnh 3:3; Lk 11:28; Jn 17:6;
Jas 2:14–20

Examples of people who obeyed God

Ge 6:9 *Noah*
Abraham: Ge 12:1–4; 17:23
The psalmist: Ps 119:30,100–106
The apostles: Ac 4:19–20; 5:29
Php 3:7–14 *Paul*

See also

2057 Christ,	8266 holiness
obedience	8336 reverence &
2425 gospel,	obedience
requirements	8354
5394 lordship	trustworthiness
8021 faith	8405 commands, in
8208 commitment to	NT
God	8460 pleasing God
8251 faithfulness to	8718 disobedience
God	

8455
obedience, of Jesus Christ

See 2057 Jesus Christ, obedience of

8456
obedience, to human authorities

Scripture teaches that all people,
Christians included, should submit
not only to God himself but also to
divinely instituted secular
authorities.

Obedience is owed to rulers

Ro 13:1–7 *See also* 1Ti 2:1–3; Tit 3:1;
1Pe 2:13–14,17

Jesus Christ expounds this principle

Mk 12:17 pp Mt 22:21 pp Lk 20:25

Obedience is owed to church leaders

Heb 13:17 *See also* 1Pe 5:5

Obedience is owed within the household

Eph 6:1–3 *See also* Pr 15:5; Col 3:20

Jesus Christ sets the example Lk 2:51

Obedience to secular authority is limited by obedience to God

Ac 5:29 *See also* Ac 4:19

See also

2036 Christ, humility	5668 children,
2520 Christ,	responsibilities
childhood	to parents
5215 authority	5959 submission
5257 civil authorities	6224 rebellion
5359 justice	against
5375 law	authority
5520 servants	8304 loyalty
5540 society	

8458

peacemakers

The commendation of peacemakers

Mt 5:9 *See also* Pr 12:20; Ro 14:19

The importance of pursuing peace

Ecc 10:4; Ro 12:18; Tit 1:6; Heb 12:14;
Jas 3:17

Examples of peacemakers

Ge 13:8–9 *Abraham;* 1Sa 25:14–31
Abigail; Est 10:3 *Mordecai;* Isa 53:5 *the
suffering servant*

See also

1620 beatitudes, the	6700 peace
3215 Holy Spirit &	6716 reconciliation
peace	6754 union with
5834 disagreement	Christ
6684 mediator	

8459

perseverance

Enduring in a course of action or
belief. In its negative sense, it can
mean being stubborn; in its positive
sense, it means continuing
commitment to the gospel of Jesus
Christ.

Human perseverance in sin

2Ki 17:41; Isa 1:5; Ro 1:32 *See also*
Ex 9:1–3; Dt 29:19; Jdg 14:17;
2Ki 13:11; Da 12:10

God's perseverance in calling Israel to obedience

Ne 9:30–31 *See also* Ex 32:14; 1Ki 3:6;
Isa 40:28; Jer 26:13; Jnh 3:10

Jesus Christ's perseverance with those who would not believe

Heb 12:1–3 *See also* Mt 17:17
pp Mk 9:19; 2Th 3:5

Christians' perseverance in faith

Col 2:6–7; 1:10–12 *See also*
Mt 24:12–13; 10:22; Jn 15:4–10;
Ro 11:22; 1Co 1:8; 2Co 10:15; Php 2:12;
Col 1:23; 2Th 3:4; Heb 6:1; 10:36–38;
2Pe 3:18

Perseverance in prayer Lk 18:1–8 *See
also* Lk 11:5–13; Ro 12:12; Eph 6:18;
1Th 5:17

Perseverance arises from suffering

Ro 5:3 *See also* Ro 12:12; 2Co 1:6;

2Th 1:4; 2Ti 3:10–11; Jas 1:2–3;
1Pe 4:19; Rev 2:2–3,19

Perseverance builds and demonstrates Christian character

Ro 5:4 *See also* 1Co 13:7; 2Co 1:21–22;
12:12; Jas 1:4; 2Pe 1:5–8

Encouragements for Christians to persevere

Ac 11:23; 13:43; 1Co 15:58; 16:13;
Php 1:27; 2Ti 1:13; Heb 2:1; 4:14;
Rev 3:11

See also

1105 God, power of	8318 patience
5480 protection	8418 endurance
5560 suffering	8476 self-discipline
5942 security	8613 prayer,
5953 stability	persistence
8120 following Christ	8704 apostasy
8248 faithfulness	

8460

pleasing God

An essential aspect of the life of
believers that is more than a matter
of external observance, but a total
and heartfelt commitment to God.

Pleasing God is commanded

Ro 12:1; Eph 5:8–10 *See also* 2Co 5:9;
Gal 6:8; Col 1:10; 3:20; 1Th 4:1;
1Ti 2:1–3; 5:4

It is more important to please God than to please people

Gal 1:10,15–16; 1Th 2:4

Pleasing God involves inward attitudes, not simply external observance

1Ch 29:17; Ps 51:16–17; Ro 14:17–18
See also Ps 5:4; 69:30–31; 147:10–11;
149:4; Pr 11:20; 12:22; 15:8; Ecc 5:4;
Isa 1:11–13; Eze 18:23; 33:11; Hag 1:7;
Mal 2:13–14; Ro 8:8; Gal 1:10; 1Th 2:4;
Heb 11:6

Sacrifices and duties please God when carried out with the right attitude

Ex 29:18; Php 4:18 *See also* Ex 29:25,41;
Lev 1:9; 3:5; Nu 15:3; 29:2; Ezr 6:10;
Heb 13:16

Results of pleasing God

Ps 37:23 *See also* 1Ki 10:9; Job 33:26;
Pr 16:7; Ecc 2:26; 7:26

Examples of actions that please God

Prayer Pr 15:8

Doing God's will Heb 13:20–21 *See also*
Mt 7:21; Eph 6:6; 1Jn 2:17

Examples of those concerned to please God by their actions

Ne 5:19; Ps 19:14 *See also* Ex 32:11;
Ne 13:31; Ps 90:17; 104:34; Da 9:17

Examples of people who pleased God

The example of Jesus Christ Mt 3:17
pp Mk 1:11 pp Lk 3:22 *See also* Mt 17:5;
Jn 5:30; 8:29; Col 1:19; 2Pe 1:17

Other examples Ge 6:8 *Noah*
Moses: Ex 33:12–13,17

Dt 33:23 *Naphtali*; 1Sa 2:26 *Samuel*;
1Ki 3:10 *Solomon*; Lk 1:30 *Mary*;
Heb 11:5 *Enoch*

See also

2057 Christ, obedience	5919 popularity
	7434 sacrifice
2339 Christ, example of	8024 faith & blessings
5763 attitudes, positive to God	8440 glorifying God
	8453 obedience
5830 delight	

8461

priorities

Scripture stresses that God must be
allowed to rule at the heart of a
person's life.

8462
priority, of God

Scripture provides examples of
individuals who have allowed God
to take priority in their lives, and
also of those who have allowed
something or someone else to take
priority.

God's glory made a priority
Mt 6:9

Commands to put God first Mt 4:10
pp Lk 4:8 *See also* Dt 6:13; 1Ch 16:29

Examples of putting God first
Ge 5:22,24 *Enoch*; Ge 6:9 *Noah*; Ge 12:4
Abraham; Jos 24:15 *Joshua*; 2Ki 20:3
Hezekiah; Da 3:16–18 *Shadrach,
Meshach and Abednego*; Da 6:10 *Daniel*;
Jn 3:29–30 *John the Baptist*

Disapproval of not putting God first
Ex 20:3 *See also* Lk 16:13

Examples of not putting God first
Ac 12:22–23 *See also* 1Ki 11:4 *Solomon*;
1Ki 15:3 *Abijah*; 2Ch 25:2 *Amaziah*;
Jer 3:10 *Judah*; Ac 5:1–5 *Ananias and
Sapphira*; Ro 16:17–18

Worship commended as the highest
human activity Ps 95:6 *See also* Ps 96:9;
99:5; Zec 14:17; Jn 4:24

Outstanding examples of worship
2Sa 6:14–15 *David was prepared to be
despised by his wife rather than inhibit his
worship. See also* Ex 3:6; Isa 6:3;
Eze 1:28; Da 6:10; Jn 9:38; Rev 1:17

God's kingdom made a priority
Mt 6:10

Commands to participate in the
kingdom Mt 6:33 *See also* Lk 19:11–27

Examples of wholehearted
participation Ac 26:19 *See also*
Heb 6:12; 12:1–2

Warning against half-hearted
participation Rev 2:4–5

Sacrifices for the kingdom advocated
Rev 2:10 *See also* Mt 5:29 pp Mk 9:47;
Mt 18:8

Examples of sacrifices for the kingdom
Heb 11:26 *See also* 2Co 11:23–30;
Php 2:21–22,30; Rev 2:13

God's will made a priority
Mt 6:10

Conformity to God's will commanded
Eph 5:17 *See also* 1Th 4:3; 5:18;
Heb 13:20–21; Jas 4:15

Outstanding examples of conformity to
God's will Mt 26:39 pp Mk 14:36
pp Lk 22:42 *See also* Jn 4:34; 6:38;
Ac 20:22–24

See also

1175 God, will of	8223 dedication
2375 kingdom of God	8334 reverence & God's nature
5024 inner being	8453 obedience
5959 submission	8622 worship
8120 following Christ	8768 idolatry
8207 commitment	

8463
priority, of faith, hope and love

Putting God first—living according
to his word—serves the glory of God
and also the best interests of
believers, by giving them true
wisdom for daily living.

The wisdom of making faith a
priority
Heb 11:6

Putting the fear of God before other
considerations Ps 31:19 *See also*
Ex 1:17; Ne 5:15; Pr 1:7

Preferring God's way to sinful advice
Ps 1:1–2
The precious wisdom of obeying God:
Pr 3:13–14; 8:19,32
Following sinful advice: Nu 31:16;
1Ki 12:28

Choosing imaginative action rather
than laziness or fearfulness Nu 13:30
See also 1Sa 25:33; Eph 5:16
Examples of failure to do this:
Mt 25:10,26–27,44–45; 26:40

Patient waiting rather than impetuous
action Ps 40:1 *See also* Ps 27:14; 37:5–6;
62:5; 123:2; Pr 3:5–6; Isa 40:31;
Hos 12:6; Jn 2:4–5; Rev 2:10

The wisdom of making hope a
priority
Heb 6:19 *See also* Ps 147:10–11

Putting true riches above earthly
wealth Lk 16:9 *See also* Dt 15:8;
Mt 6:24; 19:21 pp Mk 10:21 pp Lk 18:22;
Mt 19:29 pp Mk 10:29–30
pp Lk 18:29–30; Heb 11:26

Putting eternal joy before temporal
hardship 2Co 4:17–18 *See also*
Ac 14:22; 16:25; Ro 8:18; 2Ti 2:10;
Heb 10:34

The wisdom of making love a
priority
1Co 13:13 *Paul's concern that love, rather
than competition over spiritual gifts,
should be made a priority.*

Loyalty rather than opportunism
Pr 18:24 *See also* Ru 1:16; 2Ti 4:10
*Demas' love for this world rather than
loyalty*

Following the Spirit rather than sinful
human nature Gal 5:16 *Merely "human"
activity betrays a failure of love for God.
See also* Ps 147:10–11; Isa 31:1–3;
Ro 8:5

Inner sincerity rather than outward
appearance Ro 12:9 *See also* 1Sa 16:7;
Eph 6:5; Col 3:22

Actions rather than mere words
Jas 2:18 *See also* Mt 7:21–22; 1Jn 3:18

Peace rather than disharmony
Ro 12:18 *See also* Ro 14:19; Heb 12:14

Truth rather than falsehood Pr 12:19
See also Ac 5:4; Col 3:9

See also

1460 truth	8283 joy
5569 hardship	8292 love
6166 flesh, sinful nature	8318 patience
	8335 reverence & blessing
6644 eternal life	
8020 faith	8808 riches
8030 trust	9610 hope

8465

progress

The process of development and
growth, of special importance in the
life of believers. Scripture stresses the
importance of progress, both of the
individual believer and of the
church, and the need to work
towards that goal.

Progress in the Christian life
should be expected
2Co 3:18; Eph 4:15 *See also* Job 17:9;
Ps 84:5,7; 92:12; Pr 4:18; Ro 8:29–30

Believers are to strive for
progress in their Christian lives
Php 2:12 *See also* Ps 18:29;
1Co 9:24–27; Php 3:12–14; 1Th 3:12;
2Th 1:3; 1Ti 4:15; Heb 6:1; 1Pe 2:2;
2Pe 1:5–8; 3:18

Progress in the Christian life
brings assurance
Heb 3:14 *See also* Mt 10:22 pp Mk 13:13;
Mt 24:13; Heb 6:9–11

The church is expected to
progress
Mt 16:18; 13:31–32 pp Mk 4:30–32
pp Lk 13:18–19 Eph 4:16 *See also*
Ac 2:47; 4:4; 5:14; 6:7; 11:21

See also

4450 fruit	8026 faith, growth in
4971 seasons of life	8104 assurance
5787 ambition, positive	8162 spiritual vitality
	8266 holiness
5902 maturity	8347 spiritual growth
6744 sanctification	
7020 church, the	8443 growth

8466

reformation

The process of bringing religious
practices and beliefs back into line
with the word of God. The OT
portrays Israel as requiring
reformation at several points in her
history. God's people continue to
need to review their beliefs and
practices in the light of God's word.

The continual need to turn from
idolatry
1Sa 7:3 *Idolatry was the besetting sin of*

Israel and the point at which all reforms had to begin. See also Ge 35:2; Jos 24:14–24; Jdg 6:25–27; 2Ki 10:18–27; 11:17–18 pp 2Ch 23:16–17; 2Ch 19:3; 33:15; 1Co 10:14; 1Jn 5:21

The reform of Asa
He removed idols 1Ki 15:12–13

He repaired the altar of the temple 2Ch 15:8,18

As a result the people sought and found God 2Ch 15:9–15

The reform of Hezekiah
He removed idols and even local shrines dedicated to God 2Ki 18:4 pp 2Ch 31:1

He established worship in the renovated and consecrated temple 2Ch 29:3–7,15–28

The covenant between God and his people was renewed 2Ch 29:10–11,29–31; 30:1–27; 31:2–19

The reform of Josiah
He repaired the temple 2Ki 22:3–7 pp 2Ch 34:8–13

He ended false worship 2Ki 23:4–24 pp 2Ch 34:3–7; 2Ch 34:33

The results of Josiah's reform 2Ki 22:11–20 pp 2Ch 34:19–28 *The prevailing attitude was that God would ensure that no disaster would befall his chosen people. Now the need to turn from sin and complacency was reiterated and repentance ensued;* 2Ki 23:1–3 pp 2Ch 34:29–32; 2Ki 23:3 pp 2Ch 34:31–32; 2Ki 23:21–23 pp 2Ch 35:1–19

The reforms of Ezra and Nehemiah
The problem of intermarriage was dealt with Ezr 10:2–3 *The objection to intermarriage was based on religious not racial grounds. It led to a corruption of the faith. See also* Ezr 9:1–15; 10:5–17; Ne 13:23–27

The temple was purified Ne 13:4–13

The Sabbath-rest was reaffirmed Ne 13:15 *See also* Ne 13:16–22

Incomplete reforms
2Ki 10:28–29 *See also* 1Ki 15:14 pp 2Ch 15:17; 2Ki 3:2–3; 12:2–3

The call to reform
To Israel Jer 7:3 *See also* 2Ch 7:14; Isa 1:16–17; 55:6–7; Jer 18:11; 26:13; 35:15; Zec 1:3; Ac 3:19–26

To the church Rev 3:2–3 *See also* 1Co 5:1–13; Rev 2:5; 3:15–20

To individuals Jas 1:21 *See also* Ro 12:2; 2Co 6:14–7:1; Eph 4:22–24; Col 3:5–10; Jas 1:22–25; 4:7–10

See also

1640 Book of the Law	8144 renewal
	8148 revival
6732 repentance	8490 watchfulness
6740 returning to God	8768 idolatry
	8784 nominal
6744 sanctification	religion
7390 Levites	8831 syncretism

---

reminders

The means of calling to mind important matters or events. Scripture stresses the importance of being reminded of God's dealings with his people in the past.

The importance of being reminded of God's words and deeds
1Co 15:1; 2Pe 1:12 *See also* 2Pe 3:1

Reminders of God's covenant and faithfulness
Ge 9:12–16 *See also* Ge 17:9–14

Reminders of God's intervention in history
Jude 5 *See also* Ex 12:14–20 pp Dt 16:1–8; Ex 13:3–10; 17:14; 1Co 11:23–26; 2Pe 1:12–16

Reminders to people of their sin or shortcomings
Heb 10:3–4 *See also* Ge 41:9; Ex 30:16; Nu 5:11–15; Eze 29:16

Reminders to people to be faithful to God
Nu 15:38–40 *See also* Ro 11:22; Heb 12:1–3; 2Pe 3:1–2

Reminders to people of their potential and gifts from God
2Ti 1:6 *See also* 1Ti 4:14

Reminders to God's people on matters of faith and conduct
Ro 15:15 *See also* Dt 31:9–13; 1Co 4:17; 15:1–2; Tit 3:1–2

See also

1035 God, faithfulness	7394 memorial
	7435 sacrifice, in OT
1345 covenant	8644 commemoration
4845 rainbow	
6020 sin	8670 remembering
7355 feasts & festivals	8763 forgetting
	8764 forgetting God

---

renunciation

The deliberate rejection or disavowal, especially of a person or object.

Renunciation of the LORD
Jdg 2:12; Isa 1:28; Ac 3:13 *See also* Ex 32:8; Jos 22:16; 2Ki 22:17; 1Ch 28:9; Jer 5:19; Mt 24:10; 2Ti 2:12

Renunciation of evil
In repentance Ps 37:27 *See also* Jer 35:15; Eze 14:6; Da 4:27; 2Co 4:2; 1Ti 6:20

To find God's mercy 2Ch 7:14 *See also* Pr 28:13; Eze 18:21; Jnh 3:10

Self-renunciation and the Christian life
An integral part of discipleship Mt 16:24 pp Mk 8:34 pp Lk 9:23 *See also* Mk 10:28; Lk 5:28; 14:33; Php 3:8

The example of Jesus Christ Mk 10:45 *See also* Jn 10:17; Php 2:7–8

See also

4132 demons, malevolence	8120 following Christ
5764 attitudes, negative to God	8475 self-denial
	8481 self-sacrifice
6231 rejection of God	8704 apostasy
6652 forgiveness	8737 evil, responses to
6732 repentance	
6114 discipleship	

---

respect

An attitude of reverence and deference, reflecting an appreciation of the significance of the person or thing that is esteemed.

8470
respect, for God's character

God's revelation of himself calls for deference, honour and a response of right living.

Respect for God's name
Ps 29:2 *See also* Ex 20:7 pp Dt 5:11; Ex 23:20–21; Lev 18:21; 19:12; 22:31–33; 24:10–16; Ps 86:9–11; Jer 3:16–17; Mal 2:1–2

Respect for God's presence
Ex 3:5–6 *See also* Ex 33:19–23; Ps 89:7; Isa 6:1–5; Zep 1:7; Zec 2:13

Respect for God's word
Dt 4:2 *See also* Dt 12:32; Jos 1:7–8; Pr 30:5–6; 2Pe 1:19–21; Rev 22:18–19

Respect for God's ark and sanctuary
Lev 19:30 *See also* 1Sa 6:19–20; 2Sa 6:1–7; Ecc 5:1–2; Hab 2:20; Mt 21:12–13 pp Mk 11:15–17 pp Lk 19:45–46 pp Jn 2:13–17; Jer 7:11

Respect for God's servants
1Th 5:12–13 *See also* Ac 23:1–5; Ex 22:28; Ac 28:7–10; Php 2:29–30; 1Ti 5:17–18; Heb 13:7,17

Respect for God leads to godly living
Ex 20:20 *See also* 2Ch 6:30–31; Pr 16:6; Heb 11:7; 1Pe 1:14–17

See also

1045 God, glory of	5878 honour
1065 God, holiness of	8276 humility
	8334 reverence & God's nature
1610 Scripture	
5042 name of God, significance	8444 honouring God
	8453 obedience
5838 disrespect	8754 fear

8471
respect, for human beings

Each individual, created in the image of God, should be honoured and esteemed, and this should be worked out in every area of life.

Human beings are to be respected
They are made in the image of God Ge 9:5–6 *See also* Pr 14:31; 17:5; Col 3:9–11; Jas 3:9–10

The bounds of life belong to God
Ex 20:13 pp Dt 5:17 *See also*
Ex 21:22–25 *NIV footnote at verse 22;*
2Sa 1:14–15; 4:9–12; 1Ki 2:31–33;
Ps 139:13–16

The equality and dignity of human beings is commanded Dt 1:16–17 *See also* Ex 23:2–3; Lev 19:15; Dt 16:18–19; Pr 24:23–25; 28:21; Ac 10:24–28, 34–35; Jas 2:1–9; 1Pe 2:17

Respect in the family
Respect for parents is commanded
Ex 20:12 pp Dt 5:16 *See also* Lev 19:3;
Pr 1:8; Mal 1:6; Mt 15:4–6
pp Mk 7:10–13; Mt 19:19 pp Lk 18:20;
Eph 6:1–3; Col 3:20; Heb 12:9

Disrespect for parents is condemned
Dt 27:16 *See also* Ex 21:17; Lev 20:9;
Pr 30:17; Isa 45:10; 2Ti 3:1–2

Examples of those who respected their parents Ge 9:20–23 *Shem and Japheth;*
Ge 47:11–12 *Joseph;* 1Sa 22:3 *David;*
1Ki 2:19 *Solomon;* 1Ki 19:20 *Elisha Jesus Christ:* Lk 2:51; Jn 19:25–27

Respect in marriage Eph 5:33 *See also*
Eph 5:21–25; Col 3:18–19; 1Pe 3:6–7

Respect for children Mt 18:10 *See also*
Lev 20:1–5; Mt 18:5–6 pp Mk 9:36–37
pp Lk 9:47–48; Mt 19:13–15
pp Mk 10:13–16 pp Lk 18:15–17;
Eph 6:4; Col 3:20–21

Respect for leaders
Leaders must have gained respect
Dt 1:13–15 *See also* 1Sa 9:6; Pr 31:23;
1Ti 3:2–11

Leaders must be given respect
1Sa 26:9–11 *See also* 1Sa 24:1–7;
2Ki 3:14; Ro 13:1–7; 1Th 5:12;
Heb 13:17

Respect for old age
Lev 19:32 *See also* Job 32:4–7; La 5:12;
1Ti 5:1–2; Tit 2:2; 1Pe 5:5

Respect at the place of work
Dt 24:14–15 *See also* Lev 19:13;
Eph 6:5–9; Col 3:22–4:1; 1Ti 6:1–2;
1Pe 2:18

See also

5040 murder	5708 marriage
5061 sanctity of life	5727 old age,
5347 injustice	attitudes
5404 masters	5731 parents
5448 poverty,	8337 reverence &
attitudes to	behaviour
5520 servants	8452 neighbours,
5664 children	duty to

8472
respect, for environment

Although God created the universe and retains ultimate ownership of it, he has delegated responsibility for the well-being of the earth to the human race. This stewardship includes the care of the animal kingdom and the earth's natural resources.

God's creation is to be respected
The earth belongs to God Ps 24:1–2 *See*

also Ex 19:5–6; Lev 25:23; 1Ch 29:14;
Ps 50:9–12; 89:11; Hag 2:8

Responsibility to rule and care for the earth has been delegated to the human race Ge 1:26–28 *See also* Ge 9:1–3;
Ps 8:6–8; 115:16; Heb 2:8; Jas 3:7

God himself maintains a caring supervision of his creation Mt 6:26–30
pp Lk 12:24–28 *See also* Dt 11:10–15;
Ps 65:9–13; Mt 5:45

Respect for all nature and animals
Dt 20:19 *NIV footnote. See also*
Ex 23:4–5, 10–11; Dt 22:4, 6–7; 25:4;
Pr 12:10

Respect and care for the earth's natural resources
Ex 23:10–11 *See also* Lev 25:1–7;
Ne 10:31

See also

1325 God, the Creator	5002 human race & creation
4005 creation	5054 responsibility,
4026 world, God's creation	examples
4206 land	7428 Sabbath
4604 animals	7482 Year of Jubilee

8474
seeing God

Perceiving God in all his fulness. Scripture stresses that God, as spirit, is invisible to sinful human beings. He has, however, been revealed in Jesus Christ, who is his perfect likeness, and he will be seen in all his glory at the end of history when he comes in judgment.

No human can see the face of God in all his fulness
1Ti 6:15–16 *See also* Dt 4:10–12;
Jn 6:46; 1Ti 1:17; 1Jn 4:12

Privileged individuals may catch a glimpse of God
Ex 33:21–23 *See also* Ge 16:13–14
Hagar; Nu 12:5–8 *Moses;* Jdg 6:11–24
Gideon; Jdg 13:2–23 *Manoah and his wife*

Threat of death on seeing the face of God
Ex 33:20 *See also* Ge 32:24–30;
Ex 19:21; 24:9–11

Seeing God in a vision
Isa 6:1 *See also* 1Ki 22:19 *Micaiah*
pp 2Ch 18:18; Eze 1:1–28 *Ezekiel;*
Ac 7:55–56 *Stephen*

God may be seen in Jesus Christ
Jn 14:8–9; Col 1:15 *See also* Jn 1:1–18;
1Jn 5:20

The hope of seeing God at the resurrection
1Co 13:12 *See also* Job 19:26–27;
Ps 17:15; Mt 5:8; 1Co 13:12; Heb 12:14;
Rev 1:7

See also

1090 God, majesty of	4140 angel of the
1403 God, revelation	Lord
1469 visions	5135 blindness,
2078 Christ, sonship of	spiritual
2565 Christ, second coming	9310 resurrection

8475
self-denial

The willingness to deny oneself possessions or status, in order to grow in holiness and commitment to God. This practice is commended and illustrated by Jesus Christ himself, and underlies Christian fellowship within the church.

The wisdom of self-denial
Pr 23:20–21 *See also* Pr 25:16

Examples of self-denial in order to put God first
Da 1:8; Heb 11:25 *See also* Lev 23:29;
Jer 35:6; Da 10:3; Lk 1:15; 7:33
pp Mt 11:18

Self-denial is a requirement of following Jesus Christ
Mt 16:24 pp Mk 8:34 pp Lk 9:23
Ac 21:13; Php 3:7; 1Pe 2:11 *See also*
Mt 5:29; 6:10; 9:9 pp Mk 2:13–14
pp Lk 5:27–28 *the calling of Matthew;*
Mt 10:37–38 pp Lk 14:26–27 *the cost of being a disciple;* Mt 18:8 pp Mk 9:43;
Mt 19:21 pp Lk 18:22 *the rich young man;*
Mt 19:27 pp Mk 10:28 pp Lk 18:28 *Peter left everything to follow Jesus Christ;*
Mt 19:29 pp Mk 10:29–30
pp Lk 18:29–30 *the rewards of self-denial for the sake of the gospel;* Lk 5:11; 14:33;
21:34; Ac 20:24; Ro 6:2,6,11; 8:13; 12:1;
13:14; 1Co 6:12; 9:25–27; 2Co 8:5 *the example of the Macedonian churches;*
Gal 2:20; 5:16,23; Col 3:3,5; 2Ti 2:21;
Tit 2:12–13; Jas 4:7; 1Pe 4:2

Self-denial for the sake of others
Ru 2:11; Php 2:4 *Esther put her own life at risk for the sake of her people See also*
Ex 32:32; Est 4:16
Self-denial for the sake of those weak in their faith: Ro 14:21; 15:1; 1Co 8:13;
9:23
1Co 10:24,33; 12:15; Eph 4:2; 5:21;
Php 2:17,20–21 *the example of Timothy;*
Col 1:24; 2Ti 2:10; Tit 3:2; 1Pe 3:8; 5:5

Self-denial and the example of Jesus Christ
Mt 26:39 pp Mk 14:36 pp Lk 22:42
2Co 8:9 *See also* Ps 40:7; Isa 53:7;
Mt 11:29; Jn 13:1–17; Ro 15:3;
Eph 5:1–2; Php 2:5–8

See also

2339 Christ, example of	8339 self-control
	8356 unselfishness
2410 cross, the	8429 fasting
5959 submission	8451 mortification
8116 discipleship, cost	8468 renunciation
8120 following Christ	8481 self-sacrifice
	8827 selfishness

self-discipline

The dedicated training, through the study of Scripture, prayer and self-control, which enables Christians to be more effective witnesses to the gospel, to lead lives more pleasing to God, and to win the crown that awaits those who are victorious over sin.

Self-discipline is training oneself to be godly
1Ti 4:7 *See also* Ro 13:14; 1Co 9:24–27; Eph 4:23–24; Php 3:12–14; Col 3:12; 2Ti 1:7; Heb 5:14; 12:1

Self-discipline and the study of Scripture
Ps 119:9–11; 2Ti 3:16–17 *See also* Dt 29:29

Self-discipline involves learning through experience
Tit 2:12 *See also* Ro 5:3–5

Self-discipline should transform the whole person
A Christian's thoughts should be disciplined 2Co 10:5 *See also* Ro 12:3 *Renewal of the mind a prerequisite:* Ro 12:2; Eph 4:23 1Pe 4:7

A Christian's speech should be disciplined Ps 141:3 *See also* Jas 3:2–12

A Christian's behaviour should be disciplined Ro 14:20–21

A Christian's body should be disciplined 1Co 9:27 *See also* Ro 6:12–13; 8:13; Eph 4:22; Col 3:5; Jas 3:2

Self-discipline prevents God's discipline
1Co 11:31–32

Physical self-discipline is of some value, but only in this life
1Ti 4:8 *See also* 1Co 9:25

An elder should be self-disciplined
Tit 1:8

Examples of those who exercised self-discipline
Ge 22:9–14 *Abraham;* Ge 39:8–12 *Joseph;* 2Sa 11:11–13 *Uriah Daniel:* Da 1:8,11–13 Mt 4:4 *Jesus Christ;* 1Co 8:13 *Paul*

Self-discipline strengthens believers when faced with temptation
Mt 5:29 pp Mk 9:47; Ro 8:13; Gal 5:24

The reward for self-discipline is a crown and a prize
1Co 9:25 *See also* 1Co 9:24,27; Php 3:14; Col 2:18; 1Th 2:19; 2Ti 4:8; Jas 1:12; 1Pe 5:4; Rev 2:10; 3:11

See also
1610 Scripture
5280 crown
5596 victory
5771 abstinence
5853 experience of life
6744 sanctification

8114 discipleship
8140 prize
8230 discipline
8339 self-control
8475 self-denial
8674 study

self-examination

Reflection on one's own character, motives and actions, in order to judge whether they are truly in accordance with Christian values.

8478
self-examination, teaching on

Self-examination should take place on the basis of God's revelation of himself and the example he sets believers in Jesus Christ. It is especially important before confessing one's sins.

The importance of self-examination
Hag 1:5 *See also* Ps 4:4; 77:6; Hag 1:7; 2:15,18; 1Co 11:28; 2Co 13:5; Heb 3:12

A lack of self-examination leads to pride and self-delusion
1Co 11:28–29 *See also* Mt 7:5; Jn 8:7; Ro 2:1–4

Self-examination is not easy because of humanity's fallen nature
Ps 19:12–14 *See also* Jer 17:9

God helps believers in their self-examination
Ps 26:2 *See also* Job 7:17–18; 13:9,23; Ps 11:4–5; 139:23–24; Pr 5:21; Jer 17:10; 20:12

The purpose of self-examination is to lead people to God and amendment of life
La 3:40–42 *See also* Ps 42:5,11; 43:5; Jas 1:23–25

Self-examination is especially important when ministering to others
Gal 6:1 *See also* Ro 14:4; Gal 6:3–4; 1Ti 4:16; Jas 3:1

See also
1461 truth, nature of
6029 sin, forgiveness
6624 confession of sin

8451 mortification
8662 meditation

8479
self-examination, examples of

Scripture provides numerous examples of self-examination, and its results. In particular, self-examination is often portrayed as leading to repentance.

Self-examination in the experience of Israel
Self-examination at the entry into the promised land Jos 7:1–26; 24:14

Self-examination during the war with the Philistines 1Sa 14:24–47

Self-examination at the time of the exile Jer 31:18–20

Self-examination after returning from exile in Babylon Ne 8:9; Hag 1:5–12; 2:15–19

Self-examination by other nations
Jnh 3:1–10

Self-examination in the experience of individuals
King David Ps 51:3–6 *See also* 2Sa 12:1–13; Ps 32:3–5

Job Job 42:1–6

The psalmists Ps 119:59 *See also* Ps 42:5,11; 43:5

The lost son Lk 15:17–20

The disciples Mt 26:22 pp Mk 14:19

Judas *See also* Mt 26:25; 27:3–5

See also
6732 repentance   8820 self-confidence

self-sacrifice

The willingness to leave one's possessions or to give them to others; to deny oneself to the point of death or to give oneself in the service of God or other people.

Self-sacrifice as forfeiting one's present comfort for the sake of others
Ru 2:11 *See also* Ge 44:33–34; Heb 10:34; 11:24–27

Self-sacrifice as giving one's possessions to others
Jesus Christ commends the willingness to give away one's possessions Mt 19:21 pp Mk 10:21 pp Lk 18:22 *See also* Lk 12:33

God rewards those who give their possessions away Lk 18:28–30 pp Mt 19:27–29 pp Mk 10:28–30

Sacrificing one's possessions as demonstrated in the life of the church *See also* Ac 2:44–45; 4:32–37; 2Co 8:1–5

Self-sacrifice as leaving all and following Jesus Christ
Such sacrifice is a condition of discipleship Lk 14:33 *See also* Mt 10:37 pp Lk 14:26 *This means loving Jesus Christ over and above one's immediate family.*

Those willing to leave everything to follow Jesus Christ Lk 5:27–28; Php 3:8

Self-sacrifice as the metaphorical laying down of one's life for others
Followers of Jesus Christ are required to give themselves in the service of others Jn 12:24–25 *See also* Mt 10:38

pp Lk 14:27; Mt 16:24–25
pp Mk 8:34–35 pp Lk 9:23–24;
Lk 17:33; 1Jn 3:16–18

Examples of those who demonstrated such self-sacrifice 2Co 4:10–11 *See also* 1Co 9:19–23; 15:30–31; 2Co 11:23–29; 12:15

Self-sacrifice as the literal laying down of one's life
Jesus Christ warns his disciples to be prepared to give their lives
Mt 10:21–22 pp Mk 13:12–13
pp Lk 21:16–17

Sacrificing one's life is of no value without love 1Co 13:3

Examples of those willing to give their lives for the sake of God and others
Ac 20:23–24 *See also* Ex 32:32;
1Ch 11:15–19; Est 4:14–16; Mt 26:39
pp Mk 14:35–36 pp Lk 22:42; Php 2:17

Examples of those who gave their lives in God's service Ac 7:59–60 *See also* Jdg 11:36–38; Php 2:5–8;
Heb 11:36–38; Rev 20:4

See also

2570 Christ, suffering	8342 servanthood
8116 discipleship, cost	8356 unselfishness
8120 following Christ	8450 martyrdom
	8475 self-denial

8482

spiritual warfare

The struggle against the forces of evil, which is a constant feature of the life of faith. Scripture locates the origins of spiritual warfare in the rebellion of Satan and his angels against God and affirms the hope of God's final victory over such forces through Jesus Christ's death and resurrection.

8483
spiritual warfare, causes of

Spiritual warfare has its origin in a rebellion of many angels against God. Satan is seen as the prince of this world, leading an array of forces opposed to God. Although disarmed by Jesus Christ on the cross, they remain a powerful threat to the church and to individual believers.

Satan and his angels fall
2Pe 2:4 *See also* Isa 14:12–15;
Eze 28:12–19 *Some believe the kings of Babylon and Tyre to be types of Satan;*
1Ti 3:6; Jude 6

Satan and his angels comprise a well-organised army
Eph 6:12 *See also* Col 1:13

Satan and his angels will ultimately be fully disarmed by Jesus Christ
Col 2:15; Rev 12:7–9 *See also* Mk 3:27
pp Mt 12:29; Lk 10:18; Jn 12:31;
Heb 2:14; 1Jn 3:8

Satan persecutes the church
Rev 12:13 *The woman is here thought to be symbolic of the church. See also* Rev 2:10; 13:7 *The dragon is here thought to be symbolic of the world's persecution (empowered by Satan) of the church.*

Satan opposes the gospel
2Co 4:4 *See also* Mt 13:19 pp Mk 4:15
pp Lk 8:12; Mt 13:38–39; 1Th 2:2,18

Examples of opposition to the first Christians Ac 6:8–14; 7:54–58 *Stephen stoned to death;* Ac 8:1–3 *Saul causes havoc in Jerusalem.*
Opposition to Paul and his companions:
Ac 13:6–12,44–45; 17:13; 18:6,12
Violent hostility to Paul and his companions: Ac 9:23; 14:5,19; 16:16–24;
17:5–6; 19:23–29; 20:3; 21:27–36
Jewish plots against Paul in Jerusalem:
Ac 23:12–15; 25:3

Satan attacks individual believers
Rev 12:17 *See also* Job 2:7; Lk 22:31–32;
2Ti 3:12; 1Pe 5:8

See also

2372 Christ, victory	7505 Jews, the
4111 angels, servants	8738 evil, victory over
4116 angels opposed to God	8773 jealousy
4120 Satan	8787 opposition to God
5598 victory over spiritual forces	8794 persecution
5975 violence	8833 threats

8484
spiritual warfare, enemies in

Christians are at war with the world, the flesh and the devil. Satan empowers the world to attack believers externally, persecuting, deceiving and seducing them. Internally, sinfulness frustrates the efforts of believers to serve God fully.

The world is an enemy
Jas 4:4 *"world" here refers to the sinful human race, hostile to the truth and to the people of God. See also* Ro 12:2;
1Jn 2:15–17; 5:4

The world hates Christians
Jn 15:19–20 *See also* Mt 5:10–12
pp Lk 6:22; Jn 16:2; 17:14; 1Pe 4:12–16;
1Jn 3:13; Rev 13:7 *The beast may represent the world's antichristian persecution.*

The world has its own false teaching and religion Col 2:8 *See also* 1Ti 4:1;
2Ti 4:3–4; 1Jn 4:1; 2Jn 7–11; Jude 3–4;
Rev 13:11; 19:20 *This beast is thought to represent antichristian religion.*

The world seeks to seduce Christians
1Jn 2:16 *See also* Lk 12:15,19; 2Ti 4:10;
Tit 2:12; Heb 11:24–25; Rev 17:1–5
Babylon may represent the world's seduction.

Sinful human nature is an enemy
Gal 5:17; 1Pe 2:11 *See also* Ro 6:12;
7:14–23; 8:13; Gal 5:24; Col 3:5;
Heb 12:4; Jas 4:1

The devil is an enemy
1Pe 5:8 *See also* Mt 13:39 pp Mk 4:15

pp Lk 8:12; Jn 17:15; 2Th 3:3; Rev 2:10;
12:17

He seeks to tempt Christians 1Th 3:5
See also Ge 3:1–6; Heb 2:18; 4:15

He seeks to deceive 2Co 11:3;
Rev 12:9 *See also* Ge 3:13; 2Co 2:11; 4:4;
11:4; Rev 20:3

He constantly seeks to accuse believers Rev 12:10 *See also* Job 1:9–11;
Zec 3:1

See also

3278 Holy Spirit, indwelling	6166 flesh, sinful nature
4018 life, spiritual	6251 temptation, resisting
4027 world, fallen	7105 believers
4121 Satan, enemy of God	8345 servanthood & worship
5201 accusation	8451 mortification
5931 resistance	
6030 sin, avoidance	

8485
spiritual warfare, as conflict

The warfare believers must fight is spiritual, personal, intense and continual. It calls for courage, determination and prayer, and therefore believers must stand in God's strength and use the armour he has provided.

General descriptions of spiritual conflict
It is spiritual Eph 6:12 *See also* Zec 4:6;
2Co 10:3–4; Gal 5:17; 1Pe 2:11

It is personal Lk 22:31–32 *See also*
Ro 7:23; 2Ti 3:12; 4:18

It is strenuous Heb 12:4 *See also*
Jn 16:33; Php 1:27–30; 1Pe 4:12–13

It is continual Eph 6:13 *See also* 2Ti 2:3;
Heb 3:13; Rev 12:10

How believers are to fight
With courage 1Co 16:13 *See also*
Jos 1:9; 10:25; 2Ch 32:6–8

With determination 1Ti 6:12 *See also*
2Th 1:4; Heb 10:23; 1Pe 5:9–10

With watchfulness 1Pe 5:8 *See also*
1Co 16:13; Gal 6:1; Eph 6:18

With prayer Eph 6:18 *See also* Ex 17:11;
Mt 6:13 pp Lk 11:4; Mt 26:41
pp Mk 14:38 pp Lk 22:46; Ac 12:5;
2Th 3:2

Standing in God's strength Eph 6:10
See also 1Sa 17:45; 2Sa 22:40;
Ps 18:32–36; 118:8; Eph 3:16; Php 4:13;
2Ti 2:1

Using the armour of God Eph 6:11 *See also* Ro 13:12–14; 2Co 10:4;
Eph 6:13–17

See also

1105 God, power of	8414
2066 Christ, power of	encouragement
5544 soldiers	8418 endurance
5566 suffering, encouragements in	8459 perseverance
	8493 watchfulness, believers
5957 strength, spiritual	8618 prayerfulness
8219 courage	8672 striving with God

8486
spiritual warfare, armour

The armour of God refers to the resources that Christians possess for defending themselves against the attacks of the world, the flesh and the devil.

God is the believer's strength and shield
Ps 28:7–8 See also Ge 15:1; Dt 33:29; Ps 3:3; 7:10; 119:114

Believers should be rightly clothed for battle
Ro 13:12–14 See also Eph 4:22–24; Col 3:9,12–14; 1Pe 4:1

Believers should put on the full armour of God
The belt of truth Eph 6:14
The importance of sound teaching: a good understanding of God's truth counters Satan's deceit: Ps 119:95,116; Eph 4:14–15; Col 2:8; 2Ti 1:13–14; 1Pe 1:13

The breastplate of righteousness Eph 6:14
Assurance that believers are righteous in God's sight will counter Satan's accusations: Pr 4:23; 13:6; Isa 61:10; Zec 3:1–4

The gospel of peace Eph 6:15
The peace of God reassures and gives confidence in times of trouble: Jn 14:27; 16:33; Php 4:6–7

The shield of faith Eph 6:16
Exercising faith draws strength from God, guards against deception and helps overcome temptation: Ro 1:17; Hab 2:4; 1Pe 5:9; 1Jn 5:4

The helmet of salvation Eph 6:17
The expectation of future glory encourages the Christian soldier and helps overcome despair: 1Th 5:8–9; Tit 2:11–14; 1Jn 3:3

The Christian's spiritual weapons
2Co 10:4

The sword of the Spirit Eph 6:17
The Scriptures give readiness and confidence in battle and a sure defence against the evil one: Ps 119:11; 2Ti 3:16–17; Heb 4:12

The armour of God is worn with prayer Eph 6:18
Prayer ensures that believers recognise their need to turn to God and depend on him alone: Ps 55:16–18; Heb 4:16; Jas 5:16

See also

1460 truth	7797 teaching
1610 Scripture	8020 faith
3236 Holy Spirit &	8154 righteousness
Scripture	8422 equipping,
5292 defence, divine	spiritual
5953 stability	8498 witnessing &
6705 peace,	Holy Spirit
experience	9613 hope as
	confidence

8488

tithing

The practice of offering to God a tenth of the harvest of the land and of livestock, as holy to the LORD. The idea is also used in a more general sense, meaning offering one-tenth of one's income to the Lord.

Tithing was practised before the giving of the OT law
Ge 14:18–20 *Abraham offered a tenth of the goods taken in battle, apparently in thankfulness to God for victory. See also* Ge 28:22; Heb 7:1–3

Tithing under the law
Tithing extends to all kinds of produce and livestock Lev 27:30–32 *Cereal and fruit offerings could be commuted to money. See also* 2Ch 31:5–6; Ne 10:35–38; 13:12

All tithes were paid to the Levites Nu 18:21–24; Ne 10:37–38; Heb 7:5

Tithes were to be paid in a designated place Dt 12:5–6; 14:22–29; 26:2 *Tithes were paid in Jerusalem, or every three years in towns where the tithe feast was eaten.*

Levites offered a tenth to the LORD Nu 18:25–29; Ne 10:39

Uses of the tithe
Support of the Levites Nu 18:21 *See also* 2Ch 31:4

The tithe meal Dt 14:23

A three-yearly gift to the poor Dt 14:28–29

Tithing of minor items must not lead to neglect of major matters
Mt 23:23 *See also* Lk 11:42; 18:9–14

Freewill offerings were made in addition to the tithe
They were given freely Ex 36:3 *See also* Lev 7:12–18; Nu 15:3; Ezr 1:4; Ps 54:6; Eze 46:12

They were given according to ability Dt 16:10 *See also* Dt 16:17; Ac 11:29; 1Co 16:2; 2Co 8:12 *There is no specific command in the NT for the church to tithe, but many commands to give generously and to support the Lord's work.*

Blessing promised to those who tithe
Mal 3:10 *See also* Pr 3:9–10

Failure to tithe and abuses of the tithe
Mal 3:8–10 *See also* Lev 27:33; 1Sa 8:15,17; Ne 13:10

See also

4442 firstfruits	7402 offerings
5375 law	7550 Pharisees
5412 money	7766 priests
5446 poverty	7912 collections
5577 taxation	8260 generosity
7366 freewill offering	8434 giving

8489

urgency

The urgency of the call to repent
In the preaching of John the Baptist Mt 3:2 pp Mk 1:4 pp Lk 3:3

In the preaching of Jesus Christ Mk 1:15 *See also* Mt 4:17; Lk 13:3

In the preaching of Peter Ac 2:38 *See also* Ac 3:19

In the preaching of Paul Ac 20:21; 26:20

The urgency of the need to proclaim the gospel
2Ti 4:1–2 *See also* Jn 4:35–37; 2Co 6:2; 1Th 5:2 *in the light of the coming day of the Lord*

Examples of urgent summons by officials
Nu 22:37; 1Sa 21:8; Da 3:22

See also

2375 kingdom of	5463	proclamations
God	6734	repentance,
4903 time		importance
4924 delay	7754	preaching
5048 opportunities &	8461	priorities
salvation	8652	importunity

8490

watchfulness

The state of being alert and expectant; watching over someone in one's care or waiting for the arrival of someone important or for some significant event. Scripture lays particular emphasis on the need to watch for the second coming of Jesus Christ.

8491

watchfulness, divine

The Lord's alertness to the needs of his people, his constant care for them and his awareness of the power and evil intent of their enemies.

The Lord's watchfulness over his people in danger or trouble
Ps 121:1–8 *See also* Ex 3:16; Dt 32:9–10; Ezr 5:5; Ps 1:6; 11:4–5; 17:8; 32:6; 33:16–18; 34:7; 127:1; 145:20; Zec 9:8; 12:4; Mt 10:29–31; Jn 10:1–9; 2Ti 1:12

The Lord's watchfulness means that his people's needs are met
Ps 146:9 *See also* Ge 28:15; 48:15; Dt 2:7; 11:12; 2Ch 16:9; Job 10:12; 29:2; Jer 24:6; 31:28; Da 9:18

The watchfulness of a shepherd Ps 23:1; 28:9; Isa 40:11; Mt 2:6; Jn 10:1–9

The Lord's watchfulness means that he hears his people's prayers
Ps 34:15 *See also* 1Ki 8:28–30 pp 2Ch 6:20; 1Ki 9:3 pp 2Ch 7:16; Ne 1:6; 1Pe 3:12

The Lord's watchfulness with a view to correction
Jer 7:25–26 *See also* Jer 7:13; 11:7; 25:4; 32:33; 2Sa 22:28; Job 33:11; Jer 16:16–17

The Lord's watchfulness in seeking out those who have gone astray
Eze 34:16 *See also* Mt 18:12 pp Lk 15:4; 1Pe 2:25

People are vulnerable without the Lord's watchfulness

Mt 9:36 *See also* 1Ki 22:17
pp 2Ch 18:16; Isa 13:14; Eze 34:11–12

See also

1035 God, faithfulness	4957 night
	5148 ear
1220 God as shepherd	5149 eyes
	5537 sleeplessness
2021 Christ, faithfulness	5942 security
	5977 waiting
2330 Christ as shepherd	6738 rescue

8492
watchfulness, of leaders

Leaders must be alert to the needs of those they serve and also to the dangers that surround believers in the world. The OT teaching on watchmen provides an indication of the importance of watchfulness and the responsibility of those called to be watchful.

Leaders are required to be watchful

Eze 3:17 *See also* Eze 33:7–9; Jn 21:16

They are accountable to God Eze 3:18
See also Mk 13:34–35; Heb 13:17

They must warn against false teachers
Ac 20:31 *Elders are called overseers in Acts 20:28; 1Ti 3:2; Tit 1:7; 1Pe 5:2. See also* Jn 10:1–3; Ac 20:29; 2Ti 4:2–5; Tit 1:9–11

Examples of leaders' warnings to churches 1Co 4:14 *See also* Ro 16:17; Gal 5:21; 1Th 4:1; Tit 3:10; Rev 22:18

Leaders' watchfulness in prayer

Isa 62:6–7 *See also* 1Sa 12:23;
Ro 1:9–10; Eph 1:16; Php 1:4; 2Th 1:11

Leaders need to watch over their own lives

Ac 20:28 *See also* Mk 14:29–30;
1Ti 3:2–7; 4:15–16; Tit 1:6–8; Jas 3:1;
3Jn 9–10

Watchmen sometimes fail to be watchful

Isa 56:9–12; Eze 34:1–10; Zec 10:2–3

See also

5052 responsibility to God	7939 ministry
5802 care	8252 faithfulness, relationships
5803 carelessness	8318 patience
7734 leaders, spiritual	8611 prayer for others
7789 shepherd, church leader	8678 waiting on God
	8839 unfaithfulness

8493
watchfulness, of believers

Alertness to dangers and blessings in the Christian life, and also to opportunities to do good.

Watchfulness for dangers

1Pe 5:8 *See also* Pr 4:23

The danger of false teaching Mt 7:15
See also Ps 94:8; Pr 8:33–34; Mt 24:4–5;
Mk 8:15; Ro 16:17; 1Co 16:13

The danger of temptation Mt 26:41
pp Mk 14:38 *See also* Dt 4:15; 1Ki 2:4;
Lk 12:15; 17:1–3; 1Co 10:12; Gal 6:1;
2Jn 8

The danger of neglecting the word of God Dt 4:9 *See also* Jos 22:5; 1Ki 2:3;
Heb 2:1; 12:25; 2Pe 1:19

The danger of damage to the Lord's work Ne 4:9; 7:3

The danger of speaking sinfully
Ps 39:1; 141:3; Pr 13:3; 21:23; Jas 1:26;
3:5–8; 1Pe 3:10

Watchfulness for blessings

Ps 25:15; 59:9; 123:1–2; 130:5–6;
Isa 40:9; Mic 7:7; Lk 2:25,36–38

Watchfulness and prayer

Col 4:2–3 *See also* Mt 26:41
pp Mk 14:38; Mk 13:33 fn; Lk 21:36;
Eph 6:18; 1Pe 4:7

Watchfulness for the return of Jesus Christ

Mt 24:42–44 *See also* Mt 25:1–13;
Mk 13:32–37; Lk 12:35–40; 21:32–36;
1Th 5:4–8; Rev 16:15

Watchfulness for opportunities to serve the Lord

1Pe 3:15 *See also* Eph 5:15–16;
Col 4:5–6

Meeting the needs of others Eph 6:18
See also Mt 26:36–40; Gal 6:10; Tit 3:1

Contrast with the watchfulness of unbelievers with evil intent

Ps 37:32 *See also* 1Sa 18:9; 19:11;
Ps 10:8; Jer 20:10; Mt 26:16; Mk 3:2;
Ac 9:24

Warning against neglect of watchfulness

Rev 3:2–3

See also

1335 blessing	8344 servanthood in believers
2565 Christ, second coming	
	8453 obedience
5534 sleep, spiritual	8477 self-examination
5767 attitudes in prayer	8618 prayerfulness
6248 temptation	9610 hope
8329 readiness	

8495

witnessing

The task of declaring what has happened, especially in relation to the life, death and resurrection of Jesus Christ. Believers are given the responsibility of proclaiming the good news of Jesus Christ to the world at all times and in all places.

8496
witnessing, importance of

Sharing the good news about God and Jesus Christ with others is a work to which some believers have a special calling, but in which all believers are to take part.

Witnessing is sharing the truth of God

Ps 145:10–12; Lk 24:46–48 *See also*
1Ch 16:7–9; Ps 71:15; Mt 27:54
pp Mk 15:39 pp Lk 23:47; Jn 1:35–36;
4:29

Believers are commanded to witness

Mt 28:18–19 *See also* Isa 12:4–5;
Mt 24:14 pp Mk 13:10; Ac 1:8; 9:15–16

Special ministries of witnessing

By the prophets Jn 1:6–8 *See also*
Jer 1:4–9; Eze 33:7–9; Jnh 1:2,9;
Jn 1:15,29,36; Ac 10:43

By Jesus Christ Jn 18:37 *See also*
Jn 3:31–34; Rev 1:5; 3:14

By the apostles Ac 4:33 *See also*
Ac 2:32; 10:39–42; 13:30–31;
1Jn 1:1–3

By Christian leaders 2Ti 1:8 *Paul, in prison for his faith, encourages the young leader, Timothy. See also* Ac 8:5; Eph 4:11

Witnessing is a task for all God's people

1Pe 2:9; 3:15 *See also* Ps 26:6–7;
107:1–2
All of the people of Israel are called to be God's witnesses: Isa 43:10,12; 44:8
Isa 52:7; Ac 8:4

Witnessing is a major aspect of Christian living

Ro 10:9–10 *See also* Mt 10:32–33
pp Mk 8:38 pp Lk 12:8–9; 2Co 4:13;
1Jn 2:23; 4:15

Examples of witnessing to Jesus Christ

Mt 16:16 pp Mk 8:29 pp Lk 9:20 *Simon Peter;* Lk 2:16–17 *shepherds;* Jn 1:40–42 *Andrew;* Jn 1:49 *Nathanael;* Jn 11:27 *Martha;* Jn 20:28 *Thomas;* Ac 8:37 fn *the Ethiopian eunuch*

Witnessing recounts personal experience

Isa 63:7 *See also* Ps 66:16; Jer 51:10;
Da 4:2; Mt 9:27–31; Mk 1:40–45;
Jn 9:25; Ac 4:20

Witnessing to the resurrection of Jesus Christ

Ac 2:32 *See also* Lk 24:33–35;
Ac 5:30–32; 1Co 15:3–7

See also

2354 Christ, mission	7724 evangelists
2427 gospel, transmission	7754 preaching
	7772 prophets
3224 Holy Spirit & preaching	8025 faith, origins of
	8407 confession of Christ
7706 apostles	8424 evangelism

8497
witnessing, approaches to

Scripture provides teaching, supported by examples, concerning when believers should witness, the methods they are to use, and the manner of doing it.

When and where to witness

In the home and family Mk 5:18–19
pp Lk 8:38–39 *See also* 2Ki 5:1–3;
Jn 1:41

To individuals Jn 1:40–42 *See also* Jn 4:7–26; Ac 8:30–35

To assembled groups Ac 17:17 *See also* Ac 5:42; 16:13; 19:8–9

Methods of witnessing

Sharing personal testimony Jn 4:29 *See also* Ac 22:3–8 *Paul uses the account of his conversion in witnessing.*

Explaining the Scriptures Ac 8:30–35 *See also* Isa 53:7–8; Ps 119:172; Ac 17:1–3,10–12

Using prophetic gifts 1Co 14:24–25

Answering questions Col 4:6 *See also* Jn 9:8–11,15–17,24–25; 1Pe 3:15

Through writing Jn 20:31 *See also* Lk 1:1–4

Through holy living Mt 5:16 *See also* 1Pe 3:1–2

Through acts of devotion Mt 26:6–7 pp Mk 14:3 *See also* Lk 7:36–38; Jn 12:1–3

The manner of witnessing

With love Mk 10:21 *See also* Php 1:15–17

With urgency 2Co 5:20 *See also* Eze 33:7–9

Fearlessly Eph 6:19–20 *See also* Ac 4:29

Clearly and courteously 1Pe 3:15 *See also* Ac 26:1–3; Col 4:4–6

See also

5046 opportunities	8202 boldness
5624 witnesses to Christ	8219 courage
	8264 gentleness
6629 conversion, examples	8266 holiness
	8292 love
6717 reconciliation, world to God	8469 respect
7739 missionaries	8489 urgency

8498
witnessing, and Holy Spirit

Christian witnessing is made effective through the empowering, strengthening and guiding of the Holy Spirit. Witnessing is an aspect of spiritual warfare, and believers need supernatural aid to face Satan's opposition.

The Holy Spirit supports believers in witnessing
Ac 5:31–32 *See also* Jn 15:26–27

The Holy Spirit empowers effective witness
Ac 1:8; 1Co 2:1–5 *See also* Lk 4:14–19; 24:48–49

He confirms the testimony of believers
1Th 1:5; Heb 2:3–4

He convinces people of their need
Jn 16:7–11

He brings people to new birth Jn 3:5–8

The Holy Spirit guides believers in witnessing
Ac 8:39–40 *See also* Ac 8:29–35; 16:6–7

Witnessing and spiritual warfare
Rev 12:11 *See also* Eph 6:15–17

Witnessing and persecution
Witnessing results in persecution
Rev 1:9 *See also* Ac 4:17; 5:40; 7:54–60 *Stephen's witnessing leads him to become*

the first Christian martyr. The English word "martyr" comes from the Greek word for "witness"; Ac 22:22–25; Eph 6:19–20; Col 4:3–4; 2Ti 1:8; Rev 2:12–13; 6:9; 17:6

Supernatural help to face persecution
Mt 10:18–20 pp Mk 13:9–11 pp Lk 21:12–15; Ac 7:55 *See also* Ac 5:18–19; 18:9–10

Witness is promoted by persecution
Ac 8:1–5; Php 1:12–14

See also

2372 Christ, victory	4121 Satan, enemy of God
3030 Holy Spirit, power	5565 suffering of believers
3230 Holy Spirit & regeneration	8450 martyrdom
3248 Holy Spirit, conviction	8482 spiritual warfare
3263 Holy Spirit, guidance	8794 persecution
3293 Holy Spirit, witness of	

8600
Prayer and worship of the believer

8602
prayer

Fellowship with God through Jesus Christ, expressed in adoration, thanksgiving and intercession, through which believers draw near to God and learn more of his will for their lives. Scripture stresses the vital role of the Holy Spirit in stimulating and guiding prayer.

This set of themes consists of the following:
8603 prayer, as a relationship with God
8604 prayer, as a response to God
8605 prayer, and God's will
8606 prayer, and Holy Spirit
8607 prayer, God's promises concerning
8608 prayer, and worship
8609 prayer, as praise and thanksgiving
8610 prayer, as asking God
8611 prayer, for others
8612 prayer, and faith
8613 prayer, persistence in
8614 prayer, answers to
8615 prayer, doubts about
8616 prayerlessness
8617 prayer, advice for effective
8618 prayerfulness
8619 prayer, in the church
8620 prayer, practicalities of

8603
prayer, as a relationship with God

Prayer is based on God's love for believers. Through his grace, he gives them things which they do not deserve, while through his mercy he

shields them from those things which they do deserve.

God's children can turn to their Father in prayer

Under the old covenant Isa 64:8–9 *See also* Ps 103:13–14; Isa 63:16

Under the new covenant Mt 6:9–13 pp Lk 11:2–4 *See also* Mt 6:6; 7:7–11 pp Lk 11:9–13; Ro 8:15; Gal 4:6

Jesus Christ's prayer life with his Father Mk 14:36 pp Mt 26:39 pp Mt 26:42 pp Lk 22:42 *See also* Jn 17:1–26

It is possible to approach God in prayer because of Jesus Christ's sacrifice
Heb 10:19–22 *See also* Eph 3:12; Heb 7:15–19

Prayer reflects a longing after God
Ps 42:1–2; Jer 29:12–13 *See also* Ps 130:5–6; 145:18–19; Pr 8:17; Isa 26:9; 33:2; La 3:25

See also

1040 God, fatherhood	8135 knowing God
1250 Abba	8656 longing for God
6606 access to God	
8122 friendship with God	

8604
prayer, as a response to God

Prayer offers believers a means of acknowledging the character and purposes of God and the opportunity to seek guidance concerning his will for them.

The direction of prayer is upwards towards God
Ps 123:1–2 *See also* Ps 25:1; 86:4; 121:1–2; 143:8–10; 145:15

Fellowship with God through prayer
Ps 73:23–26 *See also* Ex 33:11; 1Ki 8:57–59; Ps 16:2; 145:17–20; Mt 18:20

The habit of prayer
Lk 5:16 *See also* Ne 2:4 *Nehemiah felt so close to God that it was automatic for him to speak to God and the king almost simultaneously*; Da 6:10–11,13

Contemplative prayer as a response to God's presence
Ps 27:4 *See also* 1Ch 16:10–11 pp Ps 105:3–4; Ps 27:8; Isa 55:6; Jer 29:13; Ac 17:27–28; Heb 11:6

Prayer of acceptance in response to God's call
1Sa 3:10 *See also* Isa 6:8; Rev 3:20

Prayer of confession
In response to God's holiness
1Jn 1:5–9 *See also* Isa 6:3–7; 55:7–9

In response to sin being exposed
Ps 51:1–2 *See also* Ps 51:3–12

Prayer of co-operation in response to God's purposes
Jn 15:7–8 *See also* Ps 119:105–106; Lk 1:38; Jn 15:16

Prayer of confidence in response to God's mercy and grace
Heb 4:16 *See also* Ne 1:4–7; Ps 123:1–2; Jas 1:5–8

See also

1055 God, grace & mercy	6602 acceptance
1065 God, holiness of	6624 confession of sin
5767 attitudes in prayer	6732 repentance
	7921 fellowship

8605
prayer, and God's will

Prayer is concerned not only with the well-being of the one who prays. A vital aspect of its purpose is to allow the will of God to be done, and to bring glory and honour to his name.

True motives for prayer
The desire that God's name be honoured Mt 6:9–13 pp Lk 11:2–4 *See also* Nu 14:13–16; Jos 7:7–9; 2Sa 7:25–26; 1Ki 18:36–37; Ps 115:1; Jn 17:1

The desire that God's will be fulfilled Mt 6:9–13 pp Lk 11:2–4 *See also* Mt 26:39 pp Mk 14:36 pp Lk 22:42; Mt 26:42; Heb 10:7 *Submission to God's will characterised Jesus Christ's prayer life.*

God answers prayer that accords with his will
1Jn 5:14–15

Petitioners may enquire of God to discover his will Ps 143:10 *See also* Ge 25:22–23; Jdg 1:1–2; 2Sa 2:1; 1Ch 14:14–15

The Holy Spirit helps believers to pray in God's will Ro 8:26–27

God's response to prayers allows believers to discern his will
2Co 12:7–9 *See also* Ex 33:18–20; 2Sa 12:15–18; Job 19:7–8; Ps 35:13–14

God does not respond to the prayers of the wicked
Jn 9:31 *See also* Ps 66:18; Pr 15:8; Isa 1:15; 59:1–2; La 3:44; 1Pe 3:12

See also

1115 God, purpose of	5959 submission
1175 God, will of	8124 guidance
	8444 honouring God

8606
prayer, and Holy Spirit

See 3221 Holy Spirit, and prayer

8607
prayer, God's promises concerning

God promises to hear and respond to the prayers of his people, when they pray in the name of his Son and according to his will.

God expects his people to make requests of him in prayer
Mt 7:7–11 pp Lk 11:9–13 *See also* Mt 21:22

God promises to answer prayer in the name of Jesus Christ
Jn 14:13–14; 15:7 *See also* Jn 15:16; 16:23–24

God promises to respond to the prayers of his people in times of need
Ps 91:14–16 *See also* Ps 50:14–15

God promises to hear the prayers of the oppressed
Ps 10:17 *See also* Ex 22:22–23,26–27; Ps 102:19–20; Isa 41:17

God promises to hear the prayers of the truly penitent
2Ch 7:14 *See also* Eze 36:37; Zec 10:6; 13:8–9

God promises to hear the prayers of his obedient people
1Jn 3:22

The need in prayer to have confidence in God's promises
Mk 11:24; 1Jn 5:14 *See also* Mt 18:19

See also

5467 promises, divine	8024 faith & blessings

8608
prayer, and worship

Worship is turning to God in awe, praise and joy, as his people realise how wonderful he is. Prayer is a natural part of worship: to know God is to want to worship him and pray to him.

Worship is a fundamental requirement of life
All nations are exhorted to worship God 1Ch 16:28–29 *See also* Ps 29:1–2; 96:9

Israel is commanded to worship God 2Ki 17:36 *See also* Ps 95:6–7; 99:4–5

Right attitudes in worship are imperative
Reverence and humility characterise acceptable worship Heb 12:28–29 *See also* Ps 5:7; 95:6; 138:2; Ecc 5:1

Honesty, without hypocrisy, characterises acceptable worship Am 5:21–24 *See also* Mt 15:7–9 pp Mk 7:6–7; Isa 29:13; Lk 18:9–14; Jn 4:24

Prayer can focus on different aspects of God's character
Prayer can focus on God's holiness Ex 15:11 *See also* Ps 77:13; 96:9; 99:5

Prayer can focus on God's glory Ps 19:1–6 *See also* Ps 29:1–2; 138:5; Ro 16:27; Php 4:20; Jude 25

Prayer can focus on God's majesty Ps 104:1–4 *See also* Ps 8:1; 76:4; 96:4–6

Prayer can focus on God's kingship Ps 97:1 *See also* Ps 9:7; 22:3; 93:1; 95:3; 102:12

Prayer can focus on God's love and compassion Ps 103:1–18 *See also* Ps 111:4; 118:1–4; 145:17–20

Prayer can focus on God's justice and righteousness Ps 97:2 *See also* Ps 7:17; 9:8; 97:6; 111:3

Prayer can focus on God's creative activity Ne 9:6 *See also* Ps 90:2; 95:3–7; 102:25–27; 104:5–9,24–26

See also

1045 God, glory of	1325 God, the Creator
1065 God, holiness of	
1075 God, justice of	8336 reverence & obedience
1085 God, love of	8622 worship
1090 God, majesty of	8632 adoration

8609
prayer, as praise and thanksgiving

Prayer embraces praising God for who he is, thanking him for what he has already done, and looking forward with joy to what he has promised to do in the future.

Scripture exhorts God's people to praise and thank him
Php 4:6 *See also* Ps 66:1; 68:4; 95:1–2; 105:1–3; Eph 5:19–20; Col 4:2; 1Th 5:16–18; Heb 13:15

Praise and thanksgiving in prayer for God's goodness towards his people
Praise and thanksgiving for deliverance and salvation Ps 65:1–5 *See also* Ps 66:5–6; 81:1–7; 124:1–8; Jnh 2:1–9

Praise and thanksgiving for provision of material needs Mk 8:6 pp Mt 15:36 *See also* Ps 65:9–13; Mt 26:26–27 pp Mk 14:22–23 pp Lk 22:19–20

Praise and thanksgiving for help in time of trouble Ps 34:1–4 *See also* Ps 30:1–12; 40:1–5; 103:1–5; 116:1–19

Praise and thanksgiving for the encouragement of other believers Php 1:3–6 *See also* Ro 1:8; 2Co 8:1; Eph 1:16; 2Th 1:3

Notable songs of praise and thanksgiving
Ex 15:1–18 *Moses, on crossing the Red Sea*
David, on his deliverance from Saul: 2Sa 22:2–51; Ps 18:1–50
1Ch 16:8–36 *David, on bringing the ark to Jerusalem;* Lk 1:46–55 *Mary, on learning that she was to be the mother of Jesus Christ*

See also

7927 hymn	8664 praise
8352 thankfulness	8676 thanksgiving
8646 doxology	

8610
prayer, as asking God

God wants his people to turn to him in prayer, individually and corporately, in times of need or crisis, and to bring requests to him as a Father.

God's people are commanded to bring their requests to him

Php 4:6 *See also* 1Ch 16:11; Mt 7:7 pp Lk 11:9; Jn 16:24; Eph 6:18–20; 1Th 5:17; Jas 5:13

Prayer for deliverance from difficulty

Ps 4:1; 107:6 *See also* Ps 40:2–3; Jnh 2:1–3; Ac 12:5

Prayer for deliverance from enemies

Ps 17:8–9; 35:4 *See also* 2Ki 19:9–11; 2Ch 14:11

Prayers of individuals in time of crisis

Jacob's prayer Ge 32:9–12

David's prayers Ps 28:1–9 *See also* Ps 4:1; 5:1–3; 30:8–10; 142:1–7

Elijah's prayer 1Ki 19:4

Jeremiah's prayer Jer 15:15–18

Jesus Christ's prayers Mt 26:39 pp Mk 14:35–36 pp Lk 22:42–44

Individual petition to God in prayer

Individual prayer for guidance Ge 24:12–14 *See also* Jdg 1:1–2; 6:36–40; 1Sa 14:41; 2Sa 2:1; 1Ch 14:14–15

Individual prayer for healing 2Ki 20:1–11 pp Isa 38:1–10

Individual prayer for the birth of a child 1Sa 1:10–11 *See also* Ge 25:21; 30:17

Corporate petition to God

Corporate prayer for deliverance Ex 2:23 *See also* Nu 20:15–16; Dt 26:6–8; Jdg 3:9; 4:3; 6:7–10; 1Sa 12:8

Corporate prayer for restoration Ps 44:23–26; 79:8–9; 80:4–7; 85:4–7

Corporate prayer for protection, especially at times of crisis Ezr 8:21–23 *See also* 2Ch 20:12–13; Ezr 10:1; Est 4:16; Ps 74:18–23; Da 2:17–18

The first Christians prayed together when they met

Ac 1:13–14 *See also* Ac 2:42,46–47; 16:13,16; 20:36; 21:5

The first Christians prayed together at times of crisis or important decisions

When threatened with punishment Ac 4:24–31 *See also* Ac 12:5,12

When Barnabas and Saul were sent off by the church at Antioch Ac 13:3

When Paul and Silas experienced persecution Ac 16:25

Prayers for mercy and grace

Ps 143:1; Heb 4:16 *See also* 2Ch 6:18–19; Ps 130:1–2; Mt 20:30–31

See also
8636 asking   8640 calling upon
                     God

8611
prayer, for others

Believers should pray, not only for their own needs, but for those of others. Scripture provides many examples of intercession, and commends it as pleasing to God.

Believers must value others

Php 2:3–4

Examples of praying for others

Moses prays for the Israelites Dt 9:18–19 *See also* Ex 32:9–14; 34:9; Nu 14:11–19; Dt 9:25–29

Samuel prays for Israel 1Sa 7:5–9 *See also* 1Sa 12:19–23

Job prays for his friends Job 42:10

Jeremiah prays for Judah Jer 7:16 *God forbade the prophet Jeremiah to pray for his people because they were unrepentant sinners. See also* Jer 11:14; 14:11

Jesus Christ intercedes for believers

Ro 8:34 *See also* Isa 53:12; Heb 7:25; 1Jn 2:1

The Holy Spirit intercedes for believers

Ro 8:26–27

Christians are to intercede for others

Christians are to pray for their enemies Mt 5:44 *See also* Lk 6:28; 23:34; Ac 7:60

Christians are to pray for one another Eph 6:18 *See also* 1Th 5:25; Phm 22; Heb 13:18–19; Jas 5:14–16; 1Jn 5:16

Christians are to prayer for rulers 1Ti 2:1–2

Examples of pleas made to Jesus Christ on behalf of others

Mt 8:5–13 pp Lk 7:1–10; Mt 15:21–28 pp Mk 7:24–30; Mt 17:14–20 pp Mk 9:14–29 pp Lk 9:37–42

Examples of notable prayers of intercession

2Ki 19:14–19 pp Isa 37:14–20 *Hezekiah for deliverance;* Ezr 8:21–23 *Ezra for a safe journey;* Da 9:1–19 *Daniel for Jerusalem;* Jn 17:6–26 *Jesus Christ for his disciples*
Paul for the believers in Ephesus:
Eph 1:15–21; 3:14–21
Col 1:9–13 *Paul for the believers in Colosse*

See also
2306 Christ, high   6655 forgiveness,
       priest   application
2360 Christ, prayers   8658 Lord's Prayer
       of
3221 Holy Spirit &
       prayer

8612
prayer, and faith

Effective prayer depends on faith, especially on a willingness to trust in God's faithfulness to his promises to his people.

Faith is necessary in order to approach God

Heb 11:6

Faith is necessary to receive benefits from God

Mk 6:5–6; Jas 5:16–18 *See also* Eph 3:12; Heb 10:22

Faith is necessary for effective prayer

Mt 21:21–22 pp Mk 11:22–24 Jas 1:5–8 *See also* Jas 5:14–15

Jesus Christ responded to people's need on the basis of faith

Mt 9:27–30 *See also* Mt 8:5–13 pp Lk 7:1–10; Mt 9:20–22 pp Mk 5:25–34 pp Lk 8:43–48; Mt 15:21–28 pp Mk 7:24–30

Examples of notable prayers of faith

1Ki 18:36–37 *Elijah, in contest with the prophets of Baal;* Jas 5:17–18 *Elijah, praying about rain;* 1Ki 17:19–22 *Elijah and the widow's son;* 2Ki 4:32–35 *Elisha and the Shunammite's son*

See also
5159 hearing   8490 watchfulness
8020 faith   8678 waiting on God
8224 dependence

8613
prayer, persistence in

An answer to prayer may not come immediately. Petitioners are to continue praying earnestly. This requires patience, determination and, at times, a willingness to wrestle with God for the desired outcome.

The principle of persistence in prayer

Prayer should be made with patience and perseverance Ps 40:1; 88:1 *See also* 1Ch 16:11; Ps 116:2

Jesus Christ taught his disciples to persist in prayer Lk 18:1–8 *See also* Lk 11:5–10

Persistence in prayer was exemplified in the early church Ac 1:14 *See also* Ac 2:42

Paul exhorted the churches to practise persistent prayer Eph 6:18 *See also* Ro 12:12; 1Th 5:17

Examples of persistence in prayer

Abraham pleads persistently for Sodom Ge 18:23–33

Jacob persists in wrestling with God Ge 32:24–32

Moses persists in interceding for Israel Dt 9:25–29 *See also* Ex 32:31–32

Hannah persistently asks for a son 1Sa 1:10–11

Elijah persists in prayer about the rain Jas 5:17–18 *See also* 1Ki 18:36–44

The psalmists persist in calling out to God Ps 88:1–18; 119:147–149; 130:1–6

Jesus Christ persisted in pursuing the Father's will Lk 22:42–44 pp Mt 26:36–43 pp Mk 14:32–40

Persistence in prayer is exemplified in waiting for God
Mic 7:7 See also Ps 27:14; 33:20; 37:7; 38:15; 40:1; Isa 26:8

See also
8459 perseverance
8653 importunity to God
8672 striving with God

8614

prayer, answers to

God has promised to answer prayer for personal or corporate needs and for the needs of others.

God answers the prayers of individuals
God answers the psalmists' prayers
Ps 145:18–19 See also Ps 3:4; 6:8–9; 30:2–3; 66:19–20; 116:1–2; 118:5; 138:3

God answers Moses' prayers
Ex 15:23–25; 17:4–7; Nu 11:10–17

God answers Hannah's prayer for a son 1Sa 1:27 See also 1Sa 1:10–20

God answers the prayers of the prophets Ps 99:6 See also 1Sa 7:9; La 3:55–57; Jnh 2:1–2; Jas 5:17–18

God answers the prayers of the kings of Israel 1Ki 9:3; 2Ch 18:31

God answers corporate petition
Answered prayer for deliverance from hardship Dt 26:7–8 See also Ex 2:23–25; 3:7–9; Nu 20:16; 1Sa 12:8; Ps 81:7

Answered prayer for deliverance from enemies 1Sa 12:10–11 See also Jdg 3:9,15; 2Ki 19:19–20; 1Ch 5:20

God answers the prayer of the oppressed
Jas 5:4 See also Ex 22:22–23; Job 34:28

God answers prayer for healing
Jas 5:14–16 See also Nu 12:10–15; 1Ki 17:21–22; 2Ki 4:32–35; 20:1–6 pp 2Ch 32:24 pp Isa 38:1–6; Mt 8:2–3 pp Mk 1:40–42 pp Lk 5:12–13; Ac 9:40

God answers prayer for others
Dt 9:18–19 See also 1Sa 7:8–9; Ac 12:5–8

See also
5225 barrenness
5333 healing
5446 poverty
6634 deliverance
7221 exodus, the
8790 oppression

8615

prayer, doubts about

Sometimes God does not seem to answer prayer, causing his people to doubt him. Scripture affirms God's faithfulness to those who pray according to his will, and points out that the human understanding of a situation is limited.

Examples of God's servants questioning his promises
Ex 5:22–23 See also Ge 15:2–3; Jos 7:7–9

Examples of God's servants questioning the tasks he has given them
Nu 11:11–15 See also 1Ki 19:4; Jer 15:15–18; 20:7–9,14–18; Jnh 4:1–3; Mt 27:46 pp Mk 15:34; Ps 22:1

Examples of God's servants expressing their anger and confusion in prayer
Job 10:2–22 See also Job 13:20–27; 14:1–22; Ps 13:1–2; 42:9–10; 44:22–26; 77:7–9; 80:4–6; 88:6–9; Hab 1:2–3

God's response to prayers of questioning or complaint
God reiterates his promises to those who question him Ge 15:2–5 See also Ex 6:1–8

God provides help for those who question him 1Ki 19:1–8

God rebukes those who question him Job 40:1–9 See also Jer 15:19–21

God explains events to those who question him Hab 1:5–11

See also
5566 suffering, encouragements in
8482 spiritual warfare
8721 doubt
8726 doubters

8616

prayerlessness

Without prayer any relationship with God is impoverished because vital communication is lost.

Reasons for prayerlessness
Unbelief Ps 14:1–4 pp Ps 53:1–4 See also Job 21:15; Ro 3:11

Self-reliance Jer 17:5 See also Zep 3:2

Worship of other gods Dt 32:17–18 See also Jer 2:5–6,8

Guilt as a result of disobedience Ge 3:9–12 *Adam and Eve did not respond to their sin by praying. On the contrary they sought to hide from God;* Jnh 1:1–6 *Jonah tried to run away from God.*

Tiredness Lk 22:45 See also Mt 26:40 pp Mk 14:37; Mt 26:43–45 pp Mk 14:40–41

Discord in relationship 1Pe 3:7

Examples of prayerlessness
Joshua, after a great victory Jos 7:2–5 *Joshua devised his own plan in attacking Ai and did not seek the LORD until after he suffered a disastrous defeat.*

King Ahaziah, turning to idols 2Ki 1:16 See also 2Ki 1:1–6

The nominal religion of Israel Isa 43:22 *This verse implies that prayer involves effort—the people only paid lip service to God.* See also Isa 1:14; 64:7

Israel trusts in other people rather than God Isa 30:1–2; 31:1

Israel's failure to repent of their sins Da 9:13 See also Isa 9:13; Jer 5:3

The lack of an intercessor among God's people Eze 22:30

Consequences of prayerlessness
Alienation from God Jn 15:6 See also Ps 73:27

God's judgment Zep 1:4–6 See also Jer 10:21

Disloyalty to Jesus Christ Mt 26:74 pp Mk 14:71 pp Lk 22:60 pp Jn 18:27 *Peter had previously failed to pray in Gethsemane.*

Spiritual poverty Jas 4:2 See also 2Ki 17:15; Jer 2:5

Ineffective ministry 1Sa 2:12 *This literally means they had no fellowship with the LORD;* 1Sa 12:23; Jn 15:4–5

Conflicts with others because of unfulfilled desires Jas 4:1–4

See also
5582 tiredness
5829 defiance
5885 indifference
6172 guilt
6178 hardness of heart
6245 stubbornness
8752 false worship
8784 nominal religion
8834 unbelief

8617

prayer, advice for effective

Scripture provides guidance concerning what attitudes and actions are appropriate for effective prayer. It also identifies a number of motives which are likely to lead to prayers being unanswered.

Hindrances to prayer
Sin Isa 59:2 See also Ps 66:18; Jer 14:10–12; La 3:42–44; Mic 3:4

Disobedience Zec 7:13 See also Dt 1:43–45; Pr 1:28–31

Selfishness Jas 4:3

Injustice Isa 1:15–17 See also Pr 21:13; Isa 58:1–7

Lack of faith Jas 1:6–7

Qualities that lead to effective prayer
Humility Lk 18:9–14 See also 2Sa 7:18; 2Ch 7:14; Ps 51:16–17; Isa 57:15; Mt 8:8 pp Lk 7:6

Obedience 1Jn 3:21–22 See also 1Sa 15:22; Jer 7:22–23

Righteousness Pr 15:29 See also 1Ki 3:11–12; Ps 34:15

Single-mindedness Jer 29:13 See also Dt 4:29; 1Ch 28:9

Faith Mt 21:21–22 pp Mk 11:22–24 See also Mt 7:7–11 pp Lk 11:9–13; Mt 8:5–13 pp Lk 7:1–10; Mt 15:21–28 pp Mk 7:24–30; Jn 14:12–14

See also
6020 sin
8154 righteousness
8276 humility
8453 obedience
8827 selfishness

8618

prayerfulness

An attitude by which a constant relationship between God and believers is developed.

Prayerfulness is a way of life
Lk 2:37 See also Ps 5:3; 55:17; 109:4;
Da 6:10–11,13

Prayerfulness arises from a desire to be with God
Ps 130:5–6 See also Ps 42:1–4; 84:1–2

Prayerfulness arises from an awareness of need that can only be met by God
1Ti 5:5 See also Ps 86:1; 105:4

Prayerfulness demonstrates a continuing trust in God
Jn 15:5–8 See also Ps 63:1–8

Prayerfulness involves a heart that is right with God
Isa 1:15–17 See also Mt 6:7; Mk 12:40
pp Lk 20:47

Prayerfulness involves the need to be alert
Mt 26:41 pp Mk 14:38 pp Lk 22:40 See
also Mic 7:7; Lk 21:36; Col 4:2

Prayerfulness needs to be maintained especially in difficult circumstances
Lk 18:1 See also Hab 3:16–19; Ac 16:25;
1Th 5:17; 1Pe 4:7

Examples of people whose prayerfulness proved effective
Hannah, who prayed for a child
1Sa 1:20 See also Isa 1:10–18

Elijah, an ordinary man who prayed
Jas 5:17–18 See also 1Ki 17:1; 18:41–46

Nehemiah, a man who discovered God's plan through prayer Ne 1:4 See
also Ne 1:5–11; 2:4–5

David, sustained through trials
1Sa 30:6 See also 2Sa 22:1–4
pp Ps 18:1–3; Ps 3:1–8

Daniel, whose patience in prayer was rewarded Da 10:12 See also Da 9:1–19

Jesus Christ, who perfectly trusted his Father Heb 5:7 See also Lk 5:16;
Jn 11:41–42

The early church, which was founded upon prayer Ac 1:14 See also Ac 2:42;
4:23–31; 6:4; 12:5

Paul, who prayed for all the churches which he founded or visited Col 1:9 See
also Ro 1:9–10; Eph 1:16; Php 1:4;
1Th 3:10; 2Th 1:11; 2Ti 1:3; Phm 4

See also
5763 attitudes,　　　8102 abiding in
　positive to God　　　Christ
8030 trust　　　　　　8164 spirituality
　　　　　　　　　　　8225 devotion

8619
prayer, in the church

The prayer life of the NT provides a pattern from which the modern church can learn, both in terms of the importance of prayer, and also matters for prayer.

Prayer was at the centre of the life of the early church
They prayed when they met together
Ac 1:14 See also Ac 2:42; 4:23–31;
12:12; 20:36; 21:5

They prayed about the selection and ordination of Christian leaders
Ac 13:2–3 See also Ac 1:24–25; 6:6;
14:23

They prayed during persecution
Ac 12:5 See also Ac 7:59–60; 12:12;
16:22–25

They prayed for healing Ac 9:40 See also
Ac 28:7–8

The apostles' teaching on prayer in church life
The importance of prayer Col 4:2 See
also Ro 12:12; Eph 6:18; 1Th 5:17;
1Ti 2:1; 1Pe 4:7

Prayer for the spread of the gospel
Col 4:3–4 See also Eph 6:19–20;
2Th 3:1

Prayer for the sick Jas 5:14

Prayer for sinners 1Jn 5:16–17 See also
Jas 5:16

Prayer for God's servants Ro 15:30 See
also 2Co 1:11

Orderly conduct of public prayer
1Co 11:4–5 See also 1Co 11:13–15

The practice of the apostles
Prayer was central to their ministry
Ac 6:3–4

They prayed for the church Col 1:9–10
See also Eph 1:16–21; 3:16–19;
Php 1:9–11; Col 1:3; 1Th 1:2;
2Th 1:11–12

See also
7028 church, life of　　8638 benedictions

8620
prayer, practicalities of

Scripture commends a life of prayer, characterised by simplicity of expression, sincerity of heart and trust in the promises of God. It gives guidance on how, when and where to pray.

Scripture stresses the importance of prayer
1Th 5:16–18 See also Ac 6:3–4;
Ro 12:12

Judgment comes on those who do not pray
Ps 79:6 See also Ps 53:4; Jer 10:21;
Zep 1:4–6; Jas 4:2

Prayers should be expressed simply
Mt 6:7–8 See also Ecc 5:1–3;
Lk 18:9–14

Prayer should not be ostentatious
Mt 6:5–6 See also Mt 14:23 pp Mk 6:46;
Lk 5:16

Physical positions for prayer
Sitting while praying 2Sa 7:18 See also
Jdg 20:26; Ne 1:4

Kneeling while praying Lk 22:41 See
also 1Ki 8:54; 2Ch 6:13; Ezr 9:5;
Ac 9:40; 21:5; Eph 3:14

Standing while praying 1Ki 8:22 See
also 1Sa 1:26; Mk 11:25

Lying prostrate while praying
2Ch 20:18 See also Ge 24:52; Nu 20:6

Praying with arms outstretched
Ex 9:29; Isa 1:15 See also 1Ki 8:54;
2Ch 6:13

Praying with hands raised 1Ti 2:8 See
also Ex 9:29; 1Ki 8:22,54; Ps 63:4;
77:1–2

Prayer can be offered at any time
Praying several times a day Da 6:10 See
also Ps 55:17; 88:1

Praying early in the morning Mk 1:35
See also Ps 5:3; 119:147

Praying all night Lk 6:12 See also
1Sa 15:11; Lk 2:37

Prayer is not confined to any single place
Jn 4:21–24

Praying inside a building Da 6:10 ;
Mt 6:6 See also 1Ki 8:28–30

Praying outside a building Mk 1:35 ;
Lk 5:16 See also Ac 10:9; 21:5

Prayer may be accompanied by fasting
Ac 13:2–3 See also Ezr 8:23; Ne 1:4;
Ps 35:13; Da 9:3; Lk 2:37; 5:33;
Ac 14:23; Mt 17:21 fn pp Mk 9:29 fn

See also
5161 kneeling　　　5921 privacy
5174 prostration　　8429 fasting
5184 standing　　　8626 worship,
5767 attitudes in　　　places
　prayer　　　　　　8629 worship, times

8622

worship

The praise, adoration and reverence of God, both in public and private. It is a celebration of the worthiness of God, by which honour is given to his name.
This set of themes consists of the following:
8623 worship, of God alone
8624 worship, reasons for
8625 worship, acceptable attitudes in
8626 worship, places of
8627 worship, elements of
8628 worship, hindrances to
8629 worship, times for
8630 worship, results of

8623
worship, of God alone

God alone is worthy of worship; the worship of other gods is forbidden. In the NT worship is offered to the Son of God.

God alone is to be worshipped
He alone is worthy of worship
1Ch 16:25 The English word "worship"
means literally "worth-ship". See also
Ps 48:1; 96:4–5; 145:3; 2Sa 22:4

The worship of God the Father Jn 4:23
See also Php 2:11

The worship of God the Son Mt 2:11;

Mt 14:33; Jn 20:28 *See also*
Mt 28:16–17; Jn 9:35–38; Php 2:9–11;
Heb 1:6; Rev 5:8–14

Angels worship God
Ps 103:20; 148:1–2 *See also* Ps 29:1–2;
Isa 6:1–4; Eze 10:1–18; Rev 4:8–9

The worship of other gods forbidden
Ex 20:3 pp Dt 5:7; 2Ki 17:35–36 *See
also* Ex 34:14; Dt 6:13–14; Ne 9:6;
Ps 86:9–10; 97:7; Ac 10:25–26;
14:13–18

The worship of angels forbidden
Col 2:18 *See also* Rev 19:9–10; 22:8–9

See also

1080 God, living	4114 angels and
1150 God, truth of	praise
2218 Christ, Son of	5878 honour
God	8632 adoration
2336 Christ,	8768 idolatry
exaltation	

8624
worship, reasons for

The supreme reason for human
existence is to worship God for his
love, greatness and saving deeds.

To worship is a divine command
Mt 4:10 pp Lk 4:8 *See also* Dt 6:13;
Ex 23:25; 2Ki 17:36; 1Ch 16:29;
Ps 22:23; 29:2; 68:26; 113:1; 117:1;
148:11–13; 150:6; 1Ti 2:8; Rev 14:7

God's people are to be a worshipping people
1Pe 2:9 *See also* Ex 19:5–6; Ps 105:1–6;
Isa 43:21; Rev 1:5–6

Worship is the response of God's people
To God's love Ex 4:31 *See also* Dt 6:5;
12:7; 26:10–11; 2Ch 7:3; Ps 95:6–7;
117:1–2; 138:2

To God's holy presence 1Ch 16:29
pp Ps 96:8–9 *See also* Ex 33:10; Lev 10:3;
Jos 5:13–15; Ps 29:2; 99:5; Rev 4:8; 15:4

To God's greatness Ps 95:1–3 *See also*
Ex 3:12; Ps 22:27–28; 66:1–4; 96:1–3;
Rev 15:3–4

To the deeds of God
Ge 8:20 *Noah's response to God's
deliverance from the flood. See also*
Ge 12:7 *God's promise of an inheritance to
Abraham*
The signs and wonders in Egypt and Sinai:
Ex 4:29–31; 12:27; 15:1,20
Ezr 3:10–11; Isa 19:21; Da 3:28 *God's
deliverance of Daniel in Babylon;*
Mt 9:7–8 pp Mk 2:12 pp Lk 5:25–26 *the
healing of the paralytic;* Ac 3:8 *the healing
of the crippled beggar*

To the fear of God Ps 22:23; Heb 12:28
See also Ps 2:11; Ac 10:2

See also

1050 God, goodness	5932 response
of	7140 people of God
1060 God, greatness	7404 ordinances
of	8352 thankfulness
1065 God, holiness	8608 prayer &
of	worship
1085 God, love of	8664 praise

8625
worship, acceptable attitudes in

True worship is not the mechanical
repetition of rituals, but should be
wholehearted and reverent. It should
be based upon trustful and obedient
lives, in that obedience is itself to be
seen as an act of worship.

Worship should be in accordance with God's commands
Ge 22:2 *See also* Ge 12:1,7–8;
Dt 30:16–20; 1Sa 15:22; Ps 40:6–8;
Jer 7:2; Da 3:28; Ac 13:2; Ro 12:1

Worship should not be mechanical
Jn 4:23–24 *See also* Heb 10:1

Worship should give God the honour due to him
1Ch 16:29 pp Ps 96:8–9

Worship of mere human devising is unacceptable
Isa 29:13 *See also* Lev 10:1; Mt 15:7–9
pp Mk 7:6–7; Php 3:3; Col 2:23

Worship should be orderly and reverent
1Co 14:40 *See also* 1Ch 16:37–42;
1Ki 18:30–39; 1Co 14:26

Worship should be grounded in godly and obedient living
Mic 6:6–8; Ro 12:1 *See also* Ps 15:1–5;
24:3–4; 1Ti 2:10

The proper attitude of worshippers
Preparation for worship 1Co 11:28 *See
also* Lev 16:3–4; 2Sa 12:20; 2Ch 7:1;
Mt 2:11

Wholeheartedness Dt 6:5 *See also*
Ex 34:14; Dt 10:12; Jos 22:5; 1Sa 12:24;
Ps 27:4; Mt 22:37 pp Mk 12:30; Lk 10:27

Confidence in approaching God
Heb 10:22–23 *See also* Ge 4:4; Jas 4:8;
Heb 7:19; 11:4

See also

7422 ritual	8453 obedience
8266 holiness	8618 prayerfulness
8333 reverence	8620 prayer,
8345 servanthood &	practicalities
worship	8748 false religion

8626
worship, places of

Under the old covenant, there were
rules governing the places where
worship might be offered but under
the new covenant the earthly
location is of no importance.

Worship at places commemorating some act of God
Ge 12:7 *See also* Ge 8:20; 26:23–25; 35:1

Worship at a place chosen by God
Dt 12:13–14 *See also* Ge 22:2;
Dt 14:23–25; 1Ch 21:18–19;
2Ch 7:15–16

Worship in certain sacred places
Dt 12:5 *See also* Ex 3:12; Dt 26:2;
1Sa 1:3,28; Isa 27:13; Jn 4:20

Worship at the Tent of Meeting
Ex 25:8–9 *See also* Ex 29:42–43; 33:10;
Lev 17:1–5

Worship at the temple in Jerusalem
1Ch 22:1 *See also* 2Ch 7:15–16;
29:27–30; Ne 8:6; Lk 1:8–10; 2:37;
Ac 8:27

Worship in a synagogue
Lk 4:16 *See also* Ac 13:15; 15:21; 17:2

Worship in the home
Da 6:10 *See also* Mt 6:6; Ro 16:5;
1Co 16:19; Col 4:15; Phm 2

The earthly location for worship is unimportant
Jn 4:21–24 *See also* Ge 24:26; 47:31;
Jdg 7:15; Job 1:20

In heaven worship is perfect
Lk 2:13; Heb 12:22; Rev 4:9–11;
5:13–14; 7:9–12; 19:4–7

See also

7239 Jerusalem	7466 temples
7302 altar	7474 Tent of
7374 high places	Meeting
7442 shrine	7766 priests
7456 synagogue	9410 heaven
7459 tabernacle, in	
OT	

8627
worship, elements of

Praise and thankfulness are
important elements of worship,
which also includes confession of
sin, the reading of Scripture and
music.

Worship with awe
Dt 10:12 *See also* Lev 10:1–3; 2Ch 7:3;
Ps 2:11; 68:35; 96:9; Ecc 5:1

Worship includes trust
Ps 4:5 *See also* Ps 37:7; Heb 11:6

Worship includes praise
Ps 22:22; 107:32; Heb 13:15 *See also*
2Ch 31:2; Ne 9:5–6; Ps 150:1–6;
Heb 2:12; Rev 7:11–12

Worship includes thanksgiving
Ps 100:4; Rev 11:16–17 *See also*
2Ch 7:3; Ps 50:14,23; Eph 5:19–20;
Php 4:6; Rev 7:11–12

Worship with joy
Ps 95:1 *See also* Ps 27:6; 43:4; 100:2;
Lk 24:52–53; Ac 2:46–47

Worship includes the confession of Jesus Christ as Lord
Heb 13:15

Worship includes confession of sin
Hos 14:2 *See also* Lev 16:21; Ne 9:2;
Ps 66:18

Worship includes the reading of God's word
Col 3:16; 1Ti 4:13 *See also* Ne 8:5–6; 9:3

Worship includes music and song

Ps 95:2–3 *See also* 2Sa 6:5; Ps 100:2; Eph 5:19–20

Worship includes dance

Ps 149:3 *See also* Ex 15:20; Ps 30:11

See also

1610 Scripture	6624 confession of
3218 Holy Spirit &	sin
praise	7927 hymn
5287 dance	7963 song
5420 music	8020 faith
5421 musical	8634 amen
instruments	8646 doxology

8628

worship, hindrances to

True worship goes beyond mere form and can therefore be hindered by a wrong relationship to God or to others.

Worship that is merely formal is unacceptable

1Sa 15:22 *See also* Isa 1:13; Eze 33:31; Hos 6:6; Mt 6:5; 2Ti 3:5

Worship is hindered by wrong relationships

To God Ps 66:18; Mt 15:7–9 pp Mk 7:6–7 *See also* Isa 29:13; Ps 32:5–6; Isa 59:2; 64:7; Jas 4:3

To others Isa 1:11–17; Mt 5:23–24 *See also* Am 5:21–24

See also

5908 motives	8752 false worship
8142 religion	8834 unbelief

8629

worship, times for

Scripture stresses the importance of regular worship, while at the same time recognising that believers may worship God spontaneously.

Examples of regular worship

On a daily basis Ac 2:46–47 *See also* Ex 29:38–43; Ps 141:2; Eze 46:13–15

Several times a day Da 6:10 *See also* 1Ch 16:37; Ps 119:164; Ac 3:1; Heb 10:25

On holy days 2Ch 8:12–13 *See also* Eze 46:3

At the three annual pilgrim festivals Dt 16:16

Passover (or the Feast of Unleavened Bread): Ex 12:1–20; Lk 2:41
Pentecost (or the Feast of Weeks): Ex 34:22; Ac 2:1
The Feast of Tabernacles (or Ingathering): Ex 23:16; Lev 23:33–36; Nu 29:12–39; Dt 16:13–15

On the Day of Atonement Lev 16:34 *See also* Ex 30:10; Lev 16:3–33; 23:26–32

On Sabbath days Lk 4:16 *See also* Lev 24:5–8; Nu 28:9–10

Examples of spontaneous worship

In response to an awareness of the closeness of God Ex 34:8; Jdg 7:15

In response to the experience of God's mercy Ex 4:29–31 *See also* 1Sa 1:19–28

In response to the presence and power of Jesus Christ Mt 28:8–9 *See also* Mt 14:33; Lk 24:52

Worship should not be dependent on circumstances

Php 4:6 *See also* Job 1:20–21; Da 6:10; Ac 16:25; 1Th 5:16–18

The continuous worship of God in heaven

Rev 4:10–11; 5:14; 7:11; 11:1; 19:4

See also

2066 Christ, power of	7354 feasts and
6686 mercy	festivals
7308 Atonement, Day	7428 Sabbath
of	8642 celebration

8630

worship, results of

Worship not only gives God what is due to him but also results in many benefits for his people.

True worship brings benefits for God's people

Blessing Ex 23:25–26 *See also* Dt 11:13–15

Guidance Ac 13:2–3 *See also* Isa 58:6–11; Nu 7:89

Deliverance Ac 16:25–26 *See also* Ps 50:14–15

Joy 1Ch 29:21–22 *See also* 2Ch 29:30; Ps 43:4; Isa 56:7; Lk 24:52

A sense of God's presence

2Ch 5:13–14 pp 1Ki 8:10–11 *See also* Ex 40:35

A deeper sense of Jesus Christ's lordship Php 2:9–11 *See also* Rev 1:10–18

Boldness to witness

Ac 4:31 *See also* Ps 57:9; Ac 18:9–10

True worship convicts sinners

1Co 14:24–25

See also

1335 blessing	7028 church, life of
3248 Holy Spirit,	8117 discipleship,
conviction	benefits
3263 Holy Spirit,	8283 joy
guidance	8495 witnessing

8632

adoration

An attitude of worship characterised by love and reverence towards God. It can also describe the love between man and woman.

Adoration of God by his people

Dt 10:12

Adoration and love for God Ps 31:23; 116:1 *See also* Dt 6:5; 11:1; Jos 22:5; Ps 18:1; 26:8

Adoration and reverence for God Ps 5:7 *See also* Ex 3:5; Dt 13:4; Jos 5:15; 1Ch 16:29; Ps 29:2; 33:8; 95:6; 99:5; Da 6:26; Jnh 1:16; Hab 2:20

Examples of adoration in worship

Moses and the Israelites:
Ex 15:1–2,6–7,11–12

1Sa 2:1–2 *Hannah;* 2Sa 22:47–51 *David;* 1Ki 8:23–24 *Solomon*
The psalmist: Ps 27:4; 63:2–5; 73:25–26; 84:1–2; 103:1–5,20–22
Lk 1:46–49 *Mary*
The inhabitants of heaven: Rev 4:8–11; 5:8–14; 7:9–12; 15:3–4; 19:6–8

Adoration also describes the love between man and woman

Pr 5:18–19; SS 1:2–4

See also

1065 God, holiness	8369 worthiness
of	8440 glorifying God
5012 heart	8608 prayer &
7960 singing	worship
8223 dedication	8622 worship
8283 joy	8664 praise
8297 love for God	8676 thanksgiving
8333 reverence	

8634

amen

A Hebrew term expressing the ideas of truth and reliability, often used in prayer and adoration.

Amen as an expression of worship

1Ch 16:36; Eph 3:21; Rev 7:11–12 *See also* Ne 5:13; 8:6 *The repetition of "Amen" here conveys Ezra's intensity of feeling as he read the Book of the Law. The response of the people represents a solemn, formal acceptance of God's command-ments;* Ps 72:19; 106:48; Ro 9:5 *"Amen" can mean either "Yes indeed, it is so" or "So be it";* Ro 11:36; 16:25–27; 1Co 14:16; Gal 1:3–5; Php 4:20; 1Ti 1:17; 6:15–16; 2Ti 4:18; Heb 13:20–21; 1Pe 4:11; 5:10–11; 2Pe 3:17–18; Jude 24–25; Rev 1:4–7; 19:4 *the worship of heaven*

Amen confirms a grace or blessing

Gal 6:18 *See also* Ro 15:33; 1Co 16:24; Php 4:23; Rev 22:20–21

Amen confirms a vow or action

Jer 28:5–6 *See also* Nu 5:20–22; Dt 27:15; 1Ki 1:32–36; Jer 11:1–5

Amen as a title of Jesus Christ

Rev 3:14 *See also* 2Co 1:18–20 *The implication is that all God's promises find their fulfilment in Jesus Christ.*

See also

1150 God, truth of	5741 vows
1335 blessing	5827 curse
1461 truth, nature of	8622 worship
2203 Christ, titles of	8646 doxology
5430 oaths, human	

8636

asking

The act of making requests of another, as an expression of dependence. Scripture encourages believers to ask things of God in prayer, and gives guidance concerning the motivation in doing so.

Asking as an aspect of human relationships

Examples of everyday requests
Jos 4:20–22; Ecc 7:10; 1Pe 3:15 *See also* Ex 3:22; Dt 32:7; 1Sa 12:19 *The people asked for a king;* 2Ki 2:3; Ne 2:1–2; Da 2:10–11; Mt 2:1–2 *the Magi seek the king of the Jews;* Lk 2:46 *Jesus Christ asks questions in the temple;* Jn 4:9; Ro 16:1–2; Gal 2:9–10; Phm 21

Examples of stronger appeals
Php 4:2–3 *See also* Ge 50:17; Ex 5:15; Lk 23:20; Ac 25:3; 1Th 4:1

Asking as an aspect of prayer

General petitions Mt 7:7–11
pp Lk 11:9–13; Php 4:6 *See also* Dt 18:16; Jdg 6:39; 1Sa 1:20; 1Ch 16:4; 2Ch 6:32–33; Job 6:8–9; Ps 5:3; Pr 30:7–8; Mt 9:37–38; 1Ti 2:1

Frequent requests for guidance or insight 2Sa 2:1; Eph 1:17 *See also* Ge 25:21–22; Jos 9:14; 1Sa 23:1–2; 2Ki 8:7–8; 1Ch 21:29–30; 2Ch 20:3; Isa 58:2; Jer 10:21; Col 1:9; Jas 1:5

The grounds for asking

According to God's will 1Jn 5:14–15

Trusting in God's great mercy *See also* Da 9:18

In the name of Jesus Christ Jn 14:13 *See also* Jn 16:23–27

In faith Mt 21:22 pp Mk 11:24; Jas 1:6

See also
5355 invitations	8611 prayer for
5806 compassion	others
5876 helpfulness	8640 calling upon
8291 kindness	God
8434 giving	8648 enquiring of
8610 prayer, asking	God
God	8652 importunity

8638

benedictions

Prayers invoking God's blessing upon others. They are often spoken at a time of impending separation, although they may sometimes constitute greetings.

Benedictions pronounced by priests
Nu 6:23–27 *See also* Dt 21:5; 1Sa 2:20; 2Ch 30:27

Benedictions pronounced by kings
1Ki 8:54–61 *See also* Ge 14:18–20; 2Sa 6:20; 2Ch 6:3–11

Benedictions pronounced by other leaders of the nation of Israel
Jos 22:6–8 *See also* Dt 33:1–29

Benedictions pronounced by family members
Ru 1:8–9 *See also* Ge 24:60; 27:27–29; 48:9–22; 49:1–28

Apostolic benedictions on the church
The blessing of grace and peace
Ro 1:7 *See also* Ro 16:20; 1Co 1:3; 16:23;

Gal 1:2–5; 6:16; Eph 1:2; 6:23; 1Ti 1:2; Rev 22:21

The blessing of spiritual growth
Heb 13:20–21 *See also* 1Pe 5:10

The blessing of God in all his fulness
2Co 13:14

See also
1335 blessing	7412 priesthood
1620 beatitudes, the	8610 prayer, asking
2360 Christ, prayers	God
of	8634 amen
3221 Holy Spirit &	8636 asking
prayer	8658 Lord's Prayer
5767 attitudes in	
prayer	

8640

calling upon God

Asking God to act, in dependence upon him and out of a sense of sometimes desperate need.

Calling upon God as an act of worship
By those who depend upon him and proclaim his name Ge 4:26 *See also* Ge 12:8; 26:25; 1Ch 16:8 pp Ps 105:1; Ps 86:5; 116:2,17; Job 27:10; 2Ti 2:22

Those who do not acknowledge God or call upon his name Ps 14:4
pp Ps 53:4; Ps 79:6; Isa 65:1; Jer 10:25; Zep 3:9

Calling upon God in time of need
Ps 50:15; La 3:55 *See also* 1Sa 12:17–18; 2Sa 22:4 pp Ps 18:3; 1Ki 18:24; 2Ki 5:11; Job 19:7; Ps 4:1; 17:6–9; 18:6; 27:7–12; 28:1–2; 55:16; 86:3,7; 91:15; 120:1; Pr 1:28; Isa 58:9; 65:24; Jer 11:14; 33:3; Joel 1:19; Hab 1:2; Zec 13:9

Calling upon God for his salvation
Ac 2:21 *See also* Joel 2:32; Ro 10:12–14

Calling upon God was part of the priestly function of intercession
Ps 99:6 *See also* Ex 17:11; 32:31–32; Nu 21:7; 1Sa 12:19,23; Jer 15:1

Examples of those who called upon God
Abraham Ge 13:4

Moses Ex 17:10–13,15; 32:11–13,30; Nu 14:13–19; Dt 9:26–29

Samuel 1Sa 7:5–9

Elijah 1Ki 18:36–37

Jonah Jnh 2:2,7

Stephen Ac 7:59–60

See also
1320 God as Saviour	8622 worship
7766 priests	8636 asking
8020 faith	8648 enquiring of
8607 prayer, God's	God
promises	8653 importunity to
8610 prayer, asking	God
God	

8642

celebration

Although there are examples of private celebrations in Scripture, most celebration is associated with

the acts of God. The enemies of God's people also celebrate, but in the end it is the triumph of God's purpose that is celebrated.

Celebrations in everyday life
Wedding: Jdg 14:10; Mt 22:2–3
Mt 14:6 pp Mk 6:21–22 *birthday;*
Lk 5:29 *for an honoured guest;*
Lk 15:22–24 *family reunion*

The Israelites celebrated God's acts
Celebrating God's gifts of harvest: Pentecost and Tabernacles Ex 23:16; 34:22; Lev 23:15–21,33–36,39–43; Nu 28:26; 29:12; Dt 16:9–10

Celebrating their deliverance from slavery in Egypt: Passover Ex 13:3 *See also* Ex 12:14; 23:15; 34:18; Nu 9:2; Dt 16:1

Celebrating the deliverance of the nation through Esther: Purim
Est 9:18–19

Religious celebrations
The bringing of the ark of the covenant to Jerusalem 2Sa 6:12–15
pp 1Ch 15:27–28

The bringing of the ark of the covenant to the temple 1Ki 8:3–6 pp 2Ch 5:4–6; 2Ch 5:12–13

The completion and dedication of the first temple 1Ki 8:63,65–66
pp 2Ch 7:8–10

The dedication of the second temple
Ezr 6:16

The reading of the law after the building of the walls of Jerusalem
Ne 8:9–12

Christians celebrate the death of Christ and his return 1Co 11:26

The enemies of God's people celebrate
Jdg 16:23 *capture of Samson;* Da 5:1 *Belshazzar's feast Death of God's witnesses:* Rev 11:3,7–10

Celebration in heaven
Creation Job 38:4–7

The repentance of sinners Lk 15:7,10

Divine deliverance through Jesus Christ Rev 5:9–10

The downfall of evil Rev 19:1–5

The final triumph of Jesus Christ
Rev 19:9 *See also* Rev 11:16–18; 15:2–4

See also
2372 Christ, victory	7354 feasts and
4410 banquets	festivals
5312 feasting	7466 temples
5420 music	7933 Lord's Supper
5710 marriage,	8283 joy
customs	8622 worship
6634 deliverance	8664 praise

8644

commemoration

The act of remembering particular people, places or events in order to reflect on and be thankful for God's faithfulness.

Commemoration of people
2Ch 35:25–27 See also Jdg 11:28–40;
1Ki 11:41 pp 2Ch 9:29

Commemoration of Jesus Christ
Lk 22:19; 1Co 11:23–26

Commemoration of places
Ge 35:1 See also Jos 4:19–24; Jdg 6:24;
2Sa 24:18

Commemoration of events
**Commemoration of God's creation of
the world** Ex 20:8–11 pp Dt 5:12–15
See also Ex 31:12–17

**Commemoration of God's acts in
history** Ex 12:14–17 See also
Ex 13:1–10; Ps 9:1–6; 126:1–3

**Commemoration of God's provision of
food** Lev 23:9–14 See also
Lev 23:15–22 pp Nu 28:26–31
pp Dt 16:9–12; Lev 23:33–43
pp Nu 29:12–39 pp Dt 16:13–17

See also

5286 custom	7406 Passover
7221 exodus, the	7428 Sabbath
7358 Feast of	7933 Lord's Supper
Tabernacles	8467 reminders
7361 Feast of Weeks	8670 remembering
7394 memorial	

8646

doxology

A form of words that offers praise to
God, especially for his work of
creation and redemption. Scripture
records a number of these forms of
praise which were used in both
public and private worship.

Doxologies used in the formal
worship of Israel
1Ch 29:10–13 See also Ps 41:13;
72:18–19; 106:48; 150:1–6

Doxologies used in the
spontaneous praise of God's
people
Ro 11:33–36 See also Ps 57:5,11;
Mt 21:9 pp Mk 11:9–10 pp Lk 19:38;
Gal 1:5; Eph 3:21; Php 4:20; 1Ti 1:17

Doxologies used as a benediction
Jude 24–25 See also Eph 3:20–21;
Ro 16:25–27; Heb 13:20–21; 2Pe 3:18

Doxologies used in heavenly
worship
Rev 5:12–13 See also Isa 6:3;
Lk 2:13–14; Rev 4:8,11; 5:9–14; 7:12;
19:1

See also

1045 God, glory of	8444 honouring God
1060 God, greatness	8624 worship,
of	reasons
2321 Christ as	8632 adoration
redeemer	8638 benedictions
4114 angels and	8664 praise
praise	8676 thanksgiving
7927 hymn	

8648

enquiring of God

Requesting from God a definite
direct response to a particular

question. In the OT, people are
frequently said to enquire of God for
knowledge or guidance, often
through the intermediacy of a priest
or prophet.

Enquiring of God for knowledge
Ge 25:22–23 See also Jdg 13:17; 18:5–6;
1Sa 10:22

Enquiring of God for guidance
2Sa 2:1 See also Jdg 20:18,23,27–28;
1Sa 23:2,4; 30:8; 2Sa 5:19 pp 1Ch 14:10;
2Sa 5:23 pp 1Ch 14:14

Enquiring of God through
intermediaries
Priests Jdg 18:5–6 See also
Nu 27:18–21; 1Sa 22:10,13–15

Prophets 1Ki 22:6–9 pp 2Ch 18:5–8
See also 1Sa 9:6–10; 28:6; 2Ki 3:11;
22:11–20 pp 2Ch 34:19–28; Jer 21:1–7;
37:6–8; Eze 14:7

Enquiring of God by casting lots
Ac 1:24–26 See also Nu 27:21 The Urim
and Thummim were sacred lots carried in
the breastpiece of the High Priest's ephod;
1Sa 10:20–22; 14:36–42

Enquiring of God in prayer
2Ch 20:1–17

Enquiring of God at the
tabernacle
Ex 33:7 See also Jdg 20:26–28;
1Ch 13:3; 2Ch 1:5

Devotion to God as a necessary
prerequisite for enquiring of him
Eze 20:30–31 See also Eze 14:1–11;
20:1–3

Failure to enquire of God
displeases him and heralds
disaster
1Ch 10:13–14 See also 1Ch 15:13;
Jer 10:21; Zep 1:4–6

The Holy Spirit and enquiring of
God
Jn 16:23–24 See also Jn 16:13–15

See also

7320 breastpiece	8124 guidance
7376 high priest	8160 seeking God
7392 lots, casting of	8605 prayer & God's
7766 priests	will
7773 prophets, role	8610 prayer, asking
7781 seer	God

8650

hands, lifting up of

A human gesture which can be a sign
of worship and adoration or indicate
the swearing of a solemn oath. God
is portrayed as raising his hands as a
sign of authority over his creation.

God's uplifted hand
God's uplifted hand signifies his power
Ps 118:16 See also Ex 24:11; Ps 89:13;
Isa 9:12,17,21; 26:11

**God's uplifted hand signifies his
judgment** Isa 5:25 See also 1Sa 6:3,5;
Isa 19:16; Mic 5:9; Zec 2:9

Hands uplifted for swearing
oaths
Oaths taken by God Eze 20:5 See also
Ex 6:8; Dt 32:40–41; Ne 9:15;
Eze 20:15; 36:7; 47:14

Oaths taken by people and angels
Ge 14:22–23; Da 12:7; Rev 10:5

Hands uplifted in worship
Hands lifted up in prayer Ps 28:2 See
also Ex 17:11–13; Ps 141:2; La 2:19;
3:41; 1Ti 2:8

Hands lifted up in praise Ps 63:4 See
also Ne 8:6; Ps 119:48; 134:2

Hands lifted up for blessing
Lev 9:22; Lk 24:50

Hands lifted up as a threat
1Sa 24:6 See also 1Sa 18:17; 22:17;
24:10; 2Sa 18:12,28; 20:21; Job 31:21

Uplifted hands as a sign of
minimal effort
Ge 41:44; Dt 28:32; Ezr 6:12; Ps 76:5

Uplifted hands as a sign of
support
Ps 91:12 See also Mt 4:6 pp Lk 4:11

See also

1265 hand of God	5865 gestures
1335 blessing	8602 prayer
1670 symbols	8622 worship
5156 hand	8632 adoration
5429 oaths	8666 praise, manner
5452 power	& methods

8652

importunity

Persistence and boldness in making
requests to God in prayer and to
other people, and persevering until a
favourable response is received.

8653
importunity, towards God

Earnestness and perseverance in
presenting requests to God on behalf
of oneself and others; seen in
persistent pleading, faithful
intercession and bold appeal.

Perseverance in prayer
Persistence in prayer Ps 55:17 See also
Ps 22:1–2; 86:3; 88:1,9; 1Th 5:17;
1Ti 5:5
Mt 7:7–8 pp Lk 11:9–10; Lk 18:1 See
also Lk 18:2–8

Faithfulness in prayer Eph 6:18 See also
Ro 1:9–10; Col 4:12; 1Th 1:2–3; 2Ti 1:3

Earnestness in prayer
Ps 119:58; 130:1–2 See also Ps 55:1–2;
61:1–2; Jnh 3:8
Lk 22:44 See also Heb 5:7

Boldness in prayer
Ge 18:27; Lk 11:8 See also Ex 33:12–16
Confidence in prayer: Eph 3:12; Heb 4:16

Further examples of importunity
in prayer
Repeated requests in prayer
Ge 18:22–32 Abraham prays for Sodom;
Jdg 6:36–40 Gideon asks for assurance;

Mt 15:22–28 pp Mk 7:25–30 *a Canaanite woman begs for Jesus Christ's help*; Mt 20:30–31 pp Mk 10:47–48 pp Lk 18:38–39 *Blind men call out to Jesus Christ*; Mt 26:44 *Jesus Christ prays in Gethsemane*; Mk 5:10 pp Lk 8:31 *Legion begs for mercy*; 2Co 12:8 *Paul pleads with God to take away his "thorn"*

Further examples of perseverance in prayer Ge 32:26 *Jacob wrestles with God*; Dt 9:18 *Moses fasts and prays because of Israel's sin*; 2Sa 12:16 *David pleads for his sick child*; 1Ki 18:28–29 *The prophets of Baal appeal unsuccessfully to their god*; Ne 1:4–6 *Nehemiah prays for God's people*; Da 10:2–3 *Daniel waits for the interpretation of his vision*; Lk 2:37 *Anna looks for God to redeem his people.*

Further examples of earnestness in prayer 1Sa 1:12–16 *Hannah prays for a child*; 1Ki 8:22 pp 2Ch 6:12 *Solomon prays at the dedication of the Temple*; Jas 5:17–18 *Elijah prays for rain to cease*; Ezr 9:5 *Ezra prays about the people's sin*; Isa 38:2–3 *Hezekiah prays for healing*; Da 9:3 *Daniel prays for Jerusalem*; Mk 5:22–23 pp Lk 8:41–42 *Jairus asks Jesus Christ to heal his daughter*; Jn 4:47 *A nobleman begs Jesus Christ to heal his son*; Ac 12:5 *The early church prays for Peter's release from prison.*

See also
5767 attitudes in prayer	8613 prayer, persistence
8239 earnestness	8618 prayerfulness

8654
importunity, towards people

Boldness, urgency and persistence in appealing to others; seen in making requests of all kinds, presenting the gospel and giving Christian instruction; seen too in God's patient and persistent pleading with people.

Making requests of others
Ge 19:3 *Lot prevails on his angelic visitors to stay with him*; Ge 39:10 *Potiphar's wife propositions Joseph*; Nu 22:37 *Balak summons Balaam*; Jdg 14:16–17 *Samson's wife presses for the answer to his riddle*; Jdg 16:6–16 *Delilah nags Samson to know the secret of his strength*; 2Ki 2:16–17 *Elisha is requested to authorise a search for Elijah*; Est 3:3–4 *Royal officials plead with Mordecai*; Est 8:3 *Esther pleads with the king*; Pr 19:7 *A poor man pleads in vain with fair-weather friends*; Jer 38:26 *Jeremiah pleads with King Zedekiah*; Lk 23:23 *The crowds call for Jesus Christ to be crucified*; Ac 12:16 *Peter knocks on the door after his release from prison*; Ac 25:3 *The chief priests urge that Paul be taken to Jerusalem*; 2Co 8:4 *The Macedonian churches ask to share in the giving to God's people*; Php 4:2 *Paul pleads with Euodia and Syntyche to agree.*

Importunity in preaching the gospel
2Co 5:20

Persistence Ac 5:42

Urgent appeal Ac 2:40

Boldness Ac 19:8 *See also* Ac 4:29,31; 9:27; 14:3; 18:26; 28:31; Php 1:14

Persuasion 2Co 5:11 *See also* Ac 18:4; 19:8; 26:28

Importunity in giving instruction
2Co 10:1; 1Th 4:1 *See also* Ro 15:15; Ac 13:43; 2Co 6:1; Gal 4:12; Eph 4:1,17; 1Th 4:10

God's persistent appeal
God's repeated call to individuals 1Sa 3:8; Jn 21:17

God's appeal to his wayward people 2Ch 36:15; Jer 7:13; Mt 21:35–37 *Finally, God sends his Son. See also* Jer 7:25; 11:7; 25:3–4; 26:5; 29:19; 32:33; 35:14–15; 44:4

See also
1095 God, patience of	8318 patience
7751 persuasion	8424 evangelism
7754 preaching	8459 perseverance
8202 boldness	8489 urgency
	8636 asking

8656
longing for God

A deep desire for God, which Scripture often compares to hunger or thirst. Only Jesus Christ can truly satisfy this longing for God.

The individual's longing for God
Ps 119:20; Isa 26:9 *See also* Ps 73:25; 119:81,131

The longing for God compared to hunger and thirst
Ps 42:2; 63:1 *See also* Ps 143:6; Am 8:11

The longing for God is satisfied through Jesus Christ
Jn 4:13–14; 6:35 *See also* Ps 42:2; Isa 55:1; Jn 6:27,50–51; 7:37; Rev 21:6; 22:17

See also
1080 God, living	5832 desire
1690 word of God	5939 satisfaction
3251 Holy Spirit, filling with	6644 eternal life
	6754 union with Christ
4018 life, spiritual	
5341 hunger	8160 seeking God
5580 thirst	8622 worship

8658
Lord's Prayer, the

The name given to the prayer Jesus Christ taught his disciples, probably as a model prayer for regular use.

Aspects of the Lord's Prayer
A recognition of God as Father and Lord Mt 6:9 pp Lk 11:2 *See also* Mt 7:21; 16:17; Lk 10:21; Eph 3:14–15

A desire for God's perfect will to be done Mt 6:10 pp Lk 11:2 *See also* Mt 12:50; 26:39,42; Ac 21:14; Col 1:9; Heb 10:9

Asking for physical provision Mt 6:11 pp Lk 11:3 *See also* Mt 6:31–32; 7:9–11

Asking for forgiveness Mt 6:12 pp Lk 11:4 *See also* Mt 6:14–15; 18:23–35; Mk 11:25; Lk 23:34; Col 3:13; 1Jn 1:9

Asking for spiritual protection Mt 6:13 pp Lk 11:4 *See also* 2Co 1:10–11; Jude 24; Rev 3:10

The doxology Mt 6:13 *NIV footnote.*

See also
1040 God, fatherhood	2375 kingdom of God
1175 God, will of	5480 protection
1205 God, titles of	6652 forgiveness
1330 God, the provider	8602 prayer
2360 Christ, prayers of	

8660
magnifying God

Giving glory to God through worship and through upright living. God's people are exhorted to praise him and to bring honour to his name.

Ways of magnifying God
Through praise Ps 103:19–22 *See also* Ps 33:1–5; 68:26; 104:1; 106:1–2; 111:1–10; 117:1–2; 135:1–3,19–21; 150:1–2; Lk 1:46; 19:37–38

In worship 1Ch 16:28–29 pp Ps 96:7–9 *See also* Ps 29:1–2; 100:1–2

Through reverence Ps 5:7 *See also* Da 6:25–27; Mal 2:4–7; Heb 12:28–29

By glorifying him Ps 34:1–3 *See also* Ps 63:3–4; 69:30–31; 86:12–13; 96:3–9; 2Th 1:11–12; 1Pe 2:11–12; Rev 4:6–11; 15:2–4

By honouring him 1Ti 6:15–16 *See also* Isa 26:13; Mal 2:1–2; Jn 5:22–23; 1Co 6:19–20; 1Ti 1:17; Rev 7:9–12

See also
7927 hymn	8440 glorifying God
8334 reverence & God's nature	8444 honouring God
	8622 worship
	8664 praise

8662
meditation

Spending time in quietness and usually alone, drawing close to God and listening to him, pondering on his word, his creation, his mighty works or other aspects of his self-revelation.

The importance of meditation
Ps 1:1–3 *See also* 1Sa 12:24; Job 37:14; Ps 19:14; 48:9; 77:11–12; 104:34; 107:43; Php 4:8; 2Ti 2:7

Meditation on the person of God
Ps 16:8; 63:6 *See also* Ps 104:34

Meditation on God's word
Ps 119:15–16 *See also* Jos 1:8; Ps 1:1–3; 119:23,48,78,95,97,99

Meditation on the works of God
Ps 77:12 *See also* Ps 111:2; 143:5; 145:5

Meditation on the creation
Ps 8:1–9 *See also* Ps 104:1–34; Pr 6:6; Mt 6:26–30 pp Lk 12:24–27

Meditation at night
Ps 119:148 *See also* Ps 16:7; 42:8; 63:6

Examples of people meditating
Jos 1:8; Ps 19:14 *See also* Job 22:22 *Eliphaz' advice to Job*; Ps 39:3; 119:78,148; Lk 2:19 *Mary*; Ac 8:27–35 *the Ethiopian eunuch*

The results of meditation
Obedience Ps 119:11 *See also* Jos 1:8; Ps 119:55

Understanding and wisdom
Ps 119:97–98 *See also* Ps 119:27

Praise and worship Ps 48:9–10; 63:5–6; 104:33–35; 119:97

Prosperity and success Jos 1:8

Delight in the Lord Ps 1:2 *See also* Ps 119:15–16,23–24,77–78

Confidence and faith Ps 16:8

See also

1403 God, revelation	8328 quietness
1610 Scripture	8603 prayer,
6636 drawing near to	relationship
God	with God

8664

praise

The celebration, honouring and adoration of God, in the power of the Holy Spirit, whether by individual believers or communities of believers.

8665

praise, reasons for

Scripture treats praise as the natural response of believers to God's person and actions.

Praise is commanded of God's people
Ps 68:32; 1Pe 2:9; Rev 19:5 *See also* Ps 30:4; 150:6; Isa 42:10; Php 2:9–11

Praise is due to God alone
Dt 10:21; 1Ch 16:25; Isa 42:8 *See also* Ps 66:4; 118:15–21; 148:13; Rev 4:11

Praise is pleasing to God
Ps 69:30–31 *See also* Ps 135:3; 147:1; Isa 43:20–21; 61:10–11; Jer 13:11

Praise as an act of witness
Ps 9:11 *See also* 2Sa 22:50; Ps 34:1–3; Isa 42:12; 2Co 9:13

Praise in response to God's nature
For his greatness Dt 32:3; Ps 150:2 *See also* 1Ch 16:25; Ne 8:6; Ps 104:1; Mt 9:8

For his righteousness Ps 98:8–9 *See also* Da 4:37

For his faithfulness Ps 57:9–10; 138:2 *See also* 1Ki 8:15–20,56; Ps 89:1

For his strength Ps 59:16 *See also* Ps 28:7; 81:1

Praise in response to God's deeds
For deliverance from enemies
Ex 18:10; Ps 18:46–48 *See also* Ge 14:20; Jdg 16:24; Ps 43:1–4; 124:1–7

For answered prayer Ps 28:6 *See also* Ps 66:19–20

For sending his Son, Jesus Christ
Lk 1:68–69; Eph 1:3 *See also* Lk 2:10–14,25–28; 24:53; 1Pe 1:3–6

See also

1050 God, goodness of	8444 honouring God
1060 God, greatness of	8624 worship, reasons
4114 angels and praise	8632 adoration
7027 church, purpose	8660 magnifying God

8666

praise, manner and methods of

Praise is the natural response of believers to God at all times and in all places, involving adoration in music and song. God himself assists believers to praise him through his Spirit.

The manner of praise
God is praised in faith Ps 28:7; 106:12

God is praised through Jesus Christ
Heb 13:15 *See also* Php 2:9–11

God can be praised at any time and in any place Ps 104:33; 145:2 *See also* Ps 146:2

God helps believers to praise him
Ps 51:15 *See also* Ps 40:3; Isa 61:3

The Holy Spirit moves believers to praise Lk 1:67; Eph 5:18–20 *See also* Lk 10:21; Ac 2:11; 10:44–46; Col 3:16–17

The methods of praise
In singing Eph 5:19 *See also* Ne 12:46; Ps 149:1; Isa 42:10; Lk 1:46–47,68; Ac 16:25; Col 3:16

With musical instruments Ps 150:3–5 *See also* 1Ch 25:3; 2Ch 7:6; Ps 33:2; 92:1–3; Isa 38:20

In dancing Ps 149:3 *See also* Ex 15:19–20; 2Sa 6:14; Ps 150:4

With thanksgiving Ps 42:4; 100:4 *See also* 2Ch 5:13

Hallelujah as a frequent expression of praise to God
Ps 106:48 *"Hallelujah" translates "praise the Lord". See also* Ps 111:1; 113:1; 135:1; 149:1; 150:1; Rev 19:3–4

Praise for his patient love Ps 106:1 *See also* Ps 117:2

Praise for his election of Israel
Ps 135:3–4 *See also* 1Ch 16:36; Ps 148:14

Praise for his sovereign rule Ps 146:10; Rev 19:6 *See also* Rev 19:1

Hosanna as an acclamation of praise
At Jerusalem Mt 21:9 pp Mk 11:9–10 pp Jn 12:13 *"Hosanna" is the Greek form of the Hebrew term seeking God's salvation. See also* Mt 21:5

The OT background Ps 118:25–26 *See also* 1Ch 16:35–36; Ps 79:9; 106:47

"Selah" in the context of praise
Following the assurance of answered prayer Ps 3:4 *There are a number of possible ways of understanding this obscure term: pausing or lifting up, perhaps*

---

indicating that the singers or musicians should sing or play "forte". See also Ps 21:2; 24:6; 32:5; 81:7; 84:8

Following an expression of deliverance
Ps 3:8 *See also* Ps 32:7; 49:15; 57:3; 68:19; 76:9; Hab 3:13

After a statement comparing God's greatness with human insignificance
Ps 9:20 *See also* Ps 39:5,11; 47:4; 52:5; 55:19; 59:5; 67:4; 75:3; 89:37; Hab 3:3

After an affirmation of security in God
Ps 46:7 *See also* Ps 46:11; 48:8; 61:4

On reflection of evil opposition Ps 54:3 *See also* Ps 62:4; 140:3,5

See also

3218 Holy Spirit & praise	7927 hymn
5287 dance	7960 singing
5421 musical instruments	7963 song
5422 musicians	8634 amen
	8646 doxology
	8676 thanksgiving

8667

praise, examples of

Scripture provides many examples of individuals who praised God. These examples illustrate the variety of ways and methods in which God can be praised, as well as the motivation for that praise.

OT examples of those who praised God
Melchizedek Ge 14:18–20

Moses Ex 15:1–2

Jethro Ex 18:9–10

David 1Ch 29:10–13

Ezra Ne 8:6

NT examples of those who praised God
Jesus Christ Lk 10:21

Zechariah Lk 1:67–68

The shepherds Lk 2:20

Simeon Lk 2:28

The disciples Lk 19:37; Ac 2:46–47 *See also* Lk 24:50–53; Ac 16:25

Those who were healed by Jesus Christ Lk 18:35–43; Ac 3:1–10

The citizens of heaven Rev 15:2–3

See also

2039 Christ, joy of	9412 heaven,
5088 David,	worship &
character	service
8609 prayer as praise	
& thanksgiving	

8668

praise, and Holy Spirit

See 3218 Holy Spirit, and praise

8670

remembering

The process of recalling the past, especially the presence and activity of God in the history of his people. Remembering God's work in the past can lead to praise and rejoicing, and to hope for the future. God himself remembers.

Divine remembering
God always remembers his covenant
1Ch 16:15 pp Ps 105:8 *See also* Ge 9:14–16; Ex 2:23–25; Ps 111:5; Lk 1:69–73

God always remembers his promises
Ps 105:42 *See also* Dt 6:20–23; Jos 1:3; 2Pe 3:9

God always remembers his people
Isa 49:15–16 *See also* Ge 7:24–8:1; 19:29; 30:22; 1Sa 1:19–20; Lk 1:54–55

Situations in which God will not remember Heb 8:10–12 *See also* Jer 31:33–34; Isa 65:16–17; Eze 18:21–24

The Holy Spirit helps believers to remember Jesus Christ and his words
Jn 14:26 *See also* Jn 2:22; 12:16; 16:4

Human remembering
Believers are to remember God's person Dt 8:18; Ps 119:55 *See also* Ps 42:5–6; Jer 51:50; Jnh 2:7

Believers are to remember God's acts in the past Isa 46:9 *See also* Dt 5:15; 7:17–18; 8:10–18; 1Ch 16:12; Mt 16:9–10

Believers are to remember God's wrath Dt 9:7–8 *See also* 2Pe 3:1–10

Believers are to remember God's commands Nu 15:38–40 *See also* Dt 8:1–2; Ps 103:17–18

Believers are to remember their responsibilities towards one another Ac 20:35 *See also* Gal 2:10; Heb 13:2–3

Believers are to remember the death of Jesus Christ 1Co 11:24–28; Lk 22:17–20

The importance of remembering
Remembering should lead to rejoicing Ps 13:5–6 *See also* Dt 26:4–11; Ps 66:5–6

Remembering should lead to repentance Rev 3:3 *See also* Eze 16:59–63; Mt 5:23–24; 26:75 pp Mk 14:72 pp Lk 22:61–62; Rev 2:5

Remembering should lead to understanding Lk 24:6–8 *See also* Jn 15:20; 16:1–4; Ac 11:15–18

Remembering should produce hope for the future La 3:21–24 *See also* Ps 42:4–11; 103:1–2; Heb 10:32–36

See also

1035 God, faithfulness	7394 memorial
1345 covenant	8355 understanding
3140 Holy Spirit, teacher	8467 reminders
4945 history	8644 commemoration
4963 past, the	8763 forgetting
6732 repentance	9610 hope
7355 feasts & festivals	

8672

striving with God

Striving with God can refer both to

the fruitless opposition of the ungodly to God's will and purposes, and to the struggle of the righteous with God, as they seek to find his will and obey it.

The striving of the wicked with God
It is the result of a guilty conscience Ac 26:14

Striving against God cannot succeed 2Ch 13:12 *See also* Pr 21:30; Isa 8:10; Ac 11:17

It leads to the destruction of those who attempt it Ps 2:2–5 *See also* Job 15:20–26,30

Ways in which the wicked strive with God
By resisting the Holy Spirit Ac 7:51

By arguing with God Ro 9:20 *See also* Job 40:2; Isa 45:9–11

Through unbelief Nu 14:1–4,10–11; 20:13; Ps 95:8–9

By attacking God's people Ac 5:39 *To attack God's people is to attempt to attack God himself. See also* 1Sa 17:45; Isa 37:22–25; Ac 9:4–5

Jacob strives with God
Ge 32:24–28 *Jacob's struggle with God represents the conflict within himself between self-will and dependence on God. As "Jacob", the supplanter, he had overcome Esau and Laban, but God demonstrates his superior power in the wrestling match so that as "Israel" he will be submissive to the divine will. See also* Hos 12:2–5

The striving of the righteous with God
The struggle for righteousness Ac 24:16 *See also* Lk 13:24; Ro 7:14–25; 1Co 9:25–27; Php 3:10–14; 1Ti 4:10; Heb 12:4

The discipline of prayer Col 4:12 *See also* Isa 64:7; Lk 22:44

The struggle to understand God's purposes Ex 5:22–23 *See also* Job 10:18; Ps 73:16; 88:14–18; Hab 1:2–4,13

See also

1130 God, sovereignty	8482 spiritual warfare
5094 Jacob	8613 prayer, persistence
5829 defiance	
5931 resistance	8653 importunity to God
6166 flesh, sinful nature	8785 opposition
8355 understanding	8823 self-righteousness
8476 self-discipline	

8674

study

The application of the mind with a view to acquiring knowledge, particularly of the Scriptures. God promises his help to those who give themselves to this work.

The study of the works of the LORD
Ps 111:2 *The works mentioned are his acts of providence and grace.*

God's people are to study in order to gain wisdom
Pr 2:1–5; 4:5 *See also* Job 28:12,20; Ps 90:12; Pr 3:13; 15:14; 23:23

The study of human activity, achievement and wisdom
Ecc 1:13–14 *See also* Ecc 1:17; 2:12; 7:25; 8:9,16; 9:1; 12:9–11 *The Teacher turned from human wisdom to searching out and setting forth proverbs; Ecc 12:12 He concluded that all human study was wearisome.*

The study of the word of God
The study of the word of God is commended 2Ti 2:15 *See also* Isa 8:20; Jer 15:16; Mt 22:29; Ro 15:4; 1Pe 2:2

Ezra studied the law of the LORD Ezr 7:10

The Bereans studied the Scriptures Ac 17:11

Some Jews studied the Scriptures without finding Jesus Christ Jn 5:39

God promises his help in the study of the Scriptures
Jn 14:26; 16:13

See also

1610 Scripture	5894 intelligence
3140 Holy Spirit, teacher	7793 teachers
5026 knowledge	7797 teaching
5035 mind	8361 wisdom
5302 education	8476 self-discipline
5514 scribes	8662 meditation

8676

thanksgiving

The offering of thanks, especially for gifts received. Scripture emphasises the importance of giving thanks to God for all his gifts and works, both as an expression of our dependence upon him and gratitude to him.

Thanksgiving is sometimes linked with praise to God
Ps 69:30 *See also* 1Ch 16:4; Ps 42:4; 100:4

The duty of thanksgiving to God
1Ti 4:3–4 *See also* Ps 107:8–9; 147:7–9; Lk 17:17–18; Ro 1:20–21; 14:6

The expression of thanksgiving to God
Through OT offerings Ps 50:14 *See also* Lev 7:12–15; Jnh 2:9

In Christian gatherings 1Co 10:16 *See also* 1Co 10:30; 14:16–17

Through song Ps 95:2 *See also* 1Ch 16:7–9; Ezr 3:11; Ne 12:8,24,27,46; Ps 147:7; Isa 51:3; Jer 30:19; Eph 5:19–20

Through prayer 1Ti 2:1 *See also* Ne 11:17; Da 6:10

Through giving 2Co 9:11–12

In conversation Eph 5:4

Believers are to give thanks in all circumstances
1Th 5:18 *See also* Php 4:6; Col 3:17

Thanksgiving for the blessings of salvation
1Co 15:57 *See also* Ro 7:24–25; 2Co 2:14 *for victory through Christ;* 2Co 4:15 *for God's grace;* 2Co 9:15 *for Jesus Christ himself;* Col 1:12; 2:6–7 *for union with Christ*

Examples of those who gave thanks to God
Jesus Christ Mt 14:19 pp Lk 9:16; Mk 8:6; Lk 24:30; 1Co 11:24

Paul Ac 28:15; Ro 6:17; Eph 1:16; 1Ti 1:12

Heavenly beings Rev 4:9; 7:12; 11:17

See also

3221 Holy Spirit & prayer	7960 singing
5476 property	8352 thankfulness
7322 burnt offering	8435 giving oneself
7364 fellowship offering	8609 prayer as praise & thanksgiving
7476 thank-offering	8622 worship
7933 Lord's Supper	8664 praise

8678

waiting on God

Being prepared to look patiently towards God for his guidance and accepting the timing he proposes. Waiting on God can lead to an atmosphere of expectation and confidence in God and a realisation of the unreliability of one's own judgment.

Waiting on God is something that is commanded
Hos 12:6 *See also* Ps 27:14; 37:7,34; 123:2; Isa 30:18

Reasons for waiting on God
Jer 14:22 *for his providence;* Ps 25:5 *for his salvation;* Ps 145:15–16 *for his blessings*

Waiting on Christ
Jas 5:7–8 *"Waiting on Christ" is often seen in terms of waiting patiently for God to bring about the end of all things through the promised second coming of Jesus Christ. See also* Lk 12:35–40; 1Co 1:7; 4:5; Tit 2:13; Heb 9:28; Jude 21

The benefits of waiting on God
It leads to expectancy Ps 5:3 *See also* Ro 8:23; 1Co 4:5; Gal 5:5; Tit 2:13

It leads to hope Ps 33:20 *See also* Ps 130:5; Isa 51:5; Mic 7:7

It leads to trust Isa 8:17

It leads to patience Ro 8:23–25 *See also* La 3:24–26; Rev 6:9–11

Examples of people who waited on God
Ge 49:18 *Jacob;* Ps 39:7 *David;* Isa 8:17 *Isaiah;* Mic 7:7 *Micah;* Mk 15:43 *Joseph of Arimathea;* Lk 2:25 *Simeon*

See also

4925 delay, divine	8331 reliability
5767 attitudes in prayer	8613 prayer, persistence
5977 waiting	8618 prayerfulness
8030 trust	8640 calling upon God
8213 confidence	9610 hope
8318 patience	
8329 readiness	

8700

Threats to the life of faith

8701

affluence

Literally, "flowing" with prosperity. Wealth is not condemned in Scripture but is seen as a good gift of God. However, affluence has its dangers.

Godly affluence
Ex 3:8 *See also* Dt 28:1–6,11; Ps 1:3; 112:3; Pr 8:18–21; 22:4; Isa 60:5; 61:6; 66:12; Mic 4:4

Examples of affluence Ge 2:8–12 *Eden;* Ge 13:2 *Abraham;* Ge 26:12–13 *Isaac;* Ge 33:11 *Jacob;* Job 42:10–12 *Job Solomon:* 1Ki 3:13; 10:23–29 2Ch 32:27–29 *Hezekiah;* Mt 27:57 *Joseph of Arimathea*

The dangers of affluence
Pride Dt 8:17–18; 1Ti 6:17 *See also* Ps 10:4–6; 73:3–6

Reliance upon riches Pr 11:28; 1Ti 6:17 *See also* Ps 62:10; Pr 23:5; Ecc 10:19; Mk 10:24 fn; Lk 12:16–21

Over-attachment to riches Mt 19:22 pp Mk 10:22 pp Lk 18:23

Greed for more riches Ecc 5:10

Temptation 1Ti 6:9–10

Cares and anxieties Mt 13:22 pp Mk 4:19 pp Lk 8:14

Spiritual complacency Rev 3:17

Contempt for God Pr 30:8–9

Contempt for the poor or unfortunate Job 12:5; Pr 22:16; Am 2:6–8; 4:1; 5:11; Lk 16:24–31; Jas 5:1–6

Affluence is temporary
It is for this life only 1Ti 6:7 *See also* Job 1:21; Ps 37:35–36; 49:10–12,16–20; Ecc 5:15

It is often lost Job 1:13–15; Ecc 5:13–14

Spiritual affluence
The riches of God Php 4:19 *See also* Ps 36:7–9; 2Co 9:9; Eph 3:8

Spiritual wealth Eph 1:3; 1Pe 1:4; Rev 2:9

The shared wealth of the church Mk 10:29–30; Ac 4:34–35; Php 4:18

The wealth of heaven Mt 6:20; Lk 12:33; Rev 7:16–17

See also

1050 God, goodness of	5858 fat
5399 luxury	6248 temptation
5413 money, attitudes	8261 generosity, God's
5446 poverty	8778 materialism
5810 complacency	8808 riches
	8848 worldliness

8702

agnosticism

The inability to decide whether or not God exists. It is characterised by indecision and compromise when faced with the challenge to wholehearted commitment, and is condemned as sinful, inexcusable and unnecessary in the light of God's clear self-revelation.

Agnosticism is inexcusable in the light of God's self-revelation
In the creation Ro 1:19–20 *See also* Ps 19:1–2; Ac 14:17

In the person of Jesus Christ Jn 1:18 *See also* Jn 14:9; Heb 1:1–3

Agnosticism is sinful
Because God calls for wholehearted commitment Jos 24:14–15 *See also* Ex 32:26; Dt 6:13–14; 30:15–19; Ac 14:15

Because God's call demands total obedience Mt 9:9 pp Mk 2:14 pp Lk 5:27–28 *See also* Mt 4:18–22 pp Mk 1:16–20

Agnosticism results in compromise
In worship 1Ki 18:21; 2Ki 17:41 *See also* 2Ki 17:29–33; 1Co 10:21

In commitment Mt 6:24 pp Lk 16:13 *in the attitude to money;* Mt 8:19–22 pp Lk 9:57–62 *in service;* 2Co 6:14 *in relationships with unbelievers;* Eph 4:14 *in accommodating false teaching*

Agnosticism as a result of ignorance
Ignorance through being uninformed Ac 17:23–30 *See also* Ac 3:17–18

Foolish ignorance of God's existence Ps 14:1 pp Ps 53:1 *See also* Ps 92:5–7; Jer 5:4

Ignorance of God's presence Ps 115:2 *See also* Ps 42:3; Joel 2:17; Mic 7:10

Ignorance as a result of rejecting God's truth Ps 10:4 *See also* Ps 36:1; Jer 5:21–24; Zec 7:11–12; Ac 2:22–23

Ignorance as a result of sin Eph 4:17–19 *See also* Isa 1:3–4; Jer 4:22

Ignorance is no defence against God's judgment Ro 1:18 *See also* Jdg 2:10–14; Isa 44:9–11

See also

1439 revelation	6257 unbelievers
2426 gospel, responses	6628 conversion, God's demand
3284 Holy Spirit, resisting	8023 faith, necessity
5811 compromise	8710 atheism
5884 indecision	8721 doubt
6181 ignorance	8834 unbelief

8703

antinomianism

A form of spiritual anarchy, which rejects the law as having any place in the Christian life, whether as instructor or as assessor. Paul's teaching that Christians are free from the law is sometimes misunderstood as antinomian. But Paul reveres God's law, and teaches believers, who are free from the law as a system of salvation, to keep it out of gratitude for salvation freely given, and because holiness as defined by the law is the Christian calling.

Antinomianism as a rejection of God's laws
Jer 2:20 See also Pr 29:18; Jer 5:5; Hos 8:12; 2Pe 2:10

Various people described as antinomian
Israel described as antinomian
Eze 20:13 See also Ex 32:25; Jer 2:23–25; Hos 8:1; Zec 7:11–12

The ungodly described as antinomian
Jude 4 See also 2Ti 3:1–5; 2Pe 2:13–15; Jude 8

The antichrist described as antinomian
2Th 2:3–10 See also Da 7:25; 8:9–12,23–25 The object of these prophecies, Antiochus Epiphanes, foreshadowed the antichrist in his behaviour.

Jesus Christ and his followers accused of antinomianism
Mt 11:19 See also Mt 12:2; Jn 9:16; Ac 6:11–14

Jesus Christ came to fulfil the law, not abolish it Mt 5:17–19

Paul rejects antinomianism
Ro 6:1–2 See also Ro 3:31; 7:7

Misunderstandings, by opponents and converts alike, about Paul's teaching on freedom from the law
Paul accused of antinomianism
Ac 21:28 See also Ro 3:8; 6:15

Paul corrects the Corinthians' interpretation of his teaching as a licence for antinomianism 1Co 10:23 The phrase "Everything is permissible" is probably the Corinthians' misinterpretation of Paul's teaching. See also 1Co 5:1–8; 6:12–13

Punishment of antinomians
Jer 6:19 See also Ezr 7:26; Am 2:4–5; Rev 22:15

See also
5375 law	8266 holiness
5794 asceticism	8453 obedience
6169 godlessness	8750 false teachings
6221 rebellion	8774 legalism
6662 freedom, abuse	8775 libertinism
6666 grace	9115 antichrist, the

8704

apostasy

A general falling away from religion or a denial of the faith by those who once held it or professed to hold it. It is frequently described in terms of spiritual adultery and thus provokes the jealous anger of God.

8705

apostasy, in OT

Israel was in danger of abandoning God from her earliest days. The OT frequently warns against apostasy and identifies its likely consequences.

Apostasy in Egypt and in the desert
Ps 78:9–41 See also Ex 32:25–29 the death of 3,000 after Aaron made the golden calf; Lev 17:7; 20:1–6; Nu 14:9–12 The people rebel against Moses and Aaron after the return of the spies; Nu 14:31–35; 25:1–4; 32:10–11; Dt 31:16–18; 32:15–21; Ps 95:7–8; 106:13–33; Heb 3:15–19

Apostasy in the time of the judges
Ps 78:55–64 See also Jdg 2:6–23; 8:27,33–34; Ne 9:26–31; Ps 106:34–39

Apostasy in the kingdom of Israel
Hos 5:3–4 See also 2Ki 17:7–20; Hos 1:2; 4:10–19; 7:4

Apostasy in the kingdom of Judah
Jer 3:1–25 See also 2Ki 23:26–27; 2Ch 29:6–9 Hezekiah's reforms to purify the temple; 2Ch 30:7–9; Isa 1:1–6; 30:1–5 Judah's alliance with Egypt; Jer 2:7–13,19–25; 5:5–7; 7:9–15; 9:2; 13:23–27; 17:5–6,13; 23:10–15 lying prophets denounced; Jer 31:22; Eze 6:9; 16:15–42; 23:1–35; Da 9:5–14

See also
6221 rebellion	7236 Israel, united
6243 adultery,	kingdom
spiritual	7245 Judah,
7145 remnant	kingdom of
7215 exile, the	8742 faithlessness
7233 Israel, northern	8768 idolatry
kingdom	

8706

apostasy, warnings against personal

It is possible for individuals to fall away from faith or turn against Jesus Christ. Scripture identifies this danger and warns against its negative consequences.

Personal apostasy described
Heb 6:4–8 See also Mt 13:20–21 pp Mk 4:16–17 pp Lk 8:13; Mt 24:10–12; Gal 1:6; 5:4; 2Th 2:3; 2Ti 4:3–4; 1Ti 4:1; 1Jn 2:19; 5:16

Warnings against personal apostasy
Heb 10:26–31 See also Mt 10:33 pp Mk 8:38 pp Lk 12:9; Jn 15:6; 2Ti 2:12; Heb 3:12; 2Pe 3:17

OT examples of personal apostasy
Dt 13:1–11 an unfruitful prophet or relative
King Saul: 1Sa 15:11,28; 16:14; 2Sa 7:15
2Ch 26:16–21 King Uzziah;
2Ch 28:19–27 King Ahaz

NT examples of personal apostasy
Mt 26:14–16 pp Mk 14:10–11 pp Lk 22:3–6 Judas; Lk 13:26–27; Jn 6:66; Ac 5:1–11 Ananias and Sapphira; 1Ti 1:19–20 Hymenaeus and Alexander; Tit 1:16; 2Ti 4:10 Demas; 2Pe 2:1–3,10–15,20–22; Jude 4,8–16; Rev 2:20–22 Jezebel

See also
6218 provoking God	8749 false teachers
6232 rejection of	8766 heresies
God, results	8839 unfaithfulness
8712 denial of Christ	

8707

apostasy, dealing with personal

Individual believers can fall away from faith and be restored. Scripture gives examples of such falling away, and offers advice on how such people should be dealt with pastorally.

Warnings of the dangers of personal apostasy
2Co 11:2–3 See also Ps 125:4–5; Lk 9:59–62; Gal 3:1–3; 4:8–10 Those who return to strict observance of Jewish days and festivals have not understood the gospel.

Warnings against leading others into apostasy
Mt 18:6 See also Pr 28:10; Gal 5:7–10

Encouragements to guard against personal apostasy
1Co 10:12–13; Heb 3:12–14 See also Ps 85:8; Mt 24:10–13,24–25 pp Mk 13:22–23; Col 1:21–23; 1Ti 6:20–21; Heb 10:35–39; 12:1–8; 2Pe 3:17–18; Rev 13:5–10

Dealing with apostate believers
Gal 6:1 See also 1Co 5:4–5; Jas 5:19–20; 1Jn 5:16–17

Examples of those who were restored from apostasy
Samson: Jdg 16:20,28–30
Ps 51:1–17 David
Peter: Mt 26:74 pp Mk 14:72 pp Lk 22:61–62 pp Jn 18:27 for the account of Peter's reinstatement see Jn 21:15–17
Ac 15:37–38 for evidence of John Mark's recovery see 2Ti 4:11

The punishment of apostates
Isa 65:12–15; Eze 3:20; 18:24–26; 2Th 2:11–12; 2Pe 2:17

Punishment through misfortune
Dt 28:63; Am 2:4–6

Punishment through defeat Nu 14:43; Jdg 2:12–15

Punishment through rejection 2Ch 24:20; Hos 4:6

See also

1461 truth, nature of	7784 shepherd
6248 temptation	8774 legalism
6730 reinstatement	8834 unbelief
6732 repentance	
7026 church, leadership	

8709

astrology

The study of the stars and planets, based on the pagan assumption that they exercise a decisive influence over human destinies. Scripture rejects such beliefs, insisting upon the total sovereignty of God over his entire creation.

Astrology is to be rejected
The worship of heavenly bodies is forbidden Dt 4:19; 2Ki 17:16 *See also* 2Ki 21:3–5 pp 2Ch 33:3–5; 2Ki 23:4,11; Job 31:26–28; Eze 8:16–18; Zep 1:5

The consultation of stars is condemned Isa 47:13 *See also* Jer 8:2

Astrology at the time of Daniel
Da 2:1–13; 4:1–7; 5:1–8

Astrologers came to worship the newborn Jesus
Mt 2:1–10

See also

1130 God, sovereignty	4251 moon
4055 heaven and earth	4281 stars
	4284 sun
4170 host of heaven	4937 fate, fatalism
4212 astronomy	8752 false worship

8710

atheism

The denial of God's existence and thus also the denial of his word, truth and authority. It is seen in the worship of created things, in human boasting and in the decision to live a life without God which results in godlessness and brings God's judgment.

Characteristics of atheism
Denying God's existence Ps 14:1 pp Ps 53:1

Worshipping created things Ro 1:25 *See also* Da 5:23; Rev 9:20

Denying God's truth Isa 32:6; Ro 1:18 *See also* Jer 5:12,31; 11:21; 14:14; 27:15

Denying God's ability to fulfil his word Jer 17:15 *See also* Isa 5:19; Ac 17:18; 1Th 4:8; 2Pe 3:3–4; Rev 11:7–10

Showing contempt for God's name Lev 19:12; Jer 5:2; Eze 36:20; 43:8

Boasting against God Ps 10:3–5 *See also* Job 15:25; Ps 12:3–4; 36:1–2; 73:11; Pr 30:9; Jer 35:13; Rev 13:6

Not turning to God in trouble Job 35:10 *See also* Job 36:13; Jer 2:8; 17:5

Living in ignorance of God Jer 5:4 *See also* Eph 2:12

Denying Jesus Christ Jude 4 *See also* 1Jn 2:22; 4:3; 2Jn 7

Atheism results in godless living
Ro 1:28–31 *See also* Ge 6:5; 1Sa 2:12; Pr 11:9; Isa 9:17; 26:10; Jer 5:5; 23:11; Mal 3:14,18; 1Ti 1:9–10; Jude 18

Atheism brings condemnation
It cannot be excused Job 12:7–8; Ac 14:17; Ro 1:19–20

It results in lack of hope Job 8:13; 15:34; 20:5; 27:8; Ps 9:17

It results in God's judgment Isa 10:6; 33:14; Jer 5:5–6,9–11,29; Ro 1:18; 1Pe 4:17; 2Pe 3:7; Jude 14–15

God desires to save the atheist
Ac 17:27 *See also* Isa 55:7; Jer 3:12; Eze 18:23; 33:11; Ro 5:6–8

See also

2545 Christ, opposition to	8622 worship
	8712 denial of Christ
6121 boasting	8778 materialism
6169 godlessness	8802 pride
6231 rejection of God	8834 unbelief
6732 repentance	9115 antichrist, the

8711

covenant breakers

Covenants were central to OT life, with the result that those who broke covenants, and especially those who violated the covenant between God and Israel, were regarded as a serious threat to social stability.

The importance of covenants
The covenant between God and his people Ge 9:16 *See also* 2Sa 23:5; Isa 24:5; 55:3

God will remain faithful to his covenant Jdg 2:1 *See also* Ps 105:8; Isa 54:10

Covenants between people
Covenants made in the sight of God were permanently binding Nu 30:2; 1Sa 23:16–18 *See also* Dt 23:21; Ecc 5:4

Condemnation of those who break covenants Hos 6:7 *See also* Pr 2:17

Examples of covenants between people Ge 21:27; Jos 24:24; 2Sa 5:3; 1Ki 5:12; 20:34; Jer 34:8

Examples of breaking the covenant with God
Coveting the possessions of others Ecc 4:4 *See also* Ex 20:17

Stealing Ex 20:15 pp Dt 5:19 *See also* Dt 23:24

Using dishonest weights or scales Lev 19:35–36; Pr 20:23 *See also* Dt 25:13–16; Hos 12:7–8; Am 8:5

Moving boundary stones Pr 23:10 *See also* Dt 19:14; 27:17

Extortion Hab 2:6 *See also* Isa 10:1–2; Eze 22:12; Am 5:11

Breach of trust Lev 6:2; Eze 16:17

Not repaying loans Ps 37:21

Not paying fair wages *See also* Ge 31:6–9

Failing to care for aliens
Aliens living in Israel were regarded as having privileged status amongst Gentiles, and were treated as covenant people in some respects: Ex 23:9; Dt 29:9–15; 31:12; Jos 8:33–35

See also

1345 covenant	8714 dishonesty
5311 extortion	8719 distrust
5466 promises	

8712

denial of Jesus Christ

The making of a conscious, informed decision not to accept Jesus Christ or his claims and teaching.

Jesus Christ was denied by the Jewish people
Jn 1:11 *See also* Mt 11:16–19 pp Lk 7:31–35; Mt 13:54–58 pp Mk 6:1–6; Mt 26:63–68 pp Mk 14:61–65 pp Lk 22:66–71; Lk 4:16–30; Jn 5:37–43; Ac 4:8–12; Ps 118:22

The consequences of denying Jesus Christ
Denying Jesus Christ results in judgment Jn 12:48 *See also* Mt 12:38–42 pp Lk 11:29–32

Denying Jesus Christ means replacement by others Ac 13:46 *See also* Mt 21:40–41 pp Mk 12:9 pp Lk 20:15–16; Ac 18:5–6

To deny Christ is to be denied by Christ 2Ti 2:12 *See also* Mt 10:32; Mk 8:38

Warnings against those who deny Jesus Christ
2Pe 2:1 *See also* 1Jn 2:22–23; 2Jn 7; Jude 4

Denial, repentance and restoration: the example of Peter
Peter's denial predicted by Jesus Christ Mk 14:29–30 pp Mt 26:31–34 pp Lk 22:31–34

Peter declares he will never deny Jesus Christ Mk 14:31 pp Mt 26:35

Peter denied that he knew Jesus Christ Mt 26:69–75 pp Mk 14:66–72 pp Lk 22:55–62 pp Jn 18:15–18 pp Jn 18:25–27

Peter's restoration to Christ Jn 21:15–19; Ac 1:15–22; 2:14–41

See also

2545 Christ, opposition to	6230 rejection
	6602 acceptance
5113 Peter, disciple	6730 reinstatement

8713

discouragement

A sense of unhappiness arising from a loss of confidence in one's own abilities, in the reliability of God or in the power of the gospel. Discouragement can occur in the Christian life, especially when there is resistance to the gospel or in instances of personal failure.

Scripture provides reassurance for those who experience discouragement.

The experience of discouragement
Job 3:20–26 See also Nu 21:4–5 *the Israelites in the desert*; Jos 2:8–11 *the Canaanites and Rahab*; 1Sa 17:10–11 *the Israelites and Goliath*; 2Ki 19:26 *God's judgment on Sennacherib*; Job 5:6–7; Ps 38:1–14; Pr 1:26–27 *Wisdom speaks to the sinner*; Ecc 2:17–20 *the Teacher's disillusion*; Isa 21:2–4; Jer 45:3 *to Baruch*; Eze 21:7 *God's judgment on Israel*; Zec 10:2; 2Co 1:8–9 *Paul*

Prayer in discouragement
Ps 42:5–11 See also Dt 26:6–7; 2Sa 22:7 *David*; 2Ch 20:9 *Jehoshaphat*; Ne 9:32; Ps 31:9–12; Isa 38:14 *Hezekiah*; Jer 8:18–19; Jnh 2:1–2

Endurance in discouragement
Isa 42:3–4 See also 2Co 6:4–10 *Paul*; 2Th 1:4; Heb 10:32; 12:3; Rev 2:3 *concerning the church at Ephesus*

Discouragement through disobedience
Jer 8:9 See also 1Sa 28:15–18; Job 15:24–25 *Eliphaz to Job*; Zep 1:17

Discouragement and discipline
Heb 12:5–7 See also Jdg 2:14–15; Isa 26:16

Effects of discouragement
Pr 17:22 See also Ex 6:9 *the Israelites in Egypt*; 2Sa 4:1; Ezr 4:4 *the rebuilding of the temple*; Job 4:5; Pr 15:13; 18:14

Resisting discouragement
Dt 1:21 See also Jos 1:9; 8:1; 1Sa 17:32 *David reassuring Saul about Goliath*; 1Ch 22:13 *David to Solomon*; 2Ch 32:7 *Hezekiah*; Jer 51:46; Lk 18:1; Jn 14:1; Gal 6:9; Eph 3:13; 2Ti 4:5

God's help in discouragement
Ro 8:35–39 See also Dt 31:6,8,23; Jos 1:9; 1Ch 28:20; 2Ch 20:15,17; Ps 34:18; Isa 40:29–31; 61:1; Lk 4:18; Jer 30:10; Jn 16:33; 2Co 7:6 *Paul*

Warnings not to discourage others
The Israelites discouraged when on the point of entering the promised land Ob 12 See also Dt 1:28 *by the spies*; Nu 32:7 *by the Gadites and Reubenites*

General warnings not to discourage others Ps 109:16; Zec 10:2; Ac 15:19 *James advises against discouraging the Gentiles*; Col 3:21

The need to stand with the discouraged
Heb 13:3 See also Job 6:14; Jer 8:21; Ro 12:15; Jas 1:27

See also
5805 comfort	8459 perseverance
5831 depression	8785 opposition
5835 disappointment	8790 oppression
8230 discipline	8794 persecution
8414 encouragement	9614 hope, results
8418 endurance	of absence

8714

dishonesty

A way of speaking or acting which leads to people being deceived, misled or cheated.

8715

dishonesty, and God's nature

Dishonesty is contrary to the will and nature of God, and so should not be found among the people of God.

Dishonesty is contrary to the will and nature of God
Nu 23:19 See also 1Sa 15:29; Ro 3:4; Tit 1:2

Dishonesty, like sin, is of satanic origin Jn 8:44 See also Ge 3:1–5

God's hatred of dishonesty
Pr 12:22 See also Ps 5:4–6; Pr 6:16–17; Isa 59:1–4, 12–15

Kinds of dishonesty
In business deals Hos 12:7 See also Dt 25:13–16; Pr 20:14; Am 8:5; Mic 6:10

In not paying debts Ps 37:21 See also Jas 5:4

In exploiting the poor Eze 22:29 See also Job 24:2–11; Isa 32:7; Jer 22:13

God's judgment on dishonesty
God's denunciation of dishonesty in general Hos 4:1–2 See also Lev 19:15; Jer 7:8–10; 1Th 4:6

The dishonesty of liars and false witnesses Pr 19:9; Ac 5:1–10 See also Dt 19:16–19; Jos 7:10–12 *regarding Achan's sin*; 2Ki 5:19–27; Ps 5:6; Isa 29:20–21; Jer 9:4–9; Rev 21:8

The dishonesty of false prophets and teachers Jer 14:14–15; 2Pe 2:1–3; Isa 9:14–15; Jer 28:15–16; Eze 13:1–23; Zec 10:2–3; 1Ti 4:1–2

God's demands for making amends for dishonesty
Lev 6:1–7; Lk 3:12–14 *This demonstrated that their repentance was genuine*; Lk 19:8 *the result of encountering Jesus Christ*; Lk 16:1–12 *Jesus Christ was not commending the steward's dishonesty but his shrewdness.*

See also
1065 God, holiness of	6130 corruption
5492 restitution	6145 deceit
5614 weights & measures, laws	8275 honesty
	8767 hypocrisy

8716

dishonesty, examples of

Examples of the dishonest behaviour condemned by God.

Dishonest words condemned
Lying Eph 4:25 See also Lev 19:11; Ps 34:13; Col 3:9–10

False witness Ex 20:16 pp Dt 5:20 See

also Mt 19:17–18; Mk 10:19; Lk 18:20; Ex 23:1,7; Mt 26:59–60; Ac 6:12–14

Swearing falsely Lev 19:12 See also Ex 20:7; Mt 5:33–37

Dishonest actions condemned
Stealing Ex 20:15 pp Dt 5:19 See also Mt 19:18 pp Mk 10:19 pp Lk 18:20; Ro 13:9

Dishonest dealing Pr 11:1 See also Lev 19:13; Dt 25:13–16; Ps 62:10; Isa 33:15–16; Tit 2:9–10

Israel condemned for dishonest gain
Bribery and extortion Eze 22:12–13 See also Jer 22:13,17–19; Eze 22:27–31; Hab 2:6–9

Cheating and dishonest scales Am 8:4–8 See also Lev 19:35–36; Mic 6:10–13; Mal 1:14 *In this case, they were cheating the LORD.*

Examples of dishonesty
Ge 26:15–22 *Abimelech's servants* Jacob: Ge 25:29–33; 27:6–29; 30:31–43 Ge 29:21–30; 31:19 *Rachel*; Ge 31:36–42 *Laban*; Jos 7:11–26 *Achan*; 1Ki 21:2–16 *Ahab and Naboth's vineyard*

See also
5238 bribery	5429 oaths
5253 cheating	5512 scales &
5310 exploitation	balances
5311 extortion	5555 stealing
5318 fraud	8751 false witness
5353 interest	8776 lies

8718

disobedience

The refusal to obey someone, especially someone in a position of authority. Scripture insists on the need to obey God at all times.

Disobedience enters people's hearts for various reasons
Disobedience comes through greed and lust Ge 3:6 See also Ge 3:11–12; Ex 16:19–20; Jos 7:20–21; 2Sa 11:2–4

Disobedience arises from impatience Ex 32:23 See also Nu 20:10–11; 1Sa 13:8–14

Disobedience comes through fear Jer 43:2–7; Jn 7:13; 12:42; Gal 2:12

Disobedience results from pride and arrogance Lev 10:1 See also Ex 5:2; 2Ch 26:16

Unbelief is disobedience
Heb 3:12 See also Jer 7:23–28; Ro 11:30–32 *Ro 11:20 makes it clear that the disobedience spoken of here was unbelief*; Heb 3:18–19; 4:2,6

Lack of love is disobedience
Jn 14:24 See also 1Jn 2:9; 3:15

Disobedience to God leads to punishment
Punishment is applied to individuals Ge 3:17–19 See also Ge 3:23–24; Lev 10:1–2; Nu 20:12; 1Sa 28:18; 2Sa 12:14; Jnh 1:10–12; Eph 5:5–6

Punishment for the disobedience of unbelief 2Th 1:8–9 See also Heb 2:2–3

Nations are also punished Ge 15:14 *See also* Ac 7:7
Dt 11:26–28; 1Sa 12:15 *See also* Ex 32:35; Dt 28:15; Isa 13:11

Disobedience, like all sin, can be forgiven Ro 5:19 *See also* Eph 2:1–5

See also

5483 punishment	8453 obedience
5813 conceit	8744 faithlessness
5883 impatience	as
6155 fall of Adam &	disobedience
Eve	8834 unbelief
6178 hardness of	8840 unfaithfulness
heart	to God
6218 provoking God	
6222 rebellion	
against God	

8719

distrust

Failure to trust another, or a tendency to be suspicious of others' abilities or intentions. Though sometimes justifiable towards other human beings, such an attitude is never acceptable towards God.

Distrust between human beings
Ge 50:15–17 *Joseph's brothers distrusted him because they could not believe he had forgiven them. See also* Ge 32:6–8 *Jacob distrusted Esau because he thought he was seeking revenge;* Jdg 11:19–20 *Sihon distrusted Israel because he suspected a trick;* Ac 15:37–38 *Paul distrusted John Mark, having been let down by him.*

Distrust of God
Israel distrusted God Zep 3:2 *See also* Dt 1:32–33; 9:23–24 *Because that generation distrusted God, they failed to enter the promised land;* Ps 78:7,22 *Israel distrusted God in spite of the miracles he had done for her.*
Israel distrusted God as a result of her idolatry: 2Ki 17:14–15; Jer 13:25

Other examples
Distrust in God involves failure to trust God's promises and placing trust in other things: Jer 13:25; Eze 33:13; Mal 3:6–10; Mt 19:22 pp Mk 10:22

Distrust by God
Job 4:18 *See also* Job 15:15; Jn 2:24

Distrust is sometimes justified
Ps 118:8 *See also* Job 39:12; Ps 5:9; 44:6; 146:3; Jer 7:4; 9:4; 12:6; Mic 7:5; Hab 2:18

See also

1415 miracles	8721 doubt
5020 human nature	8742 faithlessness
7257 promised land	8768 idolatry
8020 faith	8830 suspicion
8030 trust	8834 unbelief
8354 trustworthiness	

8720

double-mindedness

Indicative of insincerity and hypocrisy. God requires wholeheartedness and sincerity from all people, both in their dealings

with others and in their worship of him.

Double-mindedness is characteristic of sinners
Jas 4:8 *See also* Ps 119:113–115

Double-mindedness in dealings with other people
Ge 34:1–29; Jos 9:3–15; 1Sa 18:17–25; 2Sa 3:22–27; 20:8–10;
Ne 6:1–4,10–13; Mt 26:47–50 pp Mk 14:43–46 pp Lk 22:47–48; Ac 23:12–24

Double-mindedness in daily life
Mt 23:25–28 *See also* Mt 15:10–19 pp Mk 7:14–23; Lk 11:39–40

Double-mindedness in worship
Idolatry 1Ki 18:21 *See also* 2Ki 17:27–34,40–41; Hos 10:1–2

Insincerity Mt 15:1–9 pp Mk 7:1–13 *See also* Isa 29:13

Lack of faith in prayer is equated with double-mindedness
Jas 1:5–8

God requires wholeheartedness and sincerity
Towards himself 1Ch 28:9 *See also* Nu 14:20–24; Jos 14:14; 2Ch 31:21; Ro 12:9; 1Co 5:8; 2Co 1:12; 1Ti 3:8; Jas 3:13–17

Towards other people Col 3:22 *See also* 2Ch 19:8–11; Eph 6:5–9

See also

5884 indecision	8615 prayer, doubts
5891 instability	8622 worship
5920 pretence	8721 doubt
8207 commitment	8767 hypocrisy

8721

doubt

Uncertainty about the truth and reality of spiritual things, as seen especially in a lack of faith in and commitment to God.

8722
doubt, nature of

Doubt leads to insecurity and lack of trust concerning God's willingness and ability to deliver his people. It also leads to a fear of people and situations.

Doubting God's truth
Doubt as a questioning of God's words
Ge 3:1 *See also* Ge 3:4; Isa 5:19; Jer 17:15; 2Pe 3:4

Doubt as lack of faith Mt 21:21–22 pp Mk 11:23–24 *See also* Mt 17:20; Mk 6:6; 16:14; Lk 17:6

Doubt as wavering Jas 1:6 *See also* 1Ki 18:21; Ro 4:20; Eph 4:13–14

Doubt as double-mindedness Jas 1:8 *See also* 2Ki 17:40–41; Lk 16:13; 1Co 10:21; Jas 4:8

Doubt as insecurity about relationship with God
Doubting God's compassion Ps 77:7–9 *See also* Ps 90:13; Heb 12:5–6

Doubting God's concern Job 30:20; Isa 49:14 *See also* Ps 13:1–2; 22:1–2; 35:17; Isa 40:27; Jer 8:18–22; La 3:8; Hab 1:2

Doubting God's desire to deliver Jer 45:3 *See also* Ex 5:22–23; La 2:1–9; 3:13–20

Doubting God's ability to deliver Ps 78:18–22 *See also* Ex 14:10–12; Ps 78:41–43; Mt 8:26 pp Mk 4:39–40 pp Lk 8:24–25

Doubting God's justice Jer 12:1 *See also* Job 9:23; Ps 73:13–16; 82:2; Jer 15:16–18; Hab 1:13

Doubt as fear of people and situations
Mt 14:30–31 *See also* Ge 12:12–13; 19:30; 26:7; Jos 7:5; 1Sa 17:11; Isa 51:12–13

See also

1030 God,	8702 agnosticism
compassion	8720 double-
1085 God, love of	mindedness
5877 hesitation	8726 doubters
8021 faith	8754 fear
8615 prayer, doubts	8834 unbelief

8723
doubt, results of

Doubt results in uncertainty and ineffectiveness in the spiritual life of individual believers and of the believing community. God appeals to those who waver to make a clear choice.

Doubt results in spiritual uncertainty
Uncertainty about commitment
Lk 9:57–62 pp Mt 8:19–22 *See also* Ge 19:17,26; Ex 16:2–3; Mt 6:24 pp Lk 16:13; Heb 11:15

Uncertainty about God's power
Nu 13:31 *See also* Dt 1:29–33

Uncertainty about God's love Isa 40:27 *See also* Dt 1:27; Job 9:16–18; 30:21

Uncertainty about the meaning of life
Job 3:16 *See also* 1Ki 19:3–4; Ps 42:3–4; Jer 20:14–18; Jnh 4:3

Uncertainty about teaching Eph 4:14 *See also* 1Ti 6:20–21

Uncertainty about the will of God
Jdg 6:17 *See also* Jdg 6:36–40; Jn 20:25; 2Co 13:3

Doubt may result in a spiritual decline
Doubt may result in drifting from faith
Heb 2:1 *See also* 2Ch 36:12–13; Ne 9:16–17; Ps 95:8–9; La 5:20; Heb 3:12–13; 6:4–6; 2Pe 2:20–21

Doubt may result in faithless action
Isa 31:1; Ro 14:23 *See also* Ge 12:13; 16:2–3; Ex 32:1; Nu 20:11–12; Ac 7:40; Ro 14:14

Doubt brings the risk of God's judgment Nu 20:12 *See also* Nu 11:1; 14:37; Heb 6:7–8

Doubt leads to ineffectiveness in prayer
Jas 1:6–7 *See also* Mt 17:20; 21:21 pp Mk 11:23

Doubt spreads
Dt 1:28 *See also* Nu 13:32; 2Ki 17:14

God's appeal for a clear decision
1Ki 18:21 *See also* Dt 30:15–17; Jos 24:15; Jn 20:27; Jas 4:8

See also
5831 depression 5884 indecision
8704 apostasy 8839 unfaithfulness

8724
doubt, dealing with

Uncertainty may be remedied by gaining assurance from God's word, remembering God's past goodness, reflecting on his power and appealing to his unfailing love. Believers should help the weak with the patience and encouragement that reflects God's own compassion.

Doubt dealt with by holding on to God's truth
Gaining assurance from God's word
Ps 119:147; 1Jn 5:13 *See also* Ps 119:116; Jn 20:31; Ro 15:4; 2Pe 1:19

Receiving correction and understanding through God's word
2Ti 3:14–17 *See also* Ps 119:130; Pr 6:23; 1Co 10:11

Avoiding idle speculation Eph 4:14; 1Ti 6:20–21; 2Ti 2:16,23; Tit 3:9

Doubt dealt with by meditating on God's works
Remembering God's past deeds
Ps 77:10–20 *See also* Dt 7:17–19; 1Ch 16:8–12 pp Ps 105:1–6; Ps 22:4–5; 74:12–17; 143:5; Isa 46:9; Mt 16:9–10

Commemorating God's deeds
Ex 12:14 *Religious festivals such as Passover provided a permanent reminder of God's past goodness to his people. See also* Dt 16:1; Lk 22:19; 1Co 11:24–25

Reflecting on divine power Mt 11:4–6; Jn 10:38; 14:11

Doubt dealt with by trusting
Trusting in God's unfailing love
Ps 6:2–4 *See also* Ps 42:8; Isa 49:15–16; 54:10; Jer 31:3–4

Trusting in God's presence Ge 28:15 *See also* Ex 3:12; Dt 20:1; 2Ch 20:15–17; Ps 42:11; 73:23–26

Trusting in God's strength Isa 41:10 *See also* 1Ki 19:6–8; Isa 40:28–31; 43:2

Remembering God's concern for the weak
God's compassion for the weak
Eze 34:16 *See also* Isa 42:3

God's grace to those with doubts
Ex 5:22–6:1 *God responds to Moses' uncertainty by promising a demonstration of his power. See also* Nu 11:21–23; Jdg 6:39–40; Jn 20:27

Pastoral concern for those who doubt
Being patient with doubters Jude 22 *See also* Ro 14:1–4,15–17; 15:1

Encouraging those with doubts
Jdg 20:22; Job 4:3–4 *See also* 2Ch 32:6–8; Isa 35:3–4; 40:1; 1Th 3:2; Heb 10:23–25; 12:12

See also
5954 strength
8025 faith, origins of
8026 faith, growth in
8105 assurance, basis of
8414 encouragement
8670 remembering

---

doubters

Scripture provides examples of believers who express temporary doubts—in particular about the willingness and power of God to deliver his people, the nature of his purpose, and their own place within the divine plan.

Examples of those doubting their effectiveness to serve God
Moses Ex 3:11 *See also* Ex 4:1,10–13; 6:12,30; Nu 11:13–15

Gideon Jdg 6:15 *See also* Jdg 6:17,36–40

Elijah 1Ki 19:3–4 *See also* 1Ki 19:10,14

Jeremiah Jer 1:6 *See also* Jer 15:10

Those temporarily doubting God's promises
Ge 15:8 *See also* Ge 17:17–18; 18:12–15; Lk 1:18

Those doubting God's power
Abraham and Isaac doubt God's protection Ge 12:12–13 *Fearing for his safety, Abraham resorts to deception. See also* Ge 20:2; 26:7

Moses and Israel in the desert
Ex 5:22–23 *See also* Ex 14:10–11 *The Israelites doubt God's protection at the Red Sea;* Nu 11:21–22 *Moses doubts God's provision of food;* Nu 13:31–33 *The ten spies doubt God's power to give victory in Canaan;* Nu 20:7–12 *Moses strikes the rock twice.*

Others doubting God's deliverance
1Sa 17:11 *The people of Israel are dismayed by the challenge from Goliath;* Isa 7:2 *King Ahaz, afraid of the coalition of Syria and Israel turns to Assyria for help;* Mt 14:29–31 *Peter, walking on water, is afraid and begins to sink;* Ac 12:14–15 *The early church does not believe that God has released Peter from prison.*

Believers questioning God
Questioning God's actions Jdg 6:13 *See also* Nu 11:10–12; 14:3; Jos 7:7–8

Questioning God's commands
1Sa 16:2 *Samuel;* 2Ki 4:42–43 *Elisha's servant;* Isa 7:12 *Ahaz*
Jesus Christ's disciples: Mk 6:37 pp Mt 14:16–17 pp Lk 9:13
Jn 11:39 *Martha;* Ac 9:13–14 *Ananias*

Believers with doubts about Jesus Christ
Mt 11:2–3 pp Lk 7:18–19; Jn 20:25 *See also* Mt 28:17; Mk 16:11–14; Lk 24:25

See also
6257 unbelievers
8721 doubt
8834 unbelief

---

enemies

Opponents or hostile forces which pose a threat to people or nations. Scripture identifies Satan as being the particular enemy of God and notes many enemies of the people of God. Scripture urges caution and courage in dealing with such enemies. Jesus Christ had enemies, and he provides an example of Christian conduct in the face of enemies' threats.

8728
enemies, of Israel and Judah

Throughout their history, Israel and Judah contended with enemies committed to their destruction, finding refuge only in their covenant-keeping God.

Enemies of Israel
The Egyptians Ex 1:8–11; 14:9; 1Ki 14:25 pp 2Ch 12:2; 2Ch 36:3

The Amalekites Ex 17:8; Jdg 3:13

The Edomites Nu 20:18; 1Ki 11:14

Sihon, king of the Amorites Nu 21:23

Og, king of Bashan Nu 21:33

The Canaanites and the surrounding nations Jos 11:1–5

The Syrians (Arameans) Jdg 3:8; 1Ki 11:25; 20:1; 2Ki 6:8,24; 24:2; 2Ch 28:5

The Moabites Jdg 3:12; 2Ki 1:1; 24:2

The Ammonites Jdg 3:13; 10:9; 2Sa 10:6 pp 1Ch 19:6; 2Ki 24:2

The Midianites Jdg 6:1

The Philistines Jdg 10:7–8; 1Sa 4:1–2; 17:1–2; 31:1; 2Sa 5:17; 8:1; 21:15,18 pp 1Ch 20:4

The Assyrians 2Ki 15:19,29; 17:3–6; 18:13

The Babylonians 2Ki 24:1; 25:1; 2Ch 36:5–7,15–20

Those opposed to the rebuilding under Ezra and Nehemiah Ezr 4:4–6; 5:3; Ne 2:10

Haman the Persian Est 3:5–6

The Greeks Zec 9:13

The Romans Jn 11:48

Characteristics of Israel's enemies
They were often more numerous than Israel 1Sa 13:5 *See also* Na 1:12

They were often better equipped
Jos 17:16 *See also* 1Sa 13:19–22

They were cruel and oppressive
Jer 6:23 *See also* Ex 6:5–9; Dt 28:33; Jdg 6:2–6; Jer 50:42; Hab 1:6

They were cunning Ps 83:3

They were determined to destroy Israel Ps 83:4

They were often in league with each other See also Ps 83:5–8

God helped Israel against her enemies

He opposed Israel's enemies Ge 12:3 See also Ex 23:22

He protected Israel Dt 23:14; Ne 4:15; 6:16; Ps 125:2; Isa 51:22; 59:19

He delivered Israel Nu 10:9; 1Sa 12:11; 2Ki 17:39; Lk 1:71

He gave Israel victory Ex 23:27 See also Lev 26:7–8; Nu 10:35; Dt 6:19; 33:27; Ps 60:12 pp Ps 108:13; Ps 68:1; Isa 54:15

He destroyed Israel's enemies Ex 15:6 See also Dt 20:17; 30:7; Jos 10:19; 2Ch 20:29; Ps 44:5

He gave Israel rest Dt 12:10 See also Dt 25:19; 1Ki 5:3–4; 1Ch 22:9

Israel's attitude towards her enemies

Israel was not to fear them Dt 20:1–4 See also 1Sa 17:45–47

Israel was to pray for deliverance 1Ki 8:33–34 pp 2Ch 6:24–25; 1Ki 8:37–40 pp 2Ch 6:28–31; Ezr 8:22–23; Ps 74:3,10,18,22–23

Kindness was to be shown to Israel's enemies Ex 23:4–5; 2Ki 6:21–23; Pr 25:21–22; Ro 12:20

Thanksgiving for victory over Israel's enemies

Giving thanks to God was the proper response to victory Ex 15:1 See also 2Sa 8:11–12 pp 1Ch 18:11; Ps 136:24

Israel often forgot to give thanks to God Jdg 8:33–34

God used enemies to chastise Israel

Dt 28:47–48 See also Lev 26:44 Because of his covenant, the LORD was unwilling to destroy Israel completely at the hand of her enemies; Dt 28:53; Jdg 2:10–23; 6:1; Isa 8:5–8

See also

1320 God as Saviour	6700 peace
5056 rest	7233 Israel, northern
5205 alliance	kingdom
5290 defeat	7236 Israel, united
5482 punishment	kingdom
5596 victory	7245 Judah,
5605 warfare	kingdom of
6634 deliverance	

8729
enemies, of Jesus Christ

Throughout his life Jesus Christ was òpposed by both spiritual and human enemies. He overcame every enemy so that his people might be set free by his victory.

The enemies of the infant Jesus
Mt 2:13–20 See also Mt 2:14–20; Rev 12:1–5

Satan as the enemy of Jesus Christ
In the temptation in the wilderness Mk 1:12–13 pp Mt 4:1–11 pp Lk 4:1–13 See also Ge 3:15

Operating through Jesus Christ's friends Mt 16:22–23 See also Lk 22:3; Jn 13:21–27

The Jewish leaders as enemies of Jesus Christ
They plotted to kill Jesus Christ Mt 12:14 pp Mk 3:6 pp Lk 6:11 See also Ps 2:2; Isa 53:3; Mt 27:1; Jn 5:18; 7:1,19; 11:53; 1Pe 2:21–24

They had no real reason for hating him Jn 15:25 See also Ps 35:19; 69:4

Judas as the enemy of Jesus Christ
Mt 26:14–16 See also Mt 10:4,36; Mic 7:6; Mt 26:21–25,47–50; Jn 13:25–27

The enemies of Jesus Christ succeeded in killing him in accordance with God's will
Jesus Christ was crucified Ac 2:23 See also Mt 27:22; Mk 15:1; Jn 18:28–32; Ac 3:13

Jesus Christ did not retaliate but prayed for his enemies Lk 23:34

Jesus Christ can change an enemy into a friend
Gal 1:23 See also Ac 9:1–6; 22:4–5; 26:9–11; Ro 5:10; Php 3:18; Col 1:24

Jesus Christ will ultimately conquer all his enemies
1Co 15:25–26 See also Ps 2:9; Mal 3:2; Mt 22:44; Ps 110:1; Ac 2:34; Php 2:9–11; 2Th 1:6–10; 2:3–8; Heb 1:13; 10:13

See also

2315 Christ as Lamb	2585 Christ, trial
2369 Christ, responses to	4121 Satan, enemy of God
2372 Christ, victory	5798 betrayal
2545 Christ, opposition to	6626 conversion
2570 Christ, suffering	8739 evil, examples of
2575 Christ, temptation	9240 last judgment

8730
enemies, of believers

Christians must expect to face many enemies on account of their faith. Jesus Christ made it clear that such opposition was the inevitable result of commitment to him. Nevertheless, Christians are called upon to love their enemies.

Christians are enemies of the world because they belong to Jesus Christ
Jn 15:18–19 See also Ps 86:14; Jn 17:14; 2Ti 3:12; 1Pe 4:15–16; 1Jn 3:13

Opposition to Christians is opposition to Jesus Christ
Mt 25:34–40 See also Mk 9:42; Lk 17:1; Ac 9:4–5

Particular enemies of Christians
All kinds of people Mk 13:13 pp Mt 10:22 See also Jn 15:21

Family members Mt 10:34–36 pp Lk 12:51–53 See also Ge 37:1–11; Mic 7:6; Mt 10:21 pp Mk 13:12

Religious zealots Ac 4:18; 5:28; 8:3; 9:1–2; 2Pe 2:1; 3Jn 9–10

Christians may be killed by their enemies
Jn 16:2 See also Ac 7:56–60; 12:1–2; 26:9–10; Rev 6:9

Christian attitudes towards enemies

To love, do good, bless and pray for them Mt 5:44–45 See also Job 31:29–30; Lk 6:27–29,35; 23:34; Ac 7:59–60; Ro 12:14; 1Pe 3:9

To forgive them Mt 6:12–15; Lk 11:4; 23:33–34; Ac 7:59–60

To help and show kindness to them Ro 12:20 See also Pr 25:21–22; Lk 10:25–37

To show kindness to their beasts of burden Ex 23:4–5

Not to rejoice in their misfortunes Pr 24:17–18

To win them with kindness Ro 12:21 See also 1Sa 26:21

Christians have a spiritual enemy
Satan opposes Christians 1Pe 5:8 See also Job 1:7–9; Lk 22:31; 2Ti 4:17–18

The need to engage in spiritual warfare 1Pe 5:9 See also 2Co 10:4; Eph 6:10–18; 1Ti 5:14–15; 2Ti 4:7; Jas 4:7

God supports his people against their enemies
Ps 23:5; Jn 17:15 See also Dt 33:27; 1Sa 12:11; 2Sa 22:1–3; Ps 18:2; 43:1; 46:1; 59:1–2; 71:1–4; 91:1–4; 119:134; 140:1–2; 143:9; 144:11; Mt 10:28–31; Lk 1:69,71; 22:32; 2Ti 4:8

Death as the last enemy to be destroyed by Jesus Christ
1Co 15:26 See also Ps 116:8; 2Ti 1:10; Rev 20:14; 21:4

See also

5560 suffering	8484 spiritual
5944 self-defence	warfare,
6716 reconciliation	enemies
8220 courage, facing enemies	8610 prayer, asking God
8291 kindness	8785 opposition
8301 love and enemies	8794 persecution
8450 martyrdom	9020 death

8731
enemy, Satan as the enemy of God

See 4121 Satan, as the enemy of God

8733

envy

A desire for another's gifts, possessions, position or achievements, closely associated with jealousy.

Causes of envy
Envy is the result of human sin Gal 5:19–21 See also Pr 23:17;

Mt 15:19–20 pp Mk 7:21–23; Ro 1:29;
1Co 3:3; 1Ti 6:4; Tit 3:3; 1Pe 2:1–2

Envy arises from the good fortune of others Ge 26:12–14; 1Sa 18:6–8;
Ps 73:3; Mt 20:12–15

Love does not envy others 1Co 13:4

Envy arises from the spiritual abilities of others Ps 106:16–18; Ac 13:44–45
See also Nu 11:28–30; 12:2; 16:1–3;
Mt 27:18 pp Mk 15:10; Ac 17:5;
Php 1:15

Examples of envy
Cain envies Abel Ge 4:3–5
Esau envies Jacob Ge 27:41
Rachel envies Leah Ge 30:1
The brothers envy Joseph Ge 37:4

Results of envy
Job 5:2 *See also* Pr 14:30; Ecc 4:4;
Jas 3:14–16

In some cases, envy can be used by God Ro 10:19; 11:11,13–14 *Paul hopes that the Gentiles' response to the gospel might make Israel want its blessings as well. See also* Dt 32:21

Envy forbidden
Ps 37:1 *See also* Pr 3:31; 24:1; Gal 5:26

See also
5848 exaggeration	6133 coveting
5910 motives, examples	8773 jealousy
5929 resentment against people	

8734

evil

The presence of corruption, malevolence and depravity in the world, opposed to God's nature and will. Scripture stresses that evil is a force in its own right, rather than the mere absence of good, and describes its origins and the manner in which God deals with its continuing presence and power in his world. This set of themes consists of the following:
8735 evil, origins of
8736 evil, warnings against
8737 evil, believers' responses to
8738 evil, victory over
8739 evil, examples of

8735
evil, origins of

Although Scripture does not reveal the ultimate origin of evil, it identifies a number of intermediate sources.

Satan as a source of evil
Ge 3:1 *Identified later (Rev 12:9) with Satan;* Mt 4:1 pp Mk 1:13 pp Lk 4:2
Jn 8:44; 1Jn 3:8; Rev 12:9 *See also*
1Ch 21:1 *Satan incites David to take a census of Israel;* Job 1:11; 2:5; Mt 5:37;
6:13; 13:38–39 *the parable of the weeds;*
Lk 13:16 *Satan is responsible for a woman's crippling disease;* Jn 13:2 *The devil prompts Judas to betray Jesus Christ;*

Jn 17:15; Ac 5:3 *Ananias lies to the Holy Spirit at Satan's instigation;* 2Co 4:4; 12:7
Paul's thorn in the flesh from Satan;
Eph 2:2; 6:11; 1Th 2:18; 1Pe 5:8;
1Jn 3:12; 5:19; Rev 2:10; 20:2

Other evil powers
Lk 9:39 pp Mk 9:17–18; Eph 6:12;
1Ti 4:1 *See also* Jdg 9:23; 1Sa 16:14;
18:10–11; 19:9–10; Mt 12:45
pp Lk 11:26; Rev 12:7; 16:13–14

Fallen human nature as a source of evil
Ge 6:5; Mt 15:19 pp Mk 7:21–22
Jas 1:13–14 *See also* Ge 8:21; Pr 6:18;
Ecc 8:11; 9:3; Isa 59:7; Jer 4:14; 17:9;
18:12
The hypocrisy of the Pharisees and teachers of the law: Mt 23:25 pp Lk 11:39;
Mt 23:27–28
Ro 1:24; 7:14–23; 1Ti 6:10 *the love of money a root of evil;* Jas 3:6 *The tongue is a source of evil;* Jas 4:1

Physical evil is a consequence of moral evil
Ge 3:17; Ro 5:12 *See also*
Dt 28:20–24,58–59; Ps 90:8–9;
Pr 14:30; Mal 4:6; Ro 6:23; 8:19–21;
Rev 16:1,5–6

See also
4116 angels opposed to God	6020 sin
4120 Satan	6154 fall, the
4130 demons	6166 flesh, sinful nature
5033 knowledge of good & evil	6186 evil scheming
5560 suffering	6199 imperfection

8736
evil, warnings against

Scripture repeatedly warns against evil. It exposes it and reveals its consequences.

God opposes evil
Ps 34:16 *See also* Pr 6:16–19; Isa 31:2;
Mic 2:1

Warnings against specific dangers
Lev 20:23; 2Co 6:14 *See also* Eze 20:18;
Lk 12:1,15; Ac 13:40; 1Co 10:21;
2Pe 3:17

God's law given to counter evil
By exposing evil Ro 7:7 *See also* Ro 3:20;
5:20; 7:13; Gal 3:19

By leading believers away from evil
Gal 3:24 *See also* 1Ti 1:9–11

The state is ordained to restrain evil
Ro 13:1–4 *See also* Dt 17:7,12–13;
21:21; 1Ti 2:1–2; 1Pe 2:13–14

Evil rebounds on evildoers
Pr 22:8; Gal 6:7–8 *See also* Dt 19:18–19;
Est 9:25; Pr 1:29–31; 14:22; 17:13;
Hos 8:7

Evil ends in judgment
Isa 65:12; Ro 2:9 *See also* Ps 37:9;
Pr 12–15; 12:7; Mal 4:1; Ro 2:5; 6:23

See also
1025 God, anger of	5482 punishment
1310 God as judge	5978 warning
5215 authority	6187 immorality
5376 law, purpose of	6193 impenitence

8737
evil, believers' responses to

Scripture outlines several ways in which believers should respond to evil.

Evil is to be avoided
Ps 1:1; Pr 4:14; 1Th 5:22 *See also*
Job 28:28; Ps 119:115; Pr 4:27; 14:16;
Isa 52:11; Ac 2:40 *Peter's appeal to the crowd;* Ro 12:9; 13:14
Evil likened to yeast: 1Co 5:6–7; Gal 5:9
2Co 6:14–18; Eph 4:27; 5:3,6–7;
2Th 3:6; 1Pe 3:11; Ps 34:14

Evil is to be hated
Pr 8:13 *See also* Ps 97:10; Am 5:15;
Jn 3:20; Ro 12:9

Evil is to be rebuked
Mt 16:23 pp Mk 8:33; 2Ti 4:2 *See also*
1Sa 2:29; 13:13; 15:22; 2Sa 12:9 *Nathan rebukes David;* 1Ki 18:18 *Elijah rebukes Ahab;* 2Ch 16:9; 24:20; 26:18; Ezr 10:10;
Ps 141:5; Da 4:27; 5:22; Mt 14:4
pp Mk 6:18 *John the Baptist rebukes Herod;* Lk 23:40; Ac 5:3–4 *Peter rebukes Ananias;* Ac 5:9 *Peter rebukes Sapphira;*
1Ti 1:3; 5:20; Tit 1:13; 2:15

Evil is to be resisted
Pr 1:10; Gal 2:11; Eph 6:11; Jas 4:7 *See also* 1Co 5:13; Eph 5:11; Heb 12:1;
1Pe 5:9

Evil is to be repaid with good
Lk 6:35; Ro 12:20–21 *See also*
Pr 25:21–22; Ex 23:5; Lev 19:18;
Mt 5:44 pp Lk 6:27; 1Th 5:15; 1Pe 3:9

Believers should pray in response to evil
Mt 6:13 pp Lk 11:4; Ac 4:29; Heb 4:16
See also Ex 17:4; 1Ki 18:36; 2Ki 19:19;
2Ch 20:12; Ezr 8:23; Ne 1:4; Mt 26:41
pp Mk 14:38 pp Lk 22:46; Ac 12:5;
Jas 5:13

Believers should trust God in the face of evil
Ps 23:4; Mt 26:39 pp Mk 14:36
pp Lk 22:42 *See also* Ps 4:8; 20:7; 27:1;
Isa 12:2; Da 3:17–18; Hab 3:17–18;
2Ti 1:12; Heb 13:6; Ps 118:6–7

See also
8030 trust	8493 watchfulness, believers
8213 confidence	
8226 discernment	8618 prayerfulness
8485 spiritual warfare, conflict	

8738
evil, victory over

Although evil continues to be present and active in the world, Scripture gives an assurance that God will finally triumph over evil in all its forms.

Satan's power is already limited by God
Job 1:12 *See also* Ge 3:14–15; Job 2:6;
Zec 3:2; Rev 12:9

Evil spirits are subject to God's control

1Sa 16:14 *See also* Jdg 9:23; 1Sa 18:10; 19:9; 1Ki 22:23; Col 2:13–15; Jude 6

Jesus Christ's triumph over evil powers

1Jn 3:8 *See also* Mt 12:25–29 pp Mk 3:23–27 pp Lk 11:17–22; Mk 1:27 pp Lk 4:36; Lk 4:13; 10:18; Jn 12:31; 14:30; Heb 2:14–15; 1Jn 4:4; Rev 3:21

God's transforming power reverses the effects of evil in human lives

2Co 3:18; 1Jn 3:2 *See also* Jnh 3:10; Mk 5:15 pp Lk 8:35; Lk 19:8; Ac 26:17–18; Ro 6:14; 12:2; 1Co 15:10; 2Co 12:9; Col 3:10

God brings good out of evil

Ge 50:20; Ro 8:28 *See also* Ge 45:8; Job 23:10; Jn 9:3; 12:24; Ac 2:36; 3:13–16; 5:30–31; Php 1:12–14,17–18; Jas 1:2–3; 1Pe 1:6–7

The removal of the curse on creation

Ro 8:20–21 *See also* Mt 19:28; Ac 3:21; Rev 21:1,5; 22:3

Jesus Christ's victory over evil is expressed in his thousand-year reign with believers, during which Satan is bound

Rev 20:4 *See also* Rev 20:2 *Interpreters differ over whether the "thousand years" refers to a future period or to Jesus Christ's present rule in the world.*

The final defeat of all evil powers

Rev 20:4; Ro 16:20; Rev 20:10 *See also* Mal 4:1; Mt 13:41–42; 25:41; 1Co 15:25; 2Th 2:8; Rev 19:20; 21:8

Evil will be excluded from the new heaven and earth

2Pe 3:13 *See also* Isa 65:17; Rev 21:4,27; 22:15

See also

2324	Christ as Saviour
2372	Christ, victory
2565	Christ, second coming
4127	Satan, defeat of
5596	victory

8320	perfection
9105	last things
9115	antichrist, the
9155	millennium
9410	heaven
9610	hope

8739
evil, examples of

Biblical examples of evil are many and varied.

Evil disasters sent by God in judgment

Ge 7:20; 19:24
The ten plagues of Egypt: Ex 7:20; 8:6,17,24; 9:6,10,23; 10:13,22; 12:29 Nu 16:21–22; 1Sa 5:6; 2Sa 24:15; 1Ki 17:1

Other disasters

Ge 12:10; 26:1; 41:54; Am 1:1; Lk 13:4; Ac 11:28

National evil

Israel guilty of evil Ex 32:7; Nu 14:11; Dt 32:5; Jdg 2:11–15; 3:7; 4:1; 6:1; 10:6; 13:1; Ne 9:28; Isa 65:12; Am 2:4–8

Threats to Israel from other nations

Jdg 6:1; 1Sa 7:7; 2Ch 20:10–11

Judgment on other nations

1Sa 15:2; Isa 14:29–30; 15:1; 17:1; 19:1; Jer 46:10,25–26; 47:4; 48:1; 49:1–2,7–8,35–38; 50:1–2; Am 1:11,13; 2:1

Evil rulers

Of Israel 1Ki 12:31; 15:25–26,33–34; 16:12–13,18–19,30; 21:25; 22:51–52; 2Ki 10:31; 13:1–2,10–11; 14:23–24; 15:8–9,17–18,24,27–28; 17:1–2

Of Judah 1Ki 11:4; 15:1–3; 2Ki 8:16–18,26–27; 11:1; 16:2; 21:1–2,9,19–20; 23:31–32,36–37; 24:8–9,18–19; 2Ch 12:13–14

Of other nations Ex 5:2; Nu 21:23; Jdg 4:1–3; 2Ki 18:13; Isa 14:3–6,13–14; Da 4:31; 5:22

Evil religious leaders

1Sa 2:12; 1Ki 18:19; Jer 23:11; Eze 13:4; 34:2; Hos 5:1; Mic 2:6; Zep 3:4; Mt 23:15; Rev 2:14,20

Opponents of Jesus Christ

Mt 2:16; 12:14 pp Mk 3:6; Lk 4:28; Jn 5:18; 7:12,32; 8:59; 10:20,31; 19:6

Opponents of the church

Ac 4:3; 5:18; 6:9; 8:1–3; 12:1; 13:8,50; 14:5,19; 16:19; 17:5,13; 18:12; 19:29; 20:3; 21:27; 23:12

Evil influences

Nu 25:1; 31:16; Dt 18:9; Hos 7:9; 1Co 5:6; 8:10; 1Ti 4:1; 2Pe 2:18; 1Jn 2:26

See also

4815	drought
4822	famine
4957	night
5368	kingship
6169	godlessness
7227	flood, the

8751	false witness
8776	lies
8785	opposition
8794	persecution
8802	pride

8741
failure

Scripture indicates various ways in which believers may fail God, while emphasising that God will never fail his people.

God will never fail his people

1Ch 28:20 *See also* Jos 1:8–9; Ps 89:28

God's righteousness will not fail

Isa 51:6

God's compassion will not fail

La 3:22–23

God's word will not fail

Isa 55:10–11 *See also* Ro 9:6

Examples of failing God

Failing to abide in him Ps 14:3 *See also* Ps 58:3; 78:57; Jer 2:19; 3:22; 15:6; Jn 15:6; 2Pe 3:17

Failing to believe in him Jn 20:27 *See also* Nu 14:11–12; Ps 78:21–33; Heb 3:12

Failing to fear him Ge 20:11 *See also* Ex 9:30; Dt 25:18; Job 6:14; Lk 23:40

Failing to honour him Mal 2:2 *See also* Nu 20:12; 1Sa 2:29–30; Da 5:22–23; Ro 2:23

Failing to love him

1Co 16:22 *See also* Jos 23:10–13; Mt 10:37; Rev 2:4

Failing to obey him

2Ki 17:14–20; Mt 7:26

Failing to remember him

Dt 8:11; 32:18 *See also* Jdg 3:7; 8:33–34; 1Sa 12:9; Ps 78:11; 106:21; Isa 17:10

Failing to seek him

2Ch 12:14 *See also* Ps 14:2–3; 119:155; Isa 9:13; Zep 1:6

Failing to serve him

Dt 28:47–48 *See also* Job 21:14–15; Jer 2:20; Mal 3:14; Ro 1:25

Failing to trust him

Mt 6:30 pp Lk 12:28 *See also* Mt 14:31; 16:8; 17:17–20

Peter's failure of Jesus Christ

Mt 26:33–35 pp Mk 14:29–31; Lk 22:31–34; Jn 18:25–27

See also

1035	God, faithfulness
1055	God, grace & mercy
1125	God, righteousness
5484	punishment by God
5838	disrespect

5960	success
8032	trust, lack of
8359	weakness, spiritual
8451	mortification
8718	disobedience
8742	faithlessness
8764	forgetting God

8742
faithlessness

The lack or absence of faith, or the turning away from a professed commitment to God.

8743
faithlessness, nature and causes of

The abandoning of a commitment to the Lord, seen in disowning him, wandering from the truth and becoming entangled with the world, and resulting in judgment.

Warnings against faithlessness

2Ti 2:12–13 *See also* Mt 10:33 pp Lk 12:9; Lk 9:62; Heb 10:35–39; Hab 2:3–4

Ways in which faithlessness is seen

Turning away from the Lord Heb 3:12

Abandoning the gospel of grace Gal 1:6

Becoming entangled in the world 2Pe 2:20–22 *See also* Pr 26:11; 2Ti 4:10

Causes of faithlessness

False teaching 2Ti 2:17–18 *See also* Gal 1:7; 4:8–11; 1Ti 4:1–3; 2Ti 4:3–4; 2Pe 3:17

Persecution and trials Mt 13:20–21 pp Mk 4:16–17 pp Lk 8:13 *See also* Mt 24:9–13

Concern for money and possessions 1Ti 6:10 *See also* Pr 30:8–9; Mt 13:22 pp Mk 4:18–19 pp Lk 8:14

Love growing cold Mt 24:12 *See also* Rev 2:4

Sexual desire 1Ti 5:11–15

Faithlessness brings punishment

Church discipline 1Ti 1:18–20 *These men had been excluded from the church, a sanctuary from Satan's power.*

God's judgment Mt 10:33 pp Lk 12:9 *See also* Heb 6:4–6; 10:26–27

The faithlessness of those who fall away

The absence of true faith 1Jn 2:19

True faith is proved by perseverance *See also* Jas 1:2–3; 1Pe 1:5–7

Israel's faithlessness in the OT

Israel's unfaithfulness led to God's rejection Ps 78:56–59

Warnings not to repeat Israel's unfaithfulness Ps 95:7–11; Heb 3:7–12; 4:1–2

See also

1035 God, faithfulness	8459 perseverance
1310 God as judge	8704 apostasy
8021 faith	8712 denial of Christ
8230 discipline	8794 persecution
8234 doctrine	8810 riches, dangers
8316 orthodoxy, in NT	8840 unfaithfulness to God

8744
faithlessness, as disobedience

A lack of faith and obedience to God, which is seen especially in the lives of unbelievers. However, Scripture makes clear that believers can occasionally lapse into faithlessness towards God.

Faithlessness among the ungodly

In their character and lifestyle Ps 101:3–5; 119:158 *See also* Ps 10:4; 14:1; Jn 16:8–9; 2Th 3:2; Tit 1:15–16

Examples of faithless men 1Sa 25:2–3 *Nabal;* Est 3:5–6 *Haman;* Mt 2:16 *Herod the Great;* Ac 19:23–27 *Demetrius*

The faithless appear to prosper Jer 12:1 *See also* Job 21:7; Ps 73:3–5,12; Mal 3:15

Faithlessness results in judgment Pr 14:14; Jn 3:36 *See also* Ps 73:17–18,27; Mal 4:1; Mk 16:16; Jn 8:24; 2Th 2:12; Rev 21:8

Faithlessness among the Jews

Their failure to trust God for deliverance Isa 31:1 *See also* Isa 22:8–11; 30:1–2,12–13

Their rejection of the gospel Jn 12:37–38 *See also* Isa 53:1; Jn 3:11–12; 5:37–40; 8:45; 10:25–26

Specific examples Mt 13:58 pp Mk 6:5–6 *the people of Nazareth;* Mt 19:21–22 pp Mk 10:21–22 pp Lk 18:22–23 *the rich young ruler;* Ac 28:24 *Many Jews reject Paul's ministry in Rome;* 1Ti 1:13 *Paul's own persecution of the church arose from unbelief in Jesus Christ.*

Israel's estrangement from God Mt 21:43 *See also* Ps 118:22; Mt 21:41 pp Mk 12:9; Ro 9:32–33

The acceptance of the Gentiles Ro 11:17–21 *The Jews' rejection of the gospel opens the way for Gentiles to be*

incorporated into the people of God, represented here as branches grafted onto a cultivated olive tree.

Israel's faithlessness is partial and temporary Ro 11:5 *Though the people as a whole have rejected Jesus Christ, a faithful remnant remains;* Ro 11:11–12,23–27 *God's purpose for the faithful of Israel is their ultimate salvation.*

Faithlessness among believers

Lack of faith is rebuked Mt 14:30–31 *See also* Mt 6:30–32 pp Lk 12:28–30 *worrying about food and clothing;* Mt 8:24–26 pp Mk 4:38–40 pp Lk 8:23–25 *Fear during a storm at sea;* Mt 17:17–20 pp Mk 9:17–19 pp Lk 9:40–42 *inability to cast out a demon*

Causes of faithlessness Mt 16:8–10 *failure to learn from the lessons of the past;* Lk 24:25 *failure to accept teaching that has been given*

See also

1310 God as judge	8718 disobedience
2309 Christ as judge	8721 doubt
6169 godlessness	8726 doubters
7140 people of God	8834 unbelief
8710 atheism	

8746
false Christs

Mistaken and deceptive people claiming to be Jesus Christ. Jesus Christ warns his followers to be on their guard against the appearance of such people.

Jesus Christ warns that false Christs will appear

Mt 24:5 pp Mk 13:6 pp Lk 21:8 *See also* Mt 24:23 pp Mk 13:21

False Christs will perform signs and miracles in order to deceive

Mt 24:24 pp Mk 13:22

False Christs can be recognised because the return of Jesus Christ will be obvious to everyone

Mt 24:27–31 pp Mk 13:24–27 pp Lk 21:25–28 *The personal return of the Lord Jesus Christ is not described in terms of an appearance to a select group, but to the whole world. The attempt of anyone to convince others that he is Christ therefore is a sure sign of deception.*

See also

2565 Christ, second coming	8749 false teachers
	8767 hypocrisy
6145 deceit	8776 lies
8747 false gods	9115 antichrist, the

8747
false gods

Any gods other than the LORD himself. Some of these divinities took the form of images, others were mythical. Some Israelites became involved in idolatrous worship of such gods. The book of Acts records attempts to deify human beings.

False gods associated with foreign nations in the OT

Amon, the chief god of Egypt *See also* Jer 46:25

Asherah, a Canaanite goddess Ex 34:13–14 *Asherah was the consort of El, the chief Canaanite god. Wooden poles, perhaps carved in her image, were often set up in her honour and placed near other pagan objects of worship. See also* Dt 7:5; Jdg 6:25–30 *Gideon destroys an Asherah pole;* 1Ki 14:15,23; 15:13; 16:33; 18:19 *Elijah summons 400 prophets of Asherah to Mount Carmel. King Josiah's reforms:* 2Ki 23:4–7,13–16 Isa 27:9; Jer 17:2; Mic 5:14

Ashtoreth, a goddess of war and fertility Jdg 2:12–13 *Ashtoreth, the consort of Baal, was associated with the evening star and was worshipped as Ishtar in Babylon and as Athtart in Aram. To the Greeks she was Astarte or Aphrodite and to the Romans, Venus. See also* Jdg 10:6; 1Sa 7:3–4; 12:10; 31:10; 1Ki 11:5,33

Baal, a Canaanite and Phoenician god of fertility and rain Jdg 2:10–13 *Baal, meaning "lord", was pictured standing on a bull, a popular symbol of fertility and strength. Baal was associated with Asherah and Ashtoreth, goddesses of fertility.*

Baal-Zebub, a popular deity of the Philistines Mt 12:24 pp Mk 3:22 pp Lk 11:15 *Beelzebub is the Greek form of the Hebrew name "Baal-Zebub", meaning "lord of the flies". See also* 2Ki 1:1–6,16–17

Bel, the chief deity of Babylon Isa 46:1 *Bel was another name for the sun god, Marduk. Nebo, the god of learning and writing was the son of Marduk. See also* Jer 50:2; 51:44

Chemosh, the chief god of Moab 1Ki 11:7 *See also* Nu 21:29; 1Ki 11:33; 2Ki 23:13; Jer 48:7,13,46

Dagon, worshipped in Babylonia and Philistia Jdg 16:23 *See also* 1Sa 5:2–7; 1Ch 10:10

Molech, the chief deity of Ammon 1Ki 11:4–5 *See also* Lev 18:21 *The practice of sacrificing children to Molech was common in Phoenicia and the region;* Lev 20:2–5; 1Ki 11:7,33; 2Ki 23:10 *Josiah destroyed the area where the altars for child sacrifice were located;* 2Ki 23:13; Isa 57:9; Jer 32:35; 49:1,3; Zep 1:5; Ac 7:43

Tammuz, a Babylonian fertility god Eze 8:14

The worship of false gods was a snare to God's people

Their worship included disgusting rites 1Ki 14:23–24; 19:18; Jer 7:31; Hos 13:2

Numerous attempts were made to stop the worship of Baal and other false gods Jdg 6:28–32; 1Ki 18:17–40 *See also* 2Ki 10:18–28; 11:18; 23:4–5,13

Attempts to stop false worship proved unsuccessful 2Ki 21:3 *The word "Baal" was not orginally a proper name but came to be used as such. See also* 2Ch 28:1–4; Hos 13:1–2

Warnings against and condemnation of, the worship of false gods
Ps 40:4; Da 3:29 *Nebuchadnezzar came to realise the foolishness of worshipping false gods. See also* Ps 4:2; Jer 13:25; 16:19; Am 2:4; Zep 1:4

The first Christians were confronted with the worship of Greek and Roman deities
Zeus and Hermes Ac 14:12 *Zeus was the patron god of the city of Lystra and his temple was there. Paul was identified as the god Hermes (the Roman Mercury), Zeus' attendant and spokesman.*

Artemis Ac 19:24–28 *Artemis was the Greek name for the Roman goddess, Diana.*

Castor and Pollux Ac 28:11 *the two "sons of Zeus", regarded as the guardian deities of sailors*

Attempts to deify human beings
Ac 12:21–22; 14:12–15; 28:6

See also
1080 God, living	7471 temples,
4251 moon	heathen
6103 abomination	8752 false worship
6243 adultery,	8768 idolatry
spiritual	8799 polytheism
7312 Baal	8840 unfaithfulness
7324 calf worship	to God
7384 household	
gods	

8748

false religion

The worship of anything that is not God, including any form of religion that fails to do justice to the glory and majesty of God. Scripture criticises both the practices and the beliefs of false religions.

The nature of false religion
Man-made images are worshipped Ac 17:29 *See also* Dt 4:28; Ps 115:4–7; 135:15–17; Isa 44:10–20; Jer 10:3–5; 16:20; Da 3:4–7; Ac 19:26

Created things are worshipped Ro 1:25 *See also* 2Ki 21:3 pp 2Ch 33:5; Jer 8:2; 19:13; Eze 8:16

Secular authorities are worshipped Rev 13:4 *The dragon in Revelation may be understood as the devil and the beast as the antichrist: the forces at work behind the human authorities that defy the rule of God. See also* Ac 12:21–23; Rev 13:8,12

Demons are worshipped Dt 32:17 *See also* Lev 17:7 fn; Ps 106:37–38; 1Co 10:20; Rev 9:20

False religion is based on man-made traditions, myths and philosophies
Col 2:8,20–23; 1Ti 1:4; 6:20

False religious practices
Immorality 1Ki 14:23–24 *See also* Eze 16:16–17; Hos 4:13–14

Human sacrifice 2Ki 17:17 *See also* Lev 18:21; Ps 106:37–38

False religion ensnares its adherents
It offers no help in time of need
1Sa 12:21 *See also* Jdg 10:14; 1Ki 18:29; 2Ki 19:12 pp Isa 37:12; Isa 16:12; 44:17–20; 45:20; 46:7; 57:13; Jer 11:12

It prevents people from finding the truth Jnh 2:8 *See also* Mt 23:13; Lk 11:52; 2Co 4:4

It devalues, degrades and defiles 2Ki 17:15 *See also* Ps 106:39; 115:8; 135:18; Isa 44:9; Jer 2:5; Eze 20:18

It leads to immorality Nu 25:1–2 *See also* Nu 25:3,6–8; Ro 1:23–31; Rev 9:20–21

It enslaves Gal 4:8 *See also* Dt 12:30; Gal 4:3,9–10; Col 2:8

False religion receives the full force of God's anger
Jer 16:18 *See also* 1Ki 13:1–3,33–34; 2Ki 17:18–23; Jer 22:8–9; Mic 5:13–15; Na 1:14; Zep 1:4–5

See also
4130 demons	8750 false teachings
6187 immorality	8752 false worship
7348 defilement	8768 idolatry
7449 slavery,	8784 nominal
spiritual	religion
8142 religion	8807 profanity
8747 false gods	8829 superstition

8749

false teachers

Those who teach error and in so doing lead others astray. They are to be distinguished from false prophets who are equally condemned in Scripture.

The OT prophets warned God's people against being led astray by false teachers
Isa 9:16; Eze 34:2 *See also* Isa 3:12; 8:20; Jer 2:8; 10:21; 23:1; Eze 22:26; Mal 2:7–8

Jesus Christ condemned false teachers
He opposed legalism and hypocrisy Mt 5:19

He identified the teachers of the law and Pharisees as false teachers Mt 23:1–33 pp Lk 11:42–52 *See also* Mt 15:14

He warned his followers against them Mt 16:6,12 pp Mk 8:15 pp Lk 12:1

The condemnation of false teachers in the early church
Paul urges his readers to avoid false teachers 1Ti 6:3–6 *See also* Ac 20:29–31; Ro 16:17–18; 2Co 11:3–4 *The Corinthian church had been undiscerningly tolerant of Jewish deceivers in their midst;* Eph 4:14 *The Colossian heresy taught that the combination of faith in Jesus Christ with man-made regulations was necessary for salvation:* Col 2:4,8 *Paul warns against the heretical teachers in the Ephesian church:* 1Ti 1:3–4,7 1Ti 4:1–3; 6:20–21; Tit 1:10–11; Heb 13:9; 2Jn 9–10 *The Nicolaitans:* Rev 2:6,15

Rev 2:14 *the followers of Balaam;* Rev 2:20

Hymenaeus and Philetus are cited as examples of false teachers 2Ti 2:17–18

Those who teach will be judged particularly strictly Jas 3:1 *See also* 2Co 11:13–15; Gal 1:6–9; 5:10

See also
5509 rulers	7784 shepherd
5804 charm	7797 teaching
5863 flattery	8704 apostasy
7464 teachers of the	8750 false teachings
law	8751 false witness
7550 Pharisees	8766 heresies
7766 priests	

8750

false teachings

Scripture repeatedly warns against false teachings, which deny or distort some aspect of the gospel. The origin of such teachings is attributed either to human error or to demonic inspiration.

Examples of false teachings
Rev 2:14–15 *See also* Mt 5:19; 2Th 2:1–2; 1Ti 4:1–3; Rev 2:20

Qualities of false teachings
They are valueless Mt 15:9 pp Mk 7:7 *See also* Isa 29:13; Eph 5:6; Col 2:20–23; 1Ti 1:3–7

They are destructive in their nature 2Pe 2:1 *See also* Mt 7:15; Ac 20:29–30; Tit 1:10–11

They have the capacity to lead people astray Ac 20:30 *See also* Eph 4:14; 1Ti 6:20–21; Heb 13:9; 2Pe 2:14–15; 1Jn 2:26

They may be popular 2Pe 2:2 *See also* Mt 24:4–5 pp Mk 13:5–6; 2Ti 4:3; 2Pe 2:18–19; 1Jn 4:1–5

They may be accompanied by miraculous signs Mt 24:24 pp Mk 13:22 *See also* 2Th 2:9–10; Rev 13:11–15

The origin of false teachings
Demonic inspiration 1Ti 4:1–2 *See also* 2Co 11:3–4; 1Jn 4:1–3; Rev 16:13–14

Human error 2Pe 2:3 *See also* Col 2:8; 1Ti 6:20–21

Discerning false teachings
By their content 1Jn 4:2–3 *See also* 1Co 12:3; 1Jn 2:20–23; 2Jn 7–11

By the teacher's lifestyle Mt 7:15–20 *See also* 2Co 11:20; 1Jn 3:7–10; Jude 4

By their effects 1Ti 6:3–5 *See also* 1Ti 1:3–4; 2Ti 2:16–18; Rev 2:20

The antidote to false teachings
Holding fast to the true gospel 1Jn 2:24 *See also* Gal 1:6–9; 1Ti 1:18–20; 2Ti 1:13–14

Shunning false teachers Ro 16:17–18 *See also* 2Ti 3:1–9; Tit 3:9–11; 2Jn 9–11

See also
1460 truth
5441 philosophy
5794 asceticism
7774 prophets, false
8237 doctrine, false
8703 antinomianism
8749 false teachers
8766 heresies
8775 libertinism
8784 nominal religion
8831 syncretism
9115 antichrist, the

8751

false witness

The telling of lies about another so as to make them appear guilty when they are innocent. Condemned in Scripture, false witness was experienced by Jesus Christ and is to be expected by those who follow him.

False witness is condemned in Scripture
Ex 20:16 pp Dt 5:20 See also Ex 23:1; Dt 19:15–19; Ps 101:5–7; Mt 19:18 pp Mk 10:19 pp Lk 18:20

False witness arises from an evil heart
Mt 15:19–20 pp Mk 7:21–23

False witness will be subject to judgment
Ps 101:5–8; Pr 21:28 See also Pr 19:9; Da 6:24; Mt 12:35–37

Examples of those who were the victims of false witness
Jesus Christ Mt 26:59–61 pp Mk 14:55–59 See also Mt 11:18–19 pp Lk 7:33–34

Other examples 1Ki 21:8–14 Naboth; Ps 27:12 David; Da 6:24 Daniel; Ac 6:11–13 Stephen Paul: Ac 17:5–7; 24:5–9; 25:7; Ro 3:8

False witness against believers is to be expected by them
Mt 5:11–12 pp Lk 6:22–23 See also Mt 24:9–10; Ac 19:9

See also
2585 Christ, trial
5202 accusation, false
5625 witnesses, false
6145 deceit
8714 dishonesty
8776 lies
8794 persecution
5951 slander

8752

false worship

Forms of worship that are not worthy of God, especially worship offered without sincerity and obedience or that is contrary to the commands of God.

Examples of false worship
Worship conducted in disobedience to God Lev 10:1–2 See also Nu 3:2–4; 1Sa 15:1–23; 2Ki 17:33

Worship and sacrifices offered by those who were not priests
1Sa 13:11–14 See also 2Ch 26:19–20

Insincere worship Isa 29:13 See also Mt 15:8–9; Mk 7:6–7; Col 2:23

Worship lacking in due humility and reverence Mt 6:5 See also Lk 18:10–14

Worship conducted in ignorance of God Jn 4:22 See also Ac 17:22–23

Scripture vividly contrasts false worship with true worship
True worship involves the worshipper's heart, soul and mind
Dt 6:5 pp Mt 22:37 pp Mk 12:30 pp Lk 10:27

True worship is costly 2Sa 24:24; Mk 12:41–44; Ro 12:1 True worship involves the whole of a person's life and not just formal acts of worship.

True worship is in the spirit Jn 4:23–24 See also Isa 29:23; Php 3:3; 1Ti 2:9; Heb 12:28

See also
5135 blindness, spiritual
6183 ignorance, of God
7413 priesthood, OT
8218 consecration
8333 reverence
8622 worship
8714 dishonesty
8718 disobedience
8748 false religion
8768 idolatry
8784 nominal religion

8753

favouritism

The unfair treatment of a person or group in preference to another. Favouritism is shown in Scripture as causing division both in the family and in the church. It is warned against in the administration of justice. The human tendency to partiality is contrasted with God's impartial dealings.

Favouritism in family life
Isaac's preference for Esau
Ge 25:23,28

Rebekah's preference for Jacob
Ge 27:6–10

Jacob's preference for Joseph
Ge 37:3–4

Elkanah's preference for Hannah
1Sa 1:5–6

The child of a favourite wife must not receive preferential treatment
Dt 21:15–16

Favouritism in church relationships
In the treatment of widows Ac 6:1

James warned against favouring rich Christians Jas 2:1–4,8–9

Paul warned Timothy against showing favouritism 1Ti 5:21

Justice must be impartial
Lev 19:15 See also Ex 23:3; Dt 16:19; Job 13:10; Ps 82:2; Pr 24:23; 28:21; Mal 2:9

God has no favourites
Ro 2:11 See also Job 34:19; Mt 5:45

God has no favourite nation
Ac 10:34–35 See also Ro 2:10; Eph 6:8–9

God does not differentiate between Jewish and Gentile Christians
Ac 15:7–9; Ro 10:12–13

God judges all without favouritism
Dt 10:17; 2Ch 19:7; Ro 2:9; Col 3:25; 1Pe 1:17

See also
2042 Christ, justice of
5095 Jacob, life
5347 injustice
5359 justice
5765 attitudes to people
5859 favour
5863 flattery
5882 impartiality
8773 jealousy
8800 prejudice

8754

fear

An attitude of anxiety or distress, caused by concern over a threat to one's future. Scripture provides numerous examples of situations in which fear is experienced. It declares, however, that God alone is to be feared, and moments of human fear can be opportunities for deepening faith in him.

Reverent fear of God commended
Pr 1:7 See also Dt 6:13; 31:12–13; Jos 4:24; 24:14; 1Sa 12:24; Ps 2:11; 34:7–9; Pr 15:33; Ecc 12:13; Isa 33:6; Rev 14:7

Fear of natural phenomena
Ps 91:5; Jnh 1:4–5 See also Ge 19:30; Job 5:22; Ecc 12:5; Isa 7:25; Mt 8:26; Rev 11:13

Fear of the unnatural
Fear of thoughts and visions Da 4:5; Ac 10:4 See also 1Sa 3:15; Job 4:13–15; Isa 21:4; Da 8:17; 10:11–12; Mt 1:20; 28:4; Lk 1:12–13,29–30; 2:9–10

Fear of the unknown or the abnormal Mt 14:26–27 pp Mk 6:50 pp Jn 6:19–20 Ac 5:5 See also Ex 20:18; 34:30 The radiance of Moses' face reflected God's glory and made the Israelites afraid; Dt 5:5; 1Sa 4:7; Ne 6:16; Jer 10:2; Da 5:9 Belshazzar's fear at the writing on the wall; Jnh 1:10; Mt 17:6 the fear of the disciples at the transfiguration; Mt 27:54; Mk 5:33; 9:32; 16:8; Lk 5:10; 8:37 Fear seized the people when the Gerasene demoniac was healed; Lk 9:34; Jn 19:8; Ac 19:17

Fear of embarrassment or shame
Ge 3:10 See also Isa 54:4; Jn 3:20; 2Co 12:20

Fear of the future
Jer 51:46 See also Isa 41:23; Mk 10:32; Lk 12:32; Ac 27:24

Fear of persecution
Ezr 4:4; Jn 12:42–43 See also 1Ki 19:3; Jn 7:13; 9:22; 20:19; 1Pe 3:14; Rev 2:10

Fear of death
Heb 2:14–15 See also Ps 55:4–5; Mk 5:36 pp Lk 8:50; Ac 23:10

Fear of people
Of enemies Ex 14:10; 1Sa 7:7 See also Nu 22:3; Jdg 7:3; 1Sa 17:24,11; 2Sa 10:19; 2Ch 12:5; Ps 27:1–3; 56:1–4; Isa 20:5; 41:5; Jer 22:25; 41:18; Ob 9

Of one's own family Ge 32:11; 45:3;

Jdg 9:21 *See also* Ge 31:31; 32:7; 42:4; 50:19; Jdg 6:27

Of particular people 1Sa 15:24; 1Co 2:3 *See also* Ge 26:7; Ex 2:14; Dt 2:4; 1Sa 18:15 *Saul's fear of David*; 2Sa 3:11; Ne 2:2 *Nehemiah's fear before the king*; Est 7:6; Jer 26:21; 38:19; Mt 2:22; Mk 12:12; Lk 19:21; Ac 9:26 *the disciples fear of Paul, not believing his conversion*; 1Co 16:10; 2Co 7:15; Gal 2:12

Of human beings in general Pr 29:25 *See also* Dt 1:17; Isa 51:7

Fear of judgment
Eze 11:8; Ac 24:25 *See also* 1Sa 28:20; 1Ch 21:30; Isa 33:14; Jer 17:18; 30:5; 42:15–16; Eze 12:18; 27:35; Zec 9:5; 1Jn 4:18 *Christians, assured of God's love, no longer fear judgment*; Rev 18:10,15

Fear as a deterrent
Ro 13:4 *See also* Dt 13:11; 17:13; 19:20; 21:21; Job 19:28–29

Fear as an opportunity for faith
Dt 1:21; Ps 23:4; Pr 3:25–26; Mt 10:29–31 *See also* Ex 14:13; Dt 1:29; 7:18–21; 31:6; Jos 11:6; Ne 4:14; Ps 3:6; 34:4; 49:5; 56:3; Isa 10:24; 35:3–4; 41:14; 43:5; 44:8; 51:12; Jer 1:8,17; 30:10; 42:11; 46:27; Eze 2:6; 3:9; Da 10:19; Mt 8:26 pp Mk 4:40 pp Lk 8:25; Mk 6:49–51; Jn 14:27

See also

5482 punishment	8361 wisdom
5819 cowardice	8722 doubt
8020 faith	8727 enemies
8030 trust	8829 superstition
8219 courage	9210 judgment,
8334 reverence &	God's
God's nature	

8755
folly

A human attitude of lack of wisdom or contempt for wisdom, which shows itself in a lack of understanding and obedience. Scripture contrasts human foolishness with divine wisdom, and indicates the serious consequences of a rejection of the wisdom of God.

8756
folly, examples of

Human folly is seen in rebellion against God, ignoring his way and will, a failure to understand him: and moral or spiritual irresponsibility.

Examples of human folly
The folly of God's people Jer 4:22 *See also* Dt 32:6 *rejecting God*; Jer 10:8 *worshipping idols*; Hos 7:11 *seeking foreign help rather than trusting God*

The folly of Israel's leaders Jer 10:21 *The shepherds are those entrusted with the task of guiding and caring for God's people*; Eze 13:3 *See also* Mt 23:16–17

Particular demonstrations of human folly Nu 12:1–11 *Aaron and Miriam*; Saul: 1Sa 13:13; 26:21

1Sa 25:25 *Nabal. In Hebrew this name means "fool".*
David: 2Sa 24:10 pp 1Ch 21:8
2Ch 16:7–9 *Asa, king of Judah*;
Isa 19:11–13 *Pharaoh's advisors*; Mt 7:26 *the foolish builder*; Mt 25:1–3 *the foolish virgins*; Lk 12:16–21 *the rich fool*; Gal 3:13 *the Galatian Christians*

Paul's "foolishness"
2Co 11:16–21 *Paul engages in what he admits is the foolish boasting of his accomplishments in order to challenge the claims of false "apostles". See also* 2Co 11:1; 12:6,11

God's wisdom regarded as "foolishness"
1Co 1:18 *See also* Hos 9:7; Zec 11:15; 1Co 1:20–25,27; 4:10

Human wisdom is foolishness to God
1Co 3:19 *See also* Job 12:17; Isa 29:14; 44:25; 55:8; Jer 50:36; Ro 1:22

See also

1180 God, wisdom of	6121 boasting
5164 lips	6188 immorality,
5173 outward	sexual
appearance	6222 rebellion
5401 madness	against God
5575 talk, idle	8361 wisdom
5813 conceit	8759 fools
5907 miserliness	

8757
folly, effects of

The attitude that leads to a closing of the mind towards God and his truth, and a false self-confidence, which results in being easily led astray, failure to see danger, unpreparedness and ultimate ruin.

Folly gives a false basis for confidence
Contempt for God's wisdom Pr 1:7 *See also* Job 28:28; Ps 14:1; 85:8; 111:10; Pr 1:20–27; 12:1; 18:2

Blindness to God's truth Eph 5:17 *See also* Ps 92:6; Ecc 5:1–4; Jer 5:4; Lk 11:39–40 *hypocrisy in worship*; Ro 1:21; 1Co 15:36 *failure to understand the nature of death and resurrection*; 2Ti 2:23; Tit 3:9 *futile controversies*

Rebellion against God's authority Ps 107:17; Jer 5:21–25

Self-reliance Pr 28:26 *See also* Pr 11:28; 12:15; 14:12; Lk 12:20

Folly cannot be hidden
Ecc 10:3 *See also* Ps 69:5; Pr 12:23; 13:16; 15:2; 2Ti 3:9

Folly opens the way to deception
Pr 14:8

Being led astray Pr 14:15 *See also* Pr 7:7–23; 9:13–18; Ecc 7:26; Hos 7:11; Gal 3:1

Failing to see danger Pr 22:3 *See also* Ecc 4:13

Being unprepared Mt 25:10

The consequences of folly
Destruction and ruin Pr 1:32 *See also* Pr 5:23; 10:8; Ecc 7:17; 1Ti 6:9

Shame Pr 3:35 *See also* Pr 18:13; Isa 44:9; Jer 8:9

Grief to parents Pr 17:25 *See also* Pr 10:1; 15:20; 17:21

Punishment Pr 16:22 *See also* Ps 38:5; Pr 18:6; 26:3

Exclusion from God's way of salvation Isa 35:8 *See also* Mt 25:10–12

Folly is persistent
Pr 27:22 *See also* Pr 15:14; 26:11

Remedies for folly
The forgiveness of foolish actions Nu 12:11; Job 42:8; Ps 85:8; Tit 3:3–5

Discipline Pr 19:25; 21:11; 22:15; 29:15

Wisdom and instruction Pr 8:5; 14:33; Isa 29:24; Ro 2:20

See also

5029 knowledge of	6145 deceit
God	8333 reverence
5568 suffering,	8767 hypocrisy
causes	8820 self-confidence
5928 resentment	
against God	

8759
fools

Those who lack wisdom and understanding, especially in relation to God.

8760
fools, characteristics of

Scripture portrays fools as those who have rejected God and his ways and are unable or unwilling to appreciate the wisdom of knowing and obeying him.

The world regards Christians as fools
1Co 4:10 *See also* 1Co 1:26–31

The world regards the gospel as foolish
1Co 1:18 *See also* 1Co 1:20–25

Fools do not believe in God
Ps 53:1 pp Ps 14:1 *See also* Ro 1:21

Fools do not trust God Hos 7:11 *See also* 2Ch 16:7–9; Isa 19:11–13; 30:1

Fools lack knowledge of God Jer 4:22 *See also* Jer 5:4,21; Ps 92:6; Lk 24:25; Eph 5:15–17

The behaviour of fools
Fools worship idols Jer 10:8 *See also* Jer 10:14 pp Jer 51:17; Ro 1:22–23

Fools act in a godless manner Isa 32:6 *See also* Ps 94:5–8; Pr 10:23; Ecc 7:25; Jer 4:22

Fools are dishonest Jer 17:11

Fools give vent to their anger Pr 29:11 *See also* Ecc 7:9

Fools are disobedient 1Sa 13:13 *See also* 2Sa 24:10 pp 1Ch 21:8; Ps 107:17; Pr 10:8

Fools despise instruction and discipline Pr 1:22 *See also* Pr 1:28–33; 5:23; 12:15; Isa 65:2; Jer 18:12; Eze 3:7

The speech of fools
Fools speak unwisely Pr 18:6–7 *See also* Ecc 10:12; Eph 5:4

Fools are slanderous Pr 10:18 *See also* 2Pe 2:15

Fools are mockers Pr 14:9 *See also* Pr 1:22; 14:6; 23:9; 24:9

Fools love quarrelling and dissension Pr 20:3 *See also* Pr 19:1; 1Ti 1:4; 6:4; 2Ti 2:23; Tit 3:9

The words of fools are empty Pr 15:2 *See also* Pr 14:7; 26:7; Ecc 9:17; 10:14

Fools rely on themselves
Pr 12:15 *See also* Pr 14:12; 28:26

Fools rely on words, not deeds
Jas 2:20 *See also* Ecc 5:4; Lk 11:39–40

See also
5029 knowledge of God	8230 discipline
5546 speech	8361 wisdom
5789 anger	8710 atheism
5868 gossip	8714 dishonesty
6121 boasting	8718 disobedience
8030 trust	8755 folly

8761
fools, in teaching of Jesus Christ

Jesus Christ speaks about those whose words and actions demonstrate opposition to, or disregard for, the wisdom of God revealed in his words and through the Scriptures, and in parables points to the serious consequences of folly.

The foolishness of the Pharisees
Their blindness Mt 23:16–17 *The Pharisees demonstrate foolishness by attaching undue significance to what is less important whilst neglecting what really matters. See also* Mt 7:3 pp Lk 6:41; Mt 15:14 pp Lk 6:39; Mt 23:23–24

Their hypocrisy Lk 11:39–40 *The Pharisees were concerned with the externals of religion. Jesus Christ is concerned, also, with the inner life. See also* Mt 12:35–36; 23:25–28

The foolishness of the disciples
Lk 24:25 *See also* Mt 15:16–20 pp Mk 7:20–23; Mk 8:17 pp Mt 16:9; Mk 9:32; 16:12–14

Fools in Jesus Christ's parables
The rich fool Lk 12:16–21 *The foolishness of trusting in wealth and not in God. See also* Job 27:16–19; Da 4:30–31; Mt 6:19

The foolish builder Mt 7:24–27 pp Lk 6:49 *See also* Pr 1:28–33; Isa 65:2; Jer 5:21–25; 13:10; Eze 3:7

The foolish virgins Mt 25:1–13 *The foolishness of being unprepared for the coming of God's kingdom. See also* Mk 13:35–36; Lk 12:35–36

The seriousness of the term "fool"
Mt 5:22 *See also* Pr 1:32; Ecc 7:17

See also
2375 kingdom of God	7550 Pharisees
5133 blindness	8030 trust
5375 law	8721 doubt
6245 stubbornness	8767 hypocrisy
	8834 unbelief

8763
forgetting

The process of accidentally or deliberately failing to remember people, events or ideas. Scripture rebukes those who forget the past work of God in history or in their lives or who neglect their present responsibilities towards God in order to please themselves.

Causes of forgetting
Forgetting can be deliberate 2Pe 3:5

Forgetting can be caused by idolatry Jer 23:25–27 *See also* Dt 32:15–18; Jdg 3:7; Jer 18:15; Hos 2:13

Forgetting can be caused by pride Hos 13:4–6 *See also* 2Ch 26:16; Ps 10:4

Forgetting can be caused by drinking Pr 31:4–5 *See also* Ge 9:20–21; Mt 24:45–51 pp Lk 12:42–46

Forgetting can be caused by affliction Ps 102:4 *See also* Ge 41:28–31; La 3:17–20

Forgetting people
Ge 40:23 *See also* Job 19:13–15; Ps 31:11–12

Forgetting God
Dt 32:18 *See also* Jdg 2:10–13; 1Sa 12:9–10

Forgetting God's acts in the past
Ps 78:11–20 *See also* Jdg 8:33–34; Ne 9:16–17; Ps 106:7–13

Consequences of forgetting God
Forgetting God brings suffering on the individual Ps 50:22 *See also* 1Sa 12:9; Isa 17:10–11

Forgetting God brings suffering on others 2Sa 12:9 *David's forgetting of God in his adultery with Bathsheba led to her husband Uriah suffering death through David's manipulation of events. See also* Ps 106:13–15; Jer 3:21

Forgetting God brings destruction on the nation Dt 8:19–20 *See also* Isa 65:11–12; Hos 8:14

Warnings not to forget God
Dt 6:12 *See also* Dt 4:9; 8:10–14; 2Ki 17:35–38

People may sometimes feel that God has forgotten them
Ps 13:1 *See also* Ps 42:9–10; 44:23–24; Isa 49:14; Mt 27:46 pp Mk 15:34; Ps 22:1

God promises never to forget his people
Isa 44:21 *See also* Isa 49:15–16; Heb 6:10

Things God urges believers to forget
Isa 43:18 *See also* Php 3:13–15

See also
5051 responsibility	8670 remembering
7394 memorial	8718 disobedience
8248 faithfulness	8742 faithlessness
8467 reminders	8764 forgetting God
8493 watchfulness, believers	8783 neglect
8644 commemoration	8839 unfaithfulness

8764
forgetting God

Scripture warns people how easy it is to forget God in the varying circumstances of life and to fail to give him his due place, and points out the consequences of so doing.

Warnings not to forget God
Forgetting God's past acts Dt 4:9 *See also* Dt 9:7–8; Isa 51:12–13

Forgetting God's covenant Dt 4:23 *See also* 2Ki 17:38

Forgetting God's ways Isa 55:6–8 *See also* Dt 18:9–13; 1Ki 2:1–4

Reasons why people forget God
Easy circumstances Dt 6:10–12 *See also* Dt 8:10–14

Idolatry Jdg 8:33–34 *See also* Ex 32:1–8; Dt 12:29–31; 1Ki 11:4–6

Pride and stubbornness Ne 9:16 *See also* Dt 9:12–13; 2Ki 17:14–17; Jer 7:22–26

Consequences of people forgetting God
Spiritual adultery Hos 1:2 *See also* Jer 3:6–10; Hos 4:10–13; 5:4

Social decay Hos 4:1–3

The destruction of the nation Dt 8:19–20 *See also* Dt 6:14–15

The death of the sinner Ps 9:17 *See also* Job 8:11–13; Ps 50:22; Isa 65:11–12

Examples of people forgetting God
Jdg 8:33–34; 2Ki 17:7–20; Ps 78:40–43; 106:19–22; Isa 1:2–3; Jer 3:19–21

Exhortations and resolve not to forget God
Ps 103:2; 119:61,109

God's provision to help people not to forget him
His word Ps 78:5–7 *See also* Dt 31:24–27; Jer 20:9

Covenantal meals and festivals Dt 16:1–3,9–12; 1Co 11:23–26

External signs Ge 9:12–17; 17:9–13; Nu 15:37–39; Dt 11:18–20

God's challenge to those who forget him
Hos 4:1 *See also* Isa 57:11; Jer 2:31–32; Hos 2:2–13

God's call to those who forget him
Jer 3:19–22 *See also* Rev 2:4–5; 3:20

God's grace even when his people do forget him
Isa 49:15–16 *See also* Dt 4:25–31; Ne 9:29–31

See also

6020 sin	8704 apostasy
6231 rejection of God	8718 disobedience
6666 grace	8742 faithlessness
6732 repentance	8763 forgetting
8304 loyalty	8783 neglect
8670 remembering	

8765

grudge

A persistent feeling of ill will or resentment held by one person against another, often as the result of an injury or insult. Christians are not to bear grudges against others; instead they are to forgive those who have wronged them.

Examples of those who held grudges
Esau against Jacob Ge 27:41

Joseph's brothers against Joseph Ge 37:4 *See also* Ge 37:5,8,18–19,23–24; 50:15

The Israelites against Moses and Aaron Nu 11:1; 14:1–4,27

Saul against David 1Sa 18:7–9

Ahab against Elijah 1Ki 18:16–17; 21:20; 22:8

Herodias against John the Baptist Mk 6:18–19

The disciples against others Mt 26:6–9 pp Mk 14:3–5; Jn 12:3–6

The Sadducees against the apostles Ac 5:17

The Jews against Stephen Ac 7:54

Severe grudges that led to hatred and murder
That of Abel by Cain Ge 4:4–8

That of Joseph by his brothers, averted by Reuben Ge 37:18–20

That of Amnon, on the orders of Absalom 2Sa 13:22,28–32

That of John the Baptist by Herodias Mk 6:22–24,27–28

Warnings against the holding of grudges
In the OT Lev 19:18 *See also* Dt 15:10; Jdg 8:1–3; Job 5:2; 36:13; Pr 3:11; 20:22; 23:17

In Jesus Christ's teaching Mk 7:21–23 pp Mt 15:19–20

In the apostles' teaching Ro 12:17–21; 1Th 5:15 *See also* Gal 5:15,19–21; Php 2:13–15; Col 3:8; 2Ti 2:24; Jas 3:14–16; 1Pe 2:1

Christians should not hold grudges
Mt 5:43–47 *See also* Mt 18:21–35; Col 3:13

See also

5265 complaints	5875 hatred
5494 revenge	5927 resentment
5789 anger	6652 forgiveness
5799 bitterness	8733 envy

8766

heresies

Teachings held by a factional religious party which deny some aspect of established doctrine. NT writers give no toleration to heresies in the church.

Heresy as deviant teaching
Heb 13:9 *See also* Gal 1:6–7; 2Ti 4:3–4

Heresies and the factional nature of Judaism
The party of the Pharisees Ac 26:5 *See also* Ac 15:5; Php 3:5–6

The party of the Sadducees Ac 23:8 *See also* Mt 22:23 pp Mk 12:18 pp Lk 20:27

Christianity was perceived as a heresy within Judaism Ac 24:14 *See also* Ac 24:5; 28:22

Heresies within the church
The imposition of Jewish regulations on Gentile converts Ac 15:1 *See also* Gal 6:12–13; 1Ti 1:3–7; Tit 1:10

Heresies concerning the person of Jesus Christ 2Jn 7 *See also* 1Jn 2:22–23; 4:1–3

Heresies concerning the return of Jesus Christ 2Th 2:1–2 *See also* Mt 24:4–5 pp Mk 13:5–6 pp Lk 21:8; Mt 24:23–24 pp Mk 13:21–22

The origins of heresy
Erroneous human teaching Col 2:8 *See also* Eph 4:14; Col 2:20–22

Deceitful demonic power 1Ti 4:1 *See also* 1Jn 4:2–3,6

Christian opposition to heresy
Heresy warned against 2Pe 3:17 *See also* 1Ti 4:7; Tit 1:10–14

Heresy condemned 2Pe 2:3 *See also* Gal 1:8–9; 2Pe 2:17–22

See also

1460 truth	8750 false teachings
5441 philosophy	8774 legalism
8237 doctrine, false	8775 libertinism
8703 antinomianism	8784 nominal
8712 denial of Christ	religion
8748 false religion	8831 syncretism
8749 false teachers	

8767

hypocrisy

An outward pretence masking an inner reality. Scripture condemns hypocrisy, especially in matters of faith. Believers should express their commitment to God in their words and their deeds, as well as in their inner motivation.

The origin of hypocrisy
Jer 17:9 *See also* Hos 10:2 *Israel*; Mk 7:21–22 pp Mt 15:19

The expression of hypocrisy
Insincere motives Mt 6:2 *See also* Mt 6:5,16; 15:7–9; 22:18; 23:5–7

When deeds do not match words
Isa 29:13 *See also* Mt 15:7–8 pp Mk 7:6;

Pr 26:24–26; Jer 9:8; 12:2; Eze 33:31; Mt 23:28; Ro 2:17–24; Jas 2:14–26

A tendency to judge others Mt 7:5 pp Lk 6:41 *See also* Ro 2:1

The alternative to hypocrisy
Heb 10:22 *See also* Ps 24:3–4; 26:4; 32:2; Jas 3:17; 4:8; 1Pe 2:1–3

Hypocrisy is not to be found in leaders
1Ch 28:8–9 *See also* Mal 2:6 *the true priest*; 1Co 4:1–5; 1Ti 3:8; Tit 1:8; Jas 3:1

Examples of hypocrites
Israel's leaders Jer 6:13 *See also* Jer 8:8

The Pharisees Mk 12:38–40 *See also* Mt 23:1–32; Lk 12:1–2,56

Peter and Barnabas Gal 2:12–13 *By acting in this way, Peter was denying his own conviction that Gentiles could be saved by faith without having to submit to the law.*

Many false teachers Ro 16:17–18 *See also* Php 1:17; 1Ti 4:2; 2Ti 3:5; Jude 16

Examples of those who did not practise hypocrisy
Jesus Christ 1Pe 2:21–22 *See also* Isa 53:9; Jn 8:44–46

Paul and his companions 2Co 1:12 *See also* 2Co 2:17; 1Th 2:3–10

See also

5381 law, letter &	7552 Pharisees,
spirit	attitudes to
5812 concealment	Christ
5820 criticism	7733 leaders
5908 motives	8275 honesty
5920 pretence	8720 double-
6145 deceit	mindedness
6242 adultery	

8768

idolatry

The worship or adoration of anyone or anything other than the LORD God. Idolatry includes the worship of other gods, such as those of the nations surrounding Israel, images or idols and the creation itself.

8769

idolatry, in OT

Scripture provides illustrations of idolatry from various periods in the history of the people of God. Idolatry is seen as a constant temptation for believers, especially in times of national or personal stress.

Idolatry among the Gentiles
Jdg 11:24; 16:23–24; 2Ki 5:18; Isa 36:18–20; 37:38; 46:1; Eze 8:14; Ac 14:11–13; 1Co 8:5

Idolatry among God's people
In patriarchal times Jos 24:2 *See also* Ge 31:30,34 *these household gods may have been either masks or statuettes*; Ge 35:2

In the Mosaic period Ex 32:4

In the period of the judges Jdg 17:5 *See also* Jdg 10:6

In the early monarchy 1Ki 11:10 *See also* 1Ki 12:28 *The golden calves were perhaps pedestals on which the LORD was thought to sit.*

In the middle monarchy 1Ki 16:33 *An Asherah pole was probably a crude carved wooden image of a Canaanite fertility goddess. See also* 1Ki 11:7–8; 16:32

In the late monarchy 2Ki 21:2–6

After the fall of Jerusalem Eze 8:10 *See also* Eze 8:3,14,16

Objects of false worship
The sun, moon and stars Dt 4:19 *See also* Dt 17:3; Job 31:26

Other objects of worship Dt 4:28 *See also* Dt 16:22 *sacred stones;* 1Ki 12:31 *high places;* Isa 1:29 *oaks*

Practices associated with idolatry
The burning of children 2Ki 23:10

The superstitious use of religious symbols 2Ki 18:4 *See also* Jdg 8:27 *The ephod was a priestly garment sometimes subject to excessive veneration.*

Sexual deviance Dt 23:17 *See also* 1Ki 14:24; Hos 4:14

See also

4155 divination	7384 household
4281 stars	gods
5205 alliance	7442 shrine
5947 shame	7471 temples,
6243 adultery,	heathen
spiritual	8747 false gods
7312 Baal	8752 false worship
7374 high places	

8770
idolatry, in NT

The NT world included many religions which promoted the worship of idols. Idolatry was thus of continuing importance to NT writers, especially Paul.

Idolatry in the Gentile world
Ac 17:16 *See also* Ac 14:11–13; 17:22–23; 19:24; 1Co 8:5; Gal 4:8

Criticism of idolatry
Idolatry leads to other sinful behaviour Ro 1:24 *Verses 22 and 24–25 show the link between idolatry and immoral conduct.*

Idolatry is an offence against the doctrine of creation Ro 1:20 *See also* Ac 17:24–29

Idols are futile and degrading Ro 1:22–23 *See also* 1Co 8:4; 10:19; 12:2

Idolatrous worship of human beings Ac 12:22 *See also* Lk 20:24–25 *Jesus Christ opposes the hypocrisy which objected to Roman coinage as idolatrous on the grounds that the emperor's head infringed the Ten Commandments;* Ac 28:6

Demonic powers are involved with idolatry 1Co 10:20 *See also* Rev 9:20; 13:4

Food sacrificed to idols Ac 15:20 *See also* Ro 14:2–3,6; 1Co 8:4–13; 10:14–31

Encounters with idolatrous practice Ac 19:28 *See also* Ac 14:11–18; 17:18–31

Spiritual idolatry
1Jn 5:21 *"idols" here may well refer to a wide range of God-substitutes.*

The temptations of Jesus Christ present three main kinds of spiritual idolatry
Possessions Mt 4:3 pp Lk 4:3 *See also* Mt 6:24 pp Lk 16:13; Lk 18:23; Php 3:19; Col 3:5; 1Ti 6:10

Prestige and self-esteem Mt 4:6 pp Lk 4:9 *See also* Lk 3:8; 10:29; 18:11–12,21; Ro 2:19

Power Mt 4:8–9 pp Lk 4:6–7 *See also* Lk 4:54–55; 23:39; Jn 18:10–11; 19:10; Php 2:6; Jas 4:6,10

See also

2575 Christ,	8276 humility
temptation	8319 perception,
4185 sorcery and	spiritual
magic	8802 pride
8218 consecration	8829 superstition
8226 discernment	

8771
idolatry, objections to

Scripture presents idolatry as absurd and irrational, offensive to God and a source of spiritual and moral danger.

Idolatry is disparaged
The absurdity of making idols Hab 2:18 *See also* Dt 4:28; Isa 40:18–20; 41:6–7; Jer 10:3–9; Hos 10:6; Hab 2:19

Idols represent falsehood and fraud Ps 40:4 *See also* Jer 2:5; 10:14; 16:19; 51:17–18; Hos 12:1; Am 2:4

Bowing down to idols is inappropriate Ps 135:17–18 pp Ps 115:5–8 *See also* Isa 2:8; 44:15–17; 46:6; Jer 1:16; Mic 5:13

Idols contrasted with the LORD Isa 46:5 *See also* Isa 40:25–26; Jer 5:24; 10:10; Hos 2:8; Ac 17:24–25

Idolatry is forbidden by God Ex 20:3–4 pp Dt 5:7–8

Idolatry incurs severe penalties Zep 1:4 *See also* Dt 13:1–9,12–15; Isa 66:4; Am 5:27; Na 1:14

God abominates idols Eze 7:20 *Two terms, that is "idols" and "vile images", meaning "abomination" are found here in parallel. A third, punning on the word for "dung" is often used by Ezekiel for idols. See also* Dt 7:25; 2Ki 23:24; Eze 5:9,11; 6:4

Pressure to worship idols must be resisted and idols abandoned Da 3:18 *See also* Isa 2:20; 30:22; 31:7

The dangers of idolatry
Blindness Isa 44:18

Becoming like idols Ps 115:8 *See also* Jer 2:5; Hos 9:10

Spiritual adultery Dt 31:16 *See also* Jdg 8:33; Isa 1:21; Jer 13:27; Hos 1:2; 2:7; 8:9

Injustice Am 5:7

See also

1080 God, living	6218 provoking God
1130 God,	8138 monotheism
sovereignty	8462 priority of God
1185 God, zeal of	8759 fools
1240 God, the Rock	8764 forgetting God
6103 abomination	8807 profanity
6187 immorality	

8773
jealousy

A strong feeling of possessiveness, often caused by the possibility that something which belongs, or ought to belong, to one is about to be taken away. The word can be used in a positive sense (e.g., the jealousy of God), meaning a passionate commitment to something which rightly belongs to one. It can also be used in a negative sense (e.g., human jealousy), to mean a self-destructive human emotion similar to envy.

God's jealousy for his people
God's jealousy demands an exclusive response from his people Ex 20:4–6 *See also* Ex 34:14; Dt 32:16,21

God pictured as a jealous husband with an unfaithful wife Eze 16:1–63

God is jealously protective of his people Joel 2:18 *See also* Isa 26:11; Zec 1:14–15; 8:2

God's possessiveness expresses itself in judgment on his people's unfaithfulness Dt 4:24 *See also* Dt 6:15; 29:20; Jos 24:19; 1Ki 14:22; Eze 23:25; 36:6; Na 1:2; Zep 1:18; 3:8

Human jealousy is potentially destructive
Human jealousy arises from sin Mk 7:21–23 pp Mt 15:19–20

Human jealousy can be destructive Pr 14:30 *See also* Job 5:2; Pr 27:4; Ecc 9:5–6

Human jealousy is criticised by Scripture Gal 5:19–21 *See also* Ps 37:1–2; Pr 23:17; Ro 13:13; 1Co 13:4–7; Tit 3:3–5; Jas 3:14–16

Examples of jealousy
In the OT Ge 4:3–5 *Cain and Abel;* Ge 27:41 *Esau and Jacob;* Ge 30:1 *Rachel and Leah*
Joseph's brothers: Ge 37:4; Ac 7:9
1Sa 18:6–9 *Saul and David;* Isa 11:13 *Ephraim and Judah*

In the early church Ac 5:17; 13:45; 17:5; 1Co 3:3; 2Co 12:20

See also

1185 God, zeal of	6133 coveting
5762 attitudes, God	8733 envy
to people	8787 opposition to
5765 attitudes to	God
people	8827 selfishness
5789 anger	8830 suspicion

8774
legalism

The belief that salvation demands or

depends upon total obedience to the letter of the law. Examples of legalism include an excessive concern for minute details of the law coupled with a neglect of its fundamental concerns, and a preoccupation with human legal traditions.

Legalism represents a fatal misunderstanding of the purpose of OT law
Ro 9:31–32 *See also* Ro 3:20; Gal 3:10–11

Legalism is contrary to the gospel
Gal 2:16 *See also* Mt 23:13,15; Ro 3:20–24; Php 3:8–9

Paul: example of a Jewish legalist
Php 3:4–6 *See also* Gal 1:14

The ugly effects of legalism
Lack of love Mt 23:23 *Legalism actually contradicts the spirit of OT law. See also* Hos 6:6; Mic 6:7–8; Mt 23:14 fn; Lk 10:31–32; Jn 7:49

Spiritual pride Lk 18:11–12 *See also* Mt 6:1–2,5,16; 23:5–7; Lk 16:15; Ro 10:3

Formalism Isa 29:13 *See also* Mk 7:6

Degeneration into man-made rules Isa 29:13 *See also* Mk 7:7–8

Hypocrisy Mt 23:27–28 *See also* 1Sa 15:19–22; Mt 15:3–9 pp Mk 7:9–13; Mt 23:25–26; Jn 7:19

Spiritual blindness Jn 9:16

Warnings against legalism
Mt 16:6 pp Mk 8:15 *See also* Mt 16:12; Gal 4:10–11; 5:2–4

The burden of legalism
Ac 15:10 *See also* Ps 130:3; Jas 2:10

The answer to legalism: the grace of Jesus Christ
Ac 15:11 *See also* Mt 5:17; Gal 3:13; 4:21–31; Eph 2:8–9

See also

5108 Paul, life of	6676 justification
5135 blindness, spiritual	7550 Pharisees
5381 law, letter & spirit	7555 Sadducees
5588 traditions	8023 faith, necessity
6669 grace & salvation	8154 righteousness
	8767 hypocrisy
	8802 pride

libertinism

A form of abuse of Christian freedom which refuses to acknowledge any obligation for Christians to obey the law or to restrain sin.

Grace must not lead to libertinism
Ro 6:1–2,15 *See also* Ro 3:5–8; Gal 2:17–21

Believers must resist sin
Ro 6:12,14 *See also* Heb 12:1–2; 1Jn 5:16–18

The law remains valid for believers
Mt 5:17–18 *See also* Jos 23:6; 1Ch 22:12; Pr 28:7; Ro 7:12; 1Ti 1:8

The dangers of libertinism
Falling back into sin Ro 6:1–2; Heb 12:1; 1Jn 1:8–10

Disobedience towards God 1Jn 2:3–4 *See also* 1Jn 3:4; 2Co 10:6; Eph 5:6; 1Pe 2:8

Selfishness 1Jn 3:17 *See also* Lk 6:32–34; 2Ti 2:1–4; 1Jn 2:9–11

See also
6662 freedom, abuse   8750 false teachings 8703 antinomianism

lies

Statements or answers which are untrue. Lying, false witness, deceit and false dealings are all condemned in Scripture.

Lying is condemned
Ps 34:12–13; Eph 4:25; Col 3:9–10 *See also* Ex 20:16 pp Dt 5:20; Lev 19:11–12; Pr 6:16–17; 12:22; Jer 17:9–10

Examples of lying
Ge 3:4–5 *the serpent to Eve*; Ge 4:9 *Cain to the* Lord; Ge 12:11–13 *Abraham urges Sarah to lie to the Egyptians*; Ge 18:15 *Sarah to the* Lord; Ge 20:1–2 *Abraham to Abimelech*; Ge 26:6–7 *Isaac to the men of Gerar*

Jacob to Isaac: Ge 27:18–19,24

Ge 39:14–18 *Potiphar's wife to her household servants*; 2Ki 5:22–27 *Gehazi to Naaman and then to Elisha*; Ac 5:1–10 *Ananias and Sapphira*

Some Jews persuaded others to lie about Stephen: Ac 6:11,13

Ac 25:7; Ro 3:8

Lying will not go unnoticed or unpunished
Pr 19:9 *See also* Ps 5:6; 52:2–5; 55:23; 101:7; Jer 6:13–15; 23:32; Na 3:1; 1Ti 1:9–10; Rev 21:8,27; 22:15

God's people should resist the temptation to lie
Job 27:2–5; Rev 2:2

Lying can be an act of malice
Pr 26:24–28

Lying can be the sign of a dead conscience
1Ti 4:1–2

A lying spirit
1Ki 22:21–23 pp 2Ch 18:20–22

Lying is the hallmark of the devil and the antichrist
Jn 8:44 *See also* 1Jn 2:22; Rev 13:14; 20:7–10

See also

4120 Satan	8714 dishonesty
5202 accusation, false	8749 false teachers
	8750 false teachings
5863 flattery	8751 false witness
6145 deceit	8767 hypocrisy

lust

An overpowering and compulsive desire or passion, especially of a sexual nature. Scripture condemns lust of all kinds, and urges believers to show self-control.

Lust has its origins in the heart and mind
Pr 6:25–29; Mt 5:28 *See also* Ge 3:6; Job 31:1; Jas 1:13–15; 1Jn 2:16

Lust is natural to unbelievers
Ro 1:21–27 *See also* Ro 7:5; 1Co 6:9–10; 1Pe 4:3; 2Pe 2:14–18

Believers can and must fight against lust by showing self-control
Gal 5:16–21; Col 3:5 *See also* 1Co 9:27; Gal 5:24; Eph 4:22; 1Th 4:4–5; 2Ti 2:22; Tit 2:12; 1Pe 2:11

Examples of lust
Lust expressed as sexual desire Ge 39:6–12 *Potiphar's wife and Joseph*; 2Sa 11:2–5 *David and Bathsheba*

Lust for money 1Ti 6:9–10 *See also* 1Ti 3:3

The lustful desire of Israel and Judah for alliances Eze 23:1–21 *Both kingdoms sought security from such alliances, rather than trusting in God.*

See also

3233 Holy Spirit & sanctification	6133 coveting
	6237 sexual sin
5412 money	6242 adultery
5452 power	6744 sanctification
5792 appetite	8266 holiness
5832 desire	8451 mortification
5869 greed	

materialism

The outlook on life which treats material possessions as being of supreme importance or which denies the spiritual aspects of life. Scripture notes the dangers of material wealth and possessions. The accumulation of wealth can easily become a god in itself and lead people astray from the worship of the true God. Yet it is not money itself, but the love of money, which is seen by Scripture as a fundamental cause of evil.

8779
materialism, nature of

The attitude to life that places particular emphasis on immediate, physical values rather than on future, spiritual ones or that regards the material world as the only reality.

The basic features of materialism

An attitude of godlessness Ps 14:1–2 pp Ps 53:1–2 *See also* Job 35:9–10; Ps 10:4,11; Ecc 1:1–11; Lk 12:13–19; Ro 1:20–22

A denial of the resurrection Mt 22:23 *See also* Ecc 4:1–3; 9:3–6; Ac 4:1–2; 23:6–8; 1Co 15:12–17; 2Ti 2:17–19

Desire for wealth and physical gratification 1Co 15:32 *See also* Ecc 2:4–9; 9:7–10; Mt 6:19–24

Materialism condemned

Ps 52:7 *See also* Job 22:4–11; 31:25–28; Ps 49:10; Pr 18:11; 23:5; Ecc 5:10; Mt 16:26; Lk 12:23–25; 21:34; Jas 5:1–3

See also

5503 rich, the	8211 commitment to
5766 attitudes to life	world
5785 ambition	8260 generosity
5832 desire	8755 folly
5839 dissatisfaction	8809 riches
5864 futility	8848 worldliness
5874 happiness	

8780
materialism, as an aspect of sin

The pursuit of possessions and wealth and a preoccupation with physical things is futile and dissatisfying.

Materialism as the result of human sin

At the fall Ge 3:6

Among pagans Ro 1:22–23 *See also* Ps 115:2–8; Isa 44:9–11; Da 3:1,4–7; Hab 2:18; Ac 17:16; 2Ti 3:2

Within Israel itself Ex 20:4–5 *See also* Ex 32:4; Lev 26:1; Dt 4:15–19; 7:25; 1Ki 11:1–6; Ps 106:19–20; Isa 42:8; Jer 2:11–13; 1Co 10:14

Materialism and possessions

Possessions are to be seen as a gift from God 1Ch 29:12 *See also* Ge 13:2; 26:12–13; Dt 8:18; 2Ch 32:29; Ps 112:1–3; Pr 10:22; Ecc 5:19; Hos 2:8

Material goods can turn the heart away from God Dt 8:13–14; 1Ti 6:9–10 *See also* Job 31:24–28; Eze 28:5; Mt 19:21–22 pp Lk 18:22–23; Mt 26:14–16; 1Jn 3:17

Possessions and riches can make it difficult to enter the kingdom Mt 19:23–24 pp Mk 10:24–25 pp Lk 18:24–25 *See also* Mt 13:22 pp Mk 4:18–19 pp Lk 8:14; 1Ti 6:17–19; Jas 2:2–5; 5:1–6

The weaknesses of materialism

It is transitory Pr 27:24 *See also* Job 22:20; Ps 49:10,17; Pr 22:1–2; 23:5; Ecc 2:18,21,26; Jer 17:11; Lk 12:20–21; 1Ti 6:7

It does not satisfy Ecc 5:10 *See also* Ecc 4:8; 5:12; Hag 1:5–6; Mt 6:19

It can encourage greed 1Ki 21:2–4 *See also* Ex 20:17 pp Dt 5:21; Jos 7:1,20–24; 1Ki 10:23–27

It can lead to worldliness Mt 16:26 pp Mk 8:36–37 pp Lk 9:24–25 *See also* Jer 17:11; Lk 16:15,25–26; Jas 1:9–11; Rev 3:17

Jesus Christ's non-materialistic attitude

Mt 8:20 pp Lk 9:58 *See also* Php 2:5–6

Warnings to believers to guard against materialism

Lk 12:15 *See also* Jer 9:23–24; Mt 6:25–32; 1Ti 6:17–19; Heb 13:5; 1Jn 2:15–17

Godly examples of a non-materialistic attitude

Ge 13:8–9; 14:23; Ac 3:6; 4:32–37; Php 4:11–12

See also

2339 Christ, example	6133 coveting
of	6139 deadness,
5399 luxury	spiritual
5413 money,	6178 hardness of
attitudes	heart
5475 property	8206 Christlikeness
5810 complacency	8768 idolatry
5869 greed	8827 selfishness

8782

mockery

A form of ridicule directed especially against individuals, with the purpose of humiliating them. Scripture condemns mockers as arrogant, unrighteous and foolish.

Targets of mockery

God Isa 52:5 *See also* Ps 74:10,18,22

Job Job 30:1 *See also* Job 17:2; 21:3; 30:9

God's servants 2Ch 36:16 *See also* Ne 2:19; Ps 22:7; 35:15–16; 69:12; 80:6; 89:50–51; 119:51; Jer 20:7; La 3:14,63 *Christians mocked:* Ac 2:13; 17:32; 26:24

Jesus Christ Mt 20:17–19 pp Mk 10:32–34 pp Lk 18:31–33 *See also* Mt 26:67–68 pp Mk 14:65 pp Lk 22:63–65; Lk 23:11; Mt 27:27–31 pp Mk 15:16–20; Mt 27:41–44 pp Mk 15:31–32 pp Lk 23:35; Lk 23:36

Those who oppose God will become objects of mockery

Pr 3:34 *See also* 2Ki 19:20–28 pp Isa 37:22–29; Job 22:17–20; Jer 10:14–16 pp Jer 51:17–19; Eze 22:1–5

False accusations of mockery

Job 11:1–3 *See also* Job 9:21–24 *Job accuses God of mocking the plight of innocent sufferers.*

Mockery in metaphorical use

Pr 20:1

Characteristics of mockers

They are proud and arrogant Pr 21:24 *See also* Pr 3:34

They instigate strife Pr 22:10 *See also* Pr 9:7; 29:8

They do not respond to correction Pr 15:12 *See also* Pr 1:22–26; 13:1; 19:25

Scripture condemns mockers as unrighteous

Ps 1:1 *See also* Pr 14:6 *Resistance to correction accounts for the failure to find wisdom;* Pr 14:9; 24:9; Isa 57:4; Hos 7:5

Mockers will be punished

Pr 1:22–26 *See also* Pr 9:12; 17:5; 19:28–29; 21:11; 30:17; Isa 28:22; 29:20; Zep 2:10–11; Gal 6:7

See also

2530 Christ, death of	8727 enemies
5818 contempt	8759 fools
5823 cruelty	8802 pride
5879 humiliation	8815 ridicule
5893 insults	8819 scoffing
8361 wisdom	

8783

neglect

The shirking of one's duties or responsibilities, whether to God or to other people. The consequences of such neglect are often serious.

The Israelites sometimes neglected their religious duties

They neglected to support the Levites Dt 14:27 *See also* Dt 12:19; Ne 13:10

They neglected the temple Ne 13:11 *See also* 2Ch 24:5; Mal 1:6–14

Such neglect earned them the judgment of God 2Ch 29:6–9

The Israelites sometimes neglected their social obligations

They neglected to ensure justice for the poor Isa 5:7 *See also* Am 2:6–8; 4:1–3; 5:7–15

Their leaders neglected their responsibilities Isa 56:10–12 *See also* Eze 34:1–6; Am 6:1–7

God punished their neglect Zep 1:12–13 *See also* Isa 32:9–15

Neglect in the NT

Warnings against neglect 1Ti 4:14 *See also* Mt 23:23 pp Lk 11:42; Mt 25:14–30 pp Lk 19:12–26; Lk 12:35–48

Examples of neglect

The neglect of salvation Heb 2:1–4

The neglect of public worship Heb 10:25

Sodom's neglect of the poor Eze 16:49

The neglect of widows Ac 6:1–4

See also

1310 God as judge	7967 spiritual gifts,
4540 weeds	responsibility
5051 responsibility	8232 discipline,
5359 justice	family
5508 ruins	8741 failure
5803 carelessness	8763 forgetting
5810 complacency	
7259 promised land,	
later history	

8784

nominal religion

An outward show of piety which may appear to be very devout. However, the heart is far from God and this is confirmed by the person's attitudes and actions.

The nature of nominal religion

It has an appearance of devotion which masks an evil heart Jer 12:2 *See*

also Pr 26:23; Isa 58:2; Eze 33:31–32;
Mt 23:27–28

**It is based on what human beings may
think is right** Mt 15:7–9 pp Mk 7:6–7
See also Isa 29:13

**It becomes apparent by the actions of
its adherents** Tit 1:16 *See also*
Mt 7:15–23; 1Ti 1:3–7; 1Jn 2:4

**The insufficiency of nominal
religion**
1Sa 15:22 *See also* Isa 1:11–15;
Am 5:21–24; Mt 9:13; 12:7; Hos 6:6

**Those who practise nominal
religion are condemned**
Pr 15:8 *See also* Isa 66:3–4; 2Ti 3:1–5

See also

5173 outward	8774 legalism
appearance	8822 self-
5920 pretence	justification
7550 Pharisees	8823 self-
8142 religion	righteousness
8734 evil	8845 unfruitfulness
8748 false religion	9210 judgment,
8767 hypocrisy	God's

8785

opposition

The act of resisting individuals and
forces. Scripture stresses the reality of
sin and evil in the world and calls
upon believers to resist them.
Scripture also points to the existence
of evil forces that oppose God and
identifies them so that believers may
recognise and resist them. These
forces were evident in the ministry of
Jesus Christ.

8786
opposition, to sin and evil

Believers are called upon to oppose
all that is hostile to God's purposes
in the world.

God opposes evil
Mt 21:12–13 pp Mk 11:15–16
pp Lk 19:45–46 pp Jn 2:14–17 *See also*
Ex 4:24; Lev 20:3; 26:14–17; Nu 22:22;
Mal 3:2–5; Jas 4:6; 1Pe 5:5; Rev 2:16

God's people should oppose evil
Within themselves Col 3:5 *See also*
Mt 5:29–30; Ro 8:13

Among themselves Gal 2:11 *See also*
1Co 5:12–13; Eph 5:3

**Examples of failure to oppose
evil**
Within the church 1Co 5:1–2; Rev 2:20

Within the family 1Sa 3:13; 1Ki 1:6

Within the state Hab 1:4 *See also*
Jdg 5:23; 1Sa 15:9–11; Jer 5:28

**Examples of unwise opposition to
evil**
Mt 26:51–52 pp Mk 14:47
pp Lk 22:50–51; Jn 18:10–11;
Lk 9:54–55; Ac 19:13–16

Opposing evil by doing good
Commanded by God 1Pe 2:15 *See also*
Mt 5:44; Ro 12:20–21; 1Th 5:15

Exemplified in Scripture Nu 12:13;
1Sa 24:17; 26:11; 2Ki 6:22; Lk 22:51;
23:34

Motives for opposing evil
Concern for the honour and glory of
God Nu 25:6–13 *See also* 1Ki 19:10;
Eze 28:22; Jn 2:17

Concern for the good of others
Gal 2:4–5 *See also* Dt 17:12–13;
1Ti 5:20

See also

5485 punishment,	8275 honesty
legal aspects	8292 love
5731 parents	8370 zeal
5931 resistance	8451 mortification
6026 sin, judgment	8737 evil, responses
on	to
6186 evil scheming	8766 heresies
8230 discipline	

8787
opposition, to God's person and
work

The forces of evil are antagonistic
towards God, his people and his
work, and believers must oppose
them.

**Targets of opposition from evil
forces**
The Lord himself Ps 2:1–3; Heb 12:3
See also Isa 63:10; Ac 7:51; Rev 17:14

God's people Ac 8:1–3 *See also*
Nu 16:1–3; 2Sa 16:5–8; Est 3:6;
Jer 18:18; Ac 26:9–11; 2Ti 4:14–15;
Rev 13:7

God's work 1Th 2:2 *See also* Ezr 4:4–5;
Ne 4:7–8; Ac 4:18; 13:8; 1Co 16:9

Sources of opposition
The world Jn 15:18–19 *See also*
Jn 17:14; 1Jn 3:13

The flesh Gal 5:17 *See also* Mt 26:41
pp Mk 14:38; Ro 7:23

The devil 1Pe 5:8 *See also* Zec 3:1;
Mt 13:38–39; Rev 2:10; 12:4,7,9,13,17

Strategies used in opposition
Shows of strength Jdg 6:5;
1Sa 17:10–11; 2Ki 6:14

Discouraging propaganda
2Ki 18:19–22 *See also* Rev 13:4–6

Surprise Ge 39:11–12; Ps 10:8–9; 64:4

Seduction Mt 4:9; 1Jn 2:15–16;
Rev 2:14,20

Deceitfulness Jude 4 *See also* Nu 31:16;
1Sa 18:17; Ne 6:1–2; Ro 16:18;
2Co 11:13–15; 2Jn 7,8; Rev 19:20

Sustained pressure Ge 39:10;
1Sa 1:6–7; 2Ki 6:25; Ne 6:4

Motives for opposition
Jealousy 1Sa 18:9 *See also*
Ps 106:16–18; Mt 27:18 pp Mk 15:10;
Ac 5:17–18; 13:45; 17:5

Troubled conscience Jn 7:7 *See also*
Isa 30:10; Ac 26:14; 1Jn 3:12; Rev 11:10

Vested interests Ac 16:19; 19:24–27

No just cause Ps 69:4; Jn 15:25

Dealing with opposition
Being prepared 2Pe 3:17; 2Co 10:4 *See
also* Mk 13:9; Jn 16:1–4; 1Pe 4:12

Keeping a right perspective
2Ki 6:15–17; Ne 4:14; Ro 8:31

Prayer Ne 6:9 *See also* Ne 4:4; Lk 18:7;
Ac 4:23–24

Patience 2Ti 2:25

Prudence Jdg 8:1–3; Pr 15:1; Ac 22:25;
23:6; 25:11; 2Co 6:3

Perseverance 1Co 15:58; Php 1:27–28;
1Pe 5:9; Rev 1:9; 13:10; 14:12

See also

2426 gospel,	6166 flesh, sinful
responses	nature
3284 Holy Spirit,	8459 perseverance
resisting	8483 spiritual
4027 world, fallen	warfare,
4116 angels opposed	causes
to God	8493 watchfulness,
4120 Satan	believers
4132 demons,	8727 enemies
malevolence	8794 persecution

8788
opposition, to Jesus Christ
See 2545 Jesus Christ, opposition to

8790

oppression

The unfair or cruel treatment of
individuals or nations, which
prevents them from having the same
opportunities, freedom and rights as
others.

8791
oppression, nature of

Oppression leads to the exploitation
of the weak and vulnerable by the
strong.

The victims
The weak Ps 12:5 *See also* Ps 10:2;
Ecc 4:1; Eze 34:4

The poor Pr 22:22–23 *See also* Ex 23:6;
Dt 15:7; Pr 22:7,16; 28:27; Eze 22:29;
Am 2:6–7; 5:11–12; 8:4,6; Zec 7:10;
Jas 2:6

Widows and orphans Ex 22:22 *See also*
Dt 24:17; Job 24:3,9; 31:21,22;
Ps 94:5–6; Pr 23:10; Isa 1:23; Jer 7:6;
Zec 7:10; Mal 3:5; Mk 12:40

The foreigner Ex 22:21 *See also*
Ge 15:13; Ex 23:9; Lev 19:33–34;
Dt 23:7; 24:17; Ps 94:6; Jer 22:3;
Eze 22:29; Mal 3:5

Servants Dt 24:14–15 *See also* Ge 16:6;
Ex 1:11; 3:9; Lev 19:13; Isa 58:3;
Mal 3:5; Ac 7:24; Jas 5:4

Examples of oppression
Ge 16:6 *Sarah oppresses Hagar;* Ge 31:39
Laban oppresses Jacob; Ex 1:8–22 *the
Egyptians oppress Israel;* Isa 52:4 *the
Assyrians oppress Israel*

The oppressors' motives
Greed Jer 5:27–28 *See also* Pr 31:5;
Ecc 5:8–9; Isa 1:23; 10:2; Jer 22:17;
Am 4:1

8792

Lust for power Ex 1:10 *See also* 2Ch 10:14; 16:10; Pr 28:15

God's attitude to the oppressor
Ex 22:22–24 *See also* Dt 27:19; Pr 21:13; Isa 14:5–6; Jer 6:6; 22:3–5; Am 1:3,6,9,11; 2:1; Zep 3:1; Lk 20:47

The experience of oppression
It brings grief and crying to God Ps 42:9 *See also* Ex 3:7; Jdg 2:18; Ps 43:2; 137:1; Ecc 4:1

The example of Jesus Christ Isa 53:7 *See also* Mt 27:27–31 pp Mk 15:16–20; Ac 8:32–35

Following Jesus Christ 1Pe 2:21 *See also* Jn 16:33; Ac 14:22–23; 1Th 3:2–4; 2Ti 2:3; 3:12

See also
5220 authority, abuse
5242 buying & selling
5310 exploitation
5311 extortion
5446 poverty
5457 power, human
5730 orphans
5743 widows
5972 unkindness
7530 foreigners
8343 servanthood in society
8797 persecution, attitudes

8792

oppression, God's attitude to

God is concerned for the victims of oppression; he hears, sustains and delivers them. Christians are to exhibit the same concern.

God forbids the oppression of the poor and vulnerable
Zec 7:10 *See also* Pr 22:22–23

God warns the oppressor
Jer 7:5–7 *See also* Isa 33:14–15

God condemns the oppressor
Ps 72:4; Isa 10:1–3 *See also* Pr 17:5; Isa 30:12–13; Eze 22:7,13,31; Am 2:6; 5:11; Mic 2:1–3; Na 3:1,19; Lk 11:42

God's concern for the oppressed
Showing mercy to the oppressed Ps 103:6; Dt 10:18 *See also* 1Sa 2:8; Ps 146:7–9

Defending the oppressed Ps 72:4 *See also* Dt 10:18; Ps 9:9; 10:17–18; 12:5; 68:5; 146:7–9; Jer 50:33–34

Delivering the oppressed Job 5:15 *See also* Ex 3:7–9; Dt 6:21; Ps 35:10; 107:6 pp Ps 107:13, 19; Pr 20:22; Isa 14:3–4; 49:26; Ac 7:34

The oppressed turn to the LORD
In prayer Ps 10:12 *See also* Jdg 4:3; 10:9–10; 2Ch 6:38–39; Ps 42:9; 57:1; 79:11; 82:3–4; 94:1–7; Rev 6:10

In trust Ac 16:25 *See also* Job 19:25; Ps 42:1–3; 138:7; 2Co 4:17; 6:4–5; 1Pe 4:19

Christian attitudes towards the oppressed
Showing practical mercy Mt 5:7 *See also* Lev 19:10; Dt 24:19–21; Pr 31:8–9,20; Isa 58:9–10; Jer 22:3; Zec 7:9; Mt 6:3; 25:34–39; Ro 12:13; Php 4:10,15; Jas 1:27

Showing concern Heb 13:3 *See also* Ro 12:15; Gal 6:2; Col 4:18; Phm 10

See also
1025 God, anger of
1030 God, compassion
5347 injustice
5480 protection
5484 punishment by God
5560 suffering
5806 compassion
6658 freedom
6686 mercy
7222 exodus, events of
8031 trust, importance of
8614 prayer, answers

8794

persecution

Scripture indicates that believers can expect to face hardship, ridicule and oppression, from individuals and state authorities, on account of their faith. It encourages believers to remain faithful in the face of such persecution and to draw strength from the example of Jesus Christ himself.

8795

persecution, nature of

Persecution by the world and secular powers is a likely consequence of faith. Scripture identifies a number of potential sources of such persistent harassment.

Persecution is characteristic of this world
Ps 10:2 *See also* Am 1:6,9; 2:1; Hab 1:6–11; Rev 6:8; 9:7–10

Satan is the arch-persecutor of the church
Ge 3:15 *See also* Job 2:6–7; Zec 3:1; Lk 22:3–4; 1Pe 5:8; Rev 2:10,13

The agencies of persecution
The world Jn 15:18; 1Jn 3:13 *See also* Mk 12:7; Jn 5:18; 15:19; 17:14; Ac 14:22; 1Th 2:14–15; 1Jn 3:1

Earthly governments Mk 13:9 *See also* 1Ki 19:2; Ne 6:1,9; Est 3:6; Ps 119:161; Jer 38:6; Da 3:13–17; Mt 10:17; Ac 12:1–3

Religious authorities 1Th 2:13–16 *See also* Jer 26:8; Am 7:12–13; Mt 23:34–37; Ac 4:27–29; 5:17–18; 22:4
Powers that persecute the church are symbolised by beasts and Babylon: Rev 13:7,15; 17:6

Family and friends Mt 10:36 *See also* Mic 7:6; Ge 4:8; Mt 10:21; Mk 3:21; Gal 4:29

The experience of persecution
2Co 12:10 *See also* 1Sa 24:14; Ps 59:1–4; 64:1–4; 2Co 4:8–12; 11:23–26; Heb 11:32–38

Believers must expect persecution
2Ti 3:12 *See also* Mt 13:21; Mk 10:29–30; 1Th 3:4

Persecution is part of the tribulation of the church
Mt 24:7–10 *See also* 2Th 2:3–4; Rev 6:11

Persecution is sometimes part of God's judgment on his people
La 4:16–19 *See also* Jer 6:22–26; 32:26–29; 39:5–10

See also
1620 beatitudes, the
1660 Sermon on the Mount
4025 world, the
4120 Satan
5215 authority
5292 defence, divine
5680 family
5690 friends
8116 discipleship, cost
8785 opposition
8790 oppression
9140 last days

8796

persecution, forms of

Scripture identifies a number of reasons why individuals and governments may attempt to persecute believers and also the methods by which they may carry this out.

The motives for persecution
Envy Ac 5:17–18 *See also* Ge 26:14–15; 37:4,8; 1Sa 18:8–9; Ps 106:16; Da 6:1–5; Mt 27:18; Ac 13:45; Jas 3:16

Fear Lk 22:2 *See also* Ex 1:10; 1Sa 18:15,29; Mt 2:3; Ac 19:23–27

Hatred 1Jn 3:12 *See also* Ge 4:3–8; 1Ki 22:8 pp 2Ch 18:7; Jn 7:7

The means of persecution
Deception Ps 38:12 *See also* 1Ki 21:10; Ezr 4:12–13; Ps 35:11; Jer 20:10; Am 7:10; Mt 5:11; Jn 7:12; Ac 6:11; 21:21,28; 24:5

Threats Ps 10:7 *See also* Ezr 4:4; Da 3:15; Jn 9:22; Ac 4:17

Ridicule Ne 4:1–3 *See also* Hos 9:7; 1Co 4:13; Heb 13:13; Rev 2:9

Ostracism Mt 10:22 *See also* Jn 9:29,34; 12:42; 16:2

Violence Ro 8:35 *See also* Jer 38:6; Mt 10:17 pp Mk 13:9; Jn 21:18–19; Ac 5:40; 16:37; 2Co 11:25; Gal 6:17; Heb 11:36–39

How God deals with persecutors
1Ti 1:13 *See also* Da 4:34–35; Ac 12:1,21–23; Gal 1:23

See also
2426 gospel, responses
2545 Christ, opposition to
5040 murder
5560 suffering
5875 hatred
6145 deceit
8498 witnessing & Holy Spirit
8733 envy
8754 fear
8815 ridicule
8819 scoffing
8833 threats

8797

persecution, attitudes to

Scripture outlines the attitudes which believers should adopt in the face of persecution, laying particular emphasis upon the faithfulness of God, the example of Jesus Christ and the need for patience and hope by believers.

The call to endure in the face of persecution
Passively Ps 119:87 *See also*
Mt 10:22,28; 1Co 4:12; 2Th 1:4; Jas 5:8

Actively Heb 12:1 *See also* Eph 6:10–20;
2Ti 2:3; 1Pe 5:9; Rev 2:3

Attitudes believers are to adopt in facing persecution
Living holy and forgiving lives 1Pe 2:12
See also Mt 5:44; Ro 12:19–20;
1Pe 2:15,23; 3:16

Rejoicing in suffering
Ro 5:3–5 *See also* Ps 30:5; Mt 5:11–12
pp Lk 6:22–23; Ac 5:41; 16:22–25;
Ro 12:15; Col 1:24; 1Pe 1:6,8; 4:12,16

**Relying on the promise of God's grace
to endure** La 3:22–23 *See also*
Ps 18:17–19; Na 1:7–8; Ro 8:18,35–39;
2Ti 3:10–11; Heb 13:6; Rev 3:10

**Trusting in the promise of God's
presence** Heb 13:5 *See also* Ps 23:4;
Isa 43:2,5; Mt 28:20; 2Co 4:9

Praying always Eph 6:18 *See also*
Ps 35:24; 38:15–16; 129:5; 143:9;
Mic 7:7–8; Lk 6:28; 18:7–8; 1Pe 4:7

The certain prospect of victory over persecution
The triumph of Jesus Christ 1Co 15:25
See also Ob 21; Php 3:20–21;
2Th 1:6–8; Rev 11:15

The vindication of the saints Jude 24
See also Ezr 6:8; Est 6:11–13; Ps 126:1;
Da 6:26; Hag 2:22–23; 2Ti 1:12;
Rev 2:10; 7:13–17; 12:11

Believers are to take heart from the example of Jesus Christ in facing persecution
**The persecution of Jesus Christ was
predicted in the OT** Ps 22:1–18;
Isa 50:6; 53:7–12

The fulfilment of these predictions
Mt 27:26–31 pp Mk 15:15–20

**The relevance of Jesus Christ's
innocent suffering to believers**
1Pe 2:20–23 *See also* 1Pe 3:14–17
suffering for the sake of righteousness;
1Pe 4:13–14 *rejoicing at sharing in
Christ's sufferings*

See also

1035 God,	8283 joy
faithfulness	8318 patience
2570 Christ,	8414 encourage-
suffering	ment
5596 victory	8459 perseverance
5914 optimism	8482 spiritual
5959 submission	warfare
6652 forgiveness	8602 prayer

8799

polytheism

Belief in, and worship of, more than
one god. It is forbidden in Scripture
because God has revealed himself as
the one true God. Israel in the OT
and the church in the NT lived
amongst polytheistic peoples. The
Israelites shared in this worship and
so came under God's judgment.

The uniqueness of God
There is only one true God Isa 45:5–6
See also Dt 6:4; 32:39; Isa 43:10; 44:8

The contrast of the true God with idols
1Th 1:9 *See also* 1Ch 16:26 pp Ps 96:5;
Isa 40:18–19,25–26; Ac 17:29;
1Co 8:4–6; Gal 4:8

Polytheism is expressly forbidden
Warnings against worshipping idols
Ex 20:23 *See also* Ex 20:3–5
pp Dt 5:7–9; Ex 23:13; Lev 17:7

**Polytheism compromises relationship
with God** 2Ki 17:35–38 *See also*
Dt 31:16; Jer 11:10; 1Co 10:18–22

**The challenge to Israel to worship God
only** Jos 24:15 *See also* Ge 35:2–4;
Dt 12:2–4; 1Ki 18:21

Polytheism brings God's judgment
Ex 22:20; Dt 31:17–18; Jos 23:16;
Jer 11:11–13

Polytheism among Israel's neighbours
Jdg 10:6 *See also* Jdg 16:23; 1Ki 11:33;
2Ki 1:2; 17:29–33; Isa 46:1; Jer 50:2;
Eze 8:14

Polytheism among the Israelites
**They were called to destroy foreign
gods** Nu 33:51–52 *See also* Ex 23:24;
34:12–13; Dt 12:2–3

They were seduced by foreign gods
2Ki 17:15–18; Jer 2:11 *See also*
Ex 34:15–16; Nu 25:2; Dt 12:30;
32:16–17; Jdg 2:11–13; Ps 106:34–36;
Hos 2:13; 11:2

Polytheism among Israel's kings
1Ki 11:5–7 *Solomon*; 1Ki 12:28–29
Jeroboam, king of Israel; 1Ki 16:30–33
Ahab, king of Israel; 2Ki 16:3–4 *Ahaz,
king of Judah*; 2Ki 21:3–5 *Manasseh, king
of Judah*

Examples of reforming kings
1Ki 15:12–13 *Asa, king of Judah*;
2Ki 18:4 *Hezekiah, king of Judah*;
2Ki 23:12–15 *Josiah, king of Judah*

The character of polytheism in the OT
The physical representation of deities
Lev 26:1; 1Ki 14:23; Isa 48:5

Cult prostitution Dt 23:17; 1Ki 14:24

Human sacrifice Lev 18:21 *to Molech*;
Dt 12:31; 2Ki 3:26–27 *to Chemosh*;
Jer 19:5 *to Baal*; Eze 16:20–21

Self-mutilation 1Ki 18:28–29

Polytheism in the NT
It was widespread Ac 17:23 *The
Athenians were fearful of offending a god
by failing to give him attention. Any
omissions were covered in the designation
"UNKNOWN GOD". See also*
Ac 14:11–13; 19:35; 1Co 8:5–6

The worship of man-made idols
1Co 12:2 *See also* Ac 17:16; 19:26;
Ro 1:20–23; 1Co 10:19–20 *Idols in
themselves are nothing, but they represent
a demonic presence which lies behind
polytheistic worship.*

See also

1165 God, unique	8768 idolatry
7312 Baal	8829 superstition
8138 monotheism	8831 syncretism
8622 worship	8840 unfaithfulness
8747 false gods	to God

8800

prejudice

Seen mainly in Scripture as a bias
against places, peoples and ideas. It is
sometimes so firmly rooted as to
resist all contrary evidence.

Prejudice against places
Jn 1:46 *See also* Jn 7:41,52

Prejudice against people
**Prejudice due to an attitude of
superiority** Jn 7:49 *See also* 1Sa 10:27;
25:10–11; Job 30:1–10; Isa 65:5;
Lk 18:11

Prejudice based on fear or jealousy
Ex 1:9–10,12–13; 1Sa 18:8–9,29

Prejudice against Jesus Christ
Jn 12:37 *See also* Mt 9:34; Mk 6:2–3;
Jn 9:29; 10:20

Prejudice may be based on false assumptions about people's behaviour
Hostility incorrectly assumed
Ge 12:11–12 *See also* Ge 20:1–2;
26:1–11

Motives misunderstood Nu 32:5–9 *The
leaders of Reuben and Gad chose to inhabit
the fertile land in Transjordan but they
were also prepared to cross the Jordan to
help their brothers conquer the land. See
also* Nu 32:14,17; Jos 22:10–24;
2Sa 10:3

Prejudice in terms of partiality
Favouritism Ge 25:28; 37:3;
44:20,27–29

**People are often prejudiced in favour
of their own kind** Mt 5:46–47
pp Lk 6:32–34 *See also* Lk 7:29; 17:16;
Ac 10:45; Lk 11:18

**Prejudice on grounds of outward
appearance or behaviour** Jas 2:3–4 *See
also* 1Sa 16:7; 2Sa 14:25; Ecc 9:16;
Jn 8:15; Ro 14:1,3,10,13; 1Co 4:5;
Gal 2:6

Prejudice due to race Est 3:5–6 *See also*
Ezr 4:15–16; Ne 4:1–4; Est 3:8–14; 7:4;
Da 3:8–12; 6:3–9,13

Partiality forbidden Ex 23:3 *See also*
Lev 19:15; Jas 2:9

God is not prejudiced
God is impartial Ac 10:34 *See also*
Ro 2:11; Eph 6:9; Col 3:25

Job falsely accuses God of partiality
Job 9:16,20,30–31; 10:15–17

Prejudice which no contrary evidence would change
Lk 16:31 *See also* 1Sa 22:13–15;
Mt 11:21–23; 21:32; Ac 7:52; 13:41

The Sadducees' prejudice against the resurrection
Mt 22:23 pp Mk 12:18 pp Lk 20:27 *See
also* Ac 4:1–3; 23:8

8801

presumption

A form of self-confidence, which makes overconfident assumptions concerning one's importance and rights. It is criticised as a form of arrogance that is unacceptable among believers, whose lives should be characterised by humility.

Presumption is unacceptable
Ps 5:5; Isa 13:11 *See also* Nu 15:30; Dt 6:16; 18:20; Isa 45:9; Ro 2:4; 9:20; 1Co 10:9; Jas 4:13; 2Pe 2:10

Examples of presumption
Ge 11:1–4 *those preparing to build the tower of Babel in defiance of God*; Nu 14:40–45 *the Israelites, ignoring Moses' orders*; Lk 12:16–21 *the rich fool*

Humility is commended in place of presumption
Mic 6:8 *See also* Lk 14:10; 22:26; Ro 12:3; Jas 4:10; 1Pe 5:5

8802

pride

Arrogance or delusions of greatness on account of one's achievements, status or possessions. Scripture frequently speaks of God humbling the proud.

8803
pride, evil of

Pride is viewed as a great evil because it involves pretending to a greatness and glory that belong rightly to God alone.

The sinfulness of pride
It is condemned as evil 1Sa 15:23; Pr 21:4; Jas 4:16 *See also* Mk 7:22–23; Ro 1:29–30; 2Co 12:20; 2Ti 3:1–2; 1Jn 2:16

It is a characteristic of Satan Eze 28:2; 1Ti 3:6 *See also* 2Th 2:4 *the antichrist*

Warnings against pride
In the book of Proverbs Pr 16:5,18 *See also* Pr 3:7,34; 6:16–17; 11:2; 25:6–7,27; 26:12; 27:1; 29:23

Elsewhere in Scripture Ps 119:21 *See also* Lev 26:19
Proud talk: 1Sa 2:3; Ps 12:2–3; Jer 9:23–24
Ps 5:5; 40:4; 138:6; Isa 5:21;

Jer 13:15–17; Mt 23:12 pp Lk 14:11
Jesus Christ's teaching on pride; Ro 12:16; 1Co 10:12
God opposes the proud: 1Pe 5:5; Jas 4:6; Pr 3:34

The gospel excludes pride
Ro 3:27 *See also* Lk 18:9–14; Ro 4:2–3; 11:17–20; 1Co 1:26–31; Eph 2:8–9

Godliness involves rejecting pride
Pr 8:13 *See also* Ps 101:5; 131:1; Ro 12:3; 1Co 13:4; Gal 6:14

8804
pride, examples of

Scripture illustrates the many different ways in which pride manifests itself.

Pride in status
Ex 5:2 *Pharaoh;* 2Ki 5:11 *Naaman*
Hezekiah: 2Ki 20:13; 2Ch 32:25
Est 5:11–12 *Haman*
Moab: Isa 16:6; Jer 48:29
Isa 47:8 *Babylon;* Eze 16:49–50 *Sodom;*
Eze 28:2 *the king of Tyre*
Assyria: Eze 31:3,10
Da 5:23 *Belshazzar;* Ob 3 *Edom;*
Zep 2:15 *Nineveh*
Teachers of the law and Pharisees:
Mt 23:6–7 pp Mk 12:38–39
pp Lk 20:46; Lk 11:43
Ac 8:9 *Simon the sorcerer;* Rev 18:7
Babylon the Great

Pride in strength
1Sa 17:42 *Goliath;* 2Ki 14:9–10
Amaziah, king of Judah; 2Ki 18:33–35
the Assyrian commander
Israel: Isa 9:9–10; Hos 10:13
Isa 10:13 *the king of Assyria*
Nebuchadnezzar: Da 3:15; 4:30
Peter: Mt 26:33–35 pp Mk 14:29–31
pp Lk 22:33; Jn 13:37

Pride in wisdom
Isa 10:13 *the king of Assyria;* Ac 17:21;
Ro 1:22; 1Co 1:20; 3:18

Proud ambition
Isa 14:13–14 *the king of Babylon;*
2Th 2:3–4 *the antichrist*

Spiritual pride
2Ki 10:16; Job 32:1; 33:9; Isa 65:5;
Mt 6:2,3,16
Teachers of the law and Pharisees:
Mt 23:5,30; Mk 12:40 pp Lk 20:47;
Lk 16:14–15; 18:9,11–12; Jn 9:40–41
Lk 10:29 *an expert in the law*
Some Jews: Jn 8:33; 9:34; Ro 2:17–20
1Co 4:7,18; Rev 3:17 *the church in Laodicea*

8805
pride, results of

The real nature of pride can be seen in the fact that it leads to many other evils and ends in destruction.

Pride leads to other forms of evil
Self-deception Gal 6:3 *See also*
Dt 8:17–18; Isa 16:6; 47:10; Jer 49:16
pp Ob 3; 1Co 8:2; 1Ti 6:3–4

Spiritual blindness Jer 43:2 *See also*
Dt 8:14; Ne 9:16,29

A hard heart Ps 36:2 *See also* Ps 10:3; 52:1; Da 5:20

A malicious spirit Ps 119:85 *See also*
Ps 73:8; 140:5

Contempt for others Ps 123:4 *See also*
Ps 119:51; Pr 21:24

Quarrelling Pr 13:10

Violence Ps 73:6 *See also* Est 3:5–6; Ps 86:14

Injustice Ps 119:78 *See also* Ps 56:2

Oppression Ps 10:2 *See also* Ps 119:122; Hab 2:4–5

Contempt for God Ps 10:4 *See also* 2Ki 19:22

Pride may be accompanied by temporary prosperity
Ps 73:3 *See also* Ps 10:5

Pride ends in disaster
Pr 16:5,18 *See also* 2Sa 22:28
pp Ps 18:27; Job 40:11–12; Ps 31:23; 101:5; Pr 11:2; 15:25; 26:12; 29:23;
Isa 2:11–12,17; 13:11; 26:5; Zep 3:11; Mal 4:1; Lk 1:51–52; 1Ti 3:6

Examples of the proud being humbled
Pharaoh: Ex 14:28; Ne 9:10
2Ch 26:16 *Uzziah*
The king of Assyria: 2Ch 32:21; Isa 10:12,16
2Ch 32:25 *Hezekiah;* Est 7:10 *Haman;*
Isa 3:16–17 *the women of Zion*
The king of Babylon: Isa 13:19; 14:11–15
Isa 23:9; 25:10–12 *Moab;* Isa 28:1–3 *Samaria*
Babylon: Isa 47:10–11; Jer 50:31–32
Judah and Jerusalem: Jer 13:9; Eze 7:24
Eze 16:49–50 *Sodom*
The king of Tyre: Eze 28:5–9,17
Egypt: Eze 30:6; 32:12
Da 4:30–33 *Nebuchadnezzar;* Da 5:30
Belshazzar; Am 6:8; Zep 2:15 Nineveh;
Zec 9:6; 10:11 *Assyria;* Mt 11:23
Capernaum; Ac 12:21–23 *Herod;*
Rev 18:7–8 *Babylon the Great*

8807

profanity

Behaviour which dishonours God's name or brings it into disrepute. It is often the result of idolatry, injustice or irreverence. Scripture strongly admonishes God's people to avoid it.

General warnings against profanity
Lev 22:31–33 *See also* Lev 21:5–6

God's name profaned through idolatry
Through child sacrifice Lev 18:21 *See also* Lev 20:3; Dt 12:29–31; 18:9–13; 2Ki 16:1–4 pp 2Ch 28:1–4; 2Ki 17:16–17; 21:1–6 pp 2Ch 33:1–6; Ps 106:36–39; Isa 57:3–5; Jer 32:32–35; Eze 16:20–22

Through the worship of idols Eze 20:39 *See also* Jer 44:25–28; Eze 20:31; 43:6–9

God's name profaned through injustice and evil
Mal 2:10 *See also* Jer 34:12–16; Am 2:6–8; 5:7–15; Mic 6:6–8

God's name profaned through false swearing
Lev 19:12 *See also* Jer 5:1–2; Mt 5:33–37; Jas 5:12

God's name profaned through blasphemy
Isa 52:5–6 *See also* Ex 20:7 pp Dt 5:11; Lev 24:10–16; Isa 37:23; 2Pe 2:12

God's name profaned through irreverence
Lev 22:2 *See also* Eze 22:26; Zep 3:1–4; Mal 1:6–14

God's name profaned in the sight of foreign nations
Eze 39:7 *See also* Eze 20:13–44; 36:16–23; Ro 2:17–24; Isa 52:5

Penalties for profanity
Lev 20:1–5 *See also* Jer 44:25–30; Eze 13:17–23; 21:24–27; 39:1–8; Am 4:2–13; 8:4–14; Mal 2:7–9

See also

1025 God, anger of	5838 disrespect
5042 name of God, significance	5896 irreverence
5347 injustice	6026 sin, judgment on
5430 oaths, human	6130 corruption
5800 blasphemy	8444 honouring God
5818 contempt	8768 idolatry

8808

riches

Material possessions and wealth. Scripture stresses that riches originate from God: used wisely, they can be a blessing; used foolishly, they can lead people away from God.

This set of themes consists of the following:
8809 riches, nature of
8810 riches, dangers of
8811 riches, believers' attitudes towards
8812 riches, ungodly use of
8813 riches, spiritual

8809

riches, nature of

God has created an abundance of good things. Those who have material wealth should understand its true nature and acknowledge God.

God and riches
All riches belong to God the Creator Ps 24:1–2 *See also* Job 41:11; Ps 50:12; Hag 2:8

God gives of his riches 1Sa 2:7 *See also* Ecc 5:19; 1Ch 29:12; 2Ch 1:12

God gives the ability to produce wealth Dt 8:17–18 *See also* Ge 26:12–13; Dt 26:9–10

Riches may be a sign of God's blessing Pr 10:22 *See also* 2Ch 25:9; Job 1:9–10; Ps 112:1–3; 128:1–2; Pr 8:17–18

Riches should be thankfully received 1Ti 4:4–5 *See also* Mt 14:19; Ro 1:21; Col 3:17

The character of earthly riches
Riches provide great opportunity for doing good Ex 35:29; 1Ch 29:6–7; Lk 12:33; 16:9; 19:8; Ac 4:34–35

Riches do not satisfy Ecc 5:10 *See also* Pr 13:11; 27:20,24; Ecc 4:8; 6:7; Lk 12:18

Riches are insecure and uncertain 1Ti 6:17 *See also* Job 1:13–19; Pr 23:5; 27:24; Jer 48:36; Mt 6:19; 1Pe 1:18; Rev 18:14–20

Riches are for this life only 1Jn 2:17 *See also* Lk 12:13–21; 1Ti 6:6–8

See also

1325 God, the Creator	5503 rich, the
1330 God, the provider	5629 work, ordained by God
1335 blessing	5874 happiness
4035 abundance	5890 insecurity
5399 luxury	8352 thankfulness
5446 poverty	8701 affluence

8810

riches, dangers of

Material wealth can be a source of both physical and spiritual danger, against which believers are clearly warned to be on their guard.

Riches are spiritually dangerous
Love of riches a root of many evils 1Ti 6:10 *See also* Jos 7:11,20–21; 1Ti 3:3

They may lead to divided loyalty Mt 6:24 pp Lk 16:13 *See also* Mt 4:9–10; Jas 4:4

They may hinder people's response to the gospel Mt 13:22 pp Mk 4:19 pp Lk 8:14; Mt 19:21–22 pp Mk 10:21–22 pp Lk 18:22–23

They may create false security 1Ti 6:17 *See also* Job 31:24–28; Ps 52:6–7; Pr 11:28; Jer 49:4

They may make people proud Eze 28:5 *See also* Ps 62:10; Pr 18:23; 28:11; Hos 12:8

They may cause unbelief and anxiety Ecc 5:12 *See also* Job 20:17–20; Pr 15:6

They may lead people to forget God Pr 30:8–9 *See also* Dt 8:10–14; 32:15; Ne 9:25–26; Hos 13:6

Riches are physically dangerous
Working for them may cause excessive tiredness Pr 23:4 *See also* Jn 6:26–27

Enjoying them may lead to self-indulgence Jas 5:5 *See also* Hag 1:3–5; Mt 23:25; Lk 16:19–21; 1Ti 6:8–9

Misusing them may foster oppression and injustice Lev 19:13 *See also* Dt 24:12–15; Pr 22:16; Isa 1:23; Jer 22:13; Mic 6:12; Mal 3:5; Jas 2:6; 5:4

See also

5398 loss	6250 temptation, sources
5476 property	
5582 tiredness	8778 materialism
5870 greed, condemnation	8802 pride
	8821 self-indulgence
5973 unreliability	8849 worry

8811

riches, believers' attitudes towards

God entrusts some of his people with material wealth. If this is to be a blessing, it must be used in God-honouring ways.

Believers may be blessed with riches
Riches can be a blessing from God 1Ch 29:16 *See also* 1Ch 29:14–15; Job 1:9–10
Poverty is no certain mark of God's disfavour: 2Ki 4:1; Mt 8:20; Lk 6:20; 16:20–22; Ro 15:26

The attitude of believers towards riches
They acknowledge that their riches come from God 1Ch 29:12 *See also* Ecc 5:19–20

They devote their riches to God's service Pr 3:9–10 *See also* 1Ch 29:1–9; Ac 4:32–37

They support gospel work and workers Lk 8:1–3; Ac 16:15

They give to the poor 1Jn 3:17 *See also* Lk 19:8; Ac 9:36–39; Gal 2:10

They are generous 1Ti 6:18 *See also* Dt 15:10–11; 2Co 9:10–11

They remain humble Jas 1:10–11

They do not trust in riches 1Ti 6:17 *See also* Job 31:24–28; Pr 11:28; Jer 49:4

They do not set their heart on riches Ps 62:10 *See also* Lk 12:29–30

Believers value heavenly riches most
Mt 6:20–21 *See also* Lk 12:33–34; 1Ti 6:18–19

Examples of rich believers
Abraham Ge 12:1–3; 13:1–2

Solomon 2Ch 1:11–12; 9:22

Hezekiah 2Ch 32:27–29

Job Job 1:1–3

Joseph of Arimathea Isa 53:9; Mt 27:57–60 pp Mk 15:42–46 pp Lk 23:50–54 pp Jn 19:38–42

See also

5389 lending	8031 trust, importance
5413 money, attitudes	8262 generosity, human
5556 stewardship	
5558 storing	8291 kindness
7105 believers	8436 giving
7742 missionaries, support	possessions
7755 preaching, importance	8444 honouring God

8812
riches, ungodly use of

Ungodly people often make the possession of wealth a priority. They do not understand the true nature of wealth, and they do not realise that they will have to ~e God in judgment.

The ungodly grow rich
Ps 73:12 See also Lk 19:21; Jas 2:6–7

The ungodly misuse riches
They often obtain their riches unjustly Pr 10:2 See also 1Ki 20:5; Pr 13:11; 21:6; 22:16; Jer 17:11; Mic 2:1–5; 6:10–12; Hab 2:6–11

They accumulate and hoard their riches Pr 11:26 See also Job 27:16–17; Pr 3:27; Ecc 2:26; 5:10–14; Jas 5:1–3

They trust in their riches Ps 49:5–6 See also Job 31:24; Ps 52:7; Pr 11:28; Jer 9:23–24; 48:7

The ungodly suffer difficulties because of their riches
Pr 15:6 See also Pr 10:16; 13:7–8; 15:16–17

The ungodly, like all people, must leave their riches to others
Ps 49:10 See also Ps 39:6; Ecc 2:18–21; Lk 12:20

Jesus Christ warned the rich of their danger
Lk 6:24 See also Lk 12:15; 16:25

Examples of the ungodly rich
Nabal 1Sa 25:2–3

Rich young ruler Mk 10:17–23
pp Mt 19:16–24 pp Lk 18:18–25

See also
1025 God, anger of	5907 miserliness
5347 injustice	8714 dishonesty
5493 retribution	8790 oppression
5793 arrogance	9210 judgment,
5864 futility	God's

8813
riches, spiritual

Out of his infinite abundance God gives his people spiritual treasure. This, much more valuable than material wealth, is to be held in the highest esteem and sought after eagerly.

The riches of God
His wisdom and knowledge
Ro 11:33–36

His mercy, love and grace Eph 2:4; 3:8 See also Ro 2:4; Eph 2:7

His riches in Jesus Christ Col 2:2–3 See also Php 4:19; Col 1:27

God bestows spiritual riches on believers
His precious word Job 23:12;
Ps 19:9–10; 119:72,111,127

A wealth of spiritual qualities
Isa 33:5–6 See also Pr 2:1–5; 15:6; 2Co 9:10–11; Eph 1:7–8; Col 2:2–3; Jas 2:5

A glorious gospel 2Co 4:7

A costly kingdom Mt 13:44–46

A rich reward Ru 2:12 See also 1Sa 26:23; Ps 18:20; Pr 25:21–22; Col 3:24; Heb 10:35

A heavenly inheritance Ac 20:32 See also Eph 1:13–14,18; Col 1:12; 3:24; 1Pe 1:4

Christians and spiritual riches
Christians need to appreciate their spiritual riches Eph 1:7–8 See also Eph 1:18; Rev 2:9

Christians need to store up treasure in heaven Lk 12:33 See also Mt 6:20; Lk 12:20–21; 1Ti 6:19; Heb 11:26; Rev 3:18

See also
1055 God, grace & mercy	5591 treasure
1690 word of God	5705 inheritance, spiritual
2375 kingdom of God	6671 grace & Christian life
2420 gospel	8134 knowing God
5450 poverty, spiritual	8361 wisdom
5500 reward, God's people	9410 heaven

8815
ridicule

Laughing others to scorn, publicly humiliating or making fun of them in a demeaning manner.

8816
ridicule, nature of

Scripture declares that ridicule of the weak, the poor and the godly is unacceptable. Those who ridicule them invite judgment upon themselves.

Warnings against ridicule
Ridicule is foolish Pr 11:12 See also Pr 1:20–22; 14:6,9

Ridicule creates trouble Pr 9:12 See also Pr 19:29; 22:10; 29:8; 30:17; Mt 5:22 "Raca" probably means "empty-head", a term of derision.

Ridicule is a sign of the last days 2Pe 3:3–4 See also Jude 18

Examples of ridicule
Jdg 9:28–29,38; 1Sa 17:41–44; 1Ki 22:24; 2Ki 2:23–24; 18:23–25; Ne 2:19; 4:1–3

Ridicule associated with divine punishment
Isa 14:3–4 See also Isa 37:22–23; Jer 49:17; 50:13; Eze 36:1–7; Hab 2:6; Zep 2:15
Mic 2:3–4 See also Dt 28:37; 1Ki 9:6–9 pp 2Ch 7:19–22; Jer 19:8; 24:9; Eze 5:14–15; 23:32; 22:3–5; Hos 7:16; Mic 6:16

Prophets ridicule idolatry
1Ki 18:27 See also Isa 41:7,21–24; 44:12–17; 46:1–2; Jer 10:3–5

See also
5484 punishment by God	8365 wisdom, human
5550 speech, negative	8471 respect for human beings
5818 contempt	8760 fools, characteristics
5879 humiliation	8769 idolatry, in OT
5893 insults	8794 persecution
5900 laughter	
5951 slander	

8817
ridicule, objects of

Ridicule of God and of believers is to be expected, but it will bring divine retribution upon its perpetrators.

God ridiculed
Ps 74:10–18 See also 2Ki 19:4 pp Isa 37:4

Jesus Christ mocked
Lk 22:63–65 pp Mt 26:67–68 pp Mk 14:65 See also Lk 23:11; Mt 27:27–31 pp Mk 15:16–20; Jn 19:1–3; Mt 27:39–44 pp Mk 15:29–32 pp Lk 23:35–37

God's messengers scorned
2Ch 36:15–16 See also 2Ch 30:6–10; Ac 2:1–13; 17:17–18,32; Heb 11:36

God's people may suffer ridicule for their faith
Ps 22:6–8
Job's suffering increased by the ridicule of his persistent trust in God: Job 12:4; 16:10; 19:18; 30:1,9
Ps 35:15–25; 42:10; 69:10–12; 79:4; 89:50–51; 123:3–4; Jer 20:7; La 2:15–16; 3:14,63

Divine judgment because of ridicule
Zep 2:8–11 See also Pr 3:34; Isa 28:22

God ridicules his enemies
Ps 2:4–5 See also Ps 59:8

See also
1025 God, anger of	7140 people of God
2570 Christ, suffering	8728 enemies of Israel & Judah
5281 crucifixion	8782 mockery
5568 suffering, causes	8819 scoffing

8819
scoffing

Treating individuals, people, ideas or values with contempt or ridicule. Scripture indicates that God's word and his people can expect to be treated with contempt by the world.

Objects of scoffing
Nations punished by God Jer 19:8 See also 1Ki 9:6–9; Jer 49:17; 50:13; La 2:15–17; Zep 2:13–15

God's messengers 2Ch 36:15–16

Reasons for scoffing

Unbelief 2Pe 3:3–4 *See also* Ac 13:41; Hab 1:5; Jude 17–19

Arrogance Hab 1:10 *See also* Ps 73:3–8; Isa 28:14–15

Lack of wisdom Pr 29:9

God scoffs at the nations

Ps 59:5–8 *See also* Ps 2:1–6

See also

5818 contempt	8782 mockery
5893 insults	8794 persecution
5900 laughter	8815 ridicule
5951 slander	

8820

self-confidence

A positive assessment of one's own abilities and resources. Scripture censures excessive self-confidence, in that such an attitude lacks humility and fails to recognise the role of God's grace in the Christian life.

Excessive self-confidence

In one's own abilities Isa 28:15; Mt 26:33–35 pp Mk 14:29–31 pp Lk 23:33–34 pp Jn 13:37–38 *See also* Lk 22:33–34; Jdg 16:20; 1Ki 20:11; 2Ki 19:23–24; Job 8:13–14; Ps 49:5–6; Jer 17:5; Hos 12:8

Excessive self-confidence leads to pride Isa 9:9–10; Ob 3 *See also* Ge 11:4; 37:5; Ex 15:9; 2Ch 26:16; Pr 16:18; Isa 16:6; Eze 28:2; Ac 8:9; Ro 11:17–18; 1Co 5:2; 1Jn 2:16

Challenges to excessive self-confidence Ne 6:16; 1Co 4:7 *See also* Ps 49:12–13; 52:7; Pr 3:5–7; 11:28; 28:26; Isa 5:21; 14:13–15; Jer 49:7,4–5; Jas 4:13–16

Excessive self-confidence is a barrier to justification Lk 18:9–14

Accurate self-confidence

Of one's natural advantages Php 3:4–6 *See also* Ac 22:3,28

Of one's experience of God 2Co 12:2 *See also* Ac 22:4–21; 2Co 12:1; 13:5–6; Gal 1:13–17; 6:4

Of one's calling to serve 2Co 10:8 *See also* 2Co 10:13–17; Gal 2:7

Of one's service Ac 20:19; Ro 12:3 *See also* Ac 20:18,20–21; 1Co 9:15–18; 2Co 1:12; Php 2:16; 1Th 2:1–12

Of one's own weakness 2Co 11:29–30 *See also* 2Co 11:21–28; 12:9

Accurate self-estimates lead to justification Lk 18:9–14

Justified self-confidence may appear as pride 2Co 11:17–18

Jesus Christ's accurate assessment of himself

Mt 16:15–17 pp Mk 8:29 pp Lk 9:20–21 *See also* Mt 26:62–64; Jn 13:13

The proper source of all confidence

Jer 9:23–24 *See also* Ps 34:2; 44:6–7; Isa 10:15; 1Co 1:27–31

See also

5776 achievement	8213 confidence
5793 arrogance	8340 self-respect
5956 strength,	8757 folly, effects of
human	8801 presumption
5961 superiority	8802 pride
6121 boasting	8823 self-
8020 faith	righteousness

8821

self-indulgence

Throwing off restraint and discipline and yielding to the desire to gratify selfish appetites and cravings. Scripture warns against such a characteristic and urges, instead, self-control, generosity and consideration for others.

The desire to satisfy selfish cravings

Eph 2:3 *See also* Ro 7:8; 16:18; Tit 3:3; Jas 1:14; 2Pe 2:18–19; 1Jn 2:16

Examples of self-indulgent desires

Selfish ambition Jas 3:14–16 *See also* Pr 18:1; Gal 5:20; Php 1:17

The desire for one's own way Isa 56:11–12 *See also* Dt 29:19; Est 1:10–12; Jas 4:1–3

The desire for sexual gratification Gal 5:19 *See also* Ge 19:5 *Israelites' immorality with Moabite women:* Nu 25:1; 1Co 10:8 2Sa 11:2–4 *David's adultery with Bathsheba;* 2Sa 13:11–14 *Amnon's rape of Tamar;* Pr 7:16–18 *the lure of the adulteress;* 2Co 12:21 *sexual sin in the church at Corinth;* 2Pe 2:14 *sexual desires of false teachers*

The desire for wealth Jas 5:3–5 *See also* Jos 7:21 *Achan;* 1Sa 8:3 *Samuel's sons;* Jer 22:17 *Jehoiakim, king of Judah;* Hag 1:4 *the people of Judah;* Tit 1:11 *false teachers in Crete*

Indulgence in food and drink Isa 22:13 *See also* Pr 23:20; Ecc 6:7

Abandoning restraint

Eph 4:19 *See also* Ro 1:26–31; 2Ti 3:1–4; Jude 7

The consequences of self-indulgence

Self-indulgence proves futile Ecc 2:1–11 *See also* Lk 12:18–21

Self-indulgence leads to ruin Pr 21:17 *See also* Pr 6:26; 23:21,29–32; Lk 15:13–16; 1Ti 5:6

Self-indulgence brings God's judgment Ro 2:8 *See also* Pr 5:20–21; Php 3:19; Da 4:29–32 *God's judgment on Nebuchadnezzar's selfish pride;* Am 4:1–2 *God's judgment on Israel's pampered upper-class women;* Am 6:4–7 *God's judgment on Israel's self-indulgent nobility;* Lk 12:19–20

Dealing with self-indulgence **Receiving new life through Jesus Christ** Mt 23:25 *Dealing with self-indulgence requires an inner transformation. See also* Ro 12:2; Col 2:21–23

Ro 13:14 *See also* Gal 5:24; Tit 2:11–12 *Living in accordance with the Spirit:* Ro 8:5; Gal 5:16

Seeking God's will Ps 119:36; 1Pe 1:14; 4:2

Self-control 1Th 4:3–5 *See also* Pr 23:4; 1Co 9:25–27; 1Pe 4:7; 2Pe 1:6

Ruthless self-denial Col 3:5 *See also* Da 1:8; Mt 5:28–29; 1Pe 2:11

Consideration for others Gal 5:13 *See also* 1Co 10:23–24; Php 2:3–4

Generosity Dt 15:7–8; Lk 19:8

See also

5771 abstinence	8339 self-control
5832 desire	8475 self-denial
5850 excess	8777 lust
5856 extravagance	8827 selfishness
5866 gluttony	9210 judgment,
5869 greed	God's
6236 sexual sin	

8822

self-justification

A self-centred attitude by which people defend their actions and beliefs without reference to God. Scripture insists that the confidence and ultimate justification of believers lie with God, and condemns those who look elsewhere for these.

The impossibility of self-justification

Self-justification is impossible before a holy God Job 25:4 *See also* 1Sa 6:20; Mal 3:2; Rev 6:17

Justification is achieved by God, not by people Ro 5:1–2 *See also* Ro 3:27–30; Gal 2:20–21

How self-justification occurs

Self-justification occurs through ignoring God and his ways Ne 9:16 *See also* Lk 16:14–15

Self-justification occurs through pride Lk 18:9–14 *See also* Mt 23:1–7 pp Mk 12:38–39 pp Lk 20:45–46; Ro 2:17–27

Self-justification occurs through legalism Lk 10:25–29 *See also* Gal 3:1–5; 5:4

Self-justification causes separation from God and Jesus Christ

Gal 5:4 *See also* Mt 18:21–35; Lk 18:9–14

Examples of self-justification

Ge 3:8–12 *Adam;* Ex 32:19–24 *Aaron;* 1Sa 13:7–14 *Saul;* Mt 19:16–22 pp Mk 10:17–22 pp Lk 18:18–23 *the rich young man;* Php 3:4–9 *Paul as a Pharisee*

God's attitude to self-justification

God's condemnation of self-justification Ro 2:1–11

God's punishment of self-justification Pr 29:1 *See also* Ge 3:8–19; Jer 6:19–23

The true basis of justification
People are justified by God's grace alone Eph 2:8–9 *See also* Ro 3:21–24; Tit 2:11; 3:4–7

God accepts those who trust in his mercy without trying to justify themselves Ps 130:3–4 *See also* Ps 143:2; Lk 18:9–14

See also

1025 God, anger of	6676 justification
4030 world, behaviour in	6686 mercy
	8276 humility
5943 self-deception	8802 pride
6178 hardness of heart	8824 self-righteousness
6666 grace	9250 woe

8823

self-righteousness

A moral self-confidence and superiority arising from satisfaction in one's own achievements. True righteousness can only be found in a relationship with Jesus Christ.

8824
self-righteousness, nature of

Self-righteousness fosters the sinful human illusions of sinlessness, sufficiency and freedom.

The claim to self-righteousness
Ro 10:3 *See also* Lk 10:29; 18:9; Php 3:4–6

The illusion of self-righteousness
That people are sinless 1Jn 1:8 *See also* Pr 20:9; Hos 12:8

That people are guiltless Pr 16:2 *See also* Jer 2:34–35

That people are deserving Dt 9:4 *See also* Eze 28:2

The results of self-righteousness
Self-deception 1Jn 1:5–6 *See also* Pr 30:12; Jer 17:9; Mt 23:23–24,27–28; Lk 16:15; Heb 3:13

A sense of superiority Lk 18:9–11 *See also* Php 2:3; Col 2:16–18

Separation from God 1Jn 1:10 *See also* Zep 3:11; 2Co 10:18; Gal 5:4

Examples of self-righteousness
Nu 16:3 *some Israelites opposed to Moses*; 1Sa 15:13–21 *Saul*; Ps 10:5 *the wicked The Pharisees*: Lk 16:14; 18:9–14; Jn 9:39–41
Rev 3:17–18 *the church at Laodicea*

See also

5961 superiority	8767 hypocrisy
6020 sin	8802 pride
6121 boasting	8822 self-justification
6145 deceit	
8714 dishonesty	

8825
self-righteousness, and the gospel

Self-righteousness is an obstacle to the gospel, which insists that true righteousness can only be found in Jesus Christ.

The real issue of righteousness
Job 9:2 *See also* 1Sa 6:20; Job 4:17; 15:14; 32:2 *Although Elihu had misjudged Job, his main point, that only God was righteous, was correct*; Job 40:8; Ps 130:3

True righteousness is not the result of human effort
Ro 3:20 *Even though God's law tells people what God requires, human beings cannot keep it because of the weakness of their sinful human natures. See also* Ro 9:31; Gal 2:16; 3:11; Eph 2:8–9; Tit 3:5; 1Jn 2:16

Self-righteousness is a contradiction in terms
2Ch 6:36; Isa 64:6 *See also* Ezr 9:15; Ps 14:3; Ecc 7:20; Da 9:7; Ro 3:10,23

God calls people from their pretended self-righteousness
Isa 2:22 *See also* Ps 75:2–4; Jer 17:5; Mt 5:20

True righteouness
It comes from God Ro 10:3 *See also* Ps 98:2; Isa 46:13; 51:5; Jer 9:23–24; Ro 1:17

It is grounded in Jesus Christ Ac 13:39 *See also* 1Co 1:30; 2Co 5:21

It comes about by faith Ro 5:1 *See also* Gal 5:5; Eph 2:8

It is received in humility Lk 18:13–14 *See also* Ro 3:27; 4:2; 1Co 1:31; 4:7; 2Co 11:30; 12:9; Gal 6:13–14; Eph 2:9; Php 3:7–9

See also

6676 justification	8154 righteousness
8020 faith	8774 legalism

8827

selfishness

A self-centred concern for oneself, without due regard to the needs of others. Scripture treats selfishness as an aspect of sin and urges believers to care for others as well as themselves.

Selfishness is a characteristic of the sinner
Ro 8:5; 2Co 5:15 *See also* Pr 18:1; Ro 2:8; Eph 2:3

Selfishness is a characteristic of sinful society
2Ti 3:1–2 *See also* Jdg 17:6; 21:25

Expressions of selfishness
Greed Mt 23:25 *See also* Mk 12:7; Lk 12:13–21; Ac 5:3

Ambition Php 2:3 *See also* Jer 45:5; Gal 5:19–20; Php 1:17; Jas 3:14–16

Boastfulness Da 4:30

Examples of selfishness
Ge 11:4 *the builders of the tower of Babel*; Ge 13:10–11 *Lot in his choice of territory*; Eze 28:2–5 *the king of Tyre*; Eze 34:8 *Israel's leaders*; Mk 10:35 *James and John*

Self-absorption as the result of pain or depression
Job 14:22; 1Ki 19:10

Antidotes to selfishness
God's word Ps 119:36

The example of Jesus Christ Ro 15:3 *See also* Php 2:4–8

Dying to the old nature Ro 6:6 *See also* Eph 4:22; Col 3:9

Serving one another 1Pe 4:10 *See also* 1Co 10:24

Loving one another Jn 13:34 *See also* Mt 22:39; Ro 13:8–10

See also

4030 world, behaviour in	6121 boasting
	6133 coveting
5503 rich, the	6166 flesh, sinful nature
5558 storing	
5786 ambition, negative	8356 unselfishness
	8802 pride
5869 greed	8821 self-indulgence

8828

spite

The malicious desire to retaliate in words or action. It may be in response to good or evil. Believers are to rid themselves of any such vindictive spirit.

Examples of people acting out of spite
In response to good 1Ki 19:1–2 *Jezebel*; 2Ch 16:10 *Asa, king of Judah*; Est 3:6 *Haman*; Mt 14:3–12 pp Mk 6:17–29 *Herodias*; Jn 12:10 *the chief priests Stephen's persecutors*: Ac 7:54,57–58

In response to evil Ps 140:3 *See also* Ge 27:41 *Esau Joseph's brothers*: Ge 37:4,8,11,18–27 Eze 25:15 *the Philistines*; Ac 23:12–15 *some Jews*

Spite has no place in the lives of believers
Believers are to rid themselves of all spitefulness Eph 4:31 *See also* 1Co 5:8; Col 3:8; 1Pe 2:1

As a result believers are enabled not to retaliate against others Lev 19:18 *See also* Pr 20:22; 24:29; Mt 5:38–40; Ro 12:17,19–21; 1Th 5:15; 1Pe 2:21–23; 3:9

See also

5495 revenge & retaliation	5818 contempt
	5875 hatred
5510 rumours	5917 plans
5546 speech	5951 slander
5817 conspiracies	

8829

superstition

Misplaced credulity concerning the supernatural, which leads to irrational fear, misdirected reverence, false religion and magic, and which brings God's judgment. Scripture warns against and condemns such things.

Superstition causing irrational fear
Jer 10:2 *See also* Job 15:20–24; 18:11

Fear of Jesus Christ or his disciples
Mt 14:26–27 pp Mk 6:49–50 See also
Mt 14:2 pp Mk 6:14; Ac 5:13

Fear of other gods 1Ki 20:23 See also
1Ki 18:28; 20:28; Ac 17:23

Misunderstanding God's work
Ac 8:18–19 See also Lk 24:36–37;
Ac 12:15; 19:13 invoking the name of
Jesus Christ for exorcism as though it were
a magic formula; Ac 28:3–4

**Superstition leading to
misdirected reverence**
Ac 14:11–13 See also Ac 28:5–6;
Rev 22:8–9

False religion
Jdg 10:6–7 See also 1Sa 7:3–4;
1Ki 13:33; 14:15–16,22–24;
2Ch 28:2–4 pp 2Ki 16:3–4; Jer 9:14;
44:17–18; Hos 11:2

Unhelpful speculations
1Ti 1:3–4 See also Isa 65:2–3;
66:17–18; Eze 13:2,17; 1Ti 6:3–4

**The true demonic source of
superstition**
1Ti 4:1 See also Rev 9:20–21

See also
1409 dream	8333 reverence
4130 demons	8709 astrology
4155 divination	8747 false gods
4185 sorcery and	8748 false religion
magic	8750 false teachings
5423 myths	8768 idolatry
5864 futility	

8830

suspicion

The belief that people or things are
not as they appear. It may be based
on evidence, but it can also be ill-
founded, occasioned by jealousy or
malicious gossip.

Suspicion of sexual impurity
Dt 22:13–19 See also Nu 5:11–31

Suspicion of drunkenness
1Sa 1:9–18 See also Ac 2:13–15

Suspicion of espionage
2Sa 10:1–5

Suspicion of treachery
1Sa 18:6–9 See also Ex 1:9–10;
1Sa 20:24–31; 21:10–12; 29:1–11

Lack of suspicion
2Sa 15:7–12 See also 1Sa 27:1–12;
2Sa 13:1–11,23–29

Evil suspicions
1Ti 6:3–5

See also
5969 treachery	8719 distrust
6242 adultery	8721 doubt
8277 innocence	8773 jealousy

8831

syncretism

The incorporation into religious
faith and practice of elements from
other religions, resulting in a loss of

integrity and assimilation to the
surrounding culture.

Syncretism in Israel
God's claim to exclusive worship, the
basis of the rejection of syncretism
Ex 20:3 pp Dt 5:7 See also Dt 6:13–15;
Jos 24:14–15; 1Ki 18:21

Syncretism forbidden to Israel
Ex 34:15–16 See also Dt 7:1–6;
Jos 23:16; 1Sa 7:3

Israelite practice of syncretism
Jer 19:4–5 See also 2Ki 17:34–41;
21:1–7 pp 2Ch 33:1–7; Eze 8:9–16

The consequence of syncretism Jer 2:5
See also Dt 18:9–13; 2Ki 17:15–17;
Isa 2:6

Punishment for syncretism Zep 1:4–5
See also Dt 17:2–7; Jer 19:10–13;
Hos 2:2–13

Syncretism in NT times
Mediterranean society was
syncretistic Ac 14:11–13; 17:16–23;
19:13–16

NT opposition to syncretism Heb 13:9
See also 1Co 10:21; Gal 4:9–10; Col 2:18

**Monotheism is incompatible with
syncretism**
Isa 44:6 See also Dt 6:4–5; Isa 43:10–12;
1Co 8:4–6

See also
1345 covenant	7442 shrine
5441 philosophy	8138 monotheism
7312 Baal	8747 false gods
7374 high places	8768 idolatry

8832

testing

God allows his people to pass
through certain experiences, so that
he may see, and prove to them, that
their faith in him is genuine.
Believers sometimes doubt God and
test him, to see if he is true to his
word, but this is forbidden in
Scripture.

God tests his people
Jas 1:2–3; 1Pe 1:7 See also Job 7:17–18;
23:10; Ps 11:5; Isa 1:25; Zec 13:9;
Mal 3:3; Jas 1:12

**Examples of God testing his
people collectively**
Ex 16:4; Dt 8:2–3 See also Ex 20:20 at
the giving of the law; Dt 8:16 over the
gathering of manna; Dt 13:3–4 by their
attitude to a false prophet; Jdg 2:20–3:4
by leaving nations in the promised land

**Examples of God testing his
people individually**
Ge 22:1–2 See also Jdg 7:4–7 Gideon;
2Ch 32:31 Hezekiah; 2Co 12:7–9 Paul

**Jesus Christ tested the faith of
people when he was on earth**
Jn 6:5–6 See also Mt 15:22–28
pp Mk 7:25–30 a Canaanite woman;
Mk 8:17–21 his disciples

**Believers have a responsibility to
test the quality of their lives**
Ro 12:2 See also Ps 17:3

David prayed to God to test him: Ps 26:2;
139:23
La 3:40; 2Co 13:5; Gal 6:4; 1Th 5:21

**God will make a final test of
believers' lives and service**
1Co 3:12–15

**People may test God as an
expression of faith and
obedience**
Mal 3:10 See also Jdg 6:39

**People must not test God as an
expression of doubt and
disobedience**
Ex 17:2 See also Ex 17:7 fn;
Nu 14:22–23; Dt 6:16; 33:8;
Ps 78:18,41,56; 95:8 fn; Mt 4:7
pp Lk 4:12; Dt 6:16; Mt 19:3 pp Mk 10:2;
Ac 5:9; 15:10; Heb 3:8–9

The command to test the spirits
1Jn 4:1

See also
4351 refining	5593 trial
4645 fleece	8027 faith, testing of
5473 proof through	8104 assurance
testing	8124 guidance

8833

threats

Intimidating announcements of
action to be taken unless conditions
are met. God uses threats against
tyrannical and disobedient earthly
rulers as a means of restoring them
to obedience and humility in his
sight. God's people are not to
threaten others and though the
wicked will sometimes seek to
intimidate them, they are to rely on
God's protection.

God threatened Pharaoh
Ex 8:1–4,21; 9:2–3,13–14; 10:3–6

God threatened his own people
In general Jos 23:15–16 See also
Lev 26:14–20; Dt 11:26–28; 28:15–20;
1Sa 12:15,25; 1Ki 9:6–7

Regarding the Babylonian captivity
Eze 6:9–10 See also Jer 6:8; 22:5–7;
44:28–29

**Threats made by God may be
averted**
Through a faithful intercessor
Ex 32:11–14 See also Ne 1:8–9

Through turning from evil Jnh 3:10

**The result of threats inflicted by
God may be alleviated**
Through returning to the LORD
Dt 30:1–3

Through submission to God's will
Jer 27:6–13

**God's people may be threatened
by others**
Ac 9:1 See also 2Ki 18:17–35
pp Isa 36:1–20; Ne 4:7–8; Ps 55:9–11;
73:8

God's people, when threatened, are to rely on him
Ps 64:1–10 See also 2Ki 19:6–7
pp Isa 37:6–7; Ne 6:11–14;
Isa 30:17–18; Ac 4:17–21,29–30

God's people are not to threaten others
Eph 6:9 See also 1Pe 2:20–23

The rich are more likely to be threatened than the poor
Pr 13:8

See also
5828 danger
5937 rivalry
5959 submission
5978 warning
6702 peace,
destruction
8483 spiritual
warfare, causes

8650 hands, lifting
up
8727 enemies
8754 fear
8790 oppression
8794 persecution
9210 judgment,
God's

8834

unbelief

The lack of faith and trust in God
that challenges his truthfulness and
finds expression in disobedience and
rebellion.

8835
unbelief, nature and effects of

Unbelief, or the failure to trust God,
holds back his blessing and leads to
condemnation and spiritual death.

The nature of unbelief
Not trusting God Ps 78:22

Rebelling against God Heb 3:12 See also
Ps 78:40; Heb 3:16

Disobeying God Heb 11:31 NIV
footnote. See also Eph 2:2; Heb 3:18–19;
4:11

Questioning God's truthfulness
1Jn 5:10 See also Ps 106:24; 1Jn 1:10

Unbelief as the result of the devil's work
Taking away God's word Lk 8:12
pp Mt 13:19 pp Mk 4:15

Causing spiritual blindness 2Co 4:4 See
also Ro 1:21; 2Co 4:3; Eph 4:18

Unbelief as the result of not belonging to God
Jn 10:26 See also Jn 5:38; 8:44–45;
12:37–40; 1Co 2:14

Unbelief hinders Jesus Christ's miracles
Mt 13:58 pp Mk 6:5–6

The consequences of persistent unbelief
Failure to receive God's reward
Heb 3:19 The "rest" that God's people
enjoyed on entering the promised land is
here taken to symbolise the final reward
prepared by God for his people. See also
Heb 4:1–2,6; Jude 5

Exclusion from the people of God
Ro 11:20 See also Heb 6:4–6

Death in sin Jn 8:24 See also Ps 106:43;
Mk 4:12; Ac 10:43

God's wrath Jn 3:36 See also Ro 1:18;
2:5,8

Condemnation by God Jn 3:18 See also
Mk 16:16; Lk 12:46; Jn 12:48; 2Th 2:12;
Rev 21:8

See also
1025 God, anger of
1310 God as judge
5135 blindness,
spiritual
5484 punishment by
God
6026 sin, judgment
on
6125 condemnation,
divine

6245 stubbornness
8032 trust, lack of
8718 disobedience
8742 faithlessness
8840 unfaithfulness
to God
9024 death, spiritual

8836
unbelief, as response to God

The stubborn and sinful refusal to
accept God's word and his
messengers. Since the coming of
Jesus Christ it is frequently expressed
in the rejection of his person and
teaching.

Unbelief expressed towards God
Ps 78:22

Rebellion against God 2Ki 17:14–15
See also Ne 9:16; Ps 78:17–19; 95:8–11;
Isa 65:2; Jer 7:26; Ac 7:51; Heb 3:12–19

Rejection of God's promises Ps 106:24
See also Ro 4:20; 10:16; Heb 4:2

Unbelief expressed towards Jesus Christ
Rejection by those close to him Jn 1:11
See also Mt 13:54–58 pp Mk 6:1–6;
Lk 4:14–30; Jn 7:5

Rejection of his miracles Mt 12:22–24
pp Mk 3:22 pp Lk 11:14–16

Rejection of his claims Lk 22:67;
Jn 5:37–38; 6:36,64; 10:24–26; 1Pe 2:7

Rejection of his words Jn 3:11–12 See
also Jn 5:46–47; 8:45

Demands for miraculous signs Jn 4:48
See also Mt 12:38–39 pp Lk 11:29;
Mt 16:4 pp Mk 8:12; Lk 11:16

Unbelief expressed towards God's messengers
Ge 19:16 Lot; Ex 4:1 Moses; 2Ki 7:2
Elisha; 2Ch 32:15 Sennacherib of Assyria
urges the inhabitants of Jerusalem to
disbelieve Hezekiah's words; Isa 53:1
Isaiah; Mt 21:32 John the Baptist
Paul and Barnabas: Ac 13:50; 14:2
Ac 17:13 Paul and Silas
Paul: Ac 19:9; 28:24

Unbelief expressed in unrighteousness
Tit 1:15 See also Ro 1:18; 2Th 2:12; 3:2;
1Ti 1:13

Unbelief despite miraculous signs
Ne 9:16–17 See also Ex 4:8–9; Ps 78:32;
Jn 9:18; 10:31–33; 12:37

Means of overcoming unbelief
Jn 10:37–38 the evidence of Jesus Christ's
miracles; Ro 10:14–15 preaching the
gospel; 1Co 14:22–24 prophecy in
worship; 1Pe 3:1 the behaviour of a
believing spouse; 1Ti 1:13 God's mercy

See also
1418 miracles,
responses
1690 word of God
2018 Christ, divinity
2363 Christ,
preaching &
teaching
2369 Christ,
responses to
2545 Christ,
opposition to

5265 complaints
5467 promises,
divine
6178 hardness of
heart
6222 rebellion
against God
6231 rejection of
God
7773 prophets, role

8837
unbelief, and life of faith

Believers may go through periods of
doubt and indecision, especially on
account of difficulties in trusting
God or accepting certain aspects of
his will for them.

General examples of unbelief in believers
Abraham Ge 17:17 See also Ge 15:8
Sarah Ge 18:13–14
Moses Nu 11:21–22
Gideon Jdg 6:12–13,17,36–40
Elisha's servant 2Ki 4:42–44
Zechariah Lk 1:20
John the Baptist Mt 11:3

The unbelief of Jesus Christ's disciples
Unbelief concerning Jesus Christ's
power over the natural world
Mt 8:24–26 pp Mk 4:38–40
pp Lk 8:23–25; Mt 14:26 pp Mk 6:49
Mt 14:29–31; 16:8–10 pp Mk 8:17–21
See also Mk 6:37 pp Jn 6:7; Mk 6:52;
Mt 15:33 pp Mk 8:4; Jn 11:39;
Ac 12:15–17

Unbelief concerning Jesus Christ's
resurrection Mk 16:14; Lk 24:25 See
also Mk 16:9–13; Lk 24:11,37–41;
Jn 20:25

Unbelief concerning Jesus Christ's
power to heal Mt 17:17 pp Mk 9:19
pp Lk 9:41 See also Mt 17:19–20

Encouragements in overcoming unbelief
Mk 9:24; Jn 14:11 See also Mt 11:4–6;
Jn 10:37–38; 20:30–31; Ro 4:20

See also
1175 God, will of
2015 Christ,
compassion
2048 Christ, love of
2066 Christ, power of
2560 Christ,
resurrection

6257 unbelievers
8020 faith
8031 trust,
importance
8721 doubt
8726 doubters
9610 hope

8839

unfaithfulness

The failure to fulfil the obligations of
a relationship, resulting in disloyalty
to God and to others.

8840
unfaithfulness, to God

In the OT the terms of the covenant
with God were constantly broken by
Israel by acts of idolatry and

disobedience. The consequence was God's judgment, which eventually included exile.

Warnings within the covenant
Ne 1:8; Lev 26:1,14–17,31–33; Dt 4:25–27; 8:19–20; Pr 2:22; Eze 14:13; 15:8

Unfaithfulness seen in idolatry
Idolatry as marital unfaithfulness
Jer 3:20 *The covenant between God and Israel at Sinai viewed in terms of a marriage contract;* Jer 3:6–9 *See also* Jer 3:12–14; 9:2; 31:32; Hos 1:2

Idolatry as prostitution 1Ch 5:25; Hos 4:10–12; 9:1

Idolatry as abandoning God Jer 1:16 *See also* Jdg 10:13; Jer 5:19; 15:6

Unfaithfulness seen in other forms of disobedience
Trust in money and possessions
Job 31:24–28 *See also* Jer 49:4

Doing wrong to others Nu 5:5–6 *See also* Lev 6:2; Pr 11:3; 13:2; Isa 1:21–23; Hos 6:6–7

Marrying foreign wives Ezr 10:2 *See also* Ezr 9:1–4; Ne 13:27

Withholding tithes and offerings
Jos 7:1; 22:20; Mal 3:8

Breaches in the ritual law 1Sa 14:33; Mal 1:7–8

Unfaithfulness as a characteristic of God's people throughout the OT
Jer 5:11 *See also* Ac 7:37–41; Jdg 2:16–17; Ne 9:26; Hag 1:7–9

Unfaithfulness among Israel's leadership
The unfaithfulness of the priesthood
Ezr 9:1–2 *See also* 2Ch 36:14; Eze 22:26; Mal 2:7–8

Unfaithful kings
Solomon's unfaithfulness leads to unfaithfulness among his subjects:
1Ki 11:4–5,33
2Ch 12:1–2 *Rehoboam;* 2Ch 26:16–18 *Uzziah's bad example*
Ahaz: 2Ch 28:19–23; 29:19
Manasseh: 2Ki 21:9 pp 2Ch 33:9;
2Ki 21:16; 2Ch 33:19

Unfaithfulness leads to judgment
Dt 32:20; Ps 73:27; 78:56–59; Pr 21:18

Individuals judged for unfaithfulness
Jos 7:1,25; 1Ch 10:13

Wandering in the desert Nu 14:33 *See also* Nu 14:34–35

The people taken into exile Eze 39:23 *See also* 1Ch 9:1; Da 9:7

Restoration following repentance
Eze 39:25–26 *God's purpose through the exile is to bring about the eventual repentance and restoration of his people.* *See also* Lev 26:40–42; Dt 30:1–3; Ne 1:8–9

See also
1310 God as judge	7141 people of God, OT
1349 covenant at Sinai	7215 exile, the
5482 punishment	7766 priests
6189 immorality, examples	8718 disobedience
6243 adultery, spiritual	8769 idolatry, in OT
	8810 riches, dangers
	8834 unbelief

8841
unfaithfulness, to people

A breach of the trust that is expected within specific relationships, and also a failure of mutual responsibility within a community life; the breaking of the last six of the Ten Commandments.

Unfaithfulness to one another breaks God's commandments
Lev 19:18 *See also* Ex 20:12–17; Dt 5:16–21; Mt 22:39 pp Mk 12:31; Ro 1:29–31

Unfaithfulness to promises made
Nu 30:2 *See also* Nu 30:9; Jos 9:20; 1Sa 20:42

Unfaithfulness in business
Mt 25:24–26; Lk 16:3–12; 19:8

Unfaithfulness to the marriage covenant
Mal 2:14–15

The seriousness of marital unfaithfulness
Adultery in the OT punishable by death:
Lev 20:10; Dt 22:22; Jn 8:3–5
Sexual unfaithfulness is given as a possible ground for divorce in the NT because it undermines the marriage bond: Mt 5:32; 19:9

Examples of marital unfaithfulness
Jdg 19:1–2
Hosea's relationship with his faithless wife reflects God's relationship with his idolatrous people: Hos 1:2–3; 2:2,5

Unfaithfulness among family and friends
Mic 7:5–6

God's people may face opposition from their families Jer 12:6 *See also* 2Sa 15:10; Mt 10:21 pp Mk 13:12 pp Lk 21:16

Unfaithful friends cause great sorrow
Ps 55:12–14 *See also* Ps 41:9; 55:20–21
Times of trouble may prove a friend unfaithful: Job 6:14–17; Ps 38:11; Pr 25:19

Unfaithfulness to Jesus Christ during his earthly ministry
Jesus Christ deserted by his followers
Jn 6:66; 16:32 *See also* Mt 26:31 pp Mk 14:27; Zec 13:7; Mt 26:56 pp Mk 14:50

Jesus Christ betrayed by Judas
Mt 26:47–50 pp Mk 14:43–46 pp Lk 22:47–48; Jn 18:2–5

Jesus Christ denied by Peter Mt 26:74 pp Mk 14:71–72 pp Lk 22:59–61; Jn 18:26–27

Unfaithfulness to God's appointed leaders
The Israelites challenge their leaders
Ex 16:3–8 *See also* 1Sa 8:7–8

Paul's friends desert him 2Ti 1:15 *See also* 2Ti 4:9–11,16

Examples of treachery and betrayal
Jdg 16:18–19 *Samson betrayed by Delilah;* 2Sa 3:27 *Joab murders Abner;* 2Sa 4:5–6 *Ish-Bosheth assassinated by Recab and Baanah;* 2Sa 11:14–15 *David has Uriah killed in battle;* 2Sa 20:9–10 *Amasa killed by Joab;* 1Ki 21:8–10 *Jezebel's treachery towards Naboth*

See also
5675 divorce	8298 love for one another
5680 family	
5692 friends, bad	8452 neighbours, duty to
5708 marriage	
5798 betrayal	8712 denial of Christ
5973 unreliability	8714 dishonesty
6242 adultery	
8253 faithfulness, examples	

8843

unforgivable sin

The wilful, outwardly expressed and impenitent slander against the Holy Spirit, when Jesus Christ's mighty works, clearly performed by the power of the Holy Spirit, are attributed to Satan, thus subjecting Christ to public disgrace.

The unforgivable sin is slandering the Holy Spirit
Mt 12:31–32 pp Mk 3:28–29 *See also* Lk 12:10; Heb 10:26–29

The unforgivable sin is attributing Jesus Christ's miracles to Satan
Mk 3:30 *See also* Mt 12:24 pp Mk 3:22 pp Lk 11:15

See also
2369 Christ, responses to	5800 blasphemy
	5951 slander
3245 Holy Spirit, blasphemy against	6193 impenitence
	8704 apostasy
	8844 unforgiveness

8844

unforgiveness

God remains unforgiving to those described as unrepentant, who blaspheme against the Holy Spirit and who are themselves unforgiving. Being unforgiving and demonstrating true love are mutually exclusive.

The unforgiveness of God
Towards the unrepentant Dt 29:18–21 *See also* Ex 23:21; 34:7; Nu 14:18; Jos 24:19; 2Ki 24:4; Isa 30:12–14; Jer 5:7; La 3:42; Hos 1:6; Lk 18:10–14; Heb 10:28–31

Towards those whose hearts are hardened Jos 11:20; Mt 13:13–15 pp Mk 4:11–12 pp Lk 8:9–10; Isa 6:9–10; Jn 9:39–41; 20:23

Towards those who blaspheme
against the Holy Spirit Mt 12:31–32
pp Mk 3:28–29 pp Lk 12:10 *Blasphemy
against the Spirit probably involves
attributing the authenticating miracles of
Jesus Christ to the work of Satan rather
than to the power of the Holy Spirit. See
also* 1Jn 5:16

Towards those who are not forgiving
Mt 6:14–15; Jas 2:12–13 *See also*
Mt 5:23–24; 7:1–2 pp Lk 6:37–38;
Mt 18:32–35; 23:23; Mk 11:25–26 *NIV
footnote at verse 26*; Ro 14:9–13

**God's people call upon him not to
forgive the wicked**
Jer 18:23 *See also* Ne 4:5; Isa 2:9

True love is forgiving
Ro 5:8; 1Co 13:4–5 *See also* Ps 86:5;
130:3–4; Da 9:9; Mic 7:18; Ac 13:38;
Ro 15:7; 2Co 2:5–11; Eph 4:32;
Col 3:13

See also

3245 Holy Spirit,	6193 impenitence
blasphemy	6652 forgiveness
against	6686 mercy
5883 impatience	6732 repentance
5897 judging others	8282 intolerance
5972 unkindness	8843 unforgivable
6178 hardness of	sin
heart	

8845

unfruitfulness

A lack of fruitfulness, whether
material or spiritual, which is often
seen as a sign of God's disfavour or
anger.

**Unfruitfulness as a moral or
spiritual condition**
Mt 21:19 pp Mk 11:14 *See also*
Job 15:32–33; Eze 17:9; 19:10–12;
Mt 21:43; Heb 6:7–8

Reasons for unfruitfulness
Disobedience Lev 26:18–20 *See also*
Dt 11:17; 28:15–16; Ps 78:46;
107:33–34; Isa 5:10; 32:10; Hos 8:7;
Hag 2:19

A continuing preoccupation with the
world Mt 13:22 pp Mk 4:19 pp Lk 8:14

A broken relationship with Jesus
Christ Jn 15:4 *See also* Jn 15:6

Some results of unfruitfulness
Unfruitfulness condemned Isa 5:1–7

Unfruitfulness leads to rejection
Mt 3:8–10 pp Lk 3:9; Mt 7:19

Unfruitfulness retrieved
Lk 13:6–9 *The parable holds out the
possibility of restoration.*

Discipline with a view to renewed
fruitfulness Jn 15:2

See also

1025 God, anger of	8102 abiding in
4815 drought	Christ
4822 famine	8256 fruitfulness
5225 barrenness	8347 spiritual
5343 idleness	growth
5881 immaturity	8718 disobedience
6230 rejection	9165 restoration

8846

ungodliness

The state of believing in God, while
adopting a lifestyle which seems to
deny this. Believers are warned to
guard against ungodliness.

Expressions of ungodliness
A defiant spirit towards God Mt 7:6
*Jesus Christ is teaching his disciples not to
share the riches of spiritual truth with
persons who are persistently
unappreciative, vicious and defiant. See
also* Job 36:8–13; Ps 73:8–11

Mocking God and/or his people
2Pe 3:3–4 *See also* Ps 35:15–16;
Ac 13:40–41; Hab 1:5

Evil behaviour Isa 32:6–7 *See also*
Pr 11:9; Jnh 1:1–2; 1Ti 1:9–11

Examples of ungodliness
2Ch 36:15–16 *the southern kingdom of
Judah*; Ps 52:1–3 *Doeg the Edomite*;
Isa 9:13–17 *the northern kingdom of
Israel*
Judah's religious leaders: Jer 23:11–12,
15–17
Christians before conversion: 1Co 6:9–11;
Eph 2:1–3
2Ti 3:1–5 *people in general during the last
days (the time between the first and second
comings of Jesus Christ)*; Heb 12:16 *Esau*

God will judge the ungodly
In this life Pr 11:31 *See also* Pr 1:28–33;
3:33–34; Isa 10:5–7; 33:14; Ro 1:18

At the final judgment 2Pe 3:7 *See also*
Job 27:8; Pr 3:34; 1Pe 4:18; 2Pe 2:4–10;
Jude 14–15

Jesus Christ died for the ungodly
Ro 5:6–8; 11:26; Isa 59:20

**God's people must guard against
ungodliness**
By relying upon God's grace
Tit 2:11–12

By putting no confidence in ungodly
people 1Co 6:1 *See also* Ps 1:1;
Jude 3–4, 17–19

By avoiding ungodly teaching and
behaviour 2Ti 2:16 *See also* 1Ti 4:7;
6:20–21

See also

4030 world,	8744 faithlessness
behaviour in	as
5829 defiance	disobedience
6166 flesh, sinful	8782 mockery
nature	8812 riches, ungodly
6169 godlessness	use
6187 immorality	8819 scoffing
8265 godliness	9210 judgment,
8734 evil	God's

8847

vulgarity

**Believers are to avoid vulgar
intentions**
The men of Sodom had vulgar
intentions Ge 19:5

They were judged by God Ge 19:24–25;
2Pe 2:6–7; Jude 7

The men of Gibeah had vulgar
intentions Jdg 19:22,25

They were punished by the Israelites
Jdg 20:4–7,33–36,48

Such vulgarity is condemned by God
Lev 18:22; Ro 1:24–28

Paul warns against vulgar speech
Eph 4:29; 5:4; Col 3:8

**Believers are to avoid vulgar
actions**
Noah got drunk and exposed himself
Ge 9:21–22

Lot's daughters became pregnant by
their father Ge 19:31–36

**Some converts led vulgar and
depraved lives before conversion**
1Co 6:9–11

**The Cretans had a reputation for
vulgarity**
Tit 1:12,15–16

See also

4435 drinking	6237 sexual sin
5546 speech	6238 homosexuality
6188 immorality,	8308 modesty
sexual	

8848

worldliness

The sinful tendency to conform to
the world, to be contrasted with the
biblical command to maintain
contact with the world while
avoiding becoming like the world.
Believers are called to live in the
world, while not being of the world.
This attitude is supremely
exemplified in the ministry of Jesus
Christ.

**The paradox of God's love for a
sinful world**
Jn 3:16; 1Jn 2:15–16

**God's people are called to be
separate from the world, yet a
source of blessing to it**
The example of Abraham Ge 12:1–3
*The life of Abraham illustrates the
important biblical balance, called to
separation from his native environment to
be a blessing to the nations. See also*
Ge 15:7; 18:18; Gal 3:8

The example of others Ge 41:56–57
Joseph; Da 2:48–49 *Daniel and his friends*

**Conformity to the pagan
standards of the OT world
disparaged**
Lev 18:28 *with respect to sexual perversion*
With respect to concepts of leadership:
1Sa 8:5; 1Ki 21:7
1Ki 11:7–8 *with respect to idolatry;*
Isa 3:19 *with respect to pride*
With respect to self-reliance: Isa 31:1;
Zec 4:6

**God's concern for the nations of
the world**
Isa 49:6 *See also* Jnh 4:11; Rev 22:2

Jesus Christ is a model of the required balance of being in the world but not of it

He was in the world Jn 3:16–17 See also Jn 9:5; 16:28

He was not of the world Jn 8:23 See also Lk 4:5–8 pp Mt 4:8–10; Jn 17:14; 18:36; 1Jn 3:1

He was a friend of the disreputable Mt 11:19 See also Mk 2:16; Lk 7:44–48

He was concerned for outsiders Jn 10:16 See also Mt 28:19; Mk 7:24–30 pp Mt 15:21–28; Ac 1:8

Believers are called to live in the world, while not being of it

They have been chosen out of the world Jn 15:19 See also Jn 17:14,16; 2Co 6:17

They must avoid conformity with the world Ro 12:2 See also 1Th 4:3–5; 2Ti 4:10; Tit 2:12; Jas 1:27; 1Pe 1:14–16; 4:3–4; 1Jn 2:15; 5:4

They must maintain contact with the world 1Co 5:9–10 See also Jn 17:11

They must do good in the world Gal 6:10 See also Tit 2:14

See also

1335 blessing	8211 commitment to
2015 Christ,	world
compassion	8217 conformity
2324 Christ as	8269 holiness,
Saviour	separation
4030 world,	from worldly
behaviour in	8324 purity
7155 saints	8778 materialism

8849

worry

A sense of uneasiness and anxiety about the future. Scripture indicates that such anxiety is ultimately grounded in a lack of trust in God and his purposes.

The causes of worry

Being world-centred Mt 6:25 pp Lk 12:22 See also Mt 6:34; 13:22 pp Mk 4:19 pp Lk 8:14; Lk 12:29; 21:34; 1Co 7:33

Lacking confidence in God Jn 14:1 See also Mt 6:26–32 pp Lk 12:27–30; Mt 8:25 pp Mk 4:38 pp Lk 8:24; Mt 14:31; 16:8

Abandoning God Dt 28:64–65 See also La 1:3; Eze 4:16–17; 12:19

Worry leads people away from God

Ps 37:8 See also Pr 12:25; Mt 13:22 pp Lk 8:14; Lk 10:40–42

Worry is futile

Mt 6:27 pp Lk 12:25 See also Ecc 2:22–23

Remedies for worry

Being God-centred Isa 26:3; Mt 6:33 pp Lk 12:31 See also Jer 17:7–8; Ro 8:6

Prayer Ps 55:22; Php 4:6–7 See also Ps 94:18–19; 139:23; 1Pe 5:7

See also

5537 sleeplessness	8104 assurance
5559 stress	8213 confidence
5805 comfort	8219 courage
5831 depression	8721 doubt
6700 peace	8754 fear
8020 faith	8834 unbelief

9000

Last things

9010

Death

9020

death

Death in its various aspects is seen by Scripture as the opposite of God-given life.

9021
death, natural

The end of life in the present world.

Death is natural to humanity as part of the created world

Ecc 12:7 See also Ps 39:5; 104:29; Ecc 3:18–21; 2Pe 1:13–14

Death is a result of Adam's sin

Ro 5:12 There is a tension between this text and those which suggest that death is a natural aspect of being human. Some suggest that the death referred to here is spiritual rather than physical. See also Ge 2:17; 3:19; Ro 6:23; 1Co 15:21–22

Death is universal

None can escape death Ps 89:48 See also Ge 6:3; Jos 23:14; 2Sa 14:14; Job 30:23

Death comes to all kinds of people Job 21:23–26 See also 2Sa 12:15–18; 2Ki 4:20; Ps 37:35–36; 49:10; Ecc 3:19; Lk 16:22

Only two people did not die Ge 5:24; 2Ki 2:11 Enoch and Elijah died in the sense that their bodies were transformed from being suited to earthly life to life in heaven. They anticipated the death of Jesus Christ, whose body was not corrupted but transformed, and the transition to the new world of those who are alive when Jesus Christ comes again.

Death is irreversible

Heb 9:27 The idea of reincarnation, that after death people repeatedly return to this life in a lower or higher form, is incompatible with death being once for all and an entrance into heaven or hell after the judgment. See also Job 16:22; Ps 115:17

Death is an aspect of human frailty

Ps 146:3–4 See also Isa 51:12; 1Pe 1:24; Isa 40:6–8

Death occurs when God determines it

Job 14:5 See also Dt 32:39; Job 38:17; Lk 12:20; Rev 1:18

The means of death

Through old age Ge 25:8; 35:29; Jdg 8:32; 1Ki 2:10

Through disease and accident 2Ki 1:2,16–17; 20:1 pp 2Ch 32:24; Mk 5:23; Ac 20:9

Through violence Jdg 9:5,52–54; 2Sa 13:28–29; 1Ki 15:28; 2Ki 8:14–15; Mt 2:16; 14:8–11

As a judgment by God Lev 10:1–2; Nu 16:31–32; 20:23–24; 1Sa 25:38; 2Sa 6:7; 24:15; 2Ch 13:20; Ac 5:5,10; 12:21–23; 1Co 11:29–30

Through a legal penalty Ex 21:12–17; Lk 23:32,40–41

The prospect of death affects human attitudes and values

Life is short Jas 4:14 See also Job 7:6; 8:9; 9:25; Ps 39:5; 89:47; 90:10; 102:11; Ecc 6:12; Isa 38:12; 40:6–8

People fear death Ps 18:4–6; 116:3; Heb 2:15

People should prepare for death 2Ki 20:1 pp Isa 38:1 See also Ps 39:4; 90:12; Am 4:12

The expectation of death is an incentive to serve God Ecc 9:10 See also Isa 38:18–19; Jn 9:4

The expectation of death is an incentive to hold material blessings lightly 1Ti 6:7 See also Job 1:21; Lk 12:13–21; 1Co 7:29–31

Death is sometimes desired to escape problems

Nu 11:11–15; 1Ki 19:4; Job 3:11; 7:15; Jer 8:3; Jnh 4:3; Ac 16:27; Rev 9:6

Death was defeated by Jesus Christ

2Ti 1:10 See also Isa 25:8; Hos 13:14; 1Co 15:24–26; Heb 2:14; Rev 20:14

There is no death in heaven

Rev 21:4 See also Lk 20:35–36; 2Co 5:1–2

See also

2530 Christ, death of	5795 bereavement
4015 life	6020 sin
5067 suicide	6203 mortality
5281 crucifixion	7346 death penalty
5297 disease	8357 weakness
5725 old age	9040 grave, the

9022
death, of believers

Believers in Jesus Christ will depart from this present life to the joy of God's presence.

Death is a normal experience for believers

Ro 14:8 See also Heb 9:27

Death can be a blessing

Because of the prospect of heaven Php 1:21–23 See also Nu 23:10; Ps 49:15; 116:15; Lk 2:29; 2Ti 4:6–8; Rev 7:13–17; 14:13

Because it brings relief from trouble and problems 1Ki 19:4; Job 3:20; 7:15; 2Th 1:7

At death believers are with Christ

They are in his presence Lk 23:43 See also 2Co 5:8; 1Th 5:10

They are safe and secure Rev 2:11 The second death is the final banishment of unbelievers from God's presence. See also Ro 14:8; Rev 20:6

They have the prospect of a new order of things Rev 21:4 See also 2Ti 4:6–8; Rev 22:3–5

The defeat of death

Death is vanquished for believers 1Co 15:55 See also Ro 8:36; 2Ti 1:10; Heb 2:14; Rev 20:14

Death is to be reversed in resurrection Though most of the above passages suggest that eternal life in Jesus Christ's presence is experienced immediately at death, others such as the following link these blessings with resurrection at the final coming of Jesus Christ: Jn 11:23; 1Co 15:51–54; 1Th 4:16

The death of believers is likened to sleep

Implying rest, renewing and awaking Ac 7:59–60 Sleep does not imply lack of consciousness but rather rest, renewing and awaking. In the NT it is only used of believers. See also Dt 31:16; Da 12:2; Mk 5:39; Jn 11:11–14; Ac 13:36; 1Co 15:6,17–18; 1Th 4:13–16

Implying peace and comfort Lk 16:22 Abraham's side suggests a welcome to a place of peace and protection. See also Ge 49:33; 2Ki 22:20; Isa 57:1–2; Lk 16:25

Death and the recognition of others

1Th 4:17 "caught up together" implies recognition. See also Ge 25:8 "gathered to his people" (literally "to his father's kin") is a common OT expression and implies continued existence together; Job 3:13–14; Mt 17:4; Mk 9:4; Lk 16:24; 1Co 13:12

Believers can face death without fear

They die in relationship with God Heb 2:14–15 See also Ps 23:4; Pr 14:32

They die trusting the Lord Heb 11:13,21–22

They receive comfort in facing death Jn 11:25–26 See also Isa 25:8; 1Co 15:26; Rev 1:18

In death they can glorify God Php 1:20

In this believers are to be envied Nu 23:10

Believers often hated the idea of death

Job 17:13–16; Ps 9:13; Isa 38:10; Ro 8:36; 1Co 15:55–56; 2Co 4:11–12

Martyred believers are specially honoured in Scripture

Rev 12:11 See also Rev 2:13

See also
2372 Christ, victory	8754 fear
5059 rest, eternal	9310 resurrection
5535 sleep and death	9414 heaven,
6644 eternal life	community of
7903 baptism	redeemed
8450 martyrdom	9430 paradise
8481 self-sacrifice	9610 hope

9023
death, of unbelievers

The departure from the present life of unrepentant people to await final banishment from God.

Death is inevitable

Ps 49:10; 89:48 See also 2Sa 14:14; Job 30:23; Ps 37:36; Ecc 3:19–20; 8:8

The premature death of unbelievers is the consequence of sin

Pr 10:27 OT writers, for whom God's blessing on the righteous occurs mostly in the present life, often saw early or sudden death as divine judgment on the wicked. See also 1Ch 10:13; Job 22:16; Ps 9:17; 37:1–2,22,38; 55:23; 139:19; Pr 5:21–23; 11:19; 14:12; Isa 17:14; Eze 3:19; 18:4,20; Da 5:30; Lk 12:20

Aspects of the death of unbelievers

They die unforgiven Jn 8:21,24

They die without hope Pr 11:7; Ecc 8:10

God has no pleasure in their death Eze 18:23 See also Eze 18:32; 2Pe 3:9

Descriptions of the death of unbelievers

Being destroyed Mt 7:13; Ro 9:22

Perishing Jn 3:16; 2Pe 2:12

Being in fire Lk 16:22–24; Heb 10:27

Being in darkness Mt 25:30; 2Pe 2:17

The consequences of the death of unbelievers

The intermediate state of awaiting judgment Rev 20:13 See also Lk 16:23; Jn 5:29; Ac 24:15

The judgment Heb 9:27 See also Jn 5:29

The eternal consequences Da 12:2; Mt 25:41 See also Mt 18:8; 25:46; Mk 9:45–48; Gal 1:8–9; Heb 6:2; Jude 7

The challenge of the death of unbelievers

The call to prepare 2Ki 20:1 See also Ecc 7:17; 9:10; Am 4:12

The only escape is through Jesus Christ Jn 8:51 Death for believers is swallowed up in life, so that they are never personally aware of the pain and sting of death (compare Jn 11:26). See also Jn 5:24

See also
4826 fire	8734 evil
5295 destruction	8755 folly
5482 punishment	9120 eternity
6109 alienation	9210 judgment,
6732 repentance	God's
8341 separation	9510 hell
8730 enemies of	
believers	

9024
death, spiritual

A condition in this life of alienation from God because of sin. It leads ultimately to the "second death", the permanent separation of unbelievers from God.

Spiritual death means alienation from God in this life

Eph 2:1–3; Col 1:21 See also Mt 8:22; Ro 6:23; Col 2:13

Spiritual death is a result of Adam's sin

Ro 5:15–16 See also Ro 5:12

Symptoms of spiritual death

Spiritual ignorance Mt 4:16; Isa 9:2; Lk 1:79; Eph 5:8

A mind controlled by the sinful nature Ro 8:5–8 See also Pr 8:36; 14:12; 16:25; 21:16; Eph 4:18

Unbelief Jn 3:36; 1Jn 5:12

Living in sinful pleasures Lk 15:13; 1Ti 5:6

Acting in ways that lead to death Heb 6:1; 9:14

Spiritual death leads ultimately to the "second death"

Rev 2:11; 20:6,14; 21:8

A church may be spiritually dead

Rev 3:1

Deliverance from spiritual death is only through Jesus Christ

Eph 2:4–5 See also Eze 37:1–14; Lk 15:24,32; Jn 5:24–25; Ro 6:3–4,13

See also
2324 Christ as	6510 salvation
Saviour	8834 unbelief
5035 mind	9105 last things
5080 Adam	9110 after-life
5918 pleasure	9240 last judgment
6181 ignorance	

9030
dead bodies

Dead bodies were to be treated with respect

2Sa 21:12–14; Ecc 6:3

Unburied dead bodies were a sign of God's curse upon Israel

Dt 28:26; Jer 16:4

Contact with dead bodies

The high priest was not to touch a dead body Lev 21:11

Contact with a dead body made a person unclean Nu 19:11 See also Nu 9:6–10; 19:16

Jesus Christ was willing to touch a dead body Mt 9:25 pp Mk 5:41 pp Lk 8:54; Mk 9:26–27; Lk 7:14

The reluctance to approach dead bodies because of the smell Jn 11:39

See also
5137 bones	7340 clean and
5241 burial	unclean
5288 dead, the	7424 ritual law

9040
grave, the

An OT synonym for death, the natural, inevitable human destiny, though not without hope for the righteous.

The grave as a place of burial

Nu 19:16,18; Dt 34:6; 1Ki 13:31;
2Ki 21:26; Isa 22:16

The grave representing natural death

Ge 37:35; Ps 88:3 *See also* Ge 42:38;
44:29; 2Sa 22:5–6; 1Ki 2:6,9;
Job 3:21–22; 5:26; 10:19; 17:1; Ps 30:3;
89:48; Pr 5:5; 9:18; 15:24; 30:16;
Isa 28:15,18; Jer 20:17; Hab 2:5

The grave as judgment

Ps 55:15 *See also* Nu 16:30,33;
Job 24:19; 40:13; Ps 9:17; 31:17; 49:14;
Isa 5:14; 14:9,11,15

The grave represented only hopelessness and oblivion before Jesus Christ's resurrection

Job 17:13–16; Ecc 9:10 *See also* Job 7:9;
Ps 6:5; 31:17; 88:5,11; Isa 38:18

The OT hope of redemption from the grave anticipated the gospel message

Ps 49:15; 1Co 15:55 *See also* 1Sa 2:6;
Job 14:13; Hos 13:14; Ac 2:27; Ps 16:10

See also

5241 burial	9310 resurrection
9020 death	9510 hell
9050 tombs	9530 Hades
9210 judgment,	9540 Sheol
God's	9610 hope

9050

tombs

Graves or burial places, often cut out of rock. People were usually buried in family tombs and kings were often buried in royal tombs.

Tombs cut out of rock

Isa 22:15–16 *See also* 2Ki 23:16;
2Ch 16:14; Mt 27:59–60 pp Mk 15:46
pp Lk 23:53

Caves used as tombs

Ge 50:13 *See also* Ge 23:17–20;
25:8–10; Jn 11:38

Tombs sealed with a stone

Jn 11:38 *See also* Mt 27:60 pp Mk 15:46;
Mt 27:64–66; 28:2; Mk 16:3; Lk 24:2

Burial in a family tomb

Ge 23:19; 25:8–10; 47:29–30;
49:29–32; Jdg 8:32; 16:31; 2Sa 2:32;
17:23; 19:37; 21:12–14; 1Ki 13:22

Royal tombs

2Ch 16:14 *See also* 2Ch 21:20; 24:25;
26:23; 28:27; 32:33; Ne 3:16

Tombs in gardens

2Ki 21:18 *See also* 2Ki 21:26; Jn 19:41

Contact with a tomb rendered a person ritually unclean

Nu 19:16 *See also* 2Ki 23:6

Figurative use of tombs

Mt 23:27–28 *See also* Lk 11:43–44

See also

2530 Christ, death of	5320 funeral
2560 Christ,	8767 hypocrisy
resurrection	9020 death
4218 cave	9030 dead bodies
4257 pit	9040 grave, the
4354 rock	9540 Sheol
5241 burial	

9100

Aspects of the last things

9105

last things

The doctrine of the last things ("eschatology") includes the subjects of death, the second coming of Jesus Christ, the resurrection of the dead, the last judgment, heaven and hell.

Death

Physical death is universal Job 30:23
See also 2Sa 14:14; Ro 5:12

The timing of natural death is beyond human control Ecc 8:8 *See also* Ps 90:10;
Mt 6:27; Jas 4:14

Death is not to be feared by the believer Ps 23:4 *See also* Ps 116:15;
Pr 14:32; Ro 14:8; Php 1:21; Rev 14:13

For believers, death is likened to falling asleep Jn 11:11–13 *See also* Mk 5:39;
Ac 13:36; 1Co 15:6

At the second coming, believers still living on earth will not experience death 1Th 4:15–17 *See also*
1Co 15:51–52

Death is the penalty for unforgiven sin Ro 6:23 *See also* 1Ch 10:13; Pr 11:19;
Ro 5:12

The second coming of Jesus Christ

The second coming is foretold Mt 26:64 pp Mk 14:62 *See also*
Lk 21:27; Ac 1:11; Heb 9:28

The timing of the second coming is known only to God the Father Mt 24:36
pp Mk 13:32 *See also* Mal 3:1; Mt 24:44
pp Lk 12:40; Rev 16:15

God's purpose at the second coming is to gather his people together, to reward the faithful and judge the wicked Mt 16:27 *See also* Da 7:13–14;
Mt 25:31–32; Jn 14:3; 1Co 4:5;
1Th 4:16–17; 1Pe 5:4; 1Jn 3:2;
Jude 14–15

The right attitude towards the second coming 1Jn 2:28 *See also* Mk 13:35;
Ac 3:19–20; 1Ti 6:13–14; 2Pe 3:11

The resurrection of the dead

All will be raised Jn 5:28–29 *See also*
Da 12:2; Ac 24:15

Believers in Jesus Christ will be raised to eternal life Jn 6:40 *See also* Jn 11:25;
2Co 4:14; 1Th 4:16

Unbelievers will be condemned Jn 5:29
See also Mt 25:46

Believers will be given resurrection bodies 1Co 15:42–44 *See also*
1Co 15:50–53

The last judgment

All face judgment after death Heb 9:27
See also Ro 14:12; 1Pe 4:5; Rev 20:11–12

Judgment is entrusted to Jesus Christ Jn 5:22 *See also* Ac 10:42; 17:31;
Rev 1:18

Those who have not responded to Christ will be condemned Jn 12:48 *See also* 2Th 1:7–8; 2Pe 3:7; Jude 15;
Rev 20:15

Believers will not be judged for sin Jn 5:24 *See also* Jn 3:18; Ro 8:1–2,33–34

Believers will be judged on how they have lived their Christian lives 2Co 5:10 *See also* 1Co 4:5; Heb 9:28;
1Jn 4:17

Heaven

God's throne is in heaven where he is continuously worshipped Rev 4:9–10
See also Isa 6:1–3

God's will is perfectly served in heaven Mt 6:10 pp Lk 11:2 *See also* 1Ki 22:19

At Jesus Christ's second coming, a new heaven and earth will replace the old Rev 21:1

The redeemed will enjoy life in the presence of God in the new heaven 1Th 4:17 *See also* Mt 5:8; Php 3:20;
Jude 24; Rev 21:1–4

All life in heaven is sustained by God Rev 22:1–2 *See also* Jn 6:58; Rev 2:7;
21:23

Hell

Hell is the destiny of human beings who reject God Mt 25:41 *Hell was originally meant for the punishment of the devil and his angels. See also*
Mt 13:41–42; Ro 2:8; Heb 10:26–27;
Jude 6; Rev 17:8

Those in hell are finally separated from God 2Th 1:9 *See also* Mt 25:46

Hell is a place of fire, darkness and weeping Rev 20:15 *See also* Mt 8:12;
2Pe 3:7; Jude 7

Jesus Christ himself frequently warned about the dangers of hell Lk 12:5 *See also* Mt 5:29–30 *Jesus Christ is using Eastern hyperbole, not intended literally, to stress importance;* Mt 13:40

See also

1310 God as judge	9020 death
2565 Christ, second	9210 judgment,
coming	God's
5493 retribution	9240 last judgment
6644 eternal life	9310 resurrection
6720 redemption	9410 heaven
8341 separation	9510 hell

9110

after-life

Although the OT generally portrays this as a vague and shadowy existence, often associated with judgment, there are hints of the idea of resurrection to a fuller life which are developed in the NT. The NT points to judgment beyond death and to the believers' hope in resurrection, to a more complete enjoyment of God's presence and his blessings and to the promise of a new heaven and earth.

The after-life in the OT
The grave as a place of silence
Ps 115:17 *See also* Ps 6:5; 30:9;
88:10–11; Isa 38:18

The grave as a place of darkness
Job 10:21–22 *See also* 1Sa 2:9; Ps 88:12

The grave as a place of no return
Job 7:8–10 *See also* Job 16:22; Ps 146:4;
Pr 2:18–19; Ecc 12:7

The grave as a place of judgment
Ps 88:5 *See also* Ps 31:17; Pr 9:18;
Isa 14:9–11; 26:14; Eze 31:14; 32:17–32

**The grave offers peace to the
righteous** Job 3:13; Ecc 4:2; Isa 57:1–2

The hope of resurrection Da 12:2 *See
also* Job 19:26; Ps 16:10–11; 49:15;
73:24; Isa 25:7–8; 26:19

The after-life and God's judgment
Judgment beyond death is certain
Heb 9:27 *See also* 2Co 5:10;
Rev 20:12–13

There will be salvation for believers
Mt 25:19–23; Heb 9:28; Rev 11:18

**There will be separation from God for
unbelievers** Rev 20:15; 21:27 *See also*
Mt 8:12; 13:42; 22:13; 24:51; 25:30;
Lk 12:46; Rev 22:15

**The believing dead are already
with Jesus Christ**
Lk 23:43; 1Th 4:14–17 *Believers, with
Jesus Christ in spirit, await their final
resurrection which will take place when he
returns. See also* Jn 12:26; 14:3; 2Co 5:8;
Php 1:23; Heb 12:23; Rev 6:9–11

The after-life and believers' hope of resurrection
The bodily resurrection of Jesus Christ
Lk 24:39–43 *See also* Jn 20:20,26–27;
Ac 1:3; 1Jn 1:1

Believers share in Christ's resurrection
Ro 8:11 *See also* 1Co 6:14; 15:20–23;
2Co 4:14

The resurrection body of believers
Php 3:20–21 *See also* 1Co 15:23,42–55;
2Co 5:1–4

The future consummation of the believers' enjoyment of God
Future glory Ro 8:18–19 *See also*
2Co 4:17–18; 1Jn 3:2

A new heaven and earth 2Pe 3:13;
Rev 21:1

God's presence with his people
Rev 21:2–7 *The final consummation will
bring God's promises to and purposes for
his people to fulfilment;* Rev 22:14 *See
also* Ex 25:8; Rev 22:1–5

The Holy Spirit as a guarantee
2Co 1:22; 5:5; Eph 1:13–14

See also

2565 Christ, second coming	9120 eternity
	9135 immortality
4055 heaven and earth	9210 judgment, God's
6645 eternal life	9310 resurrection
9020 death	9410 heaven
9105 last things	9510 hell

antichrist, the

One who is directly and implacably
opposed to Jesus Christ.

**The antichrist will deny
fundamental truths about Jesus
Christ**
2Jn 7 *See also* Mt 24:24 pp Mk 13:22;
Mk 3:29; 1Jn 2:22; 4:3

**The antichrist as a self-
appointed rival to God**
2Th 2:3–4 *See also* Da 7:7–8,24–25;
8:9–12,23–25; 11:36–45;
Rev 13:1–10,11–18

**The coming of the antichrist is a
sign of the "last days"**
1Jn 2:18 *See also* 2Th 2:6–10

**The final defeat of the antichrist
is assured**
2Th 2:8 *See also* Da 7:26–27; 8:25;
11:45; Rev 17:7–14

See also

2012 Christ, authority	6147 deceit, practice
	8730 enemies of believers
2372 Christ, victory	
2375 kingdom of God	8746 false Christs
4120 Satan	8787 opposition to God
5290 defeat	8795 persecution
5800 blasphemy	9140 last days

eternity

In Scripture eternity is not an
abstraction but limitless time, over
which God is totally sovereign.

9121
eternity, nature of

God alone possesses lasting time, in
contrast to the fleeting time of the
human race.

Eternity from God's perspective
Ps 90:4 *See also* 2Pe 3:8

God's eternity is absolute
Ps 90:2 *See also* Ge 1:1; Jn 1:1–2;
Ro 16:26

The name of God and eternity
Ex 3:14–15 *See also* Ge 21:33; Isa 26:4;
40:28; 41:4; Rev 1:8

God's eternal attributes
His love Jer 31:3 *See also* 1Jn 4:8,16

His righteousness Isa 51:6; 2Co 9:9

His wisdom 1Co 2:7

His power Ro 1:20

Worship of God as eternal
Jude 25 *See also* 1Ch 16:36; Ro 11:36;
2Pe 3:18

Jesus Christ's eternal existence
Heb 13:8 *See also* Jn 17:5,24;
Heb 1:10–12; Ps 102:25–27; Heb 5:6;

Ps 110:4; Heb 7:24–25; Rev 1:17–18;
22:13

**The Holy Spirit's eternal
existence**
Heb 9:14

Eternity and creation
Ge 1:1 *See also* Pr 8:22–29 *Wisdom
(personified) is speaking here.*

Eternity and the human race
Ps 39:4–5 *See also* Job 10:5; 36:26;
Ecc 3:11

See also

1205 God, titles of	5001 human race, the
1510 Trinity, the	
4005 creation	9135 immortality
4903 time	9160 new heavens & new earth
4909 beginning	
4930 end	

9122
eternity, and God

Whether one considers the past or
the future, God alone is discovered
to be permanent and lasting.

**God's being, his wisdom and his
word are eternal**
God has always existed Ge 1:1 *See also*
Job 38:4; Ps 90:2; Hab 1:12; Jn 1:1–2

The eternity of God's wisdom
Pr 8:22–23 *See also* Heb 9:14; 1Pe 1:20

God's word has always expressed his
nature Ps 119:89 *See also* Ps 119:160;
Mt 24:35; 1Pe 1:23–25; Isa 40:8

God's purpose to bless is eternal
2Ti 1:9–10 *See also* Eph 1:3–11;
Tit 1:2–3; 1Pe 1:18–21; Rev 13:8

**Some aspects of the created
order are eternal**
Mic 6:2 *See also* Ge 49:26; Dt 33:15;
Hab 3:6

Eternal life
God bestows eternal life 1Jn 5:11 *See
also* Jn 3:16; 17:3

Resurrection of the body
1Co 15:42–44 *See also* 1Co 15:50–56;
2Co 5:1–5; 1Pe 1:23

God's eternal blessings
His eternal salvation Isa 45:17; Heb 5:9

His eternal covenant Isa 54:10;
Jer 32:40; Heb 13:20

His eternal glory 2Co 4:17–18 *See also*
2Ti 2:10; 1Pe 5:10

An eternal crown 1Co 9:25; 1Pe 5:4;
Rev 2:10

An eternal inheritance Heb 9:15;
1Pe 1:3–5

An eternal home Lk 16:9; Jn 14:2–3

The eternal kingdom of God
God's eternal rule 1Ti 1:17 *See also*
Ps 10:16; Jer 10:10; Rev 15:3

The Messiah's eternal kingdom
Isa 9:6–7; Lk 1:32–33

Jesus Christ's eternal kingdom
2Pe 1:11 *See also* Rev 11:15

Eternal punishment
Mt 25:46 *See also* Da 12:2; Mt 25:41; Jude 6–7,13; Rev 14:11

See also

1115 God, purpose of	5482 punishment
1140 God, the eternal	6510 salvation
1345 covenant	6638 election
2018 Christ, divinity	6644 eternal life
2375 kingdom of God	9410 heaven
3015 Holy Spirit, divinity	9510 hell

9125
footstool

Used mostly symbolically to refer to God's supreme authority over his creation. It is used especially to refer to his final victory over all those who oppose him.

The footstool as a rest for the feet
2Ch 9:18; Jas 2:3

The footstool used symbolically
God's footstool as a symbol for the ark and the temple Ps 132:7 *See also* 1Ch 28:2; Ps 99:5; La 2:1

God's footstool as a symbol for the earth Isa 66:1 *God cannot be confined to any man-made temple. See also* Mt 5:35; Ac 7:49

Defeated enemies can be regarded as a footstool Jos 10:24–25; 1Ki 5:3; Ps 66:12; Isa 51:23; Mic 7:10

Jesus Christ will make all God's enemies his footstool Heb 1:13 *This passage affirms Jesus Christ's supremacy over the angels. See also* Ps 110:1; Mt 22:44 pp Mk 12:36 pp Lk 20:43; Ac 2:34–35; Eph 1:22

Jesus Christ will complete his victory when he returns Heb 10:13 *See also* 1Co 15:25; Heb 2:8; Ps 8:6

See also

1130 God, sovereignty	5581 throne
2372 Christ, victory	7306 ark of the covenant
2545 Christ, opposition to	7467 temple, Solomon's
5151 feet	

9130
future, the

God's promises about the future are certain because it is under God's control. Christians should live on the basis that these promises, which focus on the return of Jesus Christ, will be fulfilled.

God controls the future
God knows the future Ex 3:19–20 *See also* Dt 31:21; 2Sa 7:19 pp 1Ch 17:17; Ps 139:4; Isa 42:9; 46:10; Da 2:28; Ac 2:23; 3:18

God can reveal the future Da 2:45 *See also* Ge 15:13–16; 41:25; 1Sa 9:15–16; 2Ki 8:10; Da 8:19; 10:14; Mt 2:13; Ac 18:9–10; 27:22–24

The future is unknown to human beings
Ecc 8:7 *See also* Pr 27:1; Ecc 3:22; 7:14; 9:12; 10:14; Mt 24:42–43; Ac 20:22; Jas 4:14

There is a future hope for believers
It is based on God's promise Jer 31:17 *See also* Ps 37:37; Pr 23:18; 24:14; Isa 60:15

Future blessings are guaranteed Jer 29:11 *See also* Ge 17:7; Lev 26:3–5; Dt 6:2; 30:9; Isa 30:23; 65:23; Am 9:13

Future blessings are superior to present experiences Php 1:21–23 *See also* Ge 22:17–18; Mt 19:29 pp Mk 10:29–30 pp Lk 18:29–30; Ro 8:18–25; 1Pe 5:4; 1Jn 3:2

Key aspects of future hope
Believers will go to heaven 1Pe 1:4 *See also* Lk 16:22; 23:43; Jn 14:2–3; 2Co 5:1; Col 1:5; 1Th 4:16–17

Jesus Christ will come again Ac 1:11 *See also* Da 7:13; Mt 24:30 pp Mk 13:26 pp Lk 21:27; Php 3:20; 1Th 4:16; 2Th 2:1; Heb 9:28; Jas 5:8

The dead will rise 1Co 15:52 *See also* Da 12:2; Jn 5:28–29; 6:39–40; Ac 24:15; 2Co 4:14; Rev 20:4–5,12

Final judgment 2Co 5:10 *See also* Ps 62:12; Mt 16:27; 25:31–32; Heb 9:27; 2Pe 3:7; 1Jn 4:17; Jude 14–15; Rev 20:13

The devil and evil will be destroyed Isa 25:7–8 *See also* 2Th 2:8; Heb 2:14; Rev 7:16; 11:18; 19:20–21; 20:10

God's kingdom will be fully established Rev 11:15 *See also* Isa 11:6–9; Zec 14:9; 1Co 15:24; Rev 21:1–5

Believers' responsibility towards future generations
Jos 4:6–7 *See also* Ex 12:25–27; 16:32–33; Dt 6:20–21; Jos 4:21–22; 22:27; Ps 22:30; 45:17

Jos 4:6–7 *The twelve stones taken from the bed of the river Jordan is one of several instances where God's people are told to preserve memorials of present blessings for the sake of future generations. See also* Ex 12:25–27; 16:32–33; Dt 6:20–21; Jos 4:21–22; 22:27; Ps 22:30; 45:17

Proper attitudes towards the future
Looking forwards rather than backwards Php 3:13–14 *See also* Ge 19:17; Isa 43:18–19; Col 3:1–2; Heb 12:1–2

Having perseverance and faith 1Co 15:58 *See also* Gal 6:9; Heb 11:6–8,17–19; 1Pe 1:13; Rev 3:11

Avoiding occult predictions and false prophecies Jer 27:9 *See also* Isa 44:25–26; Jer 29:8; Eze 13:3–7; Zec 10:2; Ac 16:16–18

See also

1193 glory, revelation of	4966 present, the
1427 prophecy	5498 reward
2565 Christ, second coming	5977 waiting
4915 completion	9105 last things
4963 past, the	9310 resurrection
	9410 heaven
	9610 hope

9135
immortality

The quality of enduring into eternity, which Scripture insists belongs to God alone. However, God bestows the gift of eternal life and immortality upon those who believe and trust in him.

9136
immortality, in OT

The OT stresses that God alone is immortal and indicates that this gift may be granted to human beings under certain conditions.

Immortality is an attribute of God
God is everlasting in himself Ps 90:2 *See also* Ne 9:5; Ps 41:13; Isa 9:6; 40:28; Hab 1:12

God is everlasting in his character and actions Dt 33:27 *The way in which Scripture emphasises the character of God in these contexts shows that immortality is about a quality of being as well as about infinite duration.*
The everlasting covenant: Ge 9:16; 17:7,13,19; 1Ch 16:17 pp Ps 105:10
God's everlasting rule: Ps 9:7; 10:16; 132:12; Da 7:14,27
God's unfailing and everlasting love: Ps 52:8; 103:17; Isa 54:10; Jer 31:3
God's everlasting righteousness: Ps 119:142; Da 9:24
Isa 45:17 *God's everlasting salvation;* Isa 54:8 *God's everlasting kindness;* Isa 60:19–20 *The LORD as the everlasting light*

Immortality is conditionally offered to human beings
Ge 3:22–23 *See also* Ps 6:5; 88:5,10; 115:17; Da 12:2 *The most specific OT reference to immortality. Note that while resurrection to judgment is for all, immortality is only for the righteous (Pr 12:28).*

Enoch and Elijah: two special cases
Ge 5:24; 2Ki 2:11

The confidence of believers
Ps 16:9–11 *See also* Ps 17:15; 21:6; 73:24; 133:3

God will abolish death Isa 25:8

See also

1030 God, compassion	5062 spirit
1085 God, love of	6203 mortality
1125 God, righteousness	9020 death
1140 God, the eternal	9120 eternity
1160 God, unchangeable	9210 judgment, God's

9137
immortality, in NT

In the NT, immortal life is offered to human beings through Jesus Christ and guaranteed by the Holy Spirit. It is closely associated with eternal life and resurrection, but is seen more as a quality of being rather than in terms of unlimited extent.

Immortality is an attribute of God
1Ti 1:17 See also Ro 1:23; 1Ti 6:16

Immortality is offered to human beings through Jesus Christ
2Ti 1:10 See also Jn 6:50; 8:51; 11:26; 1Co 15:22,54

Immortality is guaranteed by the Holy Spirit
2Co 5:1–5

The association of immortality with eternal life
Ro 2:7

The association of immortality with resurrection
Lk 20:36 See also 1Co 15:42–43,53–54; 1Th 4:17; Rev 20:4–6

Immortality implied by Jesus Christ's transfiguration
Mt 17:3 pp Mk 9:4 pp Lk 9:30–31 the presence of Moses and Elijah

Immortality as a quality of being
It is inseparable from God's other characteristics Ro 1:23; 1Ti 1:17; 6:16

It is inseparable from humanity's final state of existence Lk 20:36; Ro 2:7; 1Pe 1:4

See also
2424 gospel, promises	6644 eternal life
2580 Christ, transfiguration	8020 faith
	9105 last things
5059 rest, eternal	9310 resurrection
5080 Adam	9613 hope as confidence
5703 inheritance	

9140

last days

The final epoch of history which is marked by the coming of the Messiah and the establishment of God's kingdom. In the NT it is portrayed as the period between Jesus Christ's first coming and the consummation of all things at his return, and is marked by godlessness and the persecution of God's people.

OT expectation of the last days
The Messianic kingdom Isa 2:2–4 pp Mic 4:1–3 See also Isa 9:6–7; 11:1–9; 65:20–25; Jer 33:15

The restoration of Israel Jer 33:16; Hos 3:5 See also Isa 25:9; Jer 30:9; 50:4; Joel 3:1; Zec 8:23

The day of the Lord Isa 13:6–12; Eze 30:3; Joel 2:11,30–31; Am 5:18–20; Ac 2:19–20

Jesus Christ's coming introduces the last days
The timing of his revelation 1Pe 1:20 See also Gal 4:4–5

The announcement of God's kingdom Mk 1:15 See also Mt 12:28 pp Lk 11:20; Lk 4:43; 8:1

The fulfilment of Messianic promise
Lk 4:18–21 See also Isa 61:1–2; Mt 11:4–5 pp Lk 7:22

The outpouring of the Spirit
Ac 2:16–18 See also Joel 2:28–29; Eze 36:27

Revelation in the last days
Heb 1:1–2 See also Mt 13:16–17 pp Lk 10:23–24; Ro 16:25–26; Eph 3:9; Col 1:26

Redemption in the last days
Heb 9:26 See also Da 9:24; Ac 2:21; Joel 2:32; 2Co 6:2; Isa 49:8; 1Pe 1:18–20

Features of the last days
Godlessness 2Ti 3:1–5 See also Da 12:10

Deception and apostasy 1Ti 4:1 See also Mt 24:4–5 pp Mk 13:5 pp Lk 21:8; Mt 24:10–12; 1Jn 2:18–19

Scoffing 2Pe 3:3–4; Jude 18–19

Persecution Da 11:33–35; Mk 10:30; Lk 21:12–17 pp Mt 24:9–10 pp Mk 13:9–13

Jesus Christ's return brings the last days to a close
It ushers in a new era Heb 9:28 See also Mt 13:49; 24:3

It is identified with the day of the Lord 2Co 1:14; 1Th 5:2; 2Pe 3:10

Living in the last days
Heb 6:5 Between Jesus Christ's comings, believers have a foretaste of the age to come. See also Eph 1:19–21; Col 3:1–4; Heb 10:24–25

See also
1310 God as judge	9105 last things
2565 Christ, second coming	9145 Messianic age
6169 godlessness	9165 restoration
8490 watchfulness	9220 day of the Lord
8794 persecution	9240 last judgment
	9310 resurrection

9145

Messianic age

In the OT, writers look forward to the era that will be inaugurated by God's decisive intervention in human history, in order to establish his eternal kingdom under the Messiah. The Messianic age is characterised by righteousness, justice and peace, by the outpouring of the Holy Spirit and by the restoration and renewal of God's people and of creation. In the NT, the idea appears in a developed form as the "kingdom of God", inaugurated by the first coming of Jesus Christ and to be consummated at his return.

The victory of God's kingdom foreseen
Da 2:37–44 See also Zec 14:9

The victory of God's Messiah Ps 45:3–6 This psalm came to be applied to the Messiah. See also Ps 110:5–6 This psalm was also applied to the Messiah in the OT times; Isa 9:3–5; 42:13; 59:17–19

The Messiah's universal reign
Da 7:13–14
Psalms traditionally taken as referring to the Messiah: Ps 2:8–9; 72:8–11

Restoration in the Messianic age
Restoration of harmony in creation Isa 11:6–9 pp Isa 65:25

Restoration of the land's prosperity Am 9:13–15 See also Ps 72:3; Isa 4:2; Joel 3:18

Restoration and renewal of God's people Jer 3:18; Mic 4:6–8 See also Isa 60:1–3; Joel 3:16–17; Am 9:11; Ob 17–21; Ac 1:6; Zec 3:9
God's people seek him in repentance: Hos 3:5; Jer 50:4–5; Eze 11:19–20 pp Eze 36:28

Characteristics of the Messianic age
Righteousness and justice Isa 32:1 See also Ps 72:2,12–13; Isa 9:7; 11:3–5; 32:16; Jer 23:5–6 pp Jer 33:15–16

Peace and security Isa 32:17–18 See also Mic 4:3–4 pp Isa 2:4; Isa 65:20–23; Jer 23:5–6; 33:15–16; Eze 34:25–29; Zec 9:9–10

Universal acknowledgment of the Lord Jer 3:17 See also Isa 2:2–3 pp Mic 4:1–2; Isa 19:23–25; Zec 14:16

The outpouring of the Holy Spirit Joel 2:28–29 See also Isa 11:2; 32:15; 44:3; 59:21; Eze 36:27

The kingdom of God in the NT
Inaugurated at Jesus Christ's first coming Mt 12:28 pp Lk 11:20 See also Mk 1:15; Lk 4:43

Includes the restoration of all things Ac 3:21 See also Rev 21:1–4

Consummated at Jesus Christ's return Rev 11:15 See also Mt 24:30–31 pp Mk 13:26–27; Rev 12:10

See also
2230 Messiah, coming of	5359 justice
	6700 peace
2312 Christ as king	8154 righteousness
2345 Christ, kingdom of	9105 last things
	9140 last days
2375 kingdom of God	9150 Messianic banquet
2565 Christ, second coming	9220 day of the Lord

9150

Messianic banquet

A symbolic portrayal of the blessings of the age to come in which those chosen by God share in a rich feast with the Messiah. In the NT this is often pictured as a marriage supper with Jesus Christ as the groom and the church as both bride and invited guests. The feast, which will take place after the consummation of God's kingdom, is prefigured in the Lord's Supper.

The Messianic banquet promised
Isa 25:6; Lk 14:15

The significance of banqueting
As a sign of spiritual blessing Ps 23:5

See also Job 36:16; Isa 1:19; 55:1–2; Joel 2:24–26

As a sign of spiritual satisfaction
Ps 63:5 *See also* Ps 107:9; Isa 58:11; Eze 34:14; Jn 7:37–38; Rev 7:16–17

As a sign of fellowship with God
Rev 3:20 *See also* Ex 24:11 *This may have been a covenant meal to seal the covenant between God and Israel;* SS 2:4

The Messianic banquet as a wedding feast
The invitation to participate Mt 22:2; Rev 19:7–9 *See also* Mt 25:1–10; Lk 14:16; Rev 21:2,9–10

The invitation rejected Mt 22:3–6; Lk 14:16–20

The invitation given to others
Mt 8:11–12 *See also* Mt 22:7–14; Lk 13:28–29; 14:21–24

The anticipation of the Messianic banquet
Celebrating God's goodness Dt 16:15 *See also* Ne 8:10–12; Zec 14:16

It is prefigured in the Lord's Supper
Lk 22:15–16 *The Messianic banquet is here associated with the Passover meal which Jesus Christ shared with his disciples;* Mt 26:27–29 pp Mk 14:23–25 pp Lk 22:17–18; Jn 6:48–51 *See also* Lk 22:29–30; Jn 6:55–56; 1Co 11:26

See also

2230 Messiah, coming of	6638 election
4035 abundance	7020 church, the
4404 food	7933 Lord's Supper
4410 banquets	9145 Messianic age
5710 marriage, customs	

9155

millennium

The period of 1,000 years referred to in Revelation chapter 20, during which Satan is bound and believers reign with Jesus Christ. This millennium is understood in different ways: as a period of unparalleled peace and prosperity for the church and the gospel at the end of this age, after which Christ will return (postmillennialism); as the time following Christ's return when he will reign on earth (premillennialism); as a symbolic reference to the period between Christ's first and second comings (amillennialism).

Characteristics of the millennium
Satan is bound Rev 20:1–3 *"the Abyss" is the subterranean place of confinement for Satan and evil spirits. See also* Lk 8:31 pp Mt 8:29 pp Mk 5:7

Martyred believers are raised to reign with Jesus Christ Rev 20:4–6 *Those who have suffered for the gospel receive their promised reward. See also* Ro 8:17; 2Ti 2:11–12; Rev 2:10

Satan's release and final overthrow
Rev 20:7–10 *See also* Eze 38:1–4,

Eze 38:15–16,18–22; 39:2–5; Zec 14:2; Ro 16:20

The millennium will be a golden age on earth
Isa 2:2–4 pp Mic 4:1–3 *The OT looks forward to a period of universal peace and prosperity on earth. Both pre- and postmillennialists see this as a reference to Jesus Christ's future earthly reign. See also* Isa 11:6–9; 51:4–5; 65:25

The premillennial interpretation
The premillennial order of events
Rev 19:11–13 *Jesus Christ's return. Premillennialists understand the events of Revelation chapter 19 to precede those of Revelation chapter 20;* Rev 20:2–3 *Satan bound for 1,000 years;* Rev 20:4–6 *a "first resurrection" of believers to share Jesus Christ's reign over the earth;* Rev 20:7–10 *Satan's release and final overthrow;* Rev 20:11–15 *the general resurrection of all people to face God's judgment*

A first resurrection of believers
1Co 15:22–25 *This passage allows the idea of a gap between the resurrection of believers and the eternal age. See also* 1Th 4:16–17

God's future earthly reign Zec 14:9 *See also* Da 2:44; Zep 3:11; Zec 14:16–21

Believers will reign with Jesus Christ
Mt 19:28 *Premillennialists take this to refer to an earthly reign. See also* Lk 22:29–30; 1Co 6:2; Rev 5:9–10

Difficulties with premillennialism
Scriptures that depict a single resurrection of both the righteous and the wicked: Da 12:2; Jn 5:28–29
Jesus Christ's parables of the kingdom depict a single occasion of separation and judgment: Mt 13:40–43,49–50; 25:31–32

The postmillennial interpretation
The rapid spread of the gospel
Mt 24:14 pp Mk 13:10 *See also* Mt 13:31–33 pp Mk 4:31–32 pp Lk 13:18–21

A future turning to God Ps 22:27–28; Isa 19:19–24; Zec 2:11

Difficulties with postmillennialism
The fortunes of the gospel and the church appear to be at a low ebb before Jesus Christ returns: Mt 24:9–12 pp Lk 21:12–17; 2Ti 3:1–5,12–13
Jesus Christ's reign is not postponed to some future era; it has begun already: Mt 28:18; Ac 2:33–36; 7:55–56

The amillennial interpretation
Satan was defeated at Jesus Christ's first coming Jn 12:31 *See also* Mt 12:29 pp Mk 3:27 pp Lk 11:21–22; Lk 10:18–20; Col 2:14–15

Interpreting the "first resurrection"
As a reference to the soul entering heaven after death: Lk 23:43; 2Ti 4:7–8
As spiritual resurrection to new life in Christ: Ro 6:5; Eph 2:6; Col 3:1

Dangers of the amillennialist view
The future hope of believers is not only a spiritual reality: Ro 8:19–21; Rev 21:1
Though defeated, Satan should not be underestimated: 1Pe 5:8; 1Jn 5:19; Rev 12:17

See also

2372 Christ, victory	8794 persecution
2375 kingdom of God	9105 last things
	9115 antichrist, the
2565 Christ, second coming	9145 Messianic age
	9220 day of the LORD
4120 Satan	9310 resurrection
8450 martyrdom	9410 heaven

9160

new heavens and new earth

A way of referring to the new creation that will come about at the end of time. The theme of the restoration and re-creation of the world is a central aspect of the Christian hope.

The new heavens and new earth will replace the old
Isa 65:17 *See also* Heb 12:26–27; 2Pe 3:12–13; Rev 21:1

The nature of the new heavens and new earth
Their permanence Isa 66:22 *See also* Heb 12:28

The place of God's presence Rev 21:3

The effects of the fall will be reversed
Rev 21:4 *See also* Isa 65:20,23,25

See also

4055 heaven and earth	9105 last things
4203 earth, the	9165 restoration
4209 land, spiritual aspects	9410 heaven

9165

restoration

The returning of something or someone to their original state. Through the redeeming work of Jesus Christ, both humanity and creation will eventually be restored.

Restoration of human beings through the ministry of Jesus Christ
Restoration of health Lk 4:38–39; 8:43–44; 14:2–4

Restoration of life Lk 7:11–15; Jn 11:1–44

Restoration of sight Mk 8:22–25; Jn 9:1–7

Restoration of hearing Mk 7:32–35

The restoration of creation
Ac 3:21 *See also* Isa 11:6–9; 41:17–20; 55:10–13; Rev 21:1–4; 22:1–5

The restoration of Israel
Ps 14:7 *See also* Ps 69:35–36; Isa 41:13; 51:1–6; Jer 30:18–22; Eze 36:8–12; Am 9:13–15; Ro 11:25–27

Restoration in everyday life
The restoration of status Ge 40:13; Job 8:6

The restoration of fortunes Dt 30:3; Eze 16:53

The restoration of buildings 2Ch 24:4; Ezr 5:9

The restoration of authority 2Sa 8:3

See also

1115 God, purpose of	6698 newness
2321 Christ as redeemer	6740 returning to God
4005 creation	7135 Israel, people of God
5023 image of God	7145 remnant
5492 restitution	9160 new heavens & new earth
6614 atonement	
6652 forgiveness	

9170

signs of the times

Portents marking significant historical events. In Scripture the phrase refers principally to signs indicating the coming of the Messiah and the kingdom of God (both in the ministry of Jesus Christ and at the end of time).

Signs of the times signifying the future deliverance of Judah
2Ki 19:29–31 pp Isa 37:30–32 *The fruitfulness of the earth is to be a sign to Hezekiah that there will be a fruitful remnant of Judah.*

Signs of the times in the life of Jesus Christ
The virgin birth of Jesus Christ Isa 7:14 See also Mt 1:22–23

The miracles of Jesus Christ Mt 12:28 pp Lk 11:20 See also Jn 2:11,23; 3:2; 4:54; 6:2,14; 9:16; 11:47; 12:17–18; 20:30

Jesus Christ's resurrection
Mt 12:38–40 pp Lk 11:29–30 See also Mt 16:4; Jn 2:18–22

The Jews failed to perceive the signs of the times accompanying Jesus Christ's coming Mt 16:1–4 pp Mk 8:11–13 See also Lk 12:54–56; Jn 12:37

Signs of the times at the end of the age
Mt 24:3–14 pp Mk 13:3–13 pp Lk 21:7–19; Lk 21:25–28 pp Mt 24:29–30 pp Mk 13:24–26

It is impossible to predict the date of Jesus Christ's return from the signs of the times 1Th 5:1–2

Signs of the times signifying judgment
Isa 20:3–4; Mt 24:15–25 pp Mk 13:14–23 pp Lk 21:20–24 *The fall of Jerusalem is itself a sign of the judgment of all people at the end of time.*

Interpreting the signs of the times
Mk 13:28–29 pp Mt 24:32–33 pp Lk 21:29–31 See also 1Ch 12:32

See also

1416 miracles	5135 blindness, spiritual
1448 signs	
2230 Messiah, coming of	8319 perception, spiritual
2375 kingdom of God	9105 last things
	9220 day of the LORD
2565 Christ, second coming	9240 last judgment

9200

Judgment

9210

judgment, God's

God judges the world by identifying and condemning sin and by vindicating and rewarding the righteous. God exercises temporal judgment on the world and on his people; final judgment will take place when Jesus Christ returns.

The nature of God's judgment
Its certainty Ecc 12:14 See also Ps 7:11; Ecc 3:17; 11:9; Jas 5:9

Its righteousness Ge 18:25 See also Ps 9:7–8; 50:6; 96:13 pp 1Ch 16:33

Its impartiality 2Ch 19:7 See also Dt 10:17; Job 34:19; Ps 98:9; Ro 2:11; Eph 6:9

The purpose of God's judgment
To display his glory Isa 5:16 See also Ex 14:4; Isa 59:18–19; Eze 7:27; 38:23; Rev 14:7

To vindicate the righteous
1Sa 24:12–15 See also Ps 7:8–9; Isa 34:8; Jer 11:20; 51:9–10; Rev 16:5–7

To defend the weak Ps 140:12 See also Ps 82:1–4; Isa 11:4; Eze 34:16–22

To bring salvation to his people
Isa 30:18 See also Ex 6:6; Dt 32:36; Ps 76:8–9; 105:5–7 pp 1Ch 16:12–14; Isa 33:22

To punish sin Ro 2:12 See also Ps 1:4–6; Jn 12:48; Ro 5:16; Heb 10:26–30; 13:4

To turn people to God Isa 19:22 *Temporal judgments may turn people to God and so save them from eternal judgment. See also* 1Ki 8:33 pp 2Ch 6:24; 2Ch 7:13–14; Da 4:33–34; Hos 2:5–7; 1Co 11:29–32

God's judgment may be delayed
Job 24:1–4; 2Pe 3:9 See also Ps 74:10–11; 94:2–3; Hab 1:2–4,13; Ac 17:30; Ro 3:25; Rev 6:10

Examples of God's judgment
Judgment on ungodly individuals
Ac 12:23 See also 2Ch 21:18–19 Jehoram; Da 5:26–28 Belshazzar; Rev 2:22 Jezebel, the false prophetess

Judgment following particular sins
Ge 4:10–14 Cain's murder of Abel; Nu 20:12 Moses' and Aaron's disobedience; Lev 10:1–2 Nadab's and Abihu's disobedience; 1Sa 25:38–39 Nabal's contemptuous treatment of David; 2Sa 6:6–8 Uzzah's handling of the ark; 2Ki 2:23–24 youths jeering at Elisha; 2Ki 5:27 Gehazi's greed; 2Ch 26:19–20 Uzziah's pride and unfaithfulness; Ac 5:1–10 Ananias' and Sapphira's lies

Judgment on peoples and nations
Joel 3:12–13 See also Ge 6:17; 19:24–25 Egypt: Ex 7:4–5; Nu 33:4 1Sa 2:10; 5:6

Assyria: Isa 10:12; 37:36 pp 2Ki 19:35 Isa 34:5
Babylon: Jer 25:12; 51:56 Jer 25:31–33

God's judgment on his enemies
Dt 32:41–43 See also Ps 45:3–6; Isa 1:24; Eze 38:21–22; Jn 12:31; Rev 20:7–10

God's judgment on Israel
God's warning of judgment
Dt 28:15–24; Jer 1:16 See also Lev 26:15–20,33; Jer 11:7–8

Plagues Nu 16:46–47; 21:5–9; 2Sa 24:15 pp 1Ch 21:14

Drought and famine 1Ki 17:1; Hag 1:10–11

Defeat by enemies Jos 7:1–7; Jdg 2:11–16 *The cycle of sin, defeat and deliverance is repeated several times in Judges;* 2Ch 28:4–5

Exile 2Ki 17:23; Jer 11:17; La 1:5; Eze 39:23–24

God's final judgment on the whole earth
Ac 17:31 See also Da 12:2; Mt 25:31–32; Jn 12:48; Ro 2:16; 14:10; 1Co 4:5; 2Ti 4:1; 1Pe 4:5; Rev 20:11–15

See also

1075 God, justice of	5827 curse
1310 God as judge	6020 sin
2309 Christ as judge	9105 last things
4925 delay, divine	9220 day of the LORD
5482 punishment	9230 judgment seat
5493 retribution	9240 last judgment

9220

day of the LORD

The occasion of God's final intervention in human affairs to punish sin, restore the faithful of his people and establish his rule over the nations. It is linked with the Messianic hope and will be fulfilled at Jesus Christ's return. This future consummation is anticipated in historical acts of judgment and, although its time is unknown, it will be heralded and accompanied by signs and by great upheavals in nature.

The day of the LORD as a day of judgment
Of universal judgment Isa 24:21–22 See also Zep 1:14–18

Of judgment on the nations
Isa 13:9–11; Jer 46:10 See also Job 20:28–29; Isa 13:4–6 *God's judgment on Babylon*
God's judgment on Egypt: Isa 19:16–17; Eze 30:3–4
Isa 47:1; Joel 3:12–14; Ob 15 *God's judgment on Edom;* Zep 3:8; Ro 2:16; Rev 6:15–17

Of judgment on faithless Israel
Am 5:18–20 See also Isa 2:12; Joel 1:15; 2:1–2; Mt 7:22–23; Jn 12:48; Ro 2:5

The day of the LORD as a day of hope

A day of restoration for God's people
Jer 30:7–8 See also Joel 2:23–28

God will gather his people Isa 11:11; 27:12–13; Mic 4:6–7; Mt 24:30–31 pp Mk 13:26–27

God will save his people Zep 3:14–20 See also Isa 4:5–6; 26:1; Joel 2:32; 3:16–18; Ob 17; Zec 9:16–17

God will purify his people Isa 4:3–4; Zep 3:11–13; Zec 14:20–21; Mal 4:1–2

God will exalt his people Ob 21; Mic 4:8; 5:8–9; Rev 22:5

God will complete his saving work Php 1:6 The "day of Christ Jesus" is the NT equivalent to the "day of the LORD" which refers to Jesus Christ's second coming. See also Da 12:1–2; Jn 6:40; 11:24; 1Co 1:8; 2Ti 1:12; 4:8

The siege and deliverance of Jerusalem on the day of the LORD

Nations will gather against Jerusalem Eze 38:14–16; Zec 14:2; Lk 21:20; Rev 20:8–9

The LORD will fight for Jerusalem Eze 38:18–23; Zec 12:2–5; 14:3–5,12–13

The establishment of God's kingdom on the day of the LORD

God's kingdom will be universal and everlasting Zec 14:9 See also Da 2:44; 7:13–14; Rev 11:15

God will be the object of universal worship Isa 19:19–24; Zep 3:9–10; Zec 14:16

God's rule will be centred on a restored Jerusalem Isa 2:2–4 pp Mic 4:1–3; Zec 2:10–12; Rev 22:3

The fulfilment of Messianic hope on the day of the LORD

Isa 4:2 See also Isa 11:10; Jer 30:9; Hos 3:5; Am 9:11; Zec 9:9; 12:10

Being prepared for the day of the Lord

The day will come unexpectedly Th 5:2–3 See also Mt 24:43–44 pp Lk 12:39–40; Mk 13:32; 2Pe 3:10

The need to be ready for the day Th 5:4–8 See also Eze 13:5; Zep 2:1–3; Mal 4:5; 2Pe 3:11–12

Signs heralding the day may be discerned Mt 24:33 pp Mk 13:29 pp Lk 21:31; 2Th 2:3

The day of the Lord will be accompanied by signs and great upheavals in nature

c 2:19–20 See also Joel 2:30–31; Isa 13:9–10; Joel 2:10; Lk 21:11,25–26

Historical events anticipate the day of the LORD

Disaster foreshadows final judgment Isa 5:29–30 Judah invaded by Assyria; Eze 30:10 Egypt defeated by Nebuchadnezzar; Joel 2:2–4 Israel devastated by a locust swarm; Am 5:27 Israel defeated and exiled by Assyria; Mt 24:21 pp Mk 13:19 Jerusalem destroyed by the Romans

Return from exile foreshadows final restoration Isa 11:12–14; Hag 2:23; Zec 3:8

See also
1310 God as judge	9115 antichrist, the
2230 Messiah, coming of	9140 last days
	9170 signs of times
2233 Son of Man	9210 judgment,
2565 Christ, second coming	God's
	9240 last judgment
9105 last things	9310 resurrection
9110 after-life	

9230

judgment seat

The platform or throne from which kings and officials administer justice. God presently exercises judgment from his heavenly throne, symbolised in the OT by the ark of the covenant, and will one day bring all peoples before his judgment seat to give account of their lives and to receive their due reward.

Examples of earthly seats of judgment
Pr 20:8; Jn 19:13 pp Mt 27:19 See also Ex 18:13–14; 1Ki 7:7; Ps 122:5; Pr 31:23; Ac 12:21; 23:3; 25:23; Jas 2:6

God's judgment seat
God judges from his throne Ps 9:4–5 See also Ps 9:7–8; 11:4–7; 45:6; 97:2

The ark as a symbol of God's throne 2Sa 6:2 pp 1Ch 13:6 See also Ex 25:22; 1Sa 4:4; 2Ki 19:15 pp Isa 37:16; Ps 80:1; 99:1

God's future judgment 2Co 5:10 God's future judgment is exercised through Jesus Christ; Rev 20:11–13 See also Da 7:9–10; Joel 3:12; Mt 25:31–32; Ro 14:10

Believers will share Jesus Christ's judgment throne Mt 19:28 See also Lk 22:30; Rev 20:4

See also
1075 God, justice of	5581 throne
1310 God as judge	7306 ark of the
2309 Christ as judge	covenant
2565 Christ, second coming	9210 judgment, God's
5270 court	9220 day of the LORD
5359 justice	9240 last judgment
5366 king	

9240

last judgment

God's judgment of all people at the end of the age. This has been entrusted to Jesus Christ who, at his return, will reward the righteous and punish the unrighteous. Judgment will be on the basis of deeds, the response to God's revelation and faith in Jesus Christ. Believers need not fear the last judgment, but should live godly lives in anticipation of it.

The certainty of last judgment
Heb 9:27 See also Ecc 3:17; Ro 14:10–12; 2Co 5:10; 1Pe 4:5

The time of last judgment
It was anticipated in the cross Jn 12:31 Jesus Christ is speaking about his approaching death.

It will take place at the end of the age Mt 13:49 See also Mt 13:39–43

It will take place at Jesus Christ's return 2Th 1:6–7 See also Mt 25:31–33; 1Co 4:5; 2Pe 3:10; Rev 19:11

Last judgment is the prerogative of God
God as judge Da 7:9–10 See also Heb 12:23

God entrusts judgment to Jesus Christ Ac 17:31 See also Jn 5:22; Ac 10:42; Ro 2:16

The result of last judgment
Two eternal destinies Da 12:2 See also Mt 25:46

The ungodly will be punished 2Pe 3:7 See also Mt 25:41; Ro 2:5; Heb 10:26–28; 2Pe 2:4,9; Jude 6–7,15

The righteous will be rewarded 2Ti 4:8 See also Mt 25:34; 1Co 9:25; Rev 11:18

The basis of God's last judgment
It is according to works Rev 20:11–15 See also Mt 12:36–37; 16:27; Ro 2:6–10; Rev 22:12

It is according to revelation Ro 2:12 See also Mt 11:20–24 pp Lk 10:13–15 Those towns and cities which have rejected the revelation that Christ brings will face final judgment and condemnation; Mt 12:41–42 pp Lk 11:31–32 Gentiles have the light of general revelation and of conscience yet fail to live in accordance with what God has revealed: Ro 1:18–21; 2:14–15; 3:23; Gal 3:1

It is according to attitude to Jesus Christ Jn 3:18 The only basis for salvation is faith in Jesus Christ. See also Mt 10:14–15 pp Lk 10:11–12 Those towns which reject Jesus Christ's messengers will face judgment; Mt 10:32–33 pp Lk 12:8–9 Those who disown Jesus Christ will be disowned by him; Mt 25:35–40; Mk 8:38; Lk 10:16; Ac 4:12; 16:30–31

The fairness of God's last judgment
Ro 3:4–6 See also Ps 51:4; 98:9; Isa 16:5; Ro 3:19

Believers and last judgment
Believers need not fear judgment Jn 5:24 See also Ro 5:9; 1Co 11:32; 1Jn 4:17

Believers should live in the light of final judgment 1Co 3:12–15 building with materials that will last; 2Ti 4:1 holding to sound teaching; Heb 10:25 encouraging one another
Waiting with patient endurance: Jas 5:7–9; Rev 6:10–11
2Pe 3:11–13 living holy and godly lives

See also

1310 God as judge	8020 faith
1439 revelation	8442 good works
2309 Christ as judge	9105 last things
2565 Christ, second coming	9210 judgment, God's
5482 punishment	9220 day of the LORD
5498 reward	9230 judgment seat

9250

woe

An exclamation of judgment upon God's enemies, or of misfortune on oneself, or, in the ministry of Jesus Christ, of sadness over those who fail to recognise the true misery of their condition.

Woe as an exclamation of judgment on others
Woe to God's enemies Isa 33:1
Probably referring to Assyria. See also Jer 48:1–2; Na 3:1–7; Hab 2:6–20; Zep 2:5

Woe to God's faithless people Hos 7:13–16 *See also* Isa 30:1–2; 45:9–10; Jer 4:13–18; Eze 16:23–27

Woe to careless leaders of God's people Jer 23:1–2 *See also* Eze 13:1–9; 34:1–10; Zep 3:1–4; Zec 11:15–17

Woe to those who are complacent in their prosperity or religion Am 6:1–7 *See also* Am 5:18–24

Woe to those who neglect social justice Isa 10:1–4 *See also* Isa 5:8–23; Jer 22:13–19; Mic 2:1–3

Woe to a godless world Rev 8:13 *See also* Rev 12:12; 18:10,16–17,19

Woe as an exclamation of misfortune on oneself
Woe as a consequence of circumstances or events Jer 10:19
Jeremiah is describing the pain he feels at the impending destruction of his nation. See also 1Sa 4:6–8; Ps 120:5–7; Jer 4:13

Woe as a consequence of one's own sin La 5:16 *See also* Isa 3:8–9; 6:5

Woe as a consequence of God's call on one's life 1Co 9:16 *See also* Jer 45:1–5; Eze 2:9–3:11

Woe as an exclamation of sadness over others
Woe to those who do not recognise their own needs Lk 6:24–26

Woe to those whose religion blinds themselves and misleads others Lk 11:52 *See also* Mt 23:13–33; Lk 11:42–51

Woe to those who cause others to sin Mt 18:7 *See also* Lk 17:1–3

Woe to those on whom judgment is coming Lk 10:13–14 pp Mt 11:20–22

Woe to the one who betrays the Son of Man Mt 26:24 pp Mk 14:21 pp Lk 22:22

Woe to those who experience the signs of the end of the age Mt 24:19–21 pp Mk 13:17–19 pp Lk 21:23 *The word translated "how dreadful" is the same word that elsewhere is translated "woe".*

Woe may give way to forgiveness, comfort and deliverance
Isa 6:5–7 *See also* Isa 29:1–8; 40:1–2
After the woes of earlier chapters, Isaiah now prophesies the comfort that will come to God's people; Jer 45:2–5; La 3:16–26

See also

1335 blessing	5978 warning
5135 blindness, spiritual	6124 condemnation
5560 suffering	8767 hypocrisy
5805 comfort	8823 self-righteousness
5810 complacency	9210 judgment, God's
5899 lament	
5938 sadness	

9300

Resurrection

9310

resurrection

The raising of Jesus Christ from the dead by God after his suffering and death on the cross. Historical evidence for his resurrection includes the empty tomb and the appearance of the risen Christ to the disciples. It has significance both in relation to the identity of Jesus Christ and the future hope of believers.
This set of themes consists of the following:
9311 resurrection, of Jesus Christ
9312 resurrection, significance of Jesus Christ's
9313 resurrection, spiritual
9314 resurrection, of the dead
9315 resurrection, of believers

9311

resurrection, of Jesus Christ

The resurrection of Jesus Christ is of central importance to the NT. It affirms the divinity of Jesus Christ, marks the words and deeds of his ministry with God's seal of approval and opens the way to the future resurrection of believers.

Jesus Christ's resurrection was foreshadowed in the OT
In Abraham and Isaac: Ge 22:5; Heb 11:19
In Jonah: Jnh 1:17; 2:10; Mt 12:40

Jesus Christ's resurrection was predicted
In the OT 1Co 15:3–4 *See also* Isa 53:11; Hos 6:2; Lk 24:45–46; Ac 2:25–31; 13:35; Ps 16:8–11; Ac 13:34; 26:22–23

By Jesus Christ himself Mt 16:21 pp Mk 8:31 pp Lk 9:22 *See also* Mt 17:9 pp Mk 9:9; Mt 20:18–19 pp Mk 10:32–34 pp Lk 18:31–33; Mt 26:32 pp Mk 14:28; Jn 2:19–21

Jesus Christ's resurrection was anticipated by the raising of the dead
In the OT Heb 11:35 *None of the OT or NT miracles are true resurrections. Those raised resumed life as before, their bodies unchanged. Resurrection for Jesus Christ and therefore for his people means a changed body and permanent life in glory. This is the "better resurrection". See also* 1Ki 17:22; 2Ki 4:35; 13:21

In the miracles of Jesus Christ Lk 7:22 pp Mt 11:4–5 *See also* Mt 9:23–25 pp Mk 5:38–42; Mt 27:52–53; Lk 7:14–15; Jn 11:43–44

The sequence of events in Jesus Christ's resurrection
It was preceded by suffering and death Php 2:8–9 *See also* Jn 19:28–33; Heb 2:9

It took place on the first day of the week Jn 20:1–2 pp Mt 28:1–2 pp Mk 16:2–4 pp Lk 24:1–3

It was announced by angels Mt 28:5–6 pp Mk 16:5–6 pp Lk 24:4–6 *See also* Lk 24:23; 1Ti 3:16

The disciples were reluctant to believe it Lk 24:25–26 *See also* Mk 16:13–14; Lk 24:11; Jn 20:24–25

The disciples saw the evidence and were ultimately convinced Jn 2:22 *See also* Lk 24:33–35; Jn 20:8,18,26–28; Ac 2:32; 3:15; 4:33

The risen Christ appeared to many people Ac 1:3
To the disciples: Mt 28:16–17; Mk 16:14; Lk 24:50–52; Jn 20:19–23,26–31; 21:1–2; Ac 1:9–11
To Mary Magdalene: Mk 16:9; Jn 20:11–18
Lk 24:13–15 to two on the Emmaus road
To Peter: Lk 24:34; 1Co 15:5
To Paul: Ac 9:3–5 pp Ac 22:6–8, 26:12–15; 1Co 15:8
Ac 10:39–41; 1Co 15:6 *to over 500 people;* 1Co 15:7 *to James*

The resurrection was followed by Jesus Christ's entry into glory Ro 8:34 *See also* 1Co 15:24–29; Eph 1:18–21; 1Ti 3:16; Heb 1:3; Rev 1:18

Jesus Christ's resurrection body was spiritual but not ghostly Lk 24:37–39 *See also* Jn 20:27; Ac 1:4; 1Co 15:50; Php 3:21

See also

1429 prophecy, OT fulfilment	2530 Christ, death of
2018 Christ, divinity	2555 Christ, resurrection appearances
2351 Christ, miracles	
2366 Christ, prophecies concerning	2560 Christ, resurrection
2421 gospel, historical foundation	5396 lordship of Christ
2505 Christ, ascension	5471 proof
	8425 evangelism

9312

resurrection, significance of Jesus Christ's

Jesus Christ's resurrection represents a demonstration of the power of

God, the confirmation of the divinity of Jesus Christ and the grounds of hope for Christian believers.

Jesus Christ's resurrection was a demonstration of God's power
The power of God the Father
Eph 1:18–20 *See also* Mt 22:29–32; Ac 2:24; 3:15; 10:40; 13:29–30; Gal 1:1; Col 2:12

The power of the Holy Spirit Ro 1:4; 1Ti 3:16; 1Pe 3:18

The resurrection confirmed Jesus Christ as the Son of God
Jn 20:30–31 *John calls Jesus Christ's miracles "signs" (see also Jn 2:11; 6:2) and his resurrection is the climax, confirming his identity beyond all doubt; Ro 1:4 See also Ps 2:7; Ac 13:33*

The centrality of the resurrection of Jesus Christ
As the basis of faith 1Co 15:14–15 *See also* Ac 3:15; 4:33; 17:18; 24:21; Ro 10:9; 2Ti 2:8; Heb 6:1–2

As the basis of believers' justification
Ro 4:25; 8:34

As the basis of Christian hope
Ac 24:15; 1Co 15:19

As the basis of believers' resurrection
1Co 15:20–23 *The Law of Moses (Ex 23:16) provided for an offering of the firstfruits of crops to God. The firstfruits were the guarantee of the full harvest to come. The NT sees the resurrection of Jesus Christ as the firstfruits of the full ingathering of all God's people when Jesus Christ comes again. See also Jn 14:19; Ac 26:23; Ro 8:11*

See also
1105 God, power of	3030 Holy Spirit,
2066 Christ, power of	power
2218 Christ, Son of	8020 faith
God	9610 hope
2420 gospel	

9313
resurrection, spiritual

The gospel brings new life to men and women, who lived in death and darkness until they came to faith. The NT emphasis upon "being made alive in Christ" is closely linked to the resurrection of Jesus Christ.

Being made alive in Christ
Eph 2:1,4–6 *See also* Eze 37:1–14

Crossing over from death to life
Jn 5:24–26 *See also* Ro 6:3–5; 1Co 15:17; Col 2:13

Believers continue to live by the power of the risen Christ
Php 4:13 *See also* 2Co 5:17; Gal 2:20; Php 3:10

Results of being made alive in Christ
Spiritual desires Col 3:1–2

Spiritual assurance Col 3:3–4 *See also* Jn 5:24

Spiritual appetite 1Pe 2:1–3 *See also* Jn 3:3,6

Commitment to God Ro 6:13

Love for fellow believers 1Jn 3:14

Spiritual character Ro 7:4 *See also* Gal 5:22–23

See also
1055 God, grace &	6728 regeneration
mercy	8105 assurance,
2066 Christ, power of	basis of
3230 Holy Spirit &	8255 fruit, spiritual
regeneration	8292 love
3290 Holy Spirit,	8347 spiritual
life-giver	growth
4015 life	
5110 Paul, teaching	
of	

9314
resurrection, of the dead

Scripture speaks of a general resurrection of all people at the end of time, which will be followed by judgment.

The resurrection of the dead predicted
In the OT Da 12:2

By Jesus Christ Jn 5:28–29

The resurrection of the dead will occur at Jesus Christ's return
Rev 20:12–13 *See also* Ac 17:31; 1Co 15:52; 1Th 4:16

The resurrection of the dead includes both the righteous and wicked
Ac 24:15 *See also* Mt 25:31–32

Attitudes to the resurrection of the dead
Denial by false teachers 1Co 15:12 *See also* Mt 22:23 pp Mk 12:18 pp Lk 20:27; Ac 23:8; 2Ti 2:18

Ridicule from unbelievers Ac 17:18,32

Unbelief Ac 26:8 *See also* Mt 22:29–32 pp Mk 12:24–27 pp Lk 20:34–38; 1Co 15:35–44

See also
2042 Christ, justice	7555 Sadducees
of	8834 unbelief
2565 Christ, second	9105 last things
coming	9110 after-life
5288 dead, the	9135 immortality
5535 sleep and death	

9315
resurrection, of believers

The future event of finally being raised to glory with Jesus Christ. Believers may rest assured that, on account of their faith, they will share in the resurrection and glory of Christ and be with him for ever.

The nature of the resurrection of believers
A resurrection to eternal life
Jn 11:25–26 *See also* Da 12:3; Lk 20:35–36; Jn 5:24–25

Being completely united to Jesus Christ Ro 6:5 *See also* Jn 6:39,44;

Ac 26:23; Ro 6:8; 1Co 6:14; 15:20–23; 2Co 4:14; Col 3:4; 1Th 4:16; 2Ti 2:11

It leads to becoming like Jesus Christ
1Co 15:49 *See also* Ps 17:15; Mt 22:24–30 pp Mk 12:18–25; 1Co 15:51–53; Php 3:21; 1Jn 3:2

The resurrection as the future hope of believers
1Co 15:19; 1Th 4:13–14 *In the NT the death of believers is often likened to sleep. See also* Job 19:23–27; Ps 49:15; 71:20; Isa 26:19; Da 12:3; Hos 13:14; Jn 11:24; Ac 23:6; 24:15; 2Co 5:1–4; 2Ti 1:10

The resurrection as an incentive to godliness and perseverance
1Co 15:58 *See also* Lk 14:12–14; 1Co 15:30–32; 2Co 5:6–10; Php 1:20–21; Heb 11:35; 1Jn 3:3

The resurrection as an incentive to endurance of suffering
Ro 8:17; 2Ti 2:11–12 *See also* Jn 12:24–25; Ac 14:22; 1Pe 4:12–13

See also
1194 glory, divine &	6754 union with
human	Christ
5136 body	8459 perseverance
5560 suffering	9413 heaven,
6214 participation in	inheritance
Christ	9613 hope as
6644 eternal life	confidence

Heaven

heaven

God's habitation where he is worshipped and served by angels. Solely on account of the sacrifice of Jesus Christ on the cross, believers will inherit a place in heaven and there for ever enjoy perfect fellowship with God in his worship and service.

9411
heaven, nature of

Scripture refers to heaven as God's habitation but also uses the term as an alternative for God himself.

Heaven as God's habitation
It is the place where he dwells Dt 26:15 *See also* Ge 28:17; 2Ch 6:21; Ecc 5:2; Rev 13:6

It is insufficient as God's dwelling-place 1Ki 8:27 pp 2Ch 6:18 *See also* Ps 113:5–6

Heaven as the place of God's throne
Ps 11:4 *See also* Ex 24:9–11; 1Ki 22:19; Isa 6:1; 63:15; Da 7:9; Mt 5:34; 23:22; Ac 7:49; Isa 66:1; Heb 8:1; Rev 4:1–6; 20:11

Heaven as God's vantage point
Ps 33:13 *See also* Ps 53:2; 102:19–20; Ecc 5:2

Heaven as an alternative term for God

Lk 15:18 *See also* Mt 8:11; 13:11 *Matthew is writing especially for Jews who, out of reverence, tried to avoid using the word "God". Mk 4:11 and Lk 8:10 prefer "kingdom of God"*; Mt 16:19; 18:18; 21:25 pp Mk 11:30 pp Lk 20:4; Jn 3:27; 17:1

Heaven and the sovereignty of God

Heaven is the place of God's rule Da 4:26 *See also* Ps 45:6; 103:19; Ac 17:24

God's voice from heaven speaks with divine authority Dt 4:36 *See also* Da 4:31; Jn 12:28; 1Th 4:16; 2Pe 1:17–18

Heaven glimpsed by human eyes

At the baptism of Jesus Christ Mk 1:10 pp Mt 3:16 pp Lk 3:21–22 *See also* Jn 1:32

In visions Ac 7:56 *See also* 2Co 12:2–4; Rev 4:1

Prayer addressed to God in heaven

1Ki 8:30 *See also* Dt 26:15; 2Ch 30:27; Ne 1:4; Ps 20:6; Rev 5:8

The association of oaths with heaven

Mt 23:22 *See also* Ge 24:3; Da 12:7; Mt 5:34; Jas 5:12

The place of Jesus Christ in heaven

His pre-existence in heaven Jn 6:38 *See also* Jn 3:13

His ascension into heaven after his resurrection Lk 24:51 pp Mk 16:19 *See also* Eph 1:20

His place is now with God the Father Heb 9:24 *See also* Col 3:1

His second coming will be from heaven 1Th 4:16 *See also* Mt 25:31; Ac 1:11; 1Th 1:10

The new heaven

The new heaven completely replaces the old Rev 21:1 *See also* Isa 65:17; 66:22; 2Pe 3:13

The new Jerusalem is divinely created in heaven Rev 21:2 *See also* Isa 2:2–5; Heb 11:16; 13:14; Rev 3:12; 21:10

Fulness of life in heaven is wholly sustained by God Rev 21:22–23; 22:1–2 *See also* Isa 55:1; Eze 47:8–9,12; Jn 7:38–39; Rev 2:7

See also

1130 God, sovereignty	7269 Zion
1205 God, titles of	8602 prayer
1469 visions	9105 last things
2505 Christ, ascension	9160 new heavens & new earth
5429 oaths	9230 judgment seat
5581 throne	9430 paradise

9412

heaven, worship and service in

All in heaven engage continuously in the worship of God, while they perfectly carry out his will.

All heaven worships God

The multitude in heaven and the twenty-four elders Rev 19:6–7 *See also* Ne 9:6; Rev 4:6–11; 7:11–12; 11:16; 22:8–9

The redeemed 1Pe 2:9 *See also* Isa 51:11; Rev 19:5–7

The angels Lk 2:13–14; Rev 5:11–12; 7:11

God is worshipped in song Rev 15:2–3 *See also* Rev 14:3

Jesus Christ is worshipped in heaven Php 2:10–11 *See also* Da 7:14; Heb 1:6; Rev 5:8–14

All heaven serves God

God's will is perfectly done in heaven Mt 6:10 *See also* Mt 12:50

The redeemed will serve God Rev 22:3 *See also* Rev 5:10; 7:13–15

The redeemed will reign with Jesus Christ and share his authority Mt 19:28; 25:34; 1Co 6:3; 2Ti 2:12; Heb 12:28; Rev 2:26–27; 3:21; 20:6

The divine service of angels

They have divine authority Rev 8:2; 18:1; 20:1

They serve Jesus Christ Mt 25:31; 26:53; Lk 4:10; 22:43; 2Th 1:7–8; Heb 1:6; 1Pe 3:22

They serve believers 1Ki 19:5–8; Mt 24:31; Heb 1:14

They serve by encouraging Ge 21:17; Lk 22:43; Ac 27:23–24

They serve by guarding Ex 14:19; 2Ki 6:15–17; Ps 91:11; Mt 18:10; Rev 7:2–3

They serve by instructing Ge 22:11,15; Zec 6:5; Mt 1:20; 2:13; 28:5–7; Lk 1:13,19; Ac 8:26; 10:3–5

They serve by delivering believers in trouble Da 6:22; Ac 5:19; 12:7

Their service is continuous Ge 28:12; Jn 1:51

See also

1175 God, will of	7963 song
2012 Christ, authority	8626 worship, places
4110 angels	8664 praise
7720 elders in the church	

9413

heaven, inheritance of

Heaven is the secure inheritance, of priceless value, awaiting the redeemed. There, faithful service will be rewarded and the redeemed will be given resurrection bodies for service in the heavenly realm.

Believers inherit the kingdom of heaven

Their inheritance is secure Mt 25:34 *See also* Lk 12:32; 22:28–29; Jas 2:5

The value of their inheritance is beyond human calculation 1Co 2:9–10 *See also* Ac 20:32; Eph 1:18; 2:6–7

As those adopted into God's family they are heirs of God and Christ Ro 8:17 *See also* Gal 4:7; Tit 3:7; Heb 6:17

The nature of the heavenly inheritance

It is inviolable 1Pe 1:3–5 *See also* Rev 21:25,27

It is a response to faith and love Jas 2:5 *See also* Col 1:12; 3:24; Heb 11:7

It is for overcomers Rev 21:7 *See also* 1Jn 4:4; 5:3–5; Rev 2:7,11,17,26–28; 3:5,12,21

The heavenly treasure is to be sought Mt 6:19–21 *See also* Mt 13:44; 19:21; Lk 12:33; 2Co 4:18; Php 3:8; 1Ti 6:18–19; Rev 3:18

Heavenly rewards

Service will be rewarded in heaven 1Co 3:11–14 *See also* Mt 5:12 pp Lk 6:23; Rev 22:12

The prospect of heavenly rewards should be a spur to present service Php 3:14 *See also* Heb 11:26

Rewards will vary Mt 16:27 *See also* Da 12:3; Mt 25:20–23 pp Lk 19:15–19; 1Co 3:8; 2Co 9:6; Rev 22:12

Endurance for Jesus Christ's sake will be specially rewarded Mt 5:10–12 pp Lk 6:22–23

Rewards for service include crowns signifying position and authority 1Pe 5:4 *See also* 1Th 2:19; 2Ti 4:8

The redeemed will share Jesus Christ's position in glory Eph 2:6 *See also* Jn 14:3; 17:24; 1Jn 3:2; Rev 22:4

The resurrection body as a heavenly inheritance

Php 3:20–21 *See also* 1Co 15:42–44; 2Co 5:1–4

See also

2375 kingdom of God	5705 inheritance, spiritual
5280 crown	8117 discipleship, benefits
5312 feasting	8418 endurance
5498 reward	8642 celebration
5558 storing	9310 resurrection
5591 treasure	

9414

heaven, as community of the redeemed

The community of the redeemed in heaven will represent all peoples and languages. They will owe this solely to the sacrifice of Jesus Christ. They will share in the divine life in perfect fellowship with God, free for ever from suffering and death.

Heaven as a divine gift

Ro 6:23 *See also* Lk 12:32; 22:28–30; Jn 17:2

Divine preparations made for believers in heaven

Jn 14:2 *See also* 2Co 5:1; Heb 11:16

The redeemed in heaven come from all peoples

Rev 7:9–10 *See also* Isa 59:19; Mal 1:11; Mt 8:11 pp Lk 13:29; Rev 5:9

The redeemed owe their place in heaven solely to Jesus Christ

Rev 7:14 *Washing one's robes in the blood of the Lamb symbolises cleansing through the sacrifice of Jesus Christ. See also* 1Pe 1:18–19; Rev 22:14

The redeemed are identified with Jesus Christ

Jesus Christ acknowledges the redeemed as his own Lk 12:8 *See also* Mt 7:21–23

Believers possess the family likeness to Jesus Christ 1Co 15:49 *See also* 2Co 3:18; Php 3:21; 1Jn 3:2

Believers share divine life 2Pe 1:4 *See also* Rev 2:7; 3:21

Believers on earth at the second coming will be taken up to heaven

Rev 11:12 *See also* Jn 11:26; 1Th 4:16–17 *Believers living on earth when Jesus Christ returns will not experience death, but be taken straight to heaven.*

Conditions in heaven for the redeemed

Perpetual and perfect fellowship with the **Lord** Rev 21:3 *See also* Ps 17:15; Mt 5:8; Jn 14:3; 1Th 4:17; Rev 22:4

Joy in the immediate presence of God Ps 16:11 *See also* Isa 51:11; Mt 25:21; Lk 15:7,10; Jn 15:11; 1Th 2:19–20; Heb 12:2,22; Jude 24

Restfulness 2Th 1:5–7 *See also* Heb 4:3,9; Rev 14:13

There will no longer be any need for the marriage relationship Mt 22:30 pp Mk 12:25 pp Lk 20:35–36

Heaven is filled with the light of God's glory Rev 21:23 *See also* Da 12:3; Mt 13:43; 2Co 4:17; 1Pe 2:9

Believers will share Jesus Christ's glory Col 3:4 *See also* Jn 17:24; 1Th 2:12; 1Pe 5:4,10

Divine glory will banish the memory of earthly troubles Ro 8:18 *See also* 2Co 4:17; 1Pe 5:1

There will be no more death or suffering in heaven Rev 21:4 *See also* Isa 25:8; 35:10; 51:11; Lk 20:35–36; Rev 7:17

Believers are citizens of the heavenly Jerusalem

Php 3:20 *See also* Ps 87:5; Isa 35:9–10; 51:11; Gal 4:26; Heb 11:16; Rev 21:2

Their names are enrolled as citizens of heaven Lk 10:20 *See also* Php 4:3; Heb 12:23; Rev 3:5; 13:8; 14:1; 17:8; 20:12; 21:27

See also

1045 God, glory of	6644 eternal life
2024 Christ, glory of	6720 redemption
2565 Christ, second coming	7239 Jerusalem
	8283 joy
5255 citizenship	9020 death
5708 marriage	9420 book of life

book of life

Book in which the names of the living were recorded and from which

their names were removed at death. From the time of the exodus onwards, Scripture contains references to God's book of life. It is to contain only the names of the righteous and is to be opened on the day of judgment.

The privilege of having one's name in the book of life

Lk 10:20; Heb 12:22–23 *See also* Da 12:1; Php 4:3; Rev 3:5; 21:27

The unrighteous are excluded from the book of life

Ex 32:31–33 *See also* Ps 69:27–28; Rev 13:8; 17:8; 20:12–15

Other references to such a book

Ps 56:8; 139:16; Mal 3:16

See also

5232 book	9230 judgment seat
9210 judgment, God's	

paradise

The destination of the righteous after death

Lk 23:43 *This Persian term originally described a park or pleasure garden. It was used by the Jews of the Garden of Eden, and of the future blessedness of the saints. See also* 2Co 12:3–4; Rev 2:7

See also

4209 land, spiritual aspects	6644 eternal life
	9020 death
4241 Garden of Eden	9410 heaven

Hell

hell

A term used in English translations of the Bible to represent the Hebrew word "Sheol" (the place of the departed) and the Greek word "Gehenna", which came to refer to the place of punishment for the wicked after death. The Valley of Hinnom (Hebrew "Ge Hinnom", from which "Gehenna" is derived) on the south side of Jerusalem became a symbol of all that is hateful to God, on account of its use for human sacrifice.

9511
hell, as a place of punishment

The place of eternal punishment in fire and darkness intended for Satan and his angels, but also for human beings who choose to reject God.

Hell was originally created for the devil and his angels

Mt 25:41 *See also* Lk 8:31; 2Pe 2:4; Rev 20:1–3,10

Hell is a consequence of rejecting God

Mt 13:40–42 *See also* Dt 32:22 *Fire is often referred to in the OT as a symbol of divine judgment;* Mk 9:42–48; Jn 3:36; Ro 2:8; 1Th 5:9; Heb 10:26–29; 2Pe 3:7; Rev 20:15; 21:8

Jesus Christ possesses authority over hell

Mt 16:18; Rev 1:18 *The Greek word "Hades" often simply means "death". However, at points it implies the experience of punishment after death. See also* Jn 5:27; Ac 10:42; 17:31

The Valley of Hinnom as a figure of hell

The Valley of Hinnom as a geographical feature Jos 15:8; 18:16

The Valley of Hinnom as a place of child sacrifice 2Ch 28:3 pp 2Ki 16:3 *See also* 2Ki 23:10; 2Ch 33:6 pp 2Ki 21:6; Jer 32:35

The Valley of Hinnom as a place of God's judgment Jer 7:30–32 *See also* Jer 19:1–15

The Valley of Hinnom as a synonym for hell Mt 10:28 pp Lk 12:4–5 *The word used for "hell" is "Gehenna", from the Hebrew "Ge Hinnom", meaning "the Valley of Hinnom". See also* Mt 5:29–30; 18:8–9 pp Mk 9:43–48

See also

3284 Holy Spirit, resisting	6230 rejection
	9122 eternity & God
4120 Satan	9210 judgment, God's
4130 demons	
5001 human race, the	9240 last judgment
	9530 Hades
6124 condemnation	9540 Sheol
6193 impenitence	

9512
hell, as an experience

The state of final separation from God, and so from all light, love, peace, pleasure and fulfilment.

Hell is separation from God

2Th 1:8–10 *See also* Mt 7:23; 8:12; 25:32; Rev 21:8

The final state of the wicked is one of eternal punishment

Mt 25:41–46 *"eternal punishment" means the punishment that is part of, and belongs to, the final order of things that follows this present age. This is usually, though not invariably, understood as an unending process of punishment consciously experienced by the wicked. See also* Jude 7

Biblical expressions for final punishment

God's wrath Jn 3:36 *See also* Dt 32:22; Zep 1:18; Mt 3:7; Ro 2:5; 1Th 1:10; Rev 19:15–16

Torment Lk 16:23–24 *See also* Mt 8:29; Rev 14:11; 20:10

Corruption Ps 55:23; 2Pe 1:4

Destruction Gal 6:8 See also Dt 7:10; Ps 88:11; Jn 17:12; Ro 9:22; Php 3:18–19; 2Th 2:3; Rev 17:8

Unquenchable fire Jude 7 See also Isa 66:24; Mt 3:12; 18:8–9; Heb 10:27; Rev 19:20

Intense darkness, emphasising utter isolation Jude 13 See also Mt 22:13; 2Pe 2:17; Jude 6

Death Jn 8:21 See also Job 28:22; Pr 15:11; Isa 28:15; Hos 13:14; Ro 6:23; 1Co 15:26,54–55

The second death Rev 20:14–15 See also Rev 20:6; 21:8

The finality of hell
Lk 16:26 See also Heb 6:4–6; 10:26–27; Rev 16:11

See also
1025 God, anger of	5584 torture
4826 fire	6130 corruption
5295 destruction	8341 separation
5398 loss	9024 death, spiritual
5482 punishment	9040 grave, the
5493 retribution	9105 last things

9513
hell, as incentive to action

The reality of hell should affect the way people live.

The importance of making the right choice
Mt 7:13–14 See also Dt 30:19; Jer 21:8; Lk 13:23–25

A personal spiritual life is vital
It is more important than short-term worldly gain Mt 16:26 pp Mk 8:36 pp Lk 9:25 See also Lk 12:20; 16:19–25

It is not just outward appearance Mt 3:7–10 pp Lk 3:7–9

Religious activity alone is not only valueless but perilous Mt 7:21–23 See also Pr 14:12; Jer 23:11–12; Lk 13:26–28; Jn 15:6

Believers must maintain their loyalty to God
Mt 10:28 pp Lk 12:4–5 See also Dt 4:23–24; Isa 8:12–13

Temptations to sin must be dealt with drastically
Mt 5:29–30 See also Mt 18:8–9; Mk 9:43–48

Some attitudes and practices that lead to hell
Deliberately continuing in sin Heb 10:26–27 See also Nu 15:30; Heb 6:4–6; 2Pe 2:20

Lack of spiritual response Mt 22:13; 24:51; 25:30

Wilfully ignoring divine activity Mt 11:20–24 pp Lk 10:13–15 Sodom, destroyed by God, was notoriously sinful. See also Mt 23:33; 25:41–46

Contempt for fellow humans Mt 5:22 The term "fool" implied the despising of another as worthless and godless. See also Jas 3:6

See also
5818 contempt	8704 apostasy
6139 deadness, spiritual	8712 denial of Christ
6193 impenitence	8748 false religion
6248 temptation	8784 nominal religion
8408 decision-making	8848 worldliness
8489 urgency	9410 heaven

9520
Abyss, the

Derived from a Greek word meaning "something which is bottomless" and often used to refer to a place of despair in which demons are imprisoned.

The Abyss as a place of despair
Lk 8:31; Rev 9:2

The Abyss as the home of demons
Rev 9:11; 17:8

The Abyss as a prison
Rev 9:1; 20:1,3

See also
4227 deep, the	9510 hell
9020 death	
9210 judgment, God's	

9530
Hades

A term used in the NT to refer to the place in which departed spirits rest, while waiting for judgment.

Hades is the place where the dead wait for judgment
Rev 20:13–14 See also Mt 11:23 pp Lk 10:15 translated "depths"; Lk 16:23 translated "hell" Translated "grave" and rendering the Hebrew word "Sheol": Ac 2:27,31 Rev 6:8

Jesus Christ is Lord of Hades
Mt 16:18; Rev 1:18

See also
9020 death	9430 paradise
9040 grave, the	9510 hell
9110 after-life	9540 Sheol

9540
Sheol

A Hebrew term used to refer to the grave, the pit or the tomb. Some older translations have the term incorrectly translated as "hell".

Sheol is the destiny of all
Ps 89:48 See also Ge 37:35; 44:29; 1Ki 2:9; Ps 18:5; 107:20; Pr 1:12; 30:16; Eze 31:15–17; Jnh 2:2

Sheol is often described in terms suggesting a grave
Ps 88:11–12 See also Job 3:13–19; 7:9; 17:13–16; Ps 6:5; Ecc 9:10; Isa 14:9–11; 38:18

To go to Sheol was regarded as a punishment
Nu 16:33 See also 1Sa 2:6; Job 24:19; Ps 9:17; 31:17; 49:14; 55:15; Isa 14:15

There is hope even in Sheol
Job 14:13; Ps 16:10 See also Ps 30:3; 49:15; 86:13

See also
4257 pit	9110 after-life
9020 death	9510 hell
9040 grave, the	9530 Hades
9050 tombs	

9600
Hope

9610
hope

In Scripture, a confident expectation for the future, describing both the act of hoping and the object hoped for. When grounded in God, hope provides the motivation to live the Christian life even in the face of trouble.

This set of themes consists of the following:
9611 hope, nature of
9612 hope, in God
9613 hope, as confidence
9614 hope, results of its absence
9615 hope, results of

9611
hope, nature of

Hope, in its general sense, is the anticipation of a future outcome. It is a subjective expectation which may be either firmly based or misdirected.

Hope that an event will take place
1Co 9:10; 1Ti 3:14 See also Est 9:1; Lk 6:34; Ac 24:26 Felix hoped Paul would offer him a bribe; Ro 15:24 Paul hoped to visit Rome on his way to Spain; 1Co 9:15; 16:7; 2Co 1:13–14; 5:11; 11:1 Paul hopes to send Timothy to the Philippians: Php 2:19,23 Phm 22; 2Jn 12; 3Jn 14

Hope for a positive outcome
Ecc 9:4 See also Ru 1:12; 2Ki 4:28; Pr 19:18; Ro 11:14

Misplaced or vain hope
Ps 33:17; Jer 23:16 See also Job 8:13–14; 11:20; Pr 26:12; 29:20; Jer 50:7; 1Ti 6:17

Hope removed or not satisfied
Job 30:26; Jer 8:15 See also Job 6:19–20; 14:7–12; 19:10; 27:8; Isa 38:18; Jer 13:16; 14:19; La 3:18; Eze 37:11; Zec 9:5; Lk 24:21 The two disciples share their hopes with Jesus Christ on the Emmaus road; 1Th 4:13

The malicious hope of the wicked
Pr 10:28 See also Pr 11:7,23; 24:19–20; Lk 20:20; 23:8; Ac 16:19

9612
hope, in God

A total grounding of one's confidence and expectation in God's goodness and providential care even in the face of trouble.

Hope in God is commanded
Ps 131:3; 1Ti 6:17 *See also* Ps 31:24; 130:7; Ro 12:12; Heb 10:23

Hope can be placed in Scripture as the word of God
Ps 119:74 *See also* Ps 119:43,49,81, 114,147; 130:5; Isa 42:4; Ac 26:6; Ro 15:4; Col 1:5

Hope can be placed in God in the face of difficulty or trial
Ps 42:5; 2Co 1:10 *See also* Ezr 10:2; Job 5:16; 13:15; Ps 9:18; 25:19–21; 119:116; Jer 14:19; 1Ti 5:5

The outcome of hoping in God
It brings security and confidence
Ps 146:5 *See also* Job 11:18; Ps 25:3 *There is no shame for those who hope in the* Lord; Ps 33:17–18,20–22 *The* Lord *helps and protects those who hope in him;* Ps 39:7; 52:9; 71:5; 147:11; Jer 14:22; La 3:21–22; Ac 24:15; Ro 15:12; 1Ti 4:10

It leads to specific results Ps 37:9; Isa 40:31; Ro 15:13 *See also* Ps 33:22; 62:5 *rest;* Ps 71:14; Pr 24:14–16 *wisdom;* Isa 51:5; Jer 29:11; La 3:25; Mic 7:7; Zec 9:12 *restoration;* Ro 4:18 *the example of Abraham's hope;* Ro 5:2,5; 2Co 1:7; 10:15; 1Th 1:3; 2Ti 2:25; Tit 1:2 *eternal life;* 1Pe 3:5; 1Jn 3:3

See also
1050 God, goodness   5763 attitudes,
    of   positive to God
1320 God as Saviour   8020 faith
1330 God, the   8030 trust
    provider   8331 reliability
4112 angels,   8463 priority of faith,
    messengers   hope & love

9613
hope, as confidence

Hope means more than a vague wish that something will happen. It is a sure and confident expectation in God's future faithfulness and presence. The horizon of Christian hope extends beyond death into an eternity prepared by God himself, the reality of which is guaranteed by Jesus Christ.

God and Jesus Christ are the hope of believers
Ps 71:5; 1Ti 1:1 *See also* Jer 14:8; 17:13;

Mt 12:21; Isa 42:4; Ac 28:20; Ro 15:12–13; Isa 11:10; 1Ti 4:10; 1Pe 1:21

The hope of resurrection and eternal life
Ac 23:6 *The Sadducees did not believe in the resurrection whereas the Pharisees did;* Tit 1:2 *See also* Ac 2:26–27; Ps 16:9; Ac 24:15; Ro 8:24; 1Co 15:19; Tit 3:7; Heb 6:11; 7:19; 1Pe 1:3

The hope of future glory
Ro 5:2; Col 1:27; Tit 2:13 *See also* Ro 8:18–21; 2Co 3:10–12; Gal 5:5; Eph 1:12,18; 1Th 2:19; 5:8; 2Ti 4:8

Hope is a Christian virtue
Ro 5:3–4; 1Co 13:13 *See also* Ro 12:12; 15:13; 1Co 13:7; Eph 4:4; Col 1:23; Heb 3:6; 1Pe 3:15

The effect of future hope on living now
Col 1:4–5 *See also* Ro 8:22–23 *Hope induces a longing for what will be when Jesus Christ returns;* 1Th 1:3; 5:8; Heb 6:19; 1Pe 1:13; 1Jn 3:1–3

See also
1035 God,   8215 confidence,
    faithfulness   results
1190 glory   9020 death
3203 Holy Spirit &   9110 after-life
    assurance   9130 future, the
5596 victory   9160 new heavens &
6510 salvation   new earth
6644 eternal life   9310 resurrection

9614
hope, results of its absence

An absence of hope leads to a loss of vision, a sense of despondency and ultimately to despair. This contrasts sharply with the Christian hope.

Feelings produced by a lack of hope
Despair Job 17:13–15; Pr 13:12; 1Ch 29:15 *See also* Job 6:11; 7:6; Ps 88:15–18; Ecc 2:17; Isa 19:9; 38:18; 2Co 1:8

A sense of being abandoned by God
Ps 22:1–2 *See also* La 3:18; Eze 37:11

A deep longing for life to end 1Ki 19:4; Job 3:20–21; Ecc 4:1–2 *See also* Ge 27:46; Nu 11:15; Job 7:13–15; Jer 8:3; Jnh 4:3,8; Rev 9:6

The outcome of a lack of hope
The choice of trusting in God or futile self-effort Ro 4:18 *See also* Jnh 1:13–14; Jer 18:11–12; Ac 27:20

Suicide Mt 27:5 *See also* 1Sa 31:4; 2Sa 17:23; 1Ki 16:18

See also
5067 suicide   6230 rejection
5770 abandonment   8713 discourage-
5831 depression   ment
5916 pessimism   8820 self-confidence

9615
hope, results of

Hope gives believers confidence and reassurance in this present life, allowing them to lead effective lives for God. It also reassures them of the reality of eternal life, allowing them to face death with confidence.

Hope reassures believers in this present life
Hope reassures believers in their faith
Heb 3:6 *See also* Eph 1:18–19; Heb 7:18–22; 10:23

Hope encourages believers Ps 31:2 *See also* Isa 40:31; 49:23; Ro 5:3–5

Hope encourages believers to rejoice
Ro 12:12 *See also* Ro 5:1–2

Hope encourages believers to look for restoration Ps 37:9; Jer 14:8; 31:17; La 3:29–31; Hos 2:15; Zec 9:12

Hope leads to more effective Christian living and witness
Hope encourages believers to be bold
2Co 3:12

Hope encourages believers to evangelise 1Pe 3:15

Hope leads to godly living Ps 25:21; Heb 6:10–12; 1Jn 3:2

Hope equips believers for spiritual warfare 1Th 5:8

Hope enables believers to face suffering with confidence Ro 5:3–5 *See also* Ps 22:24; 147:11; Php 1:20

Hope enables believers to face the future with confidence
Hope assures believers of an eternal dimension to life 1Co 15:19

Hope enables believers to face death with confidence Ps 16:9–10 *See also* Job 19:25–27; Ps 33:18; 1Co 6:14; 2Co 4:10–14; Php 1:3–6; Rev 1:17–18

Hope assures believers of their eternal life Ac 2:26–27; Ro 8:23–25; Tit 1:1–2; 3:7; 1Pe 1:3

Hope enables believers to face the coming wrath with confidence 1Th 1:10

Hope assures believers of their heavenly inheritance 1Pe 1:3–5 *See also* Eph 1:18

See also
3203 Holy Spirit &   8202 boldness
    assurance   8283 joy
3287 Holy Spirit,   8318 patience
    sealing of   8414 encourage-
5703 inheritance   ment
6705 peace,   8459 perseverance
    experience   9413 heaven,
8104 assurance   inheritance
8117 discipleship,
    benefits

Scripture Index

How to use this book

The heart of the Dictionary of Bible Themes is the section on Bible Themes: over 2,000 themes covering the key themes of Scripture. Two ways of helping readers find their way into this section are provided:

* the Alphabetical List of Themes (pages 1–15). This provides a complete listing in one single alphabetical order of all the theme titles. Selective cross-references are also provided for ease of use, e.g., at "anxiety" the reader is directed to "worry" and at "Cephas" to "Peter".

* the Scripture Index of Themes (pages 613–1232). Verses of the Bible are listed and appearing alongside each verse are the themes associated with that particular passage.

In each case, theme name and theme number should be noted and readers should use the theme number to locate the theme in the Thematic Section.

Using the Scripture Index of Themes

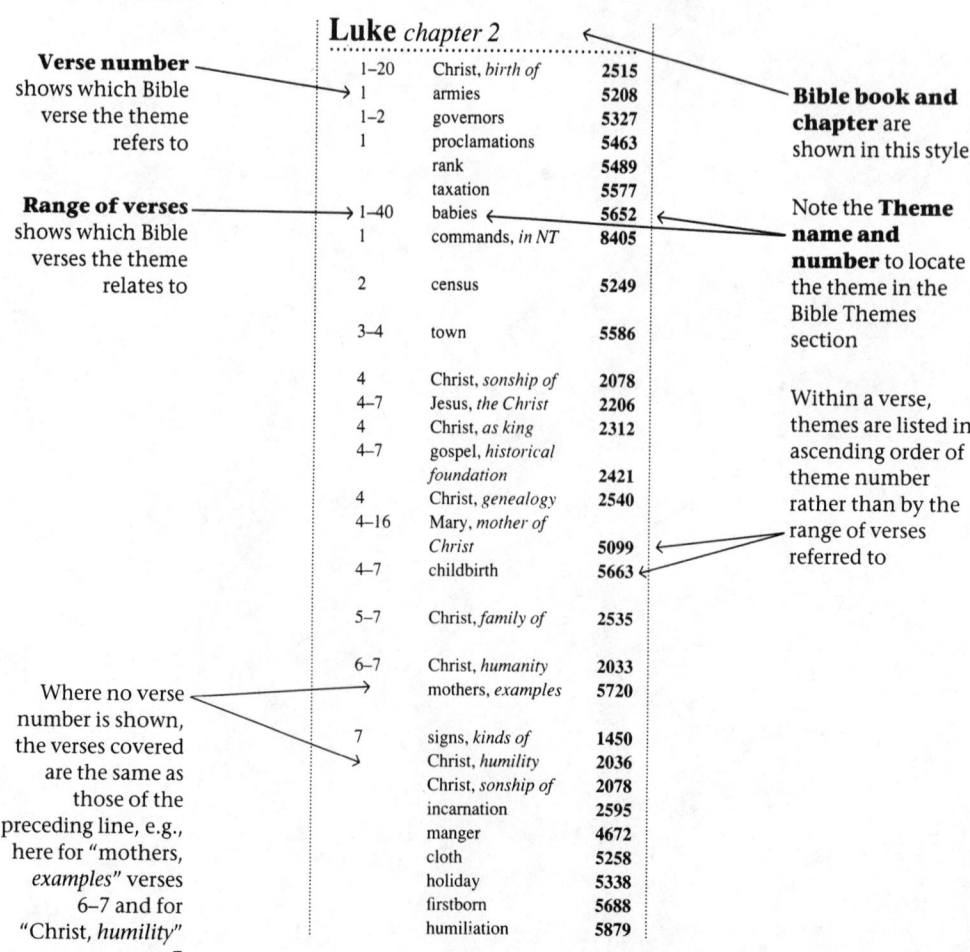

Verse number shows which Bible verse the theme refers to

Range of verses shows which Bible verses the theme relates to

Where no verse number is shown, the verses covered are the same as those of the preceding line, e.g., here for "mothers, *examples*" verses 6–7 and for "Christ, *humility*" verse 7

Luke *chapter 2*

1–20	Christ, *birth of*	2515
1	armies	5208
1–2	governors	5327
1	proclamations	5463
	rank	5489
	taxation	5577
1–40	babies	5652
1	commands, *in NT*	8405
2	census	5249
3–4	town	5586
4	Christ, *sonship of*	2078
4–7	Jesus, *the Christ*	2206
4	Christ, *as king*	2312
4–7	gospel, *historical foundation*	2421
4	Christ, *genealogy*	2540
4–16	Mary, *mother of Christ*	5099
4–7	childbirth	5663
5–7	Christ, *family of*	2535
6–7	Christ, *humanity*	2033
	mothers, *examples*	5720
7	signs, *kinds of*	1450
	Christ, *humility*	2036
	Christ, *sonship of*	2078
	incarnation	2595
	manger	4672
	cloth	5258
	holiday	5338
	firstborn	5688
	humiliation	5879

Bible book and chapter are shown in this style

Note the **Theme name and number** to locate the theme in the Bible Themes section

Within a verse, themes are listed in ascending order of theme number rather than by the range of verses referred to

Genesis

▶ Chapter 1

Genesis *chapter 14*

Genesis *chapter 15*

Genesis *chapter 27*

Genesis *chapter 28*

Exodus *chapter 21*

Exodus *chapter 24*

Exodus *chapter 31*

Exodus *chapter 32*

Leviticus *chapter 20*

Leviticus *chapter 24*

Numbers

▶ Chapter 1

Numbers *chapter 2*

Numbers *chapter 3*

Numbers chapter 21

Numbers chapter 22

Numbers chapter 23

Deuteronomy chapter 6

Deuteronomy
chapter 17

Deuteronomy
chapter 18

Deuteronomy
chapter 33

Joshua chapter 9

Joshua chapter 10

Joshua chapter 11

1 Samuel *chapter 18*

2 Samuel *chapter 23*

2 Samuel *chapter 24*

1 Kings

▶ **Chapter 1**

1 Kings *chapter 2*

1 Kings chapter 5

1 Kings chapter 6

1 Kings *chapter 17*

1 Kings *chapter 18*

2 Kings *chapter 5*

2 Kings *chapter 6*

2 Kings chapter 24

2 Kings chapter 25

2 Chronicles *chapter 19*

2 Chronicles *chapter 20*

Ezra

▶ Chapter 1

Ezra chapter 2

Ezra chapter 3

Job

Job chapter 31

Job chapter 32

Psalms

Psalm 19

Psalm *38*

Psalm *39*

Psalm 50

Psalm 51

Proverbs

▶ **Chapter 1**

Proverbs *chapter 2*

Proverbs *chapter 3*

Proverbs *chapter 6*

Proverbs *chapter 12*

Proverbs *chapter 15*

Proverbs *chapter 16*

Proverbs *chapter 17*

Proverbs *chapter 18*

Proverbs *chapter 19*

Proverbs *chapter 22*

Proverbs *chapter 25*

Proverbs *chapter 26*

Proverbs *chapter 29*

Song of Songs
▶ Chapter 1

Song of Songs
chapter 2

Song of Songs
chapter 3

Song of Songs
chapter 4

Isaiah *chapter 2*

Isaiah *chapter 11*

Isaiah *chapter 53*

Isaiah chapter 56

Isaiah chapter 57

Isaiah *chapter 60*

Isaiah *chapter 61*

Isaiah *chapter 66*

Jeremiah

▶ Chapter 1

Jeremiah *chapter 2*

Jeremiah *chapter 5*

Jeremiah *chapter 6*

Ezekiel chapter 35

Ezekiel chapter 36

Ezekiel chapter 37

Daniel *chapter 8*

Daniel *chapter 9*

Daniel *chapter 12*

Hosea

▶ **Chapter 1**

Hosea *chapter 2*

Joel *chapter 3*

Amos

▶ Chapter 1

Micah *chapter 7*

Nahum

▶ **Chapter 1**

Malachi *chapter 3*

Matthew *chapter 7*

Matthew *chapter 8*

Matthew *chapter 9*

Matthew chapter 12

Matthew *chapter 15*

Matthew *chapter 16*

Matthew *chapter 17*

Matthew *chapter 19*

Matthew *chapter 21*

Matthew *chapter 22*

Matthew *chapter 25*

Matthew *chapter 27*

Mark chapter 9

Mark *chapter 10*

Luke

▶ **Chapter 1**

Luke chapter 2

Luke *chapter 3*

Luke *chapter 4*

Luke *chapter 6*

Luke chapter 11

Luke *chapter 18*

Luke *chapter 19*

Luke *chapter 20*

Luke *chapter 21*
···

Luke *chapter 23*

John

▶ Chapter 1

John *chapter 2*

John *chapter 4*

John *chapter 7*

John *chapter 13*

John *chapter 18*

John *chapter 19*

John chapter 21

Acts

► Chapter 1

Acts *chapter 3*

Acts *chapter 5*

Acts *chapter 10*

Acts *chapter 17*

Acts *chapter 21*

Acts *chapter 25*

Acts *chapter 26*

Romans *chapter 3*

Romans *chapter 5*

Romans *chapter 7*

Romans chapter 15

1 Corinthians

▶ Chapter 1

1 Corinthians *chapter 4*

1 Corinthians
chapter 13

1 Corinthians

chapter 14

1 Corinthians

chapter 15

1 Corinthians
chapter 16

2 Corinthians

▶ **Chapter 1**

2 Corinthians *chapter 5*

2 Corinthians
chapter 12

Galatians *chapter 4*

Galatians *chapter 6*

Ephesians

▶ Chapter 1

Ephesians *chapter 3*

Ephesians *chapter 5*

Ephesians chapter 6

Philippians

► **Chapter 1**

Philippians *chapter 4*

Colossians *chapter 2*

Colossians *chapter 3*

Colossians *chapter 4*

1 Thessalonians

chapter 3

1 Thessalonians

chapter 4

2 Thessalonians

▶ Chapter 1

1 Timothy

▶ Chapter 1

1 Timothy *chapter 2*

1 Timothy *chapter 5*

1 Timothy chapter 6

Hebrews

▶ Chapter 1

Hebrews *chapter 3*

Hebrews *chapter 4*

Hebrews *chapter 7*

Hebrews *chapter 11*

James

▶ **Chapter 1**

James *chapter 5*

1 Peter

▶ **Chapter 1**

1 Peter *chapter 3*

2 Peter

► Chapter 1

1 John

▶ Chapter 1

1 John *chapter 5*

2 John

3 John

Jude

Revelation

▶ Chapter 1

Revelation *chapter 2*

Revelation chapter 8

Revelation chapter 9

Revelation chapter 10

Revelation chapter 18

Revelation *chapter 21*